EIN YAAKOV

THE ETHICAL AND INSPIRATIONAL TEACHINGS OF THE TALMUD

compiled in the sixteenth century by

RABBI YAAKOV IBN CHAVIV

a translation with commentary by

Avraham Yaakov Finkel

JASON ARONSON INC.
Northvale, New Jersey
Jerusalem

APPROBATIONS

Ein Yaakov has ignited the fire of the love of Torah in the hearts of the Jewish people for centuries.

Rabbi Finkel has rendered this precious treasure accessible to the English reading public in an excellent easy to read format in accordance with the great traditions of our people.

> — Rabbi Joshua Fishman
> Executive Vice President
> Torah Umesorah
> National Society for Hebrew Day Schools

A significant contribution toward the dissemination of Torah learning. The *aggadot* of our Sages are basic in the understanding of Jewish ethics and weltanschauung.

How symbolic that Reb Yaakov Finkel becomes the expositor of Rav Yaakov Ibn Chaviv's *Ein Yaakov* (The Eye of Jacob). A proper title for this sefer would be "Einei Yaakov" (The Eyes of Jacob).

> — Rabbi David Cohen
> Congregation Gvul Yaabetz
> Brooklyn, NY

This book was set in 9 pt. Garamond by Alpha Graphics of Pittsfield, NH and printed and bound by Book-mart Press, Inc. of North Bergen, NJ.

10 9 8 7 6 5 4 3 2 1

Library of Congress Cataloging-in-Publication Data

Ein Ya'akov. English
    The translation of the Ein Yaakov / [translated by] Avraham Yaakov Finkel.
        p.   cm.
    Ein Yaakov originally compiled by Jacob ben Solomon Ibn Habib.
    ISBN 0-7657-6082-7 (alk. paper)
    1. Aggada—Early works to 1800.   I. Finkel, Avraham Yaakov.
    II. Ibn Habib, Jacob ben Solomon, 1445?-1515 or 16.   III. Title.
BM516.E43E3713   1999
296.1'2760521—dc21
                                                        99-17829
                                                        CIP

Printed in the United States of America on acid–free paper. For information and catalog write to Jason Aronson Inc., 230 Livingston Street, Northvale, NJ 07647-1726, or visit our website: www.aronson.com.

Dedicated to the memory of my parents

✧ CONTENTS ✧

CONTENTS

CONTENTS

CONTENTS

CONTENTS

CONTENTS

CONTENTS

CONTENTS

CONTENTS

ᵔᵓ ACKNOWLEDGMENTS ᵔᵓ

How can I repay *Hashem* for all His bounties to me?
(Psalms 116:12)

I want to begin by giving thanks to *Hashem* for enabling me to complete this translation of *Ein Yaakov*—the compilation of the aggadic material of the Talmud—and thereby afford you, the discerning reader, the opportunity to savor the wisdom of our Sages straight from the source. You will delight in the poignant observations of these spiritual giants, be guided by their counsel, and inspired by their unflinching faith. In short, you will be learning Torah. And Torah learning is an affirmation of the immortality of the Jewish people; indeed, in our evening prayer the Torah is described as, "our life and the length of our days." It is my hope that the study of this essential part of the Talmud will uplift you and stimulate a thirst for greater Torah knowledge.

Three years ago, my friend Arthur Kurzweil, the astute and farsighted vice-president of Jason Aronson Inc., suggested that I undertake the translation of *Ein Yaakov*. With his heartening words I overcame my initial hesitation to undertake this project. Throughout the prolonged and laborious process of producing this work Arthur's infectious enthusiasm has kept me going. In his capacity as publisher of Anglo-Jewish literature he has the great *zechus* of introducing a generation of English-speaking Jews to the ideas of our great sages and thinkers. In so doing, he is playing a significant part in the current worldwide resurgence of Torah learning and observance. I am very grateful to him for piloting the production of *Ein Yaakov* through all its stages and for turning the manuscript into a finished book. "May *Hashem* grant you your heart's desire, and fulfill your every plan" (Psalms 20:5).

Many thanks to Elizabeth Bruno for her meticulous editing of the massive manuscript and to Dana Salzman, editorial director, for her dedication to overseeing the project. I am grateful also to Judie Tulli for creating the impressive cover design, and to the entire staff of Jason Aronson Inc. whose efforts and kindnesses are very much appreciated.

I want to thank my children, grandchildren, and great-grandchildren for being such a great source of genuine *nachas*, and for showing such a lively interest in the progress of the work. They are living proof of the verse, *Ateret zekeinim benei banim*, "Grandchildren are the crown of their elders" (Proverbs 17:6).

"*Acharon acharon chaviv.*" I must thank my dear wife, Suri, who typifies the virtue and kindness of a Jewish wife and mother. Her devotion, patience, and encouragement have helped me greatly in bringing this work to fruition. "May we merit to see children and grandchildren engaging in Torah and *mitzvot*, bringing peace upon Israel."

✆ INTRODUCTION ✆

THE KEY TO UNDERSTANDING AGGADAH

Ein Yaakov, one of the most popular classics in Rabbinic literature, is a collection of the aggadic material found in the Talmud.

What is *aggadah*? *Aggadah* is the component of the Talmud that deals with non-legal subjects. The Talmud is first and foremost a record of the discussions of Torah law (*halachah*), which took place in the great academies of Eretz Yisrael and Babylonia, from the third to the sixth centuries C.E. All present participated in exploring the meaning and ramifications of the Mishnah, arguing and reasoning together in a lively give-and-take discussion. Often in the course of these scholarly argumentations, the mention of a name, situation, or idea would lead to the introduction of a story, parable, or ethical lesson that lightened the mood and relieved the strain of the arduous halachic research. And so, embedded in the columns of intricate Talmudic legal debate we find a vast treasury of edifying narrative material, called *aggadah* or *aggadata,* that touches on all facets of life ranging from birth to death to resurrection and branches out into many fields of knowledge.

The *aggadah* sections of the Talmud have been assembled in *Ein Yaakov*, making this work a repository for the spiritual, moral, and religious values stressed by the Sages of the Talmud. Embracing more than one fourth of the more than five thousand single pages of the Talmud, *aggadah* contains a kaleidoscopic variety of inspiring tales, colorful parables, and homilies that stir the soul and fire the imagination. The teachings of *aggadah* are a window to a higher world; they elevate and inspire you. In fact, the word *aggadah* itself, derived from *aggeid*, "to bind, to draw," reflects the power of *aggadah* to draw you closer to God. The Gemara sums it up concisely, "If you want to appreciate the greatness of the Creator, study the *aggadah*, for through it you will get to know Him and cling to His ways" (*Sifrei, Eikev* 49). In a similar vein, we have the saying, "Someone who has mastered *aggadah* but not *halachah* has not even tasted the flavor of wisdom. But someone who has mastered *halachah* but does not know

the teachings of *aggadah* has not even felt the taste of the fear of God" (*Avot deRabbi Natan* 29).

THREE CATEGORIES

The vast mosaic of *aggadah* can be divided into three major categories: (1) homiletical interpretations of Scriptural verses; (2) ethical teachings and descriptions of historical events; and (3) *aggadot* dealing with metaphysical and mystical concepts.

An example of the first category is the interpretation of the verse, "This is my God, I will glorify Him" (Exodus 15:12). (How do you glorify God?) The Gemara explains the passage to mean: I will glorify Him through the performance of *mitzvot*: I will build a beautiful *sukkah*, buy a beautiful *lulav*, beautiful *tzitzit*; I will write a beautiful *sefer Torah*, and wrap it in exquisite silk wrappings (Nazir 2b).

An illustration of *aggadot* that expresses ethical concepts is the following: "If a son saw his father (unintentionally) transgressing a law of the Torah, he should not say to him, 'Father, you have violated a Torah law,' (because this would embarrass his father). He should instead ask, 'Is this what the Torah says?'" The Gemara asks, "But isn't that the same thing?" The Gemara answers, "He should tell him calmly, 'Father, it says in the Torah as follows: . . .' and the father will draw his own conclusion" (Sanhedrin 81a). A prime example of an *aggadah* that describes an historical event is the extensive account of the destruction of the *Bet Hamikdash* in Gittin 55b–58a.

The following is an illustration of an *aggadah* that imparts mystical ideas: "The height of Adam, the first man, reached from earth all the way to heaven . . . . But when he sinned, the Holy One, blessed be He, placed His hand on him and made him shorter" (Chagigah 12a).

At first glance, this *aggadah* may seem bizarre. Could Adam really have been that tall? And how can you imagine God shrinking him!

The *Nefesh Hachayim*[1] comments that this *aggadah,* like all *aggadot* of this type, should not be taken literally. He explains the profound lesson of this allegory:

When Adam was created, his intellect was so clear and all-encompassing that he could comprehend all the actions and processes of the entire universe and fathom the deepest mysteries of the heavenly realm. But when he sinned his intellect became blurred, so that his spiritual stature was diminished. In other words, before his sin, Adam was completely selfless and could see the truth in a detached manner. When he sinned, his latent egotism and self-centeredness were awakened. These selfish tendencies clouded his objectivity so that he could no longer perceive the absolute truth.

When you come across such cryptic *aggadot* you should remember that the Sages disguised their mystical aggadic teachings, framing them in parables, symbolisms, metaphors, and allegories, concealing their true intent beneath layer upon layer of profound meaning.

Now you may wonder, why, when outlining Torah law and *mitzvot*, the Gemara speaks in clear-cut, simple terms, whereas when it comes to *aggadah*, the Sages couch their teachings in vague, figurative language and obscure allusions?

Rabbi Moshe Chaim Luzatto (the Ramchal) answers by pointing out[2] that the Torah consists of two parts: a revealed portion (*nigleh*) which deals with the *halachot* of *mitzvot*, civil and criminal law, and a hidden portion (*nistar*) which focuses on esoteric subjects such as Creation, prophecy, the world to come, the coming of *Mashiach*, the Divine Throne, and similar abstruse themes. The Ramchal goes on to explain that, when expounding *halachah*, the Sages spoke in distinct, understandable terms, because every Jew has to know and understand the laws of the Torah. On the other hand, the secrets of the higher worlds and the mystical ideas of Heaven are not meant for the masses. If these teachings were formulated in plain language, evil-minded people and unscrupulous scholars might distort them to suit their nefarious purposes. So, in order to protect and preserve these teachings for posterity, the Gemara phrased them in figurative language whose true meaning was transmitted from master to disciple, so that only God-fearing Torah scholars would have the key to their meaning, while pseudo-scholars who do not have this key stumble about in the dark.

THE DOWNWARD SLIDE

As we study the aggadic tales about the lives of great masters we are overawed by their immense Torah knowledge, wisdom, steadfast rectitude, deep devotion, and boundless love of the Jewish people. But we should beware of judging them by contemporay standards. We must realize that ever since Moses reached the pinnacle of prophecy there has been a downward slide in the level of saintliness and scholarship. And so, the prophets were saintlier than the *tannaim* and *amora'im* (the teachers of the Mishnah and the Gemara) who were more sagacious than the *rishonim* and *acharonim*

(the earlier and later authorities) that came after them. They in turn were wiser than the rabbis of subsequent generations, who again were more knowledgeable than the most eminent scholars of our generation. The Gemara is quite blunt in describing the gradual decline in Torah learning, saying, "If the earlier sages were like sons of angels, we are like sons of men, and if the earlier sages were sons of men, we are like donkeys" (*Shabbat* 112b).

In light of this, we must approach the study of *aggadah*—the subject matter of *Ein Yaakov*—with humility and reverence.

RABBI YAAKOV B. SHLOMOH IBN CHAVIV

Rabbi Yaakov ibn Chaviv, the compiler of *Ein Yaakov*, was born in Zamora, Spain around 1445, and studied under R. Shmuel of Valencia. When King Ferdinand ordered the expulsion of the Jews from Spain, in 1492, R. Yaakov fled to Portugal. Soon the Inquisition spread its tentacles to that country, and the situation of the Jews in Portugal deteriorated. Before long, R. Yaakov's young son, Levi, a budding Torah scholar, along with tens of thousands of Jewish children, was abducted and forcibly baptized. R. Yaakov managed to free his son and flee together with him to Salonica, Turkey (now Greece) where he remained until his death in 1516.

R. Yaakov's complete mastery over the Talmud was soon recognized by the leaders of the Salonica community who appointed him to lecture in the local yeshivah.

In Salonica, a wealthy scholar, Don Yehudah Benveniste, offered R. Yaakov hospitality and gave him access to his well-stocked library. There he found authentic copies of the Mishnah and the Talmud and their commentaries that had been unavailable to him until that time. It was in Don Yehudah's home that R. Yaakov compiled his monumental work *Ein Yaakov*, late in life. He also added a commentary culled from the writings of the famous commentators: Rashi, Tosafot, Ramban, Rashba, Ritva, and many others. R. Yaakov died before he could complete the *Ein Yaakov*, but his son, R. Levi ibn Chaviv, finished the work. He was unable, however, to collect the *aggadot* of the Jerusalem Talmud.

Ein Yaakov gained instant popularity, and soon after its first printing (Salonica, 1516) it became the favorite textbook of businessmen and working people who were eager to learn Gemara but had neither the time nor the inclination to explore the knotty deliberations of the halachic portions of the Talmud.

Over the centuries, *Ein Yaakov* has been published close to a hundred times, with added commentaries, including *Iyun Yaakov, Etz Yosef, Anaf Yosef, Rif, Ben Yehoyada*, which is a profound commentary by the *Ben Ish Chai* of Baghdad, and *Hakotev*, R. Yaakov ibn Chaviv's own commentary.

THE TRANSLATION

In this translation I have tried to convey the sense of the Hebrew and Aramaic text as faithfully as possible, rendering it in an informal, idiomatic style, adapted to the needs of the present-day English-speaking reader. In an attempt to make the concise talmudic text intelligible I have incorporated the clarifying comments of Rashi, Maharsha, and others in the text, placing them between square brackets. The text is elucidated, so that the train of thought of the Gemara flows smoothly. With minor exceptions, *Ein Yaakov* follows the sequence of the tractates in the Talmud. Often pieces that are repetitions of material that occurred in previous *mesechtot* were omitted. To enable the reader to locate the corresponding text in the Gemara, the matching page number in the Gemara appears at the head of each page of translation. Also, the page breaks as they appear in the Gemara have been inserted in the parallel places in the English text. In addition, in order to make it easy to find a given topic I added headings for the individual *aggadot*.

MISHNAH, GEMARA, AND *BARAITA*

A few words are in order to explain the terms Mishnah, Gemara, and *Baraita*, which you will encounter on virtually every page of this book.

The Mishnah is the Oral Torah (*Torah shebe'al peh*). The Rambam, in his *Introduction to the Mishnah*, explains that every commandment God gave to Moses He gave to him together with its explanation. With the passing of time, whenever a case arose about which no one had heard the explanation directly from Moses, the Sages would decide the law by applying the Thirteen Rules through which the Torah may be interpreted. This is the Oral Torah, which was transmitted by word of mouth from generation to generation until R. Yehudah Hanassi collected all the traditions, clarifications, and explanations which had been taught by the Sages of previous generations and wrote them down in the book called the Mishnah. *Baraita(ot)* are rabbinical teachings that R. Yehudah Hanassi did not include in the Mishnah.

The Talmud, or Gemara, explains and expands upon the highly compressed information of the Mishnah and the *Baraitot*. The Mishnah and Gemara thus fuse into one work—the Talmud. Without a doubt, the Talmud is the most important factor in the physical and spiritual survival of the Jewish people in exile.

A *SHIUR* (LESSON) IN *EIN YAAKOV*

Ein Yaakov should not be read superficially like an ordinary book. If you study its pages in depth, you will see the Sages spring to life before your eyes. You will

marvel at the agility of their minds, the nimble way they respond to insuperable problems that are as current as today's headlines. You will find it to be a source of genuine joy, an enriching experience of true Talmudic delight.

When you study *Ein Yaakov* you enter the world of the Talmud; you are actually "learning Gemara" in the true sense of the word. You don't have to be a *talmid chacham* to learn *Ein Yaakov*; you can learn it even if you have never learned Gemara before. But I recommend that you set up a *shiur* with a *chavruta* (study partner) and study Gemara the way it is learned in the great *yeshivot* of the past and present where thousands of young scholars intensely argue puzzling points in the Gemara, and the sound of vigorous talmudic debate shakes the rafters of the *bet midrash*. Or you could learn *Ein Yaakov* with your older children, or with a study group. When you do, you will notice that each line of Gemara sets off a passionate discussion, ideas are tossed back and forth, points are raised and refuted in what is known as *milchamtah shel Torah*, "the battle of Torah." And in the process, new friendships are forged and old ones strengthened.

Ideally, *Ein Yaakov* should be taught by a rabbi the way it has been done ever since the work was first published. Today, as in the past, Jews with a thirst for Torah are gathering nightly in a *shul* or a private home for a *shiur* in *Ein Yaakov*. The sense of fulfillment they have of successfully learning through an entire *mesechta* (tractate) is positively exhilarating. Through the *shiur* in *Ein Yaakov* people who are total strangers are transformed into a closeknit group of friends who genuinely care for each other. Whether you learn by yourself, with a *chavruta*, or with a study group, the important thing is to maintain a regular schedule: A page or a chapter a day, or even only every Shabbat.

꿍   꿍

The Torah assures us that, "[The Torah] is not on the other side of the ocean, that you should have to cross the ocean to achieve it. [That is not necessary.] It is very close to you. It is in your mouth and in your heart, to achieve it" (Deuteronomy 30:12).

Books like *Ein Yaakov* bring the Torah close to you and make it easy for you to grasp it. If you learn it diligently, its words penetrate your heart and uplift you. Learning Torah is a rewarding experience that brings countless blessings and peace upon you and your family. As it says, "And all your children will be students of God, and your children will have abundant peace" (Isaiah 54:13).

—Avraham Yaakov Finkel

NOTES
1. By R. Chaim Berlin of Volozhin, Vilna, 1824.
2. In his *Discourse on Aggadot*.

✦ THE *AGGADOT* ✦
OF THE TALMUD

by Rabbi Avraham, son of the Rambam

Translator's note: This classic essay on the approach to the aggadot *was written about three hundred years before* Ein Yaakov *appeared. Because of its timeless significance it has been included in most editions of the work.*

ESSAY ON THE MEANING
OF THE *AGGADOT*

It is important to understand that the homiletic expositions and stories in the Talmud have underlying meanings that are shrouded in secrecy, and most of the commentators did not even attempt to probe their deeper meaning.

My father, (the Rambam), had in mind writing a commentary on the *aggadot*, as he mentions in his *Commentary on the Mishnah*. Yet in the end he decided against it, as he stated in the beginning of his *Moreh Nevuchim* (Guide for the Perplexed), applying to himself the passage, "Moses was afraid to come close to it."[1]

However, after my father's death, I decided to write a few explanatory remarks on this subject in the hope that it will be helpful to students of this field. If you follow my guidelines in understanding the aggadic teachings of the Sages, you will come to grasp their deeper meaning, and, as a result, you will not make light of them or deny that they are true. Neither will you fall into the trap of thinking that the miracles that happened to the Sages are as momentous as those that happened to Moses and Israel at the parting of the Red Sea, or as remarkable as the parting of the Jordan for Elisha and Elijah.[2] Such misconceptions arise when you take the *derash* (i.e., homiletic interpretations) literally and accept only the surface meaning of the text. But there is abundant evidence to show that the aggadic tales and teachings, aside from their plain meaning, have profound hidden significance. My father already made this clear in his book; I merely want to explain it in greater detail by classifying the *aggadot* into different categories and citing examples for each category. But first I want to make a few introductory remarks.

EVERY THEORY MUST
BE SUBSTANTIATED

To begin with, let me point out that if a person puts forward a certain theory without offering proof, expecting people to accept it at face value just because they respect him, he is sadly mistaken; his approach flies in the face of both the Torah and common sense. It goes against common sense, because he wants people to believe something without evaluating and investigating whether it squares with the facts. And it runs counter to the Torah, because it goes against the truth and is unethical. The Torah [tells us not to curry favor with anyone], saying [to a judge], "Do not give special consideration to the poor, nor show respect to the great" (Leviticus 19:15). And it says also, "Do not give anyone special consideration when rendering judgment" (Deuteronomy 1:17). And there is no difference between a person who believes an idea without supporting evidence and one who trusts a person's statement simply because he respects him and holds that it must be true since it comes from a great scholar. This does not prove that the statement is true.

Accordingly, we are not required to endorse all the theories of the Sages of the Talmud on medicine, physics, and astronomy in every respect just because we know the authors to be outstanding personalities and eminent scholars in all facets of the Torah. Of course, when it comes to Torah knowledge, the scholarship of the Sages is unsurpassed, and it is their responsibility to teach it to us, as it says, "You must keep the Torah as they interpret it for you" (Deuteronomy 17:11), but this does not necessarily apply to all other branches of knowledge. You can see that even the Sages themselves when faced with an issue that could not be proven by debate and logical arguments, said, "I swear, that even if Joshua b. Nun had said it, I would not have obeyed him!"[3] Which means, "I would not believe him although he was a prophet, since he cannot prove his point by the talmudical rules of logical argument."

Let me offer you one conclusive proof that no one will refute. It is this: We find that the Sages themselves said that the opinions expressed in the Gemara with regard to general medicine are not borne out, like for instance when the Gemara says that wearing a "preserving stone"[4] is a safeguard against miscarriage, or other things mentioned in tractate Shabbat. They tested these remedies and found them not to have any therapeutic value.

DEDICATION TO THE TRUTH

You should realize, however, that there are exceptions to the rule, (that the medical advice of the Sages is unreliable). For example, the admonition of the Sages, "If you are hungry, eat; if you are thirsty, drink; if your dish is cooked, pour it out while it is hot," is certainly true. What it means is that you should not eat until you are hungry or drink until you are thirsty, and when you sense the call of nature, you should not delay relieving yourself. This dictum is the key to healthful living; it has been verified by experience and by medical testing.

By the same token, it would be wrong to argue as follows: While Aristotle, the great philosopher, has proved by indisputable facts that the Creator exists, as well as other things that are true, he holds the false belief that the universe never had a beginning but always was, and he propounds the fallacy that the Creator does not know every detail. Now you should not say that since he erred on these points, therefore, all his theories are untrue. You should carefully examine each of this statements on its own merits and accept that which passes muster and reject that which does not hold up. You should refrain from ruling on things that cannot be decided either way, regardless of who says it. As our Sages said [about a law R. Shimon proposed], "If this is a tradition [he received from his teachers] we will accept it, but if it is only an inference, we want to raise an objection."[5] In the same way, when the Sages were faced with an issue they were unable to decide either way, they said *teiku* which means, "the question remains unsolved." Similarly, we find that when they discovered that the opinion they held was wrong, they reversed themselves, and frankly took back what they had said, like, "Bet Hillel retracted their earlier decision and decided in accordance with Bet Shammai."[6] Indeed, their dedication to the truth was so great that the Gemara tells us that Rava appointed an Amora to say in his name, "The statement I made to you was an error on my part."[7] Don't accept theories with blind faith just because the author is an outstanding scholar. You should accept teachings only on the basis of solid evidence, as my father said in his commentary. Anyone who is objective and has an open mind will agree with this.

CATEGORIES OF SCRIPTURAL INTERPRETATIONS

With God's help I will now proceed to classify the *derashot* [scriptural expositions] in the Talmud, breaking them down into five categories.

1. The first category consists of *derashot* that should be understood in their literal sense, since they contain nothing but their plain, obvious meaning. Although this category needs no illustration, I will give you an example anyway, to make it unmistakably clear. I have in mind the Gemara in Berachot 31a that expounds, "You are forbidden to fill your mouth with laughter in this world, for it says, 'When God will return the captivity of Zion . . . then our mouths will be filled with laughter' (Psalms 126:2);" (the word *then* implies that we will laugh only after the Redemption, but not while we are still in *galut* (exile).

2. The second category of *derashot* covers interpretations that have both a literal and a figurative meaning. Since the Sages meant to convey the figurative rather than the plain meaning of these sayings, they couched them in such a way that their plain meaning represents the opposite of their figurative and true meaning. Most of these have been explained in *Moreh Nevuchim* (Guide for the Perplexed, volume 3:43) and in the *Commentary on the Mishnah* [by the Rambam]. An example of this kind of rabbinic exposition is found in the Gemara in Taanit 31a, where it says, "R. Eliezer said: In days to come, the Holy One, blessed be He, will make a circle for the righteous, and He will sit among them in Gan Eden. Every one of them will point his finger at Him, as it says, 'And they will say on that day: Behold, this is our God . . . let us exult and rejoice in His deliverance'" (Isaiah 25:9).

   Of course, no intelligent person will take this *derash* in its literal sense. What R. Eliezer meant to say is that the reward of the righteous in the world to come will be that they receive from God a lucid perception of the absolute truth, something they could never attain in this world. This is the supreme and ultimate good. He therefore compares the joy of gaining this insight to a dance, and likens the blissful delight each individual experiences to the pointing with their fingers at the Holy One, blessed be He. Thus he illustrates this lofty idea through a concise allegory. This exemplifies all other interpretations of this kind.

3. The third category embraces expositions that have only a simple meaning, but this simple meaning is so puzzling that most people cannot understand it. And if you do understand it, you find that the composition of the piece is unclear and confused and its wording vague and ambiguous. Therefore, be careful when you study such expositions, and don't be hasty in figuring out what they mean, because you can easily reach the wrong conclusion and get the wrong idea.

   To give you an example, the Gemara says, "A person should always incite (*yargiz*) his *yetzer tov* (good impulse) to fight against his *yetzer hara* (evil impulse). For it says, 'Incite (*rigzu*) [your inner powers] and don't sin' (Psalms 4:5).[8] If he overcomes his evil impulse, fine. But if he cannot, he should recite the *Shema*, for the verse continues, 'Reflect in your hearts while on your beds [*mishkavchem*] (ibid.) [this alludes to the *Shema*, for it says, *beshochbecha*, you should recite the *Shema* when you retire]. If this works, fine. If not, he should remind himself of the day of death, for the verse concludes, 'and be silent' (ibid.)" (Berachot 5a).

Although this exposition means exactly what it says, it is difficult to understand it because the terms "good and evil impulse" are unfamiliar, and the suggested ways of overcoming the evil impulse are baffling. I think it is important that I explain this *derashah* to help you understand it and similar expositions in this category.

Note that the word *yargiz*, "incite," means also, "to rule, to control." The term *yetzer tov* refers to your intellect, and *yetzer hara* denotes your passions and physical desires. So the real meaning of the statement is that you should strive to make your mind control your physical desires, and that you should reflect on this all the time. If reflecting on this is enough to restrain your passions, well and good; but if not, you should reinforce your thoughts by articulating this concept, uttering passages that will make you submissive, help you subdue your passion, and stop you from having lustful thoughts. The passage you should recite is the *Shema*, because the *Shema* stresses the fact that the *yetzer tov* encourages you to believe in the Oneness of God, to love and serve Him and to trust in the principle of Divine reward and punishment. The *Shema* tells you to subdue the *yetzer hara* when it says, "Do not stray after your heart and eyes" (Numbers 15:30), and it tells you to bolster your *yetzer tov*, saying, "Be holy to your God" (ibid. v. 40).

The *derashah* continues, "If reciting the *Shema* works, fine. If not, he should remind himself of the day of death." This means that if the *yetzer hara* continues to stir your passion and is not subdued by your recitation of the *Shema*, you will overcome it by thinking of the day of death. Remembering that man is mortal is enough to break the arrogance of your *yetzer hara*, as Akavya b. Mehalalel said, "Consider three things and you will not come in the grip of sin: . . . 'Where you are going'—to a place of dust, worms and maggots. . ." (Avot 3:5).

4. The fourth category consists of metaphoric interpretations of certain verses. However, the Sages did not suggest that their figurative interpretation is the actual meaning of the verse, God forbid to think that.

An example of this kind of exposition is the Gemara in Taanit 9a, where R. Yochanan said: What is the meaning of the passage, "*Asseir te'asseir*, You shall tithe" (Deuteronomy 14:22)?

It means, "Give tithe, so that you will become rich."[9] [And there is a verse to prove it. God says: "If you give tithes,] I will pour upon you a blessing without end" (Malachi 3:10). What is the meaning of the words, "without [*beli*] end"?—Until your lips grow weary (*yivlu*) from saying, "It is enough!"[10]

Don't think like people who are unable to grasp the real truth and who think that such metaphoric interpretations are traditions like the expositions of the laws of the Torah. That is not so. The fact is that the interpretations of passages that do not involve fundamental laws and principles are not based on tradition. Such expositions were thought up by the authors according to their own understanding. Many of these interpretations are vehicles to express lofty ideas through allegories, parables, and symbolism. Take the commentary[11] on the verse, "Jethro heard . . . and he came to the desert where Moses was staying, near God's mountain" (Exodus 18:1), where R. Yehoshua asked: What did Jethro hear? and answered: He heard about the war of Amalek.[12] I have no doubt that this is merely R. Yehoshua's opinion and not a tradition. The fact that he cites evidence to support his opinion proves it, because for a tradition we need no evidence. Furthermore, the fact that all other Sages disagree with him, proves it also. If it was a tradition they would not dispute him.

The fifth category comprises *derashot* [metaphoric expositions] that contain exaggerations, like the following: Mar Zutra said, Between *Atzel* and *Atzel* there are four hundred camelloads of *derashot* (scriptural interpretations) (Pesachim 62b). Mar Zutra has in mind the verse, "Atzel had six sons, and these were their names: Azrikam, Bocheri, Ishmael, Sheariah, Obadiah, and Hanan, all these were the sons of Atzel" (1 Chronicles 8:38). The first *Atzel* is at the beginning of the verse, the second is at the end. To say that this verse has four hundred camel-loads of interpretations is clearly an exaggeration. For if in the whole book of Chronicles there are not four hundred camel-loads of scriptural interpretations, how could there be that many in one passage? Therefore, it must be an exaggeration.

AGGADIC ANECDOTES

The aggadic anecdotes can be divided into four parts:

1. True stories to serve as precedents for the purpose of deciding a law. An example is the case of a person who is sitting with his head and the greater part of his body inside the sukkah but with the table inside the house (because the

sukkah is too small). Bet Shammai declared the sukkah invalid, but Bet Hillel ruled that it was valid. Said Bet Hillel to Bet Shammai: "Did it not happen that the elders of Bet Hillel and the elders of Bet Shammai once went on a visit to R. Yochanan b. Hachoranit, and they found him sitting with his head and greater part of his body within the sukkah while his table was in the house?" [The fact that R. Yochanan sat in such a sukkah proves our view that it is valid.] Retorted Bet Shammai: "On the contrary. This incident proves that our view is right, for they told him, 'If you have always sat in a sukkah like this, you have never fulfilled the mitzvah of sukkah!'" (Ketubot 13b). [Thus the anecdote is told to serve as a precedent for a law concerning the minimum size of a sukkah.]

2. Stories that are told to teach a moral lesson, like the following: A person should always be gentle like Hillel and not impatient like Shammai. The story is told about two people who made a wager between themselves. They said: "Whoever will go and make Hillel angry will receive 400 zuz . . . and Hillel did not become angry" (Shabbat 30b). The moral of this story is that you should try to emulate Hillel and not be overly particular or become angry even when provoked, for forbearance is an admirable trait. There are many similar stories in the Talmud.

3. Anecdotes that convey a fundamental religious principle, like the following: It happened once that the people said to Choni Hame'agel: Pray that it should rain. He drew a circle around him and said, "Master of the universe! Your children have turned to me . . ." (Taanit 19a). This story shows the power of perfect faith, that God listens to the prayer of His righteous servants and answers them when they are in distress, as it says, "What nation is so great that they have God close to it, as God our Lord is, whenever we call Him?" (Deuteronomy 4:8). The prophets too, expressed this thought, saying, "Then you will call, and God will respond" (Isaiah 58:9), and also, "He will call upon Me, and I will answer him" (Psalms 91:15). A similar story is told about Nakdimon b. Gurion in Taanit 19a, and there are a great number of such anecdotes in the Talmud.

4. Tales that point out a miracle or an amazing incident, like the following story about R. Meir, R. Yehudah, and R. Yose who were traveling on the road. R. Meir deduced from the innkeeper's name that he was dishonest, and subsequent events proved him right (Yoma 83a). Many similar incidents can be found in the Talmud.

DREAMS PRESENTED AS REAL EVENTS

Then there are stories that did not actually happen but were seen in a dream. The Sages express them in terms of real events, because they believed that no reasonable person would ever mistake dreams for actual facts, like the following: R. Yishmael b. Elisha [the High Priest] said: It once happened on Yom Kippur that I entered the innermost part of the Sanctuary to burn the incense and saw the Lord of Hosts seated on a high and exalted throne . . . (Berachot 7a), and many other similar stories. And the same is true of stories that tell of visions of the prophets, how God spoke to them, and stories about demons. A naive person who thinks that these things happened exactly as they were recorded and believes things that are impossible, is foolish and ignorant of the laws of nature. For in telling the stories of miracles the Sages followed the example of the prophets who told in plain language what they saw in their visions, as my father explained it in the *Moreh Nevuchim*.

EXAGGERATIONS

There are many incidents that actually happened but were exaggerated in the belief that no reasonable person would mistake their meaning. The Rabbis condoned the use of exaggeration, saying, "The Torah used overstatement, the prophets used overstatement, and the Sages used overstatement. The Torah used hyperbole, like in the verse, "Great cities fortified to the skies" (Deuteronomy 1:28). The prophets used hyperbole, like in the verse, "The people were playing flutes and rejoicing with great joy; the ground burst from their noise" (1 Kings 1:40). The Sages exaggerated when they described the heap of ashes on the altar [saying that there were three hundred *kor* of ashes—an immense quantity—on the altar]; they exaggerated when they spoke of the golden vine [on which the people used to hang their gifts of gold for the *Bet Hamikdash*, saying that it took three hundred *kohanim* to collect those gifts]; and they exaggerated when they described the curtain that separated the Holy of Holies from the Sanctuary, [saying that it was so heavy that it took three hundred *kohanim* to immerse it in a *mikveh*] (Tamid 29a). These are just three examples in the Mishnah, but in the Gemara there are countless cases of exaggeration. To cite one example: Rabbah and R. Zeira had the Purim feast together. They became intoxicated, and Rava got up and slew R. Zeira. On the next day Rabbah prayed for R. Zeira and revived him (Megillah 7b). What it means is that Rabbah beat R. Zeira and wounded him so badly that R. Zeira was near death. The Gemara uses the phrase "he slew him" because the wound was life-threatening, or it might have been on the throat. And the word *achyei* [he revived him] means "he recovered." The term *achyei* is often used for that meaning. Many similar stories are found in the Talmud.

PARABLES

Some *aggadot* tell stories that actually took place but are told in the form of parables or metaphors so that only a person who grasps the author's intent can understand them. In some cases even fools and children can make sense of the symbolism. An example of this kind of *aggadah* is found in the following Gemara in Sukkah:

> Once there were two Kushites who served King Solomon as scribes, Elichoref and Achiyah.[13] One day Solomon noticed that the Angel of Death was sad. "Why are you sad?" he asked. "Because in heaven they have demanded from me the souls of the two Kushites who are sitting here," the Angel of Death replied. [Their time to die had arrived, but they were not at the place where they were destined to die.] To save their lives, Solomon placed them in the custody of the demons [over whom he ruled] and sent them to the sity of Luz, [where the Angel of Death has no power].[14] However, as they reached the gate of Luz, they died. The next day Solomon saw that the Angel of Death was cheerful. "Why are you cheerful?" he asked. "Because you sent the men to the place where I was ordered to take their lives, [namely, at the gate of Luz]," replied the Angel of Death. Thereupon Solomon coined the phrase: A man's feet are responsible for him; they carry him to the place where he is wanted (Sukkah 53a).

The meaning of this *aggadah* is obscure. It seems to me that it actually happened. In other words, Solomon knew that the two scribes were going to die of a sickness they had, and in an effort to save their lives he sent them to a place with a good climate where they would be cured. But they died there at God's behest, from which there is no escape. That's why Solomon said: A man's feet carry him to the place where he is wanted. You can find deeper meaning in each detail of the story, but I don't want to go into that at this time.

Don't be surprised that the Sages use parables and allegories rather than plain ordinary language; they also use this method to interpret verses of the Prophets. See the Gemara in Berachot 18a where they interpret the passage, "He (Benaiah) struck the two altar-fires of Moab" (2 Samuel 23:20) in a figurative sense,[15] although the prophets stated it in plain language as if it had no other meaning. I want to make it clear that these verses have no meaning other than the symbolism by which the Sages explained them. Now, if the words of the prophets are explained in a figurative sense, surely symbolism should be applied to the words

of the Sages that are difficult to understand. My father pointed this out in his *Shemonah Perakim*.[16]

ALLEGORIES, SYMBOLISMS, AND PARABLES

We found a source in the Talmud that proves beyond doubt that most of the sayings of the Sages are allegories and symbolisms, and should not be taken literally. The Gemara relates:

> R. Eliezer had a disciple who once rendered a halachic decision in his presence. Said R. Eliezer to his wife Ima Shalom, "I wonder whether this student will live through the year." The student, in fact, did not live out the year. "Are you a prophet [that you knew that he was going to die]" his wife asked. "I am neither a prophet nor the son of a prophet," R. Eliezer replied, "but I have this tradition: Whoever renders a halachic ruling in the presence of his rabbi is liable to the death penalty at the hands of Heaven," [and that is what this student was guilty of] . . . The name of this disciple was Yehudah ben Gurya.

The Gemara continues: The reason that the disciple's name and that of his father were mentioned is so that you should not say that the whole story is a parable. From this you can infer that in many instances the words of the Sages were not taken literally, but were seen as parables. Fix this proof in your mind and keep your eyes open to it, for it is a marvelous thing and a superb piece of evidence. (This proof was pointed out to me by a great Torah scholar.)

This last group of figurative *aggadot* is very much like the second category of *derashot* mentioned above that deals with allegorical interpretations. They are both important portions of *Aggadah*, containing magnificent and lofty concepts that could not be revealed to the masses, and, therefore, they were veiled in parables and metaphors.

COMPOSITES

One important thing for you to remember and which will be very helpful to you in determining whether a story is real, a dream, a parable, or a metaphor, is that many *aggadot* contain a mixture of all these elements. If you are going to explain an entire story according to one single form, either in its plain meaning or in any other way, you will be bewildered and confused.

An example of an aggadah with a blend of two or more meanings is the following story: Once R. Yochana b. Zakkai was traveling on the road, riding on his donkey, and R. Elazar b. Arach was driving the donkey from behind. R. Elazar said to him, "Rabbi, please teach me one chapter of the Account of the

Divine Chariot."[17] "My son," replied R. Yochanan, "Did I not teach you that the Divine Chariot should not be taught to one person unless he is a sage and understands it by himself?" R. Elazar then said, "Rabbi, allow me to say one thing that you taught me." He answered, "Go ahead and say it!" R. Elazar then expounded the Divine Chariot, and as he did, fire came down from heaven and encircled all the trees in the field. Then all the trees broke out in song, singing, "Praise God from the earth, sea giants and all watery depths . . . fruitful trees and all cedars . . . Halleluyah!" An angel then called out from the fire and said, "This exposition is truly the Account of the Divine Chariot!" R. Yochanan b. Zakkai stood up and kissed R. Elazar b. Arach on the head and said, "Blessed be the Lord, God of Israel, Who gave to our father Abraham a son who knows, understands, and is able to delve into and expound the Divine Chariot." This story and the one after it are mixtures of all these elements and forms of meaning. I cannot analyze these things in depth because they are profound mysteries that should not be revealed.

SUMMARY

I have attempted to clarify the *aggadot* for the thoughtful student by classifying the anecdotes and Scriptural expositions, citing examples for each category. I am confident that, after studying my comments, when you come across a story or a *derash*, you will have no difficulty recognizing what type of *aggadah* it is.

Knowing these things, you will avoid casting aspersions on the words of the Sages like the Karaites[18] and the fools did. This will also prevent a person from going to the other extreme of foolishly believing in impossible things and in events that never happened. In the end, he will deny the spiritual essence of God by ascribing to Him physical attributes. This comes from taking certain passages about God in a literal sense and believing that God is a tangible Being.

Think seriously about the principle I propound in this essay. It is a towering pillar and a strong wall against confusion and error.

And now be blessed by God;[19] place me like a seal on your heart[20] and like *tefillin* between your eyes.[21] Let this be a gateway and an introduction for whatever you will read or hear in the future of any *derash* (explanation of a verse) or story; you will benefit greatly from it. Join the ranks of those that recognize and understand the truth, stay away from the opponents of the truth who go after delusion and are deluded.[22]

May God in His mercy lead us in the right course and guide our steps so that we may walk in the pathways of the truth and follow His direction. May His Name be blessed. Amen.

NOTES

1. An allusion to Exodus 34:30.
2. 2 Kings 2:14.
3. Berachot 24b, where the Gemara says, "Even if R. Yehoshua b. Levi had said it . . ."
4. Also called eaglestone.
5. Yevamot 76b.
6. Pesachim 88b; Yevamot 116b; Gittin 41b; Eduyot 1, 12, 13, 14.
7. Chullin 100a; Eiruvin 16b; Gittin 43a; Sanhedrin 44a et al.
8. *Rigzu*, from the same root as *yargiz*, means both "tremble" and "incite to fight."
9. The second part of the compound verb, *asseir te'asseir*, can be read *te'asheir*, "you will become rich."
10. The words *beli* and *yivlu* have letters *bet, lamed, yud* in common.
11. Zevachim 116a.
12. Exodus 17:8–14.
13. 1 Kings 4:3.
14. Sotah 46b.
15. Ariel, translated here as "the two altar-fires of Moab," symbolizes the two Temples. *Ari*, lion, represents the Sanctuary which, like a lion, is wide in the front and narrow in the back. The reference to Moab alludes to David and Solomon who are descendants of Ruth the Moabitess.
16. The Rambam's introduction to *Perek Cheilek*, the tenth chapter of tractate Sanhedrin.
17. The first chapter of Ezekiel in which he describes his mystical vision of the Divine Throne.
18. A breakaway sect founded late in the eighth century. Karaites rejected the Oral Torah and rabbinic traditions of Talmudic law. During the last few centuries they have gradually faded into oblivion.
19. Genesis 26:29.
20. Song of Songs 8:6.
21. Deuteronomy 6:8.
22. 2 Kings 17:15.

EIN YAAKOV

∽ BERACHOT ∾

THE TIME FOR THE *SHEMA* OF THE EVENING

(2a) From what time may a person begin to recite the *Shema* of the evening?[1] From the time that the priests enter to eat their *terumah*[2] until the end of the first watch,[3] so says R. Eliezer. But the Sages say: [You are allowed to recite the *Shema*] until midnight. Rabban Gamliel says: until the first ray of dawn appears.[4] It happened one day that the sons of Rabban Gamliel came home late at night from a wedding feast and told him that they had not yet recited the evening *Shema*. He replied: If dawn has not yet broken you must still recite it. [Rabban Gamliel continued:] The *Shema* is not the only case that the Sages [permit something only until midnight, although they really hold that its time extends until dawn]. But, as a general rule, whenever the Sages say "until midnight," the mitzvah may be performed until the break of dawn.

The mitzvah of burning the fat and the pieces of the sacrifices on the altar must be performed until the break of dawn.[5] Similarly, all the offerings that must be eaten on the day that they were brought [such as thanksgiving-offerings, sin-offerings, and guilt-offerings] must be eaten before the break of dawn [of the next day]. [The Gemara asks:] If the Sages hold that the Shema may be recited until dawn, why did they say [that it may be recited only] until midnight? [The Gemara answers:] In order to keep a person away from transgression [because he may procrastinate, sleep the whole night, and miss saying the *Shema*].

[The Gemara asks:] Let's see. When do the priests enter to eat the *terumah*? When the stars come out. Then why doesn't the Mishnah come straight to the point and say: You are allowed to begin to recite the *Shema* from the time the stars come out. [The Gemara answers:] The Mishnah uses this wording [associating the Shema with the eating of *terumah*] in order to teach us something in passing: that a priest is allowed to eat *terumah* as soon as the stars appear [and he does not have to wait until he has brought his compulsory forgiveness-offering on the next day]. Because the fact that he did not yet bring the forgiveness-offering does not

disqualify him from eating *terumah*. And so we have been taught[6]: The verse, "At sunset he will be clean" (Leviticus 22:7), means that he must wait only for sunset to eat *terumah*, but he need not wait until he has brought his forgiveness-offering.

(2b) R. Yose said: Twilight is like the blink of an eye. The moment the evening comes, the day is gone; it is impossible to fix its exact time.

THE THREE NIGHT WATCHES

(3a) [The Mishnah stated]: [You may say the *Shema*] until the end of the first watch; so said R. Eliezer.

[The Gemara asks:] What is R. Eliezer's opinion? If he holds that the night has three watches,[7] then he should say, "until the end of the fourth hour"; and if he holds that the night has four watches, then he should say, "until the end of the third hour."[8] [The Gemara answers:] He actually holds that the night is divided into three shifts, but [he does not speak in terms of hours] because he wants to teach us in passing that just as the shifts change in heaven [among the ministering angels], so are there watches here on earth. For it has been taught: Rabbi Eliezer says: The night is divided into three shifts, and at each shift the Holy One, blessed be He, sits and roars like a lion, as it says, "God roars from on high, He makes His voice heard from His holy dwelling. He roars aloud over His [earthly] abode (Jeremiah 25:30)."[9] Here on earth you can tell the different watches of the night by the following signs: In the first shift the donkey brays; in the second, the dog barks; and in the third, the baby nurses from its mother's breast,[10] and the wife talks with her husband.[11]

[The Gemara inquires:] What does R. Eliezer mean by the signs he gave for the shifts here on earth? Do they take place at the beginning of the shifts? If so, he does not need a special sign to indicate the beginning of the first shift. It is nightfall! Then again, if he thinks that these signs mark the end of the watch, why does he need a special sign to mark the end of the last watch? Obviously, it is daybreak! [The Gemara answers: These signs denote the following times:] [The donkey braying] tells us when the end of the first watch is, [the baby nursing] tells us the beginning of the third watch, and [the dogs barking] marks the middle of the middle shift. And if you want, you may say: all these times mark the end of the respective shifts. And if you object that the last watch needs no sign [because you can just look out and see that it's day,] I tell you that the sign is needed for a man who sleeps in a dark room [without windows] and does not know when it is time to recite the *Shema*. When he hears a woman talking to her husband and a baby nursing from its mother's breast he knows that it's time to get up and recite the *Shema*.

R. Yitzchak b. Shmuel said in the name of Rav: The night is divided into three watches, and at each watch the Holy One, blessed be He, sits and roars like a lion and says: Woe to the children! Because of their sins I have destroyed My house, burned My Sanctuary, and exiled My children among the nations of the world.

AN ENCOUNTER
WITH ELIJAH

It was taught: R. Yose says: One day, while traveling on the road, I entered one of the ruins of Jerusalem to pray. Suddenly Elijah appeared and stood at the door to guard me and waited until I finished my prayer. After I finished, Elijah said to me: *Shalom*, peace unto you, Rabbi! I replied: *Shalom*, my Rabbi and my master![12] Said Elijah: Son, why did you enter this ruin? To pray, I answered. He said: You should have prayed on the road. I explained: I was afraid I might be interrupted by people passing by. Elijah retorted: You should have said a shorter prayer.[13] [Said R. Yose:] This conversation with Elijah taught me three things: First, that you should not walk into a ruin. Second, that you are allowed to pray on the road, and third: If you pray on the road you should say a short prayer. [Elijah] then said to me: Son, what voice did you hear in this ruin? I replied: I heard a heavenly voice. It sounded like a cooing dove, and it said, Woe to the children. Because of their sins I have destroyed My house, burned My Sanctuary, and exiled My children among the nations.

[Elijah] said to me: I swear by your life and by your head! You should know that this did not only happen just that one time, but three times each day the heavenly voice laments the destruction of the *Bet Hamikdash*. And that's not all; every time Jews go to the synagogues or to the halls of learning and answer, *Yehei shemei rabba mevorach*, "May His great Name be blessed,"[14] the Holy One, blessed be He, nods His head[15] and says: Happy is the King who is praised like this in His house! Alas, that a father has sent His children into exile among the idol worshippers! Woe to the children who have been banished from their father's table!

[The Gemara summarizes:] The rabbis have taught: There are three reasons why a person should not step into a ruin: because people should not suspect [that he was meeting a woman there for immoral purposes],

because the walls may cave in on him, and because of demons that may be living there.

MORE ABOUT
THE NIGHT WATCHES

(3b) Our Rabbis have taught: The night is divided into four watches, so says Rebbi.[16] R. Nathan says: There are only three. What is R. Nathan's reason? Because it says, "Gideon and the hundred men with him arrived at the outposts of the camp, at the beginning of the middle (*hatichonah*) watch" (Judges 7:19). And we have learned that the term *tichonah*, middle, can only be used if something precedes and something follows it. [The Gemara asks:] And how does Rebbi understand the term *tichonah*? [The Gemara answers:] He holds that *tichonah* means in the middle of one of the middle ones. R. Nathan argues: It does not say, "one of the middle ones"; it says, "the middle!" [The Gemara asks:] What is Rebbi's reason [for stating that the night has four watches?]—R. Zerika in the name of R. Ammi, quoting R. Yehoshua ben Levi, said: [Rebbi derives it from the following verses:] One verse says: "I wake up at midnight to praise You for Your just rules" (Psalms 119:62), and another verse says: "My eyes precede the watches of the night" (Psalms 119:148) [meaning, I am up even before the watches of the night are over]. How is it possible [that he woke up at midnight and still had two watches ahead of him, since the plural "watches" means at least two]? This is possible only if the night has four watches [two before and two after midnight]. But R. Nathan holds as did R. Yehoshua, who said: [The morning *Shema*] may be recited until the third hour of the day because kings usually wake up in the third hour of the day. [They sleep] six hours of the night and two hours of the day which amounts to eight hours or two watches of four hours each. [David says: I wake up at midnight, which is eight hours or two watches of four hours each before the kings rise.] R. Ashi said: One watch and a half is also called the plural "watches."

[The Gemara now brings an unrelated *halachah* from the same spokesman.] R. Zerika speaking in the name of R. Ami, quoting R. Yehoshua, also said: In the presence of the dead you should discuss only things that have to do with the dead. R. Abba b. Kahana said: This pertains only to words of Torah,[17] [which should not be discussed], but there is no harm in discussing worldly matters. But some say that R. Kahana said: This *halachah* applies *even* to words of Torah, and surely worldly matters [should not be discussed in the presence of the dead].

DAVID'S HARP

It says, "I arise at midnight to praise You for Your just rules" (Psalms 119:62). [The Gemara asks:] [What?] David did not wake up until midnight? He was up from the evening! For it says, "I rose before the *neshef* and cried for help" (Psalms 119:147). And how do we know that *neshef* means the beginning of the night? Because it says, "In the *neshef*, in the evening of the day, in the blackness of night and in the darkness" (Proverbs 7:9). [This proves that David was up from the beginning of the night; then why did he say, "I arise at midnight"?] R. Oshia answered: This is what David meant to say: It never happened that midnight should pass, and I should still be sleeping. [I was always up well before that time.] R. Zeira said: Until midnight he dozed like a horse, [that has a light sleep]; from that point on he energized himself like a lion. R. Ashi said: Until midnight he was engrossed in the study of Torah; from that point on he recited songs and praises.

[The Gemara asks:] But does *neshef* mean evening? *Neshef* means morning! For it says: "David attacked the men from *neshef* until the evening of the next day" (1 Samuel 30:17). Doesn't this imply from morning until evening, [and *neshef* means morning]. [The Gemara counters:] No. It means "from evening until evening." [Asks the Gemara:] If so, the same expression should be used and it should say, "from *neshef* to *neshef*," or "from *erev* to *erev*." Rava said: [You are right]. The *neshef* in that verse does mean morning. But there are two kinds of *neshef*:[18] the evening *neshef*, when the night is removed and the day comes, and the morning *neshef*, when the day is removed and the night comes.

[The Gemara raises a question: David said, "I arise at midnight."] How did David know exactly when midnight was, if even Moses, our teacher, did not know exactly when midnight is, for it says, "Moses said to Pharaoh in God's name: Around midnight, I will go out in the midst of Egypt" (Exodus 11:4). What does "around midnight" mean? Should we say that the Holy One, blessed be He, told him to tell Pharaoh that around midnight [the firstborn would die]? That's impossible; there is no uncertainty or approximation with God. Therefore we must say that God told him "exactly *at* midnight," but when Moses came to Pharaoh he told him, "*around* midnight," [because he could not be sure exactly when midnight was.] Now, if Moses was in doubt, how could David have known it? [The Gemara answers:] David had a sign [whereby he could tell when it was midnight]. For so said R. Abba b. Bizna in the name of R. Shimon the Pious: There was a harp hanging above David's bed, and precisely when midnight arrived a north wind came and would blow on the harp and it would play by itself. He immediately got up and studied Torah until the break of dawn. At dawn the sages of Israel came in to see him and said to him: Our Master, the King, Israel your people need sustenance. Replied David: Let them go and make a living from one another.

[Retorted the sages:] A handful cannot satisfy a lion, neither can a pit be filled with the dirt you dug out; [some of it gets lost; in other words, the commu-

nity needs outside resources to supply its needs]. Replied David: Send out the troops and attack the enemy for plunder. They immediately went to ask Achitofel's [tactical] advice and consulted the Sanhedrin [and asked for their prayers], and they inquired of the *Urim* and *Tumim*[19] [whether or not they would be victorious]. Rabbi Yosef says: What verse can we quote to substantiate this? It says, "After Achitofel were Jehoiada son of Benaiah and Abiathar, and the commander of the king's army was Joab" (1 Chronicles 27:34). In other words, Achitofel was the adviser; as it says, "In those days, the advice that Achitofel gave was accepted as if a man had asked advice of the word of God."

(4a) "Benaiah the son of Jehoiadah," this means the Sanhedrin. "And Abiathar" was the High Priest of David and represented the *Urim* and *Tumim*. And so it says, "And Benaiah the son of Jehoiadah was commander of the *Kereiti* and the *Peleiti*. Why are the Sanhedrin called *Kereiti* and *Peleiti*? *Kereiti*, because their words are very decisive (*koretim*); *Peleiti*, because they are very distinct (*mufla'im*)[20] in their words. And finally, "the commander of the king's army was Joab. [Notice the order of the verse: First Achitofel, then the Sanhedrin, then the *Urim* and *Tumim*, and finally the king's general, Joab, who was the one to lead the army into war.] R. Yitzchak b. Adda says: Which verse can be cited to support the story of David's harp? It says, "Awake, O my glory! Awake, O harp and lyre! I will wake the dawn" (Psalms 57:9).

[The Gemara now returns to the discussion of the original question as to how it is possible that David knew the exact moment of midnight and Moses did not.]

Rabbi Zeira said: Moses certainly knew the exact time of midnight, and David did too. [The Gemara asks:] Since David knew it, why did he need the harp to wake him up from his sleep? Since Moses knew, why did he say, "About midnight?" [The Gemara answers:] Moses thought that Pharaoh's astrologers might make a mistake in calculating the precise moment of midnight, and when the plague would not occur at the predicted hour they would say that Moses was a liar. For a rabbi has said: Train your tongue to say "I don't know," because eventually you are going to make a mistake, and you'll get caught. R. Ashi says: The time when Moses spoke was midnight between the thirteenth and the fourteenth day of Nisan, and he said to Israel: The Holy One, blessed be He, said: Tomorrow at the hour like[21] the midnight of tonight, I will go out into the midst of Egypt.

DAVID'S PIETY AND HUMILITY

(4a) [The Gemara continues:] David prayed: "Guard my soul for I am pious" (Psalms 86:2). There is a dispute between R. Levi and R. Yitzchak about the meaning of this prayer. One said: This is what David said to the Holy One, blessed be He: Master of the universe, am I not pious? All the kings of the East and the West sleep into the third hour of the day, but "I arise at midnight to praise You for Your just rules" (Psalms 119:62). The other said: This is what David said to the Holy One, blessed be He: Master of the universe, am I not pious? All the kings of the East and the West sit in their assemblies surrounded by their royal entourage, whereas my hands are soiled with blood of menstruation, of fetuses and placentas, in order to declare a woman clean for her husband.[22] And not only that, [I am not a dictator, but] whatever I do, I discuss with my teacher Mefiboshet, and I say to him: Is my decision right? Did I correctly convict, correctly acquit, correctly declare clean, correctly declare unclean? And I am not ashamed to ask.

R. Yehoshua b. Idi says: Which verse may be cited to support this? It says, "I will speak of Your decrees and not be ashamed in the presence of kings" (Psalms 119:46).

A Tanna taught: [The name of David's teacher] was not Mefiboshet but Ishboshet. Why then was he called Mefiboshet? Because he embarrassed David by pointing out his mistakes. [The literal meaning of Mefiboshet is, "With his mouth he puts others to shame."] Because David humbly accepted criticism he was worthy to have Kilav as a son.[23] And R. Yochanan said: His name was not Kilav but Daniel. Why then was he called Kilav? Because he put Mefiboshet to shame in matters of *halachah*. [Kilav means *kol av*, "he was always the father; always a step ahead" (Rashi).] Solomon said this about him: "My son, if your mind gets wisdom, my mind too, will be gladdened" (Proverbs 23:15). He also said: "Be wise, my son, and gladden my heart, that I may have what to answer those who taunt me" (Proverbs 27:11).

[Referring to the verse: "Guard my soul for I am pious," the Gemara wonders:] Did David really consider himself pious? Did he not say, "I would not have believed (*lulei*) that I would ever see the good reward of God in the land of the living" (Psalms 27:13). And a Tanna taught in the name of R. Yose: Why are there dots on the word *lulei*? [The dots are interpreted to mean that he was doubtful.] David said to the Holy One, blessed be He: Master of the universe, I am confident that you will pay a good reward to the righteous in the world to come, but I do not know whether I will have a share in it, [thus you see that he was not so sure of his piety. The answer is: He really considered himself to be a pious man, but] he was afraid that perhaps some sin may have caused him to lose his reward. This is consistent with a statement by R. Yaakov b. Idi. For R. Yaakov b. Idi noted a contradiction between two verses. One verse reads: [God said to Jacob,] "I am with you. I will protect you wherever you go" (Genesis 28:15). And another verse reads, "[Before meeting Esau,] Jacob was very frightened and distressed" (Genesis 32:8).

[The question is, why was Jacob afraid if God had promised to protect him? The answer is:] He was concerned that some sin may have caused God's promise to be no longer in effect. [And where do we have an example of a sin causing a promise to be rescinded?] As it has been taught: It says, [In the Song at the crossing of the Red Sea,] "Until Your people crossed, O God, until the people You gained crossed over" (Exodus 15:16). The phrase, "Until Your people crossed, O God" refers to Israel's first entrance into Eretz Yisrael. The phrase, "Until the people You gained crossed over," refers to the second entrance [in the days of Ezra]. [But the verse puts the two together.] Hence the Sages say: Israel should have been worthy to have miracles performed for them in the days of Ezra just as they happened in the days of Joshua bin Nun when they entered victoriously, but sin prevented the miracle from happening. [In the days of Ezra they entered Eretz Yisrael only by the grace of Cyrus, and they remained subjugated under Persian rule.]

THE *SHEMA* AND THE *SHEMONEH ESREI*

(4b) [The Gemara now resumes the discussion of the *Shema* and the *Shemoneh Esrei*.] It has been taught: The Sages made a fence for their words, [they took preventive measures,] so that a person, returning from the field in the evening, should not say: Let me first go home, eat a little, drink a little, sleep a little, and then I'll recite the *Shema* and the *Shemoneh Esrei*. In the meantime, he may fall asleep and sleep through the whole night without having said the *Shema* and the *Shemoneh Esrei*. Instead, say the Sages, when a man returns home from the field in the evening, he should go to the synagogue. If he knows how to read verses of the Torah, he should study *Chumash* or *Tanach*. If he can learn Mishnah, let him study Mishnah, and then let him recite the *Shema* and the *Shemoneh Esrei*. Only then should he go home, eat his meal, and say the Grace after Meals. And whoever transgresses the words of the Sages [and says: I really have time until tomorrow morning,] deserves to die [by the hand of God].

[The Gemara asks:] What is the difference that in other cases the Rabbis do not say "he deserves to die," and here the Rabbis use the expression, "he deserves to die"? [After all, he transgressed only a rabbinic ordinance.] [The Gemara answers:] If you wish, you may say: Because here we are concerned that people will fall asleep [if they don't realize that they have to recite the *Shema* first]. Or, if you prefer you may say: They want to exclude the opinion of those who say that the evening prayer is voluntary. [Therefore, the Sages want to make it very clear by their warning that you are obligated to say the evening prayer.]

The Master said [in the *Baraita* just quoted:] He should recite the *Shema* and the *Shemoneh Esrei*. This supports Rabbi Yochanan's view [who holds that even in the evening, the *Shema* comes before the *Shemoneh Esrei*; contrary to R. Yehoshua b. Levi, who holds that at night you say *Shemoneh Esrei* first and then the *Shema*]. Because R. Yochanan said: Who will have a share in the world to come? He who says the *Shemoneh Esrei* immediately after the *berachah* of *Ga'al Yisrael* [which is related to the *Shema*.][24] R. Yehoshua b. Levi says: The *Shemoneh Esrei* prayers were arranged to be said in the middle [between the morning *Shema* and that of the evening. Therefore, in the evening, the *Shemoneh Esrei* comes first, and then the evening *Shema* with the *berachah Ga'al Yisrael*]. [The Gemara asks:] What are they arguing about? [The Gemara answers:] If you wish, you may say, they disagree on the interpretation of a verse. Or of you prefer, you may say, that they argue about the rationale. For R. Yochanan argues: Although the redemption from Egypt reached its climax in the morning only,[25] it actually began the night before [therefore, even in the evening, *Ga'al Yisrael* must immediately be followed by the *Shemoneh Esrei*].

Rabbi Yehoshua, on the other hand, argues that since the main deliverance happened in the morning, [that of the evening] was no real redemption, [therefore, in the evening, *Ga'al Yisrael* must not be followed by the *Shemoneh Esrei*]. Or, if you wish you may say that they argue about the interpretation of a verse. They differ in the interpretation of the verse, "[Teach the commandment to your children] when you lie down and when you get up" (Deuteronomy 6:7). Rabbi Yochanan argues: Let's compare lying down to getting up. Just as at the time of getting up, reciting the *Shema* precedes the *Shemoneh Esrei*, so also at the time of lying down, the *Shema* comes first and then the *Shemoneh Esrei*. But Rabbi Yehoshua b. Levi argues differently. He says: Let's compare lying down to getting up. Just as in the morning, you recite the *Shema* right after you get up, so should you recite the *Shema* of the evening as the last thing you do before going to bed.

Mar b. Ravina raised the following objection: We have learned that in the evening [during the *Maariv* prayer] you should say two *berachot* before the *Shema* and two *berachot* after the *Shema*. Now if *Ga'al Yisrael* must be followed immediately by the *Shemoneh Esrei*, you are not doing that, because you have to say the *berachah* of *Hashkiveinu* (Lay us down to sleep)[26] between *Ga'al Yisrael* and the *Shemoneh Esrei*. [The Gemara answers:] I will tell you. [*Hashkiveinu* is not considered an interruption.] Since the Rabbis enacted that *Hashkiveinu* should be said, it is considered as an extension of the *berachah* of *Ga'al Yisrael* [*Hashkiveinu* also is also a prayer for the redemption and protection of Israel]. If you do not learn that way, then in the morning, how can we say the *Shemoneh Esrei* immediately after *Ga'al Yisrael*? Didn't R. Yochanan say: Before beginning the *Shemoneh Esrei* you should say, "My Lord, open my lips" (Psalms 51:17), and afterward you should say, "May the words of my mouth be acceptable" (Psalms 19:15)? [Isn't "My Lord, open my lips" an interruption between *Ga'al Yisrael* and the beginning of the *Shemoneh Esrei*?] The answer is that since the Rabbis ordained that "O Lord, open my lips" should be said, it is like an addition to, and part of, the *Shemoneh Esrei*. Here too, since the Rabbis ordained that *Hashkiveinu* should be said, it is an extension of the *berachah* of *Ga'al Yisrael*.

RECITING *ASHREI*

R. Elazar b. Avina said: Whoever recites the psalm, *Tehillah LeDavid*, "A praise by David" (Psalm 145) three times a day[27] can be confident that he is destined for the world to come. What is the reason? Shall I say because this psalm [known as *Ashrei*] is arranged according to the *alef bet* [with every verse beginning with another letter of the *alef bet*, in order]? Then why not recite Psalm 119, "Happy are those whose ways are blameless," which is arranged in alphabetical order, but which has eight verses for each letter of the *alef bet*? Shall I say that *Ashrei* is a special psalm because it contains the verse, "You open Your hand, and satisfy the desire of every living thing" (Psalms 145:16) [which speaks of God's boundless benevolence. If it is the sustenance that God gives to life,] why not recite the Great Hallel (Psalm 136) in which it says, "He gives nourishment to all flesh" (Psalms 136:25)? The question remains: Why is *Ashrei* singled out? [The Gemara answers:] Because *Ashrei* has both [the alphabetical order and verse 16 describing God's sustenance of life in general].

R. Yochanan said: Why is there no verse in the *Ashrei* that begins with the letter *nun*?[28] Because there is a verse beginning with a *nun* that predicts something that is not good for Israel. For it says, "*Naf'lah*, [which begins with the letter *nun*], She has fallen, not to rise again, the maiden of Israel" (Amos 5:2). In Eretz Yisrael they interpreted this verse differently [turning the curse into a blessing]. They said: Read, "*Naf'lah*, She has fallen, but will never fall again. Rise! Maiden of Israel!" R. Nachman b. Yitzchak says: Even though the *nun* is missing in *Ashrei*, [because David did not want to include a verse that predicts the downfall of Israel,] David will reverse that and lend support to Israel through his *ruach hakodesh*, Divine inspiration. Because the next verse in *Ashrei* reads, "God supports all that fall (*nofelim*)" (Psalms 145:14).

The Angels Michael and Gabriel

R. Elazar b. Avima further said: That which is written about Michael is greater than that which is written about Gabriel. For about Michael it says, "Then one of the Serafim flew over to me" (Isaiah 6:6) [meaning, in one flight, without stopping,] whereas about Gabriel it is written, "The man Gabriel, whom I had seen at the beginning of the prophetic vision came flying in flight," (Daniel 9:21) [the implication is that

Gabriel came in two flights, stopping in between]. [The Gemara asks:] How do you know that the word "*echad*, one" [in the passage, "one of the Serafim"] refers to Michael? Rabbi Yochanan said: It is derived by a *gezeirah shavah*,[29] (a Scriptural analogy) from the word "*echad*." The present verse says, "Then *echad*, one of the Serafim flew over to me," and in another place it says, "Now Michael, *echad*, one of the chief heavenly ministers, came to help me" (Daniel 10:13). [Just as in the second verse *echad* refers to Michael, so also in the first verse, *echad* refers to Michael.] It was taught in a *Baraita*: Michael arrived in one flight; Gabriel in two. Elijah in four, and the Angel of Death in eight; but in the time of a plague, the Angel of Death arrives in one flight.

The Bedtime *Shema*

R. Yehoshua b. Levi says: Although you have recited the *Shema* in the synagogue, it is a mitzvah to recite it again at bedtime. R. Assi says: What verse can be cited to support that? "Tremble and don't sin. Ponder it in your hearts while on your beds, and be utterly silent [when you are asleep]. *Selah*" (Psalm 4:5). But R. Nachman says: (5a) If he is a Torah scholar [who is engrossed in Torah thoughts all day] he does not have to say the Bedtime *Shema*. Abbaye says: Even a Torah scholar should recite one verse of supplication, like, for example, the verse, "In Your hands I will entrust my soul, redeem me, Lord, God of truth" (Psalms 31:6).

R. Levi says in the name of R. Shimon b. Lakish: A person should always incite (*yargiz*) his good inclination to fight against his evil inclination. For it says, "Incite [your inner powers] and don't sin" (Psalms 4:5).[30] If he overcomes his evil inclination, fine. But if he cannot, he should engage in Torah study, for it says, "Ponder it in your hearts" [get your heart involved in Torah study]. If that helps to subdue his evil inclination, fine. If not, he should recite the *Shema*, for it says, "on your beds" [this alludes to the *Shema*, because it says *beshochbecha*, "you should recite it when you retire"]. If this works, fine. If not, he should remind himself of the day of death, for it says, "and be utterly silent. *Selah*."[31]

[The Gemara continues,] Rabbi Yitzchak says, "Whoever recites the Bedtime *Shema* is as though he held a two-edged sword in his hand [to protect him against the demons], for it says, "With exalted praises to God in their mouths, and two-edged swords in their hands" (Psalm 149:6). How can you infer that this refers to the Bedtime *Shema*? Mar Zutra, and some say, Rav Ashi, says: You can infer it from the beginning of this verse, "Let the devout rejoice in glory, let them sing joyously on their beds," (Psalm 149:5) [and "on their beds" refers to the Bedtime *Shema*].

Rabbi Yitzchak says furthermore: When you recite the Bedtime *Shema*, the demons stay away from you, as it says, "And the sons of *reshef* (sparks of fire) fly, *uf*, upward" (Job 5:7). [Explains R. Yitzchak]: The word

uf refers to the Torah, for it says, "If you close your eyes, *hata'if*, [related to *uf*], it is gone" (Proverbs 23:5) [meaning, Torah requires constant study. If you merely blink your eyes you forget it. And the Torah keeps away the "*reshef*"]. R. Yitzchak asks: What is *reshef*? He answers: *Reshef* refers to demons, for it says [If Israel will ignore the Torah], "they will be consumed by *reshef*, fiery, demonic, fever, cut down by bitter plague" (Deuteronomy 32:24). [At any rate, the remedy against the demons of the night is the recitation of the Bedtime *Shema*.]

Rabbi Levi b. Chama says in the name of Resh Lakish: What is meant by the verse, "God said to Moses . . . 'I will give you the stone tablets, the Torah and the commandments that I have written for the people's instruction'" (Exodus 24:12)? He expounded: "The tablets" refers to the Ten Commandments; "the Torah" refers to the Written Torah; "the commandments" refers to the Mishnah (the Oral Torah); "which I have written" refers to the Prophets and the Writings; "for the people's instruction" refers to the Gemara. This teaches you that all of these were given to Moses on Sinai.

THE MEANING OF PAIN AND SUFFERING

(5a) R. Shimon b. Lakish said: If you study Torah, painful sufferings will leave you, as it says, "And the sons of *reshef* (sparks of fire) *uf*, fly upward" (Job 5:7). R. Shimon b. Lakish explains: The word *uf* refers to the Torah, for it says, "If you close your eyes, *hata'if*, [related to *uf*] it is gone" (Proverbs 23:5). And *reshef* refers to demons, for it says, "they will be consumed by *reshef*, fiery, demonic fever, cut down by bitter plague" (Deuteronomy 32:24). [Thus, it is the *uf*, the Torah, that chases away the *reshef*, the demons.]

R. Yochanan exclaimed: What you, R. Shimon b. Lakish, just said, even schoolchildren know that! They know that the Torah protects you from affliction. They have learned in the Torah, "If you obey God, and you will do what is just in His eyes . . . then I will not strike you with any of the sicknesses that I brought on Egypt, for I am God, your healer" (Exodus 15:26). [You don't have to cite a verse from Job to tell us that!] Instead, you should say: If a person has the opportunity to study Torah and does not study it, then the Holy One, blessed be He, will bring on him ugly and painful sufferings that will stir him up. For it says, "I was dumb, silent; I kept quiet from the good thing, and my pain was stirred up" (Psalms 39:3). "I kept quiet from a good thing" can refer only to the Torah, about which it says, "For I have given you a *good* teaching, do not forsake My Torah" (Proverbs 4:2). [In other words, I did not study Torah, therefore I was stricken with pain.]

R. Zeira, and others say, R. Chanina b. Papa, says: Let me show you that the ways of the Holy One, blessed be He, are not like the ways of flesh-and-blood people. The way of people is, if a person sells an object to someone [if he is forced to sell it out of poverty (Rashi)], the seller is sad, and the buyer is happy. But the Holy One, blessed be He, is different. He gave the Torah to Israel, and He rejoices, for it says, "For I have given you a good teaching, do not forsake My Torah." [The wording of this verse conveys God's great joy: The Torah is a beautiful thing! God tells us. Make sure you appreciate it and use it properly!]

Rava, and others say, Rav Chisda, says: If a person feels pain coming on, he should examine his way of life. For it says, "Let us search and examine our ways, and turn back to God" (Lamentations 3:40). If he searched and found nothing that he did wrong, he should attribute his pain to the neglect of Torah study, as it says: "Happy is the man whom You chastise, O God, the man whom You teach Your Torah" (Psalms 94:12). [Meaning: Happy is the man who understands that the purpose of his pain is to induce him to learn more Torah].[32] If he did attribute his suffering to neglect of Torah, but did not find this to be the cause, he should know that his sufferings are afflictions of love. For it says, "For whom God loves, He chastises" (Proverbs 3:12). [God afflicts him in this world even though he has not sinned, in order to give him a greater reward in the world to come (Rashi).]

Rava, in the name of R. Sechora, in the name of R. Huna, says: If the Holy One, blessed be He, is pleased with someone, He crushes him with pain, for it says, "God was pleased with him, therefore, he crushed him with disease" (Isaiah 53:10). Now, you might think that this is so, even if he does not accept the afflictions with love. Therefore, the verse continues: "When he offers his soul as a trespass-offering." [The Gemara expounds:] Just as a trespass-offering has to be brought willingly, so are the sufferings in this verse willingly accepted. And if he does accept them, what is his reward? The verse continues, "He will see children and have a long life." And that's not all; his learning will remain firm with him, [he will not forget it]. For the verse concludes, "The one that God desires will be successful in his learning."

[The Gemara now defines yisurim shel ahavah, afflictions of love.] There is a dispute between R. Yaakov b. Idi and R. Acha b. Chanina about the nature of afflictions of love. One of them says: Afflictions of love are the kind of pain that does not prevent a person from learning Torah. For it says, "Happy is the man whom You chastise, O God, the man whom You teach Your Torah" (Psalms 94:12). The other one says: Afflictions of love are the kind of pain that does not disrupt a person's prayers. As it says: "Blessed is God who has not turned away my prayer, or His faithful care from me" (Psalms 66:20). R. Abba the son of R. Chiya b. Abba said to them: So said R. Chiya b. Abba in the name of R. Yochanan: [You are both right]. Both are considered afflictions of love, [they interfere neither

with Torah study nor with prayer] for it says, "For whom God loves, He chastises" (Proverbs 3:12).

Why then does it say, "the man whom You teach Your Torah" [which was the basis for the opinion that the criterion for afflictions of love is that they don't interfere with Torah study]? [The Gemara answers:] Don't read telam'dennu [You teach him,], but telam'deinu [You teach us]. In other words, the concept that afflictions are beneficial, "You have taught us in Your Torah." [The Gemara asks: Where in the Torah do we find that afflictions are beneficial?] We derive it from a kal vachomer [a logical inference] from the law regarding "tooth and eye." [If a master knocks out a tooth or an eye of his Canaanite slave, then the slave has to be set free (Exodus 21:26–27).] The reasoning goes: Tooth and eye are only one limb, and yet if they are mutilated the slave goes free. Painful sufferings torment a person's entire body; imagine how much freedom is eventually obtained through them!

This is in line with what R. Shimon b. Lakish taught us. For R. Shimon b. Lakish said: The word brit, covenant, is mentioned in regard to salt, and brit is also mentioned in regard to suffering: the word brit is mentioned in regard to salt, for it says, "Do not leave out the salt of your God's brit, covenant, from your meal offerings" (Leviticus 2:13). And the word brit is mentioned in connection with suffering, as it says at the end of the Tochachah, the chapter of terrifying curses, "These are the words of the brit, covenant" (Deuteronomy 28:69). Just as in the covenant that was mentioned in connection with the salt, the salt lends a taste to the meat; so also in the covenant mentioned in connection with suffering, the sufferings wash away a person's sins.

[More on the subject of suffering:] It has been taught in a Baraita: R. Shimon b. Yochai says: The Holy One, blessed be He, gave Israel three precious gifts, and all of them are obtained only through suffering. They are: The Torah, Eretz Yisrael, and the world to come. From where do we know that the Torah is acquired only through suffering? Because it says, "Happy is the man whom You chastise, the man whom You teach Your Torah" (Psalm 94:12). From where do we know that Eretz Yisrael is acquired through suffering? Because it says, "Just as a man chastises his son, so does God your Lord chastise you" (Deuteronomy 8:5), and right after that it says, "God, your Lord is bringing you to a good land" (Deuteronomy 8:7). From where do we know that the world to come is acquired through suffering? Because it says, "For the commandment is a lamp, and the Torah is a light, and the way to life is the rebuke that chastises" (Proverbs 6:23). [The "way to life," meaning, the world to come, is reached only through reproof and suffering.]

A Tanna recited before R. Yochanan: If a person engages in the study of the Torah, and in charitable acts, (5b) and [has to endure the dreadful anguish] of having to bury his children, all his sins are forgiven.

R. Yochanan said to the Tanna: I grant you that a person merits forgiveness of his sins because of his Torah study and acts of charity, for it says, "Through kindness and truth sin will be forgiven" (Proverbs 16:6). "Kindness" refers to acts of charity, for it says, "He who strives to do charitable and kind deeds, attains life, success and honor" (Proverbs 21:21). "Truth" refers to Torah, for it says, "Buy truth and never sell it" (Proverbs 23:23). But how do you know that a person who suffers the anguish of burying his children merits forgiveness of all his sins? [The Gemara answers:] There was this old man[33] who taught him the answer in the name of R. Shimon b. Yochai: It is derived from a *gezeirah shavah*, a Scriptural analogy of the word *avon*, sin, iniquity. It says in the above-mentioned verse, "Through kindness and truth, *avon*, sin, will be forgiven." And elsewhere it says, "You atone the *avon*, sin of the fathers because of their children after them" (Jeremiah 32:18) [meaning, the sin of the father is erased through the anguish he experiences on account of his children's death].

R. Yochanan says: Leprosy and trouble with children are not considered afflictions of love. [The Gemara asks:] Can it be that leprosy is not an affliction of love? Haven't we learned in a *Baraita*: If a person has one of these four categories of leprosy,[34] it is nothing but an altar of atonement. [The Gemara answers:] R. Yochanan does not dispute that. They are indeed an altar of atonement, but they are not afflictions of love. And if you wish, I can say: The *Baraita* refers to us [in Babylonia], whereas R. Yochanan's statement refers to them [in Eretz Yisrael].[35] And if you like, I can say this: The *Baraita* [that considers it sufferings of love] refers to leprosy that is in hidden places on the body where no one can see it, whereas Rabbi Yochanan refers to visible leprosy [which makes him repulsive to others, and therefore cannot be considered as sufferings of love].

[The Gemara asks:] And is trouble with children not considered afflictions of love? Under what circumstances? Shall I say that he had children and they died? [You cannot possibly say that his pain is not considered afflictions of love,] for did not R. Yochanan himself say: This is the bone of my tenth son that I lost.[36] [If he consoled himself and others with this, surely the death of his children must have been sufferings of love. So, how could R. Yochanan say that losing children is not sufferings of love?] [The Gemara answers:] When R. Yochanan says that having trouble with children is not sufferings of love, he means the trouble and pain of a person who never had children. [But if he had children and they died, he considers it sufferings of love.]

R. Yochanan once was sick, so R. Chanina went to visit him. R. Chanina asked him: "Do you welcome this pain?" He replied: "I want neither the pain nor the reward for that pain." R. Chanina then said, "Give me your hand." So R. Yochanan extended his hand to R. Chanina,

and thereby R. Chanina made R. Yochanan stand up and cured him. [The Gemara wonders:] Why did not R. Yochanan cure himself?[37] [The Gemara answers:] I will tell you, a prisoner cannot free himself from jail." [And a sick person cannot cure himself.]

R. Elazar once was sick. When R. Yochanan came to visit him he noticed that R. Elazar was sleeping in a dark room. R. Yochanan then uncovered his arm. Light radiated from it and lit up the room.[38] R. Yochanan then noticed that R. Elazar was weeping. He asked him: Why are you crying? Is it because you did not study enough Torah? After all, we learned: It makes no difference whether you offer much or little, as long as your intention is sincerely directed toward Heaven.[39] Are you crying because you are are needy? Not everyone merits two tables, both Torah and wealth. Is it perhaps because you have no children? This is the bone of my tenth child! [He meant to console him: I lost ten children, but I am not despondent. You are not the only one with such troubles.] R. Elazar answered: I cry because of this beauty [meaning, R. Yochanan's beauty] that will decay in the earth. R. Yochanan replied: That definitely is a good reason to cry; and together they cried. Meanwhile, R. Yochanan asked him: Do you welcome your pain? Replied R. Elazar: I want neither the pain nor the reward for the pain. R. Yochanan said: Give me your hand. R. Elazar extended his hand, and R. Yochanan made him stand up and cured him.

Once four hundred jars of wine belonging to R. Huna turned sour. R. Yehudah, the brother of R. Sala the Pious, and the other scholars came to visit him and told him: Perhaps you should examine your actions [to find out why this calamity happened to you]. R. Huna exclaimed: What! Do you suspect me of wrongdoing? They retorted: Do you suspect the Holy One, blessed be He, of punishing someone unfairly? R. Huna said: If anyone has heard any rumor against me, let him speak. They told him: We heard that you do not give your tenant his share of the vine twigs.[40] R. Huna replied: Sure, I did not give him some of the twigs, but does he leave me any? He steals everything! They said to him: This is what people mean when they say, "When you steal from a thief you also get a taste of it." [Even if your tenant steals from you, you may not withhold from him his lawful share.] R. Huna then said: I promise to give it to him in the future. Some say that after he made this pledge, miraculously, the vinegar turned to wine again; others say, the price of vinegar went up, so that it was sold for the same price as wine.

PROPER PRAYER

It is taught: Abba Binyamin says: All my life, I took great pains to fulfill two things: that my prayer should be before my bed, and that my bed should be placed in the north–south direction. [The Gemara asks:]

What is the meaning of "before my bed"? Does that mean that he prayed in front of his bed? R. Yehudah said in the name of Rav: How do you know that when you pray there should be nothing between yourself and the wall? Because it says, "And Hezekiah turned his face to the wall and prayed to God" (Isaiah 38:2). [Thus you should pray in front of the wall, not in front of the bed!] [The Gemara answers:] He did not mean that he prayed *before* his bed, he meant *near* his bed [not in a spatial sense, but near in time. He was careful to pray immediately after getting up]. The other thing Abba Binyamin mentioned was that he always made sure that his bed was lined up in a north–south direction. For R. Chama b. R. Chanina said in the name of R. Yitzchak: If someone places his bed north and south he will have male children. As it says, "Your treasure will fill their stomach, you will be satiated with children" (Psalms 17:14). [The word *tzefunecha*, treasure, is cognate to *tzafon*, north. Hence, it is interpreted to mean, "If your bed is to the north, then you will have male children."] R. Nachman b. Yitzchak said: Another benefit is that his wife will not miscarry. Here it says, "Your treasure will fill their stomach," and elsewhere it says: "When she completed her pregnancy, there were twins in her stomach" (Genesis 25:24). [Here too, "will fill their stomach" means that she will carry her pregnancy to term.]

It is taught: Abba Binyamin says: When two people enter a synagogue to pray, and one of them finishes his prayer before the other and does not wait for the other but leaves, his prayer is torn in his face. For it says, "His prayer is torn in his face; do you think that because you finished your prayer the *Shechinah* leaves the land?" (Job 18:4) [Your friend is still praying; the *Shechinah* is still there. Why are you in such a hurry to leave?] [Continues Abba Binyamin]: And that's not all, but he causes the *Shechinah* to leave Israel. For the verse concludes, "Or will the rock, *tzur*, be removed out of its place." [Explains Abba Binyamin] And "the rock, *tzur*" is a reference to the Holy One, blessed be He, for it says, "You thus ignored the Mighty One (Tzur) who bore you (Deuteronomy 32:18). [The Gemara asks]: But if he waits for his friend, what will be his reward? (6a). Yose b. Chanina says: He is rewarded with the following blessings, for it says, "If only you would heed My commands! Then your prosperity would be like a river, your triumph like the waves of the sea. Your offspring would be as many as the sand . . ." (Isaiah 48:18–19).

WHEN IS THE SHECHINAH PRESENT?

It was taught: Abba Binyamin says: A person's prayer is accepted only [when he prays] in a synagogue, for it says, "God listens to the song and the prayer" (1 Kings 8:28); thus, prayer should be recited where there is song by the *chazzan* and the congregation. Rabin b.

R. Adda says in the name of R. Yitzchak: How do you know that the Holy One, blessed be He, can be found in the synagogue? Because it says, "God stands in the divine assembly" (Psalms 82:1). And how do you know that if ten people pray together that the *Shechinah* (Divine Presence) is with them? Because it says, "God stands in the divine *eidah*, assembly" [and *eidah* applies to ten men].[41] And how do you know that if three men are sitting as judges adjudicating a case that the *Shechinah* is with them?

Because it says: "In the midst of the judges He judges" (Psalms 82:1). And how do you know that if two are sitting and studying Torah together that the *Shechinah* is with them? Because it says, "Then those who revere God have been talking to one another, [meaning two,] God has heard and noted it, and a scroll of remembrance has been written at His behest concerning those who revere God and thought upon His name" (Malachi 3:16). [The Gemara asks:] What does it mean: "and thought upon His name"? R. Ashi says: This teaches us that if a person thinks of doing a mitzvah, and he was not able to do it because of an accident, then the Torah considers it as though he had actually performed it. [The Gemara continues:] And how do you know that if one person sits and studies Torah the *Shechinah* is with him? Because it says, "Wherever I allow My name to be mentioned, I will come to you [*eilecha*, you, in the singular] and bless you" (Exodus 20:21).

[The Gemara asks:] Now, since the *Shechinah* is even with one person learning, do you have to tell me that the *Shechinah* is present when two people are learning? [The Gemara answers:] There is a difference. The words of two are written down in the book of remembrance; the words of one are not written down in the book of remembrance. [Asks the Gemara:] If the *Shechinah* is present even if two are learning, why do we need a verse for three? [The Gemara answers:] I would have thought that administering justice is making peace, but is not considered Torah study. Therefore, he teaches us that, on the contrary, if three judges are rendering true justice that is Torah, and the *Shechinah* is present. [The Gemara now asks:] Since this is the case with three, why do we need a verse for ten? [The Gemara answers:] There is a difference. When there are ten people, the *Shechinah* comes even before they begin to pray; with three judges, the *Shechinah* enters only when they actually sit down to begin the legal proceedings.

GOD'S TEFILLIN

R. Abin b. R. Abba says in the name of R. Yitzchak: How do you know that the Holy One, blessed be He, puts on *tefillin*? Because it says, "God has sworn by His right hand and by the strength of His arm" (Isaiah 62:8). By "His right hand" is meant the Torah, for it says, "At His right hand was a fiery law unto them" (Deuteronomy 33:2). "His strength" means *tefillin*, as

9

it says, "God will give strength to His people" (Psalm 29:11) [and the strength is inherent in their *tefillin*]. And how do you know that the *tefillin* are a source of strength to Israel? Because it says, "When the nations of the world will see that God's name is associated with you, and they will be in awe of you" (Deuteronomy 28:10), and we are taught: R. Eliezer the Great says: This refers to the *tefillin* of the head.

R. Nachman b. Yitzchak asked R. Chiya b. Abba: What is written in the *tefillin* of the Master of the universe? He replied: "Who is like Your people Israel, one nation on earth" (1 Chronicles 7:21). [The Gemara asks:] Is the Holy One, blessed be He, praised with the praise of Israel? [The Gemara answers:] Yes, indeed. For it says, "Today you have granted praise and importance to God" and, "God has similarly granted praise and importance to you" (Deuteronomy 26:17,18). The Holy One, blessed be He, said to Israel: You have made Me a unique essence in this world [Israel acknowledges that there is only one source of existence in the universe, the Creator], and I will make you a unique entity in the world. You have made Me a unique essence in the world, for it says, "Hear, O Israel, the Lord our God, the Lord is One" (Deuteronomy 6:4). And I will make you a unique entity in the world, for it says, "Who is like Your people Israel, one nation in the world" (1 Chronicles 17:21).

R. Acha b. Rava said to R. Ashi: Granted, this explains what is written in one of [the four] compartments of the *tefillin*.[42] But what is written in the other compartments of God's *tefillin*? He replied: They contain the following passages, "For what great nation is there," "And what great nation is there" (Deuteronomy 6:7,8); "Happy are you Israel" (Deuteronomy 33:29); "Or has God ever done miracles" (Deuteronomy 4:34); and "He will make you the highest" (Deuteronomy 26:19). [The Gemara asks:] If so, you have too many compartments [aren't there only four? You gave me six verses!]. [The Gemara answers:] Therefore you must say that, "For what great nation is there" and "And what great nation is there," which are similar, are in one compartment. "Happy are you Israel" and "Who is like Your people Israel" are in one compartment; "Or has God ever done miracles" in one compartment; and "He will make you the highest" in one compartment. (6b) And [in God's arm-*tefillin*] these verses are all in one compartment.

ABSENT FROM COMMUNAL PRAYER

(6b) Rabin b. R. Adda in the name of R. Yitzchak says further: If someone who regularly goes to the synagogue misses one day, the Holy One, blessed be He, inquires about him. For it says, "Who among you reveres God and obeys the voice of His servant, [meaning, he listens to the *chazzan*], and now walks in dark-

ness and has no light?" [i.e., and now he is absent] (Isaiah 50:10). [The Gemara explains: It depends on why he was absent.] If he went to fulfill a mitzvah, he did not "walk in darkness," and he will have the light. But if he was absent because of personal business he will have no light. The passage ends, "Let him trust in the name of God." [The Gemara asks:] How does this phrase relate to the context? [The Gemara answers:] It explains why missing communal prayer because of personal business is considered "walking in darkness." It tells you that, rather than worrying about his personal affairs, he should have trusted in God and gone to the synagogue. But he did not trust in God.

R. Yochanan said: Whenever the Holy One, blessed be He, comes into a synagogue and does not find ten persons[43] there, He immediately becomes angry. For it says, "Why, when I came, was no one there. Why, when I called, would none respond?" (Isaiah 50:2).

A PERMANENT SYNAGOGUE SEAT

R. Chelbo says in the name of R. Huna: If a person has a permanent seat where he always prays, the God of Abraham will help him. And when he dies, people will mourn his passing, lamenting: Where is this humble person! Where is this pious person! He was one of the disciples of our Father Abraham! [The Gemara asks:] And how do we know that Abraham prayed in a permanent place? Because it says, "Abraham woke up early in the morning, [hurrying back] to the place where he had been standing before God" (Genesis 19:27). And "standing" means prayer, for it says, "Then Pinchas stood up and prayed" (Psalms 106:30).

R. Yochanan says in the name of R. Shimon b. Yocha'i[44]: If someone establishes a set place for prayer, his enemies will surrender to him. And so [the prophet Nathan, speaking in God's name,] said to David, "I will designate a *place* for My people Israel and will plant them firm, so that they shall dwell secure and shall tremble no more. Evil men shall not oppress them any more as in the past" (2 Samuel 7:10). [This blessing refers to the *Bet Hamikdash*.] R. Huna pointed out an inconsistency: In the present verse it says, [When the Jewish people will pray in the *Bet Hamikdash*] their enemies will not be able to "oppress them," yet elsewhere [in Chronicles, where this prophecy is repeated,] it says that the enemies will not be able "to *destroy* them" (1 Chronicles 17:9). [The question is: does prayer in the *Bet Hamikdash* protect only from total destruction or does it also shield from oppression?] [The Gemara answers:] When the *Bet Hamikdash* was first built it had the power to protect the Jewish people from any kind of pain and oppression, but later on [after the people sinned, Heaven decreed oppression for them] but their prayers in the *Bet Hamikdash* were still effective in preventing their destruction.

10

THE MAIN REWARD
FOR CERTAIN GOOD DEEDS

R. Chelbo says in the name of R. Huna: When a person leaves the synagogue he should not take large steps, [because he thereby gives the impression that he is eager to leave]. Abbaye says: This applies only when he goes away *from* the synagogue, but when he goes *to* the synagogue, it is a mitzvah to run. For it says, "Let us *run* to know God" (Hosea 6:3). R. Zeira says: At first, when I saw the scholars running to the lecture on *Shabbat* I thought that they were desecrating the *Shabbat* [because it is forbidden to run on *Shabbat*]. But now I also run to the lecture, because I have heard that R. Tanchum taught in the name of R. Yehoshua b. Levi: A person should always—even on *Shabbat*—run to hear a lecture on *halachah*, as it says, "They shall follow after God as though a lion were roaring [i.e., as though a lion were chasing them] (Hosea 11:10). R. Zeira says: The main reward people receive for attending a Talmudic lecture is for running to it. [Most people don't fully understand the subject matter, but they receive a reward for the physical effort they make in getting there (Rashi).]

Abbaye says: The reward people receive for attending the *halachah* lecture before Yom Tov [when the lecture halls are very crowded] lies in being crushed. [A person is rewarded for not being annoyed at the discomfort.] Rava says: The main reward people receive for learning Gemara is for exerting themselves to understand the *halachah*. R. Papa says: The main reward a person receives for visiting a mourner's home is for silence; [just for being there and silently sharing the mourner's grief]. Mar Zutra says: The reward people receive for observing a fast day is for the charity they give. [By giving charity they demonstrate that they understand the meaning of fasting.] R. Sheshet says: The reward of a funeral eulogy lies [not in the substance of the oration, but] in the [plaintive] tone of voice of the speaker, which moves the audience to tears. R. Ashi says: The reward of attending a wedding lies in the speeches that should bring joy to the bride and groom.

R. Huna says: Whoever prays with his back turned to the synagogue is called wicked. For it says: "The wicked walk all around" (meaning, they walk in a turned-around way) (Psalms 12:9). Abbaye says: This only applies where he does not turn his face toward the synagogue, but if he does turn his face toward the synagogue it does not matter. There once was a man who prayed in back of the synagogue and did not turn his face toward the synagogue. Elijah passed by and appeared to him disguised as an Arab merchant. He said to the man: Are you suggesting that there are two deities? [That the people in the synagogue are praying to God, and you are praying to another deity?] He then drew his sword and killed him.

One of the scholars asked R. Bibi: What is the meaning of: *Kerum zelut liv'nei adam*, "When exalted things are neglected among men" (Psalms 12:9)? He replied: *Kerum* refers to the things that should be of primary significance in our lives, but people treat them with contempt (*zelut*).[45] [I.e., prayer that rises to the most exalted heights, yet people don't treat it with the proper respect (Rashi).] R. Yochanan and R. Eliezer offer a different interpretation of this passage: As soon as a person needs the support of his fellow men, his face changes color like the *kerum*, as it says, "When a person's face turn the color of a *kerum*, he is regarded with contempt by everyone" (Psalms 12:9). [The Gemara asks:] What is a *kerum*? When R. Dimi came [to Babylonia from Eretz Yisrael] he said: There is a bird in the coastal towns called *kerum*, and as soon as the sun begins to shine, it changes into all kinds of colors. R. Ammi and R. Assi both say: [When a person needs the support of others] it is as though he is punished by two opposite punishments: by fire and by water. For it says, "When You let men ride over our heads, it is as though we had to go through fire and water" (Psalms 66:12).

R. Chelbo further said in the name of R. Huna: You should always be careful to pray the *Minchah* (afternoon) prayer, because Elijah's prayer was answered only when the afternoon offering was to be offered, as it says, "When it was time to present the *Minchah* offering, the prophet Elijah came forward and said, 'Answer me, O God, answer me'" (1 Kings 18:36,37). "Answer me" that the fire should come down from heaven, and "answer me" that people should not say that this is witchcraft. R. Yochanan said: You should also be careful to pray the *Maariv* (evening) prayer. For it says, "Take my prayer as an incense offering, my upraised hands as an evening sacrifice" (Psalms 141:2). R. Nachman b. Yitzchak says: You should be equally careful to pray the *Shacharit* (morning) prayer. For it says: "Hear my voice, O God, at daybreak" (Psalms 5:4).

CHEERING THE GROOM
AND BRIDE

R. Chelbo further said: A person who takes part in a wedding banquet and does not try to cheer the bridegroom scorns the "five voices" that are mentioned in the verse, "[Again there shall be heard in the cities of Judah and the streets of Jerusalem] the voice of joy and the voice of gladness, the voice of the groom and the voice of the bride, the voice of those who cry, 'Give thanks to the God of Hosts'" (Jeremiah 33:11). And if he does cheer the bridegroom, what reward does he get? R. Yehoshua b. Levi says: He will merit to acquire the knowledge of the Torah that was given with five voices.[46] For it says, "On the third day, as the morning dawned, there were *kolot*, "thunderclaps" [the literal meaning of *kolot* is "voices." The plural is counted as two voices,] and lightning and a thick cloud on the mountain, and the *voice of a shofar*[47] . . . and when the *voice* of the *shofar* grew louder . . . Moses spoke, and

11

God replied with a *Voice*" (Exodus 19:16). [The Gemara asks:] That's not true! [You don't have five, you have *seven* voices.] For it says, "All the people saw the *kolot*, "voices" of the thunderclaps [and the plural counts as two]" (Exodus 20:15). [The Gemara answers:] These voices don't count. They were voices that were seen *before* the Giving of the Torah.

R. Abahu says: Cheering a bridegroom is like bringing a thanksgiving offering. For it says, "They are bringing a thanksgiving offering to the House of God" (Jeremiah 33:11). [This is the continuation of the verse that mentions the five voices that are associated with the bride and bridegroom.] R. Nachman b. Yitzchak says: It is like restoring one of the ruins of Jerusalem, for [the above-mentioned verse ends] "For I will return the captivity of the land as before, so says God."

R. Chelbo further said in the name of R. Huna: If a person is filled with the fear of God, people listen to his words. For it says, "The sum of the matter, when all has been heard: fear God and observe His commandments, for this is the whole man" (Ecclesiastes 12:13). [The Gemara asks:] What does "for this is the whole man" mean? R. Elazar says: The Holy One, blessed be He, said: It means: The whole world was created only for the sake of this Godfearing person. R. Abba b. Kahana says: He is worth as much as the whole world. R. Shimon b. Azzai says: The whole world was only created to attend to his needs.

R. Chelbo further said in the name of R. Huna: If a person knows that his friend usually greets him, he should greet him first. For it says: "Seek peace and pursue it" (Psalm 34:15). [Just being peaceful is not enough; you should make an effort to promote peace.] And if his friend greets him, and he does not return the greeting he is called a robber. For it says, "It is you who have ravaged the vineyard; that which was robbed from the poor is in your houses" (Isaiah 3:14). [What can you rob from a poor man who has nothing? You can rob him of his dignity. By not returning his greeting, you rob his very essence (Rashi).]

GOD'S PRAYER

(7a) R. Yochanan says in the name of R. Yose b. Zimra: How do we know that the Holy One, blessed is He, prays? Because it says, "I will bring them to My sacred mountain, and let them rejoice in My house of prayer" (Isaiah 56:7). It does not say "in *their* house of prayer," but *"My* house of prayer." From here you see that the Holy One, blessed be He, prays. [The Gemara asks:] What does God pray? R. Zutra b. Tobi said in the name of Rav: May it be My will that My mercy should suppress My anger, and that My attribute of mercy should dominate all My other attributes, so that I may conduct Myself with My children with mercy, and that I should deal with them, not according to the strict letter of the law [but do for them more than they have rightfully earned].

AN ORDINARY PERSON'S BLESSING

We have learned in a *Baraita*: R. Yishmael b. Elisha, [the High Priest,] said: It once happened that on Yom Kippur I entered into the innermost part of the Sanctuary to burn the incense[48] and saw Akatriel Y-h, the Lord of Hosts, seated on a high and exalted throne. He said to me: "Yishmael, My son, bless Me!" I said to Him: May it be Your will that Your mercy should suppress Your anger, and that Your mercy should dominate all Your other attributes, so that You will conduct Yourself with Your children with mercy, and deal with them, not according to the strict letter of the law [but do for them more than what is due to them]. And God nodded to me with His head [as if to say, "Amen" (Rashi)]. This teaches us that the blessing given by an ordinary person should not be taken lightly.

R. Elazar says in the name of R. Chanina[49]: A blessing given by an ordinary person should not be taken lightly, because we know of two men who were prominent in their generation, who were blessed by two ordinary people, and in each case the blessing was fulfilled. They were: David and Daniel. David was blessed by Aravnah, as it says, "Aravnah said to King [David], 'May God your Lord accept you'" (2 Samuel 24:23).[50] Daniel was blessed by King Darius, as it says, "Your God, whom you serve so regularly, will deliver you" (Daniel 6:17).[51]

GOD'S ANGER LASTS AN INSTANT

R. Yochanan says in the name of R. Yose: How do you know that you should not appease someone when he is angry? For it says, "My Presence will go, and I will do according to your will" (Exodus 33:14). The Holy One, blessed be He, said to Moses: [Don't try to appease Me now]. Wait until My angry face passes, then I will do according to your will.[52] [The Gemara asks:] Is anger an attribute of the Holy One, blessed be He? [The Gemara answers:] Yes. For we have learned: It says, "God is angry every single day" (Psalms 7:12). And how long does this anger last? An instant. And how long is an instant? One fifty-eight thousand eight hundred and eighty-eighth part of an hour. And no human being has ever been able to pinpoint that instant, except the wicked Balaam, about whom it says, "He knows the knowledge of the Highest One" (Numbers 24:16). [How can this be true?] He could not even figure out what his animal wanted,[53] then how could he know the knowledge of the Most High!

So what does this mean? It comes to teach us that Balaam knew how to pinpoint the exact instant in which the Holy One, blessed be He, gets angry. And this is what the prophet meant when he said to Israel, "My people, remember what Balak the king of Moab plotted against you, and what Balaam the son of Beor answered him . . . and you will recognize the righteous acts of God" (Micah 6:5). What does this mean? R. Elazar says: The Holy One, blessed be He, said to Israel: You should know, how many righteous acts I performed for you by not being angry in the days when the wicked Balaam [wanted to curse you]. For had I allowed that latent instant of anger to emerge, not a single remnant would have been left of Israel.[54] And this is what Balaam meant when he said to Balak, "How can I pronounce a curse if God will not grant a curse? What divine wrath can I conjure if God will not be angry?" (Numbers 23:8). This teaches us that God was not angry all these days [that Balaam wanted to curse Israel].

And how long does His anger last? A moment. And how long is a moment? R. Avin says: As long as it takes to say the word *rega*, "moment." And how do you know that He is angry for only one moment? Because it says, "For His anger endures only for a moment [*rega*], but His favor is for a lifetime" (Psalms 30:6). Or if you wish you may infer it from the following verse, "Hide for just a moment, until the anger passes" (Isaiah 26:20). And when is He angry? Abbaye said: During the first three hours of the day, when the comb of the rooster is white, and it stands on one leg, that is when the moment of anger occurs. [The Gemara asks:] But the rooster stands like that all the time? [The Gemara answers:] At other times it has red streaks in its white comb, but during this time in the morning, when it is the moment of anger, it does not have any red streaks.

There was a heretic in the neighborhood of R. Yehoshua b. Levi who used to annoy him very much with his [spurious] interpretations of various verses [since he did not recognize the Oral Torah]. One day, R. Yehoshua b. Levi [decided that he wanted to curse him, and in order for that curse to take effect he would have to pinpoint the moment of God's anger]. So he took a rooster and placed it between the legs of his bed and watched it, thinking that as soon as he saw the sign he would curse the heretic. When the moment arrived he was dozing. When he woke up he said: We learn from this, that it is not right to do this [to curse people, even though R. Yehoshua did not do it for his own honor but for the honor of the Torah]. For it says, "His mercies are on all His works" (Psalm 145:9); and it also says, "It is not good for a righteous man to punish others" (Proverbs 17:26).

We learned in the name of R. Meir: [Why is the moment of anger in the morning?] At the time when the sun rises, and all the kings of the East and the West put their crowns on their heads and bow down to the sun, the Holy One, blessed be He, becomes angry.

R. Yochanan further says in the name of R. Yose: One feeling of remorse that a person brings on by himself is better than many lashings, for it says, "She [Israel] will run after her lovers [other gods,] until she will finally say, 'I will go and return to my first husband [God], for then I fared better than now'" (Hosea 2:9). [The verse praises the self-induced feeling of remorse.] Resh Lakish says: Self-reproach is better than a hundred lashings, for it says, "A rebuke enters deeper into the heart of one who understands, than a hundred stripes into a fool" (Proverbs 17:10).

WHY DO THE RIGHTEOUS SUFFER?

R. Yochanan further says in the name of R. Yose: Three things Moses asked of the Holy One, blessed be He, and they were granted to him. [We know that they were granted, because at the end of his request God replied, "I will also fulfill this request of yours" (Exodus 33:17) (Rashi).] He asked that the *Shechinah* (Divine Presence) should rest on Israel, and it was granted, for it says, "You [God] are coming with us" (Exodus 33:16). He asked that the *Shechinah* should not rest on the idol-worshipping nations, and it was granted, for it says, "So that we are distinguished, I and Your people." And he asked that he should be shown the ways of the Holy One, blessed be He, and it was granted, for it says, "Allow me to know Your ways" (Exodus 33:13). Moses said to God: Master of the universe, why is it that some righteous men prosper and other righteous men suffer? Why is it that some wicked men prosper and others suffer? [How is God's justice manifesting itself?] God replied: Listen, Moses, the righteous man who prospers is a righteous man who is the son of a righteous man; the righteous man who suffers is a righteous man the son of a wicked man. The wicked man who prospers is a wicked man the son of a righteous man; the wicked man who suffers is a wicked man the son of a wicked man.

[The Gemara now explains:] The master said above: The righteous man who prospers is a righteous man the son of a righteous man; the righteous man who suffers is a righteous man the son of a wicked man. [The Gemara asks:] But it is not that way! For we have two contradictory verses. One verse says, "He keeps in mind the sins of the fathers to their children" (Exodus 34:7), [in other words, children die because of the sins of their fathers,] and we have another verse that says, "Children shall not die for the fathers" (Deuteronomy 24:16). Thus there is a contradiction between the two verses. We answer: There is no difficulty.

The verse referring to children who do suffer for their fathers' sins, speaks about children who continue the actions of their fathers, and the verse dealing with children who do not suffer, refers to children who do not continue the actions of their fathers. [At any rate, you see that a righteous man who does not follow in his father's wicked ways does not suffer. Then how can you say that a righteous man who suffers is the son of a wicked man?] [The Gemara answers: That was not God's answer. It has nothing to do with who his father was.] This is what God told Moses: A righteous man who prospers is a completely righteous man; the

13

righteous man who suffers is a not completely righteous man. The wicked man who prospers is not a perfectly wicked man; the wicked man who suffers is a perfectly wicked man.

The saying of R. Yochanan [that all three of Moses' requests were granted] is disputed by R. Meir who says: Only two requests were granted to Moses, but one, [his request to understand God's ways] was not granted. For it says, "I will be gracious to whom I will be gracious," although you may think that this person does not deserve grace, "and I will show mercy on whom I will show mercy" even though he may not deserve it (Exodus 33:19). [Thus, God's ways cannot be known.]

[And another indication that God did not grant Moses' third request is in the verse,] "[God] said, 'You cannot see My face" (Exodus 33:20). We learned in the name of R. Yehoshua b. Korcha: This is what the Holy One, blessed is He, said to Moses: When I wanted you to see Me, you did not want to see My face, [at the burning bush where Moses hid his face (Exodus 3:6)]; now that you want, I don't want [an implied criticism of Moses]. This goes against the interpretation of this verse by R. Shmuel b. Nachmeini who said: [Moses was not criticized for hiding his face, rather, he was rewarded for it]. As a reward for three things Moses received three gifts: As a reward for "Moses hid his face" (Exodus 3:6) [at the burning bush] he was granted the radiance of his face.[55] For "because he was afraid" [for being in awe of God and not looking] he was rewarded that "[seeing his radiance, the people were afraid to come close to him"] (Exodus 34:30). And for "to look," [for not looking at the Divine] he was rewarded that "he sees a true picture of God" (Numbers 12:8). [This is the vision of God's back (Rashi).] For it says, "I will remove My hand, and you will see My back" (Exodus 33:23). R. Huna b. Bizna said in the name of R. Shimon the Pious: This means that the Holy One, blessed be He, showed Moses the knot of the *tefillin*.

THEY PRAISED GOD

(7b) R. Yochanan said further in the name of R. Shimon b. Yocha'i: Since the day that the Holy One, blessed be He, created this world, no one called Him, *Adon* (Lord), until Abraham came and called Him *Adon*, for it says, "[Abraham] said, 'My Lord, *Adonai*, God, how can I really know that [Eretz Yisrael] will be mine?'" (Genesis 15:8). Rav said: Even Daniel's prayer was answered only in the merit of Abraham, for [Daniel prayed], "And now, our God, pay heed to the prayer of Your servant and to his plea, and show Your favor to Your desolate Sanctuary, for the Lord's sake" (Daniel 9:17). He should have said: "For Your sake," but he meant, "For the sake of Abraham who referred to You as *Adon*, Lord, and proclaimed You the true Lord."

R. Yochanan said further in the name of R. Shimon b. Yocha'i: Since the day that the Holy One, blessed be He, created His world no one praised God until Leah came and praised Him. For [when Judah was born, Leah said:] "This time I will praise God" (Genesis 29:35).

THE NAMES REUBEN AND RUTH

[Leah's first-born son was Reuben.] Why was he called Reuben? R. Elazar said: Leah said: Look, what a difference there is between my son [Reuben] and [Esau] the son of my father-in-law. [The name Reuben is seen as a combination of *re'u*, "look" and *bein*, "between".] [Esau] the son of my father-in-law sold his birthright voluntarily, for it says, "He sold his birthright to Jacob" (Genesis 25:33). Yet, in spite of that, look what it says about him, "Esau hated Jacob (Genesis 27:41), and, "Esau said, 'Isn't he rightly called Jacob (Ya'akov)! He went behind my back (*akav*) twice.'" (Genesis 27:36). R. Elazar says that [Leah continued:] But my son Reuben, even though Joseph took his birthright from him against his will, as it says, "[Reuben] was the first-born, but when he defiled his father's bed,[56] his birthright was given to the sons of Joseph" (1 Chronicles 5:1), nevertheless, he was not jealous of him, for it says, "Reuben heard these words and tried to rescue Joseph [from his brothers]" (Genesis 37:21).

[The Gemara now considers the etymology of the name Ruth.] Why was she called Ruth? R. Yochanan said: Because she had the merit that David came forth from her, who [*ravah*,] satiated the Holy One, blessed be He, with songs and hymns. [The name Ruth is seen as derived from *ravah*, "to saturate, to soak."] [The Gemara asks:] How do we know that the name of a person has an effect on his actions? R. Elazar says: Because it says, "Come and see what God has done, how he has made *shammot*, desolation, on the earth" (Psalms 46:9). R. Elazar expounds: Don't read *shammot*, "desolation," but *sheimot*, "names." [Thus, the name of a person reflects the purpose and essence of his soul in this world.]

GOD'S BLESSINGS
ARE NEVER RESCINDED

R. Yochanan further said in the name of R. Yose:[57] No word of blessing that the Holy One, blessed be He, uttered, even a conditional blessing, was ever retracted by Him. How do we know this? From our teacher Moses. For it says, "[God said to Moses,] 'Just leave Me alone, and I will destroy them [Israel], obliterating their name from under the heavens. I will then make you into a nation greater and more numerous than they'" (Deuteronomy 9:14). Although Moses prayed that this decree should be rescinded, and it was indeed annulled, nevertheless, the blessing of, "I will then make you into a nation greater and more numerous than they," was fulfilled in his children. For it says,

"The sons of Moses: Gershom and Eliezer . . . And the sons of Eliezer were: Rehabiah the chief . . . the sons of Rehabiah *were very numerous*" (1 Chronicles 23:15,16). And R. Yosef learned: They were more than sixty myriads. This is inferred from the word *rivyah*, "increase," as it occurs in two different contexts. It says in the present verse, "They were very numerous (*ravu*)," and elsewhere it says, "The Israelites were fertile and prolific, and they became numerous (*vayirbu*)" [and when the children of Israel left Egypt they numbered about 600,000 adult males (Exodus 12:37)].

DAVID AND ABSALOM

R. Yochanan further said in the name of R. Shimon b. Yocha'i[58] : Bringing up a bad child in one's house is worse than the war of Gog and Magog [which will take place before the coming of *Mashiach*, and is described as a period of great suffering]. For it says, "A song of David when he fled from his son Absalom" (Psalms 3:1). And in the next verse David says, "O God, my foes are so many! Many are those who attack me." But when speaking of the war of Gog and Magog, David says, "Why do nations create such an uproar, and peoples mutter in vain" (Psalms 2:1) [In other words, David is not overly troubled by the prospect of the war of Gog and Magog.] He certainly does not describe it in terms of, "My foes are so many!"

[The Gemara now analyzes the first part of this verse,] "A song of David when he fled from his son Absalom." What! "A *song* of David" this is called? It rather should be called, "A *lament* of David." R. Shimon b. Avishalom said: [Let me explain it with a parable.] What can this be compared to? To a man who has a note coming due. Before he pays it he is depressed and worries about it. After he has paid it, he is happy and relieved. So it was with David. When the Holy One, blessed be He, told him, "I will make a calamity rise against you from within your own house" (2 Samuel 12:11), he was worried. He thought: Maybe it will be a slave or a bastard who will [revolt against me and will] have no pity on me. When he saw that it was Absalom, he was happy, [thinking that his own son would have mercy on him]. That's why he said, "A song of David."

FIGHTING AGAINST
THE WICKED

R. Yochanan further said in the name of R. Shimon b. Yocha'i: It is permitted to fight the wicked in this world. For it says, "Those who forsake the Torah praise the wicked, but those who keep the Torah fight them" (Proverbs 28:4). We also learned in a *Baraita*: R. Dosta'i b. R. Mattun says: It is permitted to fight with the wicked in this world. For it says, "Those who forsake the Torah praise the wicked . . ." And if a person should whisper in your ear and tell you: But it says,

"Do not fight with evildoers, and don't be envious of wrongdoers" (Psalms 37:1), then you should tell him: A timid person interprets the verse that way, but the real meaning of this verse is: "Don't compete with the evildoers and strive to be like them, and don't be envious of wrongdoers, trying to be like them." And so it says, "Do not envy sinners in your heart, but only God-fearing men, at all times (Proverbs 23:17).

[The Gemara interjects:] But it is not like that! For R. Yitzchak said: If you see a wicked man on whom fortune is smiling, don't start up with him, for it says, "[If you see that the evildoer] hit a streak of good luck, [don't get in his way]" (Psalms 10:5). And not only that, but even in a court case he is going to win, for it says, "Your judgments are far beyond him" (Psalms 10:5) [in other words, he places himself above the law]. And what's more, [when things are going his way] he will see his enemies fall, for it says in the same verse, "He snorts at all his foes."

[The Gemara answers:] There is no contradiction. The one [R. Yitzchak, who says you should not fight against the wicked] speaks of quarreling about personal differences; the other [R. Yochanan, who says that it is permitted to fight with the wicked] refers to a confrontation over religious issues. And if you wish I can say that both speak of fighting about religious issues, and there still is no difficulty. [It all depnds on the kind of evildoer you are contending with.] The one [R. Yitzchak] speaks of a wicked man on whom fortune is smiling; the other [R. Yochanan] speaks of a wicked man on whom fortune is not smiling. Or, if you wish, I can say that both speak of a wicked man on whom fortune is smiling, and there still is no contradiction. The one [R. Yochanan] speaks of a perfectly righteous man; [he need not be concerned about fighting the evildoer;] the other [R. Yitzchak] speaks of a man who is not perfectly righteous; [he should not take on an evildoer].

For R. Huna said: What is the meaning of the verse, "Why do you countenance treachery, and stand idly by when the one in the wrong devours the one in the right?" (Habakuk 1:13). [The Gemara asks:] Can the wicked swallow the righteous? Doesn't it say, "God will not abandon him in his hand" (Psalms 37:33)? And doesn't it also say, "No harm befalls the righteous" (Proverbs 12:21)? [The Gemara answers:] You must therefore say: [It all depends on who is the righteous one, and who is the wicked one.] The evildoer can swallow up someone who is more righteous than he is, but he cannot swallow up a perfectly righteous man. And if you want I can answer you: It is different when fortune is smiling on the wicked man; [then anything can happen].

PRAYING WITH
THE CONGREGATION

R. Yochanan further said in the name of R. Shimon b. Yocha'i: The service of the Torah is greater than the study of Torah [meaning: a person derives more benefit from serving a great Torah scholar and observing his daily conduct, than from actually studying under him]. For it says, "Elisha son of Shafat who poured water on the hands of Elijah is here" (2 Kings 3:11) [i.e., he personally attended him]. It does not say, "who learned from him" but, "who poured water." This teaches you that the service of Torah [i.e., attending to a Torah scholar] is greater than the learning of Torah.

R. Yitzchak said to R. Nachman: Why don't you come to the synagogue to pray? He replied: I cannot, [I am too weak]. R. Yitzchak suggested: Let me gather ten people, and let us pray with a *minyan* [in your house]. R. Nachman replied: It's too much trouble for me. I don't feel up to it. R. Yitzchak persisted: At least instruct the messenger of the congregation to let you know the exact time that the congreagtion is praying, so that you can pray at the same time as the congregation. R. Nachman asked: Why is this so important? R. Yitzchak replied: For R. Yochanan says in the name of R. Shimon b. Yocha'i: (8a) What is the meaning of the verse, "As for me, may my prayer to You, O God, be at an opportune time" (Psalms 69:14). When is it an opportune time? When the congregation is praying together. R. Yose b. R. Chanina says: You learn it from here, "Thus says God: In an hour of favor I answer you" (Isaiah 49:8). R. Acha b. R. Chanina says: You learn it from here, "See, God does not despise the mighty" (Job 36:5) [i.e., God never scorns the communal prayers of the congregation]. And it says, "He redeems my soul in peace, from the battle against me, because of the multitudes that were with me" (Psalms 55:19) [i.e., the multitudes that prayed with me (Rashi)].

We also learned this in a *Baraita*: R. Nathan says: How do we know that the Holy One, blessed be He, does not despise the prayer of the congregation? Because it says, "See God does not despise the mighty" (Job 36:5), and it says, "He redeems my soul in peace, from the battle against me, because of the multitudes that were with me" (Psalms 55:19). The Holy One, blessed be He, says: If a person is involved in the study of the Torah, in performing acts of kindness, and prays with the congregation, I consider it as if he had redeemed Me and My children from among the nations of the world.

R. Levi[59] said: Whoever has a synagogue in his town and does not go there to pray is called a bad neighbor. For it says, "Thus says God, 'As for My wicked neighbors who touch the heritage that I gave to My people Israel'" (Jeremiah 12:14). ["The heritage" refers to the synagogue. The wicked neighbor only "touches" it—[i.e., he treats it casually and visits it infrequently]. And that's not all; he also brings exile on himself and his children. For the verse concludes, "I am going to uproot them from their soil, and I will uproot the House of Judah out of the midst of them."

They told R. Yochanan [who lived in Eretz Yisrael] that there were old men in Babylon. He was surprised to hear that and exclaimed: It says, "In order to prolong your life and the lives of your children *on the land*" (Deuteronomy 11:21), but not outside Eretz Yisrael! When they explained to him that the old men in Babylon came early to the synagogue and left it late, he said: That is what helps them to live long. R. Yehoshua said the same to his children: Come early to the synagogue and leave it late so that you may live long.

R. Acha b. Chanina says: What verse can be cited to support this? "Happy is the man who listens to Me, coming early to My gates each day, waiting at the posts of My doors" (Proverbs 8:34). And the next verse says, "For he who finds Me, finds life."

R. Chisda says: A person should always enter two doors into the synagogue. What is the meaning of "two doors"? Say: The distance of [the width of] two doors, and then pray. [I.e., don't stay near the entrance because it looks as if you are anxious to leave (Rashi).]

WHAT DOES "IN THE TIME OF FINDING" MEAN?

"For this let every pious man pray to You in the time of finding" (Psalms 32:6). What does "in the time of finding" mean? R. Chanina says: It refers to finding a wife. For it says: "He who finds a wife has found happiness" (Proverbs 19:22). In Eretz Yisrael, when a man got married they used to ask him: *Matza* or *motzei*? "*Matza*," for it says, "He who finds [*matza*] a wife has found happiness." [Or is it perhaps] "*motzei*," for it says, "Now, I find (*motzei*) woman more bitter than death" (Ecclesiastes 7:26).[60] R. Nathan says: "In the time of finding" refers to finding the Torah, for it says, "For he who finds Me finds life" (Proverbs 9:35). R. Nachman b. Yitzchak says: "In the time of finding" refers to finding a peaceful death, for it says, "To find death" (Psalms 68:21).

We have learned a similar *Baraita*: There are 903 different kinds of death, for it says, "To find [*totza'ot*] death," and the numeric value of *totza'ot* is 903. The worst kind of death is the croup, the easiest death is "death by a kiss" [as was experienced by Moses and Aaron]. Croup is like a thorn in a ball of wool, which you have to pull out with a forceful yank, and inevitably there will be some damage to the wool. Some people say: It is like pulling a rope through the hole in a ship [which causes great friction because the rope fits very tightly into the hole (Rashi)]. On the other hand, "death by a kiss" is like lifting a hair out of a glass of milk. R. Yochanan said: "The time of finding" refers to being buried. R. Chanina said: Which Scripture can be cited to support this? "Who rejoice to exultation, and are glad to reach the grave" (Job 3:22).

Rabbah b. R. Shila: The popular saying goes: A man should pray for peace even to the last shovelful of earth that is thrown on his grave. Mar Zutra says: "The time of finding" refers to finding an outhouse. [In the marshy soil of Babylon it was difficult to dig an outhouse, and people were forced to go out into the fields to answer the call of nature; therefore a person should pray to find one near his house (Rashi).] They said in Eretz Yisrael: Mar Zutra's interpretation is the best of all.

THE FOUR CUBITS OF *HALACHAH*

Rav said in the name of Rafram b. Papa: Master, please tell us some of those fine things having to do with the synagogue that you said in the name of R. Chisda. He replied: This is what R. Chisda said: What is the meaning of the verse, "God loves the gates of Zion [*Tziyon*] more than all the dwellings of Jacob"? (Psalms 87:2). The meaning is: God loves the gates that are *metzuyanim*, designated[61] to learn *halachah*, more than the synagogues and houses of study. This is in line with the following saying of R. Chiya b. Ammi in the name of Ulla: Since the day that the *Bet Hamikdash* was destroyed, the Holy One, blessed be He, has nothing in this world except the four cubits of *halachah*. [Commenting on this,] Abbaye said: Initially, I would study at home and pray in the synagogue. However, once I heard that R. Chiya b. Ammi said in the name of Ulla: "Since the day that the *Bet Hamikdash* was destroyed, the Holy One, blessed be He, has nothing in this world except the four cubits of *halachah*," I pray only in the place where I study.

R. Ammi and R. Assi prayed only between the pillars of the *Bet Hamidrash* (study hall) where they used to learn, although there were thirteen synagogues in Tiberias.

SOUND ADVICE AND WORDS OF WISDOM

R. Chiya b. Ammi further said in the name of Ulla: You should always live in the same town as your teacher. For as long as Shimei ben Geira was alive Solomon did not marry the daughter of Pharaoh[62] [in deference to Shimei who was his teacher]. [The Gemara asks:] But we learned in a *Baraita* that you should *not* [live in the same place as your teacher]? [The Gemara answers:] That presents no difficulty. [It depends on your relationship with your teacher.] If you are submissive to him you should live close to him. But if you are headstrong, you had better keep your distance.

R. Chiya b. Ammi further said in the name of Ulla: A person who works for a living is greater than one who fears heaven. For concerning a person who fears heaven it says, "Happy is the man who fears God" (Psalms 112:1), whereas concerning one who works for a living it says, "When you eat the labor of your hands, you are happy, and it is well with you" (Psalms 128:2). The phrase "You are happy" refers to this world; "it is

well with you" refers to the world to come. [Thus he has a double blessing.] But about the man who fears heaven it does not say, "it is well with you." [He has only one blessing.]

(8b) R. Yehoshua b. Levi said to his children: Be careful to respect an old man who has forgotten what he has learned through no fault of his own, [but due to illness or the pressures of earning a livelihood (Rashi)], because it has been said: Both the whole tablets and the broken pieces of the first tablets were placed in the Ark.[63]

Rava said to his children: When you are cutting meat, don't cut it on your hand. Why not? Some people say because of danger [that they might cut themselves], and others say, in order not to spoil the meal, [for even a minor cut will cause blood to drip from the hands and make the food repulsive to the people seated at the table (Rashi)]. [Two other things] Rava told his children: Do not sit on the bed of an Aramaean woman, and do not pass behind a synagogue when the congregation is praying. What is the meaning of: Don't sit on the bed of an Aramaean woman? Some say that it means: Don't go to sleep before reciting the Bedtime *Shema* [otherwise your bed will be like that of an Aramaean]. Some say it means: Do not marry a convert. And some say it is to be taken literally: Don't sit on the bed of an Aramaean woman, because of an incident that happened to R. Papa. For R. Papa once visited an Aramaean woman [to pay her the money he owed her]. She pulled out a bed and asked him to sit down. He replied: I will not sit down until you lift up the bed [so that I can see what is underneath]. She picked up the bed, and there was a dead child. [Her scheme was to have R. Papa sit down on the bed and then accuse him of crushing and killing the child (Rashi)].

Therefore, the Sages said: It is not permitted to sit on the bed of an Aramaean woman. [The third thing Rava told his children was:] And do not pass behind a synagogue when the congregation is praying. This substantiates the opinion of R. Yehoshua b. Levi, for R. Yehoshua b. Levi said: It is forbidden for a person to pass behind a synagogue while the congregation is praying, [because it seems as if he is not interested in praying].

It has been taught in a *Baraita*: R. Akiva says: Because of three things I like the Medes:[64] When they cut meat they do it only on the table [and not on their hands]; when they kiss, they kiss only the hand [because of the saliva (Rashi)]; and when they confer with one another they will not do it indoors but they will go out into the field, [because "the walls have ears"; you never know who may be listening (Rashi)]. R. Adda b. Ahava says: Which verse supports this? It says, "Jacob sent word and summoned Rachel and Leah *to the field* where his flock was (Genesis 31:4) [and only there did he talk to them about leaving Laban]. It has been taught: R. Gamliel says: Because of three things

I like the Persians: They behave modestly during their meals, they behave modestly in the lavatory, and they behave modestly in sexual matters. R. Yosef expounded the verse, "I have summoned My consecrated ones" (Isaiah 13:3). He said: This refers to the Persians who are consecrated and destined for Gehinnom [i.e., God has summoned the rulers of Persia to destroy the Babylonian empire (Rashi)].[65]

DISCUSSION ABOUT THE EXODUS

(9a) R. Abba said: Everyone agrees that the redemption of the children of Israel from Egypt occurred in the evening. For it says, "God your Lord brought you out of Egypt at night" (Deuteronomy 16:1). Everyone also agrees that they did not actually leave Egypt until the next morning, for it says, "On the day after the Passover sacrifice, the Israelites left triumphantly" (Numbers 33:3). But there is disagreement about the definition of the term *chipazon*, "in haste," in the verse, "You must eat the [Passover offering] *in haste*." [Starting at midnight, the Egyptians were "in haste" to make the Israelites leave as soon as possible, what with all the first-born dying; and in the morning, the Israelites were "in haste" to leave. The question is: Whose "haste" is the verse referring to?] R. Elazar b. Azariah says: It refers to the haste of the Egyptians [to make the Israelites leave]. R. Akiva says: It refers to the haste of the Israelites [in the morning when they wanted to depart].

We have also learned a *Baraita* that conforms with this: It is written, "God your Lord brought you out of Egypt at night." But did they actually leave at night? Did they not, in fact, leave in the morning, as it says, "On the day after the Passover sacrifice, the Israelites left triumphantly"? This teaches you that the redemption really took effect the evening before [when the Egyptians urged the Israelites to leave; but they did not listen to them and did not leave until the next morning, in compliance with God's intructions.][66]

It says, "[God said to Moses,] 'Please [*na*], speak discreetly to the people, [and tell them to take gold and silver things from the Egyptians when they leave]'" (Exodus 11:2). In the school of R. Yannai they said: The word *na* means "please." The Holy One, blessed be He, said to Moses: Please, go and tell the children of Israel: I beg of you, borrow from the Egyptians articles of silver and gold, so that (9b) the righteous Abraham should not say: God did fulfill for them the promise of, "They will be enslaved and oppressed" (Genesis 15:13), but the other part of that promise, that "they will then leave with great wealth," He did not fulfill for them. When Moses told this to the children of Israel, they replied: What! You want us to take silver and gold? We would be happy if we could just leave ourselves! [The Gemara gives a parable:] You can compare it to a person who is locked up in a prison,

and people tell him: Tomorrow they will release you from prison and give you a lot of money. And he answered them: Please, just let me go free *today*. I don't ask for anything else!

It says, "[The Egyptians] let them have what they asked for" (Exodus 12:36). R. Ammi says: This teaches you that the borrowing was done by force. Some say, it was the Egyptians who were forced to lend it to them. Others say: No, it was the Israelites who were forced to borrow from the Egyptians. Those that say that it was the Egyptians that were forced to lend cite as proof the verse, "Housewives are sharing in the spoils" (Psalms 68:18). And those that say that it was the Israelites that were forced to borrow explain that the Israelites were reluctant to borrow because it meant carrying a great deal of excess baggage.

It says, "[The Israelites] thus drained Egypt of its wealth" (Exodus 12:34). R. Ammi comments: This teaches you that they left Egypt empty, like a bird trap without corn [for bait. A trap without bait will be empty]. Resh Lakish said: They left Egypt empty, like the bottom of the sea [where there are no fish (Rashi)].

It says, ["God said:] 'I Will Be Who I Will Be'" (Exodus 3:14). [God's name implies a double promise of Divine Presence.] The Holy One, blessed be He, said to Moses: Go and tell Israel: I was with you during this servitude while you were enslaved in Egypt, and I will be with you during the servitude of other exiles. Moses replied: Why not deal with the evil when its time comes! [Why mention other exiles? Let's cross that bridge when we come to it.] God answered: You are right, go and tell them, "*I Will Be* sent me to you" (Exodus 3:13) [and do not say, I Will Be Who I Will Be sent me].

[When he challenged the false prophets of Baal, Elijah prayed that fire should descend from heaven to prove that he was God's true prophet. He said,] "Answer me, O God, answer me!" (1 Kings 18:37). R. Abbahu said: Why did Elijah say twice "Answer me"? The two times "answer me" teach you that Elijah said to the Holy One, blessed be He: Master of the universe, [first] *answer me* that a fire should come down from heaven and consume whatever is on the altar; and *answer me* [again] that the people should not say that the fire was produced through witchcraft. For it says, "You have turned their hearts backward" (1 Kings 18:37). [You caused the people to be blind to Your Presence; now make them perceive Your Presence.]

THE *SHEMA* AND *SHEMONEH ESREI* IN THE MORNING

It has been taught: R. Meir says: The morning *Shema* may be recited from the time that you can tell the difference between a wolf and a dog. R. Akiva says: Between a regular donkey and a wild donkey. Others say: From the time that you can recognize your friend from a distance of four cubits. R. Huna says: The *halachah* is according to the others. Abbaye says: With regard to the time for putting on the *tefillin* the *halachah* is according to the others; with regard to *Shema*, you should follow the practice of the *vatikin* (pious men). [And when do the *vatikin* recite the *Shema*?] R. Yochanan says: The *vatikin* used to finish saying the *Shema* at sunrise, in order to recite the *geulah* [the *berachah Ga'al Yisrael*, which is part of the *berachot* of *Shema*] immediately before the *Shemoneh Esrei*. And when they end the *Shema* at sunrise, the result is that they say the *Shemoneh Esrei* at the first possible moment. R. Zeira said: What verse supports this, [that it is a mitzvah to pray at sunrise]? The verse, "Let them fear you with the sun [i.e., recite the *Shema* at sunrise. In other words, when the sun rises, *Shema* has already been concluded, and we begin the *Shemoneh Esrei*]. The verse continues: "Before the moon, for generations on end," (Psalms 72:5) [meaning, may this reverence continue at the *Minchah* (afternoon) prayer which should be said before sunset (Rashi)].

R. Yose b. Elyakim testified in the name of the holy congregation of Jerusalem: If you join the *berachah* of *Ga'al Yisrael* to the *Shemoneh Esrei*, [as the *vatikin* do, finishing *Shema* at precisely the moment of the beginning of sunrise (*Tosafot*),] you will be safe from harm that entire day. R. Zeira said: That is not so! For I did join in the prescribed way, and I ran into harm's way. They asked him: What happened? Do you mean the fact that you had to carry a myrtle branch to the king? [You call that being harmed?] You should have paid money for the opportunity to see the king! For R. Yochanan says: A person should make an effort to run to see the kings of Israel. And not only to see the kings of Israel, but even to see a gentile king, so that if he is found worthy [to live to see the restoration of the Jewish kingdom] he will be able to understand the difference between the kings of Israel and the kings of the gentiles.

R. Ila'a said to Ulla: When you go to Eretz Yisrael, ask how my brother R. Berona is doing, in the presence of all the scholars standing there, for he is a great man who rejoices to perform mitzvot. It happened one time that he was able to join *Ga'al Yisrael* to the *Shemoneh Esrei*, and he did not stop smiling all day.

THE FIRST TWO PSALMS ARE ONE

[The Gemara asks:] Let us see: The verse, "May the expressions of my mouth . . . find favor before You" (Psalms 19:15), is an appropriate ending of the *Shemoneh Esrei*, and it would also be a fitting phrase to start the *Shemoneh Esrei*. In what sense would it be fitting as an opening phrase? Because it suggests: I want to speak now; I want to start my *Shemoneh Esrei* [and I ask You: Please accept the words of my mouth]. [Since it is suitable as an opening and an ending of the *Shemoneh Esrei*,] why did the Sages institute it only at the *end* of

the *Shemoneh Esrei*? Let it be recited at the beginning? R. Yehudah b. R. Shimon b. Pazzi said: Since David said it only after eighteen chapters of the Psalms, [it is at the end of Psalm 19], the Sages too enacted that it should be said after eighteen *berachot*.[67]

[The Gemara asks:] But those eighteen chapters of the Psalms are really nineteen? [The Gemara answers:] "Happy is the man" and "Why are nations in an uproar" [the first verses of psalms 1 and 2] are actually one chapter. For R. Yehudah b. R. Shimon b. Pazzi said: David composed one hundred and three chapters of Psalms, and he did not say "*Halleluyah*" until he saw the downfall of the wicked, as it says, "May sinners disappear from the earth, and the wicked be no more, Bless the Lord, O my soul, Hallleluyah" (Psalms 104:35). [This verse is the last verse of Psalm 104. Therefore, the Gemara asks:] Now are these one hundred and three psalms? There are one hundred and four! [The Gemara answers:] This proves that "Happy is the man" and "Why are the nations in an uproar" [the first two psalms] are one chapter. [And how do we know that it is those two psalms that form one chapter and no other two?] Because R. Shmuel b. Nachmeini said in the name of R. Yochanan:

(10a) Every chapter that David truly loved he started with the word *Ashrei* ("Happy") and ended with *Ashrei*. He began the first chapter of Psalms with *Ashrei*, for it says, "*Ashrei*, "Happy is the man," and he concluded with *Ashrei*, for it says [at the end of Psalm 2] "*Ashrei*, Happy are all who take refuge in Him" (Psalms 2:12). [This is proof that the first two chapters are one.][68]

THE WISDOM OF BERURIAH

There were some robbers [*biryonim*[69]] in the neighborhood of R. Meir who caused him a great deal of trouble. R. Meir prayed that they should die. His wife Beruriah said to him: What do you have in mind with this prayer? Why do you pray that they should die? Is it because it says, "May *chata'im*, sinners, disappear"? It does not say *chot'im*, sinners; it says *chata'im*, sins! [Let sins disappear.] And what's more, look at the end of the verse. There it says, "and the wicked be no more." Once the sins will disappear, there will be no more wicked men! Rather pray for them that they should repent, and there will be no more wicked men. R. Meir did pray for them, and they repented.

A certain heretic said to Beruriah: It says, "Sing, O barren one, you who bore no child! (Isaiah 54:1). He asked her: Because she has no children, she should sing? She answered him: You fool! Look at the end of the verse, where it says, "For the children of the wife forlorn shall outnumber those of the married woman, so says God." But what is the meaning of a "barren woman who bore no child"? Sing, O community of Israel, you resemble a barren woman who will not give birth to children destined for Gehinnom, like you [the heretic].

A HERETIC'S QUESTION

A certain heretic said to R. Abbahu: It says, "A psalm of David when he fled from his son Absalom" (Psalm 3:1). And it also says, "A *michtam* of David; when he fled from Saul into a cave" (Psalms 57:1). Which event occurred first? [Running away from Absalom or running from Saul? Continued the heretic:] Let's see. The story of Saul happened first. Shouldn't David have written about it first? [Why is it placed in Psalm 57, whereas the running from Absalom, which happened later, is the subject of Psalm 3?] R. Abbahu replied: For you who do not derive interpretations from two verses that are joined together, there is a difficulty. But for us who derive interpretations from two verses that are joined together there is no difficulty. For R. Yochanan said: How do we know from the Torah that you can derive interpretations from verses that are joined together? Because it says, "They [the words of the Torah] are joined for all eternity, they are done in truth and uprightness" (Psalms 111:8) [although they do not seem to be in chronological order].

[For example:] Why is the chapter of Absalom (Psalm 3) joined to the chapter of Gog and Magog (Psalm 2), [even though chronologically, Absalom lived long before the war of Gog and Magog which will take place only in the times of *Mashiach*]? To teach us a lesson. If a person will tell you, is it possible that a slave should rebel against his master? [Meaning, if someone asks: how can people contradict David's prophecy about the war of Gog and Magog in Psalm 2?] you tell him, [pointing to Psalm 3]: Can a son rebel against his father? Yet, [as incredible as it sounds,] this did happen. And so [the war of Gog and Magog and the ensuing coming of *Mashiach*] will also happen.

THE SOUL IS A REFLECTION OF GOD

R. Shimi b. Ukva, some say Mar Ukva, was very often in the company of R. Shimon b. Pazzi, and he used to organize the various *Aggadot*[70] and recite them before R. Yehoshua b. Levi. While he was doing this he asked R. Shimon b. Pazzi: What is the meaning of the verse, "Bless God, O my soul, and all that is in me, bless His holy name" (Psalms 103:1)? R. Shimon b. Pazzi replied: Let me show you, how the ways of the Holy One, blessed be He, are different from the ways of man who is flesh and blood. A man is capable of drawing a picture on the wall, but he cannot give it spirit and soul, bowels and intestines. But the Holy One, blessed be He, is not so: He shapes one form in the midst of another, [an embryo inside the womb,] and gives it spirit and soul, bowels and intestines. And that is what Hannah meant when she said, "There is no holy one like God. Truly, there is none beside You. There is no *tzur* [rock] like our God" (1 Samuel 2:2).

What does "There is no *tzur* like our God" mean?— It means: There is no artist (*tzayar*) like our God. [The Gemara asks:] What did Hannah mean when she said, "Truly, there is none beside You"? R. Yehudah b. Menassiah says: Don't read: There is none *biltecha*, (beside You). Read instead: *levalotecha*, "there is nothing that can outlive You." For the ways of the Holy One, blessed be He, are not like the ways of man. A man's works outlive him, but the Holy One, Blessed be He, outlives his works.

R. Shimi said to R. Shimon b. Pazzi: [Let me rephrase my question.] This is what I meant to ask: David mentions the words, "Bless God, O my soul"[71], in five verses. Now I wonder, what do these five verses correspond to? [Answered R. Shimon b. Pazzi:] They correspond to the Holy One, blessed be He, and the soul. [This manifests itself in the following five analogies:] Just as the Holy One, blessed be He, fills the whole world, so does the soul fill the body. Just as the Holy One, blessed be He, sees, but cannot be seen, so does the soul see but cannot be seen. Just as the Holy One, blessed be He, nourishes the whole world, so does the soul nourish the whole body. Just as the Holy One, blessed be He, is pure, so the soul is pure. Just as the Holy One, blessed be He, dwells in the innermost chambers, so does the soul dwell in the innermost chambers. Therefore, David says, let the human being come that has these five qualities within him, and praise Him who has these five qualities.

ISAIAH AND KING HEZEKIAH

[The Gemara now tells a story that relates to the theme of joining *Ga'al Yisrael* to the *Shemoneh Esrei*.]

R. Hamenuna said: What is meant by the verse, "Who is like a wise man, and who knows *pesher*, how to find a compromise in any situation?" (Ecclesiastes 8:1). Who is like the Holy One, blessed be He, who knows how to reconcile two righteous men, [King] Hezekiah and [the prophet] Isaiah? Hezekiah said: Isaiah should come to me, for we find that [the prophet] Elijah went to [King] Ahab, as it says, "Elijah set out to appear before Ahab" (1 Kings 18:12). Isaiah, on the other hand, said: Hezekiah should come to me, for we find that Jehoram son of Ahab went to [the prophet] Elisha.[72] What did the Holy One, blessed be He, do? He brought sufferings on Hezekiah, [who became sick,] and then He said to Isaiah: Go visit the sick. For it says, "In those days Hezekiah fell dangerously ill. The prophet Isaiah, son of Amotz came to him and said to him: Thus says God: Set your affairs in order, for you are going to die, and you will not live." What is the meaning of the redundant phrase, "You are going to die, and you will not live"? It means: You will die in this world, and you will not live in the world to come.

Hezekiah said to Isaiah: Why do I deserve such terrible punishment? What did I do wrong? Replied Isaiah: Because you did not try to have children. Why did you never get married? Said Hezekiah: The reason was that I saw by the holy spirit that I will have bad children. Replied Isaiah: What have you to do with God's secrets! You have to do what you were commanded, and let the Holy One, blessed be He, do whatever pleases Him. Said Hezekiah: Now that you have convinced me, give me your daughter; maybe through your merits combined with mine good children will come forth from me. Isaiah answered: The decree is final. You are going to die. Said Hezekiah: Son of Amotz, finish your prophecy and leave! [Don't tell me the decree is irrevocable.] I have the following tradition from my ancestor [David[73]]: Even if a sharp sword rests on a person's throat he should not refrain from praying for mercy. The same has also been said by R. Yochanan and R. Elazar: Even if a sharp sword rests on a person's throat he should not refrain from praying for mercy, as it says, "Though He slay me, yet I will place my hope in Him" (Job 13:15).

(10b) R. Chanan said: Even if the master of dreams says to a person that tomorrow he will die, he should not refrain from praying, for it says, "In spite of all dreams, futility, and idle chatter, rather, fear God!" (Ecclesiastes 5:6) [meaning, ignore dreams, false prophets, and idle chatter (Rashi)]. "Thereupon Hezekiah immediately turned his face to the *kir* (wall) and prayed to God" (Isaiah 38:2). [The Gemara asks:] What is the meaning of *kir*? R. Shimon b. Lakish said: He prayed from the innermost chambers (*kirot*) [*kir* also means chamber] of his heart, for it says, "My bowels, my bowels, from the innermost chambers (*kirot*) of my heart I am suffering a terrible fear" (Jeremiah 4:19). R. Levi said: Hezekiah prayed about an issue with a chamber (*kir*). He said to God: Master of the universe, the Shunnamite woman made only one little chamber [as lodging for Elisha], and you restored her son to life,[74] then surely you should restore my health in the merit of my ancestor [Solomon] who covered the Sanctuary with silver and gold! "Please, O God," Hezekiah prayed. "Remember how I walked before You sincerely and wholeheartedly, and have done what is pleasing to You" (Isaiah 38:3). [The Gemara asks:] What does "I have done what is pleasing to You" mean? R. Yehudah says in the name of Rav: He joined the *ge'ullah* [the *berachah* of *Ga'al Yisrael* with the *tefillah*, [the *Shemoneh Esrei*]. R. Levi said: He hid away the Book of Cures. [He hid the book that described the remedy for every sickness. He did it in order that people should pray to God for healing (Rashi).]

The Rabbis taught: King Hezekiah did six things; for three of them the Sages praised him, and for three of them they did not praise him. For the following three they praised him: For hiding the Book of Cures, for breaking into pieces the copper snake that Moses had made[75] [because the people had made it into an idol[76]], and for dragging the bones of his father to the grave on a bed of ropes [because his father Ahaz was evil]. The following three things the Sages did not approve of: He stopped up the waters of Gichon [a

spring near Jerusalem that Hezekiah stopped up to deny the approaching Assyrian army access to a water supply (Rashi)].[77] He cut off the gold from the doors of the Sanctuary and sent it to the King of Assyria,[78] and he intercalated the month of Nisan during Nisan. [On the first day of Nisan, Hezekiah decided to add an extra month to the previous year by changing Nisan into *Adar Sheini*, the Second Adar (Rashi).][79]

The Sages did not approve of this [because you can add an extra month during Adar, but you cannot do that once the new year has begun in Nisan]. [The Gemara asks:] Didn't Hezekiah know that? Didn't he know the verse, "This month [Nisan] shall be the beginning of months to you" (Exodus 12:2), which teaches us that you can have only one Nisan and you cannot make another month Nisan? [The Gemara answers:] He made an error regarding the law that was stated by Shmuel. For Shmuel said: On the 30th of Adar it is too late to add an extra month Adar to the year [even though it is not yet Nisan], since theoretically it is possible for the 30th Adar to become the first day of Nisan [if witnesses report seeing the new moon]. Hezekiah did not consider this theoretical possibility, [and that was his error].

[Although Hezekiah's prayer was effective and it saved him, the Gemara finds a small flaw in it.] R. Yochanan said in the name of R. Yose b. Zimra: If a person prays to be helped in his own merit, his wish will be granted on the basis of someone else's merits. But if he prays to be helped on the basis of someone else's merit, his prayer will be answered in his own merit. A case in point: Moses petitioned God on the basis of the merits of others. For it says, "Remember Abraham, Isaac and Israel your servants" (Exodus 32:13), and his prayer was answered in his own merit, as it says, "He would have destroyed them, had not Moses His chosen one confronted Him in the breach to avert His destructive wrath" (Psalm 106:23).

Hezekiah, on the other hand, made his prayer dependent on his own merit, for it says, "Remember how I have walked before You" (Isaiah 38:3), and God granted his request based on the merits of others, for it says, "I will protect and save this city for My sake and for the sake of My servant David" (2 Kings 19:34). And R. Yehoshua b. Levi had this in mind when he said: What is the meaning of the verse, "Even when peace did come it was very bitter for me" (Isaiah 38:17)? He explains, it means: Even when the Holy One, blessed be He, sent Hezekiah the message of peace it was bitter for him [because it was not sent in his own merit, but in the merit of David].

ELISHA AND
THE SHUNAMMITE WOMAN
[Whenever Elisha visited the town of Shunem he would stop for a meal at the house of a Shunammite

woman. Once she said to her husband,] "I am sure it is a holy man of God who comes this way regularly" (2 Kings 4:9). R. Yose b. Chaninah said: This teaches you that a woman is a better judge of the character of a guest than a man is. [She said about Elisha:] "It is a holy man." How did she know? Rav and Shmuel gave different answers. One said: Because she never saw a fly on his table. The other said: She spread a linen sheet over his bed, and she never saw a nocturnal pollution on it. She said, "He is a holy man." R. Yose b. Chanina said: [The implication is that] he is holy but his attendant is not holy. For it says, "And Geichazi stepped forward to push her away" (2 Kings 4:27). R. Yose b. Chanina said: He grabbed her by the breasts.

[Referring to Elisha, the Shunnamite woman said:] "He comes this way tamid, regularly" (2 Kings 4:9). R. Yose b. R. Chanina said in the name of R. Elizer b. Yaakov: [We see from here,] that a person who offers hospitality to a Torah scholar and lets him enjoy his possessions is considered as if he had brought the daily burnt-offering [which is called tamid offering].

HOW YOU SHOULD PRAY

R. Yose b. R. Chanina further said in the name of R. Eliezer b. Yaakov: You should not stand on a high place when you pray, but you should pray in a low place, as it says, "Out of the depth I call You, O God" (Psalm 130:1). We also learned something similar to this in a Baraita: You should not stand on a chair or on a footstool or on a high place when you pray, but you should pray in a low place, because a person should not be haughty before God, as it says, "Out of the depth I call You, O God," and it also says, "A prayer of a lowly man when he is faint" (Psalm 102:1).

R. Yose b. R. Chanina also said in the name of R. Eliezer b. Yaakov: When you pray you should place your feet close together, for it says with reference to the angels, "Their feet were straight," (Ezekiel 1:7) [they seemed like one foot.]

R. Yose b. R. Chanina also said in the name of R. Eliezer b. Yaakov: What is meant by the verse, "Do not eat on blood"? (Leviticus 19:26). [He answered: It means:] Do not eat before you have prayed for your blood, [i.e., for your life]. R. Yitzchak said in the name of R. Yochanan, who spoke in the name of R. Yose b. R. Chanina, who in turn quoted R. Eliezer b. Yaakov: If a person eats and drinks and afterward prays, Scripture says about him, "You have cast Me behind your back" (1 Kings 14:9) [i.e., You have postponed your prayers to Me until after taking care of your physical needs]. [The Gemara adds:] Do not read geivecha, your back, but geiyecha, your pride [meaning, you began to pray with an arrogant attitude]. Says the Holy One, blessed be He: After becoming smug and self-satisfied he wants to come and accept the kingdom of heaven by reciting the Shema! [He is not in the proper frame of mind for praying.]

THE BERACHOT OF SHEMA AND TORAH STUDY

(11b) What berachot do we say in the morning [before we recite the Shema]? R. Yaakov said in the name of R. Oshaia: (11b) [The first berachah is:] "Blessed are You . . . who forms light and creates darkness." [The Gemara asks:] Why mention darkness [a term associated with bleakness and death]. Let's rather say: "Who forms light and creates brightness." [The Gemara answers:] We follow the Scriptural text [which reads, "I am God who forms light and creates darkness" (Isaiah 45:7)]. [The Gemara asks:] If you do that, why don't you also follow the Scriptural text of the rest of that passage, which says, "Who makes peace and creates evil." The verse reads, "creates evil," yet we say, "Who makes peace and creates all things."

[The Gemara answers:] We substitute "all things" for "evil" as a euphemism. [The Gemara challenges:] So do the same with the first part of the verse and say "brightness" instead of "darkness" as a euphemism! Rava replied: [There is a reason why we prefer to use the word "darkness" in the morning]. We want to mention the characteristic of the day at nighttime and the characteristic of the night in the daytime. [We believe that God is One, who dictates both day and night, both happiness and suffering.] [The Gemara asks:] Granted that we mention the characteristic of the night in the daytime, for we say [in the Shacharit (morning) prayer], "Who forms light and creates darkness." But where do you find the characteristic of the day mentioned in the nighttime? Abbaye replied: [You find it in the words of the Maariv (evening) prayer:] He causes the light to recede before darkness and darkness before light.

What berachah do we recite [before we study the Torah]? R. Yehudah said in the name of Shmuel: [Blessed are You . . .] who has sanctified us with His commandments and has commanded us to engross ourselves in the words of the Torah. R. Yochanan [wanted also to end with a berachah. He therefore] used to close the berachah as follows: Please God, our Lord, sweeten the words of Your Torah in our mouth and in the mouth of Your people, the family of Israel. May we and our offspring and the offspring of Your people, the House of Israel—all of us—know Your name and study Your Torah. Blessed are You God, who teaches Torah to His people Israel. R. Hamenuna said: [Blessed are You . . .] who selected us from all the peoples and gave us His Torah. Blessed are You God, Giver of the Torah.

BOWING IN THE SHEMONEH ESREI

(12a) Rabba b. Chinena the elder said in the name of Rav: When you recite the Shemoneh Esrei [you have to bow four times: at the beginning and the end of the first berachah and at the beginning and the end of the *berachah* of *Modim*], you should bow at the word *baruch*, "blessed," and straighten yourself at the mention of God's name. Shmuel said: What is Rav's reason for this? Because it says, "God makes those who are bent stand straight" (Psalm 146:8). The Gemara raised an objection from the verse, "You should bow down before My name," (Malachi 2:5) [which implies that you should bow—not straighten up—when mentioning God's name]. [The Gemara answers:] Does it say, "You should bow down *at* the mention of God's name?" It says, "*before* the mention of God's name" [you should bow down; but *at* the mention of His name you should stand erect]. Shmuel said to Chiya b. Rav: Come here, dear Torah scholar, let me tell you a beautiful thing your father said. This is what your father said: You should bow down at the word *baruch*, "blessed," and you should return to an upright position at the mention of God's name.

(12b) When R. Sheshet bowed down he used to bend like a cane, [in one swift motion,] but when he straightened himself he used to raise himself like a snake, [slowly; his head first and then his body, to show that while he is eager to bow down to God, he is in no hurry to get it over with].

PRAYING FOR A FRIEND
Rabba b. Chinena the elder also said in the name of Rav: If someone is able to pray for his friend and he does not, he is called a sinner, for it says, [Samuel said to the people:] "As for me, far be it from me to sin against God and refrain from praying for you" (1 Samuel 12:23). Rava said: If his friend is a Torah scholar he must pray for him to the point of making himself sick. What is the reason? Is it because it says, [Saul, angry at his servants, complained,] "None of you is sick about me [i.e., no one is concerned about my problem,] and no one reveals the secret to me"? (1 Samuel 22:8). Maybe the case of a king is different. But we derive it from the following verse, [David said about Doeg and Achitofel who were Torah scholars,] "Yet, when they were ill, my dress was sackcloth; I afflicted myself with fasting" (Psalm 35:13).

CONTRITION BRINGS
ABOUT FORGIVENESS
Rabba b. Chinena the elder further said in the name of Rav: If a person commits a sin and is ashamed of it, all his sins are forgiven. For it says, "Thus you will remember and feel shame, and you will be too abashed to open your mouth again, when I have forgiven you for all that you have done, says God, the Lord" (Ezekiel 16:63), [proof that shame and forgiveness go hand in hand]. [The Gemara asks:] Maybe a community [to which this verse refers] is different? [But how do you know that shame brings about forgiveness even for an individual? The Gemara therefore suggests a different

proof verse, stating:] But we derive it from this verse, [When Saul conjured up the spirit of the deceased Samuel,] "Samuel said to Saul, 'Why have you disturbed me and brought me up?' And Saul answered, 'I am in great trouble. The Philistines are attacking me, and God has turned away from me; He no longer answers me, either by prophets or by dreams. So I have called you to tell me what I am to do'" (1 Samuel 28:15). But Saul does not mention that he consulted the Urim and Tummim,[80] [although according to verse 6 of this chapter he did, in fact, consult the Urim].

Saul did not mention it because he had killed all the people of Nov, the city of priests, [and his silence shows that he was ashamed of what he had done]. And how do we know that God had forgiven Saul? Because it says, [Samuel said to Saul,] "Tomorrow your sons and you will be with me," (1 Samuel 28:19), and R. Yochanan said: "With me" means "you will be in my dwelling" [in Gan Eden; proof that he was forgiven]. The Rabbis said [we learn it] from here: [The Gibeonites demanded that David hand over seven of Saul's sons and said,] "And we will hang them before God in Givat Saul, the chosen of God" (2 Samuel 21:6). [It was not the Gibeonites who said, "Saul, the chosen of God."] It was a heavenly voice that came forth and declared, "Saul is the chosen of God," [proof that he was forgiven].

MENTIONING THE EXODUS IN
MESSIANIC TIMES?
MISHNAH: We have an obligation to mention the Exodus in the *Shema* every night. Said R. Elazar b. Azariah[81]: I feel as if I were seventy years old, [his beard had turned white prematurely,] and yet I have never been worthy to find a verse that proves that the Exodus from Egypt should be mentioned in the [*Shema*] of the evening until Ben Zoma expounded: It says: "You will then remember the day you left Egypt all the days of your life" (Deuteronomy 16:3). Now, if it had said, "the days of your life," it would have meant only the days; but "*all* the days of your life" [implies that you must say the *Shema* also at night. However, the Sages say: "The days of your life" refers to this world; "*all* the days of your life" [implies that we will mention the Exodus even] after the coming of *Mashiach*.

It has been taught in a *Baraita*: Ben Zoma said to the Sages: [You are saying that we will mention the Exodus even after the coming of *Mashiach*]. But is this so? Doesn't it say, "Assuredly, a time is coming—declares God—when it shall no more be said, 'As God lives, who brought the Israelites out of the land of Egypt,' but rather, 'As God lives who brought out and led the offspring of the House of Israel from the northland and from all the lands to which I have banished them'" (Jeremiah 23:7,8), [thus, after the coming of *Mashiach* the Exodus will not be mentioned any more]. The Sages replied: This does not mean that the

23

exodus from Egypt will be totally eliminated, but that the deliverance from the exile among the nations of the world will take first place and the exodus from Egypt will become secondary. In the same vein, it says, [God said to Jacob,] "You shall be called Jacob no more, but Israel shall be your name" (Genesis 35:10).

(13a) This does not mean that the name Jacob will be eliminated, but that Israel will be the main name and the name Jacob secondary. And we have another verse [that indicates that the Exodus will be overshadowed by the final redemption], for it says, "Do not recall what happened of old, or ponder what happened long ago!" (Isaiah 43:18). The phrase, "Do not recall what happened of old" refers to the exile among the nations [like Persia and Greece], and "ponder what happened long ago" refers to the exodus from Egypt. [But what are we going to rejoice about? The next verse tells us,] "I am about to do something new, even now it will come to pass." R. Yosef taught: This refers to the war of Gog and Magog [which will precede the coming of *Mashiach*]. You can compare it to a person who, while traveling along the road, came face to face with a wolf. When he escaped, he went and told everyone about his brush with the wolf. He then ran into a lion and escaped from it too. So he told everyone about his encounter with the lion. He then crossed the path of a snake, and again he escaped. Now he related his miraculous rescue from the snake, forgetting the two previous incidents. So it is with Israel: the later troubles make them forget the earlier ones.

ABRAM/ABRAHAM
AND SARAI/SARAH

"Abram, that is, Abraham" (1 Chronicles 1:27). [The Gemara expounds:] At first he became a father to Aram [Av-ram, father of Aram, the people of his own country], but at the end he became a father to the whole world, [as it says, "Your name shall be Abraham, for I have set you up as the father of a multitude of nations" (Genesis 17:5)]. [Likewise,] Sarai is the same as Sarah. At first she became a princess of her own people, but later she became a princess of the entire world. [Sarai translates "my princess;" Sarah means simply "princess."]

Bar Kappara taught: Whoever refers to Abraham as Abram violates a positive commandment, for it says, "Your name shall become Abraham" (Genesis 17:5). R. Eliezer says: He violates a negative commandment, for it says, "No longer shall you be called Abram." [The Gemara asks:] If that is so, the same should apply if someone refers to Sarah as Sarai? [The Gemara answers:] No. In the case of Sarah, the Holy One blessed be He, said to Abraham, "Sarai your wife—do not call her by the name Sarai, for Sarah is her name" (Genesis 17:15). [Only Abraham has to call her Sarah, but not necessarily everyone else.] [The Gemara asks:] If that is so, shouldn't the same apply to someone who refers to Jacob as Jacob instead of Israel? [The Gemara an-

swers:] Definitely not. There is a difference, because the Torah itself later calls him Jacob again, for it says, "God spoke to Israel in a night vision, and said, 'Jacob! Jacob!'" (Genesis 46:2). R. Yose b. Avin (some say, R. Yose b. Zevida) raised an objection by citing the following verse, "It is You, the Lord, God, who selected Abram, brought him out of Ur Kasdim and made his name Abraham" (Nehemiah 9:7). [Nehemiah refers to Abraham as Abram!] [The Gemara answers:] The prophet [Nehemiah] is praising God by putting events in chronological order and stating that originally [Abraham was called Abram].

VARIOUS ASPECTS OF THE *SHEMA* AND THE *SHEMONEH ESREI*

(13a) R. Yehoshua b. Korcha said: Why was the first section of *Shema*, "Hear, O Israel," placed before that of *Vehayah im shamo'a*,[82] "If you are careful to pay heed to My commandments"? [He answered:] So that you should first acknowledge God's absolute sovereignty [by declaring that God is One, Unique and Indivisible], and then take upon yourself the duty of performing God's commandments [which is the theme of the second section]. Why was the section of *Vehayah im shamo'a* placed before that of *Vayomer*, "And God said"? Because [the concepts in the section of *Vehayah im shamo'a* apply both in the daytime and at night particularly, "Teach your children . . . when you lie down and when you get up], whereas the section of *Vayomer* [which contains the mitzvah of *tzitzit* (tassels)] applies only to the day. [It is obligatory only at a time "when you see them," (Numbers 15:39).]

(13b) It was taught in a *Baraita*: Sumchus says: Whoever draws out the word *echad*, "One," Heaven will lengthen his days and years. R. Acha b. Yaakov said: You should draw out the *dalet* of *echad* [but not the *chet*, because the word *echad* does not mean "one" until you have uttered the *dalet*]. R. Assi said: But make sure that you don't garble the *chet* [of *echad*, omitting the vowel, since that would make the word meaningless]. R. Yirmiyah was once sitting in front of R. Chiya b. Abba, and R. Chiya noticed that R. Yirmiyah was drawing out the word *echad* very much. So he said to him: You're taking too long. Once you have acknowledged God as King over all that exists above and below and over the four directions of the universe, no more is necessary.

R. Yosef said: A person should not recite the *Shema* when lying on his back. The implication is that the *Shema* should not be said in that position, but that there is no objection to sleeping on one's back. [The Gemara asks:] But did not R. Yehoshua b. Levi strongly disapprove of anyone sleeping on his back? [The Gemara answers:] I will tell you. When it comes to sleeping, if he turn over a little, it's all right, but reading the *Shema* is forbidden even if he turns over a little [because it is an arrogant posture]. [The Gemara challenges:] But R. Yochanan did turn over a little when he read the *Shema*? [The Gemara answers:] R. Yochanan was an exception because he was a very heavy person [and it was difficult for him to move].

(14b) Ulla said: A person who recites the Shema without wearing the *tefillin* is as though he is testifying falsely against himself [because in the *Shema* he is reading, "Bind these words as a sign on your hand, and let them be an emblem in the center of your head" (Deuteronomy 6:8), and there is nothing on his hand and his head]. R. Chiya b. Abba said in the name of R. Yochanan: It is as if he offered a burnt offering without a meal-offering, and a sacrifice without a wine-offering.

R. Yochanan also said: If a person wants to acknowledge God's absolute sovereignty (15a) in the ideal way, he should first relieve himself, wash his hands, then put on his *tefillin*, recite the *Shema* and say the *Shemoneh Esrei*, and that is the perfect way of accepting God's sovereignty. R. Chiya b. Abba said in the name of R. Yochanan: Whoever relieves himself, washes his hands, puts on his *tefillin*, recites the *Shema* and says the *Shemoneh Esrei*, Scripture considers it as if he had built an altar and offered a sacrifice on it, as it says, "I wash my hands in purity and walk around Your altar, O God" (Psalm 26:6). Said Rava to him: Don't you think that if he washed his hands it is as if he immersed himself in a *mikveh*, because it says, "I will wash in purity" [i.e., my entire body], and it does not say, "I will wash my hands." [Rava interprets the verse to mean: I will do the equivalent of immersing my body in purity by washing my hands.]

Ravina said to Rava: Please, sir, look at this Torah scholar who came from Eretz Yisrael and says: If you have no water for washing your hands, you should wipe your hands with earth or with pebbles or with wood shavings. Rava replied: He is absolutely right. Does it say, "I will wash in water"? It says, "I will wash in purity," meaning, with anything that cleans.

(15b) R. Chama b. Chanina said: If someone recites the *Shema* and is careful to enunciate every letter properly [by spacing consecutive words that end and begin with the same letters[83]], Gehinnom is cooled off for him, as it says, "When the Almighty scatters the kings, it seemed like a snowstorm in Tzalmon" (Psalm 68:15). Don't read *befareis* [when He scatters]; read *befareish*[84] [when one enunciates distinctly]. And don't read *betzalmon* [in Tzalmon]; read *betzalmavet* [in the shadow of death, meaning Gehinnom. Thus, the meaning that emerges is, "If you will space the words of *Shema* properly and pronounce them clearly, then the sanctity inherent in those words will cool off Gehinnom"].

R. Chama b. R. Chanina also said: (16a) Why are tents mentioned in conjunction with streams, as in the verse, "How good are your *tents*, Jacob, your habitations Israel. They stretch out like *streams*, like gardens by the river, they are like aloes God has planted"?

(Numbers 24:5,6). This comes to tell you that, just like streams bring a person up from impurity to purity, so do the tents of Torah, [houses of learning,] lift a person from the scale of guilt to the scale of merit.

(16b) Our Rabbis taught: We consider only three people as our Fathers: [Abraham, Isaac, and Jacob, but not the twelve sons of Jacob,] and we refer to only four women as our Mothers: [Sarah, Rebeccah, Rachel, and Leah]. What is the reason? Do you think because we do not know whether we are descended from Reuben or from Simon [and that's why we cannot say with certainty that these are our Fathers]? But the same is true of the Mothers; we don't know either whether we are descended from Rachel or from Leah! [Yet we refer to all four as our Mothers; why can't we refer also to the sons of Jacob as our Fathers]? [The Gemara answers:] Because up to this point, they were held in a higher esteem [and therefore are called Fathers and Mothers]; from this point on there was not the same level of esteem.

R. Eliezer said: What is the meaning of the verse, "I bless You all my life; I lift up my hands, invoking Your name"? (Psalms 63:5). "I bless You" refers to the *Shema*; "I lift up my hands, invoking Your name" refers to the *Shemoneh Esrei*. And in the next verse David says about a person who does this [recites *Shema* and *Shemoneh Esrei*], "My soul is satiated as with fat and marrow" (Psalms 63:6). But that's not all. The person [who recites *Shema* and *Shemoneh Esrei*] inherits two worlds, this world and the world to come, as it says, "I sing praises with songs on my lips" (*ibid.*). [The plural "songs" alludes to the two worlds.]

(14a)[85] Rav said: If someone greets his friend before he has said the *Shemoneh Esrei*, it is as if he had made him a *bamah* (a self-styled altar), for it says, "O, cease to glorify man, who has only breath in his nostrils! For by what does he merit esteem?" (Isaiah 2:22). Don't read *bameh*, "by what," read instead, *bamah*.[86] Shmuel interprets the verse: [without changing the reading of *bameh*, "by what,"] By what reason do you esteem this man and not God? [Thus, under no circumstances should you greet anyone before you have said the *Shemoneh Esrei*.] R. Sheshet raised an objection: We learned in a Mishnah: In the breaks between the sections of the *Shema* you are allowed to greet someone out of respect and return a greeting. [Now, the *Shema* is said before the *Shemoneh Esrei*, and yet you are allowed to greet someone!] R. Abba explained [that Rav and Shmuel who forbid greeting someone before the *Shemoneh Esrei*] refer to a person who goes to his neighbor's house to greet him in order to ingratiate himself with him, [but if he just happens to meet someone he is allowed to greet him].

R. Yonah said in the name of R. Zeira: If someone does business before he has said the *Shemoneh Esrei*, it is as if he had built a *bamah* [a self-styled altar, something that is strictly forbidden]. So they said to him: Do you really mean to say that it is as serious as build-

25

ing a *bamah*? He replied: I only mean that it is forbidden [but it is not as bad as building a *bamah*]. What I am saying is similar to what R. Idi b. Avin said in the name of R. Yitzchak b. Ashian: You are forbidden to take care of your business before you said your prayers, for it says, "Righteousness [i.e., prayer] shall go before him as he sets out on his way" (Psalm 85:14). R. Idi b. Avin further said in the name of R. Yitzchak b. Ashian: If you pray first and then go out to do business, the Holy One, blessed be He, will take care of your business, for it says, "[If] righteousness [i.e., prayer] goes before him, He will clear the way for him" (Psalm 85:14).

SEVEN DAYS WITHOUT
A DREAM

R. Yonah said further in the name of R. Zeira: If someone goes for seven days without a dream he is called evil. For it says, "He who goes to sleep [*save'a*], satisfied, will not be reminded of evil" (Proverbs 19:23). Don't read *save'a*, [satisfied] but *sheva* [seven][87], [and the passage means: He who goes to sleep for seven days and does not have a dream is evil]. R. Acha the son of R. Chiya b. R. Abba said to him: This is what R. Chiya said in the name of R. Yochanan: Anyone who satiates himself with words of Torah before he goes to sleep will not receive any bad tidings in his dreams, for it says, "He who goes to sleep satiated will not be reminded of evil."

ADDED PRAYERS AT
THE CONCLUSION OF THE
SHEMONEH ESREI

(16b)[88] [The Gemara continues:] R. Elazar, at the conclusion of his *Shemoneh Esrei*, used to recite the following: May it be Your will, Lord our God, that our lot should be one of love, brotherhood, peace, and friendship; that our territory should be filled with students; and that our end should be successful, so that at the end we should indeed see the things we hoped for all our lives, and set our share in Gan Eden, and set us aright with good friends and the right inclination in Your world. And may we get up in the morning and find our hearts yearning to fear Your name, and may our wants and desires come before You for the good.

Rabbi Yochanan, at the conclusion of his *Shemoneh Esrei* used to add this: May it be Your will, Lord our God, to look at our shame [i.e., look how ashamed we are of our sins], and see the evil that surrounds us, and clothe Yourself in Your attribute of mercy, cover Yourself with Your strength, and wrap Yourself in Your kindness, and gird Yourself with Your graciousness, and may the attribute of Your goodness and Your humility come before You.

R. Zeira, at the conclusion of his *Shemoneh Esrei*, used to add the following: May it be Your will, Lord

our God, that we should not sin, and that we should not be ashamed and embarrassed before our fathers.

R. Chiya, after completing the *Shemoneh Esrei*, used to add the following: May it be Your will, Lord our God, that Your Torah should be our whole occupation, that our hearts should not be sick, and our eyes should not be dimmed.[89]

Rav, upon completing the *Shemoneh Esrei*, used to add the following: May it be Your will, Lord our God, to grant us long life, a life of peace, a life of goodness, a life of blessing, a life of sustenance, a life of physical health, a life in which there is fear of sin, a life in which there is no shame nor humiliation, a life of wealth and honor, a life in which we will have love of Torah and fear of heaven, a life in which our heartfelt requests will be fulfilled for the good.[90]

Rebbi, at the conclusion of his *Shemoneh Esrei*, recited this: May it be Your will, Lord our God, and the God of our forefathers, that You may rescue me from brazen men and from brazenness, from an evil man, an evil mishap, an evil companion, from the evil impulse, from an evil neighbor, the destructive spiritual impediment, a harsh trial and a harsh opponent, whether or not he is a member of the covenant.[91] [Rebbi prayed for all these things] even though there were Roman soldiers that Antoninus,[92] Rabbi Yehudah Hanassi's friend, had appointed to protect Rebbi at all times.

R. Safra, at the conclusion of his *Shemoneh Esrei*, used to add the following: May it be Your will, Lord our God, to establish peace (17a) among the heavenly family and among the earthly family [i.e., the Torah scholars], and among the students who study Your Torah, whether for its own sake or for ulterior motives; and may it be Your will that those who do so for ulterior motives will ultimately come to study the Torah for its own sake.

R. Alexandri, at the conclusion of his *Shemoneh Esrei*, used to add this: May it be Your will Lord, our God, that you should place us in a corner of light and not in a dark corner; that our hearts should not be sick and our eyes should not be dimmed. Some say that this prayer was said by R. Hamenuna, but that R. Alexandri said the following prayer: Master of the universe, it is obvious and known to You that we really want to do Your will, but what stands in the way? The yeast in the dough [i.e., the evil impulse] and the oppression of the nations of the world. May it be Your will to save us from their hand, so that we may return to perform all of Your laws with a perfect heart.

Mar, the son of R. Huna (Ravina), at the conclusion of his *Shemoneh Esrei*, said the following prayer: My God, guard my tongue from evil and my lips from speaking deceitfully.[93] To those who curse me, let my soul be silent; and let my soul be like dust to everyone. Open my heart to your Torah, then my soul will pursue Your commandments. And save me from a mishap, from the evil impulse, from an evil woman, and from all bad things that threaten to come upon the world. As for all those who design evil against me, speedily nullify their counsel and disrupt their designs. May the expressions of my mouth and the thoughts of my heart find favor before You, my Rock and my Redeemer.[94]

Rava, at the conclusion of his *Shemoneh Esrei*, recited the following: My God, before I was formed I was unworthy, and now that I have been formed, it is as if I had not been formed. I am dust in my life, and will surely be so in my death. Behold—before You I am like a vessel filled with shame and humiliation. May it be Your will, Lord, my God and the God of my forefathers, that I not sin again. And what I have sinned before You, may You cleanse with Your abundant mercy, but not through suffering or serious illness. This was the confession of R. Hamenuna Zuti on Yom Kippur.[95]

When R. Sheshet fasted, he said the following after he concluded his *Shemoneh Esrei*: Master of all the worlds, You know very well that in the time the *Bet Hamikdash* was standing, if a person sinned he brought a sacrifice, and although only its fat and blood were offered on the altar, his sin was thereby forgiven. Now I have fasted, and my fat and blood have diminished. May it be Your will, therefore, that You consider my fat and blood that have been diminished as if I had offered them on the altar, and accept me favorably.

SAYINGS OF THE RABBIS

When R. Yochanan finished the Book of Job, he used to say this: The end of man is to die, and the end of an animal is to be slaughtered. All are destined to die. Happy is the person who was brought up in a Torah environment, who exerts himself to study Torah, who gives pleasure to his Creator, and who grew up with a good name and left the world with a good name [as Job did]. Solomon had a man like that in mind when he said, "A good name is better than fragrant oil, and the day of death than the day of birth" (Ecclesiastes 7:1).

R. Meir was in the habit of saying: Put your heart and soul into learning My ways [i.e., study the Torah for its own sake], and watch at the doors of My Torah [i.e., study with single-minded determination], guard My Torah in your heart, and keep My fear before your eyes. Keep your mouth from all sin, cleanse and sanctify yourself from all sin and transgression, then I will be with you wherever you are.

The Rabbis of Yavneh used to say the following adage: I am [a Torah scholar] and I am God's creation, and my neighbor [who is an unlearned laborer] is also God's creation. My work is in the city [in the *bet midrash*], and my neighbor's work is out in the field. I get up early for my work, and he gets up early for his work. Just as he does not interfere with my work, so do I not encroach on his work. Now you might say, that I am accomplishing so much more [by studying

Torah], and he is accomplishing so much less. Therefore we learned: It makes no difference whether you do a lot or a little, as long as you are doing it for the sake of heaven.[96]

Abbaye was wont to say the following: A person should always be cunning in devising new strategies to improve his fear of heaven. [Another thing to remember is:] "A gentle response allays wrath" (Proverbs 15:1), and you should do your best to be on good terms with your brothers, your relatives and with all men, and even with the heathen in the street. That way, you will be loved in heaven above, well-liked below in this world, and respected by people. It was said about R. Yochanan b. Zakkai that no one ever greeted him first, even a heathen in the street. [R. Yochanan always was first to offer greetings.]

Rava was known to say the following: The goal of Torah wisdom is [that it should lead to] repentance and good deeds, so that a person should not study Torah and Mishnah [and become proud of his knowledge] and then despise his father and mother and his teacher or even those that are superior to him in wisdom or outnumber him, as it says, "The beginning of wisdom is the fear of God; [meaning, when you start learning, your objective should be to attain the fear of God;] all who do God's commandments gain sound understanding" (Psalms 111:10). It doesn't say, "All who *study* God's commands gain sound understanding," but "All who *do* God's commands," meaning, all who do the commands for the sake of God, but not those who do the commands for ulterior motives. And as for a person who studies the Torah for ulterior motives, [namely in order to criticize and dispute its teachings], it is better if he had not been created.

Rav was in the habit of saying the following: The world to come is not like this world. In the world to come there is no eating or drinking or procreation or business; no jealousy, hatred, or competition, but the righteous sit with their crowns on their heads, and they derive pleasure from the radiance of the *Shechinah*, as it says, "They [the seventy elders of Israel] had a vision of the Divine, and they ate and drank," (Exodus 24:11) [not in a physical sense, but the spiritual delight they derived from the radiance of the *Shechinah* is compared to the pleasure of eating and drinking (Rashi)].

THE MERITS OF WOMEN

Our Rabbis taught: The promise the Holy One, blessed be He, made to the women is greater than the promise He made to the men. For it says, "You carefree women, attend, hear My words! You confident ladies, give ear to My speech!" (Isaiah 32:9). [God addresses the women in terms of "carefree" and "confident," an allusion to their reward both in this world and the world to come.] Rav said to R. Chiya: How do women [for whom Torah study is not considered a paramount duty] earn a share in the world to come? By making their small children go to the synagogue [where they learn Torah], and by making their husbands go to the yeshivah to learn Mishnah, and by waiting for their husbands until they come home from the yeshivah.

FAREWELL WISHES
OF TORAH SCHOLARS

At the yeshivah of R. Ammi—some say of R. Chanina—when the Torah scholars finished studying with each other and gave each other permission to return [to their homes or to their countries], they bade farewell to R. Ammi as follows: May all your needs be fulfilled in your lifetime, and may your end be life in the world to come, and your hope for many generations. May your heart be engrossed in understanding, may your mouth speak wisdom and your tongue utter words of song, may your eyelids look straight before you [i.e., may you understand correctly the meaning of the Torah], may your eyes be enlightened by the light of the Torah, may your face shine like the radiance of heaven, may your lips utter knowledge, and your kidneys[97] rejoice in uprightness. May your steps run to hear the words of the aged, [i.e., never consider yourself too wise to listen to the advice of people who are older than you].

When the Rabbis took leave of the yeshivah of R. Chisda—others say, of the yeshivah of R. Shmuel b. Nachmeini—they said to him: It says, *Alufeinu mesubalim*, "May our leaders be accepted by the common people" (Psalm 144:14). Rav and Shmuel—some say, R. Yochanan and R. Elazar—offer different interpretations of this passage. According to one, *alufeinu* refers to our teachers, our leaders, may they lead us in Torah, and *mesubalim*[98] means "may we be loaded with *mitzvot*." The other says: *Alufeinu* refers to our teachers; may they instruct us in Torah and *mitzvot*, and *mesubalim* means, "we are loaded with pain," [in other words, may we have the strength to bear the frustrations of life].

(17b) [The verse continues:] "May there be no breach," meaning, "May our helpers not be like those who accompanied Saul, one of whom was Doeg the Edomite" [who was not sincere and fell into bad ways].[99] "And may there be no defection," meaning, "May our helpers not be like those in David's entourage, which included Achitofel" [who defected from David and supported Absalom's rebellion].[100] [The verse continues,] "May there be no outcry," meaning, "May our helpers not be like those in Elisha's following, which included Geichazi [who was stricken with leprosy, and had to cry, "Unclean! unclean!"]. [The verse continues,] "In our streets," meaning, "May we not have a son or student who spoils his food in public," [meaning, who misinterprets the words of the Torah in the streets].[101]

THE WORLD IS SUSTAINED
BECAUSE OF CHANINA

[The Gemara continues: The prophet says,] "Listen to Me, you strong-hearted, who are far from righteousness" (Isaiah 46:12). Rav and Shmuel—some say, R. Yochanan and R. Eliezer—offer different interpretations of this verse. One says: [The verse refers to righteous men, and it means to say:] The whole world is sustained by the righteousness of God, but the righteous are sustained by their own merits. [The phrase, "who are far from *tzedakah*" means that they don't have to depend on God's charity; they can rely on their own merits.] The other one agrees [that the passage refers to righteous men, but he interprets it as follows:] The whole world is sustained in the merit of the righteous, but they themselves are not even nourished by their own merits. This is in line with a saying by R. Yehudah in the name of Rav who said: Every single day, a heavenly voice goes forth from Mount Chorev that says: The whole world is sustained because of Chanina[102] my son, but Chanina my son, he makes do with a *kav* of carobs from one Friday until the next. [At any rate, all interpretations agree that "the strong-hearted" in the verse refers to the righteous.]

However, this is disputed by R. Yehudah [who interprets "strong-hearted" in a derogatory sense]. He says: Whom does Isaiah call "strong-hearted"? The foolish Goba'i [Gibeonites].[103] R. Yosef said: I'll prove to you [that they are fools,] because not one of them ever converted to Judaism. R. Ashi said: The people of the city of Mechasya [a suburb of Sura, the seat of one of the great *yeshivot* of Babylonia], they are the "strong-hearted." They witness the honor of the Torah twice a year [because immense crowds would gather there in R. Ashi's yeshivah in Adar and Elul to listen to his discourses on the laws of Pesach and Sukkot], and not one of them ever converted to Judaism.

DO THE DEAD HAVE
KNOWLEDGE OF THIS WORLD?

(18a) It has been taught: A person should not walk in a cemetery with *tefillin* on his head or a Torah scroll in his arm and read from it.[104] If he does, he comes under the category of, "He who mocks the poor offends his Maker" (Proverbs 17:5). [By flaunting his *tefillin* he mocks the dead who are poor in that they cannot perform *mitzvot*.]

Rachava said in the name of R. Yehudah: A person who sees a funeral passing by and does not join the procession comes under the category of, "He who mocks the poor offends his Maker." And if he does join the procession, what is his reward? R. Assi says: Scripture says about him, "He who is generous to the poor makes a loan to God" (Proverbs 19:17), [a play on the similarity of *malveh*, "to make a loan," and *melaveh*, "to escort the dead,"] and it says, "He who shows pity for the needy honors Him" (Proverbs 14:31).

(18b) The sons of R. Chiya went out to work in the fields, and, as a result, began to forget some of their learning. They tried very hard to recall it. Said one to the other: Does our [late] father know the trouble we are having? Replied the other: How could he know? Doesn't it say [about the dead], "His children honor him, and he does not know it" (Job 14:21). [So you see, after his death a person does not know what his children are doing.] Said the other: Do you really believe that he doesn't know? Doesn't it say, "He feels the pain of his flesh, and his spirit mourns in him," (Job 14:22) and R. Yitzchak commented on this: The worm is as painful to the dead as a needle in the flesh of the living? [Which proves that the dead do feel.] [He replied:] I'll tell you. It's their own pain they feel, but the pain of others they don't feel.

[The Gemara asks:] Is that so? Didn't we learn in a *Baraita*: There is a story about a pious man who gave a *dinar* to a poor man on the eve of Rosh Hashanah in a year of famine. When his wife took him to task for it he went and spent the night in the cemetery. There he heard the spirits [of two dead girls] talking to each other. Said one to the other: My dear, let's roam around the world, and let's hear from behind the curtain [that separates this world from the Divine Presence] what punishment is coming on the world [in the divine judgment decreed on Rosh Hashanah]. Said her companion: I can't go because I am buried in a mat of reeds [instead of linen shrouds]. You go by yourself, and whatever you hear you'll tell me. So the other one went, wandered around, and returned. Said her companion to her: My dear, what have you heard from behind the curtain? She replied: I heard that whoever is going to plant after the first rainfall will find his crops destroyed by hail.[105]

So the man went and did not plant until the second rainfall. As a result, everyone else's crop was destroyed, only his was not damaged [because it had barely begun to sprout when the hailstorm came]. The next year he again went and spent the night in the cemetery and heard the two spirits talking to each other. Said one to the other: Come, let's roam around the world, and hear from behind the curtain what punishment is coming on the world. Replied the other: My dear, didn't I tell you that I am not able to go because I am buried in a mat of reeds? You go by yourself, and whatever you hear, come and tell me. So the other one went, roamed around the world, and returned. She said to her: My dear, what have you heard from behind the curtain? She replied: I heard that whoever plants after the second rainfall will have his crops struck with blight [which destroys the tender shoots but does not harm the stronger stalks]. So the man went and planted after the first rainfall, with the result that everyone else's crop was blighted and his was not.

Said his wife to him: How come that last year everyone else's crop was damaged and yours was not, and

this year everyone else's crop was blighted and yours is not? So he told her everything that happened. People said that shortly afterward the wife of that pious man got into an argument with the mother of one of the girls [whose spirits the pious man had overheard talking]. The wife said to the girl's mother: Come and I'll show you your daughter buried in a mat of reeds. The next year, the pious man again spent the night of Rosh Hashanah in the cemetery and heard the two spirits talking to each other. Said one to the other: My dear, come, let's roam around the world and hear from behind the curtain what punishment is coming on the world. Said the other: My dear, leave me alone; the things we discussed have already been heard among the living. [The Gemara summarizes:] Wouldn't this story indicate that the dead know what goes on among the living, [and disprove the opinion that holds that they don't know]? [The Gemara answers:] Maybe someone else died and told them.

R. Shmuel b. Nachmeini said in the name of R. Yonatan: How do we know that the dead talk to each other? Because it says: [Shortly before Moses died,] "God said to him, 'This is the land regarding which I made an oath to Abraham, Isaac and Jacob, saying . . .'" (Deuteronomy 34:4). What is meant by "saying"? The Holy One, blessed be He, said to Moses: [When you pass away,] say to Abraham, Isaac, and Jacob: The oath that I swore to you I have already carried out for your descendants [which seems to prove that the dead know and care about what goes on in this world]. (19a) For if you should think that the dead do not know, what would be the use of Moses telling them? So you must conclude that they do know. But in that case, why does Moses have to tell them [they know anyway that God fulfilled His promise]? [The Gemara answers:] In order that they should be grateful to Moses.

R. Yitzchak said: Making disparaging remarks about the dead is like making remarks about a stone. Some say [the reason is] that the dead do not know; others say that they know but do not care. [The Gemara challenges:] Is that so? Has not R. Papa said: A certain person made a derogatory remark about Mar Shmuel [after his death], and a beam fell from the roof and broke his skull? [So you see that the dead do know and do care.] [The Gemara answers:] A Torah scholar is different, because the Holy One, blessed be He, avenges his insult. [Mar Shmuel did not necessarily know or care about it. It was God who avenged the insult to this great man.]

MAKING DISPARAGING REMARKS ABOUT TORAH SCHOLARS

R. Yehoshua b. Levi said: Whoever makes derogatory remarks about Torah scholars after their death will end up in Gehinnom, as it says, "But those who turn to their perverseness, God will make them go the way of evildoers. Peace upon Israel" (Psalm 125:5). [This means that] even at a time when there is peace upon Israel, [i.e., when the righteous have died, because their death atones for the sins of Israel and brings peace,] God will make them go the way of evildoers [to Gehinnom].

It was taught in the yeshivah of R. Yishmael: If you see a Torah scholar who has committed a transgression at night, do not think badly of him during the day, for maybe he repented. [The Gemara asks indignantly:] What! Why do you say, "Maybe"? No, he most certainly repented. [The Gemara answers:] You can only be sure that he repented if the sin he committed was between himself and God, but if he sinned against his fellow man by misappropriating money, then his repentance is not accepted until he returns the money to its owner. [Therefore, the term "maybe" is fitting.]

R. Yehoshua b. Levi further said: In twenty-four cases the Bet Din would excommunicate a person for offending a rabbi, and they are all recorded in the Mishnah. R. Elazar asked him: Where in the Mishnah? He replied: Look for them, and you'll find them. R. Elazar searched and found three cases: One case about a person who made derogatory remarks about a Torah scholar after his death, another about a person who sneered at the washing of the hands, and a third about a person who spoke to God with too much familiarity.

What was the case in the Mishnah where a person was excommunicated for making a derogatory remark about deceased Torah scholars? As we have learned:[106] [A *sotah* is made to drink the curse-bearing waters[107]]. Akavyah b. Mehalalel used to say: The water of the *sotah* is given neither to a convert nor to a freed female slave. The Sages disagree, and say that it is. The Sages said to Akavyah: There is the case of a certain Karkemit, a freed female slave in Jerusalem, who was made to drink the curse-bearing water by Shemayah and Avtalyon.[108] Akavyah replied: They gave her the water because she was like them. [They were descendants of Sennacherib,[109] thus from a family of converts.] Akavaya was excommunicated [for making this disparaging remark], and when he died in excommunication the Bet Din stoned his coffin.

[The Gemara asks:] What is the case where a person was excommunicated for sneering at the washing of the hands? [The Gemara answers:] We learned in a Mishnah: R. Yehudah said: Heaven forbid that we should say that Akavyah b. Mehalalel was excommunicated! For the doors of the Court of the *Bet Hamikdash* did not close on anyone in Israel[110] who could equal Akavyah b. Mehalalel in wisdom, purity, and piety. [In other words, he was a saintly person.] So who was, in fact, excommunicated? It was Elazar b. Chanoch, because he expressed doubt about the law of washing the hands [before meals], and when he died, the Bet Din had a large stone placed on his coffin, to teach you that if a person is excommunicated and dies in a state of excommunication the Bet Din stones his coffin.[111] [It should be noted that, although the entire incident of Akavyah b. Mehalalel was not true, and he was never excommunicated, the law still stands that one is excommunicated for denigrating a deceased Torah scholar.]

What is the case where a person was excommunicated for speaking to God with too much familiarity? [The Gemara answers:] We have learned in a Mishnah: Shimon b. Shetach sent a message to Choni HaMe'aggeil, because of the following incident[112]: [During a severe drought] the people came to Choni for help. He drew a circle on the ground, stood in the circle, and prayed for rain, whereupon God sent a torrential cloudburst. Said Choni: This is not what I asked for! If this keeps up, the world will be inundated. Thereupon, it started drizzling. Said Choni: This is not what I asked for! At last a normal, gentle rain began to fall. R. Shimon b. Shetach, objecting to the excessive familiarity Choni was exhibiting in his dialogue with God, said: You deserve to be excommunicated, and if you were not [the great] Choni I would place you under a ban. But what can I do, since you speak informally to God, and yet He fulfills your wishes. You are like a child who speaks to his father informally, and the father does what the child wants. To you applies the verse, "Your father and mother will rejoice, and she who gave birth to you will exult" (Proverbs 23:25). [Although Choni was not excommunicated we can derive from his message that a person who speaks to God in a casual manner deserves to be excommunicated.]

BIRKAT HAMAZON—
GRACE AFTER MEALS

(20b) R. Avira expounded—sometimes in the name of R. Ammi and sometimes in the name of R. Assi—as follows: The ministering angels said to the Holy One, blessed be He: Master of the universe, It is written in Your Torah, that "You show no favor or take bribes" (Deuteronomy 10:17). [Is that so?] Aren't You showing favor to Israel, for it says, "God bestows favor upon you"? (Numbers 6:26). Replied God: Why shouldn't I show favor to Israel! Look, I wrote in the Torah, "When you eat and are satisfied, you must bless God your Lord" (Deuteronomy 8:10) [I said they should bless only when they are satiated], but they are so stringent that even when they eat as little as the size of an olive or an egg[113] [they recite *Birkat Hamazon*, Grace after Meals].

(21a) R. Yehudah said: From where is it known that the grace after meals is ordained by the Torah? For it says, "When you eat and are satisfied, you must bless God your Lord" (Deuteronomy 8:10). From where do we know that the *berachah* before you study the Torah is a Biblical command? Because it says, "When I proclaim God's name, praise God for His greatness" (Deuteronomy 32:3).

(21b) R. Adda b. Ahava said: From where is it known that a person praying by himself does not recite the *Kedushah*?[114] Because it says, "I must be sanctified among the children of Israel" (Leviticus 22:32); and for any divine service at least ten men are required. From where in Scripture is this derived? Rabina'i the brother of R. Chiya derives it from an analogy between two verses that contain the word *toch*. It says in one verse, "I must be sanctified *betoch*, among, the children of Israel." In another verse we read, "Separate yourselves *mitoch*, from among, this *eidah*, community" (Numbers 16:21). Now we draw an analogy between this verse that contains the word *eidah* and another verse that also contains the word *eidah*, the other verse being, "How long shall this evil *eidah*, community, exist?" (Numbers 14:27). Now, just as the *eidah* in this verse refers to ten men [the ten spies who brought back a bad report about Eretz Yisrael], so does the other verse refer to ten men, [and the analogy of *toch* shows that *Kedushah* requires ten men].

PRAYER REQUIRES
A CLEAN ENVIRONMENT

(24b) R. Abba tried to avoid R. Yehudah because [R. Abba] wanted to go to Eretz Yisrael, but R. Yehudah had said: Whoever leaves Babylonia to go to Eretz Yisrael violates a positive commandment, for it says, "They shall be brought to Babylonia, and there they shall remain until I take note of them, declares God" (Jeremiah 27:22). [R. Abba] said: Let me go and listen from outside the yeshivah to what [R. Yehudah] is saying, and then I'll go. So he went and heard reciting in front of R. Yehudah: If a person was saying the *Shemoneh Esrei* and he broke wind, he should wait until the wind passes off and resume where he left off. Some say: If he was reciting the *Shemoneh Esrei* and he wanted to break wind, he should step back four cubits, break wind, and wait until the wind dissipates and resume his prayer, saying: Master of the universe, You created us with many openings and cavities. You are well aware of our shame and confusion, and that our end is worms and maggots! He then resumes the *Shemoneh Esrei* where he left off. R. Abba then said: If I had come only to hear this, it would have been worthwhile.

It was taught in a *Baraita* according to R. Chisda: If a person is walking in a dirty alley he should not recite the *Shema*, and that's not all, but if he was in the middle of reciting the *Shema* when he came to a dirty alley, he should stop. [The Gemara asks:] And what if he doesn't stop? R. Meyasha the grandson of R. Yehoshua b. Levi said: Scripture alludes to such a person in the following verse, "Moreover, I gave them laws that were not good and rules by which they will not live" (Ezekiel 20:25), [which is to say that by doing the mitzvah of reading the *Shema* improperly he does not merit life]. R. Assi said, the following verse [alludes to him,] "Ah, those who haul sin with ropes of falsehood" (Isaiah 5:18), [meaning, he brings sin

upon himself with a "flimsy rope," by merely uttering the words of *Shema* in an improper place (Rashi)]. R. Adda b. Ahavah said: "Because he has denigrated the word of God," (Numbers 15:31) [meaning, he denigrated the words of *Shema*]. [The Gemara asks:] And if he did stop, what reward will he get? R. Abbahu said: To him the following verse applies, "Through this word you will live long" (Deuteronomy 32:47), [by being careful to say the words of *Shema* in suitable surroundings you will live long].

HISTORICAL BACKGROUND OF
THE *SHEMONEH ESREI*

(26b) We learned: R. Yose b. R. Chanina says: The [three] *Shemoneh Esrei* prayers were instituted by the Patriarchs [Abraham, Isaac, and Jacob]. R. Yehoshua b. Levi says: The *Shemoneh Esrei* prayers were instituted [after the destruction of the *Beit Hamikdash*], to take the place of the continual sacrifices [that were brought each day, one in the morning and one in the afternoon].[115] We have one *Baraita* that supports the opinion of R. Yose b. R. Chanina, and another *Baraita* that supports R. Yehoshua b. Levi's view. The *Baraita* that reflects R. Yose b. R. Chanina's opinion states: Abraham instituted the *Shemoneh Esrei* of the morning [*Shacharit*], for it says, "Abraham got up early in the morning, and went to the place where he had stood [*amad*]" (Genesis 19:27), and *amidah*, "standing," means only prayer, as it says, "Then Pinchas stood up *vaya'amod*, and prayed" (Psalm 106:30). Isaac instituted the *Shemoneh Esrei* of the afternoon [*Minchah*], for it says, "Isaac went out *lasuach*, to converse [with God] in the field toward evening, [in the afternoon,]" (Genesis 24:63), and *sichah*, conversing [in this context] means prayer, as it says, "A prayer of the poor man when he is faint and pours forth *sicho*, his conversation to God" (Psalm 102:1). Jacob instituted the *Shemoneh Esrei* of the evening [*Maariv*], for it says, "He [Jacob] came to a familiar place, *vayifga*, and spent the night there because the sun had already set" (Genesis 28:10). And *vayifga* denotes prayer, as it says, "As for you, do not pray for this people, do not raise a cry of prayer on their behalf, do not *tifga*, plead with Me" (Jeremiah 7:16).

The *Baraita* that reflects R. Yehoshua b. Levi's opinion [that the *Shemoneh Esrei* prayers correspond to the sacrifices] states: Why did the Sages say that the morning *Shemoneh Esrei* could be said until midday? Because the continual morning sacrifice could be brought up until midday . . . And why did they say that the afternoon *Shemoneh Esrei* could be said up to the evening? Because the continual afternoon sacrifice could be brought until the evening.

THE CONFLICT BETWEEN
R. GAMLIEL AND R. YEHOSHUA

(27b) We have been taught: R. Eliezer says: If someone prays standing behind his rabbi [which shows arrogance], or greets his rabbi in a casual way,[116] or gives public Talmudic discourses without his rabbi's permission, or says something he has not heard from his rabbi [and attributes it to his rabbi (Rosh)], his irreverent behavior causes the *Shechinah* to depart from Israel.

The Rabbis taught in a *Baraita*: It happened that a student came to R. Yehoshua [who was the *Av Bet Din*, head of the *Bet Din*] and asked, "Rabbi, is the evening *Shemoneh Esrei (Maariv)* optional or mandatory?" R. Yehoshua answered, "It is optional." The same student then went to R. Gamliel [who was the *Nasi*, head of the Sanhedrin] and asked him the same question. R. Gamliel replied, "It is mandatory." Countered the student, "But R. Yehoshua told me that it is optional!" Said R. Gamliel, "Wait until tomorrow when all the great scholars assemble in the *bet midrash*." When the great scholars had assembled, this student got up and asked, "Is the evening *Shemoneh Esrei* optional or mandatory?" "It is mandatory," replied R. Gamliel. Turning to the Sages, R. Gamliel then asked, "Is there anyone here who disagrees with me [and says that it is optional]?" "No," replied R. Yehoshua.[117] "But I was told that you said that it is optional!" challenged R. Gamliel. He then said, "Stand up, Yehoshua, and let them testify against you [that you, in fact, hold that it is optional."] R. Yehoshua got up and said, "If I were alive and the witness dead, I could deny it, [and the dead could not contradict me]. But now that the witness is alive and I am alive, how can a living person contradict a living person?" [i.e., I cannot deny that I said this]. So R. Gamliel continued his lecture while R. Yehoshua remained standing, until all the scholars in the *bet midrash* began to complain. They called out to Chutzpit the *meturgeman*[118] [the person who explained the rabbi's discourse to the audience simultaneously, as the rabbi was speaking] and said to him, "Stop!" and Chutzpit stopped his exposition. Then they said, "How much longer are we going to stand by and watch R. Yehoshua's feelings being hurt? Last year on Rosh Hashanah[119] R. Gamliel treated R. Yehoshua harshly [when he ordered him to appear before him with his staff and his money on the day when Yom Kippur would fall according to R. Yehoshua's calculation].

He offended him again in the incident with R. Tzadok,[120] and now he is snubbing him again! Let's remove R. Gamliel from office!" [They deliberated,] "Whom shall we appoint to replace him? We can hardly appoint R. Yehoshua. That would be too painful for R. Gamliel, since he is his opponent. We can hardly appoint R. Akiva, because R. Gamliel may invoke punishment on him, and R. Akiva has no ancestral merit[121] [to protect him from this.] So let's appoint R. Elazar b. Azariah; he is wise and rich and he is a tenth-generation descendant from Ezra. He is wise, so that any question we ask him he will be able to answer. He is rich, so that if it is necessary to pay off the

emperor, he will be able to do so. He is a tenth-generation descendant from Ezra, so that he has ancestral merit, and R. Gamliel will not be able to invoke punishment on him." They approached R. Elazar b. Azariah and said to him, "Are you willing to become the head of the Yeshivah?" He answered, "I have to talk it over with my wife." He went and discussed it with his wife. She said to him, (28a) "Maybe they'll fire you too." He replied, ["There is a saying,] 'It is worth to use an expensive crystal goblet for only one day, even if it breaks the next day,'" [meaning, it is worthwhile to take the position even if it lasts only for one day]. She raised another objection, "But you don't have white hair," [and a person in that position should look like a venerable old man]. He was eighteen years old at that time, and miraculously, eighteen rows of hair [on his beard] turned white. That is why R. Elazar b. Azariah said: I am *like* seventy years old, but not actually seventy years old.

OPEN ADMISSION

We learned in a *Baraita*: On that day [when R. Elazar b. Azariah was installed [as *Nasi*] they removed the doorman [who had been guarding the door of the *bet midrash* during R. Gamliel's term in office,] and admission was granted to any student who wished to enter. Because R. Gamliel had issued a proclamation: Any scholar who is not truly sincere[122] may not enter the *bet midrash* [and the doorman kept out the people who did not qualify]. On that day many seats were added in the *bet midrash* [to accommodate the influx of new scholars]. R. Yochanan said: There is a difference of opinion between Abba Yosef b. Dusta'i and the Rabbis. According to one, four hundred seats were added, and according to the other, seven hundred seats were added. R. Gamliel felt bad. He said to himself: Perhaps, God forbid, I kept people from studying the Torah [by preventing them from entering the *bet midrash*]. Thereupon he was shown in a dream white barrels full of ashes [to tell him that the new scholars were like ashes and not worthy to be in the yeshivah]. [The Gemara comments:] But this was not really true, [they were, in fact, sincere scholars;] he was only shown this dream to appease him [but the Gemara seems to say that actually R. Gamliel's policy of restricted admission was incorrect].

R. GAMLIEL APOLOGIZES

We learned in a *Baraita*: The tractate *Eiduyot* [which is a collection of many *halachot*] was learned on that day; and wherever the phrase "on that day" is used in the Talmud it refers to the day [that R. Elazar b. Azariah became the *Nasi*]. And there was no *Halachah*, which until that time had been in doubt that was not clarified and decided on that day. [The Gemara now points out the noble character of R. Gamliel, stating:]

R. Gamliel, [even though he had been unseated] did not stay away from the *bet midrash* even for an hour [but continued to participate in the deliberations]. Which is evidenced in the following Mishnah: On that day, Yehudah, an Ammonite convert, appeared in the *bet midrash* and asked the Sages: Am I permitted to enter into the community of Israel [i.e., May I marry a Jewish woman]? Said R. Gamliel: [Even though you are a convert,] you are forbidden to marry a Jewish woman. R. Yehoshua said: You are allowed to marry a Jewish woman.

Countered R. Gamliel: But doesn't it say explicitly, "An Ammonite or Moabite may not enter God's marriage group"? (Deuteronomy 23:4). To which R. Yehoshua retorted: Do the original nations of Ammon and Moab still live in their native countries? After all, Sennacherib, king of Assyria, long ago came and mixed up all the nations, as it says, [The king of Assyria said:] "I have erased the borders of peoples, I have plundered their treasures and exiled their vast populations" (Isaiah 10:13). [Therefore, today we don't know who is a descendant of the original Ammonites.] And we have a principle that when in doubt we follow the majority, [and the majority of the people in the world are not Ammonites. Thus, we may assume that any person that presents himself to us belongs to the majority of nations and is not a descendant of Ammon. Therefore, even though this convert Yehudah comes from the country of Ammon, he is part of the majority and is not an Ammonite and permitted to marry a Jewish woman].

Said R. Gamliel in rebuttal: But it says, "But afterwards I will bring back the captivity of the children of Ammon" (Jeremiah 49:6), so they must have come back already, [and the convert is an Ammonite and forbidden to marry a Jewish woman]. To which R. Yehoshua replied: But it also says, "I will bring back My people Israel," (Amos 9:14) and they have not yet returned, [so that you have no proof that the prophecy regarding Ammon has been fulfilled]. They immediately ruled that the convert was permitted to marry a Jewish woman. R. Gamliel then said: I now recognize that R. Yehoshua's opinion is decisive, [and that I unduly offended him]. I will go and apologize to him. When he came to R. Yehoshua's house he noticed that the walls of the house were black. He remarked, "From the walls of your house I can tell that you must be a blacksmith." R. Yehoshua replied, "Woe to the generation whose leader you are, since I see that you have no idea what Torah scholars are going through, how hard it is for them to make a living and to sustain themselves!" R. Gamliel said, "I admit that I was wrong. Please forgive me for hurting your feelings." R. Yehoshua ignored him. R. Gamliel persisted, "Please forgive me out of repect for my father." R. Yehoshua then accepted the apology. They said, "Who will go and and tell the Rabbis [that we made up]?" A certain laundryman said, "I will go."

So R. Yehoshua sent the following message with him to the *bet midrash*: The one who used to wear the cloak should continue to wear the cloak [i.e., R. Gamliel should be reinstated as the *Nasi*;] but should the one who did not wear the cloak [i.e., R. Elazar b. Azariah] say to the one who used to wear the cloak: Take off your robe and I will wear it? [However, the scholars in the *bet midrash* had misgivings about the authenticity of the message.] So Rabbi Akiva said to the Rabbis: Let's close all the doors of the *bet midrash*, so that R. Gamliel's attendants will not be able to come and pressure the Rabbis into restoring him to office. Said R. Yehoshua: I had better go and deliver the message myself. He went, knocked on the door of the *bet midrash* and said: Let a sprinkler [the *kohen* who sprinkled the purification water] who is the son of a sprinkler, continue to sprinkle [meaning, let R. Gamliel be restored to office]. Should someone who is neither a sprinkler nor the son of a sprinkler say to a sprinkler, the son of a sprinkler: Your water is ordinary cave water [and not purification water] and your ashes are plain ashes from a stove [and not ashes from the red cow]?[123]

Said R. Akiva to him, "R. Yehoshua, we see that you have received your apology. Whatever we did we only did for the sake of your honor. Tomorrow morning you and I will go to [R. Gamliel's] house" [to tell him that he has been reinstated as *Nasi*]. They said, 'But what shall we do [with R. Elazar b. Azariah]?' We have a rule that you may raise an object to a higher degree of sanctity but you may not lower its degree of sanctity. [Since R. Elazar b. Azariah was elevated to the post of *Nasi* we cannot depose him.] If we arrange for one to lecture one week and the other to lecture the next week, they will be envious of each other. Therefore, let R. Gamliel lecture three weeks and R. Elazar b. Azariah one week. And now we understand what was meant when someone asked: 'Whose week was it?' and they answered, 'It was R. Elazar b. Azariah's week.' [We now understand that it refers to the week that it was R. Elazar b. Azariah's turn to lecture.]—And the student [who asked whether the *Shemoneh Esrei* of *Maariv* is optional or mandatory] was R. Shimon b. Yocha'i.[124]

R. NECHUNIA'S PRAYER

(28b) MISHNAH. R. Nechunia b. Hakaneh used to say a short prayer when he entered the *bet hamidrash*, and when he left the *bet hamidrash*. They asked him: What is the text of this prayer? He replied: On my way in I pray that no mistake shall happen because of me [i.e., no wrong decision be rendered,] and on my way out I thank God for my lot [that I have the opportunity to study Torah].

GEMARA: [The Gemara elaborates:] The Rabbis taught in a *Baraita*: What prayer did he say[125] on entering the *beit midrash*?—May it be Your will, Lord my

God, that no mistake should arise through me, and that I should not err in a matter of *halachah*, and my colleagues will rejoice over [my embarrassment. They would be punished for that, and I would be the indirect cause of their punishment (Rashi)]. That I should not call unclean clean and clean unclean, and that my colleagues should not err in a matter of *halachah*, and I rejoice in [their embarrassment]. What did he say on his way out of the *bet midrash*? I thank You, Lord my God, that You set my portion with those who sit in the *bet hamidrash*, and You have not set my portion with those who sit in the street corners. For I get up early and they get up early, but I get up early to learn Torah, whereas they get up early to do trivial things. I work and they work, but I work and receive a reward, whereas they work and do not receive a reward.[126] I am running and they are running, but I am running toward life in the world to come, whereas they are running toward Gehinnom.

R. ELIEZER'S ADMONITION

Our Rabbis taught: When R. Eliezer became sick, his students came to visit him. They said to him: Rabbi, teach us the ways of life, so that we may earn through them the life of the world to come. He told them: Be mindful of the dignity of your friends, and when you are praying you should be aware before whom you are standing, keep your children from engaging in idle chatter, and set them between the knees of Torah scholars, and if you do all this you will earn life in the the world to come.

R. YOCHANAN B. ZAKKAI'S LAST WORDS

When R. Yochanan b. Zakkai became sick, his students came to visit him. When he saw them, he began to cry. His students said to him: Rabbi, lamp of Israel, the right pillar [the reference is to the two pillars in the *Bet Hamikdash* called Yachin and Boaz; see I Kings 7:21], mighty hammer! Why are you crying? He replied: If they were taking me before a human king who is here today and tomorrow in the grave, who may become angry with me but whose anger will not last forever, who may imprison me, but whose imprisonment is not forever, who may put me to death but not to everlasting death, and whom I can appease with words and bribe with money, nevertheless I would be crying. Now that I am about to be taken before the King who reigns over kings, the Holy One, blessed be He, who lives and endures forever and ever; if He is angry with me His anger lasts forever, if He imprisons me His imprisonment is eternal, if he puts me to death, it is an eternal death, and whom I cannot appease with words or bribe with money.[127] [Shouldn't I cry?] And that's not all. When there are two roads

in front of me: one leading to *Gan Eden*, the other to Gehinnom, and I don't know which road are they going to take me, shouldn't I cry? They said to him: Rabbi, please bless us. He said to them: May it be God's will that your fear of God should be as great as your fear of flesh and blood. His students said to him: Is that all? [I.e., our fear of God should only be equal to our fear of man?] He said to them: I wish you would be able to attain that! And I'll prove it to you. If a person commits a sin he says: I hope that no one sees me, [but he is not afraid that God watches him. Which proves that his fear of man is stronger than his fear of God]. When he was about to die, he said to them: Clear out the vessels [so that they should not become unclean, since vessels in the house with a dead body become unclean,[128]] and prepare a chair for Hezekiah, the king of Judah, who is coming [to accompany me to heaven].

WHY EIGHTEEN *BERACHOT*?

MISHNAH. R. Gamliel said: Every day a person should say eighteen *berachot* (blessings), [the *Shemoneh Esrei*][129].

GEMARA. To what do these eighteen *berachot* correspond? R. Hillel, the son of R. Shmuel b. Nachmani, said: They correspond to the eighteen times David mentioned God's name in the Psalm, "Render unto God, you sons of the powerful" (Psalm 29). R. Yosef said: To the eighteen times God's name is mentioned in the *Shema*. R. Tanchum said in the name of R. Yehoshua b. Levi: To the eighteen vertebrae in the spinal column. R. Tanchum also said in the name of R. Yehoshua b. Levi: When you say the *Shemoneh Esrei* you should bow [at the appropriate places] to the point that all vertebrae in the spinal column are protruding through the skin. Ulla says: [To the point that the bulge that forms in the fat of your chest] is equal to the width of an *issur* [a coin]. R. Chanina said: If you simply bow your head, that is sufficient. Said Rava: This is true only if it hurts you to bow [you are trying to do more], so that it looks like you are making an effort to bow down.

[The Gemara asks:] Aren't these eighteen *berachot* really nineteen? R. Levi said: The *berachah* of *Velamalshinim* [which relates to heretics] was later inserted in Yavneh. [The Gemara asks:] What does this *berachah* correspond to? R. Levi said: In the view of R. Hillel [who mentioned the eighteen times God's name occurred in Psalm 29], it corresponds to, "The God of glory thunders" (Psalm 29:3); in the view of R. Yosef [who matched the eighteen *berachot* with the eighteen times God's name occurs in the *Shema*], it corresponds to the word *echad* (one) in the *Shema* [which is not actually a divine name, but refers to the oneness of God]. In R. Tanchum's view [who matched them with the eighteen vertebrae], it corresponds to the small vertebra in the spinal column.

THE *BERACHAH* RELATING TO HERETICS

The Rabbis taught: Shimon Hapakuli arranged the order of the eighteen *berachot* [which we say in the *Shemoneh Esrei*] before R. Gamliel in Yavneh. R. Gamliel asked the Sages: Is there anyone here who would be able to compose a *berachah* relating to the heretics?[130] Shmuel Hakatan came and composed the *berachah* [of *Velamalshinim*]. The next year [Shmuel Hakatan, while officiating as *chazzan*], forgot the text of that *berachah*. (29a) For two or three hours he tried to recall it, and they did not remove him from being the *chazzan*. [The Gemara asks:] Why didn't they remove him, seeing that R. Yehudah said in the name of Rav: If a *chazzan* makes a mistake in any of the other *berachot* we do not remove him, but if he makes a mistake in the *berachah* of the heretics he is removed, because we suspect him of being a heretic. [So why was Shmuel Hakatan allowed to remain at his post?] [The Gemara answers:] Shmuel Hakatan is different, because he himself composed it, [therefore we don't suspect that he became a heretic]. [Asks the Gemara:] But shouldn't we be concerned that he had a change of heart [and became a heretic]?

Abbaye said: We have a tradition: A good man does not turn bad. [Asks the Gemara:] Is that so? Doesn't it say, "If a righteous person turns away from his righteousness and does wrong"? (Ezekiel 18:24). [So you see that a righteous person can go bad.] [The Gemara answers:] This verse refers to a person who originally was wicked [and later repented; such a person can revert to his old ways,] but one who was always righteous does not turn bad. [The Gemara challenges this:] Is that true? After all, we learned in a Mishnah: Don't be sure of yourself until the day you die. For there was the case of Yochanan the High Priest who officiated for eighty years, and in the end of his days he became a Sadducee.[131] [So you see that even a person who was a *tzaddik* all his life can become a heretic, and Shmuel Hakatan also may have become a heretic.] Abbaye said: Yochanan is really Yannai, [Yochanan was not a *tzaddik* all his life. He was, in fact, King Yannai, who was an evil man, even though he later became a righteous man. When he ended up as a Sadducee he was reverting to his original wicked ways. But someone who was a *tzaddik* all his life would not do something like that.]

Rava said: Yannai and Yochanan are two different persons. Yannai was originally wicked, but Yochanan was originally righteous. [The Gemara analyzes:] According to Abbaye there is no problem [Yochanan/Yannai was originally evil, therefore, in the end he reverted to his evil ways, whereas Shmuel Hakatan was a *tzaddik* all his life and will not turn bad]. But according to Rava [who said that Yochanan was a *tzaddik* from the start], there is a difficulty [because Yochanan became a Sadducee, thus Shmuel

Hakatan also may have become a heretic]. Rava will tell you: It is possible that a person who was righteous from the start also may backslide and turn bad. [Asks the Gemara:] If so, why didn't they remove Shmuel Hakatan? [The Gemara answers:] Shmuel Hakatan is different, because he had already started to say the *berachah Velamalshinim*. For R. Yehudah said in the name of Rav—or some say in the name of R. Yehoshua b. Levi: [The rule that we remove a *chazzan* if he made a mistake in *Velamalshinim*] applies only if he has not yet begun to say the *berachah*, but if he has begun, [and in the middle he became confused] he is allowed to finish.

PRAYING AT THE RIGHT TIME

(29b) [We learned in the Mishnah:] R. Eliezer says: If someone makes his *Shemoneh Esrei* a *keva*, a prescribed task, his prayer is not accepted. [The Gemara asks:] What does *keva* mean? R. Yaakov b. Idi said in the name of R. Oshaia: If a person considers praying a burden [and only prays to fulfill his obligation]. The Rabbis say: If he does not pray in a beseeching manner. Rabbah and R. Yosef both say: If he does not insert a new idea into his prayer [but says it routinely].[132] R. Zeira said: I can add a new idea to my prayer, but I am afraid to do so because I may become confused and forget where I left off. Abbaye b. Avin and R. Chanina b. Avin both said: [*Keva* refers to] someone who does not pray [*Shacharit*] at sunrise and [*Minchah*] at sunset. [He prays in order to conform to the minimum requirements of the law, making no effort to pray at the optimum times.] For R. Chiya b. Abba said in the name of R. Yochanan: It is a mitzvah to pray when the sun is either rising or setting. R. Zeira said: The following verse supports this, "Let them fear You when the sun is rising [a reference to *Shacharit*], and before the moon [when the sun is setting, a reference to *Minchah*], all generations" (Psalm 72:5). However, in Eretz Yisrael they cursed anyone who delays the *Minchah* prayer until sunset. Why? Perhaps [by waiting until the last moment] he will miss the proper time.[133]

TEFILLAT HADERECH—THE WAYFARER'S PRAYER

Eliyahu said to R. Yehudah, the brother of R. Sala Chasida: Don't get angry, and that will prevent you from committing a sin. Don't get drunk, and that will also prevent you from committing a sin. And when you go on a trip, consult with your Creator [i.e., pray to God], and then set out on your journey. [The Gemara asks:] What is meant by, "Consult with your Creator, and then set out on your journey"? R. Yaakov said in the name of R. Chisda: This refers to *Tefillat Haderech*, the Wayfarer's Prayer.

(30a) [The Gemara asks:] How should you say the Wayfarer's Prayer? R. Chisda said: While standing erect. R. Sheshet said: You may say it even while walking. R. Chisda and R. Sheshet once were going on a trip together. R. Chisda stopped and began to say *Tefillat Haderech*. R. Sheshet [who was blind] asked his attendant: What is R. Chisda doing [why did he stop]? The attendant replied: He is standing and saying *Tefillat Haderech*. R. Sheshet then told his attendant: Help me stand up, and I will also say *Tefillat Haderech* while standing. [Even though I hold that it may be said while walking,] if I can do it in a better way, why do it in an inferior way?

FACING ERETZ YISRAEL
WHEN PRAYING

The Rabbis taught in a *Baraita*: A blind person or someone who cannot tell the four directions[134] should focus his thoughts on his Father in heaven. For it says, "They pray to God" (1 Kings 8:44). If he is standing outside Eretz Yisrael, he should turn toward Eretz Yisrael, for it says, "They pray to You in the direction of their land" (ibid. 48). If he is standing inside Eretz Yisrael, he should turn toward Jerusalem, for it says, "They pray to God in the direction of the city which You have chosen" (ibid. 44). If he stands in Jerusalem he should turn in the direction of the *Bet Hamikdash*, for it says, "Then they pray toward this house" (2 Chronicles 6:26). If he stands in the *Bet Hamikdash* he should face toward the Holy of Holies, for it says, "Then they pray toward this place" (1 Kings 8:35) . . . Consequently, if he is in the east he should face toward the west; if he is the west he should face toward the east; if he is in the south he should face toward the north; and if he is in the north he should face toward the south. In this way all Israel will be directing their thoughts toward the same place. R. Avin said: What verse supports this?— "Your neck is like the Tower of David, built with *talpiyot*, turrets," (Song of Songs 4:4). The word *talpiyot* is a contraction of *tel*, "the elevation," meaning the *Bet Hamikdash*, and *piyot ponim*, "toward which all mouths (*piyot*) are turned (*ponim*)" [meaning all prayers are directed].

BE IN AWE EVEN WHEN
REJOICING

(30b) MISHNAH. You should only begin to say the *Shemoneh Esrei* if you are in a humble frame of mind. The pious men of old would wait an hour before they began to pray, in order to concentrate their thoughts on their Father in heaven.

GEMARA. Abbaya was sitting in front of [his teacher] Rabbah, and Rabbah noticed that Abbaye was a bit too cheerful [as if he was not serious about

the Torah and mitzvot]. Rabbah told him: It is written, "Rejoice with trembling" (Psalm 2:11) [meaning, be respectful even when rejoicing], to which Abbaye replied, "[Your criticism is unfounded,] because I am wearing *tefillin* [and they are a testimony that I submit my heart and power to God]. R. Yirmiyah was sitting in front of R. Zeira and seemed to be overly cheerful. So R. Zeira told him, "In all sorrow there is profit" (Proverbs 14:23). R. Yirmiyah replied: [I have reason to be happy because] I am wearing *tefillin* [and the mitzvah fills me with joy].

Mar the son of Ravina made a wedding banquet for his son. He saw that the rabbis seemed overly jolly, (31a) so he brought a precious white crystal cup worth four hundred *zuz* and shattered it in front of them. That dampened their spirits. R. Ashi made a wedding banquet for his son, and when he noticed that the rabbis were becoming overly merry he brought a white crystal cup and broke it in front of them, and that subdued their spirits. At the wedding of Mar, Ravina's grandson, the rabbis said to R. Hammenuna Zuti: "Please sing a song for us!" So he sang: Woe is to us, for we all will die! The Rabbis said to him: What refrain shall we sing to this song? He replied: [Sing the following line:] Where is the Torah, and where is the mitzvah that we will need to protect us [from the judgment of Gehinnom! (Rashi)].

R. Yochanan said in the name of R. Shimon b. Yocha'i: A person is forbidden to fill his mouth with laughter in this world, [to laugh boisterously, with unbridled hilarity,] because it says, "*Then* our mouths will be filled with laughter, and our tongues with songs of joy." When will that be? At the time "When they will say among the nations, 'God has done great things for them!'" [at the ultimate redemption] (Psalm 126:2). It was told about Resh Lakish that after he heard this saying from his teacher R. Yochanan, he never again broke into uncontrolled laughter.

BIDDING FAREWELL WITH
A TORAH THOUGHT

Our Rabbis taught in a *Baraita*: You should not start praying when you are in a gloomy mood, a lazy mood, a giddy mood, a talkative mood, a frivolous mood, or while you are engaged in trivial chatter, but only when you are in a joyous mood that stems from doing a mitzvah [for example, from the joy you derive from reciting *Ashrei* (Psalm 145) (Rashi)]. In the same way, when bidding farewell to a friend, don't say goodbye while talking banalities, telling jokes, frivolous things, or making small talk; rather, tell your friend a *halachic* point. And so we find that the early prophets always ended their speeches with words of praise and comfort.

In the same vein, Mari the grandson of R. Huna the son of R. Yirmiyah b. Abba learned: When saying goodbye to a friend you should always end with a Torah insight. That way, your friend will remember you. And so we find that R. Kahana escorted R. Shimi b. Ashi from Pum Nahara to Bei Tzinita, a palm grove in Babylon, and when he arrived there he said to him: Master, is it true what people say that these palm trees of Babylon have been here from the time of Adam? R. Kahana replied: Your question brings to mind a saying of R. Yose b. R. Chanina. For R. Yose b. R. Chanina said: What is meant by the verse, "A land no man passed through, where no human being has settled"? (Jeremiah 2:6). Now, if no one passed through it, how could anyone settle there? The verse comes to teach you that whatever land Adam decreed should be settled is settled, and whatever land Adam decreed should not be settled is not settled. [So we see that R. Kahana combined his farewell with a Torah thought.]

Our Rabbis taught: When you pray you should direct your thoughts to heaven. Abba Shaul says: There is an allusion to this in the verse, "You will direct their hearts; You will incline Your ear [and listen to their prayers"] (Psalm 10:17).

It was taught in a *Baraita*: R. Yehudah says: This was the custom of R. Akiva: when he prayed together with the congregation, he used to cut it short in order not to try the patience of the congregation [who would wait until R. Akiva had finished his *Shemoneh Esrei*]. But when he prayed by himself, a person would leave him in one corner and later find him in a different corner. Why is that? Because of his bowing and bending [during the *Shemoneh Esrei*, he unconsciously moved about the room].

HANNAH'S PRAYER

R. Hamenuna said: How many important *Halachot* [about the *Shemoneh Esrei*] can we derive from the following verses relating to Hannah: [Hannah, one of Elkanah's two wives, was childless. Brokenhearted, she went to the *Bet Hamikdash* to pray to God, and we read], "Now Hannah was praying in her heart; only her lips moved, but her voice could not be heard. So Eli [the priest] thought she was drunk. Eli said to her, 'How long will you make a drunken spectacle of yourself? Sober up!' And Hannah replied, 'Oh no, my lord! I am a very unhappy woman. I have drunk no wine or other strong drink, but I have been pouring out my heart to God. Do not take your maidservant for a worthless woman; I have only been speaking all this time out of my great anguish and distress.' 'Then go in peace,' said Eli. 'And may the God of Israel grant you what you have asked of Him'" (1 Samuel 1:13–17).]

[The Gemara now expounds these verses:] "Now Hannah was praying in her heart," from this we learn that when you pray you must concentrate your thoughts. "Only her lips moved," from this we learn that when you pray you should clearly enunciate the words. "Her voice could not be heard," this teaches us that you are not permitted to raise your voice when praying the *Shemoneh Esrei*. "So Eli thought that she was drunk," we derive from this that a drunken person is forbidden to say the *Shemoneh Esrei*. "Eli said, 'How long will you make a drunken spectacle of yourself?'" R. Elazar said: From this we learn that if someone sees his friend (31b) do something improper he should admonish him. "And Hannah replied, 'Oh no, my lord,'" Ulla, and according to others, R. Yose b. R. Chanina, said: She said to Eli: You are not a master in this matter, neither does the holy spirit rest on you that you suspect me of this thing. Others say: This is what she said: You are no master, [meaning,] the *Shechinah* and the holy spirit is not with you, for you judge me in a harsh manner and do not take a sympathetic view of my conduct. Don't you know "that I am a very unhappy woman. I have drunk no wine or other strong drink."

R. Elazar said: From this we learn that a person who is unjustly accused of anything must tell his accuser that he is wrong. "Do not take your maidservant for a worthless woman." R. Elazar said: We derive from this that for a person to say the *Shemoneh Esrei* while drunk is as bad as worshipping idols. [He uses a scriptural analogy to prove his point:] It says here, "Do not take your maidservant for a worthless woman, a daughter of *belia'al*," and elsewhere it says, "Certain sons of *belia'al*, worthless men, among you have gone forth" (Deuteronomy 13:14). Just as [in Deuteronomy 13:14] the term *belia'al* is used in connection with idolatry, so here too, it denotes idolatry. [Thus, Hannah equated praying while drunk with idolatry.] "'Then go in peace,' said Eli," R. Elazar said: From this we learn that if someone falsely suspects his neighbor of committing a wrong he must make amends. And that is not all, but he also has to bless him, as it says, [after wrongly suspecting Hannah of being drunk, Eli blessed her, saying,] "And may the God of Israel grant you what you have asked of Him."

[The Gemara continues its interpretation of Hannah's plea. It says,] "And she made this vow: 'O God of *Tzeva'ot* [Master of the Legions], if You will look upon the suffering of Your maidservant and will remember me and not forget Your maidservant, and if You will grant Your maidservant a male child, I will dedicate him to God for all the days of his life; and no razor shall ever touch his head'" (1 Samuel 1:11).

[The Gemara expounds:] "And she made this vow: 'O God of *Tzeva'ot*....'" R. Eleazar said: From the day that God created His world, no one called the Holy One, blessed be He, *Tzeva'ot* until Hannah came and called Him *Tzeva'ot*. Hannah said to the Holy One, blessed be He: Master of the Universe, [considering] the legions and legions that You have created in Your world, is it so hard for You to give me one son? [R. Elazar explains it] with a parable: A king made a feast for his servants, and a poor man came, stood by the door, and said to them: Please give me a piece of bread, but no one paid attention to him, so he pushed his way into the king's chamber and said to him: Your Majesty, seeing that you made this great feast, is it so hard for you to give me one small piece of bread?

[Hannah said,] "If You will indeed look [ra'oh tir'eh,] at the suffering . . ." R. Elazar said [explaining the seemingly redundant expression ra'oh tir'eh, literally translated, "see you will see"]: Hannah said to the Holy One, blessed be He: Master of the universe, if You will look, good and well. But if You will not look, you will have to help me, regardless.

[Note: It should be remembered that the Torah says[135] that if a husband warns his wife not to closet herself with a certain man, and she violates that warning, the husband brings her to the priest. If she does not admit to having committed adultery she has to drink the "water of the sotah." If she is guilty, both she and the adulterer die, but if she is innocent she is blessed and will become pregnant. Hannah now threatened: If You will not answer my plea] I will go and be alone with a man in a room. My husband Elkanah will become jealous [and warn me not to closet myself with that man. I will then violate his warning], and I will have to drink the "water of the sotah." [Then I will be blessed and become pregnant, because I will be innocent, since I did not do anything wrong with that man.] And You cannot belie Your Torah which says, "If the woman is pure and has not been defiled she will remain unharmed and will become pregnant" (Numbers 5:28).

[The Gemara challenges this interpretation:] This explanation is satisfactory only according to the one who says [that the blessing was] that if the woman was barren [before drinking the "water of the sotah"] she will become pregnant. But according to the one who says that [the blessing was] that if she used to give birth with difficulty, she will now give birth with ease; if she had girls she will now have boys; if she had short babies she will have tall ones; if she had dark-skinned babies, she will give birth to fair-skinned ones [but the blessing was not that she will become pregnant,] what are you going to say? [Since Hannah could not hope to become pregnant by becoming a sotah, what did she imply by the redundand ra'oh tireh?]

[The Gemara answers:] As we have learned in a Baraita: It says, "[If she was pure and has not been unfaithful] she will remain unharmed and will become pregnant." This teaches that if she was barren she will become pregnant, so says R. Yishmael. Said R. Akiva to him: If that is so, any childless woman will go and seclude herself in a room with a man [and be made to drink "water of the sotah"], and if she did not commit adultery she would become pregnant! Rather, the passage means that if she used to give birth with difficulty, she now will give birth with ease; if she had short babies, she now will give birth to tall ones; if they were dark-skinned they will now be fair-skinned ones; if she

only had one child she now will have two. [But there is no promise that a barren woman will become pregnant.] This being so, what did Hannah mean when she said, "You will look upon [using the repetitive ra'oh tir'eh] . . ." ? [The Gemara answers:] The Torah uses ordinary idiomatic language, [and Hannah merely used an idiomatic expression].

[Hannah vowed:] "If You will look upon the suffering of Your maidservant and will remember me and not forget Your maidservant, and if You will grant Your maidservant . . ." R. Yose b. R. Chanina said: Hannah uses the term "maidservant" three times. What is the significance of that?—Hannah said to the Holy One, blessed be He: Master of the universe, You have created three tests for a woman [when she finds herself in a life-threatening situation] to determine wether she deserves death,[136] namely, niddah, challah, and the kindling of the Shabbat lights.[137] Have I violated any of them?

[The verse continues:] "And if You will grant Your maidservant a male child" [literally, seed of men]. What did she mean by "a male child" [seed of men]? Rav said: A man among men [one who stands out]. Shmuel said: A child who will anoint two men [as king], namely Saul and David. R. Yochanan said: A child that will be equal to two men, namely Moses and Aaron, as it says, "Moses and Aaron [are outstanding] among His priests, and Samuel, among those who call his name" (Psalm 99:6). The Rabbis say: "A male child" [seed of men] denotes a child that will blend in among men [i.e., he will be inconspicuous]. When R. Dimi came from Eretz Yisrael [to Babylon], he explained this to mean: [Hannah prayed that her child should] be neither too tall nor too short, neither too thin nor too heavy, neither too red nor too pale, that he should not be too smart, [because people will talk about him, and the evil eye may be cast on him,] and that he should not be a fool.

[When Hanna brought the young Samuel to Eli, she said to him,] "I am the woman who stood here beside you" (1 Samuel 1:26). [The implication is that while she was standing and praying, Eli was standing too.] R. Yehoshua b. Levi said: This teaches you that it is forbidden to sit within four cubits of a person who is saying the Shemoneh Esrei.

YOUNG SAMUEL'S INDISCRETION

[Hannah said to Eli,] "It was this boy I prayed for" (1 Samuel 1:27). R. Elazar said: Samuel was guilty of rendering a decision in the presence of his rabbi. [That is why Eli wanted to invoke the divine death penalty on him and pray that Hannah would give birth to another child, but Hannah said "It was this boy I prayed for. I don't want a different child." (Rashi)]

[The Gemara now explains what the decision was that young Samuel rendered.] For it says, "After slaughtering the bull, they brought the boy to Eli" (ibid. 25). [The Gemara asks: What is the connection?] Because the bull was slaughtered, that's why they brought the boy to Eli? [The Gemara answers:] This is what it means. Eli had told them: Call a *kohen*, and let him come and slaughter the animal. When Samuel saw that they were looking for a *kohen* to slaughter the animal, he said to them: Why do you have to look for a *kohen* to slaughter it? The *shechitah* may be performed by a layman![138] They brought him to Eli, who asked him: How do you know that? He replied: Does it say, "The *kohen* shall kill"? It says, "The *kohanim* shall bring forth the blood," (Levitcus 1:5) [and "bringing forth the blood" means receiving the blood].[139] The duty of the *kohen* begins with the receiving of the blood, which means that the *shechitah* may be performed by a layman.[140] Eli said to him: Well said. Nevertheless you have rendered a decision in the presence of your rabbi, and anyone giving a decision in the presence of his rabbi is liable to the death penalty [by the hand of God]. [When Hannah heard this,] she cried out: "I am the woman who stood here beside you . . ." Eli said to her: Let me punish him, and I will pray to God, and He will give you a better one than this. She retorted: "It was this boy I prayed for."

[The Gemara continues to expound:] "Now Hannah was praying in her heart" (1 Samuel 1:13) R. Elazar said in the name of R. Yose b. Zimra: She spoke about her heart. She said to Him: Master of the universe, whatever you created in a woman, You created nothing without a purpose, eyes to see, ears to hear, a nose to smell, a mouth to speak, hands to do work, legs to walk with, breasts to nurse with. These breasts that You have put on my heart, are they not to nurse with? Give me a son, so that I will nurse him with them.

R. Elazar also said in the name of R. Yose b. Zimra: If someone fasts on *Shabbat* [because he had a bad dream], a decree that may have been pronounced against him seventy years earlier, when he was still a child, is cancelled [the reason being that fasting is very difficult for him on *Shabbat*, since everyone else is enjoying himself (Rashi)]. Yet all the same, he is punished for failing to making *Shabbat* a delight. What is his remedy? R. Nachman b. Yitzchak said: Let him keep another fast [on the next day] to atone for this fast.

THEY SPOKE DEFIANTLY TOWARD GOD

R. Elazar also said: Hannah spoke brazenly toward heaven, as it says: "And she prayed to [*al*] God" (1 Samuel 1:10). [Literally, the word *al* means "upon, against." Thus she prayed *against* God.] This teaches us that she spoke brazenly toward heaven.

R. Elazar also said: Elijah spoke defiantly toward heaven, as it says, [Elijah said to God, "For You have turned their hearts backward," (1 Kings 18:37) [as if to say that it was God's fault that they worshipped idols]. R. Shmuel b. Yitzchak said: How do we know that [in later prophecies] the Holy One, blessed be He, endorsed Elijah's statement? (32a) Because it says, [God declares, "On that day, I will gather the outcasts] and those that I have caused to sin," (Micah 4:6) [because I created the evil impulse (Rashi)].

R. Elazar also said: Moses also spoke impudently toward heaven, for it says, "Moses prayed to God" (Numbers 11:2). [Although it says *el Hashem*, "to God,"] don't read *el Hashem*, "to God," but read *al Hashem*, meaning, "he argued with God." For in the yeshivah of R. Eliezer they pronounced an *alef* like an *ayin*, and an *ayin* like an *alef* [so that to them *el* and *al*[141] were interchangeable]. In the yeshivah of R. Yannai they derived it from the following phrase, "And Di-Zahav" (Deuteronomy 1:1). What do the words "And Di-Zahav" mean? In the yeshivah of R. Yannai they explained: Moses said to the Holy One, blessed be He: Master of the universe, it is the profusion of silver and gold [*zahav*] that You showered on the Jewish people until they said, Enough! [*dai*], that caused them to make the Calf.

In the same vein they said in the yeshivah of R. Yannai: A lion does not roar and go on a wild rampage over a basket of straw but over a basket of meat [and it was God who gave them the basket of meat]. R. Oshaia said: It is like the case of a man who had a lean cow with large limbs. He began to feed it *karshinin* (horse-beans), and it [became big and strong] and started kicking him. So he said to the cow: What caused you to kick me? It's the *karshinin* I fed you! [It's my own fault.] R. Chiya b. Abba said in the name of R. Yochanan: It is like the case of a man who had a son. He bathed him, anointed him, gave him plenty to eat and drink, hung a purse around his neck, and set him down in front of a house of prostitution. How could the boy help sinning?

R. Acha the son of R. Huna said in the name of R. Sheshet: This bears out the popular saying: A full stomach leads to all kinds of sin. As it says, "When they grazed they were sated; when they were sated they grew haughty, and so they forgot Me" (Hosea 13:6). R. Nachman derived it from here: "But your heart may then grow haughty, and you may forget God your Lord" (Deuteronomy 8:14). The Rabbis learned it from here, "They will eat, be satisfied, and live in luxury. They will then turn to foreign gods" (Deuteronomy 31:20). Or if you prefer, I can say from here, "Jeshurun[142] thus became fat and rebelled" (ibid. 32:15).

R. Shmuel b. Nachmani said in the name of R. Yonatan: From what verse is it known that the Holy One, blessed be He, ended up agreeing with Moses [that the wealth He showered on the Jewish people led them to sin?] Because it says, "I lavished silver and gold on her, which they used for Baal" (Hosea 2:10).

39

THE POWER OF PRAYER

[The Gemara continues to expound verses relating to the sin of the Golden Calf.] "God said to Moses, 'Go down'" (Exodus 32:7). What is meant by, "Go down"? R. Elazar said: The Holy One, blessed be He, said to Moses: Go down from your greatness. The only reason I gave you greatness was for the sake of the Jewish people. Now that they have sinned, what good are you to me! Immediately Moses became unnerved to the point that he lacked the strength to speak. However, when God said to him, "Just leave Me alone, and I will destroy them," (Deuteronomy 9:14) [giving him a hint that by praying he could avert their destruction], Moses said to himself: I see, this depends on me. And instantly he stood up and prayed fervently and pleaded for mercy. It is like the case of the king who was angry with his son and began hitting him severely. The king's friend was sitting there but was afraid to say anything, until the king said: If not for the fact that my friend is sitting here I would kill you. The friend said to himself: This depends on me. He immediately got up and saved the prince.

R. Simla'i expounded: You should always begin by telling the praises of the Holy One, blessed be He, and only then pray [for your personal needs]. How do we know that? From Moses, because it says, [Moses said:] "At that time I pleaded with God," (Deuteronomy 3:23) and the verse continues, "O God, Lord, You have begun to show me Your greatness and Your display of power. What Force is there in heaven or earth who can perfom deeds and mighty acts as You do?" And after that [Moses made his personal request,] saying, "Please let me cross [the Jordan]. Let me see the good land."

(32b) R. Elazar said: Prayer is more effective than good deeds, for no one was greater in good deeds than our teacher Moses, and yet he was answered only after he prayed, as it says, "Do not speak to me any more [about entering Eretz Yisrael]" (ibid. 26) [His good deeds did not help, but because of his prayer God granted his request—at least partially—for it says immediately afterward,] "Climb to the top of Pisgah," [and I will at least *show* you Eretz Yisrael].

R. Elazar also said: Prayer is more effective than sacrifices. For it says, "'What need have I of all your sacrifices?' says God," (Isaiah 1:11) and this is followed by, "And when you lift up your hands . . . though you pray at length I will not listen" (ibid. 15). [God says: I will not accept your sacrifices, and in addition, I will not even accept your prayer. This shows that prayer is greater. If sacrifices were greater, God would not have to state that He will not accept their prayer (Rashi).]

R. Elazar also said: Since the day on which the *Bet Hamikdash* was destroyed, the gates of prayer have been closed, as it says, "And when I cry and plead, He shuts out my prayer" (Lamentations 3:8). But although the gates of prayer are closed, the gates of tears are not closed, for it says, "Hear my prayer, O God; give ear to my cry; do not be silent to my tears," (Psalm 39:13) [but the tears are *seen* by God, you need to pray only that they should be accepted (Rashi)].

R. Elazar also said; Since the day the *Bet Hamikdash* was destroyed, an iron wall separates Israel from their Father in heaven. For [God said to Ezekiel,] "Then take an iron plate and place it as an iron partition between yourself and the city" (Ezekiel 4:3) [i.e., Jerusalem, which is the conduit for our prayers].

R. Chanin said in the name of R. Chanina: If a person prays long, his prayers will not remain unfulfilled. From where in Scripture do we know this? From our teacher Moses. For it says, [Moses said,] "I prayed to God [for forty days]" (Deuteronomy 9:26), and it says, "But God also listened to me this time" (ibid. 19). [The Gemara asks:] Is that so? But R. Chiya b. Abba said in the name of R. Yochanan: If a person prays long and looks to see if he is answered he will suffer heartache and disillusionment in the end. For it says, "An extended prayer sickens the heart" (Proverbs 13:12). What is his remedy? Let him study the Torah, for the verse ends, "But desire realized is a tree of life" [meaning, through Torah study his desires will be fulfilled]. And the tree of life means only the Torah, as it says, "[The Torah] is a tree of life to those who grasp it" (Proverbs 3:18). [At any rate, the upshot seems to be that to pray long is frowned upon. How can R. Chanin say that the prayers of a person who prays long will be fulfilled?] [The Gemara answers:] There is no contradiction. R. Chiya speaks of a person who prays long and looks for the fulfillment of his prayer; R. Chanin on the other hand, speaks of a person who prays long but does not demand an answer.

R. Chama b. Chanina said: If a person sees that his prayers are not answered he should continue to pray, as it says, "Hope to God, strengthen yourself and He will give you courage; and continue to hope to God" [even if you were not answered the first time] (Psalm 27:14).

FOUR THINGS THAT NEED ENCOURAGEMENT

Our Rabbis taught in a *Baraita*: There are four things for which you need constant encouragement; namely, for Torah study, good deeds, prayer, and for your worldly occupation [such as a craftsman, merchant, or warrior (Rashi)]. From where do we know this about Torah and good deeds? Because it says, [God said to Joshua,] "But you must be strong and resolute to observe and to do according to the Torah" (Joshua 1:7): "Be strong" in Torah, and "resolute" in good deeds. From where do we know this about prayer? Because it says, "Hope to God, strengthen yourself and He will give you courage; and continue to hope to God" (Psalm 27:14). From where about worldly occupation? Because it says, [Speaking to his troops, Jo'ab said,] "Strengthen yourselves and let us be resolute for the sake of our people" (2 Samuel 10:12).

R. Elazar also said: Fasting is more effective than charity. What is the reason? Charity you do with your money, whereas fasting you do with your body. Rava never ordered a fast on a cloudy day, because it says, "You have screened Yourself off with a cloud, that no prayer may pass through" (Lamentations 3:44).

A DIALOGUE BETWEEN
ISRAEL AND GOD

(32b) [The Gemara expounds:] "Zion says, 'God has forsaken me, God has forgotten me.'" [The prophet replies: God forbid!] "Can a woman forget her baby, or disown the child of her womb? Though she might forget, I never could forget you" (Isaiah 49:14). [The Gemara asks:] It says, "God has forsaken me, God has forgotten me." Isn't forsaking the same as forgetting? [Why the redundant phrase?] Resh Lakish said: The community of Israel said to the Holy One, blessed be He: Master of the universe, if a man takes a second wife he still remembers his first wife, but You have forsaken us and forgotten us! The Holy One, blessed be He, replied: My daughter [How can you say that. Look what I have done for you!]. I have created twelve constellations in the sky, and for each constellation I have created thirty lieutenants,[143] and for each lieutenant I have created thirty captains, and for each captain I have created thirty majors, and for each major I have created thirty colonels, and for each colonel I have created thirty generals, and to each general I attached three hundred and sixty-five thousands of myriads of stars, corresponding to the days of the solar year, and all these I have created only for your sake. And you say, "You have forsaken and forgotten me"! "Can a woman forget her baby [ullah]?" Said the Holy One, blessed be He: Can I possibly forget the elevation-offerings [olah] of rams and the first-born animals you offered to Me in the wilderness? [The community of Israel retorted:] Master of the universe, since You don't forget anything, perhaps you will not forget the sin of the Calf either?

God answered: "Indeed, these I will forget" [the word "these" alludes to the sin of the golden Calf when Israel said, "These are your gods" (Rashi)]. To which the community of Israel replied: If it is possible for You to consider something forgotten, perhaps You will forget my actions at Sinai [when I readily accepted the Torah]? God replied: "The 'Anochi' [the "I"] will not forget you" [alluding to the Giving of the Ten Commandments at Sinai when God said, "I am your Lord"]. This is consistent with what R. Elazar said in the name of R. Oshaia: What is meant by, "Indeed, 'these' I will forget"? This refers to the sin of the Calf. And "'I' will not forget you" refers to the revelation at Sinai.

THE PIOUS JEW
AND THE GENERAL

The Rabbis taught in a *Baraita*: The story is told that once a pious man was praying while on the road when a general passed by and greeted him, and, [since he was in the middle of *Shemoneh Esrei*,] the pious man did not return the greeting. So the general waited until the Jew finished his prayer. When he finished, the general said to him: Empty-headed fool that you are! Don't you know that it says in your Torah, "Only take heed and watch yourself very carefully" (Deuteronomy 4:9) and it also says, "Watch yourselves very carefully"? (ibid. 4:15) [both meaning, "don't put your life in danger"]. When I greeted you, why didn't you return my greeting? If I had cut off your head with my sword, who would have taken me to court for shedding your blood? The pious man said: Wait just a minute. Allow me to set you straight. He continued: Suppose you were standing before a king of flesh and blood, and someone came by and greeted you, (33a) would you have [turned away from the king] and answered him? No, replied the general. And if you had returned his greeting, what would they have done to you? Said the general: They would have chopped off my head. The pious man now said: Let's take this to its logical conclusion. You yourself acknowledge that you would not have turned away from a king of flesh and blood, a man who is here today and tomorrow in the grave; surely I cannot turn away when standing before the supreme King of kings, the Holy One, blessed be He, who lives and endures for all eternity. Immediately the general was placated, and the pious man was dismissed to go home in peace.

R. CHANINA AND THE LIZARD

Our Rabbis taught: The story goes that in a certain place there was a [poisonous] lizard[144] that used to hurt people. So they went to R. Chanina b. Dosa and told him about it. He said to them: Show me its hole. When they showed him the hole, he placed his heel over it. The lizard came out, bit R. Chanina b. Dosa, and it died on the spot. R. Chanina slung it on his shoulder, carried it to the *bet midrash* and said: You see, my children, it is not the lizard that kills, it is sin that kills! Which led them to coin the phrase: Woe to the person that runs into a lizard, but woe to the lizard that runs into R. Chanina b. Dosa!

GREAT IS KNOWLEDGE

[The Gemara now discusses why *Ata chonein*, "You graciously give man discerning knowledge," was made the first of thirteen personal requests of the weekday *Shemoneh Esrei*.]

R. Ammi said: Great is knowledge, for it was placed at the beginning of the *berachot* of the weekday *Shemoneh Esrei*. R. Ammi also said: Great is knowledge, for we find that [the word "knowledge" was placed between two Divine names, as it says, "For a God of knowledge is the Lord" (1 Samuel 2:3) [the word *de'ot*, knowledge, between *Kel* and *Hashem*]. And if a person has no knowledge [i.e., if he refuses to believe that there are deep mysteries beneath the surface appearance of things, and that God is the Essence of this world (Rashba)], it is forbidden to have mercy on him, for it says, "For they are a people without understanding, that is why their Maker will show them no mercy" (Isaiah 27:11).

R. Elazar said: Great is the *Bet Hamikdash* for it was placed between two Divine names, as it says, "The place You dwell in is Your accomplishment, *God*; the *Mikdash* (sanctuary) of *God* Your hands have founded" (Exodus 15:17). R. Elazar also said: Anyone who has the understanding [that God is the Essence of everything in the world] it is as though the *Bet Hamikdash* was built in his days; because understanding (knowledge) is set between two Divine names, and the *Bet Hamikdash* is set beween two Divine names.

R. Acha Karchina'ah objected to this. He said: If so, revenge should also be great, for it is also set between two Divine names, as it says, "God of vengeance, O God" (Psalm 94:1). Replied [R. Elazar:] Yes, at the appropriate time vengeance is indeed great. And this is in line with what Ulla said: Why does the verse repeat the word "vengeance"? ["God of vengeance, O God; God of vengeance *hofia*, appear!"] One for good and one for ill. For good, as it says, "[God] *hofia*, made an appearance, from Mount Paran [when He offered the Torah to Ishmael before giving it to Israel, but Ishmael turned it down.] For ill, as it says, "God of vengeance, O God; God of vengeance *hofia*, appear!"

INAPPROPRIATE PRAYERS

(33b) MISHNAH. If someone says: [Have mercy on us] as You have mercy on a bird's nest, [since the Torah commands us to send away the mother bird before taking the young from her nest[145]], or he says: For Your goodness is Your name remembered [i.e., for Your good deeds we thank You], or he says: We give thanks, we give thanks, [repeating the words,] we silence him. [The Gemara will explain.]

GEMARA. It is understandable that we silence someone who repeats, "We give thanks, we give thanks," because it seems as if he were accepting and thanking two deities. And we can also understand why we silence someone who says, "for Your good deeds we thank You," because his statement implies that for the good things that happen we should praise God, and for the seemingly bad things we should not praise Him. Whereas we learned in a Mishnah: A person is obligated to praise God for bad things,[146] just as he praises Him for good things.[147] However, why do we silence a person who says, "Have mercy on us as You have mercy on a bird's nest"? [What is wrong with saying that?]

[The Gemara answers:] This matter is disputed by two **Amora'im** in Eretz Yisrael, namely R. Yose b. Avin and R. Yose b. Zevida. One said [we silence him] because he introduces jealousy into the works of creation, [since he implies that God has mercy on the birds, but not on the animals]. The other one said [we silence him] because he suggests that the mitzvot of the Holy One, blessed be He, are motivated by compassion, while, in truth, they are absolute decrees [which we obey unquestioningly, even when we cannot fathom the reasons behind them (Rashi)].

A certain man went down to the ark to serve as *chazzan*[148] in the presence of R. Chanina and said [in the *Shemoneh Esrei*]: The great, the mighty, the awesome, the glorious, the powerful, the valiant, the fearless, the strong, the sure, and the honored. R. Chanina waited until he finished and then said to him: [Are you all through? Why did you stop when you did?] Did you finish all the praises of God? Why all these extra words? Even the three that we do say [the great, mighty, and awesome], if Moses our teacher had not mentioned them in the Torah[149] and the Men of the Great Assembly had not inserted them in the *Shemoneh Esrei*, we would not be allowed to recite even those three praises. And yet you say all this and keep going on and on! Your situation is comparable to a king who had a million golden *dinars*, and people would praise him by stating that he owns a million silver *dinars*. Is it not a disgrace for him? [Which is to say that we simply cannot begin to appreciate God, so as to praise Him (Ritva). By adding our own praises we belittle Him with faint praise.]

THE FEAR OF HEAVEN

[The Gemara cites another teaching of R. Chanina:] R. Chanina said: Everything is decreed in heaven except the fear of heaven [i.e., Heaven decrees whether you will be tall or short, rich, smart, fair or dark-complexioned, but *you* have the freedom to choose between good and evil (Rashi)]. As it says, "And now Israel, what does God want of you? Only that you fear God your Lord" (Deuteronomy 10:12). [The Gemara asks:] Is the fear of God such a small thing? [The verse makes it sound as though the fear of God is only a minor matter.] Didn't R. Chanina say in the name of R. Shimon b. Yocha'i: The Holy One, blessed be He, has in His treasury nothing except a stockpile of the fear of heaven, as it says, "The fear of God is His treasure" (Isaiah 33:6). [The Gemara answers:] Yes! [But who is saying this verse? Moses.] Well, for Moses it was a small thing. For R. Chanina said: You can compare it to the case of a person who is asked for a big article, and he has it. [Since he has it] it seems like a small article to him. If he is asked for a small article, and he does not have it, it seems like a big article to him.

THE LONG AND THE SHORT OF IT

(34a) The Rabbis taught in a *Baraita*: There are three things that are bad if you have too much of them, but if you use them sparingly they are beneficial, namely:

yeast, salt and "saying 'no'"[150] [when you are asked to lead the prayers].

The Rabbis taught: Once a student went down[151] to lead the service in the presence of R. Eliezer, and he drew out his *Shemoneh Esrei* a long time. The other students said: Rabbi, look how he is dragging out his prayer! He replied: Is he drawing it out longer than our teacher Moses did, who said, "I threw myself down before God and lay prostrate for forty days and forty nights"? (Deuteronomy 9:26). There was another story about a student who went down to lead the service in the presence of R. Eliezer. This student cut his prayer short. His students said to R. Elliezer: Look, how he rushes through his *Shemoneh Esrei*! He replied: Is he praying any shorter than Moses our teacher did who prayed, "O God, please heal her!"?[152] (Numbers 12:13). R. Yaakov said in the name of R. Chisda: If you pray for your friend you don't have to mention his name, for it says, [Moses prayed,] "O God, please heal her!" [and he did not mention the name of Miriam].

The Rabbis taught: These are the *berachot* of the *Shemoneh Esrei* at which you should bow: The *berachah* of the *Avot* [Patriarchs, the first *berachah*], beginning and end,[153] and at the *berachah* of thanksgiving [Modim], beginning and end.[154] If a person wants to bow at the beginning and end of every single *berachah*, we instruct him not to do so.

R. CHANINA B. DOSA'S AUSPICIOUS PRAYERS

(34b) MISHNAH. The story goes that R. Chanina b. Dosa used to pray for the sick and instantly knew who would live and who would die. They asked him: How can you tell? He replied: If my prayer flows smoothly from my mouth [and I do not stumble], I know that it is accepted, but if it doesn't, I know that it is rejected.

[The Gemara asks:] From where is this derived? R. Yehoshua b. Levi said: From the verse, "I create [*borei*] fruit of the lips: 'Peace, peace, for far and near,' says God, 'and I shall heal him'" (Isaiah 57:19). [*Borei* can also mean "healthy," and "fruit of the lips" refers to prayer. Thus the verse is translated, "When the prayers are healthy, i.e., when they flow smoothly, I will heal the patient."]

The Rabbis taught: It happened one day that the son of R. Gamliel became seriously ill. He sent two of his disciples to R. Chanina b. Dosa with the message: Pray to God that he may get well. As soon as R. Chanina saw them he went up to the attic and prayed for mercy. Shortly afterward he came down and said to the disciples: You can go home now. The boy has come out of his coma, and the fever has subsided. Amazed, they asked him: How do you know this, are you a prophet? He replied: I am neither a prophet nor a son of a prophet, but from past experience I know that if my prayer flows smoothly, it is accepted; but if it does not, then I know

that it is rejected. [The disciples decided to test his theory.] So they sat down and jotted down the precise time [that R. Chanina b. Dosa told them that the fever had subsided.] When they came to R. Gamliel, [and told him everything] he said to them: So help me! You did not miss the moment of his recovery by one second. At exactly the time [you noted] my son's fever abated, and he asked for a drink of water.

On another occasion it happened that R. Chanina b. Dosa went to study Torah at the yeshivah of R. Yochanan b. Zakkai. At that time the son of R. Yochanan b. Zakkai became ill. Said R. Yochanan: Chanina my son, pray that my son may live. Rabbi Chanina put his head between his knees and prayed for him, whereupon the sick boy got better. Said R. Yochanan b. Zakkai: If I, Ben Zakkai, had kept my head between my legs all day long, no attention would have been paid to me. Said his wife to him: Does this mean that Chanina is greater than you? He replied: No, he is not greater than I, but he is like a servant [who is constantly in the presence of the king, and can ask a favor at all times]. I, however, am like a minister [who appears only at fixed times to plead before the king. Therefore, he has more intimacy].

THE GLORIOUS REWARDS FOR BAALEI TESHUVAH

Rabbi Chiya b. Abba said in the name of R. Yochanan: All the [glorious things] the prophets prophesied for the future apply only to *baalei teshuvah*, [returnees to Torah life,] but as for the perfectly righteous, "No eye has seen them, O God, but You," (Isaiah 64:3) [which is to say that their reward is beyond description]. He differs on this point with R. Abbahu, for R. Abbahu said: In the place where *baalei teshuvah* are standing [in heaven] even the perfectly righteous cannot stand. For it says: "Peace, peace to him that was far off and to him that is near" (Isaiah 57:19). First peace to him that was far off, and only then, peace to him that is near. But according to R. Yochanan [who holds that the righteous are on a higher plateau] what does "a person that was far off" mean?—That refers to one who was far from transgression from the start [i.e., the perfectly righteous]. And what does "the person that is near" mean? That refers to one who originally was close to transgression and now has moved away from it [i.e., a *baal teshuvah*].

R. Chiya b. Abba also said in the name of R. Yochanan: All the prophets that prophesied about the glories of the future referred only to the days of *Mashiach*, but as for the world to come, "No eye has seen it, O God, but You," (Isaiah 64:3) [this purely spiritual world is beyond description]. He differs on this point with Shmuel, for Shmuel said: There will be no difference between the present age and the Messianic era except that our subjugation to the [gentile] kingdoms will end, as it says, "The poor will never cease to exist in the land," (Deuteronomy 16:11) [even in the Messianic age there will be poor people].

R. Chiya b. Abba said in the name of R. Yochanan: All the prophesies [about the magnificent bounties that will be showered on Israel in the future] were directed only at a person who marries off his daughter to a Torah scholar, and at one who does business with a Torah scholar, and at one who shares some of his wealth with a Torah scholar. But as for the Torah scholar himself, [his reward is beyond description,] "No eye has seen it, O God, but You" (Isaiah 64:3).

[The Gemara inquires:] What is it that no eye has seen? R. Yehoshua b. Levi said: This is the wine that has been preserved in its grapes from the six days of Creation. [This wine has a spiritual quality since it was created out of nothing (Maharsha)].[155] R. Shmuel b. Nachamani said: This is Eden, which no creature has ever seen. Perhaps you will say: Where was Adam? [Wasn't he in Eden? No.] He was in the Garden. Now you may say: The Garden and Eden are the same? [Wrong!] For it says, "A river flowed out of Eden to water the Garden" (Genesis 2:10). So you see that the Garden and Eden are two separate things.

R. Chiya b. Abba said in the name of R. Yochanan: A person should pray only in a house with windows [so that he should gaze toward heaven and become humble (Rashi)], since it says, "[Daniel's] upper chamber had windows that were open toward Jerusalem" (Daniel 6:11).

R. Kahana said: I consider a person impertinent who prays in a open valley [where people are passing]. He should pray in an enclosed and secluded spot [which is conducive to a reverent disposition (Rashi)]. R. Kahana also said: I consider it impertinent for a person to declare his sins openly, for it says, "Happy is he whose transgression is forgiven, whose sin is covered over" (Psalm 32:1).

BERACHOT FOR
PHYSICAL PLEASURE

(35a) MISHNAH. What berachah do you say before eating fruit? Over fruit of the tree you say: Who creates the fruit of the tree. GEMARA. [The Gemara asks:] From where do we derive [that you have to say a berachah before eating anything?] As the Rabbis have taught in a Baraita: It says, "All the fruit shall be holy, and it shall be [hilulim], something for which God is praised" (Leviticus 19:24).[156] The fact [that hilulim (praises) is in the plural] teaches us [that there are two praises], and a berachah is required both before and after eating. Based on this, R. Akiva stated: You are forbidden to taste anything before saying a berachah over it.

The Rabbis have taught: It is forbidden to enjoy anything in this world without saying a berachah, and if someone enjoys anything of this world without saying a berachah it is as though he misappropriated something that is sacred to God. How can he rectify this?

He should consult a Torah scholar. [The Gemara asks:] He should go to a Torah scholar? What can a Torah scholar do for him? He has violated the law! Said Rava: What it means is, that before he starts eating he should go to a Torah scholar who will teach him the berachot. He then will not misappropriate things that are sacred to God. R. Yehudah said in the name of Shmuel: Whoever enjoys anything of this world without a berachah is as if he made personal use of things that are consecrated to heaven, because it says, "The earth is God's and all that it holds" (Psalm 24:1). R. Levi pointed out a discrepancy between two texts: It says, "The earth is God's and all that it holds," but it also says, "The heavens belong to God, but the earth He gave over to man" (Psalm 115:16). He answered: There is no inconsistency. The passage, "The earth is God's" is before saying the berachah, (35b) and the verse, "The earth He gave over to man," is after saying the berachah [after saying the berachah he has permission to enjoy the food].

R. Chanina b. Papa said: To enjoy this world without saying a berachah is like robbing the Holy One, blessed be He, and the community of Israel, as it says, "He who robs his father and mother and says, 'It is no offense,' is a companion to a destroyer" (Proverbs 28:24). "Father" refers to the Holy One, blessed be He, as it says, "Is He not your father who created you" (Deuteronomy 32:6); and "mother" is none other than the community of Israel, as it says, "My son, heed the discipline of your father, and do not forsake the instruction of your mother" (Proverbs 1:8). What is the meant by "a companion to a destroyer"? R. Chanina b. Papa answered: He is the companion of Jeroboam son of Nevat who destroyed Israel's faith in their Father in heaven. [Jeroboam induced the people to worship idols, and the person who does not say a berachah will cause others to emulate him, and, like Jeroboam, will cause them to sin (Rashi).]

R. Chanina b. Papa pointed out a discrepancy: It says, "Assuredly, I will take back My new grain in its time" (Hosea 2:11), and elsewhere it says, "You will gather in your grain" (Deuteronomy 11:14). [In one passage the grain is called "My grain," in the other, "your grain."] He answered: There is no inconsistency: one verse speaks of a time when the people of Israel obey the will of God [then "you will gather your grain," because you have a right to it]; the other, when they do not obey the will of God [it will be taken from them since they have no right to it (Rashi)].

COMBINING TORAH STUDY
WITH EARNING A LIVELIHOOD

The Rabbis have taught in a Baraita: "You will gather in your grain" (Deuteronomy 11:14). What does the Torah want to teach us [by mentioning the gathering of the grain]? Since it says, "Let not this book of the Torah cease from your lips" (Joshua 1:8), I might think that this is to be taken literally, [and a person is not allowed to do anything but learn Torah]. That's why it says, "You will gather in your grain," which implies that you should combine Torah study with earning a livelihood, so says R. Yishmael. R. Shimon b. Yocha'i says: Is that possible? If a person ploughs in the ploughing season, sows in the sowing season, reaps in the harvest season, threshes in the threshing season, and winnows when the wind blows, what is to become of the Torah [when will he find the time to learn Torah]? Impossible! But when the Jewish people are doing God's will, their work is done by others, as it says, "Strangers shall stand and feed your sheep, aliens shall be your plowmen and vine-trimmers" (Isaiah 61:5). And when the Jewish people are not doing God's will, they will have to do their work themselves, as it says, "And *you* will gather in your grain."[157] Not only that, but they will have to do the work of others, as it says, "You shall have to serve your enemy" (Deuteronomy 28:48). Said Abbaye: There were many who did as R. Yishmael [combining Torah study with a worldly occupation] and were successful; others tried to emulate R. Shimon b. Yocha'i [devoting themselves to Torah study exclusively] and were not successful. [The Gemara offers an illustration:] Rava said to the disciples: I beg of you, don't show up in the yeshivah during the months of Nisan and Tishrei [Nisan being the season of the grain harvest; Tishrei, the season for pressing grapes and olives,] so that you should not be busy earning a living for the entire year. [Work hard during those two months so that you'll be free to study Torah the rest of the year.]

Rabbah b. Bar Chanah said in the name of R. Yochanan, quoting R. Yehudah b. Ila'i: Look what a difference there is between the earlier and the later generations. The earlier generations who made Torah study their steady occupation and did mundane work on an off-and-on basis were successful in both. The later generations who worked on a steady basis and studied Torah by fits and starts were not successful at either.

(40a) R. Yehudah said in the name of Rav: You are forbidden to eat anything before you feed your animals, because it says, "I will provide grass in your field for your cattle" and then, "and you will eat and be satisfied" (Deuteronomy 11:15).

A REGIMEN OF HEALTH

Rava b. Shmuel said in the name of R. Chiya: After every food eat salt, and after every beverage, drink water, then you will have no health problems.[158] It has been taught similarly: After every food eat salt, and after every beverage, drink water, and you will stay healthy. We learned in another *Baraita*: If a person eats any kind of food without taking salt after it, or drinks any kind of beverage without drinking water after it, during the day he should worry about bad breath, and

at night he should worry about *askara*, the croup.[159]

The Rabbis taught: Whoever drinks plenty of water after his meal will not suffer any intestinal illness. How much should he drink? R. Chisda says: A cup of water to a loaf of bread.

R. Mari said in the name of R. Yochanan: If you make it a habit to eat lentils once every thirty days, you will keep the croup away from your house, [because lentils prevent constipation, which is the cause of this sickness (Rashi)]. But you should not have them every day. Why not? Because they cause bad breath. R. Mari also said in the name of R. Yochanan: If you make it a habit to eat mustard once every thirty days, you will keep sickness away from your house. But don't eat it every day. Why not? Because it may cause weakness of the heart. R. Chiya b. Ashi said in the name of Rav: A person who regularly eats small fish will not suffer from intestinal disorder. And not only that, but small fish increase fertility and strengthen a person's whole body. R. Chama b. Chanina said: Someone who regularly eats black cumin will not develop heart trouble.[160] The Gemara raised an objection [citing a contradictory statement]: R. Shimon b. Gamliel says: Black cumin is one of sixty poisonous drugs, and when someone sleeps on the east side of a pile of cumin he is guilty of causing his own death [because the west wind will carry the aroma to him and poison him (Rashi), which shows that cumin is harmful]. The Gemara answers: There is no contradiction. R. Shimon b. Gamliel speaks of the aroma of cumin [which is poisonous], and R. Chama speaks of its taste.

DON'T EMBARRASS OTHERS

(43b) R. Zutra b. Tuvya said in the name of Rav; others say R. Chanan b. Bizna said it in the name of R. Shimon Chasida; still others say R. Yochanan said it in the name of R. Shimon b. Yocha'i: It is better for a person to throw himself into a fiery furnace rather than that he should embarrass his friend in public. From where do we know this? From Tamar, about whom it says, "When she was being taken out [to be burned for alleged immorality] she sent the security to her father-in-law [Judah] with the message, "I am pregnant by the man who is the owner of these articles" (Genesis 38:25). [Tamar chose to be put to death rather than identify Judah as the man by whom she was pregnant and publicly put him to shame.]

THINGS UNBECOMING FOR
A TORAH SCHOLAR

The Rabbis taught in a *Baraita*: Six things are unbecoming for a Torah scholar. He should not go out wearing perfume; he should not go out with patches on his shoes; he should not go out alone at night; he should not talk with a woman in the street; he should not be the last one to enter the *bet hamidrash*; and he should not have a meal in the company of ignorant persons. Some add: when walking he should not take big steps, and he should not walk with an erect posture.

[The Gemara now analyzes the six unbecoming things.] *He should not go out wearing perfume.* R. Abba the son of R. Chiya b. Abba said in the name of R. Yochanan: This applies only in a place where homosexuality is prevalent, [where men wear perfume to make themselves attractive (Rashi)]. Said R. Sheshet: This applies only to the scenting of clothes, but when perfume is used on the body its purpose is to dissipate perspiration [and no one will suspect him of depravity]. R. Papa said: The hair is in the same category as clothes; others, however, say, as the body.

He should not go out with patches on his shoes. This supports R. Chiya b. Abba, since R. Chiya b. Abba said: It is unbecoming for a Torah scholar to go out with patches on his shoes. Is that indeed so? R. Chiya b. Abba himself used to go out with patches on his shoes! Mar Zutra b. R. Nachman said: He was speaking of one patch on top of another. And this is unbecoming only on the upper part of the shoe, but on the sole of the shoe it makes no difference [because there it is not visible]. Even on the upper part of the shoe it applies only in the street, but in the house it does not matter. Also this applies only during the summer, but during the winter it does not matter [because the mud will hide the patches (Rashi)].

He should not go out alone at night, so as not to arouse suspicion [that he is going someplace for immoral purposes]. This is the case only if he does not have a fixed time to go to learn Torah, but if has a fixed time people know that he is going to his nightly Torah session [and will not suspect him].

He should not talk to a woman in the street. R. Chisda said: Even with his wife. We have learned similarly in a *Baraita*: Even with his wife, even with his daughter, even with his sister, because not everyone knows who are his relatives, [and they may suspect him of immorality].

He should not be the last to enter the bet hamidrash. Because people will say that he is lazy.[161]

He should not have a meal in the company of ignorant persons. What is the reason? Because he may be influenced by their ways.

Some add that he should not take big steps. Because we learned: Walking with large steps takes away one five-hundredth part of a person's eyesight. What is the remedy [if it has been damaged]? He can restore his eyesight by drinking of the wine of the *Kiddush* of Friday night.

He should not walk with an erect posture. Because we learned: If a person walks with a proud bearing even for four cubits, it is as if he pushed the feet of the *Shechinah* [he acts arrogantly against God], since it says, "The whole earth is full of His glory" (Isaiah 6:3).

THE BOUNTY
OF ERETZ YISRAEL

(44a) [The Gemara relates an incident to illustrate the excessive sweetness of the fruits of Ginnosar (Genessareth), which grow around the Yam Kinneret (Sea of Galilee).]

Rabbah b. Bar Chanah said: When we [the students] were going with R. Yochanan to eat the fruit of Ginnosar, when there were a hundred of us we used to take ten fruits for each of us, and when there were ten of us, each of us would receive a hundred fruits, and every hundred of these fruits would fill a basket of three *se'ahs* [a large amount]. We would eat all of these fruits, and after eating them we could have sworn that we had not had a bite to eat. You mean to say that you could swear that you had not tasted food? Isn't this food? Rather, put it this way: Our hunger was not stilled. [We could still eat more; that's how delicious they were.] R. Abbahu used to eat so much of the fruits of Ginnosar that a fly slipped off his forehead. [The fruit made his skin so smooth that the fly lost its hold.] R. Ammi and R. Assi used to eat so much of them until their hair fell out. R. Shimon b. Lakish ate of them to the point that he became disoriented. R. Yochanan reported this to the *Nasi*, whereupon R. Yehudah Hanasi dispatched a search party to look for him, and they brought him back to his house.

[The Gemara continues to discuss the bounty of Eretz Yisrael.] When R. Dimi came [from Eretz Yisrael] he told that King Yannai had a city on the King's Mountain where they used to take out 600,000 bowls of pieces of fish each week for the men picking figs [that's how many fig-pickers there were, an indication of the superabundance of the fig harvest]. When Rabin came [from Eretz Yisrael] he told that King Yannai had one tree on the King's Mountain from which they used to take down forty *se'ahs* of young pigeons from three broods every month. When R. Yitzchak came, he said: There was a town in Eretz Yisrael named Gufnit where there were eighty pairs of brothers who were all *kohanim* and who were married to pairs of sisters who were all daughters of *kohanim*. [Two brothers were married to two sisters; in other words, forty pairs of brothers were married to forty pairs of sisters.] The Rabbis searched from Sura to Nahardea[162] and could not find a similar case except for the two daughters of R. Chisda who were married to two brothers, Rami b. Chama and Mar Ukva b. Chama; and although they both were daughters of a *kohen*, their husbands were not *kohanim*.

HEALTHFUL AND
HARMFUL FOODS

[The Gemara now embarks on a discussion of the benefits and drawbacks of certain foods.] (44b) R. Yannai said in the name of Rebbi: Ounce for ounce, an egg is more nutritious than any other food. When Rabin came [from Eretz Yisrael] he said: A lightly roasted egg is better than six measures of flour. When R. Dimi came he said: A lightly roasted egg is better than six [measures of flour]; a fully roasted egg is better than four; and ounce for ounce a boiled egg is better than any other food, except meat.

The Rabbis learned in a *Baraita*: The spleen of an animal is good for the teeth but hard on the stomach; leek[163] is bad for the teeth but good for the stomach. All raw vegetables make a person look pale, and eating things that are not fully grown stunts a person's growth. Anything that is eaten whole [like little fish] restores vitality, and something that is near a vital organ [of a slaughtered animal] restores vitality. Cabbage is a nutritious food, and beets have therapeutic value. Woe to the house through which turnips are passing [meaning, woe to the stomach that has to digest turnips].

[Now the Gemara explains these items one by one.]

We learned in the above-mentioned *Baraita*: "The spleen of an animal is good for the teeth but hard on the stomach." [The Gemara asks:] What is the remedy? [How can you get the benefit for your teeth and avoid stomach trouble?] [The Gemara answers:] By chewing it well and then spitting it out.

"Leek is bad for the teeth but good for the stomach." What is the remedy here? [How can you have the benefits without the drawbacks?] Boil them well and swallow them [without chewing them].

"All raw vegetables make a person look pale." R. Yitzchak said, it is speaking about the first meal a person eats after blood-letting; it is then that it is unhealthful to eat raw vegetables. R. Yitzchak also said: You should not talk to anyone who eats vegetables before the fourth hour of the day [i.e., on an empty stomach.][164] What is the reason? Because his breath smells. R. Yitzchak also said: You should not eat raw vegetables before the fourth hour. It happened that Amemar, Mar Zutra, and Rav Ashi were sitting together when they were served raw vegetables before the fourth hour. Amemar and Mar Zutra ate, but Mar Zutra did not eat. They said to Mar Zutra: What is the reason that you are not eating? Is it because R. Yitzchak said that you should not talk to anyone who eats vegetables before the fourth hour? Look, we *are* eating vegetables, and yet you continue to talk to us! Mar Zutra replied: I hold like the other saying of R. Yitzchak, where he stated that you should not eat raw vegetables before the fourth hour.

"Eating things that are not fully grown stunts a person's growth." Said R. Chisda: Even a kid worth a *zuz* [i.e., a good, fat kid]. But that's only if it has not yet reached a quarter of its full size, but if it is already a quarter of its full growth it's all right to eat it.

"Anything that is eaten whole restores vitality." R. Papa said: Even tiny fishes that live in ponds.

"Something that is near a vital organ restores vitality." R. Acha b. Yaakov said: This refers to the neck of an animal [which is close to the heart]. Rava said to his servant: When you buy a piece of meat for me try to get a part from near where the *berachah* over the *shechitah* is said [i.e., from near the neck, which is the place where the *shechitah* is done].

"Cabbage is nutritious food; beets have therapeutic value." [The Gemara asks:] Is cabbage good only for food and has no therapeutic value? Haven't we learned in a *Baraita*: There are six things that provide a permanent cure for a sickness, namely: cabbage, beets, an extract of *sisin*,[165] the stomach of an animal, the womb of an animal, and the large lobe of the liver? [The Gemara answers:] Say that cabbage is *also* good for food, [in addition to its medicinal value].

"Woe to the house through which turnips are passing." Is that so? Did not Rava say to his servant: When you see turnips for sale in the market, don't bother to ask me, "What will you eat with your bread?" [You may assume that I will eat it, because it is very healthful.] Abbaye said: [It means, when turnips are cooked] without meat they are harmful. Rava said: When turnips are eaten without drinking wine afterward [they are harmful. But when you wash them down with wine they are beneficial].

ZIMMUN, THE INVITATION FOR BIRKAT HAMAZON

(45a) MISHNAH. If three people ate together they are required to [appoint one of them as a leader] to formally invite the others to join him in the recitation of *Birkat Hamazon* (Grace after Meals). [This formal invitation is called the *zimmun*.]

GEMARA. From where is this derived? R. Assi says: Because it says: "Declare the greatness of God with me, and let us exalt His name together" (Psalm 34:4). [One person invites the other two to join him in declaring God's greatness.] R. Abbahu derives the same concept from the following verse, "When I proclaim God's name, praise God for His greatness" (Deuteronomy 32:3). R. Chanan b. Abba says: From where do we know that someone who answers Amen to a *berachah* should not say it louder than the one who is reciting the *berachah*? Because it says: "Declare the greatness of God with me, and let us exalt His name together," [meaning, not louder than the other]. R. Shimon b. Pazzi said: From where do we derive that the *metargem* [the person who, in the days of the Gemara, used to translate from Hebrew into Aramaic each verse of the Torah as it was read in the synagogue], should not raise his voice louder than the reader? Because it says, "Moses spoke, and God answered with a Voice" (Exodus 19:19). The Torah did not have to say the words, "with a Voice." So what does the expression "with a Voice" teach us? [It means] that when God answered, His Voice was not louder than Moses' voice.[166] The same was taught in a *Baraita*: The *metargem* may not raise his voice louder than the reader. If the *metargem* cannot speak as loud as the reader, then the reader should lower his voice.

WHO IS AN *AM HAARETZ*?

(47b) (Referring to a *Baraita* that states that an *am haaretz*[167] may not be included in a *zimmun*, the Gemara explains:) We have learned in a *Baraita*: Who is an *am haaretz*? Anyone who does not take upon himself the added stringency of eating non-sacred [i.e., regular] food in ritual cleanness,[168] so says R. Meir. However, the Rabbis say: Anyone who does not correctly tithe his fruits is considered an *am haaretz*. But the *Kutim* (Samaritans) do tithe their produce correctly, since they are very conscientious about observing any law written in the Torah explicitly.[169] For the Rabbi said: Any mitzvah that the *Kutim* took upon themselves they are more scrupulous about than the Jews, [therefore they may be included in the *zimmun*].

The Rabbis taught in a *Baraita*: Who is an *am haaretz*? Anyone who does not recite the *Shema* morning and evening, so says R. Eliezer. R. Yehoshua says: Anyone who does not put on *tefillin*. Ben Azzai says: Anyone who has no *tzitzit*[170] on his garment. R. Natan says: Anyone who has no *mezuzah* on his door. R. Yonatan b. Yosef says: Whoever has sons and does not bring them up to study Torah. Acheirim says: Even if someone knows Tanach and the Mishnah, but he has not studied Gemara,[171] he is considered an *am haaretz*.

R. Yehoshua b. Levi said: A person should always try to get up early and go to the synagogue so that he has the special merit of being one of the first ten, since even if a hundred people will come after him he earns the reward of all of them. [The Gemara asks:] You mean to say that he actually is going to take away every one else's reward? Say instead: He will receive a reward that is equal to that of all of them.

BIRKAT HAMAZON AT KING YANNAI'S BANQUET

(48a) R. Nachman said: A boy who understands to whom the *Birkat Hamazon* is directed may be counted for *zimmun*. When Abbaye and Rava were young boys they were sitting before Rabbah. Rabbah asked them: To whom do we say *Birkat Hamazon*? They replied: To God. And where does God reside? Rava pointed to the ceiling; Abbaye went outside and pointed toward heaven. Said Rabbah to them: Both of you are going to become rabbis. As the popular saying goes: You can tell a young pumpkin by the sap that comes out of its stalk. [You could tell by Abbaye and Rava's answers that they were destined to become great rabbis.]

King Yannai[172] and his queen sat at a banquet. Since Yannai had killed the Sages there was no one [of

eminence] to recite *Birkat Hamazon*. Yannai turned to his queen and said: I wish we had someone who could lead us in *Birkat Hamazon*. She answered: Swear to me that if I bring you one of the Sages you will not harm him. Yannai swore. She then brought in Shimon b. Shetach, her brother [whom she had put into hiding]. Yannai seated Shimon b. Shetach between himself and the queen and said: Look at all the honor I am showing you. Retorted Shimon b. Shetach: You are not the one that honors me, it is the Torah that honors me, as it says, "Extol her [the Torah] and she will exalt you, she will bring you honor if you embrace her" (Proverbs 4:8).[173] Yannai said to his queen: You see [I was correct in killing the Rabbis] for the Rabbis do not accept any kind of authority. [The Rabbis are not grateful for any favors they receive (Rashi).] They then brought Shimon b. Shetach a cup of wine to recite *Birkat Hamazon*.

[Since he had not eaten with them] he said: How can I lead the *Birkat Hamazon*? What shall I say? Shall I say: Blessed is He from Whose bounty Yannai and his companions [instead of "we"] have eaten? So he drank that cup of wine, [and thus partook of the meal], whereupon they brought another cup over which he said the grace. R. Abba the son of R. Chiya b. Abba said in the name of R. Yochanan: When Shimon b. Shetach said grace after drinking a cup of wine he was acting strictly on his own opinion, [no one else agreed with him on this point (Rashi)]. For R. Chiya b. Abba said in the name of R. Yochanan: No one can say grace on behalf of others unless he has eaten a measure of grain food the size of an olive with them.

MORE ABOUT *BIRKAT HAMAZON*

(48b) R. Nachman said: Moses instituted the *berachah* of *Hazon* ["Who nourishes," the first *berachah* of *Birkat Hamazon*], at the time when the manna came down for the Jewish people. Joshua instituted the *berachah* *Al haaretz* ["For the land," the second *berachah*], when they entered Eretz Yisrael. David and Solomon instituted the *berachah* that ends *Boneh Yerushalayim*, ["Who rebuilds Jerusalem," the third *berachah*]. David instituted the words, "For Israel Your people and for Jerusalem Your city," and Solomon instituted the words, "For the great and holy House, [both in the third *berachah*]. The *berachah* of *Hatov vehameitiv*, ["Who is good and Who does good," the fourth *berachah*], was instituted in Yavneh to commemorate the people who were killed in Betar.[174] For R. Matna said: On the day when [the Romans] permitted the burial of those who were slain in Betar, the Rabbis in Yavneh ordained that *Hatov vehameitiv*, "Who is good and Who does good" should be said. "Who is good," because the bodies did not decompose, and "Who does good," because they were allowed to be buried.

The Rabbis taught in a *Baraita*: From where do we know that *Birkat Hamazon* is ordained by the Torah?

Because it says, "When you eat and are satisfied, you must therefore bless God your Lord for the good land that He has given you" (Deuteronomy 8:10). The *Baraita* expounds: "When you eat and are satisfied" this means the *berachah* of *zimmun*.[175] "God your Lord" denotes the *berachah* of *Hazon*, "Who nourishes." "For the land" denotes the *berachah* for the land. "The good" denotes "Who builds Jerusalem;" and similarly it says, "The good mountain and Lebanon" (Deuteronomy 3:25). "That He has given you" denotes the *berachah* of "Who is good and Who does good." . . . [The Gemara asks:] We have Scriptural sources for *Birkat Hamazon* after meals, but from where do we know that a *berachah* must be said before you eat?—Because it says, "That He has given you," which implies, as soon as He has given you [the food], even before you have eaten of it [you must say a *berachah*].

R. Meir says: From where do we know that that just as person must say a *berachah* when something good happens, he also has to say a *berachah* when something bad happens? Because it says, "Which God your Lord has given you" (Deuteronomy 8:10), [the name Lord signifies God as Judge, thus "your God"] means that God is your judge in every judgment He has passed on you, whether the verdict is one of happiness or of suffering.

(51a) R. Yochanan said: Whoever says *Birkat Hamazon* over a full cup of wine will receive an inheritance that is boundless, as it says, "Full with the blessing of God, he will inherit the west and the south" (Deuteronomy 33:23). R. Yose b. R. Chanina says: He has the privilege of inheriting two worlds, this world and the world to come.

WHAT IF YOU FORGOT TO SAY *BIRKAT HAMAZON*?

(53b) [We learned in the Mishnah:] If a person has eaten and forgotten to say *Birkat Hamazon*, Bet Shammai say that he has to return to the place where he ate and say grace there, whereas Bet Hillel say that he should say it in the place where he remembered. GEMARA. There once were two disciples who failed to say grace. The one who did it unintentionally followed the rule of Bet Shammai [and went back to say grace at the place where he ate]. He found a purse full of gold. The other intentionally left the place where he was eating [because he was in a hurry to go somewhere else], and, [mistakenly] relying on the rule of Bet Hillel, he said grace there. He was eaten by a lion. [Because in a case of intentional omission Bet Hillel agree that one has to return to his original place.] Rabbah b. Bar Chanah once was traveling with a caravan, and he ate a meal and forgot to say grace. He said to himself: What shall I do? If I say to the others that I forgot to say grace, they will tell me: Say it here; it makes no difference. Wherever you say grace, you are blessing the All-Merciful. I am better off telling them

that I forgot a golden dove. So he told them: Please wait for me, I forgot a golden dove, [and I must go back]. He went back and said grace, and he was rewarded that he found a golden dove. [The Gemara asks:] Why, of all things, a golden dove?—Because the community of Israel is compared to a dove, as it says, "The wings of the dove are covered with silver, and her pinions shimmer with gold" (Psalm 68:14). Just as the dove is saved only by her wings, so is Israel saved only by the mitzvot.

A *BERACHAH* COMMEMORATING MIRACLES

(54a) MISHNAH. If you see a place where miracles happened to the Jewish people, you should say: Blessed be He who perfomed miracles for our forefathers in this place. . . .

GEMARA. [The Gemara asks:] From where in Scripture is it derived [that you should say a *berachah* in a place where a miracle happened]? R. Yochanan said: Because it says, [When Jethro came to Moses in the desert and heard about the miracles of the Exodus, he said a *berachah*:] "Praised be God, who rescued you from the power of Egypt and Pharaoh" (Exodus 18:10).

[The Gemara says:] The rule laid down in the Mishnah that you should say a *berachah* in a place where a miracle happened applies only to a miracle that happened to the entire Jewish people, but you do not say a *berachah* for a miracle that happened to you alone. [The Gemara asks:] But what about the case of the person who was traveling through a place called Ever Yeminah[176] when a lion pounced on him, and who miraculously was saved. When he came to Rava, he told him: Whenever you pass that place you should say: Blessed be He who performed a miracle for me in this place. [Another such case:] Mar the son of Ravina once was going through the Plain of Aravot, and he was extremely thirsty [to the point where his life was in danger]. Miraculously a spring of water was created for him, and he drank from it. Another time he was walking in the market place of Mechuza when a wild camel attacked him. Suddenly, the wall of a nearby building caved in, and he was able to escape inside. [After that,] whenever he came to Aravot he said the *berachah*: Blessed be He who performed miracles for me in Aravot and also in the incident with the camel. Whenever he came to the marketplace of Mechuza he would say the *berachah*: Who performed miracles for me with the camel and also in Aravot. [The question is: How can our Gemara say that a *berachah* is said only for a miracle that happened to the entire Jewish people? Here we have three cases where *berachot* were said by individuals to whom personal miracles occurred.] The Gemara answers: If the miracle happened to the entire people, everyone is required to say a *berachah*; but if the miracle happened to an individual, only he is required to say a *berachah*.

[What sort of miracles is the Gemara talking about?]

We learned in a *Baraita*: If you see the place where the Jewish people crossed the Red Sea or the place where they crossed the Jordan River [in the days of Joshua], or the place where they crossed the streams of the mountains of Arnon, or the place of giant stones, or the slopes of Bet Choron, or the boulder that Og, the king of Bashan, tried to throw at the Jewish people, or when you see the stone where Moses sat when Joshua waged war against Amalek, or [the pillar of salt that was once] the wife of Lot, or when you see the wall of Jericho that sank into the ground, for all of these things you have to offer thanksgiving and praise to the Almighty.

[Now the Gemara explains what miracles happened at all these places.] I grant you, we all know about the crossing of the Red Sea, because it says, "The Israelites entered the sea bed on dry land" (Exodus 14:22). The crossing of the Jordan does not present a problem either, for it says, "The priests who bore the Ark of God's covenant stood on dry land exactly in the middle of the Jordan, while all Israel crossed over on dry land, until the entire nation had finished crossing the Jordan" (Joshua 3:17). But how do we know that a miracle happened when they crossed the streams of the mountains of Arnon? Because it says, "It is therefore told in the Book of God's Wars, *et vaheiv besufah*, "*Et* and *Heiv* in the rear" (Numbers 21:14). [The Gemara interprets the phrase as follows:] "*Et* and *Heiv* in the rear."

There were two lepers, one named *Et*, the other *Heiv*, and they were following in the rear of the camp of Israel. When the Israelites were passing the streams of Arnon, the Amorites came (54b) and made caves in the mountains [which were close to one another], and they lay there in ambush. The Amorites reckoned: When the Jews pass [down below in the narrow valley they will be at our mercy, and] we will kill them. The Amorites did not know that the Ark that was traveling in front of the nation used to level the mountains in their path. When the Ark came to the place where the Amorites were lying in ambush, the two mountains moved together, and they came into one another, crushing the Amorites, so that their blood flowed into the streams of Arnon. [But the Israelites did not see what was happening in the streams behind them.] When *Et* and *Heiv* came [trailing the camp], they saw blood coming from between these two mountains, [and they realized what had happened]. They went and told the Israelites, who then broke into song. And that is the incident that is referred to in the verse, "The outpouring of streams which inclined toward the habitation of Or, and leans toward the borders of Moab" (Numbers 21:15).

"The place of giant stones" [*avnei elgavish*]. What are these giant stones? We learned: The word *elgavish* is interpreted as a contraction of three words: *al, gav, ish*, meaning "stones that remained suspended because

of a man, and came down because of a man." They remained suspended because of a man; this man was Moses, as it says, "The *man* Moses was very humble" (Numbers 11:3), and it also says, [in connection with the plague of hail], "The thunder ceased and the hail stones that were in mid-air stopped falling to the ground" (Exodus 9:33) [because Moses prayed that the plague should stop. And the hail stones remained suspended in mid-air. Later in history,] these stones came down because of a man: This was Joshua, about whom it says, "Take Joshua son of Nun, a *man* of spirit" (Numbers 27:18). [This is what happened:] It says, "While [the Amorites] were fleeing before Israel down the slope from Bet Choron, God hurled huge stones on them from the sky" (Joshua 10:11). [These were the stones that Moses had stopped from falling during the plague of hail. God saved these stones to demolish the enemies of Israel.]

"The boulder that Og, the king of Bashan, tried to throw at the Jewish people." [For this we have no Scriptural source], but we have a tradition. [The giant] Og, King of Bashan, said: How big is the camp of Israel? Three *parsi*, [about twelve miles]. I'll go and uproot an enormous boulder the size of three *parsi*, and I'll throw it down on them and kill them. Og went and ripped out a boulder of that size and carried it on his head. But the Holy One, blessed be He, sent ants into that mountain, and they made the boulder crumble, forming a hole in which Og's head became lodged. Og tried to pull the mountain off, but his teeth extended on either side, so that he was unable to lift it off his neck. And this is what the verse means when it says, "You broke the teeth of the wicked" (Psalm 3:8), as R. Shimon b. Lakish explained it. For R. Shimon b. Lakish said: What is the meaning of the verse, "You broke the teeth of the wicked"? Do not read *shibbarta* [You broke], but *sherivavta* [that You extended]. [God extended the teeth of the wicked Og.] How tall was Moses? Ten cubits. He took an ax that was ten cubits long, jumped ten cubits, and slammed that ax into the ankles of Og [that way he was able to knock him down], and he killed him.

"The stone where Moses sat," as it says, "When Moses' hands became weary, they took a stone and placed it under him, and he sat on it" (Exodus 17:12).

"Lot's wife," as it says, "Lot's wife looked behind him, and she was turned into a pillar of salt" (Genesis 19:26).

"The wall of Jericho that sank into the ground," as it says, "And the wall collapsed" (Joshua 6:20).

[Now the Gemara asks:] We understand [why the *berachah* should be said over] all the other events, because they are miracles, but the wife of Lot [turning into a pillar of salt] was a punishment. [When you see that pillar] you should say the *berachah*: Blessed be the true Judge [the *berachah* that is said upon hearing bad news], yet our *Baraita* says that you should say a *berachah* of "thanksgiving and praise"? [The Gemara answers:] Read it like this: [When you see the place where Lot was saved and his wife was turned into a pillar of salt] you say two *berachot*. For Lot's wife you say: Blessed be the true Judge, and for Lot you say: Blessed be He who remembers the righteous. [The righteous in this case was Abraham in whose merit Lot was saved.]

R. Yochanan said: Even when the Holy One, blessed be He, is angry he remembers the righteous, for it says, "When God destroyed the cities of the plain, God remembered Abraham, and He allowed Lot to escape the upheaval" (Genesis 19:29).

"Or the wall of Jericho that sank into the ground." [The Gemara asks:] But did the wall of Jericho sink into the ground? It toppled over! For it says, "The wall collapsed" (Joshua 6:20). [The Gemara answers:] Since the height and the width of the wall of Jericho were exactly the same, it must have sunk into the ground. [The only way that the Isrealites could get into the city would be if it had sunk into the ground.]

FOUR PEOPLE WHO MUST OFFER THANKSGIVING

R. Yehudah said in the name of Rav: Four categories of people have to offer thanksgiving, namely, people who have sailed the ocean, people who have traveled in deserts, someone who was sick and became well, and someone who was imprisoned in a dungeon and was set free. How do we know that people who have sailed the ocean have to say a *berachah*? Because it says, "Those who go down to the sea in ships . . . they have seen the works of God . . . By His word He raised a storm wind . . . [Their ship] rises up to the heaven, plunging down to the depths . . . They reeled and staggered like a drunken man . . . In their distress they cried to God, and He saved them from their troubles . . . They rejoiced when all was quiet . . . *Let them give thanks to God* for His mercy" (Psalm 107:23–31).

How do we know that those who have traveled in deserts have to say a *berachah*? Because it says, "They lost their way in the wilderness . . . Hungry and thirsty their spirit failed. In their distress they cried to God . . . He showed them a direct way . . . *Let them give thanks to God* for His mercy" (Psalm 107:4–8).

How do we know that someone who was sick and became well has to say a *berachah*? Because it says, "Fools who suffered for their sinful way, and for their iniquities . . . All food was loathsome to them . . . In their distress they cried to God . . . He gave an order and healed them . . . *Let them give thanks to God* for His mercy" (Psalm 107:17–21).

How do we know that someone who was imprisoned in a dungeon and was set free has to say a *berachah*? Because it says, "They lived in the deepest darkness . . . because they rebelled against the word of God . . . He humbled their hearts through suffering . . . In their distress they cried to God . . . And He brought them

out of the deepest darkness . . . *Let them praise God* for His mercy" (Psalm 107:10–20).

What *berachah* should he say? R. Yehudah said: Blessed is He who bestows beneficent kindnesses. [The Vilna Gaon's variant reading is: *Hagomeil lechayavim tovot shegemalani kol tov*, Who bestows good things upon the guilty, Who has bestowed every goodness upon me. This is the *berachah* that we say.] Abbaye said: And he has to say this *berachah* in the presence of ten people, as it says, "Let them exalt Him in the assembly of the people" (Psalm 107:32). Mar Zutra said: And two of the ten must be rabbis, for it says, "Acclaim Him in the seat of the elders" (ibid.). R. Ashi objected: [How do you know that only two of them must be rabbis?] Maybe all ten have to be rabbis? [The Gemara answers:] Does it say, "In the assembly of elders? It says, "In the assembly of the people," [which means ten ordinary people]. [The Gemara asks further:] Maybe you need ten ordinary people and an additional two rabbis? [For a total of twelve.] [Says the Gemara:] This is a difficulty. [We don't know the answer.][177]

R. Yehudah became ill, and then he recovered. R. Chana of Baghdad and the other Rabbis came to visit him. They said to him: Blessed is God who has given you back to us, and did not give you to the dust. He said to them: You exempted me of the obligation of saying a *berachah* [since you said the *berachah* for me]. [The Gemara asks:] But didn't Abbaye say that you have to say the *berachah* in the presence of ten people? [The Gemara answers:] There were ten. [The Gemara asks further:] But *he* didn't say the *berachah*! [The Gemara answers:] There was no need, because he answered after them, Amen.

THREE THINGS THAT SHORTEN ONE'S LIFE

R. Yehudah said: Three people need special protection [against evil spirits]: a sick person, a bridegroom, and a bride. [They are not allowed to go out alone]. In a *Baraita* we learn: A sick person, a woman who just gave birth, a bridegroom, and a bride [are not allowed to go out alone]. Some add, a mourner. Some add further, Torah scholars at night [are not allowed to go out alone].

(55a) R. Yochanan and R. Eliezer both said: When the *Bet Hamikdash* stood, the altar atoned for Israel, but now a person's table atones for him [if he uses his table properly, by saying *berachot* over the food and sharing his meals with the needy]. R. Yehudah said: Three things cause a person to have his life shortened: If someone is given a Torah scroll to read and he refuses.[178] If someone is given a cup of *wine* to lead the *zimmun* of *Birkat Hamazon* [Grace after Meals], and he refuses to accept it. Or if someone conducts himself in a domineering manner. How do we know that if someone is given a Torah scroll to read and he refuses, his life is shortened? Because it says, "[The Torah] is your life and the length of your days" (Deuteronomy 30:20). [Thus if someone refuses to read from the Torah he spurns the blessing of long life.] If someone is given a cup to lead the *Birkat Hamazon* and he refuses, because it says, "I will bless those who bless you" (Genesis 12:3). If someone conducts himself in a domineering manner, because it says, as R. Chama b. Chanina said: Why did Joseph die before his brothers?[179] Because he acted in a haughty manner.

THE WISDOM OF BETZALEL

R. Yochanan said: There are three things that the Holy One, blessed be He, Himself proclaims, namely, a famine, great prosperity, and the appointment of a good leader for the community. "A famine," as it says, "God has decreed a famine" (2 Kings 8:1). "Great prosperity," as it says, "[God says,] '*I* will summon the grain and make it abundant'" (Ezekiel 36:29). "A good leader," as it says, "God spoke to Moses, saying, 'See, I have singled out by name Betzalel, the son of Uri,'" (Exodus 31:1,2) [to lead the Jewish people in building the Tabernacle].

R. Yitzchak said: You are not allowed to appoint a leader over the community unless you first consult the community, as it says, "See, God has singled out by name Betzalel, son of Uri" (Exodus 36:30). [How did that happen?] The Holy One, blessed be He, said to Moses: Moses, do you consider Betzalel to be suitable [for this task]? He replied: Master of the universe, if You consider him suitable, then I surely consider him suitable! Said God to him: Nevertheless, go and tell the people, [and see what they have to say]. He went and asked Israel: Do you consider Betzalel to be suitable? They replied: If the Holy One, blessed be He, and you consider him suitable, then surely we consider him suitable!

R. Shmuel b. Nachmani said in the name of R. Yonatan: The name Betzalel was given to him [to indicate that he would become a person of] great wisdom. [How did his wisdom become evident?] When the Holy One, blessed be He, said to Moses: Go and tell Betzalel to make Me a Tabernacle, an Ark, and vessels, [in that order—first the building, then its contents (Exodus 31:7)]. Moses reversed the order and said to Betzalel: Make an Ark, vessels, and a Tabernacle, [the Ark first and then the Tabernacle]. Betzalel said to him: Moses, our Teacher, as a rule a person first builds a house, and then he brings the contents into it, but you say: Make an Ark, vessels, and a Tabernacle. Where shall I put the vessels that you are telling me to make? Maybe the Holy One, blessed be He, said to you: Make a Tabernacle, an Ark, and vessels? Moses replied: Maybe you were in the shadow of the Almighty, and you knew.[180]

R. Yehudah said in the name of Rav: Betzalel knew how to combine the letters with which heaven and earth were created. [The Torah is the blueprint of the universe. Thus heaven and earth were created from the Torah, which consists of words that are combinations of letters. Betzalel knew how to combine these letters to create a Tabernacle that would have the proper amount of *kedushah*.] [How do we know that Betzalel knew this?] Because [when discussing the Tabernacle], the Torah says, "God has filled [Betzalel] with a divine spirit of *wisdom, understanding*, and *knowledge*" (Exodus 35:31). And another verse says, "God founded the world by *wisdom*; He established the heavens by *understanding*" (Proverbs 3:19). And it also says, "By His *knowledge* He split the deep waters [in order to make room for the earth]" (ibid. 20). [Thus we see, that wisdom, understanding, and knowledge were used to create the world, and Betzalel needed all of these in order to build the Tabernacle.]

R. Yochanan said: The Holy One, blessed be He, gives wisdom only to a person who already has wisdom, for it says, "He gives wisdom to the wise, and knowledge to those who have understanding" (Daniel 2:21). R. Tachlifa from Eretz Yisrael heard this and repeated it before R. Abahu. He said to him: You learn it from there, but we learn it from this verse, "I have placed wisdom in the heart of every wise-hearted person" (Exodus 31:6).[181]

DREAMS AND DREAM INTERPRETATIONS

R. Chisda said: It is not a good thing for a person to dream about himself when he is fasting.[182] R. Chisda also said: A dream that is not interpreted is like a letter that is not read [it is of no consequence]. R. Chisda also said: You never have a dream—either a good or a bad one—that is completely fulfilled. R. Chisda also said: A bad dream is better than a good dream. [When a person has a bad dream he will worry about it, and it prompts him to do *teshuvah*.] R. Chisda also said: The worry that you have as a result of a bad dream is enough to be considered the fulfillment of the dream, and you will not have to suffer any further ill effects from it. The happiness you derive from a good dream is the fulfillment of that dream. R. Yosef said: Even for me [R. Yosef was blind and could not really enjoy the imagery of his dreams], the happiness caused by a good dream cancels it. R. Chisda also said: A bad dream is worse than a physical beating, for it says, "God has caused things so that people would be afraid of Him" (Ecclesiastes 3:14), and Rabbah b. Bar Chanah said in the name of R. Yochanan: That is a bad dream. [A beating hurts only while it lasts, but the nagging fear induced by a bad dream persists for a long time.]

"'Let the prophet who has a dream tell the dream; and let him who has received My word report My word faithfully! How can straw be compared to grain?' says God" (Jeremiah 23:28). [The Gemara asks:] What do straw and grain have to do with a dream? R. Yochanan said in the name of R. Shimon b. Yocha'i: Just as you cannot have grain without straw [all kernels of grain are encased in straw, which is worthless], in the same way it is impossible to have a dream without some nonsense.

R. Berechiah said: Even though part of a dream may come true, all of it never comes true. How do we know this? From Joseph. For it says, ["Joseph dreamed], 'The sun, the moon, and eleven stars were bowing down to me'" (Genesis 37:9) [The sun was Jacob, the eleven stars were his brothers, the moon represented his mother Rachel,] and (55b) at that time his mother was not living any more [so that part of the dream was nonsense].

R. Levi said: A person should always anticipate that a good dream will come true even if it takes as long as twenty-two years. How do we know this? Also from Joseph. For it says, "These are the chronicles of Jacob. Joseph was seventeen years old . . ." (Genesis 37:2). And furthermore it says, "Joseph was thirty years old when he stood before Pharaoh" (Genesis 41:46). How long is it from the age of seventeen to thirty? Thirteen. Add to this the seven years of plenty and two years of famine. [After which Joseph's dreams came true. So you see that it can take as long as twenty-two years for a dream to be fulfilled.]

R. Huna said: A good person is shown a bad dream [so that he will do *teshuvah*], and a bad person is shown a good dream [to give him his reward in this world (Rashi)]. We have learned a *Baraita* to the same effect: David did not have a good dream in all his life, and Achitofel never had a bad dream in all his life.

R. Bizna b. Zavda said in the name of R. Akiva . . . in the name of a certain elder—and who was this? R. Bana'ah who said: There were twenty-four interpreters of dreams in Jerusalem. Once I had a dream, and I went to all twenty-four, and they all gave different interpretations, and all of them came true. This confirms what it says: All dreams follow the mouth of the interpreter. [The Gemara asks:] You are saying: "It says," [implying that you are quoting a Scriptural verse]. Is the saying, "All dreams follow the mouth of the interpreter" then a Scriptural verse? [Where is such a verse?] [The Gemara answers:] Yes, as R. Elazar said. For R. Elazar said: How do we know that all dreams follow the suggestion of the interpreter? Because it says, ["The butler said to Pharaoh], 'Things turned out just as [Joseph] said they would'" (Genesis 41:13). Rava added: [Don't think that whenever an interpreter says something it invariably comes true]. It only does if the interpretation fits the dream, for it says, "He interpreted each one's dream according to the content" (ibid. 12).

[The Gemara says:] It says, "The chief baker saw that [Joseph] was able to give the correct interpretation" (Genesis 40:16). How did he know? R. Elazar says: Each one had a dream, and he also dreamed the interpretation of the other one's dream.

R. Yochanan said: If somebody wakes up in the morning and thinks of a Biblical verse, [or he hears a child quoting a verse], this is a kind of minor proph-

ecy. R. Yochanan also said: Three kinds of dreams come true: an early-morning dream, a dream that someone else has about you, and a dream that was interpreted in the middle of a dream. Some say: Also a dream that was repeated, as it says, [Joseph saw significance in the fact] "that Pharaoh had the same dream twice" (Genesis 41:32).

R. Shmuel b. Nachmaini said in the name of R. Yonatan: A person is shown in a dream only the things that he thinks about during the day, as it says, [Daniel said,] "O king, the things that you think about [during the day] will come to you in your bed [in your dreams]" (Daniel 2:29). Or if you prefer, you can derive it from here, "You may know the thoughts of your mind [in your dreams]" (ibid. 30). Rava said: Proof [that a person dreams of the things he thinks about during the day is that] a person never dreams about a golden date tree, or about an elephant going through the eye of a needle [because he never thinks of impossible things].

(56a) The Roman emperor[183] said to R. Yehoshua b. Chananiah: You Jews say that you are very smart. If so, tell me what will I see in my dreams tonight? He replied: You'll see in your dream that the Persians [against whom the emperor was mounting an expedition] will force you to work for them, that they'll rob you, and force you to feed unclean animals with a golden stick, [meaning they'll humiliate you]. The emperor thought about this all day, and at night he saw it in his dream. [Which proves that a person dreams about the things he thinks of during the day.]

King Shvur (Shapur)[184] said to Shmuel: You Jews say that you are wise. So tell me what will I see in my dreams? He told him: You will see the Romans coming and taking you captive. They will put you to work grinding date pits in millstones that are made of gold, [making a mockery of you]. The king thought about it the whole day, and at night he saw it in a dream.

BAR HEDYA, THE INTERPRETER OF DREAMS

[The Gemara relates an incident to illustrate the saying that "all dreams follow the mouth of the interpreter," meaning, they are fulfilled according to their interpretation.]

Bar Hedya was an interpreter of dreams. If you paid, he gave a favorable interpretation; but if you did not pay, he gave an unfavorable interpretation. Abbaye and Rava each had a dream. Abbaye gave him a *zuz*, but Rava did not give him any money. They told him: In our dream we had to read the verse, "Your ox will be slaughtered before your eyes, [but you will not eat from it]" (Deuteronomy 28:31). To Rava [who did not pay him] he said: Your business will fail, and you will be so upset that you will have no appetite to eat. To Abbaye [who paid him] he said: Your business will prosper, and you will so overjoyed that you will not be able to eat . . . They said to him: In our dream we had to read the verse, "All the nations of the world will realize that God's name is associated with you and they will be afraid of you" (Deuteronomy 28:10). To Abbaye he said: Your name will become famous as head of the yeshivah, and you will be greatly feared. To Rava he said: The king's treasury will be broken into; you will be arrested as a thief, and everyone will draw an inference from you [saying: if Rava is suspect, then surely we are].

The next day, the king's treasury was burglarized, and they came and arrested Rava . . . Rava went to him alone and told him: "I dreamed that the outer door of my house fell off. He said to him: Your wife will die. Rava then said: I saw that my front and back teeth fell out. He said to him: Your sons and daughters will die. He said: I saw two pigeons flying. He said to him: You will divorce two wives. He said to him: I saw two turnip-tops. He said: You will be hit two times with a stick. That day Rava went and sat all day in the *Bet Midrash*. There were two blind people who were fighting with one another. Rava went to separate them, and they hit him two times. They wanted to hit him again, but Rava said: Two times is enough! I saw it in my dream. [You can't hit me again!]

Finally Rava gave Bar Hedya a fee. He said to him: I dreamed that I saw a wall fall down. He replied: You will become extremely wealthy [nothing will stand in your way]. He said to him: [In my dream] I saw my own villa collapse, and everyone came and took a brick. He said to him: Your teachings will be spread throughout the world. . . .

Bar Hedya and Rava were once traveling together in a ship. Bar Hedya said to himself: Why should I go with a person to whom a miracle will happen? [We will be in danger; he will be saved through a miracle, but I will not.] As Bar Hedya disembarked he dropped a book. Rava found it, and saw written in it: All dreams go according to the interpretation. Rava exclaimed: Wretch that you are! It all depended on you, and you gave me all this pain! I forgive you everything, except for what you said about my wife[185] [whose death Bar Hedya had predicted]. May it be God's will that you will fall into the hands of the Government, and that they will have no mercy on you! . . .

(56b) [Bar Hedya was executed by the Romans.] They tied together two cedars with a rope, and tied one of Bar Hedya's legs to one cedar and the other to the other. Then they released the rope, so that each tree rebounded to its place. He was decapitated and his body was split in two.

DREAM SYMBOLS

Ben Dama, the nephew of R. Yishmael, asked R. Yishmael: I dreamed that both my jaws fell off. [What does that mean]? He replied: Two Roman bands had a conspiracy against you, but they died. [The jaws signify the mouth with which they plotted. You have nothing to worry about].

Bar Kappara said to Rabbi; I dreamed that my nose fell off. He replied: Fierce anger[186] [i.e., a hostile decree] has been removed from you. He said: I dreamed that both my hands were cut off. He replied: You won't need your hands any more to earn a livelihood. He said; I dreamed that both my legs were cut off. He replied: You will ride [comfortably] on horseback.

R. Chanan said: Three kinds of dreams symbolize peace, namely, a dream about a river, a bird, and a pot. A river, because it says, "I will extend to her prosperity like a stream" (Isaiah 66:12). A bird, because it says, "Like the birds that fly, so will the God of Hosts protect Jerusalem" (ibid. 31:5). A pot, for it says, "God will ordain peace for us" (ibid. 26:12). [*Tishpot*, "ordain," also means putting a pot on a fire].[187]

DREAMS ABOUT PERSONALITIES

(57b) R. Yochanan said: If, when you wake up, a Biblical verse comes to mind, it is a kind of minor prophecy.

The Rabbis taught: There are three kings [that have significance in a dream]. If somebody sees King David in his dream, he may look forward to piety. If someone sees King Solomon, he may look forward to wisdom. If he sees Ahab [the evil king who met a violent death] in his dream, he should worry that he might be punished. There are three prophets [who have significance in a dream]. If somebody sees the Book of Kings [which is a book in *Nevi'im*, the Prophets] he may look forward to greatness [because it tells the stories of the kings]; if the Book of Ezekiel, he may look forward to wisdom [because Ezekiel had the prophecy of the Divine Chariot, the ultimate knowledge of the heavenly realm]. If he sees the Book of Isaiah, he may look forward to consolation [because Isaiah gave consolation to the Jewish people]. If he sees the Book of Jeremiah he should be afraid of punishment [because Jeremiah wrote the Book of Lamentations].

There are three large books in *Ketuvim*, The Writings. If someone sees the Book of Psalms in his dream he may look forward to piety. If Proverbs, he may anticipate wisdom. If Job, he should be fearful of punishment [because the Book of Job tells how Job suffered]. There are three small books in *Ketuvim* that have significance in dreams. If somebody sees the Song of Songs in a dream, he may look forward to piety [because Song of Songs describes the love between God and the Jewish people, and this love leads to piety]. If Ecclesiastes, he may expect wisdom. If Lamentations, he should worry about punishment. And if someone dreams about the Book of Esther, a miracle will happen to him [just as it did in the days of Esther].

There are three Sages [who are signifant in a dream]. If somebody sees Rabbeinu Hakadosh [Rabbi Yehudah Hanasi] in his dream he may look forward to wisdom. If Rabbi Elazar b. Azariah, he may look forward to riches, [since R. Elazar b. Azariah was very wealthy].

If R. Yishmael b. Elisha, he should be afraid of punishment.[188] There are three great scholars[189] [who are significant in a dream]. If someone sees Ben Azzai in a dream, he may look forward to piety. If Ben Zoma, he may look forward to wisdom. If Acher, he should worry that punishment may be in store for him. [Acher was Elisha b. Abuya, a rabbi who became a heretic.]

THREE OF A KIND

Three things come into the body, [they are eaten], but the body does not enjoy them: *gudgedaniot* [a kind of clover], date-berries, and unripe dates [all these things are unhealthful]. Three things do not come into the body [you don't eat them], but the body enjoys them nonetheless: washing, anointing, and sexual intercourse. Three things are a semblance of the world to come: *Shabbat*, sunshine, and *tashmish*. [The Gemara asks:] What sort of *tashmish*? Shall I say *tashmish* of the bed [i.e., sexual intercourse]? But this weakens a person. [How can something be a semblance of the world to come if it has a drawback!] But it means moving one's bowels. [This is healthful and good in every respect]. Three things refresh the spirits of a person: a beautiful sound, a beautiful sight, and a fragrant smell. Three things increase a person's self-esteem: a beautiful home, a beautiful wife, and beautiful furnishings.

There are five things that are considered one-sixtieth of something else, namely: honey, *Shabbat*, sleep, and a dream. Fire is one sixtieth of Gehinnom. [The pain caused by a burn is only one-sixtieth of the anguish of Gehinnom.] Honey is one-sixtieth of manna. [As sweet as honey is, it is only one sixtieth as pleasant as the manna was.] *Shabbat* is one-sixtieth of the [spiritual delight of the] world to come. Sleep is one-sixtieth of death. A dream is one-sixtieth of prophecy.

THE WISDOM OF BEN ZOMA

(58a) R. Hamenuna said: If someone sees a large crowd of Jews, he should say: Blessed are You God, our Lord, King of the universe, Knower of secrets. If he sees a large crowd of heathens he should say: "Your mother will be utterly ashamed, she who bore you will be disgraced. Behold the end of nations—wilderness, desert, and steppe!" (Jeremiah 50:12).

The Rabbis taught in a *Baraita*: If someone sees a large crowd of Jews he should say: Blessed is the Knower of secrets. For their minds are different from one another, and their faces are not similar to one another [nevertheless, God understands each of them]. Ben Zoma once saw a large crowd of people on one of the slopes of the Temple Mount. He said: Blessed is the Knower of secrets, and blessed is He who has created all these people to serve me. [What did he mean by that? After all, they are not his servants!] He used to say: Look how hard Adam had to work until he found a loaf of bread to eat. He plowed, he sowed, he harvested,

he bound sheaves, he threshed, he winnowed, he selected, he ground, he sifted, he kneaded, and he baked. Only after all this effort was he able to eat. But I, Ben Zoma, I wake up in the morning, and I find all of these things done for me, [and I find a finished loaf of bread all ready to eat]. And look how much effort Adam had to take until he found a garment that he could wear. He had to shear the wool, clean it, comb it, spin it, and weave it. And only after doing all that did he have a garment to wear. But I wake up in the morning, and I find all these things done for me. All kinds of skilled craftsmen come to my door, and I wake up and find everything all ready before me. [Ben Zoma thanked God for creating society in a way that we all benefit from one another. Thus every individual is served by everyone else.]

[The Gemara tells us another example of Ben Zoma's outlook on people and things.] Ben Zoma used to say: What does a good guest say? He says: Look how much trouble my host has taken for me! How much meat he has set before me! How much wine he has set before me! How many cakes he has set before me! All the trouble he took to prepare this meal he did only for my sake. But what does a bad guest say? He says: What trouble did my host go to for me? Did he serve wine, meat, or cake? And besides, whatever trouble he did take was only for the sake of his wife and children! [He didn't do it for me!] What does Scripture say about a good guest? "Remember to magnify the effort, praise the effort], about which people sing" (Job 36:24). But about a bad guest it says, "People will be afraid of him, he does not take note of any wise people" (Job 37:24).

THE *BERACHAH* WHEN SEEING KINGS AND SCHOLARS

[Speaking about David's father, Jesse, the verse says,] "In the days of Saul the man [Jesse] was already old, and he came with a group of people [to the battle field where Goliath was threatening the Jewish people]" (1 Samuel 17:12). Rava, or as some say, R. Zevid or R. Oshaiah, said: This was Jesse, David's father, who used to leave home with a crowd accompanying him, and returned home with a crowd accompanying him, and he used to expound the Torah to a crowd of people. [Jesse, one of the towering figures of his time, always was accompanied by a large entourage.] Ulla said: We have a tradition that [the law of saying the *berachah* "Blessed be the Knower of secrets" when you see] a large crowd of Jews does not apply in Babylon, [only in Eretz Yisrael]. We learned: A large crowd [where you say this *berachah*] is not less than 600,000.

The Rabbis taught in a *Baraita*: If someone sees Jewish kings he should say: Blessed is He who gave a portion of His own glory to those who fear Him. If he sees non-Jewish kings he should say: Blessed is He who gave of His glory to human beings. If he sees outstanding Torah scholars he should say: Blessed is He who has shared His wisdom with those who fear Him. Upon seeing outstanding secular scholars he should say: Blessed is He who has given of His knowledge to human beings. R. Yochanan said: A person should always try to run to see Jewish kings; and not only to see Jewish kings, even to see non-Jewish kings. For if he deserves to live to see the coming of *Mashiach* he will be able to tell the difference between the Jewish kings of the future and the kind of kings that used to reign on earth in the past.

R. SHESHET AND THE HERETIC

R. Sheshet was blind. One day, the whole town was going out to greet the king, and R. Sheshet went along with them. A certain heretic saw him and said: Whole pitchers are taken to the river [to be filled with water], but where do the broken pitchers go? [He was taunting him, as if to say: Why do you, a blind man, go to greet the king? You cannot even see him!] Replied R. Sheshet: I'll show you that I know more than you. The first troop in the parade passed by, and everyone began to shout. Said the heretic to R. Sheshet: The king has come! No, said R. Sheshet, the king has not come. The second troop passed, and the people shouted. The heretic said: The king has come! Replied R. Sheshet: The king has not come. A third troop passed. This time, everything was quiet. Said R. Sheshet: Now the king is definitely coming.

Said the heretic: How do you know? He answered: Royalty on eath is a reflection of royalty in heaven. For it says, [After God performed the great miracle on Mount Carmel through Elijah, the evil Queen Jezebel threatened to kill him. Elijah ran away into the desert and hid in a cave at Mount Horeb. It was there that God's angel told him,] "'Come out of your cave and stand on the mountain before God, and God will pass." There was a great and mighty wind splitting mountains and shattering stones, all before God. But God was not in that wind. After the wind there came an earthquake. But God was not in the earthquake. After the earthquake a fire broke out. But God was not in the fire. After the fire there was a still small voice. [That small voice signaled the Presence of God.] (1 Kings 19:11,12). [R. Sheshet meant to say that a great king does not need loud noise to announce his presence.] When the king came, R. Sheshet said the *berachah*: Who gave of His glory to a human being. The heretic scornfully said to him: You are saying a *berachah* for someone you can't even see! [The Gemara asks:] What happened to this heretic? [The Gemara answers: Some say that his own friends poked out his eyes. Others say that R. Sheshet stared at him, and the heretic turned into a pile of bones.

R. SHILA AND THE ROMAN OFFICIALS

There was a person who had sexual relations with a prostitute, and R. Shila ruled that he should be flogged. So this person went to the government and leveled false charges against R. Shila [to get even with him]. He said: There is one person among the Jews who officiates as judge without the permission of the government. A committee was sent to investigate the charge. When they came to R. Shila they asked him: Why did you sentence him to be flogged? He replied: Because he had intercourse with a donkey. The officials asked: Do you have witnesses? He answered: Yes, I have. Elijah then came in the form of a human being and testified. The officials said to R. Shila: In that case he should be put to death! [Why did you let him off so easily!] R. Shila replied: Ever since we have been exiled from our land we have no authority to impose the death penalty. But you, go ahead and do what you want with him.

While the officials were deliberating on what to do with this man, R. Shila praised God and said, "Yours, O God, are greatness, power, splendor, triumph, and majesty—yes, all that is in heaven and on earth. Yours is the kingdom, O God, and You are exalted above every leader" (1 Chronicles 29:11). The officials asked: What are you saying? He replied: This is what I said: Blessed is the All-Merciful who has modeled the government of earth after the government of heaven. He has given you sovereignty and a love of justice. They said to him: Since you have such high regard for the honor of the government, we herewith appoint you as judge. They handed him a staff [the symbol of authority] and said: You now have the right to administer the law. When R. Shila left this session, the person [whose immoral conduct had brought on the entire incident] said to him: Does God perform such miracles for liars? [You lied, because you told them that you were praising them when, in fact, you were saying a Biblical verse. And yet a miracle happened. How can God do such a thing!] He replied: Wretch that you are! Aren't [people like these officials] called donkeys? For it says, "Their flesh is like the flesh of donkeys" (Ezekiel 23:20). R. Shila saw this man running back to those officials to tell them that he had called them donkeys. R. Shila said to himself: This fellow is a pursuer [who puts my life in danger], and the Torah says: If someone comes to kill you, be quick and kill him first.[190] He hit him with the staff [the officials had given him] and killed him.

R. Shila said: Since through this verse ["Yours, God, are greatness"] a miracle was done for me, I will expound it. "Yours, God, are greatness": this refers to the work of Creation, and so it says, "Who performs deeds that cannot be fathomed" (Job 9:10). "Power": this refers to the Exodus from Egypt, as it says, "The Israelites saw the great power" (Exodus 14:31). "Splendor": this refers to the sun and moon, which stood still for Joshua [when he was fighting against the Canaanites], as it says, "And the sun stood still, and the moon halted" (Joshua 10:13). "Triumph" [*Netzach*]: this refers to the [eventual] downfall of Rome, and so it says, "Their blood [*nitzcham*, the blood of Edom, which is Rome] will be sprinkled on my garments [at the final Redemption]" (Isaiah 63:3). "Majesty" refers to the battle of the valleys of Arnon [where the mountains came together and crushed the Amorites who were lying in ambush], as it says, "It is therefore told in the Book of God's Wars, *Vaheiv* in *Sufah* (Numbers 21:14). "All that is in heaven and on earth": this refers to the war of Sisera [in which Deborah and Barak had a miraculous great victory], as it says, "The stars fought from heaven, from their courses they fought against Sisera" (Judges 5:20).

"Yours is the kingdom, O God": this refers to the war against Amalek, and so it says, "The hand [of Amalek] is on God's Throne. God shall be at war with Amalek for all generations" (Exodus 17:16). "And You are exalted": this refers to the war of Gog and Magog; and so it says, "Thus says God the Lord, 'Lo, I am coming to deal with you, O Gog, chief prince of Meshech and Tuval!'" (Ezekiel 38:3). "Above every leader": R. Chanan b. Rava said: Even the foreman of workers who dig ditches, for irrigation is appointed from heaven. We learned in a *Baraita* in the name of R. Akiva: "Yours, God, are greatness": this refers to the parting of the Sea. "Power": this refers to the slaying of the first-born. "Splendor": this refers to the giving of the Torah. "Triumph": This refers to Jerusalem. "Majesty": refers to the *Bet Hamikdash*, may it be Your will that it be rebuilt speedily in our days.

R. CHISDA'S LAMENT

(58b) Ulla and R. Chisda were walking along the road. When they passed by the doorway of R. Chana b. Chanila'i, R. Chisda broke down and sighed. Said Ulla to him: Why are you sighing? [Sighing is bad for you.] Rav said that a sigh breaks half of a person's body, as it says, "And you, son of man, groan with breaking of your loins" (Ezekiel 21:11), and R. Yochanan said that it breaks the entire body of a person, as it says, "And when they ask you, 'Why do you sigh?' answer, 'Because of the tidings that have come. Every heart shall sink and all hands hang nerveless . . .'" (ibid. 12).

R. Chisda answered: How can I not sigh when I see a house in which there were sixty cooks by day and sixty cooks at night who cooked for every needy person; and R. Chana b. Chanila'i never took his hand away from his money purse, thinking that perhaps a respectable poor man might come, and until he would reach into his purse to take money for him he'll be embarrassed. But that's not all; this house had four doors, one door open to each of the four directions, and

anyone who was hungry when he went in, went out satisfied. And in years of hunger he used to throw wheat and barley in all directions outside, so that anyone who was too embarrassed to take charity during the day would be able to come at night and find food on the street. And now this house has fallen into a heap of rubble, should I not groan?

He answered him: This is what R. Yochanan said: From the time that the *Bet Hamikdash* was destroyed, a decree has been issued against the houses of the righteous that they should also be destroyed, for it says, "In My hearing, said God of Hosts: Surely, great houses shall lie desolate, spacious and splendid ones without occupants!" (Isaiah 5:9). R. Yochanan said further: The Holy One, blessed be He, will once again bring them back to their habitation, as it says, "Those who trust in God are like Mount Zion" (Psalm 125:1). Just as the Holy One, blessed be He, will return Mount Zion to its complete habitation [i.e., the *Bet Hamikdash* will be rebuilt], so too will He bring back the homes of the righteous to their previous habitation. He saw that he had not comforted him, so he told him: It is good enough for a slave to suffer the same fate as his master. [If God's house is in ruin, then the homes of His servants should also be in ruin.]

R. Yehoshua b. Levi said: If someone sees his friend after thirty days, he says: [*Shehecheyanu*], Blessed is He who has kept us alive, sustained us, and brought us to this season. If he sees someone after a twelve-month interval he says: Blessed is He who revives the dead. Rav said: A dead person is not forgotten until twelve months go by, as it says, "I am put out of mind like the dead; I am like an object given up for lost" (Psalm 31:13), [and an object is not given up for lost until twelve months have passed (Rashi)].

BERACHOT FOR GOOD AND BAD TIDINGS

(60a) [The Mishnah says:] If something bad happens, even though there is an element of good in it, you should say the *berachah Dayan Ha'emet*, "The true Judge." [The Gemara asks:] What's the case? [The Gemara answers:] For example, if a flood inundated his land [so this year's crop is ruined]. Even though there is an element of good in it for him, because his land will become more fertilized for next year [so it will produce a better crop], nevertheless, now it is still bad for him. [Therefore he should say the *berachah* according to the present circumstances: *Dayan Ha'emet*.]

[The Mishnah said:] If something good happens, even though there is an element of bad in it, you should say the *berachah* of *Hatov veHameitiv*, "Who is good and does good." What's the case? For example, if somebody finds a valuable object. Even though this may [eventually] be bad for him, because if the king finds out about it [he will imprison him] and take it away from him. Nevertheless, for the time being it is a good thing, [and for that he has to say the *berachah* of *Hatov veHameitiv*].

The Rabbis taught: It happened once that Hillel the Elder was coming home from a trip when he heard an outcry in the city. He said: I am positive that this anguished outcry is not from my house. About this kind of person Scripture says, "He is not afraid of bad news; his heart is firm and he trusts in God" (Psalm 112:7). Said Rava: Whenever you expound this verse you can explain it from the beginning to the end or from the end to the beginning. You can explain it from the beginning to the end: "He is not afraid of bad news." Why? Because "his heart is firm and he trusts in God." You can also explain it from the end to the beginning: "A person whose heart is firm and who trusts in God, is not afraid of bad news."

A certain disciple once followed R. Yishmael b. R. Yosi in the market of Jerusalem. R. Yishmael noticed that this disciple was afraid. So he said to him: You must be a sinner, for it says, "Sinners in Zion are frightened" (Isaiah 33:14). He replied: But it says, "Happy is the man that is always afraid" (Proverbs 28:14). R. Yishmael answered him: That verse refers to words of Torah, [and it tells you always to be afraid that you might forget your learning, and therefore you should review your studies constantly. In other matters have faith in God and don't be afraid].

R. Yehudah b. Natan was walking behind R. Hamenuna. R. Yehudah b. Natan sighed, and R. Hamenuna said to him: Do you want to bring suffering on yourself? It says, "For what I feared has overtaken me, what I dreaded has come upon me" (Job 3:25). He replied: But it says, "Happy is the man that is always afraid" (Proverbs 28:14). He answered: That verse is talking about words of Torah.

A DONKEY, A ROOSTER, AND A LAMP

(60b) R. Huna said in the name of Rav who quoted R. Meir, others say that he quoted R. Akiva: A person should make it a habit always to say: Whatever God does He does for the good." We find an example of this in the following episode with R. Akiva: R. Akiva once was traveling along the road, and he had with him a donkey, a rooster, and a lamp. He arrived in a certain city, and went to look for lodging for the night, but everyone turned him away. He said: Whatever God does is for the good and spent the night out in the open field. A lion came and devoured his donkey; a cat came and ate up his rooster; and a gust of wind came and blew out the lamp. [So R. Akiva was left in the dark, without food, and without transportation.] He said: Whatever God does is for the good. That very same night an army regiment came, captured the city, and took the people into captivity. R. Akiva said [to the people who wondered about his fate that night]: Didn't

I tell you: Whatever God does is for the good? [If I had my donkey it would have brayed, the rooster would have crowed, and if the lamp had burned the soldiers would have found me and taken me prisoner.]

MANO'ACH FOLLOWED HIS WIFE

(61a) If someone counts out money from his hand into a woman's hand in order to gaze upon her, even if he is as great as Moses in Torah and good deeds, he will not escape the punishment of Gehinnom, for it says, "Hand to hand, he will not escape evil" (Proverbs 11:21), which means that [even if he is like Moses who received the Torah from the hand of God into his hand (Rashi)], he will not escape the punishment of Gehinnom.

R. Nachman said: Mano'ach [Samson's father] was an *am ha'aretz* (ignoramus), for it says, "Mano'ach followed behind his wife" (Judges 13:11). R. Nachman b. Yitzchak objected to this. He said: [If you say that he literally followed behind his wife], then, in the case of Elkanah [Samuel's father] when it says, "And Elkanah followed behind his wife," and in the case of Elisha when it says, "And he arose and followed behind her" (2 Kings 4:30), do you mean to say that they actually followed behind a woman? No, [says the Gemara], it means that they followed her words and her advice. So too, in the case of Mano'ach it means that he followed his wife's words and advice [and there is no proof that Mano'ach was an *am haaretz*]. R. Ashi said: According to R. Nachman's view that Mano'ach was an *am haaretz*, he did not even know the simple meaning of a verse of Scripture. For it says, "Rebeccah set off with her girls, and they rode on the camels, following after the man" (Genesis 24:61), after the man and not in front of the man.

R. Yochanan said: It is better to go behind a lion than behind a woman; it is better to go behind a woman than behind an idol; it is better to go behind an idol than behind a synagogue when the congregation is praying, [because by not entering he shows contempt of the synagogue]. However, this applies only if he is not carrying a load, but if he is carrying a load there is no objection [because it is obvious that he did not enter because he was carrying a load]. And also this applies only if there is no other entrance, but if there is another entrance there is no objection [because people will think that he will enter by the other door]. Again this applies only if he is not riding on a donkey; but if he is riding on a donkey, there is no objection. And again, this applies only if he is not wearing *tefillin*; but if he is wearing *tefillin* there is no objection. [People will not suspect him of disparaging the synagogue service because by wearing *tefillin* he shows that he accepts the laws of the Torah.]

THE ORGANS OF THE BODY

Rava said: The evil tendency resembles a fly and it dwells between the two openings of the heart, as it says,

"Dead flies make the perfumer's ointment fetid and putrid" (Ecclesiastes 10.1). Shmuel says: The evil tendency resembles a wheat kernel [chittah], because it says, "Sin [chatat] is crouching at the door" (Genesis 4:7).[191]

The Rabbis taught: Man has two kidneys—one prods him to do good, and the other to do evil, and it is reasonable to suppose that the good kidney is on the right side and the bad one on the left, as it says, "A wise man's mind tends toward the right, a fool's mind tends to the left" (Ecclesiastes 10:2).

The Rabbis taught: The heart discerns, the kidneys advise, the wind-pipe produces the voice, the food-pipe takes in all kinds of food (61b), the lungs absorb all kinds of moisture, the tongue shapes the words, the mouth [i.e., the lips] articulates, the liver is the source of anger, the gall lets a drop fall into the liver and soothes the anger. The spleen produces laughter, the large intestine grinds the food, the stomach brings sleep, and the nose wakes up. If the sleeper [the stomach] arouses or the awakener [the nose] sleeps, [meaning, if they reverse their functions, so that the nose induces sleep and the stomach awakens], a person's health deteriorates, and he withers away. We learned in a Baraita: If both [the stomach and the nose] induce sleep or both awaken, a person dies immediately.

THE GOOD AND EVIL INCLINATIONS

We learned in a Baraita: R. Yose Hagelili says: The righteous are controlled by their good tendency, as it says, "My heart is slain within me" (Psalm 109:22). [David, in effect, is saying: My yetzer hara is as if dead; I dominate it completely.] The wicked are controlled by their evil tendency, as it says, "The evil tendency says to the wicked, 'Do not be afraid of God'" (Psalm 36:2). Average people are controlled by both tendencies [the good and evil inclinations are fighting each other], as it says, "Because He stands at the right hand of the needy, to save him from those who control him" (Psalm 109:31) ["those" refers to both the good and the bad inclinations]. Rava said: For example, I am in the category of the average. Said Abaye to Rava: You don't allow anyone to live! [If a tzaddik like you, Rava, is only average, what is everyone else!] Rava said: A man knows about himself whether he is righteous or wicked. Rava further said: The world was created for either the completely righteous or for the completely wicked. [The wicked receive the reward in this world for the few good deeds they performed; the righteous receive their reward in the world to come (Rashi).] Rav said: The world was created only for Ahab son of Omri and for R. Chanina b. Dosa; for Ahab son of Omri [the wicked king] this world was created,[192] and for R. Chanina b. Dosa, the world to come.[193]

R. AKIVA'S MARTYRDOM

"You shall love God your Lord with all your heart, with all your soul, and with all your resources" (Deuteronomy 6:4). We learned in a Baraita: R. Eliezer the Great says: If it says "with all your soul," why does it have to say "with all your resources"? And since it says, "With all your resources" why does it have to say, "With all your soul"? To teach you that if you have a person who values his life more than his money, for him it says, "With all your soul"; and if you have a person who values his money more than his life, for him it says, "With all your resources." R. Akiva says: "With all your soul" means: [You must love God] even if it means giving up your life. [You must be ready to offer your life for the sake of God.]

The Rabbis taught: It happened once that the [Roman] government issued a decree forbidding the Jews to study the Torah. What did R. Akiva do? He gathered people together in public assemblies and taught them the Torah. When Pappus b. Yehudah found him [expounding and lecturing] he said: Akiva, aren't you afraid of the government? Replied R. Akiva: Let me explain it to you with a parable. A fox once was taking a walk by the river bank, and he saw swarms of fish moving from one place to another. Said the fox to the fish: Why are you running? They replied: We are trying to avoid the nets that people set to trap us. He said to them: Why don't you all come up on dry land, then you and I can live together just as my ancestors lived in peace with your ancestors. They answered: Are you the one they call the most clever of the animals? You are not clever, but very foolish. If we are in danger in the water, which is our natural habitat, surely will we be in danger in an environment in which we would die [on dry land]!

[Continued R. Akiva:] It is the same with us. If our lives are in danger when we sit and study the Torah, of which it says, "It is your sole means of survival and long life" (Deuteronomy 30:20), surely we will be in danger if we stopped our Torah studies. It was said that not long after this R. Akiva was arrested and thrown into prison, and Pappus b. Yehudah was also arrested and imprisoned next to R. Akiva. R. Akiva said to Pappus: Who brought you here? Pappus answered: Happy are you, R. Akiva, that you have been arrested for studying Torah. Too bad that I, Pappus, was arrested for trivial things. When R. Akiva was taken out for execution it was time to recite the Shema, and while they were combing his flesh with iron combs [he recited the Shema and] accepted God's absolute sovereignty with love. His disciples said to him: Rabbi, is one required to go this far in offering one's life? Replied R. Akiva: All my life I have been troubled by the verse, "[You shall love God] with all your soul," [which I interpret to mean], "you have to be ready to give up your soul." I said to myself: When will I ever have the opportunity to fulfill this mitzvah? Now that I have the opportunity shall I not fulfill it? He drew out the word *echad*[194] until his soul left him while he was saying *echad*.

A heavenly voice came forth and proclaimed: Happy are you, Rabbi Akiva, that your soul left you with the word *echad*. The ministering angels said to the Holy One, blessed be He: Master of the universe, is this the reward of Torah [that a great man like R. Akiva should have to die such a tragic death]? [He should have been] "from men that die by Your hand, O God," (Psalm 17:14) [and not be killed by human hands]. God responded: "Their portion is in life" (ibid.). A heavenly voice came forth and said: Happy are you Rabbi Akiva, that you are destined for life in the world to come.

THE PLAGUE IN DAVID'S TIME

(62b) "David went and stealthily cut off the corner of Saul's cloak" (1 Samuel 24:5). R. Yose b. Chanina said: Whoever treats clothes with contempt will end up being unable to enjoy his clothes, for it says, "King David was now old . . . and though they covered him with bedclothes, he never felt warm" (1 Kings 1:1) [This was his punishment for treating Saul's robe with disdain.]

[David said to Saul,] "If God incited you against me, let Him be appeased by an offering" (1 Samuel 26:19). R. Elazar said: The Holy One, blessed be He, said to David: Are you calling Me an instigator? For that I'll make you stumble over something that even schoolchildren know, namely the passage, "When you take a census of the Israelites to determine their numbers, each one shall be counted by giving an atonement offering for his life, in this manner they will not be stricken by the plague when they are counted" (Exodus 30:12). [The Torah ordains that a census should not be taken by body count; rather, each individual should give a coin, and by counting the coins the census takers arrive at the total.] Immediately, "Satan arose against Israel and encouraged David to count Israel" (1 Chronicles 21:1), and it says further, "He said [to David], 'Go and count Israel'" (2 Samuel 24:1). And when David counted them he did not take any ransom [coins] from them. It says further, "God sent a pestilence upon Israel from morning until the appointed time" (ibid. 15). [The Gemara asks:] What is the meaning of "the appointed time"? Shmuel the Elder, the son-in-law of R. Chanina, answered in the name of R. Chanina: [The plague lasted] from the time of the slaughtering of the continual sacrifice until the time of the sprinkling of the blood. R. Yochanan said: Until noon. [At any rate, we see that as a result of David's census a plague came on the Jewish people.]

"[God] said to the angel who was destroying the people, 'Enough!'" [*rav*] (ibid. 16). R. Eliezer said: The Holy One, blessed be He, said to the angel: Bring Me the greatest person [*rav*] among them, through whose death many debts will be paid [his death will be an atonement for many of their sins]. At that moment death came to Avishai ben Tzeruyah, whose greatness was equal to that of the majority of the entire Sanhedrin.

"God sent an angel to Jerusalem to destroy it, but as he was about to wreak destruction, God saw, and He relented from the evil" (1 Chronicles 21:15). [The Gemara asks:] What did God see? Rav said: He saw our father Jacob, [and in Jacob's merit God relented], as it says, "[Jacob encountered the angels of God, and] Jacob said when he *saw* them" (Genesis 32:3). Shmuel said: [God] saw the ashes of [the ram] of Isaac; [He remembered the *Akeidah*[195]], where it says, "God will *see* to the lamb for a burnt offering" (ibid. 22:8). R. Yitzchak Nafcha said: He saw the atonement money [that was donated for the construction of the *Mishkan*], as it says, "You will take this atonement money from the Israelites, and it will be a remembrance before God"[196] (Exodus 30:16). R. Yochanan said: He saw the *Bet Hamikdash*, as it says, "On God's Mountain [where the *Bet Hamikdash* is situated] He will be *seen*" (ibid. 22:14). There is a difference of opinion about this between R. Yaakob b. Idi and R. Shmuel b. Nachmani. One said that God saw the atonement money, the other that He saw the *Bet Hamikdash* [and that caused Him to spare the people from destruction]. It is likely that the view of the one who said that He saw the *Bet Hamikdash* is correct because it says, "Today, it is therefore said, 'On God's Mountain, He will be *seen*'" (ibid.)

DON'T COMPETE
WITH SCHOLARS

(63a) We have learned in a *Baraita*: Hillel the Elder said: At a time when the scholars are not teaching Torah to the people, you should disseminate Torah. When the scholars disseminate the Torah, you should modestly stay in the background so as not to compete with them. If you see a generation that has a love of Torah, spread the knowledge of Torah, as it says, "One man gives generously and ends with more" (Proverbs 11:24). But if you see a generation that has no love for Torah, then keep the Torah to yourself, as it says, "It is a time to act for God, for they have violated Your Torah" (Psalm 119:126). [Forcing Torah on people who have no understanding for it will only lead to degradation of the Torah.] Bar Kappara expounded: When goods are cheap, that's the time to buy [for the price will surely go up (Rashi)]. In a place where there is no one to do the job, you be the one. Abaye said: We can infer from this that when there is someone to do the job [i.e., when there is a scholar who teaches Torah], then you should not compete. [The Gemara asks:] That is obvious! [We all know the rule that you are not allowed to render *halachic* decisions in the presence of your rabbi (Rashi).] [The Gemara answers:] Abaye has in mind a case where the Torah scholar [is not your rabbi], and he is your equal in learning [nevertheless, you should not expound Torah in his town].

Bar Kappara expounded: Where in *Tanach* do you find a short section that contains all the basic elements of the Torah? [The verse,] "In all your ways acknowledge Him, and He will make your paths smooth" (Proverbs 3:6). [The verse means that if you are constantly aware of the presence of God, then your most mundane acts, like eating and sleeping, become mitzvot.] Rava said: Even when committing a transgression [a person should consider whether the transgression is done for the sake of heaven, as Elijah did when he transgressed by offering a sacrifice on Mount Carmel.[197] He did so in order to prove to the false prophets of Baal and their followers that God is truly the One and Only Creator. Thus, his transgression was really a mitzvah]. Bar Kappara further expounded: A person should teach his son a trade that is clean and easy. What, for example? Needle-stitching [tailoring].

It was taught in a *Baraita*: Rabbi says: A person should not invite too many friends to his house, as it says, "A person's many friends are hurtful to him" (Proverbs 18:24). It was taught in a *Baraita*: Rebbi says: A person should not appoint a manager over his household [because there are women around]. For if Potiphar had not appointed Joseph as manager over his household he would not have landed in all his trouble.

THE ORDEAL OF THE *SOTAH*

It was taught: Rabbi said: Why does the chapter of the nazirite[198] (Numbers 6:1–21) follow immediately after the chapter of the *sotah* [the suspected adulteress] (Numbers 5:31)? To teach you that whoever sees a *sotah* in her disgrace should abstain from wine. Chizkiah b. R. Parnach said in the name of R. Yochanan: Why does the section dealing with the *sotah* follow immediately after the section of *terumah*[199] and the tithes (Numbers 5:5–10)? To tell you that if someone has *terumah* or tithes and does not give them to the *kohen*, he will end up [suspecting his wife of infidelity] and needing the services of a *kohen* to administer the ordeal that the *sotah* has to submit to. For it says, "If a person withholds his hallowed things [and does not give them to the *kohen*]" (ibid. 9), and immediately after this it says, "If any man's wife goes astray" (ibid. 5:12). And later it says, "The man must bring his wife to the *kohen*" (ibid. 15). And what's more, in the end he himself will need [tithes, because he will lose his money], as it says, "If a person withholds his hallowed things he will become impoverished." Said R. Nachman b. Yitzchak: But if he does give [the *terumah* and the tithes], he will become rich, for it says, "Whatever a person gives to the *kohen*, will belong to him," which means, he will have great wealth.

R. Huna b. Berechiah said in the name of R. Elazar Hakappar: Whoever includes God's name with his suffering [meaning, he praises God for bad things, saying *Baruch Dayan Ha'emet*, "Blessed be the true Judge," or he prays to God for mercy (Rashi)], will find that his income is doubled, as it says, "The Almighty will be in your distress, and you will have double money" (Job 22:25).[200] R. Shmuel b. Nachmani said: His sustenance will fly to him like a bird, for it says, "And money will fly to you."[201] R. Tuvia said in the name of R. Yoshiah: If someone is lax in his Torah study he will have no strength in times of trouble. For it says, "If you showed yourself slack [in your Torah study], in time of trouble your strength will be small" (Proverbs 24:10). R. Ammi b. Mattenah said in the name of Shmuel: Even if he was lax in the observance of only one mitzvah [he will have no strength to withstand trouble], for it says, "If you showed yourself slack," meaning, in any case, [whether in Torah study or in a mitzvah].

CHANANIAH AND
THE TWO SCHOLARS

R. Safra said: R. Abbahu used to relate that when Chanania, the nephew of R. Yehoshua, went to Babylonia, he began to intercalate the years[202] and fix new moons outside Eretz Yisrael. The Rabbis [of the *Bet Din*] sent two scholars after him: R. Yose b. Kippar and the grandson of R. Zechariah b. Kevutal [to stop him from doing that]. When Chananiah saw them coming he asked them: Why did you come? They replied: We came to learn Torah from you. He then announced: These men are among the foremost Torah scholars of our generation. Their ancestors served in the *Bet Hamikdash* (as we have learned: Zechariah b. Kevutal says: Many a time I read to [the *Kohen Gadol*[203]] out of the Book of Daniel [on the night of Yom Kippur, when the *Kohen Gadol* was not allowed to fall asleep]).[204] Before long, [disputes arose between Chananiah and the two scholars]; he would declare something ritually clean, and they declared it unclean; he would forbid certain things, and they permitted them. Chananiah then announced: These men are worthless individuals; they are insincere.

They said to him: Once you built us up by proclaiming our greatness you cannot destroy our reputation any more; once you built a fence [by praising us] you cannot break it down [by discrediting us]. He said to them: [Why do you take issue with everything I say?] Why do you declare clean the things I declare unclean, why do you forbid the things I permit? They answered: Because you intercalate years and fix new moons outside Eretz Yisrael, [and this may be done only in Eretz Yisrael]. He replied: But did not Akiva b. Yosef intercalate years and fix new moons outside Eretz Yisrael?[205] They replied: R. Akiva was different; there was no one left in Eretz Yisrael who was his equal. He replied: I also did not leave anyone greater than me in Eretz Yisrael.

They retorted: The little kids [the young students] you left behind have become fully grown goats with horns [great Torah scholars]. They have sent us to you, and this is what they told us: Go and tell Chananiah in our name. If he listens, fine; if not, he will be excommunicated. (63b) And warn our brothers in Babylonia [not to listen to him]. If they listen to you, fine. If not, let them all go up a mountain. Let Achiah [the leader of the Babylonian community] build there a [heathen] altar, and let Chanaiah play the harp [because he is a Levite],[206] and let them all become heretics and declare that they don't have anything to do with the God of Israel. As soon as [the two rabbis finished their message], all the people started to cry and said: God forbid! We do want to have a portion in God! [In other words, they agreed not to follow Chananiah.] And why did the rabbis go to such lengths in warning the people? Because it says, "For from Zion will the Torah come forth and the word of God from Jerusalem" (Isaiah 2:3) [therefore, intercalation of years and fixing of new moons should be done in Eretz Yisrael].

[The Gemara asks:] It is understandable that if he declared something clean the two rabbis should declare it unclean, because that would be more stringent. But how was it possible that they should declare clean something he declared unclean? Have we not learned: If a rabbi has declared something unclean, his colleague is not allowed to declare it clean; if he prohibited something, his colleague is not allowed to permit it? [The Gemara answers:] The two rabbis thought that they were justified to act like this [and differ with Chananiah on all counts] in order that the people should not be swayed to follow him.

GOD, MOSES, THE TORAH, AND THE PEOPLE OF ISRAEL

The Rabbis have taught: When our Rabbis entered the Yeshivah in Yavneh[207] they found there R. Yehudah, R. Yose, R. Nechemiah, and R. Eliezer b. R. Yose Hagelili. They all began their expositions by making a few remarks in honor of the host. R. Yehudah, who was the main speaker in every place, began to lecture about the honor of the Torah, expounding the verse, "[After the sin of the golden calf,] Moses took his tent and set it up outside the camp" (Exodus 33:7). [R. Yehudah explained:] Now can't we draw a logical inference from this? We know that the Ark of God was never more than twelve *mil* away from anyone in the camp, [because the Ark was in Moses' tent outside the camp, and the camp of the children of Israel measured twelve *mil* across],[208] and yet the Torah says, "Whoever sought God would go to the Meeting Tent" (Exodus 33:7), how much more [is the description of "one who seeks God"] applicable to Torah scholars who wander from city to city and from country to country to learn Torah!

"God would speak to Moses face to face" (ibid. 11). [This is difficult to understand, since God said, "My face cannot be seen" (Exodus 33:23).] Therefore R. Yitzchak expounds: The Holy One, blessed be He, said to Moses: Moses, both I and you will explain the *Halachah* to the Jewish people. Some say that the Holy One, blessed be He, said this to Moses: Just as I have shown you a cheerful face, so should you show a cheerful face to the Jewish people [even though they sinned with the golden calf], and return your tent to its original place [inside the camp].

"[Moses] returned to the camp" (ibid.). R. Abbahu said: The Holy One, blessed be He, said to Moses: The people will now say: The Master [God] is angry [because of the golden calf], and the disciple [Moses] is angry [seeing that he moved his tent outside the camp], what will happen to Israel? If you return the tent to its place, well and good, but if not, your disciple Joshuah son of Nun will take your place. Therefore it says, "[Moses] returned to the camp." Rava said: Even though Moses returned, God's words were not said in vain, since it says, "But his aide, the young man Joshua son of Nun, did not leave the tent" (ibid.) [and ultimately succeeded Moses].

R. Yehudah spoke further about the honor of the Torah, interpreting the verse, "Pay attention [*haskeit*] and listen, Israel. Today you have become a nation" (Deuteronomy 27:9). [He expounded: How could Moses say, "Today"! Do you mean to say that the Torah was given to Israel on that day? That day was at the end of the forty years of wandering through the desert; forty years after the Giving of the Torah at Sinai!—The verse comes to teach you that the Torah is as beloved by those who study it as it was on the day it was given on Mount Sinai. R. Tanchum, the son of R. Chiya from K'far Akko, said: Proof of that is, that a person recites the *Shema* every morning and evening, and if, by mistake, he misses reading the *Shema* one evening he feels [as depressed] as if he had never read it before, [which shows his great love of Torah and *mitzvot*].

[The Gemara continues to expound the text:] The word *haskeit* [is a contraction of the words *has* (make) and *kitot* (classes)], and it means: Form groups to study Torah, since the Torah can be acquired only if you learn with a study partner, as R. Yose b. Chanina said: What is the meaning of the verse, "A sword against the people who boast [*baddim*]; they will become foolish!" (Jeremiah 50:36). A sword will come upon the Torah scholars who sit by themselves [*bad bevad*] and study Torah alone. And not only [a sword will come], but they also will become foolish. [The Gemara now wants to prove by means of analogy that *veno'alu* means foolish.] It says here, *veno'alu*, "they will become foolish," and it says [in connection with Aaron and Miriam], *no'alnu*, "we acted foolishly" (Numbers 12:11). But that's not all; [learning alone] may lead to sin, for the verse continues, "and we have sinned" (ibid). And if you prefer, I can [prove that *no'alu* means foolish] from the following passage, "The nobles of Tzo'an have been fools [*no'alu*]" (Isaiah 19:13).

Another explanation of the verse, "Pay attention [*haskeit*] and listen, Israel" is: Cut yourselves to pieces [*kittetu*] for the sake of Torah. [I.e., be ready to suffer for the sake of Torah study], as Resh Lakish expounded: From where do we know that the Torah endures only with a person who is willing to die for it? [meaning, to forgo the comforts of life]. From the passage, "This is the Torah, when a person dies in a tent [figuratively, a house of study]" (Numbers 19:14). [How can you acquire Torah? When you are ready to give up luxuries and creature comforts.]

Another interpretation of the verse, "Pay attention [*haskeit*] and listen, Israel," is: [*Haskeit* is seen as a contraction of] *has*, "be quiet and listen attentively," and *katteit*, "then analyze [and ask questions]."

They said in the yeshivah of R. Yannai: What is the meaning of the verse, "As milk under pressure produces butter, and a nose under pressure produces blood, so does anger under pressure produce strife" (Proverbs 30:33). With whom do you find the cream (milk) of Torah? With a person who spits out the milk he sucked from his mother's breasts, [meaning, to become a Torah scholar one has to begin to study in early childhood].[209] "And a nose [*af*, which also means anger] under pressure produces blood": A student who remains silent when his teacher is angry with him for the first time will be worthy to be able to distinguish between clean and unclean blood. "Anger under pressure produces strife": A student who remains silent when his teacher is angry with him a first and a second time will be worthy to decide [the intricate] legal cases dealing with financial matters and capital punishment, as we have learned.

R. Yishmael says: If you want to become wise concentrate on studying financial laws. There is no section in the Talmud that surpasses them, because they are like a flowing spring [of knowledge]. R. Shmuel b. Nachmani said: What is the meaning of the verse, "If you have been foolishly [*novalta*] arrogant, if you have been a schemer [*zamota*], then clap your hand to your mouth"? (Proverbs 30:32): Whoever demeans [*menabbeil*[210]] himself for the sake of Torah [and is not ashamed to ask questions that may sound foolish], in the end will attain great heights, but if he restrains [*zamam*[211]] himself [and is ashamed to ask questions], his hand will be on his mouth [he will be unable to answer when he is asked questions].

HOSPITALITY

Before beginning his lecture, R. Nechemiah made a few remarks about the importance of extending hospitality, expounding the verse, "Saul said to the Kenite [Jethro], 'Come, withdraw at once from among the Amalekites, so that I will not destroy you along with them; for you showed kindness to all the Israelites when they left Egypt'" (1 Samuel 15:6) [because Jethro prepared a meal for Aaron and all the elders of Israel (Rashi) (Exodus 18:12)]. [Explained R. Nechemiah:] We can draw a logical inference from this: If such a great reward was bestowed on Jethro, [that he and his people were saved] although he befriended Moses only for his own benefit, then surely [a great reward awaits] a person who invites a Torah scholar, gives him food and drink, and lets him enjoy his possessions.

R. Yose began to speak about the greatness of hospitality, expounding the verse, "Do not despise an Edomite, since he is your brother.[212] Do not despise an Egyptian, since you were an immigrant in his land" (Deuteronomy 23:8). We can draw a logical inference from this: If such a great reward was bestowed on the Egyptians, although they befriended the Israelites only for their own advantage, as it says, "[Pharaoh said to Joseph:] If you have capable men among [your brothers] appoint them as livestock officers over my [cattle]" (Genesis 47:6), then surely [a great reward is in store for] a person who invites a Torah scholar to his house, gives him food and drink, and allows him to enjoy his possessions.

R. Eliezer the son of R. Yose Hagelili began his speech by praising hospitality, expounding the verse, "God blessed Oveid-edom's[213] house . . . because of the Ark of God [which reposed in his house for three months] (1 Samuel 6:12). [He said:] We can draw a logical inference from this. If he received such a great reward for taking care of the Ark, which does not eat or drink, and all he did was sweep up in front of it and sprinkle water on the dust, then surely [a great reward is in store for] a person who invites a Torah scholar to his house, gives him food and drink, and lets him enjoy his possessions. [The Gemara asks:] What was the blessing Oveid-edom received? R. Yehudah b. Zevida said: The blessing refers to Chamot [Oveid-edom's wife] and her eight daughters-in-law, who each gave birth to six babies at a time **(64a)**, as it says, "Pe'ulletai the eighth son [of Oveid-edom] for God had blessed him" (1 Chronicles 26:5), [which proves that he had eight sons], and it says further, "All these, sons of Oveid-edom; they and their sons, strong and able men for the service—sixty-two of Oveid-edom" (ibid. 8).[214]

BIDE YOUR TIME

R. Avin Halevi said: Whoever presses his luck before its time, will forfeit it entirely, for example Absalom [who tried to dethrone his father David. He lost his life and never became king]. But whoever waits for the right time will be able to survive the hour of his bad fortune, as in the case of Rabbah and R. Yosef. For R. Yosef was called *Sinai* [because he had memorized word for word a vast number of *Mishnayot* and *Baraitot*, as they were taught on Mount Sinai], and Rabbah was called *Oker Harim*, "an uprooter of mountains," [because he was a profound thinker and had a keen analytical mind]. The time came that a new head of the yeshivah had to be appointed [in Pumbedita]. The disciples inquired of the authorities in Eretz Yisrael: Choosing between *Sinai* or *Oker Harim*, whom should we select [to head the yeshivah]? They received the following answer: Choose *Sinai* [i.e., R. Yosef], because everybody needs "the master of the wheat" [i.e., the person who has all the facts and traditions at his fingertips]. Nevertheless, R. Yosef did not accept the appointment because the astrologers had told him that he would officiate as *rosh yeshivah* for only two years [and then he would die]. So Rabbah was head of the yeshivah for twenty-two years, and R. Yosef succeeded him in office and served for two-and-a-half years. [Thus, by not accepting the post before the right time, R. Yosef gained twenty-two years of life.] During all those years that Rabbah served as *rosh yeshivah*, R. Yosef [did not conduct himself in a pretentious manner] and did not so much as order a doctor to come to his house [to draw blood, but went to the doctor's office].

R. Avin Halevi further said: What is meant by the verse, "May God answer you in the day of distress, may the name of Jacob's God make you impregnable" (Psalm 20:2). Why does it say, "Jacob's God" and not "Abraham's and Isaac's God"? This teaches you that when the owner of the beam wants to move it from one place to another, he should take hold of the heaviest part of the beam. [So too, Jacob, the immediate ancestor of the Jewish people, should be the one to pray for his children.]

R. Avin Halevi also said: If you attend a meal at which a Torah scholar is present it is as if you relished the radiance of the *Shechinah* [Divine Presence]. For it says, "Aaron and all the elders of Israel came to partake of the meal with Moses' father-in-law before God" (Exodus 18:12). [The Gemara asks:] Why does it say that they ate before God, when, in fact, they ate before Moses? [The Gemara answers:] This comes to teach you that if you partake of a meal at which a Torah scholar is present it is as if you enjoyed the radiance of the *Shechinah*.[215]

BIDDING FAREWELL

R. Avin Halevi also said: When you say goodbye to your friend, don't say: *Leich beshalom*, "Go *in* peace"; rather say, *Leich leshalom*, "Go *to* peace." For when bidding farewell to Moses, Jethro said: *Leich leshalom* "Go *to* peace" (Exodus 4:18), after which Moses became very successful. David, on the other hand, said to Absalom: *Leich beshalom*, "Go *in* peace," whereupon Absalom went and hanged himself.

R. Avin Halevi also said: When taking leave of the dead [after the funeral procession] a person should not say: *Leich leshalom*, "Go *to* peace," but *Leich beshalom*, "Go *in* peace." For it says, "[God said to Abraham:] You will join your ancestors *beshalom*, in peace" (Genesis 15:15).[216]

R. Levi b. Chiya said: After leaving the synagogue, if a person goes straight to the *bet midrash* [study hall] to study Torah he is considered worthy to greet the *Shechinah*, as it says, "They go from strength to strength, appearing before God in Zion" (Psalm 84:8) [i.e., those who go from the synagogue to the *bet midrash* are worthy to greet God in Zion].

R. Chiya b. Ashi said in the name of Rav: Torah scholars have no rest either in this world or in the world to come [because they are forever reaching higher spiritual levels], as it says, "They go from strength to strength, appearing before God in Zion."

R. Elazar said in the name of R. Chanina: Torah scholars increase peace in the world, as it says, "And all your children will be students of God, and your children [*banayich*] will have abundant peace" (Isaiah 54:13). Do not read[217] *banayich*, "your children," but *bonayich*, "your builders" [meaning, children are also builders, because by studying the Torah they are builders of abundant peace]. There is abundant peace for the lovers of Your Torah,[218] and there is no stumbling block for them (Psalm 119:165). May there be peace within your walls, serenity in your palaces. For the sake of my brothers and my comrades, I shall speak of peace in your midst. For the sake of the House of God, our God, I will request good for you (Psalm 122:7–9). God will give might to His nation, God will bless His nation with peace (Psalm 29:11).

NOTES

1. The Mishnah begins with the *Shema* of the evening because, according to the Torah, the day begins with the preceding evening. This is in keeping with the order mentioned in the verse, "It was evening and it was morning, one day" (Genesis 1:5).

2. *Terumah*, elevated gift, is the agricultural offering a farmer is required to give to a *kohen* (priest), as it says, "You must give him the first portion of your grain" (Deuteronomy 18:4). Since *terumah* is sacred, a *kohen* who is ritually unclean, (for example, if he had a leprous mark or had touched a dead small animal) is not allowed to eat *terumah* unless he has immersed in a *mikveh* and waits until nightfall, after which "he can eat the sacred offerings which are his portion" (Leviticus 22:6–7).

3. Until one-third of the night has passed, since the night is divided into three watches.

4. About 1 1/5 hours before sunrise (Rambam). R. Eliezer and R. Gamliel differ in their interpretation of the Torah words "and when you lie down" (*uveshochbecha*) (Deuteronomy 6:7). R. Eliezer explains them to mean, when *you go to bed*; therefore he says that the time expires at the end of the first watch. R. Gamliel under-

stands them to mean, when you *sleep*; hence, he fixes the whole night as the time to recite the *Shema*.

5. The fat and the pieces must be burned on the altar on the day the sacrifice was brought and the night thereafter until the dawn of the following day. This is derived from, "Do not allow the Passover sacrifice to be left lying overnight until morning" (Exodus 34:25). A burnt offering (*olah*) was entirely consumed by fire. The meat of other offerings was eaten; only the fat was burned on the altar.

6. *Sifre Emor*.

7. There is a dispute among the *Tanna'im* (teachers of the Mishnah) whether there the night is divided into three or four watches. The watches refer to groups of angels who take turns in singing God's praises.

8. He should be explicit and set a clear-cut time rather than express it in terms of night watches.

9. In the Hebrew text, the word *sha'ag*, roar, occurs three times in this verse, an allusion to the three watches.

10. The baby grows hungry.

11. The third watch is at the end of the night when people wake up and begin to talk to each other. In a figurative sense, the woman talking to her husband symbolizes the Jewish people praying to God early in the morning (*Maharsha*).

12. Overawed by Elijah's appearance, Rabbi Yose was speechless and unable to greet him. Out of great humility, Elijah greeted Rabbi Yose first.

13. *Tefillat Havineinu*, the abbreviated *Shemoneh Esrei* (*Amidah*) to be said in an emergency (*Berachot* 29a).

14. The main response in the *Kaddish*.

15. This is an anthropomorphism, and should not be taken in a physical sense. Figuratively God bemoans the exile of His people and the destruction of the *Bet Hamikdash*.

16. Rebbi is the respectful title of Rabbi Yehudah HaNasi, the Prince, who compiled and edited the Mishnah. He is also called Rabbeinu Hakadosh, our Holy Rabbi. He died around 189 C.E.

17. To study Torah in the presence of the dead is disrespectful. It is considered "taunting a poor man," because the dead cannot do mitzvot or study Torah any more.

18. The word *neshef* means "jumping away" or "to be removed" (Rashi).

19. The *Urim* and *Tumim* were inside the High Priest's breastplate (Exodus 28:30). Divine answers to questions were obtained when the letters that were engraved in the precious stones of the *eifod* lit up to form the Divine reply.

20. *Peleiti* and *mufla'im* are cognates and are derived from the same root.

21. *Kachatzos* may be translated "like midnight" or "about midnight." According to R. Ashi, Moses did not say "about midnight," for he knew when it was midnight. He said, "like midnight."

22. The menstrual flow renders a woman ritually unclean (Leviticus 15:19). Also after giving birth, a woman is ritually unclean (Leviticus 12). In case of doubt, a rabbinical authority has to be consulted. David would take time out from his busy schedule to decide such questions in order to declare a woman clean for her husband.

23. 2 Samuel 3:3.

24. The requirement to join *Ga'al Yisrael* and the *Shemoneh Esrei* is based on the proximity of the verses, "O God, my Rock and my Redeemer (*go'ali*) (Psalm 19:15), which is followed by "May God answer you" (Psam 20:2). Thus, if you pray immediately after *ga'al* (*go'ali*), God answers. (Rashi)

25. As it says, "On the day after the Passover sacrifice the Israelites left" (Numbers 33:3).

26. This is the second *berachah* after the *Shema* of the evening. It is said between *Ga'al Yisrael* and the *Shemoneh Esrei*.

27. Analogous to the three prayers of the day (Rashi).

28. *Ashrei* is arranged alphabetically, except that the verse beginning with the letter *nun* is missing.

29. Similar words in different contexts are meant to clarify one another. This rule is limited to cases that are defined by Sinaitic tradition.

30. *Rigzu*, from the same root as *yargiz*, means both "tremble" and "incite to fight."

31. The question is asked: If reminding oneself of the day of death is a foolproof method for overcoming the evil impulse, why not begin with that? Why go through all the intermediate steps? A hasidic sage answers: It is best to subdue the *yetzer hara* with joyful means, through Torah study or by reciting the *Shema*. Only as a last resort should a person frighten himself by plunging into the depressing thoughts of death.

32. The question is asked: If he neglected to study Torah, why does it say that he searched and could not find any wrongdoing? After all, the neglect of Torah is itself an obvious shortcoming. The Kotzker Rebbe answers: The very fact that he could find no wrongdoing, that he thinks he is perfect, proves that he neglected to study Torah. If he had studied Torah more thoroughly he would surely have discovered many failings.

33. There is a rule that whenever the expression "*hahu saba*, there was this old man" occurs it is a reference to *Eliyahu Hanavi*, Elijah the Prophet.

34. Listed in the Mishnah *Nega'im* 1:1.

35. In Eretz Yisrael where a leprous person had to be isolated outside the city (Leviticus 13:36), leprosy could be considered sufferings of love, since sufferings of love are designed to bring people closer together, and he had to suffer in isolation. In Babylonia a leprous person did not have to be isolated. His suffering was not as severe and could be considered sufferings of love. (Rashi).

36. R. Yochanan lost ten children, and he used to carry a small piece of a bone of his tenth child, and

would tell people: This is the bone of my tenth son.

37. He had cured R. Chiya b. Abba by grasping his hand (*Berachot* 5b).

38. R. Yochanan was very good-looking so that his skin had a radiant glow (Rashi).

39. *Menachot* 10b.

40. *Bava Metzia* 103a.

41. Referring to the spies, God said, "How long shall this evil *eidah*, assembly, exist?" (Numbers 14:27). There were twelve spies. Since Joshua and Kaleiv disagreed with the others, there were ten spies who gave a bad report about the Land, and were called "an evil *eidah*." Thus, *eidah* means ten.

42. The head-*tefillin* contain four compartments into which the following passages have been inserted: 1. "*Shema*" (Deuteronomy 6:4–9); 2. "And it will come to pass if you will hearken" (Deuteronomy 11:13–21); 3. "Sanctify" (Exodus 13:1–10); and 4. "It will come to pass when He shall bring you" (Exodus 13:11–16). The hand-*tefillin* have one compartment containing the same passages.

43. A *minyan*. Ten adult males are needed for public prayer services.

44. This segment may be found in the Gemara on folio 7b.

45. He interprets the word *kerum* as cognate to *rom*, exalted, things that are of the greatest importance. He sees *zelut* as related to *mazalzeil*, to hold in contempt.

46. The Giving of the Torah was the wedding par excellence, for it joined the people of Israel with God. That is why the "five voices" of the wedding parallel the "five voices" of the Giving of the Torah (*Maharsha*).

47. Ram's horn.

48. Leviticus 16:12, 13.

49. This paragraph is taken from *Megillah* 15a. It was inserted here because it pertains to the subject at hand.

50. Aravnah's blessing was fulfilled, as is stated in 2 Samuel 24:25, "the plague was held back from Israel" (*Maharsha*).

51. Darius said this when Daniel was thrown into the lion's den. The blessing was fulfilled because Daniel was not harmed by the lions and emerged unscathed.

52. *Panai* means both "presence" and "face." Here, *panai yeileichu* is rendered as "My angry face will go away."

53. His donkey.

54. Literally, "of the enemies of Israel." The Gemara uses this as a euphemism for Israel, because it does not want to utter this dreadful curse against Israel.

55. Exodus 34:29–35.

56. After Rachel's death, Jacob moved his bed from Rachel's tent to the tent of Rachel's handmaid, Bilhah. Resenting his mother Leah's humiliation,

Reuben placed Jacob's bed into Leah's tent (Rashi on Genesis 35:22, *Shabbat* 55b).

57. This paragraph is in *Berachot* 7a, at the bottom of the page.

58. *Ein Yaakov* now continues on page 7b, at the point where it left off.

59. In the Gemara this saying is attributed to Resh Lakish.

60. In other words: Is yours a happy or unhappy marriage?

61. *Metzuyanim*, designated, marked, is derived from *tziyun*, mark, sign, which is spelled the same as *Tziyon*, Zion.

62. The verse relating Shimei's death (1 Kings 2:46) is followed by the verse recording Solomon's marriage to Pharaoh's daughter (1 Kings 3:1).

63. *Bava Batra* 14b.

64. The people of Media, a part of the ancient Persian empire, corresponding to northwest Iran.

65. This chapter is Isaiah's prophecy about Babylon. The Persians are called "consecrated ones," because they gave permission for the second *Bet Hamikdash* to be built. The Gemara says, that in spite of that, they are destined for Gehinnom because of their persecution of the Jewish people (*Maharsha*).

66. "Not a single one of you may go out the door until morning" (Exodus 12:21).

67. The *Shemoneh Esrei* initially had eighteen *berachot*; the *berachah* of *Velamalshinim* was added later.

68. *Tosafot* asks: Why does the Gemara say: Every chapter that was dear to David he began and ended with *Ashrei*? This is the only one! Tosafot answers: The Gemara means to say that he began and ended every chapter that was dear to him with words of praise. Not only with *Ashrei*, but also with *Halleluyah*, and there are many psalms that begin and end with *Halleluyah*.

69. Members of the war party during the last siege of Jerusalem. They wanted to fight the Romans against the advice of the Rabbis (*Gittin* 56a).

70. Homiletic expositions, parables, and moral teachings of the Talmud.

71. Psalm 103:1; 103:2; 103:22; 104:1; 104:35.

72. 2 Kings 3:12.

73. 2 Samuel 24:14–17.

74. See 2 Kings, Ch. 4.

75. See Numbers 21:6–9.

76. 2 Kings 18:4.

77. 2 Chronicles 32:30.

78. 2 Kings 18:16.

79. 2 Chronicles 30:2.

80. The *Urim* and *Tummim* were placed in the High Priest's breastplate (Exodus 28:30). They would be consulted like an oracle; the High Priest would meditate on the stones of the breastplate until he reached a level of divine inspiration. He would see the breastplate with inspired vision, and the letters containing the answer would light up. The High Priest would be

able to combine the letters to spell out the answer (*Yoma* 73b).

81. This is the Mishnah that is quoted in the *Haggadah*.

82. The *Shema* is made up of three chapters: *Shema* (Hear O Israel, Deuteronomy 7:4–11); *Vehayah im shamo'a* (It shall come to pass, Deuteronomy 11:3–22); and *Vayomer* (And He said, Numbers 15:37–42).

83. Such as *bechol levavecha*, or *va'avadetem meheirah*, or *al levavechem*.

84. The words *befareis* and *befareish* are spelled the same.

85. At this point, *Ein Yaakov* backtracks to *Berachot* 14a.

86. Prayer takes the place of sacrifices. Instead of paying homage to God he paid homage to his friend, as though he were an altar.

87. *Save'a* and *sheva* are written the same.

88. *Ein Yaakov* now resumes the Gemara text on *Berachot* 16b.

89. Alluding to Lamentations 5:17.

90. Since this prayer contains a full range of people's spiritual and physical needs, it is now said on the *Shabbat* preceding *Rosh Chodesh*.

91. This is recited as part of our daily *Shacharit* (Morning) service.

92. Marcus Aurelius Antoninus, (121–180 C.E.), Roman emperor, famous for his *The Meditations* on Stoic philosophy. He was a great friend and admirer of Rabbi Yehudah Hanassi.

93. Psalm 34:14.

94. We recite this prayer (with a few minor changes) at the conclusion of every *Shemoneh Esrei*.

95. It is also part of the *Viduy* (confession) we recite on Yom Kippur.

96. *Menachot* 110a.

97. The kidneys function as advisers (*Berachot* 61a).

98. From the verb *saval*, to carry a burden, to endure, to suffer, to tolerate.

99. *Sanhedrin* 106b.

100. *Sanhedrin* 106b.

101. Some claim that the original version of the Talmud included the phrase, "like Yeshu the Nazarene," but that this was deleted by the censor.

102. The reference is to the saintly Sage R. Chanina b. Dosa.

103. *Kiddushin* 70b.

104. According to the Rosh he should not even recite Torah passages by heart in a cemetery.

105. In Eretz Yisrael there are three periods of rainfall. Crops that were planted during the first period, which begins on 17 Marcheshvan, will have grown rigid stalks by the second period and will be broken by the hailstorm that will occur at that time. However, the crops that were planted during the second period will still be very tender and will bend in the hailstorm and not be ruined by it (Rashi).

106. *Eduyot* 5:6

107. A *sotah* is a woman who was warned by her husband not to be alone with a certain man, but she violated the warning. The husband then took her to the *Bet Hamikdash* where she was made to drink the "curse-bearing" water that contained earth from the floor of the *Bet Hamikdash*, and the writing of the *sotah* chapter on a parchment was dissolved in it. If she was innocent nothing would happen to her. If she was guilty, she would die. See Numbers 5:11–31.

108. Two illustrious Sages.

109. King of Assyria, died 681 B.C.E. See *Gittin* 57b.

110. The Passover lamb was offered in three shifts. Each time the Court was filled to capacity by people who came there to offer their Passover lamb the gates were closed. Yet among this vast throng, which included many great men, there was none that could equal Akavyah b. Mehalalel. In other words, Akavyah was the greatest.

111. *Pesachim* 64b.

112. Related in *Taanit* 19a.

113. You are required to say *Birkat Hamazon* (Grace) after eating the quantity of an olive according to R. Meir, and the quantity of an egg, according to R. Yehudah; see *Berachot* 45a.

114. Sanctification, a prayer that is said during the repetition of the *Shemoneh Esrei*.

115. The text of the individual *berachot* of the *Shemoneh Esrei* was composed by the Men of the Great Assembly at the beginning of the Second Temple period and it was put into its final form after the Destruction four centuries later.

116. Instead of saying, "Greetings to you, my master."

117. Out of respect for R. Gamliel (*Tz'lach*).

118. Literally, translator.

119. *Rosh Hashanah* 25a.

120. *Bechorot* 36a.

121. He was a descendant of Sisera, the army commander of King Jabin of Canaan who was defeated by Deborah and Barak (Judges, Chapter 4).

122. Literally: Any scholar whose interior is not in harmony with his exterior, which is to say: he is putting up a front.

123. The reference is to law that provides for the purification of a person who had contact with the dead. A *kohen* sprinkled on such a person is the ashes of a red cow dissolved in "living water" (water from a spring). See Numbers 19:1–22.

124. A great Tanna, student of R. Akiva, and author of the *Zohar*. He and his son fled from the Romans and hid in a cave for thirteen years. His tomb in Meron is visited by thousands annually. He lived in the middle of the second century C.E.

125. Literally, "What prayer should a person say." According to the Rambam in his Commentary on the

Mishnah, this implies that everyone should say this prayer on entering a *bet midrash*.

126. You are rewarded for the toil of Torah study even if you do not come up with the solution to a problem. By contrast, a tailor gets paid for his labor only if the suit fits.

127. He is referring to the world to come. But in this world we *can* appease God—through prayer, and we *can* bribe Him with money—through *tzedakah* (*Maharsha*).

128. Numbers 19:14.

129. Also called *Amidah*.

130. This *berachah* was composed in response to the threat of such heretical Jewish sects as the Sadducees, Boethusians, Essenes, and the early Christians.

131. A heretical sect.

132. *Keva* also means routine, regularity.

133. At the 32-degree latitude of Eretz Yisrael, twilight lasts only a few minutes.

134. When reciting the *Shemoneh Esrei*, you should face east toward Jerusalem.

135. Numbers 5:11–31.

136. A play on the similarity between *amatecha* (your maidservant) and *mitah* (death).

137. *Shabbat* 32a: For three transgressions women die during childbirth: for being careless regarding the laws of *niddah* (menstruation), *challah* (the tithe from dough), and the kindling of the *Shabbat* lights.

138. *Zevachim* 32a.

139. *Chagigah* 11a.

140. *Zevachim* 32a.

141. *El* is written *alef—lamed*; *al* is written *ayin—lamed*.

142. A poetic name for Israel.

143. The terms *chayal, ligyon, rahaton, karton*, and *gistra* denote military ranks in ascending order (Rashi).

144. A cross between a snake and a lizard (Rashi).

145. Deuteronomy 22:6.

146. Upon hearing bad news one says: *Baruch dayan ha'emet*, Blessed is the true Judge.

147. Upon hearing good news one says: *Baruch Hatov veHameitiv*, Blessed is the One who is good and does good.

148. The reader's lectern used to be on a lower level than the synagogue, hence "he went down."

149. Deuteronomy 10:17.

150. The Gemara says that when you are asked to officiate as *chazzan*, the first time you should refuse, the second time, you should hesitate, and the third time you should comply (33b).

151. The reading lectern was at a lower level than the floor of the synagogue, which explains the expression "he went down."

152. Moses prayed for his sister Miriam, who was stricken with leprosy.

153. It ends, *Magein Avraham*, "Shield of Abraham."

154. It ends, *ulecha na'eh lehodot*, "to You it is fitting to give thanks."

155. *Maharsha* notes that the numeric value of *yayin*, "wine," equals that of *sod*, "secret, mystery," both adding up to 70. It alludes to the secrets of the Torah that are preserved and guarded and are yet to be revealed.

156. The verse refers to the fruit of the fourth year. During the first three years, fruit is considered *orlah*, and is forbidden to be eaten. The fruit grown in the fourth year (*neta reva'i*) must be brought to Jerusalem and may be eaten there.

157. Tosafot notes that this interpretation disagrees with R. Chanina b. Papa, who interprets this verse as speaking of where Israel *is* doing God's will. *Tosafot* answers that R. Shimon b. Yochai speaks of a time when they have not reached the highest level of perfection.

158. The *Shulchan Aruch* states that if the food you ate contains salt it is not necessary to eat salt afterward, and if the beverage contains water you need not drink water afterward.

159. Or diphtheria.

160. Or heartburn.

161. Rashi and *Maharsha*.

162. The seats of two prominent *yeshivot* in Babylon.

163. *Kerishin*, alternately translated as horse-beans and as vetch.

164. The first meal was taken at the fourth hour.

165. Rashi translates it *poliol*.

166. *Tosafot* explains that Moses proclaimed the last eight commandments to the people. Moses obviously had to speak in a very loud voice to be heard by all the people. God did not have to speak loudly because he was speaking only to Moses. Nevertheless, when speaking to Moses, God spoke "in a Voice," meaning, God raised His Voice to the level of Moses' volume, in order that Moses, the *metargem*, when addressing the people, should not speak louder than God, the Reader.

167. The Gemara's concept of an *am haaretz* is totally different from what today colloquially is called an *am haaretz*.

168. This applied only during the time the *Bet Hamikdash* was standing.

169. After deporting the ten tribes of Israel, the King of Assyria settled the people of Kuta in the city of Shomron (Samaria) (2 Kings 17:24–26). The Kutim or Cuthites (Samaritans) accepted only the Written Torah. They rejected *Torah Shebe'al Peh*, the Oral Law, and the enactments of the Sages.

170. Tassels.

171. Literally: He has not served Torah scholars. Rashi explains this to mean that he has not studied Gemara. The Sages of the Gemara interpret the Mishnah, which is written in a very succinct style. Without their explanations the Mishnah cannot be understood.

172. King Yannai I (Yochanan Hyrkanus) of the Hasmonean dynasty ruled Judea and also officiated as *Kohen Gadol* (High Priest). However, the rabbis were

suspicious of the purity of his lineage, and cast doubt on his qualifications to serve as *Kohen Gadol.* Infuriated by this, King Yannai had all the leading rabbis put to death in 113 B.C.E. (*Kiddushin* 66a).

173. The fearless words Shimon b. Shetach flung in the face of the murderous King Yannai are evidence of his astounding faith, rectitude, and courage.

174. After initial successes, the Jewish revolt against the Romans, under the leadership of Bar Kochba, was crushed when the Roman legions captured the fortress of Betar in 133 C.E. Bar Kochba was killed in battle, together with 580,000 Jews. The Romans did not allow the bodies of the victims to be buried, but miraculously, they did not decompose. Eventually the ban was lifted, and the dead were brought to burial.

175. According to the reading of the Vilna Gaon.

176. A region south of the Euphrates River (Rashi).

177. The *Shulchan Aruch* rules that it is better to have ten people, two of whom are rabbis. But if you don't have two rabbis, you should say the *berachah* anyway.

178. This applies if someone is called to the Torah and refuses to go.

179. Because it says, "Joseph died, [and then] all his brothers" (Exodus 1:6) (Rashi).

180. Moses reversed the order, because the Ark, which was the purpose for which the Tabernacle was erected, was uppermost in his mind (*Iyun Yaakov*).

181. Why does God give wisdom only to wise people and not to fools who need it the most? Rabbi Simchah Bunam of Pshis'cha said: Wise people know how to use wisdom; fools will waste it. Wise people use wisdom to build a Tabernacle and teach Torah; fools take wisdom and they can destroy the world with it.

182. The *Aruch* translates: Whatever a person sees in his dream when he is fasting is meaningless.

183. Presumably Trajan (53–117 C.E.), who waged war against Persia.

184. King Shapur I, who died in 272 C.E., reigned in ancient Persia.

185. Literally: "What you said about the daughter of Rav Chisda," who was Rava's wife.

186. The word *af* means both nose and anger.

187. A pot brimming with food symbolizes domestic peace; a meandering river signifies tranquility within a country; a bird that flies unencumbered across international borders represents global peace (*Ketav Sofer*).

188. R. Yishmael was the *Kohen Gadol* who died a martyr's death under the Romans.

189. The Gemara calls them *talmidei chachamim* because these three Sages never received *semichah*, official ordination.

190. This principle is derived from Exodus 22:1. When a burglar enters a house he should expect that the owner of the house will defend his property. If the burglar comes anyway, that means that he is ready to kill. If somebody is ready to kill you, you are allowed to kill him first to defend yourself.

191. *Chittah*, wheat, is seen as related to *chatat*, sin.

192. The wicked Ahab received his reward in this world—he was a very wealthy man.

193. R. Chanina b. Dosa was extremely poor and had no enjoyment of this world (*Taanit* 24b).

194. The last word of the verse *Shema Yisrael Hashem Elokeinu Hashem echad,* Hear, O Israel: God is our Lord, God, the One and Only (Deuteronomy 6:4).

195. The Binding of Isaac.

196. *Shittah Mekubetzet* explains that remembering is a form of seeing.

197. Instead of in the *Bet Hamikdash.*

198. A *nazir* assumed a vow that obligated him to abstain from wine, shaving his hair, and contact with the dead.

199. *Terumah* is the heave-offering given to the *kohen* from the yields of the yearly harvests (Numbers 18:8). Its quantity depended on the generosity of the owner, who could give one-fortieth, one-fiftieth, or one-sixtieth of his harvest.

200. The word *to'afot* is seen as related to the Aramaic *af,* to double.

201. Here, *to'afot* is seen as related to the Hebrew *uf,* to fly.

202. The Jewish calendar is based on a lunar/solar system. The Jewish year consists of twelve lunar months of a little more than 29 1/2 days. Twelve lunar months total a little more than 354 1/2 days, eleven days less than the solar year, which consists, roughly, of 365 1/4 days. Since the Festivals must be celebrated in their seasons according to the solar year—Pesach in the spring, Shavuot in the summer, Sukkot in the fall—it was essential to harmonize the lunar and solar years. This was done by intercalation, or introduction of an extra month, Adar, which made that year a leap year. There are seven such leap years, of thirteen months, in every cycle of nineteen years. In Talmudic times, the Sanhedrin fixed the new moons and intercalated the years.

203. The High Priest.

204. *Yoma* 18b.

205. *Yevamot* 122a.

206. The Levites officiated as singers and musicians during the services in the *Bet Hamikdash.*

207. *Kerem beYavneh,* literally the Vineyard at Yavneh, because the yeshivah was located in a vineyard, or because the students were seated in rows like the vines in a vineyard.

208. *Maharsha* explains that the Ark was in Moses' tent, which was located outside the camp. The camp measured twelve *mil* across. Thus the farthest distance a person had to walk to reach Moses' tent was twelve *mil.* Now the Torah describes anyone that went out to Moses' tent as "one who sought God."

209. Or, only by abandoning childish attitudes and juvenile pursuits can you become a Torah scholar (*Maharsha*).

210. From the same root as *novalta.*

211. From the same root as *zamota*.

212. Since the Edomites are descendants of Esau.

213. He was a Levite.

214. The sixty-two children are: The eight sons mentioned in the text, six more that were born to his wife in one birth, and the sextuplets that were born to each of his eight daughters-in-law, which add up to sixty-two (Rashi).

215. The Torah insights the scholar relates elevate the guests at the meal to a spiritual level that is comparable to enjoying the radiance of the *Shechinah* (*Rokeach* 329).

216. A euphemism for dying.

217. As in all cases where the Rabbis use the expression *al tikrei*, "do not read," they do not mean to alter the Masoretic text, but to suggest an additional meaning. Since the word *banayich* already appears in the verse, the repetition of the same word can only be intended to introduce a new idea—that children are also builders.

218. Not only those who study the Torah, but also those who support and respect Torah scholars (*Etz Yosef*).

❧ SHABBAT ❧

ASKING QUESTIONS ABOUT UNFAMILIAR TRACTATES

(3b) [On the preceding page of the Gemara, Rav asked Rebbi[1] a question regarding carrying on *Shabbat*, and Rebbi answered him. Thereupon] R. Chiya said to Rav: Son of distinguished ancestors! Haven't I told you that when a rabbi is busy studying one tractate you should not ask him a question about another, because he may not be well-versed in it. For if Rebbi were not a great man you would have embarrassed him, for he might have given you an incorrect answer. This time, however, he did give you the correct answer.

PREPARING FOR PRAYER

(9b) [The Mishnah said: When the time of *Minchah*[2] comes you should not sit down to get a haircut until you have prayed, nor should you enter a bathhouse or a tannery or sit down to eat or enter the courthouse for a lawsuit close to *Minchah* for fear that you forget to pray, but once you have started any of these activities you don't have to interrupt to pray.]

[The Gemara asks:] What is considered the beginning of a haircut [so that you don't have to interrupt to pray]? R. Avin said: When the barber places the barber's sheet on your knees. And when is the beginning of a bath? When you take off your coat [and begin to undress]. And when is the beginning of tanning? When a person ties an apron around his shoulders. And what is considered the beginning of a meal? Rav said: When you wash your hands. R. Chanina said: When you loosen your belt. But they do not disagree: the one refers to the Jews of Babylonia [who wore their belts very tight and had to loosen their belt before eating (Rashi)]; the other refers to the Jews of Eretz Yisrael [who did not have the custom of loosening their belt before washing (Rashi)].

(10a) [The Gemara now discusses various ways in which Sages prepared for prayer.] Rava son of R. Huna used to put on special long socks when he prayed [since he ordinarily went barefoot]. He said, "Prepare to meet your God [in prayer], Israel!" (Amos 4:12). Rava would remove his cloak [so as not to look like a prominent person], humbly clasp his hands, and pray, saying: [I conduct myself] like a slave before his master. R. Ashi said: I noticed that when there was suffering in the world, R. Kahana would throw off his cloak, clasp his hands and pray, saying: [I pray] like a slave before his master. In time of peace he would put it on, wrap something around his head and pray, saying: "Prepare to meet your God [in prayer], Israel."

JUDGING LEGAL CASES

[The Gemara continues:] Rava saw that R. Hamenuna was praying for a long time. Said he [about R. Hamenuna and people like him]: Such people turn their back on everlasting life [which is the reward for Torah study] and occupy themselves with transitory matters [praying for worldly things like health, peace, and sustenance]. But R. Hamenuna [who prolonged his prayer] held that there is a separate time for prayer and a separate time for Torah study. R. Yirmiyah was sitting in front of R. Zeira, and they were engrossed in Torah study. When it was getting late for praying, R. Yirmiyah rushed [because he wanted to leave]. R. Zeira then applied to him the verse, "If a person turns away from listening to the Torah, even his prayer is an abomination" (Proverbs 28:9).[3]

[We learned in the Mishnah that you should not enter a courthouse for a lawsuit close to *Minchah*. The Gemara digresses to expound on the subject of adjudicating legal disputes.]

R. Ammi and R. Assi used to sit and study Torah between the pillars [that supported the balcony] of the *bet hamidrash*, and every now and then they would knock at the side of the door and call out: If there is anyone who has a question about a legal dispute, let him come in! R. Chisda and Rabbah son of R. Huna were sitting and judging legal cases the whole day. They felt faint, [because they had not eaten all day, or because they were upset at not having studied Torah that day (Rashi)]. [In order to lift their spirits and show them that judges merit a great heavenly reward,] R. Chiya b. Rav of Difti quoted for them the verse, "The next day, Moses sat to judge the people. The people stood around Moses from morning to evening [waiting for him to settle their disputes]" (Exodus 18:13). [Expounds the *Baraita*:] Now, can you imagine that Moses sat and judged all day? If so, when did he have time to learn? The verse comes to teach you that if a judge passes judgment with absolute truthfulness, even for a single hour, the Torah considers it as if he became a partner with the Holy One, blessed be He, in the creation of the world. [From where do we know this?] For it says here, "The people stood around Moses from morning to evening" and elsewhere [in the chapter of Creation], it says, "It was evening and it was morning, one day" (Genesis 1:5). [The similarity of the phrases tells us that an honest judge has something in common with Creation.]

[The Gemara asks:] Until what time of the day should the judges sit in judgment? R. Sheshet said: Until mealtime. R. Chama said: What verse substantiates this? For it says, "Woe is to you, O land when your kings [i.e., your judges[4]] are like children and your ministers eat early in the morning! Happy are you, O land, when your kings [i.e., your judges] are free from lust and your ministers dine at the proper time—for strength and not with guzzling" (Ecclesiastes 10:16,17); "for strength" means [they eat after they have strengthened themselves with Torah study and not after they have guzzled wine].

MEALTIME SCHEDULE

We have learned in a *Baraita*: The first hour of the day [i.e., 6 a.m.] is the mealtime for Lydians [gladiators who are ravenously hungry]; the second hour is the mealtime for robbers [who have plied their trade all night]; the third hour for heirs [who do not have to work for a living]; the fourth hour for field workers; the fifth hour of the day is the mealtime for the average man. [Asks the Gemara:] But it isn't so! For R. Papa said: The fourth hour is the mealtime for the average man. Rather [we have to change the *Baraita* around:] The fourth hour is the mealtime for the average man, the fifth hour for field workers, and the sixth hour for Torah scholars. And if someone eats after the sixth hour it is like throwing a stone into a barrel of wine, [meaning, it is not as beneficial as if he had eaten earlier].[5] Said Abbaye: This is true only if he ate nothing at all early in the morning, but if he ate something in the morning then it does not matter [if he eats his meal after the sixth hour].

DIVINE NAMES

(10b) [We learned in a *Baraita* that it is not permissible to greet a person with "*Shalom aleichem*" ("Peace upon you") at the baths. The Gemara now comments:] This supports the following statement of R. Hamenuna in the name of Ulla: A person may not say "*Shalom aleichem*" to his neighbor in the bathhouse, because it says, "Gideon built there an altar, and he called Him '*Hashem Shalom*.'" [So we see that the name of God is *Shalom*. Therefore you are not allowed to say *Shalom aleichem* in a bathhouse.] [Asks the Gemara:] If so, it should also be forbidden to say the word *emunah* (faith) in a toilet, because it says, *Keil emunah*, "He is the faithful God," (Deuteronomy 7:9). And if you answer that indeed it is so [that you may not say the word *emunah* in a toilet], but Rava b. Mechasia said in the name of R. Chama b. Guria who quoted Rav: One is allowed to say the word *emunah* in a toilet. [The Gemara answers:] In the phrase "the faithful God," the word "faithful" is not a proper name of God, but here in the phrase "*Hashem-Shalom*," the name of *Hashem* is *Shalom*.

[The Gemara now lists several unrelated sayings by the same person.]

NOTIFY THE RECIPIENT
OF A GIFT

Rava b. Mechasia also said in the name of R. Chama b. Goria who quoted Rav: If you give a gift to your neighbor you have to notify him beforehand [that you are giving him that gift], for it says, "[*Shabbat*] is a sign between Me and you for all generations, to make you realize that I, God, am making you holy" (Exodus 31:13). We learned the same in a *Baraita*: "To make you realize that I, God, am making you holy." The Holy One, blessed be He, said to Moses: I have a wonderful gift in my treasure house, called *Shabbat*, and I want to give it to Israel. Go and let them know [that they are about to receive this gift]. From this R. Gamliel learned: If someone gives a loaf of bread to a child he must inform his mother. What shall he do to the child [to inform the mother]? Said Abaye: He should rub oil between the eyes of the child or apply paint around around the child's eyes, [so that his mother will ask him about it, and he will then tell her who did it and that this person also gave him the bread, and as a result goodwill and friendship will be furthered]. But nowadays that people are fearful of witchcraft [and the mother might suspect that someone applied the paint in order to cast a spell on the child], what should a person do [to let the mother know that he gave a gift to the child]? R. Papa said: He should rub on the child's face some of whatever he gave him. [Asks the Gemara: How can you tell me that if someone gives a gift to a friend he is required to notify him beforehand?] It is not so!

For R. Chama b. R. Chanina said: If someone makes a gift to his neighbor he does not have to notify him beforehand, for it says, "Moses did not realize that the skin of his face had become luminous when God had spoken to him" (Exodus 34:29). [So you see that Moses received a gift from God, and he did not know about it.] [Answers the Gemara:] There is no difficulty: You do not have to inform the recipient if you give him a gift that he will find out about eventually [as in the case of the radiance of Moses' skin]. However, you do have to inform the recipient if otherwise he would never find out that you gave him this gift [as in the case of the mother. She would not know who gave the bread to her child]. [The Gemara asks:] But *Shabbat* is something that would become revealed eventually [and yet God informed Israel of it]? [The Gemara answers:] The great reward that is in store for those who observe *Shabbat* would not have become known [if God had not told Moses to reveal it to the Jewish people].

R. Chisda [who was a *kohen*] was holding in his hands two [priestly] gifts of an ox.[6] He said: I will give these to anyone who comes and tells me a new teaching in the name of Rav. Rava b. Mechasya said to him: This is what Rav said: If you give a gift to your neighbor you have to notify him beforehand, because it says, "To make you realize that I, God, am making you holy" (Exodus 31:13). So he gave him [the priestly portion he had received]. Rava b. Mechasya asked R. Chisda: Are the sayings of Rav so dear to you [that you give away your priestly portion in order to hear a new insight that Rav said]? Yes, he answered. [Replied Rava b. Mechasya:] This exemplifies what Rav used to say: A coat is precious to the person who wears it, [and since you are Rav's student you cherish his teachings]. R. Chisda asked Rava b. Mechasya: Did Rav really say that? The thing you told me just now in the name of Rav is even more important to me than the first one! If I had another priestly gift I would give it to you.

TEACHINGS BY
RAVA B. MECHASYA

Rava b. Mechasya also said in the name of R. Chama b. Guria in Rav's name: A person should never show preference for one child over his other children, for because of two sela's weight of silk that Jacob gave to Joseph[7] over and above what he gave to his other children, his brothers became jealous of him, and this led to our forefathers' descent into Egypt.

Rava b. Mechasya also said in the name of R. Chama b. Guria in Rav's name: A person should always seek out as his residence a city that was recently settled. Since it was recently settled its sins are fewer, as it says, [Lot said to the angel:] "This city [Tzo'an] is near enough [*kerovah*] for refuge, and it is a small city" (Genesis 19:20). [Asks the Gemara:] What is meant by *kerovah*? Shall we say that it is near and small? Surely the angel could see that for himself! Rather, [Lot meant to say:] Since it had been recently settled[8] its sins are fewer [and therefore it is safe to flee there]. R. Avin said: From where do we know [that if a city has fewer sins its destruction is not imminent]? Because it says, [Lot said to the angel,] "Please [*na*], let me flee there" (ibid.) The numeric value of *na* is fifty-one,[9] and the city of Sodom was fifty-two years old at that time, [thus Tzo'an was settled a year after the founding of Sodom and, therefore, was safe from destruction. That is why Lot wanted to flee there.]

[The Gemara continues: We know that at the time of its destruction, Sodom was fifty-two years old,] but it had only twenty-six years of tranquility, (11a) for it says, [The five cities of the plain, which included Sodom] "had been subservient to Kedorla'omer [king of Elam] for twelve years, and for thirteen years they rebelled against him" (Genesis 14:4), [so that Sodom had twenty-five years of turmoil], and in the fourteenth year Kedorla'omer was killed [so that there was no tranquility for a total of twenty-six years, but the other twenty-six years of Sodom's existence it enjoyed peace].

Rava b. Mechasya also said in the name of R. Chama b. Guria in Rav's name: Every city whose roofs are higher than the synagogue will in the end be destroyed, for it says, "To exalt the House of our God, repairing its ruins" (Ezra 9:9).[10] However, this refers only to houses, but as for [ornamental structures like] towers and turrets we do not care [they may be higher than a synagogue]. Said R. Ashi: I prevented the town of Mechasya from being destroyed. [Rav Ashi, the *rosh yeshivah* of the Yeshivah of Mechasya,[11] did not permit houses to be built higher than the synagogue.] [The Gemara demurs:] But Mechasya was destroyed! [The Gemara answers:] It was not destroyed because of *that* sin [of having houses higher than the synagogue].

Rava b. Mechasya also said in the name of R. Chama b. Guria in Rav's name: It is better to be under Ishmaelites (Arabs) than under idolators;[12] under idolators rather than under Parsees [a Persian tribe]; under Parsees rather than under a Torah scholar [for he invokes swift punishment when angered]; under a Torah scholar rather than under an orphan or a widow [for God Himself avenges an offense against an orphan or widow].

Rava b. Mechasya further said in the name of R. Chama b. Guria in Rav's name: I can tolerate any illness, but not a stomachache; any pain, but not heartache; any ache, but not a headache; any evil, but not an evil wife.

Rava b. Mechasya further said in the name of R. Chama b. Guria in Rav's name: If all the oceans were ink, all reeds pens, the heavens parchment, and all men writers, they would not suffice to write down the depth of understanding that is required to conduct the wide-ranging, day-to-day affairs of government. What verse bears this out? "Like the heavens in their height, like the earth in its depth, is the mind of kings—unfathomable" (Proverbs 25:3).

FASTING BECAUSE
OF A BAD DREAM

R. Yehoshua b. R. Idi once happened to visit R. Ashi. A third-born calf was prepared for him, [which is considered better than the first- and second-born (Rashi)]. They said to him, "Please have some of it." "I am fasting," he replied. They asked him, "But don't you accept R. Yehudah's ruling: [If you vowed to fast a day] you may postpone that fast and keep it later?" "This is a fast on account of a [bad] dream I had," he replied, and Rava b. Mechasya said in the name of R. Chama in Rav's name: Fasting prevents the portents of a [bad] dream like fire consumes flax; and R. Chisda said: Provided the fast is kept on the day of the dream; and R. Yosef added: And even on *Shabbat* [when fasting is forbidden, a dream-fast is permitted].

GETTING READY
FOR *SHABBAT*

(12a) Rabbi Yishmael taught in a *Baraita*: A person is allowed to go out with *tefillin* on his head on the eve of *Shabbat* near nightfall,[13] [and we are not afraid that he will go out with them after nightfall]. What is the reason? Because Rabba b. R. Huna said: A person is required to touch his *tefillin* every now and then. We infer this by means of a *kal vachomer*[14] (a logical deduction) from the *Kohen Gadol*'s forehead-plate[15]: If in the case of the headplate, which contained the Divine Name only once, yet the Torah said, "It shall always be on his forehead" (Exodus 28:38), which means that the *Kohen Gadol*'s mind must not be diverted from the headplate, then surely with the *tefillin*, which contain the Divine Name many times, he is continually mindful that he is wearing them [and we need not fear that he will go out with them after nightfall].

We learned in a *Baraita*: Chanania said: You should examine [the pockets of] your garments on Friday evening before it is getting dark [to make sure that there is nothing in them, since carrying is forbidden on *Shabbat*]. R. Yosef remarked: This an important *halachah* concerning *Shabbat*.

VISITING THE SICK
ON *SHABBAT*

The Sages taught: If you come in to visit a sick person on *Shabbat*, you should say: It is *Shabbat*, a day when we do not cry out, but [I wish you that] recovery is near at hand. R. Meir said: [You should say:] The *Shabbat* will bring compassion, [i.e., the merit of honoring *Shabbat* by refraining from expressing anguish will bring healing]. (12b) R. Yehudah [when visiting the sick] said: May the Omnipresent have mercy on you and on the sick of Israel. R. Yose was wont to say: May the Omnipresent have mercy on you among the sick of Israel. Shevna, who was a respected person in Jerusalem, when entering a sickroom would say: *Shalom*, Peace, and on leaving: It is *Shabbat*, a day when we do not cry, but [I wish you that] recovery is near at hand. God's compassion is abundant, and enjoy the *Shabbat* in peace. [The Gemara asks:] With whom does the following statement by R. Chanina agree: If someone [prays for the recovery of] a sick person in his house, he should include him with the other Jewish

sick.[16] [The Gemara answers:] It agrees with R. Yose [as quoted above].

R. Chanina also said: It was with difficulty that the Sages allowed a person to comfort mourners and visit the sick on *Shabbat* [because the visitor becomes depressed and cannot fully enjoy the delight of *Shabbat*].

Rabbah b. Bar Chanah said: When we followed R. Elazar on his visits to a sick person, sometimes he would say to him [in Hebrew]: *Hamakom yifkedach leshalom*, "May the Omnipresent remember you in peace." And sometimes he would say [the same thing in Aramaic]: *Rachmana yadkerinach leshalom*, "May the Merciful remember you in peace." [The Gemara asks:] How could he do this? Did not R. Yehudah say: A person should never ask God for his needs in Aramaic. And R. Yochanan said: If a person asks God for his needs in Aramaic, the ministering angels do not intercede on his behalf because they do not understand Aramaic. [The Gemara answers:] A sick person is different because the *Shechinah* is with him [and we do not need the angels to intercede]. For R. Anan said in Rav's name: How do you know that the *Shechinah* supports a sick person? Because it says, "God supports him on his sickbed" (Psalm 41:4). We learned a proof to this in a *Baraita*: If a person comes to visit the sick he should not sit on the bed or on a chair,[17] but he should wrap himself [as a sign of respect toward the *Shechinah*] and sit in front of him, because the *Shechinah* is above the head of a sick person. For it says, "God supports him on his sickbed." And Rava said in Ravin's name: How do we know that the Holy One, blessed be He, gives the sick person his sustenance? Because it says, "God supports him on his sickbed."

READING BY THE LIGHT
OF AN OIL LAMP

[The Gemara continues:] We learned in the Mishnah: On *Shabbat* you are not allowed to read by the light of a lamp [because it is feared that you might tilt the lamp to bring the oil closer to the wick and thereby commit the transgression of "igniting a fire"]. Rava said: If the one reading by the light of the lamp is an important person, it is permitted [because an important person does not tilt a lamp on weekdays either].

An objection is raised: We learned in a *Baraita*: You may not read by the light of a lamp on *Shabbat*, because you may tilt it. Said R. Yishmael b. Elisha: I will read, and I will be careful not to tilt the lamp. Once it happened that he read [on *Shabbat* by the light of a lamp] and wanted to tilt the lamp. [Catching himself,] he exclaimed, "How great are the words of the Sages who said: You may not read by the light of a lamp [on *Shabbat*]." R. Nathan disagrees and says: He read and did tilt it, and [after *Shabbat*] he wrote in his notebook: I, Yishmael b. Elisha, read by the light of a lamp, and I tilted it on *Shabbat*. When the *Bet Hamikdash* will be rebuilt I will bring a fat sin-offering. [This shows that even an important person like R. Yishmael b. Elisha was not permitted to read by the light of a lamp.] [The Gemara answers:] R. Yishmael b. Elisha is different [than other important people], since when it came to learning Torah he considered himself an ordinary person. [When studying Torah he was oblivious of everything else, so that even on weekdays he would tilt the lamp when studying Torah.]

DEATH OF
THE YOUNG SCHOLAR

(13a) We learned in a *Baraita* that was taught by Eliyahu Hanavi[18]: It once happened that a scholar who had learned a great deal of Mishnah and *Chumash*[19] and had served the Torah scholars [meaning that he learned the interpretations of the Mishnah, what we call Gemara], died in the prime of life. His wife took his *tefillin*[20] and carried them around to the synagogues and *batei midrash* and said to the rabbis: It is written in the Torah, "This [the Torah] is your life and the length of your days" (Deuteronomy 30:20). My husband learned a lot of Mishnah, studied a great deal of *Chumash* (13b), and learned much Gemara. Why did he die in the prime of life? There was no one who could answer her. [Eliyahu, the author of this *Baraita*, said:] One time I was the guest at the home of this woman, and she told me the whole story. I said to her: My daughter! How did he conduct himself during your *niddah* period [when a woman is forbidden to her husband]? She replied: God forbid! He did not even touch me with his little finger. [Continued Eliyahu:] I asked her: And how was he to you during your "days of white garments"? [After the flow has ended a woman puts on white garments and examines herself for seven days to make sure that no stains are found. During those seven days she also is forbidden to her husband.]

[She replied:] He ate together with me, and drank together with me, and he slept together with me with physical contact, but it did not enter his mind to have marital relations. [We know that *Halachah* makes no distinction between the time when a woman is counting her seven clean days and the days she is actually menstruating.] [Replied Eliyahu:] I said: Blessed be the Omnipresent for slaying him, because he did not show proper respect for the Torah. Because the Torah says, "[A man should] not come close to a woman who is ritually unclean because of her menstruation, [both during the days of her menstrual flow and at any time before she counted the full seven clean days and immersed in a *mikvah*]. When R. Dimi came [from Eretz Yisrael], he said: [They did not have any physical contact at all.] They were in a wide bed [and nevertheless he was punished so severely]. In Eretz Yisrael they said: R. Yitzchak b. Yosef said: There was an apron separating them [so that they could not have any physical contact].

CONSTANT MIRACLES

The Sages taught: Who wrote *Megillat Taanit*? [*Megillat Taanit* is a *Baraita* that lists the days on which it is forbidden to fast and to deliver eulogies because of miraculous rescues that happened to the Jewish people on those days.] The Rabbis said: The author was Chanaiah b. Chizkiah and his group who cherished [the miracles by which the Jewish people were saved from their] troubles. R. Shimon b. Gamliel said: We also cherish the miraculous events that brought us relief from our troubles. But what can we do? If we were to write down all the days on which we saw miracles that saved us from our troubles we would never finish [because the troubles are constant and the miracles are constant. We would have to declare a Yom Tov every day (Rashi)]. To put it another way: A fool is never harmed, [he is not aware of the troubles that surround him. Similarly, we do not recognize the miracles that happen to us every day]. Or you might say: The flesh of a dead person does not feel the scalpel. [We have become inured to the persecutions that constantly befall us.] [Asks the Gemara:] But it isn't so! [How can you say that the dead do not feel.] Didn't R. Yitzchak say: Worms are as painful to the dead as a needle in the flesh of the living? For it says, "His flesh will decay upon him, and his soul feels the pain" (Job 14:22) [so we see that the soul does feel pain]! [The Gemara answers:] What we meant to say is: The dead flesh of a living person does not feel the scalpel. [Similarly, the Jewish people is insensitive to the many miracles that happen every day].

R. Yehudah said in the name of Rav: The man named Chananiah b. Chizkiyah should be remembered for good. If it had not been for him the Book of Ezekiel would have been hidden [i.e., excluded from the Bible] because the words of the Book of Ezekiel seem to contradict the words of the Torah.[21] What did he do? They brought up to him three hundred barrels of oil [for food and light] and he sat in his attic and reconciled all contradictions.

BEFORE THE DESTRUCTION OF
THE *BET HAMIKDASH*

(14a) R. Parnoch said in the name of R. Yochanan: If someone holds a Torah scroll naked [without its wrapping], he will be buried naked. [Asks the Gemara:] Naked! Do you really mean that? [No Jew —not even the most corrupt person—ever was buried naked!] Rather said R. Zera, "he will be buried naked," means he will be buried without good deeds [as though he had never performed a mitzvah]. [Asks the Gemara:] Without good deeds! Do you really mean that? [Surely, the fact that he held a Torah scroll without its wrapping does not negate all his mitzvot?] Rather say, he will be buried naked, without getting credit for that mitzvah [the mitzvah of holding the Torah scroll].

(14b) Rabbi Yehudah said in the name of Shmuel: When Solomon instituted *eruvin*[22] and the washing of the hands [before meals], a Heavenly Voice came forth and declared, "My son, if your mind gets wisdom, My mind, too, will be gladdened" (Proverbs 23:15), and "Get wisdom My son, and gladden My heart, that I may have what to answer those who taunt Me" (Proverbs 27:11).

(15a) R. Kahan said: When R. Yishmael b. R. Yose became ill, his disciples sent word to him: Our teacher, tell us the two or three things that you told us you know from your father [and you have not yet taught us]. He sent back: This is what my father said: One-hundred-and-eighty years before the destruction of the [second] *Bet Hamikdash* the wicked kingdom of Rome began its conquest of Israel. Eighty years before the destruction of the *Bet Hamikdash*, the Sages decreed that the territory of the other nations and glassware be considered unclean. Forty years before the destruction of the *Bet Hamikdash*, the Sanhedrin went into exile [they left their chamber in the *Lishkat Hagazit*[23] on the Temple Mount], and convened in the *chanuyot*.[24] Why is it important to know this? [And why did they leave the *Lishkat Hagazit* and move to the *chanuyot*?] Said R. Yitzchak b. Avdimi: This comes to teach us that they did not judge any more cases involving fines. [Asks the Gemara:] Do you really think that they stopped judging cases involving fines? [After all, there was no requirement that such cases had to be judged in the *Lishkat Hagazit*.] Say instead: They stopped adjudicating capital cases [because such cases had be judged in the *Lishkat Hagazit*].

TAKING CLOTHES
TO THE CLEANER'S

(19a) We learned in a *Baraita*: R. Tzadok said: It was the custom in R. Gamliel's house to bring white clothes to the laundry three days before *Shabbat*, but colored clothes they brought to the laundry even on Friday. From this we learn that white clothes are more difficult to launder than colored ones [therefore, a laundryman may charge more for cleaning white clothes]. Abaye once brought a colored garment to the cleaner's. He asked the cleaner: How much do you charge for cleaning it? The cleaner replied: As much as for a white garment. Answered Abaye: The Rabbis foresaw that there would be people like you, [and they determined that it takes less labor to clean colored clothes and should cost less].

Abaye said: When you bring a garment to a cleaner you should measure it when you hand it to him and again when you pick it up. If it is bigger, he ruined it by stretching it, and if it is smaller, he ruined it by shrinking it, [and you are entitled to a reduction].

WICKS FOR THE *SHABBAT* LAMP

(21a) Rami b. Chama taught: Those wicks and oils that the Sages said should not be used to light the *Shabbat* lamp, should neither be used to light in the *Bet Hamikdash*, because it says, [The Israelites were commanded to bring illuminating oil], "to keep the lamp [in the Tabernacle] constantly burning" (Exodus 27:20). He taught [this passage] and interpreted it to mean that the flame must rise by itself and not be made to rise by other means. [The forbidden wicks and oils do not burn by themselves but need constant attention.] [The Gemara raises an objection:] We learned in a Mishnah: [At the *Simchat Beit Hasho'evah*[25] four huge lamps were erected in the Women's Court of the *Bet Hamikdash*.] Wicks were fashioned from the worn-out pants and belts of the *kohanim* [which contained wool], and with these they lit the special lamps. [But the Gemara stated on 20b that wool was unfit to be used as a wick for a *Shabbat* lamp. Thus this contradicts Rami b. Chama, who said that wicks that are unfit for *Shabbat* are also unfit for the *Bet Hamikdash*.] [The Gemara answers:] The *Simchat Bet Hasho'evah* celebration was different, [because it was not a Biblical precept (Rashi)].

LIGHTING THE
CHANUKAH *MENORAH*

(21b) [The Gemara now turns from the subject of *Shabbat* lights to a discussion of the *halachot* of Chanukah and the lighting of the *Menorah*.]

Our Rabbis taught in a *Baraita*: The mitzvah of Chanukah requires one light for the entire household [meaning, one light should be lit every night for the entire household]; those who are meticulous kindle one light for each member of the household; and regarding the extremely meticulous [there is a difference of opinion]: Beit Shammai maintain: On the first day you should light eight lights, and one less each of the following days. But Beit Hillel contend: On the first day you should light one light, and on the following seven days you should increase the number by one each day. Ulla said: In Eretz Yisrael there is a dispute about this between two *Amora'im*[26]: R. Yose b. Avin and R. Yose b. Zevida. One holds that the reason of Beit Shammai is that the lights to be lit each day should correspond to the number of days [of Chanukah] that are yet to come.[27] And the reason of Beit Hillel is that it should correspond to the days that have gone by.[28] But the other maintains that Beit Shammai's reason is that it should correspond to the bulls of *Sukkot*; [Thirteen bulls were sacrificed on the first day of *Sukkot*, twelve on the second, eleven on the third, and so on; one less each succeeding day (Numbers 29:13–32).] Whereas Beit Hillel's reason is that when it comes to religious matters we increase but do not reduce.[29]

Rabbah b. Bar Chana said in the name of R. Yocha-nan. There were two learned old men in Sidon; one did like Beit Shammai, the other like Beit Hillel. The first one gave as his reason that it should correspond to the bulls of *Sukkot*, whereas the other gave as his reason that in religious matters we increase but do not reduce.

What is [the miracle of] Chanukah, [and why do we commemorate it by kindling lights]? Our Rabbis taught[30]: The eight days of Chanukah begin on the twenty-fifth of Kislev. On these days it is forbidden to deliver eulogies and to fast. For when the Greeks entered the *Bet Hamikdash* they defiled all the oils they found there. And when the *Chashmona'im* (Hasmoneans) gained the upper hand and defeated them, they searched and found only one jar of oil stamped with the seal of the *Kohen Gadol* [proof that it was undefiled]. But the oil in the jar was enough for only one day's lighting. Yet a miracle happened and it lasted for eight days, [during which time new oil was prepared]. The following year these days were established as a festival on which *Hallel* is said and [*Al Hanissim* is recited in the *Shemoneh Esrei*, in the *berachah* of] *Modim*, Thanksgiving.

(22a) R. Kahana said: R. Natan b. Minyumi expounded in the name of R. Tanchum: What is the meaning of the verse, [Joseph was thrown into a pit]. "The pit was empty, there was no water in it" (Genesis 37:24). When it says, "The pit was empty," isn't it obvious that there was no water in it? But what does the phrase, "there was no water in it" come to teach us? There was no water in it, but there were snakes and scorpions in it.

R. Yehudah said in R. Assi's name: It is forbidden to count money by the Chanukah light. When I told this to Shmuel he remarked: "Does the lamp then have sanctity?" [Certainly not.] R. Yosef objected, saying: Does blood have sanctity? For we learned in a *Baraita*: [We are commanded to cover the blood of birds and deer after slaughtering, as it says[31]:] "He shall pour out its blood and cover it [with dust]" (Leviticus 17:13): [We derive from here] that just as you use your hand to slaughter [the bird] you should use your hand to cover its blood, and you should not [kick the dust over it] with your foot, so that you should not treat *mitzvot* with contempt. The same reason applies here. [Don't count money by the Chanukah light] because *mitzvot* should not be treated with contempt.

(22b) R. Sheshet raised a question: It says, "Aaron shall light the *Menorah* . . . outside the cloth partition in the Communion Tent" (Leviticus 24:3). [He asked:] Does God then need its light? After all, during the entire forty years that the children of Israel wandered through the wilderness they traveled only by His light! [He answered:] [The *Menorah*] is a testimony to the people of the world that the *Shechinah* dwells among the Jewish people. But how was [the *Menorah*] a testimony? Said Rav: The testimony was evident in the

western branch of the *Menorah*. The same quantity of oil was poured into it as into the other [six branches]. Yet the *kohen* kindled the others from it [in the evening] and ended with it. [The lights of the *Menorah* were lit every evening and burned until morning, with the exception of the light of the western branch, which miraculously continued to burn until the following evening. The priest cleaned out the old wicks in the morning but the wick on the western branch he replaced in the evening, relit it, and lit the other six lights from it. Thus he ended the cleaning process with the western branch. This miracle was testimony that the *Shechinah* dwells among the Jewish people.]

(23a) [The Gemara asks:] What *berachah* do we recite when we light [the Chanukah lights]? We say: Who has sanctified us with His commandments, and has commanded us to kindle the Chanukah light. [The Gemara asks:] And where did He command us [to kindle the Chanukah light]? [Of course, the mitzvah of kindling the Chanukah lights is Rabbinical and not written in the Torah.] R. Ivya said: [It is included in the command of,] "Do not stray [from the word that the Rabbis teach you]" (Deuteronomy 17:11). R. Nechemiah said: [It comes under the heading of,] "Ask your father and let him tell you, and your grandfather, who will explain it" (*ibid.* 32:7).[32]

THE MITZVAH OF *PEI'AH*

R. Shimon said: There are four reasons why the Torah ordered that *pei'ah* should be left at the end of the field,[33] [instead of letting the farmer decide which portion of the field he wants to leave for the poor]: (1) As a precaution against robbing the poor, (2) against wasting the time of the poor, (3) against suspicion, and (4) against violating the command of, "Do not completely harvest the corners of your fields" (Leviticus 19:9). [The Gemara now analyzes the four reasons:] As a precaution against robbing the poor: Because the owner of the field may see a free hour [when there are no poor people in the field], and say to his poor relatives: This portion is *pei'ah*, [but now that the portion is at the end of the field the poor will see it and take their share (Rashi)]. (23b) Against wasting the time of the poor: that the poor should not have to sit and watch for the moment the owner will leave *pei'ah*. Against suspicion: that passers-by should not say, "Cursed be the man who has not left *pei'ah* in his field." [They do not realize that it has already been taken by the poor.] And against violating the command of "Do not completely harvest the corners of your field." [The Gemara asks:] Are not the other three the reasons why the Torah said, "Do not completely harvest the corners"? Rava said: [The Torah ordained that *pei'ah* should be left at the corner of the field as a precaution] against fakers [who may not leave anything and claim that they left *pei'ah* in the middle of the field].

THE REWARD FOR KINDLING
SHABBAT LIGHTS

R. Huna said: Whoever regularly fulfills the mitzvah of kindling [the *Shabbat* and Chanukah] lights will have *children* who are Torah scholars. Whoever is careful to observe the mitzvah of *mezuzah* will merit to have a beautiful dwelling. Whoever is careful to observe the mitzvah of *tzitzit* will merit to have a beautiful garment. Whoever is careful about reciting *Kiddush* will merit to fill barrels of wine, [meaning, he will become rich].

R. Huna regularly passed by R. Avin, the carpenter's house. Noticing that he used to light many *Shabbat* lights, he remarked: Two great men will come forth from this house. [His prediction came true.] R. Idi b. Avin and R. Chiya b. Avin [were born there]. R. Chisda regularly passed the house of R. Shizbi's father.[34] Noticing that he used to kindle many lights, he remarked: A great man will come forth from here. [And so it happened.] R. Shizbi was born there.

R. Yosef's wife was in the habit of kindling the *Shabbat* lights late [she waited until shortly before nightfall]. So R. Yosef said to her: We have learned, [By day, a pillar of cloud guided the Israelites along the way, and at night a pillar of fire provided them with light.] "The pillar of cloud did not move away by day, nor the pillar of fire at night" (Exodus 13:22). This teaches us that the pillar of fire arrived before the pillar of cloud departed, and the pillar of cloud appeared before the pillar of fire departed. [He indicated to his wife that she too, should kindle the lights well before the onset of *Shabbat*.] She then decided to kindle the lights very early, [while it was still day]. But an old sage told her: We have learned: [You should kindle the *Shabbat* lights before the onset of *Shabbat*], provided you don't do it too early [because then you cannot tell that they are lit in honor of *Shabbat*], or too late.

Rava said: Whoever loves the Rabbis will have sons who are rabbis. Whoever respects the Rabbis will have rabbis for sons-in-law. Whoever stands in awe of the Rabbis will himself become a Torah scholar; but if he is not suited for this, his words will be heeded like those of a Torah scholar.

GETTING READY FOR *SHABBAT*

(25b) R. Yehudah said in Rav's name: This was the practice of R. Yehudah b. Ila'i: On Friday afternoon a tub of hot water was brought to him, and he washed his face, hands, and feet. He would then sit wrapped in a fine linen robe that had *tzitzit* attached to it, and he looked like an angel of the Lord of Hosts.

It says, "My life was bereft of peace, I forgot what happiness was" (Lamentations 3:17). [The Gemara asks:] What is the meaning of, "My life was bereft from peace"? R. Abbahu said: This refers to the kindling of the *Shabbat* lights. [Jeremiah bemoans the fact that at the destruction of the *Beis Hamikdash* they could not

even afford *Shabbat* lights, which bring peace into the home.] "I forgot what happiness was," R. Yirmiyah said: This refers to the loss of baths. R. Yochanan said: This means the washing of hands and feet in hot water. R. Yitzchak Nafcha said: This refers to a beautiful bed with elegant bedding on it. R. Abba said: This refers to a neatly made bed and an adorned wife for Torah scholars.

We learned in a *Baraita*: Who is rich? He who enjoys his wealth, so says R. Meir. R. Tarfon says: He who owns a hundred vineyards, a hundred fields, and has a hundred slaves working in them. R. Akiva said: He who has a wife whose deeds are beautiful.[35] R. Yose said: He who has a toilet near his table.[36]

(26a) Rabbi Tarfon said: You should use nothing but olive oil for the *Shabbat* lights. When he heard this R. Yochanan b. Nuri got up and exclaimed: What shall the Babylonians do who have only sesame oil? And what shall the Medeans do who have only nut oil? And what shall the Alexandrians do who have only radish oil? And what shall the people of Cappadocia do who have none of these oils except naphtha? The only oils that may not be used for *Shabbat* lights are those listed by the Sages [in the Mishnah on page 20b. All other oils may be used].

WAS THE TACHASH
A UNICORN?

(28b) [According to Exodus 26:14, the covering of the Tabernacle was made of the skins of *tachash*, an animal species. The Gemara now wants to identify the *tachash*. The Gemara asks:] What about the *tachash* that existed in the days of Moses? R. Ela'a said in the name of R. Shimon b. Lakish: R. Meir used to assert that the *tachash* of Moses' times was a separate species, and the Sages could not decide whether it should be classified as a wild beast or a domestic animal. It had a single horn on its forehead, and it was made available to Moses just for that occasion to make the covering for the Tabernacle from it, and after that it was hidden. [The Gemara concludes:] Now, since he says that it had one horn on its forehead we gather that it was a clean animal [i.e., an animal whose flesh a Jew may eat]. For R. Yehudah said: The ox that Adam, the first man, brought as a sacrifice had a single horn on its forehead, for it says, "[I will exalt God's name with song . . .] that will please God more than an ox or a bull that has a horn (*makrin*) and hoofs" (Psalms 69:32). [The Gemara objects:] But *makrin*[37] implies "*two* horns"! Said R. Nachman b. Yitzchak: [*Makrin* is written without a *yud* and can be read:] *mi-keren*, "more than *a* horn." [The Gemara asks:] So let us conclude that [the *tachash*] was a domestic animal? [The Gemara answers:] Since there is a *keresh* [a kind of antelope, unicorn] that is a wild animal and has only one horn, you can say that the *tachash*, too, is a wild animal.

78

THE SEEMING CONTRADICTIONS IN ECCLESIASTES

(30b) R. Yehudah the son of R. Shmuel b. Shilat said in Rav's name: The Sages wanted to hide the Book of Ecclesiastes because its words contradict themselves. So why didn't they hide it? Because it begins with Torah teaching and ends with Torah teaching [and everything in between is also Torah teaching; the contradictions are only apparent inconsistencies]. It begins with Torah teaching, for it says, "What real gain is there for a man in all his labor he toils beneath the sun?"[38] (Ecclesiastes 1:3). On which the School of R. Yannai commented: *Beneath* the sun he has no [real gain], but he does have real gain *before* the sun [i.e., if he toils in the Torah, which existed before the sun]. Ecclesiastes ends with Torah teaching, for it says, "The sum of the matter, when all is said and done: Revere God and observe His commandments, for this is the whole of man" (Ecclesiastes 12:13). [The Gemara asks:] What is the meaning of, "for this is the whole of man"? Said R. Elazar: The whole world was created only for the sake of this kind of person. R. Abba b. Kahana said: This kind of person is equivalent to the entire world. Shimon b. Azzai—others say, Shimon b. Zoma—said: The entire world was created only to provide this kind of person with company [so that he should not be alone].

[The Gemara asks:] What are the [seeming] contradictions in Ecclesiastes?—It says, "Anger is better than laughter" (Ecclesiastes 7:3); and on the other hand it says, "I said of laughter that it should be praised" (ibid. 2:2). It says, "I praised joy" (ibid. 8:15); and on the other hand it says, "What does joy accomplish?" (ibid. 2:2). [The Gemara answers:] There is no difficulty. [You just have to put things into perspective.] Sometimes, "Anger is better than laughter": the anger that the Holy One, blessed be He, displays to the righteous in this world is better than the laughter that the Holy One, blessed be He, beams at the wicked in this world. [The suffering of the righteous in this world paves their way to the world to come. It is preferable to the prosperity the wicked enjoy in this world. Their good fortune is the reward for whatever good they did, and in the world to come they are destined for perdition.] "I said of laughter that it should be praised": this refers to the laughter the Holy One, blessed be He, laughs with the righteous in the world to come. "I praised joy": This refers to the joy you experience when you do a mitzvah.[39]

"What does joy accomplish?": this refers to joy that is not connected with a mitzvah. [The Gemara summarizes:] All this comes to teach us that the *Shechinah* does not rest on a person who is depressed, lazy, in a frivolous mood, or who is engaged in banal conversation or idle talk. [The *Shechinah*] comes to rest on a person only if he is in a joyous mood that was brought on by a mitzvah. And so it says, [When the prophet Elisha was in a glum mood he said:] "'Now then, get me a musician.' And as the musician played, the hand

of God came upon him" (2 Kings 3:15). R. Yehudah said: The same is true for the study of *Halachah*, [a lecturer should begin his discourse with a lighthearted remark to dispel the tension]. Rava said: It works also for a good dream, [if you go to sleep in a happy mood you'll have a good dream].

[Opposing the statement that a lecturer should begin with a humorous story, the Gemara says:] But that is not so, for R. Gidal said in Rav's name: If any student sits before his teacher and his lips are not dripping bitterness [caused by the awe and respect of his teacher] they shall be burned, for it says, "His lips are like lilies, [*shoshanim*], they drip flowing myrrh [*mor oveir*]" (Song of Songs 5:13). Don't read *mor oveir*, but *mar oveir*, "dripping bitterness"; don't read *shoshanim*, but *sheshonim*, "those that study." [Thus the verse is translated: The lips of those that study drip with bitterness brought on by awe and respect.] [The Gemara answers:] There is no difficulty. The teacher is the one that makes the joke; the student is the one who is in awe. And if you prefer, say that both apply to the teacher, and there still is no difficulty: Before the teacher starts [he should relax the mood of the audience with a witticism], but after he launches into his lecture [he has to be serious]. Just as Rabbah did; before he began his discourse he used to say something humorous to make the students feel at ease; then he sat down with awe and began the discourse.

CONTRADICTIONS IN THE BOOK OF PROVERBS

[The Gemara continues:] They also wanted to hide the Book of Proverbs, because its words seem to contradict each other. So why didn't they hide it? They said: [We also thought at first that the statements in Ecclesiastes were self-contradictory]. Didn't we look into the matter and figure out reasons for the apparent contradictions? So here, too, let's put our minds to it [and reconcile the contradictions]. [The Gemara asks:] Well, what are the seeming contradictions [in the Book of Proverbs]?—It says, "Do not answer a fool according to his foolishness" (Proverbs 26:4), and it also says, "Answer a fool according to his foolishness" (ibid. 5). [The Gemara answers:] There is no difficulty: one passage refers to Torah subjects [there you may answer a fool]; the other refers to general topics.

[The Gemara gives an example that shows that regarding general topics you should not answer a fool.] Like the case of a certain person who came up to Rebbi and said to him: "Your wife is my wife, and your children are mine," [accusing Rebbi's wife of adultery and his children of illegitimacy]. Rebbi calmly replied: Would you like to have a cup of wine? He drank and burst, [he died. In other words, Rebbi did not argue with a man who obviously was a fool].

[The Gemara gives another example:] A certain person came up to R. Chiya and said to him: "You should know that your mother is my wife, and you are my son!" R. Chiyah [did not argue] but said: Would you like to have a cup of wine? He drank and burst.

R. Chiya noted: It was Rebbi's prayer that helped that his children should not be considered illegitimate. For when Rebbi prayed he used to say: May it be Your will, Lord our God, that You save me today from brazen men and from brazenness.

[On the other hand, when it comes to Torah subjects you should answer a fool.] Like the time when R. Gamliel was sitting and lecturing: In time to come a woman will have a child every single day, as it says, "The women will conceive and have children at the same time" (Jeremiah 31:7).[40] A certain disciple sneered at him and said, it is written, "There will be nothing new under the sun!" (Ecclesiastes 1:9), [even after *Mashiach* comes, nature will not change]. R. Gamliel replied: Come, let me show you something similar to that even in the world as it is today. He showed him a chicken [which lays an egg every single day. Since this was a Torah subject R. Gamliel did respond to the disciple's ridicule].[41] Another time R. Gamliel sat and expounded: In future times trees will produce fruit every single day, for it says, "It shall bring forth branches and bear fruit" (Ezekiel 17:23): just as the branches exist every day, so will there be fruit every day. Again that disciple sneered at him and said: It is written, "There will be nothing new under the sun!" R. Gamliel replied: Come, let me show you something similar even in today's world. He went and showed him a caper bush [which produces berries, flowers and branches that are eaten successively[42] (Rashi)].

Another time R. Gamliel sat and expounded: In future times, Eretz Yisrael will produce [ready-made] cakes and woolen robes, for it says, "There will be a handful of grain in the land" (Psalm 72:16). [*Pisat bar*, meaning, cakes as wide as a hand. *Pisat bar* can mean also "woolen garment" (Rashi).] Again that disciple sneered at him, saying, "There will be nothing new under the sun!" Replied R. Gamliel: Come, let me show you something similar even in today's world. He went and showed him mushrooms [which resemble cakes], and as far as the robes are concerned he showed him the bark of a young palm tree [which has a soft, silklike covering on the inside]. [The foolish disciple had asked the same question three times, and R. Gamliel patiently replied each time, because when it comes to Torah matters we are not allowed to let any question go unanswered, no matter how foolish it is.]

HE TRIED
TO INFURIATE HILLEL

We learned in a *Baraita*: A person should always be gentle, like Hillel, and not impatient, like Shammai. The story is told about two (31a) people who made a wager between themselves. They said: Any person who will go and make Hillel angry will receive four hundred *zuz*. One of them said: I'll go and get him angry. That day was Friday afternoon, and Hillel was washing his head. So he went and passed by the door of Hillel's house, shouting, "Is Hillel here, where is Hillel?" [disrespectfully, without mentioning Hillel's title of *Nassi* (Prince)]. Hillel put on his robe and went out to him, saying [calmly], "My son, how can I help you?" He replied, "I have a question to ask." "Go ahead and ask, my son," prodded Hillel. "Why are the heads of the Babylonians round?" the man asked. "My son, you have asked a very important question," Hillel replied, "I'll tell you. Because they don't have good midwives." The man left, waited a while, came back, and called out, "Is Hillel here? Where is Hillel?" He put on his robe and went out to him, saying, "My son, what can I do for you?" He replied, "I have a question to ask."

"Ask, my son," Hillel said. "Why are the Tarmodeans weak-eyed?" came the question. "My son, you have asked an astute question," he replied. "I'll tell you why. Because they live in a sandy place" [and the wind is forever blowing the sand into their eyes]. He left, waited a while, came back, and called out, "Is Hillel here? Where is Hillel?" He put on his robe and went out to him, saying, "My son, what can I do for you now?" "I have a question to ask," he said. "Ask, my son," prompted Hillel. He asked, "Why are the feet of the Africans wide?" "My son, you have asked a significant question," said Hillel. "The reason is that they live in marshy places," [their wide feet help them not to sink into the swamp]. The man, [desperate that he was losing the bet,] then said, "I have many other such questions to ask, but I am afraid that you are going to get angry." Hillel put on his robe, sat down, and said to him, "Ask all the questions you have to ask." Said he, "Are you the Hillel who is called *Nassi* (Prince, Leader) of Israel?" "Yes," he replied. "If you're really the one," he retorted, "may there not be any more like you in Israel." "Why, my son?" Hillel inquired. "I lost four hundred *zuz* because of you!" he exclaimed. Replied Hillel, "Always be careful and watch your temper. It is worth that you should lose four hundred *zuz* because of Hillel, and even another four hundred *zuz*; but no matter what you do, Hillel will not lose his temper."

TEACH ME THE TORAH WHILE
I'M STANDING ON ONE LEG

We have learned: The story is told that a certain non-Jew once came to Shammai and asked him, "How many Torahs do you have? Shammai replied, "We have two: the Written Torah and the Oral Torah."[43] So the non-Jew said to him, "I believe you regarding the Written Torah, but not regarding the Oral Torah. Make me a proselyte on condition that you teach me the Written

Torah only." Shammai scolded him and sent him away in disgust. He then went to Hillel who accepted him as a proselyte [and began teaching him the Torah]. On the first day he taught him, *alef, bet, gimmel, dalet*.[44] The next day he reversed the order, [calling the same letters *tav, shin, reish, kuf*].[45] "But yesterday you did not say that!" he complained. Responded Hillel, "[How do you know that this is an *alef* and this a *bet*? Only because you took my word for it.] You trusted me when I told you *alef, bet, gimmel, dalet*. So trust me also when I'm telling you that the Oral Torah was given by God."

There is another story that a certain non-Jew once came before Shammai and said to him, "Make me a proselyte on condition that you teach me the entire Torah while I am standing on one foot." He pushed him away with a builder's ruler he was holding in his hand. The non-Jew then went to Hillel, who accepted him as a proselyte. He said to him, "[The fundamental rule of the Torah is:] Do not do to others what you do not want done to yourself; that is the whole Torah. The rest is commentary. Go and learn it."

Another story has it that a certain non-Jew was passing behind a *bet hamidrash*, where he heard a teacher reciting the verse, "These are the garments that they shall make: a breastplate and an *eifod*"[46] (Exodus 28:4). Said the non-Jew: "For whom are these?" "For the *Kohen Gadol* (High Priest)" replied the teacher. The non-Jew then said to himself: "I will go and become a proselyte, so that they should make me a *Kohen Gadol*." So he went to Shammai and said to him, "Make me a proselyte on condition that you appoint me *Kohen Gadol*." Shammai pushed him away with a builder's ruler he had in his hand. He then went to Hillel [with the same request], and he made him a proselyte. Hillel said to him, "Can you appoint any person a king unless he knows how to govern? First go and study the rules of government, [meaning, the laws of the Torah and of the priesthood]. He went and started to learn. When he came to the verse, "Any stranger [who is not a *kohen*] that comes close shall die" (Numbers 1:51), he asked, "To whom does this verse apply?" "Even to David, King of Israel," his teacher replied.

The proselyte then drew a logical conclusion: If the people of Israel who are called sons of the Almighty,[47] and because of His love for them He called them, "Israel is My firstborn son" (Exodus 4:22), yet the Torah says about them, "Any stranger [who is not a *kohen*] that comes close shall die": surely this applies to a mere proselyte who comes with his staff and his bag! He then went to Hillel and said to him, "Hillel, humble man that you are, may you be blessed for bringing me under the wings of the *Shechinah*." A while later, these three converts met in one place. They all agreed, "Shammai's short temper almost drove us out of the world, but Hillel's patience brought us under the wings of the *Shechinah*."

THE FEAR OF GOD IS SUPREME

Resh Lakish said: What is the meaning of the verse, "The faith of your times and the strength of your salvation comes through wisdom and knowledge [of Torah]; and the fear of God is His treasure" (Isaiah 33:6). "The faith" refers to the Order of *Zera'im* (Seeds), "your times" to the Order of *Mo'ed* (Festivals), "strength" to the Order of *Nashim* (Women), "salvation" to the Order of *Nezikin* (Civil Law, Damages), "wisdom" to the Order of *Kodashim* (Sacred Things), and "knowledge" to the Order of *Taharot* (Purity).[48] But [although the six Orders of the Mishnah encompass the essence of life], nevertheless, "the fear of God is His treasure," [in God's eyes it towers above all else].

[Giving a different interpretation to this verse,] Rava said: When a person is brought into the heavenly Court of Judgment he is asked: Did you deal honestly ["faith"]? Did you set aside fixed times for Torah study ["times"]? Did you have children ["strength, heirs"]? Did you hope for salvation, [the coming of Mashiach, "salvation"]? Did you study the complexities of civil law ["wisdom"]? Did you draw logical inferences from your Torah studies ["knowledge"]?[49] Yet even so [although he may have done all these good things], if "the fear of God is His treasure," good and well: if not, it is not well. You can compare it to a person who told his worker, "Bring a *kur* of wheat to the attic for me," and he went and brought it up for him. "Did you mix in a *kav* of *chumton*?"[50] he asked him. "No, I didn't," the worker replied. "Then it would have been better if you had not brought it up, [because now it is going to rot]." [The same is true for Torah without the fear of God.]

[In passing, the Gemara now points out a legal aspect of the use of *chumton*:]

In the Yeshivah of R. Yishmael it was taught: A person may mix a *kav* of *chumton* in a *kor* of grain and does not have to be concerned [that he is cheating the buyer. He need not tell him explicitly that it is not all grain. The buyer expects the *chumton* to be added as a preservative].[51]

Rabbah b. R. Huna said: Any person that has knowledge of Torah without (31b) the fear of heaven is like a treasurer who has been handed the keys to the inner chambers but not the keys to the outer chambers: how can he get in? [The fear of heaven is the outer doorway through which he must pass to reach the inner doorway to understanding the Torah.] [In a similar vein], R. Yannai proclaimed: Woe is to the person who has no courtyard but makes a gateway to the courtyard! [Torah study is only a gateway through which you enter the courtyard of fear of heaven. Woe is to the person who studies the Torah without reverence and awe of God.] R. Yehudah said: The Holy One, blessed be He, created His world only so that people should revere Him, for it says, "God has done it that men revere Him" (Ecclesiastes 3:14).

R. Simon and R. Elazar were sitting together, when R. Yaakov b. Acha passed by. So one said to the other, "Let us stand up before him, because he is a sin-fearing man." Said the other, "Let us stand up before him because he is a Torah scholar." "I am telling you that he is a sin-fearing man, and you tell me that he is [only] a Torah scholar!" the other retorted. [Says the Gemara:] I'll prove to you that it was R. Elazar who said that R. Yaakov b. Acha was a sin-fearing man [and who considered reverence of God greater than Torah scholarship]. For R. Yochanan said in R. Elazar's name: The Holy One, blessed be He, values nothing in the world as highly as the fear of Heaven, for it says, "And now, Israel, what does God want of you? Only that you remain in awe of God your Lord" (Deuteronomy 10:12), and it says, "He said to man, 'See! [hen] Fear of God is wisdom'" (Job 28:28), and in Greek hen means "one" [thus the passage means, "The one and only thing God holds dear is the fear of God." The Gemara concludes:] Indeed, it must have been R. Elazar [who said that R. Yaakov b. Acha was a God-fearing man].

IT'S NEVER TOO LATE
FOR *TESHUVAH*

[The Gemara cites another example of a bewildering verse in Ecclesiastes.]

R. Ulla expounded: What is the meaning of the verse, "Don't overdo wickedness" (Ecclesiastes 7:17)? You should not be too wicked, but to be a little wicked is all right! [The Gemara answers with an analogy:] If a person ate garlic and his breath smells, should he eat more garlic so that he will have more bad breath? [I.e., if a person transgressed a little he should not think that it is too late to repent and he may as well continue to sin. It is never too late to do *teshuvah*.]

Rava b. Ulla expounded: What is meant by the verse, "Death has no pangs [*chartzubot*] for [the wicked]; their strength is firm [*bari ulam*]" (Psalm 73:4). The Holy One, blessed be He, said: It is not enough for the wicked that they are not fearful or depressed[52] about the day of death [they are not concerned about an afterlife], but their hearts are as firm as the hall [the *ulam* of the *Bet Hamikdash*, which was very wide]. And that is what Rabbah meant when he said: What is the meaning of, "This is the way of those who are self-confident [*kesel*]" (Psalm 49:14)? The wicked know that their way leads to death, but there is fat on their loins [*kislam*]. [The kidneys, which are near the loins, are considered the seat of understanding. The fat chokes off their understanding for the need to do *teshuvah*.] Perhaps you are going to say that they don't realize [that they have to do *teshuvah*]? Therefore it says, "They talk about their end all the time" (ibid.), [they are aware of it, but it does not concern them. They still don't do *teshuvah*].

NIDDAH, CHALLAH, AND
SHABBAT LIGHTS

MISHNAH: For three transgressions women die during childbirth: for being careless regarding *niddah* [the laws of menstruation], *challah* [the tithe from dough], and kindling the *Shabbat* light. GEMARA: What is the reason for this punishment for *niddah*? Said R. Yitzchak: She transgressed through the chambers of her womb [when she was negligent regarding *niddah*], therefore she is punished through the chambers of her womb [when she dies during childbirth]. [The Gemara asks:] That is understandable of *niddah*, but what can you say of *challah* and the kindling of *Shabbat* lights? [The Gemara answers:] It is as a certain Galilean expounded before R. Chisda: The Holy One, blessed be He, said: I put a *revi'it*[53] of blood in you [the smallest amount of blood needed to sustain life], therefore I commanded you regarding blood [of *niddah*]. (32a) I called you "the first," ["Israel was holy to God, the first fruits of His harvest" (Jeremiah 2:3)], therefore I commanded you concerning the first, [the first portion of the dough, which is *challah*[54]]. The soul that I placed in you is called a lamp, therefore I commanded you concerning the lamp [i.e., the *Shabbat* lights]. If you fulfill them, good and well; but if you don't, I will take your souls.

[The Gemara asks:] And why [do they die] exactly in childbirth? [The following proverbs all carry the message that when a person is in danger, his failings are remembered and punished, and childbirth is a time of danger for a woman.] Rava said: When the ox has fallen down, sharpen the knife. Abaye said: Let the maidservant keep on misbehaving; she will be punished for everything with the same rod [the labor pains are the punishment for the sin of Eve, and punishments for her other transgressions are added to it]. R. Chisda said: Leave the drunkard alone; he will fall down by himself. Mar Ukva said: When the shepherd is lame, and the goats are running fast [so that he cannot hit them when they are acting up], at the gate of the goats' pen there are words, and in the barn there is the reckoning [when the woman is in good health, her good deeds can fend off the Accuser, but when she is in danger the Accuser cites all her past transgressions]. R. Papa said: At the door of the store [when a person earns a great deal of money] he has many brothers and friends, but at the door of losses and poverty [when he suffers financial reverses] there are neither brothers nor friends [when the woman is in danger, her heavenly defense attorneys vanish].

HAZARDOUS SITUATIONS
FOR MEN

And when are the [merits and shortcomings of] men examined? Said Resh Lakish: When they go across a bridge. [The Gemara asks:] A bridge [is that the only example], and nothing else? [The Gemara answers:]

Say, anything that is similar to a bridge [any dangerous place, such as a leaning wall]. Rav would not cross a river on a ferry if there was a heathen passenger on board. He said: Maybe his time has come for the heathen to be punished for his sins [while on the ferry], and I'll be caught along with him." Shmuel, on the other hand, would not cross a river on a ferry unless there were also heathens aboard. He reasoned: Satan has no power over two persons of different nationalities [at the same time]. R. Yannai always checked the ferry before boarding it [to make sure it had no leaks], for R. Yannai followed his hard-and-fast rule, which was: A person should never stand in a dangerous place expecting a miracle to be performed for him, because such a miracle may not happen. And if a miracle does happen to him, it will be deducted from the merits [he has earned for his good deeds]. R. Chanin said: What verse tells us this? [Jacob prayed:] "I have become diminished [i.e., my merits have decreased] because of all the kindness and faith that You have shown me" (Genesis 32:11). R. Zeira never walked under palm trees on a day that a strong south wind was blowing [for fear that a tree might fall on him].

TESHUVAH AND GOOD DEEDS SAVE FROM DEATH

Our Rabbis taught: For three transgressions women die in childbirth. R. Elazar said: For three transgressions women die young. R. Acha said: [Women die young] because of the sin of washing their children's diapers on *Shabbat*. Others say, because they call the *aron hakodesh* (the holy ark in the synagogue) a chest [which is disrespectful]. It was taught in a *Baraita*: R. Yishmael b. Elazar said: Because of two sins ignorant people die: because they call the holy ark a chest, and because they call a synagogue a *bet am* [house of the people, a demeaning expression].

R. Yitzchak the son of R. Yehudah said: A person should always pray for mercy that he should not become sick, because if he does become sick he is told: Show [a record of] the good deeds in whose merit you deserve to be healed. Mar Ukva said: From which verse is this derived? From the verse, "If you build a new house you must place a guard-rail around your roof. Do not bring blood-guilt on your house if anyone falls from it [*mimmenu*, literally 'from him']" (Deuteronomy 22:8); [in other words], it is from him [*mimenu*] that proof must come [that he is worthy to be healed from the injuries of his fall]. It was taught in the Yeshivah of R. Yishmael: It says, "If anyone [*hannofel*, literally 'the falling one'] falls from it." This unfortunate fellow was destined to have an accident since the six days of Creation, for the Torah calls him "the falling one" before he falls. But deserved good fortune is brought upon good people through good people, and deserved misfortune upon guilty people through guilty ones. [The owner of the house who is guilty of failing to make a guard-rail is God's instrument to fulfill the destiny of the victim to have a fatal accident.]

Our Rabbis taught: If a person is sick and his life is hanging in the balance, the people standing at his bedside should tell him: Make confession, for all who are sentenced to death make confession. When a person goes out into the street, he should imagine that he was arrested by an officer [to be brought to court]; when he has a headache he should imagine that he has a chain around his neck; when he goes to bed and has no strength to get up he should imagine that he was brought on the scaffold to be punished. For whoever is brought up on the scaffold to be punished, if he has great defense attorneys he will be saved, but if not, he is not saved. And these are a person's defense attorneys [in the Court of Heaven]: *teshuvah* (repentance) and good deeds. And even if nine hundred and ninety-nine [angels] are prosecuting him and one argues in his favor, he is saved, for it says, "If he has a angel,[55] one advocate against a thousand, to declare the man's uprightness, then He has mercy on him and decrees, 'Redeem him from descending into the Pit, for I have obtained his ransom" (Job 33:23,24). R. Eliezer the son of R. Yose Hagelili said: Even if that angel brings nine hundred and ninety-nine arguments against him and only one argument in his favor,[56] he is saved, for it says, "one advocate against a thousand."

WHY DO CHILDREN DIE YOUNG?

It was taught in a *Baraita*: R. Shimon b. Gamliel said: The laws of *hekdesh* (objects consecrated to the *Bet Hamikdash*), *terumot* (the first levy of the produce of the year given to the *kohen*), and tithes are basic laws of the Torah, (32b) yet the unlearned were trusted to observe them. [Strictly observant Jews eat the bread of the unlearned and assume that they gave *terumah*, *challah*, and the tithes. They also use their utensils without fearing that they consecrated them to the *Bet Hamikdash*, which would render them forbidden for secular use.]

It was taught in a *Baraita*: Rabbi Natan said: A person's wife dies as a punishment for his sin of failing to fulfill his vows, for it says, "When you have no money to pay [your vows] why should he take away your bed [meaning, your wife] from under you?" (Proverbs 22:27). Rabbi said: For failing to fulfill his vows a person's children die young, for it says, "Don't let your mouth [through vows] bring guilt on your flesh [i.e., your children], and don't tell the messenger [of the congregation who comes to collect the vow] that it was an error [that you vowed, but that you cannot pay]. Why should God be angry at your speech [your vow] and destroy the work of your hands?" (Ecclesiastes 5:5). What is the work of a man's hands? Say, it is his sons and daughters.

There is a difference of opinion between R. Chiya b. Abba and R. Yose; one holds that children die as a punishment for the neglect of *mezuzah*; while the other say that it is for the neglect of Torah study. The one who maintains that it is for neglect of *mezuzah* holds that a verse may be connected with the one preceding it, but not with a verse that comes before the preceding one; and the one who contends that it is because of neglect of Torah study holds that a verse may be connected even with the one that comes before the preceding one.[57]

There is also a difference of opinion between R. Meir and R. Yehudah: One holds that [the death of children] is for the neglect of *mezuzah*, whereas the other holds that it is due to the neglect of *tzitzit*. The view that it is for the neglect of *mezuzah* is understandable, for it says, "Write them on [parchments affixed] to the doorposts [*mezuzot*] of your house," which is followed by, "[If you do this,] you and your children will live long" (Deuteronomy 11:20,21). But what is the reason for the opinion that it is for the neglect of *tzitzit*? R. Kahana—others say, Shila Mari—said: Because it says, "Moreover, on your garments is found the lifeblood of the innocent poor" (Jeremiah 2:34), [which means, because you neglected to affix *tzitzit* to the corners of your garments, innocent children die]. R. Nachman b. Yitzchak said: The view of the one who says that it is for the neglect of *mezuzah* is based also on [the end of] this verse, "Did I not find them in a cave?" (ibid.) [which means] that they made their doors like an entrance to a cave [i.e., a place that has no doorpost and thus no *mezuzah*. And in verse 30 it says, "Did I smite your children in vain?" Thus, neglect of *mezuzah* is the reason for the death of the children].

Resh Lakish said: Whoever is careful to observe the mitzvah of *tzitzit* will have the merit that 2,800 servants will serve him, for it says, "Thus says God of Hosts: In those days, ten men from the nations of every tongue will take hold—they will take hold of every Jew by a corner of his cloak[58] and say, 'Let us go with you'" (Zechariah 8:23). [There are *tzitzit* on each of the four corners of a Jew's garment, and traditionally there are seventy languages. Thus if ten men of seventy nations are taking hold of each of the four corners of a Jew's garment, we arrive at a total of 2,800.]

THE PUNISHMENT
FOR VARIOUS FAILINGS

(32b) It was taught in a *Baraita*: R. Nechemiah said: As a punishment for a person's unwarranted hatred there will be a great deal of discord in his house, his wife will miscarry, and his sons and daughters will die young.

R. Elazar b. R. Yehudah said: As a punishment for failing to separate *challah* there will be no blessing in the [wine and oil] that have been stockpiled, and as a result prices will rise. Seed is sown and others will eat

it, as it says, "I will do the same to you. I will bring upon you terror [*behalah*], along with depression and fever, destroying your outlook and making life hopeless. You will plant your crop in vain, because your enemies will eat it" (Leviticus 26:16). Don't read *behalah* but *be-challah*, "because of failure to give *challah*" [these calamities will come upon you]. But if you do give *challah*, you will be blessed, for it says, "You shall also give to the priest the first of your dough, that a blessing may rest on your house" (Ezekiel 44:30).

As a punishment for failing to give *terumah* and tithes the heavens withhold dew and rain, [and as a result] prices rise, workers' wages are lost, people run frantically in search of a livelihood and cannot find it, as it says, "Drought [*tziyah*] and heat [*chom*] snatch away the snow waters, and the grave [snatches away] those who have sinned" (Job 24:19). [The Gemara asks:] How is it implied in the text [that these troubles come in retribution for failing to give *terumah* and tithes]? In the Yeshivah of R. Yishmael they expounded: Because of the things I commanded[59] you in the summer [to give *terumah* and tithes], but you did not do them, it will not rain during the winter. But if you do give *terumah* and tithes you will be blessed, for it says, "Bring all the tithes into the storehouse, and let there be food in My House, and thus put Me to the test—said the Lord of Hosts. I will surely open the floodgates of heaven for you and pour down blessings on you, that there will be more than enough [*ad beli dai*]" (Malachi 3:10). What does *ad beli dai* mean? Said R. Rama b. Chama: Until your lips will be exhausted [*yivlu*] from saying, "Enough!"—[*dai*].[60]

The punishment for robbery is an invasion of locusts. As a result, there will be widespread famine, and people will eat the flesh of their sons and daughters, as it says, "Listen to this message, you cows of Bashan on the hill of Samaria—who oppress the poor, who rob the needy" (Amos 4:1).[61] Said Rava: For example, this refers to these pleasure-seeking women of Mechuza (33a) who are constantly eating but don't do any work, [thus they rob their husbands, and, since they spend their time eating and drinking they drive their husbands to robbery (Rashi)]. Furthermore, it says, "I smite you with blight and mildew . . . your fig trees and olive trees were devoured by locusts" (Amos 4:9); and it also says, "What the caterpillar has left, the locust has devoured; and what the locust has left the canker-worm has eaten" (Joel 1:4). It also says, "They snatched [from the person] on the right but remained hungry, and consumed [from the person] on the left without being sated. Each devoured the flesh of his own arm [*zero'o*]" (Isaiah 9:19). Don't read "the flesh of his own arm [*zero'o*]," but "the flesh of his own children [*zar'o*]."

The punishment for the delay of justice, the perversion of justice, rendering incorrect judicial decisions [by not giving enough thought to the case at hand], and neglect of Torah study, the sword and plunder will increase, pestilence and famine will come, people will eat and will not be satisfied, and they will eat their bread by weight [rationed]. For it is written, "I will bring a vengeful sword against you to avenge My covenant" (Leviticus 26:25). Now "covenant" refers to the Torah, for it says, "If not for My covenant day and night [meaning the Torah which should be studied day and night], I would not have established the laws of heaven and earth" (Jeremiah 25:26). Furthermore it says, "I will cut off your food supply, so that ten women will have to bake bread in one oven, and they will deliver your bread by weight" (Leviticus 26:26); and it says, [these things will happen] "because they did not respect My laws" (ibid. 43) [by delaying and distorting judgment and rendering wrong decisions].

As a punishment for swearing in vain [i.e., swearing an obvious untruth; for example, that a man is a woman], for swearing falsely [i.e., an untruth that is not obvious], for profanation of God's name[62] and desecration of *Shabbat* wild beasts multiply, cattle diminish, the population decreases, and the roads become desolate, as it says, "And if these things [*be'eileh*] are not enough to discipline you" (ibid. 23); don't read *be'eileh* but *be'alah*, oaths. [The verse thus means, "If you are not disciplined with regard to vain and false oaths], and it says, "I will send wild beasts among you" (ibid. 22), [proof that wild beasts are the punishment for swearing falsely]. Now, in connection with false oaths it says, "Do not swear falsely by My name; [if you do], you will profane [*vechillalta*] your God's name (Leviticus 18:12), and with regard to the profanation of God's name it says, "So that they do not profane [*yechallelu*] My holy Name" (ibid. 22:2), and about the desecration of *Shabbat* it says, "Anyone violating it [*mechalleleha*] shall be put to death" (Exodus 31:14). Since [various forms of] the word *chillul* appear in all three places we infer that, just as false oaths are punished by wild beasts, so are the profanation of God's name and the desecration of *Shabbat*.

As a punishment for the sin of spilling of blood, the *Bet Hamikdash* was destroyed, and the *Shechinah* departed from Israel, as it says, "Do not pollute the land in which you live; it is blood that pollutes the land . . . You must not defile the land upon which you live and in the midst of which I dwell" (Numbers 35:33). So, if you do defile the land you will not live in it, and I will not dwell in its midst [meaning, the *Bet Hamikdash* will be destroyed].

Because of adultery and idol worship, and for not abiding by the laws of *shemittah* [the sabbatical year] and *yovel* [the jubilee year[63]] exile comes to the world, God sends the Jewish people into exile, and other people come and take over their homeland, for it says, "The people who lived in the land before you did all these disgusting perversions [referring to incest and adultery] and defiled the land" (Leviticus 18:27); and it says, "The land became defiled . . . and I directed My providence at the sin committed there" (ibid. 25);

and it says, "Do not cause the land to vomit you out when you defile it, as it vomited out the nation that was there before you," (ibid. 28) [proof that adultery is punished by exile].

With regard to idol worship it says, "I will let your corpses rot on the remains of your idols" (Leviticus 26:30); and it says, "I will make your sanctuaries desolate . . . and I will scatter you among the nations" (ibid. 31,33) [proof that the punishment for idolatry is exile]. Concerning *shemittah* and *yovel* it says, [If you will not observe the laws of *shemittah* and *yovel*] "Then, as long as the land is desolate and you are in your enemies' land, the land will enjoy its sabbaths" (ibid. 34), and it says, "Thus, as long as it is desolate, [the land] will enjoy the sabbatical rest [of the *shemittah* and *yovel* years] that you did not observe when you lived there" (ibid. 35).

As a punishment for obscene talk, troubles increase, harsh decrees are renewed, young Jewish men die, and orphans and widows cry out and are not answered, as it says, "That is why God will not rejoice over their young men, nor show compassion to their orphans and widows; for they all flatter the wicked, and every mouth speaks foul language. Because of that, His anger has not turned back, and His arm is still outstretched [to bring even more trouble on them]" (Isaiah 9:16). [The Gemara asks:] What is the meaning of, "His arm is still outstretched"? R. Chanan b. Rava said: Everyone knows why a bride goes under the *chuppah* [wedding canopy], yet if someone speaks about it in vulgar terms, even if a decree for seventy years of happiness had been sealed for him, it would be reversed and turned into an evil decree.

Rabbah b. Shila said in the name of R. Chisda: Whoever uses foul language, Gehinnom is made deeper for him, for it says, "Gehinnom is made deeper for the mouth that speaks improper things" (Proverbs 22:14). R. Nachman b. Yitzchak said: A person who hears such talk and does not protest will suffer the same punishment, for the verse continues, "He who infuriates God [by listening to lewd talk without protesting] will fall into it" (ibid.).

WHAT CAUSES *HADROKAN* (DROPSY)?

R. Oshaia said: Anyone who is obsessed with sin to the exclusion of everything else,[64] will find wounds and bruises breaking out all over him, for it says, "Bruises and wounds are for him who is completely absorbed with sin" (Proverbs 20:30). And that's not all; he is also punished with *hadrokan* [dropsy[65]], for the verse continues, "striking at the innermost part of the belly" (ibid.). R. Nachman b. Yitzchak said: *Hadrokan* is usually a sign of sin.

The Rabbis taught: There are three kinds of *hadrokan*: the thick swelling of the flesh is a punishment for sin; the swollen one, a blister filled with water, is caused by hunger; and the thin kind that causes the flesh to become very lean, is caused by magic. [The Gemara continues:] Shmuel Hakatan had this sickness, [obviously not from any sin]. He cried out: Master of the Universe! Who will determine the cause of my sickness? [Not knowing the symptoms, people will suspect that I sinned.] As a result, he was healed. Abaye also suffered from this sickness. Said Rava: I know that Abaye often fasts [that is why he contracted *hadrokan*]. Rava also was afflicted with it. [The Gemara wonders why Rava would have *hadrokan*. After all, he did not fast excessively. The Gemara suggests as a possible reason that he withheld his bowels, and this can cause *hadrokan*. But this could not be the case, for Rava surely was careful to respond to the call of nature,] since Rava was the one who said: More people are killed because they delay relieving themselves than die of starvation. [The Gemara answers:] Rava was different: He had no choice, because when he lectured, the scholars [used to ask him questions without letup] and forced him to delay easing himself.

The Rabbis taught: There are four signs: (1) *Hadrokan* (dropsy) is a sign of sin; (2) jaundice is a sign of unwarranted hatred; (3) poverty[66] is a sign of arrogance; (4) *askara* (diphtheria, croup) is a sign of slander. [Just like slander, *askara* begins inside the body and ends by afflicting the throat (Rashi).]

WHAT CAUSES *ASKARA* (DIPHTHERIA, CROUP)?

The Rabbis taught: *Askara* (diphtheria, croup) comes to the world (33b) because of neglect of giving tithes. [If someone eats *tevel*, untithed produce, he is liable to the death penalty at the hands of the Heavenly Court, which takes the form of diphtheria. Since the forbidden food entered his stomach by way of his throat, he is stricken with a sickness that starts in the stomach and spreads to his throat.] R. Elazar b. R. Yose said: Diphtheria comes because of slander. Said Rava—others say, R. Yehoshua b. Levi—what verse substantiates this? "But the king shall rejoice in God; all who swear by Him shall exult, when the mouth of liars is stopped [*yissacheir*]" (Psalm 63:12) [*yissacheir* is associated with *askara*, diphtheria].

The scholars of the Yeshivah asked: Does R. Elazar b. R. Yose mean to say: Diphtheria is caused *only* by slander, or perhaps that it is caused *also* by slander? [The Gemara answers:] Come and listen to the following proof: When our Rabbis entered the "Vineyard in Yavneh" [the Yeshivah of Yavneh[67]], R. Yehudah, R. Elazar b. R. Yose, and R. Shimon were there. The following question was raised: Why does *askara* begin in the intestines and end in the mouth? To which R. Yehudah b. R. Ila'i, the First Speaker on all Occasions,[68] replied: Although the kidneys produce the urge [to slander], the heart understands [i.e., the heart invents the slanderous tales], and the tongue articulates the slanderous words, it is the mouth that completes the slan-

der. R. Elazar b. R. Yose answered: [The sickness ends in the mouth] because they eat unclean food with it. [The Gemara asks:] Do you really mean that eating unclean food [is punishable by death]? [The Gemara answers: R. Elazar b. R. Yose does not mean eating non-kosher food, but] eating food that was not tithed [which is punishable by death at the hands of the Heavenly Court. At any rate, this is proof that R. Elazar b. R. Yose does not ascribe diphtheria exclusively to slander but also to other causes, such as eating food that has not been tithed]. R. Shimon answered: [The sickness ends in the mouth] as a punishment for neglecting Torah study [which is done with the mouth]. The scholars said to him: Women will prove the opposite! [Women are not obligated to study the Torah, yet they also fall victim to *askara* (diphtheria)].

[The Gemara answers:] That is because they deter their husbands from studying. The scholars asked: Gentiles will prove the opposite! [Gentiles are not obligated to study the Torah, yet they die of *askara*.] [The Gemara answers:] That is because they deter Israel from studying. The scholars asked: Then let little children [who die of *askara*] prove the opposite!—They cause their fathers to neglect their Torah studies. [The Gemara asks:] But what about young children who are learning in a yeshivah? [They do not cause their fathers to neglect their studies, and they themselves are studying, why should they be stricken with *askara*?] [The Gemara answers:] This can be explained by R. Gurion's statement. For R. Gurion—others say, R. Yosef b. R. Shemayah—said: When there are righteous men in the generation, the righteous are snatched away [by death] for the [sins of the] generation; when there are no righteous men in a generation, schoolchildren are snatched away for [the sins of] the entire generation. R. Yitzchak b. Ze'iri—others say, R. Shimon b. Nezira—said: What is the verse that supports this? "If you do not know, O fairest of women, go follow the footsteps of the sheep, and graze your kids by the tents of the shepherds" (Song of Songs 1:8).[69]

[The Gemara] interprets this: ["If you do not know" —if you do not keep My *mitzvot*, trouble is in store for you; "go follow the footsteps of the sheep"—go and ask for mercy in the merit of the Patriarchs; "and graze your kids"—the Patriarchs will be the shepherds of your children, they will save the little children,] so that the children will not be taken as a pledge for the evil leaders of the generation who do not adhere to the Torah. [The Gemara reiterates, as has been pointed out previously, that the reason for this entire discussion is] to prove that R. Elazar b. R. Yose meant [that *askara* is brought on] *also* by slander. This proves it.

THE MIRACLE OF RABBI SHIMON B. YOCHA'I

[Earlier on this page, R. Yehudah b. R. Ila'i was referred to as the "official First Speaker on all occasions."

The Gemara now inquires:] Why is it that [R. Yehudah b. R. Ila'i] is called "The First Speaker on all Occasions"? [The Gemara answers:] It happened once that R. Yehudah, R. Yose, and R. Shimon [b. Yocha'i] were sitting together, and Yehudah, the son of proselytes, was sitting by them. R. Yehudah [b. R. Ila'i] opened the discussion by observing: How beautiful are the works of this nation! [The Romans.] They have made streets, constructed bridges, and built public baths. R. Yose was silent. R. Shimon b. Yocha'i answered: Whatever they have done was only for their own benefit. They made streets in order to set harlots in them; baths in order to enjoy themselves in [them; bridges in order to collect tolls from [those who cross] them. Now, Yehudah, the son of proselytes, went and related their words [to his students or his parents, without intending the information to reach the Romans (Rashi)], but [the information] was heard by the authorities. The Romans declared: Yehudah [b. Ila'i], who exalted us, shall be exalted [to become the First Speaker on all Occasions[70]]; Yose, who was silent, shall be exiled to Tzippori (Sepphoris)[71]; Shimon, who criticized Rome, shall be put to death.

R. Shimon [b. Yocha'i] and his son [R. Elazar] went and hid in the bet hamidrash. Every day his wife brought them bread and a jug of water, which was their meal. When the decree became more severe [and an intensive search was launched to find the condemned men], he said to his son: Women are impressionable by nature. The Romans may torture her, and then she will expose us. So they went and hid in a cave. A miracle occurred and a carob tree and a well of water were created for them. They took off their clothes, sat up to their necks in sand, and learned all day. When it was time to pray, they put on their clothes and prayed. Then they got undressed again, so that their clothes should not wear out. Thus they lived for twelve years in the cave. [It was during these twelve years that R. Shimon b. Yocha'i wrote the Zohar, which deals with the hidden, mystical aspects of the Torah and is the basis of the Kabbalah]. Then Elijah [the Prophet] came and stood at the entrance to the cave and exclaimed: Who will inform bar Yocha'i[72] that the emperor is dead and his decree annulled?[73] Then they left the cave.

When they saw people plowing and sowing, they exclaimed: These people ignore eternal life [Torah study], and occupy themselves with temporal life! Anything they cast their eyes on was burned immediately. Thereupon a Heavenly Voice came forth and said to them: Have you come out of the cave to destroy My world! Return to your cave! So they went back into the cave and stayed there for another twelve months, saying: The wicked are punished in Gehinnom for twelve months, [and we should not be worse than that]. A Heavenly Voice came forth and said: Go out of your cave! So they went out. Wherever R. Elazar [R. Shimon's son] wounded [by casting a disapprov-

ing glance], R. Shimon would heal. R. Shimon said to him: My son! You and I are sufficient for the world, [meaning, it is enough that you and I are studying Torah. Not everyone can attain our lofty level of understanding]. One Friday afternoon, before sunset, they saw an old man hurrying along with two bunches of myrtles in his hand. "What are these for?" they asked. "They are in honor of Shabbat," he replied. "Wouldn't one bunch be enough?"—"One is for Zachor ('Remember') and one for Shamor ('Safeguard')."[74] Said R. Shimon to his son, "See how precious are the mitzvot to Israel." This soothed their minds.

When R. Pinchas b. Yair, R. Shimon's son-in-law, heard [that R. Shimon had emerged from the cave] he went to greet him. He took him to the bathhouse and tried to dress the wounds on his flesh. Seeing the gaps in his body [caused by sitting in the sand], he began to cry, and his [salty] tears dripped into these wounds, so that R. Shimon began to scream with pain. R. Pinchas b. Ya'ir said, "Woe to me, that I see you in such a state." "On the contrary," R. Shimon replied, "it is wonderful that you see me like this. For if you did not see me in this condition, I would not have been [as learned] as I am." [It was through his suffering that he gained his great knowledge.] For before this episode, when R. Shimon b. Yocha'i would ask R. Pinchas b. Ya'ir a question, the latter would give him thirteen answers, but after this experience, when R. Pinchas b. Ya'ir asked a question, R. Shimon b. Yocha'i would have twenty-four answers.

R. Shimon b. Yocha'i said: Seeing that such a great miracle occurred to me, let me go and make some improvement, [just as Jacob did after he was saved from Esau], for it says, [After his encounter with Esau,] "Jacob arrived whole in the city of Shechem" (Genesis 33:18), which Rav interprets to mean: Whole physically [healed from the limp that resulted from wrestling with Esau's guardian angel], whole financially, and whole in his Torah learning [in spite of the rigors of his travels he did not forget anything]. The verse ends, "He acted graciously toward the city."[75] [What did he do for the city?] Rav said: He instituted a monetary system for them [to replace their barter system]. Shmuel said: He established marketplaces for them; R. Yochanan said: He built bathhouses for them.

R. Shimon b. Yocha'i then asked: "Is there anything here that needs improvement?" The people replied, "Yes. There is a place that may be unclean, [we suspect that human remains are buried there], (34a) and the kohanim are inconvenienced by having to make a detour around it."[76] Said R. Shimon b. Yocha'i, "Is there anyone who knows if that place was ever known to be accessible [to kohanim]?" [I.e., free of graves.] There was an old man who replied, "I remember that Ben Zakkai [who was a kohen] used to cut beans of terumah[77] in this place." [He planted beans of terumah and cut them down after they had grown (Rashi).] So R. Shimon did likewise [he cut beans and threw them down at this place. Miraculously, the dead rose to the surface, and the spot was marked [Rashi]. Wherever the ground was hard [a sign that it had not been dug], he declared it clean, and wherever it was loose he placed a marker [indicating that it was unclean]. There was an old man who said [contemptuously], "The son of Yocha'i has purified a cemetery!" R. Shimon replied, "If you had not been with us, or even if you had been with us but had not voted, you could very well have made such a remark. But now that you were with us and voted with us [in favor of this action], people will say: Even prostitutes dye each other's hair [to enhance their appearance]; surely scholars should [be mindful of each other's honor]!" R. Shimon b. Yocha'i thereupon gazed at him, and the old man died. Then he went out into the street where he saw R. Yehudah b. Geirim, the son of proselytes.[78] "That man is still in the world!" he exclaimed. He gazed at him, and he turned into a heap of bones.

PRE-*SHABBAT* INSTRUCTIONS

(34a) [We learned in the Mishnah:] A person must say three things in his home on the eve of *Shabbat* just before dark: "Have you tithed? Have you prepared the *eruv*?[79] Kindle the *Shabbat* lights!" [The Gemara asks:] From where in Scripture do we know this? Said R. Yehoshua b. Levi: It says, "You will know that all is well in your tent, you will visit your home, and you will not fail" (Job 5:24). Rabbah b. R. Huna said: Although the Rabbis said: A person must say three things . . . , he should say them in a gentle tone of voice, so that his instructions will be accepted. R. Ashi said: Although I never heard this statement of Rabbah b. R. Huna, I have always followed this practice, because I thought it was the sensible thing to do.

(34b) [The Gemara asks:] What is twilight? [The Gemara answers:] From sunset on, as long as the eastern sky has a reddish glow, then, when the lower horizon is dark, but not the upper horizon, it is twilight; but when the upper horizon is as dark as the lower, it is night, so says R. Yehudah. R. Nechemiah says: [Twilight begins at sunset and lasts] as long as it takes a person to walk half a *mil*.[80] [If he begins walking at sunset, the end of a half-a-*mil* walk marks nightfall.] R. Yose said: Twilight is like the twinkling of an eye— the night comes and the day goes, and it is impossible to fix the exact time.

MIRIAM'S WELL

(35a) R. Chiya said: If you want to see the well of Miriam,[81] climb to the peak of Mount Carmel. When you look down toward the sea you will notice a round rock, shaped like a sieve. That is Miriam's well. Rav said: A moveable well is *tahor* [ritually pure, and, like a *mikveh*, may be used to cleanse people and utensils of *tumah* (contamination) [by immersing them in it]. The

only moveable well in existence is the well of Miriam. [It miraculously followed the children of Israel through the wilderness, thanks to the merit of Miriam.]

LESSON IN PREVENTIVE MEDICINE

(41a) R. Zeira avoided Rav Yehudah, because he [R. Zeira] wanted to move to Eretz Yisrael, but Rav Yehudah [was against this]. He said: Anyone who goes from Babylon to Eretz Yisrael violates a positive commandment, for it says, [After the destruction of the first *Bet Hamikdash*] "They will be brought to Babylon, and there they will remain" (Jeremiah 27:22). [R. Zeira held that this verse refers to the vessels of the *Bet Hamikdash*,[82] and that you are permitted to move to Eretz Yisrael.] He said: I'll go and hear one more Torah insight from [Rav Yehudah], then I'll go home and set out on my journey to Eretz Yisrael. R. Zeira went and found Rav Yehudah at the bathhouse, saying to his attendants: "Bring me soap, bring me a comb. [This he said in Hebrew. Then, switching to Aramaic, he continued:] Open your mouth [to allow the heat of the baths to enter your body], so that your body will give off perspiration! And drink some water that has been heated in the bathhouse." Said R. Zeira: It was worthwhile to come here just to hear these words of Rav Yehudah.

[The Gemara now analyzes what R. Zeira learned from Rav Yehudah's utterances in the baths:] It is understandable that from the fact that Rav Yehudah said [in Hebrew], "Bring me soap and bring me a comb," R. Zeira learned that you are allowed to say mundane things in the holy tongue. And when Rav Yehudah said, "Open your mouth [and draw in the heat] so that your body will give off perspiration!" he echoed Shmuel, who coined the phrase: Heat drives out heat [i.e., the vapors of the bath bring out the vapors of the body]. But, when Rav Yehudah said, "Drink the water that was warmed in the bathhouse," what is the advantage of that? [The Gemara answers:] We learned in a *Baraita*: A person who eats without drinking eats his blood [loses the vitality of his body], and that is the beginning of stomach trouble. If a person eats without walking at least four ells [after his meal], the food spoils in his intestines and is not digested, and that is the beginning of a foul mouth odor. A person who has a call of nature but eats before taking care of his bodily needs is like an oven that is stoked with new fuel on top of its ashes, and that is the beginning of constant body odor. A person who bathes in hot water and does not drink from the water that has been warmed in the bathhouse is like an oven that was heated on the outside but not on the inside. A person who bathes in warm water and does not have a cold shower afterward is like iron that was put into fire but not into cold water [to harden it]. Bathing without rubbing oil onto your body is like pouring water over [the outside of] a barrel [which will never get to the inside. It will not benefit you].

ELISHA, THE MAN OF THE WINGS

(49a) R. Yannai said: When you wear *tefillin* your body must be as clean as that of Elisha, the man of the wings. What does that mean? Abaye said: A person should not let wind while wearing *tefillin*. Rava said: A person should not sleep in them. [The Gemara asks:] Why was he called Elisha, the man of the wings? [The Gemara answers:] Because the wicked Roman government once issued a decree against the Jewish people that anyone wearing *tefillin* would have his brains pierced. In spite of that Elisha put them on and went out into the street. When a Roman inspector spotted him he ran away, and the Roman pursued him. When the Roman caught up with him, Elisha took off his *tefillin* and held them in his hand. "What do you have in your hand?" the Roman asked. "Wings of a dove," Elisha replied. He stretched out his hand, and [miraculously, instead of *tefillin*] he was holding the wings of a dove. That's why he is called Elisha, "the man of the wings." [The Gemara asks:] And why did he say wings of a dove and not of any other bird? [The Gemara answers:] Because the community of Israel is compared to a dove, as it says, "As the wings of a dove sheathed in silver" (Psalm 68:14): just as the dove is protected by its wings so is Israel protected by the *mitzvot*.

THE FATHER WHO NURSED HIS SON

(53b) The Rabbis taught: It happened once that a man's wife died and left a nursing child, and he could not afford to pay a woman to nurse the child. A miracle happened, and the man's breasts opened like the two breasts of a woman, and he nursed his son. R. Yosef said: Look! What a great man that man must have been, that such a miracle was performed for him! Said Abaye: On the contrary! Look how lowly that man must have been that the order of Creation had to be changed for him, [and God did not provide him in a natural way the means to pay for a wet nurse]. Rav Yehudah said: Look how difficult it is for a person to earn a livelihood, that the order of Creation had to be changed for this person, [and he was not granted sustenance]. R. Nachman said: The proof [that earning a livelihood is more difficult than changing the order of Creation] is that miracles that save people's lives happen quite often, whereas food rarely is created miraculously.

Our Rabbis taught: It once happened that a man married a woman who had only one hand, but he did not notice it until she died. Rabbi commented: What a modest woman this must have been that her husband did not know her handicap! Replied R. Chiya: For her it was normal [it is normal for a woman to cover herself, especially when she wants to hide a physical defect], but how modest was this man that he did not notice it until she died.

R. ELAZAR'S COW

(54b) [The Torah ordained that on *Shabbat* "your donkey and ox must rest" (Exodus 23:12). Thus you are not allowed to let your animal do any work, including carrying, on *Shabbat*. In this connection we learned in the Mishnah:] The cow of R. Elazar b. Azariah used to go out [on *Shabbat*] with a strap between her horns, but this was against the wishes of the Sages [because in their opinion this constitutes carrying]. [The Gemara asks:] Did R. Elazar b. Azariah have only one cow, [that the Mishnah says, "the *cow* of R. Elazar b. Azariah used to go out . . ."]? Didn't Rav—others say Rav Yehudah in Rav's name—say: The annual tithe of R. Elazar b. Azariah's herd was 12,000 calves? [That means he owned 120,000 calves.] [The Gemara answers:] We learned in a *Baraita*: The cow in question did not belong to R. Elazar b. Azariah, but to a female neighbor of his; but because he did not admonish her [when he saw the cow going out with the strap on *Shabbat*], it is considered his cow.

ADMONISHING WRONGDOERS

[This incident leads the Gemara into a discussion of the subject of admonishing others:] Rav, R. Chaninah, R. Yochanan, and R. Chaviva taught the following: [The Gemara notes parenthetically that in the entire Order of Mo'ed, whenever we encounter this group of Amora'im, there are those who substitute R. Yonatan for R. Yochanan.] Whoever has the power to restrain members of his household from doing wrong and does not do so, is held responsible for the sins of his household. If he can protest against the wrongdoing of the people of his city, and he does not do so, is held responsible for the sins of the people of his city. If he has the power to protest against the sins of the whole world and does not do so, he is held responsible for the sins of the whole world. R. Papa noted: The members of the staff of the *Resh Galuta* [the Leader of the Exile[83]] are held responsible for the sins of the whole world, just as R. Chanina said: Why does it say, "God will enter into judgment with the elders and nobles of His people" (Isaiah 3:14): if the nobles sinned, (55a) why are the elders faulted for that? We must say instead: [He will punish] the elders [i.e., the Sanhedrin] because they did not protest against the sins of the nobles.

THE LETTER OF LIFE ON THEIR FOREHEAD

Rav Yehudah was sitting before [his teacher] Shmuel, when a woman came and cried before Shmuel [complaining that someone had treated her unfairly], but Shmuel paid no attention to her. Rav Yehudah said to Shmuel: Don't you agree with the central idea of the verse, "If someone stops his ears at the cry of the wretched, he too will call [to God], and he will not be answered?" (Proverbs 21:13). Replied Shmuel to Rav Yehudah: Bright scholar that you are! Your teacher [meaning, I myself, since Shmuel was Rav Yehudah's teacher], is in cold water, [I won't get burned]; but the teacher of your teacher [i.e., Shmuel's teacher, Mar Ukva], he is in hot water. Mar Ukva is here in town, and he is the head of the *Bet Din* (Court), [it is Mar Ukva's obligation to help people who have been wronged. It is not my responsibility]. For it says, "O House of David,[84] thus says God: Render just verdicts early in the day; rescue him who is robbed from him who defrauded him. Else my wrath will break forth like fire and burn with none to quench it, because of their evil deeds" (Jeremiah 21:12).

R. Zeira said to R. Simon: Why don't you admonish those people on the staff of the *Resh Galuta*? Replied R. Simon: They will not accept my reprimand anyway. Said R. Zeira: Even though they will not accept your reprimand, it still is your duty to rebuke them. For R. Acha b. R. Chanina said: It never happened that the Holy One, blessed be He, issued a favorable decree and later changed it into an evil decree, except in one case, for it says, "God said to [Ezekiel], 'Pass through the city of Jerusalem, and put a mark on the foreheads of the people [the *tzaddikim*, the righteous people (Rashi)] who moan and groan because of all the abominations that are committed in it'" (Ezekiel 9:4).

[The Gemara now explains the verse:] The Holy One, blessed be He, said to the angel Gabriel: Go and mark a letter *tav* in ink on the foreheads of the *tzaddikim*, so that the angels of destruction [who will come to Jerusalem to punish the wicked] will not have any power over the *tzaddikim*; and mark a letter *tav* in blood on the foreheads of the wicked, in order that the angels of destruction will have power over them. The Attribute of Justice then said before the Holy One, blessed be He: Master of the universe, what is the difference between the people that have the mark of ink on their forehead and those that have the mark of blood? Replied He: Those are totally rightous men, whereas those are totally wicked! The Attribute of Justice continued: Master of the universe, the *tzaddikim* had the power to protest against their wickedness but they did not do so. God answered to the Attribute of Justice: I know with certainty that if they had protested, the evildoers would not have accepted their admonition.

The Attribute of Justice persisted: Master of the universe, [granted] that this was plain to You, but did the *tzaddikim* know for sure that their reproof would not be accepted by the wicked? [Certainly not.] [The Gemara tells us that God accepted the accusing argu-

ment of the Attribute of Justice], and that is why it says, [God began by ordering the angels of destruction to] "Kill off the aged, youth and maiden, women and children, but do not touch any person that bears the mark; [and at this point God accepted the complaint of the Attribute of Justice and changed the decree from good to evil, saying,] "and begin at my Sanctuary [*mikdashi*]." And it says: "So they began [to kill] the elders who were in front of the House" (Ezekiel 9:6). R. Yosef taught: Do not read *mikdashi* but *mekudashay* [those who are sanctified to Me]: this refers to the people who fulfilled the Torah completely, from *alef* to *tav*.[85] [They were punished first because they did not rebuke their wicked fellowmen.]

And immediately, [Ezekiel saw in his prophetic vision how] "Six men entered by way of the upper gate that faces north, each with his club in his hand; and among them there was another, clothed in linen, with a slate of a scribe at his waist. They came forward and stopped at the copper altar" (ibid. 2). [The Gemara asks:] Was there still a copper altar at [the time of Ezekiel]? [We know that Solomon had hidden it and replaced it with a larger altar made of stone.[86] What then is the meaning of the copper altar?] [The Gemara answers:] The Holy One, blessed be He told the [six messengers]: Begin the massacre with the Levites who sing songs before Me accompanied by copper instruments. And who were these six people? [What attributes do they represent?]

Said R. Chisda: They represent [God's] Anger (*Ketzef*), Rage (*Af*), Wrath (*Cheimah*), Destruction (*Mash'chit*), Shattering (*Meshabbeir*), and *Annihilation* (*Mechaleh*). [Asks the Gemara:] And why was the letter *tav* used [as the sign on the forehead]? Rav said: The *tav* [on the forehead of the righteous] stands for *tichyeh*, "you shall live," and the *tav* [on the forehead of the wicked] stands for *tamut*, "you shall die." Shmuel said: The *tav* stands for *tamah*, "the merit of the Patriarchs [Abraham, Isaac, and Jacob] has been exhausted." [The *tav* on the forehead of the wicked meant that they could no longer rely on the protection of the Patriarchs.] R. Yochanan said: The *tav* stands for *tachon*; "the merit of the Patriarchs will cause the righteous people to find favor in the eyes of God." And Resh Lakish said: The *tav* is the last letter of the signature of the Holy One, blessed be He. For R. Chanina said: The signature of the Holy One, blessed is He, is *EMET*,[87] [Truth]. R. Shmuel b. Nachmani said: [The *tav* signifies] the people who fulfill the whole Torah from *alef* to *tav*.

WHEN DID THE MERIT OF THE PATRIARCHS RUN OUT?

[The Gemara continues with the question:] At what point in history was the merit of the Patriarchs exhausted? Rav said: Since the days of the prophet Hosea the son of Be'eri, for Hosea says, "Now I will reveal her shame in the very sight of her lovers, and none shall save her from Me" (Hosea 2:12) [not even the merit of the Patriarchs]. Shmuel said: Since the days of Chazael, for it says, "King Chazael of Aram oppressed the Israelites throughout the reign of Jeho'achaz (2 Kings 13:22). And says further, "But God was gracious and merciful to them, and He turned back to them because of His covenant with Abraham, Isaac, and Jacob. He did not want to destroy them, and He did not cast them out from His presence *until this time*" (2 Kings 13:23) [but after that time, the merit of the Patriarchs ran out]. R. Yehoshua b. Levi said: Since the days of Elijah [the merit of the Patriarchs was used up], for it says [in connection with the great dispute between Elijah and the prophets of Baal], "When it was time to present the meal offering, the prophet Elijah came forward and said, "O Lord, God of Abraham, Isaac, and Israel! Let it be known *today* that You are God in Israel, and that I am Your servant, and that I have done all these things at Your bidding" (1 Kings 18:36). [By saying "today" Elijah implied that from that day on the merit of the Patriarchs ended.] R. Yochanan said: [It ended] since the days of Hezekiah, for the verse [foretelling the birth of King Hezekiah] states, "[In his time there will be] an abundance of service, and peace without limit, [he will sit] on the throne of David and take over his kingdom, that it may be firmly established in justice and in equity now and evermore. The zeal of the Lord of Hosts shall bring this to pass" (Isaiah 9:6). [It will come to pass through the zeal of God, but not through the merit of the Patriarchs, since that has been exhausted.]

ARE DEATH AND SUFFERING THE RESULT OF SIN?

R. Ammi said: Death is caused only by sin, and suffering is caused only by willful transgression. For it says, "The person who sins, he alone shall die; a son shall not bear the burden of a father's guilt, nor shall a father bear the burden of a son's guilt. The righteousness of the righteous shall be accounted to him alone, and the wickedness of the wicked shall be accounted to him alone." (Ezekiel 18:20). [How do we know that] death is caused only by sin? Because it says, "I will punish their transgression with the rod, and their iniquity with affliction" (Psalm 89:33).

(55b) An objection was raised: [A *Baraita* says:] The ministering angels asked the Holy One, blessed be He, "Master of the universe! Why did You decree death on Adam?" God replied, "I gave him a simple mitzvah, yet he violated it." "But Moses and Aaron fulfilled the whole Torah," the angels retorted, "nevertheless they died too." God replied, "The same fate is in store for all: for the righteous and for the wicked; for the good . . ." (Ecclesiastes 9:2). [This shows that death may strike people who have no sin, contrary to R. Ammi's opinion.] [The Gemara answers:] R. Ammi

holds the view of the Tanna of the following *Baraita*. For we have learned: R. Shimon b. Elazar said: Moses and Aaron also died through their sin, as it says, [After Moses struck the rock instead of speaking to it, God said to Moses and Aaron,] "Because you did not have enough faith . . . [you are going to die and will not bring this assembly to the promised land]" (Numbers 20:12). Therefore, if they had had enough faith, their time to leave this world would not yet have come. [Thus the deaths of Moses and Aaron were caused by their sin.]

An objection was raised: [We have learned in a *Baraita*:] There were four people who died as a result of the instigation of the serpent [which prompted Adam and Eve to sin, but who themselves were free of sin]: Benjamin the son of Jacob, Amram the father of Moses, Jesse the father of David, and Chilav the son of David. We know of all these, [not from a scriptural source but] by tradition, except for Jesse the father of David for whom we have an explicit scriptural verse. For it says, [When Absalom rose up against his father David], "Absalom appointed Amasa army commander in place of Joab. Now Amasa was the son of a man named Yitra the Israelite who had married Abigail the daughter of Nachash and [she was] a sister of Joab's mother Tzeruiah" (2 Samuel 17:25).

[Asks the Gamara:] Was Abigail the daughter of a man named Nachash? Abigail was a daughter of Jesse! For, it says [with reference to the sons of Jesse], "And their sisters were Tzeruiah and Abigail" (1 Chronicles 2:16). [Thus Abigail was a daughter of Jesse. Then how can she be called a daughter of Nachash?] The verse means to tell us that Abigail was "the daughter of the person who died because of the sin of the *nachash* (Serpent),"[88] [but who himself was free of sin]. [The Gemara now asks:] Who is the author of this *Baraita*? Shall we say the author is the Tanna of the *Baraita* that discusses the dialogue between the ministering angels and God [on the first line of 55b, where the angels asked God why He decreed death on Adam]? [He cannot be the author] because that *Baraita* says that Moses and Aaron were free of sin, [and this *Baraita* counts only four people who did not sin and does not include Moses and Aharon. Evidently the author of this *Baraita* does not agree with the *Baraita* of the "ministering angels" that Moses and Aaron never sinned].

Therefore, the author surely must be R. Shimon b. Elazar, who said [above] that Moses and Aaron died through their sin, [yet this *Baraita* tells us that there were four people who never sinned. So you see even R. Shimon b. Elazar, who says that Moses and Aaron did sin, agrees that there were people who never sinned. This proves that according to everyone, there is death without sin and there is suffering without willful transgression. And, therefore, R. Ammi's thesis, [to the effect that death comes only as a result of sin] is refuted. [The Gemara is telling us in effect that bad things happen to good people.]

91

REUVEN'S IMPETUOUS ACT

[The Torah tells us that Reuven lived with Bilhah, his father's concubine (Genesis 35:22).] R. Shmuel b. Nachmani said in R. Yonatan's name: Whoever says that Reuven sinned is making a mistake. For it says [in the same verse], "Jacob had twelve sons," which teaches us that all of Jacob's sons were equal [in righteousness]. [The Gemara asks:] But what do you do with the verse, "Reuven lived with Bilhah, his father's concubine"? [The Gemara answers:] This verse teaches us that he moved his father's bed [and placed it in Leah's tent],[89] and the verse considers that as if he had lived with her. It was taught in a *Baraita*: R. Shimon b. Elazar said: That righteous man [Reuven] was saved from that sin [he never committed that sin] and this act never happened. Is it possible that someone whose descendants will stand on Mount Eival and proclaim, "Cursed is he that lives with his father's wife" (Deuteronomy 27:20), should do such a thing himself?

[The Gemara asks:] If so, how do you explain the passage, "Reuven lived with his father's concubine"? (Genesis 35:22). [The answer is:] He stood up for his mother's humiliation. [Please note: The sisters Rachel and Leah were both married to Jacob. Leah was Reuven's mother; Rachel's maidservant was Bilhah.] Reuven said: I could live with the fact that my mother's sister [Rachel] was a rival to my mother. But that [Bilhah], the maidservant of my mother's sister, should be a rival to my mother, [now that Rachel has died, this I cannot swallow]. Thereupon Reuven took the initiative and changed his father's sleeping arrangements, [moving Jacob's bed from Bilhah's tent into Leah's tent]. Others say: He mixed up two beds, one of the *Shechinah* and the other of his father. [Rashi explains that Jacob prepared a bed for the *Shechinah* in the tents of his four wives, and in the tent where he perceived the *Shechinah*, that is where he spent the night.] And so [Jacob admonished Reuven for rearranging the beds, saying, "[Because you were] unstable as water, you will no longer be first. For when you moved your father's beds, you disgraced the *Shechinah* that went up on my bed" (Genesis 49:4).

THE TWO SONS OF ELI

[A superficial reading of the text of 1 Samuel 2:22, stating that Eli's sons "lay with the women that did service at the entrance of the Tent of Meeting" may convey the impression that they committed sinful acts.] R. Shmuel b. Nachmani said in R. Yonatan's name: Whoever says that the sons of Eli sinned is making a mistake. For it says, "Chofni and Pinchas, the two sons of Eli, were priests of God there" (1 Samuel 1:3). He agrees with Rav who says that Pinchas [the son of Eli] never sinned. Now, since in the verse Chofni is equated with Pinchas, we can say: Just as Pinchas did not sin, so Chofni did not sin either. [The Gemara asks:] If so, how do you explain the passage, "How they [the sons of Eli] com-

mitted adultery with the women" (ibid. 2:22)? [The Gemara answers:] Because they delayed their bird-offerings[90] so that the women did not return home to their husbands until they were certain that their offerings had been sacrificed, Scripture considers it as if they had violated the women.

[The Gemara elaborates:] We learned before that Rav said: Pinchas [the son of Eli] did not sin, for it says, "Achiyah son of Achituv, the brother of Ichavod who was the son of Pinchas, the son of Eli, the priest of God" (ibid. 14:3). Now, is it possible that Pinchas committed the grave sin of adultery, and Scripture would trace his grandson Achiyah's lineage to him? Look, it says, "God will leave to a person who does this [commit adultery] no descendants dwelling in the tents of Jacob and presenting offerings to the Lord of Hosts" (Malachi 2:12). [The Gemara now expounds this verse:] If this [adulterous] person is a Yisrael [not a *kohen*], he will not have a teacher who is sharp [*er*], and he will not have a descendant who will be able to answer [*onah*] among the students; if he is a *kohen*, he will not have a son who will bring an offering in the Bet Hamikdash. [So how could Pinchas have committed these sins and have a grandson Achiya who was a respectable *kohen*?] You must conclude, therefore, that Pinchas did not sin.

[The Gemara asks:] But it says, "How they lay with women" (1 Samuel 2:22). [The Gemara answers:] *Yishkevun* is written without a *vav* and can be read *yishkevon*, which translates "*he* lay" [only Chofni]. [The Gemara asks:] But it says, [Eli said:] "Don't, my *sons*! It is no favorable report I hear" (ibid. 2:24). R. Nachman b. Yitzchak said: We should read this not as *banai* "my sons", but as *b'ni*, "my son" [in the singular, meaning only the son Chofni]. [The Gemara asks:] But it says, *maavirim* "you [plural] are causing the Jewish people to transgress," [which is an indication that Pinchas also sinned]. Said R. Huna b. R. Yehoshua: It is written *maaviram*, "*he* causes them to transgress," [only Chofni—not Pinchas—sinned]. [The Gemara asks:] But it says, "Now Eli's *sons* were scoundrels" (ibid. 2:12). [The Gemara answers:] Because Pinchas should have admonished his brother Chofni for his sins but he did not, Scripture considers it as if he too had sinned. [This contradicts R. Shmuel b. Nachmani's opinion, which said above that both brothers did not sin (*Tosafot*).]

SAMUEL'S SONS

(56a) Rabbi Shmuel b. Nachmani said in R. Yonatan's name: Whoever says that the sons of [the prophet] Samuel sinned [by taking bribes and distorting justice] is making a mistake. For it says, "When Samuel grew old . . . but his sons did not follow in his ways" (1 Samuel 8:1,3). It is true that they did not follow in his [saintly] ways, but they did not sin either. [The Gemara asks:] If so, how do you explain the passage,

"They were bent on gain, they accepted bribes, and they subverted justice" (ibid.)? [The Gemara answers:] That means that they did not act like their father. For the righteous Samuel used to travel to all the places in Eretz Yisrael and judge the people in their town, as it says, "Each year he made the rounds of Bethel, Gilgal, and Mitzpah, and acted as judge over Israel" (ibid. 7:16). But his sons did not do that. They stayed in their own city, [and made people who had lawsuits come to them], in order to increase the fees of their clerks and court secretaries. [In other words, they were not corrupt, but they did establish an expensive bureaucracy.]

[The evaluation of the character of Samuel's sons] hinges on the following controversy between two *Tanna'im*: It says, "They were bent on gain." R. Meir said: [They were Levites,] and they brazenly demanded their portions of the tithes that go to the Levites. [Usually the Levi waits until the Yisrael gives him the tithe, because the Yisrael has the option to give it to any Levi he chooses. But the sons of Samuel took unfair advantage of their position to demand the tithes outright. But this is not considered taking bribes or subverting justice (Rashi).] R. Yehudah said: They forced people to sell their merchandise for them and give them the profits, [and that *is* akin to taking bribes and distortion of justice, because if these people had a court case the son of Shmuel would favor them]. R. Akiva said: They took a greater portion of the tithes than was coming to them [but that is not regarded as taking bribes]. R. Yose said: They took their gifts of tithes by force [depriving the Yisrael of his option to give the tithe to whomever he chooses, but this was not considered as taking bribes or subverting justice].

DAVID AND BATHSHEBA

R. Shmuel b. Nachmani said in R. Yonatan's name: Whoever says that David sinned [with Bathsheba, and who claims that David lived with Bathsheba before she was divorced from her husband Uriah] is making a mistake. For it says, "David was successful in all his undertakings, for God was with him" (1 Samuel 18:14). [R. Shmuel b. Nachmani asks rhetorically;] Is it possible that later in his life he should stumble into such a sin, and earlier in his life the *Shechinah* should have been with him? [No, that is impossible.] [The Gemara asks:] If so, [if he did not sin with Bathsheba, but in fact, lived with her after she had already received a valid *get*[91] from her husband], how do you interpret [the words of the prophet Nathan who chastised David] and said, "Why then have you flouted the word of God to do what is evil in His eyes?" (2 Samuel 12:9). [The Gemara answers:] David wanted to do evil, but he did not. Rav said: Rebbi (Rabbi Yehudah Hanassi),[92] who is a descendant of David, is trying to defend David by interpreting the verse in his favor. Rebbi expounds the passage, "Why then have you flouted the word of God

to do what is evil in His eyes."—The "to do what is evil" mentioned here is different than all the "to do what is evil" mentioned elsewhere in the Torah. Wherever it says in the Torah, "to do what is evil" it is written as "and he did," but here it is written as "to do." This means that David intended to do evil, but did not.

[The Gemara continues to expound Nathan's words of reproof:] Nathan said, "You have put Uriah the Hittite[93] to the sword." [The implication is: True, he was guilty of rebelling against the king's authority], but you should have had him tried him in the Sanhedrin [Court], and you did not. [Nathan further said:] "You took his wife and made her your wife." [The implication is: You had a full right to marry this woman because she had already received a valid *get*]. For R. Shmuel b. Nachmani said in R. Yonatan's name: Whoever went to war in David's army would send a [conditional] *get* to his wife [which would take effect retroactively if the husband died in battle].[94]

Since Uriah in fact fell in the war, the *get* went into effect retroactively from the time Batsheba received it. Therefore, when David lived with Bathsheba she was an unmarried woman (Rashi, *Tosafot*)]. [How do we know that every soldier wrote a *get* to his wife?] For it says, [Jesse said to his young son David when he went to visit his brothers at the front], "Take these ten cheeses [as a gift] to the captain of their thousand. Find out how your brothers are and take their *arubah* [bond]." What is the meaning of "take their *arubah*"? R. Yosef learned: David was told to take from them the thing that will cancel the marriage bond between husband and wife, [meaning a *get*]. [Which proves that soldiers would send to their wives a conditional *get*.]

[Nathan further said to David:] You have killed [Uriah the Hittite] with the sword of the Ammonites (2 Samuel 12:9). [What does that mean?]—Just as you will not be punished if the Ammonites kill with their swords, so will you not be punished for the death of Uriah the Hittite. Why not? Because Uriah rebelled against the authority of King David, [and a person who defies the King deserves the death penalty. Because when Uriah came home from the battlefront, and David told him to go home and wash up, he did not go]. Uriah said to David, "My master Joab and Your Majesty's men are camped in the open; how can I go home and eat and drink and be with my wife?" (ibid 11:11). [Uriah rebelled by referring to Joab as "my master" in the presence of the King (Rashi), or because he disobeyed the King's order to go home and wash up (*Tosafot*).]

[The Gemara continues:] Rav said: When you examine the life of David you find no shortcoming other than "the matter of Uriah the Hittite" (1 Kings 15:5) [whose case he failed to bring before the Sanhedrin for adjudication. But David did not sin with Bathsheba (Rashi)].

DID KING DAVID LISTEN TO SLANDER OR DIDN'T HE?

Abaye Keshisha (the elder) found a contradiction in Rav's statements: Did Rav really say [that David's only sin was that he failed to have Uriah condemned to death by the Sanhedrin]? But Rav said [that David was also guilty of the sin of] listening to and accepting slander. The difficulty remains unresolved.

[The Gemara now focuses on this last statement.] Rav said: David listened to and accepted slander, for it says, [David inquired if there were any descendants left of Saul to whom he could do favors for the sake of his friend Jonathan. He found Tziva, a servant of the House of Saul who told him that there still was one son of Jonathan named Mefiboshet whose feet were lame]. "The king asked Tziva, 'Where is he?' And Tziva said to the king, 'He is in the house of Machir the son of Ammiel, in Lo-devar'" (2 Samuel 9:4) [By saying Lo-devar, which means "without content," Tziva slandered Mefiboshet, implying that Mefiboshet was not a Torah scholar (Rashi).] It says further, "King David had him brought from the house of Machir son of Ammiel, *miLo-devar*, "from Lo-devar" (ibid. 5) [*miLo-devar* can be read as *malei davar*, meaning, "full of substance." Thus, David found Mefiboshet to be a great Torah scholar, and he recognized that Tziva was a liar and a slanderer]. Now, let's see. David realized that Tziva was a liar; then, when Tziva maligned Mefiboshet a second time, why did David accept his defamation?

[The Gemara now relates the circumstances surrounding the second case of slander.] [In the wake of Absalom's rebellion against David, his father, David was forced to flee from Jerusalem. On his travels he met Tziva, the servant of the House of King Saul who generously supplied him with food and wine.] It says, "The king asked Tziva, 'And where is your master's son?' [meaning Mefiboshet]. 'He is staying in Jerusalem,' Tziva replied to the king, 'for he thinks, now [that Absalom's rebellion is about to succeed] that the House of Israel will give him back the throne of [Saul] his grandfather'" (ibid. 16:3). [Tziva thus maliciously and slanderously implied that Mefiboshet was looking forward to the day that David would be forced to abdicate the throne.] And how do we know that David accepted this libelous accusation? Because it says, "The king said to Tziva, 'All that belongs to Mefiboshet is now yours!'[95] And Tziva replied, 'I bow low. Your Majesty is most gracious to me'" (2 Samuel 16:4). [The fact that David rewarded Tziva is proof of Rav's contention that David accepted and believed his slanderous reports.]

But Shmuel said: David did not accept slander. [He did not believe Tziva's slanderous tale] until he himself noticed things about Mefiboshet's behavior that made it obvious that Tziva was telling the truth. For it says, [that after the collapse of the rebellion and Absalom's death, David returned triumphantly to Jerusalem, his monarchy once again firmly established. It was then that] "Mefiboshet, the grandson of Saul, also came down to meet the king. He had not pared his toenails or trimmed his mustache or washed his clothes from the day that the king left until the day he returned safe" (ibid. 19:25). [His unkempt appearance could be interpreted as a sign of mourning David's return and bemoaning his own dashed hopes of gaining the throne, which would corroborate Tziva's accusation. Or the reason for Mefiboshet's disheveled look could be that he was waiting for David's official installation, at which time he would attend to his appearance.]

And it says further, "When he came to Jerusalem to meet the king, the king asked him, 'Why didn't you come with me [into exile], Mefiboshet?' [David wanted to determine if Tziva's accusation was true.] He replied, 'My lord the king, my own servant deceived me. I planned to saddle my donkey and ride on it and join Your Majesty [but Tziva ran off with the donkey, so that I would have to walk on foot which I cannot do (*Maharsha*)]—for I am lame. (56b) [Tziva] has slandered me to my lord the king. But my lord the king is like an angel of God, [and you know that I speak the truth]; do as you see fit. For all the members of my father's family deserved only death from my lord the king; yet you set your servant among those who ate at your table. What right have I to appeal further to Your Majesty?' The king said to him, 'You need not speak further.' [But David still had doubts. After all, Mefiboshet had no witnesses. Therefore he said,] 'I decree that you and Tziva shall divide the property.' And Mefiboshet said to the king, 'Let him take it all, as long as my lord the king has come safe'" (2 Samuel 19:25–30).

[The Gemara reveals the intent of Mefiboshet's words.] This is what [Mefiboshet] said to David: I have anxiously hoped for your return home. But since you treat me this way, I have no complaints against you, but against Him who restored [the monarchy to] you in peace. [This confirmed Tziva's accusation that Mefiboshet mourned David's return.] This is in line with the verse, "And the son of Jonathan was Meriv-baal" (1 Chronicles 8:34). Was then his name Meriv-Baal? We know that his name was Mefiboshet! But because he started a fight [*merivah*] with his *baal*, master [meaning, David], a Heavenly Voice came forth saying: You quarreler and the son of a quarreler! He was called "quarreler," as we mentioned above. He was called "son of a quarreler" as it says, "Saul advanced to the city of Amalek and he quarreled in the valley" (1 Samuel 15:5). R. Manni says: [That means] he quarreled about the subject of the valley. [When God told Saul to slay the Amalekites, Saul said: If the Torah decreed that because of one murdered man a heifer should have its neck broken in the valley,[96] then surely it is wrong to kill so many Amalekites! Thus Saul quarreled with God about his decree (*Yoma* 22b).]

[We learned at the beginning of this segment that according to Rav, David did accept slander. Now the Gemara tells us the calamities that followed in the wake of this failing.]

Rav Yehudah said in Rav's name: When David said to Mefiboshet: You and Tziva divide the land, a Heavenly Voice came forth and proclaimed: Rechav'am (Rehoboam) and Yerav'am (Jeroboam) will divide the kingdom.[97] Rav Yehudah said in Rav's name: If David had not listened to slander, the kingdom of the House of David would never have been divided, Israel would not have worshiped idols, and we would not have been exiled from our country. [The punishment for David's acceptance of slander was the division of the kingdom; this, in turn, led to the idolatry initiated by Yerav'am, who set up two golden calves as idols; the punishment for idolatry was exile.]

KING SOLOMON

R. Shmuel b. Nachmani said in R. Yonatan's name: Whoever says that Solomon sinned [through idolatry] is making a mistake, for it says, "[Solomon] was not as wholeheartedly devoted to the Lord his God as his father David had been" (1 Kings 11:4). It is true that he was not as wholeheartedly devoted to God as his father had been, but he did not sin. [The Gemara asks:] But how are we to interpret the verse, "In his old age, his wives turned away Solomon's heart" (ibid.)? [The Gemara answers:] This can be explained according to R. Natan, for R. Natan pointed out a contradiction between two verses: One verse says, "In his old age, his wives turned away Solomon's heart," but another verse says, "He was not as wholeheartedly devoted to the Lord his God as his father had been," suggesting that he was not as pious as his father, but he did not sin?

[The Gemara answers:] This is the intent of the verses: In his old age, his wives turned away his heart to go after other gods, but he did not go. [The Gemara challenges this answer:] But it says, "At that time, Solomon would build [yivneh] a high place for Kemosh the abomination of Moab (1 Kings 11:7)? [The Gemara answers:] [The use of yivneh instead of the more common banah, built,] implies that he wanted to build but did not. If so, [what about the verse], "At that time Joshua built [yivneh] an altar to God" (Joshua 8:30), [does this also mean that] he wanted to build but did not? No. He most certainly did build it. So here too, it means that [Solomon] actually built it [proof that Solomon sinned, and the Gemara's question still stands].

[The Gemara answers:] But we can prove from the following Baraita [that Solomon did not sin]: Rabbi Yose said: It says, [The righteous King Yoshiahu (Josiah) began cleansing the Land of Judah of idol worship, and] "The king [Yoshiahu] also defiled the [pagan] high places facing Jerusalem to the south of the Mount of Destruction, which King Solomon of Israel had built for Ashterot, the abomination of the Sidonians" (2 Kings 23:13). [Asks R. Yose:] Now, is it possible that Assa came and did not destroy them, then Yehoshafat, and he did not destroy them, until Yoshiyahu came and destroyed them! [Why does Scripture give only Yoshiyahu the credit for destroying them?[98]]

Of course, Assa and Yehoshafat destroyed all idols in Eretz Yisrael. [The intent of the verse is] to compare the former [the building of Solomon] to the latter [Yoshiahu's destruction of idolatry]. Just as the destruction of the idols is attributed to Yoshiahu for glory [although he destroyed only those idols that were erected after Yehoshafat's death], so it is in the case of Solomon, although he did not build the pagan shrines, it is attributed to him for shame [because he did not stop his wives from worshipping idols. But at any rate, Solomon did *not* build the pagan shrines].

[The Gemara objects:] But it says, "Solomon did what was displeasing to God"? [So you see, he did transgress!] [The Gemara answers:] Because Solomon should have restrained his wives but he did not, Scripture considers it as though he had sinned, [but he did not actually sin].

Rav Yehudah said in Shmuel's name: That righteous Solomon would have been better off working as a paid janitor in a pagan house of worship, only that it should not be said about him, "He did what was displeasing to God."

Rav Yehudah said in Shmuel's name: When Solomon married Pharaoh's daughter she brought him a thousand different musical instruments. She explained to him: This we use in the worship of this idol, that in the worship of that idol, and he did not stop her.

Rav Yehudah said in Shmuel's name: When Solomon married Pharaoh's daughter, the angel Gabriel came down and drove a post into the ocean. In the course of time, sediment collected around the post [and eventually an island was formed]. It was on this island that the great city of Rome was built [whose people oppressed the Jewish people. [The underlying idea of this allegory is that by marrying Pharaoh's daughter, Solomon planted the seeds of the destruction of the Bet Hamikdash and the ensuing exile.]

We learned in a Baraita: On the day that Yerav'am placed the two golden calves, one in Bethel and the other in Dan, a hut was built [on that sandbank in the ocean], and this developed into Greek Italy.

KING YOSHIYAHU (JOSIAH)

R. Shmuel b. Nachmani said in R. Yochanan's name: Whoever says that Yoshiyahu (Josiah) sinned is making a mistake. For it says [about Yoshiyahu], "He did what was pleasing to God, and he followed all the ways of his ancestor David" (2 Kings 22:2). [The Gemara asks:] If so, how do you interpret, "There was no king like him before who returned [*shav*] to God with all his heart and soul and resources" (ibid. 23:25)? [Which implies that he sinned before he repented.] [The Gemara answers:] This teaches you that he corrected every judgment he made from the time he was eight years old until he reached the age of eighteen [he became king and acted as judge when he was eight years old (ibid. 22:1). When he reached the age of eighteen, a Torah scroll was found (ibid. 22:8). He began to study its written and oral laws and realized that all his verdicts had been wrong (Rashi)]. He then refunded to the owners the amounts they had paid as a result of his incorrect verdicts [and this is the meaning of *shav*, he returned]. Now you might say that he took from the one [to whom he wrongly had assigned the money] and gave it to the one [he had unjustly forced to pay]. Therefore it says, "with all his resources," to tell you that he refunded from his own money.

Now, R. Shmuel b. Nachmani disagrees with Rav. For Rav said: There was no greater *baal teshuvah*[99] than Yoshiahu in his generation and a certain person in our generation; and who is that? Abba the father of R. Yirmiyah b. Abba, and some say, Acha, the brother of Abba the father of R. Yirmiyah b. Abba, (for a Master said that R. Abba and Acha were brothers). R. Yosef said: There is another great *baal teshuvah* in our generation. And who is that? Ukvan b. Nechemiah, the *Resh Galuta* (the Exilarch). He is known as "Natan, the man with the fiery sparks." [He began to emit a radiant glow when an angel touched him when his *teshuvah* was accepted, or because an angel took hold of a lock of his hair (Rashi).] R. Yosef said: I once was sitting at a lecture and dozed off, and I saw in a dream how an angel stretched out his hand and received him.

GOLDEN JERUSALEM

(59a) [When going out into the street on *Shabbat*, a woman may wear jewelry and accessories, since this is not considered carrying. The Mishnah lists several things the Rabbis forbid her to wear, for fear that she might remove them to show them to a friend, and meanwhile she will be carrying them in the street on *Shabbat*.]

The Mishnah states: [On *Shabbat*] a woman may not go out wearing "a golden city." The Gemara inquires: What does "a golden city" mean? Rabbah b. Bar Chanah said in R. Yochanan's name: It refers to a "golden Jerusalem," [a piece of gold jewelry on which the city of Jerusalem was engraved], like the one R. Akiva made for his wife.[100]

CALAMITY IN A CAVE

(60a) The Mishnah states: [On *Shabbat*] a person may not go out wearing a [wooden] sandal reinforced with iron pegs. [The Gemara asks:] What is the reason? Shmuel said: It was toward the end of the period of religious persecution that a group of people were hiding in a cave [to avoid being forced into idol worship]. The group decreed: Whoever wants to enter our cave may enter, but no one may leave the cave. [They were afraid that enemy soldiers lurking outside might spot the person leaving, and discover the cave (Rashi).] It happened that one of them had his sandals on backward, [and, noticing his footprints,] the others thought that one of them had left the cave. They imagined that he had been caught by the enemies who now were about to pounce on them. Panic-stricken they began to press against each other, [stepping on each other with the iron pegs on their sandals]. They killed more of each other than their enemies had slain of them.

R. Ila'i b. Elazar, [offering a different version], said: They were holed up in the cave, when they heard a noise coming from above the cave. Thinking that the enemy was coming, they pressed against each other. They killed more of each other than the enemy had slain of them. Rami b. Yechezkel, [offering another version], said: They were sitting in a synagogue when they heard a noise coming from behind the synagogue. Thinking that the enemy was coming, they pressed against each other and killed more of each other than the enemy had slain of them. At that time it was decreed that a person should not go out [on *Shabbat*] with iron pegs on his sandals. [The Gemara asks:] If the reason is [that the pegs might hurt people], it should be forbidden on weekdays too? [The Gemara answers:] [It is forbidden only on *Shabbat*] because the tragic incident happened on *Shabbat*, [and the decree was meant to commemorate it].

RIGHT BEFORE LEFT

(61a) We learned in a *Baraita*: When you put on your shoes, you should put on your right shoe first and then your left one. When you take them off, you should take off the left shoe first and then the right. [Since the right side is stronger, you should accord it more honor. By taking off your left shoe first you are honoring the right because your right shoe stays on your foot longer (Rashi).] When you wash, you should wash your right hand first and then your left. When you anoint yourself with oil, you should first anoint the right side and then the left. But if you want to anoint your entire body you should anoint your head first, for the head is the king of all the limbs.

METHOD FOR TALMUD STUDY

(63a) R. Kahana said: By the time I was eighteen years old I had studied the entire Talmud, yet I did not know until today that a verse cannot be taken out of its plain meaning, [meaning that even when a verse is interpreted metaphorically, we still must understand it according to its simple meaning]. What is R. Kahana trying to tell us by this statement? That a person should begin by learning a large portion of the Talmud quickly even if he does not understand it that well, then he should review it and try to gain a full understanding.

THE PROPER ATTITUDE
FOR TORAH STUDY

R. Yirmiyah said in R. Elazar's name: If two scholars sharpen each other's mind by debating *Halachah*, the Holy One, blessed be He, helps them to reach the right halachic decisions, for it says, "In your glory [vahadarecha] win success" (Psalm 45:5). Don't read *vahadarecha* but *vachadadecha*, "your sharpness." [If you are sharpening one another, you will be successful in arriving at the right decision.] And that's not all, but they will rise to prominence, for it says, "ride on triumphantly" (ibid.) Now you might think that this is true even if [a person studies Torah] not for its own sake, therefore the verse continues, "in the cause of truth," [only if he learns Torah for its own sake]. You might think that this is so even if he becomes conceited, therefore it says [in the same verse], "and humility and righteousness." But if they do this, they will deserve to receive the Torah, which was given by the right Hand,[101] as it says, "It will teach you the awesome things of Your right Hand," (ibid.) [which refers to the Torah].

R. Nachman b. Yitzchak said: They will receive the things that have been said about the Torah of the right hand. [What does that mean?] For Rava b. R. Shila said—others say, R. Yosef b. Chama—in R. Sheshet's name: What is the meaning of the verse, "In its [the Torah's] right hand there is length of days; in its left, riches and honor" (Proverbs 3:16): should we say that in its right hand there is only length of days, but not riches and honor? [Certainly the Torah confers long life as well as riches and honor.] But to those who study the Torah "with their right hand" it confers long life, and surely riches and honor; but those who study the Torah "with their left hand" will enjoy riches and honor, but not long life. [Studying Torah "with the right hand" means probing its words with great intensity, just as the right hand is the stronger one. Or it refers to people who study the Torah for its own sake. Studying Torah "with the left hand" signifies the opposite of these. (Rashi).]

R. Yirmiyah said in the name of R. Shimon b. Lakish: When two scholars are congenial with each other in their halachic discussions, the Holy One, blessed be He, listens to them, for it says, "Those who revere God have been speaking [nidberu] to one another. God listened and noted it" (Malachi 3:16). And speech [dibbur] denotes "leading one another in *halachah*." For it says, "He will lead [yadbeir] nations under us" (Psalm 47:3).

What is the meaning of "and who think about his Name"? (Malachi 3:16). Said R. Ammi: If someone only thinks of doing a mitzvah, but is unavoidably prevented from doing it, Scripture considers it as if he had done it.

R. Chinena b. Idi said: Whoever does a mitzvah as it is written in the Torah [with the right intention], will not hear bad news, for it says, "Someone who keeps the *mitzvot* will not know from evil" (Ecclesiastes 8:5). R. Assi—others say R. Chanina—said: Even if the Holy One, blessed be He, makes a [bad] decree, he [the person who keeps the *mitzvot*] is able to annul it, for it says, "The word of the King is the rule, and who can tell him what to do?" (ibid. 4). And immediately afterward it says, "Someone who keeps the *mitzvot* will not know from evil." [Even though God's word is the rule, the one who keeps the *mitzvot* can tell God to annul the decree (Rashi).]

R. Abba said in the name of R. Shimon b. Lakish: When two Torah scholars listen to each other's views in *halachah*, the Holy One, blessed be He, listens to their voices, as it says, "You who are sitting in the gardens [i.e., in the study halls], you are friends who are listening to one another, please let me hear your voices" (Song of Songs 8:13). But if they do not listen to one another they cause the *Shechinah* to move away from the Jewish people, for it says [immediately following this], "Go away, my Beloved," (ibid. 14).[102]

R. Abba also said in the name of R. Shimon b. Lakish: When two students [who do not have a teacher] become study partners in *halachah* [and try to learn as best they can], the Holy One, blessed be He, loves them, as it says, "and his banner over me was love" (ibid. 2:4) [i.e., when students gather under one banner, God loves them]. Rava said: As long as they have a basic knowledge of the subject, and as long as there is no teacher in town from whom to learn.

[Having cited a teaching of R. Abba in the name of R. Shimon b. Lakish, the Gemara proceeds to cite a number of unrelated teachings by those *Amora'im*.]

R. Abba also said in the name of R. Shimon b. Lakish: Someone who lends money to a needy person is greater than someone who performs *tzedakah*, [and actually gives him money. It is less of an embarrassment for a person to accept a loan than to accept charity]. And someone who gives money to a poor man with which to do business and enters into a partnership with him, that is the greatest form of *tzedakah*, [because he enables the poor man to earn a living].

R. Abba also said in the name of R. Shimon b. Lakish: Even if a Torah scholar is vengeful and bears a grudge like a snake, nonetheless you should wrap him around your waist, [stay close to him, because you will learn from him]. [On the other hand], if an *am haaretz* [ignorant fellow] appears to be a pious man, don't live in his neighborhood [because his piety is flawed, and you may end up emulating him (Rashi).]

DON'T KEEP A VICIOUS DOG

R. Kahana said in the name of R. Shimon b. Lakish— some say, R. Assi said in the name of R. Shimon b. Lakish—others say, R. Abba said in the name of R.

Shimon b. Lakish: Anyone who raises a vicious dog in his house keeps kindness away from his house, [because poor people are afraid to enter the house to ask for *tzedakah* (Rashi)], as it says, "He who denies [*lamos*] (63b) kindness to his friend" (Job 6:14). [He expounds:] In Greek a dog is called *lamos* [thus he translates: Through the dog he is denying kindness to his friend]. R. Nachman b. Yitzchak said: He also throws off the fear of Heaven from himself, for the verse continues, "he is abandoning the fear of the Almighty" (ibid). [The Gemara cites a story as an illustration:]

There was a [pregnant] woman who went to a house to [use the oven] to bake. The dog barked at her, [and frightened her], causing the fetus to be torn loose. The householder said to her, "Don't be afraid. His sharp teeth and his claws have been removed." "Take your comforting advice and throw it to the thorns," she shot back. "[It's too late.] I feel that I have miscarried already."

R. Huna expounded: What is the meaning of the verse, "O youth, enjoy yourself while you are young! Let your heart lead you to enjoyment in the days of your youth. Follow the desires of your heart and the glances of your eyes—but know well that God will call you to account for all such things" (Ecclesiastes 11:9). [He explains: We should split this verse.] The first clause ["Enjoy yourself . . . follow the desires of your heart" are the words of the *yetzer hara* (the evil inclination). The second clause, ["Know well that God will call you to account"] are the words of the *yetzer tov* (the good inclination). Resh Lakish said: The first clause refers to Torah study, [rejoice and be happy in your learning when you are young]. The second clause refers to good deeds, ["Know well . . ."] means that you should know that you will be judged whether you fulfilled that which you have learned].

(69b) R. Akiva once made a banquet for his son and over every glass [of wine] that he poured he offered a toast, "Wine and health to our Rabbis! Wine and health to our Rabbis and their students!"

THE WAYFARER FORGOT WHEN IT IS *SHABBAT*

(69b) If someone is traveling in the desert and does not know what day is *Shabbat*, he should count six days [from the day he realizes that he forgot when it is *Shabbat*] and observe the seventh. Chiya b. Rav said: He should observe *Shabbat* on the first day after he realizes it and then count six weekdays. [Asks the Gemara:] Regarding what essential point do they disagree? [The Gemara answers:] One Rabbi holds that he should follow the order of the world's Creation [where *Shabbat* came after six days of labor]; the other Rabbi holds that it should be done as in the case of Adam [who was created on the sixth day, so that his first full day was *Shabbat*].

WHAT IS AN *AMGUSHA*?

(75a) R. Zutra b. Tuviah said in Rav's name: If someone pulls the thread of a seam on *Shabbat* [and thereby brings the two ends tightly together], he is required to bring a sin offering [because this is considered sewing[103]]. And if someone learns even only one thing [even a Torah insight] from an *amgusha* [a pagan priest], he deserves to die. And if someone is able to calculate the cycles of the seasons and the constellations but does not do so, you may not converse with him.

What is an *amgusha*? Rav and Shmuel have different opinions about it. One says it is a sorcerer; the other says a blasphemer. It can be proved that it is Rav who asserts that it is a blasphemer, for R. Zutra b. Tuvya said in Rav's name: If someone learns even only one thing from an *amgusha* he deserves to die. Now, if you think that an *amgusha* is a sorcerer, [why should a person who learns from him deserve death?] After all, it says, "Do not learn to *do* the revolting practices of those nations" (Deuteronomy 18:9), [from which you can infer] that you may learn from them in order to understand and to judge sorcery [so that you will be able to determine whether a false prophet is a sorcerer (Rashi)]. [We must conclude therefore that it is Rav who holds that an *amgusha* is a blasphemer.] This proves it.

LEARN ASTRONOMY

R. Shimon b. Pazzi said in R. Yehoshua b. Levi's name, who quoted Bar Kappara: A person who knows how to calculate the cycles of the seasons and the constellations but does not do so, about him it says, "They never give a thought to the plan of God, and take no note of the work of His hands" (Isaiah 5:12). R. Shmuel b. Nachmani said in R. Yochanan's name: From where do we know that it is a person's duty to calculate the cycles of the seasons and the constellations? Because it says, "Since this is your wisdom and understanding in the eyes of the nations" (Deuteronomy 4:6). What kind of wisdom is recognized by the nations of the world? The science of astronomical cycles and the stellar constellations.

REMEDIES AND ANTIDOTES

(77b) Rav Yehudah said in Rav's name: The Holy One, blessed be He, did not create a single thing in His world without purpose. And so he created the snail as a remedy to place on a wound [of an animal]. He created the fly as a cure for the sting of a bee. [If you grind up a fly and place it on a bee bite, it will bring relief (Rashi).] What is the purpose of mosquitos? [Crushed] mosquitos are a remedy for snake bite. Snakes were created as a remedy for boils. A [crushed] spider is an antidote for a scorpion bite. [The Gemara asks:] How do you heal a boil with a snake? [The Gemara answers:] You take one black snake and one white snake, you cook the two dead snakes, then you rub them onto the boil

FIVE KINDS OF FEAR

The Rabbis taught: There are five kinds of fear in the world, whereby a weak creature inspires fear in a strong one: the fear the *mafgia* casts over the lion [*mafgia* is a small animal that frightens the lion with its loud shriek]; the fear a mosquito casts on the elephant [the mosquito enters the trunk of an elephant and terrifies it]; the fear of the spider on the scorpion [by entering the ear of the scorpion]; the fear the swallow casts on the mighty eagle [by getting under its wings and hampering its flight]; the fear of the *kilbit* [a small fish] on the Leviathan [a huge fish, by going into its ear].. Rav Yehudah said in Rav's name: Where do we find a verse to support this? "[God] causes the weak one to cast fear on the strong one" (Amos 5:9).

QUESTIONS AND ANSWERS ABOUT BIOLOGY

R. Zeira met [his master,] Rav Yehudah standing at the door of his father-in-law's house and saw that he [Rav Yehudah] was very cheerful, and if he would ask him all the secrets of the world he would tell him. R. Zeira said to Rav Yehudah: Why is it that the goats walk at the head of the herd in front of the sheep? Replied Rav Yehudah: It is consistent with the creation of the world, where first there was darkness and afterward there was light. [Goats are usually black; sheep are usually white.] R. Zeira continued to ask: Why is the hind part of a sheep covered with a broad tail, and why are the hind parts of goats uncovered? [Goats have thin tails.] [Rav Yehudah answered:] The animal with which we cover ourselves [the sheep whose wool we use to cover ourselves] is also covered; the animal [the goat] whose hair we do not use to cover ourselves, is uncovered.

He asked: Why is it that a camel has a short tail? [The answer is:] Because it eats thorns, [and if its tail were long it would get caught in the thorns]. [He asked:] Why does an ox have a long tail?—Because it grazes in the pasture, and it has to chase away the flies with its tail. [He asked:] Why are the feelers of a locust soft?—Because it lives among the willows, and if its feelers were hard they would break against the trees and the locust would go blind. For Shmuel said: If you want to blind a locust, just tear its feelers. [R. Zeira continued questioning:] Why is it that the lower eyelid of the hen closes over the upper eyelid? [Rav Yehudah answered:] Because during the night it rests on high beams, and if its eyelids closed downward, the smoke rising from the room below would blind it.

The Rabbis taught: There are three creatures that grow stronger as they grow older: a fish, a snake, and a pig.

DON'T LECTURE ON KABBALISTIC TOPICS

(80b) A certain man from Galilee happened to visit Babylon. The people there asked him: "Please give us a lecture on *Maasei Merkavah*" [the Works of the Chariot, the mystical first chapter of Ezekiel that deals with the mysteries of the Divine Chariot]. He said to them: "I will lecture you as R. Nechemiah lectured to his colleagues." Thereupon a hornet came out of the wall and stung him on the forehead, and he died. People said, "He brought this on himself; it's his own fault." [He should not have lectured on the mystical Chariot (Rashi).][104]

TOTAL REJECTION OF IDOLATRY

(82a) MISHNAH: Rabbi Akiva said: From where do we know that a person who carries an idol [without actually touching it] becomes unclean, just as a person that carries a *niddah*[105] [without actually touching her][106] becomes unclean? Because it says, "Cast them away [the idols] like a menstruous woman. 'Get out!' you must call to them" (Isaiah 30:22). Just as a *niddah* renders unclean a person that carries her [without touching her], so does an idol render unclean a person carrying it [without touching it].

(82b) GEMARA: Rabba said: The phrase "Cast them away [*tizreim*] like a menstruous woman," means "Separate yourself from [the idols], treat them like a stranger [*zar*]." "'Out!' you must call to them, and don't say, 'Come on in!'" [In other words, you must totally reject idolatry.]

(83b) We have learned: It says, "[After Gideon died, the Israelites] adopted Baal-berit as a god" (Judges 8:33). This refers to Zevuv, the idol of Ekron. This teaches us that everyone made an image of his idol and put it in his bag, and whenever he thought of it he took it out of his bag and embraced and kissed it.

DON'T SKIP A TORAH LECTURE

R. Chanina b. Akavya said: Why did the Rabbis rule that a Jordan riverboat [a small, canoe-like boat] can become unclean? Because it is loaded on dry land and then lowered into the river. [But a ship that stays always in the water does not become unclean.] [This gives rise to the following edifying lesson:] R. Yehudah said in Rav's name: You should never miss a lecture in the *bet midrash*, even for a single hour, [even if you are familiar with the subject matter being discussed, because invariably new aspects will come to the surface. Proof of that is the fact that] the above Mishnah [about the Jordan riverboat] was taught in the *bet midrash* for a number of years, and the reason [why the riverboat is susceptible to uncleanness] was not known until R. Chanina b. Akavya explained it, [and a student who had been absent at that moment would have missed the explanation].

[The Gemara now amplifies on this subject.] R. Yonatan said: A person should never miss a lecture in the *bet midrash* or skip Torah study even on his deathbed, for it says, "This is the Torah, when a man dies in a tent" (Numbers 14:14); even on his deathbed a person should engross himself in the study of the Torah. Resh Lakish said: The words of the Torah endure only with a person [and his descendants] if he makes sacrifices for it, as it says, "This is the Torah, when a man dies in a tent" (ibid.), [i.e., he does not indulge in worldly pleasures (Rif)].

PRE-HISTORIC AGRICULTURISTS

(85a) R. Chiya b. Abba said in R. Yochanan's name: What is meant by the verse, "Do not move your neighbor's boundary marker, which was set in place by the first settlers" (Deuteronomy 19:14)? [The first settlers [of Eretz Yisrael] were the Amorites and the Chivites (Rashi).] The passage means to say: Don't encroach on the boundary the first settlers marked off. [Don't plant too close to your neighbor's boundary, causing the roots of your plants to draw nutrients from his land and deplete it (Rashi).] [The Gemara asks:] What boundary markers did the first settlers put in place? R. Shmuel b. Nachmani said in R. Yochanan's name: It says, "These are the children of Seir the Chorite, inhabitants of the earth" (Genesis 36:20). [The Gemara asks: The verse describes the Chorites as "inhabitants of the earth"], does that mean that all other people are inhabitants of heaven? [The Gemara answers:] "Inhabitants of the earth" means that the Chorites were experts in the science of agriculture. They would be able to say: This piece of land is best suited for planting olive trees, this piece of land is best suited for planting grapevines, and this is best suited for fig trees. And the name *Chori* (Chorites) implies that they smelled the earth, [by transposing the letters of *Chori* you obtain *rei'ach*, "smell"].

[The Gemara asks:] And what about the name Chivi (Chivites)? Replied R. Papa: They would taste the earth like a snake [*chivya*, that eats dust (Genesis 3:14), to determine what would best grow in it]. R. Acha b. Yaakov said: *Chori* signifies that they became freed [*chorin*] of [tilling] their land; [they were driven out by Esau's descendants (Deuteronomy 2:12)].

WHEN DID THE GIVING OF THE TORAH TAKE PLACE?

(86a) R. Ada b. Ahavah said: Moshe went up [Mount Sinai] early in the morning and came down early in the morning. How do we know that he went up early in the morning? Because it says, "Moses got up early in the morning and climbed Mount Sinai" (Exodus 34:4). Therefore, we know that he came down early too, because it says, "Go down. You can then come up along with Aaron" (Exodus 19:24). The descent is compared

to ascent; just as he went up early in the morning, so he came down down early in the morning.

(86b) [Now the Gemara will deal with the question of what day in Sivan the Torah was given.] Our Rabbis taught: On the sixth of Sivan the Ten Commandments were given to the children of Israel. R. Yose said: On the seventh of Sivan. Rava said: [Let's put everything into perspective]. Everyone agrees that they arrived in the wilderness of Sinai on the first of the month [of Sivan], for it says, "On this [*hazeh*] day they came into the wilderness of Sinai" (Exodus 19:1). And elsewhere it says, "This [*hazeh*] month [Nisan] shall be the head month to you" (ibid. 12:1); [Since both verses use the word *hazeh*, we draw an analogy]: Just as in [12:1] the first of the month is meant, so here too [in 19:1] the first of the month is meant.

Furthermore, all agree that the Ten Commandments were given to Israel on *Shabbat*. For [in the Ten Commandments] it says, "Remember the *Shabbat* to keep it holy" (ibid. 20:8), and elsewhere it says, "Moses said to the people, 'Remember this day [as the time] you left Egypt'" (ibid. 13:3). [Moses said this while the Exodus was in progress.] Just as [in 13:3] he spoke on the very day the event was taking place, so too the commandment to keep *Shabbat*, [the fourth is the Ten Commandments], was proclaimed on that very day [on *Shabbat*; proof that the Ten Commandments were given on *Shabbat*]. [So the Rabbis and R. Yose agree that they arrived in the Sinai desert on the first of Sivan, and that the Torah was given on *Shabbat*.] On what point do they differ? They differ as to what day of the week was the first of that month [of Sivan].

[The Gemara now reconstructs the chronology of events.] R. Yose holds that the first of that month was on a Sunday, and on that Sunday Moses told them nothing, because they were exhausted from the journey. On Monday [the second of Sivan] he told them [what their historic mission was going to be, including,] "You will be a kingdom of priests to Me" (ibid. 19:3–6). (87a) On Tuesday [the third of Sivan] he told them to set a boundary around the mountain, [and warned them not to climb the mountain] (ibid. 12). On Wednesday they separated themselves from their wives.

But the Rabbis hold that the first of the month [of Sivan] fell on a Monday. On that Monday Moses did not tell them anything because they were exhausted from the trip. On Tuesday he told them, "You will be a kingdom of priests to Me" (ibid. 19:3–6). On Wednesday he told them to set a boundary around the mountain; and on Thursday they separated themselves from their wives.

An objection was raised: [The verse telling them to separate themselves from their wives] states, "Sanctify them today and tomorrow" (ibid. 10). [Obviously this refers to Thursday and Friday, because the Torah was given on *Shabbat*. This supports the view of the Rabbis,] but it goes against the opinion of R. Yose [who said they separated on Wednesday, thus], according to him, "Today and tomorrow" refers to Wednesday and Thursday. And the Torah was given only on *Shabbat*. What about Friday?] [The Gemara answers:] R. Yose can answer you: Moses added another day on his own. [God ordered the separation for Wednesday and Thursday, but Moses added an extra day, Friday, and God agreed with him.] For we learned in a *Baraita*: Three things Moses did on his own responsibility, and the Holy One, blessed be He, agreed with him: he added one day, [to the two days of separation God had ordained]; he separated from his wife [completely. He began the separation as the rest of the people did, but after the Giving of the Torah he did not go back to his wife (Rashi)], and he broke the Tablets.

[Digressing from the main theme, the Gemara now focuses on the three things Moses did on his own initiative.] "Moses added one day on his own responsibility." [The Gemara asks:] In what verse did he find a basis for adding an extra day? [The Gemara answers:] He expounded the passage, "Sanctify them today and tomorrow" (ibid. 10). He said: "Today" must be like "tomorrow." Just as tomorrow includes the previous night,[107] so today must include the previous night; but the night that preceded Wednesday passed already! Therefore, [the phrase "today and tomorrow"] must mean two days excluding today [Wednesday]. [Asks the Gemara:] And how do we know that the Holy One, blessed be He, agreed with Moses? [The Gemara answers:] Because the *Shechinah* did not come to rest on Mount Sinai until *Shabbat* morning. [If Moses' interpretation would have been wrong, the *Shechinah* would have come down on Friday.]

We learned that Moses separated from his wife on his own authority. [The Gemara asks:] What verse did he interpret [to buttress his action]? [The Gemara answers:] He applied a logical argument to himself. He reasoned: If the children of Israel with whom the *Shechinah* spoke only for a single hour, and established a set time when this was going to happen, yet in spite of that the Torah says, "Keep yourselves in readiness ... Do not come near a woman" [ibid. 19:15], I, with whom the *Shechinah* speaks constantly without a set time, surely [I should separate from my wife, for I never know when the *Shechinah* will speak to me!]. And how do we know that the Holy One, blessed be He, agreed with him? Because it says, "Go tell them to return to their tents"[108] (Deuteronomy 5:27), which is followed by, "You however, must remain here with Me." Others say: Because it says, "With him I speak face to face" (Numbers 12:8).

We learned that Moses shattered the Tablets on his own initiative. [Asks the Gemara:] On what verse did he base his action? [The Gemara answers:] He argued: If, regarding the Pesach sacrifice, which is only one of the 613 *mitzvot*, the Torah says: "No outsider may eat it" (Exodus 12:43) ["Outsider" is interpreted to mean a person who has become estranged from God, and who

has no connection with this one mitzvah], here the entire Torah is being given,[109] and all Israel are apostates [because of the sin of the golden calf], then surely they should not receive the Torah!

And how do we know that the Holy One, blessed be He, agreed with him? Because it says, "[the tablets] that [*asher*] you broke" (ibid. 34:1). Resh Lakish interpreted this to mean: [God said to Moses:] Thank you for breaking them. [The word *asher* is seen as cognate to *ishur*, approval. God approved of it, and praised Moses for breaking them (Rashi).]

[The Gemara now returns to the controversy between the Rabbis and R. Yose, where the Rabbis said that the Torah was given on the 6th of Sivan, and R. Yose said it was given on the 7th of Sivan, and that the first of Sivan fell on Sunday. The Gemara tries to offer proof:] Come and learn: It says, [God told Moses:] "They should be ready for *the* third day [when the Torah will be given]." (Ibid. 19:11.) This presents a difficulty according to R. Yose's view. [He said that they separated from their wives on Wednesday. Then the third day is Friday, and the Torah was not given until *Shabbat*!] [The Gemara answers:] We already said: Moses added an extra day on his own initiative. [Moses interpreted the verse to mean: "Prepare yourselves through three days of separation," i.e., Wednesday, Thursday, and Friday.]

We learned in a *Baraita*: It says, "Moses brought the people's reply back to God" (ibid. 19:8) [that they were ready to accept the Torah], and further it says, "Moses told God the people's response" (ibid. 9). [The response to what?] What did God say to Moses, that Moses, in turn, should convey to the children of Israel? And what answer did the people give to Moses? And what did Moses report to the Almighty? [The Gemara answers:] The second question was [whether the people would accept] the command to set a border around the mountain [and Moses reported to God that they were willing to accept that], so says R. Yose b. R. Yehudah. Rebbi explains: First Moses spelled out the punishment for not adhering to the Torah. [This they accepted], for it says, "Moses brought the people's reply back [*va'yashev*] to God" (ibid.), which denotes things [punishments] that repel [*meshavevim*] a person's mind. But afterward he explained the reward for observing the Torah, for it says, "Moses told [*va'yaggeid*] God the people's response" (ibid.), which means that he told them things [rewards] that draw the heart like a story [*aggadah*]. Others say, [It's the opposite!] First he explained the rewards, for it says, "Moses brought the people's reply back [*va'yashev*] to God," and *va'yashev* suggests words that put a person's mind at ease. Afterward he outlined its punishments, for it says, "Moses told, [*va'yageid*]," and *va'yageid* implies words that are difficult for a person to accept, like wormwood [*gidin*].[110]

[The Gemara returns to the question of when did the Giving of the Torah took place.] [To recapitulate:

All agree that the Giving of the Torah happened on *Shabbat* and that the children of Israel entered the Sinai Desert on the first of Sivan. But according to the Rabbis, that particular *Shabbat* fell on the 6th of Sivan, and thus the first of Sivan was on Monday; R. Yose holds that *Shabbat* was on the 7th of Sivan, and the first of Sivan came out on Sunday.]

[The Gemara now suggests a proof:] Come and learn: We learned in a *Baraita*: The sixth was also the sixth day of the month [Sivan] and also the sixth day of the week [Friday]; this is a difficulty according to the Rabbis, [because they say that the first of Sivan was on Monday, and if that is so, the 6th of Sivan is on *Shabbat*, and not on Friday!]. [The Gemara answers:] This *Baraita* agrees with R. Yose [who holds that the first of Sivan was on Sunday, therefore the 6th Sivan was on Friday].

[The Gemara asks:] What does that first "sixth" [in the *Baraita*] refer to? Rava said: (87b) It was the sixth day of their setting up camp. [On the first of Sivan they pitched their tents, and the sixth day of their encampment was also the sixth day of the month and the sixth day of the week.] R. Acha b. Yaakov said: It was also the sixth day of their traveling [for on the same day that they left Refidim (Exodus 19:2), they arrived in the Sinai Desert]. They disagree about precisely what laws of *Shabbat* the children of Israel received in Marah. ["It was (in Marah) that God taught them a decree and a law" (Exodus 15:25), which is interpreted to mean "certain laws of *Shabbat*."] It says, "Observe the *Shabbat* . . . as God your Lord commanded you," which R. Yehudah expounded in Rav's name: As He commanded you in Marah.

[All agree that they received some teachings about *Shabbat* in Marah], but one Rabbi holds that they were commanded about *Shabbat* in general terms, but not specifically about the prohibition against traveling beyond the *techum*[111] on *Shabbat*; the other Rabbi holds that they were commanded regarding the prohibition against traveling beyond the *techum* on *Shabbat*. [Rava is the Rabbi who asserts that it was the sixth day from their encampment, which fell on Sunday, but they left Refidim on the previous day, which was *Shabbat*. They did travel on *Shabbat* because they had not yet received the law of *techumim*. According to R. Acha b. Yaakov they traveled and encamped on the same day, i.e., Sunday, and did not travel on *Shabbat*, because they had received the law of *techumim* in Marah.]

[The Gemara presents another proof:] Come and learn: The Nisan in which the children of Israel came out of Egypt, the chronology was as follows: on the fourteenth they slaughtered their Pesach sacrifice, on the fifteenth they left Egypt, and on that evening the first-born were slain. [The Gemara asks:] Do you really mean *that* evening? [Are you implying that the death of the first-born happened *after* they left Egypt?] [The Gemara answers:] Say instead: On the previous evening, the first-born were slain, and that day [the

15th of Nisan] was a Thursday. [We must remember that Nisan always has thirty days.] Now, since the 15th of Nisan came out on a Thursday, the first day of Iyar had to be on *Shabbat*. [Note: the month of Iyar has twenty-nine days.] Therefore, the first of Sivan came out on Sunday. This presents a difficulty according to the Rabbis' view [who hold that the first day of Sivan was on Monday]. [The Gemara answers:] The Rabbis will tell you that in that year, Iyar was declared a full month [of thirty days.]

[The Gemara cites another proof:] Come and learn: It says, "In the first month of the second year [of the Exodus], on the first of the month, the Tabernacle was erected" (Exodus 40:17). [In that connection] a Tanna learned: That day took ten crowns [meaning, it was the first day with regard to ten concepts]: It was the first day of Creation, i.e., Sunday; the first day on which the princes brought their sacrifices for the dedication of the Tabernacle (Numbers 7); the first day for *kehunah* (priesthood), [the day on which Aaron and his sons began to officiate as priests]; the first day on which the communal offerings were brought; the first day that a heavenly fire came forth from Heaven [and consumed the offerings on the altar (Leviticus 9:24)]; the first day on which the *kohanim* were restricted to eating the flesh of the sacrifices within the confines of the Tabernacle [whereas before that day, they could eat it anywhere]; the first day that the *Shechinah* began to dwell among the people of Israel; the first day for the priestly blessing of Israel to be given by Aaron (ibid. 9:22); the first day that the prohibition against private altars went into effect; and it is the first of the cycle of months.

Now, since the first of Nisan of that year [the second year after the Exodus] was a Sunday [as mentioned above], that means that in the previous year [the year of the Exodus], the first of Nisan fell on Wednesday. [How do you know that?] For we learned in a *Baraita*: Between one *Shavuot* and another, and between one *Rosh Hashanah* and another there is a difference of only four days [meaning, this year's *Rosh Hashanah* falls four days later in the week than last year's],[112] and in a leap year, the difference is five days.[113] [If, as we said, the first of Nisan of the first year was on Wednesday, and Nisan has thirty days,] it follows that the first of Iyar fell on Friday. [Iyar has only twenty-nine days.] That means that the first of Sivan was on *Shabbat*. This presents a difficulty according to both R. Yose and the Rabbis. [According to R. Yose the first of Sivan was on Sunday, and according to the Rabbis it was on Monday.]

[The Gemara answers: Our calculations assumed that the year is composed of six full months of thirty days and six defective months of twenty-nine days, which gives us 354 days, and a differential of four days.] According to R. Yose's view, in that year, seven months were declared defective [which gives us a total of 353 days for the year and a discrepancy of only three days from one year to the previous year. So, if the first of Nisan of the second year was on Sunday, the year before it fell on Thursday [and since Nisan has thirty days], the first day of Iyar was on *Shabbat*. And since Iyar has twenty-nine days, the first of Sivan fell on Sunday, which is as R. Yose said it should be].

(88a) According to the Rabbis' view, there were eight months of twenty-nine days [which gives us a year of (8x29) + (4x30) = 352 days, and a discrepancy of only two days in the date from year to year. Therefore, if in the second year, the first of Nisan was on Sunday, the previous year the first of Nisan came on Friday, the first of Iyar on Sunday, and the first of Sivan on Monday, exactly as the Rabbis calculated it.]

[Another proof:] Come and learn: We learned in *Seder Olam*[114]: This is the chronology of the events that happened in the month of Nisan in which the children of Israel left Egypt: On the fourteenth day of that month they slaughtered their *Pesach* sacrifice. On the fifteenth day of that Nisan they left Egypt, and that was a Friday. [Now if the 15th was a Friday, obviously the first of Nisan was also a Friday.] And since the first of Nisan was a Friday, the first of Iyar was a Sunday (since Iyar has only twenty-nine days), and the first of Sivan fell on a Monday [which is in line with the Rabbis' calculation], but presents a difficulty according to R. Yose [who said that the first of Sivan was on Sunday]. [The Gemara answers:] R. Yose will tell you that this is consistent with the Rabbis, [but that he disagrees with them].

[The Gemara brings another proof.] Come and learn: R. Yose said: On the second day [after the children of Israel came to Mount Sinai, which was the second day of Sivan], Moses went up the mountain [and heard, "You will be a kingdom of priests and a holy nation to me" (Exodus 19:6)], and he came down [and told the people about their responsibility]. On the third day he went up [and heard the mitzvah of setting a boundary around the mountain], and he came down. On the fourth day he came down and did not go up again [until the Giving of the Torah]. [The Gemara wonders:] Since on the fourth day he did not go up, from where did he come down? [Answers the Gemara: You are right.] On the fourth day he did go up and came down. On the fifth day he built an altar and brought a sacrifice on it (ibid. 24:4). On the sixth day he had no time, [so that he did not go up]. [Why did he have no time?] Isn't it because that was when the Torah was given? [So isn't R. Yose himself telling us that the Torah was given on the 6th day of Sivan, and not on the 7th day?] [The Gemara answers:] No. The reason that Moses had no time was because he had to prepare for *Shabbat*.

[The Gemara brings a final proof.] A certain person from the Galilee expounded before R. Chisda: Blessed be the Merciful One who gave a threefold Torah [the Torah, Prophets, and Writings] to a threefold people [*Kohanim*, *Levi'im*, and *Yisraelim*], through a third-born [Moses, born after Miriam and Aaron],

on the third day [of their separation from their wives], in the third month of the year [Sivan]. [Asks the Gemara:] With whose view does this conform [that the Torah was given on the third day of separation]? [The Gemara answers:] With the Rabbis' view, [because according to R. Yose, the Torah was given on the fourth day after the separation. He said that the mitzvah of separation was given on Wednesday, and the Torah was received on *Shabbat*].

WERE THEY FORCED TO ACCEPT THE TORAH?

It says, [Before the Giving of the Torah, "They [the children of Israel] stood beneath the mountain"[115] (Exodus 19:17). Said R. Avdimi b. Chama: This teaches us that the Holy One, blessed be He, overturned the mountain (Sinai) on them like an inverted barrel and said to them: If you accept the Torah, fine. If not, here will be your burying place. Commented R. Acha b. Yaakov: This provides major grounds for protest against the Torah. [If ever the Jewish people are called before the Heavenly Tribunal to answer for their non-observance of the *mitzvot*, they can say in rebuttal that they accepted the Torah under duress (Rashi).] Countered Rabbah: Even so, they willingly accepted the Torah in the days of Achashverosh [out of love, in gratitude for the miracle of Purim], for it says, "The Jews accepted and irrevocably obligated themselves" (Esther 9:27), which means that they irrevocably obligated themselves to keep what they had accepted long before [at Sinai]; [this time, however, out of love].

TORAH, THE RAISON D'ETRE OF THE WORLD

Chizkiyah said: What is meant by the verse, "In heaven You pronounced sentence; the earth was frightened and calm" (Psalm 76:9). If the earth was frightened, why was it calm; then again, if it was calm, why was it frightened? He replied: At first it feared [that Israel would not accept the Torah], but afterward [when they accepted the Torah] it became tranquil. And why was it frightened? As Resh Lakish said: What is meant by the passage, "And there was evening and there was morning, the sixth day [*hashishi*] (Genesis 1:31). Why the extra *hei* of *hashishi* [*the* sixth day]? [The other days of Creation are described simply as "a third, a fourth, a fifth day," without the article *ha*.] It comes to teach us that the Holy One, blessed be He, stipulated with the works of Creation, and said to them: If Israel accepts the Torah, you will continue to exist; if not, I will turn you back to primordial emptiness and void. [On the sixth day, when God completed His Creation and said "*Yom hashishi, the* sixth day," He alluded to the 6th day of Sivan, the day of the Giving of the Torah. The phrase is thus made to read: "There was evening and there was morning"—only because of the sixth day of Sivan, the date the Torah was given at Sinai.]

"WE WILL DO" BEFORE "WE WILL HEAR"

R. Sima'i expounded: When the children of Israel said, "We will do" before they said, "We will hear" (Exodus 24:7), [which is the ultimate commitment of faith: We will do it, even if we don't understand it], 600,000[116] ministering angels came and placed two [spiritual] crowns [of Divine radiance] on every single Jew, one for "We will do" and one for "We will hear." But when they sinned [through the golden calf], 1,200,000 angels of destruction came down and took their crowns away, as it says, "The people took off the ornaments that they had on from Mount Chorev (Sinai)" (ibid. 33:6). R. Chama b. R. Chanina said: At Chorev the [angels] put them on, and at Chorev the [angels] took them off. At Chorev the [angels] put them on, as was stated above; at Chorev [the angels] took them off, as it says, "The people took off the ornaments" (ibid.). R. Yochanan commented: And Moses had the merit to receive all these [spiritual] crowns, for it says immediately after this, "And Moses took the *ohel*, tent" (ibid. 7), [*ohel* is seen here as cognate to *hilo*, "radiance" (Job 29:3), alluding to the fact that Moses' face was giving off rays of light (Exodus 34:29) (Rashi)]. Resh Lakish said: In time to come, the Holy One, blessed be He, will return the crowns to us, for it says, "And the ransomed of God shall return, and come with shouting to Zion, crowned with joy everlasting. They shall attain joy and gladness, while sorrow and sighing flee" (Isaiah 35:10).

R. Elazar said: When the children of Israel said, "We will do" before they said "We will hear," a Heavenly voice went forth and said: Who revealed to my children this secret that is being used by the ministering angels, as it says, "Bless God, O His angels, mighty creatures who do His bidding, who listen to the voice of His word" (Psalm 103:20). First it says, "who do" and then "who *hear*." [They are ready to spring into action even before they receive their orders, unlike servants who first want to know their assignment and then decide whether or not they will undertake it (Rashi).]

R. Chama b. R. Chanina said: What is meant by the passage, "Like the [fruitful] apple tree among the [barren] trees of the forest" (Song of Songs 2:3). Why is the Jewish people compared to an apple tree? To teach you that, just as an apple tree produces fruit before its leaves sprout, so did the children of Israel say "We will do" before they said "We will hear."[117]

There was this Sadducee [a member of a sect that did not believe in the Oral Torah] who saw Rava pondering his learning while the fingers of his hand were underneath his feet. So engrossed was he in his stud-ies that he was crushing his fingers and blood was gushing from his fingers. Exclaimed the Sadducee, "What an impetuous nation you Jews are! Your mouth comes before your ears! [You accepted the Torah (mouth) before hearing (ears) what it obligated you to do.] You still persist in your rashness! [Look what you are doing to your fingers!] First you should have listened to the Torah and then decided whether or not you could accept it." **(88b)** Replied Rava, "We who trust God [and have faith that He will not demand of us something we cannot do], of us it says, "The integrity of the upright guides them" (Proverbs 11:3). But those people that are suspicious by nature, of them it says, "The deviousness of the treacherous leads them to ruin" (ibid.).

THE GRANDEUR OF TORAH

(88b) R. Shmuel b. Nachmani said in R. Yonatan's name: What is the meaning of the verse, "You captured My heart, My sister, O bride. You have captured Me with one of your eyes" (Song of Songs 4:9). At first [by accepting the Torah], you captured Me with one of your eyes; but when you actually fulfilled the Torah, you captured Me with both your eyes. [A person can perceive something intellectually and physically. When the Jewish people accepted the Torah they perceived it intellectually, with one eye. But now that they physically are fulfilling the *mitzvot*, their closeness to God is complete—a perception with both eyes (*Maharsha*).]

Ulla said: How shameless is a bride who is unfaithful to her husband while she is standing under her bridal canopy [a reference to the sin of the golden calf, which the children of Israel worshipped while still at Sinai]. Said Mari, the son of Shmuel's daughter: What verse supports this? "While the King was yet at Sinai, [the children of Israel] gave up their fragrance as the golden calf defiled the covenant" (Song of Songs 1:12). Said Rav: But His love remained with us, because it says, "they *gave* up their fragrance"—temporarily, but it does not say, "it became [irredeemably] spoiled."

The Rabbis taught in a *Baraita*: People who suffer insults but do not insult others, who hear someone mocking them but don't answer, who do their duties out of love [of God] and rejoice in suffering [all humiliations that are visited on them], of them Scripture says, "But those that love Him are like the sun rising in full strength" (Judges 5:31).

R. Yochanan said: What is meant by, "God gave the promise, the report [i.e., the Torah that He gave to the world. It] was split up to all the nations" (Psalm 68:12)—Every single word that came forth from God was divided into seventy languages,[118] [so that the nations cannot claim: If we had heard the Torah in our language, we also would have accepted it (*Maharsha*)].

The yeshivah of R. Yishmael expounded the following verse: "My word is . . . like a hammer that shat-

104

ters the rock" (Jeremiah 23:29). Just as a hammer breaks a rock into a myriad of little chips, so was every word that came forth from the Holy One, blessed be He, divided into seventy languages.

R. Chananel b. Papa said: What is meant by, "Listen, for I am saying things that I say only among princes" (Proverbs 8:6). Why are the words of the Torah compared to a prince? It comes to tell you: Just as a prince has the power over life and death, so do the words of the Torah have the potential to cause death and restore life. This is what Rava meant when he said: For those who devote themselves to Torah study with all their might—like a person who uses his strong right hand—for them the Torah is a potion of life. But for those who don't study the Torah for the sake of Heaven but use it for other purposes, for them it is a deadly poison. Another explanation of the word *negidim*, "princes": Attached to every word that was uttered by God there were two crowns [that were plainly visible, as it says, "And all the people *saw* the sounds" (Exodus 20:15) (Rashi)].

R. Yehoshua b. Levi said: What is meant by the verse, "My Beloved is to me like a bundle of myrrh [*tzeror hamor*] that lies between my breasts" (Song of Songs 1:13). [The meaning is:] The congregation of Israel said to the Holy One, blessed be He: Master of the universe, although You have distressed [*meitzar* related to *tzeror*] me and made my life bitter [*meimar* related to *hamor*][119] [because You have removed Your glory from me in the wake of the sin of the golden calf], yet my Love lies between my breasts, [because immediately after the sin of the golden calf, You commanded us to erect the Tabernacle, where the *Shechinah* dwelled between the two staves of the Ark, that protruded through the cloth partition like two breasts (Rashi)].

[The next verse states:] "My Beloved is to me like a cluster (*eshkol*) of henna (*hakofer*) in the vineyards (*karmei*) of Ein Gedi" (ibid. 14). [The Gemara expounds:] He to Whom everything belongs (*shehakol shelo—eshkol*) should make atonement (*mechappeir—hakofer*) for me for the sin of the young goat (*gedi*, referring to the golden calf)[120], which I gathered up (*karamti—karmei*) for myself. [The Gemara asks:] What proof do you have that the word *karmei* denotes gathering? Mar Zutra the son of R. Nachman said: It says in a Mishnah: The long board on which a washer piles up [*kormim*] all the clothes.[121]

R. Yehoshua b. Levi said: What is the meaning of the verse: "His cheeks are like a bed of spices"?—With every single word that the holy One, blessed be He, uttered, the whole world was permeated with fragrance. But if the entire world was filled with fragrance after the first word, where did the fragrance of the second word go? The Holy One, blessed be He, took the wind out of His storage place, and the fragrance from the first word passed along to make room for the fragrance of the second word. [The fragrance went to Gan Eden to await those that study the Torah (Rashi)],

as it says, "His lips are like lilies (*shoshanim*) that drip fragrance as it passes on" (ibid.). Do not read *shoshanim*; read instead *sheshonim*, "those that study."

R. Yehoshua b. Levi also said: After every word that emanated from the Holy One, blessed be He, the souls of the children of Israel left them, as it says, "My soul departed when He spoke" (ibid. 5:6). [Asks the Gemara:] But if their souls left them after God's first word, how could they receive the second word? [The Gemara answers:] He brought down the dew with which He will revive the dead, and with that He brought them back to life, as it says, "You released a bountiful rain, O God; Your inheritance and the people that were weary You prepared [to receive the Torah]" (Psalm 68:10).

R. Yehoshua b. Levi also said: After every word that emanated from the Holy One, blessed be He, the children of Israel retreated twelve *mil*, but the ministering angels gently led them back [*medaddin*, to lead, like a mother who helps her child take his first steps (Rashi)]. For it says, "The ministering angels march, they march [*yiddodun yiddodun*]" (ibid.). Don't read *yiddodun* [which denotes that they themselves were moving]; read instead *yedaddun* [meaning, they were helping the children of Israel to move back].

THE DIALOGUE BETWEEN MOSES AND THE ANGELS

R. Yehoshua b. Levi also said: When Moses went up to heaven, the ministering angels said to the Holy One, blessed be He, "Master of the universe! What is this man born of a woman doing among us?" Replied God, "He has come to receive the Torah." Retorted the angels, "This cherished treasure that has been hidden by You for 974 generations before the creation of the world,[122] You want to give to one who is nothing but flesh and blood? What is man that You are mindful of him, mortal man that You take note of him! O God, our Lord, How majestic is Your name throughout the earth! It is only right that Your glory [the Torah] should be conferred on heaven" (Psalm 8:5,2). Said the Holy One, blessed be He, to Moses, "Go ahead. You answer them." "Master of the universe," replied Moses, "I am afraid they may consume me with their fiery breath." "Then hold on to my Throne of Glory," said God to him, "and give them an answer,"[123] as it says, "He makes him hold on to the face of His throne, and He spreads His cloud over him" (Job 26:9). R. Nachum said: This teaches us that the Almighty spread the radiance of His *Shechinah* and His protective cloud over Moses, [so that he could hold on to the heavenly throne].

[Now that Moses felt secure,] he said to God, "Master of the universe! The Torah that You are giving me, what is written in it? 'I am God your Lord, who brought you out of Egypt' (Exodus 20:2). Turning to the angels, Moses said, "Did you go down to

Egypt? Where you slaves to Pharaoh? Why should you have the Torah? What else does it say in the Torah? 'Do not have any other gods before Me' (ibid. 3). Do you live among people who worship **(89a)** idols [that you need to be warned against this]? What else does it say in the Torah? 'Remember the *Shabbat* to keep it holy' (ibid. 8). Do you then work [during the week] that you need the concept of *Shabbat*? What else does it say in the Torah? 'Do not take the name of God your Lord in vain' [the prohibition against swearing falsely] (ibid. 7). [Where do you come to swear? What kind of arguments do you have?] Do you have business dealings? What else does it say in the Torah? 'Honor your father and your mother' (ibid. 12). Do you have a father and a mother? What else does it say in the Torah? 'Do not commit murder. Do not commit adultery. Do not steal' (ibid. 13). Is there jealousy among you, do you have an evil impulse [that you have to be told not to do these things]?"

Immediately, they admitted to the Holy One, blessed be He [that the Torah belongs down in this world], for it says [in the final verse of the psalm], "God, our Lord, how majestic is Your name throughout the earth!" (Psalm 8:10) and it does not say any more, "Let Your glory [the Torah] be conferred on heaven" (ibid. 2). Immediately, all of the angels became Moses' friends, and each angel taught him a concept [as a gift], as it says, "You went up to the heights, you have taken captives [meaning, you convinced the angels to consent to the Giving of the Torah], you have received gifts because of man" (ibid. 68:19), meaning, as compensation for the fact that the angels [scornfully] called you a mere mortal [who is not fit to accept the Torah], you received gifts. And even the Angel of Death revealed a secret to him [that the offering of incense would halt the spread of a plague], for it says, "He offered the incense to atone for the people" (Numbers 17:12), and it says, "He stood between the dead and the living, and the plague was checked" (ibid. 15). Now how did Moses know that the incense would halt the plague, if not for the fact the Angel of Death himself had told him?

SATAN SEARCHING
FOR THE TORAH

R. Yehoshua b. Levi also said: When Moses came down from the Presence of the Holy One, blessed be He, Satan came and asked Him, "Master of the universe! Where is the Torah?" "I have given it to the earth," He replied. Satan then went to the earth and asked, "Where is the Torah?" The earth replied, "God understands its way" (Job 28:23). He then went to the sea, and it told him, "I do not have it." He went to the deep, and it told him, "It is not in me," for it says, "The deep says, 'It is not in me'; the sea says, 'I do not have it'; Destruction and Death say, 'We have only a rumor about it'" (ibid. 14, 22). Satan went back to God and

said, "Master of the universe! I have searched the entire world, but I have not found it." "Go to the son of Amram [Moses]," replied God. So he went to Moses and asked him, "Where is the Torah that the Holy One, blessed be He, gave you?" "Who am I that the Holy One, blessed be He, should give me the Torah?" answered Moses. Said the Holy One, blessed be He, to Moses, "Moses, are you a liar?" "Master of the universe," Moses replied, "You have this precious hidden treasure, that you delight in every day. Should I keep it all for my own benefit?" Said the Holy One, blessed be He, to Moses, "Moses, because you have belittled yourself, the Torah shall be called by your name, as it says, "Be mindful of the Torah of My servant Moses" (Malachi 3:22).

R. Yehoshua b. Levi also said: When Moses went up to heaven he found the Holy One, blessed be He, busy tying crowns [*taggin*] onto the letters of the Torah.[124] Said He to him, "Moses, don't they give greetings of 'Shalom' in your town?" "Does a slave say 'Shalom' to his master?" said Moses. Replied God, "[Instead of saying nothing], you should have helped Me, [by wishing Me success in My work]." The next time Moses spoke to God he said, "And now, let the power of God be great, as you have said," [Numbers 14:17]. [Meaning, I am taking the liberty of wishing You success, as You told me to do.]

SATAN'S DECEPTION

R. Yehoshua b. Levi also said: What is the meaning of the verse, "When the people saw that Moses was taking a long time [*bosheish*] to come down from the mountain" (Exodus 32:1)?—Don't read *bosheish* [delayed], but *ba'u sheish* [the sixth hour had come]. [This is what happened.] When Moses went up to heaven, he told the children of Israel: "I will return at the end of forty days, at the beginning of the sixth hour."[125] When at the end of forty days [Moses had not yet come back], Satan came and caused a mixup in the world. Said Satan to Israel, "Where is your teacher Moses?" "He has gone up to heaven," they answered. Said Satan, "The sixth hour has come [and he has not come back]," but they paid no attention to him. "He died," but they disregarded him. Then he showed them an image of Moses' deathbed [floating in the air]. That's why they said to Aaron, "We have no idea what happened to Moses, the man who brought us out of Egypt" (ibid.).

WHY IS IT CALLED
MOUNT SINAI?

One of the Rabbis asked R. Kahana: Did you hear what the name Sinai stands for? He answered: Sinai means the mountain where miracles [*nissim*] were performed for Israel. He countered: Then it should be called Mount Nisai. No, it means the mountain that became a happy sign [*siman*] for Israel. Then it should be called

Mount Simanai. Said he to him: [If you really want to know the correct derivation,] why don't you join the yeshivah of R. Papa and R. Huna b. R. Yehoshua, because they concentrate on the study of *Aggadah* [the homiletical and moral teachings of the Talmud]. For R. Chisda and Rabbah b. R. Huna both said: Why is it called Mount Sinai? Because it is the mountain where hatred [*sin'ah*] came down against idol worshipers [for their rejection of the Torah]. And so said R. Yose b. R. Chanina: [The mountain] has five names: The Wilderness of Tzin, meaning that the children of Israel were given the *mitzvot* of the Torah there [the words *Tzin* and *mitzvot* are related]; the Wilderness of Kadesh, where the children of Israel received their holiness [*kedushah*]; the Wilderness of Kedeimot, where the preeminence [*kedumah*] of Israel was established [by their acceptance of the Torah]; the Wilderness of Paran, (89b) because the children of Israel were fruitful [*paru*] and multiplied there; and the Wilderness of Sinai, because hatred (*sin'ah*) came down against idol-worshippers. And what was its real name? It was called Chorev. This is disputed by R. Abbahu, for R. Abbahu said: The real name is Mount Sinai, and why is it also called Mount Chorev? Because it brought about destruction [*churvah*] to idolators, [since through the Revelation on this mountain it became clear that there is only one God].

ISAAC STRIKES A BARGAIN WITH GOD

[We learned in the Mishnah:] From where do we derive that a scarlet string was tied to the goat that was sent to Azazel on Yom Kippur? It says, "Even if your sins are like crimson [*kashanim*], they will turn as white as snow" (Isaiah 1:18).[126] [The Gemara asks:] [Instead of] *kashanim* [like crimson threads, in the plural], it should say *kashani* [like a crimson thread, in the singular, to parallel "snow" in the other part of the verse, and which is in the singular]. Said R. Yitzchak: The Holy One, blessed be He, said to Israel: Even if your sins are like these years [*ka-shanim*] that have continued in their arranged order since the six days of Creation, they will become as white as snow.

Rava expounded: What is meant by, "'Go now, and let us reason together,' God will say" (ibid.). Instead of, "*Go* now, and let us reason together," it should say, "*Come* now, and let us reason together"? And instead of, "God will say," it should say, "God said"? [Rava answers: This is a prophecy.] In the future the Holy One, blessed be He, will say to Israel, "*Go* now to your forefathers; they will admonish you." And Israel will say to Him, "Master of the universe! To whom shall we go? To Abraham, to whom You said, 'Know for sure that your descendants will be foreigners . . . They will be enslaved and oppressed' (Genesis 15:13), and yet he did not plead for mercy for us? To Isaac, who blessed Esau with, 'The time will come when you [Esau] will

have the power' (ibid. 27:40), and yet he did not plead for mercy for us? To Jacob, to whom You said, 'I will go down to Egypt with you' (ibid. 46:4), and yet he did not plead for mercy for us? To whom shall we go? Now, we want God to be the One who will reprove us."[127] So the Holy One, blessed be He, will answer them, "Since you made yourself dependent only on Me, 'even if your sins are as crimson, they will turn as white as snow.'"

R. Shmuel b. Nachmani said in the name of R. Yonatan: What is meant by the verse, "Surely You are our Father; Abraham did not know us, and Israel did not recognize us. You, O God, are our Father, our Redeemer. Your name is everlasting" (Isaiah 63:16). In time to come, the Holy One, blessed be He, will say to Abraham, "Your children have sinned against Me." Abraham answered Him, "Master of the universe! Let them be wiped out to sanctify Your name!" Then He said, "I will tell this to Jacob who has experienced so much pain raising his children; maybe he will plead for mercy for them." So He said to Jacob, "Your children have sinned." But he too, answered Him, "Master of the universe! Let them be wiped out for the sanctification of Your name!"

[God] replied, "The grandfathers do not make sense, and there is no counsel to be gained from the children." But when He said to Isaac, "Your children have sinned," he answered, "Master of the universe! Are they my children and not Your children too? When they said 'We will do' before saying 'We will hear,' [in accepting the Torah], You called them, 'Israel, My son, My firstborn' (Exodus 4:22); and now they are *my* sons and not *Your* sons! Besides, how much have they actually sinned? [Let's see.] How long does a person live? An average of seventy years. Take off twenty years, because [for sins committed during the first twenty years, the heavenly Court] does not punish. So there are only fifty years left. Take off twenty-five for the nights [when they were sleeping and did not sin]. Now we are left with only twenty-five. Subtract twelve-and-a-half that they were praying, eating, and answering the call of nature, and there are twelve-and-a-half years left [for which You can hold them responsible]. If You are willing to bear the whole burden, fine; if not, I'll take half, and You'll take half. And if You are going to say that I should bear the whole burden, [I did that already once before]. Look, I offered myself as a sacrifice for you."

Immediately, the Jewish people will say, "You [Isaac] are our father!" Isaac will then say to them, "Instead of praising me, praise the Holy One, blessed be He," and Isaac will point upward toward God. Immediately they will lift their eyes toward heaven and exclaim, "You, O God, are our Father, our Redeemer. Your name is everlasting" (Isaiah 63:16).

R. Chiya b. Abba said in R. Yochanan's name: Jacob really was meant to go down to Egypt in iron chains, but his merit saved him [so that he went there with great honor, instead], for it says, "I drew them [not with chains], but with cords fitting for a man, with bands of love. I will be like one who lifts the yoke off their jaws [to make it easier for the animal to walk], I will give them the strength to bear the bone-breaking labor [of Egyptian slavery]" (Hosea 11:4).

THE CASE OF
THE *SHABBAT*-BREAKER

(96b) [The Gemara discusses the case of the *mekosheish*, the man who violated the *Shabbat* in the desert.] Our Rabbis taught in a *Baraita*: The man who gathered sticks on *Shabbat*[128] was Tzelofchad. And so it says, "While the children of Israel were in the desert [*bamidbar*], they discovered a man gathering sticks on *Shabbat*" (Numbers 15:32); and elsewhere it says, [Tzelofchad's daughters said to Moses], "Our father died in the desert [*bamidbar*]" (ibid. 27:3). [We derive by means of a *gezeirah shavah*[129] the word *bamidbar*, which is found in both verses], that, just as the verse, ["Our father died in the desert"] refers to Tzelofchad, so too the present verse, [about the man who gathered sticks on *Shabbat*], refers to Tzelofchad, so said R. Akiva. R. Yehudah b. Beteira said to him: Akiva, regardless whether you are right or wrong, you will have to give justification for your statement [before the heavenly Court]. If you are right, you disclosed the name of a person whose identity the Torah shielded; and if you are wrong, you have slandered a righteous man.

(97a) [The Gemara asks:] But [R. Akiva] derived it from a *gezeirah shavah* [and whatever is derived from a *gezeirah shavah* is considered as plainly stated in the Torah; thus the Torah did not shield Tzelofchad]. [The Gemara answers:] R. Yehudah b. Beteira did not learn this *gezeirah shavah* from his teachers, [and a *gezeirah shavah* can only be applied when it was received by tradition from Sinai (Rashi)]. [The Gemara asks:] Then, [in R. Yehudah's view], what sin did Tzelofchad commit [for his daughters said, "He died because of his own sin" (ibid.)]? [The Gemara answers:] He was one of the people who defiantly climbed toward the top of the mountain (ibid. 14:44).

There is a similar dispute about the verse, [After Miriam and Aaron spoke against Moses], "God displayed anger against *them*, and He went away" (ibid. 12:9). Said R. Akiva: This teaches us that [not only Miriam, but] Aaron too, was stricken with leprosy. R. Yehudah b. Beteira said to him: Akiva, regardless whether you are right or wrong, you will have to give justification for your statement before the heavenly Court. If you are right, you disclosed the name of a person [Aaron] whose identity the Torah shielded. And if you are wrong, you have maligned this righteous man. [Asks the Gemara:] But it says, "God displayed anger against *them*," [referring to both Miriam and Aaron]? [The Gemara answers:] This means that

Aaron was only reprimanded. We learned a *Baraita* that holds the view that Aaron too, was stricken with leprosy. It says, "When Aaron turned [*va-yifen*] to Miriam, he saw that she was leprous" (ibid. 10). It was taught : That means that he became free [*panah*] from his leprosy. [*Va-yifen* is a form of *panah*, meaning, "to turn, to turn away from, to be free from."]

Resh Lakish said: He who suspects an innocent person will receive bodily punishment. For it says, [When Moses received his mission to bring the children of Israel out of Egypt, he said to God], "But they will not believe me" (Exodus 4:1), [casting doubt on their faith]. But the Holy One, blessed be He, knew that Israel would believe. He said to Moses: They are believers, the children of believers, but I know that you will end up not believing. They are believers, as it says, "The people believed" (ibid. 31), the children of believers, as it says, "And he [Abraham] believed in God" (Genesis 16:6). You will end up not believing, as it says, "God said to Moses and Aaron, 'Because you have not believed in Me'" (Numbers 20:12). From where do we know that Moses was stricken [on his body for suspecting the innocent]? Because it says, "God then said to Moses, 'Place your hand [on your chest] inside your robe,' [and when he removed it from his chest it was leprous, as white as snow]'" (Exodus 4:6).

Rava—according to others, R. Yose b. R. Chanina —said: God parcels out goodness more quickly than He metes out punishment. For with regard to meting out punishment it says: "And when [Moses] removed [his hand], it was leprous, as white as snow," [it became leprous only after he removed it]. But with regard to dispensing goodness it says, "As he removed it from his chest, his skin had returned to normal" (ibid. 7). The implication is that even before his hand was fully withdrawn from his chest, his skin had already returned to normal.

"Aaron's staff swallowed up their staffs" (Exodus 7:12). R. Elazar said: This was a double miracle. [The first miracle: Aaron's staff had become a serpent; the second miracle: after turning back into a staff, it swallowed up the magicians' staffs.]

THE WATER LIBATION
ON SUKKOT

(103b) We learned in a *Baraita*: R. Yehudah b. Beteira said: It says, in connection with the offering of the second day of Sukkot, *veniskeihem*, "and their libations," (Numbers 29:19), [instead of *veniskah*][130]; in connection with the sixth day's offering it says *unesacheha*, "and its libations," (ibid. 31); [instead of *veniskah*] (ibid. 31); and in connection with the offering of the seventh day it says, *kemishpatam*, "as prescribed for them" (ibid. 33) [instead of *kamishpat*]. The difference between *veniskeihem* and *veniskah* is a *mem*; between *unesacheha* and *veniskah*, a *yud*; and between *kemishpatam* and *kamishpat*, a *mem*. *Mem*, *yud*, and *mem* together form the word *mayim*, "water." This gives us an indication that the ceremony of the water libation [which was celebrated on Sukkot][131] was a Biblical law.

MOURNING THE DEATH OF AN UPRIGHT PERSON

(105b) It was taught in a *Baraita*: Why do a person's sons and daughters die in childhood? So that he should weep and mourn for an upright man. [The Gemara asks:] You say, "So that he should weep"—How can a pledge be taken from him now [before he has done anything wrong]? [The Gemara answers: His children die] because he did not weep and mourn for an upright man; for whoever weeps for an upright man will have all his sins forgiven by virtue of the honor he accorded him.

R. Shimon b. Elazar said in the name of Chilfa b. Agra in R. Yochanan b. Nuri's name: A person who tears his clothes in anger, who breaks his vessels in anger, and who scatters his money in anger, should be considered an idol worshipper, because such is the cunning strategy of the evil impulse: Today it will tell a person: Do this! and tomorrow it will tell him: Do that! until it in the end it tells him: Worship idols! and he goes and worships them. R. Avin said: What verse substantiates this?—"There shall be no foreign god inside of you, and you shall not bow to an alien god" (Psalm 81:10). What foreign god resides inside a man's body? It is the evil impulse. But if a person does these things, [not because he is really angry] but in order to intimidate the members of his household [so that they obey him], then it is permitted. Just like R. Yehudah, [when he wanted to show his displeasure] he would pull the tassels of his garment, R. Acha b. Yaakov used to shatter broken vessels, R. Sheshet used to pour brine on his maidservant's head, R. Acha broke the lid of a pitcher.

R. Shimon b. Pazzi said in the name of R. Yehoshua b. Levi in Bar Kappara's name: If a person sheds tears over the death of a righteous man, the Holy One, blessed be He, counts them and lays them away in His treasure house, for it says, "You count my wanderings, put my tears into Your flask. Are they not in Your book?" (Psalm 56:9).

R. Yehudah said in Rav's name: If a person is neglectful about lamenting the death of a Torah scholar he deserves to be buried in the prime of life, for it says, "They buried him [Joshua] on his own property, at Timnat Serachin in the hill country of Ephraim, north of Mount Gaash" (Joshua 24:30). The name Gaash [which means "to shake"] teaches you that the mountain shook and quaked and wanted to obliterate the Israelites [because they did not eulogize Joshua appropriately].

R. Chiya b. Abba said in R. Yochanan's name: If a person is neglectful about lamenting a Torah scholar he will not live long. He is being punished measure for measure. [He did not mourn the premature death of the Torah scholar, therefore Heaven will shorten his life. (Rashi.)] And so it says, "In full measure, [according to their sins], when You send her away, You fight with her"[132] (Isaiah 27:8). R. Chiya b. Abba raised an objection to R. Yochanan's statement: It says: Israel served God during the lifetime of Joshua and the lifetime of the elders who lived on many days after Joshua" (Joshua 24:31), [thus their lives were not shortened]?—R. Yochanan replied: O, you Babylonian![133] It says "who lived on many *days* after Joshua," but not "many *years*." [R. Chiya b. Abba retorted:] If so, what about the verse, "In order to prolong your days and the days of your children" (Deuteronomy 11:21)? Does that also mean days but not years? [Replied R. Yochanan:] When it comes to blessings it is different, [then, "days" means "years"].

R. Chiya b. Abba also said in R. Yochanan's name: If a person's brother dies, (106a) all the other brothers should worry [that they too may die]. If a member of a group dies, the entire group should worry. Some say that this applies only if the oldest [or the most important member] dies; others say, only if the youngest [or the least important member] dies.

HOW TO HONOR *SHABBAT*

(113a) It says, "Honor it [the *Shabbat*] by not doing your own ways" (Isaiah 58:13). "Honor it [the *Shabbat*]": means that your *Shabbat* clothes should not be like your weekday clothes. [Just as] R. Yochanan called his clothes "My 'dignifiers.'" [Clothes confer dignity on a person.] "Abstain from doing your own ways" means that on *Shabbat* you should not walk the way you walk on weekdays. "Abstain from seeking your needs" (ibid.) means that pursuing your own business is forbidden, but taking care of the business of Heaven [charity] is permitted. "Discussing the forbidden" means (113b) that on *Shabbat* you should not talk about things you discuss on weekdays [i.e., business dealings]. Speaking about these matters is forbidden, but thinking about them is permitted.

[The Gemara asks:] All of these things are plain to understand, except for "on *Shabbat* you should not walk the way you walk on weekdays." What does that mean? [The Gemara answers:] It is like the case about which Rebbi asked R. Yishmael b. R. Yose: Are you allowed to take extra-long steps on *Shabbat*? [Is this considered pursuing your own business, which is forbidden?] He replied: Is it then permitted on weekdays [to take long steps]? I say: A very long stride takes away one five-hundredth part of a person's eyesight, but it returns when he recites *Kiddush* on Friday night [and drinks the wine]. [This is the kind of walking that should not be done on *Shabbat*.]

Rebbi[134] asked R. Shmuel b. R. Yose: Are you allowed to eat earth on *Shabbat*? [This was considered to have therapeutic value.] He answered: Is it then permitted on weekdays? I say: It is forbidden also on weekdays, because it is harmful to your health.

R. Ammi said: Anyone who eats from the earth of Babylon it is as if he ate from the flesh of his ancestors. Others say: It is as if he ate creeping animals, because it says, "[The Flood] obliterated all living things" (Genesis 7:23). And Resh Lakish said: Why is Babylon called the Land of Shinar? [Shinar comes from the root *na'ar*, "to shake out."] Because all the dead creatures of the Flood were shaken out into Babylon. [So if someone eats the earth of Babylon, he is eating earth that contains the decomposed remains of his ancestors.] R. Yochanan said: Why is Babylon called Metzullah? [Metzullah comes from the root *tzallal*, "to sink."] Because all the dead people of the Flood sank into the land of Babylon, [because of its low-lying terrain].

[We learned above:] Others say: It is as if he ate creeping animals. [The Gemara asks:] But surely these were completely dissolved [and were not present in the earth any more]? [The Gemara answers:] Since eating earth is harmful, the Rabbis forbade the eating of earth as if he were eating creeping things. [The Gemara gives an illustration of the harmful effects of eating earth:] Somebody once ate some red clay, and later he ate cress [a vegetable of the leek family]. Somehow this cress took root in the clay that was in his system; it grew into his heart and caused him to die.

THE MAGNIFICENCE OF RUTH

[When Naomi sent Ruth to the threshing floor to meet Boaz in the hope that Boaz would marry her, Naomi said:] "Wash yourself, anoint yourself with oil, and put on your clothing" (Ruth 3:3). R. Elazar said: This refers to the *Shabbat* clothes. [Of course, she was wearing clothes; then what kind of clothing could Naomi have meant? Obviously, she had to mean *Shabbat* clothing (Rashi).]

[Pursuing this theme, the Gemara quotes the verse,] "Instruct a wise man, and he will grow wiser" [he will improve on what you told him] (Proverbs 9:9). R. Elazar said: This refers to Ruth the Moabitess and the prophet Samuel of Ramah. As for Ruth, although Naomi said to her, "Wash yourself, anoint yourself with oil, and put on your clothing, and *then* go down to the threshing floor," when Ruth actually did it, it says first, "She went down to the threshing floor, and only *then*, "she did just as her mother-in-law had instructed her" (ibid. 6) [and washed and dressed herself. She realized that people would become suspicious if they saw a young woman, all dressed up, go to a threshing floor late at night].

As for Samuel, [how do we see that he reacted wisely to what someone told him?] [Young Samuel, who grew up in Eli's house, came to Eli a few times during the night and said, "I heard you calling me." Eli understood that it was God who was calling Samuel.] Although Eli said to him, "Go back to sleep. If you are called again, say, 'Speak, God, because Your servant is listening" (1 Samuel 3:9), when it actually happened, it says, "God came, and stood over Samuel, and He called as before, 'Samuel! Samuel!'" And Samuel answered, "Speak, for Your servant is listening," but he did not say, "Speak, God." [He did not have the audacity to presume that God was speaking to him.]

[The Gemara now returns to the subject of Ruth. It says,] "Off she went. She came and gleaned in a field" (Ruth 2:3). R. Elazar says: [This means that] she went from field to field until she found other reapers in a field who were decent people, [and she followed them in order to pick leftover stalks in the field]. "Boaz said to the servant who was in charge of the reapers, 'Who is this girl?'" (ibid. 5). [The Gemara asks:] Is it proper for a *tzaddik* like Boaz to inquire about a girl? Said R. Elazar: [He inquired] because he detected an act of wisdom in her conduct: If two stalks fell down she picked them up, but if she saw three stalks falling down she would not pick them up. [She was acting in keeping with the law of *leket*, the "law of the stalks that have fallen" (Leviticus 19:9), which states that if only one or two stalks fall from the farmer's hand, he may not pick them up but must leave them for the poor, but if three or more stalks fall, he may take them (*Pe'ah* 6:5); Rashi]. In a *Baraita* we learned: [Boaz inquired] because he saw modesty in Ruth: Leftover stalks that were still standing in the field she picked while she was standing; but stalks that had fallen down, she would squat down to pick up, instead of bending over.

[Boaz said to Ruth:] "Don't go to glean in another field . . . stay here close to my girls" (ibid. 8). [The Gemara asks:] Is it proper for Boaz to seek closeness to women? Said R. Elazar: [Boaz knew that this was Ruth, and knew her history.] Now, when he saw that "Orpah, [Ruth's sister-in-law], kissed her mother-in-law Naomi goodbye, [and left her], but Ruth stayed close to Naomi [even though she faced a life of poverty]" (ibid. 14), [he recognized Ruth's outstanding qualities]. Therefore, Boaz said: It is permitted to attach oneself to such a person.

"When it was time to eat, Boaz said to her, 'Come over here (*halom*)'" (ibid. 2:14). R. Elazar said: [By using the word *halom* he gave her a prophetically inspired hint], telling her in effect: The royal house of David will descend from you. [Ruth was the great-grandmother of David.] [In the present verse, Boaz used the word *halom* in reference to Ruth], and *halom* is used also in reference to David, for it says, "Then King David came and sat before God, and he said, 'What am I O Lord God, and what is my family, that You have brought me *halom*, to this point?'" (2 Samuel 7:18). [*Halom* thus refers to both Ruth and David.]

[Boaz told Ruth,] "Dip your bread into vinegar" (ibid.). Said R. Elazar: This shows us that vinegar is helpful to bring relief from the heat. [This was harvest time, in the middle of the summer, and Boaz advised her to use vinegar.] R. Shmuel b. Nachmani said: [By speaking of vinegar] he gave her a prophetically inspired hint, telling her in effect: An offspring will descend from you whose deeds will be as harsh as vinegar. And who was that? That was Menashe, [King of Yehudah (Judah), the most corrupt of all the kings of Yehudah[135]].

"So she sat down beside the reapers" (ibid.). Said R. Elazar: She sat down on one side of the reapers," [and Boaz sat on the other side, so that the reapers separated him from Ruth (Rashi)], but she did not sit among them. This was a prophetic indication to her that the monarchy of David would become split. [David's descendants would rule over Judah and Benjamin; the other ten tribes would break off and form the Kingdom of Israel. This was symbolized by the reapers who separated her from Boaz.] "He [Boaz] handed her roasted grain, and she ate, she was satisfied and had some left over" (ibid.). Said R. Elazar: "She ate"—this refers to the prosperity in the time of David. "She was satisfied"—this refers to the prosperity in the time of Solomon. "And she had some left over"—this refers to the prosperity in the days of Hezekiah. Others say: "She ate" refers to the prosperity in the days of David and Solomon. "She was satisfied" refers to the prosperity in the days of Hezekiah. "And she had some left over" refers to the prosperity in the days of Rebbi, [Rabbi Yehudah Hanassi, the compiler of the Mishnah, known also as Rabbeinu Hakadosh, who was very wealthy], for we learned: The house steward who took care of Rebbi's horses and mules was wealthier than King Sh'vur [of Persia]. In a *Baraita* we learned: "She ate" presages that you'll eat in this world; "she was satisfied," presages that you'll be satisfied in the days of *Mashiach*; "and she had some left over" is a pre-indication that in the ultimate future, even then you'll have something left over in the spiritual prosperity.

THE MIRACULOUS ANNIHILATION OF SANCHERIV'S ARMY

[The Gemara cites another verse about whose interpretation there is disagreement among the same three Amora'im. The verse concerns the army of Sancheriv that besieged Jerusalem. During the night, a miracle happened, and the entire army died in their sleep.] It says: "And beneath [*tachat*] His glory [*kevodo*] a burning will kindle like the burning of fire" (Isaiah 10:16). [It should be noted that *tachat* means both "beneath" and "instead"; *kevodo* means "glory," but it can also mean "clothing" (because garments confer honor on a person). *Kevodo* can also mean the honor of a person, meaning the human being himself.] R. Yochanan said: "Beneath His glory [*tachat kevodo*]" means, "That which is *tachat kevodo* "beneath his clothing" shall be burned, but not the clothing itself. [In other words, the bodies of Sancheriv's soldiers, which are beneath their

clothing, were burned, but their clothing remained intact].

R. Yochanan is consistent with his opinion, because R. Yochanan called his clothing "my dignifiers."[136] R. Elazar said: *Tachat* means "instead." He interprets the phrase, *Tachat kevodo*, "Instead of the bodies of these soldies there were only ashes." R. Shmuel b. Nachmani said: [He holds like R. Yochanan, that *tachat* means underneath, and like R. Elazar, that *kevodo* means "his body."] He interprets *tachat kevodo* to mean that they were burned like Aharon's two sons [Nadav and Avihu]. Just as Nadav and Avihu's death meant the burning of their soul [but their bodies remained whole], so here too, [in the case of Sancheriv's soldiers], their bodies remained intact; only their souls were taken from them, and in that sense, they were burned.

A TORAH SCHOLAR SHOULD DRESS METICULOUSLY

R. Acha b. Abba said in R. Yochanan's name: (114a) From what verse in the Torah do we know that we should change clothes when we honor to God? For it says, [The *kohen* who removes the ashes from the altar] "shall take off his clothing and put on other garments, [of lower quality]" (Leviticus 6:4). It was taught in the yeshivah of R. Yishmael: The Torah teaches you [thereby] a lesson in good manners: When you pour a cup [of wine] for your master, don't wear the same clothes you use in the kitchen when you are cooking a dish for your master. [When serving God you should dress decorously.]

R. Chiya b. Abba said in R. Yochanan's name: It is a disgrace for a Torah scholar to go out into the street with patched-up shoes. [The Gemara asks:] But R. Achah b. Chanina [who is certainly a Torah scholar] did go out into the street that way? [The Gemara answers:] R. Acha b. R. Nachman said: [When is it disgrace to go out into the street?] With one patch on top of another.

R. Chiya b. Abba also said in R. Yochanan's name: A Torah scholar who has a grease stain on his clothing deserves to die, for it says, "All those who hate Me love [i.e., deserve] death" (Proverbs 8:36). Don't read *mesan'ai*, "those who hate Me," but read *masni'ai*, "those who cause Me to be hated." [A Torah scholar who is not neat and dresses shabbily causes people to have contempt of all Torah scholars, to despise Torah learning, and causes God to be hated. People will say: If a Torah scholar looks so contemptible, I don't want to be part of the Torah community (Rashi)]. Ravina said: The above refers not to a grease stain but to a stain caused by semen. But they do not disagree: one refers to the outer garment, the other to the inner garment. [On the outer garment, even a grease stain leads to contempt of God; therefore, the outer clothing certainly should be immaculate. But on the inner garment, only a stain caused by semen brings about contempt of God.]

R. Chiya b. Abba also said in R. Yochanan's name: What is the meaning of the verse, "Just as My servant Isaiah has gone naked and barefoot for three years" (Isaiah 20:3). [He explains: "naked" is not meant literally.] "Naked" means that he went around with worn-out clothing; "barefoot" means that he went out with shoes that were patched.[137]

WHO IS CONSIDERED A TORAH SCHOLAR?

R. Yochanan said: Torah scholars are called *banna'im*, "builders," because all their lives they are busy building the world. [They are the true builders, for they make it possible for the whole world to endure.]

R. Yochanan also said [this about Torah scholars:] Who is considered a Torah scholar to whom we will return a lost article if he says he recognizes it. [The *halachah* states that you return a lost article to a Torah scholar if he merely claims to recognize it; an ordinary person must state identifying marks before the lost article is returned to him.[138]] R. Yochanan answered: A Torah scholar is someone who is so particular about his clothing that if he puts his shirt on inside out, he takes it off and puts it back on the right way, [so that the seams are on the inside. In addition to being a scholar he must be meticulous about his appearance].

R. Yochanan also said: Who is considered a Torah scholar to such a degree that he can be appointed as the leader of the community? R. Yochanan answered: This is someone whom you can ask halachic questions about any subject in the Talmud, and he answers you, even if you ask him a question about tractate Kallah [a collection of *Baraitot* that are not part of the Talmud].

R. Yochanan also said: Who is considered to be the kind of Torah scholar who deserves that the other people in the city have to do his work, [to relieve him of physical labor so that he would have the time to learn]? [He answered:] This refers to someone who neglects his personal welfare for the sake of Torah and *mitzvot*, [then the others have to make it possible for him not to be concerned with mundane things]. But they only are required to provide for his basic necessities.

R. Yochanan also said: Who is considered to be a Torah scholar? Anyone whom you can ask a *halachah* anywhere in the Talmud, and he answers you. [The Gemara asks:] What practical difference does it make if he is that kind of scholar or not? [The Gemara answers:] The question is whether he is enough of a scholar to be appointed a leader over the community. [If he knows the entire Talmud, but] is well-versed in only one tractate, he can be appointed leader in his own town, but if he is well-versed in the entire Talmud [and can answer a question about any subject in the Talmud] then he can be appointed as head of a yeshivah [and become the recognized authority over a very large area].

SAVING SACRED BOOKS FROM A FIRE ON *SHABBAT*

(115a) [This chapter deals with problems that arise when a fire breaks out on *Shabbat*. The Sages prohibited saving articles from a burning house on *Shabbat*, because if this were permitted, in his panic, a person would forget that it is *Shabbat* and try to extinguish the fire, which the Torah forbids. Now that he is forbidden to save his possessions, he will resign himself to the loss and will not put out the fire. However, the Sages made certain exceptions, which are outlined in this section.]

MISHNAH: You are permitted to save all sacred writings [Torah, Prophets, and Writings[139]], from a fire [on *Shabbat*, by moving them from the burning house into an open courtyard], whether we read these writings [publicly in the synagogue] or not. [We read the weekly Torah portion and the Haftarah from the Prophets, but we do not read from the Writings.] [You may save these sacred writings], even if they are written in any language. [Furthermore, if such writings are worm-eaten and cannot be used any more] they must be stored away or buried. And why don't we read [from the Writings] on *Shabbat*? Because, [if it were permitted, people would stay at home to read these fascinating Books, and] would neglect to come to the *Bet Hamidrash* to listen to the rabbi's *Shabbat* discourse.

BURYING THE TRANSLATION OF THE BOOK OF JOB

GEMARA: R. Yose said: It once happened that my father Chalafta visited R. Gamliel Berebbi[140] in Tiberias and found him sitting at the table of R. Yochanan b. Nizuf, holding in his hand a Targum [Aramaic] translation of the Book of Job, which he was reading. My father told R. Gamliel: I remember that R. Gamliel your grandfather[141] was standing on one of the steps leading up to the Temple Mount when they brought him a Targum translation of the Book of Job, and he told one of the builders to bury it under a row of stones. Thereupon R. Gamliel II also gave orders that this translation should be put away, and they hid it.

(115b) The text of *berachot* [like the *Shemoneh Esrei*] and amulets [verses written on parchment that were worn to ward off sickness and misfortune], although they contain letters of the Divine Name and many verses of the Torah, may not be rescued from a fire on *Shabbat*, but these parchments and the Divine Names on them must be left to burn where they are [because they are not considered sacred writings]. Therefore it was said: People who write down *berachot* are as though they were burning the Torah [because, if a fire breaks out on *Shabbat*, you are not allowed to save them]. It happened that someone was writing these [*berachos*] in Sidon. When they told R. Yishmael about it he went to investigate if indeed this was true. As R. Yishmael came up the ladder, the writer realized that he was coming, so he took a stack of written *berachot* and threw them into a large bowl of water [to destroy the evidence]. Rabbi Yishmael said to him precisely the following words: Your punishment for the second thing you did [destroying the *berachot*] is even greater than that for the first thing [writing them].

THE SEVEN BOOKS OF THE TORAH

We learned in a *Baraita*: "When the Ark went forth, Moses said, 'Arise, O God, and scatter Your enemies! Let Your foes flee before You!' When it came to rest, he said, 'Return, O God, to the myriads of Israel's thousands'" (Numbers 10:35,36).

[The *Baraita* points out:] The Holy One, blessed be He, inserted signs [in the Torah] before and after this section. [These signs are the inverted letters *nun* that precede and follow this section in the Torah scroll.] This comes to teach us (116a) that this is not the proper place for this section. [It should have been placed in the chapter that deals with the marching order of the Israelite Camp, in Numbers 2 (Rashi).] Rabbi said: That is not the reason for the signs. The reason is that these [two verses] form a separate book of the Torah [and the signs are meant as brackets, to set the book apart]. [The Gemara asks:] With whom does the following statement of R. Shmuel b. Nachmani in R. Yochanan's name agree: "Wisdom has hewn her seven pillars" (Proverbs 9:1)? This refers to the *seven* books of the Torah. With whom does this agree? With Rabbi. [According to Rabbi, those two verses constitute a separate book. Therefore, the sections of Numbers preceding and following it are also separate books, so that Numbers actually comprises three books, and the Torah has a total of seven books.]

[The Gemara asks:] Who is the Tanna that disagrees with Rabbi? [The Gemara answers:] It is R. Shimon b. Gamliel. For we learned in a *Baraita*: R. Shimon b. Gamliel said: In the future [when the evil impulse and punishment will cease to exist], this section [of these two verses] will be moved away from here and written in its right place. Then why is it written here? In order to make a break between one evil and another. What was the second evil?—"The people began to complain" (Numbers 11:1) [which follows immediately after this section of two verses]. And what was the first evil?—"They moved away from God's mountain" (Numbers 10:33), [which precedes that section]. And R. Chama b. R. Chanina interpreted that phrase to mean that they turned away from following God. [The Gemara asks:] And where is the proper place [for this two-verse section]? [The Gemara answers:] In the chapter of the banners [Numbers 2, which describes the order in which the children of Israel marched on their journey through the wilderness].

HERETICS AND *MINIM*

We learned in a *Baraita*: Blank parchments and the books of the *Minim* (heretics)[142] may not be saved from a fire [on *Shabbat*]. R. Yose said: On weekdays, you should cut out the Divine Names that are found in these books and store them, and burn the rest. R. Tarfon said: May I bury my son if I would not burn them together with their Divine Names if I got hold of them. For even if someone chased me and wanted to kill me, or a snake pursued me to bite me, I would enter a heathen temple to find refuge, but not the houses of these people; the heathens deny God because do not know of Him, but the *Minim* know about God, but deny Him. Of them it is written, "Behind the door and doorpost you have placed your mark of remembrance" (Isaiah 57:8) [meaning, the *Minim* do remember God, but they have thrown Him out the door (Rashi)].

R. Yishmael said: You can apply a *kal vachomer*, logical reasoning: If, in order to bring peace between a husband and wife, the Torah decreed: Let My Name that was written in sanctity be erased in the water, [in the case of the suspected adulteress where the *kohen* writes the curses on a parchment and dissolves the writing in the bitter water (Numbers 5:23)], these *Minim* who provoke jealousy and hatred between the Jewish people and their Father in Heaven, [surely their writings should be destroyed]. David had in mind people like that when he said, "O God, You know I hate those who hate You and loathe Your adversaries. I feel a perfect hatred toward them; I count them my enemies" (Psalm 139:21,22). And just as you may not rescue them from a fire, so may you not save them from a collapsing structure or from water or from anything that may ruin them.

R. Yosef b. Chanin asked R. Abbahu: What about the Books of *Bei Abbadon*? [I.e., books written by *Minim* for the purpose of having debates with Jews. The locale where these debates were held was called *Bei Abbadon* (Rashi).] Are you allowed to save them from a fire [because they contain Biblical verses] or not? [R. Abbahu replied:] Yes and No. He was not sure about the matter.

Rav would not set foot in a *Bei Abbadon*, and certainly not in a *Bei Nitzrefei* [a Christian place of worship. The term *Nitzrefei* is derived from *Notzri*, Nazarene, a resident of Nazareth in southern Galilee)]. Shmuel would not enter a *Bei Nitzrefei*, but he would enter a *Bei Abbadon*. Rava was asked why he did not go to the *Bei Abbadan*. He replied: Because there is a palm tree blocking the way, and I have trouble passing it. [This was just an excuse (Rashi).] They said: All right, we will remove it. [He countered: It will leave a hole,] which will make the road impassable. [Rav and Rava would not enter a *Bei Abbadon*, fearing that during a debate they would be killed (Rashi).] Mar b. Yosef said: I am well acquainted with them, and I am not afraid of them. Still, when he went there one time, they wanted to harm him.

R. Eliezer's wife, Imma Shalom, was R. Gamliel's sister. A certain heretic philosopher [who was also a judge] lived near [R. Gamliel]. (116b) The heretic judge spread the word around that he did not accept bribes, [but secretly he welcomed gratuities]. R. Gamliel and his sister wanted to expose him, so the sister brought him a golden lamp. She then appeared before him in court and said, "I want to have a share of my late father's estate." "The estate should be divided!" ruled the judge. [He ruled in her favor, because she had bribed him.] Said R. Gamliel, "But it says in our Torah: Where there is a son, a daughter does not inherit." Replied the judge, "Since you Jews were exiled from your land, the Torah of Moses has been replaced by another book that states that a son and a daughter inherit equally." The next day R. Gamliel brought him a Lybian donkey [as a bribe]. This time the judge [reversed himself because of R. Gamliel's bribe and] said, "I looked at the end of this book, and there it says, 'I did not come to subtract from the Torah of Moses or to add to it.' In the Torah it says, 'A daughter does not inherit where there is a son.'" So the sister said to the judge, "May your light shine like a lamp" [hinting at the lamp she had given him as a bribe the day before]. Said R. Gamliel, "A donkey came and knocked over the lamp."[143]

THE THREE MEALS OF *SHABBAT*
(117b) R. Chisda said: You should get up early on Friday morning to make the preparations for the *Shabbat* meals, as it says, "On Friday, they will have to prepare what they bring home" (Exodus 16:5)—they should do it immediately. R. Abba said: On *Shabbat* you are required to recite the *berachah* of *Hamotzi* over two loaves, for it says, "[they gathered] a double portion [of manna]" (ibid. 16:22). R. Ashi said: I saw that R. Kahana held two loves but he only sliced one, for he said: It is written, "*Liktu*, 'gather of it [the manna]'" (ibid. 16:16) [in the plural, alluding to the practice of taking two loaves but cutting only one loaf]. When R. Zeira recited the *Hamotzi* he cut up the entire loaf. Said Ravina to R. Ashi: It seems that he is famished. Replied R. Ashi: Since he does not [cut up an entire loaf] every day, but only today, [in honor of *Shabbat*], therefore it does not look gluttonous.

The Rabbis taught: How many meals is a person required to eat on *Shabbat*? Three. R. Chidka said: Four, [one on Friday night and three during the day]. R. Yochanan noted: Both the Rabbis and R. Chidka expounded the same Scripture to substantiate their opinions: The verse is, "Moses announced: 'Eat it [the manna] today, for today is God's *Shabbat*. You will not find anything in the field today'" (ibid 16:25). [Moses mentions the word *hayom*, "today," three times.] R. Chidka holds that the three "todays" refer to the three meals a person must eat on *Shabbat* in the daytime, aside from the meal he is required to eat at night. The

Rabbis hold that the three "todays" include the Friday night meal.

(118a) R. Shimon b. Pazzi said in the name of R. Yehoshua b. Levi who spoke in the name of Bar Kappara: A person who observes the practice of eating three meals on *Shabbat* is saved from three calamities: the pangs of the advent of *Mashiach*, the suffering of Gehinnom, and the war of Gog and Magog [prior to the coming of *Mashiach*, which is described by the prophets Zechariah and Ezekiel as a time of dreadful suffering]. We know that he will be saved from the pangs of *Mashiach*, because it says here *yom*, in connection with *Shabbat* "today" (Exodus 16:25), and it says, "Lo, I will send the prophet Elijah to you before the coming of the awesome, fearful day, *yom*, of God" (Malachi 3:23). [Thus, by observing the three meals (*yom*) he will be protected from the "fearful day" (*yom*).] [He will be shielded from] the suffering of Gehinnom: because it says here *yom*, "today," and it says, "That *yom*, (day) will be a day of wrath (Zephaniah 1:15). [He will be saved] from the war of Gog and Magog, because it says here, *yom*, (today), and it says elsewhere, "On that *yom* (day) when Gog sets foot on the soil of Israel" (Ezekiel 38:18).

TAKING DELIGHT IN *SHABBAT*
R. Yochanan said in the name of R. Yose: Someone who takes delight in *Shabbat* is given a boundless inheritance, for it says, "Then [in the days of *Mashiach*] you will indulge in spiritual pleasures, I will set you astride the heights of the earth, and let you enjoy (118b) the heritage of your father Jacob" (Isaiah 58:14). [Why Jacob?] Not like Abraham, about whom it says, "Rise, walk the land, through its length and breadth" (Genesis 13:17), [but not more than that; God's promise to Abraham was limited]; and not like Isaac about whom it says, "To you and to your offspring I will give all these lands" (ibid. 26:3) [only these lands, but not more; God's promise to Isaac also was restricted], but like Jacob about whom it says, "You shall spread out to the west, to the east, to the north and to the south" (ibid. 28:14) [a boundless promise. Similarly the person who observes the three meals on *Shabbat* will receive a boundless inheritance].

R. Nachman b. Yitzchak said: He is saved from the subjugation by the nations of the Exile. It says here, "I will set you astride the heights of the earth" and it says elsewhere, "You shall tread on their high places" (Deuteronomy 33:29) [which Rashi in Deuteronomy interprets to mean that you will tread on the necks of your enemies].

R. Yehudah said in the name of Rav: If a person savors the *Shabbat* he is granted his heart's desire, for it says, "Delight together with God, and He will grant you the desires of your heart" (Psalms 37:4). [Explains R. Yehudah] From this verse by itself we do not know what "delight" refers to; but when it says, "You shall call the *Shabbat* a delight" (Isaiah 58:13), it becomes clear that [the phrase, "Delight together with God"] refers to the mitzvah of taking delight in the *Shabbat*.

R. Chiya b. Abba said in R. Yochanan's name: If someone observes the *Shabbat* according to its laws, even if he practices idolatry like the generation of Enosh,[144] he is forgiven, for it says, "Happy is *enosh*, 'the man' who does this, . . . [who keeps the *Shabbat meichallelo* from desecrating it]" (Isaiah 56:2); do not read *meichallelo* but *machul lo*, "he is forgiven."

R. Yehudah said in Rav's name: If the Jewish people had kept the first *Shabbat*, no nation of the world would have been able to dominate them, for it says [in reference to the first *Shabbat*], "Some people went out to gather [manna] on *Shabbat*, [in violation of Moses' command], but they found nothing" (Exodus 16:27). And afterward it says, "Then came Amalek" (ibid. 17:8).[145]

R. Yochanan said in the name of R. Shimon b. Yocha'i: If Israel would observe two *Shabbat*s in succession according to its laws, they immediately would be redeemed, for it says, "For thus says God: 'As for the eunuchs who keep My *Shabbat*s,'" (Isaiah 56:4), which is followed by, "I will bring them to My holy mountain" (ibid. 7), [a reference to the days of the Redemption].

R. Yose said: May I share in the reward of those who eat three meals on *Shabbat*. R. Yose also said: May I share in the reward of those who recite the entire *Hallel*[146] every day. [The Gemara asks:] Is that so? Has not a Rabbi said: A person who says *Hallel* every day is a blasphemer [because the prophets ordained that *Hallel* be recited on Festivals and special occasions, and by saying it every day he is treating it disdainfully, singing it like an ordinary song (Rashi).] [The Gemara answers: R. Yose is not referring to *Hallel*.] He has in mind people who are reciting *Pesukei deZimra*, [specifically Psalms 148 and 150 in which God's praises reach a thundrous crescendo (Rashi)].

SAYINGS BY R. YOSE

R. Yose said: May I share in the reward of those who pray with the red glow of the sun [at dawn and at sunset]. R. Chiya b. Abba said in R. Yochanan's name: It is a mitzvah to pray with the red glow of the sun. R. Zera said: From what verse do we derive this? "Let them revere You at sunrise and before the moon shines, for generations on end" (Psalms 72:5).

R. Yose also said: May I share in the reward of those who die of stomach trouble, [its excruciating pain wipes out sin and brings about forgiveness (Rashi)], for a Rabbi said, "Most of the righteous die of stomach trouble."

R. Yose also said: May I share in the reward of those who die while engaged in the performance of a mitzvah. R. Yose also said: May I share in the reward of those who usher in the *Shabbat* in T'veriah (Tiberias) and end the *Shabbat* in Tzipori (Sepphoris). [In the low-

lying Tiberias the *Shabbat* begins earlier, while in Sepphoris, which was situated on a mountain, the *Shabbat* ends later than in other places (Rashi).] R. Yose also said: May I share in the reward of the people who gather up the students to come to the *bet hamidrash*; and not of those who tell them that it is time to go home. R. Yose also said: May I share in the reward of those who collect charity, but not of those who distribute charity [and who have the difficult task of being impartial in distributing the funds according to the needs of the recipient (Rashi)]. R. Yose also said: May I share in the reward of those who are suspected of something they did not do. R. Papa said: I once was suspected of something without foundation.

R. Yose also said: I never declined the wishes of my friends. I know myself that I am not a *kohen*, yet if my friends would ask me to go up to the platform [to recite the priestly blessing] I would go up, [although he certainly would not recite the *berachah* which a non-*kohen* is forbidden to do]. He merely would go through the motions so as not to turn down his friends (Iyun Yaakov)].

R. Yose also said: Never in my life have I said anything and taken back what I said. [If a person about whom he said something asked him whether, in fact, he had said this, he never denied it, even if it was unfavorable (Rashi).]

MERITORIOUS DEEDS

R. Nachman said: May it be a merit for me that I fulfilled the mitzvah of three meals on *Shabbat*. R. Yehudah said: May it be a merit for me that I prayed with deep concentration. R. Huna b. R. Yehoshua said: May it be a merit for me that I never walked four cubits with my head uncovered. R. Sheshet said: May it be a merit for me that I fulfilled the mitzvah of *tefillin*. R. Nachman said: May it be a merit for me that I fulfilled the mitzvah of *tzitzit*. [They never walked four cubits without wearing *tefillin* and *tzitzit* (Rashi).]

R. Yosef asked R. Yosef b. Rabbah: What mitzvah was your father especially careful of? Of the mitzvah of *tzitzit*, he replied. One day he was going up a ladder when one of the threads of his *tzitit* tore, and he would not come down until the thread was replaced.

Abbaye said: May it be counted as a merit for me that whenever I saw that a young scholar had finished a treatise of the Talmud (119a) I made a festive meal for the rabbis. Rava said: May it be counted as a merit for me that when a young scholar came before me as a litigant in a lawsuit I did not put my head down on a pillow as long as I did not try to find justification for his case. [Rava had high regard for scholars and was sure that they would not bring suit unless they thought that it had merit (Maharsha). The S'fat Emet explains that this does not mean that Rava favored the scholar, but if Rava had a number of cases on his docket, one of which was brought by a scholar, out of respect of the scholar, he would hear his case first. However, he would judge each case with complete impartiality.] Mar b. R. Ashi said: I am disqualified to judge in a scholar's lawsuit. What is the reason? Because I love him as much as I love myself, and a person is unable to find fault with himself.

HOW THE GREAT SAGES HONORED *SHABBAT*

As he ushered in the *Shabbat*, R. Chanina wrapped himself in his *Shabbat* attire and exclaimed: Let us come and go out to welcome Queen *Shabbat*. R. Yannai put on his *Shabbat* attire and exclaimed: Enter, O bride! Enter, O bride!

When Rabbah b. R. Huna visited the home of Rabbah b. R. Nachman he was offered three wafers smeared with oil. "Did you know that I was coming [that you prepared such a delicacy]?" R. Huna asked. "Are you then better than *Shabbat* about which it says, 'You call the *Shabbat* a delight'?" (Isaiah 58:13). [We did not know you were coming, but we prepared the wafers in honor of *Shabbat* (Rashi).]

R. Abba bought meat for thirteen *istira peshita*[147] from thirteen butchers,[148] and as soon as the meat was delivered he handed it to his servants, saying: Hurry up, prepare it quickly! Hurry up, prepare it quickly [in honor of *Shabbat*]!

R. Abbahu used to sit on an ivory stool and fan the fire [to prepare the food for *Shabbat*]. R. Anan used to wear overalls [to do work in preparation for *Shabbat*, so as not to soil his good clothes], for the School of R. Yishmael taught: The clothes that a person is wearing when he is cooking a dish for his master he should not wear when he is pouring a cup [of wine] for his master. R. Safra used to singe the head of [an animal, in order to prepare it for *Shabbat*]. Rava would salt a fish. R. Huna lit the lamp. R. Papa braided the wicks [for the oil lamps]. R. Chisda sliced beets. Rabbah and R. Yosef chopped wood [in honor of *Shabbat*]. R. Zeira kindled the fire for *Shabbat*. R. Nachman b. Yitzchak would constantly bring in necessities for *Shabbat* and go out [and buy more things for *Shabbat*]. He would say: If R. Ammi and R. Assi [who were the foremost scholars of that time] would come to visit me, wouldn't I bring in [the finest things to honor them]? [Therefore we want to do the same thing for *Shabbat*.] Others say: R. Ammi and R. Assi carried in necessities for *Shabbat*, saying: If R. Yochanan came to visit us, wouldn't we bring in [the finest things to honor him]?

YOSEF WHO HONORED THE *SHABBAT*

Yosef-who-honored-*Shabbat* had a gentile neighbor who was very wealthy. Astrologers told this neighbor: Yosef-who-honors-*Shabbat* will take over all your properties. So he went, sold all his properties, and with the money he bought a precious jewel, which he set in his hat. One day, while he was crossing on a ferry boat, a gust of wind blew his hat into the water, and a fish swallowed it. The fish was caught and brought to market on a Friday afternoon toward sunset. "Who is willing to buy this fish at this time?" they asked. People told them, "Go and take this fish to Yosef-who-honors-*Shabbat*. He always buys fish [on Friday]. So they took this fish to him. He bought it, opened it, found the jewel, and sold it for thirteen roomfuls of gold *dinarim*.[149] An elderly person met him and said: He who spends money to honor the *Shabbat*, the *Shabbat* will pay him back.

WHY DO THE RICH BECOME PROSPEROUS?

Rabbi asked R. Yishmael b. R. Yose: Because of what particular merit do the wealthy people in Eretz Yisrael become rich? He replied: Because they give tithes, as it says, *Asser te'asser*, "Give a tithe" (Deuteronomy 14:22). [The double expression means:] Give tithes (*asser*) in order that you may become rich (*tit'asher*). Because of what merit do people become rich in Babylonia? He replied: Because they honor the Torah. And the wealthy people in other countries, why do they deserve to be rich? Because they honor the *Shabbat*, he replied. For R. Chiya b. Abba related: I once stayed at the home of a wealthy man in Ludkia, and they brought up a golden table that had to be carried by sixteen men; sixteen silver chains were attached to it, and plates, cups, pitchers, and flasks were set on it, and on that table there were all kinds of food, delicacies, and spices. When they put the table in place they said, "The earth is God's and all that it holds," (Psalm 24:1) [and until we recite a *berachah* we are not allowed to partake of all these delicacies because all this belongs to God].

When they removed the table [after the meal] they said, "The heavens belong to God, but the earth He gave over to the children of men" (Psalm 115:16). So R. Chiya b. Abba said to him: "My son, how have you merited to obtain all this wealth?" "I used to be a butcher," he replied, "and whenever I came across a fine animal I said: This animal should be set aside for *Shabbat*." R. Chiya b. Abba said to him, "Fortunate are you that you merited such wealth, and praised be the Almighty Who bestowed it on you."

The Roman emperor [Hadrian] said to R. Yehoshua b. Chanania: "Why does the food you prepared for the Sabbath smell so good?" R. Yehoshua replied, "We have a special spice that we put into it, and its name is Sabbath." "Give me some of it," the emperor demanded. "It works for whoever observes the Sabbath, but for those who do not observe the Sabbath, it has no effect," replied R. Yehoshua b. Chanania.

THE MAGNIFICENCE
OF *SHABBAT*

The *Resh Galuta*,[150] asked R. Hamenuna: What is the meaning of the verse, "[If you call . . .] God's holy day 'honored'"?[151] Replied R. Hamenuna: This refers to Yom Kippur, on which there is neither eating nor drinking. Therefore the Torah says that you should honor Yom Kippur with festive attire. [The verse continues,] "And honor it," [referring to *Shabbat*]. [How should you honor the *Shabbat*?] Rav said: By eating earlier than you normally do [to show your eagerness]. Shmuel contends: By eating later than you normally do, [so that you honor the *Shabbat* by eating the *Shabbat* meal with greater appetite]. The sons of R. Papa b. Abba asked R. Papa: We, for example, who have meat and wine every day, how shall we make *Shabbat* a day of distinction? He answered: If you are accustomed to having your meal early, then delay it; if you are accustomed to eating later, have your *Shabbat* meal earlier.

When R. Sheshet gave his *Shabbat* discourse, in the summer he seated the rabbis [who came to listen to his lecture] on the sunny side of the lecture hall, [so that they should feel uncomfortable and leave quickly and thus have their *Shabbat* meal early]. In the winter he seated them on the shady side of the hall, [so that they would feel chilled and leave quickly and have their *Shabbat* meal early].

(119b) [When *Shabbat* was approaching,] R. Zeira used to go after pairs of scholars [who were studying Gemara together] and say to them: I implore you, don't desecrate the *Shabbat*. [Stop learning. Go ahead and indulge in the delights of *Shabbat*! (Rashi)].

Rava—others say, R. Yehoshua b. Levi—said: Even if a person is praying by himself on Friday night [and not with a *minyan*], he must recite *Vayechulu*, "Thus the heavens and the earth were finished . . ." (Genesis 2:1); for R. Hamenuna said: Whoever prays *Maariv* on Friday night and recites *Vayechulu*, the Torah considers it as if he became a partner with the Holy One, blessed be He, in the Creation, for it says *Vayechulu*, "and they were finished;" don't read *vayechulu* but *vayechalu*, "and they finished the heavens and the earth . . ." [whereby "they" refers to God and the individual who praises God and the *Shabbat* (Rashi)]. R. Elazar said: How do we know that when God speaks it is as good as done? Because it says, "By the word of God the heavens were made" (Psalm 33:6). R. Chisda said in Mar Ukva's name: Whoever prays on Friday night and recites *Vayechulu*, "Thus the heavens and the earth were finished," the two ministering angels that accompany a person place their hands on his head and say to him, "Your guilt shall depart and your sin be purged away" (Isaiah 6:7).

We learned in a *Baraita*: R. Yose b. R. Yehudah said: Two ministering angels escort a person on Friday night from the synagogue to his house, one a good angel, the other an evil angel. And when he comes home and finds the candles lit and sees that the table is set and his bed is made, the good angel declares: May the coming *Shabbat* be just like the present one. And the evil angel has no choice but to answer "amen." But if he does not find [the candles lit, the table set, and the bed made,] the evil angel wishes: May it be like this on the next *Shabbat*. And the good angel has no option but to answer "amen."

R. Elazar said: A person should set his table on Friday, even if he [is not hungry] and wants to eat only as little as the size of an olive. R. Chanina said: A person should set his table on *Motza'ei Shabbat* [after the conclusion of *Shabbat*], even if he cannot eat more than the size of an olive. [It is a mitzvah to escort the *Shabbat* on its way out with a meal, just as you would escort the king when he leaves town (Rashi).] Drinking hot water after the conclusion of *Shabbat* has therapeutic value. Eating warm bread after the conclusion of *Shabbat* also has therapeutic value. They used to prepare a choice calf for R. Abbahu at the conclusion of *Shabbat*, and he would eat one of its kidneys. When his son Avimi grew up he asked him: Why do you have to waste so much meat [why slaughter a new calf on *motza'ei Shabbat*]? Why don't you leave a kidney from the calf you prepared on Friday? So he left it over, and a lion came and ate up [the calf that would have been slaughtered on *motza'ei Shabbat*; a sign from Heaven that he should have prepared a new calf in honor of the departure of *Shabbat*].

RESPONDING "AMEN"

R. Yehoshua b. Levi said: Whoever answers [in the *Kaddish*], *Amein yehei shemei rabba mevarach*, "May His great name be blessed," with all his strength [meaning, with his full concentration], if an evil sentence has been decreed for him, it will be rescinded, as it says, "When punishment was cancelled in Israel, when people dedicate themselves—Bless the Lord!" (Judges 5:2). Why are punishments cancelled? Because the people bless God. R. Chiya b. Abba said: Even if this person was tainted with idolatry, he is forgiven: it says here, "When punishment is cancelled [*bifro'a pera'ot*]," and elsewhere it says [in connection with the sin of the golden calf], "Moses saw that the people were out of control [*parua*], since Aaron had let them get out of control [*fera'oh*]" (Exodus 32:25), [thus he was somewhat tainted with that sin. *Parua* and *fera'oh* are cognate to *befro'a pera'ot*, which implies that punishment is cancelled even for a person tainted with idolatry].

Resh Lakish said: Whoever responds "Amen" with all his strength will have the gates of Gan Eden opened for him, for it says, "Open the gates and let a righteous nation enter, a nation that keeps faith [*shomer emunim*]" (Isaiah 26:2). Do not read *shomer emunim* but *she'omerim amen*, "those that say amen." What does "amen" mean? Said R. Chanina: It is a contraction of *Keil melech ne'eman*, "God, trustworthy King."

WHY WAS JERUSALEM DESTROYED?

R. Yehudah b. R. Shmuel said in Rav's name: A fire breaks out only in a house where there is desecration of the *Shabbat*, for it says, "But if you do not obey My commandment to sanctify the *Shabbat* day and to carry in no burdens through the gates of Jerusalem on the *Shabbat* day, then I will set fire to its gates; it shall consume the palaces of Jerusalem, and it shall not be extinguished" (Jeremiah 17:27). What does "it shall not be extinguished" mean? Said R. Nachman b. Yitzchak: [The fire will break out] at a time when there will be no people around to extinguish it, [which is on *Shabbat*].

Abbaye said: The reason Jerusalem was destroyed was because of the sin of the desecration of *Shabbat*, for it says, "They have closed their eyes to My *Shabbat*s, and I was desecrated among them" (Ezekiel 22:26). [God's name was desecrated when Jerusalem was destroyed, which resulted from the violation of the *Shabbat* (Rif)].

R. Abbahu said: The reason Jerusalem was destroyed was because people neglected to read the *Shema* in the morning and the evening. For it says, "Woe to those who chase liquor from early in the morning [instead of reading the *Shema*] . . . !" And it says, "Who at their banquets have lyre and lute, timbrel, flute and wine; but who never give a thought to the deeds of God . . . Therefore My people will suffer exile, for giving no heed" [to the reading of the *Shema*] (Isaiah 5:11–13).

R. Hamenuna said: The reason Jerusalem was destroyed was because people neglected to send their children to Torah schools. For it says, "Pour out [God's wrath] because of the young children in the street" (Jeremiah 6:11). Why is God's wrath poured out? Because the children are in the streets [instead of in school].

Ulla said: The reason Jerusalem was destroyed was because people were not ashamed of each other. For it says, "They have acted shamefully; they have done abhorrent things—yet they do not feel shame . . . Surely they shall fall among the falling" (Jeremiah 6:15).

R. Yitzchak said: The reason Jerusalem was destroyed was because they made no distinction between the great and the small. For it says, "Layman and priest shall fare alike" [the great men were treated disdainfully, as if they were ordinary people]. This passage is followed by, "The land will be utterly emptied" (Isaiah 24:2,3).

R. Amram b. R. Shimon b. Abba said in R. Shimon b. Abba's name who said in R. Chanina's name: The reason Jerusalem was destroyed was because the people

did not admonish each other. For it says, "Her leaders were like deer that found no pasture" (Lamentations 1:6).[152] Just as in a herd of deer, the head of one deer faces the tail of the one in front of it, so Israel of that generation buried their faces in the earth [looked the other way], and did not admonish each other.

R. Yehudah said: The reason Jerusalem was destroyed was because the people treated Torah scholars with contempt. For it says, "But they mocked the messengers of God and disdained His words and taunted His prophets until the wrath of God arose against His people, till there was no remedy" (2 Chronicles 36:16). What does "till there was no remedy" imply? Said R. Yehudah in Rav's name: Whoever despises a Torah scholar will find no remedy for his wounds.

[It should be understood that the above-mentioned sages did not contradict each other's opinions as to the reason for the destruction of Jerusalem. All the failings they cited were factors that brought about the calamity. Each sage stressed the defect that was prevalent in his time (Iyun Yaakov).]

TORAH SCHOOLS FOR CHILDREN

Rav Yehudah said in Rav's name: What is the meaning of the passage, "Dare not touch My anointed ones, and to My prophets do no harm" (Psalms 105:15)? "Dare not touch My anointed ones" refers to schoolchildren. [It was the custom to anoint them with oil (Rashi).] "And to My prophets do no harm" refers to Torah scholars.

Resh Lakish said in the name of Rabbi Yehudah Nesiah[153]: The world endures only because of the breath of schoolchildren. Said R. Papa to Abaye: What about your breath and my breath? [We are Torah scholars, doesn't the world endure because of us?] He replied: You cannot compare breath that has been tarnished by sin to breath that has not been blemished by sin. Resh Lakish also said in the name of R. Yehudah Nesiah: We do not suspend classes of Torah schools even for the building of the *Bet Hamikdash*.

Said Resh Lakish to R. Yehudah Nesiah: I have a tradition from my ancestors—others say, from your ancestors: Any city that does not have a Torah school for children will eventually be destroyed [but ruins will be left standing]. Ravina said: It will be laid waste [and nothing will be left].

Rava said: Jerusalem was destroyed only because there were no trustworthy people left in it, as it says, "Roam the streets of Jerusalem, search its squares, look about and take note . . . if there is anyone who acts justly, who seeks integrity that I should pardon her" (Jeremiah 5:1). [The Gemara asks:] Do you mean to say there were no honest people in Jerusalem at the time of its destruction? Didn't R. Ketina say: Even at the time of Jerusalem's downfall, [when it reached its spiritual low point], honest people did not cease to live there. For it says, "For should a man seize his brother in the house of his father, saying, 'You have a garment; come be chief over us,'" (Isaiah 3:6). (120a) [This means: People said:] You possess knowledge of the secrets that are hidden from us and covered with a cloth [of mystery]. "And this stumbling block is under your hand" (ibid.). [They said:] You know the things that will cause us to stumble, and you can instruct us on how to avoid transgression. Therefore, "come and be chief over us."

[What will that person answer? He will be perfectly honest.] "He will lift up his hand on that day and swear," (ibid.). And "lifting up [yissa] one's hand" means taking an oath, as it says, "Do not take the name of God in vain" [Lo tissa]. [He will answer forthrightly:] "I am not a choveish"—I am not one who spends his time in the bet midrash. [I am unqualified and incapable of answering your questions.] "In my house there is neither bread nor clothing"—I am ignorant. I don't know the Scriptures, Mishnah, or Gemara. [Thus we see that there were people who were completely honest. Why then does Rava say that there were no honest people in Jerusalem?]

[The Gemara answers: This verse does not prove that he was honest.] Perhaps in this case it was different. For if he had lied and said, "I have studied the deeper meaning of the laws of the Torah," people would have put him to the test and told him, "Tell us [the answer to our questions]." [Retorts the Gemara:] He could have replied that he had learned and forgotten. Instead he said, "I am not one who spends his time in the bet midrash"? [We must conclude that he was scrupulously honest.] [The Gemara answers:] There is no difficulty: They were honest with regard to Torah study, but when Rava said that honest people had ceased to exist in Jerusalem, he was referring to integrity in business dealings.

(121a) We learned in a Baraita: One day a fire broke out in the courtyard of Yosef b. Sima'i in She'an, and the men of the military unit stationed in Tzippori came to extinguish it because he was the treasurer of the king. But Yosef did not allow them to put out the fire in honor of Shabbat. By a miracle, it began to rain and the fire was extinguished. In the evening he sent two sela to each of the soldiers who came to help him, and fifty to their commander. When the Sages heard of it they said: He did not need this, because we learned: If a gentile comes to extinguish a fire, we do not tell him either to extinguish it or not to extinguish it, because a non-Jew is not required to rest on Shabbat.

HOSPITALITY

(127a) R. Yochanan said: Offering hospitality to guests is as great a mitzvah as getting up early to go to the bet midrash to learn Torah, because the Mishnah mentions these two things together, stating, "for guests or because of neglect of the bet hamidrash." R. Dimi of

Nehardea said: Hospitality is a greater mitzvah than getting up early to go to the bet midrash, because the Mishnah mentions first "for guests" and only then "the neglect of the bet midrash." Rav Yehudah said in Rav's name: Hospitality is a greater mitzvah than having a revelation of the Shechinah, for it says, [when Abraham wanted to offer hospitality to the three wayfarers, he interrupted the vision of God he was having and asked God to wait for him. Abraham said,] "My Lord, if you would, please do not go away from your servant" (Genesis 18:3). R. Elazar said: Notice how the nature of the Holy One, blessed be He, differs from that of mortal man. The nature of human beings is such that an unimportant person cannot tell a great man: Wait for me until I come to you; whereas when speaking to the Holy One, blessed be He, Abraham said: Wait for me, and I will come back to you.

R. Yehudah b. Shila said in R. Assi's name in R. Yochanan's name: There are six things whose fruits a person enjoys in this world, but whose principal remains intact for him in the World to Come, [although he is rewarded for these mitzvots in this world, his reward in the World to Come is not diminished]. They are: hospitality to guests, visiting the sick, absorption in prayer, early attendance at the bet hamidrash, raising your children to study the Torah, and judging your neighbor favorably. [The Gemara asks:] Is that so? Haven't we learned in a Mishnah[154]: These are the precepts whose fruits a person enjoys in this world but whose principal remains intact for him in the World to Come. They are: the honor due to father and mother, acts of kindness, bringing peace between man and his fellow—and the study of Torah is equivalent to all of them. [This implies], only these, and not the six things R. Yochanan enumerated. [The Gemara answers:] (127b) Those that R. Yochanan mentions are included in those listed in the Mishnah.[155]

JUDGE YOUR FELLOW
FAVORABLY

The Rabbis taught in a Baraita: Someone who judges his fellow favorably is also judged favorably from Heaven. The story is told about a person who came down from the Upper Galilee and hired out to an employer in the south of Eretz Yisrael for three years. At the end of the three years, on the eve of Yom Kippur, he said to his master, "Give me my wages, and I will go and support my wife and my children." "I have no money," replied the master. "Then give me produce," the worker said. "I don't have any," the master answered. "Well, then give me a piece of land."—"I don't have any land." "Then give me cattle." "I have none." "Give me pillows and bedding." "I don't have that either." So he slung his bundle over his shoulder and went home, deeply dejected. After Yom Tov, the master took the man's wages in his hand along with three donkeys, one loaded with food, one loaded with drink, and the third loaded with all kinds of sweets, and went to the worker's house.

After they had eaten and drunk together, he gave him his wages for the three years. "When you asked me, 'Give me my wages,' and I answered you, 'I have no money,' what did you suspect me of?" the master asked. The man replied, "I thought, perhaps you came across a good deal and had used all your money to buy the inexpensive goods." "And when you asked for cattle and I said that I had none, what did you suspect me of then?" the master asked. "I thought, perhaps you had rented the animals to someone [and were unable to give them to me]," was the reply. "When you asked me for land, and I said that I had no land, what did you suspect me of?" "I thought perhaps you had leased it to others." "And when I told you that I had no produce, what did you suspect me of?" "I thought that perhaps they were not tithed." "And when I said that I had no pillows and bedding, what did you suspect me of then?" "I said to myself that perhaps you had consecrated all your property to Heaven."

"I swear," the master exclaimed. "That is exactly what happened. I had made a vow to give all my possessions to the *Bet Hamikdash* because of my son Hyrcanus who was not learning Torah. [I hoped that in the merit of my gift he would mend his ways.] But when I went to my friends in the South they absolved me of all my vows. [And that is why I can pay you now.] And as far as you are concerned, just as you judged me favorably, so may the Almighty judge you favorably."[156]

The Rabbis taught: The story is told that a certain pious man[157] ransomed a young Jewish girl from captivity. At the lodging he let the girl sleep at his feet. The next morning he immersed in a *mikveh* and learned with his disciples. He said to them, "When I made her sleep at my feet, what did you suspect me of?" They replied "[We did not suspect you at all.] We thought, there is a disciple among us whom you do not know so well, [and you did not want to leave the girl unprotected.]" "When I immersed in the *mikveh*, what did you suspect me of?" he asked. "We thought, perhaps because of the hardship of traveling you had a pollution at night," they replied. "I swear," he exclaimed, "that is what happened." And just as you judged me favorably, so may the Almighty judge you favorably."

The Rabbis taught: The scholars were once in need of something from a non-Jewish noblewoman where all the important men of Rome could be found. They said, "Who will go?" "I will go," said R. Yehoshua. So R. Yehoshua went with his disciples. When he came to the entrance to her house, he took off his *tefillin* at a distance of four cubits, entered, and locked the door in front of them. After he came out he immersed in a *mikveh* and learned with his disciples. He said to them, "When I took off my *tefillin* before entering the house, what did you suspect me of?" "We thought, you did not want sacred words to be brought into a place of uncleanness," the disciples answered. "When I locked the door, what did you suspect me of?" "We thought perhaps you had to discuss with her a confidential matter concerning the government." "When I immersed in the *mikveh* what did you suspect me of?" "We thought perhaps some saliva may have squirted from her mouth on your clothing." "I swear," he exclaimed, "that is exactly what happened, and just as you judged me favorably, so may the Almighty judge you favorably."

CARING FOR A NEWBORN ON *SHABBAT*

(129b) R. Nachman b. Yitzchak said in R. Abba b. Abbuha's name in Rav's name: All that is mentioned in the Chapter of Reproof [Ezekiel, Chapter 16, where the prophet admonishes the Jewish people], may be done on *Shabbat* for a woman who has given birth. For it says in that chapter, "As for your birth, when you were born your navel cord was not cut, and you were not bathed in water to smooth you, you were not rubbed with salt, nor were you swaddled" (Ezekiel 16:4). "As for your birth, when you were born": From this we gather that an infant may be delivered on *Shabbat*. "Your navel cord was not cut": From this we gather that the umbilical cord may be cut on *Shabbat*. "You were not bathed in water to smooth you": From this we gather that the newborn infant may be washed on *Shabbat*. "You were not rubbed with salt": From this we gather that the newborn infant may be salted on *Shabbat* [to toughen the body (Rashi)]. "Nor swaddled": From this we gather that the infant may be swaddled on *Shabbat*.

THE JOYOUS MITZVAH OF *MILAH*

It was taught in a *Baraita*: R. Shimon b. Gamliel said: Every mitzvah that the Jews accepted with joy, such as the mitzvah of circumcision, as it says, "I rejoice over Your commandment, as one who finds great spoil" (Psalms 119:162), [this refers to the mitzvah of *milah*, which is unique in that it dates back to the time of Abraham (Rashi)], they still observe with joy [by celebrating a *brit milah* with a festive meal]. Whereas every commandment that they accepted with resentment, such as the laws of forbidden marriages, as it says, "Moses heard the people weeping with their families" (Numbers 11:10), meaning, they cried over family matters [i.e., regarding incest, which was now forbidden to them], they still perform them with resentment, for there is no marriage without some quarrel.

ELISHA-THE-MAN-OF-THE-WINGS

We learned in a *Baraita*: R. Shimon b. Elazar said: Every commandment for which the Jews were willing to give their lives when the government forced them to transgress, such as idolatry and circumcision, is still strictly adhered to. By contrast, every mitzvah for which the Jews were not willing to offer their lives when the government forced them to transgress, such as the mitzvah of *tefillin*, they still observe with laxness. For R. Yannai said: *Tefillin* require a clean body, like Elisha-the-man-of-the-wings. What does this mean? Abbaye said: One should not pass wind while wearing them. Rava said: One should not fall asleep while wearing them. And why is he called "the-man-of-the-wings"? Because the Roman government once issued a decree against the Jews that whoever wore *tefillin* on his head would have his brains pierced.[158]

Yet Elisha went out into the streets wearing *tefillin*. When a Roman officer spotted him, Elisha ran away, and the officer chased him. When Elisha noticed that the officer was catching up with him, he took the *tefillin* off his head and held them in his hand. "What do you have in your hand?" the officer asked. "The wings of a dove," Elisha replied. He opened his hand, and miraculously, there were the wings of a dove in it. Therefore everyone called him "Elisha-the-man-of-the-wings." [The Gemara asks:] Why did he tell him the wings of a dove rather than that of any other bird? Because the Jewish people is compared to a dove, as it says, "like the wings of a dove sheathed in silver, and her pinions with yellow gold" (Psalm 68:14). Just as a dove is protected by its wings, so is the Jewish people protected by the *mitzvot*.

(133b) We learned in a *Baraita*: "This is My God and I will beautify Him" (*ve'anveihu*)(Exodus 15:2). This means, beautify yourself before Him with *mitzvot*: with a beautiful sukkah, a beautiful *lulav*, a beautiful shofar, beautiful *tzitzit*, a beautiful Torah scroll, written with the proper intention, with good ink, with a good pen, by an expert scribe, and wrap it with beautiful wrapping.

Abba Shaul said: *Ve'anveihu* means: Emulate Him. Just as He is merciful and compassionate, so should you be merciful and compassionate.

POSTPONEMENT OF CIRCUMCISION

(134a) Abbaye said: My mother told me that if an infant looks red all over, it is an indication that the blood is not absorbed within the organs of the body, and therefore the circumcision should be postponed until the blood is absorbed. If an infant has a yellow or greenish appearance, it is an indication that it lacks blood, and the circumcision should be postponed until the baby becomes full-blooded. For we learned in a *Baraita*: R. Natan said: I once went to the cities by the sea, and there appeared before me a woman whose first and second sons both had died as a result of their circumcision. She brought her third son to me, and when I examined him I noticed that he was quite red. I told her to postpone the *milah* until the baby's blood would

become absorbed. She did so, and then the child was circumcised, and he lived. The child was then named after me: Natan, the Babylonian. On another occasion I came to the country of Kapudkia (Cappadocia), and there appeared before me a woman whose first and second sons both had died as a result of their circumcision. She brought the third son to me, and when I looked at him I noticed that he looked greenish, and when I examined him I found that he did not have enough blood to be circumcised. So I told her to wait until the child had sufficient blood. She waited and then the child was circumcised, and the child lived. She named him after me and called him Natan, the Babylonian.

THE TORAH WILL NEVER BE FORGOTTEN

(138b) Rav said: There will come a time when the Torah will be forgotten by Israel, for it says, "Then God will smite you in an amazing way" (Deuteronomy 28:59). What is this amazing way (*hafla'ah*) [with which God will punish Israel]? But when it says, "Truly, I shall further punish this people in a most amazing way (*haflei vafeleh*); and the wisdom of its wise men shall fail, and the prudence of its prudent men shall vanish" (Isaiah 29:14), I understand that *hafla'ah* refers to the Torah. [Thus the verse "God will smite you in an amazing way (*vehiflah*)" means that God will cause the Torah to be forgotten, and that is the worst disaster that could befall the Jewish people, God forbid.]

Our Rabbis taught: When the Rabbis entered the Yeshivah in Yavneh, they said: There will come a time when the Torah will be forgotten by the Jewish people, for it says, "A time is coming—declares God my Lord—when I will send a famine upon the land: not a hunger for bread or a thirst for water, but for learning the words of God, [and there will be few people who will be able to impart it]. Men will wander from sea to sea and from north to east, they will roam about to seek the word of God, but they will not find it" (Amos 9:11,12). [Asks the Gemara:] What is the definition of] "the word of God"? [The Gemara answers:] "The word of God" alludes to *halachah*. "The word of God" alludes also to the end of time. "The word of God" alternately means prophecy.

We learned in a *Baraita*: R. Shimon b. Yocha'i said: God forbid that the Torah will be forgotten by the Jewish people, for it says, "Since it [the Torah] will not be forgotten by their descendants" (Deuteronomy 31:21). What then is the meaning of the verse, "They will roam about to seek the word of God, but they will not find it"? It means that they will not find a clear *halachah* and a lucid Mishnah in one place, [but every statement will be challenged and disputed (Rashi), as is the case in the Gemara, but, of course, the Torah will never be forgotten].

THE BANE OF CORRUPT JUDGES

(139a) We learned in a *Baraita*: R. Yose b. Elisha said: If you see a generation that suffers many troubles, go out and investigate the judges of the Jewish people, because all the troubles that come upon the world only come because of [corrupt] judges. For it says, "Hear this, you rulers of the House of Jacob, you chiefs of the House of Israel, who detest justice, and make crooked all that is straight. Who build Zion with crime, Jerusalem with iniquity! Her rulers judge for bribes, her priests give rulings for a fee, and her prophets prophesy for pay; yet they rely on God, saying: 'God is in our midst, no calamity will befall us'" (Micah 3:9–11). They are wicked, yet they rely on the Creator. Therefore, the Holy One, blessed be He, will bring on them three punishments to correspond to the three sins of which they are guilty, [i.e., her rulers taking bribes, her priests taking fees, and her prophets prophesying for pay].

As it says, "Because of your sins, Zion will be plowed like a field, and Jerusalem will become heaps of ruins, and the Temple Mount a shrine in the woods" (ibid. 12). And the Holy One, blessed be He, will not cause His *Shechinah* to rest on Israel until the evil judges and law officers will disappear from the among the Jewish people. For it says, "I will turn My hand against you, and smelt out your dross as with lye, and remove all your wastes. And I will restore your judges as of old, and your advisers as they once were" (Isaiah 1:25,26). [The verse ends, "After that you will be called City of Righteousness, Faithful City," which signifies that the *Shechinah* will rest on Jerusalem (Rashi).]

Ulla said: Jerusalem will be redeemed only because of *tzedakah* (charity), as it says, "Zion will be redeemed because of justice, and its returnees [i.e., the Jewish people who will return to Jerusalem] through the mitzvah of *tzedakah*" (ibid. 27).

R. Papa said: When the haughty [people who dress ostentatiously (Rashi)] will cease to exist, then the heretics [who try to seduce us away from the Torah] will also become extinct. When the corrupt judges will cease to exist, then foreign oppressors also will vanish. [Now the Gemara explains:] When the haughty will cease to exist, then the heretics will also become extinct, as it says, "I will smelt out your dross as with lye." When the corrupt judges will cease to exist, then foreign oppressors also will vanish, as it says, "God has removed your [corrupt] judges, He has swept away your foes" (Zephaniah 3:15).

R. Malai said in the name of R. Eliezer: What is the meaning of the passage, "God has broken the staff of the wicked, the rod of tyrants" (Isaiah 14:5)? The staff in "God has broken the staff of the wicked," refers to judges who act as a staff of support to their sheriffs by paying them exorbitant salaries to carry out their duties. "The rods of the tyrants" refers to Torah scholars who are related to these corrupt judges. [The corrupt judges use their learned relatives to endorse them, so that the scholars are like rods of support in the hands of these judges (Rashi).]

Mar Zutra said: "The rods of tyrants" refers to Torah scholars who teach civil law to people who are ignoramuses and who then become judges that judge unfairly.

R. Elazar b. Malai said in the name of Resh Lakish: What is the meaning of the verse, "For your hands are defiled with blood, and your fingers with iniquity; your lips speak falsehood, and your tongue utters treachery" (Isaiah 59:3)? "For your hands are defiled with blood" refers to judges [who take bribes]. "Your fingers with iniquity" refers to the scribes [who use their fingers to write false documents]. "Your lips speak falsehood," refers to attorneys who teach their clients to make fraudulent claims. "Your tongue utters treachery" refers to the litigants themselves who tell lies.

R. Malai said in the name of R. Yitzchak of Magdala: From the day when Joseph was separated from his brothers he tasted no wine, as it says, "[May these blessings be] on the crown of Joseph who was separated (*nezir*) from his brothers" (Genesis 49:26) [The word *nazir* also denotes a Nazirite, a person who took a vow to abstain from drinking wine.] R. Yose b. R. Chanina said: His brothers also did not taste wine, for it says, [When the brothers met with Joseph and ate with him,] "They drank with him and became intoxicated with him" (Genesis 43:34). This implies that until that day they did not drink. But the other [R. Malai] holds: They did not become intoxicated, but they did drink wine.

R. Malai said furthermore: As a reward for [Aaron's unselfishness that is evident from the verse where God says to Moses,] "When he [Aaron] sees you, his heart will be glad," (Exodus 4:14), [God testifies that Aaron was truly happy that his younger brother had been given the mission to take the Israelites out of Egypt, and that Aaron did not have a trace of jealousy or rancor in his heart], for this admirable quality he merited to wear the *choshen mishpat*, the breastplate, on his heart.

THE ADVERSITIES OF EXILE

(145b) R. Chiya b. Abba and R. Assi were sitting before R. Yochanan while R. Yochanan was sitting and dozing. R. Chiya b. Abba asked R. Assi: Why are the fowl in Babylonia fatter [than those in Eretz Yisrael]? He replied: Go to the desert of Gaza [which is in Eretz Yisrael], and I'll show you fatter ones. Why are the festivals in Babylonia much more joyous than in Eretz Yisrael? Because the people in Babylonia are poor. [They work very hard all year; therefore, they enjoy the leisure and the good food on Yom Tov all the more. Why are the scholars in Babylonia better dressed than those of Eretz Yisrael? Because they are not as learned in Torah as the scholars of Eretz Yisrael, [so they wear distinguished clothes to attain respect]. Why are idol worshippers lustful? Because they eat abominable and creeping things. Just then R. Yochanan woke up and said to them: Young men! Haven't I taught you [to keep in mind the passage], "Say to Wisdom, 'You are my sister'?" (Proverbs 7:4) [which is expounded to mean:] If something is as clear to you as the fact that you cannot marry your sister, then say it; otherwise, don't say it. They replied: Then would you please explain these things to us?

[R. Yochanan expounded:] Why are the chickens in Babylonia fat? Because they were not sent into exile. For it says, "Moab has been secure from his youth on; he is settled on his lees . . . He has never gone into exile. Therefore his fine flavor has remained, and his bouquet is unspoiled" (Jeremiah 48:11). And how do we know that the chickens of Eretz Yisrael were driven into exile? Because we learned in a *Baraita*: R. Yehudah said: For fifty-two years no man passed through Judea, as it says, "For the mountains I take up weeping and wailing, for the pastures in the wilderness a lament. They are laid waste; no man passes through . . . Birds of the sky and beasts [*behemah*] as well have fled and are gone" (ibid. 9:9). The numeric value of *behemah* is fifty-two,[159] [an allusion to the fifty-two years of desolation, as calculated in Megillah 11b (Rashi)].

R. Yaakov said in the name of R. Yochanan: [All the animals, birds, and fish returned from exile, except the Spanish colias [a species of fish]. For Rav said: The water from Babylonia flowed through underground conduits to the spring of *Ein Eitam* [a high point in Eretz Yisrael; and the fish returned to Eretz Yisrael by way of these conduits (Rashi)], but the colias, because of its soft spine, was unable to swim upward [to Eretz Yisrael].

Why are the festivals in Babylonia more joyous? Because the curse [of Hosea] did not apply to them. For Hosea said [about Eretz Yisrael], "And I will end all her rejoicing, her festivals, new moons and *Shabbat*s—all her festive seasons" (Hosea 2:13). And it says, "Your new moons and festivals fill Me with loathing, they have become a burden to Me" (Isaiah 1:14). What does "they have become a burden to Me" mean? R. Elazar said: The Holy One, blessed be He, said: Not only does Israel sin before Me, but they also cause Me the trouble to decide which evil decree to bring upon them. R. Yitzchak said: There was not a single Yom Tov [in Eretz Yisrael] when troops [of the army of occupation] did not come to Tzipori (Sepphoris) [and spoiled the Yom Tov atmosphere]. R. Chanina said: There is not a single Yom Tov that a general with his entourage did not come to Tveriah (Tiberias) [and upset the enjoyment of the Yom Tov, in fulfillment of the curse].

Why are the scholars of Babylonia better dressed? Because they are not native-born citizens [of Babylonia. They are exiles from Eretz Yisrael, and must gain recognition through their distinguished clothes]. As the saying goes, "At home, it's my name that counts; abroad, it's the clothes I wear."

It says, "In days to come Jacob shall strike root, Israel shall blossom [*yatztitz*] and bloom [*ufarach*]" (Isaiah 27:6). R. Yosef quoted a *Baraita*: This refers to Torah scholars in Babylonia who weave blossoms [*tzitzin*] and flowers [*perachim*] around the Torah, [meaning, they are outstanding scholars]. R. Yosef supports R. Yochanan's view, that the reason they wear distinguished-looking clothes is not because they are mediocre scholars. Why are idol worshippers lustful? Because they did not stand at Mount Sinai. (146a) For when the Serpent came on Eve, he infused sensuality into her. [When the Serpent enticed Eve to eat the forbidden fruit he had marital relations with her (Rashi).] But when the Jewish people stood at Mount Sinai their lustfulness left them. Since the idol worshippers did not stand at Mount Sinai they did not lose their lustfulness. R. Acha b. Rava asked R. Ashi: What about proselytes? [Their ancestors were not at Mount Sinai; at what point did their lustfulness depart?] [He replied:] Although they themselves were not present [at Sinai], their souls were present, as it says, "[Moses said:] But it is not with you alone that I am making this covenant and this dread oath. I am making it both with those who are standing here with us today before God our Lord, and with [the souls of] those who are not here with us today" (Deuteronomy 29:13,14). R. Yochanan [who said that the lust did not depart until Sinai] disagrees with R. Abba b. Kahana. For R. Abba b. Kahana said: Until three generations the lustful tendency did not leave our Patriarchs: Abraham fathered Ishmael, Isaac fathered Esau, but Jacob fathered the twelve tribes, none of whom had the slightest blemish [even before the Stand at Mount Sinai].

HE FORGOT HIS LEARNING

(147b) R. Chelbo said: The wine of Parugita[160] and the [warm springs] water of Dimsit [better known as Emmaus] ruined the Ten Tribes of Israel. [By overindulging in these luxuries they neglected their Torah studies and abandoned their faith, which led to their downfall.[161]] When R. Elazar b. Arach once visited those places [Parugita and Dimsit], he indulged [in the wine and the baths] to the point that he forgot his learning. When he returned he was called up to read from the Torah scroll, but instead of reading *Hachodesh hazeh lachem*, "This month shall mark for you" (Exodus 12:2), he read *Hacheresh hayah libbam* ["Their hearts were deaf." As a result of wallowing in luxury he had forgotten how to read correctly]. But the Rabbis prayed for him, and his learning was restored. This incident forms the background to what we have learned in a Mishnah: R. Nehorai said: Exile yourself to a place of Torah, and do not assume that the Torah will follow you [if you move to a place where there are no scholars]. For it is your colleagues who will cause your learning to remain with you, [only in association with fellow students can Torah be properly studied], and do not rely on your own understanding, [by studying alone in an environment devoid of Torah scholarship] (*Avot* 4:14). A Tanna taught: His name was not R. Nehorai but R. Nechemiah, and others say his name was R. Elazar b. Arach, and why was he called R. Nehorai? Because he enlightened [*manhir*] the eyes of the Sages in *halachah*.

VIEWING PAINTINGS

(149a) Our Rabbis taught: On *Shabbat* you may not read the caption under a mural depicting animals or under a painting of people in a historic scene [like David and Goliath, because if a person reads these captions he may tend to read business documents, which is forbidden on *Shabbat*]. And paintings themselves that portray people may not be looked at even on weekdays, because it says, "Do not turn to idols" (Leviticus 19:4). [Asks the Gemara:] How do we derive from this verse that one should not look at paintings of people? R. Chanin interpreted the passage to mean: Do not look at things that you have conceived with your own imagination. [Tosafot explains that the prohibition applies only to paintings made for idolatrous worship, but decorative art may be viewed.]

BRINGING PUNISHMENT DOWN ON ONE'S NEIGHBOR

(149b) R. Yaakov, the son of R. Yaakov's daughter, said: Whoever causes his neighbor to be punished will not be allowed to enter into the domain of the Holy One, blessed be He. [Asks the Gemara:] From where do we know this? Do you think because it says, [A brief plot summary: The evil King Ahab of Israel and his wicked wife, Queen Jezebel, wanted a field that belonged to Navot the Yezreelite. When Navot refused to sell it they had him put to death on trumped up charges and seized his field. Later Ahab wanted to go to war to capture the town of Ramot-Gilead from the King of Aram. Yehoshafat, the King of Judah, advised him to consult the prophets before going into battle. Ahab asked his false prophets, and they all told him to launch an attack.

There was one true prophet of God, however, named Michaihu ben Yimlah. When Ahab asked his advice, he told him not to go, because he would be defeated. To lend added weight to his words, Michaihu related the heavenly scene he had viewed in his prophetic vision. Michaihu told Ahab:] "God asked, 'Who will entice Ahab so that he will march and fall at Ramot-Gilead?' One [angel] said thus, and another said thus, until a certain spirit came forward and stood before God and said, 'I will entice him.' 'How?' God asked. And the spirit replied, 'I will go forth and be a lying spirit in the mouth of all his prophets.' Then God said, 'Entice him, and you will prevail. Go out and do it'" (1 Kings 22:19–22). [The Gemara asks:] Who was this

spirit? Said R. Yochanan: This was the spirit of Navot the Yezreelite. And what did God mean when He said, "Go forth"? Said Rav: [God told him:] "Leave My domain." [Since Navot brought punishment down on Ahab he had to leave the nearness of God, which proves R. Yaakov's point.]

[Says the Gemara: This verse is no proof.] Perhaps the reason [that the spirit of Navot had to leave God's nearness] was because it says, "Anyone who speaks untruth shall not stand before My eyes" (Psalms 101:7), [and the spirit of Navot suggested that the false prophets mislead Ahab. Although God was looking for a way to entice Ahab to go to war, he did not want it to be done through falsehood].

[Says the Gemara:] We can adduce a proof from the following verse, "To punish the righteous is surely not good" (Proverbs 17:26). What does that mean? If the verse says "it is not good," it means, "it is bad." Now the Gemara expounds: If a righteous man brings down a punishment on someone else, it is bad for him. And it says, "For You are a God who desires no wickedness; evil cannot abide with You" (Psalms 5:5), [which means] You are righteous, therefore, in Your nearness there dwells no person who is evil. [So we see that whoever brings punishment down on his neighbor will not be admitted to God's domain.]

WHAT BUSINESS TALK IS PERMITTED ON *SHABBAT*?

(150a) [The Gemara asks:] Is talking [about business affairs] forbidden [on *Shabbat*]? Didn't R. Chisda and R. Hamenuna both say: You are allowed to discuss charity accounts on *Shabbat*? And R. Elazar said: You may decide on the amounts of charity to be distributed to the needy on *Shabbat*. And R. Yaakov b. Idi said in R. Yochanan's name: You may take care of averting life-threatening situations and matters of importance to the community [such as petitioning governmental authorities (Rashi)] on *Shabbat*, and you may go to the synagogue to discuss communal affairs on *Shabbat*. And R. Shmuel b. Nachmani said in R. Yochanan's name: You may go to theaters, circuses, and civic centers to take care of communal affairs on *Shabbat*. In the Yeshivah of Menashe they taught that a father is allowed to arrange a match for his daughter and for his son to receive a Torah education and to be taught a trade on *Shabbat*![162] [So you see, discussions about mundane matters are permitted on *Shabbat*.] [The Gemara answers:] Scripture says, "[You should refrain] from pursuing *your own* affairs and talking about business dealings" (Isaiah 58:13). Your own business affairs you may not discuss on *Shabbat*, but the business of Heaven [charity and communal matters] you may discuss.

(150b) The Rabbis taught: It once happened that the fence in the field of a pious man broke down, and when he decided to repair it he remembered that it was *Shabbat*, and he did not repair it. Miraculously, a caper[163] bush grew up in that field, and it provided a livelihood for him and his family.

THE POWER OF
A DAY-OLD INFANT
(151b) The Rabbis taught: R. Shimon b. Gamliel said: For a day-old infant we desecrate the *Shabbat* [if necessary]; for David, King of Israel, if dead, we are not allowed to desecrate the *Shabbat*. For a day-old infant we desecrate the *Shabbat*, for the Torah says: Violate one *Shabbat* for him, so that he may live to keep many *Shabbats*. For King David, if dead, we are not allowed to desecrate the *Shabbat*, for once a person dies he is free from all *mitzvot*. Accordingly, R. Yochanan interpreted the phrase, "Free among the dead," (Psalms 88:5)—once a person is dead, he is free from all *mitzvot*.

The Rabbis also taught: R. Shimon b. Elazar said: A day-old infant need not be guarded against cats and mice, as it says, "There shall be fear and dread of you instilled in all the wild beasts of the earth" (Genesis 9:2); as long as a person is alive he inspires fear in animals; once he is dead they no longer fear him.

R. Papa said: We have a tradition that a lion never attacks two people together. But we see that it does? This can be explained with a saying by Rami b. Abba who said: An animal has no power [to attack] a person unless that person appears to it like an animal, for it says, "A man who does not understand honor is like the beasts that perish" (Psalms 49:21) [meaning, if he is killed by a beast you can be sure that he looked like a beast to the predator (Rashi)]. R. Chanina said: A person should not sleep in a house alone; and whoever sleeps in a house alone, Lilith [a demon of the night] will take hold of him.

POVERTY IS LIKE A WHEEL
(151b) We learned in a *Baraita*: R. Shimon b. Elazar said: Give [charity] as long as you find someone to whom to give it, and you have the opportunity and the means to do it. For Solomon in his wisdom said, "Remember your Creator in the days of your youth, before those days of sorrow come" (Ecclesiastes 12:1)—this refers to the days of old age. [And the verse continues], "And those years arrive of which you will say, 'I have no pleasure in them'"—this refers to the Messianic age when there will be neither merit nor guilt. On this point he disagrees with Shmuel who said: The only difference between this world and the Messianic era is that in the Messianic era the Jewish people will be no longer under the domination of other nations, as it says, "The poor will never cease to exist in the land" (Deuteronomy 15:11), [and even in Messianic times there will be needy people].

We learned in a *Baraita*: R. Elazar Hakappar said: A person should always pray for mercy to be spared from the hardship [of poverty], for if he himself does not become poor, his son will, and if his son does not become poor, his grandson will. For it says, "Because of [*big'lal*] this thing" (ibid. 10). In the Yeshivah of R. Yishmael they expounded the word *big'lal* as being related to *galgal*, "wheel," and they said that poverty is a wheel [*galgal*] that rolls around in the world, [eventually striking all people or their descendants]. R. Yosef said: We have a tradition that a Rabbinical scholar will not become poor. [Asks the Gemara:] But we see that they do become poor? [Answers the Gemara:] Even if he becomes destitute, nevertheless, he does not have to go begging from door to door. R. Chiya said to his wife: When a poor man comes, quickly offer him bread, so that others will quickly offer bread to your children. She cried out: You are cursing them! He replied: It says in the Torah, "Because of [*big'lal*] this thing"; and in the Yeshivah of R. Yishmael they expounded *big'lal* to mean that poverty is a [*galgal*], a wheel that rolls around in the world.

R. Gamliel Berebbi interpreted the verse, "God will give you mercy [i.e., He will inspire you to have mercy on others], and He will have pity on you and multiply you" (Deuteronomy 13:17)—[this teaches us that] whoever is compassionate toward others, compassion is shown to him by God, but whoever is not compassionate toward others, compassion is not shown to him by God.

TEARS OF GRIEF
AND LAUGHTER
[It says,] "Before sun and light and moon and stars grow dark, and the clouds come back again after the rain" (Ecclesiastes 12:2). [The Gemara expounds:] "Sun and light" refers to the forehead and the nose; and "the moon" refers to the soul; "the stars" refers to the cheeks; "and the clouds come back again after the rain" refers to a person's eyesight that is lost [due to the constant crying in old age over all the grief a person experiences (Rashi)]. Shmuel said: Crying in a person past forty years of age causes irreparable harm to the eyes. [As an illustration the Gemara relates:] When R. Chanina's daughter died, he suppressed his tears. His wife reproached him for his apparent insensitivity. "Have you just sent out a hen from your house?" she asked. He answered, "Shall I suffer two losses? The loss of a child and the loss of my eyesight [due to crying]?" He held like R. Yochanan who said in the name of R. Yose b. Ketzarta: There are six kinds of tears, three are beneficial, and three are harmful: those caused by smoke, by crying [for grief], and (152b) by the pain of exertion in the washroom are harmful, but those caused by medicinal eye drops, by laughter, and by plants [like onions or horseradish] are beneficial.

THE INFIRMITIES OF OLD AGE

[The Gemara continues the interpretation of Ecclesiastes 12:1, which began on 151a.] "When the guards of the house become shaky"—this refers to the sides of the body and the ribs [which sustain the body]; "and the strong men are bent"—the thighs [which become weak in old age]; "and the grinders are idle"—the teeth; "those who peer through the windows grow dim"—the eyes (Ecclesiastes 12:3).

The emperor asked R. Yehoshua b. Chanania: Why did you not come to *Bei Avidon*? [A place where the heretics debated religious doctrine with the rabbis.] He replied: The mountain is snowy [I'm an old man, my head is white], it is surrounded by ice [my beard is white], the dog does not bark any more [my voice is weak], the grinders don't grind [my teeth don't work]. In the Yeshivah of Rav they described old age as follows: I look as if I were searching for something I never lost, [an old person walks stooped over, as if he were searching for something even though he did not lose anything (Rashi)]. The Rabbis taught: R. Yose b. Kisma said: Two are better than three [a young person who walks on his two feet is better off than an old man who needs a cane], and woe for the one thing that goes and does not come back. What is that? Said R. Chisda: This is youth. When R. Dimi came [from Eretz Yisrael] he said: Youth is like a crown of roses; old age is like a crown of thistles. It was said in a *Baraita* in R. Meir's name: Chew well with your teeth, you will find it in your steps [if you chew well, your steps will be bouncy and vigorous], as it says, "For then we had plenty to eat, we were well-off, and suffered no misfortune" (Jeremiah 44:17). Shmuel said to Rav Yehudah: You sharp scholar! Open your mouth and put in your bread. Until the age of forty food is more beneficial; after that drink is more beneficial.

Rabbi asked R. Shimon b. Chalafta: Why did we not have the pleasure of your visit on the Yom Tov, as my ancestors were visited by your ancestors? He replied: The little rocks have become big hills [even a small knoll looks like a high hill, and I am likely to stumble], the near have become distant [it is difficult for me to walk even a short distance], two [legs] became three [I need a cane], and the peacemaker of the home has ceased [I can no longer fulfill my marital obligation].

[The Gemara resumes its exegesis of Ecclesiastes, with 12:4.] "The doors to the street are shut"—this refers to the openings in the body [that do not function properly in old age]; "with the noise of the handmill growing fainter"—this refers to the stomach [that does not properly digest]; "and he will wake up at the sound of the bird"—even the chirping of a bird will wake the aged from sleep. "And all the daughters of song grow dim"—even the singing of male and female singers sound to him like a monotone. In the same vein, Barzilai the Gileadite said to David, "I am now eighty years old. Can I tell the difference between good and bad?" (2 Samuel 19:36). This tells you that the opinions of old people are prone to change [due to senility, since Barzilai could not tell the difference between good and bad]. "Can your servant taste what he eats and drinks?" This tells you that the lips of old people crack. "Can I still listen to the singing of men and women?" This tells you that the aged become hard of hearing. Rav said: Barzilai the Gileadite was a liar; for there was a maidservant in the household of Rav who was ninety-two years old, and she used to taste all the dishes. Rava said: Barzilai the Gileadite was promiscuous in his younger years, and whoever wallows in immorality becomes old prematurely.

It was taught in a *Baraita*: R. Yishmael b. R. Yose said: When it comes to Torah scholars, the older they grow, the more wisdom they acquire. For it says, "With the aged there is wisdom, and with longevity there comes understanding" (Job 12:12). But the ignorant, the older they grow, the more foolish they become. For it says, "He deprives trusted men of speech, and takes away the reason of elders" (Job 12:20).

[The Gemara continues its exegesis of Ecclesiastes with verse 12:5.] "[An old man] is afraid of heights"—even a low knoll looks to him like the highest mountain. "And there is terror on the road"—when he walks on the road, his heart becomes fearful. "And the almond tree blossoms"—this refers to the lowest vertebra in the spinal column [that bulges in old people]. "And the grasshopper becomes a burden"—the buttocks of an old man become heavy. "And the desire fails"—the sexual passion ceases.

R. Kahana was arranging the verses before Rav. When he came to the above-mentioned verse, Rav uttered a deep sigh and groaned. [R. Kahana said:] This shows that Rav's desires have ceased. R. Kahana said: What is the meaning of, "For He decreed, and it was"? (Psalms 33:9)—This refers to a woman. [It is not logical for a man to desire a woman; it is so only because God decreed it (Rashi).] "He commanded and it endured" (ibid.)—this refers to [the instinct of parents to raise] children. We learned in a *Baraita*: A woman is a container full of wastes whose opening is full of [menstrual] blood, yet everyone has a passion to pursue her and seek her company.

WHAT HAPPENS AFTER DEATH?

[Returning to Ecclesiastes; it says,] "But man sets out for his eternal abode" (Ecclesiastes 12:5). R. Yitzchak said: This teaches us that every *tzaddik* is given an abode in heaven according to the honor he deserves. You may compare it to a king who enters a town together with his servants. They all enter through the same gate [similarly, all people die in the same way], but at night, each one receives accommodations according to his status [likewise, in heaven each person receives the place he has earned].

R. Yitzchak also said: What is the meaning of the verse, "For childhood and youth are futile"? (Ecclesiastes 11:10).—The things a person does in his youth [when he overindulges in sensual pleasures] weaken him in his old age. R. Yitzchak also said: Worms are as painful to the dead as a needle in the flesh of a living person, as it says, "He [the deceased] feels the pain of his flesh" (Job 14:22). R. Chisda said: The person's soul mourns for him for seven days after his death. [The soul mourns for the body that cannot enjoy the delights of Gan Eden the way the soul does (*Maharsha*), for it says, "And his spirit mourns for him" (ibid.). [And how do we know that the soul mourns for seven days?] It says, "[Joseph] observed a seven-day mourning period for his father" (Genesis 50:10).

Rabbi Yehudah said: If a person dies and leaves no one to mourn his death, ten people should go and stay in the place where he passed away. [The Rema states that the custom in such a case is that a *minyan* assembles for prayer services at the home of the deceased.] It happened that a person died in the neighborhood of Rav Yehudah. Since there were no mourners, (152b) Rav Yehudah brought ten people to be in the place where the person died. After seven days, the dead man appeared to Rav Yehudah in his dream and said to him: May your mind be at ease, because you have soothed my mind [in the hereafter]. R. Abbahu said: The deceased knows everything that is said in his presence until the cover is placed on the coffin; [according to *Tosafot*: until the headstone is placed on the grave]. R. Chiya and R. Shimon b. Rabbi disagree on this point: one holds [that the dead person knows what is said in his presence] until the cover is placed on the coffin, while the other asserts, until the flesh is decomposed. The one who says: until the flesh is decomposed derives it from the verse, "He feels the pain of his flesh, and his spirit mourns for him" (Job 15:21)—[his soul has consciousness as long as his flesh is with him]. The one who says: until the cover is placed on the coffin derives it from the verse, "And the dust returns to the ground as it was, and the spirit returns to God" (Ecclesiastes 12:7). [As soon as the body—which is dust—returns to the earth, the spirit returns to God and has no knowledge of what is said in its presence (Rashi).]

Our Rabbis taught: "And the dust returns to the ground as it was, and the spirit returns to God who gave it." [Comments the Gemara:] Give it back to Him. Just as He gave it to you—in purity, so should you return it to Him—in purity. A parable: A king of flesh and blood distributed royal garments to his servants [for them to use]. The wise ones among them [used the garments only for special occasions, and after use they] folded them carefully and placed them in chests. The fools among them went and did their work in these garments. After a time the king demanded the garments back: the wise servants returned them clean and pressed. The fools returned them soiled. The king was pleased with the wise servants, but he was angry with the fools. About the wise ones he said: Let my garments [that were returned to me in immaculate condition] be placed in my treasury, and let [the servants who took such good care of them] go home in peace. But about the fools he said: My garments should first be sent to the cleaner's, and the fools should be sent to prison. So too, the Holy One, blessed be He, says about the bodies of the righteous, [analogous to the royal garments], "May they come in peace, may they come to their permanent resting place" (Isaiah 57:2). And about their souls He says, [the phrase spoken by Abigail to David], "The soul of my master will be bound up in the bundle of life in the care of God" (1 Samuel 25:29). But about the bodies of the wicked He says, "There is no peace—says God—for the wicked" (Isaiah 48:22). And regarding the souls of the wicked He says [the continuation of Abigail's wish for David], "and the souls of your enemies He will fling away as from the hollow of a sling" (1 Samuel ibid.).[164]

We learned in a *Baraita*: R. Eliezer said: The souls of the righteous are preserved beneath the Throne of glory, as it says, "The soul of my master will be bound up in the bundle of life" (1 Samuel ibid.). But the souls of the wicked are restrained, and they wander all over. At one end of the world stands one angel and a second one stands at the other end, and they hurl the souls of the wicked at each other, for it says, "and the souls of your enemies He will fling away as from the hollow of a sling."

A DIALOGUE WITH
A DECEASED TANNA

Rabbah asked R. Nachman: [We discussed the souls of the righteous and the wicked,] but what about the soul of the average person? He replied: If I had died, I could not have given you this answer: This is what Shmuel said: Both the wicked and the average people are handed over to an angel named Dumah: the average people enjoy rest, whereas the wicked have no rest. R. Mari said: Even the righteous will ultimately turn to dust, for it says, "And the dust returns to the ground as it was."

There were diggers who were digging up R. Nachman's land. R. Achai b. Yoshiah, who was buried there [and this was not known], growled [when the diggers hurt his body]. So the diggers went and told R. Nachman, "Someone growled at us." R. Nachman went there and asked him, "Who are you?" Came the reply: "I am Achai b. Yoshiah." Said R. Nachman, "But did not R. Mari say, 'Even the righteous will eventually turn to dust.' [How is it that your body is still intact]?" "Who is this Mari?" R. Acha b. Yoshiah retorted. "I have never heard of him." Said R. Nachman, "But it is written, 'And the dust returns to the ground as it was'?" Replied R. Achai b. Yoshiah, "The person that taught you Ecclesiastes [from which you quoted this verse] did not teach you Proverbs. Because there it says, 'Envy causes the bones to rot' (Proverbs 14:30). Anyone who harbors jealousy in his heart, his bones decay, but anyone who does not harbor jealousy in his heart, his bones do not decay [and I was never envious]."

R. Nachman then poked R. Achai b. Yoshiah's body, and he saw that his body had substance. Said R. Nachman to R. Achai b. Yoshiah, "[Since your body is intact,] why don't you get up and go home?" Replied R. Achai b. Yoshiah, "Now you revealed that you have not even studied the Prophets, for it says, "You will know that I am God when I have opened your graves and lifted you out of your graves" (Ezekiel 37:13), [we don't have a right to leave our graves until the time of *Techiyat Hameitim*, the Revival of the Dead]. Said R. Nachman to R. Achai b. Yoshiah, "But it says, 'for you are dust, and to dust you will return' (Genesis 3:19), [and you are telling me that a person who has no envy does not turn to dust]?" Replied R. Achai b. Yoshia, "The verse [in Genesis] refers to one moment before the Resurrection of the Dead" [when even the *tzaddikim* will turn into dust, but then they will come to life again].

A certain heretic said to R. Abbahu: You assert that the souls of the *tzaddikim* are safeguarded beneath the Throne of Glory; then how did the sorceress who used bones to communicate with the dead[165] bring up the spirit of the prophet Samuel through magic? (1 Samuel 28:7). He replied: This happened within the twelve months of the passing of the prophet Samuel. For we learned in a *Baraita*: For twelve months after a person's demise his body remains intact, and his soul ascends and descends; after twelve months the body ceases to exist, (153a) and the soul ascends to heaven and does not return any more.

A HEART-RENDING EULOGY

R. Yehudah b. R. Shmuel b. Shilat said in Rav's name: From the eulogy that is given at a person's funeral we can tell whether or not his place is in the World to Come. [If he is a good person he will be praised, and his death will be lamented (Rashi).] [Asks the Gemara:] But that is not so? For Rav said to R. Shmuel b. Shilat: [When I die] I want you to deliver a fervent and grieving eulogy for me, because I will be present at my own eulogy, [since the soul of the deceased is present at his eulogy and hears what is being said. Now, Rav was certainly a great *tzaddik* who would surely ascend to Gan Eden. Why did he have to exhort people to give an anguished eulogy?]

[Answers the Gemara:] There is no difficulty. Sometimes it is necessary to encourage people to deliver an emotional eulogy, even if the deceased is a *tzaddik*. But when can we tell whether the deceased will go to Gan Eden? If the people are moved to tears by the fervent eulogy, then we know that his place is in the World to Come. Abbaye asked Rabbah, "You,

for example, who is disliked by all the people of Pumbedita, [Rabbah was hated because he used to admonish the people of Pumbedita for their dishonesty in business], who is going to deliver a heart-rending eulogy for you?" Rabbah replied, "If you (Abbaye) and Rabbah b. Chanan will give an emotional eulogy that will be sufficient."

R. Elazar asked Rav: Which person has a place in the World to Come? Rav replied: A person has a place in the World to Come if the eulogist exclaims, "The path that this person has chosen, follow it!" (Isaiah 30:21). R. Chanina said: If a person's teachers are satisfied with him [that is an indication that he has a place in the World to Come]. Furthermore, "And the mourners go around in the streets [extolling his good deeds]" (Ecclesiastes 12:5) [that, too, is a sign that he has a place in the World to Come].

The Galileans said: Do things in your lifetime that will be recounted in the eulogies that are given in front of your coffin; the Judeans said: Do things for which you will be eulogized by speakers standing *behind* your coffin. There is no divergence between the two views. Each used as an example the custom of his locality. [In Galilee the eulogist would stand in front of the coffin; in Judah, behind the coffin.]

REPENT ONE DAY
BEFORE YOU DIE

We learned in a Mishnah: R. Eliezer said: Repent one day before you die. R. Eliezer's students asked him: Does anyone know on what day he will die [in order to do *teshuvah* the day before]? Replied R. Eliezer: All the more reason that he should repent today, since he might die tomorrow. That way, he will spend his whole life in *teshuvah*. And Solomon, too, said in his wisdom, "Let your clothes always be white [meaning, let your soul always be pure and spotless], and your head never lack ointment" (Ecclesiastes 9:8). Rabbi Yochanan b. Zakkai said: A parable: A king summoned his servants to a banquet, without setting an exact time. The wise servants got dressed in festive attire and sat at the entrance to the royal palace, for they said: Is there anything lacking in the king's household? [We have to be ready. The feast may start at any moment.] The foolish servants went to do their menial jobs, for they said: Can there be a banquet without extensive preparations being made? [We have plenty of time.] Suddenly the king called his servants to come to the banquet. The wise ones came handsomely attired, while the fools entered wearing dirty clothes. The king was happy to see the wise servants, but angry at the foolish ones. Said the king: Those servants who dressed up for my feast should sit down, eat, and drink. But those who did not dress properly for the banquet should stand and watch.

R. Meir's son-in-law said in R. Meir's name: [If they stand and watch] they would look like waiters, [and that is not enough of a humiliation for them]. But both groups are seated at the banquet—the servants that prepared themselves will be eating, while those that did not prepare themselves will go hungry. The prepared ones will drink, the unprepared ones will go thirsty. For it says, "Assuredly, so said the Lord God: My servants [those that served Me properly during their life] shall eat [meaning, they will delight in the radiance of the *Shechinah* in the World to Come], and [those who did not prepare themselves in this life] you shall hunger [in the hereafter]; My servants shall drink, and you shall thirst; My servants shall rejoice, and you shall be shamed. My servants shall shout in gladness, and you shall cry out in anguish, howling in heartbreak" (Isaih 65:13,14). Another interpretation of the verse, "Let your clothes always be white"—this refers to *tzitzit* [because *tzitzit* are usually white], "and your head never lack ointment"—this refers to *tefillin*.

GOD HAS PITY ON DOGS

(155b) R. Yonah expounded at the entrance of the house of the Nasi: What is the meaning of the verse, "A righteous man is concerned with the cause of the wretched" (Proverbs 29:7). The Holy One, blessed be He, knows that a dog's food is meager, [people don't take pity on a dog to feed it (Rashi)], therefore He ordained that a dog's food stays in his stomach for three days [before it is fully digested].

ISRAEL IS NOT SUSCEPTIBLE TO PLANETARY INFLUENCES

(156a) It was written in R. Yehoshua b. Levi's notebook: If a person was born on a Sunday he will be completely of one type, and there will be nothing of another type in him. [Asks the Gemara:] What do you mean, "there will be nothing of another type"? Do you think [that a person who is born on Sunday is completely evil], and there is no virtue in such a person? But R. Ashi said: I was born on Sunday, [and Rav Ashi was a *tzaddik*]? Therefore, you must say that there is not a trace of evil [in a person born on Sunday]. But R. Ashi said: I and Dimi b. Kakuzta were both born on Sunday: I am the *Rosh Yeshivah*,[166] and he is the leader of the gangsters in town. [This being so, you cannot say that all persons born on Sunday are good, because the evil Bar Kakuzta was born on Sunday. Neither can you say that all are bad because R. Ashi was born on Sunday.]

[Says the Gemara:] It means that a person who is born on a Sunday is either completely virtuous *or* completely wicked. [He has free choice. But when he exercises his free choice he will become either totally virtuous or totally wicked.] The person who is born on Monday will be a bad-tempered person. Why is this so? Because the waters were divided on Monday [the second day of Creation; therefore he will be at odds with everyone]. The person who is born on Tuesday will be wealthy and promiscuous. Why? Because herbs were created on Tuesday [the third day of Creation, and herbs grow quickly, and intermingle indiscriminately]. If a person is born on Wednesday he will be wise and have a good memory. Why? Because on Wednesday, the fourth day of Creation, the luminaries were set into the sky [and it says, "Torah is a light" (Proverbs 6:23)]. If a person is born on Thursday he will be kind to others. Why? Because on Thursday, the fifth day of Creation, the fishes and birds were created [through God's lovingkindness they find their food effortlessly]. If someone is born on Friday he will be a seeker. R. Nachman b. Yitzchak explained: A seeker after *mitzvot* [just as on *erev Shabbat*, everyone seeks to make the necessary preparation for *Shabbat*]. A person who is born on *Shabbat* will die on *Shabbat*, because the *Shabbat* was desecrated in order to bring him into the world [although this is permitted, and it is a mitzvah]. Rava b. R. Shila said: [a person born on *Shabbat*] will be called a very holy person. [Not everyone born on *Shabbat* will die on *Shabbat*, but if someone was born and died on *Shabbat* that is a sign that he was a very saintly person (*Maharsha*).]

R. Chanina said to his disciples: Go and tell R. Yehoshua b. Levi [in whose (above-mentioned) notebook were written the character traits of the people born on each day of the week]: It is not the constellation on the day of birth that influences a person's life, but the hour at which he is born. [There are seven celestial bodies—the sun, the moon, and five planets—and every hour another one is dominant over the others.] A person who is born in the hour when the sun is dominant will be a bright man, he will eat and drink of his own [he will not take away anyone's food or drink, like the sun that does not encroach on the moon], and his secrets will be known to all [like the sun that shines for everyone to see], and if he is a thief he will not be successful [because the sun does not steal. It shines only in the daytime, not at night]. A person who is born under Venus will be wealthy and promiscuous. Why? Because Venus is the planet of fire [and fire denotes passion]. A person born under Mercury will be wise and have a good memory. Why? Because the planet Mercury is the scribe of the sun, [it is closest to the sun and records the orbit of the sun (Rashi)].

A person born under the influence of the moon will suffer a great deal; he will build and dismantle, dismantle and build, [just like the moon that waxes and wanes]. He will eat and drink that which is not his [like the moon that sometimes can be seen at daytime], and his secrets will remain hidden [like the moon that is actually dark, since it does not have light of its own], if he is a thief he will be successful [like the moon that takes the sun's light and makes it his own]. A person born under Saturn will be a man whose plans are thwarted. [The Hebrew name of Saturn is *Shabta'i*, which means "to frustrate."] Others say: All evil plots against him will be nullified. A person born under Jupiter [in Hebrew called *Tzedek*] will be a *tzaddik*, a righteous person. R. Nachman b. Yitzchak said: He will be a charitable person. A person born under Mars will be spilling blood. R. Ashi said: [Having a free will, he is going to choose;] he will be either a surgeon [literally, blood-letter], a robber [who kills people], a butcher, or a *mohel*. Rabbah said: I was born under Mars [and I don't do any of these things]. Replied Abaye: You, too, shed blood, [for as a judge] you punish people and have them executed.

We learned: R. Chanina said: The constellations at a person's birth make him wise and make him wealthy, and Israel's destiny is determined by the stars. R. Yochanan said: Israel can change the influence of the stars for the better [through prayer and good deeds]. R. Yochanan is consistent with his view, for R. Yochanan said: How do we know that Israel's destiny is not determined by the stars? Because it says, "Thus said God: Do not learn to go the way of the nations, and do not be dismayed by portents in the sky; let the nations be dismayed by them!" (Jeremiah 10:2)—They are dismayed but not Israel [because Israel can overcome planetary influences by prayer and doing *mitzvot*]. Rav, too, holds that Israel's destiny is not determined by the stars. For Rav Yehudah said in Rav's name: How do we know that Israel is not subject to planetary influences? Because it says [at the Pact Between the Halves], "He [God] then took [Abraham] outside" (Genesis 15:5). [This was preceded by a discussion between Abraham and God.] Abraham said to the Holy One, blessed be He: "Master of the universe! 'A servant of my household will inherit me' (ibid. 3). Replied God: "Not at all, 'One born from your own body will inherit what is yours' (ibid. 4)." "Master of the universe!" Abraham exclaimed. "I have looked at my constellation and I find that I am not destined to beget a son." Replied God, "Go beyond your astrology. Israel is not governed by the planets alone; [its fate is superseded by *mitzvot* and good deeds]. What do you think? (156b) Because [when you were born] Jupiter was in the West [where it is cold, and this causes impotence (Rashi)]? I will turn it around and place it in the East." And so it says, "Who has roused *Tzedek* (Jupiter) from the east, summoned him for his [Abraham's] sake?" (Isaiah 41:2).

From Shmuel we can also learn that Israel is not susceptible to the influences of the planets. For Shmuel and [a gentile astrologer named] Avlat were sitting together while certain people were passing on their way to a swamp. Said Avlat to Shmuel, "That man is going [to the swamp] but he will not come back, because a snake will bite him, and he is going to die." "If he is a Jew," replied Shmuel, "he will go and come back." While they were sitting there, the man went [to the swamp] and returned. [Seeing this,] Avlat got up, threw down the man's knapsack and found in it a snake

that was cut into two pieces. Said Shmuel to the man [who was saved, even though he was destined to die], "What good deed did you do to deserve this?"

The man replied, "[I am with a group of people, and] every day we placed our bread into a basket, and then we ate together; but today one of us had no bread, and he was ashamed. So I told my friends, "Let me collect the bread [into the basket]." When I came to him I pretended to take bread from him [but I really put in my own share], so that he should not be embarrassed." "You did a mitzvah," said Shmuel to him. ["That's why you were saved."] Thereupon Shmuel went out and expounded: "Charity saves a person from death" (Proverbs 11:4)—not only will it save him from an unnatural death, but also from a natural death.

And from R. Akiva we also learn that Israel is not subject to astral influences. For R. Akiva had a daughter. The astrologers told R. Akiva: On the day she will go under the bridal canopy a snake will bite her, and she will die. R. Akiva was very worried about this. On her wedding day she took her brooch and stuck it into the wall. It happened that the needle of her brooch landed in the eye of a snake and killed it. The next morning, when she pulled the brooch out of the wall, the snake came dragging after it. "What did you do [to deserve this miracle]?" her father asked. "Last night a poor man came to our door," she replied. "Everyone was busy preparing the wedding banquet, and nobody was able to hear the poor man knocking on the door. So I got up and took the portion that was given to me and gave it to the poor man." "You did a mitzvah," said R. Akiva. Thereupon R. Akiva went out and expounded: "Charity saves a person from death" (ibid.), not only from an unnatural death, but also from a natural death.

And from R. Nachman b. Yitzchak, too, we learn that Israel is not subject to what is written in the stars, [and that destiny can be overcome by *tzedakah* and good deeds]. For R. Nachman b. Yitzchak's mother was told by astrologers: Your son will be a thief. So she did not allow him to go bareheaded. She said to him, "Cover your head, so that you should have the fear of heaven, and pray for mercy." R. Nachman b. Yitzchak did not know why his mother told this to him. One day he was sitting under [someone else's] date palm learning Torah when his head covering fell off. He looked up and saw the luscious dates on the tree. [Since his head was uncovered] he was overcome by irresistible temptation. He climbed up the tree and bit off a cluster of dates with his teeth.]

NOTES

1. Rabbi Yehudah HaNasi, also called Rabbeinu Hakadosh, c. 135 C.E.—200 C.E. Compiler of the Mishnah.

2. The afternoon prayer.

3. The Rif explains that R. Zeira agrees with R. Yirmiyah that there are separate times for prayer and Torah study. But he holds that you should not interrupt your Torah study in order to pray.

4. A judge is equated to a king in the verse, "By justice a king sustains the land" (Proverbs 29:4).

5. If you throw a stone into a barrel the level of the wine rises but you don't have more wine.

6. The Torah ordains that a Jew who slaughters an ox, a sheep, or a lamb as a sacrifice is required to give to the *kohen* as his priestly portion the shoulder, the cheeks, and the stomach (Deuteronomy 18:3). The Gemara speaks of two priestly gifts because there are two shoulders and two cheeks.

7. The coat of many colors.

8. An alternate meaning of *kerovah*.

9. *Nun* = 50; *alef* = 1.

10. When "the house of our God" is exalted, the ruins are repaired. Conversely, when the synagogue is demeaned, destruction ensues.

11. A town near Sura on the Euphrates River.

12. Arameans who were more cruel (Rashi).

13. *Tefillin* are not worn on *Shabbat*. In Talmudic times the *tefillin* were worn all day, both indoors and outdoors.

14. A fortiori reasoning, a logical conclusion from minor to major; all the more.

15. The High Priest's forehead-plate, *tzitz*, was a thin gold plate, extending from ear to ear, inscribed with the words *Kodesh laShem*, "Holy to God."

16. He should pray for him as one of many other sick people.

17. Tosafot comments that this applies only to a case where the patient is lying lower than the visitor sitting on a chair. It would be disrespectful for the visitor to sit higher than the *Shechinah*, which is at the patient's head.

18. According to the Gemara in *Ketubot* 106a, Eliyahu Hanavi taught this Midrash, called Seder Eliyahu, to R. Anan, an Amora of the third century.

19. Pentateuch.

20. Tosafot HaRosh explains that the Gemara (*Menachot* 44) says that whoever wears *tefillin* merits long life. Therefore, she showed the *tefillin* to lend added weight to her question.

21. For example, Ezekiel 44:31.

22. *Eruv* (literally, "mixture") is a quantity of food, enough for two meals, placed (a) 2,000 cubits from the town boundary so as to extend the *Shabbat* limit by that distance; (b) in a room or in a courtyard to enable all the residents to carry in the courtyard on *Shabbat* from one house to another.

23. The Chamber of the Hewn Stones.

24. A place on the Temple Mount.

25. *Simchat Beit Hasho'evah* is the joyful celebration of the "drawing of the water." At the daily morning service of Sukkot, in addition to the usual wine libation, water was poured on the altar. This was drawn from the Pool of Shilo'ach on the night after the first day of Sukkot and carried to the *Bet Hamikdash* amid great rejoicing (*Sukkah* 51a, 53a).

26. Teachers of the Gemara.

27. Thus, for example, on the third day of Chanukah there are five days yet to come. Therefore you should kindle five lights.

28. Thus on the third day of Chanukah, three days have gone by. Therefore we kindle three lights.

29. *Menachot* 99a.

30. In *Megillat Taanit*.

31. *Chullin* 83b.

32. Both verses tell us that the Torah authorizes the Rabbis to enact decrees and institute *mitzvot*, so that underlying all Rabbinic *mitzvot* there is a Biblical obligation. Which is why, before performing a Rabbinic mitzvah, we can also say, "Who has commanded us to . . . e.g., wash our hands."

33. *Pei'ah* is the portion left at the end of the field. It must be left at the last edge of the field, to be reaped by the poor.

34. See *Shabbat* 116b, where *bei nasha* is translated as "his father" (Haga'ot HaBach).

35. R. Akiva's wife Rachel was a model of goodness and virtue. She married R. Akiva when he was an ignorant shepherd and encouraged him to become a Torah scholar. After an absence of twenty-four years, during which time she faithfully waited for him, he returned with 24,000 disciples and credited her for all his learning (*Nedarim* 50a).

36. In Talmudic times, when most people used outhouses that were in the fields, indoor plumbing was a sign of wealth.

37. *Makrin* means "horned," implying the normal growth of two horns (Rashi).

38. On earth where the sun shines.

39. Every mitzvah should be done with *simchah*, joy.

40. Ben Yehoyada explains that the discomfort and pain a woman experiences during pregnancy and childbirth are the results of Eve's transgression. After the ultimate Redemption and *Tikkun*, when the world is restored and Eve's transgression has been put aright, people will enjoy the epitome of happiness, which is having children, but without the attendant drawbacks and difficulties.

41. By his flippant attitude he showed that he was a fool (Rashi).

42. *Bava Batra* 28b.

43. The Written Torah is the Pentateuch. The Mishnah is the Oral Law, the explanation of the Written Torah. The Oral Torah had to be transmitted by word of mouth; it was not to be committed to writing. However, following the destruction of the Second *Bet Hamikdash* and the ensuing dispersal of the Jewish people, Rabbi Yehudah Hanasi decided to write

down the Mishnah. It was the only way to ensure that the Torah and the Jewish nation could survive.

44. The first four letters of the Hebrew alphabet.

45. Going backward, starting with the last letter of the Hebrew alphabet.

46. The *eifod* was a half-cape as wide as the body, reaching from just below the elbows to the heel that was worn by the *Kohen Gadol* (High Priest). It had a belt that was tied in front and two shoulder straps.

47. Deuteronomy 14:1.

48. The Mishnah is divided into six Orders, called *Sedarim*. "Faith" applies to *Zera'im* (Seeds), because when we plant the seeds we have faith in God that He will give us a crop. "Times" applies to *Moed*, which deals with the times of the Festivals. "Strength" applies to *Nashim* (Women), because it is derived from a root meaning inheritance, and women produce heirs. "Salvation" alludes to *Nezikin* (Civil Law), because these laws save and protect you from damages and losses. Since the subjects covered in *Kodashim* (Sacred Things) and *Taharot* (Purity) are very complex, these two orders are identified with wisdom and knowledge.

49. These six questions are Rava's way of interpreting the same verse.

50. A kind of salty earth that was used as a preservative (Rashi).

51. One *kav* = one hundred and eightieth of a *kor*.

52. *Chartzubot* is seen as a contraction of *chared* (fearful) and *atzeiv* (depressed).

53. About five fluid ounces or 150 ml.

54. Numbers 15:20.

55. For every mitzvah a person performs an angel is created who acts as his defense attorney to plead for him on the day of judgment (*Avot* 4:13).

56. Even if a person did a mitzvah imperfectly and in a flawed way, but for a small part his action was prompted by pure intentions, then this small part suffices to tip the scale in his favor (Anaf Yosef).

57. One holds that the verse, "In order to prolong your days and the days of your children" (Deuteronomy 11:21) is linked on the verse preceding it, "inscribe them on the doorposts of your house" [*mezuzah*]. The other holds that it is also linked to the verse that precedes this passage, "Teach them to your children" [Torah study].

58. It is physically impossible for 700 people to take a hold of the corner of a Jew's garment. Therefore it is interpreted to mean, "in the merit of the *tzitzit* that are on the four corners of a Jew's garment, 2,800 people will be eager to serve him" (*Maharsha*).

59. *Tziyah*, drought, is read as *tzivah*, commanded. *Chom*, heat, is equated with summer.

60. *Yivlu*, "will be exhausted," is associated with *beli*.

61. The proof comes from a combination of verses in Amos, Joel, and Isaiah, three prophets who lived at the same time. From Amos we learn that the plague of locusts comes because of oppression of the poor, from

Joel we learn the dreadful consequences of a locust infestation, and from Isaiah we learn that in the resultant famine people will eat their children.

62. If a Jew's improper actions cause defamation of the Torah, he is guilty of *chillul Hashem*, profanation of God's name.

63. Leviticus, Chapter 25. Every seventh year (*shemittah*) the land is left fallow. Every fiftieth year (*yovel*) all land is returned to its original owner, and all slaves are released (Leviticus, Chapter 25, *Arachin* 29a, Rambam, *Shemittah* 10:9).

64. Literally: Anyone who makes himself empty from all other interests to devote himself to sin.

65. An abnormal accumulation of bodily fluids (hydrops).

66. According to *Kiddushin* 49b this means poverty in knowledge of Torah. An arrogant person is too conceited to learn from anyone.

67. A town northwest of Jerusalem where R. Yochanan b. Zakkai established a yeshivah after the destruction of the *Bet Hamikdash*. The students were seated in rows like the rows of vines in a vineyard, hence the name "Vineyard of Yavneh."

68. The Gemara will explain this title later on this page.

69. The Song of Songs is a sublime allegory that compares the relationship between God and Israel to that of a loving husband angered by a straying wife who betrayed him.

70. R. Yehudah b. Ila'i was appointed head of the Great Court.

71. In Upper Galilee.

72. R. Shimon b. Yocha'i.

73. Since Antonius Pius died in 161 C.E., the conversation of the three Sages must have taken place in 149 C.E.

74. The Gemara (*Shevuot* 20b) teaches that when God gave the Ten Commandments, He miraculously caused Israel to hear simultaneously the two aspects of the *Shabbat* commandment: *Zachor* and *Shamor*. *Zachor, Remember* (Exodus 20:8), is the commandment to keep *Shabbat* in our minds and hearts by reciting the *Kiddush*. *Shamor, Safeguard* (Deuteronomy 5:12), is the injunction to avoid desecration of *Shabbat*. This is also the reason that we light two candles for *Shabbat*.

75. Usually translated, "He encamped before the city."

76. *Kohanim* (priests) are forbidden to be in contact with the dead and, therefore, may not enter a cemetery or visit a grave.

77. First portion of the crop, which must be set aside and given to a *kohen*. *Terumah* has a state of sanctity and may not be eaten by a non-*kohen*, or by a *kohen* in a state of *tumah* (contamination, uncleanness).

78. R. Yehudah b. Geirim was the one who related the R. Shimon b. Yocha'i's disparaging remarks about the Roman government, and thereby caused his suffering.

79. On *Shabbat*, it is forbidden to carry from one private domain into another. However, if an *eruv* (a quantity of food, enough for two meals) is placed in one of the houses in a courtyard, all the residents of that courtyard are permitted to carry into each other's houses.

80. A *mil* is 0.7 miles, 3,542 feet, 1.079 km. Hence, half a *mil* is 0.35 miles, 1,771 feet, .5395 km.

81. The well that miraculously followed the children of Israel on their wandering through the desert and supplied them with water thanks to the merit of Miriam.

82. *Ketubot* 111a.

83. *Resh Galuta*, or Exilarch, was the official title of the political leader of Babylonian Jewry. A descendant of King David, his authority was recognized by the Babylonian government.

84. Mar Ukva, the Head of the *Bet Din*, was a descendant of David (*Maharsha*).

85. The first and last letters of the Hebrew alphabet, as we say, "from A to Z."

86. 1 Kings 8:64 and *Zevachim* 59b.

87. The word *emet*, truth, is composed of *alef*, the first letter of the *alef bet*; *mem*, the middle letter; and *tav*, the last letter of the *alef bet*. This is consistent with the verse, "I am He—I am the first, and I am the last as well" (Isaiah 48:12) (Rashi).

88. The word *nachash* means serpent or snake.

89. After Rachel's death, Jacob moved his bed into the tent of Rachel's handmaid Bilhah. Reuven created a mixup by placing the bed in his mother Leah's tent.

90. After giving birth, a woman completed a period of purification, after which she brought an offering of two turtledoves or two pigeons.

91. A writ of divorce.

92. Also known as Rabbeinu Hakadosh, the compiler of the Mishnah, c. 135 C.E.–200 C.E.

93. Bathsheba's husband. David had written a letter to Joab ordering him to place Uriah in the front line so that he should be killed. Uriah had rebelled against the king's authority and was liable to the death penalty.

94. If the husband is missing in action, the retroactive *get* would save the wife from becoming an *agunah*, a wife tied to a husband whose whereabouts are unknown, and who therefore cannot remarry.

95. When David found Mefiboshet he gave him everything that belonged to Saul and to his entire family (2 Samuel 9:9).

96. Deuteronomy 21:1–9.

97. When Rechav'am succeeded Solomon, the kingdom was split. Rechav'am ruled over the tribes of Yehudah and Binyamin, while Yerav'am was king of the other ten tribes.

98. Assa and Yehoshafat were righteous kings. See 1 Kings 15:11 and 22:43.

99. Returnee to Torah observance.

100. *Nedarim* 50a.

101. Deuteronomy 33:2.

102. The entire Song of Songs is a sublime allegory describing the dialogue between God and Israel. To translate it in its literal sense would be false and misleading.

103. One of the thirty-nine categories of labor that is forbidden on *Shabbat*. If someone inadvertently violated these prohibitions he must bring a sin offering.

104. See *Chagigah* 11b, 13a, and 14b.

105. A woman who has her monthly period.

106. For example, carrying her on a stretcher. See Leviticus 15:23.

107. The day begins at nightfall of the preceding day. For example, Tuesday begins on Monday evening and lasts until Tuesday evening at nightfall when Wednesday begins. *Shabbat* begins on Friday at sundown.

108. A euphemism for marital relations.

109. The entire Torah is dependent on the Ten Commandments.

110. A bitter-tasting herb.

111. Literally, *techumin*. *Techum* is the boundary beyond which you may not walk on *Shabbat*, which is 2,000 cubits outside the town limits. This can be extended by another 2,000 cubits by means of an *eruv*.

112. The Jewish year is a lunar year that has 354 days, or fifty weeks and four days, which explains the difference of the four days.

113. In a leap year, one month of twenty-nine days is inserted, i.e., four weeks plus one day, so that the difference between one year and the next becomes five days.

114. The earliest Jewish history in existence, written by R. Yose B. Chalafta, a Tanna who was a student of R. Akiva. Its chronology begins with Adam and ends with the revolt of Bar Kochba (127 C.E.) against the Romans during the rule of Hadrian.

115. Literally translated; commonly rendered "at the foot of the mountain."

116. The number of adult males that left Egypt (Exodus 12:37).

117. Rabbeinu Tam notes in *Tosafot* that, contrary to what the Gemara says, apple trees produce apples after the leaves sprout. He explains that the tree referred to here is not an apple tree but rather an etrog (citron), for the Targum translates "apples" in, "Your breath is like the fragrance of apples" (Song 7:9) as "the fragrance of an etrog." An etrog stays on the tree from one year to the next, so that last year's fruit is on the tree before this year's leaves sprout.

118. According to tradition, there are seventy primary nations in the world.

119. *Tzeror hamor* alludes to *meitzar* (distressed) and *meimar* (embittered).

120. Rashi explains that *gedi*, goat, represents small cattle in general, including a calf.

121. *Kelim* 23:4.

122. Rashi explains that God intended to give the Torah 1,000 generations after Creation. But when He saw that the world could not endure without the Torah, He gave it twenty-six generations after Creation— ten generations from Adam until Noah; ten generations from Noah until Abraham; and Moses is the sixth generation after Abraham (Abraham, Isaac, Jacob, Levi, Amram, Moses). Thus the Torah really should have been given 974 generations later. Thus the angels argued: The Torah should have been with us for 1,000 generations, yet You are giving it to man after only twenty-six generations—974 generations too early.

123. God said to Moses: Hold on to the Throne of Glory, for that is the most convincing answer you can give to the angels. You are thereby telling them that by fulfilling the *mitzvot* of the Torah, man can rise to such closeness to God as to be able to hold on to the divine throne, a level angels can never attain.

124. In the script that is used for the Torah, small thin lines, called crowns or *taggin*, are placed on top of seven letters.

125. Rashi explains that Moses had told them he would come at the end of forty days, within the sixth hour. The Israelites thought that the day he went up was included in the forty days. Moses, however, meant forty full days—days and nights. The day he went up was not included, because it was not a full day.

126. Part of the crimson string was displayed in the *Bet Hamikdash*. When the goat went to its death at Azazel, the people knew that their sins were forgiven when the scarlet string in the *Bet Hamikdash* miraculously turned white (*Yoma* 66–67).

127. This explains the phrase, "God will say." He will admonish them and tell them their wrongdoing.

128. According to some, his violation was that he carried on *Shabbat*. According to others it was that he cut the sticks or bound them (*Shabbat* 96b).

129. A tradition that similar words in different contexts are meant to clarify one another.

130. On the first, third, fourth, fifth, seventh, and eighth days it says *veniskah*, "and its libation." On the second day, *veniskeihem*, and on the sixth day, *unesacheha*. On every day it says, *kamishpat*, "as prescribed"; whereas on the seventh day it says, *kemishpatam*, "as prescribed for them."

131. For a description of the joyous festivities surrounding the *nisuch hamayim* celebration see *Sukkah* 48a and 48b.

132. The reference is to Samaria, representing the Northern Kingdom of Israel (Ibn Ezra).

133. R. Chiya b. Abba was born in Babylonia but moved to Eretz Yisrael.

134. Rabbi Yehudah Hanassi, the compiler of the Mishnah.

135. See 2 Kings 21:1–16.

136. Above 113a.

137. *Maharsha* explains that, although a Torah scholar should not wear shabby clothes, Isaiah did so on God's instructions, as a sign and portent for Egypt and Ethiopia (Isaiah 20:2).

138. *Bava Metzia* 27a.

139. The Talmud was taught orally and was not yet written down in the days of the Mishnah.

140. This R. Gamliel was the grandfather of Rabbi Yehudah Hanassi. Berebbi was a title of distinction (Rashi).

141. R. Gamliel Hazaken (the Elder).

142. *Minim* probably is a reference to the early Christians. They tried to lead Jews astray through their writings and their proselytizing efforts.

143. [Because of the donkey I gave him, he overturned his verdict for which you had given him a lamp. Thus they proved that he was corrupt.]

144. Genesis 4:26. Rashi explains that idol worship was introduced in the days of Enosh.

145. Amalek is Israel's sworn enemy, the epitome of evil and the prototype of all oppressors of the Jewish people throughout its history.

146. *Hallel*, literally Praise, consists of Psalms 113 to 118. It is recited on *Rosh Chodesh* (New Moon), *Pesach*, *Shavuot*, Sukkot, and Chanukah. On *Rosh Chodesh* and from the third day of *Pesach*, Psalms 115, 1–11, and 116:1–11 are omitted.

147. A silver coin, equal to a common seal or half a *zuz*; *Ketubot* 64a, *Gittin* 45b.

148. The number thirteen is an exaggeration; it means "many butchers."

149. This is clearly an exaggeration. The number thirteen often is used to denote a large number, as in the "thirteen butchers" mentioned above (Rashi).

150. The *Resh Galuta* (Exilarch, or Leader of the Exile) was the political leader of Babylonian Jewry. The authority of the *Resh Galuta*, a descendant of King David, was recognized by the Babylonian government.

151. Since the preceding phrase reads, "If you call the *Shabbat* delight," it follows that calling God's day "honored" does not refer to *Shabbat*.

152. In Lamentations, Jeremiah bemoans the destruction of Jerusalem and the *Bet Hamikdash*.

153. R. Yehudah Nesiah II (the Prince) became *Nasi* around the year 240 C.E., when he was about twenty years old.

154. *Pe'ah* 1:1.

155. Hospitality and visiting the sick fall under the heading of kind deeds. Early attendance at the *bet hamidrash* and raising children to study the Torah are included in the study of Torah. Judging your neighbor favorably brings about peace between man and his fellow because you try to justify his actions even if they seem reprehensible. Absorption in prayer is also an act of kindness to one's own soul, as it says, "A kindly man benefits his soul" (Proverbs 11:17) (Rashi).

156. The *S'fat Emet* quoting the *She'iltot* states that the worker in this story was Rabbi Akiva before he began to learn Torah, and the master was Rabbi Eliezer b. Hyrkanus.

157. The pious man was either R. Yehudah b. Bava or R. Yehudah b. R. Ila'i (Rashi).

158. The Roman decree applied only to the head *tefillin*, about which it says, "All the nations of the world will realize that God's name is associated with you, and they will be afraid of you" (Deuteronomy 28:10). The Romans were afraid of the *tefillin* (*Maharsha*).

159. *Bet* = 2; *hei* = 5; *mem* = 40; *hei* = 5.

160. A place in the north of Eretz Yisrael.

161. In 556 B.C.E., the last of the ten tribes that composed the Kingdom of Israel were led into exile by Shalmanessar, King of Assyria. They are lost without a trace. "This happened because they did not obey the Lord their God; they transgressed His covenant. . . they did not obey and they did not fulfill it" (2 Kings 18:9–12).

162. It is a mitzvah for a father to teach his son a trade (*Kiddushin* 30b).

163. A caper is the flower bud of a low shrub of Mediterranean countries, pickled and used as a condiment.

164. Hidden in this segment is the mystery of reincarnation, whereby a soul that did not attain sufficient merit in life returns to earth up to three times in other bodies in the hope that during the subsequent lives it will be cleansed. This is alluded to in the verse, "Truly, God does all these things two or three times to a man, to bring him back from the Pit, that he may bask in the light of life" (Job 33:29,30). And in the verse, "He will fling away the lives of your enemies as from the hollow of a sling" (1 Samuel 25:29)—from one body into another, to be cleansed, as in the parable in the Gemara (*Maharsha*).

165. 1 Samuel 28:3–9.

166. Head of the Academy.

❧ ERUVIN ❧

TABERNACLE AND SANCTUARY

(2a) We find that the Tabernacle (*Mishkan*) is called Sanctuary (*Mikdash*), and the Sanctuary (*Mikdash*) is referred to as Tabernacle (*Mishkan*). [The Gemara asks:] Granted that the Sanctuary is called Tabernacle (*Mishkan*), for it says, "I will keep My Tabernacle (*Mishkani*) in your midst" (Leviticus 26:11). But from where do you know that the Tabernacle is referred to as Sanctuary (*Mikdash*)? Do you think from the verse, "The Kehatites who carried the Sanctuary (*haMikdash*) then began their march, and the Tabernacle (*haMishkan*) would be set up before they arrived [at the destination]" (Numbers 10:21)? (2b) [The Gemara demurs:] In this verse, the term *haMikdash* refers [not to the Tabernacle, but] to the holy ark, [which was carried by the Kehatites,[1] and in this context it is called *haMikdash*, (Sanctuary), because it is the most sacred of all objects in the Tabernacle (Rashi)]. [The Gemara answers:] We derive [the interchangeability of *Mikdash* and *Mishkan*] from, "They shall make Me a *Mikdash* (Sanctuary), and I will dwell among them" (Exodus 25:8), [and here *Mikdash* (Sanctuary) clearly refers to the *Mishkan* (Tabernacle)].

TOO MANY COOKS SPOIL THE BROTH

(3a) People say: If two cooks are in charge of one pot, the dish is neither cold nor hot [because each relies on the other to prepare it correctly (*Maharsha*)].

R. MEIR'S INERADICABLE INK

(13a) R. Yehudah said in the name of Shmuel, in the name of R. Meir: When I studied Torah under R. Akiva I used to put vitriol[2] into my ink, and R. Akiva did not object. But later, when I came to R. Yishmael, he [R. Yishmael] asked me, "My son, what is your occupation?" "I am a scribe," I replied. "Be painstaking in your work," he exhorted me, "for you have a holy profession. If you omit or add one single letter [in the Torah] you would destroy the entire universe, [e.g., if you omit the *alef* of *emet* (truth), you write *met* (dead),

a dreadful distortion. Or if you add a *vav* to *vayedabbeir* (He spoke), you get *vayedabberu* (they spoke), implying that that there is more than one God (Rashi)]. I then told R. Yishmael, "I have a certain ingredient called vitriol, which I add to my ink." He replied, "How can you put vitriol into ink? The Torah clearly says, [about the scroll the priest must write in the case of the suspected adulteress], 'And he shall write . . . and dissolve the writing' (Numbers 5:23), to tell you that the writing must be [done with ink that can be] dissolved," [and ink that contains vitriol cannot be dissolved].

[The Gemara asks:] What did R. Yishmael mean [when he warned R. Meir against omitting or adding letters], and what did R. Meir mean [when he replied about the ingredients of his ink? They seem to be speaking past each other]. [The Gemara answers:] R. Meir meant to say to R. Yishmael: You need not be concerned that I will omit or add letters, because I am an expert scribe. But I have gone one step further. I have even taken precautions to prevent the possibility of a fly sitting on the protruding corner of the letter *dalet* and erasing it, thereby changing it into a *reish*. [If the *dalet* of *echad*, "one," in *Hashem echad* is changed into a *reish*, the result is the blasphemous phrase, *Hashem acher*, meaning, "another God."] For I add to my ink a certain chemical called vitriol to it [to make it inerasable].

RABBI MEIR'S BRILLIANCE

(13b) R. Acha b. Chanina said: It is obvious and known to Him Who spoke, and the world came into being, that in the generation of R. Meir there was no one like him. [Asks the Gemara:] Then why was the *halachah* not decided according to his opinion? [Answers the Gemara:] Because his colleagues could not fathom the depth of his understanding. [He was so utterly persuasive that it was impossible to disagree with him.] He would bring convincing arguments to prove that something was ritually clean when, in fact, it was unclean, and that something was ritually unclean when, in fact, it was clean. We learned: His name was

137

not R. Meir but R. Nehora'i. Then why was he called R. Meir? Because he enlightened the Sages in the *halachah*. [The word *meir* means "to give light."]

Rebbi declared: The reason that I am brighter than my colleagues is that I saw the back of R. Meir [when I studied under him my seat in the Yeshivah was behind him (Rashi)]. Had I seen him from the front, I would have been even brighter, for it says, "Your eyes shall see your teacher" (Isaiah 30:20).

R. Abbahu said in R. Yochanan's name: R. Meir had a disciple named Sumchus who, for anything that was ritually unclean, offered forty-eight reasons why it should be clean, and for anything that was ritually clean cited forty-eight reasons why it should be unclean.

It was taught: There was an accomplished disciple in Yavneh who brought a hundred and fifty reasons to prove that a [dead] creeping animal was clean. [It is, in fact, unclean (Leviticus 11:29–35).] Said Ravina: I can also give you a logical reason to prove that it is clean. If a snake that kills [man and beast] and thereby brings uncleanness into the world [a corpse is unclean and spreads uncleanness to those who touch it], yet the snake itself is ritually clean [the snake is not listed among the eight unclean creeping things enumerated in Leviticus 11:29,30)], surely a creeping thing that does not kill [man and beast] and thus does not cause uncleanness, [when dead] is ritually clean. No, [says the Gemara:] This argument does not hold water. [The snake itself is not inherently unclean.] It merely acts as a thorn. [It injects its venom into its victim who then dies. But the corpse's uncleanness is not derived from the snake. Therefore you cannot draw an inference from a snake.]

BET SHAMMAI AND BET HILLEL

R. Abba said in Shmuel's name: For three years Bet Shammai and Bet Hillel argued, each one maintaining: The *halachah* is according to our view. Then a heavenly voice rang out and declared: Both, these and those, are the words of the living God, but the *halachah* is according to Bet Hillel. [Asks the Gemara:] Since both these and those are the words of the living God, why did Bet Hillel merit that we should conduct ourselves according to their opinion? [Answers the Gemara:] Because they were easygoing and modest, and when discussing their own rulings they considered Bet Shammai's opinions too. And that's not all, but they would first discuss Bet Shammai's views and only then formulate their own position. To give you an example: We have learned: If someone sits with his head and most of his body in the sukkah, but his table is in the house [it did not fit into the sukkah], Bet Shammai declares the sukkah invalid, but Bet Hillel ruled that it is valid. Said Bet Hillel to Bet Shammai: Wasn't there a story that the elders of Bet Shammai and the elders of Bet Hillel [note that Bet Hillel mentioned the elders of Bet Shammai before mentioning

the elders of Bet Hillel] went to visit to R. Yochanan b. Hachoranit and found him sitting with his head and most of his body inside the sukkah while his table was in the house? [So you see it is all right?]

Replied Bet Shammai: You cannot cite this as proof! They told him at that time: If this is the way you always conduct yourself, then you have never fulfilled the mitzvah of sukkah. [At any rate, this incident shows the modesty of Bet Hillel. The Gemara summarizes:] This comes to teach you that if a person humbles himself, the Holy One, blessed is He, raises him up; and if anyone elevates himself, the Holy One, blessed be He, humbles him. Whoever seeks greatness, greatness runs away from him; and whoever runs away from greatness, greatness pursues him. Anyone that pushes time [i.e., he is overeager to succeed], time will push him [he will never be successful]; but anyone that bides his time, time will be on his side [in due time he will achieve success].

The Rabbis taught: For two-and-a-half years Bet Shammai and Bet Hillel carried on a dispute. One side argued that it would be better for man if he had not been created than to have been created, while the other side contended that it is better for man to have been created than not to have been created. When they counted the votes they found that the majority held that it would be better for not to have been created than to have been created, but now that he has been created a person should examine his past actions [and do *teshuvah* for his shortcomings]. Others say: He should consider the consequences of his actions ahead of time.

(14a) R. Chiya taught: The reservoir that Solomon built held as much water as one hundred and fifty *mikva'ot*. Now, consider: a *mikveh* contains forty *se'ah* (120 gallons of water), as it says, "He must immerse his entire body in water" (Leviticus 15:16), meaning, in a *mikveh*. "His entire body" implies that it must contain enough water so that his entire body is covered. How much is that? A quantity of water the volume of 1 cubit x 1 cubit x 3 cubits. And the Sages have estimated that a *mikveh* must hold forty *se'ah*.

(17a) Our Rabbis learned in a *Baraita*: An army that goes out to fight an optional war [any war that was fought after the divinely ordained wars in the days of Joshua (Rashi)] is permitted to confiscate dry wood, [not to mention fresh wood]. R. Yehudah b. Teima said: They may also pitch their tents wherever they want, and they should be buried where they are killed.

AGGADIC TEACHINGS OF R. YIRMIYAH B. ELAZAR

(18b) R. Yirmiyah b. Elazar said: Only part of a person's praise should be said in his presence, but all of his praise in his absence. [Praising him fully in his presence may be interpreted as flattery (Rashi).] Only part of his praise should be said in his presence, for it says, [Speaking to Noah, God says,] "I have seen that you

138

are righteous before Me in this generation" (Genesis 7:1). [In Noah's presence God praises him only for being righteous.] But *all* of a person's praises should be said in his absence, for it says, "Noah was a righteous and faultless man in his generation" (ibid. 6:9). [In his absence he is praised fully for being both righteous and faultless.]

(18b) R. Yirmiyah b. Elazar also said: What is the meaning of the verse, "There was a freshly plucked olive leaf in its beak" (ibid. 8:11)? The dove said to the Holy One, blessed be He: May my food be as bitter as an olive, but coming directly from You, rather than sweet as honey but coming from mortal man. [How do we know that *taraf*, "freshly plucked," signifies sustenance?] It says in this verse, *taraf*, "freshly plucked," and elsewhere it says, "Provide me, *hatrifeini*, with my daily bread" (Proverbs 30:8). [So we see that both *hatrifeini* and *taraf* mean sustenance.]

R. Yirmiyah b. Elazar also said: Any house in which words of the Torah are heard at night will never be destroyed, for it says, "But none says, 'Where is my God, my Maker, who gives songs [i.e., the words of Torah] in the night'" (Job 35:10)—[A person who learns Torah at night will never face a situation where he cries out, "Where is my God," for his house will never be destroyed.]

R. Yirmiyah b. Elazar also said: since the *Bet Hamikdash* was destroyed, [and the *kohanim* stopped pronouncing the Four-Letter Divine Name when blessing the people], it is enough for the world to use only the first two letters of the Tetragrammaton. For it says, "Let all souls praise God, Ya-H, Halleluyah" (Psalms 150:6), [the Name Ya-H is sufficient (Rashi)].

R. Yirmiyah b. Elazar also said: When Babylonia was cursed, its neighbors were also cursed [as a result of this curse], but when Shomron (Samaria) was cursed, its neighbors were blessed [as a result of this curse]. When Babylonia was cursed, its neighbors were also cursed, for it says, "I will make it a home of wild beasts and swamps [predators that roam the adjacent localities causing damage]. When Shomron was cursed, its neighbors were blessed, for it says, "I will turn Samaria into a ruin in open country, (19a) into ground for planting vineyards," (Micah 1:6) [so that its neighbors could plant vineyards there].

THE THREE GATES
OF GEHINNOM

R. Yimiyah b. Elazar further said: There are three entrances to Gehinnom: one in the desert, one in the sea, and one in Jerusalem. One entrance is in the desert, for it says, "[Korach and his party] fell alive into the depths [of Gehinnom] along with all that was theirs" (Numbers 16:33). [One entrance is] in the sea, for it says: [Jonah prayed from the belly of the fish,] "From the depths of Gehinnom I cried out, and You heard my voice" (Jonah 2:3). [One entrance is in Jerusalem,] for

it says, "Declares God, who has a fire in Zion, who has a furnace in Jerusalem" (Isaiah 31:9). In the Yeshivah of R. Yishmael it was taught that "a fire in Zion" refers to Gehinnom, and "a furnace in Jerusalem" refers to the entrance to Gehinnom. [Metaphorically the three entrances represent the sins that lead to Gehinnom: "the desert" refers to the sin of quarreling, exemplified by Korach's rebellion in the desert. "The sea" refers to the sin of Jonah, who was able to admonish but failed to do so. "Jerusalem" refers to the sins of Jerusalem, "The young bully the old, the despised bully the honored . . ." (Isaiah 3:5) (Anaf Yosef).]

[Asks the Gemara:] Aren't there more entrances to Gehinnom? Has not R. Meryon said in the name of R. Yehoshua b. Levi, according to others, Rabbah b. R. Meryon learned in a *Baraita* of the Yeshivah of R. Yochanan b. Zakkai: There are two palm trees in the Valley of Ben Hinnom, and smoke rises between these palm trees. And we learned concerning [these trees]: The fronds of the palm trees of Iron Mountain may be used [as a *lulav*], and this is the entrance to Gehinnom. [Proof that there are more than three entrances.] [Answers the Gemara:] Perhaps this entrance is the same as the one in Jerusalem [because the Valley of Ben Hinnom is close to the wall around the City].

THE SEVEN NAMES
OF GEHINNOM

R. Yehoshua b. Levi said: Gehinnom has seven names: Sheol, Perdition, Pit of Destruction, Appalling Pit, Slimy Mud, Shadow of Death, and Nether World. "Sheol," for it says, "From the belly of Sheol I cried out, and You heard my voice" (Jonah 2:3). "Perdition," for it says, "Is Your kindness be recounted in the grave, Your faithfulness in perdition?" (Psalms 88:12). "Pit of destruction," for it says, "Because you will not abandon my soul to the grave, You will not allow Your devout one to witness destruction" (Psalms 16:10). "Appalling Pit" and "Slimy Mud," for it says, "He raised me from the appalling pit, from the slimy mud" (Psalms 40:3). "Shadow of Death," for it says, "Those who sat in darkness and the shadow of death" (Psalms 107:10). The fact that the name "Nether World" [is synonymous with Gehinnom] is a tradition [and is not supported by a scriptural verse].

[The Gemara asks:] Do we have no other names? What about the name Gehinnom [itself]? [The Gemara answers: The verse in Joshua 15:8 that mentions Gei ben Hinnom does not refer to Purgatory;] it refers to a valley that is as deep as the Valley of Hinnom. [An alternative reason is], because people go there to engage in incest. But isn't Gehinnom also called *Tofteh*? For it says, "The *Tofteh* has long been ready for him" (Isaiah 30:33). [Answers the Gemara: This is not a specific term for Gehinnom.] It means that anyone who is seduced (*hamitpateh*) by his evil impulse will fall into it [*hamitpateh* is seen as cognate to *Tofteh*).

139

Regarding the location of Gan Eden, Resh Lakish said: [We don't really know where it is.] If it is in Eretz Yisrael, its entrance is in Bet Shean.[3] If it is in Arabia, its entrance is Bet Gerem. If it is in between the rivers its entrance is Durmaskanin. In Babylonia, Abbaye would praise the fruit growing on the south side [of the Euphrates], and Rava praised the fruit of Harpania.

DON'T LOSE HOPE
ON THE WICKED

(21a) Rav Chisda said that Mari b. Mar expounded: What is the meaning of the verse, "God showed me two baskets of figs, placed before the Temple of God ... one basket contained very good figs, like (21b) first-ripened figs, and the other basket contained very bad figs, so bad that they could not be eaten" (Jeremiah 24:1,2). The good figs represent the perfectly righteous; the bad figs symbolize the completely wicked. Now in case you will say that their hope is lost and their prospects for the future have evaporated, therefore it says, "The baskets[4] yield their fragrance" (Song of Songs 7:14), both these and those [both the righteous and the wicked] will yield their fragrance. [Thus we may not give up hope on the wicked. They may do teshuvah and earn a place in the World to Come.]

Rava expounded: What is the meaning of the verse, "The mandrakes yield their fragrance" (ibid.)? This refers to the young men of Israel who never felt the taste of sin. "At our doors are all choice fruits" (ibid.) alludes to the daughters of Israel who tell their husbands about their openings [meaning, they tell their husbands when they begin to menstruate so that they will know to abstain from any contact]. Another interpretation of "our doors" is: They close their doors [and reserve them] for their husbands [and do not commit adultery]. "New and old, have I kept for you, my Beloved" (ibid.). The congregation of Israel says to the Holy One, blessed be He, "Master of the universe, I have imposed many more restrictions on myself than You dictated to me, and I have fulfilled them all."

BIBLICAL AND RABBINICAL
COMMANDMENTS

R. Chisda asked one of the young scholars who arranged and recited Aggadot before him: Have you heard what is meant by the phrase, "New and old" (ibid.)? He replied: ["The new"] refers to the lighter mitzvot, and "the old" refers to the more severe mitzvot. [R. Chisda] asked: Was then the Torah given at two different times [that you can speak of old and new mitzvot]? But "the old" refers to the mitzvot that were given to Moses on Sinai [the mitzvot ordained by the Torah], whereas "the new" means the new enactments that were imposed by the authorities of each generation.

Rava expounded: What is the meaning of the passage, "But more than this, my son, be careful of making many books" (Ecclesiastes 12:12)?—My son, be more careful in the observance of the mitzvot ordained by the Rabbis than in the mitzvot of the Torah; for in the mitzvot of the Torah there are positive[5] and negative[6] commandments; but when it comes to the laws of the Rabbis, whoever violates one of the Rabbinical injunctions is liable to the death penalty. Maybe you will say: If these Rabbinic injunctions are really important why were they not explicitly recorded in the Torah? [To answer you] it says, "The making of many books is without limit" (ibid. 12:12); [there is no end to the number of injunctions that can be imposed, and the Torah does not want to enumerate every conceivable case that may arise. The Torah gives us the basic guidelines, and it gave the power to enact new decrees to the Bet Din of every generation, as the need arises].

R. AKIVA'S PIETY IN PRISON

The Rabbis taught: R. Akiva was once imprisoned in jail, and R. Yehoshua Hagarsi served him. Every day, a certain quantity of water was brought to him. One day, the prison keeper met R. Yehoshua Hagarsi, and he said, "Today you are bringing more water than usual. Are you planning to dig [a tunnel] under the prison walls?" He spilled half the water and gave him back the other half. When he came to R. Akiva, R. Akiva said to him, "Don't you know that I am an elderly man, and my life depends on you?" [Then why did you did you wait so long to bring me the water? (Iyun Yaakov)]. He told him all that had happened, whereupon R. Akiva said, "Give me some water to wash my hands." Replied R. Yehoshua, "There isn't even enough water to drink; it surely will not be enough to wash your hands." "What can I do," R. Akiva said, "when for ignoring the [Rabbinic] mitzvah of washing your hands a person incurs the death penalty? It is better that I should die a natural death rather than that I should violate the opinion of my colleagues" [who instituted the washing of the hands before meals]. They said that R. Akiva did not taste anything until they brought him water, and he washed his hands. When the Sages heard of this incident they commented: If he was so conscientious in his old age, imagine how careful he must have been in his youth [to abide by the Rabbinic mitzvot]; and if he behaved like this under the rigors of prison, imagine how [exemplary] he conducted himself under normal circumstances.

Rav Yehudah said in the name of Shmuel: When Solomon instituted the laws of eruvin[7] and the washing of hands before meals, a Heavenly Voice came forth and proclaimed: My son, if your mind gets wisdom, My mind, too, will be gladdened" (Proverbs 23:15). And it also says, "Get wisdom my son, and gladden My heart, that I may have what to answer those that taunt me" (ibid. 27:11).

ISRAEL DECLARES
ITS LOVE OF GOD

Rava expounded: What is the meaning of the verse, "Come my beloved, let us go to the fields, let us lodge in the villages, let us go early to the vineyards; let us see if the vine has flowered, if its blossoms have opened; if the pomegranates are in bloom. There I will give my love to you" (Song of Songs 7:12,13)? [Rava now expounds the allegory:] "Come my beloved, let us go to the field"—the community of Israel spoke before the Holy One, blessed be He: Master of the universe, do not judge me as You would those people that live in the big cities who commit robbery and adultery, who swear vain and false oaths; "let us go to the field"—come, and I will show You scholars who study the Torah in poverty; "let us lodge in the villages"—don't read "in the villages" (bakefarim) but bakofrim, "among the disbelievers." Come and I will show you the people on whom You have bestowed a great deal of goodness, and they have denied Your existence. "Let us go early to the vineyards"—to the synagogues and the houses of learning; "let us see if the vine has flowered"—alludes to the students of the Chumash (Pentateuch);" if its blossoms have opened"—is an allusion to the students of the Mishnah; "if the pomegranates are in bloom"—alludes to the students of the Gemara. "There I will give my love to you"—There I will show You my glory and my greatness, the praise of my sons and my daughters.

SOLOMON'S WISDOM

R. Hamenuna said: What is the meaning of the verse, "[Solomon] composed three thousand proverbs, and his songs numbered one thousand and five" (1 Kings 5:12)? This teaches us that Solomon gave three thousand reasons for every word in the Torah, and for every word of Rabbinical precept he gave one thousand and five reasons.

Rava expounded: What is meant by the verse, "And besides that Kohelet was a sage, he also taught knowledge to the people, he listened and investigated, and he set forth many reasons" (Ecclesiastes 12:9)? "He taught the people knowledge" means that he punctuated the text [of Scripture and of the Mishnah (Rashi)], and he explained it with parables and comparisons.

"He listened and investigated, and he set forth many reasons"—Ulla said in the name of R. Elazar: Originally the Torah was like a basket that had no handles, until Solomon came and attached handles to it. [By instituting the laws of eruvin and of the washing of hands Solomon raised the people's meticulous observance of mitzvot (Rashi).]

DEDICATION TO
TORAH STUDY

It says, "His locks are curled and black as a raven" (Song of Songs 5:11). "His locks are curls"—R. Chisda said

in the name of Mar Ukva: This teaches us that it is possible to derive mounds and mounds of halachot from the marks on every letter in the Torah. "And black (shechorot) as a raven (ke'oreiv)"—With whom do you find the capability [to derive mounds of halachot]? With a person who (22a) gets up early (shacharit, similar to shechorot) to go to the bet hamidrash (house of study) and stays until late at night (arvit, similar to oreiv). [Such a person is able to pile up mounds of novel halachic expositions.] Rabba explained: [You can find this ability] in a person who blackens his face like a raven [i.e., who suffers poverty and hunger for the sake of Torah study]. Rava said: [You find this ability] in a person who is able to adopt a cruel attitude toward his children and his household, acting like a raven. [The raven is cruel to his brood.[8] The commentators remark that this recommendation does not apply to present-day scholars.] This was the case with R. Adda b. Matnah who went to study at the yeshivah of Rav. So his wife said to him, "What shall I do with your children? [We have nothing to eat.]" He replied: Are there no vegetables left in the swamp? [Let them eat those vegetables.] He was willing to have his children eat those vegetables rather than for him to forego the learning in the yeshivah.]

DIVINE JUSTICE

It says, "He repays those who hate Him to His face with destruction" (Deuteronomy 7:10). Says R. Yehoshua b. Levi: If it were not for the fact that the passage states it explicitly, it would have been impossible for a person to say it. For it is like a person who is carrying a burden on his face and he wants to throw it off; [it is as if God, too, were carrying a load on His face and wants to shake it off]. "He is never slow with those who hate Him"—R. Ila remarked: He is never slow with His enemies, but He will delay for the perfectly righteous. And this agrees with what R. Yehoshua b. Levi said: What is the meaning of the verse, "Observe faithfully the commandment . . . which I command you today to do them" (ibid. 11). Today [in this world] you have the opportunity to do them, but you cannot wait until tomorrow [in the World to Come] to do them. Today [in this world] you can fulfill the mitzvot, but tomorrow [the World to Come] is set aside for you to receive your reward for doing them.

R. Chaggai, others say R. Shmuel b. Nachmani, said: What is the meaning of the verse, "Slow to anger (erech apayim)" (Exodus 34:6)? [The word apayim is written in the dual form, literally "slow of angers."] It should have said erech af, "slow of anger" [in the singular]. [Answers the Gemara: Af means also "face," and apayim means "faces."] God shows His smiling Face toward the righteous, and His angry Face toward the wicked. [God gives the righteous their full reward in the World to Come, and He is patient with the wicked, hoping that they will do teshuvah. But if they don't repent He gives them their eternal punishment in the World to Come (Rashi).]

THE BODY MUST FOLLOW
THE HEAD

(41a) We learned in a *Baraita*: After the death of R. Gamliel, R. Yehoshua entered the yeshivah to revoke his ruling [to the effect that a fast that falls on Friday must be broken before *Shabbat* begins]. Thereupon R. Yochanan b. Nuri got up and said, "I propose that 'the body must follow the head' [in matters of law we must follow the decisions of the early authorities]. As long as R. Gamliel was alive, the *halachah* was decided according to his view, and now that he is dead you want to repeal his words? Yehoshua, we will not listen to you, because the *halachah* was already established according to R. Gamliel's view."

And there was no one that voiced any opposition whatsoever to this statement.

THREE CATEGORIES

(41b) We learned in a *Baraita*: There are three things that can force a person to act against his better judgment and against the will of God: Idol worshippers, an evil spirit [a demon taking possession of a person's body], and the pressure of extreme poverty. [Asks the Gemara:] What practical difference does it make [that we know these three reasons]? [Answers the Gemara:] So that people should pray [for the sinner] to be freed from these scourges. [People should realize that the transgressor is acting under duress, and that he is forced to sin (Iyun Yaakov).]

There are three kinds of people that will not see Gehinnom: One who suffers from extreme poverty, one who suffers from intestinal trouble, and one who is being harassed by creditors [or, one who is being persecuted by the Roman government (*Tosafot*), because these people suffer a great deal during their lifetime]. Some say: Also someone who has a bad wife. Why does the first Tanna not [mention a bad wife]? Because it is a mitzvah to divorce a bad wife, [thus he does not suffer a great deal]. Then why does the second Tanna mention [a bad wife]? Because sometimes it happens that the *ketubah* [the wife's marriage settlement][9] amounts to more than he can afford, or he has children from her, and is, therefore, unable to divorce her.

[Asks the Gemara:] What difference does it make [that we know the three or four reasons that a person will not see Gehinnom]? [Answers the Gemara:] So that he will accept his afflictions with love, [realizing that his suffering atones for his shortcomings and paves his way to Gan Eden]. There are three types of people that die suddenly, even while they are in the middle of a conversation: a person who suffers from abdominal pain, a woman who just gave birth, and a person suffering from dropsy [an abnormal accumulation of fluids]. For what practical purpose does the Gemara tell us this? To prepare the shrouds [so that if they die suddenly the burial will not be delayed].

MEASURING DEPTH
AND HEIGHT

(43b) We are taught: R. Gamliel had a tube through which he could see a distance of two thousand cubits on land as well as across the sea. If a person wants to measure the depth of a valley he can do so by looking through such a tube. [He first measures how far he can see through the tube. He then finds a point on the edge of the valley where he can see all the way to the bottom, which gives him the depth of the valley at that point (Rashi).] If someone wants to know the height of a palm tree he should measure his own height and the length of his shadow, as well as the length of the shadow of the tree. He will then be able to determine the height of the palm tree. [The ratio of the height of the tree to its shadow is the same as that of the man's height to his shadow.] If someone wants to prevent wild animals from seeking shelter in the shade of a grave mound, [because he is afraid that the animals will smell the corpse and mutilate it (Rashi)], he should stick a rod into the ground during the fourth hour of the day [when it is hot in the sun but cool in the shade, and the animals come to stay in the shade]. He should look in which direction the shadow falls at that hour and build the mound on the grave in the direction of the shadow [so that the mound does not cast any shadow].

LAUNCHING A
COUNTERATTACK
ON *SHABBAT*?

(45a) Rav Yehudah said in the name of Rav: If foreigners laid siege to a Jewish town it is not permitted to strike out at them or to desecrate the *Shabbat* because of them. We have learned a proof to this in a *Baraita*: If foreigners laid siege, etc. Regarding which case was this statement said? Only where the invaders came because of money matters, but if they came to take lives, then the people are permitted to strike out at them with weapons even on *Shabbat*. If the enemy attacked a town close to the border [so that if they captured it, they would overrun the entire region], then even if they did not come to take lives but only to rob straw or stubble, the people are permitted to launch an armed counterattack and desecrate the *Shabbat* in the process.

R. Yosef b. Minyumi said in the name of R. Nachman: Babylon is considered as a frontier town, and by "frontier town" he meant Nahardea [which was situated on the line separating the heathen and Jewish settlements in Babylonia].

R. Dustai of Biri expounded: What is the meaning of the passage, "David was told, 'The Philistines are raiding Ke'ilah and looting the threshing floors'" (1 Samuel 23:1). A Tanna taught: Ke'ilah was a frontier town, and they came only for the purpose of looting straw and stubble. For it says, "and looting the threshing floors," and yet it says, "David consulted God, 'Shall I go and attack those Philistines?' And God said to David, 'Go, attack the Philistines and you will save Ke'ilah'" (ibid. 2). Now, about what did David consult God? Do you think that he asked whether or not he was permitted [to counterattack since it was *Shabbat* (Rashi)]? That is not likely. The Bet Din of the prophet Samuel was then in existence, [so David would have put his question to the Bet Din since halachic queries are not put to the *Urim Vetumim*[10] (Rashi)]. Rather, he asked whether he would be successful in battle or not. This is also borne out by a precise reading of the verse. For it says, "Go, attack the Philistines, and you will save Ke'ilah." [The phrase "and you will save Ke'ilah" proves that God announced that he would be victorious.] This proves [that David asked whether he would win the battle].

RAV DISAGREES WITH SHMUEL

(53a) Rav and Shmuel hold different opinions regarding the name Cave of Machpelah. One says that the cave consisted of two chambers, one inside the other. The other said that it was built like a house with an upper story. According to the one who holds that it was built like a house with an upper story, the name *Machpelah* [which means "double"] is quite fitting. But according to the one who holds that it consisted of two chambers, one inside the other, why should it be called *Machpelah*? [The Gemara answers:] It is "doubled" because of the couples that are buried there.

It says, "Mamre, at Kiryat Arba [which is the Cave of Machpelah]" (Genesis 35:27). R. Yitzchak explained: this refers to the four couples that are buried there [*Arba* means "four"]: Adam and Eve, Abraham and Sarah, Isaac and Rebeccah, and Jacob and Leah.

It says, [In the days of Abraham there was a war among four mighty kings who fought against five subservient kings who had rebelled. The story of the war begins,] "It happened in the days of Amrafel" (Genesis 14:1). Rav and Shmuel disagree about this verse. One holds that the king's name was Nimrod, and why was he called Amrafel? Because he ordered our father Abraham thrown into the burning furnace. [The name Amrafel is seen as a contraction of *amar*, "he said," and *hipil*, "had him thrown."] But the other holds that his real name was Amrafel; and why was he called Nimrod? Because during his reign he incited the whole world to rebel against God. [Nimrod, from the root *marad*, "to rebel."]

"A new king came to power in Egypt" (Exodus 1:8). Rav and Shmuel disagree about the meaning of this verse. One holds that it was actually a new king, and the other says that [it was the old king, but] that he issued new decrees. The one who explains that it was actually a new king bases his view on the fact that it says "a *new* king," while the one who holds that [it was the old king, but that] he issued new decrees, finds support for his view in the fact that it does not say, "The old king died and a new king came to power." But according to the one who said that it was the old king but he issued new decrees, [we can ask:] But it says, "A new king came to power in Egypt who did not know Joseph"? [Is it possible that the old king did not know Joseph? Therefore it must be a new king.] [The Gemara answers:] What is the meaning of "who did not know Joseph"? [He acted] as if he had never known Joseph.

LATER GENERATIONS HAVE LESS INTELLECTUAL GRASP

R. Yochanan said: I stayed for eighteen days at R. Oshaia Beribbi and I learned from him only one thing in our Mishnah: that the word *me'abberin* ("extended"), in the phrase, "How are the *Shabbat* boundaries of cities extended?", is spelled with an *alef* rather than with an *ayin*. [The Gemara asks:] Is that so? Did not R. Yochanan say: R. Oshaia Beribbi had twelve disciples. I spent eighteen days among them, and I learned how astute and brilliant each of them was? Now is it possible that he learned how astute and brilliant each of them was but he did not learn any Gemara? [The Gemara answers:] If you wish you may say that he did learn a great deal from them, but from R. Oshaia he only learned that one word. Or if you prefer you may say: He learned only one thing regarding our Mishnah, [but concerning other Mishnahs he learned many things].

R. Yochanan further said: When we learned Torah under R. Oshaia [we were so eager to learn that] four of us crowded into the space of one cubit. Rebbi said: When we learned Torah under Rabbi Eliezer b. Shamua, six of us crowded into the space of one cubit. R. Yochanan said: R. Oshaia Beribbi in his generation was like R. Meir in his generation. Just as R. Meir's colleagues in his generation could not fathom the depth of his knowledge, so were R. Oshaia's colleagues in his generation unable to fathom the depth of his knowledge.

R. Yochanan also said: The intellectual capacity of the early Sages was like the entrance to the *Ulam* [a chamber of the *Bet Hamikdash* whose door was twenty cubits wide], and that of the later Sages was like the entrance to the *Heichal* [a chamber whose door was ten cubits wide], but ours is like the eye of a thin needle. Who is meant by "the early Sages"? R. Akiva and his generation. Who is meant by "the later Sages"? The generation of R. Elazar b. Shamua. Others say that "the early Sages" refers to the generation of R. Elazar b. Shamua, and "the later Sages" refers to the generation of R. Oshaia Beribbi. "But our intellectual capacity is like the eye of a thin needle." Said

Abaye: As for us [of the time of the later Amora'im], understanding the Gemara is as difficult as forcing a large peg into a small hole in a wall. [The intellectual capacity of succeeding generations gradually diminishes.] Said Rava: As far as we are concerned, when it comes to understanding logic it is like trying to stick your finger into hardened wax; [it does not penetrate]. Said R. Ashi: Forgetting things comes as easily to us as putting a finger into an open pit, [or, into mustard. As soon as you retract your finger the hole fills up; similarly, as soon as we finish a tractate we forget it (*Tosafot*)].

JUDEANS MORE ARTICULATE
THAN GALILEANS

Rav Yehudah said in the name of Rav: The people of Judea who were careful to express themselves in beautiful phrases retained their learning. The Galileans, however, who were not careful to speak in beautiful phrases, did not retain their learning. [The Gemara asks:] What does retaining one's learning have to do with using fancy language? Say instead: The people of Judea who spoke in a precise and articulate way [and quoted the teachings exactly as they heard them from their Rabbi], and who made mnemonic signs for themselves, retained their learning. But the Galileans who were not exact in their language and who did not make signs to memorize what they had learned, did not retain their learning. If you prefer you may say: The Judeans who learned from one Rabbi retained their learning, but the Galileans who did not learn from one Rabbi did not retain their learning. [They became confused by the different approaches of the various Rabbis to the same topic.]

Ravina said: The Judeans who shared their learning with other people retained their learning, but the Galileans who did not share their learning with others did not retain their learning. King David taught the Torah to the people, but King Saul did not learn with others. About David who learned with others it says, "Those who fear You will see me and rejoice" (Psalms 119:74). But about Saul who did not share his learning with others it says, "And wherever he turned he (53b) acted wrongly" (1 Samuel 14:47); [his halachic decisions were faulty (Rashi)].

R. Yochanan said: From what verse can we derive that the Holy One, blessed be He, forgave Saul for the sin [of killing the priests of Nov (1 Samuel 22:18)]? For it says, [Saul sought the advice of Samuel and asked the sorceress of Endor to raise Samuel's spirit. Samuel's spirit told Saul that he would die], "Tomorrow your sons and you will be with me" (1 Samuel 28:19). "With me" implies: In my heavenly dwelling place, [in Gan Eden. Thus he asured him that his sin had been forgiven].

OUTWITTED BY A WOMAN, A
GIRL, AND A BOY

R. Yehoshua b. Chanania said: In all my life, no one ever outsmarted me except for a woman, a little boy, and a little girl. What was the episode with the woman? I was once staying with a hostess who served me beans. On the first day I ate all of them and left nothing. On the second day, too, I left nothing. However, on the third day, she put too much salt on them, and as soon as I tasted it I stopped and did not touch it. "Rabbi," she asked me, "why aren't you eating?" "I have already eaten," I replied. "Then why didn't you abstain from eating the bread [at the beginning of the meal]?" "Rabbi," she continued, "could it be that you are not eating today to make up for the fact that you did not leave anything from your dish yesterday and the day before? For haven't the Sages said that the waiter who dishes out the food should not leave any food in the pot for himself, but the guests should leave something on the plate" [for the waiter? This was the woman's veiled reproach for his failure to leave her a "tip" on the two previous days]. What was the incident with the little girl? Once I was on a trip, and when I noticed a path running across a field I took that path. Suddenly a little girl called out, "Rabbi, isn't this a field?" [Who gave you the right to go through someone else's field?] I replied, "Isn't this a trodden path?" The little girl shot back, "[How do you think it became a trodden path?] It is robbers like you that made it a trodden path!"

What was the story with the little boy? I was once on a trip when I saw a young boy sitting at a crossroad. I asked him, "Son, what road do I take to go to the city?" He replied, "This road is long but short, and this road is short but long." So I took the short road. When I came close to the city I discovered that it was surrounded by gardens and orchards [so that I could not enter]. I turned back, and when reached the boy I said, "Son, didn't you tell me that this road was the short one?" "Rabbi, but didn't I also tell you that it was long?" he retorted. I kissed him on his head and said to him, "Fortunate are you, Israel, all of you are wise, both young and old."

R. Yose Hagelili was once on the road when he met Beruriah [R. Meir's wife, a very wise and pious woman]. He asked her, "By what road should we travel to Lod [Lydda]?" She replied, "Galilean fool that you are! Didn't the Sages say, 'Do not talk excessively with women'? (*Avot* 1:5). You should have asked, 'How to Lod?'"

STUDY WITH A LOUD VOICE

Beruriah once found a disciple who was studying very quietly. (54a) She reprimanded[11] him and said: Doesn't it say, "[The Torah] is arranged and preserved" (2 Samuel 23:5)—If the Torah is arranged and embedded in all your two hundred and forty-eight limbs then it will be preserved, otherwise, [if you don't use one part of your body, namely your voice], you will not retain it. We learned in a *Baraita*: Rabbi Eliezer had one disciple who learned Torah very quietly. After three years he forgot all that he had learned. We learned: Rabbi Eliezer had another disciple who deserved burning for sinning against God. "Leave him alone," the Rabbis said, "he was an attendant to a great man."

Shmuel said to Rav Yehudah: Smart man that you are, open your mouth and read the Written Torah loudly, open your mouth and read the Oral Torah [Mishnah and Gemara], loudly so that you will retain your learning and you will live long. For it says, "The [words of the Torah] are life to him that finds them [*lemotza'eihem*], healing for his whole body" (Proverbs 4:22). Don't read *lemotza'eihem*, "to him that finds them," but *lemotzi'eihem*, "him that utters them" loudly.

Shmuel further said to Rav Yehudah: Smart man that you are, "Grab and eat, grab and drink; [if you have the money, enjoy it now, and don't wait until tomorrow (Rashi)], for the world that we all must leave is like a wedding feast [it is here today and gone tomorrow" (Rashi)].

Rav said to R. Hamenuna: Son, if you have the means, go ahead and be good to yourself, for there is no pleasure in the grave, and death does not procrastinate [it comes suddenly]. If you say: I will leave my wealth for my children [rather than use it myself], who will tell you in the grave? [Who will guarantee you that they will spend the money wisely?] A person's children are like the grass of the fields, some blossom and some wither.

TORAH IS THE BEST MEDICINE

R. Yehoshua b. Levi said: If someone is walking along the road, and he has no company, he should engross himself in the study of Torah, for it says, "For they [the words of Torah] are a graceful accompaniment" (Proverbs 1:9). If someone has a headache let him engage in Torah study, for it says, "[The words of Torah] are a graceful accompaniment for your head" (ibid.). If someone has a sore throat let him study Torah, for the verse continues, "and a necklace around your throat" (ibid.). If someone has a stomachache let him study Torah, for it says, "It will be a cure for your navel" (ibid. 3:8). If a person feels pain in his bones, let him study Torah, for the verse continues, "a tonic for your bones" (ibid.). If he feels pain all over his body, let him study Torah, for it says, "It is a healing for his whole body" (ibid. 4:22).

R. Yehudah b. R. Chiyah said: Come and see that the attributes of the Holy One, blessed be He, are unlike those of mortal man. When a human being administers a medicine to his friend it may be beneficial to one organ but harmful to another. Not so the Holy One, blessed be He. He gave the Torah to Israel, and it is a life-giving remedy for the entire body, as it says, "It is a healing for his whole body" (ibid.).

ENUNCIATE TORAH THOUGHTS AND PRAYERS

R. Ammi said: What is the meaning of the passage, "It is pleasant if you retain them (the Torah) inside you, and that all of them be constantly on your lips" (ibid. 22:18)? When are the words of the Torah "pleasant"? "If you retain them inside you." And when will you retain them inside you? When they will be "constantly on your lips" [when you articulated them clearly]. R. Zeira said: This may be proved by the following verse, "A ready response is a joy to a man; and how good is a word rightly timed" (ibid. 15:23). When does a man have joy? When he has a ready response. An alternative interpretation is: When does man derive joy from a ready response? When his word is rightly timed, O, how good that is! R. Yitzchak said: You may derive it from this verse, "[The Torah] is something that is very close to you. It is in your mouth and in your heart, so that you can keep it" (Deuteronomy 30:14). When is the Torah very close to you? When it is in your mouth, [when you articulate it clearly], and in your heart with the intent to keep it.

Rava said: It may be derived from the following verse, "You have granted him his heart's desire, and You have not denied the utterance of his lips. Selah." (Psalms 21:3). When have You granted him his heart's desire? At the time when You have not denied the utterance of his lips, [because he expressed himself loudly and clearly]. Rava pointed out an inconsistency: It says, "You have granted him his *heart's* desire" [implying that he only has to think of his desire in his heart], and then it says, "You have not denied the utterance of his *lips*," [implying that it is necessary for him to verbally enunciate his desire]. [The Gemara reconciles the contradiction:] If he is deserving, "You have granted him his heart's desire," [even his unspoken wishes are answered]. But if he is not deserving then, "You have not denied the utterance of his lips," [only a request that is enunciated is answered].

It was taught in the yeshivah of R. Eliezer b. Yaakov: Wherever we find the expression of *netzach*, *selah*, or *va'ed* it means "eternity" or "forever." How can we prove that *netzach* means forever? For it says, "For I will not always contend, I will not be angry forever (*lanetzach*)" (Isaiah 57:16). How can we prove that *selah* means forever? For it says, "As we heard so we saw the city of God, Master of Legions, in the city of our God—may God establish it forever, *Selah*!" (Psalms 48:9). How do we prove that *va'ed* means forever? For it says, "God will reign forever and ever (*va'ed*)!" (Exodus 15:18).

HOW TO RETAIN
YOUR TORAH LEARNING

R. Elazar said: What is the meaning of, "[The Torah is like] a necklace around your throat" (Proverbs 1:9)? If a person adopts the characteristics of a necklace that is loose around the neck [meaning that he is congenial and easygoing], and sometimes is seen and sometimes is hidden [like the necklace that is covered by his beard and not seen most of the time, the Torah scholar does not go out often but stays indoors to concentrate on his studies (Rashi)], then he will retain his learning, but otherwise he will not.

R. Elazar also said: What is meant by the verse, "His cheeks are like beds of spices" (Song of Songs 5:13)? If a person allows himself to be treated like a garden bed on which everybody steps [he is extremely humble], and as spices whose fragrance is enjoyed by everyone [he teaches others], then he will retain his learning, but otherwise he will not.

R. Elazar also said: How do we interpret the passage, "They were stone tablets" (Exodus 31:18)? If a person makes his cheeks like stone that is not worn away [when people step on it; meaning, he tirelessly uses his facial muscles in teaching others], then his learning will be preserved, otherwise it will not.

R. Elazar also said: What is the message contained in the passage, "[The tablets were written with God's script] engraved on the tablets" (Exodus 32:16)? If the first Tablets had not been broken, the Torah would never have been forgotten by Israel. [Just as God's words were engraved on the tablets so the Torah would have been indelibly etched in our consciousness.]

R. Acha b. Yaakov said: [If the first tablets had not been broken] no nation would have had dominion over Israel, for it says, "Engraved (charut) on the tablets." Don't read charut (engraved) but cheirut (freedom); [because of the tablets Israel would have had everlasting freedom].

R. Matna expounded: What is the significance of the verse, "And from the wilderness [the Israelites went to] Mattanah" (Numbers 21:18)? If a person allows himself to be treated like a wilderness on which everybody steps, he will retain his learning; otherwise he will not.

Rava, the son of R. Yosef b. Chama, had an argument with R. Yosef. On the day before Yom Kippur, [Rava] thought: Let me go and appease him. So he went to R. Yosef, and he found his attendant mixing[12] a cup of wine for him. "Give it to me," Rava said, "and I will mix it for him." He gave it to Rava, who then mixed it. When R. Yosef [who was blind and could not see Rava] tasted it he said, "This blend tastes like that of Rava, the son of R. Yosef b. Chama," [who was an expert at mixing wine in the right proportion]. "I am right here," Rava said. "Do not sit down," R. Yosef replied, "until you explain to me the following verses. What is the meaning of the passage, "From the desert, [the Israelites went to] Mattanah, from Mattanah to Nachaliel, and from Nachaliel to Bamot. From Bamot [they went to] the Valley" (Numbers 21:18–20).

Replied Rava: This means that if a person allows himself to be treated like a desert on which everyone treads, the Torah will be given to him as a gift [mattanah]; and as soon as the Torah is given to him as a gift, he will be God's inheritance [nechalo E-l], as it says, "from Mattanah to Nachaliel." And as soon he is God's inheritance, he rises to heights of greatness [bamot means heights], for it says, "from Nachaliel to Bamot." But if he is arrogant, the Holy One, blessed be He, will humble him, for it says, "from Bamot to the Valley" [he will fall from the peak of greatness to lowly stature]. However, if he repents, the Holy One, blessed be He, will raise him, for it says, "Let every valley be lifted up" (Isaiah 40:4).

R. Huna said: What is the intent of the verse, "Your flock settled there; O God, in Your goodness You provide for the needy" (Psalms 68:11)? [The analogy is as follows:] If a person behaves like a beast that devours its prey immediately after killing it [similarly, if a student "devours" his rabbi's lecture and absorbs every word], or, as others say, if he behaves like a beast that eats his prey even when it is dirty [similarly, if a student learns Torah with total disregard of personal comfort], then he will retain his Torah learning; otherwise he will not. If he acts like this, the Holy One, blessed be He, Himself will prepare a banquet for him, for it says, "O God, in Your goodness You provide for the needy" (ibid.) [i.e., those who deserve it because of their devotion to Torah study].

R. Chiya b. Abba said in the name of R. Yochanan: What is meant by the verse, "He who tends a fig tree will enjoy its fruit" (Proverbs 27:18)? Why are the words of Torah compared to a fig tree? Just like a fig tree, (54b) whenever you want to pick figs you find them, [because its fruit ripens at different times], so it is with the Torah; every time you study it you find new insights.

R. Shmuel b. Nachmani expounded the verse, "A loving doe, a graceful mountain goat" (ibid. 5:19). He asked: Why is the Torah compared to a doe? It comes to tell you that just as a doe has a narrow womb and is loved by its mate at all times like the first time they were mating, so it is with the words of the Torah. They are loved by those who learn them at all times as much as the first time they were studied. Why [is the Torah compared to] a graceful mountain goat? Because the Torah confers grace on those that study it. "Let her breasts satisfy you at all times" (ibid.). Why are the the words of the Torah compared to a breast? Just like a breast, as often as the child sucks from it, it finds milk in it, so it is with the words of Torah. As often as you study them you find new insights in them. "Be infatuated with love of her [the Torah] always" (ibid.), like R. Elazar b. Pedat, for example. They said about R. Elazar b. Pedat that when he sat and studied Torah in the lower market of Tzippori (Sepphoris) he left his cloak in the upper market of town. [He was totally absorbed in his studies] R. Yitzchak b. Elazar said: One time a person came and wanted to take the cloak and found a poisonous snake in it. [God intervened and prevented the thief from stealing the cloak of the *tzaddik*.]

In the yeshivah of R. Anan it was taught: How do you interpret the verse, "You riders on white asses, you who sit on rich cloths, and you who walk by the way, declare it!" (Judges 5:10)? "You riders on white asses" refers to Torah scholars who wander from town to town and from province to province to study Torah and clarify its words, making them as lucid as noontime (white). "You who sit on rich cloths (*midin*)" refers to *halachic* authorities whose rulings (*din*) reflect the absolute truth. "You who walk" refers to the students of *Tanach*. "By the way" refers to the students of the Mishnah. "Declare it" refers to the students of the Talmud, whose entire conversation revolves around Torah.

R. Shizvi said in R. Elazar b. Azariah's name: How do you interpret the verse, "A negligent man never has game to roast" (Proverbs 12:27)? This means: A crooked hunter [a person who studies Torah but does not review what he has learned (Rashi)] will not live long. [*Lo yacharoch* (he will not roast) is seen as a contraction of *lo yichyeh* and *lo yaarich* (he will not live long).] R. Sheshet expounded [the verse in a positive vein to mean:] The clever hunter will singe [the wings of the birds he caught so that they will not fly away, analogous to the student who reviews the chapters he studied and thereby retains his learning]. When R. Dimi came [from Eretz Yisrael to Babylonia] he said: This is comparable to a hunter who hunts birds. If he breaks the wings of each bird as he catches it he will keep it, otherwise it will fly away. [Similarly, if a student goes over the chapters he studied, the Torah will remain fixed in his memory.]

Rava said in the name of R. Sechorah, who quoted R. Huna: What is the intent of the verse, "Wealth obtained by vain means will dwindle, but he who gathers by honest labor increases it" (Proverbs 13:11)? [Metaphorically this means:] If a person accumulates bundle after bundle of Torah, his learning dwindles; [meaning, if he studies a great deal at a time without reviewing the material, he will forget it]. But if he studies piecemeal and takes the time to go over the chapters then his knowledge will increase. Rava said: The Rabbis are aware of this [principle] but they disregard it. R. Nachman b. Yitzchak said: I followed this advice, and I remember all that I learned.

THE TRANSMISSION OF
THE ORAL TORAH

(54b) Our Rabbis taught: By what method did Moses teach the Oral Torah he had received from God? Moses learned it directly from the Almighty. Then Aaron entered [the tent], and Moses taught him the lesson [he had heard from God]. Aaron then withdrew and sat down on the left side of Moses. Thereupon Aaron's sons came in, and Moses taught them the lesson. The sons then withdrew; Elazar taking his seat on Moses' right and Itamar on Aaron's left. R. Yehudah said: Aaron was always on the right side of Moses. Then the [seventy] elders came in, and Moses taught them the same lesson. When the elders withdrew all the people entered, and Moses taught them the lesson. The result was that Aaron heard each lesson four times, his sons heard it three times, the elders twice, and all the people once. At this point Moses left, and Aaron taught [to all present] the lesson. Then Aaron went away, and his sons taught [to all present] the lesson. When his sons went away the elders taught [to all present] the lesson. As a result, everyone heard the lesson four times. Said R. Eliezer: From this we can learn that a teacher has a duty to teach his student the same lesson four times. It is logical that this is so: If Aaron who learned from Moses who had learned it from the Almighty [had to hear the lesson four times], surely an ordinary student who learns from an ordinary teacher [must be taught the lesson four times].

R. Akiva said: From where do we know that a person must repeat the same lesson to a student until he knows it? For it says, "And teach it to the Israelites" (Deuteronomy 31:19). And from where do we know that [not only do they have to know it, but that] it has to be completely clear to them? For it says, "Place it in their mouths" (ibid.) [so that they can repeat it smoothly]. And from where do we know that the teacher has to explain the reasons of the laws [and should not teach in an authoritarian way]? For it says, "These are the laws that you must place before them" (Exodus 21:1); [so that they can be easily understood, rather than teach by rote]. [The Gemara asks:] Why did not everyone come at the same time and learn [the Oral Torah] from Moses [four times]? [The Gemara answers:] In order to give honor to Aaron, his sons, and the elders. [Asks the Gemara:] If that is so, why not let Aaron come in and learn it from Moses [four times], then let Aaron's sons enter and learn it from Aaron [four times], then let the elders enter and learn it from Aaron's sons [four times], and let them in turn, teach the Oral Torah to all the people [four times]?

[Answers the Gemara:] Since Moses learned it from the Almighty, it is better for them to learn it from Moses himself. We learned above: R. Yehudah stated: Aaron was always on the right side of Moses. According to whose opinion is the following *Baraita*? If three people are going the same way, the teacher should walk in the middle, the greater scholar [of the other two] should walk on his right, and the lesser scholar should walk on his left? Can we assume that it represents the opinion of R. Yehudah and not that of the Rabbis [who hold that Aaron sat on the left of Moses]? [The Gemara answers:] We can even say that [the *Baraita*] agrees with the view of the Rabbis, [even the Rabbis agree that the right side is more esteemed, but the reason they said that Aaron sat on Moses' left was, since he had to sit on Moses' left when the two were alone, he was allowed to stay on the left] to save him the trouble of moving to the right of Moses.

THE DEDICATED
TEACHER'S REWARD

R. Pereida had a student whom he taught his lesson four hundred times before he grasped it. One day they needed Rabbi Pereida to attend to a matter involving a mitzvah. He taught the student [four hundred times] as usual, but this time the student did not master the lesson. "What is different today that you don't catch on?" asked R. Pereida. "From the moment they came and asked you to take care of the mitzvah matter my thoughts began to wander," the student replied, "for every moment I imagined: Now the Rabbi will get up; now the Rabbi will get up." "All right, pay attention, and I will teach it to you again," R. Pereida said; and so he taught him another four hundred times. A heavenly voice came forth asking him [R. Pereida], "Would you prefer to have four hundred years added to your life, or would you rather that you and your generation enter the World to Come?" Replied R. Pereida, "I prefer that I and my generation should merit to enter the World to Come." "Give him both," said the Holy One, blessed be He.

MNEMONIC SIGNS

R. Chisda said: The Torah can only be acquired if you use mnemonic signs [signs designed to help a person remember the *Halachot* and the names of the sages who taught them]. For it says, "Place [the Torah] in their mouth" (Deuteronomy 31:19). Don't read *simah* ("place it") but *simnah* ("signs"). R. Tachlifa from *Eretz Yisrael* heard this and told it to R. Abbahu who remarked: You derive [the need for signs] from that passage; but we elicit it from a different verse, "Erect markers (*tziyunim*)" (Jeremiah 31:21)—set up signs for the Torah [to help you remember it]. From where do you know that the word *tziyun* means a sign? Since it says, "Any one of them who sees a human being shall erect a marker (*tziyun*) beside it" (Ezekiel 39:15). R. Elazar said: It is derived from the following verse, "Say to Wisdom, 'You are my sister,' and call Understanding a kinswoman" (Proverbs 7:4)—devise signs to help you become thoroughly familiar with the Torah.

Rava interpreted this verse as follows: Set fixed times for Torah study [so that the students follow a set schedule, rather than study at random times (Rashi)]. (55a) This [the fact that you should make great efforts, such as devising mnemonic signs] is in keeping with the following statement of Avdimi b. Chama b. Dosa who said: What is meant by, "[The

Torah] is not in heaven, so that you should say, 'Who shall go up to heaven and bring it to us so that we can hear it and keep it?' It is not over the sea so that you should say, 'Who will cross the sea and get it for us?'"—"It is not in heaven," for if it were in heaven you would have to go up after it, and if it were "over the sea" you would have to go across the sea to get it.

Rava said: "[The Torah] is not in heaven," this means that the Torah cannot be found in a person whose haughtiness is as high as the heavens. "It is not over the sea," this means that the Torah cannot be found in a person whose smugness is as wide as the sea. R. Yochanan said: "It is not in heaven" means the Torah cannot be found among the arrogant; "It is not over the sea" means that it cannot be found among merchants and traders, [who are too busy pursuing their business to study the Torah].

(56a) Rav Yehudah said in Rav's name: In a town whose streets run uphill and downhill both men and beasts will die in the prime of their lives. [Exclaims the Gemara:] They will die? You surely don't mean that! Say instead: They will become old in the prime of their lives [because of the exertion]. R. Huna the son of R. Yehoshua said: The hills between Bei Biri and Bei Neresh made me old.

WAS RAVINA INSOLENT?

(63a) Ravina once was sitting in the presence of R. Ashi when he saw a person tying his donkey to a palm tree on *Shabbat*. [It is forbidden on *Shabbat* to make use of something that grows.] Ravina called out to him to stop, but he paid no attention to him. Ravina then declared: Let this man be placed under a ban. Ravina now asked R. Ashi: Does an act such as mine [placing this person under a ban] in your presence look like an impudence? [Ravina was a student of R. Ashi.] R. Ashi replied: [No, you did the right thing, for it says,] "There is no wisdom, no prudence, no counsel against God" (Proverbs 21:30), wherever the name of God is being profaned no respect needs to be shown to a Rabbi. [Even one's Rabbi's presence is immaterial when God's name is being desecrated. Therefore Ravina was permitted to place that person in a ban.]

HE RENDERED A DECISION
IN HIS RABBI'S PRESENCE

Rava said: A student is forbidden [to render a halachic decision] in the presence of his Rabbi, and if he does he is liable to the death penalty [at the hands of Heaven]; in his Rabbi's absence a student is still forbidden [to give a halachic decision], but if he does he is not liable to the death penalty. [Asks the Gemara:] Is it so that in his Rabbi's absence he is not liable to the death penalty? Haven't we learned in a *Baraita*: R. Eliezer said: The sons of Aaron [Nadav and Avihu] only died[13] because they ruled on a halachic matter in the presence of Moses their Rabbi. What was it that they decided on their own? They expounded the verse, "Aaron's sons shall place fire on the altar" (Leviticus 1:7). They reasoned: Although fire came down from heaven,[14] it is a mitzvah to bring an ordinary fire; [and without consulting Moses they put a fire on the altar, and for this they died]. [The *Baraita* continues:]

R. Eliezer had a disciple who once rendered a halachic decision in his presence. Said R. Eliezer to his wife Ima Shalom, "I wonder whether this student will live through the year," and the student, in fact, did not live through the year. "Are you a prophet [that you knew that he was going to die]?" she asked him. "I am neither a prophet nor the son of a prophet," he replied, "but I have this tradition: Whoever renders a halachic decision in the presence of his Rabbi is liable to the death penalty at the hands of Heaven," [and that is what this student was guilty of]. Now, regarding this incident Rabbah b. Bar Chana said in R. Yochanan's name that the name of this disciple was Yehudah ben Gurya, and that he was three *parsa'ot* [a *parsahs* equals 2.7 miles; three *parsa'ot* are 8.1 miles] away from R. Eliezer. [Thus he was not in the presence of R. Eliezer, and still he incurred the death penalty, which contradicts Rava's statement at the beginning of this discussion.]

[The Gemara reconciles the contradiction:] The disciple was, in fact, in R. Eliezer's presence when he gave the ruling, [and the distance of three *parsa'ot* refers to the disciple's place of residence]. [Asks the Gemara:] But R. Yochanan said that he was three *parsa'ot* away from R. Eliezer? [And if the student did not give his ruling at a distance of three *parsa'ot*, why mention it?] [The Gemara counters:] And according to you, [that R. Yochanan is telling us that he was three *parsa'ot* away, and that the ruling took place in R. Eliezer's absence], why did R. Yochanan find it necessary to mention this disciple's name and that of his father? [Answers the Gemara:] The reason that [all these details were given] is so that you should not say that the whole story was just a parable. [But Yehudah ben Gurya was in fact a real disciple who lived three *parsa'ot* away from R. Eliezer and who gave a halachic ruling in his Rabbi's presence. For this he incurred the Heavenly death penalty, and he did not live through the year. Thus Rava's statement is upheld.]

R. Chiya b. Abba said in R. Yochanan's name: Whoever gives a halachic decision in the presence of his Rabbi deserves to be bitten by a snake, for it says, "Then Elihu son of Berachel the Buzite said in reply, 'I am younger . . . therefore I tremble (*zachalti*), and I am afraid to speak" (Job 32:6) [i.e., he is afraid to speak before his elders]. And elsewhere it says, "With venomous creatures (*zochalei*) that crawl in the dust" (Deuteronomy 32:24) [meaning snakes]. Ze'iri said in R. Chanina's name: He is called a sinner, as it says, "I have stored Your word in my heart [meaning, although I know the *halachah* in my heart, I will not give a rul-

ing in my Rabbi's presence], so that I would not sin against You" (Psalms 119:11). R. Hamenuna pointed out a contradiction: It says: "I have stored Your word in my heart" (ibid.) [meaning, I refrained from rendering decisions], and it also says, "I proclaimed righteousness [meaning, I taught the Torah] to the multitudes" (Psalms 40:10) [in other words, I decided *halachah* for everyone]. [The Gemara answers:] This is really no contradiction: The first verse relates to the time when Ira Haya'iri [David's Rabbi[15]] was still alive, whereas the second verse relates to the time when Ira Haya'iri was no longer alive.

R. Abba b. Zavda said: Whoever gives all his priestly gifts to only one *kohen* brings famine into the world. For it says, "Ira Haya'iri was a priest to David" (2 Samuel 20:26). Was he a *kohen* only to David and not to everyone else? [How can you say that? If he is a *kohen*, he officiates for everyone!] What it means is that David sent all his priestly gifts to him, [and to no other priest]. And the next verse says, "There was a famine during the reign of David" (ibid. 21:1), [proof of R. Abba b. Zavda's statement].

R. Elazar said: [Whoever gives a halachic decision in the presence of his Rabbi] is demoted from his high station. For it says, "Elazar the priest said to the soldiers returning from the campaign . . . This is the rule that God commanded Moses" (Numbers 31:21). [Elazar instead of Moses announced this *halachah*, which dealt with the purification of vessels.] Although he told the people: The commandment was given to my father's brother [i.e., Moses], and not to me [thus he duly gave credit to Moses], nonetheless, he was still punished. For it says, "And he [Joshua] shall stand before Elazar the priest" (Numbers 27:21) [meaning, Joshua will direct his questions to Elazar and seek answers through the *Urim Vetummim*], and yet we do not find that Joshua ever had to seek Elazar's advice. [This honor was taken away from Elazar because his declaration was akin to giving a ruling in the presence of his Rabbi.]

JOSHUA'S SHORTCOMING

R. Levi said: Whoever answers a word [of *halachah*] in the presence of his Rabbi will die childless. For it says, [Eldad and Medad were speaking prophecy in the camp, whereupon] "Joshua son of Nun, Moses' young attendant, spoke up. 'My lord Moses,' he said. 'Destroy them!'" (Numbers 11:28) [Joshua, in effect, told Moses what to do.] (63b) And elsewhere is says, "Nun his son, Joshua his son" (1 Chronicles 7:27). [The genealogy ends here, because Joshua had no children.] This interpretation disagrees with R. Abba b. Papa, for R. Abba b. Papa said: Joshua was punished [to die childless] because he prevented the Jewish people from having marital relations for one night. For it says, "Once, when Joshua was near Jericho [laying siege to that city], he looked up and saw a man [an angel] standing before him, drawn sword in hand" (Joshua 5:13), and in the next verse it says, "[The angel] replied, 'No, I am captain of God's hosts. Now I have come!'" (ibid. 14). The angel told Joshua: Last night you failed to bring the continual evening sacrifice,[16] and now you are causing the people to neglect the study of the Torah. [Since you do not wage war at night you should have brought the evening sacrifice, and you should have allowed the men to study Torah instead of continuing the siege through the night.]

[Joshua asked the angel:] Because of which failing did you come, [for the failure to bring the sacrifice or for our failing to study the Torah]? Replied the angel: Now I have come, [I came for the present shortcoming, for your failure to study the Torah]. Immediately after that [when they advanced on the city of Ai], it says, "Joshua spent that night in the valley" (ibid. 8:13), which R. Yochanan explains to mean that he entered into the depths of *halachah*. [He learned his lesson from the angel, and at the next occasion, after a day of battle at Ai, he and the people studied Torah during the night.] Now we have a tradition that as long as the Holy Ark and the *Shechinah* are not in their proper place [in the Tabernacle, which was the case during the siege of Jericho, when the Ark was with them[17]], the people are forbidden to have marital relations. [And that night in Jericho, when they were laying siege to the city they failed to return the Ark to the Tabernacle in Gilgal, and therefore were prevented from having marital relations (Rashi).]

R. Shmuel b. Inia said in the name of Rav: Studying the Torah is more important than offering the daily continual sacrifices, since [the angel] said to Joshua: Now I have come, [the main reason for his coming was their failure to learn Torah, and not the failure to bring the sacrifice].

WHEN IS A PERSON CONSIDERED DRUNK?

(64a) Rav Yehudah said in the name of Shmuel: A person who drank a *revi'it* [4.42 fluid ounces] of wine is not allowed to give a halachic decision. R. Nachman said: This teaching is not a very fine one, because I myself, unless I drink a *revi'it* of wine my mind is not clear. Said Rava to R. Nachman: Why do you express yourself like this [finding fault with a halachic ruling on the basis of personal experience]? Did not R. Acha b. Chanina say: What is the meaning of the verse, "He who keeps company with harlots (*zonot*) will lose his wealth" (Proverbs 29:3)? [Which is expounded:] Anyone who says: This teaching is a fine one (*zo na'ah*) [*zonot* sounds like *zo na'ah*] or: That teaching is not a fine one, loses the wealth of Torah he has accumulated; [he will forget it]. Replied R. Nachman: All right, I take it back.

Rabbah b. R. Huna said: A person who has drunk a *revi'it* of wine [and is slightly intoxicated] is not allowed to pray, but if he does, his prayer is considered a proper one [and he does not have to repeat it]. If he is really drunk he is not allowed to pray, and if he does, his prayer is an abomination, [and when he is sober he has to repeat the prayer (*Tosafot*)]. [The Gemara asks:] When is a person considered slightly intoxicated and when is he drunk? [The Gemara answers:] The following incident will enlighten us: When R. Abba b. Shumani and R. Menashya b. Yirmiah of Difti were saying goodbye to each other at the bridge of the River Yufti they said: Let each of us say some halachic thought that the other has never heard before, for Mari the son of R. Huna has said: When saying goodbye to a friend, your parting words should be a point of *halachah*, because he will remember you by it.

One of them began: When is a person considered slightly intoxicated and when is he considered drunk? He is considered slightly intoxicated if he is capable of speaking before a king [he is able to speak coherently to a person he is in awe of]. He is considered drunk if he is unable to speak before a king [and would get confused. And if a person reaches the stage that he cannot speak clearly to the King of Kings his prayer is an abomination]. The other then began: [The property that was left by a convert who died without leaving any heirs is considered *hefker*, ownerless property]. What should a person who took possession of the property that was left by a convert do to retain that property? [It is legally his, but what should he do to ward off an *ayin hara*, the sinister influence of the evil eye?] He should use some of the money to buy a Torah scroll, [and in the merit of the mitzvah the rest of the money will be preserved].

R. Sheshet said: Even (64b) a husband [should do a mitzvah] with part of the property he inherited from his wife, [so that he will be successful with it]. Rava said: Even a person who earned a large profit in business should do a mitzvah with part of his profit. R. Papa said: Even someone who has found something should do the same thing. [All of these cases represent windfall money. Therefore there is the danger that he might lose it unless he does a mitzvah with part of it.] R. Nachman b. Yitzchak said: [He does not necessarily have to buy a *sefer Torah* with it]. Even if he uses some of the money to have a pair of *tefillin* written [this will insure that the windfall money remains in his possession]. R. Chanin, and some say it was R. Chanina, said: What verse supports this [that doing a mitzvah results in good fortune]? For it says, [Before going into battle against the Canaanites] "the Israelites made a vow to God" (Numbers 21:2), [if victorious they would consecrate all the spoils of war. Therefore they were successful in routing the enemy (Rashi)].

HALACHOT WE LEARNED FROM R. GAMLIEL

It once happened that R. Gamliel was riding on a donkey when traveling from Acco to Cheziv while R.

Ila'i was following behind him. R. Gamliel found a loaf of bread on the road and said, "Ila'i, please pick up the loaf from the road." Later he came across a non-Jew and said to him, "Mavaga'i, [his first name], please take this loaf from Ila'i. [You can keep it as a present.]" R. Ila'i then approached the non-Jew and asked him, "Where are you from?" "I come from the cities of Burgenin." "And what is your name?" "My name is Mavaga'i." "Did R. Gamliel ever meet you before [that he knew your name]?" "No," the non-Jew replied. At that time we learned that R. Gamliel could figure out [his first name] by the holy spirit.

And we learned from this incident three things: We learned that we are not allowed to pass by food [lying on the ground, but it must be picked up], and we learned [from the fact that the loaf was given to the non-Jew] that we follow the majority of the people that travel. [Since the majority of travelers were non-Jews we must assume that the loaf was dropped by one of them, and therefore it was forbidden to a Jew.] And we learned [from the fact that this incident happened after Pesach, and the loaf was given to a non-Jew] that it is permitted to derive benefit from a non-Jew's *chametz* after Pesach [by giving it to a non-Jew, because the non-Jew will show his gratitude. However, deriving benefit after Pesach from a Jew's *chametz* that was baked before or on Pesach is forbidden].

When R. Gamliel arrived in Cheziv someone approached him and asked him to annul his vow. R. Gamliel said to R. Ila'i, "Have we by any chance drunk a *revi'it* of Italian wine?" "Yes, we did," he replied. "In that case," said R. Gamliel, "let the man walk behind us until the effect of the wine wears off. [Then we will be able to annul his vow.]" The man walked behind them for three *mils* [three times 2,000 cubits] until R. Gamliel reached the Ladder of Tzur (Tyre) [a steep mountain]. When he reached the Ladder of Tzur, R. Gamliel got off the donkey, wrapped himself in his *tallit*, sat down, and annulled the vow. We learned many *Halachot* from this episode: We learned that a *revi'it* of Italian wine causes a person to get drunk; that a drunken person may not rule on halachic questions; that a journey causes the effects of wine to wear off, and that a person may not annul a vow while riding, walking, or standing, but only while sitting.

PRAY WHEN YOUR MIND IS AT EASE

R. Sheshet said in the name of R. Elazar b. Azariah: (65a) I could free the entire Jewish people from Divine judgment, since the day of the destruction of the *Bet Hamikdash* until the present time. [I would argue] that it says, "Therefore, listen to this, unhappy one, [Israel], who are drunk, but not with wine!" (Isaiah 51:21). [Since Israel is characterized as being drunk they are not responsible for their actions and cannot be judged.] An objection was raised from the follow-

ing *Baraita*: If a drunken person bought or sold something the deal is valid. If he committed a transgression that is punishable by death he should be executed; if his transgression is punishable by flogging he should receive lashes. The general rule is that a drunken person is regarded as sober in all respects except that he is exempt from prayer. So how could R. Sheshet say that he could free the Jewish people from judgment? [The Gemara answers:] He meant that he could free them from judgment if they are accused of praying [without concentration. He would then claim that a drunken person is exempt from prayer (Rashi)].

R. Chanina said: [The rule that a drunken person is regarded as sober, except that he is exempt from prayer] applies only to a person who did not reach the stage of Lot's drunkenness [total obliviousness[18]], but if he reached Lot's level of drunkenness he is exempt from everything.

R. Chiya b. Ashi said in the name of Rav: A person whose mind is not at ease should not pray, for it says, "He who is in distress shall not render judgment."[19] R. Chanina did not pray on a day when he was angry. He said: It is written, "He who is in distress shall not render judgment."

Mar Ukva did not appear in court on a day when a hot southerly wind was blowing. R. Nachman b. Yitzchak said: To study *halachah* your mind has to be as clear as a day on which a northerly wind is blowing. Abbaye said: If my [foster] mother had told me, "Hand me the *kutcha*" [a dish consisting of sour milk, bread crusts, and salt[20]], I would not have been able to study; [even a small request was enough to distract me]. Rava said: If a louse bit me I could not study. [To prevent this] the mother of Mar Brei d'Ravina prepared for him seven [clean] garments for the seven days of the week [so that he could study in comfort].

THE NIGHT IS FOR SLEEPING

Rav Yehudah said: The night was only created for sleep. Resh Lakish said: Moonlight was only created to study the Torah. When people told R. Zeira that his discourses were brilliant he replied: This came about because I studied during the day.

The daughters of R. Chisda once asked their father, "Wouldn't you like to sleep a little?" He replied, "Soon there will come days that are long and short [the days in the grave will be long for resting but short for Torah study and *mitzvot*], and we will have plenty of time to sleep." R. Nachman b. Yitzchak said: We are all day workers. R. Acha b. Yaakov borrowed [from the daytime] and paid back [at night]. [He resolved to study a number of pages each day, and if his work prevented him from studying in the daytime he made up for it at night (Rashi).]

R. Eliezer said: If someone comes home from a [dangerous] trip he should not pray for three days, [because he will be tense and on edge on account of the hardship of the trip (Rashi)]. For it says, "These I assembled by the river that enters Achava, and we encamped there for three days. I reviewed[21] the people . . ." (Ezra 8:15). [Before three days he was unable to review the people because of the hardship of the journey (Rashi).]

When Shmuel's father came back from a trip he did not pray for three days. Shmuel did not drink in a house where there was strong drink; [its odor would go to his head]. R. Papa did not pray in a house where there was fish stew; [he so disliked its pungent smell that he could not concentrate].

SAYINGS ABOUT WINE

R. Chanina said: A person who can be mollified when he is drinking wine has one of the qualities of his Creator, for it says, [When Noah came out of the ark after the Flood he offered sacrifices.] "God smelled the pleasing odor, [smell and taste being closely related], and . . . He said . . . 'Never again will I doom the earth because of man'" (Genesis 8:21), [which proves that God was appeased when He smelled the pleasing odor].

R. Chiya said: A person who keeps a cool head while drinking wine has the characteristics of the seventy elders,[22] because the numeric value of *yayin* (wine) is seventy [*yud* = 10; *yud* = 10; *nun* = 50]. The word *sod* (counsel) also has the numeric value of *yayin* (wine, 70), [*samach* = 60; *vav* = 6; *dalet* = 4]. Which tells you that as soon as wine goes in, counsel and discernment vanish. [But the person who keeps a cool head while drinking does not lose his discernment and has the charasteristics of the seventy elders (Rashi).]

R. Chanin said: The only reason why wine was created is to comfort mourners and to pay a reward to the wicked [in this world for the few good deeds they performed, so that they will perish in the World to Come], as it says, "Give strong drink to him that is going to perish [the wicked], and wine to the embittered [the mourner]" (Proverbs 31:6). R. Chanan b. Papa said: A person in whose house wine does not flow as freely as water has not reached the ultimate stage of blessedness, for it says, "And He will bless your bread and your water" (Exodus 23:25). Just as the "bread" mentioned in this verse may be bought with the money of the Second Tithe[23], so does the "water" in this passage represent a beverage that may be bought with the Second Tithe money. Thus "water" must refer to wine [since water may not be bought with Second Tithe money]. Yet the verse calls the wine "water," (65b) to suggest that if wine flows as freely as water in a person's house, his house has reached the ultimate stage of blessedness; otherwise it has not.

R. Ila'i said: There are three things by which you can tell whether a person has a decent character: by his cup [if his mind is at ease after he drank wine], by his purse [by the way he deals in money matters], and by his anger [if he controls his temper].[24] Some say: by his laughter too.

THEY RESPECTED THE RICH

(85b) Bonyis ben Bonyis once called on Rebbi. "Make way for the man worth one hundred *maneh*! [Assign him a good seat!]"[25] , Rebbi exclaimed. When another person entered he called out, (86a) "Make way for the man worth two hundred *maneh*!" [Offer him a better seat, among more distinguished people, for he is wealthier.] Thereupon Rabbi Yishmael b. R. Yose remarked, "Rebbi, the father of this man [Bonyis] owns one thousand ships sailing the seas and a corresponding number of towns on land." Replied Rebbi, "The next time you see his father tell him not to send his son to me in such shabby clothes; [his clothes fooled me]." Rebbi greatly respected wealthy people; R. Akiva also greatly respected wealthy people. Their attitude was in line with Rabba b. Mari's exposition of the verse, "May he sit forever before God; appoint kindness and truth that they may preserve him" (Psalms 61:8). He expounded: When may a person sit before God forever [and when does he deserve to be respected]? When he appoints kindness and truth that they may preserve him. [A rich man has the means to dispense kindness and food to the needy. His generosity will preserve and protect him. Based on this verse, Rebbi and Rabbi Akiva respected the wealthy because they have the resources to support many people].

WHAT CAN WE LEARN
FROM ANIMALS?

(100b) R. Yochanan said: If the Torah had not been given we could have learned modesty from the cat [which covers its excrement], not to rob from the ant [an ant does not take another ant's food], not to engage in adultery from the dove [which is faithful to its mate], and good manners from the rooster, who first courts and then mates. And how does the rooster court his mate? Rav Yehudah said in Rav's name: He tells her this: "I will buy you a coat that reaches down to your feet;" [when courting, a rooster spreads his wings and bends his hips toward the ground]. After mating [when he shakes his head downward (Rashi)], he is telling her, "May my comb drop off if I have any money and do not buy you one."

THE FOOLISH HERETIC

(101a) A certain heretic said to R. Yehoshua b. Chanania: You are a prickly shrub, since it says about you, "The best of them is like a prickly shrub" (Micah 7:4). Replied R. Yehoshua: Fool that you are! Look at what it says at the end of the passage, "The upright man is better than a protective sukkah (shelter)." [Asks the Gemara:] So what is meant by "The best of them is like a prickly shrub"? [Answers the Gemara:] Just as a prickly shrub protects a breach [in a wall] so do the best men among us protect us. Another explanation: "The best of them is like a prickly shrub (*chedek*)" because they crush (*mechaddekin*) the evildoers in Gehinnom. For it says, "Up and thresh, fair Zion! For I will give you horns of iron and provide you with hoofs of bronze, and you will crush (*vahadikot*) many peoples" (Micah 4:17).

NOTES

1. Numbers 4:4–16.

2. Sulphuric acid. Blue vitriol is copper sulfate and is used as an additive in the manufacture of ink.

3. A town in a fertile Jordan Valley, south of Teveriah (Tiberias).

4. Literally: mandrakes.

5. Things you must do.

6. Things you are forbidden to do.

7. *Eruv*, plural *eruvin*, literally "mixture." Solomon instituted the law of *Eruv chatzeirot* whereby a quantity of food enough for two meals is placed in a house in a courtyard to enable all the residents to carry from their houses into the courtyard and vice versa.

8. *Ketubot* 49b.

9. The *ketubah* is the halachically required marriage contract, which is read at the wedding ceremony. It spells out the obligations of a man to his wife and provides for the wife's support if the marriage comes to an end.

10. The High Priest wore the *Urim Vetummim* in the breastplate on which twelve brilliant stones were set. In times of doubt and national crisis the *Urim Vetummim* were consulted for information and guidance (Exodus 28:30, Numbers 27:21, 1 Samuel 28:6). Some of the letters that were engraved on the stones would light up, and by combining the letters into words the answer was elicited.

11. Literally: She kicked him.

12. Their wine was too strong to be served straight, but had to be diluted with water, one-third wine with two-thirds water (*Bamidbar Rabbah* 1).

13. Leviticus 10:1–3.

14. Ibid. 9:24.

15. 2 Samuel 20:26.

16. Numbers 28:1–8.

17. Joshua 6:9.

18. Genesis 19:30–38.

19. This passage does not appear in *Tanach*. It may be a quote from the Book of Ben Sira (Rashi).

20. *Pesachim* 42a.

21. Literally: I understood.

22. Numbers 11:16,17.

23. In the first, second, fourth, and fifth year of the seven-year *Shemittah* cycle, a Second Tithe is taken. This tithe must be eaten in Jerusalem. People that live too far from Jerusalem can turn their tithe into money, which must be spent on food that must be consumed in Jerusalem. Any food except salt and water may be bought with Second Tithe money. See Deuteronomy 14:22–26 and *Eruvin* 26b.

24. In the Hebrew the adage is more poignant: *bekoso, bekiso, beka'aso*.

25. A *maneh* was a weight in gold equal to one hundred *shekels*.

❧ PESACHIM ❧

WHAT IS THE MEANING
OF "OR"?

(2a) [The Mishnah begins:] On the evening [or] of the fourteenth of Nisan [which is erev Pesach], we must search [our homes] for chametz (leaven) by candlelight. [The Gemara asks:] What does the Mishnah mean when it says or [of the fourteenth of Nisan? [Since the word or translates as "light," does it mean the evening or the morning of erev Pesach?] R. Huna said: [Or means] light [i.e., the morning]. R. Yehudah said: Or refers to the night.

The Gemara raises a question: It says, [after Joseph's brothers bought grain in Egypt,] "With the first morning light [haboker or], the men were sent away" (Genesis 44:3). [The fact that or is synonymous with morning] proves that or means daytime. [The Gemara answers:] Does it say, "The or was morning"? No, rather it says, "The morning was or," which is like saying, "The morning began to shine." [Here or is used as the verb "to shine," but if or is used as a noun it could mean "night."] And this verse [about the brothers leaving in the morning] is consistent with what Rav Yehudah said in Rav's name: A person should always enter a town while it is light and leave when it is light, [to avoid the dangers of the night. That is why the brothers waited until morning].

DO NOT USE
COARSE LANGUAGE

(3a) R. Yehoshua b. Levi said: A person should not utter coarse language, for the Torah uses eight letters more than necessary in an effort to avoid using an uncouth term. For it says, "[God said to Noah:] 'Take seven pairs of every clean animal . . . and of every animal that is not clean'" (Genesis 7:2). [By using the phrase "that is not clean" instead of the single word temei'ah, "unclean,"[1] the Torah added eight Hebrew letters.] R. Papa says: Nine [extra letters were used], for it says, "If a man is not clean because of a nocturnal emission" (Deuteronomy 23:11). [Here the use of tamei, "unclean," would save nine letters.] Ravina said: Ten [extra letters were used], because tahor, "clean,"

is written with a vav. R. Acha b. Yaakov said: Sixteen [letters could have been saved by using the word tamei], for it says, "'It's accidental,' [Saul] thought. 'He is not clean, surely he is not clean'" (1 Samuel 20:26).

In the yeshivah of R. Yishmael it was taught: A person should always express himself in refined language. For regarding a zav [a man who has a discharge from his organ], the Torah speaks in terms of merkav, "riding," while concerning a woman [who has the same condition] the term moshav, "sitting" is used (Leviticus 15:9,20), [although the same law applies to both men and women; but it is not refined to use for women the term merkav, 'riding,' which suggests spreading the legs apart (Rashi)]. Furthermore it says, "You should choose discreet language" (Job 15:5), and it also says, "My lips utter insight in purity" (ibid. 33:3). [The Gemara asks:] Why do you cite a second verse? [What novel thought does it contribute?] [The Gemara replies:] In case you will say that [you must use refined language] only when discussing Torah law [because it is the word of God], but not when it comes to Rabbinical law, then come and listen to the following proof: For it also says, "You should choose discreet language." Now in case you still object and say that this applies only when discussing Rabbinical law, but when it comes to secular matters you do not need to use refined language, then come and listen to the following proof: For it also says, "My lips utter insight in purity."

[We learned above that the term "riding" is not used in connection with women because it has an immodest connotation.] [The Gemara asks:] Is riding not used in connection with women? But what about, "Rebecca set off with her girls, and they rode on the camels" (Genesis 24:61)? [The Gemara answers:] There it was normal for her to straddle the camel because she was afraid to fall off its high back. But what about, "Moses took his wife and sons and made them ride on a donkey [which does not have a high back]" (Exodus 4:20)?— There the term riding is used (3b) because it was normal for his sons to ride. But what about, "[Abigail] was riding on the donkey" (1 Samuel 25:20).—There it was normal for her to ride a donkey because she was afraid of the night. Or, if you prefer, say that she was not afraid of the night, but she was afraid of David [that he would kill the entire household of her husband Nabal]. Or, if you prefer, say, she was not afraid of David, but she was afraid of the mountain [as it says, "she came down a trail on the mountain" (ibid.)].

YOUR VOCABULARY SAYS
WHO YOU ARE

There were two disciples who were sitting before Hillel, one of whom was R. Yochanan b. Zakkai, (according to others they were sitting before Rebbi, and one of them was R. Yochanan). One asked: Why must we gather grapes in [ritually] clean baskets, and why don't we have to gather olives in [ritually] clean baskets?[2] [The disciple avoided using the word *tumah*, uncleanness.] The other asked: Why must we gather grapes in [ritually] clean vessels, and why may we gather olives in *tumah*, "in [ritual] uncleanness?" [This disciple did not hesitate to use the word *tumah*, uncleanness.] "I am certain," said Hillel, "that the one [who avoided saying *tumah*] will become a *halachic* authority in Israel." It did not take long before he was a *halachic* authority in Israel.

[The Gemara now cites an example of a person who used vulgar language with regard to the showbread. In Leviticus 24:5–9 we are told that every Shabbat twelve loaves of *lechem hapanim*, "showbread," were placed on the Table in the Sanctuary. The old loaves were removed and divided among the *kohanim* (priests) who were blessed with bounty when they ate it. The Gemara relates:] There were three *kohanim*: one said, "My share of the showbread was the size of a bean." The second said, "My share of the showbread was the size of an olive." The third one said, "My share was the size of the tail of a small lizard" [a disparaging way of speaking]. They investigated his ancestry and found that his genealogy was tainted, and that he was unfit to serve as a *kohen*. [The Gemara asks:] But we learned: If a *kohen* who has served at the altar wants to get married we do not have to investigate his family tree [for we may assume that his lineage was researched before and it was found to be pure. This being so, how could they now have found his lineage to be tainted]? [The Gemara answers:] Do not say that he was found to be unfit to serve as a *kohen* because of his lineage, but because of his disdainful attitude. Or, if you prefer, say, that this case was different because he harmed himself [through his improper language, and a new investigation brought to light the blemish that had been overlooked previously (Rashi)].

HE TRAPPED
THE TREACHEROUS HEATHEN

A certain heathen used to pretend to be a Jew and would go to Jerusalem to eat of the paschal lamb. He once boasted to R. Yehudah b. Beteira: "It says, 'No outsider may eat it . . . no uncircumcised man may eat [the Passover sacrifice]' (Exodus 12:43,48), and I eat from its very best parts." Said R. Yehudah b. Beteira, "Do they give you from the fat broad tail?" "No," replied the heathen. R. Yehudah b. Beteira then advised him, "When you go there next time, tell them to give you to eat from the fat broad tail." When the heathen went up [to Jerusalem] again he said to them, "Give me of the fat broad tail." He was told that the fat broad tail is sacrificed on the altar.[3] When he insisted that R. Yehudah had told him to request that portion, they investigated him and discovered that he was a heathen. Thereupon they killed him. They sent a message to R. Yehudah, "Peace unto you, R. Yehudah b. Beteira, for although you are in Netzivim your net is cast in Jerusalem."

DON'T BE A BEARER
OF BAD TIDINGS

R. Kahana was sick. So the Rabbis sent R. Yehoshua, the son of R. Idi, to find out how he was feeling. When he got there he found that R. Kahana had died. He then made a tear in his garment [as a sign of mourning] and turned the tear to his backside [so that it should not be too obvious, and to soften the shock to his colleagues], and he went along crying. "Did he pass away?" they asked him. "I did not say it," he replied, "'for he that reports bad tidings is a fool'" (Proverbs 10:18).

Yochanan Chakuka'ah went out to some villages [to check the crops]. When he came back people asked him, "Is the wheat growing well?" He replied, "The barley is growing nicely," [implying that the wheat crop had failed, but he did not give them a straight answer because he did not want to be a bearer of bad tidings]. "Go tell that to the horses and the donkeys," the people retorted derisively, for it says, 'They would also deliver barley and straw for the horses and the swift steeds'" (1 Kings 5:8). [The Gemara asks:] What then should he have said? [The Gemara answers: He should have said:] "Last year's wheat crop was plentiful," or, "The lentil crop is abundant."

(4a) [The Gemara relates how Rav avoided reporting the death of his parents.] Rav was the son of R. Chiya's brother and the son of [R. Chiya's] sister. [Aivu, Rav's father and R. Chiya were born of the same father, and Rav's mother and R. Chiya were born of the same mother.] When Rav went [from Babylonia] to Eretz Yisrael, R. Chiya asked him, "Is your father alive?" He replied, "[Ask me instead whether] my mother is alive." "Is your mother alive?" he asked. "Are you then sure that my father is alive?" he replied. [R. Chiya gathered that both had died.] Thereupon R. Chiya said to his servant, "Take off my shoes [in mourning for my brother and my sister], and carry my bathing clothes after me to the baths." From this three laws can be derived: (1) A mourner is forbidden to wear shoes; (2) when the report of a death is received after thirty days, mourning is observed for one day only [instead of seven]; and (3) a part of the day counts as a full day, [for he planned to go to the baths after an hour, without waiting a full day].

PEOPLE ON A MITZVAH MISSION ARE SAFE FROM HARM

(8b) R. Elazar said: People who are sent to perform a mitzvah will not suffer any harm, neither en route to their destination nor on their return trip. R. Elazar's statement is consistent with the teaching of Issi b. Yehudah who said: Since the Torah says, "No one will be envious of your land when you go to be seen in God's presence three times each year [in the Bet Hamikdash on the three Pilgrimage Festivals]" (Exodus 34:24).[4] This teaches that your cow will graze in the meadow, and no wild beast will hurt it; your chicken will scratch around in the dungheap and no weasel will hurt it. Now we can draw a logical conclusion from this. If [animals], that are commonly subject to harm, will not be hurt, then people, who ordinarily are not exposed to harm surely will not be hurt [when they are on a mission to perform a mitzvah]. [The Gemara inquires:] This rationale applies with respect to going to do a mitzvah, but how do I know that on his return trip no harm will befall him?

[The Gemara answers:] For it says, "You may turn around in the morning and return to your tents" (Deuteronomy 16:7). This teaches that you will go and find your tent in peace [on your return]. [The Gemara asks:] But since he is safe even on his return trip, why mention it at all with regard to going [to do a mitzvah]? [The Gemara answers: It is necessary,] for the verse, ["No one will be envious of your land when you go . . ."] forms the basis of R. Ammi's teaching. For R. Ammi taught: Whoever owns land must must visit Jerusalem on the three Pilgrimage Festivals, but anyone that does not own land need not make the Festival pilgrimage. [He derives it from the fact that God assures the pilgrims that no one will seize their land while they are in Jerusalem; thus only those who own land must make the pilgrimage.]

[The Gemara digresses on the subject of the pilgrimages to Jerusalem:] R. Avin b. Adda said in the name of R. Yitzchak: Why are there no fruits of Ginnosar [an area along the Yam Kinneret (Sea of Galilee), known for its luscious fruit] in Jerusalem? In order that the people coming on pilgrimage to Jerusalem on the Festivals should not say: It would have been worthwhile if we had come to Jerusalem only to taste its Ginnosar fruit, and that would have meant that the pilgrimage would not be for its own sake.

In the same vein, R. Dostai b. R. Yannai said: Why are there no hot springs [like those] of T'veriah (Tiberias) found in Jerusalem? In order that the people coming on pilgrimage to Jerusalem on the Festivals should not say: It would have been worthwhile for us to come to Jerusalem just to bathe in the hot springs of T'veriah, and that would have meant that the pilgrimage would not be for its own sake.

(22b) We learned in a Baraita: Shimon Ha'imsani (others say, Nechemiah Ha'imsani), expounded on every "et" (the mark of the accusative) in the Torah [to include something else], but when he came to the verse, "You should fear [et] the Lord, your God" (Deuteronomy 6:13), he stopped expounding [since he found it impossible to include someone else to be feared like God]. His students asked him, "What will be with all the ets that you interpreted?" He replied, "Just as I was rewarded for expounding them (derishah), so will I be rewarded for stopping to interpret them (perishah)" [and taking back all my expositions. Since the et in this verse does not include anyone else, none of the other ets in the Torah include anyone or anything else either (Rashi)]. [The et in this verse was left unexpounded] until R. Akiva came and taught: [In the verse,] "You should fear [et] the Lord, your God"—the word et comes to include Torah scholars [who should be revered just like God].

MURDER, IDOLATRY, AND INCEST, THE THREE CARDINAL SINS

(25a) R. Yaakov said in R. Yochanan's name: A person is allowed to cure himself with all [forbidden] things except with the wood of an asheirah, a tree that is devoted to idolatry. [The Gemara asks:] How is this to be understood? If we say [that the patient's life] is in danger, then even the wood of an asheirah may be used, [because all prohibitions are set aside when it comes to saving a life]; and if his life is not in danger then all other forbidden things too are prohibited, [not just the wood of an asheirah]? [The Gemara answers:] Actually, it means that [the patient's life is] in danger, yet even so, the wood of an asheirah may not be used to cure him. For we learned that R. Eliezer said: It says, "Love God your Lord with all your heart, with all your life, and with all your wealth" (Deuteronomy 6:5).

Now, since it says "with all your life," why does it have to say "with all your wealth"? And since it says, "with all your wealth," why does it have to say, "with all your soul"? [Why doesn't it just say: "Love God with that which is dearest to you"?] The Torah wants to teach you: there could be a person who values his life higher than his wealth, that's why it says, "with all your life," [he should be ready to give up his life for his love of God]; and there could be a person who values his wealth higher than his life, that's why it says, "with all your wealth." [But using the wood of an asheiah, which is a form of idolatry, is a contradiction of loving God. Therefore he may not use it and should rather give up his life.]

[The Gemara pursues the theme of giving up one's life.] When Ravin came [from Eretz Yisrael to Babylonia] he said in the name of R. Yochanan: A person [who is dangerously ill] is allowed to cure himself with all forbidden things, except idolatry, sexual crime, and murder. [A person must give up his life rather than commit any of the three cardinal sins.⁵] (25b) Idolatry as we discussed above. [You must love God "with all your life," implying that a person must give up his life rather than worship idols]. Regarding sexual crime and murder we have learned: Rabbi said: It says, [if a man raped a betrothed girl out in a field, the ravager shall be put to death but the girl is not to be punished,] "This is no different from the case where a man rises up against his neighbor and murders him" (Deuteronomy 22:26).

[The Gemara asks:] What is the Torah teaching us by comparing the rape of a betrothed girl to murder? [The Gemara answers:] The [simile of the case of murder] is intended to explain [the case of the betrothed girl], but at the same time it turns out [that the case of murder] is elucidated [by the case of the betrothed girl.⁶ Each case teaches us something about the other]. The murderer is compared to a betrothed girl [to teach us]: Just as a betrothed girl must be saved from being raped even if it means killing the ravager, so [in the case of a] murderer the victim must be saved even if it means killing the attacker. By the same token, the betrothed girl is compared to the murderer [to teach us]: Just as in the case of a murder, [if a person is told: Kill someone, otherwise you will be killed, he must allow himself to be killed rather than commit murder, so a betrothed girl must give up her life rather than be violated by a man.

[The Gemara asks:] And how do we know that in the case of murder itself [a person must allow himself to be killed rather than commit murder]? [The Gemara answers:] It is based on common sense. As in the case of a person who came before Rava and told him: "The governor of my town has told me to kill so-and-so. If you don't I will kill you. [What shall I do?]" Rava answered, "Let him kill you rather than you should kill another human being. How do you know that your blood is redder? Maybe his blood is redder." [Either way, a life will be lost. Who told you that your life is more dear to God than the other person's life?]

MAROR, BITTER HERBS

(39a) Rava said: What is *chazeret*? *Chassa*. What does *chassa* symbolize? That the Merciful One had pity [*chas*] on us. R. Shmuel b. Nachmani said in R. Yochanan's name: Why were the Egyptians compared to *maror* (bitter herbs) [in the verse, "They made the lives of [the Israelites] miserable" (*vayemareru*, which is from the same root as *maror*) (Exodus 1:14)]. To teach you: Just as the beginning, [the top], of this *maror* is soft while its end is hard, so were the Egyptians: their beginning

was benign but their end was hard, [at first they made the Israelites work but paid them wages, but later they enslaved them and treated them very harshly].

MARRYING A KOHEN'S DAUGHTER

(49a) We learned in a *Baraita*: R. Shimon said: A Torah scholar is not permitted to take part in a feast that is not connected to a mitzvah. What kind of feast does this refer to? R. Yochanan said: For example, the feast that is held when the daughter of a *kohen* is marrying a *Yisrael* [a non-*kohen*], or the daughter of a scholar is marrying an ignoramus. For R. Yochanan said: If the daughter of a *kohen* marries a *Yisrael*, their match will not be successful. What will happen? R. Chisda said: Either she becomes a widow or she ends up being divorced or she does not have children. [Because it says, "When a *kohen*'s daughter marries a non-*kohen*," which is followed by, "But if a *kohen*'s daughter is widowed or divorced and has no children" (Leviticus 22:12) (Rashi).] In a *Baraita* it was taught: Either he will bury her [prematurely], or she will bury him, or she will bring him to poverty. [The Gemara counters:] But this is not so! [The opposite is true.] For R. Yochanan said: If someone wants to become wealthy he should join the descendants of Aaron [meaning, he should marry the daughter of a *kohen*], for surely the combination of Torah and the priesthood will make them rich? [The Gemara answers:] There is no contradiction: one refers to a Torah scholar, [if he marries a *kohen*'s daughter the marriage will be fortunate]; the other refers to an ignoramus [whose marriage to a *kohen*'s daughter will not be blessed because it disgraces Aaron (Rashi)].

[The Gemara now cites several cases of rabbis who married a *kohen*'s daughter.]

R. Yehoshua married a *kohen*'s daughter and became ill. He said: Aaron obviously is not pleased that I joined his children, and that he should have a son-in-law such as myself. R. Idi b. Avin married a *kohen*'s daughter, and he had two sons who received rabbinical ordination: R. Sheshet b. R. Idi and R. Yehoshua b. R. Idi. R. Papa said: If I had not married a *kohen*'s daughter I would not have become wealthy. R. Kahana⁷ said: If I had not married a *kohen*'s daughter I would not have gone into exile [from my home in Babylonia to Eretz Yisrael⁸]. They said to him: But you were exiled to a place of Torah learning! [He answered:] I did not go into exile as other people do, [out of my own free will. I had to run away. He considered that a punishment which he blamed on the fact that he married a *kohen*'s daughter, and he felt unworthy of that].

INDULGING IN HEDONISTIC FEASTING

R. Yitzchak said: Anyone who partakes of a feast that is not connected to a mitzvah will eventually go into exile. For it says, "They feast on lambs from the flock and on calves from the stalls," and this is followed by, "Assuredly, right soon they shall head the column of exiles" (Amos 6:4,7).

Our Rabbis taught: Every scholar who takes part in many banquets all over [just for the pleasure of eating], in the end destroys his home, causes his wife to live like a widow [because he has to travel to distant places to earn enough money to maintain the luxurious standard of living he has become accustomed to (Rashi)], and causes his children to live like orphans. He forgets his learning, and becomes involved in many arguments [because he forgets his learning and renders incorrect decisions]. His words are disregarded, and he disgraces the Name of Heaven, the name of his teacher, and the name of his father, and he causes a bad name for himself, his children, and his children's children until the end of time. What is the bad name people call him? Said Abaye: They call his son, "the son of the stove-heater." Rava said: They call his son, "the son of the tavern dancer." R. Papa said: "the son of the plate-licker." R. Shemayah said: "the son of the one who folds his coat underneath himself and lies down on it to sleep wherever he happens to be [because he is too drunk to go home]."

MARRYING THE DAUGHTER
OF A TORAH SCHOLAR

Our Rabbis taught: A person should sell everything that he has and marry the daughter of a Torah scholar, for if he dies or goes into exile he can be sure that his children will be Torah scholars, [for his virtuous wife will educate them]. But he should not marry the daughter of an *am haaretz* [an unlearned person], for if he dies or goes into exile [and will not be there to educate his children], his children will be *ammei haaretz*.

Our Rabbis taught: A person should sell everything he has to marry the daughter of a Torah scholar, and marry off his daughter to a Torah scholar. A marriage like that may be compared to the grafting of a grapevine with a grapevine, something that is beautiful and pleasing. But he should not marry the daughter of an *am haaretz*, for this amounts to mixing the grapes of a vine with the berries of a thorn bush, something that is ugly (49b) and unbecoming.

We learned in a *Baraita*: A person should sell everything he owns to marry the daughter of a Torah scholar. If he cannot find the daughter of a scholar, he should marry the daughter of one of the great men of that generation, [i.e., people who are known for their piety and good deeds]. If he does not find the daughter of one of the great men of the generation, he should marry the daughter of one of the heads of the congregation. If he cannot find a daughter of one of the heads of the congregation he should marry the daughter of an administrator of a charity fund. If he cannot find

the daughter of a charity administrator, he should marry the daughter of a teacher of young boys. But he should not marry the daughter of an *am haaretz*, because they are loathsome and their wives are like creeping things [an allusion to the fact that they are not careful about the laws of menstruation (*Maharsha*)], and about their daughters it says, "Cursed is he who lies with any animal" (Deuteronomy 27:21).

[The Rema on Even Ha'ezer[9] explains that an *am haaretz* is not a person who lacks Torah knowledge, but one who does not observe *mitzvot* and lives licentiously. The Taz on Even Ha'ezer[10] comments that if the daughter of an *am haaretz* grows to be a devout woman who appreciates Torah learning there is no objection to marrying her.]

THE *AMMEI HAARETZ*'S HATRED
OF TORAH SCHOLARS

We learned in a *Baraita*: Rebbi said: An *am haaretz* is not allowed to eat meat, for it says, "This is the law [*Torah*] concerning mammals and birds" (Leviticus 11:46). [The Gemara interprets the word *Torah* in this context:] Someone who learns Torah is allowed to eat the flesh of an animal or a bird, but someone who does not learn Torah is not allowed to eat the flesh of an animal or fowl. [Since an *am haaretz* does not use his energy for the purpose for which he was created, he has no right to take the life of another creature to give him the energy he misuses.]

We learned in a *Baraita*: R. Akiva said: When I was an *am haaretz* [before I began learning Torah], I used to say: I wished I had a Torah scholar, so I could bite him the way a donkey bites. His disciples said to him: Rabbi, say at least [that you would have bitten him] like a dog bites! He replied: A donkey bites and breaks the bones, while a dog bites but does not break the bones. [Basically, Rabbi Akiva was a kindhearted person, but his hatred of Torah scholars was rooted in jealousy and in the fact that they kept themselves aloof from the *ammei haaretz* (R. Akiva Eiger).]

We learned: R. Meir used to say: If someone marries his daughter to an *am haaretz* it is as though he tied her up and placed her before a lion: just as a lion pounces on his prey and devours it [before it dies], and it has no shame, so too an *am haaretz* strikes his wife and has marital relations and has no shame.

We learned: R. Eliezer said: If not for the fact that we [Torah scholars] need the *ammei haaretz* to provide us with food and services [so that they earn their livelihood from us], they would kill us. R. Chiya taught: If someone learns Torah in front of an *am haaretz* [who does not learn any Torah] it is as if he cohabited with the betrothed [of the *am haaretz*] right in front of his face. [The *am haaretz* feels degraded when Torah is studied in his presence (Rashi)]. For it says, "Moses prescribed the Torah to us, an inheritance [*morashah*] for the congregation of Jacob (Deuteronomy 33:4).

Don't read *morashah* but *me'orasah* [the betrothed]. The hatred with which the *ammei haaretz* hate the Torah scholars is greater than the hatred of the heathens toward Israel, and the wives of the *ammei haaretz* hate even more than they do. We learned: A person who has studied and then abandoned the Torah [hates the Torah scholars] more than any *am haaretz* hates the Torah scholars.

We learned in a *Baraita*: Six things were said concerning an *am haaretz*: We do not appoint him to witness something in order that he should testify later; we do not accept testimony from him; we do not tell him any secrets; we do not appoint an *am haaretz* as guardian of the property of orphans; we do not appoint him administrator of a charity fund; and we should not be the traveling companion of an *am haaretz*. Some say: If we have found a lost article belonging to an *am haaretz* [for example, if an article was found after a caravan of *ammei haaretz* passed by (*Tosafot*)], we do not have to announce that we have found it. [The Gemara asks:] Why doesn't the first Tanna mention this?— [Because he disagrees. He reasons that] perhaps the *am haaretz* will have good children, and they will eventually enjoy the money that you return to him, as it says, "He, [the wicked man], will prepare it, and the righteous will wear it" (Job 27:17).

A TOPSY-TURVY WORLD

(50a) [Zechariah in his prophecy about the coming of *Mashiach* says,] "On that day, sunlight will not be held in esteem [*yekarot*], but it will be disdained [*vekipa'on*]" (Zechariah 14:6). [The Gemara asks:] What is the meaning of *yekarot vekippa'on*? Said R. Elazar: It means, that the light [of the sun], which is precious [*yakar*] in this world, will be looked down upon in the next world [for then we will have the magnificent light of the days of Creation]. R. Yochanan said: This [light is a metaphor for the Torah, and specifically it] refers to the tractates of *Nega'im* and *Ohalot* [which deal with the very complex laws of defilement through leprosy and through contact with a dead body]. In the future world these tractates will no longer be difficult to grasp [*yekarot*] but will be easy [*vekipa'on*] to understand. R. Yehoshua b. Levi said: [*Yekarot vekipa'on*] refers to the people who are honored and respected [*yekarot*] in this world, but who will be held in contempt [*vekipa'on*] in the future world.

[The Gemara proves this by citing] the story of Rabbi Yosef the son of R. Yehoshua b. Levi, who became sick and experienced a heavenly vision. When he came to, his father asked him, "What did you see there?" "I saw a topsy-turvy world," he replied, "those that are on top [in this world] occupy the lowest regions [of heaven], and those that are downtrodden [in this world] are on top [in the heavenly realm]. Replied his father, "Son, [you did not see a topsy-turvy world]; you saw a clear world, [a world of true values]. And

how do we [Torah scholars] rate there?" Replied R. Yosef, "Just as we are respected here, so are we respected there. And I heard them saying, 'Happy is the person who comes here and brings his learning with him, [meaning, during his lifetime he has learned as much as he could].' And I also heard them saying, 'No one can stand within the confines of those who died a martyr's death at the hands of the government.'" [The Gemara asks:] Who are these martyrs? Shall we say, R. Akiva and his colleagues?[11] Is their only merit that they were executed by the government, and nothing else? [Surely they had many other outstanding qualities.] [The Gemara answers:] It refers to the martyrs of Lydda.[12]

GOD'S NAME WILL BE ONE

[Zechariah continues his prophecy of the Messianic times, saying,] "God will be King over all the world; on that day God will be One and His Name will be One" (Zechariah 14:9). [The Gemara asks:] Is He then not One now? R. Acha b. Chanina said: This world is not like the World to Come; in this world, for good tidings you say the *berachah*: Who is good and does good, while for bad tidings one says: Blessed is the true Judge.[13] But in the World to Come it will be only: Who is good and does good. [There we recognize that God does only good, and thus there are no bad tidings.]

In the verse, "His name will be One," what does "One" mean? Is now His name not One? R. Nachman b. Yitzchak said: This world is not like the World to Come. In this world His name is written with *yud kei vav kei*, and it is read as *alef dalet*, *Adonai*, but in the World to Come it will all be One: it will be written with *yud kei* and read as *yud kei*.

Rava intended to lecture about [the mystical meaning of the Four-Letter Divine Name], but an elderly scholar advised him against it, saying: It is written, ["This is My name forever, [*leolam*]," (Exodus 3:15), [but *leolam* is written without a *vav* and can be read as] *le'aleim*, "it must be hidden," [you must hide My name, and don't reveal its hidden meaning]. R. Avina pointed out the following contradiction: It says, "This is My name, to be hidden," and the verse continues, "and this is how I am to be recalled for all generations." [On the one hand the name is to be concealed, and on the other hand it is to be publicly remembered!] The Holy One, blessed be He, said: My name is not read the way it is written. My name is written with *yud kei*, but it is read as *alef dalet*.[14]

DOING *MITZVOT* FOR THEIR OWN SAKE

(50b) If someone works on Friday or on the day before Yom Tov from *Minchah*[15] and onward, or on the night after *Shabbat* or after Yom Tov, or at the close of Yom

Kippur, or wherever there is the slightest suspicion of a transgression, including even a public fast day [proclaimed on account of rain, when work was forbidden[16]], he will never see a sign of a blessing [in the money he earned from that work].

Rava pointed out two contradictory verses. One verse states, "For Your faithfulness is as high as heaven" (Psalms 57:11), and another verse says, "For Your mercy is higher than the heavens" (Psalms 108:5). How can this be explained? For those who do a mitzvah for its own sake [God's mercy is higher than the heavens], and for those who do it for ulterior motives [God's mercy is only as high as heaven]. And this is consistent with Rav Yehudah's statement. For Rav Yehudah said in Rav's name: By all means a person should engage in Torah study and good deeds even if he does not do it for its own sake, because by doing good for ulterior motives he will eventually come to do good for its own sake.

PROFESSIONS THAT ARE BLESSED WITH SUCCESS

The Rabbis taught: Someone who depends on his wife's income or who earns his livelihood from a hand-mill will never be blessed with success. [The Gemara explains:] "His wife's income" means [the money she earns by going from door to door carrying a pair of scales, which she rents to people who want] to weigh something. [This is not a respectable occupation for a woman, and it pays very little (Rashi).] "Earning his livelihood from a hand-mill" means by renting it to others. [This involves a great deal of work and produces a small profit. But buying and selling mills is a profitable enterprise (Rashi).] But if his wife makes clothes and sells them, Scripture praises her, for it says, "She makes a cloak to sell" (Proverbs 31:24).

The Rabbis taught: If someone deals in wooden sticks and jars he will never be blessed with success. What is the reason? Since such business occupies much space and yields only a small profit the evil eye has power over it.

The Rabbis taught: Traders who sell their wares in market-stands and those who raise small cattle [like sheep and goats], and those who cut down beautiful trees, and those who [when dividing something with others] try to get the better share, will never be blessed with success. What is the reason? Because people gaze at them. [Market traders are exposed to the evil eye, which brings about misfortune. The other three provoke the anger of the public and bring the evil eye on themselves (Rashi).]

The Rabbis taught: The wages of four occupations never are blessed with success: the wages of scribes, the wages of interpreters [who stand next to the rabbi and interpret his lecture or sermon to the congregation], the profits of orphans [if someone invests the money of orphans and keeps half the profit for his labor], and money that is earned from trading overseas. [The Gemara now analyzes the four occupations:] I can understand that the wages of interpreters [are not blessed with success], the reason being that it looks like wages earned for work done on *Shabbat*; orphans' money, too, because they are not able to forgive if someone treated them unfairly; money earned from trading overseas, because a miracle does not happen every day [and merchants' ships are often exposed to grave danger]. But what is the reason that the wages of scribes never are blessed with success? Said R. Yehoshua b. Levi: The men of the Great Assembly[17] observed twenty-four fasts [and prayed] that those who write Torah scrolls, *tefillin*, and *mezuzot* should not become wealthy, for if they became wealthy they would stop writing.

The Rabbis taught: People who write Torah scrolls, *tefillin*, and *mezuzuot*, their wholesalers and retailers, and all who deal in religious articles, including the sellers of *techeiles* [the wool dyed blue, used for one of the threads of the *tzitzit*], never are blessed with success. But if they do their work for its own sake, [if their primary concern is to provide religious articles for the community so that the people can perform the *mitzvot*], then they will be blessed with success.

The inhabitants of Beyshan used not to go from Tyre to Sidon on Friday. [Friday was market day in Sidon, but they stayed at home in order to devote themselves to making preparations for *Shabbat* (Rashi).] Their children went to R. Yochanan and said, "Our fathers [who were wealthy] could afford [to miss the Sidon market], but for us it is impossible. [Are we permitted to go to Sidon on Friday?]" Replied R. Yochanan: "Your fathers have taken it upon themselves not to do this, [and this is binding on you as well], for it says, 'My son, heed the discipline of your father, and do not forsake the teaching of your mother (Proverbs 1:8).'"

A ROASTED GOAT ON THE NIGHT OF PESACH

(53a) R. Yose said: Tuddus of Rome [a prominent Jew who lived in Rome], accustomed the Jews of Rome to eat a *gedi mekulas*[18] on the nights of Pesach, [a goat roasted with its head, its legs, and its internal organs, the way the *korban Pesach* (the Passover sacrifice) was roasted in the days the *Bet Hamikdash* was standing]. So the Sages sent him the following message: If not for the fact that you are [the prominent] Tuddus, we would put you under a ban, because you are making Jewish people eat the meat of sacrifices outside Jerusalem [which is forbidden]. [The Gemara asks:] But this is not really meat of sacrifices? [The people certainly did not bring the goats as a sacrifice!] [The Gemara answers:] (53b) It is just like making Jewish people eat meat of sacrifices [because it looks exactly like a Passover sacrifice].

THE LESSON LEARNED
FROM THE FROGS

The scholars asked a question: Was Tuddus a great man or was he a powerful man? [Did the Sages refrain from putting him under a ban out of respect for his learning or were they afraid of him?] [The Gemara answers:] Come and listen: [Tuddus of Rome must have been a great scholar for] he also taught this: What reason did Chananiah, Mishael, and Azariah have to allow themselves to be thrown into the fiery furnace for the sanctification of God's name?[19] [Why did they not apply the rule "He shall live by it [the Torah]," (Leviticus 18:5) and not die by it? (Rashi).] They drew a logical inference from the frogs. [They reasoned:] If frogs, which are not commanded to give up their lives for the sanctification of God's name, yet it says about them, [Moses warned Pharaoh,] "They [the frogs] will come up and enter your palace . . . and your ovens and your kneading bowls " (Exodus 7:28). [Tuddus expounded:] When is the kneading bowl found near the oven? When the oven is hot. [So when the frogs jumped into the ovens it meant that they would be burned, yet they did not hesitate to do it.] We, who are commanded to sanctify God's name, surely must sacrifice our lives. [This teaching proves that Tuddus of Rome was a great scholar.]

R. Yose b. Avin said: [Tuddus] would fill the pockets of Torah scholars with merchandise [to enable them to do business]. For R. Yochanan said: Whoever puts merchandise into the pockets of Torah scholars will merit to sit in the Heavenly Academy, for it says, "Whoever distributes of his wealth [to Torah scholars] is in the [Heavenly] domain of wisdom (Ecclesiastes 7:12).

WHEN WAS FIRE CREATED?

(54a) [The Gemara asks:] Was fire created on *Motza'ei Shabbat* [after the end of *Shabbat*]? But we learned in a *Baraita*: Ten things were created on the eve of *Shabbat* at twilight. They are: The well [the Well of Miriam that accompanied the Israelites in the wilderness], the manna, the rainbow,[20] the writing [the shape of the letters], the writing instrument [used to carve out the letters of the Tablets], the Tablets,[21] the grave of Moses, the cave in which Moses and Elijah stood [when they beheld the glory of God[22]], the opening of the mouth of Balaam's donkey[23] [that began to speak], and the opening of the earth's mouth to swallow up the wicked [Korach and his company].[24] R. Nechemiah said in his father's name: Also fire and the mule [were created on the eve of *Shabbat*. [He holds that a mule is not a cross beween a horse and a donkey but that the first mule was created from the earth (Rashi).]

R. Yoshiah said in his father's name: Also the ram [that Abraham offered at the *Akeidah* (the Binding of Isaac)[25]] and the *shamir* worm [a small worm that split large stones as it crawled on them. Since no sword or iron could be used to hew the stones for the Temple's construction, the *shamir* took the place of conventional tools].[26] R. Yehudah said: Also the first pair of pliers [were created on the eve of *Shabbat*]. He used to say: You need a pair of pliers to make a pair of pliers. [You need pliers to hold the red-hot metal on the anvil as it is shaped into another pair of pliers (Rashi).] But who made the first pair of pliers? You have to say that it was created by God. So they answered: No, it is possible [for man to make a plier without another plier]. You can form it in a mold and give it its shape. So the first pair of pliers, too, was man-made.

[The point the Gemara wants to make is that R. Nechemiah said that "also fire" was created on the eve of *Shabbat*, and this contradicts the Mishnah, which says that fire was created only after the end of *Shabbat*]. [The Gemara answers:] There is no difficulty. [It depends on what kind of fire.] One is referring to our fire; the other is referring to the fire of Gehinnom. Our fire was created at the end of *Shabbat*; the fire of Gehinnom was created on the eve of *Shabbat*.

[The Gemara asks:] Was then the fire of Gehinnom created on the eve of *Shabbat*? But we learned in a *Baraita*: Seven things were created before the world was created. They are: the Torah, Repentance, the Garden of Eden, Gehinnom, the Throne of Glory, the *Bet Hamikdash*, and the name of *Mashiach*. [So you see, Gehinnom was not created on the eve of *Shabbat*. It was created even before the creation of the world!]

[The Gemara now cites proof texts:] The Torah [existed before the world was created], for it says, "God has created me [the Torah] at the beginning of His way" (Proverbs 8:22). Repentance, for it says, "Before the mountains came into being," and it says [in the next verse], "You return man to contrition, and say, 'Return you children of men'" (Psalms 90:2,3). The Garden of Eden, for it says, "And the Lord God planted a garden in Eden before the world" (Genesis 2:8). Gehinnom, for it says, "The Tofet [i.e., Gehinnom] has long been ready for him" (Isaiah 31:33). The Throne of Glory and the *Bet Hamikdash*, for it says, "O Throne of Glory exalted from of old, our Sacred Shrine!" (Jeremiah 17:12). The name of *Mashiach*, for it says, "His [Mashiach's] name will endure forever, and has existed before the sun" (Psalms 72:17). [Thus we see that Gehinnom was created before the world, and not on the eve of *Shabbat* as the Gemara stated above.] [The Gemara answers:] I will tell you: The cavity of Gehinnom was created before the world, but its fire was created on the eve of *Shabbat*.

[The Gemara asks:] Was then its fire created on the eve of *Shabbat*? But we learned in a *Baraita*: R. Yose said: The fire that the Holy One, blessed be He, created on the second day of the week will never be extinguished [because it is the fire of Gehinnom], for it says, "They will go out and gaze on the corpses of the men who rebelled against Me: Their worms will not die, nor their fire be quenched" (Isaiah 66:24). And

R. Bana'ah the son of R. Ulla said: Why doesn't it say, *ki tov*, "It was good," on the second day of Creation? Because the fire of Gehinnom was created on that day. And R. Elazar said: Even though it does not say *ki tov*, "It was good," on Monday, yet God included it as well as the entire Creation on Friday, for it says, "And God saw all that He had made, and behold, it was very good," (Genesis 1:31) [including the fire of Gehinnom; and it is considered good because the wicked are punished and purified by it (Rashi)].

[Thus the question remains: We see that the fire of Gehinnom was created on Monday, and not on the eve of *Shabbat*, as the Gemara contended above.] [The Gemara replies:] The cavity of Gehinnom was created before the world came into being, and its fire on Monday. And our fire [is divided into two]. God's intention was to create it on the eve of *Shabbat*, but it was not created until the close of *Shabbat*. For we learned in a *Baraita*: R. Yose said: Two things He intended to create on the eve of *Shabbat*, but they were not actually created until the end of *Shabbat*. [First,] at the close of *Shabbat*, the Holy One blessed be He, gave Adam a special wisdom that was a semblance of Divine wisdom, and Adam brought two stones and struck them against each other, and fire emerged for the first time. [Second,] Adam also took two animals [a horse and a donkey] and crossbred them, and a mule came forth.

TEN THINGS, SEVEN THINGS, AND THREE THINGS

The Rabbis taught: Ten things were created during the twilight of the first *Shabbat* eve. They are: The well, manna, the rainbow, writing, writing instruments, the Tablets, the grave of Moses, the cave in which Moses and Elijah stood, the opening of the donkey's mouth, and the opening of the earth's mouth to swallow up the wicked [Korach and his party].[27] Some say, also the staff of Aaron with its almonds and its blossoms.[28] Others say, also the demons; still others say, also (54b) Adam's garment, [the leather garment that God made for Adam and his wife (Genesis 3:21) (Rashi)].

Our Rabbis taught: Seven things are hidden from man. They are: the day of death; the day of consolation [when he will be relieved of his worries (Rashi)]; his final Divine judgment; no one knows what his neighbor thinks; and no one knows where he is going to earn money; and when the kingdom of David will be restored; and when the wicked kingdom [the Roman empire[29]] will come to an end.

Our Rabbis taught: There are three things that God intended to create, and if it had not occurred to Him to create them, it would be essential that He should create them. [This is just a figure of speech. The Gemara wants to emphasize that the things mentioned here are fundamentals of human society, and we simply could not exist without them.] They are: that a dead body should decay [otherwise the family would keep it unburied, and they would constantly be reminded of their sorrow]; that the dead should be forgotten [otherwise people would mourn them all their lives]; and that produce eventually should rot [otherwise farmers would hoard their produce, create a food shortage, and drive up the prices (Rashi)]. Some say: that coins should be used as currency [and replace the ancient barter system].

SHALL WE RECITE: *BARUCH SHEM KEVOD MALCHUTO?*

(56a) [We learned in the Mishnah that the people of Jericho used to "wrap up" the *Shema*, [meaning, they recited it without making the necessary pauses]. We learned in a *Baraita*: How did they "wrap up" the *Shema*? They said: "Hear O Israel, the Lord our God, the Lord is One,"[30] and did not make a pause [between *echad* (One) and *ve'ahavta* ("You shall love"). [*Shema* is the acknowledgment of God's sovereignty, whereas *ve'ahavta* tells a Jew what his duties are. They did not pause to think about these different concepts], so said R. Meir. R. Yehudah said: They did make a pause, but they did not recite *Baruch Shem kevod malchuto leolam va'ed*, "Blessed is the Name of His glorious kingdom for all eternity" [before *ve'ahavta*]. [The Gemara asks: If they did not say *Baruch Shem kevod malchuto*,] what is the reason that we do say it? [The Gemara answers:] As R. Shimon b. Lakish explained it. For R. Shimon b. Lakish said: It says, "[On his deathbed] Jacob called for his sons and said, 'Come together, and I will tell you what will happen in the end of days'" (Genesis 49:1).

Jacob wanted to reveal to his sons when *Mashiach* would come but the *Shechinah* left him, [so that suddenly he did not know]. He said: Perhaps, Heaven forbid, one among my children is unfit, as happened to Abraham who had a son Yishmael, and like my father Isaac who had a son Esau. So his sons answered him, "Hear O Israel, the Lord our God, the Lord is One, [addressing their father by his name 'Israel']; just as there is only one [God] in your heart, so is there only one [God] in our hearts. [Our faith in God is unshakable]." At that moment our father Jacob opened his mouth and said: *Baruch Shem kevod malchuto leolam va'ed*, "Blessed is the Name of His glorious kingdom for all eternity." The Rabbis said: What shall we do? Shall we recite it? But our teacher Moses did not say it. Shall we not say it? But Jacob did say it! So they enacted that it should be said quietly.

R. Yitzchak said: The yeshivah of R. Ammi taught: We can compare this to a princess who smelled a meat dish seasoned with spices. If she says that she wants to eat it she suffers disgrace [for giving in to her cravings]. On the other hand, if she does not say that she wants it she suffers pain [because her desire is unfulfilled]. [Noting her predicament,] her servants quietly began to bring the dish to her. [We are also in a predicament.

We want to say *Baruch Shem kevod malchuto* because of Jacob, yet we don't want to say so as not to slight Moses, so we say it quietly.]

R. Abbahu said: The Sages ordained that it should be said aloud because of the complaints of the *minim* [heretics, who might accuse the Jews of whispering curses against them]. But in Nahardea, where there are no heretics as of now, they say it quietly.

HIGH-HANDED HIGH PRIESTS

(57a) We learned: Abba Shaul said: There were many sycamore tree trunks in Jericho and the strong-arm bullies among the priests seized them by force. Thereupon the owners decided to consecrate the trunks to the *Bet Hamikdash*, [in effect telling the bullies that they were stealing from the *Bet Hamikdash*]. Speaking of such priests, Abba Shaul b. Botnit said in the name of Abba Yosef b. Chanin: Woe is me because of the house of Baytus! [an unscrupulous High Priest], woe is me because of their sticks [with which his servants beat the people]. Woe is me because of the house of Chanin [also a wicked High Priest], woe is me because of their whisperings! [in secret meetings where they thought up oppressive decrees]. Woe is me because of the house of Katros [again a tyrannical High Priest], woe is me because of their pens [with which they wrote evil rulings]. Woe is me because of the house of Yishmael b. Piachi, woe is me because of their fists! For these are High Priests, their sons are the Temple treasurers, their sons-in-law are the trustees, and their servants strike the people with sticks.

[Pursuing this topic, the Gemara says:] Our Rabbis taught: The court of the *Bet Hamikdash* uttered four cries: The first cry: "Leave this place, sons of Eli, who defiled the Temple of God!"[31] The second cry: "Leave this place, Yissachar of K'far Barkai, who honors himself but desecrates the sacrifices of God!" For when offering the sacrifices he used to wrap his hands in silk. [This invalidates the sacrifice, and it is a contemptuous gesture (Rashi).] [On the positive side] the Court of the *Bet Hamikdash* also cried out: "Raise up your heads, O gates of the Court, and let Yishmael b. Piachi, the disciple of Pinchas, enter and serve as High Priest!" [But above it says, "Woe is me because of the house of Yishmael b. Piachi"? Rashi explains that his sons oppressed the people but he himself was a righteous man.] The Temple Court also cried out: "Raise up your heads, O gates of the Court, and let Yochanan b. Narvai, the disciple of Pinkai enter, and let him fill his stomach with the sacrifices." It was said about Yochanan b. Narvai that he ate three hundred calves and drank three hundred barrels of wine, and he ate forty *se'ah* of young birds as a dessert. [These quantities were consumed by his entire family, which was very large (*Masoret HaShas*).] It was said: As long as Yochanan b. Narbai lived it never happened that any portion of a sacrifice became *notar*,

[was left over after the prescribed time during which it must be eaten had passed].

IS LAMB BETTER THAN GOAT MEAT?

[The Gemara asks:] What happened to Yissachar of K'far Barkai [who used to wear silk gloves when performing the service of the sacrifices? What was his punishment]? It was said, [continues the Gemara], the [Hasmonean] king and his queen were sitting [and having a discussion]. The king said, "Goat meat is better [than lamb]," while the queen said, "Lamb is better." They said, "Who is going to decide this question? The High Priest who brings sacrifices every day." So he [Yissachar, the High Priest] came to the palace. (57b) [When he heard the question], he made a contemptuous gesture with his hand [belittling the question]. He said, "If goat meat were better we would use it for the daily sacrifice." [Thus he disagreed with the king.]

Said the king, "Because he showed no respect for royalty, let his right hand be cut off." But Yissachar bribed the guard, and instead of cutting off his right hand he cut off his left hand. When the king found out he ordered that the right hand be cut off also, [clearly the Divine retribution for not wanting to perform the service directly with his hands]. R. Yosef remarked: Praised be the Merciful One who caused Yissachar of K'far Barkai to get what he deserved in this world. R. Ashi commented: Yissachar of K'far Barkai never learned the Mishnah.

For we learned, R. Shimon said: [If lambs and goats occur in the same verse in the Torah], lambs are always mentioned before goats. You may think that this is done because lambs are better, therefore it says, "If he brings a lamb as his offering" (Leviticus 4:32). [In this case the goat is mentioned in an earlier passage (ibid. 28)] to teach us that they are both the same. Ravina said: [Not only did he fail to learn the Mishnah], he did not study the Torah either. For it says, "If he brings a lamb . . . If his sacrifice is a goat" (Leviticus 3:7,12), which means that if he wishes he can bring a lamb, and if he wishes he can bring a goat [indicating that both are the same].

TEACH ME THE BOOK OF GENEALOGIES

(62b) R. Simla'i came before R. Yochanan and said, "Please teach me the Book of Genealogies."[32] Asked R. Yochanan, "Where are you from?" He replied, "From Lod [Lydda, a town in Eretz Yisrael]." "And where do you live?" "I live in Nahardea [a town in Babylonia, famous for its great yeshivah]." So R. Yochanan said, "We do not teach the Book of Genealogies either to people from Lod or from Nahardea, and surely not to you who are from Lod and live in

Nahardea!" [He was just trying to put him off.] But when R. Simla'i insisted R. Yochanan relented. "Let us learn it in three months," R. Simla'i suggested. R. Yochanan indignantly took a clod of earth and threw it at him, saying, "Beruriah, the wife of R. Meir and the daughter of R. Chaninah b. Teradyon, who studied three hundred laws from three hundred rabbis on one winter day, was unable to master the Book of Genealogies after studying it for three years, and you want me to teach it to you in three months!"

As R. Simla'i was leaving he asked R. Yochanan, "Rabbi, why is it that a Pesach sacrifice that is offered both for its actual purpose and for a different purpose is invalid, whereas a Pesach sacrifice that is offered both for those who can eat it and those who cannot eat it, is valid? "Since obviously you are a Torah scholar," replied R. Yochanan, "come and I will tell you."

Rami b. R. Yehudah said in the name of Rav: Since the day that the Book of Genealogies was hidden, the strength of the Sages has been weakened, and the light of their eyes has been dimmed [because many Torah laws it contained have been forgotten (Rashi)]. Mar Zutra said: Between *Atzeil* and *Atzeil* [in the book of Chronicles] the Sages had four hundred camel-loads of scriptural interpretations.[33]

THE SERVICE OF
THE PESACH SACRIFICE

(64a) [The Mishnah describes the technical arrangement of the slaughtering of the Pesach offering with the vast multitude standing in the Court of the *Bet Hamikdash*.] The Pesach sacrifice is slaughtered in three separate groups, for it says, "The entire community of the congregation of Israel shall slaughter [their sacrifices] in the afternoon" (Exodus 12:5). The terms "community," "congregation," and "Israel," [refer to three separate groups]. The first group entered. When the Court of the *Bet Hamikdash* was filled, they closed the doors and the *kohanim* sounded a *tekiah*, a *teruah*, and a *tekiah*.[34] The *kohanim* lined up in different rows; in their hands they held receptacles of silver and receptacles of gold [to receive the blood that was to be splashed on the Altar]. The line that was holding silver bowls had only silver, and the line that was holding gold bowls had only gold; they were not allowed to mix [silver and gold bowls]. These bowls did not have flat bottoms, for fear that the *kohanim* would put them down and the blood would congeal.

The Jew slaughtered the lamb, and the *kohein* caught the blood [in his bowl]. The *kohein* then passed it to his colleague who, in turn, passed it to his colleague who received the full bowl, and [after the blood had been splashed on the Altar] the empty bowl was passed down the line [until it reached the *kohein* who was waiting to catch the blood of the next Pesach sacrifice]. The *kohein* who was standing next to the Altar splashed it in one throw against the base of the Al-

tar.[35] The first group then left, and the second entered; when the second group left the third came in. The procedure that was followed by the first group was repeated by the second and the third. They recited the *Hallel*.[36] If they finished it [before they finished sacrificing], they repeated it, and if they repeated it [and still were not finished sacrificing], they recited it a third time, although [the sacrificing went so fast that] they never had to recite it a third time. R. Yehudah said: The third group never reached "I love Him, for God hears my voice" (Psalms 116:1), because the third group had few people [so that the sacrificing took only a short time].

THE CENSUS OF KING AGRIPPAS

(64b) The Rabbis taught: It never happened that a person was crushed in the Court of the *Bet Hamikdash* except on one Pesach in the days of Hillel when an old man was crushed, and they called it *Pesach ma'uchin*, "the Pesach of the crushed."

Our Rabbis taught: King Agrippas once wanted to count the multitudes of the Jewish people. So he said to the *Kohein Gadol*[37]: I want you to count the Pesach sacrifices. He then took a kidney from each of the sacrifices, and it turned out that there were 600,000 pairs of kidneys, [or 1,200,000 people], twice as many as those who went out from Egypt; this does not include those who were unclean [and therefore unable to bring the sacrifice], and those who were on a distant journey; and there was not a single Pesach sacrifice in which less than ten people participated, [so that there were at least 12,000,000 people]. So they called it *Pesach me'uvin*, "the Pesach of the masses."

DOES THE OFFERING
OF THE PESACH SACRIFICE
OVERRIDE *SHABBAT?*

(66a) We learned in a *Baraita*: This *halachah* was forgotten by the B'nei Beteira.[38] It once happened that the fourteenth of Nissan, *erev Pesach*,[39] [the day on which the Pesach sacrifice is brought] fell on *Shabbat* [when slaughter and cooking are forbidden], and they did not know whether or not the Pesach sacrifice overrides *Shabbat*. They said, "Is there anyone who knows whether the Pesach sacrifice overrides *Shabbat* or not?" They were told, "There is a person who has come up from Babylonia, named Hillel the Babylonian, who has studied under the two greatest men of the generation, namely, Shemaya and Avtalyon. He knows whether or not the Pesach sacrifice overrides *Shabbat*." So they sent for him and asked him, "Do you know whether the Pesach sacrifice overrides *Shabbat* or not?" He replied, "Is there then only one Pesach sacrifice during the year that overrides *Shabbat*? Surely there are more than two hundred sacrifices during the year that override *Shabbat*![40] They said, "How do you know that?"

["What Scriptural proof do you have for that?"] He answered, "It says with *bemo'ado*, 'at its proper time' (Numbers 9:3), with reference to the Pesach sacrifice, and it says *bemo'ado* 'at its proper time' (ibid 28:2) in connection with the *tamid*, the daily sacrifice.

Just as *bemo'ado* that is said in reference to the *tamid* overrides *Shabbat*, so *bemo'ado* that is mentioned in connection with the Pesach sacrifice overrides *Shabbat*. Besides, it is a matter of simple logic. If the *tamid*, the omission of which is not punished by *kareit* [premature death], overrides *Shabbat*, then surely the Pesach sacrifice, the neglect of which is punished by *kareit*,[41] overrides *Shabbat*." They immediately [stepped aside], appointed him as their leader and designated him *Nasi*, [head of the community of Israel].[42]

Thereupon Hillel sat down and lectured the whole day on the laws of Pesach. He began to criticize them, saying, "What is the cause that I, an immigrant from Babylonia, should become a *Nasi* over you? It was your laziness, because you did not serve the two greatest men of the generation, Shemayah and Avtalyon [as I did]." They then asked him [a halachic question], "Rabbi, what if a person forgot to bring a slaughtering knife on Friday, [to slaughter the Pesach sacrifice],[43] may he bring it on *Shabbat*?" "I have heard this *halachah*," Hillel replied, "but I forgot it. But leave it to the Jewish people: if they are not prophets, still, they are the children of prophets!" [We'll see what they are going to do.] The next day, whoever brought a lamb as a Pesach sacrifice stuck the knife in its wool, and whoever brought a goat [which has no wool] as a sacrifice stuck it between its horns. When [Hillel] saw what the people were doing he recalled the *halachah* and said, "That is precisely the tradition I received from Shemayah and Avtalyon."

ARROGANCE AND ANGER

(66b) Rav Yehudah said in Rav's name: Whoever is conceited, if he is a sage, his wisdom leaves him; if he is a prophet, his prophecy leaves him. If he is a sage, his wisdom leaves him; we learn this from Hillel. For the Gemara said [above], "[Hillel] began to criticize them," [a sign of arrogance], and then, [when they asked him what to do if someone forgot to bring a knife on Friday], he [was forced to admit], "I have heard this *halachah* but I forgot it."[44] If he is a prophet, his prophecy leaves him: we learn this from Deborah. For it says, "The leaders have ceased, ceased in Israel, until I arose, O Deborah, I arose, O mother in Israel!" (Judges 5:7). [This was a boastful statement.] And then it says [in the Song of Deborah], "Awake, awake, O Deborah. Awake, awake, [say your song of prophecy]" (ibid. 12). [Proof that her prophecy left her after she took too much credit for herself.]

Resh Lakish said: Anyone that gets angry, if he is a sage, his wisdom leaves him; if he is a prophet, his prophecy leaves him. If he is a sage, his wisdom leaves

him: we learn this from Moses. For it says, "Moses was angry at the generals and captains" (Numbers 31:14); this is followed by, "Eleazar the priest said to the soldiers returning from the campaign: This is the rule that God commanded Moses" (ibid. 31:21). [Why did Eleazar, and not Moses, expound the law?] Because Moses had forgotten it [after becoming angry]. If he is a prophet, his prophecy leaves him; we learn this from Elisha. Because it says: "Elisha said, 'If not for the fact I respect King Yehoshaphat of Judah I would not look at you or notice you'" (2 Kings 3:14) [this was an expression of anger]. And then Elisha said, "'Now then, get me a musician.' As the musician played the hand of God came upon him" (ibid. 15). [The fact that he needed a musician to arouse the prophecy proves that the spirit had left him after he became angry.]

R. Mani b. Patish said: Anyone who becomes angry, even if greatness has been decreed for him by Heaven, he will be stripped of his rank. From where do we know this? From Eliav, [David's older brother], for it says, "Eliav became angry with David and he said, 'Why did you come down here, and with whom did you leave those few sheep in the wilderness. I know your impudence and your impertinence: you came down to watch the fighting'" (1 Samuel 17:28). And when Samuel went to anoint a king, [and he had to choose one of Jesse's sons], about all of David's brothers it is written, "God has not chosen this one either," (ibid. 8), whereas about Eliav it says, "But God said to Samuel, 'Pay no attention to his appearance or his stature, for I have rejected him'" (ibid. 7). This shows you that God favored him until this incident, [but He rejected him because of his explosive fury].

THE RIGHTEOUS WILL REVIVE THE DEAD

(68a) What is meant by the passage, "Then lambs will graze as in their meadows [*kedobram*]" (Isaiah 5:17)? Menashia b. Yirmiyah said in the name of Rav: [Instead of *kedovram*,] read *kimedubbar bam*, "in accordance with the promise that was made [to the lambs, i.e., Israel]. [The Gemara asks:] What is that promise? Said Abbaye: [It refers to the end of the verse where it says,] "And on the ruins of the fat ones strangers shall feed," ["strangers" refers to the righteous]. Rava said to him: If it said, "On the ruins" I would accept your interpretation, but since it says "*and* on the ruins," the second clause of the verse expresses a different idea, [and does not relate to the first clause]. Rather, said Rava, the explanation is as R. Chananel said in Rav's name. For R. Chananel said in Rav's name: In time to come, the righteous will revive the dead, [just as Elijah and Elisha did]. For it says here, "Then lambs will graze as in their meadows," and it says elsewhere, "Then will Bashan and Gilead will graze as in olden days" (Micah 7:14). Now, Bashan stands for Elisha who came from

Bashan, as it says, "and Yannai and Shafat in Bashan" (1 Chronicles 5:12), and it says, "Elisha the son of Shafat is here who poured water on the hands[45] of Elijah" (2 Kings 3:11). Gilead refers to Elijah, for it says, "And Elijah the Tishbite, an inhabitant of Gilead, said to Ahab" (1 Kings 17:1). [Since the phrase "will graze" occurs in both verses, we ascribe Elijah and Elisha's power to revive the dead to the "lambs," the symbol of the righteous.]

R. Shmuel b. Nachmani said in R. Yochanan's name: In time to come, the righteous will revive the dead. For it says, "There shall yet be old men and women in the squares of Jerusalem, each with staff in hand because of their great age" (Zechariah 8:4). And it says, "and place my staff on the face of the boy" (2 Kings 4:29). [Elisha used the staff to revive the boy. Since the first verse also uses the word "staff" the implication is that the old men, i.e., the righteous, also will revive the dead.]

Ulla pointed out a contradiction between two verses. It says, "He will swallow up death forever" (Isaiah 25:8) [i.e., the reign of the Angel of Death will end], but it also says, "He who dies at a hundred years will be considered a youth" (ibid. 65:20), [so you see that people *will* die]. [The Gemara answers:] There is no contradiction: There (in 25:8) the reference is to Israel, here (in 65:20), to idol worshippers. [The Gemara asks:] What have idol worshippers to do with [the prophecy of the joyous Redemption of the Jewish people]? [The Gemara answers:] Because it says, [regarding the ultimate Redemption], "Strangers shall stand and pasture your flocks, and aliens shall be your plowmen and vine-trimmers" (ibid. 61:5).

THE LUMINARIES IN
THE WORLD TO COME

R. Chisda pointed out a contradiction between two verses. It says, "Then the moon will be ashamed, and the sun will be abashed" (ibid. 24:23), but on the other hand, it says, "And the light of the moon will become like the light of the sun, and the light of the sun will become sevenfold, like the light of the seven days" (ibid. 30:26). [The Gemara answers:] This presents no difficulty. The former refers to the World to Come [then the sun and the moon will pale into insignificance because of the lustrous radiance of the *Shechinah* (Rashi)], whereas the latter refers to the days of *Mashiach* [then the light of the moon will be like the light of the sun]. [The Gemara asks:] But Shmuel said: The only difference between this world and the world to come is that the Jewish people will no longer be dominated by other governments, [thus the potency of light of the sun and the moon will not change]. In light of Shmuel's statement, how do you explain the contradictory verses? [The Gemara answers:] Both passages refer to the World to Come; yet, there is no difficulty: The former refers to the camp of the

Shechinah; the latter, to the camp of the righteous; [for them the sun and the moon will shine with much greater brightness].

ABOUT RESURRECTION

Rava pointed out a contradiction between the following two verses. It says, "I kill and give life" (Deuteronomy 32:39). Yet it also says, "I wounded and I will heal" (ibid.). If He gives life, He surely can heal! [Then, why mention it?] But the Holy One, blessed be He, said this: The person I kill, I revive, just as I wound and heal [the same person]. [This is explained in the next paragraph.]

Our Rabbis taught: It says, "I kill and I give life." You might say that this means, I kill one person and give life to another person, in the way of the world, [where people die and people are being born]. That's why it says, "I wounded and I will heal"; just as the wounding and the healing obviously refer to the same person, [the wounded person is the one who will be healed], so do death and life refer to the same person, [the person who died will be revived]. This is a conclusive answer to those who claim that resurrection of the dead is not mentioned in the Torah. The passage can be interpreted another way: Initially, people are resurrected with the defects they had in their former life [blind, deaf, or lame], and then, "what I wounded I will heal," [i.e., after they are resurrected I will heal them of the physical defects they had in their former life].

REJOICING AND FEASTING
ON YOM TOV

(68b) We learned in a *Baraita*: Rabbi Eliezer said: On a Yom Tov a person should either eat and drink [all day], or sit and study [all day]. Rabbi Yehoshua said: Divide the day: You should devote half of the Yom Tov to eating and drinking, and half to study in the *bet midrash*. And R. Yochanan commented: Both derived it from the same verse. One verse says, "A solemn gathering dedicated to God your Lord" [i.e., studying all day] (Deuteronomy 16:8), whereas another verse says, "A solemn gathering for you" [i.e., eating and drinking all day] (Numbers 29:35). R. Eliezer says: This means, either entirely to God or entirely to yourself; while R. Yehoshua says: Divide it: Devote half to God and half to yourselves.

R. Elazar said: All agree that the Yom Tov *Shavuot* should be devoted "to yourselves" [i.e., to feasting]. What is the reason? Because it is the day on which the Torah was given, [and we show our happiness by eating and drinking]. Rabbah said: All agree that *Shabbat*, too, should be devoted "to yourselves." What is the reason? Because it says, "You shall call the *Shabbat* a 'delight'" (Isaiah 58:13). R. Yosef said: All agree that on Purim we require "for yourselves" too. Why? Because

Purim is called "Days of feasting and gladness" (Esther 9:22).

Mar the son of Ravina would fast every day of the year, except for Shavuot, Purim, and on the day before Yom Kippur. Shavuot, because it is the day on which the Torah was given; Purim, because it it is called "Days of feasting and gladness"; the day before Yom Kippur, because Chiya b. R. Difta taught: It says, "You must fast on the ninth day of the month" (Leviticus 23:14). Do we then fast on the ninth? Of course, we fast on the tenth! [Yom Kippur is on the tenth of Tishrei.] But this verse comes to tell you: whoever eats and drinks on the ninth of Tishrei, the Torah considers it as if he had fasted both on the ninth and the tenth.

On Shavuot R. Yosef used to order: Prepare me a third-born calf [i.e., the third young calved by its mother, which is considered exceptionally tender]. He explained: If not for this day [of Shavuot, and the Torah, which was given on it], how many Yosefs are there in the market! [I.e., If I had not studied the Torah and gained prominence as a Torah scholar I would be just another "Joe" in the street.]

R. Sheshet used to review all his studies every thirty days, and he used to stand and lean on the side of the doorway and exclaim, "Rejoice, my soul, Rejoice, my soul, it is for your benefit that I have studied the Torah, it is for your benefit that I have studied the Mishnah" [in other words, he studied to benefit his soul]. [The Gemara asks:] But this is not so; [the soul is not the only one to benefit from Torah study], for R. Elazar said: If not for the Torah, heaven and earth would not remain in existence, for it says, "If not for My covenant by day and by night [i.e., the Torah, which must be studied "by day and by night"], I would not have established the laws of heaven and earth" (Jeremiah 33:25). [Thus, the entire universe endures only because of Torah study. Why then did R. Sheshet think only of his own soul?] [The Gemara answers:] Initially, when a person studies he does so with himself in mind.

A LESSON IN PROPER CONDUCT

(86b) R. Huna the son of R. Natan visited the home of R. Nachman b. Yitzchak. "What is your name?" they asked him. "Rav Huna," he replied, [mentioning his title of "Rav"]. "Would you please have a seat on the couch," they said, and he sat down. Then they offered him a glass of wine, which he accepted [without waiting to be asked a second time], but he drank it in two times, without turning his face away. They asked him, "What is the reason that you called yourself *Rav* Huna?" He replied, "That is my name." [People called me *Rav* Huna since childhood, thus Rav is part of my name and not a title (Rashi).] "When we asked you to take a seat on the couch, why did you sit down immediately?" [The couch was reserved for prominent

guests. They implied that, out of modesty, he should have sat down on the floor or on a chair.] He answered, "We have a rule: You should do whatever your host asks you to do." "When you were offered a glass of wine, why did you accept it at the first invitation?" Replied Rav Huna, "You may turn down an unimportant person, but you should not turn down a great man." "Why did you drink it in two times?" He replied, "Because we learned: He who drinks his cup in one draft is a glutton; in two drafts, acts properly; in three drafts, shows arrogance. "Why didn't you turn your face away [as a sign of humility]?" He answered, "We learned in the Mishnah: A bride turns her face away [but not a man]."

R. Yishmael son of R. Yose visited the home of R. Shimon b. R. Yose b. Lakunia. They offered him a cup of wine, which he accepted at the first invitation and drank in one gulp. So they said to him, "Don't you hold that he who drinks his cup in one gulp is a glutton?" He replied, "This does not apply when your cup is small, your wine sweet, and my stomach wide" [R. Yishmael was very heavy.][46]

THE TORAH PROTECTS
THE JEWISH PEOPLE

(87a) [The Gemara wants to derive from scriptural verses that a newly married woman is torn between wanting to spend the first Yom Tov after her wedding in her father's house or staying home with her husband.] It says, "So I became in his eyes as one who finds favor (*shalom*)" (Song of Songs 8:10), which R. Yochanan interpreted: Like a bride who was found perfect (*sheleimah*) in her father-in-law's home,[47] and she is eager to tell her parents how much she is appreciated. As it says, "And in that day [of the Redemption], says God, you [Israel] will call Me *Ishi* [my Husband], and no longer will you call Me *Baali* [my Master]" (Hosea 2:18). [Both *ishi* and *baali* denote "my husband," but *ishi* suggests greater love than *baali*.] R. Yochanan said: That means: She will be like a bride in her father-in-law's house [i.e., she loves her husband, and she is happy there, hence *ishi*], and not like a bride in her father's house [where she does not feel secure and at ease].

[The Gemara now cites other verses that are expounded by R. Yochanan.] It says, "We have a little sister whose breasts are not yet formed" (Song of Songs 8:8). [Breasts are the source of nourishment. Since our spiritual nourishment is the Torah, breasts symbolize the sources of Torah, i.e., yeshivahs and their teachers.] R. Yochanan said: [The little sister without breasts] refers to the country of Elam,[48] where the people learned Torah but where Torah was not taught [there were no great yeshivahs in Elam].

It says, "I am a wall, my breasts are like its towers" (ibid. 10). R. Yochanan expounded: "I am a wall" alludes to the Torah [that protects Israel]; "and my breasts are like its towers" refers to Torah scholars. Rava interpreted the passage: "I am a wall" stands for the community of Israel; "and my breasts are like its towers" represents the synagogues and the houses of study [that insure the continued existence of Torah].

IN PRAISE OF ISRAEL'S YOUNG MEN AND WOMEN

R. Zutra b. Tuvya said in Rav's name: What is the meaning of the verse, "For our sons are like saplings well-tended in their youth, our daughters are like cornerstones trimmed to give shape to a palace" (Psalms 144:12). "For our sons are like saplings" alludes to the young men of Israel who have not tasted the taste of a sin. "Our daughters are like cornerstones" suggests the unmarried women of Israel who protect their openings for their future husbands. This is supported by another verse, "They will be filled like a dashing bowl [the bowl that is used to catch the blood of the sacrifice], like the corners of the altar" (Zechariah 9:15) [meaning, even though they are filled with desire they do not become promiscuous, but reserve themselves for their future husbands]. Or, if you prefer, you can draw a parallel from the following passages, "Our storehouses are full, supplying produce of all kinds," [an allusion to menstrual blood; meaning that when the women are menstruating they withhold themselves from their husbands]. And it says,"they are trimmed to give shape to a palace" (ibid. 13,12), which means that both the young men and the young women of Israel are praised as if the *Bet Hamikdash* had been built in their time.

THE PROPHET HOSEA IS ADMONISHED

[The Gemara cites another verse that is expounded by R. Yochanan.] It says, "The word of God came to Hosea son of Beeri, in the reigns of Kings Uzziah, Jotham, Ahaz, and Hezekiah of Judah" (Hosea 1:1). During one period of time, four prophets prophesied, and the greatest of the four was Hosea. For it says, "When God first spoke to Hosea" (ibid. 2), [expounded to mean: God spoke first and foremost to Hosea]. [The Gemara asks:] Did God then speak first to Hosea? [Was he then the first prophet?] After all, there were many prophets from Moses until Hosea. Said R. Yochanan: He was the first of four prophets who prophesied in that era, namely: Hosea, Isaiah, Amos, and Micah. [Now, this is what happened at Hosea's first prophecy:] The Holy One, blessed be He, said to Hosea, "Your children have sinned [and they deserve to be punished]."

Hosea should have answered, "They are Your children! They are the children of Your favored ones, the children of Abraham, Isaac, and Jacob. [Even though they have sinned,] show them Your mercy anyway." Not enough that Hosea did not say this, but he said to God, "Master of the universe! The whole world belongs to You. So, exchange them for another nation." Said the Holy One, blessed be He, "What shall I do with this old man? I will tell him, 'Go and marry a wife who is a harlot and have children with her who may well have been born from an adulterous relationship.' Then I will tell him, 'Send her away!' [Now I'll see] whether Hosea will be able to send her away. [I am sure that he will not send away his wife and children], any more than I will send Israel away." For it says, "God said to Hosea, 'Go, take for yourself a wife who is a harlot, and you will have children born of harlotry'" (Hosea 1:2). And it says, "So he went and married Gomer daughter of Divlaim" (ibid. 3).

[The Gemara expounds:] "Gomer," Rav said: That name suggests that all satisfied their lusts [*gomerim*] on her; (87b) "the daughter of Divlaim," this means that she was a woman with a bad reputation [*dibbah*] and the daughter of a woman with a bad reputation [*dibbah*]. Shmuel said: [*Divlaim* means:] that she was as sweet in everyone's mouth as a cake of figs [*deveilah*]. R. Yochanan said: [It means:] that everyone pushed at her like you push into a soft cake of figs. Another interpretation is: "Gomer": Rav Yehudah said: The [name Gomer hints at the fact that the enemies] tried to destroy [*ligmor*] all of the wealth of Israel in her days. R. Yochanan said: The enemies did indeed rob Israel, and they finished [*gameru*] their resources [until there was nothing left]. For it says, "For the king of Aram destroyed their wealth and trampled them like the dust that is left after threshing, [in the days of King Jehoahaz of Israel]" (2 Kings 13:7).

[Now the Gemara goes back to Hosea who had been commanded to marry the harlot Gomer, the daughter of Divlaim.] It says, "She became pregnant and gave birth to a son, and God instructed Hosea, 'Name him Jezreel; for in a little while I will remember the blood of Jezreel on the house of Jehu, and I will bring an end to the kingdom of the house of Israel." [Jezreel was the name of a valley in Eretz Yisrael, and Jehu was the king who was commanded through a prophet to kill the evil king Ahab. Jehu killed Ahab, but then emulated Ahab's sinful ways. Therefore, Jehu was not considered innocent of having murdered Ahab. Jehu himself was not punished, but Hosea prophesied that Jehu's grandson, who was as wicked as his grandfather, would be killed for the sin of Jehu and for what happened in the valley of Jezreel where Jehu killed Ahab.[49]

The name Jezreel meaning, "God will plant the Jewish people among the nations" alludes to the future exile. [The text continues], [Gomer] became pregnant again and gave birth to a daughter. God said to Hosea, 'Call her Lo-ruchamah, [meaning, "she will not have received compassion"]; I will no longer have pity on the house of Israel, that I will in any way forgive them' . . . She became pregnant again and gave birth to a son. And God said, 'Call him Lo-ammi ["not My people"] for you are not My people, and I will not be yours'" (Hosea 1:3–6,8–9).

After she gave birth to the two sons and one daughter, the Holy One, blessed be He, said to Hosea, "Shouldn't you have learned a lesson from your teacher Moses, for as soon as I spoke to him he separated himself from his wife, so you too, separate yourself from your wife." "Master of the universe," Hosea pleaded, "I have children from her, and I cannot throw her out of my house, and I cannot divorce her." Replied the Holy One, blessed be He, "Then if you, whose wife is a harlot and your children are the children of lewdness, and you don't even know if they are your children or if they are the children of another father, yet you cannot bear to part from her and the children; then Israel who are My children, the children of My tested ones, the children of Abraham, Isaac, and Jacob, [and the Jewish people is] one of the four possessions that I have acquired in this world (the Torah is one possession, for it says, 'God acquired me as the beginning of His way' (Proverbs 8:22); Heaven and earth is one possession, for it says, 'God the Most High, Possessor of Heaven and earth" (Genesis 14:19); the *Bet Hamikdash* is one possession, for it says, 'This mountain [i.e., the *Bet Hamikdash*] which His right hand had acquired' (Psalms 78:54); Israel is one possession, for it says, 'The people You have acquired' (Exodus 15:16).) Yet you say, 'Exchange them for a different people!'"

As soon as Hosea realized that he had sinned, he stood up to plead for mercy for himself. Said the Holy One, blessed be He, to him, "Instead of pleading for mercy for yourself, ask for compassion for the Jewish people, against whom I decreed three decrees because of you [i.e., (1) Jezreel, meaning exile; (2) Lo-ruchamah, meaning no compassion; (3) Lo-ammi, meaning 'they are not My people any more']." Thereupon, Hosea stood up to ask for mercy, and God annulled the decrees. And He began to bless them, as it says, "The number of the people of Israel will be like the sands of the sea . . . and instead of being told, "You are not My people," they will be called Children-of-the-Living-God. And the people of Judah and the people of Israel will assemble together . . . And I will sow her [i.e., the Jewish people] in the land as My own, and I will have compassion on the nation that was once called Lo-ruchamah, and I will say to Lo-ammi, "you are My people."

THE EVIL KING JEROBOAM'S GOOD DEED

R. Yochanan said: Lordship over many people shortens the lives of those who hold such positions of authority, for there is not a single prophet who did not outlive four kings, as it says, "The prophecy of Isaiah the son of Amoz, who prophesied concerning Judah and Jerusalem, in the days of Kings Uzziah, Jotham, Ahaz, and Hezekiah, kings of Judah" (Isaiah 1:1).

R. Yochanan said: How did [the evil] Jeroboam the son of Joash king of Israel merit to be counted together with the [righteous] kings of Judah? Because he refused to accept slander against Amos. How do we know that he is mentioned [along with the four kings]? Because it says, "The word of God came to Hosea son of Beeri, in the reigns of Kings Uzziah, Jotham, Ahaz, and Hezekiah of Judah, and in the reign of King Jeroboam son of Joash of Israel" (Hosea 1:1). And from where do we know that he refused to accept slander? Because it says, "Amaziah, the [idolatrous] priest of Bethel, [an idolatrous shrine], sent this message to King Jeroboam of Israel: "Amos is conspiring against you . . . for this is what Amos said, 'Jeroboam shall die by the sword . . .'" (ibid. 11). But Jeroboam replied to Amaziah, "Heaven forbid! That righteous man never said such a thing! And if he did say such a thing, what can I do to him! The *Shechinah* told him." [He would not have said such a thing to overthrow me. But if God told him, who am I to argue!]

Rabbi Elazar said: Even when the Holy One, blessed be He, is angry, He remembers His compassion, for it says, "I will no longer continue to have compassion on the house of Israel" (Amos 1:6). [The verse can be broken into two parts: "I will no longer continue [to be angry]," but, "I will have compassion on the house of Israel" (Rif).] R. Yose son of R. Chanina said: You can derive it from the end of this verse, "That I should in any way pardon them" (ibid.). [God hints that He will forgive them.]

R. Elazar also said: The only reason that the Holy One, blessed be He, sent the Jewish people into exile among the nations is so that converts would join them, as it says, "I will plant them for Me in the earth" (Hosea 2:25). Does a man plant a *se'ah* of good seeds unless he intends to harvest many *kur* of grain? [So, too, if God plants the Jewish people among the nations, it is because he wants to get something very precious in return: converts who will come under the wings of the *Shechinah*.] R. Yochanan said: It is from here [that we know that God wants us to bring in converts]: "I will have compassion on *Lo Ruchamah* [on her that has not obtained compassion]" (ibid.). [Meaning, on the nations who did not accept the Torah. God planted the Jewish people among the nations so that He can have compassion on the converts. The verse concludes: "I will say to those who are not My people; you are My people."]

R. Yochanan said in the name of R. Shimon b. Yochai: What is the meaning of the verse, "Do not slander a slave to his master lest he curse you, and you incur guilt" (Proverbs 30:10)? And in the next verse it says, "There is a breed of men that curses their fathers and do not bless their mother" (ibid. 11). [The Gemara asks: What is the connection between the two verses?] Because they curse their father and do not bless their mother, that's why you should not slander a slave? [The Gemara answers: It means:] Even if the slaves are a breed that curse their father and do not bless their mother, you still should not slander them. From where do we know this? From Hosea [who was admonished for slandering Israel, even though they had indeed sinned; see section above].

WHY WERE THE JEWS EXILED TO BABYLONIA?

R. Chiya taught: What is the meaning of the verse, "God understands the way to it; He knows its source" (Job 28:23)? The Holy One, blessed be He, knows that the Jewish people are unable to endure the cruel decrees of Edom [i.e., Rome], that's why He sent them into exile to Babylonia. R. Elazar said: The only reason the Holy One, blessed be He, exiled the Jewish people to Babylonia is because it is as deep as *sheol* [so that He can redeem them quickly], as He promised, "From *Sheol* [the nether world] itself I will save them, redeem them from death" (Hosea 13:14). R. Chanina said: Because the Babylonian language is similar to the language of the Torah, [thus they will not forget the Torah]. R. Yochanan said: [God exiled them to Babylonia,] because He thereby sent them back to their mother's house. [Abraham was born in Ur Kasdim,[50] Ur of the Chaldeans, Mesopotamia.] You can compare it to a man who became angry with his wife. Where does he send her? To her mother's house.

And that is in line with the saying of R. Alexandri, who said: Three returned to their original home, namely: Israel, Egypt's wealth, and the writing of the Tablets. Israel, as we have said. Egypt's wealth, [which the Israelites took with them at the Exodus[51]], for it says, "In the fifth year of King Rehoboam, King Shishak of Egypt marched against Jerusalem and carried off the treasures of the House of God and the treasures of the royal palace" (1 Kings 14:25,26). The writing of the Tablets, for it says, "[Moses said:] I broke them before your eyes" (Deuteronomy 9:16), ["before your eyes" suggests that they saw something miraculous happen, to which all eyes are turned]. [What did they see?] We learned: The Tablets were broken, but the letters flew upward toward Heaven. Ulla said: [They were exiled to Babylonia] so that they should be able to eat an abundance of (88a) dates [which grow there in profusion] and engross themselves in Torah study.

Ulla visited Pumbedita [a city in Babylonia, seat of a famous yeshivah]. When they offered him a basket [*tirama*] of dates he asked, "How many of those can be had for a *zuz*?" "Three for a *zuz*," they told him. "What!" he exclaimed, "a basketful of honey can be bought for one *zuz*, yet they Babylonians do not engage in Torah study!" [With food so affordable, they surely have plenty of time to study.] At night, [after eating too many dates], he had an upset stomach. "A basketful of deadly poison for one *zuz* in Babylonia," he moaned, "and yet the Babylonians study Torah!" [His discomfort made him see the Babylonians in a more positive light.]

THE HOUSE OF THE GOD OF JACOB

R. Elazar said: What is the meaning of the verse, "And many nations shall go and shall say, 'Come, let us go up to the Mountain of God, to the House of the God of Jacob'" (Micah 4:2). It says, "The God of *Jacob*," but not the God of Abraham and Isaac? The meaning is: [The nations will perceive the *Bet Hamikdash*], not as the House of the God of Abraham, who described the site of the *Bet Hamikdash* with the word "mountain," for it says, "On God's *Mountain* He will be seen" (Genesis 22:15). [They will perceive it] not as the House of the God of Isaac, who described that site as a "field," for it says, "And Isaac went out to meditate in the *field* toward evening" (ibid. 24:63). But they perceive the *Bet Hamikdash* as the House of the God of Jacob, who described the site of the *Bet Hamikdash* in terms of "house." For it says, "He named the place [of the Holy of Holies] *Beth El* [the House of God]" (Genesis 28:19). [Abraham's mountain, Isaac's field, and Jacob's house all refer to the Temple Mount. They symbolize the first, second, and future *Bet Hamikdash*, which will be the permanent and everlasting House of God.]

R. Yochanan said: The day of the ingathering of the exiles is as important a day as the day when heaven and earth were created. For it says, "The people of Judah and the people of Israel shall assemble together and appoint one head over them, and they will go up out of the land [of their exile], for marvelous shall be the *day* of Jezreel" (Hosea 2:2),[52] and it says, "It was evening and it was morning, one *day*" (Genesis 1:5). [Since the word "day" occurs in both verses, both events may be equated.]

WHAT IS THE SIZE OF THE EARTH?

(93b) From the crack of dawn until sunrise takes as long as a five-mile walk.[53] From where do we know this? Because it says, "As the dawn was breaking, [on the day of the destruction of Sodom], the two angels rushed Lot, saying . . ." (Genesis 19:15). [Thereupon Lot fled Sodom and escaped to Tzoar], and it says, "The sun had risen by the time Lot arrived in Tzoar" (ibid. 23). Now, R. Chanina said: I myself saw that place [Tzoar], and it is five miles [from Sodom].

(94a) Rava said: The length of the world [i.e., the distance the sun travels during daytime] is 6,000 *parsangs* [i.e., 24,000 miles], and the thickness of the heaven [*rakia*][54] is 1,000 *parsangs* [i.e., 4,000 miles]; the first one of these statements [i.e. the length of the world] is a tradition, while the other [i.e., the thickness of *rakia*] is based on calculation.

An objection was raised: Egypt was four hundred *parsangs* square. Now Egypt is one-sixtieth of Kush [Ethiopia], and Kush is one-sixtieth of the world [so the world is 60x60x400x400 *parsangs*, which is much more than the 6000 *parsangs* that Rava mentioned], and the world is one-sixtieth of the Garden, and the Garden is one-sixtieth of Eden, and Eden is one-sixtieth of Gehinnom. Thus the whole world is like a small pot cover on Gehinnom. Rava's statement [that the expanse of the world is 6,000 *parsangs*] is hereby refuted.

Come and hear [another proof]: Tanna debei Eliyahu taught: R. Natan said: The entire inhabited portion of the world is situated under one star. You can tell that this is so, because a person looks at a star, and when he goes toward the east it is still right above him, and when he goes to the four corners of the world that star is still right above him. So you see that the entire inhabited part of the world is situated under one star. This is also a refutation of Rava's statement. [If the entire world is under one star, and there are countless stars in the sky, then the rest of the world must be many time greater than the inhabited part; much greater than 6,000 *parsangs*, as Rava claims.]

IS THE ZODIAC STATIONARY OR MOVING?

Come and hear [another proof]: The constellation of Taurus is in the north, and Scorpio is in the south; and the entire inhabited part of the world lies between Taurus and Scorpio. Now, it takes the sun only one hour of the day to traverse the entire inhabited part of the world. You can tell that this is so, because at the fifth hour of the day [at 11 a.m.] the sun is still in the east, whereas at the seventh hour of the day [at 1 p.m.] the sun is already in the west. From half of the sixth hour [11:30 a.m.] until half of the seventh hour [12:30 p.m.] that is when the sun is directly above all people. [We see the sun overhead only one hour of the day; hence, the uninhabited parts of the world [the oceans, the mountains, and deserts] are eleven times as great as the inhabited part [certainly much larger than Rava's 6,000 *parsangs*]. This disproves Rava's assertion.

(94b) We learned in a *Baraita*: The Sages of Israel contend: the *galgal* [the wheel of the Zodiac that surrounds the world and on which the constellations are fixed] does not move, while the constellations move along this stationary wheel. [Each constellation pushes the sun to the next constellation, and then returns to its place on the Zodiac (Rashi).] The Sages of the nations maintain: The *galgal* [wheel of the Zodiac] revolves, and the constellations are fixed [on the *galgal* and move as an integral part of the *galgal*]. Rebbi said: We can prove that what they say is incorrect, for we never find Taurus in the south or Scorpio in the north. [And if, as they maintain, the Zodiac moves and the constellations move along with the Zodiac, the constellations would circle the earth, and sometimes Taurus would be in the north and sometimes in the south. But according to the Sages of Israel, who say that the Zodiac is fixed, and the constellations move only a short distance and then return to their original posi-

tions, Taurus is always in the north and Scorpio always in the south.]

R. Acha b. Yaakov raised an objection: Perhaps it is like the metal pivot in the hole of a millstone or like the bolt in the hinge of a door? [The pivot or bolt can be rotated without moving the millstone or the door, so there are two things that can rotate independently. In the same way, there are two *galgalim*, one in which the constellations are embedded and which does not move at all, and a second *galgal*, inside or outside this stationary *galgal*, that moves the sun along (Rashi).]

THE ORBIT OF THE SUN

The Sages of Israel assert: During the day, the sun travels below the *rakia*, and at night it moves above the *rakia*. [The *rakia* is the expanse that separates the sun from the earth.] The Sages of the nations of the world say: During the day the sun travels below the *rakia*, and at night it moves below the earth, [that's why it illuminates the inhabited part of the world]. Said Rabbi: Their view seems to be more correct than ours, because the [underground] wells are cold by day and warm at night. [At night, when the sun is below the earth, it heats the underground wells.]

We learned: R. Natan said: In the summer the sun travels high in the sky, therefore the whole world is hot while the wells are cold [the underground sources of the wells are not warmed by the sun]. In the winter the sun travels near the bottom of the sides of the sky. Therefore the whole world is cold while the wells are hot, [because the sun heats up the lower parts of the earth where the springs are].

We learned in a *Baraita*: The sun travels along four paths: During Nisan, Iyar, and Sivan [the months of spring], it travels over the mountains in order to melt the snow; in Tammuz, Av, and Elul [the summer months], over the inhabited world, to ripen the fruits; in Tishri, Marcheshvan, and Kislev [the autumn months], over the seas, to dry up the swollen rivers; in Tevet, Shevat, and Adar [the winter months], over the wilderness, so as not to dry up the seeds in the ground.

THE SON OF HOLY ONES

(104a) [At the departure of *Shabbat* and the onset of the work week we recite *Havdalah*, to be mindful of the differences between sanctity and secularity. In the *berachah* we mention several points of distinction: "between holy and secular, between light and darkness, between Israel and the nations, between the seventh day and the six days of labor." The Gemara continues:]

R. Yochanan said: [When reciting *Havdalah*], the son of holy ones [a Tanna] recited only one [point of distinction, namely, "Who separates between holy and secular"], but the people are accustomed to recite three [points of distinction]. [The Gemara asks:] Who is the son of holy ones? [The Gemara answers:] R. Menachem

b. Simai. And why did they call him the son of holy ones? Because he never looked at the figure on a coin. [He considered it a violation of the second Commandment, "Do not make any carved image or picture . . ."]

BRING CHEER ON YOM TOV

(109a) Our Rabbis taught in a *Baraita*: A person is required to bring joy to his children and his household on Yom Tov, for it says, "You shall rejoice on your festival along with your son and your daughter . . ." (Deuteronomy 16:14). [The Gemara asks:] With what does he bring them joy? [The Gemara answers:] With wine. R. Yehudah said: Men with what is appropriate for them, and women with what is appropriate for them. [The Gemara explains:] "Men with what is appropriate for them": with wine. And what is appropriate for women? R. Yosef said: In Babylonia, they would buy for their wives colorful garments; in Eretz Yisrael, ironed linen garments.

We learned in a *Baraita*: R. Yehudah b. Beteira said: When the *Bet Hamikdash* was standing there could be no rejoicing except with meat, as it says, "You shall also sacrifice peace offerings and eat there, rejoicing before God your Lord" (ibid. 27:7). But now that the *Bet Hamikdash* is no longer standing, there is no rejoicing except with wine, as it says, "Wine cheers the hearts of men" (Psalms 104:15).

R. AKIVA'S SEVEN INSTRUCTIONS TO HIS SON

(112a) Our Rabbis taught: Seven things R. Akiva commanded his son R. Yehoshua: My son, you should not sit and study in a conspicuous place in town [because many people pass there, and they will disturb you and disrupt your studies]. You should not live in a city whose municipal leaders are Torah scholars. [They will be busy studying the Torah, and they will not take care of the needs of the city.] You should not enter your own house suddenly [without knocking on the door first], and you certainly should not barge into your neighbor's house unannounced. You should not go barefoot [for this is not becoming for a Torah scholar]. Get up early in the morning and eat breakfast right away; in the summer because of the heat, and in the winter because of the cold. Treat your *Shabbat* like a weekday rather than be dependent on other people. And try to associate with a person on whom fortune is smiling. R. Papa said: But you should not buy from such a person or sell to him [since he has good luck he will outwit you and get the better of you], but you should go into partnership with him, [so that you and he will share in the same good luck]. But now that R. Shmuel b. Yitzchak has said: What is the meaning of the verse, "You have blessed his efforts" (Job 1:10)? Whoever took a small coin from Job was blessed; now, even to buy from or sell to a successful person is a good thing.

FIVE PIECES OF ADVICE BY R. AKIVA

There were five things that R. Akiva commanded R. Shimon b. Yochai, when he [R. Akiva] was in prison.[55] R. Shimon b. Yochai said to him, "Please teach me Torah." "I will not teach you," he replied. [He was afraid that R. Shimon would be imprisoned.] Said R. Shimon b. Yochai, "If you won't teach me Torah, I'll tell my father Yochai, and he will hand you over to the government."[56] "My son," replied R. Akiva, "even more than the calf wants to suck milk from the cow does the cow want to suckle its calf," [meaning, I want to teach you Torah more than you want to study. But I am afraid for your life]. Said R. Shimon b. Yochai, "Who is in danger here? Surely the calf is in danger!" [It is my life, and I am prepared to take the risk. So please teach me.]

Said R. Akiva, ["All right, I'll teach you. First:] If you wish to be strangled, hang on a large tree." [Meaning, if you have a question concerning a life-and-death situation, consult a great person.] [Second:] "When you teach your son, teach him from a corrected scroll." [The Gemara asks:] What does that mean? Said Rava, others say, R. Mesharshiya: If a child is learning new material, make sure that he learns from a corrected text, because once an error has taken hold, it becomes ingrained in the mind. [Third:] "Do not cook in a pot in which your neighbor has cooked." [The Gemara asks:] What does this allude to? [The Gemara answers:] Do not marry a divorced woman when her husband is still alive. For a Rabbi said: If a divorced man marries a divorced woman, there are four minds in the bed. [Each one is thinking about the former spouse.]

Or, if you prefer, say, that it refers even to a widow, for (112b) not all fingers are alike, [a euphemistic reference to the male organ; she will compare her present husband to her former husband, and disdain her present husband (Rashi)]. [Fourth:] If you want to have a mitzvah and also make a profitable investment, then you should lend money without interest on a field and make a deal that you receive some of its produce as partial repayment. [Fifth:] If you want to have a mitzvah and also a pure body, then marry a wife, [then you will have a pure body], and then you will have children, [and thereby you fulfill the mitzvah of "be fruitful and multiply"].

FOUR INSTRUCTIONS BY RABBEINU HAKADOSH[57]

Rabbeinu Hakadosh gave his children the following four instructions: [First:] Do not live in the city of Shachantziv because they are scoffers and will influence you to become scoffers [and that will lead you away from the Torah]. [Second:] Do not sit on the bed of an Aramaean woman. Some say, [this means:] Do not go to sleep without saying the *Shema* [as an Aramean woman does]. Others explain: Do not marry a convert, [since she often retains emotional ties to her natural relatives, and this can make for an unhappy marriage]. Others explain "Aramaean" literally, because of an incident that happened to R. Papa. [R. Papa went to an Aramaen woman to pay her the money he owed her. She asked him to sit down on a bed. He refused to sit down unless she showed him what was underneath the bed. She picked up the bed, and there was a dead child. She had plotted to have R. Papa sit down on the bed and then accuse him of crushing and killing the child.[58]] [Third:] Do not try to evade paying taxes, because if you are caught, they will take from you everything you own. [Fourth:] Do not stand before an ox when he comes up from the pasture, because Satan is dancing between his horns, [meaning, at that time the ox is very wild and dangerous]. R. Shmuel said: This refers to a black ox and in the month of Nisan [in the spring when things begin to grow the ox acts frenzied]. R. Oshaia learned: You should keep a distance of fifty cubits from an ox that is a *tam* [i.e., an ox that has not yet gored three times], and keep away as far as you can see from an ox that is a *mu'ad* [i.e., an ox that has gored three times]. A Tanna taught in R. Meir's name: Even when the ox's head is in the feeding bag, climb up to the roof and throw away the ladder from under you.

THREE INSTRUCTIONS
BY R. YISHMAEL
R. Yishmael b. R. Yose gave the following three instructions to Rebbi [Yehudah Hanasi]: [First:] Do not cause a blemish to yourself. What does that mean? Don't engage in a lawsuit with three people, because one will be your opponent and the other two will testify against you [in a fraudulent conspiracy]. [Second:] Don't negotiate to buy something when you don't have the money to buy the article. [Third:] Be meticulous in the observance of the laws of family purity.

SOUND BUSINESS ADVICE
(113a) Our Rabbis taught: There are three that you should not provoke, namely, a young gentile, a little snake, and a young student. Why? Because their kingdom is behind their ears [meaning, they will grow up and take revenge].

Rav said to his son Aivu: I have worked very hard trying to teach you Torah, but I have not been successful. So come and let me teach you some worldly wisdom: Sell what you have bought while the sand is still fresh on your feet, [meaning, as soon as you return from a buying trip, sell the goods you bought so that you can buy more goods (Rashi)]. Anything you sold, [if you find that the price has gone up] you may regret that you sold it too early, except for wine; sell it and never regret that you sold it, [because it could have turned to vinegar if you had held on to it]. First

open your purse, and then open your sacks. [Collect the money before you deliver the merchandise.] Better a *kav* [a small measure] from the ground than a *kur* [a large measure] from the roof. [Better a small profit close to home than to travel a great distance to make a large profit.] When the dates are in your container, run to the brewer [who makes beer out of them, otherwise you'll eat them and you won't have any beer]. How much should you keep at home before you go to the brewery? Up to three *se'ah*. R. Papa said: If I were not a beer brewer I would not have become wealthy. Others say, R. Chisda said: If I were not a beer brewer I would not have become wealthy. Why is a beer brewer called *sudna*? Said R. Chisda: *Sod na'eh*, "it is a pleasant secret." A brewery makes you rich, and you can practice kindness and charity through it. [Dates are inexpensive, so you can give them away to the needy.]

R. Papa said: Every bill has to be collected, [and collecting is a troublesome thing]. Each time you extend credit it is doubtful whether you will be paid, and when you are paid it is bad money [you get it in small installments, so that you cannot use it for other business].

WISE COUNSEL
R. Yochanan said three things in the name of the people of Jerusalem: When you go out into battle, don't be in the vanguard, but be among the last, so that you should be the first to come home. Make your *Shabbat* like a weekday, rather than rely on others for charity. Associate with a person on whom fortune is smiling.

R. Yehoshua b. Levi said three things in the name of the people of Jerusalem: Do not do private things in a conspicuous place like on a roof, because of an incident that happened, [i.e., the episode of David and Bathsheba, where David saw Bathsheba on her roof (2 Samuel 11:2)]. If your daughter has matured [if you can find no other match], free your slave and give him to her. And beware of your wife with her first son-in-law. What is the danger? Because she might sin with him. R. Kahana said: Because she might squander your money to shower him with gifts. [The Gemara says:] Both suspicions are valid.

VARIOUS CATEGORIES
OF PEOPLE
R. Yochanan said: There are three categories of people who will inherit the World to Come, namely: a person who lives in Eretz Yisrael, a person who raises his children to the study of Torah, and someone who recites *Havdalah* over wine on *Motza'ei Shabbat*. [The Gemara asks:] What exactly are you referring to? [The Gemara answers:] To a person who leaves over from the wine of *Kiddush* for the wine of *Havdalah*. [If he made *Kiddush* and has some wine left, he should not drink it up but should save it for *Havdalah*.]

R. Yochanan said: There are three kinds of people whose praise the Holy One, blessed be He, proclaims every day: A bachelor who lives in a large city and does not yield to the temptations of immorality. A poor man who returns a lost article to its owner, and a wealthy person who tithes his produce without publicity.

R. Safra was a bachelor who lived in a large city. (113b) A certain *amora* repeated this saying of R. Yochanan in the presence of Rava and R. Safra. [When R. Safra heard it] his face lit up. Said Rava to R. Safra: The saying does not refer to a person like you, but rather to people like R. Chanina and R. Oshaia who were shoemakers in Eretz Yisrael and sat [and repaired shoes] in the marketplace that was swarming with harlots. [The two Rabbis] made shoes for these harlots, and these women would enter their shop. The harlots would look at the Rabbis, but they would not lift their eyes to look at the harlots. When these women would take an oath they used the following formula, "We swear by the life of the holy Rabbis of Eretz Yisrael."

There are three kinds of people whom the Holy One, blessed be He, loves, namely: A person who does not fly into a rage, a person who does not become drunk, and a person who does not bear a grudge against anyone.

There are three kinds of people whom the Holy One, blessed be He, hates, namely: A person who speaks one thing with his mouth but thinks another thing in his heart; a person who knows testimony that would benefit his neighbor but does not testify for him; and a person who sees something indecent that his neighbor did, and he testifies against him alone. [What is that all about?] Like the incident where a certain Tuvyah sinned, and Zigud alone came [without a second witness] and testified against him before R. Papa. Thereupon R. Papa ordered that Zigud [the witness] be given lashes. Exclaimed Zigud, "What! Tuvyah sinned, and Zigud should get lashes!" Said R. Papa, "Yes, [you deserve to be punished.] Because it says, 'A single witness must not testify against a person' (Deuteronomy 19:15), yet you have testified against Tuvyah alone. [Your testimony is worthless], you merely gave Tuvyah a bad reputation, [and for that you deserve lashes]."

Our Rabbis learned: There are three kinds of people whose life is no life: people who are overly compassionate, people who are quick-tempered, and people who are squeamish. R. Yosef remarked, "All these characteristics are found in me."

Our Rabbis taught: There are three groups that love one another, namely: converts, slaves, and ravens. There are four types that are insufferable: a poor man who is conceited, a wealthy person who owes money and denies his liability, an old man who engages in immorality, and a communal leader who acts highhandedly. Some say: Also a person who divorces his wife once and a second time, and then marries her for a third time. [The Gemara asks:] And first Tanna? [Why doesn't he include the last case?] [The Gemara answers:] It may be that the *ketubah* [marriage settlement, the amount he has to pay upon divorce] is large [and he cannot come up with the money, so that he is forced to remarry her], or he has children from this wife, and he cannot remain divorced from her [because he has no one to take care of his children].

CANAAN'S FIVE BEHESTS

Canaan commanded five things to his sons: Love one another, love robbery, love immorality, hate your masters, and don't ever speak the truth. Six things were said about the horse: it loves promiscuity, it loves battle, it has a proud spirit, it despises sleep, it eats a great deal, and it excretes little. Some say: It also tries to kill its master in battle.

There are seven people who are banned by Heaven, namely: A Jew who has no wife; a person who has a wife but chooses to have no children; a person who has children but does not bring them up to study Torah; a person who does not put *tefillin* on his head and on his arm, who does not wear *tzitzit* on his garment and has no *mezuzah* on his door, and a person who does not wear shoes. Others say: Also a person who never partakes of a meal in honor of a mitzvah [particularly, a *se'udah* of a *brit milah* (*Tosafot* at the top of 114a)].

WHO COMPOSED THE *HALLEL*?[59]

(117a) Rav Yehudah said in Shmuel's name: The *Shirah* [the Song at the Sea (Exodus 15)] in the Torah was sung by Moses and Israel when they came out of the Red Sea. [The Gemara asks:] And who recited the *Hallel* [which we say on Yom Tov and *Rosh Chodesh*]? [The Gemara answers:] The prophets of the Jewish people ordained that the *Hallel* should be recited on every special occasion [like Yom Tov], and on times of national deliverance from peril, in gratitude for their redemption.

We learned in a *Baraita*: R. Meir used to say: All the praises of the Book of Psalms were composed by David. For it says, "The end [*kalu*] of the prayers of David son of Jesse" (Psalms 72:20). Don't read *kalu* but *kol eilu* ["all these" are the prayers of David]. [The Gemara asks:] The *Hallel* [that consists of Psalms 113–118], who composed that? R. Yose said: My son Elazar holds that Moses and Israel said it when they came out of the Red Sea, but his colleagues disagree with him. They contend that David composed the *Hallel*. But I prefer my son's opinion to that of his colleagues: Is it then possible that [in all the generations from the Exodus until King David's time] the Jewish people slaughtered their Pesach sacrifice and took their *lulav* bundles [on Sukkot] without singing a hymn to God? [Impossible! Therefore we must say that Moses composed the text of *Hallel*.]

We learned in a *Baraita*: R. Eliezer says: All the songs and praises that David sang in the Book of Psalms he said about himself, [praying that he be redeemed from foes and treachery]. R. Yehoshua says: He spoke them in reference to the Jewish community, [praying for their rescue from trouble and distress]. The Sages say: Some of them refer to the community, while others refer to David himself. [The rule is:] Those that are phrased in the singular refer to David himself [like, "Heal *me*, for *I* have sinned against You" (Psalms 41:5)], while those that are phrased in the plural refer to the community, [like, "Before *our* eyes let it be known among the nations that You avenge the spilled blood of your servant" (Psalms 79:10)].

HAPPINESS A PREREQUISITE FOR DIVINE INSPIRATION

A Psalm that is introduced with *nitzu'ach* and *niggun* [*lamenatzei'ach bineginot*][60] relates to the future, [i.e., the days of *Mashiach*]. *Maskil*[61] signifies that David spoke through an interpreter who explained the psalm. *LeDavid mizmor*,[62] "To David, a psalm," denotes that first the *Shechinah* rested on him, and then he utterd that psalm. *Mizmor leDavid*, "A psalm of David" means that first he said that particular psalm, and then the *Shechinah* rested on him. [The fact that the singing of psalms was connected with the resting of the *Shechinah*] teaches you that the *Shechinah* does not rest on a person if he is in a state of laziness, sadness, giddiness, frivolity, or engaged in idle talk, but only in connection with the joy of doing a mitzvah. For it says, "Elisha said, 'Now then, get me a musician.' As the musician played, the spirit of prophecy came over him" (2 Kings 3:15). R. Yehudah said in Rav's name: The same holds true with regard to the study of Torah [when learning, you should be in a joyful mood]. R. Nachman said: The same goes for a good dream. [If you go to sleep in a happy mood, you will have pleasant dreams.]

[The Gemara asks:] But that is not so? Did not R. Giddal say in Rav's name: If a Torah scholar sits before his teacher and his lips do not drip with trepidation, they should be burned, for it says, "His lips are like lilies [*shoshanim*]; they drip with flowing myrrh [*mor oveir*]" (Song of Songs 5:13). Don't read *shoshanim* but *sheshonim*, "those that study;" don't read *mor oveir*, but *mar oveir*, "dripping with trepidation." [So you see, those that study should be awestruck, not in a happy mood.] [The Gemara answers:] There is no difficulty: one applies to the teacher [he should be exhilarated], the other to the student [he should be awestruck]. Or, if you prefer, say: Both refer to the teacher; and there still is no difficulty: he should be in a joyful mood before he begins his lecture, but he should be overcome with awe after he begins his discourse. Just as Rabbah used to do. He would say something humorous before he launched into his lecture, and the dis-

ciples would chuckle. After that, he would sit down in great awe and begin his discourse.

HISTORIC FIGURES WHO SANG THE *HALLEL*

Our Sages taught: Who [were the historic figures that] sang the *Hallel*? R. Eliezer said: Moses and Israel sang it when they stood by the Red Sea. They exclaimed: "Not for our sake, O God, not for our sake, but for the sake of Your Name bring glory" (Psalm 115:1). And the Holy Spirit responded, "For My sake, My own sake, do I act" (Isaiah 48:11). R. Yehudah said: Joshua and Israel sang the *Hallel* when the kings of Canaan attacked them. They exclaimed, "Not for our sake" . . ." and the Holy Spirit responded, "For My sake . . ." R. Elazar Hamodai said: Deborah and Barak sang it when Sisera attacked them. They exclaimed, "Not for our sake," and the Holy Spirit responded, "For My sake, My own sake do I act." R. Elazar b. Azariah said: Hezekiah and his companions sang it when Sancheriv attacked them. They exclaimed, "Not for our sake . . ." and the Holy Spirit responded, "For My sake . . ." R. Akiva said: Chananiah, Mishael, and Azariah sang it when the wicked Nebuchadnezzer rose against them. They exclaimed, "Not for our sake . . ." and the Holy Spirit responded, etc. R. Yose Hagelili said: Mordechai and Esther sang it when the wicked Haman rose against them. They exclaimed, "Not for our sake . . ." and the Holy Spirit responded, etc. But the Sages said: The prophets of Israel instituted that the Jewish people should recite the *Hallel* at every special occasion, and at times of national deliverance from peril they should recite it in gratitude for their redemption.

MAGEIN DAVID, "SHIELD OF DAVID"

(117b) [God told Nathan to say to King David:] "I will give you great renown like that of the greatest men on earth" (2 Samuel 7:9). R. Yosef taught: This alludes to the fact that we end [the third *berachah* after the *Haftarah*] with the words *Magein David*, "Shield of David," [just as we end the first *berachah* of the *Shemoneh Esrei* with, *Magein Avraham*, "Shield of Abraham." The prophet Nathan thus says that David will be granted the same honor as "the greatest men on earth," i.e., Abraham, Isaac, and Jacob].

R. Shimon b. Lakish said: It says, [God said to Abraham] "I will make you into a great nation" (Genesis 12:2); that means that we say [in the first *berachah* of the *Shemoneh Esrei*, "the God of Abraham." It says, "I will bless you" (ibid.); that means that we say [in the same *berachah*], "the God of Isaac." It says, "and make your name great" (ibid.); that means that we say, "the God of Jacob." You might think that we end the *berachah* with all three [saying, "God of Abraham, Isaac, and Jacob"], that's why it says, "*You* shall become a blessing" (ibid.). We end the *berachah* with you [alone], and we don't end it with all of them.

THE "GREAT *HALLEL*"

(118a) Our Rabbis learned: [At the Seder, after we pour] the fourth cup of wine, we conclude the *Hallel* and recite the "Great *Hallel*," [i.e., the entire Psalm 136]; this is the opinion of R. Tarfon. Others say: [We say,] "God is my shepherd; I shall not want" (Psalm 23). [The Gemara asks:] Where does the "Great *Hallel*" begin? Rav Yehudah said: It begins with "Give thanks to God; for He is good" (ibid. 136:1) until "By the rivers of Babylon" (ibid. 137:1). R. Yochanan said: From "A song of ascents" (ibid. 120:1) until "By the rivers of Babylon." R. Acha b. Yaakov said: From, "For God has chosen Jacob for Himself" (ibid. 135:3,4) until "By the rivers of Babylon." And why is this *Hallel* called the "Great *Hallel*"? R. Yochanan said: Because the Holy One, blessed be He, sits in the heights of the world and parcels out food to all his creatures, [and the concluding verse of this psalm reads, "He gives nourishment to all flesh, for His kindness endures forever" (ibid. 136:25)].

R. Yehoshua b. Levi said: To what do the twenty-six verses [of Psalm 136] each of which ends in "His kindness endures forever" correspond? To the twenty-six generations that the Holy One, blessed be He, created in His world, and although He had not given them the Torah, He sustained them by His kindness.[63]

R. Chisda said: What is the meaning of, "Give thanks to God, for He is good"? [It means:] Give thanks to God Who collects a person's debt [if he sinned] from the good that He showered on that person: if he is a wealthy person, God takes away his ox, if he is a poor man He takes his sheep, from an orphan He takes an egg, from a widow, a chicken, [to atone for their sins. In other words: If a person must suffer loss so as to gain atonement, his loss is tailored to his means].

MAN OR WOMAN, WHO SUFFERS MORE?

R. Yochanan said: It is twice as distressful for a man to earn his livelihood as it is for a woman to give birth. For about a woman in childbirth it says, "It will be with pain [*be'etzev*] that you will give birth to children" (Genesis 3:16), whereas about earning a livelihood it says, "in anguish [*be'itzavon*]" (ibid. 17). [*Itzavon* denotes a more intense pain. The pain of childbirth is short and mixed with joy; the hardship of earning a livelihood is a constant and joyless burden (Etz Yosef)].

R. Yochanan said: Earning one's livelihood is more difficult than the redemption. For about the redemption it says, [Jacob said: "The angel who delivers me from all evil" (Genesis 48:16); so you see, for redemption only an angel was needed. However, when it comes

to earning a livelihood it says, "The *God* Who took care of me"] (ibid. 15).

R. Yehoshua b. Levi said: When the Holy One, blessed be He, said to Adam, "[The earth] will bring forth thorns and thistles for you, and you will eat the grass of the field" (ibid. 3:18), tears flowed from his eyes. He said to Him, "Master of the universe! Will I and my donkey eat out of the same trough!" [Will we be eating the same food?] But as soon as God said to him, "By the sweat of your brow will you eat bread" (ibid. 19), [and not grass,] his mind was put at ease. R. Shimon b. Lakish said: We are fortunate that we did not remain with the first [curse, in that we do not have to eat grass]. Abaye said: But we still have not been freed completely from the first curse, because we still eat herbs and vegetables of the field.

R. Shizbi said in the name of R. Elazar b. Azariah: The livelihood of a person is as difficult to provide as the parting of the Red Sea. For it says, "Quickly the crouching one is freed; he is not cut down and slain, and he shall not want for food" (Isaiah 51:14), [an allusion to sustenance], and in the next verse it says, "For I am God your Lord, Who stirs up the sea into roaring waves" (ibid. 15).

R. Elazar b. Azariah said: If a person's digestive system is blocked it is as difficult as the day of death and as the parting of the Red Sea. For it says, "Quickly the crouching one is freed, he is not cut down and slain [meaning, if that which is closed rushes to open, that person will not die, so if it does not open it is like the day of death]. And it says in the next verse, "Who stirs the sea into roaring waves" [The opening of the digestive system is like the splitting of the sea.]

MALICIOUS GOSSIP AND SLANDER

R. Sheshet said in the name of R. Elazar b. Azariah: If someone profanes the Festivals it is as if he worshipped idols. For it says, "Do not make any cast metal idols" (Exodus 34:17) and in the next verse it says, "Keep the Festival of Matzahs" (ibid. 18).

Furthermore, R. Sheshet said in the name of R. Elazar b. Azariah: If someone spreads malicious gossip against his neighbor, or listens to and accepts malicious gossip, or if someone gives false testimony about his neighbor, he deserves to be thrown to the dogs. For it says, "Cast it to the dogs" (Exodus 22:30), and in the next verse it says, "Do not accept [*sisa*] a false report" (ibid. 23:1). This can be read *lo sashi*, "do not cause someone else to hear slander," [meaning do not speak *leshon hara*, malicious gossip.]

WHY DO WE SAY THE *HALLEL*?

[The Gemara asks:] Since there is the great *Hallel*, why do we recite the regular *Hallel* [Psalms 113–118]? [The Gemara answers:] Because the following five things are mentioned in it: The exodus from Egypt, the parting of the Red Sea, the Giving of the Torah, the resurrection of the dead, and the suffering that precedes the coming of *Mashiach*. The exodus from Egypt, for it says, "When Israel went out of Egypt" (Psalms 114:1); the parting of the Red Sea, for it says, "The sea saw it and fled" (ibid. 3); the Giving of the Torah, for it says, "The mountains skipped like rams" (ibid. 4); the resurrection of the dead, for it says, "I shall walk before God in the land of the living" (ibid. 116:9); the suffering that precedes the coming of *Mashiach*, for it says, "Not for our sake, O God; not for our sake, but give honor to Your Name" (ibid. 115:1).

R. Yochanan said: "Not for our sake, O God; not for our sake," refers to our servitude to foreign nations. [We pray that God will save us from those nations, not for our sake, but for His sake.] Others say, R. Yochanan said: "Not for our sake" refers to the war of Gog and Magog, [we are asking God to save us for His sake from that catastrophic war, which will take place at the end of time, as prophesied by Ezekiel (Chapter 38)]. R. Nachman b. Yitzchak said: [We recite the *Hallel*] because it contains an allusion to the deliverance of the souls of the righteous from Gehinnom, as it says, "Please, God, save my soul" (Psalms 116:4). Chizkiah said: Because it speaks about the casting of the righteous [Chananiah, Mishael, and Azariah who were thrown] into the burning furnace, [by Nebuchadnezzar], and their emergence from it unscathed.

THEY EMERGED FROM THE FURNACE UNHARMED

Where in *Hallel* do we find mention of the casting into the furnace? In the verse, "Not for our sake, O God, not for our sake," for this is what Chananiah said; "But for Your Name's sake give glory" this Mishael said; "because of Your kindness and Your truth" Azariah said. "Why should the nations say, 'Where is their God now?'" all of them said in unison. Where in *Hallel* do we find mention of their emergence from the fiery furnace? In the verse, "Praise God, all the nations," for this was said by Chananiah; "Praise Him all peoples," was said by Mishael; "For His kindness has overwhelmed us," was said by Azariah; "And the truth of God endures forever, Halleluyah!" (Psalm 117:1) by all of them. Others maintain that it was the angel Gabriel who said, "And the truth of God endures forever," [because Gabriel was in the furnace with them. Indeed, Nebuchadnezzar saw a fourth being inside the furnace who "looked like a divine being" (Daniel 3:25)].

For when the wicked Nimrod cast our father Abraham into the fiery furnace, Gabriel said to the Holy One, blessed be He, "Master of the universe! Let me go down and cool it off and save the righteous man from the blazing furnace." Said the Holy One, blessed

be He, "I am unique in My world, and Abraham is unique in his world. It is fitting for the One Who is unique to save the one who is unique." But because the Holy One, blessed be He, does not withhold the reward that is due to any of his creatures, He said to Gabriel, "For this, [for wanting to save Abraham], you will have the merit to rescue three of Abraham's descendants." [And when the three were rescued, Gabriel said, "The truth of God endures forever," in other words, "God's promise is fulfilled."]

R. Shimon Hashiloni expounded: When the wicked Nebuchadnazzar cast Chananiah, Mishael, and Azariah into the blazing furnace, Yurkami, the angel who is appointed over the hail, said to the Holy One, blessed be He, "Master of the universe! Let me go down and cool off the furnace [with my hail], and let me save these righteous men from the blazing furnace." Said Gabriel to him, "[If you, the angel of the hail, were to cool off the furnace] it would not demonstrate the power of the Holy One, blessed be He. For you are the angel of hail, and everyone knows that water extinguishes fire. But I, the angel of fire, will go down, and I will cool off the furnace inside, (118b) and heat it on the outside [so that those who threw them in will be burned (Daniel 3:22)], and thereby I will perform a miracle within a miracle." The Holy One, blessed be He, said to Gabriel, "Go down." At that moment Gabriel began to praise God and said, "The truth of God endures forever."

WHY DID THE FISH PRAISE GOD?

R. Natan said: It was the fish in the sea that said, "The truth of God endures forever." This is in line with R. Huna's statement. For R. Huna said: The Israelites of the generation of the Exodus were lacking in faith. As Rabbah b. Mari expounded: What is the meaning of the verse, "They rebelled at the sea, at the Red Sea" (Psalms 106:7). We see from here that the Israelites rebelled at the time of the parting of the Sea and said: Just as we emerge from the sea on one side, so do the Egyptians emerge from another side. The Holy One, blessed be He, said to the angel of the sea, "Spit out the Egyptians on to the dry land [so that the Israelites will see that they were drowned]." Said the angel of the sea, "Master of the universe! Does a master give a gift to his servant and then take it back from him?" [You gave the bodies of all these Egyptians as a gift to the fish in the sea, and now You want to take back that gift?] Said God to the angel of the sea, "[There will come a time when] I will give you one-and-a-half times as many as were now consumed by the sea." He replied, "Master of the universe, can a servant claim his debt from his master?" [How will I be able to claim it from you?] Said God to him, "The River Kishon will be my guarantee." Immediately the sea ejected all the Egyptians to the dry land, and Israel came and saw them.

For it says, "The Israelites saw the Egyptians dead on the seashore" (Exodus 14:30).

[The Gemara asks:] And how did the sea get one-and-a-half as many as were now drowned? [The Gemara answers:] In connection with Pharaoh it says, "He took six hundred chosen chariots" (ibid. 7), whereas in connection with Sisera it says, "Sisera gathered . . . nine hundred iron chariots" (Judges 4:13). When Sisera came to make war against Israel and attacked them with iron spears, the Holy One, blessed be He, brought forth the stars out of their orbits against them, as it says, "The stars fought from heaven, from their courses they fought against Sisera" (ibid. 20). As soon as the stars descended on the armies of Sisera these iron spears became hot, and they went down to cool off their spears and to refresh themselves in the River Kishon. Said the Holy One, blessed be He, to the River Kishon, "Go and pay off the pledge [you gave to the sea]." Right away the River Kishon spit out the army of Sisera and threw them into the sea. And so it says, "The stream of river Kishon swept them away, that ancient stream" (ibid. 21). What does "that ancient stream" mean? The stream that became a guarantor long ago, in earlier times. At that moment the fish of the sea opened their mouths and exclaimed, "and the truth of God endures forever."

R. Shimon b. Lakish said: What is the meaning of, "He transforms the barren wife [akeret]" (Psalms 113:9). The elders of Israel said to the Holy One, blessed be He, "Master of the universe, Your children [i.e., those that have sinned during the long exile] have made me [the nobles of Israel] like a weasel that lives in the hidden recesses [ikarei] of the house. [Similarly, during the exile, the noblemen of Israel (i.e., its tzaddikim) are in hiding and do not play the leading role as they should.]

Rava expounded: What is the meaning of, "I love Him, for God has heard my voice and my supplications" (Psalms 116:1)? The congregation of Israel said: Master of the universe! When am I loved by You? When You hear the voice of my supplication. "I was brought low [dalloti], but He saved me" (ibid. 7). The congregation of Israel said to the Holy One, blessed be He: Master of the universe! Although I am poor [dallah] and lacking in mitzvot, I am dedicated to You, and therefore it is fitting that I should be saved.

THE GIFTS OF THE ROMAN EMPIRE ARE REJECTED

R. Kahana said: When R. Yishmael b. R. Yose became ill, Rebbi sent to him the following request: Please tell us two or three things that you once told us in the name of your father. R. Yishmael b. R. Yose sent back to him: This is what my father said: What is the meaning of the verse, "Praise God, all you nations" (Psalms 117:1). Why are the nations of the world mentioned in this passage? [Why should *they* praise God, "for His

kindness has overwhelmed *us*" (ibid. 2)?] This is the meaning: "Praise God, all you nations," for the mighty and miraculous deeds He performed for them; and surely we should praise Him, "for His kindness has overwhelmed us."

Futhermore R. Yishmael b. R. Yose sent word to Rebbi: In time to come Egypt will send a gift to *Mashiach* who will be inclined not to accept it from them. But the Holy One, blessed be He, will tell *Mashiach*: Accept it from them; they acted as hosts to My children in Egypt. Immediately, "Noblemen from Egypt will bring gifts [to *Mashiach*]" (Psalms 68:32). Then the kingdom of Kush [Ethiopia] will draw a logical inference: If the gifts of the Egyptians who enslaved them are accepted, then surely we, who did not enslave them, will find that our gifts are accepted. Then the Holy One, blessed be He, will tell *Mashiach*: Accept it from them. Right away, "Kush will hasten its gifts to God" (ibid.).

At that, the evil Roman Empire will draw a logical conclusion: If the gifts of Egypt and Ethiopia who are not their brothers [they are not descendants of Isaac], are accepted, then surely we, who are their brothers [Rome is Edom, which is identical with Esau who is Jacob's brother (Genesis 36:1)] will find that our gifts are accepted. But the Holy One, blessed be He, will say to Gabriel: "Rebuke the wild beast of the reeds [kaneh], the multitude [adat] of the bulls" (ibid. 31). [Which means:] "Rebuke the beast [i.e., the Roman empire], and acquire [keneih] for yourself the community [of Israel]." Another interpretation: Rebuke the beast of the reeds, [i.e., Rome], which is compared to a beast that lives among the reeds, as it says, "Wild boars [i.e., Rome] gnaw at it [the reeds],[64] and creatures of the field feed on it" (ibid. 80:14). R. Chiya b. Abba interpreted the passage in R. Yochanan's name: Rebuke the wild beast [i.e., Rome], all of whose actions are written with the same pen, [meaning, all its decrees are harmful to the Jewish people. *Kaneh* also means feather, quill, pen]. [The Gemara continues its interpretation of Psalms 68:31.] "The multitude of the bulls [abbirim] with the calves of the people." This means that [Rome] slaughtered the noble [Jewish] people [abbirim] like calves that have no owners. "They come cringing with pieces of silver" (ibid.). Which means that they [Rome] stretch out their hand to accept money [as bribes], but do not carry out what they promised to do. "He has scattered the people that delight in wars." What has caused Israel to be dispersed among the nations of the world? The wars and the battles the Jewish people fought against the nations of the world. [If King Zedekiah had not rebelled against Nebuchadnezzar, and if the Biryonim [Zealots] had obeyed R. Yochanan b. Zakkai and had submitted to the Roman overlords rather than tried to overthrow their regime, the Jewish people would not have been sent into exile (*Maharsha*).]

RICH REWARDS FOR STUDENTS OF TORAH

[R. Yishmael b. R. Yose] also sent this teaching to Rebbi: In the great city of Rome there are three hundred and sixty-five marketplaces, and in each there are three hundred and sixty-five palaces, and each palace has three hundred and sixty-five floors, and each of the floors contained enough food to feed the whole world.[65] R. Shimon b. Rabbi asked Rabbi—others say, R. Yishmael b. R. Yose—asked Rabbi: [Since the contents of one floor could feed the whole world], for whom are all these other floors? [Rabbi replied:] For you, your friends, and associates. For it says, [concerning Rome], "Her profits and her hire shall be consecrated to God. They shall not be stored or treasured; rather her profits shall go to those who sit before God, that they may eat their fill and clothe themselves elegantly" (Isaiah 23:18). What does "it shall not be stored" mean? R. Yosef learned: "they shall not be stored" means that the treasures will not be placed in a warehouse; "or treasured" means that they will not be placed in a vault [like silver and gold, but they will be accessible to the Jewish people]. What does "to those who sit before God" mean?

R. Elazar said: (119a) That refers to a person who recognizes where all his colleagues sit in the yeshivah [a sign that he regularly attends the yeshivah]. Others say: R. Elazar said: These are the people that greet their colleages in the yeshivah [i.e., they are the first to arrive at the yeshivah before the lecture begins]. What does "and clothe themselves elegantly [limechasseh atik]" mean? That refers to the person who conceals [mechasseh] the things that the Ancient of Days [the Holy One, blessed be He[66]] concealed [kissah]. And what is that? The secrets of the Torah [i.e., the mystical teachings about the Divine Chariot, described in the first chapter of Ezekiel, and the mysteries of Creation]. According to others it refers to a person who reveals the things that the Ancient of Days concealed [kissah]. And what is that? The rationale of the laws of the Torah. [Searching for the reasons behind the laws of the Torah is a commendable exercise that is rewarded with the great blessings alluded to in the verse.]

R. Kahana said in the name of R. Yishmael b. R. Yose. What is meant by, "For the Conductor [lamenatzei'ach]; a song of David"? [This is the heading of a number of psalms.] It means: Sing praises to Him Who is happy when he is defeated, [lamenatzei'ach, derived from natzach, "to overcome"]. Come and notice the vast difference between the character of the Holy One, blessed be He, and that of mortal man. When mortal man is defeated he is unhappy; but when the Holy One, blessed be He, is defeated He rejoices. For it says, "He would have destroyed them [Israel] had not Moses, His chosen one, confronted Him in the breach to avert His destructive wrath" (Psalm 106:23) [the fact that Moses was called "the chosen one" proves that God was happy to be vanquished (Rashbam)].

R. Kahana said in the name of R. Yishmael b. R. Yose, and the Rabbis said that R. Shimon b. Lakish said it in the name of R. Yehudah Nesiah: What is the meaning of the verse, "They [the Chayot angels] had the hands of a man below their wings" (Ezekiel 1:8). It is written yado, "his hand," [singular, instead of yedei, "the hands of"]. This refers to the hand of the Holy One, blessed be He, which is spread out beneath the wings of the Chayot [the angels that are described in Ezekiel 1], in order to accept baalei teshuvah and protect them from the Attribute of Unmitigated Justice [that argues against their acceptance].

WHAT HAPPENED TO EGYPT'S TREASURES?

Rav Yehudah said in Shmuel's name: Joseph gathered up all the silver and gold in the world and brought it to Egypt, for it says, "Joseph collected all the money in Egypt and Canaan" (Genesis 47:14). This tells us only about the money of Egypt and Canaan, but how do we know that he collected it from all other countries? Because it says, "[People from] all the countries came to Egypt [to buy grain]" (ibid. 41:57). And when the Israelites left Egypt they took along this vast treasure, for it says, "[The Israelites] drained Egypt of its wealth" (Exodus 12:35). R. Assi said: They emptied out Egypt, like a bird-catcher's trap without grain [to attract birds]. Rabbi Shimon said: Like a pond without fish. All this wealth remained in Eretz Yisrael until the days of Rehoboam, when Shishak, king of Egypt came and carried it off. For it says, "In the fifth year of King Rehoboam, King Shishak of Egypt marched against Jerusalem and carried off the treasures of the House of God and the treasures of the royal palace" (1 Kings 14:25,26).

Then Zerach, the king of Kush [Ethiopia], came and took it away from Shishak; then Assa came and grabbed it from Zerach king of Kush and sent it to Hadrimon the son of Tavrimon. The Ammonites came and seized it from Hadrimon son of Tavrimon. Jehoshafat came and seized it from the Ammonites, and it remained there until Ahaz ruled, when Sancheriv came and took it from Ahaz. Then Hezekiah came and took it from Sancheriv, and it remained there until Zedekiah ruled, when the Babylonians [Chaldeans] came and seized it from Zedekiah. The Persians came and took it from the Chaldeans; the Greeks came and took it from the Persians; finally the Romans came and took it from the Greeks, and it is still in the possession of Rome.

R. Chama son of R. Chanina said: Joseph hid three treasures in Egypt: one was revealed to Korach, one to Antoninus the son of Severus, and the third is hidden away for the righteous for future times.

It says, "Riches hoarded by their owner is to his misfortune" (Ecclesiastes 5:12). R. Shimon b. Lakish said: This refers to Korach's wealth. "And all the property that was at their feet" (Deuteronomy 11:6). R. Elazar said. This refers to a person's wealth, which puts him on his feet. R. Levi said: It took three hundred white mules to carry the keys to Korach's treasure house. [This is, of course, an exaggeration.] The keys to Korach's treasure house, and all the keys and locks, were made of leather [to make them lightweight, and still they were such a heavy load].

A RESPONSIVE DIALOGUE IN THE *HALLEL*

R. Shmuel b. Nachmani said in R. Yonatan's name: [The following verses in the *Hallel* were recited in a responsive dialogue among Samuel, Jesse, David, and David's brothers when the prophet announced that the young shepherd David would be the future king of Israel.]

"I thank You for You have answered me" (Psalms 118:21) was said by David. "The stone the builders despised has become the cornerstone," (ibid. 22) by Jesse [Yishai]; "This emanated from God," (ibid. 23) by David's brothers; "This is the day God has made," (ibid. 24) by Samuel. "Please God, save now!" (ibid. 25) was said by David's brothers. "Please God, bring success now!" (ibid.) was said by David; "Blessed is he who comes in the name of God," (ibid. 26) by Jesse; "We bless you from the House of God," (ibid.) by Samuel; "The Lord is God, He illuminated for us," (ibid. 27) by all of them; "Bind the festival offering with cords," by Samuel; "You are my God, and I will thank You," (ibid. 28) by David; "You are my God, and I will exalt You," by all of them.

WHO WILL SAY GRACE AT THE GREAT BANQUET?

(119b) R. Avira expounded, sometimes citing R. Ammi, sometimes citing R. Assi: What is meant by, "The child [Isaac] grew and was weaned [*vayigamal*]" (Genesis 21:8)? [He answered:] The Holy One, blessed be He, will make a great banquet for the righteous on the day He will display His love for the descendants of Isaac. After they haven eaten and drunk, the cup of wine over which Grace after meals is recited will be offered to our father Abraham, that he should say Grace, but he will answer, "I cannot say Grace, because I had a son Ishmael." Then they will give the cup to Isaac, but he will say, "I am unworthy to say Grace because I had a son Esau." Then they will offer the cup to Jacob, but he will say, "I cannot say Grace because I married two sisters during both their lifetimes, and in time to come this will be prohibited by the Torah." Then Moses will be asked, "Take the cup and say Grace." But Moses will reply, "I cannot say Grace, because I was not privileged to enter Eretz Yisrael, either in life or in death." Then Joshua will be asked, "You take the cup and say Grace." But he will answer,

"I cannot say Grace because I was not privileged to have a son." For it says, "Nun his son, Joshua his son" (1 Chronicles 7:27). [The genealogical list of Ephraim ends with Joshua, proof that he had no son.] Then they will turn to David and say to him, "You take the cup and say Grace." "I will say Grace," he will say, "and it is fitting that I say Grace, for it says, 'I will raise the cup of salvations, and invoke the name of God'" (Psalms 11:13).

NOTES

1. Unlike in the English where "not clean" and "unclean" are synonymous, the Hebrew has different terms for clean, *tahor*, and unclean, *tamei*. And the Torah wants to avoid using the distasteful term *tamei*.

2. For the answer see *Shabbat* 17a.

3. Leviticus 3:9.

4. *Pesach, Shavuot*, and *Sukkot*.

5. *Sanhedrin* 74a.

6. Literally, this comes as a teacher and is found to be a learner.

7. He was not a *kohen*.

8. *Bava Kamma* 117a.

9. *Hilchot Piryah Verivyah*, 2.

10. Even *Ha'ezer, Hilchot Piryah Verivyah* 2.

11. R. Akiva was one of the *Asarah Harugei Malchut*, the Ten Martyrs who were brutally killed by the Romans. Their deaths are memorialized in the *Eileh Ezkera* prayer during the *Mussaf* service on Yom Kippur.

12. The two brothers Lulianus and Pappus who pleaded guilty to the murder of the Emperor's daughter in order to save the entire Jewish people who were held responsible for it; see *Taanit* 18b.

13. *Berachot* 54a.

14. The Four-Letter Name is a proper Name of God and, for that reason, is not pronounced as it is spelled except during the service in the *Bet Hamikdash*. During the reading of Scripture or recitation of prayers, we pronounce the Name reverently as *Adonai*, but even that pronunciation is not used in ordinary speech. For that purpose, the term *Hashem*, literally, *the Name*, is used.

15. The afternoon service, beginning two-and-a-half hours before nightfall.

16. *Taanit* 12b.

17. A group of one hundred and twenty Sages who led the Jewish people at the beginning of the Second Temple era. They laid the foundation of the liturgy and enacted many ordinances to prevent laxity in observance of the commandments.

18. *Pesachim* 74a. *Gedi mekulas* translates "a helmeted goat," because the legs are hung on the outside of the goat, like a helmeted soldier who carries his weapon on his side (Rashi).

19. See Daniel, Chapter 3.

20. Genesis 9:13.

21. Exodus 32:16.

22. Exodus 33:22 and 1 Kings 19:9.

23. Numbers 22:28.

24. Numbers 16:30.

25. Genesis 22:13.

26. The underlying idea is that the future miracles and exceptions to God's natural order were provided for in advance when He created the world prior to the first *Shabbat*.

27. Numbers, Chapter 16.

28. Numbers 17:23.

29. Or any government that persecutes the Jewish people.

30. Deuteronomy 6:4.

31. 1 Samuel 2:22.

32. A commentary on Chronicles, a Biblical book that contains many genealogical lists.

33. The forty-seven verses between the name Atzeil in 1 Chronicles 8:38 and Atzeil in 1 Chronicles 9:44 contain a vast number of different interpretations.

34. A *tekiah* is a long, straight blast on the *shofar*; a *teruah* is a series of short blasts.

35. The base of the Altar protruded only on the north and west sides. Thus he had to splash the blood on the northwest corner of the Altar.

36. Literally, "Praise"; Psalms 113–118.

37. The High Priest.

38. They were the leaders of the community in Eretz Yisrael.

39. *Erev Pesach*, the 14th of Nissan, is the day before Passover.

40. There are fifty *Shabbatot* in the year. Every *Shabbat* the two daily burnt offerings and two *Mussaf* (additional) sacrifices are brought, which add up to two hundred sacrifices, not counting the extra sacrifices that are brought on the *Shabbat* that occurs in the middle of Pesach and Sukkot.

41. Bamidbar 9:13.

42. For this unusal display of modesty, the Sages gave high praise to the B'nei Beteira.

43. Carrying an object in a public domain is forbidden on *Shabbat*.

44. He should not have boasted about his diligence.

45. Meaning, personally attended.

46. *Bava Metzia* 84a.

47. It was customary for a newly married couple to move in with the husband's parents.

48. A province of Babylonia, where Daniel was.

49. 2 Kings, Chapter 9.

50. Genesis 11:31.

51. As it says, "The Israelites drained Egypt of its wealth" (Exodus 12:35).

52. The Targum translates Jezreel as *kenishtehon*, "ingathering."

53. One mile (*mil*) is 2,000 cubits.

54. The Rabbis thought of *rakia* (heaven) as a thick curtain that envelops the earth. When the sun is behind the *rakia*, it is invisible. At daybreak it enters an opening in the *rakia*, and from daybreak until the beginning of sunrise it passes through the thickness of the *rakia*. At sunrise it emerges from the *rakia* and shines on the earth. During the day it travels across the sky from east to west. At sunset it enters an opening in the *rakia* and traverses its thickness until it disappears entirely when the stars come out.

55. R. Akiva was imprisoned and later martyred by the Romans for defying their prohibition against teaching the Torah (*Berachot* 61b).

56. He said this merely to impress upon him the seriousness of his resolve.

57. Our holy Teacher, i.e., Rabbi Yehudah Hanasi.

58. *Berachot* 8b.

59. *Hallel*, the hymn of praise and prayer, is composed of Psalms 113 through 118. It is recited on the Festivals of Pesach, Shavuot, and Sukkot, as well as on Chanukah and Rosh Chodesh (New Moon). On Rosh Chodesh and the last six days of Pesach a shortened version of *Hallel* is recited, in which the first eleven verses of both Psalm 115 and 116 are omitted.

60. "For the conductor, upon *Neginot* [a musical instrument]" (Radak). E.g., Psalms 67:1.

61. As in Psalms 52:1.

62. E.g., Psalms 24:1.

63. There were twenty-six generations from Adam until Moses. Now, the world is sustained in the merit of the Torah. The generations that lived before the Torah was given, having no merit, were sustained solely by God's kindness.

64. In a prophetic vision Daniel saw the fourth beast, which represents Rome. This beast "devoured and crushed and stamped the remains" (Daniel 7:19), in the manner of a wild boar (Rashbam).

65. The number 365 conforms to the 365 days of the solar year, which is the basis of the gentile (Roman) calendar. The Jewish year of 354 days is a lunar year (*Maharsha*).

66. Daniel 7:9,13,22.

෴ YOMA ෴

SEQUESTERING
THE HIGH PRIEST

(2a) *Mishnah*: [On Yom Kippur the entire service in the *Bet Hamikdash* was performed by the *kohen gadol*, the high priest, who had to be in a state of ritual purity in order to officiate. Therefore,] seven days before Yom Kippur the *kohen gadol* was separated from his house and moved to the Palhedrin Chamber [to prevent him from becoming impure through contact with his wife who may be in menstruation]. And another priest was appointed to take his place in case any [impurity] should happen to him that would disqualify him for the service. R. Yehudah said: Also another wife was appointed for him in case his own wife should die, [and to officiate on Yom Kippur the high priest must be married], for it says, "He shall make atonement for himself and his house" (Leviticus 16:11); "his house" meaning "his wife." They said to [R. Yehudah]: "If so, there will be no end to the matter," [the appointed wife may also die].

TAKE YOURSELF

(3b) We learned in a *Baraita*: The expression *kach lecha*, "take yourself" (Leviticus 9:2), means "pay for it with your own funds," and *asei lecha*, "make for yourself" (Numbers 10:2), means "make it, [and pay for it from your own funds,]" but *veyikchu eilecha*, "they shall take for them" (Exodus 27:20), means "pay for it with community funds," so said R. Yoshiah. R. Yonatan said: Both *kach lecha* and *veyikchu eilecha* mean "pay for it with community funds"; then why does the Torah say *kach lecha*, "take yourself"? It is as if God said [to Moses]: I would rather that you take it [and pay for it] with your own funds than with the community's funds.

Abba Chanan said in the name of R. Elazar: One verse says, "Make yourself a wooden ark" (Deuteronomy 10:1), and another, "They shall make an ark of acacia wood" (Exodus 25:10). [In Deuteronomy it is Moses who is told to make the ark, whereas in Exodus the same command is addressed to the children of Israel.] How can both passages be reconciled? [He answered:] The verse in Exodus 25:10 refers to a time

when Israel lived up to God's will, [before the making of the golden calf, then the entire community received the command to build the ark], whereas the verse of Deuteronomy 10:1 refers to a time when Israel did not live up to God's will, [they had made the golden calf; then only Moses received the command].

WHEN DID MOSES ASCEND
MOUNT SINAI?

(4a) We learned in a *Baraita*: Moses went up [Mount Sinai] in a Heavenly cloud, he was covered by that cloud, and was sanctified in that cloud in order to receive the Torah for Israel in holiness. For it says, "God's glory rested on Mount Sinai" (Exodus 24:16). This all happened *after* the Giving of the Ten Commandments, which took place at the beginning of the forty days [during which Moses was in Heaven preparing to receive the Tablets (Exodus 24:18)]; this is the opinion of R. Yose Hagelili. R. Akiva, on the other hand, said: The verse, "God's glory rested on Mount Sinai" [does not refer to the period *after* the Giving of the Ten Commandments], but rather to the (4b) beginning of the month Sivan, [i.e., *before* the giving of the Ten Commandments]; and when it says, "the Heavenly cloud covered it [*vayechaseihu*]," it means that the cloud covered the mountain, [not Moses. He had not yet gone up the mountain]. Then it says, "On the seventh day He called to Moses." Moses was standing at the bottom of the mountain together with all Israel. [This being so, why does it say that God called only Moses and not all the people?] This was done in order to accord honor to Moses. Rabbi Nosson [who holds like R. Yose Hagelili] said that Moses was in the Heavenly cloud for six days *after* the Revelation, in order to dissolve all food and drink in his intestines so as to make him like one of the ministering angels.

R. Matyah b. Cheresh [who also agrees with R. Yose Hagelili's view] said: The purpose of Moses' six days of separation was to fill him with awe, so that the Ten Commandments should be given with awe, fear, trembling, and trepidation. For it says, "Serve God with awe, and rejoice with trembling" (Psalms 2:11). What is the meaning of "Rejoice with trembling"? R. Adda B. Matna said in the name of Rav: Where there is joy, [and the Giving of the Ten Commandments was a joyous occasion], there also should be awe.

[Returning to the original dispute, the Gemara asks:] On what essential point do R. Yose Hagelili and R. Akiva disagree? [The Gemara answers:] They are arguing about the controversy of the Tannaim of a *Baraita*: For we learned in a *Baraita*:[1] On the sixth of Sivan, the Ten Commandments were given to the children of Israel. R. Yose said: On the seventh of Sivan. According to the Tanna who holds that the Ten Commandments were given on the sixth of Sivan, Moses went up Mount Sinai [to receive the Tablets] on the seventh day. According to R. Yose, who holds that the Ten Commandments were given on the seventh of Sivan, both the Ten Commandments were given and Moses ascended the mountain on the seventh day. For it says, "He called to Moses on the seventh day" (Exodus 24:16). R. Yose Hagelili holds like the first [the anonymous] Tanna, who maintains that the Ten Commandments were given on the sixth of Sivan. Therefore, [the six days, followed by the seventh day on which God addressed Moses] happened *after* the Giving of the Ten Commandments. Consequently, when it says, "God's glory rested on Mount Sinai and the cloud covered it/him six days," "him" refers to Moses [and not to the mountain].[2] Then, "on the seventh day, He called to Moses" to receive the rest of the Torah [besides the Ten Commandments that had already been given]. For if you would think that "the glory of God rested on Mount Sinai" from the beginning of the month, so that "and the cloud covered it/him" referred to the mountain, and that "on the seventh day, He called to Moses" to receive the Ten Commandments, [that is impossible, since according to R. Yose Hagelili] they had received the Ten Commandments on the sixth of Sivan, and also, the cloud departed on the sixth day [after the Ten Commandments were given]! [Thus the seventh day must refer to the seventh day *after* the Giving of the Ten Commandments.]

R. Akiva, however, holds like R. Yose, who said that the Ten Commandments were given to Israel on the seventh of Sivan, [and the cloud covered the mountain until the sixth of Sivan, and on the seventh, God called Moses to receive the Ten Commandments]. [Now the Gemara analyzes:] According to R. Akiva [who says that the Ten Commandments were given on the seventh of Sivan] we can understand the statement[3] that Moses broke the Tablets on the seventeenth of Tammuz. We have twenty-four days in Sivan [from the seventh to the thirtieth] and sixteen days in Tammuz, which gives us a total of forty days, which is the time Moses was on the mountain, and on the seventeenth of Tammuz he came down and broke the Tablets. But according to R. Yose Hagelili who holds that after the Giving of the Ten Commandments Moses was isolated for six days in a Heavenly cloud, and then began the forty days he spent on the

mountain, the Tablets could not have been broken until the twenty-third of Tammuz! [The Gemara answers:] R. Yose Hagelili will retort: The six days of isolation are included in the forty days on the mountain. [Consequently, even according to R. Yose Hagelili, the Tablets could have been broken on the seventeenth of Tammuz.]

DON'T BLURT OUT YOUR MESSAGE

It says, "God called to Moses, and spoke to him" (Leviticus 1:1). Why is it that God first called Moses and then spoke? The Torah teaches us good manners: a person should not say something to his friend on impulse, [blurting out the message he wants to convey]; he should first tell him that he wants to speak to him. This supports the view of R. Chanina, for R. Chanina said: A person should not relate something to his friend unless he calls him first to speak to him. Rabbah said: How do we know that when a person tells something to his friend, the message must be kept confidential until the friend tells him, "Go ahead and relate it to others"? From the verse, "God spoke to him from the Communion Tent [leimor], [saying]." [Leimor is seen as a contraction of lo emor, "do not tell it [to others]" (Rashi).]

THE CHAMBER OF *PARHEDRIN*

(8b) [We learned in the Mishnah that seven days before Yom Kippur the high priest was separated and moved into the Chamber of *Parhedrin*.]

R. Yehudah asked: Was it then called the Chamber of *Parhedrin* [officials]? Was it not rather called the Chamber of *Balvati* [senators]? [The Gemara answers:] Originally, it was indeed called Chamber of *Balvati*, but because they paid money [to the Hasmonean kings] to be appointed high priest, and the high priests were changed every twelve months [because they were wicked they did not survive for more than twelve months (Rashi)], like those government officials that are rotated every twelve months [by the king], that is why it came to be called the Chamber of the *Parhedrin* [Officials].

CORRUPT HIGH PRIESTS OF THE SECOND *BET HAMIKDASH*

(9a) Rabba b. Bar Chanah said in R. Yochanan's name: What is the meaning of the verse, "The fear of God prolongs life, but the years of the wicked will be shortened" (Proverbs 10:27)? "The fear of God prolongs life" refers to the first *Bet Hamikdash*, which stood for four hundred and ten years and in which there served only eighteen high priests. "But the years of the wicked will be shortened" refers to the second *Bet Hamikdash*, which stood for four hundred and twenty years; but more than three hundred high priests served during that period.

Subtract from the four hundred and twenty years the forty years that Shimon Hatzaddik [the Righteous] served, and subtract also the eighty years during which Yochanan *Kohein Gadol* officiated, [he succeeded Shimon Hatzaddik], and the ten years of Yishmael ben Pabi, and according to others, also the eleven years of R. Elazar b. Charsum. [Thus if we subtract the total of 40 + 80 + 10 = 130 years from the 420 years we are left with 290 years], and we come to the conclusion that none of the other high priests survived a full year.

R. Yochanan b. Torta [who was a convert to Judaism] said: What can account for this? Because they bought the right to serve as high priest [and were not appointed on their merits], for R. Assi said: Martha the daughter of Baitus brought a *tarkav*-full of dinars to King Yannai to have Yehoshua b. Gamla designated as high priest.

WHY WAS SHILOH DESTROYED?
R. Yochanan b. Torta also said: Why was the Tabernacle at Shiloh[4] destroyed? Because of two evils that prevailed there: Immorality and treating holy things with contempt. Where does it say that they were guilty of immorality? For it says, "Now Eli was very old. When he heard all that his sons [Chofni and Pinchas] were doing to all Israel, and about the acts of adultery that they engaged in with women who gathered in great numbers at the entrance of the Tent of Meeting" (1 Samuel 2:22). And even though R. Shmuel b. Nachmani said in the name of R. Yochanan: Those who say that the sons of Eli sinned are mistaken; [he says that the verses should not be taken literally; what is meant is], (9b) since Chofni and Pinchas delayed the bringing of the sacrifices that the women who gave birth were required to bring,[5] Scripture considers their act of delaying as if they had committed adultery. [The other sin was:] Treating holy things with contempt. [How do we know that?] Because it says [about Eli's sons], "But even before the fat was brought on the altar, the priest's boy would come and say to the man who was sacrificing, 'Hand over some meat to roast for the priest, for he won't accept boiled meat from you, only raw.' And if the man said to him, 'Let them first bring the fat as an offering on the altar, and then you can take [of the meat] as much as you want,' he would reply, 'No, hand it over at once or I'll take it by force.' The sin of the young men against God was very great, for the men treated God's offerings with contempt" (1 Samuel 2:15–17). [A *kohein* may partake of the meat of a sacrifice only after the fat and the prescribed portions have been offered on the altar. These priests took the meat without waiting for the portions to be offered on the altar.]

WHY WAS THE FIRST *BET HAMIKDASH* DESTROYED?
Why was the first *Bet Hamikdash* destroyed? It was destroyed because of three basic sins that prevailed at

that time: the sins of idolatry, immorality, and bloodshed. Idolatry, for it says, "The bed is too short for stretching out, and the cover too narrow for curling up!" (Isaiah 28:20). [Metaphorically, the prophet announces that Eretz Yisrael will be too small to hold the multitude of enemies that will gather on its territory.] What is the meaning of "The bed is too short for stretching out"? R. Yonatan said: This bed is too short for two neighbors to stretch themselves, [meaning, God cannot coexist with any other god].[6] What is the meaning of "the cover is too narrow for curling up"? R. Shmuel b. Nachmani said: When R. Yonatan came to this verse, he would cry and say: To the One about Whom it says, "He heaps up the ocean waters like a wall" (Psalms 33:7), an idol became a partner!

The second basic sin was immorality: [How do we know that?] For it says, "God said, 'Because the daughters of Zion are so haughty and walk with heads thrown back, with roving eyes, and with floating gait, making a tinkling with their feet'" (Isaiah 3:16). [The Gemara expounds:] "Because the daughters of Zion are haughty,"—a tall girl would walk alongside a short girl [to make herself more conspicuous]. "They walked with their heads thrown back"—they would walk with a proud posture. "With roving eyes"—they put a lot of eyeshadow on their eyes. "With a floating gait"—they used to walk [flirtatiously], with the heel touching the toe. "And make a tinkling with their feet"—R. Yitzchak said: They would take myrrh and balsam and place it in their shoes, and when they came near the young men of Israel they would kick coquettishly, and they would spray the [fragrance of the perfume] on them and would thus arouse their evil impulse like the venom of a snake.

The third basic sin was bloodshed. [From where do we know that?] Because it says, "Moreover, Menasseh put so many innocent persons to death that he filled Jerusalem [with blood] from end to end" (2 Kings 21:16). They were wicked, but they placed their trust in the Holy One, blessed be He.[7] For it says, "Her rulers judge for bribes, her priests give rulings for a fee, and her prophets prophecy for pay; yet they rely on God, saying, 'God is in our midst; no calamity shall overtake us'" (Micah 3:11). Therefore, the Holy One, blessed be He, brought on them three evil decrees, to correspond with the three sins they had committed. "Therefore, because of you, Zion shall be plowed like a field, and Jerusalem shall become heaps of rubble, and the Temple Mount shall be left like stumps of trees" (ibid. 12).

WHY WAS THE SECOND *BET HAMIKDASH* DESTROYED?
[The Gemara asks:] But why was the second *Bet Hamikdash* destroyed, inasmuch as they were engaging in Torah, *mitzvot*, and acts of kindness? [The Gemara answers:] Because there was baseless hatred among them.

This teaches you that baseless hatred is as serious a sin as the three sins of idolatry, immorality, and bloodshed put together. [The Gemara asks:] And during the time of the first *Bet Hamikdash* was there no baseless hatred? Doesn't it say, "They shall be cast before the sword together with My people, oh, strike the thigh [in grief]" (Ezekiel 21:17). And R. Elazar said: This refers to people who eat and drink together and then stab each other with the daggers of their tongues! [The Gemara answers:] That hatred was not the sin of the common people; it was the sin of the princes in Israel. For it says, "Cry and wail, son of man [i.e., Ezekiel], for this is the sin that is prevalent among My people" (Ezekiel 21:17). [It says,] "Cry and wail, son of man," you might assume that all of Israel was guilty of this; therefore the passage continues, "all the princes of Israel" [meaning, the sin of unwarranted hatred was prevalent only among the leaders of Israel, but not among the average people].

WHO WAS BETTER: THE EARLIER OR THE LATER GENERATIONS?

R. Yochanan and R. Elazar both said: The former ones, [the generations that lived in the time of the first *Bet Hamikdash*], since their sins were done in the open, [meaning, they did not hide their wrongdoings]; therefore, the time of their redemption [i.e., the end of the Babylonian exile] was revealed.[8] By contrast, the sin of the later generations, [those of the second *Bet Hamikdash*], was not revealed, [meaning, their baseless hatred was hidden in their heart]. Therefore, the time of their redemption was never revealed, [and we do not know when our exile will end].

R. Yochanan said: The fingernail of the earlier generations [those of the first *Bet Hamikdash*] is better than the entire body of the later generations. Said Resh Lakish to him: On the contrary, the later generations are better than the earlier ones, because, despite the fact that they are under the domination of foreign governments, they study and observe the Torah. R. Yochanan replied: The *Bet Hamikdash* proves my point, for the first *Bet Hamikdash* was rebuilt, but not the second *Bet Hamikdash*, [evidence that the earlier generations were on a higher lever than the later ones].

They asked R. Elazar: Were the earlier generations better, or the later ones? He replied: Look at the *Bet Hamikdash*! [The fact that the first one was rebuilt, while the second one was not, is an indication that the earlier generations were greater.] Others say, he answered: The *Bet Hamikdash* is your witness [in this matter; it was restored for the earlier generations, but the second one was not restored for the later generations].

WHY WAS PROPHECY ABSENT DURING THE SECOND TEMPLE?

Resh Lakish was swimming in the Jordan River. Rabba b. Bar Chana came and gave him a hand [to help him out of the river]. Resh Lakish then said to Rabba b. Bar Chana: God hates you, [Babylonian Jews! For you remained in Babylonia and did not come up to Eretz Yisrael with Ezra]. For it says, "If she be a wall, we will build upon it a silver battlement. If she be a door, we will panel it in cedar" (Song of Songs 8:9). [He expounds:] If you had made yourself like a solid wall, and you all had come up together to Eretz Yisrael in the days of Ezra, then you would have been compared to silver that is not subject to decay. Now that you have come up piecemeal, like doors [that come in two parts], you are like cedarwood that is subject to decay, [and, as a result, there is only a partial Divine Presence in Eretz Yisrael]. What is meant by the analogy with cedarwood? Ulla said: It refers to a *sasmagur*, [a kind of worm that chops and chews up the cedar tree from within (Rashi)]. And why is the period of the second *Bet Hamikdash* compared to a *sasmagur*? R. Abba said: It refers to the *Bat Kol*, [a Heavenly Voice. Just as a small portion of the cedar is not destroyed by the worm, so did the *Bat Kol*, which was regarded as a lower grade of prophecy, remain during the time of the second *Bet Hamikdash*, even though full-fledged prophecy did not exist]. For we learned in a *Baraita*: After the later prophets, Haggai, Zechariah, and Malachi, had died, the prophetic spirit disappeared from the Jewish people, but they still made use of the *Bat Kol* [which periodically would descend from Heaven to offer guidance in human affairs].

[Now the Gemara refers back to the incident where Rabbah b. Bar Chana helped Resh Lakish climb out of the river, and Resh Lakish berated him and Babylonian Jewry. The Gemara asks:] Is it possible that Resh Lakish started a conversation with Rabbah b. Bar Chana? Resh Lakish did not even start a conversation with R. Elazar who was the teacher of all of Eretz Yisrael —the reason being that people would trust anyone Resh Lakish conversed with to the point that they gave him merchandise without witnesses, and Resh Lakish did not want to vouch for anyone's character—now, would he start a conversation with Rabbah b. Bar Chana?[9] R. Papa said: Insert the name of another person in this story. Either say that Resh Lakish was the one who was bathing, and the one who offered the hand was Ze'iri [who was a greater sage than Rabba b. Chana, and therefore Resh Lakish started a conversation with him], or say that the one who extended the hand was Rabbah bar b. Chana, and the one who was bathing was R. Elazar, [so the question does not arise].

When Resh Lakish came before R. Yochanan, [R. Yochanan] said to him: [The fact that not all the Jews from Babylonia came up to Eretz Yisrael with Ezra] is not the reason [why there was a lower degree of prophecy during the second *Bet Hamikdash*]. Even if they had all come up with Ezra, the Divine Presence would still not have rested on the second *Bet Hamikdash*, for it says, "May God expand Japheth, but may He dwell in the tents of Shem" (Genesis 9:27). **(10a)** [The implication is:] although God has expanded Japhet, [meaning, although the Persians, who are descendants of Japhet, ruled Eretz Yisrael when the second *Bet Hamikdash* was built], the Divine Presence rested only in the "the tents of Shem," [i.e., in the first *Bet Hamikdash*, which was built by Solomon, who was a descendant of Shem].

[The Gemara asks:] And how do we know that the Persians are descendants of Japhet? Because it says, "The sons of Japhet were: Gomer, Magog, Madai, Yavan, Tuval, Meshech, and Tiras" (Genesis 10:4). And R. Yosef learned in a *Baraita*: Tiras is Persia.

THE FALL OF
THE ROMAN EMPIRE

R. Yehoshua b. Levi said in the name of Rabbi: In time to come, Rome will fall into the hands of Persia. For it says, "Hear then the plan that God has devised against Edom [i.e., Rome], and what He has purposed against the inhabitants of Teman: Surely the least of the flock shall drag them away; surely their habitation shall be aghast because of them" (Jeremiah 49:20). Rabbah b. Ullah objected: How do you know that "the least of the flock" refers to Persia? Probably because it says, "The two-horned ram that you saw [signifies] the kings of Media and Persia" (Daniel 8:20). Why not say that it refers to Greece, for it says, "And the rough he-goat is the king of Greece" (ibid. 21)? When R. Chaviva b. Surmeki came up [from Babylonia to Eretz Yisrael] he reported this [objection of Rabbah b. Ullah] before a certain rabbi. The rabbi replied: Only a person who does not understand the meaning of the passage would dare raise such an objection against Rabbi. Now, what does "the least of the flock" mean? It means [Tiras], the youngest of his brothers, for R. Yosef learned that Tiras is Persia, [and Tiras is mentioned last in the list of the sons of Japheth in Genesis 10:2, therefore he is "the youngest of the brothers"].

Rabbah b. Bar Chana said in the name of R. Yochanan who quoted R. Yehudah b. Ila'i: In time to come, Rome will fall into the hands of Persia. This can be established by logical reasoning: If the Chaldeans who destroyed the first *Bet Hamikdash*, which was built by the descendants of Shem [these Chaldeans], fell into the hands of the Persians,[10] then surely the Romans who destroyed the second *Bet Hamikdash*, which was built by the Persians,[11] should fall into the hands of the Persians.

Rav said: Persia will fall into the hands of Rome. Thereupon R. Kahana and R. Assi asked Rav: Shall the builders [i.e., the Persians] fall into the hands of the destroyers [i.e., the Romans]? He replied: Yes, it is the decree of the King [God]. Others say: He replied to them: They [the Persians] too are guilty, for they destroyed the synagogues. We have learned a proof to this in a *Baraita*: Persia will fall into the hands of Rome because they destroyed the synagogues, and also because it is the King's decree that the builders fall into

the hands of the destroyers. Rav also said: The son of David [i.e., *Mashiach*] will not come until the wicked kingdom of Rome will have extended its control over the whole world for nine months. For it says, "Therefore, He will abandon [the Jewish people to their enemies] until the time that she [the Jewish people] that is now suffering the pangs of labor will have given birth; then the rest of the brothers shall return to the children of Israel" (Micah 5:2), [in other words, God's abandonment of the Jewish people will last as long as the period of pregnancy, i.e., nine months].

DON'T PLAY WITH FIRE

(11a) R. Yehudah said: It happened that a Roman police officer caught Artiban while he was checking *mezuzot* in the upper market of Tzipori (Sepphoris). He fined him one thousand *zuz*. [The Gemara asks:] But has not R. Elazar said: People who are on a mission to fulfill a mitzvah will meet no harm, [and checking *mezuzot* certainly is a mitzvah]? [The Gemara answers:] In cases where danger is to be expected it is different, for it says, "Samuel said, 'How can I go [to anoint David as king as God has commanded me to do]? If Saul hears of it, he will kill me.' God answered, 'Take a heifer with you and say, 'I have come to sacrifice to God'"" (1 Samuel 16:2).

THE HIGH PRIEST PREPARES
FOR YOM KIPPUR SERVICE

(18a) [The Gemara now focuses on the *kohen gadol*, who was secluded in the Palhedrin Chamber for seven days prior to Yom Kippur.] MISHNAH: Several of the elders of the Sanhedrin were assigned to read before the *kohen gadol* [on each of the seven days] the order of the service of Yom Kippur [as described in Leviticus, Chapter 16]. They would say to him: Master *kohen gadol*, read this chapter out loud, perhaps you have forgotten it, or perhaps you never learned it. On the morning before Yom Kippur, they would place the *kohen gadol* at the eastern gate [of the Court of the *Bet Hamikdash*], and they would pass in front of him the bulls, rams, and sheep [that were to be offered on Yom Kippur] in order that he become accustomed to seeing these animals [and should remember the order in which they were to be offered], and to familiarize him with the service of Yom Kippur. All these seven days of preparation he was allowed to eat and drink [as much as he wanted], but on the eve of Yom Kippur before sundown, they did not permit him to eat much because food makes a person drowsy. [He had to stay awake all night for fear that if he slept he might have a seminal emission, which would render him unclean and unfit to perform the service.]

[The Gemara says:] We can understand that the elders [reviewed the order of the service of Yom Kippur with the *kohen gadol*] because they assumed that perhaps he forgot it, but how could they possibly assume that he had never learned it at all? Would we ever permit the appointment of an [ignorant] *kohen gadol?* Didn't we, in fact, learn in a *Baraita:* It says [in reference to the *kohen gadol*], "The priest who is exalted above his fellows" (Leviticus 21:10), that means that [the *kohen gadol*] should be physically stronger, more handsome, wiser, and wealthier than all his colleagues. Others say: From where do we know that if he is not wealthy, his colleagues, the *kohanim,* have to give him wealth in order that he should be wealthier than they are? Because it says, "The priest who is exalted above his fellows," (i.e., he should be greater than his colleagues, *mei'echav,* [literally "from his brothers"]), through the contributions of his colleagues).

[The Gemara asks: Since the *kohen gadol* had to be wiser than his colleagues, how could they possibly assume that he had never learned the order of the service of Yom Kippur?] R. Yosef said: This is not difficult. One refers to the first *Bet Hamikdash,* the other to the second Bet Hamikdash. [There is a fundamental difference between the kind of *Kohen gadol* that served in the first *Bet Hamikdash* and the kind that served in the second *Bet Hamikdash.*] For R. Assi said: Martha, the daughter of Baitus, gave a *tarkavful* of gold dinars to King Yannai [who reigned during the second *Bet Hamikdash*] to have [her husband] Yehoshua b. Gamla appointed *kohen gadol.* [So we see that high priests in the second *Bet Hamikdash* were not appointed on their merits but through bribes, and there was reason to believe that a *kohen gadol* was ignorant.]

WHY DOES THE MISHNAH OMIT THE GOATS?

[We learned in the Mishnah that on the morning before Yom Kippur they passed before the *kohen gadol* the bulls, rams, and sheep that were to be offered, but the Mishnah does not mention the two goats that were brought on Yom Kippur.] We learned in a *Baraita:* The goats were also passed in front of him. [The Gemara asks:] Why does the Tanna of our Mishnah omit the goats? [The Gemara answers:] Since the goats were brought as an atonement for sins, if the *kohen gadol* saw them he would become depressed. [The Gemara asks:] If so, we should not pass any bulls in front of him either, since the bulls, too, come for a sin offering.[12] [The Gemara answers:] The bull atones for his own personal sins and the sins of his fellow *kohanim.* And if one of the *kohanim* had sinned, the *kohen gadol* would know about it and bring him to repentance. [That is why seeing the bulls would not depress him.] But the goats were brought as an atonement for the sins of all Israel, and the *kohen gadol* cannot possibly be aware of the sins of such a multitude of people and cannot persuade each individual to do *teshuvah.* [Therefore the sight of the goats would be a source of depression.] Ravina said: This is an example of the popular

saying: If your nephew has been appointed as tax collector, be careful not to cross in front of him when you meet him in the street, [because he knows how much you earn and how much tax you owe. Similarly in this case, the *kohen gadol* knows the transgressions of every *kohen,* and will make sure that he repents and sets things right].

THE OATH OF THE HIGH PRIEST

(18b) [After the *Kohen Gadol* learned the order of the Yom Kippur service, he was taught the offering of the incense, which was an essential part of the Yom Kippur service. It consisted of the *kohen gadol* taking a special spoon full of incense and a pan in which burning coals were placed into the Holy of Holies. There he placed the incense on the fire so that the smoke permeated the inner sanctuary.]

The Mishnah says: [On the day before Yom Kippur,] the elders of the Sanhedrin handed the *kohen gadol* over to the elders of the priesthood who took him up to the house of Avtinas [a chamber in the *Bet Hamikdash* where the ingredients of the incense were ground and mixed]. The elders of the Sanhedrin made him swear, and went away. [What was the oath they adjured him?] They said to him: Master *Kohen Gadol,* we are the representatives of the Sanhedrin, and you are our representative and the representative of the Sanhedrin. We impose an oath on you in the name of the One Whose Presence dwells in this House, that you will not deviate from any of the instructions we now give you. [They made him swear not to offer the incense according to the Sadducee manner.]

He turned aside and wept [because they had suspected him of being a Sadducee], and they turned aside and wept [because they had insinuated that he might be a Sadducee]. If he was a Torah scholar he would expound [on the laws of Yom Kippur], and if not, there were scholars who expounded before him. If he was used to reading the books of Tanach, he would read; if not, other people would read to him. What topics did they read? From Job, Ezra, and Chronicles, [because the contents of these books are stimulating and would keep him awake]. Zecharia b. Kevutal said: Many times I personally read before him from the Book of Daniel.

(19b) [We learned in the Mishnah:] He wept and they wept. [The Gemara explains:] He turned aside and cried because they suspected him of being a Sadducee, and they cried, because R. Yehoshua b. Levi said: "He who suspects an innocent person will be stricken with sickness." [The Gemara asks:] Why was it necessary [to make the *kohen gadol* take this oath]? [The Gemara answers:] They were concerned that he would prepare the incense on the outside and enter the Holy of Holies with it, the way the Sadducees did it. [The Sadducees, who did not believe in the Oral Torah, said that the *kohen gadol* should place the incense into the pan with the burning coals and then enter the Holy of Holies with the incense already burning. However, according to the Oral Torah, the *kohen gadol* must place the incense on the burning coals *after* he has entered the Holy of Holies.]

THE SADDUCEE HIGH PRIEST

The Rabbis taught in a *Baraita*: There was a Sadducee [*Kohen Gadol*] who prepared the incense on the outside [i.e., before entering the Holy of Holies, he placed the incense on the burning coals in the pan], and then brought the burning incense into the Holy of Holies. When he came out he was extremely happy. His father met him and said to him: My son, although we are Sadducees [and ignore the Oral Torah], we fear what the *Perushim* [Pharisees, people who do observe the laws of the Oral Torah] are able to do to us. He replied: All my life I was in anguish because of this verse, [God said,] "Since [on Yom Kippur] I appear over the Ark cover in a cloud" (Leviticus 16:2). I used to say to myself: When will I have the opportunity to fulfill this? Now that I [am acting as the *Kohen Gadol*] and the opportunity has come my way, shouldn't I fulfill it [the way I think it should be done]? [The Sadducees interpreted the verse to mean: Let him not come into the inner Sanctuary except with a cloud of incense, for only thus will I appear on the Ark cover. Therefore the Sadducees prepared and lit the incense before entering the Holy of Holies.]

It was said that it did not take long until he died and was thrown on a trash dump, and worms were coming out of his nose [because he smelled the fragrance of the incense outside the Holy of Holies (Ritva)]. Some say: He was stricken as he came out of the Holy of Holies. For R. Chiya said: [When he came out] a noise was heard in the Court of the *Bet Hamikdash*, for an angel had come and struck this *Kohen Gadol* on his face, and when his fellow *kohanim* came to take him out they found a mark like a calf's foot between his shoulders, for it says, "The legs of each [angel] were [fused into] a single rigid leg, and the feet of each were like a calf's hoof" (Ezekiel 1:7).

STAYING UP ALL NIGHT

[The Mishnah says:] If the *Kohen Gadol* began to doze off on the night of Yom Kippur, the young *kohanim* would snap their fingers [to keep him awake], and they would say to him: Master *Kohen Gadol*, stand up and drive away your drowsiness by stepping unto the cold floor. They would entertain him [chanting songs and psalms] until the time of the slaughtering of the daily morning offering [i.e., daybreak].

We learned in a *Baraita*: They entertained him neither with a harp nor with a lyre, but by singing. What were they singing? "Unless God builds the house, its builders labor in vain on it" (Psalms 127:1)

[implying that unless his service is totally devoted to God, it is of no value]. Some of the distinguished people of Jerusalem did not go to sleep all night in order that the *kohen gadol* should hear the echo of their voices and not be overcome by sleep.

We learned in a *Baraita*: Abba Shaul said: Even outside Jerusalem they used to stay up all night before Yom Kippur, in memory of the *Bet Hamikdash*, but this led to sinful conduct [because men and women were mingling in a lighthearted atmosphere (Rashi)]. Abbaye, some say R. Nachman b. Yitzchak, said that this refers to the city of Nehardea. For Eliya said to Rav Yehudah, the brother of R. Sila Chasida: You have wondered: Why has *Mashiach* not yet come? Now today is Yom Kippur, and yet how many immoral acts have taken place in Nehardea! He answered: What did the Holy One, blessed be He, say [about the temptations the people of Nehardea yield to]? Elijah replied: (20a) "Sin is crouching at the door" (Genesis 4:7). [They cannot help it; the *yetzer hara* (the evil tendency) causes them to sin.] And what does Satan [the Accuser] say about this? He answered: Satan has no permission to act as accuser on Yom Kippur. How do we know this? Rami b. Chama said: The numeric value of *HaSatan* [the Satan] is 364 [5 + 300 + 9 + 50]; that means on 364 days of the year he has permission to act as accuser, but on Yom Kippur he has no permission to accuse the Jewish people.

THE *KOHEN GADOL'S* RESONANT VOICE

(20b) There is a *Baraita* in accordance with Rav. What does Gevini, the announcer of the *Bet Hamikdash*, call out: Arise, all you *kohanim*, for your service, Levites for your chanting platform, and Israel for your places! His voice could be heard for three *parsangs*.[13] It happened that King Agrippa, while on the road, heard [the announcer's] voice from a distance of three *parsangs*, and when he came home he sent him gifts. Nevertheless, the voice of the *Kohen Gadol* was even more powerful than the announcer's, for a rabbi said: It has happened already that as the *Kohen Gadol* [leaned his hands on his bull and confessed his sins,] saying, "Please God, I have erred"; his voice carried as far as Jericho. And Rabbah b. Bar Chanah said in the name of R. Yochanan: The distance from Jerusalem to Jericho is ten *parsangs*: and [consider also that] on Yom Kippur the *Kohen Gadol* was weak [because of the fast], and Gevini [the announcer] was not weak; and the *Kohen Gadol* made his confession during daytime [when his voice is less audible due to interference from the light of the sun], and Gevini made his announcements at night, [when there is no such interference]. For R. Levi said: Why doesn't a man's voice carry in the daytime as far as it does at night? Because of the orbit of the sun that saws in the sky like a carpenter sawing cedars [and drowns it out]. Those minute particles of light are called *la*, "infinitesimally small," and Nebuchadnezzar had them in mind when he said, "All the inhabitants of the world are considered [*la*], of no account" (Daniel 4:32).

The Rabbis taught: If not for the [interference of the] orbit of the sun, the tumultuous noise of Rome would be heard [all over the world]; and if not for the tumultuous noise of Rome, the sound of the orbit of the sun would be heard.

The Rabbis taught: There are three voices going from one end of the world to the other: The sound of the orbit of the sun, the tumultuous noise of Rome, and the cry of the soul when it leaves the body. Some say, also the sound of childbirth (21a) and some say, also the sound of Ridiya [the angel of rain]. The Rabbis prayed for the soul when it leaves the body, and they succeeded in having that cry stopped.

THE TEN MIRACLES
Rav Yehudah said in the name of Rav: When the Jews came up [to Jerusalem] on their Yom Tov pilgrimages, they stood so crowded together in the *Bet Hamikdash* [that they could not move], but, [miraculously], when they prostrated themselves [on hearing the *Kohen Gadol* pronounce the ineffable Name] there was ample room between them, [a space of four cubits, so that one should not be able to hear someone else's confession of sins (Etz Yosef)], and the crowd spilled over into the area of eleven cubits between the back wall of the Holy of Holies [and the *Kotel Maaravi*, the Western Wall]. What does that mean? It means that, although the crowd [was so great that it] spilled over into the eleven cubits behind the back wall of the Holy of Holies, and the people were standing crammed together, yet when they prostrated themselves, there was ample space between them. This was one of the ten miracles that happened in the *Bet Hamikdash*, for we learned in a Mishnah: Ten miracles were performed for our ancestors in the *Bet Hamikdash*: No woman miscarried because of the aroma of the sacrificial meat; the sacrificial meat never became putrid; no fly was seen in the place where the meat was butchered; no seminal emission occurred to the *Kohen Gadol* on Yom Kippur; the rains did not extinguish the fire of the woodpile on the altar; no disqualification was found in the *Omer*,[14] the Two Loaves,[15] or the Showbread;[16] the people stood crowded together, yet prostrated themselves in ample space; neither serpent nor scorpion ever caused injury in Jerusalem; nor did any man say to his fellow, "The place is insufficient for me to stay overnight in Jerusalem."

[The Gemara asks: How is it that] the *Tanna* starts with [miracles that happened in] the *Bet Hamikdash* and ends with [miracles that happened] in Jerusalem? [The Gemara answers:] There are two more [miracles that happened in the *Bet Hamikdash*], for we learned in a *Baraita*: It never happened that the rains doused the fire of the pile of wood on the altar; and the column of smoke that rose from it could not be blown away even if all the winds of the of the world came storming.

THE FIRE OF THE ALTAR
(21b) R. Oshaya said: When King Solomon built the *Bet Hamikdash*, he planted there all kinds of trees of golden delights that bore fruit at the proper time, and when the wind blew on them they would fall off, as it says, "Let his fruits shake like the [fruits of] Lebanon" (Psalms 72:16), [and Lebanon symbolizes the *Bet Hamikdash* (*Gittin* 56b)]. And when the heathens entered the *Bet Hamikdash* the trees withered, for it says, "And the flower of Lebanon withers" (Nahum 1:4). But in time to come, the Holy One, blessed be He, will restore them, as it says, "It shall blossom abundantly. It shall also exult and shout; it shall receive the glory of Lebanon" (Isaiah 35:2).

[The Gemara raises a question:] The Rabbi said above: The column of smoke rising up from the pile of wood on the altar [could not be blown away]. But was there then any smoke on the altar? Haven't we learned in a *Baraita*: Five things have been said regarding the fire of the pile of wood: It was lying like a lion,[17] it was as clear as sunlight, its flame was of a tangible substance, it burned wet wood like dry wood, and it did not produce smoke. [So, how can the above *Baraita* say that the smoke could not be blown away?] [The Gemara answers:] When the *Baraita* said [that the flame on the altar produced smoke] it referred to wood from the outside that was placed on the woodpile of the altar [in addition to the holy fire that was burning there]. For it says, "Aaron's sons shall place fire on the altar, and arrange wood on the fire" (Leviticus 1:8). [This teaches us that,] although the fire comes down from heaven, it is a mitzvah to bring fire from the outside too.] [It was this extraneous fire that produced the smoke.]

[The *Baraita* said: The fire of the pile of wood was] lying like a lion. [The Gemara asks:] But haven't we learned in a *Baraita*: R. Chanina, the deputy *Kohen Gadol*, said: I myself have seen it, and it was lying like a dog? [The Gemara answers:] This is no difficulty: During the first *Bet Hamikdash* it was crouching like a lion; during the second *Bet Hamikdash*, like a dog.

[The Gemara asks:] But was the [Heavenly] fire present in the second *Bet Hamikdash*? Did not R. Shmuel b. Inia say: What is the meaning of the verse [referring to the second *Bet Hamikdash*], "Go up to the hills and get timber, and rebuild the House; then I will look on it with favor, and [*ve'ikabeid*] I will be glorified" (Haggai 1:8). It is read *ve'ekabedah*, although it is written *ve'ikabeid* [without the letter *hei*]. Then why is the letter *hei* omitted? To indicate that five things [the numeric value of *hei* is five] that were present in the first *Bet Hamikdash* were missing in the second *Bet*

Hamikdash: the Ark, the Ark-cover, the Cherubim [these three are one unit], the Heavenly fire, the *Shechinah*, the Divine inspiration [of Prophecy], and the *Urim veTummim*.[18] [So you see that there was no Heavenly fire at all in the second *Bet Hamikdash*.] [The Gemara answers:] I will tell you. [The Heavenly fire] was there [crouching like a dog], but it did not help in burning.

SIX KINDS OF FIRE

Our Rabbis taught: There are six different kinds of fire: Fire that eats but does not drink; fire that drinks but does not eat; fire that eats and drinks; fire that burns dry as well as moist things; fire that pushes away fire; and fire that eats fire. "Fire that eats but does not drink," that is our [common] fire [water extinguishes it]; "fire that drinks but does not eat," that is the fever of the sick [they are thirsty but have no appetite]; "fire that eats and drinks" refers to the fire of Elijah, for it says, "Then fire from God descended and consumed the burnt offering . . . and licked up the water that was in the trench" (1 Kings 18:38); "fire that burns dry as well as moist things," that is the fire of the pile of wood on the altar; "fire that pushes away other fire" refers to the fire of Gabriel [the angel who came down to save Chananiah, Mishael, and Azariah. He cooled the inside of the fiery furnace and heated it on the outside to burn those who threw them into it];[19] and "Fire that eats fire," that is the fire of the *Shechinah*, for a Rabbi said: [Concerning the angels who objected to the creation of man:] God stretched out His finger among them and burned them [and these angels were made of fire (Rabbeinu Chananel), thus it is "fire that eats fire"].

[The Gemara raises an objection to an earlier statement:] "But the column of smoke rising up from the pile of wood on the altar could not be blown away by all the winds of the world." [The Gemara questions:] But did not R. Yitzchak b. Avdimi say: On the night after the last day of Sukkot, [on the last day of Sukkot (*Hoshana Rabbah*), God judges mankind with regard to water supply], everyone looked at the column of smoke rising up from the woodpile of the altar. If it inclined toward the north, the poor people were happy, and the affluent were distressed, because the rains of the coming year would be abundant and their fruit would rot [and could not be stored, thus fruit prices would fall]. If the smoke slanted southward, the poor were depressed and the affluent were elated because there would be little rain, the fruit could be stored, [and prices would rise]. If the smoke inclined eastward, everyone was happy [because that meant the wind was coming from the west bringing the proper amount of rain; the fruit would not rot, and there would be no famine]; if the smoke slanted toward the west, [as a result of an east wind,] all were depressed, [because an east wind dries up the seeds and brings on famine].

[In any event, we see that the smoke on the altar moved, which contradicts the statement above.] [The Gemara answers:] It just means that it swayed back and forth, like a palm tree, but it was not scattered.

[The Gemara raises another objection:] The Rabbi said: [If the smoke slanted] toward the east [indicating a west wind], all were happy; toward the west, [indicating an east wind], all were depressed. The following *Baraita* contradicts this: The east wind is always good, the west wind always bad, the north wind is good for wheat that has grown to one-third of its normal height, and bad for olives when they are budding; the south wind is bad for wheat that has grown to one-third of its standard size, and good for olives when they are budding. And R. Yosef—according to others, Mar Zutra—suggested the following mnemonic device [to make it easy to remember]: [In the Sanctuary,] the Table was in the north, and the Menorah in the south, meaning, the north wind promotes the growth of wheat, which is food for the table; the south wind promotes the growth of olives, which is food for the Menorah. [At any rate, one *Baraita* considers the east wind good and the west wind bad; the other *Baraita* finds the east wind bad and the west wind good.] [The Gemara answers:] There is no contradiction: The statement "the east wind is good" refers to Babylonia [which is full of swamps and marshes and has a damp climate. It benefits from the dry east wind], and, "the east wind is bad" refers to Eretz Yisrael, [an arid and mountainous country that is harmed by the dry east wind].

DO NOT COUNT
THE JEWISH PEOPLE

(22b) R. Yitzchak said: It is forbidden to count the Jewish people, even for the sake of a mitzvah, for it says, "[Saul] mustered them *be-bezek*, using small bits of pottery"; (1 Samuel 11:8). [Each soldier would cast a piece of pottery into a dish. By counting the pieces Saul knew how many soldiers there were.] R. Ashi challenged this statement: How do you know that the word *bezek* means broken bits of pottery? Perhaps it is the name of a city, as in the verse, "They found Adoni-Bezek in Bezek" (Judges 1:5)? Rather the proof should be brought from here: "Saul called the people together and counted them by using *tela'im* [sheep]" (1 Samuel 15:4). [He handed a sheep to each person, and afterward these sheep were counted.]

R. Elazar said: Whoever counts the Jewish people violates a Biblical law, for it says, "The number of the people of Israel shall be like that of the sands of the sea, which cannot be measured" (Hosea 2:1). R. Nachman b. Yitzchak said: He would violate two prohibitions, for it says, "which cannot be measured or counted," [meaning, they *may* not be measured or counted]. R. Shmuel b. Nachmani said: R. Yonatan pointed out a contradiction: It says, "The number of the people of Israel shall be like the sands of the sea," [so there is a number], and it says, "which cannot be measured or counted," [the implication being that they are beyond measure or count]. [He answered:] This is no contradiction. The phrase "They cannot be measured or counted" refers to the time when Israel fulfills the will of God, [then they will be infinite in number]; the phrase "The number of the people of Israel" refers to the time when Israel does not fulfill the will of God; [they will have a number, but even then their number will be like the sands of the sea]. Rabbi said in the name of Abba Yose b. Dusta'i: There is another way of reconciling the contradiction: The phrase "Which cannot be measured or counted" refers to counting done by human beings, [who get tired of counting because the number is so great (*Maharsha*)], but the phrase, "The number of the people of Israel" refers to counting by God. [He can count them, no matter how numerous they are.]

R. Nehila'i b. Idi said in the name of Shmuel: [The passage, "Saul counted them by using sheep," teaches us that,] as soon as a person has been appointed to be a leader of a community, he becomes rich. First it says, "Saul counted them by means of broken bits of pottery," and after he was accepted as king it says, "He counted them by using sheep." [The assumption is that these were Saul's sheep, and each person was given a sheep, after which the sheep were counted.] [The Gemara asks:] Maybe each person brought his own sheep? [The Gemara answers:] If so, then what is so remarkable about it, [that the passage stresses that he counted them by using sheep? The answer is that the verse wants to tell us that since Saul became king he became rich and was able to supply each person with a sheep for the purpose of counting].

THE TRANSGRESSIONS OF SAUL AND DAVID

[The Gemara continues by expounding the next verse, which deals with the war King Saul fought against Amalek. It says,] "[Saul] battled in the valley" (1 Samuel 15:5). R. Mani said: [He argued with God] about the ceremony that happens "in the valley": When the Holy One, blessed be He, said to Saul: Go and attack Amalek, [kill alike men and women, infants and sucklings, oxen and sheep, camels and donkeys]" (ibid. 3). Saul said: If because of one person [who was killed] the Torah says: Bring a calf to a valley where its neck is to be broken [as atonement of the murder]; then surely the lives of all these Amalekites should be spared! And if you will say that people have sinned, what is the sin of the cattle [of the Amalekites, that they too should be destroyed]? And if the adults have sinned, what have the little ones done? Thereupon, a Heavenly Voice came forth and said to Saul, "Don't overdo goodness" (Ecclesiastes 7:16). And when Saul said to Doeg, "You, Doeg, go and strike down the

priests of the city of Nob" (1 Samuel 22:18), [because they had given supplies to David and his men], a Heavenly Voice came forth and said to him, "Don't overdo wickedness" (Ecclesiastes 7:17).

[Having won the battle against Amalek, Saul transgressed and left the animals alive and spared the life of Agag, the king of Amalek. It was for this sin that the kingdom was taken away from him and given to David.]

R. Huna said: How little does a person whom God supports need to worry or be concerned! Saul [who had no Divine support] sinned once, and it was counted against him [so that he lost his throne]; David [who had Divine support] sinned twice, yet it did not count against him, [and his throne was not taken from him]. What was the one sin of Saul? The episode with Agag [whom he did not kill, in violation of God's command].[20] [The Gemara asks:] But there was also the matter with Nob, the city of priests, [where Saul killed all the priests because they had given supplies to David and his men]?[21] [The Gemara answers:] The incident with Agag alone prompted God to say, "I regret that I made Saul king" (1 Samuel 15:11).

What were the two sins of David? The sin of causing the death of Uriah [the husband of Bathsheba][22] and the sin of counting the people to which he was enticed.[23] [The Gemara asks:] And what about the matter with Bathsheba [with whom he had illicit marital relations, isn't that a third sin? [The Gemara answers:] For that he was punished, for it says, "He shall pay for the lamb four times over" (2 Samuel 12:6). [When the prophet Nathan told David the parable of the rich man who had stolen the poor man's lamb, David angrily said that the rich man would have to pay for the lamb four times over. Thus, unknowingly, he pronounced his own sentence. What were the four punishments?] The child [that was born to Bathsheba], Amnon, Tamar, and Absalom [all these died during his lifetime]. [But for Uriah and for counting Israel he was not punished.] [The Gemara asks:] But he *was* punished for the sin of counting Israel! For it says, "God sent a pestilence upon Israel from morning until the set time" (2 Samuel 24:15). [The Gemara answers:] In the case of the counting, his own body was not punished.

[The Gemara asks:] But in the case of Bathsheba, his own body was not punished either! [It was his children that died.] [The Gemara says:] It is not so! He *was* punished on his own body. For Rav Yehudah said in the name of Rav: For six months David was stricken with leprosy [as a punishment for the matter with Bathsheba], the Sanhedrin separated themselves from him, and the *Shechinah* left him. For David says, "May those who fear You, those who know Your decrees return again to me" (Psalms 119:79), and he also says, "Let me again rejoice in Your help" (ibid. 51:14) [referring to the *Shechinah* that had left him].

[The Gemara demurs:] But didn't Rav say that David listened to slander, [i.e., the slander of Zibah against Mefiboshet, the son of Saul, so that he committed a third sin]? [The Gemara answers:] We hold like Shmuel who says that David never accepted slander. And even according to Rav who says that David did accept slander, he was punished for this. For Rav Yehudah said in the name of Rav: At the time when David said to Mefiboshet, [although Mefiboshet had explained that he was not against David], "I decree that you and Zibah shall divide the field" (2 Samuel 19:30), a heavenly Voice came forth and said to him: Rehoboam and Jeroboam will divide the Kingdom [into the Kingdoms of Judah and Israel, and your descendants will rule only over Judah].

KING SAUL

"When Saul was king for one year . . . " (1 Samuel 13:1). R. Huna said: [The unusual wording suggests that when he became king] he was like a one-year-old infant that has not tasted the taste of sin. R. Nachman b. Yitzchak objected to this: [You may just as well say that] the verse compares him to a one-year-old infant that is dirty with mud and excrement? Thereupon R. Nachman was shown terrifying angels in his dream. [Realizing that he had offended Saul], he said: I ask for forgiveness from you, the bones of Saul, son of Kish [for saying such harsh things about you]. But he saw again a terrifying angel in his dream. This time he said: I ask for forgiveness from you, bones of Saul, son of Kish, King of Israel. [Only then did he stop having the frightening dreams.]

R. Yehudah said in the name of Shmuel: Why did the kingdom of Saul not last? Because there was nothing unsavory in his family background, [as there was in David's ancestry, for David descended from Ruth, the Moabitess]. Because R. Yochanan said in the name of R. Shimon b. Yehotzadak: We do not appoint anyone as leader over the community unless he carries a basket of reptiles on his back [meaning, his family background is flawed], so that if he became arrogant, people could tell him: Turn around, [and look behind you. There is a blemish on your lineage. And Saul's drawback was his impeccable ancestry].

Rav Yehudah said in the name of Rav: Why was Saul punished [by being caught in a situation that led to the loss of his kingship]? Because at the beginning of his reign he waived the honor that was due to him, [and a king is not allowed to relinquish the respect due to him]. For it says, [When Saul was chosen to be the king the people acclaimed him,] "But some scoundrels said, 'How can this fellow save us?' So they scorned him and brought him no gift. But he pretended not to mind" (1 Samuel 10:27), [and that was a mistake]. And the next verse says, "Nachash the Ammonite marched up and besieged Jabesh-gilead" (ibid. 11:1). [When Saul routed the Ammonites, the people wanted to put to death the scoundrels who had disdained him, but Saul spared their lives. This was not correct, for he should have avenged their disdain of the crown.]

TAKING REVENGE AND BEARING A GRUDGE

R. Yochanan also said in the name of R. Shimon b. Yehotzadak: Any Torah scholar (23a) who takes no revenge and does not bear a grudge like a snake is no real Torah scholar.[24] [The Gemara asks:] But doesn't it say, "Do not take revenge nor bear a grudge" (Leviticus 19:18)? [The Gemara answers:] That refers to money matters, for we learned in a *Baraita*: What is called revenge and what is called bearing a grudge? If one person said to another, "Lend me your sickle," and he replied, "No," and tomorrow the second fellow comes to the first and says, "Lend me your ax," and he replies, "I will not lend it to you, just as you did not want to lend me your sickle"—that is revenge. And what is called bearing a grudge? If one person says to another, "Lend me your ax," and he replies, "No," and tomorrow the second fellow asks, "Lend me your garment," and he answers, "Here it is. I am not like you who would not lend me what I asked for"—that is bearing a grudge. [So you see, the prohibition against taking revenge applies only to monetary matters.]

[The Gemara asks:] But has not the Torah forbidden vengeance also in cases of personal insult? Haven't we learned in a *Baraita*: Concerning those who are insulted and do not take revenge by insulting others, who hear themselves reproached and do not reply, who do good deeds out of love of God [and not for the sake of reward], and accept their sufferings with joy, Scripture says, "May those that love Him be like the sun rising in might" (Judges 5:31). [The Gemara answers: That means,] that he may keep it in his heart [although he takes no action]. [The Gemara asks:] But hasn't Rava said: He who gives up his right to take revenge, the Heavenly Tribunal waives all of his sins? [The Gemara answers:] That refers to a case when the offender asks to be forgiven, and the injured party forgives him, [then all his sins are forgiven].

OFFERING THE INCENSE MAKES ONE RICH

(26a) [The privilege of offering the incense was the most sought-after service in the *Bet Hamikdash*. Therefore, a *kohen* who had already performed that function had to wait for a second opportunity until all his colleagues had their turn. The Mishnah tells us: At the third call-up the officer would announce in the Temple court: "Beginners for incense [i.e., those *kohanim* who had never offered incense], come up for a chance at offering the incense!" At the fourth call-up he would announce: Beginners and old *kohanim*! Who will take up the parts [of the sacrifice] from the ramp to the altar? [The pieces of the sacrifice had been placed on the lower part of the ramp to be brought up to the altar.]

We learned: It never happened that a *kohen* offered the incense more than once [because every *kohen* was eager to perform this function]. Why is that so? R. Chanina said: Because [the offering of the incense] makes one rich. R. Papa said to Abaye: Why does the incense make a person rich? Do you think because it says, "They shall place incense in Your presence" (Deuteronomy 33:10) and in the next verse it says, "May God bless his wealth" (ibid. 11)? If so, a burnt offering should also enrich, for it says in the same verse, "[They shall place] . . . burnt sacrifices on Your altar" (ibid. 10). He answered: Sacrifices are brought frequently, incense is not, [and presumably, wealth is promised only for that which is infrequent, otherwise every *kohen* would be rich (Rashi)].

Rava said: You will not find any Torah scholar rendering *halachic* decisions who is not an offspring of the tribe of Levi or Issachar. "Of the tribe of Levi," for it says, [in the blessing that Moses gave to the tribe of Levi], "They shall teach Your law to Jacob" (Deuteronomy 33:10); of Issachar, for it says, "Of the children of Issachar, men who knew how to interpret the signs of the times, to determine how Israel should act" (1 Chronicles 12:33). [The Gemara remarks:] Why don't you mention also the tribe of Judah about whom it says, "Judah is My law-giver" (Psalms 60:9)? [Rava replied:] I am speaking only about scholars who render practical decisions on the basis of established *halachah*, [and this applies to the descendants of Levi and Issachar, but not to descendants of Judah who were lawgivers].

THE PATRIARCHS STUDY THE TORAH

(28b) R. Chama b. Chanina said: Throughout the entire history of our ancestors, they were never without a house of study. When they were in Egypt, they had houses of study, for it says, "Go, gather the elders of Israel" (Exodus 3:16), ["elders" refers to scholars who devoted their lives to Torah study]. When they were in the wilderness they had houses of study, as it says, "Assemble seventy of Israel's elders" (Numbers 11:16). Our father Abraham was an elder who attended the house of study, for it says, "And Abraham was *zakein*, an elder, well advanced in years" (Genesis 24:1). [*Zakein* (elder) is seen as a contraction of *zeh shekanah chochmah*, "a person who has acquired wisdom through study."[25]]

Our father Isaac was also an elder who studied in a yeshivah, for it says, "It happened when Isaac was an elder [*zakein*]" (ibid. 27:1). Our father Jacob, too, was an elder who learned in a yeshivah, for it says, "Israel's eyes were heavy with age [*mizoken*]" (ibid. 48:10). Even Eliezer, Abraham's servant, was an elder who learned in a yeshivah, for it says, "Abraham said to his servant, the elder [*zekan*] of his household who was in charge of all that he owned" (ibid. 24:1). R. Elazar explains this to mean that Eliezer was proficient in the Torah of his master.

[In the Torah, Eliezer is called,] "*Damesek Eliezer*," (Genesis 15:5). [What does the word *damesek* mean?]

R. Elazar said: [Damesek is a contraction of] *doleh umashkeh*, which means, "he drew and he gave others to drink of the Torah of his master."

ABRAHAM KEPT THE ENTIRE TORAH

Rav said: Our father Abraham kept the entire Torah [even before it was given], for it says, "Because Abraham obeyed My voice, kept My charge, My commandments, My decrees, and My laws" (Genesis 26:5). R. Shimi b. Chiya said to Rav: Perhaps the verse means that he observed the seven laws [of the sons of Noah which all mankind is obligated to keep]?[26] [Rav interjects: How can you suggest that he observed only seven *mitzvot*;] he definitely fulfilled the mitzvah of circumcision? [R. Chiya counters:] Then say that he kept the seven laws and circumcision [but not to the whole Torah]. Rav answered: If that is so, why does the Torah say, "My commandments and My laws"? [This implies much more than the seven Noachide *mitzvot* and milah; it includes all 613 *mitzvot*.]

Rava or R. Ashi said: Abraham our father kept even the [Rabbinic laws] such as the law of *eruv tavshilin*,[27] for it says, "He kept . . . *toratai*, "My Torahs" [in the plural], meaning both the Written Torah and the Rabbinic laws.

THINGS THAT ARE WORSE THAN OTHERS

R. Nachman said: The sweltering heat of the sun on a cloudy day is more oppressive than direct sunlight. It is just like a jar of vinegar [which emits a stronger odor through a small hole than when entirely open; similarly, sunlight shining through small spaces between the clouds is stronger than unobstructed sunshine].

It is worse to look at the sun through breaks in the clouds than to look at the uncovered sun. An analogy is water dripping from the roof. [It is more pleasant to be in a bath than to have water dripping on your body continually.]

(29a) Lustful thoughts are more harmful than the sin itself. An analogy is the odor of meat. [The smell of roasted meat is more harmful to one's health than eating it.]

The heat at the end of the summer is more oppressive than that of the summer itself. It is just like a hot oven. [It is easy to stoke an oven that has been heated two or three times on that day. Similarly, by the end of the summer the air is very hot, and any additional heat makes life unbearable.]

A person who has a fever in the winter is in worse condition than one who is feverish in the summer. An analogy is a cold oven. [It takes a great deal of wood to stoke an oven in the cold days of winter. Similarly, a fever in the winter is a sign of serious illness.]

It is harder to relearn something old that you once knew and forgot than to learn something new. An analogy is cement made of recycled old cement [it is harder to mix than newly made cement].

ESTHER, "THE DOE OF DAWN"

It says, "For the leader, on [ayelet hashachar], a psalm of David" (Psalms 22:1). [Ayelet hashachar is a metaphor that literally means "doe of the dawn."] Just as the antlers of a deer branch off in all directions, so is the light of dawn scattered in all directions. R. Zera said: Why is Esther compared to a doe? [Psalm 22, "The Doe of the Dawn," is replete with prophetic allusions to Esther (Maharsha).] To tell you that just as a doe has a narrow womb and is desirable to her mate at all times like at the first time, so was Esther beloved by King Ahasuerus at all times like at the first time. R. Assi said: Why is Esther compared to the dawn, [in the expression "the Doe of the Dawn"]? To tell you that just as the dawn comes at the end of the night, so was the story of Esther the end of all the miracles. [The Gemara asks:] But there is the miracle of Chanukah [which happened after the miracle of Purim]? [The Gemara answers:] We are speaking about miracles that are included in the Holy Scriptures. [The Gemara asks:] This explanation is acceptable according to the opinion that Esther was meant to be written down [and included in the Holy Scriptures], but what is there to say according to the opinion that Esther was not meant to be included in the Holy Scriptures, [thus "the Doe of Dawn" could not refer to Esther]? [The Gemara answers:] R. Assi could explain [the phrase "the Doe of Dawn"] according to what R. Binyamin b. Yefet said, for R. Elazar said in the name of R. Binyamin b. Yefet: Why is the prayer of the righteous compared to a doe? To tell you that just as with the doe, as long as it grows, its antlers form additional branches every year; so it is with the righteous—the longer they pray, the more will their prayer be heard.

THE ORDER OF THE DAILY ALTAR SERVICE

(33a) Abbaye listed the order of the altar service according to the tradition [the students in the bet midrash had received from their rabbis], and according to Abba Shaul: The arrangement of the large woodpile [on the outer altar where the sacrifices were burned] comes before the arranging of the secondary woodpile [from which coal was taken into the Sanctuary] to burn the incense-offering; the arranging of the secondary woodpile for the incense-offering comes before the placing of the two logs of wood on the large woodpile; the placing of the two logs comes before the removal of the ashes from the inner altar [the small altar in the Sanctuary, used only for incense]; the removal of the ashes from the inner altar precedes the cleaning of the five lamps of the Menorah;[28] the cleaning of the five lamps comes before the [dashing of] the blood of the regular daily offering [the slaughter had taken place before the cleaning of the lamps]; the [dashing of the] blood of the regular daily offering precedes the cleaning of the [other] two lamps [of the Menorah]; the cleaning of the two lamps precedes the offering of the incense [on the inner altar]; the burning of the incense precedes the burning of the limbs [of the regular daily morning offering on the outer altar]; the burning of the limbs precedes the burning of the meal offering [that accompanied the regular daily offering];[29] the meal offering precedes the offering of the cakes [minchat chavitin, which are brought daily by the kohen gadol][30]; the offering of the cakes comes before the pouring of the wine [onto the altar that accompanies the regular daily offering]; the pouring of the wine precedes the bringing of the mussaf [additional] offering [on Shabbat, Yom Tov, and Rosh Chodesh]; the mussaf offering comes before the burning of the two pans of frankincense [that were on top of the stack of the showbreads];[31] the burning of the pans of frankincense precedes the regular daily afternoon offering, as it says, "He is to arrange the burned offering on it and burn the choice parts of the peace offerings [hashelamim] on it" (Leviticus 6:5)—"on it" [i.e., the daily regular morning offering] you are to complete all the day's offerings. [The Sages expound the word hashelamim, "the peace offering." It is interpreted as if pronounced hasheleimim, "the completions," meaning that all the services of the day should be completed after the morning regular offering, and before the afternoon regular offering (Rashi).]

THE DILIGENCE OF HILLEL

(35b) Our Rabbis taught: A poor man, a rich man, and a lustful man are summoned before the heavenly tribunal. They ask the poor man: Why didn't you involve yourself in Torah study? If he says: I was very poor, and I was busy trying to earn a livelihood, they would say to him: Were you poorer than Hillel? The story is told about Hillel the Elder that he went to work every day and earned a tarpik [equal to half a dinar], half of which he would give to the guard at the bet midrash, and the other half went for food for himself and his family. One day he did not earn anything. Since the guard at the bet midrash did not allow him to enter, he climbed up to the roof and sat on a skylight [directly above the bet midrash] to hear the words of the living God from the mouth of Shemayah and Avtalyon. Now that day was a Friday; it was in the winter, and snow fell on him. At sunrise, Shemaya said to Avtalyon: Brother Avtalyon, every day this house is light, but today it is dark. Is it a cloudy day? They looked up, and saw the form of a man in the skylight. They went up and found him covered by three cubits of snow. After removing the snow, they bathed and anointed him, and placed him in front of the fire. They said: This man deserves that *Shabbat* should be desecrated on his behalf, [since his condition is life-threatening].

R. ELAZAR B. CHARSOM'S LOVE OF TORAH

To the rich man they say: Why didn't you engage in Torah study? If he says: I was rich and was extremely busy overseeing all my properties [so that I had no time to study Torah], they would say to him: Were you richer than R. Elazar? The story is told about R. Elazar b. Charsom that his father left him a thousand cities on dry land and, to match, a thousand ships on the sea. Every day, [instead of attending to the business of his cities and ships], he would take a bag of flour on his shoulder and go from city to city and from province to province to learn Torah. One day, [passing through one of his own cities], his own employees found him [and, not knowing who he was,] put him to work for the master of the city, [i.e., himself]. He said to them, [without telling them who he was]: "Please leave me alone, so that I can go and study Torah." They replied, "By the life of R. Elazar b. Charsom, we will not let you go [until you do your quota of work]." He gave them a lot of money so that they let him go. He never took care of his properties; instead, he sat day and night engrossed in Torah study.

JOSEPH'S PIETY

To the lustful man they say: Why didn't you engage in Torah study? If he says: I was handsome and could not control my passion, they would say to him: Were you driven by your lustful instincts more than Joseph? It is said about Joseph the *tzaddik* that the wife of Potiphar every day tried to seduce him with her talk. The clothes she put on for him in the morning she did not wear in the evening; those that she wore in the evening, she did not put on in the morning. She said to him: Surrender to me! He said: No, I won't! She said: I am going to lock you up in a prison. He said: "God sets prisoners free" (Psalms 146:7). She said: I am going to bend your proud stature [i.e., disgrace you]. He answered: "God makes those who are bent stand straight" (ibid. 8). She said: I am going to blind your eyes. He replied: God restores sight to the blind" (ibid.). She offered him a thousand talents of silver to make him give in to her, "to lie next to her, to be with her" (Genesis 39:10), but he would not listen to her; not "to lie next to her" in this world, not "to be with her" in the World to Come.

Consequently, Hillel causes the poor to be blamed, R. Elazar b. Charsom causes the rich to be blamed, and Joseph causes the lustful to be blamed.

THE *KOHEN GADOL*'S CONFESSION

(36b) Our Rabbis taught in a *Baraita*: How does the *Kohen Gadol* confess? [He says:] I have been iniquitous [*aviti*], I willfully sinned [*pashati*], I have erred [*chatati*]. And similarly, in connection with the he-goat [that was to be dispatched to the cliff known as *Azazel*] it says, [in the order of "iniquities, sins, errors"], "He shall confess on it all the iniquities of the children of Israel, their willful sins and errors" (Leviticus 16:21). Similarly, with Moses it says, [in the same order], "Forgiving iniquity, willful sin, and error" (Exodus 34:7), so says R. Meir. However, the Sages say: *Avon* denotes an intentional sin, and so it says, "That person shall be utterly cut off [spiritually and] his intentional sin [*avono*] shall remain upon him" (Numbers 15:31), [and *kareit* is given only for intentional transgressions, thus *avon* is an intentional sin]. *Pesha* stands for rebellious acts, and so it says, "The king of Moab has rebelled [*pesha*] against me" (2 Kings 3:7). And it says in another passage, "Libnah rebelled [*tifsha*] at that time" (ibid. 8:22). *Cheit* refers to unintentional sins, [sins done in error], and so it says, "If an individual commits an inadvertent sin [*techeta*]" (Leviticus 4:2). [Having defined the terms *avon*, *pesha*, and *cheit*, the Sages dispute R. Meir's order, saying:] It is not logical that after the *kohen gadol* has confessed the intentional sins and rebellious acts, he should then confess the unintentional transgressions. [You don't begin by asking forgiveness for serious offenses and then mention small ones. Therefore, R. Meir's order of *aviti, pashati, chatati* is incorrect.]

Rather, this is how the *Kohen Gadol* said the confession: I sinned inadvertently [*chatati*], I sinned intentionally [*aviti*], I have committed rebellious acts [*pashati*] before You, I and my household, [listing the sins in ascending order of gravity]. And so it says in connection with David, "We have sinned inadvertently [*chatanu*] like our fathers, we have transgressed intentionally [*he'evinu*], and we have acted rebelliously [*hirshanu*], [listing the sins in the same order] (Psalms 106:6). Also Solomon said, [When the people repent and say,] "We have sinned inadvertently (*chatanu*), we have transgressed intentionally (*he'evinu*), and we have acted rebelliously (*rashanu*)" (1 Kings 8:47). So also says Daniel, "We have sinned inadvertently [*chatanu*], we have transgressed intentionally [*avinu*], and we have acted rebelliously [*hirshanu*]" (Daniel 9:5). [In all these examples there is an increase in the level of sin.] [The Sages now question their own thesis:] If so, why is it that Moses said, "Forgiving intentional sin [*avon*], rebellion [*pesha*], and error [*chata'ah*]" [in the reverse order]? [They answered:] Moses said to the Holy One, blessed be He: Master of the universe, when Israel will sin before You and then repent, consider their willful sins [both those done intentionally and done rebelliously] as errors![32]

BLESSING GOD'S NAME

(37a) We learned in a *Baraita*: Rabbi said: It says, "When I proclaim God's name, praise God for His greatness" (Deuteronomy 32:3). Moses said to the Jewish people: When I mention the Name of the Holy One, blessed be He, you should praise Him. [Therefore, on Yom Kippur, when the *Kohen Gadol* pronounces the ineffable Name of God, the people should say: Blessed is the Name of His glorious kingdom for all eternity.] Chananiah, the son of the brother of R. Yehoshua, [offers an alternate source]. It says, "The memory of the righteous shall be for a blessing" (Proverbs 10:7). The prophet [Solomon, the author of Proverbs,] says to the Jewish people: When I mention the Righteous One of all the Worlds [i.e., God], then you should say a blessing.[33]

THE GIFTS OF KING MUNBAZ, QUEEN HELENA, AND NIKANOR

King Munbaz[34] made all the handles of the vessels that were used in the *Bet Hamikdash* on Yom Kippur out of gold. His mother, Queen Helena, made a golden candelabrum [as an ornament] on the entrance to the Sanctuary. She also made a golden tablet on which was inscribed the chapter dealing with the *sotah*.[35] Miracles happened with the doors that Nicanor brought for the Court [*azarah*] of the *Bet Hamikdash*.[36] All these people are mentioned in praise.

[With regard to the golden candelabrum that Queen Helena made,] we learned in a *Baraita*: In the morning when the sun rose, it would reflect sparkling rays, and everyone [in the Temple Court] knew that the time to read the *Shema* had arrived. The Gemara raises an objection: If someone says the *Shema* in the morning together with the people of the *mishmar*[37] [of *kohanim* who were performing the service on that day] or together with the laymen *maamad* [the representatives of the people who were standing by when the offerings were made], then he has not fulfilled the mitzvah of reading the *Shema*, because the people of the *mishmar* read the *Shema* very early, [because they were afraid that the service would extend beyond the proper time for reading the *Shema*], and the men of the *maamad* read it too late, [only after the daily continual morning offering was brought. At any rate we see that neither the *kohanim* nor the laymen said the *Shema* at sunrise. So for whom was this sign of the shimmering candelabrum that the sun had risen?]. Abaye answered: For the rest of the people of Jerusalem.

THE MIRACLES OF NIKANOR'S DOORS

(38a) We learned in a *Baraita*: What miracles happened to Nikanor's doors? They said: When Nikanor had gone to Alexandria in Egypt to bring [copper] doors [for the eastern gate of the Temple Court], on his way back a storm blew up in the sea that threatened to drown him. They took one of the two doors and cast it into the sea [to lighten the load], still the storm did not subside. When they wanted to throw the other door overboard too, Nicanor stood up, held the door against himself, and said: "You'll have to throw me in with it!" At that moment the sea calmed down. Now Nikanor was dismayed that he had allowed them to throw the other door into the sea. When he reached the port of Acco, [miraculously] the door floated up from under the ship. Others say: [The miracle was that] a creature in the sea swallowed it and spat it out on dry land. Concerning this, Solomon said, "The walls of our house are made of cedar wood, our doors are made of cypresses [*berotim*]" (Song of Songs 1:17); do not read *berotim*, "cypresses," but *brit yam*, "covenant of the sea," [as though the doors had made a covenant with the sea to save them]. Therefore, all the gates in the *Bet Hamikdash* were changed for golden ones, except for the Nicanor gates, because of the miracles that happened with them. But some say: [They were not changed to gold] because their copper had a golden sheen. R. Eliezer b. Yaakov said: It was Corinthian copper, [a very pure kind of polished copper that had a golden luster, so that there was no need to change them to gold].

THE EXCLUSIVE INFORMATION OF THE GARMU FAMILY

[The previous Mishnah listed the names of the people who were praised for the contributions they made to the *Bet Hamikdash*. The present Mishnah says:] The family of Garmu, because they refused to teach anyone else how to make the showbread.[38] The family of Avtinas, because they refused to teach anyone else how to prepare the incense. Hugros of the tribe of Levi, because he knew a certain musical variation and did not want to teach it to anyone else. Ben Kamtzar, because he did not want to teach to anyone a certain special way of writing. [He knew how to write with four pens at the same time.] Concerning the first ones [that were mentioned in the previous Mishnah] it is said: "The memory of the righteous shall be for a blessing" (Proverbs 10:7). Concerning the ones in this Mishnah it is said: "But the name of the wicked shall rot" (ibid.).

[Says the Gemara:] We learned in a *Baraita*: The family of Garmu were proficient in making the showbreads [for the *Bet Hamikdash*], but they did not want to teach it to anyone else. The Sages [dismissed the family of Garmu] and sent for experts from Alexandria in Egypt. These experts knew how to bake as well [as the Garmu family], but they did not know how to scrape the loaves from the oven as well [as the Garmus], for these Alexandrian experts would heat the oven on the outside and bake on the outside, [so that the fragile loaves would not break when they removed them], whereas the Garmu family were able to heat the oven on the inside and bake on the inside [because they knew how to remove them without breaking them]. The bread made by the experts from Alexandria became moldy, whereas the bread made by the Garmu family never became moldy.

When the Sages heard about this, they said: Everything God created, He created for His honor, for it says, "Everything that is called in My Name, I have created for My honor," [and it is no honor for God that the showbread should become moldy]. So they decided to reinstall the Garmu family. The Sages sent for them, but they refused to come. When they doubled their wages, they came. Until now they used to receive twelve *manah* [i.e., twelve hundred *zuz*] per day; from that day on they received twenty-four *manah*. R. Yehudah said: Until now they received twenty-four *manah* per day; from that day on they received forty-eight *manah*.

The Sages said to them: What reason did you have for not wanting to teach your skill to others? They replied: In our father's house they knew that this *Bet Hamikdash* would be destroyed, and perhaps an unworthy person would learn it, and use this knowledge to worship idols. [Nevertheless, it appears that the Sages did not accept this reason, and therefore the Garmu family is mentioned for disgrace (Rambam).] However, because of the following matter they are mentioned for praise: Their children were never found to have white bread, so that no one should say: They are taking from the flour of the showbreads for themselves. They did this to fulfill the command, "You shall be clear before God and before Israel" (Numbers 32:22). [You should avoid doing anything—even when acting rightly—that might arouse suspicion.]

THE SECRET TECHNIQUE OF THE AVTINAS FAMILY

We learned in a *Baraita*: The Avtinas family were proficient in preparing the incense [for the *Bet Hamikdash*], but they did not want to teach their technique to anyone else. The Sages sent for experts from Alexandria of Egypt [to replace the Avtinas family]. They knew how to blend the ingredients as well as the Avtinas family, but did not know how to make the smoke rise in a straight column as well as they. The smoke of the incense of the Avtinas family would ascend straight as a pillar, whereas the smoke of the Alexandrian experts spread in every direction. When the Sages heard about this they said: Whatever God created, He created for His honor, as it says, "God made everything for His purpose" (Proverbs 16:4), [and since the Avtinas family produces a more decorous incense], they should be reinstated. The Sages sent for them, but they would not come. When they doubled their salary, they came.

Until now they used to receive twelve *manah* per day; from that day on, twenty-four. R. Yehudah said: Until now, twenty-four *manah;* from that day on, forty-eight. The Sages asked them: What reason did you have for not wanting to teach your skill? They replied: In our father's house they knew that this *Bet Hamikdash* would be destroyed, and they said: Perhaps an unworthy person would learn this art and use it to serve an idol. [Nevertheless, they are mentioned for disgrace.] However, because of the following they are mentioned for praise: It never happened that a bride of their family went out wearing perfume, and when they married a woman from someplace else they stipulated that she should not wear perfume, so that no one should say: They are applying this fragrance to themselves from the ingredients of the incense [of the *Bet Hamikdash*]. They did this in obedience to the command, "You shall be clear before God and before Israel" (Numbers 32:22).

THE DESCENDANTS OF THE AVTINAS FAMILY

We learned in a *Baraita*: R. Yishmael said: I once was traveling along the road, and I ran into one of the descendants [of the Avtinas family]. I said to him: Your ancestors wanted to increase their own glory [by demanding exorbitant fees for their services (Rif)] and diminish the glory of the Creator [by not teaching their skill to anyone else]; now [that the *Bet Hamikdash* is destroyed] the glory of the Creator is where it should be, [for the whole world is filled with His glory], but their glory has been taken away from them. R. Akiva said: R. Yishmael b. Luga told me: One day, I and one of the descendants [of the Avtinas family] went out into the field to gather herbs, and I saw him crying and laughing. I said to him, "Why did you cry?" He replied, "I reminded myself of the glory of my ancestors." "And why did you smile?" He answered, "Because the Holy One, blessed be He, will give it back to us [when the *Bet Hamikdash* will be rebuilt]." "And what reminded you just now [of the former glory of your family]?" He said, "Because I see in front of me the herb called *maaleh ashan* [the smoke-rising herb]." "Show it to me," I said. "We are sworn not to show it to anyone," he answered.

R. Yochanan b. Nuri related: I once met an old man who held in his hand a scroll containing a list of the different spices for the incense. I asked him, "What family are you descended from?" "I come from the Avtinas family," he replied. "What do you have in your hand?" "A scroll containing a list of spices for the incense." "Show it to me!" I said. He told me, "As long as my father's household was still there, they would not give it to anyone, but now [that the *Bet Hamikdash* is destroyed, and my father's family is no longer here], here it is, but be careful with it, [and don't let it fall into the wrong hands]. When I told this story to R.

Akiva, he said: From now on it is forbidden to speak disparagingly about this family. Ben Azzai said: [From the reinstatement of the Garmu and Avtinas families, you can learn not to be concerned that someone else will take away your livelihood, for:] They will call you by your name, and you will be seated in the place that is rightfully yours, (38b) and they are giving you from what belongs to you [i.e., the income Heaven decreed you will earn]. A person cannot touch that which Heaven has prepared for his fellow, and one kingdom cannot take away from another kingdom even as little as a hair's breadth. [When the time comes for one government to fall and another to take power, it will not be delayed by even a minute.]

HUGROS AND BEN KAMTZAR

We learned in the Mishnah: Hugros from the tribe of Levi knew a certain variation in song which he refused to teach to anyone else. The Rabbis taught: When he wanted to give his voice a beautiful resonance, he would put his thumb into his mouth, and place his forefinger between the two sides of his moustache, and sing so resoundingly and exquisitely that his fellow kohanim, overwhelmed by the beautiful sound, thrust back their heads and joined in.

The Rabbis taught: Ben Kamtzar did not want to teach to anyone the special way of writing he knew. They said about him that he would hold four pens between his fingers, and if there was a word of four letters, he would write it at once. [He did this with the Four-Letter Divine Name, and this was considered a superior way of writing the Name. (Rashi).] They said to him: What reason do you have for not wanting to teach it? All the others when asked this question found a reason for their refusal [i.e., lest someone use it for idolatry], but Bar Kamtzar could not find an answer, [for this cannot be used for idolatry]. Concerning the first ones [that contributed gifts to the Bet Hamikdash] it says: May the memory of the righteous be for a blessing; however, with regard to Kamtzar and the others, [even though they did have an excuse], it says, "But the name of the wicked shall rot." [The Gemara asks:] What is the meaning of "The name of the wicked shall rot"; [how can a name rot]? R. Elazar said: Rottenness and decay will enter their name; no one will name his children after them.

Ravina challenged the rule [that you should not name your child after a wicked person. He said:] There is a story about a child named Doeg b. Yosef [who lived in the time of the destruction of the Bet Hamikdash]. His father died and left him as a small child to his mother. Every day his mother would measure him with her handbreadth [tefachim] to see how much he had gained, and would donate that amount in gold to the Bet Hamikdash. And when the enemy conquered Jerusalem [and there was a terrible famine] she slaughtered her child and ate him, and concerning this woman Jeremiah lamented, "Alas, women eat their own fruit, the children that are measured in tefachim [handbreadths]" (Lamentations 2:20). Whereupon the Holy Spirit replied, [It is a punishment for,] "If a kohen and a prophet [referring to the prophet Zechariah b. Yehoiadah, the priest, who was] killed in the Bet Hamikdash" (ibid.).[39] [In any event, we see that someone named his child Doeg even though Doeg the Edomite was a wicked man, and who killed the priests of Nob (1 Samuel 23:18). [The Gemara answers:] Look what happened to the child named Doeg. [He had a terrible end.]

THE RIGHTEOUS
AND THE WICKED

R. Elazar said: A righteous person is remembered for his own good deeds, for it says, "May the memory of the righteous be for a blessing"; a wicked person is remembered also for the bad deeds of his associates, for it says, "But the name of the wicked [resha'im, in the plural] shall rot," [he and all other wicked people].

Ravina said to the scholar who used to recite Aggadic teachings before him: What is the source of the saying of the Rabbis, "May the memory of the righteous be for a blessing"? He replied: It is a Scriptural verse, "May the memory of the righteous be for a blessing" (Proverbs 10:7). Ravina said: [What I meant to ask you was:] From what verse in the Torah can this be derived? [He replied:] From the verse, "God said, 'Shall I hide from Abraham, what I am going to do?'" (Genesis 18:17). And [in the next verse] it says, "Abraham is about to become a great and mighty nation" (ibid. 18). [Upon mentioning Abraham's name, God immediately gave him a blessing.] Ravina then asked: And from what verse in the Torah do we derive that "the name of the wicked shall rot"? [He replied:] From the verse, "[Lot] pitched his tents until Sodom" (ibid. 13:12), and in the next verse it says, "But the people of Sodom were very wicked, and they sinned against God" (ibid. 13). [After mentioning the name Sodom, the verse immediately relates how wicked its people were.]

R. Elazar said: There was a tzaddik who lived between two wicked people and did not learn from their evil deeds, and there was a wicked man who lived between two tzaddikim and did not learn from their good deeds. The tzaddik who lived between two wicked people and did not learn from their evil deeds was Obadiah [who was a servant of the wicked Ahab and Jezebel].[40] The wicked man who lived between two tzaddikim and did not learn from their good deeds was Esau [who lived between Isaac and Jacob and remained an evildoer].

R. Elazar said: From the blessings of the tzaddikim you can infer the curse for the wicked, and from the curse of the wicked you can infer the blessing for the tzaddikim. From the blessings of the tzaddikim you can infer the curse of the wicked, for it says, [God says,] "I know [Abraham] that he will command his children and his household after him to keep God's way, doing charity and justice" (Genesis 18:19). This is followed by, "God then said, 'The outcry against Sodom is so great'" (ibid. 20). [From the juxtaposition of these verses we can infer that Sodom was punished because they did not "do charity and justice" like Abraham (*Maharsha*).] From the curse of the wicked we can infer the blessing for the *tzaddikim*, for it says, "But the people of Sodom were very wicked, and they sinned against God" (ibid. 13:13), [followed by,] "After Lot left him, God said to Abraham, . . . 'All the land that you see I will give to you and to your offspring forever'" (ibid. 14,15). [We can infer from the juxtaposition of these passages that Abraham was blessed because his way of life was the exact opposite of the wickedness of Sodom.]

R. Elazar also said: Even for the sake of a single *tzaddik* this world would have been created, for it says, "God saw that the light was good" (Genesis 1:4). [R. Elazar expounds,] "God saw that the light should remain in existence because there was good [i.e., a *tzaddik*]," and the word "good" refers to a *tzaddik*, for it says, "Say to the *tzaddik* that he is good" (Isaiah 3:10).

R. Elazar further said: Whoever forgets anything of his Torah [due to negligence, laziness, or indifference], causes his children to go into exile, for it says, "Because you have spurned the teaching of your God, I, in turn, will forget your children" (Hosea 4:6). R. Abbahu said: Such a person is removed from his high position, as it says, "Because you have rejected knowledge, I reject you as my priest" (ibid.).

R. Chiya b. Abba said in the name of R. Yochanan: No *tzaddik* departs this world until an equally great *tzaddik* has been created. For it says, "The sun rises, and the sun sets" (Ecclesiastes 1:5); [it rises before it sets]. [For example,] before the sun of Eli set, the sun of Samuel of Ramatayim had already risen. R. Chiya b. Abba also said in the name of R. Yochanan: The Holy One, blessed be He, saw that there are few *tzaddikim*, [and the worlds needs *tzaddikim* for its continued existence], therefore, He planted them in every generation, as it says, "For the pillars of the earth belong to God, and He has set the world upon them" (1 Samuel 2:8) [He parceled them out them among the generations, so that the world should endure.] R. Chiya b. Abba further said in the name of R. Yochanan: Even for the sake of a single *tzaddik* the world remains in existence, for it says, "The *tzaddik*, [even if he is the only one], is the foundation of the world" (Proverbs 10:25).

R. Chiyah said in his own name: We can derive it from the following verse: "He guards the feet of His pious ones," which he interprets to mean, "Because of[41] His pious ones He will preserve [the world]" (1 Samuel 2:9). [The Gemara asks:] But "pious ones" means many; [how does that prove that God preserves the

world even for *one* tzaddik]? R. Nachman b. Yitzchak said: [Although the *keri*, the traditional reading, is *chasidav*, "His pious ones"], it is written *chasido*, "His pious *one*."

R. Chiya b. Abba also said in the name of R. Yochanan: When a person has lived the greater part of his life without having sinned, he will no longer sin, for it says, "He guards the feet [i.e., the latter years] of His pious ones [so that they will not sin]" (ibid.). In the yeshivah of R. Shila they taught: Once a sin presented itself to a person a first and a second time, and he resists the temptation, he will never commit this sin, as it says, "He guards the feet of His pious ones," which is interpreted to mean: "God will protect those who resisted a sin two times."[42]

HEAVEN ASSISTS
BAALEI TESHUVAH

Resh Lakish asked: What is the meaning of the passage, "At scoffers He scoffs, but to the lowly He shows grace" (Proverbs 3:34)? It means: If a person wants to defile himself [with sin], the door is opened for him, [i.e., Heaven passively allows him to sin], but if he comes to cleanse himself [of sin], he receives active help from Heaven [in his attempt to do *mitzvot*]. In the yeshivah of R. Yishmael they taught: This may be compared to a person who sells both foul-smelling kerosene and fragrant balm. (39a) If a customer comes in to buy kerosene, the shopkeeper says to him: Measure it for yourself, [I don't want to inhale this offensive odor]. But to the customer who comes to buy balm he says: Wait for me, so that I measure it together with you, and both you and I will enjoy the fragrance. [When a person wants to commit a sin, God stands at a distance and lets him have his way; but if someone wants to do *teshuvah*, God helps him along.] In the yeshivah of R. Yishmael they taught: Sin numbs a person's heart, for it says, "Do not make yourselves unclean with them, and thus become unclean" (Leviticus 11:43). Don't read *venitmeitem* [you will become unclean], but *venitamtem* [you will become spiritually insensitive].

We learned in a *Baraita*: It says, "Do not make yourselves unclean with them, and thus become unclean." [Isn't that obvious? What does the passage come to tell us?] If a person begins by defiling himself a little, Heaven will allow him to defile himself a great deal. If he defiles himself in this world, he will become defiled in the World to Come. The Rabbis taught: [Conversely,] "Sanctify yourselves, and you will become holy" (Leviticus 11:44). This means: If a person sanctifies himself a little, [Heaven helps him] to become very much sanctified. If he sanctifies himself below, he becomes sanctified from Above; if he sanctifies himself in this world, he becomes sanctified in the World to Come.

MIRACLES DURING SHIMON HATZADDIK'S TENURE[43]

We learned in a *Baraita*: During the forty years that Shimon Hatzaddik served [as *Kohen Gadol*, when, on Yom Kippur, he put his hands into the box to draw the lots for the he-goat that would be offered on the altar[44]], the lot inscribed "For God" always came up in his right hand. [This was a sign of God's favor.] After his death, sometimes it would come up in the *Kohen Gadol*'s right hand; sometimes in his left. [During Shimon Hatzaddik's term] the strip of red wool [that was tied to the horns of the second he-goat] always miraculously turned white the moment it was pushed over the Azazel desert cliff. [This was a sign that God had forgiven Israel's sins of the past year.][45] After Shimon Hatzaddik's passing, it would sometimes turn white, sometimes not. Also, throughout those forty years, the lamp of the Menorah known as the "Western Lamp" burned for twenty-four hours, even though it was filled with enough oil for only twelve hours. [This was a sign that the *Shechinah* dwelled among Israel.] From that time on, sometimes it burned; at other times it went out. Also, the fire on the woodpile on the altar continued to burn strongly, so that the *kohanim* never had to add more wood to the pile, besides the two logs, which was a special mitzvah. From that time on, sometimes the wood on the altar would burn strongly, sometimes not, so that the *kohanim* could not do without adding wood to the pile all day. [During Shimon Hatzaddik's term,] a blessing was bestowed on the *Omer*,[46] the Two Breads (offered on *Shavuot*[47]), and the showbreads, so that every *kohen* who received a piece of it the size of an olive, ate it and became satisfied, and some *kohanim* ate of it and even left over some of it. But after the period of Shimon Hatzaddik, a curse was sent upon the *Omer*, the Two Breads, and the showbreads, so that every priest received only a piece as small as a bean: the decent ones withdrew altogether, while the gluttons snatched and devoured it. Once one of the gluttons snatched his portion and that of his colleague, and they nicknamed him *ben chamtzan*, (39b) "the grabber," until his dying day.

Rabbah B. Shilah said: What verse proves that *chamtzan* is a derogatory nickname? The passage, "My God, rescue me from the hand of the wicked, from the grasp of an unjust and [*chomeitz*], a violent person" (Psalms 71:4). Rava said, we know it from here, "Learn to do good, devote yourself to justice, aid the [*chamotz*], the oppressed" (Isaiah 1:17), meaning, aid him who is *chamotz*, oppressed, but don't aid the oppressor.

HARBINGERS OF CALAMITY

The Rabbis taught: In the year that Shimon Hatzaddik passed away, he predicted that he would die. They asked him: How do you know? He replied: On every Yom Kippur I was met by an old man dressed in white and wrapped in white who would enter [the Holy of Holies] with me and leave with me, but today I was met by an old man dressed in black and wrapped in black who entered [the Holy of Holies] with me but did not leave with me. After Sukkot, Shimon Hatzaddik was sick for seven days; then he died. After his death, the *kohanim* stopped enunciating God's ineffable Name when they blessed the people. [They did not feel worthy of it, but pronounced it the way we pronounce the Name.]

We learned in a *Baraita*: The last forty years before the destruction of the *Bet Hamikdash*, the lot [on the he-goat, marked "for God"] did not come up in the *kohen gadol*'s right hand, the red strip of wool that was tied on the he-goat did not turn white anymore, the "Western Lamp" did not miraculously burn until the next day, and the doors of the Sanctuary opened by themselves, [an omen that the enemies would overrun the *Bet Hamikdash*], until R. Yochanan b. Zakkai scolded them, saying: Heichal! Heichal! O you Sanctuary! Why do you foreshadow your own downfall? I know that you will be destroyed, because it is already predicted in the prophecy of Zechariah, the grandson of Ido, "Throw open your gates, O Lebanon, and let fire consume your cedars!" (Zechariah 11:1), [but you don't have to invite disaster. Lebanon is a nickname for the *Bet Hamikdash*].

R. Yitzchak b. Tavlai said: Why is the *Bet Hamikdash* called Lebanon? Because it makes the sins of Israel white, [*Levanon* is seen as related to *lavan*, "white"]. R. Zutra b. Tuvyah said: Why is the *Bet Hamikdash* called "Forest," as it says, "the Lebanon Forest House" (1 Kings 10:21)? To tell you that, just as a forest produces sprouts, so does the *Bet Hamikdash* produce sprouts. For R. Hoshaya said: When Solomon built the *Bet Hamikdash* he planted all kinds of precious golden fruit trees that bore fruit in their season, and when the wind blew on them, their fruits would fall off, for it says, "Let his fruit thrive like the forest of Lebanon" (Psalms 72:16). And these golden fruits provided a livelihood for the *kohanim*. But when the heathens entered the *Heichal*, the fruits dried up, for it says, "The blossoms of Lebanon wither" (Nahum 1:4). But at the time of the ultimate Redemption, the Holy One, blessed be He, will restore the *Bet Hamikdash* to us, for it says, "It shall blossom abundantly, it shall also exult and shout; it shall receive the glory of Lebanon" (Isaiah 35:2).

THE SEVEN SONS OF KIMCHIT

(47a) The story is told about R. Yishmael b. Kimchit that once [on Yom Kippur][48] he talked in the street to an Arab, and some saliva from the Arab's mouth sprayed on his clothes. [As a result, he became defiled and disqualified to perform the service as *Kohen Gadol*], so his brother Yesheivav took over and served in his place. Thus their mother saw two of her sons officiate as *Kohanim Gedolim* on the same day. Furthermore, the story is told about R. Yishmael b. Kimchit that once [on Yom Kippur] he went out into the street and talked to a lord, and some saliva from the lord's mouth sprayed on his clothes, [so that he became defiled, and was unable to perform the Yom Kippur service]. Thereupon his brother Yosef took over and served in his place, and his mother had the privilege of seeing two of her sons serve as *Kohanim Gedolim* on Yom Kippur. The Rabbis taught: Kimchit had seven sons, and all of them served as *Kohanim Gedolim*. So the Sages asked her: What have you done to merit such [eminence]? She replied: All of my life, the beams of my house never saw the braids of my hair, [a sign of modesty]. They said to her: [There must be another reason,] because many women did that, but they did not have seven sons like yours.

OFFERING THE INCENSE
ON YOM KIPPUR

(51b) The Mishnah says: [When offering the incense,] the *Kohen Gadol* walked across the *Heichal*[49] until he came to the two curtains that separated the *Heichal* from the Holy of Holies, and between the two curtains there was [a space of] one cubit. R. Yose said: There was only one curtain, as it says, "This curtain will divide between the Sanctuary and the Holy of Holies" (Exodus 26:33).

[According to the opinion that there were two curtains,] the outer curtain [facing the *Heichal*] was folded back by a clasp on the south side [allowing for an opening for the *Kohen Gadol* to pass through], and the inner curtain [facing the Holy Ark] was kept open on the north side. [The *Kohen Gadol* entered on the south side and] walked between the two curtains until he reached the north side. When he reached the north side [he entered the Holy of Holies through the folded-back inner curtain]. He then turned around and walked south [toward the Ark] with the inner curtain on his left side, until he reached the Ark. When he reached the Ark he placed the pan of burning coals between the two carrying poles.[50] He piled up the incense on the coals, whereupon the entire House became filled with smoke. He came out [of the Holy of Holies] in exactly the same manner that he came in, [he did not turn around but walked backward with his face turned toward the Ark]. And in the outer Chamber [the *Heichal*] he said a short prayer. He did not say a lengthy prayer so as not to frighten the people of Israel [who were anxiously awaiting his return].

THE HIDDEN ARK
OF THE COVENANT

(52b) [The Gemara asks:] Which *Bet Hamikdash* is the Mishnah referring to? If you say, the first *Bet Hamikdash*; was there then a curtain? [In the first *Bet Hamikdash* there was a wall of cedar planks,[51] not a curtain.] If you say, the second *Bet Hamikdash*; was there then an Ark? For we learned in a *Baraita*: When the Ark was hidden, there was hidden along with it the jar containing the *manna*,[52] and a bottle containing the anointing oil [with which the *kohanim* were installed], the staff of Aaron with its almonds and blossoms,[53] and the chest that Philistines had sent as a gift to the God of Israel, as it says, "Take the Ark of God and place it on a cart, and put next to it in a chest the gold objects you are paying Him as a sign of guilt. Send it off, and let it go its own way" (1 Samuel 6:8), [proof that the chest was next to the Ark, and when the Ark was hidden the chest was hidden along with it].

[The Gemara asks:] Who hid it? Yoshiahu (King Josiah) hid it. What prompted him to hide it? He saw the verse, "God will bring you and your elected king to a nation unknown to you and your fathers" (Deuteronomy 28:36). [He hid the Ark in anticipation of the coming exile.] Therefore he hid it, [somewhere underground in the *Bet Hamikdash*], for it says, "He said to the Levites, consecrated to God, the teachers of all Israel, 'Hide the Holy Ark in the House that Solomon son of David, king of Israel, built. You no longer will carry it on your shoulders. [This is not to say that your service is over. On the contrary.] Now serve the Lord your God and His people Israel'" (2 Chronicles 35:3). [How do we know that the other objects were hidden along with the Ark?] R. Elazar said: It is derived from a *gezeirah shavah*[54] of *shammah*, "there"; *dorot*, "generations"; and *mishmeret*, "to be kept."[55] [The question of the Gemara was: Since there was no Ark, how could the Mishnah, which speaks of the Ark, refer to the second *Bet Hamikdash*?] [The Gemara answers:] The Mishnah does speak of the second *Bet Hamikdash*. And what does "when he reached the Ark" mean? It means, "when the *Kohen Gadol* reached the *place* of the Ark." [The Gemara asks:] But the Mishnah says, "He placed the pan of burning coals between the two carrying poles [of the Ark]." [That does not sound as if there was no Ark!] [The Gemara answers:] Say: He placed it "as if it were between the two carrying poles."

HE DID NOT TURN HIS BACK

(53a) [We learned in the Mishnah:] The *Kohen Gadol* came out of the Holy of Holies in exactly the same way as he came in, walking backward. [The Gemara asks:] How do we know that this is the proper way to exit? R. Shmuel b. Nachmani said in the name of R. Yonatan: It says, "Solomon came to the *bamah* [the high place, to bring sacrifices on the altar that was there], that was in Gibeon Jerusalem" (1 Chronicles 35:3). What does Gibeon have to do with Jerusalem? [They are two different places!] The passage compares his departure from Gibeon, going to Jerusalem, with his entrance to Gibeon, coming from Jerusalem, meaning, just as when he entered Gibeon coming from Jerusalem his face was turned toward the *bamah* that was there, so also when he was leaving Gibeon to return to Jerusalem [he did not turn around, but backed away], his face was still turned toward the *bamah*.

In the same way, the *kohanim* officiating and the *levi'im* as performing their service on their platform, and the Israelites in the *Azarah* [Temple Court, attending the offering of the continual daily sacrifice as representatives of the people], when they left they would not turn around and walk out, but would turn their faces, still looking at the altar as they were leaving. Similarly, a disciple when leaving his rabbi should not turn around and walk out, but should keep his face turned toward his rabbi as he leaves.

And so, when R. Elazar would walk away from R. Yochanan [his rabbi, he always made certain to be in the proper position]. If R. Yochanan had to leave first, R. Elazar would remain in his place, his head bowed respectfully, until R. Yochanan was out of his sight. If R. Elazar had to leave first, he would walk backward until R. Yochanan could no longer see him. When Rava took leave of R. Yosef [his teacher, who was blind], he would walk backward until he would bump his feet, and R. Yosef's doorway became full of bloodstains. [But R. Yosef was not aware of what was happening.] (53b) When the people told R. Yosef what Rava was doing, he said to Rava, "May it be the will of God that your head should rise above the entire city." [He blessed him that he might become *rosh yeshivah*. His blessing came true.]

THE *KOHEN GADOL*'S PRAYER

[We learned in the Mishnah that the *Kohen Gadol* said a short prayer in the Outer Chamber.] What did he pray? Rava the son of R. Adda and Ravin the son of R. Adda both said in the name of Rav: He prayed: "May it be Your will, O Lord our God, that this year should be full of rain, and that it should be hot." [The Gemara asks:] But is a hot year a good thing? Rather say: If it is destined to be a hot year, may there be plenty of rain. R. Acha, the son of Rava, added the conclusion of the prayer in the name of R. Yehudah. [The *Kohen Gadol* prayed:] "May the monarchy never depart from the House of Judah, and may the house of Israel need not be dependent on one another for their livelihood, and do not accept the prayers of the wayfarers, [for they don't want it to rain]."

R. Chanina b. Dosa once was traveling along the road when it started to rain. He said: Master of the universe! Everyone is happy about the rain, but Chanina is suffering! Immediately the rain stopped. When he arrived home he said: Master of the universe! Everyone is in distress, and Chanina is at ease, [for I have no planted fields! Is it right that it should not rain, just so that I should be happy?]. Immediately it began to rain again. R. Yosef said: How can you consider the prayer of the *Kohen Gadol* effective when you see the impact R. Chanina b. Dosa's prayer has!

The Rabbis taught: It happened that one *Kohen Gadol* extended his prayer. The other *kohanim* took a vote and decided to go in after him. Just as they were about to enter [the *Heichal*], he came out. They said to him: Why did you pray for so long? He replied: Do you find it so hard to take that I prayed for you, and for the *Bet Hamikdash* that it should not be destroyed? They told him: Please, don't make a habit of doing that, for we have learned: The *Kohen Gadol* did not say a lengthy prayer so as not to frighten the people [who might think that he had died in the Holy of Holies].[56]

WHERE WAS THE HOLY ARK HIDDEN?

(53b) [The Mishnah says:] Once the Ark had been taken away, [at the destruction of the first *Bet Hamikdash*], there was a stone [where the Ark had formerly stood] that had been there since the days of the early prophets [Samuel and David, (Rashi)[57], which was called *Shetiyah*[58] [Foundation of the World], with a height of three fingers above the ground, on which the *Kohen Gadol* would place the shovel of burning coals [and burn the incense].

[The Gemara notes:] The Mishnah does not say: "Once the Ark has been hidden away," but "Once the Ark had been taken away." This is in keeping with the opinion that the Ark went into exile to Babylonia [along with the Jewish people]. For we learned in a *Baraita*: R. Eliezer said: The Ark went into exile to Babylonia, as it says, "At the turn of the year, King Nebuchadnezzar sent to have [King Jehoiachin] brought to Babylon together with the precious vessels of the House of God" (2 Chronicles 36:10), ["the precious vessels" refers to the Ark]. R. Shimon b. Yochai said: The Ark went into exile to Babylonia, for it says, "'Nothing will be left behind,' says God" (Isaiah 39:6), referring to the Ten Commandments that were in the Ark. R. Yehudah said: The Ark was hidden in its original place, for it says, "The poles [of the Ark] projected so that the ends of the poles were visible in the Sanctuary, but they could not be seen outside; and there they remain to this day" (1 Kings 8:8).

[The Gemara notes:] The fact that we say that R. Shimon b. Yochai holds that the Ark was taken away disagrees with what Ulla says, for Ulla said: R. Matyah b. Cheresh asked R. Shimon b. Yochai in Rome: Since R. Eliezer has taught us once and a second time that the Ark was taken to Babylonia, [the first time was the verse quoted earlier, "He sent to have him brought to Babylon together with the precious vessels of the House of God" (i.e., the Ark).] But what was the second time? Because it says, "Gone from the daughter of Zion all her splendor" (Lamentations 1:6). What does *hadarah*, "all her splendor," mean? Read *chadarah*, meaning, "the treasure that was hidden in the innermost *cheder*," chamber (i.e., the Ark; it is gone]. [In any event, R. Matyah asked R. Shimon b. Yochai:] According to your opinion, what happened to the Ark? He answered: I believe that the Ark was hidden in its original place, for it says, "The poles [of the Ark] projected . . . and there they remain to this day," [so it is hidden in the Sanctuary].

R. Nachman said: We are taught that the Ark was hidden in the storage room for the wood. R. Nachman b. Yitzchak said: This is confirmed by a Mishnah that says: It once happened that a *kohen* was playfully relaxing when he noticed that one of the tiles on the floor seemed to be raised. He came and began to tell his friend, but before he could finish his story he died. As a result, everyone knew positively that the Ark was hidden there. [The Gemara asks:] What was he doing there? R. Chelbo said: He was playing with his ax. [He died before revealing the location of the elevated tile, and they understood from his tragic death that they should not try to find it (Ben Yehoyada).][59] In the yeshivah of R. Yishmael a different version of the story was taught: Two *kohanim* who had a blemish, [and therefore could not do any other service], were busy removing worms from the wood when one of them dropped his ax, and it fell on the place where the Ark was hidden. Immediately, a flame shot out and consumed him.

SHETIYAH, THE FOUNDATION OF THE WORLD

(54b) [We learned in the Mishnah that in the second *Bet Hamikdash*, on the place where the Ark stood in the Holy of Holies, there was a stone called *Shetiyah*, where, on Yom Kippur, the *Kohen Gadol* would burn the incense.]

We learned in a *Baraita*: [Why was it called *Shetiyah*, Foundation Stone?] Because it was from this central point that the entire world was founded, [this was the nucleus around which the world was formed].[60] This statement is in accordance with the opinion that the world was created from Zion, [Eretz Yisrael was created first, and the rest of the world was stuck to it on all sides (Rashi)]. For we learned in a *Baraita*: R. Eliezer said: The world was created from its middle, [meaning, the first spot of the world was its middle, and afterward the sides were added on]. For it says, "The earth runs into a main mass, and its clods are stuck around it" (Job 38:38). R. Yehoshua said: The world was created from its sides. [Originally, there were four masses of matter, which then converged on the center (Rashi).] For it says, "He commands the snow, 'Become land!,' and to the light rain and to the heavy dowpour He also says, 'Convert to land!'" (Job 37:6). [The snow and the rains, which come from the four directions, were ordered to solidify and to fuse into one planet (Rashi).] R. Yitzchak Nappacha said: The Holy One, blessed be He, cast a stone into the sea, from which

the world was then founded, for it says, [God says to Job,] "Do you know into what foundations the pillars of the world were sunk, or who threw into [the sea] its cornerstone?" (Job 38:6). But the Sages said: The world was started from Eretz Yisrael, for it says, "A psalm of Asaf. Almighty God has spoken . . . From Zion, perfect in beauty, God appeared" (Psalms 50:1,2). [The Sages expound this to mean:] From Zion the beauty of the world was perfected, because God allowed to world to spread from the central point that is Zion.]

We learned in a *Baraita*: R. Eliezer Hagadol said: It says, "These are the heavenly bodies and the earthly creatures that were created on the day that God brought the earth and heaven into being" (Genesis 2:4). [The Gemara expounds: We see from this passage that there were two things that came into being:] The heavenly bodies were created from the heavens, and earthly things were created from the earth. The Sages, however, said: These and those, both came from Eretz Yisrael, for it says, "Almighty God has spoken and called the earth into being from sunrise to sunset, [the stars and galaxies, whatever exists in the cosmos], from Zion, perfect in beauty, God appeared" (Psalms 50:1,2). This is interpreted to mean, "From Zion the beauty of the world was perfected."

LEADING AWAY THE HE-GOAT

(66a) [The Mishnah says: After making his confession,] the *Kohen Gadol* handed the he-goat to the one who was appointed to lead it to Azazel in the wilderness. Anyone is fit to lead it, [even an Israelite], but the *kohanim* established a rule not to allow an Israelite to lead it. R. Yose said: It once happened that Arsela led it, and he was an Israelite. They built a ramp, [an elevated walkway leading from the Temple Courtyard to outside Jerusalem], because of the Babylonian Jews who used to pull at the man's hair, calling out to him, "Take our sins and leave! Take our sins and leave!"

THE LEVITES DID NOT WORSHIP THE GOLDEN CALF

(66b) Rav Yehudah said: The tribe of Levi did not take part in the worship of the golden calf, for it says, "Moses stood at the camp's entrance and announced, 'Whoever is for God, join me!' All the Levites gathered around him." (Exodus 32:26). Ravina was sitting and repeated this teaching. However, the sons of R. Papa b. Abba challenged him: [It says concerning the Levites,] "He was the one who said of his father and mother, 'I do not see them,' not recognizing brother or child." (Deuteronomy 33:9). [The verse refers to the sin of the golden calf, when the Levites avenged God and put to death those who worshipped the idol, even if they were their closest relatives; proof that there were Levites who did worship the golden calf.] The Gemara answers: When the verse speaks of "his father," it refers to the father of his mother who was a *Yisrael*; and when it says, "his brother," it refers to a half-brother, [who has the same mother but a different father] who was a *Yisrael*; and when it says, "his son," it means the sons of his daughter, which she had from a *Yisrael*. [Thus the Levites themselves indeed did not worship the golden calf, in accordance with Ravina.]

THE STRIP OF RED WOOL

We learned in a *Baraita*: In the beginning they used to tie the strip of red wool atop the outside of the Sanctuary doors. [This strip of red wool would miraculously turn white if God had chosen to forgive Israel's sins. They tied it to the outside, so that everyone could see the great miracle.] If it became white, everyone rejoiced; if it did not whiten, they were sad and ashamed. Therefore, they instituted that it should be tied to the inside of the Sanctuary doors. But [there were *kohanim* near the entrance] who would peek in and still could see it; and if it became white they rejoiced; and if it did not, they were ashamed. Thereupon, they enacted that half of the red strip should be tied to the rock [from which the he-goat was hurled down] and half to the horns of the he-goat.

R. Nachum b. Papa said in the name of R. Elazar Hakappar: In the beginning they used to tie the strip of red wool to the inside of the Sanctuary, and once the he-goat reached the wilderness, it became white. For it says, "If your sins are like crimson, they will turn snow-white" (Isaiah 1:18).

DON'T CRITICIZE LAWS YOU DON'T UNDERSTAND

(67b) We learned in a *Baraita*: It says, "Follow My laws and be careful to keep My decrees" (Leviticus 18:4). "Follow My laws" refers to such commandments, which, even if they were not written in the Torah, common sense tells us should have been written in the Torah. And they are the following: [the laws prohibiting] idolatry, immorality, bloodshed, robbery, and blasphemy. "Be careful to keep My decrees" refers to *mitzvot* Satan [i.e., the evil tendency] argues against [and says that they are irrational and should not be obeyed], like the prohibition against eating pork, against wearing *shaatnez* [garments made from a mixture of wool and linen],[61] the law of *chalitzah* for a sister-in-law,[62] the purification of the leper, and the mitzvah of the he-goat that is to be sent away. And perhaps you will say that these are meaningless ceremonies; therefore the Torah says [concerning these decrees], "I am God your Lord" (Leviticus 19:3), meaning, I, God, have ordained them, and you don't have the right to find fault with them.

SHIMON HATZADDIK MEETS ALEXANDER THE GREAT

(69a) A *kohen* is not permitted to wear the priestly garments outside the *Bet Hamikdash*; however, inside the *Bet Hamikdash*, whether during or outside the time of service, he is permitted to wear them, because it is permitted to make personal use of the priestly garments. [The Gemara asks:] Are the *kohanim* really not allowed to wear the priestly garments outside the *Bet Hamikdash*? But we have learned in a *Baraita*: The twenty-fifth of Tevet is the "Day of Mount Gerizim," [a festive day] on which no eulogies should be given. It was on that day that the Samaritans asked Alexander the Macedonian for permission to destroy the House of God, and he gave them permission to do it. People came and told this to Shimon Hatzaddik, the *Kohen Gadol*. What did Shimon Hatzaddik do? He put on his priestly garments and wrapped himself in his priestly garments, and he took with him some of the distinguished men of Israel. Carrying torches in their hands, Shimon Hatzaddik and his companions walked all that night toward Alexander and the Samaritans, and Alexander and his troops and the Samaritans were marching [toward Shimon Hatzaddik], on their way to destroy the *Bet Hamikdash*. At dawn, Alexander asked the Samaritans, "Who are these people with the torches that are coming toward us?" The Samaritans replied, "Those are the Jews who rebelled against you."

When Alexander reached the town of Antiparas the sun rose, and the two groups met. When Alexander saw Shimon Hatzaddik he descended from his chariot and bowed down before him. The Samaritans said to him, "A great king like yourself should bow down before this Jew?" He replied, "The image of this person appears before whenever I go out into battle, and it brings me victory." Alexander then asked Shimon Hatzaddik and his companions, "Why did you come?" They answered, "Is it possible that these idol worshippers should fool you into destroying the House where prayers are offered for you and your kingdom that it should never be destroyed!" Alexander said to them, "What idol worshippers do you mean?" They replied, "We are referring to these Samaritans who are standing before you right now." Said Alexander, "I am handing them over to you to do with them as you please." Immediately, they pierced the soles of their feet and they tied them to the tails of their horses and dragged them over thorns and thistles until they came to Mount Gerizim, [the mountain venerated by the Samaritans who had tried to destroy the *Bet Hamikdash*]. Once they reached Mount Gerizim, they plowed it and planted it with horse beans [an animal food], just as the Samaritans wanted to do with the House of God. And that day they made a festive day [on which no eulogies should be given].

[To summarize, the Gemara is asking: This story shows that Shimon Hatzaddik wore the priestly garments outside the *Bet Hamikdash*, yet the *Baraita* above stated that this is forbidden?] [The Gemara answers:] If you wish you can say: The garments he wore were fit to be priestly garments, but they were not actual priestly garments. Or, if you like you can say: "It is a time to act for God, they have voided Your Torah" (Psalms 119:126), which is interpreted to mean: When it is a time to act for God and save the *Bet Hamikdash*, then it is permitted to break the laws of the Torah, [and therefore Shimon Hatzaddik was allowed to wear the priestly garments outside the *Bet Hamikdash*].

THE *KOHEN GADOL* READS FROM THE TORAH

(69b) [Once the *Kohen Gadol* had been informed that the goat had reached the desert, he would read the portion of the Torah [Leviticus, Chapter 16, describing the Yom Kippur service].

[The Gemara asks:] Where did they read from the Torah [on the occasion of *Hakheil*, which is the mitzvah to read the Book of Deuteronomy once in seven years, in the presence of all Israel, men, women, and children (Deuteronomy 31:10–13)]? [They read it] in the *Azarah*, the Temple Courtyard. R. Eliezer b. Yaakov said: They read it on the Temple Mount [outside the Temple], for it says, "[Ezra] read from [the Torah] facing the square before the Water Gate" (Nehemiah 8:3). [The Water Gate was a gate that opened from the Temple Mount into the Courtyard. Since Ezra read the Torah "before the Water Gate," he read it on the Temple Mount, and so too, the reading of *Hakheil* was on the Temple Mount.] R. Chisda said: It was read [not in the Temple Court, but] in the Women's Court.

[After the completion of the Second *Bet Hamikdash*, Ezra gathered the entire people on Rosh Hashanah and read and explained to them the Torah. Before beginning to read, Ezra said a *berachah*,] "He blessed the Lord, the great God," (Nehemiah 8:6). [The Gemara asks:] What is meant by "great" [in reference to God]? R. Yosef said in Rav's name: He exalted God by pronouncing the Ineffable Four-Letter Name. R. Giddal said: [Ezra said,] "Blessed be the Lord, the God of Israel, from this world to the world to come" (1 Chronicles 16:36). Abaye said to R. Dimi: Perhaps it means that he exalted Him by using the Ineffable Name? He answered: The Ineffable Name may not be pronounced outside the *Bet Hamikdash*, [and this happened on the Temple Mount, outside the *Bet Hamikdash*]. Is that so? [Is it true that the Ineffable Name may not be enunciated outside the Temple?] Doesn't it say, "Ezra the scribe stood on a wooden tower made for the purpose . . . [and Ezra praised God]" (Nehemiah 8:4)? And R. Giddal himself said: "He exalted Him by pronouncing the Ineffable Name" [and this was outside the Temple Court]? [The Gemara answers:] It was a one-time special ruling, for that occasion only, [not to be taken as a precedent].

THE *YETZER HARA* OF IDOLATRY

[The Gemara now explains the importance of this prayer, and what they were praying for.] "And they cried in a loud voice to the Lord their God" (ibid. 9:4). What did they cry? Rav, and according to others, R. Yochanan, said, they cried: Woe, woe, it is he [the *yetzer hara*, the evil impulse of idolatry] that has destroyed the *Bet Hamikdash*, burnt the Sanctuary, caused the death of all the *tzaddikim*, and has driven the Jewish people into exile from their land, and he is still frolicking among us! [O God,] You only gave us this evil impulse so that we may be rewarded for overcoming it. Well, we want neither the *yetzer hara* of idolatry nor the reward for resisting it. Thereupon a note fell down from heaven on which the word *Emet*, "Truth," was written, [as if to say, "I truly agree with you"].

R. Chanina said: From this we can learn that the seal of the Holy One, blessed is He, is *Emet*. They fasted for three days and three nights, after which the *yetzer hara* of idolatry was handed over to them, [to do with it as they please]. At that moment out of the Holy of Holies there came forth a form of a young fiery lion. The prophet Zechariah said to the Jewish people: That apparition is the *yetzer hara* of idolatry, for it says, "This is wickedness, he said" (Zechariah 5:8). As they were grabbing the *yetzer hara*, a hair of his tresses was pulled out. The *yetzer hara* cried out and his voice traveled for four hundred *parsangs*. They said: What shall we do? Maybe, God forbid, Heaven will have mercy on him! The prophet said to them: Throw it into a leaden pot, and seal its opening with lead, because lead absorbs the sound of the voice. For it says, "'That,' he said, 'is wickedness'; and, thrusting it down into the tub, he pressed the leaden weight into its mouth" (ibid.). Then they said: Since this is a favorable time, let us pray to be freed also of the *yetzer hara* [the evil impulse] of sensual desire. They prayed for mercy, and he was handed over to them. The prophet said to them: If you kill this impulse, the world will end, [because without sexual desire, life is not propagated].

They imprisoned him for three days, and then looked in all of Eretz Yisrael for a fresh egg but could not find one [because procreation of the species had ceased]. They said: What shall we do now? Shall we kill him? The world would come to an end. Shall we pray for partial mercy, [to allow him to stay alive but not to entice people to immorality]? They do not grant partial requests in Heaven. [By definition, if sexual lust exists, it arouses desire. But it can be kept within the bounds of morality.] Thereupon they darkened his eyes, [i.e., they curbed the sexual *yetzer hara*'s unbridled passion], and let him go. It helped to the extent that the *yetzer hara* no longer entices people to commit incest.

THE WORDS OMITTED
BY JEREMIAH AND DANIEL

In Eretz Yisrael they taught the following version of Ezra's *berachah*: R. Giddal said: "Ezra blessed . . . the great God" (Nehemiah 8:6), meaning that He exalted Him by pronouncing the Ineffable Name. R. Matna said: He said, "Our God, the great, mighty, and awsome God" (ibid. 9:32). R. Matna's interpretation seems to agree with what R. Yehoshua b. Levi said. For R. Yehoshua b. Levi said: Why were they called Men of the Great Assembly?[63] Because they restored the crown of the Divine attributes to its ancient glory. [They restored to the *Shemoneh Esrei* the Divine attributes that Jeremiah and Daniel had omitted.] For Moses had come and said, "He is the great, mighty, and awesome God" (Deuteronomy 10:17). Then Jeremiah came and demurred, saying: Heathens are carousing in his Sanctuary! So, where are His awesome deeds? Thus Jeremiah left out the attribute "the Awesome" [he prayed, "O great and mighty God" (Jeremiah 32:17)]. Daniel came and objected, saying: Heathens are enslaving His children! So where are His mighty deeds? Thus Daniel omitted the attribute of "Mighty." [He prayed: "O Lord, great and awesome God" (Daniel 9:4).]

But the Men of the Great Assembly came and said: On the contrary! These are the very things that demonstrate His might and His awful powers, in that He suppresses His wrath [for the many years that the nations oppressed the Jewish people], and He is slow to show His anger toward the wicked [who are persecuting the Jews]. They demonstrate His awful powers, for if it had not been for the nations' fear of God, how could one small people survive among so many nations! [The Gemara asks:] But how could Jeremiah and Daniel omit phrases that were instituted by Moses? R. Elazar said: Since they knew that the Holy One, blessed be He, desires the truth, they did not want to ascribe things to Him that [on the surface] appeared to be untrue.

SAYINGS ABOUT
TORAH SCHOLARS

(71a) [The Gemara cites several verses in which the word *chayim*, "life," has different connotations.] It says, "I shall walk before God in the land of life [*hachayim*]" (Psalms 116:9). Rav Yehudah said: "The land of life" means a place where there are markets [where a person can buy food that sustains life]. Another passage states, "For they [the words of the Torah] will bestow on you lengths of days, years of life and peace" (Proverbs 3:2). [The Gemara asks:] Are there then years that are years of life, and years that are not years of life? R. Elazar said: "Years of life" means the years of a person's life that have changed from bad to good, [for example, a person who was poor and becomes wealthy feels as though he was born to a new life (Rashi)].

[The Torah exclaims,] "O men [*ishim*], I call out to you" (Proverbs 8:4). [What is meant by *ishim*?] R. Berechiah said: The Torah is calling out to Torah scholars, "O men [*ishim*]," [and instead of using the word *anashim* for "men" it uses *ishim*, which sounds like *ishah*, "woman"]. For Torah scholars resemble women, [in that they are soft-spoken and not robust], and nonetheless, they show their strength like men [in the realm of Torah].

R. Berechiah also said: If someone wants to pour wine on the altar [to accompany his offering], he should fill the throats of Torah scholars with wine, [meaning, he should bring the wine to scholars]. For it says, "O men [*ishim*] I call to you" [*ishim* also means fire-offerings].

R. Berechia further said: If a person sees that his son is not learning Torah as well as he should, his son should marry the daughter of a Torah scholar,[64] [then his grandchildren will grow up to become Torah scholars]. For it says, "If [a tree's] roots are old in the earth, and its stump dies in the ground, [i.e., his children are not studying Torah properly], then at the (71b) scent of water [i.e., Torah] it will bud and produce branches like saplings" (Job 14:8,9).

A CRUSHING REPARTEE

The *Kohen Gadol* made a feast [the night after Yom Kippur or the next day: not on Yom Kippur] for his friends for having left the *Bet Hamikdash* safely, [for the Torah warns that if he performs any part of the service improperly, he is liable to lose his life].

We learned in a *Baraita*: It happened with one *Kohen Gadol*, when he left the Sanctuary [after the Yom Kippur service], that everyone was following him. But when the people saw Shemayah and Avtalyon [the great mentors of Hillel and Shammai], they left the *Kohen Gadol* and followed Shemayah and Avtalyon. Later, Shemayah and Avtalyon came to take leave of the *Kohen Gadol*. The *Kohen Gadol* [venting his bitterness at being slighted], said to them, "May the descendants of the heathens come in peace!" [Shemayah and Avtalyon were descendants of Sancheriv, King of Assyria.] They answered him, "May the descendants of the heathens who act like Aaron, come in peace, but may this descendant of Aaron not come in peace, because he does not act like Aaron!" [Aaron pursued peace, but this *Kohen Gadol*, by his caustic remark, showed that he was not a worthy descendant of Aaron.]

THE BOARDS OF
THE TABERNACLE WERE
"STANDING UP"

(72a) R. Chama b. Chanina said: What is the meaning of the verse, "Make the boards of the tabernacle out of acacia wood, standing up" (Exodus 26:15)? It

EIN YAAKOV

means that they should be made to stand the way they grew, [what was the top of the tree should be on top]. A different interpretation of "standing up" is that the boards should hold up, [support], their gold covering [which was fixed to them with nails]. A third interpretation of "standing up" is this: Perhaps you will say that since the Tabernacle was hidden away, that the boards have disappeared and the hope of their restoration is lost, and that which we look forward to is gone, [since they are made of wood, which decays]; therefore it says "standing up," meaning, they will last forever and ever.

THE THREE CROWNS

(72b) R. Yochanan said: There were three crowns [on the vessels of the Sanctuary]: that of the Altar, that of the Ark, and that of the Table. [They symbolize the three crowns of Israel: the crowns of priesthood, Torah, and royalty, respectively.] The crown of the Altar, [priesthood], Aaron deserved and took it [for himself and his descendants]. The crown of the Table, [royalty], David deserved and took it [for himself and his descendants]. However, the crown of the Ark [the Torah] is still lying there, and whoever wants to take it, may come and take it. [The priesthood and royalty are hereditary; not so the Torah—it can be acquired by each person.] Perhaps you will say that [the crown of Torah] is inferior, [and that is why there are few takers], therefore it says, "[The Torah says] 'Through me kings reign'" (Proverbs 8:15), [consequently, the Torah is greater than royalty].

R. Yochanan pointed to the following contradiction: The Hebrew word for crown, zeir, [spelled zayin, reish], can also be read zar, which means "strange." This teaches us: If a person deserves it, the Torah becomes a crown for him; if not, the Torah is estranged from him; [he will forget what he learned]. R. Yochanan pointed out another contradiction: It says, [God said to Moses], "Make yourself a wooden Ark" (Deuteronomy 10:1), and it also says, "They shall make an Ark of acacia wood" (Exodus 25:10). [The command was given to Moses, yet it was also given to the people.] This teaches us that the people of his city are commanded to do the work of the Torah scholar for him. [Although the command was given to Moses, the people did the work for him.]

It says, "Cover the Ark on the inside and outside with gold" (ibid. 11). Rava interpreted it metaphorically to mean: Any Torah scholar whose inside is not like his outside, [who is not sincere], is no scholar. Abaye, and, according to others, Rabbah b. Ulla, said: He is called loathsome, for it says, "[He puts no trust in His holy ones,] what then of one loathsome and foul, a man who drinks wrongdoing like water!" (Job 15:16). [Torah is compared to water; thus, he learns Torah but has iniquity in his heart.]

THE PROPER ATTITUDE TOWARD TORAH STUDY

R. Shmuel b. Nachmani said in the name of R. Yonatan: What is the meaning of the verse, "What good is money in the hand of a fool, when he has no mind to purchase wisdom?" (Proverbs 17:16). It means: Woe to the scholars, if they engage in Torah study but have no fear of heaven! [In the same vein,] R. Yannai used to call out: I pity the person who has no courtyard, but makes a gate for his courtyard! [The Torah is the gate that should lead to the courtyard, which is the fear of heaven. What good is Torah study without the fear of heaven?] Rava said to his students: I ask of you, please, do not inherit a double Gehinnom! [If you work hard at studying the Torah without fulfilling it, you miss the pleasures of this world, and you do not deserve to enter the World to Come [Rashi].]

R. Yehoshua b. Levi said: What is meant by the verse, "This is the Torah that Moses set [sam] before the children of Israel" (Deuteronomy 4:44)? [The word sam, when written with a samach, means both medicine and poison.] The verse means: If a person merits it, the Torah becomes a healing medicine for him; if not, a deadly poison. Rava had this in mind when he said: To those who study it the right way, [with a devout attitude], it is an elixir of life; to those who do not study it the right way, it is a deadly poison.

R. Shmuel b. Nachmani said: R. Yonatan pointed to the following contradiction: It says, "The orders of God are upright, gladdening the heart" (Psalms 19:9), but it also says, "The word of God is tried [tzerufah]" (Psalms 18:31). [He reconciled the verses:] If he deserves it, it gladdens him; if not, it tries him. Resh Lakish said: It can be derived from the text of the last passage: If he deserves it, it purifies him for life; if not, it purifies him [through suffering that ends in] death [tzaraf also means both "to try" and "to purify"].

It says, "The fear of God is pure, enduring forever" (Psalms 19:10). R. Chanina said: This refers to a person who studies the Torah in purity. What does that mean? It means that he gets married and afterward studies the Torah, [so that he is not distracted by impure thoughts]. "The testimony of God is trustworthy, making the simple one wise" (ibid. 8). R. Chiya b. Abba said: This means that the Torah may be trusted to testify about those who study it, [as to who practices what he studies and who does not].

HOW WERE THE URIM AND TUMMIM CONSULTED?

[We learned in the Mishnah:[65]] [All year round,] the Kohen Gadol performs the service in eight garments, and an ordinary kohen in four garments: in a tunic, pants, a hat, and a belt. In addition to these, the Kohen Gadol wore: a breastplate, an eifod,[66] a cloak, and a headplate. Only when wearing these [eight] garments

208

can the *Kohen Gadol* be asked to consult the *Urim* and *Tummim*.[67] The *Urim* and *Tummim* are consulted only on behalf of a king, the Court, or someone whom the public needs.

(73a) We learned in a *Baraita*: How were the *Urim* and *Tummim* consulted? The one asking the question [i.e., the king or the head of the *Bet Din*] had his face turned toward the one who was being consulted [i.e., the *Kohen Gadol*], and the one being consulted directed himself toward the *Shechinah* [i.e., the *Urim* and *Tummim* and the Ineffable Name written on it]. The inquirer said: [as was the case with David, who inquired of the *Urim* and *Tummim*,] "Shall I pursue those raiders? Will I overtake them?" (1 Samuel 30:8). And the one who was consulted answered, "So says God, 'Go ahead! You will succeed!'" R. Yehudah said: He does not have to say, "So says God," but only "Go ahead! You will succeed!" The question should not be asked in a loud voice, for it says, "He shall inquire for him [alone]" (Numbers 27:21), [so that only he can hear it]. On the other hand, he should not just mentally reflect on the question, for it says, "He shall inquire for him" [i.e., he should articulate the question]. He should put the question in the way Hannah said her prayer, for it says, "Now Hannah spoke in her heart, only her lips moved, but her voice could not be heard" (1 Samuel 1:13). One should not ask two questions at the same time, [but after he receives the answer to the first question, he should put the second]. If one did ask two questions at the same time, only one question [the first] would be answered. For it says, [David asked two questions,] "Will the citizens of Ke'ilah deliver me into [Saul's] hand? Will Saul come down, as Your servant has heard?" And God replied, "He will come down" (ibid. 23:11).

[The Gemara asks:] But you said: Only the first question will be answered? [But this was the answer to the second question?] [The Gemara answers:] (73b) David asked in the wrong order and received his answer in the right order. [He should have asked first: "Will Saul come down?" and then, "Will they deliver me into his hands?"] And when he realized that he had asked in the wrong order, he repeated the questions in the right order. For it says, "Will the citizens of Ke'ilah deliver me and my son into Saul's hands?" And God answered, "They will" (1 Samuel 23:12). However, if both questions had to be asked at the same time [because of an emergency], then both were answered, as it says, "David inquired of God, 'Shall I pursue those raiders? Will I overtake them?'" And He answered him, 'Pursue, for you shall overtake, and you shall rescue'" (1 Samuel 30:8). And although a decision of a prophet could be retracted, [like Jonah's decree that Nineveh would be destroyed], the decision of the *Urim* and *Tummim* could not be rescinded. For it says, "The judgment of the *Urim*" (Numbers 27:21), [and a judgment cannot be rescinded].

THE NAME "*URIM* AND *TUMMIM*"

[The Gemara asks:] And why were they called *Urim* and *Tummim*? They were called *Urim*, [from *or*, "light"], because they would cause the words [on the breastplate] to light up, and *Tummim* [from *tamim*, "complete"], because they completely fulfilled the words [of their message]. Now if you should ask: Why didn't the *Urim* and *Tummim* fulfill their words at Givat Binyamin (Judges, Chapter 20)? Because the Israelites did not specifically inquire [whether the battle would end in victory or defeat; therefore, the *Urim* and *Tummim* answered with an ambiguous "March against them"]. Later, when they asked in clear-cut terms, the *Urim* and *Tummim* approved and gave a definitive answer, "The Israelites inquired of God, (and Pinchas son of Elazar son of Aaron the priest ministered before him in those days), "Shall we again take the field against our kinsmen the Benjaminites, or shall we not?" God answered, "Go up, for tomorrow I will deliver them into your hands."

How did the *Urim* and *Tummim* spell out the message? R. Yochanan said: The individual letters stood out. Resh Lakish said: The letters making up the words moved together [to form the words of the message]. [The Gemara asks:] But the letter *tzadi* does not appear [in the names of the twelve tribes; what if the message required a *tzadi*]? R. Shmuel b. Yitzchak said: The names Avraham, Yitzchak, and Yaakov [were also engraved on the stones of the breastplate, and Yitzchak has a *tzadi*]. [The Gemara asks:] But the *tet*, too, was missing? R. Acha b. Yaakov said: The words Avraham, Yitzchak, and Yaakov [were also engraved on the stones of the breastplate, and Yitzchak has a *tzadi*]. [The Gemara asks:] But the *tet*, too, was missing? R. Acha b. Yaakov said: The words *shivtei Yeshurun* [the tribes of Jeshurun] were also etched into the stones [and *shivtei* is written with a *tet*].

THE HUNGRY EYE

(74b) [The Gemara expounds the verse,] "In the desert He fed you manna . . . in order to send you hardship" (Deuteronomy 8:16). [What kind of hardship was eating the good-tasting manna?] R. Ammi and R. Assi [each offered a different explanation]. One said: You cannot compare a person who eats and has bread in his basket [to eat the next day] to one who eats but has no bread in his basket. [Since the manna that came down was enough only for that day, and none was left for the next day, it was a hardship of sorts.] The other said: You cannot compare a person who sees what he is eating to a person who does not see what he is eating. [The manna tasted like whatever a person wished, but he could not see the dish he was tasting; he only saw manna. And that was the hardship.] R. Yosef said: This gives you an indication that blind people, no matter how much they eat, are not satisfied [because they cannot see their food]. Abaye said: Therefore, a person should have his meal only in the daytime, [or by candlelight so that he should see it and be satisfied]. R. Zeira said: What verse supports that? "Feasting the eye is more important than the pursuit of desire" (Ecclesiastes 6:9). Resh Lakish elaborated: Sometimes the sight of a woman can be more gratifying than the act itself, for it says, "Feasting the eye is more important than the pursuit of desire."

It says, "If a person ogles his cup of wine, it goes down smoothly" (Proverbs 23:31). Rav Ammi and R. Assi [each offered a different interpretation]. One said: To a person who gazes at his cup of wine, [i.e., drinks excessively], all forbidden relationships seem like smooth, level land [i.e., permissible]. The other said: To a person who ogles his cup of wine, the possessions of the whole world seem like level land, [meaning, he has no inhibitions and will end up stealing from others to finance his drinking habit].

DIFFERENT INTERPRETATIONS OF BIBLICAL VERSES

R. Ammi and R. Assi gave different interpretations of the verse, "If there is anxiety in a man's heart, let him suppress it [yash'chenah]" (Proverbs 12:26). One said: [Yash'chenah means:] he should drive these worrisome thoughts from his mind, [from the expression masiach daas, "divert attention"]. The other said: [It means:] He should talk about his worries to his friends [from sach, "to talk"].

R. Ammi and R. Assi gave different interpretations to the following verse, "And the serpent's food shall be dust" (Isaiah 65:25). One said: A snake may eat all the delicacies in the world; still, all it tastes is dust. The other said: Even if a snake eats all the delicacies in the world it will not be satisfied until it eats dust.

We learned in a Baraita: R. Yose said: Come and see what a difference there is between the ways of mortal man and the ways of the Holy One, blessed be He. If a person is angry with his neighbor he will do all he can to inflict the greatest possible harm on him. No so, the Holy One, blessed be He. He cursed the serpent, ["Dust you shall eat all the days of your life" (Genesis 3:14); still, when a snake goes up to the roof, it finds its food there. When it goes down on the ground, it finds its food there. [God's curses have a good side.] He cursed Canaan, ["He shall be a slave's slave to his brothers" (Genesis 9:25)], but he eats what his master eats, drinks what his master drinks. He cursed the woman [with menstrual discomfort and birth pains], yet all are running after her. He cursed the earth, ["It will bring forth thorns and thistles" (ibid. 3:18)], yet all are nourished from it.

THE MANNA AS ARBITER

We learned in a Baraita: R. Yose said: Just as the prophet would tell the Jewish people what was in the innermost recesses of their hearts, so would the manna reveal the deepest secrets. How is that? If two people came to Moses with a lawsuit, one saying: You stole my slave, the other saying: You sold him to me, Moses would say to them: Let's postpone judgment until tomorrow. The next morning, if the slave's omer [i.e., his portion of manna][68] was in the house of his master, that was proof that the other one had stolen him; if it was found in the house of his second master, it was proof that the first one had sold him to the second one. So also, if a man and a woman came before Moses for a legal decision, the husband saying: She was unfaithful to me, [therefore, if I divorce her I do not have to pay her marriage settlement [ketubah], and she stating: He wants to desert me; [I have conducted myself properly, and if he wants to divorce me, I am entitled to my marriage settlement]. Moses would say to them: Let's postpone judgment until tomorrow. The next morning, if her portion of manna was found in front of her husband's house, that was proof that she had been unfaithful to him, [and that his conduct was impeccable, and, since they were still married he deserved to have her omer fall at his doorstep]. But if her omer was found in front of her father's house, that would be proof that the husband had behaved improperly, [and therefore had lost his right to her portion of manna].

THE DISCERNING MANNA

It says, "At night, when the dew would fall on the camp, the manna would descend on it" (Numbers 11:9); [in other words, the manna fell on the camp]. But it also says, "The people will go out and gather" (Exodus 16:4); [they collected the manna right outside the camp]. Yet a third verse says, "The people had to wander about and search for it" (Numbers 11:8); [they had to make an effort to find it]. How do we reconcile these three verses? [The Gemara answers:] For the tzaddikim the manna fell at the entrance of their home; the average people would have to go outside of the camp to collect the manna; but the wicked ones would have to wander about and actually search for the manna.

The manna is described as "bread" (Exodus 16:4); it is also called "cakes" (Numbers 11:8), [i.e., an unbaked dough], and it also says, "They would grind it" (ibid.) [before they ate it]. How do we reconcile these three verses? [The Gemara answers:] Tzaddikim found the manna in the form of ready-made bread; the average people received it as dough ready to be put into the oven [requiring a slight effort]. The wicked ones had to grind the manna in a hand mill.

"It tasted like an oil wafer [leshad]" (ibid.). R. Abbahu said: [What is the meaning of leshad?] Just as a nursing infant tastes many flavors in the breast [*shad*], [depending on what the mother had eaten], so did the Jewish people find many tastes in the manna when they ate it.

EATING AT REGULAR HOURS

It says, "Moses said, 'In the evening, God will give you meat to eat, and in the morning there will be enough bread to fill you up'" (Exodus 16:8). We learned in a *Baraita* in the name of R. Yehoshua b. Korchah: "The meat, which they requested improperly; [they had enough cattle and did not have to ask for more], was given to them at an improper time, [the quail came in the evening,[69] too late to prepare it for dinner]. (75b) The bread, which they requested properly [because a person cannot exist without bread], was given to them in a proper fashion, in the morning [in time for breakfast]. With this, the Torah teaches us a lesson in proper conduct: that you should eat meat only at night. [The Gemara asks:] But didn't Abbaye say: If a person has a meal to eat, he should eat it only in the daytime? [The Gemara answers:] He meant: like in the daytime, [he should eat it at night by the light of a torch or a candle, so that he sees what he is eating].

R. Acha b. Yaakov said: At first the Jewish people were like hens that picked in the pile of rubbish, [eating at all times of the day], until Moses came and set regular hours for their meals [in the morning and evening].

[As regards the manna:] One verse calls it "bread," another verse calls it, "oil," and a third verse describes it as "honey."[70] R. Yose b. R. Chanina explained: To the young people it tasted like bread, to the elderly it tasted like oil, and to the children it tasted like honey.

MANNA, "ANGEL FOOD"

Our Rabbis taught: It says [about the manna], "Each man ate the bread of the mighty [*abirim*]" (Psalms 78:25). This was bread that the angels eat [a spiritual kind of food], so said R. Akiva. When this interpretation was told to R. Yishmael, he said [to his disciples]: Go and tell my colleague Akiva: Akiva, you have made a mistake. Do the ministering angels then eat bread? After all, it says, [Moses said, "For forty days and forty nights,] I did not eat any bread nor drink water, [I was like an angel]" (Deuteronomy 9:18). So how do I interpret "the bread of *abirim*"? It means: (Manna was) food that was completely absorbed by the two hundred and forty-eight limbs [*eivarim*] of the body, [and no waste matter was eliminated].

WHY DID THE MANNA COME DOWN IN DAILY RATIONS?

(76b) The disciples of R. Shimon b. Yochai asked him: Why didn't the manna come down for the children of Israel, a year's supply, all at one time, [just as grain is harvested once a year]? He replied: I will give you a parable: You can compare it to a king of flesh and blood who had one only son whom he provided with sustenance once a year. As a result, the son would visit his father only once a year. Thereupon the king decided to provide him with a daily allotment. Now the son would come to visit his father every day. The same way with the children of Israel. If a person had four or five children he would worry, saying: Maybe the manna will not come down tomorrow, and my children will all starve to death. Consequently, each day every person would turn his thoughts toward his Father in Heaven. Another reason [why the manna fell every day] is, so that it should be fresh and warm: [if harvested once a year it would become stale]. Another reason is, so that they should not have to carry around a year's supply of manna on their journey.

HOW BIG WAS THE ACCUMULATION OF THE MANNA?

It happened that R. Tarfon, R. Yishamael, and the elders were sitting and studying the chapter of the manna, R. Elazar Hamoda'i sitting among them. R. Elazar Hamoda'i began to expound and said: The manna that came down to Israel was sixty cubits[71] high! R. Tarfon said to him: Moda'i, how much longer will you pile up words and bring them up upon us? [From where do you know that this is so?] He replied: My teacher, I derive it from a combination of scriptural verses. First, it says, [concerning the flood], "The waters had surged upward fifteen cubits, and all the mountains were covered" (Genesis 7:20). If you say the level of the water was fifteen cubits above the lowland and, at the same time, fifteen cubits above the mountains, did the water stand like walls, [one wall higher than the other]? And besides, how could the Ark rise to the top of the mountains? Therefore, you must say that first all the underground springs opened up, [and filled up all the valleys] until the water level reached the top of the mountains. Afterward, the rain from above added fifteen more cubits above the mountains. Now, which measure is greater, that of reward or that of punishment? Surely you must agree that the measure of reward is greater than that of punishment. [We can apply this rule to the punishment of the flood,] for with the flood it says, "The windows of heaven were opened" (ibid. 11); whereas with the measure of goodness, [i.e., the manna], it says, "So He commanded the skies above, He opened the doors of heaven and rained manna upon them for food, giving them heavenly grain" (Psalms 78:23). [Note the relationships: flood—windows; manna—doors. And we learned in a *Baraita*: How many windows are there in a door? Four. [So, since two doors[72] of heaven were opened for the manna], there was a total of eight windows. [At the flood only two windows of heaven were opened, [so we find that the measure of goodness of the manna was four times as great as the measure of punishment of the flood. Now, the two windows of the flood produced fifteen cubits of water]. Consequently, the manna that fell on Israel was [4 x 15] not less than sixty cubits high.

We learned that Issi b. Yehudah said: The manna that came down for Israel would accumulate to a height where all the kings of the east and the west could see it, for it says, "You spread a table before me in full view of my enemies," (Psalms 23:5). [This refers to children of Israel when they ate the manna in the wilderness, and all the kings could see it.] The verse continues, "You anoint my head with oil, my cup is filled." Abaye said: We learn from this that the cup of David [over which he will say Grace at the great banquet that God will make for the *tzaddikim*][73] in the World to Come will hold 221 lugin, because it says, "My cup is full [*revayah*]," and the numeric value of *revayah* is 221.

[The Gemara asks:] How can R. Elazar Hamoda'i compare [the flood and the manna]? During the flood it rained for forty days, [to reach a height of fifteen cubits]; the manna fell for just a short while [so how could it become so high?]; or, [conversely we can ask], the water of the flood was distributed evenly over the whole world [and therefore it reached only fifteen cubits], but when the manna fell, it came down on the children of Israel alone; therefore it should be much higher than sixty cubits! [The Gemara answers:] The basis of R. Elazar Hamoda'i's calculation is a *gezeirah shava* [scriptural analogy] of *petichah* ["opening"], which occurs both in connection with the flood and the manna.[74]

TELLTALE NAMES

(83b) R. Meir, R. Yehudah, and R. Yose were traveling on the road. (R. Meir used to find significance in people's names, whereas R. Yehudah and R. Yose paid no attention to names.) When they came to a certain town they looked for an inn. When they found one they asked the innkeeper, "What is your name?" He replied, "My name is Kidor." R. Meir said to himself, "His name tells me that he is a wicked person, for it says, 'For they are a generation [*ki dor*] that turns the wrong way' (Deuteronomy 32:20)." [Before the onset of *Shabbat*,] R. Yehudah and R. Yose gave him their wallets for safekeeping, but R. Meir did not. He placed his wallet in a pitcher and buried it near the grave of the innkeeper's father. That night, the father appeared to the innkeeper in a dream and told him, "Go and take the purse that is next to my head." In the morning, the innkeeper told the Rabbis, "This is what I saw in my dream." Rabbi Meir replied, "Dreams that you dream Friday night [when you are at rest and you have all kinds of fantasies] are meaningless."

R. Meir went to the grave and watched the wallet all that day, and after *Shabbat*, brought it home. The next morning, the two Rabbis said to the innkeeper, "Give us our purses." He replied, "You never gave me your purses." R. Meir then said to them, "Why don't you pay attention to people's names? [His name would have given you a clue to his character.]" They said, "Why didn't you tell us that [he was a swindler]?" He replied, "I only had a suspicion. Did I say that you can make a definite assumption that a person is a thief [on the basis of the sound of his name? That's why I had no right to tell you]." [Now they wanted to get their purses back.] So they took the innkeeper to a tavern and invited him for a drink, [hoping that he would get drunk and admit the theft of the wallets. It did not help,] but they noticed that he had some lentils on his moustache. They went to his wife and told her, ["Your husband said you should give us the two wallets, and a sign is that you served him lentils for lunch."] They got their wallets back and went away. The innkeeper killed his wife because of that.

The *Baraita* had this incident in mind when it said: The failure to wash his hands before the meal caused a person to eat pork.[75] The failure to wash his hands after the meal, before reciting Grace, caused a person to be killed. [This refers to our case. If Kidor had washed his hands after his meal, he would have wiped his mouth and removed the lentils. Then the Rabbis would not have had a sign to claim their wallets from the wife, and Kidor would not have killed her.] After this incident, they, too, paid attention to people's names. When they came to a house whose owner's name was Balah they did not go in, saying: This person has to be a wicked man, for it says, "Then I said about her that was worn out [*balah*] by adultery" (Ezekiel 23:43).

A MAD DOG

The Rabbis taught: Five things were said about a mad dog: its mouth is open, its saliva is dripping, its ears are drooping, its tail hangs between its thighs, and it walks on the side of the road. Some say: It barks, but its voice cannot be heard. What causes rabies in dogs? Rav said: It is caused by witches who are practicing their witchcraft on them. Shmuel said: A rabid dog is possessed of an evil spirit. What is the difference between these two opinions? The difference is (84a) whether you should kill a mad dog by throwing something at it [to avoid direct contact]. [If rabies is caused by an evil spirit, and someone kills the dog with a hand-held instrument, the evil spirit may enter that person by way of the instrument. If it is caused by witchcraft, there is no danger of contagion through contact. (Rashi)] There is a *Baraita* according to Shmuel: A mad dog should be killed by throwing something against it, [like an arrow or a knife]. For whoever is touched by a rabid dog becomes dangerously ill, and whoever is bitten by it, dies. If someone was touched by a rabid dog, what should he do? He should cast off the clothes that were touched by the dog and run. A mad dog once brushed against Rav Kahana the son of R. Yehoshua in the marketplace; he stripped off his garments and ran, saying: I fulfilled in my own person, "Wisdom preserves the life of him who possesses it" (Ecclesiastes 7:12).

FOR WHAT SINS DOES YOM KIPPUR PROVIDE ATONEMENT?
(85b) [The Mishnah says:] If a person says, "I will sin and repent; I will sin and repent," they [the Heavenly Court] do not assist him in achieving repentance. If he says, "I will sin, and Yom Kippur will provide atonement," Yom Kippur does not provide atonement. For sins between man and God, Yom Kippur provides atonement; but for sins between man and his fellow man, Yom Kippur does not provide atonement, until he appeases that person. This was expounded by R. Elazar b. Azariah: "From all of your sins before God, shall you be cleansed" (Leviticus 16:30). "From your sins before God," i.e., for sins between man and God, Yom Kippur provides atonement; but for sins between man and his fellow man, Yom Kippur does not provide atonement until he appeases that person. R. Akiva [read the phrase as, "Before God shall you be cleansed," and] said: Fortunate are you, O Israel! Before Whom do you cleanse yourselves? Who cleanses you? Your Father in Heaven! As it says, "I will sprinkle pure water on you, and you shall be cleansed" (Ezekiel 36:25). And He also says, "The *mikveh* of Israel is God" (Jeremiah 17:13). Just as a *mikveh* purifies the contaminated, so does the Holy One, blessed be He, purify Israel.

FOUR KINDS OF ATONEMENT
(86a) R. Matya b. Cheresh asked R. Elazar b. Azariah in Rome: Have you heard of the four kinds of atonement on which R. Yishmael used to expound? He replied: There are only three, for repentance [the fourth kind] is required for each kind of atonement. [What is this all about? Here are the three kinds of atonement:] If a person transgressed a positive commandment, [for example, he had a mitzvah to eat matzah on Pesach, and he did not eat it], and repented, then he is forgiven on the spot, [for this is the least serious offense], as it says, "Turn back, you wayward children, I will heal you from your rebelliousness!" (Jeremiah 3:22). If a person violated a prohibition, [e.g., by eating forbidden foods, which is a more grievous sin], and repented, the repentance suspends the [punishment], and Yom Kippur effects full atonement. For it says, "Because on this day you shall have all your sins atoned" (Leviticus 16:30). If he has committed a sin that is punishable by *karet* [spiritual excision, premature death], or for which he is condemned to death by *Bet Din*, and he repents, then repentance and Yom

Kippur effect only suspension [of judgment and punishment], and suffering cleanses him from sin [and brings about complete *teshuvah*]. For it says, "I will punish their transgression with the rod, their iniquity with afflictions" (Psalms 89:33). However, if a person has been guilty of the sin of *chilul Hashem*, of causing the desecration of the Name of God, [by sinning and causing others to sin, which is the most serious form of transgression], then *teshuvah* has no power to suspend punishment, Yom Kippur has no power to atone, and suffering cannot wipe out his guilt, but all of them together effect suspension of punishment. Complete atonement comes only with the sinner's death, as it says, "Then God of Hosts revealed Himself to my ears: 'This iniquity [of *chilul Hashem*] shall never be forgiven you until you die'" (Isaiah 22:14).

CHILUL HASHEM—DESECRATION OF GOD'S NAME
What is meant by *chilul Hashem*, causing the desecration of God's Name? Rav said: For example, if I buy meat from the butcher and do not pay him right away, [he would suspect me of wanting to avoid paying him, and he might emulate me by becoming lax about stealing]. Abaye said: This applies only in a place where the storekeepers do not come around to collect their bills; but in a place where they do go out to collect their bills, it does not matter [if you don't pay at once]. Ravina said: And Mata Mechasya [Ravina's hometown] is a city where the storekeepers go around to collect their bills. Whenever Abaye bought [a zuz's worth of] meat from a store that was owned by two partners, he would pay a zuz to each of the partners; [he was afraid that if he paid only one partner, the other would not know about it and suspect him of avoiding payment]. Afterward he would bring both partners together and straighten out his account. R. Yochanan said: In my case, [it would be a *chilul Hashem*] if I walked four cubits without uttering Torah thoughts or wearing *tefillin*, [because people might not know that I am very weak, and emulating me, might become negligent in their observance of *mitzvot* (Rashi)].

Yitzchak who learned in the yeshivah of R. Yannai said: If a person's friends are embarrassed about his reputation, that constitutes a *chilul Hashem*. What is an example of this? R. Nachman b. Yitzchak said: For instance, if people say about a person: May God forgive So-and-so [for what he did]. Abaye explained: As we learned: It says, "Love God your Lord" (Deuteronomy 6:5). This means that you should cause the Name of Heaven to be beloved. A person should study the *Chumash*, the Mishnah, and learn Gemara; he should be honest in business, and speak gently to people. What do people say about such a person? "Fortunate is the father who taught him Torah. Fortunate is the teacher who taught him Torah. Woe to the people that did not learn Torah; for this person has studied Torah, look how fine his ways are, look how correct his deeds are!" About this person Scripture says, "You are My servant, Israel in whom I glory" (Isaiah 49:3). But if a person studies the Torah and the Mishnah, and learns Gemara, but is dishonest in business and does not speak gently to people, what do people say about him? "Woe to him who studied Torah, woe to his father who taught him Torah, woe to his teacher who taught him Torah! This man who studied Torah; look how corrupt his deeds are, how ugly his ways are." About such a person Scripture says, "They came to those nations [into exile], they desecrated My holy Name, in that it was said of them, 'These are the people of God, yet they had to leave their land'" (Ezekiel 36:20). [The nations attributed the exile of Israel to God's weakness, and that is a *chilul Hashem*.]

THE GREATNESS
OF REPENTANCE

R. Chama b. Chanina said: Great is repentance, for it brings healing to the whole world, as it says, "I will heal their rebelliousness, I will love them freely" (Hosea 14:5). R. Chama b. R. Chanina pointed out a contradiction: [In the first past of the verse] it says, "Turn back, you rebellious children" (Jeremiah 3:22), the implication being that their sin is attributed to youthful rebelliousness [which has been forgotten]; while [in the second part] it says, "I will heal their rebelliousness" (ibid.) [which implies that they retain a mark of their former sin]. This is no difficulty: The first part refers to repentance prompted by love of God [then no trace of sin remains]; the second part refers to repentance motivated by fear [then a stain remains]. Rav Yehudah pointed out this contradiction: It says, "Turn back, you rebellious *children*, I will heal your rebelliousness" (ibid.). But it also says, "For I [God] have become *Master* over you, and I have taken you, one from a town and two from a family" (Jeremiah 3:14). [The first verse describes the relationship of God to Israel as a father to his children; the second verse, as a master to a servant.] There is no contradiction: The first verse speaks of repentance out of love or out of fear; the second verse speaks of repentance brought on by suffering.

Rabbi Levi said: Great is repentance, for it reaches up to the Throne of Glory, as it says, "Return, O Israel, to God your Lord" (Hosea 14:2). (86b) Rabbi Yochanan said: Repentance is so great that it supersedes even a prohibition of the Torah. For it says, "The prophet is saying, 'If a man divorces his wife, and she leaves him and marries another man, may he ever go back to her?'[76] Would that not bring profound guilt on the land [if he took her back]? But you [Israel] have committed adultery with many lovers [i.e., worshipped many idols]; but I still say, 'Come back to Me'" (Jeremiah 3:1).

R. Yonatan said: Repentance is so great that it brings about redemption [before the preordained time], for it says, "A redeemer shall come to Zion, and to those of Jacob who repent of willful sin" (Isaiah 59:20). He expounds: "How is it that a redeemer shall come to Zion [prematurely]?" Because of "those of Jacob who repent of willful sin."

Resh Lakish said: Great is repentance, for, because of it intentional sins are counted as errors. For it says, "Return, O Israel, to God your Lord; for you have stumbled because of your sin" (Hosea 14:2). [The Gemara asks:] "Sin" means an intentional transgression, yet he calls it "stumbling," [and "stumbling" implies error]. But is that so? Has not Resh Lakish said that repentance is so great that because of it intentional sins are counted as merits, as it says, "And when a wicked man turns back from his wickedness and practices justice and charity, he shall live because of them" (Ezekiel 33:19), [the implication is that *teshuvah* turns intentional sins into merits; and you say that they are counted only as errors]? That is no contradiction: The latter verse speaks of repentance out of love [then intentional sins convert to merits]; the first of repentance out of fear, [then intentional sins are counted as errors].

R. Shmuel b. Nachmani said in the name of R. Yonatan: Great is repentance, because it prolongs the life of a person, as it says, "If a wicked man returns from his wickedness . . . he will live longer" (Ezekiel 33:19).

R. Yitzchak said: In Eretz Yisrael they said in the name of Rabbah bar Mari: Come and see how the conduct of mortal man differs from that of the Holy One, blessed be He. The conduct of mortal man is, that when he is angered, it is doubtful whether he can be appeased by [the offender] or not. And even if he can be appeased, it is doubtful whether he can be appeased by mere words [of apology]. But with the Holy One, blessed be He, [even] if a person commits a sin in secret, He is appeased by words alone, as it says, "Take words with you, and return to God" (Hosea 14:3). Furthermore, He even counts it as a good deed, for it says, "and take that which is good" (ibid.). Still more, Scripture accounts it to him as if he had sacrificed bulls, for it says, "Let the words of our lips compensate for the sacrificial bulls" (ibid.). Perhaps you will say [this refers to] obligatory bulls? Therefore it says "I will heal their rebelliousness, I will love them freely" (Hosea 14:5), [meaning, God considers our *teshuvah* as a freely donated offering, which is more fully accepted by God than an obligatory one (Rashi)].

We learned in a *Baraita*: R. Meir used to say: Great is repentance, for on account of a single individual who repented, the sins of the whole world are forgiven, for it says, "I will heal their rebelliousness, I will love them freely, for My anger is turned away from him" (Hosea 14:5). It does not say "from them," but "from him."

WHAT IS A *BAAL TESHUVAH*?

[The Gemara asks:] What is an example of a *baal teshuvah*? Rav Yehudah said: If the temptation [to commit his original transgression] returns to him on two more occasions, and he overcomes it and does not sin [that is a sign that he is a *baal teshuvah*]. Rav Yehudah, pointing with his hand, said: [If he is tempted to sin again] with the same woman, at the same time [of his life, when he is still young], in the same place. Rav Yehudah said: Rav pointed out a contradiction: It says, "Happy is he whose transgression is forgiven, whose sin is covered over" (Psalms 31:1), and it also says, "He who covers up his sins will not succeed" (Proverbs 28:13). That is no difficulty. One verse speaks of sins that are public knowledge. [A person should publicly acknowledge such wrongdoings and not cover them up.] The other verse speaks of sins that are not known. [Those he should not publicize, but confess only to God.] R. Zutra b. Tuvyah said in the name of R. Nachman: One verse speaks of sins a person committed against his fellow; [those he should not conceal, so that people will help him to obtain forgiveness from the person he has offended]. The other verse speaks of sins against God; [those he should conceal from the public and confess only to God].

We learned in a *Baraita*: R. Yose b. Yehudah said: If a person commits a transgression for the first time, he is forgiven; the second time, he is forgiven; the third time, he is also forgiven; but if he commits it the fourth time, he is not forgiven. For it says, "Thus says God, 'For three transgressions of Israel [I have looked away], but for four I will not pardon them'" (Amos 2:6). And it also says, "Truly, God does all these things with a man two or three times" (Job 33:29). [The Gemara asks:] What novel idea does the verse in Job contribute? [The Gemara answers:] If you only had the verse in Amos you would have said that it applies only to a community [that sins the first, second, and third time], but not to an individual. Therefore, the second verse is cited, "Truly, God does all these things to an man two or three times," [to tell you that even an individual who sins the first, second, and third time is forgiven].

The Rabbis taught: The sins that a person confessed on Yom Kippur, he should not confess on the next Yom Kippur. But if he repeated the sins during the year, he should confess them on another Yom Kippur. And if he did not commit the sins again, but still confessed them again, about such a person Scripture says, "Like a dog that returns to his vomit, so [is a] fool who repeats his foolishness" (Proverbs 26:11). R. Elazar b. Yaakov said: On the contrary, such a person is all the more praiseworthy, for it says, "For I recognize my transgressions, and am ever conscious of my sin" (Psalms 51:5). If so, how do I explain, "Like a dog that returns to his vomit," etc.? [This can be explained] in accordance with R. Huna, for R. Huna said: Once a person committed a sin and repeats it, it becomes permitted to him. [Asks the Gemara:] What! Permitted! Do you really think that is the meaning? Rather, say: It seems to him as if it were permitted; [he has no qualms about repeating the sin; and in that respect he is like a dog returning to his vomit].

MUST THE SIN BE SPECIFIED?

We learned in a *Baraita*: R. Yehudah b. Bava said: [When a person confesses] he has to specify the details of his sin, for it says, "[Moses said,] 'The people have committed a terrible sin by making a golden idol'" (Exodus 32:31) [Moses specified their sin "by making a golden idol."] R. Akiva said: It is not necessary to specify the sin, for it says, "Happy is he whose transgression is forgiven, whose sin is covered over" (Psalms 32:1), [and not specifically mentioned]. If so, why did Moses say specifically, "by making a golden idol"? This can be explained in accordance with R. Yannai. For R. Yannai said: Moses said to the Holy One, blessed be He: The silver and gold that you gave to Israel in such abundance until they said: "It's enough!"[77], that is what caused them to make the golden idol. [In other words, Moses said these words in defense of the Jewish people.]

MOSES AND DAVID

The Jewish people had two good leaders: Moses and David. Moses said to God: Let my wrongdoing be written down clearly, as it says [with reference to the *Mei Merivah*, the "Waters of Dispute," God said,] "You did not have enough faith in Me to sanctify Me" (Numbers 20:12). David asked that his wrongdoing [with Bathsheba] should not be written down, for it says, "Happy is he whose transgression is forgiven, whose sin is covered over" (Psalms 32:1). The different requests of Moses and David can be compared to the case of two women who were given stripes by the *Bet Din*; one of them had been guilty of adultery, and the other had eaten unripe figs of the seventh year. [The produce of the Sabbatical year may not be wasted,[78] and eating unripe figs is tantamount to wasting them, because they are not eaten in the proper fashion. The offense of the second woman is not nearly as grave as that of the first.] The woman who had eaten the unripe figs said to the *Bet Din*: I beg of you, please tell everyone why I am receiving these lashes, so that people should not say that I was punished for the same sin the other woman was punished for. Therefore, they brought unripe figs of the Sabbatical year and hung it around her neck, and they called out: This woman has received lashes because of a violation of the laws of the Sabbatical year. [Similarly, the children of Israel committed the grave sin of accepting the bad report the spies had told about Eretz Yisrael. In contrast, Moses' sin of the Waters of Dispute was not nearly as serious. That is why Moses asked that his sin be spelled out clearly.]

APHORISM

It is a mitzvah to expose hypocrites, in order to prevent a desecration of God's Name, [because people will follow their example]. For it says, "If a righteous man abandons his righteousness and does wrong, then I put a stumbling block before him, [so that he will be exposed, and everyone will know that he is a wicked man]" (Ezekiel 3:20).

The repentance of even the completely wicked puts off punishment, even though their sentence has been sealed.

The tranquility of the wicked brings trouble in its wake; [in their spare time they think up sins they will commit].

Power buries its possessors, [it causes premature death].

Everyone comes into this world naked and leaves this world naked. O, if only his departure would be like his arrival! [That he leave this world as blameless as when he entered it.]

Whenever Rav went to the *Bet Din* to act as judge, he would say: By his own choice he [meaning himself] is going to meet death [Divine punishment for rendering wrong judgment], and moreover, the needs of his household he does not provide [a judge did not get paid for his services], for he returns home empty-handed. I only wish that when I come home from the *Bet Din* I will be as righteous as when I left for the *Bet Din*, [that I will not render any wrong decisions].

(87a) When Rav saw a crowd following him [out of respect], he would say: "Though his eminence ascends as high as the sky, his head reaching the clouds, he will perish forever, like his own dung; those who saw him will ask, 'Where is he?'" (Job 20:6,7). When the people carried R. Zutra [who was very old] on a chair on their shoulders on the *Shabbat* before Yom Tov [when he would lecture on the laws of the Yom Tov], he would say, "Power does not last forever, or a crown for all generations" (Proverbs 27:24).

THE MERIT OF THE FATHERS

"To show favor to an evildoer is not good" (Proverbs 18:5). [What does this mean?] It is not good for the evildoers if God shows them favor in this world. It was not good for Ahab that he was shown favor in this world. [When the depraved king Ahab was told by Elijah that he would perish, he tore his clothes and repented (1 Kings 21:27), whereupon God said to Elijah,] "Since he has humbled himself before Me, I will not bring the evil in his days" (ibid. 29). [The deferment of his punishment was not good for Ahab, because it gave him the opportunity to sin even more, and he thereby lost his share in the World to Come (*Maharsha*).]

[The verse, "To show favor to an evildoer is not good" ends with the words,] "It turns aside the judgment of a righteous person" (Proverbs 18:5), which

means, "It is good for the righteous that they are not favored in this world," [for thereby they have a greater share in the World to Come]. It was good for Moses and Aaron that they were not shown favor in this world, as it says, [God said to Moses and Aaron,] "You did not have enough faith in Me to sanctify Me . . . Therefore, you shall not bring this assembly to the land that I have given you" (Numbers 20:12).

We can infer from this that if they had shown full faith, their time to leave this world would not yet have come. Happy are the righteous! Not only do they acquire merit for themselves, but they confer merit on their children and grandchildren to the end of all generations. [The Gemara proves it:] For Aaron had several sons who deserved to be burned like [his sons] Nadav and Abihu, as it says, "Elazar and Ithamar, [Aaron's] remaining sons" (Leviticus 10:12), [the implication being that they, like their brothers, deserved to be burned, but survived (Rashi)], but it was the merit of their father Aaron that saved them. Woe is to the wicked! Not only do they bring guilt upon themselves, but they confer guilt on their children and grandchildren until the end of all generations. There were many descendants of Canaan [the son of Ham who was cursed by Noah] who were fit to be relied upon [in religious matters] like Tabi, the slave of R. Gamliel,[79] but the guilt of their ancestor caused them [to remain slaves].

HELPING OTHERS DO *MITZVOT*

Anyone who helps others do *mitzvot* will never be the cause of sin, and anyone who causes others to commit sins is not given the opportunity to do *teshuvah*. Why is it that if a person helps others do *mitzvot*, he will never be the cause of sin? So that he should not be in Gehinnom [for his sins] and his disciples in Gan Eden, for it says, "Because You will not abandon my soul to the grave, You will not allow Your devout one[s] to witness destruction" (Psalms 16:10). ["Your devout one(s)" refers to the students who will not be allowed to see their teacher go into Gehinnom while they are in Gan Eden (*Maharsha*).]

"Anyone who causes others to sin is not given the opportunity to do *teshuvah*," so that this person should not be in Gan Eden while his disciples are in Gehinnom. For it says, "A man oppressed by blood-guilt [i.e., he caused others to sin] will flee until the grave; no one will support him" (Proverbs 28:17).

WHEN DOES YOM KIPPUR PROVIDE ATONEMENT?

[The Mishnah said on 85b,] If a person says "I will sin and repent; I will sin and repent," the Heavenly Court does not give him the opportunity to repent. [If he says,] "I will sin, and Yom Kippur will provide atonement," Yom Kippur does not provide atonement. For sins between man and God, Yom Kippur provides atonement; but for sins between man and his fellow man, Yom Kippur does not provide atonement, until he appeases that person. Thus did R. Elazar b. Azariah expound, "From all your sins before God, shall you be cleansed" (Leviticus 16:30)—for sins between man and God, Yom Kippur provides atonement; but for sins between man and his fellow man, Yom Kippur does not provide atonement until he appeases that man. R. Akiva said: Happy are you, O Israel! Before Whom do you cleanse yourselves? Who cleanses you? Your Father in Heaven! As it says, "And I will sprinkle pure water on you, and you shall be cleansed" (Ezekiel 36:25), and he also says, "The *mikveh* of Israel is God" (Jeremiah 17:3); just as a *mikveh* purifies the contaminated, so does the Holy One, blessed be He, purify Israel.

(87b) [We learned in the Mishnah:] If a person says: I will sin and repent; I will sin and repent, the Heavenly Court does not give him the opportunity to repent. [The Gemara asks:] Why does it say "I will sin and repent" twice? [The Gemara answers:] This is in accordance with what R. Huna said in the name of Rav. Once a person has committed a transgression and repeated that transgression, it becomes permissible to him. [Asks the Gemara:] Do you really think it becomes permissible? [The Gemara answers:] It appears to that person like something permissible. [Therefore, he does not feel the need to do *teshuvah*.]

[We learned in the Mishnah:] If he says, "I will sin, and Yom Kippur will provide atonement," Yom Kippur does not provide atonement. [Asks the Gemara:] Shall we say that our Mishnah is not in accordance with the view of Rabbi? For we learned in a *Baraita*: Rabbi says: For all transgressions in the Torah, whether one repented of them or not, whether positive or negative, Yom Kippur provides atonement. [The Gemara answers:] You can say that this Mishnah agrees even with Rabbi. If a person depends on Yom Kippur for his atonement at the time that he commits the transgression, then even according to Rabbi, Yom Kippur does not provide atonement.

R. Yosef b. Chavu pointed out to R. Avahu a contradiction: We learned in our Mishnah: For sins between man and his fellow man, Yom Kippur does not provide atonement. But it says, [Eli said to his sons,] "If a man sins against a man, then God will accept his prayers [and will forgive him]" (1 Samuel 2:25) [which seems to indicate that he can obtain forgiveness without appeasing the neighbor he has wronged]. [Answers the Gemara:] *Elohim* here means judge, [and the verse means: If a person sins against his neighbor, he needs the ruling of a judge to determine the damages he has to pay, and he then can obtain atonement]. [Asks the Gemara:] If so, [how do you understand the second clause of that verse,] "But if he sins against God, who can pray for him [*yitpallel*]?" [The verb *palleil* may mean either "to judge" or "to pray, appease, forgive."

If we translate this verse as "who can judge him?" this is hard to understand. God has many ways to judge him!] [The Gemara answers:] [*Palleil* means "to appease,"] and this is what the verse means to say: If a man sins against his fellow man, and he appeases him, then God will forgive him; but if a man sins against God, who will seek appeasement for him? There is only one thing that will help: repentance and good deeds.

HOW TO ASK FORGIVENESS

R. Yitzchak said: Whoever offends his neighbor, even if he only slighted him with words, he has to appease him, as it says, "My child, if you have been a guarantor for your friend, if you have given your handshake for a stranger, you have been trapped by the words of your mouth . . . Do this therefore, my child and be rescued, for you have come into your fellow's hand. Go humble yourself before him, and placate your fellow" (Proverbs 5:1–3). If you are holding his money, open your palm and return the money to him, and if you are not holding any of his money, but you offended him, send many friends [to intercede on your behalf to get him to forgive you for slighting him].

R. Chisda said: He should try to appease him three times, each time with three people. For it says, "He then goes around [*yashor*] to people and says, 'I have sinned; I have made crooked that which was straight; but to no avail, [I regret that I did it]'" (Job 33:27), [*yashor* is seen as derived from *shurah*, "group"; and Job mentions three expressions of asking forgiveness].

R. Yose b. Chanina said: Anyone who asks forgiveness of his neighbor need not do so more than three times, as it says, [The brothers said to Joseph,] "Kindly [*ana*] forgive [*sa na*] the spiteful deed of your brothers, so now please forgive [*sa na*]" (Genesis 50:17). [The brothers asked Joseph's forgiveness using the expression *na*, "please," three times.] And if the person [whom he has wronged] has died, he should bring ten persons and make them stand by his grave and say: I have sinned against the Lord, God of Israel, and against this person whom I have hurt.

R. Yirmiyah had offended R. Abba. Thereupon R. Yirmiyah went and sat down at the door of R. Abba [to ask his forgiveness]. When the maid poured out the water, some drops fell on R. Yirmiyah's head. He said: They have made a pile of refuse of me, and he applied to himself the verse, "From the trash heaps He lifts the destitute" (1 Samuel 2:8). R. Abba heard [about the humiliation R. Yirmiyah had suffered] and came out toward him, saying: Now I have to come forward and ask you for forgiveness, as it says, "Go humble yourself [before him] and placate your fellow" (*Mishlei* 6:3).

When R. Zeira had any complaint against a person, he would repeatedly pass in front of that person, making himself available to that person, so that he should come forward to appease him.

Rav had a complaint against a certain butcher. When the butcher did not come to Rav on the eve of Yom Kippur to ask his forgiveness, he said: I will go to him and appease him. R. Huna met Rav on his way to the butcher and asked: Where are you going? He replied: To appease So-and-so. R. Huna said: You are going to cause the butcher's death [because you are degrading yourself by asking his forgiveness when he should have appeased you. That will bring punishment down on him, and his life will be taken]. Rav went there anyway, and he stood next to this butcher who was sitting and chopping the head of an animal. He raised his eyes and saw Rav. He then said to him: You are Abba [contemptuously calling Rav by his first name]. Go away! I will have nothing to do with you! While he was chopping the head, a bone jumped off, stuck in his throat, and killed him.

Rav was reciting certain [introductory] verses before Rabbi [began his lecture], and just then R. Chiya (87b) entered, whereupon Rav started again from the beginning. When Bar Kappara entered, he started again from the beginning; when R. Shimon the son of Rabbi entered, he started again from the beginning. But when R. Chanina entered, he said: How many times shall I go back? He did not repeat it again. R. Chaninah resented it. Rav went to him on thirteen eves of Yom Kippur [to ask his forgiveness], but R. Chanina did not accept his apology. [The Gemara asks:] Why did Rav do that [appease him thirteen times]? Did not R. Yose b. R. Chanina say: If a person asks forgiveness of his neighbor, he should not ask more than three times? [The Gemara answers:] Rav was different, [he imposed stringencies on himself beyond the requirements of the law]. [The Gemara asks:] How could R. Chanina act so unyieldingly? Did not Rava say: Anyone who is willing to forgive and to forget, all his transgressions are forgiven? [The Gemara answers:] R. Chanina had seen in a dream that Rav was hanging high from a palm tree, and we have a tradition that any person that hangs high from a tree in a dream will become a head of a yeshivah. R. Chanina [who was the *rosh yeshivah*[80]] concluded that Rav would become the head of the yeshivah [which meant that he, R. Chanina, would die]. Therefore, he did not accept his appeasement, so that Rav would go to teach Torah in Babylonia [and not take his place. Rav indeed became the *rosh yeshivah* of Sura]. He said: I will push him aside, so that I will not be pushed aside.

NOTES

1. *Shabbat* 86b.

2. *Vayechaseihu* may be translated "covered him," Moses, or "covered it," the mountain, since *har*, "mountain," is also masculine.

3. *Taanit* 26a.

4. This sanctuary was set up by Joshua after Eretz Yisrael had been conquered (Joshua 18:1). It stood for

369 years until it was destroyed by the Philistines (1 Samuel, Chapter 4).

5. After giving birth to a boy or a girl, a woman has to bring a sheep as a burnt offering and a dove as a sin offering. If she cannot afford a sheep she brings two doves (Leviticus 12:6–8). By delaying the bringing of these doves, Eli's sons forced the women to stay in Jerusalem and prevented them from returning home and resuming family life. Scripture considers that as if they had committed adultery. (Leviticus 12:6–8)

6. The reference is to Menasseh, the idolatrous king who placed an idol in the *Bet Hamikdash*.

7. *Ein Yaakov* follows the arrangement of the text suggested by the Bach. The Bach is an abbreviation of Bayit Chadash, a commentary on the Tur Shulchan Aruch by R. Yoel Sirkis (1561–1640). The Bach also wrote emendations to the Talmud which appear in the margin of the Talmud pages.

8. "When Babylon's seventy years are over . . . I will fulfill My promise to bring you back to this place" (Jeremiah 29:10).

9. Tosafot comments that Resh Lakish did not initiate a conversation, but he certainly did reply when someone addressed him. See *Zevachim* 5a.

10. Belshazzar, the son of Nebuchadnezzar, was defeated by the Persian Kings Darius and Cyrus (Rashi).

11. King Cyrus of Persia encouraged the Jews to return to Eretz Yisrael and to rebuild the *Bet Hamikdash* (2 Chronicles 36:22,23).

12. The bulls were brought as a sin offering to atone for himself, his family, and his fellow *kohanim* (Leviticus 16:6,11).

13. A *parsang* is a Persian mile, or about 4,000 yards.

14. Leviticus 23:19. The *Omer* is the sheaf of barley offered in the *Bet Hamikdash* on the morning of the sixteenth of Nissan, after which the people were allowed to eat the new grain crop. Had a ritual defect been found in the barley, the offering could not have been brought that year.

15. Leviticus 23:17. The Two Loaves had to be baked before the onset of Shavuot, and offered on Shavuot itself. If they became disqualified by a defect, replacements could not be baked.

16. The Showbread was baked on Friday and placed on the Table in the Sanctuary on *Shabbat* where they remained until they were replaced by new loaves on the next *Shabbat*. If a defect were found, the mitzvah could not be performed because new loaves could not be baked on *Shabbat*.

17. A large piece of coal shaped like a crouching lion fell from heaven in the days of Solomon and stayed on the altar until Menasseh removed it (Rashi).

18. The mystical divine names of God that were placed inside the fold of the breastplate of the *Kohen Gadol*. He would meditate on these names to attain inspiration.

19. Daniel 3:22; *Pesachim* 118a,b.

20. 1 Samuel, Chapter 15.

21. 1 Samuel 22:19.

22. 2 Samuel 11:2–27.

23. 2 Samuel 24:1.

24. Maharsha explains this by referring to the curse of the serpent, "I will plant hatred between you and the woman, and between your offspring and her offspring. He will strike you in the head, and you will strike him in the heel" (Genesis 3:15). Man will try to crush the snake's head, which is a mortal blow, whereas the snake takes revenge by striking only the heel, which is not a lethal injury. Similarly, the scholar should take revenge very mildly.

25. Sifra, *Kedoshim* 3:7.

26. The seven Noachide *mitzvot* are: the command to administer justice, the prohibitions of blasphemy, idolatry, murder, immorality, theft, and eating flesh torn from a living animal.

27. Literally, "mixing of dishes." If Yom Tov falls on Friday you are not allowed to prepare food for *Shabbat*. You may start on *erev* Yom Tov to prepare a dish for *Shabbat* and then continue cooking for *Shabbat* on Yom Tov. This is called *eruv tavshilin*.

28. The Menorah in the *Bet Hamikdash* had seven lamps. The lamps that had burned all night had to be cleaned in two steps, first five and then the remaining two (*Yoma* 14a).

29. Numbers 28:5.

30. Leviticus 6:13.

31. Two pans of frankincense were placed on top of the stack of showbread every week. On Shabbat the incense was burned on the outer altar, after which the *kohanim* ate the showbread (*Menachot* 96b).

32. R. Akiva Eiger points out that Moses is referring to *teshuvah* that is done out of fear of punishment; but if a person does *teshuvah* out of love of God, his intentional sins are accounted as merits.

33. This is the source for our custom to answer *Baruch Hu uvaruch Shemo*, "Blessed be He, and blessed be His Name," upon hearing God's Name in a *berachah*. (Shulchan Aruch, Orach Chaim 124:5).

34. King of Adiabene, a kingdom in northern Mesopotamia (now Iraq); its capital was modern Irbil. Several decades before the destruction of the second *Bet Hamikdash*, he and his mother embraced Judaism. According to Rashi in *Bava Batra* 11a, Munbaz was a descendant of the Hasmonean dynasty.

35. Numbers 5:11–31. The chapter of the suspected adulteress had to be written on a parchment, and the writing had to be dissolved in water that she was made to drink. The *kohen* who wrote the parchment could copy it from this gold tablet, and did not have to take out a *sefer Torah*.

36. The miracles will be discussed further on.

37. One of eight divisions of *kohanim* that performed the services of the *Bet Hamikdash* in rotation.

38. Exodus 25:30 and Leviticus 24:5–9. Twelve loaves of *lechem hapanim* were arranged in two stacks on the Table in the Sanctuary on *Shabbat* and eaten by the *kohanim* on the following *Shabbat*. Since they were thin and fragile, it required great skill to prepare and bake them.

39. The prophet Zechariah ben Yehoiadah, the priest, admonished the people, whereupon they pelted him with stones and killed him in the Court of the *Bet Hamikdash* (2 Chronicles 24:20–22).

40. 1 Kings 18:3.

41. *Raglei*, "the feet of . . . ," is translated "because of the pious ones."

42. *Raglei*, "the feet of," is translated in the sense of "times" (e.g., *shalosh regalim*), "three times," in "Why have you beaten your donkey these three times [*shalosh regalim*]?" (Numbers 23:32).

43. Shimon Hatzaddik (The Righteous) was the *Kohen Gadol*, as well as the spiritual and political leader of the people during the fourth century B.C.E., when Eretz Yisrael was under the domination of Greece. He used his power to strengthen the study and observance of the Torah throughout the land.

44. Leviticus 16:8.

45. In accordance with the verse, "Even if your sins will be as scarlet, they will turn as white as snow" (Isaiah 1:18).

46. The *Omer* is one-tenth of an *ephah*, (about two quarts) of barley offered on the sixteenth of Nissan, after which the new grains of that year were permitted for use (see Leviticus 23:10).

47. Leviticus 23:17.

48. According to Rashi it happened on Yom Kippur. Yerushalmi says that it happened on *erev* Yom Kippur. Maharsha agrees with Yerushalmi, since he holds that it seems rather unlikely that the *Kohen Gadol* would go for a stroll and talk to an Arab in the street on Yom Kippur.

49. The Sanctuary of the *Bet Hamikdash* consisted of two chambers: The *Heichal* or *Kodesh*, which contained the seven-branched Menorah, the Table of the showbreads, and the golden-incense Altar. The *Kodshei Kodashim*, the Holy of Holies, was the seat of the Holy Ark containing the Tablets on whose cover were the two *keruvim*, cherubs; it faced west. The two chambers were separated by two curtains that ran from the north to the south wall. The large Altar [Copper Altar] on which the sacrifices were offered was in the *Azarah* [Court] in front of the *Heichal*.

50. Exodus 25:10–22. Since the Ark was missing in the second *Bet Hamikdash*, the *Kohen Gadol* put the pan with coals in the place where the two carrying poles would have been.

51. 1 Kings 6:16.

52. Exodus 16:33.

53. Numbers 17:25.

54. If a similar word occurs in two different passages in the Torah, the laws of one passage are applied to the subject of the other.

55. The word *shammah*, "there," occurs in Exodus 30:6 in relation to the Ark, and in Exodus 16:33 in relation to the manna, indicating that the jar of manna was hidden with the Ark. In both Exodus 16:33 and Exodus 30:31 (which deals with the anointing oil) the word *dorot*, "generations," appears, indicating that the bottle of oil was hidden with the jar of manna. Lastly, both in Exodus 30:31 (anointing oil) and Numbers 17:25, which refers to Aaron's staff, the word *mishmeret*, "to be kept," occurs, indicating that Aaron's staff was hidden together with the oil. The upshot is that the Ark, the manna, the oil, and Aaron's staff all were hidden together.

56. During much of the Second Temple period, unqualified individuals officiated as *Kohen Gadol*. Often such people died in the Holy of Holies on Yom Kippur when they altered the process of burning the incense.

57. *Sotah* 48b.

58. It is generally believed that the great stone in the Dome of the Rock is the *Shetiyah* Stone (Radbaz 639, 691).

59. The *Shiltei Hagiborim* holds that the Ark was hidden beneath the Holy of Holies, but that there was a tunnel built by Solomon that led from the storage room for the wood to the Holy of Holies.

60. This suggests that the Holy of Holies lies at the root of creation of material reality.

61. Deuteronomy 22:11.

62. If a man died childless, his brother is obligated to marry his deceased brother's widow (*yibbum*). If he is not ready to marry his brother's widow, the act of *chalitzah* must be performed whereby the widow removes her brother-in-law's shoe, spits on the ground, and makes a prescribed declaration. (See Deuteronomy 25:5–10.) She thereby becomes free to marry. Today, in all such cases, *chalitzah* is always performed.

63. This group led the Jewish people at the beginning of the Second Temple era. It included Ezra, Mordechai, Haggai, Zechariah, Malachi, and Shimon Hatzaddik. They laid the foundation of the liturgy and enacted many ordinances to strengthen the observance of the *mitzvot*.

64. According to the Maharsha.

65. *Yoma* 71b.

66. An apron-like garment that covered the *Kohen Gadol*'s back from below his elbows to his knees, with a belt woven into it to be tied around the front.

67. The *Urim veTummim* was a slip of parchment on which the Ineffable Four-Letter Name of God was written. It was inserted in the fold of the breastplate. Twelve precious stones were attached to the front of the breastplate. When the *Urim veTummim* were consulted, the letters etched on the stones lit up and spelled out a message.

68. Each person received exactly one *omer* of manna each day, a measure of about one quart (Exodus 16:16). Miraculously, it would fall in the house of the person who was entitled to it.

69. Exodus 16:13.

70. Exodus 16:4, 31; Numbers 11:8.

71. A cubit is approximately eighteen inches, so sixty cubits would be 108 inches.

72. The plural "doors" implies a minimum of two.

73. See *Pesachim* 119b.

74. "The windows of the heavens were opened [*niftachu*]" (Genesis 7:11), and "He opened [*patach*] the doors of heaven" (Psalms 78:23).

75. During a time of persecution, a certain Jewish restaurant owner served non-kosher food to non-Jews and kosher food to his Jewish customers. One day, a Jew ordered a meal and failed to wash his hands. The restaurateur, taking him for a non-Jew, served him pork (Rashi).

76. A man may not remarry the wife he divorced if she had married someone else in the interim (Deuteronomy 24:4).

77. The name of the place Di Zahav (Deuteronomy 1:1) is read as *dai zahav*, "enough of gold" (Rashi on Chumash).

78. Leviticus 25:6.

79. R. Gamliel called him a *talmid chacham*, a Torah scholar (*Sukkah* 20b).

80. *Ketubot* 103b.

∾ SUKKAH ∾

DID MOSES AND ELIJAH ASCEND TO HEAVEN?

(5a) We learned in a *Baraita*: R. Yose said: The *Shechinah* never came down to this earth, and Moses and Elijah never ascended to the highest levels of Heaven. For it says, "The heavens belong to God, but the earth He gave over to man" (Psalms 115:16). [The Gemara asks:] But did not the *Shechinah* come down to earth? Doesn't it say, in fact, "God came down on Mount Sinai" (Exodus 19:20)? [The Gemara answers:] That was above ten handbreadths. [The Gemara asks:] But it says, "His feet will stand on that day on the Mount of Olives" (Zechariah 14:4)? [Thus He will be below ten handbreadths.] [The Gemara answers:] This will be ten handbreadths above the ground. [Asks the Gemara:] But did not Moses and Elijah ascend to Heaven? Doesn't it say, in fact, "And Moses went up to God" (Exodus 19:3)? [The Gemara answers:] That was to a level of ten handbreadths [below the highest sphere of Heaven]. But doesn't it say, "It happened when God took Elijah up to Heaven in a whirlwind" (2 Kings 2:11)? [The Gemara answers:] That was to a level of ten handbreadths [below the highest sphere of Heaven]. But doesn't it say, "[Moses] took hold of the Throne [of Glory], while God spread His cloud over him" (Job 26:9)? And R. Tanchum expounded: This teaches us that the Almighty spread some of the radiance of His *Shechinah* and His cloud over him [Moses], [proving that Moses did ascend to Heaven]? [The Gemara answers:] That was at a level of ten handbreadths [below the highest sphere of Heaven]. [The Gemara asks:] Nevertheless, it says, "[Moses] took hold of the Throne [of Glory]," [obviously, he did reach the loftiest level]?[1] [The Gemara answers:] The Throne was lowered for Moses' sake until it came down to a level of ten handbreadths [below the highest sphere of Heaven], and then Moses took hold of it.

PRAYERS ARE LIKENED TO A SHOVEL

(14a) R. Elazar said: Why are the prayers of the righteous compared to a shovel? [The verb *atar*, "to pray," is derived from *eter*, "shovel."] To teach you that just as a shovel turns the grain from one place to another in the barn, so do the prayers of the righteous turn the mind of the Holy One, blessed be He, from the attribute of harshness to that of mercy.

A SUKKAH ON THE DECK OF A SHIP

(23a) We learned in a *Baraita*: A sukkah that was built on the deck of a ship, R. Gamliel declares invalid, and R. Akiva says it is valid. It happened once when R. Gamliel and R. Akiva were sailing on a ship [on Sukkot], that R. Akiva got busy building a sukkah on the deck of the ship. The next day, the wind blew it away. R. Gamliel said to him: "Akiva, where is your sukkah?"

VISITING YOUR RABBI ON YOM TOV

(27b) We learned in a *Baraita*: It once happened that R. Ila'i went to visit R. Eliezer, his teacher, in Lod (Lydda) on a Yom Tov. [He left on *erev* Yom Tov, to be able to visit his rabbi on the first day of Yom Tov.] R. Eliezer said to him: Ila'i, you are not one of those who are resting on the Yom Tov [as they should]. For R. Eliezer used to say: I praise the people who are lazy, and who do not leave their homes on Yom Tov, [although they only stay at home because they are lazy], for it says, "You and your family should rejoice [on Yom Tov]" (*Devarim* 14:25). [The Gemara asks:] Is that so? For did not R. Yitzchak say: How do we know that a person is required to visit his rabbi on Yom Tov? For it says, [When the Shunammite woman went to see the prophet Elisha, her husband asked her,] "Why are you going to him today? It is not a New Moon or *Shabbat*!" (2 Kings 4:23). This implies that on [a holy day, like] the New Moon and on *Shabbat* a person is required to visit his rabbi. This is not difficult. [He is obligated to visit his rabbi] when he can go and return to his house on the same day, [and enjoy part of the Yom Tov day together with his wife]. [R. Eliezer who said that he should not visit his rabbi on Yom Tov] speaks of a case when he cannot go and come back on the same day. [Then he should stay at home and enjoy the Yom Tov together with his wife and family.]

HE CHANGED THE SUBJECT

We learned in a *Baraita*: It happened that R. Eliezer spent the *Shabbat* [of Sukkot] in Upper Galilee in the sukkah of R. Yochanan b. R. Ila'i in Kisri or, as some say, in Kisarion. When the sun reached the sukkah, R. Yochanan asked R. Eliezer: Am I allowed to spread a sheet over the sukkah [to provide shade. Is this considered erecting a temporary tent, which is forbidden on *Shabbat*, or not]? He answered: There was not one tribe in Israel that did not produce a judge. [He changed the subject.] When the sunlight reached halfway across the sukkah, R. Yochanan asked R. Eliezer: Am I allowed to spread a sheet over the sukkah? He replied: There was not a tribe in Israel from which there did not come prophets. From the tribes of Judah and Benjamin kings came forth that were appointed by prophets, [for example, Saul and David who were appointed by Samuel]. When the sun reached the feet of R. Eliezer, R. Yochanan took a sheet and spread it over the sukkah. [Thereupon] R. Eliezer put on his cloak and left, [he did not want to endorse R. Yochanan's action]. The reason that he changed the subject was not because he wanted to evade giving an answer, but because he never said anything that he did not hear from his rabbi, [and he had not heard from his rabbi a halachic ruling on this question].

HE ONLY REPEATED HIS RABBIS' TEACHINGS

(28a) We learned in a *Baraita*: It once happened that R. Eliezer spent *Shabbat* in Upper Galilee, and they asked him thirty halachic questions regarding the sukkah. Of twelve of these he said: I heard them from my rabbis; of eighteen he said: I have not heard them, [and he did not answer them]. R. Yose b. R. Yehudah said: It was the opposite: Of eighteen of them he said: I heard them from my rabbis; of twelve he said: I have not heard them from my rabbis. They said to him: Is everything you say in *Halachah* only what you have heard from your rabbis? To this he replied: Now you are forcing me to say something that I have not heard from my rabbis: [The following things I have not actually heard from my rabbis, but I have observed them doing them, and I follow their ways:] In all my life, no one ever arrived before me in the *bet midrash* [house of learning]; I never slept or took a nap in the *bet midrash*; I was always the last one to leave the *bet midrash*; I have never spoken idle talk; and I have never said anything that I have not heard from my rabbis.

(21b) R. Acha b. Adda said in the name of R. Hamenuna who quoted Rav: How do we know that

even the casual conversation of Torah scholars requires study? Because it says, "Whose leaf never withers" (Psalms 1:3), [even the most insignificant part of the tree has value].

R. ELIEZER IMITATED HIS TEACHER'S WAYS

(28a) They said about R. Yochanan b. Zakkai that in all his life he never spoke idle talk; he never walked four cubits without thinking Torah thoughts or without *tefillin*; no one ever arrived before him in the *bet midrash*; and he was always the last to leave. He never slept or took a nap in the *bet midrash*. But he never thought Torah thoughts in dirty alleys; no one ever found him sitting silently, but only sitting and learning out loud; and no one but himself opened the doors for the students. He never in his life said anything he had not heard from his rabbi, [his rabbi being Hillel the Elder]. He never said to his disciples: It is time to stop learning, except on *erev* Pesach [in order to start the *seder* on time] and on *erev* Yom Kippur [when it is a mitzvah to eat a meal during the day]. And his disciple R. Eliezer followed his example.

R. YOCHANAN B. ZAKKAI'S AWESOME GREATNESS

We learned in a *Baraita*: Hillel the Elder had eighty disciples, thirty of whom were worthy that the *Shechinah* rest on them as it did on Moses our Teacher; thirty of them were worthy that the sun should stand still for them as it did for Joshua the son of Nun,[2] and the remaining twenty were in between these two levels.

The greatest of his disciples was Yonatan b. Uziel; the smallest [of the eighty disciples] was R. Yochanan b. Zakkai. They said about R. Yochanan b. Zakkai that he did not leave [unstudied] the Scripture, Mishnah, Gemara, *halachot*, *aggadot*, exegetical details of the Torah [*dikdukei Torah*], rabbinical enactments [*dikdukei Soferim*], logical deductions [*kal vachomer*], analogies [*gezeirah shavah*], calendrical computations, numeric values of letters [*gematria'ot*], the speech of the ministering angels, the speech of spirits, the speech of palm trees, washer's parables, fox fables, great things, and small things. "Great things" refers to *Maaseh Merkavah*, [the mystical secrets of the Divine Chariot as described in Ezekiel 1]; "small things" refers to the questions of Abaye and Rava, [the later Amora'im]. [This vast knowledge of R. Yochanan b. Zakkai] is the fulfillment of the verse, "I endow those who love me with substance; and I will fill their treasuries" (Proverbs 8:21). Now, if the smallest of [Hillel's disciples] was so great, how much greater was the knowledge of the greatest of his disciples? They said of Yonatan b. Uziel [who was the greatest of the disciples], that when he would sit and immerse himself in the Torah, every bird that flew above him was immediately consumed by fire.

SOLAR AND LUNAR ECLIPSES

(29a) The Rabbis taught: When the sun is in eclipse, it is a bad omen for idol worshippers; when the moon is in eclipse, it is a bad omen for Israel, because the people of Israel base their calendar on the moon and the idol worshippers base theirs on the sun. If the sun is in eclipse in the east [i.e., in the morning], it is a bad omen for people who live in the east. If it is in eclipse in the west, it is a bad omen for those who live in the west; in the middle of the sky [i.e., at noon], it is a bad omen for the whole world. If its surface is red like blood, it is a sign that the sword is coming to the world; if it is [dark grey, overcast] like sackcloth, it is a sign that the arrows of famine are coming to the world; if it looks like both, the sword and the arrows of famine are coming to the world. If the solar eclipse occurs at sunset, disaster will be postponed; if it is at sunrise, it will come soon. But some say that the order is reversed [if it occurs at sunset, shortly before its disappearance, disaster will come soon. If it occurs at dawn, when the sun still has an entire day ahead of it, the calamity will be postponed (Rashi)].

And there is no nation that is struck by disaster unless its gods [guardian angel (Rashi)][3] are struck along with it, as it says, "I will perform acts of judgment against all the gods of Egypt" (Exodus 12:12). But when Israel fulfills the will of God, they don't have to be afraid of all these omens, as it says, "Thus says God: Do not learn from the way of the nations; do not be frightened by the signs of the heavens, although the nations are frightened by them" (Jeremiah 10:3). The idolators will be frightened, but Israel will not be frightened.

We learned in a *Baraita*: An eclipse of the sun occurs because of the following four things: Because of an *Av Bet Din* [Dean of the Sanhedrin] who died and was not eulogized properly; because of the betrothed girl who cried out in the city, and no one came to save her; because of homosexuality; because of two brothers who were killed at the same time. And because of the following four things the moon and the stars go into eclipse: Because of people who write forged documents; because of people who give false witness; because of people who raise small livestock in Eretz Yisrael [they cannot be prevented from grazing in the fields of others]; and because of people who cut down good trees [even their own trees, for they destroy the ecological balance and they are ungrateful for God's bountiful blessings (Rashi)].

SINS THAT CAUSE FINANCIAL LOSSES

Because of the following four reasons the property of householders winds up in the hands of the government: Because of people who hold on to bills that have been paid, [expecting to collect on them again]; for lending money at interest; (29b) because of people who had the power to protest [against sinful acts] and did not protest; because of people who publicly pledge to give a specific amount for charity and do not give.

Rav said: Because of the following four reasons the property of householders is lost [i.e., confiscated by the king's treasury agents]: For not paying a worker on time; for withholding a worker's wages; for casting off one's responsibilities and placing them on others; and because of arrogance. Arrogance is as bad as all other evils combined, but concerning humble people it says, "But the humble shall inherit the earth, and delight in an abundant peace" (Psalms 37:11).

THE KING PAID THE TOLL

(30a) R. Yochanan said in the name of R. Shimon b. Yocha'i: What is the intent of the verse, "For I am God, Who loves justice and hates a burnt-offering [bought] with robbery" (Isaiah 61:8)? You can compare this to a human king who passed through a toll collector's booth and says to his servants, "Pay the toll." They reply, "But all the toll collections belong to you, O King!" He answered, "All travelers will learn from me not to avoid paying taxes." So the Holy One, blessed be He, said, "For I am God, . . . Who hates a burnt-offering [bought] with robbery" (Isaiah 61:8); "Let My children learn from Me and keep away from robbery," [although everything belongs to God, and even a stolen burnt-offering was God's to begin with].

We also learned: R. Ammi said: A dried-out *lulav*[A] is invalid because it is not *hadar*, "beautiful" [as decreed in Leviticus 23:40]; a stolen one is invalid because it constitutes a mitzvah fulfilled through a transgression.

REMEMBERING THE *BET HAMIKDASH*

(41a) [The Gemara asks:] How do we know that we should do something to remember the *Bet Hamikdash*? R. Yochanan replied: Because it says, "For I will make a cure for you, and I will heal you from your wounds— declares God; for they called you 'Outcast!'[saying,] 'She is Zion—no one cares about her!'" (Jeremiah 30:17). The implication is that we should care about her [and remember her].

ONE *LULAV* FOR FOUR RABBIS

(41b) It once happened that R. Gamliel, R. Yehoshua, R. Elazar b. Azariah, and R. Akiva were traveling on a ship [on Sukkot] and only R. Gamliel had a *lulav*, which he had bought for one thousand *zuz*. R. Gamliel took it in hand and fulfilled the mitzvah with it; he then gave it as a gift to R. Yehoshua who took it, fulfilled the mitzvah with it and gave it as a gift to R. Elazar b. Azariah; who took it, fulfilled the mitzvah with it, and gave it as a gift to R. Akiva; who took it, fulfilled the mitzvah with it, and then gave it back to R. Gamliel.

[The Gemara asks:] Why is it necessary to mention that R. Akiva gave it back to R. Gamliel? [The Gemara answers:] We are taught something in passing, namely, that a gift made on condition that it should be returned is a valid gift. This conforms with what Rava said, for Rava said: [If a person says to his neighbor,] "Take this *etrog* [as a gift] on condition that you return it to me," and the neighbor took it and fulfilled the mitzvah with it; then, if he gave it back, he has fulfilled his obligation, but if he did not give it back, he has not fulfilled his obligation [because he did not comply with the condition; so retroactively, when he took it, he in fact stole it, and a stolen *lulav* is invalid].

[The Gemara asks:] Why is it necessary to mention that R. Gamliel bought the *lulav* for one thousand *zuz*? [The Gemara answers:] In order to let you know how precious the *mitzvot* were to them.

TRAINING CHILDREN TO OBSERVE THE *MITZVOT*

(42a) We learned in a *Baraita*: A minor who knows how to shake the *lulav* is required [by Rabbinic law] to fulfill the mitzvah of *lulav* [as a means of training him to observe the *mitzvot*. The same reason applies to the examples that follow.] If he knows how to put on a *tallit*, he is required to fulfill the mitzvah of *tzitzit*. If he knows how to take care of *tefillin*, his father should buy *tefillin* for him. When he begins to talk, his father should teach him Torah and teach him how to read the *Shema*. [The Gemara asks:] What is meant by "teaching him Torah"? R. Hamenuna said: He should teach him to recite the verse, "The Torah that Moses commanded to us is the heritage of the Congregation of Jacob" (Deuteronomy 33:4). And what is meant by teaching the child the *Shema*? He should teach him the first verse, "Hear, O Israel, God is our Lord, God is the One and Only" (Deuteronomy 6:4).

A DISPUTE ABOUT *ARAVAH*[5]

(44a) We learned: R. Yochanan and R. Yehoshua b. Levi had a dispute. One held that the *aravah* ceremony is an enactment of the prophets [Chaggai, Zechariah, and Malachi, the prophets of the second *Bet Hamikdash*]. The other held that the *aravah* ceremony is only a custom of the prophets. [The Gemara observes:] It can be proved that it was R. Yochanan who said, "It is an enactment of the prophets," since R. Avahu said in the name of R. Yochanan: The ceremony of the *aravah* is an enactment of the prophets. That proves it.

THE GREATNESS OF R. SHIMON B. YOCHA'I AND HIS SON

(45b) Chizkiah said in the name of R. Yirmiyah who quoted R. Shimon b. Yocha'i as saying: I am able to release the whole world from Heavenly judgment from the day I was born until now, [through the merit he earned by his suffering when he was hiding in a cave for thirteen years (*Maharsha*)], and if my son Elazar were with me, we could free the world from judgment from the day of Creation to the present time. And if Yotam the son of Uziah [the righteous King of Judah] were with us, we could release the world from Heavenly punishment] from the creation of the world until its ultimate end.

Chizkiah also said in the name of R. Yirmiyah who quoted R. Shimon b. Yocha'i as saying:] I have seen the group of saintly people [who stand in the presence of the *Shechinah*], but they are few in number. If there are a thousand, I and my son [Elazar] are among them; if a hundred, I and my son are among them; and if there are only two, they are I and my son.

[The Gemara asks:] Are there really only that few? Didn't Rava, in fact, say: Seated in the row immediately in front of the Holy One, blessed be He, are eighteen thousand *tzaddikim*, for it says, "Around [Him] there are eighteen thousand" (Ezekiel 48:35)? [The Gemara answers:] That is no difficulty. R. Shimon b. Yocha'i referred to *tzaddikim* who contemplate the *Shechinah* through a transparent partition; Rava referred to *tzaddikim* who behold the *Shechinah* through an opaque partition. [The Gemara asks:] But are those who contemplate Him through a lucid partition so few? Did not Abaye say: The world never has less than thirty-six *tzaddikim* who are admitted to the nearness of the *Shechinah* every day, for it says, "Praiseworthy are those who yearn [*lo*] [for Him]" (Isaiah 30:18), and the numeric value of *lo* is thirty-six [*lamed* = 30; *vav* = 6]? [The Gemara answers:] This presents no difficulty: The number of thirty-six refers to those who may enter into the nearness of the *Shechinah* with permission; the two [R. Shimon b. Yocha'i and his son] may enter without permission.

THERE IS NO LIMIT TO HOW MUCH YOU CAN LEARN

(46a) R. Zeira, and according to others, R. Chanina b. Papa, said: Come and see, what a difference there is between the norms of mortal man and the norms of the Holy One, blessed be He. By the norms of mortal man, an empty vessel holds what is put into it, and a full vessel cannot hold anything that is added to it. But by the norms of the Holy One, blessed be He, a full vessel holds whatever is added to it, while an empty vessel cannot hold what is put into it. For it says, "It shall be if you listen diligently" (Deuteronomy 28:1), [literally, "if listening, you will listen"]. Which means, if you listen, [i.e., if you make a practice of listening and learning], you will continue to listen [your mind ("a full vessel") will be able to absorb more and more knowledge], but if [you do not make it a practice to listen and learn], then you will not listen [a person who was not trained in his youth to study the Torah ("an empty vessel") will not be able to grasp it later in life]. Another interpretation: If you will listen to the old [i.e., if you review the material you have learned], you will be able to listen to the new [your previous knowledge will help you understand new learning]. "But if your heart will stray and you do not listen" (Deuteronomy 30:17) [i.e., if you do not review your lessons], you will gain no further knowledge.

THE WATER LIBATION[6]

(48a) [The Mishnah says:] How is the water libation done? A golden flask holding three *lugim*[7] was filled from the Shilo'ach [a fresh-water spring near the Temple Mount]. When they reached the Water Gate [one of the southern gates of the Temple Courtyard], they sounded a *tekiah* [a long blast], a *teruah* [a series of short blasts], and a *tekiah*. The *kohen* then went up the ramp of the Altar and turned to his left. There were two silver bowls there. R. Yehudah says: They were made of plaster, but [they looked like silver] because their surfaces were darkened from wine. Each had a hole (48b) like a thin nose, one wider [for the wine] and the other narrower, [for the water, because water flows more freely than wine], so that both would drain out at the same time [onto the Altar, and from there into the *shitin*, a pit deep beneath the Altar]. The western one was for water; the eastern one was for wine. If the *kohen* [inadvertently] poured the water into the bowl for wine, or the wine into the bowl for water, he fulfilled the obligation. R. Yehudah said: He would pour with one *log* all eight days. [R. Yehudah differs with the first Tanna on two counts: He holds that the water libation was one *log*, while the first Tanna holds three *lugim*. In addition, R. Yehudah maintains that the water-libation ceremony was performed all eight days—seven days of Sukkot and one of Shemini Atzeret; whereas the first Tanna holds that it was done only on the seven days of Sukkot (Rashi)]. To the *kohen* who poured the libation they would say, "Raise your hand!" [so that all could see that he was pouring it into the bowl].[8] For once a *kohen* [who was a Sadducee] poured it over his feet [instead of pouring it into the proper bowl], and all the people pelted him with their *etrogim*.

SHITIN, THE DEEP PITS BENEATH THE ALTAR[9]

(49a) Rabbah b. Bar Chana said in the name of R. Yochanan: The *shitin*, the deep pits beneath the Altar, were placed there [by God Himself] at the six days of Creation, for it says, "The rounded shafts for your libation's abysslike trenches, handiwork of the Master Craftsman" (Song of Songs 7:2). "The rounded shafts" refers to the *shitin*; "abysslike trenches" implies that these pits are dug into the earth and descend into the abyss. "Handiwork of the Master Craftsman" means

that they are the product of the craftsmanship of the Holy One, blessed be He.

It was taught in the yeshivah of R. Yishmael: [The Torah begins with the word] *Bereishit*, "In the beginning" (Genesis 1:1). Don't read *bereishit* but *bara shit*, "He created the *shitin*, the pit [underneath the Altar]."

We learned in a *Baraita*: R. Yose said: The *shitin* are hollow and they go down all the way to the very depth of the earth. For it says, "I will now sing on behalf of my Beloved, my Beloved's song about His vineyard: My Beloved had a vineyard in a fertile corner. He fenced it around and cleared it of stones; He planted it with the choicest vines and built a tower inside it; He even hewed a wine press in it" (Isaiah 5:1,2). "He planted it with the choicest vines" refers to the *Bet Hamikdash*; "He built a tower inside it" refers to the Altar, "and He even hewed a vat in it" refers to the *shitin*.

EXEGESIS OF SONG OF SONGS 7:2

(49b) Rava expounded: What is meant by the verse, "Your footsteps were so lovely when shod in pilgrim's sandals, O daughter of nobles!" (Song of Songs 7:2). How beautiful are the steps of Israel when they go up to Jerusalem on the Pilgrimage Festivals. "O daughter of nobles" means, daughter of our father Abraham, who is called a noble, as it says, "The nobles of the people gathered, the people of the God of Abraham" (Psalms 47:10). It says, "the God of Abraham"; why not the God of Isaac and Jacob? It comes to tell you that, [the gentiles who converted will be protected by] "the God of Abraham" who was the first convert.

It was taught in the yeshivah of R. Anan: What is the intent of the words, "Your rounded thighs" (Song of Songs 7:2)? Why are the words of the Torah compared to a thigh? To teach you that just as the thigh is hidden, so should the words of the Torah be hidden, [taught in privacy, without publicity]. And that is the underlying thought of what R. Elazar said. For R. Elazar said: What is the meaning of the verse, "He has told you, 'O man, what is good! What does God require of you but to do justice, to love kindness and to walk humbly with your God?'" (Micah 6:8)? "Do justice" means to act justly; "to love kindness" refers to acts of lovingkindness; "to walk humbly with your God" refers to escorting the dead and providing for a bride. Now we can make a logical deduction: If concerning things that are normally done in public [i.e., weddings and funerals] the Torah tells us to do them in private, surely things that are normally done behind closed doors [like giving alms to the poor should be done in secret].

CHARITY AND ACTS OF KINDNESS

R. Elazar said: Giving *tzedakah* [charity] is greater than offering all the sacrifices, for it says, "Doing what is right and just is preferable to God than an offering" (Proverbs 21:3). R. Elazar also said: Acts of kindness are greater than charity, for it says, "Sow charity for yourselves, and you will reap according to kindness" (Hosea 10:12). [The verse speaks of "sowing charity" and "reaping kindness."] If a person sows, it is doubtful whether he will eat the harvest or not; but when a person reaps, he will certainly eat it. R. Elazar further said: Charity is rewarded according to the kindness with which it is given, for it says, "Sow charity for yourselves, and you will reap according to [the] kindness [with which you give your charity]."

We learned in a *Baraita*: In three respects acts of kindness are greater than charity: Charity you can give only with your possessions, but acts of kindness you can do both with your person [eulogizing and escorting the dead, gladdening a bride and groom], and with your possessions [by lending money, things, or clothes]. Charity you can give only to the needy; acts of kindness you can perform both to the rich and the poor. Charity you can give only to the living; acts of kindness you can perform both to the living and the dead [by attending their funeral and burial].

R. Elazar said furthermore: If a person does charity and justice, it is as if he had filled the whole world with kindness, for it says, "If a person loves righteousness and justice, then the kindness of God fills the earth" (Psalms 33:5). Lest you say that whoever wants to jump at the mitzvah [of *tzedakah* and *chesed*] may jump at it, [and he will be able to give his *tzedakah* to a worthy recipient, and will have the full merit of his *tzedakah*], Scripture says, "How precious is Your kindness, O God!" (Psalms 36:8), [a person has to make a great effort to attain the mitzvah of *tzedakah*]. You might think that this applies also to a God-fearing person; therefore Scripture expressly says, "The kindness of God is forever and ever upon those who fear Him" (Psalms 103:17).

R. Chama b. Papa said: If a person has charm, that is a sign that he is God-fearing, for it says, "The grace of God is forever and ever upon those who fear Him."

R. Elazar further said: What is the intent of the verse, "She opens her mouth with wisdom, and the Torah [teaching] of kindness is on her tongue" (Proverbs 31:26)? Is there then a Torah of *chesed* [kindness] and a Torah that is not of kindness? The meaning is: the Torah that is studied for its own sake is a Torah of *chesed*; whereas a Torah that is studied for an ulterior motive is a Torah that is not of *chesed*. Some say: If a person learns Torah in order to teach others that is a Torah of *chesed*; if he learns Torah without the intent of teaching it to others, that is a Torah that is not of *chesed*.

UNCOVERED LIQUIDS

(50a) [Introductory note: Wine and water, if left uncovered for the amount of time it would take a snake to emerge from a nearby hole and drink, may not be drunk for fear that a snake may have drunk from them and left some of its venom behind. And so we learned in the Mishnah that if the water and the wine for the libation were left uncovered, they are unfit for the Altar.] We learned in a *Baraita*: Liquid that has passed through a strainer [to remove the venom] is forbidden because of the law forbidding uncovered liquids. R. Nechemiah however said: When does this apply? Only when the lower vessel [underneath the strainer] was uncovered, but when the vessel underneath the strainer is covered, although the strainer itself was uncovered, the law of "uncovered liquids" does not apply, since the venom of a snake is like a sponge that floats on the surface and remains in the strainer.

THE REJOICING OF *BET HASHO'EVAH*

(51b) [The Mishnah says:] Whoever did not see the rejoicing of *Bet HaSho'evah* [literally, the place of water drawing; the festivities that preceded the water drawing] never saw rejoicing in his life. Whoever did not see Jerusalem in her splendor, never saw a desirable city in his life. Whoever did not see the *Bet Hamikdash* in its completed state never saw a magnificent building in his life. [The Gemara asks:] Which *Bet Hamikdash* are you referring to? [To the one built by Solomon, Nehemia, or Herod?] Abaye, and some say, R. Chisda, said: We are referring to the *Bet Hamikdash* built by Herod [the second *Bet Hamikdash*, which was rebuilt by Herod]. How did he build it? Rabbah replied: Of yellow and white marble. Some say: of yellow, blue, and white marble; one row of stones protruding, and one row of stones receding, in order to provide a hold for the plaster. Herod planned to cover the stones with gold, but the Rabbis told him: Leave it alone, because it is more beautiful this way, for [the diverse colors of the marble] make it look like the waves of the sea.

[We learned in the Mishnah:] Two *kohanim* stood at the Upper Gate that descends from the *Ezrat Yisrael* [Courtyard of the Israelites] to the *Ezrat Nashim* [the Women's Courtyard], with two trumpets in their hands. [When] the Temple Crier called out, they sounded a *tekiah*, a *teruah*, and a *tekiah*. When they reached the tenth step, they sounded a *tekiah*, a *teruah*, and a *tekiah*. When they reached the Courtyard, they sounded a *tekiah*, a *teruah*, and a *tekiah*. They would continue sounding *tekiah* until they reached the gate leading out to the east. When [the procession carrying the water] reached the gate leading out to the east, they turned to the west and said, "Our forefathers [in the days of the first Temple] who were in this place [turned] their backs toward the Sanctuary and their faces to the east and bowed eastward to the sun.[10] But as for us—our eyes are toward *Yah*." R. Yehudah said: They repeated and said, "We are for *Yah*, and toward *Yah* are our eyes."

THE HUGE SYNAGOGUE OF ALEXANDRIA

We learned in a *Baraita*: R. Yehudah said: Whoever has not seen the double colonnade [in the basilica-synagogue] of Alexandria in Egypt has never seen the glory of Israel. It is told that it was in the shape of a large basilica, one colonnade inside the other, and it seated twice as many people as went out of Egypt [in the Exodus, i.e., 2 x 600,000]. There were seventy-one golden armchairs corresponding to the seventy-one elders who were like the Sanhedrin, and each chair was made of no less than twenty-one talents of gold. In the center of the synagogue there was a wooden platform where the sexton of the Synagogue stood, holding a flag. When it was time to answer *Amen* [when the *chazzan* ended a *berachah*, and the people in the vast synagogue could not hear him], he waved the flag, and the entire congregation answered *Amen*. They did sit indiscriminately, but the goldsmiths sat separately, silversmiths separately, blacksmiths separately, coppersmiths separately, and weavers separately, so that when a poor man entered the synagogue he recognized the people of his trade and turned to that section [to apply for a job]. That way he was able to support himself and his family.

THE TRAGIC END OF THE JEWS OF ALEXANDRIA

Abaye said: They were all killed by Alexander of Macedonia [the Vilna Gaon corrects this to read Trajan, referring to the Roman emperor who launched a murderous attack on the Jews of Alexandria between 115 and 117 C.E.]. [The Gemara asks:] Why were they punished so severely? [The Gemara answers:] Because they violated the verse, "You must never again return on that path [to Egypt]" (Deuteronomy 17:16), and they did return. When [the Emperor] came and found the Jews reading the passage, "God will bring upon you a nation from afar" (ibid. 28:49), he said: Under normal circumstances it would take me ten days to arrive here by boat, but a strong wind blew up and brought me here in five days! [Since he considered the verse and the blowing wind auspicious omens,] he attacked them and killed them.

THE FESTIVITIES OF *BET HASHO'EVAH*

[We learned in the Mishnah:] At the conclusion of the first day of Sukkot [the *kohanim* and Levites] went down [from the Temple Courtyard] to the Women's Courtyard, where they made a great improvement. [Every year they built a balcony out of wooden boards from which the women could view the festivities without mingling with the men, thereby preventing frivolity.] [In the Women's Courtyard] there were golden candelabra with four golden bowls on top of them, four ladders for each candelabrum, and four youths from

among the young *kohanim* each holding a thirty-log pitcher of oil—for a total of one hundred and twenty *lugin*—which they poured into one of the bowls.

From the worn-out trousers of the *kohanim* and their belts they made wicks, which they would kindle. There was not a courtyard in Jerusalem that was not illuminated by the light of the *Bet Hasho'evah*, [since the candelabra were fifty cubits high, and the Temple Mount was higher than the rest of Jerusalem].

Devout men and men of good deeds would dance before the people with flaming torches in their hands [which they would juggle], and would sing songs and praises; and the Levites with harps, lyres, cymbals, trumpets, and countless musical instruments stood on the fifteen steps that descended from the Courtyard of the Israelites to the Women's Courtyard—corresponding to the fifteen Songs of Ascent in Psalms. On these steps the Levites would stand with musical instruments and chant songs.

SEPARATE SEATING

[The Gemara asks:] What was the great improvement [they made in the Women's Courtyard]? R. Elazar replied: Like the one about which we learned: Originally the walls of the Women's Courtyard were smooth, but later the Court was surrounded with a balcony, and it was enacted that the women should sit above and the men below.[11]

We learned in a *Baraita*: Originally the women used to sit inside the Women's Courtyard and the men were outside, but when this caused frivolity it was enacted that the women should sit outside and the men inside. However, when this still led to levity, it was instituted that the women should sit above [on the balcony] and the men below. [The Gemara asks:] But how could they do this? [How could they alter the original design of the *Bet Hamikdash*?] Doesn't it say, [when David gave the plans for the *Bet Hamikdash* to Solomon, he said,] "All this that God made me understand by His hand on me, I give you in writing—the plan of all the work" (1 Chronicles 28:19)? Rav replied: They found a scriptural verse and expounded it: [Prophesying about the death of *Mashiach*, the son of Yosef, who will perish in the war of Gog and Magog, Zechariah states:] (52a) "The land will mourn, each of the families by itself: the family of the house of David by itself, and their wives by themselves" (Zechariah 12:12). They said: We can draw a logical inference: If in the future, [at the death of *Mashiach*, the son of Yosef, referred to in the passage], when they will be busy mourning, and the evil inclination has no power over them [because a grieving person is not lighthearted], Scripture nevertheless says that men and women should be separate, surely now [at the festivities of the Water-Drawing] when the people are rejoicing and the evil inclination has power over them, [men and women should be separate].

THE SLAYING OF
THE EVIL IMPULSE

[The Gemara asks:] What is the reason for the mourning [mentioned in Zechariah 12:12]? R. Dosa and the Rabbis have different opinions about it. One holds that the people mourn the slaying of *Mashiach*, the son of Yosef [the forerunner of *Mashiach*, the son of David, the herald of the true Messianic age]. The other maintains that they mourn the slaying of the evil impulse. It is understandable according to the one who holds that the reason is the slaying of *Mashiach*, the son of Yosef, since that is in keeping with the verse, "They will look toward Me because of those whom they have stabbed; they will mourn over him as one mourns over an only child" (Zechariah 12:10). But according to him who explains the reason to be the slaying of the evil impulse, is that an occasion for mourning? It should be an occasion for rejoicing! Then why did they cry? It can be explained as R. Yehudah expounded: In the Messianic age, the Holy One, blessed be He, will bring the evil inclination and slaughter it in the presence of righteous and the wicked. To the righteous it will look like a high mountain, and to the wicked it will look like a thread as thin as a hair. Both the righteous and the wicked will weep; the righteous will weep, saying: How were we able to overcome such a towering mountain? The wicked will weep, saying: How is it that we were unable to subdue such a thin thread? And the Holy One, blessed be He, will be astonished together with them, for it says, "Thus says God, Master of Legions: Just as it will be wondrous in the eyes of the remnant of this people in those days, so will it be wondrous in My eyes" (Zechariah 8:6). [Thus the slaying of the *yetzer hara* is also an occasion for mourning.]

R. Assi said: In the beginning the evil inclination is as thin as the thread of a spider, but in the end it becomes like the wagon-rope. [If a person continues to give in to his evil impulse, he becomes addicted to it and cannot shake it off anymore.] For it says, "Woe to those who pull iniquity upon themselves with cords of falsehood, and sin like the rope of a wagon" (Isaiah 5:18).

MASHIACH'S REQUEST

We learned in a *Baraita*: The Holy One, blessed be He, will say to *Mashiach*, the son of David (may he reveal himself speedily in our days!), "Ask anything of Me, and I shall give it to you," as it says, "I am obliged to say that God said to me, 'You are My son, I have begotten you this day. Ask of Me and I will make nations your inheritance'" (Psalms 2:7,8). But when he will see that *Mashiach*, the son of Yosef, is slain, he will say to Him, "Master of the universe, all I ask from you is the gift of life." God will answer him, "As regards life, your father David has already prophesied this about you, for it says, 'Life he requested of You, You gave it to him, length of days, for ever and ever'" (Psalms 21:5).

THE SEVEN NAMES OF
THE EVIL IMPULSE

R. Avira or, as some say, R. Yehoshua, expounded: The evil impulse has seven names. The Holy One, blessed be He, calls it *Evil*, as it says, "For the inclination of man's heart is evil from his youth" (Genesis 8:21). Moses called it the Uncircumcised, for it says, "Circumcise the foreskin of your heart" (Deuteronomy 10:16), [the heart is the seat of the evil impulse]. David called it Unclean, for it says, "Create a pure heart for me, O God" (Psalms 51:12), which implies that there is an unclean one. Solomon called it the Enemy, for it says, "If your enemy [i.e., your evil impulse] is hungry, give him bread to eat [engross yourself in Torah study]; if he is thirsty, give him water [i.e., Torah] to drink. You will be heaping live coals on his head, and God will reward you" (Proverbs 25:21,22). Don't read *yeshaleim lach*, "He will reward you," but rather, *yashlimenu lach*, "he will cause you to be at peace with yourself." Isaiah called it the Obstacle, for it says, "He will say, 'Pave, pave! Clear the road! Remove the obstacle from My people's path!'" (Isaiah 57:14). Ezekiel called it Stone, for it says, "I will remove the heart of stone from your body and give you a heart of flesh" (Ezekiel 36:26). Joel called it the Hidden One, [because the *yetzer hara* is hidden inside a person's heart], as it says, "I will drive the hidden one far from you" (Joel 2:20).

THE GREATER THE MAN, THE
STRONGER HIS *YETZER HARA*

We learned in a *Baraita*: The passage, "I will drive the hidden one far from you" (ibid.) refers to the evil impulse that is hidden in a person's heart. [The verse continues,] "I will banish it to a parched and desolate land." This means, to a place where there are no people [for the *yetzer hara*] to entice. "With its face to the Eastern Sea" (ibid.), [suggests] that the *yetzer hara* set its eyes on the First Temple [which is compared to the sea, since masses of people converged on it, like rivers flowing into the sea (Rashi)] and destroyed it and killed the Torah scholars that were there. "And its rear to the Western Sea" (ibid.) [indicates] that the *yetzer hara* set its eyes on the Second Temple and destroyed it and killed the Torah scholars that were in it. "Its stench will go up, and its foul smell will rise" (ibid.) [signifies] that the *yetzer hara* leaves the other nations alone and entices only Israel.

Abaye explained: The evil impulse incites Torah scholars more than anyone else. To illustrate, it happened that Abaye heard a certain man say to a woman, "Let's get up early and go on our way together." Abaye said to himself, "I will follow them in order to prevent them from sinning." He followed them for three *parsangs* across pastures. When they parted company [each having to go in a different direction], he heard them say, "We each have a long road ahead of us, and we enjoyed each other's company, [too bad we have to go our separate ways]." Said Abaye, "If I were in his place, I could not have controlled myself." Absorbed in deep and agonizing thought, he leaned against a doorpost when a certain old man [the prophet Elijah] came up to him and taught him, "The greater the man, the stronger is his evil impulse."

R. Yitzchak said: A person's evil impulse grows stronger by the day, for it says, (52b) "Every product of the thoughts of his heart was nothing but evil, all the day" (Genesis 6:5); [meaning, as the days go by, man gets progressively worse]. R. Shimon b. Lakish said: A person's evil impulse grows stronger by the day, and it tries to kill him, as it says, "The wicked [impulse] watches for the righteous and seeks to kill him" (Psalms 37:32), and if the Holy One, blessed be He, did not help him, he would not be able to resist it. For it says, "But God will not forsake him to his hand, nor let him be condemned when he is judged" (ibid. 33).

MORE ABOUT
THE *YETZER HARA*
In the yeshivah of R. Yishmael it was taught: If that contemptible scoundrel [the evil impulse] meets you, drag him to the *bet midrash*, [subdue him by learning Torah]. If he is made of stone, he will crumble; if he is made of iron, he will disintegrate. If he is made of stone, he will crumble, for it says, "Ho, everyone who is thirsty, go to the water [the Torah]" (Isaiah 55:1), and it also says, "Stones are worn away by water" (Job 14:19). If he is made of iron, he will disintegrate, for it says, "Behold, My word is like fire—so says God— and like a hammer that shatters rock" (Jeremiah 23:29), [i.e., the hammer is shattered by the hard rock it strikes (*Tosafot*)].

R. Shmuel b. Nachmani said in the name of R. Yochanan: The evil impulse seduces a person in this world and testifies against him in the World to Come, as it says, "If one indulges his servant from youth, he will end up being ruled [*manon*] by him" (Proverbs 29:21). For according to the Atbach system of R. Chiya, a witness [*sahadah*] is called *manon*.[12]

A TRAVELER, A GUEST,
A MASTER OF THE HOUSE
(52b) R. Huna pointed out a contradiction: It says, "For a spirit of harlotry misled them" (Hosea 4:12) [i.e., an undefined spirit]. But it also says, "For a spirit of harlotries is in their midst" (ibid.5:4) [i.e., a spirit that is deeply imbedded in their personality]. [He reconciled the verses:] At first [the *yetzer hara*] only causes them to go astray, but in the end it enters into their hearts and takes possession of them]. Rava noted: At first [the evil impulse] is called a passing wayfarer, then he is called a visitor, and in the end, he is called a man

[i.e., master of the house]. For it says [in Nathan's parable], "One day a *wayfarer* came to the rich man, but he was reluctant to take from his own sheep or cattle to prepare for the *visitor* that had come to him; so he took the poor man's lamb for the *man* who had come to him" (2 Samuel 12:4).

R. Yochanan remarked: Man has a small organ. When he satisfies it, it is hungry; but when he keeps it hungry, it is satisfied. [The more a person satisfies his sensual appetite, the greater his desire becomes,] as it says, "When they were starved, they became sated" (Hosea 13:6).

SEVEN SHEPHERDS
AND EIGHT PRINCES
It says, "And this will assure peace: Should Assyria invade our land and tread upon our palaces, we will set up against him seven shepherds or eight princes" (Micah 5:4). [The Gemara asks:] Who are the seven shepherds? [The Gemara answers:] David in the middle, Adam, Seth, and Methuselah on his right [these are righteous men who lived before the Flood]; Abraham, Jacob and Moses on his left And who are the eight princes?—Jesse, Saul, Samuel, Amos, Zephaniah, Zedekiah, Elijah, and Mashiach.

THE CHANTS OF THE REJOICING
OF *BET HASHO'EVAH*
(53a) Our Rabbis taught: [At the festivities of the *Bet Hasho'evah* [the Drawing of the Water] some of the celebrants would chant: "Happy is our youth that has not shamed our old age" [We did not trangress in our youth and, as such, are not ashamed in our old age]. These were the devout and men of good deeds. Others used to chant: "Happy is our old age, which has atoned for our youth." These were the *baalei teshuvah*. Both groups would chant together, "Happy is he who did not sin, but if he has sinned let him repent, and He will forgive him."

We learned in a *Baraita*: It was said about Hillel the elder, when he used to rejoice at the *Simchat Bet Hasho'evah*, he used to chant, "If I am here, everyone is here; but if I am not here, who is here?" [When saying "I" he was referring to the *Shechinah* (Rashi).] He also used to say, "To the place that I love, there my feet carry me." And so also says the Holy One, blessed be He, "If you will visit My House, I will visit your house; but if you do not visit My House, I will not visit yours," for it says, "Wherever I allow My name to be mentioned [i.e., in the *Bet Hamikdash*, where the Four-Letter Divine Name was used in prayers and blessings] I will come to you and bless you" (Exodus 20:21).

Hillel once saw a skull floating on the water, [a skull he recognized as that of a murderer]. He said to it: Because you drowned others, they drowned you, and those who drowned you will be drowned eventually.

[The underlying thought is that God punishes man "measure for measure."]

HIS FEET ARE RESPONSIBLE FOR HIM

R. Yochanan said: A man's feet are responsible for him; they carry him to where he is wanted. [His feet will lead him to the place where he is destined to die (Rashi).]

Once there were two Kushites who served King Solomon as scribes, Elichoref and Achiyah, sons of Shisha.[13] One day, Solomon noticed that the Angel of Death was sad. "Why are you sad?" he asked. [Because in heaven they have demanded from me the souls of the two Kushites who are sitting here. Their time to die has arrived, but they are not at the place where they are destined to die.] To save their lives Solomon placed them in the custody of the demons [over whom he ruled] and sent them to the city of Luz [where the angel of Death has no power (*Sotah* 46b)]. However, as they reached the gate of Luz they died. The next day Solomon saw that the Angel of Death was cheerful. "Why are you cheerful?" he asked. "Because you sent the men to the place where I was ordered to take their lives, [at the gate of Luz]," replied the Angel of Death. Thereupon Solomon coined the phrase: A man's feet are responsible for him; they carry him to the place where he is wanted. ["Feet" in this context means circumstances (Aruch Laneir).]

RABBIS PERFORMING ACROBATIC FEATS

We learned in a *Baraita*: They said about R. Shimon b. Gamliel that when he rejoiced at the *Simchat Bet Hasho'eva* he used to take eight lighted torches and throw them in the air, catching one and throwing one, and they did not touch one another [an amazing feat of juggling], and when he prostrated himself [in the Temple Courtyard] he used to press both his thumbs against the floor, bow down [his body supported only by his thumbs], and kiss the ground and raise himself [while his body was supported by his thumbs], a feat no one could duplicate. And this was meant by *kidah* [falling on the face, whereby the body remains suspended horizontally, braced by the thumbs, and only the face touching the ground].

Levi showed in the presence of Rabbi how *kidah* was performed, and as a result, he became lame. [The Gemara asks:] Was this really the cause of his lameness? Did not R. Elazar say: A person should never complain against heaven, for there was a great man who did complain against Heaven and as a result became lame; and who was this man? R. Yehoshua b. Levi. [He criticized God for failing to have mercy on His people.] [The Gemara answers:] Both factors cause his lameness [his complaint was the reason for his disability;

the demonstration of *kidah* was the circumstance that brought it about].

At the *Simchat Bet Hasho'evah*, Levi used to juggle in the presence of Rabbi eight knives; Shmuel used to juggle before King Sh'vur [Shapur of Persia] with eight glasses filled with wine [without spilling any of it]; and Abaye before Rabbah with eight eggs, or, as some say, with four eggs.

THEY WERE KEPT BUSY AROUND THE CLOCK

We learned in a *Baraita*: R. Yehoshua b. Chananiah said: When we were rejoicing at the *Simchat Bet Hasho'evah*, our eyes saw no sleep. How was this? The first hour we were busy with the daily morning sacrifice; from there we went to pray; after that we went to the offering of the additional [*Mussaf*] sacrifice; this was followed by the *Mussaf* prayer; after that we went to the *bet midrash* [to learn]; then we went to eat and drink; then came the [*Minchah*] afternoon prayer; after that the daily evening sacrifice, followed by the rejoicing of *Simchat Bet Hasho'evah*, which lasted throughout the night. [The Gemara asks:] This cannot be true. [How can a person go without sleep night after night, for so many days!] Did not R. Yochanan say: If someone says, "I swear that I will not sleep for three days in a row," he is flogged [for taking a false oath, because it is impossible to go without sleep for three days], and he is allowed to go to sleep immediately. [The Gemara answers:] R. Yehoshua b. Chanania meant to say, "We did not enjoy a good night's sleep," because they dozed on each other's shoulders.

R. Chisda said to one of the Rabbis who arranged the *Aggadas* in front of him: Have you heard corresponding to what did David compose the fifteen Songs of Ascent [Psalms 120–134]? He replied: Thus said R. Yochanan: When David dug the *shitin* [the Pits, deep below the Altar], the waters of the Abyss came up and threatened to flood the world. David then sang the fifteen Songs of Ascent, and as a result the waters receded. [R. Chisda asked:] If so, they should be called Songs of Descent instead of Songs of Ascent? He replied: Since you mentioned it, I reminded myself that [R. Yochanan] said it like this: When David dug the *shitin*, the waters of the Abyss came up and threatened to flood the world. David asked, "Is there anyone who knows whether it is permitted to write the Ineffable Name (53b) on a piece of pottery and throw it into the Abyss so that its waters should recede?" [Would it be permitted in this case to cause the Divine Name to be erased?] No one answered. Said David, "If there is anyone here who knows the answer and does not speak up, may he be suffocated."

Achitofel[14] then drew a logical conclusion: If, in order to bring peace between man and wife, the Torah said: Let My name that was written in sanctity [on a scroll][15] be blotted out by the water, it surely may be done for the sake of bringing peace to the world! Achitofel therefore said to David: It is permitted! David then wrote the Divine Name on a piece of pottery, threw it into the Abyss, and its waters receded sixteen thousand cubits. When David saw that it had receded so much, he said, "The nearer the water is to the earth the more moisture the earth receives." He then composed the fifteen Songs of Ascent, which raised the water fifteen thousand cubits, [which is why they are called "Songs of *Ascent*"], leaving it one thousand cubits [below the surface]. Ulla noted: You can infer from this that the thickness of the earth's crust is one thousand cubits, [and below that is the Abyss]. [The Gemara asks:] But we see that with very little digging you reach the water table? R. Mesharshiya answered: That is because of the high level of the source of the Euphrates. [The source of the Euphrates is situated very high in the mountains, and through hydraulic pressure its water flows close to the surface of the earth (Rashi).]

THE SONGS OF THE INTERMEDIATE DAYS [CHOL HAMO'ED]

(55a) We learned in a *Baraita*: What psalms did they chant on the Intermediate Days [of Sukkot at the *Mussaf* offering]? On the first day [of Chol Hamo'ed] they said [the psalm beginning with the words], "Render unto God, you sons of the powerful" (Psalms 29:1); on the second day, [the psalm containing the words,] "But to the wicked, God said" (Psalms 50:16); on the third day, "Who will rise up for me against evildoers?" (Psalm 94); on the fourth day, "Understand, you boors among the people" (ibid. 8); on the fifth day, "I removed his shoulder from the burden" (Psalms 81:7); on the sixth day, "All the foundations of the earth collapse" (Psalms 82:5); and if *Shabbat* fell on any of these days [when Psalm 92 has to be read], Psalm 82 [the last one] should be set aside.

THE SEVENTY BULLS OF SUKKOT

(55b) R. Elazar said: What do the seventy bulls[16] [that were offered during the seven days of Sukkot] symbolize? The seventy national groups [of the world]. What does the single bull of the Eighth Day [Shemini Atzeret] symbolize? God's one, chosen nation, Israel. You can compare this to a mortal king who said to his servants, "Prepare for me a great banquet," but on the last day said to his close friend, "Prepare for me a modest meal so that I can enjoy your company."

R. Yochanan remarked: Woe to the idol worshippers, for they have suffered a loss and don't even realize what they have lost [by the destruction of the *Bet Hamikdash*]. When the *Bet Hamikdash* was standing, the Altar atoned for their sins, but now [that it no longer exists] who shall atone for their sins?

MIRIAM, THE DAUGHTER OF BILGAH

(56b) Our Rabbis taught: It happened that Miriam the daughter of Bilgah [a family of *kohanim*, who held one of the twenty-four watches taking turns serving in the *Bet Hamikdash*] became an apostate and married an officer of the [Syrian] Greek kings. When the Greeks entered the Sanctuary [in the days of Matityahu the *Kohen Gadol*] she stamped with her sandal against the Altar, crying out, "Lukos! Lukos! [Wolf! Wolf!] How long will you consume Israel's money and yet not stand by them in the time of oppression!"[17] When the Sages heard about this event [after the miraculous victory in the days of Chanukah], they fastened the ring [of the watch of Bilgah, as a punishment for this incident],[18] and closed its window.

Some, however, say that Bilgah's watch [was punished] because they were once late in coming [to do the service] and so Yeshevav, their fellow watch, filled in for them. Although the neighbors of the wicked usually are worse off for having such neighbors, the neighbors of Bilgah [i.e., Yeshevav] benefited, because [after the imposition of the penalty], Bilgah was required to divide the bread in the southern part of the Courtyard [even when it was the incoming watch, consequently Bilgah always seemed to be leaving the Temple], while Yeshevav always did it in the north, [and the north was considered superior to the south].

[The Gemara asks:] This is quite understandable according to him who said that [Bilgah was penalized] because they were late in coming, and for that reason the whole watch was punished; but according to the one who said that they were punished because Miriam the daughter of Bilgah left the fold, do we punish a father for the sins of his daughter? "Yes, we do," explained Abaye. "As the saying goes, 'The child's talk in the marketplace is either of his father or of his mother.'" [The Gemara asks:] But may we penalize the entire watch because of her father or mother? Replied Abaye, "Woe to the wicked and woe to his neighbor." [The neighbors of the wicked suffer the same fate, and Miriam would not have degraded the Altar unless she had heard her family speak that way.] "It is well with the righteous and well with his neighbor, as it says, 'Tell [each] righteous man that he shall fare well; for they shall eat the fruit of their deeds'" (Isaiah 3:10).

NOTES

1. *Shabbat* 88b.
2. Joshua 10:12f.
3. Every nation has a guardian angel in heaven. The guardian angel of the enemy nations in heaven will be demolished, and the nations they represented on earth will be crushed. This is alluded to in the verse, "I destroyed his fruit above and his trunk below" (Amos 2:9). (*Sefer Chasidim* 1160)

4. The Four Species that are taken and waved every day of Sukkot, except on *Shabbat*, are: the *lulav* (palm branch), *hadasim* (myrtle twigs), *aravot* (willow branches), and an *etrog* (citron).

5. At the *aravah* ceremony, willow branches were carried around the Altar in the *Bet Hamikdash* on Sukkot. The first six days of Sukkot one circuit was made; on the seventh day, seven circuits.

6. A special libation [pouring of water on the Altar] was done only during the seven days of Sukkot. All other libations in the *Bet Hamikdash* consisted of wine poured on the Altar, but on Sukkot water was poured simultaneously with the wine libation as part of the daily burnt-offering in the morning.

7. A *log* has the volume of six eggs, or at least 30.6 fluid ounces; some say that it is much more.

8. During the Second *Bet Hamikdash*, the heretical sect of the Sadducees, who rejected any law not explicitly stated in the Torah, found followers among some of the *kohanim*. Since the water libation is an oral tradition transmitted to Moses and not explicitly mentioned in the Torah, the Sadducean *kohanim* refused to perform it properly.

9. The *shitin* were the deep pits beneath the Altar into which the wine and the water flowed after the libation.

10. Ezekiel 8:16.

11. The *mechitzah* or dividing wall and the galleries separating men and women in the synagogues are derived from the great improvement instituted in the *Bet Hamikdash*.

12. In the Atbach system, letters from *alef* to *yud* whose combined numeric values add up to 10, and letters from *chaf* to *kuf* whose combined numeric values add up to 100, are interchanged. Thus *alef* (1) interchanges with *tet* (9) [AT]; *bet* (2) with *chet* (8) [BACH], etc. Also *mem* (40) interchanges with *samach* (60), since together they add up to 100. Furthermore, *hei* (5) and *nun* (50), which have no mate in the single and double digits, interchange with each other. Consequently, *sahadah* (witness) converts to *manon*; *samach* (60) interchanges with *mem* (40); *hei* (5) with *nun* (fifty); *dalet* (4) with *vav* (6); *hei* (5) with *nun* (50)].

13. 1 Kings 4:3.

14. David's teacher, *Avot* 6:3.

15. Numbers 5:23. In the case of the *sotah* [the suspected adulteress], the *kohen* writes prescribed curses containing God's Name on a scroll and dissolves the writing in the bitter waters. The woman then had to drink the water. If she was innocent, she would remain unharmed and would become pregnant.

16. On the first day of Sukkot, thirteen bulls were brought, and one less on each successive day, for a total of seventy bulls (13 + 12 + 11 + 10 + 9 + 8 + 7 = 70) (Numbers 29:12–16). On Shemini Atzeret, the eighth day, only one bull was brought (ibid. 36).

17. *Maharsha* explains Miriam's outburst as an allusion to the daily offerings. Wolves are known to eat sheep, and the Altar consumed the two sheep of the *tamid* offering every day.

18. Twenty-four rings were affixed to the floor of the Temple Courtyard where the slaughtering was done. The rings could be raised so that the animal's head could be inserted in them and locked in place during slaughtering. The ring assigned to the watch of Bilgah was permanently stapled to the floor so that it could not be raised. This forced Bilgah to use the ring of another watch and thus suffer embarrassment.

ᦆᦆ BEITZAH ᦿᦿ

AN EGG THAT WAS LAID
ON *SHABBAT*

(4a) [In the Gemara we find the following dispute between Rav and R. Yochanan: In a case when *Shabbat* is immediately followed by a Yom Tov, Rav says: An egg laid on *Shabbat* may not be eaten on Yom Tov; whereas R. Yochanan holds: An egg laid on one is permitted on the other.]

[The Gemara continues:] The host of R. Papa—some say, a stranger—came to R. Papa to ask a question about some eggs that were laid on a *Shabbat* that was followed immediately by a Yom Tov [the Yom Tov fell on Sunday]. His question was, "Is it permitted to eat these eggs tomorrow, [on Sunday, which is Yom Tov]?" R. Papa answered him, "Go away now, and come back tomorrow," because Rav did not appoint an interpreter[1] for himself from the first day of Yom Tov until the end of the second day. He was concerned that [he might render incorrect halachic decisions] while under the influence of wine or strong drink, [and R. Papa did not want to render a decision on *Shabbat* for the same reason]. When the questioner came back the next day, R. Papa said to him, (4b) "If I had given you my decision right away, [in my intoxicated state,] I would have made a mistake and told you that in a dispute between Rav and R. Yochanan the *halachah* is according to R. Yochanan [who permits such eggs]; whereas Rava said:[2] In three cases the *halachah* is according to Rav, regardless whether he is lenient or stringent, [and this case is one of the three. Thus, the eggs laid on Shabbat may not be eaten on Yom Tov]."

R. ELIEZER'S
PROLONGED LECTURE

(15b) The Rabbis learned: It once happened that R. Eliezer was sitting and lecturing on the laws of Yom Tov the whole day [of Yom Tov]. When the first group of students left [the *bet midrash*], he said, "These are people who own large vats of wine"; [i.e., they are only interested in eating and drinking, and don't want to study Torah]. When the second group left, he said, "These are people who own barrels of wine." When the third group left, he said, "These are people who measure their wine by pitchers." When the fourth group left, he said, "These are people of small bottles of wine." When the fifth group left, he said, "These are people of cups of wine." When the sixth group began to leave, [he became upset seeing the *bet midrash* becoming empty], so he said, "These are people who should be cursed." When he looked at the students who remained, he noticed that their faces were turning pale, [they thought that he was angry at the sixth group because they waited so long before leaving to go to eat, and he surely would be furious with them (Rashi)]. So he said to them, "My children, I am not talking to you, but to those six groups who have left. They are turning their back on eternal life and involve themselves with transient [material] life." When he finished his lecture, he said to them, [quoting Nehemiah], "Go eat rich foods and drink sweet drinks and send portions to those who have nothing prepared, for the day is holy to our Lord. Do not be sad; the enjoyment of God is the source of your strength" (Nehemiah 8:10).

TWO WAYS OF CELEBRATING
YOM TOV

The Master said: "They are turning their back on eternal life and involve themselves with transient life." [The Gemara asks:] But isn't enjoying the Yom Tov a mitzvah, [so how can he characterize it as "transient life"]? [The Gemara answers:] R. Eliezer follows his own stated view, for he said: Rejoicing on Yom Tov [by eating and drinking] is optional. For we learned in a *Baraita*: R. Eliezer said: On Yom Tov a person has the choice: either he eats and drinks all day, or devotes all day to prayer and Torah study. R. Yehoshua said: Divide it: Devote half of the day to God, and half of it to yourselves [i.e., to enjoying good meals with family and friends]. R. Yochanan said: Both [R. Eliezer and R. Yehoshua] base their opinions on the same Scriptural verses: One verse [refers to Yom Tov as] "An assembly to *the Lord, your God*" (Deuteronomy 16:8), while another verse [describes it in terms of] "It shall be an assembly for *you*" (Numbers 29:35). How can we satisfy both these contradictory passages? R. Eliezer holds: You either devote the entire day to God or the entire day to yourselves, whereas R. Yehoshua contends: Divide it: Devote half of the day to God and half to your own enjoyment.

[The Gemara asks:] What is meant by the phrase [mentioned above], "Send portions to those who have nothing prepared"? R. Chisda said: Send portions to a person who did not prepare an *eruv tavshilin*,[3] [and thus cannot prepare meals for Shabbat]. Others say: [Send portions] to a person who was unable to prepare an *eruv tavshilin* [for example, he lost something on *erev* Yom Tov and spent the entire day looking for it (Rashi)]; but a person who had the opportunity to make an *eruv tavshilin* but did not do it is negligent.

[The Gemara asks:] What is the meaning of, "the enjoyment of God is the source of your strength"? R. Yochanan said in the name of R. Eliezer b. R. Shimon: The Holy One, blessed be He, said to Israel: My children, borrow on my account and celebrate the holiness of the day, and trust in Me, and I will pay; [I will make sure that you will be able to repay your debts].

R. Yochanan further said in the name of R. Eliezer b. R. Shimon: If a person wants to make sure that his property will remain in his possession, he should plant an *eder* tree [a holm oak, a high and majestic tree. His name and the property on which it stands will then be associated with the tree, so that no one will dispute his ownership]. For it says, "You are mighty [*adir*] on high, O God" (Psalms 93:4), [the name *eder* is related to *adir*, suggesting strength, endurance, and permanence]. A different reason why it is called *eder* is because *adra* [the Aramaic name of the tree] implies what its name denotes, because people say: Why is it called *adra*? Because it lasts for generations [*dori*]. We learned also in a *Baraita*: A field in which there is an *eder* tree cannot be robbed or forcibly bought, and its fruits are protected [the scent of the *eder* seeds kills any kind of infestation of insects and vermin (Rashi)].

A PERSON'S INCOME IS FIXED ON ROSH HASHANAH

R. Tachlifa, the brother of Rabina'i Chozaah, taught: (16a) All of a person's sustenance [for the entire year] is determined for him [during the ten days] between Rosh Hashanah until Yom Kippur, except for the money he spends for *Shabbat* and Yom Tov, and to pay the tuition for his children's Torah education. If he spends less [for any of these] he is given less, and if he spends more he is given more. R. Abbahu said: What verse is the basis for the [amount of a person's income for the year being fixed on Rosh Hashanah]? "Blow the *shofar* at the moon's renewal, when it [the moon] is hidden on out festive day" (Psalms 81:4). On what Yom Tov is the moon covered [and not easily visible]? This can only be referring to Rosh Hashanah [which falls on the first of Tishrei, when the moon is in

eclipse]. And it says [the next verse, in regard to Rosh Hashanah], "Because it is a decree [*chok*] for Israel, a judgment [day] for the God of Jacob" (ibid. 5). And where do we find that *chok* signifies a person's sustenance? For it says, "They ate the food allotment [*chukam*] that Pharaoh gave them" (Genesis 47:22).

Mar Zutra said: We derive from here [that *chok* denotes sustenance], "Allot me my daily bread [*chuki*]" (Proverbs 30:8).

HILLEL AND SHAMMAI'S VIEWS ON *SHABBAT*

We learned in a *Baraita*: They told about Shammai the Elder that all his life he ate in honor of *Shabbat*. If he found a beautiful animal, he said, "let this be for *Shabbat*." If afterward he found a better-looking animal, he set aside the second one for *Shabbat* and ate the first one, [thus he always ate in honor of *Shabbat*]. But Hillel the Elder had a different approach, for whatever he did was done for the sake of Heaven; [he had faith that he would find the proper provisions for *Shabbat* later in the week]. As it says, "Blessed is the Lord, day by day" (Psalms 68:20). We also learned in a *Baraita*: Bet Shammai said: From the first day of the week set aside [food] for *Shabbat*, but Bet Hillel said: "Blessed is the Lord, day by day."

THE GLORIOUS GIFT OF *SHABBAT*

R. Chama b. Chanina said: If you give a gift to your neighbor you do not have to let him know [that you were the one who gave it to him], for it says, [When God made Moses' face radiant], "Moses did not realize that the skin of his face had become luminous" (Exodus 34:29), [thus God gave him the radiance but did not tell him]. An objection was raised [from the following *Baraita*]: It says, [in regard to mitzvah of observing *Shabbat*], "To make you realize that I, God, am making you holy" (Exodus 31:13). The Holy One, blessed be He, said to Moses: Moses, I have a precious gift in My treasury: its name is *Shabbat*, and I want to give it to Israel. Go and tell them about it. Based on this, R. Shimon b. Gamliel said: If someone gives a piece of bread to a child he must tell his mother [that he gave her child this present]. [This contradicts R. Chama b. Chaninah's statement that the recipient of a present need not be told who the giver was.]

[The Gemara answers:] This is no difficulty: [The gift of the radiance of Moses' face] was a gift that eventually would become known; [people would tell Moses about it. A gift like that the giver does not have to announce to the recipient]. But in the case of a gift that will not eventually become known, [like the gift of a piece of bread to a child, the donor should inform the mother of the child]. [The Gemara asks:] But isn't *Shabbat* also a gift that was bound to become known?

[Yet Moses was told to inform Israel that God was giving them the gift of Shabbat?] [The Gemara answers:] The rich reward that is in store for the observers of Shabbat would not eventually have become known. [It was this reward that Moses was told to convey to Israel.]

R. Yochanan said in the name of R. Shimon b. Yocha'i: All the *mitzvot* that the Holy One, blessed be He, gave to Israel, He gave them publicly, except for *Shabbat*, which He granted them confidentially. For it says, "[*Shabbat*] is a sign between Me and the children of Israel" (Exodus 31:17). [The Gemara asks:] If it is something private, then the idolators should not be punished for *Shabbat* [because they were not aware of *Shabbat*. Nevertheless, the Gemara[4] tells us that the nations will be admonished and punished for not accepting and fulfilling the Torah, apparently including the mitzvah of *Shabbat*. If they did not know about *Shabbat*, why should they be punished for not observing it?]. [The Gemara answers:] He publicized *Shabbat* [to the nations], but He did not let them know the enormous reward that awaits the observers of *Shabbat*. [The reward was conveyed to Israel privately.]

Or if you prefer, say: Its reward too was made known to the nations, but the *nashamah yeteirah*, the "additional soul" [the feeling of spiritual elevation] a Jew receives on *Shabbat* was not made known to them. For R. Shimon b. Lakish said: On the eve of *Shabbat*, the Holy One, blessed be He, gives a Jew a *neshamah yeteirah*, and at the conclusion of *Shabbat* He takes it away from him, for it says, "On the seventh day, He rested and was refreshed" [*vayinafash* (Exodus 31:17), [this is homiletically interpreted to mean: Once *Shabbat* has passed and a person has rested, woe that the additional soul is no longer here [*vay avedah nefesh*, which is seen as a contraction of *vayinafash*].

(16b) There was a certain blind man who used to recite *Baraitas* before Mar Shmuel; [he had commited them to memory in their precise wording]. [Once on a Yom Tov] Mar Shmuel noticed that he looked downcast. "What seems to be the trouble?" he asked him. "I have not prepared an *eruv tavshilin*," he replied. "Then rely on mine," Mar Shmuel answered. [When preparing his *erruv tavshilin*, Mar Shmuel, the Rabbi of Nahardea, had in mind all those who forgot to set an *eruv tavshilin* (Rashi).] The next year he noticed him downcast again. "What is troubling you?" he asked. "I have not prepared an *eruv tavshilin*," he replied. This time Mar Shmuel answered, "You are negligent. [I did not intend for people who are neglectful to benefit from my *eruv tavshilin*.] Everyone else is permitted to rely on my *eruv tavshilin* [if they unintentionally forgot], but for you it is forbidden."

HE EVADED THE QUESTION

(21a) R. Ivia the Elder asked R. Huna: Is it permitted to slaughter on a Yom Tov an animal half of which is owned by a non-Jew and half by a Jew? [Work on Yom Tov is forbidden, just as on *Shabbat*, but it is permitted to slaughter, to cook, and to carry on Yom Tov, since these acts are needed to prepare food. Since half the animal belongs to a non-Jew, is this considered slaughtering for a non-Jew, which is not permitted on Yom Tov?][5] R. Huna replied: It is permitted. R. Ivia the Elder asked: Why is this different than vows and free-will offerings [which are also a partnership: part of a vow offering is enjoyed by the owner and part of it is offered on the Altar, and they are forbidden to be slaughtered on Yom Tov. Why then is the slaughter of an animal permitted that is partially owned by a non-Jew]?

He replied: "A raven flies." [This was an evasive answer; he tried to sidestep the question.] When R. Ivia left, R. Huna's son, Rabbah, said to his father: "Was this not R. Ivia the Elder whom you have praised as a great man? [Why then did you snub him and evade his question?]" Replied R. Huna, "[I did not mean to embarrass him,] but what else could I have done? Today I am [exhausted from giving a lecture, and I need some food to invigorate me, as it says,] 'Sustain me with dainty cakes, refresh me with fragrant apples' (Song of Songs 2:5),[6] and he asked me something that requires intense reflection, [and I simply don't feel up to it]."

THEY APPEASED
THE MARAUDERS

It once happened that Shimon HaTemani did not come to the *bet midrash* on the eve of Yom Tov. The next morning R. Yehudah b. Bava met him and asked, "Why didn't you come to the *bet midrash* last night?" He replied, "A band of marauders invaded our town wanting to ransack the entire city; so we slaughtered a calf for them and fed them, and they left peacefully." Said R. Yehudah to Shimon HaTemani, "I wonder if your gain is not nullified by your great loss [i.e., the punishment for desecrating the Yom Tov], for the Torah says, [You are allowed to do work on Yom Tov] 'for yourselves' (Exodus 12:16), but not for idolators, [and you slaughtered the calf on Yom Tov for the heathen marauders]."

R. ELAZAR B. AZARIAH'S COW

(23a) [The Mishnah says:] R. Elazar b. Azariah's cow was led out on *Shabbat* with a leather strap between its horns. [He considered it an ornament, which may be carried on *Shabbat*; the Sages, however, regarded the strap as a burden and prohibited it.]

[The Gemara asks: Since the Mishnah calls it "R. Elazar b. Azariah's cow,"] does that mean that R. Elazar b. Azariah had only one cow? But didn't Rav—and some say, Rav Yehudah in Rav's name—say: R. Elazar b. Azariah gave as tithe thirteen thousand calves every year from his herd? [The Gemara answers:] It was not his cow, [that was led out with a strap on *Shabbat*] but that of his lady neighbor, and because he did not keep her from doing that it is referred to as his cow.

(24b) Rav said: A person should not miss even a single hour of study in the *bet hamidrash*, for I and Levi were both present when Rabbi taught this lesson. In the evening he said: [Fish brought by a gentile on Yom Tov] are permitted to be eaten, but the next morning he said: They are [only] permitted to be received [but not eaten]. I who was present in the *bet hamidrash* recanted, but Levi who was not present did not recant.

A LESSON IN GOOD MANNERS

(25b) We learned in a *Baraita*: When eating garlic or onion, a person should not begin to eat from the top but from the leaves; and if he does he is a glutton. Similarly, a person should not drink his cup of wine in one draught, and if he does he is a guzzler.

Our Rabbis taught: Whoever drinks his cup of wine in one draught is a glutton, in two draughts is well-mannered, in three draughts is arrogant.

WHY WAS THE TORAH GIVEN TO ISRAEL?

It was taught in the name of R. Meir: Why was the Torah given to Israel? Because they are bold, [and the Torah was meant to tame them]. [Elaborating on this idea, the Gemara continues:] It was taught in the yeshivah of R. Yishmael: It says, "From His right hand He presented the fiery Torah to them" (Deuteronomy 33:2). [The Gemara expounds:] The Holy One, blessed be He, said: It is fitting that they be given the fiery Torah [to subdue their bold personality]. Some say: The [Jewish] people are bold by nature, and if the Torah had not been given to Israel, no nation could have resisted them. This is in line with what R. Shimon b. Lakish said: There are three that stand out for their boldness: Israel among the nations, the dog among the animals, and the rooster among birds. It was taught in a *Baraita*: Also the goat among small livestock, and some say: Also the caper bush among shrubs, [for it produces new berries every day].

THE SCRUPULOUSLY HONEST STOREKEEPER

(29a) [The Mishnah says:] A person may say [on Yom Tov] to a storekeeper, "Fill this container for me [with oil or wine]," but let him not express his order in terms of a measurement, [he should not say, for example, "Give me a quart of oil," because that is business terminology]. R. Yehudah says: If the container was of a specific measure, [and it was used for measuring], he may not fill it up. The story is told that Abba Shaul b. Botnit [a Tanna who was a storekeeper] used to fill up

his various measures on the day before Yom Tov and give them to his customers on Yom Tov [because we are not allowed to measure on Yom Tov]. Abba Shaul [a Tanna of the third and fourth generations] says: He even did this on Chol Hamo'ed[7] [in order that the foam might settle (Rashi)], to make sure the customer received a full measure. But the Sages say: We should do this [filling the customers' containers the night before] also on an ordinary day, in order to make sure that the last drop of oil flows from the measuring vessel into the customer's container.

[The Gemara gives another reason:] We learned in a *Baraita*: [Abba Shaul b. Botnit filled up the measures the night before on Chol Hamo'ed], in order not to be distracted from his Torah studies.[8]

Our Rabbis taught: [Abba Shaul b. Botnit] once collected three hundred jugs of wine from the froth of the measures, [and he felt that this wine really did not belong to him], and his colleague [R. Elazar b. R. Tzadok] collected three hundred jugs of oil from the drops of [oil that remained in] the measuring cups [when he poured the oil into the customers' containers, and he too believed that this oil did not belong to him]. They brought these jugs to [donate them to] the treasurers of the *Bet Hamikdash* in Jerusalem. The Sages told them, "You don't have to do this. [It was not your fault. The customers who did not want to wait for the foam to settle and for the last drop of oil to run out of the measuring cup renounced all claims to the wine and oil.]" They replied: "Nevertheless, we don't want any part of something that technically does not belong to us." The Sages retorted, "Since you want to be strict with yourselves, apply it to a project that benefits the community." For we learned in a *Baraita*: If a person robbed [many people, and he wants to repent], but he does not know whom he robbed [and to whom to make restitution], he should apply it to projects that benefit the community. What are such projects? Said R. Chisda: The construction of wells, ditches, and water reservoirs [to supply water to the community].

JEWS ARE COMPASSIONATE

(32b) R. Natan b. Abba said in the name of Rav: The rich men of Babylonia will go down to Gehinnom [because they are not compassionate], for Shabtai b. Marinus once came to Babylonia and begged them to furnish him merchandise [which he would sell and share the profit with them], and they turned him down; [when he asked for food] they did not give him that either. He said: These people are descendants of the "mixed multitude,"[9] for it says [about the Jewish people], "[God] will give you mercy and be merciful to you [as He swore to your forefathers]" (Deuteronomy 13:18). [This teaches you that] if someone is compassionate toward others, you can be sure that he is a descendant of our father Abraham; and if someone is not compassionate toward others, you can be sure that he is not a descendant of our father Abraham.

R. Natan b. Abba also said in the name of Rav: If someone is dependent on someone else's table, the world looks dark to him, for it says, "He wanders about for food—where is it?—he realizes that the day of darkness is ready, at hand" (Job 15:23). R. Chisda said: His life is no life.

The Rabbis taught: There are three whose life is no life, namely: A person who is dependent on someone else for his meals, a person who has a domineering wife, and a person who suffers physical pain. Some say: Also a person who owns only one shirt, [since he cannot change he is tormented by lice (Rashi)]. [The Gemara asks:] And why doesn't the first Tanna mention this? [The Gemara answers:] Because he [holds that a person who owns only one shirt] can examine his clothes and delouse them.

NOTES

1. Rav used to appoint an interpreter who clarified and elaborated on Rav's teachings to the public.

2. *Beitzah* 5b.

3. Literally, "a mixture of dishes." The *halachah* states that on a Yom Tov that falls on Friday no food may be prepared for *Shabbat. Eruv tavshilin* is a symbolic act through which meals may be prepared on a Yom Tov that falls on Friday for the following *Shabbat.* The method is to prepare a dish on Thursday for *Shabbat* that enables all the cooking done on Friday to be regarded as a continuation of the cooking begun on Thursday.

4. *Avodah Zarah* 2b.

5. "The only work that you may do is that which is needed so that everyone will be able to eat" (Exodus 12:16).

6. Rav Huna was appointed Rosh Yeshivah on that day (Aruch).

7. The intermediary days of Pesach and Sukkot.

8. Abba Shaul b. Botnit was a Tanna during the Second Temple period, known for his scrupulous integrity. Many people came to ask him halachic questions, especially on Chol Hamo'ed when they were off from work (Rashi).

9. A multitude of people of various nationalities converted to Judaism and accompanied the Jews out of Egypt (see Exodus 12:35).

ꙅ ROSH HASHANAH ꙮ

THE CLOUDS
OF GLORY DEPARTED

(2b) When Aaron died, Sichon [the Canaanite king] was still alive, for it says, (3a) "The Canaanite king of Arad heard" (Numbers 33:40). What report did he hear? He heard that Aaron had died and the clouds of glory [that enveloped and protected the Jewish people on their wandering through the wilderness] had disappeared, [and now they were exposed to all enemies]. Sichon took this to be a sign from Heaven that he had permission to wage war against Israel.

The above will help us understand the verse, "The people saw [vayiru] that Aaron had died" (ibid. 20:29). Expounding this passage R. Abahu remarked: Don't read vayiru, "they saw," but vayeira'u, ["they became visible," because the clouds of glory had departed. But now it does not make sense to say, "They became visible (ki) that Aaron had died." To solve this problem he translates ki] in accordance with the linguistic rule of Resh Lakish who stated: The word ki [in addition to its usual translation of "that"] has four other meanings, namely: "if," "perhaps," "but," and "because" [in our case it means "because," and the passage is rendered, "The people became visible because Aaron had died," and the clouds of glory had disappeared]. [The Gemara asks:] How can you prove that Sichon was alive when Aaron died by citing a verse that says that a Canaanite king attacked Israel? [The Gemara answers:] We learned in a Baraita: Sichon, Arad, and Canaan are one and the same. He was named Sichon because he resembled a sa'yach, [a wild young horse] of the desert, he was called Canaan after his kingdom, and his real name was Arad. Others say: He was called Arad because he acted like an arad [a wild donkey] of the desert, he was named Canaan after his kingdom, and his real name was Sichon.

DID DARIUS/CYRUS HAVE A
CHANGE OF HEART?

[The Gemara derives from scriptural verses that the reigns of Jewish kings are counted as beginning from Nisan, and those of non-Jewish kings as beginning from Tishrei.]

R. Abbahu said: Darius/Cyrus was a virtuous king,[1] and therefore they counted the years of his reign like those of the Jewish kings [beginning with Nisan].

R. Yosef challenges this statement. [He wants to prove that the years of the reign of Darius/Cyrus are reckoned from Tishri.] First of all, [if we count his years from Nisan], then there would be a contradiction between two verses. For it says, "This Temple was completed by the third day of the month of Adar, during the sixth year of the reign of King Darius" (Ezra 6:15), and in this context we learned: At that time, in the following year, [which would be Adar of the seventh year of Darius], Ezra went up from Babylonia accompanied by the exiles. Now it also says, "He arrived in Jerusalem in the fifth month of the seventh year of king [Darius]" (ibid. 7:8), and if they reckoned the years of the non-Jewish kings from Nisan, [as you say,] it should be "in the eighth year" [because Nisan falls between Adar and Av, the fifth month]. Furthermore, there is no logical connection; [R. Abbahu] refers to Cyrus, and the text cited speaks of Darius! [The Gemara answers:] We learned in a Baraita: Cyrus, Darius, and Artachshasta [Artaxerxes] are one and the same person. He was called Cyrus [Koresh] because he was a virtuous [kosher] king [note the inversion of Koresh–kosher], Artachshasta after his kingdom, and Darius was his real name.

[The Gemara asks:] The difficulty still remains, [for in Ezra 7:8 his reign is counted from Tishrei, whereas in Haggai 1:15 it is counted from Nisan]? R. Yitzchak answered: This is no difficulty. The verse [in Haggai, which counts his years from Nisan, like the Jewish kings] refers to a time when he was a virtuous king, the other verse [Ezra 7:8, which counts his years from the first of Tishrei, the fixed date for non-Jewish kings] refers to a year later, when [Cyrus's (Darius's)] attitude toward the Jewish people changed.

R. Kahana raised a strong objection: Did Cyrus (Darius) really have a change of heart? Doesn't it say, (4a) [Darius said,] "And whatever they require— young bulls, rams, and sheep for burnt-offerings for the God of heaven, wheat, salt, wine, and oil according to the specifications of the kohanim who are in

Jerusalem—shall be supplied to them, day by day, without fail" (Ezra 6:9)? [Which proves that he gave generously toward the service in the *Bet Hamikdash*. Why do you say that his attitude changed?] Replied R. Yitzchak: Rabbi, I'll use your own package [i.e., I'll use the verse you cited] to refute your argument, for the next verse states,] "so that they may offer pleasing offerings to the God of heaven and pray for the welfare of the king and his children" (ibid. 10), [which proves that he had a selfish motive]. [R. Kahana retorted:] Do you mean to say that a person who acts this way [doing good for ulterior motives] does not act properly? Surely we learned in a *Baraita*: If a person says, "I am donating this *sela* for charity in order that my children should live, and also in order that I should merit life in the World to Come," we consider him a perfectly righteous man! [The Gemara answers:] This presents no difficulty; The last statement applies to a Jew [who will not rebel against God if his condition is not fulfilled and will not regret the charity he gave], whereas the *Baraita* speaks of a heathen [who will regret his good deed if his condition is not met]. Therefore, Cyrus's (Darius's) generosity, which had a condition attached to it, was not a commendable deed.

If you prefer you may say that we know that Darius (Cyrus) had a change of heart because it says, [Darius specified how the Temple should be built: He ordered: There shall be] "three rows of marble and one row of new wood, with expenses provided for by the royal palace" (Ezra 6:4). Why did he order the *Bet Hamikdash* to be built this way [with a row of wood]? He reasoned: If the Jews will rise up against me, I will burn the Temple down, [proof that he changed for the worse]. [The Gemara asks:] But did not Solomon do the same thing? For it says, "He then built a wall around the inner courtyard, three rows of hewn stone and a row of cedar beams" (1 Kings 6:36)? [The Gemara answers:] Solomon placed the wood above the ground, whereas Darius anchored it in the foundation [which weakened the foundation and made it easier to be destroyed]; Solomon placed the wood in the building, Darius did not place it in the building; Solomon insulated the wood with plaster [making it fireproof], Darius did not cover it with plaster.

R. Yosef, and some say, R. Yitzchak, said: How do we know that he had a change of heart? We infer it from the verse, [Nehemiah said,] "The king said to me, with the *shegal* sitting beside him" (Nehemiah 2:6). What does *shegal* mean? Rabbah b. Lima said in Rav's name: a she-dog [which he used for immoral purposes].[2] [The Gemara disputes this:] But if that is so, how do we interpret the verse, [Daniel berated King Belshazzar when he interpreted the handwriting on the wall,] "You exalted yourself against the Lord of Heaven, and the vessels of His House were brought before you, and you, your nobles [*sheglatach*], and your concubines drank wine from them" (Daniel 5:23). Now how can *shegal* in this context stand for a dog? Does a

dog drink wine? [The Gemara answers:] This is no difficulty: He had taught it to drink. [The Gemara asks:] But what about the verse [which describes the subservience of the nations to Israel in the days of *Mashiach*], "Daughters of kings are your visitors, the *shegal* stands erect at your right in the golden jewelry of Ophir" (Psalms 45:10). Now, if *shegal* is a dog, what promise is the prophet predicting for Israel, [respect of a gold-bedecked dog]? [The Gemara answers:] This is what the passage means: Because the Torah is as beloved by Israel as a *shegal* is to the idol worshippers you have earned as a reward the gold of Ophir. Or if you prefer, say that generally *shegal* does mean "queen," but, [as an exception to the rule], in this case Rabbah b. Lima had a tradition that it means "dog," and the reason why in the text it is called *shegal* is because the king loved [this dog] as much as a queen, or maybe, because he put it on the queen's seat.

Or, if you prefer, say that we know that he had a change of heart because it says, [King Artaxerxes ordered his treasurers to grant Ezra whatever he requested for the building of the *Bet Hamikdash*,] "up to one hundred talents of silver, up to one hundred *kors* of wheat, up to one hundred *bats* of wine[3] up to one hundred *bats* of oil, and unlimited salt" (Ezra 7:22). At first there was no limit, [originally he said, "and whatever they require shall be supplied to them" (ibid. 6:9)], but now he set a limit [which proves that he had a change of heart]. [The Gemara suggests:] Perhaps at first he did not know what would be needed for the service in the *Bet Hamikdash*, [and he said to give them any amount in order to establish what they would need. After he determined their daily requirement, he ordered that it be appropriated to them. So this verse does not prove that he changed for the worse].

IN WHAT MONTH WAS THE WORLD CREATED?

(10b) We learned in a *Baraita*: R. Eliezer says: In Tishri the world was created; in Tishri the Patriarchs [Abraham and Jacob] were born; on Pesach Isaac was born; on Rosh Hashanah Sarah, Rachel, and Hannah were remembered [by God, and they became pregnant]; on Rosh Hashanah Joseph was released from prison; on Rosh Hashanah [six months before the redemption] the slavery of our ancestors in Egypt ended; in Nisan they were delivered; and in Tishri they will be redeemed at the ultimate redemption. R. Yehoshua says: In Nisan the world was created; in Nisan the Patriarchs were born; in Nisan the Patriarchs died; on Pesach Isaac was born; on Rosh Hashanah Sarah, Rachel, and Hannah were remembered [by God, and became pregnant]; on Rosh Hashanah Joseph was released from prison; on Rosh Hashanah the slavery of our ancestors in Egypt ended; and in Nisan they will be redeemed at the ultimate redemption.

[The Gemara seeks to derive these statements from

scriptural verses:] We learned in a *Baraita*: R. Eliezer says: From where do we know that the world was created in Tishri? Because it says, "God said, 'Let the earth sprout vegetation; seed-bearing plants, fruit-bearing trees yielding fruit, each after its kind" (Genesis 1:11). In what month does the earth produce grass and the trees are full of fruit? You must say that this is Tishri. [Another proof that the world was created in Tishri is the fact that the vegetation needed rain,] and Tishri is the rainy season, so the rain came down, and the plants began to sprout. For it says, "A mist ascended from the earth and watered the whole surface of the soil" (ibid. 2:11).

R. Yehoshua says: From where do we know that the world was created in Nisan? Because it says, "The earth brought forth vegetation, plants yielding seed after its kind, and trees [that are about to] yield fruit" (ibid. 2:12). In what month is the earth full of grass and the trees are beginning to produce fruit? You must say that this is Nisan. That time is the period when cattle, wild animals, and birds mate, as it says, "The rams have mounted the sheep" (Psalms 65:14).[4] [The Gemara asks:] And how does [R. Eliezer] explain the phrase, "trees that are about to yield fruit" [(1:12), which happens in Nisan]? [The Gemara answers: According to R. Eliezer] this denotes a blessing for future generations, [that the trees will continue to produce fruit forever]. [The Gemara asks:] And what does R. Yehoshua do with the phrase, "fruit-bearing trees," [(1:11) implying that the trees are full of fruit, which happens in Tishri]? [The Gemara answers:] He explains it in accordance with the following saying by R. Yehoshua b. Levi: All creatures of creation were brought into being full-grown, [and the trees were full of fruit], they gave their consent to being created, and they were created with their pattern, for it says, "Thus the heaven and the earth were finished and all their array [*tzeva'am*]" (Genesis 2:1). Don't read *tzeva'am*, but *tzivyonam*, "their pattern." [But ever since Creation, trees have begun to form fruit in Nisan.]

WHEN WERE
THE PATRIARCHS BORN?

R. Eliezer said: How do we know that the Patriarchs were born in Tishri? For it says, "They gathered before King Solomon—every man of Israel—for the festival of Sukkot, in the month of Etanim, which is the seventh month. [Why is the seventh month—Tishri—called the month of Etanim?] It is the month in which the *etanim*, the strong ones of the earth [i.e., the Patriarchs], were born. [The Gemara asks:] And how do you know that *etan* means strong? Because it says, "Strong [*etan*] is your dwelling" (Numbers 24:21). It also says, "Listen, you mountains [*harim*], [and *harim* is cognate to *horim*, "Patriarchs"] to the grievance of God, and you strong rocks [*etanim*] the foundations of the earth!" (Micah 6:2). Furthermore it says [proving that the

Patriarchs are called "mountains"] "The voice of my Beloved! There He comes leaping over mountains, bounding over hills" (Song of Songs 2:8). He leaps over mountains [*harim*] [to bring the redemption earlier] in the merit of the Patriarchs [*horim*], He bounds over hills, in the merit of the Matriarchs.

R. Yehoshua says: How do we know that the Patriarchs were born in Nisan? For it says, "In the four hundred and eightieth year after the Children of Israel's exodus from the land of Egypt, in the fourth year, in the month of Ziv"—that is Nisan, the month in which the splendid ones [*zivtanei*] of the world were born. [The Gemara asks:] But how will [R. Yehoshua who says the Patriarchs were born in Nisan] explain the phrase "month of *Etanim*" ["of the strong ones," which signifies that the Patriarchs were born in Tishri]? [The Gemara answers:] It is is called Month of *Etanim* because it is "strong in *mitzvot*" [the *shofar*, Yom Kippur, sukkah, and *lulav*]. And what does R. Eliezer [who holds that the Patriarchs were born in Tishri] make of the phrase "in the month of Ziv" [which indicates that they were born in Nisan]? He will say that it is called Ziv, "splendor," because it is the month in which the trees are colorfully blooming. For Rav Yehudah has said: If you go for a walk in the month of Nisan and you see trees in bloom, you should say, "Blessed is He who has not left His universe lacking anything, and He created in it good creatures and good trees, to cause mankind pleasure with them."

[The Gemara observes:] He who holds that the Patriarchs were born in Nisan holds that they died in Nisan, and he who holds that they were born in Tishri holds that they died in Tishri. For it says, [Moses said,] "I am a hundred and twenty years old today" (Deuteronomy 31:2). [The word "today" seems to be superfluous in this context. Then why was it included in the text?] Moses implied that, "Today, this very day, my days and years have reached completion." This teaches that the Holy One, blessed be He, fills the years of the righteous from day to day and from month to month, as it says, "I shall fill the number of your days" (Exodus 23:26).

PROOF THAT ISAAC
WAS BORN ON PESACH

[The Gemara asks:] How do we know that Isaac was born on Pesach? Because it says, [The angel said to Abraham,][5] I will return to you at this time next year, and Sarah will have a son" (Genesis 18:14). Now let's analyze. What Yom Tov was it when the angel said this? Shall I say that it was Pesach, and he referred to Shavuot [which is fifty days later]? Could Sarah give birth fifty days after conception? Shall I say then that it was Shavuot, and the angel referred to Tishri [which is five months later]? The question remains; could she bear a child after a five-month pregnancy? The only alternative is that the angel predicted it on Sukkot, and he was referring to Pesach [which is six months later]. All the same, could she bear a child in six months?

[The Gemara counters:] We learned in a *Baraita* that that particular year was a leap year [so that the interval between Sukkot and Pesach was seven months]. [But the Gemara rejects this explanation:] If we subtract the days of uncleanness, [for Sarah became *niddah*[6] on that day[7]], there is even less than seven months? Mar Zutra answered: Even the one who maintains that a woman who gives birth after nine months does not give birth before the ninth month is complete, admits that if she gives birth after seven months she can give birth before the seventh month is complete. For it says, "And it happened with the passage of the [*tekufot*] period of days" (1 Samuel 1:20); the minimum of *tekufot* are two and the minimum of days is two. [A *tekufah* is three months, hence Hannah gave birth after six months and two days.][8]

THEY WERE REMEMBERED ON ROSH HASHANAH

We learned: On Rosh Hashanah Sarah, Rachel, and Hannah were remembered by God, [and they became pregnant]. How do we know this? R. Elazar said: We derive it from two places where *pekidah*, and two places where *zechirah* [both meaning "remembering"], are mentioned. It says regarding Rachel, "God remembered [*vayizkor*] Rachel" (Genesis 30:32), and it says concerning Hannah, "God remembered her [*vayizkerah*]" (1 Samuel 1:19). Now we also find the word *zechirah* in connection with Rosh Hashanah, as it says, "a remembrance [*zichron*] with shofar blasts" (Leviticus 23:24). [Thus we can make an equation: Just as this *zechirah* takes place on Rosh Hashanah, so too the *zechirah* of Rachel and Hannah occurred on Rosh Hashanah.]

In the same vein, we compare the *pekidah* of Hannah to the *pekidah* of Sarah. The *pekidah* of Hannah is, "For God had remembered [*pakad*] Hannah" (1 Samuel 2:21); the *pekidah* of Sarah is, "God remembered [*pakad*] Sarah as He had said" (Genesis 21:1). [In summary: Hannah, Rachel, and Rosh Hashanah all have *zechirah* in common, which proves that they were remembered on Rosh Hashanah. Both Hannah and Sarah have *pekidah* in common, so that we can say that Sarah, like Hannah, was remembered on Rosh Hashanah.]

JOSEPH WAS RELEASED ON ROSH HASHANAH

We learned: On Rosh Hashanah Joseph was released from prison. How do we know this? Because it says, "Blow the shofar at the moon's renewal, at the time appointed for our festive day. Because it is a decree for Israel, a judgment day for the God of Jacob. (11b) He

appointed it as a testimony for Joseph when he went out over the land of Egypt [after his release]" (Psalms 81:4–6).

THE FUTURE REDEMPTION

We learned: On Rosh Hashanah, [six months before the redemption,] the slavery of our ancestors in Egypt ended. [How do we know this?] It says, "I shall take you out from under the burdens [*sivlot*] of Egypt" (Exodus 6:6), and it says elsewhwere, "I removed his [Joseph's] shoulder from the burden [*seivel*] [when he was released from prison on Rosh Hashanah]" (Psalms 81:7). [Hence, just as Joseph's *seivel* ended on Rosh Hashanah, so did our ancestors' *sivlot* end on Rosh Hashanah.]

We learned: "In Nisan our ancestors were redeemed," as the Torah relates [in the story of the Exodus]. "In Tishri they will be delivered at the ultimate redemption." This is derived by an analogy of the word shofar found in two places. It says in one place [with reference to Rosh Hashanah] "Blow the shofar at the moon's renewal" (ibid. 4), and elsewhere [concerning the ultimate redemption] it says, "On that day a great shofar will be blown" (Isaiah 27:13). [Thus the redemption will occur on Rosh Hashanah, in Tishri.]

We learned: R. Yehoshua said: In Nisan our ancestors were delivered, and in Nisan they will be delivered at the ultimate redemption. How do we know this? The Torah calls the night of Pesach, "A night of watching for God to take them out of the land of Egypt" (Exodus 12:42). This means that the night of Pesach is a night that has been set aside and guarded [for the ultimate redemption to occur] from the six days of Creation. And what does R. Eliezer [who holds that the ultimate redemption will be in Tishri] say to this? [He says "a night of watching" means] the night of Pesach is a night during which the Jewish people are guarded against evil spirits.

FOUR JUDGMENT DAYS

(16a) [The Mishnah says:] There are four times during the year that the world is judged: On Pesach it is judged regarding the outcome of grain crops; on Shavuot regarding fruit of the trees; on Rosh Hashanah all the people of the world pass before God, one by one, as it says, "He Who fashions the hearts of them all, Who comprehends all their deeds" (Psalms 33:15); and on Sukkot judgment is rendered in respect of rain.

[The Gemara asks:] Which grain [is the Mishnah referring to]? Do you think the grain that is already grown, [and which was planted in the fall, before the rainy season]? If so, when were all the adversities judged which this grain crop went through until this point? So we are to assume that it refers to the grain that is going to be planted later, [in the next fall]. [The Gemara now asks:] Does that mean that grain is judged only once a year? But we learned in a *Baraita*: If some disaster [like hail or a draught] or misfortune strikes the grain before Pesach, it was decreed on the previous Pesach [before it was planted]; if the incident happened after Pesach, it was ordained on the Pesach after which it was planted. If an accident or misfortune happens to a person before Yom Kippur, it was decreed on the Yom Kippur a year before; if a tragedy occurred after Yom Kippur, it was judged on the Yom Kippur that just passed.

Rava said: [Contrary to the earlier implication,] we learn from this that two judgments are passed on the grain crop, [a judgment on Pesach that applies to the period from the time of the sowing of the grain [which is done in the fall] until it is standing in the field, and what happens after that until harvest time is determined on the next Pesach]. Abaye advised: Therefore, if a person sees that seed that generally matures slowly [like wheat and spelt, which are planted in Marcheshvan (October)] are thriving, [so he knows that the judgment of last Pesach was a favorable one, he should [cash in on that good judgment] by planting the quick-ripening seeds [like barley, which is sown in Shevat or Adar (January or February)], so that by the time of judgment on the next Pesach it will be well along [and resistant to any adversity].

FOUR DIFFERENT OPINIONS

[The Gemara asks:] Who is the author of our Mishnah? It agrees neither with R. Meir, nor with R. Yehudah, nor with R. Yose, nor with R. Natan. [What did these Sages say?] For we learned in a *Baraita*: All are judged on Rosh Hashanah, [including the grain, the fruit, and the water], and their final verdict is sealed on Yom Kippur, so says R. Meir [but our Mishnah says that grain, fruit, and water are judged at different periods]. R. Yehudah says: All have their preliminary judgment on Rosh Hashanah, and the final verdict is sealed each in its time respectively: on Pesach regarding the grain crop, on Shavuot regarding fruit, on Sukkot in respect of rain, and man is judged on Rosh Hashanah and his verdict is sealed on Yom Kippur. R. Yose says: Man is judged every day, for it says, "You inspect him every morning" (Job 7:18). R. Natan says: Man is judged every moment, for it says, "And you observe him every moment" (ibid.). [None of these opinions coincide with our Mishnah.]

If you should suggest that our Mishnah does agree with R. Yehudah [who says that everything is initially judged on Rosh Hashanah], and the "four times" the Mishnah mentions refer to the final verdict, then there is a difficulty regarding the judgment of man, [because the Mishnah says that man's judgment is on Rosh Hashanah, and according to R. Yehudah it is on Yom Kippur]. [So who is the Tanna of our Mishnah?] Rava said: The Tanna of our Mishnah follows the view of the yeshivah of R. Yishmael, for it was taught in the yeshivah of R. Yishmael: At four times in the year the world is judged: On Pesach regarding the grain crop; on Shavuot regarding the fruit of the trees; on Sukkot concerning the water; and man is judged initially on Rosh Hashanah and his final verdict is sealed on Yom Kippur, but our Mishnah refers only to the beginning of the judgment [but the final verdict is rendered on Yom Kippur].

R. Chisda said: What is the reason of R. Yose [who said that man is judged every day]? [The Gemara says:] Why do you ask? He stated his reason: Because it says, "You inspect him every morning." [The Gemara clarifies:] We mean to ask as follows: [Granted that he has this verse,] but why doesn't he follow R. Natan's line of thinking [who said that man is judged every moment]? [The Gemara answers:] He bases his view on, "He observes him every moment"] and "observing" is not the same as "judging." If so, [the Gemara challenges,] "inspecting" is not the same as "judging" either!

R. Chisda said: The opinion of R. Yose is based on the following verse, "To do the judgment of his servant and the judgment of his people Israel, every single day" (1 Kings 8:59). Furthermore, said R. Chisda: [Something else can be learned from this verse:] If both a king and a congregation are coming to court, the king's case should be heard first, for it says, "To do the judgment of his servant and the judgment of his people Israel," [the servant, i.e., the king, is mentioned before the people]. Why is the king judged first? If you want I can answer: because it is not respectful to have the king wait outside, or if you prefer, I can say: It is to the king's advantage to be judged first, before the Divine anger is intensified.

R. Yosef said: On the basis of whose view do we pray daily for the sick and for infirm scholars? [The Gemara is amazed:] On the basis of whose view, you ask? [The answer should be obvious!] Of course, according to R. Yose's view, [who holds that man is judged every single day, thus he can pray to be judged favorably]. Or if you prefer, I can say, even according to the Rabbis' view [who hold that man is judged on Rosh Hashanah], if you bear in mind R. Yitzchak's dictum. For R. Yitzchak said: Crying [to God from the depth of your heart] is effective whether before the final judgment is pronounced and even after it has been pronounced.

OMER, TWO LOAVES, AND THE POURING OF WATER

We learned in a *Baraita*: R. Yehudah said in the name of R. Akiva: Why did the Torah command us to bring an *Omer*[9] on Pesach? Because Pesach is the season [that God judges] the grain crop. Therefore, the Holy One, blessed be He, said: Bring before Me the *Omer* offering on Pesach so that the grain in the fields will be blessed. Why did the Torah command us to bring the offering of two loaves[10] on Shavuot? Because Shavuot is the time of judgment for the fruit of the trees; therefore, the Holy One, blessed be He, said: Bring before Me the two loaves on Shavuot so that the fruit of the trees will be blessed. [The reason that wheat represents a blessing for fruit is because before the two loaves were brought, first fruits [bikkurim] could not be offered in the Bet Hamikdash (Rashi).] Why did the Torah command us to pour water [on the Altar][11] on Sukkot? The Holy One, blessed be He, said: Pour out water before Me on Sukkot, so that your rains of this year will be blessed. Also recite before Me [on Rosh Hashanah] Malchiyot, Zichronot, and Shofarot:[12] Malchiyot, [Kingship], so that you should make Me king over you, Zichronot [Remembrances], so that I should remember you in a favorable way; and through what? Through the shofar.

WHY DO WE BLOW THE SHOFAR?

R. Abbahu said: Why do we blow on a ram's horn? The Holy One, blessed be He, said: Sound before me a ram's horn so that I may remember, for your sake, the Akeidah [the binding] of Isaac, and I will consider it as if you had bound yourselves before Me.

R. Yitzchak said: Why do we blow the shofar on Rosh Hashanah? [The Gemara is surprised at the question:] [You ask], why do we blow? God told us to blow! [The Gemara explains:] He meant to ask, why do we blow the teruah?[13]—[Again the Gemara is surprised:] Why do we blow the teruah? [That is obvious!] The Torah says, "a remembrance with teruah blasts" (Leviticus 23:24)! [The Gemara explains:] What he means is: Why do we blow a tekiah and teruah sitting [before the Shemoneh Esrei of Musaf] (16b) and then again blow a tekiah and teruah while standing [during the Shemoneh Esrei of Musaf]? [The Gemara answers:] In order to confuse Satan. [When he sees how devoutly the Jewish people observe the mitzvot, he will be speechless, unable to bring charges against them (Rashi).]

R. Yitzchak also said: If the shofar is not blown at the start of the year, bad things will happen in the end.[14]

SAYINGS BY R. YITZCHAK

R. Yitzchak said: Every year that starts out poorly [meaning, in which the Jewish people view themselves as impoverished and in need of God's mercy (Rashi)] will become rich at the end, [will end with good fortune], as it says, "From the beginning [meireishit] of the year to year's end" (Deuteronomy 11:12). Meireishit can be read merashit, which means "being poor." "To year's end" is expounded to mean "the year has good prospects."[15]

R. Yitzchak said furthermore: A person is only judged based on his actions up to that point in time, [and not for evil deeds he will commit later in life], as it says, [An angel called to Hagar,] "God has heard the boy's voice there where he is" (Genesis 21:17). [Hagar's son Ishmael was saved because at that moment he was still an innocent child.]

R. Yitzchak said additionally: Three things summon up a person's sins, namely, a shaky wall [if he passes under a shaky wall Heaven reviews his past actions to determine if he is worthy to be saved]; being overconfident about the effectiveness of his prayers [i.e., he thinks of himself as being so righteous that he expects his prayers to be answered]; and calling down Divine judgment on one's neighbor. For R. Chanan said: Whoever calls down Divine judgment on his neighbor is himself punished first [for his own sins], for it says, "Sarah said to Abraham, 'The outrage against me is upon you . . . Let God judge between me and you!'" (Genesis 16:5), and later it says, "Abraham came to eulogize Sarah and to bewail her" (ibid 23:2) [proof that Sarah died first].

R. Yitzchak further said: There are four things that cancel an evil decree against a person, namely: charity, prayer, changing one's name, and changing one's conduct. "Charity," because it says, "Charity saves from death" (Proverbs 10:2). "Prayer," because it says, "Then they cried out to God in their distress, and He rescued them from their straits" (Psalms 107:6). "Changing one's name," for it says, "God said to Abraham, 'Sarai your wife—do not call her by her name Sarai, for Sarah is her name'" (Genesis 17:15); and the verse continues, "I will bless her, and make her bear you a son." "Changing one's conduct," for it says, [about the people of Nineveh,] "God saw their deeds, that they had repented from their evil way, and God relented concerning the evil He had said He would bring upon them" (Jonah 3:10). Some say that changing one's place of residence also [helps to have an evil decree cancelled,] for it says, "God said to Abram, 'Go away from your land,'" (Genesis 12:1), and in the next verse it says, "I will make you into a great nation." [The Gemara asks:] Why doesn't the other list changing one's place of residence?—In that case it was the merit of Eretz Yisrael that helped him.

R. Yitzchak also said: A person is required to go and visit his rabbi on Yom Tov, for it says, [The husband of the Shunnamite woman said to his wife,] "Why are you going to [Elisha] today? It is not Rosh Chodesh [New Moon] or a Shabbat!" (2 Kings 4:23); this implies that on New Moon and Shabbat a person should go. [Shabbat is the collective name for Shabbat and Yom Tov.][16]

THREE BOOKS ARE OPENED ON ROSH HASHANAH

R. Kruspeda'i said in the name of R. Yochanan: Three books are opened on Rosh Hashanah: one of the totally wicked [people who have more sins than mitzvot], one for the totally righteous [people who have more mitzvot than sins], and one for those in between. The totally righteous are inscribed and sealed immediately in the Book of Life; the totally wicked are inscribed and sealed immediately in the Book of Death; the sentence of the in-between people is left pending from Rosh Hashanah until Yom Kippur. If they deserve it, they are inscribed in the Book of Life; if they don't deserve it, they are inscribed in the Book of Death. R. Avin said: What verse supports this?—"May they be erased from the book of life, and let them not be inscribed with the righteous" (Psalms 69:29). "May they be erased from the book" refers to the book of the wicked; "of life" refers to the book of the righteous; "and let them not be inscribed with the righteous;" refers to the book of the in-between people. R. Nachman b. Yitzchak derives it from here: [Moses said to God,] "If not, erase me now from the book that You have written" (Exodus 32:32). "Erase me now" refers to the book of the wicked; "from Your book" refers to the book of the righteous; "that You have written" refers to the book of the in-between.

THREE GROUPS
ON JUDGMENT DAY

We learned in a *Baraita*: Bet Shammai say: There will be three groups on the Day of Judgment [when it will be decided whether or not they will arise from the dead]: one group of perfectly righteous, one of perfectly wicked, and one intermediate group. The perfectly righteous are inscribed and sealed right away to arise from the dead for everlasting life; the perfectly wicked are inscribed and sealed right away for Gehinnom, for it says, "Many of those who sleep in the dusty earth will awaken: these for everlasting life and these for everlasting shame" (Daniel 12:2). Those of the intermediate group will go down to Gehinnom (**17a**) and scream [in pain for a short while], and rise again, as it says, "I will bring that third [group] into fire and purify it as one purifies silver, and I will refine it as one refines gold; they will call out in My Name, and I will answer them" (Zechariah 13:9). Hannah had them in mind when she said, "God brings death and gives life, He lowers to the grave and raises up" (1 Samuel 2:6). Bet Hillel says: [Since with the intermediary group merits and failings are evenly balanced,] He who is full of mercy will tip the scale of justice toward the side of mercy, [and they will not have to go to Gehinnom]. And David said about them, "I love [God], for He has heard my voice, my supplications" (Psalms 116:1), and, as a matter of fact, the entire psalm is devoted to them, including, "I was brought low, but He saved me" (ibid. 5).

EVILDOERS WILL GO DOWN
TO GEHINNOM

Both sinners of Israel who [willfully] transgress with their bodies [the Gemara will explain what is meant by that] and sinners of the gentiles who [willfully] transgress with their bodies go down to Gehinnom and are judged there for twelve months. After the twelve months, their bodies are consumed and their souls are burned, and the wind scatters [their ashes] under the soles of the feet of the righteous, for it says, "And you will trample the wicked, for they will be ashes under the soles of your feet" (Malachi 3:21). But the *Minim* [i.e., Jewish followers of the Nazarene, who distorted and misrepresented the words of the Torah]; and the informers and the scoffers, who deny the Torah and do not believe in the resurrection of the dead; and those who spread their fear in the land of the living; and those who sinned and caused others to sin, as did Jeroboam, the son of Nevat and his colleagues—these people will go down to Gehinnom and will be punished there from generation to generation, as it says, "They will go out and see the corpses of the men who rebelled against Me, for their decay will not cease and their fire will not be extinguished and they will lie in disgrace before all mankind" (Isaiah 66:24); Gehinnom will come to an end but they will not, as it says, "Their form is doomed to rot in the grave" (Psalms 49:15). Why such a severe punishment? Because they laid hands on *zevul* [God's dwelling place; through their sins they destroyed the *Bet Hamikdash* (Rashi)]. For it says "that there will be no dwelling [*zevul*] for Him" (ibid.), and *zevul* refers to the *Bet Hamikdash*, as it says, [Solomon said,] "I have surely built a house of habitation [*zevul*] for Him" (1 Kings 8:13). Hannah referred to these people when she said, "May those that contend with God be crushed" (1 Samuel 2:10). R. Yitzchak b. Avin said: And their faces are as black as the bottom of a pot. Rava said: Among them you have some of the best-looking people of Mechuza, [hedonists who indulge in the pleasures of life], and they are called "sons of Gehinnom."

WHEN *MITZVOT* AND SINS ARE
EVENLY BALANCED

The Master said above: Bet Hillel says: [If merits and failings are evenly balanced,] He Who is full of kindness will tip the scale of justice toward the side of kindness. [The Gemara asks: How can this be?] After all, it says, [in reference to the intermediate group,] "I will bring that third group into fire" (Zechariah 13:9). [How then can Bet Hillel say that they can escape that fate]? [The Gemara answers:] That refers to sinners of Israel who willfully transgress with their bodies.—You say sinners of Israel who sin with their bodies! But you said that there is no remedy for them, [after the fires of Gehinnom they turn to dust]? The Gemara responds: There is no remedy for them when their sins outnumber their good deeds. Here we speak of people whose sins and merits are evenly balanced but whose sins include those that are committed by sinners of Israel who sin with their bodies. In that case they cannot escape the punishment of "I will bring that third group into fire." On the other hand, [if their *mitzvot* and sins are evenly balanced, and they don't include any sins that are committed by sinners of Israel who sin with their bodies], then He Who is abundant in kindness will tip the scale of Justice to the side of kindness. And David said about them, "I love God, for He hears my voice" (Psalms 116:1).

Rava expounded: What is meant by the verse, "I love God, for He hears my voice"? The Community of Israel said to the Holy One, blessed be He: Master of the universe, when do I know that I am truly loved by You? When You are listening to the voice of my supplication. "I was brought low [*daloti*], but He saved me"—Although I am poor [*dallah*] in *mitzvot*, [like the intermediate group whose *mitzvot* do not outnumber their sins], yet it is fitting to save me.

WHO ARE JEWS THAT SIN WITH THEIR BODIES?
[The Gemara inquires:] What is meant by "sinners of Israel who transgress with their bodies"? Rav said: The skull that did not put on *tefillin* [i.e., a person who never put on *tefillin* throughout his entire life]. And who are the sinners among the gentiles who transgress with their bodies? Rav said: Those who are guilty of incest [which is prohibited by one of the seven Noachide commandments]. And who is meant by "those who spread their fear in the land of the living"? R. Chisda said: This refers to a communal leader who inspires fear among the congregation, not for the sake of God.

Rav Yehudah said in the name of Rav: A leader who inspires excessive fear in the community not for the sake of God will not have a son who is a Torah scholar, as it says, "Therefore, if he frightens people, he will not see [among his sons] any who have a wise heart" (Job 37:24).

HOW DOES GOD TIP THE SCALES OF JUSTICE?
[We learned above:] Bet Hillel says: [If a person's merits and failings are evenly balanced,] He Who is full of mercy will tip the scales of justice toward the side of mercy. [The Gemara asks:] How is this done? R. Eliezer says: He pushes down the scale of merit, [lending more weight to the *mitzvot*], for it says, "He will once again show us mercy, He will [overrate our *mitzvot*] so that they will outweigh our iniquities" (Micah 7:19). R. Yose b. Chaninah says: He raises the scale of iniquities, [lessening the impact of our sins], as it says, "He lifts up [the scale of] iniquity and overlooks transgression" (ibid. 18).

It was taught in the yeshivah of R. Yishmael: A person's first sins are put aside [and are left pending]. And this is because of the Divine attribute of Mercy.

[If, without counting the first sins, in the final tally his *mitzvot* outweigh his sins, then the first sins are not placed on the scale.] Rava said: However, the sin itself is not erased. And if by placing these first sins on the scale he has more sins than *mitzvot*, then his first sins are counted.

WHOSE TRANGRESSIONS ARE OVERLOOKED?
Rava said: If a person is willing to overlook injustices that are done to him, then his own iniquities are overlooked. For it says, "Who is a God like You, Who forgives iniquity and overlooks transgression" (Micah 7:18). Who is forgiven his iniquity? A person who overlooks offenses that were committed against him.

R. Huna the son of R. Yehoshua was not feeling well. R. Papa went to visit him. When he saw that his condition was critical he said to those present, "Prepare the shrouds." In the end he recovered, and R. Papa was embarrassed to see him. He said to him, "What did you see [in the hereafter]?" R. Huna replied, "Yes, what you thought was true. [I was indeed in the hereafter,] but the Holy One, blessed be He, said to the angels: Since he does not insist on having things his way, don't be strict with him," as it says, "He forgives iniquity and overlooks transgression." Who is forgiven his inquity? A person who overlooks offenses that were committed against himself." [The verse concludes,] "for the remnant of His heritage." R. Acha b. Chanina said: This phrase is like a fat tail of a sheep with a thorn in it, [a proverb meaning, the phrase contains a comforting message but also a warning], for, "He overlooks transgression for the remnant of His heritage" implies that He does this only for the remnant, but not for his entire heritage. [And what is meant by, "for the remnant of His heritage"?] (17b) It means, "for a person who makes himself like a remnant, [by being meek and humble]."

THE THIRTEEN ATTRIBUTES OF MERCY
[In the Torah the Thirteen Divine Attributes of Mercy are introduced with the passage,] "God passed before him [Moses] and proclaimed:" (Exodus 34:6). R. Yochanan said: Were it not written in Scripture, it would be impossible for us to say it. This passage teaches us that God wrapped himself [in a *tallit*] like one leading the congregation in prayer and showed Moses the order of prayer. He said to him: Whenever Israel sins, let them perform before Me this order of prayer, [the order of the Thirteen Attributes of Mercy] and I will forgive them. [The Thirteen Attributes of Mercy are: 1. God, 2. God, 3. Omnipotent, 4. Merciful and 5. Kind, 6. Slow to Anger, 7. Abundant in Kindness and 8. in Truth. 9. He remembers deeds of love for thousands of generations, 10. Forgiver of In-

iquity, 11. Rebellion and 12. Error. 13. Who does not clear of guilt [those who do not repent (Exodus 34:6,7)].

[The Gemara now analyzes a few of the Thirteen Attributes of Mercy:] God, God. [Why does the verse start with "God, God"? [Hashem, God, represents the Attribute of Mercy, and "God, God" implies,] I am [the attribute of Mercy] before a person sins, and I am the same Hashem after he sins and repents.

[The verse continues,] "Omnipotent, Merciful, and Kind." Rav Yehudah said: A covenant has been made with the Thirteen Attributes that if the Jewish people mention them in their prayers,[17] they will not remain unanswered. For it says, "Behold! I seal a covenant" (ibid. 10).

Ilfa pointed out a contradiction between two verses: It says, "Abundant in Kindness" and then it says, "and in Truth." How can this be? [How can God be kind and at the same time rigorously adhere to the truth?] [He reconciled the two:] At first [He judges with] the Attribute of Truth, but in the end, with Kindness. [In the same vein] R. Elazar contrasted two contradictory passages: It says, "Yours, O Lord, is kindness," and the verse continues, "for You repay each man according to his deeds" (Psalms 62:13). [How can this be? Aren't kindness and retaliation opposites?]—At first God repays each man according to his deeds, but in the end, "Yours, O Lord, is kindness."

R. Huna noted a similar contradiction: It says, "God is righteous in all His ways," and the verse concludes, "and kind in all His deeds" (Psalms 145:17). How can [God be righteous and kind at the same time]?—At first He rules with righteousness, but in the end [when He sees that the world cannot exist under strict justice (Rashi)] He rules with kindness.

THE POWER OF *TESHUVAH*

R. Yochanan said: *Teshuvah* is so great that it has the power to annul a person's guilty verdict. For it says, "Make fat that people's heart, stop its ears, and seal its eyes, lest, seeing with its eyes, and hearing with its ears, it also grasp with its mind, and repent and be healed" (Isaiah 6:10) [which shows that repentance has the power to heal, i.e., to annul an evil verdict]. R. Papa said to Abaye: Perhaps [repentance annuls an evil verdict] only before the verdict was pronounced, [but not after sentencing]? He replied: It says, "and be healed." What is a thing that is in need of healing [i.e., in need of an annulment]? You can only say: a guilty verdict, [after it was pronounced].

An objection was raised [against this opinion] from the following *Baraita*: If a person repents during the ten days between Rosh Hashanah and Yom Kippur, his sins are forgiven. If he does not repent during those ten days, his sin are not forgiven, even if he offered all the rams of Nevayot.[18] [This contradicts R. Yochanan who said that *teshuvah* brings about forgiveness at any

time.] [The Gemara answers:] There is no contradiction: The latter case refers to the sins of an individual; [his *teshuvah* effects forgiveness only during the Ten Days of Penitence], while the former refers to the sins of a community, [its *teshuvah* effects forgiveness at any time].

An objection was raised from the following *Baraita*: It says, "The eyes of the Lord your God are always upon [Eretz Yisrael]," (Deuteronomy 11:12), sometimes for the people's benefit, and sometimes to their detriment. How can it be sometimes for their benefit? Let's say that on Rosh Hashanah the Jewish people were in the category of the totally wicked, and Heaven decreed that very little rain should fall that year, but later on they repented. What should be done? God cannot increase the rainfall allotted for that year because the decree has already been made. Therefore, God makes [the little rain] fall at the right time on the land [fields, vineyards, and gardens] that needs it, according to the region [to get the maximum benefit from the sparse rainfall].

How can it be sometimes to the people's detriment? Let's say that on Rosh Hashanah the Jewish people were in the category of the completely righteous, and Heaven decreed abundant rainfall for that year, but later on they fell into error. To reduce the total amount of rainfall is impossible, because the decree has already been made. Therefore, the Holy One, blessed be He, makes it rain not in the proper season and on land that does not require rain [on forests and deserts]. Now, [according to your opinion that for a community a decree can be changed for good at any time], then why not, [in the first case], annul the decree and increase the amount of rain? [The Gemara answers:] The case there is different, namely that the small amount of rain was sufficient, [but if there was no such solution, then *teshuvah* can bring about an increase in the amount of rain].

Another objection was raised from the following *Baraita*: It says, "Those who go down to the sea in ships, who ply their trade in the mighty waters; they have seen the works of the Lord . . . By His word He raised a storm wind that made the waves surge . . . They reeled and staggered like a drunkard . . . In their adversity they cried to God . . . Let them give thanks to God for His kindness and His wondrous deeds for mankind" (Psalms 107: 23–31). The Psalmist inserted signs [of an inverted letter *nun*] before and after each of these verses. These signs have the same intent as the words *ach* and *rak* in the Torah [which signify that something is to be excluded from the text]. The signs come to tell you that [the crying was limited, in the sense that], if they cried before the final verdict, they were answered; but if they cried after the final verdict, they were not answered. [This contradicts the view that for a community a decree can be changed for good at any time.] [The Gemara answers:] Those on a ship are considered as individuals [whose *teshuvah* annuls a decree only during the Ten Days of Penitence].

BALURIA, THE PROSELYTE'S QUESTION

Come and learn: Baluria, the proselyte, asked R. Gamliel: It says in your Torah, "God, Who does not show favor" (Deuteronomy 10:17), but it also says, "May God bestow favor on you" (Numbers 6:26). [The two verses seem to contradict each other?] R. Yose Hakohen joined the conversation and said to her: Let me explain it to you with a parable. Suppose a person lent his neighbor one hundred dollars and fixed a term for repayment in the presence of the king, while the borrower swore by the life of the king that he would repay the loan. When the time arrived he did not repay him, and he went to the king to excuse himself. The king told him: My embarrassment I am willing to forgive you, but I cannot forgive you the wrong against your neighbor. You have to go and ask his forgiveness. Here, too, the verse [where God is said to show favor] speaks of offenses a person committed against God; [those God will forgive]. The other verse [where He does not show favor] speaks of offenses a person committed against his fellow man. But when Rabbi Akiva came [he suggested a different interpretation]. (18a) He taught: One verse refers to the time before final judgment is rendered, [when God does show favor]; the other to the time after final judgment, [when He does not show favor. Thus, after judgment the decree cannot be annulled]. [The Gemara points out that] this refers to a decree of an individual, [not that of a community, which can be reversed at any time, as we learned above].

Regarding the final judgment of an individual there is a difference of opinion among Tannaim. For we learned in a *Baraita*: R. Meir used to say: Two men are stricken with the same illness, or two men enter a courthouse to be judged for the same crime; yet one recovers, and the other does not, one is acquitted, and the other is not. Why should one recover and the other not; and why should one be acquitted and the other not? Because the one prayed and was answered, and the other prayed and was not answered. Why was one answered and the other not? One prayed with full concentration and was, therefore, answered; the other did not pray with full concentration and was, therefore, not answered. R. Elazar said: The one prayed before his final verdict was pronounced, [that's why he was answered]; the other after his final verdict was pronounced, [that's why he was not answered].

R. Yitzchak said:[19] Crying to God [from the depth of your heart] is effective before the final judgment is pronounced and even after it has been pronounced.

TORAH AND KINDNESS OVERTURN AN EVIL DECREE

[The Gemara asks:] But can the final judgment of a community be annulled [as you claim that it can]? Don't we have a passage that says, "Cleanse your heart of evil, O Jerusalem" (Jeremiah 4:14), and another passage, "Even if you were to wash with niter and use much soap, your guilt is sealed before Me" (ibid. 2:22); and does not the first verse refer to the time before the final judgment is pronounced, and the second verse after? [Thus, after the final judgment, the decree of a community cannot be reversed?] [The Gemara answers:] No, both refer to the time after the final decree has been pronounced. [Then why does one verse say that the judgment can be rescinded and the other that it cannot?] There is no contradiction. In the one case the final decree was pronounced together with an oath, [then it cannot be rescinded]; in the other case the final decree was not accompanied by an oath, [then it can be rescinded]. This is in keeping with the saying of R. Shmuel b. Ammi. For R. Shmuel b. Ammi—or as some say R. Shmuel b. Nachman—said in the name of R. Yonatan: How do we know that a final decree accompanied by an oath is never annulled? Because it says, "Therefore I have sworn concerning the house of Eli that the sin of the house of Eli would never be atoned for by sacrifice or meal offering" (1 Samuel 3:14). [God swore that none of Eli's descendants would reach old age.][20]

[Commenting on this verse,] Rabbah said: With sacrifice and meal offering it cannot be atoned for, but it can be atoned for with Torah. Abaye said: With sacrifice and meal offering it cannot be atoned for, but it can be atoned for with Torah and acts of kindness. Both Rabbah and Abaye were descendants of the house of Eli. Rabbah, who applied himself to Torah study, lived forty years; Abaye, who devoted himself to Torah and to acts of kindness, lived sixty years.

Our Rabbis taught: There was a family in Jerusalem whose members died at eighteen years of age. They came and told R. Yochanan b. Zakkai. He said to them: Perhaps you are descendants of the house of Eli, about whom it says, "All those raised in your house will die as young men" (1 Samuel 2:33)? Go and study Torah and you will live. So they went and studied Torah and lived, and they used to call that family after him, "the Rabban Yochanan family."

WHEN IS GOD ACCESSIBLE?

R. Shmuel b. Inia said in the name of Rav: How do we know that the final decree on a community is never sealed? [The Gemara asks:] How can you say, never sealed? Doesn't it say, "Your guilt is sealed before Me" (Jeremiah 2:22)? [The Gemara answers:] He meant to say: How do we know that although the decree against a community is sealed, it can still be annulled? [The Gemara answers:] Because it says, "As is the Lord our God, whenever we call to Him" (Deuteronomy 4:7). [The Gemara asks:] But it also says, "Seek God when He can be found" (Isaiah 55:6) [this implies, only when He is accessible, but God cannot always be found]. [The Gemara answers:] This verse speaks of an individual, the other verse of a community.

248

[The Gemara asks:] And when can an individual find God? [The Gemara answers:] In the ten days between Rosh Hashanah and Yom Kippur. [The Gemara cites a verse in support of this statement.] It says, "About ten days later God struck Nabal and he died" (1 Samuel 25:38). [David had sent ten young men to the wealthy but boorish Nabal to ask for food and supplies. Nabal gave each of them a meal, but he refused to supply food for David and his men.] Why did God wait ten days? Rav Yehudah said in the name of Rav: They match the ten meals Nabal gave to David's men. R. Nachman said in the name of Rabbah b. Abbuha: These were the ten days between Rosh Hashanah and Yom Kippur. [God vainly hoped that he would repent.]

LIKE SHEEP PASSING IN FRONT OF THEIR OWNER

[We learned in the Mishnah:] On Rosh Hashanah all mankind passes before God like *benei maron*. The Gemara asks: What is the meaning of the phrase "like *benei maron*"? [The Gemara answers:] Here [in Babylonia] we translate it: "Like sheep [passing single file before their owner]." Resh Lakish said: Like climbing Bet Choron [a narrow mountain pass with steep inclines on both sides that could only be negotiated in single file]. Rav Yehudah said in the name of Shmuel: Like the soldiers of the house of David who passed muster one by one before the king. Rabbah b. Bar Chanah said in the name of R. Yochanan: [Although they pass single file] they are all inspected with a single glance. R. Nachman b. Yitzchak said: We derive the same concept from the verse, "He Who fashions their hearts together, Who comprehends all their deeds" (Psalms 33). What does that mean? Shall I say that it means that God has created all creatures and given them all identical minds? But we see that this is not so! What it means is this: The Creator sees their hearts together and discerns all their deeds.

THE MESSENGERS OF THE BET DIN

[Originally, the fixing of Rosh Chodesh, (the first day of the month), was dependent on the testimony of witnesses who had observed the first appearance of the moon, whereupon Rosh Chodesh would be proclaimed by the Bet Din in Jerusalem. A month might have twenty-nine or thirty days, so that the new month might be proclaimed on the thirtieth or the thirty-first day respectively.]

[We learned in the Mishnah:] Messengers were dispatched [to let the outlying communities know] on which day Rosh Chodesh was proclaimed. This was done on six occasions: They were sent out after Rosh Chodesh of the month of Nisan was proclaimed, [so that the people should know] on what day to celebrate

Pesach. They were sent out for Av, because of the fast of Tishah be'Av; for Ellul, because of Rosh Hashanah, [which usually falls thirty days after Rosh Chodesh Elul, although occasionally the Bet Din might fix Rosh Hashanah thirty-one days after Rosh Chodesh Ellul]; for Tishri, to let them know when to observe Yom Kippur and Sukkot; for Kislev because of Chanukah [which starts on the 25th of Kislev], and for Adar because of Purim, [which is celebrated on the 14th of Adar]; and when the *Bet Hamikdash* stood the messengers also used to go out for Iyar because of the *Pesach Sheini* [the second Pesach. People who are ineligible to bring the pesach offering may bring a *Pesach Sheini* on the 14th of Iyar].[21]

THE FOUR FASTS

[The Gemara asks:] Why were the messengers not also sent out to announce Rosh Chodesh of Tammuz and Tevet, [because of the fasts of the 17th of Tammuz and the 10th of Tevet? And proof that these fasts must be observed can be adduced from the following:] (18b) For R. Chanah b. Bizna said in the name of R. Shimon Chasida: What is meant by the verse, "Thus says God, Master of Legions: The fast of the fourth month [Tammuz], and the fast of the fifth [Av] and the fast of the seventh [Tishri] and the fast of the tenth [Tevet] will be for the House of Judah for joy and for gladness" (Zechariah 8:19).[22] Zechariah calls these days both days of fasting and days of joy, implying that if there is peace they will be days of joy and gladness, but if there is no peace [i.e., if the Jewish people are under foreign domination] they will be fast days. [So now that the Temple is destroyed and these fasts must be observed, why were the messengers not dispatched for Tammuz and Tevet?]

R. Papa answered: What it means is this: If there is peace they will be for joy and gladness; in times of persecution they will be fast days; at times when there are neither persecutions nor peace, then it is up to the individual whether or not he wants to fast, [and therefore no messengers were sent out for Tammuz and Tevet]. [The Gemara asks:] If that is the case, [why did they dispatch messengers] for Tishah be'Av? R. Papa replied: The fast of Tishah be'Av is different, since many calamities happened on that day, as a Master has said: On Tishah be'Av the first and the second *Bet Hamikdash* were destroyed, and Beitar was captured,[23] and the city of Jerusalem was ploughed.[24] [Therefore, Tishah be'Av is observed by all.]

We learned in a *Baraita*: R. Shimon said: There are four interpretations Rabbi Akiva gave with which I disagree. He said, [expounding the verse in Zechariah 8:19, quoted above], "The fast of the fourth month"—this refers to the ninth of Tammuz, on which the wall of the city was breached,[25] as it says, "By the ninth of the fourth month, the famine in the city became critical; there was no food left for the common people. Then [the wall of the city] was breached" (Jeremiah 52:7). Why is it called the fourth month? Because Tammuz is the fourth in the order of months. "The fast of the fifth month"—this refers to Tishah be'Av, [the ninth of Av] on which the House of our God was burned. Why is it called the fifth month? Because Av is the fifth in the order of months. "The fast of the seventh"—this refers to the third of Tishri, the day on which Gedaliah ben Achikam was killed.[26]

Who killed him? Yishmael ben Netaniah killed him, and [the fact that the fast of Gedaliah is listed among the fasts that commemorate the destruction of the Temple] teaches us that the death of the righteous is equal to the burning of the House of our God. Why is it called the seventh month? Because Tishri is the seventh in the order of months. "The fast of the tenth month"—this refers to the tenth of Tevet, the day on which the king of Babylonia began to lay siege to Jerusalem, as it says, "In the ninth year, on the tenth of the month, the word of God came to me: Son of Man, record this day, this exact day; for on this very day the king of Babylonia has laid siege to Jerusalem" (Ezekiel 24:1,2). Why is it called the tenth month? Because Tevet is the tenth in the order of months. [The Gemara asks:] But shouldn't this last fast have been listed first, [since the event it commemorates occurred before the others]? But why was it placed last? [The Gemara answers:] So that the months are arranged in their proper order. [This is Rabbi Akiva's view.]

But I, continues R. Shimon, don't interpret the verse like this. My interpretation is: "The fast of the tenth month" refers to the fifth of Tevet, [not the tenth], the day on which the report reached the Captivity[27] that the city had been conquered, for it says, "It happened in the twelfth year of our exile, on the fifth day of the tenth month, that a fugitive came to me from Jerusalem and reported: 'The City has been conquered'" (Ezekiel 33:21), and they gave the day of the report the same status as the day of the burning [of the Bet Hamikdash].

My view is more logical than R. Akiva's, [because I list the fasts in chronological order], placing the first [event referred to by the prophet, namely, the siege of Jerusalem] first, and the last last, [i.e., the report of the destruction of the Temple in Tevet, the tenth month], whereas he places the first last [i.e., the first calamity mentioned in the verse, that of breaching the wall, he places before the siege], and last first, [he identifies the last calamity mentioned in the verse, i.e., the calamity of the tenth month, as the siege, which happened first]. He follows only the order of the months, while I follow both the order of the months and the chronological order of the calamities. [This is one of the four interpretations in which R. Shimon disagreed with R. Akiva. The others are found in the Tosefta on Sotah, Chapter 6, and Sifre on Deuteronomy 6:4, and on Genesis 21:9 (Rashi).]

THE EVIL DECREE WAS LIFTED

(19a) On the twenty-eighth of Adar, the Jews received glad tidings—that they need no longer refrain from studying the Torah. For the Roman government[28] had issued a decree forbidding the Jews to engage in Torah study, to circumcise their sons, and requiring them to desecrate the Shabbat. What did Yehudah b. Shamua [a student of R. Meir] and his colleagues do? They went and consulted a certain noblewoman whom all the Roman dignitaries used to visit. She advised the sages: "Come and make a demonstration of your sorrows at nighttime." They went and demonstrated at night, crying, "Alas, in heaven's name, are we not your brothers? Are we not the sons of one father, and are we not the sons of one mother? Why are we different from every nation and tongue, that you issue harsh decrees against us?" The decrees were thereupon annulled, and that day was declared a Yom Tov.

THERE WAS NO PROPHET LIKE MOSES

It says, "The words of God are pure words; like purified silver, clear [ba'alil] to the world, refined sevenfold" (Psalms 12:7). Rav and Shmuel [interpreted the phrase "refined sevenfold" as signifying seven times seven, i.e., forty-nine]. One said: Fifty gates of understanding were created in the world, and all but one were given to Moses, as it says, "You have made him little less than God" (ibid. 8:6). Now, Kohelet (Solomon) tried to be like Moses, as it says, "Kohelet sought to find words of delight" (Ecclesiastes 12:10) but a bat kol [a heavenly voice] went forth and said to him, "Words of truth have been recorded properly [in the Torah]" (ibid.), stating, 'No other prophet like Moses has arisen in Israel'" (Deuteronomy 34:10) [thus you should not aspire to become like him].

The other said: Among the prophets indeed none did arise [like Moses], but among kings [like Solomon] there did arise. But how will he interpret the passage, "Kohelet sought to find words of delight"? [The Gemara answers:] Kohelet tried to reach legal decisions by his own intuition, without witnesses or warning,[29] Whereupon a bat kol [a heavenly voice] went forth and said, "Words of truth have been recorded [in the Torah], stating, "A case must be established on the basis of [at least] two or three witnesses" (Deuteronomy 19:15).

GOD WILL NEVER FORGIVE THOSE WHO KILLED JEWS

(23a) R. Yochanan said: Every cedar tree that the nations have uprooted from Jerusalem will be restored to it by the Holy One, blessed be He, in time to come. For it says, "I will plant cedars, acacia in the wilderness" (Isaiah 41:19), and "wilderness" refers to Jerusalem, as it says, "Zion has become a wilderness, Jerusalem a wasteland" (ibid. 64:9).

R. Yochanan also said: If someone learns Torah but does not teach it to others, it is like a myrtle in the wilderness [where no one enjoys its fragrance; a waste of his talent]. Others say: A person who studies Torah and teaches it in a place where there are no Torah scholars, is like a myrtle in the wilderness, which is very precious [to a person traveling through the hot and dry desert].

R. Yochanan further said: Woe to the idol worshippers. [They are going to wake up one day realizing that their evil is so great] that there is no remedy for them. For it says, "In place of the copper I will bring gold, and instead of the iron I will bring silver; in place of the wood, copper, and in place of the stones, iron" (ibid. 60:17). But what can they bring to replace R. Akiva and his companions [whom they killed]? Concerning these idolators it says, "Though I will cleanse [the nations by forgiving many of their sins], the bloodshed [they perpetrated against Israel] I will not cleanse, when God dwells in Zion, [at the End of Days they will be punished]" (Joel 4:21).

THE DISPUTE BETWEEN
R. GAMLIEL AND R. YEHOSHUA

[The Mishnah says:] It once happened that two witnesses came and said: We saw [the new moon] in the morning in the east (25a) and in the evening [we saw the new moon] in the west. R. Yochanan b. Nuri said, "These are false witnesses" [what they say they saw is impossible, since the moon does not travel from east to west in twelve hours (Rashi)]. However, when they came to Yavneh [to the Sanhedrin], R. Gamliel [the *Nasi*, leader of the Sanhedrin] accepted their testimony [because he ignored their morning sighting]. On another occasion two witnesses came and said, "We saw the moon at its proper time [on the thirtieth of the month], but on the night between the thirtieth and thirty-first it was not visible [although it was a clear night]."

R. Gamliel accepted their testimony since it squared with his calculations, and he declared Rosh Chodesh on the thirtieth day, but R. Dosa b. Harkinas said, "They are false witnesses, [since it is impossible that the moon should appear on the thirtieth day, and not be visible on the following night]. How can you testify that a woman gave birth, and the next day we see that she is still pregnant?" [Similarly, if the moon was seen on the thirtieth, it should be visible on the thirty-first.] R. Yehoshua [who was the *Av Bet Din*, the second in command], said [to R. Dosa b. Harkinas], "I agree with you." [They are false witnesses, and Rosh Chodesh should have been declared on the thirty-first. Consequently, Yom Kippur will be a day later.] Thereupon R. Gamliel sent a message to R. Yehoshua, "I

order you to come to me with your staff and money on the day when Yom Kippur will fall according to your computation."

R. Akiva went and found R. Yehoshua upset, so he said to him, "I can expound the verses to prove that whatever R. Gamliel has done is valid, for it says, "These are God's appointed festivals, holy convocations, that *you* are to designate in their appropriate time" (Leviticus 23:4)—whether *you* designate them in their expected time or not in their expected time, I have no festivals but these. [Meaning, the decision whether Rosh Chodesh should be on the thirtieth or thirty-first day is at the discretion of the Bet Din.]

R. Yehoshua came to [discuss the matter with] R. Dosa b. Harkinas, who said to him, "If we are going to question the decisions of R. Gamliel's Bet Din, then we must question the decisions of every Bet Din from the days of Moses until now; as it says, "Moses, Aaron, Nadab, and Abihu and the seventy elders of Israel went up" (Exodus 24:9). Why are the names of the elders not expressly mentioned? Only to teach us that every three people who arose as a Bet Din for Israel are considered like the Bet Din of Moses" [since apparently most of the members of the Bet Din of Moses also were not very distinguished].

Then R. Yehoshua took his staff and his money in his hand and went to Yavneh to R. Gamliel on the day when Yom Kippur fell according to his computation. R. Gamliel stood up and kissed him on his head and said, "Come in peace, my master and my disciple! My master in wisdom and my disciple in the sense that you accepted my words."

TREAT YOUR LEADERS
WITH RESPECT

[The Gemara says:] We learned in a *Baraita*: Why were not the names of the elders expressly mentioned [in Exodus 24:9]? So that nobody should say [about a judge]: Is so-and-so like Moses and Aaron? Is so-and-so like Nadab and Abihu? Is so-and-so like Eldad and Meidad? [He is just an ordinary person. Why should I accept him as my judge? We tell him: Perhaps the seventy elders were also ordinary people. After all their names are not mentioned in the Torah. Therefore, you have to bow to the rulings of your judge.] Furthermore it says, "Samuel said to the people: It is God Who produced Moses and Aaron" (1 Samuel 12:6), and it says in the same paragraph, "So God sent Jerubaal and Bedan and Jephthah and Samuel" (ibid. 11). Jerubaal is Gideon. Why is he called Jerubaal? Because he fought with Baal. Bedan is Samson. Why is he called Bedan? Because he came from Dan. Jephthah is Jephthah.

(25b) And it also says, "Moses and Aaron were among his priests, and Samuel among those who invoke His name" (Psalms 99:6). So we see that Scripture places three of the most insignificant leaders on the same level as three of the most respected personalities. This comes to tell you that Jerubaal in his generation is like Moses in his generation; Bedan in his generation is like Aaron in his generation; Jephthah in his generation is like Samuel in his generation; and to teach you that the most insignificant person, once he has been appointed as leader of the community, becomes like the most powerful ruler. It also says, "You shall come to the *kohanim*, to the Levites, and to the judge who will be in those days" (Deuteronomy 17:9). Can we imagine that a person should go to a judge who does not live in his days? The intention is that you must be satisfied to go to the judge who officiates in your days. [God will lead him on the right path so that he will make the right decisions.] It also says, "Do not say, 'How was it that former times were better than these,' for that is not a question prompted by wisdom" (Ecclesiastes 7:10). [To say: "The judges of earlier times were better than those of the present" is not a wise statement.]

[We learned in the Mishnah:] R. Yehoshua took his staff and his money in his hand. Our Rabbis taught: When R. Gamliel saw him, he stood up and kissed him on his head, saying: Come in peace, my master and my disciple! My teacher, because you have taught me Torah publicly, and my disciple, because I issued a decree and you fulfilled it like a disciple. Happy is the generation in which the great ones respect the lesser ones, and all the more so the lesser respect the greater ones. [The Gemara asks:] You say: all the more so! It is the duty [of the lesser ones to respect the greater ones. We don't need to derive this by inference!] [The Gemara answers:] What is meant is that because the greater ones respect the lesser ones, the lesser ones apply the lesson to themselves.

EVERYTHING DEPENDS
ON FAITH

(29a) [The Mishnah says:] It says, [Shortly after the Exodus, Amalek attacked Israel in Rephidim. Moses told Joshua to choose men and prepare for battle against Amalek. Moses, Aaron, and Chur went up to the top of the hill.] "As long as Moses held his hands up, Israel would be winning, but as soon as he let his hands down, the battle would go in Amalek's favor" (Exodus 17:11). [The Mishnah asks:] Now did the hands of Moses wage war or cause [Amalek to suffer] defeat?—Certainly not. The Torah wants to tell you that as long as [Moses held his hands up], Israel looked upward and subjected their hearts to their Father in Heaven, and as a result, they prevailed, but otherwise they suffered defeat. The same lesson can be derived from the following: It says, [The people spoke out against God and Moses, whereupon God sent poisonous snakes, and a number of Israelites died. When Moses prayed for the people, God said to Moses,] "Make yourself [the image of] a poisonous snake, and place it on a pole. Everyone who is bitten shall look at it and live" (Numbers 21:8). [The same question is asked:]

Now did the snake kill or did the snake keep alive? No, it did not. The Torah wants to tell you that when Israel looked upward and subjected their hearts to their Father in Heaven [meaning, they thought of God and repented], they were healed, but otherwise they perished.

THE PSALM OF THE DAY

(31a) We learned in a *Baraita*: R. Yehudah said in the name of R. Akiva: What psalm did the Levites say on the first day of the week [during the offering of the regular morning sacrifice]?—[The psalm beginning with the verse,] "The earth is God's and its fullness" (Psalm 24). Why this psalm? Because God created the world, and gave it to man and ruled alone over the world. What did they say on the second day of the week?—[The psalm beginning with,] "Great is God and much praised in the city of our God, Mount of His Holiness" (Psalm 48). Why this psalm? Because [on the second day of Creation] He divided His works [between the heavenly and the earthly components of the universe] and reigned over both. [The psalm specifies Jerusalem, because the division between Jerusalem and the rest of the world is as great as that between heaven and earth (Rashi).]

On the third day they said: "God stands in the Divine assembly, in the midst of judges shall He judge" (Psalm 82). Because [on the third day of Creation] He revealed the earth in His wisdom and He prepared dry land for His community. [The continued existence of the world depends on the maintenance of justice and equity. Therefore the psalm speaks of justice (*Maharsha*).] On the fourth day they said, "O God of vengeance, Lord!" (Psalm 94). Because [on the fourth day of Creation] God created the sun and the moon, [but man came to regard the luminaries as gods that should be worshipped]. And [God is called 'God of vengeance'] for in the future He will punish those who worship the sun and the moon.

On the fifth day they said, "Sing joyously to the God of our might" (Psalm 81). Because [on the fifth day of Creation] He created fishes and birds [whose beauty and colorful variety stir people] to praise His name. On the sixth day they said, "God is king, He is robed in grandeur" (Psalm 93). Because [on the sixth day of Creation] He completed His works and reigned over them. On the seventh day they said, "A psalm, a song for the Sabbath day" (Psalm 92). [The psalm makes no mention at all of *Shabbat*. What is the connection?] The psalm refers to the World to Come, to the day that will be all *Shabbat*, [when the world will come to an end and will be destroyed before the resurrection of the dead (Rashi)].

R. Nechemiah [disagreeing with R. Akiva] said: Why would R. Akiva make a distinction between these psalms? [The psalms for the first six days he takes as referring to the past, whereas the psalm for *Shabbat* he takes as referring to the future?] [R. Nechemiah now repeats the entire *Baraita*, and concludes:] On the seventh day, the Levites said, "A psalm, a song for the Sabbath day," because God rested [on the first *Shabbat* of Creation. Thus the psalms of all seven days refer to the days of Creation].

The dispute [between R. Akiva and R. Nechemiah centers around something R. Katina taught]. For R. Katina said: The world will last six thousand years, and for one thousand years it will be desolate, for it says, "God alone will be exalted on that day" (Isaiah 2:11), [and a "day" of God lasts a thousand years].[30] Abbaye disagreed and said: It will be desolate for two thousand years, for it says, "He will heal us [i.e., resurrect the dead] after two days [after two thousand years of desolation]" (Hosea 6:2). [R. Nechemiah holds like Abbaye, and therefore he cannot say that two thousand years are a *Shabbat day*.]

THE GRADUAL WITHDRAWAL OF THE *SHECHINAH*

R. Yehudah b. Idi said in the name of R. Yochanan: [Before the destruction of the first *Bet Hamikdash*], the *Shechinah* withdrew from Israel in ten stages. Parallel with this, the Sanhedrin made ten stops on its way into exile [before and after the destruction of the second *Bet Hamikdash*]. We know from Biblical verses that the *Shechinah* withdrew from Israel in ten stages: It went from the Ark cover to one of the Cherubs and from the Cherub to the threshold of the *Bet Hamikdash*, and from the threshold to the court, and from the court to the [outer] Altar, from the Altar to the roof [of the *Bet Hamikdash*], and from the roof to the wall [of the courtyard], and from the wall to the city [of Jerusalem], and from the city to the Mount of Olives [which is at the outskirts], and from the Mount of Olives to the wilderness, and from the wilderness it went up to its heavenly abode, as it says, "I will go, I will return to My place" (Hosea 5:15). From the Ark cover to the Cherub and from the Cherub to the threshold, as it says, "It is there that I will set My meetings with you . . . from atop the cover [of the Ark]" (Exodus 25:22), and it says, "Then the glory of the God of Israel ascended from atop the Cherub on which it had been, going to the threshold of the Temple" (Ezekiel 9:3).

And from the threshold to the courtyard, as it says, "The Temple was filled with the cloud, and the courtyard was filled with the glow of the glory of God" (ibid. 10:4). From the courtyard to the Altar, as it says, "I saw the Lord standing upon the Altar" (Amos 9:1). From the Altar to the roof [of the *Bet Hamikdash*], as it says, "Better to dwell on a corner of a roof than to dwell with a contentious wife in the house of a friend" (Proverbs 21:9). [Metaphorically, the *Shechinah* is saying that it would rather be outside on a roof rather than live with the cantankerous wife, Israel, who placed an idol in the Sanctuary (Rashi).] From the roof to the wall, as it says, "Behold, the Lord standing on a plumbed wall" (Amos

7:7). From the wall to the city, as it says, "The voice of God calls out to the city" (Micah 6:9). From the city to the mountain, as it says, "And the glory of God ascended from over the midst of the city and stood upon the mountain that is east of the city" (Ezekiel 11:23). From the mountain to the wilderness, for it says, "It is better to live in the desert" (Proverbs 21:19). And from the wilderness it went up to its heavenly abode, as it says, "I will go, I will return to My place, until they will acknowledge their guilt" (Hosea 5:15).

R. Yochanan said: The *Shechinah* lingered for Israel's sake in the wilderness for six months in the hope that they would repent. When it saw that they did not repent, God said: Let them suffer anguish, as it says, "The eyes of the wicked would look with longing, heaven would be denied them. Their hope would become despair" (Job 11:20).

Parallel with this, the Sanhedrin made ten stops on its way into exile. We know this from sources in the Gemara, namely: from the Chamber of the Hewn Stone [in the inner courtyard] to Chanut [a place on the Temple Mount], and from Chanut to Jerusalem, from Jerusalem to Yavneh, (31b) from Yavneh to Usha, from Usha back to Yavneh, from Yavneh back to Usha, and from Usha to Shfar'am, from Shfar'am to Bet She'arim, from Bet She'arim to Tzipori (Sepphoris), from Tzipori to Tveriah (Tiberias), and Tveriah is the lowest-lying of all of them, [situated on Yam Kinneret, (The Sea of Galilee), below sea level. Figuratively, in Tveriah the prestige of the Sanhedrin fell to its lowest level]. For it says, "You will sink down, from the ground will you speak" (Isaiah 29:4).

R. Elazar says: The Sanhedrin moved six times, for it says, "For He has brought down those who dwell on high, in an exalted city, He has lowered it, He has lowered it to the ground, He has brought it down to the dust" (ibid. 26:5).[31] R. Yochanan said: And from that [lowly] position they will be redeemed in the future, for it says, "Shake the dust from yourself; arise and sit [on your throne] Jerusalem; undo the straps on your neck, O captive daughter of Zion!" (ibid. 52:2).

MALCHIYOT, ZICHRONOT, AND SHOFAROT

Our Rabbis taught: From where do we know that we have to say the *berachah* of the Patriarch [at the beginning of the *Shemoneh Esrei*]? Because it says, "Render to God, you sons of the powerful" (Psalms 29:1). ["The powerful" refers to the Patriarchs, who were "powerful" in their righteousness.] And from where do we know that we say the *berachah* of God's might? Because it says, "Render to God honor and might" (ibid.). And from where do we know that we say the *Kedushah* (Sanctification)? Because it says, "Render to God the honor due His Name, bow to God in the beauty of holiness" (ibid. 2). And from where do we learn that [in the *Mussaf Shemoneh Esrei* on Rosh Hashanah] we should say the verses of *Malchiyot*, *Zichronot*, and *Shofarot*, [kingship, remembrance, and shofar]? R. Eliezer says: Because it says, [In reference to Rosh Hashanah,] "There shall be a rest day for you, a remembrance with shofar blasts, a holy convocation" (Leviticus 23:24). [The Gemara analyzes:] "A rest day" signifies the sanctification of the day; "a remembrance" alludes to the *Zichronot* [remembrance verses]; "with shofar blasts" alludes to the *Shofarot* [the shofar verses]; "a holy convocation" reminds us to sanctify Rosh Hashanah by abstaining from work. And from where do we know that we say *Malchiyot* [kingship verses]? We learned in a *Baraita*: Rabbi says: "I am the Lord your God" (Leviticus 23:22), followed immediately by, "In the seventh month." The closeness of these two verses alludes to *Malchiyot*.

WHY DON'T WE SAY *HALLEL* ON ROSH HASHANAH?

(32b) On Rosh Hashanah we do not recite *Hallel*.[32] What is the reason? R. Abbahu said: The ministering angels said to the Holy One, blessed be He, "Master of the universe, why don't the Jewish people sing songs of praise to You on Rosh Hashanah and Yom Kippur?" Replied God, "Is it possible that the King should be sitting on the throne of justice with the books of life and death open before Him, and the Jewish people should sing hymns of praise?"

NOTES

1. Literally, "Koresh was a kosher king"; he was called Koresh because he was kosher (Rashi). Note: Koresh and kosher are made up of the same letters.

2. A non-Jew is forbidden to commit immorality, since it is one of the seven Noachide commandments (Rashi).

3. The *kor* and the *bat* are measures of volume.

4. Most commentators translate it, "The meadows are clothed with flocks."

5. *Lamo'ed* is usually translated as "at the appointed time." But *mo'ed* also means Yom Tov, hence the Gemara renders it "at the next Yom Tov."

6. A woman in her period of menstruation is forbidden to have physical contact with her husband.

7. *Bava Metzia* 16a.

8. *Niddah* 38b.

9. The *Omer* offering consisted of a measure of the first reaping of barley, which was offered on the sixteenth of Nisan, the second day of Pesach. Before the bringing of the *Omer* new cereals of that year were forbidden for use (Leviticus 23:10,11).

10. On Shavuot two loaves of wheat flour from the new crop were brought into the *Bet Hamikdash*. They were called *Bikkurim*, the first-harvest offering (Leviticus 23:17).

11. The ceremony of the Pouring of the Water on the Altar as described in *Sukkah* 48a is derived from allusions in Torah verses.

12. These are three sections that have been inserted in the *Shemoneh Esrei* of *Mussaf* on Rosh Hashanah. In the verses of *Malchuyot* we accept God as our sovereign King and ruler of the universe; in the verses of *Zichronot* we affirm our belief in Divine Providence, that all of man's deeds are remembered by God; and in the verses of *Shofarot* we relive the Giving of the Torah on Mount Sinai amidst powerful blasts of the shofar.

13. *Teruah* is the staccato sound of nine very short blasts. *Tekiah* is the straight unbroken sound.

14. This does not refer to a year when Rosh Hashanah falls on *Shabbat*, in which case it is forbidden to blow the shofar (*Tosafot*).

15. As in Jeremiah 29:11.

16. If his rabbi lives close by he must visit him every *Shabbat* and Rosh Chodesh; if he lives far away, he must go to visit him only on Yom Tov (R. Chananel).

17. On public fast days we read the chapter in the Torah containing the Thirteen Attributes of Mercy.

18. The best rams; compare Isaiah 60:7.

19. *Rosh Hashanah* 16a.

20. 1 Samuel 2:33.

21. Unlike the first Pesach offering, the second Pesach has no Yom Tov associated with it, and although no *chametz* may be eaten with the offering, those who bring a *Pesach Sheini* may eat *chametz* on that day.

22. The Babylonians breached the walls of Jerusalem in the fourth month [17 Tammuz]; they destroyed the Temple in the fifth month [9 Av]; Gedaliah was murdered in the seventh month [3 Tishri], and the siege began in the tenth month [10 Tevet]. Those days were established as fasts.

23. During the Bar Kochba revolt, after a heroic struggle, Beitar was conquered by the Romans on Tishah be'Av, in 133 C.E.

24. *Taanit* 29a.

25. We observe the fast commemorating the same event on the seventeenth of Tammuz.

26. Gedaliah was appointed governor of Judah by Nebuchadnezzar, the Babylonian king. He was slain by Yishmael, a member of the former royal family of Judah.

27. The captives who were driven into exile to Babylonia along with King Yechoniah of Judah, eleven years before the destruction of the Temple.

28. At the time of the Roman military campaign against the Parthians who had invaded Syria (163–164 C.E.).

29. A verdict may only be reached on the basis of the testimony of two witnesses, and after the perpetrator has been duly warned.

30. Based on, "For in Your sight a thousand years are like yesterday that has passed" (Psalms 90:4).

31. The six exiles are: 1. He has brought down; 2. lowered it; 3. lowered it; 4. to the ground; 5. brought it down; 6. to the dust (Rashi).

32. *Hallel* means praise; it is recited in the morning service on Rosh Chodesh, Chanukah, and Festivals.

✧ MEGILLAH ✧

THE FIVE HEBREW FINAL LETTERS

(2b) R. Yirmiyah—others say, R. Chiya b. Abba—said: The final forms of the letters *mem, nun, tzadi, pei,* and *kaf* were introduced by the prophets, [and before that, only the middle forms were used in all cases]. [The Gemara objects:] Can you really say this? Doesn't it say, "These are the commandments" (Leviticus 27:34), [meaning, "these and no others," and no innovations may be introduced]? Thus a prophet is not permitted to initiate anything new from now on. [So how can you say that the prophets introduced the final letters?] Besides, [there is another difficulty], for R. Chisda said: The letters *mem* and *samach* on the Tablets (3a) were held in place by a miracle. [It says that the writing was "engraved through the Tablets" (Exodus 32:16), which means that the writing penetrated through the stone; the stone was bored clean through.]

Now, since the *samach* and the final *mem* are completely closed, their inner parts were floating in air and needed a miracle to stay in place. This proves that the final *mem* was already known when the Torah was given, and was not initiated by the prophets.] [The Gemara answers:] Yes, both the middle and the final forms of the letters *mem, nun, tzadi, pei,* and *kaf* were known, but they did not know which form should be used in the middle of a word and which at the end of a word. The prophets then came and decreed that the open forms should be used in the middle of a word and the closed forms at the end of a word.

[The Gemara counters:] This is well and good, but still it says, "These are the commandments," which implies that a prophet is not permitted to initiate anything new from now on. [So how can you say that the prophets ordained where the open and closed forms should be placed?] [The Gemara answers:] Rather, they had forgotten [where each form had to be placed], and the prophets reestablished [the correct way of placing the letters. So they did not innovate anything].

WHO WROTE THE TARGUM?

R. Yirmiyah—others say, R. Chiyah b Abba—also said: The Targum[1] translation of the Torah was writ-ten by Onkelos the convert[2] under the guidance of R. Eliezer and R. Yehoshua. The Targum of the Prophets was written by Yonatan b. Uziel according to the teachings of Haggai, Zechariah, and Malachi. When [Yonatan b. Uziel authored his translation of the Prophets], Eretz Yisrael shook over an area of four hundred *parsah* by four hundred *parsah*,[3] and a heavenly voice came forth and said: Who is this person who has revealed My secrets to mankind? Yonatan b. Uziel stood up and said: I am the one who revealed Your secrets to mankind. You are fully aware that I have not done it for my own honor, and I have not done it for the honor of my father's house. Rather, I have done it for the sake of Your honor, to keep dissension from spreading in Israel. [He clarified obscure passages, leaving no doubt about their meaning, in order to prevent conflict among commentators who otherwise might offer different interpretations (Rashi).] And Yonatan b. Uziel also wanted to reveal the Targum of the Writings. But a heavenly voice came forth and said to him: You have done enough! [The Gemara asks:] Why [was he prevented from translating the Writings]? Because the Writings contain hints to the coming of *Mashiach* at the end of days, [in the Book of Daniel (Rashi)].

[The Gemara asks:] Was the Targum of the Torah actually written by Onkelos the convert? Didn't R. Ika b. Avin say in the name of R. Chananel who quoted Rav: What is the meaning of the verse, "They read in the scroll, in God's Torah, clearly, with application of wisdom, and they helped [the people] understand the reading" (Nehemiah 8:8)? [The phrase] "They read in the scroll, in God's Torah"—this refers to the [Hebrew] text of the *Chumash* [i.e., the five books of the Torah]; "clearly"—this refers to the Targum; "with application of wisdom"—this refers to the breaking of the text into sentences; "and they helped [the people] understand the reading"—this refers to the cantillation marks [which serve as punctuation marks, like commas, colons, and periods]. Some say that it refers to the tradition that tells us which vowels [go with the consonants of each word]. [The fact that the verse in Nehemiah refers to the Targum proves that it existed long before Onkelos. Obviously, he was not the au-

255

thor.] [The Gemara explains: The original Targum] was forgotten, and [Onkelos] revived it.

[We learned above that when Yonatan b. Uziel wrote the Targum of the Prophets, Eretz Yisrael shuddered. The Gemara now asks:] Why is it that when the Targum of the Torah was written, Eretz Yisrael did not shudder, and when the Targum of the Prophets was written Eretz Yisrael did shudder? [The Gemara answers:] The text of the Torah [has a plain meaning which] is understandable, [so that the Targum did not reveal any hidden secrets], but the text of the Prophets contains some subjects that are understandable but others that are veiled and obscure. [The land shuddered because the Targum revealed many subjects that should have remained hidden.] For example, it says, "On that day, the wailing in Jerusalem will be as great as the wailing of Hadadrimmon in the valley of Megiddon" (Zechariah 12:11). And R. Yosef commented: If not for the Targum of this verse, I would not know what it meant, [since there is no mention anywhere in *Tanach* of a mourning for a man named Hadadrimmon in the valley of Meggidon]. The Targum explains that on that day the mourning in Jerusalem will be as great as the mourning for Ahab, the son of Omri who was killed by Hadadrimmon ben Tavrimon in Ramot Gilead, and like the mourning for Josiah the son of Ammon who was killed by Pharaoh, the Lame, in the valley of Megiddo.[4]

DANIEL'S VISION

[The Gemara quotes another statement by R. Yirmiyah—some say, R. Chiya b. Abba.] It says, "I, Daniel, alone saw the vision; the people who were with me did not see the vision, but a great fear fell upon them, and they fled into hiding" (Daniel 10:7). Who were these men? R. Yirmiyah—some say, R. Chiya b. Abba—said: They were Chaggai, Zechariah, and Malachi. They were superior to Daniel [in one aspect], and he was superior to them [in another aspect]. They were superior to him, because they were prophets and he was not. [He was, in fact, a prophet, but, unlike Chaggai, Zechariah, and Malachi, he never was given a mission to bring a prophetic message to the people (Rashi).] And he was superior to them in that he saw the vision and they did not.

[The Gemara asks:] But if they did not see the vision, why were they frightened? [The Gemara answers:] Although they did not see the vision, their representative angel[5] did see it. Ravina said: From this we learn that if a person is terrified even though he has not seen anything frightening, his representative angel has seen something. What should he do? He should recite the *Shema*. And if he is standing in a filthy place [where it is forbidden to say the *Shema*]? He should move away four *amot* (cubits) from that place. And if he cannot move, he should say, "The goat in the slaughterhouse is fatter than me." [He

should tell his tormentor to go there and find a more suitable victim.]

THE READING OF
THE *MEGILLAH*
TAKES PRECEDENCE

We learned in a *Baraita*: The *kohanim* at their service [of offering the sacrifices in the *Bet Hamikdash*], and the Levites on their platform [where they chanted the psalm of the day during the offering of the daily continual sacrifice], and the Israelites at their station [attending the offering of the sacrifices as representatives of the entire nation]—all should interrupt their service to come and hear the reading of the *Megillah*. The scholars of the yeshivah of Rabbi found support in this *Baraita* for their ruling that you should interrupt your Torah study to come and listen to the reading of the *Megillah*. For they drew a [*kal vachomer*] logical inference from [the interruption of] the Temple service, namely: If the Temple service, which is stringent [is interrupted for the reading of the *Megillah*], surely Torah study [which is not as stringent as the offering of sacrifices, must be interrupted for the reading of the *Megillah*!].

JOSHUA'S ENCOUNTER
WITH AN ANGEL

[The Gemara questions this premise:] But is it true that the Temple service is more stringent than Torah study? Doesn't it say, "Once, when Joshua was near Jericho, he looked up and saw a man standing before him, drawn sword in hand. Joshua went up to him and asked him, 'Are you one of us or of our enemies?' He replied, 'No, I am a captain in God's army. Now I have come!' Joshua threw himself face down to the ground" (Joshua 5:11–14). [The Gemara digresses:] How could Joshua have done this, [prostrating himself in front of a stranger]? Didn't R. Yehoshua b. Levi say: It is forbidden to greet another person at night, for fear that he might be a demon, [and it surely is forbidden to prostrate oneself before a demon, since that would amount to idol worship]. [The Gemara answers:] The case [of Joshua] was different, for the stranger had told him, "I am a captain in God's army. Now I have come." [So Joshua knew that he was not a demon.] [The Gemara suggests:] Maybe [the stranger] was lying? [The Gemara answers:] We have a principle that demons do not mention God's Name in vain, [and he said, "God's army," so he could not have been a demon.]

[After this brief digression, the Gemara returns to the main theme.] The angel chided Joshua: This afternoon you failed to bring the daily afternoon sacrifice, and now [at night] you neglected the study of the Torah. Joshua asked the angel: For which of [these two offenses] have you come? He answered, "Now I have come." [Meaning, for the present offense, i.e., the neglect of Torah study. Which proves that the study of Torah is greater than the Temple service.] Immediately [after hearing the angel's reprimand], "Joshua lodged that night in the valley." R. Yochanan said: (3b) This teaches us that he spent the night exploring [the "valley," i.e.,] the profundities of *Halachah*.

And R. Shmuel b. Unya said: Torah study is more important than the offering of the daily sacrifices, for [the angel said], "Now I have come." [The angel admonished Joshua for the offense of neglecting Torah study rather than for failing to offer the sacrifice. This contradicts the scholars of the yeshivah of Rabbi who contend that sacrifices are more important than Torah study.]

The Gemara answers: There is no contradiction: In the case of Joshua the whole nation neglected to study Torah, whereas the ruling of the yeshivah of Rabbi refers to the study of an individual.

WOMEN REQUIRED TO HEAR
THE *MEGILLAH*

(4a) R. Yehoshua b. Levi said: Women are obligated in the reading of the *Megillah*, for they were included in that miracle. [They were saved by the miracle, and Esther played a leading role in it.]

R. Yehoshua b. Levi also said: A person is required to read the *Megillah* on the night of Purim, and repeat it on the day of Purim, for it says, "O my God, I call out by day, but You answer not; and by night, but there is no respite for me" (Psalms 22:3) [This psalm is a preindication of the miracle of Purim.] The students took this to mean that the *Megillah* should be read at night, and that the Mishnah [of tractate *Megillah*] should be studied by day. [They understood the term *lishnotah*, "to repeat it," to mean "to study its Mishnah."] R. Yirmiyah said to them: It has been explained to me by R. Chiya b. Abba that when R. Yehoshua b. Levi said *lishnotah* he meant that the *Megillah* should be repeated, as people say, "I will finish this section, and then I will repeat it."

The same ruling was stated by R. Chelbo who said it in the name of Ulla from Biri: A person is required to read the *Megillah* on the night of Purim and repeat it on the day of Purim, as it says, "So that my soul might sing to Your honor [by day], and not be stilled [by night], O Lord, my God, forever will I thank you" (Psalms 30:13). [This psalm refers to the miracle of Purim (Rashi).]

ROMAN THEATERS WILL
BECOME *YESHIVOT*

(6a) R. Abahu said: It says, "Ekron will be uprooted" (Zephania 2:4). This refers to Caesarea of the Romans, which is situated on sandy beaches. And Caesarea was a thorn in the side of Israel in the days of the Greeks.

And when the Hasmonean dynasty gained the upper hand and defeated the Greeks, they renamed it "the captured tower of Tzur."

R. Yose b. Chanina said: What is the meaning of the verse, "I will remove his blood from his mouth, and his abominations from between his teeth, and then he, too, will remain for our God" (Zechariah 9:7)? "I will remove his blood from his mouth"—this refers to their altar [on which they threw the blood of the sacrifices to their idols]. "And his abominations from between his teeth"—this refers to their House of Galya. "And then he too will remain for our God"—this refers to the synagogues and the houses of study in Edom [i.e., the Roman empire]. [The verse continues,] "He will be like a master in Judah, and Ekron will be like the Jebusite." This refers to the theaters and circuses in Edom where the leaders of Judah will publicly teach the Torah.

R. Yitzchak said: Leshem is Pamias [i.e., Banias, the source of the Jordan River (Rashi)]. Ekron shall be uprooted—this refers to Caesarea of the Romans, which was the capital of kings. Others say: Kings were trained there. Others say: Kings were appointed there.

Regarding Caesarea [probably meaning Rome] and Jerusalem: If someone tells you that both of these cities are destroyed, do not believe it. If he says that both are flourishing, do not believe it. If he says that Caesarea is destroyed and Jerusalem is flourishing or that Jerusalem is destroyed and Caesarea is flourishing, you may believe it. For it says, "I shall be filled with her that is laid waste" (Ezekiel 26:2).—If this one is filled [i.e., flourishing], then the other is destroyed; and if the other is filled, then this one is destroyed.

R. Nachman b. Yitzchak said this idea is implied in the verse, [God told Rebecca that the twins she is carrying—Jacob and Esau—will bring forth two nations—Israel and Edom (Rome). They cannot flourish simultaneously; one of them will always have the upper hand]. "One people shall be mightier than the other" (Genesis 25:23).

PREDICTIONS ABOUT
THE MURDEROUS CHARACTER
OF GERMANY

R. Yitzchak also said: What is the meaning of the verse, "Shall grace be granted to the wicked one who did not learn righteousness?" (Isaiah 26:10). Isaac said to God: Master of the universe, grant grace to Esau. God replied: He is a wicked man. Isaac then said to God: He has not learned righteousness. God answered: "In the land of the upright he will act with corruption" (ibid.), [meaning, he will destroy Jerusalem (Rashi)]. Isaac then said to God: If so, "Let him not see the majesty of God" (ibid.).

Rabbi Yitzchak said [on the same theme]: What is the meaning of the verse, "God, do not grant the desires of the wicked, do not let their plans succeed, that they might become exalted" (Psalms 140:9). Jacob said to the Holy One, blessed be He: Master of the universe: Do not grant the desires of Esau the wicked. "Do not let his plans succeed"—this refers to **(6b)** Germamya [Germany],[6] for if they would march forth they would destroy the whole world.[7]

And R. Chama b. Chanina said: There are three hundred crowned heads in Germamya of Edom, and there are three hundred and sixty-five nobles in Rome, and every day one group engages another in battle, and one of them is killed, and then they are busy appointing another king [to replace the one who was killed].

IF YOU WORK HARD
YOU WILL SUCCEED

R. Yitzchak said furthermore: If someone tells you, "I worked hard at studying Torah, but I did not understand it," don't believe him. And if someone tells you, "I gained understanding of the Torah without exerting myself," do not believe him either. But if he tells you, "I have toiled in the study of Torah, and I have succeeded," you may believe him. This is true regarding Torah study, but when it comes to business, success depends on the assistance from heaven. [A person's efforts alone do not guarantee success.] And even regarding Torah study, it is true only of gaining a clear understanding of the meaning, but in regard to remembering what you have learned, your success depends on help from heaven.

DON'T ANTAGONIZE
THE WICKED

Rabbi Yitzchak also said: If you see a wicked person on whom fortune is smiling, don't provoke him, for it says, "Do not contend with wicked men" (Psalms 37:1). And that's not all, but he may even be successful in his undertakings, for it says, "His ways are always successful" (ibid. 10:5). And not only that, but he will win his court case, for it says, "Your judgments are far beyond him" (ibid), [i.e., God's justice does not affect him]. And not only that, but he sees his enemies' downfall, for it says, "He snorts at all his foes" (ibid.).

[The Gemara asks:] Is that so, [that you should not provoke the wicked]? Didn't R. Yochanan say in the name of R. Shimon b. Yochai: It is permissible to antagonize the wicked in this world, for it says, "Those who forsake the Torah praise the wicked, but those who heed the Torah fight them" (Proverbs 28:4). And we learned in a *Baraita*: R. Dostai b. Matun said: It is permissible to provoke the wicked in this world. And if someone whispers to you and says: But it says, "Do not anger the wicked and do not be zealous against evildoers" (Psalms 37:1), you should know that only a person with a guilty conscience interprets the verse like that. Rather, [the correct meaning of the verse is,] "Do not compete

with the wicked," [meaning, do not try] to be like the wicked. "And do not be envious of evildoers."

THE GREEK TRANSLATION OF
THE BIBLE (SEPTUAGINT)

(9a) We learned in a *Baraita*: R. Yehudah said: Even when our Rabbis permitted the use of Greek, they only permitted its use for writing the Torah, and they did so only because of the incident with Ptolemy [of Egypt]. [The Gemara asks:] What happened there?

As it was taught in a *Baraita*: It happened that King Ptolemy gathered seventy-two sages and placed them in seventy-two houses without telling them why he had brought them together. He went to each one of them and told him, "Translate for me [into Greek] the Torah of your Master Moses." God then prompted each of them, and they all reached the same idea about how to translate a number of words in the Torah [whose literal translation might be misunderstood by King Ptolemy]. They wrote for him [in Greek], "God created in the beginning" (Genesis 1:1) [instead of "In the beginning created God," for Ptolemy might think that God was created by a being called "In the beginning."]

They also wrote, "I shall make man with an image and form" instead of "Let *us* make man in *our* image and *our* likeness" (Genesis 1:26), [which Ptolemy might interpret as proof that there is more than one God.] They also wrote, "He completed on the sixth day, and He rested on the seventh day" (Genesis 2:2), instead of "He completed on the seventh day," which Ptolemy might interpret to imply that God worked on the seventh day. They wrote, "He created him male and female" (ibid. 5:1), rather than "He created them," [which Ptolemy might have misunderstood to mean that two men were created, each with male and female features]. They also wrote, "Come, let Me descend and let Me confuse their speech," (ibid. 11:7), rather than, "Let us descend and let us confuse their speech," to avoid the mistaken notion of multiple deities.

They also wrote, "Sarah laughed among her relatives" (ibid. 18:12), rather than "Sarah laughed within herself," in order to avoid the charge of favoritism being leveled against God, since Abraham had also laughed (Genesis 17:17) but was not admonished, whereas Sarah was rebuked. They also wrote, "For in their fury they killed an ox and willfully they uprooted a trough," (ibid. 49:6), [rather than "they killed a man," which would have given rise to the charge that our ancestors were murderers]. They also wrote, "Moses took his wife and his sons and transported them on a carrier of men" (Exodus 4:20), [instead of "on a donkey," so that Ptolemy should not say that Moses did not even own a horse or a camel (Rashi)]. They also wrote, "And the length of time that the Israelites lived in Egypt and in other lands was four hundred and thirty years" (Exodus 12:40), [adding the phrase "and in other lands," since a chronology based on the years mentioned in the Torah would add up to only a 210-year sojourn in Egypt. The 430 years mentioned in the verse are calculated from the Covenant of the Parts (Genesis 15:13), when the bondage in Egypt was announced to Abraham].

They also wrote, "He sent the important men of Israel" (Exodus 24:5) [instead of "the young men of Israel," so that Ptolemy should not say that Moses did not send distinguished people to offer sacrifices and to welcome the *Shechinah* (Rashi)]. They also wrote, "And against the great men of the children of Israel He did not stretch out His hand [to harm them]" (ibid. 11). [To be consistent, they used the term *zaatutei* in both verses.] (9b) They also wrote, [Moses said,] "I have taken not one precious object of theirs" (Numbers 16:15). [They substituted *chemed*, "a precious object," for *chamor*, "a donkey," so that Ptolemy could not infer that Moses might not have taken a donkey, but he did take other things from them.] They also wrote ". . . the sun and the moon and the stars, which the Lord your God has apportioned to give light to all the peoples under the entire heaven" (Deuteronomy 4:19). [They inserted the words, "to give light," to avoid the mistaken notion that the nations of the world are allowed to worship the sun, the moon, and the stars.]

They also wrote, "And he will go and serve other gods, or prostrate himself to the sun or to the moon . . . that I have not commanded that they be served" (Deuteronomy 17:3). [They added the phrase "that they be served" so that Ptolemy should not mistakenly conclude that God did not command that the sun and the moon come into being, but that they arose through another power or by themselves.] And [in the list of non-kosher animals, instead of "the rabbit" (Leviticus 11:6)] they wrote, "the short-legged one." They did not write the literal translation "the rabbit," because the name of Ptolemy's wife was Rabbit. They changed it to "the short-legged one" so that Ptolemy should not say: The Jews are making fun of me, and therefore wrote my wife's name in the Torah [among the non-kosher animals].

WHY ONLY GREEK?

[Our Mishnah said:] R. Shimon b. Gamliel said: Even books of Scripture the Sages did not permit to be written in any foreign language other than Greek. R. Abahu said in the name of R. Yochanan: The *halachah* is like R. Shimon b. Gamliel. R. Yochanan said: What reason does R. Shimon b. Gamliel have [for permitting only Greek]? Because it says, "May God expand Japheth, and may he dwell in the tents of Shem" (Genesis 9:27) This means: The words [the language] of Japheth will be in the tents of Shem. [Greece (Yavan) is a descendant of Japhet, and the Jewish people are descendants of Shem. Thus the verse is interpreted to mean that Greek may be used in the tents of Shem, i.e., the Torah.]

[The Gemara asks:] Why don't you say that it refers to the languages of Gomer and Magog[8] [who are also descendants of Japhet (Genesis 10:2)]? [The Gemara answers:] R. Chiya b. Abba said: The reason [that R. Gamliel allowed only Greek] is because it says, "May God expand [*yaft*] Japheth," [and *yaft* alludes to] *yafyuto*, "the beauty of Japheth" [i.e., the Greek language, which is the most beautiful of the Japheth languages]; it shall be [used] in the tents of Shem.

VAYEHI INTRODUCES A PAINFUL STORY

"And it was in the days of Achashverosh" (Esther 1:1). R. Levi said, and some say it was R. Yonatan: The following teaching is a tradition handed down to us from the Men of the Great Assembly.[9] Wherever Scripture uses the term *vayehi*, "and it was, and it happened," it indicates that what follows is a distressing story. [For example:] "It was in the days of Achashverosh" (Esther 1:1)—there was Haman. "And it was in the days when the judges ruled" (Ruth 1:1)—there was famine. "It was when man began to increase on the earth" (Genesis 6:1) is followed by, "God saw that the wickedness of man was great" (ibid. 5). "And it was when they migrated from the east" (ibid. 11:2) is followed by, "Come, let us build a city, [and the Tower of Babel]" (ibid. 4). "It was in the days of Amraphel" (ibid. 14:1) is followed by, "They waged war" (ibid. 2). "And it was when Joshua was in Jericho" (Joshua 5:13) is followed by, "He looked up and saw a man standing before him, drawn sword in hand." [This was an angel who had come to admonish him.] "And God was with Joshua" (ibid. 6:27) is followed by, "And the children of Israel committed a transgression" (ibid. 6:27).

"And there was a man from Ramataim (1 Samuel 1:1) is followed by, "for he loved Hannah, but God had closed her womb" (ibid. 5). "And it was when Samuel grew old" (ibid. 8:1) is followed by, "and his sons did not follow in his ways" (ibid. 3). "And it was that David succeeded in all his undertakings [and God was with him]" (ibid. 18:14), which was the cause that "Saul kept a jealous eye on David" (ibid. 8). "And it was when the king [David] was settled in his house" (2 Samuel 7:1), followed by [God said to David,] "But you will not build the house, [i.e., the Temple]" (1 Kings 8:19).

[The Gemara raises an objection: How can you say that *vayehi*, "and it was," always introduces a distressing story?] Doesn't it say, "It was in the four hundred and eightieth year after the children of Israel's exodus from the land of Egypt" (I Kings 6:1). And it [also] says, [when Jacob met Rachel for the first time], "And it was when Jacob saw Rachel" (Genesis 29:10). And it also says, "And it was evening, and it was morning, one day" (ibid. 1:5); and there is the second day [of Creation], and the third day [of Creation], and there are many other passages [where the phrase "and it was" does not preface a distressful event].

R. Ashi clarified: [The rule is:] Whenever *vayehi*, "and it was," is used, it may preface either a happy or a painful event, but the expression "and it was in the days of" always introduces a distressing event. This expression occurs five times in Scripture, namely, "And it was in the days of Achashverosh" (Esther 1:1); "And it was in the days when the judges ruled" (Ruth 1:1); "And it was in the days of Amraphel" (Genesis 14:1); "And it was in the days of Ahaz" (Isaiah 7:1); "And it was in the days of Jehoiakim" (Jeremiah 1:3), [and all of these augur woeful times].

THE REWARD
FOR TAMAR'S MODESTY

[The Gemara now quotes another tradition related by R. Levi.] R. Levi said: It is a tradition that has been handed down to us from our ancestors that Amotz and Amatziah were brothers. [Amotz was Isaiah's father; Amatziah was a king of Judah (Rashi).] [The Gemara asks:] What [novel lesson] does this teach us? [The Gemara answers:] As R. Shmuel b. Nachmani said in the name of R. Yochanan: [It teaches us] that a bride who is modest in her father-in-law's house is rewarded by having kings and prophets among her descendants. From where do we derive this? From Tamar, for it says, "Judah, [Tamar's father-in-law,] saw her, and because she had covered her face, he assumed that she was a prostitute" (Genesis 38:15).

Now, because she had covered her face, that is why he assumed that she was a prostitute? Rather, what it means is, because she always covered her face in her father-in-law's [Judah's] house [out of modesty], and Judah, therefore, did not even know what she looked like, she was rewarded by having kings and prophets among her descendants. [Who were these kings and prophets?] The kings came from David, [who was one of Tamar's descendants];[10] and prophets came from Amotz, for R. Levi said: It is a tradition that has been handed down to us from our ancestors that Amotz and Amatziah were brothers. And it says, "The vision of Isaiah son of Amotz" (Isaiah 1:1). [Consequently, Isaiah was a nephew of King Amatziah, who, like all kings, was a descendant of Tamar. Tamar thus counted Isaiah the prophet among her descendants.]

THE ARK TOOK UP NO SPACE

R. Levi also said: It is a tradition that has been handed down to us from our ancestors: The Ark [miraculously] did not take up any room. We learned this also in the following *Baraita*: The Ark that Moses built had ten *amot* (cubits) of empty space on all sides. And it says, "Inside the Partition [that separated the Holy from the Holy of Holies there was the area of the Holy of Holies which was] twenty cubits in length and twenty cubits in width" (1 Kings 6:20). And it says that the wing of one cherub was ten cubits and the wing of the

other cherub was ten cubits. Where then was there room for the Ark itself [if the wings of the cherubs occupied the entire twenty cubits inside the Holy of Holies?] We must conclude, therefore, that the Ark stood by a miracle [without taking up any room].

DISCOURSES ABOUT
THE BOOK OF ESTHER

R. Yonatan opened his lecture [on the Book of Esther] by expounding the verse, "I will rise up against them—declares the Lord of Hosts—and will wipe out from Babylonia name and remnant, child and grandchild—declares God" (Isaiah 14:22). "Name" refers to [Babylonia's] script; "remnant" refers to her language, [meaning, the Babylonian language will become extinct]; "child" refers to their kingdom; "grandchild" refers to Vashti [who was Nebuchadnezzar's great-granddaughter].

R. Shmuel b. Nachmani opened his lecture [on the Book of Esther] by expounding the verse, "In the place of the thornbush, a cypress will rise, and instead of the nettle, a myrtle will rise. This will be a commemoration for God, an eternal sign never to cease" (Isaiah 55:13).

"In the place of the thornbush"—this alludes to the wicked Haman who declared himself an idol, for it says, "upon all the thorns and all the bushes" (ibid. 7:19). "A cypress will rise"—this refers to Mordechai who is called the finest of all spices, as it says, "You must take the finest spices, [*mor deror,*] [pure myrrh]." And the Targum translates *pure myrrh* as *meira dachya* [which sounds like Mordechai]. "Instead of the nettle [*sirpad*]"—this means, instead of the wicked Vashti, granddaughter of the wicked Nebuchadnezzar who burned the resting place of the House of God, [*sirpad* is seen as a contraction of *saraf refidah*, "he burned the resting place"], as it says, "His resting place was gold" (Song of Songs 3:10). "A myrtle will rise"—this refers to the righteous Esther who was called Hadassah, as it says, "He brought up Hadassah" (Esther 2:7). "This will be a commemoration for God"—this refers to the reading of the *Megillah*. "An eternal sign never to cease"—this refers to the days of Purim.

R. Yehoshua b. Levi opened his lecture [on the Book of Esther] by expounding the verse, "As happy as God was to be good to you and increase you, so will He be happy to exile you and destroy you" (Deuteronomy 28:63). [The Gemara asks:] Does God rejoice at the downfall of the wicked? Doesn't it say, "As they went out before the front-line troops, they said, 'Give thanks to God, for His mercy endures forever!'" (2 Chronicles 20:21)? On which R. Yochanan commented: Why is the phrase "for He is good" not mentioned in this praise? [This praise usually reads, "Give thanks to God, *for He is good*, for His mercy endures forever."[11] It can also be translated "for it is good," which suggests that God should be praised for the downfall of the wicked (Rashi). It is omitted] because the Holy One, blessed be He, does not rejoice at the downfall of the wicked.

[As proof of this R. Yochanan added:] What is the meaning of the verse, "One did not come near the other all through the night" (Exodus 14:20).[12] [When the Egyptians were drowning in the Red Sea,] the ministering angels wanted to sing a song of praise. God exclaimed: My creatures are drowning in the sea, and you want to sing a song of praise? [Proof that God does not rejoice at the downfall of the wicked. But what about the verse, "He will be happy to exile you and destroy you"?]

R. Elazar explained: God does not rejoice [at the downfall of the wicked], but he makes others rejoice. [When the Jews deserved to be destroyed in the days of Haman, their enemies were happy (Rashi).] The text itself supports this, for the verse states, "so He will make others rejoice [yasis]," and it does not say, "He Himself rejoices" [yasus]. This proves [what we said].

R. Abba b. Kahana opened his lecture on the Book of Esther by expounding the verse, "To the man who pleases Him He has given wisdom, knowledge and enjoyment" (Ecclesiastes 2:26)—This refers to the righteous Mordechai. [The verse continues,] "but to the sinner He has given the urge to gather and amass"—this refers to Haman. [The verse continues,] "that he [the sinner] may hand it over to one who is pleasing to God"—this refers to Mordechai and Esther, for it says, "And Esther put Mordechai in charge of Haman's property" (Esther 8:2).

Rabbah b. Ofran opened his lecture on the Book of Esther by expounding the verse, "And I will set My throne in Elam, and wipe out from there king and princes" (Jeremiah 49:38). "King"—this refers to Vashti; "and princes"—this refers to Haman and his ten sons.

R. Dimi b. Yitzchak opened his lecture on the Book of Esther by expounding the verse, (11a) "For we are slaves, though even in our bondage God has not forsaken us, but has disposed the kings of Persia favorably toward us" (Ezra 9:9). When did this take place? In the time of Haman.

R. Chanina b. Papa opened his lecture on the Book of Esther by expounding the verse, "You have let men ride over us; we have endured fire and water, and You have brought us through to prosperity" (Psalms 66:12). "We have endured fire"—in the days of the wicked Nebuchadnezzar; "and water"—in the days of Pharaoh. "And You have brought us through to prosperity"— in the days of Haman.

R. Yochanan opened his lecture by expounding the verse, "He was mindful of His steadfast love and faithfulness toward the House of Israel; all the ends of the world have seen the salvation of our God" (Psalms 98:3). When did all the ends of the world see the salvation of our God? In the days of Mordechai and Esther.

Resh Lakish opened his lecture by expounding the verse, "Like a roaring lion and a growling bear, so is a wicked ruler over a poor people" (Proverbs 28:15). "A roaring lion"—this refers to the wicked Nebuchadnezzar, about whom it says, "The lion has left his den" (Jeremiah 4:7), "And the a growling bear"—this refers to Achashverosh, for Daniel said in a prophecy concerning the kingdom of Persia, "Then behold! another beast, a second one, similar to a bear" (Daniel 7:5). And R. Yosef taught: This refers to the Persians who eat and drink like a bear and are fat like bears and are hairy like bears, and can never sit still like a bear. "The wicked ruler" refers to Haman; "over a poor people"—refers to the Jews who were poor [in their observance of the] mitzvot.

R. Elazar opened his lecture by expounding the verse, "Through laziness the ceiling [mekareh] sags, and through the idleness of the hands the house caves in" (Ecclesiastes 10:18). Because of the laziness of the Jews who did not engage in Torah study, the enemy of God [a euphemism for God Himself] became poor. [Because the Jews in the time of Haman neglected their Torah studies, it was as if God became weak and was unable to save them.] The word moch means "poor," as in the verse, "If [a person] is too poor [moch] to pay the endowment valuation" (Leviticus 27:8). The word mekoreh definitely means God, like "[God] Who sets the rafters [hamekareh] of His lofts in the water" (Psalms 104:3).

R. Nachman b. Yitzchak opened his lecture by expounding the verse, "A song of ascents: Had not God been with us . . . let Israel declare it now! Had not God been with us when a man assailed us" (Psalms 124:10). Note, it says "a man assailed us" and not "a king"; [this is a reference to Haman].

Rava opened his lecture by expounding the verse, "When the righteous become great the people rejoice, but when the wicked dominate, the people groan" (Proverbs 29:3). "When the righteous become great"— this refers to Mordechai and Esther. "The people rejoice," as in "The Jews enjoyed light, gladness, happiness, and honor" (Esther 8:16). "But when the wicked dominate, the people groan"—this refers to Haman, as it says, "The king and Haman sat down to feast, but the city of Shushan was dumbfounded" (ibid. 3:15). R. Mattenah began his lecture with the verse, "What nation is so great that they have a God close to it, as God our Lord is whenever we call Him?" (Deuteronomy 4:7). R. Ashi began his lecture with the verse, "Or has God proved Himself, to come and to take a nation for Himself from out of the midst of another nation" (ibid. 4:34).

EXPOUNDING *MEGILLAT* ESTHER

(11a) [The Gemara continues the exposition of *Megillat* Esther that began above (10b).] "It was [vayehi] in the days of Achashverosh" (Esther 1:1). Rav said: The word *vayehi* is a combination of *vay*, "woe," and *hi*, "mourning." It was [in the days of Haman that the agonizing prophecy came true] that stated, "You will [try to] sell yourselves to your enemies as slaves and maids, but no one will want to buy you" (Deuteronomy 28:68).

Shmuel opened his lecture on the Book of Esther by expounding the verse, "I will not grow so disgusted with them nor so tired of them that I would destroy them and break My covenant with them, for I am the Lord their God" (Leviticus 26:44). "I will not grow so disgusted with them"—this refers to the times of the Greeks; "nor so tired of them"—this refers to the times of Nebuchadnezzar; "that I would destroy them"—in the days of Haman; "and break My covenant with them"—during the period of the Persians; "for I am the Lord their God" during the times of Gog and Magog, [the climactic war that will introduce the End of Days and the Messianic era].

In a *Baraita* [we learned a different interpretation of this verse:] "I will not grow so disgusted with them" in the times of the Chaldeans, for I provided Daniel, Chananiah, Mishael, and Azariah [to lead] them. "Nor did I grow tired of them" in the times of Haman, for I provided Mordechai and Esther [to guide them]. "That I would destroy them," during the persecution of the Greeks, for I provided Shimon the Righteous, Mattityahu the High Priest, and the Hasmonean and his sons [to lead them]. "To break My covenant with them" in the times of the Persians,[13] for I provided for them the scholars of the yeshivah of Rabbi and the Sages of the various generations. "For I am the Lord their God" in time to come, when no nation or people will be able to dominate the Jews.

R. Levi opened his lecture on *Megillat* Esther with the verse, "If you do not drive out the land's inhabitants before you, those who remain shall be barbs in your eyes and thorns in your sides, causing you trouble in the land that you settle" (Numbers 33:55). [Alluding to the fact that King Saul, in violation of God's command, spared the life of Agag, King of Amalek (1 Samuel, Ch. 15). Israel was punished through Haman, a descendant of Agag, who indeed was a "thorn in their side, causing great trouble."]

R. Chiya opened his lecture on *Megillat* Esther expounding the verse [immediately following the above-mentioned verse], "I will then do to you what I originally planned to do to them" (Numbers 33:56).

ACHASHVEROSH

"It was in the days of Achashverosh" (Esther 1:1). R. Levi explained the name Achashverosh as a contraction of *achiv shel rosh*, "brother of the head," and, "who had the same character as the head." [The Gemara explains:] He was called "brother of the head" because he was the brother of the wicked Nebuchadnezzar who was called "the head," as it says, "You are the head of gold" (Daniel 2:38). Achashverosh had the same char-

acter as the head [Nebuchadnezzar] in the sense that [Nebuchadnezzar] murdered and [Achashverosh] tried to murder; [Nebuchadnezzar] destroyed the Temple, and [Achashverosh] tried to destroy the Temple. For it says, "During the reign of Achashverosh, at the beginning of his reign, they drew up a [false] accusation against the inhabitants of Judah and Jerusalem" (Ezra 4:6) [The slanderous accusation was meant to give Achashverosh a pretext to halt the construction of the second *Bet Hamikdash* that had been started under Cyrus (Rashi).]

Shmuel said: [The name Achashverosh indicates] that in his time the faces of the Jews became as black as the bottom of a pot. [The name Achashverosh is seen as a combination of *shachor*, "black," and *esh*, "fire."] R. Yochanan said: [He was called Achashverosh] because everyone who remembered him said, "O, my aching head!" [Achashverosh is seen as a contraction of *ach*, "woe," and *rosh*, "head."] R. Chanina said: [The name Achashverosh indicates] that everyone became poor in his time, [since the name is a blend of *ach*, "woe," and *rosh*, "poor"]. For it says, "And King Achashverosh levied taxes" (Esther 10:1).

[It says,] "That is [*hu*] the Achashverosh" (Esther 1:1). [This tells us that] Achashverosh was just as wicked at the beginning of his reign as at its end. [We find the same idiom used in the verse, "that is [*hu*] the Esau, the father of Edom" (Genesis 36:43) [which tells us] that Esau remained in his wickedness from beginning to end. [Another example is,] "He is [*hu*] King Ahaz" (2 Chronicles 28:22), which means that he remained wicked from beginning to end.

[Similarly,] "these are Dathan and Aviram" (Numbers 26:9), [teaches that Dathan and Aviram persisted in their wickedness from beginning to end]. [By the same token,] "Abram, [*hu*] that is Abraham" (1 Chronicles 1:27) tells us that Abraham remained a righteous man from beginning to end. [And the verse,] "They are [*hu*] Moses and Aaron" (Exodus 6:27) means that Moses and Aaron were righteous from the beginning of their lives until the end. [The verse,] "and David, he [*hu*] was the youngest" (1 Samuel 17:14) tells us that David kept his humility from beginning to end. Just as he humbled himself in his youth before someone who was greater than he in Torah scholarship, so too when he was king he humbled himself before someone who was greater than him in wisdom. [David learned only two things from his adviser Achitofel, yet he called him "his teacher, his guide, his intimate" (*Avot* 6:3).]

[The verse in Esther 1:1 continues,] "who ruled." Rav said: [This means that Achashverosh] ruled on his own. [He seized control of the Persian empire and was not of royal lineage (Rashi).] Some interpret this as a praise [of Achashverosh], for it implies that no one else was as suited for the throne as he was. Others interpret it as a slur, because it implies that he was not really fit to be king, but he paid a lot of money and thereby rose to power.

ACHASHVEROSH RULED THE WORLD

[It says in the *Megillah*,] "[Achashverosh ruled] from Hodu to Kush" (Esther 1:1). Rav and Shmuel [disagreed about the meaning of this phrase]. One said that Hodu is at one end of the world and Kush is at the other, [thus Achashverosh ruled the entire world]. The other said: Hodu and Cush were adjacent to each other [and the verse uses them as an example]. Just as he ruled over Hodu and Kush, so he ruled from one end of the world to the other.

A similar idiomatic form is used in the verse, "For he [King Solomon] ruled over the entire area beyond the [Euphrates] River, from Tifsach to Azzah" (1 Kings 5:4). Rav and Shmuel [disagreed about the meaning of this verse]. One said that Tifsach was at one end of the world and Azzah was at the other. The other said that Tifsach and Azzah were adjacent to each other, [and the verse uses them as an example to tell us that] just as he ruled over Tifsach and Azzah so he ruled over the entire world.

THREE WORLD RULERS

We learned in a *Baraita*: Three kings dominated the entire world, namely, Ahab, son of Omri, Nebuchadnezzar, and Achashverosh.[14] [Ahab was a world ruler] for it says, [Obadiah said to Elijah, "As the Lord your God lives, there is no nation or kingdom where my master [Ahab] has not sent to look for you; and when they said, 'He [Elijah] is not here,' he [Ahab] made that kingdom or that nation swear that they could not find you" (1 Kings 18:10). Now if Ahab did not rule over them, how could he have made them swear? [Proof that Ahab ruled every nation in the world.] Nebuchadnezzar [was a world ruler] for it says, "The nation or the kingdom that does not serve him—King Nebuchadnezzar of Babylonia—and does not put its neck under the yoke of the king of Babylonia, I will attend to that nation with the sword and with famine and with pestilence—declares God" (Jeremiah 27:8).

Achashverosh [was a world ruler] as we mentioned earlier, [that he ruled from one end of the world to the other].

OTHER MIGHTY RULERS

(11b) [The Gemara asks:] Are there no others [who ruled the entire world]? Surely there is Solomon? [Why doesn't the *Baraita* include him?] [The Gemara answers:] [Unlike those mentioned in the *Baraita*] Solomon did not stay in power until his death. [The Gemara demurs:] This explanation is acceptable according to the one who says that Solomon was a king and then became a commoner.[15] However, according to the one who says that he was a king, then became a commoner, and then regained his throne, what can you say? [Why wasn't he listed as a world ruler?] [The

Gemara answers:] Solomon was an exception in that he reigned over beings of the upper world [i.e., demons] as well as over the creatures of the lower world, for it says, "Solomon sat on the throne of God" (1 Chronicles 29:23).

[The Gemara asks:] But what about Sennacherib? [He, too, ruled over the entire world.] For it says, "Which among all the gods of those countries saved their countries from me?" (Isaiah 36:20). [Why is he not mentioned in the *Baraita*?] [The Gemara answers:] There was Jerusalem, which he did not conquer. [Thus he did not rule over the entire world.]

[[The Gemara asks:] And what about Darius? [He was a world ruler,] for it says, "King Darius wrote to all nations, peoples, and languages who dwell in the entire earth, 'May your peace be abundant!'" [An indication that all nations were his subjects. Why is he not included in the *Baraita*?] [The Gemara answers:] There were seven provinces over which he did not rule, for it says, "It pleased Darius to appoint over the kingdom one hundred and twenty satraps to be in charge of the whole kingdom" (ibid. 2), [but Achashverosh ruled over 127 provinces].

[The Gemara asks:] What about Cyrus? [He surely was a world leader,] for it says, "Thus said King Cyrus of Persia, 'The Lord God of Heaven has given me all the kingdoms of the earth'" (Ezra 1:2). [Why doesn't the *Baraita* mention him?] [The Gemara answers:] There he was merely boasting, [but he did not actually rule all nations of the world].

(12a) R. Nachman b. R. Chisda expounded the verse, "So says God to Cyrus, His anointed one, whose right hand I have held" (Isaiah 45:1). [The Gemara asks:] Was Cyrus [actually anointed with the oil used to anoint the Jewish kings, that he should be called] the "anointed one"? Rather, [the passage means that] God said to the Messiah: I complain to you about Cyrus. I said, "He will build My house and gather My exiles, [and he will personally take part in the building of the *Bet Hamikdash*]," but Cyrus only said, "Any one of you of all His people, the Lord his God be with him, and let him go up [and rebuild the *Bet Hamikdash*]" (2 Chronicles 36:23). [Cyrus is criticized for failing to order the Jews to return to Eretz Yisrael and personally to supervise the rebuilding of the Temple.]

THE ROYAL BANQUET

(12a) It says, "He displayed the vast riches of his kingdom and the splendid glory of his majesty" (Esther 1:4). R. Yose b. Chanina said: This shows that Achashverosh wore the garments of the *Kohen Gadol* [which had been looted from the Temple by Nebuchadnezzar's army (Rashi)]. For it says here, "the splendid glory [*tiferet*] of his majesty" and it says [in reference to the holy garments of the *Kohen Gadol*], "for glory and for splendor [*tiferet*]" (Exodus 28:2).

[It says further,] "for many days, a hundred and eighty days" (Esther 1:4), followed by, "And at the end of this period the king gave a banquet for seven days in the court of the king's palace for all the people who lived in the fortress of Shushan, high and low alike." Rav and Shmuel differed about this. One said [that Achashverosh's conduct indicates that] he was a clever king. The other said that he was a foolish king. [It should be noted that before giving the above-mentioned banquet for the people of Shushan, Achashverosh made a lavish feast for the nobles and officials of the provinces (v. 3).] The one who said that Achashverosh was a clever king holds that he acted wisely by first inviting those who lived far away, for he could win the loyalty of the inhabitants of his own city any time he wanted. The one who said Achashverosh was a foolish king holds that he should have invited the people of his city first, so that if the distant provinces rebelled against him, the residents of Shushan would have rallied to his support.

WHY DID THEY
DESERVE PUNISHMENT?

R. Shimon b. Gamliel's disciples asked him: Why did the enemies of Israel [a euphemism for "the Jewish people"] deserve extermination? He said to them: You tell me! They replied: Because they enjoyed the banquet of that wicked man [Achashverosh]. He said to them: If so, only the Jews of Shushan should have been ordered killed, [for only they attended the banquet], but the Jews in the rest of the realm should not have been ordered killed. The disciples then said to him: You tell us [why all the Jews deserved death]. He answered them: Because they bowed down to the [golden] idol [that Nebuchadnezzar had set up].[16] The disciples asked him: [If the Jews were guilty of idol worship, why were they saved]; does [God] play favorites? He replied: The Jews only pretended to worship the idol [out of fear of being thrown into the fiery furnace],[17] so, too, the Holy One, blessed be He, only pretended to exterminate the Jewish people [to cause them to repent]. And so it says, "For He does not willfully bring grief" (Lamentations 3:33).

THE WINE SERVED
AT THE BANQUET

It says, "The drinks were served in gold vessels—vessels of varied [shonim] design" (Esther 1:7). [The Gemara asks:] It should say meshunim [which is the proper term for "varied," rather than shonim, which means "repeat"]. Rava said: A heavenly voice went forth and said to them: Your predecessors [i.e., Belshazzar and his company] were destroyed [because they used] the vessels [of the Bet Hamikdash], and you [Achashverosh] are repeating [shonim] [their transgression] by also drinking from them.

[The verse continues,] "Royal wine was served in abundance [rav]." Rav said: [It is obvious that at a royal banquet wine flows freely. Why mention it? The word rav wants to tell us that] each person was served wine that was older than he was in years; [rav signifies not the quantity but the quality of the wine, that it was aged].

[The next verse reads,] "And the drinking was according to the law" (Esther 1:8). R. Chanan said in the name of R. Meir: According to the law of the Torah. Just as the law of the Torah requires that [at a meal] there should be more food than drink,[18] [for it says, "Eat bread with salt, drink water in small measure" (Avot 6:4)], (Etz Yosef)], so too at the banquet of that wicked man [Achashverosh] more food was served than drink.

[The verse continues:] "There was no coercion." R. Elazar said: This teaches us that each person was served the wine of his region.

[The verse continues:] "For the king had given orders to every palace steward to comply with each man's wishes." Rava said: To comply with the wishes of Mordechai and Haman. For Mordechai is described as man, as it says, "A Jewish man" (Esther 2:5). And Haman is also described as man, for it says, "A man, an adversary and an enemy!" (ibid. 7:6).

VASHTI'S HUMILIATION

[The text continues:] "In addition, Queen Vashti gave a banquet for women, in the royal palace of King Achashverosh" (Esther 1:9). [It should have said, "in the [privacy of the] house of the women" [rather than "in the royal palace"]. Rava said: Both of them [Achashverosh and Vashti] had immorality in mind; [for that reason she held the women's banquet in the king's palace]. As the popular saying goes, "He uses large pumpkins and his wife uses (12b) small pumpkins." [Whatever immorality a man commits, he can expect his wife to do the same (Rashi).]

[The next verse reads,] "On the seventh day, when the king was merry with wine" (Esther 1:10). [The Gemara asks:] And wasn't he merry with wine before the seventh day? [Why mention the seventh day?] Rava answers: The seventh day was Shabbat, [when the difference in conduct between Jews and idolators is most glaring]. For when Jews eat and drink they begin to discuss words of Torah and sing praises to God. But when idolators sit down to eat and drink they discuss vulgarities. And so it was at the banquet of the wicked [Achashverosh]. Some of the guests would say that the women of Media are the most beautiful, while others would argue that Persian women are the most beautiful.

So Achashverosh said to them: The vessel that I use [i.e., my wife Vashti] is neither Median nor Persian, but Chaldean, [yet she is the most beautiful woman]. Would you like to see her? "Yes," they replied, "but

MEGILLAH

only if she appears naked, [to prove that her beauty is not artificially enhanced by her royal finery and jewelry (*Maharsha*)]. [And why was Vashti disgraced in this manner, especially on *Shabbat*?] For [the heavenly tribunal] metes out punishment measure for measure; [the way that a person treats others he will be treated]. [Vashti's debasement] teaches us that that the wicked queen used to bring Jewish girls, strip them naked, and make them work on *Shabbat*. That's why it says, "Some time afterward, when the anger of King Achashverosh subsided, he remembered Vashti and what she had done, and what had been decreed against her" (Esther 2:1)—as she had treated [Jewish girls], so was she treated.

VASHTI DETHRONED

It says, "And Vashti refused" (Esther 1:12). Now, let's see: She was an indecent woman, as the master said above, "Both of them [Achashverosh and Vashti] had immorality in mind." So, why did she refuse to come [and display her beauty]? R. Yose b. Chanina said: This teaches us that she broke out in leprosy, [a skin disease; so she did not want to expose herself]. In a *Baraita* it was taught that the angel Gabriel came and made her a tail.

[The verse ends,] "The king was furious, and his rage burned in him" [The Gemara asks:] Why did he become so angry? Rava answered: Because Vashti sent him a message: You stable boy of my father [Belshazzar]! My father could drink as much as a thousand men could guzzle and not get intoxicated, whereas you [Achashverosh] get drunk after just a little wine! As soon as he heard this [insult] his rage burned in him.

"Then the king spoke to the sages who knew the times" (Esther 1:13). Who were these sages? The Rabbis. "Who know the times"—Who know how to intercalate years[19] and calculate the months in the Jewish calendar.

"What," he asked, "shall be done, according to the law, to Queen Vashti?" (ibid. 15). [Achashverosh] said to them, "Judge her for me!" [The Rabbis] said among themselves, "What shall we do? If we tell him to kill her, tomorrow he will become sober, and will hold us responsible for her death. Shall we tell him to let her go? We cannot do that either, for she showed contempt of the crown. So they [diplomatically] said to [Achashverosh:] From the day that the Temple was destroyed, and we were exiled from our land, the ability to give advice has been taken from us, and we no longer know how to judge capital cases. Go to Ammon and Moab who have remained settled in their places like wine that has settled on its lees, [therefore, their wise men have the calm composure to offer sage counsel].

The advice the Rabbis gave to Achashverosh was sound, for it says, "Moab has been secure from its youth on; he is settled on his lees, and has not been poured from vessel to vessel—he has never gone into exile. Therefore his fine flavor has remained, and his bouquet is unspoiled" (Jeremiah 48:11).

It says, "And Memuchan said" (Esther 1:16). We learned in a *Baraita*: Memuchan is Haman. And why was he called Memuchan? Because he was destined [*muchan*] for punishment [to be hanged]. R. Kahana said: From this we see that a vulgar fellow elbows his way to the front. [Memuchan is listed as the last of the seven officers that were consulted (v. 14), yet he was the first to offer advice.]

[Following Memuchan/Haman's advice, Achashverosh sent dispatches throughout his empire stating,] "Every man should wield authority in his own home" (Esther 1:22). Rava commented: If it had not been for these first dispatches, no Jew[20] would have survived [in the Persian empire]. [Reading the first dispatch] the people said: What a silly command is he sending us that every man should rule in his own home? Of course he should! Even a lowly weaver is the commander in his house! [Therefore, when his second dispatch arrived calling for the extermination of the Jews, they considered it as just another one of the king's senseless decrees and totally ignored it.]

ACHASHVEROSH THE FOOLISH KING

[Achashverosh was advised,] "Let Your Majesty appoint officers in every province of your realm to assemble all the beautiful young maidens. . . . The proposal pleased the king, and he acted upon it" (Esther 2:3,4). Rav said: What is the meaning of the verse, "Every clever person acts with knowledge, but a fool broadcasts his stupidity" (Proverbs 13:16)? "Every clever person acts with knowledge"—this applies to David, for it says, "[David's] servants said to him, "Let a young maiden be sought for my master, the king [to serve him]" (1 Kings 1:2). [Since David sought only one maiden,] whoever had a daughter brought her to him [thinking she might become the queen]. "But a fool broadcasts his stupidity"—this applies to Achashverosh, for it says, "Let Your Majesty appoint officers . . . to assemble all the maidens." Whoever had a daughter hid her from him, [because all would be violated, and only one would be chosen as a wife (Rashi)].

MORDECHAI'S ANCESTRY

"There was a Jewish man in Shushan the capital named Mordechai, son of Yair, son of Shimi, son of Kish, a Benjaminite" (2:5). [The Gemara asks:] What is the verse telling us [with this genealogy]? If the verse comes to trace Mordechai's lineage, it should trace it back all the way to Benjamin. What is so special about these three, [that they are mentioned and the others

265

not]? [The Gemara answers:] We learned in a *Baraita*: All the names [mentioned in the verse, Yair, Shimi, and Kish,] are nicknames of Mordechai himself. He is called "son of Yair," for he was a son who lit up [*he'ir*] the eyes of the Jews through his prayer. He is called "son of Shimi," for he was a son whose prayers God heard [*shama*]. And he is called "son of Kish," for he knocked [*hikish*] on the Gates of Mercy, and they were opened for him.

[The Gemara asks:] The verse calls him a "Yehudi" [Jew], which implies that he came from the tribe of Judah. But it also calls him a "Yemini" [Benjaminite], implying that he came from the tribe of Benjamin. [Well, what tribe did he belong to?] R. Nachman said: Mordechai was crowned with good names, [of his father's and mother's tribes]. Rabbah b. Bar Chanah said in the name of R. Yehoshua b. Levi: Mordechai's father was from the tribe of Benjamin, and his mother from the tribe of Judah. The Rabbis explained: The families [of Judah and Benjamin] used to argue with each other [about Mordechai's ancestry]. The family of Judah would say, "I am responsible for Mordechai's birth, for King David [a descendant of the tribe of Judah] did not have Shimi ben Gera executed, [Mordechai's ancestor who deserved the death penalty for cursing David.[21] David spared his life, thereby making it possible for Mordechai to be born].

The family of Benjamin would say, "He is actually descended from us." Rava said: The community of Israel used the two nicknames in a disparaging way, [each blaming the other for causing trouble for the Jewish people]. [They said,] "Look what a man from Judah has done to us, and how a Benjaminite paid us back." "What a man from Judah has done to us," (13a) for King David [who was from the tribe of Judah], failed to execute Shimi, who was the forebear of Mordechai who provoked Haman, [and caused all our troubles.] "How a Benjaminite paid us back," for Saul [who was from the tribe of Benjamin], spared the life of Agag who was the progenitor of Haman who oppressed the Jews.

WHO IS A JEW?

R. Yochanan said: As a matter of fact, Mordechai descended from the tribe of Benjamin. So why is he called a *Yehudi*, Jew, a man from the tribe of Judah? Because he repudiated idolatry [when he refused to bow down to Haman who considered himself a god]. For whoever renounces idolatry is called a Jew, *Yehudi* [a name whose letters contain the Four-Letter Name of God]. For it says, [concerning Chananiah, Mishael, and Azariah, who refused to bow down to Nebuchadnezzar's idol], "[Some Chaldeans maligned the Jews to Nebuchadnezzar saying,] 'There are certain Jewish men, *Yehuda'in* . . . your god they do not worship, and to the golden statue they do not prostrate themselves'" (Daniel 3:12).

This is in line with R. Shimon b. Pazi's statement, for R. Shimon b. Pazi said: When my father began to expound on Chronicles, he would say: All of your words, [meaning, many of the names mentioned in Chronicles] refer to a single person, and we know how to interpret them. [For example:] It says, "And his Jewish wife bore Yered, the father of Gedor, and Chever the father of Socho, and Yekusiel, the father of Zano'ach; and these are the sons of Bityah, the daughter of Pharaoh whom Mered married" (1 Chronicles 4:18). Why does the verse call her "Jewish" [when in fact she was Pharaoh's daughter, as the verse later states]? Because she repudiated idolatry. For it says, "Pharaoh's daughter went to bathe in the Nile" (Exodus 2:5), and R. Yochanan explained this to mean that she went to cleanse herself from the idolatry of her father's house. [She immersed herself in order to become a convert to Judaism (Rashi).]

[The Gemara later explains that Yered, Chever, and Yekusiel, the sons of Bityah, all refer to Moses. The Gemara now asks:] Did she then give birth to Moses? She [only] raised him! [The Gemara answers:] This comes to teach you that whoever raises an orphan boy or girl in his house, Scripture considers him as the orphan's father.

[R. Shimon b. Pazi explains how all the names mentioned in the verse actually refer to Moses:] Yered, this really is Moses. So why is he called Yered? Because in his days manna came down [*yarad*] [from heaven] for Israel. Why is he called *Gedor*? Because he fenced in [*gadar*] the breaches of Israel, [referring to the Torah, which was given through Moses]. He was called Chever, because he joined [*chibbeir*] Israel to their father in Heaven. He was called Socho, because he was like a protective covering [*sukkah*] for Israel. He was called Yekusiel, because in his days Israel hoped to God [*kivu laKeil*]. He was called Zano'ach because he caused Israel's sins to be discarded through his prayers; [*zano'ach* means to discard]. The verse mentions "father" three times, because he was a father [i.e., master] in Torah, a father [i.e., master] in wisdom, and a father [i.e., master] in prophecy.

[The verse (1 Chronicles 4:18) continues,] "These are the sons of Bityah, the daughter of Pharaoh whom Mered married." But was his name actually Mered? Wasn't his name Caleb?[22]—The Holy One, blessed be He, said: Let Caleb who rebelled [*marad*] against the advice of the spies come and marry Bityah, the daughter of Pharaoh, who rebelled against the idol worship of her father's house.

WHY WAS ESTHER CALLED HADASSAH?

[The Gemara continues expounding the *Megillah*, focusing on the verse that says that Mordechai "had been forced to leave Jerusalem" (Esther 2:6). Rava said: He went into exile voluntarily, [to join the Sanhedrin in order to remain in the company of the Torah scholars who were forced into exile (Rif)].

"He had raised Hadassah, she is [also known] as Esther" (Esther 2:7). [The Gemara remarks:] She is called Hadassah [Myrtle], and she is called Esther. [What was her real name?] [The Gemara answers:] We learned in a *Baraita*: R. Meir said: Her real name was Esther, and why does the verse call her Hadassah [Myrtle]? Because the righteous are called myrtles [*hadas*], and so it says, "He was standing among the myrtle bushes that were in a pool of water" (Zechariah 1:8). [In his vision Zechariah saw the *Shechinah* standing among the righteous.]

R. Yehudah says: Her real name was Hadassah, and why does the verse call her Esther? Because she concealed [*masteret*] the facts about herself, as it says, "But Esther did not reveal her kindred or her people" (Esther 2:20).

R. Nechemiah said: Her true name was Hadassah, and why does the verse call her Esther? Because the nations of the world called her by the name *Istahar*,[23] [meaning "moon," as if to say: She is as beautiful as the moon (Rashi)].

Ben Azzai said: Her name was actually Esther, and why does the verse call her Hadassah? Because she was of medium height—neither tall nor short, but medium like a myrtle [*hadas*].

R. Yehoshua b. Korcha said: Esther had an olive complexion [like a myrtle leaf, and was not very pretty], but she was blessed with great charm.

DID MORDECHAI MARRY ESTHER?

[The verse continues:] "For she had neither father nor mother, and when her father and mother died Mordechai adopted her as his daughter" (Esther 2:7). [The Gemara asks: Since we know that she was an orphan,] why does the verse reiterate, "And when her father and mother died"? R. Acha said: [This teaches us that Esther was an orphan from birth, for] when Esther's mother was pregnant her father died. When she gave birth to her, her mother died.

"Mordechai adopted her as his daughter"—A Tanna taught in the name of R. Meir: Do not read "as his daughter,[*bat*]" but rather "as his home, [*bayit*]" [i.e., as his wife. And proof that *bat*, "daughter," is used instead of *bayit*, "home, wife"] can be found in the verse, "But the poor man had only one little ewe lamb that he had bought. He raised it and it grew up together with him and his children: it used to share his morsel of bread, drink from his cup, and nestle in his bosom, it became like a daughter to him" (2 Samuel 12:3). [The Gemara analyzes:] Because it shared his morsel of bread it became like a daughter to him? Rather, [the verse does not mean "like a daughter" but] "like a home" [i.e., a wife].

It says, "along with the seven attendants from the king's palace" (Esther 2:9). Rava explained: This teaches us that she used them to count the days of the week. [To keep track of which day was *Shabbat* she used a different attendant each day of the week.]

[Hegai, the guardian of the women,] "treated Esther and her maids with special kindness" (ibid.) Rav said: He fed her Jewish [i.e., kosher] food. Shmuel said: He gave her fatty pork. [She ate it but was not punished because she was forced to eat it (Rashi).] R. Yochanan said: He fed her grains, [and grains are nutritious for the righteous] as it says [about Daniel and his three companions], "So the steward took away their food . . . and gave them grains" (Daniel 1:16).

"Esther won the admiration of all who saw her" (Ester 2:15). R. Elazar said: This teaches that whoever saw her took her for a member of his own nation.

MODESTY, A GENETICALLY TRANSMITTED TRAIT

R. Elazar said: What is the meaning of the verse, (13b) "He does not withdraw His eyes from the righteous" (Job 36:7)? [God does not ignore the deeds of the righteous. He rewards them measure for measure, even many generations later (Rashi), for example:] As a reward for the modesty that was displayed by Rachel she merited that the [modest] Saul[24] descended from her. And as a reward for Saul's modesty he merited that [the modest] Esther descended from him.[25] And what was the modesty of Rachel? For it says, "Jacob told Rachel that he was her father's brother" (Genesis 29:12). Was he then her father's brother? Was he not, in fact, the son of Rebeccah, her father's sister? Rather, [this is what happened:] He asked [Rachel], "Will you marry me?" She replied, "Yes, but you should know that my father is a swindler, and you will not be able to outfox him." Jacob replied, "If he is a swindler, I am his brother in swindling." [That is what Jacob meant when he said that he was "her father's brother."]

Rachel then asked him, "Is a righteous person permitted to engage in trickery?" He replied, "Yes, for it says, 'With a pure person you act in purity, and with a corrupt person you act perversely'" (2 Samuel 22:27). Jacob asked her, "What trick does he have up his sleeve?" She answered, "I have an older sister, [Leah], and my father will not let me get married before he marries her off." [He will surely try to switch her for me.] So Jacob gave Rachel signs [through which she could identify herself to him]. When the wedding night came, [and Rachel realized that her father was about to substitute Leah for her], she said to herself, "Now my sister will be humiliated, [for she will not have the signs Jacob gave me to identify myself]." Right away, Rachel gave to Leah the signs that Jacob had given her. That's why it says, "In the morning, [Jacob discovered that] it was Leah" (Genesis 29:25).

Are we to infer from this that until that morning she was not Leah? [Of course not!] Rather, because of the signs that Rachel had given to Leah, Jacob did not know [until the morning that it was Leah and not Rachel]. Therefore she was rewarded that the [modest] Saul descended from her. [The Gemara asks:] And what modesty did Saul display? For it says, [When young Saul approached Samuel for advice where he could find his father's lost donkeys, the prophet anointed him king. When his uncle asked him what Samuel had said, he replied,] "'He told us that the donkeys had been found,' but he did not tell him about the matter of the kingship of which Samuel had spoken" (1 Samuel 10:16). Therefore he was rewarded that [the modest] Esther descended from him. And what was Esther's modesty? For it says, "Esther told nothing of her kindred or her people" (Esther 2:20). [Esther modestly concealed the fact that she was of royal lineage (Etz Yosef).]

R. Elazar taught: When the Holy One, blessed be He, assigns greatness to a person, He assigns it to his descendants for all generations, for it says, "He will seat them there forever [with kings on thrones], and they will become exalted" (Job 36:7). But if he becomes haughty, the Holy One, blessed be He, lowers him, as it says [in the next verse], "And if they are bound in shackles, caught in the chains of poverty" (ibid. 8).

THE PLOT

[The Gemara continues to expound the *Megillah*:]

It says, "In those days, while Mordechai was sitting in the palace gate, Bigtan and Teresh became angry . . . and plotted to do away with King Achashverosh" (Esther 2:21). R. Chiya b. Abba taught in the name of R. Yochanan: The Holy One, blessed be He, caused a master to be angry with his servants to fulfill the will of a righteous man. And who [was this righteous man]? Joseph. As it says, [Referring to Joseph, the wine steward said,] "And there was a young Hebrew man with us" (Genesis 41:12).[26] And [where do we see that] God made servants become angry with their master? For it says, "Bigtan and Tersh became angry . . . and plotted to do away with King Achashverosh," in order to perform a miracle for a righteous man. And who [was that righteous man]? Mordechai, as it says, "Mordechai learned of it" (Esther 2:22).

R. Yochanan said: Bigtan and Tersh were two Tarsians, and [Mordechai overheard how] they were conversing in the Tarsian language, telling each other, "Ever since [Esther] came to the palace, we have not had a night's sleep. Come let's place poison into [the king's] cup of water, so that he will die." But they did not realize that Mordechai was a member of the Great Sanhedrin[27] and knew the seventy languages [of the world]. One said to the other, "But my watch is not the same as your watch?" The other answered, "I will take my watch and your watch" [and while I am filling in for you, you can put the poison into the cup]. And this is implied by the verse, "The matter was in-

vestigated, and it was found—that he was not on his watch," [that one of the two was missing, and this led to the discovery of the conspiracy].

GOD CREATES THE CURE
BEFORE THE AFFLICTION

[The Gemara continues to expound:] "After these events King Achashverosh promoted Haman" (Esther 3:1). [The Gemara asks:] After which events? Rava said: "After the Holy One, blessed be He, had created [through the plot of Bigtan and Teresh] a cure for the disaster [which was about to strike]."[28] For Resh Lakish said: "The Holy One, blessed be He, does not afflict Israel unless He has created a cure for them beforehand, as it says, 'When I heal Israel,' and only then, 'the sin of Ephraim will be revealed'" (Hosea 7:1). [Their sin will be revealed through the punishment God brings down on them (Rashi)]. But this is not true of the other nations—God smites them first, and only afterwards does He heal them. As it says, "God will first afflict and then heal the Egyptians" (Isaiah 19:22)—first affliction and then healing.

It says, "But he disdained to lay hands on Mordechai alone. Having been told who Mordechai's people were, Haman plotted to do away with all the Jews—Mordechai's people—throughout the kingdom of Achashverosh" (Esther 3:6). [The verse lists first Mordechai, then Mordechai's people, and then all the Jews.] Rava comments: At first [Haman intended to do away with Mordechai alone, then Mordechai's people, then he also wanted to exterminate the people of Mordechai. And who are considered the people of Mordechai? The Sages. In the end, [Haman decided] to destroy, kill and annihilate all the Jews.

HAMAN, THE MASTER
SLANDERER

It says, "He [Haman] cast *pur*, which means 'the lot'" (Esther 3:7). We learned in a *Baraita*: When the lot fell on the month of Adar, Haman was very happy. He said: The lot fell for me in the month in which Moses their teacher died. He did not realize that while Moses died on the seventh of Adar, he was also born on the seventh of Adar.

[Haman said to Achashverosh,] "There is a certain people" (ibid. 8). Rava said: "There is no one who could slander as expertly as Haman." For Haman said to Achashverosh, "Come let us start to fight against them." Replied Achashverosh, "I am afraid, for whoever starts a fight with them is punished by their God." Haman argued, "They have been lax in their observance of the *mitzvot*,"[29] [therefore, their God will not punish you]. Achashverosh answered him, "There are rabbis among them who will pray for mercy for them." Haman countered, "They are one people," [meaning, the rabbis are equally lax in the observance of *mitzvot*, so their prayers will not be answered.] [Haman continued,] "Perhaps you will fear that [by exterminating them] I will depopulate certain regions of your empire? [Don't worry about that, for] they are scattered and dispersed among the nations." [Haman continued,] "Should you say that they are productive, [and their destruction will cause a loss of income for your treasury? On the contrary], they are separate [*meforad*], like a *pereidah*, "a mule" which does not have offspring. And if you think that there is one small province that belongs to them, I am telling you, 'they are in all the provinces of your realm'" (ibid.).

[Haman continued,] "And their laws are different from those of all the other nations" (ibid.). They do not eat our food, they do not drink with us, they do not marry our daughters, neither do they give their daughters to us in marriage. [Haman continued,] "And they do not keep the king's laws,"—they avoid the king's service all year with the excuse, "today is the Sabbath or today is Passover," and they pay no taxes to the king.

"And it is not in Your Majesty's interest to tolerate them" (ibid.). For they eat and drink and mock the king. For even if a fly falls in a glass of wine of one of them, he removes the fly and drinks the wine, but if my lord, the king, were to touch this person's glass, he would throw it to the ground and not drink from it.

HAMAN AND ACHASHVEROSH, PARTNERS IN CRIME

[Haman continued,] "If it please Your Majesty, let an edict be drawn for their destruction, and I will pay ten thousand talents of silver" (ibid. 3:9). Resh Lakish expounded: It was well known beforehand to He Who spoke and the world came into being that Haman would one day pay *shekalim* for the purpose of destroying the Jews. God therefore ordained that the Jews should give their *shekalim* before Haman gave his. And so we have learned in the Mishnah[30]: On the first of Adar [the Sanhedrin] makes announcements regarding the payment of the *shekalim*[31] and the prohibition against having different species of seeds in your field.[32]

It says, "The king said to Haman, 'The money and the people are yours to do with as you see fit'" (ibid. 3:11). R. Abba b. Kahana said: (**14a**) "To what can the dialogue between Achashverosh and Haman be compared?" [We can gather from it that Achashverosh was as eager to kill the Jews as Haman was.] We can compare it to two people, one of whom had a pile of dirt in his field, and the other had a ditch in his field. The owner of the pile of dirt said to himself, "I wish I could buy that ditch, [so I can dump the pile of dirt into the ditch and clear my field]." The owner of the ditch said to himself, "I wish I could buy that pile of dirt [so I can fill my ditch]." One day they met. The owner of the ditch told the owner of the dirt, "Sell me your pile of dirt." The owner of the dirt replied, "Take it for free!" [Both Haman and Achashverosh wanted to do away with the Jews. And when Haman offered money for the right to exterminate them, Achashverosh was happy to agree and turned down the money.]

It says, "So the king removed his signet ring from his hand" (ibid. 3:10). R. Abba b. Kahana said: The removal of the signet ring [which symbolized that Haman had full authority to act] had a greater effect on the Jews than [the admonitions of] the forty-eight prophets and the seven prophetesses who prophesied to Israel. For they were all unable to bring the Jews back to the ways of righteousness, whereas the removal of the signet ring brought them back to the ways of righteousness.

WHY DON'T WE SAY *HALLEL* ON PURIM?

The rabbis taught: Forty-eight prophets and seven prophetesses prophesied to Israel, and they did not take away from or add to what is written in the Torah, except for enacting the mitzvah of reading the Megillah. [The Gemara asks:] On what scriptural basis [did they ordain the reading of the Megillah]? R. Chiya b. Avin said in the name of R. Yehoshua b. Korcha: [They drew a logical inference:] Now, if the Jews who were delivered from bondage in Egypt to freedom sang the Song of the Sea [in praise of God], then surely [God should be praised by reading the Megillah] when they were saved from death [at the hands of Achashverosh and Haman]. [The Gemara asks:] If so, we should also say *Hallel* on Purim. [The Gemara answers: We don't say *Hallel* on Purim] because we do not recite *Hallel* for a miracle that took place outside Eretz Yisrael. [The Gemara rebuts:] So how can we sing songs of praise [*Hallel* on Pesach] for the Exodus which was also a miracle that occurred outside of Eretz Yisrael? [The Gemara answers:] As we learned in a *Baraita*: Before the children of Israel entered Eretz Yisrael, songs of praise could be sung in all countries. However, once they entered Eretz Yisrael, all the other countries were no longer fit for singing songs of praise. R. Nachman [gave a different answer]: The reading [of the Megillah] is equivalent to reciting *Hallel*. Rava said: Granted, that when commemorating the Exodus we should say *Hallel*, which includes the verse, "Give praise, you servants of God,"[33] for [after the Exodus] they were no longer slaves of Pharaoh. But here, [regarding the miracle of Purim], could we say, "Give praise, you servants of God" [which implies that after the fall of Haman we were servants of God alone] and no longer the servants of Achashverosh? But we were still servants of Achashverosh; [we were only saved from death (Rashi)].

MORE THAN FORTY-EIGHT PROPHETS

Were there no more than forty-eight prophets? Doesn't it say, [about Elkanah,] "There was a man from Ramatayim Tzofim" (1 Samuel 1:1)? [which is interpreted to mean that Elkanah was] one of two hundred prophets[34] [tzofim] who prophesied in Israel." [The Gemara answers:] Yes, there were many [more] prophets who prophesied, as we learned in the *Baraita*: Many prophets prophesied for Israel—twice as many as the number of people who left Egypt.[35] However, only those prohecies that contained a message for future generations was written down, whereas those that did not hold such a message were not written down.

[The Gemara now focuses on the verse 1 Samuel 1:1 cited above:] R. Shmuel b. Nachmani said: Ramatayim Tzofim means: A man who came from two heights that faced each other. R. Chanan said: It means: A man who descended from people who stood at the heights of the world. And who are they? The sons of Korach, as it says, "And the sons of Korach did not die" (Numbers 26:11). It was taught in the name of our teacher, Rabbi: A high place was set aside for them in Gehinnom, and they stood on it.[36]

THE SEVEN PROPHETESSES

Who were the seven prophetesses? Sarah, Miriam, Deborah, Hannah, Abigail, Chuldah, and Esther. How do we know that Sarah was a prophetess? For it says, "[Haran] who was the father of Milkah and Yiskah" (Genesis 11:29). R. Yitzchak said: "Yiskah is Sarah, and why is she called Yiskah?" For she saw [from *sachah*, to look, to gaze] with holy inspiration, as it says, "God said to Abraham, 'All that Sarah tells you, heed her voice'" (ibid. 21:12). Another explanation is: She is called Yiskah, because everyone gazed [*sochin*] at her beauty.

How do we know that Miriam was a prophetess? Because it says, "Miriam the prophetess, Aaron's sister took . . . " (Exodus 15:20). [Why is she referred to as] Aaron's sister and not as Moses' sister? R. Nachman said in the name of Rav: Because she prophesied when she was [just] Aaron's sister, [before Moses was born]. She said: "In the future, my mother will give birth to a son who will save Israel." When Moses was born, the whole house was filled with light. [Seeing this] her father rose and kissed her on the head and said to her, "My daughter, your prophecy has been fulfilled." But when they placed Moses into the river,[37] her father rose and tapped her on the head and said, "My daughter, where is your prophecy?" Therefore, it says, "[The child's] sister stood herself at a distance to know what would happen to him" (Exodus 2:4), which is interpreted to mean: to know what would be the outcome of her prophecy.

How do we know that Deborah was a prophetess? Because it says, "Deborah, a prophetess, the wife of Lapidot" (Judges 4:4); [the word *lapidot* means "flames."] [The Gemara asks:] What is the meaning of "a woman of flames"? This teaches us that she made wicks for the Tabernacle [in Shiloh].[38]

"She [Deborah] sat under a palm tree" (Judges 4:5). Why under a palm tree? R. Shimon b. Avshalom said: [She sat and judged under a palm tree] because she did not want to violate the prohibition against *yichud*, a married woman being alone in a room with a man. Another reason [why she sat under a palm tree was], because just as a palm tree has only one heart, [its trunk grows straight up without spreading into branches], so too, the Jewish people in that generation had only one heart for their Father in heaven.

How do we know that Hannah was a prophetess? For it says, "And Hannah prayed, 'My heart rejoices in God, my horn is exalted through God'" (1 Samuel 2:1). [She said,] "My horn is exalted" and not, "My flask is exalted," implying that the reign of the kingdom of David and Solomon who were anointed with a horn[39] would last a long time. However, the reigns of Saul and Yehu who were anointed with a flask[40] did not endure.

[Hannah prayed,] "There is none as holy as God, truly, there is none beside you; there is no Rock like our God" (1 Samuel 2:2). R. Yehudah b. Menashya said: Do not read: *biltecha*, "there is none beside You," but rather, *levalotecha*, "to survive You." Come and see how much the nature of man contrasts with the nature of God. The nature of man is that his works outlast him, but God outlasts His works.

"And there is no Rock like our God." Do not read, "there is no *tzur* [Rock], but rather, "there is no *tzayar*, (artist) like our God." In the ways of the world, when a man draws a figure on a wall he is unable to endow it with breath, soul, internal organs and intestines. But God creates a form inside another form [a child in the mother's womb] and endows it with breath, soul, internal organs and intestines.

How do we know that Abigail was a prophetess? For it says, (14b) [Abigail blessed David, saying,] "May my lord's soul be bound up in the bond of life" (1 Samuel 25:29). As Abigail left David she said to him, "And when God will have done good to my lord . . . then remember your maid" (ibid. 30), [she discreetly hinted, that if her husband Nabal died, David should marry her (Rashi)]. R. Nachman said: This bears out the popular saying: "While a woman talks she spins." [Abigail foretold that after Nabal's death she would become David's wife; an indication of her prophetic vision.] Others say, [R. Nachman meant the adage:] The goose stoops as it goes, but its eyes peer far ahead.

How do we know that Chulda was a prophetess? For it says, [King Joshiah sent a delegation to inquire of God regarding the Torah scroll that had been found.] "So Chilkiyahu the priest, and Achikam, Achbor, Shafan, and Asayah went to Chuldah the prophetess" (2 Kings 22:14). [The Gemara asks:] But if Jeremiah was still alive, how could she prophesy? [It would be an insult to the towering prophet Jeremiah for a minor prophetess to prophesy.] Jeremiah began to prophesy in the thirteenth year of King

Joshiah, and the Torah scroll was found in the eighteenth year of Joshiah's reign (Rashi)].[41] [The Gemara answers:] The yeshivah of Rav said in the name of Rav: Chuldah was a relative of Jeremiah, and therefore he did not mind that she prophesied.

[The Gemara asks:] But Joshiah himself, how could he ignore Jeremiah and send his representatives to Chuldah instead? [The Gemara answers:] In the yeshivah of R. Shila they said: "He sent his emissaries to Chuldah because women are more compassionate."

JEREMIAH BROUGHT BACK THE TEN TRIBES

R. Yochanan said: [Joshiah sent the delegation to Chuldah because] Jeremiah was not there at the time, for he went to bring back the ten tribes [that had been led into exile by Sennacherib]. And how do we know that they returned? Because it says, "For the seller shall not return to the sale" (Ezekiel 7:13), [meaning, if someone sold property, it would not revert back to him in the Yovel year for the observance of Yovel will be discontinued].[42] Is it possible that after the observance of Yovel had already come to an end, the prophet Ezekiel would prophesy that it will be discontinued? Rather, this teaches us that Jeremiah brought back [the ten tribes], and Joshiah, son of Amon ruled over them.

[How do we know that Joshiah ruled over them?] For it says, "[Joshiah] said, 'What is this tombstone that I see?' The people of the city said to him, 'It is the grave of the man of God who came from Judah and prophesied about these things that you have done upon the altar of Beth-el'" (2 Kings 23:17).[43] What was Joshiah [who was the king of Judah] doing at the altar in Beth-el [which was in the kingdom of Israel, the country of the ten tribes]? This teaches that Jeremiah brought back the ten tribes and Joshiah ruled over them. R. Nachman said: [Proof that Jeremiah brought them back can be drawn] from here: "Also Judah, there is triumph in store for you, when I return the captivity of My people" (Hosea 6:10).

[How do we know that Esther was a prophetess?] For it says, "And it was on the third day and she [Esther] clothed herself in royalty" (Esther 5:1). [The Gemara asks:] It should have said "in royal apparel"? [The Gemara answers:] The verse hints that a spirit of holiness clothed her. For it says here: "and she clothed," and elsewhere it says, "And the spirit clothed Amasai" (1 Chronicles 12:19).

TEACHINGS ABOUT THE SEVEN PROPHETESSES

R. Nachman said: Eminence is unbecoming to women, [for it tends to make them haughty]. For there were two prophetesses who were famous and their names had distasteful meanings. One was named Deborah [Hebrew for bee], and the other was named Chuldah [which means weasel in Hebrew]. Regarding Deborah it says, "She sent and called Barak" (Judges 4:6), but she did not go to him. Regarding Chuldah it says, "Tell the man who sent you to me" (2 Kings 22:15), and she did not say, "Tell the king." [In both cases eminence gave rise to arrogance.]

R. Nachman also said: Chuldah was a descendant of Joshua. [We derive this from the following verses:] It says regarding Chuldah, "[Chuldah the prophetess, the wife of Shalum son of Tikvah] son of Charchas" (2 Kings 22:14), and elsewhere, [concerning Joshua] it says, "They buried him on the boundary of his portion, in Timnat Cheres" (Judges 2:9). [Cheres is the same as Charchas.]

WHO WAS THE PROPHET MALACHI?

(15a) Rav[44] said: [The prophet] Malachi is really Mordechai; and why was Mordechai called Malachi? Because he was second to King [Achashverosh. He was like a malach, an angel or messenger, meaning a person of great importance (Maharsha)].

We learned in a Baraita: R. Yehoshua b. Korcha said: Malachi is really Ezra, but the Sages say: Malachi was his real name. It is likely that the one who said that Malachi is Ezra is correct, for in the prophecy of Malachi it says, "Judah has broken faith, abhorrent things have been done in Israel and in Jerusalem. For Judah has profaned the holy [nation] of God, which he loved, and has married the daughter of a foreign god" (Malachi 2:11). Now who was it that made Jewish husbands separate from their gentile wives? It was Ezra, as it says, "And Shechanyah, son of Yechiel, of the family of Eilam, spoke up and exclaimed to Ezra, 'We have trespassed against our God by bringing into our homes alien women'" (Ezra 10:2). [Since both Malachi and Ezra decry intermarriage with gentile women, there is reason to believe that they are one and the same person.]

The Sages taught: There were four exceptionally beautiful women in the world: Sarah, Rachav, Abigail and Esther. According to the one who said that Esther had an olive complexion,[45] omit Esther from the list and insert Vashti.

CONTINUATION OF EXPOSITION OF THE MEGILLAH

"When Mordechai learned all that had happened, Mordechai tore his clothes . . . and he cried a loud and bitter cry" (Esther 4:1). What did Mordechai say [when he cried out]? Rav said: [Mordechai cried,] "Haman is more arrogant than Achashverosh!" Shmuel said: [Mordechai cried,] "The Upper King [i.e., God] has overcome the Lower King [i.e., Achashverosh]." [A euphemism, meaning, "Achashverosh has thwarted the will of God."]

[It says in the Megillah,] "When Esther's maidservants and chamberlains came and informed her, the queen was greatly agitated" (Esther 4:4). What is meant by "greatly agitated"? Rav said: "She began to menstruate." R. Yirmiyah said: "Her bowels loosened."

"Thereupon Esther summoned Hatach" (ibid. 5). Rav said: "Hatach was, in fact, Daniel." And why was Daniel called Hatach? Because they cut him down from his greatness; [Hatach is seen as related to *chatach*, (to cut)]. Shmuel said: [Daniel was called Hatach,] "Because all affairs of the kingdom were decided by him." [*chatach* also means "to decide."]

[Esther sent Hatach to Mordechai,] "to find out the why and wherefore of it all" (ibid.); [literally, "what this [*zeh*] and why this [*zeh*]."] R.Yitzchak said: She asked him: Perhaps the Jews have transgressed the Five Books of the Torah about which it says, "they [the Ten commandments] were written on this [*zeh*] side and on that [*zeh*] side" (Exodus 32:15). [With the double use of *zeh*, "this," Esther alluded to the Ten Commandments.]

"And they told Mordechai what Esther had said" (Esther 4:12). But Hatach himself did not go to Mordechai. It does not say, "And he [i.e., Hatach] told Mordechai," but "they told." [Hatach did not himself want to report the bad news that Esther refused to carry out Mordechai's request.] This teaches us that you should not personally report bad news.

It says, "And Mordechai passed [*vaya'avor*] and did everything as Esther had commanded" (ibid. 4:17). [*Vaya'avor* also means, "he transgressed."] Rav said: He transgressed by fasting on the first day of Pesach. [One day of the three-day fast that Esther had declared fell on the first day of Pesach]. Shmuel said: "*Vaya'avor*, (he passed) signifies that Mordechai crossed the river [that divided the city in order to assemble the people]."

TEACHINGS BY R. ELAZAR IN THE NAME OF R. CHANINA

R. Elazar said in the name of R. Chanina: "The blessing of a ordinary person should never be taken lightly by you, for we know of two great men in their generation who were blessed by two ordinary people, and in each case the blessing was fulfilled. They were David and Daniel. David was blessed by Aravnah, as it says, 'Aravnah said to the king [David], "May God, your Lord, respond to you with favor"' (2 Samuel 24:23). Daniel was blessed by Darius, who said [when Daniel was thrown into the lion's den], "May your God, Whom you serve continually, save you" (Daniel 6:17).

And R. Elazar [also] said in the name of R. Chanina: "A curse of an ordinary person should not be taken lightly, for Avimelech cursed Sarah, 'This will serve you as a covering of the eyes'" (Genesis 20:16), and it was fulfilled in her descendants, as it says, "When Isaac was old and his eyes were too dim to see" (ibid. 27:1).

And R. Elazar [also] said in the name of R.Chanina: "Come and see, how greatly the ways of man differ from

the way of God. The way of man is first to place a pot on the fire and then to pour water into it. But God first gives water and then prepares the pot, in fulfillment of the verse, "At the sound when He gives a multitude of waters in the heavens" (Jeremiah 10:13). [God first creates the vapors that rise from the ground, and only then forms the clouds that store the rains.]

Another teaching from R. Elazar in the name of R. Chanina: When a righteous person dies, he only is lost to his generation, [for his soul lives on]. You can compare it to a person who lost a precious pearl. Wherever it is, it is still a pearl, [it still exists]. It is lost only to its owner.

Another teaching from R. Elazar in the name of R. Chanina: Whoever quotes a saying and names the one who said it brings redemption to the world, as it says, "Esther told the king in the name of Mordechai . . ." (Esther 2:22) [that he had discovered the plot against the king's life. This set into motion the series of events that culminated in the Haman's downfall and the redemption of Purim.]

Another teaching from R. Elazar in the name of R. Chanina: What is the meaning of the phrase, [Haman said,] "But none of this is of any value to me" (Esther 5:13)? This teaches us that all the treasures of the wicked Haman were engraved on his heart,[46] and as soon as he saw Mordechai sitting at the palace gate, he said, "But none of this is of any value to me." [The Gemara asks:] Because he saw Mordechai sitting at the palace gate he said, "But none of this is of any value to me"? [The Gemara answers:] Yes, as R. Chisda explained: For Mordechai came from a rich background, and Haman came from a poor background. [Although Haman now was fabulously wealthy, previously he had sold himself as a slave to Mordechai.] (15b) R. Papa said: They called Haman, "a slave who sold himself for loaves of bread."

THE REWARD OF THE RIGHTEOUS

R. Elazar further said in the name of R. Chanina: In time to come, the Holy One, blessed be He, will be a crown on the head of every righteous person. For it says, "In that day, the Lord of Hosts shall become a crown of beauty and a diadem of glory to the remnant of His people" (Isaiah 28:5). What is meant by the phrase, "a crown of beauty [*tzvi*] and a diadem [*tzefirat*] of glory"? It teaches that this is the reward for those who do His will [*tzivyono*], [*tzivyono* similar to *tzvi*], and for those who await [*metzapeh*] His glory; [*metzapheh* similar to *tzefirat*]. You might think that this applies to anyone [who does God's will]? Therefore the verse tells us, "to the remnant of His people." Which is to say: This reward is only for a person who makes himself like a remnant [i.e., who is humble]. [The next verse continues,] "and a spirit of judgment"—this refers to a person who judges his evil inclination [and forces it to repent (Rashi)]; "for him who sits in judgment"—this refers to a person who judges truthfully; "and of valor"—this refers to a person who overcomes his evil tendency; "for those who repel attacks"—this refers to the scholars who debate issues of the Torah; "at the gate"—this refers to the Torah scholars who come early in the morning and stay late into the evening in the synagogues and study halls.

[The Gemara expounds the next verse:]

The Attribute of Justice said to the Holy One, blessed be He: Master of the universe! Why are the Jews different from the nations of the world; [why are only the Jews rewarded like this]? The Holy One, blessed be He, replied: Israel engages in Torah study, whereas the nations of the world do not. Said the Attribute of Justice to God: [Accordingly, regarding the wicked in Israel who are sent to Gehinnom it says,] "But these are also muddled with wine and dazed by liquor . . . they stumble [paku] in judgment [peliliah]" (ibid. 7). The word paku, "stumbled" certainly is a reference to Gehinnom, as it says, [Abigail begged David not to kill Nabal, saying], "let this not be a cause for stumbling [lefukah] to you" (1 Samuel 25:31). And the word peliliah, certainly refers to judges, for it says, "And he shall pay the amount determined by the judges [biflilim]" (Exodus 21:22)

CONTINUING THE EXPOSITION OF THE MEGILLAH

"[Esther] stood in the inner court of the king's palace" (Esther 5:1). R. Levi said: "When she reached the chamber of the idols, the Divine Presence left her. She prayed, "My God, my God, why have You abandoned me?" (Psalms 22:2).[47] Could it be that [You left me because] You judge an unintentional offense like an intentional one, or forced actions like willful ones? [Even though I am going to Achashverosh of my own free will, I am forced to do it in order to save the Jewish people.] Or [did you abandon me] because I called Achashverosh a dog, for it says, "Save my life from the sword, my only one from the clutches of a dog" (ibid. 21). She therefore took it back and called him a lion, for it says, "Deliver me from a lion's mouth; from the horns of wild oxen rescue me" (ibid. 22).

THE LENGTH OF THE SCEPTER

"As soon as the king saw Queen Esther standing in the courtyard, she won his favor, and the king extended the golden scepter to her" (Esther 5:2). R. Yochanan said: Three ministering angels came to her help at that time; one held her neck straight, one made her charming, and one extended the king's scepter toward her. [The Gemara asks:] How far was the scepter extended? R. Yirmiyah answered: It was two amot long, and the angel stretched it to twelve amot. And some say: to sixteen amot. And some say: to twenty-four amot. We leaned in a Baraita: It was lengthened to sixty amot.

We find that the same thing happened to the arm of Pharaoh's daughter; [it was miraculously extended when she reached for the baby Moses as he lay in a basket in the River Nile].[48] And you find the same with the teeth of the wicked [that they were extended to sixty amot].[49] For it says, "You have broken [shibbarta] the teeth of the wicked" (Psalm 3:8). Do not read shibbarta, read shirbavta, "You extended." Rabbah b. Efron said in the name of R. Eliezer who heard it from his teacher, who [in turn] heard it from his teacher: [The scepter] was lengthened to two hundred amot.

WHAT LED ESTHER TO INVITE HAMAN?

"The king said to her, 'What troubles you, Queen Esther? . . . Even to half the kingdom, it shall be granted you'" (Esther 3:5). Achashverosh offered her "half the kingdom," but not the entire kingdom, and not something that divides [i.e., something situated in the middle of] the kingdom. And what is that? Building the Bet Hamikdash; [this request he would not grant her.]

"Esther replied, 'Let Your Majesty and Haman come today to the feast that I have prepared for him'" (ibid. 5:4). The Rabbis taught in a Baraita: What was Esther's reason for inviting Haman? R. Eliezer says: She set a trap for him, as it says, "May their table become a trap for them" (Psalms 69:23). R. Yehoshua said: She learned this [tactic] in her father's house, as it says, "If your enemy is hungry, give him bread to eat . . . and God will reward you." (Proverbs 25:22). R. Meir said: [She invited Haman] so that he would not seek counsel and rebel [against the king]. [He was successful in all his undertakings and might want to overthrow the king (Rashi).] R. Yehudah said: [She invited Haman] so that they should not realize that she was Jewish. R. Nechemiah said: [She invited Haman] so that the Jews should not say, 'We have a sister in the king's palace' [who will protect us], and so they would neglect to pray for mercy. R. Yose said: [She invited Haman] so that he would be available to her at all times, [and she might be able to trip him up in front of the king]. R. Shimon b. Menasya said: [She thought:] Perhaps God would feel her plight, [how she debased herself by inviting this villain] and perform a miracle for us. R. Yehoshua b. Korcha said: [She said to herself:] I will make eyes at Haman, so that the king [will become jealous] and have us both killed. R. Gamliel said: Esther knew that Achashverosh was a fickle king. [If Haman was present when she convinced the king to kill him, the execution would be carried out before the king could change his mind (Rashi).]

R. Gamliel added: "We still need the reason of R. Eliezer the Modean [to explain why Haman alone was invited (*Maharsha*)]." For we learned in a *Baraita*: R. Eliezer the Modean said: [By inviting Haman] she made the king jealous of him and she made the other nobles jealous of him. Rabbah said: [She invited Haman because she reasoned:] "Pride goes before ruin" (Proverbs 16:18). Abaye and Rava both said: [She had in mind the verse,] "When they are hot I will set out their drink [which will lead to their downfall]" (Jeremiah 51:39). Rabbah b. Abuha once met the prophet Elijah and asked him: Which of all these reasons was the one that actually prompted Esther [to invite Haman]? Elijah replied: "She was motivated by all the reasons given by all the *Tanna'im* and *Amora'im*."

THE TABLES ARE TURNED

"That night the sleep of the king was disturbed" (Esther 6:1). R. Tanchum said: The sleep of the King of the world was disturbed, [God was aroused to take revenge (Rashi)]. And the Rabbis said: The creatures of the higher and lower worlds were disturbed; [the angels disturbed Achashverosh's sleep, accusing him of being ungrateful to Mordechai who had saved his life (Rashi). Rava said: It means literally that King Achashverosh's sleep was disturbed. A thought occurred to him. He said to himself: What is the meaning of Esther inviting Haman? Perhaps they are conspiring against me to kill me? He thought again: If so, is there no one who loves me who would have informed me [of their plot]? He thought again: Perhaps there is a person who did me a favor, and I never rewarded him, and that's why people are reluctant to reveal it to me. Right away, "he ordered that the book of records, the annals, be brought, and they were read to the king" (ibid. 6:1); The [use of the grammatical form, "they were read" rather than "they read"] teaches us that they were read of themselves.

"There it was found written" (ibid. 2). [The Gemara asks:] It should have said, "A writing was found." [The Gemara answers:] This [phraseology] shows (16a) that Shimshai, the king's scribe [Haman's son] kept erasing [the record of Mordechai saving the king's life], and the angel Gabriel kept writing it [into the book]. R. Assi said: R. Shila from Kfar Tamarta derived a lesson from this: If a writing on earth that relates the merits of Israel cannot be erased, then surely such a writing in heaven [will not become erased].

[After being told that Mordechai had saved his life, Achashverosh asked his servants,] "What honor or advancement has been conferred on Mordechai for this?" [The servants replied,] "Nothing at all was done for him" (ibid. 6:3). Rava said: Not because they loved Mordechai [did the servants tell the king that he was never rewarded], but because they hated Haman.

[Haman had come to inform the king that he planned to hang Mordechai on the gallows] "he had prepared for him" (ibid. 6). We learned in a *Baraita*: The [seemingly superfluous phrase] "for him" implies that Haman prepared the gallows "for himself."

[Achashverosh asked Haman, "What should be done to a man whom the king wants to honor?" Haman suggested a suitable reward, whereupon the king said, "Quick then! Get the garb and the horse as you have said, and] do this for Mordechai" (ibid. 10). Haman asked Achashverosh, "Which Mordechai?" Achashverosh replied, "The Jew." Haman retorted, "There are many Mordechais among the Jews." The king answered, "The one who sits at the King's gate." Haman, [trying to worm out of it] said, "It is sufficient to give him one village or one river [from which to collect taxes]." Achashverosh shot back, "Omit nothing from all that you proposed! And give him that too!"

"So Haman took the attire and the horse" (ibid. 11). Haman went out and found that Mordechai's disciples were sitting before him, and he was demonstrating to them the laws of *kemitzah*. [50] When Mordechai saw that Haman was coming toward him leading the horse, he became afraid and said to the disciples, "This wicked man is coming to kill me. Get away from here, so that you too won't get burned by his fury [literally: coal]." Thereupon Mordechai wrapped himself in his robe and stood up to pray.

HAMAN MEETS MORDECHAI

Haman came and sat before them and waited until Mordechai finished his prayers. He asked him, "What subject were you discussing?" Mordechai answered, "When the Holy Temple stood, the Torah ordained that if a person brought a meal offering, he had to bring a fistful of fine flour on the altar and would obtain atonement through it." Haman said to him, "Your fistful of flour has come and pushed aside my ten thousand talents." Mordechai retorted, "Villain! If a slave acquires property, to whom does the slave belong; and to whom does the property belong? [Of course, to the master. You sold yourself as a slave to me, [51] therefore that was my money, not yours]!"

Haman then said to Mordecahi, "Arise, put on these garments, and ride this horse, for the king wants you to do so." Mordechai answered, "I can't until I go to the bathhouse and have my hair cut, for it is not proper to wear the king's garments in this state." In the meantime, Esther sent an order to close all the bathhouses and all the barbershops [so that Haman would have to attend to Mordechai personally]. Haman therefore personally took him to the bathhouse and bathed him. He then went to his house and brought scissors to cut his hair. After he cut Mordechai's hair, he sighed. Mordechai asked him, "Why are you sighing?" Haman replied, "A man whom the king considered more important than all his other nobles should now become a bathhouse attendant and a barber?" Mordechai shot back, "Villain! Weren't you once a barber in the village of Kartzum?" Indeed we learned in a *Baraita*: Haman was the barber in the village of Kartzum for twenty-two years.

After cutting Mordechai's hair, Haman dressed him. Haman then told him, "Mount [the horse] and ride." Mordechai replied, "I can't because I am weak from the days of fasting." So Haman bent down and Mordechai [stepped on his back] and mounted the horse. As he mounted, he kicked Haman. Haman asked, "Doesn't it say, 'If your enemy falls, don't rejoice.'" [Why did you kick me?] (Proverbs 24:17)? Mordechai answered, "Villain! That refers to a Jewish enemy, but about your kind it says, 'And you shall tread on their backs'" (Deuteronomy 33:29).

HAMAN PARADES MORDECHAI THROUGH THE CITY SQUARE

"And he proclaimed before him, 'This is what is done for the man whom the king wants to honor'" (Esther 6:11). As he was leading Mordechai through the street where Haman lived, [Haman's] daughter who was standing on the roof, saw it. However, she thought that the one riding on the horse was her father, and the one leading him was Mordechai. She took the chamber pot and emptied it out on her father's head, [thinking that he was Mordechai]. He looked up at her, and when she saw that it was her father, she threw herself from the roof to the ground and killed herself. And this is what the verse is referring to when it says, "Then Mordechai returned to the king's gate," R. Sheshet said: He returned to his sackcloth and fasting. [The verse continues,] "while Haman hurried home, in mourning with his head covered" (ibid. 12)—"in mourning," for his daughter; "with his head covered," because of what happened to him, [the rubbish that had landed on his head].

HAMAN RETURNS HOME

[At home] "Haman told Zeresh, his wife, and all his close friends all that had happened to him. His wise men and his wife said to him . . ." (ibid. 13). [The Gemara asks:] Why is it that they are first called "his friends" and later [in the same verse] they are called "his wise men"? R. Yochanan said: Because whoever says something wise—even if he is a non-Jew—is called [in Scripture] "a wise man."

[The wise statement was,] "If Mordechai is of Jewish descent, you will not overcome him; you will surely fall before him" (ibid.). They told him: If Mordechai is a descendant of one of the other tribes, you will overcome him. But if he is a descendant of Judah, Ephraim, Menashe, or Benjamin, you will not be able to overcome him. Judah [cannot be vanquished], for it says [about Judah], "Your hand shall be on your enemies' necks" (Genesis 49:8). The tribes [Benjamin,

Ephraim, and Menashe] cannot be vanquished either for it says about them, "Before Ephraim, Benjamin and Menashe arouse Your strength; it is for You to save us" (Psalms 80:3).

[They ended their statement,] "You will surely fall before him" (ibid.). [Literally: "Fall you will fall."] R. Yehudah b. Ila'i expounded: Why did they use a double expression of falling? Because they told Haman: The [Jewish] nation is compared to dust and is compared to the stars. When they sink they sink to the dust, [everyone steps on them (*Maharsha*)], but when they rise they rise to the stars, [and Mordechai is on the rise].

"While they were still speaking with him, the king's chamberlains arrived and hurriedly brought Haman to the banquet that Esther had prepared" (Esther 6:14). This teaches us that they brought him to the palace in a state of panic, [and he did not have time to cleanse himself of the trash his daughter had cast on his head (Rashi)].

HAMAN'S DOWNFALL

[At the banquet Esther requested:] "Let my life be granted as my wish, and my people's [life] as my petition. For we have been sold, my people and I, to be destroyed . . . for the adversary [Haman] is not worthy of the king's damage" (ibid. 7:4). Esther said to Achashverosh, "This adversary [Haman] is not concerned with damage done to the king. He was jealous of Vashti and had her killed, and now he is jealous of me and wants to kill me."

"King Achashverosh said, and he said to Queen Esther, 'Who is it that has dared to do this?'" (ibid. 5). [The Gemara asks:] Why does the verse repeat the word "said"? R. Abahu said: At first [Achashverosh, thinking that she was a commoner] spoke to her through a spokesman, but when she told him, "I am of royal descent, I come from the house of Saul," he immediately spoke directly to her, as it says, "He said to Queen Esther."

"Esther replied, 'The oppressor and enemy is this evil Haman!'" (ibid.) R. Elazar said: This teaches us that she was actually pointing at Achashverosh, but an angel came and pushed her hand toward Haman.

"The king rose in his fury . . . and went to the palace garden, [while Haman remained to beg for his life]. When the king returned from the palace garden to the banquet room . . ." (ibid. 7:7). The verse compares his returning to his rising. Just as his rising [to go to the garden] was in fury, so was his returning [from the garden] in fury. For [Achashverosh] went out and found ministering angels in the form of men uprooting the trees of the garden. He said to them, "What are you doing?" They answered, "Haman has ordered us [to do this]." [Achashverosh] then came into the house where, "Haman was falling on the couch on which Esther reclined" (ibid 8). [The Gemara asks:]

Why does the text say "Haman was falling *nofeil*"? It should have said, "had fallen, *nafal*." [The Gemara answers:] This teaches us that [Haman wanted to get up] but an angel came and pushed him back onto her [to make Achashverosh think that he was attacking the queen]. [When Achashverosh saw this] he said, "Grief inside, and grief outside!" [Haman is attacking the queen inside and destroying my garden outside.] "The king then said, 'Does he mean to ravish the queen in my own palace?'"

Then Charvonah, one of the chamberlains said, 'Furthermore, the gallows that Haman made for Mordechai is standing in Haman's house, it is fifty cubits high" (ibid. 9). R. Elazar said: Charvonah, the wicked, was also implicated in the plot [to hang Mordechai]. When he saw that the plot was not successful, he immediately abandoned [Haman's side and supported Mordechai]. This is alluded to in the verse, "When He punishes [the wicked] without mercy, those who benefit from him [his former allies] flee quickly" (Job 27:22).

[Achashverosh ordered Haman to be hanged on the gallows he had put up for Mordechai,] "and the king's fury abated [*shachachah*]" (Esther 7:10). [The Gemara asks:] Why [does the verse] use a double form of the word, [*shachachah*] "abated," where it could have said *shachah*? [The Gemara answers: There were two furies that subsided:] One was the fury of the King of the universe, [Who was angry because the Jews had bowed down to the idol of Nebuchadnezzar (*Maharsha*)], the other was the anger of Achashverosh. Others say: One was Achashverosh's anger over what [Haman had planned to do to] Esther, the other was his anger over what Haman had done to] Vashti.

JOSEPH AND HIS BROTHERS

[After revealing himself to his brothers,] "[Joseph] gave each of his brothers an outfit of clothes. To Benjamin, however, he gave 300 pieces of silver and five outfits" (Genesis 45:22).

[The Gemara asks:] Is it possible that this righteous man [Joseph] should stumble and make the same mistake that brought about his own suffering? [I.e., the mistake of arousing jealousy by favoring one brother over the others.] For Rava b. Mechasya said in the name of R. Chama b. Gurya who quoted Rav: Because of two *sela*'s weight of fine wool that Jacob gave to Joseph over and above what he gave to his other sons,[52] his sons became jealous of Joseph, which set into motion a chain of events that led to our forefathers' going down to Egypt. [Why then, did Joseph repeat the same mistake by giving Benjamin five outfits?]

[The Gemara answers:] R. Binyamin b. Yefet said: [By giving him five outfits] Joseph hinted to Benjaminn that he would have a descendant [Mordechai] who would leave the king's presence wearing five royal garments, as it says, "Mordechai left the king's pres-

ence in royal robes of blue and white, with a magnificent crown of gold and a mantle of fine linen and purple" (Esther 8:15).

[After meeting his brothers,] "Joseph embraced the neck [*tzaverei*] of his brother Benjamin and wept" (Genesis 45:14). [Literally, *tzaverei* means "necks" in the plural.] [The Gemara asks:] How many necks did Benjamin have? R. Elazar said: The plural form teaches us that Joseph wept for the first and the second Temples that were destined to be in the territory of Benjamin, and were destined to be destroyed.

[The verse continues,] "and Benjamin wept on his neck." He wept over the Tabernacle of Shiloh which was destined to be in the territory of Joseph and was destined to be destroyed.

[Joseph told his brothers,] "You and my brother Benjamin can see with your own eyes" (Genesis 45:12). [Why did Joseph address Benjamin apart from his brothers?] R. Elazar said: Joseph told his brothers: Just as I bear no malice toward Benjamin who was not involved in my sale, so I bear no malice toward you. [The verse continues,] "that my mouth is speaking to you." [Why this awkward phraseology?] Joseph implied: What I speak with my mouth, I feel with my heart, [meaning, I am sincere].

"Joseph sent the following to his father: Ten male donkeys loaded with Egypt's finest products" (ibid. 23). [The Gemara asks:] What is "Egypt's finest product"? R. Binyamin b. Yefet said in the name of R. Elazar: He sent him old wine which the elderly enjoy.

[When Jacob died, the brothers were afraid that Joseph still held a grudge against them.] "His brothers then came and threw themselves at his feet" (Genesis 50:18). R. Binyamin b. Yefet said in the name of R. Elazar: This bears out the popular adage, "When the fox is successful, bow down to him." [How can you compare Joseph to] a fox? In what way was he less worthy than his brothers? [The Gemara suggests a different saying.] Rather, [R. Elazar said this,] he meant to apply it to the verse, "And Israel bowed down toward the head of the bed" (Genesis 47:31). R. Binyamin b. Yefet said in the name of R. Elazar: When the fox is successful, bow down to him.

"Thus [Joseph] comforted them, and spoke to their heart" (ibid. 50:21). R. Binyamin b. Yefet said in the name of R. Elazar: This teaches us that he spoke to them words that are accepted by the heart [i.e., encouraging words]. He said: If ten lights could not put out one light, [i.e., you could not destroy me when you sold me], how can one light put out ten lights [by seeking revenge]?

LIGHT, GLADNESS, HAPPINESS, AND HONOR

[After Haman's death,] "The Jews enjoyed light, gladness, happiness and honor" (Esther 8:16). R. Yehudah expounded: "Light" refers to Torah, and so it says, "For a commandment is a lamp, and Torah is light" (Proverbs 6:23). "Gladness" refers to the festivals, and so it says, "You shall be glad on your festival" (Deuteronomy 16:13). "Happiness" refers to circumcision, and so it says, "I rejoice over Your word [*imratecha*]" (119:162). [The *mitzvah* of *milah* is introduced by *vayomer*, "God *said* to Abraham" (Genesis 17:9), in contrast to other *mitzvot* which are introduced by *vayedabbeir*, "God spoke."] "And honor" refers to *tefillin*, and so it says, "All the nations of the world will see that the name of God is proclaimed over you, and they will be in awe of you" (Deuteronomy 28:10). And it was taught in a *Baraita*: Rabbi Eliezer the Great said about this verse: This refers to the head *tefillin*.

THE TEN SONS OF HAMAN

"And Parshandata, and Dalfon . . . the ten sons of Haman" (Esther 9:7–10). R. Adda of Yaffo said: The names of the ten sons of Haman and the word "ten" [which follows,] must be said [by the reader of the Megillah] in one breath. What is the reason? Because they all died at the same moment. R. Yochanan said: The letter *vav* of Vayzata [the last name on the list] must be elongated [when writing the Megillah] like a pole [used by the boatmen on the river] Librut. What is the reason? Because all of them were hanged on one pole [one above the other].

[Dispatches were sent to all the Jews] "with words of peace and truth" (Esther 9:30). R. Tanchum, and others say R. Assi said: This teaches us that the Megillah scroll requires etched lines [on the parchment], like an actual Torah scroll.

"Esther's words confirmed these regulations for Purim" (ibid. 32). [The Gemara asks:] Was it Esther's word alone [that led to the miracle] and not the fasts? R. Yochanan said: [The end of the previous verse should be combined with the beginning of the present verse,] "The matter of the fasts and lamentations [as well as] Esther's words confirmed these regulations."

CONCLUSION OF THE *MEGILLAH*

[The Megillah ends,] "For Mordechai the Jew was viceroy to King Achashverosh and was highly regarded by the Jews and popular with most of his brethren" (Esther 10:3). It says, "popular with most of his brethren," implying that he was not popular with *all* of his brethren. This teaches us that some members of the Sanhedrin turned away from him, [for by accepting public office he neglected his Torah studies (Rashi)].

R. Yosef said: [We can infer from this that] the study of Torah is greater than the [potential] saving of lives.[53] For at first Mordechai's name is listed [in Scripture] after four sages, but in the end [after the miracle of Purim] he is listed after five sages. At first it says, "Those who came with Zerubabel were: Jeshua, Nehemiah, Seraiah, Reelaiah, Mordechai-bilshan" (Ezra 2:2). And in the end it says, "Those who came with Zerubabel were: Jeshua, Nehemiah, Azariah, Raamiah, Nachmani, Mordechai-bilshan" (Nehemiah 7:7).

SENDING DELICACIES TO FRIENDS, AND GIFTS TO THE POOR

[Having reached the end of the exposition of the verses of *Megillat* Esther, *Ein Yaakov* now focuses on the *mitzvot* associated with Purim that are mentioned in Chapter 9 of the *Megillah*. These *mitzvot* are discussed earlier in the tractate, beginning on 7a:] (7a) "They were to observe [these days] as days of feasting and gladness, and as an occasion of sending delicacies to one another and gifts to the poor" (Esther 9:22). R. Yosef said: [The mitzvah] of "sending delicacies to one another" entails sending two portions to one person. [The mitzvah] of "gifts to the poor" requires giving two gifts to two people, [meaning, one gift to each of two people].

R. Yehudah HaNasi sent R. Oshaya the thigh of a calf born third to its mother [which is choice, quality meat] and a bottle of wine. R. Oshaya sent back to him a message, saying, (7b) "Our teacher, by giving us these gifts you have fulfilled the mitzvah of sending portions to one another and gifts to the poor."

Rabbah sent with Abaye to Mari b. Mar a basket filled with dates and a cup filled with flour of roasted wheat. Abaye said to Rabbah, "Mari will say [about you]: When the farmer becomes king he does not remove the sack [he used to feed his animals] from around his neck" [meaning, although you have become head of Pumbedita, you are still sending only ordinary gifts (Rashi)]. Mari sent Rabbah in return a basket filled with ginger and a cup filled with long peppers. Abaye said to Mari, "Rabbah will say: I sent him sweet things, and he sends me back bitter things!"

Abaye said: When I left Rabbah's house to go to Mari, I was full. When I arrived at Mari's house, they brought me sixty plates with sixty kinds of cooked food, and I ate sixty pieces from them. The last dish was called pot roast, and I liked it so much that I wanted to eat the plate too! Abbaye added: This proves the popular adage: A poor person does not know when he is hungry. Or the other saying: There is always room for sweet things.

Abaye b. Avin and R. Chanina b. Avin exchanged their Purim meals with one another.

DRINKING WINE ON PURIM

Rava said: A person is required to drink [wine] on Purim until he does not know the difference between "blessed is Mordechai" and "cursed is Haman." Rabbah and R. Zeira had their Purim feast together. After they became intoxicated, Rabbah got up and killed R. Zeira. The next day he asked for divine mercy for him, and he came back to life. The next year, Rabbah said to R. Zeira, "Come, let us have the Purim feast together." He answered, "Miracles don't happen all the time!"[54]

R. Ashi was sitting before R. Kahana [his teacher]. It was getting dark, and students had not arrived. R. Kahana asked him: Why have the students not arrived? [R. Ashi replied:] Perhaps they are busy with the Purim feast. [R. Kahana then said:] Couldn't they have had it last night? [R. Ashi] replied: Has the master not heard what Rava said, that if you eat your Purim meal at night you have not fulfilled your obligation? [R. Kahana said:] Did Rava say that? [R. Ashi] answered: Yes. He then repeated it after him forty times until he had committed it to memory.

(16b) Rav said, and some say [that it was] R. Shmuel b. Marta who said it: The study of Torah is greater than building the *Bet Hamikdash*. For as long as Baruch b. Neriah was alive, Ezra [who was his disciple] did not leave him to go to Eretz Yisrael.

Rabbah said in the name of R. Yitzchak b. Shmuel b. Marta: The study of Torah is greater than honoring one's parents, for all of the years that our father Jacob was in the yeshivah of Ever he was not punished [for failing to honor his father and mother].

HALLEL MUST BE RECITED IN SEQUENCE

(17a) [The Mishnah says:] A person who reads the *Megillah* out of sequence has not fulfilled his obligation.

[The Gemara says:] We learned in a *Baraita*: The same is true of *Hallel*,[55] of the reciting of *Shema*, and of the *Shemoneh Esrei* [they all must be recited in sequence].

[The Gemara asks:] From where do we know that *Hallel* [must be said in sequence]? Rabbah said: For it says, "From the rising of the sun to its setting the name of God is praised" (Psalms 113:3). [Just as sunrise and sunset are always in sequence, so too the praise of God [i.e., *Hallel*] must be in sequence (Rashi).] R. Yosef said: For it says [in *Hallel*], "This is the day God has made" (ibid. 118:24). [Just as the hours of the day are not reversed, so too the psalms of *Hallel* may not be reversed (Rashi).] R. Avya said: It says [in *Hallel*], "The Name of God shall be blessed" (ibid. 118:24). [Just as God's Name never changes, so must His praise remain unchanged and said in the proper sequence (Rashi).] R. Nachman b. Yitzchak, and some say it was R. Acha b. Yaakov, said: [We can derive it] from here, "from now to eternity" (the continuation of the above verse), [*Hallel* must forever remain unchanged.]

THE SHEMA MUST BE RECITED IN SEQUENCE

The *Shema* must be recited in sequence, for we learned in a *Baraita*: *Shema* must be recited as it is written [in Hebrew]; so says Rabbi. But the Sages say: It may be recited in any language. What is the reason for Rabbi's ruling [that *Shema* may only be read in Hebrew]? For it says, (17b) "And they [these words] shall be" (Deuteronomy 6:6), which implies that [the words of *Shema*] shall always be as they are now [i.e., in Hebrew]. And what is the reason for the ruling of the Sages [that *Shema* may be recited in any language]? It says, "Hear" (ibid. 4), which implies in any language that you understand. [The Gemara asks:] And how does Rabbi interpret this "Hear"? [The Gemara amswers:] According to Rabbi, that verse is needed to teach us that when reciting *Shema* you must let your ears hear what your mouth is saying. And the Sages hold according to the opinion that states that even if a person recited *Shema* without making his words audible, he nevertheless fulfilled his obligation.

[The Gemara asks:] But how do the Sages deal with the words, "and they shall be" [which Rabbi interpreted to imply that *Shema* must be read only in Hebrew]? [According to the Sages] these words are needed to teach that you may not read *Shema* out of sequence. [The Gemara asks:] And from where does Rabbi know that you may not read *Shema* out of sequence? [The Gemara answers:] He derives it from the [additional *hei* in the word] *hadevarim*, which could have been written *devarim* [without a *hei*]. [And how do the Sages interpret the additional *hei*?] The Sages do not derive any teaching from [the *hei* of] *hadevarim*.

[The Gemara asks:] Can we assume that according to Rabbi the entire Torah may be read in any language? [This must be so], for if it enters your mind to say that the entire Torah must be read in Hebrew, why was it necessary for Scripture to write "and they shall be" [to teach that *Shema* must be read in Hebrew]? [The Gemara answers:] Even if you hold that the entire Torah must be read in Hebrew, "and they shall be" is still necessary [as regards *Shema*]. For it might occur to you to interpret "Hear" as the Sages did [i.e., that *Shema* may be read in any language]. The Torah therefore wrote, "and they shall be."

[The Gemara asks:] Can we assume that according to the Sages the entire Torah must be read only in Hebrew? [This must be so,] for if it enters your mind to say that according to the Sages the entire Torah may be read in any language, why was it necessary to write "Hear" [to teach that *Shema* may be read in any language]? [The Gemara answers: Even if you hold that the entire Torah may be read in any language, "Hear" is still necessary [as regards *Shema*]. For it might occur to you to interpret "and they shall be" as Rabbi did [i.e., that *Shema* may be read only in Hebrew]. The Torah therefore wrote "Hear" [to teach that *Shema* may be read in any language].

THE SHEMONEH ESREI

[The Gemara asks:] From where do we know that the *Shemoneh Esrei* [must be recited in the set order]? We learned in a *Baraita*: Shimon HaPakuli set the order of the eighteen *berachot* [of the *Shemoneh Esrei*] before R. Gamliel in Yavneh. R. Yochanan said, and some say that it was taught in a *Baraita*: One hundred and twenty elders, [the members of the Great Assembly], among whom were many prophets, instituted the order of the eighteen *berachot* of the *Shemoneh Esrei*.

The Rabbis taught: From where do we know that we should recite a *berachah* that mentions the Patriarchs? [The first *berachah* recalls the the greatness of the Patriarchs Abraham, Isaac, and Jacob.] For it says, "Mention before God the powerful of the earth" [a reference to the Patriarchs] (Psalms 29:1). And from where do we know that we should recite a [second] *berachah* that mentions God's Might? For the verse continues, "Bring to God honor and might." And from where do we know that we should recite a [third] *berachah* that describes God's Holiness? For it says, "Bring to God the glory of His name, bow to God in the splendor of holiness" (ibid.)

And what prompted [the Sages] to say the *berachah* of Insight after the *berachah* of Holiness? Because it says, "They shall sanctify the Holy One of Jacob and stand in awe of the God of Israel" (Isaiah 29:23). Which is followed by the passage, "and the confused shall acquire insight" (ibid. 24).

And what prompted them to say the *berachah* of Repentance after the *berachah* of Insight? For it says, "And his heart will understand and he will [then] repent and be healed" (ibid. 6:10).

[The Gemara asks:] If the order of this verse is the reason, then the *berachah* of Healing should be said immediately after the *berachah* of Repentance [because that is their order in this verse]. Why, then, is the *berachah* of Repentance followed, not by the *berachah* of Healing, but by the *berachah* of Forgiveness?

[The Gemara answers:] Don't imagine such a thing, for it says, "Let him turn back to God, [in repentance], and He will have mercy on him, and to the Lord, for He freely forgives" (Isaiah 55:7). [So you see that repentance is followed by forgiveness, not healing.] [The Gemara now asks:] But why do you rely on this verse and not on the other [which places healing after repentance]? [The Gemara answers:] There is a different verse that says, "He forgives all your sins, heals all your diseases. He redeems your life from the Pit" (Psalms 103:3–4). This teaches you that redemption and healing follow after forgiveness. [That's why the *berachah* of Repentance is followed by Forgiveness and then Healing.] [The Gemara asks:] But it says, "He will repent and be healed." [Therefore, Repentance should be followed by Healing, not by Forgiveness.] [The Gemara answers: The healing mentioned in that verse is not a cure for physical sicknesses; rather it refers to the healing powers of forgiveness.]

[The Gemara asks:] What prompted the Sages to say the *berachah* of Redemption as the seventh blessing? Rava said: Because Israel is destined to be re-

deemed in the seventh year [of the seven years before the coming of *Mashiach*]. [The Gemara asks:] But the master has said that in the sixth year [of those seven years] sounds [of the blowing of the shofar] will be heard; in the seventh year there will be wars; and at the end of the seventh year, the son of David [*Mashiach*] will come. [The Gemara answers:] The war [that will break out in the seventh year] is also considered the beginning of the redemption.

[The Gemara asks:] And what prompted them to say the *berachah* of Healing as the eighth blessing? R. Acha said: Because the mitzvah of circumcision that requires healing is designated for [the child's] eighth day; therefore they made Healing the eighth *berachah*.

And why did they make the *berachah* of the Years [of Prosperity] the ninth blessing? R. Alexandri said: This *berachah* was instituted against those who drive up the prices of food, as it says, "Break the strength of the wicked" (Psalms 10:15). And David included this verse in the ninth psalm, [that's why this *berachah* is in the ninth place. The Gemara counts the first two psalms as one; therefore, Psalms 10 is counted as Psalms 9 (Rashi)].

And why did they place the *berachah* of the Ingathering of the Exiles after the blessing of the Years [of Prosperity]? For it says, "But you, O mountains of Israel, will give forth your branch and bear your fruit for My people Israel, for their return is near" (Ezekiel 36:8). [In the verse the ingathering of the exiles is preceded by a bountiful harvest.]

[The reason the *berachah* of the Ingathering is followed by the *berachah* of Restoration of Justice is this:] Once the exiles are assembled, judgment will be visited on the wicked, as it says, "I will turn My hand upon you, and smelt out your dross as with lye" (Isaiah 1:25), and the next verse says, "I will restore your judges as of old" (ibid. 26).

[Why is the *berachah* against Heretics next? Because] once judgment has been visited on the wicked, all the heretics will cease to exist and the wanton sinners are included with them, for it says, "But the heretics and sinners shall all be crushed, and those who forsake God shall perish" (ibid. 28).

[Why is the *berachah* for the Righteous next? Because] once the heretics perish, the horn [i.e., prestige] of the righteous will be raised, as it says, "All the horns of the wicked I will cut, but the horns of the righteous shall be lifted up" (Psalms 75:11). And the righteous converts are included with the righteous, as it says, "Stand up for a white head and give respect to the old" (Leviticus 19:32), and in the next verse it says, "When a convert dwells among you" (ibid. 33). [The righteous converts are mentioned in the *berachah* for the righteous.]

Where will the prestige of the righteous be exalted? In Jerusalem. As it says, " Pray for the peace of Jerusalem; may those who love you be at peace" (Psalms 122:6). [The lovers of Jerusalem are the righteous

(*Maharsha*).] [That's why the *berachah* for the rebuilding of Jerusalem follows after the *berachah* for the Righteous.]

[The *berachah* for the coming of Mashiach follows next because] once Jerusalem is built, David [i.e., *Mashiach*] will come, as it says, **(18a)** "Afterwards, [after Jerusalem is rebuilt], the children of Israel will return [to the *Bet Hamikdash*] and will seek the Lord their God and David their king" (Hosea 3:5).

[The *berachah* of Acceptance of Prayer is next because] once David comes, prayer will come, for it says, "I will bring them to My sacred mountain and let them rejoice in My house of prayer" (Isaiah 56:7).

And once prayer comes, the service in the *Bet Hamikdash* will be restored, for it says, "Their burnt offerings and sacrifices shall be welcome on My altar" (ibid.). [That's why the *berachah* for the Temple Service comes after the *berachah* for Prayer.]

[The *berachah* of Thanksgiving is next because] once the Temple service is restored, thanksgiving comes, as it says, "He who offers thanksgiving honors Me" (Psalms 50:23); [offering is followed by thanksgiving].

[The Gemara asks:] What prompted the Sages to arrange the Priestly Blessing after the *berachah* of Thanksgiving? [The Gemara answers:] For it says, "Aaron lifted his hands toward the people and blessed them. He then descended [from the altar where] he had performed the sin offering, the burnt offering, and the peace offerings" (Leviticus 9:22). [Aaron blessed the people after offering the sacrifices.]

[The Gemara asks:] Why don't we say the Priestly blessing] before the *berachah* of the Temple Service, [for they are mentioned in that order in the verse]? [The Gemara answers:] That would not be logical. For it says, "He then descended [from the altar where] he had performed the sin offering . . . Does it then say "to perform"? It says, "where he *had* performed," [which implies that he blessed the people *after* having performed the sacrificial offering].

[The Gemara asks:] Then say the Priestly Blessing immediately after the *berachah* for the Temple Service. [Why was the *berachah* of Thanksgiving placed between them?] [The Gemara answers:] You cannot possibly think so, for it says, "He who offers thanksgiving," [which indicates that thanksgiving must follow the Temple service].

[The Gemara asks:] Why base yourself on this verse [that connects thanksgiving and Temple service]? Base yourself on the other verse [that connects the priestly blessing with the Temple service]. [The Gemara answers:] It is more logical to connect thanksgiving and the Temple service for they are one and the same concept; [Thanksgiving is also a form of Divine service (Rashi)].

[The Gemara asks:] Why did they arrange the *berachah* "Establish Peace" after the Priestly Blessing? [The Gemara answers:] For it says, "[The priests] will thus link My name with the children of Israel, and I will bless them" (Numbers 6:27). [This verse follows after the verses of the Priestly Blessing.] And the blessing of the Holy One, blessed be He, is peace, as it says, "God will bless His nation with peace" (Psalms 29:11).

WE ARE FORBIDDEN TO CHANGE THE TEXT OF PRAYERS

[The Gemara asks:] Now that one hundred and twenty elders [i.e., the Men of the Great Assembly], among whom were many prophets, drew up the *berachot* of the *Shemoneh Esrei* in the proper order, what did Shimon HaPakuli arrange? [The Gemara answers:] They had forgotten [the order of the *berachot*], and he arranged them again [in the proper order]. From this point on, it is forbidden to [add to] the praises of the Holy One, blessed be He. For R. Elazar said: What is the meaning of the verse, "Who can tell the mighty acts of God, proclaim all His praises?" (Psalms 106:2).—For whom is it fitting to tell the mighty acts of God? Only for one who can express *all* of His praise. [Since no one is capable of expressing all of God's praise, you should only recite the established *berachot*, without adding your own words of praise.]

Rabbah bar bar Chanah said in the name of R. Yochanan: He who praises God excessively will be uprooted from the world. For it says, "Can [God] be told [of all His praises] that I may express [an abundance of praise]; if a man says [to do this] he will be swallowed up" (Job 37:20).

R. Yehudah, a resident of Kfar Giboraya—and some say a resident of Kfar Gibbor Chayil—expounded: What is the meaning of the passage, "To You, silence is praise" (Psalms 65:2)?—The best medicine of all is silence. When R. Dimi came [to Babylonia] he said: In the west [i.e., Eretz Yisrael] we have a saying: "A word is worth a *sela*, silence is worth two."

R. Acha said in the name of R. Elazar: How do we know that the Holy One, blessed be He, called Jacob [by the title] "El"? For it says, "And the God of Israel called him [Jacob] 'El'" (Genesis 33:20). If you would think [that the verse means that] Jacob called the altar [that he had erected] "El," it should have said, "And Jacob called it 'El.'" Rather, the verse means: "and He called Jacob 'El.'" Who called him "El"? The God of Israel.

YOU MUST STAND WHEN READING THE TORAH

(21a) [The Mishnah says:] One who reads the *Megillah* either standing or sitting has fulfilled the obligation [even if reading on behalf of the congregation].

[The Gemara comments:] We learned in a *Baraita*: This [ruling, that one may read the *Megillah* sitting] does not apply to the Torah reading; [you may not read the Torah for a congregation while sitting (Rashi)]. From where in Scripture do we derive this? R. Abahu said: For it says, [God said to Moses,] "And you, stand here with Me" (Deuteronomy 5:28). And R. Abahu, expounding this verse, said: Were it not that this verse is written like this, it would not be possible to say it, [we would not be allowed to apply such corporeal terms to God]: as it were, the Holy One, blessed be He also was standing, [because He said, "with Me." Similarly, when reading the Torah to the congregation, the reader must stand].

R. Abahu also said: From where do we derive that a teacher should not sit on a couch and teach Torah while his students are sitting on the ground? For it says, "And you, stand here with Me." [Rather, both teacher and students should be seated on couches or both on the ground.]

The Rabbis taught: From the days of Moses until R. Gamliel they studied the Torah while standing. When R. Gamliel died, feebleness descended on the world, and they would learn the Torah sitting. And so we learned in a Mishnah: Ever since R. Gamliel died, the honor of Torah ceased [since people were no longer able to accord it the honor of studying while standing].

MOSES'S POSITION WHEN LEARNING TORAH

[The Gemara tries to reconcile an apparent discrepancy:] One verse says, "I [Moses] sat on the mountain" (Deuteronomy 9:9), and another verse says, "I [Moses] stood on the mountain" (ibid. 10:10). Rav said: Moses would stand while learning [Torah from God], but he would sit while reviewing by himself [what he had learned (Rashi)]. R. Chanina said: Moses was neither standing nor sitting, but bowing. R. Yochanan said: The word "sat" should be understood as "stayed," as in the verse, "You sat [stayed] in Kadesh many days" (Deuteronomy 1:6). Rava said: Moses studied the easy parts standing, and the difficult parts he studied sitting.

TO WHAT DO THE TEN VERSES CORRESPOND?

(21b) [We learned in the Mishnah:] On Monday, Thursday, and at *Minchah* on *Shabbat*, three people are called up to the Torah. [The Gemara asks:] To what do these three people correspond? [The Gemara answers:] They correspond to Torah, Prophets, and Writings. Rava said: They correspond to *Kohanim*, Levites, and Israelites.

[The Gemara asks:] Regarding the *Baraita* quoted by R. Shimi that not less than ten verses should be read in the synagogue, to what do these ten verses correspond? [The Gemara answers:] R. Yehoshua b. Levi said: They correspond to the ten unoccupied men of the synagogue.[56] R. Yosef said: They correspond to the Ten Commandments that were said to Moses at Sinai.

R. Levi said: They correspond to the ten "praises" said by David in Psalms [146-150, which begin and end with *Halleluyah*]. R. Yochanan said: They correspond to the ten utterances with which the world was created. What are these ten utterances? [The ten times that the Torah says,] "And [God] said" in the portion of *Bereishit* [in the story of Creation (Genesis 1:1-31)]. [The Gemara challenges:] But there are only nine! [The Gemara answers:] The word *bereishit*, "In the beginning," is also an utterance [of Creation], for it says, "By the word of God the heavens were made, and by the breath of His mouth all their hosts" (Psalms 33:6).

SYNAGOGUES OR STUDY HALLS—WHICH IS GREATER?

(27a) Bar Kappara expounded: What is the meaning of the verse, "He [Nebuchadnezzar] burned the house of God, the king's house, and all the buildings of Jerusalem; and every great house he burned in fire" (2 Kings 25:9)? "The house of God"—this refers to the *Bet Hamikdash*; "the king's house"—this refers to the king's palace; "and all the buildings of Jerusalem"—this should be understood according to its plain meaning. "And every great house he burned in fire"—R. Yochanan and R. Yehoshua gave different interpretations of this: One of them said it refers to a place where they made the Torah great [i.e., the study halls], and the other said it refers to a place where they made prayer great [i.e., the synagogues]. The one who said that "great" refers to Torah finds support in the verse, "Let the Torah be made great and glorious" (Isaiah 42:21). The one who says that "great" refers to prayer finds support in the verse, "Tell me, please, the great things that Elisha has done" (2 Kings 8:4); and the great things that Elisha did he accomplished through prayer.

You may assume that it is R. Yehoshua b. Levi who said that "every great house" refers to places where they made the Torah great. For R. Yehoshua b. Levi said that a synagogue may be converted into a study hall, [thus a study hall has greater sanctity]. This is clear proof.

SELLING A TORAH SCROLL

The students asked: Is it permitted to sell an old Torah scroll in order to buy with its proceeds a new one? Come and learn: R. Yochanan said in the name of R. Meir: You may not sell a Torah scroll, except [if you use the funds] to learn Torah or to take a wife. From this we can infer that selling one Torah scroll [to buy] a new Torah scroll is permissible. [The sanctity of learning Torah is comparable to the sanctity of a Torah scroll itself.]

[The Gemara asks:] Perhaps Torah study has a higher degree of sanctity than a Torah scroll, for learning Torah brings you to the performance of *mitzvot*. Taking a wife also has a higher degree of sanctity than a Torah scroll; [and marriage has an overriding purpose] for it says, "He did not create the world to be empty, He fashioned it to be inhabited" (Isaiah 45:18), but to exchange an old Torah scroll for a new one, is perhaps not permitted? [The question remains unresolved.]

We learned in a *Baraita*: A person may not sell a Torah scroll, even if he does not need it. [He may sell it only in order to learn Torah or to marry.] R. Gamliel went one step further and said: Even if a person has nothing to eat and sold a Torah scroll or his minor daughter as a maidservant, he will never see a sign of blessing [from that money].

HOW DID THEY ATTAIN LONG LIFE?

R. Zakkai's disciples asked him, "In the merit of what good deed did you attain long life?" He replied, "During my entire life I never urinated within four cubits of my place of prayer, and I never called a friend by a nickname, and I never missed reciting *Kiddush* of the *Shabbat* day [over wine]."

[He continued,] "I had an elderly mother, and once I did not have wine for *Kiddush*. She sold her headdress and brought me wine for *Kiddush* of the day. We learn in a *Baraita*: When R. Zakkai's mother died, she left him three hundred barrels of wine, and when he died, he left his children three thousand barrels of wine.

R. Huna once came before Rav wearing a straw belt. Rav asked him, "What is the meaning of this? [Why are you wearing a makeshift belt?]" R. Huna replied, "I did not have wine for *Kiddush*, so I pawned my belt and used the money I borrowed to buy wine. Rav said to him, "May it be the will of God that you be [one day] completely covered with silk." [Rav's blessing came true] when R. Huna's son Rabbah was married. R. Huna, who was a very short person, went to rest on a sofa [during the wedding]. His daughters and daughters-in-law came [and did not notice that he was sleeping on the sofa since he was so short]. They placed their silk wraps on top of him until he was completely covered with silk. When Rav heard [that his blessing had come true], he was annoyed [with R. Huna] and said: Why didn't you say when I blessed you, "The same to you, Sir"? [Perhaps it was a favorable moment, and the blessing would have been fulfilled for me too (Rashi).]

R. Elazar b. Shamua's disciples asked him, "In the merit of what good deed did you attain long life?" He replied, "During my entire life I never used a synagogue as a shortcut, and I never stepped over the heads of [the people of] the holy nation, [i.e., the students in the *bet hamidrash*. It was customary for them to sit on the ground, and R. Elazar never pushed them aside in order to get to his seat (Rashi)]. And I never lifted my hands [to recite the priestly blessing] without saying a *berachah*."[57]

R. Pereida's disciples asked him, "In the merit of what good deed did you attain long life?" He replied, "During my entire life no one was ever in the *bet midrash* before me, and I never recited *Birkat Hamazon*[58] in the presence of a *kohen*, [but I gave the *kohen* the honor to lead the recitation of *Birkat Hamazon*]. I never ate the meat of an animal whose priestly gifts [the right foreleg, the jaw, and the stomach] had not been separated." As R. Yitzchak said in the name of R. Yochanan: It is forbidden to eat [meat] from an animal whose gifts were not separated. R. Yitzchak also said: To eat [meat] from an animal whose gifts were not separated is like eating *tevel* [untithed produce]. But the *halachah* is not in accordance with his opinion.

[R. Pereida mentioned,] "I never recited Grace after Meals in the presence of a *kohen*." [The Gemara asks:] Is this really a commendable practice? But R. Yochanan said: Any Torah scholar [who allows] someone else to recite Grace after Meals [in his presence], even if that person is an unlearned *Kohen Gadol*, deserves death [by the hand of Heaven]. For it says, "All who hate me [i.e., the Torah] love death" (Proverbs 8:36). Don't read *mesanai*, "those that hate me"; read instead *masni'ai*, "those that make me hated." [By honoring an unlearned *kohen*, the Torah scholar makes people disdain the Torah.] [The Gemara answers:] R. Pereida was referring to a *kohen* who was his equal [in learning].

R. Nechunia b. Hakanah's disciples asked him, "In the merit of what good deed did you attain long life?" He replied, "In all my life I never derived honor from the shame of my fellow, and I never went to bed with my fellow's curse on me [i.e., I never retired before appeasing those who were angry with me]. And I was generous with my money.

[R. Nechunia said:] I never derived honor from the shame of my fellow—as in this incident involving R. Huna, who was carrying a spade on his shoulder. R. Chana b. Chanilai came along and tried to carry it for him. Rav Huna said to him, "If you are used to carrying [garden tools] in your own town, then go ahead and carry my spade. But if not, I am not willing to be honored through your embarrassment."

[R. Nechunia also mentioned:] I never went to bed with my fellow's curse on me—as illustrated by Mar Zutra. When he went to bed, he would say: I forgive anyone who has given me trouble. [R. Nechunia forgave even those who had cursed him.]

[R. Nechunia mentioned also:] I was liberal with my money. As the master has said: Job was generous with his money, for he would let the storekeeper keep the change.

R. Akiva asked R. Nechunia the Great, "In the merit of what good deed did you attain long life?" [R. Nechunia's] servants came and struck him, [for asking an impertinent question], so he went and sat on top of a palm tree and asked [R. Nechunia], "Rabbi! If it says, 'lamb' [in the verse, 'The *one lamb* shall you offer in the morning' (Numbers 28:4)], why does it also say 'one'?" [Lamb alone implies a single lamb.] He replied, "The word "one" teaches us that [the offering must be] the single most outstanding lamb in its flock." [Recognizing R. Akiva's erudition, he then said to his servants, "He is a Torah scholar. Leave him alone!"]

R. Nechunia said, [in reply to R. Akiva's original question as to how he had merited to live so long], "During my entire life, I never accepted gifts, as it says, 'One who hates gifts will live' (Proverbs 15:27); I did not insist on retribution against those who wronged me; and I was liberal with my money."

"I never accepted gifts"—as illustrated by R. Elazar. When they sent him gifts from the *nassi*'s[59] household he would not accept them. And whenever they invited him to a banquet, he would not go. He would tell them, "Don't you want me to live? For it says, 'One who hates gifts will live.'" R. Zeira, whenever they sent him gifts from the *nassi*'s household, would not accept them, but when they invited him to a banquet, he would go. He explained, "They are honored by my presence." [He felt that he was not receiving anything; rather that he was doing them a favor by attending their banquet.]

"I did not insist on retribution against those who wronged me"—as Rava said: Anyone who does not insist on retribution, the Heavenly Tribunal waives all of his sins, as it says, "He forgives transgression and passes over sin" (Micah 7:18). Whose transgression does he forgive? One who passes over sins [committed against himself].

Rabbi asked R. Yehoshua b. Korcha: In the merit of what good deed did you attain long life? He replied: Do you begrudge me my life? Said Rabbi: My teacher! It is Torah, and I need to learn [from you; perhaps I can emulate your practices (Rashi)]. He answered: In all my life I never looked at the image of a wicked person, for R. Yochanan said: You may not gaze at the face of a wicked person. For it says, [King Yehoshafat of Judah and the wicked King Yehoram of Israel came to consult the prophet Elisha, who told the idolatrous Yehoram,] "Were it not that I respect King Yehoshafat of Judah, I wouldn't look at you or notice you" (2 Kings 3:14). R. Elazar said: [A person who gazes at a wicked man becomes blind, as it says, "Isaac had grown old and his eyesight was fading" (Genesis 27:1). Because Isaac gazed at the wicked Esau, [his eyesight faded]. [The Gemara asks:] Is this what caused [Isaac's blindness]? Didn't R. Yitzchak say: Don't take lightly the curse of an ordinary person, for Avimelech cursed Sarah, and his curse was fulfilled in her offspring. For it says, [Avimelech said to Sarah when giving her the gift of a thousand pieces of silver], "Let this be an eye covering [i.e., compensation] for you" (Genesis 20:16). Don't read *kesut*, "covering"; rather read the word as *kesiyat*, "blindness." [Thus, we see that Isaac's blindness was the result of Avimelech's curse and was not

caused by his gazing at Esau.] R. Elazar answered: Both [the gazing on Esau and the curse of Avimelech] brought on Isaac's blindness.

Rava said: [We can derive it from here:] "It is not good to look at the face of a wicked person" (Proverbs 18:5).

When [Rabbi] was about to leave [R. Yehoshua], [Rabbi] said to [R. Yehoshua]: My teacher! Bless me. [R. Yehoshua] answered: May it be [God's] will that you reach half my age. [Stunned, Rabbi exclaimed:] And not your full age? [Why do you begrudge me that I live as long as you?] R. Yehoshua answered: Should those that come after you tend cattle? [If you live as long as I, your children will not be able to inherit your office of *nasi*, and will always live in your shadow (Rashi).]

Avuha b. Ihi and Minyamin b. Ihi [were discussing the matter of gazing]. One said: I will be rewarded [in the world to come] because I never gazed at a Kuthean. The other said: I will be rewarded [in the world to come] because I never formed a partnership with a Kuthean.

R. Zeira's students asked him: In the merit of what good deed did you attain long life? He replied: During my entire life, I never intimidated the members of my household; I never walked in front of one greater than myself; I never thought [about Torah matters] in filthy alleyways; I never walked four *amot* without thinking Torah thoughts and without wearing *tefillin*; I never slept in the study hall, neither a regular sleep nor a short nap; I never derived pleasure from my colleague's blunder; and I never called my colleague by his nickname. And some say [that R. Zeira said]: I never called my colleague by his surname [if it had an unflattering connotation].

THE *SHECHINAH* IS WITH US IN EXILE

(29a) We learned in a *Baraita*: Come and see how much the Holy One, blessed be He, loves the Jewish people. For wherever they were exiled, the *Shechinah* went with them. When they were exiled from Egypt, the *Shechinah* was with them, as it says, "Did I not appear to your ancestor's family when they were in Egypt?" (1 Samuel 2:227). When they were exiled to Babylon, the *Shechinah* was with them, as it says, "Because of you I was sent to Babylon" (Isaiah 43:14).[60] When they were exiled to Edom (Rome) the *Shechinah* was with them, for it says, "Who is this [Redeemer—i.e., the *Shechinah*] that comes from Edom, with sullied garments from Botzrah?" (ibid. 63:1). And also in the future when they will be redeemed, the *Shechinah* will be with them, as it says, "God will then return with your returning exiles" (Deuteronomy 30:3). It does not say *veheishiv*, "and He will bring back"; rather, *veshav*, "He will return together with them from the exiles."

[The Gemara asks:] Where [is the *Shechinah*] in Babylon? Abaye said: In the synagogue of Hutzal and in the synagogue "that was moved and settled" in Nahardea.[61] But don't think that [the *Shechinah* is] in both synagogues. Rather, [the *Shechinah*] is sometimes in one and sometimes in the other.

Abaye said: May I be rewarded because whenever I am within a *parsah*[62] [of either of these two synagogues], I go out of my way to pray there.

THE *SHECHINAH* APPEARED IN THE SYNAGOGUE

Shmuel's father and Levi were once sitting in the synagogue "that was moved and settled" in Nehardea. The *Shechinah* came, and they heard the sound of a commotion, so they got up and left.

R. Sheshet [who was blind] was sitting in the synagogue "that was moved and settled" in Nehardea. The *Shechinah* came, but he did not leave. The ministering angels then came and began to frighten him [trying to make him leave]. He said to God: Master of the universe! If one is afflicted [R. Sheshet] and one is not afflicted [the angels], who must step aside for whom? Said God [to the ministering angels]: Leave him alone!

THE SANCTITY OF THE SYNAGOGUE

[Speaking about the Jews in exile, God told Ezekiel,] "Yet I have been for them a small sanctuary in the countries where they arrived" (Ezekiel 11:16). R. Yitzchak expounded: This refers to the synagogues and study halls of Babylon. R. Elazar said: This refers to the house of our teacher, [Rav, who was R. Elazar's teacher] in Babylon.

Rava expounded the meaning of the verse, "God! You have been an abode for us in all generations, [even after the destruction of the *Bet Hamikdash*]" (Psalms 90:1). This refers to the synagogues and study halls [where God dwells at all times]. Abaye said: At first I used to study at home and pray in the synagogue. However, after I understood the full significance of King David's words, "God! I love the shelter of Your house and the place of Your glory's residence" (ibid. 26:8), I study only in the synagogue.

SYNAGOGUES AND STUDY HALLS TRANSPLANTED TO ERETZ YISRAEL

We learned in a *Baraita*: R. Elazar Hakapar said: The synagogues and study halls outside of Eretz Yisrael will be transplanted to Eretz Yisrael in time to come, [in the days of *Mashiach*], for it says, "Just like Mount Tabor among the mountains and Mount Carmel came across the sea [to Sinai at the giving of the Torah], so will [Pharaoh] come into the sea [after his defeat by

Nebuchanezzar]" (Isaiah 46:18). Now, we can draw a logical inference from this: If Mount Tabor and Mount Carmel, which came to Sinai only temporarily to learn Torah, were [rewarded] nevertheless and transplanted to Eretz Yisrael, the synagogues and study halls in which Scripture is read and Torah is taught surely will be moved to Eretz Yisrael.

HAUGHTINESS IS A CHARACTER FLAW

Bar Kappara expounded: What is the meaning of the verse, "Why are you so hostile [*teratzedun*], O you lofty mountains?" (Psalms 68:17); [the mountains were envious of Mount Sinai]. A Heavenly voice went forth and said [to the mountains of the world]: Why do you want to sue [*tirtzu din*] Mount Sinai? Compared to Sinai you are all blemished. [Proof that the mountains were "blemished" may be inferred from this:] Here the mountains are described as "lofty" [*gavnunim*], and elsewhere [among the blemishes that render a *kohen* unfit for the Divine service] the Torah lists, "misformed eyebrows, [*gibben*], or cataracts" (Leviticus 21:20). [Since *gibben* denotes blemish, *gavnunim*, from the same root, means blemished.] R. Ashi said: From this we see that a person who is conceited is a blemished person. [Being boastful about their lofty peaks the mountains were considered blemished, and the lowly Mount Sinai was chosen.]

GOD'S HUMILITY

(31a) R. Yochanan said: Wherever you find the power of the Holy One, blessed be He, mentioned in Scripture, you also find His humility mentioned. This is written in the Torah, repeated in the Prophets, and stated a third time in the Writings. It is written in the Torah, "God your Lord is the ultimate Supreme Being and the master of all natural forces" (Deuteronomy 10:17). And immediately after this it says, "He brings justice to the orphan and the widow." This is repeated in the Prophets, "For thus said the exalted and uplifted One, Who abides forever and Whose name is holy" (Isaiah 57:15). And immediately after this it says, "Yet I am with the contrite and the lowly in spirit." This is stated a third time in the Writings, for it says, "Extol He Who rides upon the highest heavens, God is His name" (Psalms 68:5). And immediately after this it says, "The father of orphans, the champion of widows" (ibid. 6).

THE HONOR OF ROLLING UP THE TORAH SCROLL

(32a) R. Shefatiah said in the name of R. Yochanan: If ten people have read from the Torah [meaning, if ten people got together to read from the Torah, because the Torah is not read if there are fewer than ten people present, and three to seven were called for an *aliyah* (Rashi)] the most distinguished among them rolls up the Torah scroll, and the one who rolls up the Torah receives the reward of all those who took part in the reading. For R. Yehoshua b. Levi said; If ten people have read from the Torah, the one who has rolled up the Torah scroll receives the reward of all those who took part in the reading. [The Gemara asks:] Do you think that he receives the reward of all of them [and all the others lose their reward]? [The Gemara rephrases:] Say, rather, [the one who rolls up the Torah scroll] receives a reward that is equal to [the reward of] all the others.

FOLLOWING THE ADVICE
OF A HEAVENLY VOICE

R. Shefatiah also said in the name of R. Yochanan: From where do we know that we may [follow the advice] of a heavenly voice? [If a person is in doubt about whether or not to take a certain course of action and then hears a voice saying, "Yes" or "No," he may follow that advice. This is not the kind of sorcery forbidden by the Torah (Rashi).] For it says, "Your ears will heed the command spoken from behind you: 'This is the road to follow'" (Isaiah 30:21). However, this applies only if one heard a male voice in a town, or a female voice in the fields— and even then only if the voice says, "Yes, yes," or it say, "No, no." [The word is repeated.]

READING FROM THE TORAH
WITH THE *TROP*

R. Shefatiah also said in the name of R. Yochanan: Whoever reads from the Torah without the [traditional] melody [as indicated by the cantillation marks (*trop*)] or recites Mishnah without song, about him the verse says, "So I too gave them laws that were not good, and rules by which they could not live" (Ezekiel 20:25). Abaye disputed this: Because a person does not know how to sing pleasantly you apply to him the verse, "rules by which they could not live"? Rather, this verse should be applied to a situation as described by R. Mesharshiyah who said: Two Torah scholars who live in the same city and do not join together in discussing matters of *halachah*, about them Scripture says, "So I too gave them laws that were not good and rules by which they could not live."

CONCLUSION

"Moses related [the rules of] God's festivals to the children of Israel" (Leviticus 23:44). [This teaches us that] it is a mitzvah to read from the Torah each and every [festival portion] at its appropriate time.

NOTES

1. The Targum is the Aramaic interpretive translation of the *Tanach*.

2. A nephew of the Roman emperor Hadrian at the time of the destruction of the second *Bet Hamikdash*.

3. The entire area of Eretz Yisrael (Rashi on Numbers 13:25).

4. See 2 Kings 23:29.

5. Every person has an angel that represents him in heaven (Rashi).

6. A reference to Germany (R. Yaakov Emden).

7. Rabbi Eliyahu Dessler in his *Michtav MeEliyahu* (vol. 2, page 50) explains that [Germany], the nation that descends from Esau/Edom, is driven by insatiable pride and arrogance. German haughtiness comes to the fore in that nation's innate murderous instinct, which is expressed in the maxim, "Only I, and none but me!" (Isaiah 47:8,10). Since the character of the Jewish people is marked by meekness and submission, the diametric opposite of German arrogance, it is the object of the Germans' burning hatred.

8. Identified as France and Spain by Abarbanel on Genesis 10:2.

9. A group of 120 sages who led the nation at the end of the Babylonian exile and the beginning of the era of the second *Bet Hamikdash*. Its members included the prophets Haggai, Zechariah, and Malachi, as well as Mordechai.

10. For the genealogical line, see Ruth 4:18–22.

11. Psalms 106:1, 107:1, 118:1.

12. The plain meaning of the verse relates that the Egyptians and the Israelites could not approach one another all that night.

13. According to another version: the Romans.

14. Alexander the Great also ruled over the entire world, but the *Baraita* does not list him because it only mentions rulers whose names are found in Scripture (*Tosafot*).

15. See *Gittin* 68b.

16. Daniel 3:1.

17. Daniel 3:6.

18. Numbers 28:12,14.

19. To add an additional month to the year in order to bring the lunar year into harmony with the solar year.

20. The Gemara uses the euphemism, "the enemies of Israel."

21. 2 Samuel 19:24.

22. See verse 15.

23. According to Rashi, Istahar is derived from the Aramaic *sihara*, "moon."

24. Saul was of the tribe Benjamin, the son of Rachel.

25. Esther was the daughter of Mordechai's uncle, and the Targum (Esther 2:5) traces Mordechai's ancestry back to Saul.

26. Pharaoh was angry with his wine steward and chief baker and sent them to prison where they met Joseph, who correctly interpreted their dreams. The wine steward in this verse recommended Joseph to Pharaoh as an interpreter of dreams. This led to Joseph's rise to power (Genesis, Chapters 40 and 41).

27. Literally: one who sat in the Chamber of the Hewn Stone, a chamber on the Temple Mount where the Great Sanhedrin held its deliberations.

28. The cure was Mordechai's discovery of the plot which indirectly led to his rise and Haman's downfall.

29. In the verse, the word *yeshno*, "there is" is read as *yashenu*, "they have fallen asleep," i.e., they have become lax.

30. *Shekalim* 1:1.

31. Each adult male Jew had to give half a *shekel* to the *Bet Hamikdash* treasury to be used to buy communal sacrifices. The merit of the *shekalim* negated the influence of Haman's *shekalim*.

32. *Kilayim*, Leviticus 19:19.

33. Psalm 113:1.

34. Ramatayim sounds like *matayim*, "two hundred."

35. There were about 600,000 adult males who left Egypt (Exodus 12:37).

36. At the time of Korach's rebellion against Moses.

37. Exodus 1:22 and 2:3.

38. See Joshua 18:1.

39. 1 Samuel 16:13 (David); 1 Kings 1:39 (Solomon).

40. 1 Samuel 10:1 (Saul); 2 Kings 9:1 (Yehu).

41. Jeremiah began to prophesy in the thirteenth year of King Joshiah, and the Torah scroll was found in the eighteenth year of his reign. Menasseh had systematically destroyed all the Torah scrolls, so that the people were completely unfamiliar with its contents, and this discovery was a surprising revelation to everyone. The king was upset by the passage in Deuteronomy 28:36, predicting the exile of the nation and its king.

42. In the *Yovel*, the Jubilee, any field sold during the previous forty-nine years is returned to its original owner. *Yovel* was only observed when all of Israel resided in Eretz Yisrael. Thus, if Jeremiah had not brought back the ten tribes, the observance of Yovel would have been discontinued even before Ezekiel prophesied that it would cease, and his prophecy would be meaningless.

43. After the discovery of the Torah scroll, Josiah destroyed all the idols in the country. In Beth-el he burned the bones of the idol worshipers on the altar that Jeroboam had erected (Rashi). This was foretold by the prophet from Judah mentioned in verse 17.

44. In the Talmud this statement is attributed to R. Nachman.

45. Above 13a.

46. His thoughts were constantly focused on his wealth (Maharal).

47. This psalm contains many allusions to Esther (*Maharsha*).

48. Exodus 2:5; *Sotah* 12b.

49. We read in *Berachot* 54a that the giant Og, king of Bashan, was carrying a huge boulder on his head, aiming to throw it down on the Israelites encamped in the wilderness. God performed a miracle. Ants bored a hole in the boulder so that it sank around Og's neck. Then God extended Og's teeth so that he could not lift the boulder off his neck.

50. The fistful of grain that the *kohen* took from the *omer* which was brought in the *Bet Hamikdash* on the 16th of Nisan. The day this incident occurred was the 16th of Nisan, and Mordechai was teaching the law applicable on that day.

51. Above, 15b.

52. The reference is to the colorful coat Jacob gave to Joseph. This made the brothers envious and in their envy they sold Joseph (Genesis 37:3).

53. The actual saving of a life supersedes all laws of the Torah except for the three cardinal sins: idolatry, murder, and immorality.

54. Maharsha explains that this incident is not to be taken literally. Upon Rabbah's urging, R. Zeira drank too much, whereupon R. Zeira became critically ill. Rabbah then prayed that R. Zeira should not die, and he recovered.

55. Songs of praise, comprising Psalms 113–118. *Hallel* is recited on Pesach, Shavuot, Sukkot, Chanukah, and Rosh Chodesh.

56. Ten men who are supported by public funds, who refrain from other employment so that they are available for a *minyan* in the synagogue at the times for prayer.

57. See *Sotah* 39a.

58. Grace after Meals.

59. The *nassi*, literally "prince," was the president of the Sanhedrin in Eretz Yisrael.

60. *Shilachti*, "I sent," is translated as *shulachti*, "I was sent." (See Redak on Isaiah 43:14.)

61. King Yechoniah and the exiles built this synagogue with stones and earth they had brought with them from Jerusalem.

62. A Persian mile, about 4,000 yards.

ᥱ TAANIT ᥫ

GOD'S POWER MANIFEST IN THE RAIN

(2a) The Mishnah says: We mention the Power of Rain [i.e., the manifestation of God's power through rain] in the *berachah* of the Revival of the Dead, [the second *berachah* of the *Shemoneh Esrei*, by inserting the words: *Mashiv haruach umorid hageshem*, "He makes the wind blow, and He makes the rain fall"]. The Gemara asks: How do we know that the "Power of Rain" has to be mentioned in the *Shemoneh Esrei*? The Gemara answers: For we learned in a *Baraita*: It says, " . . . to love God your Lord, and to serve Him with all your heart" (Deuteronomy 11:13). What does "to serve Him" mean? Does it mean [serving Him] through prayer or through sacrifices? That's why the verse says, "serve Him with all your heart." Now how do you serve God with your heart? Your answer must be: through prayer. And the next verse reads, "Then I shall provide rain for your land" (ibid. 14). [Which proves that the "Power of Rain" should be mentioned in the *Shemoneh Esrei*, the epitome of prayer.]

[The Gemara asks:] Why does the Mishnah use the expression "We begin to mention the Power of Rain"? Let it say instead, "We begin to mention Rain." R. Yochanan said: Because rain comes down through the power [of God], for it says, "Who performs great deeds that are beyond comprehension" (Job 5:9). And the next verse says, "Who gives rain upon the face of the earth" (ibid. 10). [The Gemara asks:] How is the idea [that God's power is manifest in rain] implied in these verses? Rabbah b. Shila replied: We can derive it from a *gezeirah shavah* [the rule that similar words in different contexts are meant to clarify each other], applied to the word *cheiker* in verses dealing with Creation. Here it says, "Who performs great deeds that are beyond comprehension [*cheiker*]." And elsewhere it says, "Did you not know? Did you not hear? The Lord is the eternal God, the creator of the ends of the earth; He does not weary, He does not tire; there is no calculating [*cheiker*] His understanding. He gives strength to the weary and grants abundant power to the powerless" (Isaiah 40:28). And about Creation it says, "Who sets mountains with His strength, Who is girded with might" (Psalms 65:7). [Job 5:9,10, which speaks of rain, uses the word *cheiker*; and Isaiah 40:28, which refers to Creation, uses both *cheiker* and "power." Therefore, just as God displayed "power" at Creation, so is His "power" evident in rain.]

THREE KEYS

R. Yochanan said: Three keys the Holy One, Blessed be He, has kept under His control and not delegated to an agent, namely: the key of rain, the key of childbirth, and the key of the revival of the dead. The key of rain, for it says, "God will open His good treasury in heaven to give your land rain at precisely the right time" (Deuteronomy 28:12). The key of childbirth, for it says, "God remembered Rachel. He heard her prayer and opened her womb" (Genesis 30:22). The key of the revival of the dead, for it says, "Then you will know that I am God, when I open your graves" (Ezekiel 37:13). In Eretz Yisrael they said: Also the key of sustenance [God kept under His control], for it says, "You open Your hand and satisfy the desire of every living being" (Psalms 145:16).

WIND AND DEW

(3a) We learned in a *Baraita*: The Sages did not make it mandatory for us to say, "He makes the wind blow and He makes the dew descend" [even throughout the winter (Rashi)], but if a person wants to mention it, he may do so. What is the reason? R. Chanina said: Because [God] never withholds the [wind and the dew, because without dew the world could not exist]. And how do we know that [God] never withholds the dew? For it says, "Elijah the Tishbite, a resident of Gilead, said to Ahab, 'As the Lord the God of Israel lives—before Whom I stand—I swear there will not be dew nor rain during these years, except by my word'" (1 Kings 17:1). And further it says, [God said to Elijah,] "Go, appear before Ahab, then I will send rain upon the earth" (ibid 18:1). But [God] did not mention [that He would restore] dew. Why? (3b) Because [God] never withholds dew. [The Gemara asks:] But if dew is never held back why did Elijah swear [that dew would not descend]?

[The Gemara answers:] This is what Elijah meant to say: Even the dew of blessing would not fall either, [meaning, dew would fall, because the world cannot exist without dew, but not enough dew would fall to make things grow]. [The Gemara asks:] Then why wasn't the dew of blessing restored [along with the rain]? [The Gemara answers: There was no point in saying it to Ahab] because he could not have told the difference [and it would not have convinced him of God's power]. [The Gemara asks:] How do we know that [God] never withholds the winds? R. Yehoshua b. Levi said: For it says, "'For I have scattered you like the four directions of the heavens,' says God" (Zechariah 2:10). What is God telling the Jewish people? Shall we say, God is telling them: I have scattered you to the four corners of the earth? If that is the case, Scripture should have said not "like the four" but "to the four." But this is what He meant: Just as it is impossible for the world to exist without winds, so too the world cannot exist without the Jewish people.

R. Yehudah said: Wind that comes after rain is as beneficial as the rain itself; clouds after rain are as beneficial as the rain itself; sunshine after rain is twice as beneficial as the rainfall. [The Gemara asks:] What does this exclude? [Meaning, what is not as good as rainfall?] [The Gemara answers:] Flashes of light that occur at night and sunshine between rainclouds, [these are not as beneficial as rainfall].

Rava said: Snow is as beneficial to a mountain as five rainfalls to the earth. For it says, "He commands the snow, 'Fall to the ground.' And [also says this] to showers of light rain, and showers of His mighty downpour of rain" (Job 37:6); [the verse mentions five forms of rain].

Rava also said: Snow is beneficial to the mountains, heavy rain to trees, gentle rain to the produce in the field. (4a) A light drizzle [urpila] is beneficial even to the seeds underneath a hard clod of earth; [they immediately begin to sprout (Rashi)]. What is urpila? It is a contraction of: Uru pili, "Wake up, [and sprout] through the cracks!"

TORAH SCHOLARS

Rava also said: A young Torah scholar is like a seed under a hard clod of earth; once he has sprouted he grows fast.

R. Ashi said: If a young Torah scholar gets angry it is the [zeal for the] Torah that inflames him, as it says, "Behold, My word is like fire, says God" (Jeremiah 23:29).

R. Ashi said: A scholar who is not as hard as iron is not a true Torah scholar, for it says, [the continuation of the above verse], "and like a hammer that shatters rock!" (ibid.). R. Abba said to R. Ashi: You have learned it from that verse, but learn it from the

following verse, "A land whose stones are iron" (Deuteronomy 8:9). Don't read avaneha [its stones]; read instead boneha, "its builders." [Torah scholars are the ones that build the future of the Jewish people. They must be unyielding and steadfast.] Ravina said: Despite that, he must train himself to be gentle, for it says, "Banish anger from your heart, and remove evil from your flesh" (Ecclesiastes 11:10).

THREE WHO MADE
IMPROPER REQUESTS

R. Shmuel b. Nachmani said in the name of R. Yonatan: There were three people who asked for things in an improper way. [Despite that] two were answered in a proper manner, but one was answered in an improper manner. [Who are the three people that made improper requests?] Eliezer, the servant of Abraham; Saul, the son of Kish; and Jephtah the Gileadite. [The Gemara explains:] Eliezer, the servant of Abraham [asked in an improper manner], for it says, "If I say to a girl, 'Tip over your jug, and let me have a drink,' and she replies, 'Drink, and I will also water your camels,' she will be the one whom You have designated for Your servant Isaac" (Genesis 24:14). [How could Eliezer say that?] She might have been lame or blind. Nevertheless, he was answered properly, in that [God made] Rebecca appear on the scene. Saul the son of Kish [made an improper request] for it says, "The king [Saul] will enrich whoever kills [Goliath] with great wealth and give his daughter to him in marriage, and he will free his father's family from royal service in Israel" (1 Samuel 17:25). [How could Saul say such a thing?] He might have been a slave or a bastard. He too was answered properly in that [the person who slew Goliath] turned out to be David.

Jephtah [made an improper request] for it says, "Jephtah made a vow to God and said, 'If You will indeed deliver the Ammonites into my hand, then whatever comes out of the door of my house to meet me on my safe return from the Ammonites . . . shall be offered by me as a burnt offering'" (Judges 11:30,31). It might have been an unclean thing [a dog or a pig]. And [God] answered him in a disapproving manner, for it so happened that his only daughter [came running out to meet him]. This [incident] is what the prophet had in mind when he said, "Is there no balm in Gilead? Can no physician be found?" (Jeremiah 8:22). [The reference is to Pinchas, who was in Gilead and who could have annulled Jephthah's vow. But Jephthah in his pride refused to go to Pinchas, and Pinchas, who was a prophet, found it below his dignity to go to Jephthah. As a result of their intransigence, Jephthah's daughter tragically was forced to spend the rest of her life in isolation.[1]]

And it also says, [in regard to human sacrifices], "which I never commanded, never decreed, and which never came to My mind" (Jeremiah 19:5). [This alludes to three incidents:] "Which I never commanded" refers to the sacrifice of the son of Mesha, king of Moab, as it says, "So he took his first-born son who was to succeed him as king, and offered him up on the wall as a burnt offering" (2 Kings 3:27). "Which I never decreed" refers to the story of the daughter of Jephthah, [for the vow he made was invalid from the start]. "And which never came to My mind" refers to Isaac the son of Abraham. [God never intended for Abraham to sacrifice Isaac; He only meant to test him.]

ISRAEL'S IMPROPER REQUEST

R. Berechiah said: The congregation of Israel also made an improper request, yet God granted that request. For it says, "Let us know, let us strive to know God like the dawn whose emergence is certain; then He will come to us like the rain, like the late rain that satiates the earth" (Hosea 6:3). The Holy One, blessed be He, said: My daughter, you are asking for something [rain] which sometimes is desirable and at other times is not desirable, [it depends on the season], but I will be to you something that is desirable at all times, as it says, "I will be to Israel like the dew" (Hosea 14:6). The people of Israel made another improper request. They said to Him: Master of the universe, "Place me like a seal on Your heart; like a seal on Your arm" (Song of Songs 8:6). The Holy One, blessed be He, said: My daughter, you are asking for something that sometimes can be seen and at other times cannot be seen. [The heart and the arms are usually covered.] However, I will make of you something that can be seen at all times. For it says, "Behold, I have engraved you upon the palms of My hands" (Isaiah 49:16); [they are always visible].

THE MIRACULOUS RAINFALL
IN THE DAYS OF JOEL

(5a) [The Mishnah says:] Until when do we pray for rain? [Meaning, until when do we say *vetein tal umatar*, "and give dew and rain," in the weekday *Shemoneh Esrei*?] R. Yehudah says: Until Pesach is over. R. Meir says: Until the end of Nisan, as it says, "He has brought down the rain for you—the early rain and the late rain—in the first [month]" (Joel 2:23).

[The Gemara says:] R. Nachman said to R. Yitzchak: Does the early rain then fall in Nisan? [But we know that] the early rain falls in Marcheshvan! For we learned in a *Baraita*: The early rain falls in Marcheshvan, and the late rain falls in Nisan. R. Yitzchak answered: This is what R. Yochanan said: [Normally the late rain falls in Nisan,] but during the days of [the prophet] Joel, the son of Pethuel [both the early and the late rains fell in Nisan], as it says, "What the cutting-locust has left, the locust has devoured. What the locust has left, the grub has devoured, and what the grub has left, the hopper has devoured" (Joel 1:4). [There were seven years of famine, followed by four years of a plague of

locusts, after which God took pity on the Jewish people and, miraculously, both the early and the late rains fell in Nisan to bring an end to the famine.] That year, the entire month of Adar passed, and it still did not rain. It only began to rain on the first of Nisan. The prophet then told the Jewish people: Go and plant your fields. They replied: If a person has a *kav* of wheat or two *kabim* of barley, should he eat them and keep alive, or plant them and die? [Even at best, it will take a long time for the grain to ripen.] He answered: Go out and plant your fields anyway.

A miracle happened. They suddenly discovered grain hidden in the cracks of the walls and the antholes [where mice had hidden it (Rashi)]. They went out and planted on the second, third, and fourth of Nisan, and the second rain came down on the fifth of Nisan. On the sixteenth of Nisan they offered the *Omer*.[2] It turned out that grain and the *Omer* that usually take six months to ripen, ripened in eleven days [from the fifth to the sixteenth of Nisan]. About that generation it says, "They who sow in tears [because they had nothing to eat] shall reap with songs of joy. Though he goes along weeping, carrying the measure of seeds, he shall come back with songs of joy, carrying his sheaves" (Psalms 126:5).

[The Gemara asks:] What is the meaning of, "Though he goes along weeping, carrying the measure of seeds"? [Since the first segment of the verse refers to the farmer; this part must refer to something else.] R. Yehudah said: When the ox is ploughing, on his forward run it cries; but on his return it can already eat the sprouts from the furrows. And that is alluded to with the words, "he shall come back with songs of joy." What is meant by "carrying his sheaves"? R. Chisda said, others say it was taught in a *Baraita*: The stalk of grain alone measured a span,[3] and the ear measured two spans; [a miracle, since usually the stalk is three or four times the size of the ear (Rashi)].

R. Nachman asked R. Yitzchak: What is meant by the verse, "For God has called for a famine, and it is coming to the land for seven years" (1 Kings 8:1). What did they eat during these seven years? R. Yitzchak replied: This is what R. Yochanan said: During the first year, they ate what was stored up in the houses; in the second year, what was in the fields; in the third, the flesh of kosher animals; during the fourth, the flesh of non-kosher animals; during the fifth, the flesh of repulsive, creeping creatures; during the sixth, the flesh of their sons and daughters; and during the seventh, the flesh of their own arms, and thereby the verse came true, "Everyone will eat the flesh of his own arm" (Isaiah 9:19).

THERE IS A JERUSALEM
IN HEAVEN

R. Nachman also asked R. Yitzchak: What is the meaning of the verse, "There is something holy in your midst, and I will not enter the city" (Hosea 11:9). [Surely it cannot mean,] because there is something holy in your midst, therefore, [God says:] I will not enter the city! R. Yitzchak replied: This is how R. Yochanan explained it: The Holy One, blessed be He, said, "I will not enter the heavenly Jerusalem until I can enter the earthly Jerusalem," [meaning, until there is holiness in the Jerusalem on earth]. [The Gemara asks:] Is there a Jerusalem above? [The Gemara answers:] Yes. For it says, "The built-up Jerusalem is like the city with which it is joined together" (Psalms 122:3) [meaning, Jerusalem on earth is modeled after its prototype in heaven].

THE SIN OF IDOLATRY

R. Nachman further asked R. Yitzchak: What is the meaning of the verse, "They are uniformly foolish and stupid, the vanities for which they are punished are [nothing but] wood" (Jeremiah 10:8). He replied: This is how R. Yochanan explains it: There is one thing that brings about the suffering of the wicked in Gehinnom, and that is idol worship. [And how do we know that this verse speak of idol worship?] It says here, "The vanities for which they are punished," and elsewhere, it says, [speaking of idols], "They are vanity, the work of deception" (Jeremiah 10:15).

R. Nachman further asked R. Yitzchak: What is meant by the verse, "For My people has committed two sins" (ibid. 2:13)? Only two sins? Did the prophet ignore the twenty-four sins [listed in Ezekiel 22? Alternately, the sins mentioned in the twenty-four books of *Tanach* (Rashi)]. R. Yitzchak replied: This is how R. Yochanan explains it: [The prophet is focusing on one major sin, which is as grave as two sins]. There is one sin (5b) that is equal to two, and that is idol worship. For it says, "For My people has committed two sins: They have forsaken Me, the source of living waters, to dig for themselves cisterns, broken cisterns that cannot hold the water" (Jeremiah 2:13). [This is a double sin: Forsaking God, and worshipping a worthless idol.] And it says about the non-Jews, [that they never abandoned their false god], "Traverse the isles of the Kittites and observe, send forth unto Kedar and consider deeply . . . Has a nation ever exchanged its gods, though they are not [genuine] gods? Yet My people has exchanged its Glory for something that is useless" (ibid. 10,11). A Tanna explained: The Kittites worship fire, the Kedarites worship water, and although they know that water extinguishes fire they have not changed their gods, but My people has changed their God for something that is useless.

SAMUEL, SAUL, AND DAVID

R. Nachman also asked R. Yitzchak: What is meant by the verse, "When Samuel became old" (1 Samuel 8:1)? Did Samuel ever reach old age? He was only fifty-two years old when he died! For a Tanna taught us in

a *Baraita*: If someone dies when he is fifty-two years old, he has died at the age of Samuel of Ramah. He replied: This is how R. Yochanan explains it: Old age came upon him prematurely, for it says, [God said], "I regret that I have made Saul king" (1 Samuel 15:11). Samuel complained to God, "Master of the universe! You have made me the equal of Moses and Aaron, as it says, 'Moses and Aaron were among His priests, and Samuel among those who invoke His name' (Psalms 99:6). Just as the work of Moses' and Aarons's hands did not go to waste in their lifetime [i.e., Joshua, their student, outlived both of them], so let not the work of my hands go to waste in my lifetime; [don't let Saul die in my lifetime]." The Holy One, blessed be He, replied, "What shall I do? Should Saul die right away? Samuel won't allow it. Should Samuel die young? People will murmur that he died because of his sins. Should neither Saul nor Samuel die? The time has come for David to begin his reign, and one reign may not encroach on another even by a hair's breadth."

So the Holy One, blessed be He, said: I will make Samuel prematurely old, [so that Saul will outlive Samuel, and because of Samuel's old appearance people will not say that he sinned and therefore died young]. This is alluded to in the verse, "Saul was sitting in Gibeah under the tamarisk tree in Ramah" (1 Samuel 22:6). How does Gibeah come to Ramah, [Gibeah is in Benjamin while Ramah is in Ephraim]? The verse comes to teach you that it was the prayer of Samuel of Ramah that accomplished that Saul should live [as king] in Gibeah for an additional two-and-a-half years. [The Gemara asks:] Does one person get pushed aside because of another? [Meaning, did Samuel have to die because of David? Since David had to become king, Saul had to die before David was crowned, and Samuel had to die before Saul.]

[The Gemara answers:] Yes, for R. Shmuel b. Nachmani said in the name of R. Yonatan: What is meant by the verse, "Because I have made My words clear-cut through the prophets, I have slain them through the utterances of My mouth" (Hosea 6:5). It does not say that they were slain because of their misdeeds; rather, "through the utterances of My mouth," [i.e., by a Divine decree, as in the episode with Samuel (Rashi)]. So you see that one person is pushed aside for the sake of another.

JACOB OUR FATHER
NEVER DIED

R. Nachman and R. Yitzchak were sitting at a meal, and R. Nachman said to R. Yitzchak: Please tell us some Torah thoughts. R. Yitzchak replied: This is what R. Yochanan said: You should not talk during a meal. We are concerned that the [food enters] the windpipe before it reaches the gullet, which may be life-threatening, [because the person may choke]. After they ended the meal R. Yitzchak added: This is what R. Yochanan said: Jacob our Father never died. R. Nachman objected: Was it for nothing that they eulogized, embalmed, and buried him? R. Yitzchak replied: I derive it from a Scriptural verse, for it says, "But you, have no fear, My servant Jacob—declares God. Be not dismayed, O Israel! I will deliver you from far away, your children from their land of captivity" (Jeremiah 30:10). The verse compares Jacob to his children [the Jewish people]. Just as the children of Jacob will be alive [at the time of the Redemption], so Jacob, too, will then be alive. [Hence, he never died.]

R. Yitzchak said: Anyone who says, "Rachav, Rachav"[4] instantly experiences a seminal emission. R. Nachman said: I say it, and it does not affect me at all. R. Yitzchak replied: When do we say this, [that a person has a seminal emission by merely repeating her name,] if he knows her and recognizes her.

MAY YOUR OFFSPRING BE LIKE YOU

When [R. Yitzchak and R. Nachman] parted, R. Nachman asked R. Yitzchak, "Please, Master, bless me." He replied, "Let me tell you a parable: To what can we compare this? To a man who was traveling in the desert. Hungry, tired, and thirsty, he came to a tree whose fruit were very sweet, its shade pleasant, and there was a stream of water flowing beneath it. He ate from its fruit, drank from the water, and rested in its shade. When he was about to continue his journey, he said, 'Tree, O tree, how can I bless you? Shall I say: May your fruits be sweet? They are sweet already. That your shade should be pleasant? It is already pleasant. That a stream of water may flow beneath you? A stream of water flows beneath you already. Therefore [I say], May it be God's will, that all the trees planted from your seed (6a) should be like you.' You, too, [R. Nachman, said R. Yitzchak,] With what shall I bless you? With the knowledge of the Torah? You already have the knowledge of Torah. With riches? You have riches already. With children? You have children already. Therefore, I say, May it be God's will that your offspring will be like you."

SPOTTY RAINFALL

(6b) R. Chisda said: If rain fell on some parts of the country, and not on other parts, that is not considered the fulfillment of the curse of, "He will shut up the skies so there will be no rain" (Deuteronomy 11:17), [for the wet areas will supply food to the drought-stricken parts]. [The Gemara challenges this:] But it is not that way! Doesn't it say, "I therefore held back the rain from you three months before the harvest: I would make it rain on one town and not on another; one field would be rained on, while another, on which it did not rain, would wither" (Amos 4:7). And [referring to this verse,] R. Yehudah said in the name of

Rav: Both [the rain and the lack of it] are a curse! [So, how does R. Chisda say that a partial rainfall is not a curse?] [The Gemara answers:] There is no contradiction. In the one case [where partial rainfall is a curse] the verse speaks of an excessive amount of rain that fell [on some parts of the country and destroyed the crops]; in the other case [where partial rain is not a curse] the verse refers to a normal amount of rain [that fell on parts of the country]. R. Ashi said: This is borne out by a precise reading of the verse, for it says, timateir, [which is seen as a contraction of tehei mekom matar], "it will be a place flooded by rain." This proves it.

THE BERACHAH OVER RAIN

R. Abahu said: When do we begin to recite the berachah over rain? When the bridegroom goes out to meet the bride, [when a drop of rain that falls into a puddle meets the droplets splashing upward]. [The Gemara asks:] What is the berachah? R. Yehudah said in the name of Rav: We thank You, O Lord, our God, for every single drop that you have brought down for us. R. Yochanan ended the berachah like this, "Were our mouths full of song as the sea, and our tongue as full of joyous song as its multitude of waves, and our lips as full of praise as the breadth of the heavens . . . !"[5] until: "Let Your mercy not forsake us as Your kindness has not abandoned us. Blessed are You, O God, to Whom most thanksgiving is due." [The Gemara asks:] "Most thanksgiving" and not "all the thanksgiving"? Rava replied: Say, "O God, to Whom thanksgiving is due."

THE IMPORTANCE OF RAIN

R. Abahu said: The day when rain falls is greater than the day of the Revival of the Dead, for the Revival of the Dead is only for the righteous, whereas rain benefits both the righteous and the wicked. And he disagrees with R. Yosef, for R. Yosef said: Since rain is equal to the Revival of the Dead, [the Sages] established that it should be mentioned in the berachah of the Revival of the Dead [in the Shemoneh Esrei].

Rav Yehudah said: The day when rain falls is as great as the day when the Torah was given. For it says, "My teaching shall drop like the rain" (Deuteronomy 32:2), and "teaching" surely means Torah, for it says, "For I have given you a good teaching, do not forsake My Torah" (Proverbs 4:2). Rava said: It is even greater than the day on which the Torah was given, as it says, "My teaching shall drop like the rain." [When making an analogy,] what is being compared to what? Surely, the smaller thing [the teaching, i.e., the Torah] is compared to the greater, [the more obvious, i.e., the rain]. [The underlying meaning is: The Torah is as essential to a Jew's spiritual existence as rain is to his physical existence (Maharsha).]

Rava pointed out a contradiction: On the one hand it says, "My teaching shall drop like rain" (Deuteronomy

32:2). On the other hand, this is followed by, "My saying shall flow down like the *dew*" (ibid.). [The Gemara answers:] If the scholar is a worthy [God-fearing] person then [the Torah] is to him like dew [which is always a blessing]; but if not, it destroys him, [just like a powerful rainstorm crushes the crops].

TORAH STUDY

We learned in a *Baraita*: R. Banaah used to say: If a person studies Torah for its own sake, his Torah learning becomes a potion of life for him, for it says, "It is a tree of life for those who grasp it" (Proverbs 3:18); and it says further, "It will be health to your navel" (ibid. 8). [Just as a fetus in the mother's womb is nourished through the navel, so are we nourished through the Torah (Ralbag).] And it also says, "For one who finds me [the Torah] finds life" (ibid. 8:35). But if a person studies Torah not for its own sake, it becomes a deadly poison for him, as it says, "My teaching shall drop [*yaarof*] like rain," and *arifah* surely means death, as it says, "They shall break the neck [*ve'arfu*] of the calf there in the valley" (Deuteronomy 21:4).

R. Yirmiah said to R. Zeira: Master, please come and teach us [some *halachot*]. R. Zeira replied: I don't feel well; I can't. R. Yirmiyah then said: Please, Master, perhaps you can teach us something in *Aggadah* [which is easier]? R. Zeira replied: This is what R. Yochanan said: What is meant by the verse, "For a man is a tree in the field" (Deuteronomy 20:19)? Is a man a tree? [We must say that the verse wants to compare man to a tree.] It says about trees, "From it you will eat, and you shall not cut it down" (ibid.), but it also says about trees, "you shall destroy it and cut it down." How does this apply to a human being? If you have a Torah scholar who is a worthy [God-fearing] person, learn [eat] from him and do not cut him down; but if he is not worthy [God-fearing], destroy him and cut him down.

R. Chama b. R. Chanina said: What is meant by the verse, "Iron sharpens iron" (Proverbs 27:17)? It teaches you that just as with iron, one blade sharpens another, so it is with two Torah scholars—one sharpens the other's mind through *halachah*. Rabbah bar Bar Chana said: Why are the words of the Torah compared to fire? For it says, "'Behold, My word is like fire,' declares God" (Jeremiah 23:29). This teaches you that just as fire does not burn alone [you have to rub a few pieces of wood against each other to start a fire], so, too, the words of Torah do not endure with a person who studies alone. This agrees with what R. Yose b. Chaninah said: What is meant by the verse, "A sword upon those who are alone; and they will become foolish" (Jeremiah 50:36)? This means: A sword upon the enemies of Torah scholars [a euphemism, meaning the scholars themselves], who study on their own. And not only [don't they advance] but they become foolish, as it says, "they will become foolish," and worse than that,

they are guilty of sin. For it says here, "They will become foolish," and elsewhere it says, "we have been foolish and we have sinned" (Numbers 12:11). If you wish, you can derive it from the following verse, "The officers of Zoan have become foolish . . . they have led Egypt astray" (Isaiah 19:13).

R. Nachman b. Yitzchak said: Why are the words of the Torah compared to a tree, as it says, "It is a tree of life for those who grasp it"? It teaches you that, just as small pieces of wood are needed to ignite large ones, so it is with Torah scholars: the younger ones sharpen the minds of the older ones, [because they ask stimulating questions]. This agrees with what R. Chanina said: I have learned a great deal from my teachers, and from my colleagues more than from my teachers, but from my students I learned more than from anyone.

R. Chanina b. Papa pointed out a contradiction. It says, "Bring forth water for the thirsty!" (Isaiah 21:14), [implying, the teacher should search out the student], and it also says, "Ho, everyone who is thirsty, go to the water" (ibid. 55:1), [implying, the student should pursue the teacher]. [The Gemara resolves the contradiction:] If he is a worthy [God-fearing] student, "Bring forth water for the thirsty," but if he is not, then, "Ho, everyone who is thirsty, go to the water."

R. Chanina b. Chama pointed out a contradiction. It says, "Let your springs [of Torah knowledge] spread outward" (Proverbs 5:16), but it also says, "Let them [your wisdom] be yours alone" (ibid. 17). [The Gemara answers:] If he is a worthy student, "Let your springs spread outward," but if he is not, then, "Let them be yours alone."

TORAH IS LIKE WATER, WINE, AND MILK

R. Chanina b. Idi said: Why are the words of the Torah compared to water—as it says, "Ho, everyone who is thirsty, go to the water"? It teaches you that just as water flows from a higher to a lower level, so do the words of the Torah endure only with a person who is humble. R. Oshiah said: Why are the words of the Torah compared to these three liquids: water, wine, and milk—as it says, "Ho, everyone who is thirsty, go to the *water*," and it says, "Go and buy *wine* and *milk* without money" (Isaiah 55:1)? This is meant to teach you that just as these three liquids can only be preserved in ordinary [earthenware] vessels, so too the words of Torah are retained only by a person who is humble. This is exemplified by the story about the daughter of the Roman Emperor. Once, when seeing R. Yehoshua b. Chanania, she sighed, "O, such glorious wisdom in such an ugly vessel!" [She was repelled by his appearance.] He replied, "Doesn't your father keep wine in an earthenware vessel?" She asked, "Where else should he keep it?" R. Yehoshua retorted, "You who are nobles should keep it in vessels of gold and silver!" She then went and told this to her father, so he ordered the wine put into vessels of gold and silver, and it became sour.

When the Emperor heard this, he asked his daughter, "Who gave you this idea?" She replied, "R. Yehoshua b. Chananiah." So the Emperor summoned him and asked him, "Why did you tell my daughter to put wine into gold and silver vessels?" He replied, "The way she spoke to me, that's how I answered her." [She thought that wisdom and good looks should go together, and I wanted to show her that the opposite is true.] [The princess now asked,] "But are there not good-looking people who are learned?" R. Yehoshua b. Chananiah answered, (7b) "If these [handsome] people were ugly they would be even more learned." [They would be humble, and humility fosters learning.] Another explanation [as to why the Torah is compared to water, wine, and milk] is: Just as these three liquids become spoiled through disregard, [if you don't pay attention to them, they will spill or dirt will drop into them], so too are the words of Torah: if you don't pay attention to them [and constantly review them] you will forget them.

MORE ABOUT RAIN

R. Chama b. Chanina said: The day when rain falls is as great as the day when heaven and earth were created. For it says, "Pour out, O heavens, from above, and let the upper heights drip righteousness; let the earth open up and salvation and goodness will flourish; let it make them sprout together; I am God, Who created it" (Isaiah 45:8). It does not say, "I created *them*" [i.e., heaven and earth], but "I created *it*" [the rain, which shows that God takes pride in creating the rain].

R. Oshiah said: The day when rain falls is so great that even salvation sprouts from it. For it says, "Pour out, O heavens, from above, let the earth open up and salvation . . . will flourish" (ibid.).

WHY RAIN IS WITHHELD

R. Tanchum b. Chanilai said: Rain only falls if the sins of Israel have been forgiven. For it says, "God, You have favored Your land [with rain], You have returned the captivity of Jacob. You have forgiven the iniquity of Your people, pardoned all their sins" (Psalms 85:2,3). Ze'iri of Dihavat said to Ravina: You have learned it from this verse; we derive it from the following source, [Solomon prayed at the completion of the *Bet Hamikdash*,] "May You hear from Heaven and forgive the sin of Your servants . . . and may You give rain upon Your land" (1 Kings 8:36).

R. Tanchum the son of R. Chiya of Kfar Akko said: Rain is withheld only if the enemies of Israel [a euphemism, meaning Israel itself] are condemned to be destroyed, as it says, "As drought and heat snatch melting snow, so the grave snatches sinners" (Job 24:19).

Ze'iri of Dihavat said to Ravina: You have learned it from this verse; we derive it from a different verse, "He will shut up the skies so that there will be no rain . . . and you will soon perish" (Deuteronomy 11:17).

R. Chisda said: Rain is held back only because people are neglecting the duty of giving *terumah* and *maaser*,[6] as it says, "As drought and heat snatch melting snow." [The Gemara asks:] How do you derive that from this verse? In the yeshivah of R. Yishmael it was taught: [You can infer:] Because you have not carried out the *mitzvot* that I commanded you to do in the summer [i.e., giving *terumah* and *maaser* at harvest time], you will be denied the water of melting snow in the winter.

R. Shimon b. Pazzi said: Rain is held back only because of people who talk evil gossip, as it says, "The north wind prevents the rain, because [God] shows an angry face when there is whispered slander" (Proverbs 25:23). R. Salla said in the name of R. Hamenuna: Rain is held back only because of people who are insolent, for it says, "The showers have been withheld, and the late rain did not happen; yet you had the boldness of a harlot woman, you refused to be ashamed" (Jeremiah 3:3).

R. Salla further said in the name of R. Hamenuna: A person who is insolent will end up stumbling into sin, for it says, "Yet you had the boldness of a harlot woman." R. Nachman explained: It is evident that he has already stumbled into sin, for it says, "You *had* the boldness," and not, "You *will have*." Rabbah the son of R. Huna said: If a person is insolent, you are allowed to call him "wicked," for it says, "A wicked man is brazen-faced" (Proverbs 21:29). R. Nachman the son of R. Yitzchak said: You may even hate him, for it says, "The boldness of his face is transformed" (Ecclesiastes 8:1). Do not read *yeshune*, "transformed"; read instead *yesane*, "hated."

R. Katina said: Rain is held back only because of neglect of Torah, as it says, "Through laziness the ceiling sags [*yimach*]" (ibid. 10:18). [He expounds:] Because of the laziness among the Jewish people in that they did not engage in Torah study, the enemy of God [a euphemism, meaning God Himself] becomes impoverished, [and "unable" to provide rain]. *Mach* actually means "poor," as it says, "If a person is too poor [*mach*] to pay the assessment" (Leviticus 27:8). The ceiling actually symbolizes God, for it says, "He Who roofs His upper chambers with water" (Psalms 104:3). R. Yosef derived [that the lack of rain is tied to the neglect of Torah study] from the following verse, "Thus, they have never seen the light; the skies are patchy [with clouds], which a wind comes and clears away" (Job 37:21).

[The Gemara expounds:] "Light" surely means Torah, as it says, "For the mitzvah is a lamp, and the Torah is light" (Proverbs 6:23), [and they neglected to study the Torah]. [The verse continues,] "The skies are patchy [with clouds]"—with reference to this it was taught in the yeshivah of R. Yishmael: Even when the sky is full of patches of white clouds ready to bring down the dew and the rain, [because of neglect of Torah study], a wind passes and disperses them.

R. Ammi said: Rain is held back only because of the sin of robbery. For it says, "With clouds [*kapayim*] He conceals the rain" (Job 36:32). [R. Ammi interprets the verse to mean:] Because of the sin of the hands [i.e., robbery; *kapayim* also means hands], God hides the rain. And *kapayim*, "hands," means "robbery," for it says, "and from the robbery that is in their hands" (Jonah 3:8). And "light" surely stands for rain, for it says, "He scatters the rain clouds of His lightning" (Job 37:11). What is the remedy, [if there is no rain]? A person should pray more. For it says, "He commands [the rain] upon those who entreat Him" (ibid. 36:32), and "entreat" means prayer, as it says, "And you [Jeremiah]—do not pray for this people . . . and do not entreat Me" (Jeremiah 7:16).

R. Ammi also said: What is meant by the verse, "If the sword is blunt, and he has not honed the edge, nevertheless it strengthens the warrior. Wisdom is a more powerful skill" (Ecclesiastes 10:10)—If you see that the sky is as hard as iron,[7] so that neither dew nor rain fall, it is due to the deeds of the generation that is corrupt. For it says, "For they did not turn their face to God but became corrupt." [This is a metaphoric interpretation of "he has not honed the edge."] What is the remedy? Let them strengthen themselves through prayers [for mercy], for it says, "nevertheless, [even though they sinned], it [prayer] strengthens the warrior. Wisdom is a more powerful skill"—[this last phrase signifies:] all the more so [would the rain have fallen] if their deeds had been righteous to begin with.

[Each of the above-mentioned Sages attributes the lack of rain to the failing that was most prevalent in his generation.]

THE STUDENT HAD
TROUBLE UNDERSTANDING

Resh Lakish said: If you see a student (8a) who finds studying as hard as iron, [he cannot grasp the subject matter], it is because the basic principles are not systematically organized in his mind. For it says, "He has not honed the edge." What is the remedy? He should spend more time studying in the yeshivah. For it says, "It strengthens the warrior." [But the verse concludes,] "Wisdom is a more powerful skill," which means, it would have been much better if he had studied in a systematic fashion from the start. For example, Resh Lakish would review the Mishnah forty times, corresponding to the forty days in which the Torah was transmitted to Moses, and only then would he appear before R. Yochanan [to study Gemara]. R. Adda b. Abbahu used to review the Mishnah twenty-four times, corresponding to the [twenty-four books of *Tanach*] Torah, Prophets, and the Writings, and only then would he come before Rava [to learn Gemara].

Rava said: If you see a student to whom studying comes as hard as iron, it is because his teacher did not [encourage him] with a smiling face, as it says, "He has not honed the edge," [here interpreted as "his face had an unkind expression"]. What is his remedy? The student should send friends [to appease the teacher], as it says, "it strengthens the warrior" [here expounded as, "He should overwhelm his teacher with warriors, i.e., his friends]." [The verse concludes,] "Wisdom is a more powerful skill" [meaning,] he would have been better off if his conduct toward his teacher had been proper to start with, [then the teacher would have had a friendly attitude toward him].

R. Ammi also said: What is the meaning of the verse, "If the snake bites because it was not charmed [*lachash*], then there is no advantage to the charmer's art" (Ecclesiastes 10:11)? [R. Ammi expounds:] If you see a generation over which the heavens are the color of rust [and covered with a blanket of smog] like copper, so that neither dew nor rain falls, it is because that generation does not have enough people who pray the silent [*Shemoneh esrei belachash*]; [*lachash*, "to charm," means also "to whisper"]. What is their remedy? Let them go to a person who knows how to pray properly, as it says, "Let his friend speak on his behalf" (Job 36:33).[8] The phrase "There is no advantage to the charmer's art" means: If a person is able to pray [the *Shemoneh Esrei*] properly but does not do so, what benefit does he have from remaining silent? But if he prayed [the silent *Shemoneh Esrei*] but was not answered, [i.e., the rain did not come], what is his remedy? He should go to the most devout man of that generation, [and ask] that he should pray for the generation, as it says, "He commands [the rain to fall] because of the *mafgia*" (ibid.); and *pegiah* means fervent prayer, as it says, "And you [Jeremiah]—do not pray for this people; do not speak up for them with a cry and a prayer, and do not entreat [*tifga*] Me" (Jeremiah 7:16). But if he did pray, and was successful, and as a result, became conceited, then he brings anger upon the world, for it says, "He acquires [God's] anger, because he is rising in stature and becomes conceited" (Job 36:33).

Rava said: Two Torah scholars who live in the same city, but cannot agree and cooperate on points of *halachah*, arouse [God's] anger and bring it on themselves, as it says, [Rava's interpretation of Job 36:33,] "Talk to your friend, otherwise you are provoking the wrath [of God], and you are bringing it on yourself" (ibid.).

THE BANE OF
EVIL TALEBEARING

Resh Lakish said: What is the meaning of the passage, "If the snake bites because it was not charmed, then there is no advantage to the charmer's art" (Ecclesiastes 10:1)? In time to come all animals will gather around the snake and say to it, "The lion claws [its prey] and devours it; the wolf tears it and devours it; but you snake, what benefit do you derive [from biting and killing people]?" The snake answers, "There is no advantage to the charmer's art" [literally, "to the man of the tongue," meaning, "Do people, then, derive physical pleasure from slandering each other?].

R. Ammi said: A person's prayer is only answered if he puts his whole heart into it, as it says, "Let us lift our hearts with our hands to God in heaven" (Lamentations 3:41). Shmuel b. Nachmani then appointed an interpreter [to explain what he was saying], and he expounded as follows: "They deceived Him with their speech, lied to Him with their words; their hearts were not steadfast with Him; they were untrue to His covenant. Nevertheless, He, being merciful, is forgiving of iniquity" (Psalms 78:36–38). [Which proves that God accepts a person's prayer even if his heart is not in it.] [The Gemara answers:] There is no contradiction: One refers to prayer by an individual, the other to the prayer of the community. [The prayer of an individual must be fervent and sincere if it is to be answered, but God accepts any kind of communal prayer.]

THE WELL AND THE WEASEL
R. Ammi also said: Rain falls only for the sake of people who are honest in their business dealings, for it says, "Truth will sprout from earth, and justice will look down from heaven" (Psalms 85:12).

R. Ammi further said: Come and see how great are the people who have faith in God. This is borne out by the story of the Weasel and the Well: [A girl fell into a well. A young man who happened to pass by agreed to rescue her if she would marry him. They appointed as witnesses to their pledge a passing weasel and the well. The young man reneged on his promise and married someone else. The couple had two children: one was killed by a weasel, the other fell into a well and died. Realizing that this was a sign from heaven, the wife demanded to hear the truth. She then told her husband to divorce her and marry his intended. He did, and the marriage was blessed with children and much happiness.][9] [R. Ammi summarizes:] Now if this is the case with a person who trusts in a weasel and a well, [making them his witnesses], surely if a person places his faith in the Holy One, blessed be He, [making God his witness, he can be certain that ultimately the truth will come out].

TZADDIKIM ARE JUDGED SEVERELY
R. Yochanan said: Whoever leads a righteous life [on earth below] is judged more strictly in heaven above. [A tzaddik is judged more sternly because his reward in the World to Come is far greater than that of ordi-

nary people], as it says, "Truth will sprout from earth, and justice will look down from heaven." [If he is a perfect tzaddik, he will be judged with unmitigated justice.] R. Chiya b. Avin in the name of R. Huna [derived this lesson] from the following verse, "As You are feared, so is Your fury" (Psalms 90:11). [The more God-fearing a tzaddik is, the more rigorously he is judged.] Resh Lakish said: [It may be inferred from here,] "You have eliminated those who rejoiced in doing righteousness, who would invoke Your ways [in prayer]; You became enraged because we had sinned. We had always relied on them and been saved" (Isaiah 64:4). R. Yehoshua b. Levi said: Whoever joyfully accepts the suffering that befalls him brings salvation to the world, as it says, "We had always relied on them and been saved."

PRAY FOR ONE THING AT A TIME
(8b) In the days of R. Shmuel b. Nachmani there was a famine and an epidemic. People asked: What shall we do? Shall we pray that God should take away both scourges? That is not possible. Let us then pray that God should eliminate the epidemic, and we will have to endure the famine. But R. Shmuel b. Nachmani told them: Let us pray the God eliminate the famine, because when the Merciful One grants abundance, He grants it to the living. For it says, "You open Your hand, and satisfy the desire of every *living* thing" (Psalms 145:16), [so He will keep us alive and well]. How do we know that [it is not proper] to pray for two things at the same time? Because it says, "So we fasted and implored our God for this" (Ezra 8:23). "*This*" implies that they had other things [to pray for, but they prayed for only one thing]. In Eretz Yisrael they said in the name of R. Chaggai that it could be inferred from here, "To pray for mercy from before the God of Heaven concerning this secret" (Daniel 2:18). "*This*" suggests that there were other things too [to pray for].

GOOD INTENTIONS COUNT AS GOOD DEEDS
In the days of R. Zeira the government passed a decree ordering the Jews to convert, and they also prohibited Jews to observe fast days. [They did not want the Jews to fast and thereby cause the decree of forced conversions to be annulled (*Maharsha*).] R. Zeira said to his colleagues: Let us now resolve to fast, and when the decree will be lifted we will observe the fast. His colleagues asked him: How do you know that this is effectual? He replied: Because it says, "He said to me, 'Do not fear, Daniel, for from the first day that you set your heart to understand and to fast before your God, your words have been heard'" (Daniel 10:12). [A good intention counts as a good deed, even if you are prevented from carrying it out (*Maharsha*).]

RAIN AND SUNSHINE

R. Yitzchak said: If it rains on Friday, even if there is a drought as bad as in the days of Elijah,[10] it must be considered a sign of God's displeasure [because people are unable to do their shopping for the *Shabbat* meals]. This is what Rabbah b. Shila had in mind when he said: A rainy day is as hard to bear as the day when Court is in session. [On Mondays and Thursdays the Bet Din convened to settle disputes between people. This gave rise to tumultuous scenes, crowded streets, and traffic jams.] Ameimar said: Were it not for the fact that the world needs rain, I would pray that rainfall should be abolished [because it causes inconvenience].

R. Yitzchak further said: Sunshine on *Shabbat* is an act of generosity toward the poor [they enjoy it free of charge], for it says, "But a sun of righteousness will shine for you who fear My name [i.e., *Shabbat* observers], with healing in its rays" (Malachi 3:20).

R. Yitzchak also said: A rainy day is so great that even the money in one's pocket is blessed, [even craftsmen whose work does not depend on rain are blessed (Rashi)], as it says, " . . . to give your land rain at precisely the right time, and to bless everything you do" (Deuteronomy 28:12).

BLESSING ON THINGS HIDDEN FROM SIGHT

R. Yitzchak also said: Blessing is bestowed only on things hidden from sight, [i.e., things that have not been counted, weighed, or measured]. For it says, "God will grant a blessing in your granaries [*baasamecha*]" (ibid. 28:8). [R. Yitzchak associates *baasamecha* with *samui*, "hidden."] In the yeshivah of R. Yishmael it was taught: Blessing is bestowed only on something that the eye does not look at. For it says, "God will grant a blessing in your granaries."

We learned in a *Baraita*: If someone enters the barn to measure the grain, he should say [before he starts measuring]: May it be Your will O God, our Lord, that You should send blessing on the work of our hands. When he begins to measure, he should say: Blessed be He Who sends blessing on this pile of grain. If he measured and then said the *berachah*, his *berachah* is in vain, because blessing is not granted on something that has been weighed, measured, or counted; but only on something that is hidden from the eye.

MORE ABOUT RAIN

R. Yochanan said: The day on which it rains is as great as the day of the Gathering of the Exiles [of Israel]. For it says, "O God, return our captivity like *afikim* in the desert" (Psalms 126:4). And *afikim* means rain [streams that are formed by rain (Rashi)], as it says, "The channels [*afikei*] of the sea appeared" (2 Samuel 22:16), [proof that *afikim* refers to water].

R. Yochanan further said: The day on which it rains is great, for on that day even armies stop fighting, as it says, "When you saturate the rows [of grain], even the legions have to rest" (Psalms 65:11).

R. Yochanan further said: Rain is held back only because of people who pledge charity publicly and fail to pay. For it says, "Like clouds, wind—but no rain—is one who boasts of gifts not given" (Proverbs 25:14).

GIVE TITHES AND YOU WILL BECOME RICH

R. Yochanan further said: What is meant by the verse, **(9a)** *aseir te'aseir*, "You shall tithe" (Deuteronomy 14:22)? [The double expression[11] means:] If you give tithes you will become rich. [The word *te'aseir*, "you shall tithe," can be read *te'asheir*, "you will become rich."] R. Yochanan met the young son of Resh Lakish[12] [the boy was a nephew of R. Yochanan] and said to him, "Tell me the verse [you have learned today]." The boy replied, "You shall tithe." Now the boy asked, "Why the double expression *aseir te'aseir*?" R. Yochanan answered, "If you give tithes you will become rich." The boy then asked, "From where do you know this?" R. Yochanan replied, "Go and test it yourself." The boy now asked, "Is it permitted to test the Holy One, blessed be He, inasmuch as it says, 'Do not test God your Lord' [Deuteronomy 6:16]?"

R. Yochanan replied, "R. Oshaiah said, 'The case of tithing is the exception [to the prohibition].' For it says, 'Bring all the tithes into the storage house, and let it be sustenance in My Temple. Test Me, if you will with this, says God, Master of Legions, [see] if I do not open up for you the floodgates of the heavens and pour down upon you blessing without [*beli*] end'" (Malachi 3:10). What is the meaning of the words, "without end"? R. Ammi b. Chama said in the name of Rav: [There will be so much blessing] until your lips will be worn out from saying "It's enough" [*beli* is seen as related to *yivlu*, "worn out"]. The boy said to R. Yochanan: If I had learned this verse [in my studies], I would need neither you [to explain this to me] nor R. Oshaiah, your teacher; [I would have known on my own that it is permitted to test God when it comes to tithing].

RESH LAKISH'S ASTUTE YOUNG SON

On another occasion R. Yochanan met the young son of Resh Lakish sitting and reciting the verse, "A man's folly corrupts his way, and his heart rages against God" (Proverbs 19:3); [when a corrupt man is punished for his wickedness he is angry with God]. Hearing this, R. Yochanan sat down and wondered, "Is there anything written in the Writings that is not alluded to in the Torah?" [since the Torah is the basis of all the books of Tanach]. The boy replied, "Is then this verse not alluded to in the Torah? Because it says, [when Joseph's brothers discovered that their money had been returned to them,] "Their hearts sank. 'What is it that God has done to us?' they asked each other with trembling voices" (Genesis 42:28). [They had sold their brother Joseph, and now they blamed God for their misfortune.] [Amazed at the acute answer,] R. Yochanan lifted his eyelids, and stared at the boy, [he had drooping eyelids, which had to be lifted with silver tweezers to enable him to see].[13] Right away, the boy's mother came and took the child away, saying, "Go away from him, he should not do to you as he did to your father." [An unfortunate remark by R. Yochanan led to Resh Lakish's premature death (*Bava Metzia* 84a).]

RAIN MAY FALL FOR ONE PERSON

R. Yochanan also said: Rain may fall even for the sake of a single individual, but general prosperity is granted only for the sake of the many. That rain may fall for the sake of even one person we derive from the verse, "God will open His good treasury in heaven to give *your land* [*artzecha*] rain" (Deuteronomy 28:12); ["your land" is in the singular]. General prosperity is granted for the sake of the many, for it says, [regarding the manna,] "I will make bread rain down *to you* [*lachem*]" (Exodus 16:4); [*lachem*, "to you," is in the plural].

An objection was raised: We learned: R. Yose b. R. Yehudah says: There were three major leaders who came to the aid of the Jewish people: Moses, Aaron, and Miriam, and because of them three beautiful gifts were given: the well, the clouds of glory, and the manna. The well [of water that accompanied the children of Israel on their wandering through the wilderness] came in the merit of Miriam, the clouds of glory [that surrounded and protected them] came in the merit of Aaron, and the manna fell in the merit of Moses. When Miriam died the well disappeared, as it says, "Miriam died there" (Numbers 20:1); and the next verse reads, "The people did not have any water"; and the well returned in the merit of Moses and Aaron. When Aaron died the clouds of glory disappeared, as it says, "When the Canaanite king of Arad heard . . . and he attacked them" (ibid. 21:1). What [report] did he hear [that gave him the courage to mount an attack]? He heard that Aaron had died, and that the clouds of glory had disappeared. He then thought that he had permission to attack Israel. That's why it says, "The people realized that Aaron had died" (ibid. 20:29). And R. Avahu explains: Do not read *vayir'u*, "they saw, realized" but *vayeira'u*, "they became visible." [When the protective cover of the clouds of glory departed the people became visible and exposed.]

The well and the cloud returned because of the merit of Moses, but when Moses died all of them disappeared, as it says, "I removed the three shepherds in one month" (Zechariah 11:8). Did then all three die in one month? Did not Miriam die in Nisan, Aaron in

Av, and Moses in Adar?—This teaches us that [when Moses died] the three beautiful gifts that were given because of them were lost and they all disappeared in one month. [The Gemara asks: The upshot of all this is] that sustenance [manna] was granted because of one individual, [Moses]! [But R. Yochanan said that prosperity is granted only for the sake of the many, not because of an individual.] [The Gemara answers:] The case of Moses is different. Since he prayed on behalf of the many, he himself is considered the equivalent of the community at large.

R. PAPA'S DISTRESS

R. Huna b. Mano'ach, R. Shmuel b. Idi, and R. Chiya of Vastanya used to attend the lectures of Rav. When Rava died, they began attending R. Papa's lectures, and whenever he told them a *halachah* that did not seem reasonable to them, they would wink at one another. [R. Papa noticed it] and was upset about it. (9b) He had a dream in which the verse, "I removed the three shepherds in one month" was read to him. [R. Papa took this as a sign that the three scholars would die at the same time for showing him disrespect.] The next day, when the three scholars left [after the lecture], R. Papa told them, "Go in peace" [meaning, "Please don't come back!" [He wanted to fulfill the dream by removing them from the *bet midrash* without actualizing the dream through their death. R. Papa thus saved their lives.]

R. Shimi b. Ashi always attended the lectures of R. Papa and would constantly ask him questions. One day he noticed that R. Papa put down his head,[14] saying *Tachanun*. [It was customary to add personal requests when reciting *Tachanun*.] He heard him pray, "May God protect me from the humiliation I suffer at the hands of Shimi." Shimi immediately resolved to remain quiet, and he stopped asking him questions.

THE INEXPENSIVE DATES OF BABYLON

When Ulla came to Babylon and saw that they were selling a basketful of dates for one *zuz*, he exclaimed, "A basketful of honey [dates] sells for a mere *zuz* [the cost of living is so low], and still the people of Babylonia don't occupy themselves enough with learning Torah!" [Ulla ate those dates, and] during the night he suffered terrible stomach cramps [diarrhea (Rashi).] He then exclaimed, "A basketful of knives sells for a *zuz*, [in other words: the cheap food is useless], and in spite of that the Babylonians find so much time to learn Torah!"

WHERE DOES THE RAIN COME FROM?

We learned in a *Baraita*: R. Eliezer said: The whole world receives only the rain that comes up from the ocean [i.e., from the water below the sky and not from the water above the sky that was separated on the second day of Creation (Rashi)]. For it says, "A mist rose up from the earth, and it watered the entire surface of the ground" (Genesis 2:6). R. Yehoshua said to R. Eliezer: But isn't the water of the ocean salty, [and rainwater is not salty]? R. Eliezer replied: The [water of the ocean] becomes sweet in the clouds. R. Yehoshua said: The entire world is irrigated from the water above the sky, as it says, "From the rain of heaven will [the land] drink water" (Deuteronomy 11:11), [i.e., from the water that was separated on the second day of Creation]. But what does R. Yehoshua do with the verse, "A mist rose up from the earth" [which indicates that the water comes from the earth]?

[R. Yehoshua explains:] This teaches us that the clouds grow in strength as they rise toward heaven and then open their mouths like a waterbag and receive the rainwater from heaven, as it says, "They [i.e., heaven] will pour rain into its clouds" (Job 36:27). [The clouds rise from the earth but are filled with water from above.] The clouds are perforated like a sieve, and they come and sprinkle water onto the ground, as it says, "A sprinkling of water from the clouds of heaven" (2 Samuel 22:12). And there is only one hair-breadth of space between one drop and another. This comes to teach you that the day when it rains is as great as the day when heaven and earth were created, for it says, "Who performs great deeds that are beyond comprehension, [and] wonders beyond number" (Job 5:9) and it says [in the next verse], "Who gives rain on the face of the earth" (ibid. 10); and it also says, "Did you not know? Did you not hear? The Lord is the eternal God, the Creator of the world . . . there is no calculating His understanding" (Isaiah 40:28). [Both the rain and Creation are "beyond comprehension." Hence the analogy.]

ERETZ YISRAEL WAS CREATED FIRST

(10a) Eretz Yisrael was created first, and the rest of the world came afterward. For it says, "Before He made the Land [of Israel], and then the area outside the Land" (Proverbs 8:26). Eretz Yisrael is watered first, and the rest of the world is watered afterward. For it says, "Who gives rain upon the face of the Land [of Israel], and sends water over the outlying fields" (Job 5:10). Eretz Yisrael is watered by the rain, and the rest of the world is watered by what is left over. You can compare this to a person who makes cheese; [when the cheese is ready] he takes the edible part, and leaves the refuse behind. Eretz Yisrael is watered by the Holy One, blessed be He, Himself, and the rest of the world is irrigated through a messenger, for it says, "Who gives rain upon the face of the Land [of Israel], and *sends* water over the outlying fields [i.e., the area outside Eretz Yisrael]" (Proverbs 8:26).

R. Yehoshua b. Levi said: The whole world gets its rain from the leftover rain of Gan Eden. For it says, "A river flowed out of Eden to water the garden. From there it divided and became four major rivers" (Genesis 2:10). We learned in a *Baraita*: With the leftovers of a *kur* [a vessel used for watering an area of a *kur*], an area of three *kav* can be watered. [Gan Eden is sixty times the size of the world; and three *kav* are one-sixtieth of a *kur* (Rashi).]

The Rabbis taught: Egypt is four hundred *parsang* by four hundred *parsang*,[15] and it is one-sixtieth of Ethiopia. Ethiopia is one-sixtieth of the world, and the world is one-sixtieth of the Garden of Eden, and the Garden is one-sixtieth of Eden, and Eden is one-sixtieth of Gehinnom; thus the world compared to Gehinnom is only like a cover to a pot. Others say that Gehinnom is immeasurable; and some say that Eden is immeasurable.

JACOB'S AND JOSEPH'S ADVICE

(10b) "Jacob said to his sons, 'Why do you make yourselves conspicuous?'" (Genesis 42:1). Jacob was telling his sons: [Even though you have enough food,] do not make it obvious to the children of Esau or the children of Ishmael that you are satiated, so that they should not become jealous of you.

[Joseph told his brothers as he sent them off to bring their father,] "Do not become agitated on the way" (ibid. 45:24). R. Elazar said: Joseph said to his brothers: On the way, don't get involved in discussions of *halachah*, for you may [become distracted and] lose your way. [The Gemara asks:] But it's not that way! Didn't R. Ela'i b. Berechiah say: If two Torah scholars are traveling on the road, and they do not discuss Torah topics, they deserve to be burned. For it says, "As they [Elijah and Elisha] were walking and conversing, behold!—a chariot of fire and horses of fire appeared and separated between the two of them" (2 Kings 2:11). [And R. Ela'i expounds:] The only reason they were not burned was because they spoke about Torah themes, but if they had not discussed [Torah issues] they would have deserved to be burned! [Then how could Joseph have told his brothers not to speak about Torah?] [The Gemara answers:] There is no contradiction. [The case of Elijah and Elisha] speaks of reviewing subjects you have studied; [Joseph cautioned his brothers not] to study in depth [which requires great concentration].

We learned in a *Baraita*: [Joseph's admonition,] "Do not become agitated on the way" means: Do not take big strides, and enter the city when the sun is still shining. [The Gemara explains:] "Do not take big strides," for the Master said: Big strides take away one five-hundredth part of your eyesight. "Enter the city when the sun is still shining"—as R. Yehudah said in the name of Rav: A person should always leave the city by daylight and return by daylight, as it says, "The day dawned, and the men were sent off" (Genesis 44:3).

EAT VERY LITTLE
WHILE TRAVELING

R. Yehudah said in the name of R. Chiya: When traveling you should not eat any more than you would eat in years of famine. Why? Here [in Babylonia] they give as the reason that [the rigors of traveling brings on] digestive problems, but in Eretz Yisrael they say: it is in order to make sure that you don't run out of food. What is the difference between the two reasons? The difference (11a) shows up when someone is aboard ship. [Sailing is very relaxing so he need not be concerned about digestive troubles; but he doesn't know how long the journey will take and may run out of food,] or when someone travels from one inn to another inn [food is readily available, but the strain of the trip may bring on stomach trouble]. R. Papa ate a loaf of bread for every *parsang* he walked. [Why did he eat so much?] Because he held that the reason for eating very little was in order to avoid digestive trouble, [and being a very heavy person, R. Papa was not afraid of indigestion (Rashi)].

R. Yehudah also said in the name of Rav: Whoever starves himself in years of famine is saved from unnatural death [by the sword or starvation (Rashi)], for it says, "In famine He will deliver you from death" (Job 5:20). It should have said: "from famine." [R. Yehudah explains:] This is what the passage means: As a reward for starving himself in years of famine [out of solidarity with his suffering fellow men, even though he himself had enough food], a person will be saved from unnatural death.

Resh Lakish said: A person may not have marital relations during years of famine. For it says, "Joseph had two sons *before* the famine years came" (Genesis 41:50). A Tanna taught: Childless people may have marital relations in years of famine.

SHARING IN THE SUFFERING
OF OTHERS

We learned in a *Baraita*: When the Jewish people is suffering and one of them separates himself from them, [and does not share in their pain], the two angels that accompany every person come and place their hands on his head and say, "So-and-so who has separated himself from the community shall not witness its consolation." We learned in another *Baraita*: When the community is steeped in suffering, a person should not say, "[This is none of my concern.] I'll go to my house, I'll eat and drink, and all will be well with me." Scripture describes such a person, as saying [in times of adversity], "Yet behold! There is joy and gladness, slaying of cattle and slaughtering of sheep, eating meat, and drinking wine, [saying,] 'Eat and drink, for tomorrow we die'" (Isaiah 22:13). And what follows after this verse? "This became revealed in My ears, so says God, Master of Legions, that this sin will never be atoned for until you die." ["Eat, drink, for tomorrow we die"]

is the slogan of common people, [at least they still fear death], but what does Scripture say about the attitude of the wicked? It says, "Come, I will get wine, and we will guzzle liquor together; and tomorrow will also be like this!" (ibid. 56:12), [they refuse to consider the consequences of their wrongdoing].

And what does the next verse say? "The righteous one perishes, . . . and no one gives thought that because of the evil [deeds of the wicked] the righteous one was taken away" (ibid. 57:1). [The *tzaddik* is taken away, because God does not want him to pray for the wicked (Rashi).] [The right attitude is,] a person should share in the suffering of the community. This is what we find in regard to Moses our teacher, that he suffered along with the community, as it says, [Moses was holding up his hands during the battle with Amalek,] "When Moses' hands became weary, they took a stone and placed it under him, so that he would be able to sit on it" (Exodus 17:12). [The *Baraita* asks: Did Moses have to sit on a stone?] Didn't he have a cushion or a pillow to sit on? Moses said, "[I insist on sitting on a stone.] Since the children of Israel are in anguish, [being attacked by Amalek], I will share in their anguish."

[The *Baraita* continues:] Anyone who suffers along with the community will merit to witness its consolation. Perhaps a person [who is enjoying himself in the privacy of his home while others are suffering] will say, "Who is there to testify against me?" The stones of a person's house and its beams will testify against him, as it says, "For a stone will shout from the wall, and a sliver will answer it from the beams" (Habakkuk 2:11).

[The *Maharsha* points out that the following Gemara refers to transgressions in general.]

In the yeshivah of R. Shila it was taught: The two ministering angels who accompany every person testify against him. For it says, "For He will order His angels to you" (Psalms 91:11). R. Chidka said: A person's own soul testifies against him, as it says, "Guard the doorways of your mouth for the one who lies in your bosom [i.e., your soul]" (Micah 7:5), [meaning, "Be careful not to speak lies and evil gossip for your own soul will testify against you" (*Maharsha*)]. Others say: A person's own limbs testify against him, for it says, "You are My witnesses, so says God" (Isaiah 43:10).

A DEBATE ABOUT
ABSTAINING AND FASTING

Shmuel said: Whoever fasts (voluntarily) is called a sinner. Shmuel holds the same opinion as the following Tanna: For we learned in a *Baraita*: Elazar haKappar Berebbi says: Why does it say [concerning a *nazir*],[16] "[The offering] shall make atonement for him, for having sinned against his soul" (Numbers 6:11). What sin did [a *nazir*] commit against his soul? [He is called a sinner] because he has denied himself [the enjoyment] of wine. We can now draw a logical inference [a *kal vachomer*]: If a *nazir* who abstained only from wine is called a sinner, a person who mortifies himself by [fasting and] abstaining from all [food and drink is surely considered a sinner]. R. Elazar said: [On the contrary, one who fasts] is considered holy, for it says, "Holy shall he be, the hair on his head being left to grow untrimmed" (ibid. 6:5). If a *nazir* who abstained only from wine is called holy, surely a person who [fasts and] denies himself the enjoyment of all [food and drink] is called holy.

[The Gemara asks:] How will Shmuel [who says that one who fasts is called a sinner] explain that the Torah calls a *nazir* holy? [The Gemara answers: He will say that] the concept of holiness refers to the *nazir*'s hair, [his hair is holy, he is not]. And R. Elazar [who says that fasting makes a person holy], how will he explain that a *nazir* is called a sinner? [He will say that] this applies to a *nazir* who defiled himself [by contact with the dead].

[The Gemara asks:] Did R. Elazar really say [that fasting is commendable]? Didn't he say: A person should always regard himself (11b) as if holiness rests within his innards, as it says, "The Holy One is in your midst" (Hosea 11:9). [And since his intestines have sanctity, he is obligated to guard them and not to weaken them by fasting.] [The Gemara answers:] This is no contradiction: R. Elazar says fasting is commendable for a person who is strong enough to endure fasting, and he says that fasting is reprehensible for a person who is too weak to fast.

Resh Lakish said: [A person who fasts] is considered devout, for it says, "He who weans himself [by abstaining from food and drink] is devout" (Proverbs 11:17).[17] R. Yirmiah b. Abba said in the name of Resh Lakish: A Torah scholar may not afflict himself by fasting [voluntarily] because [he becomes weak] and is unable to learn Torah. R. Sheshet said: A young Torah scholar who accepts [a voluntary] fast, may a dog eat his meal.

THE FAIRNESS
OF DIVINE JUSTICE

[At this point the *Ein Yaakov* goes back to page 11a in the Gemara.] It says, "A God of faith without injustice, righteous and fair is He" (Deuteronomy 32:4). [The Gemara expounds:] "A God of faithfulness": Just as the wicked are punished in the World to Come even for the smallest transgression they committed, so too the righteous are punished in *this* world for the slightest transgression they committed. "Without injustice": Just as the righteous will receive their reward in the World to Come, even for a minor mitzvah they performed, so too are the wicked rewarded in *this* world even for a minor mitzvah that they performed. "Righteous and fair is He": The Sages said: When a person leaves this world all his deeds are enumerated before

him, and he is told: Did you do such and such a thing in such and such a place on such and such a day? He will answer: Yes. Then they tell him: Sign, and he signs. For it says, "He seals [a judgment] with the hands of every man" (Job 37:7). But not only that, the person acknowledges that the judgment was fair, and he says: You have judged me correctly, to fulfill the verse, "You are justified when You speak" (Psalms 51:6).

THREE TEACHINGS
BY R. ELAZAR

(14b) R. Elazar said: An important person should not put on sackcloth unless he is confident that his prayers will be answered like Jehoram, the son of Ahab. [Jehoram was a wicked king, but when faced with famine and tragedy he confessed that the calamity was due to his and his people's wickedness, and he prayed] as it says, "It happened when the king heard the woman's words that he rent his garments while he was passing on the wall, and the people saw that there was sackcloth on his flesh underneath" (1 Kings 6:30). [His prayer was answered; the famine miraculously ended.]

R. Elazar further said: Not everyone is answered through rending his garments, nor is everyone answered through falling on the face [i.e., putting the head down in supplication]. Moses and Aaron were answered through falling on the face; Joshua and Caleb were answered through rending their garments. Moses and Aaron through falling on the face, for it says, "Moses and Aaron fell on their faces" (Numbers 14:5). Joshua and Caleb [who were not as saintly as Moses and Aaron were answered only after] rending their garments, for it says, "And Joshua the son of Nun and Caleb rent their clothes" (ibid. 6). R. Ze'ira, and some say R. Shmuel b. Nachmani, took issue with this, saying: If the verse had stated "Joshua and Caleb rent their clothes" it would be as you say, but since it says, "*and* Joshua," they may have done both [falling on their faces and rending their garments. The *vav* connects this verse with the previous verse, which relates that Moses and Aaron fell on their faces].

R. Elazar also said: [In the Messianic age] not all will stand up [before the Jewish people]; neither will all prostrate themselves. Kings will stand up and nobles will prostrate themselves. Kings will stand up, for it says, "Thus said God, the Redeemer of Israel and their Holy One, (15a) to the despised soul, to the one loathed by nations, to the servant of rulers: Kings will see you and stand up" (Isaiah 49:7). Nobles will prostrate themselves, for the verse continues, "nobles and they will prostrate themselves" (ibid.). R. Ze'ira, and some say, R. Shmuel b. Nachmani, objected: If the verse had stated, "And nobles will prostrate themselves" it would be as you say, but since it says, "Nobles *and* they will prostrate themselves," they will perhaps do both [stand up *and* prostrate themselves].

R. Nachman b. Yitzchak said: I will add to the above: [In time to come,] not everyone will share in the light, neither will everyone share in the joy. Light is set aside for the righteous and joy for the upright. Light is set aside for the righteous, for it says, "Light is sown for the righteous" (Psalms 97:11). Joy for the upright, for it says, "and for the upright of heart, joy" (ibid.).

FAST DAYS BECAUSE
OF DROUGHT

(15a) [The Mishnah says:] What is the order of service on fast days [for rain]? The Ark is taken out to the town square; wood ashes are placed on the Ark and on the heads of the *Nasi*[18] and the *Av Bet Din*.[19] Everyone else puts ashes on his own head. The elder among them addresses them with impassioned words of reproof [encouraging them to repent], saying: My brothers, when Scripture speaks of the people of Nineveh, it does not say, "God saw their sackcloth and their fasting" but, "God saw their deeds, that they repented from their evil ways" (Jonah 3:10). And in the Prophets it says, "Rend your hearts and not your garments" (Joel 2:13).

(16a) [The Gemara asks:] Why do they go outside to [pray for rain in] the city square? R. Chiya b. Abba said: [They mean to say by that:] We have prayed in the privacy [of the synagogue] but we were not answered, let us therefore humiliate ourselves [by praying] in public [showing the world that we are in deep distress]. Resh Lakish said: [It is as if they said:] We have gone into exile [from the synagogue into the street]; may our exile atone for us. [The Gemara asks:] What is the difference [whether praying outside as humiliation or as exile]? The difference shows up when they move from one synagogue to another. [Which would be a form of exile, but not a humiliation.]

And why do they take out the Ark to the city square; [after all, it is possible to pray without the Ark]? R. Yehoshua b. Levi said: It is to convey the idea: We had a vessel [the Ark], which we kept hidden [in the synagogue], and now, because of our sins, it has been disgraced [by being put on public display].

And why do they wear sackcloth? R. Chiya b. Abba said: As if to say: Look, we are considered animals, [because sackcloth is made of goats' hair (Rashi). They want to convey the thought: God, you have pity on animals, have pity on us too (Ben Yehoyada)]. And why do they place ashes on the Ark? R. Yehudah b. Pazzi said: [It is like putting ashes on the *Shechinah*.] They do it because God says, "I am with him in distress" (Psalms 91:15), [I share the suffering of the Jewish people]. Resh Lakish said: [As if to say,] "In all their troubles He was troubled" (Isaiah 63:9). R. Zeira said: The first time I saw the rabbis placing ashes on the Ark my whole body trembled [at the enormity of placing ashes, as it were, on God].

And why does everyone put ashes on his head? Concerning this matter there is a difference of opinion between R. Levi b. Chama and R. Chanina. One says: [To indicate] that we are as insignificant as ashes. The other says: That [God] may remember for our sake the ashes of Isaac.[20] What is the difference between them? The difference is whether you could use ordinary dust. [For self-abasement ordinary dust would do, but for recalling the ashes of Isaac only ashes could be used.]

Why did they go to the cemetery? There is a dispute about this between R. Levi b. Chama and R. Chanina. One says: [As if to say:] We are like the dead before You. The other says: In order that the dead should plead for mercy on our behalf. What is the difference between the two opinions? The difference is with regard to going to a non-Jewish cemetery. [The first reason would apply, but we cannot expect gentile dead to pray on our behalf.]

[The same two Tanna'im have a dispute about the following unrelated subject:] What is the meaning of the name "Mount Moriah" [the site of the *Bet Hamikdash*]?[21] Concerning this there is a dispute between R. Levi b. Chama and R. Chanina. One says: Because from this mountain teaching went forth to Israel, [taking Moriah as derived from *yarah*, "to teach"]. The other says: Because it is the mountain that inspired reverence [of God] among the heathens, [taking Moriah as derived from *yarei*, "to fear"].

THE SPEECH OF
ADMONISHMENT

[We learned in the Mishnah:] The elder among them addresses them with impassioned words of reproof. We learned in a *Baraita*: If there is an elder present, he addresses them; if not, a scholar addresses them; and if there is no scholar present, then a tall, impressive-looking person addresses them. [The Gemara asks:] When you refer to an elder, do you mean an elder who is not a scholar? Abbaye replied: This is what it means: If there is present an elder who is also a scholar, then he addresses them; if not, a [younger] scholar addresses them, and if not, a tall, impressive-looking person addresses them. [What does he say?] "My brothers, neither sackcloth nor fasting will cause [God to have pity on us]. Only repentance and good deeds arouse God's pity. For we find when Scripture speaks of the people of Nineveh it does not say, 'God saw their sackcloth and their fasting' but, 'God saw their good deeds that they repented from their evil way'" (Jonah 3:10). [What did the King of Nineveh order the people of Nineveh to do?] "Both man and animal shall cover themselves with sackcloth" (ibid. 8). What did the people of Nineveh do? They separated the mother animals from their young, [whereupon the animals started bellowing mournfully]. They then said, "Master of the universe! If You do not have mercy on us, then we will not have mercy on them, [and You do want us to have pity on them, for it says, 'His mercy is on all His creatures'" (Psalms 145:9)].

[The King of Nineveh further commanded,] "They shall cry out mightily to God" (ibid.). What did they say? They said: Master of the universe! If one person is long-suffering and the other is quick-tempered, if one is righteous and the other is not, who listens to whom? [Usually, the long-suffering person yields to the quick-tempered one; the righteous gives in to the wicked. The implication being, You, God, should yield to our prayer.]

[The King of Nineveh also decreed,] "Every man shall turn back from his evil way, and from the robbery that is in their hand" (Jonah 3:8). What is meant by "from the robbery that is in their hands"? Shmuel said: Even if a person had stolen a beam and built it into a building, he would tear down the building and return the beam to its owner.

THE EVIL DECREE WAS LIFTED

(18a) [The Gemara listed a number of days on which fasting is not permitted because of their festive character. One of these days is the twenty-eighth of Adar,] about which we learned in a *Baraita*: On the twenty-eighth of Adar, the good news reached the Jews that they were no longer forbidden to study the Torah. For the Roman government had issued a decree prohibiting the Jews to learn Torah and to circumcise their children, and forcing them to desecrate *Shabbat*. What did Yehudah b. Shamua and his colleagues do? They went and consulted a certain Roman noblewoman whom all the Roman dignitaries used to visit. She advised them, "Come tonight and hold a demonstration voicing your plight." They went and demonstrated that night, crying, "Woe, in heaven's name, are we not your brothers? Are we not the sons of one father [Adam], and are we not the sons of one mother [Eve]? Why are we different from every nation and tongue that you issue harsh decrees against us?" Thereupon the decrees were annulled, and that day was declared a festive day.[22]

THE DEATH OF THE RIGHTEOUS IS AVENGED

(18b) Why is Turainus Day celebrated [as a festive day]? [The background to the story: Lulianus and Pappus were two righteous Jewish brothers. When the king's daughter was found murdered, the Jews were falsely accused of the crime, whereupon the king threatened to take dreadful revenge against the Jews. To save the community, Lulianus and Pappus, although innocent, selflessly confessed to the murder and were executed.] This is what transpired: When Turainus was about to execute Lulianus and his brother Pappus in Ludkia, he said to them, "If you are of the descendants of Chananiah, Mishael, and Azariah, let your God come and save you from my hands, just as He saved Chananiah, Mishael, and Azariah[23] from the hands of Nebuchadnezzar" [who cast them into the fiery furnace, and they emerged unscathed]. They replied, "Chananiah, Mishael, and Azariah were perfectly righteous men, and they deserved that a miracle should happen to them, and Nebuchadnezzar was a decent king, who deserved that a miracle should come about through him. But you, you are a vulgar, wicked man! You don't deserve that God should perform a miracle through you. Anyway, we deserve to die [at the hands of Heaven for our failings]. And if you don't kill us, God has many other ways to kill us; he has plenty of bears, lions, and leopards that can attack and kill us. The only reason that He has handed us over into your hand is so that at some future time He will take vengeance on you for shedding our blood." In spite of this, he killed them. It was reported that no sooner had he left [the place of execution] than two Roman officials appeared and split open his skull with clubs.

THE STORY OF NAKDIMON BEN GURION

We learned in a *Baraita*: It happened once when all the people of Israel came to Jerusalem for Yom Tov,[24] that there was not enough drinking water. So Nakdimon b. Gurion [a very wealthy man] went to one of the [Roman][25] lords and said to him, "Lend me twelve wells of water for the pilgrims, and I will repay you twelve wells of water; and if I don't, I will repay you instead twelve *kikar* of silver" [a tremendous amount of money], and he set a time limit for repayment. When the time came to repay the loan and no rain had fallen, the lord sent him a message in the morning, "Repay me either the wells of water or the money you owe me." Nakdimon replied, "I still have time; the whole day belongs to me."

At noon [the Roman] again sent him a message, "Pay me back either the water or the money you owe me." Nakdimon replied, "I still have time today." In the afternoon, the Roman again sent the same message. Nakdimon again replied, "I still have time today." So the Roman lord scoffed at him and said, "The whole year there hasn't been any rain; (20a), do you really expect it to start raining now?" Having said this, the lord happily went to the bath house, [confident that Nakdimon would not be able to return the wells and would have to pay the money].

While the lord joyfully went to the bath house, Nakdimon sorrowfully entered the *Bet Hamikdash*. He wrapped himself [in his cloak], and stood up and prayed, saying, "Master of the universe! It is obvious and known to You that I have not taken out this [loan] for my honor nor for the honor of my family, but only for Your honor have I done this so that there should be enough water for the people who came to Jerusalem for Yom Tov." Immediately the clouds gathered in the sky, and rain fell until the twelve wells were filled to overflowing. As the lord came out of the bath house, Nakdimon b. Gurion came out of the *Bet Hamikdash*. When they met, Nakdimon said to the lord, "Pay me for the surplus water that you received [over and above the amount I borrowed]."

The Roman replied, "I realize that it is only for your sake that the Holy One, blessed be He, interfered with the workings of His world [and broke the drought]. But my claim against you for the money is still valid, for the sun has already set, [so your loan is past due]. Consequently, the rain that fell is my water [and you still owe me the money]." Nakdimon went back into the *Bet Hamikdash*, wrapped himself, and stood up to pray. He said, "Master of the universe! Make it known that You have beloved ones in Your world." Immediately the clouds scattered, and the sun shone through, [showing that it was still day, and Nakdimon had repaid the loan before the deadline]. Thereupon the lord told him, "If not for the fact that the sun broke through the clouds, I still would have a claim against you enabling me to extract my money from you." We learned in a *Baraita* that his real name was not Nakdimon but Boni. Why did people call him Nakdimon? Because the sun pierced [*nikderah*] through the clouds because of him.

THREE FOR WHOM THE SUN MIRACULOUSLY SHONE

The Rabbis have taught: For the sake of three people the sun [miraculously] shone, namely: Moses, Joshua, and Nakdimon b. Gurion. We know that it happened for the sake of Nakdimon ben Gurion from the above story. In the case of Joshua we know it because it says, "Then the sun stood still, and the moon stopped" (Joshua 10:13). But from where do we know that the sun [miraculously] shone for the sake of Moses? R. Elazar said: We derive it from a *gezeirah shavah* [an analogy based] on the word *acheil* [appearing in two different verses]. It says [concerning a war fought by Moses], "This day I shall begin [*acheil*] to place dread and fear of you" (Deuteronomy 2:25), and [concerning a war fought by Joshua] it says, "This day I will begin [*acheil*] to exalt you" (Joshua 3:7). [Since *acheil* appears in both verses, we say that whatever happened in the war of Joshua also happened in the war of Moses; thus, just as the sun stood still for the sake of Joshua, so it also stood still for Moses.]

R. Shmuel b. Nachmani said in the name of R. Yochanan: We derive it from a *gezeirah shavah* based on the word *teit*. It says [concerning Moses], "This day I shall begin to place [*teit*] the dread and fear of you," and it says [about Joshua], "On the day God delivered [*teit*] the Amorites before the children of Israel" (Joshua 10:12). [Similarly, this teaches us that just as the sun stood still in Joshua's war, so it also stood still in the war fought by Moses.] R. Yochanan said: [We don't have to rely on a *gezeirah shavah*]. It can be inferred from the passage itself [which is addressed at Moses], "When they hear of your reputation they will tremble and be anxious before you" (Deuteronomy 2:25). When did they tremble and were anxious before Moses? When the sun [miraculously] shone longer for Moses.

GENTLE LIKE A REED

We learned in a *Baraita*: A person should always be gentle and flexible like a reed [in his relationships with others] and never hard and unyielding like a cedar tree. [To illustrate this,] R. Elazar son of R. Shimon once left his teacher's house in Migdal Gedor, leisurely riding on his donkey by the river bank, feeling extremely contented and self-satisfied because he had learned so much Torah. (20b) Suddenly he came face to face with a very ugly person[26] who greeted him, "Greetings to you, Rabbi." But R. Elazar did not return the greeting. Instead he said, "You good-for-nothing, how hideous you look! Are all the people in your town as ugly as you are?" The person replied, "I don't know, [I cannot say anything unflattering about other people]. But you, go and tell the Craftsman that made me [i.e., God], 'How ugly is the vessel You made.'" When R. Elazar realized that he had done wrong, he got off his donkey, prostrated himself before the man, and said to him, "I realize that I have sinned against you. Please forgive me." The man refused, saying, "I am not going to forgive you until you go to the Craftsman who made me and tell Him what an ugly vessel He has made." R. Elazar walked behind the man until the city where the townspeople came out to greet R. Elazar. They called out, "Greetings to you, our Rabbi, our Rabbi! Our teacher, our teacher!" The man [who was walking in front of R. Elazar] asked the people, "Whom are you calling, 'our Rabbi, our Rabbi'?" They answered, "The person who is following behind you." He retorted, "If that is a rabbi, there should not be any more like him in Israel!" The people asked him, "Why are you saying this [about R. Elazar]?" He replied, "because he did such and such to me." The people begged him, "Even so, forgive him, for he is a great Torah scholar." The man replied, "For your sake I will forgive him, provided that he should not get into the habit [of insulting people]," [meaning, he should not get into the self-admiring frame of mind that prompted the disparaging remark (*Maharsha*)]. Immediately after this incident, R. Elazar son of R. Shimon taught, "[In dealing with other people] a person should always be gentle like a reed and not unyielding like a cedar."

DON'T GO IN HARM'S WAY

In Nahardea there was a shaky wall that had been in the same condition for thirteen years. Nevertheless, Rav and Shmuel would not go past it. One day, R. Adda b.

Ahavah came to Nahardea, and [walked together with Rav and Shmuel]. Shmuel remarked to Rav, "Let's walk around the wall." Replied Rav, "Today it is not necessary, for R. Adda is with us, and his merits are so great that we don't have to be afraid [that the wall will collapse]."

R. Huna had many barrels of wine stored in a dilapidated house, and he was afraid to take them out lest the house collapse in the process. He brought R. Adda b. Ahavah to the house and engaged him in *halachic* discussion until R. Huna's men finished emptying the house, [for he was sure that as long as R. Adda b. Ahavah was in the house nothing would happen]. As soon as R. Adda left the house, the walls caved in. When R. Adda b. Ahavah noticed what had happened he was upset because he agreed with R. Yannai's statement that "a person should not stand in a dangerous place and say, 'A miracle will occur for me,' for perhaps a miracle will not occur. And if a miracle does occur, his merits will be diminished." [By having this miracle performed for him in this world he will have fewer merits in the World to Come.] R. Chanan said: This is supported by the verse, [Before his encounter with Esau, Jacob prayed, "I [i.e., my merits] have been diminished by all the kindnesses and by all the truth that you have done for Your servant" (Genesis 32:11).

R. ADDA B. AHAVAH'S VIRTUOUS PRACTICES

[The Gemara asks:] What were the virtues of R. Adda b. Ahavah? [The Gemara answers:] It has been taught: The disciples of R. Adda b. Ahavah asked him to what he attributed his longevity. He replied, "I was never angry in my house, and I never walked in front of any person who is greater than myself [in wisdom]. I have never thought about Torah subjects in unclean alleys, and I have never walked four cubits without thinking Torah thoughts or without wearing *tefillin*. I have never slept in the *bet midrash*, neither regularly nor took a nap; I have never derived pleasure from the disgrace of a friend; and I have never called my friend by a nickname [that had a derogatory overtone] or, as some say, by a nickname given to the entire family."

R. HUNA'S GOOD DEEDS

Rava said to Rafram b. Papa: Tell me some of the good deeds R. Huna did. Rafram replied, "Of his childhood I do not remember anything, but of his old age I recall that on stormy days they used to drive him around in a golden carriage, and he would inspect every part of the city and order that any shaky wall be torn down. If the owner of the wall could afford it, he would have to rebuild it himself; if not, R. Huna would rebuild it at his own expense."

On the eve of every *Shabbat* [Friday] he would send a messenger to the marketplace, and any leftover veg-etables he bought up and had them thrown in the river [so that they would not be put on sale again the following week]. [The Gemara asks:] Should he not have distributed these vegetables among the poor? [The Gemara answers:] He was afraid that the poor would rely on him and not buy [their own vegetables]. [The Gemara asks:] Why didn't he give the vegetables to the domestic animals? [The Gemara answers:] Because he held that food fit for human consumption may not be given to animals [since this would be treating food in a degrading fashion, which is forbidden (Rashi)]. So why did he buy the vegetables at all?—Because he was afraid that [if he did not,] the following week the farmers might not bring enough produce to market [which would drive up the prices.]

Whenever R. Huna discovered a new medicine, he would fill up a jar with it and place it by the door and announce, "Anyone who needs it, come and take of it." Some say that he knew a medicine for the disease caused by the demon Shivta [that strikes people who don't wash their hands before eating], and he used to hang a jug full of water and announce, "Whoever needs it may come and wash his hands to save his life from danger!" Before he sat down for a meal he would throw open the door and announce, "Whoever is in need can come and eat!" Rava said, "All of these good practices I could carry out myself except for the last one, [of throwing open the door] (21a) because there are a great many poor people in Mechuza, and I could not feed them all."

ILFA AND R. YOCHANAN

Ilfa and R. Yochanan studied Torah together. When their poverty became unbearable they said to one another, "Let's leave the *bet midrash* and go into business, so that one may be fulfilled by the verse, 'There will not be any more poor among you'" (Deuteronomy 15:4). Before they had gone far, they sat down beneath a shaky wall and began to eat their meal. Soon two angels appeared, and R. Yochanan heard one say to the other, "Let's throw down the wall and kill them, for they are about to forsake eternal life [of Torah] and involve themselves in the temporary life [of business]." The other angel replied, "Leave them alone, because the hour of death of one of them has not yet arrived,[27] [he is destined to become a great man]." R. Yochanan heard this, but Ilfa did not. R. Yochanan said to Ilfa, "Did you hear anything?" "No," replied Ilfa. So R. Yochanan said to himself, "Since I heard it and Ilfa did not, it must be that I am the one who still has much to accomplish." R. Yochanan then said to Ilfa, "I am going back [to study Torah], so that in me will come true the verse, 'The poor will never cease to exist in the land'" (ibid. 11).

R. Yochanan returned to his studies but Ilfa did not. By the time Ilfa returned [from a business trip (Rashi)], R. Yochanan had been appointed head of the yeshivah, and the local people said to Ilfa, "If you had stayed with us and studied Torah, we would have appointed you *rosh yeshivah*," [since Ilfa was a greater scholar than R. Yochanan (Rashi)]. Ilfa then balanced himself at the top of a ship's mast and declared, "If anyone asks me a question regarding a statement of R. Chiya and R. Oshaiah,[28] and I am unable to answer it from our Mishnah, I will throw myself from the mast and drown, [implying, "No one—not even R. Yochanan—is as well-versed as I am. Why then does he deserve to be the *rosh yeshivah* and not I?" (R. Chananel)]. [In response to Ilfa's challenge, a certain old man came forward and recited a *halachah* from the Tosefta: If a person says [in his will]: Give my sons one *shekel* a week, but if they need to be given a *sela* [more than a *shekel*], we give them a *sela* . . . " [and Ilfa proceeded to show that it is the opinion of R. Meir].

NACHUM OF GAMZU'S AFFLICTIONS

People said about Nachum of Gamzu that he was blind in both eyes, both his hands and legs were amputated, and his whole body was covered with sores, that he was lying in a tottering house, and the legs of his bed were standing in buckets of water to prevent the ants from crawling on him. One time, his disciples wanted to move his bed and then clear the things out of his house, but he said to them, "My children, first clear out the things from the house and then move out my bed, for I am confident that as long as I am in the house it will not collapse." So they first cleared out the things and then moved out the bed, whereupon the house immediately caved in. His disciples then asked him, "Rabbi, since you are so perfectly righteous, why has all this suffering come upon you?" He replied, "It's all my own fault. I was once traveling to my father-in-law, and I had with me three donkeys, one loaded with food, one loaded with drink, and a third loaded with all kinds of delicacies. Suddenly a poor man approached me and said, 'Rabbi, please give me some food.' I replied, 'Wait until I unload my donkey.' But before I finished unloading, the poor man died [from hunger]. So I fell on his face and cried out, 'May my eyes which had no pity on your eyes become blind; may my hands which had no pity on your hands be cut off; may my legs which had no pity on your legs be amputated,' and I was not satisfied until I said, 'May my whole body be covered with sores.'" Hearing this his disciples moaned, "How dreadful that we have seen you like this!" Nachum answered, "It would have been worse if you had not seen me like this!" [i.e., if I had not received my punishment in this world (*Maharsha*)].

IT'S ALL FOR THE BEST

Why was he called Nachum of Gamzu? Because whatever happened to him he would say, *Gam zu letovah*,

"It's all for the best." Once the Jews wanted to send a gift to the Roman Emperor, and Nachum was chosen to go [to deliver it to the palace] for he had experienced many miracles. They sent with him a bag full of precious gems and pearls. On the way he spent the night in an inn, and during the night the people stole the jewels and replaced them with earth. When Nachum arrived at the palace they untied his bag and found that it was full of earth. The Emperor [was furious] and wanted to kill the Jews for mocking him. Nachum merely said, "*Gam zu letovah*, It's all for the best."

The prophet Elijah then appeared in the guise of a Roman senator and remarked, "Perhaps this is some of the earth of their father Abraham, for when he threw earth [against the armies of the four kings][29] it turned into swords, and when he threw straw it turned into arrows, as it says, 'Who made [his enemies] like dust before his sword, like straw blown about [before] his bow?'" (Isaiah 41:2). Now there was one nation the Emperor previously had been unable to subdue, but when they tried some of this earth against it they were able to conquer it. They took Nachum to the imperial treasury and filled his bag with precious stones and pearls and sent him on his way with great honor.

On his return trip he spent the night in the same inn, and they asked him, "What gift did you bring to the Emperor that they showed you such honor?" He replied, "I brought what I had taken from here." The innkeepers thereupon tore down the inn and took the earth to the Emperor and said to him, "The earth that was brought to you belonged to us." They tested it, and when they found that it did not work they put the innkeepers to death.

IT IS THE PERSON THAT HONORS THE PLACE

R. Nachman b. R. Chisda said to R. Nachman b. Yitzchak, "Please come and sit a little closer to us," [since R. Nachman b. Yitzchak was sitting among people that were below his stature]. R. Nachman b. Yitzchak replied, "We have learned: R. Yose says: It is not the place that honors the person, it is the person that honors the place." We find an example of this with regard to Mount Sinai: As long as the *Shechinah* rested on it the Torah says, "Even the cattle and sheep may not graze near the mountain" (Exodus 34:4), [for the *Shechinah* honored the mountain], but as soon as the *Shechinah* departed from the mountain it says, "But when the trumpet is sounded with a long blast [as a sign that *Shechinah* has withdrawn], they will then be allowed to climb the mountain" (ibid. 19:13).

We find the same in connection with the Tabernacle in the wilderness. As long as it remained pitched the Torah commanded, "to send out of the camp everyone who had a leprous mark or a male discharge" (Numbers 5:2); but once the curtain [of the Tabernacle] was rolled up [to be transported to a new site], both those with male discharge and a leprous mark were permitted to enter the place. To this R. Nachman b. R. Chisda replied: If so, I will come and sit closer to you. Answered R. Nachman b. Yitzchak: It is more appropriate that a scholar, the son of a less distinguished scholar, should go to one who is a scholar and is the son of a more distinguished scholar, than that the latter should go to the former. [*Rav* Chisda, the father of R. Nachman, was a more distinguished scholar than Yitzchak, the father of R. Nachman who did not have the title of *Rav*.]

KIND DEEDS
PREVENTED CALAMITIES

Once a plague raged in Sura, but it did not spread to the neighborhood where Rav lived. People thought that this was due to the special merit of Rav. In a dream it was explained to them that this was too insignificant a matter to require the merit of a person as great as Rav, but that they were saved from the plague in the merit of a certain person who was in the habit of lending his shovel and spade for burials. [His kindness was rewarded measure for measure in that the people of the neighborhood were spared from death and burial (Rashi).]

Once a fire broke out in Derokeret but it did not spread to the neighborhood of R. Huna. People thought that this was due to the special merit of R. Huna. In a dream it was explained to them that this was too insignificant a matter to require the merit of a person as great as R. Huna, but that it was because of a certain woman who would heat her oven on the eve of *Shabbat* and allow her neighbors to use it. [Her kindness of making her heated oven available to others was rewarded measure for measure by sparing her neighborhood from fire.]

ABBA UMANA,
THE RIGHTEOUS SURGEON

Abba Umana was a surgeon [who practiced bloodletting], and every day he would be greeted by a heavenly Voice [saying, "Peace to you"], while Abaye received such greetings only on the eve of every *Shabbat*, and Rava would receive such greetings only [once a year] on the eve of every Yom Kippur. Abaye felt downcast because [of the greater honor shown to] Abba Umana. [He wanted to emulate him so as to likewise receive a heavenly greeting every week], but people told him: You cannot do what Abba Umana does. What did Abba Umana do that earned him this special merit? When performing his bloodletting procedure he would treat men and women in separate compartments. He also had a special hospital gown for bloodletting that was slit at the shoulder, and whenever a female patient came to him he would place the gown on her shoul-

ders [and insert the bloodletting cup through the slit] in order not to see her [uncovered shoulder]. He also had a private place where the patients deposited their fees. Those that could afford it put their fees there, and those that could not afford to pay were not put to shame. Whenever a young Torah scholar came to consult him, not only would he accept no fee, but he would also give him some money, saying, "Go and regain your strength."

One day Abaye sent two scholars to test Abba Umana. He received them and gave them food and drink, and in the evening he prepared woolen mattresses for them to sleep on. **(22a)** In the morning, the scholars rolled up the mattresses and took them to the market [as if to sell them]. There they met Abba Umana and said to him, "Sir, how much are these mattresses worth?" [They wanted to test whether he would suspect them of stealing the mattresses (Rashi).] He gave them an estimate, and they said, "Perhaps they are worth even more?" He replied, "That is the price I paid [for similar mattresses]." They then told him, "These mattresses really belong to you. We took them from you [in order to test you]. Please tell us, [when you noticed that the mattresses were gone,] what did you suspect us of?" He replied, "I said to myself, perhaps you needed money to redeem captives, and you were embarrassed to tell me." They told him, "Now take them back." He replied, "No, for the moment I noticed that they were missing I dismissed them from my mind and resolved to give them to charity."

[We learned above that Rava received heavenly greetings only on the eve of every Yom Kippur while Abaye received such greetings on the eve of every *Shabbat*. The Gemara says:] Rava felt bad because Abaye was shown greater honor. Therefore he was told in a dream: "You should be satisfied that your merit protects the entire city."

THE JAILER WHO HAD A SHARE
IN THE WORLD TO COME

R. Beroka Choza'ah regularly visited the marketplace at Bei Lapat where Elijah the prophet often appeared to him. Once he asked Elijah, "Is there anyone in this market who has a share in the World to Come?" "No, there isn't" was the reply. Meanwhile he saw a person who was wearing black shoes [a type not worn by the Jews of that region], and who was not wearing *tzitzit*[30] on his clothing. "This man has a share in the World to Come," Elijah exclaimed. R. Beroka called him but he did not come, so he ran after him and asked him, "What is your occupation?" "Go away, and come back tomorrow," the man answered. The next day R. Beroka repeated his question, and the man replied, "I am a jailer, and I make sure to keep the male and the female prisoners separate from each other. At night I place my bed between the men's and the women's sections in order that they will not come to sin. And when

I see a Jewish girl prisoner on whom the gentile jailers have cast their eyes I risk my life to save her."

R. Beroka then asked the man, "Why do you wear black shoes, and why aren't you wearing *tzitzit?*" He replied, "I mingle with the gentiles [and I have to disguise myself] so that they should not realize that I am a Jew. Then, if a harsh decree is enacted against the Jews they will tell me about about it, and I will be able to report it to the rabbis so that they pray to God, and the evil decree is nullified." R. Beroka asked the man, "Yesterday when I asked you what your occupation is, why did you tell me to go away and come back tomorrow?" He answered, "They had just passed an evil decree against the Jews, and I was first going to let the rabbis know so that they could pray to God."

Meanwhile two men were passing by, and Elijah said, "These two have a share in the World to Come." R. Beroka asked them, "What is your occupation?" "We are jesters," they replied, "and when we see people who are depressed we cheer them up, and also, when we see two people quarreling we try very hard to make peace between them."

[We learned in the Mishnah:] A fast is proclaimed and the shofar is blown on account of the sword [i.e., the threat of an invading army].

[The Gemara comments:] We learned in a *Baraita*: The word "sword" mentioned in the Mishnah means not only an impending attack by hostile forces, but even a friendly army passing through on its way to wage war against a third country constitutes a danger [and requires a fast and the blowing of the shofar]. For there could not be a more friendly army than that of Pharaoh Necho [whose army only wanted to pass through Eretz Yisrael on its way to do battle with Assyria],[31] and even so King Josiah [of Judah] suffered a terrible fate at the hands of Pharaoh Necho. For it says, (22b) [When Josiah marched against Necho to prevent him from passing through,] "[Necho] sent messengers to [King Josiah] saying, 'What is there between me and you, O King of Judah? I do not march against you this day but against the kingdom that wars with me, and God has told me to hurry. Refrain, then, from interfering with God Who is with me, so that He does not destroy you'" (2 Chronicles 35:21).

[The Gemara asks:] What is meant by "God Who is with me"? R. Yehudah said in the name of Rav: [Necho meant his] idols. Josiah said to himself: Since he [Pharaoh Necho] is relying on his idols I will surely triumph over him. [But when Josiah went to fight against Pharaoh Necho he suff·red a terrible defeat. It says,] "The archers shot King Josiah, and the king said to his servants, 'Get me away from here, for I am badly wounded!'" (ibid. 24). [The Gemara asks:] What is the meaning of "for I am badly wounded"? R. Yehudah said in the name of Rav: This teaches us that [the arrows] had pierced his whole body like a sieve.

R. Shmuel b. Nachmani said in the name of R. Yonatan: Why was Josiah punished? Because he should have consulted Jeremiah [whether or not to fight Necho], and he did not [but relied on his own judgment]. [The Gemara asks:] On what verse did Josiah base his decision to fight Pharaoh Necho?—On [the Divine promise], "No sword shall cross your land" (Leviticus 26:6). What sword? Is the verse referring to a hostile army? [No, for] that has been promised already [in the same verse], "I will grant peace in the land." Therefore Josiah concluded that God promised that even a friendly army will not pass through Eretz Yisrael. But he did not realize that since his generation [had sinned], God did not fulfill his promise for them.

When King Josiah was dying, Jeremiah came to visit him and saw that his lips were moving [and he was trying to say something]. Jeremiah thought that perhaps, God forbid, Josiah was saying something improper because of his terrible pain. He bent down [to listen] and heard that he was accepting God's judgment, saying, "God is righteous, for I disobeyed His word" (Lamentations 1:18). Thereupon Jeremiah applied to him the verse, "The breath of our nostrils, God's anointed [is King Josiah]" (ibid. 4:20). [King Josiah was as dear to us as the breath of our nostrils (Targum Eichah).]

R. Yose said: A person may not afflict himself by fasting, for he may [become too weak to earn a living] and will need the support of other people, and they may not have pity on him [because they will accuse him of bringing his weakness on himself (*Maharsha*)]. R. Yehudah said in the name of Rav: R. Yose's reason is because it says, "Man became a living soul [i.e., living being]" (Genesis 2:7), which he interprets to mean: Keep alive the soul that I gave you.

RAINFALL AT THE PROPER TIME

We learned in a *Baraita*: It says, "I will provide your rains in their proper time" (Leviticus 26:4). This means that the earth will not be drenched with rain nor will it be parched, but the rain will come in just the right amount. For overabundant rain makes the earth muddy, and it yields no fruit. Another explanation: (23a) "In their proper time" means that it will rain only [at times when it does not inconvenience people, namely] on Wednesday night [when people stayed indoors because of a demon that roamed the streets on that night (Rashi)][32] and on Friday night [when everyone stayed at home]. And that's how it happened in the days of Shimon b. Shetach. [The Gemara proves that even though it rained only twice a week, in a time of blessing such rainfall is sufficient to produce a good crop.] At that time it rained on Wednesday and Friday evenings so that the wheat kernels were as large as kidneys, and barley grains were like the pits of olives, and the lentils were as big as coins. They preserved some of them to show future generations [that the observance of the Torah produces bountiful crops and

EIN YAAKOV

that the paltry size of their grain kernels] was due to their sinful conduct. For it says, "Your sins have overturned these, and your transgressions have withheld bounty from you" (Jeremiah 5:25). So it happened also in the days of Herod when the people were involved in the rebuilding of the *Bet Hamikdash*. At that time it rained only at night, and in the morning the wind would scatter the clouds. The sun began to shine, and the people were able to go to work. This showed them that the work they were doing was finding favor in Heaven.

CHONI HAME'AGEL, THE CIRCLE DRAWER

We learned in a *Baraita*: It once happened that the greater part of the month of Adar had passed and no rain had fallen yet. The people turned to Choni Hame'agel and asked him to pray for rain. He prayed, but no rain fell. So he drew a circle and stood inside it, the same as Habakkuk did, as it says, "I will stand on my watch, take up my station at the siege" (Habakkuk 2:1). [Choni] called out, "Master of the universe, Your children have turned to me because I am like a member of Your household. I swear by Your great name that I will not move from here until You have mercy on Your children." A light rain began to fall, and his disciples said to him, "Rabbi, we want to live to see you, and [if you don't pray for more rain] we will end up dying [from hunger]. We believe that this rain fell only to release you from your oath [and allow you to move]." So Choni continued to pray, "It is not for this that I have asked, but rain to fill cisterns, ditches, and pools."

Thereupon the rain began to come down in torrents, until every drop was as large as the opening of a barrel, and the Sages estimated that each drop contained no less than a *log*[33] of water. His disciples then said to him, "Rabbi, we want to live to see you and not to die; it seems to us that the rain is coming down to obliterate the world." Choni then said [to God], "It is not for this that I have prayed, but for rain of goodwill, blessing, and bounty." Then it began to rain in the normal way. [But it rained so much that the water started to rise, and] the people were forced to go up to the high ground of the Temple Mount to escape the flooding] because of the abundant rain. [His students] then told Choni, "Just as you prayed for the rain to fall, pray for the rain to stop." He replied, "I have a tradition that you should not pray that an abundance of good be taken away. Even so, bring me a bull to be brought as an offering."

They brought him a bull for an offering, and he placed his two hands on it and said, "Master of the universe! Your people Israel that you have brought out from Egypt cannot tolerate too much goodness nor can they endure too much punishment. When You were angry with them they could not bear Your fury; and

now that You have showered too much goodness on them they cannot endure it either. May it be Your will that the rain stop, and that there should be relief to the world." Immediately the wind began to blow, the clouds were scattered, and the sun began to shine. When the people went out into the fields they brought back mushrooms, [a sign that the rain was a blessing]. Thereupon Shimon b. Shetach {who served as *Nasi*, (President of the Sanhedrin)] sent a message to Choni, saying, "If not for the fact that you are Choni, I would have placed you under the ban of *nidui*," [because Choni spoke to God in a very demanding and insistent way (Rashi)].

"[And what's more,] if our time had been similar to the time when Elijah received from God the key to rain [i.e., control over rainfall, and Elijah had made an oath that there would be no rain],[34] would not God's name be desecrated through you [Choni]? [For Choni would have made an oath not to move from the circle until it rained, while Elijah had sworn that it would *not* rain. Thus, either Elijah or Choni would have made a vain oath and created a desecration of God's name (Rashi).] But what shall I do, since you pressure God, and He grants your desire like a son who pesters his father, and who pampers him. Thus the son will say, 'Father, bathe me in hot water, bathe me in cold water, give me nuts, almonds, apricots, and pomegranates,' and he indulges him. About you Scripture says, 'Your father and your mother will be glad, and the one who bore you will rejoice'" (Proverbs 23:25).

We learned in a *Baraita*: This was the message the Sanhedrin sent to Choni Hame'agel: [They applied the following verses to Choni Hame'agel:] "You will decree and it will be done, and light will shine upon your affairs" (Job 22:28). "You will decree and it will be done" means, you decree [on earth] below [that the rain should come], and the Holy One, blessed be He, fulfills your word [in heaven] above. "And light will shine upon your affairs" means, you lit up [i.e., you brought relief through your prayer to] a generation that was in darkness [because it suffered from drought]. "When people are downtrodden you would say, 'Arise!'" (ibid. 29) means, you have lifted up through your prayer a generation that had sunk low. "And He will save those with downcast eyes" (ibid.) means, you raised through your prayer a generation that was low on account of its sin. "Those who are not innocent will be saved," (ibid. 30) means, you have saved through your prayer a generation that is not innocent. "They will be delivered through the pureness of your hands" (ibid.). Through what were they delivered? Through the work of your pure hands.

ASLEEP FOR SEVENTY YEARS

R. Yochanan said: Throughout his life this righteous man [Choni Hame'agel] had difficulty understanding the following verse: "A song of ascents. When God will return the captivity of Zion, we will be like dreamers" (Psalms 126:1), [meaning, the Babylonian exile, which lasted seventy years, is compared to a person who spent seventy years dreaming]. Choni wondered: How can a person sleep and dream for seventy years straight? One day as he was traveling on the road, he saw a man planting a carob tree. He said to him, "Let's see; it takes seventy years for a carob tree to bear fruit. Are you sure you will live seventy more years so that you will be able to enjoy its fruit?" The man replied, "When I came into this world I found a carob tree that others had planted for me [even though they did not expect to see the fruit of their labor]. Just as my ancestors planted the tree for me, I plant this tree for my descendants."

Choni sat down to have a meal, and he fell into a deep sleep. As he slept, a rock formation rose up around him that shielded him from view, and he slept for seventy years. When he awoke [at the end of seventy years], he saw a man picking fruit from the carob tree, and he asked him, "Do you know who planted this tree?" The man replied, "My grandfather." Choni then said to himself, "Obviously, I must have slept for seventy years!" He saw his donkey that had given birth to generations of donkeys. He then returned home and inquired if his son was still alive. He was told that his son was no longer living, but that his grandson was alive. He then said to them, "I am Choni Hame'agel!", but no one believed him. He went to the *bet midrash*, and there he overheard the scholars say, "The learning is as clear to us as in the days of Choni Hame'agel, for whenever he came to the *bet midrash*, any difficulty the rabbis had he would clear up for them." So he told them, "I am that person!" but the scholars did not believe him, and they did not accord him the proper respect. He became deeply depressed and prayed to God that he might die, and so he died. Rava said: [Choni's story exemplifies the popular saying:] Give me companionship or give me death.

THE RIGHTEOUS
ABBA CHILKIAH

Abba Chilkiah was the grandson of Choni Hame'agel, and whenever the world needed rain the Rabbis sent a message to him [to ask that he should pray for rain]. Once there was a great need for rain and the Rabbis sent a delegation of two rabbis to him with the request that he should pray for rain. They came to his house but did not find him home. So they then went out into the field where they found him hoeing. They greeted him (23b) but he did not return their greeting. At the end of the day he gathered some wood and placed the wood and the rake on one shoulder and his cloak on the other shoulder. The whole way home he walked barefoot, but whenever he came to a stream he put on his shoes [to cross the stream]. When he came a stretch of thorns and thistles he picked up his clothing; when he reached the city, his wife, nicely dressed, came out

to greet him. When he arrived home, his wife entered the house first, then he came in, and only then did he allow the scholars to enter. He sat down to eat but did not invite the scholars to join him. He shared the meal among his children, giving the older son one portion and the younger son two. He then said to his wife, "I know that the rabbis have come for rain; let us go up on the roof and pray [where no one sees us], perhaps the Holy One, blessed be He, will have mercy and rain will fall without making it appear as if it came about through us."

They went up on the roof and stood at different corners. The clouds first appeared in the corner where his wife was standing; [her prayers were answered before his]. When he came down from the roof, he asked the scholars, "Why have you come?" They replied, "The Rabbis have sent us to ask you to pray for rain." Abba Chilkiah exclaimed, "Blessed be God who has made you no longer dependent on Abba Chilkiah. [The rain must have come in someone else's merit]." They said, "We know that the rain came because of your prayers, but please explain the meaning of the strange things we observed you doing throughout the day:

When we greeted you in the morning, why didn't you react?"

[He replied,] "I am a laborer hired by the day, and I feel that I may not waste a moment from my work."

"Why did you put the wood on one shoulder and your cloak on the other shoulder [and not as a cushion under the wood]?"

"Because it was a borrowed cloak; I borrowed it only for the purpose of wearing it and not to serve as cushion for the wood."

"Why did you put your shoes on in the water but walked barefoot the rest of the way?"

"When I was on the road I could see where I was going, [and I could avoid stepping on anything that might hurt me], but I could not see what was in the water, [so I had to put on my shoes to protect my feet]."

"Why did you pick up your garments whenever you came upon thorns and thistles? [Weren't you afraid to scratch your skin on the thorns?]"

"The body heals itself, but my clothing does not."

"Why did your wife get dressed up to greet you when you entered the city?"

"So that I should not look at other women."

"Why did she enter the house first and then you after her and then we?"

"Because I did not know who you were, [that's why I had to place myself between you and my wife]."

"Why didn't you invite us to eat with you?"

"Because I did not have enough food for all."

"Why did you give one portion to the older son and two portions to the younger son?"

"Because the older one stays at home [and probably helped himself when he was hungry], and the other stays away in the synagogue to learn [all day]."

"Why did the cloud first appear in the corner where your wife was standing and then in your corner?"

"Because she stays at home and gives food to the poor people, which they can enjoy immediately; whereas I only give money, which cannot immediately be enjoyed. Or, it may have to do with the wicked people who live in our neighborhood. I prayed that they should die, whereas she prayed that they should repent, which indeed happened."

CHANIN[35] HANECHBA, THE HIDDEN ONE

Chanin Hanechba was the son of the daughter of Choni Hame'agel. When the world needed rain, the Rabbis would send the schoolchildren to him. The children would grab onto the hem of his coat and cry out, "Father, father, give us rain!" Chanin would then pray, "Master of the universe, bring rain for the sake of these children who are unable to tell the difference between the Father Who gives rain and the father who cannot!" Why was he called Chanin Hanechba [the hidden one]? Because he humbly used to hide himself [when he prayed for rain, so that people should not realize that the rain came in answer to his prayer (Rashi)].

HE PRAYED IN SOLITUDE

(23b) R. Zerika said to R. Safra: Come and see the difference between the mighty men [i.e., the righteous] of Eretz Yisrael and the pious men of Babylonia. When the world needed rain, the pious men of Babylonia, R. Huna and R. Chisda, would say: Let us all gather together and pray, perhaps God will be swayed by our prayers and send rain; [they prayed in public, and the people would realize that it was because of their prayers that the rain came]. But the mighty men of Eretz Yisrael, for example, R. Yonah, the father of R. Mani [prayed for rain in solitude]. When the world needed rain he would go into his house and say [as an excuse]: Give me my sack, and I will go and buy a zuz worth of grain. [He did not even tell his family that he was going to pray for rain.] When he left his house, he would go to a low-lying place [to pray], for it says, "From the depth I called You, O God" (Psalms 130:1). Standing in a secluded spot and covering himself with his sack he prayed, and the rains came. Upon returning home, his family would ask him, "Where is the grain [you went to buy]?" And he would reply, "[I did not buy the grain because] I said to myself, now that the rains have have come there will be an abundance of grain [and prices will go down]."

HIS WISHES CAME TRUE

It also happened that R. Mani, R. Yonah's son, was being harassed by the people of the Nasi's [the head of the Sanhedrin's][36] household. So he stretched out on

his father's grave and cried, "Father, Father, the people of the Nasi's household are tormenting me!" One day, when the Nasi and his entourage were passing R. Yonah's grave, the legs of the horses stuck to the ground. They could not move until they agreed to stop annoying R. Mani.

Another anecdote: R. Mani who often attended R. Yitzchak b. Eliashiv's lectures once complained to him, "The rich members of my father-in-law's family are annoying me." R. Yitzchak b. Eliashiv declared, "They should become poor," and so they indeed became poor. Later on R. Mani came back and complained, "Because of their poverty they are pressuring me to support them." R. Yitzchak b. Eliashiv declared, "They should become rich again," whereupon they became rich.

On another occasion R. Mani complained to R. Yitzchak b. Eliashiv, "I do not find my wife attractive anymore." R. Yitzchak asked what her name was and then said, "Chanah should become beautiful," whereupon she became beautiful. R. Mani later came back to complain, "Now that she is pretty, she has become domineering." Said R. Yitzchak, "In that case, let Chanah become ugly again!" and his words came true.

Two students who used to attend the lectures of R. Yitzchak b. Eliashiv said to him, "Please pray for us that we should become wise." R. Yitzchak replied, "I once had the power [to pray and receive whatever I wanted], but I no longer possess that power." [Alternatively: I stopped using this power, for I don't want to bother God to change the course of nature (Maharsha).]

A UNIQUE DONKEY

(24a) R. Yose had a donkey. When he rented it out for the day, the people who rented it would return it toward evening. They would send the rental fee on the back of the donkey, which would make its way home to its master's house. However, if they had overpaid or underpaid, the donkey would not move. One day, a pair of shoes were left on the donkey's back, and it would not move until they removed the shoes, and only then did the donkey go home.

HE GAVE EVERYTHING TO CHARITY

Eliezer[37] of Bartosa [was exteremely generous to the point that] the communal charity collectors would avoid him so that he would not give away everything he had, [and they did not want to take all his money]. One day he was going to the market to shop for a trousseau for his daughter. When the charity collectors spotted him they ran away, but he ran after them and told them, "I command you to tell me: What [charitable project] are you involved in?" They replied, "We are collecting money for the wedding of two orphans." He said, "I swear that they take precedence over my daughter." He then gave them all the money he had with him, except for one *zuz*. With this *zuz* he bought some wheat, which he deposited in a grain silo. When his wife came home she asked her daughter, "What did your father bring home?" She replied, "Whatever my father brought he put in the silo." So she went and opened the door of the silo. She noticed that the wheat was piled up high, and that it was bulging out through the hinges of the door. The door would not open because of all the wheat. When R. Eliezer came home from the *bet midrash*, his wife told him, "Come and see what the One Who loves you has done for you." He replied, "I swear, that all this wheat shall be dedicated for sacred purposes, and you have no more right to it than any poor person in Israel." [He did not want to derive any benefit from something he obtained through a miracle, since to do so would detract from his merits in the World to Come[38] (Rashi).]

THEY FASTED AND PRAYED, BUT THE RAIN DID NOT COME

R. Yehudah Nesiah (the Prince) ordained a fast [because of a drought], but no rain fell. He remarked: What a great difference is there between Samuel of Ramah [the prophet Samuel] and Yehudah the son of Gamliel, [himself]![39] [Samuel prayed and the rains came,[40] but my prayers for rain are not answered]. Woe to the generation that finds itself in such a predicament [that they rely on me, and I cannot produce rain]! Woe to person in whose days this has happened! He became very depressed, and then it began to rain, [for God is close to the brokenhearted].[41]

Once the House of the *Nasi* [the head of the Sanhedrin] ordained a fast [because of a drought] and did not inform R. Yochanan and Resh Lakish of this. In the morning, however, they did let them know [that today is a fast, and that they should not eat]. So Resh Lakish asked R. Yochanan: But we did not take upon ourselves yesterday to fast today? [A fast should be undertaken during *Minchah* of the previous day.][42] R. Yochanan answered: We are subject to the decrees of the *Nasi*, [and therefore we do not have to commit ourselves to this fast on the previous day].

On another occasion the House of the *Nasi* proclaimed a fast but no rain fell. Thereupon Oshaiah, the youngest of the scholars in the yeshivah, expounded the verse, "If a sin is committed unintentionally by the community [because of their] leadership . . ."[43] (Numbers 15:24), [meaning, if the Bet Din rendered an erroneous ruling, and the community acted on this erroneous ruling they are required to bring an offering]. Oshaiah said: This can be compared to a girl who is engaged and still lives in her father's house. If her eyes are beautiful, her body needs no examination [you may assume that she is pure], but if her eyes are not beautiful, then her body needs examination; [an implied criticism of the *Nasi* who is considered "the eye of the community": It is because of the failings of the *Nasi* that it does not rain]. The servants of the *Nasi* [took offense at this] and came and tied a cloth around Oshaiah's neck and began choking him and tormented him. The people of the city then told the servants of the *Nasi*: Leave him alone! He used to criticize us too, but once we saw that his criticism was for the sake of Heaven we left him alone, so you too should leave him alone.

Rabbi decreed a fast [because of a drought], and no rain fell. So Ilfa—some say, Rav Ilfa—went down to lead the congregation in prayer, and as soon as he said the words, "He makes the wind blow," the wind began to blow; and as soon as he said, "and He makes the rain fall," it began to rain. Rabbi then asked him, "What is your special merit?" He replied, "I live in a village where poverty is rampant, where they do not even have wine to make *Kiddush* and *Havdalah* on *Shabbat*. So I go to great trouble to obtain wine for *Kiddush* and *Havdalah*, and I help the entire community fulfill their duty of *Kiddush* and *Havdalah*." [Because of this merit his prayers were answered immediately.]

Rav once came to a certain community and enacted a fast, but the rains did not come. The *chazzan* went down to officiate, and as soon as he said the words, "He makes the wind blow," the wind began to blow, and as soon as he said, "He makes the rain fall," it began to rain. Rav asked him, "What is your special merit?" He replied, "I am a teacher of little children, and I teach the children of the poor as well as those of the rich; I take no tuition from those who cannot afford to pay. I also have a fishpond, and any boy who does not want to learn I bribe with the fish from the pond, and I coax him until he becomes eager to learn."

R. Nachman once ordained a fast, and he prayed but it did not rain. He exclaimed: Take Nachman and throw him down from the high wall to the ground! [Meaning: Dismiss me from my prominent position; I don't deserve it, for my prayers are not answered!] He became deeply dejected, and then it began to rain.

Rabbah once decreed a fast and prayed but no rain came. So the people pointed out to him that when Rav Yehudah ordered a fast it *did* rain. [Why are your prayers not answered?] Rabbah retorted, "What shall I do? Is it because of learning? Our learning is on a higher level than Rav Yehudah's, for in Rav Yehudah's time all studies were concentrated on (24b) the Order of *Nezikin* [the fourth order of the Mishnah that deals with damages, civil law, and criminal law], while we are well-versed in all six orders of the Mishnah. And when Rav Yehudah came to a difficult Mishnah in the Order of *Taharot* (Purifications) that states: A woman who is pickling vegetables [in vinegar, oil, or brine] in a pot . . . , (*Taharot* 2:1) or as some say, the Mishnah that states: If olives are pickled [in vinegar or wine] together with their leaves . . . (*Uktzin* 2:1), he exclaimed: I see in these *Mishnayot* the highly intricate debates of Rav and Shmuel, [Rav Yehudah was over-whelmed by the profundity of the subject matter (Rashi)]. Yet," continued Rabbah, "we have [here in town] thirteen *yeshivot* that are studying the tractate *Uktzin*, [proof that our learning is on a higher level than Rav Yehudah's]. But [even so], when Rav Yehudah took off one shoe [signifying the beginning of a fast], rain fell; and we cry all day, and our prayers are not answered. Is it because of any wrongdoing? Then if anyone knows that we have done anything wrong, let him tell me." Rabbah concluded, "The true reason that the rain does not come is this: What can the leaders of the generation do when their generation does not deserve that it rains?"

THE FAMINE WAS RESCINDED

Rav Yehudah once saw two people throwing bread at each other, and he cried out: It seems that there must be plenty of bread around [if people use bread to play ball]. He gave an angry look and, as a result, a famine set in. Thereupon the Rabbis told R. Kahana the son of R. Nechunia, who was Rav Yehudah's attendant, "You who are close to Rav Yehudah, get him to go out to the market so that he sees how much the people suffer from the famine." He persuaded Rav Yehudah, and he went out to the market. Noticing a large crowd of people, Rav Yehudah asked, "What is going on here?" They told him, "These people are standing on line to buy some spoiled dates that are for sale." Said Rav Yehudah, "Evidently there is a famine." He then told his attendant, "Take off my shoes." As soon as he had taken off one shoe, it began to rain. As he was about to take off the other shoe, Elijah appeared and said, "The Holy One, blessed be He, said, 'If you take off the other shoe, I will destroy the world,'" [since God had already answered his prayer, taking off the other shoe would be too much of an imposition (*Maharsha*)].

R. Mari, the son of the daughter of Shmuel, said: Once I was standing at the bank of the river Papa, and I saw angels dressed like sailors that were bringing sand and loading it into ships. [Miraculously,] the sand turned into fine flour. When the people came to buy it I called to them: Don't buy this flour because it came into existence through a miracle, [and we should avoid deriving benefit from things that are the result of a miracle]. The next day, boats arrived from the city of Parzina carrying wheat, and this everyone bought [since it did not originate from a miracle].

Rava once came to the town of Hagrunia and en-acted a fast [because of drought conditions] but no rain fell. So he said to the people, "Continue fasting through the night." The next morning he told them, "If any-body saw anything in a dream tell it." So R. Elazar of Hagrunia related, "In my dream I saw my-self calling out, 'Good greetings, to the good rabbi from the good Master Who from His bounty showers good on His people.'" Rava then exclaimed, "It seems that this is a favorable time [for our prayers to be ac-cepted]." So he prayed and rain did come.

RAVA AND KING SHAPUR

Rava's Bet Din once sentenced a man to be flogged be-cause he had lived with a non-Jewish woman. Rava ordered the sentence to be carried out, and the man died. When King Shapur heard about it he wanted to punish Rava. Ifra Hormuz, the mother of King Shapur [who had a special liking for Rava (Rashi)], told her son, "Do not interfere with the Jews because whatever they ask of their God is granted them." The king asked her for an example, and she said, "They pray, and it begins to rain." He replied, "That must have been in the rainy season. Let them pray for rain now, in the *tekufah* of Tammuz [the summer solstice, in the dry season]." Ifra Hormuz sent a message to Rava, "Con-centrate your thoughts, and pray for rain." Rava prayed but it did not rain. He then said, "Master of the uni-verse, 'We have heard, O God, our fathers have told us, the deeds You performed in their time, in days of old' (Psalms 44:2), but we have not seen it with our eyes, [You are not performing miracles for us]." There-upon it began to rain so heavily that the gutters of Mechuza emptied their waters into the river Tigris. Rava's father then appeared to him in a dream and said, "Is there anyone who is causing so much trouble for God? [You have asked for an unnecessary miracle, only to prove your power to the king.] [I advise you,] don't sleep in your bed tonight; [it is unsafe]." Rava slept in a different place that night, and the next morning he discovered that his bed had been slashed with knives. [Demons had come to kill him because he had caused God to perform an unnecessary miracle, and when they did not find him they cut up his bed (Rashi).]

R. Papa once ordered a fast, and he felt very faint. He broke his fast, and then prayed but the rain did not come. So R. Nachman b. Ushpazarti told him, "If you would eat another spoonful of grits, the rain would surely come." [He said it sarcastically, criticizing him for breaking his fast and praying afterward (Rashi).] R. Papa was very embarrassed and felt bad, and then the rain came.

RABBI CHANINA BEN DOSA

R. Chanina b. Dosa was once traveling on the road when it began to rain. He exclaimed, "Master of the universe, everybody is comfortably settled at home, while Chanina [who is getting wet] is suffering." [His cry was heard in Heaven,] and the rain stopped. When he came home he exclaimed, "Master of the universe, everybody is filled with anxiety [because they need the rain for their crops], while Chanina is at ease [because I don't own any fields. Why should they be distressed because of me?]" So it started to rain again. Said R.

Yosef: Of what use was the prayer of the *Kohen Gadol* [on Yom Kippur] against R. Chanina b. Dosa? For we have learned in a Mishnah:[44] [On Yom Kippur] the *Kohen Gadol* uttered a short prayer in the outer chamber [of the *Bet Hamikdash*]. What did he pray? Rava son of R. Adda and Ravin son of Adda both said in the name of Rav Yehudah: May it be Your will, O Lord our God, that this year may be one of rain and of heat.

[The Gemara asks:] Is then excessive heat beneficial? Shouldn't it be considered something harmful? [The Gemara answers: This is how the prayer was meant:] If it is a very hot year, it should be compensated by an overabundance of rain and dew, [and the *Kohen Gadol* added,] and let the prayers of the people who are on the road when it rains [who pray for the rain to stop] not be answered by You [because the farmers need the rain]. [Thus R. Yosef said that the *Kohen Gadol*'s prayer was ineffective in the face of the more powerful prayer of R. Chanina b. Dosa.]

R. Acha the son of Rava said in the name of Rav Yehudah that the *Kohen Gadol*'s prayer included also: A ruler should never cease from the house of Judah, and Your people Israel should never have to depend on one another for their livelihood, nor on a different nation.

AN OVEN FULL OF BREAD

Rav Yehudah said in the name of Rav: Every day a Heavenly Voice is heard declaring: The whole world is sustained in the merit of Chanina my son, and Chanina my son is satisfied with a *kav*[45] of carobs from one *Shabbat* eve to the next.

Every Friday his wife would light the oven and throw twigs inside so that smoke would rise from the chimney, and the neighbors would think that she was baking bread for *Shabbat*, because she was embarrassed [that she had no food to cook for *Shabbat*]. She had a bad neighbor who said to herself: I know that they don't have anything; what is producing all that smoke? She went and knocked on the door. R. Chanina's wife, embarrassed that she had no bread, hid in a small room. When the neighbor saw that nobody answered the door she entered and found the oven filled with bread, and the kneading bowl full of dough. She called out to R. Chanina's wife, "Bring a shovel, for your bread is getting burned!" R. Chanina's wife replied: "I just went to get it." We learned in a *Baraita*: She actually had gone to get a shovel to remove the bread, because she was accustomed to miracles.

THE HEAVENLY GIFT WAS TAKEN BACK

Once R. Chanina's wife asked her husband, "How long do we have to suffer such poverty?" "What shall we do?" R. Chanina retorted. "Pray to God that He should give you something," she replied. He prayed, and a heavenly hand came down and gave him a leg of a golden table. R. Chanina then saw in a dream that in the World to Come all the righteous people will be sitting at golden tables with three legs while he will be eating at a table that has only two legs. So he asked his wife, "Will you be satisfied that everyone else will be eating at a table with three legs and we at a table that has one leg missing?" She asked, "What shall we do?" She asked [rhetorically], "Pray that the leg be taken away." He prayed and the leg was taken back. We learned in a *Baraita*: The second miracle [of the leg being taken back] was greater than the first [of the giving of the leg], for there is a tradition that things are given from Heaven but not taken back.

VINEGAR BURNS AS BRIGHTLY AS OIL

Once on a Friday evening R. Chanina noticed that his daughter was sad. Concerned, he asked her, "My daughter, why are you sad?" She replied, "I accidentally exchanged the vinegar can for the oil can and I lit the *Shabbat* lights with vinegar." So he asked her, "He Who commanded the oil to burn will also command the vinegar to burn." We learned in a *Baraita*: The light continued to burn until the conclusion of *Shabbat* when they used the light for *Havdalah*. [He was careful to light a new *Havdalah* candle and extinguish the original *Shabbat* candle because he did not want to derive benefit from a miracle (Rashi).]

OTHER MIRACLES

R. Chanina b. Dosa had a herd of goats. When people told him that the goats were causing damage to other people's property he exclaimed: If it is true that they are causing damage, let them be devoured by bears, but if not, let each one toward evening bring a bear on its horns. Toward evening, each goat brought a bear balanced on its horns.

R. Chanina had a neighbor who was building a house, but the beams did not reach the walls. So she came to R. Chanina and said, "I have built a house, but the beams will not reach the walls." He asked her, "What is your name?" She replied, "Eichu." He then said, "Eichu, let your beams become longer and reach the wall." Thereupon the beams extended. Some say that pieces were [miraculously] inserted in the empty space, which made the beams reach the walls. We learned in a *Baraita*: Plimo said: I saw the house and noticed that the beams projected one cubit on either side, and people told me: This is the house that R. Chanina covered with beams through his prayer.

HE RESIGNED HIMSELF TO HIS LOT

R. Elazar b. Pedat lived in great poverty. He once underwent a bloodletting and did not have anything to eat afterward. He took the peel of a garlic and put it in his mouth; he felt faint and fell asleep. The Rabbis who came to see him [to find out how he was feeling] noticed that he was crying and laughing in his sleep, and that a ray of light emanated from his forehead. When he awoke they asked him, "What is the reason that first you cried and then you laughed?" He replied, "Because the Holy One, blessed be He, was sitting by my side, and I asked Him, 'How much longer will I have to suffer in this world?' He answered me, 'Elazar my son, would you prefer that I should turn the world back to its beginnings? Perhaps you will then be born in a time of prosperity?' I replied, 'I see that even after You change the whole world, it is still questionable that my life will improve, [for you said "perhaps"].' I then asked Him, 'Which is greater, the number of years that I have already lived, or the years that I have left to live?' He replied, 'The years that you have lived.' I then said to him, 'If so, since I have passed the half-way point of my life, I do not want You to change the workings of the world.'

God answered, 'As a reward for resigning yourself to your lot you will be given in the World to Come thirteen rivers of balsam oil as clear as the Euphrates and the Tigris, which you will be able to enjoy.' [The spiritual rewards of the world to come are presented in terms of a metaphor we can understand (*Maharsha*).] I asked, 'Master of the universe! Is that all?' He replied, 'And what shall I give to your friends? [I cannot take away the reward from other people and give it to you.] I asked God, 'I am asking for the reward of the wicked who will not obtain a reward in the World to Come.' Thereupon God snapped His finger against my forehead [which caused his face to radiate], and He said, 'Elazar my son, I have shot My arrows against you.'" [An expression of God's love and affection. He cried when he heard that he had passed the half-way point of his life; he laughed when he heard the fabulous reward that awaited him in the World to Come (Rashi).]

R. Chama b. Chanina decreed a fast but no rain fell. The people said to him: When R. Yehoshua b. Levi enacted a fast rain *did* fall. R. Chama replied: I am one person, and the son of Levi is another person, [he is a greater person than I]. Go and ask him to come here, and together we will concentrate. Perhaps the entire community will feel brokenhearted, and in that merit the rain will come. They prayed but no rain fell. R. Yehoshua b. Levi asked them: Are you all in agreement that in our merit the rain should fall? They replied: Yes. He then cried out: Heaven, heaven, cover your face [with clouds that will bring rain]. But it did not cover its face. He then said: How impudent is the face of heaven [that it does not cover itself in front of the entire community]! At last the sky became covered with clouds, and it began to rain.

Levi once ordained a fast but it did not rain. He then prayed: Master of the universe! You ascended and took Your seat on high, and You have no compassion on Your children. Thereupon it began to rain, but Levi became lame in his leg [for speaking harshly to God]. R. Elazar said: A person should not speak in a reproachful tone to God, for a great man spoke in a reproachful manner to God and he became crippled, and this is Levi. [The Gemara asks:] Was this really the cause of his lameness? Wasn't the reason for his disability that he injured himself when demonstrating to Rabbi how the *kohanim* used to perform the *kidah* [a difficult form of prostration]?[46] [The Gemara answers:] Both things caused his lameness.

THE SAGES PRAYED FOR RAIN

R. Chiya b. Luliani heard the clouds saying to each other: Let us go and pour out our water on the nations of Ammon and Moab [and leave Eretz Yisrael without any rain]. [Turning to the clouds,] R. Chiya exclaimed: When the Holy One, blessed be He, went to the other nations offering them the Torah, no nation was willing to accept it, until He offered it to Israel and they accepted it. And now, you clouds, would desert Israel and pour rain on the lands of Ammon and Moab? Deposit your rain here. And they poured out their rain on the spot [and did not proceed to Ammon and Moab].

R. Chiya b. Luliani expounded: What is meant by the verse, "A righteous man will flourish like a date-palm, like a cedar in the Lebanon he will thrive" (Psalms 92:13)? Why is he compared to both a date-palm and a cedar? [He answered:] If a righteous man would be compared only to a date-palm and not a cedar, I might think that just as the stem of a date-palm (25b) does not grow new shoots once it is cut down, so too the stem of a righteous man, God forbid, does not renew itself, [meaning, he will not be resurrected at the Revival of the Dead (Rashi)], therefore he is compared to a cedar [which does regrow new shoots]. If he would have been compared only to a cedar tree and not to a palm tree, I might have thought that, just as a cedar does not produce fruit, so too a righteous man, God forbid, does not produce fruit, [meaning, he will not receive a reward in the World to Come (Rashi)]. That's why the verse compares the righteous man both to a date-palm and a cedar tree.

We learned in a *Baraita*: R. Eliezer once decreed thirteen fasts, but no rain fell. After the thirteenth fast, when the people began to go home from the synagogue, he said to them, "Have you prepared graves for yourselves? [There is a drought, and people are going to die!]" So the entire congregation broke out into loud weeping, and because of that, rain began to fall [because God listens to the brokenhearted].

Another time it happened that R. Eliezer lead the congregation in prayer and said the twenty-four *berachot* [which are said on a fast day for rain],[47] but his prayer was not answered. R. Akiva followed him at the lectern and said: Our Father, our King, we have no King except for You. Our Father, our King, for Your sake, have pity on us; and it began to rain. The people now thought that R. Akiva was greater than R. Eliezer. But a Heavenly Voice came forth and declared: The prayer of R. Akiva was answered, not because he is greater than R. Eliezer, but because R. Akiva has a more forgiving nature.

SHMUEL HAKATAN'S PARABLES

Shmuel Hakatan [the Little] enacted a fast, and rain began to fall before sunrise, [the people had not yet begun to fast]. The people thought that this was due to the exemplary conduct of the congregation, but Shmuel told them: [The opposite is true; it is a sign of God's disapproval]. I will explain it to you with a parable. You can compare it to a servant who asked his master for something, and the master says: Give it to him; I don't want to hear his voice beseeching me. [That's why God gave the rain, before you prayed for it.]

Another time Shmuel Hakatan ordained a fast, and after sunset, [after an entire day of fasting and praying], rain fell. The people thought that this was due to the merit of the community. But Shmuel told them: [This is not a sign of God's favor; on the contrary]. I will explain it to you with a parable. You can compare it to a servant who asked his master for something, and the master said: Keep him waiting until he becomes submissive, and feels pain, and then give it to him. [Here too, since God waited for an entire day of the community's fasting and agonizing before granting their request, it is a sign of God's displeasure.] [The Gemara asks:] According to Shmuel Hakatan, what kind of rainfall would be a sign that God approved of the conduct of the community? [The Gemara answers:] If the congregation began to say [the prayer,] "He makes the wind blow," and the wind blew, and if they recited, "and He makes the rain descend," and the rain came down, [that would be a sign of Divine approval].

IT RAINED IN LUD

[The Mishnah[48] said:] One time a fast day was decreed in Lud, and rain fell before midday. Thereupon R. Tarfon said to the people: Go, eat and drink, and observe the day as a Yom Tov. The people ate and drank and observed the day as a Yom Tov, and in the evening they recited the great *Hallel* [Psalms 136].

[The Gemara asks:] Why didn't they say *Hallel* immediately, as soon as it began to rain? Abaye and Rava both said in answer to this question: We say *Hallel* only **(26a)** in a contented mood and on a full stomach. [The Gemara asks:] Is that so? Did not R. Papa once come to the synagogue at Abi Gobar[49] and ordain a fast, and when rain fell before noon, he told them: First recite the great *Hallel*, and after that eat

and drink! [The Gemara answers:] It is different with the people of Mechuza, for drunkenness is very common among them, [and they are liable to become drunk during the meal and forget to say *Hallel*].

THE TWENTY-FOUR MA'AMADOT

[The Mishnah explains what is meant by *Ma'amadot*:] This is the purpose of the institution of *Ma'amadot*. [It is based on the verse describing the *tamid*, the daily continual offering,] "Command the children of Israel and tell them: Be scrupulous in presenting to Me the offering of food due Me at the stated times . . ." (Numbers 28:1). [This verse clearly shows that the offering of the *tamid* offering is the responsibility of the entire Jewish people every day. And theoretically every Jew would have to be present at the offering of the communal offerings, which is technically not feasible.] So how can a person's offering be brought on the altar when he is not present? Because of this, the early prophets [i.e., the prophet Samuel and King David (Rashi)] divided all Israel into twenty-four *mishmar* groups [of *kohanim*, Levites, and Israelites], and each *mishmar* group was represented in the *Bet Hamikdash* in Jerusalem by all its *kohanim* and Levites and a *ma'amad* of Israelites. [Thus each week a different *mishmar* group of *kohanim* and Levites and a *ma'amad* of Israelites had the responsibility of standing in the court of the *Bet Hamikdash* beside the altar as representatives of all Israel when the communal offerings were brought.]

When the time came for the *mishmar* group to go up to Jerusalem, all the *kohanim* and the Levites [of that *mishmar*] went up to Jerusalem and the Israelites of the *mishmar* [members of that week who did not go up to Jerusalem] assembled in the synagogues of their cities and read [each day] in the Torah the story of Creation (Genesis 1) [to make the people mindful of the interconnection of the Temple service and the existence of the world]. On Sunday they read,[50] "In the beginning" and "Let there be a firmament"; on Monday they read, "Let there be a firmament," and "Let the waters be gathered into one area"; on Tuesday, "Let the waters be gathered" and "Let there be luminaries"; on Wednesday, "Let there be luminaries" and "Let the waters teem"; on Thursday, "Let the waters teem" and "Let the earth bring forth"; on Friday, "Let the earth bring forth" and "Thus the heaven and the earth were finished." A large section [comprising at least six verses] could be read by two people, and a short section [that had only three verses] could be read by only one person. These sections were read from a *sefer Torah* at *Shacharit*, and at *Mussaf* [on days when a *Mussaf* offering was brought], but at the *Minchah* service [they did not take out a *sefer Torah*] but they said the section by heart, like those who read the *Shema* by heart. On Friday they did not assemble in the synagogue at

Minchah [to recite the appropriate reading], out of respect for *Shabbat* [i.e., in order to prepare for *Shabbat*].

WHY DID THEY READ THE STORY OF CREATION?

(27b) [The Gemara asks:] From where in Scripture do we derive [that the men of the *mishmar* group who did not go up to Jerusalem assembled in the synagogue and read the story of Creation? What is the relevance of the story of Creation]? R. Yaakov b. Acha said in the name of R. Assi: If not for the *ma'amadot* [i.e., the offering of the *tamid*, the continual offering,] heaven and earth would cease to exist. [The world exists only in the merit of the Jewish people, and without sacrifices to atone for their sins, the Jewish people cannot exist, hence without sacrifices the world cannot endure (Rashi).] For it says, "[Abraham] said, 'O Lord God! Whereby shall I know that I will inherit [Eretz Yisrael]?'" (Genesis 15:8). Abraham said: Master of the universe, perhaps if Israel will sin against You, You will destroy them like the generation of the Flood and the generation of the Dispersion of Babel?[51] God answered: No, I will not. Abraham then said: Master of the universe! "Let me know whereby I shall inherit [the Land]." God replied, "Bring to Me three heifers, three goats and three rams . . . ," (ibid. 9), [implying that in the merit of the sacrifices the Jewish people will exist forever]. Abraham said: Master of the universe! That is fine as long as the *Bet Hamikdash* is standing, but what will happen when the *Bet Hamikdash* is destroyed? Replied God: That's why I have instituted the order of sacrifices, and whenever they read it I will consider it as if they had offered them before Me, and I will forgive all their sins.

FOUR FASTS IN ONE WEEK

We learned in a *Baraita*: The men of the *ma'amad* prayed that the sacrifices their colleagues were bringing should be favorably accepted, and the men of the *mishmar* [who did not go up to Jerusalem] gathered in their synagogues and observed four fasts, on Monday, Tuesday, Wednesday, and Thursday of that week. On Monday they fasted for people who are crossing the sea [that they should arrive safely]; on Tuesday, for people who travel through the desert; on Wednesday, that children should not be stricken with diphtheria; on Thursday, for pregnant women and nursing mothers, that pregnant women should not suffer a miscarriage and that nursing mothers should be able to nurse their babies. On Friday they did not fast in honor of *Shabbat* [so as not to enter *Shabbat* famished]; and needless to say, they did not fast on *Shabbat*. [The Gemara asks:] Why did they not fast on Sunday? R. Yochanan said: Because of the Christians. [They may resent it if the Jews fast on their day of rest.] R. Shmuel b. Nachmani said: Because Sunday is the third day after man was

created. [Man was created on Friday.] Resh Lakish said: [They did not fast on Sunday] because [on Sunday God removes] the extra soul [every Jew receives on *Shabbat*]. For Resh Lakish said: Every Jew receives an additional soul on Friday, but at the close of *Shabbat* it is taken back, as it says, "He rested and was refreshed [*vayinafash*]" (Exodus 31:17), which is expounded: After *Shabbat* has ended, a Jew cries *vay avedah nefesh*, "Woe! I lost my extra soul!"

THEY OUTWITTED THE GUARDS

(28a) Our Rabbis have taught: What is the story behind the names of the families of *Gonvei Ali* and *Kotz'ei Ketziot*? It is told that once the government made a decree forbidding the Jews to bring wood to the altar and to [fulfill the mitzvah of] bringing their first-fruit to Jerusalem.[52] The authorities placed guards on the roads, as Jeroboam the son of Nevat had done, to prevent the Jews from going to Jerusalem on the festival pilgrimages.[53] What did the God-fearing people of that generation do? They took the baskets of first-fruit, covered them with dried figs, and carried them with a pestle [a tool used for pressing figs] on their shoulder. At the checkpoint, the guards asked, "Where are you going?" They replied, "We are going to make two cakes of dried figs with this pestle on our shoulder in the mortar we have over there." Once they passed the checkpoint they decorated the first-fruit baskets and brought them to Jerusalem. [Hence the name *Gonvei Ali*, "those who outwitted the guards with a pestle."] We learned in a *Baraita*: We find a similar story with regard to the family of Salmai Hantufati.

The Rabbis taught: What is the story in connection with the family of Salmai Hantufati? It is told that once the government issued a decree forbidding the Jews to bring wood to the altar, and they placed guards on the roads, as Jeroboam the son of Nevat had done, to prevent the Jews from going to Jerusalem on the *Yamim Tovim*. What did the God-fearing people of that generation do? They brought the logs of wood and made ladders out of them, which they carried on their shoulders and marched along. At the checkpoint the guards asked them, "Where are you going?" They replied, "We are going to take down some pigeons from the dovecot up ahead. That's why we are carrying the ladders." Once they passed the checkpoint, they took apart the ladders and brought the wood to Jerusalem [to be used on the altar]. Scripture has them and people like them in mind when it says, "Remembrance of a righteous one brings blessing" (Proverbs 10:7), and of Jeroboam and his cohorts it says, "But the name of the wicked will rot" (ibid.).

FIVE CALAMITIES

[The Mishnah (26a) stated:] Five tragedies happened to our ancestors on the seventeenth of Tamuz, and five disasters happened on the ninth of Av. On the seventeenth of Tamuz the Tablets were shattered [by Moses because of the sin of the golden calf], the daily continual offerings were discontinued, a breach was made in the wall of Jerusalem, Apostomos burned the Torah scroll, and placed an idol in the *Bet Hamikdash*. On the ninth of Av it was decreed that our forefathers should not enter Eretz Yisrael, [when they cried without a cause upon hearing the evil report of the spies][54] the first and the second *Bet Hamikdash* were destroyed, the city of Betar was captured [in the Bar Kochba uprising against the Romans, and thousands were killed in the ensuing massacre], and the city of Jerusalem was ploughed up [and leveled like a field].

(28b) [The Gemara asks:] How do we know that the Tablets were shattered on the seventeenth of Tamuz? For we learned in a *Baraita*:[55] On the sixth of Sivan the Ten Commandments were given to Israel. R. Yose says: On the seventh of Sivan. The Tanna who says that they were given on the sixth holds that on the seventh Moses went up the mountain [to receive the Tablets]. And the Tanna who holds that the Tablets were given on the seventh of Sivan holds that they were given on the seventh, and on the same day Moses went up the mountain. For it says, "[God] called to Moses on the seventh day" (Exodus 24:16), and then it says, "Moses arrived in the midst of the cloud and ascended the mountain; and Moses was on the mountain for forty days and forty nights" (ibid. 18). [Since Moses went up on the seventh of Sivan and stayed there for forty days, we can make the following calculation:] There are twenty-four days more days in Sivan, and sixteen more days in Tamuz, which add up to forty days [that Moses was on the mountain]. Thus, it was on the seventeenth of Tamuz that he came down from the mountain and broke the Tablets, as it says, "As soon as Moses came near the camp and saw the calf and the dancing . . . he threw down the Tablets out of his hands and shattered them at the foot of the mountain" (Exodus 32:19).

THE NOBLE ROMAN OFFICER

We learned in a *Baraita*: When Turnus Rufus the wicked destroyed the *Bet Hamikdash*, the [Romans] condemned R. Gamliel to death. A high-ranking officer came to the *bet midrash* and announced, "I'm looking for the man with the nose! I'm looking for the man with the nose!" [Meaning, the most prominent personality in the yeshivah, just as the nose is the most prominent feature of the face. Surreptitiously he meant to warn him that his life is in danger (Rashi).] R. Gamliel took the hint and went into hiding. Thereupon the officer secretly visited him and asked him, "If I save your life, will you promise me a share in the World to Come?" R. Gamliel replied, "Yes." The officer then asked him, "Will you swear it to me?" He swore it to him. The officer then climbed up to the

roof and threw himself down and died. There was a [Roman] tradition that whenever a death sentence was pronounced, and one of the signers of the warrant died, that sentence was annulled. [They considered the man's death as a sign that the sentence was unjust (Rashi).] Thereupon a heavenly voice came forth and declared: This officer is destined to have a share in the World to Come.

THEY RETURNED THE KEYS

We learned in a *Baraita*: At the time of the destruction of the first *Bet Hamikdash*, groups of young priests, holding the keys of the *Bet Hamikdash* in their hands, climbed up to the roof of the Sanctuary and exclaimed: Master of the universe! Since we were not privileged to be faithful treasurers, we herewith return the keys. They then threw the keys upward toward heaven, and a semblance of a hand appeared and took hold of the keys. At that the young priests jumped from the roof and fell into the flames. Isaiah had these priests in mind when he lamented, "A prophecy concerning the Valley of Vision [i.e., Jerusalem]: What happened to you now that you have all gone up to rhe roofs, you who have been full of commotion, a tumultuous city, an exuberant town? Your slain are not slain by the sword, nor did they die in war" (Isaiah 22:1,2). Concerning God the prophet also says, "For it is a day of turmoil and trampling and confusion unto my Lord, God, Master of Legions in the Valley of Vision; [God Himself] is crying at the wall and shouting at the mountain" (ibid. 5).

[We learned in the Mishnah:] As the month of Av arrives we cut down on rejoicing. Rav Yehudah the son of R. Shmuel b. Shilat said in the name of Rav: Just as with the beginning of Av we restrain our rejoicing, so with the beginning of Adar we increase rejoicing. R. Papa said: Therefore, if a Jew has a lawsuit against a non-Jew, he should try to postpone it, because [in Av] the Jew's luck is bad. He should rather go to court in Adar when his luck is good.

THE HAPPIEST DAYS
IN THE YEAR

[We learned in the Mishnah (26b):] R. Shimon b. Gamliel said: There were no happier holidays in Israel than the fifteenth of Av and Yom Kippur. On these days the girls of Jerusalem used to come out wearing white dresses—borrowed ones—in order not to embarrass the girls that did not have white dresses of their own. [Before being worn] all these borrowed dresses had to be immersed in a *mikveh*, [since a dress might have been worn by a woman who was ritually unclean]. The Jewish girls used to come out and dance in the vineyards, saying: Young man, take a look and see whom you choose for yourself [as a wife]. Don't pay attention to beauty, but set your sights on [good] family. "Grace is deceptive and beauty is illusory; a woman who fears God—she should be praised" (Proverbs 31:30). And it says further, "Extol her for the fruit of her hand, and let her be praised in the gates by her very own deeds" (ibid. 31).

Furthermore, it also says, "O maidens of Zion, go forth and gaze upon King Solomon, wearing the crown that his mother gave him on his wedding day, on his day of bliss" (Song of Songs 3:11). "On his wedding day"—this refers to the day of the Giving of the Torah. "His day of bliss" refers to the building of the *Bet Hamikdash*, may it be speedily be rebuilt in our days! [The entire Song of Songs is a sublime allegory describing the love of Israel for God.]

WHY WAS THE FIFTEENTH OF AV A YOM TOV?

[The Mishnah stated above: R. Shimon b. Gamliel said: There were no happier holidays than the fifteenth of Av and Yom Kippur. The Gemara explains:] It is understandable that Yom Kippur [is considered a joyous Yom Tov], because it is a day of forgiveness and pardon, and it commemorates the giving of the second Tablets of the Law [which occurred on that day]. But what is the significance of the fifteenth of Av? Rav Yehudah said in the name of Shmuel: Because on that day the tribes were permitted to intermarry.[56] [The Gemara asks:] From what passage did the Sages derive this? [The Gemara answers:] They expounded the verse, "This is what God has commanded concerning the daughters of Zelaphehad: They may marry anyone they wish provided they marry into the clan of their father's tribe" (Numbers 36:6). [The word "this" implies that] this restriction shall be limited to this generation only.

R. Yosef said in the name of R. Nachman: [The cause of the celebration of the fifteenth of Av is] because it is the day on which the tribe of Benjamin was permitted to re-enter the congregation of Israel, as it says, [After the incident with the concubine at Gibeah,][57] "The men of Israel had taken an oath at Mizpah, saying, "None of us will give his daughter as a wife to [the tribe of] Benjamin" (Judges 21:1). [The Sages ruled that the oath applied only to the first generation, but subsequent generations were permitted to give their daughters in marriage to Benjamin, and this decision was reached on the fifteenth of Av.] On what verse did they base their ruling? Rav said: It says, "None of *us*" will give his daughter as a wife; but this oath does not apply to our children.

Rabbah b. bar Chanah said in the name of R. Yochanan: [The cause of the celebration is:] Because it was on this day that the death sentence was lifted against the surviving members of the generation that wandered in the wilderness for forty years.[58] We have learned that as long as those destined to die in the wilderness had not yet died, God did not speak directly

to Moses, for it says, [Moses said,] "So it was only after all the men of war had stopped dying . . . that God spoke to me saying" (Deuteronomy 2:16,17). It was only then that God resumed speaking lovingly to Moses as he used to.

Ulla said: [The fifteenth of Av is considered a Yom Tov,] because that was the day on which Hoshea the son of Elah removed the guards that Jeroboam had stationed on the roads to prevent the people from going to the *Bet Hamikdash* on the three pilgrimage festivals, and [Hoshea b. Elah] proclaimed: (31a) Let them go to whichever temple they wish, [to the *Bet Hamikdash*, or *lehavdil*, to the idolatrous shrines in Bethel and Dan].

R. Matnah said: [The fifteenth of Av was proclaimed a Yom Tov] because it was on that day permission was granted [by the Romans] to bury the dead that were killed in Betar. R. Matnah said furthermore: On the day that those killed in Betar were permitted to be buried, the Rabbis at Yavneh [i.e., the Bet Din of R. Gamliel the Elder] instituted the recitation of the *berachah Hatov vehameitiv*, "Who is good, and Who does good" [the fourth *berachah* in *Birkat Hamazon*, Grace after Meals]. "Who is good" because their bodies did not decay, "and Who does good" because permission was granted for their burial.

Rabbah and R. Yosef both said: [The reason that the fifteenth of Av is a Yom Tov is] because it is the day that they stopped cutting wood to be burned on the altar. [By the middle of Av the heat of sun begins to wane. Wood cut after that date is not dry enough to prevent infestation of worms, and wormy wood is unfit for the altar (Rashi).] We learned in a *Baraita*: R. Eliezer Hagadol says: After the fifteenth of Av the strength of the sun grows weaker; therefore, they stopped cutting wood for the altar, because the wood is not dry enough [and prone to becoming wormy, which makes it unfit for the altar]. R. Menashya commented: And they called that day the Day of Breaking the Ax. From that day on, [since the nights grow longer], if a person increases his time of learning at night, God will lengthen his life, but if a person does not increase his time of learning [after the fifteenth of Av], his life will be taken away. What is meant by "taken away"? R. Yosef said: It means that his mother will bury him; [he will die before his time].

THEY ALL DANCED IN BORROWED DRESSES

[We learned in the Mishnah:] On these days the girls of Jerusalem used to come out wearing white dresses—borrowed ones—in order not to embarrass those that did not have white dresses of their own. [The Gemara comments:] We learned in a *Baraita*: The daughter of the king borrowed the dress from the daughter of the *Kohen Gadol*, the daughter of the *Kohen Gadol* from the daughter of the deputy *Kohen Gadol*, and the daughter of the deputy *Kohen Gadol* would borrow from the daughter of the *kohen* who was anointed for battle [in time of war], and the daughter of the latter from the daughter of an ordinary *kohen*, and the daughters of all Israel would borrow from one another, in order not to embarrass those girls who did not own [a white dress].

[The Mishnah said:] All dresses required immersion in a *mikveh*, [because the owner may have been ritually impure]. R. Elazar said: Even clothes that were folded and stored in a box [an indication that they were new and unquestionably ritually pure] had to be immersed [in order not to embarrass anyone].

[The Mishnah stated:] The Jewish girls used to come out and dance in the vineyards. [The Gemara comments:] We learned in a *Baraita*: Whoever was unmarried would go to that place [and choose a wife for himself].

[The Mishnah stated:] What did the girls say? "Young man, take a look and see whom you are choosing for yourself [as a wife]." We learned in a *Baraita*: [There were three groups of girls:] The attractive ones among them would say, "Look for beauty, for the most important feature of a woman is her beauty." The girls of distinguished ancestry would say, "Look for good family, because the primary purpose of a wife is raising children," [and a girl who has had a good upbringing will tend to raise her children well]. The unattractive girls among them would say, "Marry a woman for the sake of Heaven, but adorn us with golden jewelry, [and beautiful clothes; then we, too, will look appealing]."

Ulla Bira'ah said in the name of R. Elazar: In days to come, the Holy One, blessed be He, will make a circle for the righteous, and He will sit among them in Gan Eden. Every one of them will point with his finger toward Him, as it says, "And they will say on that day, 'Behold, this is our God; we hoped to Him that He would save us; this is God to Whom we hoped, let us exult and rejoice in His deliverance'" (Isaiah 25:9).

NOTES

1. Rashi, quoting *Bereishit Rabbah*, Chayei Sarah.

2. The *Omer* is the sheaf of barley offered on the sixteenth of Nisan. Before the offering of the *Omer*, the new crop of grain of that year was forbidden for use. (See Leviticus 23:10.)

3. A span is the distance between the tips of the thumb and little finger, and is equivalent to nine inches.

4. Rachav was one of the four most beautiful women in the world (*Megillah* 15a).

5. We say this in the *Nishmat* prayer on Shabbat.

6. *Terumah* is the heave-offering from the yearly harvest that must be given to the *kohen*; *maaser* is the tithe of the harvest that must be given to the Levite.

7. An allusion to "I will make your skies like iron" (Leviticus 26:19).

8. This verse is in Job's "Song of the Rain" (36:23–33). The conventional translation of the phrase is "Its thunder announces it."

9. Rashi and Aruch, s.v. *cheled* (p. 142b).

10. See 1 Kings 17:7, ff.

11. Literally: "Tithe you shall tithe."

12. The boy was a nephew of R. Yochanan, since his father, Resh Lakish, married R. Yochanan's sister (*Bava Metzia* 84a).

13. *Bava Kamma* 117a.

14. "Burying" one's face in submissive supplication.

15. A *parsang* is four *mil*, and a *mil* is an eighteen-minute walk.

16. A person who has taken the vow to become a *nazir*, to abstain from wine and let his hair grow, as outlined in Numbers 6.

17. Resh Lakish interprets *gomeil* as "he weans," as in *vayigamal*, "he was weaned" (Genesis 21:8).

18. President of the Great Sanhedrin in Jerusalem.

19. Dean of the Sanhedrin.

20. The *Akeidah*, the Binding of Isaac (Genesis 22).

21. 2 Chronicles 3:1.

22. The same event is related in *Rosh Hashanah* 19a.

23. The colleagues of Daniel.

24. On the three *Regalim* (Pilgrimage Festivals), Pesach, Shavuot, and Sukkot, all Jews were required to come to Jerusalem to the *Bet Hamikdash* to bring sacrifices (Deuteronomy 16:16).

25. This happened shortly before the destruction of the second *Bet Hamikdash*, when Eretz Yisrael was under Roman domination (*Maharsha*).

26. This was the prophet Elijah in the disguise of an ugly man who came to teach R. Elazar a point concerning his relations with his fellow men (Rashi).

27. Literally: Time stands still for him.

28. R. Chiya and R. Oshaya composed the *Baraitot* under the guidance of R. Yehudah Hanasi (Rabbeinu Hakadosh) to explain the statements of the Mishnah. R. Chiya's *Baraitot* comprise the Tosefta. Their *Baraitot* are quoted in the Gemara with the introductory phrase *tanu rabbanan*, "Our Rabbis taught." See *Chullin* 141a.

29. Midrash *Tanchuma* on Genesis 14.

30. As commanded in Numbers 15:38 and Deuteronomy 22:12.

31. 2 Kings 23:29.

32. *Pesachim* 112b.

33. The volume of six eggs; about 549 cubic centimeters.

34. 1 Kings 17:1ff.

35. In *Ein Yaakov* the name is Chanin, whereas in the Gemara his name is written Chanan.

36. R. Yehudah III.

37. *Ein Yaakov* gives his name as Eliezer Ish Bartota; the Gemara identifies him as Elazar Ish Bartota.

38. *Taanit* 20b.

39. Rabbi Yehudah Nesiah was the son of the son of Rabban Gamliel III. He succeeded his father as *Nasi*

in ca. 200 C.E. He was known as R. Yehudah Nesiah
to distinguish him from his illustrious grandfather, R.
Yehudah HaNasi, the compiler of the Mishnah.

40. 1 Samuel 12:17.

41. Psalms 34:19.

42. *Taanit* 11b.

43. Literally, "the eyes of the community."

44. *Yoma* 53b.

45. A liquid measure equal to the volume of
twenty-four average chicken eggs.

46. *Sukkah* 53a.

47. *Taanit* 15a.

48. *Taanit* 19a.

49. A place near the city of Mechuza.

50. Each person called to the Torah had to read a
minimum of three verses. Since three persons (a Kohen,
Levi, and Yisrael) were called up, there were not enough
verses in any one section to accommodate them. Therefore a second section was read each day. Even then (as on
Sunday and Monday) a verse had to be repeated because
the two sections did not have the necessary nine verses.

51. Genesis 6:9ff and Genesis 11:1–9.

52. Deuteronomy 26:1–11.

53. Pesach, Shavuot, and Sukkot.

54. Numbers 14:1.

55. *Shabbat* 86a.

56. The Torah (Numbers 36:6,7) states that a
woman of the generation that entered the Land under
Joshua who had inherited land was forbidden to marry
out of her tribe to prevent her inherited property from
being transferred to her husband's tribe upon her
death. This prohibition applied only to the generation
that entered Eretz Yisrael, and it was left to the Sages
to determine when it was no longer in force.

57. Judges, Chapter 19.

58. After the spies returned from their expedition
to Eretz Yisrael and discouraged the people from entering the Land, God swore that all the men between
the ages of twenty and sixty had to die during the forty
years of wandering. In the fortieth year no one died,
and on the fifteenth of Av they realized that the decree had expired.

ᵒ⁄⧾ MO'ED KATAN ᵒ⧾

MARKING GRAVES

(5a) [Tractate *Mo'ed Katan* deals with the restrictions of work pertaining to the intermediate days (Chol Hamo'ed) of Pesach and Sukkot. The first Mishnah states that] on Chol Hamo'ed graves may be marked, [so that people who want to be ritually pure should not become contaminated by walking on them].

[The Gemara remarks:] R. Shimon b. Pazzi said: Where do we find a hint in Scriptures that graves should be marked? For it says, [that in the Messianic era, following the war of Gog and Magog,] "The passersby will traverse the land, and when they see a human bone they will build a marker near it" (Ezekiel 39:15). Said Ravina to R. Ashi: But who told us this [in the Torah] before Ezekiel came? R. Ashi replied: According to your view, how do you explain the statement by R. Chisda, namely: This law we did not learn from the Torah of Moses our Teacher, but we did learn it from the words of the prophet Ezekiel b. Buzi, who stated, "Any estranged person of uncircumcised heart or uncircumcised flesh shall not enter My sanctuary" (Ezekiel 44:9). [Would you ask here too:] Who told us this before Ezekiel came? We must say therefore that we learned it by oral tradition [from Sinai], and then Ezekiel came and gave us a verse on which to base it.

WEIGH YOUR ACTIONS

R. Yehoshua b. Levi said: Whoever calculates his actions [weighing the cost of a mitzvah against its reward, and the reward of a sin against its cost] will be rewarded to see the salvation of the Holy One, blessed be He, for it says, "One who orders [*vesam*] his way, I will show him the salvation of God" (Psalms 50:23). Read not *vesam*, but *vesham*, "he evaluates," his ways. R. Yannai had a student who used to ask him very difficult questions during his daily lecture, but at his discourses on the *Shabbat* that fell on a Yom Tov [when a large crowd filled the *bet midrash*] he did not ask him any questions, [so as not to embarrass him in front of the large audience in case he did not have the answer]. (5b) R. Yannai said about this student, "Someone who evaluates that which he is doing I will show the salvation of God;" [the student evaluated whether it was worthwhile for him to ask questions or not].

WHY NO WEDDINGS ON CHOL HAMO'ED?

[The Mishnah says:] A person is not permitted to marry a woman on Chol Hamo'ed, whether she is a virgin or a widow, nor may he fulfill the mitzvah of *yibbum* [i.e., the obligation to marry the widow of one's brother, if the deceased brother died childless],[1] because it is a reason for rejoicing for the groom. But a person may remarry a woman whom he had previously divorced.

[The Gemara asks:] What difference does it make if the groom rejoices? [Is it then forbidden to rejoice on Yom Tov!] Rav Yehudah said in the name of Shmuel, and so said R. Elazar in the name of R. Oshaia, and some say, R. Elazar said it in the name of R. Chanina: [The reason one may not marry on Chol Hamo'ed is] because we are not allowed to mix the rejoicing of one mitzvah [marriage] with the rejoicing of another [Yom Tov]. Rabbah the son of R. Huna said: It is forbidden, because he completely forsakes rejoicing with the Yom Tov and concentrates on rejoicing with his wife. Abbaye said to R. Yosef: The reason offered by Rabbah the son of R. Huna is the same as that given by Rav. For R. Daniel b. Kattina said in the name of Rav: From where do we know that one is not permitted to marry on Chol Hamo'ed? Because it says, "You shall rejoice with your festival" (Deuteronomy 16:14), [the implication being:] Rejoice exclusively with your festival, but not with your wife. Ulla said: [The reason it is not permitted to marry on Chol Hamo'ed is] because of the trouble [of preparing for the wedding feast]. R. Yitzchak Nappacha said: [The reason why the Sages prohibited marrying on Chol Hamo'ed is, because if it were permitted, people would set their wedding date on Chol Hamoed [when everyone is off from work], and this would mean that people would postpone raising a family and delay fulfilling the commandment of "be fruitful and multiply."

YOU SHOULD NOT MIX ONE REJOICING WITH ANOTHER

(9b) [The Gemara asks:] From where do we know the *halachah* that you are not allowed to mix one rejoicing with another? [The Gemara answers:] For it says, [When the *Bet Hamikdash* was completed] "At that time Solomon instituted the celebration—and all Israel was with him—a great assemblage coming from the Approach of Chamat to the Brook of Egypt[2]—before the Lord our God, for seven days [before Sukkot, to celebrate the inaugural of the *Bet Hamikdash*] and seven [more] days [to celebrate Sukkot], fourteen days in all" (1 Kings 8:65). Now if it is true that one joy may be mixed with another, should Solomon have waited until Sukkot, and celebrated Sukkot and the inauguration of the *Bet Hamikdash* simultaneously? [The fact that he celebrated the inauguration separately, is proof that we should not mix one joy with another.]

[The Gemara asks:] Perhaps postponing [a wedding and scheduling it on Chol Hamo'ed] is forbidden, but when it happens that they fall together it is permitted? [The Gemara answers: If so,] Solomon should have left a small part of the *Bet Hamikdash* unfinished, [and completed it shortly before Yom Tov, so that the inauguration would take place concurrent with the Yom Tov]. [The Gemara counters:] But perhaps he could not do that, because it is not proper to take a break in the building of the *Bet Hamikdash* and not complete it! [Thus you have no proof that mixing one joy with another is forbidden.]

[The Gemara asks:] Then he could have left unfinished one cubit of the scarecrow spikes, [that were installed on the roof of the Temple to discourage birds from soiling the roof. These spikes were not an intrinsic part of the *Bet Hamikdash*; therefore delaying the installation of them would not be improper]. [The Gemara answers:] The scarecrow spikes were an intrinsic part of the *Bet Hamikdash*, [so Solomon did not have the option to delay their installation. Thus we have no proof from the *Bet Hamikdash* for the rule that we do not mix one joy with another]. Rather we derive it from a redundant passage. It says, [they celebrated] "fourteen days"; why does it have to say also, "seven days and seven days"? We can infer from this that the first seven days were separate from the second seven days [which teaches us that we do not mix one joy with another].

THEY ATE ON YOM KIPPUR

R. Parnach said in the name of R. Yochanan: That year [when they celebrated the inauguration of the *Bet Hamikdash* for seven days before Sukkot] they did not observe Yom Kippur [because on each of these seven days they rejoiced and feasted, and Yom Kippur is five days before Sukkot]. Afterward they were worried that perhaps the enemies of Israel [a euphemism, meaning

Israel itself] deserved to be destroyed [for violating Yom Kippur]. Thereupon a Heavenly Voice came forth and declared: All of you are going to earn the life of the World to Come [because you feasted for the sake of a mitzvah]. [The Gemara asks:] And from where do we know that they were forgiven? R. Tachlifa taught: It says, "On the eighth day [Solomon] sent the people off, and they blessed the king and went to their homes, joyous and glad-hearted over all the goodness that God had shown to His servant David and to His people Israel" (1 Kings 8:66).

[And we expound:] "To their homes" means that they went home and found their wives in a state of purity; "joyous" means that they had enjoyed the radiance of the *Shechinah*; "glad-hearted" means that each wife became pregnant and gave birth to a male child; "over all the goodness" means that a Heavenly Voice had come forth and declared: All of you are going to earn the life of the World to Come; "that God had shown to His servant David and His people Israel": We can understand that "all the goodness shown to His people Israel" means that God had forgiven them for eating on Yom Kippur, but what does "all the goodness shown to His servant David" refer to? Rav Yehudah said in the name of Rav: At the moment that Solomon wanted to bring the Ark into the *Bet Hamikdash*, the gates stuck together. Solomon offered twenty-four prayers but he was not answered. Then he said, "Raise up your heads, O gates, you everlasting entrances, so that the King of Glory may enter. Who is this King of Glory? God, the mighty and strong, God, the strong in battle" (Psalms 24:7ff), but again he was not answered. But as soon as he said, "God, Lord, do not turn back the request of Your anointed one; remember the righteousness of Your servant David" (2 Chronicles 6:41,42), he was answered immediately, [and the gates opened]. At that point the faces of David's enemies turned colors [in shame] like the bottom of a pot, because it became apparent to all that God had forgiven David for that certain sin.[3]

RECONCILING CONTRADICTORY PASSAGES

R. Yonatan b. Asmai and R. Yehudah b. Gerim were studying the chapter concerning vows[4] at the yeshivah of R. Shimon b. Yochai. They said goodbye to him in the evening, but returned in the morning and said goodbye again. He said to them, "Didn't you say goodbye last night?" They replied, "You taught us that a student who takes leave from his master and remains overnight in the city must take leave from him once again, for it says, "On the eighth day [the twenty-second of Tishri] he sent the people off, and they blessed the king" (1 Kings 8:66), and then it says, "On the twenty-third day of the seventh month [Tishri] he sent the people off" (2 Chronicles 7:10). [Did he send them off on the 22nd or the 23rd?] We learn from here that a student who takes leave of his master and stays overnight must take leave of him again the next day. R. Shimon b. Yochai said to his son: These [R. Yonatan b. Asmai and R. Yehudah b. Geirim] are outstanding scholars; go to them that they may bless you. He went and found them as they were discussing two contradictory passages. It says, "Weigh the course of your feet, and all your ways will be established" (Proverbs 4:26).

[If two *mitzvot* present themselves to you at the same time, choose to do the more important one (Rashi).] And it says, "Lest you weigh the path of life" (ibid. 5:6), [do the mitzvah without regard to its importance]. [The Gemara answers:] It is not difficult to explain. The verse that tells you to choose the more important mitzvah applies in a case where someone else will do the other mitzvah. (9b) The verse that tells you not to pick and choose, applies in a case where you do not know if there is someone else who can do it, [then you should do the mitzvah when it presents itself without waiting for a more important mitzvah to come your way].

[As R. Shimon b. Yochai's son was standing there] he heard them discuss a contradiction in two other verses: It says, "It [the Torah] is more precious than pearls, and all your desires cannot compare to it" (Proverbs 3:15), implying that your personal interests cannot be compared to the Torah, but that *mitzvot* are comparable to the Torah, [which suggests that a person should set aside Torah study to do a mitzvah]. On the other hand it says, "All desires cannot compare to it" (ibid. 8:11), implying that nothing—not even *mitzvot*—can compare to the Torah, [which suggests that a person should not set aside Torah study to do a mitzvah]. [The Gemara answers:] One verse (3:15) refers to a mitzvah that cannot be done by anyone else [then you should aside your Torah studies to do it]; the other verse (8:11) refers to a mitzvah that someone else can do [then you should continue learning].

A BIZARRE BLESSING

[The two scholars then turned to R. Shimon b. Yochai's son and asked him,] "What can we do for you?" He replied, "Father told me that I should go to you and ask you for a blessing." So they said to him as follows, "May it be God's will that you sow and not mow; that you bring in things but not take them out, [which they understood to mean that they should buy merchandise but not be able to sell it]; that you send out things but not bring in [which they understood to mean that they should sell merchandise but not reap any profit]; your house should be destroyed and your temporary dwelling should be inhabited; your table should be turned over, and you should not see a new year."

When he came to his father he told him, "Not only didn't they give me a blessing, they caused me a great deal of grief." His father asked him, "What did they say to you?" "Such and such is what they said." "Those are all blessings," said the father, [and he explained:] "You should sow and not mow" means that you should have children and they should not die. "You should bring in things and not take them out" means that you bring daughters-in-law into your house, and your sons do not die, so that their wives will not leave again. "You should send out things but not bring in" means that you should marry off your daughters, and their husbands should not die so that your daughters will not come back to you. "Your house should be destroyed and your temporary dwelling should be inhabited" means that this world is no more than a temporary dwelling, and the World to Come is a permanent home, as it says, "In their imagination [*kirbam*] their houses are forever" (Psalms 49:12); don't read *kirbam*, but *kivram*, "their graves." [Thus the passage reads,] "Their grave is their house forever."

[So their blessing was: Your house should be destroyed—you should not reach the World to Come so quickly; your temporary home should be settled—you should live a long life in this world.] "Your table should be turned over" means that you should have many children [who create turmoil and commotion at the table]; "You should not see a new year" means that your wife should not die, and you should not have to marry a new wife [and live through the first year of marriage during which you must gladden your wife].[5]

[Maharsha explains that they formulated their blessing in these cryptic terms, in order that his father, the saintly R. Shimon b. Yochai, would have to explain the meaning and thereby personally bestow the blessing on them.]

WAS THIS BLESSING A CLICHÉ?

R. Shimon b. Chalafta was saying goodbye to Rav. Said Rav to his son, "Go to him that he should bless you." R. Shimon blessed him, "May it be God's will that you should not embarrass others and not be embarrassed yourself." When he came to his father, he asked him, "What did he say to you?" The son replied, "He said some commonplace things," [and repeated the blessing]. Rav answered his son, "He gave you the same blessing that God gave the Jewish people two times over!" For it says, "And you will eat, eat and being satisfied, and you will praise the name of God your Lord . . . and My people *will not be ashamed evermore*. Then you will know that I am in the midst of Israel, and that I am the Lord your God, there is none other; and My people *will not be ashamed evermore*" (Joel 2:26,27).

TO TEACH OR NOT
TO TEACH IN PUBLIC

It happened one time that Rabbi decreed that students should not be taught outside in the marketplace. He expounded the passage, "Your rounded thighs are like jewels [i.e., the Torah], the work of a master's hand; [the work of the Master Craftsman]" (Song of Songs 7:2). Just as the thigh is always hidden [by the clothes], so also should the Torah be studied in a discreet way.

R. Chiya [disregarding the decree,] taught his two nephews, Rav and Rabbah son of Bar Chana, out in the marketplace. Rabbi heard about it and was upset. When R. Chiya came to visit him, he said to him "Iyya [referring to him disparagingly as Iyya instead of Chiya], who's calling you outside?" [in other words, "You are wanted outside"]. R. Chiya realized that Rabbi had taken his conduct as a personal affront, and as a result he considered himself in a state of *nezifah* [being shunned] for thirty days. On the thirtieth day [before the end of the day], Rabbi sent for him to come, then sent him a second message not to come. [The Gemara asks:] What did he have in mind when he sent the first message, and what made him change his mind? First he thought that "part of the day counts as the whole day," [and once the thirtieth day has begun the thirty-day period of *nezifah* (being shunned) had been completed]. And later he concluded that this rule did not apply in this case.

In the end, however, R. Chiya did come on the thirtieth day. So Rabbi said to him, "Why did you come?" R. Chiya replied, "Because you sent for me." "But then I sent you a message not to come!" He replied, "The first message I received, the second one I did not." Rabbi then applied to him the verse, "When God favors a man's way, even his foes will make peace with him" (Proverbs 16:7) [which means, it was providential that you received only the first message]. Rabbi then asked him, "Why did you transgress my order [by teaching in a public place]?" R. Chiya replied, "Because it says, 'Wisdom [of the Torah] should be sung out in the street' (ibid.1:20)." Rabbi answered, "If you studied the Torah once, you did not study it a second time; and if you studied it a second time, you did not study it a third time; and if you studied it a third time, your teachers did not explain it to you, because the verse, "Wisdom should be sung out in the street," has to be interpreted in the sense in which Rava expounded it. [Meaning, Rabbi expounded the verse in a way that supports what Rava teaches us; because Rava was born a century after Rabbi's death].[6] For Rava expounded the verse to mean: If a person studies the Torah indoors, the Torah will proclaim him as a scholar outside. [The Gemara asks:] But it also says, "From the beginning I did not speak in secrecy" (Isaiah 48:16) [which suggests that Torah may be taught out in the open]. [The Gemara answers:] This refers to the "Kallah" assemblies [when large audiences gather to listen to lectures twice a year before the Yamim Tovim. But when a teacher speaks to his student it should be done in private]. [The Gemara asks:] But R. Chiya [who holds that you should teach outside], what does he do with the verse, "Your rounded thighs are like jewels" [which

compares the Torah to the thigh, which is always hidden, as Rabbi expounded]? [The Gemara answers:] He interprets the verse as referring to charity and acts of kindness; [these should be done privately, but not the teaching of Torah].

THE MEANING OF CUSHITE [ETHIOPIAN]

R. Zutra b. Tuvyah was arranging scriptural verses before Rav Yehudah. When he came upon the passage, "These are the last words of David [he uttered through divine inspiration]" (2 Samuel 23:1), he said to Rav Yehudah: It says "the last words," so there must have been some beforehand; so which are David's first words [of prophecy]? Rav Yehudah kept quiet, and did not answer. R. Zutra, [thinking that he had not heard the question,] repeated: It says "the last words" so there must have been first words [of prophecy]? Which are those first words? Rav Yehudah replied: What do you think; if someone does not know the explanation of this verse, he is not an eminent scholar? R. Zutra realized that Rav Yehudah was offended [by his repetition], and he considered himself in a state of *nezifah* [being shunned] for one day. [The Gemara asks:] As long as the question was brought up, what indeed were David's first [prophetic] words? [The Gemara answers,] "David spoke to God the words of this song on the day that God delivered him from the hand of all his enemies and from the hand of Saul" (2 Samuel 22:1). The Holy One, blessed be He, said to David: David, you are reciting a song on Saul's downfall? Had you been Saul and he David, I would have given up many a David for his sake; [for he was a more righteous man than you (Rashi)]. That's why it says, *Shiggaion* [an error] of David, which he sang to God, concerning Cush the man from Benjamin [i.e., Saul]" (Psalms 7:1).

[The Gemara asks: Why is Saul referred to as Cush?] Was Cush his name? [The Gemara answers:] Just as a Cushite [an Ethiopian] stands out for his skin color, so did Saul stand out for his good deeds. In a similar vein we explain the verse, "Miriam and Aaron spoke against Moses concerning the Cushite woman he had married" (Numbers 12:1). Was her name Cushit? Wasn't her name Zipporah? But just as a Cushite [Ethiopian] woman stands out for the color of her skin, so did Zipporah stand out for her kind deeds. Another example: It says, "And Eved-Melech the Cushite heard . . . " (Jeremiah 38:7). Was his name Cushi? Wasn't his name Zedekiah? But just as a Cushite [Ethiopian] stands out for the color of his skin, so did Zedekiah stand out for his good deeds. Similarly, it says, "To Me, O children of Israel, you are just like the Cushites [Ethiopians], declared God" (Amos 9:7). Wasn't their name children of Israel? But just as a Cushite [Ethiopian] is different with his skin, so are the children of Israel different in their conduct from all other nations.

A *TZADDIK* CAN ANNUL GOD'S DECREE

R. Shmuel b. Nachmani said in the name of R. Yochanan: What is the meaning of the verse, "These are the last words of David: The words of David son of Jesse, the words of the man who lifted up the world" (2 Samuel 23:1)? It means, [Through his words and actions] David raised up the heights of repentance; [he taught us what *teshuvah* is. He repented of the sin with Bathsheba, and God forgave him, proof that even the worst sinner can repent and will be granted forgiveness by God]. [The Gemara continues to expound:] "The God of Israel has said—the Rock of Israel has spoken to me—[Become a] ruler over men; a righteous one who rules through the fear of God" (ibid. 3). What does this mean? R. Abbahu said: It means this: "The God of Israel has said—the Rock of Israel has spoken to me [David]": I [God] rule over men; who rules over Me? The *tzaddik*, [the righteous one rules over Me], for I make a decree and the *tzaddik* annuls it [through his prayer].

DAVID'S EXEMPLARY CHARACTER TRAITS

[The Gemara continues to expound:] It says, "These are the names of David's warriors: One who sat in the assembly, a sagacious man, head of the captains—he is Adino the Eznite, who stood over eight hundred corpses at one time" (ibid. 8). What does this mean? Said R. Abbahu: It means: These are the various aspects of David's strength: "He sat in the assembly" means, when David was sitting in the house of study [giving a Torah discourse] he did not sit on mattresses and pillows [as befitting a king] but on the ground. As long as his teacher Ira the Jairite[7] was alive, he [Ira] used to sit on mattresses and pillows while teaching the Rabbis. When he passed away, David [took over] and taught the Rabbis while sitting on the ground. So the Rabbis said to him: Please sit on mattresses and pillows; but he refused to do so.

"A sagacious man [*tachkemoni*]"; Rav explained: The Holy One, blessed be He, said to David: Since you have humbled yourself, you shall be like Me [*tihyeh kamoni*, which sounds like *tachkemoni*], so that when I make a decree you will be able to annul it.

"Head of the captains" [literally, "head of the Three"] means: head of the three Patriarchs, [David will walk in front of them in the World to Come (Rashi)].

"He is Adino the Eznite" means, when David was sitting and studying the Torah he would make himself flexible [*adin*] like a worm, but when he went to war he would toughen himself like a piece of wood [*etz*], [hence Eznite].

"Who stood over eight hundred corpses at one time" means, when he threw his spear he slew eight hundred at one time, and yet he sighed [in frustration] over the two hundred [he missed]. For it says, "How could one pursue a thousand?" (Deuteronomy 32:30). A Heavenly Voice came forth and said: [You could have slain one thousand,] "if not for the matter of Uriah the Hittite [Bathsheba's husband]" (1 Kings 15:5).

THE BANNED SCHOLAR

(17a) There was a young Torah scholar about whom objectionable rumors were circulating [alleging immoral conduct on his part (*Tosafot*)]. Rav Yehudah said: What shall we do? Put him under a ban? The Rabbis need him [as a teacher]. Not put him under a ban? It would cause a disgrace to God's Name, [if the Rabbis don't act if one of their colleagues is accused of wrongdoing]. So he said to Rabbah b. bar Chana: Did you hear anything that pertains to this situation? He replied: This is what R. Yochanan says: What is the meaning of the text, "For the lips of the *Kohen* should safeguard knowledge, and people should seek Torah from his mouth; for he is an messenger of God, Master of Legions" (Malachi 2:7). [It teaches us that] if a teacher is like a messenger of God, then seek Torah from his mouth, but if he is not, don't seek Torah from his mouth. [On the basis of this,] Rav Yehudah put the scholar under a ban.

Later on Rav Yehudah became sick. The Rabbis came to visit him, and this scholar came along with them. When Rav Yehudah saw him he smiled. So the scholar said: Not enough that you placed me under a ban, but you are laughing at me too, [adding insult to injury]! Replied Rav Yehudah: I am not laughing at you. But I am happy that I will be able to say when I go to the World to Come, that even toward a great person like you I showed no partiality. Rav Yehudah passed away. This scholar then came to the *bet midrash* and said: Please lift my ban. The Rabbis said to him: There is no one here equal in rank to Rav Yehudah who could lift your ban, but go to R. Yehudah Nesiah (the grandson of Rabbeinu Hakadosh), and he will be able to lift the ban. So he went to him. R. Yehudah Nesiah said to R. Ammi: Please look into this case, and if it is necessary to lift the ban, lift it. R. Ammi studied the case and concluded that the ban should be lifted.

Thereupon R. Shmuel b. Nachmani stood up and said: [How can you take this matter so lightly!] Even when the maidservant of Rabbi's house put someone under a ban, the Sages did not treat it lightly for a full three years; surely a ban imposed by our colleague Rav Yehudah should not be treated lightly. R. Zeira observed: Why did Providence have it that suddenly today this aged Rabbi—R. Shmuel b. Nachmani—should show up at the *bet midrash*, when it has been many years that he has not come? It is a sign that this person's ban should not be lifted. As a result, they did not lift the ban. The scholar left, and as he was walking along and crying, a wasp came and stung him in his male organ, [in retribution for his immoral behavior (*Tosafot*)], and he died.

They took him to the burial cave of the pious, but he was not accepted for burial. [A snake appeared and refused to let them in (Rashi).] They then took him to the burial cave of the judges [a stage below the pious], and there he was accepted. Why was he accepted there? Because he had acted as R. Ilai said. For we learned in a *Baraita*: R. Ilai says: If a person feels that his *yetzer hara* [his carnal impulse] is getting the best of him, he should go away to a place where they don't recognize him, put on black clothes and wrap himself in a black robe, and then do whatever his heart desires, but at least he will not desecrate the name of Heaven openly.

[The Gemara mentioned above that when the maidservant of Rabbi's house placed someone under a ban the Rabbis respected it for three years. The Gemara now asks:] What was the story of the maidservant of Rabbi's house? [The Gemara answers:] The maidservant of Rabbi's house saw a certain person hitting his grown-up son. She said: That person should be banned because he is guilty of the transgression of, "Do not place a stumbling block before the [morally] blind" (Leviticus 19:14), [this means setting up another person to commit a sin]. For it is taught: "Do not place a stumbling block before the blind"—this verse refers to one who beats a grown-up son [which will cause him to become enraged and curse or strike back at his father].

THEY PRONOUNCED A BAN

Resh Lakish was once guarding an orchard, when a fellow came by and began eating some figs. Resh Lakish screamed at him, but the man paid no attention to him, so Resh Lakish called out, "Let this person be put under a ban." The man replied, "On the contrary, let that person [Resh Lakish] be put under a ban." [He argued that Resh Lakish had no right to put him under a ban claiming,] "If I owe you money [because I stole your figs], does that mean that I deserve to be placed under a ban?" [And the law is, if a person places someone under a ban who does not deserve it, then that person himself must be banned.] Thereupon Resh Lakish came to the *bet midrash* [and reported the incident]. They told him, "The ban he pronounced is valid; your ban is not valid." [Resh Lakish asked,] "How can it be rectified?" [They replied,] "Go and find the person who pronounced the ban and ask him to withdraw it." [Said Resh Lakish,] "I don't know who he is!" They said [to Resh Lakish], "Go to the *Nasi* [the Exilarch] and ask him to lift your ban." For we learned in a *Baraita*: If someone is placed under a ban and does not know who banned him, let him go to the *Nasi*, and let him lift his ban.

MATCHES ARE MADE IN HEAVEN

(18b) Rav Yehudah said in the name of Shmuel: Every day a Heavenly Voice comes forth and proclaims: The daughter of So-and-so is destined to be the wife of So-and-so. Rav Yehudah further said in the name of Rav: Forty days before the embryo is formed a Heavenly Voice comes forth and proclaims: The daughter of So-and-so is designated to be the wife of So-and-so; such and such field is destined to become the possession of So-and-so. [So we see that it is predestined from Heaven whom a person will marry; why then is Shmuel concerned that someone else will marry her first? How can anyone change a Heavenly decree? The Gemara answers:] Shmuel is concerned that someone else will change the Divine decree through prayer. This is illustrated by what happened to Rava: Rava overheard a person pray, "May this girl be destined for me." Rava said to him, "Don't pray like this; if it is decreed that you should marry her, you will not lose her anyway, and if not, you will end up denying God, [for if she will marry someone else, you will say that God does not have the power to answer your prayer]. Later he overheard him praying that [if I cannot marry this woman,] either I should die before her, [and I should not live to see her married to someone else,] or she should die before me. Rava said to him: "Didn't I tell you not to pray this way?" [And that is why Shmuel ruled that it is permitted to marry a woman on Chol Hamo'ed; because he was concerned that if he delays, a rival suitor may marry her before he does.]

Rav said in the name of R. Reuven b. Itztrobeli: We can prove from verses in the Torah, the Prophets, and the Writings that it is decreed by God who should become your wife. From the Torah, [When Eliezer came to get Rebeccah for Isaac,] "Then Laban and Bethuel answered and said, 'The matter stemmed from God'" (Genesis 24:50). From the Prophets, [When Samson wanted to marry a Philistine woman,] "His father and mother did not know that it was from God" (Judges 15:4). And from the Writings, "A house and wealth are an inheritance from fathers, but an intelligent woman comes from God" (Proverbs 19:14).

Rav in the name of R. Reuven b. Itztrobeli also taught: A person is not suspected of doing something unless he actually did it; and if he did not do all of it, then he did part of it; and if he did not intend to do it, then he had seen others do it and enjoyed [watching them].

R. HUNA'S PASSING

(25a) When [the great *amora*] R. Huna passed away, [his disciples] thought [it would be proper] to place a Torah scroll on his bier. R. Chisda, however, said to them: Should we do for him now [after his passing] something he did not approve of during his lifetime? For R. Tachlifa said: I myself once saw that R. Huna wanted to sit down on his couch, but there was a Torah scroll lying there, so he put an overturned vessel on the floor and placed the scroll on it. Obviously, he held that it was forbidden to sit on a couch on which a Torah scroll was lying. [Therefore the Torah scroll should not be placed on his bier.]

[When they tried to move the bier] it did not fit through the doorway. So they thought of lowering it from the roof. Said R. Chisda: This is what I learned from him: The proper respect of a Torah scholar demands that his bier should be taken out of the house through a door. They then wanted to transfer R. Huna to a smaller bier [which could pass through the door], but R. Chisda told them: This is what I learned from him: The proper respect of a Torah scholar demands that he should remain on the first bier.

For R. Yehudah said in the name of Rav: From where do we derive that a Torah scholar should be removed on his first bier? For it says, [After the Ark was captured by the Philistines it was subsequently returned by them. On its final journey to the City of David, "They placed the Ark of God upon a new wagon and carried it from the house of Abinadab which was in Gibeah" (1 Samuel 6:3); [this was the wagon the Philistines had used originally to return the Ark (Rashi). Proof that a Torah scholar should be removed on his first bier]. They finally broke the door and carried him out.

R. Abba, the first to eulogize R. Huna, said: Our Rabbi was worthy that the *Shechinah* should rest on him, but the fact that he lived in Babylon [and not in Eretz Yisrael,] precluded it, for the *Shechinah* does not manifest itself outside Eretz Yisrael]. [Upon hearing this statement,] R. Nachman, son of R. Chisda—some say it was R. Chanan, son of R. Chisda—broke in and said: It says, "The word of God came to Ezekiel son of Buzi, the Kohen, in the land of the Chaldeans" (Ezekiel 1:3), [which seems to indicate that the *Shechinah* appears even outside Eretz Yisrael]. His father [R. Chisda] tapped him on the foot, [trying to silence him], whispering to him, "Haven't I told you not to bother everyone [with this question]? [R. Abba is right. The *Shechinah* does not manifest itself outside Eretz Yisrael.] Ezekiel received the spirit of prophecy in Babylon because he had already been a prophet in Eretz Yisrael."

R. HUNA'S BURIAL
When they brought the remains of R. Huna to Eretz Yisrael [for burial], people told R. Ammi and R. Assi: R. Huna is coming. [They took this to mean that R. Huna was alive and was coming to settle in Eretz Yisrael.] They said: When we were [studying] in Babylon we were not able to raise our heads because of him, [his greatness was so overwhelming], and now that we have come here he is following us. The people then told them that it was his coffin that had arrived. R. Ammi and R. Assi went to pay their respects, but R. Ila and R. Chanina did not go out. Some say, R. Ila went out, but R. Chanina did not.

The Sages of Eretz Yisrael deliberated: Where should [a great sage like R. Huna] be laid to rest? They decided [that he should be interred] alongside R. Chiya [in Tveriah (Tiberias)], for both R. Huna and R. Chiya spread Torah in Israel. Now the question arose:] Who will bring the coffin into the cave of R. Chiya? [Overawed by the saintliness of R. Chiya, no one dared enter the cave.] R. Chaga said: I will carry him there, for I allowed myself to be tested by R. Huna when I was only eighteen years old; I never experienced a seminal discharge, and he made me his attendant; and therefore I am familiar with his saintly way of life. [Let me give you an example:] One day the strap of his *tefillin* accidentally turned over, [so that the white side was seen on the outside], and because of that he fasted forty fasts. R. Chaga then brought him into the burial cave. Yehudah [the son of R. Chiya] was reposing on the right of his father, and his twin brother Chizkiah on the left of his father. Said Yehudah to Chizkiah: Stand up from your resting place; it is not good manners that R. Huna should be left standing [while we are lying]. As Chizkiah rose, a column of fire rose up with him. Seeing this, R. Chaga was overcome with fright, set up the coffin [to shield himself from the fire], and left. The reason why R. Chaga was not harmed [by the fire] was because he raised the coffin of R. Huna [which protected him].

IMPASSE AT THE BRIDGE
When Rabbah the son of R. Huna and R. Hamenuna passed away [in Babylon], they brought the remains of both of them to Eretz Yisrael [for burial]. (25b) When they came to a narrow bridge, [and both coffins could not pass side by side], both camels that were carrying the coffins remained standing. An Arab who happened to see this asked in surprise, "What's going on? What is the meaning of this?" They replied that the deceased Rabbis were according honor to each other: as if one was saying to the other, "You go ahead," and the other replying, "No, you go ahead first." Said the Arab, "If you ask me, I'd say that the one who is himself a great man and the son of a great man should go first." No sooner did the Arab say this, than the camel bearing Rabbah b. R. Huna's remains passed over the bridge. [Rabbah was the son of the illustrious R. Huna, whereas R. Hamenuna was not of such distinguished ancestry.] Thereupon the Arab's molars and front teeth fell out. [Although the Arab had made a sensible suggestion, he was punished for having the impudence to voice his opinion in the presence of the numerous great rabbis who escorted the deceased (*Iyun Yaakov*).]

EULOGIES
[At the funeral] a certain young disciple delivered a eulogy, beginning as follows:

A tree of ancient roots came here from Babylon,[8]
Along with him came R. Hamenuna, a giant
in Torah.

Our tragedy is twofold with the loss of these two great *tzaddikim*;

Upon seeing the ruins coming from Shine'ar [Babylon].

God was angry at His world, and therefore he seized these two great souls in retribution. He is awaiting their arrival with happiness. The One Who is riding in the high heavens rejoices with delight, welcoming the souls of the pure and righteous *tzaddikim*.

When Ravina passed away, a certain funeral orator paid tribute to him, beginning as follows:

O palm trees, sway your heads in sorrow, and grieve

Over a *tzaddik* who is likened to a palm tree.[9]

Mourn and lament night and day,

Over one who spent nights like days learning Torah without respite. [Ravina together with R. Ashi edited and compiled the entire Babylonian Talmud.]

R. Ashi asked Bar Kipok [a famous orator], "What eulogy would you deliver at my funeral?" He replied, "I would say,

If among the cedar trees fire rages, how can the lowly hyssop on the wall survive?

If Leviathan[10] is caught in the fisherman's net, what hope is there for the fishes in the pond?

If in a rushing stream fish are hooked, what awaits the fish in the marsh?

Bar Avin [another noted eulogist] remarked, "God forbid that I should associate the righteous with harsh terms like 'fire' and 'hooks.'" "Then what would you say?" "I would say":

Let us weep for the [loss of] the mourners suffered,

but not for what is lost:

He will find his resting place,

It is we who are left with the anguish and the grief.

R. Ashi was disappointed [with the allegories they used, one referring to him in terms of "fire" and "hooks," the other comparing him to a lost soul, implying that his lifelong work would be lost (Rashi)].[11] As a result they became crippled, so that on the day [when R. Ashi died] they were not able to come to deliver a eulogy for him. And that is what R. Ashi had in mind when he said: Neither Bar Kipok nor Bar Avin can give *chalitzah* [12] [because they are crippled].

When Rava once came to River Diglat (Chidekel), [which posed a grave danger when it overflowed its banks,] he said to Bar Avin: Stand up and say a prayer. He rose and began:

When the third river [the Chidekel][13] overflowed,

God, remember the covenant You made and have mercy.

Although we may have strayed like a wife that strays from her husband,

Do not forsake us by testing us with the bitter waters [that a suspected adulteress is made to drink].[14]

R. Chanin, the son-in-law of the *Nasi*'s family, was childless. He prayed, and his prayer was answered. However, the day his son was born R. Chanin himself passed away. [At the funeral] the speaker began his eulogy by saying:

From the height of joy we were plunged into deep sorrow,

Happiness now joined affliction.

At the time of his elation, the father sighed his last breath. At the sweet child's birth he lost his cherished father.

They named the child Chanan after his father.

When R. Yochanan passed away, R. Yitzchak b. Elazar opened his eulogy by saying: This day is as unbearable for Israel as the day when the sun set at noon. For it says, "And it shall be on that day . . . that I will make the sun set at noon" (Amos 8:9). Said Yochanan: This refers to the day of King Josiah's death [who was killed at thirty-nine years of age, in the battle at Megiddo].[15] When R. Yochanan died, R. Ammi [who was a disciple of R. Yochanan] observed seven days of mourning, and the *sheloshim* [thirty days]. R. Abba the son of R. Chiya b. Abba said: What R. Ammi did [was not required by *halachah*]. He did it on his own initiative. For R. Chiya b. Abba said in the name of R. Yochanan: Even for his rabbi who taught him Torah one sits in mourning only one day.

When R. Zeira passed away, the speaker opened his eulogy as follows:

The land of Shin'ar [Babylon] was his birthplace,

But in Eretz Yisrael his glory reached its peak.

"Woe is me!" does Tveriah [Tiberias] lament,

For she has lost her most precious treasure.

When R. Abahu died, the pillars of Kisri [Caesarea] were shedding tears; when R. Yose died, the gutters on the rooftops of Tzipori [Sepphoris] ran with blood; when R. Yaakov died, the stars were visible in the daytime; when R. Assi died, all trees were uprooted; when R. Chiya b. Abba died, fiery stones came down from the sky; when R. Menachem b. Simai died, all graven images were erased and their surfaces became completely smooth; when R. Tanchum son of R. Chiya died, all human statues were dislodged from their bases; when R. Eliashiv died, seventy homes were broken into by thieves in the city of Nahardea. When R. Hamenuna died, hailstones came down from the sky; when Rabbah and R. Yosef died, the bridges of the Euphrates River collapsed, and the rocks that supported the bridges were thrown together; when Abaye and Rava died, the bridges of the River Chidekel collapsed and the rocks were thrown together; when R. Mesharshia died, the palm trees sprouted thorns. [According to the Me'iri, all these outlandish phenomena are metaphors the orators used to describe the great loss that was felt at the death of these *tzaddikim*.]

TEARING *KERIAH*

[At the loss of a relative a rent [*keriah*] must be made in one's garment.] We learned in a *Baraita*: (26a) The following *keriot* may not be mended: a *keriah* for his father or mother, or for his rabbi who taught him Torah, for a *Nasi*, an *Av bet din*, or upon hearing tragic news, or on hearing God's name being cursed, or upon seeing a Torah scroll being burned, or upon seeing the ruins of the cities of Judea, of the *Bet Hamikdash* or of Jerusalem. You should rend first for the *Bet Hamikdash* and then extend the *keriah* for Jerusalem.

[The Gemara asks:] From where do we derive that a person should tear *keriah* over the death of his father, mother, and rabbi who taught him Torah?—For it says, [when Elijah ascended to heaven alive in a whirlwind,] "Elisha was watching and shouting, 'Father! Father! Israel's chariot and horsemen'" (2 Kings 2:12). [The Gemara expounds:] "My Father! My Father" [teaches us to tear *keriah* on the loss of] father and mother; "Israel's chariot and horsemen" [teaches us to tear *keriah* on the loss of] the rabbi who taught him Torah. [The Gemara asks:] How is this implied in this passage? [The Gemara answers:] As R. Yosef explained it, quoting Targum Onkelos's translation of the phrase, "My Father! My Father! Israel's chariot and horsemen": My Rabbi! My Rabbi! Who was a better protector for the people of Israel with his prayer than chariots and horsemen.

[The Gemara asks:] And from where do we infer that these [tears] may not be mended?—From the conclusion of the above verse, "[Elisha] took hold of his garments and tore them into two pieces" (ibid.). When it says, "he tore his garments," don't I realize that they were torn apart? Why then does the verse say, "into two pieces"? It wants to teach us that these garments must remain torn forever.

Resh Lakish asked R. Yochanan: But Elijah is still alive, [he ascended alive to heaven! Why did Elisha tear *keriah* for him at all]? R. Yohanan replied: Since it says, "And then he saw him no more" (ibid.), in Elisha's eye he was as if dead.

[The Gemara asks:] And from where do we derive that for the death of *Nasi* or a Chief Justice, or upon hearing tragic news [you also have to tear *keriah*]?—From the verse, [When David learned how Saul and Jonathan had been killed by the Philistines,] "David took hold of his clothes and tore them; and so did all the men with him. They lamented and wept, and they fasted until evening, for Saul and his son Jonathan, and for the nation of God, and for the House of Israel, for they had fallen by the sword" (2 Samuel 1:11). [And the Gemara explains:] "Saul" refers to the death of a *Nasi*; "Jonathan" refers to the death of a Chief Justice; "for the nation of God and for the House of Israel" refers

to tragic news, [that for all of these one has to tear *keriah*].

Rav b. Shabba said to R. Kahana: Perhaps they tore *keriah* only because all these tragic things [the death of Saul and Jonathan] happened at the same time? R. Kahana replied: By repeating "for this" and "for this" and "for that" Scripture indicates that each tragedy warrants *keriah* by itself.

[The Gemara asks:] From where do we know that *keriah* should be torn on hearing God's name blasphemed? [The Gemara answers:] From the verse, "Eliakim son of Hilkiah, who was in charge of the palace, as well as Shebna the scribe and Joah son of Asaph the recorder, came to Hezekiah with rent garments, and told him the words of Rabshakeh" (2 Kings 18:37). [They were distressed at hearing the blasphemous challenge uttered by Rabshakeh, the general of Sennacherib's Assyrian army.]

And from where do we derive that *keriah* should be torn for a Torah scroll [being burned]?—From the verse, "It happened that whenever Jehudi would read three or four columns, [of the Book of Lamentations in which Jeremiah prophesies the destruction of the *Bet Hamikdash*, King Jehoiakim] would cut it out with a scribe's razor and throw it into the fire that was in the fireplace" (Jeremiah 36:23). [The Gemara asks:] What is meant by "three or four columns"? [The Gemara spells out:] When they told King Jehoiakim that Jeremiah had written the Book of Lamentations, he asked: What is written there? They answered, "Alas—she [Jerusalem] sits in solitude" (Lamentations 1:1). The King replied: I am the King; [it does not affect me, only the city]. Then they quoted the second verse, "She [Jerusalem] weeps bitterly in the night" (ibid.2). He replied again: I am the King. They then cited the third verse, "Judah has gone into exile because of suffering." (ibid. 3) [He replied again:] I am the King. [This does not concern me.] They continued with the fourth verse, "The roads of Zion are mourning," but again he replied: I am the King.

But when they quoted the fifth verse, "Her enemies are now her masters," (ibid. 5), he asked: Who said that? They cited the remainder of the verse, "For God has afflicted her for her many transgressions," [implying that it was God Who said it]. He then immediately began to cut out the Divine names mentioned in Lamentations and burned them in the fire. That is the intent of the verse, "The king and all his servants who heard all these words did not fear and did not tear their clothes" (Jeremiah 36:24). [Comments the Gemara:] This implies that they should have torn their clothes [at witnessing the destruction of the scroll].

SHE MOURNED TOO MUCH

(27b) Rav Yehudah said in the name of Rav: Whoever mourns too much over a death will weep over another death. There was a certain woman who lived in the neighborhood of R. Huna who had seven sons. It happened that one of them died, and she did not stop crying over him. R. Huna sent word to her, "Don't act like this." But she did not listen. He then sent a message to her, "If you listen to me, fine; but if you don't, did you prepare shrouds for another son?" The next son died, and eventually they all died, and she kept on crying. R. Huna sent her another message: "[If you don't stop,] you had better prepare shrouds for yourself." And she died.

"Do not weep for a dead man, and do not lament for him" (Jeremiah 22:10). [The Gemara expounds:] "Do not weep for a dead man" means, do not weep excessively. "And do not lament for him" means, not more than the proper measure. What is considered appropriate? Three days for weeping, seven days for lamenting, and thirty days to refrain from cutting the hair and putting on pressed clothes. After that, the Holy One, blessed be He, says: Don't be more compassionate toward the deceased than I.

THE DEATH OF THE RIGHTEOUS ATONES

(28a) R. Ammi said: Why does the Torah place the report of Miriam's death[16] immediately after the [chapter of the] red heifer [whose ashes are used in purifying a person who was contaminated by contact with a corpse]?[17] [What is the connection?] To tell you that just as the red heifer brings about atonement, so does the death of the righteous atone [for his generation].

R. Elazar said: Why does the Torah mention in the same verse the report of Aaron's death and the taking off of the priestly garments?[18] To tell you that just as the priestly garments atone, [for example, the Breastplate of Judgment atoned for miscarriage of justice, and the Robe atoned for the sin of slander (Rashi)], so does the death of the righteous atone [for his generation].

THE SPAN OF OUR LIFE

The Rabbis taught: If a person dies suddenly [without having been sick], he is considered as being yanked away [an unfavorable sign]. If he was sick one day before he died, he is considered as being hauled away, [quickly, but not as precipitously]. R. Chanina b. Gamliel says: This case is termed "death by a plague," as it says, "Son of man, behold, I am taking from you the darling of your eyes [your wife] in a plague" (Ezekiel 24:16). And it says, [Ezekiel said:] "I told this to the people in the morning, and in the evening my wife died" (ibid. 18), [thus she was sick for one day, and her death is termed "a plague"]. If a person was sick for two days and then dies, that death is called "being pushed out" of this world, [not as abrupt as the first two]. [If he dies] after three days of sickness, it is a death of reproof; after four days, it is a sign of being snubbed; but if a person dies after an illness of five days,

it is the ordinary death of all people. Said R. Chanin: What text substantiates this? The verse, "God spoke to Moses, 'Behold, your days are drawing near to die,' [Hein karevu yamecha lamut]" (Deuteronomy 31:14). "Behold" [Hein] means "one" in Greek [ena]; "drawing near" [karevu in the plural] is two; "your days" [yamecha in the plural] are two, which adds up to five [days].

If a person dies at the age of fifty, that is death by karet ["to be cut off," premature death as punishment for certain grave sins[19]]; at the age of fifty-two, that is the age of the prophet Samuel of Ramah; at sixty, that is death by the hand of Heaven. Mar Zutra said: From where can this be derived? [From the verse,] "You will go to the grave in ripe old age" (Job 5:26), since the numeric value of "in ripe old age [bechelach]" amounts to sixty.[20] If a person reaches the age of seventy, that is old age; if he reaches eighty that is considered the age of strength, as it says, "The span of our life is seventy years, or, given the strength, eighty years" (Psalms 90:10).

Rabbah said: From fifty up to sixty years of age, that is death by karet, and the reason that the Baraita above did not mention this is out of respect for the prophet Samuel of Ramah [who died at fifty-two years of age]. When R. Yosef reached the age of sixty he gave a festive meal for the Rabbis. He said: [Today] I have passed the age limit of karet. Abaye said to him: It is quite true that you have escaped the limit of karet in regard to age, but have you yet passed the limit of days of sickness? [A sudden death, death by being "hauled away," "pushed out," or "by plague," as mentioned above]? R. Yosef replied: Be happy with the half you hold in your hand; [at least I escaped the karet of age]. R. Huna died suddenly, so the Rabbis were very worried [that this was a bad sign]. But two sages who came from Hadayev taught: The above Baraita [regarding sudden death being a bad omen] applies only to a person who has not reached the age of eighty, but if he has reached eighty and then dies a sudden death, that is "dying by a kiss."[21]

IT DEPENDS ON MAZZAL

Rava said: The length of your life, how many children you will have, and your livelihood do not depend [entirely] on your merit, but [also] on mazzal [i.e., the constellation under which you were born].[22] To illustrate, take R. Rabbah and R. Chisda. Both were devout and righteous rabbis; proof of that is that either of them could make it rain through their prayers. Nevertheless, R. Chisda lived to the age of ninety-two, whereas Rabbah only lived forty years [length of life]. In R. Chisda's house sixty weddings were held, but in Rabbah's house there were sixty tragedies [children]. In R. Chisda's house there was the finest white bread to feed the dogs, and the dogs did not want it; but at Rabbah's house there was not enough barley bread for the family [sustenance].

Rava also said: The following three things I requested from Heaven; two of them were granted, and one was not: I prayed to be given the wisdom of R. Huna and the wealth of R. Chisda, which were granted me; but the humility of Rabbah son of R. Huna I was not granted.

IS DEATH PAINFUL?

R. Seorim the brother of Rava, while sitting at the bedside of Rava, noticed that he was waning and in the throes of death. Rava said to R. Seorim, "Please tell the Angel of Death not to make me suffer." Answered R. Seorim, "Aren't you a close friend of the Angel of Death? [Why don't you tell him yourself?]" Said Rava, "Since my fate has already been sealed, the Angel of Death does not care about me any more." R. Seorim then said to Rava, "[After your demise,] please come to me in a dream." Rava later appeared to R. Seorim in a dream. R. Seorim asked him, "Tell me, did it hurt [when you passed away]?" Replied Rava, "No more than the prick of a cupping needle" [an instrument used for bloodletting].

Rava, while sitting at R. Nachman's bedside saw him waning and in the throes of death. Said R. Nachman to Rava, "Please tell the Angel of Death not to make me suffer." Replied Rava, "Aren't you a distinguished person? [Why don't you tell him yourself]?" Retorted R. Nachman, "Who is distinguished, who is worthy, who is commendable [before the Angel of Death? Whom does he really care about]?" Said Rava, "[After your demise,] please come to me in a dream." R. Nachman later appeared to Rava in a dream. Rava asked him, "Tell me, did it hurt [when you passed away]?" He replied, "It was as painless as taking a hair from the milk. Yet, if the Holy One, blessed be He, would tell me, 'You have a chance to go back to the world you came from,' I would not want to go back, because the fear [of the Angel of Death] is too great."

ENCOUNTERS WITH THE ANGEL OF DEATH

R. Elazar was eating terumah [the heave offering given to the kohanim] when the Angel of Death appeared to him. Said R. Elazar, "Don't you see that I am eating terumah, and terumah is holy food? [And if I were to die, the terumah would be defiled, something that should not be done]" Thereby the critical moment passed, [and he lived on]. R. Sheshet set eyes on the Angel of Death in the market. Said R. Sheshet to him, "Do you want to grab me here in the market, as if I were an animal? Come to my house, [and take my life there]!" He thereby overcame the Angel of Death. R. Ashi set eyes on the Angel of Death in the market. Said R. Ashi, "Give me thirty more days [of life] to give me a chance to review all my learning, as you say [in

Heaven], "Happy is the man who arrives here with his learning in his hand."[23] On the thirtieth day the Angel of Death appeared again, so R. Ashi said, "What's the rush? Wait at least until the day is over!" The Angel of Death replied, "You are holding back R. Huna b. Natan from succeeding you as Nasi, and we have a rule: No kingdom can infringe on the term of another kingdom even as much as a hair's breadth." [R. Huna b. Natan's time to become Nasi has come, therefore it is time for you to pass on.]

However, the Angel of Death could not overpower R. Chisda, for he kept on studying all the time. The Angel of Death climbed up and sat down on top of the cedar tree next to the bet midrash. The tree split [and made a loud noise], so that R. Chisda stopped learning for a moment. At that, the Angel of Death instantly overpowered him.

The Angel of Death could never come close to R. Chiya. So one day he disguised himself as a poor man. He came and knocked on the door and asked for a slice of bread. They handed him some bread. He then said to R. Chiya, "You are demonstrating that you have pity on the poor. Why don't you take pity on me, [the Angel of Death. Why are you making it so hard for me to take your life?]" The Angel of Death revealed himself to R. Chiya, and showed him his fiery rod [to prove his identity]. At that, R. Chiya surrendered his soul to the Angel of Death.

LAMENTS AND DIRGES

(28b) [The Mishnah says:] Women are allowed to wail and lament [in unison] on Chol Hamo'ed, but they may not [mournfully] clap their hands.

[The Gemara comments:] What did the women say [in their dirge]? Rav said, "Woe to him that departed; woe to the bearers of the casket." Rava said: The women of Shechantziv say, "Woe to him that departed; woe to the bearers of the casket." And they also lamented, "Take the bone pin out of the jaw, and let water be put into the vessel," [meaning, body and soul are now separated; the soul being the vessel going back to the Divine source (Aruch)]. Rava said: [At the death of a poor man] the women of Shechantziv lamented, "Borrow silken shrouds for him who is free of all possessions." Rava also said: The women of Shechantziv used to say, "O mountains, cover yourselves with beautiful garments, for the person who is about to be buried at your feet was a son of distinguished ancestry."

Rava also said: The women of Shechantziv used to say [in their dirge,] "Our brothers, the merchants are searched by the customs inspectors [whether they are trustworthy]." Rava also said: The women of Shechantziv used to say [in their dirge], "He rushed and ran after money all his life, and now he has to borrow the fare for the ferry" [to take him from this world to the World to Come (Maharsha)]. Rava also said: The women of Shechantziv used to say this, "His death was like everyone else's death, but his suffering was the interest he paid." [Some people merely pay back the loan by returning the soul they borrowed, while others have to pay interest on their loan by suffering the pain of lingering illness (R. Chananel).]

THEY COMFORTED R. YISHMAEL

We learned in a *Baraita*: When the sons of R. Yishmael died, four elder Rabbis came to comfort him: R. Tarfon, R. Yose Hagelili, R. Elazar b. Azariah, and R. Akiva. [On the way there] R. Tarfon said to them, "You all know that R. Yishmael is a great sage and well-versed in *Aggadic* exposition. So no one should break in while another is speaking, [and begin a halachic discussion. For then R. Yismael will join in the debate, and a mourner is not allowed to learn Torah (Rashi)]." Said R. Akiva, "And I'll be the last one to speak." R. Yishmael himself opened [the conversation][24] and said, [referring to himself and blaming himself for his misfortune,] "His sins were many, tragedies came one after another, so that he had to trouble the Rabbis time and again [to come and comfort him and eulogize his sons (*Iyun Yaakov*)]!"

R. Tarfon responded and said, [Moses said about the death of the sons of Aaron,] "As far as your brothers are concerned, let the entire family of Israel mourn for the ones whom God burned" (Leviticus 10:6). Now we can draw a logical inference from this: If Nadab and Avihu [Aaron's sons] who performed only one mitzvah [after being installed as *kohanim*], as it says, "The sons of Aaron brought the blood to him" (ibid. 9:9), [and for this single mitzvah all Israel mourned them], the sons of R. Yishmael [who performed numerous *mitzvot* on behalf of the people], surely they should be mourned universally.

R. Yose Hagelili then responded, [It says about Abijah son of Jeroboam,] "'All of Israel will lament for him and bury him' (1 Kings 14:13). Just think about it: If Abijah, the son of Jeroboam who did only one good thing, as it says, 'Because something good has been found in him' (ibid.), was mourned by all of Israel, surely the sons of R. Yishmael should be mourned universally." [The Gemara asks:] What was the one good thing Abijah did? R. Zeira and R. Chanina b. Papa gave different explanations: One said that he left his post [as guard to prevent the people from making festival pilgrimages] and went himself to Jerusalem; the other said that he eliminated the guards his father Jeroboam had stationed on the roads to prevent the people from making festival pilgrimages to Jerusalem.

Next R. Elazar b. Azariah reponded and said, "'You [Zedekiah] will die peacefully, and like the burnings performed for your forefathers, the earlier kings who were before you, so will they burn you'" (Jeremiah 34:5). [Zedekiah was buried with proper honors, including the burning of the king's bedding and private utensils at his funeral—so that no commoner could

ever make use of these utensils (Rashi).] We can draw a logical inference from this: If Zedekiah, King of Judah, who performed only one mitzvah, namely that he pulled Jeremiah out of the slime pit (Jeremiah 38:10), was to be mourned with such honor, surely the sons of R. Yishmael [should be mourned with great honor].

R. Akiva then responded and said, "'On that day the mourning will become intense in Jerusalem, like the mourning of Hadadrimmon [and the mourning] at the Valley of Megiddon'" (Zechariah 12:11). On this R. Yosef commented: If not for the translation of the Targum, I would not know what this passage meant. How does the Targum translate it? "On that day the mourning in Jerusalem will be as great as the lament over Ahab son of Omri whom Hadadrimmon son of Tabrimmon had slain[25] and as the lament over Josiah son of Amon whom Pharaoh Neco had slain in the Valley of Megiddon."[26] Now we can draw a logical inference. If Ahab who did only one good thing, as it says, "The war intensified on that day, and the king [Ahab] was propped up in his chariot in the presence of Aram. He died in the evening" (1 Kings 22:35); [the good deed was that Ahab, although mortally wounded, had himself propped up so that his soldiers would not be demoralized and flee], yet he was deeply mourned, surely the sons of R. Yishmael should be intensely lamented.

Rava said to Rabbah b. Mari: It says about Zedekiah, "You will die peacefully" (Jeremiah 34:5), but then it also says, "He [Nebuchadnezzar] blinded Zedekiah's eyes" (ibid. 39:7), [do you call this dying in peace?]. He replied: This is how R. Yochanan explained it: Nebuchadnezzar died in Zedekiah's lifetime, [giving Zedekiah the satisfaction of witnessing his enemy's death]. Something else Rava asked Rabbah b. Mari: It says, [about King Josiah,] "Therefore, behold, I will gather you in to your forefathers—you will be gathered to your grave in peace" (2 Kings 22:20). But it also says, "The archers shot at King Josiah. The king said to his servants, 'Remove me, for I am gravely wounded'" (2 Chronicles 22:20). And Rav Yehudah said in the name of Rav: They riddled his body like a sieve. [Do you call this dying in peace?] Rabbah b. Mari replied: This is how R. Yochanan explained it: This means that the *Bet Hamikdash* was not destroyed in his lifetime.

R. Chanina said: The departure of the soul from the body (29a) is like a knot in a rope being squeezed through a small hole in the ship's mast. R. Yochanan said: Like a heavy rope being pulled through a round hole.

R. Levi b. Chita said: When taking leave of the dead one should not say to him, "Go to peace," *lech leshalom*, but "Go in peace," *lech beshalom*. But when taking leave of a living friend you should not say, "Go in peace," *lech beshalom*, but "Go to peace," *lech leshalom*. When taking leave of the dead one should not say, "Go to peace," *lech beshalom*, because it says [about Abraham], "You shall join your fathers in peace, [*beshalom*]" (Genesis 15:15). When taking leave of a living friend you should not say, "Go in peace," *lech beshalom*, but "Go to peace," *lech leshalom*, because Jethro said to Moses *lech leshalom*, "Go to peace" (Exodus 4:18), and Moses went and was successful. By contrast, David said to Absalom, *lech beshalom*, "Go in peace" (2 Samuel 15:9), and he was hanged.

And R. Levi said further: Whoever comes out of the synagogue and goes to the *bet hamidrash*, or from the *bet hamidrash* to the synagogue, will be privileged to be admitted to the Presence of the *Shechinah*. For it says, "They advance from strength to strength; each one will appear before God in Zion" (Psalms 84:8). R. Chiya b. Ashi said: Torah Sages have no rest even in the World to Come, as it says, "They advance from strength to strength, each one will appear before God in Zion."

NOTES

1. Deuteronomy 25:5ff.
2. From north to south.
3. Concerning Bathsheba.
4. Numbers 30:1–17.
5. Deuteronomy 24:5.
6. Rabbi died about 200 C.E., and Rava lived 299–352 C.E.
7. 2 Samuel 20:26.
8. Rabbah b. R. Huna's father was the Exilarch of Babylonian Jewry; his family traced its ancestry to King Jehoiachim of Judah.
9. Psalms 92:13.
10. A huge fish; Isaiah 27:1, Psalms 74:14, Job 40:25.
11. Rashba suggests that R. Ashi was disappointed at the insensitivity of the two orators. They should have responded, "God forbid! Who thinks about such things!" Instead, they blurted out their eulogy as if they had prepared it in advance.
12. The ceremony whereby the widow of a husband who has died childless takes off the shoe of the brother of her late husband. She thereby gains the right to remarry. (See Deuteronomy 25:5–9.)
13. Genesis 2:14.
14. Numbers 5:11–31.
15. 2 Chronicles 25:23–25.
16. Numbers 20:1.
17. Numbers 19:1–22.
18. Numbers 20:26.
19. Sins such as eating *chametz* on Pesach, eating or working on Yom Kippur, transgressing the law of circumcision, and incestuous or immoral relations are punishable by *karet*.
20. Bet = 2; chaf = 20; lamed = 30; chet = 8.
21. R. Huna died when he was more than eighty years old, in 297 C.E.
22. The Me'iri sharply rejects the belief that *mazzal* plays a role in the fate of man. He says, "A person should never refrain from praying for God's mercy. Prayer and righteousness overpower any planetary configuration. Don't pay attention to this Gemara; it is the opinion of a single individual, and in no way does it represent the traditional Jewish view."
23. The Maharsha in *Bava Batra* 10a explains that the expression "his learning is in his hands" refers to the learning that he had committed to writing.
24. Comforters are not allowed to say anything before the mourner begins to speak.
25. 1 Kings 22:34ff.
26. 1 Kings 23:29.

❧ CHAGIGAH ❧

TWO LEARNED DUMB MEN

(3a) There were two dumb [but not deaf] men in the neighborhood of Rabbi, sons of the daughter of R. Yochanan b. Gudgada, and according to others, sons of the sister of R. Yochanan. Whenever Rabbi came into the *bet midrash* they sat down in front of him, shook their heads, and moved their lips. Rabbi prayed for them, and when they were cured, people suddenly realized they had mastered *Halachah, Sifra,*[1] *Sifrei,*[2] and the entire Talmud.

ABRAHAM, THE FIRST CONVERT

Rava expounded: What is the meaning of the verse, "How lovely are your footsteps when shod in sandals, O daughter of nobles" (Song of Songs 7:2)? It means: How lovely are the feet of Israel when they go up on the festival pilgrimage. "O daughter of nobles" means: daughter of Abraham our Father, who is called a noble, for it says, "The nobles of all the peoples gathered, [to join] the people of the God of Abraham" (Psalms 47:10). ["The nobles" refers to gentiles who converted. Like Abraham they left their family and heritage to follow God (Rashi).] It says, "[to join] the people of the God of Abraham" and not the God of Isaac and Jacob, because Abraham was the first convert.

R. Kahana said: R. Natan b. Minyomi expounded in the name of R. Tanchum: What is the meaning of the verse, [When the brothers threw Joseph into the well,] "the well was empty; there was no water in it" (Genesis 37:24). Since it says that the well was empty, don't we know that there was no water in it? So what is meant by "there was no water in it"? The verse wants to tell us that, true, there was no water in it, but it was infested with snakes and scorpions.

R. ELAZAR B. AZARIAH'S LECTURE

Our Rabbis taught: It happened once that R. Yochanan b. Beroka and R. Elazar Chisma went to pay [a Yom Tov] visit to R. Yehoshua in the city of Peki'in. Said R. Yehoshua to them, "What new Torah thought did you hear in the *bet midrash* today?" They replied: "We are your students, and we are drinking from your waters," [implying that a student has no right to expound before his master (Rashi)]. R. Yehoshua answered: "Even so, it is impossible that there should be a session in the *bet midrash* without a novel Torah thought being developed. Tell me, whose turn was it this *Shabbat* [to give the discourse]?" [There was an arrangement whereby R. Gamliel lectured on two Shabbatot, and R. Elazar b. Azariah lectured every third *Shabbat*.][3]

[The students replied:] "It was the *Shabbat* of R. Elazar b. Azariah." "And what was the theme of his discourse?" They answered, "He lectured on the chapter of *Hakheil* [the public reading of the Torah at the end of the Sabbatical year," (Deuteronomy 31:12)]. "And how did he expound it?" [They replied, "He expounded the verse,] 'You must gather together the people, the men, women, children,'(ibid.) as follows: It is understandable that the men must come in order to learn, the women, in order to hear, but what is the purpose of bringing the little ones?—In order that those who bring them should be rewarded." Said R. Yehoshua, "You had such a precious pearl in your hand, and you wanted to withhold it from me!"

R. Elazar further expounded: It says, "You have singled out God today . . . and God on His part has singled you out today" (Deuteronomy 26:17,18).—The Holy One, blessed be He, said to Israel: You have made Me a unique object of praise, and I shall make you a unique object of My praise in the world. Israel has made God a unique object of praise, for it says, "Hear O Israel, the Lord our God, the Lord is the One and Only" (Deuteronomy 6:4). And God has made Israel a unique object of praise in the world, for it says, (3b) "And who is like Your people Israel, a unique nation on earth" (1 Chronicles 17:21).

R. Elazar b. Azariah[4] also expounded the passage, "The words of the wise [i.e., the Torah] are like goads, and [like] nails well planted are the saying of the people of assemblies [i.e., Torah scholars], coming from one Shepherd" (Ecclesiastes 12:11).—Why are the words of the Torah compared to a goad? To teach you that just as a goad guides the cow [that pulls the plow] and makes it follow the furrow in order to produce life-giving [grain] for the world, so do the words of the Torah steer those who study them, away from the ways of death, and direct them to the ways of life.

Now you might think, that just as the goad is movable so are the words of the Torah movable [and changeable], therefore it says, "like nails" [they are unalterable and lasting]. But in case you think that, just as a nail diminishes [when it is knocked into the wall it makes a hole] and does not increase, so do the words of the Torah diminish [your income when you spend your time studying] and do not increase; therefore the passage says, "well planted"—just as a plant flourishes and increases, so do the words of Torah flourish and increase, [and by learning Torah you gain abundant blessings].

[The passage mentioned,] "the people of assemblies": This refers to Torah scholars who sit in groups and are studying the Torah; some of them declaring clean, and others declaring unclean; some prohibiting, and others permitting; some pronouncing a person fit [to act as a *kohen* or as a witness], others pronouncing him unfit. Someone might say: [Since there are so many conflicting views,] what is the point of learning Torah? Therefore it says, "all coming from one Shepherd." One God gave them, one leader [Moses] uttered them from the mouth of the Lord of all creation, blessed be He; for it says, "God spoke *all* these words" (Exodus 20:1); [meaning all the various rabbinical interpretations emanate from God]. Therefore, you [the student] should open your ears like a funnel [to take in the Torah teachings] and acquire an open mind to understand why some Rabbis declare clean and others declare unclean; why some Rabbis prohibit and others permit; why some Rabbis pronounce a person fit, while others pronounce him unfit.

[On hearing this exposition, R. Yehoshua] exclaimed to his students, "Happy is the generation in which R. Elazar lives. That generation is not an orphan generation!"

R. YOSE'S MISSTEP

[The Gemara asks:] Why didn't [R. Yochanan b. Beroka and R. Elazar Chisma] tell R. Yehoshua right away the new explanation they heard in the *bet midrash*? [Why did they hem and haw, saying, "We are your students, etc."?][5] [The Gemara answers:] It was because of a certain incident. For we learned in a *Baraita*: It once happened that R. Yose b. Durmaskit went to pay a [Yom Tov] visit to R. Elazar in Lud. Said R. Elazar to R. Yose, "What new Torah thought did you hear in the *bet midrash* today?" He replied [promptly], "There was a vote taken, and it was decided that [Jews living east of the Jordan River in the territories of] Ammon and Moab [that were originally captured by Sichon and Og and subsequently conquered by the

children of Israel (Rashi)], should give the tithe of the poor in *Shemittah*, the Sabbatical year, because these territories did not have the status of Eretz Yisrael, and thus did not have to observe *Shemittah*]."

R. Elazar [angrily] said to R. Yose, "Yose, stretch out your hands, and go blind." [He was upset because R. Yose attributed the passing of this law to a vote taken at this seesion, while in fact, it had been enacted long ago by the Men of the Great Assembly (Rashi)]. R. Yose stretched out his hands and lost his sight. R. Elazar wept and said, "The secret of God is [revealed] to those who fear him, and His covenant to inform them" (Psalms 25:14), [implying that the Rabbis at the *bet midrash* had ruled correctly]. He said to R. Yose, "Go tell the Rabbis [in the *bet midrash*]: Don't be concerned about [the correctness of] your vote [that Ammon and Moab do not have the status of Eretz Yisrael]. For I have a tradition from R. Yochanan b. Zakkai who heard it from his teacher, and his teacher from his teacher, that it is a *halachah* of Moses from Sinai that [those living in] Ammon and Moab are required to give the tithe of the poor in the Sabbatical Year, [because *Shemittah* does not apply there].

[The Gemara asks:] What is the reason?—Because many cities that were conquered by those who went out from Egypt [in the time of Joshua] were not conquered again by those who returned from the Babylonian exile [under Ezra]. Because the first sanctification of Eretz Yisrael [under Joshua] lasted only temporarily [until the first exile], but not for the future; [but the territory sanctified by the returnees from Babylon was sanctified forever]. Therefore, the returnees from Babylon decided to leave the lands of Ammon and Moab unconsecrated [so that the laws of *Shemittah* should not apply there], in order that the poor people may be sustained [from the tithe of the poor given in the lands of Ammon and Moab] in the Sabbatical year. We learned in a *Baraita*: After R. Elazar calmed down, he prayed, "May it be His will that Yose's sight be restored." And it was restored.

YIREH—YEIRA'EH

(4b) R. Yochanan b. Dahavai said in the name of R. Yehudah: A person who is blind in one eye is exempt from appearing [in the Bet Hamikdash on the three Pilgrimage Festivals],[6] for it says, *yeira'eh* "[all your males] *should be seen* [by the Shechinah in the Bet Hamikdash]" (Deuteronomy 16:17), [which can be read as] *yireh*, "He [who comes to the Bet Hamikdash] *will see* [the Shechinah]"; in other words, just as God comes to see you, so He comes to be seen [by you]. Just as He comes to see with both eyes, so must he be seen with both eyes. [Therefore, a person who is blind in one eye is exempt from going up to the Bet Hamikdash.]

When R. Huna came to the above verse of *yireh*, *yeira'eh*, he cried and said: [Can you imagine!] A slave whose master was anxious to see him, [for God wants the Jewish people to come to the *Bet Hamikdash*], yet [the slave sank so low] that his master should alienate himself from him! For it says, "When you come to appear before Me; Who asked you to trample My courtyards?" (Isaiah 1:12).

VERSES THAT MOVED
THE RABBIS TO TEARS

Whenever R. Huna came to the following verse he used to cry: "You shall sacrifice peace offerings and eat [them] there" (Deuteronomy 27:7). [He would say:] The slave whose master longed to have him eat at His table, [God invited Israel to eat sacrifices], should become alienated from him. For it says, "Why do I need your numerous sacrifices? says God" (Isaiah 1:11).

When R. Elazar came to the following verse he cried: [When Joseph revealed himself to his brothers,] "His brothers could not answer him, so dumbfounded were they on account of him" (Genesis 45:3). If a human being's rebuke rendered them dumbfounded, how much greater will be the effect of the rebuke of the Holy One, blessed be He!

R. Elazar wept also when he came to the following verse, [When the sorceress, at Saul's behest, raised the spirit of Samuel from the dead,] "Samuel complained to Saul, 'Why did you disturb me, to raise me up?'" (1 Samuel 28:15). Now, if Samuel, the righteous, was afraid of the Judgment, surely we should be afraid [of Judgment Day]! [The Gemara asks:] How do we know that Samuel was afraid of Divine judgment? For it says, "The woman said to Saul: I saw a great man ascending from earth" (ibid. 12). "Ascending" [*olim* in the plural] implies two: one was Samuel, but who was the other? Samuel went and brought Moses with him. He said to him: Maybe, God forbid, I am being summoned to Judgment. Please come with me, [as my defense counsel (Rif)], because there is nothing written in the Torah that I did not fulfill, [which proves that Samuel was concerned about his judgment].

When R. Ami came to the following verse, he began to cry: "Let him put his mouth to the dust—there may yet be hope" (Lamentations 3:29). He said: So much [suffering, yet all the verse promises is a] "maybe"! [There still is no guarantee of salvation.]

R. Ami used to cry when he came to the following verse, "Seek God, all you humble of the land who have fulfilled His law; seek righteousness, seek humility. Perhaps you will be concealed on the day of anger" (Zephania 2:3). R. Ami said: So many admirable qualities, and [the prophet promises] only "perhaps"!

When R. Assi came to the following verse, he broke into tears: "Despise evil and love good, and establish justice by the gate, then perhaps the Lord, God of Legions, will grant favor" (Amos 5:15). [R. Assi cried:] After so much righteousness, Scripture promises only "perhaps"!

HER LIFE WAS SHORTENED
BY MISTAKE

When R. Yosef came to the following verse, he wept: "There are some who are swept away [to die] for lack of justice" (Proverbs 13:23). [The Gemara asks:] Is it possible that a person dies before his time has come? [The Gemara answers:] Yes, as is illustrated by the case of R. Bibi b. Abaye, who was often visited by the Angel of Death. The Angel of Death once said to his messenger, "Go and bring me Miriam, the women's hairdresser."[7] He went and brought him Miriam, the children's nurse [taking her life instead of Miriam the hairdresser's]. Said the Angel of Death to his messenger, "Didn't I tell you to bring Miriam the women's hairdresser?" The messenger replied, "In that case, I will take her back, [bring her back to life]." Said the Angel of Death, "No, once you brought her to me, let her be included with the dead." [The story proves that it is possible for a person to die before his time.]

The Angel of Death asked the messenger, "[Since her time to die had not yet come,] how were you able to take her life? He replied, "She was holding a shovel in her hand and was using it (5a) to sweep the oven. She took the shovel and put it on her foot and thereby burned herself. As a result, her luck turned bad, so I was able to take her life." Said R. Bibi b. Abaye to the Angel of Death, "Do you have permission to do such a thing?" He answered, "Doesn't it say, 'There are some who are swept away [to die] for lack of justice'?"

R. Bibi retorted, "But after all, it says, 'A generation goes, and a generation comes'" (Ecclesiastes 1:4), [implying that a generation leaves only when it is complete]. The Angel of Death explained, "I take charge of the souls [of people that died prematurely] until the generation is completed, and only then the souls are handed over to the angel called Dumah who is appointed over the dead. Said R. Bibi to the Angel of Death, "What happens to the years [that were taken from the person who died prematurely]?" He replied, "If there is a Torah scholar who acts with forbearance, I add those years to his life instead."

VERSES THAT MOVED
R. YOCHANAN TO TEARS

When R. Yochanan came to the following verse he was moved to tears: [God said to Satan,] "You incited Me against him, to destroy him, for no reason!" (Job 2:3). [Said R. Yochanan:] What hope can there be for a slave who has a master who is swayed when people incite him.

Also, when R. Yochanan came to the following verse he broke into tears: "Behold, He cannot have faith even in His holy ones" (Job 15:15). [Said R. Yochanan:] If He does not trust His holy ones, whom will He trust? One day while traveling, R. Yochanan saw a man picking figs; he was taking those that were unripe and left those that were ripe. Said R. Yochanan, "Aren't the ripe ones better?" He replied, "I need them for a trip; the [unripe ones] will keep, the others won't." Said R. Yochanan: This is what the verse refers to when it says, "Behold, He cannot have faith even in His holy ones." [God is afraid that the *tzaddikim*, like ripe figs, will lose their virtue; therefore, He removes them from this world at a young age.]

[The Gemara asks:] Is that so? For there was a certain disciple in the neighborhood of R. Alexandri who died at a young age, and [R. Alexandri] said: If this scholar had lived a righteous life, he still would have been alive. How does R. Alexandri know that he died because of his transgressions, [perhaps he was free of sin but] he was one of those about whom it says, "He cannot have faith even in His holy ones," [and he died young because he was prone to sin later in life]? [The Gemara answers: R. Alexandri knew that] this person rebelled against his teachers, [therefore he died because of his sin].

When R. Yochanan came to the following verse, he was moved to tears, "I will draw near to you for the judgment, and I will be a swift witness against the sorcerers; against the adulterers; against those who swear falsely; against those who withhold the wage of the worker" (Malachi 3:5). [He said:] A slave whose master hastens to judge him and rushes to testify against him, does he have a chance to be acquitted?

R. Yochanan b. Zakkai said: Woe is to us, for the verse places side by side minor offenses and grave sins, [placing withholding wages on the same level as adultery].

Resh Lakish said: Whoever subverts the judgment of a convert is considered as if he subverts the judgment of God Himself, for it says [in the above text], "against those who wrong [*umatei*] the stranger" (ibid.); [the word *umatei* can be read as *umati*, "those who wrong *Me*"].

R. Chanina b. Papa said: If a person does something wrong and regrets it, he is forgiven immediately. For it says [in the same verse], "[against those] who do not fear Me" (ibid.). "But if they do fear Me, they are forgiven at once."

When R. Yochanan came to the following verse, he cried, "For God will judge every deed—even everything hidden—whether good or evil" (Ecclesiastes 12:14), [i.e., even errors you committed inadvertently]. Said R. Yochanan: A slave whose master counts his unintentional sins as intentional, what hope is there for him? [The Gemara asks:] What is the meaning of "even everything hidden"? Rav said: This refers to a person who kills a louse in front of his neighbor, which makes him sick to the stomach. [He is punished for his insensitivity.] Shmuel said: This refers to a person who spits in front of his neighbor and nauseates him.

[The Gemara asks:] What is meant by "whether good or evil" (ibid.)? R. Yannai said: This refers to a person who gives alms to a poor man publicly, [he is punished for doing a good deed in callous manner].

This is similar to the case where R. Yannai saw a person give a *zuz*[8] to a poor man publicly. Said R. Yannai to him: It would have been better if you had not given him at all, than to give him and put him to shame. [He, too, did a good deed in an insensitive manner.] In the yeshivah of R. Shila it was taught: This refers to a man who gives alms to a woman secretly, for he raises suspicion about her. [People will think that she received money in exchange for immorality.]

Rava said: It refers to a person who sends to his wife on Friday afternoon meat that has not been cut up, [the veins and the forbidden fat have not been removed. In her rush to prepare for *Shabbat*, she will forget to remove them]. [The Gemara asks:] Is that so? But Rava himself used to send [to his wife meat that had not been cut up]! [The Gemara answers:] The daughter of R. Chisda [Rava's wife] is different, for he knew that she was an expert [and would notice that the veins had not been removed, but generally, women are not experts at this].

When R. Yochanan came to the following verse he wept, "When they [the Jewish people] are then beset by many evils and troubles" (Deuteronomy 31:21). He said: Is there any remedy for a slave whose master brings on him many evils and troubles? [The Gemara asks:] What is the difference between "evils and troubles" [isn't that a redundant phrase]? Rav said: The Torah speaks about evils that clash with each other; for instance, if a person is stung by a wasp and a scorpion, [the remedy for a wasp bite is hot water, and for a scorpion's bite cold water. The reverse is dangerous. Therefore when both happen simultaneously there is no remedy (Rashi quoting *Avodah Zara* 28b)].

Shmuel said: [the phrase "whether good or evil"] refers to a person who gives money to the poor only when the poor man has hit bottom. [Had he given him money earlier, his help would have been far more beneficial, for the poor man could have bought food at a cheaper price.]

Rava said: This is implied by the popular saying: A *zuz* to buy food cannot be found, but in an emergency it can be found.

[The Gemara continues:] It says, "I will then display anger against them and abandon them. I will hide My face from them, and they will be devoured [by their enemies]" (Deuteronomy 31:17). R. Bardela b. Tavyumi said in the name of Rav: A person from whom God does not hide His face [i.e., one who has abundant good fortune] is not one of [the children of Israel]; a person who is not devoured by his enemies (5b) is not one of [the children of Israel. According to the *Me'iri* this statement was said in a sarcastic vein.]

GOD HIDES HIS FACE

The Rabbis said to Rava: It seems to us that God does not hide His face from you, and neither are you "devoured by your enemies." [Your prayers are answered, and the government does not confiscate your possessions.] Replied Rava: Do you have any idea how much money I must send secretly to King Shapur? Nevertheless, since the Rabbis had already directed their suspicions on Rava, messengers came from King Shapur, and they confiscated his property. Said Rava: This is what we learned in a *Baraita*: R. Shimon b. Gamliel said: Wherever the Rabbis cast their eyes, either death or poverty follows.

It says, "On that day I will utterly hide My face" (Deuteronomy 31:18). Rava said: The Holy One, blessed be He, says: Although I hide My face from them, I shall speak to them in a dream. [Rava infers this from the words "on that day," but at night, in a dream, God will appear to them (Rashi).] R. Yosef said: [No matter what,] God's hand is always stretched out over us, as it says, "With the shade of My hand I covered you" (Isaiah 51:16).

THE IMPUDENT HERETIC
R. Yehoshua b. Chananiah was once at the court of the emperor [Hadrian]. A certain heretic [a follower of the Nazarene who was standing there] showed him by gestures: "[You belong to the people] whose God has turned His face from them." R. Yehoshua motioned in reply: "His hand is always stretched out over us." The emperor asked R. Yehoshua, "What did he show you?" Replied R. Yehoshua, "'A people whose God has turned His face from them.' And I showed him, 'His hand is always stretched out over us.'"

The people then asked the heretic, "What did you show him?" "A people whose God has turned His face from them." "And what did he show you?" "I don't know," the heretic stammered. Said the emperor, "A person who does not understand what he is shown by gesture dare make motions in the presence of the emperor!" They led him out and executed him.

When R. Yeshua b. Chanania was lying on his deathbed, the Rabbis said to him: What will happen to us in our disputations with the heretics? [None of us can shut them up as decisively as you can.] He replied: "Counsel has been lost from the children; their wisdom has gone stale" (Jeremiah 49:7). This means that as soon as the counsel has been lost from the children [of Israel], the wisdom of the nations of the world goes stale. [God will never allow the gentiles to gain the edge over the Jewish people.] Or, if you prefer, you may derive it from here, [Esau said to Jacob,] "Let's get going and move on. I will travel alongside you" (Genesis 33:12), [meaning, the gentiles will keep abreast of Israel but they will not gain the upper hand].

Once, while he was going up the stairs of Rabba b. Shila's house, R. Ila heard a child reading the verse, "For behold, He forms mountains and creates the wind; he recounts to a person what his conversations were" (Amos 4:13). He said: A slave whose master controls his conversation, what hope can there be for him? [The

Gemara asks:] What is meant by the phrase "What his conversations were"? Rav said: Even the lighthearted conversation between a man and his wife [before intimacy] will be mentioned to him at the time of his death.

THREE TEARS
It says, "My eyes will drip tears, for the flock of God will have been captured" (Jeremiah 13:17). [In the Hebrew text, "tears" is mentioned three times.] R. Elazar said: What is the significance of these three "tears"? One for the first *Bet Hamikdash*, one for the second *Bet Hamikdash*, and one for the people of Israel who have been exiled from their land. But some say: one tear is for the neglect of Torah study. It is all right according to the view that one tear is for Israel who have become exiled from their land, for it agrees with the passage, "for the flock of God will have been captured." But according to the view that it was for the neglect of Torah study, how do you explain the verse, "for the flock of God will have been captured"? [The Gemara answers:] Since Israel have become exiled from their land, there can be no greater neglect of Torah study than that.

We learned in a *Baraita*: About the following three things the Holy One, blessed be He, weeps every day: about a person who has the ability to occupy himself with the study of Torah and does not; about a person who is unable to occupy himself with the study of Torah and does [and professes to be a rabbi]; and about a leader who intimidates the community.

Rebbi was holding the Book of Lamentations and reading in it. When he came to the verse, "He cast down from heaven to earth the glory of Israel" (Lamentations 2:1), it fell from his hands. Commented Rebbi: It fell from the highest roof to the deepest pit.

VISITING A TORAH SCHOLAR
Rabbi [Yehudah Hanasi (the Prince)] and R. Chiya were once traveling together. When they came to a certain town they asked, "Is there a Torah scholar here? We would like to pay our respects to him." They were told, "There is a Torah scholar here in town, but he happens to be blind." Said R. Chiya to Rebbi, "Stay here. [Since you are the *Nasi*[9]] it is below your dignity to visit him. I will go by myself to visit him." But Rebbi insisted and went with him. When they left [the blind scholar], he said to them, "You have visited a person who is seen but cannot see; may you deserve to visit Him who sees but cannot be seen."

Said Rabbi to R. Chiya, "If I had listened to you [and had not come along with you], I would have missed this blessing." They then asked the blind scholar, "From whom did you hear [that visiting a scholar is such a great mitzvah]?" He replied, "I heard it at the lecture of R. Yaakov. For R. Yaakov of K'far

Chitya used to visit his teacher every day. When R. Yaakov became old, the teacher said to him, 'Please don't exert yourself to come to visit me. You are too old to walk here every day.' R. Yaakov replied, 'Do you think so little of the passage concerning the Rabbis, 'A person will have eternal life, he will not see the pit; when he sees wise men at their death' (Psalms 49:10,11)? Now if a person who sees a wise man on his deathbed deserves to live, surely a person who comes to see a wise man while he is alive deserves to live."

THE "ONE-DAY SCHOLAR"

R. Idi, the father of R. Yaakov b. Idi, used to be on the road [traveling to the yeshivah] for three months, and he would spend one day at his Rabbi's yeshivah.[10] The Rabbis called him the "one-day scholar." He became heartsick about this and applied to himself the verse, "I have become like one who is a laughingstock to his fellow" (Job 12:4). Said R. Yochanan to him, "I beg of you, do not bring down punishment on the Rabbis." R. Yochanan then went to the *bet midrash* and expounded: "They seek Me every day and desire to know My ways" (Isaiah 58:2). Do they seek Him only by day, and not by night? Therefore, the verse comes to tell you that whoever studies the Torah even one day in the year, Scripture considers it as if he studied the whole year. The same holds true regarding punishment. For it says, [Moses said to the returning spies,] "Like the number of days that you spied out the Land, forty days, a day for a year, a day for a year, shall you bear your iniquities—forty years" (Numbers 14:34). Did they then sin for forty years? Didn't they, in fact, sin only forty days? Therefore, it comes to teach you that whoever commits a transgression even one day in the year, Scripture considers it as if he had transgressed all year round.

SIN-OFFERINGS
AND BURNT-OFFERINGS

R. Levi pointed out a contradiction: It says, "Visit your Neighbor's [i.e., God's] house sparingly" (Proverbs 25:17), [meaning, you should not bring too many sacrifices in the *Bet Hamikdash*], and it says, "I enter Your house with burnt-offerings" (Psalms 66:13) [implying that it is a good thing to bring many offerings]. He explained: There is no contradiction, one verse deals with sin-offerings and guilt-offerings, [telling you to avoid transgressions so that you will not have to bring sin and guilt offerings]; the other refers to burnt-offerings and peace-offerings [which are brought on joyous occasions]. Similarly we learned in a *Baraita*: "Visit your Neighbor's house sparingly." This verse speaks of sin-offerings and guilt-offerings. How do you know this? Perhaps it deals with burnt-offerings and peace-offerings? When it says, "I enter Your house with burnt-offerings, I will fulfill to You my vows" it clearly refers to burnt-offerings and peace-offerings. How then shall I explain the verse, "Visit your Neighbor's house sparingly"? We must conclude that this verse speaks of sin-offerings and guilt-offerings.

A CROOKED THING CANNOT BE
MADE STRAIGHT

(9b) We learned in a *Baraita*: It says, "A crooked thing cannot be made straight, and what is not there cannot be counted" (Ecclesiastes 1:15). "A crooked thing cannot be made straight"; this refers to a person who neglected to read the morning *Shema* or the evening *Shema*, or he neglected to say the morning *Shemoneh Esrei* or the evening *Shemoneh Esrei*. "And what is not there cannot be counted"; this refers to a person whose friends wanted to include him in the performance of a mitzvah, and he refused to go.

Bar Hei Hei said to Hillel: What is meant by the verse, "Then you will return and see the difference between the righteous and the wicked, between the one who serves God and the one that does not serve Him" (Malachi 3:18)? [Bar Hei Hei asked:] The "righteous" is the same as "the one that serves God"; the "wicked" is the same as "the one that does not serve Him"? Replied Hillel: The one that serves God and the one that does not serve Him, both are perfectly righteous. [So what is the difference between them?] You cannot compare a person who repeats the chapter he studied one hundred times to one who repeats it a hundred and one times. Said Bar Hei Hei to Hillel: And because he is missing that one time you call him "one that does not serve Him"? Hillel answered: Yes, go and learn it from the mule-drivers' market. If you hire a mule to carry a load for ten parsangs the driver will charge you a *zuz*; for eleven *parsangs* he charges two *zuz*.

Elijah said to Bar Hei Hei, according to others he said it to R. Elazar: What is meant by the verse, "Behold I would refine you, but not like silver; I have chosen for you the crucible of hardship" (Isaiah 48:10)? It teaches that the Holy One, blessed be He, reviewed all the good qualities in order to give them to Israel, and He found no better quality than poverty. Shmuel, and others say R. Yosef, said: The people have a saying for it: Poverty looks good on Israel like a red strap on white horse.

R. Shimon b. Menasya said: To whom does the verse, "A crooked thing cannot be made straight" refer? It refers to a man who has forbidden sexual relations and begets a bastard. For if you would say that it refers to theft and robbery, he can return the stolen article and set things straight. R. Shimon b. Yochai said: Nothing is called crooked except that which was straight at the beginning and has become crooked afterward. And what is this? A Torah scholar who stops studying the Torah.

SUBJECTS THAT MAY
NOT BE EXPOUNDED

(11b) The Mishnah says: The subject of forbidden sexual relations may not be taught in the company of three people [i.e., a teacher addressing two students], nor the subject of Creation [i.e., the mysteries of the universe] in the presence of two, nor the Account of the Divine Chariot[11] in the presence of one unless he is a sage and can understand it by himself. Whoever seriously inquires into four things would be better off if he had not come into this world, namely: What is above [the universe], what is underneath it, what happened before [Creation], and what [will happen] after [Creation]. And whoever has no consideration of the honor of his Maker would be better off if he had not come into the world.

[The Gemara asks:] First you say: "[A person should not study] the Account of the Divine Chariot [by himself]." [Obviously he is a person who is able to understand it.] And then you say, "unless he is a sage and can understand it by himself"! [The Gemara answers:] This is the meaning: forbidden sexual relations may not be expounded [by a teacher] to three [students], nor [may a teacher expound] the subject of Creation to two [students], nor may [a teacher] teach the Account of the Divine Chariot to one [student], unless [the student is one] who understands [and does not have to ask questions].

"A teacher may not expound the subject of Creation to two students." [The Gemara asks:] From where in Scripture is this derived? [The Gemara answers:] The Rabbis taught: It says, "For inquire [she'al] now regarding the early days" (Deuteronomy 4:32); [she'al, "inquire," is in the singular; therefore we infer that] one person may inquire, but not two.

You might think that one person may inquire about what happened before Creation. Therefore it says, "[For inquire . . .] from the day that God created man on the earth" (ibid.), [you may inquire only about what happened after Creation].

You might think that it is also forbidden to inquire about what happened during the six days of Creation, [because man was created on the sixth day of Creation]. Therefore it says, "Regarding the early days that preceded you" (ibid.), [i.e., concerning the first day of Creation and onward you are permitted to inquire].

You might think that a person may also inquire concerning what is above and what is below, what happened before and what will happen after. Therefore it says, "from one end of the heaven until the other end of the heaven" (ibid.), which means: [regarding the things that are found] from one end of the heaven to the other you may inquire, but you may not inquire into what is above, what is below, what went before, and what will be after.

(12a) [The Gemara asks:] But now that we derive from the passage, "from one end of heaven to the other" [that we may not inquire into things that are outside the realm of Creation], why do we need the phrase, "from the day that God created man on the earth" [which tells us the same thing]? [The Gemara answers:] We need this verse to substantiate the statement by R. Elazar who said: The first man's height reached from earth all the way to heaven, for it says, "From the day that God created man on earth and from one end of heaven" (ibid.); but when he sinned, the Holy One, blessed be He, placed His hand on him and made him shorter, as it says, "Back and front You have restricted me, and You have laid Your hand upon me" (Psalms 139:5).

Rav Yehudah said in the name of Rav: The first man stretched from one side of the world to the other side of the world [i.e., when lying down he extended from east to west]. For it says, "from the day when God created man on the earth, and from one end of heaven to the other end of heaven" (Deuteronomy 5:32); but when he sinned, the Holy One, blessed be He, placed His hand on him and made him shorter, as it says, "And You have laid Your hand on me." [Asks the Gemara:] If so, there is an apparent contradiction between the verses! [One verse says that he reached from the earth to heaven; the other verse that he extended from east to west.] [Answers the Gemara:] There is no contradiction. They both have the same dimension. [The distance from east to west is the same as from earth to heaven.]

[The *Nefesh Hachayim* explains that this *Aggadah* should not be taken literally. It means that Adam's intellect was so clear and all-encompassing that he could comprehend the actions and processes of the entire universe.]

THE TEN CREATIONS
OF THE FIRST DAY

Rav Yehudah also said in the name of Rav: Ten things were created on the first day, and they are: heaven and earth, *Tohu* (chaos) and *Bohu* (desolation), light and darkness, wind and water, the twenty-four hours of day and night. Heaven and earth, for it says, "In the beginning God created heaven and earth" (Genesis 1:1). *Tohu* and *Bohu*, for it says, "And the earth was [*tohu*] and [*bohu*]" (ibid. 2). Light and darkness: darkness, for it says, "And darkness was on the surface of the deep" (ibid.); light, for it says, "God said, 'Let there be light'" (ibid. 3); wind and water, for it says, "And the wind of God hovered on the surface of the waters" (ibid. 2); the twenty-four hours of day and night, for it says, "There was evening and there was morning, one day" (ibid. 5).

We learned in a *Baraita*: What does *tohu* mean? *Tohu* is a green ray that circles the entire world, and from it darkness came forth, for it says, "He made darkness His concealment, around Him" (Psalms 18:12). *Bohu* means the damp stones that are sunk in the deep of the earth from which water gushes forth, as it says, "He shall measure it with a line of chaos and with weights of emptiness" (Isaiah 34:11).

THE LIGHT OF THE FIRST DAY

[The Gemara asks:] Was light really created on the first day? Doesn't it say, "God set them [the luminaries] in the firmament of heaven" (Genesis 1:14), and then it says, "There was evening, there was morning, a *fourth* day" (Genesis 1:17)! [The Gemara answers:] This can be explained according to R. Elazar, for R. Elazar said: The light that the Holy One, blessed be He, created on the first day was a kind of light by which a person could see from one side of the world to the other; but when the Holy One, blessed be He, saw the generation of the Flood and the generation of the Dispersion,[12] and saw that they were corrupt, He took the light and hid it from them for it says, "He withheld the light from the wicked" (Job 38:15). And for whom did he save it? For the righteous in time to come, for it says, "And God saw the light that it was *tov* (good)" (Genesis 1:3); and *tov* applies to the righteous, for it says, "Tell each righteous man that [his deeds are] [*tov*,] good" (Isaiah 3:10). When God saw the light that He had set aside for the righteous, He was happy, for it says, "Because of the light of the righteous He will rejoice" (Proverbs 13:9).

The Tanna'im disagree [with regard to the light of the first day]. R. Yaakov holds that the light the Holy One, blessed is He, created on the first day [was so magnificent] that a person could look and see by it from one side of the world to the other. But the Sages say: The luminaries are identical with the light of the first day, but they were not hung up [in the sky] until the fourth day. [The Baal Shem Tov asks: Where did God hide the light of the first day? He hid it in the Torah; and by studying the Torah with the proper intent you can discover the light God has concealed in it.]

THE TEN INSTRUMENTS
OF CREATION

R. Zutra b. Tuvyah said in Rav's name: With ten things the world was created: With wisdom, understanding, knowledge, strength, rebuke, might, righteousness and judgment, kindness and compassion. With wisdom and understanding, [how do we know this?] For it says, "God founded the earth with wisdom; He established the heavens with understanding" (Proverbs 3:19). With knowledge, for it says, "Through His knowledge the depths were cleaved" (ibid. 20). With strength and might, for it says, "Who sets mountains with His strength, Who is girded with might" (Psalms 65:7). With rebuke, for it says, "The pillars of the heavens shuddered and were shocked by His rebuke" (Job 26:11). With righteousness and justice, for it says, "Righteousness and justice are the founda-

tions of Your throne" (Psalms 89:15). With kindness and compassion, for it says, "Remember Your mercies, O God, and Your kindnesses, for they are old as time" (ibid. 25:6).

[The Maharsha explains that these ten things parallel the ten *sefirot* and the ten Divine utterances with which the world was created.]

Rav Yehudah said in the name of Rav: When the Holy One, blessed be He, created the world, it kept spreading like two spools of thread [that keep on rolling], until the Holy One, blessed be He, rebuked it and brought it to a standstill, for it says, "The pillars of the heavens shuddered and were shocked by His rebuke" (Job 26:11). And Resh Lakish, giving a similar interpretation, said: What is meant by, "I am *El Shaddai*, God Almighty" (Genesis 17:1)? [It means], I am He that said to the world *dai*! Enough! [Stay in one place!] Resh Lakish said: "When the Holy One, blessed be He, created the sea, it kept spreading until the Holy One, blessed be He, rebuked it and it became dry. For it says, "He rebukes the sea and dries it up, and makes all the rivers parched" (Nahum 1:4).

WHICH CAME FIRST:
HEAVEN OR EARTH?

The Rabbis taught: Bet Shammai say: Heaven was created first, and afterwards the earth was created, for it says, "In the beginning God created heaven and earth" (Genesis 1:1). Bet Hillel say: Earth was created first and afterward heaven, for it says, "On the day that the Lord God made earth and heaven" (ibid. 2:4). Bet Hillel said to Bet Shammai: According to your opinion, does a person first build the attic and then the house! [Scripture says otherwise,] for it says, "Who builds His chambers in the heavens and founded His vault on the earth [which was already created]" (Amos 9:6). So Bet Shammai said to Bet Hillel: According to your opinion, [that earth was created first], does a person first make a footstool and then a chair? [He does not, because the size of the footstool depends on the height of the chair.] And so it says, "The heaven is My throne and the earth is My footstool" (Isaiah 66:1) [first heaven, then earth].

But the Sages say: Both [heaven and earth] were created at the same time, as it says, "Also, My hand has laid the foundation of the earth, and My right hand has measured out the heavens; I call to them and they stand together" (ibid. 48:13). How do Bet Shammai and Bet Hillel explain the argument of the Sages; how do they explain the term "together"? [They will say] that it means that they work in harmony together [but not that they were created simultaneously]. [The Gemara asks:] But the two verses contradict each other! Resh Lakish answered: At Creation, God first created heaven and then earth, but when He set them up, He first set up the earth and then heaven.

[By the way,] what is the meaning of the word *Shamayim* [heaven]? R. Yose b. Chanina said: It [is a contraction of] *sham mayim*, "there is water in that place." In a *Baraita* it was taught: It is a contraction of *esh* and *mayim*, "fire and water"; this teaches us that the Holy One, blessed be He, brought them together and mixed them, and made the sky out of them.

R. Yishmael asked R. Akiva, when they were traveling on the road, saying: For twenty-two years you were an attendant of Nachum Ish Gamzu, the sage who gave an explanation for the word *et* each time it occurred in the Torah. [Tell me,] what explanation did he give of the *et* in *et hashamayim*, "the heaven," and *et haaretz*, "the earth" (Genesis 1:1)? Replied R. Akiva: If it had said *shamayim va'aretz* [omitting the *et*], you would think *shamayim* and *eretz* were names of the Holy One, blessed be He. Now that it says *et hashamayim* and *et haaretz*, you know that "heaven and earth" really means heaven and earth.

THE PILLARS OF THE WORLD

(12b) We learned in a *Baraita*: R. Yose says: Woe is to the people who see but do not know what they are looking at; who stand but do not know what they are standing on. What does the earth stand on? On pillars, as it says, "Who shakes the earth from its place, and its pillars tremble" (Job 9:6). The pillars stand on the waters, as it says, "To Him who spread out the earth upon the waters" (Psalms 136:6). The waters rest on the mountains, as it says, "Water would stand upon the mountains" (ibid. 104:6). The mountains on the wind, for it says, "For behold! He forms mountains and creates the wind" (Amos 4:13). The wind on the storm, for it says, "Stormy wind fulfilling His word" (Psalms 148:8). The storm is suspended from the arm of the Holy One, blessed be He, as it says, "And under His arms is the world" (Deuteronomy 33:27). But the Sages say: The world rests on twelve pillars, as it says, "He set up the borders of nations to parallel the number [of the twelve tribes] of the children of Israel" (ibid. 32:8). Others say: on seven pillars, for it says, "She carved out its seven pillars" (Proverbs 9:1). R. Elazar b. Shamua says: [The world rests on] one pillar, and *Tzaddik* is his name, for it says, "A *tzaddik* ["righteous one"] is the foundation of the world" (ibid. 10:25).[13]

THE SEVEN HEAVENS

R. Yehudah said: There are two heavens, for it says, "To God belong the heaven and the heaven of heaven" (Deuteronomy 10:14). Resh Lakish said: There are seven heavens: *Vilon, Rakia, Shechakim, Zevul, Ma'on, Machon, Aravot.* Vilon (Curtain) serves no purpose other than that it comes in the morning [into its pouch so that the light becomes visible] and goes out in the evening [so that we can no longer see the light (Rashi)], and it renews every day the work of Creation, as it says,

"Who spreads the heavens like a thin curtain and stretches them like a tent to dwell in" (Isaiah 40:22).

Rakia (Firmament) is where the sun, moon, the stars, and the constellations are placed, as it says, "God placed them in the heavenly sky [*rakia*]" (Genesis 1:17). *Shechakim* (Clouds) is where millstones are grinding manna for the righteous. For it says, "He had already commanded the skies [*shechakim*] above, and opened the doors of heaven, and rained upon them manna to eat, and gave them heavenly grain" (Psalms 78:23,24). *Zevul* (Lofty Dwelling) is where the heavenly Jerusalem[14] and the *Bet Hamikdash* and the altar are built. And [the angel] Michael, the great Prince, stands and offers sacrifices on it, for it says, [Solomon says,] "I have surely built a house of habitation [*zevul*] for You, the foundation for Your dwelling forever" (1 Kings 8:13).

And how do you know that *zevul* is called heaven? Because it says, "Look down from heaven and see, from your abode [*zevul*] of holiness and splendor" (Isaiah 63:15). *Ma'on* (Dwelling) is the place where there are groups of heavenly angels that utter songs of praise at night and are silent by day out of respect for the Jewish people [who sing God's praises by day]. For it says, "In the day, God will command His kindness [when the Jewish people are praying], and at night His song is with me [with the angels]" (Psalms 42:9).

[The Gemara briefly digresses:] Resh Lakish said: Whoever engages in Torah study at night, the Holy One, blessed be He, will spread over him a thread of kindness[15] the next day. For it says, "In the day, God will command His kindness." And why is it that in the day God will command His kindness? Because, "at night His song was with me," [at night he was studying Torah, which is God's song]. Others say: Resh Lakish said: Whoever engages in Torah study in this world, which is like the night, the Holy One, blessed be He, will spread over him a thread of kindness in the World to Come which is like the day, as it says, "In the day, God will command His kindness, and at night His song is with me."

R. Levi said: Whoever stops learning Torah and engages in idle talk, will be fed coals of juniper [a slow-burning plant], as it says, "Those who cut short [the study of the words written on] the Tablets, and turn to idle talk, juniper roots will be their food" (Job 30:4).

[At this point the Gemara resumes the discussion of the seven heavens:] And how do we know that *Ma'on* is called heaven? Because it says, "Look down from your holy *Ma'on* [Dwelling] in heaven" (Deuteronomy 26:15).

Machon (Established Residence) is the [heaven where there are the storage houses of snow, hail, harmful dew, [to beat down the produce (Rashi)] raindrops, the chamber of the whirlwind and the storm, and the cave of vapor. And the doors of all these storehouses are of fire, as it says, "God will open His good treasury in heaven" (Deuteronomy 28:12), ["good treasury" implies that there also is a bad treasury of harmful dew, storm, etc.]. [The Gemara asks:] But are these treasuries in heaven? Surely they are on earth! For it says, "Praise God from the earth; sea giants and ocean depths, fire and hail, snow and vapor, stormy wind fulfilling His word" (Psalms 148:7,8). Said R. Yehudah in Rav's name: Originally they were in heaven, but David prayed for them and had them brought down to the earth. He said to God: Master of the universe, "You are not a God who desires wickedness, no evil sojourns with You," (ibid. 5:5) [so bring them down to earth]. [In other words,] You are a righteous God, let no evil reside with You. And how do we know that *Machon* is called heaven? For it says, "May You hear from heaven, the *machon* of Your abode."

Aravot is the place where right, justice, and righteousness dwell; the treasuries of life, peace, and blessings; the souls of the righteous, and the souls that will eventually be created; and the dew with which the Holy One, blessed be He, will revive the dead. How do we know that right and justice dwell there? Because it says, "Right and justice are Your throne's foundation" (Psalms 89:15). Righteousness, for it says, "He donned righteousness like armor" (Isaiah 59:17). The treasuries of peace, because it says, "Gideon built an altar and called it, 'God is the source of our peace'" (Judges 6:24). The treasuries of life, for it says, "For with You is the source of life" (Psalms 36:10). The treasuries of blessing, for it says, "He will receive a blessing from God" (ibid. 24:5). The souls of the righteous, for it says, [Abigail said to David,] "May my lord's soul be bound up in the bond of life, with the Lord your God" (1 Samuel 25:29). The souls that will eventually be created, for it says, "When the spirit that envelops them is from Me, and I made their souls" (Isaiah 57:16). And the dew with which the Holy One, blessed be He, will revive the dead, for it says, "A generous rain did You lavish, O God, when Your heritage was weary You established it firmly" (Psalms 68:10).

In [*Aravot*, the seventh heaven,] there also are the Ofanim, the Serafim, the holy Chayot,[16] the ministering angels, and the Throne of Glory; and the King, the living God high and exalted dwells over them in *Aravot*, as it says, "Extol Him who rides upon *Aravot*, whose name is Yah" (ibid. v. 5). And how do we know that *Aravot* is called heaven? We derive it from the word *rochev*, "riding," which occurs in two Biblical passages. Here it says, "Extol Him who who rides [*rochev*] upon *Aravot*" and elsewhere it says, "He rides [*rochev*] across the heavens to help you" (Deuteronomy 33:26). And darkness, clouds, and a thick fog surround Him, for it says, "He made darkness His concealment, around Him His shelter—the darkness of water, the clouds of heaven" (Psalms 8:12).

[Asks the Gemara:] But is there darkness in the presence of God? Doesn't it say, "He reveals the deep and the mysterious; He knows what is in the darkness,

and light dwells with Him"? (Daniel 2:22). [The Gemara answers:] There is no contradiction here: This [last] verse refers to the inside chamber, the other verse to the outside chamber, [these are metaphors that refer to different degrees of love of God].[17]

R. Acha b. Yaakov said: The is still another heaven above the heads of the Chayot, for it says, "There was a likeness of an expanse above the heads of the Chayah, like the color of the awesome ice, spread out over their heads from above" (Ezekiel 1:22). Up to this point, [the seven heavens,] you have permission to speak; beyond this point, [regarding the eighth heaven,] you do not have permission to speak, for so it is written in the Book of Ben Sira: Do not ponder things that are beyond your comprehension, and do not contemplate things that are hidden from you. Reflect on things that are permitted to you,[18] but stay away from esoteric subjects.

STUDYING THE "ACCOUNT OF THE DIVINE CHARIOT"

[We learned in the Mishnah:] We should not teach the Account of the Divine Chariot[19] in the presence of one. R. Chiya taught: But you are permitted to teach him the headings of the chapters. R. Zeira said: The headings of the chapters may be taught only to a head of a Bet Din or to someone who is God-fearing. Others say: [He has to have both qualifications: He has to be a head of a Bet Din, and] he also must be God-fearing. R. Ammi said: We teach the mysteries of the Torah only to a person who has five characteristics, [that is, if he is], "Captain of fifty, a respected person, adviser, teacher of the wise, and a comprehender of mysteries" (Isaiah 3:3). And R. Ammi further said: We should not teach Torah to an idol worshipper, for it says, "He issued His commands to Jacob, His statutes and rules to Israel. He did not do so for any other nation; of such rules they know nothing" (Psalms 147:20).

R. Yochanan said to R. Elazar: Come and I will teach you the subject of the "Divine Chariot." R. Elazar replied: I am not old enough. When he was old enough, R. Yochanan had passed away. R. Assi then said to him: Come I will teach you the Account of the Divine Chariot. He replied: If I had been worthy, I would have been taught by your master R. Yochanan.

R. Yosef was studying the Account of the Divine Chariot; the elders of Pumbeditha were studying the [mystical aspects] of Creation. They said to R. Yosef: Would you teach us the Account of the Divine Chariot? He replied: If you teach me first the subject of Creation. After the Elders of Pumbeditha finished teaching him [the mystical aspects of Creation], they said to him: Now you teach us the Account of the Divine Chariot. But R. Yosef replied: Regarding the Account of the Divine Chariot we have learned, "Keep the honey and milk under your tongue" (Song of Songs 4:11) [which means], the things that are sweeter than honey and milk [like the Account of the Divine Chariot], keep them under your tongue; [don't teach them to others].

R. Abbahu said: We infer [that you should not teach the Account of the Divine Chariot to others] from here: "Let the lambs [*kevasim*] be your clothing" (Proverbs 27:26). [Instead of *kevasim* read *kevushim*, "hidden things," in other words:] Things that are the mystery of the world, keep them hidden under your coat, [don't divulge them]. The elders of Pumbeditha said to R. Yosef: We have learned already [in the chapter of Divine Chariot] as far as the verse, "Then He said to me 'Son of Man stand on your feet,'" (Ezekiel 2:1). R. Yosef replied: If you learned that, you have learned a great deal, because this portion includes the [verses Ezekiel 1:27,28] of the Account of the Divine Chariot the Rabbis prohibited.

R. Yehudah said: There is one man in particular who should be remembered for a blessing, namely, Chananiah b. Chizkiah. For if it had not been for him, the Book of Ezekiel would have been hidden [and not included in Scripture], because it contains statements[20] that seem to contradict the laws of the Torah [if they are not explained well]. What did he do? He had three hundred jars of oil brought up to his chamber, and he stayed there until he explained all of them.

The Rabbis taught: There once was a small child who was reading the Book of Ezekiel in his teacher's house, and he understood the meaning of *Chashmal* [a type of angel mentioned in the chapter of the Divine Chariot in Ezekiel 1), whereupon a fire came forth from the *Chashmal* and consumed him. So the Rabbis wanted to hide the Book of Ezekiel, but Chananiah b. Chizkiah said to them: If this boy was a child prodigy, does that mean that everyone is a sage? [The boy was an exception, but ordinary people are not in any danger if they read the Book of Ezekiel.]

WHERE DO BRAZEN PEOPLE COME FROM?

(13b) It says, "Who were cut down before their time" (Job 22:16). We learned in a *Baraita*: R. Shimon HeChasid said: This refers to the 974 generations which God decreed should come into being before the world was created, but which were not created. [God originally planned to give the Torah to the thousandth generation from Adam.[21] When He foresaw that the world could not exist without Torah for so long, He gave the Torah to the twenty-sixth generation from Adam. The other 974 generations were destroyed (Rashi).]

[However, God did not destroy them irrevocably. But instead of making them generations for themselves,] He planted some of them in every single generation, and these are the shameless people in every generation.

R. Nachman b. Yitzchak said: On the contrary, the words *asher kummetu* [translated above as "which were

cut down"] signify a blessing. The phrase refers to Torah scholars who stay awake at night to study Torah in this world. In return, the Holy One, blessed be He, reveals to them mystical secrets in the world to come, for the [above-mentioned verse ends,] "The foundations [i.e., the mysteries of the Torah] will be poured out to them like a river" (Job 22:16).

THE CREATION OF ANGELS

Shmuel said to Chiya b. Rav: Great Torah scholar, come let me tell you some of the beautiful things that your father used to say: Every single day ministering angels are created from the stream of fire[22] who sing God's praise and afterwards expire, for it says, "They are new every morning; great is Your praise [because of them]" (Lamentations 3:23). In this he differs with R. Shmuel b. Nachmani, who said in the name of R. Yonatan: From every single word that is uttered by the Holy One, blessed is He, an angel is created, for it says, "By the word of God the heavens were made, and by the breath of His mouth all their hosts" (Psalms 33:6), [thus we see that the angels were created by God's word, and not from the stream of fire].[23]

ISAIAH'S EIGHTEEN CURSES

When R. Dimi came [from Eretz Yisrael to Babylonia], he said: Eighteen curses did Isaiah pronounce on Israel, and he was not calmed until he pronounced on them the verse, "The youngster will bully the old, and the base will bully the respectable" (Isaiah 3:5). What are the eighteen curses? The following: "For behold, the Lord, God, Master of Legions will remove from Jerusalem and from Judah prop and stay, every prop of bread and every support of water; hero and man of war, judge, prophet, diviner, and elder; captain of fifty, respected person, adviser, teacher of the wise, and comprehender of mysteries. I will make youngsters their leaders, and mockers will rule them" (Isaiah 3:1–4).[24] "Stay" refers to the masters of the Scriptures; "prop" refers to the masters of the Mishnah, like R. Yehudah b. Teima and his colleagues.

R. Papa and R. Yehudah disagree on this point: One says: there were six hundred orders of the Mishnah; the other says: there were seven hundred orders of the Mishnah. [Of course, we only have six. The Maharsha explains that they had the same Mishnah we have, but they subdivided it into 600 or 700 orders.] "Every prop of bread"—this means the masters of the Talmud, as it says, "Come and partake of My bread, and drink of the wine that I mixed" (Proverbs 9:5) [for we can rely on their rulings as we rely on bread to fill us (Rashi)].

"Every support of water" this means the masters of *Aggadah*, who draw the heart of a person like water by means of *Aggadah*. "Hero"—this means the masters of traditions [i.e., scholars who transmit halachic rulings that they heard from their teachers]. "Man of war"—this means a person who knows how to debate Torah topics [and arrive at the truth]. "Judge"—this means a judge who renders judgment that is truly righteous. "Prophet"—is meant literally. "Diviner"—this means a king, as it says, "There is a charm on the lips of a king" (Proverbs 16:10). "Elder"—this means a person who has the wisdom to give advice. "Captain of fifty"—do not read "captain of fifty, *chamishim*" but "captain of the *Chumashim*"—this means a person who knows how to debate questions relating to five *Chumashim* [the five Books of the Torah].

Another interpretation of "captain of fifty" is as R. Abbahu said: From here we learn that we do not appoint a translator[25] for a congregation if he is less than fifty years old. "Respected person"—this means a person in whose merit the entire generation is nourished (Rashi), like R. Chanina b. Dosa who was respected on high [for in his merit the entire world was nourished[26]]. And he is respected below [in this world], like R. Abbahu who was respected at the court of Caesar.[27] "Adviser"—this means a person who is able to intercalate years[28] and to fix the months. "Teacher"—that is a student who makes his teachers wise. "Wise"—when he begins a Torah lecture all are speechless, [overwhelmed by what he is saying]. "One who comprehends"—this means a person who has the ability to draw an inference from something he knows. "Mysteries"—this refers to a person who is worthy to receive words of the Torah (like the Account of the Divine Chariot) that were given in a whisper.

"I will make youngsters their leaders"—R. Elazar said: These are people that are emptied of *mitzvot*. "And mockers will rule over them"—R. Acha b. Yaakov said: This means foxes, the sons of foxes. [The Gemara continues:] But all this did not satisfy Isaiah until he said to them, "The young will bully the old"—meaning, the people that are emptied of *mitzvot* will behave rudely toward people who are full of good deeds like a pomegranate [is full of seeds]. "And the base will bully the respectable"—means a person who takes grave laws of the Torah very lightly will behave rudely toward people who take even the easiest laws very seriously.

WERE THERE HONEST PEOPLE LEFT IN JERUSALEM?

R. Ketina said: Even at the time of the downfall of Jerusalem, there still were honest people there. [Proof of this is] the verse, "When a man will grasp his relative, a member of his father's house, [saying], 'You have a garment; become a leader over us!'" (Isaiah 3:6). This means: You have Torah knowledge within your grasp. "And let this obstacle be under your control" (ibid.)—What does "this obstacle" refer to? It refers to Torah, because a person cannot grasp the true meaning of

Torah learning unless he first makes mistakes and learns from them.

"He will swear on that day, saying, 'I cannot become a patron, with no food or clothing in my own house [i.e., I have no knowledge of Torah], do not make me a leader of people'" (ibid. v. 7). "He will swear" [*yisa*] refers to an oath, and so it says, "Do not take the name of the Lord, your God in vain [*sisa*]" (Exodus 20:7). "I cannot become a patron"—[Don't ask me to teach you Torah, because] I was never a student at a *bet midrash*. "With no food or clothing in my house"—meaning, I have no knowledge of Scriptures, Mishnah, or Gemara. [Asks the Gemara: How does this prove that he is an honest person?] Perhaps this case is different, because if he had said to them: I have knowledge; [I will become your teacher], they would have said to him: So, tell us some Torah insights! [Therefore he had no choice but to confess that he had no Torah knowledge.]

[The Gemara counters: The fact that he said: I have no knowledge shows that he is an honest man,] because he could have said: I have learned but I have forgotten everything. Why did he say: I was never a student at a *bet midrash*? It must mean: I never learned at all. [We must conclude, therefore, that he is honest]. [The Gemara asks:] Is that so? Has not Rava said: Jerusalem was not destroyed until there were no more honest people in it. For it says, "Roam the streets of Jerusalem, look about and take note, search its squares; if you can find a man [of authority], if there is one who dispenses justice and seeks truth, then I will forgive her" (Jeremiah 5:1). [Why do you say that there were honest people left?] [The Gemara answers:] There is no contradiction: (14b) One verse [Isaiah 3:6] refers to Torah learning; the other verse [Jeremiah 5:1] refers to business dealings. In regard to Torah learning they were honest; [they truthfully said that they had never learned], but in regard to business dealings there were no honest people left.

HE EXPOUNDED ON THE "DIVINE CHARIOT"

Our Rabbis taught: Once R. Yochanan b. Zakkai was traveling on the road, riding on his donkey, and R. Elazar b. Arach was driving the donkey from behind. R. Elazar said to him, "Rabbi, please teach me one chapter of the Account of the Divine Chariot." "My son," replied R. Yochanan b. Zakkai, "Did I not teach you that the 'Divine Chariot' should not be taught to one person unless he is a sage, and understands it by himself? R. Elazar then said, "Rabbi, allow me to say to you one thing that you taught me." He answered, "Go ahead and say it!" R. Yochanan got off the donkey at once, wrapped himself in his *tallit*, and sat down on a stone beneath an olive tree. R. Elazar said to him, "Rabbi, why did you get off the donkey?" He replied, "Would it be right that, while you are expounding on the 'Divine Chariot,' and the *Shechinah* is with us, and the ministering angels accompany us, that I should ride on a donkey?"

Immediately, R. Elazar b. Arach began to expound the Account of the Divine Chariot, and as he did, fire came down from heaven and encircled all the trees in the field. Then all the trees broke into song. What was the song they sang? "Praise God from the earth, sea giants and all watery depths . . . fruitful trees and all cedars . . . Halleluyah!" (Psalms 148:7,9,14). An angel then called out from the fire and said, "This exposition is truly the Account of the Divine Chariot!" R. Yochanan b. Zakkai stood up and kissed R. Elazar b. Arach on the head and said, "Blessed be the Lord, God of Israel who gave to our father Abraham a son who knows, understands, is able to delve into and expound the Divine Chariot. There are people who preach well but do not practice what they preach; others perform well but preach poorly. But you preach eloquently, and you practice what you preach. Praiseworthy are you, our Father Abraham, that R. Elazar b. Arach is one of your offspring."

THE FOUR WHO ENTERED *PARDES*, "THE GARDEN"[29]
Our Rabbis taught: There were four people who entered *Pardes*, "the Garden,"[30] namely: Ben Azzai, Ben Zoma, Acher,[31] and R. Akiva. R. Akiva said to them: When you come to the pure [transparent] marble stones, [meaning, a high level in the spiritual world] do not say: Water, water! [even though the stones are as clear as water]. For it says, "One who tells lies shall not be established before My eyes" (Psalms 101:7). [And now you are standing before God, so be sure not to say anything that is untrue.]

Ben Azzai gazed toward the *Shechinah* and died. Of him it says, "Difficult in the eyes of God is the death of His loved ones" (Psalms 116:15). Ben Zoma gazed toward the *Shechinah* and went mad. About him it says, "When you find honey, eat what is sufficient for you, lest you be satiated and vomit it up" (Proverbs 25:16). Acher "destroyed the plants" [became an apostate]. Rabbi Akiva [was the only one who] entered whole and came out whole.

(15a) Acher "destroyed the plants." Of him it says, "Let not your mouth bring guilt on your flesh" (Ecclesiastes 5:5). What did Acher see that made him renounce Judaism? He saw that permission was given to the angel Metatron, [one of the highest angels,] to sit and write down the merits of Israel. Said Acher: It has been taught that in Heaven no one ever sits, since there is no weariness there [yet I saw the angel Metatron sitting]. Perhaps, God forbid, there are two divinities that guide the world? [Since Metatron caused Acher to reject Judaism,] he was whipped with sixty fiery lashes.

They said to Metatron: What is the reason you did not stand up before [Acher] when you saw him? [For

if he had risen before him, Acher would not have rejected Judaism.] They gave him permission to erase the merits of Acher. A heavenly voice then announced: "Return, you wayward children" (Jeremiah 3:22)— except for Acher [for he saw the *Shechinah*, yet he rebelled against God]. Acher then said: Since I have been driven from the World to Come, let me at least enjoy this world. So Acher went to evil ways. He visited a prostitute, and she said, "Are you not Elisha b. Abuyah?" But when he tore a radish from the ground on *Shabbat* and gave it to her, she said, "You must be *acher* [i.e., someone else. Elisha b. Abuyah would never desecrate *Shabbat*]."

ACHER AND RABBI MEIR
After he renounced Judaism, Acher asked [his former student] R. Meir a question: "What is the meaning of the verse, 'God has made the one as well as the other' [Ecclesiastes 7:14]?" R. Meir answered, "It means that for everything God created, He also created a counterpart. He created mountains, and He created hills; He created seas, and He created rivers." Acher said to R. Meir, "Your rabbi, R. Akiva, did not explain it like this, but as follows: He created righteous people, and he created wicked people. He created Gan Eden, and He created Gehinnom. Everyone has two portions, one in Gan Eden and one in Gehinnom. Since a righteous person deserves it, he takes his own portion and his fellow's portion in Gan Eden. Since a wicked person is guilty, he takes his own portion and his fellow's portion in Gehinnom." R. Mesharshiya said: What passage confirms this? Regarding the righteous it says, "They will inherit a double portion in their land" (Isaiah 61:7). Concerning the wicked it says, "Devastate them with double disaster" (Jeremiah 17:18).

After he renounced Judaism, Acher asked R. Meir, "What is the meaning of the verse, 'Gold and glass cannot approximate it, nor can its exchange be in golden articles' [Job 28:17]?" R. Meir answered, "It is a reference to the words of the Torah, which are difficult to acquire like vessels gold and fine gold, but which are easily broken like vessels of glass." Said Acher to R. Meir, "R. Akiva, your rabbi, did not explain it like this, but as follows: Just as vessels of gold and vessels of glass, although they may be broken, can be repaired, so too, a Torah scholar, although he has sinned, can set himself right [by doing *teshuvah*]." To which R. Meir retorted, "Then you, too, do *teshuvah*!" Acher answered, "I have already heard from behind the heavenly Curtain: 'Return, you wayward children'—except for Acher."[32]

Our Rabbis taught: Once on a *Shabbat*, Acher was riding on a horse and R. Meir was walking behind him to learn Torah from him. At one point Acher said, "Meir, turn back, since I have measured with my horse's footsteps that the *techum Shabbat* [the boundary beyond which it is forbidden to go on *Shabbat*] ends here."

R. Meir replied, "You, too, turn back [and do *teshuvah*]!" Acher replied, "Have I not already told you that I have heard from behind the heavenly Curtain, 'Return, you wayward children—except for Acher!'" R. Meir took hold of him and brought him to a *bet midrash*. Acher said to a child, "Tell me the verse [you learned today]."[33] The child answered, "There is no peace for the wicked" (Isaiah 48:22). He then took him to another *bet midrash*. Acher said to a child, "Tell me the verse [you learned today]." The child answered, "Even if you were to wash with niter and use much soap, your iniquity has become a stain before Me—the word of my Lord, God" (Jeremiah 2:22).

He then brought him to another *bet midrash*, where Acher said to a child, "Tell me your verse." The child replied, "And you, that are spoiled, what will you do? If you wear scarlet, if you don a golden ornament, if you paint your eyes with mascara, you will be beautifying yourself in vain" (Jeremiah 4:30). He took him to still another *bet midrash*, until he took him to thirteen different houses of learning: the response was always the same, [indicating a rejection of Acher]. In the last *bet midrash*, when he said to the child, "Tell me your verse," the child quoted, "But to the wicked [*velarasha*], God said, 'To what purpose do you recount My decrees [Psalms 50:16]?'" That child had a speech defect, so that it sounded as if he had said, "But to Elisha God said," [*velerasha* sounded like *uleElisha*]. Some say that Acher had a knife on him, and he cut up the child and sent him to the thirteen houses of learning; and others say that he said, "If I had a knife in my hand I would rip him to pieces."

ACHER'S DEATH

When Acher died, they said in heaven: We cannot sentence him to Gehinnom, and we cannot allow him to enter the World to Come. We cannot sentence him to Gehinnom because he immersed himself in Torah study, and we cannot let him enter the World to Come because he sinned. R. Meir said: It would be better that he should be sentenced [to Gehinnom, so that his soul should be cleansed], and he could then be admitted to the World to Come. When I die I will cause smoke to rise from his grave [as a sign that Acher was judged and punished for his sins in Gehinnom]. When R. Meir died, smoke rose up from Acher's grave. R. Yochanan said: What a mighty deed for a person to throw his rabbi into the fire! [R. Meir meant to benefit Acher's soul, but people would not understand it (*Maharsha*).] Continued R. Yochanan: There was one person among us [i.e., Acher], and we could not save him, [and bring him to the World to Come]. If I take him by the hand, [and bring him to the World to Come,] who will snatch him away from me? When I die I will stop the smoke from rising from his grave, [as a sign that he was forgiven and was admitted to Gan Eden]. And when R. Yochanan died, the smoke stopped rising from Acher's

grave. One of the official mourners [at R. Yochanan's funeral] began his eulogy: Even the guard at the gate of Gehinnom could not stop you, [R. Yochanan, when you came to take out Acher]!

Acher's daughter came to Rebbi[34] and asked him to support her. Rebbi asked her, "Whose daughter are you?" She replied, "I am Acher's daughter." Said Rebbi, "Are there still children of Acher left in the world? Doesn't it say, 'He will have neither child nor grandchild among his people, no survivor in his habitations'" (Job 18:19)? She answered, "Remember the Torah he learned; don't remember his deeds." Thereupon a fire came down and scorched Rebbi's bench. [The fire symbolizes the Torah which is called the "fiery Torah" (Deuteronomy 33:2) (*Maharsha*).] Rebbi began to cry and said, "If such great things happen to people who dishonor the Torah, how much more wonderful things will happen for those who honor the Torah!"

HOW COULD R. MEIR LEARN TORAH FROM ACHER?

How was R. Meir permitted to learn Torah from Acher? After all, Rabba b. Bar Chana said in the name of R. Yochanan: What is the meaning of the verse, "For the lips of the Kohen should safeguard knowledge, and people should seek Torah from his mouth; for He is an angel of God, the Master of Legions" (Malachi 2:7). [This means that] if the teacher is like an angel of God, people should seek Torah from him; but if not, they should not seek Torah from him. [So how was R. Meir permitted to learn Torah from Acher?] Resh Lakish answered: R. Meir found support for his view in the verse, "Incline your ear and hear the words of the wise; set your heart to My knowledge" (Proverbs 22:17). It does not say, "set your heart to *their* knowledge," but to "*My* knowledge." [In other words: You may listen to the wisdom of an unworthy wise man, but ignore his deeds, and follow God's teaching instead.]

R. Chanina said: R. Meir derived it from here, "Hear, O daughter, and see, and incline your ear; forget your people and your father's house" (Psalms 45:11). [Meaning, listen to the words of the wise, but repudiate their actions if they are wicked.] [The Gemara asks:] But the passages contradict each other! [Malachi 2:7 says that your teacher must be like an angel, whereas Proverbs 22:17 and Psalms 45:11 indicate that you may learn from a teacher even if his actions are flawed.] [The Gemara answers:] There is no contradiction: In one case, [the last two verses], refer to an adult [who will not be influenced by the bad deeds of the teacher]; the first verse refers to a child, [whose teacher's conduct must be impeccable]. When R. Dimi came [to Babylonia] he said: In Eretz Yisrael they say: R. Meir ate the date, and threw away the pit, [i.e., he absorbed Acher's knowledge, and overlooked his bad conduct].

HE ATE THE FRUIT AND DISCARDED THE PEEL

Rava expounded: What is meant by the verse, "I went down to the nut grove to see the budding of the valley" (Song of Songs 6:11)? Why are Torah scholars compared to the nut? To tell you that just as in the case of the nut, even if it is soiled with mud and filth, yet its core does not become repulsive; so in the case of a Torah scholar, although he may have sinned, yet his Torah is not tainted. Rabbah b. Shila once met Elijah. He asked him, "What is the Holy One, blessed be He, doing?" He replied, "He is repeating teachings in the name of all the Rabbis, but He does not repeat any of R. Meir's teachings." Asked Rabbah b. Shila, "Why?" "Because he learned Gemara from Acher." Said Rabbah b. Shila, "What's wrong with that? R. Meir found a pomegranate, he ate the fruit inside, and the peel he threw away!" [I.e., he only learned the good things.] Elijah answered, "[Since you spoke up for R. Meir,] God is at this very moment quoting a saying by R. Meir [which has to do with a person who was hanged for a sin he committed]. [Says God,] Meir my son says: When a person suffers, what does the *Shechinah* say? My head is heavy. My arm is heavy. Now, if the Holy One, blessed be He, feels such pain over the blood of the wicked [man who was hanged], how much more anguished is He over the blood of the righteous that is shed.

THE TORAH PROTECTS THE GOD-FEARING STUDENT

Shmuel found Rav Yehudah leaning on the door lock and weeping. He said to him, "You bright scholar, why are you crying?" He replied, "Is it a small thing that is written about the Rabbis? 'Where is the one who counts? Where is the one who weighs? Where is the one who counts the towers?'[Isaiah 33:18]." [He explained:] "Where is the one who counts?"—[meaning Torah scholars,] for they counted the letters of the Torah. "Where is the one that weighs?"—for the Torah scholars drew *a fortiori* logical conclusions from the lenient to the rigorous things in the Torah. "Where is the one who counts the towers?"—for they taught three hundred *halachot* regarding a "tower that floats in the air".[35] And R. Ammi said: Three hundred questions did Doeg and Achitofel raise concerning a "tower that floats in the air." Yet we learned in a Mishnah: Three kings and four commoners have no share in the World to Come.[36]

[Cried Rav Yehudah:] [They were all great Torah scholars, and yet the Torah they learned did not save them], then what shall become of us? Shmuel said to him: You bright scholar! [They have no share in the World to Come] because they were corrupt from the start [that's why their Torah knowledge did not protect them]. But what about Acher? Why did his Torah learning not protect him? Because he never stopped singing Greek songs, [and thereby he violated the prohibition against music after the destruction of the Temple (Rashi)]. They said about Acher that, [before he became an apostate], when he used to get up to leave the *bet midrash* many heretical books fell from his lap [which proves that his character was flawed from the outset, and that is why his Torah learning did not save him].

Nimus the weaver asked R. Meir: Does all wool that is dipped into the dyeing kettle come up with the right color? [He implied: Does the Torah protect every student from sin?] R. Meir replied: If the wool was pure when the sheep was sheared, the color will take [i.e., if the student was God-fearing when he began to study, he will be protected (Rashi)]; if the wool was not clean when the sheep was sheared, the color will not take [meaning, if he was not God-fearing to begin with, the Torah he learned will not protect him].

R. AKIVA EMERGED UNHURT

R. Akiva entered [the *Pardes*] whole and came out whole. And Scripture says of him, "Draw me after you, let us run, the King will bring me to his chambers" (Song of Songs 1:4) [R. Akiva indeed entered the *Pardes*, which is God's chamber.] The ministering angels tried to push away R. Akiva, but the Holy One, blessed be He, said to them: Leave this old man alone, for he is worthy to make use of My glory, [i.e., to use God's holy Name to enter the heavenly realm of the *Pardes* (Maharsha)].

(16a) From what verse did R. Akiva learn [where the *Shechinah* is, and to be careful not to gaze at it, and to avoid the mistake the others made]? Rabbah b. Bar Chanah said in R. Yochanan's name, the verse, "He approached [*ata*] with some of the holy myriads" (Deuteronomy 33:2)—He is a Sign [*ot*, similar to *ata*], among His holy myriads, [so that R. Akiva knew not to look there]. R. Abbahu said: "[God is] preeminent among ten thousand" (Song of Songs 5:10)—He is the Emblem among the ten thousand. Resh Lakish said, "The Lord of Hosts is His name" (Isaiah 47:2)—He is the Lord among His hosts. R. Chiya b. Abba said in the name of R. Yochanan, from the verse, "'God is not in the wind,'" [Elijah was told]. After the wind came an earthquake. 'God is not in the earthquake.' After the earthquake came a fire. 'God is not in the fire.' After the fire came a still, thin sound. And behold, God was passing" (1 Kings 19:11,12), [and R. Akiva knew that at that point he was not to gaze in the direction of the *Shechinah*[37]].

COMMITTING A SIN IN SECRET

[We learned in the Mishnah:] Whoever is disrespectful of his Maker would be better off if he had never come into the world. [Asks the Gemara:] What does this mean? [How did he show disrespect?] R. Abba said: It refers to a person who stares intently at the rainbow, for it says, "Like the appearance of a rainbow that would be in the clouds on a rainy day, so was the appearance of the brilliance all around. That was the appearance of the likeness of the glory of God" (Ezekiel 1:28). R. Yosef said: It refers to a person who commits a sin in secret. For R. Yitzchak said: If someone commits a sin in secret, it is as though he pushed the feet of the *Shechinah*. [He is saying, in fact: God does not see me in my hiding place.] For it says, "This said God, 'The Heaven is My throne, and the earth is My footstool'" (Isaiah 66:1).

Is that so? Didn't R. Ila'i the elder say: If a person sees that his evil inclination is getting the best of him, let him go to a place where no one knows him and put on black clothes and wrap himself in black clothes, and let him do what his heart desires. [His loneliness and his drab clothes will make him depressed and dampen his desire so that he will not sin; and if he does sin, at least no one knows him,] but he should not desecrate God's name publicly. [Thus R. Ila'i seems to suggest that a person who cannot control himself should commit a sin in secret, which contradicts the statement that this person pushes the feet of the *Shechinah*.] [The Gemara answers:] There is no contradiction: One case speaks of a person who is able to overcome his evil impulse, [but he prefers secretly to give in to his desire. He is the one that pushes the feet of the *Shechinah*]. The other case speaks of a person who is unable to subdue his evil impulse. [He should yield to it, but in a secret place.]

DON'T BELIEVE THE BLANDISHMENTS OF THE EVIL IMPULSE

R. Yehudah b. Nachmani, the *meturgeman* [i.e., the person who explained the expositions] of Resh Lakish, expounded: Anyone that stares intently at the following three things, his eyesight will become weak: the rainbow, the *Nasi* [the Prince], and at the *Kohanim*. [The Gemara explains:] At the rainbow, because it says, "Like the appearance of a rainbow that would be in the clouds on a rainy day . . . That was the appearance of the likeness of the glory of God" (Ezekiel 1:28). At the *Nasi*, because it says, [God said to Moses,] "You shall place some of your majesty on him [Joshua]" (Numbers 27:20). Anyone who gazes at the *Kohanim*—during the time when the *Bet Hamikdash* was standing—when they stood on their platform and blessed the Jewish people enunciating the *Shem Hameforash* [the Four-Letter Name of God].

R. Yehudah b. Nachmani, the *meturgeman* of Resh Lakish, expounded: What is meant by the verse, "Do not trust a friend; do not rely on an official [*aluf*]" (Michah 7:5)? If the evil impulse says to you, "Go ahead and sin; the Holy One, blessed be He, will forgive you,"

don't believe it, for it says, "Do not trust one [who appears to be] a friend," and *rei'a* means the evil impulse, for it says, "For the inclination of man's heart is evil [*ra*] from his youth" (Genesis 8:21), [*rei'a* and *ra* are written with the same letters]. And the "official" refers to none other than the Holy One, blessed be He, for it says, "You are the Master [*Aluf*] of my youth" (Jeremiah 3:4). [In other words: Don't rely on God to forgive you.]

Perhaps you will say: Who will testify against me? The stones of a person's home, and the beams of a person's house will testify against him, for it says, "For a stone will cry out from a wall, and a sliver will answer it from the beams" (Habakkuk 2:11). But the Sages say: A man's soul testifies against him, for it says, "Guard the doorways of your mouth from the one who lies in your bosom" (Michah 7:5). What is it that lies in a person's bosom? You must say, it is his soul. R. Zerika said: Two ministering angels that accompany him testify against him, for it says, "He will charge His angels for you, to protect you in all your ways" (Psalms 91:11). But the Sages say: A person's limbs testify against him, as it says, "You are My witnesses—the word of God" (Isaiah 43:12).

HE WAS WRONGFULLY PUT TO DEATH

(16b) R. Yehudah b. Tabbai swore: May I not see the consolation of the Jewish people[38] if I did not have a *zomeim* witness[39] put to death as a demonstration against the Sadducees who say: A *zomeim* witness is not put to death unless [through his false testimony] the accused had already been put to death. Said R. Shimon b. Shetach to him: May I not see the consolation of the Jewish people if you did not shed innocent blood. For the Sages said: *Zomemim* witnesses are not put to death until *both* of them have been proved *zomemim*; and they are not flogged until *both* of them have been proved *zomemim*; and they are not ordered to pay money [as damages] until *both* of them have been proven *zomemim*, [but here only one of the witnesses was a *zomeim*, and yet you had him put to death].

Right away, R. Yehudah b. Tabbai took it upon himself never again to render a decision except in the presence of Shimon b. Shetach [who would correct him if he made a mistake]. And all his life Yehudah b. Tabbai prostrated himself on the grave of the executed man, and his voice could be heard. The people thought that it was the voice of the dead man. So R. Yehudah b. Tabbai told them: It is my voice you are hearing; and you'll know this by the fact that on the day after I die, my voice will not be heard anymore. R. Acha the son of Rava said to R. Ashi: Perhaps [it was the voice of the dead man, and it stopped because R. Yehudah b. Tabbai] appeased him, or the deceased summoned him to [the heavenly] court [and there the matter was settled].

THE MIRACLE
OF THE SHOWBREAD

[The Mishnah said:] Menachem went out and Hillel entered. [The Gemara asks:] Where did Menachem go? Abbaye said: He went off on bad ways. Rava said: He went off in the [Roman] King's service. We also learned this in a *Baraita*: Menachem went off in the King's service, and eighty pairs of disciples dressed in silk came along with him.

(26b) R. Yehoshua b. Levi said: A great miracle happened with the showbread. It was [fresh] when it was set down [on the Table], and it was just as fresh when it was taken away [a week later] as when it was set down.

THE FIRE OF GEHINNOM

(27a) R. Abbahu said in the name of R. Elazar: The fire of Gehinnom has no power over Torah scholars. You can prove it with a logical deduction drawn from the salamander: If a person smears himself with the blood of a salamander [a creature born in a fire that burns for seven years without interruption], which is only an offspring of fire, fire has no power over him; then surely fire has no power over a Torah scholar whose entire body is fire, for it says, "Behold, My word is like fire, says God" (Jeremiah 23:29).

Resh Lakish said: The fire of Gehinnom has no power over the transgressors of Israel. You can prove it with a logical deduction drawn from the altar of gold. If the altar of gold, on which there is [a covering of] only a *dinar* thickness of gold, is not damaged by so many years of the fire, how much less so the transgressors of Israel who are full of good deeds as a pomegranate [is full of seeds], for it is written, "Your brow behind your veil is like a pomegranate split open" (Song of Songs 4:3). Don't read "your brow" [*rakatech*] but "your worthless ones" [*rekanim shebach*].

NOTES

1. Halachic Midrash on Leviticus.
2. Halachic Midrash on Numbers and Deuteronomy.
3. *Berachot* 28a.
4. According to Rashi, R. Elazar; according to Maharsha, R. Joshua.
5. See beginning of this section.
6. Pesach, Shavuot, and Sukkot.
7. Tosafot, s.v. *hava shechiach*, identifies Miriam, the women's hairdresser, *Miriam megaddela seiór neshaya*, as the mother of the Nazarene. Perhaps the name Miriam Megaddela is associated with the name Mary Magdalene. (Compare *Shabbat* 104b in the uncensored Talmud edition.)
8. A small coin.
9. Prince.
10. He left right after Pesach, traveled for three months, spent one day at the yeshivah, and traveled

for three months to be home in time for Sukkot (Rashi).
11. Ezekiel 1:4f, 10, and Isaiah 6.
12. The generation that rebelled against God and built the Tower of Babel to wage war against God. God dispersed them over the face of the earth and gave them different languages (Genesis 11:1–9).
13. The Maharsha explains that this does not refer to physical pillars but to spiritual concepts. The three pillars of the world are justice, truth, and peace. They rest on water, the symbol of Torah. Water rests on mountains, which are symbolic of the righteous. The mountains rest on the wind, i.e., the soul, which chooses good over evil. The wind rests on the storm, i.e., the *yetzer hara*, which has to be overcome. Finally, the storm rests on the arm of God, meaning that man cannot conquer the *yetzer hara* unless God helps him do it.
14. The Maharsha explains that the heavenly Jerusalem, the counterpart of the earthly Jerusalem, was never destroyed and never will be destroyed.
15. Usually when a person stays up all night he looks pale and haggard, but when he studies Torah at night God will give him a "thread of kindness," which will make him look and feel refreshed and vigorous (*Maharsha*).
16. These are various groups of angels whose essence cannot be defined in human terms.
17. The Maharal in *Be'er Hagolah* emphasizes that this Gemara is not to be taken literally. When discussing the heavens the text uses metaphors to describe the essence of spiritual entities. The true meaning of these concepts is completely beyond our limited comprehension.
18. The study of wonders of nature, so that you will recognize the greatness of the Creator revealed in nature.
19. The first chapter of Ezekiel, which deals with mystical concepts of the Divine Throne and angels.
20. For example, in Chapter 44.
21. As it says, "The word He commanded for a thousand generations" (Psalms 105:8).
22. Mentioned in Daniel 7:10.
23. It should be understood that this Gemara alludes to profound mystical concepts that transcend our understanding and should not be taken at face value.
24. The Vilna Gaon notes that this verse contains only seventeen curses. He explains that the eighteenth curse is in the next verse, "When a man will grasp his relative, a member of his father's house, saying, 'You have a garment; become a chief over us.'"
25. A *meturgeman*, translator, translated the Torah reading into Aramaic during the service.
26. *Taanit* 24b–25a.
27. *Sanhedrin* 14a.
28. The duration of a lunar month is about 29½ days, and the lunar year of twelve lunar months, is

12 x 29.5, or about 354 days. The solar year has 365 days. Thus the lunar year is about eleven days shorter than the solar year. If nothing is done to adjust the lunar calendar, the Yamim Tovim would move through the four seasons of the year. The situation is corrected by periodically inserting a thirteenth lunar month, Adar II, in a procedure called intercalation. As a result, Pesach always occurs in the spring, as the Torah demands (Deuteronomy 16:1).

29. This is one of the best-known and most profound aggadic sections in the Gemara.

30. They entered heaven by using mystical Divine names (Rashi). Tosafot comments that they did not actually ascend to heaven; it only appeared to them that they did.

31. Acher is Elisha b. Abuyah. He is known as Acher (another person) because he turned his back on Judaism and became an apostate.

32. One of the great Hasidic masters said: Acher was a fool. When he heard that he lost his share in the the World to Come he could have done *teshuvah* out of pure, selfless love of God, without any thought of reward. He would have attained the highest level of service of God.

33. The verse a small child would recite was considered to be an omen for the future.

34. R. Yehudah Hanasi.

35. The "tower that flies in the air" refers to laws of a levitically unclean object in an enclosed space that opens to the public domain, as discussed in tractate *Ohalot*. It is interesting to note that the Geonim, who lived over 1,000 years ago, theorized how these laws apply to a space station, which they described as a "tower that floats in the air."

36. The three kings are: Jeroboam, Ahab, and Menashe. The four commoners are: Balaam, Doeg, Achitofel, and Gechazi (*Sanhedrin* 90a).

37. When R. Akiva entered Heaven and saw the great commotion of myriad of angels, he did not mistake this to be the *Shechinah*. He realized that God is only One. Whereas Acher, being terrified by the hosts of angels he saw, mistakenly thought that this was Divinity, and was misled into believing that there are two divine Powers (*Maharsha*).

38. A form of oath.

39. *Eidim zomemim*, "plotting witnesses," are witnesses whose testimony has been refuted by other witnesses, [*mazimim*], who testified that the *zomemim* were with them at another place at the time of the crime. The Torah says, "You must do the same to them as they plotted to do to their brother" (Deuteronomy 19:19). The Sages derived from this that the law of retaliation applies only where the sentence has not been carried out on the basis of their testimony. However, if it has, the *zomemim* witnesses are not punished (*Makkot* 5b). The Sadducees disputed this and maintained that the *zomemim* are punished when the sentence of their intended victim was in fact carried out.

✂ YEVAMOT ✂

[The tractate *Yevamot* deals with the subject of *yibbum*,

HOW TO SHOW RESPECT FOR THE *BET HAMIKDASH*

(6a) We learned in a *Baraita*: It says, "Every person must respect his mother and father" (Leviticus 19:3). I would think that if a father tells his son [who is a *kohen*], "Defile yourself [by contact with the dead],"[1] or, "Do not return [a lost object],[2] the son must obey his father [because the mitzvah of respecting your father should override these prohibitions]. That is why it says, "Every person must respect his mother and father, and [nevertheless,] keep My Sabbaths, I am God your Lord"—you are all obligated to honor Me, [and *Shabbat* takes precedence].

We learned in a *Baraita*: I would think that a person should be in awe of the *Bet Hamikdash*. That is why it says, "Keep My Sabbaths and be in awe of My sanctuary. I am God" (Leviticus 19:30). [The Gemara elaborates:] In connection with *Shabbat* the verse uses the term *tishmoru*, "keep," and in the same verse, in connection with the sanctuary, the term *tira'u*, "be in awe," is used. [The Gemara draws an analogy from this to teach us:] Just as the term *tishmoru*, "keep," used in relation to *Shabbat* (6b) does not mean that you should be in awe of *Shabbat* but rather in awe of Him who ordered you to observe *Shabbat*; so also the word *tira'u*, "be in awe," used in connection with the sanctuary does not mean that you should be in awe of the sanctuary but rather that you should be in awe of Him who gave the commandment regarding the sanctuary, [and the *Bet Hamikdash* is the vehicle to inspire you with this awe].

[The Gemara asks:] How does "being in awe of the *Bet Hamikdash*" manifest itself? [The Gemara answers:] A person should not enter the Temple Mount with his walking stick, or wearing his shoes, or carrying his purse, or with dust on his feet; he should not use [the *Bet Hamikdash*] as a shortcut; and, of course, he should not spit there. I would think that all this applies only when the *Bet Hamikdash* was standing. How do I know that these prohibitions are in force even when the *Bet Hamikdash* is no longer standing? For it says, "Keep My Sabbaths, and be in awe of My sanctuary" (Leviticus 19:39)—just as the word *tishmoru*, "keep," as men-

tioned in connection with *Shabbat* goes on forever [even in exile], so, too, the *tira'u*, "being in awe," mentioned in connection with the *Bet Hamikdash* applies to the site of the *Bet Hamikdash* even when it is no longer standing.

BET HILLEL AND BET SHAMMAI DIFFER REGARDING *YIBBUM*

[The tractate *Yevamot* deals with the subject of *yibbum*, the obligation of a childless man's brother, the *yavam*, to marry his dead brother's wife, his *yevamah*. If the *yavam* does not wish to take his brother's wife, the *chalitzah* ceremony must be performed. The *yevamah* is then free to remarry. A brief outline of the basic laws of *yibbum* is given in Deuteronomy 25:3–10.]

[The Mishnah says: If the wife of the deceased brother was a forbidden relative of her brother-in-law[3]—for example, if she was his daughter—the brother-in-law cannot marry his daughter. Now, if the deceased had more than one wife,] Bet Shammai permits the *tzarah* [i.e., "co-wife"] to marry her brother-in-law through *yibbum*. But Bet Hillel forbids it. (13b) If the *tzarah* [co-wife] performs *chalitzah* [with the brother-in-law], Bet Shammai considers her ineligible to marry a *kohen* [since her *chalitzah* was legal, and any woman who performed a legal *chalitzah* is, like a divorced woman, forbidden to marry a *kohen*].[4] But Bet Hillel considers her to be eligible [to marry a *kohen*, because Bet Hillel holds that her *chalitzah* was uncalled for, since she was not allowed to marry her brother-in-law in the first place, and therefore the *chalitzah* was of no consequence].

If the *tzarah* [co-wife] married [through *yibbum*] her deceased husband's brother, [and he dies,] Bet Shammai declares her eligible to marry a *kohen* [because her *yibbum* marriage was legal]. But Bet Hillel declares her ineligible to marry a *kohen* [because, in Bet Hillel's view, her *yibbum* marriage was illegal, so that she is considered a harlot, and as such, forbidden to marry a *kohen*]. Although the one school prohibits what the other permits, and permits what the other prohibits, nevertheless, the students of Bet Shammai did not refrain from marrying women from the families of Bet Hillel; neither did Bet Hillel refrain from marrying women from the families of Bet Shammai. In the same way, differences of opinion regarding issues of ritual cleanness and uncleanness where one school declared clean what the other declared unclean [did not cause a rift between the students], for they never hesitated to borrow vessels from each other and use them to prepare food that was ritually clean.

(14b) The Mishnah wants to tell us that, in spite of their halachic differences, they loved and respected each other, as it says, "Only love truth and peace!" (Zechariah 8:19).

RABBI DOSA AND
THE THREE SAGES

(16a) In the days of R. Dosa b. Harkinas they permitted the tzarah [co-wife of a deceased husband who was married to his brother's daughter] to marry the yavam, her brother-in-law [through yibbum, in accordance with the ruling of Bet Shammai, mentioned above]. This was very upsetting to the Sages, [since they disagreed with this ruling but did not want to act against R. Dosa] because R. Dosa was a great scholar. [The Sages thought that he was the one who had made this ruling], and because of his blindness he had stopped coming to the bet midrash. The Sages said, "Who will go and discuss with R. Dosa [why he ruled like Bet Shammai]?" R. Yehoshua said, "I will go." "And who else will go?" "R. Elazar b. Azariah." "And who else?" "R. Akiva."

So [these three Sages] went and stood in front of R. Dosa's door. His maid entered and told R. Dosa, "Rabbi, the Sages of Israel have come to visit you." "Show them in," he said to her, and they entered. He grabbed hold of R. Yehoshua and offered him a seat on a golden couch. Said R. Yehoshua to R. Dosa, "Rabbi, won't you tell your other disciple to be seated too." "Who is he?" R. Dosa inquired. "R. Elazar b. Azariah." R. Dosa replied, "Does Azariah, our colleague, have a son?" He then applied to him the following verse, "I have been a youth and also aged; but I have not seen a righteous man forsaken, nor his children begging for bread" (Psalms 37:25). [I have been a youth—in Azariah's days; and also aged—in R. Elazar's days, but I have not seen a righteous man—Azariah—forsaken, nor his children—R. Elazar—begging for bread; because both father and son were very wealthy (Maharsha).] He then took hold of him and sat him down on a golden couch also. "Rabbi," said R. Yehoshua, "won't you tell the other disciple to sit down?" "And who is that?" "Akiva b. Yosef." Exclaimed R. Dosa, "Are you the Akiva b. Yosef whose fame has spread all over the world! Sit down, my son, sit down. May there be many like you in Israel."

They began to discuss with R. Dosa various issues of halachah until they got around to the topic of "the

tzarah of the daughter." They asked him, "What is halachah regarding the tzarah of a daughter?" [Is she allowed to marry the yavam, her brother-in-law, through yibbum?] Replied R. Dosa, "About this law there is a dispute between Bet Shammai and Bet Hillel." "And according to whose opinion is the halachah decided?" they asked. "The halachah is according to the opinion of Bet Hillel," R. Dosa answered. So they retorted, "But we heard that you said that the halachah is like Bet Shammai!"

Thereupon R. Dosa said, "Did you hear 'Dosa [permitted the tzarah]' or 'ben Harkinas'?" They replied, "By the life of our Rabbi, we heard it indefinite; without hearing which particular son of Harkinas had said it." "I have a younger brother named Yonatan," R. Dosa said to them, "who has a sharp mind [and who sticks to his opinion even if the majority is against him (Rashi)]. He is one of the disciples of Shammai, [and he is the one that ruled that the tzarah of a daughter is permitted to marry her brother-in-law through yibbum]. You should be careful that he should not overpower you when you discuss these halachot with him, for he has three hundred reasons why a tzarah of a daughter is permitted [to marry her brother-in-law through yibbum]. But I call heaven and earth as witnesses that on this mortar-shaped seat sat the prophet Haggai, and he pronounced the following three halachot: (1) The tzarah of a daughter is forbidden [to marry her brother-in-law, which proves that the halachah is like Bet Hillel]; (2) that Jews living in the lands of Ammon and Moab [east of the Jordan] should give the tithe of the poor in the Shemittah year [the Seventh Year of the cycle];[5] (3) that proselytes may be accepted from the Karduyim and the Tarmodiyim.

We learned in a Baraita: When the three Sages entered [R. Dosa's house] they all came in through the same door, but when they left they went out through three different doors [in order to spread out and find R. Dosa's brother, Yonatan (Tosafot)]. R. Akiva met Yonatan. Yonatan gave R. Akiva all his proofs [to the effect that a tzarah of a daughter should be permitted to marry her brother-in-law], and R. Akiva was unable to disprove him. Yonatan then exclaimed, "Are you the Akiva whose fame reaches from one end of the world to the other? You may consider yourself fortunate that you have achieved such a reputation, while in fact you have not reached the level of scholarship of a cow herder." R. Akiva humbly replied, "Not even that of a sheep herder!"

AMMON AND MOAB SEARCHED
FOR THE TORAH SCROLL

(16b) R. Shmuel b. Nachmani said in the name of R. Yochanan: What is meant by the verse, "The enemy spread out his hand on all her treasures" (Lamentations 1:10)?—This refers to Ammon and Moab. At the time when the heathens entered the *Bet Hamikdash*, all went after gold and silver, but Ammon and Moab went searching for the Torah scrolls. They said: The scroll where it is written, "An Ammonite and Moabite man may not enter God's congregation" (Deuteronomy 23:4) must be burned.

It says, "God commanded against Jacob that his enemies should surround him" (ibid., v. 17). Rav said: Like, for instance, Humania against Pum Nahara. [Both were towns in Babylonia, and Humania was inhabited by Greeks who constantly harassed the impoverished Jews of Pum Nahara.]

SANCTIFY YOURSELF
BY ABSTAINING FROM
PERMITTED THINGS

(20a) [The Mishnah mentioned a category of *yevamot* who are "forbidden to marry their *yavam* due to holiness." The Gemara explains: "Forbidden due to holiness" refers to the secondary degrees of relationships forbidden by rabbinical rulings.[6] [The Gemara asks:] And why are these restrictions characterized as "forbidden due to holiness"? Abaye explained: Because whoever lives up to the rulings of the Rabbis is called a holy man. Said Rava: According to your interpretation, then, whoever does not live up to the rulings of the Rabbis is merely not called a holy man, but you cannot call him wicked either! [But surely such a person *is* a wicked man!] Therefore, Rava explained: ["Forbidden due to holiness"] means: A person should sanctify himself by abstaining from things that are permitted. [And marriages that are forbidden by the Rabbis are termed "forbidden due to holiness" because they are preventive measures designed to keep a person away from contracting unions that are Biblically forbidden.]

CAUTIONARY RULES TO
PROTECT THE TORAH

(21a) Rava said: Where in the Torah do we find a hint regarding incestuous relations of the second degree?— It says, [in reference to incest,] "For all those [*ha'eil*] abominations were done by the people who were in the land before you, and the land became contaminated" (Leviticus 18:27). The expression *eil*, "those," denotes "grave" ["all those *grave* abominations"]; this implies that there are milder ones. And what are they? The cases of incest of the secondary degree. [The Gemara asks:] How do you know that *eil* denotes something grave?—Because it says, "And he took away the mighty [*eileih*] of the land" (Ezekiel 17:13).

Shall we say that this contradicts the opinion of R. Levi, for R. Levi said: The punishment for dishonest weights and measures is more severe than that for marrying forbidden relatives, for in the case of forbidden unions the Torah uses the term *eil*, and in the case

of the dishonest weights the term *eileh* is used. ["All who do this, [*eileh*], are an abomination to God your Lord"(Deuteronomy 25:16).] *Eil* denotes severity; *eileh* denotes greater severity. [The additional *eh* of *eileh* is seen as an indication of more severe punishment for false weights and measures.] [The Gemara asks:] But in connection with forbidden unions it also says *eileh*?[7] [The Gemara answers:] This *eileh* was written to exclude the sin of false weights from *karet* [the punishment of premature death].[8]

[The Gemara asks:] If forbidden relations are punishable by *karet*, [and false measures are not,] then in what way are false measures more severe than forbidden relations? [The Gemara answers:] In the case of incest it is possible to do *teshuvah* [as long as no child was born of the forbidden union, a person can do *teshuvah*], but for false measures he cannot do *teshuvah*. [Since he does not know whom he cheated, he cannot make restitution. And it is essential that restitution is made before he can do *teshuvah*.] Rav Yehudah said: [The prohibition of relations of the second degree] may be derived from here, "He [Solomon] listened and sought out, and arranged many proverbs" (Ecclesiastes 12:9).

Explaining this verse, Ulla said in the name of R. Elazar: Before Solomon's time, the Torah was like a basket without handles; when Solomon came, he attached handles to it, [to protect it from falling. In the same way, Solomon prohibited incest of the second degree as a cautionary rule to safeguard against transgression of the laws of the Torah itself]. R. Oshaia said: [the prohibition of incestuous relations of the second degree] may be derived from here, "Avoid it; do not pass through it; veer away from it and pass it by" (Proverbs 4:15). [The verse alludes to the Torah. We should add restrictions to it, like the prohibition of incestuous relations of the second degree, so as to avoid violations of the laws of the Torah itself.]

Said R. Ashi: R. Oshaiah's interpretation may be presented as an allegory of a man who guards an orchard. If he watches it from the outside, all of it is protected. If he watches it from the inside, the section in front of him is protected, but the section behind him is not protected. [The Gemara comments:] R. Ashi's analogy is inappropriate. In the case of the orchard, the section in front of him, at least, is protected; whereas here, if it were not for the prohibition of the incestuous relations of the second degree, a person would engage in incestuous relations forbidden by the Torah.

R. Kahana said: It may be derived from the last verse in [the chapter about incestuous relations,] "You shall safeguard My charge" (Leviticus 18:30)—meaning: Make a protection for My protection, [i.e., enact additional provisions to safeguard God's original commandments].

Said Abaye to R. Yosef: R. Kahane's verse [in Leviticus 18] surely is Torah law; [then why are these forbidden relations described as prohibitions of the second degree?]. R. Yosef answered: It is indeed Torah law, but the Rabbis have expounded it. [Countered Abaye:] Well, the entire Torah was expounded by the Rabbis, [and no one would characterize those laws as "second degree"]! But the fact is that the prohibitions [of incest of the second degree] were enacted by the Rabbis, and the verse quoted is used only as a slight allusion.

INTERPRETATION OF DEUTERONOMY 25:6

(24a) The Rabbis expounded the verse [defining yibbum], "It shall be the firstborn—if she can bear—shall succeed to the name of his dead brother; so that his name not be blotted out from Israel" (Deuteronomy 25:6). "It shall be the firstborn"—this tells us that the oldest brother [of the deceased husband] has the duty to marry the yevamah through yibbum. "If she can bear" excludes a woman who cannot bear children. "Shall succeed to the name of his dead brother"—with regard to inheritance. [The yavam who marries the yevamah is entitled to his deceased brother's] entire inheritance [and does not have to share it with his other brothers]. [The Gemara asks:] You say "with regard to inheritance," [taking the yavam as the subject of "shall succeed"]. Perhaps it means "with regard to the name" [and the subject of "shall succeed" is the firstborn child that will be born from the yibbum]? [For example, if the deceased was called] Yosef, the child should be named Yosef; if Yochanan, the child should be named Yochanan!

[The Gemara answers:] Here it says, "Shall succeed to the name of his dead brother," and elsewhere it says, [concerning Ephraim and Menashe,] "They will be included under the names of their brothers with regard to their inheritance"(Genesis 48:6). Just as the "name" that was mentioned there [in Genesis] has to do with inheritance, so, too, the "name" that is mentioned here has to do with inheritance. "So that his name not be blotted out"—this exempts from yibbum and chalitzah the wife of a eunuch, [since he cannot have children] his name is anyhow blotted out.

Rava said: Although throughout the Torah no verse ever loses its plain meaning, here we have a gezeirah shavah [the rule that similar words in different contexts are meant to clarify one another. In this case, the word "name"], that has entirely stripped the text of its plain meaning, [which is that the child should be named after the deceased father, yet the gezeirah shavah teaches us that this is not necessary].

SINCERE CONVERTS

(24b) R. Nechemiah used to say: "Lion-proselytes" [people like the Samaritans converted because "God let lions loose against them"],[9] and "dream-proselytes" [who converted on the advice of a dreamer], and the proselytes of Mordechai and Esther [i.e., people who converted out of fear][10] are not legitimate converts unless they become converted at the present time. [The Gemara asks:] How can you say "at the present time"? Say, "unless they become converted like [those who convert] at the present time," [when converts are motivated solely by sincere love of God and His Torah].

Our Rabbis taught: No converts will be accepted in the days of Mashiach, [when Israel will be prosperous and universally respected, and prospective converts may be motivated by selfish considerations]. In the same way, no converts were accepted in the times of David and Solomon [Israel's golden age]. R. Elazar said: What verse confirms this view?—"Behold, he will be a convert who is converted for My own sake; he who lives with you will be settled among you" (Isaiah 54:15)—only "he who lives with you" in your poverty [when you are in exile], will be settled among you, but no other [prospective converts].

THE PROSPECTIVE PROSELYTE

(47a) Our Rabbis taught: Nowadays, if a person wants to become a convert, we ask him: What is your reason for wanting to become a convert? Don't you know that the Jewish people at the present time are beset with afflictions, pushed around, oppressed, driven from place to place and tormented? If he replies: I know all that, and I feel unworthy [to join in their suffering. I only wish I could be part of it (Rashi)], he is accepted at once, and is made aware of some of the easier and of some of the more severe mitzvot. (47b) What is the reason?—So that if he decides to back out, let him do it now. For R. Chelbo said: Converts are as difficult for Israel as a sore [sapachas], because it says, "For God will show mercy to Jacob. He will choose Jacob again, and grant them rest on their land. The proselyte will join them and will be attached [venispechu] to the House of Jacob" (Isaiah 14:1), [venispechu is from the same root as sapachat].[11]

He is then made aware of the sin of neglecting the mitzvah of leket, shik'chah, pei'ah,[12] and the Tithe for the Poor. Why just these mitzvot? R. Chiya b. Abba replied in the name of R. Yochanan: Because a Noachide [i.e., a descendant of Noah] would rather be killed than spend so much as a perutah [a small coin] that is not returnable. [Therefore these mitzvot are the most difficult for him to accept.] He is then told about the punishment for transgressing the commandments. This is what he is told: You should realize that before you made the decision to convert, if you ate [cheilev,] forbidden fat, you would not be punished by karet [premature death]; if you desecrated Shabbat, you would not be punished by stoning. But now, if you eat cheilev, you will be punished by karet; if you desecrate Shabbat, you will be punished by stoning. Just as he is made aware of the punishment for the transgressions of the *mitzvot*, so is he informed of the reward for fulfilling the *mitzvot*. He is told: You should realize that the World to Come was made only for the righteous, and that Israel nowadays are unable to bear either too much prosperity [because they will be tempted to sin] or too much suffering. But you should not frighten him off too much, and you should not go into great detail about the *mitzvot*.

R. Elazar said: What verse corroborates this? It says, "When [Naomi, Ruth's mother-in-law,] saw that [Ruth] was determined to go with her [and convert to Judaism], she stopped arguing with her" (Ruth 1:18). [What was their debate?] Naomi told Ruth, "We are forbidden on *Shabbat* to walk beyond the *Shabbat* boundary." Ruth countered, "Where you go, I will go" (Ruth 1:16). "With us, it is forbidden for a man to be alone with a married woman!"—"Where you lodge, I will lodge" (ibid.). "We have been commanded six hundred and thirteen *mitzvot*!"—"Your people are my people" (ibid.). "We are forbidden to worship idols!"—"Your God is my God" (ibid.). "The Bet Din [Court] has four death penalties!"—"Where you die I will die." "The Bet Din has at its disposal two cemeteries [one for those who were executed by stoning or burning— for the gravest offenses; the other, for those executed by decapitation or strangulation—for lesser offenses]. "And there I will be buried," was Ruth's answer. Right away, "Naomi realized that Ruth was determined to go with her, she stopped arguing with her" (Ruth 1:18).

WOMEN CAPTIVES

(48a) [During a war, a soldier, inflamed by the passion of battle, may be attracted to a woman prisoner. In order to cool his ardor, the Torah ordains that she must shave her head, let her nails grow, and weep for her father and mother for a full month to make her look less pleasing. After that, if he still wants her, and after she converts to Judaism, he may marry her (Deuteronomy 21:10–14)].

We learned in a *Baraita*: It says, "She must let her nails grow" [literally "make her nails"] (Deuteronomy 21:12). [What does "make her nails" mean?] R. Eliezer said: She should cut them. R. Akiva said: She should let them grow.

We learned in a *Baraita*: It says, "She should weep for her father and her mother" (48b) (ibid. 21:13). Rabbi Eliezer said: "her father and her mother" means her actual father and mother. R. Akiva said: "Her father and her mother" refer to idolatry, for so it says, "They say to the wood, 'You are my father,'" (Jeremiah 2:27).

THE PROPHET ISAIAH
AND KING HEZEKIAH

[Explanatory note: The righteous King Hezekiah of Judah did not get married because he saw in a vision that he would have corrupt children. Isaiah chided him that he had no right meddling in God's affairs, and that, as a result of failing to fulfill the command to multiply, he would become sick and die. When he became deathly ill he prayed fervently to God and was told by Isaiah that fifteen years had been added to his life. Hezekiah then married Isaiah's daughter, and they had a son, Menashe, who was thoroughly depraved and even killed his grandfather Isaiah. In the end Menashe did *teshuvah* (2 Kings 20:1–6, *Berachot* 10a).]

(49b) We learned: R. Shimon b. Azzai said: I found a scroll in Jerusalem in which the lineage of families was recorded, and in it was written, "So-and-so is a *mamzer*, an offspring of a married woman's adulterous union." There was also written in that scroll, "The teaching of R. Eliezer b. Yaakov is small but pure," [i.e., it is mentioned infrequently, but wherever it is mentioned the *halachah* is according to him (Rashi)]. It also said there: "[King] Menashe killed [the prophet] Isaiah [who was his grandfather]." [Menashe was angered by Isaiah's prophecy of the impending destruction of Jerusalem.] Rava said: [Menashe] put Isaiah on trial [on the trumped-up charge of being a false prophet] and then had him executed. [Menashe] said to [Isaiah]: Your teacher Moses said, "A man cannot see Me and still exist" (Exodus 33:20), yet you say, "I saw the Lord sitting upon a high and lofty throne" (Isaiah 6:1). Your teacher Moses said, "What nation is so great that they have a God close to it, as God our Lord is, whenever we call Him?" (Deuteronomy 4:7), and you say, "Seek God when He can be found, call upon Him when He is near" (Isaiah 55:6); [so He is not always accessible.]

Moses your teacher said, "I will make you live out full lives," (Exodus 23:26), yet you said [to my father Hezekiah], "Thus said God . . . I am going to add fifteen years to your life" (Isaiah 38:5); [if his time is up, there can be no additional years]. Isaiah then said to himself, "I know that no matter what I tell him, Menashe will not accept it; and if I did answer, [and he executes me,] he would be guilty of willful murder. [Now, at least he thinks that he was justified in sentencing me to death.] So Isaiah uttered the Divine Name and was swallowed up by a cedar tree. They brought in the cedar and began to saw it. When the saw reached Isaiah's mouth, he died. [This was his punishment] for speaking about Israel in disparaging terms, saying, [not on God's orders, but in exasperation], "I dwell among a people with impure lips" (Isaiah 6:5).

[The Gemara asks:] But what about the contradictory verses [about which Menashe questioned Isaiah]? [The Gemara answers:] [The fact that Isaiah said,] "I saw the Lord" (Isaiah 6:1) can be explained by the following *Baraita*: All the prophets looked through a dim glass [and thought they saw Divinity, but they did not], but Moses looked through a clear glass [and understood that he could not see God]. Regarding

[Isaiah's exhortation,] "Seek God when He can be found" (Isaiah 55:6), this verse applies to an individual [for whom there are special times when God is more accessible]; the other verse (Deuteronomy 4:7), [which implies that God is accessible all the time], applies to communal prayer. [The Gemara asks:] When is the special time for an individual? R. Nachman replied in the name of Rabbah b. Abuha: During the ten days between Rosh Hashanah and Yom Kippur.

With regard to, "I will make you live out full lives" (Exodus 23:26); [how could Hezekiah be given fifteen additional years, when his time was up?]. There is a disagreement among Tanna'im. For we learned in a *Baraita*: R. Akiva expounded: "I will make you live out full lives," (50a) refers to the number of years a person is allotted at birth. If he deserves it, he is allowed to live out those years. If he is unworthy, some of those years are taken away. But the Sages said: If he deserves it, years are added to his life, ["full lives" means additional years]; if he is unworthy, his lifespan is shortened. They said to R. Akiva: [You say, it is impossible to add to the allotted years,] but it says, "I am going to *add* fifteen years to your [Hezekiah's] life!" [implying an addition to the allotted years]. Replied R. Akiva: This means that the years that were deducted from Hezekiah's lifespan were given back to him. I will prove to you [that these fifteen years were allotted to him when he was born], because a prophet foretold [in the days of Jeroboam, many generations earlier,] "Behold, a son will be born to the House of David, Josiah will be his name" (1 Kings 13:2). Now, Menashe [Josiah's grandfather] was not yet born [when his father Hezekiah became terminally ill and was informed that he would live for another fifteen years. So the original years allotted to Hezekiah at his birth extended past the year of his illness to include the year of Menashe's birth], and the fifteen years that were added were the ones that had been taken away earlier.

And what about the Rabbis? [How do they explain that additional *new* years were added to Hezekiah's life? They will answer:] Does it then say, [The prophet said,] "A son will be born to Hezekiah"? No, it says, "A son will be born to the House of David" (1 Kings 13:2). This son [Josiah] could be born from Hezekiah and from someone else [of the House of David].

MARTHA BRIBED THE KING

(61a) [We learned in the Mishnah:] It happened that Yehoshua b. Gamla [who was a *kohen*] betrothed [the widow] Martha, the daughter of Baitus, and was appointed by the King as *Kohen Gadol*. [A *Kohen Gadol* is not allowed to marry a widow.] He married her, [because a *kohen* who betrothed a widow and afterward was appointed *Kohen Gadol* is allowed to consummate the marriage].

[The Gemara notes:] [Yehoshua b. Gamla] was "appointed" as *Kohen Gadol* [by the King], [the im-plication being,] but not with the consent of all the other *kohanim*. R. Yosef said: I see a conspiracy here, for R. Assi said: Martha the daughter of Baitus brought a large basket full of *dinarim* [as a bribe] to King Yannai before he appointed [her husband] Yehoshua b. Gamla as the *Kohen Gadol*.

R. Nachman said in the name of Shmuel: Although a man may have many children [and has fulfilled the command of "be fruitful and multiply,"] he should not remain without a wife, for it says, "It is not good for man to be alone" (Genesis 2:18).

THREE THINGS MOSES DID ON HIS OWN

(62a) The Rabbis taught: Three things Moses did on his own initiative, and his decision conformed with God's intention: He separated from his wife, he broke the Tablets [when he came down from Mount Sinai and saw the people worshipping the golden calf],[13] and he added one day [to the days of preparation for the Receiving of the Torah].[14]

"He separated from his wife"—what was his reasoning? He said: We find that the *Shechinah* spoke to the children of Israel only one time, and God set a specific time [when He would speak to them], yet the Torah says [to them], "Do not come near a woman" (Exodus 19:15). I, to whom God may speak at any given time, and there is no fixed time [when God will speak to me], how much more so that I should separate from my wife. And his decision conformed with God's will, for it says, [after the Giving of the Torah, God said to Moses], "Go tell them to return to their tents.[15] You, however, must remain here with Me" (Deuteronomy 5:27,28).

"He broke the Tablets"—what was his reasoning? He said: We find in connection with the *korban Pesach* [the Paschal lamb], which is only one of the 613 commandments, that the Torah says, "No person who has defected from Judaism may eat it" (Exodus 12:43). How much more should this apply to the entire Torah when all Israel have turned away from God [and worshipped the golden calf. Consequently, he broke the Tablets]. And this conformed to God's will, for it says, [God said to Moses concerning the Tablets] ". . . that you broke, [*asher shibbarta*]" (Exodus 34:1), and Resh Lakish understood [the word *asher* to mean that God said to Moses:] *yiyasheir kochacha*, "I thank you for breaking them." [Proof that God agreed with Moses' decision to break the Tablets.]

"He added one day on his own initiative [to the preparation to the Giving of the Torah]"—what was his reasoning? God told Moses, "Sanctify them today and tomorrow" (Exodus 19:10) [which implies] that "today" and "tomorrow" must have the same characteristics. Just as "tomorrow" includes the previous night,[16] so "today" must also include the previous night. But since today's previous night is already gone,

Moshe understood that [when God said "today" He meant] two days besides "today." [Hence, there would be three days of preparation, and on the fourth day would be the Giving of the Torah.] We see that God agreed with him, for the *Shechinah* did not come down on Mount Sinai until *Shabbat* [which was the fourth day, after three days of preparation.][17]

R. AKIVA'S 24,000 STUDENTS

(62b) We learned in a *Baraita*: R. Yehoshua said: If a person got married while he was young, he should marry again when he gets older. Even though he had children while he was young, he should continue having children even as he grows older. For it says, "In the morning sow your seed, and in the evening do not be idle, for you never know which is going to succeed—the one or the other—or if both are equally good" (Ecclesiastes 11:6). R. Akiva said: If a person learned Torah while he was young, he should continue learning Torah even as he grows older; if he had students when he was young, he should make sure to have new students when he gets older. For it says, "In the morning sow your seed . . ."

It was said that R. Akiva had twelve thousand pairs of students who came from [all over the country], from Gevat all the way to Antiparas. All of them died in one season because they did not treat each other with respect. As a result, the world was desolate [for lack of Torah learning], until R. Akiva came to the Rabbis in the south and taught them the Torah [and created a new chain in the transmission of the Torah]. They were R. Meir, R. Yehudah, R. Yose, R. Shimon, and R. Elazar b. Shamua, and they were the ones who restored the Torah at that [critical] time. We learned: All of R. Akiva's students died between Pesach and Shavuot.[18] R. Chama b. Abba—some say, R. Chiya b. Avin—said: All died a painful death. What did they die from? R. Nachman replied: From the croup.

THE BLESSINGS OF MARRIED LIFE

R. Tanchum said in the name of R. Chanila'i: Any man who does not have a wife is living without happiness, without blessing, and without goodness. "Without happiness," for it says [concerning Yom Tov], "and rejoice with your household" (Deuteronomy 14:26), [and *bayit*, "house," means your wife]. "Without blessing," for it says, "to bring a blessing to rest upon your house [i.e., through your wife]" (Ezekiel 44:30). "Without goodness," for it says, "It is not good for man to be alone" (Genesis 2:18). In Eretz Yisrael they used to say: [An unmarried man] is without Torah and without a protective wall [against sin]. "Without Torah," for it says, "If I would not have a wife, my help [i.e., the Torah] is taken away from me" (Job 6:13). [Meaning, if I have to do the household chores,

I will have no time to learn Torah and will forget all I learned (Rashi).] "He is considered without a protective wall [against sin]" for it says, "Woman surrounds [and protects] her husband" (Jeremiah 31:21). Rabba b. Ulla said: [An unmarried man is] without peace, for it says, "You will know that your tent is at peace, and you will visit your home and find nothing amiss" (Job 5:24). [Meaning, you will be at peace if you have a tent, i.e., a wife (Rashi).]

LOVE AND HONOR YOUR WIFE

Our Rabbis taught: If a person loves his wife as he loves himself, and honors her more than he honors himself, and raises his sons and daughters on the right path and marries them off close to the age of maturity, about such a person Scripture says, "You will know that your tent is at peace" (Job 5:24). A person who loves his neighbors, and one who is close to relatives, and one who marries his sister's daughter, (63a) and one who lends a *sela* to a poor man in his time of need, about such a person Scripture says, "Then you will call, and God will respond; you will cry out and He will say, 'Here I am'" (Isaiah 58:9).

R. Elazar said: Any man who does not have a wife is not considered a man, for it says, "He created them male and female . . . and named them Man [*Adam*]" (Genesis 5:2). [Only when man was united with woman were they called *Adam*, man.]

R. Elazar further said: Any man who does not own land is not considered a man. [According to the Maharsha, this refers to a person who does not have a place to live], for it says, "As for the heavens, the heavens are God's; but the earth He has given to man" (Psalms 115:6).

R. Elazar further said: What is meant by the passage, [God said,] "I will make a compatible [*kenegdo*] helper for him" (Genesis 2:18)? [*Kenegdo* can mean also "against." How can she be his helper and, at the same time, be against him?]—If he merits it, his wife is a help to him; if he does not merit it, she opposes him.

Others say: R. Elazar pointed out a contradiction: It is written *kenegdo*, which means "opposite, but in support of him," but we can read it *kenigdo*, which means, "castigating and striking."—If a person merits it, his wife will be a support for him; if he does not merit it, she will end up striking him.

R. Yose met Elijah and asked him: It says, "I will make a helper for him." In what way does a wife help her husband?[19] Replied Elijah: If a man brings wheat, does he chew the wheat? [His wife grinds and bakes it for him.] If he brings flax, can he wear the flax? [His wife changes the flax into a garment.] Doesn't this prove that a wife brightens her husband's eyes and puts him on his feet?

R. Elazar further said: What is meant by the verse, [When God brought Eve to Adam,] "Adam said, 'Now this is bone from my bones and flesh from my flesh'"

(Genesis 2:23). ["Now" implies] that Adam lived with every animal, but he was not satisfied until he lived with Eve, [and then he said: "Now, this time . . ."].

R. Elazar further said: What is the meaning of the verse, God told Abraham, "All the families of the earth will be blessed [venivrechu] through you" (Genesis 12:3)? [R. Elazar sees venivrechu as derived from the same root as lehavrich, "to graft," and he explains the verse to mean,] "The Holy One, blessed be He, said to Abraham, 'I have two shoots [non-Jews] that I would like to graft onto you: Ruth the Moabitess [the forebear of King David] and Naamah the Ammonitess [a convert who was the mother of King Rechavam and the forebear of the righteous King Hezekiah].'" "All the families of the earth"—even families that live anywhere in the world receive blessing only for Israel's sake. "Through him [Abraham] all the nations of the world will be blessed" (Genesis 18:18)—even the ships that sail from Gaul to Spain are blessed only for Israel's sake.

BUSINESS OR FARMING?

R. Elazar further said: In the future, all craftsmen will become farmers, for it says, "All who grasp an oar, rowers and all sailors of the sea will come down from their ships and stand on the ground [and turn to farming]" (Ezekiel 27:29).

R. Elazar further said: There is no occupation that is worse than farming, for it says, [in the above verse,] "They will come *down*." R. Elazar once saw a field that was ploughed to its width.[20] R. Elazar told the farmer: [No matter what you do,] even if you ploughed it lengthwise, it is still more profitable to engage in business. Rav was passing between fields of grain. When he saw the ears waving in the wind, he exclaimed: No matter how [proudly] you sway, engaging in business brings more profit than you can produce.

Rava said: If you have one hundred *zuz* invested in business, you have meat and wine every day, but if the hundred *zuz* are invested in land, all you have is salt and unripe vegetables. What's more, [when you own a farm] you'll have to sleep on the ground all night [to protect your crops], and you'll become involved in fights [with your neighbors].

R. Papa said: You should plant crops [for your own family's needs], and don't buy [grain in the market], even if the cost is the same; there is a blessing in the crops you raise yourself. Sell your possessions, [and do business with the proceeds] rather than fall into poverty. But sell only furnishings, but don't sell your clothes, because you might not find just what you need. If you find a small hole in the wall, stop it up right away, so that you won't have to do a major repair job. [If it is too late to stop up the hole,] repair it, so that you won't have to demolish the wall and rebuild it, for whoever gets involved in construction becomes poor.

BE CAREFUL WHEN CHOOSING A WIFE

Be quick when it comes to buying land, but be slow and careful when it comes to choosing a wife. It is better to marry a woman who is below you on the social ladder, [rather than a woman who has a higher social status, because she may look down on you]. However, you should go up a step in choosing your *shoshvin*, [a friend to be your best man, so that you should follow his example].

Rav was once taking leave of R. Chiya, when R. Chiya said to him: May the Merciful One deliver you from a fate that is worse than death. [Rav said to himself:] But is there anything worse than death? He went out and thought about it. He then found the verse, "Now I find the woman [with a bad character] more bitter than death" (Ecclesiastes 7:26). [So R. Chiya's blessing was that Rav should not end up with a wife who had a bad character.]

HE MARRIED A SHREW

Rav's wife used to torment him constantly. If he told her, "Prepare me lentils," she would prepare him beans. If he asked her for beans, she prepared him lentils. When his son Chiya grew up, he used to switch his father's instructions [so his mother mistakenly would prepare exactly what Rav wanted]. "Your mother has improved," Rav remarked to his son. Replied the son, "I switched your orders." So Rav told him, "Now I understand what people say, 'You can learn something from your son.'" [Rav had never thought of this ploy.] "But you should not continue to do this, because it says, "They train their tongue to speak falsehood, striving to be iniquitous" (Jeremiah 9:4).

R. Chiya's wife nagged and pestered him constantly. Nevertheless, whenever he found a suitable present for her he would wrap it in a cloth and bring it to her. Said Rav to him, "But look how she is annoying you!" R. Chiya replied, "It is enough that our wives raise our children, and they save us (63b) from sinful [thoughts]."

Rav Yehudah was teaching his son R. Yitzchak the passage, "I find the woman more bitter than death." R. Yitzchak asked: "Like who, for example?" "Like your mother," he replied. [The Gemara asks:] But on a different occasion R. Yehudah taught his son R. Yitzchak, "A person finds true contentment only with his first wife, for it says, 'Your source will be blessed, and you will rejoice with the wife of your youth'" (Proverbs 5:18), and when his son asked him, "Like who, for example?" he answered, "Like your mother." [There seems to be a contradiction between the two ways R. Yehudah described his wife.] [The Gemara answers:] She was a cantankerous woman, but she could easily be appeased with a kind word.

[The Gemara asks:] What is an example of a bad wife? Said Abaye: A woman who prepares a tray [of food for her husband] and also has her mouth ready [to torment him]. Rava said: A woman who prepares a tray for him and then turns her back on him [and does not join him].

R. Chama b. Chanina said: When a man marries a woman, his sins are wiped out [mitpakekin],[21] for it says, "He who has found a wife has found goodness, and obtains [vayafeik] favor from God" (Proverbs 18:23). [mitpakekin is considered as having the same meaning as vayafeik, and is translated, "he obtains from God the burying of his sins."]

THE GOOD AND THE BAD WIFE

In Eretz Yisrael they used to ask a man who had married, "Matza or motzei?" By matza they meant: Does the verse "He who has found [matza] a wife has found goodness" apply to you? By motzei they meant: Or does the verse, "I find [motzei] the woman more bitter than death" apply to you? [In other words, does your wife have a good or a bad character?]

Rava said: It is a mitzvah to divorce a bad[22] wife, for it says, "Drive away the scoffer and strife will depart, and arguments and shame will come to an end" (Proverbs 22:10). Rava further said: If a person has a bad wife, but the amount of her ketubah [the amount the husband has to pay if he divorces her] is very large, and he cannot afford it], then he should marry another wife, [and the competition will cause his first wife to improve]. As people say: A co-wife [is more effective in correcting a bad wife] than [punishing her with] a thorn. Rava further said: A bad wife is as bad as a stormy day, for it says, "An annoying dripping on a stormy day and a quarrelsome wife are alike" (Proverbs 27:15).

Rava further said: Come and see how precious is a good wife and how troublesome is a bad wife. How precious is a good wife, because it says, "He who has found a wife has found goodness" (ibid. 18:23). If we take this verse literally, we see how precious is a good wife that the passage praises her. And if this passage refers to the Torah, [we can say,] how precious is a good wife, that the Torah is compared to her. How evil is a bad wife, for it says, "I find the woman [with a bad character] more bitter than death" (Ecclesiastes 7:26). If we take this passage literally, then we can say: How evil is a bad wife, that the verse despises her; and if the verse refers to Gehinnom, then we can say: How evil is a bad wife that Gehinnom is compared to her!

It says, "Behold, I bring against them an evil from which they will not be able to escape" (Jeremiah 11:11). R. Nachman said in the name of Rabbah b. Abuha: [A man who is married to] a bad wife, the amount of whose ketubah is very large [so that he cannot afford to divorce her] finds himself in the situation described in this verse.

It says, "The Lord has delivered me into the hands of those I cannot withstand" (Lamentations 1:14). R.

Chisda said in the name of Mar Ukva b. Chiya: [A man who is married to] a bad wife, the amount of whose ketubah is very large, is caught in a similar situation. In Eretz Yisrael they said: [An example of this verse is] a person who has no land of his own, [and whose food supply is dependent on fluctuating market prices of grain and produce over which he has no control].

A DEGRADED NATION

It says, "Your sons and daughters will be given to a foreign nation" (Deuteronomy 28:32). R. Chanan b. Rava said in the name of Rav: This refers to the father's wife [a stepmother]. "I will provoke them with a degraded nation" (ibid. 32:21). R. Chanan b. Rava said: An example of that is a bad wife the amount of whose ketubah is very large. R. Elazar (Eliezer) said: "A degraded nation" refers to the Sadducees.[23] For so it says, "The degraded one says in his heart, 'There is no God'" (Psalms 14:1). We learned in a Baraita: "A degraded nation" refers to the people of Barbaria and Martena'i who go naked in the streets; for there is nothing more despicable in the eyes of God than a person who walks around naked in the streets. R. Yochanan said: This phrase refers to the Parsees, [evil Persians who humiliated and persecuted the Jews (Rashi)].

When they told R. Yochanan that these Parsees had come to Babylonia, he staggered from fright and fainted. But when he was told that they accept bribes [to annul a ruling] he recovered and sat up. The Parsees proclaimed three decrees against the Jews: They prohibited the consumption of kosher meat; this was the Divine punishment because people neglected to give the priestly gifts.[24] They prohibited the use of public bathhouses; this was the Divine punishment because people neglected the laws of immersing in a mikveh. They dug up the bodies from their graves; this was the Divine punishment because people were rejoicing on the pagan festivals, as it says, "The hand of God will be against you and your parents" (1 Samuel 12:15). [How can the parents be punished if they are already dead?] Said Rabbah b. Shmuel: The punishment is that their graves are dug up. For the Master said: Because of the sins of the living the dead are dug out of their graves.

Rava said to Rabbah b. Mari: It says, "They will not be gathered together nor buried; they will be like dung upon the face of the earth" (Jeremiah 8:2). And it also says, "Yet death will be preferable to life" (ibid. v.3). [If their bodies are not buried, how can death be preferable to life?] He replied: It would be better for the wicked to die rather than live in this world and sin and, as a result, fall into Gehinnom.

SAYINGS FROM THE BOOK OF BEN SIRAH

It is written in the Book of Ben Sirah: A good wife is a precious gift to her husband; she will be put in the bosom of a God-fearing man. A bad wife is a plague for her husband. What is the remedy for such a person? He should divorce her and be cured from his plague. A beautiful wife is her husband's delight; [he feels as if] the days of his life are doubled. Turn away your eyes from a pretty woman, lest you get trapped in her net. Do not go to her husband to drink wine and beer with him, because through the looks of a pretty woman many were destroyed, and strong ones were killed because of her. Many were the wounds of the peddler [who sells perfume to women], and who is tempted to behave indecently [and is beaten by the husband]; like a spark ignites the coal [so does his evil impulse incite him to sin]. As a cage is full of birds, so are the houses [of the harlots] full of treachery (Jeremiah 5:27). Do not worry about tomorrow's trouble, for you never know what the day will bring. Maybe by the time tomorrow arrives you won't be here anymore, and you worried about a world that was not yours. Keep away many people from your house, and do not bring everyone into your house. Many people should seek your welfare, but reveal your secret only to one of a thousand.

A JEW HAS TO GET MARRIED

R. Assi said: *Mashiach* will not come before all the souls are removed from the *Guf* [the place in Heaven that holds the souls of the unborn people], for it says, "The souls will keep *Mashiach* from coming, and the souls that I have made [are a prerequisite for the coming of *Mashiach*]" (Isaiah 57:16).[25]

We learned in a *Baraita*: R. Eliezer said: Any Jew who does not get married [and have children] is considered as if he spills blood. For it says, "He who spills human blood shall have his own blood spilled by man" (Genesis 9:6), and the next verse says, "Now be fruitful and multiply." R. Yaakov said: It is as though he diminished the Divine image, for it says, "For God made man in His own image" (ibid.), and immediately after that it says, "Now be fruitful and multiply."

Ben Azzai said: It is as though he [both] spills blood and diminished the Divine image; for it says, "Now be fruitful and multiply." They said to Ben Azzai: There are some people who make beautiful speeches and their deeds reflect the speeches they made. Others act admirably but do not make eloquent speeches. You, Ben Azzai, however, you gave an eloquent speech [about the sin of not having children,] but you don't act accordingly; [you did not get married, and you do not have children]. Ben Azzai replied: What shall I do, since my soul is passionately in love with the Torah, and the world can be populated through others.

THE MITZVAH OF "BE FRUITFUL AND MULTIPLY"

Our Rabbis taught: It says, "When [the Ark] came to rest, [Moses] said, 'Reside tranquilly, O God, among the ten thousands of Israel's thousands'" (Numbers 10:36). **(64a)** This teaches us that the *Shechinah* does not rest on less than [a group of] twenty-two thousand Jews.[26] Suppose Israel comprised twenty-two thousand less one person, and one individual did not get married, does he not [by the fact that he did not have a child] push away the *Shechinah* from Israel [for he could bring the twenty-thousandth into the world]! Abba Chanan said in the name of R. Eliezer: He deserves the death penalty, for it says, [Nadab and Abihu died,] "and they had no children" (Numbers 3:4). From this we can infer that if they had had children they would not have died. Others say that such a person causes the *Shechinah* to leave Israel, for it says, [God promised Abraham,] "I will be a God to you and to your offspring after you" (Genesis 17:7). I.e., as long as there is offspring, there is a place for the *Shechinah* to rest; but if there is no offspring, on whom should the *Shechinah* rest? On wood and stones?

CHILDLESSNESS

We learned in a *Baraita*: If a person married a woman and lived with her for ten years, and she did not give birth to a child, he must divorce her and give her her *ketubah*,[27] since it is possible that it is he who did not merit to have children from this woman. Although we cannot bring an explicit proof from the Torah for this law of waiting ten years, we can find a hint for it. It says, "After Abram had lived in Canaan for ten years, [he took Hagar as a wife, since he did not have children from Sarah]" (Genesis 16:3). [The explicit wording "lived in Canaan"] teaches you that the time that Abram had spent outside of Eretz Yisrael does not count toward the ten years, [since living outside Eretz Yisrael is considered a sin, we assume that this caused his infertility]. Therefore, [if we can attribute the infertility to something else,] we can say that it is not part of the ten years. Thus, if the husband or the wife were sick, or if both were in prison [and living together], the years of sickness or the time spent in prison are not counted toward the ten years.

WHY WERE OUR PATRIACHS BARREN?

R. Yitzchak said: Our father Isaac was incapable of having children, for it says, "Isaac pleaded with God opposite [*lenochach*] his wife [because they did not have children]" (Genesis 25:21). It does not say, "concerning [*al*] his wife" but "opposite [*lenochach*] his wife." From here we see that both [Isaac and Rebeccah] were barren [and both Isaac and Rebeccah prayed to be healed from their own condition.] [The Gemara asks:] If so, instead of, "God granted his plea" (ibid.) it should say, "God granted their plea." The Gemara answers:] Because the prayer of a *tzaddik* [Isaac] who is the son of a *tzaddik* [Abraham] is not like the prayer of a *tzaddik* who is the son of a wicked man. [Rebeccah's father, Bethuel, was a wicked man.]

R. Yitzchak further said: Why were our forefathers incapable of having children? Because the Holy One, blessed be He, desires to hear the prayer of the righteous. R. Yitzchak further said: Why is the prayer of the righteous compared to a pitchfork? [The word *vayetar*, "he pleaded," in the above passage is from the same root as *atar*, "pitchfork."] Just as a pitchfork turns over the grain and moves it about from one place to another, so does the prayer of the righteous change the attributes of the Holy One, blessed be He, from anger to mercy.

R. Ammi said: Abraham and Sarah both were *tumtum* [a person whose male or female organs are covered up], for it says, "Look to the rock (64b) from which you were hewn [a reference to someone whose male organ was formed (Rashi)], and to the hollow of the pit from which you were dug" [i.e., the female organ that was formed] (Isaiah 51:1). This is followed immediately by, "Look to Abraham your forefather and to Sarah who bore you." [Proof that the verse referring to male and female organs being formed applies to Abraham and Sarah.]

R. Nachman in the name of Rabbah b. Abuha said: Our mother Sarah had a physical deformity that prevented her from having children, for it says, "Sarai was barren; she had no child" (Genesis 11:30). [Why the redundant "she had no child"?]—She did not even have a womb.

During the days of David, the lifespan of a generation was reduced, for it says, "The days of our years among them are seventy years" (Psalms 90:10).

THE MITZVAH TO HAVE CHILDREN

(65b) [The Mishnah says:] A man has the obligation to fulfill the mitzvah to have children, but not a woman. R. Yochanan b. Beroka [disagreed and] said: It says about both the man and the woman, "God blessed them. God said to them, 'Be fertile and become many'" (Genesis 1:28); [both have the duty to have children].

[The Gemara asks:] From what verse is it derived [that only the man, and not the woman, has the duty to procreate]? R. Ila'i in the name of R. Elazar b. Shimon replied: From the verse, "Fill the earth and conquer it [*vechivshuha*]" (ibid.); it is the nature of a man to conquer, but it is not the nature of a woman to conquer. [The Gemara disputes this:] On the contrary! The word *vechivshuha*, "and conquer it," is addressed to both the man and the woman.[28] R. Nachman b. Yitzchak said: It is written *veshivshah*, "And you [the man, (in the singular)] shall conquer it." R. Yosef said: It can be derived from here, [God said to Jacob,] "I am God Almighty. Be fruitful and increase [*pereih ureveih*, in the singular]" (Genesis 35:11), and it does not say *peru urevu*, [in the plural].

PEACE IS A GREAT THING

R. Ila'i said in the name of R. Elazar b. Shimon: Just as it is a mitzvah for a person to admonish only when he will be obeyed,[29] so is it a mitzvah not to admonish when he will not be obeyed. R. Abba said: It is wrong [to admonish when you will not be obeyed], for it says, "Do not rebuke a scoffer, lest he hate you; rebuke a wise man, and he will love you" (Proverbs 9:8).

R. Ila'i further said in the name of R. Elazar b. R. Shimon: You are allowed to stretch the truth for the sake of peace, for it says, [The brothers instructed messengers to tell Joseph,] "Before he died, your father gave us final instructions. He said, 'This is what you must say to Joseph: Forgive the spiteful deed and the sin your brothers committed'" (Genesis 50:16,17). [Jacob never gave such instructions. The brothers invented the statement for the sake of preserving the peace between themselves and Joseph.] R. Natan said: It is a mitzvah [to tell a white lie for the sake of peace], for it says, [When God told Samuel to anoint David as king, "Samuel asked: How can I go? If Saul finds out he will kill me" (1 Samuel 16:2), [whereupon God told him to claim that he had come to bring an offering to God].

At the yeshivah of R. Yishmael they taught: Peace is a great thing, for even the Holy One, praised be He, modified [Sarah's statement]; for initially it says: [Doubting that she could have a child, Sarah said,] "My husband is old!" (Genesis 18:12), while afterward, [when God told Abraham about Sarah's doubt, He changed her statement of, "My husband is old," which Abraham might resent, to,] "I am old," [in the interest of preserving domestic peace].

WAS DAVID'S LINEAGE QUESTIONABLE?

(76b) [The Mishnah says:] A [male convert from] Ammon and Moab is not allowed [to marry a Jewish woman],[30] and this prohibition is forever, [meaning, all his descendants are equally forbidden], but their women are permitted immediately [after conversion to marry a Jew].

[The Gemara asks:] From where do we derive [that the women are permitted immediately]? R. Yochanan replied: From the verse, "When Saul saw David going out to attack the Philistine [Goliath], he asked his army commander Abner, 'Whose son is that boy, Abner?' And Abner replied, 'By your life, Your Majesty, I do not know'" (1 Samuel 17:55). [The Gemara asks:] Did Saul not know who David was? Doesn't it say [earlier], "[Saul] took a strong liking to him, and made him one of his arms-bearers" (ibid. 16:21)! Shall we say that Saul was asking who his father was? Do you mean to say that he did not know David's father? But it says, "In the days of Saul the man was old, and would come among people" (ibid. 17:12), and Rav, and some say, R. Abba, said: This refers to Jesse, David's father, who came in and went out with the army; [he was a commander of 600,000 soldiers (Rashi)].

[The Gemara says:] Saul wanted to know whether David was a descendant of Peretz or of Zerach [the sons of Yehudah and Tamar].[31] If he decended from Peretz he would be king, because a king breaks [poretz, a play on the name Peretz] someone else's fence [to clear a way for himself], and no one can stand in his way. However, if he is a descendant of Zerach, he would only be an important person. [The Gemara asks:] What prompted Saul to make inquiries about David's ancestry? [The Gemara answers:] Because it says, [When David went forth to fight Goliath,] "Saul clothed David in his own battle garments [madav]" (ibid. v. 38), and madav means that Saul was the same size [middah] as David. And about Saul it says, "From his shoulder up he was taller than any of the people" (ibid. 9:2). Saul wondered: What does the fact that my clothes fit him portend? Surely he is destined to become the king, [and if he is a descendant of Peretz he would indeed be a king].

Doeg the Edomite then said to Saul: Instead of asking whether David is fit to be a king or not, ask whether or not he is allowed to enter the assembly of Israel. Why should he be disqualified? Because he is a descendant of Ruth the Moabitess. [And the Torah says: No Ammonite or Moabite shall be admitted into the assembly of God" (Deuteronomy 23:4).] Said Abner: We learned: "An Ammonite" [is forbidden], but not an Amonitess; "a Moabite" [is forbidden], but not a Moabitess. [Therefore, Ruth the Moabitess was allowed to marry Boaz, and David's lineage, which reaches back to Ruth, is unblemished.] [Said Doeg:] If this is so, [that the masculine form of a word excludes the women], in the case of a mamzer [the offspring of adultery or incest[32] who is not allowed to marry a Jew] we should also exclude a female mamzer? [Abner answered:] The word mamzer means mum zar, "a strange blemish" [anyone—male or female—who has that blemish is forbidden].

[Doeg asked:] Then we should say that the law, "Do not despise an Egyptian" applies only to an Egyptian, man, but not an to an Egyptian woman?[33] [Abner answered:] Here [in the case of Ammonites and Moabites] it is different, because the Torah gives the reason [for the restriction], "Because they did not greet you with bread and water when you were on the way out of Egypt" (ibid. v. 5). It is the custom for men to greet [wayfarers] with bread and water, but it is not the custom for women to greet them, [for it is immodest, and that is why the women were excluded from the prohibition]. [Doeg said:] The men should have greeted the men, and the women the women! Abner remained silent, [unable to refute this argument]. Thereupon King Saul said [to Abner], "Go find out whose son is this lad" (1 Samuel 17:56).

Why is it that in the previous verse (v. 55) Saul calls David na'ar, "boy," and here he calls him elem, "lad"?

[Elem also means "hidden."] This is what Saul implied: You [Abner] have overlooked a halachah, [it was hidden (elem) from you]. Go and ask in the bet midrash [whether a Moabite woman is allowed to marry a Jew, and then we will know whether or not David is acceptable]. Abner asked the question and was told: "An Ammonite," but not an Ammonite woman; "a Moabite," but not a Moabite woman (Deuteronomy 23:4). (77a) Doeg then raised all the objections [that he had asked to Abner], and the Bet Din too remained silent [and, like Abner, had no answer].

They then wanted to announce publicly that [since David was a descendant of Ruth the Moabitess] he was unfit to enter the assembly of God. Immediately, [an incident happened]: "Amasa was the son of a man named Ithra the Israelite who consorted with Abigail daughter of Nahash" (2 Samuel 17:25). But elsewhere it says, "Abigail bore Amasa; the father of Amasa was Jether the Ishmaelite" (1 Chronicles 2:17). [Why is he called both Ithra the Isaelite and Jether the Ishmaelite?] Rava explained: This teaches us that he girded his sword like an Ishmaelite and exclaimed: Whoever does not obey this halachah shall be stabbed with this sword. I have this tradition from the Bet Din of Samuel of Ramataim [the prophet Samuel]: An Ammonite, but not an Ammonite woman; a Moabite but not a Moabite woman. [And therefore, David's ancestry is flawless.] [The Gemara asks:] But could Jether the Ishmaelite be trusted? Has not Rabbi Abba said in the name of Rav: If a Torah scholar teaches a halachah before a question involving that halachah comes up, then we listen to him; but if not, we don't listen to him. [If a question has arisen, and then he claims to have a tradition from his teachers, we don't give him credence.] [The Gemara answers:] Here the case is different, because Samuel and his bet din were still alive, [therefore, Jether would not make an untrue statement, knowing that it could easily be verified].

However, Doeg's question still remains unanswered, [the question that the Ammonite and Moabite women should have greeted the women of Israel with bread and water, and since they did not, the prohibition should apply to them as well]. [The Gemara answers:] Here [in Babylonia] they explained it with the verse, "The honor of a princess is to stay inside" (Psalms 45:14). [A woman should stay indoors. This gave them a valid excuse for not going out to greet the women of Israel. In Eretz Yisrael they said—others say, R. Yitzchak said: It says, "[The three angels in disguise] asked [Abraham], 'Where is your wife Sarah?' 'Here in the tent,' he replied" (Genesis 18:9), [because a woman's place is in the tent. And that is why the Ammonite and Moabite women did not go out to greet the women of Israel].

Rava expounded: What is meant by the passage, "You have released my bonds" (Psalms 116:16)? David said to the Holy One, blessed be He: Master of the universe! [By permitting Ammonite and Moabite women to enter the assembly of Israel] you released me from two bonds [i.e., two women in my ancestry] that tied me down: Ruth the Moabitess[34] and Naamah the Ammonitess, [the wife of Solomon and mother of Rehoboam, the grandson of David].

Rava expounded: What is the meaning of the verse, "Much have You done, O You, Lord, my God, Your wonders and Your thoughts are for us" (Psalms 40:6)? It does not say "for *me*" but "for *us*." This teaches us that Rehoboam was sitting on David's lap when David said to him: Those two verses refer to us. [The verses, "The honor of a princess is to stay inside" and "Where is your wife Sarah" were the justification for permitting Ammonite and Moabite women to marry Jews.]

Rava expounded: What is meant by the passage, "Then I said: 'Behold I have come!' with the Scroll of the Book that is written for me" (Psalms 40:8)? David said [when he was anointed king]: I thought that I came to my kingship only now, and I did not realize that the Scroll of the Book [i.e., the Torah] writes about me. For there it says: [the angels said to Lot, "Take your wife and your two daughters] *who are found!*" (Genesis 19:15). [Lot's two daughters are the mothers of Ammon and Moab,[35] and David descends from Ruth the Moabitess.] And here it says, "I have *found* David My servant; with My holy oil I have anointed him" (Psalms 89:21). [The word "found" occurring both in Genesis 19:15 and in Psalms 89:21 connects the two verses.]

DAVID'S DECREE AGAINST THE GIBEONITES

(78b) R. Chana b. Adda said: David issued the decree forbidding *netinim* [i.e., Gibeonites] to intermarry with Jews, as it says, "So the king [David] called the Gibeonites and spoke to them.—Now the Gibeonites were not of the children of Israel" (2 Samuel 21:2).[36] [The Gemara asks:] Why did David issue this decree against them? [The Gemara answers:] Because it says, "In the days of David there was [once] a famine for three years, year after year" (ibid. v. 1). In the first year David said to the people: Perhaps [the drought has come] because there are idol worshippers among you, for it says, ". . . and you worship other gods, bowing down to them. God's anger will then be directed against you, and He will lock up the skies so that there will be no rain" Deuteronomy 11:16,17). They searched, but they did not find any idol worshippers. In the second year he said: Perhaps there are among you people who are guilty of immorality, for it says, "The raindrops have been withheld, and the late rain did not happen, yet you had the boldness of a harlot woman" (Jeremiah 3:3). They searched, but did not find any transgressors. In the third year he said to them: Perhaps there are people among you who publicly pledge to donate to charity, but do not give it, for it

says, "[Like] clouds and wind without rain, [so is] one who lauds himself for a false gift" (Proverbs 25:14). They searched but did not find any.

David then said: This must hinge entirely on myself. Immediately, "David inquired of God" (2 Samuel 21:1). What does that mean? Resh Lakish said: He asked the Urim and Tummim.[37] How is this implied? R. Elazar replied: We infer it through an analogy of two places where the word *penei* occurs. It says here, "David inquired [*penei*] of God" and elsewhere it says, "He shall seek the decision of the Urim before [*lifnei*] God" (Numbers 27:21). [Since *penei* and *lifnei* have the same root, we conclude that, "David inquired [*penei*] of God" means asking through the Urim and Tummim.] "And God answered [David], '[The famine] is on account of Saul and his bloody house, because he killed the Gibeonites'" (2 Samuel 21:1). [The verse gives two reasons:] "On account of Saul"—because he was not eulogized properly; "and his bloody house, because he killed the Gibeonites)."—[The Gemara asks:] Where do we find that Saul killed the Gibeonites! [Scripture does not mention any such thing!]—The truth is, that since Saul killed the inhabitants of Nob, the city of *kohanim*[38] who were supplying the Gibeonites with water and food, [leaving them without a livelihood], Scripture considers it as if he had killed the Gibeonites.

[The Gemara asks:] On the one hand God is exacting a punishment because Saul was not eulogized properly, and on the other hand He exacts a punishment because Saul killed the Gibeonites? [A punishment for Saul's good deeds and his bad deeds. Isn't this a contradiction?] Yes, this is so, for Resh Lakish said: What is the meaning of the verse, "Seek God, all you humble of the land who have fulfilled His law [*mishpato paalu*]" (Zephaniah 2:3)?—At the same place where a person is judged [*mishpato*] for his bad deeds, his good deeds [*pa'alo*] are remembered.

David said: [How can we rectify these two failings?] As for Saul, (79a) twelve months have already gone by, and it is not customary to make a funeral address any longer.[39] But regarding the *netinim* [Gibeonites], let us call them and appease them [for the wrong that was done to them]. Immediately, "the king called the Gibeonites and spoke to them . . . 'What can I do for you, and how can I atone for [this sin], so that you will bless the heritage of God, [and pray that the drought will end?' The Gibeonites replied, 'We have no claim of silver or gold against Saul nor against his house, and we have no [innocent] man in Israel to put to death.' . . . 'Let seven men of [Saul's] sons be delivered to us and we will hang them up for the sake of God'" (2 Samuel 21:2–6). David tried to appease them, but they would not be pacified. David then said: There are three characteristics by which the nation of Israel is known: Jews are merciful, modest, and benevolent. "Merciful," for it says, "He will give you mercy, and be merciful to you and multiply you" (Deuteronomy 13:18). "Modest," for it says, "So that awe of Him shall be upon your faces" (Exodus 20:17). "Benevolent," for it says, "So that he [Abraham] will command his children and his household after him, and they will keep God's way, doing charity and justice" (Genesis 18:19). Whoever has these three characteristics is fit to be part of the Jewish people; whoever does not have these qualities is not fit to join the Jewish people. [Since the Gibeonites showed themselves to be merciless and cruel, David decreed that they are forbidden to intermarry with the Jewish people.]

[The Gemara continues with this theme:] "So the king [David] took the two sons of Rizpah daughter of Aiah, whom she bore to Saul—Armoni and Mephibosheth—and the five sons of Michal daughter of Saul, whom she bore to Adriel son of Barzilai the Meholathite" (2 Samuel 21:8). Why these seven? R. Huna said: They passed [all the sons and grandsons of Saul] before the Holy Ark. Whomever the Ark seized was meant to die, and whomever the Ark allowed to go on was meant to be left alive.

R. Huna b. Kattina raised an objection: [If it was decided through the Ark,] how is it that it says, "The king had pity on Mephibosheth son of Jonathan son of Saul" (ibid. v. 7)? [The Gemara answers:] He did not make him pass at all before the Ark. [The Gemara asks:] Was David allowed to show favoritism [in a case involving the death penalty]? [The Gemara answers:] He did pass him before the Ark, and the Ark actually did seize him, but David prayed for him, and the Ark let him go. [Asks the Gemara:] Nevertheless, there still is favoritism involved! [If the Ark seized Mephibosheth, and David released him, someone else would be killed in his place.] Rather, David prayed that the Ark should not seize him.

[The Gemara asks:] But it says, "Fathers shall not be put to death because of their sons, and sons shall not be put to death because of their fathers" (Deuteronomy 24:16)! [Why then were Saul's descendants killed for the sin of Saul?] R. Chiya b. Abba said in the name of R. Yochanan: [Legally this was not right,] but it is better that one letter [i.e., the above law] in the Torah should be eliminated, than that the name of God should be desecrated publicly, [because the nations of the world would say that the Jews do not have high moral standards, since these Gibeonite converts were wronged, and no one avenged them (Rashi)].

[The Gemara continues:] "Rizpah daughter of Aiah [the mother whose two sons were hanged] took a sackcloth and spread it for herself over a rock, from the beginning of the harvest until rain fell down on from heaven [on the corpses]; she did not allow the birds of the heaven to descend upon them during the day, nor the beasts of the field during the night" (2 Samuel 21:10). [Thus they remained on the gallows for several months.] [The Gemara asks:] But it says, "You may not allow his body to remain on the gallows overnight" (Deuteronomy 21:23)! R. Yochanan answered in the name of R. Shimon b. Yehotzadak: It is better

that one letter [i.e., the above law] in the Torah should be eliminated, and the name of God should be sanctified in public. Because the passers-by would say, "Who are these people [hanging on the gallows]?" And they would be told, "These are royal princes." "And what have they done?" "They acted unfairly against self-made converts." [The Gibeonites deceived Joshua into accepting them as converts.] The passers-by then said, "There is no other nation in the world that is more fitting to join than Israel. For if this is the punishment meted out to princes for their injustice, how much greater would commoners be punished for injustice. And if they are punished like that for harming self-made converts, then all the more so will they be punished for doing harm to regular converts."

Immediately, one hundred and fifty thousand converts joined Israel, for it says, "Solomon had seventy thousand who carried burdens, and eighty thousand who hewed in the mountains, [and these were all converts]" 2 Kings 5:29). Perhaps these workers were native-born Jews? That is not logical, for it says, "But Solomon did not enslave anyone of the children of Israel" (ibid. 9:22). [The Gemara asks:] Perhaps these [150,000 men were no slaves] but hired native-born Jewish workers? [How do you know that they were slaves and converts?] Rather we infer it from here, "Solomon counted all the converts who lived in the Land of Israel . . . and they were found to be one hundred fifty-three thousand six hundred. He made seventy thousand of them [carriers of] burden and eighty thousand of them hewers in the mountain" (2 Chronicles 2:16,17).

[The Gemara returns to the above statement by R. Chana b. Adda that it was David who issued the decree forbidding the *netinim* (Gibeonites) to intermarry with Jews.]

[The Gemara asks:] Was it David who made the decree against the *netinim*? Surely Moses issued that decree, for it says, "from woodchopper to waterdrawer" (Deuteronomy 29:10). [By singling out woodchoppers and waterdrawers, Moses indicated that these groups are not considered as full-fledged converts, but rather as slaves, and as such forbidden to intermarry with Jews. Since Joshua made the Gibeonites woodchoppers and waterdrawers, we know from Moses' precedent that they are forbidden to intermarry with Jews (Rashi).] [The Gemara answers:] Moses issued the decree only for his generation, whereas David decreed it for all generations, [that Gibeonites are forbidden in perpetuity]. [The Gemara asks:] But wasn't it Joshua who made the decree against them? For it says, "That day Joshua made them woodchoppers and waterdrawers for the assembly and for the Altar of God" (Joshua 9:27). [Thus Joshua gave them the status of slaves, and slaves are forbidden marry Jews.] [The Gemara answers:] Joshua issued this decree for as long as the *Bet Hamikdash* was standing, whereas David made the decree [that they should retain this status] even when there is no longer a *Bet Hamikdash*.

WHY WAS THE TITHE TAKEN AWAY FROM THE LEVITES?

(86a) We learned in a *Baraita*: *Terumah*[40] belongs to the *kohen*, and the first tithe belongs to the Levite, so said R. Akiva. R. Elazar b. Azariah said: (86b) [The first tithe] belongs to the *kohen*. [The Gemara asks, surprised:] He says: It belongs to the *kohen*. Does he mean to say: Only to the *kohen*, but not to the Levite? [The Gemara answers:] Say: The first tithe belongs *also* to the *kohen*. [The Gemara asks:] What is R. Akiva's reason [for saying that the tithe belongs to the Levites]? Because it says [with reference to the first tithe], "Speak to the Levites and say to them" (Numbers 18:26); thus the passage clearly speaks about Levites. But what about R. Elazar b. Azariah? [How does he explain this passage?] He holds as does R. Yehoshua b. Levi. For R. Yehoshua b. Levi said: In twenty-four places in Scripture *kohanim* are called Levites, and the following is one of them, "But the *kohanim* the Levites the descendants of Zadok" (Ezekiel 44:15). [Zadok was a *kohen*, yet his descendants are called Levites.]

There was a certain garden from which R. Elazar b. Azariah [who was a *kohen*,][41] used to receive the first tithe. R. Akiva went and moved its entrance so that it faced a cemetery, [to prevent R. Elazar b. Azariah from entering the garden].[42] R. Elazar b. Azariah remarked: Akiva has his shepherd's bag, [where a shepherd keeps his food for the day],[43] but I [need the tithe] for my livelihood!

It was said: Why were the Levites punished [by Ezra][44] in that the first tithe was taken away from them [and given to the *kohanim*]? R. Yonatan and Savya [disagree on this point]. One holds: because they did not come up with Ezra [in the return to Eretz Yisrael from the Babylonian exile]. The other holds: In order that the *kohanim* could rely on the tithe during their uncleanness [when they are not allowed to eat *terumah*]. And from where do we know that the Levites did not go up to Eretz Yisrael in the time of Ezra?—For it says, "I assembled them at the flowing river, at the Ahava, and we encamped there for three days. I then reviewed the people and the *kohanim*, but I could find no Levites there" (Ezra 8:15).

R. Chisda said: Initially, officers were appointed from the Levites only, for it says, "And the Levite officers are before you" (2 Chronicles 19:11); but nowadays, officers are appointed from the Israelites only, for it says: and officers over you shall come from the majority,[45] [and there are more Israelites than Levites].

THE RIGHT OF EMINENT DOMAIN[46]

(89b) R. Yitzchak said: From where in Scripture do we know that the Bet Din is empowered to declare someone's property *hefker*, "ownerless"? For it says, "Anyone that failed to come within three days, in accordance with the counsel of the officers and the el-ders, all his property would be destroyed, and he would be isolated from the congregation of the exile" (Ezra 10:8). R. Elazar stated that the inference [that the Bet Din has the power to declare someone's property *hefker*] is drawn from, "These are the heritages that Elazar the *Kohen* and Joshua son of Nun, and the heads of the fathers' houses of the tribes of the children of Israel apportioned for inheritance" (Joshua 19:51). Now, what do "heads" have to do with "fathers"? [It could simply have said: "the heads of the tribes."] This comes to teach us that just as fathers may leave to their children whatever they wish, so, too, may the heads [of the Bet Din] distribute to the people whatever they wish.

ELIJAH ON MOUNT CARMEL

(90b) Come and learn: It says, "It is to him [the prophet] that you must listen" (Deuteronomy 18:15)—even if he tells you to transgress one of the commandments of the Torah; for example, in the case of Elijah on Mount Carmel [where he brought a sacrifice on a *bamah*, a makeshift altar, while it was forbidden to offer sacrifices outside the *Bet Hamikdash* on pain of *karet*, premature death], obey him in every respect in accordance with the needs of the hour! [So you see that a prophet—and the Rabbis—can set aside a law of the Torah.] [The Gemara answers:] A prophet is different [from the Rabbis], for about a prophet it says, "It is *to him* that you must listen." [The Gemara suggests:] So let us derive [Rabbinic law] from it! [The Gemara answers:] A protective measure is different; [here an exception may be made. By bringing the sacrifice, Elijah turned the people away from idolatry and caused them to worship God].[47]

SHELTERING A RUNAWAY SLAVE

(93b) We learned in a *Baraita*: It says, "If a slave seeks refuge with you from his master, you must not turn him back over to his master" (Deuteronomy 23:16). Rabbi explained: The passage deals with a man who bought a slave on the condition that he would set him free, [a slave like that may not be turned over to his master, but must be set free]. What are the circumstances of this case? R. Nachman b. Yitzchak said: In the case where the buyer gave [the slave] a written declaration, stating: As soon as I buy you, your person will become yours, as of now.

HE DID NOT GIVE CREDIT TO THE AUTHOR

(96b) R. Elazar came and related a *halachah* in the *bet midrash*, but did not report it in the name of R. Yochanan [who originally said it]. When R. Yochanan heard it, he was upset. So R. Ammi and R. Assi went over to him and, [trying to placate him] they said, "[Why are you so upset?] Don't you remember what happened at the synagogue in Tiberias when R. Elazar and R. Yose had a debate about a door bolt that had a knob on one end, [arguing about whether it is *muktzeh*[48] or not], and the discussion became so heated that they ripped a Torah scroll in anger?" [The Gemara asks:] Can we assume that Tanna'im should rip a Torah scroll! Say: A Torah scroll was ripped [accidentally] in the excitement. R. Yose b. Kisma who was present at that incident said, "I would be surprised if this synagogue will not turn into a house of idol worship!" And that is what happened. [By reminding R. Yochanan of the dreadful consequences of unbridled emotions, they tried to appease him.] When they told him this, he became even angrier and exclaimed, "Are you turning my students into my colleagues?" [R. Elazar and R. Yose had no right to fight, but I am angry because my student does not show proper respect for me.]

R. Yaakov b. Idi then came in and [used a different approach to mollify R. Yochanan, quoting the verse:] "As God had commanded Moses His servant, so Moses commanded Joshua; and so Joshua did. He did not omit a thing of all that God had commanded Moses" (Joshua 11:15). Could it be that each time Joshua said something [to the children of Israel], he told them, "This is what Moses told me"? But this is what happened: Joshua was sitting and expounding without mentioning names, and everyone understood that it was the Torah of Moses. The same is true of your disciple R. Elazar; he lectures without mentioning names, but everyone knows that it comes from you. Thereupon R. Yochanan reproached [R. Ammi and R. Assi], "Why don't you know how to placate like our friend, the son of Idi, does?"

[The Gemara asks:] Why was R. Yochanan angry in the first place? Because R. Yehudah said in the name of Rav: What is the meaning of the verse, "May I dwell in Your tent forever [*olamim*]" (Psalms 61:5). [*Olamim* literally means "worlds."] Is it possible for a person to live in two worlds? This is what David said to the Holy One, blessed be He: Master of the universe! May it be Your will (97a) that my teachings be taught in my name in this world, [thereby I will be living in this world and in the World to Come]. For R. Yochanan said in the name of R. Shimon b. Yocha'i: When a [deceased] Torah scholar's teachings are taught in his name in this world, his lips move softly in the grave. R. Yitzchak b. Ze'ira—others say, R. Shimon Nezira—said: On what verse is this based? [On the verse,] "Your mouth like the choicest wine, let it flow smoothly for my Beloved, moving softly the lips of those that are asleep" (Song of Songs 7:10) —like a heated mass of grapes. Just as a heated mass of grapes begins to ooze as soon as a person puts his finger on it, so it is with Torah scholars. When someone repeats a teaching in their name, their lips begin to move softly in the grave.

THE PROPHET JONAH

(98a) "The word of God came to Jonah a second time, saying" (Jonah 3:1). [R. Akiva comments:] The *Shechinah* spoke only a second time to him, but not a third time. But it says, "He [Jeroboam son of Jehoash] restored the boundary of Israel from the approach of Hamath until the Sea of Arabah, like the word of the Lord, God of Israel, which he had spoken by the hand of His servant Jonah son of Amitai the prophet" (2 Kings 14:25). [So you see, He spoke to Jonah a third time!] Ravina replied: [R. Akiva meant to say] that the *Shechinah* spoke to Jonah only twice concerning Nineveh. R. Nachman b. Yitzchak said: The verse means to say, "Like the word of the Lord . . . which He had spoken by the hand of His servant . . . the prophet"—just as the destiny of Nineveh was changed from bad to good, so was the destiny of Israel in the days of Jeroboam son of Jehoash changed from bad to good, [for the next verse reads, "For God had seen that Israel's suffering was very severe . . . so he saved them . . ."].

THE FAVORS OF THE WICKED ARE BAD FOR THE RIGHTEOUS

(103a) R. Yochanan said: That wicked man [Sisera, the general of the Canaanite army] had sexual relations seven times [with the virtuous Jael][49] on the day [he fled from Deborah and Barak].[50] For it says, "At her feet he knelt, he fell, he lay. At her feet he knelt, he fell; where he knelt, there he fell, vanquished" (Judges 5:27).[51] [The Gemara asks:] But surely [Jael] derived pleasure from the sin! R. Yochanan said in the name of R. Shimon b. Yocha'i: All the favors of the wicked (103b) are bad for the righteous. For it says, [God said to Laban,] "Be careful not to say anything, good or bad, to Jacob" (Genesis 31:24). Now it is perfectly understandable that [God warned Laban not to say] anything "bad," but why not "good"? We can learn from this that the favors of the wicked are bad for the righteous.

[The Gemara challenges:] I can well understand [that God warned Laban not even to say anything good], because Laban might mention the name of his idol; but here [in the incident with Jael] what bad outcome could result from it? [The Gemara answers:] Because he instilled sensual passion in her. For R. Yochanan said: When the Serpent had intercourse with Eve [after she ate of the forbidden fruit] he instilled sensuality in her. When the children of Israel stood at Mount Sinai [and received the Torah] their sensuality ended; the sensuality of the idol worshippers who did not stand at Mount Sinai never ended.

A HEAVENLY DECREE CAN BE OVERTURNED

(105a) It says, [the angel Gabriel[52] said to Daniel,] "However I will tell you what is inscribed [as a Heav-

enly decree] in truthful writing" (Daniel 10:21)—
[The Gemara asks:] Is there then [in Heaven] a writing that is not truthful? [The Gemara answers:] This is not difficult to explain. The "truthful writing" refers to a Divine decree that was accompanied by an oath, [this can never be revoked]; but a decree that was not accompanied by an oath can be revoked [through *teshuvah*]. As R. Shmuel b. Ammi said in the name of R. Yonatan: From where do we know that a Heavenly decree that is accompanied by an oath cannot be cancelled? Because it says, "Therefore I have sworn concerning the house of Eli that the sin of the house of Eli[53] would never be atoned for by sacrifice or meal offering," (1 Samuel 3:14). Rabbah explained: It will not be atoned for "by sacrifice or meal offering," but it will be atoned for by the words of the Torah [i.e., if the descendants of Eli study the Torah]. Abbaye expounded: It will not be atoned for "by sacrifice or meal offering," but it will be atoned for by acts of kindness.

[The Gemara explains why Rabbah and Abbaye were seeing this verse in a positive light.] Rabbah and Abbaye were both descendants of the house of Eli. Rabbah, who busied himself with studying the Torah, lived for forty years, but Abbaye, who both studied the Torah and performed acts of kindness, lived sixty years.

We learned in a *Baraita*: There was a certain family in Jerusalem whose members died when they reached the age of eighteen. They went to R. Yochanan b. Zakkai and told him about it. He said: Maybe you are descendants of the family of Eli about whom it says, [Because of the sin of the sons of Eli,] "All those raised in your house will die as [young] men" (1 Samuel 2:33). Go and occupy yourselves with the study of the Torah, and you will live. They went and studied Torah, and they lived longer lives. [Because of that,] they were called "the Yochanan family," after his name.

R. Shmuel b. Unya in the name of Rav: How do we know that a Divine decree against a community is never sealed [and can always be revoked]? [The Gemara asks:] You mean to say, it is never sealed? But it says, "Even if you were to wash with niter and use much soap, your iniquity has become an indelible stain before Me" (Jeremiah 2:22). But [the question R. Shmuel asked is this:] From where do we know that even if the decree was sealed, it can be torn up? [The Gemara answers:] For it says, ". . . as God our Lord is, whenever we call Him" (Deuteronomy 4:7) [implying, God is always accessible; even after the decree is sealed He will tear it up]. [Asks the Gemara:] But it says, "Seek God when He can be found" (Isaiah 5:6) [implying that God is accessible only at certain times]? [The Gemara answers:] This is no contradiction: The verse in Isaiah pertains to an individual who prays to God; the verse in Deuteronomy applies to a community that prays together, [then God is accessible at all times]. [The Gemara asks:] And when [is God most accessible] to an individual? R. Nachman replied in the name of

Rabbah b. Abuha: In the ten days between Rosh Hashanah and Yom Kippur.

HE OFFENDED R. YISHMAEL B. R. YOSE

(105b) R. Chiya and R. Shimon b. Rabbi were sitting and learning together, when one of them began to expound: When a person is praying [now that the *Bet Hamikdash* is destroyed] he should direct his eyes toward the *Bet Hamikdash*, for it says, "My eyes and My heart shall be there forever" (1 Kings 9:3). The other said: He should direct his heart upward [toward heaven], for it says, "Let us lift our hearts with our hands to God in heaven" (Lamentations 3:41). As they were speaking, R. Yishmael b. R. Yose came into the *bet midrash*. "What is the subject of your discussion?" he asked. "The subject of prayer," they replied. He said, "This is what my father R. Yose said: When you are praying, you should direct your eyes toward the the site of the *Bet Hamikdash* below, and your heart toward heaven above. Thereby both verses are fulfilled." While this conversation was going on, Rebbi entered the *bet midrash* [to give a lecture]. [Since R. Chiya and R. Shimon b. Rebbi] were of slight build, they quickly sat in their seats, [since during Rebbi's lecture everyone was required to sit in his place on the floor]. But R. Yishmael b. R. Yose, being obese, could only move to his seat with slow steps, [inconveniencing the students already seated]. "Who is this person that walks above the heads of the holy people" exclaimed Avdan [a disciple of Rebbi].[54] He replied, "I am Yishmael b. R. Yose, and I have come to learn Torah from Rebbi." "Are you worthy to learn Torah from Rebbi?" Avdan said. "Was Moses then worthy to learn Torah from the Almighty?" R. Yishmael retorted. "Are you Moses!" Avdan shot back. "Is then your teacher God?" R. Yishmael retorted. R. Yose commented, "Rebbi got what was coming to him when R. Yishmael, responding to Avdan, [called Rebbi 'your teacher' and not 'my teacher.'" [Rebbi deserved this slight for failing to come to the defense of R. Yishmael when Avdan offended him.]

In the meantime, a [young] *yevamah*[55] came before Rebbi [to have a *chalitzah* performed]. Rebbi said to Avdan, "Go out and have her examined [by women] to ascertain if she has the marks of adulthood that qualify her for *chalitzah*. After Avdan left, R. Yishmael said to Rebbi, "This is what my father R. Yose said: [In the Torah chapter on *chalitzah*] it says the word "man,"[56] [meaning, the Torah requires the *yavam* (brother-in-law) to be an adult], but as for the *yevamah*, regardless whether she is an adult or a minor, the *chalitzah* is valid. "Come back!" Rebbi called out to Avdan. "There is no need [for an examination to determine whether she is an adult], because the elder Torah scholar, R. Yose, ruled [that the *chalitzah* of a minor is valid]."

Avdan then tried to go back to his place in the *bet midrash* [and, in the process, pushed his way through the students sitting on the floor]. [Seeing this,] R. Yishmael b. R. Yosi said, "The one who is needed by the holy people may step over the heads of the holy people, but how dare one [such as you] who is not needed by the holy people step over the heads of the holy people!" Thereupon Rabbi rebuked Avdan, "Stay where you are! [Do not move forward to your seat."]

It was taught: At that moment Avdan became leprous, his two sons drowned, and his two daughters-in-law made a declaration of *mi'un*[57] [so that he lost them too]. Said R. Nachman b. Yitzchak: Blessed is the Merciful One, for putting Avdan to shame in this world [thereby cleansing him of his offense against Rabbi Yishmael, and enabling him to enter the World to Come free of sin].

WISE COUNSEL

(109a) Bar Kappara taught: A person should cling to three things and stay away from three things. The three things he should cling to are: *Chalitzah*,[58] making peace among people, and the annulment of vows.

"He should perform *chalitzah* [rather than *yibbum*]," because of what Abba Shaul said. For we learned in a *Baraita*: Abba Shaul said: If a *yavam* marries his *yevamah* because of her beauty, or in order to gratify his desire, or for any other ulterior motive, [rather than for the mitzvah of *yibbum*], it is as though he violated the law of incest, [it is as though he were marrying his brother's wife, which is forbidden].[59] And it seems to me that a child of such a union is a *mamzer* [a child born of an incestuous or adulterous union].

"Making peace among people," because it says, "Seek peace and pursue it" (Psalms 34:15). (109b) And R. Abbahu said that we infer it through the analogy of the word "pursuit" [how great the reward is for making peace among people]. Here it says, "Seek peace and *pursue* it," and elsewhere it says, "One who *pursues* righteousness and kindness will find life, righteousness, and honor" (Proverbs 21:21).

"The annulment of vows," in accordance with R. Natan, for we learned: R. Natan says: If someone makes a vow, it is as if he had built a *bamah* [a high place (altar), after such altars were forbidden].[60] [And if he does not have the vow anulled] but fulfills it, it is as though he offered a sacrifice on the *bamah*; [thus he is comitting two sins (Rashi)].

[Bar Kappara said that a person] should stay away from the following three things: From *mi'un*,[61] from taking deposits from people, and from acting as a co-signer for a loan.

"From *mi'un*," because she might have second thoughts when she grows up; [the emotions of a minor girl are not stable].

"From taking deposits from people" applies to deposits made by people of your own town, who are com-

fortable walking into your house without knocking; [the concern is that they may take back the deposited article, forget it, and demand it again].

"From acting as a co-signer for a loan." This refers to a Shaltzion kind of co-signer. [Shaltzion was a place where debts were collected, not from the borrower, but straight from the co-signer (Rashi).] For R. Yitzchak said: What is meant by the verse, "One will be utterly broken by co-signing for a stranger, but a hater of handshakes will be secure" (Proverbs 11:15)?—Evil upon evil will befall those who accept converts, and those who are a Shaltzion kind of co-signers, and those that stick to the study of *halachah* [but do not practice it].

"[Evil will befall] those who accept converts" is derived from a saying by R. Chelbo, for R. Chelbo said: Converts are as difficult for Israel as a sore on the skin.[62]

"[Evil will befall] those who are Shaltzion kind of co-signers," because in Shaltzion they disregard the creditor and go straight to the co-signer [to collect the debt].

"[Evil will befall those] that stick to the study of *halachah*," for we learned in a *Baraita*: R. Yose said: Anyone that says: I will not study the Torah, will not get the reward of the study of the Torah. Isn't that obvious? What it means is: Anyone that says: I will concentrate only on the study of Torah, [but I will not observe its laws] gets only the reward of studying the Torah. This too is obvious! It means that he does not even get the reward for the study of the Torah. What is the reason? R. Papa said: It says, "Learn them so that you will be able to keep them" (Deuteronomy 5:1). If the intent of his learning is to be able to fulfill the *mitzvot*, he gets the reward for learning Torah; but if he has no intention of carrying out the *mitzvot*, his learning is not considered learning at all. And if you wish I can explain it as we said at the outset: Anyone that says: I only want to study the Torah, but I will not do the *mitzvot*, all he gets is the reward for Torah study [and no reward for doing the *mitzvot*]. You asked: Isn't that obvious?—[The answer is:] We are talking about someone who teaches others, and the others *are* keeping the *mitzvot*. I would have thought that he also gets a reward [for fulfilling *mitzvot*] because he is causing others to keep the *mitzvot*, therefore [R. Yose] informs us that he does not. And if you wish I may say that the phrase "anyone that sticks to the study of *halachah*" applies to a judge before whom a lawsuit is brought, and he knows of a *halachah*, and thinks [based on his own judgment] that this *halachah* is comparable to the case at hand, and although he has a teacher, he does not consult him [to make sure that his opinion is correct. He is the one that is criticized in the statement, "evil will befall one that sticks to the study of *halachah*"].

R. Shmuel b. Nachmani said in the name of R. Yonatan: A judge should always view himself as if a sword were lying between his thighs, and as if

Gehinnom were open beneath him, as it says, "There is Solomon's couch, [i e , God's *Bet Hamikdash,*] encircled by sixty warriors of the warriors of Israel [i.e., the judges of Israel, who worry] . . . because of the terror by night [i.e., because of the terror of Gehinnom, which is like "the night"] (Song of Songs 3:7,8).

ANY MARRIAGE IS BETTER THAN BEING SINGLE

Ravina asked Rava: What is the law if a husband transfers to his wife [through an agent] the possession of a *get* at a time when they are having a fight? [Is the divorce], since she is quarreling with her husband, an advantage to her, [or is it a disadvantage to her] because she possibly prefers the physical pleasure [even of an unhappy marriage to the loneliness of being single]?

Come and learn what Resh Lakish said: [This is what women say:] "It is better to live together [even with constant bickering] than to live alone like a widow."

Abbaye said: Even with a husband the size of an ant she can sit in the company of the distinguished ladies.

R. Papa said: Although her husband may be a wool carder [a lowly occupation], she calls him to the threshhold of her door [to show that she is married], and [proudly] sits down next to him.

R. Ashi said: Even if her husband's lineage is blemished, she requires no lentils for her pot, [i.e., she is willing to forgo all luxuries, as long as she is married].

WHEN IS A DROWNING VICTIM'S WIFE ALLOWED TO REMARRY?

(121a) It happened that a man drowned in the marsh of Samki, [a marsh so large that you could not see the other end of it, but it was highly unlikely that he survived], and, therefore, R. Shila allowed his wife to marry again [even though technically, since you cannot see the boundaries of the swamp, he may have emerged alive on the far end]. Rav [who was upset about R. Shila's ruling] said to Shmuel: Come let us place him under a ban. Replied Shmuel: Let's first hear what he has to say. They then sent to him the following inquiry: [If a man was lost after falling into] water whose far end you cannot see, is his wife permitted to remarry or not?

R. Shila sent his reply: She is forbidden to remarry. [Then they asked him:] How about the marsh of Samki, is it considered water whose far end you can see, or water whose far end you cannot see? He replied: It is water whose far end you cannot see. [So they asked:] If so, why did you allow his wife to get married? [He replied:] I made a mistake. I thought that since the water is marshy and stationary, it is the same as "water whose far end you can see," [and he could not have been swept away to the far end and still be alive. But I realize now] that it is not so, since occasionally there are waves, he may have drifted away and still be alive. [At any rate, there was no reason to place R. Shila under a ban, because he did not show disrespect of the *halachah*.] Shmuel praised Rav, applying to him the verse, "No iniquity will befall the righteous" (Proverbs 12:21); Rav applied to Shmuel the verse, "Salvation lies in much counsel" (ibid. 11:14) [because Shmuel gave him the right advice].

R. Ashi said: The rabbinic law concerning a person who was lost in waters whose far end you cannot see, that his wife is not allowed to remarry refers only to an ordinary person but if he was a Torah scholar [his wife is allowed to remarry] because if indeed he did come up [and is alive someplace] we would know about it. However, [says the Gemara, in reality] that is not the case. The *halachah* is that it makes no difference whether the lost person is an ordinary person or a Torah scholar, if the wife did get married after the husband's disappearance [we don't force her to separate]; but to begin with, we don't allow her to get married.

We learned in a *Baraita*: R. Gamliel said: I was once sailing on a ship and saw in the distance another ship sinking in the ocean. I felt sorry for the Torah scholar I knew was on that ship. Who was that Torah scholar? R. Akiva [who apparently had drowned]. When I landed [and students came to ask me questions, there was R. Akiva!]. He came and sat down, and we began to discuss issues of *halachah*. So I said to him, "My son, who brought you up?" "I happened to grab a board from the shipwreck," he replied, "and as each wave came I bowed my head and let it sweep over me [and did not resist it, and that is how I survived]. From here the Sages understood that if wicked people attack you, [instead of resisting] you should bow your head. [R. Gamliel continued:] So I said: How great are the words of our Sages, for they said: [If a man is lost in] waters whose far end can be seen, the wife is allowed to remarry; in waters whose far end cannot be seen, she is not allowed to remarry; [survival is always a possibility].

We learned in a *Baraita*: R. Akiva said: I once was sailing on a ship and saw in the distance another ship that was going down in the ocean. I felt sorry for a Torah scholar that I knew to be a passenger on that ship. And who was that? R. Meir. When I landed at Kapudkia, R. Meir came in to discuss halachic questions with me [as if nothing had happened]. I asked him, "My son, who brought you up?" He told me, "One wave carried me to the next, until I was cast up on dry land." [Continued R. Gamliel:] So I said: How great are the words of our Sages who said: [If a man is lost] in waters whose far end can be seen, the wife is allowed to remarry; in waters whose far end cannot be seen, she is not permitted to remarry.

NECHUNIAH'S DAUGHTER

(121b) We learned in a *Baraita*: It once happened that the daughter of Nechuniah the well-digger fell into a large well. [Nechuniah used to dig wells as a favor to the pilgrims who came to the *Bet Hamikdash* on the three Festivals, to supply them with drinking water (Rashi).] [Assuming that she had drowned,] they came and told R. Chanina b. Dosa about it. After the first hour, he said, "Don't worry; all is well." After the second hour, he said, "Don't worry. She's all right." After the third hour, he said, "She has come up already." He asked the girl, "My daughter, who pulled you out?" She replied, "A ram came suddenly appeared led by an old man, [and he saved me]." [It was the ram of Isaac led by Abraham (Rashi).] The people said to R. Chaninah b. Dosa, "You are a prophet!" He replied, "I am neither a prophet nor the son of a prophet, [but I knew] that [it is impossible] that the unselfish task that this righteous man has undertaken [digging wells for the pilgrims] should bring about a tragedy for his own child." R. Acha said: In spite of this, Nechunia's son died of thirst. For it says, "His [God's] surroundings are exceedingly turbulent [*nis'arah*]" (Psalms 50:3). This teaches that the Holy One, blessed be He, deals sternly with those "surrounding Him" [i.e., the righteous], even to a hair's breadth [*sa'arah*]. R. Chanina said: It is derived from here, "God is dreaded in the great counsel of the holy [angels], and is awesome over all who surround Him" (ibid. 89:8).

(122a) [The Mishnah says:] It happened at Tzalmon[63] that a man declared: I am So-and-so, the son of so-and-so; a snake has bitten me, and I am dying. They went [to examine the body], but they did not recognize him. Nevertheless, they permitted his wife to remarry [on the basis of what he had told them].

NOTES

1. A *kohen* is forbidden to defile himself by contact with the dead (Leviticus 21:1ff).

2. The Torah forbids ignoring a lost object (Deuteronomy 22:1).

3. For example, if the deceased married his niece.

4. Leviticus 21:7.

5. These lands were conquered by Moses and included in Eretz Yisrael. After the destruction of the first *Bet Hamikdash* they lost their sanctity. This sanctity was not restored; therefore, during the time of the second *Bet Hamikdash*, the people living there were permitted to plant during the *Shemittah* year, since the laws of *Shemittah* did not apply there any longer. The Sages enacted that the people in these lands were required to give the tithe of the poor during the *Shemittah* year in addition to the "first tithe." This was done for the benefit of the poor in Eretz Yisrael who would not receive their normal support during the *Shemittah* year when the land was left fallow.

6. Included among these are: His mother's mother, his father's mother, the daughter-in-law of his son, and the daughter-in-law of his daughter, and others. The relations forbidden by the Torah are listed in Leviticus 18.

7. Leviticus 18:26.

8. Since the word "abomination" occurs in connection both with forbidden relations and false measures, you might think that both carry the same penalty, and the former is punishable by *karet*. Therefore the word *eileh* comes to exclude false measures from *karet*.

9. 2 Kings 17:25–35.

10. Esther 8:17.

11. Leviticus 13:2. Tosafot explains that the mitzvah to love a convert is so difficult to adhere to that the Jewish people are not fulfilling it properly and are punished for it. Another explanation is that converts are so much more meticulous in the observance of *mitzvot* than Israel, that their exemplary conduct holds an implied reproach for Israel's laxness.

12. *Leket*, not to gather the gleanings of the harvest (Leviticus 19:9); *Shik'chah*, not to take the forgotten sheaf (Deuteronomy 24:19); *Pei'ah*, not to reap the corner of your field (Leviticus 23:22); the Tithe for the Poor (Deuteronomy 14:28,29).

13. Exodus 32:19.

14. Exodus 19:10 and 15.

15. A euphemism for marital relations.

16. A day begins at nightfall of the previous evening.

17. See *Shabbat* 86a.

18. That is why we observe certain rules of mourning during that period: no weddings are held, and no haircuts are taken.

19. The question holds a veiled reproach, as if to say: God did man no favor by giving him a wife. By bringing sin into the world, the woman did more harm than good, for now man has to work hard to earn a living. Elijah showed him that even if crops would grow by themselves, he still needs a wife to prepare his food and make his clothes.

20. Alternately, a field that was plowed across its width.

21. Literally, "stopped up."

22. The Rambam characterizes a bad wife as one who has deviant beliefs and does not behave modestly (*Hilchot Geirushin* 10).

23. A deviant sect that rejected the Oral Law.

24. When an animal is slaughtered, the *kohen* must be given the foreleg, the jaw, and the maw (Deuteronomy 18:3).

25. The first part of the verse speaks of the coming of *Mashiach*.

26. "Ten thousands" and "thousands" are both plural, and the plural form means no less than two; hence twenty-two thousand.

27. Her marriage settlement to which she is entitled when her husband divorces her or upon his death.

28. *Vechivshuha* is the plural of the second-person imperative.

29. For it says, "You must admonish your neighbor" (Leviticus 19:17).

30. Deuteronomy 23:4.

31. Genesis 38:29.

32. Deuteronomy 23:3.

33. Deuteronomy 23:8.

34. Ruth 4:13, 17ff.

35. Genesis 19:37,38

36. Netinim are descendants of the Gibeonites who misled Joshua; see Joshua 9:3ff.

37. The breastplate of the *Kohen Gadol* contained the Urim and Tummim by means of which the *Kohen Gadol* sought answers of God on difficult questions affecting the community. The breastplate held twelve gemstones on which the letters of the *alef bet* were engraved. The *Kohen Gadol* with inspired vision would pose a question, and the letters containing the answer would appear to light up. With his divine inspiration, the *Kohen Gadol* would then be able to combine the letters to spell out the answer.

38. Because they were protecting David.

39. In fact, thirty years had elapsed since Saul's death (Rashi).

40. *Terumah* is the gift to be given to the *kohen* from the annual produce. The quantity was one-fortieth, one-fiftieth, or one-sixtieth of the crop, depending on the generosity of the farmer. (See Numbers 18:8ff).

41. The tenth generation from Ezra (*Berachot* 27b).

42. A *kohen* is not allowed to enter a cemetery because of the prohibition against defiling himself by contact with the dead (Leviticus 21:1ff).

43. R. Akiva was a shepherd before becoming the towering Torah scholar.

44. *Sotah* 47b; *Chullin* 131b.

45. This verse does not appear anywhere in Scripture.

46. The power of the court to take private property for public use.

47. See 1 Kings 18:31ff.

48. Things that are *muktzeh* [set aside] may not be handled on *Shabbat* or Yom Tov.

49. Jael's intention was to exhaust him in order to enable her to kill him (Rashi) (Judges 4:21).

50. Judges 4:1ff.

51. The words "knelt" and "fell" each occur three times, and "lay" occurs once.

52. According to most commentators.

53. The sinful behavior of the sons of Eli.

54. The students were all sitting on the floor. R. Yishmael had to push aside the students in order to make his way to his seat in the front row.

55. A brother's childless widow; see Deuteronomy 25:5–10.

56. Deuteronomy 25:7.

57. A fatherless minor girl who was married off by her mother or her brothers has a right to reject [*mi'un*] her marriage. The *mi'un* nullifies the marriage and frees her from the requirement of *yibbum* and a *get*.

58. The ceremony that releases a *yevamah* from the obligation of *yibbum* (Deuteronomy 25:5–9).

59. Leviticus 18:16. Even after the brother's death. The only exception is *yibbum*, if the brother dies without children (Deuteronomy 25:5).

60. After the *Bet Hamikdash* was built it was forbidden to build a *bamah*.

61. See note 29.

62. *Yevamot* 47b. Tosafot explains that the mitzvah to love a convert is so difficult to adhere to that the Jewish people are not fulfilling it properly and are punished for it. Another explanation is that converts are so much more meticulous in the observance of *mitzvot* than Israel that their exemplary conduct holds an implied reproach for Israel's laxness.

63. A town in the Lower Galilee.

ᥬᥭ KETUBOT ᥬᥭ

THE GREAT DEEDS
OF THE *TZADDIKIM*

(5a) Bar Kappara expounded: The deeds of the righteous are greater than the creation of heaven and earth, for concerning the creation of heaven and earth it says, "My *hand* has laid the foundations of the earth, and My right *hand* has measured out the heavens" (Isaiah 48:13), ["hand" in the singular]. But regarding the acts of the righteous it says, "The place You dwell in is Your accomplishment, God, the shrine Your *hands* have founded" (Exodus 15:17), [regarding the establishment of the *Bet Hamikdash* which is the accomplishment of the *tzaddikim*, it says "Your hands," in the plural]. An objection was raised by a certain Babylonian by the name of R. Chiya: It says, "The dry land —His *hands* [in the plural] fashioned it" (Psalms 95:5); [so we see that in the creation of the world also two hands are mentioned]. [The Gemara answers:] Even though it is read *yadav*, "His hands,"] it is written *yado*, "His hand," [in the singular].

[The Gemara asks:] But it says *yatzaru*, "they fashioned it" [in the plural, so it must refer to two hands]? Replied R. Nachman b. Yitzchak: [Only one hand was involved; the plural] refers to fingers, as it says [regarding Creation], "When I behold Your heavens, the work of Your fingers, the moon and the stars that You have set in place" (ibid. 8:4). Another objection was raised: It says, "The heavens declare the glory of God, and the firmament tells of the works of His *hands*" (ibid. 19:2); ["hands" in the plural—hence two hands were involved in Creation]. [The Gemara answers: The meaning of the phrase "the works of His hands" does not refer to God's Creation; rather, it refers to the accomplishments of the righteous.] The intent of the verse is: The *mitzvot* that the *tzaddikim* perform, who bears witness to them? [The heavens themselves attest to the works of the *tzaddikim* who pray for rain, and God answers their prayers] by providing rain.

WHY DO FINGERS HAVE A TIP?

Bar Kappara also expounded: What is meant by the verse, "You must keep a spike with your weapons

[*azeinecha*]" (Deuteronomy 23:14)? Do not read *azeinecha*, "your weapons," but *oznecha*, "your ear." [By this is meant,] that if a person hears something improper, he should use his fingers to stop up his ears. And this is what R. Elazar said: Why are the fingers shaped like a peg? [The Gemara asks:] What is the point of this question? Shall I say that R. Elazar was wondering why the fingers are separated and not joined together? [That could not have been the issue,] because every finger has its own function [in connection with the service in the *Bet Hamikdash*]. For a Master said: The little finger is used for measuring the span, [the distance between the thumb and the little finger[1]]; the finger next to it is used for taking the *kemitzah*;[2] the middle finger is needed for the measurement of the cubit;[3] the forefinger [had the significance that the *kohen* dipped his forefinger in the blood of the sin offering and sprinkled it];[4] and the thumb [which was used in the service of cleansing the *metzora* [leper].[5] But this is what R. Elazar meant to ask: Why are the fingers tapered and come to a point like a pointed peg? The reason is that if a person hears something improper, he should be able to use his fingers to stop up his ears. In the yeshivah of R. Yishmael they taught: Why is the entire ear hard and the lobe soft? So that if a person hears something improper, he should bend his lobe into his ear. We learned in a *Baraita*: A person should not allow his ears to listen to banalities, because the ears are easily burned, [and when he has sinned with his ears, the punishment will begin from there].

THE *BERACHAH* AT THE
WEDDING CEREMONY

R. Nachman said: Huna b. Nasan related to me the following *Baraita*: From where do we derive that the *berachah* at the wedding ceremony has to be recited in the presence of ten people? Because it says, [when Boaz wanted to marry Ruth,] "He then took ten men of the elders of the city and said, 'Sit here,' and they sat down" (Ruth 4:2). R. Abbahu said: It is derived from, "In congregations bless God, the Lord, you who are from the fountain of Israel" (Psalms 68:27). [A congregation comprises at least ten people. Therefore, the blessing said at a wedding, which is the celebration of the "fountain of new life," requires the presence of ten people.] [The Gemara asks:] And how does R. Nachman expound the verse quoted by R. Abbahu, [Psalms 68:27]? [The Gemara answers:] He needs this verse for the following *Baraita*: R. Meir used to say: From where do we derive that even embryos in the womb of their mothers sang the Song of the Sea [when the children of Israel crossed] the Red Sea? Because it says, "In congregations bless God, the Lord, you who are from the fountain of Israel" [i.e., the unborn children who are in the womb—the fountain of life—also participated in blessing God].

COMFORTING THE BEREAVED

(8b) R. Chiya b. Abba taught Tanach to the sons of Resh Lakish, and according to others, he taught them Mishnah. It happened that R. Chiya b. Abba's son died. On the first day [of mourning], Resh Lakish did not go [to comfort] him. On the second day, Resh Lakish took with him Yehudah b. Nachmani, who was his *meturgeman*.[6] Resh Lakish said to Yehudah b. Nachmani: Get up and say a few words of consolation regarding the death of the child. He began by quoting the verse, "When God saw this, He was offended, angered by His sons and daughters" (Deuteronomy 32:19). [He expounded: This means:] In a generation in which the parents offend God, He is angry at the children, and they die when they are young. Some say, that [the son who died] was a grown-up,[7] and that Yehudah b. Nachmani quoted [to the bereaved father] the verse, "Therefore, my Lord shall not rejoice over their young men, and He shall not pity their orphans and widows, for they are all hypocritical and evil, and every mouth utters obscenity. Yet despite all this, His anger has not subsided, and His hand is still outstretched [against them in punishment]" (Isaiah 9:16). What is meant by the phrase, "His hand is still outstretched against them"? Said R. Chanan b. Rav: [The verse is referring to the following sin:] Everybody knows for what purpose a bride is getting married, but if someone discusses it and speaks about it in frivolous terms—even if a divine decree of seventy years of happiness was sealed for him, it will be changed to evil.

[The Gemara asks:] They came to comfort R. Chiya b. Abba; but they did the opposite, they hurt him! [The Gemara answers:] They meant to say to R. Chiya b. Abba: You have been found worthy enough to suffer for the sins of the generation. [A righteous person suffers as a means of atonement for the entire community.] Resh Lakish then said to Yehudah b. Nachmani: Get up and say a few words in praise of the Holy One, blessed be He. He began by saying, "Blessed are You, O Lord our God, King of the universe, the God who is great with an abundance of greatness, mighty and strong in a multitude of awe-inspiring deeds, who

revives the dead with His utterance, who does great things that are unfathomable and wondrous deeds without number. Blessed are You, God, who revives the dead."

Resh Lakish then said to him: Now say a few comforting words to the mourners. He began by saying: Our brothers who are weary, who are afflicted with this sorrow, pay attention and ponder this: Death is something that will always be with us, [therefore, don't weep excessively]; such is the way since the days of Creation. Many have drunk [from the cup of anguish], and many will drink [from this cup]. As the former generations drank from it, so will the later generations drink from it. Our brothers, may the Master of consolation comfort you. Blessed be He who comforts the mourners. Abbaye, [criticizing these words of consolation,] said: It was appropriate for him to say, "Many have drunk," but he should not have said, "many will drink from this cup" [in the future]. It was appropriate for him to say, "as the former generations drank," but he should not have said, "so will the later generations drink" [in the future].

For R. Shimon b. Lakish[8] said, and so it was taught in the name of R. Yose: A person should never open his mouth to the Satan [i.e., a person should never talk about a bad thing happening to himself].[9] R. Yosef said: What verse supports this? [When Isaiah said,] "We would have been like Sodom, we would have resembled Gomorrah" (Isaiah 1:9), what did God answer him? "Hear the words of God, O chiefs of Sodom" (ibid. v. 10). [Because Isaiah compared Israel to Sodom, God Himself refers to them as "chiefs of Sodom."]

Resh Lakish then said to Yehudah b. Nachmani: Get up and address a few words of blessing to the people who came to comfort the mourners. He began by saying: Our brothers, who practice kindness, sons of people who practice kindness, who continue the covenant of Abraham [who was the epitome of kindness], about whom it says, "I have given him [Abraham] special attention so that he will command his children and his household after him . . . to do charity and justice" (Genesis 18:19). Our brothers, may God, the Master who repays, reward you for your kindness. Blessed are You, God, who repays kind deeds. Resh Lakish then said: Now say a few words of blessing for all Israel. He began by saying: Master of the universe! Redeem, save, rescue, and help Your people Israel from a plague, from the sword, from being plundered, from wind blasts, from withering of the crops, and from any misfortune that may come upon the world. Before we call out to You, may You answer us. Blessed are You, God, who holds back the plague.

INEXPENSIVE SHROUDS
FOR THE DEAD

We learned in a *Baraita*: Originally, the funeral expenses were harder on the relatives than the actual death of the person [because the dead were buried in expensive shrouds]. It came to the point that the relatives would just abandon the deceased and run away, [without burying him], until R. Gamliel came and instituted a simple style. He made sure that when he died they would take him out in a simple linen shroud, and from then on all the people followed his example and carried out the dead in linen shrouds. R. Papa said: Nowadays, it is customary to take out the dead even in shrouds made out of canvas worth only a *zuz*.[10]

THEY WROTE A *GET* BEFORE GOING TO WAR

(9a) R. Shmuel b. Nachmani said in the name of R. Yonatan: (9b) Whoever went to war in David's army wrote a *get*[11] for his wife [so that if he did not return from battle, and there were no witnesses to his death, she is divorced retroactively from the date of the *get*. Thus she will not become an *agunah*, [a wife tied to a husband whose whereabouts are unknown].[12] [We know this] because it says, [during Saul's war against the Philistines, Jesse sent David to the battlefield, and told him,] "Inquire after the welfare of your brothers, and take their pledges" (1 Samuel 17:18). What is meant by, "and take their pledges"? Things that are pledged between husband and wife [i.e., their betrothals]. These young David was told to take away by means of their *get* documents].

DANCING FOR THE BRIDE

(16b) Our Rabbis taught: What do we sing to the bride when we dance for her? Bet Shammai said: (17a) We describe her as she is, [without embellishments or overstating her qualities]. Bet Hillel said: [We sing,] "What a beautiful and charming bride she is!" Bet Shammai said to Bet Hillel: What if the bride is lame or blind; would you still sing to her, "What a beautiful and charming bride she is"? But the Torah says, "Keep away from anything false (Exodus 23:7)!" Replied Bet Hillel: According to your view, if a person has bought bad merchandise in the market, should you praise it in the eyes of the buyer or point out its faults? Surely you will agree that you should praise it in the eyes of the buyer. [Based on Bet Hillel's statement,] the Sages coined the saying: You should always be genial toward other people. When R. Dimi came [from Eretz Yisrael] he said: This is what they sing to a bride in Eretz Yisrael, "She needs no eye makeup, no cosmetics, and no braiding [of the hair], and still she is a graceful gazelle."

When the Rabbis ordained R. Zeira they sang for him, "There is no makeup, no cosmetics, and no braiding [of the hair], and he still is a graceful gazelle," [meaning, he is a man of unimpeachable integrity, free of false pretenses and hypocrisy (*Maharsha*)]. When the Rabbis ordained R. Ammi and R. Assi, they sang for

them, "Ordain for us men of such caliber, yea, men of such caliber, but do not ordain for us perverters [of *halachah*] and people who are unfamiliar with the law." Others say: [They sang,] "Do not ordain 'two-bit[13] scholars' and ignorant people." When R. Abbahu came from the yeshivah to the court of the emperor, the maids of the palace came out to greet him, singing, "Prince of his people! Leader of his nation! Radiant light! Welcome in peace."

It was said about R. Yehudah b. Ila'i that he used to take a myrtle twig and dance with it before the bride, chanting, "Beautiful and graceful bride." R. Shmuel b. R. Yitzchak used to dance with three myrtle twigs, [juggling the twigs (Rashi)], to which R. Zeira remarked: [By his undignified performance] the old man debases the honor of the Torah. When R. Shmuel b. Yitzchak died, a pillar of fire set him apart from the rest of the world. And we have a tradition that a pillar of fire will form an enclosure for no more than one or two outstanding personalities in a generation; [it happens only to very great *tzaddikim*]. R. Zeira said: The myrtle branch [*shutitei*, with which he danced before the bride] served the old man [to have such a miracle happen to him]. Others say: His custom [*shit'tei* of dancing before the bride] served the old man. And according to others, the fact that he made a fool of himself [*shetutei*, juggling before the bride] served the old man.[14] R. Acha would carry the bride on his shoulders and dance [with her]. The Rabbis asked him: May we do the same? He replied: If the bride is on your shoulders like a beam, [arousing no sensual thoughts,] then it is permitted, if not, you may not [carry her]. R. Shmuel b. Nachmani said in R. Yonatan's name: It is permitted to gaze at the face of a bride for seven days after her marriage, in order to make her beloved to her husband. [When the husband sees that all are gazing at her, he appreciates her beauty (Rashi).]

FUNERAL AND BRIDAL PROCESSIONS

We learned in a *Baraita*: A funeral procession has to make way for a bridal procession, and both of them must make way for the King of Israel. They said about King Agrippa that he made way for a bridal procession, and the Sages praised him for it. [The Gemara analyzes this *Baraita*:] "The Sages praised him"—this implies that he acted correctly. [The Gemara now asks:] But R. Ashi said: Even the one who says that if a Nasi is willing to give up the honor that is due to him, he can do so, [agrees that] if a king wants to give up the honor due to him, he cannot relinquish his honor, for a Tanna interpreted [the double imperative *som tasim* in the verse, "You shall surely set over yourself a king" (Deuteronomy 17:15) to imply that you must be in awe of him. [Then how could the Rabbis praise King Agrippa for making way for a bride?] [The Gemara answers:] It happened at a crossroads, [thus it was not obvious that the King was making way, but it looked as if he was headed in the direction he chose.]

We learned in a *Baraita*: The study of Torah should be interrupted for a funeral procession and for escorting the bride [to the *chuppah*].[15] They said about R. Yehudah b. Ila'i that he would interrupt his Torah studies for a funeral procession and for escorting the bride to the *chuppah*]. But this applies only if there are not enough people [attending the funeral]; but if there are enough people, you should not interrupt your Torah studies. How many are considered enough? R. Shmuel b. Unia said in the name of Rav: Twelve thousand people, and six thousand people to announce the funeral. And some say: Twelve thousand people, including six thousand to announce the funeral. Ulla said: "Enough people" means, for example, when there are enough people to form a line from the city gate to the gravesite. R. Sheshet—and some say R. Yonatan—said: The departure of the Torah [i.e., the funeral of a Torah scholar should be attended by as many people] as were present at the giving of the Torah. Just as the giving of the Torah took place in the presence of 600,000 people, so should its departure [the funeral of a Torah scholar] take place in the presence of 600,000 people. And this applies only to a person who studied the Torah and the Mishnah [but did not teach others], (17b) but for a person who taught others there is no limit.

DEATH PENALTY

(30a) Abbaye said: The term *ason* [a tragic happening] (Exodus 21:22,23) is used in connection with the death penalty enacted by the Bet Din, and the word *ason* [a tragic happening] is also used in reference to death at the hands of Heaven (Genesis 42:4). [Obviously, the Torah wants to compare the two.] Just as in the tragic happening that involves the death penalty at the hand of the Bet Din, [the person who is executed] is exempt from all money payments,[16] so too if someone is liable to death at the hand of Heaven, he is exempt from all money payments. [In Genesis 42:4 we are told that Jacob did not send Benjamin to Egypt along with his brothers, "lest disaster [*ason*] befall him."]

R. Adda b. Ahava raised an objection: How do you know that Jacob was afraid of [Benjamin] being harmed by cold and heat, phenomena that are caused by Heaven? Perhaps he was referring to lions or robbers, calamities that are initiated by man? [Therefore, Abbaye has no proof that *ason* refers to accidents that come about through the hand of God.] [The Gemara says:] Did Jacob then limit his concerns to one type of misfortune and not to another? Of course, Jacob was concerned with every kind of harm. [Thus *ason* includes

harm at the hand of heaven, and Abbaye's proof is sound.]

[In the Gemara above, R. Adda b. Ahava took it for granted that cold and heat are acts of God, and lions and thieves are acts of man. The Gemara now questions this:] But are cold and heat caused by Heaven? Haven't we learned in a *Baraita*: Everything happens by the hand of Heaven, except [sickness due to] cold and heat, for it says, "Cold and heat are in the path of the crooked, he who values his life will keep far from them" (Proverbs 22:5), [therefore, you should guard your health]. And also, are lions and thieves "acts of man"? Did not R. Yosef say, and did not R. Chiya teach likewise: Since the day the *Bet Hamikdash* was destroyed, although there is no longer a Sanhedrin, the four death penalties of the human court did not cease. What do you mean: did not cease! [Capital punishment] certainly was discontinued!

(30b) [It means:] Punishment that is comparable to capital punishment has not ceased; [although the Bet Din does not enforce the death penalty, God enforces it through comparable forms of death]. [For example:] If someone would have been sentenced to death by stoning, now, either he will fall off a roof or a wild beast will trample him. Someone who would have been sentenced to burning, nowadays will be consumed by a fire or bitten by a snake. Someone who would have been sentenced to decapitation, now either is arrested by the Roman government [and they execute him], or robbers attack him [and kill him]. Someone who would have been sentenced to die by choking, either is drowned in a river or dies from the croup. [So we see, that all such calamities are brought about by God. Then how can R. Adda b. Ahava say that thieves and wild beasts are "acts of man"?] [The Gemara answers:] It should be reversed: Lions and thieves are acts of God; [sickness due to] cold and heat are due to human [carelessness].

CHILD NEGLECT

(49b) When people would bring before Rav Yehudah [a case of a father who refused to support his young children] he used to tell them: The *yarod* [a dragon or snake (Rashi)] gives birth and casts the responsibility of caring for his young on the people of the town. When they brought such cases before R. Chisda he used to tell them: Turn a pail upside down and make the father stand on it in public and announce about himself: The raven takes care of its young, but this man [meaning, himself] does not take care of his children! [The Gemara asks:] But does a raven care for its young? Doesn't it say, "[God] gives to an animal its food, to young ravens that cry out" (Psalms 147:9)? [The Gemara answers:] This presents no difficulty: The latter [Psalms 147:9] refers to very young ravens which are white [and at that stage are disliked by their parents]; the former [in R. Chisda's statement that ravens do care for their young] refers to older birds, [and those are liked by their parents].

WHO DOES CHARITY ALL THE TIME?

(50a) "Praiseworthy are those who act justly, who do charity at all times" (Psalms 106:3). [Asks the Gemara:] Is it possible to do charity at all times? Our Rabbis in Yavneh—others say, R. Eliezer—said: This refers to a person who supports his sons and daughters when they are young. [This is a charitable act, and they depend on him all the time.] R. Shmuel b. Nachmani said: This refers to a person who raises an orphan boy and girl in his house and marries them off.

"Wealth and riches are in his house, and his beneficence lasts forever" (ibid. 112:3). R. Huna and R. Chisda [both expounded this verse]. One said: It applies to a person who studies the Torah and teaches it to others. Whereas the other said: This applies to a person who writes the Torah, the Prophets, and the Writings and lends them to others.

"And may you live to see your children's children, peace upon Israel!" (Psalms 128:6). R. Yehoshua b. Levi said: When your children have children, then there will be peace upon Israel, for [your children] will not be subject to *chalitzah* or *yibbum*[17] [which often causes friction]. R. Shmuel b. Nachmani said: When your children have children, there will be peace upon Israel's judges, because there will be no cause for quarreling [as to who is next in line to inherit the estate].

DON'T LET THE WAITER GO HUNGRY

R. Yitzchak b. Chananiah said in the name of R. Huna: All dishes may be held back from the waiter [until the end of the meal] with the exception of meat and wine [which arouse his appetite, and denying him these would be painful to him]. R. Chisda said: This applies only to fat meat and old wine. Rava said: Fat meat may not be withheld all year round, but old wine [may not be withheld only during summer months]. Abbahu b. Ihi and Minjamin b. Ihi [both had servants]. One used to give his servant from every type of dish [before the meal]; the other gave his servant only from one type of dish [that was brought to the table, and gave him the other dishes after he finished serving the meal]. Elijah the prophet came to visit the first one, but he did not come to the other.

There were two pious men—others say it was R. Mari and R. Pinchas, the sons of R. Chisda—one used to allow his servant to eat from every dish before he began serving; the other only allowed the servant to eat after he finished serving. To the one who gave to the servant first, Elijah appeared; to the other, Elijah

did not appear [because he caused the servant to have hunger pangs].

THE KING WAS SERVED TAINTED MEAT

Amemar, Mar Zutra, and R. Ashi once were sitting at the gate of King Yezdegerd's[18] palace, when the King's steward passed by [carrying the King's meal]. When R. Ashi noticed that Mar Zutra suddenly (61b) turned pale, [craving the food], he took with his finger some food from the platter and put it in Mar Zutra's mouth.[19]

"You have ruined the King's meal!" the steward cried.

[Suddenly the royal guards appeared.]

"Why did you do this?" they asked R. Ashi.

"The person who prepared this dish is unfit to be the royal chef," replied R. Ashi.

"Why do you say that?" the guards asked.

"Because I saw a piece of leprous swine meat in it," R. Ashi answered.

They inspected the meat, but could not find a trace [of leprosy].

R. Ashi then took the [chef's] finger and placed it on one of the chunks of meat. "Did you inspect this piece?" he asked.

They inspected it and found it to be diseased [as R. Ashi had said]. Later on, the Rabbis asked, "Why did you rely on a miracle?" R. Ashi replied: [It was really not a miracle,] for I saw the spirit of leprosy floating over Mar Zutra [after he tasted the dish, so I realized that the meat was contaminated with leprosy]."

CRAVING THE FRUIT MADE HER SICK

A Roman once said to a woman, "Will you marry me?" but she turned him down. He then went and bought some pomegranates, opened them, and ate them in her presence. She continuously swallowed the saliva that welled up in her mouth [as a result of watching him eat the mouth-watering delicacy], but he did not give her any of the fruit until her body blew up. At this point he said to her, "If I am going to heal you, will you marry me?" "Yes," she replied. Again he bought some pomegranates, opened them and ate them in her presence. "Spit out at once all the saliva that wells up in your mouth. Keep on spitting, [and make sure not to swallow it]," he said. She kept on spitting until she expectorated something that looked like a green palm branch, after which she recovered.

THE HARMFUL EFFECTS OF SIGHING

(62a) Rav said: Sighing breaks down half of the body, for it says, "And you, Son of Man, sigh! With a shattering of the loins and with bitterness sigh" (Ezekiel 21:11). [The loins are in the middle of the body.] R. Yochanan said: Sighing destroys the entire body, for it says [in reference to the destruction of Jerusalem], "And it shall be that when they say to you, 'For what are you sighing?' you shall say, 'Because of the report that is coming, when every heart will melt, all hands will weaken, every spirit will grow faint, and all knees will melt like water'" (ibid. v. 12). [The Gemara asks:] But how does R. Yochanan explain the phrase, "a shattering of the loins" [which indicates that only half the body is shattered]? [The Gemara answers: R. Yochanan will say that] when the entire body starts breaking down it begins from the loins. [The Gemara asks:] And how does Rav explain the phrase, "and every heart will melt, all hands will weaken, and every spirit will grow faint" [which implies that sighing destroys the entire body]? [The Gemara answers: Rav will say,] that the report of the destruction of the *Bet Hamikdash* is different, since that catastrophe was so appalling [that it broke the entire body].

A Jew and a gentile were once walking on the road together, but the gentile could not keep up with the Jew. The gentile reminded the Jew of the destruction of the Temple, which made the Jew sigh and feel faint, but the gentile still could not keep up with him. "Don't you have a saying," asked the gentile, "that sighing breaks half of a person's body; [then why are you still walking faster than me]?" "That applies only to a new disaster," the Jew replied, "but this one is already old; [we have become inured to it; it does not affect us that much]. As people say: A woman who has lost several children is not so overcome with grief when it happens again."

HE FORGOT TO COME HOME

(62b) Yehudah, the son of R. Chiya, the son-in-law of R. Yannai, was always sitting and learning in the yeshivah, but every Friday evening when the sun began to set he came home. Whenever he arrived, the people saw a pillar of light in front of him. One day he became so involved in his studies [that he forgot to come home]. When R. Yannai did not see the sign, he said to those around him: Turn over his bed [a sign of mourning], for if Yehudah were alive he would not have neglected [to come home] to fulfill the mitzvah of performing his marital duty. This statement was "like an error that proceeded from the ruler" (Ecclesiastes 10:5), for as a result of R. Yannai's remark, Yehudah died. [An ominous prediction, even when made in error, will come true.]

THEY WENT TO LEARN TORAH
AFTER THEIR WEDDING

Rabbi [Yehudah Hanassi] was busy making preparations for the wedding of his son who was getting mar-

ried to the daughter of R. Chiya, but when the time came to write the *ketubah* [the marriage contract] the bride died. Rebbi said: Is this a sign that there is a blemish [on one of our families]? They immediately sat down to research the genealogy of both families. It turned out that Rebbi was a direct descendant of Shefatiah ben Avital [a son of David],[20] whereas R. Chiya was a descendant of Shim'i, the brother of David. [Thus Rabbi's son was of royal lineage whereas his bride was not (Rashi).]

Later on Rabbi was busy making preparations for the marriage of his son to the daughter of R. Yose b. Zimra. It was agreed that [before the wedding] he should spend twelve years learning Torah at the yeshivah. When the girl was introduced to him, he said, "Let's make it six years." When she was brought before him a second time, he said, "I'd rather marry her first and then go to the yeshivah to learn." He was a little embarrassed before his father, [for having changed his mind,] but his father told him, "My son, you are following the line of thought of your Creator [in moving up your wedding date, For God, too, hastened his union with the Jewish people], for at first it says, "O bring them [to *Eretz Yisrael*] and plant them on the mount You possess [where they will build the *Bet Hamikdash*]" (Exodus 15:17), and then it says, "They shall make Me a sanctuary [in the wilderness, before arriving in *Eretz Yisrael*], and I will dwell among them" (ibid. 25:8).

[After he was married,] he spent twelve years at the yeshivah. By the time he came back, his wife could not have children any more [since she had lived without a husband for more than ten years].[21] "What shall we do?" Rebbi said. "If he gives her a divorce, people will say: This poor girl waited all these years for nothing!" If he marries another wife [in addition to her], people will say: This one is his wife and that one his mistress" [and it is not fair that after sacrificing the best years of her life so that her husband could learn Torah, she should be considered a mistress]. Therefore he prayed for her, and she was cured [and was able to have children].

R. Chanania b. Chachinai [who attended the wedding of R. Shimon b. Yochai] prepared to leave for the yeshivah toward the end of the wedding. "Wait for me," R. Shimon b. Yochai said, "until I am able to come along with you at the end of the week of festivities."[22] However, he did not wait but went away and spent twelve years studying at the yeshivah. By the time he returned, the streets of the city had changed so drastically that he was unable to find his way home. He went and sat down at the river bank where he heard someone call out to a girl, "Daughter of Chachinai! Daughter of Chachinai! Fill up your pitcher, and let's go!" He said to himself, "I'm sure this girl is ours," and he followed her. When they reached the house his wife was sitting and sifting flour. He attracted her attention, and when she saw him she was so overcome with joy that she fainted. He prayed, "Master of the universe! Is this the reward for that poor woman [who sacrificed herself to allow her husband to learn Torah]?" Thereupon she revived.

R. Chama b. Bisa went [away from home and] studied at the yeshivah for twelve years. When he came back he said, "I will not act like b. Chachinai [who startled his wife by his sudden appearance]. "So he stopped at the local *bet midrash* and sent word to his family that he had arrived. Meanwhile, his son, R. Oshaia [whom he did not recognize], entered the *bet midrash*, sat down before of him, and asked him questions on a halachic theme. R. Chama, noticing how brilliant the boy was, felt very depressed. He said to himself, "If I had stayed at home [and taught my young son Torah], he would be just as bright as this boy." When R. Chama entered his house, his son also came in. [Taking him for a stranger,] R. Chama got up for him, thinking that he had come to ask him another halachic question. His wife then said [with a twinkle in her eye,] "Have you ever heard of a father getting up for his son!" [R. Chama now realized that the boy was indeed his son Oshaia.] Rami b. Chama applied to him the verse, "A three-ply cord is not easily severed" (Ecclesiates 4:12). The three-ply cord refers to: R. Oshaia, son of R. Chama, son of Bisa.[23]

R. AKIVA'S VIRTUOUS WIFE

R. Akiva was a shepherd of Ben Kalba Savua [one of the wealthiest men in Jerusalem before the destruction of the Second Temple]. Ben Kalba Savua's daughter, seeing how modest and congenial the shepherd was, said to him, "If I betroth myself to you, will you go to the yeshivah to learn Torah?" "Yes, I will," R. Akiva replied. They were secretly betrothed, and she sent him off to the yeshivah. When Kalba Savua heard what she had done he threw her out of his house and vowed that she was not to have any benefit from his possessions. R. Akiva left and spent twelve years at the yeshivah. When he came back he brought with him twelve thousand disciples. As he approached his house he overheard an old man say to his wife, "How much longer (63a) will you lead the life of a widow?" "If he would listen to me," she replied, "he would continue learning another twelve years." R. Akiva said to himself, "Since she has given me permission, I will act accordingly."

So he left again, and spent twelve more years at the yeshivah. This time he returned bringing with him twenty-four thousand disciples. Hearing of his arrival, his wife went to meet him. Her neighbors suggested, "Borrow some decent clothes to wear." But she replied, "The righteous one knows [the needs of] his animal's soul" (Proverbs 12:10). When she came close to him, she fell on her face and kissed his feet. His attendants tried to push her aside, but R. Akiva cried to them, "Leave her alone! My [Torah] and your [Torah] are due

to her!" [The Torah I learned and taught to you came about because she induced me to go to learn Torah.] When her father heard that a great scholar had come to town he said, "Let me go to see him, perhaps he will nullify the vow [I made against my daughter]." When he came, R. Akiva asked, "Would you have made your vow if you had known that [your daughter's husband] was a great scholar?" "If he had known even one chapter, even one *halachah* [I would not have made the vow]" the father answered. "I am the one," Rabbi Akiva said. The father fell down on his face and kissed R. Akiva's feet, and he also gave him half of his wealth. R. Akiva's daughter did the same thing [her mother had done] to Ben Azzai. This proves the popular saying: "Sheep follows sheep; like mother, like daughter."

R. Yosef the son of Rava was sent by his father to the yeshivah of R. Yosef and arranged with him that he should stay there for six years. After three years had elapsed, on the day before Yom Kippur, he decided to go home and visit his family. When his father heard that he was coming [before the stipulated time], he took a weapon [to show his displeasure] and went to meet him. "You have remembered your wife," he reproached him. Others say that he said, "You have remembered your dove" [which means the same thing.] Both became so upset by the ensuing argument that neither the one nor the other ate the final meal before the fast.

THE PLIGHT OF NAKDIMON B. GURION'S DAUGHTER

(66b) Our Rabbis taught: It happened that R. Yochanan b. Zakkai was leaving Jerusalem riding on a donkey, and his disciples were following him. [R. Yochanan b. Zakkai lived during the dreadful time of the destruction of the *Bet Hamikdash*.] He saw a young woman picking barley grains out of the dung of Arab cattle. As soon as she saw him, she covered her hair and stood in front of him. "Rabbi, please feed me," she said. "My daughter," he asked her, "who are you?" "I am the daughter of Nakdimon b. Gurion," she replied. "What happened to your father's fortune?" he asked. "Rabbi," she answered, "don't they have a saying in Jerusalem, 'The salt of wealth is decrease'" [meaning, you preserve your wealth by giving charity]. Others say, "benevolence" [i.e., you preserve your money by doing kind deeds with it]. "My father did not give enough charity, and that is why he lost his money." R. Yochanan b. Zakkai then asked, "And what happened to your father-in-law's money?" She replied, "One destroyed the other" [i.e., the two fortunes were mixed up, and when the one was lost the other disappeared along with it]. "Rabbi," she continued, "do you remember when you signed my *ketubah* [marriage contract]?" "I remember," he said to his disciples, "when I signed the *ketubah* of this young woman I read in it that her father gave her thousands upon thousands of gold coins, besides the amount she received from her father-in-law." R. Yochanan b. Zakkai then burst into tears and said, "How praiseworthy is Israel! When they do the will of God, no nation or people has power over them; but when they fail to do the will of God, He delivers them into the hands of a depraved nation, and not only into the hands of a depraved nation but into the power of the beasts of a depraved nation."

[The Gemara asks: How can you say that] Nakdimon b. Gurion did not give enough charity! Haven't we learned in a *Baraita*: They said about Nakdimon b. Gurion that when he left his house to go to the *bet midrash* (67a) they used to spread a runner of fine woolen cloth for him to walk on, and the poor people followed behind him and rolled it up [to keep it for themselves]. [The Gemara answers:] If you prefer, say: He did it for his own glory. Or, if you prefer say: He did not give as much as he should have. As the saying goes, "According to the camel is the burden" [The wealthier a person is, the more he has to contribute to charity.]

We learned in a *Baraita*: R. Ealzar b. R. Tzadok said: May I [not] see the consolation of Zion if I have not seen [the daughter of Nakdimon b. Gurion picking barley grains from between the hoofs of horses in Acco. [When I saw her suffering] I applied to her the text, "If you do not know, O fairest of women, [i.e., if you, Israel, do not observe the Torah, you will end up] following the tracks of the sheep, and feeding your kids [*gediyotayich*] by the tents of the shepherds" (Song of Songs 1:8). Don't read *gediyotayich*; read instead *geviotayich*, "your body."

HELPING ORPHANS
TO GET MARRIED

We learned in a *Baraita*: If an orphan boy and an orphan girl applied for sustenance [from the communal charity fund], the orphan girl should be supported first and the orphan boy afterward [if there is enough money left]. Because it is not unusual for a man to go begging, but it is unusual for a woman to do so.

If an orphan boy and an orphan girl (67b) applied [to the charity fund] for a grant to be able to get married, we must first help the orphan girl to marry and then the orphan boy, because it is a greater shame for a woman than for a man [to be unmarried].

We learned in a *Baraita*: If an orphan comes and applies for [assistance] to get married, [the administrators of the charity fund] must rent a house for him, they must buy bedding and supply household utensils; and then they must marry him off, for it says, "Sufficient for his requirement, for whatever he needs," (Deuteronomy 15:8). "Sufficient for his requirement" refers to the house; "for whatever he needs" refers to a bed and a table; "he" refers to a wife. For it says, "I will make him a helper corresponding to him" (Genesis 2:18).

SUPPORT HIM ACCORDING
TO HIS LIFE STYLE

Our Rabbis taught: "Sufficient for his requirement" means that you are commanded to support [a poor man], but you are not commanded to make him rich. "For whatever he needs" includes even a horse to ride on and a slave to run in front of him, [if that was what he was accustomed to before he became impoverished]. It was told about Hillel the Elder that he bought for a poor man of noble descent a horse to ride on and a slave to run in front of him. One day he could not find a slave to run in front of him, so Hillel himself ran in front of him for three miles.

Our Rabbis taught: It once happened that the people of the Upper Galilee bought for a poor man of noble descent from Tzipori a pound of meat every day. [The Gemara asks:] A pound of meat! What's so special about that? R. Huna replied: It was a pound of poultry [which was very expensive, and this man was used to eating fancy food]. And if you prefer, say: [They bought] ordinary meat for a pound of coins. R. Ashi explained that this happened in a small village, and every day they had to spoil an animal for his sake. [After they gave him his pound of meat, the rest of the animal had to be discarded because there were no buyers for the meat.]

A poor man once applied to R. Nechemiah [for support]. "What do you usually have for your meals?" R. Nechemiah asked. "Fat meat and old wine," he replied. "Will you be satisfied to share my meals of lentils?" The poor man agreed and lived on his lentils, but [soon thereafter] he died. [R. Nechemiah] said: Woe for this man whom Nechemiah has killed! [Says the Gemara:] On the contrary! He should have said: Woe for R. Nechemiah who killed this man! [R. Nechemiah is to be pitied, for that person himself is to blame for his death.] He should not have cultivated such gourmet tastes.

A poor man once applied to Rava [for support]. "What do you usually have for your meals? Rava asked. "Fat chicken and old wine," he replied. "Don't you give any thought to being a burden to the community [by demanding such expensive food]?" Rava asked. "Do I eat of theirs?" the poor man retorted. "I eat what God provides. For we learned: It says, 'The eyes of all look to you with hope, and You give them their food in his proper time' (Psalms 145:15). Since it does not say 'in *their* time' but 'in *his* time' we can infer that the Holy One, blessed be He, provides for every individual his food according to his particular life style."

Meanwhile Rava's sister, who had not seen him for thirteen years, came to visit him and brought with her a fat chicken and old wine. "What an amazing thing this is!" Rava exclaimed. Turning to the poor man he said, "I apologize to you, [for what I said]; please go ahead and eat."

ABOUT GIVING CHARITY

The Rabbis taught: If a person has no means and does not want to be supported out of the charity fund, he should be granted the money he needs as a loan, which is then converted into a gift, so says R. Meir. The Sages say: He should be given the money as a gift, [not as charity, and if he does not accept the gift] it should be offered to him as a loan. [The Gemara asks:] You say: "as a gift"! But he surely won't accept it! Rava replied: You should begin by offering it as a gift.

If a person has the means but does not want to support himself [out of his own funds, but prefers to deprive and starve himself], he is given what he needs as a gift, and then he is made to repay it. [The Gemara asks:] If he is made to repay it, he surely will not accept help again! R. Papa replied: It is collected after his death. R. Shimon said: If he has the means but does not want to support himself, the community is not required to help him. If he has no means and refuses to be supported [by charity], we say to him: Bring a security and you will receive [a loan]. That way he will preserve his dignity. [He will accept the money without shame, even if he has no security, in the belief that it is given as a loan (Rashi).]

In Mar Ukva's neighborhood there lived a poor man, and every day Mar Ukva used to throw four *zuz* through a gap of the poor man's door hinge. One day the poor man said, "Let me find out who is doing me this favor." It so happened that on that day Mar Ukva stayed longer than usual at the *bet midrash*, so his wife [went to meet him] and walked home with him. As soon as the poor man noticed them bending down to throw the coins through the door, he came outside, but they ran away from him and fled into a furnace from which the cinders had just been removed. Mar Ukva's feet were burning, so his wife told him, "Lift up your feet and put them on mine." He felt bad about it, [thinking that his wife's feet were protected from the heat because her merits were greater than his]. She explained, "You see, I am usually at home, [and the bread and the food I give to the poor] they can enjoy right away, [but you give them money, and they first have to go out and buy food with it, that's why my merits are greater]."

[The Gemara asks:] And why did they run away from the poor man in the first place? Because Mar Zutra said in the name of Rav—others say R. Chanan b. Bizna said in the name of R. Shimon Chasida, still others say R. Yochanan said it in the name of R. Shimon b. Yochai: A person should let himself be thrown into a fiery furnace rather than expose his neighbor to public shame. From where do we know this? From the conduct of Tamar. For it says, "As she was taken out [to be burned], she sent word to her father-in-law" (Genesis 38:25). [Tamar did not name Judah publicly. She reasoned, "If he admits it voluntarily, well and good: if not, let them burn me, but let me not publicly disgrace him."][24]

In Mar Ukva's neighborhood there lived a poor man, to whom he used to send four hundred *zuz* on every *erev Yom Kippur*. One time he sent his son to deliver the money. He returned with the money and said, "This person does not need [your help, so I did not give him the money]."[25] "What makes you think so?" the father asked. "I saw that they were pouring old wine for him," the son replied. Said Mar Ukva, "If he is used to such luxuries, I will double the amount of money I am sending him."

When Mar Ukva was on his deathbed he said, "Please bring me my *tzedakah* accounts." When he found that he had donated seven thousand *Sianki dinars* [a vast amount] he exclaimed, "It is a light meal for a long journey," and he immediately gave half of his fortune to charity. [The Gemara asks:] How could he do such a thing! Did not R. Ila'i say: It was decreed in Usha that if a person wants to spend liberally on charity, he should not spend more than one fifth [of his resources]? [The Gemara answers:] This applies only while he is alive, [for he may become poor and need the money], but when he is about to die it does not matter.

THEY PRETENDED TO BE POOR

R. Abba used to wrap some coins in his scarf and drop the scarf behind him in order that the poor could take the money without him seeing their faces. He did however look sideways to guard against cheats [who pretended to be poor and took the money]. R. Chanina had a poor man to whom he regularly sent four *zuz* every Friday. One Friday he sent the money through his wife, who came back with the money and told him that the man did not need charity. "What gave you that idea?" R. Chanina asked. She replied, "I heard that he was asked, 'How do you want your meal to be served? (68a) On a white linen tablecloth or on a colored silk tablecloth?'" R. Chanina said, "This is what R. Yochanan had in mind when he said, 'Come, let's be grateful to the [poor people] who deceive, for if not for the cheats, we [who do not respond to every request for *tzedakah*] would be sinning every day. For it says [about people who turn their back on a poor man], "He may appeal against you to God, and it will be a sin upon you" (Deuteronomy 15:9).

In addition, R. Yehoshua b. Korcha said: Whoever turns a deaf ear[26] to a request for *tzedakah* is considered as though he worshipped idols, for [concerning *tzedakah*] it says, "Beware lest there be a lawless [*beliyaal*] thought in your heart . . . so that you are mean to your impoverished kinsman and give him nothing" (ibid.). And in connection with idolatry it says, "Lawless [*beliyaal*] men have emerged from your midst" (ibid. 13:14). Just as in Deuteronomy 13:14 the sin is idolatry, so, too, in the case of withholding *tzedakah*, the sin is idolatry. [But thanks to the cheats who fraudulently ask for charity we have an excuse for not responding to an appeal for a donation.]

The Rabbis taught: A beggar who feigns blindness, or pretends to have a swollen belly, or to be crippled will not pass from this world before he will actually get this condition.

AN INFORMAL GREETING

(69a) R. Anan sent the following message to R. Huna: "Greetings to our friend Huna! When this woman [the bearer] presents herself to you, please obtain for her one-tenth of her father's estate [for her dowry]." R. Sheshet was sitting in front of R. Huna [when he received this message. Rav Huna was extremely upset because he was addressed as "our friend Huna" rather than "Rav Huna"]. R. Huna instructed R. Sheshet, "Go and tell R. Anan the following—and whoever does not tell him exactly what I said shall be under the ban— 'Anan, Anan, should I collect from real estate or from movable goods? [Pointedly addressing him as Anan, rather than Rav Anan.] Furthermore, in a house of mourning, who sits at the head of the table?'" R. Sheshet went to R. Anan and said to him, "You are my teacher, and R. Huna is the teacher of my teacher [i.e., R. Huna is your teacher], and he will put under a ban anyone who does not convey his message to you exactly the way he said it; and if he had not threatened with a ban I would never have said what I am about to say: 'Anan, Anan, should I collect from real estate or from movable goods? Furthermore, in a house of mourning, [marzicha], who sits at the head of the table?'" R. Anan now went to Mar Ukva and said, "Look at the way R. Huna addressed me in his message, calling me 'Anan, Anan'. Also, I do not know what he meant by marzicha." Said Mar Ukva, "Tell me exactly (69b) what transpired." R. Anan told him the background of the entire incident [and the exact text of the message he sent to R. Huna]. Exclaimed Mar Ukva, "How does a person who does not know what marzicha means have the audacity to address R. Huna as 'our friend Huna'!"

[Focusing on the second question, the Gemara asks:] What does marzicha mean? Marzicha means mourning, for it says, "For thus said God: Do not go to a house of mourning [marzei'ach]" (Jeremiah 16:5).

[Referring to the question R. Huna sent to R. Anan,] R. Abbahu said: From where do we know that a mourner sits at the head of the table? For it says, "I would choose their way, I would sit at the head, I would rest like a king among his troops, as one who consoles [yenachem] mourners" (Job 29:25). [This is no proof;] yenachem means, "one who consoles mourners" [sits at the head of the table]! R. Nachman b. Yitzchak replied: The word yenachem can be read as yenucham, which means "one who is comforted," [he sits at the head of the table]. Mar Zutra said: We derive it from here, "The banquets of the haughty will cease [vesar mirzach

seruchim]" (Amos 6:7), [which is expounded to mean:] He whose soul is bitter and distracted [mar-zach, i.e., the mourner] becomes the head [sar] of the celebrated men [seruchim] who come to comfort him.

LIKE A BRIDE

(71b) It says, "So I became in his eyes as one who finds favor [shalom]" (Song of Songs 8:10). R. Yochanan expounded: Like a bride who was found perfect [sheleimah] in her father-in-law's house and is eager to tell her parents how much she is appreciated. And it says, "And in that day [of the Redemption], says God, you [Israel] will call me Ishi [my Husband], and no longer will you call me Baali [my Master]" (Hosea 2:18). [Both ishi and baali denote "my husband," but ishi suggests greater intimacy than baali.] R. Yochanan said: That means: She will be like a bride in her father-in-law's house [since she loves her husband, she is happy there; hence ishi], and not like a bride in her father's house [where she does not feel secure and at ease].

ACTS OF KINDNESS
FOR THE DEAD

(72a) We learned in a Baraita: R. Meir used to say: What is meant by the verse, "It is better to go to the house of mourning than to go to a house of feasting, for that is the end of all man, and the living should take it to heart" (Ecclesiastes 7:2)? [Specifically, what is meant by the phrase,] "and the living should take it to heart"? [After all, God wants people to serve Him out of love, not out of fear of death (Etz Yosef).] [R. Meir answered:] It refers [not to death itself but] to rituals that are associated with death. A person should realize that if he mourns for other people, others will mourn for him; if he takes care of the burial of other people, others will take care of his burial; if he bewails the death of other people, others will bewail his death; if he escorts others to the grave, others will escort him; if he carries the casket of others, others will carry his casket.

THE AIR OF ERETZ YISRAEL
MAKES YOU SMART

(75a) It says, "But of Zion it can be said, 'This man and that man were born there,' and He the Most High, maintains her thus" (Psalms 87:5). [In time to come, when the gentiles will see a Jew they will say, "This is a son of Zion! Let us bring him to Zion!" (Rashi).]

R. Meyasha, the grandson of R. Yehoshua b. Levi, expounded: Regardless whether a person was born in Eretz Yisrael or is anticipating going to Eretz Yisrael, [he is considered a son of Zion]. Commented Abbaye: And one scholar who lives in Eretz Yisrael is smarter than two of us [Babylonian scholars]. Said Rava: But if one of us [Babylonian scholars] goes to Eretz Yisrael, he will be brighter than two of them. For example, when R. Yirmiyah lived here [in Babylonia] he did not understand what the Rabbis were saying, but when he went up to Eretz Yisrael he referred to us as "foolish Babylonians."

PROTECTION AGAINST INFECTIOUS DISEASE

(77b) R. Yochanan proclaimed: Be cautious of the flies that hover over a man who suffers from ra'atan[27] [because they carry the disease]. R. Zera never sat near a person infected with ra'atan if the wind blew over both of them, [a precaution against airborne bacteria]. R. Elazar never entered the tent of a ra'atan patient. R. Ammi and R. Assi would not eat any of the eggs coming from the alley where a ra'atan patient lived. R. Yehoshua b. Levi, however, [had a different approach]. He attached himself to ra'atan sufferers and studied the Torah [with them], for he said, [a person who studies Torah is compared to] "A beloved doe, inspiring favor" (Proverbs 5:19). If the Torah inspires favor for those who study it, would it not also protect them [from sickness]?

R. YEHOSHUA B. LEVI AND THE ANGEL OF DEATH

When R. Yehoshua b. Levi was about to die, the Angel of Death was instructed: Go and carry out whatever he wishes. When the Angel of Death came and showed himself to him, R. Yehoshua b. Levi said, "Show me my place in Gan Eden." The Angel of Death replied, "Very well; I agree." Said R. Yehoshua b. Levi, "Give me your knife, since I am afraid that you may frighten me [and kill me] on the way." He handed him the knife. When they arrived there he lifted him up and showed him [his place in Gan Eden]. Suddenly R. Yehoshua b. Levi jumped over the wall [into Gan Eden] and came down on the other side. The Angel of Death grabbed R. Yehoshua b. Levi by the hem of his cloak, but he exclaimed, "I swear that I will not go back." Said the Holy One, blessed be He, "If he ever made an oath and had it annulled [then this oath will be annulled] and he must return, but if not, he does not have to return." [He was allowed to stay in Gan Eden.] The Angel of Death then said to R. Yehoshua b. Levi, "Give me back my knife." But he did not want to return it to him. Thereupon a Heavenly Voice went forth and said to him, "Give him back his knife. He has to use it on mortal men."

Elijah the prophet announced the arrival of R. Yehoshua b. Levi, "Make room for the son of Levi! Make room for the son of Levi!" When R. Yehoshua b. Levi entered [Gan Eden] he found R. Shimon b. Yochai sitting on thirteen golden stools. R. Shimon b. Yochai said to R. Yehoshua b. Levi, "Are you the son of Levi?" "Yes," he replied. "Has a rainbow ever appeared during your lifetime?" R. Shimon b. Yochai asked. "Yes," he replied. "If that is so," R. Shimon b. Yochai retorted, "you are not the son of Levi" [i.e., you are not worthy of the announcement Elijah made about you and the honor bestowed on you. Because the rainbow is the sign of the covenant that God will not destroy the world. It should not appear in the lifetime of a perfect tzaddik, since his merit alone is enough to save the world, and the sign of the rainbow is not needed. Since you did see a rainbow you cannot be such a great tzaddik (Rashi). [The Gemara says:] Actually, that was not the case; there never was a rainbow in his lifetime. But R. Yehoshua b. Levi [humbly] thought, "It is not proper to take credit [for the fact that there was no rainbow]."

R. CHANINA B. PAPA AND THE ANGEL OF DEATH

R. Chanina b. Papa was a friend of the Angel of Death, and when he was about to die, the Angel of Death was instructed to grant him whatever he wished. He went to his house and revealed himself to him. "Allow me thirty days in which to review my studies," R. Chanina b. Papa requested. "For it says: Praiseworthy is the man who arrives in the World to Come with his learning intact." The Angel of Death left him, and after thirty days appeared to him again. R. Chanina b. Papa said to him, "Show me my place [in Gan Eden]. "All right, I will," he replied. "Give me your knife, since I am terrified that you may kill me on the way," R. Chanina b. Papa demanded. "Do you plan to do to me as your friend [R. Yehoshua b. Levi] has done?" the Angel of Death countered, [for, if he had had the knife, he would not have allowed R. Yehoshua b. Levi to jump into Gan Eden (Maharsha)]. "Bring a Torah scroll," the other suggested, "and see if there is anything written in it that I have not fulfilled." [The Angel of Death asked, "Have you [risked your life] and attached yourself to ra'atan sufferers and studied the Torah with them [as R. Yehoshua b. Levi did? Yet he tricked me into giving him my knife; you, who are not as pious, are even more likely to outwit me]."

Nevertheless, when R. Chanina b. Papa died, a pillar of fire separated him from the people, and we have a tradition that a pillar of fire will form an enclosure for no more than one or two outstanding personalities in a generation. R. Alexandri drew close to the deceased and said, "[Allow the pillar to depart] for the honor of the Sages," but he did not listen. "Do it for the honor of your father," but he did not listen. "Remove the pillar of fire for your own honor [so that people can come close to eulogize you and take care of your burial]," whereupon the pillar of fire left. Abbaye said: [The reason why there was a pillar of fire was] to keep away anyone who did not fulfill the Torah as he did. Said R. Abba b. Mattena to him: It would keep away you too, since you did not build a guardrail around your roof [in violation of Deuteronomy 22:8]. [The Gemara comments:] This was not so. Of course he had a guardrail, but just then the wind had blown it down.

R. Chanina said: Why are there no *ra'atan* sufferers in Babylon? Because they eat beets, and drink beer made from *cuscuta* of the *hizmi* shrub. R. Yochanan said: Why are there no sufferers from leprosy in Babylon? Because they eat beets, drink beer, and bathe in the waters of the Euphrates.

PERMIT YOUR STUDENTS
TO SERVE YOU

(96a) R. Chiya b. Abba said in the name of R. Yochanan: If a person denies his student the privilege of serving him, it is considered as if he denied him a kindness. For it says, "Is my own help not with me? . . . He withholds kindness from his friend" (Job 6:13,14), [i.e., by denying him the opportunity to help you, you are withholding kindness from him (Rashi)]. R. Nachman b. Yitzchak said: He even causes [his student] to lose the fear of Heaven, for the verse continues, "and he forsakes the fear of the Almighty" (ibid.).

RABBI YEHUDAH
HANASI'S DEATH

(103a) The Rabbis taught: When the time of Rebbi's [R. Yehudah Hanasi] passing drew near, he said, "I need to see my sons." When they entered he told them, "Be mindful of the respect you owe your mother. Let the light be lit, the table set, the bed made, each in its accustomed place. Yosef Chofni and Shimon Efrati who served me during my lifetime shall serve me after I am dead."

[The Gemara now analyzes the individual points of Rebbi's instructions.] "Be mindful of the respect you owe your mother." [The Gemara asks:] Isn't this a Torah commandment, since it says, "Honor your father and your mother" (Exodus 20:12)? [The Gemara answers:] She was their stepmother. [The Gemara asks:] But isn't honoring a stepmother also a Torah commandment? For it was taught: "Honor your father and your mother"; "your father" [the word *et*] includes your stepmother; "and your mother" [*et*] includes your stepfather, and the extra *vav* [of *ve'et imecha*] includes your older brother. [So you see, honoring a stepmother is also a Torah command.] [The Gemara answers:] The Torah command to honor a stepmother applies only during one's father's lifetime, but not after his death. [Therefore Rebbi had to instruct them to honor their stepmother after his death.]

[Rebbi further instructed:] "Let the light be lit, the table set, and the bed made, each in its accustomed place." Why did Rebbi request these things? [The Gemara answers:] Because [after his death] he would

come and visit his house on every *erev Shabbat*.[28] On a certain *erev Shabbat* a neighbor came to the door and spoke in a loud voice. Rebbi's maidservant told her, "Be quiet, Rebbi is sitting in there." When Rebbi heard [that his visit was publicized] he stopped coming, in order not to cast aspersions on earlier *tzaddikim* [who were not granted the privilege of visiting their homes].

[Rebbi said in his final instructions:] "Yosef Chofni and Shimon Efrati who served me during my lifetime shall serve me after I am dead." At first it was thought that Rebbi meant "they shall serve me in this world" [i.e., they should take care of his funeral]. But when it turned out that they had died and were buried before Rebbi, everyone realized that Rebbi meant that they should serve him in the World to Come. [If they had died already] why did Rebbi find it necessary to tell them to serve him after his death? So that people should not say: [They died at a young age] because they had transgressed, and they only lived in the merit of Rebbi, [and now that Rebbi died, they also died. By saying that they should serve him in the World to Come Rebbi implied that they were not guilty of any sin].

Rebbi then said to his sons, "I need to see the Sages of Israel." When the Sages entered he told them, "Do not arrange special memorial meetings for me in the small towns, [but rather in the larger cities to ensure that adequate honor is paid to the Nasi as the personification of Torah (*Maharsha*)]. (103b) Make sure that the yeshivah will resume normal functioning after thirty days [of mourning]. Shimon my son is a scholar, and my oldest son Gamliel shall be the *Nasi* [President of the Sanhedrin] and Chanina b. Chama shall be the head of the yeshivah."

[Rebbi ordered:] "Do not arrange special memorial meetings for me in the smaller towns"—at first the Sages thought that Rebbi wanted to save [the people of the small towns] the trouble [of attending the memorial services]. But when they saw that when memorial services were held in the large cities everybody came [even the people from the villages and the small towns] they realized [that the reason Rebbi wanted to be eulogized in the large cities was] because of the honor [of the Torah that he personified].

"Reopen the yeshivah after thirty days [of mourning]." [Rebbi gave this instruction] because he said: I am not greater than Moses our teacher, about whom it says, "The children of Israel mourned Moses in the west plains of Moab for thirty days" (Deuteronomy 34:8). Therefore, for the first thirty days you should mourn both day and night; however, after the thirty days, either mourn in the daytime and study at night, or mourn at night and study in the daytime, until you complete a full year of mourning.

[The Gemara now briefly digresses:] On the day Rebbi died, a Heavenly Voice came forth and said: Whoever was present at the passing of Rebbi is destined to have a share in the World to Come. A certain laundryman used to come to Rebbi every day, but on that particular day he failed to make his customary call. When he heard [what the Heavenly Voice] had said, he became terribly upset [for having missed the funeral]. He went up the roof, fell to the ground, and died. A Heavenly Voice then announced: This laundryman, too, is destined to have a share in the World to Come.

[The Gemara resumes its analysis of Rebbi's instructions.] [Rebbi said:] "Shimon my son is a scholar." [The Gemara asks: Since he did not appoint Shimon as Nasi] what was the point of him mentioning this? [The Gemara answers:] This is what he meant to say: Although my son Shimon is a scholar, my son Gamliel shall be the Nasi [because he is the firstborn]. Said Levi: That is obvious! [Why did Rebbi have to give special instruction for that?] Replied R. Shimon b. Rebbi [sneeringly], "It was necessary to mention it for yourself and for your lameness.[29] [Levi became lame when he demonstrated the kidah[30]]. [The Gemara asks:] Why didn't R. Shimon b. Rebbi understand Levi's question? Doesn't it say explicitly, "But he gave the kingship to Jehoram for he was the firstborn" (2 Chronicles 21:3)? [Thus the firstborn is heir to the post; then why did Rebbi have to give special instruction on that score, as Levi asked?]

[The Gemara answers:] Jehoram was the greater among his brothers in all respects and therefore truly represented his ancestors, [thus he deserved to be the heir to the throne]. But R. Gamliel did not properly represent his ancestors, [because his younger brother Shimon was a greater scholar. Therefore, Rebbi had to give special instruction that, in spite of this, R. Gamliel should become the Nasi]. [The Gemara asks:[If he was not qualified on all counts,] then why did Rebbi ordain that he should become the Nasi? [The Gemara answers:] True, that in wisdom he did not represent his ancestors, but with regard to piety he was a true representative of his ancestors, [and that is why Rebbi appointed him as the Nasi].

[Rebbi declared in his instructions:] "Chanina b. Chama shall be the head of the yeshivah." But R. Chanina did not accept the position of rosh yeshivah because R. Afess was two-and-a-half years older than he; and so R. Afess officiated as head of the yeshivah. R. Chanina sat outside [the bet midrash, because he did not want to be subordinate to R. Afess], and Levi came and joined him. When R. Afess passed away, R. Chanina was appointed as rosh yeshivah. Since Levi now had no companion to sit with outside the bet midrash, he [left Eretz Yisrael] and came to Babylon. And that is the incident that was referred to [in Shabbat 59a]: When Rav was told that a great scholar who was lame had arrived in Nahardea and expounded that a lady is permitted to wear a crownlike headdress on Shabbat [when carrying of objects in a public domain is forbidden], he said, "Evidently R. Afess has passed away, and R. Chanina became the new rosh yeshivah,

so that Levi had no one to sit with outside the bet midrash, and therefore he decided to come here."

[The Gemara asks:] [How did Rav know that R. Afess had died,] perhaps it was R. Chanina who died, and R. Afess remained in office; and since Levi lost his study partner [R. Chanina], he came to Babylon? [The Gemara answers:] If you prefer, I can say: [If R. Chanina had died, and R. Afess were still the rosh yeshivah], Levi would have bowed to the authority of R. Afess, [so he would not have come to Babylon]. And if you prefer, I can say: Once Rabbi declared that R. Chanina b. Chama should become rosh yeshivah, it is impossible that he should not become rosh yeshivah, [thus Rav knew that R. Afess was the one who had died]. For it says about tzaddikim, "You [the tzaddik] would utter a decree and it would be done" (Job 22:28).

WHY DID R. CHIYA NOT BECOME ROSH YESHIVAH?

[The Gemara asks:] But why didn't Rebbi appoint R. Chiya as rosh yeshivah?[31] [The Gemara answers:] Because R. Chiya passed away before Rebbi. [The Gemara asks:] How could that be? Didn't R. Chiya say: I saw Rebbi's tomb and I shed tears over it." [The Gemara answers:] We have to reverse the names [and say that Rebbi shed tears over R. Chiya's tomb]. [The Gemara asks:] But did not R. Chiya say: On the day that Rebbi died, holiness ceased to exist? [Proof that R. Chiya lived at the time of Rebbi's passing.]—We have to reverse the names.—But haven't we learned in a Baraita: When Rebbi lay [deathly] ill, R. Chiya came to visit him and found him crying. "Rebbi, why are you crying," he asked. "Didn't we learn in a Baraita: If a person dies with a smile on his face, it is a good omen for him; if he dies crying, it is a bad omen for him; his face upward, it is a good omen; his face downward is a bad omen; facing the people is a good omen, facing the wall is a bad omen; if his face is yellowish, it is a bad omen; if bright red, it is a good omen; if he dies on erev Shabbat, it is a good omen [because he is entering into a state of rest]; on motza'ei Shabbat,[32] it is a bad omen. If he dies on erev Yom Kippur, it is a bad omen; on motza'ei Yom Kippur, it is a good omen [since on Yom Kippur all his sins were forgiven]. Dying of an intestinal disease is a good omen because most tzaddikim die of digestive disturbances. [So you see, crying is a bad omen! Then why are you crying?]

Rebbi replied: I am crying because of the Torah and the mitzvot I will not be able to fulfill anymore. [In short, the above is proof that when Rebbi was dying R. Chiya was still alive.] [The Gemara answers:] If you wish I can answer: Reverse the names [and say: Rebbi came to visit R. Chiya]. And if you prefer, I can say: There is no need to reverse the names, [and Rebbi died before R. Chiya].—Then why didn't Rebbi appoint R. Chiya as rosh yeshivah?] Since R. Chiya was engaged in doing important *mitzvot*, Rabbi thought: I don't want to disrupt the beneficial work he is doing.

R. CHIYA'S MONUMENTAL ACHIEVEMENT

And what this [beneficial work] was becomes evident in the following story:[33] Once when R. Chiya and R. Chanina were involved in an argument, R. Chanina said to R. Chiya, "How [dare you] argue with me? [I am such an outstanding scholar that] if, God forbid, the Torah should be forgotten in Israel, I would be able to restore it with my logical reasoning!" Replied R. Chiya, "[What I am doing is even greater.] I see to it [that it will never come to the point that] the Torah will be forgotten in Israel. [How so?] I bring flax seed, which I sow. I weave nets from the flax plants for hunting. With the nets I trap deer. The flesh of the deer I feed to orphans. From its hide I prepare scrolls, and I go into a town where there is no teacher. I then write down the five books of the Torah and I teach one to each of five children. Then I teach one of the six Orders of the Mishnah to each of six children, and I tell each of them: Teach your book to the others, [and the others will teach theirs to you]. And that was what Rebbi had in mind when he exclaimed, "How great are the accomplishments of Chiya."[34] Said R. Shimon b. Rebbi to Rebbi: "[Are his deeds] greater than yours?" "Yes," Rebbi replied. Asked R. Yishmael b. R. Yose, "Even greater than my father's deeds?" Replied Rabbi, "God forbid, I would never say a thing like that."

RABBI INSTRUCTS HIS SON

[The Gemara resumes the discussion of Rebbi's deathbed instructions.] Rebbi then said, "I want to see my younger son." R. Shimon entered, and Rebbi transmitted to him the orders of wisdom [i.e., the mystical teachings of Kabbalah and metaphysics (Iyun Yaakov)]. "I want to see my older son," Rebbi said. R. Gamliel entered, and Rabbi transmitted to him the rules of the office of *Nasi*. "My son," he said, "conduct your office of *Nasi* with authority.[35] And inspire fear among the students [so that they respect you]."

[The Gemara asks:] Is that right? [Is it proper to intimidate Torah students?] Doesn't it say, "He honors those that fear God" (Psalms 15:4), and we learned[36] that this refers to Jehoshaphat, King of Judah, who, whenever he saw a Torah scholar, would rise from his throne, embrace him and kiss him, and call him, "My rabbi, my rabbi, my teacher, my teacher"? [The Gemara answers:] This is no difficulty. The latter case refers to privacy, [in privacy even a king should honor a Torah scholar]; the former case applies in public, [when a ruler has to maintain the dignity of his office and must inspire respect among the people].

THE ANGELS OVERPOWERED THE *TZADDIKIM*

We learned in a *Baraita*: Rebbi lay ill in Tzipori, but a burial place was reserved for him in Bet She'arim. But we learned in a *Baraita*: It says, "Righteousness, righteousness shall you pursue" (Deuteronomy 16:20) —follow Rebbi to his Bet Din in Bet She'arim, [proof that Rebbi lived in Bet She'arim and not in Tzipori]? [The Gemara answers: Rebbi did indeed live in Bet She'arim, but when he became sick he was taken to Tzipori (104a) because it is situated at a higher altitude, and its air is invigorating.]

On the day that Rebbi died the Rabbis declared a public fast and prayed for heavenly mercy. They said [metaphorically]: Whoever says that Rebbi has died will be stabbed with a sword. [He lives on in the Mishnah, which he compiled.]

Rebbi's maid went on the roof and prayed, "The angels desire Rebbi, and the mortals desire Rebbi. May it be the will of God that the mortals overpower the angels." But when she saw how many times Rebbi had to go to the toilet,[37] and suffered taking off the *tefillin* and putting them on again, she prayed, "May it be the will of God that the angels overpower the mortals." Since the Sages prayed continuously, preventing Rebbi from dying, she threw a jar from the roof to the ground, momentarily distracting the Sages from their prayers. At that moment, Rebbi's soul departed.

The Sages told Bar Kappara to go and see how Rebbi was faring. When he entered the room he found that Rebbi had passed away. He tore his garment but he turned the tear backward [in order that no one should be able to tell]. When he returned he began his eulogy, "The angels and the *tzaddikim* took hold of the Holy Ark [i.e., Rebbi]. The angels overpowered the *tzaddikim*, and the Holy Ark was captured." The Sages asked him, "Does that mean that he passed away?" "You said it," he replied, "I never said it."

REBBI RAISED HIS TEN FINGERS

When Rebbi passed away, he raised his ten fingers and said, "Master of the universe, it is obvious and known to You that with my ten fingers I have toiled in the study of the Torah, and I did not enjoy any worldly pleasure even with my little finger. May it be Your will that there will be peace in my final resting place." Thereupon a Heavenly Voice came forth, declaring, "He will come in peace; they will rest on their resting places" (Isaiah 57:2). [The Gemara asks:] It should have said, "On *your* resting place"! [The Gemara answers: The plural form] bolsters R. Chiya b. Gamda's view. For he said in the name of R. Yose b. Shaul: When a *tzaddik* leaves this world, the angels say to the Holy One, blessed be He, "Master of the universe, the *tzaddik* So-and-so is coming." And He answers them, "Let the *tzaddikim* get up from their resting places, go forth to meet him, and say to him, 'Come in peace,' [and afterward], "they will return to repose on their resting places.'"

R. Elazar said: When a *tzaddik* leaves this world, three groups of ministering angels come out to welcome him. One group exclaims, "Come in peace!" The other group declares, "He who walks in his integrity" (Isaiah 57:2). The third group says, "Enter in peace; they will rest on their resting places." But when a wicked man perishes from the world, three groups of angels of destruction come out to meet him. One says, "There is no peace for the wicked" (Isaiah 48:22). The second group says, "You should die in sorrow" (ibid. 50:11). The third group says, "Go down and be laid to rest among the uncircumcised" (Ezekiel 32:19).

THE BANE OF TAKING A BRIBE

(105a) Rav Yehudah said in the name of R. Assi: The judges in Jerusalem who issued decrees received their salaries [amounting to] ninety-nine *maneh*[38] from the Temple fund [which consisted of offerings by the people. This was consecrated money]. Karna[39] used to take an *istara*[40] from the party who was innocent, and an *istara* from the party who was guilty, and then he would decide their case. [The Gemara asks:] How could he do this? Doesn't it say, "Do not take bribes" (Exodus 13:8)? Karna was only taking payment for the time he was taking off from his job, for he had a job to smell the wine in the wine cellars, [and he could tell which wine was about to go sour and, therefore, should be sold immediately (Rashi)], and for this he was paid a fee. A similar situation arose with R. Huna. Whenever he was asked to judge a case, he said: [I am busy watering my field right now]. If you bring me a person who will draw the water in my place, I will judge your case.

R. Abbahu said: Come and see how blind are the eyes of those that take a bribe. If a person has pain in his eyes he will pay money to a doctor, although it is doubtful whether or not he will be cured. Yet these people take something worth a *perutah* [a small coin] and blind their eyes with it, for it says, "Bribery blinds the clear-sighted" (Exodus 23:8).

Our Rabbis taught: "Bribery makes the wise blind" (Deuteronomy 16:19). Surely it will make the foolish blind. "It perverts the words of the righteous" (ibid.), and surely the words of the wicked. [The Gemara asks:] Can fools and wicked men become judges? [How can they expect to be offered bribes?] But this is what is meant: "Bribery makes the wise blind"—even a great sage who takes bribes will not leave this world without suffering from numbness of the mind. "It perverts the words of the righteous"—even a perfect *tzaddik* who takes bribes will not leave this world without suffering confusion of the mind.

When R. Dimi came [from Eretz Yisrael to Babylon] he said that R. Nachman b. Kohen expounded:

"Through justice a king establishes a land, but a man of graft tears it down" (Proverbs 29:4). If the judge is like a king who does not need anything, then he "establishes the land"; but if the judge is like a priest who goes around among the threshing floor [asking for *terumah*, the priestly share of the harvest, he cannot help being partial, and] he "tears it down."

Rabbah b. Shilah said: A judge who is in the habit of borrowing things is unfit to be a judge. However, this applies only if he owns nothing to lend to others, but if he has something to lend to others, [his habit of borrowing] makes no difference. [Asks the Gemara:] Is that so? Rava said: What is the reason [for the prohibition against taking bribes even if the judge is sincerely trying to render a fair judgment]? Because once a person receives a gift from somebody he establishes a bond, and the giver becomes like himself, and no one ever finds fault with himself. What is the meaning of the word *shochad*, "bribe"? *She-hu chad*, "the recipient and the giver are like one person."

R. Papa said: A person should not act as a judge for someone he loves and not for someone he hates. For no one can find fault with someone he loves or the merit of someone he hates. Abaye said: If a Torah scholar is loved by his townspeople, their love is not because they consider him a better man but because he does not admonish them for ignoring their religious duties.

Our Rabbis taught: "Do not accept bribery" (Exodus 23:8). The verse did not have to mention a bribe of money, but it wants to tell us that even accepting a bribe of words [or deeds] is forbidden, for the Torah does not say, "Do not accept *betza*, a monetary bribe," [but any kind of bribe is prohibited]. What is meant by a "bribe of words"? Like the bribe that was offered to Shmuel. He was once crossing the river on a narrow bridge when a man came over to him and lent him a hand to help him across. "What is your business here?" Shmuel asked. "I have a lawsuit," the man replied. "I am unfit to be your judge, [since I received a favor from you]," Shmuel answered.

Amemar was once hearing a lawsuit when a feather landed on his head. A man came and removed it. "What is your business here?" Amemar asked. "I have a lawsuit," the man replied. "I am unfit to judge your case," Amemar answered.

Mar Ukva once spit some saliva, and a man came and covered it. "What is your business here?" Mar Ukva asked him. "I have a lawsuit," the man replied. "[Since you did me a favor,] I am disqualified to judge your case," Mar Ukva told him.

R. Yishmael son of R. Yose had a tenant farmer who used to bring him a basket of fruit every Friday [as rent from R. Yishmael's orchard]. Once he brought it on Thursday. "Why did you change your routine today?" "I have a lawsuit," the tenant replied, "and I thought that since I am coming to you anyway, I might as well bring the fruit today [and save myself a trip]." R.

Yishmael did not accept it from him and said, "I am unfit to hear your case." He then appointed two rabbis to judge the case. As he was making the arrangements for the court case, he said to himself: [I wish] my tenant would use such-and-such an argument [for then he would win the lawsuit], or if he argued like that [he would win the lawsuit]. [Analyzing his thoughts,] he said: "Imagine the misery that awaits those that accept bribes! Here I did not take the fruit he wanted to give me, and even if I had taken it, I would only have taken fruit that belonged to me to begin with, [yet I am hoping that my tenant is going to win]. How much more [biased] would be a person who accepts an outright bribe!"

A man once brought to R. Anan a bunch of small swamp fish. "What is your business here?" he asked. "I have a lawsuit," the man replied. R. Anan did not accept it from him. "I am not fit to judge your case," he said. "I am not asking you to decide my case," the man said, "but will you at least accept my offering, so that I should not be prevented from bringing my first fruit?[41] For we learned in a *Baraita*: It says, 'A man came from Baal-Shalisha, and he brought to the man of God food from the first fruits: twenty loaves of barley bread—and some fresh kernels in their husks' (2 Kings 4:42). But how could Elisha [who was not a kohen][42] eat the first fruits? The verse implies that if someone brings a gift to a Torah scholar, it is as if he had offered first fruits."

Replied R. Anan, "Normally I would not have accepted your gift, but now that you have given me a good reason for taking it, I will accept it." He then sent the man to R. Nachman with the following message: R. Nachman, would you please judge the case of this man, since I, Anan, am disqualified from acting as a judge for him. R. Nachman thought: Since he sent me such a message, he must be a relative of his, [and it is forbidden to be a judge or a witness in a case involving a relative]. At that time, R. Nachman trying an orphan's lawsuit, [which placed him in a dilemma as to which case to decide first].

He thought: (106a) Judging an orphan is a positive Torah commandment ["Judge honestly"],[43] but respecting the wish of a Torah scholar is also a positive Torah commandment. [He decided that] the positive commandment of showing respect to a Torah scholar takes precedence. He therefore set aside the case of the orphan and took up the case of that man. When the other party to the lawsuit noticed the honor [R. Nachman] was showing his opponent [to the point of postponing an orphan's case], he was dumbfounded [and could not present his side of the dispute].

R. Anan used to receive regular visits from Elijah the prophet, who would learn with him *Seder Eliyahu*. After this incident, Elijah no longer appeared. R. Anan fasted and prayed, and finally Elijah returned. However, when Elijah came this time, he frightened R. Anan very much. [He found fault with R. Anan for

accepting the gift that initially was intended as a bribe, and for wording the message to R. Nachman in a way that caused him to delay the orphan's lawsuit (*Maharsha*).] So R. Anan made a box and sat in it until they finished learning *Seder Eliyahu*. And that is why people speak of *Seder Eliyahu Rabbah* [the greater *Seder Eliyahu*, which R. Anan learned before this incident], and *Seder Eliyahu Zuta*, [the small *Seder Eliyahu*, which he learned inside the box].

THE FAMINE IN
R. YOSEF'S TIME

[The Gemara now derives an unrelated fact from the above-quoted verse about the twenty loaves.] In R. Yosef's time there was a famine. The Rabbis said to R. Yosef, "Please pray for heavenly mercy." Replied R. Yosef, "After the majority of the prophet Elisha's disciples left, and twenty-two hundred disciples remained [for whom Elisha had to provide food during the famine], yet Elisha did not pray for relief of the famine; then how can you expect me to pray for heavenly mercy? [The Gemara asks:] From where do you know that so many disciples remained? [The Gemara answers:] Because it says, "[A man brought twenty loaves of barley bread and some fresh kernels in their husks. Elisha said, 'Give it to the men.'] His servant said, 'How can I place this before a hundred men?'" (2 Kings 4:43). Now what is meant by the phrase, "before a hundred men"? Do you think that all the food was to be set before one hundred men? [That is not likely,] for in a year of famine [twenty loaves of bread] is far too much for one hundred men. We must therefore say that a single loaf was placed before one hundred men. [There were twenty loaves of barley, one loaf of bread of first fruit, and one loaf of fresh kernels—a total of twenty-two loaves, each loaf for one hundred men, which proves that there were twenty-two hundred men (Rashi).]

When the majority of the disciples departed from the yeshivah of Rav there were still twelve hundred left; when the disciples departed from the yeshivah of R. Huna there remained eight hundred. When R. Huna gave his lecture he was surrounded by thirteen *amora'im* [who would repeat and explain his words to the masses of students]. When the scholars who attended R. Huna's lectures stood up to leave and shook out their garments [it was customary to sit on the floor during the lecture], the dust rose and darkened the light of day, and the people in Eretz Yisrael said, "They have risen after the lecture of R. Huna the Babylonian."[44] When the disciples departed from the yeshivah of Rabbah and R. Yosef, there remained four hundred disciples who called themselves orphans. When the disciples took leave from the yeshivah of Abaye—others say, from the yeshivah of R. Papa; still others say, from the yeshivah of R. Ashi—there remained two hundred disciples, and these called themselves orphans of the orphans.

THE SAD LOT OF A POOR MAN
(110b) Shmuel said: Any change in the diet, [even changing from an inferior one to a better one] causes intestinal trouble. It says in the Book of Ben Sira: "All the days of a poor man are bad" (Proverbs 15:15); [because he is hungry all the time]. [The Gemara asks:] But on *Shabbat* and Yom Tov [the poor people are generally provided with substantial meals, then not all their days are bad]? [The Gemara answers:] This can be explained according to Shmuel. For Shmuel said: Any change in the diet leads to stomach trouble [and the rich food on *Shabbat* and Yom Tov is harmful to them]. Ben Sira said: Also the nights [of a poor man are bad]. His roof is lower than all roofs, so that the rain of the other roofs runs off on his roof, and his vineyard is on the height of the mountain so that the soil of his vineyard is washed down into the vineyards of others.

LIVE IN ERETZ YISRAEL
We learned in a *Baraita*: You should always live in Eretz Yisrael, even in a city where most of the population are non-Jews, but you should not live outside of Eretz Yisrael even in a city where most of the population are Jews. For whoever lives in Eretz Yisrael is considered as though he has a God; and whoever lives outside Eretz Yisrael is considered as though he has no God. [How do we know that whoever lives in Eretz Yisrael is regarded as though he has a God?] For it says, "To give you the land of Canaan, and to be a God for you" (Leviticus 25:38). [The Gemara asks:] But can you say that a person who lives outside Eretz Yisrael has no God? [After all, God reigns over the entire world.] [The Gemara answers:] It comes to teach you that living outside Eretz Yisrael is comparable to worshipping idols. [If a person lives among heathens he will be influenced by them.] We find a similar situation in connection with David. [David said to Saul], "They have driven me away this day from attaching myself to the heritage of God [i.e., Eretz Yisrael] as if to say, 'Go worship the gods of others!'" Now, did anyone say to David, "Serve the gods of others?" But the text means to tell you that whoever lives outside Eretz Yisrael is compared to one who worships idols.

THE THREE OATHS
R. Zeira was trying to avoid Rav Yehudah because he wanted to go to Eretz Yisrael, [and Rav Yehudah frowned on this]. For Rav Yehudah said: Anyone that goes from Babylonia to Eretz Yisrael violates a positive commandment, for it says, (111a) "They will be brought to Babylonia, and they will remain there until the day that I take note of them, says God" (Jeremiah 27:22), [and that day has not yet come]. [The Gemara asks:] What about R. Zeira? [How can he go against this passage?] [The Gemara answers:

He will say:] That verse refers to the holy vessels of the *Bet Hamikdash* [that Nebuchadnezzar brought from Jerusalem to Babylonia (ibid. v. 19ff); they are the ones that must remain in Babylonia]. And Rav Yehudah? [Why does he forbid going to Eretz Yisrael when the verse he cites refers only to the holy vessels?] He has another verse [to support his view], "I adjure you, O maidens of Jerusalem, by the gazelles or by the hinds of the field: Do not wake or rouse love until it pleases God [i.e., until the time comes that God wants to redeem us]" (Song of Songs 2:7). And R. Zeira? [How can he say that it is permitted to go to Eretz Yisrael in the face of this oath?] He says: That verse is only telling us that Israel should not take up arms and go en masse [and by force] to Eretz Yisrael, [but an individual is permitted to go to Eretz Yisrael].[45] And Rav Yehudah [how can he say that even an individual should not go to Eretz Yisrael]? He says: There is another verse, "I adjure you . . ." (ibid. 3:5) [which refers to individuals]. And R. Zeira? [How can he go to Eretz Yisrael when there are two verses saying "I adjure you"]?

[R. Zeira says:] That verse is needed for the statement by R. Yose b. R. Chanina. For R. Yose b. R. Chanina said: [There are, in fact, three verses repeating the oath, "I adjure you . . ." (Song of Songs 2:7, 3:5, and 5:8).] And what is the purpose of those three oaths? One, that Israel should not go up [to Eretz Yisrael] with force; the second, that the Holy One, blessed be He, adjured Israel that they should not rebel against the nations; and the third, that the Holy One, blessed be He, adjured the nations that they should not oppress Israel too much. [In any event, all three verses are used, and there is no verse to indicate that an individual should not go to Eretz Yisrael]. [This being so,] from where does Rav Yehudah infer that it is prohibited? From, "Do not awake or rouse love" [which is considered as two oaths, and which occur in each of the three verses—enough to satisfy the three concepts of R. Yose b. R. Chanina and to forbid an individual to go to Eretz Yisrael].

And R. Zeira? [He will say: Even though each of the three oaths can be considered as two, I need all six.] For R. Levi said: Why do we need these six oaths? Three for the three concepts just mentioned by R. Yose b. R. Chanina, and the others, [one] that [the prophets] should not reveal the end of the *galut* [and the coming of *Mashiach*]; [two] that the people should not, through their sins, delay the coming of *Mashiach*; and [three] that they should not reveal to the nations the secret [of calculating the Jewish calendar, or alternately, the reasons of the laws of the Torah (Rashi)].

[The Gemara returns to the above-quoted verse:] "By the gazelles and by the hinds of the fields" (ibid.). R. Elazar expounded: The Holy One, blessed be He, said to Israel: If you uphold the oath, fine; but if not, I will give away your flesh like that of the gazelles and the hinds of the field.

THE BENEFITS OF LIVING
IN ERETZ YISRAEL

R. Elazar said: Any person that lives in Eretz Yisrael lives without sin, for it says, "None who lives there shall say, 'I am sick'; the people living there shall be forgiven of sin" (Isaiah 33:24). Said Ravina to R. Ashi: We interpret this verse as referring to people who suffer from disease [i.e., "The sick who live in Eretz Yisrael have their sins forgiven, because their suffering wipes our their transgressions" (*Maharsha*)].

R. Anan said: Whoever is buried in Eretz Yisrael is as if he were buried under the altar, for regarding the altar it says, "Make an earthen [*adamah*] altar for Me" (Exodus 20:21); and it says, "His Land [*admato*] will atone for His people" (Deuteronomy 32:43), [which shows that the entire territory of Eretz Yisrael has the same power of granting atonement as the altar, which symbolizes atonement].

Ulla regularly traveled to Eretz Yisrael, but he died outside of Eretz Yisrael. When the people reported this to R. Elazar he cried out, "That you, Ulla, should have died in an unclean land!" "But his coffin is being brought to Eretz Yisrael," the people assured him. He replied, "Receiving him in his lifetime, is not the same as receiving him after his death."

A certain man [who lived in Eretz Yisrael and whose brother had died childless outside of Eretz Yisrael] wanted to fulfill the obligation of *yibbum* [marrying his brother's childless widow][46] at Bei Chozaah [in Babylonia]. He came to R. Chanina to asked him whether it was permitted to leave Eretz Yisrael and settle abroad in order to carry out the *yibbum*. R. Chanina replied, "His brother married a heathen, and he died. Blessed be the Almighty who killed him; and this one wants to follow him!" [His brother did not really marry a heathen, but since he left Eretz Yisrael, he and his wife are considered idol worshippers, as was mentioned above (*Maharsha*).]

ERETZ YISRAEL
AND BABYLONIA

Rav Yehudah said in the name of Shmuel: Just as it is forbidden to leave Eretz Yisrael for Babylonia, so is it forbidden to leave Babylonia for other countries [because in Babylonia there were many *yeshivot*, and Torah learning flourished there]. Both Rabbah and R. Yosef said: It is even prohibited to leave Pumbeditha [a great center of Torah learning] and to settle in Bei Kubi [a village near Pumbeditha]. A man once moved from Pumbeditha to Bei Kubi, and R. Yosef placed him under a ban. A man once moved from Pumbeditha to Istunia, and he died. Abaye said: If this young scholar had wanted it, he still could have lived, [if only he had not moved away from Pumbeditha].

Both Rabbah and R. Yosef said: The suitable persons of Babylonia are accepted in Eretz Yisrael; the suitable persons of all the other countries are accepted in Babylonia. [The Gemara asks:] In what respect [are suitable persons accepted]? Do you think with respect to purity of lineage, [that women from Eretz Yisrael are preferred as marriage partners because their descent is known]? But did not the Master say: [Babylonia ranks higher than Eretz Yisrael in regard to purity of lineage, indeed,] all countries are like dough compared to Eretz Yisrael [i.e., a mixture, and we cannot be certain of the purity of the lineage], and Eretz Yisrael is like dough compared to Babylonia? [For nowhere is the lineage more pure than in Babylonia. Then how can you say that only suitable persons of Babylonia are accepted in Eretz Yisrael?] We must therefore say that "suitable persons are accepted" refers to burial; [people from Babylonia would bury their deceased in Eretz Yisrael, and people from distant countries would bury their deceased in Babylonia near the great Torah institutions of that country].

Rav Yehudah said: Whoever lives in Babylonia is considered as if he lived in Eretz Yisrael, for it says, "Woe! escape O Zion, you who dwell with the daughter of Babylonia!" (Zechariah 2:11).

Abaye said: We have a tradition that Babylonia will not witness the suffering that will precede the coming of *Mashiach*. This was explained to refer to Hutzal in Benjamin, and [in the days of *Mashiach*] it will be called the Corner of Refuge.

REVIVAL OF THE DEAD

R. Elazar said: The dead outside Eretz Yisrael will not be revived [during the resurrection of the dead]. For it says, "I will bestow splendor [*tz'vi*] upon the Land of Life" (Ezekiel 26:20), which is interpreted to mean that the dead of the land that I desire [*tzivyoni*] will be revived, but the dead of the land that I do not desire will not be revived.

R. Abba b. Mammel raised an objection: [How can you say that the dead outside of Eretz Yisrael will not be revived,] when it says, "May Your dead come to life, may my corpses arise" (Isaiah 26:19). Does not the phrase "May Your dead come to life" refer to the dead of Eretz Yisrael, and "may my corpses arise" to the dead outside Eretz Yisrael? [Thus all the dead will be revived.] And how do I interpret the verse, "I will bestow splendor [*tz'vi*] upon the Land of the Living" [which implies only the dead of Eretz Yisrael will be revived? That verse refers to Nebuchadnezzar about whom the All-Merciful said: I will bring against him a king who is as light-footed as a deer [*tz'vi*].[47] [R. Elazar] replied: Rabbi, I infer from a different passage [that only the dead of Eretz Yisrael will rise again], "Who gives a soul to the people upon it [i.e., Eretz Yisrael] and a spirit to those who walk on it" (Isaiah 42:5).

[The Gemara asks:] But it says, "May my corpses arise" [which means, all the dead will arise]?—[R. Elazar answers:] That verse refers to babies that were born dead [they, too, will be revived, but only in Eretz Yisrael]. [The Gemara asks:] But R. Abba b. Mammel [who said that the dead outside Eretz Yisrael will be revived], what does he do with the verse, "Who gives a soul to the people upon [Eretz Yisrael]"? He needs it for an exposition of R. Abbahu who said: Even a Canaanite slave girl who lives in Eretz Yisrael is assured to have a share in the World to Come. For it says here [in connection with afterlife], "to the people [*am*] upon Eretz Yisrael" and it says elsewhere [regarding slaves], [Abraham said,] "Stay here with [*im*] the donkey" (Genesis 22:5). And the Gemara expounds: people that are like a donkey.[48] [So we see that *am*, people, refers even to a slave girl, and if she lives in Eretz Yisrael she, too, has a share in the World to Come.]

"And a spirit to those who walk on it [i.e., Eretz Yisrael]" (Isaiah 42:5). R. Yirmeyah b. Abba said in the name of R. Yochanan: Whoever walks four cubits in Eretz Yisrael is assured a share in the World to Come. [This being so, it is difficult to understand] how R. Elazar can say that *tzaddikim* who died outside of Eretz Yisrael are not resurrected. R. Ila'i said: [They will be resurrected,] but their remains will first have to roll to Eretz Yisrael [and there they will come back to life]. R. Abba Sala Rabbah challenged this statement: [How can you say that!] Rolling to Eretz Yisrael is terribly painful for the *tzaddikim*! Abaye replied: There will be tunnels for them in the ground [so that they can walk upright to Eretz Yisrael, and there they will emerge alive (Rashi)].

THEIR REMAINS WERE BROUGHT TO ERETZ YISRAEL

[On his deathbed, Jacob said to Joseph,] "Let me lie with my fathers. Carry me out of Egypt, and bury me in their grave" (Genesis 47:30). Said Karna: There is a deeper meaning behind these words. Our father Jacob knew that he was a perfect *tzaddik*, and, since the dead outside Eretz Yisrael will also be revived, why did he trouble his children [to carry him from Egypt to Eretz Yisrael]? Because he wanted to avoid the hardship of having to walk through the tunnels to Eretz Yisrael.[49] Similarly it says, "Joseph made his brothers swear . . . you must bring my remains out of this place" (Genesis 50:25). And R. Chanina said: There is an underlying meaning to these words. Joseph knew that he was a perfect *tzaddik*, and, since the dead outside Eretz Yisrael will also be revived, why did he trouble his brothers to carry him four hundred *parsang* [from Egypt to Eretz Yisrael]? Because he wanted to avoid the pain of walking through the tunnels to Eretz Yisrael.

The brothers of Rabbah sent a letter to Rabbah [who lived in Babylonia, imploring him to join them in Eretz Yisrael], arguing: Jacob knew that he was a perfect *tzaddik* . . . [yet he insisted on being buried in Eretz Yisrael]. Ilfa added that the brothers mentioned

in their letter also the following incident: A man wanted very badly to marry a certain woman [who lived outside Eretz Yisrael], and he wanted to leave Eretz Yisrael [to marry her and settle in her country]. But when he heard [how much suffering a soul has to endure in order to get to Eretz Yisrael to be resurrected], he dropped the idea and remained single until the day he died. [The letter goes on: Perhaps you think that you have nothing to learn in Eretz Yisrael?] Although you are a great scholar, [you will agree that] you cannot compare a person who studies by himself to a person who studies under a master. Perhaps you will say that there is no master [in Eretz Yisrael who can teach you anything]? Let me tell you, there is a master for you in Eretz Yisrael, namely, R. Yochanan.

And if all this is not enough to persuade you to come, at least let us give you some advice [on how to conduct yourself outside Eretz Yisrael]. Be careful regarding three things: Don't sit for too long, because you might develop hemorrhoids. Don't stand too much, because standing is harmful to the heart. Don't walk too much, because excessive walking is harmful to the eyes. Rather divide your time equally: one-third of your time sitting, one-third standing, and one-third walking. Standing is better than sitting when you have nothing to lean on. [The Gemara asks:] How can you say that standing is better; [you just said that standing is harmful to the heart]! [The Gemara answers:] This is what is meant: Better than sitting (111b) with nothing to lean on is standing with something to lean on.

WILL ILLITERATES BE RESURRECTED?

R. Elazar said: Ignorant people will not be revived, for it says, "They are dead, never to live; lifeless, never to arise" (Isaiah 26:14). We have learned a proof to this: "They are dead, never to live." You might think that this applies to all, therefore it says, "lifeless, never to arise," meaning, those that are [spiritually] lifeless and negligent in the study of the Torah [will not be revived]. R. Yochanan said to him: It is no honor for God that you should say such a thing. [After all, the ignorant are also God's creatures.] I say the passage [does not refer to the ignorant] but to a person who is so [spiritually] lifeless and lax that he worships idols; [he is the one that will not be resurrected]. R. Elazar replied: I have another text that supports my contention. For it says, "For Your dew is like the dew of light, and the earth shall bring the dead to life" (Isaiah 26:19), which means that a person who makes use of the light of Torah study will be revived by the light of Torah, but a person who does not make use of the light of Torah study will not revive by the light of the Torah.

When R. Elazar noticed that R. Yochanan was chagrined [about his exposition that the ignorant will not be resurrected], he said: Rabbi, I have found a remedy for them in a verse in the Torah, [so that they, too, can be resurrected]. It says, "But you, who are attached to God your Lord, are all alive today" (Deuteronomy 4:4). How is it possible to attach yourself to the *Shechinah*, about which it says, "For God your Lord is like a consuming fire" (ibid. v. 24)? This is what the text means: Anyone who gives his daughter in marriage to a Torah scholar, or who does business in partnership with a Torah scholar, [so that the scholar can devote his time to Torah study], or who lets Torah scholars derive benefit from his resources, Scripture considers it as though he attached himself to the *Shechinah*; [and in that merit, "you are all alive today"—you will be revived to eternal life; and not just scholars, but anyone that assists Torah scholars will be resurrected].

There is a similar interpretation of the verse, "To love God your Lord, to obey Him, and to attach yourself to Him" (ibid. 30:20). How is it possible for a human being to attach himself to the *Shechinah*? This is what it means: Anyone who gives his daughter in marriage to a Torah scholar, or who does business in partnership with a Torah scholar, or who lets Torah scholars derive benefit from his resources, Scripture considers it as if he attached himself to the *Shechinah*.

IN TIME TO COME . . .

R. Chiya b. Yosef said: In time to come the *tzaddikim* will sprout through the soil and come up in Jerusalem, for it says, "May people sprout from the city like the grass of the earth" (Psalms 72:16), and "the city" can refer only to Jerusalem, for, [speaking about Jerusalem,] Scripture says, "And I shall protect this city" (2 Kings 19:34).

R. Chiya b. Yosef also said: In time to come the *tzaddikim* will rise in the clothes [they wore when they were alive].[50] We can logically infer this from a kernel of wheat. If a kernel of wheat that is planted naked, sprouts with many covers, how much more so the *tzaddikim* who are buried in their shrouds.

R. Chiya b. Yosef further said: In time to come Eretz Yisrael will grow ready-made cakes and silk garments, for it says, "There will be abundant grain on the earth" (Psalms 72:16). The Rabbis taught: "There will be abundant grain on the earth of the mountaintops" (ibid.). This is an indication that in time to come wheat will rise as tall as a palm tree and will grow on mountaintops. And in case you think that it will be difficult to harvest it, it says [in the same verse], "Its fruit will rustle like the [cedars of] Lebanon" (ibid.); the Holy One, blessed be He, will bring a wind from His treasure house that will blow over the wheat and loosen its fine flour. A man will go out into the field, and all he has to do is pick up a handful [of flour], and this will be enough to nourish him and his entire household.

It says, "Wheat as fat as kidneys" (Deuteronomy 32:14). This indicates that in time to come a kernel of wheat will be as large as the two kidneys of a big bull. And this should come as no surprise, for a fox once made his den in a turnip, and what was left of the turnip weighed sixty Tzipori pounds.

We learned in a *Baraita*: R. Yosef said: It once happened in Shichin that a man left his son three twigs of mustard. One of them split off the stalk and it was found to contain nine *kav* of mustard, and the timber was enough to cover a potter's shack.

R. Shimon b. Tachlifa related: Our father left us a head of cabbage, and we had to climb up and down a ladder [to gather its top leaves].[51]

It says, "You will drink blood of grapes like delicious wine" (Deuteronomy 32:14). This indicates that the World to Come is not like this world. In this world there is the toil of harvesting and of pressing the grapes. But in the World to Come a person will bring one grape on a wagon or a ship, put it in the corner of his house, and draw [wine] from it as if it were a large barrel [it does not need pressing], while the stalk of the grape will be used to make fire for cooking. There will not be a grape that will not contain thirty *se'ah* of wine. For it says, "You will drink blood of grapes like delicious wine [*chamer*]." Don't read *chamer*, "wine," but *chomer* [a measure of thirty *se'ah*].

THE ABUNDANT HARVEST
OF ERETZ YISRAEL

When R. Dimi came [from Eretz Yisrael to Babylonia] he said: What is meant by the passage [in Jacob's blessing to Judah], "He loads down his donkey with a [single] grapevine" (Genesis 49:11)? There is not a vine in Eretz Yisrael that does not require all the inhabitants of one city to harvest it [*ayar*, "donkey," and *ir*, "city," are written with the same consonants]. "[He loads down] his young donkey with a single vine branch" (ibid.)—there is not a fruitless tree in Eretz Yisrael that will not produce a load [of fruit] for two female donkeys. Now you might say that it does not contain wine. That is why the verse continues, "He washes his clothes in wine" (ibid.). And you might say that the wine is not red; that is why it says, "[he washes] his cloak in the blood of grapes" (ibid.). And you might say that it does not intoxicate; that is why it says *suto* ["his cloak," related to *sut*, "shake, excite"]. You might say that it is tasteless; that is why it says, "His eyes are red [*chachlili*] from wine" (ibid. v. 12)—every palate [*cheich*] that tastes it says: [Give it] to me [Give it] to me! [*li! li!*]![52] You might think the wine is suitable for young people but not for the elderly; therefore it says, "his teeth are white from milk." Don't read *leven shinayim*, "white teeth," but *leven shanim*, "an elderly person."

[The Gemara asks:] What is the plain meaning of this verse: ["His eyes are red from wine, his teeth are whiter than milk" (Genesis 49:12)]? When R. Dimi came [from Eretz Yisrael to Babylonia] he explained:

The community of Israel said to the Holy One, blessed be He: Master of the universe, wink at me with your eyes, which will be sweeter to me than wine, and show me your teeth [i.e., smile at me], which will be sweeter than milk. This interpretation supports R. Yochanan who said: Showing your teeth to your neighbor [in a broad smile] is better than giving him a drink of milk, for it says, "his teeth are whiter than milk." Don't read *leven shinayim*, "white teeth," but *libbun shinayim*, "showing the teeth" [i.e., smiling].

R. Chiya b. Adda who tutored the children of Resh Lakish once stayed away for three days and did not come [to teach the children]. "Why did you take off?" Resh Lakish asked him [when he came back]. "My father left me a trellis, [a framework on which grapevines are trained to grow flattened out]," he replied, "and on the first day I cut three hundred bunches of grapes, each of which yielded one bottle[53] of wine. On the second day I cut three hundred [smaller] bunches, only two of which yielded one bottle. On the third day I cut three hundred bunches, and it took three bunches to produce one bottle [of wine], and so I renounced ownership [and gave away] more than half of it. "If you had not taken a leave of absence [from teaching my children]," said Resh Lakish, "it would have produced much more." ["You see, the longer you stayed away from Torah, the less wine the grapes produced" (Rashi).]

Rami b. Yechezkel once visited B'nei B'rak where he saw goats grazing under a fig trees. He noticed that honey was dripping from the figs, which mingled with the milk flowing from the goats. He remarked: This is the literal fulfillment of "[a land] flowing with milk and honey" (Exodus 3:8).

R. Yaakov b. Dosta'i related: Lod is three miles away from Ono. One day I got up early in the morning and walked the entire distance trudging up to my ankles in honey of figs. Resh Lakish said, I myself saw the flow of honey and milk of Tzipori and it covered an area of sixteen by sixteen miles. Said Rabbah b. Bar Chanah: I saw the flow of milk and honey in all of Eretz Yisrael, (112a) and it covered an area as large as from Bei Mikse to the Fort of Tulbanke, which is an area twenty-two *parsang* long and six *parsang* wide.

R. Chelbo, R. Avira, and R. Yose b. Chanina happened to be at a certain place where each of them was offered a peach as big as a pot of *K'far Hino* (a village). And how much does a pot of *K'far Hino* hold? Five *se'ah*. One-third of it they ate, one-third they gave away, and one-third they gave to their animals. A year later,[54] R. Elazar came to the same place, and he too was offered [peaches]. He took them in one hand, [they were so small that he could hold a few of them in one hand] and exclaimed, "A fruitful land into a salty waste because of the evil of its inhabitants" (Psalms 107:34). [The peaches shrank because of the sins of the townsmen.]

R. Yehoshua b. Levi once visited Gabla where he saw bunches of grapes that stood there like calves.

"Calves among the vines!" he exclaimed. "These are bunches of grapes," the people explained. "Land, O Land!" he cried. "Keep your fruit for yourself! For whom are you giving forth your fruit? For those Arabs who live here[55] because of our sins?" At the end of the year R. Chiya came to the same place, and he saw [bunches of grapes] standing like goats. "Goats among the vines!" he exclaimed. "Go away!" the people said, "don't you treat us as your friends did," [who caused the clusters that were the size of calves to shrink to the size of goats].

AN INTRICATE CALCULATION

Our Rabbis taught: In a blessed year, a field in Eretz Yisrael that measured *bet se'ah*[56] produced fifty thousand *kor* of grain, whereas the same field in Tzo'an [in Egypt] in its prosperous times produced no more than seventy *kor*. For we learned in a *Baraita*: R. Meir said: I saw in the valley of Bet She'an [which is considered outside of Eretz Yisrael (Rashi)] that a field of a *bet se'ah* produced seventy *kor*. Now, there is no country anywhere that is more fertile than Egypt, for, [when the Torah wants to describe the fertile Jordan valley it says,] "Like the garden of God, like the land of Egypt" (Genesis 26:12). And in all of Egypt there is not a more fertile spot than Tzo'an where the Egyptian kings resided, for it says, "For its princes were in Tzo'an" (Isaiah 30:4). [And if a field in Bet She'an yielded seventy *kor*, then surely a field in Tzo'an produced that much.]

[Now consider this:] In all of Eretz Yisrael there is no place more rocky than Chevron where the dead were buried. And yet, Hebron was seven times more fertile than Tzo'an, for it says, "Hebron was built seven years before Tzo'an in Egypt" (Numbers 13:22). Now what is meant by "built"? Do you think that it is to be taken literally? [That is not likely.] Do you think that a person [Ham] would build a house [let alone a whole city] for his younger son [Canaan] before he built one for his older son [Mitzrayim], since it says, "The sons of Ham were Cush, Mitzrayim, Put, and Canaan" (Genesis 10:6)? The word "built" must therefore mean that it was seven times more prolific than Tzo'an [thus Hebron yielded seven times seventy *kor* = 490 *kor*]. This refers to [Hebron's] rocky soil, but soil that is not rocky yields [ten *kor* more, which gives us five hundred *kor*]. Furthermore, this refers to times when the land is not blessed, but when it is blessed it says, "Isaac farmed in the area. That year, he reaped a hundred times as much" [i.e. $100 \times 500 = 50,000$ *kor*, the yield of a *bet se'ah* in Eretz Yisrael, which is what the Gemara set out to prove].

ERETZ YISRAEL,
THE BOUNTIFUL

We learned in a *Baraita*: R. Yose said: If you planted one *se'ah* of wheat in Judah it would yield five *se'ah*:

One *se'ah* of flour, one *se'ah* of fine flour, one *se'ah of bran*, one *se'ah* of coarse bran, and one *se'ah* of coarse meal.

A certain heretic once said to R. Chanina: You do well praising your country. My father left me a field of a *bet se'ah* [in Eretz Yisrael], and it supplies me with oil, wine, grain, peas, and beans, and my cattle graze on it.

A certain Amorite [one of the early inhabitants of Eretz Yisrael] asked a Jew, "How many dates do you harvest from this palm tree on the bank of the Jordan?" "Sixty *kor*," replied the Jew. "You have not improved the land," the Amorite exclaimed. "You have made it worse! We used to harvest a hundred and twenty *kor* from it." "I was only speaking of the yield on one side of the tree," the Jew explained.

R. Chisda said: What is the meaning of the verse, "I gave you a cherished land, the heritage of the deer, coveted by the multitude of nations" (Jeremiah 3:19)? Why is Eretz Yisrael compared to a deer? To tell you that just as the skin of a deer [once it has been removed] cannot hold its body [because it draws together], so, too, [all the storehouses of] Eretz Yisrael cannot hold its produce. Another explanation: Just as the deer is the swiftest of animals, so does the produce of Eretz Yisrael ripen sooner than that of all countries. Now you may think that, just as the deer is swift but its flesh is not fat, so is Eretz Yisrael swift to ripen but its fruit is not plump. Therefore it says, "A land flowing with milk and honey" (Exodus 3:8), [to tell you that its fruit is] richer than milk and sweeter than honey.

THEY CHERISHED
ERETZ YISRAEL

When R. Elazar went to Eretz Yisrael he said, "I have escaped one [curse]." [The Gemara will explain this.] When he was ordained he said, "I have escaped two [curses]." When he was made a member of the council that decides on the intercalation of the month[57] he said, "I have escaped three [curses]." For it says, "My hand will be against the prophets who see worthless visions . . . they will not be among the counsel of My people" (Ezekiel 13:9); this refers to the council that intercalates the month, [and when he became a member of that council he escaped that curse]. "Nor will they be inscribed in the record of the House of Israel" (ibid.); this refers to ordination, [and when he was ordained he was saved from that curse]. "Nor will they enter upon the soil of Israel" (ibid.) is to be understood according to its literal meaning. [When he came to Eretz Yisrael he escaped that curse.]

When R. Zeira came to Eretz Yisrael and he could not find a bridge to cross the river, he held onto a rope bridge [i.e., a narrow board that extends across the river, and a rope is strung between two poles on either bank of the river. By holding onto the rope with both hands a person can inch his way across the board (Rashi)] and crossed. Seeing this, a certain heretic scoffed, "What an impetuous people you are! Your mouth comes before your ears! [You accepted the Torah (mouth) before hearing (ears) what it obligated you to do.] You still persist in your rashness, [for you are risking your life crossing this rope bridge]." Replied R. Zeira, "A place that Moses and Aaron were not worthy to enter, how do I know that I am worthy to enter it? [That's why I rushed to enter Eretz Yisrael on this rickety contraption.]" R. Abba used to kiss the rocks of Akko. R. Chanina used to remove obstructions [from the roads of Eretz Yisrael out of his love of the country]. R. Ammi and R. Assi (112b) used to get up [from their seats to move] from the sun to the shade [during the summer], and from the shade to the sun [in the winter, in order not to complain about the weather of Eretz Yisrael (Rashi)]. R. Chiya b. Gamda [out of love of Eretz Yisrael] used to roll himself in the dust of Eretz Yisrael, for it says, "For your servants have cherished her stones and favored her dust" (Psalms 102:15).

R. Zeira said in the name of R. Yirmeyah b. Abba: In the generation when the son of David [*Mashiach*] will come there will be many people who hate Torah scholars. When I repeated this statement to Shmuel he said to me: There will be one calamity after another, for it says, "A tenth part will remain in it [Eretz Yisrael], and it too will be ravaged" (Isaiah 6:13). R. Yosef said: There will be plunderers after plunderers. R. Chiya b. Ashi said in the name of Rav: In time to come, all fruitless trees in Eretz Yisrael will bear fruit, for it says, "The trees have borne their fruit; the fig tree and the vine have given forth their wealth" (Joel 2:22).

NOTES

1. The measurement of the breastplate.

2. The *kohen* scooped out the flour of the meal offering with the three middle fingers, using the thumb and the little finger to rub off any flour sticking out at the ends.

3. A cubit was the distance from the elbow to the tip of the middle finger. The cubit was the unit of measurement for the building of the *Bet Hamikdash*.

4. Leviticus 4:6.

5. Leviticus 8:23,24.

6. A *meturgeman* explained to the large audience the discourse a lecturer had given in a low voice.

7. That is why Yehudah b. Nachmani chose a verse about young men.

8. This is Resh Lakish.

9. "Talk of the devil and he's sure to appear!"

10. A small coin.

11. Bill of divorce.

12. An *agunah* is not alllowed to remarry until her husband's death is established.

13. Literally, "one-fifth scholars."

14. In Aramaic, the three words, myrtle twig, custom, and foolishness sound alike.

15. Wedding canopy.

16. In Exodus 21:22, where there is no fatality, a payment of money must be made. In verse 23, where there is a fatality, the death penalty is inflicted by the Bet Din, and no money payment has to be made, on the principle: If a person incurs two punishments—the death penalty and money liability—for the same offense, he is liable only for the more severe one.

17. If a married man died childless, his widow must marry her husband's brother. This is called *yibbum*. If he does not want to marry her, the *chalitzah* ceremony is performed, after which she is free to remarry (Deuteronomy 25:5–10).

18. A Persian king who had a favorable attitude toward the Jews.

19. Mar Zutra did not swallow the King's food, but in order to avoid the danger resulting from the craving, he was permitted to taste the food (*Maharsha*).

20. 2 Samuel 3:4.

21. *Yevamot* 34b.

22. The week of *Sheva Berachot*, literally, Seven Blessings; during this period the seven blessings recited under the wedding canopy are repeated at each meal attended by the newly married couple.

23. If three generations have studied the Torah, the Torah becomes hereditary in that family and will stay in that family forever (*Bava Metzia* 85a).

24. *Sotah* 10b.

25. Etz Yosef.

26. Literally, who closes his eyes.

27. A skin disease; the disease with which Pharaoh was stricken (Genesis 12:17) (*Bereishit Rabbah* and Rashi).

28. *Shabbat* Eve.

29. As if to say, "Your question is not very perceptive."

30. Falling on the face, whereby the body remains suspended horizontally, braced by the thumbs, and only the face touching the ground (*Sukkah* 53a).

31. Rabbi held him in the highest regard (*Menachot* 88a).

32. The termination of *Shabbat*.

33. *Bava Metzia* 85b.

34. Why did R. Chiya have to do all the work himself? Couldn't he have bought ready-made books of Torah and Mishnah? In order for the Torah to take hold in the younger generation every step in the teaching process—from the very beginning—must be taken purely for the sake of Heaven, without infusion of alien ideologies (*Maharsha, Bava Metzia* 85b).

35. Alternately: Surround yourself with men of high caliber (Rashi). Or, raise the prestige of your office (Aruch, s.v. *dam*).

36. *Makkot* 24a.

37. He was suffering from loose bowels (*Bava Metzia* 85a).

38. One *maneh* is equivalent to one hundred *shekels*.

39. A judge in Babylonia.

40. I.e., a *sela*, or two *shekels*.

41. The first fruits [*bikkurim*] were brought to the *Bet Hamikdash* and given to a *kohen* (Deuteronomy 26:2f).

42. He was from the tribe of Gad (*Pesachim* 68a).

43. Deuteronomy 1:16.

44. To be taken in an allegorical sense: When R. Huna's great students dispersed and spread Torah in Eretz Yisrael, the awesome knowledge they had gained in R. Huna's yeshivah became apparent to all (Chiddushei Geonim, Darash Moshe).

45. Maharsha: Every Jew certainly has the right to go to Eretz Yisrael. The prohibition is against going all together and rebuilding the walls of Jerusalem by force. As for Nehemiah who said, "Come, let us build the wall of Jerusalem" (Nehemiah 2:17), he acted with the permission of King Artaxerxes.

46. Deuteronomy 25:5ff.

47. *Tz'vi* means both splendor and deer.

48. *Am* and *im* are written the same.

49. *Ein Yaakov*. The standard Gemara text reads: Because he might not be worthy to walk through the tunnels.

50. Tosafot quoting *Talmud Yerushalmi*.

51. There is a profound idea underlying these seeming exaggerations: At Creation it was God's intention for the earth to bring forth the final product—ready-made cake and clothes—so that man would be free to devote his life to spiritual pursuits. When Adam sinned mankind was cursed, "By the sweat of your brow you will eat bread." Toil and drudgery became his lot. However, in the end of days, Adam's sin will be rectified, and the earth will produce ready-made cake and clothes as God originally intended. The Gemara proves that this is possible by citing cases of outsized turnips and enormous cabbages (*Baal Haflaah*).

52. *Chachlili* is seen as a contraction of *cheich li li*, "palate, to me, to me."

53. Two *se'ah*.

54. At the end of that year the fruit shrank because of the evil inhabitants (*Maharsha*).

55. These were decent Arabs who occupied the land because we were expelled on account of our fruits (*Maharsha*).

56. An area of fifty by fifty cubits in which one *se'ah* of seed can be sown.

57. To decide when an additional month, Adar, has to be inserted into the calendar in order to bring the lunar and the solar year into harmony.

৵ NEDARIM ৵

PRONOUNCING GOD'S NAME IN VAIN

(7b) R. Chanin said in Rav's name: If someone hears his neighbor utter God's name in vain, he must place him under a ban; and if he does not, he himself deserves to be placed under a ban, because wherever God's name is mentioned freely, without restraint, poverty will prevail. And poverty is equated with death, for it says, "[While Moses was still in Midian, God said to him,] 'Go return to Egypt. All the men who seek your life have died'" (Exodus 4:19). [This refers to Moses' archenemies, Dathan and Abiram, who later took part in Korach's rebellion; so they did not actually die, but they had become poor. God assured Moses that they could not harm him, since being poor, they were as if dead, completely without influence, and nobody would listen to their incitement (Ran).] And we learned in a *Baraita*: Wherever the Sages placed their eyes [in a stern way, to punish], death or poverty followed.

R. Abba said: I was standing before R. Huna when we heard a woman pronounce God's name in vain. So he placed her under a ban, but he immediately lifted the ban in her presence. We can learn from this three things: First, if a person hears someone utter God's name in vain, he is obligated to put him under a ban. Second, if someone was placed under a ban, and he was there, the ban must be lifted in that person's presence. Third, no time needs to pass between the placing of the ban and its annulment [if the person repented (Rambam)].

R. Giddal said in the name of Rav: (8a) From where do we know that a person can take an oath to fulfill a mitzvah, [and we are not afraid that he will break the oath if he fails to do the mitzvah (Etz Yosef)]? For it says, "I have sworn, and I will fulfill to keep your righteous ordinances" (119:106). [The Gemara asks:] But aren't we all bound by the oath at Mount Sinai [to keep all the *mitzvot*, and you cannot take an oath to do something you already swore to do]? [The Gemara answers:] What R. Giddal meant to say is that a person is allowed to take an oath in order to spur himself [to do *mitzvot*, and this is not considered uttering God's name in vain].

R. Giddal also said in the name of Rav: If someone says to his neighbor: Let's get up early and study this chapter, the one that suggested it has to get up first, for it says, [Ezekiel said:] "He [God] said to me, 'Arise and go out to the valley and there I will speak with you.' So I arose and went out to the valley and behold— the glory of God was standing there" (Ezekiel 3:22). [God suggested it, and He was there before Ezekiel.]

THE HEALING SUN RAYS

(8b) R. Chanina said in the name of R. Miashia who had it from R. Yehudah b. Ila'i: What is the meaning of the verse, "But a sun of righteousness will shine for you who fear My name, with healing in its rays" (Malachi 3:20)? This refers to people who fear to utter God's name in vain. "A sun of righteousness with healing in its rays." Abbaye said: We can infer from this that the sun rays have healing power. He differs on that point with R. Shimon b. Lakish who said: There is no Gehinnom in the World to Come, but the Holy One, blessed be He, will take out the sun from its sheath: the righteous will be healed, and the wicked will be judged and punished by it. [While Abbaye applies the verse to this world, R. Shimon b. Lakish applies it to the World to Come.] The righteous will be healed by it, for it says, "But a sun of righteousness will shine for you who fear My name, with healing in its rays." And that is not all, but they will be rejuvenated by it, because the verse continues, "and you will go out and flourish like the calves of the stall" (Malachi 3:20). The wicked will be judged by it, for it says, "For behold! That day [i.e., the sun] is at hand, burning like an oven, when all the wicked people and all the evildoers will be like straw; and that coming day [i.e., the sun] will burn them to ashes, says God, Master of Legions, so that it will not leave them a root or branch" (ibid. v. 19).

THE COMMENDABLE *NAZIR*

(9b) We learned in a *Baraita*: R. Shimon Hatzaddik said: All my life I never have eaten from a guilt-offering that was brought by a *nazir*[1] who had defiled himself, except in one instance. Once a *nazir* came from the south, and I saw that he had beautiful eyes, a handsome appearance, and his thick locks of hair were arranged in jet-black ringlets. I said to him, "My son, what made you commit yourself to destroy your beautiful hair?" [Because at the end of the term of his vow, a *nazir* has to shave off his hair.][2] The *nazir* replied, "Back home I was a shepherd for my father. Once when I went to draw water from a well I gazed at my reflection in the water. At that moment my evil impulse seized me and tried to drive me from the world [i.e., destroy my place in the World to Come through the sin of pride]. But I said to my lust, 'Evil creature! Why do you boastfully intrude into a world that is not yours, [you are proud of something] that is destined to become dust, worms, and maggots? I swear that I will [become a *nazir* so that I will be forced to] shave off [this beautiful hair] for the sake of heaven.'"

[Said R. Shimon Hatzaddik:] I immediately got up and kissed his head, saying, "My son, may there be many *nezirim* [nazirites] like you in Israel! The Torah has you in mind when it says, 'When a man or a woman expresses a *nazirite* vow to God' (Numbers 6:2)." [You have the right motive for becoming a *nazir*, namely to subdue your *yetzer hara*.][3]

R. Mani objected: [We were told above that it was Shimon Hatzaddik's custom not to eat from the guilt-offering of a *nazir* who had become unclean.] In what respect is a guilt-offering of an unclean *nazir* different, that he did not eat from it: is it because it comes as a result of a sin? Then he should not have eaten from any guilt-offerings,[4] since they all are brought because of a sin? [Then why was he more reluctant to eat from a guilt-offering of an unclean *nazir* than from any other guilt-offering?] R. Yonah answered: This is the reason: When people regret their bad deeds they become *nazirites* [intending to be extremely self-disciplined for thirty days], but when [during the term of *nezirut*] they become unclean [through accidental contact with the dead] and have to start counting another thirty days of *nezirut*, they regret their commitment, and [since their intent is not sincere, it is as though they brought *chullin* [a profane sacrifice] to the Temple court. [But R. Shimon Hatzaddik was sure that this particular young man did not regret his vow of *nezirut*, and therefore he ate from his guilt-offering.]

ABSTAINING FROM WINE IS SINFUL

(10a) The Rabbis taught: R. Elazar Hakappar Berabbi said: It says [regarding the *nazir*], "And he shall make an atonement for having sinned against a soul" (Numbers 6:11). Against which soul has the *nazir* sinned? [Against his own soul,] because he tormented himself by abstaining from wine. And we can draw a logical inference from this: If a person who torments himself

only in regard to wine is called a sinner, how much more so is a person called a sinner if he mortifies himself by abstaining from everything. Thus, anyone who fasts [as an ascetic practice] is called a sinner. [The Gemara asks:] But this verse [Numbers 6:11] refers to an unclean *nazir*? [How can you infer from it that every *nazir* is a sinner?] [The Gemara answers:] Because he sinned twice, [(1) by becoming a *nazir* in the first place, and (2) by defiling himself during his term of *nezirut* (Ran)].

BASHFULNESS

(20a) We learned: Don't fall into the habit of making vows, for you will end up violating your oaths, [and since oaths involve pronouncing God's name they are more serious than vows (Ran)]. Don't become close with an *am haaretz*[5] for it will come to the point that he will give you *tevel* [produce from which no priestly gifts and tithes have been separated] to eat, and do not associate with a *kohen* who is an *am haaretz*, for in the end he will give you *terumah* to eat [the priestly gift that a non-*kohen* is forbidden to eat].[6] And do not converse excessively with a woman,[7] for it will lead you to immorality.

We learned in a *Baraita*: It says, "Moses said to the people, 'Do not fear, for in order to elevate you has God come; so that awe of Him shall be on your faces'" (Exodus 20:17). This means shamefacedness. "So that you shall not sin" (ibid.)—This teaches us that shamefacedness leads to fear of sin. Based on this is the saying: It is a good sign for a person to be shameful. Others say: A person who has a sense of shame will not easily sin; and, if a person is not shamefaced, it is a sure sign that his ancestors were not present at Mount Sinai [at the Giving of the Torah, when Moses said the above-mentioned words].

REFRAIN FROM MAKING VOWS

(22a) It says, "There is one who speaks harshly like piercings of a sword, but the tongue of the wise heals" (Proverbs 12:18). Whoever utters a vow deserves to be pierced by a sword, "but the tongue of the wise heals," [because they can annul his vow]. We learned in a *Baraita*: R. Natan said: Vowing is like building a personal altar [which is forbidden], and keeping the vow [rather than having it annulled] is like bringing a sacrifice on that altar.[8]

Shmuel said: Even if a person fulfills his vow he is considered wicked. Said R. Abbahu: Where do we find a proof for this? "If you refrain from vowing, there will be no sin in you" (Deuteronomy 23:23). [Consequently, if you do *not* refrain from vowing, and even if you fulfill your vow, you *do* have a sin.] The Torah uses the word *techdal*, "refrain," in connection with a vow, and elsewhere it says, "There the wicked *chadelu*, 'refrain' from agitation" (Job 3:17), [where *chadelu* is associated with the wicked. This gives us a hint that he who does not refrain from making vows is considered wicked].

THE EVILS OF ANGER

R. Shmuel b. Nachmani said in the name of R. Yonatan: If a person becomes angry, the various [agonies of] Gehinnom gain a hold on him [even in this world (Rosh)], for it says, "By expelling anger from your heart, you will remove evil from your flesh" (Ecclesiastes 11:10). And "evil" can only mean Gehinnom, for it says, "Everything God made He made for His sake, even the wicked for the day of evil" (Proverbs 16:4). And not only this, but he will also suffer from abdominal disease, for it says, [When you are sent into exile among the nations,] "There God will give you a heart of anger, failing of eyes, and suffering of soul" (Deuteronomy 28:65). Now what [sickness] is it that causes failing of eyes and a suffering soul? Abdominal troubles.

[The Gemara cites a story that involves "a heart of anger."] When Ulla went up to Eretz Yisrael [from Babylonia], he was accompanied by two Jews from Choza'i. Suddenly, one of them [angrily] got up and slit the other's throat. The murderer then said to Ulla, "Did I do the right thing?" [Afraid that if he disapproved the murderer would kill him too,] Ulla replied, "Yes, and widen the gash where you slaughtered him."[9] When Ulla came before R. Yochanan, he asked him, "Perhaps, God forbid, I encouraged trangressors [by telling him to widen the cut]?" Replied R. Yochanan, "You did it to save your life." R. Yochanan then began to wonder: Let's see: the passage, "There [in the lands of the Exile] God will give you a heart of anger" (Deuteronomy 28:65) refers to Babylonia. [But this murder happened in Eretz Yisrael. How could one Jew become so angry at another Jew in Eretz Yisrael that he would actually kill him?] Ulla replied, (22b) "[The murder did not happen in Eretz Yisrael]. At that time we had not yet crossed the Jordan [into Eretz Yisrael]."

Rabbah b. R. Huna said: When a person becomes angry, even the *Shechinah* is not important to him. For it says, "The wicked man, at the height of his fury, [says,] 'He will not avenge!' All his schemes are: 'There is no Divine Judge'" (Psalms 10:4). R. Yirmeyah of Difti said: [The person who loses his temper] forgets his learning, and he gradually becomes more and more foolish. For it says, "Anger lingers in the bosom of fools" (Ecclesiastes 7:9), [all that remains is his anger (Rosh)]; and it says, "The fool broadcasts his foolishness" (Proverbs 13:16). R. Nachman b. Yitzchak said: [The fact that he becomes angry] is an indication that his sins outnumber his merits, for it says, "A hot-tempered man commits many offenses" (Proverbs 29:22).

R. Adda b. Chanina said: If the Jewish people had not sinned, they would have received only the Five Books of the Torah and the Book of Joshua, because [the Book of Joshua] tells how Eretz Yisrael is to be divided among the tribes of Israel. [But since the other Books contain mainly admonitions and reproof for sins Israel committed, if Israel had not sinned, these books would not be needed.] For it says, "For with much wisdom comes much anger" (Ecclesiastes 1:18), [meaning, the wisdom and the chastisements of the prophets were given to Israel because they caused God much anger (Ran)].

THE IMPORTANCE OF THE MITZVAH OF *MILAH*

(31b) [The Mishnah says:] R. Elazar b. Azariah said: The foreskin is so repulsive, that it is a term used to disparage the wicked, for it says, "For all the nations are uncircumcised, and the House of Israel is of uncircumcised heart" (Jeremiah 9:25). R. Yishmael said: [The mitzvah of] *milah* is so great that thirteen covenants were made on it. [In Genesis 17:1–21, the chapter where Abraham is given the mitzvah of *milah*, the word *brit*, "covenant," occurs thirteen times.] R. Yose said: [The mitzvah of] *milah* is so great that it sets aside [the laws of] *Shabbat*. [*Milah*, which entails the forbidden labor of causing a wound, is performed on *Shabbat*.][10] R. Yehoshua b. Korcha said: [The mitzvah] of *milah* is so great that when Moses neglected it he was not given a reprieve even for a single hour. [The Gemara will discuss this later.]

R. Nechemiah said: [The mitzvah of] *milah* is so great that it pushes aside the law that forbids removing a leprous spot, [because if the spot is on the foreskin it may be removed together with it]. Rabbi said: [The mitzvah of] *milah* is so great that Abraham our Father, in spite of all the *mitzvot* he fulfilled was not called perfect until he circumcised himself, for [in introducing the mitzvah of *milah*, God said to Abraham,] "Walk before Me and become perfect" (Genesis 17:1). Another proof: The mitzvah of *milah* is so great, that if not for *brit milah* the Holy One, blessed be He, would not have created His world, for it says, "Thus said God, 'If not for My covenant [*briti*] day and night [a reference to *brit milah*], I would not have set up the laws of heaven and earth'" (Jeremiah 33:25). Rebbi said: [The mitzvah of] *milah* is so great that it equals all other *mitzvot* in the Torah put together, for it says, "This is the blood of the covenant [*brit*] that God is making with you regarding all these words" (Exodus 24:8).[11]

TZIPPORAH CIRCUMCISED HER SON

[The Gemara now explains the statement in the Mishnah that Moses was not given a reprieve when he neglected the mitzvah of *milah*. The Mishnah is referring to the incident when Moses set out to return to Egypt with his wife and two sons, and was confronted by an angel who wanted to kill him for failing to circumcise his son. Tzipporah then took a sharp stone and performed the *milah* on her son Eliezer, whereupon God spared Moses' life (Exodus 4:24–26).]

We learned in a *Baraita*: R. Yehoshua b. Korcha said: [The mitzvah of] *milah* is so great that all the merits Moses amassed were not able to protect him when he was lax in performing the mitzvah of *milah*. For it says, "God confronted Moses, and [an angel] wanted to kill him" (Exodus 4:24). R. Yose said: God forbid [to say] that Moses was lax in fulfilling the mitzvah of *milah*. This is what he was thinking: If I circumcise my son now and then [right away] go on my [mission to Egypt as I am commanded to do], it would endanger the life of the infant. For it says, [in the episode when Simon and Levi attacked the men of Shechem,] "On the third day [after their circumcision] when the people were in agony" (Genesis 34:25). [So we see that for the first three days after circumcision the person undergoing it is very weak.] [Moses reasoned:] If I circumcise him and wait three days, [and then begin my journey, that would not be right] because the Holy One, blessed be He, told me, "Go return to Egypt [immediately]" (Exodus 4:19). [Therefore, he did not circumcise the child and left for Egypt.]

[The Gemara asks:] Then why was Moses punished? (32a) [The Gemara answers:] Because he began making arrangements for the night's lodging, [instead of performing the *milah* without delay].[12] For it says, "It was on the way, in the lodging" (Exodus 4:24). [The phrase hints that he was punished because he busied himself with the lodging arrrangements instead of the *milah*.] R. Shimon b. Gamliel said: It was not Moses that the angel wanted to kill but the infant, for it says, [after she performed the *milah*, Tzipporah said,] "You are a bridegroom of blood to me" (ibid. v. 23), [meaning, "you are to me a bridegroom who was almost killed"]. Go out and see: who is called a bridegroom. [It cannot be Moses; he is her husband!] Surely we must say that it refers to the infant, [and he is called bridegroom in the sense that he is the main participant in the mitzvah of *milah*. So you see, the angel wanted to kill the infant, not Moses].

AF AND CHEIMAH, TWO AVENGING ANGELS

R. Yehudah b. Bizna expounded: At the time when Moses our Teacher was lax in performing the mitzvah of *milah*, Af and Cheimah [two avenging angels named Anger and Rage] came and swallowed him up, leaving only his legs [a euphemism for his membrum (Ran), as an indication that the punishment related to his postponement of the *milah*]. Immediately, "Tzipporah took a stone knife and cut off her son's foreskin, throwing it down at his feet . . . So [the angels] released [Moses]" (ibid. v. 24). At that moment, Moses attempted to kill them, for it says, [God had to say,] "Let go of Af and

leave Cheimah alone!" (Psalms 37:8). Some say that he did kill Cheimah, for it says, [God said,] "I don't have Cheimah" (Isaiah 27:4) [implying, Cheimah has been killed]. [The Gemara asks: How can you say Cheimah was killed when later, after the sin of the golden calf, Moses said,] "For I was terrified of Af and Cheimah" (Deuteronomy 9:19)? [So Cheimah was not killed?] [The Gemara answers:] There are two angels called Cheimah, [and Moses was afraid of the other angel Cheimah]. Or if you prefer, say: [Moses was afraid of] the army of Cheimah, [but Cheimah himself was killed].

THE EMINENCE OF THE MITZVAH OF *MILAH*

We learned in a *Baraita*: Rebbi said: Great is the mitzvah of *milah*, because no one occupied himself with fulfilling *mitzvot* like Abraham our Father, yet he was called perfect only by virtue of *milah*. For, [in introducing the mitzvah of *milah*] God said to Abraham, "Walk before Me and become perfect" (Genesis 17:1). And the next verse says, "And I will set My covenant between Me and you" (ibid. v.2), [meaning, "become perfect by fulfilling the mitzvah of *milah*"]. Another explanation: Great is the mitzvah of *milah* for it weighs as much as all the other *mitzvot* in the Torah, as it says, "For according to these words [i.e., the entire Torah] have I sealed a covenant [*brit*] with you and Israel" (Exodus 34:27). [In other words, *brit milah* is equal to all the *mitzvot* of the Torah.] Another explanation: The mitzvah of *milah* is so great, that if not for the mitzvah of *milah* heaven and earth could not endure. For it says, "If My covenant [*briti*] with the day and with the night would not be [referring to *milah*], I would not have set up the laws of heaven and earth" (Jeremiah 33:25). Now this statement disagrees with R. Elazar, for R. Elazar said: The Torah is so great, that if not for the Torah, heaven and earth could not endure. For it says, "If My covenant with the day and with the night [referring to Torah study], I would not have set up the laws of heaven and earth."

Rav Yehudah said in the name of Rav: When the Holy One, blessed be He, said to Abraham our Father, "Walk before Me, and become perfect" (Genesis 17:1), he began to tremble. "Perhaps there is something unseemly about me [that God has to tell me to perfect myself]?" But when God continued, "I will set My covenant between Me and you" (ibid. v. 2), his mind was set at ease, [because he realized that his imperfection was due to his lack of *brit milah*].

PURE AND SIMPLE FAITH

[When God promised Abraham that he would have children, it says] "[God] then took [Abraham] outside and said, '. . . count the stars . . . that is how numerous your descendants will be'" (Genesis 15:5). [What is the significance of the phrase, "He took him outside"?] Abraham had said to God: Master of the universe! I have gazed at the constellation [under which I was born], and I see that I am not destined to have a son beside Ishmael. Replied the Holy One, blessed be He: Abraham! Go "outside" of your astrology. [That is why it says, "he took him outside."] Israel is not ruled by the constellations.

R. Yitzchak said: Whoever conducts himself with pure and simple faith, the Holy One, blessed be He, will act toward him with full faith. And so it says, "With the devout You deal devoutly; with the one who is strong in his wholeheartedness You act wholeheartedly" (2 Samuel 22:26). R. Oshaia said: Whoever acts in pure faith will have good fortune, as it says, "Walk before Me, and become perfect, [meaning, have perfect faith in Me]" (Genesis 17:1), and this is followed by, "You shall be the father of a multitude of nations" (ibid. v. 4), [as the reward for your perfect faith].

Ahava the son of R. Zeira learned: Anyone who does not use black magic to foretell the future is brought into an area [in Heaven] close to God where not even the ministering angels are allowed to enter. For it says, "For there is no divination in Jacob and no sorcery in Israel. A time will come when it is said to Jacob and Israel, what has God wrought?" (Numbers 23:23). [Meaning, for not engaging in magical practices, a person will be brought into an area close to God that is forbidden to angels, and a time will come when the angels will have to ask that person, "What is God doing?"]

ABRAHAM'S SHORTCOMING

R. Abbahu said in R. Elazar's name: Why was Abraham our Father punished and his descendants enslaved in Egypt for two hundred and ten years? Because he pressed Torah scholars into military service, [to fight in the war against the four kings], for it says, "He armed his students who had been born in his house" (Genesis 14:14). Shmuel said: Because he went too far in questioning the ways of God. For it says, [When God promised Abraham that his children would inherit Eretz Yisrael, he asked,] "How can I really know that it will be mine?" R. Yochanan said: Because he kept people from entering under the wings of the *Shechinah* [i.e., from believing in God]. For it says, [After his victory over the four kings, Abraham returned all the captured property, thereupon,] "The king of Sodom said to Abram, 'Give me back the people. You can keep the property'" (ibid. v.21). [Abraham should have insisted on taking the people with him in order to teach them monotheism.]

"He armed [*vayarek*] his students who were born in his house" (ibid. 14:14). Rav said: The word *vayarek* implies that he emptied them of their Torah [by pressing them into the military (Ran)]. Shmuel said: He made them shine with gold [to entice them to go to

war against the four kings]. [The verse ends,] "All his 318 fighting men." R. Ammi b. Abba said: Eliezer was equivalent to all of them. Others say, the number of 318 refers to Eliezer himself, for the numeric value of Eliezer is 318.[13] [Thus Abraham took only Eliezer to fight against the four kings.]

TEACHINGS BASED ON *GEMATRIA*

[The Gemara cites other teachings of R. Ammi b. Abba based on *gematria*.] R. Ammi b. Abba said also: Abraham was three years old when he recognized God as his Creator, for it says, "All this is because [*eikev*] Abraham obeyed My voice" (Genesis 26:5), and the *gematria* of the word *eikev* is 172.[14] [Thus, Abraham obeyed God for 172 out of the 175 years of his life; therefore, at three years of age he recognized God.]

R. Ammi b. Abba further said: (32b) The numeric value of *haSatan* [Satan] is 364.[15] [This is an indication that Satan accuses on 364 out of the 365 days of the solar year. The one day he is silenced is Yom Kippur (Ran).]

R. Ammi b. Abba said also: First his name was written Abram, [with the *gematria* of 243];[16] then his name was changed to Abraham [with the *gematria* of 248].[17] At first God gave him mastery over 243 of his limbs, and in the end He made him ruler over all of his 248 limbs. The additional five limbs are: his two eyes, two ears, and the membrum.

R. Ammi b. Abba further said: What is meant by the verse, "There was a small town with only a few inhabitants, and a mighty king came upon it and surrounded it, and built great siege works over it. Present in the city was a poor wise man who by his wisdom saved the town. Yet no one remembered that poor man" (Ecclesiastes 9:14,15). [This is an allegory:] "A small town" refers to the body; "with only a few inhabitants" refers to the limbs; "and a mighty king came upon it and surrounded it" refers to the evil impulse; "and built great siege works against it" refers to the sins a person commits. "Present in the city was a poor wise man" refers to the good impulse; "who by his wisdom saved the town" refers to repentance and good deeds. "Yet no one remembered that poor man"—for when the evil impulse gains the upper hand, no one remembers the good impulse.

"Wisdom strengthens the wise man more than ten rulers who are in the city" (ibid. 7:19). "Wisdom strengthens the wise man" refers to repentance and good deeds; "more than ten rulers" namely: the two eyes, two ears, two hands, two feet, membrum, and mouth. [Repentance and good deeds give a person the strength to control all of these.]

R. Zechariah said in the name of R. Yishmael: The Holy One, blessed be He, wanted to bring forth the priesthood from Shem, as it says, "[Shem, who is referred to as] Malki-tzedek king of Salem was a priest to God, the Most-High" (Genesis 14:18). However, since Shem blessed Abraham before he blessed God, God decided to bring it forth from Abraham. For it says, [after the war against the four kings, Shem blessed Abram, saying,] "Blessed be Abraham to God the Most High, Possessor of heaven and earth, and blessed be God Most High, who delivered your enemies in your hand" (ibid. v. 19). Said Abraham to Shem: Is it proper to bless a servant before blessing his master? Immediately the priesthood was given to Abraham, for it says, "This is the speech of God to my master [i.e., Abraham], 'Sit at My right, until I will make your enemies as footstools at your feet'" (Psalms 110:1). [This is a reference to Abraham's war against the four kings. And imediately after that it says,] "God has sworn and will not relent, 'You [Abraham] shall be a priest forever, because of the words of Malki-tzedek'" (ibid. v. 4), [meaning, because Malki-tzedek blessed Abraham before blessing God, the priesthood was taken from him]. That is why it says, [about Malki-tzedek (Shem),] "He was a priest to God, the Most High"—the implication being, *he* was a priest, but not his descendants.

AIDS TO UNDERSTANDING
THE TORAH

(37b) Rav said: What is the meaning of the verse, "[Ezra brought out the Torah scroll and,] they [the Levites] read in the scroll, in God's Torah, clearly, with the application of wisdom, and they helped the people understand the reading" (Nehemiah 8:8)?—"They read in the scroll" refers to the Torah text; "clearly" refers to Targum [the Aramaic translation and commentary]; "with the application of wisdom" refers to the division between the verses, [since the Torah is written without punctuation marks]; "and they helped the people understand the reading" refers to the cantillation signs; others say, it refers to the *Masorah* [the traditional spelling of the words].

R. Yitzchak said: [It refers to] the pronunciation of certain Scriptural words and the enhancements of the text, and letters that we must read although they are not written, and letters that we must not read although they are written, all these [were not innovated by the *Soferim*, the Sages of the *Mesorah*; rather they] were *halachot* handed down to us by Moses from Mount Sinai. Examples of pronunciation of certain words: *eretz* at the end of a sentence is pronounced *aretz*; *shamayim* and *mitzrayim* could be read *shamim* and *mitzrim*, but tradition from Sinai tells us to pronounce them *shamayim* and *mitzrayim*. Examples of textual enhancements: [Abraham said to the angels:] "Eat your meal, [*achar*,] after that, go on" (Genesis 18:4). [*Achar*, "after that," seems superfluous. It could have said, "Eat your meal, and go on." *Achar* was inserted as a textual enhancement (Ran)].

"MOSES PRESCRIBED THE
TORAH TO US"[18]

(38a) R. Chama b. R. Chanina said: Moses became wealthy merely from the chips [that were left when he carved out] the second Tablets, [and the Tablets were made of sapphire]. For it says, "God said to Moses, 'Carve [*pesol*] for yourself two stone tablets like the first ones'" (Exodus 34:1). [Why does it say, "for yourself" when the Tablets are for all Israel?—The Gemara expounds: God said:] The chips [*pesolet*] should belong to you.

R. Yose b. Chanina said: At the outset the Torah was given only to Moses and his descendants, for it says, "Write these words *for yourself*" (ibid. v. 27) and, "Carve *for yourself* two stone tablets like the first ones": Just as the chips are yours, so is the writing yours. But Moses graciously gave it to Israel, and about him Scripture says, "The gracious person will be blessed, for he gives of his bread to the poor" (Proverbs 22:9). R. Chisda raised an objection: [Moses said,] "At that time God commanded me to teach you rules and laws" (Deuteronomy 4:14). [So you see, God commanded Moses to give the Torah to Israel.] [The Gemara answers: The verse is to be understood as follows:] God commanded [the Torah to me, and I decided to teach it to you.] [The Gemara raises another objection:] It says, "See! I have taught you rules and laws as God my Lord has commanded me" (ibid. v. 5)? [Proof that God commanded Moses to teach it to Israel]? [The Gemara answers: We can read the verse as follows:] God commanded the Torah to me, and I decided to teach it to you. [A further objection:] It says, "Now write for yourselves this song [i.e., the Torah]" (ibid. 31:19); ["for yourselves" shows that it was given to all Israel, and not just to Moses]?

[The Gemara answers:] It refers to the Song of Moses,[19] [but the rest of the Torah was initially given to Moses alone]. [The Gemara rejects this:] But it says in the same verse, "So that this song will be a witness for the Israelites," [now if this refers to the song alone, how is the song a witness that Israel has to observe the Torah]? [So what did R. Yose b. R. Chanina mean by the statement that God gave the Torah only to Moses and his descendants? The Gemara answers:] Moses was given the ability to deduce a *halachah* that was not stated explicitly from one that was stated, [and this ability he graciously taught to Israel].

THE FOUR QUALIFICATIONS
FOR A PROPHET

R. Yochanan said: The Holy One, blessed be He, allows His *Shechinah* to rest only on a person who is strong, wealthy, wise, and humble, and we derive all these requirements from Moses.[20] We know that Moses was strong, because it says, "[Moses] spread the tent over the tabernacle" (Exodus 40:19); and a Tanna said: Moses our teacher spread it himself, and it says, "Each beam [of the tabernacle] shall be ten cubits long" (ibid. 26:16), [this was the height of the tabernacle; so for Moses to spread the tent over it, he must have been very tall and strong]. [The Gemara asks:] Maybe he was tall but weak.—But the fact that Moses was strong can be proved from this verse, [Moses said,] "I grasped the two tablets, and threw them down from my two hands, breaking them before your eyes" (Deuteronomy 9:17). Now we learned: The tablets were six handbreadths in length, six in width, and three in thickness. [Thus they were very heavy, and Moses had to hurl them with great force in order to shatter them, which proves that he was very robust.]

How do we know that Moses was wealthy? Because it says, "Carve for yourself two Tablets," which was interpreted to imply, "The chips are yours," [and the Tablets were made of sapphire].

How do we know that Moses was wise? For Rav and Shmuel both said: Fifty gates of wisdom were created in this world, and all but one were given to Moses, for it says, "You have made him [Moses] slightly less than the angels, and crowned him with soul and splendor" (Psalms 8:6).

How do we know that Moses was humble? Because it says, "Now the man Moses was exceedingly humble" (Numbers 12:3).

ALL THE PROPHETS
WERE WEALTHY

R. Yochanan said: All the prophets were wealthy. How do we know this? From Moses, Samuel, Amos, and Jonah. We know that Moses was rich, because [Moses defended himself, saying,] "I did not take a single donkey from anyone]!" (Numbers 16:15). If Moses meant to say that he never rented a donkey without paying for it, is it a defense for Moses to say that he is not a person who rents without paying for it? But Moses was saying that he never needed to rent a donkey [because he owned so many of them; proof that he was rich]. [The Gemara asks:] Maybe he did not rent a donkey because he was poor [and had no possessions so that he did not need a donkey to carry them]? But how do we know that he was wealthy? From the verse, "Carve for yourself two stone tablets . . . The [sapphire] chips are yours to keep."

How do we know that Samuel was wealthy? Because [Samuel said,] "Here I am; testify about me in the presence of God and in the presence of His anointed: Whose ox have I taken? Whose donkey have I taken?" (1 Samuel 12:3). If Samuel implied that he never rented an ox without paying for it—does Samuel have to tell us that he never rented anything without payment! Therefore he must have meant that he never needed to rent an ox or a donkey [because he owned them himself, which shows that he was wealthy]. [The Gemara asks:] Maybe the reason that he did not rent a donkey was because he was poor? [So what proof do you have that he was rich?] Rather the proof is from this verse, [Samuel judged Israel, circling the whole country,] "Then he would return to Ramah, for his home was there" (1 Samuel 7:17). Rava commented that wherever he went his house [and all his belongings] went with him, [so that he would not have to borrow anything; a sign that he was a rich man].

Rava said: The things that are said in regard to Samuel are greater than the things said about Moses. For about Moses it says, "I did not take a single donkey from anyone," meaning, even for payment. But in the case of Samuel, even if they insisted on renting him the animal without payment, he did not accept it. For it says, "They said, 'You have not robbed us; you have not even taken anything from us when we wanted [to give it to you]'" (1 Samuel 12:4).

We know that Amos was wealthy because it says, "Amos said and replied to Amaziah, 'I am not a [false] prophet [who prophesies for money], nor am I the son of a prophet, but I am a cattle herder and a tender of sycamore trees'" (Amos 7:14), as R. Yosef explained it: [He implied:] I am a cattleman and own sycamore trees in the valley, [I am a wealthy man; I do not need the people's money].

We know that Jonah was a wealthy man, because it says, "He went down to Jaffa and found a ship bound for Tarshish; he paid its fare and boarded it" (Jonah 1:3). R. Yochanan explained: He rented the whole ship, [for he wanted the ship to sail at once, without waiting for passengers and cargo]. R. Romanus said: The rental of the ship amounted to four thousand golden *dinars* [a clear indication that Jonah was wealthy].

R. Yochanan further said: At first [during the forty days that Moses was on Mount Sinai], he studied the Torah and forgot it, [because it is impossible for the human mind to absorb the entire contents of the Torah in such a short time (*Maharsha*)] until God gave it to him as a gift, for it says, "When [God] finished speaking to Moses on Mount Sinai, He gave him two tablets of the Testimony [as a gift]" (Exodus 31:18).

THE MITZVAH OF VISITING
THE SICK

(39b) R. Shimon b. Lakish said: Where do we find an indication in the Torah that it is a mitzvah to visit the sick? [During the rebellion of Korach and his party, Moses said,] "If these men die like all other men, and share the common fate of man, then God did not send me. But if God creates something entirely new . . ." (Numbers 16:29). How do you derive it from this? [It is alluded to in the seemingly redundant phrase, "and share the common fate of man."] As Rava expounded: [Moses said] "If these men die like all other men" who are lying sick in bed, "and share the common fate of man," meaning, and people come to visit them, then they will say that "God did not send me on this mission." [So we see that the norm was for people to visit the sick.]

THE FATE OF KORACH
AND HIS PARTY

Rava continued his exposition: "But if God creates something entirely new [to punish Korach], then you will know that I [Moses] did not make up anything myself" (ibid. v. 30)—If Gehinnom is already created, fine; and if not, God will create Gehinnom [expressly for Korach]. [The Gemara asks:] Is that so? But we learned differently in a *Baraita*: There are seven things that were created before the world: The Torah, repentance, the Garden of Eden, Gehinnom, the Throne of Glory, the *Bet Hamikdash*, and the name of *Mashiach*. We know that the Torah [was created before the world] for it says, "God made me as the beginning of His way" (Proverbs 8:22). [The Torah was the blueprint of the universe.] Repentance, because it says, "Before the mountains were born . . ." (Psalms 90:2), and after this it says, "You reduce man to pulp and You say, 'Repent, O sons of man'" (ibid. v. 4). The Garden of Eden, for it says, "God planted a garden before the world" (Genesis 2:8).[21] Gehinnom, for it says, "For Hell has been prepared from yesterday" (Isaiah 30:33). The Throne of Glory, for it says, "Your throne is established of old" (Psalms 93:2). The *Bet Hamikdash*, for it says, "O Throne of Glory exalted from of old, is the place of our Sanctuary" (Jeremiah 17:12). The name of *Mashiach*, "May his name [*Mashiach*'s] endure forever, before the sun was created his name flourished" (Psalms 72:17).[22]

[In any event, we see from this *Baraita* that Gehinnom was created before the world. Then how could Moses think that it would be created specifically for Korach?] This is what Moses meant: If an opening has already been created [for Gehinnom here to swallow up Korach and his party], fine; if not, let God create an opening right here. [The Gemara asks:] But it says, "There is nothing new beneath the sun" (Ecclesiastes 1:9)? [The Gemara answers:] This is what Moses said: If the opening is not around here, make it close to here. [But nothing new was created.]

THE SUN AND THE MOON
DEFEND MOSES

Rava, others say R. Yitzchak, lectured: What is meant by the passage, "The sun and the moon stood still in their abodes [*zevul*]" (Habakkuk 3:11)? [*Zevul* is one of the seven levels of heaven.] [The Gemara asks:] What are the sun and the moon doing in *zevul*? We know that they were set in [the lower level of heaven called] *rakia*! [The Gemara answers:] This teaches us that the sun and the moon ascended from the *rakia* to the *zevul* and said to God: Master of the universe! If You will vindicate Moses [in his confrontation with Korach's

rebellion], we will give light; if not, we will not shine. At that moment God shot arrows and spears at them and reprimanded them, "Every day people bow down to you, and yet you give your light to the world. You did not protest when My honor is disgraced, but now that the honor of a mortal man is attacked you do protest!" Since then, every day the sun and the moon do not shine until they are shot with arrows and spears, [because they accepted God's rebuke,] as it says, "They go by the light of Your arrows, by the lighning flash of Your spear" (ibid.). [The sun and moon shine only because God forces them to; otherwise they would refuse to shine in defense of God's honor, to protest against idolators who bow down to them.]

A VISITOR TAKES AWAY A
SIXTIETH OF THE SICKNESS

We learned in a *Baraita*: The mitzvah of visiting the sick has no prescribed measure. What is meant by "no prescribed measure"? R. Yosef initially thought it meant that there is no measure for its reward. Said Abaye to him: [Why single out the mitzvah of visiting the sick?] Is there then a measure for the reward for any mitzvah? After all, we learned in a Mishnah: Be as scrupulous in performing a "minor" mitzvah as a "major" one, for you do not know the reward given for the respective *mitzvot*.[23] But Abaye explained: ["No prescribed measure"] means: Even an older person must visit a young person [who is not yet bar/bat mitzvah].[24] Rava said: ["No prescribed measure"] means even a hundred times a day, [provided it does not inconvenience the patient]. R. Acha b. Chanina said: Whoever visits a sick person takes away a sixtieth of his suffering. Abaye said to Rava: If that is the case, let sixty people visit him [at the same time] and make him feel better immediately!

He replied: The sixtieth we are talking about is similar to the "tenth" that was discussed in the yeshivah of Rabbi, and it applies only when the visitor and the sick person were born under the same constellation. For we learned in a *Baraita*: [In the case of a woman who got married and stipulated in her *ketubah* that all her daughters should receive a dowry from her husband's estate,] Rabbi said: A daughter who must be given a dowry from her brothers' estate [which they inherited from their father] receives a tenth of the estate. So they asked Rabbi: According to you, if a man leaves ten daughters and one son, the son receives nothing! Rabbi replied: The first daughter to get married receives a tenth of the estate; the second, a tenth of what is left; the third, a tenth of the remainder; and [after they all received their share] they pool their money and divide it equally, [but a substantial amount[25] is left for the brother. Similarly, in the case of visiting the sick, each visitor takes one-sixtieth of what the previous visitor left over, and the sick person would not recover completely].

PRAYING FOR THE SICK

R. Chelbo became sick, whereupon R. Kahana went and announced, (40a) "R. Chelbo is sick!" But no one came to visit him. So R. Kahana said to everyone, "Didn't it happen once that one of R. Akiva's disciples fell ill, and the Sages did not come to visit him? So R. Akiva himself came to visit him, and because they swept and sprinkled the floor for him, [on R. Akiva's orders (Eitz Yosef)] the [disciple] recovered. 'My Rabbi,' the disciple exclaimed, 'you restored me to life!' As he left the disciple R. Akiva lectured, 'Anyone who does not visit someone who is sick, it is as if he shed blood.'"

When R. Dimi came [from Eretz Yisrael to Babylonia] he said: Whoever visits a sick person causes him to live, and someone who does not, causes him to die. How does he cause this? Do you think that that a person who visits someone who is sick prays that he should live; whereas he who does not, is in essence praying that he should die? Can it enter your mind that not visiting a sick person is tantamount to praying that he should die! This is what R. Dimi meant: Someone who does not visit a sick person prays neither that he should live nor that he should die. [A person who is in the throes of death and suffering a great deal would benefit from a prayer that he should die quickly (Ran).]

Whenever Rava fell sick, on the first day he would ask his family, "Don't tell anyone, so that I should not have bad luck" [as it says: You should not invite bad luck by ominous words[26] (Etz Yosef)]. But after that he said to them, "Go out and announce in the street [that I am sick]; those that hate me let them rejoice; and it says, 'When your foe falls be not glad . . . lest God see it, and be displeased, and He turn His anger from him to you' (Proverbs 24:17), [and that will be good for me]; and those that love me will pray for me."

THE REWARD FOR VISITING THE SICK

Rav said: Anyone who visits a sick person will be saved from harsh judgment in Gehinnom. For it says, "Praiseworthy is he who cares for the poor [dal], on the day of evil God will deliver him" (Psalms 41:2). "The poor" [dal] refers to the sick, as it says, "He will end my life with sickness [mi-dallah]" (Isaiah 38:12); or from this verse, "Why are you so indisposed [dal], O son of the King?" (2 Samuel 13:4). And "evil" refers to Gehinnom, for it says, "Everything God made, He made for His sake; even the evildoer for the day of evil [i.e., retribution]" (Proverbs 16:4).

Now, if someone visits the sick, what will be his reward? [The Gemara asks: Why do you ask,] what will be his reward! We just finished saying: He will be saved from the harsh judgment of Gehinnom. [The Gemara says:] What will be his reward in *this* world? "God will preserve him and keep him alive, and he will be praised on earth; and You will not give him over to

the desires of his enemies" (Psalms 41:3). [The Gemara expounds:] "God will preserve him"—from the evil impulse; "and keep him alive"—[save him] from suffering; "and he will be praised on earth"—everybody will honor him; "and You will not give him over to the desires of his enemies"—he will have friends like Na'aman's friends who [advised him on how to find] a cure for his leprosy,[27] but he should not have friends like Rehoboam's friends, who caused his kingdom to be divided.

[Prompted by this last remark the Gemara briefly digresses:] We learned in a *Baraita*: R. Shimon b. Elazar said: If older people tell you to tear down, and the young tell you to build, tear down and don't build, because the destruction of the elders [who are wise will result in] building, while the building of the [inexperienced] young leads to destruction.[28] An example of this is the case of Rehobo'am the son of Solomon [who ignored the advice the elders gave him and took counsel with the young men,[29] and as a result the kingdom was divided].

[The Gemara returns to the topic under discussion:] R. Sheshet the son of R. Idi said: A person should not visit the sick during the first three hours of the day and not during the last three hours of the day, so that he should not be discouraged from praying for that person. For during the first three of hours of the day a patient feels much better, [so that the visitor will think there is no need to pray for him]. During the last three hours of his sickness the patient feels worse [and the visitor will think that praying is hopeless].

Ravin said in Rav's name: From where do we know that God nourishes the sick? [A person who is sick and has no appetite, is sustained by God.] For it says, "God will fortify him on his bed of misery" (Psalms 41:4). Ravin also said in Rav's name: How do we know that the *Shechinah* hovers over the bed of a person who is ill? For it says, "God will fortify him on his bed of misery" [so He is there to give him strength]. We learned similarly: If you come to visit a sick person you should not sit on the bed, and not on a chair or a bench,[30] [in a way that you sit above the patient] but you should wear dignified clothes and sit [level with the sick person] on the ground, because the *Shechinah* hovers above the bed of a sick person, as it says, "God will fortify him on his bed of misery."

IF YOU HAVE KNOWLEDGE YOU HAVE EVERYTHING

(40b) R. Ammi said in Rav's name: What is the meaning of the verse, "And you, Son of Man, make for yourself implements of exile" (Ezekiel 12:3)? This refers to a lamp, a plate (41a), and a blanket, [the bare necessities for a wanderer]. It says, "[You will serve your enemies] . . . lacking everything" (Deuteronomy 28:48). R. Ammi said in Rav's name: This means without a lamp or table. R. Chisda said: It means without a wife. R. Sheshet said: Without an attendant. R. Nachman said: Without knowledge. A *Baraita* explained it to mean: Without salt or fat. Abbaye said: We have a tradition that no one is considered poor except a person who lacks knowledge. In Eretz Yisrael they have a saying: If you have knowledge you have everything; if you don't have knowledge, what have you got? If you acquired knowledge, what else do you need? If you have not acquired knowledge, what good are all your possessions?

R. Alexandri said in the name of R. Chiya b. Abba: A sick person does not recover from his sickness until all his sins are forgiven, for it says, "Who forgives all your sins; Who heals all your diseases" (Psalms 103:3); [the suffering he endured wiped out his sins (Iyun Yaakov)]. R. Hamenuna said: He regains his youth, for it says, "His flesh has revived from its trembling, and he will return to his days of youthfulness" (Job 33:25). "You have upset all his restfulness by his sickness" (Psalms 41:4). R. Yosef said: This means that [the sick person] forgets his learning. [R. Yosef spoke from personal experience, for] R. Yosef had had a severe illness that caused him to forget his learning, but Abbaye retaught him what he had forgotten. That is the reason why we often find in the Gemara that R. Yosef will say, "I have not heard this *halachah*," and Abbaye will remind him, "You yourself taught it to us, and you derived it from such-and-such *Baraita*."

Rebbi interpreted a *halachah* thirteen different ways, and taught R. Chiya only seven of these. Later on Rebbi became sick [and forgot his learning]. Thereupon R. Chiya reminded him of the seven interpretations he had taught him, but the other six were lost. There was a certain laundryman who had overheard Rebbi when he was reviewing these interpretations to himself. So R. Chiya went and learnt them from the laundryman and then taught them to Rebbi. When Rebbi met the laundryman he said, "You have taught both Chiya and myself." Others say that he said, "You taught Chiya, and he taught me."

R. Alexandri also said in the name of R. Chiya b. Abba: The miracle that is done for a sick person is greater than the miracle that was performed for Chananiah, Mishael, and Azariah.[31] For the miracle of Chananiah, Mishael, and Azariah concerned a manmade fire that can be put out by people, whereas the fire [fever] of a sick person is a heavenly fire; who can put that out?

R. Alexandri also said in the name of R. Chiya b. Abba—others say, R. Yehoshua b. Levi said: When a person's end approaches, all have power over him, [even a fly can kill him], as it says, [Thinking that he was going to die, Cain said,] 'Whoever finds me will kill me'" (Genesis 4:14). Rav derived it from this verse, "To fulfill Your decree they stand until this day, for all are Your servants" (Psalms 119:91), [all forces of nature are God's messengers to carry out His death sentence].

Rabbah b. Shilah was told that a certain tall man had died. [This is what happened:] The man was riding on a little mule and when he came to a bridge the mule was startled and jumped and threw the man, and he was killed. Rabbah then applied to him the verse, "To fulfill Your decree they stand until this day."

Shmuel saw a scorpion being carried across the river on the back of a frog. Then it stung a man so that he died. Seeing this Shmuel cited the verse, "To fulfill Your decree they stand until this day."

THE RADIANT FACE OF R. YEHUDAH B. ILA'I

(49b) R. Yehudah [b. Ila'i] was sitting in front of R. Tarfon who commented, "Your face shines today." He replied, "Your servants went out to the field yesterday and brought us beets, which we ate unsalted. If we had salted them, my face would have been even more shiny."

A Roman noblewoman berated R. Yehudah, "You who are a Sage [who decides *halachah*]; how dare you be a drunkard!" [His ruddy complexion gave her that impression (Rashi).] He replied, "Please believe me that I never taste wine except that of *Kiddush* and *Havdalah* and the four cups on Pesach, and they give me such a severe headache that I have to bandage my temples from Pesach until Shavuot." [The Gemara explains that his face was radiant, because] "A man's wisdom makes his face shine" (Ecclesiastes 8:1).

A certain heretic [Sadducee] said to R. Yehudah, "Your face has that prosperous glow [of a rich man]. You must be either a moneylender or a breeder of swine." He replied, "Both of these occupations are forbidden to Jews; but there are twenty-four bathrooms between my house and the *bet midrash*, and I use them whenever I have a call of nature. [I have a radiant complexion because I take care of my health.]"

When R. Yehudah went to the *bet midrash* he used to carry a pitcher on his shoulders [to use as a seat], saying, "Great is labor, for it honors the worker." R. Shimon used to carry a basket on his shoulders [to sit on], saying, "Great is labor, for it honors the worker." [Carrying a pitcher or a basket is not below a scholar's dignity. On the contrary, physical labor is to be admired.]

R. Yehudah's wife bought wool and made an elegant cloak. When going to the market she wore it, and when R. Yehudah went [to the synagogue] to pray he wore it. [R. Yehudah b. Ila'i was very poor.] When he put it on he said, "Blessed is He who has wrapped me with a robe." Once R. Shimon b. Gamliel proclaimed a public fast [for relief of a national calamity], but R. Yehudah did not attend the special fast service. When R. Shimon b. Gamliel heard that R. Yehudah had nothing to wear he sent him a cloak. R. Yehudah did not accept the cloak. (50a) He lifted the mat on which he was sitting [and by a miracle there appeared a treasure chest filled with gold]. "See what I have here," R. Yehudah exclaimed to the messenger. "[I have all this wealth] but I do not want to benefit from this world."

ciples wanted to push her away. But R. Akiva said, "Leave her alone! My learning and all of your learning belong to her!" When Kalba Savua heard [how his son-in-law had turned out] he asked to have his vow annulled. Rabbi Akiva annulled it for him, and he shared his wealth with him.

RABBI AKIVA AND HIS EXEMPLARY WIFE

[The Gemara now tells the story of another great Tanna and his wife who were also poverty-stricken.]

R. Akiva [who was then only a poor, unlearned shepherd] was betrothed to [Rachel] the daughter of Kalba Savua, [one of the wealthiest men in Jerusalem]. When Kalba Savua heard about it he disinherited her. Nevertheless, she went ahead and married him in the winter, [because in former times there was an interval between *kiddushin/erusin*, "betrothal," and *nisuin/ chuppah*, "marriage"]. They slept in the straw, and when he got up he had to pick pieces of straw from her hair. R. Akiva said to her, "If I had the money I would make for you a golden head ornament with Jerusalem engraved on it."[32] Elijah appeared to them in the guise of a man [to console them by showing them that there were people who were even more destitute than they were]. He knocked on their door and cried out, "Please, can you spare a little bit of straw? My wife just gave birth, and I have nothing to bed her down on." "You see!" Rabbi Akiva said to his wife, "here is a man who doesn't even have straw!" [Taking the initiative, Rachel said,] "Go to the yeshivah and become a Torah scholar!" So he went and spent twelve years studying under R. Eliezer and R. Yehoshua. At the end of twelve years, he returned to his house [but before entering] he heard from the back of the house how a wicked neighbor was taunting his wife, "Your father did the right thing [disinheriting you]! First of all, your husband is not your kind, and to make things worse, he left you a living widow all these years!" She replied, "If my husband would listen to me, he would stay in the yeshivah yet another twelve years."

[When R. Akiva heard this] he said to himself, "Since she is giving me permission, I'll go back." He went back and stayed there yet for another twelve years. When the twelve years were over, he returned accompanied by twenty-four thousand pairs of disciples. Everyone came out to pay homage to him, and his wife also came out to welcome him. But that wicked neighbor said to her, "Where do you think you are going? [You are not dressed properly to greet such a great scholar (Ran).]" "The righteous one knows his animal's soul" (Proverbs 12:10), she replied. [Meaning, R. Akiva knows why I don't have dignified clothes.] She went to see him, but the dis-

HOW DID R. AKIVA BECOME WEALTHY?

[The Gemara now wants to dispel the notion that R. Akiva became wealthy by deriving benefit from his Torah learning (*Maharsha*):] From six incidents did R. Akiva become wealthy: (1) From Kalba Savua; (2) From the figurehead of a ram that was on a ship. Because every ship used to have a wooden figurehead on its bow in the form of a ram as a good-luck charm, and they would fill this hollow ram with gold coins (Ran). Once such a wooden ram was forgotten on the beach, and R. Akiva came and found it [full of gold coins]. (3) From a treasure chest of a ship. For R. Akiva once gave four *zuz* to the sailors of a ship and told them, "Pick me up some piece of merchandise." However, all they found was an old chest that had washed up on the shore. So they brought that to him and said to him, "Master, sit on this chest in the meantime, [and wait while we try to get you the merchandise you want]." [When R. Akiva opened it up] he found that it was full of golden *dinars*. For one time a ship had sunk, and all the treasures of the passengers had been deposited in that chest, and it was found at that time. (4) From the incident with the noblewoman.[33] (5) (50b) From the wife of Turnus Rufus.[34] (6) From Keti'a b. Shalom.[35]

[The Gemara relates a similar story.] R. Gamda gave four *zuz* to sailors and asked them to purchase something for him. When the sailors could not obtain what R. Gamda had requested, they bought him a monkey. The monkey escaped and fled into a hole. When they dug after it they found the monkey lying on precious gems, and they brought the gems to R. Gamda.

The daughter of the Emperor said to R. Yehoshua b. Chananiah: "Such splendid wisdom in such an ugly vessel!" [R. Yehoshua b. Chananiah was very ugly.] He replied, "You'll find the answer in your father's palace. Where do they store the wine?" "In earthenware jars," she replied. "But ordinary people store their wine in earthenware jars too! You should store your wine in vessels made of silver and gold!" So she went and had the wine poured into silver and gold vessels, but it turned sour. Now R. Yehoshua b. Chananiah told her, "It's the same thing with the Torah." "But aren't there handsome men who are also Torah scholars?" she asked. "If they were ugly they would be even greater scholars," he retorted.

A LAVISH WEDDING BANQUET

Rebbi made a wedding banquet for his son R. Shimon. He wrote on the front of the wedding hall: "Two hundred and forty-thousand *dinars* were spent on wedding expenses." He did not invite Bar Kappara [because Bar Kappara was a merrymaker, and Rabbi was afraid that he would make him laugh, as will be explained later (Ran)].[36] Bar Kappara, [deeply hurt], said, "If those who transgress God's will [are so fortunate that they can make such an extravagant wedding], imagine [the reward that is in store] for those who do His will!" [When Rebbi realized that Bar Kappara was upset,] he invited him. Bar Kappara then said, "If those who do God's will [are so richly rewarded] in this world, imagine the abundant reward that awaits them in the World to Come!"

[Why was Rebbi afraid to laugh?] On the day that Rebbi laughed, punishment would come on the world. [Rebbi suffered for thirteen years excruciating pain from bladder stones, and during that time there never was a drought (*Bava Metzia* 85a).] So he said to Bar Kappara [who was a merrymaker], "Don't make me laugh, and I will give you forty measures of wheat." He replied, "You should see to it (51a) that I get whatever measure I want." So he took a large basket, smeared it with tar on the outside [so that the wheat kernels should not fall out], and placed it on his head [like a mask]. He then went up to Rebbi and said, "Please fill it with forty measures of wheat that I demand from you." Thereupon Rebbi burst out laughing and said, "Didn't I warn you not to make jokes?" Bar Kappara answered, "I am merely asking for the wheat you owe me." Bar Kappara then said to Rebbi's daughter, "Tomorrow I will drink wine to your father's dancing, and your mother will fill my cup."

Ben Elasah, the son-in-law of Rebbi who was a very wealthy man was invited to the wedding of R. Shimon b. Rebbi. [At the wedding] Bar Kapparah asked Rebbi, "What is meant by *to'eivah*, 'abomination' [referring to homosexuality (Leviticus 20:13)]?" Whatever interpretation Rebbi offered, Barra Kappara refuted. Finally, Rebbi said, "Well then, you explain it to me!" He replied, "Let your wife come and pour me a glass of wine." She came and did so. Bar Kappara then said to Rebbi, "Come and dance for me, then I will tell it to you." This is what the Torah says: *to'eivah—to'eh atta—bah*, "You stray in regard to her; [you turn away from permitted relations and seek forbidden ones" (Ran)]. At the second glass of wine Bar Kapparah said to Rebbi, "What is meant by *tevel*, 'perversion' [referring to bestiality (Leviticus 18:23)]?" He gave the same answers as before, until Bar Kappara said, "Do something for me, and I will tell you." When Rebbi complied, he told him, "*Tevel hu* means *tavlin yesh bah*, 'Is there any *tavlin* [spice] in it [the animal]'? Is intimacy with it preferable to permitted intimacy [how can a person do a thing like that (Ran)]?" Then Bar Kappara asked

Rebbi, "And what is the meaning of *zimmah*, 'depravity' [referring to incest with one's wife's daughter (ibid. v. 17)]?" He explained, "*Zimmah* means *zo mah hi*, Who is she?" [in a prosmiscuous society a girl does not know who her father is; as a result, a father may marry his daughter, and a brother, his sister (Ran)]. Ben Elasah could not stand all this repartee, so he and his wife left the wedding.

THE TORAH IS A GIFT

(55a) What is the meaning of, "From the wilderness *Mattanah*; and from *Mattanah*, *Nachaliel*, and from *Nachaliel* to the heights" (Numbers 21:18,19)? It means that when a person makes himself like the wilderness, which is free to all [meaning, he teaches Torah free of charge], the Torah is presented to him as a gift [*mattanah*], as it says, "And from the wilderness—a *Mattanah*, a gift." And once he has the Torah as a gift, God gives it to him as an inheritance [*Nachaliel*], [it will stay with him; he will never forget it]. And when God gives it to him as an inheritance, he rises to greatness, for it says, "and from *Nachaliel* to the heights." But if he prides himself on his learning, the Holy One, blessed be He, will lower him, as it says, "And from the heights—the valley." And that's not all, but he is made to sink into the earth, as it says, "which is pressed down into the surface of the wasteland" (ibid.). But if he repents, the Holy One, blessed be He, will raise him up again, as it says, "Every valley will be raised" (Isaiah 40:4).

R. TARFON'S BRUSH WITH DEATH

(62a) R. Tarfon went into a field after the harvest season was over and ate some fruit [thinking that the fruit was unwanted by the owner and free to all].[37] The owner [who saw R. Tarfon eating the fruit] grabbed him and put him in a sack and carried him off to throw him into the river. "Woe is to Tarfon," he wailed, "who is about to be killed by this man!" When the owner heard [that it was R. Tarfon who was in the sack] he let him go and ran away. R. Abbahu said in the name of R. Chananiah b. Gamliel: All his life that *tzaddik* [R. Tarfon] was distressed about this episode, saying, "Woe is me that I made use of the crown of Torah" [to save his life by revealing that he was a Torah scholar]. For Rabbah b. Bar Chanah said in R. Yochanan's name: Whoever uses the crown of Torah [for his own benefit] will be uprooted from the world.

This follows from a logical deduction: [At the great feast of King Belshazzar of Babylonia he ordered that the holy vessels that had been removed from the *Bet Hamikdash* be brought in to be used by the guests. Later that night the "handwriting on the wall" appeared, and that very night Belshazzar was slain.] Now, Belshazzar used the holy vessels that had lost their sanctity, for it says, "Robbers will come into it [the Temple] and profane it" (Ezekiel 7:22), this teaches us that the moment the robbers took the vessels, they lost their sanctity. Even so, Belshazzar was uprooted from the world, for it says, "That very night, Belshazzar was slain" (Daniel 5:30). How much more so a person who uses the crown of the Torah, which lasts forever, [it never loses its sanctity]!

[The Gemara asks:] Since R. Tarfon ate the fruit after the harvest season had ended, why did the owner attack him? [The Gemara answers:] Because someone had been stealing his grapes the whole year, and when he found R. Tarfon in his field, he thought that he was the thief. If that is the case, why was R. Tarfon distressed about revealing his identity? [Why didn't he offer to pay for the fruit he ate, instead of telling him his name? But, then again, since the owner suspected him of stealing grapes throughout the year, he would have had to pay a vast sum to appease him.] [The Gemara answers:] Since R. Tarfon was very wealthy, he should have paid him that sum to pacify him.

LEARN TORAH OUT OF LOVE
We learned in a *Baraita*: It says, "[You must make the choice] to love God your Lord, to obey Him, and to attach yourself to Him" (Deuteronomy 30:20). [This means] that a person should not say: I will learn *Chumash*,[38] so that people should call me a learned man [who knows the basic laws]; I will learn Mishnah so that people will call me rabbi; I will learn Mishnah and Gemara in depth so that I should become the head of a yeshivah. Rather, you should learn out of love, and the honor will come in due time. For it says, "Bind them [the words of the Torah] on your fingers, inscribe them on the tablet of your heart" (Proverbs 7:3), [so that you will never forget them, like a person who ties a string around his finger as a reminder (Gra)]. And it also says, "Its ways are ways of pleasantness" (ibid. 3:17), [a person who learns Torah becomes a more pleasant person], and, "It is a tree of life for those who grasp it, and its supporters will be happy" (ibid. v. 18).

R. Elazar b. Tzadok said: Perform *mitzvot* for the sake of their Maker, [because God commanded them], and speak of them for their own sake [and not for the sake of a reward]. Do not make the Torah a crown for self-glorification, nor a spade with which to dig [do not study the Torah for ulterior motives]. And this follows from logical reasoning: If Belshazzar, who used holy vessels that had lost their sanctity, was uprooted from the world, how much more so a person who uses the crown of Torah [whose sanctity is everlasting].

Rava said: If a scholar comes to a place where he is not known, he may tell people who he is, for it says, [Obadiah, introducing himself to Elijah, said,] "Your servant has feared God since my youth" (1 Kings 18:12). [The Gemara asks: If a person is allowed to identify himself,] why was R. Tarfon distressed about revealing

his name to the owner of the field? [The Gemara answers:] He was very wealthy, and he should have appeased him with money [rather than disclose his name].

Rava pointed out a contradiction between two verses: It says, "Your servant has feared God since my youth," and another passage says, "Let another praise you, but not your own mouth" (Proverbs 27:2). [The Gemara answers:] One verse refers to a place where you are known, [there you should not praise yourself]; the other, to where you are unknown.

Rava said: A young Torah scholar is allowed to say, "I am a Torah scholar; decide my case first; [I have to go back to learn (*Maharsha*)]." For it says, "And David's sons were priests" (2 Samuel 8:18). Were they then priests? [Of course not, but they were Torah scholars, and as such they enjoyed the same privileges as the priests (Ran).] Just as a priest receives his portion first, so is a Torah scholar entitled to get preferential treatment. And how do we know that a *kohen* goes first? For it says, "You must [strive to] keep him holy, since he presents the food offering to God" (Leviticus 21:8), which was expounded in the yeshivah of R. Yishmael: "You must keep him holy"—in everything that has to do with holiness [we show deference to the *kohen*]: (62b) he is the first to be called up to the reading of the Torah; he is the first to recite *Birkat Hamotzi* over the bread before the meal and to lead in *Birkat Hamazon* after the meal, and when someone divides something with a *kohen*, [for example, a property], the *kohen* has the right to choose which portion he wants (Ran).

A TORAH SCHOLAR IS EXEMPT FROM PAYING TAXES
Rava further said: [If the central government imposed a tax on a town that is under Jewish control], a Torah scholar is permitted to say: I will not pay the tax that was levied on the town [since the town benefits from my Torah learning]. For it says, "[King Artaxerxes wrote to Ezra: We also declare to you that concerning all the *kohanim* . . . and whoever serves in this Temple of God,] it shall not be lawful to impose upon them any levy, tax, or duty" (Ezra 7:24). And Rav Yehudah explained: *mindah* [levy] is the king's share of the crops, *belo* [tax] is a head tax, and *halach* [duty] is a tithe of the herds to be paid to the royal treasury.

(64b) R. Yochanan said in the name of R. Shimon b. Yocha'i: Wherever the Torah mentions the term *nitzim* [quarreling] or *nitzavim* [standing] it always refers to Dathan and Abiram, [Moses' archenemies]. [The Gemara asks:] If that is so, how do you explain the verse, "While Moses was still in Midian, God said to him, 'Go return to Egypt. All the men who seek your life have died'" (Exodus 4:19)? [I.e., Dathan and Abiram, who reported to Pharaoh that Moses had killed an Egyptian. God told Moses that they had died, but in Numbers 16:1 we are told that they took part in Korach's rebellion.] Resh Lakish said: [They did not really die;] they became poor, [and one who is poor is as if dead; he has lost all influence].

We learned in a *Baraita*: Four are considered dead: A poor person, a leper, a blind person, and a person who has no children. A poor person, for it says, "All the men who seek your life have died." A leper, for it says, [When Miriam was afflicted with leprosy, Moses prayed], "Let [Miriam] not be like a corpse" (Numbers 12:12). A blind person, for it says, "He has placed me in darkness, like the eternally dead" (Lamentations 3:6). A person who has no children, for it says, [Rachel who was childless said to Jacob], "Give me children, otherwise I am dead!" (Genesis 30:1).

ANNULMENT OF VOWS

(65a) We learned in a *Baraita*: If someone made a vow not to benefit from his neighbor, he can have the vow nullified only in his [neighbor's] presence. From where in Scripture is this derived? R. Nachman said: For it says, "While Moses was still in Midian, God said to him, 'Go return to Egypt, for all the men who seek your life have died'" (Exodus 4:19). This is what God said, "In Midian you vowed [to Jethro not to return to Egypt]; go and annul your vow in Midian." [The Gemara asks: How do we know that he vowed in Midian?] Because it says, "Moses desired [*va'yoel*] to dwell with the man [Jethro]" (Exodus 2:21); now *alah* [the root of *va'yoel*] means oath, as it says, "He had him take an oath [*alah*]" (Ezekiel 17:13).

ZEDEKIAH'S REBELLIOUS ACT

[The Gemara brings another proof:] It says, "He [King Zedekiah] also rebelled against King Nebuchadnezzar who made him swear allegiance by God" (2 Chronicles 36:13). [The Gemara asks:] In what way did Zedekiah rebel? [The Gemara answers:] Zedekiah found Nebuchadnezzar eating a live rabbit. "Swear to me, that you will not reveal this to anyone," he exclaimed, "so that I will not be made a laughingstock." Zedekiah swore. Later he regretted it and had his oath annulled, and then told everybody. When Nebuchadnezzar found out that they were ridiculing him he ordered the Sanhedrin and Zedekiah to appear before him. "Have you seen what Zedekiah has done?" he asked. "Didn't he swear by the name of Heaven not to divulge it?" "He had his oath annulled," they replied. "Can an oath be annulled?" he asked. "Yes," they answered. "Must it be done in the presence [of the person to whom the oath was sworn] or can it be done in his absence?" "Only in his presence." "In that case, how could you annul his oath? Why didn't you tell Zedekiah [that the annulment had to be executed in my presence]?" Immediately, "The elders of the daughters of Zion sit on the ground, they are silent" (Lamentations 2:10), [the rabbis were speechless]. R. Yitzchak said: This teaches us that they pulled the

cushions out from under them [and sat on the floor in shame].

SHE MISUNDERSTOOD

(66b) A Babylonian man went up to Eretz Yisrael and married a woman [who did not understand very well his Babylonian-Aramaic dialect.] "Boil me a couple of lentils," he requested, [meaning "some lentils"], but she [took it literally] and boiled him two lentils. So he became angry at her. The next day he said, "Boil me a *griva* of lentils, [a "gallon," thinking that she would boil a plate full, but again she took him literally] and cooked up a gallon. Then he said, "Go and bring me two *botzinin* [in Aramaic, "melons"; in Hebrew, "candles"]. She went and brought him two candles. Angrily he told her, "Go and break them on the head of the *bava*!" [In Aramaic, "on the lintel of the door."] But she thought that he wanted her to break them on the head of Bava b. Buta [the leading Sage]. Now Bava b. Buta was sitting near the door [of his house], busy judging a lawsuit. So she went and broke the two candles on his head. "Why did you do this?" he asked her, and she replied, "That is what my husband told me to do." Responded Bava, "You performed the will of your husband. May God give you two sons like Bava b. Buta [who will spread the light of Torah like the two candles you broke (Ran)]."

WHY WAS
THE LAND DESTROYED?

(81a) Shmuel said: Untidiness of the head leads to blindness; wearing unclean clothes brings on madness; untidiness of the body produces rashes and sores. They sent the following message from Eretz Yisrael: Be careful about personal hygiene; be careful to learn Torah in the company of other people [it promotes clearer understanding]; be careful to teach Torah to the children of poor people because from them the Torah will come forth; [they do not have many distractions, and they are humble (Ran)]. For it says, "Water shall flow from his wells [*midalyav*]" (Numbers 24:7)—from the *dallim* [the poor] Torah shall come forth. And why is it that Torah scholars as a rule do not have children who are Torah scholars? R. Yosef explained: Because children of Torah scholars [do not apply themselves, thinking] that the Torah is their legacy. R. Shisha the son of R. Idi said: In order that they should not become overbearing toward the community.[39] Mar Zutra said: Because they are arrogant toward the community.[40] R. Ashi said: Because they call other people names, such as "donkey." Ravina said: Because they do not recite the Blessings of the Torah in the morning service.

For Rav Yehudah said in the name of Rav: What is the meaning of the verse, "Who is the wise man who will understand this? . . . For what reason was the land destroyed?" (Jeremiah 9:11). This question was put to the sages, the prophets, and the ministering angels, but none of them give a satisfactory answer until God Himself explained it. For it says, "God said, 'Because they have forsaken My Torah that I put before them; moreover, they did not heed My voice nor follow it'" (ibid. v. 12). [The Gemara asks:] "They did not heed My voice" has the same meaning as "nor follow it" [why is it repeated]? Rav Yehudah said in the name of Rav: It means that they did not recite the proper *berachah* before they began to learn. [On the surface it appeared that they adhered to the Torah, but God revealed that they studied for selfish reasons and did not appreciate the Torah enough for its intrinsic worth to recite a *barachah* over it (Ran).]

NOTES

1. A *nazir* is a person who has taken a nazirite vow, usually for thirty days. During the term of his *nezirut* he may not drink any wine or grape beverage or eat grapes; he may not cut his hair, and he may not have contact with the dead. If he becomes ritually contaminated through contact with a corpse, he must bring a guilt-offering. See Numbers 6:9–12.

2. Numbers 6:18.

3. Your evil impulse.

4. Such as guilt-offerings for thefts, for misuse of sacred objects, or the guilt-offering of a *metzora* (leper).

5. A person who through ignorance is careless about the observance of the laws of Levitical purity and about giving the required gifts to the *kohen* and the Levite.

6. According to the Ran, the statement is addressed to a *kohen*, and the apprehension is that the unlearned *kohen* will give him unclean *terumah* to eat, which is forbidden even to a *kohen*.

7. *Avot* 1:5.

8. By making a vow and placing voluntary restrictions on himself a person wrongly assumes that he is doing a mitzvah. Just as the Torah forbids offering sacrifices outside the *Bet Hamikdash*, so it forbids self-imposed constraints (Ran).

9. Once he had slaughtered his victim he was in fact dead, and widening the gash did not hasten his death. Ulla said this in order to show his approval and thereby save his own life (Me'iri).

10. Derived from, "And on the eighth day, the child's foreskin shall be circumcised" (Leviticus 12:3), which is expounded to imply "the eighth day—even if it falls on *Shabbat*."

11. The saying by Rebbi is added by Ran and Tosafot.

12. The place of lodging was close enough to Egypt that the short trip would not endanger the child's health (Ran).

13. Alef = 1; lamed = 30; yud = 10; ayin = 70; zayin = 7; reish = 200. 1 + 30 + 10 + 70 + 7 + 200 = 318.

14. Ayin = 70; kuf = 100; beit = 2. 70 + 100 + 2 = 172.

15. Hei = 5; sin = 300; tet = 9; nun = 50. 5 + 300 + 9 + 50 = 364.

16. Alef = 1; bet = 2; reish = 200; mem = 40. 1 + 2 + 200 + 40 = 243.

17. Alef = 1; bet = 2; reish = 200; hei = 5; mem = 40. 1 + 2 + 200 + 5 + 40 = 248.

18. Deuteronomy 33:4.

19. Parashat Haazinu, Deuteronomy 32:1–43.

20. Why are wealth and strength qualifications for receiving the *Shechinah*, when they are not marks of spiritual greatness? People are impressed by wealth and power. If a Divine message is proclaimed by a prophet who is wealthy and powerful, people pay attention and obey. Therefore God chooses a person who has these characteristics in addition to being wise and humble (Ran in *Derashot HaRan*).

21. Commonly translated, "a garden in Eden to the east."

22. The underlying idea of this *Baraita* is that these seven things are essential elements for the existence of the world.

23. *Avot* 2:1.

24. Alternately: A great person must visit one who is not as great.

25. About 35 percent.

26. *Moed Katan* 18a.

27. See 2 Kings 5:1–20.

28. An analogy: A person wants to add a second story to his house. The inexperienced young contractor, not realizing that the foundation cannot support two stories, will go ahead only to find that the entire structure will collapse. The wise old contractor will first tear down the house, reinforce the foundation, and then build the two stories (*Maharsha*).

29. 1 Kings 12:8.

30. The Gemara refers to a case where the sick person is lying on the ground; then the visitor should not sit above the patient. But when the sick person is lying on a bed the visitor is permitted to sit on a chair.

31. Nebuchadnezzar ordered that these three Jews (known in Babylonian as Shadrach, Mesach, and Abed Nego) be thrown into a furnace, but God saved them from the flames (Daniel 3:22–26).

32. Later on, Rabbi Akiva did indeed buy this ornament for her (*Shabbat* 59a).

33. Once when R. Akiva needed money for the upkeep of his yeshivah he borrowed it from a noblewoman. At her request, God and the sea were to guarantee the repayment of the loan. When the money was due, R. Akiva was sick. The noblewoman then demanded that God and the sea should repay the loan. God gave the emperor's daughter a fit of insanity, which caused her to throw a treasure chest into the sea, which washed up in front of the noblewoman. When R. Akiva recovered, he repaid the loan. The noblewoman told him what had happened and gave him the

money she found in the chest over and above the amount of the debt (Ran).

34. A Roman governor of Judea. After her husband's death, she converted to Judaism and married R. Akiva, making him immensely wealthy (*Avodah Zarah* 20a).

35. Ketia b. Shalom was condemned to death by the Romans for advocating that the emperor should spare the Jews. On the way to his execution he be-

queathed his wealth to R. Akiva (*Avodah Zarah* 10b).

36. According to Shittah Mekubetzet they simply forgot to invite him.

37. Literally, "after the knives used for cutting off the fruit from the trees are folded up and put away."

38. The Pentateuch.

39. As a preventive measure.

40. As a punishment.

❧ NAZIR ❧

HOW TO GLORIFY GOD

(2b) We learned in a *Baraita*: The verse "This is my God, I will glorify Him" (Exodus 15:2) means, I will glorify Him through the performance of *mitzvot*: I will build a beautiful *sukkah*, [I will buy] a beautiful *lulav*, beautiful *tzitzit*, I will write a beautiful *sefer Torah*, and wrap it in exquisite silk wrappings.

ABSALOM HAD A HAIRCUT ONCE A YEAR

(4b) [Where does it say in Scriptures that a *nazir* for life [may have his hair trimmed]? Our Rabbis taught: Rebbi said: Absalom was a *nazir* for life,[1] for it says, "It happened at the end of forty years that Absalom said to the king, 'I would like to go now and pay my vow that I made to God in Hebron'" (2 Samuel 15:7). He used to cut his hair every twelve months, for it says, "When he would have his head barbered, at the end of every year [*yamim*] he would have his hair barbered" (ibid. 14:26). [Being a *nazir*, Absalom was permitted to cut his hair only annually, when it became uncomfortably heavy.] (5a) We derive the meaning of *yamim* from *yamim* as it is used in the context of houses in a walled city.[2] Just as there it means [a full year of] twelve months, so too here it means twelve months.

WHY IS A *NAZIR* CALLED A SINNER?

(19a) We learned in a *Baraita*: R. Eliezer Hakappar Berabbi said: Why does it say, [regarding the *nazir*], "He shall make an atonement for having sinned against a soul" (Numbers 6:11). Against what soul has the *nazir* sinned? [Against his own soul,] because he tormented himself by abstaining from wine. And we can draw a logical inference from this: If a person who torments himself only in regard to wine is called a sinner, how much more so is he called a sinner if he mortifies himself by abstaining from everything. [The Gemara asks:] But this verse refers to an unclean *nazir*? [How can you infer from it that every *nazir* is a sinner?] [The Gemara answers:] R. Eliezer Hakappar

holds that a ritually clean *nazir* is also a sinner, and the reason why the Torah teaches this in the context of an unclean *nazir* is that he repeats his sin, [first he sinned by abstaining from wine, and he repeated it by being careless about contact with the dead so that he became defiled].

BAD INTENTIONS REQUIRE ATONEMENT

(23a) Our Rabbis taught: It says, "Her husband has revoked [her vows]; and God will forgive her" (Numbers 30:13). The verse is speaking about a woman whose husband nullified her [nazirite] vow without her knowledge, [and she broke her vow], implying that she needs atonement and forgiveness [although, she did not really break her vow]. When R. Akiva came to this verse he cried: If a person who intended to take swine's meat but by chance took lamb's meat needs atonement and forgiveness, [like the woman who intended to break her nazirite vow by drinking wine, when she was not really a nazirite], surely a person who intended to take swine's meat and actually took it needs atonement and forgiveness!

A similar conclusion can be drawn from the following verse, "If a person will sin . . . but did not know and became guilty, he shall bear his iniquity" (Leviticus 5:17). If, when speaking about a person who intends to take lamb's meat and by chance took swine's meat—for example, in the case of someone who ate a slice of fat about which he is unsure whether it is permissible fat or forbidden fat [*cheilev*]—the Torah says, "he shall bear his iniquity"; surely a person who intended to take swine's meat and actually took it [shall bear his iniquity].

Isi b. Yehudah gave the following interpretation: "But he did not know and became guilty, he shall bear his iniquity." If, when speaking about a person who intends to take lamb's meat but took swine's meat—for example, in the case of someone who ate one of two slices of fat, one of which is forbidden fat [*cheilev*] and the other permitted fat, [and he does not know which of the two he ate]—the Torah says, "he shall bear his iniquity"; surely this is true of a person who intended to take swine's meat and actually took it. For this let the weepers moan.

Rabbah b. Bar Chanah said in R. Yochanan's name: What is the meaning of the verse, "For the ways of God are straight; the righteous walk in them, and the sinners will stumble over them" (Hosea 14:10)? You can explain it with the following example: Two people roasted their paschal lamb. One eats it to fulfill his obligation; the other eats it with the intention of having his fill of [roasted meat]. The one who eats it to fulfill the mitzvah is referred to in the phrase, "the righteous walk in them"; the one who eats it to have his fill is cited by the phrase, "the sinners will stumble over them." Resh Lakish retorted: How can you call such a person a sinner? Granted that he did not do the mitzvah in the preferred manner, but he did eat the paschal lamb!

THE REWARD FOR *MITZVOT*

(23b) R. Nachman b. Yitzchak said: A transgression done with good intention is better than a mitzvah performed with bad intention. But has not Rav Yehudah said in the name of Rav: A person should always engross himself in Torah and *mitzvot*, even if he does so for an ulterior motive, because if he starts doing a mitzvah for an ulterior motive he will eventually do it for its own sake? [So you see that a mitzvah done for an ulterior motive is greater, and you said a transgression done with good intention is greater?] Say instead: [A transgression done with good intention is] as good as a mitzvah done for an ulterior motive.

[The Gemara said above:] Rav Yehudah said in Rav's name: A person should always engross himself in Torah and *mitzvot*, even if he does it for an ulterior motive . . . For as a reward for the forty-two sacrifices the wicked Balak offered [when Balaam tried to curse Israel,[3] and he certainly did not offer them with the intention of doing a mitzvah], he merited to have Ruth as his descendant, for R. Yose b. R. Chanina said: Ruth was an offspring of Eglon [the grandson of Balak], king of Moab.

R. Chiya b. Abba said in the name of R. Yochanan: How do we know that the Holy One, blessed be He, does not withhold the reward even for [a decent act as minor] as using a tactful language? The older daughter of Lot called her son Moab [*mei'av*, "from my father"],[4] and the Torah says, "Do not distress Moab, and do not provoke them to fight" (Deuteronomy 2:9). Only provoking war with Moab was forbidden, but Israel was permitted to harass them short of war. By contrast, the younger daughter called her son Ben-Ammi [son of my people, a more tactful expression]; therefore it says, "Do not harass them, [the Ammonites] and do not provoke them to fight" (ibid. v. 19)—they were not even allowed to harass them.

R. Chiya said in the name of R. Yehoshua b. Korcha: A person should always be eager to do a mitzvah as soon as possible, for as a reward for being ahead of her sister by one night,[5] the older daughter of Lot (24a) merited to enter the genealogy of Jewish kings four generations earlier. [Obed, Jesse, David, and Solomon are descendants of Ruth the Moabitess, (who was an offspring of the older daughter), while Rehoboam was the son of Naamah, the Ammonitess, who was a descendant of the younger daughter (Rashi).]

R. MEIR'S QUARRELSOME STUDENTS

(49b) We learned in a *Baraita*: After the death of R. Meir, R. Yehudah said to his disciples: Do not permit the disciples of R. Meir to enter our yeshivah, because they are argumentative and do not come to learn Torah, but to get the better of me by quoting *halachot*. Sumchus pushed his way in and entered. He said to them: This is what R. Meir taught me: A *nazir* must shave off his hair [and must begin counting his nazirite days anew] for defilement through contact with a corpse or contact with the flesh of a corpse the size of an olive. R. Yehudah became angry and said, "Didn't I tell you not to allow the students of R. Meir to enter here, because they are argumentative? If he has to shave off his hair for being in contact with a piece of flesh of corpse the size of an olive, surely he has to shave for touching the corpse itself! [There is no need to mention that.] (50a) R. Yose remarked: People will say, "Meir is dead, Yehudah is angry, Yose keeps quiet, what will become of the Torah?" [And so R. Yose explained the reason that it was necessary to mention the corpse itself.]

WAS SAMUEL A NAZIRITE?

(66a) [The Mishnah says:] Samuel the prophet was a *nazir*, according to R. Nehora'i's[6] view. For it says, [Hannah, Samuel's mother, made a vow that if God would give her a son], "a razor [*morah*] shall not come upon his head" (1 Samuel 1:11), [i.e., he would become a *nazir*. [How do we know that this is the implication of *morah*?] It says with reference to Samuel the word *morah*, and it says with reference to Samson the word *morah* (Judges 13:5). Just as the word *morah* in the case of Samson refers to a *nazir*, [for it says, "the lad shall be a *nazir* of God from the womb" (ibid.), so, too, the word *morah* in the case of Samuel refers to a *nazir*. R. Yose disputed this: Does not the word *morah* denote "fear of a human being"? [And Hannah vowed that her son would be afraid of no one.] Replied R. Nehora'i: But it says, "Samuel said, 'How can I go? If Saul finds out he will kill me?'" (1 Samuel 16:2), which clearly shows that he was afraid of human beings. [Consequently, *morah* refers to *nezirut*.]

Rav said to his son Chiya: (66b) Grab the cup and lead in saying *Birkat Hamazon* [Grace after Meals, and

416

let the others answer Amen]. And so did R. Huna say to his son Rabbah. [The Gemara asks:] Does this mean that it is better to say the *berachah* [than to answer Amen]? Haven't we learned in a Baraita: R. Yose says that the one who answers "Amen" performs a greater mitzvah than the one who recites the *berachah*; and R. Nehora'i said to him: I swear to you, that this is so. You can find proof of this in the well-known fact that weak soldiers begin a battle, but it is the experienced ones that gain the victory. [Similarly, the one who answers "Amen" after the *berachah* is greater.] [The Gemara answers:] There is a dispute among Tanna'im on this issue. For we learned in a *Baraita* [that the one who says the *berachah* is greater]: Both the one who says the *berachah* and the one who responds "Amen" are included in the verse ["Declare the greatness of God with me" refers to the one who says the *berachah*; "and let us exalt His Name together" (Psalms 34:4) refers to the one who answers "Amen."] Except, the one who says the *berachah* will be rewarded first. R. Elazar said in the name of R. Chanina: Torah scholars increase peace in the world, as it says, "And all your children will be students of God, and your children will have peace" (Isaiah 54:13).

NOTES

1. By taking the vow of *nezirut* a *nazir* takes on the obligation to abstain from wine, shaving the hair, and contact with the dead. Generally, the term of *nezirut* is for thirty days, but a person can vow to be a *nazir* for life, the so-called *nezirut Shimshon*. The main purpose of the *nazir* vow is to be a discipline against sexual temptation and to avoid pride.

2. Leviticus 25:29.

3. Numbers 23–24.

4. She crassly publicized that she had conceived him from her father.

5. Genesis 19:32–34.

6. This is R. Meir (*Eruvin* 13b).

ᏬᏈ GITTIN ᏋᏗ

DON'T BROWBEAT YOUR HOUSEHOLD

(6b) R. Chisda said: A person should never intimidate his household. The concubine of Gibea was terrified by her husband, and as a result, many thousands were killed in Israel.[1] Rav Yehudah said in the name of Rav: If a person browbeats his household he will eventually commit three [major] sins: immorality,[2] bloodshed,[3] and the desecration of *Shabbat*.[4] Rabbah b. Bar Chanah said: The three things that a person must say in his home on the eve of *Shabbat* just before dark: Have you tithed? Have you prepared the *eruv*? Kindle the *Shabbat* lights! (7a) should be said in a gentle way, so that they should obey him willingly. R. Ashi said: Although I never heard this statement of Rabbah b. Bar Chanah, I followed that practice because I thought it was the sensible thing to do. R. Abbahu said: A person should never instill fear of himself in his household, for there was a great man who tyrannized his household, and because of that his servants gave him something to eat that was strictly forbidden, and that person was R. Chanina b. Gamliel. [The Gemara asks:] You mean to say, they actually fed it to him? Look, God prevents even the animal of a *tzaddik* from committing an offense;[5] surely God will protect the *tzaddik* himself from stumbling into sin! [The Gemara answers:] Say instead, they *wanted* to feed him [something that was strictly forbidden]. And what was the strictly forbidden thing they wanted to offer him? A piece of flesh from a living animal. [A piece of meat had been misplaced, and out of fear of his master's rage the servant wanted to substitute a piece cut from a living animal (Rashi).]

GUARD YOUR TONGUE

Mar Ukva [the Exilarch, head of Babylonian Jewry] asked R. Elazar for advice: There are certain people who are publicly reviling me, and I am able to have the government arrest them. Am I allowed to do so? R. Elazar drew lines on paper and wrote [the verse], "I said, I will guard my ways from sinning with my tongue, I will guard my mouth with a muzzle, even

while the wicked one stands before me" (Psalms 39:2). He added, "This means, 'although the wicked harrasses me I will guard my mouth with a muzzle.'" [In other words, you are not allowed to report them to the government.] Mar Ukva sent him another letter, stating: They are harrassing me very much; I simply cannot take it, [I cannot concentrate on my Torah studies (Iyun Yaakov)]. R. Elazar replied, [quoting the verse], "Wait silently for [the salvation] of God, and wait longingly [*hitcholel*] for him" (Psalms 37:7). He added, "This means, 'wait for God, and He will cast them like slain enemies [*chalalim*] before you; go to the *bet midrash* early every morning and stay there until late in the evening [to study Torah], and they will disappear by themselves.'" No sooner had R. Elazar spoken these words than Geniva [his main adversary] was put in chains [and led to his execution].

NO BOISTEROUS SINGING

The following question was submitted to Mar Ukva: Where does it say that [after the destruction of the *Bet Hamikdash*] you are not allowed to sing [when having a good time drinking in a tavern]? He replied, quoting the following verse, "Rejoice not, Israel, like the exultation of the peoples, for you have strayed from your God" (Hosea 9:1). [The Gemara asks:] Shouldn't he rather have quoted the verse, "They shall not drink wine with music; liquor shall become bitter to those who drink it" (Isaiah 24:9)? [The Gemara answers:] If he had quoted that verse I would have thought that only musical instruments are forbidden, but that singing was permitted. That's why he quoted the other verse [to tell that singing is also forbidden].

FORBEARANCE AND RESTRAINT

R. Huna b. Natan asked R. Ashi: What is the meaning of the verse, "Kinah, Dimonah, Ad'adah" (Joshua 15:20)?[6] He replied, "The text is listing settlements in Eretz Yisrael." "Do you think that I don't know that these are settlements in Eretz Yisrael?" the other retorted, ["I am asking you what lesson can be derived from these names"]. "For R. Gevihah from Argizah interpreted these names as follows: Whoever has a grievance [*kinah*] against his neighbor and yet remains silent [*domeim*], He that endures forever [*adei'ad*] will take up his cause." Replied R. Ashi: If that is so, [if you feel the need to find allusions in these names,] then shouldn't the passage "Ziklag, Madmannah, Sansannah" (ibid. v. 31) also teach a lesson? R. Huna b. Natan replied: If R. Gevihah from Argizah were here, he would derive a lesson from it. R. Acha from Choza'ah interpreted the passage as follows: If a person has a justifiable complaint against his neighbor for taking away his livelihood [*za'akat legimah*] and yet remains silent [*domeim*], He who dwells in the thornbush[7] [*shocheni s'neh*] will take up his cause.

NO LAURELS FOR
THE BRIDEGROOM

The Exilarch [Mar Ukva] asked R. Huna: Where does it say in the Torah that [after the destruction of the *Bet Hamikdash*] a bridegroom should not wear a wreath on his head? R. Huna replied: This prohibition was instituted by the Rabbis. For we learned in a Mishnah:[8] During the invasion of Eretz Yisrael by Vespasian [which preceded the destruction of the Temple] they decreed that [bridegrooms] should not wear wreaths and that drums with bells should not be played [at weddings]. R. Huna then got up to relieve himself. Thereupon R. Chisda [who was R. Huna's disciple and did not want to speak in his master's presence], said [to the Exilarch]: There is basis in Scripture for it, "Thus says the Lord God: Remove the turban, lift off the crown! This will not remain like this:[9] The degraded will be exalted, and the exalted will be degraded" (Ezekiel 21:31). Now you may ask, what has the turban [which is worn by the High Priest] to do with a crown? It comes to teach you that as long as the turban is worn by the High Priest [i.e., while the *Bet Hamikdash* is standing], a crown [or wreath] may be worn by anyone [referring to the wreath of the bridegroom], but when the turban has been removed from the head of the High Priest [after the destruction of the Temple], the crown must be removed from the head of everyone. Meanwhile, R. Huna came back and found them discussing it. He said: I swear that the prohibition is a rabbinical enactment;[10] however, just as your name is Chisda [charm], your words are charming [a nice interpretation, but it is not the true meaning]. Ravina found Mar the son of R. Ashi weaving a bridal crown for his daughter. He said to him, "Don't you believe in the interpretation of the passage, 'Remove the turban, lift off the crown?'" He replied, "Men are comparable to the High Priest, but it does not refer to women."

What is meant by the words in the above passage, "This is not this" [i.e., "this will not remain like this"]? R. Avira expounded, sometimes in the name of R. Ammi and sometimes in the name of R. Assi: When the Holy One, blessed be He, said to Israel, "Remove the turban, lift off the crown," the ministering angels said to the Holy One, blessed be He: Master of the universe, will "*this*" happen to Israel who said at Mount Sinai "We will do" before "We will hear"[11] [thereby showing their unquestioning dedication to God]? [Replied the Holy One, blessed be He:] Should "*not this*" be the fate of Israel who degraded the exalted and exalted the degraded, for they placed an idol in the Sanctuary.

GIVING *TZEDAKAH*

R. Avira also gave the following exposition, sometimes in the name of R. Ammi and sometimes in the name of R. Assi: What is meant by the verse, "Thus said God: Even if they are full and many—even so they will be cut down and pass on. I will afflict you, and I will not afflict you again" (Nahum 1:12)? If a person sees that his livelihood is exactly what he needs ["if they are full"], he should give charity from it, and all the more so if his income is plentiful ["and many"]. And what is meant by "they will be cut and pass on"? In the yeshivah of R. Yishmael it was taught: Whoever shears off part of his wealth and gives it to charity will be delivered from the judgment of Gehinnom. You can compare it to two sheep crossing a river, one sheared and the other not sheared; the sheared one makes it across, the unsheared one does not; [his fleece is waterlogged]. (7b) "I will afflict you" (ibid.). Mar Zutra said: Even a poor man who is supported by charity should give charity. "I will not afflict you again" (ibid.). R. Yosef taught: If he does that, he will suffer poverty no more.

ARE THE PERSIANS WORSE
THAN THE ROMANS?

(16b) Rabbah b. Bar Chanah was sick one day, and Rav Yehudah and his disciples went to visit him. They asked him the following question: If two people bring a *get* from a foreign country, is it necessary for them to declare: In our presence it was written, and in our presence it was signed; or is it not necessary? He replied: It is not necessary. For if they would say that he divorced her in our presence, would we not believe them [since the testimony of two witnesses is fully believed]? In the meantime (17a) a Persian gentile came and took away their lamp.[12] So Rabbah b. Bar Chanah exclaimed, "Merciful One! Let us be either under Your protection [in Eretz Yisrael] or [if we have to be in Exile, let us be] under the protection of the son of Esau [the Romans; for they treat us with more respect than the Persians do]. [The Gemara asks:] Does this then mean that the Romans are better than the Persians? But hasn't R. Chiya taught: What is meant by the verse, "Only God understands its way, and He knows its place" (Job 28:23)? It means that the Holy One, blessed be He, knew that Israel could not endure the evil decrees of the Romans [against the Torah]; therefore He exiled them to Babylonia. [Proof that the Persians are not as bad as the Romans?] [The Gemara answers:] This is no difficulty. The statement [that the Babylonian exile is better] refers to the period before the Persians conquered Babylonia; the statement [that Roman rule is more benign] refers to the period after the Persians took over Babylonia.

THE SCORCHING EAST WIND

(31b) "And it was when the sun shone that God designated a stifling east wind [*charishit*]" (Jonah 4:8). [The Gemara asks:] What does the word *charishit* mean? Rav Yehudah said: When [the east wind] blows it makes furrows [*charishah*] in the sea. Said Rabbah to him: If that is so, why does the verse continue, "the sun beat down on Jonah's head, and he fainted" (ibid.)? [The text stresses how hot it was, not how forcefully the wind blew.] Rabbah said: Rather [*charishit* means that] when the east wind blows it silences [*charash*] all the other winds [which have a cooling effect]. And that is the intent of the passage, "Your clothes feel warm when the land is silenced from the south" (Job 37:17). This was explained by R. Tachlifa b. R. Chisda in the name of R. Chisda: When are your clothes warm? [When is it very hot?] At the time when the land from the south is silent, which means when the east wind blows, it silences all other winds before it. [The east wind silences the cooling wind that comes from the south; and as a result, hot weather dominates.]

R. Huna and R. Chisda were sitting together when Geniva[13] passed by close to them. One said to the other, "Let's rise before him; he is a Torah scholar." Said the other, "Should we rise before a quarrelsome person?" When Geniva came up to them, he asked, "What is the topic of your discussion?" "We are talking about winds," they replied. He said to them, "The following was said by R. Chanan b. Rava: There are four winds that blow every day, and the north wind blows with all of them [and has a moderating effect on them]. If not for that, the world could not exist even for one hour. The south wind is the harshest of all of them, and if not for the [angel] *Ben Netz*, "Son of the Hawk," who restrains it, it would destroy the whole world. For it says, "Is it by your wisdom that the hawk hovers, spreads its wings toward the south?" (Job 39:26).

Rava and R. Nachman b. Yitzchak were once sitting together, when R. Nachman b. Yaakov passed by in a golden coach, wearing a blue cloak. Rava went over to greet him, but R. Nachman b. Yitzchak did not, for he said to himself: Perhaps it is one of the people of the court of the Exilarch, and Rava needs him, but I don't [because R. Nachman b. Yitzchak was himself a son-in-law of the Exilarch (Rashi)]. When he saw that the person in the coach was R. Nachman b. Yaakov he

went over to him and took off his jacket [because it was hot], and said, "The demon-wind is blowing [referring to the east wind]." Rava said: This is what Rav said: [When this wind blows] a pregnant woman can lose her child. Shmuel said: Even a pearl in the sea rots away. R. Yochanan said: Even the seed in a woman's womb becomes spoiled. R. Nachman b. Yitzchak said: All three, [Rav, Shmuel, and R. Yochanan] derived it from the same verse, "For though he flourishes among the marshes, an east wind will come, a wind from God ascending from the wilderness, and its fountainhead will become parched and his spring will dry up; and it will plunder the treasure of every splendid article" (Hosea 13:15). "The fountainhead" refers to the womb of the woman; "the spring" refers to the seed in the woman's womb; "the treasure of every splendid article" refers to the pearl in the sea.

SHE INADVERTENTLY SWORE FALSELY

(35a) Rav Yehudah said in the name of Rav: It happened once during a year of famine that a man deposited a golden *dinar* with a widow, and she placed it into a container of flour. She inadvertently baked the flour [with the *dinar*] into a bread, which she gave to a poor person. In due time, the owner of the *dinar* came and said to her, "Give me back my *dinar*." She replied, "May one of this woman's sons [meaning, "my sons"] die of poisoning if I derived any benefit from your *dinar*." It was said that before long one of her children died. When the Sages heard about this they said: If such a thing happens to a person who swears the truth, imagine how severely will be punished a person who swears falsely! [The Gemara asks:] Why was she punished at all? [She swore the truth; she did not derive any benefit from the *dinar*!] [The Gemara answers:] She did derive benefit from the *dinar*, because she gained the place of the *dinar*, [she saved the dough of the space that was taken up by the *dinar*]. [The Gemara asks:] Then how could the Sages characterize her as someone who had sworn the truth [if, in fact, she did not swear the truth]? [The Gemara answers:] The Sages meant to say: [If such a thing happens to a person who] thinks she was swearing truthfully, imagine how severely will be punished . . .

THE SIN OF THE GOLDEN CALF

(36b) Ulla said: How shameless is a bride who is unfaithful to her husband while she is standing under her bridal canopy, [a reference to the sin of the golden calf, which the children of Israel worshipped while still at Mount Sinai]. Said Mari, the son of Shmuel's daughter: What verse supports this? "While the King was yet at Sinai, [the children of Israel] gave up their fragrance as the golden calf defiled the covenant" (Song of Songs 1:12). Said Rav: But His love remained with us, because it says, "they gave up their fragrance"—temporarily, but it does not say, "it became [irredeemably] spoiled."

We learned in a *Baraita*: People who suffer insults but do not insult others, who hear someone mocking them but don't answer, who do their duty out of love [of God] and rejoice in suffering [all humiliations that are visited on them], of them Scripture says, "But those that love Him are like the sun rising in full strength" (Judges 5:31).

(38b) Rabbah said: For the following three reasons people lose their wealth: for setting free their heathen slaves,[14] for inspecting their property on *Shabbat*, and for having their main *Shabbat* meal at the time when the lecture is given in the *bet midrash*. R. Chiya b. Abba said in R. Yochanan's name: There were two families in Jerusalem: one had their main meal on *Shabbat* [at the time of the lecture], the other had their main meal on Friday [during daytime, which is forbidden, because as a result they had no appetite for the *Shabbat* meal on Friday night (Rashi)]. Both families passed from the scene without a trace.

HE RETRACTED HIS RULING

(43a) Rabbah b. Bar Huna lectured: Just as if a person marries half a woman, she is not legally married to him; so, too, if a person marries a woman who is half a slave and half free,[15] she is not legally married. R. Chisda said to him: How can you compare the two cases? In the former case [half of the woman] was not acquired, [and that is why she is not legally married], whereas in the latter case the whole woman was acquired. Thereupon Rabbah b. Bar Huna appointed an interpreter [to explain his words to the scholars in the *bet midrash*]. He quoted the verse, "Let this obstacle be under your hand" (Isaiah 3:6), and expounded it, "A person does not fully understand the true meaning of the words of the Torah until he has stumbled over them." [I too have stumbled when I made this ruling, and I take back what I said. (Rashi)] I say: Even though, if a person marries half a woman, she is not legally married; if he marries a woman who is half slave and half free, she *is* legally married.

THEY USED WITCHCRAFT TO STIR THE POT

(45a) The daughters of R. Nachman were able to stir a boiling pot with their bare hands [and they did not get burned. People who saw it thought that they were so pious that fire had no power over them; but that was not the case at all (Rashi). R. Ilish asked: It says, "One [righteous] man in a thousand I have found, but one [righteous] woman among these I have not found" (Ecclesiastes 7:28), yet here are the daughters of R. Nachman [who apparently did reach a very high level

of piety]! It happened that the daughters of R. Nachman were taken captive and [R. Ilish] was captured with them. One day R. Islish was sitting next to a person who knew the language of the birds. A raven came and gave that man a message. "What is the raven saying?" R. Ilish asked. The man replied, "It says, 'Run away, Ilish! Run away, Ilish!'" Ilish said, "The raven is a liar, I don't trust it." Then a dove came and called out. "What does it say?" R. Ilish again asked. The man answered, "It says, 'Run away, Ilish! Run away, Ilish!'" Said R. Ilish, "The community of Israel is compared to a dove.[16] This tells me that a miracle will happen."

He then said to himself, "I will go and look up R. Nachman's daughters, and if they remained steadfast in their faith I will take them with me." He then said to himself, "Whatever concerns women have they discuss in the outhouse." He overheard them say, "These captors are our husbands now, just as our husbands back in Nahardea used to be. Let's tell our captors to take us away from here, so that our husbands will not come and find out where we are and ransom us." R. Ilish escaped together with the man who understood the language of the birds. A miracle happened to R. Ilish; he crossed the river on a ferry, [and his pursuers were left standing at the bank of the river], but the other man was arrested and executed. When R. Nachman's daughters eventually came back home,[17] he said, "[Don't be fooled into thinking that they are saintly women]. They used witchcraft to stir the boiling pot."

RESH LAKISH OUTWITTED THE LYDIANS

(47a) Resh Lakish [who in younger years, before he became a great Torah scholar, was a bandit] once sold himself to the Lydians.[18] He took with him a bag with a stone in it. He said to himself: It is a well-known fact that before they kill a person they grant him his last wish, whatever that may be, in order that [the victim] should forgive them for shedding his blood. When Resh Lakish's last day arrived, they asked him, "What would you like us to do for you?" "I want you to let me tie your arms and set you down and let me give each of you one and-a-half blows with my bag. He tied them, set them down, and when he gave each one a blow with his bag he knocked them out. [One of them] ground his teeth at him. "Are you laughing at me?" Resh Lakish asked. "You still have half a blow coming to you!" He then killed all of them and ran off. Once when he sat down [on the ground] to a meal, his daughter asked him, "Don't you want a pillow to recline on?" He replied, "My belly is my cushion." When he died, all he left was a small measure of saffron, and he applied to himself the verse, "They leave their possessions to others" (Psalms 49:11).

RABBI MEIR COULD
NOT BE DISSUADED

(52a) A certain administrator of an orphan's estate that was in the neighborhood of R. Meir sold land of the estate, and [with the proceeds he] bought slaves, but R. Meir stopped him from doing that. In his dream R. Meir heard a voice saying, "I want to destroy, and you want to build?" [By forbidding the sale of the land, R. Meir kept the estate intact.] But R. Meir paid no attention to the voice, for he said: Dreams do not mean a thing, one way or the other. [The Gemara now cites another incident to show that R. Meir could not be dissuaded either by dreams or by Satan himself from following the right course:] There were two men who, at Satan's instigation, quarrelled with each other every Friday afternoon. R. Meir once happened to come to that place and stopped them from quarrelling for three Fridays in a row. When he finally made peace between them, he heard Satan say, "Woe is to me, for R. Meir drove me out of my house!"

(55b) [The Mishnah says:] At the time of the war of Titus against the Jews of Eretz Yisrael when Jews were being murdered there were no [gentile] extortionists [who forced a Jew to sell his land at a quarter less than the real value]. However, once the slaughter of the Jews stopped there were [gentile] extortionists.

KAMTZA AND BAR KAMTZA

R. Yochanan said: Let me give you an example of what is meant by the verse, "Praiseworthy is the man who always fears, but he who is stubborn of heart will fall into misfortune" (Proverbs 28:14). [The following story shows that a person must be extremely cautious and realize that stubbornness brings in its wake the greatest disaster.] Through Kamtza and Bar Kamtza Jerusalem was destroyed. Because of a rooster and a hen Tur Malka was devastated. Because of a rod of a carriage Betar was ruined. [The Gemara now explains:] "Through Kamtza and Bar Kamtza Jerusalem was destroyed." [This is what happened.] There was a person who had a friend named Kamtza and an enemy named Bar Kamtza. He once made a banquet and said to his servant, "Go and bring me Kamtza." [By mistake] the servant went and brought Bar Kamtza. When the host entered and found Bar Kamtza sitting at his banquet, he said, "The person sitting here is an enemy of mine. What is he doing at my banquet? Get out of here!" So Bar Kamtza said to him, "Since I am here, let me stay. I will pay for whatever I eat and drink." (56a) He replied, "No, I won't let you stay." "I will pay for half the banquet," Bar Kamtza pleaded. "No," was the answer. "I will pay for the whole banquet, just let me stay." He still said no, grabbed him by the arm, and threw him out.

Bar Kamtza now said to himself, "Since the Rabbis were there and did not protest, that shows that they approved of what he did. I will go and denounce them to the Roman authorities." He went and said to the Emperor, "The Jews have rebelled against you." "How do you know that?" the Emperor asked. He replied, "Send an offering to their Temple, and see if they will sacrifice it for you on the Altar."[19] So the Emperor sent with him a beautiful calf. On the way to the *Bet Hamikdash* Bar Kamtza made a blemish on its upper lip, or as some say, in the white of the eye; in a place that we consider a blemish but the Romans do not. The Rabbis thought that they should bring this sacrifice [in spite of the blemish] in order to preserve the good relations with the government [and prevent the bloodshed that might result from their refusal]. Said R. Zechariah b. Avkulas, "People will say that you can bring a blemished animal on the Altar." So they considered killing Bar Katza[20] [so that he should not report that they refused to offer the sacrifice]. R. Zechariah now again said, "People will say that you killed him because he made a blemish on a sacrifice." R. Yochanan said: Through the timidity of R. Zechariah b. Avkulas [in allowing Bar Kamtza to go back and report that the sacrifice was not offered] the *Bet Hamikdash* was destroyed, our Sanctuary was burned, and we were exiled from our land.

The Emperor then sent Nero the Caesar to destroy Jerusalem. When he arrived, he shot an arrow toward the east, and it landed in Jerusalem. He shot another toward the west; it too landed in Jerusalem. He shot in the four directions, and every time it landed in Jerusalem [which to him was an auspicious omen that he would conquer Jerusalem]. He found a Jewish child and said to him, "Please repeat to me the verse you have learned today" [as an indication of what was in store for him]. The boy said, "I will take My vengeance on Edom [i.e., Rome] through My people Israel" (Ezekiel 25:14). Nero concluded: The Holy One, blessed be He, wants to destroy His House, and He wants to blame me for it.[21] He got up, ran away, and converted to Judaism, and R. Meir was one of his descendants.

He then sent Vespasian the Caesar to destroy Jerusalem. He besieged Jerusalem for three years. There were three wealthy people [in Jerusalem]: Nakdimon b. Gurion, Ben Kalba Savua, and Ben Tzitzit Hakeset. Nakdimon b. Gurion got his name because the sun continued shining [*nakedah*] for his sake.[22] Ben Kalba Savua got his name because whoever entered his house hungry like a dog [*kelev*] came out satiated [*savua*]. Ben Tzitzit Hakeset got his name because [he was so rich that] his *tzitzit* never touched the floor since he was always sitting on cushions [*keset*]. Others say that he owed his name to the fact that his seat [*kisei*] was among the prominent people of Rome.

One of these three men said to the Rabbis: I will provide the city with wheat and barley. The second said: I will provide it with wine, salt, and oil. The third said: I will supply it with firewood. [They had stored these provisions in anticipation of the Roman siege.] The Sages praised especially the one who had the foresight to put away wood, since R. Chisda would give all his keys to his servant except the key to the woodshed, for R. Chisda said: One storehouse of wheat requires sixty storehouses of wood [to process it into bread]. The three men had stored enough supplies to sustain Jerusalem for twenty-one years.

[At that time there was a civil war raging in Jerusalem among three Jewish factions: moderates who were followers of the Rabbis; the corrupt and assimilated Sadducees who were Roman sympathizers and opponents of the Rabbis and *halachah*; and the Zealots [*Kana'im*], extreme nationalists who advocated open warfare to overthrow Roman domination. The violent and militant members of the Zealot party were called *Biryonim*.]

The *Biryonim* were then [in control of] the city, [and did not allow anyone to leave the city]. The Rabbis said to the *Biryonim*, "Let us go out and make a truce with the Romans." They did not let them, but, on the contrary, said, "Let's go out and fight the Romans." The Rabbis said, "You will not succeed." The *Biryonim* then went and burned down the storehouses of wheat and barley [in order to force the people into an immediate armed confrontation with the Romans]. As a result there was a famine in Jerusalem.

THE GREAT JERUSALEM FAMINE

Martha the daughter of Baitus was one of the richest women in Jerusalem. She sent her servant to buy fine flour. By the time he got to the market it was all sold out. He told her, "There is no fine flour, but there is white flour." "Go and get me some," she said. By the time he got there, it was all sold out. He came back and said, "There is no white flour, but there still is dark flour." "Go and get me some," she said. By the time he got there, it was all sold out. He came back and said, "There is no dark flour, but there is barley flour." She said, "Go and get me some." By the time he got there, this too was sold out. She had already taken off her shoes, but she said, "Let me go myself and see if I can find anything to eat." [She was going barefoot,] so a piece of manure stuck to her foot, and she died from the shock.

R. Yochanan b. Zakkai applied to her the verse, "The most pampered, delicate woman, who is so refined that she does not let her foot touch the ground" (Deuteronomy 28:56). Some say that she ate one of the figs R. Tzadok had thrown away, and because of her squeamishness she died. For R. Tzadok fasted for forty years that Jerusalem should not be destroyed. [He was so skinny that] when he ate something, you could see it go down his throat. When he decided to try and eat they would bring him figs, and he would only suck the juice and throw away the rest [because he could not digest solid food]. When Martha was dying she took all her gold and silver and threw it out into the street and said, "What do I need this for?" She thereby fulfilled the prophecy, "They will throw their silver in the streets" (Ezekiel 7:19).

GIVE ME YAVNEH AND ITS TORAH SCHOLARS!

(56a) Abba Sikra, the head of the *Biryonim* [the militant branch of the Zealot party] of Jerusalem was the nephew of Rabban Yochanan b. Zakkai. Rabban Yochanan b. Zakkai sent him a message, saying, "Come to me secretly." [Risking his life,] Abba Sikra came. R. Yochanan said, "How long are you going to keep this up, [thwarting the efforts to make peace, thereby causing people to die of starvation]?" He replied, "What can I do? If I say anything [to the *Biryonim* about making a truce with the Romans], they'll kill me." R. Yochanan b. Zakkai said, "Find some way for me to get out of the city, [so that I can negotiate with the Romans]. Maybe something can still be saved." Abba Sikra replied, "Pretend that you are sick, and let everyone come and visit you. Then bring something that has a foul odor and put it in your bed, so that they will think that you have died. [He had to use a ruse because the *Biryonim* permitted no one except the dead to leave the city.] Let only your students carry your coffin, and don't allow anyone else to carry you, so that they should not notice that you are still light—for everybody knows that a live person weighs less than a corpse."

R. Yochanan b. Zakkai followed Abba Sikra's strategy. R. Eliezer carried the coffin on one side, and R. Yehoshua on the other. When they came to the gate, [the *Biryonim* guards who were suspicious] wanted to pierce the coffin with a spear. Abba Sikra said to them, "[Do you want the Romans] to say about you, 'They even pierce their own rabbi!'" The guards then wanted to push the coffin, but Abba Sikra said to them, "[Do you want the Romans] to say about you, 'They push their own rabbi!'" The *Biryonim* guards then opened the gate, and [R. Yochanan b. Zakkai] got out.

When he reached the Roman headquarters he said to Vespasian, "Peace to you, Emperor! Peace to you, Emperor!" Replied Vespasian, "You forfeit your life for two reasons: first, I am not an emperor, and you call me emperor; [you ridiculed me]; and second, if I am an emperor, why did you not come to pay your respects until now?" R. Yochanan replied, "Concerning your statement that you are not an emperor, (56b) the truth is that you will become an emperor, since if you were not a ruler, Jerusalem would not be given over into your hands. For it says, 'Lebanon will fall by a mighty one [*adir*]' (Isaiah 10:34). And we know that *adir* refers specifically to a king, as it says, '[Israel's] king [*adiro*] will be from their midst' (Jeremiah 30:21). And furthermore, we know that Lebanon refers to the *Bet Hamikdash*,[23] for it says, [Moses pleaded for permission to see] 'This goodly mountain and Lebanon' (Deuteronomy 3:25).

Now, regarding your question that if you are an emperor, why I did not come until now? The answer is that the *Biryonim* among us did not allow it." Vespasian said, "If you had a barrel of honey, and there was a snake coiled around it, wouldn't you break the barrel in order to rid yourself of the snake?" [Although you would lose much of the honey, you would at least salvage some of it. Similarly, you should have burned down Jerusalem to get rid of the *Biryonim* and save the people from starvation.] R. Yochanan b. Zakkai was silent and did not know what to answer. R. Yosef, some say R. Akiva, said: We can apply to R. Yochanan b. Zakkai the verse, "Who makes wise men retreat, and makes their knowledge foolish" (Isaiah 44:25). He should have said to him: We take a pair of pliers and grab the snake and kill it, and leave the barrel undamaged. [I would rather get rid of the *Biryonim* and leave Jerusalem intact.]

Just then, a messenger arrived from Rome saying: Arise, for Caesar is dead, and the senators in Rome have decided to appoint you as the Head of State. Vespasian had just put on one shoe and wanted to put on the other, but it did not fit anymore. He tried to take off the other one, but it did not come off. [Thinking that his feet were swollen, he exclaimed:] What is the meaning of this? R. Yochanan b. Zakkai calmed him: Don't worry. You just received good tidings, and it says, "Good news will fatten a bone" (Proverbs 15:30). What should you do to remedy the condition? Let someone whom you dislike pass before you, as it says, "A broken spirit will dry up the bone" (ibid. 17:22). Vespasian did so, and he was able to put on the other shoe. He then said to R. Yochanan b. Zakkai: Since you are so wise, why didn't you come to me until now? He replied: Didn't I tell you, [because of the problem with the *Biryonim*]? Vespasian shot back: I also answered you [that you should have burned down Jerusalem].

Vespasian then said: I am going back to Rome, and I will send someone else to take my place. However, go ahead and ask me a favor, and I will grant it. [Seeing that Jerusalem was lost, R. Yochanan wanted to preserve the spiritual heritage of the Jewish people,] so he said: Give me the city of Yavneh and its Torah scholars [at least the Torah will survive and continue to flourish],[24] and the family of Rabban Gamliel [who are the leaders of the Jewish people and descendants of David], and give us some of your physicians to heal R. Tzadok. R. Yosef, some say, R. Akiva, applied to him this verse, "Who makes wise men retreat and makes their knowledge foolish" (Isaiah 44:25). He should have said to him: Let the Jews go this time altogether [and lift the siege of Jerusalem]. However, R. Yochanan b. Zakkai thought that he would not grant him that much, and so he would not be able to save even a little.

How did the doctors heal R. Tzadok? The first day they gave him water in which bran had been soaked; the next day water that had bran and a little flour mixed into it; the next day water mixed with flour, so that his stomach gradually expanded.

TITUS'S PUNISHMENT

Vespasian went back to Rome and sent the wicked Titus [to destroy Jerusalem]. Titus said, "Where is their God, the Rock in whom they trusted?" (Deuteronomy 32:37). This is the same wicked Titus who blasphemed and cursed God. What did he do? He grabbed a prostitute by the hand and entered into the Holy of Holies and spread out a Torah scroll and sinned with her on it. He then took a sword and slashed the curtain. Miraculously, blood gushed forth from the curtain, and he thought that he had killed God, as it says, "Your enemies have roared inside Your meeting place [i.e., the *Bet Hamikdash*], they take their signs for true signs" (Psalms 74:4). [They construed their success as a sign that their cause was just.] Abba Chanan said: "Who is like You, O Strong One, God?" (ibid. 89:9). Who is like You, mighty in self-restraint, that You heard the blaspheming and cursing of that wicked man and keep silent? In the yeshivah of R. Yishmael they expounded: "Who is like You among the powers, [*eilim*] God?" (Exodus 15:11). Who is like You among the silent ones [*illemim*]. [God has the strength to remain silent in the face of Titus's provocation.]

What did Titus do? He took the curtain, shaped it like a basket, and took all the vessels of the *Bet Hamikdash* and put them in it. He then put them aboard a ship to sail to his city to glorify himself with them, as it says, "And then I saw the wicked buried and newly come while those who had done right were gone from the holy place and were forgotten in the city" (Ecclesiastes 8:10). [The Gemara expounds the verse as referring to Titus:] Don't read *kevurim*, "buried," but *kevutzim*, "gathered"; don't read *veyishtakechu*, "were forgotten," but *veyishtabbechu*, "and glorified." [The verse now takes on a new meaning: The wicked Titus gathered all the vessels; he came from the *Bet Hamikdash*, and glorified himself with them in their city.]

Some say that *kevurim* means "buried" because even things that were buried were revealed to Titus [so that he was able to loot the *Bet Hamikdash* completely]. A storm blew up that threatened to sink the ship. Titus said: Evidently the God of the Jews has power only over water. When Pharaoh came He drowned him in the sea. Sisera was overcome by water,[25] and now He wants to drown me also in water. If He is a great warrior, let Him come up on dry land and wage war against me. A voice came forth from Heaven and said: Wicked one, son of a wicked one, descendant of the wicked Esau, I have an inferior creature in My world called a gnat.—

Why is it called inferior? Because it only eats but does not excrete.—Go up on the dry land and wage war against it! When Titus landed a gnat came and entered his nose, and kept knocking against his brain for seven years. One day, as he was passing a blacksmith's shop, the gnat heard the noise of the hammer and stopped knocking.

Titus said: I see, there is a remedy. So every day he brought a blacksmith to hammer for him. If he was a non-Jew he would pay him four *zuz* for doing this; if he was a Jew, he would say: It should be enough of a reward for you to see your enemy [suffer so much]. He did this for thirty days; then the gnat got used to the noise and resumed the knocking. We learned in a *Baraita*: R. Pinchas b. Aruva said: I was together with the public figures of Rome, [and from them I found out that] when Titus died they opened his skull and they found something the size of a swallow weighing two *sela*. Alternately, it has been taught: the size of a year-old dove[26] weighing two pounds. Abaye said: We learned: It had a copper beak and iron claws. When he was dying he said: Burn me, and scatter my ashes over the seven seas, so that the God of the Jews should not be able to find me and bring me to trial.

Onkelos son of Kalonikos who was Titus's nephew wanted to convert to Judaism. He went and, through sorcery, raised Titus from the dead. He asked him: Who is most highly respected in the World to Come? Titus replied: Israel. He further asked him: What about me joining them? Titus replied: They have many commandments, and you will not be able to fulfill them. Go and fight them, and you will gain prominence, for it says, "Her tormentors become her master" (Lamentations 1:5); whoever makes the Jews suffer gains prestige. He asked him: (57a) How are you being punished [in the hereafter]? Titus replied: With the punishment I decreed on myself. Every day my ashes are collected, and sentence is passed on me, and I am burned, and my ashes are scattered over the seven seas. Then Onkelos went and raised Balaam from the dead through sorcery. He asked him: Who is most highly respected in the World to Come? He replied: Israel. What about me joining them? He replied, "You must never seek peace or good relations with them, as long as you exist" (Deuteronomy 23:7). Onkelos then asked: How are you being punished?

He replied: I am being cooked in boiling semen [in retaliation for giving the advice that led Israel to behave immorally with the Moabite girls].[27] He then went and raised other sinners of Israel from the dead through sorcery. He asked them: Who is most highly respected in the World to Come? They replied: Israel. What about me joining them? They replied: Seek their welfare, and don't seek to harm them. Whoever touches them touches the apple of God's eye. He asked: How are you being punished? They replied: We are being cooked in boiling manure, for a Rabbi has said: Whoever ridicules the words of the Sages is punished in Gehinnom with boiling manure. [The Gemara observes:] Go and look at the difference between Jewish sinners and the prophets of the nations that worship idols. [The Jewish sinners told Onkelos to convert; whereas the prophets of the heathen nations, although they knew the truth, still told him not to associate with Jews.] We learned in a *Baraita*: Look how serious are the consequences of putting a person to shame. God stood up for Bar Kamtza [who had been humiliated] and made him the instrument with which He destroyed the *Bet Hamikdash*.

THE DESTRUCTION OF TUR MALKA

[The Gemara stated above on 55b:] The destruction of Tur Malka was brought about by a rooster and a hen. [How so?] In those days it was the custom that when they led a bride and a bridegroom to the wedding canopy they would carry in front of them a rooster and a hen, as if to say: May you be fruitful and multiply like fowl. One day a company of Roman soldiers was passing [such a wedding procession] and took away the rooster and the hen. The Jews jumped on the Romans and beat them, so they went and reported to the Emperor: The Jews are rising up against you. Thereupon he marched against the Jews. One of the Jews was a great warrior named Bar Deroma who was able to jump a *mil*, and he killed the Romans. The Emperor took off his crown and placed it on the ground [as a sign of submission to God] and said: Master of the universe, please do not deliver me and my kingdom into the hands of one single individual. [Bar Deroma would have been able singlehandedly to defeat the Roman forces,] but his own words made him stumble, for he said, "You, O God, who have forsaken us, and You do not go forth, O God, with our legions" (Psalms 60:12), [implying: I myself crushed the enemy with my own strength, without God's help. His pride was his undoing].

[The Gemara asks:] But David himself said this [in Psalms, and it was not held against him]? [The Gemara answers:] David was wondering: [Is it possible that God has forsaken us?] Bar Daroma's [downfall came when he] went to a toilet, and a snake came. From fright his intestines were dislodged, and he died. The Emperor said: Since a miracle happened to me, I will leave the Jews alone this time. So he left them and went away. The Jews, [instead of thanking God,] celebrated, ate and drank, and lit many torches until there was so much light that the writing on a coin could be read a mile away. Said the Emperor: The Jews are making fun of me, [they are feasting as if they had gained victory]. Therefore, he came back and attacked them. R. Assi said: Three hundred thousand soldiers with drawn swords entered Tur Malka, slaughtering the Jews for three days and three nights, while on the other side of the mountain there was singing and merriment. And the people who were celebrating on one side of the mountain had no idea what was occurring on the other side of the mountain.

It says,"God consumed without pity all the dwellings of Jacob" (Lamentations 2:2). When Ravin came he said in R. Yochanan's name: This refers to the six myriad cities King Yannai had in the King's Mountain, and each of them had as many inhabitants as the number that went out of Egypt [600,000], except for three cities that had populations twice that number. These were K'far Bish, K'far Shichlayim, and K'far Dichraya. K'far Bish [evil village] was so called because they never offered hospitality to visitors. K'far Shichlayim [village of watercress] was given that name because they supported themselves raising *shichlayim* [watercress]. K'far Dichraya [village of males], according to R. Yochanan, owed its name to the fact that the women would have a boy and then a girl and then stopped having children. Ulla said: I have seen that place, and it would not hold even six hundred thousand reeds. A certain heretic said to R. Chanina: You are telling us lies [when you say the towns had such large populations]. He replied: Eretz Yisrael is called "land of the deer" (Jeremiah 3:19). Just as the skin of a deer cannot hold its flesh; [when the hide has been removed it shrinks], so it is with Eretz Yisrael: If Jews are living there it expands, but when there are no Jews it shrinks.

THE TRAGIC END OF BETAR

We learned above (55b):] Because of a rod of a carriage Betar was destroyed. [How did that happen?] It was the custom in Betar that when a boy was born the parents would plant a cedar tree, and when a girl was born they planted a pine tree. When they got married the tree was cut down, and a bridal canopy was made of the branches. One day the Emperor's daughter was riding through town when a shaft of her carriage broke, so [her servants] cut down a cedar tree and brought it to her [to replace the broken shaft]. Seeing this, the Jews attacked the princess's party and beat them. They then reported to the Emperor that the Jews were rebelling, and he marched against them.

"[God] cut down, in burning anger, all the dignity of Israel," [literally "all the horns of Israel"] (Lamentations 2:3). R. Zeira said in the name of R. Abbahu who quoted R. Yochanan: This alludes to the eighty thousand hornblowers at the head of the Roman legions that invaded Betar where they killed men, women, and children when they captured it until their blood flowed into the Mediterranean Sea. Do you think Betar was close to the sea? It was a whole *mil* away. R. Elazar the Great said: There are two rivers in the valley of Yadayim—one of them flowing in one direction; the other, in the other direction. The Sages said that at that time they contained two parts water and one part blood [from the victims of Betar]. We learned in a *Baraita*:

For seven years the gentiles were able to cultivate their vineyards with no other fertilizer than Jewish blood.

NEVUZARADAN'S MASSACRE

(57b) R. Chiya b. Avin said in the name of R. Yehoshua b. Korcha: One of the elder citizens of Jerusalem told me that in that valley Nevuzaradan the captain of the guard [of Nebuchadnezzar] killed two hundred and eleven myriad,[28] and in Jerusalem he killed ninety-four myriad[29] on one stone,[30] until their blood flowed and mingled with the blood of Zechariah [son of Yehoyada the *kohen* who had been killed on orders of King Joash (2 Chronicles 24:22)]. Thereby was fulfilled the prophecy, "Blood touches blood" (Hosea 4:2). Nevuzaradan noticed that the blood of Zechariah was seething and bubbling and asked: What is this blood? They told him: It is the blood of sacrifices that has been poured here. [We did not perform the offering properly, and that is why it is churning.] He brought blood of other sacrifices, and it did not bubble up. He said: If you are telling me the truth, fine. But if you don't, I will comb your flesh with iron combs. They confessed: What shall we say. We had a prophet among us who would rebuke us in the name of heaven [not to worship idols]. We rose up against him and killed him. Many years have passed, yet his blood has not come to rest.

Nevuzaradan said to them: I will appease him. He brought the great Sanhedrin [of seventy-one members] and the small Sanhedrin [of twenty-three members] and killed them to appease him, but the blood did not rest. He then slaughtered young men and women, but the blood did not rest. He then killed young schoolchildren, but the blood still did not rest. So he said: Zechariah, Zechariah, I have already destroyed the best; do you want me to kill them all? When he said that, the blood rested. At that moment Nevuzaradan had a fleeting thought of repentance and remorse. He said to himself: If the Jews were punished so severely for killing one person, I who murdered so many people, how infinitely greater will be my punishment? So he ran away, disposed of his property, and converted to Judaism. [The Gemara briefly digresses on the subject of converts.] Naaman was a *ger toshav* [a non-Jew who renounces idolatry, but does not observe *mitzvot* other than the seven Noachide commandments]; Nevuzaradan was a *ger tzedek*, a righteous convert [who accepts all the *mitzvot* of the Torah and is a full-fledged Jew]. Descendants of Haman learned Torah in B'nei B'rak; descendants of Sisera taught Torah to children in Jerusalem; descendants of Sennacherib gave public Torah lectures. And who were they? Shemayah and Avtalyon.[31] [Returning to its theme, the Gemara says that the massacre of Nevuzaradan] was predicted in the prophecy, "I have placed her blood upon the smooth rock, that it not be covered" (Ezekiel 24:8).

TRAGEDIES OF THE DESTRUCTION OF THE TEMPLE

[Isaac said when Jacob was standing before him,] "The voice is Jacob's voice, but the hands are the hands of Esau" (Genesis 27:22). [The Gemara expounds:] "The voice" [portends the lament of the Jews] when Emperor Hadrian killed in Alexandria of Egypt twice the number of Jews that left Egypt. "Is Jacob's voice" portends [the wailing caused] by Emperor Vespasian who killed in the city of Betar four hundred thousand myriad, or as some say, four thousand myriad. "The hands are the hands of Esau" alludes to the Roman empire, which has destroyed our *Bet Hamikdash* and burned our Sanctuary and driven us out of our land. Another interpretation is: "The voice is Jacob's voice"—No prayer is answered unless there is a descendant of Jacob praying for that purpose. "The hands are the hands of Esau"—If a war ends in victory you can be sure that a descendant of Esau was involved in it. R. Elazar, [reflecting on the malice evidenced in the story of Kamtza and Bar Kamtza and the slander that led to the destruction of the *Bet Hamikdash*,] summarized, "Hide yourself from the scourging of the tongue" (Job 5:21); this means, stay away from strife that arises because of the tongue [i.e., libel and talebearing].

R. Yehudah said in the name of Rav: What is the meaning of the verse, "By the rivers of Babylon, there we sat and also wept when we remembered Zion" (Psalms 137:1)? [How could David who wrote Psalms mention the Babylonian exile, which happened five hundred years later?] This teaches us that the Holy One, blessed be He, showed David the destruction both of the first Temple and of the second Temple. Of the first Temple, for it says, "By the rivers of Babylon, there we sat and also wept"; of the second Temple, for it says, "Remember God, for the offspring of Edom [i.e., Rome] the day of Jerusalem's fall, for those who said, 'Destroy! Destroy! to its very foundation'" (ibid. v. 7).

Rav Yehudah said in the name of Shmuel, some say in the name of R. Ammi, and other say it was taught in a *Baraita*: On one occasion, four hundred boys and girls were abducted for immoral purposes. Since they understood what it was they were going to be used for they asked the oldest among them: If we drown in the sea, will we still be able to attain life in the World to Come? The oldest among them expounded the verse, "God promised, 'I will bring you back from Bashan, I will bring you back from the depths of the sea'" (Psalms 68:23). "I will bring you back from Bashan [at the time of the resurrection]"—from between the lions' teeth.[32] "I will bring you back from the depths of the sea"— those who drown in the sea, [meaning, even those who did not merit a Jewish burial, who drowned in the sea, or whose bodies were burned by our enemies and whose ashes were scattered will be revived at the resurrection of the dead]. When the girls heard this they all jumped into the sea. The boys drew an inference for themselves:

If these girls who will be forced into a natural form of immorality killed themselves, we who will be forced into unnatural forms of immorality surely should kill ourselves. The boys then threw themselves into the sea. In regard to such children Scripture says, "Because for Your sake we allow ourselves to be killed all the time, we are considered as sheep for slaughter" (Psalms 44:23).

HANNAH AND HER SEVEN SONS

Rav Yehudah, however, said that this text refers to the story of the woman [Hannah] and her seven sons [that happened in the days of Chanukah]. They brought the first son in front of the Emperor[33] and said to him: Bow down to the idol! He replied: It says in the Torah, "I am the Lord your God" (Exodus 20:2). So they led him away and killed him. Then they brought the next son in front of the Emperor and said to him: Bow down to the idol! He replied: It says in the Torah, "Do not have any other gods before Me" (ibid. v. 3). They led him away and killed him. Then they brought the next son and said to him: Bow down to the idol! He replied: It says in the Torah, "Whoever sacrifices to any deity other than God must be condemned to death" (ibid. 22:19).

They led him away and killed him. They then brought the next son and said: Bow down to the idol! He replied: It says in the Torah, "Do not bow down to any other god" (ibid. 20:5). So they led him away and killed him. They then brought the next son and said to him: Bow down to the idol! He replied: It says in the Torah, "Listen, Israel, God is our Lord, God is One" (Deuteronomy 6:4). They led him away and killed him. They then brought out the next son and said to him: Bow down to the idol! He replied: It says in the Torah, "Realize today and ponder it in your heart: God is the Supreme Being in heaven above and on earth below—there is no other" (ibid. 4:39). So they led him away and killed him.

They then brought out the next son and said to him: Bow down to the idol! He replied: It says in the Torah, "Today you have declared allegiance to God . . . God has similarly declared allegiance to you today" (Deuteronomy 26:17,18). We have already taken an oath to the Holy One, blessed be He, that we will not exchange Him for any other god, and He has also sworn to us that He will not exchange us for any other people. The Emperor said [to the youngest son]: I will throw down my signet ring, and you pick it up, so it will look as if you are bowing down, and the people will say that you obeyed my order, [because it was embarrassing to him that all the children were defying him].

The boy answered: A pity on you, King! A pity on you, King! If you are so worried about your own glory, how much more should I be worried about the glory of the Holy One, blessed be He. When they took him out to kill him, the mother said: Let me hold him and kiss him. She then said to him: My son, go and tell your father Abraham: You bound one son upon the altar; I bound seven children on seven altars. Then she went up to the roof and threw herself down [because she realized that now she would be forced to bow down to the idol] and died. Thereupon a heavenly voice came forth saying, "A mother of children shall rejoice" (Psalms 113:9).

R. Nachman b. Yitzchak said: [The above-mentioned verse, "Because for Your sake we allow ourselves to be killed all the time" (Psalms 44:23)] refers to Torah scholars who kill themselves [i.e., deny themselves the comforts of life] in order to study Torah. This agrees with the saying of R. Shimon b. Lakish who said: The words of the Torah will endure only with someone who kills himself for the Torah [i.e., subdues his desire for the pleasures of the world], as it says, "This is the Torah, when a man shall die in the tent" (Numbers 19:14).

ten in this Book of the Torah God will bring upon you" (Deuteronomy 28:61). Said the other: How far am I from that verse? He replied: Wait just a minute, you'll get there in one or two columns. He shot back: If I had come across that verse, I wouldn't need you [I would have understood myself that it refers to these terrible things].

Rav Yehudah said in the name of Shmuel, quoting R. Shimon b. Gamliel: What is suggested by the verse, "My eyes have brought me grief over all the daughters of my city" (Lamentations 3:51)? There were four hundred synagogues in the city of Betar, and in every one there were four hundred teachers of children; and each one of them had four hundred students. When the enemy entered they pierced them with their spears, and when they conquered the whole city they wrapped them in their scrolls and set them afire.

ROMAN ATROCITIES

Rabbah b. Bar Chanah said in the name of R. Yochanan: Forty se'ah (58a) tefillin boxes were found on the heads of the victims of Betar. R. Yannai b. R. Yishmael said: There were three crates, each containing forty se'ah [of tefillin boxes]. In a Baraita it was taught that there were forty crates, each containing three se'ah. However, there is no argument; the one was referring to the head-tefillin, the other to the arm-tefillin.[34]

R. Assi said: Four kav of brain were found on one stone. Ulla said: Nine kav. R. Kahana—some say Shila b. Mari—said: Where is this indicated in Scripture? In the verse, "O violated daughter of Babylon, praised be the one who repays you in the manner that you treated us. Praised be the one who will clutch and smash your infants against the rock" (Psalms 137:8,9) [in retaliation for what was done to us].

"The precious children of Zion, who are comparable to fine gold—alas, they are now treated like earthen jugs, work of a potter" (Lamentations 4:2). [The Gemara asks:] What is meant by "comparable to gold"? Do you think [it is meant to be taken literally] that they were covered with gold? [That is not likely.] For in the yeshivah of R. Shila they taught that two measures of gold came down to the world; one of them is in Rome, and the other in the rest of the world, [so there would not be enough gold to cover all the children of Zion]. What it means is that with their beauty they outshone fine gold. Originally, the Roman aristocrats used to keep a beautiful golden amulet set in a ring in front of them when they had relations with their wives [to impart beauty to their children]. But after they captured the Jewish people, they would take Jewish children and would tie them to the foot of their bed, and they would have relations [in the presence of this beauty instead of the amulet]. One man asked another: Where is this alluded to in the Torah? He replied: It says, "Even any illness and any blow that is not writ-

THE BRILLIANT
YOUNG PRISONER

Our Rabbis have taught: R. Yehoshua b. Chananiah once came to the great city of Rome, and the Jews there told him: There is in prison a young boy with beautiful eyes who is very good-looking, and the locks of his hair are in curls. He went and stood by the entrance to the dungeon, and said, "Who delivered Jacob to plunder and Israel to looters?" (Isaiah 42:24). The child answered him, "Was it not God, He against whom we have sinned? They did not wish to go in His ways, and did not listen to His Torah" (ibid.). R. Yehoshua b. Chananiah said: I am certain that this child will become a halachic authority in Israel. I swear that I will not budge from here until I ransom him, no matter how much they demand of me. They said that he did not leave before he had ransomed him for a large sum of money, and it was not too long before the boy became a great Torah scholar. And who was [this boy]? He was R. Yishmael b. Elisha.

THE CAPTIVE BROTHER
AND SISTER

Rav Yehudah said in the name of Rav: The son and the daughter of R. Yishmael b. Elisha were captured and sold to two different masters. A while later the two masters came together, and one said: I have a slave of unsurpassed beauty. The other said: I have a female slave who is the most beautiful in the world. So they said: Let us marry them to each other and divide the children. They put them in a room together. The boy sat in one corner and the girl in the other. The boy said to himself: I am a kohen, a descendant of High Priests; am I destined to marry a female slave? She said to herself: I am a daughter of a kohen, a descendant of High Priests; am I to be married to a slave? They cried all night long. When dawn came they recognized each other and fell into each other's arms. They wept bitterly until they both died. It is for them that Jeremiah lamented, "Over these do I weep; my eye continuously runs with water" (Lamentations 1:16).

Resh Lakish said: There was a woman named Tzofnat bat Peniel. She was called Tzofnat because everyone looked [*tzofin*] at her beauty, and they called her "the daughter of Peniel" because she was the daughter of the *Kohen Gadol* who officiated in the inner Sanctuary [*penim*]. Her captors tormented her all night. The next day they dressed her in seven wraps and took her out to sell her. A very ugly person came and said: Let me see her beauty. They said to him: Fool, if you want to buy, buy her. There is no woman as beautiful as this woman. He said: Never mind, [I want to see for myself]. He took six wraps off her, and she herself tore off the seventh and rolled in the dust, saying: Master of the universe! If you don't have pity on us, why don't You have pity on the holiness of Your Name, [it is a desecration of God's name that a Jewish woman is so humiliated]. It is for her that Jeremiah lamented, "O daughter of my people, don sackcloth and wallow in the dust; mourn as if for an only child, make yourself a bitter lament, for the plunderer came upon us suddenly" (Jeremiah 6:26). It does not say "upon you," but "upon us," meaning, "the plunderer came upon Me and you." [God suffers along with the Jewish people.]

THE PERFIDIOUS APPRENTICE

Rav Yehudah said in the name of Rav: What is meant by the passage, "They steal a man and his household, a person and his heritage" (Micah 2:2)? There was a person—a carpenter's apprentice—who desired his master's wife. One time his master wanted to borrow some money from him. So he said to his master, "Send your wife to me, and I will lend her the money; [it does not befit you to come and borrow money from your apprentice]." So he sent his wife, and she stayed with him for three days. [After three days] the carpenter came to his apprentice. "Where is my wife whom I sent to you?" he asked. The apprentice replied, "I sent her away immediately, but I heard that the young boys were joking with her on the road. [Therefore you should suspect that she sinned with one of them.]" "What do you think I should do?" the carpenter said. "If you listen to my advice," he replied, "you should divorce her." "But I would have to pay a lot of money for her marriage settlement," the carpenter said. "I will lend you the money for her *ketubah* so that you can divorce her," the apprentice replied.

So the carpenter divorced her, and the apprentice went and married her. When the time for payment of the debt arrived, and the carpenter did not have any money to pay, the apprentice said to him, "Come and work for me [for the money you owe me]." So the apprentice and the carpenter's ex-wife sat down to eat and drink while the carpenter waited on them, and

tears would flow from his eyes and fall into their cups. [And that is what is meant by, "They steal a man and his household, a person and his heritage." The man's wife and his possessions, all were stolen.] The decree [of the destruction of Eretz Yisrael] was sealed for outrages such as this. Others say, however, that she committed adultery with the apprentice before she got her divorce, and that was the cause of all the destruction.

THE FOREMOST TORAH SCHOLAR AND LEADER

(59a) Rabbah the son of Rava, some say R. Hillel the son of R. Vallas, said: From the time of Moses until Rebbi we never had someone who was both the greatest Torah scholar and the greatest leader. [The Gemara asks:] Is that true? Didn't Joshua have both these qualities? [The Gemara answers:] There was Elazar in his time [who was the *Kohen Gadol*, and he was also a great Torah scholar]. But Elazar [was the greatest scholar and leader] after Joshua's death?—There was Pinchas in his time [who also became the *Kohen Gadol*]. But wasn't there Pinchas [after Elazar's death]?—There were the Elders [who were his equals in learning]. But wasn't there Saul [who was outstanding in Torah and leadership]? Samuel lived in his generation. But Samuel died before Saul? [When we said that he was outstanding in Torah and leadership] we meant during his entire lifetime [and Saul attained this distinction only after Samuel's death]. But wasn't there David? [He was a great in Torah scholar and a great ruler.] There was Ira HaYe'iri[35] [a great Torah scholar who lived in his time]. But he died before David? We meant [that he was the epitome of Torah learning and leadership] throughout his entire lifetime. But there was Solomon? There was Shimi b. Gera.[36] But he was killed? We meant matchless greatness throughout his entire lifetime. But there was Hezekiah? [He was a great Torah scholar and a great king?]—Shevna,[37] [who was a greater scholar, lived at the same time]. But he was killed, [so Hezekiah outlived him]? We meant, throughout his entire life. But there was Ezra? There was Nehemiah son of Hacaliah with him. R. Acha son of Rava said: I can say something very similar: From the time of Rebbi until R. Ashi there was no one who was superior both in Torah learning and leadership. Is that true? Wasn't there Huna b. Natan [who incorporated both these qualities]? You cannot compare Huna b. Natan [to R. Ashi], for he was subordinate to R. Ashi.

KEEPING THE PEACE

[The Mishnah says:] The following are some of the enactments the Sages made to keep the peace: A *kohen* is called up first to read from the Torah,[38] afterward a Levite, and after him a Yisrael, in order to keep the peace, [to avoid fighting about who should be honored first].

(59b) [The Gemara asks:] From where in Scripture do we know [that a *kohen* should be called up first, then a Levite, then a Yisrael]? R. Mattenah said: Because it says, "Moses then wrote down this Torah. He gave it to the priests, the descendants of Levi" (Deuteronomy 31:9). Don't we know that the *kohanim* are descendants of Levi? We must say, therefore, that the text comes to tell us that first a *kohen* is called and then a Levite. R. Yitzchak Nafcha said: We derive it from the following verse, "The *kohanim* from the tribe of Levi shall then come forth" (ibid. 21:50). Don't we know that the *kohanim* are descendants of Levi? The verse means to tell us that a *kohen* is called first and afterward a Levite. R. Chiyah b. Abba derived it from here, "You must strive to keep [the *kohen*] holy" (Leviticus 21:8). This implies [that you should give him priority] in any matter involving holiness.

(60b) [The Mishnah says:] An *eruv*[39] should be placed in the house where it is always deposited; [its location should not be changed], in order to keep the peace. What is the reason for that? Do you think it is out of respect of the owner of the house [who will be offended when it is taken away]? If so, what about the shofar [that was blown on every Friday afternoon to announce the approach of *Shabbat*], which originally was deposited in Rav Yehudah's house and later in Rabbah's house, after which it was moved to R. Yosef's house, and from there to Abbaye's house and finally to Rava's house?[40] The real reason is so as not to arouse suspicion. [People coming into the house where the *eruv* used to be located and not finding it will suspect the residents of the court of carrying on *Shabbat* without an *eruv* (Rashi).]

(61a) We learned in a *Baraita*: We should support the gentile poor together with the Jewish poor, and we should visit the gentile sick along with the Jewish sick, and we should take care of the gentile dead along with the Jewish dead [if the gentiles are found murdered together with Jews].

RABBIS ARE CALLED KINGS

(62a) R. Huna and R. Chisda were sitting outside when Geniva happened to be passing by. One said to the other, "Let's stand up for him, for he is a Torah scholar." Replied the other, "Shall we stand up for a troublemaker?" Meanwhile Geniva came up to them. "Peace to you, kings!" he said, "Peace to you, kings!" "From what verse do you derive that rabbis are called kings?" they asked. "Because it says, 'Through me [i.e., through the wisdom of the Torah], kings will reign'" (Proverbs 8:15). "And from where do you know that a king should be given a double greeting?" they asked. "From what Rav Yehudah said in the name of Rav: How do we know that a double greeting should be given to a king? Because it says, "A spirit then garbed Amasai, the head of the captains, 'We are yours, David, and we are with you, son of Jesse! Peace! Peace unto you!'(2

Chronicles 12:19)." They said to Geniva, "Can we offer you some refreshments?" He replied, "This is what Rav Yehudah said in the name of Rav: You are not allowed to taste anything before you have fed your animal, for it says first, 'I will grant forage in your fields for your animals' and only then, 'and you will eat and be satisfied'" (Deuteronomy 11:15).

THE UNIQUE QUALITIES OF THE SAGES

(67a) We learned in a *Baraita*: Issi b. Yehudah enumerated the specific commendable qualities of the various Sages. [He gave the following descriptions:] R. Meir was a wise man and a scribe [by profession].[41] R. Yehudah was a wise man when he so desired; [when he thought things through and was not too hasty he was wise (Rashi)]. R. Tarfon was like a pile of nuts. [When someone asked him a question his answers came in a torrent, like a collapsing pile of nuts (Rashi).] R. Yishmael was like a well-stocked store; [where the merchant does not keep the customer waiting until the merchandise is back-ordered. So too R. Tarfon; whenever he was asked a question he always had the answer ready]. R. Akiva was a neatly arranged warehouse, [his learning was broken down into clearly defined areas of study]. R. Yochanan b. Nuri was like a spice salesman's basket; [he had his answers readily available]. R. Elazar b. Azariah was like a basket full of spices. [He had a vast amount of knowledge, but it was not as sharply delineated as that of R. Yochanan b. Nuri.] The *halachot* taught by R. Eliezer b. Yaakov were small in number, but of the finest quality; [invariably, the *halachah* is decided according to his opinion]. R. Yose always had sound reasons to back up his teachings. R. Shimon would grind a lot and let out a little. [What does this mean?] A Tanna explained that he used to forget little, and whatever slipped his mind was only the bran [i.e., matters that were not accepted as *halachah*]. In the same vein R. Shimon said to his students: My children, follow my teachings, for my teachings are the very best of the essential teachings of R. Akiva.

R. AMRAM CHASIDA CAUGHT A COLD

(67b) R. Amram Chasida, [a very pious man, used to impose many halachic stringencies on the servants of the Exilarch]. The servants [who resented this] mistreated him and made him lie down in the snow. [As a result, he caught a cold.] The next day the servants said to him: What would you like us to bring you? He knew that whatever he told them, they would do just the opposite, so [instead of ordering fat meat and undiluted wine, which are the remedies for a cold,] he requested lean meat broiled on coals and diluted wine. Sure enough, they brought him fat meat broiled on coals and undiluted wine. When Yalta [a distinguished lady, the wife of R. Nachman and the daughter of the Exilarch] heard what had happened to R. Amram Chasida she took him to the bathhouse. They placed him in the bath and left him there until the water turned the color of blood [from his reddish perspiration brought on by the meat and the wine he had consumed], and his skin was dotted with round spots. R. Yosef used to cure a cold by working in a mill [to warm himself]; R. Sheshet, by carrying heavy beams. He used to say: Work is a wonderful way to make you feel warm.

THE PERCEPTIVE R. SHESHET

The Exilarch said to R. Sheshet [who was blind], "Why is it that you never join us for a meal?" He replied, "I don't think your servants are reliable; I suspect them of feeding people limbs cut off from a living animal."[42] Retorted the Exilarch, "On what do you base your accusation?" Answered R. Sheshet, "I'll show you." He then told his attendant, "Go and steal me a leg of an animal." When he brought the leg, R. Sheshet said [to the servants of the Exilarch], "Lay out in front of me the pieces of the animal you are about to serve." They brought three legs and put them down in front of him. Said R. Sheshet, "Did this animal have only three legs?" They then went and cut a leg off a [live] animal and brought it. R. Sheshet then said to his attendant, "Now pull out the leg you stole." So he placed it on the table. "Do we now have an animal with five legs?" R. Sheshet exclaimed. The Exilarch said to R. Sheshet, "[You proved your point.] Since our servants indeed cannot be trusted, let them prepare the food in front of your attendant, and then you'll be able to eat with us." "All right," R. Sheshet replied.

The servants [taking advantage of R. Sheshet's blindness] brought up a table and placed before him a portion of meat that contained a very small bone that causes people to choke when they swallow it. R. Sheshet immediately felt the bone, took the entire piece of meat, and wrapped it in his scarf. When the meal was over the servants said to R. Sheshet, **(68a)** "A silver cup was stolen from us, [and you seem to be carrying something in your scarf. We'd like to see what you have]." As they searched him they found the meat wrapped in his scarf. So they said to the Exilarch, "You see, he did not come here to eat, but only to annoy us." Replied R. Sheshet, "I did come to eat, but as soon as I tasted the meat I sensed that it came from an animal that has boils." They said to him, "We did not prepare an animal with boils today." Replied R. Sheshet, "Go ahead and examine the place on the skin where my piece of meat came from, because R. Chisda said that a white spot on dark skin or a dark spot on white skin is the symptom of disease." They examined the skin and found that [there were boils]. When R. Sheshet was about to leave, they dug a hole and spread a mat over it.

They then suggested to R. Sheshet, "Perhaps you would like to lie down and rest a little [on this mat]?" R. Chisda [tried to warn R. Sheshet] by snorting behind him. R. Sheshet, sensing that something was wrong, said to a little boy, "Tell me the last verse you learned today," [as a portent for what was in store for him]. The boy said, "Turn to your right or to your left" (2 Samuel 2:21). R. Sheshet then said to his attendant, "What do you see strange?" He replied, "There is a mat thrown across the path." R. Sheshet said, "Let's move to the side." After they left the Exilarch, R. Chisda said to R. Sheshet, "How did you know [that they had set a trap for you]?" He replied, "To begin with, you yourself warned me by snorting, and then there was the verse the little boy quoted, and furthermore, the servants of the Exilarch are suspected of playing tricks."

SOLOMON AND ASHMEDAI, KING OF THE DEMONS

It says, "I provided myself with *sharim* and *sharot* and with every human luxury, *shidah* and *shidot*" (Ecclesiastes 2:8). [The Gemara explains:] "*Sharim* and *sharot*" means various musical instruments; "every human luxury" refers to pools and baths; "*shidah* and *shidot*": here in Babylonia we translate it as "male and female demons." In Eretz Yisrael they say it means royal carriages.

R. Yochanan said: There were three hundred types of demons in Shichin, but I really do not know what a demon is.[43] The Master said: In Babylonia they translate it as "male and female demons." [The Gemara asks:] What did Solomon need demons for? [The Gemara answers:] "When the Temple was being built it was built of complete quarried stone; hammers, chisel, or any iron utensils were not heard in the Temple when it was being built" (1 Kings 6:7).[44] [Solomon] said to the Rabbis: How shall I build the *Bet Hamikdash* [if I cannot use any metal tools]? They replied: There is the *shamir* [a small worm that could split large stones as it lay on them][45] that Moses brought [to engrave] the stones of the *ephod*.

Solomon asked the Rabbis: Where do I find this *shamir*? They replied: Bring a male and a female demon and tie them together; perhaps they know it and, [being under pressure], they will tell you. So he brought a male and female demon and tied them together, but they told him: We don't know, but maybe Ashmedai, the king of the demons, knows. Solomon said to them: Where is he? They answered: He is on such-and-such mountain. He has dug a pit there, fills it with water, covers it with a stone, and seals it with his special seal. Every day he goes up to heaven where he learns in the heavenly yeshivah, and then he comes down to earth and studies in the yeshivah down on earth. He then goes and examines his seal, lifts off the stone and drinks. Afterward he closes it, seals it again, and goes away.

Solomon then sent Benayahu son of Yehoyada and gave him a chain on which the Divine Name was engraved. He also gave him a ring that had the Divine Name engraved on it, and fleeces of wool and bottles of wine. [Benayahu's task was to drain the water from the pit, and fill it with wine without breaking the seal.] Benayahu went and dug a pit lower down the mountain and let the water [of Ashmedai's pit] flow into it [by way of a tunnel that he had dug connecting the two pits]. He then stuffed up the hole in Ashmedai's pit with the fleeces of wool. Now he dug a pit higher up on the mountain [above Ashmedai's pit, again connecting the two pits with a tunnel] and poured the wine into it [which flowed into Ashmedai's pit], and then filled up the two pits [he had dug with earth, so that Ashmedai should not detect any tampering]. He then went and sat on a tree. When Ashmedai came he inspected the seal, then took off the stone, and found it full of wine. He said: It says, "Wine makes a scoffer; strong drink makes one cry out; and whoever errs after it will not grow wise" (Proverbs 2:1); and it also says, "Harlotry and wine and fresh wine capture the heart" (Hosea 4:11). I will not drink it. However, when he became thirsty he could not resist the temptation. He drank it, became intoxicated, and fell asleep.

Immediately Benayahu came down from the tree and threw the chain around Ashmedai's neck and locked it securely. When Ashmedai woke up he started to struggle, but Benayahu said to him: The Name of your Master is on you! The Name of your Master is on you! [If you break the chain you will be erasing God's Name.] As he was dragging Ashmedai by the chain they came to a palm tree. Ashmedai scratched himself on it, and the tree fell down. He came to a house and knocked it down. He came to a hut that belonged to a poor widow. She came out (68b) and pleaded with Ashmedai [not to rub against her hut]. He bent to one side so as not to destroy her hut, but in the process broke a bone. He said: This is borne out by the verse, "Soft words break bones" (Proverbs 25:15). [Because of the widow's soft words he broke a bone.] He saw a blind man who was lost on the way, and he put him back on the right track. He saw a drunken man who had lost the way, and he put him back on the right path. He saw a bride being escorted to the wedding canopy by a happy throng, but Ashmedai cried. He heard a man say to a shoemaker: Make me a pair of shoes that will last seven years, and he laughed. He saw a sorcerer practicing magic, and he laughed. [The reason for his bizarre behavior will be explained shortly.]

When they finally arrived in Jerusalem, three days went by before he was brought before Solomon. On the first day he asked: Why doesn't the King want to see me? They replied: Because he drank too much. So Ashmedai took a brick and placed it on top of another. When they told this to Solomon he said to them: This is what he meant to tell you: Give him more to drink.

On the next day he said to them: Why doesn't the King want to see me? They replied: Because he ate too much. Now he took one brick off the other and placed it on the ground. When they told this to Solomon he said: This is what he meant to say: Give him less to eat. After three days Ashmedai was brought before Solomon. Ashmedai took a reed and measured four cubits and threw it in front of Solomon. He said: Think about it; when you die you will occupy no more than four cubits in this world. Now, you have conquered the whole world, yet you are not satisfied until you defeat me also?

Replied Solomon: I want nothing from you. What I want is to build the *Bet Hamikdash*, and I need the *shamir* to do it. Ashmedai said: It is not in my hands; it is under the control of the Prince of the Sea who gives it only to the wild hen because the Prince of the Sea believes the oath the wild hen has made to return the *shamir* to him. What does the wild hen do with the *shamir*? It takes it to a barren mountain [where nothing grows] and puts it on the peak of the mountain, and the mountain splits. It then takes seeds from trees and throws them into the crack, and things begin to grow. They searched and found a nest of a wild hen with little chicks in it. They placed a clear glass bowl over the nest. When the bird came it was unable to get in [to feed the chicks because the glass bowl was in its way]. So it went and brought the *shamir* and placed it on the glass bowl. At this point, Benayahu started to scream; the bird [got frightened and] dropped the *shamir*, and he took it. The bird then went and committed suicide because it was unable to keep the oath it had made [to the Prince of the Sea to return the *shamir*].

Benayahu now asked Ashmedai: When you saw that blind man who had lost his way, why did you put him on the right path? He replied: They were calling out in heaven that he is a perfect *tzaddik*, and that whoever does him a favor deserves [a share in] the World to Come. And when you saw the drunken man wandering about, why did you show him the way? He replied: They called out in heaven that he is thoroughly evil, and I wanted to do him a favor so that he used up whatever reward is due to him in this world [so that he has nothing left for the hereafter]. When you saw that wedding procession why did you cry? He said: Her husband is going to die within thirty days, and this bride will have to wait for thirteen years until her husband's brother [who is now just an infant] is old enough [to give her *chalitzah*[46] and enable her to marry again]. [Benayahu continued to ask:] When you heard that person say to the shoemaker: Make me shoes to last seven years, why did you laugh? Relied Ashmedai: This person does not even have seven days to live, and he wants shoes to last for seven years! [Asked Benayahu:] When you saw that sorcerer working his magic, why did you laugh? Ashmedai answered: He was sitting on a royal treasure [of gold and silver]; he should have had an intimation of what was underneath him.

[Even though Solomon had the *shamir*] he did not let Ashmedai go until he finished building the *Bet Hamikdash*. One day when Solomon was alone with Ashmedai, Solomon asked him: It says, "[God] has *to'afot* and *re'eim* [to carry out His mission]" (Numbers 24:8). And we interpret *to'afot* to refer to ministering angels, and *re'eim* to refer to demons. [I can understand that angels are different than people,] but in what sense are you demons superior to us humans? Said Ashmedai: Take the chain [that has God's name engraved on it] off me, and give me your ring, and I will show you. Solomon removed the chain and gave him the ring. Ashmedai then swallowed the ring, and, placing one wing on the earth and one on the sky, he threw Solomon four hundred miles. Solomon had this incident in mind when he said, "What profit does man have for all his labor which he toils beneath the sun?" (Ecclesiastes 1:3). And, "This was my reward for all my endeavors" (ibid. 2:10). What does "this" refer to? Rav and Shmuel offered different opinions: One said that it meant [that all he had left was] his staff; the other, that it meant his apron.[47] He had to go from door to door begging. Wherever he went he would say, "I, Kohelet, was king over Israel in Jerusalem" (ibid. 1:12).

When he came to the Sanhedrin [claiming to be King Solomon], the Rabbis said: Let's see. A person who is insane does not repeat the same absurdity over and over again; [he will have a number of different delusions]. What is the meaning of this? They asked Benayahu: Did the King summon you lately? He replied: No. They then asked the queens: Does the King come to you these days? They replied: Yes, he does come. The Sanhedrin then sent a message to the queens: Examine his feet [because the feet of a demon resemble the feet of a rooster]. The answer was: He comes wearing slippers, and he visits the women in the time of their separation, and he also visits his mother Bathsheba. They then brought the real Solomon and gave him the ring on which God's name was engraved. When Solomon came into the palace, Ashmedai saw him and flew away. In spite of this, Solomon was still frightened of Ashmedai, and that is why it says, "There is Solomon's bed, encircled by sixty warriors of the warriors of Israel. All trained in warfare, skilled in battle, each with sword on thigh because of terror by night" (Song of Songs 3:7,8).

Rav and Shmuel [had differing opinions about Solomon]. One said that Solomon was originally [the great] king, but after [the episode with Ashmedai it was not the same anymore. Compared to the glory of his earlier years] he was now like a commoner. The other said that originally he was [the great] king, then [on his wanderings] he was a commoner, and [when he returned] he was a great king once again.

SEVEN IDOL-WORSHIPPING KINGS

(88a) R. Yehoshua b. Levi said: Eretz Yisrael was not destroyed until seven kings of Israel worshipped idols, namely: Jeroboam son of Nebat, Baasha son of Achiah, Achab son of Omri, Jehu son of Nimshi, Pekach son of Remaliah, Menachem son of Gadi, and Hoshea son of Elah, as it says, "She who has given birth to seven children is distressed, her soul is distraught, her sun set while it was still daytime; she was shamed and disgraced" (Jeremiah 15:9). R. Ammi said: From what Torah passage do we know [that Eretz Yisrael was destroyed because of idolatry]? From the verse, "When you beget children and grandchildren . . . and they make a carved image . . . you will surely perish from the land" (Deuteronomy 4:25).

R. Kahana and R. Assi said to Rav: It says in connection with Hoshea son of Elah, "He did what was evil in the eyes of God, albeit not like the kings of Israel that were before him" (2 Kings 17:2); and immediately after that it says, "Shalmaneser king of Assyria went up against him, [and Israel was exiled]" (ibid. v. 4). [It seems paradoxical: Because he was not as bad as other kings, that is why Israel was exiled during his reign?] Rav replied: Jeroboam had stationed guards to prevent Israel from going to Jerusalem for the three pilgimage Festivals, and Hoshea b. Elah abolished them [so that the people now were free to go to Jerusalem]. Nevertheless, the people did not go up to Jerusalem for the Festivals. So God said that for the number of years that they did not go up to Jerusalem for the Yamim Tovim they should go into captivity.

THE *CHARASH* AND THE *MASGEIR*

R. Chisda said in the name of Mar Ukva, or, others say, R. Chisda said in the name of R. Yirmeyah: Mereimar expounded: What is the meant by the passage, "God hastened the calamity and brought it upon us; for God our Lord is *tzaddik* [righteous]" (Daniel 9:14). Is it because God is righteous that He hurried to bring upon us the calamity? The text means: God did a great kindness [*tzedakah*] to Israel that [eleven years] before [Jerusalem was destroyed and] Israel went into exile under King Zedekiah, the [partial] captivity of Yechoniah (Jehoiachin) was already established [in Babylonia, so that the Torah scholars who went with him would be able to teach Torah to the people that were to go into exile together with Zedekiah]. For it says about the captivity of Yechoniah (Jehoiachin), "[Nebuchadnezzar] exiled Jehoiachin to Babylonia . . . and the *charash* and the *masgeir*, one thousand" (2 Kings 24:14); [an allusion to the Torah scholars and Torah leaders who went with Jehoiachin]. They were called *charash* [dumb] because when they opened their mouths the audience was dumbstruck with awe. And they were called *masgeir* [closer] because if a halachic problem was closed to them, no one else was able to solve it. How many were there? One thousand. Ulla said: [God's righteousness] consists in that He caused Israel to be sent into exile two years before [the numerical value of] *venoshantem* (Deuteronomy 4:25) was reached.[48] (88b) R. Acha b. Yaakov said: We can learn from this that when God says "quickly" he means 852 years, [for it says, "You will surely perish *quickly*," which happened after 852 years].

SETTLE DISPUTES IN RABBINICAL COURTS

R. Tarfon used to say: Even if you find that non-Jewish courts of law have the same laws as Jewish law, you should not avail yourself of them, for it says, "These are the laws that you must set before them" (Exodus 21:1). [The Torah stresses,] "before them" [the Sanhedrin], implying "but not before a non-Jewish court." Another explanation of "before them" is "but not before laymen."

DIFFERENT STANDARDS AND PRINCIPLES

(90a) We learned in a *Baraita*: R. Meir used to say: Just as men differ in their squeamishness regarding food so they differ in their tolerance of lewdness in their wives. Some people, if a fly falls into their cup, will discard [the beverage] and not drink it. This is in line with the conduct of Pappus b. Yehudah who used to lock his wife inside the house whenever he went out [to prevent her from talking to others; a deplorable act, which leads to marital discord and infidelity (Rashi)]. Another person, if a fly falls into his soup, will throw away the fly and then drink the soup. This is the way most people handle the situation. [As far as their wives are concerned,] they do not mind if their wives talk with their brothers and relatives. Then there is the person who, if a fly falls into his soup, will [leave it there] and eat it with the soup. This person has the habit of an immoral person. He will not mind seeing his wife with her hair exposed, spinning cloth in the street with her (90b) arms uncovered, and bathing with the men. [The Gemara asks:] You mean to say: bathe together with men? [The Gemara answers: It means:] [She bathes] in the same place as the men do [and enters while the men are getting dressed (Rashi)].

It is a Torah command to divorce a wife who does that, as it says, "If she is displeasing to him or if he has evidence of immodesty on her part . . . he sent her from his house, she may go and marry another man" (Deuteronomy 24:1,2). Scripture calls him "another" to tell us that the [second husband] is not a match of the first one: [the first husband] turned a bad woman out of his house, and the [second husband] took her into his house. If the second has merit he will also send

her away, as it says, "And the latter husband hated her" (ibid. v.3), and if he does not, she will bury him, as it says, "or if the latter husband dies" (ibid.). He deserves to die, since the first husband ousted a bad woman from his house and the second took her into his house.

It says, "For he who hates should divorce" (Malachi 2:16). R. Yehudah said: This means that if you hate your wife you should divorce her. R. Yochanan said: It means: He who divorces his wife is hated [by God]. But they do not really disagree, since the one speaks of the first marriage, and the other of the second. For R. Elazar said: If a man divorces his first wife, even the Altar sheds tears, for it says, "And this is a second sin that you commit: covering the altar of God with tears, crying and moaning, so that He will no longer turn to your offering, or take it with favor from your hand. You say, 'Why is this?' It is because God has testified between you and the wife of your youth whom you have betrayed, though she is your companion and the wife of your covenant" (Malachi 2:13,14).

NOTES

1. Judges, Chapters 19 and 20.
2. If the wife failed to immerse in the *mikveh*, she will be afraid to tell him, and he will have forbidden marital relations with her.
3. Terrified, she will run away, and in her utter consternation will have an accident and be killed.
4. Out of fear of her husband's tantrum she will sometimes light the *Shabbat* candles or cook the *Shabbat* meal after twilight.
5. The donkey of R. Pinchas b. Ya'ir refused to eat grain that had not been tithed (*Chullin* 7a).
6. These are names of cities in the territory of the tribe of Judah.
7. God who appeared to Moses in the thornbush (Exodus 3:4).
8. *Sotah* 49a.
9. Literally: "This is not this."
10. And the verse is Ezekiel's prophecy that the High Priest will cease to perform his service and King Zedekiah will lose his crown and be led off to Babylonia (Rashi).
11. Exodus 24:7.
12. It was a Persian festival on which they allowed light to be lit only in their places of idol worship (Rashi).
13. Geniva was involved in a bitter dispute with the Exilarch, Mar Ukva; see above, 7a.
14. In violation of, "You shall have them serve you forever" (Leviticus 25:46).
15. If her owner said: I set half of you free.
16. "My love, My dove" (Song of Songs 5:2).
17. They were ransomed against their will (*Maharsha*).
18. A tribe of cannibals (Rashi).

19. If a gentile brings an offering we are allowed to accept it and bring it on the Altar (*Chullin* 13b).

20. The rule is: If someone tries to kill you, be quick and kill him first. And Bar Kamtza through his denunciation was a mortal threat to the community.

21. Literally: He wants to wipe His hand.

22. See *Taanit* 19b.

23. *Levanon* is derived from *lavan*, "white." The *Bet Hamikdash* purifies and cleanses Israel from their wrongdoings, rendering them "white."

24. R. Yochanan b. Zakkai's request to set up a yeshivah in Yavneh was of crucial importance. It was the instrument through which God ensured the continued existence of the Jewish people during the long exile.

25. The Kishon Brook swept the kings of Canaan away (Judges 5:21).

26. The dove that lodged in his brain is symbolic of the Jewish people, which is compared to a dove (Psalms 74:19). It tells us that ultimately the Jewish people will overcome and outlive their enemies.

27. Numbers 31:16.

28. 2,110,000.

29. 940,000.

30. Nevuzaradan, chief of the guards, servant of King Nebuchadnezzar burned the First Temple on the Ninth of Av, 3338/-423 BCE. (2 Kings 25:11,12).

31. Leaders of the Sanhedrin and teachers of Hillel and Shammai.

32. Bashan is seen as a contraction of *bein shinei*, "between teeth."

33. Antiochus Epiphanes.

34. The head-*tefillin* are bigger, because the four scriptural passages they contain are inserted in four separate compartments; whereas in the arm-*tefillin* the four passages are contained in one compartment (Rashi).

35. 2 Samuel 20:26.

36. 2 Samuel 19:17.

37. *Sanhedrin* 26a.

38. In the days of the Mishnah, the person who was called up to the Torah did the reading himself.

39. Two or more Jews who share one court may not carry anything from one house into the other on *Shabbat* unless they establish an *eruv*. By contributing their share toward the *eruv*, which consists of a loaf of bread that is deposited in one of the houses, all houses in the court are considered common to all, and objects may be carried from one house to the other.

40. According to Tosafot, the shofar was a collection box for donations.

41. *Sotah* 20a.

42. Which is forbidden, being one of the seven Noachide laws that were given to all mankind.

43. Alternately: I do not know who the mother of all these demons is (Rashi).

44. Solomon did not use iron tools because iron implements and swords are made to shorten men's lives (*Mechilta*).

45. *Avot* 5:8.

46. The ceremony of taking the shoe off the brother of a husband who has died childless, whereby his widow is allowed to marry again (Deuteronomy 25:5–9).

47. Alternately: his cup from which to drink water.

48. The numerical value of *venoshantem* is 852. [Vav = 6; nun = 50; vav = 6; shin = 300; nun = 50; tav = 400; mem = 40.] The first *Bet Hamikdash* was destroyed 850 years after the children of Israel crossed the Jordan into Eretz Yisrael (−1273–423 C.E.). Because of these two years, the prophecy of *venoshantem*, [i.e., 852], "you will have been long in the land" (Deuteronomy 4:25), was not fulfilled; and as a consequence, the prophecy of "you will be destroyed" (ibid. v. 26) was not fulfilled either.

✎ SOTAH ❧

A MATCH MADE IN HEAVEN

(2a) We learned in a *Baraita*: Rabbi says: Why is the chapter of the *nazir*[1] placed next to the chapter of the *sotah* [the woman suspected of marital infidelity (Numbers 5 and 6)]? To teach you that whoever sees a *sotah* in her degradation should abstain from wine.

R. Shmuel b. Yitzchak said: When Resh Lakish began to expound on the subject of *sotah* he would say: A person is given the wife he deserves [a modest wife is matched to a *tzaddik*, a wanton wife to a wicked man (Rashi)]. For it says, "For the rod of wickedness shall not rest on the lot of the righteous" (Psalms 125:3), [meaning, a bad wife shall not be matched to a righteous person]. Rabbah b. Bar Chanah said in the name of R. Yochanan: Making matches is as difficult as parting the Red Sea, for it says, "God settles the solitary into a family, He releases those bound in fetters" (Psalms 68:7). [The passage compares establishing a family to releasing Israel from Egyptian bondage.] [The Gemara asks:] Is that so? [Are people matched according to their deeds?] Didn't Rav Yehudah say in the name of Rav: Forty days before the creation of a child a Heavenly voice comes forth and proclaims: The daughter of so-and-so shall marry so-and-so, the house of so-and-so shall belong to so-and-so, the field of so-and-so is for so-and-so! [Since the marriage partner is selected before birth, it cannot depend on a person's deeds?] [The Gemara answers:] This presents no difficulty. The [saying about marriage being pre-ordained in heaven] refers to a first marriage, whereas [the saying that one gets the mate he deserves] refers to a second marriage.

IMMORALITY

(3b) R. Chisda said: Immorality in a house is like a worm in a sesame plant, [it destroys it]. R. Chisda also said: Anger in a house is like a worm in a sesame plant. Both these sayings refer to a woman, [because she is the mainstay of the home], but in the case of a man it does not have the same effect.

R. Chisda further said: In the beginning, before Israel committed immorality, the *Shechinah* dwelled [in the house of] each single individual, as it says, "God your Lord walks in the midst of your camp" (Deuteronomy 23:15), but when they committed immorality the *Shechinah* left them, for it says, "So that He will not see anything lascivious among you and turn away from you" (ibid.).

R. Shmuel b. Nachmani said in the name of R. Yonatan: If a person performs one mitzvah in this world, it leads the way for him to the World to Come, as it says, "Your righteous deed will precede you" (Isaiah 58:8). If a person commits one transgression in this world, it clings to him and ushers him into Judgment Day, as it says, "Their course twists and turns, they run into the desert and perish" (Job 6:8). R. Elazar says: [Sin] clings to him like a dog, for it says, "[Joseph] would not pay attention to [Potiphar's wife]. He would not even lie next to her or spend time with her" (Genesis 39:10): "he would not lie next to her"—in this world; "or spend time with her"—in the World to Come, [so that he would not be with her in Gehinnom (Etz Yosef)].

WASHING HANDS

(4b) R. Avira expounded, sometimes in the name of R. Ammi and at other times in the name of R. Assi: Whoever eats bread without first washing his hands is as though he had relations with a prostitute. For it says, "Because for the sake of a licentious woman to a loaf of bread" (Proverbs 6:26). Rava said: [If your interpretation is right,] the phrase "Because for the sake of a licentious woman to a loaf of bread" should have read, "For the sake of a loaf of bread to a licentious woman"! But, said Rava, the meaning is: Whoever has relations with a prostitute will end up begging for a loaf of bread. R. Zerika said in the name of R. Elazar: Whoever shows contempt of the washing of the hands [before and after meals] will be uprooted from the world. R. Chiya said in the name of Rav: When washing before the meal you should lift up your hands; when washing the hands after the meal [*mayim acharonim*] you should keep your hands downward. We learned also in a *Baraita*: When washing before the meal you should lift up your hands, for fear that the water passed beyond the wrist and flowed back, rendering them unclean. R. Abbahu says: Whoever eats bread without having dried his hands [after washing them] is as though he eats unclean bread. For it says, "Thus will the children of Israel eat their food: unclean among the nations where I will banish them" (Ezekiel 4:13).

ARROGANCE AND CONCEIT

[The Gemara now continues the discussion of the last segment of Proverbs 6:26 quoted above.] What is the meaning of the verse, "An adulterous woman can ensnare a precious soul" (Proverbs 6:26)? Said R. Chiya b. Abba in the name of R. Yochanan: Any person who is conceited will end up committing adultery with a married woman, as it says, "An adulterous woman can ensnare a precious soul." Rava said: [If that is the correct interpretation,] instead of "a precious soul" it should have said "a haughty soul." And furthermore, it should have said: a haughty soul can ensnare an adulterous woman! But, said Rava, the meaning is: Whoever has relations with a married woman, even though he studied Torah, of which it says, "It is more precious than pearls" (Proverbs 3:15), which means that it is more precious than the High Priest who enters the Holy of Holies; she will pursue him to the judgment of Gehinnom.

R. Yochanan said in the name of R. Shimon b. Yochai: A person who is conceited is as though he worships idols. For it says, "Every haughty person is an abomination to God" (Proverbs 16:5), and it also says, "Do not bring any abomination into your house [i.e., idolatry]" (Deuteronomy 7:26). R. Yochanan himself said: He is as though he denied the fundamental principle of Judaism, [the Oneness of God], for it says, "Your heart may grow haughty, and you may forget God your Lord" (ibid. 8:14). R. Chama b. Chanina said: He is as though he had violated all laws against sexual immorality [listed in Leviticus 18]. For it says here, "Every haughty person is an abomination to God," and elsewhere it says, "[They did] all these abominations [i.e., disgusting sexual perversions]" (Leviticus 18:27). Ulla said: [A haughty person] is as though he had erected a pagan altar, for it says, "Cease to glorify man who has breath in his nostrils [i.e., is puffed up with pride], for with what [bameh] is he deemed worthy?" (Isaiah 2:22). Don't read bameh; read instead bamah [a pagan altar].

[The Gemara now focuses on the second segment of Proverbs 16:5 mentioned above.] What is the meaning of, "Hand to hand—evil will not be exonerated" (Proverbs 16:5)? Rav said: Whoever has relations with a married woman, even if he proclaims God as the Most High, Possessor of heaven and earth as our father Abraham did, about whom it says, "I have lifted my hand [in an oath] to God Most High, Possessor of heaven and earth!" (Genesis 14:22), he will not escape the punishment of Gehinnom. The students of the yeshivah of R. Shila disputed this saying: [If Rav's interpretation is correct], instead of "Hand to hand . . ." it should have said: Of God's hand he will not escape punishment. But the meaning is: Although he received the Torah like our teacher Moses [from God's hand into his hand], about whom it says, "From his right hand he brought the fire of a religion to them" (Deuteronomy 33:2), [the adulterer] will not escape the punishment of Gehinnom. R. Yochanan argued: [If that is the correct interpretation,] instead of "Hand to hand" it should have said: hand from hand [the adulterer received Torah like Moses]. But, said R. Yochanan, (5a) the meaning is: Even if the adulterer gives charity in secret [from hand to hand], about which it says, "A gift given in secret will cover up [God's] anger" (Proverbs 21:14), he will not escape the punishment of Gehinnom.

THE BANE OF HAUGHTINESS

From where in Scripture do we know that haughtiness is forbidden? Rava said in the name of Ze'iri, from the following verse, "Listen and be attentive: Do not be haughty" (Jeremiah 13:15). R. Nachman b. Yitzchak said: From, "Your heart may then grow haughty, and you may forget the Lord your God" (Deuteronomy 8:14), and it says, "Be careful that you do not forget the Lord your God" (ibid. v. 11). [The phrase "be careful" should be understood in the sense that] R. R. Avin explained it in the name of R. Ila'i: Wherever it says "be careful", "lest," and "do not," it refers to a prohibition. [Thus, haughtiness leads to forgetting God, which is prohibited in v. 11.]

R. Avira expounded, sometimes in the name of R. Ammi and sometimes in the name of R. Assi: Whoever is haughty will in the end be demoted, as it says, "They are exalted briefly, and then they will be demoted" (Job 24:24). Now you might think that they continue to exist [after their demotion]; therefore, the verse continues, "and they are gone." However, if the haughty person corrects his way [and becomes humble], he will live a full life, as it says, "They are crushed like all [kakol] who are swept away, [i.e., they die like all other men, without any particular suffering]" (ibid.), like Abraham, Isaac, and Jacob, with whom the expressions bakol, mikol, kol, "all" are associated.[2] Otherwise, "They are snapped off like the top of a stalk" (ibid.). [The Gemara asks:] What does "like the top of a stalk" mean? R. Huna and R. Chisda explain it: One says: like the beard of a grain stalk, and the other says: it means like the ears of grain themselves. We understand the one who says: like the beard of a grain stalk, since it says, "like the top of a stalk"; but according to the one who says that it means like the ears of grain themselves, why does it say, "Like the top of a stalk"? R. Assi said, and so it was taught in the yeshivah of R. Yishmael: Like a man who enters his field; he will first pick the tallest ears [similarly, the haughty will die before their time].

[God says,] "I am with the despondent and lowly of spirit" (Isaiah 57:15). R. Huna and R. Chisda explain it. One says that it means the despondent is with Me [I lift up the despondent to dwell with Me]; and the other explains it to mean that "I am with the despondent" [I lower My *Shechinah* down to his level]. It is likely that "I come down to the despondent" is the correct interpretation. For we know that God ignored all the mountains and hills and [came down] to make His *Shechinah* rest on [the lowly] Mount Sinai, but He did not raise Mount Sinai [to His level]. R. Yosef said: A person should learn from his Creator's attitude [to love the humble], for God ignored all mountains and hills and made His *Shechinah* rest on [the lowly] Mount Sinai; and He ignored all beautiful trees and made His *Shechinah* rest on the lowly thorn-bush.[3]

R. Elazar said: A haughty person deserves to be cut down like an *Asherah* tree [a tree or orchard worshipped as an idol].[4] It says concerning arrogance, "And the haughty ones are brought down" (Isaiah 10:33), and elsewhere it says, "Cut down their *Asherah* trees" (Deuteronomy 7:5). R. Elazar further said: A haughty person's dust will not be stirred [at the Resurrection]. For it says, "Awake and shout for joy, you who rest in the dust" (Isaiah 26:19)—it does not say: you that lie in the dust, but, "you who rest [*shochenei*] in the dust," as if to say: one who during his lifetime made himself a neighbor [*shachein*] to the dust [i.e., he lowered himself by being humble]. R. Elazar also said: The *Shechinah* laments over every haughty person, as it says, "He moans from afar about the haughty" (Psalms 138:6).

R. Avira, others say R. Elazar, expounded: Come and see how the way of God differs from the way of human beings: The way of human beings is for a high-ranking person to take notice of another high-ranking person and not of a lowly person. Not so is the way of the Holy One, blessed be He. He is exalted and He takes notice of the lowly, for it says, "For though God is exalted, He notes the lowly" (Psalms 138:6).

R. Chisda, others say Mar Ukva, said: Concerning an arrogant person, the Holy One, blessed be He, declares: I and he cannot both live in the same world. For it says, "He who slanders his neighbor in secret—him I will cut down [with rebuke]; one with haughty eyes and an expansive heart, him I cannot bear" (ibid. 101:5). Don't read, "him [*oto*] I cannot bear," but, "with him [*ito*] I cannot [dwell]." There are some who apply this passage to talebearers, for it says, "he who slanders his neighbor in secret, him I will cut down."

R. Alexandri said: A haughty person becomes upset at the slightest wind [i.e., adversity], as it says, "But the wicked [i.e., arrogant] will be like the driven sea that cannot rest" (Isaiah 57:20). If the sea, which contains so many *log* of water, is stirred by a slight breeze,

how much more so a human being who contains no more than a *revi'it* of blood[5] [is shaken by the slightest wind of adversity].

R. Chiya b. Abba said in the name of Rav: A Torah scholar should possess an eighth of an eighth of pride, [a small amount of pride in order to command respect]. Said Huna the son of R. Yehoshua: [This little bit of pride] adorns a Torah scholar like a beard of an ear of grain. Rava said: A Torah scholar who is haughty deserves to be put in a ban, and if he has no pride at all, he also deserves to be banned, [because people will not obey his directives]. R. Nachman b. Yitzchak said: He should not possess any pride at all; not even a small amount of it. Can we then take lightly the verse, "Every haughty heart is an abomination of God" (Proverbs 16:5)?

Chizkiya said: A person's prayer is not accepted unless he makes his heart tender like flesh, [and not hard like a rock]. For it says: "It shall be that every New Moon and on every Sabbath all flesh shall come to prostrate themselves before Me [in prayer], says God" (Isaiah 66:23); [the prayers of those who are humble and tender-hearted like flesh will be answered, but not the prayers of the haughty]. R. Zeira said: Regarding flesh it says, "and it is healed" (Leviticus 13:18), [only a person whose heart is tender like flesh will be healed, but not an arrogant person], but concerning man it does not say: And he is healed. R. Yochanan said: The word *adam*, "man," is made up of the initials of the words *afar*, "dust"; *dam*, "blood"; and *marah*, "gall." The word *basar*, "flesh," is composed of the initials of *bushah*, "shame"; *seruchah*, "stench"; and *rimmah*, "worm." Others say: *bushah*, "shame"; *sheol*, "grave"; and *rimmah*, "worm"; because *sheol* is written with a *shin* [like *basar*, and *seruchah* with a *samach*].

R. Ashi said: Whoever is haughty will in the end be demoted. for it says, (5b) "For a *se'et* and for a *sapachat* [marks of leprosy]" (Leviticus 14:56), and *se'et* definitely means elevation, for it says, "Against all the lofty mountains and against all the towering [*nisa'ot*] hills" (Isaiah 2:14). *Sappachat* clearly means a subordinate thing, as it says, "Please attach me [*sefacheini*] to one of those priestly divisions to eat a morsel of bread" (1 Samuel 2:36). [In other words: haughtiness brings subservience in its wake.] R. Yehoshua b. Levi said: Come and see how greatly God regards meek people, since when the *Bet Hamikdash* stood if a person brought a burnt-offering he received the reward of a burnt-offering; a meal-offering, he received the reward of a meal-offering [but not more than that]; but if a person is meek, Scripture considers it as though he had offered all of the sacrifices. For it says, "The sacrifices God desires are a broken spirit" (Psalms 51:19). But that is not all; for even his prayer is not despised, for the verse continues, "A heart broken and humbled God will not despise."

R. Yehoshua b. Levi further said: A person who calculates his ways in the world [i.e., the cost of a mitzvah against its eternal reward] will be worthy to see the salvation of the Holy One, blessed be He. For it says, "One who orders [*vesam*] his way, I will show him the salvation of God" (Psalms 50:23). Don't read *vesam*, "who orders," but *vesham*, "who calculates" his way.

THEY ADMITTED
THEIR WRONGDOING

(7b) Our Rabbis have taught: [The judge] tells [the *sotah*] Biblical anecdotes and stories from the Torah that happened in ancient times [about *tzaddikim* who were not embarrassed to admit their wrongdoing], about people who exemplified the verse, "Wise men said it and did not hide it from their fathers" (Job 15:18); men such as Judah who confessed and was not ashamed [to admit the episode with Tamar].[6] What was the outcome? He earned life in the World to Come. Reuben, too, confessed and was not ashamed [to admit the matter with Bilhah].[7] What was the outcome? He earned life in the World to Come. [The Gemara asks:] And what was their reward? What was their reward, [you ask]! I just finished saying [that their reward was life in the World to Come]! [The Gemara means:] What was their reward in *this* world? [The Gemara answers:] It says, "To them alone the land was given; no stranger passed among them" (Job 15:19). It is understandable that Judah was rewarded; we find that he confessed, for it says, "Judah recognized and admitted, 'She is more righteous than I am'" (Genesis 38:26). But where do we find that Reuben confessed?

As R. Shmuel b. Nachmani said in the name of R. Yochanan: What is meant by, "May Reuben live and not die . . . and this for Judah" (Deuteronomy 33:6,7)? All the years that the Israelites were in the wilderness, Judah's bones kept turning in his coffin[8] until Moses stood up and asked for mercy for him. He said to God: Master of the universe! Who caused Reuben to confess his sin? None other than Judah; [his admission of guilt inspired Reuben to confess]. [Continued Moses,] "And this for Judah" [meaning: is it fair to Judah that his bones should be turning in his coffin?]. Thus when Moses prayed, "Hearken O God, to Judah's voice" (ibid.), each of Judah's limbs entered its socket [and stopped rolling in the coffin]. But the angels did not permit him to enter the heavenly Academy [where the Torah scholars are studying; so Moses prayed,] "And return him to his people" (ibid.). Once he was there, Judah was unable to participate in the debate the rabbis were engaged in, [so Moses prayed,] "May he be able to triumph [in the Torah debate]" (ibid.). Even so, Judah did not merit to say things the others accepted, [so Moses prayed,] "May You be a helper against his adversaries" (ibid.). [At any rate, R. Shmuel b. Nachmani infers from a verse in the Torah that Reuben confessed his guilt.]

[The Gemara asks:] We understand that Judah confessed so that Tamar should not be burned, but why did Reuben confess? After all, R. Sheshet declared: A person who publicly specifies his sins is shameless! [The Gemara answers:] Reuben confessed in order that [his father] should not suspect his brothers [of his offense].

MEASURE FOR MEASURE

(8b) We learned in a *Baraita*: Rabbi Meir used to say: From where do we know that the measure a person uses in regard to his own actions is the measure God uses to determine what will happen to him? Because it says, "With the same measurement [*se'ah*] that a person sinned he will receive his punishment" (Isaiah 27:8).[9] [The Gemara says:] This proves only that God repays serious sins measure for measure [a *se'ah* is a large measurement], but from where do we infer that He repays even for a *tarkav*, a *kav* and half a *kav*, a quarter, an eighth, a sixteenth, a thirty-second of a *kav* [meaning, for very minor sins]? For it says, "For all tumultuous battles [*sa'on*] are fought with an uproar" (Isaiah 9:4). [*Sa'on* is taken as related to *se'ah*, "measurement," and the phrase is expounded: Every tiny measure is accounted for.] And from where do we know that minor transgressions accumulate and are added to the grand total? For it says, "Adding one thing to another to reach a conclusion" (Ecclesiastes 7:27).

And so we find in the case of the *sotah* that with the very measure that she used she was measured: She stood by the door of her house to be seen by the man; therefore a *kohen* makes her stand by the Nikanor Gate [the main entrance to the Court of the *Bet Hamikdash*] and show her disgrace to everyone. She wound a beautiful scarf around her head; therefore a *kohen* takes her head covering off her head and places it under her feet. She made up her face for him; therefore (9a) her face turns green [when she drinks the bitter water]. She painted her eyes for him; therefore her eyes bulge [from drinking the bitter water]. She braided her hair for him; therefore a *kohen* loosens her hair. She signaled to him with her finger; therefore her fingernails fall off. She put on a special belt for him; therefore a *kohen* takes a plain rope and ties it above her breasts. She thrust her thigh toward him; therefore her thigh collapses. She received him upon her body; therefore her stomach swells. She gave him the world's delicacies to eat; therefore her offering consists of animal fodder [barley flour].[10] She gave him choice wine to drink in expensive goblets; therefore a *kohen* gives her bitter water in a earthenware cup. She acted in secret, and "He that dwells in the secret place of the Most High" (Psalms 91:1) will direct His face against her [to punish her (Rashi)], as it says, "The adulterer's eye awaits the night, saying, 'No eye will see me!' and he applies himself to sin in concealment" (Job 24:15). Another explanation is: She acted in secret; God proclaims it in public, as it says, "[Though] he covers his hatred by darkness, his evil will be revealed in public" (Proverbs 26:26).

[Earlier the Gemara cited three verses that conveyed the idea that God's punishment is exacted measure for measure. The Gemara now asks:] Since we derived [the principle that small sins accumulate and are added to the total] from the verse, "Adding one thing to another to reach a conclusion" (Ecclesiastes 7:27), why do we need the verse, "For all tumultuous battles are fought with an uproar" (Isaiah 9:4) [to tell us that every sin is accounted for]? [The Gemara answers:] To tell us that the punishment will be in line with the sin. But since that is derived from, "For all tumultuous battles are fought with an uproar," why do we need, "With the very same measurement that a person sinned will he receive his punishment" (Isaiah 27:8)? [The Gemara answers:] We need that passage for the inference of R. Chanina b. Papa who said: The Holy One, blessed be He, does not exact punishment of a nation until it is sent into exile, for it says, "It receives its measure of punishment when it is sent away."

[Asks the Gemara:] Is that so? Has Rava not said: What is the significance of the three cups [Pharaoh's butler saw in his dream]?[11] [A cup symbolizes the "cup of affliction."] One of those [bitter] cups Egypt drank in the days of Moses; one she drank in the days of Pharaoh-Neco [when Egypt was defeated by Babylonia];[12] and one Egypt and all its neighbors were forced to drink in the days of *Mashiach*. [So you see that Egypt's punishment is administered in three stages, and not at the time of its banishment into exile?] Perhaps you will say that the first cup [in the days of Moses] totally destroyed Egypt, and that other people came afterward and settled there, [and they drank the second bitter cup; and then other people came and settled in Egypt, and they will drink the third cup; and every nation received their punishment at the time of their final destruction]. That cannot be so. [We know that the present-day Egyptians are the descendants of the earlier Egyptians,] for R. Yehudah said: Minyamin, an Egyptian convert, was a colleague of mine among the students of R. Akiva, and he told me, "I am a first-generation Egyptian, and I married a first-generation Egyptian woman; I will marry off my son to a second-generation Egyptian woman[13] so that my grandson may be permitted to enter God's marriage group. [Children born to Egyptians in the third generation after becoming proselytes may enter God's marriage group.[14] So we see that the Egyptians of R. Yehudah's time were descendants of the original Egyptians, for if they were not, why would Minyamin have to wait for the third generation to enter God's marriage group?]

[The Gemara answers:] This is what R. Chanina b. Papa actually said: The Holy One, blessed be He, does not exact punishment of a *king* until the time of his banishment into exile, as it says, "He receives his measure of punishment when he is sent away." Amemar derived this teaching of R. Chanina b. Papa from the following verse: What means the verse, "For

I, God, have not changed, and you, the sons of Jacob will not perish" (Malachi 3:6)?—"For I, God, have not changed [*shaniti*]"—I have never struck a nation and repeated it, [*shaniti* means both "change" and "repeat"]. "And you, the sons of Jacob will not perish"—that is what is meant by, "I will use up My arrows on them" (Deuteronomy 32:23)—My arrows, I will use up on them, but [the sons of Jacob] will never cease to exist. R. Hamenuna said: The Holy One, blessed be He, does not punish a person until his measure of guilt is full, as it says, "After his satiety has been gained, misfortune will strike him" (Job 20:22).

R. Chanania b. Papa expounded: What is meant by the text, "Sing joyfully, O righteous, because of God; praise is fitting for the upright" (Psalms 33:1)? Don't read *navah*, "praise is fitting," but *neveih*, "the Dwelling that deserves praise." This alludes to Moses and David over whose works [in erecting the Sanctuary] their enemies had no power. About [the *Bet Hamikdash* that was prepared by] David it says, "Her gates have sunk into the earth" (Lamentations 2:9) [so that the enemy could not carry them away]. Concerning Moses, a Tanna said: After the first *Bet Hamikdash* was built, the Tabernacle with its fastenings, beams, bars, pillars, and bases was hidden away. Where were they hidden? R. Chisda said in the name of Avimi: Beneath the underground vaults of the Sanctuary.

THEY CRAVED
FORBIDDEN THINGS

We learned in a *Baraita*: The *sotah* set her eyes on a man who was not proper for her; what she wanted she was not given [she is forbidden to marry her lover], and what she had was taken from her; [if she drinks the water she dies, and if she admits her guilt, she is forbidden to live with her husband and forfeits her marriage settlement]. For whoever sets his eye on something that does not belong to him will not obtain what he desires, and what he possesses is taken away from him. (9b) [The Gemara is now giving eleven examples of this.] This concept is found with the Serpent [in the Garden of Eden], which craved something that was not proper for it, [it lusted after Eve]; what it wanted it did not get, and what it had was taken away from it. [What did it have that was taken away?] The Holy One, blessed be He, said: I declared that the Serpent should be the king of all the animals, but now, "Cursed are you more than all the livestock and all the wild beasts" (Genesis 3:14). I declared that it should walk with an erect posture, but now, "On your belly you shall crawl" (ibid.). I said that it should eat the same food as man eats, but now it has to eat dust. The Serpent said: I will kill Adam and marry Eve but now, [God said,] "I will plant hatred between you and woman, and between your offspring and her offspring" (ibid. v. 15). We find this concept also with Cain, Korach, Balaam, Doeg, Achitophel, Gechazi, Absalom,

Adonijah, Uzziah, and Haman; they all craved something that was not proper for them; what they desired they did not get, and what they possessed was taken away from them.

SAMSON

[The Mishnah says:] Samson followed after the desire of his eyes; therefore the Philistines gouged out his eyes. For it says, "The Philistines seized him and gouged out his eyes" (Judges 16:21). Absalom was proud of his hair, therefore he was hanged by his hair. And because he was intimate with ten concubines of his father,[15] therefore he was stabbed with ten spears. For it says, "Ten soldiers, the armor-bearers of Joab, circled around and struck at Absalom until he died" (2 Samuel 18:15). And because Absalom deceived three: his father, the Bet Din, and all of Israel, therefore three staves were thrust through his heart, as it says, "[Joab] then took three staves in his hand and thrust them into Absalom's heart—yet he was still alive in the thick growth of the elm tree" (ibid. v. 14).

[The Gemara says:] Our Rabbis taught: Samson rebelled [against God] through his eyes, for it says, "Samson said to his father, 'Take her for me, for she is pleasing in my eyes'" (Judges 14:3); therefore the Philistines put out his eyes, as it says, "The Philistines seized him and gouged out his eyes." Is this indeed so? [How can you say that Samson did something wrong,] when it says, "His father and mother did not know that it was from God, [that God had arranged this match so that he should be able to take revenge against the Philistines]" (Judges 14:4), [so it was God's will]? [The Gemara answers:] When he went he followed his personal impulse [and not God's will].

We learned in a *Baraita*: Rabbi says: Samson's decline began in Gaza, therefore he received his punishment in Gaza. Samson's decline began in Gaza, for it says, "Samson went to Gaza and there he saw a prostitute" (ibid. 16:1). Therefore he was punished in Gaza, for it says, "They brought him down to Gaza" (ibid. v. 21). [The Gemara asks:] But it says, "Samson went down to Timnah, and in Timnah he saw a Philistine woman" (ibid. 14:1), [and this happened before the encounter with the prostitute in Gaza]! [The Gemara answers:] His decline began in Gaza, [and not in Timnah, because the woman in Timnah he had married legally].

"It was after this that [Samson] loved a woman in Nachal Sorek, and her name was Delilah" (ibid. 16:4). We learned: Rabbi said: If her name had not been Delilah, it would have been appropriate to call her Delilah. [Delilah comes from the root *dal*, meaning poor, weak.] Indeed she weakened his strength, she weakened his heart, and she weakened his actions. That she weakened his strength we infer from the following verse, "His strength departed from him" (ibid. v.

19). That she weakened his heart is evident from the following verse, "Delilah saw that he had told her all that was in his heart [about the source of his strength]" (ibid. v. 18). That she weakened his actions can be gathered from the fact that the *Shechinah* left him, for it says, "But he did not know that God had left him" (ibid. v. 20). "Delilah saw that he had told her all that was in his heart."

[The Gemara asks:] How did she know [that he was telling the truth this time]? [After all, he had told her several lies about the source of his strength, and she had caught him lying?] R. Chanin said in the name of Rav: One can tell when a person speaks the truth from his heart. Abbaye said: She realized that this *tzaddik* would not take God's name in vain. When he said, "I am a Nazirite of God" (ibid. v. 17), she knew that he was telling the truth.

"The spirit of God began to resound in him in the camp of Dan, between Zora and Eshtoal" (ibid. 13:25). R. Chama said in the name of R. Chanina: Jacob's prophecy became fulfilled, for it says, "Let Dan be a snake on the road" (Genesis 49:17), [a reference to Samson who waged battle like a snake]. "The spirit of God began to resound in him in the camp of Dan"— R. Yitzchak of the yeshivah of R. Ammi said: This teaches that the *Shechinah* would ring before him like a bell, [meaning, the *Shechinah* would accompany him on his travels]. For it says here: "to resound" [*lefa'amo*], and elsewhere it says, [in the description of the garments of the *Kohen Gadol*], "A golden bell [*pa'amon*] and a pomegranate" (Exodus 28:34). "Between Zorah and Eshtaol"—R. Assi said: Zorah and Eshtaol are two great mountains, and Samson uprooted them and ground one into the other.

[The angel who announced Samson's birth said,] "And he will begin to save Israel from the hand of the Philistines" (ibid. 13:5). R. Chama b. Chanina said: (10a) The oath Abimelech [the king of the Philistines made to Abraham] became null and void, [the oath being,] "That you will not deal falsely with me, with my children, or with my grandchildren" (Genesis 21:23), [because the Philistines had violated the oath by oppressing the Israelites, therefore Samson had the right to strike back].

"Then Samson called out to God, and he said, 'O Lord, God, remember me now and strengthen me only this one time, O God, and let me take revenge from the Philistines for one of my two eyes" (ibid. 16:28). [For sanctifying one eye he wished to be paid in this world; he asked for the strength to bring down the stadium on the Philistines. The reward for sanctifying the other eye he left for the World to Come (Rashi)] (ibid. 16:28). Rav said: Samson spoke to the Holy One, blessed be He: Master of the universe! Remember the twenty years that I ruled Israel, and never did I order anyone to bring me a stick from one place to another.

"Samson went and caught three hundred foxes" (ibid. 15:4). Why did he pick foxes in particular? R.

Aivu b. Nigdi said in the name of R. Chiya b. Abba: Samson said: Let this fox, who walks backward,[16] take revenge from the Philistines who went back on the oath [of Abimelech to live in peace with Israel]. We learned in a *Baraita*: R. Shimon HeChasid said: The distance between the shoulders of Samson was sixty cubits,[17] as it says, "Samson slept until midnight. He arose at midnight, and he grasped the doors of the city gate along with the two doorposts. He carried them off together with the bar, and he placed them on his shoulders" (ibid. 16:3). And there is a tradition that the gates of Gaza were not less than sixty cubits in width.

R. Yochanan said: Samson judged Israel as their Father in heaven does. For it says, "Dan shall judge his people, like the One" (Genesis 49:16). R. Yochanan also said: Samson [*Shimshon*] was named by the name of the Holy One, blessed be He, for it says, "For the Lord God is a sun [*shemesh*] and a shield" (Psalms 84:12). [*Shemesh* also has the connotation of protection.] [The Gemara asks:] If that is so, one should be forbidden to erase his name? [The Gemara answers:] The word *shemesh* is not a name of God; it describes an attribute of God. Just as God protects the whole world, so Samson protected Israel during his generation.

R. Yochanan further said: Baalam limped on one leg, for it says, "And he went with a limp [*shefi*, dislocated]" (Numbers 23:3). Samson limped on both legs, for it says, "a viper [*shefifon*] on the path" (Genesis 49:17).

FIVE PEOPLE
WITH SPECIAL POWERS

Our Rabbis have taught: There were five people that were created with various powers, and all of them were punished through their special powers: Samson with his enormous physical strength; Saul with his neck;[18] Absalom with his hair;[19] Zedekiah with his eyes; and Asa with his legs. Samson was punished in his strength, as it says, "His strength left him" (Judges 16:9). Saul was punished in his neck, as it says, "Saul took his sword and fell on it [and it pierced his neck]" (1 Samuel 31:4). Absalom was punished in his hair, for it says, "His head became entangled in the elm tree" (2 Samuel 18:9). Zedekiah was punished in his eyes, for it says, "[Nebuchadnezzar] blinded Zedekiah's eyes" (2 Kings 25:7). King Asa was punished in his legs, as it says, "Only in his old age he became sick in his legs" (2 Kings 15:23). Rav Yehudah said in Rav's name: He suffered from *podagra* [gout]. Mar Zutra the son of R. Nachman asked R. Nachman: What is *podagra* like? He answered: Like a needle in raw flesh. How did he know this? Some say he suffered from it himself; others say he heard it from his teacher; and others say, "The secret of God is to those who fear Him, and His covenant to inform them" (Psalms 25:14), [meaning, he knew it by divine inspiration]. Rava expounded: Why was King Asa punished [with *podagra*]? Because he

drafted Torah scholars to do forced labor,[20] for it says, "King Asa mustered all Judah, with no exemptions" (1 Kings 15:22). What does "with no exemptions" imply? Said Rav Yehudah in the name of Rav: [He drafted] even a bridegroom from his chamber and a bride from her wedding canopy.

WHERE WAS TIMNAH LOCATED?

It says, "Samson went down to Timnah" (Judges 14:1), and it says, "Tamar was told that her father-in-law [Judah] was going up to Timnah to shear his sheep" (Genesis 38:13). [Both Samson and Judah were in Eretz Yisrael, yet one traveled *down* to Timnah and the other traveled *up*!] Rabbi Elazar explained: Samson disgraced himself with that journey, [it was in Timnah that he married a Philistine woman], therefore it says that he went down. Yehudah was elevated through his journey to Timnah [for it was there that he met Tamar, and from that union was born Peretz who was the ancestor of David], therefore it says that he went up. R. Shmuel b. Nachmani said: There are two towns named named Timnah; to reach one you had to go down, to reach the other you had to go up. R. Papa said: There is only one place named Timnah; [it was situated halfway up a mountain slope], so if you approached it from the top of the mountain you were traveling down; if you approached from the foot of the mountain you were traveling up, like Vardinia, Bibari, and Shuka deNaresh, [towns situated halfway up a mountain].

"[Tamar] sat at the entrance of Einayim [Eyes]" (Genesis 38:14). R. Alexandra'i said: This teaches us that [Tamar] seated herself at the doorway [of the tent] of our Father Abraham, the place that all eyes aspired to see, [for it was a place where the whole world found love, warmth, and hospitality]. R. Chanin said: It was a place named Einayim; and it is mentioned in Scripture, "Tapuach and Einam" (Joshua 15:34). [Einam is equated with Einayim.]

HOW DID ABRAHAM
MAKE GOD KNOWN?

[Having mentioned the tent of Abraham, the Gemara elaborates on that theme:]

"[Abraham] planted an *eshel* [tamarisk] tree in Beersheba" (Genesis 21:33). Resh Lakish said: This teaches that Abraham made an orchard and planted in it all kinds of delectable fruits [for wayfarers to enjoy]. R. Yehudah and R. Nechemiah [differed on this point]. One said that it was an orchard; the other, that it was an inn.[21] We can understand the one who says it was an orchard, since it says, "he planted"; but according to the one who says it was an inn, how do you explain the phrase "he planted"; [do you plant an inn?] [The Gemara answers:] Yes, we find "to plant" used [in the sense of building] in the passage, "He will plant the tents of his palace" (Daniel 11:45).

"There [Abraham] called [*vayikra*] in the name of God, Lord of the universe" (Genesis 21:33). Resh Lakish said: Don't read, *vayikra*, "he called [the place]" (10b) but *vayakri*, "he caused the name of God to be uttered by every person that passed by." How did he do that? After the guests finished eating and drinking, they got up to bless and thank Abraham, but he said to them: [Why are you thanking me?] Did you eat *my* food? The food you ate belongs to the God of the universe. You should thank, praise, and bless Him who spoke and the world came into being.

JUDAH AND TAMAR

It says, "Judah saw her [Tamar], and because she had covered her face he assumed that she was a prostitute" (Genesis 38:15). [The Gemara asks:] Because she covered her face he assumed she was a prostitute! R. Elazar said: She had covered her face in her father-in-law's [Judah's] house, [that's why Judah never saw her and did not recognize her]. For R. Shmuel b. Nachmani said in the name of R. Yonatan: Every daughter-in-law who is modest in her father-in-law's house merits that kings and prophets descend from her. How do we know this? From Tamar. Prophets descended from her, because it says, "The vision of Isaiah son of Amoz" (Isaiah 1:1). And kings descended from her through David. And R. Levi said: We have a tradition from our fathers that Amoz [the father of Isaiah] and Amaziah [King of Judah] were brothers. [Since Amaziah was a descendant of David and Amoz, the father of the prophet Isaiah was his brother; so we see that both prophets and kings descended from Tamar.][22]

[The Torah tells us that Judah was told: "Your daughter-in-law Tamar has become pregnant as a result of immoral behavior." Judah said: "Take her out and have her burned, [because she is a daughter of a *kohen*]!" (Genesis 38:24)].

[The text continues:] "When she [Tamar] was being taken out [*mutzeit*] [to be burned], she sent to her father-in-law [the proofs] with the message, . . ." (Genesis 38:25). Instead of *mutzeit*, "being taken out" [literally, "she was found"], the verb should have been *mitvatzeit*, to signify that she was taken out forcibly. R. Elazar said: [The verb *mutzeit* alludes to the fact that something was found.] After her proofs were found, [the seal, the wrap, and the staff that Judah had given her], the angel Samael [i.e., the angel of Esau, Satan] came and took them away [because he wanted Tamar to be burned so that David and *Mashiach* would never be born], but the angel Gabriel came and restored them.

This is borne out by the verse, "For the conductor, regarding the silent distant dove, to David a *michtam*" (Psalms 56:1). Expounded R. Yochanan: When Samael [Satan] came and took away her proofs she became like a silent dove. "To David a *michtam*" means: [a psalm dedicated to the one who is worthy to have as a de-

scendant] David who was humble [*mach*] and perfect [*tam*] to all. Another explanation of *michtam* is: his wound [*makkah*] was whole [*tammah*]; there was no need to circumcise David for he was born already circumcised. Another explanation of *michtam* is: Just as when he was young David humbled himself in the presence of someone greater than he was in order to learn Torah from him, so did he act humbly when he was king. [His humility (*mach*) was perfect (*tam*).]

"[Tamar] sent [the proofs] to her father-in-law with the message, 'I am pregnant by the man who is the owner of these articles'" (Genesis 38:25). [The Gemara asks: Why did she speak in such a roundabout way?] Why didn't she say straightforwardly ["You Judah are the father of my child, and here are your articles as proof"]? R. Zutra b. Tuvyah said in the name of Rav, others say R. Chana b. Bizna said in the name of R. Shimon Chasida, others say R. Yochanan said in the name of R. Shimon b. Yochai: It is better for a person to cast himself into a fiery furnace rather than put his fellow to shame in public. From where do we know this? From Tamar. [She was willing to allow herself to be burned rather than openly embarrass Judah by saying, "These articles are yours." She showed the objects to Judah. If he was going to admit that he was the father, fine. If not, she would rather be burned than shame him in public (Rashi).]

[Tamar said,] "Please identify [these objects]. Who is the owner of this seal, this wrap, and this staff?" (ibid.). Said R. Chama b. Chanina: With the words, "please identify" Judah announced to his father [Jacob a bad tiding], and with the same phrase of "please identify" something was announced to him. He announced to his father [Joseph's disappearance], when he said to Jacob, "Please identify it. Is it your son's coat or not?" [Recognizing it as Joseph's coat, Jacob cried out, "A wild beast must have eaten him. Joseph has been torn to pieces!"] And with the phrase "please identify" an announcement was made to Judah, "Please identify who is the owner of this seal, this wrap, and this staff." The term *na*, "please," is clearly an expression of request. She said to him, "Please, I beg of you, recognize the face of the Creator, [and don't deny that the articles are yours,] and don't hide your eyes from me."

"Judah immediately recognized them. He called out, 'She is more righteous than I am!'" (ibid. v. 26). This is what R. Chanin b. Bizna said in the name of R. Shimon Chasida: Joseph who sanctified the heavenly name in private [when he rebuffed Potiphar's wife's advances] merited that one letter of God's name should be added to his name, as it says, "He appointed it as a testimony for Joseph" (Psalms 81:6), [in this verse the letter *hei*—one of the letters of God's name—is inserted in the name Yosef to read Yehosef].

Judah, however, who sanctified the heavenly name in public merited that his name should encompass all four letters of the Divine name. [Yehudah is spelled:

yud, hei, vav, dalet, hei.][23] When he acknowledged and said, "She is more righteous than I am," a heavenly Voice came forth and proclaimed: You rescued Tamar and her two sons from the flames. I swear, I am going to rescue through your merit three of your descendants from the fire. Which descendants? Chananiah, Mishael, and Azariah.[24] [Judah said,] "She is more righteous than I am." How did he know [that Tamar was pregnant by him and not by someone else]? A heavenly Voice came forth and proclaimed: From Me come forth secrets.

[The text continues,] "He was not intimate with her anymore" (Genesis 38:26). [Literally: "He knew her not again."] Shmuel the elder, the father-in-law of R. Shmuel b. Ammi, said in the name of R. Shmuel b. Ammi: Once he knew [that she was righteous and pure] he did not separate from her again. [How can this be gathered from the text?] It says here, "He knew her not again [*yasaf*]," and elsewhere it says, [regarding the Receiving of the Torah,] "it was a great voice that never ended [*yasaf*]" (Deuteronomy 5:19), hence, "he knew her not again [*yasaf*]" really means "he never ended his relationship with her."

ABSALOM

[The Mishnah stated:] Absalom was proud of his hair. We learned in a *Baraita*: Abasalom rebelled [against his father] through his hair. For it says, "There was no one in all of Israel as praiseworthy for his beauty as Absalom. . . . When he would have his head barbered—at the end of every year he would have his hair barbered, because it became heavy upon him,[25] and when he had it barbered—the hair of his head weighed two hundred shekels by the king's weight" (2 Samuel 14:26). We learned: This was the way the people of Tiberias and Tzipori used to weigh things. Because of his glorious hair he was hanged by his hair, as it says, "Absalom [who rebelled against David, his father] chanced upon David's servants. Absalom was riding on a mule, and the mule came under the thick branches of a large elm tree; his head became entangled in the elm, and he was suspended between the heavens and the earth, while the mule that was under him moved on" (2 Samuel 18:9). Absalom drew his sword trying to cut himself loose. But it was taught in the yeshivah of R. Yishmael: Suddenly he saw Gehinnom split open beneath him, [and he realized that by cutting himself loose he would fall into it].

[David had given strict orders that Absalom was not to be harmed. Nevertheless, Joab and ten of his soldiers killed Absalom as he was hanging from the tree.] "The king trembled [when he received the news]. He went up to the upper chamber of the gateway and wept; and thus he said as he went: 'My son, Absalom! My son, my son, Absalom! If only I could have died in your place! Absalom, my son, my son!'" . . . "The king wrapped his face, and the king cried out in a loud voice,

'My son, Absalom! Absalom, my son, my son!'" (ibid. 19:1,5). [The Gemara asks:] Why did David say "my son" eight times? [The Gemara answers:] Seven times to raise him from the seven chambers of Gehinnom, and regarding the eighth time, some say [he said it] to unite his head [which was cut off] with his body; others say [he said it] in order to bring him to the world to come.

[It says,] "Absalom had taken in his lifetime and erected for himself the pillar that is in the Valley of the King, for he said, 'I have no son; this is in order that my name should be remembered.' He called the pillar by his name, and it is called 'Absalom's Monument' until this day" (ibid. 18:18). [The Gemara asks: What does [*lakach*] "had taken" mean? Resh Lakish said: Absalom made a bad purchase for himself [*lakach* means both "took" and "bought"]. "He erected for himself the pillar that is in the Valley of the King"— R. Chanina b. Papa said: This is an allusion to the profound plan of the King of the universe, [for David knew that he had to endure Absalom's rebellion in order to atone for his sin with Bathsheba]. For it says, [the prophet Nathan said to David,] "So says God: Behold! I shall raise evil against you from your own household" (ibid. 12:11). We find a similar passage [Jacob sent Joseph to his brothers, and that mission led to the bondage in Egypt], "So he sent him from the depth of Hebron" (Genesis 37:14).

R. Chanina b. Papa said: [the meaning is:] It was through the deep plan of that righteous man [Abraham] who was buried in Hebron; as it says, "God said to Abraham, 'Know for sure that your descendants will be foreigners in a land that is not theirs'" (Genesis 15:13) [and Joseph's trip was the opening stage of the exile in Egypt].

[Absalom erected the monument] "because he said I have no son" (2 Samuel 18:18). [The Gemara asks:] You say he does have any sons? But it says, "To Absalom were born three sons and one daughter!" (ibid. 14:27). R. Yitzchak b. Avdimi said: He did not have a son who was fit to reign as king. R. Chisda said: We have a tradition that whoever sets fire to his neighbor's crops will not have a son to inherit his estate, and Absalom had burned Joab's crops, as it says, "[Absalom] said to his servants, 'Take note of Joab's field that is next to mine, where he raises barley, and go and set it on fire'" (ibid. v. 30).

THE REWARD FOR GOOD DEEDS

(11a) [The Mishnah said: The principle of measure for measure applies not only to punishment,] it applies to good things as well; [good deeds also are rewarded measure for measure. For example:] Miriam waited a short while for [the infant] Moses, as it says, "His sister stationed herself at a distance" (Exodus 2:4); therefore, in return, all Israel waited for her seven days in the wilderness, as it says, "And the people did not move until Miriam was able to return home [after her recovery from leprosy]" (Numbers 12:15). [Another example:] Joseph had the merit of burying his father. Now none of his brothers was greater than Joseph [for he was the viceroy of Egypt, so that his father was buried with great honor and pageantry], as it says, "Joseph went up to bury his father, and with him went all of Pharaoh's servants . . . his brothers and his father's family also went . . . a chariot brigade and horsemen . . . an imposing retinue" (Genesis 50:7–9).

In return, Joseph was granted the greatest possible honor, since none other than Moses occupied himself with his burial. Moses in turn earned merit by taking care of the bones of Joseph—and there was no one in Israel greater than he—as it says, "Moses took the bones of Joseph with him" (Exodus 13:19). In return, Moses was granted the greatest possible honor, since none other than the *Shechinah* took care of his burial, as it says, "[God] buried him in the valley" (Deuteronomy 34:6). This applies not only to Moses but to all *tzaddikim*, for it says, "Your righteousness will precede you and the glory of God will gather you in [when you die]" (Isaiah 58:8).

[The Mishnah said:] "The concept of measure for measure applies to good deeds as well [as to bad deeds]. [For example:] Miriam waited a short while for Moses; therefore, all Israel waited for her for seven days in the wilderness [until she recovered from leprosy]." [The Gemara asks:] How can you compare this? Miriam waited [for Moses] only for a short while, while the Israelites waited for her for seven days? [Is this measure for measure? She received much more than she gave!] Abaye said: Read the Mishnah: When it comes to good deeds the concept of measure for measure does *not* apply, [rather, the reward outweighs the good deed by far]. Said Rava to him: But the Mishnah states that the *same* principle [of measure for measure] applies to good deeds [as to bad deeds]? But, said Rava, we must understand the Mishnah as follows: The same idea of measure for measure also applies to good deeds, in the sense that the reward will be of the same category as the good deed that was done. However, the reward for a good deed will be far greater than the good deed; whereas the punishment that is meted out for a bad deed is exacted measure for measure.

[The Gemara mentioned above:] It says, [When the infant Moses was put in a box and placed in the bulrushes,] "His sister stationed herself at a distance to know what would be done to him" (Exodus 2:4). R. Yitzchak said: [Each word of] this verse refers to the *Shechinah*: "Stationed herself," as it says, "God came and stood" (1 Samuel 3:10). "His sister," as it says, "Say to wisdom, 'You are my sister'" (Proverbs 7:4). "At a distance," as it says, "From the distance God appeared to me" (Jeremiah 31:2). "To know," for it says, "For God is the God of knowledge" (1 Samuel 2:3). "What," for it says, "What does God want of you?" (Deuteronomy 10:12). "Would be done," for it says,

"God will certainly make [do] for my lord an enduring house" (1 Samuel 25:28).[26] "To him," for it says, "[Gideon] called Him; 'God [is the source of our] Peace'" (Judges 6:24).

PRELUDE TO
EGYPTIAN OPPRESSION

It says, "A new king came into power in Egypt who did not know of Joseph" (Exodus 1:8). Rav and Shmuel have different opinions about this passage. One says that it really was a new king, while the other holds that [it was the same old king] but that he issued new decrees. The one who holds that it was a new king does so because it says "a *new* king," and the one who maintains that [it was the same king] but that he issued new decrees argues that does not say anywhere that he died and a new king ascended to the throne. . . .

[What is meant by] "Who did not know of Joseph" [if it is the same old king, he certainly did know Joseph]? [The Gemara answers:] He pretended that he had never heard of him. "He announced to his people, 'The Israelites are becoming too numerous and strong for us'" (ibid. v. 9). A Tanna taught: Pharaoh was the first to conceive the plan [to enslave the Israelites], and therefore he was the first to be punished, for it says, "When the frogs emerge they will be over you [Pharaoh], your people, and your officials" (ibid. 7:29). [The frogs came first to Pharaoh and then to the rest of Egypt.] [The Gemara continues, it says that Pharaoh declared,] "Come, let us deal wisely with him" (ibid. 1:10). It should have said "Let us deal wisely with *them*"!

R. Chama b. R. Chanina said: [Pharaoh was really trying to catch one person in his net.] He meant to say: Let us deal wisely with the redeemer of Israel. [We know that God retaliates measure for measure.] So with what shall we punish Israel? Shall we punish them with fire? If we do that, [we know God will retaliate tit for tat] for it says, "For behold, God will arrive in fire," and it also says, "For God will enter into judgment with fire" (Isaiah 66:15,16). [Shall we punish them] by the sword? [That would not do either, for the verse continues,] "With his sword against all mankind" [God would bring down the sword on us]. But come and let us punish them with water, said Pharaoh, [by casting every boy that is born into the Nile]. [This way God will not be able to retaliate against us, for He has already sworn that He would never again bring a flood on the world. For it says, "For like the waters of Noah shall this be to Me: Just I have sworn that the waters of Noah would never again pass over the earth" (ibid. 54:9). But they did not realize that He would not bring a flood on the entire earth, but on one nation He could bring a flood.

Another miscalculation: God would not flood them, but they would go and fall into the water. And that is exactly what the verse says: "The Egyptians were fleeing toward the water [in confusion], but God swamped the Egyptians in the middle of the sea" (Exodus 14.27). R. Elazar said in reference to this: What is meant by, [Jethro said: Now I know that God is the greatest of all deities,] "for I recognize Him in the evil that they had plotted [zadu] to do to them" (Exodus 18:11)?— In the very pot in which they were preparing to cook Israel they themselves were cooked. From where do we know that zadu means cooking? Because it says, "Jacob was simmering [vayazed] a stew" (Genesis 25:29).

R. Chiya b. Abba said in the name of R. Sima'i: There were three people who were consulted [by Pharaoh regarding how to deal with the children of Israel]: Balaam, Job, and Jethro. Balaam who gave the advice [to cast every boy that was born into the Nile] was killed; Job who kept quiet was tormented with pain; Jethro who ran away merited that his descendants should sit in the Chamber of the Hewn Stone [in the Temple as members of the Sanhedrin]. For it says, "And the families of scribes[27] who dwelt at Jabez— Tirathites, Shime'athites, and Suchthites.[28] These were the Kenites who descended from Hammath, the father of the house of Rechab" (1 Chronicles 2:55). And it also says, "The children of the Kenite, Moses' father-in-law [i.e., Jethro]" (Judges 1:16). [So we see that members of the Sanhedrin were descendants of Jethro.]

[Pharaoh said,] "If there is a war, they may join our enemies and wage war against us, and go up from the land" (Exodus 1:10). It should have said: "driving us from the land"? R. Abba b. Kahana said: It is like a person who curses himself and hangs the curse on someone else.

THE EGYPTIAN BONDAGE

"[The Egyptians] appointed taskmasters over him" (ibid. v. 11). It should have said: "over them" [not over him, Pharaoh]? It was taught in the yeshivah of R. Elazar b. R. Shimon: This teaches us that [the burden was placed on Pharaoh], for the Egyptians took a brick-mold and hung it around Pharaoh's neck; and if any Israelite complained that he was too delicate for this kind of work, he was told: "Are you more delicate than Pharaoh, [yet he carries a brick-mold around his neck]."

[Missim] "taskmasters"—i.e., something that shows the way, a pattern. [By carrying the brick-mold, Pharaoh showed the Israelites what he wanted them to do.] "To afflict him with their burdens" (ibid.). It should have said: "To afflict them"? The meaning is to afflict Pharaoh [by carrying the brick-mold, in order to crush the Israelites with heavy labor].

"They built storage cities [miskenot] for Pharaoh, Pithom, and Raamses" (ibid.). Rav and Shmuel [offer different interpretations of this passage]. One holds they were called miskenot, because they endangered [mesakenot] their owners; [it was because of the enslavement of the Israelites that the Egyptians eventually

were drowned in the Red Sea]. The other says the cities were called miskenot because it reduced their owners to poverty [memaskenot]; [at the Exodus the Israelites drained Egypt of its wealth].[29] A master said [as a general observation:] Whoever occupies himself with building and construction becomes poor.

"Pithom and Raamses"(ibid.). Rav and Shmuel [have different opinions about the meaning of this passage]. One said: Its real name was Pithom, and why was it called Raamses? Because one building after another collapsed [mitroses]. The other said: Its real name was Raamses, and why was it called Pithom? Because as they were building, it would gradually sink into the ground [pi tehom].

"But the more [the Egyptians] oppressed him, the more he will multiply and the more he will spread" (ibid. v. 12). It should have said, "The more they multiplied and the more they spread"? Resh Lakish said: The Holy Spirit announced [what was going to happen. They Egyptians said: "Lest they multiply and spread," but God replied: On the contrary! They will continue to multiply and spread forever!]

"[The Egyptians] became disgusted [vayakutzu] because of the children of Israel" (ibid.). This teaches us that the Israelites were like thorns [kotzim] in their eyes.

"The Egyptians enslaved the children of Israel with crushing (116b) harshness [farech]" (ibid. v. 13). R. Elazar said: They enslaved them with gentle words [peh rach, "a gentle mouth"]. R. Shmuel b. Nachmani said: [They enslaved them] with back-breaking work [perikah].

"They embittered their lives with hard labor involving mortar and bricks, as well as all kinds of work in the field" (ibid. v. 14). Rava said: At first it was mortar and brick, but afterward they made them do all kinds of work in the field; [they gradually increased the workload]. The verse concludes, "All the work they made them do was with crushing harshness." R. Shmuel b. Nachmani said in the name of R. Yonatan: They switched men's work for women and women's work for men. And even the one who explained farech above [v. 13] to mean peh rach, "gentle words," agrees that in the present verse farech definitely means harshness, [because they made them do work they were not accustomed to].

THE MERIT OF
THE RIGHTEOUS WOMEN

R. Avira expounded: As a reward for the righteous women who lived in that generation our forefathers were delivered from Egypt. When the women went to draw water, the Holy One, blessed be He, prepared for them small fishes in their jugs so that their jugs would come up half full of water and half full of fishes. They then set two pots on the fire, one for hot water and one for the fish. These they would carry to their husbands in the field; they would wash them, anoint them, feed them, give them to drink, and they would have relations with them [in the hidden places] between the boundaries of the field. For it says, "When you lie between the boundaries" (Psalms 68:14), [which the Gemara interprets to mean:] As a reward for "your lying between the boundaries" Israel merited the spoils of Egypt, for the verse continues, "[You will be like] the wings of a dove that is coated with silver and her pinion with brilliant gold" (ibid.).

When the women became pregnant they returned home, and when it was time for them to give birth they would give birth in the field under the apple tree [to hide from the Egyptians who would cast their babies into the river], for it says, "Under the apple tree I made you come forth [from your mother's womb]" (Song of Songs 8:5). The Holy One, blessed be He, would send an angel from heaven who cleansed the babies, and straightened their limbs like a midwife who straightens the limbs of a baby, as it says, "As for your birth: On the day you were born your umbilical cord was not cut, nor were you washed with water to smooth your skin" (Ezekiel 16:4). [The angel] would give them two round cakes, one of honey and one of oil, as it says, "He let them suckle honey from the bedrock and oil from the flinty cliff" (Deuteronomy 32:13).

When the Egyptians realized what was going on, they would come to kill the infants, but a miracle happened and they were swallowed up in the ground. The Egyptians then brought oxen to plough over them, as it says, "On my back the plowers plowed" (Psalms 129:3). After the Egyptians left the little babies came popping up out of the earth, breaking through the earth like grass in a field, as it says, "I made you as numerous as the plants of the field" (Ezekiel 16:7). And when these children had grown up they came to their homes in flocks, as the verse continues, "You increased and grew, and you came to have great charm" (ibid.). Do not read baadi adayim, "with great charm," but be'edrei adarim, "in flocks." And when God revealed Himself at [the parting of] the Red Sea, they were the first ones to recognize Him, for it says, "This is My God, [whom I have seen earlier,] and I will praise Him" (Exodus 15:2).

SHIFRAH AND PU'AH, THE VIRTUOUS MIDWIVES

"The king of Egypt said to the Hebrew midwives" (ibid. 1:15). Rav and Shmuel [offer different interpretations of this verse]. One said: The midwives were mother and daughter, and the other says they were daughter-in-law and mother-in-law. According to the one who said they were mother and daughter, they would be Jochebed and Miriam; and according to the one who said they were mother-in-law and daughter-in-law, they would be Jochebed and Elisheba [Aaron's wife].[30] There is a Baraita that supports the view that it was a mother and daughter team, for we learned in

a Baraita: Shifrah [one of the midwives] is Jochebed; and why was she called Shifrah? Because she made the limbs of the baby straight [meshapperet]. Another explanation of the name Shifrah is that the children of Israel were fruitful [sheparu] and multiplied in her days. Puah [the other midwife] is Miriam; and why was she called Puah? Because she would speak very sweetly [po'ah] to the baby. Another explanation of the name Puah is that she used to cry out [po'ah] with divine inspiration and say: My mother will give birth to a son who will save Israel.

[Pharaoh said to the midwives:] "When you deliver Hebrew women, you must look carefully at the birthstool [ovnayim]" (Exodus 1:16). [The Gemara asks:] What does ovnayim mean? R. Chanan said: Pharaoh gave the midwives an important clue and told them: When a woman crouches to deliver her child, her thighs grow cold like stones [avanim], [thus you can prevent a woman from secretly giving birth and then claiming that she had a miscarriage. This sign will enable you to know the exact moment of birth (Rashi)]. Another explanation of the word ovnayim is in accordance with the verse, "So I went down to a potter's shop, and behold, he was working on the potter's wheels [ovnayim]" (Jeremiah 18:3). Just as a potter's wheel has a thigh on one side and a thigh on the other side and the wooden block [he is sitting on] is in between; so also with a woman, there is a thigh on one side, a thigh on the other side, and the infant in between.

"If the [infant] is a boy, kill it, but if it is a girl, let it live" (Exodus 1:16). R. Chanina said: Pharaoh gave the midwives an important sign, namely: if it is a boy, his face is turned downward [at birth] and if a girl, her face is turned upward.

"The midwives feared God and did not do as the Egyptian king had ordered them. They helped the infant boys to live" (ibid. v. 17). We learned: not only did they not kill the children, but they supplied them with water and food.

"The midwives said to Pharaoh, 'Behold the Hebrew women are not like the Egyptians, for they are chayot.'" [The Gemara asks:] What does chayot mean? Do you think that they are midwives themselves [chayot means midwives]? Doesn't a midwife need another midwife to deliver her child! [But the meaning is,] they said to Pharaoh: This nation is compared to animals [chayot and animals give birth on their own]—Judah is called "a young lion" (Genesis 49:9); Dan is likened to "a snake on the road" (ibid. v. 17); Naphtali is called "a deer running free" (ibid. v. 21); Issachar, "a strong-boned donkey"; Joseph, "a first-born ox" (Deuteronomy 33:17); Benjamin, "a vicious wolf." Those sons of Jacob that Scripture compares to animals are described as such; the others are mentioned in general terms in the text, "Oh, how your mother was a lioness, crouching among lions" (Ezekiel 19:2).

"Because the midwives feared God, He gave them great families of their own" (Exodus 1:20). Rav and Shmuel have differing opinions about this. One said God gave them royal families; the other said He gave them priestly and Levite families. The one who said priestly and Levite families refers to Aaron and Moses [sons of Jochebed/Shifrah]; and the one who said royal families refers to David who descended from Miriam/Puah, for it says, "When Azubah died, Caleb married Ephrath [i.e., Miriam], who bore him Hur (I Chronicles 2:19), and it says, "David was the son of a certain Ephrathite" (1 Samuel 17:12), [which proves that King David descended from Miriam]. It says, "Caleb son of Hezron fathered children by Azubah [his] wife, and by Jerioth; and these are her sons: Jesher, Shobab, and Ardon" (1 Chronicles 2:18).

[The Gemara asks:] Caleb son of Hezron? He was the son of Jephuneh![31] [The Gemara answers: True, his father's name was Hezron, but he is called son of Jephuneh] because he was a son who turned away [panah] from the counsel of the spies. [The Gemara asks: But it seems that someone else was Caleb's father,] for it says that he was the son of Kenaz, "Othniel, son of Kenaz, Caleb's younger brother, conquered it" (Judges 1:13). Rava said: Caleb was the stepson of Kenaz. (12a) This can be proved by the passage, "Caleb son of Jephuneh the Kenizzite" (Joshua 14:6), [but not the son of Kenaz, implying that Caleb was raised by Kenaz, but Kenaz was not his real father]. We can infer from [the fact that Azubah was Caleb's wife] that Azubah is identical with Miriam. And why was she called Azubah? [Since Miriam was a sick girl] she was rejected [azavuhah—no one wanted to marry her]. [It says,] "Caleb fathered [holid] children by his wife Azubah" (1 Chronicles 2:18). [The Gemara asks:] "He fathered [holid] her"? [The Hebrew word holid can be translated to mean that Caleb fathered Azubah.]

But he married her! R. Yochanan said: [It was as though he fathered her, for] anyone who marries a woman for the sake of heaven, the Torah credits it to him as though he had fathered her, [and Caleb married Miriam for the sake of heaven, overlooking her infirmity]. [Miriam was also named] "Jerioth" because her face was [as pale] as curtains [yeriot]. "And these were her sons [baneha]" (ibid.). Don't read baneha [her sons] but boneha [her builder, a reference to her husband Caleb who built up her self-esteem; and the names that follow allude to him]. "Jesher"—Caleb was called by that name because he kept himself straight [yishar, and opposed the spies]. [He was called] "Shobab" because he turned his impulse aside [shibbev, and was not taken in by the designs of the spies]. [He was called] "Ardon" because he overcame [radah] his evil impulse. Others say, because his face looked like a rose [vered].

"Ashchur, the father of Teko'a, had two wives, Helah and Naarah" (1 Chronicles 4:5). [The Gemara expounds:] Ashchur is Caleb, and why is he called Ashchur? Because his face turned black [hush'charu] from fasting [to be saved from the counsel of the spies]. "The father"—Caleb became like a father to Miriam, [taking care of her during her sickness]. "Teko'a"—he attached [taka] his heart to his Father in heaven [so as not to be a party to the evil report of the spies]. "Had two wives"—Miriam became like two women. "Helah and Naamah"—she was not Helah and Naamah at the same time, but originally she was Helah [a sick woman, cholah], and in the end she became Naarah [a young girl, when she was healed]. "And the sons of Helah were: Zereth, Zohar, and Ethnan" (1 Chronicles 4:7). [These are all nicknames of Miriam. She was called] Zereth because all her friends were jealous [tzarah] of her beauty. [She was called Zohar] because her face was as radiant as the noon [tzoharayim]. Ethnan, because whoever saw Miriam would bring a present [etnan] to his own wife, [because the sight of Miriam would arouse his passion (Rashi)].

"Pharaoh then gave orders to all his people: Every boy who is born must be cast into the Nile" (Exodus 1:22). R. Yose b. R. Chanina said: He issued the same decree to his own people.[32] R. Yose b. R. Chanina further said: Pharaoh issued the decrees in three stages: first, "If the infant is a boy, kill it" (ibid. v. 16); then, "Every boy who is born must be cast into the Nile"; and finally he issued the same decree on every baby born in Egypt.

THE BIRTH OF MOSES

"A man of the house of Levi [Amram] went and married Levi's daughter" (ibid. 2:1). [The Gemara asks: It says, "Amram went."] Where did he go? R. Yehudah b. Zevina said: He went [and acted] on the advice of his daughter. We learned in a Baraita: Amram was the leader of his generation; when he saw that Pharaoh decreed that every boy who is born must be cast into the Nile he said to himself: Should we labor for nothing? [What is the point of having children?] Thereupon he divorced his wife. All the men of Israel then followed suit and divorced their wives. His daughter [Miriam] then said to him: Father, your decree is harsher than the wicked Pharaoh's decree; because Pharaoh decreed only against the males, whereas you decreed against the males and the females [neither boys nor girls will be born]. Pharaoh decreed only regarding this world [because the children that are killed live on in the World to Come], whereas you decreed regarding this world and the World to Come [since unborn children cannot come to the World to Come]. Furthermore, if the wicked Pharaoh makes a decree it is doubtful whether or not his decree will be carried out, but you are a tzaddik, and your decree will surely come to fruition, for it says, "You would utter a decree and it would be done" (Job 22:28). [At his daughter's urging Amram] got up and took his wife back; then everybody followed suit and took their wives back.

"He married Levi's daughter" (Exodus 2:1)—[The Gemara asks: In view of the above,] shouldn't it say, "he remarried"? R. Yehudah b. Zevina said: Amram acted as though he was marrying her for the first time; he made her sit under a canopy, and Aaron and Miriam danced before them, and the ministering angels chanted, "A joyful mother of children!" (Psalms 113:9).

"Levi's daughter." [The Gemara comments:] This is strange! She was one hundred-and-thirty years old,[33] and the text refers to her as "a daughter"! [The Gemara now explains that Jochebed was born as they were entering Egypt.] For R. Chama b. R. Chanina said: "Levi's daughter" refers to Jochebed who was conceived on the way to Egypt and who was born between the walls [as they were entering Egypt], as it says, "[Jochebed] who was born to Levi in Egypt" (Numbers 26:59); her birth was in Egypt but she was not conceived in Egypt.[34] Rav Yehudah said: [She is called "daughter"] because she regained her youthful appearance, [her wrinkles disappeared, and she was again a young woman (Rashi)].

"The woman became pregnant and had a son" (Exodus 2:2). [The Gemara asks:] But [when Amram took her back] she was already pregnant three months! R. Yehudah b. Zevina said: The passage is trying to tell us to compare the birth to the conception. Just as the conception was painless so was the delivery painless. This teaches us that righteous women were not subject to the decree and the curse of Eve [of the great pain of giving birth].[35]

"She realized that [the child] was good" (ibid.). We learned in a Baraita: R. Meir said: His name was Tov [good]. [We should remember that he was given the name Moses by Pharaoh's daughter.] R. Yehudah said: His name was Toviah; R. Nechemia said: She realized that he was worthy of prophecy; others say: ["The child was good" means that] he was born circumcised. And the Sages state: [She realized that he was good because] at the time he was born the whole house was filled with light—it says here, "She realized that he was good" and elsewhere it says, "God saw the light that is was good" (Genesis 1:4), [so we see that the concepts of "good" and "light" go hand in hand].

"She kept him hidden for three months" (ibid.). [She was able to hide him for three months] because the Egyptians counted the time of her pregnancy only from the time that she was remarried, but she had become pregnant three months earlier.

"When she could no longer hide him" (ibid. v. 3). Why? She should have continued hiding him! Because whenever the Egyptians heard that a woman had given birth they would bring one of their babies there so that it should cry and scream, in order that the newborn child should hear it and cry together with it, as it says, "Seize for us foxes, even the small foxes that destroy the tiny grapes" (Song of Songs 2:15); [a reference to the tiny Egyptian babies that caused the Jewish babies to reveal their hiding places].

MOSES SAVED BY PHARAOH'S DAUGHTER

"She took a box of bulrushes" (Exodus 2:3). Why bulrushes? R. Elazar said: From this you can infer that the righteous love money more than their own body. [She used bulrushes, which are less expensive than the more sturdy wood.] And why is this so? Because they never stretch out their hands to take things that do not belong to them, [so whatever they have is precious to them]. R. Shmuel b. Nachmani said: [She used bulrushes] because they are pliable and can withstand a collision with soft and hard materials. "She coated it with clay and tar" (ibid.). We learned: The clay was on the inside of the box and the tar on the outside, so that the righteous child should not smell the bad odor of the tar.

"She placed the child in it, and she placed it in the bulrushes near the bank of the Nile" (ibid.). R. Elazar said: In the Red Sea. R. Shmuel b. Nachmani said: (12b) It means reeds, as it says, "The reeds and the bulrushes will wither" (Isaiah 19:6).

"Pharaoh's daughter went to bathe in the Nile" (Exodus 2:5). R. Yochanan said in the name of R. Shimon b. Yocha'i: This passage teaches us that she went down there to cleanse herself of her father's idols; and so it says, "When my Lord will have washed the filth of the daughters of Zion" (Isaiah 4:4). "While her maids [holechot] walked along the Nile's edge" (ibid.). R. Yochanan said: The term holechot, "walked," is associated with death, and so it says, "Look, I am going [holeich] to die" (Genesis 25:12). [Why did the maids of Pharaoh's daughter die?] "She saw the box in the bulrushes" (ibid.). When the maids saw that she wanted to rescue Moses they said to her: Princess, it is customary that when a human king makes a decree, although no one heeds it, at least his children and the members of his household obey it. But you are violating your father's decree! At that moment Gabriel came and beat them to the ground, [and they died, hence the term holechot, "they went to die"].

"She sent her handmaid [amatah] to fetch it" (ibid.). R. Yehudah and R. Nechemiah differ [in their interpretation of the word amatah]. One said that the word means [she stretched out] her hand, and the other said it means that she sent her handmaid. The one who said that it means "her hand" bases his opinion on the word amatah [which can also mean "arm"]. The one who said that it means "her handmaid" did so because the text does not say yadah, "her hand." [The Gemara asks:] But according to the one who said that it means "her handmaid," you just said that Gabriel came and struck them all dead to the ground? [So how could she send a handmaid?]

[The Gemara answers:] Gabriel left her one maid, because it is not proper for a princess to be unattended. [The Gemara asks:] But according to the one who said that it means "her hand" it should have said unambiguously yadah ["her hand"]! [The Gemara answers:]

It teaches us that her arm became extended; for a master said [when discussing how Achashverosh's scepter miraculously was lengthened]:[36] You find the same thing happening with the arm of Pharaoh's daughter, and similarly with regard to the teeth of the wicked [being lengthened], as it says, "You have broken [shibbarta] the teeth of the wicked" (Psalms 3:8); and Resh Lakish said: Don't read shibbarta; read instead sherivavta, "that you have lengthened."[37]

"Opening the box she saw the child" (Exodus 2:6). [Literally: "She saw him the child."] [The Gemara asks:] It should have said "she saw the child"? R. Yose b. R. Chanina said: She saw the Shechinah with him. [The passage is interpreted to mean, "She saw Him with the child."]

"The boy began to cry" (ibid.). [The Gemara asks: In the same verse] the text calls him a both child and a boy! A Tanna taught: He was a child but his voice sounded like that of a grown boy, so says R. Yehudah. R. Nechemiah said to him: If so, [if his voice was abnormal] then you are implying that Moses had a physical flaw [which would disqualify him from officiating as a Levite in the Bet Hamikdash]? [The text refers to him as a boy] to teach us that his mother made for him a [chuppah], a semblance of a young man's marriage canopy in the box, saying: Perhaps I may not be worthy to live to see his marriage [chuppah] canopy.

"She had pity on him and said, 'This one is one of the Hebrew boys'" (ibid.). How did she know this? R. Yose b. R. Chanina said: Because she saw that he was circumcised. "This one is"—R. Yochanan said: Unknowingly she saw with prophetic insight that "this one" is in the river, but no other child will fall into the river [because on that day Pharaoh's decree to drown all boys was revoked]. And this is what R. Elazar had in mind when he said: What is meant by the verse, "If people say to you, 'Enquire of the fortunetellers and the diviners who chirp and snort'" (Isaiah 8:19)? They foresee and do not know what they foresee; they mutter and do not know what they mutter. [They receive a nebulous prophetic suggestion, but it is so vague as to be unintelligible.] When they saw that Israel's savior would be punished through water, they got up and decreed: "Every boy who is born must be cast into the Nile" (Exodus 1:22).

[But they were misled,] because once Moses was placed into the water they said: We do not see that sign any longer, [for, once he was in the river the prophecy had come true to a certain extent], so they told Pharaoh to cancel the decree. But they did not know that Moses was destined to be punished through the Mey Merivah, the Waters of Dispute,[38] [and that was what they actually saw in regard to water]. That is what R. Chama b. Chanina said: What is meant by the passage, "These are the Waters of Dispute [Mey Merivah] where the Israelites disputed with God" (Numbers 20:13)? That is the water that Pharaoh's astrologers saw and about which they were mistaken.

And that is what Moses had in mind when he said, "Six hundred thousand men on foot [ragli] are the people in whose midst I am" (Numbers 11:21), [ragli can also mean "because of me"]. Moses said to Israel: Because of me [floating in the box on the Nile], all of you were saved, [since that brought about the cancellation of Pharaoh's decree].

R. Chanina b. Papa said: The day [that Moses was rescued by Pharaoh's daughter] was the twenty-first of Nisan, and the ministering angels said to the Holy One, blessed be He: Master of the Universe! Shall the person that is destined to sing for You the Song of the Sea on this day [the twenty-first of Nisan] be punished on this day? R. Acha b. Chanina said: The day [that Moses was rescued by Pharaoh's daughter] was the sixth of Sivan, and the ministering angels said the Holy One, blessed be He: Master of the universe! Shall the person who will receive the Torah on this day [the sixth of Sivan] be punished on this day?

[The Gemara calculates:] It is understandable according to the one who said that his rescue was on the sixth of Sivan, [for the Torah says that Moses' mother kept him hidden for three months and then placed him in the Nile].[39] Hence [his rescue] took place three months after his birth. And a master said: Moses died on the seventh of Adar and was born on the seventh of Adar; and from the seventh of Adar to the sixth of Sivan is three months. But according to the one who says that his rescue took place on the twenty-first of Nisan, how could it have happened? [He was rescued three months after he was born, and from the seventh of Adar to the twenty-first of Nisan is only one month and fourteen days!] [The Gemara explains:] That year was a leap year [when a second Adar is inserted], so we have the greater part of the first Adar and the greater part of Nisan and the full second Adar in between. [That is what the Torah calls three months.]

"[The infant's] sister said to Pharaoh's daughter, 'Shall I go and call a Hebrew woman to nurse the child for you?'" (Exodus 2:7). [The Gemara asks:] Why is it that she emphasized "a Hebrew woman"? [The Gemara answers:] It teaches us that they carried Moses around to all the Egyptian women but he would not nurse from them. The Holy One, blessed be He, said: Shall the mouth that is destined to speak with Me nurse an unclean thing? [Egyptian women eat unclean food, traces of which shows up in the milk.] And this is the meaning of the passage, "To whom shall He teach knowledge, and to whom shall He explain a message?" (Isaiah 28:9). [The verse concludes,] "To [the tiny children] who are weaned from mother's milk, removed from the breasts."

"'Go,' replied Pharaoh's daughter. The young girl [almah] went and got the child's own mother" (ibid. v. 8). R. Elazar said: It teaches us that she went quickly like a young girl [almah]. R. Shmuel b. Nachmani said: [She is called] almah, [from the root alam "to hide,"] because she concealed [the fact that she was the baby's sister, and she was bringing the baby's mother].

"'Take [*heilichi*] this child and nurse it,' said Pharaoh's daughter [to the mother]" (ibid. v. 9). R. Chama b. Chanina said: Pharaoh's daughter prophesied but did not know what she was prophesying. She said: *Heilichi*, "take," [which can be seen as a contraction of] *hei shelechi*, "take what is yours." The verse continues, "And I will pay your fee." R. Chama b. Chanina said: Not only do the *tzaddikim* get back what they lost but they are even paid for it. [Not only did she get Moses back; she even was paid to take him back.]

"Miriam the prophetess, the sister of Aaron, took the drum in her hand" (Exodus 15:20). [The Gemara asks:] Why does the Torah call her Aaron's sister? Isn't she the sister of Moses too? R. Amram said in the name of Rav, others say R. Nachman said in the name of Rav: The Torah wants to teach us that she prophesied even while she was still only Aaron's sister, [before Moses was born]. (13a) She foretold: My mother will give birth to a son who will save Israel. When Moses was born and the whole house was filled with light, [Miriam's] father stood up and kissed her on her head and said to her: My daughter, your prophecy came true. But when the time came that he had to be tossed into the river [and they put him into that little box] her father got up and hit her on her head, saying: Where is your prophecy now? This is what the text says, "[The child's] sister stationed herself at a distance to see what would happen to him" (Exodus 2:4)—what would be the outcome of her prophecy.

JACOB'S FUNERAL

[The Mishnah said:] Joseph earned the merit of being the one to bury his father. [The Gemara asks:] Why is it that the first passage [reporting Jacob's funeral] states, "Joseph went up to bury his father, and with him went all of Pharaoh's servants, the elders of his household, as well as all the other elders of Egypt," and this is followed by, "All of Joseph's household—his brothers and his father's household [also went]" (Genesis 50:7); [here Pharaoh's servants precede Joseph's brothers]. Yet when they came back from the funeral it says, "Joseph returned to Egypt—he and his brothers and all who had gone up with him to bury his father" (ibid. v. 14); [the order is reversed]? R. Yochanan said: At first, before [the servants of Pharaoh] saw the honor of Israel they did not treat them with respect, [they placed themselves ahead of the brothers].

But on the way back, when they saw how they were honored they treated them with respect. For it says, "They came to the Barn of Atad (Thorns)" (ibid. v. 10). [The Gemara asks:] Do people store thorns in a barn? R. Abbahu said: It teaches us that they surrounded Jacob's coffin with crowns like a barn is surrounded with a hedge of thorns, because the sons of Esau, Ishmael, and Keturah also came. We learned: They all

came to wage war [to prevent Jacob from being buried in the Cave of Machpelah (*Maharsha*)], but when they saw Joseph's crown hanging on Jacob's coffin, each one took off his crown and hung it on Jacob's coffin. We learned: All in all, thirty-six crowns were hung on Jacob's coffin.

"They held a very great and solemn funeral oration" (ibid.). We learned: Even the horses and donkeys were involved in the lamentation, [they were draped in black]. When the funeral procession arrived at the Cave of Machpelah, Esau came and wanted to prevent the burial there. He said to them: "Mamre at Kiryat Arba is the same as Hebron" (Genesis 35:27). Now R. Yitzchak said: Kiriyat Arba is called by that name because four [*arba*] couples were buried there: Adam and Eve, Abraham and Sarah, Isaac and Rebeccah, and Jacob and Leah. [This is how R. Yitzchak interpreted it, but Esau said:] Jacob buried Leah in the portion that belongs to him, and the one remaining plot belongs to me. The brothers replied: You sold your share. He retorted: I admit that I sold my birthright; [the first-born has a right to a double share of the inheritance.[40] This additional share is what I sold,] but I did not sell my simple share of the inheritance, and this last portion in the Cave of Machpelah is mine].

They replied: You are making a mistake. You also sold your simple share of the inheritance! For it says, "[Jacob said], "You must bury me in the grave that I dug [*kariti*] for me" (ibid. 50:5). And R. Shimon b. Yehotzadak said: The word *kirah* denotes selling [*mechirah*], and in the coastal towns they use the term *kirah* instead of *mechirah*, "sale." Esau answered: Let me see the title! They replied: The title is in Egypt. Who should run and get it? Let Naphtali go, because he is a fast runner, for it says, "Naphtali is a hind let loose; he delivers words of beauty" (ibid. 49:21). R. Abbahu said: Don't read "words of beauty" [*imrei shefer*] but *imrei sefer*, "words of a document" [i.e., the title].

Chushim the son of Dan was there. Since he was hard of hearing he asked: What is going on, what is the commotion all about? They said: Esau is holding up the burial until Naphtali comes back from Egypt. Chushim shot back: Is my grandfather to lie in disgrace until Naphtali returns from Egypt? He took a club and clobbered Esau on the head so that his eyes dropped out and fell to Jacob's feet. Jacob opened his eyes and laughed, and this is what Scripture means when it says, "The righteous one will rejoice when he sees vengeance, he shall bathe his feet in the blood of the wicked one" (Psalms 58:11). At that moment the prophecy of Rebeccah was coming true, for she said, [referring to Jacob and Esau], "Why should I be bereaved of both of you on the same day?" (Genesis 27:45). Although they did not both die on the same day, still both were buried on the same day.

[The Gemara asks: Why did the brothers allow Joseph to carry the entire responsibility for their father's burial?] If Joseph had not taken care of Jacob's burial, would not his brothers have taken care of it? After all, it says, "For his sons carried him to the land of Canaan" (ibid. 50:13) [which proves that they were all involved]? [The Gemara answers: They would have wanted to assume the entire obligation,] but they said to themselves: Let us leave it to Joseph; for our father's honor will be greater when he is attended by kings rather than by ordinary people.

JOSEPH'S CASKET

[The Mishnah discussed the concept of measure for measure, citing as an example Joseph who personally took care of his father's burial,] and none other than Moses busied himself with Joseph's burial. [The Gemara comments:] We learned in a *Baraita*: Come and see how beloved were the *mitzvot* by our teacher Moses; for, while all the children of Israel were busy with the spoils of Egypt he was busy with *mitzvot* [taking Joseph's coffin out of Egypt]. For it says, "The wise of heart will seize good deeds" (Proverbs 10:8). But how did Moses know where Joseph was buried? It was told that Serach the daughter of Asher was left from the previous generation, so Moses went to her and asked, "Do you know where Joseph was buried?" She replied, "The Egyptians made a metal casket for him, which they placed in the Nile so that its waters should be blessed." [The fertile Nile valley is irrigated by the rising waters of the river.]

Moses went and stationed himself on the bank of the Nile and exclaimed, "Joseph, Joseph! The time has come which the Holy One, blessed be He, has sworn, 'I will redeem you', and the oath which you [Joseph] have adjured the children of Israel[41] [has reached the time of fulfillment]. If you will show yourself, fine; otherwise, we will be free of your oath." Immediately, Joseph's casket floated to the suface. Now don't be surprised that iron should float, for it says, "It happened as one of them was felling a beam that the iron [axhead] fell into the water . . . [The disciple cried out,] 'Woe is me, master, it is borrowed!' The man of God asked him, 'Where did it fall?" and he showed him the place. [Elisha] then cut a piece of wood and threw it there, and the blade floated up" (2 Kings 6:5,6). Now doesn't it stand to reason—if iron floated on account of Elisha who was a disciple of Elijah who was the disciple of Moses, surely [iron will float] on account of Moses our teacher!

R. Nathan said: Joseph was buried in the royal cemetery, and Moses went and stood by the cemetery of the kings and exclaimed, "Joseph! the time has come which the Holy One, blessed be He, has sworn, 'I will redeem you', and the oath that you adjured the children of Israel [has reached the time of fulfillment]. If you will show yourself, fine; otherwise, we are free of your oath.'" At that moment Joseph's casket started to shake. Moses took it and carried it with him. All the years that the Israelites were wandering in the wilderness, the *aron* [coffin] of Joseph and the *aron* [Ark][42] of the *Shechinah* were carried side by side, and onlookers used to ask: What is the significance of these two arks? They were answered: One is of the dead and one of the *Shechinah*. [They then would say:] Is it proper for a corpse to be carried alongside the *Shechinah*? They were told: [In this case it is proper, for] (13b) this one [Joseph] fulfilled all that is written in the other, [the Ten Commandments that were in the Holy Ark].

[The Gemara asks: You are implying that] if Moses had not busied himself with Joseph's remains, the Israelites would not have attended to it. But it says, "Joseph's bones which the children of Israel had brought up from Egypt they buried in Shechem" (Joshua 24:32), [evidence that after Moses' passing the children of Israel did take care of Joseph's remains and brought them to Eretz Yisrael]. In addition, if the Israelites had not attended to Joseph's remains, would not his own children have done so? [Why did his children allow anyone else to take care of their father's burial?] But it says, "And [Shechem where Joseph was buried] became a heritage for the children of Joseph" (ibid.) [so we see that Joseph was very dear to them; why then did they allow the entire people to attend to his burial]? [The Gemara answers: The children of Joseph] said to each other: Let us leave our father to be attended by the multitude, for it will be a greater honor for him than to be attended by a few people. And they also said: Leave him! His honor will be greater when the burial is performed by the great [like Moses] rather than by the small!

"They buried [Joseph] in Shechem" (Joshua 24:32). Why in Shechem of all places? R. Chama b. R. Chanina said: From Shechem they stole him,[43] and to Shechem we will return what is lost. [The Gemara asks:] The verses contradict each other. One verse says, "And *Moses* took the bones of Joseph with him" (Exodus 13:19), and another verse says, "The bones of Joseph which *the children of Israel* brought up" (Joshua 24:32). R. Chama b. R. Chanina said: Any person that does something but does not finish it, and someone else comes and finishes it, the Torah credits it to the one that completes it as though he had done the entire thing. [Since the children of Israel completed the burial, the bringing up of Joseph's remains was attributed to them.]

R. Elazar said: [A person who starts something but does not finish it] is also demoted from his greatness, for it says, "It was at that time that Judah went down from his brothers" (Genesis 38:1); [meaning, he was demoted]. Judah initiated the plan of saving Joseph when he said, "What gain will there be if we kill our brother" (Genesis 37:26), but he did not follow through on it and bring him back safely]. R. Shmuel b. Nachmani said: [If a person does not finish what he set out to do], he will even bury his wife and children; for it says, "Judah's wife, Bat Shua died" (ibid. 38:12), and it says, "Er and Onan [Judah's sons] died" (ibid. 46:12).

Rav Yehudah said in the name of Rav: Why was Joseph referred to in terms of "bones" during his lifetime? [Joseph said, "You must bring my bones up out of here" (ibid. 50:25)]. Because he did not protest when his father's honor was being belittled when his brothers said to him, "your servant, our father" (ibid. 44:31). Rav Yehudah also said in the name of Rav, others say that it was R. Chama b. R. Chanina: Why did Joseph die before his brothers? Because he assumed an attitude of superiority.

"Joseph had been brought down to Egypt" (ibid. 39:1). R. Elazar said: Don't read "had been brought down" [*hurad*] but "he brought down" [*horid*], because he brought down Pharaoh's astrologers from their lofty positions [when they could not interpret Pharaoh's dreams but he could].

THE FINAL DAYS OF MOSES

[The Mishnah said:] Whom do we have greater than Moses who was attended at his death by God Himself, as it says, "He buried him in the land of Moab" (Deuteronomy 34:6). [Moses said,] "And God said to me, 'Enough!'" (ibid. 3:26). R. Levi said: Moses used the term "enough!" to make an announcement [to the rebellious Korah and his party], and with the word "enough!" an announcement was made to him. He used the term "enough!" to make an announcement, for [he said to Korah and his rebellious party], "Enough! you sons of Levi" (Numbers 16:7); and with "enough" an announcement was made to him, [when God said to him, "Enough! Don't speak to Me any more about this" (Deuteronomy 34:6)]. Another explanation of the word *rav* "enough," is: You now have a master [*rav*] over you, namely Joshua [who is about to become the new leader]. Another explanation of *rav* is, [God said:] Do not implore Me any more [asking to be allowed to enter Eretz Yisrael], so that the people should not say: How stubborn is the Master, and how persistent is the disciple [Moses]. Why did Moses receive such a severe punishment [for striking the rock instead of speaking to it]? In the yeshivah of R. Yishmael it was explained: According to the camel's strength is the load it has to carry; [the greater a person, the more sternly he is judged].

"[Moses said to the people,] 'I am one hundred and twenty years old today'" (Deuteronomy 31:2). What is the meaning of "today"? [It means:] Today [the seventh of Adar] my days and years are completed, [for the seventh of Adar was also Moses' birthday]. This teaches you that the Holy One, blessed be He, completes the years of the righteous from day to day, and from month to month, for it says, "I will fill the number of your days" (Exodus 23:26). [Moses continued,] "I can no longer go out and come in" (Deuteronomy 31:2). What did he mean by "go out and come in"? Do you think it should be taken literally, [that he was physically weak]? But it says, "Moses was one hundred

and twenty years old when he died; his eye had not dimmed and his vigor had not diminished" (ibid. 34:7). It also says, "Moses ascended from the plains of Moab to Mount Nebo" (ibid. v. 1); and we learned in a *Baraita*: There were twelve steps, and Moses bounded them with one step! [So it cannot mean that he was frail and infirm.] R. Shmuel b. Nachmani said in the name of R. Yonatan: It means that Moses was no longer able "to go out and come in" in the words of the Torah, implying that the gates of wisdom were closed to him.

"So Moses and Joshua went and stood in the Tent of Meeting" (Deuteronomy 31:14). We learned: That *Shabbat* was a *Shabbat* when both leaders were teaching together, [the first part of the day Moses expounded, the last part of the day Joshua lectured], and the office was taken from one and transferred to the other.

We learned in a *Baraita*: R. Yehudah said: If we did not have a Scriptural verse to tell us this, it would be impossible to say the following: Where did Moses die? In the portion of Reuben, for it says, "Moses ascended from the plains of Moab, to Mount Nebo. And Nebo was located in the portion of Reuben, for it says, "The children of Reuben built . . . and Nebo" (Numbers 32:37). And where was Moses buried? In the portion of Gad, for it says, [in the blessing to Gad,] "He [Gad] chose the first portion for himself, for that is where the lawgiver's [Moses'] plot is hidden" (Deuteronomy 33:21). [Moses died in the portion of Reuben and was buried in the portion of Gad.] The distance between these two portions is about four miles. Who carried him those four miles? The passage comes to teach us that Moses was placed on the wings of the *Shechinah*, and the ministering angels declared, "He carried out God's justice and His ordinances with Israel" (ibid.). And what did the Holy One, blessed be He, say? Rav said: [God said,] "Who will stand up for Me against evil men? Who will stand up for Me against wrongdoers?" (Psalms 94:16). But Shmuel said: [God declared,] "Who is like the wise man? And who knows what things mean?" (Ecclesiastes 8:1). R. Yochanan said: [God declared,] "Where can wisdom be found?" (Job 28:12). R. Nachman said: [God proclaimed,] "So Moses, servant of God, died there" (Deuteronomy 34:5). Samalion said: [God said:] Alas! Moses died there, the great Sage of Israel![44]

We learned in a *Baraita*: R. Eliezer the Elder said: A heavenly Voice made a proclamation that was heard over an area of twelve square miles, the size of the camp of Israel, stating: "Moses died there, the great Sage of Israel!" Some say that Moses never died; for it says here, "Moses died there [*sham*]," and elsewhere it says, "And he was there [*sham*] with God forty days and forty nights" (Exodus 34:28); [the word *sham*, "there," appears in both verses]. Just as in the latter verse [Moses did not die] but was standing and serving God, so too in the former verse it means that he was standing and serving God.

"He buried him in the valley, in the land of Moab, opposite Beth Peor" (Deuteronomy 34:6). R. Berechyah said: The Torah gives us a hint within a hint [at the location of his grave], yet "no one knows his burial place to this day" (ibid.). The wicked [Roman] government once sent the following message (14a) to the governor of Bet Peor: Show us where Moses is buried. [An expedition was sent to search for it.] When they stood above the location, it seemed to be below; when they stood below, it seemed to be above. They then split up into two groups; to those that went to the top it seemed to be on the bottom; to those that went below it seemed to be on top. This bears out the passage, "No one knows his burial place." R. Chama b. R. Chanina said: Even Moses our teacher himself does not know where he is buried, for it says here, "No one [ish] knows his burial place," and [ish refers to Moses], for it says elsewhere, "And this is the blessing that Moses the man [ish] of God bestowed" (ibid. 33:1). R. Chama b. R. Chanina also said: Why was Moses buried opposite Beth Peor? [Why was he not buried in Eretz Yisrael as Joseph was?] To atone for the episode at Peor [where the Israelites behaved immorally with the daughters of Moab who seduced them to worship their idols].[45]

R. Chama b. R. Chanina further said: What is meant by the passage, "You shall walk after the Lord, your God" (Deuteronomy 13:5)? How is it possible for a human being to walk after the Shechinah? Doesn't it say, "For the Lord, your God is a consuming fire" (ibid. 4:24)? This is what it means: You should follow the attributes of the Holy One, blessed be He. Just as He clothes the naked, as it says, "God made garments of skin for Adam and his wife" (Genesis 3:21), so should you also clothe the naked. The Holy One, blessed be He, visited the sick, for it says, "God appeared to [Abraham] in the Plains of Mamre" [when he was recovering from his circumcision] (Genesis 18:1); so should you also visit the sick. The Holy One, blessed be He, comforted mourners, for it says, "After Abraham died, God blessed Isaac" (ibid. 25:11); so should you, too, comfort mourners. The Holy One, blessed be He, buried the dead, for it says, "He buried him in the valley"; so you, too, should bury the dead.

"God made garments of skin for Adam and his wife"—Rav and Shmuel offer different interpretations of this verse. One said: It means that the garments were made of a material that comes from skin [meaning wool]. The other said: It was a material that feels pleasant on the skin, [meaning linen, which is worn close to the skin].[46]

R. Simlai expounded: The Torah begins with an act of kindness and ends with an act of kindness. It begins with an act of kindness, for it says, "God made garments of skin for Adam and his wife." It ends with an act of kindness, for it says, "He buried him in the valley."

R. Simlai expounded: Why did Moses our teacher desire to enter Eretz Yisrael? Did he want to eat of its fruits or be satisfied with its goodness? [Surely not.] But this is what Moses said: Israel was given many mitzvot that can only be fulfilled in Eretz Yisrael. I want to enter Eretz Yisrael so that they should all be fulfilled by me. The Holy One, blessed be He, said to him: You are just seeking to receive the reward for fulfilling those mitzvot. I will consider it as if you had performed them. For it says, "Therefore, I will assign him a portion from the multitudes, and he will divide the spoils with the mighty—in return for having poured out his soul for death and being counted among the wicked, for he bore the sin of the multitudes and prayed for the wicked" (Isaiah 53:12). [The Gemara applies this verse to Moses:] Therefore I will assign him a portion from the multitudes—it is possible to think that his reward will be with the multitudes of later generations and not [like the reward of] the former generations [Abraham, Isaac, and Jacob]; therefore the verse continues, "and he will divide the spoils with the mighty," meaning, with Abraham, Isaac, and Jacob who were mighty in observing the Torah and the mitzvot.

"In return for having poured out his soul for death"—because he was ready to sacrifice his life, as it says, [after the sin of the golden calf, Moses said to God,] "Now, if You would, please forgive their sin. If not, You can blot me out from the book [of life] that You have written" (Exodus 32:32). "And being counted among the wicked"—because he was counted among those who were condemned to die in the wilderness. "For he bore the sin of the multitudes"—because he obtained forgiveness for the sin of the golden calf. "And prayed [yafgia] for the wicked"—because he pleaded for mercy on behalf of the sinners in Israel that they should repent. The word pegiah means prayer, as it says, "And you [Jeremiah]—do not pray for this people; do not speak up for them with a cry and a prayer, and do not entreat [tifga] Me" (Jeremiah 7:16).

DUST AND ASHES

(17a) R. Akiva expounded: When husband and wife are worthy of it, the Shechinah dwells among them; when they are unworthy, fire consumes them.[47] Rava said: If the fire [of domestic strife] is caused by the wife, it is more intense and flares up more easily than if it is caused by the husband. Why is this so? Because in the word ishah [wife], the alef and the shin which form eish [fire], are adjacent to each other, while in the word ish, the alef and shin are separated by a yud.

Rava said: Why does the Torah require that dust should be used in the ceremony of the sotah [the suspected adulteress]?[48] If she is proven to be innocent, she will have children who are like our father Abraham who said, "I am mere dust and ashes!" (Genesis 18:27); and if she is not innocent she will return to dust, [she will die from drinking the water].

Rava expounded: For saying, "I am mere dust and ashes" Abraham was rewarded that his descendants received two *mitzvot* [which are associated with dust and ashes], namely, the ashes of the red cow[49] and the dust of the ceremony of the *sotah*. [The Gemara asks:] But there is [another mitzvah associated with dust, namely, that of] covering the blood of slaughtered fowl. [Why didn't the Gemara mention that mitzvah too?][50] [The Gemara answers:] In the case of the mitzvah of covering the blood there is no benefit [to the one who performs it]. Now Rava said that Abraham's descendants were rewarded by two *mitzvot*, which means they derived benefit from them. But since the mitzvah of covering the blood does not bring any physical benefit, it was not mentioned. By contrast, the mitzvah involving the dust of *sotah* entails the benefit that if she is proven innocent and pure, domestic peace will return, and she will become pregnant.[51] The benefit inherent in the ashes of the red cow is that by means of the ashes a person who is ritually unclean becomes clean].

Rava expounded: For saying [to the king of Sodom], "Not a thread nor a shoelace! I will not take anything that is yours!" (Genesis 14:23), Abraham was rewarded that his descendants received two *mitzvot*, namely the thread of blue wool [in the *tzitzit*][52] and the straps of the *tefillin*. [The Gemara asks:] We understand that the mitzvah of *tefillin* is considered a reward, for it says, "Then all the nations of the world will realize that the name of God is associated with you, and they will be afraid of you" (Deuteronomy 28:10), and it has been taught: R. Eliezer the Elder said: This refers to the head-*tefillin*. But what physical benefit is there in wearing the blue thread of the *tzitzit*?

[The Gemara answers:] Because we learned: R. Meir used to say: Why was the color blue chosen for the mitzvah of *tzitzit*? Because blue resembles the color of the sea, and the sea looks like the color of the sky, and the sky is similar to the color of the Throne of Glory, for it says, "They saw a vision of the God of Israel, and under His feet was something like a sapphire brick, like the essence of a clear [blue] sky" (Exodus 24:10). And it says, "The appearance of a sapphire stone in the likeness of a throne" (Ezekiel 1:26). [Thus the benefit of keeping the mitzvah of *tzitzit* is that we have the *Shechinah* among us.]

THE EFFECTS OF
THE BITTER WATER

(20a) [The Mishnah says:] No sooner did [the *sotah*] finish drinking [the bitter water] than her face turned green, her eyes began to bulge, the veins in her face and body swelled, and the people there exclaimed: Remove her, so that the Temple Court should not be defiled! If she had a special merit, then the effects of the water would be deferred. Some merits defer the effects for one year, others for two years, and some for

three years. Because of that Ben Azzai said: A father is required to teach his daughter Torah, so that if she ever has to drink the bitter water, she will know that the reason its effect was delayed was that she had merits. [If she did not know this, she might think that the bitter water was ineffective and would continue to behave immorally. However, if she knows that it was her merit that postponed the effects, but that they may erupt at any time, she will worry and stop her loose behavior.] R. Eliezer says: Whoever teaches his daughter Torah teaches her immorality.[53] R. Yehoshua says: A woman would rather have one *kav* [meaning, live on a meager income] and have sexual gratification [from her husband], than nine *kav* [live a life of luxury] and sexual restraint [and abstinence because her husband is often away from home].[54] He used to say: A pious person who is a fool, a wicked man who is shrewd, an overly pious woman, and people who pretend to be pious, all these bring destruction on the world.

TORAH STUDY GREATER THAN
DOING *MITZVOT*

(21a) [The Mishnah said:] Some merits [of the *sotah*] defer the effects of the bitter water for three years. [The Gemara asks:] What kind of merit? Do you think the merit of studying the Torah? [That could not be,] for she is in the category of one who is not obligated to do a mitzvah but does it voluntarily. [Women are not required to study the Torah; therefore her merit of studying voluntarily is not strong enough to suspend the effects of the water.] We must therefore say that she had the merit of doing a mitzvah. But does the merit of doing a mitzvah protect her to such an extent [as to suspend the effects of the water]?

But we learned in a *Baraita*: This is what R. Menachem the son of R. Yose expounded: It says, "For the mitzvah is a candle, and the Torah is light" (Proverbs 6:23)—the verse compares the mitzvah to a candle and the Torah to light; the mitzvah to a candle, to tell you that just as a candle burns only for a limited time, so too, the fulfillment of a mitzvah protects only for a limited time; and the Torah is compared to light to tell you that, just as light shines forever, so does the Torah protect forever. And it says, [in reference to the Torah], "When you walk, it will lead you; when you lie down, it will watch over you; and when you wake up, it will talk with you" (ibid. 6:22). "When you walk it will lead you"—in this world; when you lie down it will watch over you"—in death; "and when you awake it will talk with you"—in the World to Come, [proving that the Torah protects forever].

This can be illustrated with a parable: A person is walking in darkness in the middle of the night. He is afraid of thorns, pits, thistles, wild beasts, and robbers, and he does not know the way. If he gets ahold of a burning torch he is saved from thorns, pits, and thistles, but he is still afraid of wild beasts and robbers, and he still does not know which way to go. As soon as dawn breaks, he is saved from wild beasts and robbers, but he still does not know which way to go. However, when he comes to a fork in the road [and reads the road sign] he is saved from everything; [the torch represents the *mitzvot*, the light of dawn symbolizes the Torah, and the fork in the road denotes the day of death. At any rate we see that the merit of Torah study is greater than that of *mitzvot*]. Another explanation of the above verse is: A transgression can erase [the reward of] a mitzvah, but not [the reward] of Torah study. [Just like a candle, a mitzvah can be extinguished, but the reward of the light of Torah cannot be extinguished], for it says, "Vast floods cannot quench love [i.e., Torah]" (Song of Songs 8:7).

[Since we see that a mitzvah has no great protective power, how did it have the power to suspend the effects of the water?] R. Yosef said: A mitzvah protects you [from punishment] and saves you [from the evil impulse] as long as you engage in the process of doing it; but when you are no longer engaged in it, it still protects you from punishment but it does not save you [from the *yetzer hara*] anymore, [therefore, the merit of the mitzvah has the power to protect the *sotah* from the effects of the water]. And as far as Torah is concerned, regardless whether you are busy studying it or not, the Torah you learned protects you [from punishment] and saves you [from the *yetzer hara*].

Rava challenged this: If that is so, Doeg and Ahitophel certainly engaged in the study of Torah; then why did it not save them from being seduced by their *yetzer hara*, for they became sinners [Rashi's interpretation]? But, said Rava, while you are engaged in learning Torah it protects you [from punishment] and saves you [from the *yetzer hara*], and when you are not busy learning Torah it protects you [from punishment] but does not save you [from the *yetzer hara*, and that is why Doeg and Achitofel, even though they learned Torah, were not saved from their *yetzer hara*]. By contrast, a mitzvah, whether you are busy doing it or not, protects you [from punishment, and that is why the *sotah* was protected from the effects of the water], but it does not save you [from the *yetzer hara*].

Ravina said: It definitely is the merit of Torah study [that made the water suspend its effects]. As for your question that a woman is not obligated to study Torah, [and therefore, her merit is not so strong,] I can answer you: True, women themselves are not commanded to study Torah; however, when they make sure that their sons study Chumash and Mishnah and they wait for their husbands until they come home from studying at the *bet midrash* should they not share the reward their husbands receive? [And the husbands are obligated to study Torah and are rewarded accordingly, so that the woman's share is strong enough to suspend the effects of the water.]

[The Gemara asks:] What does the expression, "the fork in the road" [in the phrase: When he reaches a

fork in the road he is saved from everything] stand for? R. Chisda said: It refers to a Torah scholar on the day of his death, [who has never strayed from the Torah. He is saved from everything]. R. Nachman b. Yitzchak said: It refers to a Torah scholar who has reached the level of fear of sin. Mar Zutra said: It refers to a Torah scholar who is able to interpret a law according to the *halachah*.

Another explanation [of the verse, "The mitzvah is a candle, and Torah is light"] is: A transgression cancels the merit of a mitzvah, but not the merit of Torah study. R. Yosef said: R. Menachem b. R. Yose explained this verse as though it were given on Sinai, and if Doeg and Ahitophel had interpreted it the same way, they would never have pursued David, saying, "God has forsaken him, pursue and catch him, for there is no rescuer" (Psalms 71:11). [They thought, since David sinned with Bathsheba he had lost all his merits, and they would be able to catch him.] On what verse do they base their view? On the verse, "Let Him not see anything shameful among you, and turn away from you" (Deuteronomy 23:15). But they did not know that a transgression erases [the merit] of a mitzvah, but not [the merit] of Torah study; [and since David was protected by the merit of his Torah study they could not catch him].

[The Gemara asks:] What is the meaning of the passage, "If a man offered all his wealth for that love [i.e., the Torah], he would be ridiculed and scorned" (Song of Songs 8:7)? Ulla said: You should not emulate Shimon the brother of Azariah, nor R. Yochanan of the family of R. Yehudah Hanasi [the Prince], but you should emulate Hillel and Shevna. [Shimon studied Torah and was supported by his brother Azariah; R. Yochanan was supported by R. Yehudah Hanasi. As a result, Azariah and R. Yehudah Hanasi received a share of the reward of the Torah learning of Shimon and R. Yochanan.] For when R. Dimi came [from Eretz Yisrael to Babylonia] he reported that Hillel and Shevna were brothers; Hillel [who lived in poverty] immersed himself in Torah study, and Shevna engaged in business. At the end Shevna said to Hillel: Come, let's be partners and share everything; [I will support you, and for that let me have a share of your Torah learning]. A heavenly Voice came forth and proclaimed, "If a man offered all his wealth for the love [of the Torah], he would be ridiculed and scorned" [meaning, a person should not give away the merit he earned by learning Torah to others who will support him, but he should rather learn Torah in poverty].

TEACHING TORAH TO WOMEN

(21b) [We learned in the Mishnah:] R. Eliezer says: Whoever teaches his daughter Torah teaches her immorality. [The Gemara asks:] How can it even enter your mind to say [that by teaching her Torah he teaches her] immorality! [The Gemara answers:] Read instead:

.

It is *as though* he taught her immorality. R. Abbahu said: What is R. Eliezer's reason? He bases it on the verse, "I am wisdom; I dwell in cleverness" (Proverbs 8:12). That means that as soon as the wisdom of Torah enters a person, a certain cleverness enters along with it, [and R. Eliezer was afraid that if a woman learns Torah, she will become clever and use her cunning for the wrong purposes]. And the Rabbis [who disagree with R. Eliezer], what do they do with the phrase, "I am wisdom"? They need it to substantiate the view of R. Yose b. R. Chanina; for R. Yose b. R. Chanina said: The Torah remains only with a person who stands naked [*arum*] because of it, [i.e., who retreats from all worldly concerns in order to learn Torah, even if it means being impoverished], as it says, "I am wisdom; I dwell in nakedness [*ormah*]." [*Ormah* can be translated as both cleverness and nakedness.] R. Yochanan said: The Torah remains only with a person who considers himself as if he is nothing, as it says, "[But as for] wisdom, it can be found in nothingness" (Job 28:12).

[We learned in the Mishnah:] R. Yehoshua said: A woman prefers one *kav* with sensuality to nine *kav* with restraint. What does he mean by that? This is what he means to say: A woman would rather have one *kav* [meaning, to live on a meager income] and have sexual gratification [in her marriage] than nine *kav* [i.e., living in luxury] but practice sexual restraint and abstinence [because her husband is often away from home].

FOOLS, FRAUDS, AND FELONS

[The Mishnah said:] A pious person who is a fool, a shrewd wicked man, a woman who is overly pious, and people who pretend to be pious, all these bring destruction on the world. [The Gemara asks:] What is meant by a pious person who is a fool? [The Gemara answers:] For example, a woman is drowning in the river, and he says: It is improper for me to look at her and save her.[55] What is meant by a shrewd wicked man? R. Chanina said: R. Yochanan says: A person who presents his case to the judge before the other party to the lawsuit arrives. [He is trying to sway the judge, which is forbidden.] R. Abbahu says: [A shrewd wicked man is] a person who gives a *perutah* [a small coin] to a poor man in order to bring his assets to two hundred *zuz*. [A person who owns less than two hundred *zuz* is considered a poor man; once he owns two hundred *zuz* he loses the status and the entitlements of a poor man.] For we learned in a Mishnah: Someone who has two hundred *zuz* may not take gleanings [*leket*], forgotten sheaves [*shikchah*], and the produce of the corner of the field [*pei'ah*], or the tithe of the poor [*maaseir ani*],[56] but if he has one *zuz* less than two hundred, even if a thousand people give him [their gifts to the poor] at the same time, he is allowed to accept.[57] [The shrewd wicked man gives the poor man one coin, thereby disqualifying him from taking these

gifts, and now the wicked man's own poor relatives will come and take those gifts (Rashi).]

R. Yosef b. Chama said in the name of R. Sheshet: [A shrewd wicked man] is a [corrupt] person who [pretends to be pious] and influences others to follow in his ways. R. Zerika said in the name of R. Huna: It is a person who is lenient with himself [when interpreting *halachah*] and strict with others. Ulla said: It is a person (22a) who learned Chumash and Mishnah but did not attend Torah scholars, [and learn from them the reasons behind the laws of the Mishnah. Lacking this knowledge he gives incorrect halachic rulings]. For we have learned: If a person has studied Chumash and Mishnah but has not served under Torah scholars, R. Eliezer said: Such a person is an *am haaretz* [i.e., a person who is negligent about the observance of the laws of ritual purity and tithing]. R. Shmuel b. Nachmani said: He is a boor. R. Yannai said: He is like a Samaritan [whose bread and wine are forbidden to be consumed]. R. Acha b. Yaakov said: He is like a magician [who fools the people with sleight-of-hand tricks]. R. Nachman b. Yitzchak said: It is likely that R. Acha b. Yaakov's description is the most accurate, because there is a popular saying: The magician mumbles his incantation and doesn't know what he is saying; the pseudo-scholar, too, rattles off his Mishnah without knowing what it means.

WHO IS AN *AM HAARETZ*?[58]

Our Rabbis taught: Who is an *am haaretz* [and therefore cannot be trusted to observe the laws of ritual purity and the tithes]? Anyone that does not recite the *Shema* in the morning and evening with its accompanying *berachot*, so says R. Meir. The Sages say: Anyone that does not put on *tefillin*. Ben Azzai says: Anyone that does not have *tzitzit* on his garment. R. Yonatan b. Yosef says: Anyone that has sons and does not bring them up to study Torah. Others say: Even a person who learned Chumash and Mishnah but did not serve under a Torah scholar is considered an *am haaretz*. If he learned Chumash but not Mishnah, he is considered a boor. If he learned neither Chumash nor Mishnah, Scripture says about him, "I will sow the House of Israel and the House of Judah the seed of man and the seed of cattle" (Jeremiah 31:26).

It says, "Fear God, my child, and the king. Do not mix with people who are inconsistent [*shonim*]" (Proverbs 24:21). R. Yitzchak said: This refers to people who learn *halachah* [without having served under a Torah scholar, and who are uninformed about the underlying reasons of the rulings of the Mishnah]. [The Gemara asks:] This is obvious! [The Gemara answers: No, it is not, because] you could have argued that the verse referred to people who repeat a sin [*shonim* also means "repeat"], based on R. Huna's teaching, for R. Huna said: When a person commits a transgression and repeats it, it appears to him as if it were permitted.

Therefore, R. Yitzchak lets us know [that "repeating a sin" is not the meaning of *shonim* in this text].

We learned: Scholars bring destruction on the world. [The Gemara asks:] How can it even enter your mind to say that scholars bring destruction on the world! Ravina answered: It refers to scholars who render [erroneous] halachic decisions based on superficial knowledge of the Mishnah [without knowing the underlying reasons]. There is a *Baraita* to the same effect: R. Yehoshua said: How can you say that Torah scholars are destroyers of the world! On the contrary, Torah scholars are the builders of the world! For it says, "The ways [*halichot*] of the world are his" (Habakkuk 3:6). [*Halichot* is read as *halachot*, and the passage can be paraphrased, "The world endures because of those who study *halachot*."] [The Gemara answers:] The text refers to pseudo-scholars who render halachic decisions based solely on a cursory reading of the Mishnah [without an understanding of the complex reasoning that led to the ruling of the Mishnah].

HYPOCRITICAL WOMEN
[We learned in the Mishnah:] . . . an overly pious woman causes the destruction of the world. [The Gemara says:] The Rabbis taught: A girl who prays constantly, a frivolous widow, and "a minor whose months are not completed"[59] cause the destruction of the world, [because they use their piety to cover up their shameful behavior]. [The Gemara asks:] Is that so? But R. Yochanan said: We can learn fear of sin from a girl, and to trust that [good deeds] will be rewarded from a widow! Fear of sin from a girl—for R. Yochanan heard a girl prayerfully fall on her face, saying: Master of the universe! You created Gan Eden and Gehinnom, You created evildoers and *tzaddikim*. May it be Your will that no one should stumble because of me [and forfeit his share in Gan Eden, and land in Gehinnom]. [We can learn from a widow] to trust that [good deeds] will be rewarded—for there was a certain widow who lived near a synagogue, yet she used to come every day to pray at the yeshivah of R. Yochanan. So he said to her, "My daughter, isn't there a synagogue in your neighborhood?" She replied, "Rabbi, [if I pray there,] I will not receive the reward for walking the extra distance [to pray in your yeshivah]." [So we see that both the girl and the widow are held up as examples of righteouness conduct?]

[The Gemara answers:] When the Mishnah says [that they bring destruction on the world] it has in mind women like Yochni the daughter of Retivi [a widow who, by using witchcraft, created difficulties for women in labor and then offered to pray for their easy delivery (Rashi); in other words, the Mishnah refers to women who use their piety as a smokescreen to cover their depraved character]. [The Gemara asks:] What does the Mishnah mean when it speaks of "a minor whose months are not completed"? In Babylonia

they explained that it refers to a yeshivah student who rebels against his teacher [such a student's life is cut short]. R. Abba said: It refers to a student who is not qualified to decide halachic questions but decides them anyway. For R. Abbahu said in the name of R. Huna who said it in the name of Rav: What does, "For she has felled many victims; the number of her slain is huge" mean (Proverbs 7:26)? "For she has felled many victims" refers to a student who is not qualified to decide halachic questions but decides them. "The number of her slain is huge" refers to a scholar who is qualified to decide halachic questions but does not decide them. (22b) At what age is a scholar qualified? After he has studied Torah for forty years. Is that so? Hasn't Rava decided questions of *halachah*, [and he died at forty years of age, so he could not have studied Torah for forty years]?[60] [The Gemara answers:] If a scholar is as astute as the local chief rabbi, [he is allowed to rule on halachic matters].

FALSE PIETY
[The Mishnah said:] People who pretend to be pious bring destruction on the world. [The Gemara comments:] Our Rabbis have taught: There are seven types of [false] *perushim* [Pharisees]:[61] There is the *shichmi* Pharisee, the *nikfi* Pharisee, the *kiza'i* Pharisee, the *meduchya* [pestle] Pharisee, the Pharisee who constantly calls out, "Let me know what my duty is, and I'll do it!", the Pharisee out of love, and the Pharisee out of fear. The *shichmi* Pharisee [wants to impress others with his piety]. He acts like Shechem [who was circumcised for selfish reasons].[62] The *nikfi* Pharisee knocks [*menakef*] his feet together [taking tiny steps, walking with overdone humility]. The *kiza'i* Pharisee—R. Nachman b. Yitzchak said: He is the one who makes his blood flow [*makiz*, when he knocks his head] against the walls [because he closes his eyes so as not to look at women]. The *meduchya* [pestle] Pharisee Rabbah b. Shila said: [His head] is bowed [in a show of sanctimonious modesty] like a pestle in a mortar. The Pharisee who constantly calls out, "Let me know what my duty is, and I'll do it!" [The Gemara asks:] But that is commendable! No, he really is saying, "What is there for me to do that I have not done already!" [as if he had fulfilled every obligation].

The Pharisee out of love and the Pharisee out of fear—Abbaye and Rava said to the Tanna [who was reporting this *Baraita*:] Do not mention the Pharisee out of love and the Pharisee out of fear. [They thought it meant "out of love of the reward for the *mitzvot*" and "out of fear of punishment for violating the commandments."] For Rav Yehudah said in the name of Rav: A person should always engage in Torah and *mitzvot*, even if he is not doing it for the sake of Torah, because if you begin by doing *mitzvot* for the wrong motives, you will eventually perform them for the right ones. R. Nachman b. Yitzchak said: What is hidden is hidden, and what is revealed is revealed; [but nothing is hidden from the Heavenly Tribunal], and it will exact punishment from people who wrap themselves in a *tallit* [and sanctimoniously play the part of a sage]. King Yannai told his wife: Do not fear the Pharisees,[63] nor the non-Pharisees, but only the hypocrites, who masquerade as Pharisees. For their deeds are like Zimri's but they demand a reward like that of Pinchas.[64]

THE *SOTAH* WHO
WAS INNOCENT

(26a) We learned in a *Baraita*: [It says, regarding the *sotah* who was made to drink the water], "If the woman is pure and has not been defiled, she will remain unharmed and will become pregnant" (Numbers 5:28); so that if she was sterile, she will conceive, so says R. Akiva. R. Yishmael said to him: In that case, all sterile women will seclude themselves [with a man, become a *sotah*, drink the water] and conceive, and since this one did not seclude herself, she will lose out! [By not becoming a *sotah* she will remain sterile!] If so, what is the sense of "she will remain unharmed and will become pregnant"? [The verse means:] If until now she gave birth with pain, she will now give birth with ease; if until now she had only girls, she will now give birth to boys; if she had short children, she will have tall ones; if dark ones, she will have fair ones.

THE SONG OF THE SEA

[The Mishnah says:] On that day[65] R. Akiva expounded: "Moses and the children of Israel then sang this song to God. They said:" (Exodus 15:1). There was no need for the phrase, "They said:", so why was it written? It teaches us that the Israelites responded to each sentence after Moses.

(30b) We learned in a *Baraita*: On that day R. Akiva expounded: When Israel came up out of the Red Sea they decided to sing a song of praise, and how did they sing the song? Like an adult who leads in reading the *Hallel* on behalf of the congregation, and the congregation responds by saying *Hallelujah* after each verse. [This was the pattern that was followed at the singing of the Song of the Sea.] Moses began by saying, "I will sing to God," and they responded "I will sing to God." Moses went on to say, "for His great victory," and they would chant [the refrain], "I will sing to God." R. Eliezer the son of R. Yose Hagelili says: [The pattern of the Song was] like when a minor reads the *Hallel* for a congregation. [A minor cannot exempt the congregation from reciting the *Hallel*, therefore,] the congregation must repeat everything he says. Thus, Moses said, "I will sing to God," and they responded, "I will sing to God"; Moses then said, "for His great victory," and they repeated, "for His great victory."

R. Nechemiah says: [The pattern of the Song was:] Like a *chazzan*[66] who leads the congregation [in the *berachot* before the *Shema*] in the synagogue; he begins first, and they respond after him. [The *chazzan* would recite the *berachot* before the *Shema*, which the congregation would repeat; then they would read the *Shema* together with the *chazzan*. So, too, at the Song of the Sea, Moses and the people were divinely inspired, so that they all sang the same Song simultaneously (Rashi).] [The Gemara asks:] On what essential point do they disagree? R. Akiva holds that the phrase, "They said:" (Exodus 15:1) refers to the first words of the Song, [they always responded with the refrain, "I will sing to God."] R. Eliezer the son of R. Yose Hagelili holds that "They said" refers to every phrase Moses said, [they repeated every line Moses said.] R. Nechemiah holds that *vayomeru*,"they said," implies that they all sang together with Moses, and *leimor*, "saying," denotes that Moses began first.

We learned in a *Baraita*: R. Yose Hagelili expounded: When Israel came up out of the Red Sea they decided to sing a song of praise, and how did they sing the song? The infant was lying on his mother's lap, and the newborn was sucking at his mother's breast, but once they saw the *Shechinah*, the infant raised his neck and the newborn removed his mouth from his mother's breast, and they exclaimed, "This is my God, I will exalt Him" (ibid. v. 2). As it says, "Out of the mouths of babes and sucklings You have established strength" (Psalms 8:3). R. Meir used to say: From where do we know that even the embryos in their mothers' womb uttered a song? For it says, (31a) "In assemblies [when Israel assembled at the Red Sea] bless God, the Lord, O you who are from the wellspring of Israel" (Psalms 68:27) [i.e., even those who are still in the womb]. [The Gemara asks:] But [the embryos] could not see [the *Shechinah*], then how could they say, "This is my God"?! R. Tanchum said: Their mothers' abdomens became transparent like a piece of glass, and they were able to see [the *Shechinah*].

LOVE AND FEAR OF GOD

[We learned in the Mishnah on 27b:] On that day R. Yehoshua b. Hurkenos expounded: Job served the Holy One, blessed be He, only out of love, as it says, [Job said, "Were He to kill me, I would still yearn for Him [*lo*]" (Job 13:15).] But it is still doubtful whether the meaning is "I would yearn for Him" or "I would not yearn for Him," [because when *lo* is spelled with a *vav* it means "for Him," but when spelled with an *alef* it means "not"]. Therefore, there is another verse where Job says, "Until I perish I will not renounce my claim of innocence from myself" (ibid. 27:5). This teaches that Job served God out of love; [for only a person who serves God out of love will make such a statement (*Maharsha*)]. R. Yehoshua b. Chananiah said: Who will remove the dust from your eyes, R. Yochanan b. Zakkai! [If only you were still alive!] For you have been expounding all your life that Job served God only out of fear, as it says, "That man [Job] was wholesome and upright, he feared God and shunned evil" (ibid. 1:1). Did not R. Yehoshua [b. Hurkenos], your student's student,[67] teach that he served God out of love? (31a) [The Gemara asks: How can there be a doubt whether *lo* is spelled with a *vav* or with an *alef*?] Why don't we check the text and see whether *lo* is written with a *vav* or an *alef*? If it is written *lamed alef*, then it means "not," and if it is written *lamed vav*, it means "for Him."

[The Gemara asks:] Is it then a rule that wherever *lo* is written *lamed alef* that it means "not"? After all it says, "In all their troubles there was trouble for Him [*lo*]" (Isaiah 63:9), where *lo*, for Him," is spelled *lamed alef*. Are you going to say that the meaning of *lo* is "not," [and the verse supposedly is telling us that when the Jewish people are troubled God does *not* feel their affliction]? And if you say that this is the meaning of the verse, then how do you explain the continuation of the verse, "So an angel from before Him saved them"? [which clearly indicates that God shares the anguish of the Jewish people, and that *lo*, although written *lamed alef*, means *lamed vav*, "for Him."] But we must say that *lo* [spelled *lamed alef*] can be interpreted either as "not" or as "to him." [That is why R. Yehoshua b. Hurkinos was not sure whether Job meant "I yearn for Him" or "I do not yearn for Him."]

We learned in a *Baraita*: R. Meir says: It says, with reference to Job, "He feared God" (Job 1:1), and it says about Abraham, "I know that you fear God" (Genesis 22:12); just as "fearing God" that is mentioned regarding Abraham was out of love, so, too, "fearing love" mentioned in connection with Job means out of love. [The Gemara asks:] How do we know [that Abraham served God out of love]? For it says, "Offspring of Abraham who loved Me" (Isaiah 41:8). [The Gemara asks:] What is the difference between a person who serves God out of love and one who serves Him out of fear?

[Says the Gemara:] It is mentioned in the following *Baraita*: R. Shimon b. Elazar says: A person who is motivated by love of God is greater than one who is motivated by fear of God, because with the latter the merit lasts only for one thousand generations, but with the former the merit endures for two thousand generations. It says here, "But for those who love Me, . . . I show love for thousands of generations" (Exodus 20:6). And it says [concerning those who serve God out of fear], "He safeguards the covenant and the kindness for those who love Him and for those who observe His commandments [out of fear], for a thousand generations" (Deuteronomy 7:9). [The Gemara asks:] But in this latter verse it also says, "For those who love Him . . . for a thousand years" [which seems to indicate that even for a person who serves out of love the merit lasts only for one thousand generations]? [The Gemara answers:] In the first verse, the words "thousands" is adjacent to "them that love Me" [which indicates that if a person

serves out of love, his merit is preseved for two thousand years] whereas in the second verse "thousand" is connected to "keep His commandments" [which signifies that if a person serves out of fear, his merit endures for only one thousand generations].

There were two disciples who were sitting in front of Rava. One said to him: I dreamed that they read to me the verse, "How abundant is Your goodness that You have stored away for those who fear You" (Psalms 31:20). The other said: I dreamed that they read to me the verse, "But all who take refuge in You will rejoice, they will sing joyously forever, You will shelter them, and those who love Your name will exult in You" (ibid. 5:12). Rava replied: Both of you are completely righteous rabbis; one serves God out of love, and the other out of fear.

SING YOUR PRAISES
IN A LOW VOICE

(32b) The Rabbis taught: R. Shimon b. Yochai said: When a person relates praises about himself he should say it in a low voice; however, when he makes derogatory statements about himself he should raise his voice. That a person should announce his praises in a low voice can be inferred from the confession that is made when removing the tithes[68] [wherein we state that we have fulfilled all our obligations, and the Torah does not say *ve'anita*, that we should announce this in a loud voice]. And that he should make derogatory statements about himself in a loud voice can be derived from the declaration made at the offering of the first fruits. [where we state, "An Aramaean [Laban] tried to destroy my forefather" (Deuteronomy 26:5). Thus we say that we had an ancestor Laban who was evil, and the Torah tells us to declare this in a loud voice, "Then you shall call out [*ve'anita*] and say" (ibid.).

[The Gemara asks:] Is it true that a person should announce his disgrace in a loud voice? But R. Yochanan said in the name of R. Shimon b. Yochai: Why did the Rabbis arrange that the *Shemoneh Esrei* should be recited quietly? In order not to embarrass people who committed sins [who want to confess their transgressions]. For the Torah did not set aside separate areas on the Altar for sin-offerings and burnt-offerings, [so that onlookers should not be able to identify the person who brings a sin-offering, so as not to embarrass him. In view of this, how could R. Shimon b. Yochai say that a person who relates shameful things about himself should do so in a loud voice]? [The Gemara answers:] Don't say that he should relate loudly "shameful things," but "his troubles," as we learned in a *Baraita*: It says, "[A leper] must call out, 'Unclean! unclean!'" (Leviticus 13:45)—it is necessary for the leper to announce his distress publicly so that the public should pray for his recovery. [So, too, a person should announce his troubles so that people will pray on his behalf.]

DO THE ANGELS UNDERSTAND ARAMAIC?

(33a) [The Mishnah said that the *Shemoneh Esrei*[69] may be recited in any language.] [The Gemara comments:] Since in the *Shemoneh Esrei* you are praying for our needs, you may pray in any language you wish. [The Gemara asks:] Is it true that the *Shemoneh Esrei* may be said in any language? But Rav Yehudah said: A person should never pray for his needs in Aramaic, since R. Yochanan said: If anyone prays for his needs in Aramaic, the ministering angels do not pay attention to him, [and do not convey his prayer to God], because the angels do not understand Aramaic. [So how can the Mishnah say that you may pray in *any* language?] [The Gemara answers:] This presents no difficulty. If a person prays by himself, he should not use Aramaic; but if he prays with a congregation [he may pray even in Aramaic, because he does not need the help of the angels to convey the prayer into the Presence of God. The fact that the prayer was said together with a congregation gives it the power to rise to God's Presence].

[The Gemara asks:] Is it true that the ministering angels do not understand Aramaic? But we learned in a *Baraita*: Yochanan, the *Kohen Gadol* [when he entered the Holy of Holies on Yom Kippur] heard a heavenly Voice proclaiming [in Aramaic], "The young men who went to wage war against Antioch were victorious." [Young *kohanim* of the Hasmonean family went into battle against the Greeks before Yom Kippur. The battle took place on Yom Kippur, and Yochanan the *Kohen Gadol* heard the heavenly Voice while performing the service in the Holy of Holies (Rashi).] And the heavenly Voice, which was the voice of an angel, spoke Aramaic! It also happened with Shimon Hatzaddik that he heard a heavenly Voice emanating from inside the Holy of Holies, proclaiming [in Aramaic], "The decree that the enemy intended to enact against the *Bet Hamikdash* has been rescinded."

King Gaskalgus [Caligula] was killed at that time, and all his decrees were abolished. They wrote down the exact time [when the heavenly Voice spoke], and it coincided with the time of the king's death. And the heavenly Voice [which was that of an angel] spoke in Aramaic! [Again proof that the angels speak Aramaic.] [The Gemara answers:] If you prefer, say that a heavenly Voice is different, [the angel in charge of the heavenly Voice does understand Aramaic], because it is meant to be understood [by everyone, so the angel knows all languages]. Or if you wish, say that the angel in charge of the heavenly Voice was Gabriel; for the Gemara says:[70] Gabriel came and taught [Joseph] the seventy languages. [So Gabriel knows all languages, including Aramaic, but the other angels do not.]

THE CROSSING OF THE JORDAN

(33b) The Rabbis taught: How did Israel cross the Jordan [when they left the wilderness and entered Eretz Yisrael]? [While they were journeying in the wilderness,] the Ark always traveled behind two banners [i.e., tribal divisions][71]; but on the day of the crossing it traveled in front, as it says, "Behold, the Ark of the Covenant of the Master of all the earth is passing before you in the Jordan" (Joshua 3:11). [While they were traveling,] the Levites always carried the Ark; but on this day the *kohanim* carried it, as it says, "It shall happen, just as the soles of the feet of the *kohanim*, the bearers of the Ark of God, Master of the entire earth, rest in the waters of the Jordan . . ." (ibid. v. 13).

We learned in a *Baraita*: R. Yose said: In three places we find that the *kohanim* carried the Ark: when they crossed the Jordan, when they marched around Jericho,[72] and when they returned the Ark to its permanent place [in the Holy of Holies in Solomon's Temple].[73] (34a) As soon as the feet of the *kohanim* touched the water, the water flowed backward, for it says, "When the bearers of the Ark arrived at the Jordan, and the feet of the *kohanim*, the bearers of the Ark, were immersed in the edge of the water . . . the waters descending from upstream stood still and they rose up in one column" (Joshua 3:15,16).[74] And how high was that column? A height of twelve *mil* and a width of twelve *mil*, equal to the size of the camp of Israel. [They crossed the Jordan in the formation in which they were camped, twelve *mil* by twelve *mil*. Thus, the time it took them to cross was the time it took to travel twelve *mil*. Therefore, the water piled up to a height of twelve *mil*, until the last person crossed the Jordan.] This is the opinion of R. Yehudah.

R. Elazar b. R. Shimon asked him: According to you, [comparing the water to the people], which is faster, man or water? Certainly water flows faster [than a person can walk]. Therefore, if the water began to flow again after reaching a height of only twelve *mil*, it would have drowned some people who had not crossed yet. We must therefore say that the water was piled up in stacks to a height of more than three hundred *mil*, until all the kings of the East and West saw it, for it says, "It happened when all the Amorite kings who were on the western side of the Jordan and all the Canaanite kings who were by the sea heard that God had dried up the waters of the Jordan for the sake of the children of Israel until they had crossed, their hearts melted, and there was no longer any spirit in them because of the children of Israel" (ibid. 5:1). And also Rahab the woman innkeeper said to Joshua's messengers, "For we have heard how God dried up the waters of the Sea of Reeds" (ibid. 2:10). And she continued, "We heard it, and our hearts melted—no spirit remained in any man because of you" (ibid. 11).

While they were still in the Jordan, Joshua told them: You should know on what condition you are crossing the Jordan. It is on condition that you drive out the inhabitants of the land, for it says, "You must drive out the land's inhabitants ahead of you" (Numbers 33:52). If you do this, fine; otherwise the water will return and drown you [*oteichem*]. What does *oteichem* mean? I and you [will drown and not enter Eretz Yisrael]. While they were still in the Jordan, Joshua told them, "Each of you lift a stone onto his shoulder, corresponding to the number of tribes of the children of Israel" (Joshua 4:5). [These stones were placed in the Jordan at the point where the *kohanim* were standing.] And he continued, "So that this will be a sign in your midst, when your children ask tomorrow, saying, 'Of what significance are these stones to you?' . . ." (ibid. v. 6).

It was to be a monument for the children that their fathers had crossed the Jordan. While they were still in the Jordan, Joshua told them, "Pick up twelve stones from the spot exactly in the middle of the Jordan, where the *kohanim*'s feet are standing; take them along with you and deposit them in the lodging place" (ibid. v.3). You might think that they were to deposit them wherever they would camp for the night; therefore the text states, "where you will spend *this* night." [Thus there were two sets of twelve stones: one was left in the Jordan as a memorial; the other they carried with them and deposited in Gilgal.]

R. Yehudah said: Abba Chalafta, R. Elazar b. Matya, and R. Chanania b. Chachinai saw those twelve stones [which were lifted out of the Jordan], and they estimated that each one weighed about forty *se'ah*. And we have a tradition that the weight a person can lift up on his shoulder is a third of the weight he can carry [if someone else would put it on his shoulder. Consequently, each person could have carried a weight of one hundred and twenty *se'ah*.] From this we can figure out how heavy a cluster of grapes was [that was carried by the spies], for it says, "The cluster of grapes . . . which was carried on a pole by two" (Numbers 13:23). [The Gemara asks:] Once the text told us that they carried it on a pole, don't I know that it was carried by two men? Why then does it say that it was "carried on a pole by two"?—[It means:] It was carried on two poles. [Four people carried that cluster of grapes.]

R. Yitzchak said: It was a level on top of another level. [There were two parallel poles, carried by four people. Underneath these poles there were two more parallel poles, each carried by four people, running diagonally across. Thus the poles formed a letter X (Rashi).] How was everything carried? Eight spies carried the grape cluster, one carried a pomegranate, and one carried a fig,[75] and Joshua and Caleb did not carry anything. Either because they were the most respected among them [and it would not befit them], or because they were not part of the conspiracy of the spies.

[The Gemara now returns to the debate above between R. Yehudah who said that the water of the Jordan piled up to a height of twelve *mil*, and R. Elazar b. R. Shimon who held that it reached a height of three hundred *mil*.] R. Ammi and R. Yitzcha Nafcha have a difference of opinion about this. One said: According to R. Yehudah's opinion, (34b) the children of Israel crossed the Jordan in the formation in which they were encamped [twelve *mil* by twelve *mil*]. According to R. Elazar b. R. Shimon who holds that the pillar of water reached a height of three hundred *mil*, they crossed over in single file [and the water reached a much greater height because it took much longer for the people to get across]. The other said: According to both R. Yehudah and R. Elazar b. R. Shimon they crossed over in the formation of their encampment. R. Yehudah holds that man moves as fast as water, [and a twelve-*mil* height was enough to allow everyone to cross over. R. Elazar b. R. Shimon holds that water flows at a quicker rate; therefore a greater height of water was needed to allow everyone to cross over].

THE CHAPTER OF THE SPIES

[God said to Moses,] "Send out men for yourself" (Numbers 13:2). Resh Lakish said: ["For yourself" implies that God said: You should send according to the way you understand it. I am not commanding you to send spies, but the people are demanding it,[76] so I will not prevent you from sending them.] Will a person choose a bad portion for himself? [Will God choose a bad land for himself? (*Maharsha*).] And this is why it says, [Moses said,] "It appeared to me to be a good thing" (Deuteronomy 1:23). Resh Lakish said: It appeared to be a good thing to Moses, but not to God.

[The people demanded of Moses to send spies,] "to explore the land" (ibid. 22). R. Chiya b. Abba said: The intention of the spies was to look for the shame of Eretz Yisrael. It says here, "to explore [*veyachperu*] the land," and elswhere it says, "The moon will be shamed [*vechafera*], and the sun will be humiliated" (Isaiah 24:23).

"Their names were as follows: From the tribe of Reuben, Shamua son of Zakur" (Numbers 13:4). R. Yitzchak said: We have a tradition that has been handed down to us from our ancestors that the names of the spies reflect their action, but we know the explanation of only one of them: Setur ben Michael (ibid. v. 13). He was named Setur because he contradicted [*satar*] the Holy One, blessed be He. [With his report he implied that God had lied.] The name Michael hints that he suggested that God was weak [*mach*], [and unable to help them conquer Eretz Yisrael]. R. Yochanan said: We also can explain the name Nachbi ben Vofsi (ibid. 14). [He was named Nachbi] because he hid [*hechevi*] the words of the Holy One, blessed be He, [meaning, he did not report things accurately]; and Vofsi, because he stepped on [*pasa*] the attributes of the Holy One, blessed be He, [he misrepresented the attributes].

"On the way through the Negev he came to Hebron" (ibid. v. 22). It should have said, "*they* came to Hebron"! Rava said: This teaches us that Caleb separated himself from the conspiracy of the spies and prostrated himself on the graves of the patriarchs [in Hebron] and said to them: My fathers, pray on my behalf that I should be saved from the conspiracy of the spies. Joshua [did not need a prayer because] Moses had already prayed on his behalf, as it says, "Moses gave Hoshea son of Nun the [new] name Joshua [Yehoshua]" (ibid. v. 16), meaning, May God save you [yoshiacha] from the designs of the spies. [The Gemara now proves that "he came to Hebron" is indeed referring to Caleb.] And this is meant by the passage, [God said,] "My servant Caleb, since he had a different idea . . . I will bring him to the land to which he came and his descendants will possess it" (ibid. 14:24); [and Caleb received Hebron,[77] so "the land to which he came" must have been Hebron].

"[In Hebron the spies saw the giants] Achiman, Sheshai, and Talmai, the children of Anak" (Numbers 13:22). Achiman means that he was the strongest [meyuman] of his brothers. Sheshai means that he made the land into ditches [shechitot]; [wherever he stepped he made a mark in the ground]. Talmai means that [when he walked] he made furrows [telamim] in the earth. Achiman built Anat, Sheshai built Alash, and Talmai built Telbesh. "The children of Anak"—this means that they were so tall, it seemed as if they wore the sun like a necklace [anak].

THE FERTILE SOIL OF HEBRON

"Hebron was built seven years before Zo'an in Egypt" (ibid.). [The Gemara asks:] What does the term "was built" mean? Should we say that it was actually built [seven years before Zo'an]? How is that possible? How can it be that a person should build a house for his younger son before his older son? For it says, "The sons of Ham were: Cush, Mitzrayim, Put, and Canaan" (Genesis 10:6); [Canaan was younger than Mitzrayim [Egypt]. How is it possible that Hebron in Canaan was built before Zo'an in Mitzrayim?]. But the verse means that Hebron was seven times more productive than Zo'an. Now there is no rockier place in all of Eretz Yisrael than Hebron, and that is why they bury the dead there; and there is no more fertile land among all the countries than the land of Egypt, for it says, "Like a garden of God, like the land of Egypt" (ibid. 8:10); and in all of Egypt the best place was Zo'an, for it says, "For its princes are in Zo'an" (Isaiah 30:4). Even so, Hebron was seven times more fruitful than Zo'an.

[The Gemara asks:] Is it then true that Hebron has stony soil? But it says, "After a period of forty years had gone by, Absalom said to the king, 'I would like to go now to Hebron and fulfill my vow that I made to God [and bring a sacrifice]'" (2 Samuel 15:7). [Why did he want to go to Hebron? There was no altar in Hebron!] R. Ivya—others say Rabbah bar Bar Chana—said: He went to Hebron to get sheep for his sacrifice. [So you see Hebron was pasture land; not stony soil.] And we learned in a Baraita: The best rams come from Moab, and the best lambs come from Hebron. [The Gemara answers:] From the question itself we can infer the answer. [The fact that they raised cattle in Hebron proves that the soil was rocky and not fertile enough to grow crops.] Because the topsoil [in rocky terrain] is very thin, it is used for pasture land, and the cattle grow fat there.

THE SPIES'
UNFAVORABLE REPORT

It says, "They came back from exploring the land" (Numbers 13:25), and the text continues, (35a) "They went and came to Moses." [The Gemara feels that "they went" is superfluous.] R. Yochanan said in the name of R. Shimon b. Yochai: The passage wants to compare the way they went to the way they came back. Just as on their return they had bad intentions [to bring back lies about Eretz Yisrael], so, too, when they set out on their mission they went with bad intentions [to spread lies about Eretz Yisrael]. "They reported to him and said, 'We arrived at the Land to which you sent us, and indeed it flows with milk and honey, . . . But the people that dwells in the Land is powerful'" (ibid. v. 27,28). [They began by giving a true description of the Land, but then they changed their story.] R. Yochanan formulated a principle in the name of R. Meir: Any slander that does not begin with something true will not endure, [because people will see through the lie].

"Caleb hushed the people toward Moses" (ibid. v. 30). [What does "toward Moses" mean?] Rabbah said: He won them over with words. [This is what happened.] Joshua began to say good things about Eretz Yisrael. So the people cried out: This person who has no children, [who will inherit a share of the Land] he should speak to us? Caleb said [to himself]: If I begin to talk [in the same vein as Joshua] they'll also heckle me, and interrupt me, and not let me speak. So he told them, [using a different tactic]: Is this the only thing that Amram's son[78] has done to us! The people listening thought that he was about to make derogatory remarks about Moses, so they kept quiet. [Once he had their attention] he told them: He brought us out of Egypt, split the Red Sea for us, and gave us manna to eat. If he would tell us: Prepare ladders and climb up to heaven, shouldn't we listen to him? "We will surely go up and conquer [the Land]," he said. "We can do it!" (ibid.).

"But the men who had gone up with [Caleb] said, 'We cannot go up to that people for it stronger than we!'" (ibid. v. 31). R. Chanina b. Papa said: The spies meant something deeper when they said, "It is stronger than we." They did not mean "stronger than we" but "stronger than He" [i.e., the people is stronger than God]. They implied: Even the owner of the house cannot remove his own belongings from there, [meaning, God is helpless against the people of the Land].

"It is a land that devours its inhabitants" (ibid. v. 32). Rava expounded: The Holy One, blessed be He, said: I intended this as a favor for the spies, but they interpreted it in a bad sense. I intended it for their good, because wherever the spies came the prominent people of that locality died, so that everyone should be busy with their funeral, and they would not have time to inquire about the spies, [so that the spies were able to return unharmed]. Some say that [not all the prominent people died] but that Job died, and all were busy with his funeral. But the spies interpreted it in a bad sense, saying, "It is a land that devours its inhabitants."

[The spies said,] "We looked like grasshoppers to ourselves, and so we looked to them!" (ibid. v. 33). Said R. Mesharshiya: The spies proved that they were liars. We can understand that they said, "We looked like grasshoppers to ourselves"; that makes sense. But when they said, "so we looked to them," how could they know what the people were thinking! [The Gemara argues:] This does not prove that the spies were lying. For when they made the meals to comfort the mourners [after the funerals mentioned above] they ate the meals underneath a cedar tree, and when the spies saw them they climbed the trees and sat there. Then they overheard them say, "We are seeing people in the trees that look like grasshoppers." [So the spies reported the truth.]

"The entire community broke into loud cries, and the people wept that night" (ibid. 14:1). Rabbah said in the name of R. Yochanan: That night was the night of Tishah b'Av,[79] and the Holy One, blessed be He, said: They are now crying for nothing, [for they believe the lies of the spies,] but I will set aside this day for them as a day of weeping for generations to come.

"As the whole community was threatening to stone them [Joshua and Caleb] to death, the glory of God appeared in the Tent of Meeting to all the Israelites" (ibid. v. 10). R. Chiya b. Abba said: [The juxtaposition of the two segments of the verse] teaches us that they took stones and intended to hurl them at God Himself.

"The people who spread the evil report about the Land died in a plague before God" (ibid. v. 37). R. Shimon b. Lakish said: They died an uncommon death.[80] R. Chanina b. Papa said: R. Shila of K'far Tamrata expounded: It teaches that their tongues were stretched so that they reached down to their navels, and worms were crawling out of their tongues and entered their navels, and out of their bodies into their tongues. R. Nachman b. Yitzchak said: They died of askara [a disease associated with choking; it is a punishment for slandering].[81]

[After this lengthy digression the Gemara now resumes the discussion of the crossing of the Jordan.] When the last of the Israelites emerged from the Jordan, the waters returned to their natural flow, as it says, "It happened when the kohanim, the bearers of the Ark

of the Covenant of God, ascended from the middle of the Jordan and the soles of the kohanim's feet were removed to the dry ground: The waters of the Jordan returned to their place and flowed—as they had yesterday and before yesterday—upon all its banks" (Joshua 4:18). [The Gemara understands that this is what happened: After the last person had crossed to the west bank of the Jordan, the kohanim who were still standing in the dry Jordan bed, took a step back onto the east bank.] Therefore, the Ark and the kohanim that carried it were on one side of the Jordan, [the east bank], and the entire people of Israel on the other side, [the west bank]. [How did the Ark get across to the west bank?] The Ark lifted those that carried it and passed over the Jordan, [flying across the river], as it says, "It happened when the entire people had completed crossing that the Ark of God and the kohanim passed over [flying across the river] in front of the people" (ibid. v. 11). [The purpose of this miracle was to impress upon the entire people the great holiness of the Ark (Ben Yehoyada).]

UZZAH'S ERROR
And because of this Uzzah was punished, [for he failed to apply the lesson everyone had learned at the crossing of the Jordan]. For it says, [When David transported the Ark into Jerusalem he placed it on a wagon pulled by oxen.] "They came to the threshing floor of Nacon, and Uzzah reached out to the Ark of God and grasped it, for the oxen had dislodged it, [and he thought the Ark would fall to the ground]" (2 Samuel 6:6). The Holy One, blessed be He, said to him, "Uzzah, the Ark is able to carry those that carry it; surely it can protect itself from falling!"

"God became angry at Uzzah and struck him there for the blunder [shal]" (ibid. v. 7). R. Yochanan and R. Elazar [offer different interpretations of the word shal]. One said [it means]: "for the blunder [shalu.]" The other said [it means]: He relieved himself in the presence of the Ark.[82] [At any rate, Uzzah did not respect the great holiness of the Ark.]

"And Uzzah died there by the Ark of God" (ibid.). R. Yochanan said: Uzzah entered the World to Come, for it says, "by the Ark of God"—just as the Ark endures forever, so did Uzzah enter the World to Come [and lives on forever].

"David was upset [vayichar] [with himself, for having failed to take the necessary precautions][83] because God had inflicted a breach against Uzzah" (ibid. v. 8). R. Elazar said: His face looked like a wafer baked on coals [chararah]. [The Gemara asks:] Does this mean that wherever it says vayichar, "he was upset," his face looked like a chararah? [The Gemara answers:] Normally vayichar goes together with af, which means "he was angry," but here it says vayichar without the word af.

Rava expounded: Why was David punished [that Uzzah should die because of him]? Because he called the words of the Torah "songs."[84] For David said, "Your statutes were songs to me when I was afraid, [running from my enemies]" (Psalms 119:54). The Holy One, blessed be He, said to him: The Torah, about which it says, "You close your eyes, and they are gone" (Proverbs 23:5), [meaning, if you are distracted for just an instant, Torah leaves you. It requires constant diligence]; how could you call it "songs"! I will make you stumble on something even schoolchildren know. For it says, "[Moses] did not give [any wagons] to the descendants of Kehot, since they had the responsibility for the most sacred articles, which they had to carry on their shoulders" (Numbers 7:9), and yet David brought [the Ark] in a wagon, [and this error led to Uzzah's death].

[The Gemara relates an earlier incident of disrespect toward the Ark. In the days of Eli, the Ark had been captured by the Philistines. They returned the Ark and brought it to Bet Shemesh. The people of Bet Shemesh saw the Ark coming,] "And God punished some of the people of Bet Shemesh because they looked at the Ark of God" (1 Samuel 6:19). [The Gemara wonders:] Did God punish them just for looking at the Ark! R. Abbahu and R. Elazar [have different opinions about this]. One said: They kept on harvesting while they bowed down [before the Ark, displaying a disrespectful attitude]. The other said: They spoke about [the Ark] with contempt. [They said to the Ark:] (35b) Who caused you to be angry that you did not protect yourself [and prevent your capture]? And who came to appease you that caused you to come back?

"[God] struck among them seventy men, fifty thousand men" (1 Samuel 6:19). R. Abbahu and R. Elazar [give different interpretations of this]. One said that actually, only seventy people were killed, each of whom was equal to fifty thousand. The other said that fifty thousand people were killed, each of whom was as eminent as a member of the Sanhedrin, which comprised seventy members.

[The Gemara now goes back to the story when David brought the Ark to Jerusalem. It says there,] "Whenever the bearers of the Ark walked six paces, [David] slaughtered an ox and a fattened ox" (2 Samuel 6:13), and [when this event is recorded in 1 Chronicles] it says, "They offered seven bulls and seven rams" (1 Chronicles 15:26)? [How do we resolve this discrepancy?] Said R. Papa b. Shmuel: At each pace an ox and a fat ox were offered, and at each six paces seven bulls and seven rams. R. Chisda said to him: According to this, you filled up all of Eretz Yisrael with altars! But this is how it was done: At each six paces an ox and a fat ox were offered, and after every six sets of six steps they brought seven bulls and seven rams.

[The Gemara now points out another discrepancy:] It says, [regarding the incident with Uzzah], "They came to the threshing-floor of Chidon" (1 Chronicles 13:9), and [when the original story is told] it says, "They came to the threshing-floor of Nacon" (2 Samuel 6:6). R. Yochanan said: At first it was called Chidon and afterward Nacon.[85]

HOW WAS THE TORAH INSCRIBED ON THE STONES?

[After digressing with the discussion of the sin of Uzzah, the Gemara now returns to the topic of the Israelites crossing the Jordan.] From the episode [of the crossing of the Jordan] we can gather that there were three sets of stones: one that Moses erected in the land of Moab, as it says, "On the other side of the Jordan in the land of Moab, Moses began explaining [bei'eir] the Torah" (Deuteronomy 1:6). [And how do we know that he wrote it on stones?] Because elsewhere it says, [with reference to the stones they were to be set up after crossing the Jordan it says], "You shall inscribe on the stones all the words of this Torah, well clarified [ba'eir]" (ibid. 27:8). We conclude from the analogy of bei'eir—ba'eir in both verses that just as they wrote on stones after crossing the Jordan, so too Moses wrote the Torah on stones. The second set was that which Joshua erected in the middle of the Jordan, as it says, "Joshua set up twelve stones in the middle of the Jordan" (Joshua 4:9). The third set was that which he erected in Gilgal, as it says, "The twelve stones that they had taken from the Jordan, Joshua erected in Gilgal" (ibid. v. 20).

We learned in a Baraita: How did the Israelites write the Torah [on the stones]? R. Yehudah said: They wrote it on the stones, as it says, "You shall inscribe on the stones all the words of this Torah." After that they covered them over with plaster. R. Shimon said to him: According to you, how did the nations of that time learn the Torah? [The Torah was written on the stones in seventy languages in order that the nations should not be able to claim that they did not have the opportunity to learn it. But if it was covered with plaster how could the nations learn the Torah?] R. Yehudah replied: The Holy One, blessed be He, gave the nations at that time an extra level of intelligence, and they sent their scribes who peeled off the plaster and copied the Torah and carried it to their people. At that moment their fate was sealed against them to descend to the pit of perdition, because they had the opportunity to learn but they did not. [To summarize: R. Yehudah said that the Torah was written on the stones and then covered with plaster.]

R. Shimon said: First they plastered the stones, and then they wrote the Torah on the plaster. And on the bottom of the stones they wrote, "So that they will not teach you to act according to all their abominations" (Deuteronomy 20:18).[86] From this we may infer that if they repented they would be accepted. Rava b. Shila said: What is R. Shimon's reason [for saying that they wrote it on plaster]? Because it says, "The nations will be burned for plaster" (Isaiah 33:12). [R. Shimon interprets this to mean:] They will be destroyed on account of the Torah that was written on plaster [and which they did not follow]. And how does R. Yehudah [who says that the Torah was covered with plaster] understand this verse? [He interprets it:] The nations will be destroyed like plaster. Just as plaster has no remedy except to burn it, so is there no remedy for those nations except burning [in Gehinnom, if they cling to their abominations and do not repent].

[The Gemara asks:] According to whom—[R. Yehudah or R. Shimon]—is the following Baraita: It says, "When you will go out to war against your enemies . . . you will capture its captivity" (Deuteronomy 21:10)—this comes to include Canaanites who reside outside Eretz Yisrael; so if they repent they will be accepted. (36a) According to whom? According to R. Shimon.

[The Gemara continues its discussion of the crossing of the Jordan.] Come and see how many miracles happened on that day: Israel crossed the Jordan [which dried up]; [on the same day] they came to Mount Gerizim and Mount Ebal [traveling a distance of] more than sixty mil; on the way no creature was able to stand up against them, and whoever tried to resist them immediately was overwhelmed with fright. For it says, "I will cause [the people] who are in your path to be terrified of Me, and I will throw all the people among whom you are coming into a panic" (Exodus 23:27). And it says further, "Fear and dread will fall upon them . . . Until Your people crossed, O God!" (ibid. 15:16). This alludes to their first entry [into Eretz Yisrael in the days of Joshua].

[And the verse continues,] "Until the people You gained crossed over." This alludes to the second time they came to Eretz Yisrael [when they returned in the days of Ezra]. [From the fact that the Torah equates the two entries into Eretz Yisrael] we can deduce that the Jews were worthy that miracles should happen when they came the second time [under Ezra] just as when they came the first time [with Joshua]; but the sins [the Jews had committed during the period of the first Temple] prevented miracles from occurring, [and they were allowed to return only by the grace of King Cyrus of Persia].

After [they crossed the Jordan] they brought the stones [which they had lifted out of the Jordan], built the altar, and covered it with plaster, and wrote on these stones the entire Torah in seventy languages, as it says, "well clarified" (Deuteronomy 27:8). Then they brought burnt offerings and peace offerings; they ate and drank and were merry; they pronounced the blessings and the curses [on Mount Gerizim and Mount Ebal];[87] they dismantled the altar [and carried the stones with them]; and they came and spent the night in Gilgal, as it says, "Bring [the stones] across with you and set them in the lodging place where you will spend the night" (Joshua 4:3). You might think [that they had to take the stones with them] to any place were they camped; therefore it says, "where you will

spend [the first] night," and then it says, "And those twelve stones that they had taken from the Jordan, Joshua erected in Gilgal" (ibid. v. 20).

We learned in a Baraita: The hornets did not cross over the Jordan with them. [The Gemara asks:] But that is not so! For it says, "I will send hornets ahead of you [to aid you]" (Exodus 23:28). R. Shimon b. Lakish said: [The hornets] stood by the bank of the Jordan and from there threw their poison [into the Canaanites], which blinded their eyes above and made them impotent by attacking their organs below. For it says, "Yet I destroyed the Amorite before them—[the Amorite] whose height was like the height of a cedar tree, and who were mighty as oaks—and I destroyed his fruit from above and his roots from below" (Amos 2:9). R. Papa said: There were two kinds of hornets, one in the days of Moses [that attacked their enemies east of the Jordan], and the other that Joshua used in his battles; the former did not cross the Jordan, but the other did.

BLESSINGS AND CURSES

[The Mishnah on 32a describes how the blessings and curses were proclaimed on Mount Gerizim and Mount Ebal:] Six tribes ascended Mount Gerizim, and six tribes ascended Mount Ebal, and the kohanim and the Levites together with the Ark were standing below between [the two mountains], the kohanim surrounding the Ark, the Levites surrounding the kohanim, and Israel on the slopes of the two mountains, as it says, "And all Israel, its elders, officers, and judges stood on either side the Ark . . . half of them on the slope of Mount Gerizim and half of them on the slope of Mount Ebal" (Joshua 8:33). [The Levites] turned their faces toward Mount Gerizim and opened with the blessing, "Blessed be anyone who will not make a sculptured or molten image,"[88] and [the people on both mountains] answered: Amen. They then turned to face Mount Ebal and opened with the curse, "Cursed be anyone who makes a sculptured or molten image," and [the people on both mountains] answered: Amen. [They continued] until they concluded all the blessings and the curses. After that they brought the stones,[89] built the altar and covered it with plaster, and wrote on it the entire Torah in seventy languages, as it says, "well clarified" (Deuteronomy 27:8). Then they took the stones and went and spent the night in their place [in Gilgal].

[The Gemara asks:] What is the meaning of the word vehachetzyo, "and the other half of them [on the slope of Mount Ebal]"? [The article ha seems to indicate that the verse refers to a specific half mentioned somewhere else. What is it referring to?] R. Kahana said: Just as they were divided here [on the two mountains],[90] so were they divided on the stones of the ephod.[91] An objection was raised: [We learned in a Baraita:] The Kohen Gadol wore two precious stones on his shoulders, one on each side; on them were engraved the names of the twelve tribes, six on each stone, as it says, "Six of their names on one stone, and the names of the six remaining ones on the other stone, according to the order of their birth" (Exodus 28:10). This indicates that the second six had to be engraved according to their birth, but the first six did not have to be engraved according to their birth, because the name of Judah was written [out of order] in the first position: [Judah, Reuben, Simon, Levi, Dan, Naphtali. The second stone had: Gad, Asher, Yissachar, Zebulon, Joseph, Benjamin, in the order of their birth]. The names comprised fifty letters, twenty-five on each stone.

R. Chanina b. Gamliel says: (36b) They were not written [on the stones of the *ephod*] in the order that they are listed in the Book of Numbers (Numbers 1:5–15), but in the order they are listed in Exodus (Exodus 1:2–4). And how [are they inscribed]? The sons of Leah [on one stone—*not* in the order of their birth: Reuben, Simon, Levi, Judah, Issachar, Zebulon]; [and on the other stone,] the sons of Rachel: Benjamin at the top of the list, and Joseph at the bottom of the list, with the sons of Bilha and Zilpah in the middle, [as follows: Benjamin, Dan, Naphtali, Gad, Asher, Joseph]. [The Gemara asks:] But how does R. Chanina b. Gamliel explain "according to their birth" [since he does not arrange them according to seniority]? [The Gemara answers:] It means that they must be written in the way their father called them and not in the way Moses called them: Reuben and not Reubeni; Simon and not Simeoni, Dan and not haDani, Gad and not haGadi. This disproves the above statement of R. Kahana [who said that the tribes were divided on the *ephod* as on the two mountains. But neither of the arrangements mentioned in the *Baraita* has any connection with the division of the tribes on the two mountains. Thus *vehachetzyo* cannot refer to the way they were divided on the stones of the *ephod*]. The refutation stands.

[[The Gemara asks:] If so, what then is the meaning of *vehachetzyo*, "and *the* other half of them" [on the slope of Mount Ebal]? We learned in a *Baraita*: [The *hei* of *vehachetzyo*] teaches you that the [number of people] in the six tribes on the slope of Mount Gerizim was larger than those on Mount Ebal, because part of the tribe of Levi [which was one of the tribes on Mount Gerizim] stood on the bottom between the two mountains [with the Ark]. [The Gemara asks:] Just the opposite! Since [part of] Levi was on the bottom, there should be fewer people [on Mount Gerizim]! [The Gemara answers:] This is what the *Baraita* means to say: Even though part of the tribe of Levi was down below, [the number of people on Mount Gerizim was greater] because the tribe of Joseph [which comprised Ephraim and Menasseh] was very numerous, as it says, "The children of Joseph spoke to Joshua, saying, 'Why have you given me an inheritance of only a single lot and a single portion, seeing that I am a numerous

people?' . . . Joshua said to them, 'If you are such a numerous people, ascend to the forest'" (Joshua 17:14,15). He said to them: Go and hide in the forests so that no one will cast an evil eye on you [because you are so numerous]. They replied: The evil eye has no power over the children of Joseph, for it says, "Joseph is a fruitful son, like a fruitful vine by the fountain" (Genesis 49:22), and R. Abbahu said: Don't read *alei ayin*, "by the fountain," but *olei ayin*, "overcoming the [envious] eye." R. Yose b. R. Chanina said: It can be derived from here, [Jacob blessed Ephraim and Menasseh, saying], "May they proliferate abundantly like fish within the land" (ibid. 48:16). Just as the water covers the fish in the sea so that the [evil] eye cannot harm them, so, too, the [evil] eye cannot harm the offspring of Joseph. [And that is why the people on Mount Gerizim outnumbered those on Mount Ebal.]

THE FIFTY LETTERS

[The Gemara stated above that the inscription on the stones of the *ephod* was fifty letters, twenty-five on each stone. The Gemara asks:] How can you say that there were fifty letters? [The letters in the names of the tribes] amount to only forty-nine! R. Yitzchak said: A letter was added to the name Joseph, for it says, "He appointed it as a testimony for Joseph [spelled *Yehosef* with an extra *hei*]" (Psalms 81:6). R. Nachman b. Yitzchak objected: They had to be inscribed "according to their birth" [and the name *Yosef* was given at birth without a *hei*]! But [the answer is] that throughout the whole Torah the name of Benjamin is written without a *yud* between the *mem* and the *nun*; but on the *ephod* it was spelled with a *yud* [between the *mem* and the *nun*], as it says, "And his father called him Benjamin" (Genesis 35:18), [spelled with an extra *yud*. Therefore we have fifty letters].

JOSEPH'S TEMPTATION

R. Chana b. Bizna said in the name of R. Shimon Chasida: Because Joseph sanctified God's name in private, [by resisting the advances of Potiphar's wife,] one letter [i.e., the letter *hei*] from the name of the Holy One, blessed be He, was added to his name [*Yehosef*]. Because Judah openly sanctified God's name,[92] all the letters of God's name are present in the name of *Yehudah* (Judah), [*yud*, *hei*, *vav*, and *hei*]. How did Joseph sanctify God's name? As it says, [in the episode where Potiphar's wife tried to seduce Joseph], "One such day, Joseph came to the house to do his work" (Genesis 39:11). R. Yochanan said: This teaches us that both [Joseph and Potiphar's wife] had the intention of acting immorally. "Joseph came to the house to do his work"—Rav and Shmuel [disagree in their interpretation]. One said that it really means he came to do his work; but the other said that he came to live with her. "None of the household staff was inside" (ibid.). [The Gemara asks:] Is it possible that there was no one else in a huge mansion like that of the wicked Potiphar? It was taught in the yeshivah of R. Yishmael: That day was a festival, and everyone had gone to their pagan temple, but she claimed that she was sick because she thought that this was a perfect opportunity for her to seduce Joseph. "She grabbed him by his cloak, saying . . ." (ibid. v. 12).

At that moment the image of his father appeared to him through the window and said, "Joseph, your brothers will have their names inscribed on the stones of the *ephod*, and yours among them. Do you wish that your name should be erased, and you be called a companion of harlots?" As it says, "The companion of harlots will lose his wealth" (Proverbs 29:3). Immediately, "He drew his bow with strength" (Genesis 49:24). R. Yochanan said in the name of R. Meir: This means that he held back his passion. "His arms were bedecked with gold" (ibid.), [is interpreted to mean:] Joseph pressed his fingers into the ground in order [to cause himself pain so that his desire should recede]. [The verse continues,] "From the hands of the mighty power of Jacob" —Who caused his name to be engraved on the stones of the *ephod* [and not to be erased]? The mighty power of Jacob. [The verse continues,] "From there he shepherded the stone of Israel"—From there Joseph was worthy to become the shepherd of Israel, [and to be inscribed on the stones of the *ephod*], as it says, "Give ear, O Shepherd of Israel, take care of the sheep of Joseph" (Psalms 80:2). [The fact that Israel is called "the sheep of Joseph" proves that Joseph was the shepherd of Israel.]

BENJAMIN'S TEN SONS
We learned in a *Baraita*: Joseph was worthy that twelve tribes should issue from him, just as his father Jacob fathered twelve tribes, as it says, "These are the chronicles of Jacob; Joseph at the age of seventeen . . ." (Genesis 39:11); [the Gemara connects the name Jacob with Joseph and expounds that Joseph too should have had twelve sons], but his power to beget was reduced [through the incident with Potiphar's wife, and he had only two sons]. [The other ten] were fathered by his brother Benjamin, and all the sons of Benjamin were named after [events in the life of] Joseph. For it says, "The sons of Benjamin were: Bela, Becher, Ashbel, Gera, Naaman, Eichi, Rosh, Muppim, Chuppim, and Rosh" (Genesis 46:21). He was called Bela, because Joseph was swallowed up [*nivla*] among the nations [when he was sold into slavery]; Becher was so called because Joseph was the firstborn [*bechor*] of his mother; Ashbel, because God sent Joseph into captivity [*sheva'o el*]; Gera, because Joseph had to live [*gar*] in lodgings [in a strange land]; Naaman, because Joseph was especially pleasant [*na'im*]; Echi and Rosh, [Benjamin said:] he is my brother [*achi*] and my leader

[*rosh*]; Muppim and Chuppim, because [Bejamin said:] Joseph did not see my marriage canopy [*chuppah*], and I did not see his *chuppah*. [The name Muppim is explained in Midrash Tanchuma: [Joseph's] mouth [*peh*] was like that of our father Jacob, because he knew all the Torah that Jacob had taught him (Rashi)]. Ard, because Joseph went down [*yarad*] to live among the nations. Others explain the name Ard, because Joeph's face was like a rose [*vered*].

PHARAOH'S SECRET
R. Chiya b. Abba said in the name of R. Yochanan: When Pharaoh [appointed Joseph as viceroy] and told him, "Without your say, no man will lift a hand or foot in all Egypt" (Genesis 41:44), Pharaoh's astrologers complained, "What! A slave who was bought for twenty pieces of silver you put in charge of us!" "I see in him characteristics of a king," Pharaoh replied. "If that is the case," they answered, "he should at least know the seventy languages [of the world]." The angel Gabriel came and taught Joseph all seventy languages, but he could not grasp them. So one letter of the name of the Holy One, blessed be He, [the letter *hei*], was added to his name, and that gave him the ability to learn the seventy languages [which he needed to become viceroy]. For it says, "He appointed it as a testimony for Joseph [written: *Yehosef*, with an extra *hei*], when he went out over the land of Egypt, where I [Joseph] heard a language unknown to me" (Psalms 81:6).

The next day, in whatever language that Pharaoh spoke to Joseph, he replied to him; but when Joseph spoke to Pharaoh in the holy tongue, he did not understand what he was saying. So Pharaoh asked Joseph to teach it to him, [because to be king of Egypt he was required to know all the languages]. Joseph tried to teach it to him, but he could not learn it. So Pharaoh said to Joseph, "Swear to me that you will not reveal to anyone the fact that I do not know Hebrew," and Joseph swore. When Joseph asked Pharaoh, [for permission to take Jacob's remains to Eretz Yisrael, saying], "My father bound me by an oath [that I should move his body to Eretz Yisrael]" (Genesis 50:5)], Pharaoh replied, "Go and ask to be released from your oath." [He did not want Joseph to leave Egypt.] Joseph answered, "[In that case,] I will at the same time ask to be released from the oath I made to you [not to reveal your ignorance of Hebrew]." Hearing this, Pharaoh reluctantly told him, "Go and bury your father just as he had you swear" (ibid. v. 6).

WHEN DID JUDAH SANCTIFY GOD'S NAME?
[The Gemara mentioned earlier that because Judah openly sanctified God's name, all the letters of the divine name are present in the name Yehudah (Judah).

The Gemara now asks:] What did Judah do to sanctify God's name? [The Gemara answers:] We learned in [the last part of the following] *Baraita*: R. Meir said: When the children of Israel were standing by the Red Sea, the tribes were fighting with each other, each wanting to go into the sea first. (37a) Then the tribe of Benjamin jumped ahead and went first into the sea [while the waters were still raging], as it says, "There Benjamin, the youngest, rules them" (Psalms 68:28)—don't read *rodeim*, "rules them," but *rad yam*, "descended into the sea." The leaders of Judah then hurled stones at them, [out of envy,] as the verse continues, "The princes of Judah stoned them" (ibid.). Because of that the righteous Benjamin was worthy to become the host of the Almighty [the Holy of Holies was built in the territory of the tribe of Benjamin]. For it says, "[God] dwells among [Benjamin's] slopes" (Deuteronomy 33:12).

R. Yehudah said to R. Meir: That is not the way it happened; but one tribe said: I do not want to enter the sea first; and another tribe said: I do not want to enter the sea first. However Nachshon son of Aminadav [of the tribe of Judah] jumped into the Red Sea first, for it says, "Ephraim has surrounded me with falsehood, and the House of Israel with deceit, but Judah descended [into the sea, because his faith was] with God" (Hosea 12:1). Concerning this it says in Psalms, [Nachshon ben Aminadav prayed,] "Save me, O God, for the waters have reached my neck! I am sunk in the mire of the shadowy depths, and there is no foothold . . . Let not the rushing current sweep me away, nor let the shadowy depths swallow me" (Psalms 69:2,16). At that time Moses was saying a lengthy prayer, so the Holy One, blessed be He, told him, "My dear ones are drowning in the sea, and you are saying a lengthy prayer to Me!" Moses said, "Master of the universe! What shall I do?" God replied, "Speak to the Israelites, and let them start moving. Raise your staff and extend your hand over the sea. You will split the sea . . ." (Exodus 14:15). Because of [Nachshon's act] Judah was worthy to be the rulers over Israel, as it says, "Judah became His sanctuary; the rulers over Israel. The sea saw and fled" (Psalms 114:2). Why did Judah become His sanctuary and the rulers over Israel? Because the sea saw [Nachshon of the tribe of Judah] and fled.

THE TRIBES AT MOUNT GERIZIM AND MOUNT EBAL

[The Gemara now resumes the discussion of Israel's stand at Mount Gerizim and Mount Ebal.] We learned in a *Baraita*: R. Eliezer b. Yaakov says: It is impossible to say that the tribe of Levi was at the bottom [of the two mountains, as the verse in Joshua 8:33 implies], because it says [in the Torah that Levi was standing] above [on Mount Gerizim].[93] And you cannot say that Levi was above [on the mountain], because it says

[in Joshua 8:33] that they were standing at the bottom. So how can we reconcile this contradiction? The elders of the *kohanim* and Levites were below and the rest above [on the mountain]. R. Yoshiah said: All the Levites who were qualified to carry the Ark [meaning, Levites between the ages of thirty and fifty] were standing below together with the Ark, and the rest of the tribe of Levi was above. Rabbi says: All the tribes were standing below. They turned toward Mount Gerizim and opened with the blessing, and then they turned toward Mount Ebal and opened with the curse. And what does *al*, "on" [in, "They shall stand *al* [on] Mount Gerizim"][94] mean? It means: "Next to it." [Six tribes were standing closer to Mount Gerizim and six closer to Mount Ebal.] As we learned in a *Baraita*, [an example where *al* means "next to"]: It says, "Place frankincense *al* [next to] these stacks [of loaves]" (Leviticus 24:7).

Rabbi says: *al* means "next to." You are assuming that *al* translates as "next to"; but perhaps it is not so, and the meaning is literally "on top [of the loaves]"? Since it says, "Shield [*al*] the Ark with the cloth partition [that divided the Holy of Holies, which contained the Ark from the rest of the Sanctuary]" (Exodus 40:2), [and the partition was not on, but next to the Ark, which proves that *al* with reference to the mountains does not mean "on the mountain" but "next to"].

[The Mishnah stated: They turned toward Mount Gerizim and opened with the blessing. Then they turned toward Mount Ebal and said the corresponding curse. The Torah[95] mentions eleven specific curses and a twelfth general curse.] Our Rabbis taught: Each of the eleven blessings was preceded by the general blessing [thus the general blessing was repeated eleven times]. And the general curse was recited before each of the eleven specific curses. [Each mitzvah has four components: to learn, to teach, to observe, and to do.[96] Consequently, each of the things mentioned was first said in terms of "to learn," then in terms of "to teach," then "to observe," and then "to do."] Thus there were four covenants [i.e., the general blessing, the specific blessing, the general curse, and the specific curse] attached to each of the four duties ["to learn", "to teach," "to observe," and "to do"]. (37b) So we have a sum total of sixteen covenants.

We find the same thing at Mount Sinai and again at the plains of Moab [where Moses repeated the Torah]. [And how do we know that the concept of blessings and curses applies also to Mount Sinai?] For it says, [following the blessings and curses in the plains of Moab (Deuteronomy 28)], "These are the words of the covenant that God commanded Moses to seal with the children of Israel in the land of Moab, beside the covenant that He sealed with them in Horeb" [i.e., Sinai] (Deuteronomy 28:69). [Just as the covenant in the plains of Moab was associated with blessings and curses, so was the covenant of Horeb–Sinai accompanied by blessings and curses.] Consequently, there were forty eight covenants connected to every mitzvah; [sixteen at Gerizim and Ebal, sixteen at Sinai, and sixteen at the plains of Moab]. R. Shimon excludes Mount Gerizim and Mount Ebal [from these forty-eight covenants] and instead inserts the Tent of Meeting in the wilderness [where Moses received the Torah and transmitted it again to Israel].[97] They differ on the same point as the Tanna'im of the following Baraita: R. Yishmael said that the general concept [of each mitzvah] was proclaimed at Sinai, and the details were given later in the Tent of Meeting, [so that Sinai and the Tent of Meeting cannot be counted as two separate discussions of mitzvot. Therefore, the Tanna of the Mishnah holds as does R. Yishmael, and does not count the Tent of Meeting and includes the plains of Moab].

R. Akiva said that both the general concept and the specific details of the mitzvot were given at Sinai and repeated in the Tent of Meeting, and restated a third time in the plains of Moab, [and R. Shimon holds as does R. Akiva and omits the plains of Moab]. [The Gemara continues:] There is not a single mitzvah in the Torah that was not affirmed with forty-eight covenants. R. Shimon b. Yehudah of Kfar Acco said in the name of R. Shimon: There is not a single mitzvah in the Torah that was not affirmed with forty-eight covenants that were made for 603,550 people, [the total number of men between the ages of twenty and sixty that were in the wilderness. Thus each person had forty-eight covenants for his own mitzvot, and forty-eight covenants for each of the other people for whom he accepted responsibility].[98]

Rabbi added: According to R. Shimon b. Yehudah there is not a single mitzvah in the Torah that was not affirmed with forty-eight covenants times 603,550. Consequently, each person had 603,550 mitzvot. [The Gemara asks:] What is Rabbi adding? [The Gemara answers: We have a rule that a Jew is reponsible for the conduct of his fellow Jews.] The point at issue is whether he is responsible for someone else's individual obligations [if so, he is responsible only for the mitzvot of 603,550 people]; or—as Rabbi contends—whether he is responsible even for someone else's obligation to be responsible for the mitzvot of others, [in which case the number of 603,550 must be squared].

R. Yehudah b. Nachmani, who retold R. Shimon b. Lakish's lectures to the students, expounded: All the eleven blessings and curses [that were said on Mount Gerizim and Mount Ebal, even though they seem to deal with different transgressions] are related to the prohibition against living with a married woman. It says, "Cursed is the man who makes a graven or molten image" (Deuteronomy 27:15). [The Gemara asks:] Is it enough of a punishment that he should be cursed? [He has denied the fundamentals of the Jewish faith!] We must say therefore that it refers to a person who lived with a married woman, and they had a child, [and, being the offspring of a forbidden union, that

child becomes a mamzer, and is not allowed to marry a Jewish woman], so he went to live among the heathens and ended up worshipping idols. God says: Cursed are the father and mother of this man because they caused him to go astray. [And the other ten curses also result from adulterous unions (Rashi).]

(38b) R. Yehoshua b. Levi said: From where is it known that the Holy One, blessed be He, yearns to hear the priestly blessing? For it says, "[The priests] will link My name with the children of Israel, and I will bless them" (Numbers 6:27). [God could bless Israel Himself, but he designated the kohanim to bless because He yearns to hear their blessing (Maharsha).] R. Yehoshua b. Levi also said: Every kohen who blesses is blessed himself, but if he does not pronounce the blessing, he is not blessed, for it says, "I will bless those who bless you" (Genesis 12:3). R. Yehoshua b. Levi also said: We give the cup of blessing for the recital of Birkat Hamazon [99] only to a person of generous character. For it says, "One with a generous eye will be blessed [yevorach], for he has given of his bread to the poor" (Proverbs 22:9). Don't read yevorach, "will be blessed," but yevareich, "will bless" [i.e., recite Birkat Hamazon].

R. Yehoshua b. Levi also said: From where is it known that even birds recognize miserly people; [they don't want to eat their food]? For it says, "In the eyes of every winged creature the outspread net means nothing" (ibid. 1:17). R. Yehoshua b. Levi said further: Whoever enjoys the hospitality of miserly people violates a prohibition, for it says, "Do not eat the bread of a miser, and do not lust for his delicacies. For as one who fantasizes in his soul, so is he. 'Eat and drink,' he will tell you, but his heart will not be with you" (ibid. 23:6). R. Nachman b. Yitzchak said: He violates two prohibitions: "Do not eat" and "do not lust." R. Yehoshua b. Levi said further: The need for the heifer whose neck is to be broken[100] arises only because of miserliness. For it says, "The elders of the city who are closest to the [unidentified] corpse shall speak up and say, 'Our hands have not spilled this blood'" (Deuteronomy 21:7). But can it enter our mind that the elders of a Court of Justice are murderers! But the implied meaning is: [The man found murdered] did not come to us for help and we sent him away without supplying him with food; we did not see him and let him go without escort, [but if anyone else was miserly and did send him away without food, "atone for Your people Israel" (ibid. v. 8) (Maharsha)].

NO TALKING DURING TORAH READING

(39a) Rava b. R. Huna said: Once the Torah scroll is unrolled it is forbidden to talk even about Torah topics, for it says, "And when [Ezra] opened [the Torah scroll] all the people stood" (Nehemiah 8:5), and "standing" means standing silently. For it says, "So I waited for they did not speak, they stood still and did not respond any more" (Job 32:16). R. Zeira said in the name of R. Chisda: We can derive [that talking is forbidden during the Torah reading] from the verse, "And the ears of all the people were attentive to the Torah scroll" (Nehemiah 8:3).

BIRKAT KOHANIM, THE PRIESTLY BLESSING

R. Elazar b. Shamua's disciples asked him, "What did you do to merit long life?" He replied, "I never used the synagogue for a shortcut. I never stepped over the heads of the holy people [i.e., he never stepped across the rows of students who were sitting on the floor, trying to get to his seat in the front of the *bet midrash*. He either came early, or sat outside]. I never raised my hands to pronounce *Birkat Kohanim* [the priestly blessing] without reciting the *berachah* beforehand" [R. Elazar b. Shamua was a *kohen*]. What *berachah* did he say? R. Zeira said in the name of R. Chisda, "Blessed are You God, our Lord, King of the universe, Who has sanctified us with the holiness of Aaron and has commanded us to bless His people Israel with love."[101] When the *kohen* moves his feet [to go up to the platform] for the *Birkas Kohanim* what does he say? May it be Your will, God our Lord . . .

R. ABBAHU'S HUMILITY

(40a) R. Abbahu said: At first I used to think that I was humble, but when I saw R. Abba of Acco give an explanation, and his *amora* [the person who announced his lecture aloud to the students] offered a different explanation, and R. Abba was not upset, I realized that I was not humble. How was R. Abbahu's humility evident? The wife of R. Abbahu's *amora* said to R. Abbahu's wife, "My husband does not need your husband [to teach him; he is just as learned as your husband], and when my husband bows down [to receive instruction from him] he only does so out of respect [because R. Abbahu is highly esteemed by the Roman officials]." When R. Abbahu's wife told this to her husband, he said to her, "Why should it bother you? The main thing is that through my Torah knowledge and his scholarship God is praised." When the Rabbis offered him the post of *rosh yeshivah* he declined and said, "There is a greater scholar than I for the position," for he knew that R. Abba of Acco had many creditors [pressing him for payment, and that he was in need of the money that the position of *rosh yeshivah* would earn for him].

R. Abbahu and R. Chiya b. Abba once came to a place. R. Abbahu expounded on *aggadah* [teachings on ethics and morality] and R. Chiya on *halachah* [complex legal issues]. Everyone came to listen to R. Abbahu, [because *aggadah* is heartwarming], and R. Chjiya felt slighted. R. Abbahu, [trying to console him,] told him: Let me give you a parable. Two mer-

chants came to town; one was selling precious stones, the other was selling inexpensive notions and trinkets. Whom do all the people jump on? Surely on the one who is selling inexpensive notions and trinkets! Every day R. Chiya used to accompany R. Abbahu to his lodging because R. Abbahu was respected by the Roman officials; but on that day R. Abbahu accompanied R. Chiya b. Abba to his lodging, but he still was not pacified.

R. Yitzchak said: You should always be in awe of the congregation, for the *kohanim* [while reciting *Birkas Kohanim*] are facing the people, and their backs are turned toward the *Shechinah* [the Ark, which contains the Torah scrolls]. R. Nachman said: We derive it from the following passage, "King David stood up on his feet and said, 'Hear me, my brothers and my people!'" (1 Chronicles 28:2). If [he calls them] "my brothers," why does he address them as "my people"; if "my people," why "my brothers"? R. Elazar said: David told the people: If you listen to me, you are my brothers; if you don't, you are my people, and I will govern you with the rod.

(40b) The Rabbis taught: From where is it known that *Amen* was not said in the *Bet Hamikdash*? For it says, "Rise up and bless God your Lord, from this world to the World to Come!" (Nehemiah 9:5). [This response was said after every *berachah* in the *Bet Hamikdash* (Rashi).] And from where do we know that every *berachah* must be followed by an expression of praise? For it says, "Let them bless Your glorious name, which is exalted above every blessing and praise!" (ibid.), which means: On every *berachah* give praise.[102]

THE KING READS FROM THE TORAH

(41a) [Once every seven years the entire nation gathered at the Temple to hear the king read from Deuteronomy.][103] [The Mishnah elaborates on this law:] How was this reading of the king done? At the conclusion of the first day of Sukkot, in the eighth [year], right after the end of the seventh year [of the *shemittah* cycle],[104] a wooden platform was erected in the Temple Court, and the king would sit on that platform, as it says, "At the end of seven years, at the time of the Sabbatical year, during the Sukkot festival . . . you shall read the Torah before all Israel" (Deuteronomy 31:10,11). The attendant [of the synagogue on the Temple Mount] takes a Torah scroll and hands it to the head of the synagogue; the head of the synagogue hands it to the *Kohen Gadol*; who passes it on to the king. The king stands up and accepts the Torah scroll and reads from it while seated. King Agrippa [a descendant of Herod the Edomite][105] stood up to accept the Torah scroll, and [respectfully] remained standing while reading from it.

The Sages praised him for honoring the Torah. When he came to the verse concerning the king, "You must not put a foreigner over you [as king], who is not your brother" (Deuteronomy 17:15), he wept, [because this verse disqualified him to be king]. However, the people called to him, "Do not fear, Agrippa; you are our brother, you are our brother!" [because his mother was Jewish]. [The Mishnah continues:] The king reads from the beginning of Deuteronomy up to the *Shema* (Deuteronomy 6:4–9); he reads the *Shema*; [he then skips and reads] the chapter of "And it will come to pass that if you continually hearken" (ibid. 11:13–21); the chapter "You shall tithe" (ibid. 14:22–29); "When you have finished tithing" (ibid. 26:12–15); the chapter of the king, (ibid. 17:14–20); and the blessings and curses (ibid. 28), until he finishes the entire chapter [of the blessings and curses].

THE EVIL OF FLATTERY

(41b) [The Mishnah said: When King Agrippa came to the verse, "You must not put a foreigner over you [as king]" he wept. The Gemara comments:] We learned in a *Baraita* in the name of R. Natan: At that moment [when the people called to him, "You are our brother!"], the Jewish people became liable to destruction because they flattered Agrippa. R. Shimon b. Chalafta said: From the day that flattery began to prevail, justice became perverted, the general conduct began to deteriorate, and nobody could tell another person, "My conduct is better than yours." [The moral climate declined.] R. Yehudah bar Maarava, others say, R. Shimon b. Pazi, said: It is permitted to flatter the wicked in this world, for it says [concerning the World to Come], "A vile person will no longer be called generous, and it will not be said that a miser is magnanimous" (Isaiah 32:5). This implies that it is permitted in this world. R. Shimon b. Lakish said: We can derive this from the following passage, [when Jacob met Esau, he said], "Seeing your face is like seeing the face of the Divine, you have received me so favorably" (Genesis 33:10); [he thereby flattered the evil Esau].

He differs on this point with R. Levi, for R. Levi said: To what can we compare [this conversation between] Jacob and Esau? To a person who invited his neighbor to a meal, and [the invited guest] noticed that [the host] wanted to poison him. So he told him, "The dish that I am eating tastes just like the dish I was served at the royal palace." The [host] said to himself, "Obviously, he must know the king. I had better not harm him." So he did not kill him. [The same way, Jacob spoke of "seeing the Divine," not in order to flatter Esau, but to frighten him.] R. Elazar said: Any person who has the trait of flattery brings anger on the world, as it says, "And those that are flatterers at heart will bring on [God's] anger" (Job 36:13). Not only that, but their prayers are not accepted, as the verse continues, "They should not cry out to Him when He afflicts them, [for their prayers will not be accepted]."

R. Elazar also said: Any person who is a flatterer is cursed even by the embryo in his mother's womb. For it says, "If someone tells a wicked person, 'You are righteous', the peoples will curse [*kov*] him, the nations [*le'umim*] will damn him" (Proverbs 24:24). The word *kov* means "curse" as it says, "Whom God has not cursed [*kabo*]" (Numbers 23:8). And *le'umim* refers to embryos, for it says [regarding the unborn Jacob and Esau in Rebekkah's womb], "One *le'om* will be stronger than the other *le'om*" (Genesis 25:23). R. Elazar said further: Any person who flatters [the wicked] will go to Gehinnom, as it says, "Woe to those who speak of evil as good, and of good as evil" (Isaiah 5:20). What does it say after that? "Therefore, just as a tongue of fire consumes straw, and a flame destroys stubble, so will their root become rot" (ibid. v. 24).

R. Elazar said further: If someone flatters a wicked person, he will eventually fall into his hand. If he does not fall into his hand, he will fall into the hand of his sons, and if he does not fall into his sons' hand, he will fall into his grandsons' hand. For it says, [Hananiah, a false prophet, prophesied wrongly that the people and the vessels of the Temple that had been taken into exile would soon return to Jerusalem]. "Thereupon Jeremiah the prophet said [to Hananiah], 'Amen, may God do so! May God fulfill your words'" (Jeremiah 28:6). [The fact that Jeremiah did not denounce Hananaiah was a form of flattery.] And it says, (42a) "[Jeremiah] was in the Benjamin Gate, but an official was there—his name was Irijah son of Shelemiah son of Hananiah, [the false prophet; thus Irijah was Hananiah's grandson]— and seized Jeremiah the prophet saying, 'You are deserting to the Chaldeans!' Jeremiah replied, 'Falsehood! I am not deserting to the Chaldeans!' But he did not listen to him, and Irijah seized Jeremiah and brought him to the officers" (Jeremiah 37:13,14). [Thus, because Jeremiah flattered Hananiah, his downfall came at the hand of Hananiah's grandson.]

R. Elazar also said: Any community that flatters [evildoers] will eventually be driven into exile. It says here, "For the flatterer's clan will be forlorn [*galmud*]" (Job 15:34), and elsewhere it says, "And you will say in your heart, 'What caused all these things to come about? For I have been bereaved and alone [*galmudah*], an exile and a wanderer'" (Isaiah 49:21).

R. Yirmeyah b. Abba said: Four categories of people will not [be admitted into] the presence of the *Shechinah*, namely: scoffers, flatterers, liars, and slanderers. Scoffers, for says, "God removes His hand from those that mock and scorn" (Hosea 7:5). Flatterers, for it says, "A flatterer will not come before Him" (Job 13:116). Liars, for it says, "One who tells a lie shall not be established before My eyes" (Psalms 101:7). Slanderers, for it says, "For You are not a God who desires wickedness, [referring to slander], no evil sojourns with You" (ibid. 5:5)—meaning: You are righteous, O God, someone who is evil may not live with You.

473

THE "*KOHEN* ANOINTED FOR BATTLE"

[Before every battle, a *kohen* who was specifically appointed for this purpose, addressed the troops in order to inspire them with courage and prepare them for war. This *kohen* was anointed with the anointing oil and was called *Meshu'ach Milchamah*, "the Anointed for Battle."[106] The present Mishnah elaborates on this subject:] When the *kohen* who was designated as the "Anointed for Battle" addresses the people, he must speak to them in the Holy Tongue, [quoting the verses of the Torah verbatim], as it says, "When you approach [the place of] battle, the *kohen* shall step forward" (Deuteronomy 20:2), i.e., the Anointed for Battle. [The passage continues,] "And he begins to speak to the people"—in the Holy Tongue. "He shall say to them, 'Listen Israel, today you are about to wage war against your enemies'"—"against your enemies," but not against your brothers; [this battle is not like the battle that] the tribe of Judah fought against the tribe of Simon, or Simon against Benjamin, because in a battle [against another tribe] if you fall into your adversary's hand, he will have mercy on you.

For it says, [concerning the battle between Israel and Judah, where Israel was victorious and took many prisoners, but released all of them], "The men who had been mentioned by name then got up and gave assistance to the captives—they dressed all their unclothed people from the spoils. They dressed them, gave them shoes, fed them, gave them to drink, anointed them, and led all the faint ones on donkeys. They brought them to Jericho, the city of palms, to their kinsmen, and then returned to Samaria" (2 Chronicles 28:15). "Against your enemies"—so that if you fall into their hands, they will not have mercy on you. [The *kohen* continued,] "Do not be faint-hearted, do not be afraid, do not panic, and do not break ranks" (Deuteronomy 20:3). "Do not be faint-hearted"—at the neighing of the horses and the brandishing of the swords. "Do not be afraid"—of the banging of the shields and the sound of the marching boots. "Do not panic"—at the sound of the trumpets. "Do not break ranks"—at the sound of the battle cries. "God the Lord is the One who is going with you" (ibid. v. 4)—They are trying to win, relying on the strategy of their mortal generals, but you are relying on the might of God. The Philistines came relying on the might of Goliath. But what was his end? In the end he fell by the sword, and they fell with him.[107] The Ammonites came relying on the might of Shovach [the commander of Haddadezer's army].[108] But what became of him? In the end he fell by the sword, and they fell with him. But you, Israel, you are not like that. "God your Lord is the One who is going with you. He will fight for you"—this alludes to the Holy Ark [that went with them into battle].

It says, "[The *kohen* anointed for battle] said to them, '*Shema Yisrael*, Listen, Israel.'" [The Gemara asks:] Why does he begin with these words? R.

Yochanan said in the name of R. Shimon b. Yochai: The Holy One, blessed be He, said to Israel: Even if you only fulfilled the mitzvah of reading the *Shema* [which begins with *Shema Yisrael*] morning and evening, you will not fall into the hands of your enemy. We learned in a *Baraita*: He addresses them twice: once when they are on the boundary [about to leave the country to go to war], and once on the battlefield. What does the *kohen* say on the boundary? (42b) [He says:] "Listen to the regulations of battle and return home," [referring to those who had reason to be exempt from serving in the army].[109] What does he say on the battlefield? [He says:] "Do not be faint-hearted, do not be afraid, do not panic, and do not break ranks before them." These four expressions correspond to four devices the nations of the world use to scare their enemies: they crash their shields, they sound trumpets, they shout battle cries, and they trample on the ground.

DAVID AND GOLIATH

[The *kohen* said:] "The Philistines came relying on the might of Goliath." Why was he called Goliath? R. Yochanan said: Because he had the audacity [*giluy panim*] to challenge the Holy One, blessed be He. For it says, [Goliath said], "Choose for yourselves a man [*ish*], and let him come down to me!" (1 Samuel 17:8). And the word *ish*, "man," denotes none other than the Holy One, blessed be He, as it says, "God is an *ish milchamah*, a Master of war" (Exodus 15:3). The Holy One, Blessed be He, thereupon declared: For that I will bring about his downfall at the hand of someone who is referred to as a "son of an *ish*," as it says, "David was the son of an *ish Efrati*, the son of a man from Efrat" (ibid. v. 12).

R. Yochanan said in the name of R. Meir: In three places, Goliath's own words foretold his downfall. First: When he said, "Choose for yourselves a man, and let him come down to me." [He predicted that David would bring him down.] Second: When he said, "If he can fight me and kill me" (ibid. v. 9), [his words foreshadowed that David would kill him]. And third: When he said, "Am I a dog that you come after me with sticks?" [he again suggested his downfall]. [The Gemara asks:] But didn't David use a similar phrase when he said, "You are coming against me with a sword, a spear, and a javelin" (ibid. v. 45), [isn't that too a bad omen]? [The Gemara answers:] David used this as a preface to what he intended to say: "But I am coming against you with the name of God, Master of Legions, the God of the battalions of Israel that you have ridiculed" (ibid. v. 45).

[It says,] "The Philistine [Goliath] would approach [the Israelite camp] early morning and evening" (ibid. v. 16). R. Yochanan said: He came to prevent them from reciting the *Shema* in the morning and evening.

"He presented himself for forty days" (ibid.). R. Yochanan said: Corresponding to the forty days [during which Moses remained on the mountain] when he received the Torah.[110]

"A champion [beinayim] went forth from the Philistine camp" (ibid. v.4). [The Gemara asks:] What does beinayim mean? Rav said: [Goliath] was built [mevuneh] without any blemish. Shmuel said: He was the middle one [beinoni] of his brothers. In the yeshivah of R. Shila they explained: He was built like a building [binyan]. R. Yochanan said: He was the son of a hundred men [who had lived with his mother], one of whom was his father [ben nana'i]. "His name was Goliath of Gath" (ibid.). R. Yosef taught: ["of Gath" was added to indicate that] all men pressed his mother like a gat, a wine press [i.e., they lived with her].

[The mother of Goliath was Orpah, the sister-in-law of Ruth.[111] In 2 Samuel 21:18 Orpah is called Harafah. The Gemara continues: It says,] "These four were born to Harafah [i.e., Orpah] in Gath, and they fell by the hand of David and the hand of his servants" (2 Samuel 21:22). Who were these four? R. Chisda said: They were: Saph, Madon, Goliath, and Ishbibenob (ibid. v. 18, 20, 19, and 16). "And they fell by the hand of David and by the hand of his servants," for it says, "Orpah kissed her mother-in-law [Naomi, and left], but Ruth clung to her [mother-in-law]" (Ruth 1:14). R. Yitzchak said: The Holy One, blessed be He, said: May the children of [Orpah] the one who kissed [Naomi and left] fall by the hand of the descendants of [Ruth], who clung to [Naomi]; [David was an offspring of Ruth].

Rava expounded: As a reward for the four tears that Orpah shed [when she left] her mother-in-law she merited that four mighty warriors descended from her. [And how do we know that she shed four tears?] For it says, "They raised their voice and wept again" (Ruth 1:14). ["Again" signifies that she cried twice, and each time one tear dropped from each eye (Rashi).]

[In the description of Goliath's armor], the written text says, "cheitz, 'the arrow' of his spear" (1 Samuel 17:7), but we read it as "eitz, 'the shaft' of his spear." [Why is it written cheitz?] R. Elazar said: [Cheitz is cognate to chatzi, "half"]. The verse tells us that the text has not told us even half of the praise of the strength of that wicked man Goliath. [Why does the verse tell only a small part of the prowess of Goliath?] To teach us that it is forbidden to tell the praises of wicked people. Then Scripture should not have mentioned his strength at all! [The Gemara answers: The purpose of praising Goliath is] that it implies a praise of David [who defeated a giant as powerful as Goliath].

[We learned in the Mishnah that in his address to the troops the kohen said:] The Ammonites came, relying on the might of Shovach. [The Gemara remarks:] Here the name is written Shovach, but [elsewhere it written] Shofach![112] Rav and Shmuel [have different opinions about this]. One said that his real name was

Shovach, and why was he called Shofach? Because whoever saw him was so terrified that he was poured out [nishpach] in front of him like [water from] a pitcher. The other said: His real name was Shofach, and why was he called Shovach? Because he was built like a pigeon house [shovach]; [that is how tall he was].

[The Gemara continues by citing another difference of opinion between Rav and Shmuel, this one regarding a verse that describes the strength of Nebuchadnezzar's army.] It says, "Their quiver [ashpato] is like an open grave, they are all mighty men" (Jeremiah 5:16). Rav and Shmuel—others say, R. Ammi and R. Assi—have a difference of opinion about this verse. One says: [It means:] When they shot an arrow they would make piles [ashpatot] upon piles of corpses. Now perhaps you will attribute it to the fact that they were skilled in warfare, [and not to their strength], that is why it says, "they are all mighty men"—they were able to do this by virtue of their strength. The other explained the verse: At the time when they relieved themselves they made piles upon piles of excrement. Now you might say that this was due to a stomach disorder; that is why it says, "they are all mighty men." [It was because of their large and powerful physique that they produced so much waste.] R. Mari said: We can infer from this that a person who passes stool excessively is ill in his intestines and should do something for it before the ailment worsens.

[The Gemara follows up with another exposition by R. Ammi and R. Assi.] It says, "When there is worry in a man's heart, he should suppress it [yash'chenah]" (Proverbs 12:25). R. Ammi and R. Assi [offer different interpretations]. One says: He should banish it [yis'chenah] from his thoughts. The other says: He should talk about it [yasichena] to someone else, [and that will relieve his anxiety].

THE LINEAGE OF PINCHAS

[The kohen proclaimed to the assembled troops:] "But you, Israel, are not like that . . . God the Lord is the One who is going with you. He will fight for you!" (Deuteronomy 20:4). This alludes to the Holy Ark that went with them into battle. [The Gemara asks:] Why the wordiness? [Why did he say: God is the One who is going with you; why not simply: God is with you?] [The Gemara answers:] Because the Four-Letter Divine Name and other Divine appellations[113] were [written on the Tablets of the Covenant (43a) that were] lying in the Ark. And so it says [that when the Israelites went to war to take revenge against the Midianites], "Moses sent forth the 1,000 men from each tribe as an army, them and Pinchas, . . . the sacred vessels and the signal trumpets" (Numbers 31:6)—"them" refers to the Sanhedrin; "Pinchas" was the kohen Anointed for Battle; "the sacred vessels" refers to the Ark and the Tablets that were in it; "and the signal trumpets" refers to shofarot.

We learned in a *Baraita*: Pinchas had good reason to go to war against the Midianites. He wanted to avenge what they had done to his mother's father [Joseph]. For it says, "The Midianites sold [Joseph] into Egypt" (Genesis 37:36). [The Gemara asks:] Do you mean to say that Pinchas was a descendant of Joseph? But surely it says, "Aaron's son Eleazar married one of the daughters of Putiel [who is identified with Jethro], and she bore him Pinchas" (Exodus 6:26). Does the *Baraita* not indicate that he was a descendant of Jethro? [And why is Jethro called Putiel?] Because he fattened [*pittem*] calves for idol worship. [Thus Pinchas was a descendant of Jethro, not of Joseph!]

[The Gemara answers:] No, [he was a descendant] of Joseph, [and Joseph is called Putiel] because he repressed [*pitpeit*] his evil impulse [when Potiphar's wife tried to seduce him]. [The Gemara asks:] But did not the other tribes despise Pinchas, saying: Look at this son of Putti whose mother's father [Jethro] fattened calves [to sacrifice them] for idol worship, and he went and killed a prince in Israel![114] [Proof that he is a descendant of Jethro!] We must therefore say that if his mother's father was a descendant of Joseph, his mother's mother was an offspring of Jethro, [consequently, he was a descendant of both]. This is also borne out by a precise reading of the text, "Eleazar the son of Aaron married one of the daughters of Putiel"; [since he is not called Putel but rather Putiel, with an extra *yud*], we can infer that the name can refer to both Joseph and Jethro. This inference can indeed be drawn.

A HOUSE, A VINEYARD, AND A WIFE

(44a) [Before the army went into battle, an announcement was made that anyone who had built a new house, planted a vineyard, or betrothed a woman should go home (Deuteronomy 20:5–7).]

The Rabbis taught: The text mentions first, "who has built"; then, "who has planted"; and then, "who has betrothed." The Torah teaches you thereby the way you should act; that first a person should build a house for himself, then plant a vineyard, and then marry a wife. So, too, Solomon in his wisdom said, "Prepare your work outside, and provide for yourself in the field; afterwards build your house" (Proverbs 24:27). "Prepare your work outside" refers to building a house; "provide for yourself in the field" means planting a vineyard; "afterwards build your house" means starting a family. Another interpretation is: "Prepare your work outside"—learn Scripture; "provide for yourself in the field"—study Mishnah; "afterwards build a house"—learn Gemara. Another explanation is: "Prepare your work outside"—Scripture and Mishnah; "provide for yourself in the field"—Gemara; "afterwards build a house"—do *mitzvot* and good deeds. R. Eliezer, son of R. Yose HaGelili says: "Prepare your work outside"—learn Scripture, Mishnah, and Gemara; "provide for yourself in the field"—do *mitzvot* and good deeds; "afterwards build your house"—expound the Torah [simply for the love of learning] and receive the reward.

HOW DOES AN EMBRYO DEVELOP?

(45b) [If a corpse is found between two cities, the elders and judges must go and measure the distance to the cities around the corpse. The elders of the city closest to the corpse must then bring a female calf to a barren valley, axe the back of its head [*eglah arufah*], and make a solemn declaration (Deuteronomy 21:1–9).]

[The Mishnah asks:] From what part [of the body of the corpse] do they measure [the distance to the closest city]? R. Eliezer says: From the navel. R. Akiva says: From the nose. R. Eliezer b. Yaakov says: From the place where he was slain—i.e., from the neck, [assuming that his head was chopped off].

[The Gemara asks:] On what essential point do they disagree? [The Gemara answers:] R. Akiva holds that the essence of life is in the nose, while R. Eliezer b. Yaakov maintains that the essence of life is in the navel [because the beginning of life flows through the navel]. Shall we say [that they differ on the same issue] as the Tannaim [in the Gemara[115] in *Yoma* where the following question is raised]: From what part of the body does the development of the embryo begin? [The Gemara answers:] From the head; and so it says, "You withdrew me [*gozi*] from the innards of my mother" (Psalm 71:6), and it says further, "Tear out [*gozi*] your hair, and throw it away" (Jeremiah 7:29) [thus *gozi* refers to the place where the hair grows, i.e., the head]. Abba Shaul says: From the navel, and [from there] it spreads its extensions in all directions.

You can even say that Abba Shaul agrees with R. Akiva, because R. Abba Shaul's statement refers only to the formation of the embryo, that when an embryo is formed it is formed from the middle, but as to where the source of life is [and where life ends, and a person becomes a corpse], all agree that it is in the nose. For it says, "All in whose nostrils was a lifegiving breath" (Genesis 7:22). R. Eliezer b. Yaakov said: [They measure] from the place where he was slain—from the neck. [The Gemara asks:] What is the reason of R. Eliezer b. Yaakov?—Because it says, "To place you with the necks of the corpses of the wicked" (Ezekiel 21:34); [the corpse is identified with the neck].

THE *EGLAH ARUFAH*

(46a) R. Yochanan b. Shmuel said: Why does the Torah say that the female calf should be brought to a barren valley? The Holy One, blessed be He, said: Let something that did not produce fruit [a calf less than a year old cannot have young], have its neck severed in a place that does not produce fruit [a barren valley], and atone for one who was not allowed to produce fruit [because he was killed]. [The Gemara asks:] What does the "fruit" [of the slain person] refer to? Do you think that it refers to children? In that case, if the person found dead was old or castrated, we should not perform the ceremony of *eglah arufah*! [Severing a calf's neck. And that cerainly is not so.] Therefore we must say that "fruit" refers to the performance of *mitzvot*; [the slain person was not allowed to do more *mitzvot*].

[The Mishnah on 45b taught: After breaking the calf's neck with a hatchet from behind,] the elders of that city wash their hands with water in the place where the calf's neck was broken and declare, "Our hands have not spilled this blood, and our eyes have not witnessed it" (Deuteronomy 21:7). But can it enter our mind that the elders of a Court of Justice are murderers? What they meant to say is: The man found dead did not come to us for help, and we sent him away without food; [we did not in any way indirectly cause his death, by sending him away without food, so that he was too weak to fight off his attacker]. We did not see him leave, and let him go without escort. Then the *kohanim* proclaim, "Forgive Your people, whom You, God, have liberated. Do not allow the guilt for innocent blood to remain with your people Israel" (ibid. v. 8). The *kohanim* did not have to say the words [appearing at the end of that verse], "The blood shall thus be atoned for" (ibid.). But the Holy Spirit announces [through Moses], "When they act like this, the blood will be atoned for."

THE MITZVAH
OF ESCORTING SOMEONE

(46b) We learned in a *Baraita*: R. Meir used to say: [The court] has a right to force a person to escort a traveler, because the reward for the mitzvah of escorting someone is boundless, as it says [in connection with the conquest of the city of Bethel], "The patrols saw a man leaving the city. They said to him, 'Just show us the secret entrance to the city, and we will treat you kindly'" (Judges 1:24). And it continues, "He showed them the secret entrance to the city" (ibid. 25). And what was the kindness they did to this man? "They put the town to the sword, but they let the man and all his relatives go free" (ibid.). "The man went to the Hittite country. He founded a city and named it Luz, and that has been its name to this day" (ibid. v. 26).

We learned in a *Baraita*: That is the same Luz where they make the dye for the *techeilet* [the turquoise blue used to dye the string of the *tzitzit*];[116] that is the same Luz against which Sennacherib marched without disturbing it, against which Nebuchanezzar marched without destroying it, and even the Angel of Death has no right to enter it. [So how do the people of that city die?] When the old people there become tired of life, they go outside the wall and die out there. Isn't it a *kal vachomer* [a logical inference that the reward for escorting is boundless]? If this Canaanite [who showed Jewish patrols the secret entrance by merely pointing in the direction], who did not say a word or take one step, brought deliverance for himself and his offspring for all generations to come, a person who does the mitzvah of escorting by actually going along with another person, how much greater will his reward be!

[The Gemara asks:] How did this Canaanite show the patrols the way? Chizkiyah said: He just twisted his mouth [in the direction of the secret entrance]. R. Yochanan said: He pointed it out to them with his finger. The following *Baraita* supports R. Yochanan's view: Because this Canaanite pointed with his finger, he saved himself and his children for all generations to come.

R. Yehoshua b. Levi said: If someone is on the road and has no companion, he should think Torah thoughts, [and they will protect him], for it says, "For [the words of Torah] are a graceful wreath upon your head and a necklace around your throat" (Proverbs 1:9). R. Yehoshua b. Levi said further: Because of the four steps that Pharaoh accompanied Abraham, as it says, "Pharaoh gave men orders concerning Abram, and they escorted him and his wife" (Genesis 12:20), he was allowed to enslave Abraham's children for four hundred years.[117] R. Yehudah said in the name of Rav: If someone accompanies his neighbor four cubits in a city, no harm will come to [the neighbor on his journey]. Ravina accompanied Rava b. Yitzchak for four cubits in the city; [after he left the city] he ran into a dangerous situation and was saved. The Rabbis taught: A teacher should escort his student as far as the outskirts of the city; a person should escort his colleague until the *Shabbat* boundary [i.e., 2,000 cubits beyond the city limits, the distance you are permitted to walk on *Shabbat*]; the distance a student should accompany his teacher has no limit. [The Gemara asks:] How far should this be? R. Sheshet said: Up to a *parsah*. And this applies only to the rabbi who is not his exclusive teacher, but if he is his primary teacher, he should escort him a distance of three *parsah*.

R. Kahana once accompanied R. Shimi b. Ashi from Pum Nahara to Bei Tzinita in Babylonia [a place known for its many date palm groves]. When they arrived there, R. Kahana said to R. Shimi b. Ashi, "Is it true what people say, that those palm trees of Babylonia date back to the time of Adam?" He replied, "You have reminded me of something R. Yose b. R. Chanina said, namely: What is meant by the verse, [referring to the wilderness of Sinai], "A land through which no man passed, and where no person has settled" (Jeremiah 2:6)? If no man passed through there, how could anyone settle there, and if no one settled there, how could anyone pass through there? [Isn't the text redundant?]

[R. Yose b. R. Chanina explains: It means:] Any part of the earth about which Adam decreed that it should be inhabited has become inhabited, and any part about which he decreed that it should not be inhabited remained uninhabited, [and Adam did not decree that this place should be inhabited; therefore these palm trees must date back to Adam, since no one else could have planted them]. R. Mordechai accompanied R. Ashi from Hagronya all the way to Bei Kipai; others say, to Bei Dura. [The Gemara mentions these cases to teach us how much the rabbis exerted themselves to fulfill the mitzvah of escorting a teacher.]

R. Yochanan said in the name of R. Meir: If someone does not accompany his friend, he is considered as if he shed blood; for if the citizens of Jericho had escorted Elisha, he would not have incited the bears to attack the children. As it says, "[Elisha] went up from there to Bethel. As he was going up the road, some little boys came out of the city and taunted him, saying, "Go away, baldhead! Go away, baldhead!" (2 Kings 2:23). What they meant to say was, "Go away, you who have made this place bald [unprofitable] for us." [Elisha had turned the brackish water of Jericho into sweet water,[118] and thereby caused a loss of income for the boys who sold sweet water.] What does "little boys" mean? R. Elazar said: [They were, in fact, adults, but they are called] ne'arim [boys] because they were menu'arim, "empty" of mitzvot; [and they are called] ketanim [little] because they had little faith, [and did not trust that God would provide for them from another source].

We learned in another Baraita: They were young boys but they behaved like little children. R. Yosef objected to this: Maybe they were called ne'arim because they came from a town named Ne'arim? [And Ne'arim is indeed the name of a town, for] doesn't it say, "Once when the Arameans had gone out on a raiding party they carried off a na'arah ketanah, a young girl from the Land of Israel" (2 Kings 5:2); note a contradiction: She is described as a na'arah [a girl over the age of twelve], and, at the same time, as a ketanah [a girl under the age of twelve]! R. Pedat answers: She was indeed a little girl, but she came from a town called Ne'urin. [So we see that there is a town named Ne'urim. Perhaps here too, ne'arim ketanim means "little boys from Ne'arim"?] [The Gemara answers:] In the verse about the girl, the town she came from is not mentioned, [it just says "from the Land of Israel," so na'arah could be the name of a town]. But in the verse about the boys, their hometown [Jericho] is mentioned, [so they could not be from the town of Na'arah].

ELISHA AND THE BEARS

[It says, that when the boys taunted Elisha,] "He turned around and saw them, and cursed them in the name of God" (2 Kings 2:24). [The Gemara asks:] What did he see in them [that prompted him to curse them, pronouncing God's name]? Rav said: [He did not utter a curse at all]. He just looked at them [and thought of God's name]. As we learned in a Baraita: R. Shimon b. Gamliel says: Whenever a Sage wants to rebuke someone, his gaze alone is enough to cause death or poverty. Shmuel said: He saw [with prophetic insight] that their mothers had conceived them on Yom Kippur, [when marital relations are forbidden]. R. Yitzchak Nafcha said: He saw that they were wearing their hair long in the style of the heathens. R. Yochanan said: He saw these boys had no freshness of mitzvah in them. [The Gemara asks:] Maybe their children would have freshness of mitzvah? R. Elazar said: He saw [with prophetic vision that there would be no freshness of mitzvah] in them nor in their descendants until the end of all generations.

[The verse continues,] "Two bears then came out of the forest, and tore apart forty-two of the boys" (ibid.). (47a) Rav and Shmuel [differ in their interpretations]; one said it was a miracle [that the bears appeared], and the other said it was a miracle within a miracle. The one who said it was a miracle did so because there was a forest but there were no bears in that forest, [and miraculously the bears emerged]. The one who said it was a miracle within a miracle did so because there was neither a forest nor were there any bears. [The Gemara asks: According to this interpretation,] let the bears appear miraculously, but what do you need the forest for! [The Gemara answers: Without a forest to retreat to,] the bears would have been afraid [to attack the children].

"[The bears] tore apart forty-two boys" (ibid.). R. Chaninah said: Because Balak the king of Moab offered forty-two sacrifices,[119] [his ambition to destroy Israel was fulfilled in a small way when] forty-two children were cut off from Israel. [The Gemara asks:] That cannot be the reason; for Rav Yehudah said in the name of Rav: A person should always occupy himself with Torah and mitzvot, even if he does it for ulterior motives; because from doing it for selfish reasons, eventually he will come to do it for the sake of Heaven. [What is the source of this principle?] Because as a reward for the forty-two sacrifices that Balak, king of Moab, offered, [although his purpose was to induce God to curse Israel], he merited that Ruth should come forth from him, and Ruth was the ancestor of Solomon, about whom it says, "Solomon offered up a thousand elevation-offerings on that Altar" (1 Kings 3:4). And R. Yose b. Choni said: Ruth was the daughter of Eglon, king of Moab, the son of Balak; [so you see, having Ruth as a granddaughter was Balak's reward, not the death of the boys]. [The Gemara answers:] Nevertheless, his desire was to curse the people of Israel, [and he was rewarded through the death of the boys].

ELISHA AND GECHAZI

[The Gemara now focuses on the miracle Elisha performed in sweetening the water of Jericho.] "The people of the city [of Jericho] told Elisha, 'Behold living in this city is pleasant, as my master can see, but the water is bad, and the land causes bereavement'" (2 Kings 2:19). [The Gemara asks:] If the water supply was bad and the land caused bereavement, what did they find pleasant in this city? R. Chanin said: It is the charm a hometown holds for its inhabitants.

R. Yochanan said: There are three blind loves: The love people have for their hometown, [even though others find many drawbacks in it]; the love a husband has for his wife, [even though others do not find her attractive]; and the appeal an object holds for the one who bought it, [even though others may not think it was a good buy].

Our Rabbis taught: Elisha suffered from three illnesses: he was stricken with one illness because he incited the bears against the children; with the second because he pushed away [his servant] Gechazi with both his hands; and the third illness was the one of which he died. For it says, "Elisha became ill with the disease of which he was to die" (2 Kings 13:14).

We learned in a *Baraita*: [When you must criticize a person,] always let your left hand repel, [the weaker hand], and let your right hand bring closer. Do not act like Elisha who rebuffed Gechazi with both his hands. [The Gemara asks:] What is the story of Elisha [and Gechazi]?—[Naaman, the commander of the army of Aram, was stricken with leprosy, and by following Elisha's instructions he was healed. He offered a gift, which Elisha refused. As Naaman left, Gechazi followed him and said, "My master now requests some small gift."] "Naaman said, 'Please! Take two talents of silver!'" and it says, "[Elisha] said to [Gechazi], 'Did not my heart go along when a man got down from his chariot to meet you? [Through prophetic vision I knew exactly what happened. Elisha chided Gechazi for asking for gifts, saying,] Is this a time to take money in order to buy clothing and olive groves and vineyards, sheep and oxen and male and female slaves?'" (2 Kings 5:26).

[The Gemara asks:] Had Gechazi really taken that much? [Why did Elisha accuse him of taking eight things: silver, clothing, sheep, oxen, male and female slaves, olive groves and vineyards,] when all Gechazi took was silver and garments! R. Yitzchak said: At that time Elisha was busy teaching his students [including Gechazi] the chapter of "Eight Swarming Animals."[120] So Elisha said to Gechazi, "You evildoer, [I mentioned eight things that you took to allude to the reward that is in store for you for studying the chapter of "Eight Swarming Animals"]. Is it now, in this world, the time to take the reward for studying the chapter of 'Eight Swarming Animals'?" [Elisha cursed Gechazi,] "'Naaman's leprosy shall therefore cling to you and to your offspring, forever!' And when [Gechazi] left his presence, he was snow-white with leprosy" (2 Kings 5:27), [which proves that Elisha totally rebuffed Gechazi].

"There were four men who were lepers at the city gate" (ibid. 7:3). R. Yochanan said: These were Gechazi and his three sons. "Elisha went to Damascus" (ibid. 8:7).—Why did he go there? R. Yochanan said: He went to persuade Gechazi to do *teshuvah* [repent], but Gechazi refused. Elisha said to him, "Do *teshuvah*, Gechazi." He replied, "I have learned from you: If someone sinned and caused others to sin, it becomes impossible for him to do *teshuvah*." What did Gechazi do [to cause others to sin]? Some say, he attached a magnet to the [two golden calves] of Jeroboam,[121] and suspended them between heaven and earth, [and the people worshipped the calves because they seemed to be hovering in space]. Others say, he engraved the name of God on [the mouth of one of the the golden calves] so that it would exclaim, "I [am the Lord your God]" and "You shall have no other god beside Me." Still others say: He chased away Elisha's students, for it says, [after Gechazi left Elisha,] "the prophet's disciples said to Elisha, 'Behold, the place where we sit before you [i.e., the *bet midrash*] is too cramped for us'" (2 Kings 6:1); this implies that up to that time it was not cramped, [because Gechazi used to chase away the students that came to learn].

We learned in a *Baraita*: R. Shimon b. Elazar said: [Not only in dealing with strangers should you remember the saying of "let your left hand repel, and let your right hand bring closer"]; this rule applies even to your sexual impulse, to your child, and to your wife. [If the sexual impulse is totally repressed, no children will be born; if a child is admonished too sternly, he will run away and do harm to himself; if a wife is rebuked too harshly, she will look for immoral ways to find happiness (Rashi).]

THINGS THAT CAME TO AN END

[The Mishnah says:] When murderers increased [in Eretz Yisrael], the ceremony of the *eglah arufah* was discontinued, [because it was held only when the murderer was totally unknown, but at a certain point in history the number of murderers increased, and their identity was known. So there was a strong likelihood that they were the perpetrators of any unsolved murder. When did this happen?] When Eliezer ben Dinai, who originally was called Techinah ben Perishah, appeared on the scene. [When he became a murderer] they gave him the nickname Ben Haratzchan [Son of the Murderer].[122] When adulterers increased [in the time of the second Temple], the ceremony of the bitter water was discontinued, and it was R. Yochanan b. Zakkai who discontinued it. For it says, "I will not punish your daughters [through the bitter water] when they commit harlotry, [nor] your daughters-in-law when they commit adultery, for the men are secluded with harlots and sacrifice with prostitutes" (Hosea 4:14), [and the bitter water has an effect on the suspected adulteress only if her husband is free of guilt].

[Other aspects of Jewish life that came to an end were:] When Yose b. Yoezer, leader of Tzeredah and Yose b. Yehudah, leader of Jerusalem died, the "clusters" ceased,[123] [both these leaders reached the peak in Torah learning and noble character traits], as it says, "There is no cluster to eat; my soul yearns for a ripe fruit" (Micah 7:1); [and the text continues, "The devout one has disappeared from the land, and one upright among men is no more"]. Yochanan the *Kohen Gadol* halted the recital of the confession made at the presentation of the tithe.[124] He also abolished the "wakers"[125] and the "knockers."[126] (47b) Until his days, the hammer would pound [in the workshops] in Jerusalem on the intermediate days of Yom Tov, but he put an end to it [because the noise constitutes a disrespect of the holiday]. And in his days there was no need to inquire about *demai*, [whether produce had been tithed, because he instituted that anyone who bought produce from a person who could not be trusted to have tithed, must tithe the produce himself].

(48a) [The Mishnah says:] When the Sanhedrin ceased to function [in Jerusalem, several years before the destruction of the Second Temple], singing in the banquet halls was abolished, as it says, "They drink their wine without song, liquor has become bitter to those who drink it" (Isaiah 24:9). When the early prophets died, the Urim and Tumim ceased.[127] When the [Second] Temple was destroyed, the *shamir* [the worm that could split the hardest stone] was lost; and the *nofet tzufim*, "the drippings of the honey comb" [i.e., honey of exquisite aroma, fragrance, and texture], disappeared; and men of faith were no more, as it says, "Save, O God, for the devout one is no more, for men of faith have vanished from mankind" (Psalms 12:2). R. Shimon b. Gamliel said: R. Yehoshua testified that since the *Bet Hamikdash* was destroyed there is not a day without a curse, the dew no longer comes down for blessing, and flavor has been taken away from fruits. R. Yose said: Also the richness has been taken out of the fruit [i.e., its nutritional value].

During the siege of Vespasian [which ended in the destruction of the *Bet Hamikdash*], the Sages decreed a ban on the special crown worn by bridegrooms, and on the *eirus* [a drum with a single bell]. This was done to dampen the rejoicing in light of the impending destruction of the *Bet Hamikdash*. During the siege of Titus, the Sages decreed against the use of crowns worn by brides, and that nobody should teach his son the wisdom of the Greeks. During the final phase of the siege [when the *Bet Hamikdash* was already destroyed], they decreed that a bride should not go out into the city under a canopy. But our Rabbis [meaning R. Yehudah Hanasi, the compiler of the Mishnah] permitted a bride to go out into the city under a canopy, [for the sake of modesty, because the canopy shelters the bride from the gaze of the onlookers].

When R. Meir died, the composers of parables came to an end. When Ben Azzai died, the diligent scholars disappeared. When Ben Zoma died, the expounders of the text disappeared. When R. Akiva died, the glory of the Torah disappeared. When R. Chanina b. Dosa died, men of wondrous deeds disappeared [he was a miracle worker].[128] When R. Yose Katintan died, pious men disappeared. Why was he called Katintan? Because he was the least [*katan*] of the pious men. When R. Yochanan b. Zakkai died, the splendor of wisdom disappeared; [he was a great Torah scholar and had mastered the secular sciences]. When Rabban Gamliel the Elder died, the glory of the Torah vanished; [after his death, people were no longer able to stand while learning Torah, but sat down]; purity and abstinence also died. When R. Yishmael b. Pavi died, the radiance of the priesthood vanished; [he was a very wise and wealthy man who invited many *kohanim* to his table]. When Rebbi [Rabbi Yehudah Hanasi] died, humility and fear of sin disappeared.[129]

[The Gemara comments:] R. Pinchas b. Yair says: When the *Bet Hamikdash* was destroyed, scholars became embarrassed and members of the nobility covered their head in shame [in the face of the taunts of ignorant people who had lost all respect of their piety and learning], and men of merit [righteous people] were impoverished, and strong-arm men and slanderers became powerful. And there is no one to look out for Israel's plight and no one to pray on their behalf. And [at a time like this] whom can we rely on? Only on our Father in Heaven.

CORRUPTION LEADS TO MORAL DECAY

[*Ein Yaakov* now goes back to 47b:]

When pleasure-seekers increased, justice became distorted [because judges took bribes], personal conduct deteriorated, and God has no satisfaction with this world. When more and more judges were biased in their judgment, the command [given to judges], "Do not show favoritism in judgment" (Deuteronomy 1:17) went by the wayside, and the application of, "do not be impressed by any man [when you sit] in judgment" (ibid.) stopped. [The result was that] people threw off the yoke of heaven and placed on themselves the yoke of mortal man. Since the whispering conversation in court [between judges and defense lawyers discussing the case at hand prior to the presentation of the evidence, in order to work out a deal][130] increased, the divine anger increased, and the *Shechinah* departed, because it says, "In the midst of [honest] judges [God] will judge" (Psalms 82:1). When there was an increase of [judges about whom it says,] "Their hearts lust for unjust gain" (Ezekiel 33:31), there was an increase of people "who call evil good and good evil" (Isaiah 5:20). When people "who call evil good and good evil" increased, [cries of] "Woe, woe"[131] increased in the world.

When people who draw out their saliva [speaking slowly and swallowing before uttering each word, a mannerism that shows conceit] increased, there was a growth in arrogant people, the number of students dwindled, and the Torah went around in search of students willing to learn it. When the number of arrogant people grew, the daughters of Israel began to marry arrogant men, because our generation looks only at the surface. [The Gemara asks:] Is that so? But surely a master has said: An arrogant person is not accepted even by the members of his own household, as it says, "An arrogant man does not stay at home" (Habakkuk 2:5)—meaning, even in his own home! [So how does a Jewish girl marry such a person?] [The Gemara answers:] At first [the girls] run after the [arrogant man], but in the end, [when they get to know him better], they become disgusted with him.

When there was an increase in [judges] who enlisted the assistance of householders to do their investing for them, bribery and miscarriage of justice increased, and goodness among the people ceased to exist. When there was an increase in judges who said, "I accept your favor, and I appreciate your favor," there was a corresponding increase of "Every man did as he pleased" (Judges 17:6), the lower class of people became elevated, the eminent were brought low, and the powers that be became mired deeper and deeper in corruption. When selfish and opportunistic people increased, callous and tight-fisted people who refused to lend money to others increased. They were violating the command, "Be careful that you do not [hold back a loan from someone who needs it]" (Deuteronomy 15:9).

When Jewish daughters began to behave [in seductive ways] "walking with outstreched necks and winking eyes" (Isaiah 3:16), the need increased for the bitter water [to test the *sotah*], but it was discontinued. As more and more people accepted gifts from other people, the days of human life became fewer, and man's years were shortened, as it says, "One who hates gifts will live" (Proverbs 15:27). When the people increased who relied on their own understanding to interpret the *halachah* rather than listen to the rabbi's teaching, disputes [as to what the *halachah* is] increased in Israel. When the disciples of Shammai and Hillel increased who did not serve their teachers properly, dissension [on points of *halachah*] increased, and the Torah became like two *Torot*.

SINGING LEWD SONGS IS FORBIDDEN

[The Mishnah said:] When the Sanhedrin ceased to function [in Jerusalem before the destruction of the Temple] singing in the banquet halls was abolished. [The Gemara asks:] How do we know that the verse, "They drink their wine without song" (Isaiah 24:9) refers to the time when the Sanhedrin ceased to function? R. Huna b. R. Yehoshua said: For it says, "[When] the elders [and members of the Sanhedrin] are gone from the gate [i.e., from the seat of the Sanhedrin], the young men [will no longer] sing their song" (Lamentations 5:14). Rav said: The ear that listens to songs [that have vulgar and obscene lyrics] should be torn off. Rava said: If there is [this type of sensual] song in a house, there will be destruction in the end. For it says, "There is the sound of singing in the window; desolation will be in its doorway, for the cedarwork will be removed [*eirah*]" (Zephaniah 2:14).

[The Gemara asks:] What is the meaning of "the cedarwork will be removed [*eirah*]"? R. Yitzchak said: Can a house covered with cedar beams be considered a city [*ir*]? But the meaning is, even a house covered with cedar beams [if improper songs are sung in it] will crumble [*mitro'ei'a*]. R. Ashi said: We can infer from this passage that when a house begins to fall apart, it begins at the doorway, for it says, "Desolation will be in its doorway." Or, if you prefer, say from here, "The gate is stricken with destruction" (Isaiah 24:12). Mar b. R. Ashi said: I have seen the destructive forces that demolish a house, and they gore like an ox.

R. Huna decreed that all singing of worldly songs should stop. Thereupon [the land was blessed with such abundance that] a hundred geese could be bought for one *zuz*, and a hundred *se'ah* of wheat for a *zuz*, and there were no buyers. R. Chisda came and overlooked [the singing of worldly songs]. Thereupon people who were willing to pay [the exorbitant price of] a *zuz* for a goose could not find one. R. Yosef said: When men sing and women respond in the refrain, it causes a breakdown of the standards of modesty; when women sing and men respond it is like flax, which will explode into fire at the slightest spark. [The men's *yetzer hara* will be inflamed by such singing.] [The Gemara asks:] What is the practical difference [whether we call it breakdown of modesty or "fire and flax," since both are forbidden]? [The Gemara answers:] If we can abolish only one of the two, we should abolish the practice where women do the singing, and men join in the refrain. [It is the more serious infraction.]

FIVE TRAGEDIES

R. Yochanan said: Anyone who drinks wine to the accompaniment of four kinds of musical instruments brings five kinds of tragedies on the world. For it says, "Woe to those who arise early in the morning to pursue liquor, who stay up late at night while wine inflames them. There are harp and lyre and drum and flute and wine at their drinking parties, but they would not contemplate the deeds of God" (Isaiah 5:11,12). What does it say after that [to indicate the five tragedies]? "Therefore My people is being exiled because of ignorance" (ibid. v. 13)—they cause exile in the world; "its honored ones dying of starvation"—they bring hunger into the world; "and its multitude parched for thirst"—they cause Torah to be forgotten by its students; "man will be humbled and people will be brought lower" (ibid. v. 15)—they cause humiliation to God, and "Man" refers to the Holy One, blessed be He, Himself, for it says, "God is a Man of war" (Exodus 15:3); "and the eyes of the lofty will be brought low" (Isaiah 5:15)—they cause the humiliation of Israel. And what does it says after that? **(48b)** "Therefore, the netherworld has enlarged its appetite and opened its mouth wide without limit" (ibid. v.14); [having brought the five tragedies on the world, they will end up in Gehinnom].

WHEN DID THE *URIM* AND *TUMIM* CEASE?

[The Mishnah said:] When the early prophets died, the Urim and Tumim ceased. [The Gemara asks:] Who are the early prophets? R. Huna said: They are David, Samuel, and Solomon. R. Nachman said: Even in the time of David [when they had Urim and Tumim], sometimes the Urim and Tumim answered the questions, and sometimes the questions remained unanswered; for Zadok the *Kohen* inquired [as to what David should do when he was running away from Absalom], and he received an answer, but when Abiathar the *Kohen* asked the question he was not answered, as it says, "And Abiathar came up" (2 Samuel 15:24) [meaning, he had to resign as *Kohen Gadol*, because he did not receive an answer from the Urim and Tumim].

Rabbah b. Shmuel objected [to R. Huna's statement]: It says, "[Uzziah] used to seek out God in the days of Zechariah, a man who had understanding in the visions of God" (2 Chronicles 26:3). [What does "understanding in the visions of God" mean?] Don't you think that God showed Uzziah[132] answers through the Urim and Tumim? [And Uzziah lived much after Solomon, which refutes R. Huna!] [The Gemara answers:] No, [he had understanding of the visions of God, not though Urim and Tumim, but] through the prophets.

Come and hear the following proof: When the first *Bet Hamikdash* was destroyed the [forty-eight] cities with pasture land [which were given to the Levites][133] were abolished, the Urim and Tumim ended, and no longer was there a king from the house of David, and if anyone will whisper in your ear and ask you a question, quoting, "Hattirshatha [Nehemiah][134] told them [regarding *kohanim* who could not prove their lineage] that they should not eat of the most-holy offerings until there would arise a *Kohen* to inquire of the Urim and Tumim" (Ezra 2:63); [so you see, they will say that he expected the Urim and Tumim to respond to questions even during the time of the second *Bet Hamikdash*!]. Answer the person [who asks you this question that this is just an expression about the distant future,] as someone says to his neighbor, "Until the dead are revived and *Mashiach*, son of David, comes!" [At any rate, during the time of the first *Bet Hamikdash* there was the Urim and Tumim, which

contradicts R. Huna who said that after Solomon's death the Urim and Tumim ceased.] But R. Nachman answered: Who are the early prophets? [The prophets who lived during the First Temple era], excluding the later prophets, Haggai, Zechariah, and Malachi [who lived during the Second Temple era, when there was no Urim and Tumim]. For we learned in a *Baraita*: After the death of the later prophets, Haggai, Zechariah, and Malachi, the high level of prophecy called *Ruach Hakodesh* departed from Israel; nevertheless, they still used the *Bat Kol* [a Heavenly Voice].

THE *SHAMIR*

[The Mishnah said:] When the Second Temple was destroyed, the *shamir* was lost. [The Gemara says:] The Rabbis taught: The *shamir* [is the worm] Solomon used to build the *Bet Hamikdash*. For it says, "When the Temple was being built, it was built of complete quarried stone; hammers, chisels, or any iron utensils were not heard in the Temple when it was being built" (1 Kings 6:7). The words should be understood exactly as they are written: [the stones were taken out of the quarry and placed directly in the *Bet Hamikdash*], so says R. Yehudah. R. Nechemiah asked him: How can you possibly say that [no metal tools were used in the building of the *Bet Hamikdash*]! After all, it says, [with reference to Solomon's palace], "All these were built of valuable stones . . . filed smooth with a file!" (ibid. 7:9). If so, what does R. Nechemiah do with the verse, "Hammers, chisels, or any iron utensils were not heard in the Temple when it was being built"? [It means] that they prepared [the stones] outside the *Bet Hamikdash* [using metal tools], and then brought them inside.

Rabbi said: I agree with the interpretation of R. Yehudah [that no metal tools were used at all] with reference to the stones of the *Bet Hamikdash*, and I agree with R. Nechemiah that metal tools were used in the construction of Solomon's palace. [The Gemara asks:] According to R. Nechemiah [who says that metal tools were used in the construction of the *Bet Hamikdash*], what did Solomon need the *shamir* for? [The Gemara answers:] It was needed, as we learned in a *Baraita*: On the precious stones [which were used in the breastplate and the *ephod*, and on which letters were engraved] you may not write with ink because it says, "[they shall appear] like the engraving on a signet ring" (Exodus 28:11); neither may you scratch into them with a knife, because it says, "in their wholeness" (ibid. v. 20), [so that no filings should be missing]. But he wrote with ink on the stones, and placed the *shamir* on them, and then the writing split of itself, like a fig tree that has a tendency to split in the summer, and nothing at all is lost; or like a field that splits after a heavy rain, and nothing at all is lost.

We learned in a *Baraita*: The *shamir* is a creature about the size of a barley seed, and it was created on the sixth day of Creation.[135] There is no material in the world that can withstand it. Then how is it stored? They wrap it in sponges of wool and put it in a lead pipe filled with bran of barley.

MEN OF FAITH

[The Mishnah said:] When the *Bet Hamikdash* was destroyed, men of faith were no more. [The Gemara comments:] R. Yitzchak said: These are people who had faith in the Holy One, blessed be He. For we learned in a *Baraita*: R. Eliezer HaGadol says: Anyone who has bread in his basket and asks "What shall I eat tomorrow?" is a person of little faith. And that is what R. Elazar said: What is meant by the verse, "For who is scornful on the day of small things?" (Zecharaiah 4:10).—What has caused the full reward of great *tzaddikim* in the World to Come to be diminished? The smallness of their faith; they failed to trust in the Holy One, blessed be He, [to provide their needs]. Rava said: [The verse] refers to the little children of the wicked in Israel (49a) [who died in infancy]; they tear up the decree against their fathers in the World to Come. They say to God, "Master of the universe! Since You intend to punish our fathers in the hereafter, why did You cause them sorrow [over our death] in this world?" [So please rescind the evil decree against them!]

R. Ila'i b. Berechiah said: If it had not been for the prayer of David, all Israel would be rag sellers [because of their sins]. For [David] says, "Grant them respect, O God" (Psalms 9:27).

TORAH SCHOLARS

R. Ila'i b. Berechiah also said: If it had not been for the prayer of Habakkuk, [Torah scholars would be so poor] that two Torah scholars would have to share one garment, and learn Torah that way. For it says, "O God, I have heard Your message, and I feared Your deeds, in the midst of the years, bring them back to life" ([Habakkuk 3:2). Do not read, "in the midst of years" [*bekerev shanim*], but *bekeiruv shenayim*, "in the closeness of two scholars." [Habakkuk is saying: I have heard your message, I feared Your words of Torah, which is learned in the closeness of two scholars under one garment; but I pray that You will make them prosper.]

R. Ila'i b. Berechiah said further: If two Torah scholars are walking on the road together, and they do not discuss Torah topics, they deserve to be burned by fire, for it says, "As they [Elijah and Elisha] were walking and conversing, behold!—a chariot of fire and horses of fire [appeared]" (2 Kings 2:11). The reason that they were not burned was that they were discussing Torah thoughts. It follows that if they had not been discussing Torah themes, they would have deserved to be burned.

R. Ila'i b. Berechiah also said: If two Torah scholars who live in the same city do not get along and do not agree to study together, one of them will die, and the other will go into exile. For it says, [Moses set aside three cities] "For a murderer to flee there, who will have killed his fellow without knowledge" (Deuteronomy 4:42), and "knowledge" means Torah. For it says, "My people has been eliminated for lack of knowledge . . . and you have forgotten the Torah of your God" (Hosea 4:6).

R. Yehudah son of R. Chiya said: Any Torah scholar who studies the Torah in poverty, his prayers will be answered, as it says, "The people in Zion who dwell in Jerusalem [this refers to those who learn in the *yeshivot* in Jerusalem (Rashi)]. You will not have to weep; He will surely show you grace at the sound of your outcry, when He hears you, He will answer you" (Isaiah 30:19). Immediately after this it says, "God will give you bread in adversity and water in affliction" (ibid. v. 20). R. Acha b. Chanina says: Neither will the partition [that separates mortal man from God] be closed to him, for it says, "Your Teacher will no longer be hidden behind His garment" (ibid.). ["Teacher" is a reference to God.] R. Abbahu says: A Torah scholar is rewarded in that he is satiated with the splendor of the *Shechinah*, for it says, "Your eyes will behold your Teacher" (ibid.).

HOW DOES THE WORLD CONTINUE TO EXIST?

[The Mishnah said:] R. Yehoshua testified that since the *Bet Hamikdash* was destroyed, there is not a day without a curse. [The Gemara comments:] Rava said: And the curse of each day is worse than that of the day before, as it says, [in the *Tochachah*, the series of dreadful curses], "In the morning you will say, 'If it were only night,' and in the evening you will say, 'If it were only morning'" (Deuteronomy 28:67). Which morning and which evening [will they be longing for]? Do you think for the morning of the next day? Nobody knows if it will be better [that they should wish for it]. Therefore it must be the morning of the previous day. [They will pray that the next day will not be worse than the previous day.]

[The Gemara asks:] If every day is worse than the previous day,] in what merit does the world continue to exist? [The Gemara answers:] In the merit of reciting *Kedusha DeSidra* [the *Kedushah* in *Uva leTzion Go'el*, which we say in Hebrew and in its Aramaic translation. Translating a verse constitutes Torah study, so that every Jew praises God and learns Torah each day], and the merit of the response *Yehei Shemei Rabba*, "May His great Name be blessed," which is said in the *Kaddish* after a public lecture on *Aggadah* on *Shabbat* [when large groups assemble to learn Torah, and then praise God. It is in these two merits that the world endures]. For it says, "The land whose darkness is like pitch-blackness, a shadow of death and without order [*sedarim*]" (Job 10:22). [It is so dark because there are no *sedarim*, set times for Torah study.] Hence, if there is Torah study, its light will brighten the gloomy darkness.

LOVE OF CHILDREN
AND GRANDCHILDREN

[The Mishnah said:] Since the destruction of the *Bet Hamikdash*, the dew no longer comes down for blessing, and flavor has been taken from fruits. [The Gemara comments:] We learned in a *Baraita*: R. Shimon b. Elazar says: [When people ceased to conduct themselves with] purity, taste and fragrance was removed from fruits; when they stopped tithing, the [nutritious] richness was removed from the grain. R. Huna once found a juicy date and wrapped it in his scarf. His son Rabbah came in and said to him, "I smell the fragrance of a juicy date." He replied, "My son, [if you can sense the fragrance of fruit, that is an indication that] there is purity in you." So he gave the date to his son. Meanwhile, Abba [the son of Rabbah] came in, and Rabbah gave it to him. R. Huna then said to Rabbah, "My son, you have made me happy [that you have such purity that you smelled that date] but at the same time you have dulled my teeth [because you gave your son the date I gave you; you showed thereby that you love your son more than you love me.]" [Observes the Gemara:] That is one of the facts of life, as the adage goes: The love that a father has for his son, that is the love the son will lavish on his children, [but not on his father].

R. Acha b. Yaakov raised R. Yaakov, the son of his daughter. When R. Yaakov grew up, [the grandfather] said to him, "Bring me a glass of water." He replied, "I am not your son. [I do not have the duty to honor you.]" That is what people say: [Grandchildren will say to their grandfather,] "Raise me, raise me" [but when it comes to showing respect they will say,] "I am the son of your daughter; [I don't have to honor you; I am not your son]."

ANARCHY BEFORE
THE COMING OF *MASHIACH*

[The Mishnah says:] From the day the *Bet Hamikdash* was destroyed, the Sages began to act like schoolteachers [meaning, the level of Torah learning declined], schoolteachers like synagogue attendants, synagogue attendants like ordinary people, and ordinary people (49b) grew worse steadily. And no one seeks to reverse the downward trend toward ignorance. [At a time like this,] on whom can we rely? Only on our Father in Heaven. [At the end of the *Galut*, before the coming of *Mashiach*,] when the footsteps of *Mashiach* can be heard, insolence will increase; inflation will soar; the vine will yield its fruit, but wine will be expensive [because everyone wants to become drunk]; the dominant power in the world will promote the denial of God; no one will be able to reprove another [for every-

one will be guilty of the same transgressions]; the meeting place [of Torah scholars] will be used for immorality; the Galilee will be destroyed, and the Gablan will become desolate. The people who live on the border will go around begging from town to town, and will not be pitied. The wisdom of the Torah scholars will rot, those who fear sin will be despised, and the truth will be hidden. Young people will shame old men, and old men will stand up before youngsters. A son will degrade his father, a daughter will rebel against her mother, a daughter-in-law against her mother-in-law, and a man's enemies will be the members of his household.[136] The face of the generation will be like the face of a dog.[137] A son will not be ashamed before his father. [At such a time,] on whom can we rely? Only on our Father in Heaven.

HATRED BETWEEN BROTHERS

[The Mishnah said:] During the siege of Titus, the Sages decreed that nobody should teach his son the wisdom of the Greeks. [The Gemara comments:] We learned in a *Baraita*: When the Hasmonean family fought one another, Hyrkanus was outside [Jerusalem] and Aristobulus was inside [Jerusalem]. Every day [the treasurer of the Temple] lowered down a basket with *dinars* and received in return animals for the daily sacrifices. An old man, learned in Greek wisdom, told [the besiegers] in cultured Greek [which the people in Jerusalem did not understand], "As long as they continue the Temple service, they will not be delivered into your hands." The next day, the defenders lowered the basket with *dinars*, but they sent up a pig. When the pig reached the middle of the wall, it stuck its hooves into the wall, and there was an earthquake that shook Eretz Yisrael over an area of four hundred square *parsah*. At that time the Sages declared: Cursed should be the man who breeds pigs, and cursed should be the man who teaches his son Greek wisdom!

The Rabbis taught: When R. Eliezer died, the Torah scroll was hidden away. [He had memorized a great many *halachot*, and he could quote them flawlessly.] When R. Yehoshua died, good advice and clear thinking ceased to exist. [He was very skillful at refuting the arguments of heretics.] When R. Akiva died, the arms of the Torah disappeared, and the wellsprings of wisdom were stopped up. [The depth of understanding of the meaning of each letter of the Torah was lost.] When R. Elazar b. Azariah died, the crowns of wisdom vanished; [he was a very wealthy man], for "The crown of the wise is their wealth" (Proverbs 14:24). When R. Chanina b. Dosa died, men of great deeds ceased. [He was a saintly miracle worker.] When Abba Yose b. Katinta died, pious people ceased. Why was he called Abba Yose b. Katinta? Because he was the smallest [*katan*] among the pious. When Ben Azzai died, there were no more diligent Torah students. When Ben Zoma died, there were no more expounders. When R. Shimon b. Gamliel died, the locusts came and the troubles increased [a veiled reference to the intensification of the Roman oppression. The Romans swarmed like locusts, denuding the land of its wealth]. When Rebbi [R. Yehudah Hanasi, the editor of the Mishnah] died, troubles multiplied.

[The Mishnah said:] When Rebbi died, humility and the fear of sin disappeared. [The Gemara says:] R. Yosef told the Tanna [who was writing down this Mishnah]: Do not write that humility disappeared, because I am still here, [and I have humility]. R. Nachman told the Tanna: Do not write that the fear of sin disapppeared, because I am still here, [and I have fear of sin].[138]

R. Pinchas b. Yair used to say: Watchfulness leads to zeal, zeal to cleanliness, cleanliness to restraint, restraint to purity, purity to holiness, holiness to humility, humility to fear of sin, fear of sin to saintliness, saintliness to the possession of the holy spirit, the holy spirit to the revival of the dead; and the revival of the dead comes through Elijah of blessed memory. May the Almighty make us worthy to witness his coming speedily in our days. Amen.

NOTES

1. A *nazir*, or nazirite, is a person who took a special vow to attain a higher degree of holiness. He must abstain from drinking wine, he must let his hair grow, and he may not come into contact with the dead. Ordinarily the *nazir* vow is for a term of thirty days.

2. Genesis 24:1; 27:33; 33:11.

3. Exodus 3:2.

4. See Exodus 34:13.

5. The minimum quantity of blood needed to sustain life (Rashi).

6. Where he openly admitted, "She is more righteous than I am!" (Genesis 38:26).

7. Genesis 35:22.

8. The remains of all of Jacob's sons were carried out of Egypt.

9. Usual translation: According to its measure [of sin] He contends against her farmland.

10. Numbers 5:15.

11. Genesis 40:11.

12. Jeremiah 46:2.

13. A daughter of an Egyptian father and mother who both have converted.

14. Deuteronomy 23:9.

15. 2 Samuel 15:16.

16. When hunted, a fox does not turn tail and run, but backs away.

17. About one hundred feet. The Maharal takes "shoulders" allegorically as the spiritual source of Samson's strength.

18. "He was taller than any of the people from his shoulder upward" (1 Samuel 10:23).

19. 2 Samuel 16:26.

20. To dismantle the fortress Baasa, the king of Israel, had built to prevent Asa, the king of Judah, from leaving or entering Jerusalem. (See 1 Kings 15:16-22.)

21. The word *eshel* is an acronym of the initials of *achilah* ("food"), *shetiah* ("drink"), and *leviyah* ("escorting the guests, giving them personal attention")—the three kindnesses Abraham lavished on his guests (Rashi).

22. See Genesis 38:29 and Ruth 4:18-22.

23. Leah, Yehudah's mother, gave him his name at birth with prophetic inspiration (Maharsha and Rif).

24. Daniel's companions, known in Aramaic as Shadrach, Meshach, and Abed-Nego; see Daniel 3.

25. Being a lifetime nazirite, Absalom was permitted to cut his hair once every twelve months.

26. This is the proof text cited in Ein Yaakov. The Gemara quotes, "For the Lord God will not do anything happen unless He has revealed his secret to His servants the prophets" (Amos 3:7).

27. Meaning, members of the Sanhedrin (Rashi).

28. These names allude to their great scholarship in Torah.

29. Exodus 12:36.

30. Exodus 6:23.

31. Numbers 13:6.

32. On the day Moses was born, the astrologers told Pharaoh: Today the savior of the Israelites will be born, but we do not know if he is a Jew or an Egyptian. So Pharaoh decreed that every baby born that day—both Jewish and Egyptian—had to be cast into the Nile (Midrash Tanchuma).

33. The children of Israel stayed in Egypt for 210 years. At the time of the Exodus, Moses was eighty years old (Exodus 7:7). Thus 130 years elapsed from their entry into Egypt until the birth of Moses. Jochebed was born as they entered Egypt, and when Amram took her back she was pregnant with Moses. Which means that she was 130 years old when Moses was born (Rashi).

34. The Torah states that seventy people of Jacob's family entered Egypt, but it lists only sixty-nine (Genesis 46:27). Jochebed, who was born as they were entering Egypt, is the seventieth.

35. Genesis 3:16.

36. *Megillah* 15b.

37. See *Berachot* 54b.

38. Where Moses was punished for striking the rock to produce water rather than speaking to it (Numbers 20:13,24).

39. Exodus 2:2,3.

40. Deuteronomy 14:17.

41. "When God will indeed remember you, then you must bring my bones up out of here" (Genesis 50:25).

42. In Hebrew *aron* means both the Holy Ark and coffin.

43. See Genesis 37:14-29.

44. Samalion takes *vayamot*, "he died," as a contraction of *vay*, "woe, alas" and *met*, "he died."

45. Numbers 25:1–9.

46. It could not mean leather, because at that time no animal had been killed yet (*Maharsha*).

47. *Ish* [husband] is spelled *alef, yud, shin. Ishah* [wife] is spelled *alef, shin, hei.* If we join the *yud* of *ish* and the *hei* of *ishah* we obtain the Divine Name *Yud-Hei,* an indication that the *Shechinah* literally dwells among them.

But if the *yud* is removed from *ish,* and the *hei* from *ishah,* only *alef* and *shin* are left, which form the word *esh,* fire.

48. Numbers 5:17.

49. Numbers 19:1–22.

50. Leviticus 17:13.

51. Numbers 5:28.

52. Numbers 15:38.

53. This refers to the Oral Torah, i.e., the Talmud, "because most women do not have the proper mindset for studying the Talmud, but they extrapolate and draw foolish conclusions on their own, according to their limited understanding. But a woman who studies the written Torah earns a reward" (Rambam, *Hilchot Talmud Torah* 1:13).

54. *Tosafot* 21b.

55. Tosafot quoting Yerushalmi cites another example: He sees a child drowning in the river and says: Before I jump in to save the child, let me first take off my *tefillin.* By the time he has done that the child has drowned.

56. Leviticus 23:22.

57. *Pe'ah* 8:8.

58. *Am haaretz,* literally "earthy people," were the common people, most of whom followed the Sages who were called *perushim* [Pharisees]. The *ammei haaretz* were unlearned and therefore prone to error in some areas of *halachah.*

59. Explained below.

60. *Rosh Hashanah* 18a.

61. The *Perushim* [Pharisees] were the Torah Sages, and the majority of the people followed them. The word *perushim* means "those who separate themselves," for they adhered to the most stringent requirements of the laws of ritual purity, and therefore had to refrain from many activities and avoid contact with the common people who were less meticulous in their observance of these laws.

62. Genesis 34.

63. The tyrannical King Yannai was an archenemy of the Pharisees [the Rabbis] and tortured and killed 800 of them. Before he died in 76 BCE he advised his wife, Queen Shelomit, to make peace with the Pharisees.

64. Numbers 25:10–15.

65. Wherever the phrase "on that day" occurs in the Mishnah it always refers to the momentous day when R. Elazar b. Azariah was appointed *Nasi,* head of the Sanhedrin, in place of Rabban Gamliel (see *Berachot* 27b).

66. The *chazzan* was the teacher of young boys who usually held class in the synagogue and acted as the *chazzan* for the people who came to pray (Rashi).

67. R. Yehoshua b. Hurkinos was R. Akiva's disciple, who was R. Yochanan b. Zakkai's disciple.

68. Deuteronomy 26:12–15.

69. Also called *Amidah.*

70. *Sotah* 36b.

71. Numbers 10:11ff.

72. Joshua 6:6.

73. 1 Kings 8:3.

74. The water did not spill over; rather, it formed a large pillar (Redak).

75. As mentioned in Numbers 13:23.

76. Deuteronomy 1:22.

77. Joshua 14:14.

78. By saying "Amram's son" instead of "Moses" he implied that he was against Moses and hated him so much that he was unable to enunciate his name.

79. The ninth of Av, the day on which both temples were destroyed. The day is observed as a fast.

80. The word *bamageifah,* literally "by the plague," suggests that they died an unusual and unnatural death.

81. Its symptoms match those of diphtheritic croup.

82. *Shal* is seen as related to *nashal,* "to fall, to drop off."

83. Malbim.

84. What is wrong with calling Torah "a song"? You sing a song only when the mood strikes you, but Torah should be on your mind at all times (*Maharsha*).

85. Chidon means spear, because Uzzah was killed there. Nacon means correct, because the Ark stayed for six months in the house of Obed-Edom, and his family was blessed abundantly for it (Rashi).

86. They were commanded to destroy only those of the seven nations that resided in Eretz Yisrael. Those living outside its borders could remain alive if they repented and abandoned their depraved ways (Rashi).

87. The Vilna Gaon says that this is impossible, since the blessings and curses were pronounced before the building of the altar. He deletes "and the curses"; "the blessings" refers to *Birkat Hamazon,* the Grace after Meals.

88. The opposite of Deuteronomy 27:15.

89. Deuteronomy 27:2.

90. Simon, Levi, Judah, Issachar, Joseph, and Benjamin on Mount Gerizim; Reuben, Gad, Asher, Zebulon, Dan, and Naphtali on Mount Ebal (Deuteronomy 27:12,13).

91. On the two shoulder straps of the *ephod* worn by the *Kohen Gadol* there were two precious stones on which were engraved the names of the twelve tribes, six on each stone (Exodus 28:9–12).

92. This will be explained later.

93. Deuteronomy 27:12.

94. In Deuteronomy 27:12.

95. Deuteronomy 27:15–26.

96. Deuteronomy 5:1 and 11:19.

97. Leviticus 1:1.

98. Numbers 1:46.

99. A cup of wine is used when Grace after Meals is said.

100. See Deuteronomy 21:1–9.

101. According to Turei Even, R. Elazar b. Shamua instituted this *berachah*.

102. The praise is: "Blessed is the name of His glorious kingdom for all eternity" (*Taanit* 16a).

103. Deuteronomy 31:10–13.

104. Every seventh year is a *shemittah* year, a Sabbatical year. It is a year of remission, when all loans are cancelled.

105. His mother was Jewish, but his father was an offspring of Herod, who descended from Edomite slaves.

106. Deuteronomy 20:2–10.

107. 1 Samuel 17.

108. 2 Samuel 10:14–19.

109. As outlined in Deuteronomy 20:5–8.

110. Goliath's power of uncleanness tried to overcome Moses' power of holiness. But the power of holiness and purity won because Goliath mocked the army of God for forty days, but only in the daytime, whereas Moses remained on the mountain forty days and forty nights (*Maharsha*).

111. Ruth 1:4.

112. Shobach in 2 Samuel 10:16; Shofach in 1 Chronicles 19:16.

113. Such as: Lord, Almighty.

114. Pinchas zealously took up God's cause when he killed Zimri ben Salu (Numbers 25:1–15).

115. *Yoma* 85a.

116. Numbers 15:38.

117. The four-hundred year bondage was not decreed because Pharaoh escorted Abraham. It was decreed at the Covenant between the Halves, when God said to Abraham, "Your descendants will be foreigners in a land that is not theirs for four hundred years. They will be enslaved and oppressed" (Genesis 15:12). But God did not specify in which land. For accompanying Abraham, Pharaoh merited that Israel should be enslaved in Egypt (*Maharsha*).

118. 2 Kings 19–23.

119. Numbers 23:1, 14, 29.

120. *Mishnah Shabbat*, Chapter 14; Leviticus 11:29ff.

121. 1 Kings 12:28.

122. Some say that originally he was one of the leaders of the Zealots in the revolt against the Romans before the destruction of the Second Temple. He later became a notorious bandit.

123. With them began the period, during the Second Temple era, of the *Zugot* [Pairs], whereby the leadership of the people was shared by the *Nasi* (President) and the *Av Bet Din* (Dean of the Sanhedrin).

124. Deuteronomy 26:13–16.

125. The Levites used to proclaim, "Awake, why do you sleep, O God?" (Psalms 44:24).

126. They used to make an incision on the calf between its horns before it was brought on the altar. He abolished it because it looked as if the animal had a blemish.

127. The ineffable Divine Name was placed inside the folds of the breastplate of the *Kohen Gadol*. When the *Kohen Gadol* consulted the Urim and Tumim, the letters on the stones of the breastplate containing the answer would light up. The *Kohen Gadol*, with Divine inspiration, would be able to combine the letters to spell out the answer (Exodus 28:30).

128. See *Taanit* 24b, 25a.

129. Since Rabbi Yehudah Hanasi was the compiler of the Mishnah, he could not have written about his own death. The Rambam says that this phrase was added by one of Rabbi Yehudah Hanasi's disciples.

130. This is against Torah law.

131. This cry occurs six times in Isaiah 5.

132. Rashi explains in his commentary on 2 Chronicles 26:5 that Zechariah is identical to Uzziah, King of Judah.

133. Numbers 35:2.

134. See Nehemia 8:9.

135. *Avot* 5:8.

136. Micah 7:6.

137. When a man walks his dog, the dog always looks back to see whether the master is still following him. Before the coming of *Mashiach*, the so-called leaders of the generation, rather than guide the people and teach them right from wrong, continually check with their constituents in a doglike manner, to ensure that the views they are about to expound are popular with the people.

138. R. Yosef and R. Nachman told the Tanna to make sure to mention both Rebbi's humility and his fear of sin. R. Yosef said: There are humble people who are not pious; like myself, for example. R. Nachman said: There are pious people who are not at all humble; take me, for example. Rebbi's greatness was that he was a man of both humility and piety, and when he died there were no more people who combined both these qualities (Rabbi Shimon Schwab).

ᥩ KIDDUSHIN ᥤ

IF A MAN TAKES A WIFE

(2b) We learned in a *Baraita*: Rabbi Shimon said: Why does the Torah say, "If a man takes a wife" (Deuteronomy 22:13), and not, "If a woman is taken by a man"? Because it is the way of a man to look for a wife, but it is not the way of a woman to look for a husband. You can compare it to a person who lost an article: who goes looking for the lost item? Surely the loser will look for the thing he has lost. [Ever since Adam has lost his rib, every man is trying to retrieve it by looking for a wife.]

DREADFUL CONSEQUENCES OF AN INVALID DIVORCE

(13a) Rav Yehudah said in the name of Shmuel: Anyone who does not fully know the laws of divorce and betrothal should not be involved in deciding questions concerning these issues. R. Assi said in the name of R. Yochanan: [An unqualified person will render wrong decisions regarding a *get*. As a result, the *get* is invalid: the woman is not properly divorced and is still married. If she marries someone else, she is committing adultery, and her children will be *mamzeirim*.] Unqualified persons who render rulings on matters involving adultery do more harm to the world than was experienced by the generation of the flood, for it says, "By swearing [falsely], lying, murdering, robbing, and committing adultery they spread forth [*paratzu*], and crime follows crime" (Hosea 4:2).

How is [the disastrous harm done by unqualified persons executing divorces] implied in the verse? As R. Yosef translates [*paratzu* in the sense of "multiplied"]:[1] They have children by their neighbor's wives [whose *gittin* are invalid], thereby adding sins to their sins. And the next verse says, "Therefore the land will be destroyed, and all who dwell in it will be enfeebled, along with the beasts of the field, the birds of the heavens, and even the fish of the sea will perish" (ibid. v. 3). Whereas in the generation of the flood the decree of destruction did not apply to the fish of the sea, for it says, "Everything on dry land died" (Genesis 7:22), and not the fish in the sea; in the case [of adultery and

bringing *mamzeirim* into the world] even the fish of the sea are included in the decree of destruction. [So we see that unqualified persons administering *gittin* bring punishment on the world worse than the flood.]

[The Gemara asks:] Perhaps the punishment mentioned [in Hosea 4:3] is meted out only if *all* of the sins listed in the first verse are committed, [but not adultery alone]? [The Gemara answers:] Don't let this enter your mind, for it says, "For due to swearing falsely the land has become desolate" (Jeremiah 23:10), [which shows that for one crime alone the land is punished]. [The Gemara asks:] You could say perhaps swearing falsely alone [is a reason for destruction of the land], and all the other transgressions combined bring on destruction, [but not adultery alone]? (13b) [The Gemara answers:] Does it then say, *uparatzu, "and* they spread forth," [which would indicate that the transgressions are combined]; it says *paratzu,* "they spread forth" [an independent phrase, denoting that the crime of causing adultery alone warrants the destruction of the land].

THE HEBREW SLAVE

(22a) We learned in a *Baraita*: It says, [If the Hebrew slave likes his master and does not want to leave], "because he has it so good with you" (Deuteronomy 15:16): ["with you" denotes that] he has to be treated as your equal with regard to food and drink, that you should not eat white bread and he coarse bread, you drink old wine and he new wine, you sleep on soft material and he on straw. The Sages said: From here we can infer that whoever buys a Hebrew slave is like buying a master over himself.

(22b) It says, [if the Hebrew slave does not want to go free after serving for six years,] "his master shall pierce his ear with an awl" (Exodus 21:6). R. Yochanan b. Zakkai used to explain this verse with an allegory: Why was the ear singled out from all the other limbs in the body [to be pierced]? The Holy One, blessed be He, said: The ear that heard My voice on Mount Sinai when I proclaimed, "For the children of Israel are servants to Me, they are My servants" (Leviticus 25:55), and not servants of servants, and yet this man went and acquired a master for himself, [when he had the opportunity to go free]—this ear should be pierced!

It says, "The master shall bring him to the door or to the doorpost [and pierce his ear with an awl]" (Exodus 21:6). R. Shimon b. Rebbi used to explain this verse with an allegory: Why were the door and the doorpost singled out from all the other places in the house? The Holy One, blessed be He, said: The door and the doorpost that were witnesses in Egypt when I passed over the lintel and the doorpost and proclaimed, "For the children of Israel are servants to Me, they are My servants," and not servants of servants, and I took them out from bondage to freedom, yet this man went and acquired a master for himself. His ear should be pierced in front of the lintel and the doorpost.

RAV ACHA B. YAAKOV, THE DRAGON SLAYER

(29b) We learned in a *Baraita*: If a father wants to learn, and his son also wants to learn, the father takes precedence over his son. R. Yehudah said: If the son is studious and will be more successful in his learning than the father, [and the father cannot afford the tuition for both], the son takes precedence over him, [and the father should work and support his son (Rashi)]. Like the story of R. Yaakov the son of R. Acha b. Yaakov. R. Acha b. Yaakov sent his son R. Yaakov to learn under Abaye. When the son returned, the father saw that he did not have a clear grasp of the subject matter. So he told him, "I will be more successful than you. You stay here, and I will go instead of you." Abaye heard that R. Acha b. Yaakov was coming. Now there was a demon that haunted the *bet midrash* of Abaye, and [unlike most demons] it would harm people even in the daytime, and even if two people were walking together. Abaye said, "Make sure that no one invites R. Acha b. Yaakov to their home tonight, [so that he will be forced to sleep in the *bet midrash*]. Maybe in the merit of his piety a miracle will happen, [and we will get rid of this demon]." So R. Acha b. Yaakov went and spent the night in the bet midrash, and the demon appeared in the form of a seven-headed dragon. Every time R. Acha b. Yaakov bowed down during his prayer, one head fell off. The next morning R. Acha b. Yaakov chided the Rabbis, "If a miracle had not occurred, you would have endangered my life!"

LEARNING TORAH OR GETTING MARRIED?

We learned in a *Baraita*: If a person is faced with the choice of learning Torah or getting married, he should first learn Torah and then get married. But if it is impossible for him to live without a wife, he should first get married and afterward learn Torah. Rav Yehudah said in Shmuel's name: The *halachah* is: First

he should get married, and afterward learn Torah. R. Yochanan said: Should he have a millstone around his neck [a family to support] and learn Torah! [No, he should learn first and then get married.] But R. Yochanan and Rav Yehudah do not contradict each other: One refers to Babylonian scholars; the other to the scholars of Eretz Yisrael. [The Babylonian scholars used to go to learn in Eretz Yisrael. They were not burdened with the troubles of support and could get married before learning Torah. The scholars of Eretz Yisrael learned Torah in their hometown where they live with their families. If they got married first, they would be burdened with responsibilities of support and would be distracted from their learning. They had to learn Torah first (Rashi).]

THE PROPER AGE FOR MARRIAGE

R. Chisda praised R. Hamenuna to R. Huna, calling him a great man. R. Huna said to R. Chisda: When R. Hamenuna comes to visit you bring him to me. When he arrived, R. Huna saw that R. Hamenuna did not wear a *suddar* cloth on his head. [Married men used to wear such a head covering (Rashi).] R. Huna asked him, "Why don't you wear a *suddar* on your head?" "Because I am not married," he replied. So Rav Huna turned his face away, saying, "Make sure that you don't appear before me again before you are married." [The Gemara notes:] R. Huna was acting like this for he said: If a man is already twenty years old and is not married, he spends all his days in sin. Do you really mean in sin? Can such a thought even enter your mind? But say, he is plagued with improper thoughts all his days. Rava said, and we learned the same thing in the *Baraita* that was taught in the yeshiva of R. Yishmael: Until a man is twenty years old, the Holy One, blessed be He, is sitting and waiting for him to get married. Once he reaches the age of twenty and does not get married, He exclaims, "Let his bones swell!"

R. Chisda said: The reason that I am better than my colleagues is that I got married at the age of sixteen, and if I had married when I was fourteen (30a) I would have been able to tell Satan, "An arrow in your eye!" [meaning, I would have been able to taunt Satan—the evil impulse—and I would not have been afraid that he would make me sin (Rashi)]. Rava said to R. Natan b. Ammi: While you have your son under your thumb—between sixteen and twenty-two—marry him off. Others say: between eighteen and twenty-four.

This is the subject of a dispute among Tanna'im. R. Yehudah and R. Nechemiah differ on the interpretation of the passage, "Train the youth in the way he should go [i.e., marry him off]" (Proverbs 22:6). One says it means between the ages of sixteen and twenty-two; the other, between eighteen and twenty-four.

TEACHING TORAH
TO CHILDREN
AND GRANDCHILDREN

R. Yehoshua b. Levi said: Anyone who teaches Torah to his grandson is as though he had received it direct from Mount Sinai, for it says, "Teach your children and grandchildren," which is followed by, "The day you stood before God your Lord at Horeb" (Deuteronomy 4:9). R. Chiya b. Abba found R. Yehoshua b. Levi walking down the street with a sheet on his head [instead of a turban], as he was taking a child to the synagogue [for study]. R. Chiya b. Abba asked him, "What's the rush, [that you walked out without the headgear befitting someone of your stature]?" R. Yehoshua replied, "Is it then a small thing when it says, 'Teach your children and grandchildren,' which is followed by, 'The day that you stood before God your Lord at Horeb'?" [Taking my grandson to his Torah class is as though I were standing at Sinai!]

From then on R. Chiya b. Abba did not eat the small piece of roasted meat [he normally had for breakfast] until he reviewed the previous day's lesson with a child and taught him an additional verse. R. Safra said in the name of R. Yehoshua b. Chanania: What is the meaning of the verse, "Teach [the words of the Torah] thoroughly [veshinnantam] to your children" (ibid. 6:7)? Don't read veshinnantam, but veshilashtam, "divide into three": a person should divide the years of his life, devoting a third to the study of Scripture, a third to Mishnah, and a third to Talmud. [The Gemara asks:] But does a person know how long he is going to live? [The Gemara answers:] It means days, [the days of the week: two days devoted to Scripture, two days to Mishnah, and two days to Talmud (Rashi)].[2]

THEY COUNTED THE LETTERS
OF THE TORAH

The early Sages were called soferim[3] because they were careful to count [sofer] all the letters in the Torah [to ensure the absolute correctnes of the text]. And so they said that the vav in the middle of the word gachon (Leviticus 11:42), [in the verse,"You may not eat any creature that crawls on its belly "(gachon)], marks the halfway point of all the letters of the Torah; the words darosh darash ["Moses inquired insistently" (Leviticus 10:16)] mark the midway point of the words of the Torah; vehitgalach ["He shall shave himself" (Leviticus 13:33)], the halfway point of the verses. The letter ayin in yaar [forest] in the verse "The boar of the forest [yaar] ravages it" (Psalms 80:14) marks the midway point of the letters of Psalms. The verse, "Nevertheless, He the Merciful One is forgiving of iniquity" (Psalms 78:38) is the midway point of the verses of Psalms.

We learned in a Baraita: There are 5,888[4] verses in the Torah; the Book of Psalms has an additional eight verses;[5] Daniel[6] and Chronicles have eight verses less than are found in the Torah.

IMPRESS THE TORAH
ON YOUR CHILDREN

Our Rabbis taught: "Teach [the Torah] thoroughly [veshinnantam] to your children" (Deuteronomy 6:7), [veshinnantam from the root shanan, "to be keen"]. This means that the words of the Torah should be clear in your mouth, so that if a person asks you something, you should not hesitate, but be able to answer him immediately. For it says, (30b) "Say to wisdom, 'You are my sister,' and call understanding a friend'" (Proverbs 7:4), [a person should be as well-versed in the Torah as he is familiar with the fact that his sister is forbidden to him (Rashi)]. And it also says, "Bind them on your fingers; inscribe them on the tablet of your heart" (ibid. v. 3), and it also says, "Like arrows in the hand of a warrior, so are the children of youth [meaning, students]" (Psalms 127:4), and it also says, "Your arrows are sharp—nations fall beneath you" (Psalms 45:6), and furthermore it says, "Praiseworthy is the man who fills his quiver with them; they shall not be ashamed when they speak with enemies at the gate" (ibid. 127:5). [The combination of these verses leads to the conclusion that students—who are referred to as arrows—and the person who teaches them must be sharp (Maharsha).]

[The Gemara asks:] What is meant by "with the enemies at the gate"? R. Chiya b. Abba said: Even a father and son, or a teacher and his student who study Torah together become enemies of each other [they are arguing about Torah issues, and one does not want to accept the other's reasoning], yet they do not move away from there until they come to love each other. For it says, "Therefore it is said in the Book of the Wars of God: Et vaheiv besufah—A war that is fought while learning together the Book of God ends in love" (Numbers 21:14).

TORAH IS THE CURE FOR
THE YETZER HARA

We learned in a Baraita: The word vesamtem ["You shall place these words of Mine upon your heart" (Deuteronomy 11:18)] reads like sam tam, [the Torah is] "a perfect remedy." It can be compared to a person who hit his son and wounded him badly. When he put a bandage on his wound he said, "My son! As long as this bandage [which has healing medication] is on your wound, you may eat and drink whatever you please; you may bathe in hot or cold water without fear. But if you take it off, your wound will begin to fester." So too said the Holy One, blessed be He, to Israel, "My children! I created the yetzer hara [the evil impulse], and I created the Torah as its antidote. [The yetzer hara is symbolized by the wound; the Torah by the medicated bandage.] If you study the Torah, you will not fall into the clutches of the yetzer hara, for it says, "If you do good [and study the Torah], you will be able to subdue your evil impulse" (Genesis 4:7). But if you do not study the Torah, you will be handed over into the hands of the *yetzer hara*, for it says, "Sin [i.e., the *yetzer hara*] is lying in wait at the door" (ibid.). And that is not all, but the *yetzer hara* spends all his energy on making you sin, for it says, "his [the *yetzer hara*'s] desire is toward you" (ibid.). But if you want, you can overpower him [by learning Torah], as it says, "yet you can conquer him" (ibid.).

THE *YETZER HARA*

Our Rabbis taught: The *yetzer hara* is so bad that even its Creator calls it evil, as it says, "The *yetzer* [impulse] of man's heart is evil from his youth" (Genesis 8:21). R. Yitzchak said: The *yetzer hara* renews [its battle to incite man to sin] every day. For it says, "His *yetzer* . . . was only evil every day" (ibid. 6:5). And R. Shimon b. Levi said: A person's *yetzer hara* strengthens itself every single day and wants to kill him, for it says, "The wicked one watches for the righteous and seeks to kill him" (Psalms 37:32), and if not for the help of the Holy One, blessed be He, we would never be able to resist it, for it says, "But God will not forsake him to his hand" (ibid. v. 33).

The yeshivah of R. Yishmael taught: My son, if this despicable creature [the *yetzer hara*] meets you, drag him into the *bet midrash* [and start learning Torah]: if the *yetzer hara* is like a stone, it will dissolve; if like iron, it will break apart, for it says, "Behold my word is like fire—says God—and like a hammer that shatters a rock" (Jeremiah 23:29). If it is like a stone, it will dissolve, for it says, "Ho, everyone who is thirsty, go to the water [the Torah]" (Isaiah 55:1); and it says, "Stones are worn away by water" (Job 14:19).

TEACH YOUR SON A TRADE

[A father is obligated] to teach his son a trade. Said Chizkiyah: It says, "Enjoy life with the wife you love" (Ecclesiastes 9:9). If it literally means a wife, this teaches that, just as you are obligated to marry off your son, so are you obligated to teach him a trade, but if "wife" is referring to Torah, then just as you are obligated to teach your son Torah, so are you obligated to teach him a trade. Some say, you are also obligated to teach your son how to swim. What is the reason? Because his life may depend on it. R. Yehudah said: A father who does not teach his son a trade is as though he taught him how to become a robber. [Without a trade, he will have to resort to robbery to support himself.] On what point do they differ? [What novel thought does Rabbi Yehudah add?] They differ when he teaches him business. [The first Tanna includes business, but R. Yehudah by insisting on a trade shows that he does not consider business enough, since business may be slow sometimes, and he will then resort to robbery; whereas a trade always provides an income (Rashi).]

HONOR YOUR FATHER AND YOUR MOTHER

Our Rabbis taught: It says, "Honor your father and your mother" (Exodus 20:12), and it says, "Honor God with your wealth" (Proverbs 3:9). [By using the same terminology,] the Torah compares the honor you owe your father and mother to the honor you have to give to the Almighty. It also says, "Every person must respect his mother and his father" (Leviticus 19:3), and it says, "God your Lord you shall respect, Him you shall serve" (Deuteronomy 10:20). [Here the same word, "respect," is used.] The Torah equates the respect you owe your parents with the respect you must show God. Furthermore it says, "Whoever curses his father or mother shall be put to death" (Exodus 21:17). And furthermore it says, "Anyone that curses God shall bear his sin" (Leviticus 24:15). By using the same terms the Torah compares cursing of parents with cursing the Almighty. But when it comes to hitting [the prohibition against hitting one's parents] it is impossible to create equality [because the Almighty cannot be struck]. And it is logical [to establish an equality between parents and God], because these three—God, the father, and the mother—are partners in the creation [of the child].

The Rabbis taught: There are three partners in the creation of man—the Holy One, blessed be He, the father, and the mother. When a person honors his father and his mother, the Holy One, blessed be He, says: I consider it as though I lived among them, and they had honored Me.

It was taught: Rabbi said: It is revealed and known to Him who created the world that a son honors his mother more than his father (**31a**) because she persuades him with gentle words; therefore the Holy One, blessed be He, placed the honor of the father before that of the mother [in the verse, "Honor your father and your mother" (Exodus 20:12]. It is revealed and known to Him who created the world that a son respects his father more than his mother, because he teaches him Torah; therefore the Holy One, blessed be He, placed the respect of the mother before that of the father [in the verse, "Every person must respect his mother and his father" (Leviticus 19:3)].

A Tanna recited a *Baraita* before R. Nachman: When a person causes anguish to his father and his mother, the Holy One, blessed be He, says: It was proper that I did not dwell among them, for if I dwelled among them, I would be anguished to see a child treat his parents this way.

R. Yitzchak said: Anyone who commits a transgression in a hidden place is as though he pressed against the feet of the *Shechinah*, for it says, "Thus said God, 'The heaven is My throne and the earth is My footstool'" (Isaiah 66:1). [By sinning in a secret place he is saying that God is not in that place. Thus he is "sqeezing the feet of the *Shechinah*" out of that place.] R. Yehoshua b. Levi said: A person is forbidden to walk with a haughty posture, for it says, "The whole world is filled with His glory" (Isaiah 6:3) [and the person who walks proudly erect is as if he were pushing the *Shechinah* away]. R. Huna the son of R. Yehoshua was careful not to walk four cubits bareheaded. He said: The *Shechinah* is above my head, [therefore it is not proper to walk four cubits with my head uncovered].

A son of a widow asked R. Eliezer: If my father says, "Bring me a drink of water," and my mother says, "Bring me a drink of water," which one should I give first? R. Eliezer told him: Leave your mother's honor for a moment and fulfill the honor you owe your father, because both you and your mother are obligated to show respect to your father. The same son then went to R. Yehoshua who gave him the same answer. "Rabbi," he said to him, "what if she is divorced [and does not have to respect my father anymore]?" He replied, "From the sight of your eyelashes I can tell that you are the son of a widow. [Due to the excessive crying over the loss of his father his eyelashes had become very thin.] Pour some water for them into a bowl and coo to them like to a chicken. [He gave a sarcastic answer, because he had asked a theoretical question and should not have framed his question as an actual case (Rashi).]

Ulla Rabbah expounded at the entrance to the Nasi's house. What is meant by the verse, "All the kings of the earth will acknowledge You, God, because they heard Your statements" (Psalms 138:4). It does not say "Your statement" but "Your statements" [in the plural]. When the Holy One, blessed be He, said, "I am God your Lord" and "Do not have any other gods before Me" (Exodus 20:2,3), all the nations of the world said: He is looking only for His own honor. But when He said, "Honor your father and your mother" (ibid. v. 12), they retracted and recognized the correctness of the first commands. [Therefore, the kings acknowledged God when they heard all these statements.] Rava said: We can infer it from the following verse, "Your very first utterance is truth" (Psalms 119:160). Your first utterance, and not Your last utterance? But from Your last utterance it can be seen that the first utterance is also true. [From "Honor your father and mother" the nations realized that the first commandments were true.]

THE STORY OF DAMA
BEN NETINAH

They asked the following question to R. Ulla: To what length does a person have to go in fulfilling the mitzvah of honoring parents? He replied: Let us examine what a certain non-Jew in Ashkelon by the name of Dama ben Netinah once did. The Sages once wanted to buy something from him on which he would have earned a profit of 600,000 [golden dinars]. And the key to the chest that contained the items the Sages

wanted to buy was underneath the pillow on which his father was sleeping, and so he did not disturb him.

R. Yehudah said in the name of Shmuel: They asked R. Eliezer: What is the limit of the mitzvah of honoring parents? He replied: Let us see what a certain non-Jew did in Ashkelon by the name of Dama ben Netinah. The Sages wanted to buy from him jewels for the *eifod* [of the *Kohen Gadol*] for a profit of 600,000—according to R. Kahane it was a profit of 800,000—but since the key [to the chest that contained these jewels] was lying under his father's pillow while he was asleep, he did not disturb him.[7] The next year the Holy One, blessed be He, gave him his reward. A red cow [which is used for purification][8] was born in his herd. When the Sages of Israel came to buy it he said to them, "I know that even if I asked you all the money in the world [for this cow], you would pay me. But I ask of you only the money I lost because of the honor I accorded to my father." R. Chanina commented: If someone [like Dama ben Nesinah] who is not commanded [to honor his parents], and does it anyway received such a rich reward; someone who is commanded and fulfills the command, how much more so will that person be rewarded! For R. Chanina said: The person who does something he is commanded to do is greater than the person who does something he is not commanded to do. [Because someone who is commanded to do a mitzvah worries that he does not fulfill it properly; someone who does a mitzvah voluntarily does not have such concerns (Tosafot). Also someone who is commanded to do a mitzvah has to overcome his *yetzer hara* that tells him not to do it, while a volunteer has no opposition on the part of the *yetzer hara* (Yavetz).]

R. Yosef [who was blind] said: Originally, I thought that if someone told me that the *halachah* agrees with R. Yehudah, who says that a blind person is exempt from fulfilling the *mitzvot*, I would make a banquet for the Rabbis, because [being blind] I am not required to do the *mitzvot*, but I would do them anyway. However, now that I have heard R. Chanina's statement that someone who is commanded to do a mitzvah and does it is greater than someone who does a mitzvah although he is not commanded to do it; on the contrary, if someone told me that the *halachah* does not agree with R. Yehudah, [and a blind person *is* obligated to fulfill all the *mitzvot*], I would make a banquet for the Rabbis.

HONORING FATHER
AND MOTHER

When R. Dimi came [from Eretz Yisrael to Babylon] he said: He [Dama ben Netinah] was once wearing a gold embroidered cloak and was sitting among the Roman nobles, when his mother came and ripped it off him, hit him on the head, and spat in his face,[9] yet he did not embarrass her.

Avimi, son of R. Abbahu, taught the following: It is possible for a son to serve his father a *pasyunu* [a delectable fatty bird, similar to quail], and to be punished for it [if, while serving his father, his facial expression shows that he begrudges him the delicacies]. Then again, another son may put his father to work at turning a grindstone, (31b) and nevertheless this brings him to the World to Come, [for he spoke to his father with sensitivity and dignity].[10]

R. Abbahu said: For example, my son Avimi is fulfilling the mitzvah of honoring father and mother. [How did Avimi fulfill the mitzvah in a superior way?] Avimi had five sons, each of whom received ordination while R. Avimi's father [R. Abbahu] was still alive. Yet when R. Abbahu came to see Avimi in his home, Avimi himself got up to open the door. He would call out, "Yes! Yes! I'm coming to open the door," until he got to the door. One day his father asked for a drink of water. By the time Avimi brought it, his father had fallen asleep. So he stood there, bent over, waiting until his father would wake up. During the time [that he stood bent over, ready to serve his father] he received Heavenly help and succeeded in expounding the psalm, "A song of Asaph, O God! The nations have entered into Your inheritance" (Psalms 79), [which he did not understand before].

R. Abbahu asked Abbaye: Take me, for example. Before I return from the yeshivah, my father prepares a cup and my mother mixes the wine; what should I do? Abbaye told him: From your mother you should accept it, but not from your father; for since he is a Torah scholar he will feel hurt [if you accept something from him].

R. Tarfon had an elderly mother; and whenever she wanted to go to bed he would bend down, and she would climb into bed by stepping on him, and whenever she wanted to climb out of bed, she stepped on him. He went into the *bet midrash* and praised [the fact that he was able to fulfill the mitzvah of honoring his mother in such a manner]. They said to him: You did not even reach half of what the mitzvah of honoring parents requires of you. Did she ever throw a purse into the sea in front of you, and you did not embarrass her?

When R. Yosef heard his mother's footsteps he used to say, "I have to stand up; the *Shechinah* is approaching."

R. Yochanan said: Happy is the person who never saw his parents, [for it is impossible to give them all the respect that they deserve]. [R. Yochanan's statement can be explained by the fact that] R. Yochanan's father died when his mother was pregnant with him, and his mother died when he was born. The same happened to Abbaye.

We learned in a *Baraita*: What is "fear" and what is "honor"? [The Gemara is referring to the verses, "Every person must fear his mother and father" (Leviticus 19:3) and "*Honor* your father and mother" (Exodus 20:12).] "Fear" means that a son should not stand in his father's place, nor sit in his father's seat, nor contradict his words, nor side with his father's opponents in a Torah debate. "Honor" means that he should give his father food and drink, he should help to dress his father, cover him, and lead him in and out. A question was raised: (32a) Who should pay [for the expenses of the father's food and drink]? Rav Yehudah said: The son must pay for it. R. Natan b. Oshaya said: The money should come from his father.

R. Eliezer was asked: How far does the honor of parents extend? He answered: To the point that a parent could take a wallet full of money, throw it into the sea in front of their child, and the child would not embarrass them.

SHOULD RABBAN GAMLIEL SERVE DRINKS?

(32b) It once happened that R. Eliezer, R. Yehoshua, and R. Tzadok were sitting at the wedding banquet of Rabban Gamliel, while Rabban Gamliel was standing over them and serving drinks. He offered a drink to R. Eliezer, but he did not accept it. When he offered it to R. Yehoshua, he did accept it. R. Eliezer said, "How could you do such a thing, Yehoshua! We should be sitting while Rabban Gamliel [who is the *Nasi*] is standing and serving us!" R. Yehosha replied, "We find that even a greater person than Rabban Gamliel stood and served his guests. After all, Abraham was the leading personality of his generation, and it says about Abraham, [with reference to the three angels who appeared to him,] 'He stood over them as they ate' (Genesis 18:8). And maybe you want to tell me that they appeared to him as angels, [and that is why he served them]; [that is not true,] they appeared to him only as Arabs[11] [and nevertheless, he served them]. Then should we not allow Rabban Gamliel to serve us drinks?" Said R. Tzadok to them, "How long are you going to ignore the honor of God, and involve yourself with the honor of man? The Holy One, blessed be He, causes the wind to blow, the clouds to rise, the rain to fall, the earth to yield, and sets a table for each and every individual; and we should not allow Rabban Gamliel to stand and serve us drinks?"

STAND UP BEFORE THE AGED

We learned in a *Baraita*: It says, "Stand up before the aged, and give honor to the old" (Leviticus 19:32). I might think that this includes even an elderly person who is a sinner and an ignoramus, therefore it says, "and honor the *zaken*." And *zaken* refers to someone who is wise, for it says, "Assemble seventy of Israel's elders [*zekeinim*]" (Numbers 11:16). R. Yose Hagelili said: Zaken means "a person who has acquired wisdom."[12] For it says, "God acquired me [the wisdom of the Torah] as the beginning of His way" (Proverbs 8:22). I might think that you should stand up for him even if you are at a great distance; therefore it says, "Stand up . . . and honor"—you only have to stand up when there will be honor, [meaning within four ells, so that it is obvious that you rise in his honor, which would not be discernable at a greater distance]. You might think that "honor" means honoring him by giving him money? Therefore it says, "Stand up . . . and honor." Just as standing up does not cost any money, so too "honor" implies honoring him without giving him money. You might think that you should stand up for him even in a bathroom or a bathhouse? Therefore it says, "Stand up . . . and honor," implying that you should rise only in a place where there is going to be honor. I might think that perhaps you could close your eyes to make believe that you do not see him [so that you would not have to stand up for him]? Therefore it says, "Stand up . . . you shall thus fear your God" (ibid.)—of anything that is known to the heart only it says, "you shall fear your God." R. Shimon b. Elazar says: How do we know that an elderly person should not trouble the people [to make them rise, if he can take a different route and avoid passing the crowds]? Because it says, "the aged . . . you shall thus fear." Isi b. Yehudah says: "Stand up before the aged" implies any elderly person [not only a scholar].

STANDING UP BEFORE TORAH SCHOLARS

(33a) Craftsmen [who are employed] are not permitted to stand up before Torah scholars during their work, [because their time is not their own]. [The Gemara asks:] You mean to tell me they should not stand up? Surely we learned in a Mishnah: All workmen while at work should stand up to greet the people who are bringing the *bikkurim* [first fruits] to Jerusalem and should call out to them, "Our brothers from such and such town, we welcome you!" [so we see that even while working they stand up to greet these people]. R. Yochanan said: Before *them* [i.e., the people bringing the *bikkurim*] they must stand up, but for Torah scholars they should not stand up.

R. Yose b. Avin said: [Based on this,] let us look and examine how important a mitzvah is [when it is being done] in its time, because the craftsmen do stand up for the people who are involved in doing the mitzvah of bringing the *bikkurim*, but they do not stand up for Torah scholars. [The Gemara suggests:] But perhaps it is different here [in the case of *bikkurim*]; for if they are not welcomed, they will feel slighted and will not bring *bikkurim* again.

R. Yochanan used to rise before elderly non-Jews, saying: How many troubles and trials did they go through, [and how many miracles did they experience during their lifetime]. Rava did not stand up before them but he did show them respect [by rising slightly from his seat]. Abaye used to give his hand to the elderly [so that they could lean on him]. Rava sent his messenger [to give a hand but he did not do it himself]. R. Nachman [who was the head of the Bet Din] sent his court officers to help up the elderly, [but he himself would not go], for he said, "If not for the Torah, there would be many Nachman b. Abba in the marketplace!" [He felt that it was demeaning for a man of his position to go himself.]

(33b) R. Aivu said in the name of R. Yanai: A Torah scholar is permitted to stand up before his teacher only once in the morning and once in the evening, so that his teacher's honor will not be greater than the honor accorded to Heaven. [Because we rise to pray in God's honor only mornings and evenings.] R. Elazar said: Any Torah scholar who does not stand up before his teacher is called wicked; he will not live long, and he will forget his learning. For it says, "It will not be well[13] with the wicked, and he will not long endure—like a shadow—because he does not fear God" (Ecclesiastes 8:13). Now I do not know what this fear is referring to. But when it says, "Stand up before the aged . . . thus you shall fear your God" (Leviticus 19:32), we realize that fear means rising [before one's teacher].

HOW LONG DID THE MANNA DESCEND?

(38a) It says, "The children of Israel ate the manna for forty years, until they came to inhabited territory. They ate the manna until they came to the edge of the land of Canaan" (Exodus 16:35). ["Inhabited territory" refers to the land of Sichon and Og, whereas the "edge of the land of Canaan" refers to the Plains of Moab where Moses died. So when did the manna stop?] It is impossible to say that they ate the manna only until they came to "inhabited territory" since it also says, [they continued to eat the manna] "until they came to the edge of the land of Canaan." By the same token, it is impossible to say that they ate the manna until they were about to enter Eretz Yisrael, when it stopped the moment they came to inhabited territory! How can we reconcile this? [The Gemara answers:] Moses died on the seventh of Adar, and then the manna no longer came down from heaven. However, they used the manna in their vessels until the sixteenth of Nisan. [Thus, "until they came to inhabited land" refers to the entire time they ate it, although it came down only "until they came to the edge of the land of Canaan."]

We learned in another *Baraita*: "The children of Israel ate the manna for forty years." [The Gemara asks:] Did they really eat it for forty years? Surely they ate it only for forty years less thirty days. [They entered the wilderness of Sin on the fifteenth of Iyar (Exodus 16:1) and received the manna on the following day (ibid. 6–13). Since they ate it until the sixteenth of Nisan, forty years later, they ate it for forty years less one month.] [The Gemara answers:] This teaches you that the cakes they took out of Egypt also tasted like manna, [so they really ate manna for a full forty years.]

THE SEVENTH OF ADAR, MOSES' BIRTHDAY AND *YAHRZEIT*

We learned in another *Baraita*: On the seventh of Adar Moses died, and on the seventh of Adar he was born. How do we know that he died on the seventh of Adar? Because it says, "It was there in the land of Moab that God's servant Moses died" (Deuteronomy 34:5). Then it says, [following the death of Moses,] "The children of Israel mourned Moses for thirty days" (ibid. v. 8). And it says, "It happened after the death of Moses, servant of God, that God said to Joshua, 'Moses My servant has died. Now arise, cross this Jordan'" (Joshua 1:2). Thereupon Joshua ordered the officials of the people, "Circulate in the midst of the camp, and command the people saying, 'Prepare provisions for yourselves, because in another three days you will be crossing this Jordan'" (ibid. v. 11). [And when did they cross the Jordan?] "The people ascended from the Jordan on the tenth of the first month" (ibid. 4:19). [Thus we have thirty days of mourning and three days until the crossing of the Jordan (v. 11).] Subtract these thirty-three days [from the tenth of Nisan]; thus you will find that Moses died on the seventh of Adar. And how do we know that Moses was born on the seventh of Adar? Because it says, [Moses said,] "I am a hundred and twenty years old today, I can no longer go out and come in" (Deuteronomy 31:2). He did not have to say "today" [that is obvious]. What does the verse teach us by stating this extra "today"? It teaches that the Holy One, blessed be He, sits and completes the years of the righteous exactly from day to day and month to month, as it says, "I shall fill the number of your days" (Exodus 23:26). [Therefore, since he died on the Seventh of Adar, he was born also on the Seventh of Adar.]

THE REWARD FOR *MITZVOT*

(39b) [The Mishnah says:] Whoever performs one [particular] mitzvah will have it good [in this world], he will live to a ripe old age, and he will inherit the land [meaning, the World to Come]. But whoever does not perform one [particular] mitzvah will not have it good, will not live to a ripe old age, and will not inherit the land [i.e., the World to Come].

The Gemara points out a contradiction: We learned [in the Mishnah *Pei'ah* 1:1]: These are the precepts whose fruits a person enjoys in this world but whose principal remains intact for him in the World to Come. They are: the honor due to father and mother, acts of kindness, hospitality to guests, bringing peace between man and his fellow—and the study of Torah is equivalent to all of them. [But our Mishnah promises the same reward for only one specific mitzvah.] Rav Yehudah answers: This is what the Mishnah means to say: [If a person has an equal amount of good and bad deeds,] and does one mitzvah that tips the scale, then

because of that one mitzvah he will have it good [in this world], and he is considered as though he had fulfilled the entire Torah.

[The Gemara asks:] This implies that for the other *mitzvot* [mentioned in *Pei'ah* 1:1: honoring parents, acts of kindness, hospitality, etc., a person does not need a majority of *mitzvot*], but even if he has more transgressions than *mitzvot*, as long as he has just one of these *mitzvot* to his credit he is rewarded with both worlds. [That cannot possibly be!] R. Shemayah said: The Mishnah wants to teach us that if a person has an equal amount of *mitzvot* and transgressions, and among his *mitzvot* is one of the *mitzvot* listed in *Pei'ah* 1:1, then that single mitzvah tips the scale to the mitzvah side [even though he does not have a majority of *mitzvot*].

At any rate we have learned that if someone [has as an equal number of *mitzvot* and transgressions] and then does one mitzvah to tip the scale, he will have it good in this world. The Gemara points out the following contradiction: We learned: If someone has more merits than sins, life is made difficult for him [in this world in order to cleanse him of his sins, so that he will enjoy undiminished spiritual delight in the World to Come], and [his suffering makes it appear] as though he had burned the whole Torah, and did not leave even a single letter. And if someone had more sins than good deeds, he has it good in this world [as a reward for his good deeds, so that he will experience nothing but punishment in the World to Come]; and [his good fortune makes it seem] as though he had fulfilled the whole Torah and did not leave one letter [that he did not carry out]!

[The contradiction is that the Mishnah in *Pei'ah* taught that if he has a majority of one mitzvah, he has it good in this world; whereas this Tanna teaches us that if he has a majority of one mitzvah, he is being punished in this world to pave the way for total bliss in the World to Come]. Abaye said: When our Mishnah says, "If someone does one mitzvah, he has it good" it means that the ultimate good is being prepared for the person who has a majority of *mitzvot*. How? By making life difficult for him in this world. And anguish in the World to Come is being prepared for the person who has a majority of transgressions. He has it good in this world as a reward for his good deeds.

Rava said: The Mishnah [that says that if he has a majority of *mitzvot* he is being punished in this world] is in accordance with R. Yaakov, who says that there is no reward given for *mitzvot* in this world; [the reward for *mitzvot* is reserved exclusively for the World to Come]. For we learned in a *Baraita*: R. Yaakov said: There is not a single mitzvah that is mentioned in the Torah together with its reward, where this reward does not pertain to the World to Come. For example, regarding honoring one's father and mother it says, "You will then live long and have it well" (Deuteronomy 5:16). Regarding the sending away of the mother bird it says, "[If you do this] you will have it good, and will live long" (ibid. 22:7).

[The promise of "you will live long" cannot refer to this world, says R. Yaakov, for] if a father tells his son, "Climb up that tall building, and bring down little birds for me," and the son climbs to the top of the building [thereby fulfilling the mitzvah of honoring his father], takes the little birds, but first sends away the mother bird [thereby fulfilling the mitzvah of sending away the mother bird], and on his way down falls off the building and dies, where is the promised good life, and where is the promise of a long life? It must be therefore, that the promise of "you will have it good" refers to the world that is completely good [i.e., the World to Come], and "you will live long" refers to the world that lasts forever.

[The Gemara asks:] Maybe such an event [as mentioned by R. Yaakov] never happened [and the promise of a good and long life refers to this world]? [The Gemara answers:] R. Yaakov actually witnessed such an incident. [The Gemara asks:] Maybe the reason that the son slipped and fell was that he was thinking sinful thoughts [and that is why he was punished]? [The Gemara answers:] The Holy One, blessed be He, does not consider a person's intent to commit a sin as if he had actually done it. [So he should not have been punished.] [The Gemara asks:] Perhaps he was planning to worship idols? [And idolatry is the exception, for even the mere intention to worship idols is punished,] for it says, "Thus I will hold the House of Israel accountable for their thoughts, because they have all been estranged from Me through their idols" (Ezekiel 14:5). [So the son deserved to be punished. Then what is R. Yaakov's basis for saying that there is no reward for *mitzvot* in this world?] [The Gemara answers:] R. Yaakov also understood [that he must have been planning to worship idols, otherwise he would have been protected]. But this is R. Yaakov's point: If you think that *mitzvot* are rewarded in this world, why did not the fulfillment of the mitzvah protect him from thoughts about idolatry entering his mind?

[The Gemara asks:] But R. Elazar said: Someone who is engaged in doing a mitzvah does not get hurt, [and the son was doing two *mitzvot*: honoring his father and sending away the mother bird; how could he have been hurt?] [The Gemara answers:] When you are on the way to do a mitzvah it is different, [but he fell on his way down]. [The Gemara asks:] But R. Elazar said: Someone who is engaged in doing a mitzvah does not get hurt, either on his way there or returning? [The Gemara answers:] It was a shaky ladder, so that injury was bound to happen, and the rule is that where injury is bound to happen you don't rely on miracles. For it says, "Samuel said, 'How can I go [to anoint David]? If Saul finds out, he will kill me'" (1 Samuel 16:2). [Samuel knew that there is no heav-

enly protection for a person engaged in performing a mitzvah if injury is bound to happen.]

ACHER'S APOSTASY

[R. Meir's teacher was Elisha b. Abuyah, a great scholar who at one point in his life went astray and turned his back on the Torah. He was then called Acher, "the other one." The turning point in his life came when he saw an incident like the one witnessed by R. Yaakov.]

R. Yosef said: If Acher had interpreted the verse [that promised a good and long life for the mitzvah of honoring parents and sending away the mother bird] like R. Yaakov, his daughter's son, [as referring to the World to Come], he would not have sinned. [Acher interpreted it as referring to this world, and, thinking that there was no reward for *mitzvot*, he became an apostate.] [The Gemara asks:] What exactly did Acher see? Some say he saw an incident similar to this [a man falling off a roof while fulfilling the two *mitzvot*]. Others say he saw the tongue of Chutzpit the Meturgeman (Interpreter),[14] [one of the Ten Martyrs killed by the Romans], dragged around by a pig. "The mouth that gave forth pearls licks the dust!" he exclaimed. Thereupon he went out, and began to sin.

THREE WHO RESISTED TEMPTATION

R. Tobi son of R. Kisna pointed out a contradiction to Rava: We learned in our Mishnah: Whoever performs one mitzvah will have it good. That is, only if he actually performs a mitzvah, but if he merely refrains from sinning, he will not be rewarded. But we learned in a *Baraita*: If he sits passively and commits no transgression he is rewarded as though he had fulfilled a mitzvah! Replied Rava: The *Baraita* refers to a case where a person was tempted to commit a transgression and resisted. As in the case of R. Chanina b. Pappi. When an influential noblewoman demanded that he commit immorality, he pronounced an incantation, whereupon his body broke out in boils and scabs [to discourage her]. But she did something [through witchcraft], and he was healed. So he fled and hid in a bathhouse [that was inhabited by demons] so that when even two people entered, even in the daytime,[15] they would be hurt. The next morning the Rabbis asked him, "Who guarded you?" He replied, **(40a)** "Two royal guards watched over me all night." They said to him, "Could it be that you were tempted with immorality and you resisted?" For we learned in a *Baraita*: If someone is tempted with immorality and withstands it, a miracle is performed for him.

It says, "Bless God, O His angels; the strong warriors who do His bidding, to obey the voice of His word" (Psalms 103:20). This refers to someone like R.

Tzadok and his companions. An influential noble-woman demanded that R. Tzadok commit immorality. He said to her, "I feel very weak right now, I can't. Perhaps there is something to eat?" She said, "I have some food, but it is not kosher." So he replied, "What difference does it make; if a person is going to commit immorality, he might as well eat this." She went and stoked the oven, and when she wanted to put the meat into it, R. Tzadok jumped into it. "What are you doing?" she cried out. He retorted, "One who commits immorality will fall into the fire [of Gehinnom]." She then said, "If I had known that immorality is such a grave matter to you, I would not have caused you all this agony." R. Kahana was selling baskets when an influential noblewoman demanded that he commit immorality. Said he to her, "Let me go and groom myself first." So he went up to the roof and jumped down, but Elijah came and caught him. Elijah chided him, "You should know that you made me fly four hundred *parsah* [to catch you. You should not have been calling on women to sell your baskets]!" R. Kahana retorted, "What got me into this trouble? Is it not poverty [that forces me to sell baskets to women]?" So Elijah gave him a measuring cup full of gold *dinars*.

THE *TZADDIK*
WHO BENEFITS OTHERS

Rava pointed out a contradiction to R. Nachman: We learned in a Mishnah (*Pei'ah* 1:1): These are the precepts whose fruits a person enjoys in this world but whose principal remains intact for him in the World to Come. They are: the honor due to father and mother, acts of kindness, bringing peace between man and his fellow—and the study of Torah is equivalent to them all. Concerning honoring father and mother it says, "so that your days will be lengthened [in the World to Come], and so that it will be good for you [in this world]" (Deuteronomy 5:16). Regarding acts of kindness it says, "One who pursues righteousness and kindness will find life [in the World to Come], righteousness and honor [in this world]" (Proverbs 21:21). About bringing peace it says, "Seek peace and pursue it" (Psalms 34:15). And R. Abbahu said: We compare "pursuing" in this verse to "pursuing" in the passage, "One who pursues righteousness and kindness." [Therefore, just as the latter is rewarded in both worlds, so is the former.] Regarding the study of Torah it says, "For it is your life [in this world] and the length of your days [in the World to Come]" (Deuteronomy 30:20).

[Rava's question is:] But concerning the mitzvah of sending away of the mother bird it also says, "So that it will be good with you and will prolong your life" (Deuteronomy 22:7). Why wasn't this mitzvah listed [in the Mishnah in *Pei'ah*]? R. Nachman answered: The Tanna lists some of the *mitzvot* and leaves out others.

[Rava challenges this:] The Tanna says, "*These* are the precepts" [which means these exclusively], yet you say that he lists some of them and leaves out others!" Rava said: R. Idi explained to me [why "sending away the mother bird"] is not on this list. It is based on this verse, "You can say of the *tzaddik* when he is good, that they shall eat the fruit of their deeds" (Isaiah 3:10). Is there then a *tzaddik* who is good and a tzaddik who is not good?—If he is good to Heaven and good to man, it is a good *tzaddik*—if he is good to Heaven but not good to man, it is a *tzaddik* who is not good.

[The verse, "that they shall eat the fruit of their deeds"] refers to the *tzaddik* who is good to Heaven and good to man; but when a person sends away the mother bird he is "good only to Heaven," but not "good to man," since no one benefits from it. [That is why the Mishnah does not list this mitzvah.] In a similar vein it says, "But woe to the wicked person who does evil, for the recompense of his hand will be dealt to him" (ibid. v. 11). Is there then a wicked man who does evil and a wicked man who does not do evil?—If he is evil to Heaven and evil to man [like a murderer or a robber], that is a wicked man who is evil; if he is evil to Heaven but not evil to man [e.g., he desecrates *Shabbat* or eats forbidden foods], that is a wicked man who is not evil. [To summarize, the Mishnah enumerates only *mitzvot* that benefit others.]

GOOD INTENTIONS
ARE REWARDED

The merit of *mitzvot* has both principal and bears fruit, for it says, "You can say of the *tzaddik* when he is good that they shall eat the fruits of their deeds" (Isaiah 3:10). Transgression has principal but no fruit; [the transgressor is not punished for more than his sin] for it says, "But woe to the wicked person who does evil" (ibid. v. 11). [The Gemara asks:] But how do you explain the verse, "They [the wicked] will eat of the fruit of their way and will be sated with their own schemes" (Proverbs 1:30)? [The Gemara answers:] If someone committed a transgression that produces fruit it has fruit [as when a prominent person sins, and others follow his example]; that which does not produce fruit has no fruit.

A good intention [even if it is not carried out], the Holy One, blessed be He, combines it with the good deed, [and both the intention and the good deed are rewarded]. For it says, "Then those who fear God spoke to each other, and God listened and heard, and a book of remembrance was written before Him for those who fear God and those who give thought to His name" (Malachi 3:16). What is the meaning of "who give thought to His name"? Said R. Assi: Even if someone just thinks of doing a mitzvah but is unavoidably prevented from doing it, Scripture considers it as if he had done the mitzvah. However, if someone had the intention to transgress but was unable to carry it out, the

Holy One blessed be He, does not consider it as if he had actually transgressed. For it says, "Had I perceived iniquity in my heart, the Lord would not have listened" (Psalms 66:18).

[The Gemara asks:] Then how do you interpret the verse, "Behold I am bringing evil upon this nation, even for the fruits of their thoughts" (Jeremiah 6:19)?—A bad intention that produces fruit [that is carried out], the Holy One, blessed be He, combines with the deed; a bad intention that does not result in fruit, [it was just a bad thought], the Holy One, blessed be He, does not combine with the deed. But what about the verse, "Thus I will hold the House of Israel to account for their thoughts" (Ezekiel 14:5)? Said R. Acha b. Yaakov: That verse refers to idolatry, for a Master said: The sin of idolatry is so grave that whoever denies it is as though he admits the truth of the whole Torah, [that is why the mere intention of idolatry counts as the deed itself].

Ulla said: [This can be explained] according to R. Huna, for R. Huna said: Once a person does wrong and repeats it, it becomes permitted to him. Do you mean to say, it becomes permitted to him! But we must say that it appears to him as something permitted, [and once he reaches this stage, he is punished for the intention. At this point, if he intended to sin, but did not, it is not because he repented but because circumstances prevented it (Rashi)]. R. Abbahu said in the name of R. Chanina: It is better for a person to commit a transgression secretly than to desecrate God's name.

THE SIN OF DESECRATING GOD'S NAME

We learned in a Mishnah: When it comes to the sin of desecrating the name of God,[16] regardless of whether it was done unintentionally or intentionally, its punishment is not put on credit. What is meant by "the punishment is not put on credit"? Mar Zutra explained: Heaven does not act like a storekeeper [who extends credit over a period of time, and then collects the entire outstanding debt all at once. God does not allow the sins of desecration of His name to accumulate, but punishes right away]. Mar the son of Ravina said: This comes to teach us that if a person's sins and mitzvot are equally balanced, and among the sins is that of desecration of God's name, the scale is automatically tipped to the side of the sins.

ONE MITZVAH TIPS THE SCALE

Our Rabbis taught: (40b) A person should always consider himself as though his mitzvot and sins were equally balanced; so that if he fulfills one mitzvah, how fortunate is he, for he has tilted the scale to the mitzvah side. By the same token, if he commits one transgression, woe is to him, for he has tilted the scale to the

side of guilt. For it says, "A single sinner can ruin a great deal of good" (Ecclesiastes 9:18). This means that because of a single sin he loses a great deal of good, [because he now has a majority of transgressions]. R. Elazar b. R. Shimon said: [Your actions have global ramifications,] because the whole world is judged according to its majority, and an individual, too, is judged by his majority of his good or bad deeds. Therefore, if he does just one mitzvah, how fortunate is he, for he has tipped the scale to the side of merit, for himself and the entire world; if he commits one transgression, woe is to him, for he may have depressed the scale to the side of guilt, for himself and the whole world. For it says, "A single sinner can ruin a great deal of good." Because of a single sin he committed, a great deal of good is lost to him and to the world.

R. Shimon b. Yochai said: Even if someone was a perfect tzaddik all his life but rebelled [against God] at the end, he will lose the reward for all his previous mitzvot, as it says, "The righteousness of the righteous person shall not rescue him on the day of his rebelliousness" (Ezekiel 33:12). And even if a person is wicked all his life and repents at the end, we no longer remind him of his previous transgressions, for the verse continues, "and as for the wickedness of the wicked person—he shall not stumble over it on the day of his repentance of his wickedness" (ibid.). [The Gemara asks: Why do we say that the rebellious tzaddik loses everything?] Let it at least be half mitzvot and half transgression! Said Resh Lakish: We are talking about a person who [completely changed his life] and regretted his former good deeds, [and if he regrets them, he loses them].

TZADDIKIM ARE COMPARED TO A TREE

[The Mishnah says:] Anyone that engages in the study of Torah and Mishnah and is well-mannered will not easily sin, as it says, "A three-ply cord is not easily severed" (Ecclesiastes 4:12). But anyone that does not engage in the study of Torah and Mishnah and is not well-mannered, is not considered a civilized person.

[The Gemara comments:] R. Elazar b. R. Tzadok said: To what are tzaddikim compared in this world? To a tree standing in a place of purity, some of whose branches extend over an impure area. If you trim those branches, the tree is completely surrounded by purity. It is the same with tzaddikim. The Holy One, blessed be He, brings suffering on the tzaddikim in this world, [thereby cleansing them of the few sins they committed], so that they should inherit the World to Come. For it says, "Though your beginning was insignificant, your end will flourish exceedingly" (Job 8:7). And to what are the wicked compared in this world? To a tree standing in a place of uncleanness, some of whose branches extend over an area of purity. If you trim those branches, the tree is completely surrounded by uncleanness. Thus, the Holy One, blessed be He, bestows prosperity on the wicked in this world, [as a reward for the few good deeds they performed], in order to destroy them and lower them to the bottom rung of Gehinnom, as it says, "There is a way that seems right to a man, but at its end are the ways of death" (Proverbs 14:12).

WHICH IS GREATER:
LEARNING OR PRACTICE?

R. Tarfon and the elders were sitting in the upper floor of Nit'zah's house in Lod one day, when this question was presented to them: Which is greater: Learning or doing [mitzvot]? Replied R. Tarfon: Doing [mitzvot] is greater. R. Akiva said: Learning is greater. Then all of them answered, saying: Learning is greater, because it leads to doing [mitzvot]. We learned in a Baraita: R. Yose said: Learning is greater because it preceded the mitzvah of challah[17] by forty years, [the Torah was given two months after the Exodus, whereas the mitzvah of challah went into effect only upon the Israelites' entry into Eretz Yisrael, forty years later]. [The Torah] preceded terumot[18] and tithes by fifty-four years [the obligation of terumot and tithes began only after the Land was conquered and divided among the tribes, fourteen years after their entry into the Land]. The Torah preceded shemittah [the Sabbatical year] by sixty-one years, [for they started counting the seven-year cycle fourteen years after their entry, 40 + 14 + 7]. And it preceded the Yovel [Jubilee] by one-hundred-and-three years, [since the Yovel began forty-nine years after the initial fifty-four years, 54 + 49]. [The Gemara asks:] One hundred-and-three? It should be one-hundred-and-four! [The Yovel is the fiftieth year, and presumably, its laws become effective at the end of the year.][19]

[The Gemara answers:] This Tanna is of the opinion that the laws of Yovel [i.e., the release of slaves and land] go into effect at the beginning of the year. And just as learning Torah came before the actual doing [of mitzvot], so does the judgment [in the World to Come] of a person's learning take precedence over that of his practice, in accordance with R. Hamenuna. For R. Hamenuna said: The first thing about which a person is judged [in the hereafter] is his Torah learning, for it says, "The refusal to learn Torah is the beginning of judgment" (Proverbs 17:14). And just as the judgment of learning comes before the judgment of actions, so does the reward for learning precede the reward for practice. For it says, "He gave them the lands of nations, and they inherited the toil of regimes, so that they might safeguard His statutes and observe His teachings" (Psalms 105:44,45).

HE IS NOT CIVILIZED

[We learned in the Mishnah:] Anyone that does not engage in the study of Torah and Mishnah and is not well-mannered is not considered a civilized person. [The Gemara comments:] R. Yochanan said: Such a person is not fit to serve as a witness. [Since he has a low self-esteem he has no qualms about testifying falsely.] Our Rabbis taught: Someone who eats in the market is like a dog, and some say he is unfit to testify [for he has no shame, and can easily be persuaded to lie]. R. Idi b. Avin said: The halachah agrees with the latter opinion.

Bar Kappara expounded: (41a) A hot-tempered person gains nothing but the harmful effect his anger [has on his health], but a good-natured person enjoys the fruit of his kind deeds. And anyone that does not engage in the study of Torah and Mishnah and is not well-mannered, vow not to have any benefit from him, for it says, "Praiseworthy is the man . . . who has not joined the company of the insolent" (Psalms 1:1), and this fellow is in the category of "company of the insolent." [Since he does not learn and is not mannerly, he can do nothing but scoff, mock, and sneer.]

LITERAL TRANSLATION
IS MISLEADING

(49a) R. Yehudah said: Whoever translates a verse literally is a liar, and if he adds words to it [that distort the true meaning], he is a blasphemer and a libeler.[20]

TEN MEASURES CAME DOWN
TO THE WORLD

Ten measures of wisdom came down to the world; the land of Israel took nine, and the rest of the world took one. Ten measures of beauty came down to the world; Jerusalem took nine, and one went to the rest of the world. Ten measures of wealth came down to the world; nine were taken by the Romans, and one was left for the rest on the world. Ten measures of poverty came down to the world; nine were taken by Babylonia, and one by the rest of the world. Ten measures of arrogance came down to the world; nine were taken by Elam, and one by the rest of the world. [The Gemara asks:] But did not arrogance come down to Babylonia? Surely it says, "Then I raised my eyes and saw, and behold, two women were emerging [from the Bet Hamikdash] with wind in their wings, for they had wings like a stork's wings, and they lifted the ephah between the earth and the heavens. I said to the angel who was speaking to me, 'Where are they taking the ephah?' he said to me, 'To build her a house in the land of Shinar [another name for Babylonia[21]]'" (Zechariah 5:9).

R. Yochanan said: [The two women] symbolize hypocrisy and arrogance, which came down to Babylonia! [So why do you say arrogance came to Elam?] [The Gemara answers:] Yes, originally it did come down to Babylonia, but it traveled on to Elam. This is also borne out by a precise reading of the phrase, "to build her a house" [which implies that it was only an intention, but it was not carried out]. This proves it. [The Gemara still believes that arrogance is the mark of Babylonia:] This is not so. For a Master said: A sign of arrogance is poverty, and poverty is found in Babylonia! [The Gemara answers:] The poverty [which is indicative of arrogance] refers to poverty of Torah; [an arrogant person is too conceited to ask others to teach him], as it says, "We have a little sister, and she has as yet no breasts" (Song of Songs 8:8), which R. Yochanan expounds: This refers to Elam, which merited to learn Torah, but not to teach Torah [because of their arrogance, but Babylonia did produce great teachers of Torah like Ezra].[22]

Ten measures of strength came down to the world; nine were taken by Persia, and one by the rest of the world. Ten measures of vermin came down to the world; nine were taken by Media, etc. Ten measures of witchcraft came down to the world; nine were taken by Egypt, etc. Ten measures of plagues came down to the world; nine were taken by swine, etc. Ten measures of immorality came down to the world; nine were taken by Arabia, etc. Ten measures of impudence came down to the world; nine were taken by Mishan, etc. Ten measures of talk came down to the world; nine were taken by women, etc. Ten measures of drunkenness came down to the world; nine were taken by Kushites, etc. Ten measures of sleep came down to the world; nine were taken by slaves, and one by the rest of the world.

THEY GRABBED AT
THE SHOWBREAD

(53a) [During Shimon Hatzaddik's lifetime, a blessing was bestowed on the *Lechem Hapanim* (the showbread), so that every *kohen* was able to receive a piece as big as an olive and satisfy his hunger with it. After his death, a curse was sent on the *Lechem Hapanim* so that every *kohen* received only a piece as small as a bean.] The modest [and well-mannered *kohanim*] withdrew their hands from it, but the gluttons among them grabbed [the shares of other *kohanim*]. It happened one time that one *kohen* grabbed his own and his neighbor's share; he was nicknamed Ben Chamtzan [the Snatcher] until his dying day. Rabbah son of Bar Shila said: What verse do we have [to show that *chamtzan* denotes a violent man]? The verse, "My God, deliver me from the wicked one's hand, from the palm of the schemer and the violent one [*chometz*]" (Psalms 71:4). Rava said: From here, "Learn to do good, seek justice, vindicate the victim of violence [*chamotz*]" (Isaiah 1:17).

REVERE GOD
AND TORAH SCHOLARS

(57b) We learned in a *Baraita*: Shimon Ha'Imsani, others say, Nechemiah Ha'Imsani, interpreted every *et* in the Torah, [explaining how each *et* meant to add

something], but when he came to the verse, *Et Hashem . . . tira*, "You shall revere God" (Deuteronomy 10:20), he stopped. [He could not add anything to this *et*, for there is nothing to revere other than God.] His students asked him, "What will be with all the *et*'s that you did interpret?" He replied, "Just as I was rewarded for interpreting them [*derishah*], so will I receive a reward for abstaining [*perishah* from further interpretations]." [The passage was left uninterpreted] until R. Akiva came and expounded it: The *et* in "You shall revere God" is to include Torah scholars.[23]

[In *Ein Yaakov* 52b comes after 57b]

R. MEIR'S
CONTENTIOUS STUDENTS

(52b) We learned in a *Baraita*: After the death of R. Meir, R. Yehudah said to his disciples: Do not permit the disciples of R. Meir to enter our yeshivah, because they are argumentative and do not come to learn Torah, but to get the better of me by quoting *halachot*. But Sumchus pushed his way in and entered. He said to them: This is what R. Meir taught me: If a *kohen* betrothes a woman with his share [of the meat of sacrificial offerings], regardless of whether they are the most-holy offerings or offerings of lesser holiness, he has not betrothed her. [Hearing this,] R. Yehudah became furious [with his students] and exclaimed, "Didn't I tell you not to let R. Meir's students come in here because they are argumentative and do not come to learn Torah, but to get the better of me by quoting *halachot*! How can a woman be in the Temple Courtyard in the first place! [Most-holy offerings must be eaten in, and may not be removed from, the Temple Courtyard, and women are not allowed to enter the Temple Courtyard.] R. Yose said: [R. Yehudah is in error, and if I do not speak up,] people will say: Meir is dead, Yehudah is angry, and Yose remains silent: what will become of the Torah? Cannot a person accept *kiddushin* on his daughter's behalf in the Temple Courtyard? And cannot a woman empower a messenger to receive her *kiddushin* in the Temple Courtyard? And what if she pushes her way in [and accepts the *kiddushin*, is she not betrothed? Of course she is]? [R. Yose meant to say: In his anger R. Yehudah made an error, and if I don't defend R. Meir and set the record straight, what is to become of the Torah?]

THE RABBIS' FIELD

(59a) R. Giddal was negotiating about buying a tract of land, when R. Abba went and bought it. So R. Giddal went and complained about him to R. Zeira. R. Zeira, in turn, went and complained to R. Yitzchak Nappacha. "Wait until [R. Abba] comes up to us [to Eretz Yisrael] for Yom Tov," R. Yitzchak Nappacha replied. When R. Abba came up, R. Yitzchak Nappacha met him and asked him, "If a poor man is looking over a cake [to buy it], and someone else comes and snaps it up, what is the law?" "He is a wicked man," R. Abba repleid. "Then why did you act this way [toward R. Giddal]?" R. Yitzchak Nappacha asked. "I did not know that he was negotiating about the parcel of land," R. Abba retorted. "Then let him have it now," he proposed. "I don't want to sell it to him, because it is the first field I ever bought, and it is not a good omen [for a person to sell his first purchase]. But if he wants it as a gift, let him take it." However, R. Giddal did not want to take possession of the land, because it says, "One who hates gifts will live" (Proverbs 15:27). And R. Abba did not take possession of it because R. Giddal had been bidding for it; and so neither took possession of it, and it was called "The Rabbis' field" [free to be used by yeshivah students].

KING YANNAI AND THE SAGES

(66a) It once happened that King Yannai [who was a kohen from the Hasmonean dynasty] went to Kuchlit in the wilderness and conquered sixty towns there. On his return he was very happy, and invited the Sages [to a banquet to celebrate his victories]. He told them, "Our ancestors [who were very poor] used to eat meluchim [an unappetizing herb] when they were involved in the building of the [second] Bet Hamikdash. Let us also eat meluchim in memory of our ancestors, [and to thank God for our prosperity]." So they served meluchim on golden tables, and they ate them. However, there was a person there, a scoffer, an evil-minded good-for-nothing, named Elazar ben Po'erah [a cunning Sadducee leader] who said to King Yannai, "O King Yannai! The hearts of the Pharisees [i.e., the Torah Sages] are against you." "Then what shall I do, [to see whether you are right]?" King Yannai asked. "Place the headplate[24] [of the Kohen Gadol] on your forehead [and see if the Sages allow you to do that],"[25] Elazar ben Po'erah advised. So King Yannai put the headplate on his forehead. Now, there was an elderly Sage named Yehudah b. Gedidiah. He called out, "King Yannai, the crown of royalty is enough for you! Leave the crown of priesthood to the descendants of Aaron!"[26] —for it was reported that Yannai's mother was taken captive in Modi'in [before she got married to a kohen, and a son of woman who once was a captive woman and then married a kohen is unfit to be a kohen].

The charge against his mother was investigated and proven to be unfounded, so Yannai was incensed at the Sages of Israel. Elazar b. Po'erah then said to King Yannai, "O King Yannai! An ordinary Jew has to tolerate such ridicule. But you, a King and a Kohen Gadol, should you suffer such indignities?" Asked Yannai, "What shall I do?" "If you listen to my advice," Elazar b. Po'erah replied, "Kill them all." "But what will become of the Torah, [if all the Torah scholars are killed]?" Yannai exclaimed. Elazar ben Po'erah retorted, "Look, the Torah is wrapped up and lying in the corner: whoever wants to study it can come and learn! [We don't need the Sages to teach us!]" Said R. Nachman b. Yitzchak: Then and there, heretical ideas took hold of Yannai, for he should have answered, "This applies to the Written Torah; [it is available for anyone to study], but what about the Oral Torah [Mishnah and Gemara; it can only be taught by the Sages]!" Right away, the evil was unleashed through Elazar b. Po'erah. All the Sages of Israel were killed, and the world was devoid [of Torah] until Shimon b. Shetach came [he survived because he was the brother of Yannai's wife] and restored the Torah to its original glory.

IS THIS KOHEN'S SERVICE VALID?

(66b) [The Gemara asks:] If a kohen performed the service [in the Bet Hamikdash thinking that he is a qualified kohen and later discovered that] he is the son of a divorced woman[27] or the son of a chalutzah,[28] how do we know that his service is [retroactively] valid? Rav Yehudah said in the name of Shmuel: Because it says: [concerning Pinehas], "And it shall be for him and his offspring after him a covenant of eternal priesthood" (Numbers 25:13); this includes both fit and unfit offspring. Shmuel's father said: We can infer it from [Moses' blessing to Levi], "Bless O God, his resources [cheilo], and favor the work of his hands" (Deuteronomy 33:11). Accept even the profaned [chullin] in their midst; [even the service of someone who is a chalal is valid under certain circumstances]. R. Yannai said: We can derive it from here: "If you are unable to reach a decision . . . you shall come to whomever will be the kohen in those days" (ibid. 17:8). Could you think that you should go to a kohen who does not live in his days? We must therefore say that this refers to someone who at the time of the service was kohen, [and who later found out that he was a chalal; even so his service at that time was valid].

[The Gemara asks:] How do we know that if a kohen performed the service in the Bet Hamikdash thinking that he had no blemish and then discovers that he did have a blemish,[29] that his service [retroactively] is invalid? Rav Yehudah said in the name of Shmuel: Because it says [concerning Pinehas], "Behold! I give him My covenant of peace [shalom]" (Numbers 25:12). [He expounds:] When the kohen is shaleim, "perfect, without blemish," but not when he has a defect. [The Gemara asks:] But it says shalom, "peace," and not shaleim, "perfect"! Said R. Nachman: The vav of shalom is broken [in the middle, which gives us the right to interpret it as meaning "perfect, without defect"].

ERETZ YISRAEL HIGHER THAN ALL COUNTRIES

(69a) We learned in a Baraita: It says, "[If you are unable to reach a decision in a case involving capital punishment . . . You must set out and go up to the place that God your Lord shall choose" (Deuteronomy 17:8). This teaches that the *Bet Hamikdash* is higher than the rest of Eretz Yisrael, and Eretz Yisrael is higher than all other countries. [The Gemara asks:] It is understandable that the *Bet Hamikdash* is higher than the rest of Eretz Yisrael, for it says, (69b) "If there is a dispute in your settlements, then you must set out and go up" (ibid.), [from any point in Eretz Yisrael]. But how do we know that Eretz Yisrael is higher than all other countries? Because it says, "Therefore, behold, the days are coming—the word of God—when people will no longer swear, 'As God lives, Who brought the children of Israel up from the land of Egypt,' but rather, 'As God lives who brought up and brought back the offspring of the House of Israel from the land of the North and from all the lands wherein He had dispersed them'" (Jeremiah 23:7,8).

ILLEGITIMATE CHILDREN WENT UP WITH EZRA

(70a) R. Elazar said: Ezra did not go up from Babylonia until he made it like pure sifted flour; [he carefully verified the purity of the lineage of the families, since many had intermarried,] and then he went up to Eretz Yisrael.

[The Mishnah said: *Mamzerim* went up with Ezra from Babylonia to Eretz Yisrael.] [The Gemara asks:] How do we know that *mamzerim* went up to Eretz Yisrael? Because it says, "Sanballat the Horonite and Tobiah the Ammonite slave heard it" (Nehemiah 2:10), and further it says, "But even in those days the aristocrats of Judah wrote many letters addressed to Tobiah . . . for many people in Judah had sworn allegiance to him, because he was the son-in-law of Shechaniah son of Arah, and his [i.e., Tobiah the Ammonite slave's] son Jehohanan had married the daughter of Meshullam son of Berechiah" (ibid. 6:17,18). [Since the Tanna cites this verse to prove that *mamzerim* went up with Ezra, obviously he holds that the child born of the union of heathen or a slave and the daughter of a Jew is a *mamzer*.]

[Continues the Gemara:] This explanation is acceptable according to those who hold the view that the offspring of such a union is a *mamzer*, but according to those who say that the offspring is not a *mamzer*, what proof do you have [that there were *mamzerim* that went up with Ezra]? Besides, how do you know that Tobiah and Yohohanan had sons; maybe they did not have any children? And furthermore, [assuming they did have children], how do you know that they had these children in Babylonia and then came to Eretz Yisrael? Perhaps they had these children in Eretz Yisrael? But we can derive from the following verse [that *mamzerim* came up with Ezra from Babylonia], "These are the ones who went up from Tel-melah, Tel-Harsha, Cherub, Addon, and Immer, [towns in Babylonia] and

could not declare their fathers' families and their descent, whether they were from Israel" (ibid.7:61).

Tel-Melah [literally: a pile of salt] refers to people whose deeds are like those of the people of Sodom, which was turned into a pile of salt, [an allusion to the fact that they had illicit relationships and produced *mamzerim*]. Tel-Harshah [a mound of silence] refers to those who cry out "Father!" and their mother silences them [because they are not sure who their father is]. "They could not declare their fathers' families and their descent, whether they were from Israel"—This refers to children that were picked up from the streets who knew neither their father nor their mother. "Cherub, Addon and Immer"—R. Abbahu said this, [changing the meaning to *amar Adon cherub*]: God said: I said that Israel should be as dear to me as a cherub, but they behaved like a panther [an animal that does not care with what animal it mates, and copulates even with animals of a different species]. According to others, R. Abbahu said: God said: Although they behaved promiscuously like a panther, still they are as cherished by me as a cherub.

OBJECTIONABLE MATCHES

Rabbah b. Bar Chanah said: Whoever marries a woman who is not fit for him [because of her flawed ancestry], the Torah considers it as if he had plowed under the whole world and seeded it with salt, as it says, "These are the ones who went up from Tel-Melah, Tel Harsha." [Harsha is seen as derived from *charash*, "to plow"; and Tel-Melah means, "a pile of salt."]

Rabbah b. R. Adda said in the name of Rav: Whoever marries a woman for the sake of money [overlooking her tainted ancestry], will have unworthy children, as it says, "They betrayed God for they begot alien children" (Hosea 5:7). And if you are going to say that the money for which he married her will stay with him, therefore the verse continues, "now in one month will their portions will be devoured." And if you are going to say that only his share will be lost but not hers [because she did nothing wrong by marrying a man of impeccable descent], therefore it says, "*their* portions will be devoured." And if you are going to say that it will take a long time [until their capital evaporates], therefore it says, "in one month." How is "one month" to be understood? R. Nachman b. Yitzchak said: The month will come, and the month will pass, and before you know it their money is gone.

Rabbah b. R. Adda also said—according to others, R. Salla said in the name of R. Hamenuna: If someone marries a woman who is not fit for him [because of her ancestry], Elijah ties him down, and the Holy One, blessed be He, gives him lashes. And a Tanna learned regarding all these individuals [*kohanim*, Levites, and Israelites who take wives that are not suitable for them] that Elijah writes [the following statement,] and the Holy One, blessed be He, signs it: Woe to him who disqualifies his children and who taints the reputation of his family by marrying a woman who is not suitable for him. [The Gemara remarks:] A person who constantly declares others to be of unfit ancestry is himself of questionable lineage, because a person of flawed lineage will never praise anyone else. Shmuel summed it up, "He charges others with his own defects."

HE CHARGES OTHERS WITH
HIS OWN DEFECTS

[The Gemara tells a story to illustrate this adage.] One day a certain person from Nehardea entered a butcher store in Pumbedita. "Give me meat," he demanded. They replied, "Wait until we finish serving the servant of Rav Yehudah b. Yechezkel, then we'll take care of you." Impatiently the fellow called out, "Who is this Yehudah ben Shweskel to go before me and be served ahead of me!" [He contemptuously mispronounced the name Yechezkel as Shweskel.] When Rav Yehudah heard about it, he immediately placed the fellow under a ban. They told Rav Yehuda, "Besides, this fellow is in the habit of calling people slaves"; whereupon Rav Yehudah publicly announced that he was a slave. The fellow then went and sued Rav Yehudah to appear in court before R. Nachman. When the summons was presented to Rav Yehudah, he went to R. Huna and asked him, "Shall I go or not?" R. Huna replied, "You do not have to go, because you are an important personality. But out of respect for the Nasi [R. Nachman was the son-in-law of the *Nasi*, the head of Babylonian Jewry[30]], you should go.

When Rav Yehudah b. Yechezkel arrived there, he found R. Nachman building a guardrail around his roof.[31] So Rav Yehudah said, "Don't you accept R. Huna b. Idi's statement in Shmuel's name: Once a person is appointed as head of a community, he may not do manual labor in the presence of three people"? Replied R. Nachman, "I am only making a little bit of a *gundrita* [a high-sounding word for guardrail]." Retorted Rav Yehudah, "What is wrong with the word *maakeh* [the Hebrew for guardrail] as written in the Torah, or *mechitzah*, the Rabbinical term for the same word, [that you use such a pompous term]?" R. Nachman said, "Please have a seat on this *karpita* [a bombastic word for bench]." Retorted R. Yehudah, "Do you dislike *itztaba*, the word the Rabbis use for bench, or *safsal*, the informal term for bench?" [Trying to placate him], R. Nachman said, "Please have an *etronga* [etrog, citron]." Replied Rav Yehudah, "This is what Shmuel says, 'Whoever says *etronga* [instead of *etrog*] is one-third filled with conceit. Either call it *etrog*, as the Rabbis call it, or *etroga* as the people call it.'" [Said the host to the guest,] "Will you have *anbaga* [a cup of wine]?" "Are you unhappy with *ispargus*, as the Rabbis call it, or *anpaka* as it is popularly called?"

"Let my daughter Donag come and serve drinks," R. Nachman suggested." R. Yehudah answered, "This is what Shmuel says, 'A man should not ask a woman to serve him.'" "But she is only a child," R. Nachman countered. Rav Yehudah insisted, "Shmuel says explicitly that a man may not be served by a woman at all, whether adult or child." [Trying to change the subject, R. Nachman asked,] "Would you at least send regards to my wife Yalta?" Rav Yehudah shot back, "This is what Shmuel says, 'Listening to a woman's voice is indecent,' [and if I ask her how she is feeling, she will answer me]." R. Nachman suggested, "But you can send the regards through a messenger." Rav Yehudah replied, "Shmuel said, (70b) 'You should not ask about the welfare of a woman' [because it may lead to improper familiarity]. And you should not even ask a husband how his wife is feeling.'" R. Nachman's wife sent a him a message, "Dispose of this case for him, so that he should not make you look like an ignoramus."

[Taking his wife's advice, and getting down to business, R. Nachman said to Rav Yehudah b. Yechezkel,] "What brings you here?" "You sent me a summons to appear in your court," Rav Yehudah replied. "If I don't even know the idioms you use in your speech, would I send you a summons?" R. Nachman exclaimed. So Rav Yehudah pulled the summons from his bosom and showed it to R. Nachman, saying, "Here is the man, and here is the summons!" To this R. Nachman replied, "Since you have come already, let us discuss the case, so that people should not say that the Rabbis favor each other. So would you please tell me, why did you put that person under a ban?" "Because he hurt the feelings of a messenger of the Rabbis." "Then you should have condemned him to flogging; for Rav punished with flogging a person who hurt the feelings of a messenger of the Rabbis." "I gave him a more severe punishment," replied Rav Yehudah, [because he insulted the Rabbi himself].[32]

[R. Nachman now asked,] "Why did you publicly announce that he was a slave?" Replied Rav Yehudah, "Because he is in the habit of calling other people slaves. And we learned: Anyone who finds others unfit, is himself unfit. And such a person will never praise anyone else. As Shmuel said: He charges others with his own defect. [If he calls others slaves, that is proof that he is himself a slave.]" R. Nachman remarked, "Shmuel merely said that we should suspect such a person [of being a slave], but not that we should publicly announce it"?

While they were discussing the case, suddenly the person [who had made the contemptuous remark] arrived from Nahardea and said to Rav Yehudah, "How dare you call me a slave! I who am a descendant of the royal House of the Hasmoneans!" Replied Rav Yehudah, "This is what Shmuel said: Whoever says that he is a descendant of the House of the Hasmoneans proves that he is a slave." [Because Herod, an Edomite slave, killed all the descendants of the Hasmoneans and assumed the monarchy (Rashi).] R. Nachman said, "Do you not agree with what R. Abba said in the name of R. Huna who quoted Rav: Any Torah scholar who quotes a halachic precedent he learned from his master, if he quoted this teaching before judging the case at hand [which involves himself], then we rule accordingly; but if he never quoted the teaching before the present case, we do not rule according to him, [and this is the first time you mentioned this statement of Shmuel to us.]"

"But R. Matna backs me up," replied Rav Yehudah. Now R. Matna had not been to Nehardea for thirteen years, but just on that day he showed up in that city. So Rav Yehudah b. Yechezkel asked R. Matna, "Do you remember what Shmuel said when he was standing with one foot on the ferry and one foot on land? "This is what Shmuel said," he replied. "Anyone that claims to be a descendant of the Hasmonean royal dynasty is a slave, because no one remained of the Hasmonean dynasty except one young girl who climbed up to the roof and called out, 'Anyone who claims that he is a descendant of the Hasmonean royal family is a slave!' Then she fell from the roof and died."

Thereupon the man [who had insulted the messenger of Rav Yehudah b. Yechezkel and had called others slaves] was declared a slave. On that day many *ketubot* [marriage contracts] were torn up in Nahardea [of people who were related to this man, because the marriages were invalidated]. When Rav Yehudah left R. Nachman's house people were running after him to stone him [because he had proved their tarnished ancestry, and had caused the break-up of their marriages]. So Rav Yehudah told them, "If you'll keep quiet, fine. Otherwise I am going make public about you what Shmuel said: There are two kinds of families in Nahardea—one is called *Bei Yonah*, [House of the Dove]; the other, *Bei Urvati*, [House of the Raven]— and a sign of their status is: the unclean bird [the raven is non-kosher] marks the family with the tainted ancestry; the clean bird [the dove] indicates the pure family. [And if you don't stop threatening me, I am going to reveal which families are which.]" When they heard this, they threw away the stones in their hands, which caused a blockage in the flow of the King's River.

PURE FAMILY TREE

Rav Yehudah said in the name of Shmuel: Pash'chur the son of Immer[33] had four hundred slaves—others say, four thousand slaves—and all of them married into families of *kohanim*; and any *kohen* who is insolent surely is a descendant of them. But Rav Yehudah disagreed with R. Elazar. For R. Elazar said: If you see a *kohen* who is insolent, do not suspect that his lineage is impure, for it says, "Your people are like those who quarrel among the priests" (Hosea 4:4). [Thus *kohanim* tend to be quarrelsome and insolent.]

R. Avin b. R. Adda said in the name of Rav: Whoever marries a wife who is not fit for him [because of her blemished ancestry], when the Holy One, blessed be He, causes His *Shechinah* to rest on Israel, He will testify about all the tribes [that they are His people]; but He will not testify about him, for it says, "The tribes of God are a testimony for Israel" (Psalms 122:4). When are the tribes a "testimony for Israel"? When they are "the tribes of God." R. Chama b. R. Chanina said: When the Holy One, blessed be He, causes His *Shechinah* to rest on Israel, it is only on families that are of pure descent, for it says, "At that time—the word of God—I will be a God for all the families of Israel" (Jeremiah 30:25). It does not say "for all Israel" but "to all the *families* of Israel, and they will be a people for Me" [only families of indisputable lineage].

PROSELYTES

Rabbah b. R. Huna said: There is one great advantage born Jews have over proselytes, for regarding Israel it says, "I will be a God to them, and they will be a people to Me" (Ezekiel 37:27); [God draws Israel near, even if they are distant from Him], whereas regarding proselytes it says, "For who would bolden his heart to approach Me?—the word of God. You will be a people unto Me, and I will be a God unto you" (Jeremiah 30:21). [The proselyte must take the first step coming closer to God; then God draws proselytes near to Him.] R. Chelbo said: Proselytes are difficult for Israel like a *sapachat* [a rash], for it says, "The proselyte will join them and be attached [*venispechu*] to the House of Jacob" (Isaiah 14:1), and it says further, "for swellings, for *sapachat* [rashes]" (Leviticus 14:56). [Since proselytes are very careful in observing their newly acquired *mitzvot*, their exemplary conduct constitutes a veiled accusation against many Jews who are lax in their observance (Tosafot).]

R. Chama b. R. Chanina said: When the Holy One, blessed be He, (71a) will purify the tribes, He will begin with the tribe of Levi, for it says, "He will sit smelting and purifying silver; He will purify the children of Levi and refine them like gold and like silver, and God will deal with them in righteousness" (Malachi 3:3). R. Yehoshua b. Levi said: Money purifies *mamzerim*; [people who married into Jewish families by means of their wealth will not be cast out]. For it says, "He will sit smelting and purifying silver." [The Gemara asks:] What is the meaning of, "and God will deal with them in righteousness [*tzedakah*]"? Said R. Yitzchak: The Holy One, blessed be he, dealt charitably [*tzedakah*] with Israel, in that a family that intermingled can remain in the fold [and does not have to be broken up].

Rav Yehudah said in the name of Shmuel: All countries are like dough compared to Eretz Yisrael, and Eretz Yisrael is like dough compared to Babylonia. [Dough is a mixture of various ingredients; compared to Eretz Yisrael, the families of other countries are of mixed descent. And the genealogy of the families of Eretz Yisrael is an impure blend when compared with that of the Babylonian families, which were of pure birth.]

THE PRONUNCIATION OF THE DIVINE NAME

Rabbah b. Bar Chanah said in the name of R. Yochanan: The Sages are permitted to transmit to their disciples the [pronunciation of] the Four-Letter Divine Name once every seven years—others say, twice every seven years. R. Nachman b. Yitzchak said: It is likely that the opinion that it was once every seven years is correct. For it says, "This is My Name forever [*le'olam*]" (Exodus 3:15). [Since *le'olam* is written without a *vav*] it can be read as *le'aleim*, "to conceal." [The implication: God's Name is to be hidden.] Rava wanted to give a public lecture [on the Divine Name], but an elderly scholar told him, "It says *le'aleim* [it should be kept secret. Don't give public lectures about it]. "R. Avina contrasted two verses: It says, "This is My Name" and "This is My remembrance" (ibid.). [The implication is that God gave Moses two names.] The Holy One, blessed be He, said: I am not to be called the way My name is written. My Name is written in the Torah with *yud—hei*, but I am referred to by *alef—dalet*.

Originally the Divine Twelve-Letter Name was disclosed to everyone, but when unscrupulous people increased [who used the Name indiscriminately], it was divulged only to the pious among the *kohanim* [to be uttered at the Blessing of the *Kohanim*], and they would mumble it quickly[34] while their fellow *kohanim* were chanting the Blessing of the *Kohanim*. We learned in a *Baraita*: R. Tarfon [who was a *kohen*] said: I once went up the platform after my mother's brother [to bless the assembled], and when I turned my ear to hear what the *Kohen Gadol* was saying, I heard him mumble the [Twelve-Letter] Name during the chanting of the *kohanim*. Rav Yehudah said in Rav's name: The Forty-Two Letter Name is revealed only to a person who is pious, humble, middle-aged, who does not lose his temper, who does not get drunk, and who is yielding. And anyone who knows [the Forty-Two Letter Name] and is careful [not to use it impulsively] and keeps it in purity, is beloved above and cherished below; he will inspire people with awe, and will inherit both this world and the World to Come.

HE REFUSED TO MARRY R. YOCHANAN'S DAUGHTER

(71b) Ze'iri was avoiding R. Yochanan, because R. Yochanan was pressuring him to marry his daughter [who was born in Eretz Yisrael. Ze'iri, being a Babylonian, refused on the grounds that he preferred to marry a woman of Baylonian birth, since Babylonian Jews were of pure lineage (Rashi)]. One day, as they were walking together, they reached a stream, and Ze'iri carried R. Yochanan on his shoulders across the stream. Said R. Yochanan to Ze'iri, "The Torah that I teach you is good enough for you, but our daughters are not? What is the reason that you refuse to marry her? If you are going to tell me because we learned in the Mishnah that ten classes of people went up from Babylonia [to Eretz Yisrael, including *kohanim*, Levites, Israelites and people of blemished extraction. Do you think that all the unfit ones left Babylonia and went to Eretz Yisrael]? By the same token, did then all the *kohanim*, Levites and Israelites, go up? [Of course not.] Well, just as some fine *kohanim*, Levites, and Israelites, remained in Babylonia, so did some of the impure families remain in Babylonia, [so that there is no difference between Babylonia and Eretz Yisrael as far as purity of lineage is concerned. Therefore, my daughter is from as fine a family background as any Babylonian girl]. However, R. Yochanan overlooked what R. Elazar said: Ezra did not leave Babylonia until he made it like finely sifted flour, [making sure that only families of unmixed genealogy were left in Babylonia].

THE MARK OF UNBLEMISHED ROOTS

Ulla visited Rav Yehudah in Pumbeditha. He noticed that R. Yitzchak the son of Rav Yehudah, although a grown man, was not married. Ulla asked Rav Yehudah, "Why have you not found a wife for your son?" Replied Rav Yehudah, "I don't know where to find one [that is of pure lineage]." "Are we then so sure what our family background is?" wondered Ulla. "Maybe we are descendants of those about whom it says, 'They ravaged women in Zion; maidens in the towns of Judah?'" (Lamentations 5:11). "Then what shall I do?" asked Rav Yehudah. "Look for a family that is quiet and peaceful; [because contentiousness is a sign of impure lineage]. Use the test the people of Eretz Yisrael employ: When two people were quarreling they would see which of the two would become silent first, and they would say: The quiet one is of more distinguished ancestry."

Rav said: In Babylonia, silence and peacefulness is considered the mark of a family's pure lineage. [The Gemara asks:] But Rav cannot have said this! For Rav visited the family of Bar Shefi Chala, and he investigated them; surely that means that he researched their family background. [The Gemara answers:] No, he inquired to see if they were quiet, gentle people. Rav Yehudah said in Rav's name: If you see two families constantly feuding with each other, there is a flaw in the ancestry of one of them; and [by inciting them to quarrel, Heaven] prevents them from marrying with each other.

THE PERSIAN BEAR

(72a) [In a prophetic vision concerning the Persian empire, Daniel saw a beast,] "and there were three ribs in its mouth between its teeth" (Daniel 7:5). R. Yochanan commented: This refers to the towns of Chalazon, Hadayav, and Netzivin, which Persia sometimes swallowed [and dominated] and sometimes spat out [i.e., was unable to dominate]. [The verse begins,] "Then behold! another beast, a second one, similar to a bear" (ibid.). R. Yosef taught: This refers to the Persians who eat and drink like a bear; and are fleshy like a bear; they grow their hair unkempt like a bear, and are restless like a bear. When R. Ammi saw a Persian riding he used to say, "There goes a roving bear."

Rebbi [who lived in Eretz Yisrael] asked Levi [on his return from Babylonia], "Give me a description of what Persians look like." "They look like the warriors of the House of David," replied Levi. "Describe to me the Guebers [a ferocious people living on the borders of Persia]."—"They resemble angels of destruction." "Characterize for me Ishmaelites."—"They look like demons of the latrine." "Describe to me the Torah scholars of Babylonia"—"They are like the Ministering Angels."

When Rebbi was dying he said: The town Homnia in Babylonia is populated completely by Ammonites [who are non-Jews]. Misgaria in Babylonia is inhabited completely by *mamzerim*. There is a town in Babylonia named Birka where there are two brothers who exchange their wives. There is Birta diSatya in Babylonia where today they have turned away from God: a fishpond overflowed on *Shabbat*, and they went and caught fish on *Shabbat*. Thereupon R. Acha b. R. Yoshiah placed them under a ban, and they turned their back on Judaism and became apostates. There is a town in Babylonia named Akra diAgma where Adda b. Ahava lives. (72b) Today he sits in the bosom of Abraham [i.e., today is his *brit milah*].[35] Today Rav Yehudah was born in Babylonia. For a Tanna said: On the day that R. Akiva died, Rabbi was born; on the day that Rebbi died, Rav Yehudah was born. On the day that Rava died, R. Ashi was born. This comes to teach you that a *tzaddik* does not leave the world until another *tzaddik* like him is created. As it says, "The sun rises, and the sun sets" (Ecclesiastes 1:5). Before Eli's sun went down, the sun of Samuel of Ramot rose, as it says, "The lamp of God had not yet gone out, and Samuel was lying in the Temple of God" (1 Samuel 3:3).

EZEKIEL'S LAMENT

It says, "God has commanded against Jacob that his enemies should surround him" (Lamentations 1:17). Rav Yehudah said: Like Homnia [a town inhabited by Ammonites, which surrounded] the town of Pum Nahara [which had a Jewish population].

[Ezekiel said,] "As I was prophesying, Pelatiah son of Benaiah died; and I fell on my face and I cried out in a loud voice, and said, "Alas, Lord God!" (Ezekiel 11:13). Rav and Shmuel differ in their interpretation of Ezekiel's crying. One says: It was [in Pelatiah's] favor, [and the prophet bemoaned his premature death], and the other says: It was to Pelatiah's disgrace [and the prophet lamented the fact that he died too easily]. The one who says that it was in Pelatiah's favor gives the following background information: The governor of Meshan was the son-in-law of Nebuchadnezzar. Nebuchadnezzar sent word to him: From all the prisoners you have captured you did not send any to serve us. The governor then wanted to send him some of the Jewish captives, but Pelatiah son of Benaiah said to him, "We who are of higher rank let us stay here, and let our slaves go there [to serve Nebuchadnezzar]."

Therefore the prophet [Ezekiel] lamented, "The person who has done such a favor for Israel should die in the prime of life!" The one who says that it was to Pelatiah's disgrace [that the prophet lamented, crying that Pelatiah died too easily,] explains: It says, [Ezekiel said,] "A wind then lifted me up and brought me to the East Gate of the Temple of God, which faces eastward; and behold at the entrance of the gate there were twenty-five men; in their midsts I saw Jaazaniah son of Azzur and Palatiah son of Benaiah, leaders of the people" (Ezekiel 11:1). And it says, "Then He brought me to the inner courtyard of the Temple of God, and behold, at the entrance of the Sanctuary of God, between the Entrance-hall and the Altar, there were some twenty-five men, with their back to the Sanctuary of God, with their faces turned eastward" (ibid. 8:16). If the prophet tells us that they were facing eastward, don't I know that their back was turned to the Sanctuary [which is to the west of the Courtyard]? Why then does it say, "with their back to the Sanctuary of God"? This comes to teach us that they were uncovering themselves, showing the most disgraceful form of contempt toward the Most High. And therefore the prophet laments, "Should the person who did this evil in Israel die peacefully in his bed!"[36]

NO NEED TO CHECK
HER GENEALOGY

(76a) [The Mishnah says: If it was established that if the daughter of a *kohen* has a grandfather who served at the altar, then it is obvious that he is of pure lineage,] and there is no need to investigate from the altar and upward [check this *kohen*'s mother and grandmother's pedigree since this was done when he was admitted to the service at the altar]; from the *duchan* and upward, [similarly, if a *kohen* wants to marry the daughter of a Levite, and her father or grandfather was a Levite who sang on the *duchan* platform, no further investigation is needed]; from the Sanhedrin and upward, [if either her father or grandfather was a member of the Sanhedrin, no further genealogical investigation is required, because only persons of unblemished family background were admitted to the Sanhedrin]. And a *kohen* is permitted to marry the daughter of anyone whose ancestors served as public officers or administrators of charity funds, without further research. R. Yose says: Also [if she has in her ancestry] a person who was a judge in the old Bet Din of Tzippori [the ancestry of the judge need not to be investigated, since this was done when he was appointed]. R. Chanina b. Antigonus said: Also [if she had an ancestor] who was registered as an officer in the King's army [no further genealogical research is needed].

(76b) [We learned in the Mishnah:] From the Sanhedrin and upward [no search is needed]. [The Gemara asks:] What is the reason? For R. Yosef taught: Just as the *bet din* must be pure in righteousness, so must [its members] be free from any tainted ancestry. Mereimar said: From what verse is this derived? From the verse, "You are completely fair, my beloved, and there is no blemish in you" (Song of Songs 4:7). [The Gemara asks:] Perhaps this blemish is to be taken literally, [a physical blemish]? R. Acha b. Yaakov said: It says, [God tells Moses regarding the seventy elders who were selected to become the first Sanhedrin], "Take them to the Tent of Meeting and have them stand there with you" (Numbers 11:16). "With you" implies that they should be like you, [of flawless ancestry].

THE WARRIORS IN KING DAVID'S ARMY

[The above Mishnah said:] Also if she had an ancestor who was registered as an officer in the King's army, no further genealogical check was needed. [The Gemara says:] Rav Yehudah said in the name of Shmuel: [This refers to the officers] in the army of King David, [because only people of pure lineage were chosen]. Said R. Yosef: What verse teaches us this? "According to their genealogical lists, the number of soldiers for battle was twenty-six thousand" (1 Chronicles 7:40). And what is the reason [that pure lineage was required]? Said Rav Yehudah in Rav's name: So that their own merit and that of their ancestors should stand them in good stead in the battle. [The Gemara asks:] How about Zelek the Ammonite [who was one of David's warriors];[37] surely his name indicates that he was a descendant of Ammon [a non-Jewish nation]? [The Gemara answers:] No. It means that he lived among the Ammonites. But how about Uriah the Hittite;[38] surely that means that he was a descendant of Chet? No. It means that he lived among the Hittites. But there was Ittai the Gittite.[39] And if you will answer that it means that he was a Jew who lived in Gat, that cannot be so, for R. Nachman said: Ittai the Gittite

[who was an idol worshipper] came and destroyed the idol. Furthermore, Rav Yehudah said in Rav's name: David had four hundred children, all sons of "beautiful women captives,"[40] all with hair trimmed in front and long in the back, and all rode around in chariots of gold and went at the head of the army, and they were the tough warriors of the House of David! [Being sons of non-Jewish women, their lineage was blemished, yet they served in King David's army!] [The Gemara answers:] They merely went to frighten [the enemy, but did not actually fight in the army].

TEMPTED BY SATAN

(81a) Rabbi Meir used to sneer at people who committed immorality, [saying that it is easy to subdue your carnal instinct, if only you want to do so]. Then one day, Satan appeared to him in the guise of a woman, standing on the opposite bank of the river. [There was a narrow plank bridge and a rope strung across the river to enable people to walk across while holding on to the rope.] R. Meir started across, but when he reached midpoint, his *yetzer hara* left him. Satan [the personification of the *yetzer hara*] said to R. Meir: "If not for the fact that in Heaven it was announced, 'Beware of R. Meir and his Torah,' your life would be worth to me no more than two small coins." [Implying: It is not so easy to subdue the *yetzer hara*. Therefore don't sneer at people who succumb to its wiles.]

Rabbi Akiva used to sneer at people who committed immorality. Then one day, Satan appeared to him in the guise of a woman, sitting on top of a palm tree. R. Akiva started to climb up the tree, but when he got midway the *yetzer hara* let go of him. [Satan] said to R. Akiva: "If not for the fact that in Heaven it was announced, 'Beware of R. Akiva and his Torah,' your life would be worth to me no more than two small coins."

PLIMO AND SATAN

Plimo used to [curse Satan] every day, saying, "An arrow in Satan's eye!" Once on *erev* Yom Kippur, Satan appeared to him in the guise of a poor man. He came and knocked on the door. Plimo gave him some bread. Said the poor man, "On a day like today, when everybody is inside their home, you leave me standing outside!" So he brought him into the house and gave him bread to eat. But the poor man said, "On a day like today, when everybody sits around the table, I should sit alone?" So he seated him at the table. As he was sitting there, he caused himself to break out in festering sores, and behaved in an obnoxious manner. Plimo said to him, (81b) "Sit properly." Said he, "Let me have a glass of wine"; so they poured him a glass of wine. He coughed and spit into the cup. When they reprimanded him [for his repulsive behavior], he pretended that he was dead. The family then heard people say, "Plimo has killed a man! Plimo has killed a man!" Plimo ran away and hid in a toilet [at the outskirts of the city]. Satan followed him, [and when Plimo saw him], he fell in front of him. When Satan noticed how much Plimo was suffering, he revealed himself to him, and said to him, "Why did you curse me, saying, ["A curse in Satan's eye!"]? "What else shall I say [to prevent you from enticing me to sin]?" countered Plimo. "You should say, 'Let the Merciful One denounce Satan!'"[41]

UNINTENTIONAL SINS REQUIRE ATONEMENT

We learned in a *Baraita*: It says, [If a woman makes a vow, and her husband annuls it,] "Since her husband has annulled [her vow], God will forgive her, [if she broke the vow]" (Numbers 30:13). [The Gemara asks:] Of what case does the Torah speak? [The question is: If she broke a vow that was annulled, why does she need forgiveness?] [The Gemara answers:] The Torah has in mind a woman who made a nazirite vow, and when her husband found out about it he annulled it. However, the woman did not know that her husband had annulled her vow [and thought that she still was bound by the vow], yet she drank wine and defiled herself through contact with the dead [both of which are forbidden to a *nazir*. Now, since her vow has been nullified, she did not actually transgress; still the Torah says, "God will forgive her"—she still needs forgiveness].

When R. Akiva came to this verse he wept, saying: If a person who had the intention to eat swine's meat, but actually ate sheep's meat, nevertheless the Torah says that he needs an atonement, how much more so does he need an atonement if he wanted to eat swine meat and in fact did eat it. In the same vein, it says, "If a person sins . . . without knowing for sure, he still bears responsibility [and must bring a sacrifice]" (Leviticus 5:17). [The verse refers to a person who had in front of him *cheilev* (forbidden fat) and *shuman* (permitted fat). If he ate *cheilev*, thinking that he was eating *shuman*, he must bring an *asham taluy*, "guilt-offering in case of doubt."] When R. Akiva came to this verse he wept, saying: If a person who had the intention of eating *shuman* but instead ate *cheilev*, yet the Torah says, "Without knowing for sure, he still bears responsibility," surely a person who intended to eat *cheilev* and actually did eat *cheilev* [bears responsibility and must bring a sacrifice]. Issi b. Yehudah said: It says, "Without knowing for sure, he still bears responsibility"—the fact [that a person is held responsible even for unintentional sins] should be a source of anguish to all tenderhearted people.

GOOD AND BAD VOCATIONS

(82a) [The Mishnah says:] R. Meir says: A person should teach his son a clean and easy occupation, and pray to the One to Whom all wealth and possessions belong [that he should be successful]; for every trade has the potential to bring poverty or wealth. For neither poverty nor wealth is the result of the trade, but everything is in accordance with a person's merits. R. Shimon b. Elazar says: Have you ever seen a wild beast or a bird that has a trade? And yet they are fed without difficulty. Now they were created only to serve me, whereas I was created to serve my Master. Does it not stand to reason that I should earn my livelihood without difficulty! But I have acted sinfully and thereby I have ruined my livelihood. [Through Adam's sin man has lost his privilege of being sustained without effort (Maharsha and P'nei Yehoshua).]

Abba Gurion of Tzidon says in the name of Abba Guria: A person should not teach his son to be a donkey driver, a camel driver, a wagon driver, sailor, shepherd, or shopkeeper, because these occupations involve larceny. R. Yehudah said in [Abba Guria's] name: Most donkey drivers are wicked, whereas most camel drivers are upright people [exposed to the rigors of desert travel, camel drivers become God-fearing]; and most sailors are pious [because their daily peril causes them to turn to God for help]. The best doctors are destined for Gehinnom[42] [because they are not humble; also because they sometimes cause the death of their patients, and because they refuse to treat the poor who are unable to pay them]. The worthiest of butchers is Amalek's partner. [In an effort to avoid financial loss he is tempted to sell meat of questionable *kashrut*.]

TORAH THE BEST OCCUPATION

R. Nehorai said: I will put aside every occupation in the world and teach my son nothing but Torah, because you enjoy its reward in this world while the principal remains intact for him in the World to Come. All other occupations are not like that; for when a person becomes sick or grows old or becomes afflicted and cannot work, he must die of starvation. But the Torah is not like that; it protects him from all evil in his youth and gives him a future and hope in his old age. About youth it says, "But those whose hope is in God will have renewed strength" (Isaiah 40:31). About old age it says, "They will still be fruitful in old age" (Psalms 92:15). And so it says about our Father Abraham, "Abraham was old . . . and God blessed Abraham with everything" (Genesis 24:1). We find that our Father Abraham observed the whole Torah before it was given, for it says, "Because Abraham obeyed My voice, and kept My charge, My commandments, My decrees, and My laws" (ibid. 26:5).

LOWLY PROFESSIONS

We learned in a *Baraita*: Whoever has dealings with women acquires bad habits, [and you should stay away from him]. For example: goldsmiths [who fashion

509

women's jewelry], people who comb wool [for ladies'
garments], people who clean handmills [used by house-
wives], peddlers, weavers, barbers [because women take
their children to them], launderers, bloodletters, bath
attendants, and tanners. None of these is eligible to
be appointed king or *Kohen Gadol*. What is the reason
for this? Not because they are of unfit descent but
because of their demeaning profession. We learned in
a *Baraita*: Ten things were said about a bloodletter:
He struts arrogantly,[43] he has a snobbish attitude, he
pompously leans back when he sits, he has an envious
eye and casts an evil eye [on healthy people, hoping
that they become sick and need his services], he eats a
great deal [he joins his patients in their meals] but
defecates very little; he is suspected of adultery [with
women patients], robbery [women steal from their
husbands to pay him], and bloodshed [by drawing too
much blood].

(82b) We learned in a *Baraita*: Rabbi said: No profession can disappear from the world [i.e., every trade
—clean or repulsive—is needed for society to func-
tion]. Happy is the person who sees his parents
enagaged in a respectable trade, and woe to him who
sees his parents engaged in a lowly craft. The world
cannot exist without a perfume maker and without a
tanner. Happy is the person whose trade is making
perfume; woe is to the person who is a tanner by trade.
The world cannot exist without males and without
females. Happy is the one whose children are boys; woe
is to him whose children are girls. R. Meir said: You
should always teach your son a clean and easy profession; and you should pray to the One to whom all
wealth and possessions belong [that he should be suc-
cessful]. For every trade has the potential to bring
poverty or wealth. It all comes from the One who to
whom all the wealth belongs. For it says, "'Mine is the
silver, and Mine is the gold,' so says God, the Master
of Legions" (Haggai 2:9).

[The Mishnah said:] R. Shimon b. Elazar says:
Have you ever seen a wild beast or a bird that has a
trade . . . [The Gemara comments:] We learned in a
Baraita: R. Shimon b. Elazar said: Never in my life
have I seen a deer engaged drying figs [in the field], a
lion carrying burdens, or a fox who is a storekeeper;
yet they are sustained without any trouble, although
they were created only to serve me, whereas I was created to serve my Maker. Now if these who were created only to serve me are sustained without trouble, I,
who was created to serve my Maker, surely should be
sustained without trouble. But I have acted sinfully
and thereby I have ruined my livelihood, for it says,
"Your sins have turned away these things" (Jeremiah
5:25).

R. Nehorai said: I will put aside every occupation
in the world and teach my son nothing but Torah,
because a person enjoys its reward in this world while
the principal remains intact for him in the World to

Come. For every occupation in the world supports a
person only when he is young, but in his old age [when
he cannot work anymore] he suffers from hunger. Not
so the Torah. It stands by him when he is young and
gives him future and hope in his old age. About his
young years it says, "But those whose hope is in God
will have renewed strength" (Isaiah 40:31). About old
age it says, "They will still be fruitful in old age, vigorous and fresh they will be" (Psalms 92:15).

NOTES

1. Quoting Targum Yonatan ben Uziel; as in
yifrotz, "increased" (Exodus 1:12).
2. Tosafot holds that each day should be divided
into three.
3. 1 Chronicles 2:35.
4. Mesoret Hashas notes that there are 5,845
verses; Yalkut in *Parashat Eikev* counts 5,855, and Zeit
Raanan counts 5,842. The reason for the discrepancies
may be that in Eretz Yisrael certain verses were divided
into smaller segments, so that they counted more verses.
5. Tosafot asks s.v. *yeter alav*, that even if Psalms
were be divided into verses of no more than three
words, there would still be more verses in the *Chumash*.
6. The Vilna Gaon's version.
7. R. Moshe Feinstein asks in *Dibros Moshe* 50:17:
Would not any normal father be happy to be awakened to have his son earn such a phenomenal profit?
Wouldn't he be upset for not being awakened? R.
Moshe concludes that Dama's father was not completely normal and would not have appreciated his son
making a profit.
8. Numbers 19:1–10.
9. According to Tosafot she was mentally disturbed.
This would tie in with Rabbi Moshe Feinstein's view
that Dama's father was not normal either.
10. Rashi quotes a Yerushalmi: The father asked
the son who served him the quail, "Where did you get
these delicacies?" Replied the son abruptly, "What do
you care, old man! Chew and eat!" In the other case,
the son was working the millstone when the king re-
cruited his elderly father to work in a labor detail. Said
the son, "Father, you stay here and grind, and I will
go in your place to serve the king, because there is no
end to that type of servitude."
11. This is derived from the fact that he told them
to wash their feet (ibid., v. 4). He thought that they
were Arabs who worship the dust of their feet (Rashi).
12. *Zaken* is seen as a contraction of *zeh shekanah
chochmah*, "a person who has acquired wisdom."
13. "Well" or "good" refers to Torah, for it says,
"For I have given you a good teaching, do not forsake
My Torah" (Proverbs 4:2). Hence, he will forget his
learning (Rashi).
14. The interpreter explained the expositions of
the Tanna'im to the public.

15. Demons usually attack not more than one person, and only at night.

16. Desecrating the name of God involves conduct that makes onlookers think that people who claim to be observant Jews act in an improper manner. A person who profanes God's name by being rude or dishonest commits the most serious of all sins because of the effect it has on others.

17. *Challah* is the portion of dough that must be given to the *kohen* (Numbers 15:17–21). Today *challah* portion is separated and burned.

18. *Terumah* is the offering of the produce given to the *kohen* (Numbers 18:8ff).

19. Leviticus 25:8:18.

20. For example: The verse Exodus 23:2, literally translated, might mean, "Do not testify as a witness in a court case," whereas the real meaning is, "When testifying, don't yield to the majority to pervert the law, but tell only the truth" (Rashi).

21. See Genesis 10:10.

22. "For Ezra [who came from Babylonia] set his heart to expound the Torah of God and to fulfill and to teach its statute and law in Israel" (Ezra 7:10).

23. *Pesachim* 22b.

24. On his forehead the *Kohen Gadol* wore a narrow gold plate called a *tzitz*, on which was inscribed the phrase *kodesh laHashem*, "Holy to God."

25. His status as *kohen* was questionable.

26. The *kohanim* are the descendents of Aaron.

27. A *kohen* is forbidden to marry a divorced woman or a *chalutzah*. A son of such a forbidden union is a *chalal* and unqualified to perform the Temple service.

28. If a husband dies childless, his brother must marry the widow. If he does not wish to do so, the ceremony of *chalitzah* must be performed, which frees the woman—the *chalutzah*—to marry anyone except a *kohen* (Deuteronomy 25:5–9).

29. A *kohen* who has a blemish may not offer a sacrifice (Leviticus 21:17–21).

30. *Gittin* 67 (Rashi).

31. Deuteronomy 22:8.

32. Tosafot *Yevamot* 52a.

33. The *kohen* who put Jeremiah in prison because of his dreadful prophecies about the destruction of Jerusalem (Jeremiah 20:2).

34. Literally: swallow it.

35. Or, it refers to his death.

36. The fact that the twenty-five men are mentioned in both verses proves that they refer to the same incident.

37. 2 Samuel 23:37.

38. 2 Samuel 23:19.

39. 2 Samuel 15:19.

40. See Deuteronomy 21:10–15.

41. Zechariah 3:2.

42. This refers to a doctor who thinks that he is the best doctor. He is destined for Gehinnom, because he relies completely on his own judgment and refuses to consult other doctors, which often leads to tragic results (*Maharsha*).

43. Literally: he walks on his side.

৩ BABA KAMMA ৯

PREVENTION OF ACCIDENTS

(15b) We learned in a *Baraita*: From where do we derive that you should not keep a mean dog or a shaky ladder in your house? For it says, "Do not allow a dangerous situation to remain in your house" (Deuteronomy 22:8).

(16b) "Hezekiah passed away and was buried in the choicest section of the tomb of the children of David" (2 Chronicles 32:33). R. Elazar said: This means near the best of the family, meaning near David and Solomon.

JEREMIAH, VICTIM OF MALICIOUS SLANDER

[Jeremiah, speaking of his opponents[1] who viciously slandered him, says,] "They have dug a pit [*shuchah*] to ensnare me, and concealed traps for my feet" (Jeremiah 18:22). R. Elazar said: They maliciously accused him of [having illicit relations with] a prostitute. R. Shmuel b. Nachmani said: They falsely accused him of [having adulterous relations] with a married woman. [The Gemara asks:] I understand the view of the one who says that he was accused of having a liaison with a prostitute, because *shuchah* [pit] is used in connection with a prostitute in the verse, "For the harlot is a deep pit [*shuchah*]" (Proverbs 23:27). But according to the view that he was accused of having relations with a married woman, why the analogy with *shuchah*? [The Gemara answers:] Is then a married woman [when committing adultery] different from a prostitute?

Rava expounded: What is meant by the concluding verse, "May they be made to stumble before You. At the time of Your anger act against them!" (Jeremiah 18:23)? Jeremiah said to the Holy One, blessed be He, "Master of the universe! Even when they do charity, make them stumble [by causing them to give charity] to people who do not deserve it, so that they will not be rewarded for giving charity."

THEY PAID TRIBUTE TO KING HEZEKIAH

[Concerning Hezekiah it says,] "All of Judah and the inhabitants of Jerusalem paid tribute to him when he died" (2 Chronicles 32:33). This indicates that they set up a yeshivah near his grave. Regarding this there is a difference of opinion between R. Natan and the Rabbis: One said: for [they learned there] for three days (17a), and the other said: for seven days, and others said: They learned there for thirty days. We learned in a *Baraita*: "They paid tribute to him when he died," speaking of Hezekiah, King of Judah. This means that there marched in front of [his bier] thirty-six thousand people [who had torn their clothes as a sign of mourning] so that their shoulders were bare, so said R. Yehudah. But R. Nechemiah said to him: Didn't they do the same thing when Ahab died, [and he was an evil king]?—[In the case of Hezekiah] they placed a Torah scroll on his coffin and announced, "The one who reposes in this [coffin] has fulfilled all that is written in this [Torah scroll]." [The Gemara asks:] But don't we do the same nowadays even [for a Torah scholar]? [The Gemara answers:] We only bring out the Torah scroll, but we do not place it on the coffin; or if you prefer, say: We do place the Torah scroll on the coffin but we do not announce: "The one who reposes in this coffin has fulfilled. . . . "

Rabbah b. Bar Chanah said: I once was walking along with R. Yochanan in order to ask him questions about this matter, but he had to go to the bathroom. When he came out, and I asked him the question he did not answer until he had washed his hands, put on his *tefillin*, and said the *berachah*. Then he said to us: Even if we sometimes say, "He has fulfilled what is written . . ." we never say, "He has taught what is written. . . ." ["He has taught" was said only about Hezekiah; and nowadays we do not say "He has taught" out of respect for Hezekiah, because teaching is greater than fulfilling the *mitzvot* (Rashi).] [The Gemara asks:] But did not a Tanna say, "Torah study has an advantage because it leads to the performance [of *mitzvot*; thus, since performance is the aim of Torah study, performance is greater than study]! [The Gemara answers:] This is not difficult: the latter statement refers to an individual learning Torah; [there performance is superior to studying]; the former refers to a person who teaches Torah; [and teaching others is superior to performance. Therefore, we do not say, "He has taught"].

513

LEARNING TORAH
AND GIVING *TZEDAKAH*

R. Yochanan said in the name of R. Shimon b. Yochai:
What is meant by the verse, "You will be so fortunate
to sow upon all waters, sending the ox and the donkey
to roam freely" (Isaiah 32:20)? Whoever engages in
learning Torah and giving charity deserves the inheritance of two tribes [because Joseph is compared to an
ox (Deuteronomy 33:17), and Issachar is compared to
a donkey (Genesis 49:14)]. For it says, "You will be
so fortunate to sow upon all waters." And sowing [in
this connection] denotes *tzedakah*, "charity," as it says,
"Sow for yourselves *tzedakah*, and you will reap according to kindness"; and water symbolizes Torah, for it
says, "Ho, everyone who is thirsty, go to the water"
(Isaiah 55:1).

[If he gives charity,] he is worthy of a canopy like
Joseph, for it says, "A charming son is Joseph . . . each
of the girls climbed heights to gaze" (Genesis 49:22),
[because Joseph was charitable by sustaining his brothers in Egypt (Etz Yosef)]. [And anyone that learns
Torah] deserves the inheritance of Issachar, about
whom it says, "Issachar is a strong-boned donkey"
(ibid. v. 14).

Some report the following version: His enemies
will fall before him, for it says [in Moses' blessing to
Joseph], "With them shall he gore nations to the end
of the earth" (Deuteronomy 33:17). And he is worthy of understanding like Issachar, for it says, "Of the
children of Issachar, men with understanding for the
times, to know what Israel should do" (1 Chronicles
12:33).

(21a) R. Sechorah said in the name of R. Huna who
quoted Rav: If someone lives in someone else's premises
without the owner's knowledge, he is not required to
pay him rent, for it says, "The gate is stricken with
desertion [*she'iah*]" (Isaiah 24:12). [Meaning: If a house
is uninhabited, a demon called *She'iah* ruins it. Therefore, by living in the house the tenant prevents it from
going to ruin, and that is why he is exempt from paying rent.] Mar b. R. Ashi said: I saw [this demon
She'iah] and it damaged the house as though it was
gored by an ox.

THE FLAX CAUGHT FIRE

(22a) We learned in a *Baraita*: A camel carrying a load
of flax passes through a public road. The flax enters
a store, catches fire by coming into contact with the
storekeeper's candle, and sets the whole building
ablaze. In a case like that the owner of the camel is
liable. However, if the storekeeper left his burning
candle outside his shop, he is liable. R. Yehudah says,
if it is a Chanukah *menorah* [that was left burning out-
side], the owner is exempt [from paying for damages
because it is a mitzvah to place the *menorah* outside
in order to proclaim the miracle of Chanukah].

IF YOU WANT TO BE PIOUS

(30a) We learned in a *Baraita*: The pious men of earlier generations used to hide their thorns and broken
pieces of glass in their fields three handbreadths below the surface in order that they should not stand in
the way of the plough. R. Sheshet used to burn them;
Rava used to throw them into the Tigris. Rav Yehudah
said: If a person wants to be pious, he should be especially careful to observe the laws [that are discussed]
in the Order of *Nezikin* [which deals with monetary
matters and disputes]. Rava said: He should observe
the rules of tractate *Avot* [i.e., ethical guidelines].
Others said: He should concentrate on matters [that
are discussed] in tractate *Berachot* [namely, the various *berachot* that should be recited].

GREETING QUEEN *SHABBAT*

(32a) We learned in a *Baraita*: [If two people are passing each other on a public thoroughfare, one of them
running and the other walking, and the one walking
was injured by the other], Issi b. Yehudah says that
the man who was running is liable, because he acted
in an unusual way; but Issi agrees that if this happened
on *erev Shabbat* before sunset, the one running would
be exempt, because running at that time is permissible. [The Gemara asks:] Why is it permissible on
erev Shabbat? [The Gemara answers:] It is in accordance
with R. Chanina, who used to say, (32b) "Come, let
us go forward to greet the bride, the queen!" [He would
go out into the field to welcome *Shabbat*.] Some said
[explicitly], " . . . to greet *Shabbat*, the bride, the
queen!" R. Yannai would wrap himself [in his *Shabbat*
attire], remain standing [and would not go out into
the field], and say, "Enter, O bride! Enter, O bride!"

ULLA'S CONDOLENCE

(38a) R. Shmuel b. Yehudah lost a daughter. So the
Rabbis [in Babylonia] said to Ulla [who came from
Eretz Yisrael], "Let us go and console him." But Ulla
answered them, "I don't approve of the kind of consolation the Babylonians use. In fact, I consider it outright blasphemy, for they say, 'Well, what could we
have done,' which implies that if they could have done
something [against God's will], they would have done
it." So he went alone to console the mourner and said
to him: It says, [Moses said,] "God said to me, 'Do
not attack Moab, and do not provoke them to fight'"
(Deuteronomy 2:9). [Why did God need to warn Moses
against attacking Moab?] Would it enter Moses' mind
to wage war without God's consent? But Moses [did
want to go to war against Moab], and he drew the following logical inference: If in the case of the Midianites
who came only to help the Moabites,[2] the Torah decreed, "Attack the Midianites and kill them" (Numbers 25:17), (38b), how much more so should this

decree apply in the case of the Moabites themselves [who originated the idea of inviting Balaam to curse Israel]!

But the Holy One, blessed be He, said to Moses: Your thinking does not coincide with Mine. Two good doves I have to bring forth from Moab: Ruth the Moabitess and Naamah the Ammonitess, [and therefore you cannot kill them]. [Ruth was the ancestor of David, and Naamah was the wife of Solomon.] [Concluded Ulla:] "Now can we not draw a logical inference from this and say: If for two good doves the Holy One, praised be He, saved two great nations and did not destroy them, then surely He would have spared the life of your daughter if she had been righteous and deserved to have worthy offspring."

THE WELL-DIGGER'S DAUGHTER

(50a) [The Gemara related that Nechunia the well-digger selflessly dug wells to provide water for the pilgrims who traveled to Jerusalem for the three *Yamim Tovim* (Pilgrimage Festivals).]

Our Rabbis taught: It happened that the daughter of Nechunia the well-digger once fell into a deep well [he had dug]. People came and told R. Chanina b. Dosa about it, [asking him to pray for the child]. During the first hour he said to them, "Don't worry, she will be all right." During the second hour he said, "She still is fine." But in the third hour he said, "She has come out of the well already." When they asked the girl, "Who brought you up?" she replied, "A ram [the ram of Isaac][3] materialized, and an old man [Abraham] was leading it." They then asked R. Chanina B. Dosa, "Are you a prophet [that you knew she had been saved]?" He replied, "I am not a prophet, neither am I the son of a prophet. But I said to myself, 'Can it be that the very thing that this *tzaddik* was taking so much pains with [to dig to provide water for the pilgrims], one of his children should stumble into?'"

Said R. Acha, "Nevertheless, [at a later time] Nechunia's son died of thirst, confirming what is said in the verse, 'Our God will come and not be silent; a fire will consume before Him, and His surroundings are extremely turbulent' (Psalms 50:3). This teaches us that the Holy One, blessed be He, is particular with [the *tzaddikim*] who are close to him, down to a hairbreadth, [so that the slightest transgression is punished]." R. Nechunia derives this priciple from the following verse, "God is dreaded in the great counsel of the holy [angels], and is awesome over all who surround Him" (Psalms 89:8).

R. Chanina said: If anyone says that the Holy One, blessed be He, is complacent when it comes to dealing out justice, his life will be discarded, [because with his attitude he is guiding people to sin]. For it says, "The deeds of the Mighty One are perfect, for all His ways are just" (Deuteronomy 32:4). R. Chana, or according to others, R. Shmuel b. Nachmani, said: Why does it say, (50b) *Erech apayim*, "slow to anger" [*apayim* is in the plural], and not *erech af* [in the singular]? [The plural implies that God is slow to repay both good and bad deeds, thus] He is slow in punishing the wicked and slow in rewarding the *tzaddikim* [the reward does not follow immediately after the good deed].

HE THREW STONES INTO PUBLIC GROUNDS

We learned in a *Baraita*: A person should not throw stones from his own property into public grounds. It happened that a person was throwing stones from his property into public grounds. A pious man who happened to be passing by said to him, "Fool, why are you throwing stones from ground that does not belong to you into ground that does belong to you?" The man laughed at him. As time went by, he had to sell his field, and when he was walking on those public grounds, he stumbled over his own stones. He then exclaimed, "That pious man was right when he said to me, 'Why are you throwing stones from ground that does not belong to you into grounds that belong to you!'"

A BAD LEADER FOR A BAD FLOCK

(52a) A certain Galilean in one of his lectures before R. Chisda said: When the shepherd becomes angry with his herd, he blinds the leading ram [so that it stumbles and falls into a ditch, and the herd will follow along. So, too, when God is angry with Israel he appoints unworthy leaders for them who guide them into pitfalls (Rashi)].

"IT WILL BE GOOD FOR YOU"

(54b) R. Chanina b. Agil asked R. Chiya b. Abba: Why is it that in the first Ten Commandments [in the commandment to honor father and mother (Exodus 20:12)] the phrase "that it will be good for you" is not mentioned; whereas in the second Ten Commandments (55a) (Deuteronomy 5:16) this phrase is inserted [in the same commandment]? R. Chiya b. Abba replied: Instead of asking me why the phrase "it will be good for you" is mentioned [in Deuteronomy], ask me whether or not this phrase was mentioned [on the actual Tablets], since I do not know whether it was mentioned [on the Tablets] or not. I advise you to go to R. Tanchum b. Chanila'i who was close to R. Yehoshua b. Levi, who was well-versed in *aggadah* [homiletic explanations]. So he went to R. Tanchum who told him: From R. Yehoshua b. Levi I have not heard anything about this matter. But R. Shmuel b. Nachum, the brother of the mother of R. Acha b. R.

Chanina, or as other say, the father of the mother of R. Acha b. R. Chanina, told me: Because the first Tablets containing the Commandments were destined to be broken. [The Gemara asks:] And if so, what does that have to do with including the phrase "it will be good for you"? Replied R. Ashi: [If this had been written on the first Tablets, which were broken,] God forbid, goodness would have ceased in Israel.

DREAMING OF THE LETTER *TET*

R. Yehoshua said: If someone sees the letter *tet* in a dream, it is a good omen. Why is that? If you think because it is the first letter of the word *tov*, "good," then why not say that it is the first letter of *teteitiha*, "I will sweep it clean with the broom of destruction" (Isaiah 14:23)? We are speaking here [of where he saw in his dream only] one *tet*, [and *teteitiha* has two *tets*]. Still, why don't you say [that the *tet* refers to the word *tum'ah*, "defilement, contamination," as in "Her impurity [*tumatah*] is on her hems" (Lamentations 1:9).— We are speaking of [where he saw in a dream] a *tet* and a *bet*. Then, why don't you say [that it refers to] "Her gates have sunk [*tave'u*] into the earth" (ibid. 2:9) [where *tave'u* has a *tet* and a *bet* and refers to downfall]?—The reason that a *tet* is a good omen is that the first time the letter *tet* occurs in the Torah is in the word *tov*, "good" (Genesis 1:4), for from the beginning of Genesis up to the verse, "God saw that the light was good [*tov*]", no *tet* occurs. R. Yehoshua b. Levi also said: If someone sees the word *hesed* [eulogy] in a dream, it means that mercy has been bestowed on him from Heaven, and he has been delivered [from trouble]. But this applies only if he saw the word *hesed* spelled out in script, [but not if he saw a eulogy being given].

HE HAD BLACK SHOELACES

(59b) Eliezer Ze'ira once put on a pair of black shoes [tied with black shoelaces, a sign of mourning, instead of the customary white shoelaces] and stood in the marketplace of Nehardea. When the officers of the Exilarch [the head of Babylonian Jewry] met him there, they asked him, "What reason do you have for wearing such shoes?" He replied, "I am mourning [the destruction] of Jerusalem." They said to him, "Are you such a prominent scholar that you should mourn for Jerusalem [in such a conspicuous manner]?" Thinking this to be a blatant display of self-importance, they brought him in and put him in prison.[4] He said to them, "But I am a great Torah scholar." They asked him, "How can we tell?" He replied, "Either you ask me a [difficult] halachic question, or I will ask you one." They replied, "We had rather you ask us." He then asked them, "If a person destroys unripe dates, what amount of damages does he have to pay?" They answered, "He has to pay the value of the unripe dates [which are worthless]." Asked Eliezer, "But would they

not eventually have grown into ripe dates?" [Therefore, let him pay for the ripe dates of which the owner was deprived.] They replied, "You are right. He has to pay the value of ripe dates."

Eliezer countered, "But, after all, he did not take ripe dates, [why should he pay for them]? They then said to him, "So you tell us." He answered, "[The damages are determined by assessing the depreciation of a grove of] sixty [date trees that was caused by the destruction of the unripe dates of one tree]."[5] They said, "What authority do you have to back you up?" He replied, "Well, Shmuel is alive and his Bet Din is still around." They sent this question to Shmuel who answered, "The statement [Eliezer Ze'ira] made to you [that the damages are determined by the depreciation of a grove of] sixty [date trees] is correct." [When they heard this] they released him, [and it was therefore appropriate for him to mourn for Jerusalem in such a conspicuous manner].

CALAMITY STRIKES
TZADDIKIM FIRST

(60a) R. Shmuel b. Nachmani said in the name of R. Yochanan: Disaster comes on the world only when there are wicked people in the world, yet its first victims are the *tzaddikim*, for it says, "If a fire gets out of control and spreads through thorns" (Exodus 22:5). When does a fire get out of control? Only when there are thorns nearby. ["Thorns" is a metaphor for the wicked.] It always strikes the *tzaddikim* first, for the verse continues, "and a stack of grain was consumed" [the "stack of grain" symbolizes the *tzaddikim*]. It does not say: "it will consume a stack of grain" but "the stack of grain was consumed" to tell you that the stack of grain [i.e., the *tzaddikim*] was consumed first.

R. Yosef taught: What is meant by the verse, [Before the Slaying of the Firstborn, Moses told the people,] "And as for you, you shall not leave the entrance of your house until morning" (Exodus 12:22)? Once permission is given to the Destroyer [i.e, the Angel of Death], he makes no distinction between righteous and wicked people, and what is more, he begins with the *tzaddikim*, for it says, "I will cut off righteous and wicked from among you" (Ezekiel 21:8) [the righteous are mentioned before the wicked]. R. Yosef cried at this, saying, "To such an extent are the *tzaddikim* compared to nothingness, [that they are punished even before the wicked]!" But Abaye comforted him, "It is for their benefit, [so that they will not see the evil that is about to happen], as it says, 'Because of the impending evil the righteous one was gathered in'" (Isaiah 57:1).

Rav Yehudah said in the name of Rav: (60b) A person should always enter a town by daytime and leave by daytime, as it says, "And as for you, you shall not leave the entrance of your house until morning" (Exodus 12:22).

516

WHEN PLAGUE
AND FAMINE STRIKE

We learned in a *Baraita*: When the plague is raging in town, stay indoors, for it says, "And as for you, you shall not leave the entrance of your house until morning." And it also says, "Go my people, enter your rooms and close your doors behind you" (Isaiah 26:20). And it says further, "Outside, the sword will bereave, while indoors, there will be terror" (Deuteronomy 32:25). [The Gemara asks:] Why the quotation of two additional verses? [The Gemara answers:] You might say that the advice to stay indoors refers only to the night, but not to the day; therefore, come and listen to the verse, "Go my people, enter your rooms and close the doors behind you" (Isaiah 26:20) [even in the daytime]. And you might say that these fears apply only if there is no terror indoors, whereas where there is terror indoors it is much better to go out and sit in the company of other people; therefore, listen to the verse, "Outside, the sword will bereave, while indoors, there will be terror" (Deuteronomy 32:25), which implies that even where the terror is indoors, the sword [of the Angel of Death] will bereave [more] outside. In times of an epidemic Rava used to keep the windows closed, for it says, "For death has ascended through our windows" (Jeremiah 9:20).

We learned in a *Baraita*: When there is a famine in town, move to another place, for it says, "There was a famine in the land, and Abram went down to Egypt to sojourn there" (Genesis 12:10). And it further says, [The four lepers at the gate of Samaria said to each other,] "If we propose to enter the city, there is a famine in the city, and we will die there" (2 Kings 7:4). Why two quotations?—Since you might think that the advice [to move away] applies only where there is no danger to life [in the new location], whereas if there is danger to life in the new place you should not move away; therefore, listen to the continuation of the verse, [The four lepers said,] "So let us now go and throw ourselves upon the army of Aram; if they let us live, we will live, and if they put us to death, we will die" (ibid.). [Hence, you should move away even if the new location is unsafe.]

We learned in a *Baraita*: When there is a plague in town, a person should not walk in the middle of the road, because the Angel of Death walks then in the middle of the road. For since he has been given permission [to rampage] he struts along conspicuously. But when there is peace in town, a person should not walk at the side of the road, because as long as the Angel of Death has no permission [to deal death] he sneaks by in hiding.

We learned in a *Baraita*: When there is an epidemic in town, a person should not enter the synagogue by himself, since the Angel of Death stores there his instruments. This is true only where no students are being taught there, or where ten males do not pray there together.

We learned in a *Baraita*: When dogs howl, [that is a sign that] the Angel of Death has come to town. But when dogs cavort, [that is a sign that] Elijah the prophet has come to town. However, this is so only if there is no female among them, [for then they do it because of the female].

A NO-WIN SITUATION

R. Ammi and R. Assi were once sitting before R. Yitzchak. One of them said, "Will you please expound a *halachah* for us?" Said the other, "Will you please expound an *aggadah*?"[6] When he began to expound an *aggadah*, the one [who wanted to hear *halachah*] interrupted him. When he began to comment on *aggadah*, the one [who wanted to hear *halachah*] prevented him. So he told them, "This may be compared to a man who has two wives; one wife is young and the other is old. The young one used to pluck out his white hairs to make him appear young, while the old one used to pluck out his black hairs to make him appear old. The result was that he became completely bald."

He then said to them: Under the circumstances, I will tell you something that will be of interest to both of you. It says, "If a fire gets out of control and spreads through thorns" (Exodus 22:5). The phrase "gets out of control" implies "[the fire started] by itself." [The verse continues,] "The one who started the fire must make restitution." [Metaphorically this is explained:] The Holy One, blessed be He, said: I am obligated to make restitution for the fire that I started. It was I who kindled the fire in Zion, for it says, "He kindled a fire in Zion which consumed its foundations" (Lamentations 4:11). And in time to come I will also build Zion up by fire, for it says, "And I will be for it a wall of fire all around, and for glory will I be in its midst" (Zechariah 2:9). On the halachic side he said: Why does the verse begin with the damage done by one's property; ["got out of control" implies an article spontaneously caught fire], and ends with damage done by the person [it says, "the one who started the fire"], in order to teach you that damage by done by fire implies human agency.

HIS SINFUL BEHAVIOR
STRUCK ROOTS

(67b) We learned in a *Baraita*: R. Akiva said: Why has the Torah ordained that if a thief slaughtered or sold [a sheep or an ox] he must repay five oxen for each ox, and four sheep for each sheep?[7] Because [when he stole and then sold the animal] his sinful behavior struck roots in him. (68a) . . . As Rava said elsewhere: Because he doubled his sin.

MARKING THE VINEYARD

(69a) [Note: The fruit of the first three years of a newly planted tree is termed *orlah* and may not be eaten.[8] The fruit of the fourth year, called *neta reva'i*, must be eaten in Jerusalem or redeemed. In the fifth year the fruit may be eaten without restrictions.] We learned in the Mishnah: In the fourth year of a vineyard [when its fruit must be redeemed before it may be eaten] the owners used to mark it with clods of earth, to compare its fruit to the earth: just as you can only benefit from the earth after plowing, planting, and harvesting, so too the fruit of this vineyard may be enjoyed only after redemption. The owners used to mark with broken pieces of earthenware the fruit that was *orlah* [the fruit of the first three years, which had to be destroyed], to signify that just as potsherds are of no benefit, so, too, no benefit may be derived from the fruit of *orlah*. A field of graves used to be marked with lime [to alert passersby who would become unclean upon entering]. Lime is white, the color of the bones [that are buried there]. The lime was dissolved in water to give it more brightness and then poured out [around the graves].

THE THIEF AND
THE HOLDUP MAN

(79b) The students of R. Yochanan b. Zakkai asked him: Why does the Torah impose a heavier penalty on a thief than on a robber? [A thief must make double restitution for the stolen article or animal,[9] and if he subsequently slaughtered or sold the animal, he has to pay four or five times the value of the stolen sheep or ox.[10] By contrast, a robber has to return only the stolen article or its value.][11] R. Yochanan b. Zakkai replied: The robber puts the honor of the servant [i.e., the people he robs] on the same level as the honor of his master [i.e., God; by robbing his victim in broad daylight, the holdup man shows that he fears neither his victim nor God]. The thief, on the other hand, does not put the honor of the servant on the same level as the honor of his master; [by committing his crime surreptitiously he shows that he is afraid of his victim but not of God]. He acts as if the eye of God were not seeing, and the ear of God were not hearing. As it says, "Woe is to those who try to hide in depth to conceal counsel from God, and their deeds are done in darkness; they say, 'Who sees us, and who knows of us?'" (Isaiah 29:15). Or as it says, "And they say, 'God will not see, nor will the God of Jacob understand'" (Psalms 94:7); or, as it says again, "For they have said, 'God has forsaken the earth, and God does not see'" (Ezekiel 9:9).

We learned in a *Baraita*: R. Meir said: The following parable was related in the name of R. Gamliel: [The thief and the robber] may be compared to two people who lived in the same town. Both made a banquet. One invited the townspeople but did not invite the the royal family, while the other invited neither the townspeople nor the royal family. Which should receive the heavier punishment? Of course the one who invited the towns-

people but did not invite the royal family, [meaning, the thief who fears man but not God].

R. Meir also said: Note how highly labor is regarded, for if a thief steals an ox [and slaughtered it], thereby precluding it from doing labor,[12] he has to pay fivefold, whereas if he steals [and slaughters] a sheep that does not do any labor, he has to pay only fourfold. R. Yochanan b. Zakkai said: Note how highly human dignity is regarded, for if a thief steals an ox that walks on his own feet, he has to pay fivefold, but if he steals a sheep that he has to carry on his shoulders, he has to pay only fourfold.

HATRED BETWEEN
ROYAL BROTHERS

(82b) The Rabbis taught: When the members of the Hasmonean family fought against each other, Hyrkanus was inside [the walls of Jerusalem], and [his brother] Aristobulus was outside [laying siege to Jerusalem].[13] Each day [the treasurer of the Temple] lowered down a bucket full of coins and received in return sheep for the daily sacrifices. An old man [on the inside] who was well-versed in Greek wisdom sent out a secret message [the besiegers] in cultured Greek [which the people in Jerusalem did not understand], "As long as they continue the Temple service, they will not be delivered into your hands." The next day, the defenders lowered the bucket with coins, but the besiegers sent up a pig. When the pig reached the middle of the wall, it stuck its hooves into the wall, which brought on an earthquake that shook Eretz Yisrael over an area of four hundred *parsahs* by four hundred *parsahs*. On that occasion the Sages declared: Cursed be the man who breeds pigs, and cursed be the man who teaches his son Greek wisdom. It was in reference to this terrible civil war that we learned that the *Omer*[14] was once brought from as far away as the gardens of Tzerifin, and the two loaves[15] from the Valley of Ein Socher. [They had to be brought from such distant places because the troops that besieged Jerusalem had destroyed the crops in the nearby fields (Rashi).]

STUDYING GREEK CULTURE

[The Gemara asks:] But is the study of Greek wisdom really forbidden? Didn't we learn in a *Baraita*: Rabbi said, (83a) "Why speak Syrian in Eretz Yisrael? Speak either Hebrew or Greek." And R. Yose said, "Why speak Aramaic in Babylonia? Speak either Hebrew or Persian." [So you see, the Greek language is permitted?] [The Gemara answers:] I'll tell you. The Greek language is one thing, but Greek wisdom is something else altogether. [The Gemara asks:] But is Greek wisdom forbidden? Did not Rav Yehudah say in the name of Shmuel who quoted R. Shimon b. Gamliel, "The words, 'My eyes have brought me grief over all the daughters of my city' (Lamentations 3:51), apply to the thousands of children in my father's family; five hundred of them learned Torah and the other five hundred learned Greek wisdom, and of all of them only two survived: I who live here and my cousin who lives in Asia." [Which proves that Greek wisdom was permitted.]

[The Gemara answers: Greek wisdom is indeed forbidden, but] R. Gamliel's family was an exception, because [as representatives of the Jewish people] they had constant dealings with the government, [therefore they were permitted to learn Greek culture and etiquette], as we learned in a *Baraita*: A person who takes a Roman-style haircut [a straight fringe on the forehead, shaved above the ears and in the back] emulates the ways of the Amorites [which the Torah forbids].[16] [But] Avtulmus b. Reuven was permitted to wear his hair Roman style because [as spokesman for the Jewish community] he was in close contact with government officials. The same way, the members of the family of R. Gamliel were permitted to be well-versed in Greek civilization because of their close association with government circles.

Our Rabbis taught: You should not keep a dog unless it is kept on a chain. If you live in a city that is near the border [where there is a threat of marauders], you may keep a dog if you restrain it on a chain during the day, but you may let it loose at night.

THE BLIND ARE EXEMPT FROM OBSERVING *MITZVOT*

[Note: If a person injures someone, he has to pay compensation for five things: for the damage he inflicted, for pain, medical expenses, loss of time, and for the humiliation the injured suffered.]

(87a) We learned in a *Baraita*: R. Yehudah says: A blind person [who was injured] is not entitled to compensation for humiliation. In the same vein, R. Yehudah exempted a blind person from all *mitzvot* in the Torah. Said R. Shisha son of R. Idi: The reason for R. Yehudah's ruling is because it says, "This is the commandment, the decrees and the laws" (Deuteronomy 6:1). Whoever is eligible to be appointed as judge [who adjudicates the laws] has the obligation of observing the *mitzvot* and the decrees, but whoever is not eligible to be appointed as judge is exempt from observing the *mitzvot* and the decrees, [and a blind person cannot be appointed as judge].

R. Yosef [who was blind] used to say: Originally I thought that if someone would tell me that the *halachah* agrees with R. Yehudah who says that a blind person is exempt from fulfilling the *mitzvot*, I would make a banquet for the Rabbis, because [being blind] I am not required to observe, but I would do them anyway. However, now that I have heard R. Chanina's statement that someone who is commanded to do a mitzvah and does it is greater than a person who does a mitzvah although he is not commanded

to do it;[17] on the contrary, if someone would tell me that the *halachah* does not agree with R. Yehudah, [and a blind person *is* obligated to fulfill all *mitzvot*], I would make a banquet for the Rabbis, because if I am required to do the *mitzvot* my reward will be greater.

THE OFFENDER MUST PLACATE THE INJURED PERSON

(92a) [The Mishnah says:] Even though [the person who injured someone] pays compensation, he is not forgiven [by Heaven] until he asks [the injured person] for forgiveness, as it says, [After Abimelech, king of Gerar, took Sarah, God told him in a dream that he would die. God then said,] "Now return the man's wife, for he is a prophet. He will pray for you, and you will live" (Genesis 20:7). [The implication is that Abimelech had to ask Abraham for forgiveness so that he would pray that he might live.] And how do we know that if the injured person does not forgive the offender he is branded as cruel? Because it says, "Abraham prayed to God, and God healed Abimelech" (ibid. 20:17). [The fact that Abraham prayed for Abimelech proves that he forgave him, and every Jew should follow Abraham's example (Iyun Yaakov).]

[The Gemara says:] We learned in a *Baraita*: All the various fixed amounts [that were set as compensation for smacking a person, pulling his hair, spitting at him, uncovering the head of a woman, etc.] represent only payment due for humiliation.[18] But as far as the hurt feelings of the injured person are concerned, even if the offender would offer [on the altar] all the "rams of Nebaiot,"[19] he is not forgiven until he asks forgiveness [of the person he insulted]. For it says, "Now return the man's wife for he is a prophet, and he will pray for you," [and Abraham would not have prayed unless he was placated]. [The Gemara asks:] Is it only the wife of a prophet he has to return, and the wife of another person he does not have to return?

R. Shmuel b. Nachmani said in the name of R. Yonatan: It says, "Return the man's wife"—regardless of who the man is. And in regard to your [Abimelech's] statement: "Will You even kill an innocent nation? Didn't [her husband] tell me that she was his sister? She also claimed that she was her brother" (ibid. v. 4,5).[20] [You should be aware that] "he is a prophet" who has taught: When a stranger comes to town you should ask him whether he needs food and drink; but you certainly shouldn't ask him [personal questions such as] whether the lady that is with him is his wife or his sister! [The fact that God told Abimelech, "You will die because of the woman (Sarah) you took" (Genesis 20:3)] teaches us that a descendant of Noah [a non-Jew] is liable to the death penalty if he had the opportunity to learn but did not do so [and committed a crime through ignorance, as Abimelech did].

PRAYING FOR SOMEONE ELSE

Rava asked Rabbah b. Mari: From where in Scripture do we derive the following teaching of our Rabbis: If a person prays for someone else while he himself is in need of the same thing, he will be answered first? Rabbah b. Mari replied: From the verse, "God returned the fortune of Job [that he had lost], when he prayed for his friends" (Job 42:10). Rava said to Rabbah b. Mari: You say it is derived from that passage, but I say it is from this verse, "Abraham prayed to God, and God healed Abimelech, as well as his wife and slavegirls" (Genesis 20:17), and immediately after that it says, "God remembered Sarah as he had said" (ibid. 21:1), meaning, since Abraham had prayed for Abimelech. [Thus Sarah became pregnant because Abraham prayed for Abimelech.]

TOGETHER WITH THE THORNS THE CABBAGE IS PULLED

Rava furthermore asked Rabba b. Mari: From where in Scripture is derived the popular saying: Together with the thorns the cabbage is pulled out [i.e., the good are made to suffer along with the bad]? He replied: From the verse, "'Why should you contend with Me? You have all rebelled against Me, [including the prophet]' says God" (Jeremiah 2:29). He said to him: You say it is derived from that text, but I say it is derived from this text, [God said to Moses,] "How long will you [which includes Moses] refuse to keep My commandments and My laws?" (Exodus 16:28).

WHY WAS JUDAH MENTIONED TWICE?

Rava again asked Rabba b. Mari: It says, "And from the least of his brothers [Joseph] took five men and presented them to Pharaoh" (Genesis 47:2). [Joseph chose the weakest so that Pharaoh would not recruit them for his army.] Who were the five? He replied: This is what R. Yochanan said: He chose the ones whose names were mentioned twice [in the blessing of Moses (Deuteronomy 43:2–29): Dan, Gad, Zebulun, Naphtali, and Asher. They were the weakest of the tribes, and Moses repeated their names in order to give them added strength (Rashi)]. [Rava asked:] But is not Judah's name repeated too, [and the tribe of Judah was very powerful and did not need strengthening]? Rabba b. Mari replied: His name was repeated for a different reason, as R. Shmuel b. Nachmani said in the name of R. Yonatan: What is meant by [Moses' blessing,] "May Reuben live and not die, and may his population be included in the count . . . and this for Judah" (Deuteronomy 33:6,7)? All the years that the Israelites were in the wilderness, Judah's bones kept turning in his coffin[21] until Moses stood up and asked for mercy for him. He said to God: Master of the universe! Who caused Reuben to confess his sin?[22] None other than Judah; [his admission of guilt[23] inspired Reuben to confess].

[Continued Moses,] "And this for Judah" [meaning: is it fair to Judah that his bones should be turning in his coffin?]. Thus when Moses prayed, "Hearken O God, to Judah's voice," (ibid.) each of Judah's limbs entered its socket [and stopped rolling in the coffin]. But the angels did not permit him to enter the heavenly Academy [where the Torah scholars are studying; so Moses prayed,] "And return him to his people" (ibid.). Once he was there, Judah was unable to participate in the discussions the rabbis were engaged in, [so Moses prayed,] "May he be able to triumph [in the Torah debate]" (ibid.). Even so, Judah did not merit to say things the others accepted, [so Moses prayed,] "May You be a helper against his adversaries" (ibid.). [And that is the reason why Judah's name is mentioned twice in Moses' blessing.]

Rava said again to Rabbah b. Mari: Where do we find support for the popular saying, "Poverty follows the poor"? He replied: We learned in a Mishnah:[24] The rich used to bring the *bikkurim* [first fruits] in baskets of gold and silver [and took the baskets back with them], but the poor brought them in willow baskets, and the *kohen* kept the *bikkurim* together with the baskets. Said Rava: You derive it from here, but I derive it from this verse, (92b) "[The leper] must call out, 'Unclean! Unclean!' " (Leviticus 13:45). [Not only does he suffer the disease, but he also has to announce his disgrace.]

THE IMPORTANCE OF A WHOLESOME BREAKFAST

Rava said again to Rabbah b. Mari: From what verse do we derive the teaching of the Rabbis:[25] Have an early breakfast in the summer because of the heat, and in the winter because of the cold; as the popular saying has it: Sixty men may run after a person who had an early breakfast, but they'll never catch up with him? He replied: For it says, "They will not hunger, and they will not thirst; heat and sun will not afflict them" (Isaiah 49:10). Rava said: You derive it from this verse, but I derive it from this one, "You will serve the Lord your God" (Exodus 23:25)—this refers to reciting the *Shema* and the *Shemoneh Esrei*; [and the verse continues], "He will bless your bread and your water"—this refers to bread and salt and a pitcher of water, [in other words, if you pray in the morning and then have a wholesome breakfast,] then, "I will banish sickness [*machalah*] from among you." And we learned in a *Baraita*: *Machalah* [sickness] means gall, and why is it called *machalah*? Because eighty-three diseases stem from it, and the numeric value of *machalah* is eighty-three [mem = 40; chet = 8; lamed = 30; hei = 5]. But they are all neutralized by having for breakfast bread and salt with a pitcher of water.

POPULAR SAYINGS

Rava furthermore asked R. Rabbah b. Mari: From where can we derive the Rabbis' adage: If your neighbor calls you a donkey, put a saddle on your back [meaning, agree with him, for it says, (After running away from Sarah, Hagar had an encounter with an angel who asked her,)] "'Hagar, maid of Sarai! From where are you coming?' And she replied, "'I am running away from my mistress Sarai'" (Genesis 16:8). [Hagar used the same demeaning terminology the angel had used.]

Rava again said to Rabba b. Mari: From where can we derive the popular saying that goes, "If there is a blemish on your reputation, you be the first one to tell it"? He replied: For it says, [Eliezer introduced himself, saying,] "I am Abraham's servant" (ibid. 24:34).

Rava again said to Rabba b. Mari: What verse is the basis of the popular adage, "Although a duck keeps its head down while walking, it looks far ahead [for food]"? For it says, [Abigail said to David,] "And when God has prospered my lord [David], remember your maid [Abigail]" (1 Samuel 25:31). [She prophesied that her husband Nabal would die, and she hinted that when that would come to pass, David should remember her beauty and consider marrying her (Rashi).]

Rava again said to Rabbah b. Mari: In what verse do we find support for the popular adage: Sixty pains reach the teeth of the person who hears the noise made by someone else eating while he does not eat? He replied: For it says, "But me—I, your servant—Zadok the Kohen, Benaiah son of Jehoiada, and your servant Solomon he did not invite" (1 Kings 1:26). [Thus he complained about the fact that he was not invited to the feast.] Rava said: You derive it from this verse, but I derive it from here, "Isaac brought [Rebeccah] into his mother Sarah's tent, and married Rebeccah. She became his wife, and he loved her. Isaac was then consoled for the loss of his mother" (Genesis 24:67). And in the next verse says, "Abraham married another woman whose name was Keturah." [The juxtaposition of the two verses suggests that Abraham married Keturah because he envied Isaac's marital bliss, which bears out the adage about the pain a person experiences when hearing of someone else being content while he is not content.]

Rava said again to Rabba b. Mari: What is the scriptural basis for the familiar saying, "Although the wine belongs to the owner, the drinkers should thank the waiter"? For it says, [God said to Moses,] "Lay your hands on him [Joshua] . . . so that the entire Israelite community will obey him" (Numbers 27:18,20). And it also says, "Joshua son of Nun was filled with a spirit of wisdom, because Moses had laid his hands on him. The Israelites therefore listened to him" (Deuteronomy 34:9). [Although the spirit of wisdom comes from God, Moses is given all the credit.]

Rava also said to Rabbah b. Mari: What verse supports the popular adage, "A bad palm will make its

way to a grove of unproductive trees"? He replied: This concept [that like meets like] is mentioned in the Torah, repeated in the Prophets, and mentioned a third time in the Writings; it is also taught in a Mishnah and in a Baraita. It is mentioned in the Torah in the passage, "Esau went to Ishmael" (Genesis 38:9); in the Prophets, "Boorish men collected around Jephthah and ventured forth with him" (Judges 11:3); in the Writings, "Every fowl dwells near its kind and man near his equal" (Ben Sira 13:15).[26] We learned in the Mishnah, "Anything that is attached to an article that is subject to the law of defilement will itself become defiled, but anything that is attached to an article that cannot become tamei [ritually unclean, such as smooth pieces of wood] remains clean. [Thus if a metal hook was stuck into a piece of wood, the hook does not become tamei]" (Keilim 12:2); in a Baraita, "R. Eliezer said: Not for nothing did the crow join the raven, but because it is the same kind."

Rava further said to Rabba b. Mari: What verse corroborates the popular saying, "If you will join me in lifting the burden, I will lift it; otherwise I will not lift it"? [A person does not want to enter into a risky venture unless his friend joins him.] He replied: For it says, "Barak said to [Deborah], 'If you go with me, I will go; but if you do not go with me I will not go'" (Judges 4:8).

Rava also asked Rabba b. Mari: Where in Scripture can we find a verse that supports the common saying: When a dog is hungry it will even swallow rocks? For it says, "The sated soul will trample a honeycomb, but to the hungry soul, all bitter is sweet" (Proverbs 27:7).

Rava also said to Rabbah b. Mari: From what verse can be derived the common adage: "If you call out to your neighbor to admonish him, and he does not respond, you may allow a big wall to fall on him"? He replied: Because it says, "Because I tried to cleanse you but you would not be cleansed, you will not again be cleansed of your contamination until I place My wrath upon you" (Ezekiel 24:13).

Rava further said to Rabbah b. Mari: From what verse can we infer the familiar aphorism: "Don't throw a stone into the well from which you once drank water"? [Don't show contempt toward your benefactor.] He replied: From the passage, "Do not despise the Edomite since he is your brother. Do not despise the Egyptian, since you were a stranger in his land [and 'enjoyed' Egyptian hospitality]" (Deuteronomy 23:8).

Rava again asked Rabbah b. Mari: From where can we derive the following saying, "When we were young we were esteemed like men; now that we are old we are looked down upon like children"? He replied: It says, [At the time of the Exodus,] "God went before them by day with a pillar of cloud, to guide them along their way. By night it appeared as a pillar of fire, providing them with light" (Exodus 13:21), but afterward it says, (93a) "I will send an angel before you to safeguard you on the way" (ibid. 23:20). [At the Exodus God Himself guided the children of Israel, but after the sin of the golden calf, God sent an angel to protect them.]

Rava further said to Rabba b. Mari: From where can we derive the saying, "A rich man leaves a trail of fragrant wood"? [By associating with the rich you will become rich yourself.] He replied: For it says, "Lot who accompanied Abram also had sheep, cattle and tents" (Genesis 13:5) [and Abraham was very wealthy].[27]

SARAH BLAMED ABRAHAM

R. Chanin said: Whoever invokes Divine judgment on his neighbor will himself be punished first, for it says, [When Hagar looked at Sarai with contempt,] "Sarai said to Abram, 'The outrage against me is all your fault . . . Let God judge between me and you!'" (Genesis 16:5), and subsequently it says, "Abraham came to eulogize Sarah and to weep for her" (ibid. 23:2). However, this applies only if that person could have obtained justice in an earthly court of law.[28] R. Yitzchak said: The one who cries for Divine justice fares worse than the person on whom he calls down the Divine judgment. We have learned a proof to this in a *Baraita*: Both the one who invokes Divine judgment and the one against whom it is invoked are punished by the divine court; only the one who calls down the judgment is punished first.

R. Yitzchak further said: Do not take lightly the curse of an ordinary man, for Abimelech [the Philistine king] invoked a curse on Sarah and it was fulfilled in her offspring. For he said [to Sarah], "Let this be for you a covering of the eyes" (Genesis 20:16). What he meant to say was: Since you have covered the truth from me and not informed me that [Abraham] is your husband and thereby caused me all this trouble, let it be the will of Heaven that you will be stricken with "a covering of the eyes" [i.e., blindness]. And this actually came true in her son, for it says, "And it came to pass when Isaac had become old and his eye dimmed from seeing" (Genesis 27:1). R. Abbahu said: It is always better to be one of the persecuted rather than one of the persecutors, since there are no more persecuted birds than pigeons, and of all birds they are the only ones that are fit for the altar.

ROBBERS AND USURERS WHO WANT TO MAKE AMENDS

(94a) We learned in a *Baraita*: R. Eliezer b. Yaakov says: If someone stole a *se'ah*[29] of wheat and kneaded it and baked it and separated *challah* [from the dough],[30] how can he recite a *barachah* over it; surely he would not be saying a *berachah* but a blasphemy. To a person like that the following verse applies, "The robber who pronounces a *berachah* blasphemes God" (Psalms 10:3).

(94b) Our Rabbis taught: If robbers and usurers [repent and] are ready to make restitution, you should not accept it from them. Anyone that does accept it from them, the Sages do not take kindly to his action. R. Yochanan said: This Mishnah was taught in the days of Rebbi, for we learned in a *Baraita*: It once happened that a person wanted to make restitution. So his wife told him, "Good-for-nothing! If you are going to make restitution, even your belt does not belong to you anymore." As a result, he had second thoughts about doing *teshuvah*. It was at that time that the Rabbis announced: If robbers and usurers [repent and] are ready to make restitution, you should not accept it from them, and anyone that does accept it from them, the Sages do not take kindly to his action.

THE INSCRIPTION ON THE COINS

(96b) We learned in a *Baraita*: What was [inscribed on] the coin of Jerusalem?—The names David and Solomon were engraved on one side; the words "Jerusalem the Holy City" on the other side. What was the coin of Abraham our Father?—An old man and an old woman [Abraham and Sarah] on one side, and a young man and a young woman [Isaac and Rebeccah] on the other side.

R. KAHANE'S ENCOUNTER WITH R. YOCHANAN

(117a) A certain person who wanted to point out his neighbor's straw to [government agents to be confiscated] appeared before Rav who warned him, "Under no circumstances should you point out his straw [to government agents]." He defiantly replied, "I am too going to show it to them!" Just then R. Kahane was sitting before Rav, and he struck [the rebellious fellow] on his throat and broke his neck. Rav applied [to the informer] the following passage, "Your children have fainted, they lie at the head of all the streets like a wild bull trapped in a net" (Isaiah 51:20)—just as a wild bull, once he is caught in the net, is shown no mercy, so too the property of Israel, once it comes into the hands of heathens, they show no mercy. [Rav indicated that R. Kahane had acted properly in killing the informer.] Rav said to R. Kahane, "Kahane, until now we were under the domination of the Persians who were unconcerned when murders occurred, but now we are ruled by the Greeks who do care about bloodshed, and they will cry, 'You are a murderer!' Therefore, hurry up and leave [Babylonia] and go to Eretz Yisrael, but take it upon yourself that you will not ask any questions of R. Yochanan for seven years" [as an atonement for the murder however justified it was (Iyun Yaakov)].

When he arrived in Eretz Yisrael [and entered the yeshivah] he saw that Resh Lakish was reviewing for the students the day's lecture that he had heard from R. Yochanan. [After the lecture] R. Kahane asked [the students], "Where is Resh Lakish?" They replied, "Why do you want to know?" He answered, "I have such-and-such question, and want to suggest such-and-such solution." When they told this to Resh Lakish, Resh Lakish went and told R. Yochanan, "A lion has come up from Babylonia; let the Master prepare himself well for tomorrow's lecture." The next morning they placed R. Kahane in the first row in front of R. Yochanan. But when R. Yochanan expounded on one *halachah* after another, and R. Kahane did not raise any questions, he was moved back through seven rows until he was sitting in the last row. R. Yochanan then said to Resh Lakish, "The lion you told me about turned out to be a fox!" [Yesterday's brilliant remarks were not his own insights but comments he happened to have heard from his master (Ben Yehoyada)].

R. Kahane then prayed, "May these seven rows [that I was demoted] be in the place of the seven years that Rav said [I am not permitted to speak to R. Yochanan]." He immediately rose and said to R. Yochanan, "Will you please start the lecture again from the beginning." As soon as R. Yochanan repeated the first halachic exposition, R. Kahane raised a difficulty; at the next halachic point he again posed a brilliant question. This continued until he was placed again in the first row.

R. Yochanan was sitting on seven cushions, and each time R. Kahane asked him a question [he could not answer], one cushion was pulled out from under him, and this continued until he remained sitting on the bare floor. Since R. Yochanan was then a very old man, and his eyebrows were drooping [over his eyes], he said to one of his disciples, "Pick up my eyebrows, so that I can see him." So he picked up his eyebrows with a silver stick. R. Kahane had a cut lip [from an old wound] which gave him the appearance of constantly smiling. R. Yochanan thought that R. Kahane was laughing at him. He became dejected, and as a result, R. Kahane died. The following day R. Yochanan said to the Rabbis, "Did you see how that Babylonian was making fun of us?" But they replied, "This was his natural appearance. [It just seemed that he was laughing.]" R. Yochanan then went to the cave [where R. Kahane was buried] and saw (117b) a snake [which held its tail in its mouth] blocking the entrance. He said, "Snake, snake, open your mouth, and let the Master go to the student!" But the snake did not open its mouth. He then said, "Let the student go to his fellow student!" But it still did not open its mouth, until he said, "Let the student go to the Master!" At last the snake opened its mouth [and allowed him to enter].

R. Yochanan prayed for mercy, and brought R. Kahane back to life. He said to him, "[I am sorry.] Had I known that this is the natural expression of your face, I would not have become dejected, [and this would not

have happened]. Now, please come along with me." Replied R. Kahane, "If you are able to pray for mercy that I will not die again [if you become upset when I ask you a difficult question], then I will go with you; but if not, I will not go, for you might get angry at me again, [and it is not every day that a miracle occurs]." He woke him up completely and asked him regarding all the [halachic] cases about which he was in doubt, and R. Kahane answered them for him. This episode is what is meant when R. Yochanan said: I thought that the Torah belongs to the Sages of Eretz Yisrael, but now I see that it belongs to the Sages of Babylonia.

ROBBERY IS LIKE TAKING A LIFE

(119a) R. Yochanan said: Robbing someone of a *perutah* is like taking his life, for it says, "Such are the ways of all who pursue unjust gain; they take the souls of its possessors" (Proverbs 1:19). And it also says, "They will consume your harvest and your bread, [and it will seem to you as if] they consumed your sons and your daughters [because you cannot feed them]" (Jeremiah 5:17). And furthermore it says, "Because of the *chamas* [violence] against the children of Judah, because they shed innocent blood in their land" (Joel 4:19), and it says further, [David inquired of God why there was a famine for three years. God said,] "It is for Saul and for the House of Blood, for having killed the Gibeonites" (2 Samuel 21:1). [The Gemara asks:] Why is it necessary to quote the additional verses? [The Gemara answers:] Because [if only the verse "they take the soul of its possessors" was cited], you might say that this applies only to his own soul [i.e., the soul of the victim] but not to the soul of [the victim's] sons and daughters; hence the verse, "They consumed your sons and daughters." Now you might say that this applies only where no money was given [by the robber for the article he took], but where money was given, [but the deal was made under coercion, by the threat of violence] this would not apply, hence the verse, "Because of the *chamas* [implying buying something from an unwilling seller by threatening violence,] against the children of Judah, because they shed innocent blood in their land."

Now you might say that these verses apply only where the robbery was actually committed by hand, but not where the robber was only the indirect cause of it; hence the verse, "It is for Saul and the House of Blood, for having killed the Gibeonites." Where do we find that Saul killed the Gibeonites? We must say, therefore, that because Saul killed [the inhabitants of] Nob, the city of the priests[31] who used to supply [the Gibeonites] with water and food,[32] Scripture considers it as though he had killed them, [although he only indirectly deprived the Gibeonites of their source of water and food].

ACCEPTING DONATIONS FROM WOMEN

(119a) Treasurers for charity may accept small donations from women [without their husband's knowledge], but not large amounts. Ravina [who was a treasurer for charity] came once to the city of Mechuza, and the housewives of Mechuza handed him chains and bracelets, which he accepted from them. Said Rabbah Tosfa'ah to him, "Haven't we learned in a *Baraita*: Treasurers for charity may accept small donations from women but not large amounts?" Replied Ravina, "For the people of Mechuza [who are very wealthy] these things are considered small amounts."

NOTES

1. The men of Anatot; see Jeremiah 11:21.
2. Numbers 22:4.
3. Genesis 22:13.
4. Wearing clothes befitting a person of higher status is an act of arrogance.
5. We compare the value of a grove of sixty trees bearing unripe dates with its value now that the unripe dates of one tree have been destroyed. See *Bava Kamma* 58a.
6. Homiletical, non-halachic teaching.
7. Exodus 21:37.
8. Leviticus 19:23ff.
9. Exodus 22:3.
10. Exodus 21:37.
11. Leviticus 5:23.
12. Oxen were used for plowing and pulling wagons.
13. The same story is related in *Sota* 49b, but there the roles are reversed: Aristobulus was inside Jerusalem, and Hyrkanus on the outside laid siege to the city.
14. The *Omer* is the measure for the offering of barley meal of the first reaping. It was brought on the second day of Pesach. See Leviticus 23:10–12.
15. On Shavuot two loaves of wheat meal of the new harvest were brought as a *bikkurim* [first-harvest] offering. See Leviticus 23:17.
16. Leviticus 18:3.
17. The person who does a compulsory mitzvah has to overcome his *yetzer hara* that tries to persuade him not to do it. The person who does a mitzvah voluntarily has no such inner opposition.
18. *Bava Kamma* 90a, 90b.
19. Isaiah 60:7.
20. Abraham meant to say: She is my sister in prophecy, i.e., my equal in prophecy. Sarah meant to say: He is my brother, i.e., my equal in prophecy (Etz Yosef).
21. The remains of all of Jacob's sons were carried out of Egypt.
22. Genesis 35:22.
23. Genesis 38:26.
24. *Bikkurim* 3:8.
25. *Bava Metzia* 107b.
26. The Book of Ben Sira (Joshua ben Sira, c. 200 B.C.E.), is one of the Apocrypha, books excluded from the Bible.
27. Genesis 13:2.
28. And Sarah could have appealed to the Court of Shem (Tosafot).
29. About forty pounds.
30. Numbers 15:19–21.
31. 1 Samuel 22:11–19.
32. The Gibeonites were employed in Nob as hewers of wood and drawers of water (Joshua 9:27).

ᨠ BABA METZIA ᨢ

THE WORKER'S RIGHT
TO RESIGN

(10a) Rav said: A worker has the right to quit even in the middle of the work day. R. Nachman replied: Yes, but as long as he has not quit [and continues to work at his job], his hand is like his employer's hand, [and what he acquires, the employer acquires]. But when he does quit, the reason why his act of cancelling his commitment is effective is, because it says, "For the children of Israel are servants to Me, they are My servants" (Leviticus 25:55)—but not the servants of servants; [and the employer is himself a servant of God. Therefore, no agreement can bind a Jew to work against his will].

HE IDENTIFIED THE LOST *GET*

(19a) Rabbah b. Bar Chanah lost a *get*[1] in the *bet midrash*. [He was the messenger who had to deliver the *get* to the woman. When the *get* was found] he said to the finder, "If you [attach importance to] a distinguishing mark, I have one; however, if you attach importance to recognition by sight, I can recognize the *get* [by the hand-writings of the scribe and the witnesses, and by its general appearance]. Thereupon they returned the *get* to him. He then said, "I do not know whether it was returned to me because of the distinguishing marks [I identified], and they hold the view that [the indication of] distinguishing marks [entitles the loser to recover the lost article] in accordance with Torah law, or whether it was returned to me because I was able to recognize it by sight, and recognition by sight is acceptable only from a Torah scholar [who can be trusted], but not from an ordinary person."

EXAMINE THE CLAIMANT

(27b) It says, [If you see your fellow's ox or sheep gone astray, . . . and you do not know the owner] you must bring the animal home [and keep it] "until your fellow comes looking for it [*derosh*], then you shall give it back to him" (Deuteronomy 22:2). [The Gemara asks:] Now would it ever enter your mind that he could give it back *before* the owner came looking for it? [After all, the passage clearly states that you do not know to whom the animal belongs? The Gemara answers:] This is what the verse means: Check him out carefully [*dorsheihu*] to make sure that he is not a fraudulent claimant.[2]

DON'T LEND A BORROWED
SEFER TORAH

(29b) The Master said: If you borrowed a *sefer Torah* [Torah scroll] from your neighbor, you may not lend it to someone else. [The Gemara asks:] Why just a *sefer Torah*; surely the same applies to any article? For R. Shimon b. Lakish said: Here[3] Rebbi has taught: A borrower is not allowed to lend [the article he borrowed], neither is a renter allowed to re-rent [the item he rented]. [The Gemara answers:] It is necessary to state it specifically in reference to a Torah scroll, because you could have argued: A person is pleased that a mitzvah is performed with his possession; therefore we are told that this is not so, [and you may not lend to someone else a borrowed *sefer Torah*].

DON'T SQUANDER
YOUR INHERITANCE

(29b) R. Yochanan said [sarcastically]: If a person inherits a great deal of money from his father, and he wants to lose it, he should wear linen garments, use glassware, and hire workers and not stay with them. [R. Yochanan meant to warn people against doing these things, for they would cause them to lose their money.] "He should wear linen garments"—this refers to linen garments manufactured in Rome [which are very expensive and not durable]. "He should use glassware"—white glassware [which was rare and very costly]. "He should hire workers and not stay with them"—this refers to (30a) workers who carelessly drive oxen [through the vineyards] and can cause serious damage [to the crops and to the oxen].

ACTS OF KINDNESS

(30b) R. Yosef taught: It says, [Jethro counseled Moses:] "Show them the path they must walk, and the things they must do" (Exodus 18:20). "Show them" means, show them how to earn a livelihood; "the path" refers to acts of kindness; "in which they must walk," refers to visiting the sick [for if you visit the sick you have to walk from your house to the house of the sick (Rif)]; "in which" refers to burial; "and the things" refers to the law; "they must do" refers to acts beyond the strict letter of the law.

The Master said: "In which they must walk" refers to visiting the sick. [The Gemara asks:] Is this not included in acts of kindness? [The Gemara answers]: It is necessary [to mention visiting the sick] for a person who was born on the same day, under the same constellation. For a Master taught: A person born on the same day, under the same constellation [as the patient he is visiting] receives one-sixtieth of the patient's sickness, yet even so, he should go and visit him. "In which" refers to burial. But isn't that, too, included in acts of kindness?—It is necessary with regard to an old man for whom [burying the dead] is undignified [nevertheless, he should do it]. "They must do" refers to acts beyond the strict letter of the law. For R. Yochanan said: Jerusalem was destroyed only because they judged in accordance with the strict interpretation of the Torah law. [The Gemara asks:] Should they then have judged with brute force? [The Gemara answers:] Put it this way: Because they insisted on the strict interpretation of the Torah law and did not judge with lenience, going beyond the letter of the law.

ADMONISH YOUR NEIGHBOR

(31a) One of the Rabbis said to Rava: It says, "Do not hate your brother in your heart. You must admonish [hoche'ach tochiach] your neighbor" (Leviticus 19:17). [Why the duplication hoche'ach tochiach?] Could you say perhaps that hoche'ach means admonish him once, and tochiach, admonish him twice? He replied: Hoche'ach implies even a hundred times. Regarding tochiach: I know only that the teacher must admonish the student; from where do we know that the student must admonish his teacher [if he has reason to do so]? From the passage, "Hoche'ach tochiach," which implies in any case where admonition is called for.

FATHER OR TEACHER,
WHO COMES FIRST?

(33a) [The Mishnah says:] If someone found two lost objects or animals: his own and that of his father, [and both need attention], his own comes first. His own and his teacher's, his own comes first. His father's and his teacher's, his teacher's comes first, because his father brought him into this world; whereas his teacher

taught him wisdom, which brings him to the World to Come. But if his father is a sage, then his father's lost object takes precedence. If his father and his teacher are each carrying a burden, he should first help his teacher put down his load and then help his father unload. If his father and his teacher are both in captivity, he should first redeem his teacher and then his father. But if his father is a sage, he should first redeem his father and then his teacher.

[The Gemara asks:] From where in Scripture is it derived [that taking care of your own lost object takes precedence]? Rav Yehudah said in Rav's name: It says, "There will not be any more poor among you" (Deuteronomy 15:4), [implying: see to it that you don't become poor]. Therefore, yours comes before anyone else's. But Rav Yehudah also said in Rav's name: Whoever lives by this rule [and always places his own interests before anyone else's] will eventually become poor.

Our Rabbis taught: The teacher [who takes precedence] is the one who taught him wisdom [i.e., Gemara, the discussion of the meaning of the Mishnah (Rashi)], but not the one who taught him Chumash and Mishnah: this is the opinion of R. Meir. R. Yehudah said: Any teacher who has taught him most of his knowledge [regardless whether Chumash, Mishnah, or Gemara]. R. Yose says: Even if he explained to him the meaning of only one single Mishnah, he is considered his teacher. Rava said: For example, R. Sechora who explained to me the meaning of the words zohama listron [a utensil mentioned in Keilim 25:3, a large spoon used for removing the scum of the soup (Rashi), is considered a teacher].

STUDYING GEMARA IS SUPREME

We learned in a Baraita: Those that study only Chumash are to be commended halfheartedly; those that study Mishnah are praiseworthy and are rewarded for it; those that study Gemara—there is nothing greater than that. But you should always run to learn the Mishnah more than the Gemara. [The Gemara asks:] This in itself is a contradiction! You say: Studying Gemara—there is nothing greater than that. And then you say: You should always run to learn the Mishnah more than the Gemara! Replied R. Yochanan: (33b) This Mishnah [which says that there is nothing greater than the study of Gemara] was learned in the time of Rabbi [Yehudah Hanassi].[4] [When he stated that] everyone dropped studying the Mishnah and took up Gemara. Therefore, later he taught them: You should always run to learn the Mishnah more than to learn the Gemara. [The Gemara asks:] From what verse is it inferred [that the study of Gemara is of unsurpassed greatness]? As R. Yehudah b. R. Ila'i expounded: What is meant by, "Proclaim to My people their willful sins, to the house of Jacob their transgressions" (Isaiah 58:1)? "Proclaim to My people their willful sins" refers to Torah scholars, whose unintentional sins are considered as willful sins, [for if they had studied Gemara they would not have erred]. "To the house of Jacob their sins" refers to the ignorant whose willful sins are considered unintentional errors, [because they did not know better]. And that is the meaning of what we learned in a Mishnah: R. Yehudah said: Be meticulous in the study of the Talmud, for a careless misinterpretation is considered tantamount to willful transgression.[5] [Hence, the study of Gemara overrides all other studies.]

R. Yehudah b. R. Ila'i expounded: What is meant by, "Listen to the word of God, you who are zealous regarding His word; Your brethren who hate you and shun you say, 'God is glorified because of my reputation'—but we will see your gladness, while they will be shamed" (Isaiah 66:5)?[6] "You who are zealous regarding His word" refers to Torah scholars [who study Gemara]. "Your brethren" refers to students of Scripture. "Who hate you" refers to people who study only Mishnah; [they look askance at Gemara scholars who are against studying only Mishnah (Rashi)]. "And shun you" refers to the ignorant [who despise all Torah scholars]. Now you might think that the hope [for joy of Gemara scholars] is lost and their prospects have vanished; therefore the verse continues, "but we will see your gladness" [we, meaning all groups will enjoy gladness]. Now you might think that Israel will be ashamed; therefore it says, "while they will be shamed" —the idolators will be shamed while Israel will rejoice.

BLESSING COMES ON THINGS THAT ARE NOT MEASURED

(42a) R. Yitzchak said: You should always have your money readily available, as it says, "Wrap up the money in your hand" (Deuteronomy 14:25), [so that, if a good business opportunity comes along, you have the money available to take advantage of it].

R. Yitzchak also said: You should always divide your money three ways: one-third should be invested in land, one-third in business, and one third should be in cash.

R. Yitzchak further said: A blessing is found only in something that is hidden from sight, [whose exact quantity the owner does not know]. For it says, "God will command the blessing for you in your storehouses [ba'asamecha]" (Deuteronomy 28:8). [R. Yitzchak translates ba'asamecha as derived from samui, "hidden things."] The yeshivah of R. Yishmael taught: A blessing comes only in things over which the eye has no power, for it says, "God will command the blessing for you in your hidden things" (ibid.).

We learned in a Baraita: When a person goes to measure the grain in his barn he should say, "May it be Your will, O Lord our God, to send a blessing on the work of our hands." When he begins to measure, he should say, "Blessed is He Who sends blessing on this heap." But if he measured first and prayed afterward, it is a vain prayer, because blessing is not found in things that are already weighed, measured, or counted, but only in things that are hidden from the eye, for it says, "God will command His blessing for you in your hidden things."

YOUR "YES" SHOULD BE HONEST

(49a) We learned: Concerning a verbal transaction, [where no deposit was given]: Rav said: [If it is not carried out,] it involves no breach of faith. R. Yochanan said: It does involve breach of faith. An objection was raised: R. Yose b. R. Yehudah said: Why does the Torah say, "You must have an honest efah [a dry measure] and an honest hin [a liquid measure]" (Leviticus 19:36). Surely a hin is included in an efah [then why does the Torah mention hin]? It comes to teach you that your "yes" [hen] should be honest, and your "no" should be honest. [Thus we see that a verbal agreement must be kept, which contradicts Rav.] Abbaye said: It means that a person should not say one thing and think something else. [When he makes a deal he should not have in mind to back out of it. But if he made a verbal agreement and retracts when the market price changes, he is not guilty of breach of faith (Rashi).]

HURTING SOMEONE'S FEELINGS

(58b) Our Rabbis taught: It says, "Do not wrong one another" (Leviticus 25:17). This is the prohibition against hurting people with words. [The Gemara asks:] Are you saying that the passage forbids hurting someone with spoken words, but perhaps that is not so, and the verse means to forbid cheating with money? [The Gemara answers:] When it says [earlier], "When you make a sale to your fellow or purchase something from your fellow, do not wrong one another" (ibid. v. 14), the verse already prohibited cheating with money. Then what is, "Do not wrong one another" referring to? To hurting someone with words alone. For example: If a person is a newly observant Jew, you are not allowed to tell him, "Remember your past deeds." If someone is a descendant of converts, you should not say to him, "Remember the deeds of your ancestors." If someone is a convert and now is coming to study Torah, you should not say to him, "Shall the mouth that ate unclean and forbidden foods, abominable and creeping things, come to study the Torah that was uttered by the mouth of the Almighty?"

If a person was afflicted by a disease, or buried his children, you should not speak to him the way Job's friends spoke to [the suffering] Job, "Behold, was your fear of God not your foolishness,[7] and so too your hope and the wholesomeness of your ways? Remember, please, which innocent person ever perished? Where have upright people ever been obliterated?"

(Job 4:6,7). [He said, in effect, "If you were truly innocent, these tragedies would have never befallen you," which is an example of hurting with words.] If there were donkey drivers who were looking to haul someone's grain, don't tell them, "Go to so-and-so who sells grain," knowing full well that this person never sold grain in his life. R. Yehudah said: You should not pretend to be interested in buying merchandise when you have no money, [since it disappoints the seller it is considered "hurting with words"]. The concept of "hurting with words" depends on a person's intent, which is hidden from anybody else. And regarding anything that depends on a person's intent it says, "And you shall fear your God" (Leviticus 25:17). [Only God knows what is in your mind.]

R. Yochanan said in the name of R. Shimon b. Yocha'i: Hurting someone with words is a greater sin than cheating him with money. For concerning hurting with words it says, "And you shall fear your God," but not concerning cheating financially. R. Elazar said: [Hurting with words is a greater sin because it] affects the victim himself, whereas defrauding him affects only his money. R. Shmuel b. Nachmani said: Money that was defrauded can be restored, but for hurt feelings there is no remedy. [Appeasing him does not alleviate the pain (*Shittah Mekubetzet*). Therefore hurting with words is a more serious transgression.]

A Tanna recited the following *Baraita* in front of R. Nachman b. Yitzchak: Making your neighbor's face turn white with shame in public is tantamount to committing murder. Replied R. Nachman b. Yitzchak: What you are saying is correct, because I have seen the red leave the face [of a person who has been shamed], and he turned white; [the blood rushing away from the face is akin to bloodshed].

Abbaye said to R. Dimi [who came from Eretz Yisrael]: What are they careful about in Eretz Yisrael? He replied: They are careful not to embarrass people. For R. Chanina said: All people go down to Gehinnom except three. [The Gemara asks:] Do you actually mean everyone goes down to Gehinnom! Rather what R. Chanina means to say is: All who [have sinned enough to warrant] going down to Gehinnom come out soon, except for three who go down but do not come up [soon but stay there a long time (Tosafot)], namely: Someone who lives with another man's wife, someone who shames his neighbor in public, and someone who calls his neighbor an embarrassing nickname. [The Gemara asks:] Isn't calling by a nickname the same as shaming; [why are they considered as two]? [The Gemara answers:] Even if the neighbor is used to being called by a demeaning nickname, [and does not feel humiliated when hearing it], still it is reprehensible to do that. [And that is why they are considered two separate things.]

PUBLICLY EMBARRASSING OTHERS

Rabba b. Bar Chanah said in R. Yochanan's name: (59a) It is better for a person to live with a doubtful married woman [e.g., a divorced woman whose *get* may be invalid], rather than that he should publicly put his neighbor to shame. From where do we know this? From the following verse as expounded by Rava: [David says,] "But when I limped [because I married Batsheba[8] (Rashi)] they rejoiced and gathered; the wretched gathered against me—I know not why, they tore at me and would not be silenced" (Psalms 35:15). David cried out to the Holy One, blessed be He, "Master of the universe! You know perfectly well that if they would tear my flesh, the blood would not pour forth to the earth, [because of all the insults they hurl at me, my blood is drained from my flesh]. What's more, even while they are engaged in studying the tractates *Nega'im* and *Ohalot* [two very intricate tractates dealing with leprous diseases and purity, which have no bearing on adultery or the death penalty], they taunt me, saying, 'David, if a person lives with a married woman what death penalty is he liable to?' I reply, 'He is put to death by strangulation, but he has a share in the World to Come. But a person who publicly puts his neighbor to shame has no portion in the World to Come.'" [Which proves Rabbah b. Bar Chanah's point.]

Mar Zutra b. Tuvyah said in Rav's name—others say, R. Chana b. Bizna in the name of R. Shimon Chasida— still others say, R. Yehudah said in the name of R. Shimon b. Yocha'i: A person should rather throw himself into a fiery furnace than embarrass his neighbor in public. From where do we know this? From Tamar, about whom it says, "When she was being taken out [to be burned for alleged immorality] she sent the security to her father-in-law [Judah] with the message, "I am pregnant by the man who is the owner of these articles" (Genesis 38:25). [Tamar chose to be put to death rather than identify Judah as the man by whom she was pregnant and publicly put him to shame.]

WHEN SHOULD YOU FOLLOW YOUR WIFE'S ADVICE?

R. Chanina b. R. Idi said: What is meant by the verse, "Do not wrong one another [*amito*]"? It means: Do not wrong a people that is with you in learning and good deeds. [*Amito* is read as two words: *am ito*, "the people with him".] Rav said: You should always be careful not to hurt your wife's feelings. Since she cries easily [and is very sensitive], she is quickly hurt.

R. Elazar said: Since the destruction of the *Bet Hamikdash*, the gates of prayer are locked, for it says, "Though I would cry out and plead, He shut out my prayer" (Lamentations 3:8). But even though the gates of prayer are locked, the gates of tears are not closed, for it says, "Hear my prayer, O God, give ear to my outcry, be not mute to my tears" (Psalms 39:13).

Rav further said: Whoever follows his wife's advice will go down to Gehinnom, for it says, "There had never been anyone like Ahab who sold himself to do what was evil in the eyes of God, because Jezebel his wife had incited him" (1 Kings 21:25). [Scripture blames Jezebel for Ahab's corruption and ruin.] R. Papa said to Abaye: But people say: If your wife is short, bend down and listen to her, [so you *should* follow her advice]!—There is no difficulty: On general matters [you should not follow your wife's advice], but on matters of the household [you should consult your wife, since there she is the expert]. According to others: On religious matters [you should not follow your wife's advice], but on secular matters you should.

THREE SERIOUS CRIMES

R. Chisda said: All gates [of prayer] are closed, except for the gates through which pass the cries of people who have been wronged, for it says, "Behold, the Lord standing by a wall of wrongs [*anach*], and in His hands were the wrongs" (Amos 7:7). [Anach, usually translated as "plumbline," is seen here as related to *ona'ah*, "wrong": God will answer the cries of people who have been wronged and defrauded.] R. Elazar said: All [sins] are punished through an agent, except for the wrong of overreaching, [which is punished by God Himself], for it says, "And in His hands were the wrongs." R. Abbahu said: There are three [crimes] for which the Curtain of Heaven is not closed, [meaning, there is no partition that stands between God and these crimes; He is constantly aware of them, and will punish the perpetrators]. They are: Overreaching, robbery, and idol worship. Cheating—because it says, "In His hands was the wrong [of overreaching]." Robbery—because it says, "Corruption and thievery are heard in [Jerusalem] before Me *continually*—hence disease and affliction" (Jeremiah 6:7). Idolatry—because it says, "The people who *continually* anger Me to My face [by setting up idols even in Jerusalem, and even in the Temple itself (Radak)]" (Isaiah 65:3).

SUSTENANCE IS THE BASIS OF DOMESTIC PEACE

Rav Yehudah said: You should always make sure to provide for your family, because domestic strife usually erupts when there is no sustenance, as it says, "He endows your realm with peace, and satisfies you with choice wheat" (Psalms 147:14). Said R. Papa: The popular saying puts it this way: When the barley is gone from the pitcher, strife comes knocking at the door. R. Chinena b. Papa said: You should always make sure to provide food for your family, because Israel was called poor only on account of the lack of grain. For it says, "It happened that whenever Israel would sow,

Midian . . . would encamp against them and destroy the produce of the land . . . " and the next verse states, "Israel became very impoverished because of Midian" (Judges 6:3–6).

BLESSING IS BESTOWED BECAUSE OF YOUR WIFE

R. Chelbo said: You should always be careful to give your wife the honor due to her, because your home is blessed only because of your wife, for it says, "He [metaphorically referring to God[9]] treated Abram well because of her" (Genesis 12:16). And with that in mind Rava said to the people of Mechuza: Honor your wives, so that you will become rich.

THE TORAH IS NOT IN HEAVEN

[The following *aggadah*, which demonstrates the extraordinary greatness of the Sages, is one of the most famous anecdotes in the Gemara.] We learned in a Mishnah:[10] Someone built a [portable] oven [by assembling parts]. He placed a layer of sand between the parts [which did not bond together. He then coated the assembled oven on the outside with clay, the same way all ovens are coated]. R. Eliezer said: An oven like this is not susceptible to *tum'ah* [uncleanness, because it is not a whole oven but a combination of separate parts, since the sand does not fuse the parts together]. The Sages said: An oven like this is susceptible to *tuma'ah*, [because the clay coating unites the parts into a complete vessel]. (59b) And this was called "the oven of Achna'i."[11] [The Gemara asks:] Why was it called "the oven of Achna'i"? R. Yehudah said in Shmuel's name: Because the Sages encircled the problem of this oven with various proofs like an *achna'i*, [a snake that coils itself], and proved that it is susceptible to *tum'ah*.

We learned in a *Baraita*: On that day [when the vote was taken], R. Eliezer advanced every conceivable argument, but the other Sages would not accept them. So he said to them, "If the *halachah* agrees with me, let this carob tree [outside the *bet midrash*] prove it!" Instantly the carob tree uprooted itself and moved a hundred—some say four hundred—cubits from its place. The Sages said, "You cannot bring a proof from a carob tree!" R. Eliezer said to them, "If the *halachah* agrees with me, let the stream of water prove it!" Immediately, the water in the stream started flowing backward. They retorted, "You cannot bring proof from a stream of water!" R. Eliezer persisted, "If the *halachah* agrees with me, let the walls of the *bet midrash* prove it!"

Thereupon the walls began to tilt as if to fall. At this point R. Yehoshua scolded the walls, saying, "When Torah scholars are involved in a halachic argument, what right do you have to interfere?" Out of respect for R. Yehoshua they did not collapse, and out of respect for R. Eliezer they did not straighten up, and they remain in their tilted position to this day. Finally, R. Eliezer said, "If the *halachah* agrees with me, let the heavens prove it." Thereupon a heavenly voice was heard saying, "How can you argue with R. Eliezer? The *halachah* is as he states in every instance!" But R. Yehoshua stood up and exclaimed, "[The Torah] is not in heaven!" (Deuteronomy 30:12). What did R. Yehoshua mean by this? R. Yirmeyah explains: He meant to say that the Torah has already been given us at Mount Sinai, and hence we do not pay heed to heavenly voices, because You have already written, " . . . to follow the majority" (Exodus 23:2).

[The underlying thought of this *aggadah* is that since the Torah was given to us, the rules of *halachah* are immutable and cannot be overturned by miracles, heavenly signs, or any other outside influences. No one, be he ever so great, can stand above the rules of halachic decision-making laid down by the Torah and the Sages.]

R. ELIEZER EXCOMMUNICATED

R. Natan met Elijah [the Prophet], and asked him, "What did the Holy One, blessed be He, do when this happened?" [Replied Elijah,] "He smiled and said, 'My sons have overcome Me in debate, My sons have overcome Me in debate!'" It was said: On that day, all the articles [that had fallen into this oven], which had been declared *tahor* (clean) by R. Eliezer, [were declared *tamei* (unclean)] and were brought and burnt in fire. [As a result of R. Eliezer's refusal to accept the majority opinion,] they took a vote and decided to pronounce a ban against him. They then said, "Who will go and inform him?" "I will go," replied R. Akiva, "lest a person who is unworthy of such a mission will go and thus destroy the whole world." What did R. Akiva do? He put on black garments and wrapped himself in black [as a sign of anguish and mourning], and sat at a distance of four cubits from R. Eliezer. "Akiva," said R. Eliezer to him, "What is the matter?" He replied, "Rabbi, it seems to me that your colleagues are shunning you." [Realizing that he had been banned,] he tore his garment, removed his shoes, and sat on the ground, while tears were flowing from his eyes. The world was then stricken [with a calamity]: a third of the olive crop, a third of the wheat harvest, and a third of the barley harvest [was lost]. Some say, the dough in women's hands became spoiled.

We learned in a *Baraita*: Great was the calamity on that day, for everything on which R. Eliezer fixed his gaze burned up. R. Gamliel [the *Nasi* and the power behind the ban against R. Eliezer] was sailing in a ship [on the day the ban was proclaimed]. A huge wave rose up and nearly drowned him. "It seems to me," he said, "that this must be on account of R. Eliezer b. Hyrkanos," whereupon he rose to his feet and declared, "Master of the universe, it is known and revealed before You that I acted, not to safeguard my honor, nor to safeguard the honor of my father's house, but for Your Own honor, so that dispute may not run rampant in Israel." At this, the raging sea became calm.

Ima Shalom was R. Eliezer's wife, and the sister of R. Gamliel. After this incident she did not allow R. Eliezer to "put down his head" [i.e., to recite the *Tachanun* prayer of supplication that is said after the *Shemoneh Esrei* on weekdays, but not on Rosh Chodesh[12] and Yom Tov. She was afraid that R. Eliezer might cry out to God about his chagrin at being excommunicated, and that God, in answer to his prayer, would punish R. Gamliel, her brother]. Now a certain day happened to be Rosh Chodesh, but she thought that the previous month had twenty-nine days, and that the thirtieth day was Rosh Chodesh on which R. Eliezer could not say *Tachanun* in any case, so that she did not watch him that day. But the previous month actually had thirty days, and Rosh Chodesh fell on the thirty-first, so that he was allowed to say *Tachanun* on the thirtieth day. According to others, [she was distracted because] a poor man came to the door, and she took out some bread to him. When she returned she found that he had put down his head [and was reciting *Tachanun*]. "Arise," she cried out. "You have killed my brother!" Meanwhile an announcement was issued from the house of R. Gamliel that he had died. "How did you know that?" R. Eliezer asked his wife. She replied, "I have a tradition from the house of my ancestor [King David]: All [heavenly] gates are closed, except for the gates of prayers [of those who cry because of hurt feelings]."[13]

THE SIN OF HURTING
A CONVERT'S FEELINGS

Our Rabbis taught: Whoever hurts the feelings of a convert violates three negative commandments, and whoever oppresses him transgresses two. What are the three negative commandments against hurting a convert's feelings? "Do not hurt the feelings of a convert" (Exodus 22:20); "When a proselyte comes to live in your land, do not hurt his feelings" (Leviticus 19:33); and "Each of you shall not aggrieve his fellow" (ibid. 25:17), and a convert is included in "fellow." [The Gemara objects:] But against oppression there are also three injunctions, namely, "Do not oppress [the convert]" (Exodus 22:20); "Do not oppress a convert" (ibid. 23:9); and "When you lend money to My people, to the poor man among you, do not press him for repayment" (ibid. 22:24), which also includes a convert. [The Gemara answers:] Say that both are forbidden by three negative commandments.

We learned in a *Baraita*: R. Eliezer Hagadol said: Why has the Torah warned us against hurting the feelings of a convert in thirty-six, or as others have it, in forty-six places? Because he has an innate leaning toward evil, [and if his feelings are hurt, he may relapse]. [The Gemara asks:] What is meant by, "[Do not hurt the feelings of a stranger or oppress him,] for you were foreigners in Egypt"? It has been taught: R. Natan said: Do not taunt your neighbor with the defect you yourself have. [Remember, you were once foreigners yourselves.] And so a popular adage has it, "If someone's relative was hanged, don't say to him, 'Please hang up this fish for me.'"

UNFAIR AND
DECEPTIVE PRACTICES

(60a) [The Mishnah says:] R. Yehudah said: A storekeeper may not hand out parched corn or nuts to little children, because he gets them used to shopping in his store [when their mother sends them to buy something and thereby encroaches on the income of the other merchants]. The Sages permit it. He may not reduce the price [and undercut the competiton]. But the Sages say: More power to him [for bringing down the cost of living]. A storekeeper may not sift ground beans [in order to raise the price], so says Abba Shaul. The Sages permit it [because the buyer estimates the difference between sifted and unsifted beans]. But they admit that he may not pick out the refuse from the top of the bin [leaving the refuse underneath], since that would be deceiving the eye, [for the buyer thinks that the contents of the entire bin have been sifted]. [Old] slaves, cattle, or vessels may not be made to look attractive [when offered for sale, because that would be deception].

(60b) A certain old [Canaanite] slave dyed his hair and beard [black to make him look young] and came to Rava, saying, "Buy me." Replied Rava, "[It says:] Let the poor be the members of your own household" (*Avot* 1:5), [meaning, I prefer to support the poor of my own people]. The Canaanite then went to R. Papa b. Shmuel, who bought him. One day R. Papa said to him, "Bring me a drink of water." Thereupon he went and washed the dye out of his hair and beard and said, "See, I am older than your father. [You cannot ask me to do such lowly chores]." So R. Papa applied to himself the verse, "The righteous one is spared affliction, [meaning Rava], but the wicked one comes in his place" (Proverbs 11:8).

HONESTY IN WEIGHT
AND MEASURES

(61b) [The Gemara asks:] Why is it necessary for the Torah to state, "Do not steal" (Leviticus 19:11)? [After all, it can be derived from the injunction against usury and cheating, which are themselves forms of stealing]?[14] [The Gemara answers:] The verse means to say: "Do not steal," even in order to cause [momentary] vexation to your friend [at his loss, but you plan to return it]. "Do not steal" includes even a situation where you steal with the intention of repaying double; [you want to give the other person a gift but you know

that he would never accept it; you therefore steal from him so that the Bet Din would find you liable to make double restitution. This is forbidden].[15]

R. Yeimar said to R. Ashi: Why is it necessary for the Torah to specify an injunction against false weights,[16] [surely this is included in the prohibition against charging interest and cheating]? [R. Ashi replied: It is mentioned specifically] to forbid the placing of weights in salt [which will make them heavier, and using them when buying something by weight (Rashi)]. [The Gemara asks:] But that is plain robbery! [Why does the Torah have to make special mention of that?] [The Gemara answers:] It comes to teach us that he transgresses from the time he rigs the weight, [even before he actually used it].

We learned in a *Baraita*: It says, "You shall not commit a perversion in justice, in measures of length, weight or volume" (Leviticus 19:35). "In measure of length" refers to measuring land, and it forbids measuring for one in the summer and for the other in the winter. [In measuring land he is using a rope to divide a parcel equally between two brothers. In the summer the rope is dry and shrinks, so that one brother will receive less land; while in the winter the rope is moist and expands, allotting more land to the other brother.] "In weight" forbids the placing of weights in salt; and "in volume" teaches that he should not cause foam to form, [for when the foam settles, there is less liquid in the measure]. And from this we can draw a *kal vachomer* [logical] conclusion: If the Torah objected to a false *mesurah*, which is only a thirty-sixth of a *log*, how much more so a *hin*, half a *hin*, a third of a *hin*, and a quarter of a *hin*; a *log*, half a *log*, or a quarter of a *log*.[17]

THE EXODUS AS REASON FOR
OBSERVANCE OF *MITZVOT*

Rava said: Why does the Torah mention the Exodus in conjunction with interest, *tzitzit*, and false weights?[18] The Holy One, blessed be He, said: I am the One who in Egypt distinguished between a firstborn and one who was not a firstborn,[19] I am the One who will mete out punishment to a person who claims his money belongs to a non-Jew and lends it to a Jew on interest. [A non-Jew is permitted to charge interest. This Jew misled people, saying that his money belonged to a non-Jew, and lent it to Jews on interest.] Or someone who places his weights in salt, or who attaches to his garment a thread of *tzitzit* that was dyed in artificial blue [and fools the people, claiming that it is genuine *techeilet*, which is made of the blood of the rare *chalazon* and is very expensive].

Ravina came to Sura on the Euphrates. R. Chanina of Sura on the Euphrates asked him: Why did the Torah mention the Exodus in conjunction with the prohibition against eating non-kosher small crawling creatures?[20] He replied: The Holy One, blessed be He, said: I who distinguished between a firstborn and one who was not firstborn, I will know and punish a person who mixes the innards of non-kosher fish with those of kosher fish and sells them together to a Jew. He said to him: My question is not why the Exodus is mentioned, but rather why it says [in connection with the prohibition against eating small creatures, "For I am God who *elevates* you from the land of Egypt" (Leviticus 11:45) [whereas in connection with interest, etc., it says, "who *brought you out* of Egypt"]?

Ravina told him: This comes to teach us what was taught by the yeshivah of R. Yishmael, namely: The Holy One, blessed be He, said: If I had taken out the people of Israel for no other reason than this, that they should not defile themselves by eating crawling things, it would be sufficient; [by not eating these loathsome creatures they become spiritually elevated]. He countered: Is then the reward [of abstaining from eating crawling things] greater than the reward [of obeying the *mitzvot* concerning] interest, *tzitzit*, and weights? [Why does the Torah point to abstaining from crawling things as being sufficient grounds for the Exodus?] Ravina replied: Although their reward is not greater [than keeping these other *mitzvot*], it is more disgusting for a person to eat these creatures, [and since the Jewish people are elevated above such revolting things, they are worthy to be redeemed].

YOUR OWN LIFE
TAKES PRECEDENCE

(62a) We learned in a *Baraita*: If two people are traveling through a desert, and one has a pitcher of water. [It comes to the point that] if both drink, they will both die, but if one drinks, he can reach the nearest village [and survive]. Ben Petirah taught: It is better that both should drink and die, rather than that one should watch his friend die. Until R. Akiva came and taught: It says, "Let your brother live with you" (Leviticus 25:36), [which implies that] your life takes precedence over his life. ["With you" denotes that your brother takes second place to you.]

ILL-GOTTEN GAINS
WILL BE LOST

(70b) It says, "One who multiplies his wealth through interest and increase gathers it for the patron of the poor" (Proverbs 28:8). [God will transfer his ill-gotten profits to generous people (Ibn Ezra).] What is meant by "the patron of the poor"? Rav said: Someone like King Shapur [a Persian king who took money from the Jews and gave it to poor heathens (Rashi)].

(75b) R. Shimon said: Those who lend money on interest lose more than they gain. And not only that, they consider Moses to be a fool and his Torah to be untrue, for they say: If Moses had known that there is

so much profit in usury, he would not have written in the Torah that it is prohibited.

When R. Dimi came [from Eretz Yisrael to Babylonia] he said: How do we know, if someone is owed a *maneh* by his neighbor, and he knows that his neighbor does not have the money to repay him, that the creditor is not allowed to pass before the debtor [because it will make him feel uncomfortable]? Because it says, "Do not press him for repayment" (Exodus 22:24). R. Ammi and R. Assi both said: [When he does appear before the debtor,] it is as if he is putting him through two kinds of suffering, for it says, "You have let men ride over us; we have endured fire and water" (Psalms 66:12).

NEVER LEND MONEY
WITHOUT WITNESSES

Rav Yehudah said in the name of Rav: Whoever has money and lends it to someone without witnesses transgresses the law of "Do not place a stumbling block before the [morally] blind" (Leviticus 19:14) [because he may cause the debtor to deny that he borrowed the money]. Resh Lakish said: The creditor [who lent money without witnesses] brings a curse on himself, [because when he comes to collect the debt, and the debtor denies having borrowed the money, the people will curse the creditor thinking that he wants to collect money he is not owed], for it says, "May the lying lips be silenced which speak falsehood about a righteous one with arrogance and contempt" (Psalms 31:19).

The Rabbis said to R. Ashi: Ravina fulfilled everything the Sages decreed. R. Ashi, [wanting to test Ravina], sent to him on Friday afternoon [shortly before Shabbat] the following message, "Please send me ten *zuz* [as a loan], because I came across a small parcel of land, which I want to buy." He replied, "Bring witnesses, and we will draw up a note." "Does that apply even to me?" Rav Ashi sent back. "To you more than to anyone else," he retorted. "Being very involved in your learning, you are liable to forget [that you borrowed the money], and I would draw a curse on myself."

IT WAS THEIR OWN FAULT

Our Rabbis taught: There are three people who voice their grievances [in the Bet Din] and are not answered, [because they brought their troubles on themselves], namely: someone who has money and lends it without witnesses; someone who acquires a master for himself [the Gemara will explain]; and a husband who is bossed by his wife. [The Gemara asks:] "Someone who acquires a master for himself"—what does that mean? Some say it refers to a person who says that his money really belongs to a gentile, [because he does not want to appear as such a wealthy person. The gentile may hear what he said and may take away the money from him]. Others say that it is referring to someone who signs his property over to his children in his lifetime. Others say: It is referring to someone who is unsuccessful in one city and refuses to move to another city where perhaps he will do better.

BEYOND THE LETTER
OF THE LAW

(83a) Some porters [carelessly] broke a barrel of wine belonging to Rabbah b. Bar Chanah. [Since they refused to pay for the damage] he took their garments. They in turn went and complained to Rav. "Give them back their garments," Rav said to Rabbah b. Bar Chanah. "Is that the law?" he questioned. [Since they were negligent, they are legally required to pay for the damage.] "Yes," Rav replied. "Because it says, 'In order that you may walk in the way of the good'" (Proverbs 2:20). [You should go beyond the letter of the law and be forgiving.] Rabbah b. Bar Chanah returned the garments, [but the porters were not satisfied]. They said, "We are poor people. We worked so hard all day, we are hungry, and we have nothing to eat. Do we get absolutely nothing?" "Go pay them," said Rav. "Is that the law?" he asked. "Yes, 'and keep the paths of the righteous,'" (the conclusion of Proverbs 2:20).

THE SUN RISES FOR *TZADDIKIM*

(83b) R. Zeira expounded—others say, R. Yosef learned: What is the meaning of the verse, "You bring on darkness and it is night when all the beasts of the forest stir" (Psalms 104:20)? "You bring on darkness and it is night" refers to this world, that is compared to the night. "When all the beasts of the forest stir" refers to the wicked who are like the beasts of the forest; [in this world they can do whatever they want]. "The sun rises and they are gathered in, and couch in their dens" (ibid. v. 22). "The sun rises"—for the *tzaddikim* [in the World to Come]; "and [the wicked] are gathered in"— to Gehinnom; "and couch in their dens" (ibid. v. 22)— there is not a single *tzaddik* who does not have a dwelling befitting his stature [in the World to Come]. "Man then goes out to his work, and to his labor until the evening" (ibid. v. 23). "Man then goes out to his work" means, the *tzaddikim* go forth to receive their reward; "and to his labor until the evening" refers to a person who has completed his service [to God] until the evening [i.e., until the day of death].

R. SHIMON B. ELAZAR
ARRESTS THIEVES

R. Elazar b. R. Shimon met a Roman officer who was in charge of arresting thieves. "How do you detect them?" he asked him. "Aren't they like wild animals about which it says, 'You bring on darkness when all the beasts of the forest stir'?" (Psalms 104:20). Others say, he quoted the verse, "He lurks in hiding like a lion in his lair" (ibid. 10:9). R. Elazar continued, "Perhaps you are arresting innocent people and letting the guilty go free?" The officer replied, "What shall I do? I follow the Emperor's orders, and I am doing the best I can." Said E. Elazar b. R. Shimon, "Come, I will teach you what to do. Go into a restaurant at the fourth hour of the day [about 10 A.M., when everyone is having breakfast]. If you see someone dozing with a cup of wine in his hand, ask around about him. If he is a Torah scholar, [you can understand that he is tired] because he woke up very early to learn Torah; if he is a laborer, he woke up early to do his work; if he is a night worker [and nobody heard him banging his hammer during the night, the reason that he is sleeping now is,] he may have been rolling sheet metal at night [which makes no noise]. But if this person is none of the above, he is a thief; arrest him, [because he was up during the night burglarizing homes]."

When the Roman authorities heard about Rabbi Elazar b. R. Shimon's astute advice they said, "Let the reader of the letter become the messenger." [I.e., the one who gave the advice should carry it out.] Thereupon R. Elazar b. R. Shimon was put in charge of catching thieves. R. Yehoshua b. Korcha [who was very upset at this] sent word to him, "Vinegar, son of wine, [wretched son of a *tzaddik*]! How much longer are you going to hand over the people of our God to be executed?" R. Elazar sent back the message, "[What am I doing wrong?] I am pruning the thorns from the vineyard!" Retorted R. Yehoshua b. Korcha, "[That is not your responsibility.] Let the owner of the vineyard [God] Himself prune the thorns."

THE IMPUDENT LAUNDRYMAN

One day a certain laundryman met R. Elazar b. R. Shimon, and called him to his face, "Vinegar, son of wine!" Rabbi Elazar b. R. Shimon said to himself, "Since he is so brazen, he must be a vile criminal." So he gave an order to have him arrested. When he relaxed somewhat he went to have him released, but he was unable to free him. He then applied [to the laundryman] the verse, "One who guards his mouth and tongue guards himself from trouble" (Proverbs 21:23). [The Romans] hanged him, and R. Elazar b. R. Shimon stood under the gallows and cried. Said [his disciples] to him, "Rabbi, don't feel bad. [He was a depraved fellow], for he and his son had relations with a betrothed girl on Yom Kippur." [According to Torah law, having relations with a betrothed girl is punishable by stoning, and the corpse of one who was stoned is hanged. Thus the laundryman got the punishment that was coming to him.]

When R. Elazar heard this, he put his hand on his heart and said, "Rejoice, my heart! If in matters where you were in doubt [whether or not the person was guilty], he proved to be thoroughly wicked, how much more are you right in cases when you are certain [about something]!" [He said to his body,] "I am sure that neither worms nor decay will have power over you." [He was sure that he was free of any wrongdoing.] Nevertheless, he later began to worry about the death that he had caused. So they gave him a sleeping potion and brought him into a marble operating room. They opened his abdomen,[21] and many basketfuls of fat were excised from him,[22] which they then placed in the sun during Tammuz and Av [the hottest months of the year], and the fat did not decay. [The Gemara asks:] But fat never decays! [The Gemara answers:] If it has red streaks [of flesh] running through it, it does decay; but here, although it did have red streaks, it did not decay. [When he came out of the anesthesia], Rabbi Elazar b. R. Shimon applied to himself the verse, "My flesh, too, rests in confidence" (Psalms 16:9).

The same thing happened to R. Yishmael b. R. Yose. [He, too, was put in charge of catching thieves.] (84a) One day Elijah met him and admonished him, "How much longer are you going to hand over the people of our God to be executed?" "What can I do," he replied. "It is an imperial decree." Replied Elijah, "Your father [who defied Emperor Hadrian] ran away to Asia. You run away to Ludkia!"

When R. Yishmael b. R. Yose and R. Elazar b. R. Shimon met [and stood waist to waist], a yoke of oxen could pass below them without touching them [that is how obese they were]. A certain [Roman] noblewoman said to them, "Your children are not yours," [because you could not possibly live with your wives on account of your physical build]. They replied, "Our wives' girth is even greater than ours." [Or: Our wives' desire is greater than ours.] "If so, all the more reason that your children aren't yours," she retorted. Some say, this is what they told her; "For as a man is, so is his strength" (Judges 8:21). Other say, this is what they said: "Love suppresses the flesh." [The Gemara asks:] But why did they have to answer her at all? Doesn't it say, "Do not answer a fool according to his foolishness" (Proverbs 26:4)? [The Gemara answers:] They wanted to make it clear to her, so that she should not malign the reputation of their children.

R. YOCHANAN'S SPECIAL RADIANCE

R. Yochanan said: I am the only one left of the beautiful people of Jerusalem [people whose faces radiated with a special glow (Rashi)]. [Comments the Gemara:] If a person wants to see this radiance of R. Yochanan, he should take a silver cup straight out of the silversmith's furnace [while it is still glowing], fill it with the pits of a red pomegranate, surround the top with a crown of red roses, and place it between the sun

and the shade; and this radiance is only a semblance of R. Yochanan's beauty.

[The Gemara asks:] Is that so? For did not a Master say: The beauty of R. Kahane is only a small portion of R. Abbahu's; the beauty of R. Abbahu is only a small portion of Father Jacob's; our Father Jacob's beauty was only a small portion of Adam's; and R. Yochanan is not mentioned at all in this category! [The Gemara answers:] R. Yochanan is different, [he did have this luminous glow,] but he did not have a beard.

R. Yochanan used to go and sit at the gate of the *mikveh*. He would say, "When the daughters of Israel will come up from performing the mitzvah of immersing in a *mikveh*, let them see my face, that they should have sons that are as beautiful and as learned as I am." Said the Rabbis to him, "Aren't you afraid of an evil eye?" He replied, "I am an offspring of Joseph against whom an evil eye is powerless." For it says, "A charming son is Joseph, a charming son by the well" (Genesis 49:22), on which R. Abbahu commented: Don't read *alei ayin*, "by the well," but rather, *olei ayin*, "above the [influence of the evil] eye." R. Yose b. R. Chanina derived it from, [Jacob's blessing to Joseph's sons], "And may they proliferate abundantly like fish within the land" (Genesis 48:16): just as fish in the seas are covered by water, and the evil eye has no power over them, so, too, the children of Joseph—the [evil] eye has no power over them.

R. YOCHANAN AND RESH LAKISH

One day R. Yochanan was bathing in the Jordan. Resh Lakish saw him and gracefully jumped into the Jordan after him. Said R. Yochanan to him, "Your strength should be used for Torah."[23] Retorted Resh Lakish, "Your beauty should be for women." R. Yochanan said to him, "If you will abandon your ways, I will give you my sister [in marriage] who is even more beautiful than I am." Resh Lakish agreed; he then wanted to turn around to collect his weapons but suddenly he could not jump as far as he did before, [for as soon as he committed himself to live by the spiritual values of the Torah his physical strength waned (Rashi)]. R. Yochanan taught him Chumash and Mishnah, and Resh Lakish became a Torah scholar [and the study partner of R. Yochanan].

One day [Resh Lakish and R. Yochanan] had a dispute in the *bet midrash* [about a Mishnah in *Keilim* that says:] A sword, a knife, a dagger, a spear, a handsaw, and a scythe, at what point can they become *tamei* [unclean]? When their manufacturing process is completed, [and they are finished utensils]. And at what point are they considered finished utensils? R. Yochanan said: When they are hardened in the furnace. Resh Lakish said: When they have been made to shine by dipping them in water. [Referring to Resh Lakish's past,] R. Yochanan said to Resh Lakish, "A robber knows his trade. [As a former bandit you are an expert on weapons' production.]" [Deeply hurt,] Resh Lakish retorted, "What good have you done me? [When I was the head of a gang of bandits] they called me Master, and here they call me Master!" R. Yochanan shot back, "I did you a lot of good, for I brought you under the wings of the *Shechinah*!" R. Yochanan was very saddened [by Resh Lakish's remark, and as a result,] Resh Lakish became sick. R. Yochanan's sister [Resh Lakish's wife] came and cried to him, "[Please pray for my husband!] Do it for the sake of my children!" He replied, "Leave your orphans; I will sustain them!" (Jeremiah 49:11). "Don't let me become a widow!" she cried. "Your widows can depend on me" (ibid.), R. Yochanan replied. [He refused to listen to her plea.] Subsequently Resh Lakish died.

R. Yochanan was very upset [when he realized how much he missed Resh Lakish as a study partner]. Said the Rabbis, "Who will go and console R. Yochanan? Let R. Elazar b. Pedat go [and be his new study partner]; he is very clever." So he went and sat before him, [and they tried learning together]. Anything that R. Yochanan said, R. Elazar b. Pedat told him, "You are right. There is a *Baraita* that supports your view." [Exasperated,] R. Yochanan exclaimed, "And you want to replace Resh Lakish! When I said something to Resh Lakish [he did not tell me, 'You are right']; he would ask me twenty-four questions, and I would give him twenty-four answers, and as a result, the entire subject became clearer. And what do you say, 'You are right. There is a *Baraita* that supports your view.' Don't I know myself that what I am saying is right?" So R. Yochanan went and ripped his clothes, crying, "Where are you, O son of Lakish. Where are you, O son of Lakish!"[24] He kept on crying until he lost his mind. [Seeing him in this condition,] the Rabbis prayed for mercy for him, and he died.

R. ELAZAR'S AGONY
AND VINDICATION

(84b) [At this point the Gemara returns to the story of R. Elazar b. R. Shimon (on 84a) whose judgment proved to be correct even in a doubtful case.] In spite of that, R. Elazar b. R. Shimon still did not feel totally secure, [worrying that perhaps he had made a mistake once and arrested an innocent person], and so he inflicted suffering on himself. At night they would spread sixty sheets for him, and in the morning they would remove sixty buckets of blood from under him. Every morning his wife would prepare for him sixty different types of fig pudding. After he ate them he felt better. His wife did not allow him to go to the *bet midrash*, so that he would not be taunted by the other scholars. At night, R. Elazar b. R. Shimon said to his afflictions, "My brothers and good friends, come to me!" In the morning he would tell them, "Please, go away, because you will prevent me from learning To-

rah!" When his wife heard him say this one day, she cried out, "You yourself are bringing these afflictions on you! You are wasting my father's money [with the special care and food you need]!" So she left him and went to her father's house.

[Meanwhile, a storm had blown up at sea, and a boat coming from R. Elazar's town was in danger of sinking. The sailors began praying and finally cried out in desperation, "Save us, O God, for the sake of R. Elazar b. R. Shimon!" The storm subsided (Tosafot)], and when the ship safely sailed into port, sixty sailors presented R. Elazar b. Shimon with sixty slaves, each bearing sixty purses of money, and they made for him the sixty different types of fig pudding that he ate.

One day, his wife said to her daughter, "Go and see how your father is feeling." She went, and R. Elazar said to her, "Tell your mother that we are wealthier than her parents." And he applied to himself the verse, "She [the Torah] is like a merchant's ship; from afar she brings her sustenance" (Proverbs 31:14), [meaning, the sailors who were saved in the merit of his great Torah scholarship had brought him wealth]. He ate [the fig pudding], drank, and became better. [Since his wife was not there to stop him,] he went to the *bet midrash*, where he was asked questions by sixty [women] about different types of blood [discharge they had experienced], and he declared them all clean, [and told them they needed no immersion in a *mikveh*]. The Rabbis grumbled about this, saying, "Is it possible, that [out of sixty cases] there was not at least one about which there was some doubt?" He retorted, "If I am right, all these women will [give birth] to boys; if not, let there be at least one girl among them." All the children born were boys, and they were named Elazar after him.

We learned in a *Baraita*: [Seeing how thoroughly grounded R. Elazar b. R. Shimon was in the laws of clean and unclean blood discharges,] Rabbi said: How many children did this evil [Roman] government prevent from being born! [If they had not put him in charge of arresting thieves, he would have been available for consultation, and with his extensive knowledge would have permitted many women to their husbands.]

HIS DELAYED BURIAL

When R. Elazar b. R. Shimon was near death he told his wife, "I know that the Rabbis are angry with me [for turning over many of their relatives], and they will not properly prepare my body for burial. So I want you to put me in the attic; and don't be afraid." R. Shmuel b. Nachmani said: I heard from R. Yonatan's mother who was told by the wife of R. Elazar b. R. Shimon that she kept his body lying in the attic not less than eighteen and not more than twenty-two years. When she went up she examined his hair, and if a single hair had fallen out there would still be blood. One day she saw a worm come out of his ear. She was very upset, but he appeared to her in a dream and told her, "It is nothing to be upset about. This is a punishment, for one day I heard a young scholar being insulted, and I did not protest as I should have." Whenever two people came to his house for a lawsuit, they would stand at the door and state their cases. A voice would then come out of the attic, declaring, "So-and-so, you are liable; so-and-so you are cleared of all charges." Now one day the wife of R. Elazar b. R. Shimon had an argument with a neighbor. Angrily the neighbor shouted, "Let her be like her husband who was not worthy of burial!" When the Rabbis heard this, they said, "It is degrading to the deceased that everyone is talking about this!"

According to others, R. Shimon b. Yochai [R. Elazar's father] appeared to the Rabbis in a dream and said to them, "I have one pigeon among you, and you do not allow it to come to me!" Then the Rabbis went to take care of his burial, but the people of the town of Achberia refused to let them take R. Elazar b. R. Shimon's body away; because all the years R. Elazar b. R. Shimon slumbered in the attic no wild beast ever came into the town. But once—on *erev* Yom Kippur—when everybody was busy, the Rabbis hired some people from Biri [a neighboring town]. They brought up his bier and carried it to the cave [in Meron] where his father was buried. When they arrived, they found a snake lying in the entrance to the cave [with its tail stuck in its mouth]. They called out, "Snake, snake, open your mouth and [make room] to let the son enter to join his father!" It allowed them to enter.

R. ELAZAR B. R. SHIMON,
THE SUPERIOR TORAH SCHOLAR

[After R. Elazar b. R. Shimon was buried], Rebbi [R. Yehudah Hanasi] proposed to marry R. Elazar b. R. Shimon's widow. She sent a message back to him, "Shall a vessel that was used for holy food be used for profane purposes?" In Eretz Yisrael a similar saying goes, "On the hook where the master of the house hangs his weapons should the lowly shepherd hang his pouch?" He sent back the following message, "Granted that he topped me in Torah scholarship, but did he also outdo me in good deeds?" She answered, "That he was greater than you in Torah learning I do not know, [I am no expert on Torah], but you yourself admit it. But I do know that he outstripped you in good deeds, since he took upon himself to suffer agonizing afflictions."

What is referred to when we say that R. Elazar b. R. Shimon was a greater Torah scholar than Rebbi? [The following incident will shed light on this:] R. Shimon b. Gamliel [the father of Rebbi] and R. Yehoshua b. Korcha were sitting on chairs [in the *bet midrash*, since they were the foremost Torah scholars of their time], and R. Elazar b. R. Shimon and Rebbi [R. Yehudah Hanasi] were sitting on the floor when halachic issues were being debated. The Rabbis said,

"We are drinking from their waters [i.e., benefit from their astute insights], and they are sitting on the floor!" So they prepared chairs for them, and they were invited to be seated. However R. Shimon b. Gamliel complained, "[Why did you place my son on a chair!] I have one pigeon among you, and you want to crush it?" [He was afraid that, sitting in full view on the podium, his son might be hurt by the evil eye.]

So Rebbi was brought down, [and R. Elazar b. R. Shimon remained sitting on the chair]. Thereupon R. Yehoshua b. Korcha said, "Is it right that the one that has a father [i.e., Rebbi] should live, and the one that does not have a father [R. Elazar][25] should die [through the evil eye]?" So they took down R. Elazar b. R. Shimon also, but he was unhappy about that. He said, "Do you think that I am just like him [Rebbi]?" Up to that time, whenever Rebbi said a *halachah*, R. Elazar b. R. Shimon supported it, but from that time on, whenever Rebbi would say, "I have a question," [before he could formulate his question,] R. Elazar b. R. Shimon would say, "I know you are going to raise such-and-such question, [but your question is unfounded,] and this is the answer. Are you going to bombard us with a barrage of frivolous questions?"

[Since R. Shimon b. Elazar anticipated all his objections,] Rebbi felt disheartened and went to his father to complain about it. His father said, "My son, don't feel bad. R. Elazar is a lion the son of a lion, and you are a lion the son of a fox."[26] [R. Elazar's father, R. Shimon b. Yochai, was a greater scholar than Rebbi's father, R. Shimon b. Gamliel.] And this is what Rebbi had in mind when he said, "There were three people who were truly humble, namely: my father, (85a) the B'nei Beteirah, and Jonathan the son of Saul." R. Shimon b. Gamliel [Rebbi's father's humility] is mentioned above. "The B'nei Beteirah's humility," as a Tanna taught: Originally the B'nei Beteirah were appointed as the leaders of the Jews of Eretz Yisrael, [but when they saw that Hillel who came from Babylonia outranked them in Torah scholarship, they relinquished their position and made Hillel the *Nasi*].[27] "Jonathan the son of Saul" for he told David, "You will reign over Israel, and I will be second to you" (1 Samuel 23:17).

[The Gemara asks:] How does that prove [his modesty]? Perhaps Jonathan the son of Saul [said this] because he saw that the people were behind David, [and he joined David's bandwagon]; the B'nei Beteirah too, [perhaps they abdicated] because [they were embarrassed when] they saw that Hillel could answer questions that baffled them. But regarding R. Shimon b. Gamliel [his statement can only be explained by saying that he] truly was a very humble man.

"SUFFERING IS
A PRECIOUS THING"

[Noting that as a reward for the pain R. Elazar b. R. Shimon had suffered, his body did not decompose for many years,] Rebbi said, "Suffering is a precious thing." He therefore undertook to mortify himself for thirteen years, six years through a stone in the urinary tract, and seven years through a disease in the mouth [scurvy]; others reverse it. [The severe pain Rebbi endured can be understood from the following:] The horse steward of Rebbi was richer than King Shavur. When he gave fodder to the horses, their neighs could be heard for three miles. He always fed the horses when Rebbi went to the toilet, but Rebbi's voice lifted in pain was louder than that of the horses, so that even seafarers heard it. Despite that, the suffering of Elazar b. R. Shimon was better than Rebbi's, for R. Elazar b. R. Shimon's sufferings came to him through love and left him in love, [he welcomed them as a means toward spiritual elevation, and he sent them away when they interfered with his studies]. By contrast, the sufferings of Rebbi came to him through a certain incident, and also left him through an incident.

WHY DID REBBI'S SUFFERINGS COME AND LEAVE?

"They came to him to him through a certain incident." What is that incident? [Explains the Gemara:] There was a calf that was being led to the slaughterhouse. It broke loose and hid its head under Rebbi's cloak, crying bitterly. Rebbi said to the calf, "Go, this is the purpose for which you were created." So they said in Heaven, "Since he had no mercy, let us bring suffering on him." "The pain also left him through an incident." One day the maidservant of Rebbi was sweeping the floor. There were some baby weasels there, and she swept them up too. "Leave them alone," said Rebbi to her. "It says, 'His mercies are on all His works' (Psalms 145:9)." So they said in Heaven, "Since he has pity, let us have pity on him."

During all the years that R. Elazar suffered, nobody died prematurely. During all the years that Rebbi suffered the world did not need rain, for Rabbah b. R. Shilah said: The day of rain is as difficult for the world to endure as the day of judgment. And Amemar said: If not for the fact that the world needs rain, the Rabbis would pray and do away with it. Despite the fact that it did not rain all those years, whenever a radish was pulled from the ground they would find the hole full of water.

THE WAYWARD SON BECAME A TORAH SAGE

Rebbi happened to be in the city of R. Elazar b. R. Shimon. He said to the people, "Did that *tzaddik* leave a son?" "Yes, he does have a son," the answer was. "However, any prostitute that can be hired for two *zuz*, hires him for eight [he is so handsome]." They brought him before Rebbi who ordained him as rabbi [raising his self-esteem rather than admonishing him, hoping

to induce him to live up to the distinguished title (Rashi)]. He placed him under the care of R. Shimon b. Issi b. Lakunia, his mother's brother [who would teach him Torah]. Every day [the son of R. Elazar] would say, "I want to go home," but his uncle told him, "They made you a scholar, let you wear a gold-trimmed cloak [at your ordination], and they call you 'Rabbi,' and you are saying, 'I want to go home!'" Impressed, the young man replied, "I swear that I am through with the things I have been doing until now. [I commit myself to the Torah.]"

When he became a great Torah scholar he sat in the yeshivah of Rebbi. Rebbi heard his voice and observed, "This voice sounds like the voice of R. Elazar b. R. Shimon." "He is his son," the disciples told him. Rebbi, [realizing how successful his tutor had been] applied to him the verse, "The fruit of a righteous one is a tree of life, and a wise man acquires souls" (Proverbs 11:30). [One that teaches Torah acquires his student as a son (Rashi).]

[Accordingly, the passage,] "The fruit of a righteous one is a tree of life" applies to R. Yose the son of R. Elazar b. R. Shimon. "And a wise man acquires souls" applies to R. Shimon b. Issi b. Lakunia [his teacher]. When R. Yose b. R. Elazar died he was brought to the cave [in Meron] where his father and grandfather were buried, but a snake was blocking the entrance to the cave. "Snake! Snake!" they called out. "Open your mouth and let the son join his father," but it refused to let them in. People began to think that it was because his father was a greater man [and the son was not worthy to buried there]. But a heavenly voice came forth and declared, "It is not because one is greater than the other, but because [R. Shimon b. Yochai and R. Elazar b. R. Shimon] suffered while hiding from the Romans in a cave [for thirteen years],[28] and R. Yose b. R. Elazar did not."

Rebbi once happened to visit the town of R. Tarfon. He asked the people, "Did that *tzaddik* who used to swear by the life of his children, leave a son?"[29] They answered, "He did not leave a son, but he has a grandson, and every prostitute who sells herself for two *zuz* would hire him for eight he is so handsome." So they brought him before Rebbi, who said to him, "If you are going to do *teshuvah*, I will give you my daughter [in marriage]." He did do *teshuvah*. Some say, he married [Rebbi's daughter] and divorced her; others say that he never married her, so that people should not say that he only did *teshuvah* because he wanted to marry Rabbi Yehudah Hanasi's daughter.

[The Gemara asks:] But why did Rebbi go to such lengths [of giving his daughter to a person of questionable reputation]? [The Gemara answers: Rebbi would do anything in such a case,] for Rav Yehudah said in Rav's name—others say, R. Chiya b. Abba said in R. Yochanan's name—others say R. Shmuel b. Nachmani said in R. Yonatan's name: If a person teaches Torah to his neighbor's son, he will be rewarded to sit in the yeshivah of heaven, for it says, "If you will make people repent, you will stand directly before Me" (Jeremiah 15:19). And whoever teaches Torah to the son of an unlearned person, even if the Holy One, blessed be He, makes a [evil] decree, He will rescind it for the sake of that person. For it says, "If you produce what is noble out of the worthless, you shall be like My mouth [you can make Me retract what I have decreed]" (ibid.).

THE TORAH RETURNS TO ITS FAMILIAR LODGING

R. Parnach said in the name of R. Yochanan: If a person is himself a Torah scholar, and his son is a Torah scholar, and his grandson too, the Torah will never leave his offspring, as it says, "And as for Me, this is My covenant with them, said God: My spirit which is upon you and My words that I have placed in your mouth will not be withdrawn from your mouth nor from the mouth of your offspring nor from the mouth of your offspring's offspring, [meaning, three generations] said God, from this moment and forever" (Isaiah 59:21). What is meant by, [the second] "said God"? The Holy One, blessed be He, said, I am the guarantor in this matter. What is meant by, "from this moment and forever"? R. Yirmeyah said: From this point forward the Torah comes back to its [familiar] lodging.

R. Yosef fasted forty fasts and prayed for himself that the promise of "the Torah will not be withdrawn from your mouth" might be fulfilled. He fasted another forty fasts and prayed that the promise of "the Torah will not be withdrawn from your mouth nor from the mouth of your offspring" would come true. He then fasted another one hundred fasts that the promise of "the Torah will not be withdrawn from your mouth, nor from the mouth of your offspring, nor from the mouth of your offspring's offspring" might be fulfilled. He said: From this point forward, the Torah comes back to its [familiar] lodging.

ONE HUNDRED FASTS

When R. Zeira went up to Eretz Yisrael he fasted a hundred fasts that he should forget the study method of the Babylonian Gemara so as not to become confused [when learning the approach to Talmud study of R. Yochanan, which was totally different from the adversarial style of question-and-answer followed in Babylonian yeshivot].[30] He also fasted a hundred fasts that R. Elazar should not die in his lifetime so that he should not be burdened with the responsibility of caring for the community [of Teveriah (Tiberias)]. He fasted a hundred more fasts that the fire of Gehinnom should not affect him. Every thirty days he used to test himself [to see if he was fire-resistant]. He would light up the oven and sit on it, but the fire had no effect on him. One day, the Rabbis looked at him [an evil eye resulted], and he burned his legs, and after that they called him "The short one with the burned legs." [He was of short build.]

WHY WAS ERETZ YISRAEL RUINED?

Rav Yehudah said in the name of Rav: What is the meaning of the verse, "Who is the wise man who will understand this? Who is he to whom the mouth of God speaks, that he may explain this? For what reason was the Land destroyed?" (Jeremiah 9:11). This question (85b) was asked to the Sages, but they could not answer it; to the prophets, but they could not answer it either; until the Holy One, blessed be He, Himself explained it to us. [Why was Eretz Yisrael lost?] As it says, "God has said: Because they forsook the Torah I had set before them" (ibid. v. 12). Rav Yehudah said in the name of Rav: That means that [when they learned Torah] they did not first say the berachah, ["Who has selected us from all the peoples and gave us His Torah," an indication that they did not value the Torah as our God-given heritage and did not study it for its own sake but for ulterior motives].

R. Chama said: What is meant by, "Wisdom will reside in an understanding heart, but within fools it will be publicized" (Proverbs 14:33)? "Wisdom will reside in an understanding heart" refers to a Torah scholar who is the son of a Torah scholar. "But within fools it will be publicized" refers to a Torah scholar who is the son of an unlearned person. Said Ulla: The popular saying goes, "A coin in an empty pitcher makes a lot of noise."

R. Yirmeyah asked R. Zeira: What is meant by the verse, "Small and great are equal there [in the World to Come], and the slave is free from his master" (Job 3:18). Don't we know that both the great and the small are there? But what it means is this: A person who humbles himself for the sake of the Torah in this world will become great in the hereafter; and a person who assumes the role of a slave for Torah in this world will become free in the hereafter.

R. CHIYA, THE CONSUMMATE EDUCATOR

Resh Lakish used to go around and mark the graves of the Rabbis [to warn kohanim not to go there and become tamei (unclean)]. When he came to the burial cave of R. Chiya [in Teveriah (Tiberias)] he could not find his grave. [Thinking that this was attributable to some lapse on his part,] he was deeply saddened and exclaimed, "Master of the universe! Did I not debate Torah as vigorously as R. Chiya?" A heavenly voice came forth and said, "Granted, you did debate the Torah as energetically he did, but you did not spread Torah like R. Chiya."

[The Gemara now explains how R. Chiya spread Torah.] Whenever R. Chanina and R. Chiya were having a halachic dispute, R. Chanina said to R. Chiya, "How can you dispute what I am saying! [You should know that,] God forbid, should the Torah be forgotten in Israel, I with my power of logical reasoning could bring it back." Replied R. Chiya, "How can you dispute what I am saying! [You should know that] I am the one who made sure that the Torah will never be forgotten in Israel! What did I do? I went and planted flax; [from the flax strings] I made nets, [with the nets] I caught deer, with the meat I fed orphans, and from the deerskins I prepared scrolls on which I wrote the five Books of the Torah, each on a separate scroll. Then I would go to a town [that had no teacher for young children], and teach five children, each one a different book of the *Chumash*. Then I would take six children and teach each of them a different order of the Mishnah. I would tell them, 'Until I come back, teach each other the *Chumash* and the Mishnah.' And that is how I insured that the Torah will never be forgotten in Israel."

[By starting from scratch and taking each step in the teaching process purely for the sake of God he made sure that the Torah would endure.] This is what Rebbi had in mind when he said, "How great are the deeds of Chiya!" R. Yishmael b. R. Yose asked Rebbi, "Were they even greater than yours, master?" "Yes," Rebbi replied. "Were they even greater than my father's deeds?" asked R. Yishmael b. R. Yose. "No," replied Rebbi. "God forbid! Let no one in Israel say such a thing." [R. Chiya's deeds were great, but not as great as your father's achievements.]

A CELESTIAL
SEATING ARRANGEMENT

R. Zeira said: Last night R. Yose b. R. Chanina appeared to me in a dream, and I asked him, "Next to whom are you seated [in the yeshivah of heaven]?" "Next to R. Yochanan" he replied. "And R. Yochanan, next to whom is he seated?" "Next to R. Yannai." "And R. Yannai?" "Next to R. Chanina." "And R. Chanina?" "Next to R. Chiya." So I said to him, "Does not R. Yochanan deserve to sit next to R. Chiya?" He told me, "In the place of fiery sparks and flaming tongues, who will allow to let a blacksmith's son enter?" [R. Yochanan is compared to a blacksmith's bellows that blows the fire and ignites a potential desire for Torah learning. But R. Chiya, who had already kindled the fire of Torah learning in countless students, did not need R. Yochanan's bellows to inspire him (*Maharsha*).]

HIS BLINDNESS WAS CURED

R. Chaviva said: R. Chaviva b. Surmaki told me, "I saw one of the Torah scholars to whom Elijah the prophet frequently appeared, and one morning [the scholar's] eyes were clear, but that evening they looked as if they had been burned by fire. I asked the Torah scholar, 'What happened?' He replied, 'I have asked Elijah to show me the Rabbis as they go up to the heavenly yeshivah. So Elijah told me, 'You may look at all these personalities, with the exception of the carriage of R. Chiya; when it passes by, do not look at it.' 'How do I know which is R. Chiya's carriage?' 'All the other carriages are accompanied by heavenly angels as they go up and down, except the carriage of R. Chiya; it goes up and down by itself; [his merit is so great, he does not need the help of angels].'" [Continued the Torah scholar,] "I could not control my curiosity and gazed at R. Chiya's carriage. Immediately two sparks of fire shot out and blinded me. The next day I went to the grave of R. Chiya, prostrated myself, and cried out, 'Please have mercy! I am learning your *Baraitot* all the time! [Rabbi Chiya compiled the *Baraitot*.[31]] Thereupon I was healed.'"

AN ATTEMPT
TO BRING *MASHIACH*

Elijah used to appear often in the yeshivah of Rebbi [R. Yehudah Hanasi]. One day—it was Rosh Chodesh [the first day of the new month]—Rebbi waited for Elijah, but he did not appear. [When he did come,] Rebbi asked him, "Why did you not come until now?" Elijah replied, "[I was busy.] I had to wake up Abraham, wash his hands, allow him to pray, and he would have to go to sleep afterward. I had to do the same for Isaac and again for Jacob." Questioned Rebbi, "Why not wake them all up at the same time?" Replied Elijah, "If they all prayed simultaneously, they would inject so much mercy into the world that *Mashiach* would come before his time. [That is why I am not allowed to wake them up at the same time.]

Rebbi said to Elijah, "Is there anyone alive now that could arouse such heavenly mercy [with his prayers]?" Replied Elijah, "Yes. There is R. Chiya and his sons." Immediately Rebbi proclaimed a fast, and R. Chiya and his sons were asked to lead the prayer service. As R. Chiya came to the words [in the *Shemoneh Esrei*] "He makes the wind blow," the wind began to blow; and when he uttered the words, "and makes the rain descend," it began to rain. However, when he was about to say, "Blessed are You God, Who revives the dead," the world began to shudder, and they said in Heaven, "Who has revealed this secret to the world [that R. Chiya could bring *Mashiach*]?" "It was Elijah," came the answer. They brought Elijah and gave him sixty flaming lashes. Elijah came down and appeared in the form of a fiery bear, and chased everyone away.

THE BOOK OF ADAM

(85b) Shmuel Yarchinaah[32] was Rebbi's personal physician. When Rebbi contracted an eye disease, Shmuel wanted to inject a certain medicine into his eyes. But

Rebbi objected, "I cannot bear it." "Then I will apply an ointment to it," Shmuel suggested. But Rebbi said, "I cannot bear that either." So Shmuel poured some medication into a tube and placed it under his pillow. Thereupon he was healed. [The strong therapeutic vapor of the medication penetrated his eyes (Rashi).] Rebbi tried very hard to confer rabbinical ordination [semichah] on Shmuel, but things just did not work out, [either because the times were unsettled, or he could not convene the required quorum of Sages (Rashi)]. Said Shmuel to Rabbi, "Don't feel bad; [I was not meant to be ordained]. I have seen the Book of Adam,[33] and it is written there, "Shmuel Yarchinaah (86a) will be called 'Sage' but not 'Rabbi', and Rabbi [Yehudah Hanasi] will be healed through Shmuel."

It also says in that book that Rabbi and R. Natan will be the last of the Mishnah period, [the last of the Tanna'im. R. Yehudah Hanasi compiled and edited all the accumulated Mishnah teachings], and R. Ashi and Ravina will be the last of the Amora'im. [They collated all the debates of the previous Amoraim and arranged them into the mesechtot of the Gemara.] The sign [that Ravina and R. Ashi closed the Talmud] is the verse, "Until I came to the sanctuaries [mikdeshei] of God; I contemplated [avinah] their end" (Psalms 73:17). [Mikdeshei sounds like Ashi; avinah resembles Ravina, the two Sages who brought the teachings of the Gemara to "their end" and marked the close of the era of the Amora'im.]

RABBAH B. NACHMANI'S DEATH

R. Kahana said: I was told by R. Chama, the son of Chassa's daughter, that Rabbah b. Nachmani died as a result of fright of government agents [who were chasing him]. [This is the story: Thousands of people used to gather at the great yeshivot in the months of Nissan and Tishri to listen to the lectures about the forthcoming Yamim Tovim. Since the householders were away from home attending lectures, the agents of the tax bureau were unable to collect the monthly installment of taxes.] Certain informers denounced Rabbah b. Nachmani to the government, saying, "There is one man among the Jews who prevents twelve thousand Jews from paying taxes, one month in the spring and one month in the fall [when he gives his lectures]." A royal officer was dispatched to arrest Rabbah b. Nachmani, but he could not find him. Rabbah b. Nachmani meanwhile ran away from Pumbedita to Akra, from Akra to Agma, from Agma to Shechin, from Shechin to Tzarifah, from Tzarifah to Eina Demaya, and from Eina Demaya back to Pumbedita.

In Pumbedita the royal officer found him, for by chance he stayed at the same inn where Rabbah was hiding. The waiters put a tray before the officer, poured him two glasses of wine, and then took away the tray. [During the time of the Gemara there were demons

that were provoked when certain things were done in pairs. By serving the officer two drinks, the innkeeper unintentionally aroused the ire of the demons and placed him in danger (Rashi).] Suddenly the officer's face turned backward.[34] [Terrified] the waiters said to Rabbah, "What shall we do with him? He is a royal officer, [and we may be held responsible!]." Replied Rabbah, "Bring back the tray, and let him drink one more glass. Then take away the tray, and he will be cured." They did exactly what Rabbah told them to do, and the officer was cured. "I know," said the officer, "that the person I am looking for is right here." He searched for him and found him. He then said, "I will go away from here; if they kill me, I will not reveal [where he is], but if they are going to torture me, I will tell them."

They brought Rabbah b. Nachmani before him, and he led him into a chamber and locked the door. Rabbah b. Nachmani prayed for mercy, whereupon the walls of the chamber caved in, and he fled to Agma. He sat down on a stump of a fallen palm tree and began to learn Torah. [This is what he saw in a dream:] There was a dispute in the yeshivah of Heaven [about the signs of leprosy]:[35] [Background information: If someone develops baheret (a shiny spot), he has to show it to a kohen; he is then quarantined for seven days. After the seven days, if the hair on the shiny spot turns white, he is declared unclean.[36] If the hair was white before the shiny spot appeared, it is not a sign of uncleanness. What happens if we are not sure when the hair turned white? This was the question being debated.] The Holy One, blessed be He, said: He is tahor [clean], but the entire yeshivah of Heaven ruled: He is tamei [unclean]. Who shall decide it? they said.

It was decided: Let Rabbah b. Nachmani decide, for he said: I am the sole person that is an expert on the laws of nega'im and oholot [laws dealing with the tum'ah of a dead human being and the tum'ah caused by tzaraat, (leprosy)]. They sent the Angel of Death for Rabbah b. Nachmani, but he could not come near him because he did not stop learning even for an instant, [and when a person is learning Torah, the Angel of Death has no power over him]. Meanwhile, a wind blew and the reeds began to stir. Rabbah b. Nachmani thought that a company of soldiers was coming to arrest him. He said: I'd rather die than fall into the hands of the government. [This momentary distraction gave the Angel of Death the opportunity to seize Rabbah b. Nachmani.] As he was dying he said [in regard to the dispute in heaven,] "Tahor! Tahor! He is clean!" Thereupon a heavenly voice came forth and declared, "Fortunate are you, Rabbah b. Nachmani, your body is pure, and your soul has left your body in purity!"

A message came down from heaven to Pumbedita [the city where Rabbah b. Nachmani was rosh yeshivah]. It read, "Rabbah b. Nachmani has gone up to the yeshivah of Heaven." So Abaye and Rava and all the

Torah scholars went to prepare him for burial, but they could not find his remains. They went to Agma and saw a swarm of birds forming a shade with their wings to protect something. They said, "That must be the place." They eulogized him for three days and three nights. Another message came down from heaven: Any person that leaves now will be put under a ban, [for he has not been eulogized sufficiently]. They eulogized him for an additional seven days. This time a message came down from heaven: Now you may return to your homes in peace. On the day that Rabbah b. Nachmani died, a hurricane blew up that lifted an Arab who was riding on his camel and carried him from one side of the River Papa to the other. "What is happening here?" the Arab wondered. "Rabbah b. Nachmani has died," they told him. "Master of the universe!" the Arab exclaimed. "The whole world is Yours, and Rabbah b. Nachmani is Yours. You love Rabbah, and Rabbah loves You. Then why are you destroying the world?" When he said this, the hurricane settled down.

R. Shimon b. Chalafta was obese.[37] One day he felt very hot, so he sat on the peak of a mountain and said to his daughter, "Daughter dear, please fan me a little bit, and I will give you some fragrant spices." As he was talking, a cool breeze began to blow, so he said, "How many pounds of spices do I owe the Master of this breeze?"

THE BANQUET
OF KING SOLOMON

(86b) [We learned in the Mishnah:][38] It once happened that R. Yochanan b. Matya said to his son, "Go out and hire workers." He went and agreed to supply them with meals. When he came back, his father told him, "Even if you prepare for them meals as sumptuous as the banquets of King Solomon in his heyday, you have not given them enough food, for they are the children of Abraham, Isaac, and Jacob."

[The Gemara asks:] Are we implying that the meals of Abraham, Isaac, and Jacob were better than those of Solomon? But it says, "Solomon's provision for one day was: thirty *kor* of fine flour, sixty *kor* of flour, ten fattened oxen, twenty oxen from the pasture, and a hundred sheep and goats, besides gazelle, deer, yachmur, and fattened fowl" (1 Kings 5:2,3). And Gurion b. Astion said in the name of Rav: [The fine flour and the flour] were used just for the cook's dough [loaves of dough that were placed on the pots to absorb the vapor and foam]. R. Yitzchak said: All of this was used just to make the pudding. R. Yitzchak said further: Solomon had a thousand wives, and each one of them made this entire meal in her home every single night. Why? Because each one thought that perhaps Solomon would come and dine with her that day. But concerning Abraham it says, [when he welcomed the three wayfarers,] "Abraham ran to the cattle and chose a tender choice calf" (Genesis 18:7). And R. Yehudah in the

name of Rav commented: "a calf" means one; "tender"—two; "choice" three. [Three calves for three people is very generous, but it does not even come close to the quantities of food used for Solomon's pudding!] [The Gemara answers:] In the case of Abraham there were three animals for three people, whereas the food prepared for Solomon's banquet was for all Israel and Judah, and it says, "Judah and Israel were numerous, like the sand that is by the sea" (1 Kings 4:20). [Now we understand the statement that since they are the children of Abraham, Isaac, and Jacob, a banquet like Solomon's would not be sufficient.]

[The Gemara asks:] What is meant by "fattened fowl"? Rav said: They would force-feed the fowl. Shmuel said: They were naturally fat. R. Yochanan said: They would bring an ox from the pasture that had never done any labor, and a hen that had never hatched. R. Yochanan said: The best of cattle is an ox, and the best of fowl is a chicken. Amemar said: [What type of chicken?] A fat black hen that is always around the wine-press and feeds on the pits, and that is so fat that it cannot step over a stick.

THE MEAL ABRAHAM SERVED
HIS GUESTS

It says, "Abraham ran to the cattle and chose a tender and choice calf" (Genesis 18:7). R. Yehudah said in the name of Rav: "A calf" is one; "tender"—two; "choice"—three. [The Gemara asks:] But perhaps he only brought one, [and the verse uses a colloquial expression,] as people say: a tender and choice calf? If so, the verse should have said: a tender, choice calf; why does it say *"and* choice"? We can infer from this [that it means another calf]. [The Gemara asks:] Then perhaps it means two [because it does not say *"and* tender"]? [The Gemara answers:] Since "and choice" denotes another, "tender" also denotes another, [so we have three calves]. Rabbah b. Ullah—others say: R. Hoshaia, and still others say: R. Natan b. Hoshaia—raised an objection: It says, "He gave it to a young man who rushed to prepare it" (ibid.); ["it" implies one calf, not three]. [The Gemara answers:] He gave each calf to a different young man. [The Gemara asks:] "[Abraham] fetched some cream and milk, and the calf that he prepared, and he placed it before [his guests]" (ibid. v. 8) [only one calf]. [The Gemara answers:] [It means:] As soon as each calf was ready, he brought it separately. [The Gemara asks:] Why three whole animals? Should not one be enough? R. Chanan b. Rava: In order to serve them three tongues with mustard [a great delicacy].

ABRAHAM AND
THE THREE ANGELS

R. Tanchum b. Chanila'i said: A person should never deviate from the custom [of the place where he is staying as a guest]. For when Moses went up to heaven he did not eat any bread, and when the ministering angels came down to earth they did eat bread [each following the custom of the place he was visiting]. [The Gemara asks:] How can angels eat?—But say, they made it appear as though they were eating and drinking.

Rav Yehudah said in Rav's name: Whatever Abraham did for the angels by himself, the Holy One, blessed be He, did for Abraham's children Himself, and whatever Abraham did by sending a messenger, the Holy One, blessed be He, did for His children also only through a messenger. For example: "Abraham [himself] rushed to the cattle," therefore, "God [Himself] caused a wind to start blowing, sweeping quail up from the sea [for the people to eat]" (Numbers 11:31). "[Abraham himself] fetched some cream and milk," therefore, [God said,] "I will make bread [manna] rain down to you from the sky" (Exodus 16:4). "[Abraham himself] stood over them as they ate under the tree" (Genesis 18:8); therefore, [God said to Moses,] "I [Myself] will stand before you there on the rock at Horeb" (Exodus 17:6). "Abraham [himself] went with them to send them on their way" (Genesis 18:16); therefore, [at the Exodus,] "God went before them by day with a pillar of cloud" (Exodus 13:21). By contrast, [Abraham ordered,] "Let some water be brought" (Genesis 18:4) [through a servant]; therefore, "You [Moses] must strike the rock, and water will come out of it for the people to drink" (Exodus 17:6), [they received the water not directly from God, but through Moses].

On this point [Rav Yehudah] disputes R. Chama b. Chanina, for R. Chama b. R. Chanina said, and the yeshivah of R. Yishmael supports it: As a reward for three things [that Abraham did,] his descendants merited three things: As a reward for "and he fetched some cream and milk" they received the manna; as a reward for "and he stood over them" they received the pillar of cloud;[39] and as a reward for "let some water be brought" they merited the Well of Miriam [which accompanied them on their wandering through the wilderness and supplied them with water]. [Thus in R. Chama b. R. Chanina's view "let some water be brought" was a commendable thing, since it was rewarded by the Well of Miriam.]

"Let some water be brought, and wash your feet." R. Yannai b. R. Yishmael said: [The three wayfarers said to Abraham,] "Are you accusing us of being Arabs who bow down to the dust of their feet [that you tell us to wash our feet]? You yourself have a son Ishmael who is doing this!" [worshipping idols].

"God appeared to [Abraham] in the Plains of Mamre while he was sitting in the entrance of the tent in the hottest part of the day" (Genesis 18:1). [The Gemara asks:] What is meant by "the hottest part of the day"? R. Chama b. R. Chanina said: It was the third day after Abraham's circumcision, and the Holy One, blessed be He, came to inquire after Abraham's health.

God took the sun out of its pouch [to make it an extremely hot day], so that Abraham should not be troubled by passing wayfarers. [When Abraham saw that no guests were coming,] he sent Eliezer outside [to see if there were any travelers on the road], but he did not find anyone. Said Abraham, "I don't believe you."—This proves the saying they have in Eretz Yisrael, "You can't believe a slave."—So Abraham himself went out and saw the Holy One, blessed be He, standing at the door. Thus it says, [Abraham said,] "If you would, do not go on without stopping by me" (Genesis 18:3). For when God saw Abraham tying and opening [the bandage of his circumcision] He said, "It is not proper to stand here."

That is why it says, "[Abraham] lifted his eyes and he saw three strangers standing a short distance from him. When he saw them he ran to greet them" (ibid. v. 2): [they were standing there,] because at first when they saw that he was in pain, they said to themselves: It is not proper to stop by here now, [and they began to move away. That is why it says first, "they were standing there" and then, "he ran to greet them"]. [The Gemara asks:] Who were these three men?—[The angels] Michael, Gabriel, and Raphael. Michael came to announce the news [that Isaac would be born a year later]; Gabriel, to overturn Sodom; and Raphael, to heal Abraham. [The Gemara asks:] But doesn't it say, "The *two* angels came to Sodom in the evening" (Genesis 19:1), [not just one]? [The Gemara answers:] Michael went along with Gabriel to rescue Lot. This is also borne out by a precise reading of the text, for it says, "*He* overturned the cities" (ibid. v. 25), and not, *they* overturned. Which proves [that Michael just came along to rescue Lot].

[The Gemara asks:] Why does it say with reference to Abraham, [the angels said,] "Do as you say" (ibid. v. 5), [the angels immediately accepted his invitation], whereas with regard to Lot it says, (87a) "[Lot] urged them very much" (ibid. 19:3)? [It took Lot a while to convince them to come in.] R. Elazar said: This teaches that you may decline a request of a person of lesser stature, but not the request of an important person.

[Abraham said to the angels,] "I will get a morsel of bread" (ibid. 18:5), but it also says, "Abraham ran to the cattle" (ibid. v. 7). Said R. Elazar: We see from here that *tzaddikim* say a little but do a lot; whereas the wicked promise a great deal and don't even do a little. How do we know this [about the wicked]? From Ephron. At first it says, [Ephron said,] "Four hundred silver shekels worth of land, [ordinary shekels, that is all I am going to charge]" (ibid. 23:14), but in the end, "Abraham understood what Ephron meant. He weighed out for Ephron four hundred shekels in negotiable currency" (ibid. v. 16), evidence that he refused to accept anything but *kanteri* [i.e., the most expensive currency available, money that is accepted universally]. For there are places where they call shekels *kanteri*.

ABRAHAM AND SARAH

[Abraham asked Sarah to make cakes of *kemach solet*, "ordinary meal, fine flour" (ibid. v. 6), [which seems to be self-contradictory]. Said R. Yitzchak: This shows that a woman treats guests more frugally than a man does [Abraham asked for fine flour, and she used ordinary flour].

[Abraham said to Sarah,] "Knead it and make cakes" (ibid.). But it also says, "He fetched some cream and milk and the calf" (ibid. v. 8); but he did not bring them bread! Efraim Makshaah, a student of R. Meir, said in R. Meir's name: Our Father Abraham ate even *chullin* [unconsecrated food] only when he was *tahor* [ritually clean], and that day Sarah had her female period. As a result, the bread had become ritually unclean, and he would not give his guests something he himself would not eat].

[The angels said,] "Where is your wife Sarah? And he said, "Behold—in the tent" (ibid. v. 9). This tells us that our Mother Sarah was a modest woman. Rav Yehudah said in Rav's name, some say R. Yitzchak said: The ministering angels knew full well that our Mother Sarah was in the tent, so why [did they draw out the fact that she was] in the tent? In order to make her appreciated by her husband [by highlighting her modesty]. R. Yose b. R. Chanina said: They wanted to send her the cup of wine of *Birkat Hamazon*.[40]

DOMESTIC PEACE IS
A PRECIOUS THING

We learned a *Baraita* in the name of R. Yose: Why are there dots in the Torah on the letters *alef, yud, vav* [which spell *ayo*, "where"] of the word *eilav*, "to him" [in the verse, "They said *eilav* to him, 'Where is your wife Sarah?'"]? To teach us a lesson in manners: that a person should ask the host about the woman of the house. [The Gemara asks: How can that be?] Did not Shmuel say: It is not proper to inquire about a woman? [The Gemara answers:] To ask a husband how his wife is, that is different; [it is permitted].

"Sarah laughed to herself, saying, 'Now that I am worn out, shall I once again regain my youth?'" (Genesis 18:12). R. Chisda said: After the flesh is withered and there are many wrinkles, the flesh became youthful again, the wrinkles were smoothed, and beauty was restored.

It says, [Sarah said to herself,] "My husband is old!" (ibid. v. 12) But it also says, [God said to Abraham that Sarah said,] "I am so old" (ibid. 13). God did not tell Abraham precisely what she had said. In the yeshivah of R. Yishmael they taught: You see how precious peace is, for even the Holy One, blessed be He, altered Sarah's words for the sake of peace. For it says, "Sarah laughed, saying, 'Now that I am worn out shall I once again regain my youth, and my husband is old?' "God said to Abraham, [that Sarah said,] 'since I am so old.'" [God did not mention that

she also asked, "How can I have a child when *my husband* is so old."]

THE SKEPTICS WERE SILENCED

"[Sarah] said, 'Who would have even suggested to Abraham that Sarah would be nursing *children?*'" (ibid. 21:7). [The Gemara asks: It says, "children" in the plural.] How many children then did Sarah nurse? R. Levi said: On the day that Abraham weaned his son Isaac he made a great banquet, and all the people of the world were skeptical, saying, "Have you seen that old man and woman? They picked up an abandoned child off the street and say it is their son. And to top it off they are giving this big party to substantiate their claim." What did our Father Abraham do? He invited all the important people of his time, and our Mother Sarah invited their wives. Each one brought her child along, but not the wet nurse. A great miracle occurred to our Mother Sarah. Her breasts opened like two wells, and she nursed all the children. But the skeptics still were not convinced. "Granted that Sarah miraculously gave birth at the age of ninety," they mocked, "but how could Abraham father a child at a hundred years of age?" Suddenly, the facial features of Isaac changed, and he looked exactly like Abraham. Now all the skeptics cried out, "Abraham is Isaac's father" (Genesis 25:19).

THEY PRAYED FOR OLD AGE
AND SICKNESS

Until the time of Abraham there was no old age [the hair did not turn white (*Maharsha*)]. Anyone who wanted to speak to Abraham would speak to Isaac, and vice versa [because they looked alike]. Then Abraham prayed [that people should be able to tell the difference between himself and Isaac], and the marks of old age manifested themselves. For it says, "Abraham was old, well advanced in years" (Genesis 24:1). Until the time of Jacob nobody became sick before he died; [people died suddenly, without warning]. Then Jacob prayed [that a person should become sick before he died so that he could convey his last wishes to his children], and sickness came into being, for it says, "Joseph was told that his father [Jacob] was sick" (ibid. 48:1). Until the time of Elisha no sick person ever recovered, but Elisha prayed and he did recover. For it says, "Elisha became ill with the disease from which he was to die" (2 Kings 13:14); which implies that he was sick on previous occasions, [but had recovered].

Our Rabbis taught: Elisha was sick three times: once when he pushed away Gechazi with both hands;[41] a second time when he caused bears to attack children;[42] and a third time with the sickness of which he died, as it says, "Elisha became ill with the disease from which he was to die."

A FIELD CLOSE TO THE CITY

(107a) Rav Yehudah said to Ravin b. R. Nachman: Ravin, my brother, do not buy a field close to the city; for R. Abbahu said in the name of R. Huna who quoted Rav: A person is forbidden to stand [and gaze] at the field of his neighbor when the grain is full-grown [so that the produce should not be harmed by an evil eye cast by people walking by]. [The Gemara asks:] But that is not so! For R. Abba met Rav's disciples and asked them: How did Rav expound the following verses, "Blessed will you be in the city, and blessed in the field. Blessed will you be when you come and blessed when you go" (Deuteronomy 27:3,6)? They answered him: This is what Rav said: "Blessed will you be in the city"—that your house should be close to the synagogue. "Blessed in the field"—that your field should be close to the city.[43] "Blessed will you be when you come"—when a person comes home he should not find his wife in doubt of being *niddah*.[44] "And blessed when you go"—that your children should be exactly like you.

R. Abba said to Rav's disciples: R. Yochanan did not interpret these verses like this, but rather: "Blessed will you be in the city"—that a person should have a toilet close to his house, but not a synagogue. For R. Yochanan holds that you are rewarded for walking [a long distance] to a synagogue.[45] "Blessed in the field"—that your land should be divided into three portions: a third should be planted with grain, a third with olives, and a third with grape vines. [If one crop fails, he will be saved by diversifying (Rashi).] "Blessed will you be when you come and blessed when you go"—Your leaving the world should be the same as your entering the world: Just as you entered the world without sin, so should you leave the world without sin.

(107b) [To recapitulate: We have two contradictory statements by Rav: He expounded the verse to mean that it is a blessing to have a field close to the city, whereas R. Huna said in the name of Rav that you should not buy a field close to city because of an evil eye. The Gemara says:] There is no difficulty. If the field is surrounded by a wall [so that no one can see the crops], it is a blessing to have it near the city, [for it is protected from an evil eye]; but if the field is not surrounded by a wall, it is better to have it away from the city [where it is not exposed to an evil eye].

MEDICAL ADVICE

"God will take all sickness from you" (Deuteronomy 7:15). Rav said: This is referring to the [evil] eye [which is the source of all sickness (Rashi)]. This is in line with Rav's opinion [expressed elsewhere]. For Rav once went to a cemetery where he said certain incantations, [whereby he was able to ascertain why the person buried there had died], and then he concluded: Ninety-nine out of one hundred people die because of

ayin hara (the evil eye), and one of natural causes. Shmuel [who was a great physician] said: The verse refers to wind. This is in line with Shmuel's view, for he said: All die because of the wind [i.e., natural causes]. [The Gemara asks:] But according to Shmuel, what about the people that were executed [by decapitation] by the government? [Obviously, they did not die from the wind!] [The Gemara answers:] Those, too, if not for the wind [that affects their wound], a potion could be concocted [from herbs that would make the severed head grow together with the rest of the body,] and they would recover. R. Yose b. R. Chanina said: The verse is referring to bodily secretions, for a master said: In a small quantity, the dirt of the nose and the dirt of the ear is beneficial; in large amounts it is dangerous.

R. Chanina said: The verse is referring to the cold. Because R. Chanina said: Everything is from Heaven except cold drafts; [this is not the same as the wind mentioned by Shmuel; according to Shmuel a wind that is not cold also is harmful (Rashi)]. For it says, "Cold drafts that come in the path of the crooked;[46] who values life will keep far from them" (Proverbs 22:5), [which proves that a person can avoid catching a cold. Nevertheless, God promises to take away even colds]. R. Elazar said: It refers to [diseases of] the gall. We learned in a *Baraita*: The word *machalah*,[47] "sickness," refers to the gall; and why is it called *machalah*? Because [a diseased gall] makes the entire body sick. Another explanation: [The numeric value of] *machalah* is 83, which alludes to the fact that eighty-three diseases stem from the gallbladder, and all of these sicknesses can be rendered harmless by eating bread together with salt and drinking a pitcher of water in the morning.

THE BENEFITS OF A WHOLESOME BREAKFAST

Our Rabbis taught: Thirteen things were said about eating bread for breakfast: It protects a person from the heat and the cold, from harmful winds and demons. It makes a fool wise, will make a person win a lawsuit, [having had a wholesome breakfast he will be at ease and argue his case more convincingly]. It will enable him to learn and to teach the Torah, his words will be listened to respectfully, and he will remember what he learned. He will not perspire excessively, he will be together with his wife and will not lust after other women; [eating a healthful breakfast] kills worms in the intestines. Some say, it rids a person of jealousy and promotes love, [because a good breakfast puts a person in a contented frame of mind].

Rabbah said to Rava b. Mari: What scriptural verse is the basis for the popular adage: Sixty runners may run but they will not be able to overtake a person who had breakfast in the morning? Also the saying of the Rabbis: Get up in the morning and eat breakfast—in the summer it protects you from the heat; in the winter it protects you from the cold? Rava b. Mari replied: Because it says, "They will not hunger, and they will not thirst; heat and sun will not afflict them" (Isaiah 49:10). In other words, "Heat and sun will not afflict them" because "they will not hunger, and they will not thirst." Rabbah said to him: You derive it from this verse; but I will prove it from the following verse, "You will serve God your Lord, and He will bless your bread and your water. I will banish sickness from among you" (Exodus 23:25). "You will serve the Lord your God"—this refers to the reciting the *Shema* and the *Shemoneh Esrei*; "and He will bless your bread and your water"—refers to bread and salt and a pitcher of water; and if in fact you do this, "I will banish sickness from among you."

HE REFUSED TO CHOP
DOWN HIS TREES

Rabbah b. R. Huna owned a forest on the bank of a river. He was asked to cut it down, [so that the people who pulled the barges on the river should have space to walk on the river bank]. He replied, "Let the owners of the forests upstream and downstream from mine first clear [their portion], then I will cut down mine." [The Gemara asks:] How could he demand such a thing? Doesn't it say, "Improve yourself and improve each other" (Zephaniah 2:1), which Resh Lakish interpreted to mean: First correct yourself, and then correct others [i.e., do the right thing yourself before demanding it from others]. [The Gemara answers:] The forests upstream and downstream belonged to Parzak, the Persian general, [and since Rabbah b. R. Huna knew that Parzak never was going to cut down his portion, it made no sense for him to cut down his trees, for the barge pullers would not be able to pass anyhow]. Therefore Rabbah said: If they cut down their forests, I will cut down mine; otherwise, why should I? For if they can still pull their ropes, they have enough room to walk, (108a) and if not, they cannot walk on this bank in any case [and they have to walk on the other bank; and it is useless for them to cross the river just to be able to walk on the cleared portion of my forest].

Rabbah b. R. Nachman was sailing in a small boat when he saw a forest on the river bank. "Whose forest is this?" he asked. "It belongs to Rabbah b. R. Huna," he was told. When he heard this he quoted, "And the hand of the officers and the chiefs has been foremost in this transgression" (Ezra 9:2). "Cut it down! Cut it down!" he ordered. When Rabbah b. R. Huna came and found it cut down he exclaimed, "Whoever cut it down, may his branches be cut down [i.e., may his children die]!" It was said that during the entire lifetime of Rabbah b. R. Huna, none of the children of Rabbah b. R. Nachman remained alive.

THE EXQUISITE FRAGRANCE
OF GAN EDEN

(114a) Rabbah b. Abbuha met Elijah standing in a non-Jewish cemetery. (114b) He asked him, "Are you not a *kohen*?[48] Why then are you standing in a cemetery?" Elijah replied, "Have you not learned the laws of *Taharot* [the sixth order of the Talmud, dealing with the laws of purity]? For it has been taught: R. Shimon b. Yocha'i said: The graves of non-Jews do not defile." He replied, "I can barely study four of the Orders [*Moed* (Festivals), *Nashim* (Women), *Nezikin* (Damages), *Kodashim*, (Consecrated Objects)]; how can I study all six [also *Zera'im* (Seeds) and *Taharot* (Purifications), which have no practical application outside Eretz Yisrael]?" "Why not?" asked Elijah. "I am busy trying to eke out a living," Rabbah b. Abbuha replied. Elijah then led him to Gan Eden and told him, "Take off your robe, and pick up some of these leaves." So he picked them up and took them with him. As he was going out, he heard someone saying, "Would anyone consume his portion in the World to Come the way Rabbah b. Abbuha did?" Hearing this, he shook his robe, and the leaves fell off. Yet even so, since he had carried the leaves in his robe, their fragrance was clinging to it, and so he sold it for twelve thousand *dinars*, which he donated to his sons-in-law. [He sold the robe and donated the proceeds because he did not want to derive any benefit from the fragrance of Gan Eden (*Maharsha*). This *aggadah* wants to show the great reward that is in store for Torah scholars, for if the mere fragrance of dry fallen leaves of Gan Eden is so valuable, imagine how infinitely greater is the value of the fruits of Gan Eden themselves (Etz Yosef).]

(115a) We learned in a *Baraita*: It says, "When you make any kind of loan to your neighbor, do not go into his house to take something as security" (Deuteronomy 24:10). The implication is that you may not enter the debtor's house, but you may enter the house of the cosigner of the loan, and so it says, "Take the garment of one who co-signs for a stranger" (Proverbs 20:16), and it says, "My child, if you have been a guarantor for your friend, if you have given your handshake for a stranger, you have been trapped by the words of your mouth. Do this therefore, my child, and be rescued; for you have come into your fellow's hand. Go humble yourself before him, and placate your fellow" (ibid. 6:1.2). Thus, if you owe [the creditor] money, [because you guaranteed a loan] pay him; if not [but you have harmed him with words, by slander or insult], bring many of your friends [to help you appease him].

NOTES

1. A bill of divorcement.
2. *Darash* means both "to look for, to seek" and "to investigate."
3. *Gittin* 29a.

4. R. Yehudah the Prince, the compiler of the Mishnah, c. the first half of the third century C.E.

5. *Avot* 4:16.

6. They believe that they are the ones that truly bring glory to God (Rashi).

7. Since you are so quick to lose heart, it would seem that your professed piety was not genuine (Rashi).

8. Batsheba was a doubtful married woman, because every soldier in David's army before going to the battlefront wrote a conditional *get* for his wife, so that if he was killed, she would be divorced retroactively and would not require *yibbum*. Consequently, when Batsheba was with David it was doubtful whether or not she was divorced: if Uriah was killed, she was divorced; if not, she was not divorced; and Uriah was, in fact, killed (Rashi).

9. Maharsha.

10. *Keilim* 5:10.

11. Some say that Achna'i was the name of the person who built this kind of oven (Tosafot, Gra, Tiferet Yisrael).

12. The first day of the new month.

13. Hurt feelings make a person weep, and the gates of tears are never closed; see above 59a (Rashi).

14. The "Do not steal" of the Ten Commandments is the prohibition against kidnapping (*Sanhedrin* 86a).

15. Exodus 22:3.

16. In Leviticus 19:36.

17. One *hin* = twelve *lugim* = 6.072 liter.

18. Interest: Leviticus 25:36,38. *Tzitzit*: Numbers 15:38,41. False weights: Leviticus 19:36.

19. If an Egyptian woman had sons from many different fathers, those who were firstborn of their father died, and only God knows who was his father's firstborn (Rashi).

20. Leviticus 11:44,45.

21. One of the first cases of abdominal surgery and the use of anesthesia in history. R. Elazar b. R. Shimon lived c. 150 C.E.

22. Rabbi Eleazar b. Shimon was morbidly obese; see 84a.

23. Resh Lakish was very strong and, as a young man, was associated with bandits and became the leader of a gang.

24. Resh Lakish's full name was R. Shimon b. Lakish.

25. His father, R. Shimon b. Yochai, had died.

26. This proves the point that R. Elazar b. R. Shimon was a greater Torah scholar than Rebbi.

27. *Pesachim* 66a.

28. *Shabbat* 33b.

29. When making a point, R. Tarfon often said, "May I bury my children, if what I say is not true!"

30. *Sanhedrin* 24a.

31. *Baraitot* are the *halachot* that were not included in the Mishnah by Rabbi Yehudah Hanasi.

32. Shmuel Yarchinaah is the great Amora Shmuel. He is called Yarchinaah, the Astronomer, for his extensive knowledge of astronomy (*Berachot* 58b).

33. Adam, the first man, encompassed the souls of all mankind, and all future events of the universe were shown to Adam and recorded in his Book (Maharal).

34. A condition similar to *caput obstipum rheumaticum*.

35. Leviticus 13.

36. Leviticus 13:25.

37. This incident is cited here as a follow-up to the *aggadah* that appeared earlier about R. Eliezer b. R. Shimon, who was also obese (Rashi).

38. 83a.

39. Exodus 17:6.

40. Grace after Meals.

41. 2 Kings 5:26,27.

42. 2 Kings 2:24.

43. Rav's interpretation contradicts his statement quoted by R. Huna that, if the field is close to the city, it is going to be harmed by an evil eye. The Gemara will resolve this contradiction at the top of 107b.

44. A woman in the period of menstruation.

45. *Sotah* 22a.

46. Commonly translated: "Thorns and snares are in the path of the crooked."

47. Exodus 23:25.

48. Elijah is identical with Pinechas, Aaron's grandson (Rashi).

ᕤBAVA BATRAᕥ

THE GLORY OF THE SECOND
BET HAMIKDASH

(3a) It says, "The glory of this latter Temple will be greater than that of the first" (Haggai 2:9). There is a difference of opinion between Rav and Shmuel—and according to others, between R. Yochanan and R. Elazar—[about the meaning of the word "greater" in this context]. One says that it refers to the size of the building; the other that it refers (3b) to the number of years it stood [the first Temple stood 410 years; the second, 420 years]. And both are right [the second Temple was larger and stood ten years longer than the first].

WHY DID HEROD REBUILD
THE *BET HAMIKDASH*?

[Herod was an Edomite slave who was appointed by the Romans as king over Eretz Yisrael. Eager to be accepted by the Jews, he married Miriam (Mariamne), the granddaughter of Hyrkanus who was of Hasmonean lineage.]

[The Gemara says:] Herod was a slave of the Hasmonean Court, and he wanted to marry a certain young girl [of the Hasmonean royal family]. One day he heard a voice from heaven that said: Any slave that tries to rebel now will be successful. So he rose up and murdered the entire Hasmonean family, except for that young girl. When she realized that he wanted to marry her, she went up to the roof and cried out, "Anyone who will come and claim, 'I am a descendant of the Hasmonean family,' is a slave, since I am the only survivor, and I am throwing myself down from this rooftop!" Herod preserved her body in embalming honey for seven years. Some say that he had relations with her [although she was dead]; others say that he did not. According to those who say that he had relations with her, his reason for preserving her body was to gratify his lust. According to those who said that he did not have relations with her, his reason for preserving her body was that people would say that he married a princess of Hasmonean lineage. Herod said, "Who is it that expounds the verse, 'You must appoint a king from

among your brethren' (Deuteronomy 17:15) [which disqualifies me, an Edomite slave, from being king]? It is the Rabbis."

He therefore went and killed [most of] the Rabbis. However he left Bava b. Buta alive in order to use him as an adviser. (4a) [However, even Bava b. Buta was not spared from Herod's cruelty.] Herod put a crown of porcupine skin around his eyes, [and the sharp spines] blinded him. One day Herod, [pretending to be an ordinary citizen], sat down before Bava b. Buta and said, "Rabbi, do you realize all the terrible things this no-good slave Herod is doing?" "What should I do to him?" Bava b. Buta replied. Said Herod, [trying to trap him], "I want you to curse him." Replied Bava b. Buta, "[How can I curse him?] It says, 'Even in your thoughts do not curse a king'" (Ecclesiastes 10:20). Retorted Herod, "But he is no king; [he does not meet the criteria of a Jewish king.]" Replied Bava b. Buta, "He certainly is no less than a rich man, and the same verse continues, 'and in your bedchamber do not curse the rich.' He surely is no different than a leader, and it says, 'Do not curse a leader of your people' (Exodus 22:27)."

Said Herod, [trying to goad Bava b. Buta into making a derogatory remark about him], "This applies only to a person who acts like 'one of your people,' [who observes the Torah], but this [Herod] does not act like a Jew, [therefore you definitely are allowed to curse him]." Said Bava b. Buta, "I am afraid of him." Herod continued, "But no one can tell him; it is just you and I sitting here." Bava b. Buta replied, "For a bird of the skies may carry the sound, and some winged creature may betray the matter" (Ecclesiastes 10:20). Herod then confessed, "I am Herod. If I had known that the Rabbis are so careful [not to curse a leader], I would not have killed them. Now please tell me what can I do to rectify what I have done?"

Replied Bava b. Buta, "Since you snuffed out the light of the world, [for that is what the Rabbis are called], as it says, 'For a mitzvah is a lamp, and the Torah is light' (Proverbs 6:23), you should involve yourself in [enhancing] the light of the world [i.e., the *Bet Hamikdash*], for it says, "All the nations will be illuminated by it [the *Bet Hamikdash*]" (Isaiah 2:2).[1] According to another version Bava b. Buta replied to Herod, "Since you have blinded the eye of the world [i.e., the Sanhedrin, which is called "the eye of the world"], as it says, [concerning a case where the community unintentionally sinned because the Sanhedrin inadvertently made a wrong ruling,] 'If because of the eyes of the assembly it was done unintentionally' (Numbers 15:24), you should involve yourself in [enhancing] the eye of the world [i.e., the *Bet Hamikdash*], as it says, "I am going to desecrate My Sanctuary, your pride and glory, the delight of your eyes" (Ezekiel 24:21).

"I am afraid of the Roman government," Herod countered. Replied Bava b. Buta, "Send a messenger [to Rome]. It will take a year until he gets there, he will be there for a year, and it will take him a year to come back. In the interim you will be able to demolish the *Bet Hamikdash* and build a new one." That is what he did, and [at the end of the three years] he received word [from Rome]: If you have not yet torn it down, don't do it. If you have already torn it down, don't rebuild it. If you have torn it down and rebuilt it, you are one of those bad slaves who do first and then ask permission. Even if you flaunt your sword [and are proud of your royal title], we have your genealogical record here. You are neither a king [*raka*] nor the son of a king [*raka*] but Herod, a slave who freed himself. [The Gemara asks:] How do we know that *raka* denotes royalty? For it says, [David said,] "But today I am *rach* [gentle] even though anointed king" (2 Samuel 3:39). Or, if you prefer, you can derive it from this verse, [Joseph rode in the royal chariot,] "and those going ahead of him announced, '*Avrech*! The Viceroy!'" (Genesis 41:43); [*avrech* is seen as related to *raka*].[2]

It was said: Someone who has not seen the new Temple that Herod built has never seen a magnificent building. What did he build it with? Rabbah said: He used green and white marble. Some say he used white, blue, and green marble, the stones alternately protruding and receding in order to hold the cement. He planned to cover it with gold, but the Rabbis advised him, "Leave it the way it is. It looks more beautiful this way; it has the effect of the surging waves of the ocean."

[The Gemara asks:] How could Bava b. Buta do a thing like that, [giving good advice to a depraved individual like Herod? He surely remembered that] Rav Yehudah said in the name of Rav—others say in the name of R. Yehoshua b. Levi: Daniel was punished [as will be explained later] because he gave valuable advice to Nebuchadnezzar. For it says, "Nevertheless, [despite that you had such a terrible dream foretelling the end of your reign,] O king, let my advice be acceptable to you: Redeem your sins through righteousness and your iniquities through kindness to the poor; perhaps there will be an extension to your tranquility" (Daniel 4:24). And then it says, "All this be-

fell King Nebuchadnezzar" (ibid. v. 25), and then, "At the end of twelve months . . . " (ibid. v. 26). [His reign was extended for twelve months because he followed Daniel's advice.] [Since Daniel was punished for giving advice to Nebuchadnezzar, how could Bava b. Buta counsel Herod?] It could be that [he was allowed to advise Herod] because Herod was a non-Jewish slave and as such obligated to keep *mitzvot*. Or if you prefer say, it is different when it comes to the *Bet Hamikdash*, for without the king it would not have been rebuilt at all.

[The Gemara asks:] How do we know that Daniel was punished? Do you think because it says, "Then Esther summoned Hatach" (Esther 4:5), and Rav said Hatach is the same as Daniel? That is a fitting answer for those who hold that he was called Hatach because he was demoted from his position [*hatach*, "to cut down"; then this was his punishment]. But according to those who believe that he was called Hatach because all government matters were decided on his recommendation [*hatach*, meaning "to decide"], how do you know that he was punished altogether? [The Gemara answers:] The punishment was that he was thrown into the lions' den.

[*Ein Yaakov* now returns to 3b.] [The Gemara asks:] And how could Bava b. Buta advise Herod to demolish the *Bet Hamikdash*? Surely R. Chisda said: A synagogue should not be torn down until a new one has been built to replace it! [The Gemara answers:] If you prefer I can say that this rule does not apply to royalty, since a king does not go back on his word. For this is what Shmuel said: If a king gives orders to move a mountain, it will be moved, for a king does not go back on his word. Or you if you prefer say that Bava b. Buta noticed a crack [that eventually would have caused the entire structure to collapse, and that is why he advised Herod to demolish the *Bet Hamikdash*].

(7b) There was a certain pious man with whom Elijah used to converse regularly, but after that man built a watchman's booth [where the watchman sits and ensures that no undesirables enter the court], Elijah did not speak to him anymore, [because he prevented the cries of the poor people from being heard].

SHOULD TORAH SCHOLARS BE EXEMPT FROM PAYING TAXES?

R. Yehudah Hanasi made the Rabbis pay [a share of] the tax for the expense of building [a protective] wall around the city. Resh Lakish said to him, "The Rabbis don't need the protection [of a wall], for it says, 'Were I to count them, they would outnumber the grains of sand'" (Psalms 139:18). Now who does this verse refer to? Do you think the *tzaddikim*, and that they outnumber the grains of sand? When you consider that all of Israel are "like the sand on the seashore" (Genesis 22:17), how can the *tzaddikim* alone be more numerous than the grains of sand? But the verse refers to the deeds of the *tzaddikim*, and their deeds will outnumber the grains of sand. Now, if the grains of sand, which are fewer than the deeds of the *tzaddikim*, protect the land against the sea, how much more should the deeds of the *tzaddikim* [protect them from the enemy. So they don't need the protection of the wall, and, therefore, they should not have to pay the tax].

When Resh Lakish came before R. Yochanan, the latter told him, "Why didn't you derive it from this verse, "I am a wall, and my breasts are like towers" (Song of Songs 8:10), where "I am a wall" refers to the Torah, "and my breasts are like towers" (8a) refers to the students of Torah, [who therefore do not need a wall of stones]. Resh Lakish, however, expounds this verse the way Rava did, namely, "I am a wall" refers to the community of Israel, "and my breasts are like towers" refers to synagogues and houses of learning. R. Nachman son of R. Chisda levied a tax on the Rabbis. Said R. Nachman b. Yitzchak to him: What you have done goes against the Torah, the Prophets, and the Writings.

Against the Torah, for it says, "Although He shows love to the nations, all Your holy ones are in Your hand. They follow Your footsteps, and uphold Your word" (Deuteronomy 33:3). Moses said to the Holy One, blessed be He: Master of the universe! Even at a time when You seem to be showing love to the nations of the world [by letting them subjugate Your children], all Your holy ones are in Your hand [You will still protect the *tzaddikim* and Torah scholars]. "They follow in Your footsteps"—R. Yoseph learned: This refers to the Torah scholars who bruise their feet going from town to town and from country to country to learn Torah. "And uphold Your word"—means that they are constantly involved in discussing the words of God. [So you see that they enjoy God's special protection, and therefore you should not levy a tax against them to build a protective wall.]

[R. Nachman b. Yitzchak] went against the Prophets, for it says, "Although they pay tribute [*yitnu*] to the nations, now I will gather them; but [first] they will be humbled [*vayacheilu*] somewhat by the burden of the king and princes" (Hosea 8:10). Ulla said: This verse was really said in Aramaic [in Aramaic *yitnu* means "learn" and *vayacheilu* means "they become free"]. Thus the verse translates: If they all learn Torah, I will gather them soon; and if only a small portion of them are Torah scholars, they will be freed from the taxes of the king and princes. [Therefore you should not have imposed a tax on the Torah scholars.] [R. Nachman b. Yitzchak violated] the Writings, for it says, "It shall not be lawful to impose upon [whomever serves in the Temple of God, including Torah scholars] any levy, tax, or duty, [*minda, belo,* and *halach*]" (Ezra 7:24), and Rav Yehudah said: *Minda* means the king's tax; *belo,* the head tax; and *halach,* the tax on farm products.

HE DID NOT WANT TO BENEFIT FROM THE TORAH

Rebbi [R. Yehudah Hanasi] opened his granaries in a year of food shortages and announced: Only those who have learned Torah, Mishnah, Gemara, and *aggadah* may enter, but admission is denied to unlearned people. R. Yonatan b. Amram, [who was known for his humility, disguised himself and] pushed his way in and said, "Rebbi, please give me food." Said Rebbi, "My son, did you learn Torah?" He replied, "No." "Did you learn Mishnah?" "No." "If so," said Rebbi, "how can I give you food?" "Feed me [as God feeds] the dog and the raven," R. Yonatan b. Amram pleaded.[3] So Rebbi gave him some food. After he left, Rebbi regretted it, and he said, "Woe is me, that I have given my food to an ignorant person." R. Shimon the son of Rebbi suggested, "Perhaps that was Yonatan b. Amram, your student, who never wants to derive benefit from his Torah knowledge?" They investigated and found that it was indeed so. Rebbi then announced, "The granary is open to everyone!" Rebbi [in barring the unlearned] was acting in accordance with his own principle: The ignorant are the cause of all misfortune in the world.

REDEMPTION OF CAPTIVES

Ifra Hurmiz, the mother of King Shvur, sent a purse with gold dinars to R. Yosef requesting that it should be used for a mitzvah of major importance. R. Yosef was pondering what should be considered a mitzvah of major importance when Abaye said to him: Since R. Shmuel b. Yehudah has taught that orphans should not be taxed even for the redemption of captives, we can infer (8b) that redemption of captives is a mitzvah of major importance.

Rava asked Rabbah b. Mari: From where do we derive the saying of the Rabbis that the redemption of captives is a mitzvah of major importance? He replied: For it says, "And if they tell you, 'Where shall we go?' say to them, 'Thus said God: Whoever is destined for death, to death; whoever for the sword, to the sword; whoever for famine, to famine; and whoever for captivity, to captivity'" (Jeremiah 15:20), and [commenting on this] R. Yochanan said: Each punishment mentioned in the verse is harsher than the one before it, thus [to be killed by] the sword is worse than natural death. That this is so can be proved by common sense, or if you prefer, by citing a Scripture. Common sense tells you that death by the sword is worse than natural death because the sword mutilates the body, and natural death does not. Or if you prefer, you can prove it from the verse, "Precious in the eyes of God is the [natural] death of his faithful ones" (Psalms 116:15). That famine is harsher than the sword can be proved by common sense, because death by famine brings a great deal of suffering, whereas death by the sword does not bring prolonged suffering. If you prefer, you can prove it from Scripture, "More fortunate were those slain by the sword than those slain by famine" (Lamentations 4:9). Captivity is harder than all of them, because it includes the suffering of all of the other punishments. [Consequently, the redemption of captives is a major mitzvah.]

COLLECTORS OF CHARITY

The Tanna said: We never give a position of authority over the community to less than two people. From where is this derived? R. Nachman said: It says, "And *they* [the skilled workers] shall take the gold [to make Aaron's vestments]" (Exodus 28:5); ["they" implies at least two]. This is proof that one single individual may not wield authority over the community, but that one single individual may be trusted to be treasurer of a charity fund, [because when making Aaron's vestments, each skilled worker took the gold he needed without giving an account]. This supports R. Chanina who said: It once happened that Rebbi appointed two brothers as treasurers of the charity fund [although two brothers count as one person].

[The Gemara asks:] What authority is there involved [in collecting charity, about which you said that the collectors must go in pairs, and that they may not go by themselves]? [The Gemara answers:] The reason was stated by R. Nachman in the name of R. Abbahu: Because the collectors can take [*tzedakah* money by force if the householder refuses to donate] and take collateral for a *tzedakah* contribution even on *erev Shabbat* [when the householder can claim that he cannot contribute because he is busy preparing for *Shabbat*]. [The Gemara asks:] Is that so? Doesn't it say, "I shall punish all his oppressors" (Jeremiah 30:20); said R. Yitzchak b. Shmuel b. Marta in the name of Rav, even collectors of *tzedakah* [who take *tzedakah* by force. So you see it is forbidden to take collateral]? [The Gemara answers:] There is no difficulty. [R. Abbahu] speaks about [collecting from] a wealthy person [who refuses to contribute, then the collector may force him to give a collateral]. [Rav] speaks about [collecting from] a poor man, [who is unable to contribute; if the collector forces him to give a collateral, he is an "oppressor who will be punished." For example, Rava compelled R. Natan b. Ammi [who was very wealthy] to donate four hundred *zuz* for *tzedakah*.

THEY WILL SHINE
LIKE THE STARS

It says, "The wise will shine like the radiance of the firmament" (Daniel 12:3)—this applies to a judge who has the wisdom to decide a case fairly and objectively. "And those who teach righteousness to the multitudes [will shine] like the stars, forever and ever" (ibid.): these are the collectors of *tzedakah*. However, in a *Baraita* we learned: "The wise will shine like the radi-

ance of the firmament"—this applies to a judge who has the wisdom to decide a case fairly and objectively. "And those who teach righteousness to the multitudes [will shine] like the stars, forever and ever"—applies to the teacher of young children. Like who, for example? Said Rav: Like R. Shmuel b. Shilas. For Rav once found R. Shmuel b. Shilas in a garden. "Have you left your post that you have held so faithfully?" He replied, "It has been thirteen years since I last saw my garden, and even now my thoughts are with my students." [The Gemara asks:] And what [reward is in store] for the Rabbis? Ravina said, "And may those that love Him be like the sun rising in might" (Judges 5:31).

TO INVESTIGATE OR
NOT TO INVESTIGATE?

(9a) R. Huna said: If a poor person asks for food, we investigate to see whether he really needs it, [of course this does not apply in a situation where it is obvious that he is famished]. However we do not investigate if a person comes with no clothing and says that he needs clothing. If you wish I can derive this from Scripture, and if you prefer I can show you that it is based on common sense. The common-sense reason that we do not investigate a person who is asking for clothing is that he is being humiliated; [he is standing there without clothing, while his credibility is being scrutinized], but not the person who is asking for food. Or if you prefer to hear the verse, it says, "Surely you should break [*paros*] your bread for the hungry" (Isaiah 58:7). *Paros* is written with the letter *sin*,[4] [and we read it as if it had a *shin*, *parosh*] and translate it, "If it is clear [that he is hungry] then give him from your bread." But with regard to clothing it says, "When you see a naked person clothe him" (ibid.)—immediately.

Rav Yehudah, however, said [the opposite]: You have to investigate if a person asks for clothing, but you do not investigate if he asks for food. If you wish I can base it on a verse; or if you prefer, on common sense. Common sense dictates that a person asking for food is suffering from hunger, but a person who has no clothes is not suffering. If you prefer a verse: in regard to food it says, "Surely you should break your bread for the hungry." "Break off"—right away. However in regard to clothing it says, "When you see a naked person, clothe him"—when you are convinced [that he is in need of clothing]. We learned a *Baraita* that agrees with Rav Yehudah: If a poor man says he wants clothing, we investigate him; if he says he wants food, we don't investigate.

REFLECTIONS ON *TZEDAKAH*

A poor person who used to go from door to door to collect for himself came to R. Papa asking for money [from the charity fund], but he would not give him anything. Said R. Samma the son of R. Yeiva to R. Papa: If you are not going to give him anything, no one else will give him anything either, and he will starve to death. [Replied R. Papa:] But we learned that if the poor man is going from door to door, we are not required to give him anything [from the charity fund]. He answered: We are not required to give him a substantial amount, but we must give him a small donation.

R. Assi said: A person should see to it that he gives at least one-third of a shekel to *tzedakah* every year, as it says, "We also instituted commandments upon ourselves to give one-third of a shekel yearly toward the service of the Temple of our God" (Nehemiah 10:33). R. Assi said furthermore: *Tzedakah* is equivalent to all other *mitzvot* together, for it says [in regard to the mitzvah of *tzedakah*], "We also instituted commandments: it does not say "a commandment," but "commandments" [in the plural].

R. Elazar said: Someone who influences others to give *tzedakah* is greater than the person who gives *tzedakah* himself. For it says, "The product of *tzedakah* [i.e., causing others to give *tzedakah*] shall be peace; and the effect of giving *tzedakah*, quiet and security forever" (Isaiah 32:17), [peace is a greater blessing than quiet and security].

Rava said to the people of Mechuza: I beg you, please be charitable to one another so that you will live in peace with the government. R. Elazar further said: When the *Bet Hamikdash* stood, a person used to donate his half *shekel* [and through that he had a share in the continual offering] and received atonement. Now that the *Bet Hamikdash* no longer stands, if a person gives *tzedakah*, fine; and if not, the idolators will come and take it by force. And even though [he lost his money to the idolators] God will consider it as if he gave *tzedakah*, for it says, "your oppressors for *tzedakah*" (Isaiah 60:17)—the money your oppressors take from you is considered *tzedakah*.

(9b) R. Elazar said: A person who gives *tzedakah* in secret is greater than Moses our teacher, for Moses said, "For I was terrified because of the anger and the blazing wrath" (Deuteronomy 9:19); and about a person who gives *tzedakah* secretly it says, "A gift given in secret will subdue anger" (Proverbs 21:14). R. Elazar differs on this point with R. Yitzchak, for R. Yitzchak said: *Tzedakah* given in secret subdues anger but not blazing wrath, since the verse continues, "and a present in the bosom [will appease] strong wrath" (ibid.) [which we can interpret to mean: Although a present is placed in the bosom, wrath is still strong]. Others say, R. Yitzchak said: A judge who takes a bribe brings strong wrath on the world, for it says, "A present in the bosom brings strong wrath in its wake."

R. Yitzchak further said: Whoever gives a small coin to a poor man is rewarded with six blessings, and someone who only comforts him with words [and is unable to give him a coin] receives eleven blessings [so that, if he gives a coin and comforts him, he will receive seventeen blessings]. How do we know that whoever gives a coin to a poor man receives six blessings? Because it says, "Surely you should break your bread for the hunger and bring the moaning poor to your home . . . when you see a naked person clothe him" (Isaiah 58:7); [the next verse lists six blessings— "Then your light will burst forth like the dawn, . . ."] (ibid. v. 8). And someone who comforts him with words receives eleven blessings, because it says, "And [when you] offer your soul to the hungry [taking a genuine interest in his plight (Redak)] and satisfy the afflicted soul; then your light will shine [even] in the darkness, and your deepest gloom will be like noon. Then God will guide you always, sate your soul in time of drought and strengthen your bones . . . Ancient ruins will be rebuilt through you, and you will restore generations-old foundations . . ." (ibid. 10–12).

R. Yitzchak also said: What is meant by the verse, "One who pursues *tzedakah* and kindness will find life, *tzedakah*, and honor" (Proverbs 21:21)? [Assuming that "he will find *tzedakah*" means that he will find people who will give him *tzedakah*, the Gemara asks:] Because he has always given *zedakah*, does he deserve to become a recipient of *tzedakah*? [The Gemara answers: "He will find *tzedakah*"] means, if a person does his best to give *tzedakah*, the Holy One, blessed be He, will supply him with the means to give *tzedakah*. R. Nachman b. Yitzchak said: The Holy One, blessed be He, will send him people who are truly deserving recipients of *tzedakah*, so that he will be rewarded [in the World to Come] for having given *tzedakah*.

What does this exclude? It excludes the kind of people Rabbah had in mind when he expounded: What is the meaning of the verse, [Jeremiah cursed the people of Anatot who wanted to kill him:] "May they be caused to stumble before You, at the time of Your anger, act against them!" (Jeremiah 18:23). Jeremiah said to the Holy One, blessed be He: Master of the universe! Even at a time when they subdue their evil impulse, and they try to give *tzedakah*, make them stumble through people who are not worthy to receive *tzedakah*, so that they should not receive the reward for the mitzvah of giving *tzedakah*. [And only people who "pursue *tzedakah* and kindness" will be privileged to find worthy recipients for their charitable contributions.]

R. Yehoshua b. Levi said: Anyone who continually gives *tzedakah* will have children who are Torah scholars, who are wealthy, and who know the expositions and *aggadic* teachings of the Sages. "Children who are Torah scholars" because it says, (10a) "He finds life" (Proverbs 21:21) [and the Torah is often referred to as life]. "Children who are wealthy," because it says, "[he will find] *tzedakah* [meaning, he will have the wherewithal to give *tzedakah*]. "Children who know the expositions and *aggadic* teachings" because it says, "[he will find] honor," and it says, "The wise inherit honor" (ibid. 3:35); [they will be respected for their oratory skills].

R. AKIVA'S ANSWER
TO TURNUS RUFUS

We learned in a *Baraita*: R. Meir used to say: If an unbeliever wants to criticize you, he might ask the following question, "If your God loves the poor, why doesn't He sustain them?" You should answer him, "[God wants to give us the opportunity to give *tzedakah*,] so that through the poor we should be saved from the punishment of Gehinnom." This question actually was asked by Turnus Rufus to R. Akiva, "If your God loves the poor, why doesn't He support them?" Replied R. Akiva, "In order that we should be saved from the punishment of Gehinnom, [through the *tzedakah* we give them]." "On the contrary," said Turnus Rufus. "[Giving charity] will bring you to Gehinnom! I'll give you a parable. Let's say a king was angry with his servant and put him in jail. He ordered that no food or drink should be given to him, but someone went and gave him food and drink. If the king finds out, wouldn't he be angry at him? Now you are called "servants" as it says, 'The children of Israel are My servants' (Leviticus 25:55), [and you are in prison (meaning, in exile); hence, by feeding the poor you are violating God's will].

R. Akiva answered, "I will tell you another parable. Let's say a king was angry with his son and put him in jail. He ordered that no food or drink should be given to him, and someone went and gave him food and drink. If the king finds out, wouldn't he send him a present [for having pity on his son]? Now we are called 'sons' as it says, 'You are sons of God'" (Deuteronomy 14:1). Retorted Turnus Rufus, "You are called both sons and servants. When you are fulfilling God's will you are called 'sons,' and when you are not fulfilling God's will you are called 'servants.' At the present time [that your Temple is destroyed and you are under Roman domination] you are not fulfilling God's wish, [therefore you are considered "servants" and should not be giving charity, as indicated by the parable]." R. Akiva replied, "It says, 'Surely you should break your bread for the hungry, and bring the oppressed poor to your house' (Isaiah 58:7), [and "oppressed" means oppressed by the government]. When can we bring the 'oppressed poor to our house'? Now [that we are under foreign domination]; and it says [at the same time], 'Surely you should break your bread for the hungry.'"

THE MAGNIFICENCE
OF *TZEDAKAH*

R. Yehudah b. Shalom lectured: Just as a person's income for the year is determined on Rosh Hashanah, so are his losses determined on Rosh Hashanah. If he merits, [those losses will take the form of the *tzedakah* he gives, and they will be] "the bread you break for the hungry," but if he does not merit, "he will bring the oppressed poor to his house" [a reference to the tax collectors who will take his money]. An illustration of this is the case of the nephews of R. Yochanan b. Zakkai. He saw in a dream that they were going to lose seven hundred *dinars* in the coming year. [During the course of the year] he urged them to give this amount of money for *tzedakah*, [and they gave it,] until on *erev* Rosh Hashanah they were short seventeen *dinars* [of the 700 *dinars*; they had given only 683 *dinars*]. On *erev* Yom Kippur, government agents seized seventeen *dinars*. R. Yochanan b. Zakkai told them, "Don't be afraid [that they will take more]; you had seventeen *dinars*, and those they took." They asked him, "How did you know all this?" "I saw it in a dream," he replied. "Then why didn't you tell us, so that we could have given the whole amount to *tzedakah*?" He replied, "I wanted you to give *tzedakah* purely for the sake of the mitzvah [and not because of the decree I saw in my dream]."

WITHHOLDING *TZEDAKAH*

R. Papa was climbing up a ladder when his foot slipped, and he almost fell. He said, "If I had fallen [off the ladder] I would have been punished like a violator of *Shabbat* or an idolater [these were punished by *sekilah* (stoning), and falling to death is a substitute for *sekilah*]."[5] Chiya b. Rav from Difti said to him: Maybe [you almost fell because] a poor man appealed to you, and you did not give him anything. For we learned in a *Baraita*: R. Yehoshua b. Korchah said: If someone looks away [when a poor man appeals to him for] *tzedakah*, it is as if he worshipped idols. It says in one place, "Beware lest there be a lawless thought in your heart [of denying a loan to the poor before the Sabbatical year]" (Deuteronomy 15:9); and it says elsewhere, "Lawless men have emerged from your midst [who seduce the people to worship idols]" (ibid. 13:14). Just as "lawless" in the last verse refers to idolatry, so does "lawless" in the first verse refer to a sin [i.e., denying *tzedakah*] that is equivalent to idolatry.

TZEDAKAH SAVES FROM DEATH

We learned in a *Baraita*: R. Eliezer b. R. Yose said: All *tzedakah* and acts of kindness that Israel perform in this world bring about great peace and create angels who defend Israel before their Father in heaven, as it says, "For thus says God: Do not go to a house of mourning, and do not go to eulogize nor to shake [your head in sorrow] for them; for I have revoked My peace and kindness and mercy from this people" (Jeremiah 16:5). "Kindness" refers to acts of kindness; "mercy" refers to *tzedakah*, [and the passage means: God revoked His peace, which is the product of acts of kindness and *tzedakah*, because they no longer do them].

We learned in a *Baraita*: R. Yehudah said: Great is charity, for it brings the redemption closer, for it says, "Thus said God, 'Observe justice, and do *tzedakah*, for My salvation is soon to come and My righteousness to be revealed" (Isaiah 56:1). He also used to say: Ten strong things were created in the world: A mountain is strong, but iron can cut it. Iron is hard, but fire softens it. Fire is strong, but water extinguishes it. Water is strong, but the clouds contain it. The clouds are strong, but the wind scatters them. The wind is strong, but a body can contain it [in the lungs]. The body is strong, but fear can crush it. Fear is strong, but wine allays fear. Wine is strong, but sleep dissipates it. Death is stronger than all, and *tzedakah* saves from death, as it says, "*Tzedakah* saves from death" (Proverbs 10:2).

R. Dostai b. Yannai lectured: Come and see the difference between a mortal king and the Holy One, blessed be He. The nature of a mortal king is that when a person brings him a present, it may or may not be accepted; and even if it is accepted, it is uncertain whether or not he will be granted an audience with the king. Not so the Holy One, blessed be He. If a person gives just a small coin to a poor man, he is considered worthy to receive the presence of the *Shechinah*, for it says, "As for me, through *tzedakah* I will merit to behold Your face, upon awaking I will be sated by Your image" (Psalms 17:15). R. Elazar would first give a coin to a poor man and only then go to pray, because, he said, it says, "Through *tzedakah* I will merit to behold Your face, upon awaking I will be sated by Your image." What is meant by the words, "Upon awaking I will be sated by Your image?" R. Nachman b. Yitzchak said: [It means: As a reward for staying awake I will be sated by Your image,] and it refers to Torah scholars who keep away sleep from their eyes, [while learning Torah late into the night,] in this world, and whom the Holy One, blessed be He, will satiate with the splendor of the *Shechinah* in the World to Come.

THE PERFECT WAY OF GIVING *TZEDAKAH*

R. Yochanan said: What is the meaning of the verse, "One who is gracious to the poor has lent to God" (Proverbs 19:17)? If this were not an explicit verse, it would be impossible to say such a thing: it is as if we were saying in regard to God, "A borrower is a slave to the lender" (ibid. 22:7).

R. Chiya b. Abba said: R. Yochanan pointed out a contradiction between two passages. It says, "Wealth will not avail in the day of wrath, but *tzedakah* saves from death" (ibid. 11:4), and it also says, "Treasures of wickedness will not avail, but *tzedakah* rescues from death" (ibid. 10:2). Why is the phrase about *tzedakah* mentioned twice? One verse refers to saving from an unnatural death; the other refers to saving from the punishment of Gehinnom. Which verse speaks of saving from the punishment of Gehinnom? The one that uses the word "wrath," for it says, [concerning the day of Final Judgment,] "A day of wrath is that day" (Zephanaiah 1:15).

And what kind of *tzedakah* saves a person from an unnatural death [that the other verse is referring to]? (10b) When a person gives *tzedakah* without knowing to whom he is giving, and the poor man receives it without knowing from whom he gets it. [This is the perfect way of giving *tzedakah*.] "Giving without knowing to whom you are giving" excludes the practice of Mar Ukva [who used to leave money on the doorstep of poor people in his neighborhood—he knew to whom he was giving it]. "The poor man receives without knowing from whom he gets it" excludes the practice of R. Abba [who used to drop coins behind him for the poor to pick up—the poor knew from whom they were getting it]. [The Gemara asks:] So how should you give *tzedakah*? You should put the money into a *tzedakah* box.

An objection was raised: [How can you say that everyone should put money in a *tzedakah* box?] Haven't we learned in a *Baraita*: What should a person do that he may have male children? R. Eliezer says: He should give generously to the poor. R. Yehoshua says: He should make his wife happy before they fulfill their mitzvah together. R. Eliezer b. Yaakov says: You should not put a coin into a *tzedakah* box unless the person in charge of distributing the funds is as great a *tzaddik* as R. Chanina b. Teradion.[6] [Then how can you recommend that everybody should put money in a *tzedakah* box; obviously not every treasurer is as great a *tzaddik* as R. Chanina b. Teradion!] [The Gemara answers:] Not that he has to be as great a *tzaddik* as R. Chanina b. Teradion, but as trustworthy as R. Chanina b. Teradion.

R. Abbahu said: Moses said to the Holy One, blessed be He, "Master of the universe! How is the glory of Israel going to be elevated?" God replied, "Through 'When you take a census' (Exodus 30:12)." [Literally: "when you lift the head." When a census was taken, each person contributed half a shekel. The *shekalim* were then counted and used for *tzedakah* purposes. In other words, the mitzvah of *tzedakah* has the ability to elevate the Jewish people.] R. Abbahu also said: Solomon the son of David was asked: How great is the power of *tzedakah*? He replied: Take a look at what my father David wrote in Psalms, "He who has distributed widely to the destitute, his *tzedakah* endures forever, his pride will be exalted with glory" (Psalms 112:9). R. Abba derives the power of *tzedakah* from the following passage, "He shall dwell in heights; in rocky fortresses is his stronghold; his bread will be granted, his water assured" (Isaiah 33:16). Why will he dwell in heights; in rocky fortresses is his stronghold? Because his bread he gave to the poor and his water could be relied on by the destitute.

A TOPSY-TURVY WORLD

R. Abbahu also said: They asked Solomon the son of David: Who will be able to enter the World to Come?

He replied: [An elderly person who is respected in this world because of his wisdom, as it says,] "There will be honor for His elders" (Isaiah 24:23). This is similar to what R. Yosef b. R. Yehoshua said. He was sick and had an out-of-body experience [where the soul briefly leaves the body and then returns]. His father asked him, "What did you see [in your out-of-body state]? He replied, "I saw a topsy-turvy world; those that are on top in this world [respected for their wealth and power] are at the bottom [in the World to Come]; and those that are on the bottom in this world [the poor and downtrodden], are on top." His father told him, "[You did not see an upside-down world] but an unconfused, sensible world."

[He then asked,] "And how do we Torah scholars rate there?" "Just as Torah scholars are respected in this world, so are they in the World to Come. And I heard them say, 'Praiseworthy is he who comes to this world and has his learning with him.' I also heard them say, 'Those that were killed by the [Roman] government [are on such a lofty level in heaven] that no living being can stand close to them.'" Who are the martyrs that were killed by the Roman government? Do you think R. Akiva and his colleagues? Is their martyrdom the only reason that no one can come close to them? Obviously, even without that [they would have attained this lofty position in heaven. They were all towering *tzaddikim*!]. Rather it is referring to the martyrs of Lud.[7]

TZEDAKAH WILL UPLIFT A NATION

We learned in a *Baraita*: R. Yochanan b. Zakkai said to his students: My sons, what is meant by the verse, "*Tzedakah* will uplift a nation, but the kindness of the gentiles is imperfect" (Proverbs 14:34)? R. Eliezer answered and said: "*Tzedakah* will uplift a nation"—this refers to Israel about whom it says, "Who is like Your people, like Israel, a unique nation on earth?" (2 Samuel 7:23). "But the kindness of the gentiles is imperfect" Why? Because all the *tzedakah* and kindness the gentiles do they only do in order that they should live long, for it says, "So that they may offer pleasing offerings to the God of heaven and pray for the lives of the king and his children" (Ezra 6:10). [The Gemara asks:] But if someone gives *tzedakah* with that intent, is it not considered real *tzedakah*? Surely we learned in a *Baraita*: If someone says: I am giving this *sela* for *tzedakah* for the purpose that my children should live or that I should be worthy to have a share in the World to Come, he is a nevertheless considered a real *tzaddik*. [Then why do we say that the kindness of the gentiles is imperfect because they do it to attain long life?] [The Gemara answers:] There is no difficulty: in the one case we speak of a Jew; [he gives *tzedakah* for the sake of the mitzvah, regardless of what

he says]. In the other case we speak of a gentile; [he only gives charity for the condition he stipulated; if his condition is not fulfilled, he regrets having given charity].

R. Yehoshua answered and said, "*Tzedakah* will uplift a nation"—this refers to Israel about whom it says, "Who is like Your people, like Israel, a unique nation in the world." "But the kindness of the peoples is flawed"—All the charity and kindness the gentiles do is counted as imperfect because they only do it in order that their kingdom should exist longer, for it says, [Daniel advised Belshazzar,] "Nevertheless, O king, let my advice be acceptable to you: Redeem your sins through righteousness and your iniquities through kindness to the poor; perhaps there will be an extension to your tranquility" (Daniel 4:24). R. Gamliel responded and said: "*Tzedakah* will uplift a nation" refers to Israel about whom it says, "Who is like Your people, like Israel, a unique nation on earth" (2 Samuel 7:23). "But the kindness of the gentiles is imperfect"—All the charity and kindness the gentiles do is counted as flawed because they only do it to boast about it, and whoever is boastful will end up in Gehinnom, for it says, "The boastful, willful man, scoffer is his name; the arrogant evildoer, he is a willful [*evrah*] man" (Proverbs 21:24). And *evrah* denotes Gehinnom, as it says, "A day of *evrah* [wrath] is that day" (Zephaniah 1:15). Said R. Gamliel: We still have to hear our colleague from Modiim's interpretation.

R. Eliezer from Modiim says: "'*Tzedakah* will uplift a nation" refers to Israel about whom it says, "Who is like Your people, like Israel, a unique nation on earth." "But the kindness of the gentiles is considered deficient"—all the charity and kindness of the nations of the world is flawed because they do it only to offend us, as it says, [Nebuzaradan, the chief of Nebuchadnezzar's guards, after he released Jeremiah from his chains said to him,] "God brought it about and did as He said, because you sinned to God and did not heed His voice, so this matter befell you" (Jeremiah 40:3). [Even when he did an act of kindness, his purpose was to humiliate Israel.] R. Nechuniah b. Hakanah answered and said: [The verse is to be read like this,] "*Tzedakah* as well as kindness will uplift a nation [i.e., Israel], and as far as the gentiles are concerned, their conduct is flawed.

Said R. Yochanan b. Zakkai to his students: I like R. Nechuniah b. Hakanah's interpretation better than my own and yours, because he attributes to Israel not only *tzedakah* but also kindness, and to the gentiles he ascribes imperfection. This statement of R. Yochanan b. Zakkai implies that he too offered an exposition of the verse. How did he interpret it? We learned in a *Baraita*: R. Yochanan b. Zakkai said: Just as a sin-offering makes atonement for Israel, so does charity atone for the nation of the world.

HE FED THE HUNGRY
DURING A FAMINE

(11a) The Rabbis taught: The following story is told about Benjamin the *Tzaddik* who was in charge of the *tzedakah* fund. One day—it was a year of famine—a woman came to him asking for food. "I swear," he said, "there isn't a penny in the charity fund." "Rabbi, if you don't give me food," she said, "a woman and her seven children will starve to death." Thereupon he gave her money from his own pocket. A while later he became seriously ill and was close to death. The angels in heaven said to the Holy One, blessed be He, "Master of the universe! You said that he who saves one Jewish life is considered as if he had saved the entire world; should Benjamin the *Tzaddik* who saved the lives of a woman and her seven children die at such a young age?" Immediately his verdict [in heaven] was torn up. We learned that twenty-two years were added to his life.

THE WISE KING MONOBAZ

We learned in a *Baraita*: King Monobaz[8] spent his own fortunes and the fortunes of his forebears to feed the hungry in the years of drought. His brothers and his father's family rebuked him, "Your fathers saved, and added to the treasures, while you squander them." He replied, "My fathers saved up for this world below; I save up for the world above, as it says, "Truth will sprout from earth, and righteousness will peer from heaven" (Psalms 85:12). My fathers stored in a place where human hands can wreak havoc, but I have stored in a place where no human hands can interfere, as it says, "Righteousness and justice are the foundations of His Throne" (ibid. 97:2), [*tzedakah* and justice are hidden away beneath God's Throne].

My fathers stored something that produces no fruits, but I have stored something that does produce fruits, as it says, "Tell each *tzaddik* that it is good, for they shall eat the fruit of their deed [in this world, while the principal remains intact for the World to Come]" (Isaiah 3:10). My fathers accumulated treasures of money, but I have accumulated treasures of souls, for it says, "The fruit of a *tzaddik* is a tree of life, and a wise man acquires souls" (Proverbs 11:30). My fathers gathered for others, but I have gathered for myself, for it says, "And for you it will be an act of *tzedakah*" (Deuteronomy 24:13). My fathers piled up for life in this world, but I have piled up for life in the hereafter, as it says, "Your righteous deeds will precede you, and the glory of God will gather you in [when you die]" (Isaiah 58:8).

PROPHECY GIVEN TO WISE MEN

(12a) R. Avdimi of Haifa said: Since the day the *Bet Hamikdash* was destroyed, prophecy has been taken away from the prophets and has been given to wise men. [The Gemara asks:] Is then a wise man not fit to be a prophet? [Meaning, were not wise men prophets before the *Bet Hamikdash* was destroyed?] [The Gemara answers:] This is what R. Avdimi meant to say: Even though prophecy has been taken away from prophets [who were not wise men],[9] from the wise men it has not been taken away; [they are the only ones who retained prophecy]. Ameimar said: A wise man is greater than a prophet, as it says, "A prophet has a heart of wisdom" (Psalms 90:12).[10] Usually when making an analogy, you compare the smaller to the greater. [Therefore, when it says that a prophet has a heart like that of a wise man, it means that a wise man is greater than a prophet.]

Abaye said: You can prove [that wise men still have prophecy] by the fact that very often a great Torah scholar will make an [original] statement, and the same thing is then reported in the name of another great scholar, [hence both must have had prophetic insight]. Rava said: What does that prove? Perhaps both were born under the same constellation, [and they think along the same lines, and that is why they both came to the same conclusion]. No, said Rava. The proof is that a great scholar will say something, and then the same is reported (12b) in the name of R. Akiva b. Yosef [who is a much greater scholar, and thus you cannot say that they were born under the same constellation].

Said R. Ashi: What is the problem? Perhaps just in this one instance we say that they think along similar lines. But, said R. Ashi: the proof is that sometimes a great scholar said something, and later we find out that the same thing was a *halachah* that was taught to Moses at Mount Sinai. [The Gemara asks:] Maybe [he just stumbled across the *halachah* by chance], like a blind man who finds a window, [but that does not prove that he had prophecy]. [The Gemara answers: You cannot say that.] Does he not give an explanation [for his statement]? [Therefore, if his statement coincides with the *halachah* of Moses, it proves that God directed his thinking process through a form of prophecy.]

PROPHECY GIVEN TO FOOLS
AND CHILDREN

R. Yochanan said: Since the day the *Bet Hamikdash* was destroyed, prophecy has been taken away from prophets and has been given to fools and children. Where do we find that prophecy was given to fools? As in the case of Mar the son of R. Ashi. He was standing in the marketplace of Mechuza when he heard a certain madman exclaim, "The person who will be appointed as head of the yeshivah of Mata Mechasya signs his name Taviumi." He said to himself, "Which one of the Rabbis signs his name Taviumi? I do. Apparently, my time has come." So he hurried to Mata Mechasya. By the time he got there, the Rabbis had voted to name R.

Acha of Difti as *rosh yeshivah* [but they had not actually appointed him]. When the Rabbis heard that Mar the son of R. Ashi had arrived, they sent a pair of rabbis to him to consult him [and to get his consent to appoint R. Acha as *rosh yeshivah*]. He detained them, so they sent two more rabbis. He detained them too; this went on until there were ten rabbis. As soon as he had a *minyan* of ten, he began to lecture and expound, because you do not begin a discourse with less than a *minyan* in attendance, [and thereby became the de facto *rosh yeshivah*].[11]

R. Acha applied to himself the saying: If things go bad for a person, his fortune will not change for the better quickly; and if a person is in luck, his fortune will not go bad overnight. [He conceded the fact that Mar the son of R. Ashi would be the *rosh yeshivah*.] [The Gemara asks:] Where do we find that prophecy has been given to children? [The Gemara answers:] A case in point is that of the daughter of R. Chisda. She was sitting on her father's lap, and in front of him were sitting Rava and Rami b. Chama. He said to her, "Which one would you like to marry?" "I would like to marry both," she replied. Rava immediately retorted, "Let me be the second one." [Evidently he assumed that the child had the power of prophecy.][12]

HOSEA, THE FIRST OF THE PROPHETS

(14b) The Rabbis taught: [When you write] the books of the Prophets on one scroll they should be written in the following order: Joshua, Judges, Samuel, Kings, Jeremiah, Ezekiel, Isaiah, and the Twelve Prophets. [The Gemara asks:] Let us see. It would seem that Hosea [the first of the Twelve Prophets] came before all the prophets, for it says, "God began by speaking to Hosea" (Hosea 1:2). Is it possible to say that God spoke first to Hosea? Were there not many prophets from Moses until Hosea? R. Yochanan explained: The passage means that Hosea was the first of the four prophets that prophesied in that era,[13] namely: Hosea, Isaiah, Amos, and Micah. [The Gemara says:] So, let Hosea come first, [why is Isaiah placed before Hosea]? [The Gemara answers:] Since we want to put Hosea's prophecy together [on the same scroll] with the other minor prophets, Haggai, Zechariah, and Malachi, and they were the last of the prophets,[14] his book was placed together with them. [The Gemara asks:] Why not write Hosea as a separate book, [and place it before Isaiah]?

[The Gemara answers:] Since it is a small book [only fourteen chapters, if it were written together with the major prophets and placed between Jeremiah and Isaiah],[15] it would pale into insignificance. [The Gemara continues:] Let us look at this. [Chronologically] Isaiah preceded Jeremiah and Ezekiel. Then why should not Isaiah be placed first? [The Gemara answers:] Because Kings ends with the destruction of the

Bet Hamikdash [since it relates the exile of the ten tribes], and [the majority] of Jeremiah deals with the destruction of the *Bet Hamikdash* and ends with words of consolation; and Isaiah consists largely of consolation; therefore we place destruction next to destruction and consolation next to consolation.

[When you write the] Books of the Writings on a scroll, they should be written in the following order: Ruth, Psalms, Job, Proverbs, Ecclesiastes, Song of Songs, Lamentations, Daniel, Esther, Ezra, Chronicles. [Most of these are in chronological order: Ruth was written by Samuel; Psalms by David; Proverbs, Ecclesiastes, and Song of Songs by Solomon; Lamentations by Jeremiah; Daniel lived after Jeremiah; Esther was written in the the days of Achashverosh in Persia; Ezra under Darius II who succeeded Achashverosh (Rashi).] [The Gemara asks:] According to the one who holds that Job lived in the time of Moses, should not the Book of Job come first? [The Gemara answers:] We do not want to begin with a tragedy. But the story of Ruth is also filled with tragedy [famine, exile, the death of Elimelech and his sons]? It is a tragedy that has a good ending. For R. Yochanan said: Why was she called Ruth? Because David who gratified [*rivah*] God with his songs and praises descended from her. [Therefore the Writings could begin with Ruth.]

WHO WROTE THE BOOKS OF *TANACH*?

[The Gemara asks:] Who wrote the Books of *Tanach*? Moses wrote his own book [the Five Books of the Torah], the chapter of Balaam [16] and Job. Joshua wrote his own book and the last eight verses of the Torah [that describe the passing of Moses]. Samuel wrote his own book as well as Judges and Ruth. David wrote Psalms [however he incorporated in it] the psalms of the ten elders, namely, Adam, Melchizedek, Abraham, Moses, Heiman, Yedutun, Asaph, (15a) and the three sons of Korach. Jeremiah wrote his own book, Kings, and Lamentations. Hezekiah and his colleagues wrote Isaiah,[17] Proverbs, Song of Songs, and Ecclesiastes. The Men of the Great Assembly wrote Ezekiel, the Twelve Prophets, Daniel, and the Book of Esther. Ezra wrote his own book [which includes Nehemiah], and the genealogies of the Book of Chronicles, down to himself. This supports Rav's view, for Rav Yehudah said in Rav's name: Before Ezra went up to Eretz Yisrael from Babylonia he recorded his genealogy. And who finished [the Book of Chronicles]? Nehemiah the son of Chachaliah.

WHO WROTE THE FINAL EIGHT VERSES OF THE TORAH?

We learned above: Joshua wrote his own book and the last eight verses of the Torah. The following *Baraita* supports this view: It says, "It was there that God's servant Moses died" (Deuteronomy 34:5). Now is it possible that after Moses was dead, he wrote the words, "he died"? [That would not be true! So how could he have written this verse?] We must say therefore that up to this point Moses wrote the text; from this point on, Joshua wrote. This is the opinion of R. Yehudah; others say, of R. Nechemiah. Said R. Shimon: Is it possible that even one letter was missing from the Torah scroll that Moses wrote? Doesn't it say, [Moses said to the Levites who carried the Ark,] "Take this Torah scroll" (ibid. 31:26), [and a Torah scroll that is incomplete is not valid? Therefore, when he handed them the Torah scroll it must have been complete, and written by Moses in its entirety.]

We must say, therefore, that up to the last eight verses God told Moses what to write, and Moses would verbalize the words and then write them; from that point on, God would say the words, and Moses would write them with tears. [He wept because he felt the throes of death setting in. Therefore, it was not untrue for him to write "Moses died," since he was at the point of death (Maharal).] Just as God dictated to Moses, so did the prophets dictate their message, as it says, "Baruch replied to them, 'From his mouth he [Jeremiah] would dictate all these words to me, and I would write them on the book with ink'" (Jeremiah 36:18).

[The Gemara asks:] According to whom is the following statement by R. Yehoshua b. Abba in the name of R. Giddal in the name of Rav: The last eight verses of the Torah must be read by one person [at the Torah reading in the synagogue, and may not be split into two portions, to show that they are different from the rest of the Torah]? We should say that is according to R. Yehudah [who said that Joshua wrote them, and therefore they are different], and not according to R. Shimon [who holds that Moses wrote these verses himself, albeit with tears in his eyes]. [The Gemara answers:] You could even say that it follows R. Shimon's opinion, and since they are different [in the sense that Moses wrote them while in tears], they are different [in that they must be read to or by one person only].

We learned that Joshua wrote his own book. [The Gemara asks: But it says in the Book of Joshua,] "Joshua, the servant of God, died" (Joshua 24:29)? [How could he have written that?] [The Gemara answers:] Elazar finished it. But it also says [in Joshua], "And Elazar the son of Aaron died" (ibid. v. 33)? Pinchas [the son of Elazar] finished it.

We learned that Samuel wrote his own book. But it says, "And Samuel died" (1 Samuel 28:3)? It was completed by Gad the Seer and Nathan the Prophet. We learned that David wrote Psalms, including the psalms of the ten elders [and the *Baraita* (on 14b) lists the names of the ten elders]. [The Gemara asks:] Why is not Ethan the Ezrahite mentioned [the author of Psalm 89]? Rav said: Ethan the Ezrahite is Abraham [and Abraham is listed in the *Baraita*]. For it says here,

"Ethan the Ezrahite" (Psalms 89:1) and it says elsewhere, "Who inspired the one from the east [*mimizrach*] at whose [every] footstep righteousness attended?" (Isaiah 41:2), [a reference to Abraham who came to Canaan from Aram to the east].

[The Gemara asks:] The *Baraita* lists Moses [among the ten elders whose psalms were included in the Book of Psalms] and also Heiman. But did not Rav say that Moses and Heiman are one and the same, based on the fact that the name Heiman is found in Psalms [88:1] and elsewhere it says [about Moses] "He is like a trusted [*neeman*] servant in all My house" (Numbers 12:7)? [The name Heiman is seen as related to *neeman*.] [The Gemara answers:] There were two people named Heiman. [The Heiman mentioned in Psalms is a different person altogether.]

WHO WAS JOB?

We learned in the *Baraita* that Moses wrote the Torah and the chapter about Balaam and the Book of Job. This confirms the opinion of R. Levi b. Lachma who said that Job lived in the time of Moses. Rava, however, said that Job lived in the time of the spies [who were sent by Moses to explore the Canaanite territory], for it says regarding Job, "There was a man in the land of Utz whose name was Job" (Job 1:10). And [in connection with the spies it says,] "See whether the land has trees [*eitz*] or not" (Numbers 13:20). [The Gemara asks:] How can you compare the two? In one verse it says Utz, in the other *eitz*! [The Gemara answers:] This is what Moses said to Israel: [In the land of Canaan] there is a man [Job] who lives as long as a tree[18] and protects his generation like a tree [that provides sheltering shade. Which proves that Job lived in the time of Moses].

One of the Rabbis who was sitting before R. Shmuel b. Nachmani remarked in a discourse: Job never existed; the Book of Job is to be understood as a parable [designed to teach people how to act when misfortune strikes]. R. Shmuel b. Nachmani replied: According to your theory, what is the meaning of the verse, "There was a man in the land of Utz whose name was Job"? [The fact that the verse states his name and residence indicates that he did exist!] He retorted: If that is so, what about the verse, [when Nathan came to reproach David about the matter of Bathsheba, he said,] "But the poor man had nothing except one small ewe" (2 Samuel 12:3). Surely this is nothing but a parable [that Nathan used to make his point]. So, too, Job is simply a parable. R. Shmuel b. Nachmani countered: If so, why are Job's name and the name of his city mentioned?

R. Yochanan and R. Elazar both stated that Job was one of the people who returned to Eretz Yisrael from Babylonia [with Ezra], and he had a *bet midrash* in T'veriah [Tiberias, hence Job was a Jew]. An objection was raised from the following *Baraita*: The lifespan of

Job extended from the time that Israel entered Egypt until they left it; [thus he could not have been one of the returning exiles]. (15b) [The Gemara answers:] The *Baraita* means to tell us that he lived as long as the time Israel was in Egypt [i.e., 210 years]. An objection was raised from the following *Baraita*; [to refute the assumption that Job was a Jew]: Seven prophets prophesied to the nations of the world: Balaam and his father; Job; Eliphaz the Temanite; Bildad the Shuchite; Zophar the Naamatite; and Elihu, son of Berachel the Buzite. [This would suggest that Job was a non-Jewish prophet.]

[The Gemara asks:] According to your premise, [that Job was not a Jew], was not Elihu, son of Berachel a Jew, inasmuch as it says clearly that he was a member of the family of Ram (Job 32:2), [and the fact that the text mentions his lineage indicates that he was a Jew]. We must say therefore that Elihu was a Jewish prophet who prophesied to the nations of the world. So too here we can say that Job [was a Jew] who prophesied to the nations of the world.

[The Gemara asks:] But did not all the prophets prophesy to the nations of the world? [Then why did the *Baraita* single out the seven prophets? It must be because they were non-Jews.] [The Gemara answers:] The prophecies of the Jewish prophets were primarily addressed to Israel, but these seven prophets [some of whom could be Jews] are singled out because their prophecies were directed at the nations of the world; [thus the fact that Job is one of the seven prophets does not prove that he was a non-Jew].

An objection was raised [from the following *Baraita*]: There was a pious man among the gentiles named Job. He came to this world so that God should repay him in this world for all the good things he did. When the Holy One, blessed be He, brought suffering on him he began to curse and blaspheme. The Holy One, blessed be He, then doubled his reward in this world, so that he should be denied access to the World to Come, [as it is told at the end of the Book of Job]. [But a Jewish *tzaddik* receives his reward in the hereafter,[19] so you see that Job was not a Jew!] [The Gemara answers:] There is a difference of opinion between *Tanna'im* on this point, for we learned: R. Eliezer said: Job lived in the time of the Judges, because Job said to his friends, "Behold, all of you have seen it [the lot of the wicked], so why is it that you embrace folly?" (Job 27:12). Which was the generation that embraced folly? You must say, the generation of the Judges, [when there was a complete breakdown of morality, and a total lack of respect of the authority of the judges. Therefore we have reason to believe that Job lived in the time of the Judges].

R. Yehoshua b. Korcha says: Job lived in the days of Achashverosh, because it says, "There were not found any women as beautiful as the daughters of Job anywhere in the land" (Job 42:15). What was the generation in which people went out to look for beautiful women? You must say that this was the generation of Achashverosh.[20] [The Gemara asks:] Maybe Job lived in the time of David, for it says, "They sought a beautiful girl [for David] throughout the boundary of Israel" (2 Kings 1:3)? [The Gemara answers:] In the case of David they searched only throughout Eretz Yisrael, whereas in the case of Achashverosh they searched in the entire land [of Persia and Media].

R. Natan said: Job lived in the time of the Queen of Sheba [and King Solomon], for it says, [a messenger reported to Job the loss of his oxen and donkeys, saying,] "The Sabeans came and took them" (Job 1:15). The Sages said: Job lived in the time of the Chaldeans [Nebuchadnezzar], for it says, [Another messenger reported the loss of Job's camels, saying,] "The Chaldeans came and formed three divisions . . . and seized the camels" (ibid. v. 17). Some say that Job lived in the time of Jacob and married Dinah the daughter of Jacob. [This is evident] because it says in the Book of Job, "Job said [to his wife, when she challenged his faith, 'You talk as any impious woman [*nevalot*] might talk!'" and it says elsewhere [in connection with the rape of Dinah], "[Shechem] had committed an outrage [*navalah*] against Israel" (Genesis 34:7). [Job's use of the term *nevalot* is a hint that Job's wife was Dinah, and he lived in the time of Jacob.]

[The Gemara summarizes:] All of these *Tanna'im* agree [with R. Yochanan and R. Elazar] that Job was a Jew, except for those that say [that he lived in Jacob's days, for then it was impossible for him to be a Jew]. [This must be so, for] if you think that all these Tanna'im consider him a non-Jew, how is it possible that after the death of Moses, the *Shechinah* should rest on a non-Jew, [and all agree that Job was a prophet], bearing in mind that a Master has said: Moses requested that the *Shechinah* should no longer rest on gentiles, and his request was granted, as it says, "I and Your people will be distinguished from every nation on the face of the earth" (Exodus 33:16). [And since these *Tanna'im* hold that Job lived after Moses, they must agree that Job was a Jew.]

R. Yochanan said: The generation of Job was deeply involved with promiscuity. [The proof is that] it says in the Book of Job, [Job said to his friends,] "Behold, all of you have seen it [*chazitem*], then why is it that you embrace folly?" (Job 27:12). And elsewhere it says, [The nations of the world say to the Jewish people,] "Turn away, turn away from God, O nation whose faith in Him is perfect. Turn away, turn away, and let us lewdly gaze [*nechezeh*] at you!" (Song of Songs 6:13). [By using the term *chazitem* Job alluded to lewdness.] [The Gemara asks:] Maybe the term *chazitem* refers to "prophetic vision," as in, "The vision [*chazon*] of Isaiah son of Amotz" (Isaiah 1:1)? [The Gemara answers:] If that is so, [and Job's friends saw prophetic vision,] why does Job tell them, "Why do you embrace folly?" [No, *chazitem* alludes to promiscuity.]

R. Yochanan further said: What is the significance of the verse, "And it happened in the days when judges were judging" (Ruth 1:1)? It was a generation in which the people passed judgment on their judges. If a judge rebuked a person, saying, "Take that splinter out from between your eyes," [indicating he had done a relatively minor transgression], he would impudently retort, "Take the beam from between your eyes!" ["You have sinned much worse!"] If a judge said, "Your silver has become impure," he would shoot back, "The wine [that you sold] was diluted with water" (Isaiah 1:22).

R. Shmuel b. Nachmani said in the name of R. Yonatan, Anyone that says that the Queen of Sheba was a queen only because she was married to a king, but did not have her own kingdom, is making a mistake. The term *malkat Sheva* (1 Kings 10:1) means "the kingdom of Sheva"; [she was the sole ruler over the kingdom].

THE BOOK OF JOB

[The Gemara continues by expounding the beginning of the Book of Job.] "It happened one day [on Rosh Hashanah]: The angels came to stand before God, and the Satan, too, came among them. God said to the Satan, 'From where have you come?' And the Satan answered, 'From wandering and walking about the earth'" (Job 1:7). [The Gemara, noting that the term "walk" is used in the Torah in reference to Abraham,[21] says:] Satan said to God: Master of the universe! I have traveled around in the whole world, and I have not found anyone that You can trust like Your servant Abraham. For You said to him, "Rise, walk the land, through its length and breadth, for I will give it all to you" (Genesis 13:17). Despite the fact [that You promised him all of Eretz Yisrael], when he could not find a burial plot for his wife Sarah and had to buy it for four hundred shekels of silver, he did not question what You did to him. "Then God said to the Satan, 'Have you noticed My servant Job? There is none like him on earth, a blameless and upright man who fears God and shuns evil!'" (Job 1:8). [The Gemara asks:] What is meant by "he shuns evil"? R. Abba b. Shmuel said: Job was liberal with his money. The standard practice at that time was that if a person owed half a *perutah* to a worker [a *perutah* is the smallest coin and cannot be divided], he bought something for a *perutah* and gave the worker half of it, but Job gave him the whole *perutah*.

Said R. Yochanan: Scripture pays greater tribute to Job than to Abraham. For about Abraham it says, "For now I know that you fear God" (Genesis 22:12), whereas Job is described as "a blameless and upright man who fears God and shuns evil" (Job 1:1).

"The Satan answered God, 'Does Job not have good reason to fear God? Why, it is You who have fenced him round, him and his household and all that he has. You have blessed his efforts, and his livestock have spread throughout the land'" (ibid. 1:9). [The Gemara asks:] What is meant by "You have blessed his efforts"?

R. Shmuel b. Yitzchak said: Whoever took a *perutah* from Job [and invested it] was fortunate with it. What is meant by "his livestock have spread throughout the land"? R. Yose b. Chanina said: The livestock of Job defied the laws of nature. Normally wolves kill goats; in Job's herds the goats killed the wolves.

[The Satan said to God,] "'But lay Your hand upon all that he has, and he will surely blaspheme You to Your face.' God replied to the Satan, 'See, all that he has is in your power; only do not lay a hand on him' . . . One day, as his sons and daughters were eating and drinking wine in the house of their eldest brother, a messenger came to Job and said, 'The oxen were plowing, and the she-donkeys were grazing alongside them'" (ibid. 11–14). [The Gemara asks:] What is meant by, "The oxen were plowing, and the she-donkeys were grazing alongside them"? R. Yochanan said: From here we see that the Holy One, blessed be He, gave Job a taste (16a) of the World to Come. [The donkeys were grazing in grass that grew immediately from the seeds that were sown while the oxen were plowing. Which is similar to what will happen in the World to Come, where women will become pregnant and instantly give birth.[22] (Rashi).]

"This one was still speaking when another came and said, 'God's fire fell from heaven . . . ' This one was still speaking when another came and said, 'A Chaldean formation of three columns made a raid on the camels and carried them off.' This one was still speaking when another came and said, 'Your sons and daughters were eating and drinking wine in the house of their eldest brother, when suddenly a mighty wind came from across the desert. It struck the four corners of the house so that it collapsed on the young people and killed them. . . . Then Job stood up, ripped his shirt, and tore [the hair off] his head. . . . He said, 'Naked did I emerge from my mother's womb, and naked shall I return there. God has given, and God has taken away, blessed be the name of God.' Despite all this, Job did not sin or ascribe impropriety to God. It happened one day: The angels came to stand before God, and the Satan, too, came along with them . . . and God said to the Satan, 'Where have you been?' And the Satan answered God, 'I have been roaming all over the world' (Job 1:16–2:2). He said: I traveled around in the whole world, and I have not found anyone that You can trust like Your servant Abraham. For You said to him, 'Rise, walk the land, through its length and breadth, for I will give it all to you' (Genesis 13:17). Yet, despite the fact [that You promised him all of Eretz Yisrael], when he could not find a burial plot for Sarah, he did not question God's actions."

SATAN, THE EVIL IMPULSE, AND THE ANGEL OF DEATH ARE IDENTICAL

"Then God said to the Satan, 'Have you noticed My servant Job? There is none like him on earth . . . and he still maintains his unshakeable faith. You incited Me against him to destroy him for no good reason!'" (Job 2:3). Said R. Yochanan: If this were not written expressly in Scripture, we would not dare to say such a thing. [God is presented as if He were a human being who yields to pressure against his better judgment.] We learned in a *Baraita*: Satan's strategy is to come down to earth and persuade a person [to transgress]; then he goes up to heaven and arouses God's anger [by reporting his sins], and when he then receives permission [to kill the person], he takes his life. [In Job's case, Satan could not come up with any sin; therefore it says, "to destroy him for no good reason."]

"The Satan answered God and said, 'Skin for the sake of skin' . . . And God said to the Satan, 'Behold, he is in your hand, only spare his life.' The Satan departed from the presence of God and afflicted Job with severe boils" (Job 2:4–7). R. Yitzchak said: The suffering Satan endured was worse than that of Job. Satan was like a servant who is told by his master: Break the barrel, but don't spill a drop of wine!" Resh Lakish said: The Satan, the *yetzer hara* [the evil impulse], and the Angel of Death are one and the same. He is called Satan, for it says, "The Satan departed from the presence of God" (ibid. v. 70). He is called *yetzer hara* [the evil impulse], for it says [concerning the evil impulse], "Every impulse of his innermost thought was only [*rak*] for evil, all day long" (Genesis 6:5). And it says here, [God speaking to Satan,] "Only [*rak*] spare his life" (Job 2:6), [the word *rak*, "only," occurring in both verses]. Satan is identical with the Angel of Death, for it says, "Only spare his life" so we see that Job's life was in Satan's hands.

THEY MEANT TO ACT FOR THE SAKE OF HEAVEN

R. Levi said: Both Satan [in the present instance] and Peninah [when she provoked Hannah][23] meant to act for the sake of heaven. Satan, when he saw that the Holy One, blessed be He, favored Job, [praising him more profusely than Abraham], said: Heaven forfend, God will forget His love for Abraham. Peninah [when she provoked Hannah], as it says, "Her rival [Peninah] would taunt her to make her miserable" (1 Samuel 1:6), [did so in order that Hannah would implore God to give her children]. When R. Acha b. Yaakov gave this interpretation in the city of Papunia, Satan came and kissed his feet.

JOB SINNED IN HIS THOUGHTS

[The Gemara continues:] "Despite everything, Job did not sin with his lips" (Job 2:10). Rava said: He did not sin with his lips; however, he did sin in his thoughts. What [sinful thing] did he have in mind? "The earth is handed over to the wicked one [Satan]. He covers the faces of its judges [they do not want to

see the evil]. If this is not so, then who [does it]?" (ibid. 9:24). Rava explained: Job wanted to turn the dish upside down [and say that God is punishing him unjustly]. Abaye said: Job meant to say this only in reference to Satan. [He knew that God is just, but he thought that Satan could influence Him to punish someone for no good reason.] On this point there is a difference of opinion between *Tanna'im*. [Job said:] "The earth is handed over to the wicked" [which suggests that there is no justice]. R. Eliezer said: Job wanted to turn the dish upside down, [stating: there is no justice in the world]. R. Yehoshua said: Job was only referring to Satan.

[Job said,] "You know that I will not be found guilty, yet none can save from Your hand" (ibid. 10:7). Rava said: Job wanted to release the whole world from judgment. He said: Master of the universe, You created an ox with split hoofs, and you created a donkey with solid hoofs; You created Gan Eden, and You created Gehinnom; You created *tzaddikim*, and You created wicked people; who can stop you? [Meaning: Who can change the way You created people? You preordained whether a person will be righteous or wicked. Therefore, You cannot judge and punish the wicked.]" And Job's friends told him, "[By saying this,] you undermine piety and diminish prayer to God" (ibid. 15:4). True, God created the evil impulse, but He also created the Torah as an antidote to the *yetzer hara*, [so that a person does have free choice. By learning Torah he can overcome the *yetzer hara*].

Rava expounded: What is meant by the verse, "The blessings of the forlorn would be upon me" (ibid. 29:13)? This teaches us that Job would take away by force a field belonging to orphans, improve it, and then return it to them. "And I would bring joyous song to a widow's heart" (ibid.)—whenever there was a widow that no one wanted to marry, he used to associate his name with her, [saying that she was his relative, or pretending to court her], and before long someone would come and marry her. [The Gemara continues:] Job said, "If only my anger could be weighed, and my calamity placed on a scale" (ibid. 6:2), [meaning: If only I could weigh my suffering against how much I sinned].

Rav said: Job deserves to have dust thrown into his mouth for making himself a colleague of God, [by investigating God to see whether his suffering counterbalances his sins]. [Job says,] "There is no arbitrator between us who might impose his authority on both of us" (ibid. 9:33). Rav said: Job deserves to have dust thrown in his mouth: Does a servant have a right to argue with his master, [and ask for an arbitrator]? [Job says,] "I forged a covenant for my eyes, not to gaze at a maiden" (ibid. 31:1). Rav said: Job deserves to have dust thrown into his mouth; granted, Job did not look at other women, but Abraham did not even look at his own wife, as it says, [Abraham said to Sarah, when they approached Egypt,] "Now I realize that you are a woman of beautiful appearance" (Genesis 12:11). This implies that until then he did not know what she looked like.

[Job said,] "As a cloud disperses and is gone, so does one who descends to the grave not rise" (Job 7:9). Rava said: From here we see that Job denied the resurrection of the dead. "He shattered me in a tempest; He multiplied my wounds without cause" (ibid. 9:17). Rava said: Job blasphemed [mentioning the word] tempest, and God answered him with the word tempest. He blasphemed [mentioning the word] tempest, for it says, "He shattered me in a tempest." Job said to God: Perhaps a tempest passed before You and caused you to mistake *Iyov* [Job] for *oyeiv* [enemy]. [Attributing a mistake to God is blasphemy.] God answered him through a tempest, for it says, "God then responded to Job from out of the whirlwind [*se'arah*] and said, ... Gird your loins like a warrior, and I will ask you, and you will inform Me'" (ibid. 38:1,3).

God said to him: I have created many hairs[24] in man, and for each hair I have created a separate follicle, so that two hairs should not be nourished from one follicle; for if two hairs would come out of one follicle, it would weaken a person's eyesight. I do not mistake one follicle for another; do you think that I would mistake *Iyov* for *oyeiv*? [The Gemara continues: "Who fashioned a channel for the torrent, or a path for thunderclouds?" (ibid. v. 25). [God said to Job:] I created many drops in the clouds, and for each drop I created a separate mold, so that no two drops should come from the same mold; since, if two drops would emerge from the same mold, they would turn the earth into mud, and it would not produce fruit. I do not confuse one drop with another; do you think I would confuse *Iyov* with *oyeiv*? "Or a path for thunderclouds." Many thunderclaps have I created in the clouds, and for each thunder there is a separate path, so that two thunderclaps should not travel along the same path, for if two traveled by the same path, they would demolish the entire world. Now, I do not mix up one thunderclap with another; do you think that I would mix up *Iyov* and *oyeiv*?

[God said to Job,] "Do you know the time when the mountain goats give birth, or anticipate when the gazelles calve?" (Job 39:1). "The mountain goat is cruel toward her young, and when she crouches (16b) to deliver them, she goes up to the top of a mountain, so that the young should fall down and die. And I summon an eagle to catch it with its wings and place it before her. If the eagle would come a moment earlier or a moment later, the young would be killed. Now, I do not err between one moment and another; do you think that I would err between *Iyov* and *oyeiv*?" "Or anticipate when the gazelles calve? The gazelle has a narrow womb, and when it crouches to deliver her young I prepare a snake that bites her at the opening of her womb, and she delivers her offspring without difficulty. If the snake would come one moment too

soon or one moment too late, the gazelle would die. I do not confuse one moment with another, do you think that I would confuse *Iyov* with *oyeiv*?" "Job does not speak with knowledge, his words lack understanding!" (ibid. 34:35). Rava said: From here we can infer that a person cannot be held totally responsible for the things he says when he is in distress.

HOW DID JOB'S FRIENDS KNOW OF HIS TROUBLE?

"Job's three friends heard about the total calamity that had befallen him, and each one came from his place ... They gathered together to mourn with him and comfort him" (ibid. 2:11). [The Gemara asks:] What is meant by "They gathered together"? Rav Yehudah said in the name of Rav: This teaches that they all entered [the town] through the same gate at the same time, although—according to a *Baraita*—they lived at a distance of three hundred *parsah* from each other. [The Gemara asks:] So how did each one of them know [that Job was suffering]? Some say that each one of them had a crown [on which the faces of the friends were engraved, and if one of them was stricken by misfortune, the expression on his face changed (Rashi)]. Others say that they had certain trees, and when one of the trees withered they knew that the one that was represented by that particular tree was ill. Rava said: This led to the popular saying, "Give me a friend like Job's friends, or give me death!"

JOB'S DAUGHTERS

[Originally, Job had seven sons and seven daughters. In the end, when God blessed him, and everything he had was doubled, he had fourteen sons, but only three daughters. The Gemara's discussion focuses on this.]

It says, "Man began to increase [*larov*] on the face of the earth, and daughters were born to them" (Genesis 6:1). R. Yochanan says: [The word *larov* tells us that] the world population began to increase [*riviah*], [because "daughters were born." Since girls mature earlier than boys, the more women there are, the more children are born]. Resh Lakish says: [*Larov* suggests that] strife [*merivah*] came into the world. Said Resh Lakish to R. Yochanan: According to your view that population growth came into the world, [and to have daughters is a blessing]; why did not God double the number of Job's daughters? He replied: Although they were not doubled in number, they were doubled in beauty; [the three daughters that he was given were so gorgeous that it was as if he had six daughters].

For it says, "He had fourteen sons and three daughters. The first he named Jemimah, the second Ketziah, and the third Keren-Happuch" (Job 42:13,14). Jemimah, because she was beautiful like the day [*yom*]; Ketziah, because she gave off a scent of cassia [*ketziah*]; Keren-Happuch, because her complexion resembled that of a horn of a *keresh* [antelope], so they explained it in the yeshivah of R. Shila. In Eretz Yisrael they ridiculed this explanation: A horn of a *keresh* would be a flaw, [they said, since it is swarthy]! Said R. Chisda, [she was called Keren-Happuch] because she was like the best kind of garden spice.[25] [*Puch* means mascara, a beautifying cosmetic] as it says, "If you paint your eyes with mascara [*puch*]" (Jeremiah 4:30).

HOW WAS ABRAHAM BLESSED?

A daughter was born to R. Shimon b. Rebbi, and he was upset. His father said to him: Increase has come to the world. Bar Kappara said to him: Your father has given you a hollow consolation. It is impossible for the world to exist without either males or females. However, happy is he who has sons; woe to the one who has only daughters. The world cannot exist without either a spice dealer or a tanner. Woe is to the one who is a tanner; happy is he who is a spice dealer. Regarding [the question whether or not a daughter is a blessing], there is a difference of opinion among *Tanna'im*. It says, "God had blessed Abraham with everything [*bakol*]" (Genesis 24:1). What is meant by *bakol*, "with everything"? R. Meir said: He was blessed in not having a daughter. R. Yehudah said: He was blessed in having a daughter. Others say that Abraham had a daughter whose name was Bakol [and Bakol was God's blessing].

R. Elazar Hamoda'i said: Abraham [was blessed in that he] was an expert in the knowledge of astrology, and all the kings of the East and the West used to come early in the morning [to seek his advice]. R. Shimon b. Yocha'i said: Abraham had a precious jewel hanging from his neck, and any sick person who looked at it was healed immediately. When Abraham passed away, the Holy One, blessed be He, placed it in the sun. Abaye said: This is confirmed by the popular saying: "The sun rises, the patient rises"; [during the morning hours most patients appear improved]. Another explanation [of God's blessing to Abraham] is that Esau did not rebel [against God] as long as he was alive. Another explanation is that Ishmael repented while Abraham was still alive.

[The Gemara asks:] How do we know that Esau did not rebel during Abraham's lifetime? Because it says, "Esau came home exhausted from the field" (Genesis 25:29). And we learned that on that day Abraham our father had died, and Yaakov our father made a stew of lentils to console his father Isaac. Why did he cook lentils? In Eretz Yisrael they say in the name of Rabbah b. Mari: Just as a lentil is round, so mourning makes the rounds and strikes everyone. Others say: Just as a lentil does not have a mouth [i.e., split], so does a mourner not have a mouth [he does not speak]. What practical difference does it make [what the reason is that Jacob cooked lentils]? The difference is whether we offer eggs as a consolation meal; [eggs do not have a mouth, but are not perfectly round].

[Returning to the topic of Esau,] R. Yochanan said: The wicked Esau committed five sins on the day [that Abraham died]. He raped a betrothed girl, he committed murder, he denied God, he denied the revival of the dead, and he rejected his birthright. [So we see that he began to sin only after Abraham's death.]

And from where do we know that Ishmael repented while Abraham was still alive? We know it from a conversation that took place between Ravina and R. Chama b. Buzi when they were once sitting before Rava while he was dozing. Ravina said to R. Chama b. Buzi: "Is it really true that you said that wherever the Torah uses the term *geviah*, 'to breathe his last,' it refers to the death of a *tzaddik*?" "That is correct," he replied. "But what about the generation of the Flood; [it says about them *vayigva*, 'they breathed their last,' and they were corrupt]?" he asked. He replied, "I meant that only when *geviah* is mentioned in conjunction with *asifah* "to be gathered in" [it refers to a *tzaddik*]." He retorted, "But in connection with Yishmael it says both *geviah* and *asifah* [and he was not a *tzaddik*]!"

Just then Rava woke up. "Children," he said. "This is what R. Yochanan said: Ishmael repented during his father's lifetime. And how do we know that he repented? Because it says, 'Isaac and Ishmael his sons buried him [Abraham]' (ibid. 25:9); [From the fact that Isaac is mentioned first, even though he was younger, we can infer that Ishmael allowed him to go first, which indicates that he repented]. [The Gemara suggests:] Perhaps the Torah lists them in the order of their wisdom? [The Gemara answers:] If that is so, then why in the verse, "Esau and Jacob his sons buried him" (ibid. 35:29), are they not listed in the order of their wisdom? We must conclude, that the fact that the Torah lists Isaac first shows that Ishmael pushed him forward, and since he pushed him forward we infer that he repented in Abraham's lifetime, [which was God's blessing to Abraham].

BAKOL, MIKOL, KOL

Our Rabbis taught: There were three to whom the Holy One, blessed be He, granted (17a) an inkling of the World to Come while they were still in this world, namely, Abraham, Isaac, and Jacob. [Only a semblance; the reward of the World to Come itself cannot be conceived by the human mind (Maharal).] We know this of Abraham, because it says, [God blessed Abraham] [*bakol*], "with everything" (Genesis 24:1); Isaac, because [Isaac said: I ate] *mikol* "of everything" (ibid. 27:33); Jacob, because [Jacob said:] I have *kol* "everything" (ibid. 33:11). [*Kol* in the context of these verses implies perfection, a total unflawed blessing; thus they experienced the absolute good.] There were three over whom the *yetzer hara* [the evil impulse] had no power. namely, Abraham, Isaac, and Jacob. [We know this] because it says regarding them: *bakol*, *mikol*, and *kol*.

Some include also David, for it says, [David said,] "My heart has died within me" (Psalms 109:22), [his *yetzer hara* has been completely extinguished]. [The Gemara asks:] What about the other Tanna? [Doesn't David himself attest that he conquered his *yetzer hara*?] [The Gemara answers:] That Tanna interprets David's statement as an expression of the searing pain he has suffered all his life.

Our Rabbis taught: There were six over whom the Angel of Death had no power; [rather, they died by being kissed by the *Shechinah* (Rashi)], namely: Abraham, Isaac, and Jacob, Moses, Aaron, and Miriam. We know this of Abraham, Isaac, and Jacob, because it says in connection with them: *bakol, mikol, kol* [the *kol* encompassing all the good of the world]. Mose, Aaron and Miriam, because it says in connection with them, [that they died,] "at the word of God" [literally: "by the mouth of God" [(Numbers 33:38; Deuteronomy 38:5).] [The Gemara asks:] But it does not say, "at the word of God" in connection with Miriam's death? R. Elazar said: Miriam also died by a kiss, as we derive from the use of the word *sham*, "there" [in connection with her death], and with that of Moses.[26] [The Gemara asks:] And why does not the Torah say expressly that she died "by the mouth of God"? Because it would be disrespectful of the *Shechinah* to use the phrase "by the mouth of God" [in connection with a woman].

Our Rabbis taught: There were seven on whose bodies the worms had no effect, namely: Abraham, Isaac, and Jacob; Moses, Aaron, and Miriam; and Benjamin son of Jacob. The former six for the reasons stated above, and Benjamin son of Jacob, because it says regarding him, [in Moses' blessing of the tribes,] "To Benjamin he said, 'God's beloved one shall dwell securely beside him" (Deuteronomy 33:12) [i.e., Benjamin, you can dwell securely, knowing that the worms will have no effect on you because you are so close to God]. Some say that David is also included, since David said about himself, "My flesh, too, will rest in confidence" (Psalms 16:9). The other Tanna [who does not include David] explains this verse to mean that David was praying [that his flesh "*should* rest in confidence"].

Our Rabbis taught: There were four who died through the advice of the Serpent; [the advice the Serpent gave to Eve, which brought death into the world; if not for that they would not have died, for they had not committed any sin (Rashi)]. They were: Benjamin the son of Jacob, Amram the father of Moses, Jesse the father of David, and Kilav the son of David. Regarding all of these we only have traditions, except for Jesse the father of David about whom we have an explicit verse. For it says, "Amasa was the son of a man named Ithra the Israelite, who consorted with Abigail daughter of Nachash, the sister of Joab's mother Zeruiah" (2 Samuel 17:25). [The Gemara asks:] Was Abigail the daughter of Nachash? Wasn't she the daughter of Jesse, for it says, "[Jesse's sons'] sisters were Zeruiah and Abigail" (1 Chronicles 2:16)? Why is she described as

the daughter of Nachash? Because she is the daughter of the one [Jesse] who died through the advice of the *nachash*, the Serpent [and not because of any sin he committed].

YEHOSHUA B. GAMLA, FOUNDER OF UNIVERSAL EDUCATION

(21a) Rav Yehudah said in the name of Rav: Truly, this man should be remembered for blessing: His name is Yehoshua b. Gamla,[27] for if not for Yehoshua b. Gamla, Torah would have become forgotten among the Jewish people. In earlier times—since the Torah makes fathers responsible to teach their own children—those without fathers, or whose fathers were unlearned, went untaught. On what did they base their attitude [of not caring about someone else's children's education]? On the verse, "Teach them [*otam*, the words of the Torah] to your children" (Deuteronomy 11:19). [*Otam* is written without a *vav*, and can be read as] *atem*, "you"— [*you*, the father, should teach your children]. They then instituted that teachers of children should be appointed in Jerusalem. On what verse did they base their action? On the verse, "For from Zion the Torah will come forth, and the word of God from Jerusalem" (Isaiah 2:3).

There still was the problem, for if a child had a father, the father would take him to Jerusalem to learn Torah; but if a child did not have a father, the child did not go to Jerusalem to learn. They then enacted that a central yeshivah should be established in each province for boys of sixteen or seventeen years of age. [That was no solution either, for] if a teacher became angry with a boy [and tried to discipline him], he would rebel and leave the yeshivah. [If a child has been nurtured in a Torah atmosphere since first grade, he will not rebel. But if a boy enters yeshivah only at sixteen, after he has been exposed to alien ideologies, he will be unwilling to accept the teacher's discipline.] Finally Yehoshua b. Gamla introduced a new plan, [the first comprehensive system of education in history]. He arranged for teachers to be placed in every district and every town, and that children should be taught from the age of six or seven.

GUIDELINES FOR EDUCATORS

Rav said to R. Shmuel b. Shilat:[28] Do not accept any students before they are six years old; from six years and up you can accept them, and force-feed them Torah as you force a yoke onto an ox's neck. Rav further said to R. Shmuel b. Shilat: When you have to hit a student, hit him only with a shoelace [i.e., gently; by hitting harder you don't accomplish anything]. [The child who is paying attention will do so by himself, and if a child is not paying attention, [don't expel him]. Let him at least be in the company of friends who are learning, [eventually he will apply himself to his studies].

Rava further said: The maximum number of students to be allocated to a teacher is twenty-five. If there are fifty students, we appoint two teachers. If there are forty, we appoint an assistant at the expense of the town. Rava said also: If there is a teacher who is adequate, and there is another who has the ability to teach more, we do not discharge the first one, for fear that the second one will be overconfident and, as a result, become lax in his duties and teach less. R. Dimi from Nehardea said: On the contrary, the second one will try even harder, because "rivalry among scholars increases wisdom."

Rava further said: If there are two teachers, one of whom has the ability to cover a lot of ground, but he is not careful about avoiding mistakes; and the other is very careful that the students do not make mistakes, but he makes slower progress; you should appoint the one who covers a lot of ground and is not so meticulous, since mistakes will be straightened out in time. R. Dimi from Nehardea, however, said: On the contrary, you should appoint the one who is thorough although he does not cover that much ground, for "a mistake once entered remains." For it says, [in connection with the attempt to destroy Amalek, Israel's archenemy], "Joab and all of Israel stayed there for six months until he had destroyed all the males of Edom" (1 Kings 11:16).

When Joab came before David, David said to him, (21b) "Why did you do this? [Why did you kill only the males? Why didn't you kill the females too?]" Joab replied, "Because it says, 'You shall wipe out the males [zachar] of Amalek" (Deuteronomy 25:19). Said David, "But we read 'zeicher, wipe out the memory of Amalek [meaning both males and females].'" Joab replied, "I was taught to read zachar, 'the males of Amalek.'" Joab then went to his teacher and asked him, "How did you teach me?" The teacher replied, "Zachar, the males of Amalek." [Realizing that the survival of Amalek and the murder of countless Jews resulted from his teacher's mistake,] Joab drew his sword and wanted to kill him. Cried the teacher, "Why are you doing this?" Joab retorted, "Because it says, 'Cursed be the one who is negligent in doing God's work' (Jeremiah 48:10)." The teacher pleaded, "Leave me alone; let it be enough that I am cursed!" To which Joab responded, "[The verse ends,] 'Cursed be the one who withholds his sword from bloodshed!'" Some say he killed him, and others say that he did not.

R. ADDA B AHAVAH'S UNTIMELY DEATH

(22a) R. Dimi from Nehardea brought a boatload of dried figs. [He wanted to sell the figs in Mechuza, the town where Rava officiated as rosh yeshivah.] The Resh Galuta [Exilarch] said to Rava, "Go and check whether he is a Torah scholar; if he is, then reserve the market for him [i.e., announce that no one should sell figs until R. Dimi sold out his shipment]. So Rava told his disciple R. Adda b. Ahava, "Go and smell his jar" [i.e., test him to see whether or not he is a Torah scholar]. He went and asked R. Dimi the following question: If an elephant swallowed a basket woven of willow twigs and expelled it with its excrement, is it still considered a basket and as such susceptible to tumah (ritual uncleanness), or is it considered refuse matter, which is not susceptible to tumah? R. Dimi did not know what to answer. He asked R. Addah b. Ahavah, "Are you by any chance Rava [the rosh yeshivah of this city]?"

R. Adda b. Ahavah took his cane and tapped R. Dimi on the shoe [in a playful manner], and said, "There is a great difference between me and Rava, but in any event, I can be your teacher, and so Rava is the teacher of your teacher." They did not give him exclusive rights to the market to sell his figs, so R. Dimi suffered a loss. R. Dimi complained to R. Yosef [Rava's teacher]. "See how they have treated me," he said. Responded R. Yosef, "He who did not delay taking revenge for the shame that was inflicted on the king of Edom will not delay taking revenge for the wrong done to you." For it says, "Thus says God, 'For three transgressions of Moab [I have looked away], but for four I will not pardon them—for their burning the bones of the king of Edom into lime'" (Amos 2:1).

Not long after that R. Adda b. Ahavah died. R. Yosef said, "I am afraid that I brought about the punishment [of his untimely death] because I cursed him." R. Dimi of Nehardea said, "I am afraid that I am the one who brought this punishment on him, because when he made me lose my figs [I became angry at him]." Abaye said, "No, I am the one that brought the punishment down on him, because I resented it when] he would say to the students, 'Rather than chew on bones in the yeshivah of Abaye, why don't you eat fat meat in the yeshivah of Rava?'" [The learning in Rava's yeshivah is on a higher level. Abaye felt that his resentment had caused R. Adda b. Ahavah's untimely death.]

Rava said, "I am afraid that I am the one that caused his demise, because when he went to the butcher store to buy meat, [and Rava's servant was there to buy meat for Rava,] he used to say, 'Serve me, [a student of Rava], before you serve the servant of Rava, because I am greater than [the servant].'" [Rava thought that his resentment had caused R. Adda b. Ahavah's death.] R. Nachman b. Yitzchak said, "I brought on his calamity." How so? R. Nachman b. Yitzchak was appointed to give a sermon for the community every Shabbat. Every time before going to deliver his lecture, he used to review it with R. Adda b. Ahavah, and only then would he give his speech. One day R. Papa and R. Huna the son of R. Yehoshua stalled R. Adda b. Ahava and delayed him because they were not present at Rava's concluding lecture on the tractate *Bechorot* [and wanted to ask him about it].[29] They said to him: Tell us what did Rava discuss in his lecture about the *halachot* of the "Tithing of Cattle" [the last chapter in tractate *Bechorot*]? R. Adda b. Ahavah told them exactly what Rava had said on that subject.

Meanwhile, R. Nachman b. Yitzchak [who was waiting for R. Adda b. Ahavah] was late for his lecture. So the disciples came and said, "Rabbi, please come [and give the lecture], it is late! Why are you still sitting here?" He replied, "I am sitting and waiting for the coffin of R. Adda b. Ahavah." [He was so incensed at R. Adda b. Ahavah's delay that he cursed him.] Shortly thereafter the news spread that R. Adda b. Ahavah had passed away. [The Gemara remarks:] It is likely that his death was due to R. Nachman b. Yitzchak's [curse, because it happened immediately after it].[30]

WHICH WAY DO WE FACE WHEN PRAYING?

(25a) R. Yehoshua b. Levi said: Let us be grateful to our ancestors [the Men of the Great Assembly][31] for teaching us which direction we should face when praying, as it says, "And the heavenly legion bows to You" (Nehemiah 9:6) [i.e., the sun and the moon that rise in the east bow down toward the west; therefore, we, too, should pray facing west]. R. Acha b. Yaakov objected to this interpretation. He said: Perhaps [when the sun rises in the east it is not moving westward with its back toward the east, but it is leaving the east] like a servant who leaves his master after receiving a gift from him. The servant walks backward facing his master, bowing as he goes [so, too, the sun travels toward the west with its back toward the west, and its face toward the east, and we should face toward the east when praying]?

[Says the Gemara:] This is indeed a difficulty. R. Hoshaia was of the opinion that the *Shechinah* is everywhere, [not just in the west]. For R. Hoshaia said: What is meant by the verse, "You alone are God; You made the heavens, the most exalted heavens and all their legion" (ibid.). [You are unique.] Your messengers are not like the messengers of mortal man. Messengers of mortal man [after accomplishing their mission], report back to the place from which they have been sent but Your messengers report the accomplishment of their mission at the very place where they were sent, [for the *Shechinah* is everywhere]. For it says, "Did You dispatch lightning bolts, so that they would go forth, and then say to You, 'Here we are'?" (Job 38:35). It does not say, "so that the lighting bolts come back and say, 'Here we are,'" but "so that they go forth and say," which shows that the *Shechinah* is everywhere.

R. Yishmael, too, believes that the *Shechinah* is everywhere. For it was taught in the yeshivah of R. Yishmael: How do we know that the *Shechinah* is ev-

erywhere? Because it says, "Just then the angel who was speaking to me was going forth, and another angel was going forth toward him" (Zechariah 2:7). [If the *Shechinah* is only in one place, the second angel has to come from the same direction as the first angel, i.e., *behind* the first angel.] But it does not say, "another angel came *behind* him," but "another angel came *toward* him" [from the opposite direction]. This shows that the *Shechinah* is everywhere. R. Sheshet, too, believed that the *Shechinah* is everywhere, because R. Sheshet [who was blind] said to his attendant: [When I get ready to say the *Shemoneh Esrei*,] you may place me in any direction except toward the east; not because the *Shechinah* is not in the east, but because the idolaters made it a point to pray toward the east. However, R. Abbahu said: The *Shechinah* is in the west. For R. Abbahu said: What is the meaning of the word *Uriyah* ["west" in the Persian language (Rashi)]? It stands for *avir kah*, "the air of God."[32]

THEORIES ABOUT THE WINDS AND THE PATH OF THE SUN

R. Yehudah said: What is the meaning of the verse, "My lesson shall drop [*yaarof*] like rain" (Deuteronomy 32:2)? [Moses compares the Torah to the four winds: just as the world cannot exist without the four winds, so the world cannot exist without Torah.] *Yaarof* refers to the west wind [which brings the rain] and which comes from the back [*oref*] of the world. "My saying shall flow [*tizzal*] like the dew" (ibid.)—this refers to the north wind, which [brings drought and famine, and as a result the price of produce rises and] the value of gold declines; and so it says, "To those who pour [*hazalim*] gold from the purse, [because it is cheap]" (Isaiah 46:6). "Like a downpour [*se'irim*] on the herb" (Deuteronomy 32:2); this refers to the east wind that roars through the world like a demon. "Like a shower on the grass" (ibid.); this refers to the south wind that brings on showers and makes the grass grow.

We learned in a *Baraita*: R. Elazar says: The world (25b) is like a balcony [that is enclosed on three sides and open to the fourth], and the north side is the open side, and when the sun reaches the northwest corner [of the horizon before sunset], it turns around and rises above the firmament [where it becomes invisible, and returns to the east where it reappears in the morning]. R. Yehoshua says: The world is like a tent [that has four walls], and the north side, like the other sides, is closed. When the sun reaches the northwest corner [at sunset, it leaves the tent] and moves behind the north wall of the tent, [traveling from the west to the east during the night. It reenters the tent in the morning, rising in the east], as it says, "It goes toward the south and circles toward the north" (Ecclesiastes 1:6). "It goes to the south"—during the day; "and circles toward the north"—during the night. "It goes round and round, and on its rounds the wind returns" (ibid.)—this refers to the eastern and western skies. Sometimes the sun circles them on the outside, [namely, in the winter, when the sun is not seen in the eastern and western skies], and sometimes the sun crosses them, [in the summer, when the sun travels from the eastern to the southern sky and then to the western sky].

R. Yehoshua used to say: We have found a verse that supports the theory of R. Elazar, [that the world is like a three-walled balcony], for it says, "A tempest emerges from the inner chamber" (Job 37:9)—this is the south wind; "and cold weather from the constellations"—this is the north wind; [the cold enters because the north side has no wall, which proves R. Elazar's theory]; "By God's breath He makes ice" (ibid. 37:10)—this is the west wind; "and an expanse of water comes in a heavy downpour" (ibid.)—this is the east wind. [The Gemara asks: How can you say that it is the east wind that brings this rain?] Did we not learn [in the name of Rav] that the south wind brings showers and makes grass grow? [The Gemara answers:] This is no difficulty. When the rain falls gently it comes from the south, but when the rain comes in torrents, it comes from the east.

R. Chisda said: What is meant by, "Out of the north the gold will come" (ibid. 37:22)? This refers to the north wind, which makes the gold flow, and so it says, "To those who pour gold from the purse" (Isaiah 46:6). [The north wind causes a drought, which drives up the price of food, which, in turn, cheapens the value of gold.]

Rafram b. Papa said in the name of R. Chisda: From the day the *Bet Hamikdash* was destroyed, the south wind has not brought rain, as it says, "He snatched from his right and remained hungry; he consumed on his left, but they are not sated" (Isaiah 9:19); and it says further, "North and south—You created them" (Psalms 89:13). [When you face east, north is on your left, south on your right.]

Rafram b. Papa further said in the name of R. Chisda: From the day the *Bet Hamikdash* was destroyed, rain no longer comes down from the "good treasury," that is mentioned in the verse, "God will open for you his good treasury in heaven" (Deuteronomy 28:12). When Israel does the will of God and are settled in their land, then rain comes down from the "good treasury"; but when Israel is not settled in their land, then the rain does not come down from the "good treasury."

TURN SOUTH FOR WISDOM,
NORTH FOR WEALTH

R. Yitzchak said: If you want to become wise, you should turn to the south [when saying the *Shemoneh Esrei*]; if you want to become rich, you should turn toward the north. And a sign [by which to remember this] is that the table [in the Tabernacle] is on the north side and the menorah is on the south side [of the Sanctuary. The table symbolizes wealth, the menorah rep-

resents wisdom]. R. Yehoshua b. Levi however, said: You should always turn toward the south [the side of wisdom], because when you acquire wisdom you will also acquire wealth, [because when you are wise, you are happy with your lot, and you feel rich (*Maharsha*)]. For it says, "Length of days is at its [wisdom's] right; at its left, wealth and honor" (Proverbs 3:16).

[The Gemara asks:] But did not R. Yehoshua b. Levi say that the *Shechinah* is in the west? [Yet here he says that you should turn to the south, the side of wisdom!] [The Gemara answers:] He means that you [should face west but] turn a little toward the south. Said R. Chanina to R. Ashi: You who live north of Eretz Yisrael [he lived in Babylonia], should face south [toward Jerusalem when you say the *Shemoneh Esrei*]. [The Gemara asks:] How do we know that Babylonia is to the north of Eretz Yisrael? From the verse, "From the North the evil will be released upon all the inhabitants of the land" (Jeremiah 1:14).

THE TERRITORY SUBJECT
TO TITHING

(56a) R. Acha b. Ivya was sitting in front of R. Assi, and he declared in the name of R. Assi b. R. Chanina: A *chatzuba* forms a partition in the estate of a convert. [The Gemara asks:] What is a *chatzuba*? Rav Yehudah said in the name of Rav: The plant Joshua used for a hedge to mark the boudaries [between the tribes and between the individual families] in Eretz Yisrael. Rav Yehudah further said in the name of Rav: Joshua listed [in the Book of Joshua][33] only the towns that were situated on the borders. Rav Yehudah said in the name of Shmuel: All the territory that the Holy One, blessed be He, showed to Moses [before his death on Mount Nebo][34] is subject to the mitzvah of tithing [i.e., from the produce grown in those places tithes must be separated]. [The Gemara asks:] What part of Eretz Yisrael does this exclude? [What part of the land that was promised to Abraham][35] was not shown to Moses?] [The Gemara answers:] It excludes the land of the Keni, Kenizi, and Kadmoni (Genesis 15:19).

HE AVOIDS TEMPTATION

(57b) It says, "One who walks with righteousness . . . shuts his eyes from seeing evil" (Isaiah 33:15). R. Chiya b. Abba said: This verse refers to a person who does not look at women while they are washing clothes [by the river]. [The Gemara asks:] What is the circumstance of this case [that he is praiseworthy for closing his eyes]? If there is another road, [but he passes by the river in order to look at them], he is wicked [even if he closes his eyes, because he should have kept away from temptation (Rashbam)].[36] If there is no other road, he has no choice; [he has to look where he is going]. [The Gemara answers:] The verse refers to a case where there is no other road. Nevertheless, he has to force himself to look away [from the women, and if he does, he is praised for his righteousness].

A TORAH SCHOLAR'S DINNER TABLE

R. Yochanan asked R. Banaah: How long should the undergarment of a Torah scholar be? He replied: Long enough to cover his whole body, so that no part of it can be seen [it should cover his feet]. How long should the overcoat of a Torah scholar be? Long enough that no more than a handbreadth of his undergarment should be exposed underneath. How should the table of a Torah scholar be set? Two thirds of the table should be covered with a tablecloth, and one third should be left uncovered to put the dishes and the salads on [so that the tablecloth should not get dirty]; and the ring [that was used to hang up the tabletop after the meal] should be attached to the outside [the uncovered part]. [The Gemara asks:] But have we not learned that the ring should be on the inside [the covered part, where the people are sitting]?

[The Gemara answers:] That is no difficulty. In the case [where the ring should be on the outside, it is assumed that] there is a child at the table [who would play with the ring and shake the table if it is within his reach], and in the other case [we assume] that there is no child. Or if you prefer, I can say that in both cases [we assume] there is no child, and still there is no difficulty: in one case [we assume] that there is a waiter [and the ring should be inside, because if it is on the outside, it would get in his way]. Or if you prefer, I can say that in both cases [we assume] that there is a waiter, and still there is no difficulty: the case where the ring is on the inside refers to the night, [when otherwise it might get in the waiter's way]; the case where the ring is on the outside refers to the daytime [when the waiter can see it and avoid it].

The table of an unlearned person is like (58a) a fireplace with pots all around, [because he puts the tablecloth and the bread in the middle and the unappetizing cooking pots all around]. What marks the bed of a Torah scholar? Nothing is found under it except sandals in the summer and shoes in the rainy season. [Shoes were worn in the summer and sandals in the rainy season because of the mud, and whichever footgear was not in use was stored under the scholar's bed.] By contrast, the bed of an unlearned person looks like a storeroom packed with odds and ends.

HE SAW ABRAHAM AND SARAH

R. Banaah used to mark the caves [where the dead were buried, so that people should not walk there unwittingly and become *tamei* (unclean) (Rashbam)]. When he came to the cave of Abraham,[37] he found Eliezer, the servant of Abraham, standing at the entrance. "What is Abraham doing?" R. Banaah asked. Replied

Eliezer, "He is sleeping in the arms of Sarah, and she is looking with devotion at his head." Said R. Banaah to Eliezer, "Go and tell him that Banaah is standing at the entrance [and would like to come in]." Said Abraham to Eliezer, "Let him come in. It is a known fact that there is no *yetzer hara* [lust] in this world [of the hereafter, and therefore, I am not doing anything immodest by sleeping in the arms of Sarah].

So R. Banaah went in, measured the cave, and came out again. When he came to the cave of Adam, [who is also buried in the Cave of Machpelah], a heavenly voice came forth and said, "You have seen the image of My likeness [meaning: You have seen Abraham who looked like Adam]. My image [i.e., Adam who was created in the image of God] you may not look at." "But I need to mark off the measurements of the cave," said Banaah. "The measurements of the outer cave [where the Fathers and the Mothers are buried, and which you have taken already], are the same as those of the inner cave [where Adam is buried]," the voice replied. R. Banaah said, "I looked at the heels of Adam, and they looked like two spheres of the sun."

[The Gemara observes:] Compared to Sarah, everyone looked like a monkey; and compared to Eve, Sarah looked like a monkey; and compared to the *Shechinah*, Adam was like a monkey. The beauty of R. Kahana was similar to the beauty of R. Abbahu; the beauty of R. Abbahu was similar to the beauty of our father Jacob; the beauty of our father Jacob was similar to the beauty of Adam.

R. BANAAH'S INGENUITY

There was a sorcerer who used to dig up graves [in order to remove the shrouds from the corpses]. When the sorcerer came to the grave of R. Tovi b. R. Mattenah [and raised him from the dead], R. Tovi grabbed his beard and held on to it until Abaye appeared and told R. Tovi to let the sorcerer go. The next year the sorcerer came again to R. Tovi's grave, and once again [the dead R. Tovi] grabbed the sorcerer's beard. Abaye came again, but [R. Tovi] did not let go of the beard until Abaye brought a pair of scissors and cut off the sorcerer's beard.

A father said on his deathbed, "I leave a barrel of dust to one of my sons, a barrel full of bones to another son, and a barrel full of raw wool I leave to the third son. They could not figure out what he meant, so they came to R. Banaah and asked him. He said to them, "Did your father leave any land?" "Yes," they replied. "Did he leave any cattle?" "Yes." "Did he leave bedding?" "Yes." "If so," said R. Banaah, "this is what your father had in mind [when he said, "barrels of dust, bones, and raw wool"].

There was a man who heard his wife say to her daughter, "Why are you not more discreet when you engage in illicit relations? I myself have ten children, and only one is from your father." When the man was dying he said, "I am leaving all my possessions to one son." No one knew which son he had in mind, so they asked R. Banaah, who advised the sons, "All of you, go and knock on your father's grave until he rises from his grave and reveals to you to which one of you he left his estate." All of them went and knocked on the grave, but the one who was his real son did not go. Said R. Banaah to them, "The entire estate belongs to this one." [The fact that he did not want to knock on his father's grave showed that he loved his father more than the others and, therefore, was really his son (Rashbam).]

[Resenting this judgment] the others went and denounced R. Banaah to the government, saying, "Someone among the Jews extorts money from people without witnesses and without any evidence." Thereupon they arrested him and threw him into prison. His wife [using a ploy,] then came to the authorities, complaining, "I had a slave, they cut off his head, removed his skin, ate his flesh, filled the skin with water and gave the students to drink from it, and they have not paid me the value of the slave or his wages." They did not know what to make of this, so they said, "Let us bring the wise man of the Jews; he will explain it to us." So they called R. Banaah, and he told them, "She was referring to a canteen made of goat skin." [She meant that her goat was stolen and slaughtered, and from its hide the thieves made a bottle from which they drank.]

So they said, "Since he is so wise, let him sit on the bench and be a judge." R. Banaah saw that there was a saying written on the gateway of the courthouse that read: Any judge who is sued in court by someone, is not qualified to be a judge. Said R. Banaah, "If that is so, then any stranger can come (58b) and sue a judge, and thereby disqualify him. What it should say is: Any judge who is sued in court and against whom a verdict is brought in, is not qualified to be a judge, [because this shows that he is dishonest]." So they added to the saying on the gateway the words: However, the Jewish sages say: A judge who is sued in court and against whom a verdict is brought in, is not qualified to be a judge.

He saw another saying that read: I, Blood, am at the head of all causes of death [i.e., an excess of blood is the major cause of death; hence bloodletting was recommended]. I, Wine, am at the head of all life [wine invigorates those who drink it]. "If that is so," R. Banaah remarked, "what if a person falls from a roof or from a date palm and gets killed, does he die from an excess of blood? What's more, if a person is near death, do they give him wine to drink to keep him alive? Of course not. This is what you should write: I, Blood, am at the head of all sickness; I, Wine, am at the head of all medicine [wine taken in moderation prevents disease]." Therefore they added to their inscription: However, the Jewish sages say: I, Blood, am at the head of all sickness; I, Wine, am at the head of all medicine.

COMMEMORATING THE DESTRUCTION OF THE *BET HAMIKDASH*

(60b) We learned in a *Baraita*: After the destruction of the second *Bet Hamikdash*, many people became ascetics, abstaining from meat and wine. R. Yehoshua approached them, saying: My children, why don't you eat meat and drink wine? They replied: How can we eat meat of which sacrifices were brought on the altar that is no more; and how can we drink wine, which used to be poured as a libation on the altar that is no more? R. Yehoshua said to them: If that is so, we should not eat bread either, because the meal offerings have ended. [They replied: You are right.] We can make do with fruits. Said R. Yehoshua: But we really should not eat fruit either, because there is no longer the offering of *bikkurim* [first fruits]. They retorted: Well, we can survive on other fruits [because *bikkurim* were brought only from the Seven Species].[38] Said R. Yehoshua: But we should not drink water, because we do not have the ceremony of the Pouring of the Water [on Sukkot] anymore. To this they had nothing to say, so he said to them: My children, come and listen to me. Not to mourn at all is impossible, because the calamity did happen. To mourn too much is also impossible, because we do not impose a hardship that the majority cannot bear. For it says, "You are cursed with a curse, yet you continue to steal from Me [the tithe], the entire nation!" (Malachi 3:9). [If "the entire nation" can bear the curse, the curse takes effect; otherwise it does not (R. Gershom).]

The Sages said therefore: [This is how you should show your sorrow:] If you paint your house, you should leave a little unpainted [as a sign of mourning for Jerusalem]. How much should you leave? R. Yosef said: A square cubit. R. Chisda said: The bare spot should be opposite the door [so that you see it when you come in]. You may prepare all you want for a meal, but you should leave out a minor item [as a sign of mourning]. What, for example? R. Papa said: an appetizer of salted fish. Similarly, a woman may wear all her jewelry, but she should leave off one or two things. For it says, "If I forget you, O Jerusalem, let my right hand forget its skill. Let my tongue adhere to my palate, if I fail to recall you, if I fail to elevate Jerusalem above my foremost joy" (Psalms 137:6). What is meant by "elevating Jerusalem above my foremost joy"? R. Yitzchak said: We do this by placing ashes on the head of the bridegroom. R. Papa asked Abaye: Where should the ashes be placed? He replied: On the place where the *tefillin* are worn. For it says, "To give [the mourners of Zion] splendor instead of ashes" (Isaiah 61:3) ["splendor" is a reference to *tefillin*; proof that it was the custom to put the ashes on the place of the *tefillin*]. [The Gemara sums up:] And whoever mourns for Zion will be privileged to see her joy, as it says, "Rejoice with Jerusalem, and be glad with her . . . all you who mourned over her" (ibid. 66:10).

We learned in a *Baraita*: R. Yishmael b. Elisha said: Since the the *Bet Hamikdash* was destroyed it would be fitting that we should take upon ourselves not to eat meat or drink wine; only we do not impose a hardship on the community unless the majority of the people can bear it. And since the Roman government has gained power and issues evil decrees against us, forbids us to learn Torah and do *mitzvot*, and does not permit us to perform *milah*, it would be fitting for us to take upon ourselves not to get married and have children, and the offspring of our father Abraham would come to an end in a natural way [rather than at the hands of our enemies]. However, just leave Israel alone: it is better that they should err [and get married] rather than transgress intentionally. [If we forbade them to get married, they would disobey and get married anyway. Therefore we don't issue such a decree (Rashbam).]

THE WONDROUS VOYAGES OF RABBAH B. BAR CHANAH

(73a) [The following astonishing tales of Rabbah b. Bar Chanah are among the most famous *aggadot* in the entire Talmud. They are allegories and metaphors that allude to profound concepts and are not meant to be taken literally. Unwilling to make these ideas public knowledge, the Sages concealed them in the figurative language of *aggadah*.]

Rabbah [b. Bar Chanah] said: Sailors told me: The wave that sinks the ship seems to have a white fringe of fire at its tip. If you strike it with a club that has engraved on it, "I am that I am; *Kah*; the Lord of Hosts, Amen, Amen, *Selah*," it begins to subside. [Interpretation: The waves of the ocean are symbolic of the nations of the world; Israel is compared to the sand of the sea. The nations are trying to destroy Israel, but, just as the waves that are buffeting the shore dissolve when they touch the sand, so the nations that try to obliterate Israel are doomed to oblivion. With the help of God, Israel will overcome all its enemies (Maharsha).]

Rabbah [b. Bar Chanah] said: Sailors told me: There are three hundred *parsahs*[39] between one wave and the next, and the height of each wave is also three hundred *parsahs*. They related: It once happened on a voyage, that a wave lifted us up so high that we could see the resting place of the smallest star, and it appeared to me like a field that is large enough to plant forty measures of mustard seeds. And if the wave had lifted us up any higher, we would have been burned by the heat of the star. And one wave shouted to the next: My friend, have you left anything in the world that you have not flooded, so that I can still come and destroy it? The other wave answered: Go and see the power of your Master. Without His permission, I cannot cross the sand [of the shore] even for the width of a thread. For it says, "Will you not fear Me? says God.

Will you not tremble before Me? For I have set sand as boundary against the sea, as a permanent law that cannot be broken. Its waves rage forth but cannot succeed, they roar but cannot cross it" (Jeremiah 5:22). [An allegory of what the nations of the world—the waves—say to each other in their ongoing onslaught at the sand of the shore—Israel (*Maharsha*).]

Rabbah b. Bar Chanah further said: I saw Hurmin the son of Lilith [demons] running along the battlements of the walls of Mechuza. Chasing him underneath was a cavalryman. Riding on horseback he could not catch up with him. Once they saddled two mules for Hurmin, which stood (73b) on two bridges of the Rognag River. He jumped back and forth from one to the other, holding two glasses of wine in his hand, pouring the wine from one into the other, without spilling a drop. This happened on a day that was so stormy that "Those who go down to the sea in ships . . . rise heavenward and descend to the depths" (Psalms 107:26). When the king's agents heard about Hurmin's stunts, they killed him. [The king was afraid that Hurmin would eventually depose him (Rashbam). Interpretation: Hurmin represents the *yetzer hara*. He was running on the wall, i.e., the Torah, trying to dissuade Israel from observing the *mitzvot*. The cavalryman symbolizes the *tzaddikim* who run to do the *mitzvot*. Hurmin's juggling the cups of wine without spilling a drop indicates that every misdeed the nations perpetrated against the Jewish people will be accounted for and duly punished (*Maharsha*).]

Rabbah b. Bar Chanah further said: I saw a *re'em* [unicorn or rhinoceros] that was one day old. It was the size of Mount Tabor—four *parsahs*; the length of its neck was three *parsahs*; and the resting place of its head [when it lies down] was one *parsah* and a half. The excrement it expelled was enough to clog the River Jordan. [Interpretation: The day-old *re'em* is indicative of someone who just started to learn Torah and thinks that he is an accomplished scholar. His neck of three *parsahs* says that his head is in the clouds. He can create temporary problems, but soon the river will be unblocked and the pure water will flow (Gra).]

Rabbah b. Bar Chanah further said: I saw a frog as big as the Fort of Hagronia that contained sixty houses. Along came a whale that swallowed the frog. Then came a raven that swallowed the whale. It flew up a tree and sat there. Imagine how big that tree must have been! R. Papa b. Shmuel said: If I had not been there myself, I would not have believed it. [Interpretation: This allegory refers to the succession of nations that ruled over Eretz Yisrael during the second *Bet Hamikdash*. The frog alludes to Greece; the whale, to Rome; the raven represents Ishmael, the Arab conquerors. The mighty tree that carries all these is the promise God has made to Israel that they will survive all oppressors and continue to exist until the coming of *Mashiach* (*Maharsha*).]

Rabba b. Bar Chanah further said: Once we were traveling on a ship and saw a large fish in whose nostrils a small creeping creature had entered, [and the fish died]. The ocean disgorged the dead fish and dumped it on the shore. [It was such a large fish] that sixty cities were destroyed [when the fish landed on them]. However, sixty cities ate from its flesh, and sixty cities salted the flesh that remained, and from one of its eyeballs three hundred barrels of oil were filled. When we came back after twelve months we saw that the people were sawing its bones into beams to make huts, and they began to rebuild those destroyed towns. [Interpretation: This tale alludes to the Purim story. The big fish is Haman; the small creature that caused the death of the fish is Mordechai. The destruction Haman planned had a constructive ending, and the Jews benefitted from the threat against them. Each year on Purim the miracle is relived and renewed (Maharsha).]

Rabbah b. Bar Chanah said furthermore: It happened once that we were traveling on a ship when we saw a fish whose back was covered with sand, and grass was growing there. Thinking that it was an island, we went up and baked and cooked on its back. However, when its back became hot, the fish decided to turn over, and if our ship had not been close by, we would have drowned. [Interpretation: The Jewish people traveling on the sea of their long and anguished galut [exile] sometimes experience periods of tranquility. They think they are on an island of safety, and are lulled into a false sense of security, thinking that they are standing on dry land. Then suddenly, the fish turns around, and their illusion evaporates. Fortunately, God's help is nearby, and Israel realizes that teshuvah is the key to their survival (Maharsha).]

Rabbah b. Bar Chanah further said: We once traveled aboard ship, and the ship sailed between one fin [at the head of the fish] and another fin [at its tail]. This went on for three days and three nights; the fish was swimming upward [against the wind], and we were sailing downward [with the wind]. Now if you think that the ship did not sail all that fast, when R. Dimi came he said that it traveled sixty parsahs in the time it takes to heat up a kettle of water, and if a soldier shot an arrow, we were quicker than the arrow. And R. Ashi said: That fish was one of the small fishes. [Interpretation: Again a reference to the miracle of Purim, which falls in the month of Adar in the sign of Pisces [Fishes]. For three days the fate of the Jews was hanging in the balance, the three days and three nights that the Jews fasted (Maharsha).]

Rabbah b. Bar Chanah also told: Once we were sailing aboard ship, and we saw a bird standing up to its ankles in water while its head reached to the sky. So we said to ourselves: The water probably is not too deep. We wanted to go into the shallow water to cool ourselves a little. But a heavenly voice rang out and said: Do not go down there! A carpenter dropped an axe here seven years ago, and that axe still has not reached bottom. And this is not only because the water is so deep, but also because the current is very strong. R. Ashi said: The bird [that stands in this bottomless water up to its ankles and its head reaches to the sky] was Ziz-Sadai, as it says, "And Ziz-Sadai is with Me" (Psalms 50:11). [Interpretation: The Torah is called a bird because of the constant sound of wisdom that emanates from it. Its ankles in the water refer to the revealed aspect of the Torah; at first glance you may think the Torah is only ankle deep but in reality it is extremely profound and difficult to fathom. The bird's head that reaches to the sky is the hidden aspect of the Torah, the wisdom of Kabbalah. God says, "it is with Me"; it is beyond human comprehension. If someone claims to understand Kabbalah he proves that he definitely does not (Maharsha).]

Rabbah b. Bar Chanah further said: We were once traveling in the desert and saw geese whose feathers fell out because of their fatness, and streams of fat dripped from them. So I said to them, "Will we have a portion of you in the World to Come?" [In the World to Come the tzaddikim will partake of a lavish feast.] One goose raised its wing, another raised its thigh. When I came before R. Elazar, he said to me: Israel will be held accountable for the suffering of these geese who languish because of their obesity; [they will be relieved from their pain only when Mashiach comes and they become food for the tzaddikim. But the transgressors who prevent Mashiach from coming will be held accountable for the suffering of the geese (Rashbam)]. [Interpretation: Geese are symbolic of knowledge. At the time of Mashiach, knowledge will be available to all. By raising their wings and thighs the geese implied that the study of Torah must lead to action, to the performance of mitzvot. Mashiach will come only through the mitzvot, which we do with our hands and feet (Maharsha).]

Rabbah b. Bar Chanah related: We were once traveling in the desert, and an Arab merchant came along with us. He would take a handful of earth, smell it, and say, "This is the way to such a place, and this is the way to such a place." We said to him, "How far are we from water?" He replied, "Give me some earth." When we gave it to him he said to us, "Eight parsahs." When we gave him some earth again later, he told us that we were three parsahs away from water. [In order to test him] I switched the samples of earth that were given him, but I could not stump him. [Interpretation: The Arab merchant epitomizes a great tzaddik and Torah scholar. The question, "How far are we from water?" means "What must I do to prepare myself for the lofty mysteries of the Torah you are going to reveal to me?" (Maharsha).]

[Rabbah b. Bar Chanah continued:] The Arab said to me, "Come and I will show you the people that died [during the forty years of wandering in the wilderness]." I went with him, and saw them; and they looked as if they were ecstatically happy. (74a) All of them were lying on their backs. The knee of one of them was raised, and the Arab merchant was able to pass under the leg, riding on a camel, holding his spear upright, and he did not touch the leg of the deceased. [Interpretation: The generation that wandered in the wilderness were spiritual giants of a magnitude that is far beyond our comprehension (*Maharsha*).]

[Rabbah b. Bar Chanah continues:] I cut off one corner of the *tallit* of one of those people [in order to learn how they made the *tzitzit*], but [our camels] would not move on. The Arab said to me, "If by any chance you took something from them, return it. We have a tradition that if someone takes something from them, we cannot move on." I went and returned the *tzitzit* [without examining them], and then we were able to move on. When I came before the Rabbis [and told them that I had not checked the *tzitzit*], they [were very upset and] said to me, "Every Abba is a donkey [Rabbah b. Bar Chanah was the garbled form of his real name, Rav Abba b. Bar Chanah], and every Bar Bar Chanah is a fool. What *halachah* did you want to learn by cutting off those *tzitzit*? You wanted to find out whether the *halachah* is like Bet Shammai or Bet Hillel." [Bet Shammai holds that the *tzitzit* should have four threads doubled over, making a total of eight threads. Bet Hillel contends that there should be three threads doubled over, making a total of six threads.][40] "You should have counted how many strings and how many spaces between the knots there are!"

Rabbah b. Bar Chanah said: The Arab merchant also told me, "Come, let me show you Mount Sinai." When I arrived there I saw that it was surrounded by scorpions, and they stood there looking like white donkeys. I heard a heavenly voice crying, "Woe is me that I have sworn to exile My people, and now that I have made the oath, who can absolve Me from that oath?" When I came before the Rabbis they said to me, "Every Abba is a donkey! Every Bar Bar Chanah is a fool!" You should have cried out, "*Mufar lach*, I annul Your oath!" [Why didn't Rabbah b. Bar Chanah take God's hint?] He thought that the oath God had in mind was His oath never again to bring a Flood over the earth. [Rabbah b. Bar Chanah did not want to annul that oath, and bring about another Flood.] And the Rabbis? [Why were they upset with Rabbah b. Bar Chanah?] Because they argued: If the oath [referred to the Flood], why did the heavenly voice say, "Woe is Me"? [God is never happy when people suffer, even when they deserve to suffer. Therefore, God would never have said, "Woe is me that I cannot punish them" (Rashbam).]

[Rabbah b. Bar Chanah said:] The Arab merchant said to me, "Come, let me show you the opening in the ground that swallowed the men of Korach."[41] I saw two cracks in the ground, from which smoke belched forth. The Arab took a piece of wool shearings, soaked it in water, attached it to the point of a spear, and in-serted this wool into the cracks. When he took it out it was charred. So he said to me, "Listen carefully. What do you hear?" I heard them say, "Moses and his Torah are truth, and we are liars!" The Arab said to me, "Every thirty days Gehinnom returns them back to this place like meat that is stirred in a pot, and they say, 'Moses and his Torah are truth, and we are liars!'"

[Rabbah b. Bar Chanah continues to relate what the Arab merchant told him.] He said, "Come, let me show you where heaven and earth touch each other." I followed him and saw that heaven was made up of many windows. I took my bread basket, and I placed it in a window of heaven, [and then I prayed]. After praying I looked for the basket but could not find it. I said to the Arab, "Are there thieves here?" He answered, "It is the rotating heavenly belt [of the Zodiac that took the basket with it]. Wait here until tomorrow, and you will find it." [Interpretation: Heaven and earth represent the contrasting ideas of whether a person's fate is determined by his destiny or by his own actions. Rabbah b. Bar Chanah changed his outlook on life. He put away his bread basket and decided not to work for a living any more but to rely on the power of prayer. When his fortune did not improve he wondered "Are there thieves here that steal my prayer?" He was told to be patient. There is a cycle in the world, and eventually your prayers will be answered: "tomorrow you will find it" (*Maharsha*).]

R. Yochanan related: Once we were traveling aboard ship, and we saw a fish that raised its head out of the sea. Its eyes were like two moons, and water streamed from its nostrils like from the two rivers of Sura.

R. Safra related: Once we were traveling aboard ship and we saw a fish that raised its head out of the sea. It had horns on which were engraved the words: I am a only a small creature of the sea. I am three hundred *parsahs* long, and I am now going into the mouth of Leviathan. R. Ashi said: That fish is a sea-goat that searches for its food [by digging in the sea bed] with its horns.

R. Yochanan related: We were once traveling aboard ship when we saw a treasure chest that had precious stones and pearls set in it, and it was surrounded by a kind of fish called *karsha*. A diver (74b) went down to haul in the treasure chest, but a fish noticed him and wanted to dislocate the diver's thigh. So the diver poured out a bottle of vinegar and, repelled by the smell of the vinegar, the fish swam away. A heavenly voice rang out and said to us, "What business do you have with the chest of R. Chaninah b. Dosa's wife,[[42]] for in it blue wool will be kept for the *tzaddikim* of the World to Come.

R. Yehudah Hindo'ah related: Once we were traveling aboard ship when we saw a precious stone that was surrounded by a sea monster. A diver went down to retrieve it. The sea monster came and wanted to swallow the whole ship when a raven appeared and bit off its head, so that the water turned into blood.

A second sea monster came and took the precious stone and hung it on the dead sea monster, and it came back to life. Again it came and wanted to swallow the ship. The raven came once more and bit off its head. The diver took the precious stone and threw it onto the ship. [We then made an experiment.] We had with us some salted birds [for food]. As soon as we placed the precious jewel on them, the birds came to life, and they took the stone and flew off with it. [Interpretation: The precious stone is the Torah; the diver searching for it is the Jewish people. The sea monster that is trying to deny us the jewel of the Torah is the Christian Church. The raven that bit off the sea monster's head represents the Islam that challenged Christianity. The second sea monster that took the stone and brought life to the first one suggests the righteous gentiles who merit life in the World to Come. The salted birds stand for the Torah scholars who, in spite of incredible hardship, take the jewel of the Torah and fly away with it, surviving all the persecutions (*Maharsha*).]

THE LEVIATHAN

[The Leviathan and the banquet for the *tzaddikim* in the World to Come that are the subject of the following *aggadot* are not to be understood in a physical sense. They refer to lofty spiritual levels in Gan Eden. The reward of the World to Come cannot be explained in terms we can comprehend, because there is nothing in this world to which it can be compared. Since eating is a form of great enjoyment, it is used as a metaphor for the delight the *tzaddikim* experience by being close to the splendor of the *Shechinah*; it is nourishment of the soul. Their joy is beyond description (Maharal).]

We learned in a *Baraita*: It happened that R. Eliezer and R. Yehoshua were traveling aboard ship. R. Eliezer was sleeping and R. Yehoshua was awake. R. Yehoshua shivered and R. Eliezer woke up. R. Eliezer said to R. Yehoshua, "What is the matter, Yehoshua? Why are you shivering?" "I saw a great light in the sea," R. Yehoshua replied. "You may have seen Leviathan," R. Eliezer suggested, "for it says, [in the description of Leviathan], 'His eyes are like the glimmer of the dawn' (Job 41:10)."

R. Ashi said: R. Huna b. Natan told me the following: We were once traveling on foot through the desert, and we had with us a leg of beef. We cut it open, and removed the forbidden fat and the *gid hanasheh* [the sciatic nerve].[43] We then placed it on the grass and while we were gathering firewood, the leg regained its original form, and we roasted it. When we came back to the scene after twelve months we saw that the same coals were still smoldering. When we came and told this to Amemar, he said, "That grass was *samtre*, and the coals were the coals of *rotem* wood [which keeps smoldering for a long time]."

THE MALE AND
FEMALE LEVIATHAN

It says, "God created the great sea monsters" (Genesis 1:21). Here in Babylonia they explained it to mean: the *re'em* [rhinoceros] of the sea. R. Yochanan [in Eretz Yisrael] said: This refers to Leviathan, the [male] straight monstrous fish; and the Leviathan, the [female] curved monstrous fish. For it says, "On this day God will bring punishment with His harsh, great mighty sword, upon the Leviathan, the straight monstrous fish, and upon the Leviathan, the curved monstrous fish" (Isaiah 27:1).

Rav Yehudah said in the name of Rav: Whatever the Holy One, blessed be He, created in this world, He created both male and female. This is true for Leviathan, He created the straight male monstrous fish and the curved female monstrous fish. And if they had mated with each other [and had offspring], they would have destroyed the whole world. What did the Holy One, blessed be He, do? He made the male sterile and killed the female, and preserved it in salt as food for the *tzaddikim* in the World to Come. For it says, "He will kill the great sea monster that is in the ocean" (ibid.). And also the behemoth of a thousand mountains[44] [are prepared for the *tzaddikim* in the hereafter]. These, too, were created male and female, and if they had mated with each other and had offspring], they would have destroyed the world. What did the Holy One, blessed be He, do? He made the male sterile and made the female emotionless and preserved it for the *tzaddikim* in the World to Come. For it says, [in the description of the behemoth, "Behold now, his strength is in his loins, and his might is in the navel of his abdomen" (Job 40:16). [The Gemara expounds:] "His strength is in his loins"— this refers to the male; "and his might is in the navel of his abdomen"—this refers to the female. [The Gemara asks:] In the case of Leviathan, why could not God have made the male sterile and cooled the ardor of the female; [why did He kill the female]?

[The Gemara answers:] Fishes are so unrestrained, cooling the female would not have helped to prevent their propagation. [The Gemara asks:] Why did God not do it the other way round, [making the female sterile, and cooling the ardor of the male. That certainly would have prevented reproduction]? [The Gemara answers:] If you wish, say: [It is because] a female fish tasted better. Or if you wish, say: Because it says, "Leviathan You fashioned to sport with" (Psalms 104:26). It would not have been proper [to use this expression if the one that remained alive was the female]. [The Gemara asks:] In the case of the behemoth, could God not have salted the female? [The Gemara answers:] Salted fish is tasty; salted meat is not. [The Maharal points out that the Leviathan and the behemoth are not physical beings; the male and female aspect of them means that they are two spiritual entities that complement each other. On this point he disagrees with the Maharsha, who contends that we must believe that all of this does exist in reality.]

Rav Yehudah further said in the name of Rav: When the Holy One, blessed be He, wanted to create the world, He said to the angel of the sea: Open your mouth and swallow all the waters of the world, [and let the dry land become visible]. The angel said to God: Master of the universe! Is it not enough that I take care of my own water? Right away, God kicked him and killed him, for it says, "With His strength He divides the ocean, and with His understanding He crushes *Rahav*" (Job 26:12). R. Yitzchak said: From this we can deduce that the angel of the sea is called Rahav. And if not for the fact that the water covered the corpse of Rahav, no living thing could have tolerated its stench, for it says, "They will neither injure nor destroy in all of My sacred mountain, for the earth will be as filled with knowledge of God as water covers the sea" (Isaiah 11:9). Don't read, "covers the sea" [for the sea itself is water]; rather it means, "as water covers the angel of the sea." [The killing of the angel of the sea meant that he was reduced from a spiritual being and given a physical form, hence the foul odor his corpse emitted.]

DEFEAT OF THE LEVIATHAN

Rav Yehudah said also in the name of Rav: The Jordan originates from the cave of Panias [Banias]. We learned likewise in a *Baraita*: The Jordan springs from the cave of Panias and passes through the Sea of Sivchi and the Sea of Tiberias and meanders down to the Great Sea, from which it continues to roll down until it reaches the mouth of the Leviathan. For it says, "He feels secure that he can gulp the Jordan into his mouth" (Job 40:23). Rava b. Ulla objected: This verse refers to "the behemoth of a thousand hills" [not to the Leviathan]! Rava b. Ulla explained: When does the behemoth of a thousand hills feel secure? When the Jordan flows into the mouth of the Leviathan. [As long as the Leviathan is alive, the behemoth feel safe.]

When R. Dimi came [from Eretz Yisrael] he said in the name of R. Yochanan: The verse, "For He founded [Eretz Yisrael] upon seas, and established it upon rivers" (Psalms 24:2), speaks of the seven seas and four rivers that surround Eretz Yisrael. These are the seven seas: The Sea of Tiverias, the Sea of Sodom,[45] the Sea of Cheilat,[46] the Sea of Chilta, the Sea of Sivchi, the Sea of Aspamia, and the Great Sea.[47] The four rivers are: the Jordan, the Yarmuk, the Kirmiyon, and the Fuga.

When R. Dimi came he said in the name of R. Yonatan: in time to come Gabriel will organize **(75a)** a hunt for the Leviathan, for it says, "Can you pull the Leviathan with a fishhook? Can you embed a line in his tongue?" (Job 40:25). And if the Holy One, blessed be He, will not help Gabriel, he will be unable to triumph over him. For it says, "Only his Maker can direct His sword up close" (ibid. v. 19). [Gabriel's battle with the Leviathan foreshadows the ultimate war against the forces of evil (Hakotev).]

When R. Dimi came he said in the name of R. Yochanan: When the Leviathan is hungry he exhales a fiery breath that makes all the waters of the deep boil, as it says, "He bubbles up the deep sea like a seething pot" (ibid. 41:23). And if not for the fact that he inserts his head into Gan Eden, no living thing would be able to tolerate the stench of its breath. For it says, "He ferments the sea like a boiling concoction" (ibid.). When he is thirsty, he makes furrows in the sea bed, for it says, "In his wake a path shines" (ibid. v. 24). R. Acha b. Yaakov added: [After the Leviathan finished drinking,] the deep does not regain its strength [i.e., its previous water level] for another seventy years, for it says, "He makes the deep sea look like an old man" (ibid.), and old age is no less than seventy years.

THE GREAT BANQUET FOR THE *TZADDIKIM*

Rabbah said in the name of R. Yochanan: In time to come, the Holy One, blessed be He, will make a great banquet for the *tzaddikim* from the flesh of the Leviathan, for it says, "Friends [*chabarim*] will make a feast [*yichru*] of him" (ibid. 40:30). *Keirah* means a banquet, for it says, "So he prepared a large meal [*keirah*] for them, and they ate and drank" (2 Kings 6:23). "Friends" means Torah scholars, for it says, "Those who dwell in the gardens of [*chaveirim*], Torah scholars that listen to Your voice, let Me hear it" (Song of Songs 8:13). The rest of the Leviathan's flesh will be distributed and sold in the markets of Jerusalem, for it says, "They will divide him among *kena'anim*" (Job 40:30). And *kena'anim* means merchants, for it says, "A trader [*kena'an*] with scales of deceit in his hands" (Hosea 12:8). If you prefer, you can prove it from here, "Whose merchants were princes and whose traders [*kinaneha*] were the elite of the land" (Isaiah 23:8).

Rabbah further said in the name of R. Yochanan: In time to come, the Holy One, blessed be He, will make a *sukkah* for the *tzaddikim* from the skin of the Leviathan, for it says, [God says to Job,] "Can you complete all the *sukkot* [with the skin of the Leviathan, as I can]?" (Job 40:31). If a person deserves it, a *sukkah* will be made for him from the Leviathan's skin; if he does not deserve it, only a shade will be made for him, for it says, [God says to Job,] "Can you make a shade out of his head?" (ibid.). If he is worthy, they will make a shade for him, but if he not worthy even of a shade, they will make a necklace for him [out of the skin of the Leviathan], for it says, "A necklace around your neck" (Proverbs 1:9). If he is not even worthy of this, an amulet [that people used to tie around their necks] will be made for him, for it says, [God says to Job,]

"Can you bind it on your maiden?" (Job 40:29). The rest of the Leviathan, the Holy One, blessed be He, will spread on the walls of Jerusalem, and its radiance will shine from one end of the world to the other, as it says, "Nations will walk by your light and kings by the brilliance of your shine" (Isaiah 60:3).

IN TIME TO COME . . .

It says, "I will set your walls with *kadkod* stone, and your gates with carbuncle stones" (Isaiah 54:12). Shmuel b. Nachmani said: There is a dispute between two angels in heaven, Gabriel and Michael [regarding the meaning of *kadkod*]. Others say: The dispute is between two *Amora'im* in Eretz Yisrael. And who are they? Yehudah and Chizkiah, the sons of R. Chiya. One says: *Kadkod* means onyx; the other says: jasper. The Holy One, blessed be He, said to them: I will give you both.[48]

"[I will make] your gates with carbuncle stones." We have to interpret this phrase the way R. Yochanan explained it when he once sat and expounded: In time to come, the Holy One, blessed be He, will bring precious stones and pearls that are thirty cubits by thirty cubits each, and will cut out of them an opening of ten cubits by twenty, and will place them in the gates of Jerusalem. One Student laughed when he heard this, "You can't even find a pearl the size of a dove's egg, and you say that we will find gems that are so big!" A while later, this student happened to be on a voyage out at sea where he saw angels busy cutting gemstones and pearls the size of thirty by thirty cubits, into which they reamed holes the size of ten cubits by twenty. He asked them, "For whom are these?" They replied, "The Holy One, blessed be He, in time to come will install them in the gates of Jerusalem." When the student came back, he said to R. Yochanan, "Rabbi, expound! It is fitting for you to expound. Whatever you have said I have seen with my own eyes." Replied R. Yochanan, "You good-for-nothing! And if you had not seen it, would you not have believed it? You are mocking the words of the Sages!" He set his eyes on the student, and the student turned into a heap of bones.

An objection was raised: [How can R. Yochanan say that the stones were so big, when it says that God says,] "I will lead you very high *komemiyut*" (Leviticus 26:13). [How high?] R. Meir says: Two hundred cubits; twice the height of Adam. R. Yehudah says: A hundred cubits, corresponding to the height of the *Bet Hamikdash*, and its walls, for it says, "For our sons are like saplings, nurtured from their youth; our daughters are like cornerstones crafted in the form of the *Bet Hamikdash*" (Psalms 144:12). [The walls of the *Bet Hamikdash* were a hundred cubits high, but according to R. Yochanan the stones of the gate were only twenty cubits high.] [The Gemara answers:] R. Yochanan was referring to windows for fresh air; [not the gates].

Rabbah said in the name of R. Yochanan: In time to come, the Holy One, blessed be He, will make seven canopies for every *tzaddik*, for it says, "And God will create over every structure of Mount Zion and over those who assemble in it a cloud by day, and smoke and a glow of gleaming fire by night, for this will be a canopy over all the honor" (Isaiah 4:5). This teaches us that the Holy One, blessed be He, will make a canopy for each person according to his degree of eminence. [The Gemara asks: One of the canopies mentioned in the verse is smoke.] Why is smoke needed for a canopy? R. Chanina said: Whoever looked with a begrudging eye toward Torah scholars in this world will have his eyes filled with smoke in the World to Come. Why is fire needed for a canopy?—R. Chanina said: This teaches us that those of lower rank will be burned by [envy] of their neighbor's [more distinguished] canopy. Woe for such shame! Woe for such disgrace!

In a similar vein you can say: [God instructed Moses,] "Invest [Joshua] with some of your splendor" (Numbers 27:20), but not *all* your splendor. The elders of that generation said: The face of Moses was like the sun; the face of Joshua was like the moon. [Joshua's radiance was of a lower intensity than that of Moses.] Woe for such shame! Woe for such disgrace, [that there has been such a decline in knowledge and glory within the span of one generation (Rashbam)].

R. Chama b. Chanina said: The Holy One, blessed be He, made ten canopies for Adam in Gan Eden, for it says, [Ezekiel said to Hiram, king of Tyre,] "Were you in Eden, the Garden of God; was your canopy of every precious stone—*odem*, *pitedah*, and *yahalom*; *tarshish*, *shoham*, and *yoshfeh*; *sapir*, *nofech*, and *barkas*—and gold? (Ezekiel 28:13). Mar Zutra says: Eleven canopies; for it says, "every precious stone" [in addition to the ten mentioned in the verse]. R. Yochanan said: The least of all these was gold, since it is mentioned last. [The Gemara asks:] What is implied by, "The work of your drums and the wind instruments with holes was in you" (ibid.)? Rav Yehudah said in the name of Rav: The Holy One, blessed be He, said to Hiram, king of Tyre,[49] "When I created the world I looked at you, [and saw that you would rebel against Me]; therefore, I created many holes in man [so that he can relieve himself, and will realize that he is dependent on God for his health]. Others say [this is what God said,] "I looked at you, Hiram [(75b)], and as a result, I decreed death on Adam. [The hollow "drums" and the "holes of the wind instruments" allude to the opening of the grave (Rashbam).]

[The Gemara asks: In the verse, "God will create . . . a canopy over those who assemble in Mount Zion" (Isaiah 4:5)], what does the phrase "those who assemble in it [*mikra'eha*]" refer to? Rabbah said in the name of R. Yochanan: The Jerusalem of the World to Come is not like the Jerusalem of this world. To the Jerusalem of this world, whoever wishes can go there, but to the Jerusalem of the World to Come only those that are invited[50] will be able to go.

Rabbah said in the name of R. Yochanan: In time to come, *tzaddikim* will be called by the name of the Holy One, blessed be He. For it says, "Everyone that is called by My name, and whom I have created for My glory, whom I have fashioned, even perfected" (ibid. 43:7). R. Shmuel b. Nachmani said in the name of R. Yochanan: The following three were called by the name of the Holy One, blessed be He: *Tzaddikim*,[51] *Mashiach*, and Jerusalem. *Tzaddikim*, as mentioned above. *Mashiach*, for it says, [referring to *Mashiach*], "This is the name people will call him: God is our righteousness" (Jeremiah 23:6). Jerusalem, because it says, "The circumference of the city [Jerusalem] is thus eighteen thousand [cubits], and the name of the city from that day on shall be 'God-Is-There'" (Ezekiel 48:35). Do not read "there" [*shamah*] but "its name" [*shemah*; God-Is-Its-Name]. R. Elazar said: In time to come the angels will say "Holy" before *tzaddikim* as they do before the Holy One, blessed be He. For it says, "Of every remnant that will be in Zion, and every remaining one in Jerusalem, 'Holy' will be said of him" (Isaiah 4:3).

THE JERUSALEM OF
THE FUTURE

Rabbah further said in the name of R. Yochanan: In time to come, the Holy One, blessed be He, will elevate Jerusalem three *parsahs* high, as it says, "Jerusalem will become lofty, and it will become settled in its place" (Zechariah 14:10). "In its place" means "like her place"; [the height of Jerusalem will be the same as the area it occupies now]. How do I know that the area it occupies now is three *parsahs*? Rabbah said: A certain old man told me, "I saw the first Jerusalem, and its area was three *parsahs*. And in case you will say [that a height of three *parsahs*] will make it difficult to climb up there, [let me allay your concerns,] for it says, "Who are these who fly like a cloud, like doves to their cote window?" (Isaiah 60:8). R. Papa said: From this you can infer that a cloud rises three *parsahs*.

R. Chanina b. Papa said: The Holy One, blessed be He, wanted to give Jerusalem a fixed size, for it says, [Zechariah had a vision of a man holding a measuring line]. "I asked, 'Where are you going?' He answered me, 'To measure Jerusalem, to see how wide its breadth and how long its length'" (Zechariah 2:6). The ministering angels said to the Holy One, blessed be He, "Master of the universe! There are many great cities You created in Your world that belong to the nations of the world, and you did not limit the measurements of their length and their width. Are You going to fix the measurements of Jerusalem, the city upon which Your name rests, where Your *Bet Hamikdash* stands and Your *tzaddikim* reside?" Thereupon [an angel] said, "Run, speak to that young man over there and tell him, 'Jerusalem will be settled beyond its walls, because of the multitude of people and livestock within it'" (Zechariah 2:8).

Resh Lakish said: In time to come, the Holy One, blessed be He, will add to Jerusalem a thousand gardens, a thousand towers, a thousand palaces, a thousand mansions, and each of these will be as big as Tzipori [Sepphoris] in its good times. We learned in a *Baraita*: R. Yose said: I saw Tzipori in its good times, and there were one hundred and eighty markets where ready-made dishes were sold.

[Ezekiel had a vision of the future *Bet Hamikdash*. He saw that along the walls there were three levels of cells, one on top of the other], "And the cells were arranged cell upon cell, thirty-three in number" (Ezekiel 41:6). What is meant by "thirty-three in number"? R. Levi said in the name of R. Papi, in the name if R. Yehoshua b. Sichnin: If [in time to come] there will be three Jerusalems [meaning, the Jerusalem of the future will be three times the size of the present one], each building will contain thirty dwellings, one on top of the other; if there will be thirty Jerusalems, each building will contain three dwellings, one on top of the other.

THE ULTIMATE CALCULATION

(78b) [Concerning the war between Sichon and Moab, where the king of Sichon conquered the mighty city of Cheshbon, the Torah states,] "Regarding this the poets [*moshelim*] would say: Come to Cheshbon—let it be built and established as the city of Sichon. For a fire has come forth from Cheshbon, a flame from the city of Sichon. It consumed Or of Moab, the masters of Arnon's heights. Woe to you, Moab, you are lost, O people of Chemosh! He made your sons fugitives and your daughters captives, of the king of the Amorite Sichon. Their sovereignty over Cheshbon was lost, it was removed from Dibon, and we laid waste to Nophach, which reaches up to Medeba" (Numbers 21:27–30). [Why does the Torah tell us all this? The Rabbis expound the verses as follows:] R. Shmuel b. Nachmani said in the name of R. Yochanan: What is meant by "Regarding this the poets [*hamoshelim*] would say"? *Hamoshelim*[52] refers to those who subdue their *yetzer hara* [evil impulse]. "Come to Cheshbon" means, come, let us make the ultimate calculation:[53] let us weigh what we lose by not doing a mitzvah, against the reward we gain by doing it; and the loss we incur by a transgression against the little temporary enjoyment it brings.

"Let it be built and established as the city of Sichon"—if you will do this [and make this calculation], you will be built in this world and established in the World to Come. "The city [*ir*] of Sichon"—[The Gemara expounds that *ir* can be punctuated to be read as *ayar*, "young donkey."] If a person acts like a young donkey that is easily swayed by gentle talk [of sin]; what becomes of him? "A fire comes forth from Cheshbon"—A fire will come out from [the *tzaddikim*] who do make the proper calculation [*cheshbon*], and consume those who do not calculate [the wicked]. "A flame from the city of Sichon"—From the city of the *tzaddikim* who are compared to trees [*sichin*].

"It consumed Ar of Moab"—This refers to a person who follows his evil impulse like a young donkey [*ayar*] follows gentle talk [of sin]. "The masters of Arnon's heights"—this refers to people who are conceited, for it has been said: Whoever is conceited will fall into Gehinnom. "The sovereignty [*vaniram*]"[54]— The wicked says: There is no High One [*ein Rom*]. "Cheshbon was lost"—[the wicked says:] There is no reckoning [*cheshbon*], [we do not have to render an account for our actions]. "It was removed from Dibon" —the Holy One, blessed be He, said: Wait until judgment comes [*yavo din*]. "And we laid waste to Nophach" (79a)—until the fire comes that does not need any fanning [*nifuach*]. "Up to Medeba"—until their souls melt [*da'avon*]. Others say: [God allows the wicked to have their way] until the time comes that He does what He desires to do to the wicked.

Rav Yehudah said in the name of Rav: Any person that strays from the words of the Torah is consumed by fire, for it says, "I will direct My attention against them; they have strayed from the fire [i.e., the Torah], but now fire will consume them" (Ezekiel 15:7). When R. Dimi came [from Eretz Yisreal] he said in the name of R. Yonatan: Whoever strays from the words of the Torah falls into Gehinnom, for it says, "A person who wanders from the intelligent way will rest in the congregation of the *refa'im*" (Proverbs 21:16). And *refa'im* means Gehinnom, for it says, "But he does not know that *refa'im* are there, that those she invites are in the deepest grave" (ibid. 9:18).

A *TZADDIK* RESEMBLES A DATE PALM AND A CEDAR

(80b) [The Gemara asks:] Does not the stump of the cedar tree grow shoots? Surely R. Chiya b. Luliani expounded: What is meant by, "A righteous man will flourish like a date palm, like a cedar in the Lebanon he will grow tall" (Psalms 92:13)? Why are both the date palm and the cedar mentioned? If the cedar only had been mentioned and not the date palm, I might have said that just as the cedar produces no edible fruit, so will the *tzaddik* produce no fruit; therefore the date palm is mentioned. And if the date palm only had been mentioned and not the cedar, I might have said that just as the stump of a date palm does not produce shoots [after the trunk has been cut], so too the *tzaddik*, when he dies, will not leave children who are as great as he was. Therefore the cedar is also mentioned. [Doesn't this prove that the stump of a cedar does grow shoots?] [The Gemara answers:] We are dealing here with other kinds of cedar trees, for Rabbah b. R. Huna said: There are ten kinds of cedar trees, for it says, "In the wilderness I will set cedar, acacia, myrtle and pine tree; I will place cypress, fir and box tree together in a

desert . . . " (Isaiah 41:19). Aren't these only seven kinds of cedar? When R. Dimi came [from Eretz Yisrael to Babylonia] he said: They added to the above-mentioned seven species: pistachio trees, oaks, and corals.

HONEST WEIGHTS AND MEASURES

(88b) Our Rabbis taught: From where do we know that you may not give a leveled measure where the practice is to heap it up, and that you may not give a heaped-up measure where the custom is to level it? Because it says, "You must have a perfect and honest measure" (Deuteronomy 25:15). And from where do we know that where the practice is to heap it up, if someone says: I will give a level measure, and reduce the price; or where the practice is to give a level measure, if someone says: I will heap up and and raise the price; that we should not listen to him? Because it says, "You must have a perfect and honest measure." R. Yehudah of Sura expounded: "You will not have anything [of value] in your house" [i.e., you will be poor] (ibid. v. 14). Why? Because you had "different weights" (ibid. v. 13). But [if you keep] a perfect and honest weight, you will have [wealth]; [if you keep] a perfect and honest measure, you will have [prosperity].

We learned in a *Baraita*: "You must have" (ibid. v. 15). This teaches us that market inspectors are appointed to check out measures, but not to regulate prices. The officials of the *Nasi*'s House appointed market inspectors to oversee both measures and prices. Thereupon Shmuel said to Karna: Go and teach them the statute that market inspectors are appointed to check out measures but not to regulate prices. But Karna went and lectured them that market inspectors should be appointed to oversee both measures and prices. Shmuel said to him: Is your name Karna? Let a horn [*karna*] grow out of your eye, and a lump grew on his eye. But whose opinion did Karna follow? The view of Rami b. Chama in the name of R. Yitzchak who said: Inspectors should be appointed to deal with both measures and prices, [to protect the public] from defrauders.

(89b) We learned in a *Baraita*: The measure leveler should not be made thick on one side and narrow on the other, [because the thick side cannot scrape the grain as evenly as the thin side. If the merchant uses the thin side when selling and the thick side when buying, he is dealing unfairly]. You should not level the measure quickly with one swift strike, [because then the flour is not measured accurately,] and this benefits the buyer and causes a loss to the seller. You should not level the measure very slowly, [alternately lifting the leveler and pressing it down], since this benefits the seller and shortchanges the buyer. Concerning these deceitful practices R. Yochanan b. Zakkai said: Woe is to me if I speak about them, and woe is to me if I do not speak about them. If I speak about them, the cheats might learn new tricks. If I do not speak about them, the scoundrels might say: Torah scholars are naive; they are not familiar with our shady practices. The question was raised: In the end, did R. Yochanan speak about these double-dealings or not? Shmuel b. R. Yitzchak said: He did speak about them, and he did so on the basis of the following passage, "For the ways of God are straight; the righteous walk in them, and sinners will stumble over them" (Hosea 14:10).

STOCKPILING PRODUCE

Our Rabbis taught: Concerning people who stockpile produce [in order to get a better price for it later], lend money at interest, make measures smaller, and concerning people who drive up prices, Scripture says, "[You who say,] 'When will the month pass, so that we can sell grain; the Sabbatical year, so that we can open the [stores of] grain; reduce the *ephah* and increase the shekel [by charging interest], and distort the scales of deceit'" (Amos 8:5). And further it says, "God has sworn by the glory of Jacob: 'I will never forget all their deeds'" (ibid. v. 7). Who, for example, is a person that stockpiles fruit? R. Yochanan said: Someone like Shabtai the fruit hoarder.

The father of Shmuel used to sell out all his produce when it was in season, [to let the poor benefit from the low prices]. Shmuel his son used to hold on to his fruit until it was out of season and expensive and then sell it at the original low market price. They sent the following message [from Eretz Yisrael]: What the father did is better than what the son did. What is the reason? Once the price goes up, it is very difficult to bring it down, [as Shmuel tried to do. But Shmuel's father made sure that there was an abundant supply at the beginning of the season, thereby keeping the prices down for the rest of the year].

Our Rabbis taught: You are not allowed to export from Eretz Yisrael staples that are basic necessities, such as wine, oil, and flour. R. Yehudah b. Beteirah permits it in the case of wine, because [if there is less wine] there will be less frivolity.

DO NOT MOVE AWAY
FROM ERETZ YISRAEL

(91a) Our Rabbis taught: You are not allowed to move away from Eretz Yisrael unless [the prices become so inflated] that you have to pay a *sela* for two *se'ah* of grain; [normally the price is one *sela* for four *se'ah* of grain]. R. Shimon said: [When do we say that you may leave because of inordinate inflation,] if you cannot find anything to buy [even at the inflated price]. However, if there is produce available, then even if you have to pay a *sela* for a *se'ah*, you should not leave Eretz Yisrael, [because there are many *mitzvot* you can fulfill only in

Eretz Yisrael, and because living in Eretz Yisrael brings you closer to God (Ramban)].

R. Shimon b. Yochai used to say: Elimelech[55] [and his sons] Machlon and Kilyon were the great men of their generation, and they were also the leaders of their generation. Then why were they punished? Solely because they left Eretz Yisrael and moved to a foreign country, for it says, [When Naomi and Ruth arrived in Bethlehem,] "The entire city was tumultuous over them, and the women said, 'Is this Naomi?'" (Ruth 1:19). [The Gemara asks:] What does "Is this Naomi" mean? R. Yitzchak said: They said: Did you see what happened to Naomi because she left Eretz Yisrael and moved to a foreign country? R. Yitzchak said also: On the very day that Ruth the Moabitess came to Eretz Yisrael, the wife of Boaz died. People have a saying for it: Before a person dies, someone has been appointed already to run his household. [Ruth became the wife of Boaz.][56]

BOAZ IS IBZAN

Rabbah the son of R. Huna said in the name of Rav: Ibzan [one of the judges in the Book of Judges][57] is Boaz. What does he want to teach us by telling us this? The same that Rabbah the son of R. Huna taught us elsewhere: Boaz prepared for his sons one hundred and twenty wedding banquets, for it says, "And he [Ibzan] had thirty sons, and he sent out thirty daughters [to marry into other families]; he brought thirty daughters for his sons from without [from other families]. He judged Israel for seven years" (Judges 12:9). For each of his sixty children he made two feasts [one on their betrothal (*eirusin*) and one on their marriage (*nisuin*) (Rashbam)], one in his own house and one in the house of the in-laws. [By telling us that Boaz is Ibzan, Rabbah the son of R. Huna teaches us that Boaz married Ruth although he had many children and was of advanced age.]

To none of these feasts did he invite Manoah,[58] because he said: How is this barren mule ever going to pay me back? [Before Samson was born, Manoah had no children to whose weddings he could invite Boaz.] All of his sixty children died during his lifetime, [as a punishment for having said this about Manoah (Maharal)]. And this is meant by the popular saying: If you had sixty children, but they all died in your lifetime, what good were they? Marry again, and father one that will be more stalwart than the sixty. [The sixty children that Ibzan/Boaz had did not do as well as the one child, Oved, he had from Ruth who was the ancestor of David (Rashbam).]

R. Chanan b. Rava said in the name of Rav: Elimelech and Salmon[59] and Peloni Almoni [the unnamed kinsman], and the father of Naomi all were sons of Nachshon ben Aminadav.[60] What does this come to teach us? That even if someone has ancestral merit [like Elimelech who was the son of the great *tzaddik*

Nachshon ben Aminadav], it cannot help him when he leaves Eretz Yisrael.

THE NAMES OF ABRAHAM'S AND SAMSON'S MOTHERS

R. Chanan b. Rava said furthermore in the name of Rav: The name of Abraham's mother was Amatlai the daughter of Karnevo; the name of Haman's mother was Amatlai the daughter of Orvati. A sign to help you remember which is which is: Unclean goes to unclean; clean goes to clean. [Haman's grandmother's name was Orvati, which reminds you of *orev*, a raven, which is an unclean bird; Abraham's ancestor's name was Karnevo, which reminds you of *kar*, a pillow that is stuffed with wool from sheep, which is a clean animal.] The name of David's mother was Nitzvat the daughter of Adael. The mother of Samson was named Tzlelponit, and his sister, Nashyan. [The Gemara asks:] What difference does it make [what their names were]? [The Gemara answers:] That we should be able to answer the heretics [when they ask us what their names were, and say that their names were handed down to us orally by the prophets (Rashbam)].

R. Chanan b. Rava further said in the name of Rav: Abraham our father was imprisoned for ten years [by Nimrod]. Three years in Kuta, and seven years in Kadro.[61] R. Dimi of Nehardea, however, says the opposite, [seven years in Kuta, three in Kadro]. R. Chisda said: The city Ivra Ze'ira deKuta is Ur Kasdim [Abraham's birthplace].[62]

R. Chanan b. Rava further said in the name of Rav: On the day when Abraham our father passed away, all the great men of the nations of the world stood in line and said: Woe to the world that has lost (91b) its leader, and woe to the ship that has lost its helmsman.

"Yours, God, is the kingdom, and You elevate everyone to a position of preeminence" (1 Chronicles 29:11). R. Chanan b. Rava said in the name of Rav: [The word "everyone" implies that] even the person in charge of distributing irrigation water is appointed to his position by Heaven.

WHY WERE ELIMELECH AND HIS SONS PUNISHED?

[The above Gemara said that Elimelech and his sons were punished because they left Eretz Yisrael. However,] R. Chiya b. Avin said in R. Yochanan's name: God forbid [to say that they left because of economic considerations]. Even if they had found only bran, they would not have left the country. [But even bran was not available, in which case they were certainly permitted to leave Eretz Yisrael.] Why then were they punished? Because they should have offered special prayers for the entire generation, which they did not do. For it says, "When you cry out, let your cohorts rescue you!" (Isaiah 57:13). [Meaning: When you pray

for others, God will save you together with your entire community.]

Rabbah b. Bar Chanah said in the name of R. Yochanan: [The restriction that you are not allowed to leave Eretz Yisrael] applies only in a case when money is cheap [in ample supply] but food is expensive. But in a case when money is scarce, then even if you can buy four *se'ah* of grain for a *sela* [which is the normal price], you are allowed to leave Eretz Yisrael. For R. Yochanan said: I remember the time when you could buy four *seah* of grain for a *selah*, and there were a lot of people that were swollen from starvation in Tveriah, because they did not even have an *issar* [a small coin] to buy food.

R. YOCHANAN REMEMBERED

R. Yochanan further said: I remember the time when workmen did not take jobs on the east side of the city; [they were so famished] that the aroma of freshly baked bread that pervaded the air there would cause them to die.

R. Yochanan further said: I remember the time when [the abundance and the quality of the fruit in Eretz Yisrael were so great] that when a child broke a carob in half a stream of honey would flow down both of his hands. And R. Elazar said: I remember that when a raven would take a piece of meat, a line of fat would come trickling down the wall [where it was sitting].

R. Yochanan further said: I remember the time when a boy and a girl of sixteen and seventeen years of age would go for a walk together and did not sin.

R. Yochanan further said: I remember the time when people [were so undaunted that] they said in the *bet midrash*: Anyone that agrees with idol worshippers falls into their hands, and anyone that trusts them will find that they will take whatever he owns.

MACHLON AND KILION

[Why is it that in the Book of Ruth, the sons of Elimelech are called] "Machlon and Kilion" (Ruth 1:2), and in another place they are referred to as "Joash and Saraph" (1 Chronicles 4:22)? Rav and Shmuel both explained it. One said: Their names were Machlon and Kilion, but they were called Joash and Saraph; Joash, because they gave up hope [yo'ash] that God would redeem Israel, and Saraph, because they were condemned to be burned [sereifah] by the Almighty [for leaving Eretz Yisrael]. The other says: Their true names were Joash and Saraph, but they were called Machlon and Kilion. Machlon, because they desecrated [challeil] their bodies [by leaving Eretz Yisrael]; and Kilion, because they were condemned to destruction [kilayon] by the Almighty.

We have a *Baraita* that agrees with the one who says that their real names were Machlon and Kilion, for it has been taught: How do you expound the verse, "Jokim, the men of Cozcba, and Joash and Saraph, who had dominion in Moab and Jashubi-lehem. These are ancient traditions" (1 Chronicles 4:22). "Jokim" is Joshua who kept [*heikim*] his oath to the men of Gibeon.[63] "The men of Coziba" refers to the men of Gibeon who lied [*kizvu*] to Joshua.[64] "And Joash and Saraph"—these are Machlon and Kilion. And why were they called Joash and Saraph? Joash, because they gave up hope that God would redeem Israel; Saraph, because they were condemned by the Almighty to be burned. "Who had dominion in Moab" means that they married Moabite women. "And Jashubi-lehem" refers to Ruth the Moabitess who returned [*shavah*] and became attached [to Israel] in Bethlehem of Judah.[65] "These are ancient traditions" means: These things [i.e., the entire chain of events: Machlon and Kilion leaving Eretz Yisrael, and Ruth's marriage to Boaz, which led to the birth of David and will bring on the coming of *Mashiach* (Rashbam)] were predetermined by God, the Ancient of Days.[66]

[The Gemara continues by expounding the next verse, which states,] "They were the potters [*hayotzerim*] who dwelled in Netaim and Gederah; they resided there in the service of the king" (1 Chronicles 4:23). "They were the potters" refers to the sons of Jonadab the son of Rechab who kept [*natzeru*] the oath of their father [not to drink wine or to build houses].[67] "Who dwelled in Netaim" alludes to King Solomon who resembled a young tree [*netiah*] in his kingdom; [he was crowned when he was only twelve years old]. "And Gederah" alludes to the Sanhedrin who built fences around the laws [*gederot*][68] to prevent breaches in Israel. "They resided there in the service of the king"— this refers to Ruth the Moabitess who lived to see the kingdom of Solomon, the grandson of her grandson, for it says, "He [Solomon] then sat upon his throne and placed a chair for the mother of the king" (1 Kings 2:19); and R. Elazar said: for the mother of the kingdom [for Ruth the mother of the Davidic royal dynasty].

THE OLDER, THE BETTER

We learned in a *Baraita*: [When a sabbatical year is followed by a jubilee year,[69] during both these years it is forbidden to plant crops]. It says, "You will be eating your old crops" (Leviticus 25:22), without any kind of preservative. What is implied by "without any preservative"? R. Nachman said: It will be free of worms. R. Sheshet said: It will be protected from blight. We have a *Baraita* that supports R. Sheshet's view and one that bolsters R. Nachman's interpretation. The *Baraita* that supports R. Nachman [that the crops will be free of insect infestation] states: It says, "You will be eating your old crops"; you might think that [when the ninth year comes] Israel will be eagerly awaiting the new crop, because the old crop has been consumed by insects; therefore it says, "until the crops [of the ninth year] are ripe," which means: until the new crop ripens in its natural way, [and the old crop will not have been eaten by insects]. The *Baraita* that backs R. Sheshet's view [that the crops will be free of disease] states: It says, "You will be eating your old crops"; you might think that Israel will be eagerly awaiting the new crop because the old crop was ruined by blight; therefore it says, "until the crops [of the ninth year] are ripe"; which means: until the new crop ripens in its natural way, [and the old crop will not have become tainted by disease].

We learned in a *Baraita*: It says, "You will continue eating the previous year's crops long after their time" (Leviticus 26:10). This teaches us that the older produce gets, the better it will be. [The Gemara remarks:] This is true only of things that usually are put in storage [like wine and wheat], but how do we know that things that are not usually put into storage [like fruit, will also improve with time]? [The Gemara answers:] Because it says, "You will eat [*yashan noshan*] "old, very old" (ibid.), which means: irrespective [of what foodstuff it is, it will always be better when it is older].

[The verse continues,] "And you will eventually have to clear out the old crops because of the new" (ibid.). This teaches that the granaries were filled with the old crop and the silos were full with the new crop, and Israel would say: How can we clear out one before the other? [The old crop is better than the new! But the Torah says: It will pay to store the new crop, because it, too, will improve with age (Rashbam).]

R. Papa said: Everything improves with age, except dates, beer, and small sardines.

HIS WIFE WILL CUT HIM DOWN TO SIZE

(98a) R. Chiya b. Yosef said: [If someone sells wine and it turns sour,] the condition of the wine depends on the buyer's luck [and is not the fault of the seller's pitcher]. For it says, "Surely, wine is treacherous, if the person is arrogant" (Habakkuk 2:5). [Meaning: An arrogant person who pretends to be upright, is like wine that turned sour and became vinegar.] R. Mari said: A haughty person is not even accepted by the members of his own household, for it says, "An arrogant man does not stay at home" (ibid.). This means that he is not tolerated by his wife; [she will cut him down to size (Rashbam)]. Rav Yehudah said in the name of Rav: Anyone who is not a scholar and wraps himself in a scholar's cloak [i.e., plays the part of a Torah scholar] is not admitted inside the confines of the Holy One, blessed be He, for it says here, "He does not stay at home [*yinveh*]" and elsewhere it says, "To Your holy dwelling place [*nevei*]" (Exodus 15:13).

UNACCEPTABLE BEHAVIOR

(98b) It says in the Book of Ben Sira, "I have weighed everything on the scale, and I found nothing lighter [i.e., worse] than bran, yet even worse than bran is a son-in-law who lives in the house of his father-in-law; worse than such a son-in-law is a guest who brings along another guest; and worse than such a guest is a person who answers before he has heard the question, for it says, "He who answers before he has heard, it will be foolishness and humiliation for him" (Proverbs 18:13).

THE PRIEST OF MICAH'S IDOLATROUS TEMPLE

(109b) [The Gemara now focuses on the shocking incident of "Micah's Idol," which is related in Judges 17 and 18. Micah, who had a temple of idolatry, hired a Levite to be his high priest, for a priest had to be from the tribe of Levi. This Levite turned out to be none other than a grandson of Moses.]

[The Gemara asks:] Is not the mother's family considered family? Surely it says, "There was a young man from Bethlehem in Judah, of the family of Judah; he was a Levite but he lived there, [in the territory of Judah]" (Judges 17:7). [The Gemara asks:] Doesn't this passage contradict itself? First it says that the young man was "of the family of Judah"[70] obviously he was from the tribe of Judah—and then it says that "he was a Levite," which suggests that he was from the tribe of Levi! We must say therefore that the father was from the tribe of Levi, and the mother was of the tribe of Judah, and even so the text speaks of him in terms of "the family of Judah"! [So we see that the mother's family is considered family!]

Rava b. R. Chanan said: No, [he actually was from the tribe of Judah, and "he was a Levite" means that] his first name was Levi. [The Gemara asks:] If so, what do you make of Micah's words, "Now I know that God will be good to me, for this Levite has become my priest" (ibid.v. 13)? [If the young man was from the tribe of Levi, Micah had reason to be happy; but if he was from Judah, and only his first name happened to be Levi, why was Micah jubilant?] [The Gemara answers:] Yes; [his name was Levi, and he was from the tribe of Judah], and Micah was happy that he happened to get his hands on a man whose name was Levi, [for now he could advertise that he had a Levi as *Kohen Gadol*, and the public would not read the fine print and realize that he was not from the tribe of Levi, but from Judah (Ritva)].

[The Gemara asks:] But was Levi really his name? Surely his name was Jonathan, for it says, "Jonathan, son of Gershom, son of Manasseh—he and his children—were priests for the tribe of the Danites" [after they captured the idol from Micah] (ibid. 18:30). [So Levi was not his first name, but his tribe. And this being so, we have an indication that the mother's

family is considered family.] [Says Rava:] But even according to your premise [that his name was Jonathan son of Gershom,] was then Gershom the son of Manasseh? Surely he was the son of Moses, for it says, "The sons of Moses were Gershom and Eliezer" (1 Chronicles 23:15). But because he [Jonathan] did the same wicked things as Manasseh [son of Hezekiah and who worshipped idols although his father Hezekiah was a great *tzaddik*],[71] the verse connects him to Manasseh.[72] Here, too [concerning the young man], we can say that he did come from the tribe of Levi, but the text identifies him as a member "of the family of Judah" because he acted as wickedly as Manasseh who was of the tribe of Judah,[73] [thus the verse does not prove that the mother's family is considered family].

R. Yochanan said in the name of R. Shimon b. Yochai: From here we can infer that every moral breakdown is attributed to the one who initiated it [i.e., Manasseh]. R. Yose b. R. Chanina said: We derive it [that depravity is attributed to the depraved] from here, "He [Adonijah] was very handsome, and his mother bore him after Absalom" (1 Kings 1:6). Was not Adonijah the son of Haggith and Absalom the son of Maachah? But because Adonijah acted like Absalom who rebelled against the kingdom, therefore the verse associates him with Absalom.

MARRY INTO A RESPECTABLE FAMILY

R. Elazar said: You should always associate with a good family; for Moses who married the daughter of Jethro [the Midianite priest who worshipped idols] had a grandson Jonathan [who worshipped idols], whereas Aaron who married [Elisheba] the daughter of [the righteous] Aminadab had a grandson Pinechas [who zealously defended God's honor].[74] [The Gemara asks:] But didn't Pinechas, too, descend from Jethro? Surely it says, "Aaron's son, Eleazar, married from the daughters of Putiel, and she bore him Pinechas" (Exodus 6:25), [and Putiel is identified with Jethro; thus Pinechas is a grandson of Jethro, while Jonathan is only a great-grandson of Jethro. Nevertheless, Pinechas was a *tzaddik*. This disproves your theory about marrying into a good family]. Doesn't this mean that Pinechas descended from Jethro [and why is Jethro called Putiel?], because he fattened [*pitteim*] calves for idol worship?

[The Gemara answers:] No, [Putiel] means that Pinechas descended from Joseph who quelled [*pitpeit*] his passion.[75] [The Gemara asks: But this cannot be so,] for the tribes taunted Pinechas, saying, "Look at that son of Puti[el]! His mother's father [Jethro] fattened calves for idol worship, and he kills a leader of a tribe in Israel [Zimri]!"[76] (110a) We must therefore say [that Pinechas' mother was not a daughter of Jethro, but one of Jethro's descendants, and she also descended from Joseph]. Now, if his mother's father descended from Joseph, his mother's mother [but not his mother] descended from Jethro; if his mother's father descended from Jethro, his mother's mother descended from Joseph. This is also borne out by a precise reading of the verse, for it says that Eleazar married, "from the daughters of Putiel" [in the plural, one a descendant of "Jethro who fattened [*pitteim*] calves"; the other of "Joseph who quelled [*pitpeit*] his passion"].

Rava said: Before a person takes a wife he should check out the character of her brothers [for the children take after their mother's brothers], for it says, "Aaron married Elisheba, daughter of Aminadav, sister of Nachshon" (Exodus 6:23). Since it says, "daughter of Aminadav" is it not obvious that she was the sister of Nachshon? Why does it say expressly, "sister of Nachshon"? This gives you a hint that before a person takes a wife he should check out the character of her brothers. It was taught: Most children take after the brothers of their mother.

JONATHAN DID *TESHUVAH*

[The Gemara resumes the discussion of Jonathan son of Gershom, who became a priest in Micah's idolatrous temple.] It says, [The people of Dan who had come to the temple said to the Levite,] "Who brought you here [*halom*]? What are you doing here [*bazeh*]? What do you have here [*poh*]?" (Judges 18:3). The Danites said to Jonathan [by implication]: Arc you not a descendant of Moses about whom it says, "Do not come any closer [*halom*]!" (Exodus 3:5)? Are you not a descendant of Moses about whom it says, "What is that [*zeh*] in your hand" (ibid. 4:2)? And are you not a descendant of Moses to whom God said, "You, however, must remain here with Me [*poh*]"? (Deuteronomy 5:28)? To think that you, [a grandson of Moses,] should become a priest of idolatry! Jonathan replied: I have the following tradition from my grandfather's family: A person should rather hire himself out to *avodah zarah* than to be dependent on other people. He thought that *avodah zarah* meant idol worship, but this is not so; in this saying *avodah zarah* means "work that is strange to him, below his status." It is as Rav said to R. Kahana: Flay a carcass in the street as long as you earn a living, and don't say, "I am an important person, and the work is unsuitable for me"; [there is nothing undignified in making an honest living]. When David saw that Jonathan had an intense fondness for money, he put him in charge of the treasury, for it says, "Shebuel son of Gershom son of Moses was chairman of the treasury" (1 Chronicles 26:24). Was then his name Shebuel? Surely it was Jonathan [since Gershom had only one son]! R. Yochanan said: [He was called Shebuel,] because he returned [*shav*] to God [*El*] with all his heart, [he repented].

A SON TAKES HIS FATHER'S PLACE

(116a) R. Yochanan said in the name of R. Shimon b. Yochai: The Holy One, blessed be He, bristles with anger against anyone who does not leave a son to fall heir to his possessions. For it says, "If a man dies and has no son, his inheritance shall pass [*vehaavartem*]" (Numbers 27:8). And it says also, "A day of fury [*evrah*] is that day" (Zephaniah 1:15); [*vehaavartem* and *evrah* are linguistically related]. It says, "Those who have no one to take their place, and they do not fear God" (Psalms 55:20). R. Yochanan and R. Yehoshua b. Levi [differ about the interpretation of this text]. One says that it refers to whoever does not leave behind a son. The other says that it refers to whoever does not leave behind a disciple. It can be proved that it was R. Yochanan who said "a disciple," for it was R. Yochanan who used [to carry with him a tooth of his tenth dead son with which he consoled parents who had lost a child], saying,[77] "This is the tooth of my tenth son [whom I have buried]." [If he believed that a person who does not leave a son does not fear God, he would not have shown the tooth and thereby branded himself as a person who is not God-fearing.] So it is proven that it was R. Yochanan who said "a disciple."

[The Gemara reasons:] But since R. Yochanan said "a disciple," R. Yehoshua b. Levi must be the one who said "a son"! Why then do we find that R. Yehoshua b. Levi did not go to a house of mourning [to console the mourners] unless the deceased died without leaving any sons? [He did not want to neglect his Torah studies (Rashbam).] For it says, "Weep rather for the one that went away" (Jeremiah 22:10), and Rav Yehudah said in the name of Rav: [This means:] The one who goes from the world without leaving male children. [Now, if R. Yehoshua b. Levi held that such a person was not God-fearing, he would not have gone to console the mourners.] We must say, therefore, that R. Yehoshua b. Levi is the one who said: "a disciple." And if R. Yehoshua said "a disciple," R. Yochanan must have said: "a son." If so, we find that R. Yochanan contradicts himself; [we said above that he could not have said "a son"]. [The Gemara answers:] There is no contradiction: R. Yochanan made one statement in his own name; the other [that God is angry with anyone who did not leave a son] he made in his teacher's name [but he himself did not share that view].

HE COMMENTED ON DEATH, POVERTY, AND SICKNESS

R. Pinchas b. Chama expounded the following text, "When Haddad heard in Egypt that David had been laid to rest with his forefathers and that Joab, the commander of the army, had died . . . " (1 Kings 11:21). Why is the phrase "laying to rest" used in connection with David, and that of "death" in relation to Joab? "Laying to rest" was used in connection with David, because he left a son; "death" was used in relation to Joab because he left no son. [The Gemara asks:] Did Joab not leave a son? Surely it says, "Of the sons of Joab—Obadiah son of Jehiel" (Ezra 8:9)! [The Gemara answers:] We must explain the different expressions by saying: Because David left a son like himself, the expression "laying to rest" was used, but since Joab did not leave a son like himself, the expression "died" is used.

R. Pinchas b. Chama expounded: Poverty in a person's home is worse than fifty plagues. For it says, "Pity me, pity me, O you my friends, for the hand of God has afflicted me" (Job 19:21). [At the Exodus the Egyptians were stricken with ten plagues, through "one finger of God."[78] Since Job was afflicted with "the hand of God" he suffered fifty plagues (Rashbam).] His friends answered him, "Be careful, do not turn to wrongdoing, for this is what you have chosen over poverty" (ibid. 37:21). [You had rather have fifty plagues than poverty.]

R. Pinchas b. Chama expounded: Whoever has a sick person in his house should go to a Sage who will plead for heavenly mercy for him, as it says, "The king's wrath is like angels of death, but a wise man will appease it" (Proverbs 16:14).

THE CHILDREN
OF JOSEPH'S COMPLAINT

(118a) It says, "The children of Joseph spoke to Joshua, saying, 'Why have you given me an inheritance of only a single lot and a single portion, seeing that I am a numerous people, for God has blessed me to such an extent?'" (Joshua 17:14). But according to the one who said [that the land was divided] in accordance with the number of those who entered the land, why did the children of Joseph complain? Surely they all received the shares that were coming to them! [The Gemara answers:] They complained because of the many minors they had in their tribe [meaning, orphans who were under the age of twenty years when they entered the land, and who had no father who would leave them his share upon his death].

Abaye said: From [the complaint of the children of Joseph] we can infer [that there was not even one] that did not receive a share in the land. For, if you should think that there was one who did not receive a share, would he not have complained? [And since the Torah does not tell us of any such complaint, we must conclude that, with these exceptions, all received their shares.] And if you will say that the Torah tells us only of those who complained and could be helped, but it does not tell us about anyone who complained but could not be helped, [but that there were in fact many others who complained]. That cannot be, because the children of Joseph complained, and it did not benefit them, yet the Torah tells us about their complaint. [The Gemara anwers: The reason the Torah writes about the children of Joseph's complaint is,] because it wants to give us a piece of good advice, namely, that

a person should be vigilant against an evil eye. And this is what Joshua had in mind when he answered the children of Joseph, "If you are such a numerous people, ascend to the woods" (ibid. v. 15). He implied: Go and hide in the woods so that an evil eye should have no power over you.

JOSHUA AND CALEB INHERITED
THE SHARES OF THE SPIES

(118b) The shares [in Eretz Yisrael] of the spies were taken by Joshua and Caleb.[79] From where in Scripture is this derived? Ulla said: From the verse, "Among the men who went to explore the land, only Joshua son of Nun and Caleb son of Yefuneh remained alive" (Numbers 14:38). What does the phrase "remained alive" signify? Do you think it means that [the other spies died] and they remained alive; we have another verse that tells us that, "Not a single man survived, with the exception of Caleb son of Yefuneh and Joshua son of Nun" (ibid. 25:65); [and we do not need two verses to tell us the same thing]. What then is meant by "they remained alive"? It means that they lived on their portion [i.e., Joshua and Caleb lived on spies' portion of the land].

The murmurers [i.e., the people who complained after hearing the bad report about the land given by the spies][80] and the company of Korach[81] had no share in the land. [The Gemara asks:] But have we not learned in a Baraita: The shares of the spies, the murmurers, and the company of Korach, were taken by Joshua and Caleb? [So they did have shares.] [The Gemara answers:] This presents no difficulty: The Tanna of our Baraita compares the murmurers to the spies [just as the spies had a share in the land, so had the murmurers]; while the other Tanna does not compare the murmurers to the spies, as we learned in the following Baraita: [The daughters of Tzelofchad said,] "Our father died in the desert" (Numbers 27:3)—this refers to Tzelofchad; "and he was not among company" (ibid.) refers to spies; "that protested against God" (ibid.) refers to the murmurers; "in the company of Korach" (ibid.) has the literal meaning. Thus one Tanna compares the murmurers to the spies, [since both are mentioned in the same verse], and the other Tanna does not, [since it does not say about the murmurers, "and who protested . . . "].

R. Papa further said to Abaye: But according to the one who compares the murmurers to the spies, could it be that Joshua and Caleb took almost all of Eretz Yisrael? [The murmurers comprised most of the children of Israel.][82] Abaye replied: We mean the murmurers in the company of Korach.

GOOD THINGS COME ABOUT
THROUGH GOOD MEN

(119a) R. Chidka said: Shimon Shikmona was my colleague among the disciples of R. Akiva. And this is what Shimon Shikmoni said: Moses our teacher knew that the daughters of Tzelofchad were going to inherit [a share in the land],[83] but he did not know whether or not they were entitled to the extra share of the first-born. It would have been appropriate that the Torah section about the laws of inheritance should be written through Moses, but the daughters of Tzelofchad merited that it was written through them, [because of their insistence on a share in Eretz Yisrael]. Moses knew also that the man who gathered sticks on *Shabbat*[84] was to be put to death, for it says, "Anyone violating [*Shabbat*] shall be put to death" (Exodus 31:14); but he did not know by which kind of death he was to die [stoning or strangling]. And it would have been appropriate that the section of the man who gathered sticks should be written through Moses, but since he was guilty [of violating *Shabbat*] it was written through him. This teaches you (119b) that good things are brought about through good people, and punishment is brought about through bad people.

THE GRIEVANCE OF TZELOFCHAD'S DAUGHTERS

"You will bring them and plant them on the mount You possess" (Exodus 15:17). It does not say: You will bring *us*, but "You will bring *them*." This teaches that [the people who left Egypt at the Exodus] prophesied and did not know what they were prophesying, [that their descendants and not they themselves would enter Eretz Yisrael].

[It says, when the daughters of Tzelofchad voiced their grievance,] "They stood before Moses, before Elazar the *kohen*, and before the leaders and the entire assembly" (Numbers 27:2). Is it possible that they stood before Moses, and he did not say anything to them, that they stood before Elazar, the *kohen*, and he did not say anything to them, [that they still asked the others? If Moses did not know, surely the others would not know!]. So why did they still petition the leaders and the entire assembly? But the passage should be expounded as if it were reversed: [They stood before the assembly, before the leaders, before Elazar, the *kohen*, and before Moses], so says R. Yoshiah. Abba Chanan said in the name of R. Eliezer: [Moses, Elazar, and the leaders] were all sitting together in the *bet midrash*, and the daughters of Tzelofchad came and submitted their petition to all of them.

[The Gemara asks:] On what essential point do R. Yoshia and Abba Chanan disagree? [The Gemara answers:] R. Yoshiah holds the view that honor may be shown to a disciple in the presence of his teacher, [and you are allowed to ask a student before you ask his teacher. Therefore he says that they went first to the others and then to Moses]. Abba Chanan contends that honor may not be shown to a student in the presence of his teacher, [and Tzelofchad's daughters directed their grievance at Moses].[85] [The Gemara asks:] Surely this is a contradiction between two *halachot*! [May a student be honored in front of his teacher or not?] [The Gemara answers:] This presents no difficulty. The one case is where the teacher shows the student respect, [then the teacher will be pleased if others honor the student]. The other, where the teacher does not, [in which case a student may not be honored in front of his teacher].

TZELOFCHAD'S DAUGHTERS

It was taught: The daughters of Tzelofchad were wise women, they knew how to expound the Scriptural text, and they were devout women. That they were wise is evident from the fact that their grievance was well-timed; for R. Shmuel b. R. Yitzchak said: At that moment Moses our teacher was sitting and lecturing on the section in the Torah on *yibbum*,[86] which starts with the verse, "When brothers live together" (Deuteronomy 25:5). They said to him, "If we are considered like a son [since a widow who has either a son or a daughter does not require *yibbum*], let us be equal to a son when it comes to inheritance; and if not [if we are not considered our father's heirs], then let our mother be bound by the law of *yibbum* [and let our late father's brother marry our mother. Their line of reasoning shows that they were very wise women]. Immediately, "Moses brought their claim before God" (Numbers 27:5).

That they knew how to expound the Scriptural text is apparent from the fact that they expounded the passage, "If a man will die and he has no son" (Numbers 27:8), [and drew the inference that if there is a son, a daughter does not inherit] for they said, "If our father had had a son, we would not have said anything." [The Gemara asks:] But did we not learn in a *Baraita*: "a daughter"? R. Yirmeyah said: Delete the word "daughter"; [it is an error]. Abaye said: [You do not have to delete it, because they said:] Even if a son of his had had a daughter, we would not have said anything, [for they knew that when it comes to inheritance a son's daughter takes precedence over a daughter of the deceased]. They were devout women, since they married only men that were worthy of them.

MOTHERHOOD AT A HUNDRED AND THIRTY YEARS OF AGE

We learned in a *Baraita*: R. Eliezer b. Yaakov said: Even the youngest of Tzelofchad's daughters was not less than forty years old when she got married; [she waited for a worthy husband]. [The Gemara asks:] Is that so? Surely R. Chisda said: If a woman gets married at less than twenty years of age, she bears children until sixty; after twenty she bears children until forty; but when she gets married after forty, she can no longer bear children. [If they were devout, why did they wait until they were forty years old, knowing that they could no longer bear children?] [The Gemara answers:] Since they were devout women a miracle was performed for them, as it happened with Yocheved [the mother of Moses]. For it says, "A man from the house of Levi went and married Levi's daughter" (Exodus 2:1).

(120a) Is it possible that a woman of a hundred and thirty years of age should be called "daughter" [and not "woman"]? [And how do we know that she was a hundred and thirty years old?] R. Chama b. R. Chanina explained: The "daughter of Levi" in this verse refers to Yocheved whose mother became pregnant with her on the way [when Jacob and his family went to Egypt], and who was born between the walls of Egypt; for so it says, "Yocheved, daughter of Levi, who was born to Levi in Egypt" (Numbers 27:59)—her birth was in Egypt, but she was not conceived in Egypt.[87] And why is she referred to as "daughter"? Rav Yehudah b. Zevida: This teaches us that signs of youth reappeared in her: her body became smooth again, her wrinkles vanished, and her beauty was restored.

[The Gemara asks:] Instead of "he married" it should say, "he married her *again*"! [Amram had married Yocheved before, and fathered Aaron and Miriam. When Pharaoh decreed that all newborn boys had to be drowned, he left his wife. He only remarried her later upon the urging of Miriam].[88] Rav Yehudah b. Zevida said: This teaches us that he made a wedding ceremony for her with a wedding canopy, while Aaron and Miriam sang for her, and ministering angels chanted, "A glad mother of children!" (Psalms 113:9).

TZELOFCHAD'S DAUGHTERS WERE ALIKE

[The names of the daughters of Tzelofchad are listed in different order in Numbers 27:1 and 36:11.] Further on, when the Torah relates their marriages [in Numbers 36:11], their names are listed according to their age, and here [in Numbers 27:1] when they petitioned Moses [on a matter of law], they are listed according to their wisdom. This supports R. Ammi's way of thinking. For R. Ammi said: At a yeshivah [where law is being studied], you should show preference to wisdom [when making the seating arrangements: a brilliant young scholar should get a better seat than an older person who is only an average scholar]; whereas at a banquet you should show preference to age [in the seating arrangements]. Said R. Ashi: Wisdom is given priority at study sessions only if a person is an outstanding scholar; and age is the determining factor at a banquet only if the elderly man is a distinguished person. In the yeshivah of R. Yishmael it was taught: The daughters of Tzelofchad were all alike, [and that is why the two verses list them in random order, and no support for R. Ammi's statement can be adduced]. For it says, "They became [*vatih'yena*]" (Numbers 36:11), which implies "all of them were equal [in wisdom]."

THE FIFTEENTH OF AV AND YOM KIPPUR

(121a) We learned in a Mishnah: R. Shimon b. Gamliel said: There were no greater festive days for Israel than the fifteenth of Av and Yom Kippur. For on these days [all] the daughters of Jerusalem would go out in white dresses—borrowed ones—in order not to embarrass those that [had to borrow] because they did not have white dresses of their own.[89] It is understandable that Yom Kippur should be a day of rejoicing because it is the day of forgiveness and atonement,[90] and it is the day on which the second Tablets were given.[91] But what is the significance of the fifteenth of Av? Rav Yehudah said in the name of Shmuel: It was the day on which the tribes were permitted to intermarry with one another. [Until that time there was a temporary restriction that every daughter who inherited an inheritance could marry only someone of her own tribe (Numbers 36:8). This restriction applied only to the generation that entered Eretz Yisrael. It was lifted when the last of that generation had died.] [The Gemara asks:] How did they know [that they could permit intermarriage among the tribes]? They expounded, "This is the word" (ibid. v. 6), "this" shall only apply to *this* generation [the one that left Egypt, but not to the next generation].

Rabbah b. Bar Chanah said in the name of R. Yochanan: [The 15th of Av] was the day on which the tribe of Benjamin was allowed to intermarry with the congregation of Israel. [They were forbidden to do so after the dreadful episode described in Judges 19ff.], for it says, "The men of Israel had taken an oath at Mizpah, saying, 'None of us will give his daughter as a wife to Benjamin'" (Judges 21:1). [The Gemara asks:] On what basis did they permit the tribe of Benjamin to intermarry with them? They expounded: "Of us," [in the phrase "none of us" to imply,] but not of our children. [The oath applied only to those who had taken it, but not to their children. Therefore their daughters could marry men from Benjamin.] R. Dimi b. Yosef said in the name of R. Nachman: [The 15th of Av] was the day on which the dying in the desert came to an end,[92] for a Tanna said: Before the dying in the wilderness ended, (121b) God did not speak to Moses [in a direct manner; only through an angel or the *Urim veTumim*], for it says, "It was at this time that all the men of war among the people finished dying" (Deuteronomy 2:16); and immediately after that it says, "God spoke to me"; but until that time there was no direct communication between God and Moses.

Ulla said: The 15th of Av was the day that Hoseah the son of Elah dismissed the guards that Jeroboam son of Nevat [the idolatrous king of Israel] had placed on the major highways to prevent Israel from going to Jerusalem on the pilgrimage festivals.[93] R. Mattena said: [The 15th of Av was] the day on which permission was granted to bury the dead defenders of Beitar [who were killed when the Romans overran that city].[94] For R. Mattena said:[95] On the day the slain of Beitar were allowed to be buried, the *berachah*, "Who is good and Who does good" [which is said in *Birkat Hamazon*] was instituted in Yavneh. "Who is good" was instituted because the corpses did not decompose; and "Who does good" because permission was obtained to bury them.

Rabbah and R. Yosef both said that the 15th of Av was the final day for cutting wood for the fire on the altar. For it was taught: R. Eliezer HaGadol said: When the 15th of Av arrives, the intensity of the sun begins to wane; therefore they stopped cutting wood for the woodpile on the altar. [Wood cut after the 15th of Av tends to be damp and produces heavy smoke; it is also considered to be wormy, and such wood is unsuitable for the altar.] R. Menashe said: They called the 15th of Av "the day of breaking the ax." [The reason for their joy was that they had completed doing a great mitzvah (Rashbam).]

From that day on, [the days are growing shorter; therefore] if a person adds from the night to the day [and devotes the added night hours to learning Torah], he will lengthen his life;[96] and a person who does not add hours from the night to the day [for the purpose of learning Torah] shortens his life. What does "shortens" mean? R. Yosef taught: His mother will bury him; [he will not live out his full life].

FROM ADAM TO ETERNITY

Our Rabbis taught: There were seven people who together encompass the existence of the world [their combined ages extend from Creation until the end of days. Each one learned from the other and carried on the tradition]. For Methuselah saw Adam, Shem saw Methuselah, Jacob saw Shem, Amram saw Jacob, Achiyah HaShiloni [the prophet, teacher of Elijah][96] saw Amram, Elijah saw Achiyah HaShiloni, and [Elijah] is still alive. [The Gemara asks:] Did Achiyah HaShiloni really see Amram? Surely it says, "Not a single man survived, [of the generation that wandered in the wilderness] with the exception of Caleb son of Yefuneh and Joshua son of Nun" (Numbers 26:65). [If Achiyah HaShiloni saw Jacob, he was in Egypt; then how could he have lived to enter Eretz Yisrael and see Elijah?]

R. Hamenuna replied: The decree [that all had to die in the wilderness] did not apply to the tribe of Levi, [and Achiyah HaShiloni was a Levite, hence he could have entered Eretz Yisrael].[98] For it says, "Your corpses will fall in this desert. This will happen to all of you who were recorded in the various lists, from the age of twenty years and up" (Numbers 14:29). That means that [the decree applied to] any tribe whose members were counted from age twenty and up. But the tribe of Levi, whose members were counted [for the service in the *Bet Hamikdash*] from age thirty and upward,[99] was excluded from the decree.

[The Gemara asks: Besides Caleb and Joshua,] did no one from the other tribes enter Eretz Yisrael? Surely we learned in a *Baraita*: Yair and Machir the sons of Menasseh were born in the days of Jacob, and they did not die before Israel entered the Eretz Yisrael; for it says, "The men of Ai struck down about thirty-six of them" (Joshua 6:5). And it was learned: This means that exactly thirty-six men were lost, so says R. Yehudah. R. Nechemiah said to him: Does it then say "thirty-six"? No, it says, "like thirty-six"! This refers to Yair son of Menasseh, who was equal to the majority of the Sanhedrin, [which had seventy-two members; thus a majority is thirty-six. So you see that Yair who was not a Levite did enter Eretz Yisrael, since he was not killed until the war at Ai]. R. Acha b. Yaakov said: The decree [to die in the desert] did not apply to anyone who was less than twenty years old [when he left Egypt]; nor to anyone who was over sixty years old when he left Egypt. [Since Achiyah was over sixty years old at the Exodus, he could enter the land.]

HOW WAS ERETZ YISRAEL APPORTIONED?

A question was raised: Was Eretz Yisrael first divided [into twelve equal parts,] according to the number of tribes, [who then subdivided the land according to the number of its men,] or was it divided according to the number of men that comprised the people of Israel, [each individual receiving an equal share]? (122a) Come and hear the following proof: "According to the lot shall one's inheritance be divided, whether [a tribe] is large or small" (Numbers 26:56). [Proof that it was first divided into twelve parts and only then allocated to the individuals.]

We learned in another *Baraita*: In time to come Eretz Yisrael will be divided among thirteen tribes. For the first time they entered Eretz Yisrael, it was divided only among twelve tribes, and the division was based on the monetary value of the land, for it says, "whether large or small," [meaning that a person who received a fertile piece of land had to pay monetary compensation to someone who received a barren parcel]. As R. Yehudah said: [For example,] a *se'ah* in Judea is worth five *se'ah* in Galilee. And it was divided by drawing lots, for it says, "Only by lot shall the land be divided" (ibid. v. 55). And it was divided only on the instruction of the *Urim veTummim*,[100] for it says, "According to the utterance [*pi*] of the lot."

[The Gemara asks:] How could this be? [Either by lot or by the *Urim veTummim*; it cannot be both! And what if the lot and the *Urim veTummim* contradict each other?] [The Gemara answers:] Elazar was wearing the *Urim veTummim*, while Joshua and all Israel stood in front of him. A box containing twelve slips of paper, each with the name of a different tribe on it, and another box with twelve slips of paper, each with a different land area on it were placed before him.

Elazar would look at the *Urim veTummim*, and would see which letters were lit up [on the breastplate. And when he saw the letters ZEVULUN glowing] he exclaimed, "Zevulun is going to come out of this box! And the boundary of Acco is going to come up out of the other box!" He then shook the box with the names of the tribes, and Zevulun came up in his hand. He then shook the box with the boundaries, and the boundaries of Acco came up in his hand, [just as he had predicted]. Elazar would look again at the *Urim veTummim* and exclaim: Naphtali is going to come up now, and the boundaries of Ginnosar are coming up out of the other box!" He shook the box with the tribes, and Naphtali came up in his hand. He then shook the box of the boundaries, and the boundary of Ginnosar came up in his hand.

The same would be done for every tribe. However, the division in the World to Come will not be like the division in this world. In this world, if a person owns a field of grain, he does not own an orchard; if he owns an orchard, he does not possess a field of grain. But in the world to come [i.e., in the Messianic era], there will not be a single person who will not possess land in the mountains, lowland, and valleys, for it says, "The gate of Reuben, one; the gate of Judah, one; the gate of Levi, one" (Ezekiel 48:31) [meaning, everyone's share will be the same]. The Holy One, blessed be He, Himself, will parcel it out among them; for it says, "'And these are their portions,' declares God" (ibid. v. 29). At any rate, the *Baraita* teaches us that first the land was divided only among twelve tribes, from which we can gather that the division was according to the number of tribes. This proves it.

ONE PORTION FOR
THE KING *MASHIACH*

We learned in the above-mentioned *Baraita*: In time to come, Eretz Yisrael will be divided [not among twelve, but] among thirteen tribes. To whom will the extra portion go? R. Chisda said: It will go to the King [*Mashiach*], for it says, "The servant of the city [i.e., King *Mashiach* who bears the burden of responsibility for the people] shall be served by all the tribes of Israel" (Ezekiel 48:19), [meaning: all the tribes shall yield to him a part of their land, and that he will have the thirteenth portion]. R. Papa said to Abaye: [How do you know that "he shall be served" means that they have to give him a piece of their land;] maybe it means that they should serve him as a student serves his master? Abaye replied: That is not logical. [It probably means giving him a piece of land,] for it says so almost explicitly, "And the remaining area shall be for the prince, on the one side and on the other, of the sacred portion and the property of the city" (Ezekiel 48:21); [meaning, the land that the tribes trim off from their portion will go to the Messianic King who controls the city and the country (Rabbeinu Gershom)].

A FAIR DISTRIBUTION
OF THE LAND

[The above-mentioned *Baraita* stated] that Eretz Yisrael was divided according to the value of the land, for it says, "Whether large or small," [which was interpreted to mean that a person who received a fertile piece of land had to compensate someone whose share consisted of barren or rocky soil]. [The Gemara asks:] Why does the *Baraita* state that he has to pay compensation? Does it mean that the quality of his soil is better? [Of course, in such a case compensation must be paid.] Are we talking about fools? [It is self-understood that if someone is allotted a fertile field, he receives a smaller area than a person who is allotted a barren field. We do not need the *Baraita* to tell us this.] But the *Baraita* wants to teach us that monetary compensation should be paid by people whose land is closer to Jerusalem to people whose land is farther away from Jerusalem. This is the subject of a dispute among *Tanna'im*, for R. Eliezer says that compensation for distance has to be made with money; whereas R. Yehoshua says that compensation has to be made with land. [A larger portion of land is assigned to a person whose parcel is farther from Jerusalem.]

THE SHARES OF JOSHUA
AND CALEB

We learned: It says, "Only [*ach*] by a lottery system shall the land be divided" (Numbers 26:56). [The word *ach*, "only," usually comes to exclude something, and in the present verse] Joshua and Caleb are excluded. [The Gemara asks:] In what respect were they excluded? Do you think that they did not receive any part of Eretz Yisrael at all? [Surely that cannot be.] If they received the shares that were not intended for them at the outset [i.e., the shares of the spies],[101] then certainly they received their own shares? What the verse wants to exclude is that they did not take their shares by means of lots, but rather by the command of God. How do we know that Joshua took his share by the command of God? Because it says, "By the word of God they gave [Joshua] the city that he requested, Timnat-Serach in Mount Ephraim" (Joshua 19:50).

(122b) [The Gemara briefly digresses:] Here it is spelled *Serach*, and [in Judges 1:35] it is spelled *Cheres*! R. Elazar said: This teaches us that at first [before it came into Joshua's possession] its fruits were as dry as a potsherd [*cheres*]; and afterward [after it passed into Joshua's hands] its fruits [were so rich and juicy] that if you were not careful, they would spoil [*serach*] quickly. [The Gemara returns to its main theme:] How do we know that Caleb took his share by the command of God? For it says, "They granted Hebron to Caleb, as Moses had spoken;[102] and he drove the three sons of the giant from there" (Judges 1:20). [The Gemara asks:] But was not Hebron a city of refuge [for unintentional murderers and which belonged to the Levites],[105] whereas Caleb was from the tribe of Judah]? Abaye replied: Caleb was given the suburbs [of Hebron], for it says, "But the fields of the cities and its villages they gave to Caleb son of Yefuneh as his possession" (Joshua 21:12).

RACHEL AND LEAH

(123a) [Jacob said to Joseph,] "And as for me, I have given you Shechem—one portion more than your brothers which I took from the hand of the Amorite with my sword and my bow" (Genesis 48:22). Did Jacob then take [Shechem] with his sword and his bow? Surely it says, "For I do not trust in my bow, nor does my sword save me" (Psalms 44:7)! But "my sword" means "prayer," and "my bow" means "supplication."

R. Chelbo questioned R. Shmuel b. Nachmani: What reason did Jacob have for taking away the birthright from Reuben and giving it to Joseph? [He retorted:] You ask, what reason did he have? Surely the reason is stated explicitly, "When he [Reuben] defiled his father's bed, his birthright was given to the sons of Joseph" (1 Chronicles 5:1)! [The Gemara explains:] R. Chelbo meant to ask: Why did he give the birthright to Joseph [and not to another son]? [R. Shmuel b. Nachmani answered:] Let me give you a parable: You can compare it to a man who raised an orphan in his house. Later on, the orphan became very wealthy and said, "Now let me pay back the man who raised me; I want him to enjoy some of my wealth." [The man represents Joseph; the orphan stands for Jacob. Joseph supported Jacob during his stay in Egypt, and now Jacob wanted to return the favor and give him the birthright (Rashbam).]

R. Chelbo countered: And if Reuben had not sinned, would Jacob have given him nothing at all? [If Jacob really wanted to show his appreciation to Joseph, he would have given him something that belonged to himself, rather than give him Reuben's birthright.] But R. Yonatan your teacher[104] did not explain it like this. Rather he said: The birthright was originally that Rachel was destined to have the firstborn, as it says, "These are the chronicles of Jacob: Joseph" (Genesis 37:2). [Jacob should have married Rachel first, and then Joseph would have been the firstborn,] but Leah got ahead of her through her prayers for mercy, [and she became Jacob's first wife]. But because of Rachel's extraordinary modesty, the Holy One, blessed be He, ultimately restored [the right of the firstborn to her son Joseph].

[The Gemara asks:] What is meant by "Leah got ahead of her with her prayers for mercy"? It says, "Leah's eyes were weak [rakkot]" (ibid. 29:17). What is meant by rakkot? Do you think that it means that her eyes were actually weak? [That cannot be so.] The Torah does not even use a demeaning term to describe unclean animals, for it says, "of the clean animal, and of the animal that is not clean" (ibid. 7 8), [rather than the derogatory term temei'ah, "unclean"]; would the Torah speak disparagingly of the righteous [and use the term "weak"]? But, said R. Elazar, rakkot means that from her would come forth [kohanim and Levites][105] who receive many [aruchot] priestly gift offerings.

Rav said: Her eyes were in fact weak, but that casts no reflection on her; rather it is an expression of high praise. For she would hear at the crossroads how people would be gossiping, "Rebecca has two sons, and Laban has two daughters; the older daughter should be married to the older son, and the younger one to the younger son." Leah would sit down at the crossroads and inquire, "What kind of person is the big brother?" They told her, "He is a bad man. He robs and pillages." She then asked, "What is the younger one like?" "He is a scholarly man, who stays in tents," she was told. [Hearing this,] she cried until her eyelashes fell out. And that is what the verse has in mind when it says, "God saw that Leah was hated, and He opened her womb" (ibid. 29:31). What could be the meaning of the phrase, "Leah was hated"? God saw that the actions of Esau were hated in Leah's eyes. Therefore, "He opened her womb," [and that is why Leah deserved to have the firstborn, although originally Rachel was predestined to give birth to the firstborn].

[The Gemara asks:] How did Rachel's extraordinary modesty manifest itself? [The Gemara answers:] It says, "Jacob told Rachel that he was her father's brother, and that he was Rebecca's son" (ibid. 29:12). [The Gemara asks:] Was he not the son of her father's sister? But [this is how the dialogue unfolded:] Jacob said to Rachel: "Will you marry me?" She replied, "Yes, I will. But you should know that my father is a cheat, and I am afraid that you will not be able to outwit him." Said Jacob, "What is he up to?" She replied, "I have a sister who is older, and he will not allow me to get married before her." Jacob answered, "I am his brother in shrewdness; [I can be just as devious and tricky as he is.]" She answered, "But is a tzaddik permitted to be deceitful?" "Yes," he replied. "With the pure be straightforward, with the crooked act deviously" (2 Samuel 22:27).

Jacob then gave her certain signs [by which she could identify herself to him in the dark of night, so that her father should not substitute Leah for her]. When they were about to lead Leah to him, Rachel thought, "My sister will be terribly embarrassed," so she handed her the signs. And in reference to this it says, "In the morning, [Jacob discovered that] it was Leah!" (Genesis 29:25), which seems to imply that until the morning he did not know that she was Leah. [Wasn't she there all the time?] But because of the signs that Jacob had given to Rachel, which she, in turn, had handed to Leah, he did not know who she was until the morning.

SEVENTY PEOPLE
ENTERED EGYPT

Abba Chalifa Karuia asked R. Chiya b. Abba: [Regarding Jacob's children] the Torah says that there were seventy when they entered Egypt,[106] but if you count them one by one, you find only sixty-nine names![107] R. Chiya b. Abba explained: Dinah had a twin sister, for it says, "With [ve'et] his daughter Dinah" (Genesis 46:15); [et denotes the inclusion of something; in this case, a twin sister]. [Abba Chalifa asked:] If that is so, did Benjamin also have a twin, for it says, (123b) "He saw [et] Benjamin, his brother, his mother's son" (ibid. 43:29)? R. Chiya b. Abba said: I had this beautiful pearl, [the answer to this question. I tried to keep it to myself,] but now you forced me to reveal it. [This was merely an expression designed to pique the students' interest.] R. Chama b. Chanina said: [The seventieth person] was Yocheved [the mother of Moses] who was conceived on the way[108] [from Canaan to Egypt] and born between the walls of Egypt. For it says, "Who was born to Levi in Egypt" (Numbers 26:59), which implies that her birth was in Egypt but her conception was not in Egypt.

JOSEPH'S FLAME WILL CONSUME
THE SEED OF ESAU

R. Chelbo again asked R. Shmuel b. Nachmani: It says, "It was, after Rachel had given birth to Joseph, that Jacob said to Laban, 'Let me leave; I would like to go home to my own land'" (Genesis 30:25). Why did he ask this just when Joseph was born? He replied: Jacob our father saw that the children of Esau would fall only into the hands of the children of Joseph, for it says, "The house of Jacob will be fire, the house of Joseph a flame, and the house of Esau for straw; and they will ignite them and devour them" (Obadiah 1:18). R. Chelbo challenged this, citing the passage, "And David smote them [Amalek, a descendant of Esau,][109] from twilight until the evening of the next day" (1 Samuel 30:17). [David who crushed the descendants of Esau was not a descendant of Joseph, but of Judah! How can the Sages say that Esau's offspring will be defeated by the descendants of Joseph?] R. Shmuel b. Nachmani replied: The person who taught you the Prophets obviously did not teach you the Writings, for there it says, [concerning the battle against Amalek,[110]] "When [David] went to Ziklag, people of Manasseh defected to him: Adnach, Yozavad, Yediael, Michael, Yozavad, Elihu, and Tzilletai, who were captains of thousands from Menasseh (1 Chronicles 12:21). [Thus, Amalek was defeated due to the assistance David received from the captains of Manasseh who were descendants of Joseph.]

R. Yosef raised an objection citing the following verse, "Also, some of them—of the sons of Simeon—five hundred men, went to Mount Seir, with Pelatiah,

Neariah, Refayah, and Uziel, the sons of Yishi, at their head. They smote the remnant of the Amalekites who had survived and dwelt there, up to this day" (ibid. 4:42,43), [which proves that the offspring of Esau was beaten by the descendants of Simeon, and not the descendants of Joseph!]. Rabba b. Shila replied: [The verse says that they were the sons of Yishi, and] Yishi was a descendant of Menasseh [son of Joseph], for it says, "The sons of Menasseh were Chefer and Yishi" (1 Chronicles 5:24),[111] [and Menasseh was Joseph's son].

DISINHERIT A
WAYWARD CHILD?

(133b) [The Mishnah says:] If someone wants to leave his entire estate to strangers, leaving nothing to his children, his act is legally valid, [and his estate is given to the strangers], but the Sages do not look favorably on his action; [they are angry with him because he circumvents the intent of the Torah]. R. Shimon b. Gamliel says: If his children did not behave properly, the father will be remembered for good [if he disinherited his children].

[The Gemara says:] Yosef b. Yo'ezer had a son who did not conduct himself properly. He [Yosef b. Yoezer] had a bag full of money, and he consecrated it to the Bet Hamikdash. The son went and married the daughter of the person who made the myrtle crowns for King Jannai. When his wife gave birth to a son, he bought her a fish. As he opened it he found a precious pearl inside. "Don't take it to the king," his wife said. "They will make you a low offer and force you to sell it at that price. Take it to the treasurer of the Bet Hamikdash, and don't be the one to appraise its value, for making of an oral offer to the Bet Hamikdash is as binding as the actual delivery of an article in ordinary transactions, [and if you underestimated its value you cannot raise the price]. Instead, let the treasurers set the price; [they are God-fearing people who will not cheat you].

When he brought it to the Bet Hamikdash they assessed its value at thirteen bags of dinars. The treasurers said to him, "We can pay you seven now, but we don't have the other six. We will have to owe them to you." Said he, "Give me the seven that you have in the treasury, and the balance of six I herewith consecrate to the Bet Hamikdash." So the bookkeepers of the Bet Hamikdash recorded: Yosef b. Yoezer donated one bag of dinars; his son donated six. [This shows that by disinheriting his son he caused him to do teshuvah.]

Shmuel said to Rav Yehudah: Bright scholar! Stay away from a place where [the Bet Din] takes away an inheritance from a legal heir and transfers it to someone else, even if it is from a bad son to a good son [because a bad son may have decent descendants]; and certainly stay away from a place where they take from a son and give it to a daughter.

SHAMMAI CONFRONTS
YONATAN B. UZIEL[112]

Our Rabbis taught: It happened that a certain person whose children did not behave themselves bequeathed his entire estate to Yonatan b. Uziel. What did Yonatan b. Uziel do? He sold one-third of the estate [and kept the proceeds for himself]; he took another third and consecrated it to the *Bet Hamikdash*; and the remaining third he gave back to the sons of the deceased. Shammai confronted him with his staff and bag [i.e., he scolded him for violating the father's intention. He argued that by giving the money to the son, Yonatan b. Uziel had foiled the father's wish, and that, therefore, the gift to the son was invalid (Rashbam)]. Yonatan b. Uziel said to Shammai, "Shammai! If you can nullify [the third] that I sold and [the third] that I consecrated to the *Beth Hamikdash*, [and you cannot, because I had a right to do that,] then you can also invalidate the gift that I made to the descendants. **(134a)** If not, you cannot take back from the children that which I returned to them, [because the money I gave them was mine, not their father's]." Shammai exclaimed, "The son of Uziel defeated me! The son of Uziel defeated me!"

A FIRSTBORN GIRL
IS A GOOD SIGN

(140b) [The Mishnah says:] If a person [whose wife is pregnant] says: If my wife gives birth to a male child, he will receive a *maneh* [a hundred *zuz*]; if she gives birth to a boy, he receives a *maneh*. If he says: If my wife gives birth to a girl, she [the girl] will receive two hundred *zuz*; and she gives birth to a girl, the girl receives two hundred *zuz*.

(141a) [The Gemara asks:] Does this tell us that he would rather have a daughter than a son? Surely R. Yochanan said in the name of R. Shimon b. Yochai: If a person does not leave a son to inherit him [and his estate is given to his daughter], it is a sign that the Holy One, blessed be He, is filled with anger toward this person. For it says, "If a man will die and he has no son, you shall cause his inheritance to pass over to his daughter" (Numbers 27:8), and the phrase "to pass over" [*vehaavartem*] alludes to anger [*evrah*], for it says, "A day of fury [*evrah*] is that day" (Zephanaiah 1:15). [So we see that a son is preferable to a daughter; why then is he giving his daughter two hundred *zuz* and his son only one hundred?] [The Gemara answers:] When it comes to inheritance, a son has preference [because the son carries on his name through his estate, whereas when a daughter marries, her estate is transferred to her husband's family and tribe]. However, when it comes to having more spending money, he prefers a daughter. [He would rather leave his money to his daughter, since it is more difficult for a woman to earn a living.]

Shmuel said: The Mishnah [about a person who prefers a daughter] deals with a case where his wife is giving birth for the first time. And his attitude is explained by R. Chisda, for R. Chisda said: If a daughter is born first in a family, it is a good sign for the [future] children. Some say, because she will help raise her younger brothers; and others say, because the father will not be affected by an evil eye [people will not be jealous if the firstborn is a daughter]. R. Chisda said: As for me, I cherish my daughters more than my sons. [They married the greatest sages of that generation: Rava, Rami b. Chama, and Mar Ukva b. Chama (Tosafot).]

If you prefer, say that our Mishnah [that says that a daughter is preferable to a son] is in accordance with the view of R. Yehudah. Where does R. Yehudah express this view? Do you think it refers to R. Yehudah where he expounds the word *bakol*? For we learned: "God blessed Abraham [*bakol*], "in every way" (Genesis 24:1); R. Meir said, [this means that] he did not have a daughter; [he only had sons]. R. Yehudah said, [this means that] he had a daughter who was named Bakol. [The Gemara objects:] From this statement you can infer only that, according to R. Yehudah, God did not withhold even a daughter from Abraham; this does not prove, however, that a daughter is better than a son! But it refers to the following statement by R. Yehudah: We learned: It is a mitzvah for a person to support his daughter; and how much more so to support his sons, because the sons learn Torah; this is R. Meir's view. R. Yehudah said: It is a mitzvah for a person to support his sons; and how much more so to support his daughters, so that they should not be humiliated [by having to depend on charity. Hence our Mishnah follows R. Yehudah's view that a father will give more money to his daughter than to his son].

DIFFERENT CATEGORIES
OF SAGES

(145ᴜ) [The following *Baraita* describes different categories of sages and to what they can be compared:] We learned in a *Baraita*: A person who owns many fields and vineyards and who is known to be a wealthy cattle rancher exemplifies an expert in the field of *Aggadah* [who addresses a wide audience so that his wisdom is known to all]. A person who is rich in money [like a banker] and rich in olive oil [i.e., people who earn profits all the time] is comparable to an expert in *pilpul* [in brilliant reasoning. With his keen logical arguments he is always ready to clarify halachic points]. A person whose wealth is measured [who owns grain elevators], and a person whose produce is stored away [to be sold at an opportune time], is comparable to someone who has accumulated a vast reservoir of halachic rulings [and when called upon has the answers at his fingertips]. But everyone needs the owner of wheat, the master of Gemara [where difficulties and apparent contradictions are resolved, and where, through Talmudic give-and-take, the *halachah* emerges].

ALL THE DAYS OF
A POOR MAN ARE BAD

R. Zeira said in the name of Rav: What kind of person is alluded to by the verse, "All the days of a poor man are bad" (Proverbs 15:15)? This refers to a master of Gemara [who lives under constant strain, trying to analyze legal points and clarify halachic questions]. "But a good-hearted person feasts perpetually" (ibid.) refers to a master of Mishnah [who learns in a more superficial way]. Rava, however, maintains the opposite: ["All the days of a poor man are bad" refers to a master of Mishnah; he feels bad because halachic rulings cannot be made on the basis of the Mishnah; and "a good-hearted person" refers to a master of Gemara who understands the underlying reasons of the Mishnah and therefore is qualified to give halachic rulings (Rashbam).] And this is what R. Mesharshia said in the name of Rava: What is meant by the passage, "He who moves about stones will be saddened by them; but he who splits logs will be warmed by them" (Ecclesiastes 10:9)? "He who moves about stones will be saddened by them" refers to the masters of the Mishnah [who feel bad because they are not qualified to render halachic decisions]. "But he who splits logs will be warmed by them" refers to a master of Gemara [who delves into the subject matter and derive genuine pleasure from understanding it in depth].

R. Chanina said: "All the days of a poor man are bad" refers to a person who has a bad wife; "but a good-hearted person feasts perpetually" refers to someone who has a good wife.

R. Yannai said: "All the days of a poor man are bad" refers to a person who is very squeamish; "but a good-hearted person feasts perpetually" refers to a nonchalant person.

R. Yochanan said: "All the days of a poor man are bad" refers to a person who is compassionate [he takes his neighbors' suffering to heart]; "but a good-hearted person feasts perpetually" refers to a callous person. R. Yehoshua b. Levi said: "All the days of a poor man are bad" refers to a cantankerous person; "but a good-hearted person feasts perpetually" refers to a congenial person.

R. YITZCHAK B. AVDIMI'S
WEATHER PREDICTIONS

(147a) Our Rabbis taught: Achitofel [David's adviser who sided with Absalom in his rebellion against David][113] charged his sons with the following three things: Do not get involved in any conflict; do not rebel against the kingdom of the House of David; and if the weather on Shavuot is fine, sow wheat [for it will be a good growing season that year]. Mar Zutra said: He said, "If the weather is cloudy." The Nehardeans said in the name of R. Yaakov: "Fine" does not mean absolutely cloudless, and "cloudy" does not mean completely overcast; but even if it is a partly cloudy day and a north wind is blowing, it is also considered "fine" [and the wheat harvest will be good that year].

R. Abba said to R. Ashi: [We do not rely on forecasts based on weather conditions on Shavuot;] we trust in the weather predictions of R. Yitzchak b. Avdimi, who said: At the close of the last day of Sukkot, everyone used to look at the smoke of the woodpile on the altar of the *Bet Hamikdash*. If it leaned toward the north [and a south wind was blowing], the poor were happy and the farmers were were sad, because that meant that there would be heavy rainfall and the crops would spoil, [and the farmers would have to sell their produce at a cheap price]. If the smoke blew to the south, the poor were sad and the farmers were happy, because [the north wind was a portent] that the rainfall would be sparse that year, and the [meager] crops could be preserved [and sold at higher prices]. If the smoke blew toward the east, everyone was happy, [because a west wind brings moderate rainfall, abundant crops, and stable prices]. If the smoke veered toward the west, everyone was sad, [because the east wind causes drought, famine, and skyrocketing prices].

Abba Shaul said: Beautiful weather on Shavuot is a good sign for the entire year. R. Zevid said: If the first day of Rosh Hashanah is warm, it will be a warm year; if cold, it will be a cold year. [The Gemara asks:] What is the relevance [of this weather information]? [The Gemara answers:] (147b) [It makes a difference] with regard to the prayer of the *Kohen Gadol* on Yom Kippur, [where he prayed for "a year that is dewy and rainy if it is hot." He had to revise this prayer if on Rosh Hashanah the direction of the smoke indicated heavy rainfall].

TALEBEARING

(164b) A folded promissory note[114] was once brought before Rebbi who said, "There is no date on this note." R. Shimon, son of Rebbi, remarked, "Maybe it is hidden between the folds?" When he tore the seams, he found the date. Rebbi turned around and gave R. Shimon a resentful look. [Rebbi thought that Shimon had written it, knowing full well that he was opposed to writing "folded and bound" documents, which were a constant source of errors (Rashbam).] "I did not write it," said R. Shimon; "R. Yehudah Chayta wrote it." "Cut out the talebearing!" Rebbi snapped.

On another occasion R. Shimon, son of Rebbi, was sitting in his father's presence when he [R. Shimon] finished one of the five books of the Book of Psalms. Said Rebbi, "How flawless is this writing!" "I did not write it," replied R. Shimon, "R. Yehudah Chayta did." "Cut out the talebearing!" Rebbi exclaimed. [The

Gemara asks:] [In the case of the folded document] we can well understand [Rebbi's admonition] since there was talebearing; but what talebearing was there in this case [he praised the writer of the Book of Psalms]? [The Gemara answers:] Because of the teaching of R. Dimi, brother of R. Safra, who taught: You should never relate the good qualities of your friend, because by pointing out his good qualities you will inevitably mention his shortcomings.

R. Amram said in the name of Rav: There are three transgressions nobody can avoid committing every single day: Immoral thoughts; praying intently [with the expectation that his prayers will be answered; as if he is testing God]; and talebearing. [The Gemara asks:] You mean to say that a person cannot avoid talebearing? [That is not difficult! Anybody can keep away from talebearing!] (165a) [The Gemara answers: R. Amram means:] A slight suggestion of slander[115] [no one can avoid].

(175b) [The Mishnah says:] R. Yishmael says: Whoever wants to become wise should study monetary laws [civil laws], for there is no section in the Torah that is more comprehensive than they; they are like a gushing spring. And whoever wants to study monetary laws should wait upon Shimon b. Nannas [and learn from him].

NOTES

1. Usually translated as "all the nations will stream [*naharu*] to it." The Gemara associates *naharu* with the Aramaic *nehora*, "light."

2. Rashi explains *avrech* as a composite of *av*, "father in wisdom," and *rach*, "tender in years."

3. Referring to the verse, "He gives an animal its food, to young ravens that cry out" (Psalms 147:9).

4. In our text *paros* is written with a *samach*.

5. *Sanhedrin* 45a.

6. In the Gemara his name is R. Chananiah b. Teradion.

7. Two brothers, Lulianus and Pappus, who took upon themselves the guilt for the death of the Emperor's daughter, so as to save the people as a whole; *Taanit* 18b.

8. King of Adiabene, a vassal state of the Parthian kingdom. He and his mother, Queen Helena, converted to Judaism (first century C.E.).

9. God sometimes confers prophecy on a temporary basis on a person who is not a wise man (Ramban, Maharsha, Ritva).

10. Commonly translated, "then we shall acquire a heart of wisdom."

11. The Ben Yehoyada points out that since Mar the son of R. Ashi had the prophecy that he was going to be the *rosh yeshivah*, he was afraid that if R. Acha were appointed to the post, he would meet with misfortune in order that the seat would become vacant for him. He appropriated the post for himself in order to

avoid such a tragedy.

12. The prophecy did come true (*Yevamot* 34b).

13. The period of the kings Uziah, Yotam, Ahaz, and Hezekiah.

14. They prophesied at the end of the second *Bet Hamikdash*, under the rule of King Darius of Persia (not to be confused with Darius the Mede who conquered Babylonia).

15. It should be remembered that the order given in the *Baraita* was: Jeremiah, Ezekiel, Isaiah.

16. Numbers 23 and 24. Since the chapter of Balaam is part of the Torah, obviously Moses wrote it; why mention that fact? Since Balaam was a prophet, one might think that Moses was instructed by God merely to record Balaam's prophecy. The Sages tell us that Moses prophetically received Balaam's prophecy directly from God, just as he received all of the Torah prophetically directly from God.

17. Prophets used to record their prophecies shortly before their death. Since Isaiah was murdered by Menashe, he did not write his Book (Rashi).

18. Job lived 210 years.

19. "Tomorrow—the hereafter—is reserved for receiving the reward for doing the *mitzvot*" (*Eruvin* 22a).

20. Esther 2:3.

21. Genesis 17:1.

22. "The pregnant and those in labor together" (Jeremiah 31:8).

23. 1 Samuel 1:6.

24. The word *se'arah* also means "hair."

25. According to Tosafot it means that she had a radiant complexion.

26. Numbers 20:1 and Deuteronomy 34:5.

27. A *Kohen Gadol* during the reign of King Yannai, who ruled until 77 B.C.E.

28. R. Shmuel b. Shilat was a dedicated teacher of young children (see *Bava Batra* 8b).

29. Others say that R. Papa and R. Huna were not present at the meeting when R. Nachman b. Yitzchak was appointed to give the weekly sermon, and they delayed R. Adda b. Ahavah because they did not know that R. Nachman b. Yitzchak was reviewing his lecture with R. Adda b. Ahavah (Rashi).

30. Tosafot explains that each of the Rabbis feared that he had caused R. Adda b. Ahavah's untimely death because it says: Whoever causes his neighbor to be punished will not be allowed to enter the domain of the Holy One, blessed be He (*Shabbat* 149a).

31. The Sanhedrin of Ezra the Scribe, which over the years included 120 Sages, many of them prophets, promulgated many ordinances, and ordained and authored the *Shemoneh Esrei* and other *berachot* and prayers.

32. Tosafot remarks that all these *Amara'im* disagree with the *Baraita* that says: When praying you are required to face in the direction of Jerusalem (*Berachot* 30a).

33. Chapters 15–19.

34. Deuteronomy 34:1–3.

35. Genesis 15:18–21.

36. It should be noted that Rashi's commentary on *Bava Batra* ends on 29a because of his death. At that point it is continued by his grandson and disciple, the Rashbam (R. Shmuel b. R. Meir).

37. The Cave of Machpelah in Hebron.

38. The Seven Species for which Eretz Yisrael is praised are: wheat, barley, grapes, figs, pomegranates, olives, and dates.

39. A *parsah* is about two-and-one-half miles.

40. *Menachot* 41b.

41. Numbers, Chapter 16.

42. A saintly woman who was very poor, yet turned down great wealth when she learned that it was deducted from her portion in the World to Come.

43. This nerve must be removed before the hindquarter of any animal may be eaten (Genesis 32:33).

44. Because they graze a thousand mountains in one day (Psalms 50:10).

45. The Dead Sea.

46. Perhaps Eilat, now known as the Gulf of Akaba.

47. The Mediterranean Sea.

48. "Like this one says and like that one says," *kedein ukedein*, or *kadkod* for short.

49. Hiram, the king of Tyre, the epitome of pride and haughtiness, considered himself God.

50. *Mikra'eha* means both "the assembled" and "invited guests."

51. For a *tzaddik* to be named by God's name means that he is called "a *tzaddik* for God"; all his deeds were done for the sake of God and to reflect glory on God (*Maharsha*).

52. *Moshel* means both "to make parables" and "to rule, to master."

53. *Cheshbon* means "calculation, reckoning."

54. *Vaniram* is seen as an abbreviation of *ein rom*, "there is no High One."

55. Naomi's husband; see Ruth 1:1–5.

56. Ruth 4:13.

57. Judges 12:8.

58. See Judges 13:2–24.

59. Ruth 4:20.

60. Exodus 6:23.

61. Kardo in the Gemara's version.

62. Genesis 11:31.

63. Joshua 9:15,26.

64. Ibid.

65. Jashubi-lehem is a combination of *shavah* and [Beth]*lehem*.

66. See Daniel 9:22.

67. Jeremiah 35:6ff.

68. Cautionary rules so that the people do not actually violate any of the commandments. For example, the Rabbis forbade even the handling of certain utensils on *Shabbat* [*muktzeh*], lest one use them to perform a labor forbidden on *Shabbat*.

69. The seventh year of the *shemittah* cycle followed by the eighth year, which is the fiftieth year of the *yovel* cycle.

70. This is the version in Ein Yaakov; in the Gemara there is a variant reading.

71. 2 Kings 21:1–17.

72. God in His foreknowledge knew that Manasseh son of Hezekiah would arise later who would be corrupt and worship idols (Iyun Yaakov).

73. In Judges 18:30, *"Yonatan ben Gershom ben Menashe,"* the *nun* in *Menashe* is raised above the other letters, as though hanging between the *mem* and the *shin*; so that it reads Moshe, to indicate that Yonatan was a grandson of Moses. (Rashbam; compare *Sefer Chasidim* 137.)

74. Numbers 25:11ff.

75. Genesis 39:7ff.

76. Numbers 25:6ff.

77. *Berachot* 5b.

78. Exodus 8:15.

79. For the story of the spies, see Numbers, Chapters 13 and 14.

80. Numbers, Chapter 14.

81. Numbers, Chapter 16.

82. Numbers 14:2.

83. The daughters of Tzelofchad whose father had died petitioned Moses to be given the right to inherit a share in Eretz Yisrael. See Numbers 27:1–5 and 36:1–10.

84. Numbers 15:32–34. Some say that the violation consisted of carrying on *Shabbat*; according to others it was cutting the sticks or binding them (*Shabbat* 96b).

85. This is Rabbeinu Gershom's interpretation of the Gemara. Rashbam offers a different explanation.

86. Marriage with a brother's childless widow (see Deuteronomy 25:5–10).

87. The Israelites were in Egypt for 210 years. Yocheved was born at the beginning of the 210 years, and Moses was eighty years old at the time of the Exodus. Consequently, Yocheved was 210–80 = 130 years old when she gave birth to Moses (Rashbam).

88. *Sota* 12b.

89. Compare *Taanit* 31a.

90. Leviticus 16:29ff.

91. According to *Seder Olam*, Moses spent three times forty days on Mount Sinai, beginning on the 6th of Sivan until his descent on the 10th of Tishri when he brought down the second Tablets, and that day was designated as Yom Kippur (Rashbam).

92. After the sin of the spies, God decreed that the children of Israel would wander in the wilderness for forty years, during which time that entire generation would die (Numbers 14:35). When by the 15th of Av of the fortieth year the dying stopped, the people rejoiced.

93. Pesach, Shavuot, and Sukkot.

94. At the end of the Bar Kochba uprising, in 133 C.E.

95. *Berachot* 48b.

96. Proverbs 3:2.

97. 1 Kings 11:29; 14:4,5.

98. 1 Chronicles 26:20.

99. Numbers 4:23, 29, 35.

100. The breastplate of the *Kohen Gadol* was folded in half to form a pocket. Into it a slip of parchment was inserted containing the Divine Name. It was called *Urim veTummim*, and it would cause the individual letters of the tribal names to light up. If read in the proper sequence, these letters presented complete and true answers to important questions the *Kohen Gadol* would ask of God.

101. See above 118b.

102. Deuteronomy 1:36.

103. Numbers 35:9–34.

104. R. Yonatan was R. Shmuel b. Nachmani's teacher.

105. Levi was her son.

106. Genesis 46:27.

107. Genesis 27:8ff.

108. See 120a above.

109. Genesis 36:12.

110. 1 Samuel 30:1ff.

111. The passage in 1 Chronicles 5:24 reads, "And these were the heads of their fathers' houses: Efer and Yishi."

112. The greatest of Hillel's disciples (ca. 30 B.C.E.). Author of Targum Yonatan b. Uziel.

113. 2 Samuel 15:12–34.

114. A legal document, called *get mekushar*, "folded and bound." After a few lines of writing, an equal space was left blank. Then the lines were folded onto the blank space, and one witness signed on the backside of the paper. After a few more lines, the process was repeated, and in the end the document was stitched together. Originally this was done for the benefit of the wives of *kohanim*. *Kohanim* are known to be high-strung, and in a fit of rage a *kohen* might divorce his wife. When he has second thoughts, he cannot remarry his divorced wife, because a *kohen* is forbidden to marry a divorcée. Preparing a "folded and bound" document will take a long time, enough to allow the *kohen* to reconsider before it is too late. Later the same procedure was used for promissory notes, bills of sale, and other legal documents.

115. For example, to say: "There is fire in the oven of so-and-so," suggesting that they are wealthy and eating all the time.

⸂SANHEDRIN⸃

THE EXILARCH, HEAD OF BABYLONIAN JEWS

(5a) We learned in a *Baraita*: [When Jacob blessed Judah, he said,] "The scepter will not depart from Judah" (Genesis 49:10)—this refers to the Exilarchs of Babylonia who rule over Israel with royal scepters [the symbol of supremacy. The Exilarch or *Resh Galuta*, the head of Babylonian Jewry, was appointed and given authority by the government].

[The verse continues,] "nor a lawgiver from among his descendants," this refers to the descendants of Hillel [who was the leader of the community in Eretz Yisrael][1] who teach Torah in public [but have no political power].

(5b) It has been taught: A disciple should not render a halachic ruling in the place where his teacher resides, unless there is a distance of three *parsahs* between them, which is the area occupied by the camp of Israel in the desert.

JUSTICE SHOULD BE DONE

(6b) R. Eliezer, son of R. Yose Hagelili, says: Once a case is brought before the court, the judges are forbidden to negotiate a settlement. A judge that makes a settlement is a sinner, and whoever praises a judge that made a settlement blasphemes, for it says, "He that blesses an arbitrator [*botze'a*] blasphemes God" (Psalms 10:3). But let the law cut through the mountain; [justice should be done, no matter what]. For it says, "Judgment belongs to God" (Deuteronomy 1:17). That is what Moses used to say: Let the law cut through the mountain. But his brother Aaron loved peace and sought to make peace between neighbors, as it says, "The teaching of truth was in his mouth, and injustice was not found on his lips; he walked with Me in peace and with fairness, and turned many away from iniquity" (Malachi 2:6).

[The Gemara now cites alternate interpretations of the word *botze'a* in Psalms 10:3.] R. Eliezer said: [The verse applies to something else altogether.] If someone stole a *se'ah* of wheat, ground and baked it, and separated *challah*[2] from it; how could he recite a

berachah? This person is not saying a blessing; he is showing contempt of God! About such a person the Psalmist says, "The robber [*botze'a*] praises himself that he has blasphemed God" (Psalms 10:3).

R. Meir says: This verse refers to Judah, for it says, [when the brothers threw Joseph into the pit,] "Judah said to his brothers, 'What gain [*betza*] will there be if we kill our brother; [let us sell him to the Ishmaelites]'" (Genesis 37:26). [And the verse Psalms 10:3 is saying] that anyone who praises Judah is blaspheming God, for it says, "He who praises the *botze'a* [i.e., Judah], blasphemes God"; [since Judah saw that the brothers were following his advice, he should have told them to take Joseph back to his father (Rashi)].

[Challenging R. Eliezer's opinion that a judge is forbidden to make a settlement,] R. Yehudah b. Korchah said: It is a mitzvah to make a settlement, for it says, "In your gates judge with truth, justice, and peace" (Zechariah 8:16). How is this possible? Where there is justice there is no peace [between the litigants; the one who loses is resentful], and where there is peace there is no justice! What kind of judgment goes hand in hand with peace? It is: reaching a compromise. And so it was in the case of David, as it says, "David administered justice and kindness to all his people" (2 Samuel 8:15). How is this possible? Where there is harsh justice there is no kindness, and where there is kindness there is no harsh justice! What kind of justice goes hand in hand with kindness? It is: reaching a compromise.

But the first Tanna [who holds the view that arbitration is forbidden], what does he do with the verse, "David administered justice and kindness"? He interprets the verse as follows: David judged on the basis of rigid law: he cleared the innocent and convicted the guilty; but when he saw that a poor man had been sentenced to pay damages he used to help him out of his own pocket. Thus he fulfilled the requirements of both justice and kindness—justice to the one, by seeing to it that he received the money that was due to him; and kindness to the other, by helping him out of his pocket. That is why it says about David, "David administered justice and kindness to *all* his people."

Rebbi found fault with this interpretation. He said: In that case, it should have said: "kindness to the poor" rather than "to all his people"! Therefore, said Rebbi, even if he had not helped the poor from his own pocket, he would still have administered justice and kindness: justice to the one, by ruling that he was to receive the money due to him; kindness to the other, by removing the stigma of theft from his house.

THE GOLDEN CALF

(7a) All the above *Tanna'im* [that offered the various interpretations of "The *botze'a* (robber) praises himself that he has blasphemed God" (Psalms 10:3)] dispute the exposition of R. Tanchum b. Chanilai, who said that the verse refers to the story of the golden calf. For it says, "When Aaron saw this, he built an altar before [the calf]" (Exodus 32:5). What did he see? R. Binyamin b. Yefet said in the name of R. Elazar: He saw Chur[3] being killed [for trying to prevent the making of the golden calf], and he said to himself: If I do not obey them [and refuse to make the golden calf], they will do to me what they did to Chur; and thereby will come true the verse, "Should a *kohen* and a prophet be slain in the Sanctuary of God?" (Lamentations 2:20); and they will never be forgiven. Better let them worship the golden calf [which involves only the transgression of idolatry], and this they can rectify through *teshuvah.* [Aaron thus made a compromise and ruled that he was permitted to make the golden calf. This concession is criticized in Psalms 10:3. (Rashi).]

MAY A JUDGE RECOMMEND A SETTLEMENT?

(6b) R. Shimon b. Menasia said, [speaking to a judge:] When two people come before you for judgment, before you have heard their case; or even afterward, if you have not made up your mind as to who is right; you are allowed to recommend that they reach a settlement. But if you have already heard their case and have made up your mind as to who is right, you are not allowed to tell them to work out a deal, for it says, "The beginning of a quarrel is like releasing water; before the argument breaks out, abandon it" (Proverbs 17:14). [Which means:] Before the dispute has come out into the open [and was brought into court], you can withdraw from it [and suggest a settlement]; but after the case has been brought into court, [and you have made up your mind as to who is guilty,] you cannot drop it anymore [and propose a compromise].

Resh Lakish said: When two litigants appear before you in court, one mild-mannered, the other tough, then, before you have heard their case, or even after, as long as you are in doubt as to who is right, you may tell them, "I don't want to take your case"; for perhaps the tough one will be guilty and cause you untold trouble. But once you have heard their case and know who is guilty, you cannot withdraw and say, "I don't want to get involved in your dispute." For it says, "Do not be intimidated by any man" (Deuteronomy 1:17).

R. Yehoshua b. Korchah said: From where do we know that a student who is present when his master is judging a case [of a poor and a rich litigant], and he sees a point of defense for the poor litigant and against his rich opponent, that he should not keep quiet? Because it says, "Do not be intimidated [*taguru*] by any man." R. Chanin said: This means: Do not hold back your words because of anyone; [he sees *taguru* as cognate to *agar*, "to collect"]. Furthermore, witnesses should know for Whom they are testifying, and before Whom they are testifying, and Who will punish them [if they are lying]. For it says [concerning the witnesses], "The two men [and those] who have the grievance shall stand before God" (Deuteronomy 19:17). Judges should also know whom they are judging, before Whom they are judging, and Who will punish them [if they distort the law]. For it says, "God stands in the Divine assembly, in the midst of judges shall He judge" (Psalms 82:1). In the same vein we read concerning Yehoshafat [the righteous king of Judah], "He said to the judges, 'Take care in what you do, for it is not for man's sake that you judge, but for God's'" (2 Chronicles 19:6). Now a judge might say: What do I need all this trouble for? [I may not decide a case correctly, and then I will be punished by God.] That is why it says, "He is with you in the matter of judgment" (ibid.), which means that a judge has to decide only according to what he actually sees with his own eyes. [If a judge rules on the basis of the information he elicits, he is not faulted if he judges wrongly, because he did what the law expects him to do (Rashi).]

WISE SAYINGS

(7a) R. Hamenuna said: The first thing a person is judged for in the World to Come is regarding the study of Torah, for it says, "The beginning of *madon* [quarrel or judgment] concerns the releasing water" (Proverbs 17:14), [and the Torah is compared to water]. R. Huna says [with regard to this verse]: A quarrel is like water breaking through a crack in a dam; the crack widens as the water gushes through it. Abbaye the Elder said: A quarrel is like the boards of a wooden bridge. The longer they lie in place, the more rigid they become; [the longer a quarrel lasts, the more adamant and unyielding the opposing parties become].

There was a person who used to go around saying: Happy is the person who hears himself being disdained and ignores it; for a hundred evils will pass by him [without affecting him]. Shmuel said to Rav Yehudah: There is a verse that tells us the same idea, "The one who releases the water of [quarrel] causes the beginning of a hundred quarrels [the numeric value of *madon*, "quarrel," is 100].

There was a person who used to go around saying: Don't be surprised if [a person who trangresses two or three times is not punished], because a thief is not executed for two or three burglaries [but eventually he will get caught and be punished]. Shmuel said to Rav Yehudah: This idea is hinted at in the following verse, "Thus said God, 'For three transgressions of Israel [I have looked away], but for four I will not pardon them'" (Amos 2:6).

Another person used to say: Seven pits are dug for an upright man, [and he will escape], but only one pit for the evildoer, [and he will stumble into it]. Said Shmuel to Rav Yehudah: This is implied in the following verse, "For though the righteous one may fall seven times, he will arise" (Proverbs 24:16).

Another person used to say: Let the person whose coat was taken away by the court [as payment for his debt], sing a song and go on his way. [He should be happy that his wrongdoing has been set right.] Said Shmuel to Rav Yehudah: There is a verse for this, [Jethro said to Moses,] "And this entire people, [even the ones who lost a court case,] will then also be able to go home in peace" (Exodus 18:23).

Another used to say: When a woman falls asleep, the basket [with her paraphernalia] falls off her head; [i.e., laziness leads to ruin]. Said Shmuel to Rav Yehudah: This idea is suggested in the verse, "Through slothfulness the ceiling sags" (Ecclesiastes 10:18).

Another person used to say: The person on whom I relied raised his fist at me. Shmuel said to Rav Yehudah: There is a verse that tells us that, "Even my ally in whom I trusted, who ate my bread, has raised his heel to trample me" (Psalms 41:10).

Yet another person used to say: When the love between myself and my wife was ardent, we found room to sleep on the blade of a sword; now that our ardor has cooled, a bed of sixty cubits is not large enough for us. Said R. Huna: This is alluded to in the Torah. At the outset [when Israel was faithful to God,] God said, "I will commune with you there, speaking to you from above the Ark cover" (Exodus 25:22). [And how big was the Ark? Two-and-a-half cubits long and a cubit and a half wide.] We learned: The height of the Ark was nine handbreadths, and the height of the cover measured one handbreadth; ten handbreadths in all; [thus, the *Shechinah* descended to ten handbreaths from the ground]. It says, furthermore, "The Temple that Solomon built for God, sixty cubits was its lengths, twenty its width, and thirty cubits its height" (1 Kings 6:2). But later on [when Israel turned away from God, it says, "Thus says God, 'The Heaven is My throne and the earth is My footstool; what house could you build for Me?'" (Isaiah 66:1). [So we see that when the love had faded, even the vast Temple was not big enough.]

AN HONEST
AND IMPARTIAL JUDGE

R. Shmuel b. Nachmani said in the name of R. Yonatan: A judge who passes judgment in absolute truth, [who conducts his own investigation, not relying only on the testimony of the witnesses (Rashi)], causes the *Shechinah* to dwell in Israel, for it says, "God stands in the Divine assembly, in the midst of judges He shall judge" (Psalms 81:1). But a judge who does not pass judgment in absolute truth causes the *Shechinah* to depart from Israel, for it says, "Because of the plundering of the poor, because of the cry of the needy, 'Now I will arise!' God will say" (ibid. 12:6). R. Shmuel b. Nachmani also said in the name of R. Yonatan: A judge who judges unfairly and thereby takes property from one and gives it to the other, the Holy One, blessed be He, will take away his life, for it says, "Do not rob the destitute, because he is destitute, and do not oppress the poor man in the gate [of judgment]. For God will take up their grievance; He will take away the life of those who will steal from them" (Proverbs 22:22,23).

R. Shmuel b. Nachmani further said in the name of R. Yonatan: A judge should always imagine that there is a sword placed between his thighs, and Gehinnom lying wide open under him. (7b) For it says, "Behold the resting place of Him to Whom peace belongs [i.e., the *Shechinah*] with sixty myriads of Israel's mighty [the Torah scholars] encircling it. All of them gripping the sword of tradition, skilled in the battle of Torah, each with his sword ready at his side, because of the fear of the night" (Song of Songs 3:7,8)—which means, because of the terror of Gehinnom, which is equal to the night.

R. Yoshiah—others say, R. Nachman b. Yitzchak —expounded: What is meant by the verse, "O House of David, thus says God: Administer justice in the morning and save the robbed from the hand of the oppressor" (Jeremiah 21:12)? Does a judge conduct a trial only in the morning and not during the whole day? The meaning is this: If the case that you are about to decide is as clear to you as the morning, give your verdict; if not, do not give it.

R. Chiya b. Abba says in the name of R. Yonatan: We know this from the following verse, "Say to wisdom: 'You are my sister'" (Proverbs 7:4)—If a case is as clear to you as the law that you are forbidden to marry your sister, give your verdict; otherwise, don't.

R. Yehoshua b. Levi said: If ten people judge a case, the responsibility rests on all of them. [The Gemara asks:] Isn't that obvious? [The Gemara answers:] No, this needs to be said in reference to a case where a student sits in the presence of his master [and notices that his master is rendering a wrong verdict. If he does not point it out to him, he is held responsible].

Whenever a lawsuit was brought before R. Huna he used to gather ten scholars from the yeshivah, in order—as he put it—that each of them should carry a chip of the beam [i.e., each should share in the responsibility]. Whenever R. Ashi was consulted about a *tereifah*[4] animal, he would gather all the slaughterers from Masa Mechasya, in order—as he put it—that each of them should carry a chip of the beam.

When R. Dimi came [from Eretz Yisrael] he said: R. Nachman b. Kohen explained the following verse, "Through justice a king establishes a land, but a man of graft tears it down" (Proverbs 29:4). If a judge is [thoroughly familiar with the law, and,] like a king, [does not need to consult anyone], then he establishes the country; but if he [has to ask others regarding the law] like a *kohen* who goes around the barns [asking for his priestly share], he tears the country down.

AN UNQUALIFIED JUDGE

The family of the *Nasi* appointed a judge who was not a scholar, so the Rabbis said to Yehudah b. Nachmani, who was the interpreter[5] of Resh Lakish: Go and become the interpreter of this judge [and repeat what he is saying]. Standing next to him, Yehudah bent down to hear what he wanted to say, but the judge did not say a word. So Yehudah b. Nachmani began to speak, saying, [about this judge] "Woe to him who says to wood, 'Wake up!' and to silent stone, 'Arise!' Will it teach? Behold it is coated with gold and silver, and there is no spirit within it'" (Habakkuk 2:19). He continued, "But the Holy One, blessed be He, will punish those that appointed him [as judge], for it says [in the next verse], 'But God in His holy Sanctuary; let all the world be silent before Him,' [for He will punish those that appointed such a judge]."

Resh Lakish said: Whoever appoints a judge that is unworthy, is considered as if he had planted an *asheirah* [a tree that was used for pagan worship].[6] For it says, "Appoint for yourselves judges and police officers in all your cities" (Deuteronomy 16:18), and soon after that it says, "Do not plant for yourself an *asheirah* of any kind of tree." R. Ashi said: And if such an [unworthy judge is appointed] in a place where there are Torah scholars, it is as though the *asheirah* were planted next to the altar, for it says, "near the altar of the Lord your God" (ibid.).

It says, "Do not make a representation of anything that is with Me. Do not make silver or gold gods for yourselves" (Exodus 20:20). Does that mean that that only gods of silver and gold may not be made, while idols of wood and stone are permitted? R. Ashi said: The verse refers to judges who were appointed [by bribing the king] with silver and gold.

EXEMPLARY JUDGES

Whenever Rav came to sit in judgment he used to say [about himself]: Of his own free will [the judge] goes to meet death [of Divine punishment for judging wrongly]; the needs of his household he neglects, and empty-handed he returns home. I wish that he came home as blameless as when he left! [What a dangerous and unrewarding job it is to be a judge!] Whenever he saw a group of people following him he would quote the verse, "Though his eminence ascends to heaven, and his head touches the clouds, he will perish forever in his own dung" (Job 20:6,7). Mar Zutra Chasida, when the servants carried him on their shoulders [to the *bet midrash*][7] on the *Shabbat* before the Yom Tov, where he would lecture on the laws of the forthcoming Yom Tov], used to say: "For strength endures not forever. Does the crown [of wealth] last from generation to generation?" (Proverbs 27:24). [He said this in order to quell any feelings of pride that might take hold of him.]

INSTRUCTIONS TO JUDGES

Bar Kappara lectured: From where in Scripture do we derive the saying of the Rabbis: Be thoughtful in judgment? From the verse, "Do not climb up to My Altar with steps" (Exodus 20:23), which is followed by "These are the laws" (ibid. 21:1). [The closeness of the two verses indicates that when deciding the law a judge should proceed prudently, go at a slow pace, and avoid taking big steps, like a *kohen* ascending the Altar.] R. Elazar said: From where do we know that a judge should not step over the heads of people? [At a lecture the audience would sit on the floor, and someone trying to reach his seat would have to step over the heads of people.] For it says, "Do not climb to My Altar with steps," which is followed by "These are the laws" [an indication that judges should not step over the heads of the people to get to their seats]. The verse continues, "that you must set before [the people].

[The Gemara asks:] It should have said: that you must teach them; ["set before" implies something tangible!] R. Yirmeyah—others say, R. Chiya b. Abba—said: This refers to the paraphernalia of the judges [which are tangible articles]. R. Huna, when he was about to sit in judgment, used to say: Bring out the equipment of my office: a rod [for beating a person who refuses to obey a court order], a shoe [for *chalitzah*[8]], a shofar [which was blown for excommunication], and a strap [for administering thirty-nine lashes].[9]

It says, "I then gave your judges instructions" (Deuteronomy 1:16). R. Yochanan said: This is a warning to the judges to use the rod and the strap with caution [only for the sake of carrying out justice, but not as a demonstration of their power]. [The verse continues,] "Listen to [every dispute] among your brethren and judge honestly." R. Chanina said: This is a warning to the Bet Din not to listen to the claims of one litigant in the absence of his opponent; and a warning to the litigant not to explain his case to the judge before his opponent shows up. It says *shamoa*, "listen," which can be read also as *shammei'a*, "make your words heard among your brethren" [which implies that the litigants should explain their side of the argument only when both are present]. R. Kahana said: We derive this from the verse, "Do not accept [tissa] a false report" (Exodus 23:1), [referring to the judge], which can be read tassi, "make accept" [referring to the litigant, that he should not try to make the judge accept his side of the dispute before his opponent appears]. The verse quoted above [Deuteronomy 1:16] continues, "judge honestly."

Resh Lakish says that it means: Make your judgment righteous, and then render your verdict. The verse continues, "between each man and his brother, [even] where a proselyte [is concerned]." R. Yehudah said: This refers to a dispute between brothers; for example, about dividing the main floor of a house and the attic. [The judge should not say: What difference does it make who takes what? He should order the occupant of the main floor to pay compensation to the one to whom he assigns the attic.] [The verse continues, "[even] where a proselyte [geiro] is concerned." R. Yehudah [translates geiro as "dweller" and says it refers to household articles]. This refers to a dispute as minor as one concerning a stove and an oven. [The judge should make the one who gets the more valuable stove pay compensation to the one who gets the oven.] The verse continues, "Do not give anyone special consideration when rendering judgment." R. Yehudah said, this means: Do not favor anyone, [even if he is your friend]. R. Elazar said: Do not discriminate against him [if he is your enemy].

An erstwhile host of Rav brought a case before him to be tried and said, "Weren't you my guest once?" "Yes, I remember," replied Rav. ["And how can I help you?"] "I have a lawsuit, [and I want you to decide it]," the man answered. Said Rav, (8a) "I am sorry, but I am disqualified to hear your case, [because you reminded me of the favor you once did me]." Turning to R. Kahana he said, "Go ahead, you try this case." Seeing that the man relied heavily on his acquaintance with Rav, and was confident of winning the case, R. Kahana told him, "If you agree to abide by my judgment, fine; if not, you can put Rav out of your mind, [because I will excommunicate you]."

The verse continues, "Listen to the great and small alike." Resh Lakish said: This teaches us that you should treat a lawsuit involving one perutah with the same seriousness as you would a case involving a hundred manah. [The Gemara asks:] What are the practical ramifications of this rule? Do you think that it tells us to consider and investigate disputes about small and large amounts with equal care? This is obvious! [The Gemara answers:] It tells the judge to assign priority to whichever case comes first, [even if the first case on the docket is a case involving a perutah. The text continues, "Do not be impressed by any man, since judgment belongs to God." R. Chama b. R. Chanina said: The Holy One, blessed be He, said: It is not enough

for the wicked judges that they take away money from one person and give to another unjustly, but they inconvenience Me to return it to its owner. The text continues, "If any case is too difficult, bring it to me [Moses], and I will hear it." R. Chanina—others say, R. Yoshiah—said: Because of this utterance Moses was punished. [He should have said: Bring it before the Shechinah. His punishment was that when the daughters of Tzelofchad asked him about their father's inheritance, he did not know the answer, and had to ask God,] for it says, "Moses brought their case before God" (Numbers 27:5).

It says, "I then gave your judges instructions" (Deuteronomy 1:16), and [two verses after that, it says,] "At that time I gave you instructions" (ibid. v. 18). [The judges are instructed in the first verse; to what purpose were the people instructed in the other?] R. Elazar said in R. Simlai's name: These verses are a warning to the congregation to respect their judges, and a warning to the judges to be patient with the congregation [particularly, if litigants take exception to their ruling]. To what extent [should a judge submit to abuse]? Like a father carries an infant (Numbers 11:12).

A LEADER MUST HAVE CLOUT

One passage reads, "You [Joshua] will come with this people to the land" (Deuteronomy 31:7), [implying that Joshua is on the same level as the people]; and another passage reads, "You [Joshua] will bring the children of Israel to the land" (ibid. v. 23), [suggesting that he is their leader]. [How can this inconsistency be reconciled?] R. Yochanan said: [In the first verse] Moses said to Joshua: [You will come with the people,] you should be together with the elders of the generation; [listen to their advice and do not order them around]. But [in the second verse] it was the Holy One, blessed be He, who said [to Joshua]: Take a stick and hit them over the head [meaning: assert your authority]! There can be only one leader for a generation, not two.

SAVING OTHERS FROM EMBARRASSMENT

(10b) We learned in a Baraita: The year can be intercalated [i.e., turned into a leap year by inserting a second month of Adar][10] only by members of the Bet Din that were appointed for that purpose by the Nasi (11a) the night before [the intercalation meeting]. It once happened that R. Gamliel [who was the Nasi] said: Send me seven scholars early in the morning to the upper chamber [where the Bet Din was scheduled to convene to intercalate the year]. When he came in the morning and found eight scholars, he said, "Who is the one that came here without permission? He should leave!" Shmuel Hakatan [the Little][11] then got up and said, "I am the one who came without permission. I did not come to take part in the intercalation, but because I needed to learn the practical application of these laws." Rabban Gamliel replied, "Sit down, my son, sit down. You are worthy to intercalate all [leap] years, but the Sages decreed that the year may be intercalated only by members of the Bet Din that were appointed for that purpose." [The Gemara interjects:] In reality, it was not Shmuel Hakatan that came without permission, but someone else; he only wanted to save the uninvited person from embarrassment [and therefore took the blame on himself].

A similar incident happened once when Rebbi was giving a lecture and noticed the smell of garlic. He said, "Will the one who ate garlic please leave." R. Chiya got up and left; then all the other disciples got up and left. In the morning, R. Shimon, the son of Rebbi, met R. Chiya and asked him, "Are you the one who [ate the garlic and] caused my father grief yesterday?" He replied, "God forbid, that such a thing should happen in Israel; [the reason that I walked out was in order to save the person who actually ate the garlic from embarrassment].

And from whom did R. Chiya learn to act like this? From R. Meir, for we learned: One day a woman appeared in the *bet midrash* of R. Meir and said, "Rabbi, one of the disciples here has married me by having sexual intercourse with me."[12] [She did not know who it was, and she wanted a *get* (divorce), in order to be able to remarry.] R. Meir then got up and gave her a *get* [bill of divorce, taking the blame upon himself]. Thereupon all the disciples got up and did likewise. And from whom did R. Meir learn this? From Shmuel Hakatan [in the story mentioned above about the intercalation of the year]. And Shmuel Hakatan? From Shechaniah son of Yechiel, who said to Ezra, "We have transgressed against God and have taken in alien women of the peoples of the land! But now there is hope for Israel concerning this" (Ezra 10:2). [Although only a fraction of the people married alien wives, and Shechaniah was certainly not among them, he nevertheless said "*we* have transgressed," in order to minimize the embarrassment of the true culprits.]

And from whom did Shechaniah learn this? From Joshua, for it says, [after Achan took of the consecrated property,] "God said to Joshua, 'Raise yourself up! Why do you fall on your face? Israel has sinned'" (Joshua 7:10,11). Joshua asked, "Master of the universe! Who is the one that sinned?" Replied God, "Am I an informer? Go and cast lots [to find out]." [God thus saved the sinner from embarrassment by not revealing his identity.] Or, if you prefer, say that Joshua learned it from Moses. For it says, [after a few people went out to collect the manna on *Shabbat*, which they were forbidden to do, God told Moses to say to the children of Israel,] "How long will you refuse to keep My commandments and My laws?" (Exodus 16:28), [although Moses did not transgress he is included, in order to avoid pointing the finger at those that sinned].

TWO WHO WERE WORTHY TO BE PROPHETS

[The Gemara now presents another teaching concerning Shmuel Hakatan:] The Rabbis taught: Since the death of the last prophets, Haggai, Zechariah, and Malachi, the holy spirit [of prophecy] left Israel; but they would still draw on the *Bat-Kol* [a heavenly voice, a lower grade of prophecy] for guidance. Once when the Rabbis were assembled on the upper floor of Gurya's house in Jericho, a *Bat-Kol* came forth from heaven, saying, "There is one among you who deserves that the *Shechinah* should rest on him as it did on Moses, but his generation does not deserve it." The Sages who heard it focused their eyes on Hillel the Elder, [thinking that the *Bat-Kol* meant him]. And when Hillel the Elder died, they eulogized him and said, "What a pious man he was! What a humble man he was; a true disciple of Ezra!" [Meaning, he followed in Ezra's footsteps; Ezra lived three centuries before Hillel.]

On another occasion the Rabbis assembled on the upper floor in Yavneh, when a *Bat-Kol* came forth from heaven, saying, "There is one among you who deserves that the *Shechinah* should rest on him, but his generation does not deserve it." The Sages who heard it focused their eyes on Shmuel Hakatan, [thinking that the *Bat-Kol* meant him]. And when he died they eulogized him, saying, "What a pious man he was! What a humble man he was; a true disciple of Hillel!" [It is evident that Shmuel Hakatan actually did have prophetic inspiration, because] before he passed away he predicted, "Shimon and Yishmael will die by the sword" [Shimon refers to R. Shimon b. Gamliel, the *Nassi*; Yishmael refers to R. Yishmael b. Elisha, the *Kohen Gadol*, who were among the Ten Martyrs killed by the Romans (Rashi)]; and his friends will be executed [i.e., R. Akiva and R. Chanina b. Teradion]. The enemy will pillage the rest of the people, and many troubles will come down upon the world. When R. Yehudah b. Bava died a martyr's death they wanted to eulogize him with the same praises, but the political climate precluded that; [if they had said something favorable about the martyr, the government would have regarded it as sedition], for no eulogies were delivered over people who were martyred by the [Roman] government.

SEMICHAH, RABBINICAL ORDINATION

(13b) Abaye asked R. Yosef: From what verse do we derive that it takes three [judges] to confer the title of Elder [i.e., a judge of the Bet Din]? Do you think, from the verse, "He [Moses] then laid his hands on him [Joshua]" (Numbers 27:23). If so, one person should be enough! And if you will say that Moses was equivalent to the seventy-one [judges of the great Sanhedrin], then seventy-one judges should be required [for *semichah*]! The difficulty remained unanswered.

R. Acha son of Rava said to R. Ashi: Do the hands literally have to be placed on the head [in order for the *semichah* to become effective]? [No], he replied; we confer the title on him. He is called Rabbi and granted the authority to adjudicate cases of fines and penalties.

[The Gemara asks:] Cannot one person alone grant ordination? Surely Rav Yehudah said in the name of Rav: May this man—R. Yehudah b. Bava—be remembered for blessing! For if not for him the laws of fines and penalties would have been forgotten in Israel! Forgotten? They could have studied these laws [so they should not be forgotten]! But (14a) [what Rav Yehudah meant to say was that if the system of *semichah* had been terminated] these laws might have been abolished. Because once the wicked [Roman] government decreed that whoever ordained a scholar should be put to death, and whoever received ordination should be put to death, the city where the ordination took place should be wiped out, and the *Shabbat* boundaries[13] in which *semichah* was conferred should be uprooted.

What did R. Yehudah b. Bava do? He went and sat between two great mountains, that were situated between two large cities; [and not inside a city, so that if the ordination was discovered it would not be destroyed], between the *Shabbat* boundaries of the cities of Usha and Shefaram; and there he ordained five elders. They were: R. Meir, R. Yehudah, R. Shimon, R. Yose, and R. Eliezer b. Shamua. R. Ivya includes also R. Nechemiah. When the Romans found out about it [and came to arrest them], R. Yehudah b. Bava pleaded, "My children, run away!" "But what will become of you?" they retorted. ["You are an old man, unable to flee."] "I will lie down before them motionless like a stone, [and allow them to cool their rage on me, so that they will not chase after you" (Iyun Yaakov)].

The story has it that the Romans did not budge from that spot until they stuck three hundred iron spears into his body, turning it into a sieve. [All of which goes to prove that even one person alone is authorized to confer rabbinic ordination.] [The Gemara challenges this proof:] There were actually some other people together with R. Yehudah b. Bava [when he ordained the five scholars], but out of respect for him they were not mentioned; and three ordained rabbis are required to give *semichah*]. [The Gemara asks:] Was R. Meir really ordained by R. Yehudah b. Bava? Surely Rabbah b. Bar Chanah said in the name of R. Yochanan: Anyone that says that R. Meir was not ordained by R. Akiva is making a mistake. [The Gemara answers:] True, R. Akiva did ordain R. Meir, but the ordination was not recognized [because R. Meir was very young at the time]; whereas when R. Yehudah b. Bava ordained him later in life the ordination was accepted.

R. Yochanan was very eager to ordain R. Chanina and R. Hoshaia, but since he never managed to find two other rabbis to participate in the ordination, [and three ordained rabbis are required for it], he was very distressed. R. Chanina and R. Hoshaia said to him, "Master, don't feel bad, for we are descendants of the house of Eli," [and therefore ineligible for ordination]. For R. Shmuel b. Nachmani said in the name of R. Yonatan: From what verse do we derive that a descendant of the family of Eli cannot be ordained? From the verse, [the man of God said to Eli,] "There will be no *zaken* [old man] in your family for all time" (1 Samuel 2:32). What does the word *zaken* mean [in this context]? Do you think, literally, "old man"? But it says, in the next verse, "All those raised in your house will die as [young] men" (ibid. v. 33) [which would be redundant]. We must say therefore that *zaken* refers to ordination [i.e., there will be no ordained rabbi in your family].

R. Zeira used to hide himself to avoid being ordained, because R. Elazar had said: "Stay always out of the limelight, and you'll live long." But when he heard another saying of R. Elazar, namely: "You do not attain high office unless all your sins are forgiven," he made every effort [to obtain ordination]. When they ordained R. Zeira they sang, "Neither paint nor cosmetics not hair dye, yet beaming with charm" [a refrain of a chant in honor of the bride]. When R. Ammi and R. Assi were ordained the rabbis sang: "Men like these, yea, only men like these ordain for us. But ordain no distorters of Torah, no counterfeiters of Torah!" When R. Abbahu went from the yeshivah to the Emperor's palace, the ladies of the court would come out and sing: "Great man of his people! Leader of his nation! Radiant light! Welcome! Come in peace!"

MOSES CAST LOTS

(17a) The Rabbis taught: It says, "Two men [Eldad and Medad] remained in the camp" (Numbers 11:26). Some interpret this to mean that their ballots were left in the urn. [The Gemara explains:] For when the Holy One, blessed be He, said to Moses, "Gather to me seventy men from the elders of Israel" (ibid. v. 16), Moses said to himself: How shall I do it? Shall I appoint six from each [of the twelve] tribes, there will be two more than I need [seventy-two instead of seventy]; if I select five, [I will have sixty, and] I will be lacking ten. Now if I choose six from one tribe and five from another [taking six from each of ten tribes (sixty) and five from two tribes (ten), for a total of seventy,] I will cause jealousy among the tribes. [The two tribes will feel victimized.]

What did he do? He selected six men from each tribe and brought seventy-two strips of paper. On seventy he wrote the word *zaken*, "Elder," and two he left blank. He then mixed them up, put them into an urn, and said to the seventy-two people, "Draw your ballots." To each who drew a ballot with the word *zaken* he said, "Heaven has sanctified you." To those who drew a blank he said, "Heaven does not want you; what can I do?" [This is what happened: Eldad and Medad stayed behind and did not pick a ballot, for fear that they would draw a blank. Of the seventy that did pick a ballot two people drew blanks. When the verse says "there remained" it means: there remained in the urn the ballots of two men, who were meant to be chosen, namely, Eldad and Medad (Rashi).]

We find a similar situation [where Moses had no choice but to cast lots] in the following verse:[14] [When God chose the Levites to serve in the Tabernacle, He said to Moses,] "You shall take five shekels for each individual, according to the head count" (Numbers 3:47). Moses said to himself: How shall I handle this situation? If I say to a [firstborn], "Give me [the five shekels] for your redemption," he may answer, "A Levite has already redeemed me. [What makes you say that I am one of the 273 leftovers; maybe I am one of the 22,000 that were redeemed by the Levites!]" What did Moses do? He brought 22,000 strips of paper and wrote on each, "Levite," and on another 273 strips he wrote "five shekels." Then he mixed them up, placed them into an urn, and said to all the firstborns, "Draw your ballots!" To each who drew a strip marked "Levite" he said, "A Levite has redeemed you." To each who drew a strip marked "five shekels" he said, "Pay your redemption money and go!"

THE PROPHECY OF ELDAD
AND MEDAD

[The Gemara resumes the discussion of the verse, "Two men remained in the camp" (Numbers 11:26). According to one opinion Eldad and Medad's ballots remained in the urn.] R. Shimon said: [The passage means that] Eldad and Medad remained in the camp. For when the Holy One, blessed be He, told Moses, "Assemble seventy of Israel's elders" (ibid. v. 16), Eldad and Medad said, "We are not worthy of such a high appointment," [and that is why they remained in the camp]. So the Holy One, blessed be He, said, "Because you have humbled yourselves, I will add glory to your greatness." And what glory did God add to their greatness? The seventy elders prophesied [at that moment] but did not keep the spirit of prophecy, but Eldad and Medad prophesied and did not lose their prophetic inspiration. And what did they prophesy? They said, "Moses will die, and Joshua will bring Israel into the land."

Abba Chanin said in the name of R. Eliezer: They prophesied about the quail, [when, in response to the complaints of the children of Israel, God was about to send them quail],[15] they said, "Come up, quail! Come up, quail!" R. Nachman said: They prophesied regarding Gog and Magog. [The war before the final redemption will be fought against the kingdoms of Gog and Magog. Israel's victory will usher in the Messianic age.] For it says, "Thus said the Lord God: Are you the one of whom I spoke in earlier days, through My servants, the prophets of Israel, who prophesied in those days,

[shanim,] years [ago], that I would bring you against them? It shall be on that day that Gog comes against the soil of Israel" (Ezekiel 38:17). Do not read shanim, "years," but shenayim, "two" [meaning, two prophets who prophesied]. And which two prophets said the same prophecy at the same time? Eldad and Medad.

We learned before: The seventy elders prophesied [at that moment] but did not keep their spirit of prophecy; but Eldad and Medad prophesied and did keep their prophetic inspiration. From what verse do we infer that the others did not keep it? Do you think from the verse, "They prophesied velo yasafu [and they did not continue]" (Numbers 11:25)? If so, how do you explain the passage, "God spoke in a loud voice velo yassaf" (Deuteronomy 5:19)? Does that also mean "it did not continue"? [That cannot be; the voice of the Shechinah continues forever!] You must say, therefore, that velo yassaf means, "it did not stop" [hence you cannot infer from this verse that the elders' prophetic inspiration stopped]. But [how do we know that their prophecy stopped]? [The Gemara answers:] Here, [speaking of the seventy elders] it says, "And they prophesied" [in the past tense], whereas there [regarding Eldad and Medad] it says, "they were prophesying" (ibid. v. 27), which means that they continued to prophesy; [in other words, they did not stop].

[The Gemara asks:] According to the one who holds the view that they prophesied that Moses would die, we can understand that [upon hearing their prophecy] Joshua exclaimed, "My lord Moses, 'Stop them!'" (Numbers 11:28), but according to those who believe [that they prophesied about the quail or Gog and Magog, why did Joshua say, "My lord Moses, 'Stop them!'"? [The Gemara answers:] Because they did not act properly, for [in prophesying in front of Moses] they were like a student who decides halachic questions in the presence of his master.

[The Gemara asks:] According to the two opinions that hold that they prophesied about the quail or Gog and Magog we can understand that Moses said, "I only wish that all of God's people would have the gift of prophecy!", but according to the one who holds that they prophesied that Moses would die, [why would Moses utter such a wish]? Was he pleased with this prophecy? [The Gemara answers:] They did not complete their prophecy in his presence. [The Gemara asks: Joshua asked Moses to stop them from prophesying.] How was Moses going to stop them? [The Gemara answers:] Joshua said to Moses: Put them in charge of communal work, and they will stop prophesying by themselves; [communal work entails sorrow, grief, and bickering, and prophecy can be attained only in a spirit of happiness (Tosafot)].

TEN THINGS A CITY
MUST PROVIDE

(17b) A Torah scholar is not allowed to live in a city where the following ten things are not available: A Bet

Din that is empowered to administer lashes and impose penalties; a charity fund that is collected by two and distributed by three; a synagogue; a bathhouse; a public toilet; a *mohel*; a cupper;[16] a notary; a *shochet*; and a teacher of children. They said in the name of R. Akiva that a city also must have a variety of fruits, because eating fruit promotes good eyesight.

HIERARCHY OF LEADERS

(18a) Our Rabbis taught: [Jethro advised Moses:] "You must appoint them over the people as leaders of thousands, leaders of hundreds, leaders of fifties, and leaders of tens" (Exodus 18:21). The leaders of thousands numbered six hundred [because the people of Israel numbered 600,000]; those of hundreds, 6,000; those of fifties, 12,000; and those of tens, 60,000. Accordingly, the total number of judges in Israel was 78,600.

KING JANNAI AND
SHIMON B. SHETACH

(19a) [The Mishnah says]: The king may neither judge nor be judged. [The Gemara comments:] R. Yosef said: This applies only to the kings of Israel, but the kings of the House of David may judge and be judged, as it says, "O House of David, thus said God: Administer justice diligently" (Jeremiah 21:12); and if they may not be judged, how could they judge others? Surely it says, "Improve yourselves and improve each other" (Zephanaiah 2:1), which Resh Lakish interpreted to mean: First perfect yourself, and then perfect others, [therefore, if he can be a judge, he can judge others].

[The Gemara asks:] What is the reason that the Kings of Israel may neither judge nor be judged? [The Gemara answers:] Because of an incident that happened. A slave of King Jannai [of the Hasmonean royal dynasty] killed a man. Shimon b. Shetach [the leading sage of the period and a brother of the queen] said to the Sages, "Let us look King Jannai straight in the eye, and let us judge him." So they sent a message to the king, stating, "Your slave has killed a man." Thereupon he sent the slave to them to stand trial. But they sent him another message, "You, too, must come here, for the Torah says, 'If the owner was warned [that his ox was in the habit of goring, but did not take precautions . . .]" (Exodus 21:29), which means that the owner of the ox must come and stand by his ox, [and the same applies to a slave that killed a man].

Following suit, the king came and sat down. "Stand up, King Jannai," said Shimon b. Shetach, "and let the witnesses testify against you; but you should know that it is not before us that you stand up, but before Him who spoke and the world came into being, as it says, "The two men who have the dispute shall stand before God" (Deuteronomy 19:17). King Jannai replied, "I will not rise just because you say so, but if all your colleagues, [the members of the Sanhedrin] decide that I have to rise, then I will rise."

(19b) Shimon b. Shetach turned to his right and then to his left, but they all looked down [and did not say anything, afraid to express their opinion]. Shimon b. Shetach said to them [sarcastically], "You seem to be absorbed in deep thoughts! May the Master of all thoughts [God] come and punish you." That instant Gabriel came and struck them to the ground, and they died. It was then that the Sages decreed: A king [who is not of the House of David][17] may neither act as judge nor be judged; he may neither testify as a witness, nor be testified against.

HOW COULD DAVID
MARRY TWO SISTERS?

[The Gemara said that David married Merav and Michal, both daughters of Saul.] The disciples of R. Yose asked him: How could David marry two sisters while they were both living?[18] R. Yose answered: He married Michal after the death of [her sister] Merav. R. Yehoshua b. Korcha said: His marriage to Merav was an error, [and therefore invalid. Hence he was allowed to marry her sister Michal]. For it says, [David sent a message,] "Give me my wife Michal, whom I married to myself with one hundred foreskins of the Philistines" (2 Samuel 3:14), [referring to the killing of Goliath]. [The Gemara asks:] How do you infer from this verse [that the marriage to Merav was an error]? R. Papa answered: Because David said, "my wife Michal" but not "my wife Merav." Why was his marriage to Merav an error? Because it says, "The king [Saul] will enrich whoever kills [Goliath] with great wealth and give him his daughter [in marriage]" (1 Samuel 17:25).

Now David went and killed Goliath, [and when he expected to marry Merav,] Saul said to him: I owe you a debt [of money, and with that debt you betrothed Merav,] but if a person betroths a woman with a debt, she is not betrothed [because he is not really giving her anything]. So Saul went and gave Merav as a wife to Adriel, as it says, "But it happened that when the time came to give Merav daughter of Saul to David, she was given instead to Adriel the Mecholatite as a wife" (1 Samuel 18:19). Then Saul said to David, "If you still want me to give you Michal as a wife, go and bring me another hundred foreskins of the Philistines." David went and brought them to him, [and he betrothed Michal with the hundred foreskins]. Saul then said, "I now owe you the repayment of a loan [the riches I promised you for killing Goliath], and a *perutah* [a small coin, the estimated value of the foreskins. So it is as if you betrothed Michal with the loan and a *perutah*].

Now Saul held that when a person betroths a woman with a loan and a *perutah* he mainly has in mind the loan [and therefore she would not be betrothed, as mentioned above]. But David thought that when someone betroths with a loan and a *perutah*, he primarily has in mind the *perutah*, [consequently the betrothal is valid]. Or, if you prefer, say: all agree that where a loan and a *perutah* are offered, the thoughts are on the *perutah*. But Saul believed that the hundred foreskins had no value [thus there was no *perutah* and, therefore, no betrothal]; while David thought that the foreskins could be used as food for dogs and cats [and were worth at least a *perutah*, and the betrothal was valid].

[The Gemara asks:] R. Yose [who holds that both Merav and Michal were legally married to David, and that he married Michal after Merav's death], how does he interpret the verse, "Give me my wife Michal" [which seems to imply that only Michal—and not Merav—was his wife]? [The Gemara answers:] R. Yose follows his own line of thinking. For we learned in a *Baraita*: R. Yose used to interpret the following confused passages: It says, "So the king took the two sons of Ritzpah daughter of Aiah, whom she bore to Saul—Armoni and Mefiboshet—and the five sons of Michal daughter of Saul, whom she bore to Adriel son Barzilai the Mecholatite" (2 Samuel 21:8). But was Michal really given to Adriel; was she not given to Palti son of Layish, as it says, "Saul had given his daughter Michal, David's wife, to Palti son of Layish" (1 Samuel 25:44)? [Why does it say that Michal bore five sons to Adriel?] But Scripture compares the marriage of Merav to Adriel to that of Michal to Palti, to teach you that just as the marriage of Michal to Palti was illegal [since she was already married to David], so was the marriage of Merav to Adriel illegal [because she too was married to David]. [R. Yose expounds the phrase, "Give me my wife Michal," not to exclude Merav, but to imply that just as Michal was legally David's wife, so was Merav.]

[The Gemara asks:] But R. Yehoshua b. Korcha [who holds that Merav's marriage to Adriel was valid]. What does he do with the verse, "And the five sons of Michal daughter of Saul whom she bore to Adriel" [which we interpreted to mean that the marriage of Adriel and Merav was just as illegal as that of Palti to Michal, because both women were married to David]? R. Yehoshua b. Korcha will answer you: Michal did not really give birth to them. Merav was the one who gave birth to them. [Then why does it say that Michal gave birth to them?] Merav gave birth to them, and Michal brought them up; that is why they were called by her name. This teaches you that whoever brings up an orphan in his home, the Torah considers it as if he had fathered him.

RAISING AN ORPHAN IS LIKE GIVING BIRTH TO HIM

R. Chanina said: We derive this from the following verse, [When Ruth gave birth to a child,] "The neighborhood women gave him a name, saying, 'A son is born to Naomi'" (Ruth 4:17). Did then Naomi give birth to

him? Surely it was Ruth who gave birth to him! But Ruth gave birth to him, and Naomi brought him up; therefore the child was called after Naomi's name.

R. Yochanan says we derive it from the following verse, "While his Jewish wife [i.e., Bitiah, Pharaoh's daughter] gave birth to [the names that follow all refer to Moses,] Jered, the father of Gedor; and Chever, the father of Socho; and Yekutiel, the father of Zano'ach. These are the sons of Bitiah the daughter of Pharaoh, whom Mered married" (1 Chronicles 4:18). Mered was Caleb, and why was he called Mered? [*Mered* means "to rebel."] Because he rebelled against the counsel of the other spies.[19] But did Bitiah give birth to Moses? Surely Yocheved gave birth to him! True, Yocheved gave birth to him, but Bitiah raised him.[20] That is why he was called after her.

R. Elazar says we derive it from the following verse: "With Your powerful arm You redeemed Your nation, the sons of Jacob and Joseph, Selah" (Psalms 87:16). Were they then born to Joseph? Weren't they born to Jacob? The text means to say that they were born to Jacob but Joseph sustained them; that's why they were named after him.

R. Shmuel b. Nachmani said in R. Yonatan's name: Anyone that teaches Torah to his neighbor's son, the Torah considers it as if he had fathered him, for it says, "These are the children of Aaron and Moses" (Numbers 3:1), and the following verse reads, "These are the names of Aaron's sons," [and the children of Moses are not mentioned,] to teach you that Aaron fathered his sons, but Moses taught them; that is why they are called by his name.

It says, "Therefore, thus said God to the House of Jacob who redeemed Abraham" (Isaiah 29:22). Where do we find that Jacob redeemed Abraham? Rav Yehudah answered: It means that Jacob redeemed Abraham from the suffering that goes with raising children. [Abraham really should have had many children,[21] but this came true in Jacob.] In reference to this it says, "Jacob will not be ashamed now, and his face will not pale now" (ibid.). "He will not be ashamed" of his father; "and his face will not pale now" because of his grandfather, [whom he saved the trouble of raising children].

THEY SUBDUED THEIR PASSION

(20a) R. Yochanan said: What is meant by the verse, "Many women have amassed achievement, but you surpassed them all" (Proverbs 31:29)? "Many women" alludes to Joseph and Boaz [who overcame their passion in the face of strong temptation]; "But you surpassed them all" refers to Palti ben Layish [the husband of David's undivorced wife Michal, who was faced with an even stronger temptation, yet he abstained from having marital relations with her].

R. Shmuel b. Nachmani said in R. Yonatan's name: What is meant by the verse, "Grace is false and beauty vain, a woman who fears God she should be praised" (ibid. v. 30)? "Grace is false" refers to [the temptation] of Joseph; "and beauty vain" refers to Boaz; "who fears God should be praised" refers to the [restraint shown by] Palti ben Layish; [he endured the most difficult test of all].

Another interpretation: "Grace is false" refers to the generation of Moses [they studied Torah fairly well]; "and beauty vain" refers to the generation of Joshua [their Torah study was adequate]; "fear of God should be praised" refers to the generation of Hezekiah [when Torah study reached a peak and was learned more intensely than in the days of Moses and Joshua]. Another interpretation: "Grace is false" refers to the generation of Moses and Joshua, "and beauty vain" to the generation of Hezekiah [when Torah study was at a passable level], while "fear of God should be praised" refers to the generation of R. Yehudah b. R. Ila'i. For in his time [poverty prevailed] to such a point that six of his students had only one garment to cover themselves, and still they avidly studied Torah.

ABNER'S DEATH

Our Rabbis taught: Wherever the custom is for women to follow the coffin, they may do so, and where it is customary for them to walk in front of the coffin, they may do that too. R. Yehudah said: Women should always walk in front of the coffin, for we find that David followed behind the coffin of Abner, as it says, "King David himself walked behind the bier" (2 Samuel 3:31), [and if the women had followed behind the bier, David would not have walked there]. The Rabbis said to R. Yehudah: David went to that funeral only to pacify the people, and they were indeed appeased. For David went back and forth from the men to the women, and from the women to the men, [to show everyone that he attended the funeral,] for it says, "All the people and all of Israel realized on that day that it was not ordered by the king to kill Abner the son of Ner" (2 Samuel 3:37). [So the fact that David walked behind the coffin does not prove that it was customary for the women to walk in front of the coffin.]

Rava expounded: What is meant by the verse, "All the people came to [comfort] David by bringing him a meal [lehavrot]" (ibid. v. 35)? The word is written lehachrot[22] [to destroy him], but we read it lehavrot. At first they came to destroy him [because they suspected him of arranging Abner's death,] but after [they realized that he was not involved in it] they brought him the mourner's meal.

R. Yehudah said in the name of Rav: Why was Abner punished? [What sin did he commit?]—Because he should have protested to Saul [and, being an influential public figure, he could have prevented the killing of the kohanim of the city of Nob],[23] but he did not. R. Yitzchak however said: He did protest, but

nobody paid attention to him. And both infer their opinions from the same verse, namely, "The king lamented a dirge for Abner, and said, 'Should Abner have died the death of a knave? Your hands were not bound and your feet were not placed in chains'" (2 Samuel 3:33). The one who says that he did not protest, interprets it like this: "Your hands were not bound and your feet were not placed in chains," so why did you not protest against Saul? Therefore, "as one who falls before villains have you fallen" (ibid.)

The other, who holds that Abner did protest but was not listened to, interprets it as an expression of David's bewilderment: "Should Abner have died the death of a knave?" Since you did protest to Saul, "Why did you fall like one who falls before villains?" [The Gemara asks:] According to the one who holds that Abner did protest, why was he punished? R. Nachman b. Yitzchak says: Because he delayed the crowning of David by two and a half years. [Abner made Saul's son, Ishboshet king over Israel. If not for that, David would have been crowned two and a half years earlier.]

APPOINTING A KING

(20b) R. Yose said: Whatever was set forth in the chapter concerning the king,[24] a king is permitted to do, [i.e., take away your sons to work and fight in his army, take away your daughters to serve as cooks and bakers, confiscate your fields . . .]. R. Yehudah said: [Samuel] stated that portion only in order to inspire the people with awe, [but the king is not really allowed to do these things], for it says, "You shall surely set over yourself a king" (Deuteronomy 17:15), meaning that you should be in awe of him. [We find another difference of opininion in this regard:] R. Yehudah said: Three mitzvot were given to Israel when they entered Eretz Yisrael: (1) to appoint a king (ibid.); (2) to wipe out the seed of Amalek (ibid. 25:19); and (3) to build the Bet Hamikdash, [the three mitzvot to be fulfilled in that order]. R. Nehorai said: The section [about appointing a king was not meant as a mitzvah]; it was said only because God foresaw that Israel eventually would demand a king, as it says, "You will eventually say, 'We would like to appoint a king'" (ibid. 17:14).

We learned in a Baraita: R. Eliezer said: The elders of the generation [of Samuel who demanded a king] made a proper request, for it says, [they said,] "Give us a king to judge us" (1 Samuel 8:6). But the common people among them spoiled it, for it says, "They said, 'We will be like the other nations; our king will judge us and will go forth before us'" (ibid. v. 20). [The elders wanted a king who would administer justice, whereas the common people demanded a king to lead them in battle.]

We learned in a Baraita: R. Yehudah said: Three mitzvot were given to Israel when they entered Eretz Yisrael: (1) to appoint a king; (2) to wipe out the seed of Amalek; and (3) to build the *Bet Hamikdash*; and we do not know which of them comes first. But when it says, "For the hand is on the throne of God; God maintains a war against Amalek, from generation to generation" (Exodus 17:16), that tells us that first they had to appoint a king; because "throne" represents a king, as it says, "Solomon sat upon the throne of God as king" (1 Chronicles 29:23). But I still do not know which of the other two comes first, the destruction of the progeny of Amalek or the building of the *Bet Hamikdash*.

Therefore, when it says, "When He has granted you safety from all your enemies around you," followed by, "There will be a site that God will choose as the place dedicated to His name" (Deuteronomy 12:10,11), [safety from all enemies before erecting the Temple], that tells us that destroying the seed of Amalek has priority. And that is what it says about David, "It happened after the king was settled into his home, and God had given him respite from his enemies all around," and the text continues, "that the king said to Nathan the prophet, 'See now, I am living in a house of cedar while the Ark of God dwells within the curtain [and has no dwelling place]!" (2 Samuel 7:1,2). [After defeating his enemies David wanted to build the *Bet Hamikdash*.]

SOLOMON'S SHRINKING REIGN

[Having mentioned the throne of Solomon, the Gemara begins a discussion of his reign.] Resh Lakish said: At first, Solomon reigned over the higher [spiritual] beings, for it says, "Solomon sat upon the throne of God as king" (1 Chronicles 29:23); afterward [when he sinned] he reigned only over the lower beings, as it says, "For he ruled over the entire area beyond the [Euphrates] River, from Tifsach to Gaza" (1 Kings 5:4), [over the lower world, but not over the higher beings]. Rav and Shmuel differ about the interpretation of this passage. According to one, Tifsach was situated at one end of the world and Gaza at the other. According to the other, Tifsach and Gaza were two adjacent towns, and the verse means that, just as he reigned over these, so did he reign over the whole world. Later on, he ruled only over Israel, for it says, "I, Kohelet, was king over Israel in Jerusalem" (Ecclesiastes 1:12).

Subsequently, his reign shrank to Jerusalem only, as it says, "The words of Kohelet, son of David, king in Jerusalem" (ibid. v. 1). And later yet, he reigned only over his couch, as it says, "Here is Solomon's couch," (Song of Songs 3:8); [the couch is the only thing that is his]. And ultimately, he reigned only over his staff, as it says, "This was my reward for all my endeavors" (Ecclesiastes 2:10). Rav and Shmuel [differ about this]: One says: His staff [was all he had left]; the other: His robe.[25]

[The Gemara asks:] Did Solomon regain his power [after Ashmedai removed him from office,] or not? Rav

and Shmuel [differ about this:] One holds that he did; the other, that he did not. The one who holds that he did not, agrees with the opinion in the Gemara that Solomon first was a king, then became an ordinary person, [and did not return to power]. The one who holds that he did, agrees with the opinion that he first was king, then deposed, and finally reinstated as king.

DAVID'S WIVES

(21a) [We learned in the Mishnah:] The king should not marry more than eighteen wives. [The Gemara asks:] From where do we know this? [The Gemara answers:] From the verse, "Sons were born to David in Hebron: his firstborn was Amnon, [born] to Achinoam of Jezreel; his second son was Chileab, [born] to Abigail, the [former] wife of Nabal the Carmelite; the third was Absalom, the son of Maachah, daughter of Talmai, king of Geshur; the fourth was Adonijah, the son of Chagit; the fifth was Shefatiah, the son of Avital; the sixth was Yitre'am [born] to Eglah, David's [main] wife. These were born to David in Hebron" (2 Samuel 3:2–5); [thus David had six wives]. And the prophet said to David later on [after the episode with Bathsheba], "And if this were not enough I would have increased for you this much [*kaheinah*] and this much again [*vechaheinah*]" (ibid. 12:8); each *kaheinah* alluding to six wives, [and he had six wives already], which gives us a total of eighteen.

[The Gemara asks:] [You say David had six wives?] But what about Michal, the daughter of Saul, [and she is not mentioned among the six]? Rav said: Eglah is another name for Michal. And why was she called Eglah? Because she was loved by him like a calf [*eglah*] by its mother. And the same metaphor is used in the following verse, [Samson said to the Philistines after Delilah told them the answer to the riddle,] "Had you not plowed with my calf [Delilah], you would not have solved my riddle" (Judges 14:18). [The Gemara asks:] But did Michal have children? Doesn't it say, "Michal, daughter of Saul had no child until the day of her death" (2 Samuel 6:23), [yet the verse says Yitre'am was born to Eglah/Michal]. R. Chisda said: She had no child *until* the day of her death, but on the day of her death she did; [she died in childbirth].

[The Gemara asks: But concerning the eighteen wives a king is allowed to have,] doesn't it say, "David took additional concubines and wives from Jerusalem" (ibid. 5:13), [so he did have more than eighteen]? [The Gemara answers:] To make up the eighteen. [The Gemara asks:] What are wives and what are concubines? R. Yehudah said in Rav's name: Wives have a *ketubah* and *kiddushin* [a marriage contract and a legal marriage]; concubines have neither. R. Yehudah further said in Rav's name: David had four hundred children, and all were children of "beautiful women captives";[26] they wore long hair, and rode around in golden carriages. They all were high-ranking military officers, and were men of power in the House of David.

AMNON AND TAMAR

R. Yehudah said also in the name of Rav: Tamar [a daughter of David and a sister of Absalom and Amnon] was the daughter of a "beautiful woman captive." For it says, [Tamar said to Amnon who desired her,] "So now, speak to the king, for he would not withhold me from you in marriage" (2 Samuel 13:13). Now, if you should think that Tamar was the daughter of a married wife, how would David allow Amnon to marry his sister? We must infer therefore that Tamar was the daughter of a "beautiful woman captive," [and her mother Maachah gave birth to her before she converted. Since a child follows the status of the mother, Tamar was considered neither Jewish nor a daughter of David, nor a sister of Amnon (Rashi)].

"Amnon had a friend named Jonadab, the son of David's brother Shim'ah, and Jonadab was a very cunning man" (ibid. v. 3). R. Yehudah said in the name of Rav: He was cunning to do evil, [for he advised Amnon on how to seduce Tamar].

(21b) "Adonijah son of Chagit exalted himself saying, 'I will be king!'" R. Yehudah said in the name of Rav: This teaches us that he tried to fit the crown on his head but it would not fit, [and only a person whom the crown fits is qualified to become king]. "He provided himself with chariot and riders and fifty men to run before him" (ibid.). [The Gemara asks:] What is so special about [fifty men escorting a prince]? R. Yehudah said in Rav's name: They all had their spleens removed and the flesh of their soles cut off [to enable them to run faster].

KING SOLOMON

Rav Yehudah pointed out a contradiction: It says, "Solomon had forty thousand stables of horses for his chariots" (1 Kings 5:6). And in another verse it says, "Solomon had four thousand stables of horses and chariots" (2 Chronicles 9:25). How do we reconcile this contradiction? [The answer is that one verse refers to stables and the other to the horse stalls in the stables. And it could be either way.] If we say that he had forty thousand stables, each had four thousand stalls; and if we say that he had four thousand stables, each of them had forty thousand stalls.

R. Yitzchak pointed out the following contradiction: It says, "Silver was not considered of any worth in the days of Solomon" (1 Kings 10:21). But then it says, "King Solomon made silver in Jerusalem [as common] as stones" (ibid. v. 27) [so it did have some value]. This is no difficulty. The first verse [where silver was worthless] refers to the time before Solomon married the daughter of Pharaoh; the second verse [where silver had some value] refers to the time after he married

her [which was a wrongful act; therefore the prosperity dwindled and silver attained some value].

R. Yitzchak said: When Solomon married Pharaoh's daughter, the angel Gabriel came down and stuck a reed into the sea, and it gathered a sand bank around it on which the great city of Rome was built. [His sinful conduct lay the groundwork for the destruction of the *Bet Hamikdash* by Rome.]

R. Yitzchak said furthermore: Why doesn't the Torah give the reason for all the *mitzvot*? Because the reasons for two laws were revealed, and the great man of the world [Solomon] stumbled over them. It says, "[The king] should not have many wives, [and the Torah gives the reason,] so that they not make his heart go astray" (Deuteronomy 17:17). And King Solomon said: I will take many wives, and I will not let my heart go astray. Yet we read, "So it was when Solomon grew old his wives swayed his heart after the gods of others" (1 Kings 11:4). It also says, "[The king] should not accumulate many horses, [the reason being,] so as not to bring the people back to Egypt to get more horses" ((Deuteronomy 17:16). And Solomon said: I will accumulate many horses, and I will not cause [Israel] to return to Egypt." Yet we read, "A chariot could be brought out of Egypt for six hundred pieces of silver" (1 Kings 10:29).

THE KING'S TORAH SCROLLS

[The Mishnah said:] A king has to write a Torah scroll for himself. When he goes to war, he must take it with him; when he returns, he must bring it back with him. When he sits in judgment, it must be with him. When he sits down to eat, it should be in front of him, for it says, "It shall be with him, and he shall read from it all the days of his life" (Deuteronomy 17:19).

[The Gemara notes:] Rabbah said: Even if a person inherits a Torah scroll from his ancestors, it is a mitzvah for him to write one of his own, for it says, "Now write for yourselves this song" (ibid. 31:19), [and "song" refers to the Torah]. Abaye raised an objection: [It says in our Mishnah:] "A king has to write a Torah scroll for himself," and cannot fulfill the mitzvah with a *sefer Torah* he receives from someone else. The implication is that only a king is required to write a Torah, but not an ordinary person. [Consequently, if an ordinary person inherits a *sefer Torah*, he has fulfilled the mitzvah. Yet Rabbah said that even an ordinary person must write his own?] [The Gemara answers:] No. [Even an ordinary person should write one himself,] but the Mishnah teaches us that a king has to write two Torah scrolls, as we learned in the following *Baraita*: It says, "He must write the repetition of this Torah" (Deuteronomy 17:18), meaning, he should write for himself two copies; one that he must carry with him wherever he goes and one that remains in his treasury. The one he carries with him he should write in the form of an amulet [i.e., in miniature], and attach it to his arm, as it says, "I have set God before me always, because He is at my right hand I shall not falter" (Psalms 16:8). While he is wearing this Torah scroll he may not enter the bathhouse or the toilet, for it says, "This scroll must always be with him, and he shall read from it" (Deuteronomy 17:19)—in those places where it is appropriate to read it.

THE LANGUAGE AND WRITING SYSTEM OF THE TORAH

Mar Zutra, some say Mar Ukva, said: Originally the Torah was given to Israel in [the ancient] Hebrew script [which is different from our contemporary Hebrew script] and in *Leshon Hakodesh* [the holy Hebrew language]. Later, in the time of Ezra, the Torah was given in *Ashurit* writing [the square Hebrew characters of our *sefer Torah*] and the Aramaic language. In the end, the Jews chose for themselves the *Ashurit* script and the holy Hebrew language, and left for the *hedyotot* the [ancient] Hebrew script and the Aramaic language.

[The Gemara asks:] Who are the *hedyotot*? R. Chisda said: The Kutim [i.e., Samaritans]. And what is meant by [ancient] Hebrew script? R. Chisda said: The *libuna'ah* characters [large letters, like those used in amulets (Rashi)].

We learned in a *Baraita*: R. Yose said: If Moses had not lived before Ezra, Ezra would have been worthy to receive the Torah for Israel. It says about Moses, "Moses went up to God" (Exodus 19:3), and it says about Ezra, "He, Ezra went up from Babylonia" (Ezra 7:6). [We compare the two, and we say:] Just as the going up of Moses was to receive the Torah, so was the going up of Ezra for the sake of Torah, [meaning, he could have received the Torah]. [We note another parallel between Moses and Ezra,] for regarding Moses it says, "At that time, God commanded me to teach you rules and laws" (Deuteronomy 4:14), and regarding Ezra it says, "For Ezra set his heart to expound the Torah of God and to fulfill and to teach its statute and law in Israel" (Ezra 7:10).

And even though the Torah was not given through him, the writing was changed through him, [which is an element in the giving of the Torah,] for it says, **(22a)** [concerning a letter that was written in the time of Ezra,] "The text of the letter was written in Aramaic script and translated into Aramaic" (Ezra 4:7). And it says also, [in reference to the writing that appeared on the wall at King Belshazzar's banquet,] "They could not read the writing and make its interpretation known to the king" (Daniel 5:8).[27] And another verse says, "[The king] must write a copy [*mishneh*] of this Torah" (Deuteronomy 17:18)—in a script that eventually will be changed [in the days of Ezra; *mishneh* is derived from *shanah*, which means "to repeat" and "to change"]. [The Gemara asks]: Why is the writing [we now have] called *Ashurit*? [The Gemara answers:] Because it came with them from *Ashur* [Assyria].

We learned in a *Baraita*: Rebbi said: Originally the Torah was given to Israel in this [*Ashurit*] writing. When they sinned it was forgotten [and changed to a different writing], but when they repented [in the days of Ezra], the *Ashurit* characters were restored to them. For it says, "Return to the fortress [the *Bet Hamikdash* in Jerusalem], you prisoners of hope! Today, too, I am telling you, 'I will bring back the Mishnah'" (Zechariah 9:12). [I will restore the writing that was changed (*shanah*).] And why then is it called *Ashurit*, [since Rabbi believes that it was the original writing and did not come with them from *Ashur* (Assyria)]? Because it is the best of all writing systems.

R. Shimon b. Elazar said in the name of R. Eliezer b. Parta, who quoted R. Elazar Hamoda'i: The writing of the Torah was never changed, for it says, "The *vavei* [hooks] of the pillars" (Exodus 27:10). Just as the word "pillars" never changed, neither did the *vavim*. [The word *vav* meant "hook" when the Torah was given. It is also the sixth letter of the *alef bet* and is shaped like a hook, which proves that the script never changed.] It says furthermore, [Mordechai wrote letters] "to the Jews in their own script and language" (Esther 8:9)—just as their language had not changed, neither had their script. [The Gemara asks:] But according to that, how do we interpret the words, "He shall write for himself *mishneh* [a copy] of this Torah" (Deuteronomy 17:18) [which was expounded to mean: "in a script that eventually will be changed"]?

[The Gemara answers: The word *mishneh* comes] to tell us that the king has to write two Torah scrolls [*mishneh* means "repetition," "double," and "change"]; one to carry with him wherever he goes, the other to remain in his treasury. The one that he carries with him should be written like an amulet [in miniature] and attached to his arm, as it says, "I have set God before me always; because He is at my right hand I shall not falter" (Psalms 16:8). [The Gemara asks:] But the other [who derives from the words *mishneh Torah* that the *Torah* script *was* changed, and thus we have no text to teach us that the king must have two Torah scrolls; hence he did not have a scroll to carry with him], how does he interpret the verse, "I have set God before me always"? He expounds it like R. Chanah b. Bizna who said in the name of R. Shimon Chasida: When praying you should imagine that you are facing the *Shechinah*, as it says, "I have set God before me always."

THE HEARTBREAK OF DIVORCE

R. Shaman b. Abba said: Come and see how painful it is to divorce. [The Sages] permitted King David to have *yichud* [private meetings with a woman; in David's case, with Avishag, his attendant],[28] but he was not permitted to divorce [one of his eighteen wives, which would have enabled him to marry her].

R. Elazar said: Anyone that divorces his first wife, even the altar sheds tears because of him, for it says,

"And this is the second sin that you commit: covering the altar of God with tears, crying and moaning, so that He will no longer turn to your offering, or take it with favor from your hand" (Malachi 2:13). And immediately after that it says, "You say, 'Why is this?' It is because God has testified between you and the wife of your youth whom you have betrayed, though she is your companion and the wife of your covenant" (ibid. v. 14).

GRIEVING FOR THE LOSS OF A SPOUSE

R. Yochanan, others say, R. Elazar said: The death of a man's wife can be attributed to his failure to pay his debts. For it says, "If you have no money to pay, why should he take your bedding from beneath you?" (Proverbs 22:27). R. Yochanan further said: A person whose first wife has died, is as despondent as if the *Bet Hamikdash* had been destroyed in his days, for it says, "Son of man, behold, I am taking from you the darling of your eyes in a plague. You shall not lament and you shall not weep, and your tears shall not come forth" (Ezekiel 24:16–18). And it says, "I told this to the people in the morning. In the evening, my wife died" (ibid.). And then it says, "Behold, I am profaning My Sanctuary, the pride of your strength, the darling of your eyes" (ibid. v. 21); [the death of his wife is juxtaposed with the profaning of the Sanctuary].

R. Alexandri said: For a man whose wife has died during his lifetime the world is steeped in darkness, for it says, "Light becomes darkness in his tent; his lamp will flicker out in his presence" (Job 18:6), ["tent" is a symbol for wife]. R. Yose b. Chanina said: His steps become short, for it says, "His powerful strides will be constrained" (ibid. v. 7). R. Abbahu said: His astuteness fails, as it says, "His counsel will overthrow him" (ibid.).

Rabbah b. Bar Chanah said in R. Yochanan's name: Joining couples is as difficult as the splitting of the Red Sea, as it says, "God settles the solitary into a family, He releases those bound in fetters" (Psalms 68:7). [It is as difficult to make a match between two single individuals as to release the children of Israel from Egypt.]

Do not read *motzi asirim*, "releasing those bound," but *kemotzi asirim*, "like releasing those bound;" and do not read *bakosharot*, "in fetters," but *bechi veshirot*, "weeping and singing"; [the Egyptians were weeping, while the Israelites were singing" (*Maharsha*)]. Is it really that difficult? Did not Rav Yehudah say in Rav's name: Forty days before the embryo is formed, a heavenly voice goes forth and says: The daughter of so-and-so for so-and-so? [Since matches are preordained, why is making a match difficult?] This is no difficulty: the latter applies to the first marriage; the first statement to the second marriage.

R. Shmuel b. Nachman said: Everything can be replaced, except the wife of one's youth, as it says, "A

wife of one's youth, can she be despised?" (Isaiah 54:6). Rav Yehudah taught his son R. Yitzchak: A person finds delight only with his first wife, as it says, "Your source will be blessed, and you will rejoice with the wife (22b) of your youth" (Proverbs 5:18). "Like who, for example," his son R. Yitzchak asked. "A woman like your mother," Rav Yehudah replied. [The Gemara asks:] Is that so? Didn't Rav Yehudah teach his son R. Yitzchak the verse, "And I have discovered more bitter than death: the woman who is snares, whose heart is nets, whose arms are chains" (Ecclesiastes 7:26), and his son asked him, "What woman is like that, for example?" He answered, "One like your mother." [So we see that he did not love her that much.] [The Gemara answers:] True, she was a quick-tempered woman, but she was easily placated with kind words.

R. Shmuel b. Unya said in the name of Rav: [Before she is married] a woman is an unfinished vessel, and she makes a covenant only with the person that makes her into a finished vessel [i.e., the person that has the first relations with her]. For it says, "For your husband is your maker; the Lord of Hosts is His name" (Isaiah 54:5).

We learned: The death of a man is felt by no one as keenly as by his wife, as it says, "Elimelech, Naomi's husband, died" (Ruth 1:3). [Naomi is mentioned in conjunction with Elimelech's death to convey this thought.] And the death of a woman by no one as keenly as her husband, for it says, [Jacob said,] "But as for me,—when I came from Paddan, Rachel died on me" (Genesis 48:7).

THEY SOUGHT GOOD COMPANY

(23a) We learned in a *Baraita*: This is what the prudent people of Jerusalem used to do: They would not sign their name [as a witness] to a document without knowing who would sign with them, [for if one of the witnesses is disqualified, all are disqualified, which would be a source of embarrassment]; they would not sit in judgment unless they knew who were to be their colleagues on the bench; and they would not go to a banquet unless they knew who would be seated at their table.

SCHOLARS OF ERETZ YISRAEL AND BABYLONIA

(24a) R. Oshaia said: What is meant by the verse, "I took for myself two staffs—one I called 'Noam' [Pleasantness] and the other I called 'Chovelim' [Destroyers]" (Zechariah 11:7)? *Noam* refers to the Torah scholars of Eretz Yisrael, who treat each other kindly when engaged in halachic debate; *Chovelim* refers to the Torah scholars of Babylonia who hurt each other's feelings when discussing *halachah*. [They are more aggressive when refuting a colleague's arguments.]

It says, "He said, 'These are the two anointed men [*yitzhar*] who are standing by the Lord of all the land'" (ibid. 4:14). [Earlier it says,] "There are two olive trees over it" (ibid. v. 3). R. Yitzchak said: *Yitzhar* [pure oil] applies to the Torah scholars of Eretz Yisrael who are gentle to each other when engaged in halachic debate, like olive oil; whereas "two olive trees over it" applies to the Torah scholars of Babylonia who are as bitter to each other in halachic discussions as an olive tree [whose wood has a pungent taste].

HYPOCRISY AND ARROGANCE

It says, "Then I raised my eyes and looked, and behold two women were emerging with wind in their wings, for they had wings like a stork's wings, and they lifted the *ephah* between the earth and the heavens. I said to the angel who was speaking to me, 'Where are they taking the *ephah*?" He said to me, 'To build her a house in the land of Shinar'"[29] (Zechariah 9:5–11). R. Yochanan said in the name of R. Shimon b. Yochai: The two women personify the hypocrisy and arrogance that are rampant in Babylonia. [The Gemara asks:] Is it true that arrogance is common in Babylonia? Didn't we learn: Ten measures of arrogance came down on the world, of which Elam took nine and the rest of the world one? [The Gemara answers:] Yes, originally it came down on Babylonia, but it was dragged to Elam. This is also borne out by a precise reading of the text, for it says, "to build her a house in the land of Shinar [i.e., Babylonia]"; [only one built a house, proof that the other did not settle there].

[The Gemara asks:] But isn't arrogance widespread in Babylonia, too? Didn't we learn: "The sign of arrogance is poverty"; and poverty surely is sweeping Babylonia! [Thus there must be a great deal of arrogance there.] [The Gemara answers:] The poverty mentioned here [as an indication of haughtiness] refers to poverty of Torah learning, [and Elam is known for that,] for it says, "We have a little sister, and she has no breasts" (Songs of Songs 8:8), to which R. Yochanan commented: This alludes to Elam whose students had the advantage of learning Torah but did not teach others.

[The Gemara asks:] What is the significance of the name *Babel*, [which means "mixture"]?[30] R. Yochanan replied: [That the Talmud] is a blend of Torah, Mishnah, and Gemara. [The Gemara continues:] It says, "He has placed me in darkness like the eternally dead" (Lamentations 3:6). R. Yirmeyah said: This refers to the Babylonian Talmud, [which has sustained us and kept us spiritually alive during the darkness of the long *galut*].

THE KINDHEARTED
TAX COLLECTOR

Rav Yehudah said: A shepherd [of whom it is not known whether he leads his flock into strange pastures] is ineligible [to be a witness or a judge], whereas a tax collector, unless he is known to be dishonest, is eligible. The father of R. Zeira was a tax collector for thirteen years, and when the district governor would come to a town, if [R. Zeira] saw the rabbis of the town, he would tell them, "Go my people, enter your rooms" (Isaiah 26:20); [i.e., stay indoors, otherwise the governor will think that the city is heavily populated and will impose high taxes]. When [R. Zeira] saw crowds of people in the street, he would tell them, "The governor is coming to town, and [if he sees you,] he will slaughter the father in front of the son, and the son in front of the father, [meaning, he will charge exorbitant taxes], (26a) whereupon they all went into hiding. And when the governor came, [and wanted R. Zeira to collect an excessive amount of taxes,] he used to say, "From whom can I collect so much tax? [You see, the town's population is very small]." Before he died he said: Take the thirteen *ma'ah* that are tied in my sheets and return them to so-and-so, for I took them [as tax] and do not need them.

CONFRONTATION OF RESH
LAKISH AND TWO RABBIS

(26a) R. Chiya b. Zarnuki and R. Shimon b. Yehotzadak went to Assia to declare that the current year should have an extra month. As they were going they met Resh Lakish who joined them, saying, "I will come along and see how they do it." On the way they passed a man who was ploughing. [It happened to be a Sabbatical year when farm work is forbidden.] Resh Lakish told the two Rabbis, "That person ploughing must be a *kohen*," [because *kohanim* were suspected of not observing the laws of *shemittah*].[31] [Trying to find an excuse for the man,] the Rabbis said, "He may say, 'I am only a hired laborer working for a non-Jewish employer.'" Down the road he saw a man pruning his vineyard. Again he said, "This person must be a *kohen*." The Rabbis replied, "He may say that he needs the twigs to make a bale [*akkeil*] for the wine press," [which is permitted in the Sabbatical year]. Resh Lakish retorted, "A person knows in his heart whether he is doing it for *akkeil* [to make a bale] or *akalkalot* [for a forbidden purpose]."

[The Gemara asks:] Which one did Resh Lakish see first? [The one who was pruning or, as related in the Gemara, the one plowing?] Do you think that he first saw the person who was plowing; then the Rabbis could have offered the same excuse for the one pruning, [saying that he was working for a non-Jew]. Therefore, he first must have seen the man who was pruning, [and they told him that he needed the twigs to make the bale]; and then he must have seen the man plowing, [and for that they could not offer the defense of making a bale, so they had to come up with the defense that he was working for a non-Jew]. [The Gemara asks:] Why [did Resh Lakish assume that the man he saw at work] was a *kohen*? [The Gemara answers:] Because *kohanim* are suspected of violating the laws of *shemittah*.

[The Gemara now resumes the story about Resh Lakish accompanying R. Chiya b. Zarnuki and R. Shimon b. Yehotzadak on their journey to intercalate the year. Seeing how Resh Lakish criticized the two people,] they said, "He is a troublemaker."

When they reached their destination, they went up to the second floor and took away the ladder [preventing Resh Lakish from joining them]. So Resh Lakish went to R. Yochanan and asked, "Are people who are suspected of violating the law of the Sabbatical year [since they defended these transgressors] qualified to intercalate[32] the year?" Having second thoughts, he said, "That would be no problem, [they could intercalate the year anyway,] because it is comparable to the case of the three cow herders [who are ignorant of the *halachah*] on whose calculations the Rabbis relied.[33] Afterward, he reconsidered and said, "There is no comparison between the two cases; in the case of the cow herders, it was the Rabbis who made the decision to intercalate; whereas in the case at hand, [the judges that intercalate the year,] are a bunch of wicked men, and a band of sinners cannot be counted [as a Bet Din to intercalate a year]. R. Yochanan objected to this [offensive language,] saying, "That is the trouble!" [You should not have called them a bunch of wicked men.] When R. Chiya b. Zarnuki and R. Shimon b. Yehotzadak came before R. Yochanan they complained, "[True, you did protest when Resh Lakish called us wicked men,] but when he called us cow herders you did not say anything!" R. Yochanan replied, "And if he had called you shepherds [which is even more derogatory], what could I have told him?"

SHEVNA'S BETRAYAL

[Resh Lakish called the Rabbis "a band of wicked men." The Gemara now asks:] Where in Scripture is the phrase "a band of wicked men" mentioned? [The Gemara answers:] Shevna [a deputy of King Hezekiah][34] expounded the Torah before a hundred and thirty thousand, whereas Hezekiah expounded it only before a hundred and ten thousand. When Sancheriv [King of Assyria] came and laid siege to Jerusalem, Shevna wrote a note and shot it on an arrow [across the wall into Sancheriv's camp, stating:] "Shevna and his followers are willing to make peace; Hezekiah and his followers are not." Concerning this it says, "For, behold, the wicked bend the bow, ready their arrow on the bowstring, to shoot in the dark at the upright of heart [i.e., Hezekiah]" (Psalms 11:2). Hezekiah became afraid, thinking: Perhaps, God forbid, the Holy One, blessed be He, is with the majority; and since the majority wants to surrender to the enemy, should we also surrender? The prophet then came to Hezekiah and told him, "Just because everyone thinks that they are a [le-gitimate] group, that is no reason for you to consider them [authentic] spokesmen" (Isaiah 8:12): they are nothing but a band of wicked people, and a band of wicked people has no standing [when it comes to making decisions].

[Later on,] when Shevna [haughtily] hewed out a grave for himself in the royal section of the burial ground, the prophet came and said to him, "What have you here, and whom have you here, [what business do you have] carving out for yourself a tomb here? Behold, God is going to make you wander an intense wandering, [literally: make you a wandering of a man]" (Isaiah 22:16). Rav inferred from this that it is worse for a man to be sent into exile than for a woman, [because a woman in exile arouses compassion so that she is offered help and shelter]. [The verse continues,] "God will send you circling afar [*ato*]" (ibid.). R. Yose b. R. Chanina said: This teaches us that Shevna broke out with leprosy: [Proof of this is that] here it says *ato*, and concerning a leper it says, "He must cover [*yateh*] himself up to his lips" (Leviticus 13:45). [The prophet continues,] "[God] will wind you around like a turban and hurl you like a ball into a land without obstacles, [where it will keep rolling endlessly]; there you will die, and there [will die] your chariots of honor—O shame of your master's house" (Isaiah 22:18).

We learned in a *Baraita*: [Shevna] sought to bring shame on his master's house; therefore his own glory was turned to shame. For when he went out [on his way to surrender to Sancheriv] Gabriel came and closed the gate in front of his company, [so that Shevna went on alone]. (26b) When [the Assyrians] asked him, "Where is the rest of your people?" he replied, "They [changed their mind;] they went back." "Then you were making fun of us all along," the Assyrians said. So they drilled holes in his heels, tied him to the tails of horses, and dragged him over thorns and thistles. R. Elazar said: Shevna was a pleasure-seeker. For here it says, "Go and approach that manager [*sochen*], Shevna" (Isaiah 22:15), and elswhere it says, "And [Avishag] became the king's attendant [*sochenet*]," [she warmed him in his old age, and gave him pleasure (Rashi)] (1 Kings 1:4).

It says, "When the foundations [*hashatot*] are destroyed, what has the righteous man accomplished?" (Psalms 11:3). Rav Yehudah and R. Eyna [offer different interpretations of *hashatot*. According to one it means: If Hezekiah and his followers had been destroyed, where would we have seen the reward God promised him? According to the other it means: If the *Bet Hamikdash* had been destroyed [by Sancheriv] what would the Righteous One [meaning, God] have accomplished; [how would God's glory be demonstrated]? Ulla interpreted it: If the plans of that wicked man [Shevna] had not been foiled, how would the righteous [Hezekiah] have been rewarded?

[The Gemara now shows how all three interpretations fit into the text.] We can understand the last interpretation, namely: If the plans of that wicked man had not been foiled . . . That is why it says, "When *hashatot* are destroyed" [because *shatot* means thoughts].[35] We can also accept the interpretation that [*hashatot*] refers to the *Bet Hamikdash*, for we learned in a Mishnah: There was a certain stone in the Holy of Holies since the days of the First Prophets [on which rested the Ark] that was called *shetiyah*, [so the word *hashatot* can refer to the *Bet Hamikdash*]. But according to the opinion that *hashatot* refers to Hezekiah and his followers: where do we find that the *tzaddikim* are referred to as *shatot*? In the verse, "For the foundations of the earth are the Lord's, and upon them He set [*va'yashet*] the world" (1 Samuel 2:8); [and "a *tzaddik* is the foundation of the world" (Proverbs 10:25)]. Or if you prefer, you can derive it from this verse, "His counsel is wondrous and His wisdom [*tushiyah*] abundant" (Isaiah 28:29) [referring to the Torah and the *tzaddikim* who study it, for they are the underpinnings [*shatot*] of the world].

R. Chanin said: Why is the Torah called *tushiyah*? Because [constant intensive] Torah study weakens [*mateshet*] a man's strength. Ulla said: Anxiety about one's livelihood makes a person forget his learning, for it says, "[God] crushes the [worrisome] thoughts of the skilled [i.e., the Torah scholars, by providing them with sustenance; for nervousness] would have hampered the scholars' progress in Torah study" (Job 5:12). Rabbah said: But if a person is studying Torah for its own sake, his anxieties about earning a livelihood will not interfere with his studies. For it says, "Many designs are in a man's heart, but the counsel of God, only it will prevail" (Proverbs 19:21): thoughts that contain the word of God [i.e., the Torah] will remain forever, [if it is learned for its own sake].

PUNISHMENT FOR
THE SINS OF OTHERS

(27b) It says, "Fathers shall not die because of sons" (Deuteronomy 24:16). What does this teach us? Do you think it teaches that fathers shall not be put to death for sins committed by their sons, and sons for sins of their fathers? But we know this from the end of that passage, "A man should be put to death for his own sin." Therefore, "Fathers shall not die because of sons" must mean: fathers shall not be put to death on the testimony of their sons, and, by the same token, "sons shall not die because of fathers" must mean: nor sons on the testimony of their fathers. [The Gemara asks:] Are then children not put to death for the sins of their fathers? Doesn't it say, "He keeps in mind the sins of the fathers to their children" (Exodus 34:7? [The Gemara answers:] That passage refers to children who follow their father's [evil] example, as we learned: "Because the sins of their forefathers are with them as well, they will disintegrate" (Leviticus 26:35); that is, if they follow their forefathers' [evil] example.

[The Gemara suggests:] But perhaps this refers even to children who do not follow their forefathers' [evil] example, [that they are nevertheless held responsible for their forefathers' sins]? [The Gemara answers:] Since it says, "A man shall be put to death for his own sin" (Deuteronomy 24:16), it includes those who follow their forefathers' [evil] example. And when they do not follow the example of their fathers, do they really not suffer for the sins committed by others? But it says, "They will stumble over one another" (Leviticus 26:37); meaning, one will stumble through the sin of the other; which teaches that all [Israel] are held responsible for one another, [thus one person may have to suffer for someone else's sins]? [The Gemara answers:] That saying refers to a case where they had the opportunity to protest [against other people's wrongdoing] but did not; [then they are held responsible].

WARNING TO WITNESSES

(29a) [The Mishnah says that before the trial begins, the witnesses are made aware of the awesome seriousness of testifying falsely and warned to tell the truth.]

[The Gemara asks:] What did the judges tell the witnesses to inspire them with awe? R. Yehudah said: This is what they said: [They quoted the verse,] "Like clouds and wind without rain, [so is] one who lauds himself for a false gift" (Proverbs 25:14); [implying that witnesses who give false testimony cause the rain to be withheld; the clouds may gather but the rain will not fall (Rashi)]. Said Rava: [This warning is useless,] for they may say to themselves [the popular adage: Seven years of famine do not pass the gate of a person who has a trade [i.e., the worst famine does not affect a person with a profession]. But, said Rava, this is what they told them, "A maul, a sword, and a sharp arrow is someone who bears false witness against his fellow" (ibid. 25:18). [I.e., testifying falsely results in a plague from which they cannot escape.] R. Ashi said: [Even this is not enough to frighten them,] for they might say: Although an epidemic may last for seven years, no one dies before his time! But, said R. Ashi, Natan b. Mar Zutra told me: We warn them by telling them: False witnesses are disdained by those who hired them, as it says, [Jezebel hired false witnesses to testify against Nabot,] "Then seat two unscrupulous people opposite him, who will testify against him [Nabot], saying, "You cursed God and the king!" (1 Kings 21:10). [Jezebel who hired the false witnesses, called them "unscrupulous people," proof that she held them in contempt.]

COURTROOM PROCEDURE

(30a) We learned in a *Baraita*: R. Nechemiah said: This was the way the fair-minded in Jerusalem conducted [a trial]: first the litigants were told to state their cases, then the witnesses were brought in to give their testimony. After that [the witnesses] were told to leave, and the case was discussed.

(31a) Our Rabbis taught: From where do we know that when one of the judges goes out he should not say: I argued for acquittal of the defendant, but my colleagues found him guilty; so what could I do, since they were in the majority? We know it from the verse, "Do not go around a gossipper among your people" (Leviticus 19:16), and another passage says, "He who reveals a secret is a talebearer" (Proverbs 11:13).

A rumor was making the rounds that a certain scholar had revealed something that was said in the *bet midrash* twenty-two years earlier. So R. Ammi expelled him from the *bet midrash*, saying: This man divulges secrets.

SEEK OUT THE MOST EMINENT BET DIN

(32b) Our Rabbis taught: "Righteousness, righteousness shall you pursue" (Deuteronomy 17:20). This means: go after a distinguished Bet Din to have your case tried; for example, the [Bet Din] of R. Eliezer in Lydda or that of R. Yochanan b. Zakkai in Beror Chail.

[Having mentioned Beror Chail, the Gemara briefly digresses to relate a historical note about that town.] Our Rabbis taught: [At the time when the Romans prohibited circumcision, when people heard] the noise of grindstones in Burni, it was the secret sign to announce that a *brit milah* was about to take place; [they were grinding medicinal herbs for treating the wound]. The light of a candle [by day, and many candles at night] at Beror Chail was the secret sign to announce that a [wedding] banquet was being held.

Our Rabbis taught: "Righteousness, righteousness shall you pursue" means that you should follow the Torah sages [with your court cases] to their *yeshivot*, [where the Bet Din was in session]; for example, R. Eliezer to Lod; R. Yochanan b. Zakkai to Beror Chail; R. Yehoshua to Peki'in; R. Gamliel to Yavneh; R. Akiva to B'nei B'rak; R. Chanina b. Teradyon to Sichni; R. Yose to Tzipori; R. Yehudah b. Beteirah to Netzivin; R. Chanina, the nephew of R. Yehoshua, to the Exile [to Pumbedita in Babylonia]; Rebbi to Bet She'arim; the Sages to the Chamber of the Hewn Stones [in the *Bet Hamikdash*, the seat of the Great Sanhedrin].

LIKE A HAMMER THAT SHATTERS THE ROCK

(34a) It says, "One thing has God spoken, these two I have heard" (Psalms 62:12). This means that several teachings may be derived from one verse, but a single teaching cannot be derived from different verses. In the yeshivah of R. Yishmael it was taught: "Behold, My word is like fire—the word of God—and like a hammer that shatters the rock" (Jeremiah 23:29)—just as the hammer smashes [the rock] into a multitude of

fragments, so too may a Biblical verse be interpreted many different ways.

EVEN THE SINNERS IN ISRAEL ABOUND IN *MITZVOT*

(37a) It says, "Your navel is like a round goblet [*aggan hasahar*]; let mixed wine not be lacking" (Song of Songs 7:3). "Your navel" refers to the Sanhedrin. Why was it called "navel"? Because it was situated [in the *Bet Hamikdash*] at the center of the world. Why is it described as *aggan*? Because it protects [*meigin*] the whole world. Why *hasahar* [moon]? Because [its members were seated in a semicircle, like the crescent moon, so they could see each other and speak face to face]. Why, "let mixed wine not be lacking"? If one of them had to leave, they had to make sure that twenty-three were left, corresponding to the number of the minor Sanhedrin, then he could leave; otherwise he could not go out.[36]

"Your belly is like a heap of wheat" (ibid.). Just as everyone benefits from a heap of wheat, so do all benefit from the wise insights of the Sanhedrin. "Hedged about with roses" (ibid.). Even an unimposing barrier like a fence of roses is enough [to the Jewish people] to deter them from trespassing against [the laws of the Torah]. This ties in with a story about a certain heretic who said to R. Kahana: You contend that a husband is permitted to stay alone with his wife during the period of her menstruation: can a fire be near flax without igniting it? He replied: The Torah testifies about us, "Hedged about with roses"—even through a hedge [as flimsy as a hedge] of roses they will make no breach.

Resh Lakish said: [R. Kahana could have cited the following verse,] "Your cheeks [*rakateich*] are like a slice of pomegranate" (ibid. 6:7).—Even the unworthiest [*reikanim*] among you are as full of *mitzvot* as a pomegranate of seeds, [and they can be trusted not to violate the law]. R. Zeira said: It can be inferred from here, [when Jacob approached Isaac to receive the blessing,] "[Isaac] smelled the fragrance of his garments [*begadav*]." (Genesis 27:27). Do not read *begadav*; read instead *bogedav*, "his transgressors." [Even the transgressors of Israel emit the fragrance of *mitzvot*.]

In the neighborhood of R. Zeira there lived some vulgar people. He reached out to them, hoping to induce them to do *teshuvah*; but the Rabbis objected to this. When R. Zeira died, the crude fellows said, "Until now we had 'the little man with the singed legs'[37] to pray for us, but who will pray for us now?" Thereupon they searched their souls and repented.

ADMONISHING THE WITNESSES

[The Mishnah says:] How did the Sanhedrin inspire the witnesses with awe in capital cases? The witnesses were led into the Sanhedrin hall and intimidated.

They were told: Perhaps what you said is based on an assumption or a rumor, or is evidence you heard from another witness, or even from a trustworthy person? Perhaps you are not aware that ultimately we will interrogate you and submit you to cross-examination and probing questions? You should know that capital cases are not like monetary cases. In civil cases [if a witness gives false testimony, it is sinful,] but he can make monetary restitution [to the person who suffered a loss because of the false testimony, and his sin is thereby forgiven]. But in capital cases [the false witness] is held responsible for the blood [of the person executed] and of the descendants [he could have had] until the end of time. For so do we find in the case of Cain [who killed his brother Abel] that it says, "The *bloods* of your brother are screaming to Me" (Genesis 4:10), where "bloods," *demei*, is written in the plural—implying: his blood and the blood of his potential descendants. [Alternatively: "The *bloods* of your brother" means that his blood was splattered over trees and stones.][38]

And that is why Adam was created alone, to teach you that whoever destroys one soul of Israel, the Torah considers it as if he had destroyed a complete world. [For we see that all mankind descends from Adam.] Conversely, whoever saves one life of Israel, the Torah considers it as if he had saved a complete world. Another reason why Adam was created alone is to preserve peace among men, so that one person should not say to his neighbor: My father was greater than yours; [Adam was everyone's ancestor]. Also, that the heretics should not say: There are many reigning powers in heaven, [and each created a man of its own]. Furthermore, to proclaim to the world the greatness of the Holy One, blessed be He. For if a person strikes many coins from one mold, they all look alike, but the King Who reigns over kings, the Holy One, blessed be He, fashioned every person in the mold of Adam, the first man, and yet not one of them looks like the other.

Therefore, every single individual is required to say: The world was created for my sake. [In other words, the life of each person is very precious. Therefore, you witnesses should be extremely careful not to cause a life to be destroyed through fale testimony.] Perhaps you will say: (37b) Why should we get involved in all this trouble [of testifying even truthfully, and cause a person to be executed]? To answer that it says, "[In a case] where he was a witness who saw or knew something, and he does not testify, he must bear his guilt" (Leviticus 5:1); [refusing to testify about an incident you witnessed is a sin]. Perhaps you will say: [We had rather be guilty of not testifying than] being instrumental in causing the accused's death? For that it says, "When the wicked perish there is glad song" (Proverbs 11:10), [and therefore if you are telling the truth, you certainly should testify].

THE MURDERER WAS BITTEN BY A SNAKE

[The Gemara says:] Our Rabbis taught: What is an example of testimony based on assumption [mentioned in the Mishnah]?—The judge says to the witnesses [to a murder]: Perhaps you saw [the suspect] running after this fellow into a ruin; you chased him, and found him sword in hand with blood dripping from it, and the murdered person struggling in the throes of death: If that is all you saw, you have seen nothing, [because that is only circumstantial evidence].

We learned in a *Baraita*: R. Shimon b. Shetach said: May I see the consolation of Zion[39] if I did not see a person chasing after a man into a ruin, and when I ran after him and saw him, sword in hand with blood dripping from it, and the murdered person struggling in the throes of death, I called out to him, "You wicked man! Who killed this man; either I or you!" [Obviously you are the murderer.] But what can I do, since your life is not in my hands, for it says in the Torah, "The accused shall be put to death only on the testimony of two witnesses" (Deuteronomy 17:6). May God, Who knows the thoughts [of man], exact retribution on the person who has killed his neighbor! The Sages said that before they left that spot a snake came and bit [the murderer], and he died.

[The Gemara asks:] Was this murderer liable to the punishment of death by a snake bite [which is similar to burning; whereas a murderer is to be put to death by decapitation]? Surely R. Yosef said, and so it was taught in the yeshivah of Chizkiah: From the day the *Bet Hamikdash* was destroyed, although the Sanhedrin was abolished, the four methods of execution were not abolished. How can you say [that the four methods of execution] were not abolished, when they *were* abolished with the disbanding of the Sanhedrin!

[Explains the Gemara:] The heavenly judgment that takes the place of the four methods of execution has not been discontinued. If a person committed one of the [eighteen] sins that are punishable by stoning, he either falls from the roof or is trampled to death by wild beasts. If a person did one of the [ten] sins that are punishable by burning, either he falls into a fire or is bitten by a snake [death by venom is akin to burning]. If a person did one of the [two] sins that are punishable by decapitation, either he will fall into the hands of the [Roman] government [who slay him] or he will be attacked by a band of robbers. A person who did one of the [six] sins that are punishable by strangulation, either is drowned in a river or dies of choking. [At any rate, the above-mentioned murderer should not have died from a snake bite, but rather by something similar to decapitation, which is a lighter punishment than burning.] [The Gemara answers:] I will tell you: that person was liable to be burned for a different crime [which was punishable by burning, in addition to the crime of murder], for we learned: If someone is liable to two death penalties, he is executed by the more severe method.

CAIN'S FRATRICIDE

[We learned in the Mishnah: The judges warned the witnesses: You should know that capital cases are not like monetary cases . . . for in the case of Cain who killed his brother . . . his blood was splattered on trees and stones.] Rav Yehudah, the son of R. Chiya, said: [the word *blood* teaches us that Cain inflicted many wounds and stabs on his brother's body, because he did not know from where the soul leaves the body, until he reached his throat [and that killed him]. Rav Yehudah, the son of R. Chiya, also said: Since the day the earth has opened its mouth to receive the blood of Abel it has never opened it again. For it says, "From the edge of the earth we have heard songs, 'Glory for the righteous'" (Isaiah 24:16), [the songs come] from the *edge* of the earth, but not from the *mouth* of the earth.

Chizkiah his brother raised an objection to this: It says, "The earth opened its mouth [and swallowed Korach and his company]" (Numbers 16:32) [so you see, the earth did open its mouth]! He answered: It opened only to inflict punishment, but not for good things [such as to sing songs of praise for the righteous]. R. Yehudah the son of R. Chiya also said: Exile atones for half of the sins. Originally, [Cain said], "I am to be restless and isolated [*na* and *nod*] in the world" (Genesis 4:14); but later [after he went into exile] it says, "He settled in the land of Nod" (ibid. v. 16); [*nod* without *na*, for his exile atoned and erased half of his punishment (Rashi)].

EXILE BRINGS
ABOUT ATONEMENT

Rav Yehudah said: Exile atones for three things [the sword, famine, and pestilence]. for it says, [with reference to the siege of Jerusalem by Nebuchadnezzar,] "Thus says God, 'Whoever will remain in this city will die by the sword, by famine and by pestilence; but whoever leaves and surrenders to the Chaldeans who are besieging will live, and his life will be his spoils'" (Jeremiah 21:8–9), [because he went into exile he will be saved from the three scourges]. R. Yochanan said: Exile atones for everything, for it says [concerning Yechoniah the son of King Yehoyakim], "Thus said God, 'Inscribe this man to become childless, a man who will not succeed in his life, for none of his descendants will ever succeed in being a man who sits on the throne of David, and ever to rule over Judah'" (Jeremiah 22:30).

And after Yechoniah went into exile, it says, "The sons of Yechoniah: Assir Shealtiel his son" (1 Chronicles 3:17). He was called Assir [imprisoned], because his mother conceived him in prison; Shealtiel[40] because God did not plant him in the way that others are planted. We have a tradition that a woman cannot conceive while standing upright, (38a) yet she conceived in a standing position. [Yechoniah's prison cell was very narrow so that he could not lie down. His wife was hoisted down into this cell, and there she conceived Assir Shealtiel.][41] Another explanation: He was called Shealtiel [which means: "God asked"], because God asked the Heavenly Court to be released from His vow [to punish Yechoniah with childlessness]. [Shealtiel had a son called Zerubavel.] He was called Zerubavel because he was conceived in Babylonia [*zara Bavel*], but his real name was Nehemiah the son of Chachaliah. [So we see that as a result of Yechoniah's exile his curse of infertility was annulled, and he had a son.]

WHERE WINE ENTERS,
COUNSEL DEPARTS

Yehudah and Chizkiyah, the [twin] sons of R. Chiya, once were sitting at a meal in the presence of Rebbi and did not say a word. Said Rebbi: Give the young men plenty of strong wine to drink so that they should say something. When they came under the influence they began by saying: The son of David [i.e., *Mashiach*] will not come before the two ruling dynasties in Israel will have come to an end, namely, the dynasty of the Babylonian Exilarch and that of the *Nasi* [Prince] in Eretz Yisrael. For it says, "He [*Mashiach*] shall be a sanctuary, but also a striking stone and a stumbling rock for the two houses of Israel" (Isaiah 8:14). Rebbi [who was the *Nasi* in Eretz Yisrael and a descendant of David] cried out to them: My children, you are throwing thorns into my eyes [when you say such harsh things]! Said R. Chiya to Rebbi: Please don't feel bad. You see, the numeric value of the letters of *yayin* [wine] is seventy,[42] and the word *sod* [counsel] has the same numeric value.[43] When *yayin* [wine] goes in, *sod* [counsel] goes out.

HOW WAS GOD'S
RIGHTEOUSNESS MANIFEST?

R. Chisda said in the name of Mar Ukva, or, others say, R. Chisda said in the name of R. Yirmeyah: Mereimar expounded: What is meant by the passage, "God hastened the calamity and brought it upon us; for God our Lord is a *Tzaddik*, [Righteous One]" (Daniel 9:14)? Is it because God is righteous that He hurried to bring upon us the calamity? The text means: God did a great kindness [*tzedakah*] to Israel that [eleven years] before Jerusalem was destroyed and Israel went into exile under King Zedekiah, the [partial] captivity of Yechoniah [Jehoiachin] was already established [in Babylonia, so that the Torah scholars who went with him would be able to teach Torah to the people that were to go into exile together with Zedekiah].

For it says about the captivity of Yechoniah (Jehoiachin), [Nebuchadnezzar] exiled Yechoniah to Babylonia . . . and the *charash* and the *masgeir*, one thousand" (2 Kings 24:16), [an allusion to the Torah scholars and Torah leaders who went to Babylonia with Yechoniah]. They were called *charash* [dumb] because when they opened their mouths [giving Torah discourses] the audience was dumbstruck with awe. And they were called *masgeir* [one who closes] because if a halachic problem was closed to them, no one else was able to solve it. And how many were there? One thousand. Ulla said: [God's righteousness] was evident in that He caused Israel to be sent into exile two years before the numeric value of] *venoshantem* ["you have been established for a long time"] (Deuteronomy 4:25) [i.e., 852 years] was reached.[44] R. Acha b. Yaakov said: From here you can see that when God says in the Torah that something will occur "quickly" it will happen after 852 years. [The next verse reads, "you will perish quickly," which would be after *venoshantem*, i.e., 852 years.]

WHY WAS ADAM CREATED ALONE?

Our Rabbis taught: Adam was created alone. Why? So that the heretics should not say: There are many reigning powers in Heaven, [and each one created his own man]. Another answer is: [Man was created alone] for the sake of the *tzaddikim* and for the sake of the wicked; [for if there were many first men,] the *tzaddikim* might say: We are descendants of a primordial *tzaddik*, [thus righteousness is in our genes and, therefore, we do not have to avoid temptation. When the *tzaddik* sees that he has the same ancestor as his wicked neighbor, he will be careful not to fall into sin]; and that the wicked should not say: We are descendants of a primeval wicked man, [our wickedness is a hereditary trait, and we are doomed to sin. When a wicked man sees that he issues from Adam just like his righteous neighbor, he realizes that he has the potential to become a *tzaddik* too].

Another answer is: [Man was created alone] for the sake of the different families, so that they should not quarrel with each other [and say: We are of a superior race because we are descendants a different first man than you are]. You see that now, when Adam was created alone, [and all know that they are the progeny of the same ancestor,] the world is full of strife; imagine how much more dissension there would be if two men had been created! Or you could say [that man was created alone] because of robbers and extortionists, [who will claim: Your land really belongs to the descendants of our first ancestor and not to the offspring of your first ancestor]. You see that now, when Adam was created alone, people rob and extort; think how much more robbery there would be if two had been created.

WHY NO TWO PEOPLE LOOK ALIKE

[The Gemara comments:] Our Rabbis taught: Man was created alone to proclaim the greatness of the King Who reigns over kings, the Holy One, blessed be He. For if a person strikes many coins from one mold, they all look alike, but the Holy One blessed be He, fashioned all men in the mold of Adam, yet not one person is identical to the other, for it says, "[At the time of death] the mold of a person changes like clay, and, [nevertheless, at the time of the resurrection] they will stand with their garments" (Job 38:14). And why do no two people look alike? Because a person might see a beautiful house or an attractive woman and say, "She is mine" [and no one will be able to refute him, because they don't know who he is]. For it says, "As light [another person's facial expression] is withheld from the wicked, and their raised arm is broken, [their ability to rob is foiled]" (ibid. 15).

We learned in a *Baraita*: In three things a person is different from his neighbor: in voice, appearance, and thoughts. In voice and appearance, to prevent immorality [a person should be certain in darkness and daylight that the woman he is with is his wife]; in thoughts, because of robbers and extortionists [if a person knew what his neighbor was thinking, a robber would know where his intended victim hides his treasures].

THE CREATION OF ADAM AND EVE

Our Rabbis taught: Adam was created on the eve of *Shabbat*. Why? [For if man had been created on the first day of creation,] the heretics might say: The Holy One, blessed be He, had a partner [Adam] in His work of creation. Or you might say: [Adam was the last of all creations] in order that, if a person becomes conceited [because he has a divine soul], we tell him: A mosquito was created before you. Another answer is: That Adam should be able to begin life by doing a mitzvah [of observing *Shabbat*]. Another answer is: That he should be able to start the meal immediately, [meaning, he should find the whole world ready for him to enjoy]. You can compare it to a king of flesh and blood who built a palace and furnished it, prepared a lavish feast, and when everything was ready he brought in the guests, as it says, "With all forms of wisdom did she build her house; she [i.e., God's wisdom] carved out its seven pillars. She prepared her meat, mixed her wine, and also set her table. She has sent out her maidens to announce on top of the city heights" (Proverbs 9:1–4).

[The Gemara now expounds each segment of the verse separately:] "With all forms of wisdom did she build her house"—that is the attribute of the Holy One, blessed be He, Who created the world with His wisdom.[45] "She [i.e., God's wisdom] carved out its seven pillars"—these are the seven days of Creation.

"She prepared her meat, mixed her wine, and also set her table"—these are the seas and the rivers and all the other essentials of the world. "She has sent out her maidens to announce"—this refers to Adam and Eve. "On top of the city heights": Rabbah b. Bar Chana contrasted two verses: It says here, "On top of the city heights" (Proverbs 9:3); but elsewhere it says, "On a chair at the city heights" (ibid. v. 14); ["on top" is higher than "on a chair" (Rashi)]. [He explained:] At first He placed Adam on top of the highest places, but after he sinned [by eating from the Tree of Knowledge he was demoted] to sit on a [lower] chair.

[The Gemara continues by expounding the next verse,] "Whoever is a simpleton, let him turn here! As for one who lacks an understanding heart, she says to him" (ibid. v. 4)—[After Adam sinned,] the Holy One, blessed be He, said: Who enticed him to turn and eat from the Tree? The woman [who lacks an understanding heart] enticed him. For it says, "He who commits adultery with a woman is lacking an understanding heart" (ibid. 6:32) [and it is the woman who brought about his lack of understanding].

We learned in a *Baraita*: Rabbi Meir used to say: The dust of which Adam was molded was gathered from all parts of the world. For it says, [Adam said,] "Your eyes saw my unshaped form" (Psalms 139:16); and it says further, "The eyes of God, they scan the whole world" (Zechariah 4:10). [In other words: Adam's unshaped form came from the earth of the whole world that God's eyes saw.] R. Oshiya said in Rav's name: [The earth for] Adam's body, [which ranks lower than his spirit] (38b) came from Babylonia, [which is a low-lying country]; [the earth] for his head [the most distinguished part of the body] came from Eretz Yisrael, [the loftiest of countries]; [the earth] for his limbs came from other countries. R. Acha said: Adam's buttocks came from the earth of Akra di Agma [a deep valley in Babylonia].

CHRONOLOGY OF ADAM'S FIRST DAY

R. Yochanan b. Chanina said: The day consists of twelve hours. In the first hour [of the sixth day of Creation] Adam's dust was collected; in the second hour, it was kneaded into a shapeless hunk; in the third hour, his limbs were shaped; in the fourth, a soul was infused into him; in the fifth, he stood up on his feet; in the sixth, he named all the animals; in the seventh, Eve became his bride; in the eighth, they went to bed as two people, and when they left the bed they were four [Cain and his twin sister were born]; in the ninth, he was commanded not to eat from the Tree; in the tenth, he sinned; in the eleventh, he was tried; in the twelfth, he was driven out of the Gan Eden and left. For it says, "As for man, in glory he shall not repose" (Psalms 49:13). [Meaning, Adam, in his grandeur in Gan Eden only remained there the first day, but he did not stay overnight.] Rami b. Chama [expounding the rest of the verse,] said: A wild beast never attacks a person unless he appears to it like an animal, for it says, "If a person is overwhelmed by a wild beast, it is because he looks to it like an animal" (ibid.).

GOD CONSULTS WITH THE ANGELS

Rav Yehudah said in Rav's name: When the Holy One, blessed be He, wanted to create Adam, He first created a group of ministering angels and said to them, "Is it your wish that we should make a man in our image?" Replied the angels, "Master of the universe! What will be the deeds of this man?" "Such-and-such will be his deeds," God answered. Hearing this, they exclaimed, "What is frail man that You should remember him, and the son of mortal man that You should be mindful of him?" (Psalms 8:5). [Don't create man.] Thereupon God placed His little finger among them and obliterated them with fire. The same thing happened to a second group of angels. The third group said to Him, "Master of the universe! What did the previous groups accomplish by suggesting" [that you should not create man? Therefore we say to You,] "The whole world is Yours, and whatever You want to do with Your world, do it."

[Ten generations later,] at the Age of the Flood and the corrupt generation of the Dispersion,[46] the same angels said to God, "Master of the universe! Were not the first angels right [in suggesting that man should not be created]?" Replied God, "Until your old age I am unchanged, [i.e., I am waiting until the time of the Giving of the Torah,] and until your hoary years I will carry you" (Isaiah 46:4). [True, mankind sins, but it is all worthwhile, because there is Israel who will receive the Torah (*Maharsha*).]

Rav Yehudah said in Rav's name: Adam reached from one end of the world to the other, as it says, "Since the day that God created man on earth, [reaching] from one end of the heavens to the other" (Deuteronomy 4:32). But when he sinned, the Holy One, blessed be He, laid His hand on him and diminished him, as it says, "Back and front You have restricted me, and You have laid Your hand upon me" (Psalms 139:17).

ARGUING WITH NON-BELIEVERS

We learned in a Mishnah: R. Eliezer said: A person should be diligent to learn the Torah and know how to refute the arguments of a non-believer. R. Yochanan commented: This was taught only with respect to a non-Jewish heretic, but a Jewish heretic [who learned the Torah but, driven by lust, turned his back on the Torah,] will use your arguments to support his fallacious points. [Don't have anything to do with him.]

R. Yochanan said: For any passage the non-believers used in support of their heretical views, the answer disproving their untruths can be found right there in the same verse. [For example:] "God said: Let us make Man" (Genesis 1:26) [in the plural, implying that there is more than one Creator. This is refuted by]—"So God created [singular] Man in His image" (ibid. v. 27). [Another example: God said,] "Come, let us [plural] descend and there confuse their language" (Genesis 11:7), [refuted by]—"God descended [singular] to look at the city and the tower" (ibid. v. 5).

[Another example:] "Because this was the place where God was revealed [plural[47]] to him" (Genesis 35:7), [disproved by]—"God who answered [singular] me in my time of distress" (ibid. v. 3). [Another example:] "What nation is so great that they have God close [plural[48]] to it, as God our Lord is [singular] whenever we call on Him" (Deuteronomy 4:7). [Another example:] "And who is like Your people, like Israel, a unique nation on earth whom God went forth [plural] to redeem unto Himself [singular] for a people" (2 Samuel 7:23). [Yet another example:] "I watched as thrones [plural] were set up, and the One of Ancient Days [God] sat" (Daniel 4:9).

[The Gemara asks:] Why were all these phrases written in the plural? This can be explained by R. Yochanan's teaching. For R. Yochanan said: The Holy One, blessed be He, does nothing without consulting His heavenly Court, for [when Nebuchadnezzar related his dream to Daniel, it says,] "The matter is by the decree of the angels, and the sentence is by the word of the holy ones" (Daniel 4:14). [So we see, God consults with the angels.] [Says the Gemara:] This explanation accounts for [the plural forms] of all the other verses, but how do you explain [the plural of] the thrones in heaven? [The Gemara answers:] One throne was for God and one for David. And so it has been taught: One for Him and one for David, so says R. Akiva. R. Yose complained to him: Akiva, how can you profane the *Shechinah* [by placing a human being next to God]? Rather, [God sits on] one [throne] for justice and on another for mercy.

[The Gemara asks:] Did R. Akiva accept this interpretation? [The Gemara answers:] Come and hear! It has been taught: One is for justice and one for mercy; this is R. Akiva's opinion; [so we see that R. Akiva accepted the interpretation]. R. Elazar b. Azariah said to him: Akiva, what are you learning *aggadah* for? You should learn the laws of *Negaim* and *Ohalot!*[49] [You don't understand the correct meaning of *aggadah*!] One was a throne for God; the other a footstool: a throne for God to sit on and a footstool to place His feet. [Obviously, these are all symbolic images.]

R. Nachman said: A person who knows how to debate the non-believers like R. Idit should reply to their challenges; otherwise he should not try to counter [their arguments]. Once a certain heretic said to R. Idit: It says, "To Moses He said, 'Go up to God'" (Exo-

dus 24:1). It should say instead, "Go up to Me"! Replied R. Idit: [The being that spoke was not God;] it was the angel Metatron,[50] whose name is the same as that of God.[51] For it says, "For My name is within him" (Exodus 23:21). Countered the heretic: If that is the case, we should worship him [i.e., the angel Metatron]! Replied R. Idit: No, it says in the same verse, *al tammeir bo,*[52] "Do not exchange Me for him, [the angel Metatron]."

Asked the heretic: [The verse continues,] "for he cannot not forgive your willful sin." If so, [if Metatron has no power of its own], why do we need him altogether? R. Idit answered: [You are right.] It is because of our strong faith that we do not accept him even as a messenger on our behalf, for it says, "[Moses said to God,] 'If Your Presence does not accompany us, do not make us leave this place'" (Exodus 33:15). [The heretic contended that there are two deities, but R. Idit proved that God is One, and Metatron was an angel who was not even accepted as a messenger.]

A heretic once said to R. Yishmael b. R. Yose: It says, "God made sulphur and fire rain down on Sodom and Gomorrah—it came from God" (Genesis 19:24). It should have said: "it came from Him"! [The fact that God is mentioned twice seems to indicate that there are two deities!] A certain laundryman said to R. Yishmael b. R. Yose: Let me answer him. [He then said:] It says, "Lemech said to his wives, 'Adah and Tzillah, hear my voice; wives of Lemech, listen to my speech'" (Genesis 4:23). Instead of "wives of Lemech" he should have said: "my wives"! We must say therefore that sometimes the Torah expresses itself this way; so here, too, it is an idiomatic expression of the Torah. Said R. Yishmael b. R. Yose to the laundryman: From where do you know this interpretation? Replied the laundryman: I heard it at a public lecture of R. Meir.

As R. Yochanan said: R. Meir's lectures consisted of one-third *halachah*, one-third *aggadah* [in which he explained verses of the Torah and Tanach], and one-third parables. R. Yochanan also said: R. Meir had three hundred parables of foxes, but we have only three left. **(39a)** [The three parables that we know explain the following verses:] (1) "The fathers eat sour grapes, but the teeth of the sons are set on edge" (Ezekiel 18:2); (2)"Honest balance, honest weight" (Leviticus 19:36); (3) "The righteous one is removed from affliction, but the wicked one comes in his place" (Proverbs 11:8).

WHY WAS ADAM'S RIB REMOVED SURREPTITIOUSLY?

The Roman Emperor[53] once said to R. Gamliel: "Your God is a thief. For it says, 'God cast a deep sleep upon the man [Adam] . . . and He took one of his ribs' (Genesis 2:21)." Said R. Gamliel's daughter to her father, "Let me answer him." Turning to the emperor she said, "Give me a judge [to avenge a wrong that was done to me]." "What do you need a judge for?" asked the emperor. "Thieves broke into our house last night and stole a silver pitcher; however, they left a golden one in its place." The emperor shot back, "I wish that such thieves would come to us every day!"

Said R. Gamliel's daughter to the emperor, "Was it not better for Adam that God took one rib and gave him a wife who takes care of him?" Replied the emperor, "What I meant to say was: Why didn't God remove the rib openly? [Why did He put Adam to sleep?]" Replied R. Gamliel's daughter, "Bring me a piece of raw meat." When they brought her the meat, she placed it under some hot ashes [to roast it], then took it out and offered it to the emperor to eat. "It is disgusting," said the emperor. She replied, "By the same token, Eve would have been repulsive to Adam if she had been taken from him openly."

RABBAN GAMLIEL DEBATES THE ROMAN EMPEROR

The Roman Emperor also said to R. Gamliel, "I know what your God is doing." R. Gamliel pretended to be fainting and sighed. Said the emperor, "Why are you sighing?" Replied R. Gamliel, "I have a son in one of the distant isles of the sea, and I am longing to see him. Please tell me about him." Replied the emperor, "How should I know where he is!" "If you don't know what is going on here on earth, how can you claim to know what is going on in Heaven?" R. Gamliel retorted.

On another occasion the Roman Emperor said to R. Gamliel, "It says, 'He counts the number of the stars' [Psalms 147:4]. What's so exceptional about that? I also can count the stars?" R. Gamliel brought a bunch of quinces,[54] put them into a sieve, spun them around, and said, "Count them." Said the emperor, "Hold them still for a moment." "But the heavens revolve around the same way, [so how can you possibly count the stars]!" R. Gamliel snapped back. According to others, the emperor told R. Gamliel, "I know how many stars there are." So R. Gamliel asked him, "Please tell me how many molars and [other] teeth are there in your mouth?" Placing his hand in his mouth he started to count them. Said R. Gamliel, "If you don't know how many teeth you have in your mouth, how can you claim to know what is in Heaven!"

Said the emperor again to R. Gamliel, "The Creator of the mountains did not create the wind, for it says, 'For behold, He forms mountains and creates winds'"(Amos 4:13). [The emperor claimed that there is a creator of the physical world, symbolized by the mountains; and a creator of the realm of the spirit, exemplified by the wind (Maharsha).] Replied R. Gamliel, "If that is so, concerning man it says, "He created . . . " (Genesis 1:27) and "He formed . . . " (ibid. 2:7); would you also say that the One who created one part of man did not create another part of him?

[Taking it one step further:] There is a part of the human body no larger than the size of a handbreadth by a handbreadth, which contains two holes [the eye and the ear]. Are you going to say that the Creator of the eye did not create the ear? For it says, "He who implants [nota] the ear, will He not hear? He who fashions [yotzeir] the eye, will He not see?" (Psalms 94:9); [nota for the ear; yotzeir for the eye]. Said the emperor, "Yes, [I do believe that there are two creators]." Replied R. Gamliel, "[Do you mean to say that] when a person dies both creators reach an agreement, [that the eye and the ear should stop living at the same time? That is absurd!]"

A certain sorcerer[55] said to Ameimar, "The upper half of your body is under the control of Hurmiz [Ormuzd],[56] while your lower part is controlled by Ahurmiz.[57] Ameimar said to the sorcerer, "If so, how does Ahurmiz [the ruler of the lower part of the body] permit Hurmiz [the ruler of the upper part of the body] to bring water down through his territory? [When you eat and drink, the waste passes through the digestive organs in the lower part of the body.]"

The Roman Emperor once suggested to R. Tanchum, "Come, let's get together and become one nation." "All right," replied R. Tanchum. "But we who are circumcised cannot change to become like you; you should circumcise yourself and become like us." The emperor replied, "Your point is well taken. But we have a rule, that whoever gets the better of the emperor is thrown into the den of wild animals." So they threw R. Tanchum in, but the animals did not devour him. A certain heretic said, "The reason they did not eat him is that they are not hungry." They then threw the heretic into the den, and he was eaten up.

The Roman Emperor said to R. Gamliel, "You people say that wherever ten Jews gather, the Shechinah is found. How many Shechinahs are there?" R. Gamliel called the servant of the emperor and tapped him on the neck, saying, "Why do you allow the sun to shine in the emperor's palace?" Said the servant, "The sun shines on the whole world!" R. Gamliel responded, "If the sun, which is only one of the millions of servants of the Holy One, blessed be He, shines on the whole world, surely the Shechinah of the Holy One, blessed be He, Himself [can rest in many different places at the same time]!"

R. ABBAHU SQUELCHES THE HERETIC

A heretic said to R. Abbahu, "Your God is a jokester; [He makes fun of His prophets]. For He said to Ezekiel, 'Lie on your left side' (Ezekiel 4:4), and then He said, 'Lie on your right side' (ibid. v. 6). Just at that moment a student came in and asked R. Abbahu, "What is the reason for the mitzvah of the Sabbatical year?" R. Abbahu said [to the student and the heretic,] "I am going to give an answer that will satisfy both of you. The Holy One, blessed be He, said to Israel: Plant for six years, but leave the land fallow in the seventh year, that you should know that the earth is Mine.[58] They, however, did not do that. They sinned and were sent into exile. Now if the people of a province rise up against the king, and the king is a cruel monarch, it is standard practice for him to kill all of the subjects of that province; if he is compassionate, he kills half of them; but if he is a very merciful king, he chastises the leaders. So, too, the Holy One, blessed be He, made Ezekiel suffer [by commanding him to lie on his right and left sides for a long time] in order to cleanse Israel from their sins.

A certain heretic said to R. Abbahu: Your God is a *kohen*, for it says, "Have them bring Me a *terumah* [offering]" (Exodus 25:2). [*Terumah* usually refers to the portion of the harvest that is given to the *kohen*.][59] [Pursuing this senseless premise, the heretic asked R. Abbahu:] When God buried Moses,[60] how did He cleanse Himself [from the uncleanness that results from contact with a corpse]?[61] [Continued the heretic:] If you will say, He immersed Himself in a *mikveh*, surely it says, "Who measured the waters in the palm of His hand?" (Isaiah 40:12); [so there is not enough water for God to immerse Himself in!]. Replied R. Abbahu, [giving the fool a foolish answer]: God immersed Himself in fire, for it says, "Behold, God will arrive in fire" (ibid. 66:15). Asked the heretic: Is then immersion in fire valid? Replied R. Abbahu: On the contrary, the preferred form of purification is by immersion in fire, for it says, "Something that you did not put in the fire to cleanse it, you shall pass through the water" (Numbers 31:23).[62]

A heretic once said to R. Avina: It says, [David said,] "Who is like Your people, like Israel, a unique nation on earth" (2 Samuel 7:23). What is so special about the Jewish people? You are also mingled among the nations of the world; [you are no better than we are]! For it says, "All nations are like nothing before Him" (Isaiah 40:17), [including the Jewish people]! Replied R. Avina: One of your people [the heathen prophet Balaam] has already testified about us, for he said, (39b) "It is a nation that is not counted among other nations" (Numbers 23:9), [and the verse you mentioned does not include the Jewish people].

R. Elazar pointed out a contradiction between two verses: It says, "God is good to all" (Psalms 145:9); but another verse says, "God is good to those who trust in Him" (Lamentations 3:25)! You can compare it to a person who has an orchard. When he irrigates, he [is not selective] but allows the water to reach all the saplings. But when he digs [around individual trees, which takes a special effort], he only digs around the best trees. [Similarly, when God gives sustenance to the world, He gives it to everyone. But He protects from calamities only those that trust in Him.]

REJOICING AT THE DOWNFALL
OF THE WICKED

[It says, after the death of the wicked King Ahab,] "The rejoicing passed through the camp" (1 Kings 22:36).

R. Acha b. Chanina said: When the wicked perish there is rejoicing" (Proverbs 11:10); therefore, when Ahab son of Omri perished there was rejoicing. [The Gemara asks:] But does the Holy One, blessed be He, rejoice over the downfall of the wicked? Doesn't it say [when King Yehoshafat led his troops into battle, he appointed men to sing to God]. "As they went out before the front-line troops they said, 'Give thanks to God, for His mercy endures forever!'" (2 Chronicles 20:21). Commented R. Yonatan: Why is the phrase *ki tov*, "for He is good," omitted from this chant of thanksgiving, [whereas in Psalms 107:1 it is included]? [He answered: This verse refers to victory on the battlefield where people die,] and the Holy One, blessed be He, does not rejoice in the downfall of the wicked.

For R. Shmuel b. Nachman said in R. Yonatan's name: What is meant by, [In the night before the Parting of the Red Sea it says,] "One camp did not draw near the other all night" (Exodus 14:20)? At that moment, [as the sea began to split,] the ministering angels wanted to sing hymns of praise to the Holy One, blessed be He, but He chided them, saying: The Egyptians who are My creations are drowning in the sea, and you want to sing praises to Me! [Don't do that.] [The camps that did not draw near are understood to be camps of angels who call to each other as they utter songs of praise].[63]

Said R. Yose b. R. Chanina: God Himself does not rejoice [when the wicked perish] but he causes others [who take the life of the wicked] to rejoice. This is borne out by a precise reading of the verse, for it says *yasis*, "God will cause others to rejoice" [by destroying you] (Deuteronomy 28:63); but it does not say *yasus* [thus, He Himself will not rejoice]. Which proves that God does not delight in the downfall of the wicked.

AHAB'S DEATH

[The Gemara continues by relating the circumstances surrounding Ahab's death:] It says, [after Ahab was killed,] "The dogs licked up [Ahab's] blood, and the harlots bathed [in it]" (1 Kings 22:38). R. Elazar said: The death of Ahab was a clear fulfillment of two prophecies: one of Michaihu, the other of Elijah. The prophecy of Michaihu was, "If you indeed return in peace, then God did not speak through me" (1 Kings 22:28). The prophecy of Elijah was, "In the place where the dogs licked up the blood of Navot, the dogs will lick up your blood" (ibid. 21:19). [Concerning the two harlots,] Rava said: They were [pictures of] harlots. [What is this about?] Ahab was a passionless man by nature, so his wife Jezebel, in order to arouse his passion, painted pictures of two harlots on his chariot, so that he should look at them and become aroused. ["The harlots bathed in his blood" therefore means that their pictures were covered with his blood.]

[Continuing the story of Ahab's death, the Gemara quotes,] "Then a man drew his bow [*letumo*] at random, and he hit the king of Israel" (ibid. v. 34). R. Elazar said: The word *letumo* means "without intention." Rava said: *letammeim*, in order to fulfill the two visions, that of Michaiah and that of Elijah.

THE PROPHET OBADIAH

It says, [when there was a famine in the days of Ahab,] "Ahab summoned Obadiah who was in charge of the [royal] household. Obadiah revered God greatly" (1 Kings 18:3). [The Gemara asks:] What is the verse telling us? [What is the connection between the facts that Ahab summoned Obadiah, and that Obadiah was very God-fearing?] R. Yitzchak answered: Ahab said to Obadiah: About Jacob it says, [Laban said,] "I have learned by divination, that God has blessed me on account of you" (Genesis 30:27), and about Joseph it says, "God blessed the Egyptian's house on Joseph's account" (ibid. 39:5), [so you see, if there is a *tzaddik* in the house, blessing comes to the house,] but my house has not been blessed! Could the reason be that you are not a God-fearing man? Thereupon a heavenly voice came forth, declaring, "Obadiah revered God greatly, but the household of Ahab is not suited for blessing." [That is the connection between the two parts of the verse.] R. Abba said: Scripture attributes greater fear of God to Obadiah than it does to Abraham, since the word "greatly" is not written to describe Abraham's piety,[64] while "greatly" is written in connection with Obadiah's reverence of God.

R. Yitzchak said: Why did Obadiah merit to become a prophet, [in spite of the fact that he was an Edomite convert]?[65] Because he hid a hundred prophets in caves, as it says, "It was when Jezebel [Ahab's wife] had decimated the prophets of God, Obadiah took a hundred prophets and hid them, fifty men to a cave, and sustained them with bread and water" (1 Kings 18:4). Why fifty to a cave; [why not a hundred in one cave]? Said R. Elazar: He must have learned this from Jacob, as it says, [Jacob divided the people with him into two camps, saying: If Esau attacks one camp, . . .] "at least the other camp will survive" (Genesis 32:9). R. Abbahu said: It was because one cave could not hold more than fifty people.

WHY DID OBADIAH PROPHESY AGAINST EDOM?

[The Book of Obadiah begins,] "The vision of Obadiah, thus says the Lord God concerning Edom" (Obadiah 1:1). [The Gemara asks:] Why is it that Obadiah prophesied specifically about Edom? [We find no other prophet who prophesied concerning only one nation (Aruch Laneir).] R. Yitzchak said: The Holy One, blessed be He, said: Let Obadiah who has lived with two wicked people [Ahab and his wife Jezebel] and yet did not learn from their wicked deeds, come and prophesy against the wicked Esau, [the ancestor of Edom][66] who lived in the house of two righteous persons [Isaac and Rebeccah] yet did not learn from their good deeds.

Efraim Maksha'ah, the disciple of R. Meir, said in the name of R. Meir: Obadiah was a convert who descended from Edom. [The fact that Obadiah was chosen to prophesy the downfall of Edom gave rise to the saying:] From the wood of the forest itself comes the [handle of the] ax [that chops down the trees].

We also read, "[David] struck Moab. He measured his captives with a rope, laying them down on the ground" (2 Samuel 8:2); [David was a descendant of Ruth the Moabitess.] R. Yochanan said in the name of R. Shimon b. Yochai: That's why people say: From the wood of the forest itself comes the handle of the ax [that chops down the trees]. When R. Dimi came from Eretz Yisrael he said [in the same vein]: The hip begins to decay from within, [and the fall of Moab was precipitated by a descendant of Moab].

[The Gemara now relates how when Israel behaved in a corrupt way, they were unsuccessful in their battle against Moab:] It says, [Yehoram son of Ahab and Yehoshafat King of Judah together with the King of Edom defeated Mesha, King of Moab. Seeing that he was losing the battle, Mesha] "took his firstborn son, who was to reign after him, and sacrificed him as a burnt-offering upon the wall" (2 Kings 3:27). Rav and Shmuel differ about this. One says: [Mesha offered his son] to God. The other: to an idol. [The Gemara asks:] I can understand the view that he offered his son to God. That's why the verse continues: [because of this sacrifice,] "a great wrath took effect against Israel" (ibid.), [although misguided, Mesha's intentions were commendable; whereas Israel's idolatrous actions were contemptible].

But according to the one who says that Mesha offered his son to an idol, why was there a great wrath against Israel? [The Gemara answers: This is in accordance with R. Yehoshua b. Levi's teaching. For R. Yehoshua b. Levi contrasted two verses. It says, "You did not even act according to the laws of the nations around you" (Ezekiel 5:7). But elsewhere it says, "You acted according to the laws of the nations around you" (ibid. 11:22). [How do we reconcile the two verses?] You did not conduct yourself like the upright people among the nations;[67] but you acted like the corrupt people among them.[68]

[When the tide of battle turned against the Israelites,] "they turned away from Mesha and returned to the land" (2 Kings 3:27). [It should say: "to *their* land; why "to the land"?] Said R. Chanina b. Papa: ["To the land" denotes that] at that time the Israelites sank to the lowest level [of degradation].

[To end the chapter on an uplifting note, the Gemara cites an unrelated teaching by R. Chanina b. Papa:] "The girl was very beautiful, and she became King [David's] attendant" (1 Kings 1:4). R. Chanina b. Papa said: She did not reach half the beauty of Sarah, for it says *ad meod*, "approaching the point of great beauty," but not attaining it. [Only Sarah attained such beauty.][69]

SANCTIFICATION OF THE NEW MOON

(42a) R. Acha b. Chanina said in the name of R. Yochanan: Whoever blesses the new moon in its proper time is regarded like one who greets the *Shechinah*. For one verse says, "*This* month" (Exodus 12:2), [referring to the new moon]; and elsewhere, [when the Israelites witnessed God's majesty at the Parting of the Sea, it says,] "*This* is my God and I will glorify Him" (ibid. 15:2). [Since both verses begin with "this" we equate them.] In the yeshivah of R. Yishmael it was taught: Had Israel been privileged to greet the countenance of their Father in Heaven only once a month, it would have been sufficient for them, [meaning, if we had no other mitzvah than blessing the new moon, it would have been enough, because through the cyclical renewal of the moon we come recognize the greatness of the Creator]. Abaye said: Therefore you must recite *Kiddush Levanah*[70] while standing [in honor of the *Shechinah*]. Mereimar and Mar Zutra allowed themselves to be carried on the shoulders when they recited *Kiddush Levanah*.

R. Acha said to R. Ashi: In Eretz Yisrael they used to say the following *berachah*: Blessed be He who renews the months. Replied R. Ashi: Such a [short] *berachah* [without the mention of God's name] our women can say [even at night in the dark. It is too simple (*Maharsha*)]. Instead we should recite the *berachah* the way R. Yehudah formulated it: Blessed are You God, . . . Who with His utterance created the heavens, and with the breath of His mouth all their legion. A decree and a schedule did He give them that they not alter their assigned task. They are joyous and glad to perform the will of their Owner—the Worker of truth whose work is truth. To the moon He said that it should renew itself as a crown of splendor for those borne [by Him] from the womb [i.e., the Jewish nation],[71] those who are destined to renew themselves like it, and to glorify their Molder for the name of His glorious kingdom. Blessed are You, God, Who renews the months.

[The Gemara now presents two additional but unrelated teachings by R. Acha b. R. Chanina:] It says, "For through wise strategies [*tachbulot*], you can wage war for your benefit" (Proverbs 24:6). R. Acha b. R. Chanina said in the name of R. Assi in R. Yochanan's name: In whom do you find [the right technique to win] the battle of Torah [i.e., interpret and apply its laws correctly]? Only in a person who possesses bundles [*chavilot*][72] of *Mishnayot*. R. Yosef applied to himself the verse, "Many crops come through the power of the ox" (ibid. 14:4). [The ox is the symbol of Joseph (see Deuteronomy 33:17).]

[We learned in the Mishnah that when deliberating capital cases] the judges drink no wine the whole day. [The Gemara asks:] And why not? R. Achah b. Chanina said: Because it says, "It is not proper . . . for *roznim* to imbibe strong drink" (ibid. 31:4); meaning: those who are delving into the secrets [*razo*] of the world [i.e., capital cases, for a person's soul is a deep mystery (*Maharsha*)] should not get drunk.

THE CONDEMNED MAN'S FINAL DRINK

(43a) R. Chiya b. R. Ashi said in R. Chisda's name: The person that is being taken to be executed is given a cup of wine with a grain of frankincense [immediately before the execution] in order that his mind should be numbed, [and he should not suffer great mental anguish before his death], for it says, "Give strong drink to the woebegone and wine to the embittered" (Proverbs 31:6). And we learned in a *Baraita*: The worthy women of Jerusalem used to donate [the wine and the incense] and bring it [for this purpose]. [The Gemara asks:] If the worthy women did not donate it, who paid for it? It is certainly logical that it should be paid out of public funds [and not charged to the estate of the deceased], since it says, "Give strong drink," which implies that it is paid out of public funds.

GOD DESIRES A HUMBLE SPIRIT

(43b) R. Yehoshua b. Levi said: Whoever overcomes his evil impulse and confesses the sins of his past, Scripture considers it as if he had honored the Holy One, blessed be He, both in this world and the World to Come. For it says, "He who offers [his evil impulse and makes] confession honors Me [*yechabdonneni*]" (Psalms 50:23). [The unusual double *nun* in *yechabdonneni* alludes to this.]

R. Yehoshua b. Levi also said: When the *Bet Hamikdash* was standing, if a person brought a burnt offering, he was rewarded for that burnt offering; if he brought a meal offering, he was rewarded for a meal offering; but if someone is humble, Scripture considers it as if he had brought all the sacrifices, for it says, "The sacrifices God desires are a broken spirit" (Psalms 51:19). And not only that, but his prayer is never spurned, for it says, "A broken and humbled heart, O God, You will not disdain" (ibid.).

THE CONDEMNED MAN'S CONFESSION

[The Mishnah said:] When the [condemned man] was about ten cubits away from the place where he was to be stoned, they said to him, "Confess the sin [for which you are being put to death], and all your other sins. For it is the custom for all who are executed to confess, because he who confesses has a share in the World to Come." And so we find concerning Achan[73] [who stole of the forbidden property of Jericho], that Joshua said to him [when they cast lots, and Achan was shown to be the guilty party], "My son, please give honor to the Lord, God of Israel, and confess to Him" (Joshua 7:19). Whereupon Achan answered Joshua, "Indeed I have sinned against the Lord, God of Israel; such and such I have done" (ibid. v. 20). And from where do we know that his confession brought about forgiveness, [and he had a share in the World to Come]? For it says, "Joshua said, 'Just as you have caused us trouble, so will God cause you trouble today'" (ibid. v. 25)—implying, today, in this world, you will be troubled, but you will not be troubled in the World to Come.

[The Mishnah continues:] If the condemned man does not know how to say the confession, they instruct him to say: May my death atone for all my sins. R. Yehudah said: If the condemned person is convinced that he is being put to death on the basis of testimony by false witnesses, he says: May my death atone for all my sins, except for the sin for which I am about to be executed. The Sages said to R. Yehudah: If you allow him to say this, then anyone who is being put to death will say this in order to clear his name, [and this would amount to a defamation of the witnesses and the judges. Therefore he must confess to the sin for which he is being executed].

ACHAN'S THEFT

[The Gemara comments on the verse, where Joshua said to Achan, "My son, please [na] give honor to the Lord."] Our Rabbis taught: The word na always denotes supplication. [Since Joshua said "na," it would seem that he was asking a favor of Achan. Why did Joshua need Achan's confession?] When the Holy One, blessed be He, said to Joshua, "Israel has sinned [because someone took from the forbidden property]" (Joshua 7:11), Joshua said to God, "Master of the universe, who is the one that sinned?" "Am I a slanderer?" replied God. "Go and cast lots." Joshua went and cast lots, and the lot fell on Achan. Said Achan to Joshua, "Are you proving my guilt on the basis of a lot, [and will you execute me without the testimony of witnesses]? You and Elazar the kohen are the two foremost men of the generation, yet if I would cast lots between you, the lot would definitely fall on one of you." [A lot is not reliable evidence.]

Joshua told him, "Please, I beg of you, do not denigrate the lots, for Eretz Yisrael is going to be divided by lots, [and it is important that the people have faith in the lots]; as it says, 'The land shall be divided through a lottery system' (Numbers 26:55). Therefore, confess your sin." [Thus Achan's confession was to the benefit of Joshua and all Israel. And that is why Joshua used the word "na," a term of supplication.] Ravina said: Joshua bribed Achan with words. He said: Are

we asking from you anything more than a confession? Confess to God, and free yourself! [Joshua meant: Free yourself from punishment in the World to Come, but Achan took it to mean that he would go scot-free in this world]. Immediately, "Achan answered Joshua and said, 'Indeed I have sinned against the Lord, God of Israel; such and such I have done'" (Joshua 7:20).

R. Assi said in R. Chanina's name: [Achan's choice of words] teaches us that he had stolen consecrated property on three occasions: two times in the days of Moses[74] and once in the days of Joshua, for he said, "I have sinned [this time], and such and such I have done [on two previous occasions]." R. Yochanan said in the name of R. Elazar b. R. Shimon: He sinned five times: Four times in the days of Moses, and once in the days of Joshua. For it says, "Indeed I have sinned . . . such and such I have done." ["I have sinned" counts as one; "and such" counts as two; and the second "and such" counts as another two, for a total of five times: one in the days of Joshua, and four in the days of Moses (Yad Ramah).]

[As a result of Achan's theft in the days of Joshua, Israel was punished collectively by suffering defeat in the battle for the city of Ai. The Gemara asks: If Achan sinned in the days of Moses,] why were the Israelites not punished on those occasions [for his sins]? R. Yochanan said in the name of R. Elazar b. R. Shimon: Because God did not punish Israel for transgressions that were done privately, until they crossed the Jordan.

This statement is the subject of a dispute between Tanna'im: It says, "The hidden sins are for the Lord, our God [to punish], but the revealed [sins] are for us and our children [to prevent] forever" (Deuteronomy 29:28). Why are there dots [written in the sefer Torah] over the words lanu ulevaneinu, "for us and our children," and on the ayin of the word ad, "forever"? R. Yehudah said: This teaches that God did not punish Israel collectively for a sin that was done by an individual privately, until they crossed the Jordan, [but once they crossed the Jordan all Israel was held responsible for the private sins of an individual]. Said R. Nechemia to R. Yehudah: Did God ever punish [all Israel] for the private sins of an individual? Doesn't it say, "[The hidden sins are for the Lord] . . . forever"? [Meaning: Israel will never be punished collectively for the private sins of an individual.]

But just as God did not punish [the entire people] for secret transgressions [at any time], so too did He not punish them collectively for overt transgressions until they crossed the Jordan. [The dots on the letters tell us that overt transgressions were punished collectively only after they crossed the Jordan.] (44a) [The Gemara asks:] If so, in the case of Achan, why were all the people punished; [after all, he transgressed secretly]? [The Gemara answers:] Because his wife and children knew about his sin, [and since it was known to three people it must have been known to many; therefore it was not a secret transgression (Me'iri)].

[The Gemara continues by expounding other verses on the subject of Achan's transgression: It says, after Israel lost the battle at Ai,] "God said to Joshua . . . 'Israel has sinned'"[75] (Joshua 7:11). R. Abba b. Zavda said: Even though they sinned they are still called "Israel." [The name Israel symbolizes the greatness of the Jewish people.] R. Abba said: This is what people say: A myrtle, although it stands among willows, is still a myrtle, and is still called a myrtle.

[The verse continues,] "They have also violated My covenant that I commanded them; they have also taken from the consecrated property; they have also stolen; they have also denied; they have also placed [it] in their vessels" (ibid.). R. Ila'a said in the name of R. Yehudah b. Masparta: This teaches that Achan transgressed the five books of the Torah, because the word *gam*, "also," occurs five times in this verse.

ACHAN'S PUNISHMENT

The Resh Galuta [Exilarch] once said to R. Huna: It says, "And Joshua took Achan son of Zerach and the silver and the garment and the bar of gold, [the three articles he had taken,] and his daughters and his ox and his ass and his flock and his tent and all that belonged to him, and all of Israel with him, and they brought him up to the Valley of Achor . . . Then all of Israel pelted him with stones, burned them with fire, and stoned them with stones" (Joshua 7:24,25). The Resh Galuta asked: If Achan sinned, what was the crime of his sons and daughters [that they were put to death]? R. Huna replied: On your theory, if he sinned, how did all of Israel sin, that it says, "and all of Israel with him"? But all Israel were taken there to witness the punishment as a deterrent, so his daughters too were made to witness the execution as a deterrent. [Only Achan was put to death, and all of his property was destroyed.]

"They burned them with fire and stoned them with stones" (ibid.). Were they both burned and stoned? Ravina explained: Those things that were fit for burning [like silver, gold, and garments] were burned; those that were fit for stoning [the animals] were stoned [along with Achan himself].

[Achan admitted what he had done,] "I saw among the spoils a lovely Babylonian garment and two hundred shekels of silver" (ibid. v. 21). Rav said: It was an upper garment of very fine, pure wool. Shmuel said: It was a coat dyed with alum.

"And they spread them out before God" (ibid. v. 23). R. Nachman said: Joshua came and threw them down before God, exclaiming, "Master of the universe! Over such trivial items should the majority of the Sanhedrin [of seventy-one members] be killed?" As it says, "The men of Ai struck down about thirty-six of them" (ibid. v. 5) [literally: "like thirty-six"]. We learned

in a *Baraita*: Thirty-six people were slain, so says R. Yehudah. R. Nechemiah said to him: Were there then actually thirty-six? After all, it says "like thirty-six." Rather, this phrase refers to Ya'ir son of Menashe, who was equivalent to [like] the majority of the Sanhedrin.

JOSHUA CHALLENGES GOD

R. Nachman said in Rav's name: What is the following verse referring to: "A pauper utters supplications, but a rich one answers with brazen words" (Proverbs 18:23). "A pauper utters supplications"—this refers to Moses [who pleaded with God];[76] "but a rich one answers with brazen words" refers to Joshua. [The Gemara asks:] Why do you say that? Do you think, because it says, "They spread them out [the articles that Achan had taken] before God"? (Joshua 7:23), which R. Nachman interpreted: Joshua came and threw the articles down before God, [challenging God: Is it worthwhile that for these measly things the majority of Sanhedrin should be killed!]. [The Gemara asks:] But didn't Pinchas do the same thing? For it says, "And Pinchas stood up and executed judgment [*va'yefalleil*], and the plague was halted" (Psalms 106:30).

On which R. Elazar commented: It does not say *va'yitpalleil* [he prayed], but *va'yefalleil* [he judged]. This means that Pinchas brought charges against his Creator. [After he killed Zimri and Kozbi,][77] Pinchas threw down their corpses before God and cried out: Master of the universe! Is it worthwhile that over these two, twenty-four thousand of Israel should be killed? For it says, "Those that died in the plague were twenty-four thousand" (Numbers 25:9). [So we see that Pinchas, too, challenged God, and he was praised for it.] Rather, we can infer [that Joshua spoke brazenly to God] from the following verse: [After the defeat at Ai,] "Joshua said, 'Alas, my Lord, God. Why did You bring this people across the Jordan!'" (Joshua 7:7). [The Gemara asks:] But Moses reproached God in a similar way, saying, "Why do You mistreat Your people!" (Numbers 25:9). Rather, [Joshua spoke audaciously to God when he said], "If only we had been content to dwell on the other side of the Jordan!" (Joshua 7:7).

JOSHUA FAULTED FOR THE DEFEAT AT AI

"God said to Joshua, 'Arise!' [literally: 'Get up to you']" (ibid. v. 10). R. Shila expounded [the redundant words "to you"]: The Holy One, blessed be He, said to Joshua: That which you did is worse than that which they did. [In other words: The defeat at Ai is your fault:] I commanded, "When you cross the Jordan, you shall [immediately] set up the stones [on which the Torah is written]" (Deuteronomy 27:4), yet you went a distance of sixty *mils* [into the country[78] before you set up the stones]. After R. Shila went out, Rav appointed an interpreter to speak for him, who expounded: It says, "As God had commanded Moses His servant, so Moses commanded Joshua; and so Joshua did. He did not omit a thing of all that God had commanded Moses" (Joshua 11:15), [so how can R. Shila say that Joshua did not set up the stones as he was commanded!]. [The Gemara asks:] If so, [if Joshua is innocent,] what is the meaning of "Get up to you"? [since by the expression "to you," Joshua tacitly is blamed for the defeat at Ai]?

[The Gemara answers:] God told Joshua: You were the indirect cause of the defeat at Ai, because you issued the ban prohibiting them to take of the spoils of Jericho. [You thereby sparked Achan's transgression and the ensuing tragedy.] And that is why God said to Joshua when they laid siege to Ai [a second time], "You shall do to Ai and its king as you did to Jericho and its king, except that you may plunder its spoils and its animals for yourselves" (Joshua 8:2), [and don't place a ban on the spoils of Ai as you did on the spoils of Jericho].

TORAH STUDY GREATER THAN OFFERING THE *TAMID*

"It happened when Joshua was in Jericho that he raised his eyes and saw, and behold!—a man was standing opposite him with his sword drawn in his hand. Joshua went toward him and said to him, 'Are you with us or our enemies?' He said, 'No, for I am the commander of God's legion; now I have come.' Joshua fell before him to the ground and bowed down" (Joshua 5:13,14). [The Gemara asks:] How could Joshua do this [bow down]? Didn't R. Yochanan say: A person is forbidden to say "*Shalom*"[79] to someone else at night for fear that he might be a demon. [The Gemara answers:] This case was different, for he identified himself as "the commander of God's legion." But perhaps he lied?— We have a tradition that demons do not utter the name of God in vain, [and he said: God's legion]. (44b) The angel said to Joshua, ["Now I have come" (ibid.), implying,] Before nightfall you omitted to bring the evening *tamid*[80] and "now," at night, you neglected to study the Torah, [and therefore you deserve to be punished. Instead of spending the night at the battlefront, Joshua should have stayed with the troops in the main encampment and studied Torah with them (Rashi)].

Joshua asked him, "For which of these two things did you come [to warn me]?" "Now I have come" replied the angel. [I came for the neglect of Torah, which is happening now.] Immediately,[81] "Joshua spent the night in the midst of the valley" (ibid. 8:13), on which R. Yochanan commented: "In the midst of the valley" means that he spent the night delving into the depths of Torah study. R. Shmuel b. Unya said in Rav's name: The study of Torah is even greater than the offering of the *tamid*, for the angel said, "Now I have come" [to warn Joshua, not because of the *tamid*, but for neglecting Torah study].

THE ANGEL GABRIEL

[The Gemara cites another incident involving an angel.] Abaye asked R. Dimi: According to you in Eretz Yisrael, what does the following verse have reference to? "Do not be quick to enter into strife, unless you know what you will do in the end, when your fellow humiliates you. Pursue your quarrel with your friend, but do not give away the secrets of another" (Proverbs 25:8–9); [i.e., Don't get into a fight, but if you must, have the argument with your opponent; don't reveal any secrets involving someone else]. R. Dimi replied: [It refers to the following:] When the Holy One, blessed be He, said to Ezekiel: Go and say to Israel, "Your father was an Amorite and your mother a Hittite" (Ezekiel 16:3),[82] the angel Gabriel said to the Holy One, blessed be He: Master of the universe! If Abraham and Sarah came and stood before You, would You say this to them and embarrass them? "Pursue your quarrel with your friend [Israel], but do not divulge the secret of someone else [Abraham and Sarah]!"

[The Gemara asks:] Does the angel Gabriel have permission to such an extent, [as to argue with God and speak so audaciously]! Yes, he does. Because R. Yose b. R. Chanina said: He has three names: Piskon, Itmon, and Sigron. He is called Piskon [from *pasak*, to argue] because he argues with God; Itmon [from *atam*, to shut], because he closes up the sins of Israel [and prevents them from having an effect]; Sigron [from *sagar*, to lock], because he closes his mouth in defense of Israel, no one else speaks up for them.

It says, [Job's friends asked him,] "Did you arrange your plea to God before your trouble came upon you?" (Job 36:19). R. Elazar said: A person should always pray even before trouble befalls him; for if not for the fact that Abraham prayed before the trouble arrived between Beth-el and Ai[83] [when he foresaw the affliction that would result from Achan's theft], not one Jew would have survived. Resh Lakish [interprets the conclusion of the verse, which reads, "Whoever gives strength to his power"] saying: Someone who prays with strong concentration in this world, will have no adversaries in the world above. R. Yochanan said: A person should always pray that all [angels] should be on his side, so that he should have no antagonists among the angels above.

ACHAN AND ZIMRI ARE ONE AND THE SAME

[The Mishnah said:] From where do we know that [the condemned man's] confession made atonement for him? Our Rabbis taught: From the verse, "The sons of Zerach: Zimri, Etan, Heman, Calcol, and Darda— five in all" (1 Chronicles 2:6).[84] [Zimri is identical with

Achan (Rashi).] Why does it say "five in all" [isn't that obvious!]—Because all five have a portion in the World to Come. [Thus Zimri who is Achan also has a share in the world to come.] [The Gemara asks:] Here he is called Zimri, and elsewhere he is called Achan.[85] Why is this so? Rav and Shmuel have different opinions about this: According to one, his real name was Achan, and why was he called Zimri? Because he acted like Zimri, [who behaved immorally, and brought punishment on Israel through his sin].[86] According to the other, his real name was Zimri, and why was he called Achan? Because he rolled Israel's sins down on them [and brought punishment upon them].[87]

IF THE WITNESSES DISAVOWED THEIR TESTIMONY

We learned in a *Baraita*: It once happened that a person who was taken to be executed [because he was convicted of a sin that is punishable by death] said: If I am guilty of this sin [for which I am being executed] then my death should not atone for any of my sins; but if I am innocent of this sin, then my death should atone for all my sins. [He was trying to make the point that he was definitely innocent of the sin for which he was being executed. He continued,] It is not the fault of the Bet Din and all Israel, but may the witnesses [who testified falsely against me] never be forgiven. When the Sages heard this, [and sensed a tinge of doubt,] they said: It is impossible to set aside the verdict, because the sentence has been passed. He must therefore be executed, and the weight of responsibility will forever rest on the necks of the witnesses. [The Gemara asks:] It is self-understood that the sentence has to be carried out. Is he then to be believed [when he says that the witnesses were false. Why did the Sages give any credence to his words at all]? [The Gemara answers:] In this case the witnesses themselves changed their mind and disavowed their testimony [after the sentence was passed; nevertheless the sentence must be carried out].

[The Gemara asks:] What difference does it make that they retracted their testimony? Once a witness testified, he cannot testify again [and contradict his first testimony. The Bet Din assumes that the witnesses are changing their story because they don't want him to die on their account]. [The Gemara answers:] It is necessary to state this even where the witnesses give a reason for their original testimony [and say they gave the false testimony because the defendant was their enemy; nevertheless the sentence is carried out, and the responsibility rests on the witnesses], as in the case of Baya the tax collector [where the son of Shimon b. Shetach was executed on the basis of the testimony of false witnesses, even though they disavowed their testimony and said they testified falsely because they hated him].[88]

THE DECEASED SHOULD NOT REMAIN UNBURIED OVERNIGHT

[The Mishnah said: All who are stoned must afterward be hanged.] How is the condemned man hanged [after he was stoned]? A large pole is sunk into the ground, with a wooden beam projecting from its side. His two hands are brought together one over the other, and he is hanged from the wooden beam. . . . Immediately afterward he is let down. If he is left hanging overnight, a negative commandment is transgressed, for it says, "You may not allow his body to remain on the gallows overnight, but you must bury it on the same day, since a person who has been hanged is a curse to God" (Deuteronomy 21:23). What does this mean? People seeing him on the gallows will wonder: Why was this person hanged? Because he cursed the name of God. This then turns out to be an insult to God, [because people are reminded of his blasphemy]. R. Meir explained ["a curse to God":] When a person is in pain [referring to a person who is put to death because of his sin,] what expression does the *Shechinah* utter?—"My head feels heavy; My arm feels heavy; [I feel sick about it]."

Now if God is distressed about the blood of the wicked that is shed, how much more so over the blood of the *tzaddikim*! And not only [did the Sages say, that the body must not be left hanging overnight,] but anyone who leaves his dead overnight transgresses a negative commandment. However, if he kept the dead overnight for the sake of his honor, to prepare a coffin or a shroud for him, then he does not transgress this commandment. And they did not bury [the executed person] in the burial place of his ancestors, but two burial places were prepared by the Bet Din: one for those who were executed by decapitation or strangulation; the other for those who were put to death by stoning or burning.[89] Once the flesh was completely decomposed in the grave, the remains were gathered and buried in their proper place [in the family plot]. [After he was put to death,] the relatives came and greeted the judges and the witnesses wishing them *shalom*, as if to say: We hold no grudge against you, because you rendered a true judgment. (46b) And the relatives observed no mourning [they do not sit *shivah*, because outward expression of grief is forbidden], but they do maintain a sorrowful frame of mind, because grief is harbored in the heart.

[The Gemara says:] Our Rabbis taught [an explanation of "A person who has been hanged is a curse to God"]: There is a parable: There were two twin brothers who lived in the same city; one was appointed to be the king, whereas the other became a robber. The king commanded that [the twin brother] be hanged. But whoever saw him hanging exclaimed: The king is hanged! So the king gave a command to take him down from the gallows. [Man is created in the image of God, therefore it is an insult to God when His image is hanging on the gallows (Rashi).]

R. Yochanan said in the name of R. Shimon b. Yochai: How do we know from the Torah that a person who leaves his deceased relative unburied overnight transgresses thereby a negative commandment? From the passage, "You must bury [*kavor tikberenu*] him on the same day" (Deuteronomy 21:23). [The double expression denotes that the command concerns all dead, not only those executed by the Bet Din (Rashi).] From here we learn that a person who leaves a body unburied overnight transgresses a negative commandment.

THE MITZVAH OF BURIAL IN THE GROUND

Some say that R. Yochanan said in the name of R. Shimon b. Yochai: Where do we find an allusion in the Torah that it is a mitzvah to bury the dead? Because it says, "You must bury him." This is an allusion in the Torah to the mitzvah of burial.

King Shvur [a Persian ruler] asked R. Chama: From what verse in the Torah is burial of the dead derived? R. Chama remained quiet and did not answer. So R. Acha b. Yaakov exclaimed: The world has been handed over to fools! He should have answered, "You must bury him." [The Gemara says: That is no proof.] This could be explained [by King Shvur] to mean that he should be placed in a coffin [and entombed, but it does not necessarily mean interment in the ground]. [The Gemara suggests:] He should have brought a proof from *kavor tikberenu* [stating that the double expression signifies burial in the ground]. [The Gemara rejects that:] The king would not have understood such an inference; [he wanted a clear-cut Scriptural statement]. [The Gemara asks:] Why didn't he answer that it says in the Torah that the *tzaddikim* [the Patriarchs] were all buried in the ground?

[The Gemara answers:] King Shvur would say that this was only a custom. [The Gemara suggests: He could have cited] the fact that God buried Moses [which indicates that it is God's will]? King Shvur might answer: God buried him, so that Moses should not be treated differently from the customary way. Come and hear the following proof: It says [about Abijah son of Jeroboam], "All of Israel will lament for him and bury him" (2 Kings 14:13). He might answer again: so that he should not be treated differently from the customary way. But it says [concerning the wicked,] "They will not be eulogized nor buried; like dung upon the face of the earth will they be" (Jeremiah 16:4)? The king will still say that their punishment is to be buried, and thereby treated differently from the customary way. [That is why R. Chama did not give any of these answers to King Shvur; but we who do understand rabbinical expositions derive the mitzvah of burial in the ground from "You must bury him."]

DO EULOGIES HONOR THE LIVING OR THE DEAD?

The question was raised: Is a eulogy given in honor of the living or of the dead? What is the practical difference? If the deceased had said: Do not eulogize me; [then, if the eulogy is in honor of the living, the deceased cannot prevent it; on the other hand, the heirs can dispense with it]. Or, [another practical difference is] with regard to collecting the cost of the eulogy from the heirs. [If the eulogy is in honor of the dead, they must pay for it, even if they do not want to have a eulogy. If it is in honor of the living, the heirs can forgo it.] Come and hear the following proof: It says, "Abraham came to eulogize Sarah and to weep for her" (Genesis 23:2). Now, if you say that it is an honor of the living, can you say that for Abraham's honor Sarah's body was kept unburied until Abraham came back [from the *Akeidah*]?[90] [The Gemara answers:] Sarah herself was pleased that Abraham should attain honor through her.

Come and hear the following proof: It says [concerning Abijah, son of Joroboam,] "All of Israel will lament for him and bury him" (1 Kings 14:13). Now, if it is for the honor of the living, were [Abijah's relatives] worthy of honor? [The entire family of Jeroboam, except Abijah, were wicked!] [The Gemara answers:] The *tzaddikim* are pleased that people [in general] should be honored because of them.

Come and hear the following proof: It says, "[The wicked] will not be eulogized nor buried" (Jeremiah 16:4); [and if the eulogy is in honor of the living, why are the surviving *tzaddikim* denied this honor?]. Because the *tzaddikim* do not want to be honored through the wicked.

Come and hear the following proof: It says, "You [Zedekiah] will die peacefully, and like the burnings performed for your forefathers, so will they burn for you;[91] and they will lament you, saying, 'Woe, master'" (Jeremiah 34:5). Now, if you say the eulogy is in honor of the living, of what benefit is this to Zedekiah? The prophet Jeremiah told Zedekiah: Israel will be honored through you, as they were honored through your parents.

(47a) Come and hear the following proof: It says, [Who may sojourn in Your tent?] "One in whose eyes a contemptible person is repulsive" (Psalms 15:4). This refers to Hezekiah, King of Judah, who had the remains of his father Achaz dragged around on a bed made of ropes, [to humiliate him, because he was an idol worshipper. Hezekiah thereby demeaned himself for the greater glory of God]. Now if respect paid to the dead is only in honor of the living, why did he disgrace himself? [The Gemara answers:] He did it in order that his father should obtain forgiveness [by having his body disgraced]. [The Gemara asks:] And for the sake of his father's atonement could he set aside the honor of Israel? [The Gemara answers:] Israel was pleased to give up their honor for the sake of the atonement of Achaz [Hezekiah's father].

Come and hear the following proof: [Rabbi Yehudah Hanassi died in Tzipori but he was buried in Bet She'arim]. He said to his sons: Don't eulogize me in the small towns [on the way to Bet She'arim, but only in the larger cities where the people from the entire area will gather to hear the eulogy]. Now, if you assert that eulogies are held in honor of the living, what difference did it make to him? [The Gemara answers:] He thought that Israel would attain more honor through him [if larger crowds would attend his funeral orations].

Come and hear the following proof: R. Natan said: it is a good omen for the deceased when he is punished in this world after death [for he obtains forgiveness thereby]. For example, if a person dies and is not eulogized or buried properly, or if a wild beast drags him along, or if it rains on his bier, it is a good sign [that his sins are forgiven]. We can deduce from this that the funeral observances [and the mourning period] are in honor of the deceased, [otherwise, why should any of these distressing circumstances bring about atonement?]. This is conclusive proof.

DON'T BURY A WICKED MAN BESIDE A *TZADDIK*

R. Acha b. Chanina said: From what verse can we deduce that a wicked person may not be buried beside a *tzaddik*? From the verse, [It happened that troops from Moab would raid the land when] "some people were burying a man, and just then they saw the troop coming, so they threw the man into Elisha's grave. The man's body rolled over and touched the bones of Elisha. The man thereupon came back to life and rose up to his feet" (2 Kings 13:21). [This man was a false prophet,[92] and since God does not tolerate the burial of a wicked man next to a *tzaddik*, He revived him.] Said R. Papa to R. Acha b. Chanina: Perhaps this man's revival was only to fulfill the request [Elisha made of Elijah], "May twice as much of your spirit pass on to me" (2 Kings 2:9). [Since Elijah revived one person,[93] Elisha should have revived two, but until then he had revived only one—the son of the Shunamite woman.[94] But his incident does not prove that a wicked man may not be buried next to a *tzaddik*.]

Replied R. Acha b. Chanina: If [fulfillment of Elisha's request] is the reason, why does the *Baraita* say that the revived man only stood on his feet [for a few minutes] and did not return home? [You cannot call that fulfillment of "twice as much of Elijah's spirit"!] [The Gemara asks: If this is not a case of revival,] where does it say that Elisha's request was fulfilled and he did revive two people? [The Gemara answers:] As R. Yochanan said: Elisha healed the leprosy of Naaman,[95] and leprosy is as bad as death, as it says, [when Mirian was stricken with leprosy Moses

prayed,] "Let her not be like a corpse" (Numbers 12:12).

And just as we may not bury a wicked person next to a *tzaddik*, so may we not bury an extremely wicked person next to a mildly wicked one.

WHO INHERITS AN EXECUTED REBEL?

[The *halachah* states that if someone rebels against a Jewish king he is put to death.][96] (48b) We learned in a *Baraita*: The property of those executed by the government [for sedition] belongs to the King; the property of those executed by the Bet Din [for a sin punishable by death] belongs to their heirs. R. Yehudah said: Even the propety of those executed by the government goes to their heirs. The Sages said to R. Yehudah: But doesn't it say, [God said to Elijah, concerning King Ahab,] "Behold he is at the vineyard of Naboth, which he has gone down to inherit" (1 Kings 21:16). [At Jezebel's instigation, Naboth was falsely accused of cursing the King, whereupon he was put to death. The verb "to inherit" indicates that taking possession of his field had the outward appearance of legality; proof that the property of those executed by the government goes to the king.] Replied R. Yehudah: Naboth was Ahab's cousin, and therefore, Ahab was a legitimate heir, [if there were no closer relatives].

[The Sages asked:] But Naboth had in fact many sons [who should have inherited his estate]? R. Yehudah said: Ahab had both Naboth and his sons killed [so that Ahab was the closest surviving heir]. For it says, [God said,] "Did I not see the blood of Naboth and the blood of his sons?" (2 Kings 9:26). And the Rabbis [who say that Naboth did have sons; how do they explain this verse]? [They will answer:] This refers to the sons Naboth could have had, if he had not been killed.

[The Gemara says:] We can understand the view of [the Sages] who hold that the property [of those executed for sedition] belongs to the king; that's why it says, [that the false witnesses testified,] "Naboth cursed God and the King" (1 Kings 21:13), [mentioning the king]. But according to the view [of R. Yehudah] that their property goes to their heirs, [and Ahab took possession of Naboth's vineyard because he was the legitimate heir], why did the false witnesses have to add that he cursed the king, [since cursing God alone was enough reason to have him executed]? And according to your view, [that the witnesses accused him of sedition,] why did they mention that he cursed God? The reason they said both things was in order to infuriate the judges even more. So here, too, the witnesses added that he cursed the king in order to infuriate the judges even more.

[The Gemara continues:] We can understand the view that his property goes to the King; that's why it says, "Joab fled to the Tent of God and took hold of the horns of the Altar [which gave him immunity from the death sentence]" (1 Kings 2:28); and it says further, [when ordered to leave the Tent of God,] "Joab replied, 'No; for I shall die here'" (ibid. v. 30). [He refused to be tried by the King so that his estate would not revert to the King.] But according to the view [of R. Yehudah] that his estate goes to his heirs, what difference did it make to Joab? [The Gemara answers:] By holding on to the horns of the Altar he would live long enough [for his message to reach King Solomon, and for him receive an answer].

THE AFFLICTIONS DAVID WISHED ON JOAB

"Benaiah sent back word to the King [Solomon] saying, 'Thus spoke Joab, and thus did he answer me'" (1 Kings 2:30). [The Gemara explains:] He said to him, "Go and tell the King: You cannot punish me twice. If you kill me, you also must accept on yourself the curses your father pronounced against me [for murdering Abner.[97] If Solomon executed Joab, the curses would be transferred to Solomon]. But if you are unwilling to accept the curses, then you will have to let me live and let me suffer from your father's curses." It says, "The King then said to [Benaiah], 'Do as he said—strike him down there [at the Altar] and bury him'" (ibid. v. 31). [Solomon thereby accepted the curses.]

[The Gemara briefly digresses at this point:] Rav Yehudah said: All the curses David called down on Joab were fulfilled in David's own descendants. It says, "May the house of Joab never be without someone suffering from a discharge, a leper, those who lean on crutches, who fall by the sword, and who lack food" (2 Samuel 3:29). "Someone suffering from a discharge" was fulfilled in Rehoboam, for it says, "King Rehoboam then hastened to mount his chariot [merkavah] to flee to Jerusalem" (1 Kings 12:18); and elsewhere it says, "Every saddle [merkav] upon which the person with the discharge rides shall be unclean" (Leviticus 15:9). [It is derived from the fact that both verses contain the word merkav/merkavah.]

"A leper" was fulfilled in Uzziah, for it says, "But as he became strong, his heart became haughty to the point of destructiveness, and he betrayed the Lord his God—he entered the Sanctuary of God to burn incense upon the Incense Altar" (2 Chronicles 26:16). And it says further, "A leprous growth appeared on his forehead" (ibid. v. 19). "Those who lean on crutches" was fulfilled in Asa, for it says, [about Asa,] "Only in his old age his legs failed" (1 Kings 15:23). And Rav Yehudah said in the name of Rav: He suffered from gout in the feet. Mar Zutra the son of R. Nahman asked R. Nahman: What are the symptoms of gout? He answered: It feels like a needle being stabbed into raw flesh. How did R. Nachman know that? Either he

himself suffered from it, or, if you prefer, say that he had it by tradition from his teacher, or you may say, he knew it because "The secret of God is [revealed] to those who fear Him, and His covenant to inform them" (Psalms 25:14); [he received a Divine revelation].

"Who fall by the sword" was fulfilled in Josiah.[98] For it says, "The archers shot at King Josiah" (2 Chronicles 35:23), on which Rav Yehudah commented in the name of Rav: They perforated his body like a sieve. "Who lack food" was fulfilled in Yechoniah [Jehoiachin], for it says, "His allowance was a regular allowance given to him by the king [Evil-merodach of Babylonia]" (2 Kings 25:30). [We infer from this that during Yechoniah's imprisonment under Nebuchanezzar's rule he did lack food (Maharsha).] R. Yehudah said in the name of Rav: A popular saying has it: (49a) It is better to be cursed rather than to curse someone else, [because in the end, the curse reverts back to the one who uttered it or to his descendants (Rashi)].

THE INTERROGATION OF JOAB

[After this digression, the Gemara resumes the account of Joab's capture that began on 48b.] Joab was brought before the Bet Din. "Why did you kill Abner?"[99] [Solomon] asked him. "I was the avenger of [my brother] Asahel's blood,"[100] he replied. "But Asahel was a pursuer,"[101] [Solomon argued; thus Abner killed him in self-defense]. "Abner could have saved himself by disabling him, maiming one of his limbs; [he did not have to kill him,]" Joab countered.[102] "Maybe he was unable to [injure one of his limbs]," Solomon contended. "If he could aim exactly at Asahel's fifth rib," Joab answered back, "(as it says, 'Abner struck him with the back of his spear into the fifth rib' [2 Samuel 2:23], about which R. Yochanan said: It was at the fifth rib where the gall bladder and the liver are attached); couldn't he have aimed at one of his limbs?"

Thereupon [Solomon] said, "Let's drop [the killing of] Abner; why did you kill Amasa?"[103] Joab replied, "Amasa rebelled against the King." For it says, "So Amasa went to muster the men of Judah, but he was late for the appointed time which the King had set for him" (2 Samuel 20:5). Retorted Solomon, "Amasa interpreted the words ach, 'but,' and rak, 'only' [both signifying limitation]." This is what happened: Amasa found that the men of Judah had just started studying a tractate [and did not want to interrupt their studies]. He said: It says, "Any man who will rebel against your [Joshua's] utterance and will not listen to your words, in whatever you may command him, will be put to death" (Joshua 1:18).

Now, you might think that this applies even [when the transgression is committed] for the sake of Torah study: that's why it says, "Only, [rak] be strong and courageous" (ibid.); [rak implying a limitation. Thus you may disregard the king's command when you are engaged in Torah study]. In Amasa's opinion, Torah study takes precedence to the orders of the king; therefore, he did not disobey the king's orders [by being late]. [Continued Solomon,] "But you, Joab, did disregard the king's orders." For it says, "The news [that Solomon had been anointed king] reached Joab, [and he was frightened,] for Joab had sided with Adonijah, although he had not sided with Absalom [when he rebelled against his father David]" (1 Kings 2:28).

Why is "although he had not sided with Absalom" mentioned? [It seems to be irrelevant.] Rav Yehudah said: He wanted to join Absalom's [rebellion against David,] but he did not. And why did he not join? R. Elazar said: David still had vitality left in him, [but as soon as he became infirm, Joab teamed up with Adonijah's revolt]. R. Yose son of R. Chanina said: [Joab was frightened and did not join Absalom's rebellion because] David's general staff was still in operation. For Rav Yehudah said in the name of Rav: David had four hundred children, all born to him by *yefot to'ar*;[104] they had long hair and used to march at the head of the troops. These were the gallant champions of David's army.

This [view of Joab] is opposed by R. Abba b. Kahana, who said: If it had not been for David, [who studied Torah continuously,] Joab would not have triumphed in war; and if not for Joab, David could not have engrossed himself in [full-time] Torah study. For it says, "David administered justice and kindness to his entire people. Joab son of Zeruiah was in command of the army" (2 Samuel 8:15,16); meaning, why was David able to administer "justice and kindness to his entire people"? Because "Joab was in command of the army." And why was Joab in command of the army [and victorious in war]? Because "David administered justice and kindness to his entire people."

JOAB KILLED ABNER AND AMASAH

"Joab then left David's presence and sent messengers after Abner. They brought him back from Bor-hasirah" (ibid.3:26). What is the meaning of the name Bor-hasirah? R. Abba b. Kahana said a *bor* [well] and a *sirah* [thorn bush] were the causes of the killing of Abner.[105]

"Joab led [Abner] aside to the middle of the gate [as if] to talk to him casually" (2 Samuel 3:27). R. Yochanan said: He judged him according to the law of the Sanhedrin; ["gate" is often used for Bet Din].[106] Joab asked Abner, "Why did you kill Asahel?" "Because Asahel pursued me," Abner replied. "Then you should have saved yourself by injuring one of his limbs!" Joab retorted. "I could not do that," replied Abner. "If you could aim exactly at his fifth rib, couldn't you have struck him in one of his limbs?" countered Joab.

"[As if] to talk to him casually" (ibid.). Rav Yehudah said in Rav's name: He spoke to him about the taking off of the shoe [in the *chalitzah* ceremony].[107] He struck him there in the fifth rib" (ibid.). R. Yochanan said: In the fifth rib, where the gall bladder and liver are attached.

"God will thus return his blood upon his head because he struck two men who were more righteous and better than he" (1 Kings 2:32). "Better," because they interpreted correctly the words *ach* and *rak* [as denoting limitation, so that the king's orders must not be obeyed if they involved a violation of a Torah law]; whereas Abner did not [use this interpretation, and when the king ordered him to place Uriah in the front line so that he would be killed, he did obey].[108] "More righteous," because they received verbal orders [to kill the priests of Nob, yet they disobeyed the king]; whereas Abner was ordered in a letter [to have Uriah killed, and a verbal order by the king is stronger than a written command], and nevertheless he carried out the order.

"Amasa was not vigilant of the sword in Joab's [left] hand" (2 Samuel 20:10). Rav said: Because he did not suspect him. "And he [Joab] was buried at his house in the desert" (1 Kings 2:34). Was then this house in the desert? Rav Yehudah said in Rav's name: It was like a wilderness; just as a wilderness is ownerless and free for all, so was Joab's house open to all [to the needy to find food and shelter]. Or you might say: "Like a wilderness" means, just as a wilderness is free from robbery and immorality [because nobody lives there], so was Joab's house free from robbery and immorality. "Joab sustained the rest of the city" (1 Chronicles 11:8). R. Yehudah said: Even a meal of small fishes he would just taste and then distribute to the poor; [even a small snack he would share with the poor].

A *KOHEN*'S ADULTEROUS DAUGHTER

(52a) We learned in a *Baraita*: R. Meir used to say: Why does it say [in regard to the promiscuous daughter of a *kohen*], "She has defiled her father's [position]" (Leviticus 21:9)? If until that time her father was regarded as holy, he is now regarded as profane; if he was treated with respect, he is now treated with contempt; and people say: Cursed is the person who brought a child like this into the world; cursed is the person who raised a child like this; cursed is the person that has offspring like this. R. Ashi said: In accordance with whose opinion is a wicked man called "the son of a wicked man," even if he is really the son of a *tzaddik*? It is in accordance with the above Tanna.

NADAV AND AVIHU

We learned in a *Baraita*: Abba Yose b. Dustai said: [When Nadav and Avihu, Aaron's two sons, entered the Sanctuary to bring an unauthorized offering,][109] two streaks of fire burst forth from the Holy of Holies splitting into four, and two entered into each of their nostrils and burned them [entirely]. [The Gemara asks:] But it says, "It consumed them" (Leviticus 10:2), [which seems to imply an exclusion: "It consumed *them*," but not something else]. [The Gemara answers:] "It consumed them" implies "them," but not their garments.

Moses and Aaron once were walking along, with Nadav and Avihu following behind them, and all Israel behind them. Said Nadav to Avihu, "When are these two old men going to die, so that you and I are going to become the new leaders of the generation." But the Holy One, blessed be He, said to them, "We shall see who will bury whom." R. Papa said: People have a saying for this: There are many old camels that are carrying the hides of younger ones" [many old people outlive the young].

R. Elazar said: (52b) How is a Torah scholar regarded by an unlearned person? At first he appears to him like a golden pitcher; if he makes small talk with him, like a silver pitcher; if the scholar starts receiving favors from him, like an earthen pitcher [the unlearned person loses all respect]—once it breaks it cannot be repaired.

THE SEVEN LAWS OF MORALITY FOR MANKIND

(56a) Our Rabbis taught: Seven commandments were given to the descendants of Noah [i.e., all mankind]: the duty to establish a justice system; the prohibition of blasphemy; idolatry; adultery; bloodshed; robbery; eating flesh cut from a living animal. (56b) R. Chananiah b. Gamliel said: They are also forbidden to drink the blood of a living animal. R. Chidka said: They are forbidden to castrate. R. Shimon added witchcraft. R. Yose said: Everything that is mentioned in the segment on witchcraft is forbidden to the descendants of Noah, namely, "Among you, there shall not be found anyone who passes his son or daughter through fire, who practices stick divination, who divines auspicious times, who divines by omens, who practices witchcraft, who uses incantations, who consults mediums and oracles, or who attempts to communicate with the dead. Anyone involved in these practices is repulsive to God, and it was because of repulsive practices such as these that God your Lord is driving out [these nations] before you" (Deuteronomy 18:10–12). [This was the punishment God meted out to these nations,] and God would not punish them unless He had first forbidden them to do these things.

From what verse are these [seven commandments] derived? R. Yochanan said: From the verse, "The Lord God commanded the man [Adam], saying, 'You may freely eat from every tree in the Garden'" (Genesis 2:16). [The command was given to Adam, and, therefore, to all mankind.] "[He] commanded"—refers to the establishment of a justice system; and so it says,

"For I have loved him, because he commands his children and his household after him that they keep the way of God, doing charity and justice" (Genesis 18:19) ["command" is associated with "justice"]. "The Lord"— is [a prohibition] against blasphemy, and so it says, "One who pronounces blasphemously the Name of God shall be put to death" (Leviticus 24:16). "God"—is a prohibition against idolatry, and so it says, "You shall not recognize the gods of others in My presence" (Exodus 20:3). "The man"—refers to bloodshed [murder], and so it says, "Whoever sheds the blood of man, by man shall his blood be shed" (Genesis 9:6). "Saying"—refers to adultery, and so it says, "Saying: If a man divorces his wife, and she goes from him and became another man's" (Jeremiah 3:1).[110] "From every tree in the Garden"—but not of robbery. [Since it was necessary to permit Adam to eat from the trees, we gather that without permission it is forbidden to take things that belong to someone else (Rashi).] "You may freely eat"—but not flesh cut from a living animal.

STRIKING A JEW IS LIKE STRIKING THE *SHECHINAH*

(58b) R. Chanina said: He who slaps a Jew in the face is as though he slapped the *Shechinah*, for it says, "A person that strikes a man [i.e., a Jew] hits the Holy One" (Proverbs 20:25). Resh Lakish said: Whoever raises his hand against his neighbor [in a threatening gesture], even if he did not strike him, is called a wicked man, for it says, "[Moses] said to the wicked one, 'Why would you strike your fellow?'" (Exodus 2:13). It does not say "why did you strike" but rather, "why would you strike," which indicates that although he had not yet struck him he was called a wicked man. Ze'iri said in R. Chanina's name: He is called a sinner? For it says, [in reference to the wayward sons of Eli who intimidated the people into giving them larger portions than those apportioned to them by the Torah,] "The [kohen's attendant] would say, 'No, give [the meat] now, or else I will take it by force'" (1 Samuel 2:16).

And in the next verse it says, "The sin of the attendants was very great before God." R. Huna said: His hand should be cut off, as it says, "The raised arm [of the wicked] be broken" (Job 38:15). R. Huna had the hand cut off [of a person who was in the habit of hitting other people]. R. Elazar said: The only thing that can be done with such a person is to bury him, for it says, "As for the strong-armed man, for him is the earth" (Job 22:8). R. Elazar also said, [giving the verse a different interpretation]: Land was given only to the robust and sturdy [who have the strength needed to till the soil], for it says, "As for the man who has strong arms, his is the earth" (ibid.). Resh Lakish said: What is meant by the verse, "He who works his soil will be sated with bread" (Proverbs 12:11)? If a person makes himself a slave to his land [working hard cultivating the soil], he will be sated with bread; if not, he will not be sated with bread.

(59a) R. Meir used to say: From what verse do we know that a gentile who undertakes the study and observance of the Torah is like a *kohen gadol?* From the verse, "You shall observe My decrees and My laws, which man shall carry out and by which he shall live" (Leviticus 18:5). It does not say: priests, Levites, and Israelites, but "man": this teaches you that a gentile who takes up the study and observance of the Torah is like a *kohen gadol*. [The Gemara comments:] That refers to the case where the gentiles engross themselves in the study of their own seven laws; [but not in laws that do not apply to them].

ADAM WAS NOT ALLOWED
TO EAT MEAT
(59b) Rav Yehudah said in Rav's name: Adam was not permitted to eat meat, for it says, "God said, 'Behold, I have given you every seedbearing plant on the face of the earth . . . it shall be to you for food. For every beast of the field . . . " (Genesis 1:29,30), implying: but the beasts of the field shall not be food for you. But when the descendants of Noah appeared on the scene, it was permitted, for it says, "Like plant vegetation I have given you now everything" (ibid. 9:3); [now meat became permitted]. Now you may think that the prohibition of flesh cut from a living animal does not apply to the descendants of Noah; therefore the Torah teaches, "Nevertheless, you may not eat flesh of a creature that is still alive"[111] (ibid. v. 4), [which is addressed to all mankind].

We learned in a *Baraita*: R. Shimon b. Menassia said: What a pity that a great servant was lost to the world, for if the serpent had not been cursed, every Jew would have had two useful serpents: one he would have sent to the north and one to the south to bring him precious gems and costly pearls. And not only that, but he could have attached a strap under its tail with which it would bring up earth for his garden and his wasteland.

An objection was raised: R. Yehudah b. Teima said: [We learned that] Adam was sitting comfortably in Gan Eden, while ministering angels roasted meat and cooled wine for him. When the serpent looked in and saw his glory, it became envious of him; [so you see that he was allowed to eat meat]. [The Gemara answers:] This refers to meat that came down from heaven. [The Gemara asks:] But does meat come down from heaven? [The Gemara answers:] Yes; as in the story of R. Shimon b. Chalafta, who was walking on the road when a pack of hungry lions set upon him and began to roar at him [threatening to devour him]. He quoted, "The young lions roar after their prey" (Psalms 104:21). Thereupon two sides of beef came down from heaven. The lions ate one and left the other. This R. Shimon b. Chalafta brought to the *bet midrash*. He

asked: Is this fit to be eaten or not? The rabbis answered: Nothing unclean comes down from heaven.

TURNUS RUFUS
QUESTIONS R. AKIVA
(65b) Turnus Rufus [a Roman governor] asked R. Akiva the following question, "Why is the Sabbath different from any other day of the week?" Retorted R. Akiva, "Why are you different from other people?" [Why do you have more power than anyone else?] He answered, "Because my master, the Emperor, has so decreed." "The Sabbath too," R. Akiva shot back, "is different because our Master has ordained [that it should be so]." Said Turnus Rufus, "I meant to ask you: Who told you that the day you have chosen is actually Sabbath?" R. Akiva answered, "We can prove it from the river Sabbation [which flows all week with a powerful current, churning large boulders, but rests on *Shabbat*]; we can prove it also from the *baal ov* [who can conjure up the dead on any day of the week except *Shabbat*]; we can prove it from your father's grave [the whole week smoke rises up from it, as a sign that he is being burned in Gehinnom; but on *Shabbat* when the sinners in Gehinnom are granted respite, his grave is tranquil]." Turnus Rufus said to R. Akiva, "You have disgraced, shamed, and cursed my father [by giving this proof]."

OCCULT PRACTICES
We learned in a *Baraita*: It says, "Anyone who attempts to communicate with the dead" (Deuteronomy 18:11): this means a person who deprives himself of food and spends the night in the cemetery in order that an unclean spirit [the demon of the graveyard] should help him [with his witchcraft]. And when R. Akiva reached this verse, he used to cry: If someone who starves himself so that an unclean demon should cling to him, is successful in having his wish fulfilled, someone who fasts that the spirit of purity [prophecy] should attach itself to him—surely his wish should be granted! But what should I do? [Why doesn't it work?] It is because of our sins, as it says, "Your iniquities have separated between you and your God" (Isaiah 59:2).

Rava said: If the *tzaddikim* would [be free of all sin], they would have the power to create new worlds, for it says, "Your iniquities have separated between you and your God." Rabbah created a person [by using the *Sefer Yetzirah*[112]] and sent him to R. Zeira. R. Zeira spoke to him, but he did not answer, [because the power of speech comes only from God (*Maharsha*)]. Said R. Zeira, "I see that you were created by one of our colleagues. Go back to your dust!"

R. Chanina and R. Oshaia spent every Friday delving into the *Sefer Yetzirah* [Book of Creation], and they were able to create a calf that had reached one-third of its growth [i.e., a fat and tasty animal] and ate it.

Our Rabbis taught: A *menachesh* [a person who acts on the basis of good or bad omens] is a person who says: If your bread falls out of your mouth it is a bad sign; if your staff has fallen out of your hand; your son called after you; a raven screamed after you; a deer has crossed your path; a snake appeared at your right side, or a fox emerged at your left; [all these are bad omens]. (66a) [When the tax collector comes] he will say: Don't start with me; or he will say [to the tax collector:] It is morning, it is Rosh Chodesh, or the close of *Shabbat* [please don't make me start the day, the month, or the week with the unpleasant obligation of paying taxes; it is a bad portent].

Our Rabbis taught: It says, "Do not act on the basis of omens. Do not act on the basis of auspicious times" (Leviticus 19:26). This refers to people who practice fortune-telling with cats, birds, fish, and stars.

BEWITCHED
(67b) Ze'iri happened to go to Alexandria in Egypt and bought a donkey. When he wanted to give it water to drink, it vanished, and in its place there was a plank of a bridge; [using witchcraft they had turned a plank into a donkey, and anything created by witchcraft dissolves when touched by water]. [When Ze'iri wanted to get his money back,] the sellers told him: If you were not Ze'ri, we would not refund the money to you: does anyone buy anything in this town without checking it out with water? [The town was known to be a hotbed of witchcraft.]

Yannai happened to stop at a certain inn. When he asked for a drink of water they brought him *shatita* [a drink made of water mixed with flour]. Seeing that the lips of the woman who was bringing him the drink were moving [mumbling a magic formula], he [unobtrusively] spilled a little of it, and it turned into scorpions. Then he said, "I have taken a little of your drink, now you take from my drink." So he gave her from his drink, and she turned into a donkey. He then rode on her into the market. Her friend came and [whispered an incantation] whereupon she turned back into a woman. People then saw him riding on a woman's back in the marketplace.

WHERE DID ALL
THE FROGS COME FROM?
[At the plague of frogs, it says,] "And the frog ascended and covered the land of Egypt" (Exodus 8:2). R. Elazar said: There was actually only one frog, but it produced many others, which filled the land of Egypt. This subject is debated by *Tanna'im*. R. Akiva said: There was one frog that filled all of Egypt [by multiplying profusely]. R. Elazar b. Azariah disagreed and told him: Akiva, what are you doing, involving yourself in *aggadah* [the homiletical and narrative portions of the Gemara]. Stop engaging in this field of study. Immerse

yourself in the tractates of Plagues and Tents [that deal with the more complex subjects of uncleanness due to leprosy and contact with a corpse]. What happened was that one frog croaked and all the others came.

R. ELIEZER'S FINAL WORDS
(68a) When R. Eliezer became sick, R. Akiva and his colleagues came to visit him. He was sitting in a bed with a canopy, and they were sitting in the vestibule in front of his room. It was late Friday afternoon, so Hyrkanus, the son of R. Eliezer, came in to take off his father's *tefillin*, [because *tefillin* may not be worn on *Shabbat*]. But his father admonished him, and Hyrkanus left the room feeling reprimanded. On his way out he commented to his colleagues, "It seems to me that my father's mind is not clear, [and that he is close to death]. But R. Eliezer said to them, "The minds of Hyrkanus and his mother are disturbed, because they neglect to attend to the things that must be taken care of before *Shabbat* and which are punishable by death [if they are done on *Shabbat*[113]], and they are concerned about [my wearing the *tefillin* on *Shabbat*], which is forbidden merely as a rabbinical ordinance."

Since all the Sages saw that R. Eliezer's mind was very clear, they entered his chamber but sat down at a distance of four cubits [because he had been placed under a ban].[114] "Why have you come?" R. Eliezer asked them. "To learn Torah from you," they replied. "And why did you not come until now?" he asked. "Because we did not have time," they retorted. [That was just an excuse; the true reason was the ban (Yad Ramah).] He then said to them, "I will be surprised if these people will die a natural death." R. Akiva asked him, "What will my death be?" R. Eliezer replied, "Your death will be worse than theirs." He then placed his two arms on his heart and moaned, "Woe is to my two arms that are like two Torah scrolls that are rolled up, [their words are covered, so will my knowledge be covered after I die].

"Much Torah have I learned from my teachers, and much Torah have I taught. Much Torah have I learned from my teachers, but I did not take away from their Torah even as much as a dog licking from the sea; [compared to their vast erudition, my knowledge is minimal]. I have taught a great deal of Torah, but my students have diminished the distance between us as much as a painter's brush that is dipped into a paint tube. I learned three hundred *halachot* concerning a leprous plague, and no one ever questioned me about these *halachot*. And not only that, but I have learned three hundred *halachot*—and some say, three thousand—about the planting of cucumbers, [how, by means of sorcery a person can fill overnight an entire field with cucumbers], and no one, except Akiva b. Yosef, ever asked me concerning these *halachot*.

"One time we were both walking together on a road when he asked me, 'Rabbi, teach me [how through sorcery one can] plant cucumbers.' So I uttered an incantation, and instantly the whole field filled up with cucumbers. Then he said, 'Rabbi, you have taught me how to plant them; now teach me how to pick them.' So I said something, and instantly all the cucumbers were gathered in one place." The students then asked him [whether the following types of vessels can become unclean]: a ball, a shoemaker's form, an ornamental amulet, a leather bag containing pearls, a small weight that was carried inside a leather sack. He replied: They can become unclean, and when they are unclean, they can be purified just as they are, [and their stuffing does not have to be removed]. Then they asked, "What about a shoe that is on the form?" [An object can accept *tum'ah* only after it is completely finished; an unfinished object cannot accept *tum'ah*. The question was whether or not a shoe on the form is considered a finished product.] R. Eliezer told them, [It is not a finished object; therefore,] "It is clean." And with the word "clean" on his lips, his soul left him in purity.

R. Yehoshua then stood up and declared, "The vow [by which he had been placed under a ban] is annulled; the vow is annulled!" On the conclusion of *Shabbat*, R. Akiva met his casket as it was being carried from Kisri [Caesarea] to Lod [Lydda]. Overcome with grief, he struck his flesh until his blood started flowing down on the earth. Then R. Akiva began his eulogy as the Sages were gathered around R. Eliezer's remains, crying out, "'Father! Father! Israel's chariot and horsemen!' [2 Kings 2:12]. I have a large number of coins, but no banker that will change them." [I.e., I have many halachic questions to ask, but no one to answer them (Rashi).]

JUVENILE FATHERS

(69b) From where do we know that in the earlier generations a boy of eight years could father children? From the verse, (a) "Bezalel, son of Uri, son of Chur of the tribe of Judah" (Exodus 38:22), and it says, (b) "When Azuvah died, Caleb married Efrat, who bore him Chur" (1 Chronicles 2:19). Now how old was Bezalel when he built the Tabernacle? Thirteen years, for it says, (c) "All the wise people came—those performing all the sacred work, every man from the work that they were doing" (Exodus 36:4), [and a person is not called a man before he is thirteen years old]. And we learned in a *Baraita*: (d) In the first year of the Exodus, Moses built the Tabernacle; in the second year he erected it and sent out the spies. And it says, (e) "Caleb said, . . . 'I was forty years old when Moses the servant of God sent me from Kadesh-barnea to spy out the land' (Joshua 14:7) . . . 'and now, behold, I am eighty-five years old today'" (ibid. 10).

Now, how old was Caleb when he was sent as a spy? Forty. Subtract fourteen, Bezalel's age at the time; this leaves twenty-six years [as Caleb's age at Bezalel's birth]. Now, subtract two years for the three pregnancies; it follows that each must have fathered a son at the age of eight. [(A) and (b) show that Caleb was Bezalel's great-grandfather. (C) and (d) show that Caleb was twenty-six when Bezalel was born. Within those twenty-six years three generations—Chur, Uri, and Bezalel—were born; hence their fathers must have been eight years old when they begat them (*Maharsha*).]

THE BOON AND BANE OF WINE

(70a) R. Chanan said: The only reason that wine was created was to console the mourners and to reward the wicked [for the little good they do in this world (Rashi)]. For it says, "Give strong drink to the evildoers [as compensation for those few good deeds] and wine to those of embittered soul" (Proverbs 31:6). R. Yitzchak said: What is the meaning of, "Do not look at wine becoming red" (ibid. 23:31)? Don't get involved with wine, for it reddens the face of the wicked in this world, and makes them pale [with shame] in the World to Come. Rava said: "Do not look at wine [*ki yit'addam*]": do not get involved with it, because it leads to bloodshed [*dam*].

R. Kahana pointed out a contradiction: The Torah's word for wine is *tirosh*, but it is written *tirash* [without a *vav*] (Genesis 27:28,37).—If a person merits it [and uses wine properly], he will rise to become the leader; if not, he becomes poor.[115] Rava pointed out a contradiction: It says, "Wine gladdens [*yesammach*] man's heart" (Proverbs 104:15), but it is written *yeshammach* [which has the connotation of *shemamah*, desolation].—If a person uses wine in moderation, it makes him glad; but if drinks excessively, it ruins him. And this is what Rava meant when he said: [The moderate use of] wine and aromatic spices helped me gain wisdom.

R. Amram son of R. Shimon b. Abba said in the name of R. Chanina: What is meant by the verse, "Who cries, 'Alas!'? Who cries, 'Woe'? Who is contentious? Who prattles? Who is wounded for naught? Whose eyes are red? Those who linger over wine; those who come to inquire over mixed drinks" (Proverbs 23:29,30)?—When R. Dimi came [from Eretz Yisrael], he said: In Eretz Yisrael they say: The one who explains this passage saying that the second part of the verse follows the first part does it correctly. [Who has all these shortcomings? Those who linger over wine . . .]. But the passage may also be explained conversely, that the first part is the result of the second part. [The verse tells us that it is fitting to linger over wine for someone who is in mourning, or for an evil person who is at odds with everybody.]

Ovar the Galilean expounded: [In the chapter about Noah's downfall as a result of his drunkenness] there are thirteen words that begin with the letters *vav yud*, which form the word *vay* [an outcry of woe]. "*And*

Noah, the man of the earth, debased himself *and* planted a vineyard. *And* he drank from the wine, *and* became drunk, *and* he uncovered himself with his tent. *And* Ham, the father of Canaan, saw his father's nakedness, *and* told his two brothers outside. *And* Shem and Japheth took the garment, *and* they laid it upon both their shoulders, *and* they walked backwards, *and* covered their father's nakedness. *And* Noah awoke from his wine, *and* he realized what his small son had done to him" (Genesis 9:20–24).

"And Noah, a man of the earth, debased himself and planted a vineyard" (ibid.). R. Chisda said in R. Ukva's name, and others say, Mar Ukva said in R. Zakkai's name: [Why was Noah called "a man of the earth"?—The Holy One, blessed be He, said to Noah: Noah, shouldn't you have learned a lesson from Adam, whose downfall came as a result of wine? [And Adam, too, is called "a man of the earth" because he was created from the dust of the earth.] This goes according to the view that the forbidden tree from which Adam ate was a vine. For we learned in a *Baraita*: R. Meir says: The tree from which Adam ate was a vine, (70b) because there is nothing that brings as much trouble to the world as wine does; [through Adam's sin, wine introduced the concept of death to the world]. R. Yehudah says: The Tree of Knowledge was the wheat plant, because a baby cannot say "father" and "mother" until he has reached the stage that he is eating wheat. [Thus wheat generates knowledge.] R. Nechemiah said: It was a fig tree, because the thing with which Adam and Eve sinned [the fig] became the agent through which the damage was repaired [the fig leaves]; for it says, [after Adam and Eve sinned,] "They sewed together fig leaves and made themselves loincloths" (Genesis 3:7).

SOLOMON REPRIMANDED
BY HIS MOTHER

"The words of Lemuel [Solomon] the king, the speech of reproof with which his mother disciplined him" (Proverbs 31:1), [because she saw him indulging in excessive eating and drinking]. R. Yochanan said in the name of R. Shimon b. Yochai: This teaches that his mother tied him to the whipping post and said to him, "What is it my son? And what is it, O son of my womb? And what is it, O son of my vows?" (ibid. v. 2). By "what is it my son" she meant to say: Everybody knows that your father was a God-fearing man, and therefore they will say that it is your mother who caused you to go astray. By "what is it, O son of my womb" she meant to say: All the other wives of your father, as soon as they became pregnant, they did not have relations with the king anymore; but when I became pregnant I pushed myself to be intimate with David, in order that I should have a strong and healthy son.[116] By "and what is it, O son of my vows" she meant to say: All the wives of your father's household made

vows and prayed that they should have a son worthy to be king, but I vowed and prayed that I should have a son who is diligent and filled with the knowledge of the Torah and fit to be a prophet.

[She then admonished him,] "It is not proper for kings who belong to God, it is not proper for kings to drink much wine, and for princes to imbibe strong drink" (ibid. v. 4). [The Gemara explains:] She told him: Why do you act like all the other kings who drink wine and become intoxicated, and who say: What do we need God for? By "and for princes [*rozenim*] to imbibe strong drink" (ibid.), she meant to say: Is it right that someone to whom all the mysteries [*razei*] of the world are revealed should drink wine and become intoxicated? Others say: Someone to whose door all the princes [*rozenim*] come should drink wine and become intoxicated? R. Yitzchak said: From where do we know that Solomon repented and agreed with his mother? Because it says, "Surely I am more foolish than *ish*, and do not have the understanding of a man [*adam*]" (ibid. 30:2). *Ish* refers to Noah about whom it says, "Noah, the man [*ish*] of the earth debased himself" (Genesis 9:20). "And do not have the understanding of *adam*" refers to Adam; [both Adam and Noah had their downfall because of wine, and I did not learn my lesson to keep away from wine].

(71a) R. Zeira said: Whoever sleeps in the *bet midrash*, his knowledge will be torn to shreds, [he forgets his learning, and his memory becomes erratic,] for it says, "And slumber will clothe you in tatters" (Proverbs 23:21).

THE WAYWARD AND
REBELLIOUS SON

[We read in the Torah that the parents of a "wayward and rebellious son" must bring him to the Bet Din and declare, "This son of ours is wayward and rebellious. He does not listen to our voice, and is an exceptional glutton and drunkard." He is then to be stoned to death (Deuteronomy 21:18–21).]

We learned in a *Baraita*: R. Yehudah said: If his mother is not like his father in voice, appearance, and stature, he does not become a rebellious son. Why is that so? Because it says, "He does not listen to our voice" (Deuteronomy 21:18), ["voice" is in the singular; therefore they must both have similar voices].[117] And since they must be alike in voice, they must also be alike in appearance and stature. [The Gemara asks:] With whom does the following *Baraita* agree: There never has been a "wayward and rebellious son" [in the Torah sense, that had to be executed], and there never will be. Why then was the law written? That you may study it and receive a reward.—It agrees with R. Yehudah, [since it is impossible that both parents should be exactly alike]. If you prefer, say that the *Baraita* agrees with R. Shimon, for we learned in a *Baraita*: R. Shimon said: [Can you imagine] that because a son ate a *tartemar*[118] of meat and drank a half a *log* of Italian wine, his father and mother shall have him stoned? But it never happened and never will happen. Why then was this law written? That you may study it and receive a reward. R. Yonatan said: I have seen [a rebellious son who was executed] and sat on his grave.

THE APOSTATE CITY
[The Torah states that if lawless people have convinced the majority of a city to worship idols, the city and its inhabitants must be destroyed (Deuteronomy 13:13–19).] [The Gemara asks:] With whose view does the following *Baraita* agree: There never was an "apostate city" and there never will be.—It agrees with R. Eliezer, for we learned in a *Baraita*: R. Eliezer said: A city in which there is even a single *mezuzah* cannot be condemned to be destroyed as an "apostate city." Why is that so? Because it says, [concerning an "apostate city,"] "Gather all the city's goods to its central square, and burn the city along with all its goods" (Deuteronomy 13:17). But if in it there is a single *mezuzah*, this is impossible, [because a *mezuzah* contains God's name,] and it says, [that you must obliterate all traces of idolatry in Eretz Yisrael, but] "You may not do this to the Lord your God" (ibid. 12:4), [which is the commandment not to erase God's name]. R. Yonatan said: I saw an "apostate city" [that was destroyed] and sat on its ruins.

THE TORAH ANTICIPATED THE OUTCOME
(72a) It has been taught: R. Yose Hagelili said: Can it be that the Torah ordained that the [rebellious son] should be brought before the Bet Din to be stoned just because he ate a *tartemer* of meat and drank a *log* of Italian wine? [He answers: The Torah does not punish him for his present offense, but] it anticipates his mature personality. For in the end, after wasting his father's wealth, he still will want to satisfy his cravings, but being unable to do so, he will then stand at the crossroads and rob people, [and when his victim resists he will kill him (Rashi)]. So the Torah says: Let him die while he is still innocent, rather than let him die guilty. For the death of the wicked is beneficial for them [for they cannot add to their sins] and for the world [because now people are safe]; the death of *tzaddikim* is painful for them [because they can no longer do *mitzvot*] and for the world [because the *tzaddikim* protect and counsel their generation]. Tranquility of the wicked is harmful to them and the world, but pleasing to the *tzaddikim* and the world, [because they have time to learn Torah]. Wine and sleep are beneficial for the wicked and for the world [while they are asleep they cannot do any harm]; but harmful to the *tzaddikim* and the world [because they do not engross themselves in Torah study].

When the wicked split up it is beneficial for them and for the world [because they cannot get together to concoct sinister plans], but when *tzaddikim* separate they hurt themselves and the world.

DON'T DELAY MARRYING OFF YOUR DAUGHTER
(76a) It says, "Do not defile your daughter to make her a harlot" (Leviticus 19:29). R. Eliezer said: This refers to a father who marries his [young] daughter to an old man; [since she does not accept him, she will engage in extramarital relations (Rashi)]. R. Akiva said: This refers to a father who delays marrying off his daughter who has reached maturity. R. Kahana said in the name of R. Akiva: The only poor in Israel is the crafty wicked man and he who delays marrying off his daughter who has reached maturity. [The Gemara asks:] But is not a person who delays *himself* a crafty wicked man? [Why does it say: "*and* who delays . . . "?] Abaye answered: (76b) This is what R. Kahana meant to say: Which poor man is a crafty wicked man? One who delays marrying off his daughter who has reached maturity. [Because of his poverty he delays her marriage so that he may benefit from her labor.] R. Kahana also said in the name of R. Akiva: Stay clear of a person who dispenses advice for his own benefit.

Rav Yehudah said in Rav's name: A person who marries his daughter to an old man or takes a wife for his son who has not reached maturity, or returns a lost article to a Cuthean; about him the Torah says, "He may say, 'I will have peace, even if I do as I see fit. Let me add some moisture to this dry [practice]!' God will not agree to forgive such a person" (Deuteronomy 29:18).

A TACTFUL REMINDER
(81a) [Rav Yehudah disagreed with his father and told him that he was wrong. Thereupon] Shmuel said to Rav Yehudah: You brilliant scholar! Don't speak to your father that way, [telling him bluntly that he made a mistake, because you embarrass him]. And so we learned in a *Baraita*: If a son saw his father [unintentionally] transgressing a law of the Torah, he should not say to him, "Father, you have violated a Torah law," but he should say, "Is this what the Torah says?" [The Gemara asks:] But isn't that the same thing? [The Gemara answers:] He should tell him calmly, "Father, it says in the Torah as follows: . . . " [and the father will draw his own conclusion].

CRITERIA FOR RIGHTEOUSNESS
R. Acha b. Chanina lectured: The passage, "If a man is righteous and practices justice and righteousness: he does not partake on the mountains"? (Ezekiel 18:5), means that he did not draw on the merits of his ances-

tors, [but is sustained by his own merits].[119] "He does not lift his eyes toward the idols of the house of Israel" (ibid.) means that he did not walk with a proud bearing. "He does not defile his neighbor's wife" (ibid.) means that he never competed professionally with his neighbor. "And does not approach an impure woman" (ibid.) means that he never derived any benefit from a charity fund. And it says, "He is a righteous man, he shall surely live" (ibid. v. 9). When R. Gamliel read this verse, he cried and said, "Only if a person fulfills *all* of these shall he live, but not if he did just one of them." R. Akiva told him, "If that is so, the verse, 'Do not become defiled through all these things' (Leviticus 18:24), [referring to forbidden sexual relations], would mean that a person becomes defiled only if he engages in *all* forbidden relations, [not just in one of them]? But it means [he becomes defiled] if he transgresses even one of them; so here, too, even if he fulfills just one of them, [he shall live]."

THE JUDICIAL SYSTEM
(88b) We learned in a *Baraita*: R. Yose said: Initially there were not many disputes in Israel; there was one Bet Din of seventy-one judges that sat in the Hall of Hewn Stones, and there were two courts of twenty-three judges—one sitting at the entrance of the Temple Mount, and one sitting at the entrance of the [Temple] Courtyard, and other courts of twenty-three judges were sitting in all cities throughout Eretz Yisrael. When a question came up, the local Bet Din was asked. If the local judges had heard the correct ruling about this matter, they would tell it to the litigants; and if not, the litigants went to the Bet Din nearest to their town. If those judges had heard the correct ruling, they would tell it to the litigants; if not, the litigants would go to the Bet Din situated at the entrance of the Temple Mount. If those judges had heard the correct ruling, they would tell it to the litigants; if not, the litigants would go to the Bet Din seated at the entrance of the Temple Courtyard.

The one who disagreed with his colleagues would say: This is how I expounded, and this is how my colleagues expounded. If those judges had heard the correct ruling, they would tell it to the litigants; if not, they all went to the High Court in the Hall of the Hewn Stones, where the Sanhedrin was in session from the time the morning *tamid* [the daily morning offering] was offered until the afternoon *tamid* was offered. On *Shabbat* and Yom Tov the Sanhedrin sat in the *cheil* [a spacious open area surrounded by walls, because on these days the Hall of Hewn Stones was too crowded (Rashi)].

The question was then put to them. If the members of the Sanhedrin had heard the correct ruling, they would rule accordingly; if not, they took a vote: if the majority voted the object "unclean," they declared it unclean; if "clean," they declared it clean. But when

the students of Shammai and Hillel who did not have proper training increased in number, halachic disputes mounted in Israel, and the Torah became like two Torahs [because of the many conflicting rulings].

THE QUALIFICATIONS OF A JUDGE
From there [the Sanhedrin] the judges sent a message to [the lower courts in] all Israel stating: Whoever is wise, humble, and well-liked by the people should be appointed judge in his city. From there [the municipal courts] the [judges] were promoted to the Bet Din of the Temple Mount [when there was a vacancy]; from there to the Bet Din in the Temple Courtyard; and from there to the Sanhedrin in the Hall of Hewn Stones [if one of its members died].

They sent a message from Eretz Yisrael: Who is worthy of a share in the World to Come? A person who is modest and humble, who bends his head when entering and leaving the house, who constantly studies Torah and does not think highly of himself because of it. [Hearing this message,] the Rabbis focused their eyes on R. Ulla b. Abba [because he fit that description].

A TRUE AND A FALSE PROPHET
(89a) [The Mishnah said:] A false prophet—one who prophesies something he has not heard or something that was not told to him [although it was told to another prophet]—is put to death at the hands of man.

[For a better understanding of the following discussion a brief historical summary is in order: The evil King Ahab of Israel and his wicked wife Jezebel desired a vineyard that belonged to Navot the Jezreelite. When Navot refused to sell it, they had him put to death on trumped-up charges and confiscated his vineyard. Subsequently, Ahab made a pact with the righteous King Yahoshafat of Judah to go to war together and capture the town of Ramot-Gilead from the King of Aram. Yehoshafat advised Ahab to consult the prophets before going into battle. Ahab sought the advice of four hundred of his false prophets and was encouraged to launch the attack. To underscore his advice, one false prophet named Tzidkiah ben Kenaanah made horns of iron and told Ahab, "Thus said God, 'With these you will gore Aram!'" (1 Kings 22:11)

However, there was one true prophet of God, named Michaihu ben Yimlah, who predicted Ahab's death in battle. To lend added weight to his words, Michaihu related to Ahab a heavenly scene he had viewed, stating, "God asked [the angels], 'Who will entice Ahab so that he will march and fall at Ramot Gilead?' One angel said thus, and another said thus, until a certain spirit came forward and said, 'I will entice him. I will be a lying spirit in the mouth of all his prophets.'" R.

Yochanan said: This was the spirit of Navot the Yezreelite.]

[The Gemara now discusses the subject of the false prophet.] The Rabbis taught: Three are executed by man [for offenses related to prophecy. They are executed by strangulation], and three by the hands of Heaven: One who prophesies something he has not heard; for example, Tzidkiah ben Kenaanah, for it says: "Tzidkiah ben Kenaanah made himself iron horns, and said, 'Thus has God said: With these you will gore Aram'" (1 Kings 22:11). [The Gemara asks:] But what else could Tzidkiah have done, since the spirit of Nabot misled him, for it says, "And God said, 'Who will lure Ahab to go to war and fall at Ramot-Gilead?' . . . Then the spirit [of Nabot] came forward and stood before God and said, 'I will lure him!' And God said, 'You will lure him, and you will succeed! Go forth and do it!'" (1 Kings 22:20–22). [So you see that Tzidkiah ben Kenaanah was duped into prophesying the success of Ahab's campaign. Why then should Tzidkiah be held responsible for it?]

[Digressing briefly,] Rav Yehudah said: What did God mean when He said, "Go forth"? He meant to say, "Leave My domain." What was this "spirit" of which the verse speaks? The spirit of Nabot the Jezreelite [who wanted to take revenge on Ahab for taking his life. He was ordered to leave God's nearness because he had brought punishment on Ahab].[120]

[The Gemara asked above: What could Tzidkiah ben Kenaanah have done, since the spirit of Nabot misled him? The Gemara answers:] He should have paid close attention [to the utterances of the false prophets], bearing in mind the saying of R. Yitzchak: The same prophetic message may go out to several prophets; however, each prophet will express it differently. For example: the prophet Obadiah said, "The wickedness of your heart has misled you" (Obadiah 1:3), while Jeremiah put it, "Your tyranny has beguiled you, the wickedness of your heart" (Jeremiah 49:16). But since the four hundred "prophets" [that Ahab consulted] all proclaimed the same "prophecy," word for word, [namely, "Go to war! You will be victorious!"] Tzidkiah could have gathered that what they said was worthless.

[The Gemara asks:] But perhaps Tzidkiah ben Kenaanah did not know the rule of R. Yitzchak? [The Gemara answers:] Yehoshafat was there and warned them, for it says, "Yehoshafat said, 'Is there no other prophet of God here of whom we may inquire?'" To which Ahab replied, "But there are all these [four hundred whose prophecy you just heard]!" Retorted Yehoshafat, "I have a tradition from my grandfather's house, that the same prophetic message may be revealed to several prophets, but no two prophets use the same phrase in expressing the prophecy." [Thus Tzidkiah ben Kenaanah should have known better.]

THE PUNISHMENT FOR UNAUTHORIZED PROPHECIES

[The Mishnah said:] Someone who prophesies that which was not said to him [even though the prophecy was presented to another prophet,] is liable to the death penalty at the hand of man. [The Gemara comments:] For example, Chananiah ben Azur [who lived in the days of Jeremiah and prophesied that the Babylonian exile would not occur. This is what happened:] Jeremiah was standing in the upper marketplace of Jerusalem and proclaimed, "Thus said God, Master of Legions: Behold I am breaking the strength of Elam" (Jeremiah 49:35). Based on this, Chananiah drew a *kal vachomer* inference:[121] If Elam, which [fought against Israel] only to help Babylonia, yet the Holy One, blessed be He, said, "Behold, I am breaking the strength of Elam"; all the more [will God destroy] the Chaldeans [i.e., Babylonians] themselves!

So he went to the lower marketplace and declared, "Thus said God . . . , 'I have broken the yoke of the king of Babylonia!'" (ibid. 28:2), [although he never received this prophecy]. R. Papa said to Abaye: But this illustration does not apply, since this prophecy was not [told to anyone else,] not even to his colleague [Jeremiah]? [Jeremiah received the prophecy only concerning Elam, but not regarding Babylonia.] Abaye answered: Since the Sages say that we can expound the Torah by means of *a fortiori* reasoning, it is as though [the prophecy about Elam] had been told to Jeremiah. [But it was never given to Chananiah ben Azur. Therefore the illustration does apply.]

Someone who prophesies in the name of an idol [is strangled]; like the prophets of Baal.

Someone who keeps his prophecy to himself [and does not proclaim it,] is liable to death at the hands of Heaven]; like Jonah ben Amittai.[122]

Someone who disregards the words of a prophet [his death is at the hands of Heaven], like (89b) the friend of Micah [the prophet. When Ahab won the battle against Ben-hadad, king of Aram, he spared the king's life, contrary to the command of the prophets]. It says, "A certain man [Micah] of the disciples of the prophets, said to his friend, 'By the word of God, please hit me!' But the man refused to hit him" (1 Kings 20:35).

[The Sages explain that Micah wanted to come to Ahab with a bloody face and tell Ahab: The man I was supposed to watch hit me and ran away. Ahab would then rule that the man should be killed. Micah would then tell Ahab: So, why don't you kill Ben-hadad who killed so many of our people! But Micah's friend refused to hit him, disregarding the words of a prophet.] The verse continues, "[Micah] then said to him, 'Because you did not obey the voice of God, behold, when you go away from me a lion will strike you down!'" [Since Micah was a known prophet, his command in God's name had the force of a Divine command. The friend was killed by a lion; so we see that his death came at the hands of Heaven.]

A prophet who trangresses his own prophecy, [his death is at the hands of Heaven]. Like Iddo the prophet, for it says, [when Jeroboam invited the prophet Iddo to join him at his meal, the prophet refused, saying,] "For thus it has been commanded to me by the word of God, ['Do not eat a meal and do not drink water']" (1 Kings 13:9). Afterward it says, [that a certain old (false) prophet said,] "I am also a prophet like you, and an angel spoke to me by the word of God, saying, 'Bring him back with you to your house, so that he may eat a meal and drink water'" (ibid. v. 18). [He was lying. Instead of investigating the "prophet's" message, Iddo accepted it at face value.] Then it says, "So [Iddo] returned with him and ate a meal in his house and drank water" (ibid. v. 19), [transgressing his own prophecy]. Afterward it says, "He went and a lion encountered him on the way and killed him" (ibid. v. 24), [proving that if a prophet transgresses his own prophecy, he dies at the hands of Heaven].

WITHHOLDING
A PROPHETIC MESSAGE

A Tanna recited a *Baraita* before R. Chisda: If someone receives a prophetic message and suppresses it [i.e., does not publicize it], he receives lashes [to force him to proclaim his prophecy (Tosafot)] . R. Chisda retorted: Do you mean to say that a person who eats [wormy] dates out of a sieve is to be flogged?[123] [How do we know about it? He ate the whole date! By the same token, who can tell whether he received a prophetic message?] Who could possibly warn him [not to suppress his prophecy]? Abaye said: His fellow prophets would know and could warn him. [The Gemara asks:] How would they know? Abaye said: Because it says, "For God will not do anything unless He has revealed His secret to His servants the prophets" (Amos 3:7).

[The Gemara asks:] But perhaps [the people repented and] the Heavenly decree of doom was rescinded, and that is why he suppressed his prophecy? [The Gemara answers:] If the Heavenly Court rescinded the decree, all the prophets would have known about it. [The Gemara asks:] But in the case of Jonah, the decree of destruction of Nineveh was reversed [when the people repented], yet God did not tell Jonah about it! [The Gemara answers:] Originally Jonah was told that Nineveh would be overturned,[124] but he did not know whether for good or for evil [whether "overturned" meant from evil to good, or that Nineveh would be destroyed].

If someone disregards the words of a prophet, [his death is at the hands of Heaven]. [The Gemara asks:] But how does the person know [that someone claiming to be a prophet is a true prophet]? [The Gemara answers:] If he gives him a sign. [The Gemara asks:] But Micah [mentioned above] did not give a sign, yet his friend was punished [for not obeying him]![125] [The Gemara answers:] Where he was established as a prophet, it is different; [he does not have to give a sign. And Micah was a well-known prophet]. Because if you are not going to say so, how could Isaac listen to Abraham at Mount Moriah [and allow himself to be sacrificed]? Similarly, how could the people trust Elijah at Mount Carmel and sacrifice outside the *Bet Hamikdash* [which is forbidden under normal circumstances]? But because they were established prophets it is different.

PRELUDE TO THE *AKEIDAH*[126]

[Having mentioned the *Akeidah*, the Gemara now continues by discussing that event.] "It happened after these things that God tested Abraham" (Genesis 22:1). [The Gemara asks:] After which things? R. Yochanan said in the name of R. Yose b. Zimra: *After* the words of Satan, [who tried to find fault with Abraham,] as it says, "The child [Isaac] grew and was weaned. [Abraham made a great feast on the day that Abraham was weaned]" (ibid. 21:8). So Satan said to the Holy One, blessed be He, "Master of the universe! You graciously granted this old man a child at the age of one hundred years, yet of all this feast that he prepared he did not have even one dove or pigeon to offer to You!"[127] Replied God, "All this honor he is doing in honor of his son. Yet if I were to tell him, 'Sacrifice your son to Me' he would do it at once." Thereupon, "God tempted Abraham . . . And He said, "Please [*na*] take your son" (ibid. v. 2). R. Shimon b. Adda said: The word *na* signifies supplication. [Thus God begged Abraham to do His bidding.]

You can compare it to a king of flesh and blood who had fought many battles, which he won with the help of one mighty warrior. One day, the king was faced with a crucial battle. So he said to the warrior: I beg of you, win this battle for me, so that people should not say that the earlier wars were easy, [but when he has to fight a tough battle he caves in]. So too, the Holy One, blessed be He, said to Abraham, "I have subjected you to many tests, and you passed them all. I beg of you, please withstand this test, so that people should not say that the earlier tests were of no consequence."

[The following dialogue ensued between God and Abraham:] [God said to Abraham,] "Take your son." [Abraham replied,] "I have two sons, [Isaac and Ishmael]." "Your only one." "Each is the only one to his mother." "The one you love." "I love both of them." [Finally God said,] "Isaac."

And why the long dialogue? [Why did God not come straight to the point and say: "Take Isaac"?] So that Abraham should not become deranged by the shock of the sudden command to sacrifice his son Isaac.

On the way Satan met him and said to him,[128] "If He tests you with one thing [like destroying your own child], will you become wearied? . . . Behold, you have rebuked many, and have strengthened weak hands. Your words would would raise one who stumbled; you would brace buckling knees. And now when it befalls you, you become frightened? It touches you, and you are bewildered?" (Job 4:2–5). [Satan argued: God will not be satisfied with Isaac; He will yet demand your life, and then you will have to defy Him. You had better defy Him now (Etz Yosef).] Abraham replied, "I have walked in my perfect innocence" (Psalms 26:2).

Retorted Satan, "You are a fool for being God-fearing" (Job 4:6). Abraham replied, "Remember please, which innocent person ever perished?" (ibid. v. 7); [I firmly believe in the justice of God's ways]. When Satan saw that he was not getting anywhere, he said to Abraham: "A message surreptitiously reached me" (ibid. v. 12). I have heard from behind the Heavenly Curtain [that separates the *Shechinah* from the physical world]: The lamb will be for a burnt offering, but Isaac will not be for a burnt offering. [But Abraham did not believe Satan. After the *Akeidah*, when things turned out the way Satan had said,][129] Abraham told Satan: This is the punishment of a liar that even when he tells the truth, nobody believes him.

[The Gemara cites another exposition of the word "after" in the verse "It happened *after* these events."] R. Levi said: ["After" does not mean "after the dialogue with Satan"] but "*after* Ishmael's words to Isaac." Ishmael said to Isaac: I am better than you in the fulfillment of *mitzvot*, because you were circumcised when you were only eight days old [and could not protest], but I was circumcised when I was thirteen years old; [I could have protested, but I submitted to it]. Replied Isaac: Are you trying to provoke me from merely one limb? If the Holy One, blessed be He, would tell me: "Sacrifice yourself to Me," I would willingly obey. Thereupon, "God tested Abraham" (Genesis 22:1).

EVERYONE HAS A SHARE IN THE WORLD TO COME

[The Mishnah says:] All Israel, [even sinners,] have a share in the World to Come, for it says, "Your people [Israel] are all righteous; they shall inherit the land [i.e., a share in the hereafter] for all time. They are the shoot that I planted, My handiwork in which I glory" (Isaiah 60:21). However, the following do not have a share in the World to Come [if they do not repent]: A person who says that the resurrection of the dead is not alluded to in the Torah, or that the Torah is not given by God, or an *apikoros* [i.e., someone who belittles a Torah scholar].[130] R. Akiva says: Also a person who reads un-Jewish [heretical] books, or one who mumbles magic formulas over a wound, reciting the verse, "I will not strike you with any of the sicknesses I brought on Egypt" (Exodus 15:26).

Abba Shaul says: Also a person who pronounces the name of God the way it is spelled. [The Mishnah now gives specific examples:] Three kings and four ordinary people have no share in the World to Come: The three kings are Jeroboam, [who led the people to idolatry], Ahab,[131] and Menasheh [who worshipped idols].[132] R. Yehudah says: Menasheh does have a share in the World to Come, for it says, [When Menasheh was taken captive by the Assyrians and led in chains to Babylonia,] "he prayed to Him, and He granted his prayer, heard his plea, and returned him to Jerusalem to his kingdom" (2 Chronicles 33:13). [The fact that God answered Menasheh's prayer is an indication that he regained his share in the World to Come]. The Sages said to R. Yehudah: [This verse implies that] he was returned only to his kingdom, but not to the World to Come. The four ordinary people [who do not have a share in the World to Come] are: Balaam [who cursed Israel in the wilderness],[133] Doeg [who slandered David and caused the destruction of Nob, the city of *kohanim*],[134] Achitofel [David's adviser who deserted him],[135] and Geichazi [Elisha's servant who led others to sin].[136]

QUID PRO QUO

[The Gemara asks:] Why such a severe punishment [for denying the resurrection of the dead]? The Tanna of a *Baraita* explains: Since this person denied the resurrection of the dead, he will have no share in it, because all punishments of the Holy One, blessed be He, are meted out measure for measure. For R. Shmuel b. Nachmani said in the name of R. Yochanan: How do we know that the Holy One, blessed be He, repays measure for measure? Because it says, "Elisha said, 'Hear the word of God . . . This time tomorrow, a seah of flour will sell for a shekel at the gate of Shomron!'" And then it says, "The aide on whose arm the king was leaning answered the man of God, 'Even if God were to make windows in the sky, could this come to pass?' To which [Elisha] retorted, 'You will see it with your own eyes, but you will not eat of it'" (2 Kings 7:1,2). (90b) And it says further, "That is exactly what happened to him: The people trampled [the aide] to death in the gate" (ibid. v. 20).

[The Gemara asks:] But perhaps the aide died as a result of Elisha's curse [rather than by Divine retaliation]? For Rav Yehudah said in the name of Rav: The curse of a Sage, even if undeserved, comes true. [The Gemara answers:] If so, [if he died as a result of Elisha's curse], the text should simply say, "They trampled him to death." Why does it mention "in the gate"? To tell us that he died because of the matter [of his insolent outburst] at the gate.

ALLUSIONS TO THE RESURRECTION IN THE TORAH

R. Yochanan said: Where do we find a hint to the resurrection of the dead in the Torah? For it says, [in respect to the tithe that the Levites must give to the *kohanim*], "You must give it as God's elevated gift to Aaron the *Kohen*" (Numbers 18:28). But was Aaron going to live forever? Why, he never even entered Eretz Yisrael that they should give him *terumah*![137] But this teaches us that Aaron will come back to life again at some point in the future, and the people of Israel will then give him *terumah*. Which is a hint to the resurrection of the dead in the Torah.

[The Gemara briefly digresses to discuss certain aspects of *terumah*.] In the yeshivah of R. Yishmael, a Tanna taught that the words "to Aaron" indicate [that *terumah* must be given to someone] like Aaron: just as Aaron was a *chaver*,[138] so, too, his children must be *chaverim* [in order to receive *terumah*]. R. Shmuel b. Nachmani said in the name of R. Yonatan: From where do we know that we do not give *terumah* to a *kohen* who is an *am haaretz*?[139] For it says, "[Hezekiah] ordered the people, the inhabitants of Jerusalem, to deliver the portions of the *kohanim* and the Levites, so that they might devote themselves to God's Torah" (2 Chronicles 31:4). [From this we see that] any *kohen* who devotes himself to God's Torah is entitled to a *terumah* portion; any *kohen* that does not, is not entitled to a *terumah* portion.

R. Acha b. Ada said in the name of Rav Yehudah: Giving *terumah* to a *kohen* who is an *am haaretz*, is like placing it before a lion. Just as you cannot be sure whether or not the lion will tear at its prey and devour it right away [or leave it to decompose], so, too, if you give *terumah* to a *kohen* who is an *am haaretz*, you cannot be sure whether he will eat it in Levitical purity or uncleanness. R. Yochanan said: [A person who gives *terumah* to a *kohen* who is an *am haaretz*] may even cause his death, for it says, [concerning *kohanim* who eat *terumah* that is *tamei*, defiled,] "Lest they die for it, since they have profaned [the sacred offering]" (Leviticus 22:9). In the yeshivah of R. Eliezer b. Yaakov, a Tanna taught: [By giving *terumah* to a *kohen* who is an *am haaretz*,] one may even cause him to bear the guilt of sin, for it says, [concerning *kohanim* who eat *terumah* when they are ritually unclean], "If they eat the sacred offerings, they will bear the guilt of sin" (Leviticus 22:16).

[The Gemara now resumes the discussion about allusions to the resurrection of the dead.] We learned in a *Baraita*: R. Sima'i said: Where do we find an allusion to the resurrection of the dead in the Torah? For it says, "I also made My covenant with [the Patriarchs, promising them] to give them the land of Canaan" (Exodus 6:4). It does not say "to give *you*" but rather "to give *them* [the Patriarchs]." Which gives us an allusion in the Torah to the resurrection of the dead. [God's promise can only be fulfilled if the Patriarchs are revived.]

The heretics [Sadducees] asked R. Gamliel: Where in Scripture do we see that the Holy One, blessed be He, resurrects the dead? He answered them by quot-

ing proof texts from the Torah, the Prophets, and the Writings, but they did not accept his proofs. He quoted from the Torah the verse, "God said to Moses, 'You are soon to lie with your fathers and rise up'" (Deuteronomy 31:16).[140] [The heretics rejected this saying:] Perhaps this verse means, "And the people will rise up." He quoted from the Prophets the verse, "May Your dead revive! May my corpses arise, awake and shout for joy, you who rest in the dirt! For Your dew is like the dew on fresh growth; may You topple the lifeless [wicked] to the ground" (Isaiah 26:19).

[The heretics challenged him on this, saying:] Perhaps this refers to the dead whom Ezekiel brought back to life [in the Valley of the Dry Bones]?[141] He quoted from the Writings the verse, "[The words of] your palate shall be like the finest wine, let it flow to my Beloved sweetly, stirring the lips of those asleep [in the dust]" (Song of Songs 7:10). [The heretics rejected this, saying:] Perhaps the passage means merely that their lips will flutter, [not that they will be revived], which would be consistent with R. Yochanan who said in the name of R. Shimon b. Yehotzadak: Whenever a *halachah* is quoted in the name of [a deceased scholar] in this world, his lips flutter in the grave, as it says, "stirring the lips of those asleep [in the dust]."

[Rabban Gamliel was unable to convince them] until he quoted the verse, "The land that God swore to your ancestors, [promising that] He would give it to *them*" (Deuteronomy 11:21). It does not say "to *you*" but rather "to *them*." Which provides an allusion to the resurrection of the dead in the Torah. [The promise can only be kept if the ancestors are revived.] Some say that R. Gamliel proved it from the following verse, "Only you, the ones who are attached to God your Lord, are all alive today" (ibid. 4:4). [Why the superfluous word "today"? It tells us:] Just as you are all alive today, so will you all be alive in the World to Come [i.e., at the resurrection].

The Romans asked R. Yehoshua b. Chananiah: Where in Scripture does it say that the Holy One, blessed be He, resurrects the dead, and that He knows what will happen in the future? He replied: Both concepts can be derived from the following verse: "God said to Moses, 'You are soon to lie with your fathers and rise will this people and go astray . . .'" (Deuteronomy 31:16). ["You are soon to lie with your fathers and rise" shows that Moses will be resurrected. "This people will go astray" proves that God knows the future (Rashi).] The Romans contended: Perhaps the verse means, "and rise will this people and go astray" [which does not prove resurrection]? R. Yehoshua replied: Accept at least the answer to half of your question, namely, that God knows the future. The same was taught also by R. Yochanan in the name of R. Shimon b. Yochai: From where do we know that the Holy One, blessed be He, resurrects the dead and knows what the future holds? For it says, "You are soon to lie with your fathers and rise . . ."

Similarly we learned in a *Baraita*: R. Eliezer the son of R. Yose said: In this matter [of the resurrection of the dead] I proved the books of the heretics [i.e., Samaritans] to be forgeries. For they used to say that there is no hint about resurrection of the dead in the Torah. I said to them: You have tampered with your Torah,[142] but it is of no avail to you. For you say that there is no allusion to the resurrection of the dead in the Torah. But what about the verse, [referring to an individual who commits idolatry,] "That person shall be utterly cut off [*hikkaret tikkaret*], his sin shall remain upon him" (Numbers 15:31). Now, since he "shall be utterly cut off" means that he will die in this world, when will his sin remain upon him? Don't you agree that it must be in the World to Come [i.e., at the resurrection of the dead]? R. Papa said to Abaye: Couldn't R. Eliezer have derived both [punishment in this world and in the World to Come] from "that person shall be utterly cut off" [literally: "cut off, he shall be cut off"; cut off in this world and cut off in the World to Come (Rashi)]? [Replied Abaye:] They would have countered: The Torah uses the conventional way of speaking, [and people repeat themselves for added emphasis].

REBBIS DEBATING SKEPTICS

Queen Cleopatra asked R. Meir: I know that the dead will come back to life, because it says, "Let men sprout up in the city [Jerusalem] like country grass" (Psalms 72:16). [At the time of the resurrection, the bodies of the *tzaddikikim* will move through tunnels to Jerusalem (Rashi).][143] But [please tell me,] when they rise from the dead, do they rise naked or in their clothes? Replied R. Meir: You find the answer by drawing a logical inference from a wheat kernel: If a kernel of wheat that is buried [i.e., planted] naked, sprouts forth covered with several garments, then surely will the righteous who are buried in their clothes [rise up fully clothed].

Caesar said to R. Gamliel, "You people contend that the dead will return to life. [How is that possible?] The dead turn to dust, and can dust come alive?" (91a) Caesar's daughter said to [R. Gamliel], "Leave it to me. I will answer him." [She then said,] "Let's say in our town there are two potters, one who creates pottery out of water, and the other from clay: which one would you say is the greater craftsman?" Replied Caesar, "The one who creates pottery out of water." [Making pottery out of clay any potter can do.] She retorted, "By the same token, if [God] creates a human being out of water [a drop of semen], He surely can create him out of clay [or dust]."

In the yeshivah of R. Yishmael they offered [a different version of Caesar's daughter's reply]: It can be inferred from glassware. If glassware, which is shaped by the breath of a human being [a glassblower], can be repaired if it is broken [by melting the pieces and reshaping them], surely a human being that is formed by the breath of the Holy One, blessed be He,[144] [can be restored to life after he has crumbled to dust].

A certain heretic said to R. Ami, "You people maintain that the dead will live again. [How is that possible?] After all, the dead turn to dust, and can dust come alive? Replied R. Ami, "Let me give you a parable. You can compare it to a human king who told his servants to build him a great palace in a place where there was no water or earth [for making bricks and mortar]. They went and built it, [using rocks]. After a while, the palace collapsed, so the king ordered them to rebuild it in a place where water and earth were available. They replied, "We cannot build it." Now the king became angry with them and said, "If you could build a palace in a place where there was no water or earth [for making bricks], surely you can build it now that you have plenty of water and earth!" [God, who created the world out of nothing, surely can form man out of dust (Rashi).]

Continued R. Ami, "And if you don't believe it, go out into a field and see a mole-like creature that one day is half flesh and half earth, and the next day it has evolved into a rodent that is all flesh.[145] [So you see that life can emerge from earth.] Perhaps you will say that the gradual changeover takes a long time, [whereas the resurrection must take place instantly]; then go up to the mountain where one day you will see just one *chilazon*,[146] and on the next day, after the rain falls, the whole mountain is crawling with *chilzonot*, [which demonstrates God's ability to revive the dead very quickly].

A certain Sadducee said to Geviha ben Pesisa, "Woe to you, you wicked people, for you say that the dead will be restored to life. If even the living [ultimately] die, how can the dead come back to life?" Geviha replied, "Woe to you, you wicked people, for you say that the dead will *not* be restored to life. Now, if even those who did not exist come to life [i.e., babies that are born], doesn't it stand to reason that those who once lived surely will live again?" The Sadducee retorted, "How dare you call us 'wicked people'! If I get up, I will give you a kick that will straighten out your hump!" [Gaviha was a hunchback.] Gaviha calmly replied, "If you do that, you will be called a master surgeon and be able to charge a big fee [for your services]!"

DEFENDING OUR CLAIM
TO ERETZ YISRAEL

We learned in a *Baraita*: On the twenty-fourth of Nisan the tax collectors were withdrawn from Judah and Jerusalem. For when the Africans[147] came to plead against the Jews before Alexander of Macedonia, they said, "The land of Canaan belongs to us, for it says [in the Torah of the Jews], 'The land of Canaan with its various boundaries'" (Numbers 34:2). And Canaan was our ancestor.

[They argued: The Torah itself describes the land the Jews were about to enter as the land of Canaan. The land is ours since we are the descendants of Canaan; the Jews seized it unlawfully (Rashi).] Thereupon Geviha b. Pesisa said to the Sages, "Give me permission to go and debate them before Alexander of Macedonia. If they defeat me, you can say, 'You have defeated an ignorant individual, [so you have not proved anything].' And if I defeat them, you can say, 'The Torah of Moses has defeated you!'"

The Sages then authorized him, and he went and debated [the Africans]. He asked them, "From where do you bring proof [to substantiate your claim]?" "From the Torah," they replied. "I, too, will bring you proof only from the Torah," he responded. "For it says, '[Noah] said: Cursed is Canaan. A slave of slaves shall he be to his brothers' (Genesis 9:25). Now, if a slave acquires property, to whom does the slave belong, and to whom the property? [Clearly, to his owner. Therefore, even if the land was given to the Canaanites, it belongs to their masters the Jews, the descendants of Shem.] And that's not all; it is now many years that you have not served us, [so that you owe us for centuries of labor you did not perform for us]."

Alexander said to them, "Answer him!" "Give us three days' time," they requested. So he granted them the extension during which they searched but could not come up with an answer. [Realizing that they had lost,] they immediately ran away, leaving behind their planted fields and vineyards. And that year was a Sabbatical year [when it is forbidden to till the land, so that the produce from the fields abandoned by the Africans was a welcome bonus].

On another occasion the Egyptians brought suit against the Jews before Alexander of Macedonia. They argued, "It says in the Torah of the Jews, 'God made the Egyptians respect the people, and they lent them [gold and silver and clothing that they never returned]; and they drained Egypt of its wealth' (Exodus 12:36). [We demand:] Give us the silver and gold that you took from us!" Hearing this, Geviha b. Pesisa said to the Sages, "Give me permission to go and debate them before Alexander of Macedonia. If they defeat me, you can say, 'You defeated an ignorant individual.' And if I defeat them, you can say, 'The Torah of Moses has defeated you!'"

The Sages then authorized him, and he went and debated the Egyptians. He said to them, "From where do you bring proof [that we took gold and silver from you in Egypt]?" "From the Torah," they replied. "Then I, too, will bring you proof from the Torah," he retorted. "For it says, 'The length of time that the Israelites stayed in Egypt was four hundred and thirty years' [Exodus 12:40]. So pay us the wages for the labor of the six hundred thousand men you enslaved for 430 years." Alexander of Macedonia said to them, "Answer him!" They said to Alexander, "Give us three days' time [to think of an answer]." He granted them the extension during which they searched but could not come up with an answer. [Realizing that they had lost,] they abandoned their planted fields and vineyards and ran away. And that year was a Sabbatical year.

On yet another occasion, the descendants of Ishmael and the descendants of Keturah[148] brought suit against the Jews before Alexander of Macedonia. They argued, "The Land of Canaan belongs to us and to the Jews, for it says, 'And these are the descendants of Ishmael the son of Abraham'" (Genesis 25:12), and it also says, 'These are the descendant of Isaac the son of Abraham'" (ibid. v. 19). Said Geviha ben Pesisa to the Sages, "Give me permission to go and debate them before Alexander of Macedonia. If they defeat me, you can say, 'You defeated an ignorant individual.' And if I defeat them, you can say, 'The Torah of Moses has defeated you.'" The Sages then authorized him, and he went and debated them. He said to them, "From where do you bring proof?" "From the Torah," they replied. "I, too, will bring proof only from the Torah," he retorted. "For it says, 'Abraham gave all that he owned to Isaac. And to the sons of the concubines that he had taken Abraham also gave gifts. Then, while he was still alive, he sent them to the country of the East, away from his son Isaac' (ibid. 25:5,6). Now, if a father gave an inheritance to his sons in his lifetime and sent one son away from the other [to prevent a dispute about the inheritance], does one son have any claim on the other? [Of course not! Therefore, you have no claim on Eretz Yisrael.]"

BODY AND SOUL

Antoninus[149] said to Rebbi: The body and the soul have an alibi to free themselves from punishment on Judgment Day. How so? The body can say: The soul is the one that has sinned. For from the day it left me, I have been lying like a silent rock in the grave, [unable to sin]. And the soul can say: It is the body that has sinned, for from the day I left it, I have been flying in the air like a bird, [unable to sin].

Rebbi answered: Let me give you a parable. To what can this be compared? To a king who had a beautiful orchard that contained (91b) luscious figs, and he posted in it two guards, one lame and the other blind. Said the lame one to the blind one: I see luscious figs in the orchard. Come, put me on your shoulders, and together we will pick the figs and eat them. The lame one climbed on the blind one's back, and they picked the figs and ate them. A while later, when the king, the owner of the orchard, came [and found that his figs were gone,] he said to the guards, "What happened to my luscious figs?" Said the lame one, "Do I have feet to take me to the fig trees?" Said the blind one, "Do I have eyes to see where the figs are?" What did the owner do? He placed the lame one on the shoulders of the blind one, and judged them jointly. So, too, on the Day of Judgment, the Holy One, blessed be He, brings the soul, puts it back into the body, and judges them jointly. As it says, "He will summon the heavens above and the earth, for the trial of His people" (Psalms 50:4). "He will summon the heavens above"—this refers to the soul; "and the earth, for the trial of His people"—this refers to the body.

ANTONINUS QUESTIONS REBBI

Antoninus asked Rebbi, "Why does the sun rise in the east and set in the west?" Replied Rebbi, "If it were the other way around, you would have asked me the same question, [you are asking a frivolous question]!" "This is what I meant to ask you," said Antoninus, "[Since the sun rises in the east,] why does it set in the west, [rather than in the east, circling the globe above the horizon and setting in the same place where it rose (Rashi)]?" Rebbi replied, "[It sets in the west] in order to greet its Maker," [since the *Shechinah* dwells in the west].[150] For it says, "And the hosts of the heavens [i.e., the sun] bow to you" (Nehemiah 9:6).[151] [Antoninus] answered, "[If that is the reason,] the sun should travel to the middle of the sky, greet the *Shechinah*, and set at high noon; [why does it wait until it is in the west to pay its respects]?" Rebbi replied, "Because of workers and wayfarers."[152]

Antoninus also asked Rebbi, "When does the soul enter the body? Is it at the moment of conception or when the embryo takes form?" "When the embryo is formed," Rebbi replied. Said Antoninus, "Can a piece of meat stay for more than three days without salt and not decompose? [So, too, if the human seed is not given a soul at conception, it would spoil and could not grow into an embryo.] Rather you must say that the soul enters at the moment of conception." Rebbi said, "This thing Antoninus taught me, and Scripture bears it out, for it says, "Your providence watched over my spirit [i.e., my soul]" (Job 10:12).

Antoninus also inquired of Rebbi: When does the evil impulse begin to have influence over a person: at the formation of the embryo or at the moment of birth? Rebbi replied, "At the moment of the formation of the embryo." Antoninus challenged him, "If so, the unborn child would rebel in its mother's womb and leave the womb prematurely. Rather, the evil impulse begins to have influence over a person at the moment of birth." Rebbi said, "This thing Antoninus taught me, and Scripture substantiates it, for it says, 'Sin crouches at the door [of the womb]'" (Genesis 4:7).

THE WORLD TO COME

Resh Lakish pointed out a contradiction between two verses: On the one hand it says, "Behold I will bring them from the north country and gather them from the ends of the earth. Among them will be the blind and the lame, the pregnant and the birthing together; a great congregation will return there" (Jeremiah 31:7);

[implying that at the resurrection of the dead they will return to life with their infirmity]. On the other hand it says, "Then the lame man will skip like a gazelle, and the tongue of the mute will sing glad song; for water will have broken out in the wilderness, and streams in the desert" (Isaiah 35:6) [suggesting that the handicapped will be cured of their infirmity]. How can the two verses be reconciled? [Resh Lakish answered:] They will rise at the resurrection with their impairment, and then they will be healed.

Ulla pointed out a contradiction between two verses: On the one hand it says, "He will eliminate death forever, and the Lord God will wipe tears from all faces" (Isaiah 25:8), [implying that in the World to Come there will be no death]. But on the other hand is says, "For the youth of one hundred years will die . . . never again will come from there a young child or old man who will not fill his days (ibid. 65:20),[153] [suggesting that people will die in the World to Come]. How can these verses be reconciled?—It is no difficulty. The first verse [which says that death will end] refers to Jews, whereas the second verse [which predicts death after uncommonly long life] refers to idol worshippers. [The Gemara asks:] How do idol worshippers get to the World to Come in the first place? [The Gemara answers:] The verse speaks about those of whom it says, "Foreigners will stand and tend your flocks, and the sons of strangers will be your plowmen and your vineyard workers" (Isaiah 61:5).

Rav Chisda pointed out a contradiction between two verses: On the one hand it says, "The moon will be humiliated and the sun will be shamed, for God, Master of Legions, will have reigned on Mount Zion and in Jerusalem" (ibid. 24:23). But on the other hand it says, "The light of the moon will be like the light of the sun, and the light of the sun will be seven times as strong, like the light of seven days" (ibid. 30:26).—There is no difficulty. The second verse [which describes the increased brightness of the sun and the moon] speaks of the Messianic era, whereas the first verse speaks of the World to Come [where the light of the sun and the moon will pale in comparison to the dazzling radiance of the righteous (Rashi)].

[The Gemara asks:] And according to Shmuel who says, "There is no difference between this world and the Messianic era except that the subjugation of the Jews in the lands of the exile will end,"[154] it is still no difficulty. [Both verses refer to the World to Come]. The verse that describes the increased brightness of the luminaries refers to the camp of the righteous, whereas the second verse refers to the camp of the *Shechinah* [where the splendor of the *Shechinah* will dim the light of the sun and moon].

Rava pointed out a contradiction between two verses: On the one hand it says, [God says,] "I deal death, and I give life" (Deuteronomy 32:39), [implying that a person who was deformed will be resurrected with his deformity]. But on the other hand it says [in the same verse], "I wounded, and I will heal" [suggesting that the handicapped *will* be healed of their deformities]. The Holy One, blessed be He, said: What I put to death, I bring to life—and then what I have wounded I will heal. [Meaning: The handicapped are resurrected in their impaired state, and afterward God will heal them (Rashi).]

We learned in a *Baraita*: It says, "I deal death, and I give life." This could be interpreted to mean that God causes one person to die and gives life to another, in the natural pattern of life, [where one person dies and another is born, and the verse would not refer to the resurrection of the dead]. Therefore the Torah says, "I wounded, and I will heal." Just as the wounding and healing [clearly] refer to the same person, so, too, death and life mentioned in this verse refer to the same person, [the person who died will be resurrected]. This gives the lie to those who say that the resurrection of the dead is not indicated in the Torah.

BIBLICAL ALLUSIONS TO THE RESURRECTION OF THE DEAD

It was taught in a *Baraita*: R. Meir said: Where do we find an allusion to the resurrection of the dead in the Torah? In the verse, "Then Moses and the children of Israel will sing this song to God" (Exodus 15:1).[155] It does not say "he sang," but "he will sing." This is an allusion to the resurrection of the dead in the Torah. In the same vein you may cite the verse, "Then Joshua will build an altar to God" (Joshua 8:30). It does not say "he built" but "he will build." This is an allusion to the resurrection of the dead in the Torah.

[The Gemara raises an objection:] If that is so, [what about the verse,] "Then will Solomon build a high place for Kemosh, the abomination of Moab" (1 Kings 11:7), does that also mean that Solomon will build [a shrine to an idol when he is resurrected? That is out of the question!]. [The Gemara answers that here the future tense is used to indicate] that Scripture counts it as though he had built it.[156]

R. Yehoshua b. Levi said: Where do we find an allusion to the resurrection of the dead in the Torah? For it says, "Praiseworthy are those who dwell in Your house; they will praise You continually" (Psalms 84:5). It does not say "they praised You" but "they *will* praise You." This is an allusion to the resurrection of the dead in the Torah.

R. Yehoshua b. Levi also said: Whoever sings God's praise in this world, is worthy to sing it in the World to Come, for it says, "Praiseworthy are those who dwell in Your house, they will praise You continually [in the World to Come]."

R. Chiya b. Abba said in the name of R. Yochanan: Where do we find an allusion to the resurrection of the dead in the Torah? In the verse, "Your watchmen raise their voices; as one they will sing! For every eye will behold God's return to Zion" (Isaiah 52:8). It does not

say "they sang" but "they *will* sing." This is an allusion to the resurrection of the dead in the Torah. R. Chiya b. Abba also said in the name of R. Yochanan: In time to come all prophets will sing praise in unison, for it says, "Your watchmen [which also translates "your seers" or "your prophets"] raise their voices, as one they will sing."

DO NOT WITHHOLD TORAH FROM ANYONE

[The Gemara briefly turns to an unrelated subject.] Rav Yehudah said in the name of Rav: Whoever fails to teach a student a *halachah*, is as if he robs the student of his ancestral heritage, for it says, "The Torah that Moses commanded us is the inheritance of the congregation of Jacob" (Deuteronomy 33:4), which means that it is a heritage to all of Israel since the six days of Creation.[157]

R. Chana b. Bizna said in the name of R. Shimon Chasida: Whoever fails to teach a student a *halachah* [is so blameworthy] that even the unborn children in their mother's womb curse him. For it says, "One who withholds produce [*bar*] (92a) will be cursed [*yikevuhu*] by the nation [*le'om*]" (Proverbs 11:26). And the word *le'om* [in this context] can mean only "fetuses," as it says, [when Rebeccah was carrying the unborn Jacob and Esau, God told her,] "One nation [*le'om*] will be mightier than the other" (Genesis 25:23). And *yikevuhu* can only signify cursing, for it says, "How can I curse [*ekov*] whom God has not cursed" (Numbers 23:8). And *bar* refers only to Torah, for it says, "Nourish[158] yourselves *bar* [with the Torah], lest He become angry" (Psalms 2:12).

[The Gemara asks:] But if the teacher does teach his student Torah, what is the teacher's reward? Rava said in the name of R. Sheshet: He is entitled to blessings like Joseph. For it says, "Blessing will be on the head of the provider [*mashbir*]" (Proverbs 11:26). And *mashbir*, "the provider," can refer only to Joseph, for it says, "Joseph . . . was the provider [*mashbir*] to all the people of the land" (Genesis 42:6).

R. Sheshet said: Whoever teaches Torah in this world will be rewarded by teaching it in the World to Come, for it says, "One who sates [teaches Torah in this world] will sate others with Torah [in the hereafter]" (Proverbs 11:25).

VARIOUS TEACHINGS OF R. ELAZAR

R. Elazar said: Every leader who leads the community with gentleness merits to lead them in the World to Come. For it says, "For he who has mercy on them [in this world] will lead them [in the World to Come], and along streams of water will he guide them" (Isaiah 49:10).

R. Elazar further said: Great is understanding, for it was placed [in a verse] between two Divine Names, for it says, "For the God of understanding is the Lord" (1 Samuel 2:3).

R. Elazar also said: Great is the Sanctuary, for it was placed [in a verse] between two Divine Names, for it says, "The dwelling place that You have made, O God, the Sanctuary, my Lord, that Your hands have established" (Exodus 15:17).

R. Elazar also said: If a person has understanding it is as though the Sanctuary was built in his days, for understanding was placed [in a verse] between two Divine Names [as mentioned above], and the Sanctuary was also placed between two Divine Names [as mentioned above].

R. Elazar also said: If a person has no understanding [he does not use his God-given intellect], it is forbidden to have mercy on him. For it says, "For it is not a nation of understanding, therefore, its Maker will not show it mercy, and its Creator will not be gracious to it" (Isaiah 27:11).

R. Elazar also said: Whoever gives his bread to someone who does not have understanding will be stricken with suffering, for it says, "Those who eat your bread made a *mazor* in your place, there is no understanding in him" (Obadiah v. 7). The word *mazor* here can only mean "suffering," as it says, "Ephraim saw his ailment, and Judah his suffering [*mezoro*]" (Hosea 5:13). [Because you gave bread to one who has no understanding you will be hurt in the end.]

R. Elazar also said: Any person who lacks understanding eventually goes into exile, for it says, "Therefore, My people has gone into exile from lack of understanding" (Isaiah 5:13).

R. Elazar also said: A house where words of Torah are not heard at night[159] will be consumed by fire. For it says, "Total darkness lies in wait for his hidden treasures [of Torah thoughts]; an unfanned fire will consume him; misfortune will befall the remnant [*sarid*] in his tent" (Job 20:26). And *sarid* can only refer to a Torah scholar, as it says, "Among the remnants [*seridim*] whom God summons" (Joel 3:5).

R. Elazar also said: Whoever does not benefit Torah scholars from his property will never see a sign of blessing, for it says, "There was no remnant to his food, therefore he will not achieve his prosperity" (Job 20:21),[160] and "remnant" refers to Torah scholars, for it says, "Among the remnants whom God summons."

R. Elazar also said: Whoever does not leave over bread on his table will never see a sign of blessing, for it says, "There was no remnant to his food, therefore he will not achieve his prosperity." [The Gemara asks:] But did not R. Elazar say, "If a person leaves over pieces of bread on his table, it is as if he worships idols! For it says, 'Those who set a table for Gad, who fill a libation to Meni'[161] (Isaiah 65:11)." [The Gemara answers:] It is no difficulty: In his second statement [where he forbids leaving pieces of bread], a whole loaf is left together with the pieces; [then it looks like a gift to a pagan deity]. In his first statement, [where

he criticizes a person who does not leave pieces of bread on his table,] there is no whole loaf left with it.

R. Elazar also said: Whoever obscures his speech, [putting up a false front], is as though he worships idols. For it says here, [about Jacob posing as Esau,] "He will realize that I am a deceiver" (Genesis 27:12). And it says elsewhere, [concerning idol worship,] "They are vanity, the work of deception" (Jeremiah 10:15).

R. Elazar also said: Always be unassuming, then you will live long. R. Zeira said: We have learned this also in a Mishnah: In a dark house we do not make a window to examine its signs of leprosy.[162] [If you are withdrawn and timid, people will not cast "the evil eye" on you (*Maharsha*).]

AFTER THE RIGHTEOUS
ARE RESURRECTED

It was taught in the yeshivah of Elijah: The righteous that the Holy One, blessed be He, will bring back to life [in the Messianic era] will not return to dust [between the end of the Messianic era and the World to Come], as it says [regarding the Messianic era,] "And those who remain in Zion and are left in Jerusalem—all who are inscribed for life in Jerusalem—shall be called holy" (Isaiah 4:3). Just as the Holy One [God] endures forever, so will the [righteous who are resurrected at that time] endure forever.

(92b) Now you may ask: In those [one thousand] years during which the Holy One, blessed be He, will renew His world[163]—as it says, "God alone will be exalted on that day" (Isaiah 2:11)—what will the righteous be doing?—The Holy One, blessed be He, will make them wings like eagles, and they will soar above the water, as it says, "Therefore we [i.e., the righteous] are not afraid though the earth reels, though mountains topple into the sea" (Psalms 46:3). Now you may say that they will suffer pain [from having to fly for one thousand years]? Therefore, Scripture says, "But they who trust in God shall renew their strength, they shall sprout wings like eagles, they shall run and not grow weary, they shall march and not grow faint" (Isaiah 40:13).

WHO WERE THE PEOPLE
EZEKIEL RESURRECTED?

[The Gemara asks:] Should we not infer the opposite from the dead Ezekiel brought back to life?[164] [The Gemara answers:] This Tanna holds that [the story of the resurrection of the dry bones by Ezekiel] was only a parable [foreshadowing the return of the people of Israel to their land, and no inference can be drawn from it]. For we learned in a *Baraita*: R. Eliezer says: The dead that Ezekiel resurrected stood up, sang songs of praise, and died again. What song did they sing? "God deals death with justice and brings to life with mercy."

R. Yehoshua said: They sang the following song, "God deals death and gives life, casts down into the grave and raises up" (1 Samuel 2:6). R. Yehudah said: It is true; it is a parable. R. Nechemiah said to R. Yehudah: If it is true, then why do you call it a parable; and if it is a parable, why do you say, "it is true"? What you should say is: Truly, it was a parable. R. Eliezer the son of R. Yose Hagelili said: The dead that Ezekiel resurrected went up to Eretz Yisrael, got married, and fathered sons and daughters. R. Yehudah b. Beteira stood up and said: I am one of their descendants, and these are the *tefillin* my father's father left me from them.

And who were the dead Ezekiel resurrected? Rav said: They were the men of the tribe of Ephraim who miscalculated the end of the Egyptian slavery, [and were killed after escaping from Egypt prematurely].[165] For it says, "The sons of Ephraim: Shuthelach, his son Bered, his son Tachath, his son Zavad, his son Shuthelach, also Ezer and Elead. The men of Gath, born in the land, killed them . . ." (1 Chronicles 7:20). And it says [in the next verse], "And Ephraim, their father, mourned many days, and his brothers came to comfort him."

And Shmuel says: The [dead that Ezekiel resurrected] were the people who refused to believe in the resurrection of the dead, as it says, "He said to me, 'Son of man, these bones—they are the whole House of Israel. Behold, they are saying: Our bones are dried up, and our hope is lost; we are doomed!'" (Ezekiel 37:11). [In spite of their disbelief, they were resurrected, as a sign to all Israel that the dead will come back to life (Rashi).]

R. Yirmeyah b. Abba says: The [dead that Ezekiel resurrected] were people who lacked even the slightest droplet of a mitzvah, as it says, "O dry bones, hear the word of God" (ibid. v. 4), [to show that even such sinners will be resurrected if they repent (*Maharsha*)].

R. Yitzchak Nafcha says: They were the people who covered the entire Sanctuary with pictures of abominable creatures and creeping things. For it says, "So I entered and I saw, and behold there was every sort of image—disgusting creeping things and animals and all the idols of the House of Israel—were carved upon the wall all around" (Ezekiel 8:10). And it says there [in connection with the dry bones], "He led me all around them" (ibid. 37:2).[166] [Even such people were revived to show that nothing stands in the way of genuine repentance (*Maharsha*).]

R. Yochanan says: They were the dead in the Plain of Dura. And R. Yochanan explained: The Plain of Dura extends from the Eshel River to Rabbat. [What happened there?] Among the exiles Nebuchadnezzar drove into exile there were young men who put the sun to shame with their beauty. When the Chaldean women looked at them they experienced untimely menstrual flow [from ardent desire]. They told this to their husbands, and their husbands told the king. The king then issued an order to have these young men executed [in the Plain of Dura]. But the Chaldean women continued to experience untimely flow. Thereupon the king ordered the corpses trampled beyond recognition.

CHANANIAH, MISHAEL, AND AZARIAH IN THE FIERY FURNACE

Our Rabbis taught in a *Baraita*: When the wicked Nebuchadnezzar threw Chananiah, Mishael, and Azariah into the fiery furnace, the Holy One, blessed be He, said to Ezekiel: Go and resurrect the dead in the Plain of Dura [i.e., the young men Nebuchadnezzar had executed]. As soon as he began to bring them back to life, the bones came and slapped the wicked [Nebuchadnezzar] on his face.[167] Nebuchadnezzar asked, "What kind of bones are these?" They told him, "[Ezekiel,] the friend of the [three men[168] you have thrown onto the furnace,] is resurrecting the dead in the Plain of Dura. [Recognizing God's greatness,] Nebuchadnezzar instantly lifted his voice in tribute to God, "How great are His signs; how mighty His wonders! His kingdom is an everlasting kingdom, and His dominion endures throughout generations" (Daniel 3:33). R. Yitzchak said: Molten gold should be poured into the mouth of that evil man [Nebuchadnezzar]! If an angel had not come and struck him on the mouth, he almost would have surpassed all the songs and praises that David said in the Book of Psalms.

We learned in a *Baraita*: Six miracles happened on the day [that Nebuchadnezzar threw Chananiah, Mishael, and Azariah into the fiery furnace],[169] namely: (1) the furnace [which was below ground level] rose to the surface [so that everyone could see their miraculous rescue], (2) the wall of the furnace cracked open [for the same reason], (3) its foundations caved in [from the intense heat, killing those that had thrown Chananiah, Mishael, and Azariah into the furnace (Rashi)], (4) the image [Nebuchadnezzar had erected to be worshiped] was overturned on its face, (5) four kings and their entourage [who had come to assist in the proceedings] were burned, (6) Ezekiel resurrected the dead in the Plain of Dura. And all these miracles are known only from tradition, except for the miracle of the burning of the four royal parties, which is recorded in Scripture. For it says, "King Nebuchadnezzar sent word to gather the satraps, prefects, governors, treasurers, judges, officers, and all provincial officials to attend the dedication of the statue . . ." (Daniel 3:2), and it says further, [that certain Chaldeans denounced Chananiah, Mishael, and Azariah, saying,] "There are certain Jews . . . who pay no heed to you; they do not worship the statue of gold you have set up" (Daniel 3:8–12). And it says [that when Chananiah, Mishael, and Azariah emerged unscathed from the furnace,] "the satraps, the prefects, the governors, and the royal companions gathered around to look at those men . . . on whose bodies the fire had had no effect" (ibid. v. 27).

At the yeshivah of R. Eliezer b. Yaakov it was taught: Even in times of danger a person should not lose his self-composure, [so as not to appear alarmed and dismayed,] for it says, "So these men, in their shirts, trousers, hats, and other garments, were bound and thrown into the burning fiery furnace" (ibid. v. 21).

R. Yochanan said: (93a) The righteous are greater than the ministering angels. For it says, [when seeing the three men walking around unhurt in the furnace, Nebuchadnezzar said,] "But I see four men walking around and unharmed in the fire, and the fourth looks like an angel" (Daniel 3:25). [The angel is mentioned in fourth place, after the three righteous men.]

R. Tanchum b. Chanilai said: When Chananiah, Mishael, and Azariah came out unharmed from the fiery furnace, all the nations of the world came and struck the Jews on their faces [i.e., reproached them], saying: You have such a [mighty] God, and yet you bow to [Nebuchadnezzar's] idol! [Ashamed, the Jews who had bowed down, repented and] declared, "To You, O God, is the righteousness, and to us is the shamefacedness, as of this very day" (ibid. 9:7).

R. Shmuel b. Nachmani said in the name of R. Yonatan: What is meant by the verse, [God says,] "I said: Let Me be exalted by the palm tree, let Me take hold of its branches" (Song of Songs 7:9). "Let Me be exalted by the palm tree"—this is Israel;[170] but now, all that has come up in My hand is the single branch of Chananiah, Mishael, and Azariah.

R. Yochanan said: What is the meaning of, "I saw [a vision in] the night. There was a man riding on a red horse, and he was standing among myrtle bushes that were in a pool of water" (Zechariah 1:8)? What does "I saw [a vision in] the night" mean?—The Holy One, blessed be He, wanted to turn the whole world into darkness [because the Jews had bowed down to Nebuchanezzar's idol]. "There was a man riding"—"a man" can refer only to the Holy One, blessed be He, for it says, "God is a man of war, God is His name" (Exodus 15:3). "On a red horse" signifies that the Holy One, blessed be He, wanted to plunge the entire world into [red] blood. But as soon as He looked at Chananiah, Mishael, and Azariah [who would rather die than bow down], He was placated, for it says, "and he was standing among the myrtle bushes [haddassim] that were in a pool of water [metzulah]." Now, haddassim [in this context] can refer only to the righteous, for it says, "[Mordechai] brought up Hadassah, she is [the righteous] Esther" (Esther 2:7); and the word metzulah refers to Babylonia, for it says, "[I am God] Who says to the depths [tzulah],[171] 'Dry up, and I will dry out your rivers'" (Isaiah 44:27). Immediately, the red [fury] of God's anger [symbolized by the red horse, abated] and turned white [i.e., was placated]. R. Papa said: This shows that a white horse is a favorable omen in a dream.

[The Gemara asks:] And where did these illustrious men [i.e., Chananiah, Mishael, and Azariah] go [after this episode]?[172] Rav said: They died through an "evil eye." Shmuel said: They drowned in the spittle [the gentiles spat on the Jews when they scorned them for bowing to the idol (Rashi)].[173] R. Yochanan said: They went up to Eretz Yisrael, married, and fathered sons and daughters.

This is also the subject of a dispute among Tannaim. R. Eliezer said: They died through an evil eye. R. Yehoshua said: They drowned in spittle, and the Sages said: They went up to Eretz Yisrael, married, and fathered sons and daughters. For it says, "Listen now, O, Joshua the High Priest: You and your companions who are sitting before you, for they are men of miracle" (Zechariah 3:8). Who are the men for whom a miracle was performed? Chananiah, Mishael, and Azariah.

WHERE WAS DANIEL?

[The Gemara asks:] Where was Daniel [when his three friends were thrown into the furnace]? Rav said: [He was sent by Nebuchadnezzar] to dig a great river in Tiberias. Shmuel said: He was sent to purchase grain for animal feed. R. Yochanan said: He was sent to purchase Alexandrian hogs [which were larger] for breeding purposes. [The Gemara asks:] Is that so? But we learned in a Baraita: Todos the doctor said: No cow or pig leaves Egypt without having its womb removed so that it should not reproduce. [The Gemara answers:] Daniel brought young ones, which the Egyptians let pass [without removing their womb].

The Rabbis taught: Three were involved in the scheme [to keep Daniel away from Babylonia at the dedication of the idol]: The Holy One, blessed be He, Daniel, and Nebuchadnezzar. The Holy One, blessed be He, said: Let Daniel be away from Babylonia, so that people do not say, "In his merit Chananiah, Mishael, and Azariah were saved." Daniel said: I will go away from here, so that I will not become the fulfillment of the verse, "The carved images of their gods you shall burn in fire" (Deuteronomy 7:25).[174] And Nebuchadnezzar, [knowing that Daniel would refuse to bow down, and he would have to throw him into the furnace,] said: Let Daniel go away from here, so that people should not say, "He burned his own god in fire." And from where do we know that Nebuchadnezzar worshipped Daniel? For it says, "Then King Nebuchadnezzar fell upon his face and prostrated himself before Daniel" (Daniel 2:46).

TWO FALSE PROPHETS

[The Gemara tells about two false prophets who were thrown into the fiery furnace.] "Thus said God, Master of Legions, God of Israel, concerning Achav son of Kolayah and Tzidkiah son of Maaseiah, who prophesy falsely to you in My name" (Jeremiah 29:21). And it says, "And all the exiles of Judah in Babylonia shall use a curse derived from their fate, 'May God make you like Tzidkiah and Achav, whom the king of Babylon roasted in the flames!'" (ibid. v. 22). Note that the text does not say "whom he burned" but "whom he roasted." R. Yochanan said in the name of R. Shimon b. Yochai: This teaches that Nebuchadnezzar made them like roasted kernels of grain. [The next verse says,] "Because they did vile things in Israel, committing adultery with the wives of their fellows."

What did they do? They went to Nebuchadnezzar's daughter. Achav said to her, "Thus said God: Be responsive to Tzidkiah [when he makes immoral advances to you]," while Tzidkiah said to her, "Thus said God: Be responsive to Achav [when he makes immoral advances to you]." She went and told her father, who said, "The God of the Jews hates immorality, [He would never give such an order]. When they come to you again, send them to me." When they came, she sent them to her father. "Who told you [to tell this to my daughter]?" he asked. "The Holy One, blessed be He," they replied. "But I asked Chananiah, Mishael, and Azariah about it, and they told me that [immorality] is strictly forbidden," the king retorted. [Achav and Tzidkiah] answered, "We too are prophets, just like them. To them God did not tell it, to us He did." Said Nebuchadnezzar, "I want to test you, just as I tested Chananiah, Mishael and Azariah [by throwing them into the fiery furnace]." [Achav and Tzidkiah] countered, "They were three, while we are two, [and three have more merits than two]." Nebuchadnezzar said, "Then choose anyone you wish to be thrown into the furnace together with you."

They replied, "We want Joshua the High Priest"; they thought: let Joshua come [and join us], for his merit is great, and he will protect us. They brought Joshua the High Priest [from Eretz Yisrael to Babylon], and cast the three of them into the furnace. [Achav and Tzidkiah] were burned, and as for Joshua the High Priest, only his clothes were singed, as it says, "He showed me Joshua, the High Priest, standing before the angel of God, and the Satan was standing on his right to accuse him" (Zechariah 3:1). In the next verse it says, "God said to the Satan: May God denounce you, O Satan . . . Indeed, this [man] is like a firebrand saved from the fire!"[175] Nebuchadnezzar said to Joshua, "I know that you are a righteous man, [because you were not harmed by the flames,] but why should the fire have even the slightest effect on you, [singing your clothes,] whereas Chananiah, Mishael, and Azariah were not affected by the fire at all?"

He replied, "They were three, whereas I was only one." Said Nebuchadnezzar, "But Abraham, too, was only one, [and when he was thrown into a furnace by Nimrod, he came out unharmed with his clothes intact]!" Joshua answered, "There were no wicked people with Abraham in the furnace, thus no permission was granted to the fire [to do any harm], but here there were wicked people with me, thus permission was granted to the fire [to burn them, and so it singed my clothes]. As the saying goes: If you have two dry pieces of wood, and one that is wet, the dry ones will set the wet one on fire."

[The Gemara asks:] Why was Joshua punished [that his clothes were scorched]?[176] [The Gemara answers:] R. Pappa said: Because his sons married women who are not permitted to *kohanim*,[177] and he did not protest against them, as it says, "But Joshua was wearing filthy clothes" (Zechariah 3:3). Now, was Joshua [the High Priest] in the habit of wearing filthy clothes? [That cannot be the meaning of the passage.] Rather, this teaches us that his sons married women who are not permitted to *kohanim*,[178] and he did not protest against them.

THE SIX BLESSINGS OF RUTH'S DESCENDANTS

R. Tanchum said: Bar Kappara expounded in Tzipori: What is meant by the following verse: [Ruth is telling Naomi what Boaz had given her,] "He gave me these six barleys"? (Ruth 3:17)? What are "six barleys"? Do you think it means literally "six grains of barley"? But was it the style of the wealthy Boaz to give a present of only six grains of barley? [Impossible!] (93b). And if you say it means that he gave her six *se'ahs* of barley [the smallest measure used on the threshing floor (Rashi)], is it typical of a woman to carry a load as heavy as six *se'ahs* of barley? But he actually did give her six grains—not as a gift, but] as a token that she was destined to have six descendants who would each be blessed with six blessings. And these are the six descendants: David, *Mashiach*, Daniel, Chananiah, Mishael, and Azariah.

DAVID'S BLESSINGS

The six blessings of David are implied in the verse [that relates that Saul who was depressed asked his servants to find someone to play the harp to cheer him up, and] "one of the young servants spoke up and said, 'Behold! I have seen a son of Jesse the Bethlehemite, who knows how to play; he is a mighty man of valor, and a warrior, who understands a matter, and is a handsome man, and God is with him'" (1 Samuel 16:8); [the verse lists the qualities with which David was blessed]. And Rav Yehudah said in the name of Rav: The praises in this verse were said by Doeg with an evil intent, [to spark Saul's jealousy]. Doeg said, "He knows how to play"—[he hinted] David knows how to ask penetrating halachic questions; "mighty"—he knows how to answer [complex Torah questions]; "a warrior"—he knows how to engage in the give-and-take of Torah disputations; "who understands a matter"—he understands how to infer one thing from another; "a handsome man"—he makes a convincing case for his views; "and God is with him"—the *halachah* is always decided according to his opinion.

Replying to each of these praises, Saul said, "My son Jonathan can do that too." But when Doeg said, "God is with him" [i.e., the *halachah* is always decided according to David's view]—a claim that even Saul himself could not make—Saul felt downcast and became jealous of David. For regarding Saul it says, "Wherever he turned he inspired terror," (1 Samuel 14:47) and about David it says, "David was successful in all his ways, and God was with him" (1 Samuel 18:14).

[The Gemara asks:] From where do we know that Doeg was the one who praised David?—It says here, [in the verse quoted above,] "*One* of the young servants spoke up," implying "the number-one servant." And it says elsewhere, "Now there [in Nob] on that day was one of Saul's servants, who lingered before God. His name was Doeg the Edomite; he was the chief of Saul's shepherds" (ibid. 21:8), [proof that Doeg was "the number one" among Saul's servants].

THE BLESSINGS OF *MASHIACH*

The six blessings of the second of Ruth's descendants [*Mashiach*] are enumerated in the verse, "The spirit of God will rest upon him—a spirit of wisdom and understanding, a spirit of counsel and strength, a spirit of knowledge and fear of God" (Isaiah 11:2).

[The Gemara briefly digresses, focusing on the next verse which says,] "He [*Mashiach*] will be imbued [*vaharicho*] with a spirit of fear of God" (ibid. v. 3). R. Alexandri commented: This teaches us that God loaded [the *Mashiach*] with commandments and suffering like a millstone [*rechayim*]. Rava said: *vaharicho* means "he judges by smelling [*meriach*]." [He can "smell" who is guilty and who is innocent.] For the verse continues, "He will not need to judge by what his eyes see nor decide by what his ears hear. Yet he will judge the destitute with righteousness and decide with fairness for the humble of the earth."

[Parenthetically, the Gemara relates the case of a false *Mashiach* who was unmasked when he was unable to "judge by smell."] Bar Kosiva[179] ruled for two-and-a-half years. He declared to the Rabbis, "I am the *Mashiach*." They said to him, "It says about the *Mashiach* that he judges by smelling. Let us see whether Bar Kosiva can do that." When they saw that he was unable to judge by smell, [they realized that he was a false *Mashiach*;] so they put him to death.

DANIEL, CHANANIAH, MISHAEL, AND AZARIAH'S BLESSINGS

The six blessings of Daniel, Chananiah, Mishael, and Azariah appear in the verse, [Nebuchadnezzar told

Ashpenaz, his chief of staff, to bring him of the royal seed and of the nobles of the children of Israel,] "youths in whom there was no blemish, who were good looking, skillful in all wisdom, discerning in knowledge and perceptive in learning, and who have the stamina to stand [and serve] in the king's palace, and to teach them the script and language of the Chaldeans . . . among them were Daniel, Chananiah, Mishael, and Azariah" (Daniel 1:3–6). [The Gemara asks:] What is meant by "in whom there was no blemish"? R. Chama b. R. Chanina said: They did not even have a scar from a bloodletting needle. What is meant by, "who have the stamina to stand in the king's palace"? R. Chama b. R. Chanina said: [While serving in the palace, they restrained themselves from laughter, conversation, and sleep, and suppressed the call of nature, out of respect for the king].

It says, "Among them were, from the children of Judah, Daniel, Chananiah, Mishael, and Azariah" (ibid. v. 6). R. Elazar said: All of them were from the tribe of Judah. But R. Shmuel b. Nachmani said: Daniel was from the tribe of Judah; Chananiah, Mishael, and Azariah were from other tribes.

[The Gemara asks:] What is meant by, "I will give them an everlasting name that will never be cut off" (Isaiah 56:5). R. Tanchum said: Bar Kappara expounded in Tzipori: This alludes to the Book of Daniel, which was named after him, [to perpetuate his name and the memory of his deeds].

WHAT WAS NEHEMIAH'S LAPSE?

Now, think about it. The whole subject matter of the Book of Ezra was recorded by Nehemiah the son of Chachaliah. So why is the book not named after Nehemiah the son of Chachaliah [who wrote it]?[180] R. Yirmeyah b. Abba said: [It was not named for Nehemiah] because he took credit for his achievements, as it says, "Remember in my favor, O my God, all that I did for this people" (Nehemiah 5:19, 13:31).

[The Gemara asks:] But did not David say something similar, "Remember me, O God, when You show Your people favor, recall me with Your salvation" (Psalms 106:4), [and it was not held against him]? [The Gemara answers:] David was praying for Divine mercy, [whereas Nehemiah asked to be rewarded for his great accomplishments]. R. Yosef said: [Nehemiah's lapse was that] he spoke disdainfully of his predecessors. For it says, [Nehemiah said,] "The former governors who preceded me imposed burdens on the people and took bread and wine from them, in addition to forty shekels . . . but I did not do so, because of my fear of God" (Nehemiah 5:15). He even denigrated Daniel, who was surely greater than he.

And from where do we know that Daniel was greater than Nehemiah? For it says, "I Daniel alone saw the vision, whereas the men who were with me did not see the vision, but a great fear fell upon them, and they fled into hiding" (Daniel 10:7). It says, "the men who were with me did not see the vision." Now, who were these men? R. Yirmeyah, and some say, R. Chiya b. Abba, said: They were the prophets Haggai, Zechariah, and Malachi. [Since Daniel was greater than these three prophets, he surely was greater than Nehemiah who was not a prophet (Rashi).]

(94a) In one respect Haggai, Zechariah, and Malachi were greater than Daniel, and in another respect he was greater than them. They were greater than Daniel since they were prophets whereas he was not. He was greater than them since he saw the vision, and they did not. [The Gemara asks:] But since they did not see the vision, why were they terrified [as was mentioned in the verse quoted above]? [The Gemara answers:] Although they themselves did not see anything, their representative angel[181] did see the vision. Ravina remarked: This proves that when a person is frightened [for no apparent reason], even though *he* has not seen anything, his representative angel has. What is the remedy [for such unfounded fears]? He should jump four cubits from where he is standing; alternatively, he should recite the *Shema*.[182] And if he is standing in a dirty place [where it is forbidden to recite the *Shema*], he should recite the following formula, "The goat in the butcher store is fatter than I. [Go there, and leave me alone! (Rashi).]"

THE COMING OF *MASHIACH*

[In Isaiah 9:5 we are told that God intended to appoint King Hezekiah to be *Mashiach*. It says,] "To him who increases [*lemarbeh*] [God's] authority; and for him [there shall be] boundless peace" (Isaiah 9:6). R. Tanchum said: In Tzippori, Bar Kappara expounded this verse as follows: Why is it that whenever the letter *mem* appears in the middle of a word it is always open, but the letter *mem* in the word *lemarbeh* ["to him who increases"] is closed?[183] [The *mem* is closed to tell us that] the Holy One, blessed be He, wanted to designate Hezekiah the *Mashiach*, and he wanted to make Sancheriv, [the king of Assyria who laid siege to Jerusalem, take on the role of] Gog and Magog.[184] However, the Divine Attribute of Justice said before God, "Master of the universe! If David who uttered so many songs and praises before You was not made the *Mashiach*, are You going to appoint as *Mashiach* Hezekiah who did *not* sing songs of gratitude to You in spite of all the miracles You performed for him? [That would be unjust.] Thereupon God reconsidered, and because of this, the letter *mem* in *lemarbeh* was closed [to indicate that God's plan to usher in the Messianic era was "closed," and did not materialize].

Right away the earth exclaimed, "Master of the universe! Let *me* sing a song of praise to You, instead of this righteous man Hezekiah; just make him the *Mashiach*!" The earth then started to sing to God, as it says, "From the edge of the earth we have heard songs,

'Glory for the righteous'" (Isaiah 24:16). Then the Angel of the World [i.e., an angel into whose hands the entire world has been given (Rashi)] said to God, "Master of the universe! Fulfill the wish of the righteous [Hezekiah, and make him the *Mashiach*]." A heavenly voice then rang out and said, "It is My secret; it is My secret!" (ibid.), [i.e., the time of the coming of *Mashiach* is a secret known only to Me; only I know why his arrival is delayed, and why Hezekiah cannot become *Mashiach* (Rashi)]. [Hearing that the coming of *Mashiach* was postponed, the prophet Isaiah lamented, "Woe is to me! Woe is to me, how long [must we wait]" (ibid.). A heavenly voice proclaimed, "With the treachery of the treacherous have they dealt treacherously!" (ibid.). Rava, some say R. Yitzchak, [interpreted this passage to mean that *Mashiach* will not arrive] until a series of plunderers will come and ravage the Jewish people.

[The following verse expresses a similar idea:] It says, "The prophecy concerning Dumah: He calls out to Me because of Seir: "Watchman, what of the night? Watchman, what of the night?" (Isaiah 21:11). R. Yochanan said: The angel appointed over the souls of the dead is named Dumah. [This verse tells that] all the souls gathered before Dumah and said to him, "Watchman, what of the night? Watchman, what does He say [about the end of the exile, and the coming of *Mashiach*]?" The Watchman [i.e., God] replied, "The morning comes, and also the night" (ibid.); [i.e., the redemption will surely come, but a long exile will precede it]. "If you really desire [the redemption], repent; this will bring [the redemption]" (ibid.).

JETHRO PRAISED GOD

A Tanna taught in the name of R. Pappias: It is a disgrace for Hezekiah and his companions that they did not recite songs of praise to God until the earth itself broke into song, as it says, "From the edge of the earth we have heard songs, saying, 'Glory for the righteous!'" (Isaiah 24:16).

In the same vein, it says, [when hearing the report of the Exodus,] "Jethro said, 'Blessed is God, Who has rescued you from the hand of Egypt and from the hand of Pharaoh'" (Exodus 18:10). A Tanna taught in the name of R. Pappias: It is a disgrace for Moses and the six hundred thousand Jews [who were redeemed from Egypt] that they did not say, "Blessed is God" [to praise God for their rescue] until Jethro [who was a non-Jew] came and said, "Blessed is God [for having saved you."[185]

[In this context it says that] "Jethro rejoiced [*vayichad*]" (ibid. v. 9). Rav and Shmuel [dispute the meaning of *vayichad*]. Rav said: Jethro passed a sharp [*chadah*] knife over his flesh [i.e., he circumcised himself]. Shmuel said: Jethro's flesh bristled with goosebumps [*chidudim*], [he was upset when he learned of the downfall of Egypt]. Commenting on this, Rav said: This is an example of the popular adage: Don't belittle an Aramean [i.e., a non-Jew] in front of a proselyte until the tenth generation, [for deep down it will hurt his feelings].[186]

HEZEKIAH AND SANCHERIV

It says, "Therefore, the Lord, God, Master of Legions, will send a leanness among his fat ones" (Isaiah 10:16). What is meant by "leanness among his fat ones"?—The Holy One, blessed be He, said: Let Hezekiah who has eight names come and punish Sancheriv who also has eight names.

Hezekiah had eight names, for it says about him, "For a child is born to us, a son is given us; and [God's] authority is upon his shoulder; his name is called Wondrous Adviser, Mighty Warrior, Everlasting Father, Prince of Peace" (Isaiah 9:5).[187] [The Gemara asks:] But what about the name Hezekiah itself, [shouldn't that count as the ninth name]? [The Gemara answers:] Hezekiah is a merely a contraction of the words *chizko Yah*, "God strengthened him," [but not his real name]. Alternatively, Hezekiah denotes that he strengthened [*chizeik*] Israel in their devotion to their Father in Heaven.

Sancheriv had eight names, for he is referred to as: Tiglat Pileser,[188] Pilneser,[189] Shalmaneser,[190] Pul,[191] Sargon,[192] Asnapar,[193] Rabba,[194] and Yakira,[195] [the Great and Venerated]. [The Gemara asks:] But what about the name Sancheriv itself, [shouldn't that count as the ninth]? The Gemara answers: The nickname Sancheriv means to tell you that his conversation [*sicho*] was quarrelsome [*riv*], [but it was not a real name]. An alternative explanation: It indicates that he spoke impudently against God and dared Him [to stop him (Isaiah 36:18–20)].

R. Yochanan said: For what reason did that wicked man [Sancheriv] deserve to be called Asnapar, the Great and Venerated?—It is because he never spoke disdainfully about Eretz Yisrael. For it says, [Sancheriv said,] "Until I bring you to a land that is like your land" (2 Kings 18:32).[196]

Rav and Shmuel disagree on the implication of this verse: One said that Sancheriv was a clever king; the other, that he was a foolish king. According to the one who said that he was a clever king, Sancheriv reasoned: If I tell the Jews "I will bring you to a land that is better than yours," they will say, "You are a liar! [No land is better than Eretz Yisrael.]" [By not disdaining Eretz Yisrael, he proved himself to be clever.] But the one who said that Sancheriv was a foolish king argues: If the land of exile was no better than their own, what inducement [did he offer]?

THE LOST TEN TRIBES

[While Sancheriv failed to conquer Jerusalem and exile the people in the Kingdom of Judah, he did triumph over the Northern Kingdom of Israel and exiled the Ten Tribes who lived there.]

[The Gemara asks:] To what place did [Sancheriv] carry off [the Ten tribes]? Mar Zutra said: He exiled them to Africa. R. Chanina said: He banished them to the Mountains of Selug.

[We learned above that Sancheriv did not speak disdainfully about Eretz Yisrael], but [when Sancheriv exiled the Ten Tribes of] Israel, they *did* speak disparagingly about Eretz Yisrael. For when they came to came to a place named Shosh they said: This land is as good [*shaveh*] as our land. And when they came to a place named Almin, they said: This land is like our world [*almin*], [i.e., Eretz Yisrael]. And when they came to a place named Shosh Trei they said: This land is twice as good as our land.[197]

THE DESTRUCTION OF SANCHERIV'S ARMY

[Sancheriv had laid siege to Jerusalem, but God sent an angel who killed 185,000 Assyrian warriors (Isaiah 37:36). Isaiah foretold the destruction of the Assyrian army by fire:]

"Beneath his honor a burning will burn like a blaze of fire" (Isaiah 10:16). R. Yochanan explained: ["His honor" refers to the soldier's clothes;] that which was "beneath his honor" [i.e., only the Assyrian soldiers' bodies] was burned [not their clothes]. According to R. Yochanan "honor" does not mean a person's actual honor, [i.e., his body]; rather, it refers to his clothing]. For R. Yochanan used to call his clothes "the things that honor me." But R. Elazar said: "Beneath his honor" should be taken literally, [i.e., that which was beneath their bodies, namely their souls] was burned, [but their bodies remained intact], just like the burning of the two sons of Aaron.[198] Just as in the case of the death of Aaron's sons the soul was burned, and the body remained intact, so here, too, [when Sancheriv's army perished,] the soul of each soldier was burned, while his body remained intact.

A Tanna taught in the name of R. Yehoshua b. Korchah: Pharaoh, who personally blasphemed God, was punished by God Himself, [and not through an angel]. Sancheriv, who blasphemed God (94b) through a messenger, [showing greater contempt][199] was punished by God through a messenger [which is an added indignity]. [Specifically,] Pharaoh blasphemed God directly, for [he himself said,] "Who is God that I should obey Him?" (Exodus 5:2). Therefore, he was punished by God Himself, for it says, "God swamped the Egyptians in the middle of the sea" (ibid. 14:27). And it says furthermore, "You trampled them in the sea with Your [steed-like] clouds" (Habakkuk 3:15). But Sancheriv blasphemed God through a messenger, for it says, "By the hand of your messengers you have insulted my Lord" (2 Kings 19:23). Therefore God [slighted him by] punishing him through a mere angel, as it says, "An angel of God went out and struck down one hundred eighty-five thousand [people] of the Assyrian camp" (ibid. v. 35).

THE WICKED SANCHERIV
R. Chanina b. Papa contrasted two verses: One verse says, [Sancheriv boasted,] "I shall enter His ultimate height [i.e., the *Bet Hamikdash*]" (Isaiah 37:24). But in another verse it says, "I shall enter His ultimate abode [i.e., God's dwelling in heaven]" (2 Kings 19:23). That wicked man [Sancheriv] in fact said: First I will destroy God's dwelling place below on earth, and afterward I will destroy God's dwelling place on High.

R. Yehoshua b. Levi said: What is meant by the verse, "Now, could it be that without [the consent] of God I have come up to this place to destroy it? Indeed, God told me, 'Go up against this land and destroy it!'" (2 Kings 18:25). What is the meaning of this? [How could Sancheriv claim that God had told him to destroy Jerusalem?] He based his claim on the fact that he heard the prophet Isaiah declare, "Because this people has rejected the gently flowing water of the Shiloah and instead rejoiced with Rezin and the son of Remaliah, therefore, behold the Lord is bringing upon them the mighty and abundant waters of the Euphrates River—the king of Assyria" (Isaiah 8:6). [Sancheriv took this as an order to conquer Eretz Yisrael.]

R. Yosef said: If not for the Targum, [the interpretive Aramaic translation] of this verse, I would not know what it meant. [The Targum interprets the verse as follows:] Since this people has despised the kingship of the Davidic dynasty, which leads them gently like the waters of the Shiloah that flow gently, and has [instead] preferred [the monarchy] of Rezin and the son of Remaliah.[200]

[The Gemara compares the righteous King Hezekiah of the Kingdom of Judah with the wicked Pekach son of Remaliah, ruler of the Northern Kingdom of Israel.]

R. Yochanan said: What is the meaning of the passage, "God's curse is on the house of the wicked; He blesses the abode of the righteous" (Proverbs 3:33)? The segment "God's curse is on the house of the wicked" refers to Pekach son of Remaliah, who ate forty *se'ahs* of young birds for dessert. [His curse was that, no matter how much he ate, he was never satiated (Rashi).] The second segment of the verse, "He blesses the abode of the righteous" refers to Hezekiah, King of Judah, who ate only a mere *litra* of vegetables for his entire meal. [He was satisfied after eating a very frugal meal.]

WHY WAS SANCHERIV PUNISHED?
[After this digression the Gemara resumes the discussion of Sancheriv's mistaken idea that God had authorized his invasion of Eretz Yisrael.]

[Isaiah prophesied,] "Therefore, behold, the Lord is bringing upon them the mighty and abundant waters of the [Euphrates] River, the king of Assyria" (Isaiah 8:7). And it says [in the next verse], "[The river] shall pass through Judah, flooding as it passes, and reaching to the neck." [The Gemara asks:] In light of this prophecy, why was Sancheriv punished? [The Gemara answers: In these verses] the prophet was prophesying about the fate of the Ten Tribes [that comprised the Northern Kingdom of Israel, not about the Kingdom of Judah and Jerusalem]. Sancheriv, however, resolved to conquer all of Jerusalem. The prophet then came [and predicted that Sancheriv would fail,] telling him, "For there is no weariness [*muaf*] for the one who oppresses her" (ibid. v. 23). R. Elazar b. Berechiah explained this verse to mean: The nation that is tired out [*ayef*] by the intensive study of the Torah, [meaning, the Kingdom of Judah under their righteous King Hezekiah] will not be delivered into the hands of the one who oppresses it [i.e., Sancheriv].

[The Gemara asks:] What is the meaning of the last segment of this verse: "The first time he dealt mildly, [exiling only] the land of Zebulun and the land of Naphtali, but the last time he dealt harshly, [exiling those who lived] by the way of the sea, beyond the Jordan River in the region of the nations" (ibid.)? [The meaning is this: The fate of the Kingdom of Judah] will not be like the fate of the "first ones" [i.e., the Ten Tribes] who took the yoke of the Torah lightly, [rejecting it, and who were subsequently exiled]. Rather, the "last ones" [i.e., the Kingdom of Judah under Hezekiah], who took the yoke of the Torah seriously, they deserve to have miracles performed for them as great as the miracles that were performed for those who crossed the Red Sea and the Jordan.[201] If Sancheriv changes his mind [and calls off his attack on Jerusalem], fine; if not, I will make him the butt of the nations' ridicule, [so humiliating will be his defeat].

GOD SWEARS TO DESTROY SANCHERIV'S LEGIONS
[After praising Hezekiah for his righteousness and for the way he restored the observance and study of the Torah, Scripture says,] "After these events and this truth, Sancheriv king of Assyria came. He entered into Judah and encamped against all the fortified cities, intending to breach [and capture] them for himself" (2 Chronicles 32:1). [The Gemara asks sarcastically:] Was this a fitting reward for such an outstanding personality [as Hezekiah]? [The Gemara answers, by expounding the verse:] "After these events and this truth"—after what events and to which truth does the verse refer? Ravina said: ["This truth" refers to God Whose very Essence is Truth, and the verse means:] After the Holy One, blessed be He, anticipated events

by swearing [to bring Sancheriv to Jerusalem and bring about his defeat there], He reasoned: If I tell Hezekiah that I am going to bring Sancheriv to Jerusalem and deliver him into your hand, Hezekiah will reply: I want neither [a victory over] him, nor the terror [of his invasion]. Immediately, the Holy One, blessed be He, precluded this, swearing: I will bring [Sancheriv] to Jerusalem! For it says, "God, the Lord of Hosts swore, saying, 'Surely as I have designed, so shall it happen; what I have planned, that shall come to pass, [namely] to break Assyria in My land, to crush him on My mountain. His yoke shall drop off them, and his burden shall be removed from their shoulder'" (Isaiah 14:24,25). [God brought Sancheriv to Jerusalem in order to destroy him, in fulfillment of His oath [truth], as a demonstration of His power and might (*Maharsha*).]

R. Yochanan said: The Holy One, blessed be He, said: Let Sancheriv and his legions come [and attack Jerusalem], and they will become a feeding trough for Hezekiah and his legions, [their skeletons will become feeding troughs for the animals of Hezekiah's army (Rashi)].

HEZEKIAH'S MAGNIFICENT ACHIEVEMENTS

It says, "It will be on that day that He will lift [Assyria's] affliction from your shoulders, and his yoke from upon your neck, and the yoke will be broken because of the oil" (Isaiah 10:27). R. Yitzchak Nafcha said: [This means that] the yoke of Sancheriv was broken by the oil of Hezekiah that burned [in the lamps of] the synagogues and study halls [by whose light the people studied the Torah until late into the night]. [The Gemara asks:] What did Hezekiah do [to arouse such an avid interest in Torah study]? He placed a sword over the entrance of the study hall and proclaimed, "Whoever does not engage in the study of Torah shall be pierced by this sword!" As a result, they searched from Dan [in the north] to Beersheba [in the south] and did not find a single unlearned person; and they searched from Gevas to Antipras [two border towns (Rashi)] and did not find a boy or girl, man or woman who was not knowledgeable in even the knotty laws of defilement and purification.

And concerning this generation it says, "It shall be on that day that each man will raise a heifer and two sheep . . ." (Isaiah 7:21); [after Sancheriv's defeat, the Jewish people will be satisfied with the basic necessities, and devote themselves to Torah study]. And it says also, "It will happen on that day: Where there had been a thousand vines, worth a thousand silver pieces, it will become thorns and weeds" (ibid. v. 23). This means that even though [the Jews will possess land so valuable] that a thousand vines are worth a thousand pieces of silver, nevertheless, the land will be abandoned to grow thorns and weeds, [because the people will be involved in Torah study].

[Regarding Sancheriv, it says,] "Your spoils will be gathered like the gathering of locusts, like the roar of water rushing into pools" (Isaiah 33:4). [The underlying idea of the verse is this:] The prophet Isaiah said to Israel: Gather the spoils [from Sancheriv's army]. They asked: Should each one gather booty for himself or should it be divided equally among us? Isaiah replied: "Like the gathering of locusts"; just as when the locusts gather, each locust takes for himself [and does not share with the others], so, too, you should take your spoils, each person for himself. They objected: But the wealth of the Ten Tribes is mixed up in the spoils, [so taking it would amount to stealing the property of our brothers]![202] Isaiah replied: "Like the roar of water rushing into pools"—just as pools purify the unclean, so, too, when possessions belonging to Jews fall into the hands of idolators, they immediately become purified [of any prohibition, and are considered legitimate spoils of war].

SANCHERIV'S TEN ADVANCES

R. Huna said: The wicked Sancheriv made ten marches on the day [he invaded Judah and advanced toward Jerusalem]. For it says, "[Sancheriv] has come to Ayat! He passed through Migron! He deposits his belongings at Michmas! They have crossed Mabarah! They have lodged at Geva! Ramah has quaked! Givat Shaul has fled! Cry out, Bat Galim! Hear, O Laish! O you poor Anatot! Madmenah has moved away! The inhabitants of Gevim have mustered themselves! This very day he intends to stand in Nob, waving his hand [contemptuously] at the Mount of the daughter of Zion, at the hill of Jerusalem!" (Isaiah 10:28–32). [The Gemara asks:] But these are more than ten; [the verse lists twelve places]. [The Gemara answers:] The words, "Cry out, Bat Galim, hear, O Laish" were said by the prophet to the people of Israel, [they do not refer to places]. When he said, "Cry out, Bat Galim" [daughter of the waves], he meant, "Cry out, daughter of Abraham, Isaac, and Jacob who performed [as many] *mitzvot* as there are waves in the sea!" And when Isaiah said, "Hear, O Laish" he meant, "Do not be afraid of this one [Sancheriv]; instead, be afraid of the wicked Nebuchadnezzar, who is compared to a lion [*laish*]; [he will eventually destroy Jerusalem]." For it says, "The lion [meaning, Nebuchanezzar] has left his den" (Jeremiah 4:7).

(95a) What did Isaiah mean by "O poor Anatot"? He meant that the prophet Jeremiah the son of Chilkiah from Anatot is destined to prophesy [concerning the tragic fate of Judah and Jerusalem]. For it says, "The words of Jeremiah son of Chilkiah, of the *kohanim* who were in Anatot in the land of Benjamin" (Jeremiah 1:1). [So there are three places that do not refer to locations?]

[Before answering this question, the Gemara asks:] Are the prophesies of Isaiah and Jeremiah the same?

654

In Jeremiah's prophecy the aggressor is referred to as an *ari*, whereas in Isaiah's prophecy he is described as a *laish*? R. Yochanan explained: [In Scripture, the lion is referred to by six names: *ari*, *kefir*, *lavi*, *laish*, *shachal*, and *shachatz*. If so, there were fewer than ten places, [since Bat Galim, Laish, and Anatot are not names of localities]! The Gemara answers: "They have crossed Mabarah" [*Avru Mabarah*] counts as two localities.

SANCHERIV'S FATAL MISTAKE

[The Gemara asks:] What is the underlying meaning of the verse, "Yet today [Sancheriv] will stand in Nob" (Isaiah 10:32)? R. Huna said: Only that day was left for [the punishment of] the sin of Nob.[203] [When Sancheriv's army was still a great distance from Jerusalem,] his astrologers told him, "If you go and attack Jerusalem today, you will conquer it; if you do not, you will not conquer it." Thereupon he advanced with such speed that should have taken ten days he covered in a single day. When the Assyrian army arrived at the gates of Jerusalem, they piled up a stack of carpets for Sancheriv. When he mounted it he sat higher than the wall of the city and was able to see all of Jerusalem. As he surveyed the city, it appeared small to him. "Is this the city of Jerusalem," he exclaimed, "for which I rushed my entire army, and for which I conquered all this territory? Why, it is smaller and weaker than all the cities of the nations I have conquered with my might!" He then got up, contemptuously shook his head, and waved his hand at the Temple Mount in Zion and at the Courtyard of the *Bet Hamikdash* in Jerusalem.

Therepon his soldiers said to him, "Let us launch an attack right now!" Replied Sancheriv, "You are too tired [from the long march]; but tomorrow let each of you bring me a [loose] stone of this wall, [and we will then breach it]."

Right away, "It was that very night that an angel of God went out and struck down one hundred and eighty-five thousand men of the Assyrian camp. The rest arose early in the morning and behold—they were all dead corpses!" (2 Kings 19:35). [By letting the critical day pass, Sancheriv missed his opportunity, and Jerusalem was saved.] R. Papa said: There is a popular saying for this: Justice deferred is justice erased. [If a court case is shelved, it will be called off eventually.]

DAVID'S NARROW ESCAPE

[David, fleeing from Saul, was offered food and a sword by the *kohanim* of Nob. Doeg the Edomite, a servant of Saul, saw this and reported it to Saul, whereupon Saul ordered Doeg to kill all the *kohanim* of Nob. The Gemara relates how David was punished for indirectly triggering the massacre.]

It says, "Yishbi-benob, one of the children of Harafah [Orpah],[204] and whose spear weighed three hundred copper weights, and who was girded with new [armor], declared that he would kill David" (2 Samuel 21:16). What is meant by "Yishbi-benob"? Rav Yehudah said in Rav's name: It means "a man who came [*ish sheba*] on account of the massacre at Nob [*benob*]." For the Holy One, blessed be He, said to David, "How long will this sin remain in your hand [unpunished]? It was through you that Nob the city of *kohanim* was massacred, and it was through you that Doeg the Edomite was driven from the World to Come,[205] and it was through you that Saul and his three sons were killed[206] [as punishment for ordering the killing of the *kohanim* of Nob]. Now, [what punishment do you choose]? Do you choose that your descendants should be wiped out, or that you yourself should be delivered into the enemy's hand?"

David replied, "Master of the universe! It is better that I should be delivered into the enemy's hand, and let my children not be annihilated."

[The Gemara relates how David's punishment was carried out.] One day, when David went to Shekor Bazai, Satan appeared, disguised as a deer. David shot an arrow at the dear, but missed. Chasing after the deer, he wandered into the land of the Philistines. When Yishbi-benob saw him, he exclaimed, "This is the person that killed my brother Goliath!" Yishbi then bound David, doubled him up, and threw him under an olive press, [and sat on it so as to crush him (Rashi)]. However, a miracle happened, and the ground under him became soft [and gave way, which saved David's life]. This is what David had in mind when he wrote, "You have widened my stride beneath me, and my ankles have not faltered" (Psalms 18:37).

Now, the day David was captured was Friday toward evening, and Avishai son of Tzeruiah, [David's nephew and one of his gallant officers,] was washing his head with four measures of water, [in preparation of *Shabbat*]. Suddenly he noticed bloodstains [in the water]. Others say that a dove came, flailing about with its wings. Avishai said to himself, "Israel is compared to a dove, for it says [about Israel], "You will be like the wings of a dove, covered with silver" (Psalms 68:14). This must be a sign that David, the king of Israel is in trouble. Avishai then went to David's house, but did not find him there.

[Avishai wanted to use David's mule to rush to his aid,] but he said to himself, "We have learned: A person is forbidden to ride on the king's horse, to sit on his throne, and to use his scepter. But does this apply in a time of danger?" He went and asked this question to the scholars in the study hall. They told him, "In a time of danger it is permitted [to ride the king's horse]."

Avishai then mounted David's mule and rode off. Miraculously, the earth shrank under him [so that he reached the land of the Philistines in a very short time]. As Avishai was riding, he saw Orpah, the mother of Yishbi-benob, spinning. As soon as she saw him, she broke the thread of the spindle and hurled the spindle at him, trying to kill him. [When she saw that she had missed,] she said with false innoncence, "Young fellow, please bring me the spindle [which I accidentally dropped]." He threw the spindle at the top of her head and killed her. When Yishbi-benob saw Avishai approaching, he said to himself, "Now that there are two against me [David and Avishai], they will kill me." [So, before Avishai arrived] he threw David high up in the air, stuck his spear into the earth, and announced, "David will fall on the spear and be killed!" Avishai, [seeing David in mortal danger], pronounced the Divine Name, whereupon David remained suspended in the air between heaven and earth.

[The Gemara asks as an aside:] Why didn't David pronounce the Name himself?—Because a captive cannot free himself from prison. [He needs outside help.]

[While David was suspended above the spear] Avishai asked him, "What are you doing there? [How did you get into this predicament]?" "The Holy One, blessed be He, said such-and-such to me, and I replied such-and-such," David answered [referring to the options God had offered him, and that he had made the choice to fall into the hands of his enemy rather than have his children pay for his sin]. Avishai said to David, "Reverse your prayer [and ask that your descendants should suffer instead of yourself, as people say,] "Let your grandson sell wax [i.e., be poor], as long as you yourself don't suffer" [i.e., don't sacrifice the present for the sake of the future]. "If so," said David, "please help me [to reverse it]." [Avishai prayed for him;] and so it says, "Avishai the son of Tzeruiah helped David" (2 Samuel 21:17). R. Yehudah said in the name of Rav: Avishai helped David by praying for him [to have his verdict reversed].

Avishai pronounced the Divine Name and brought him down safely. [The two men fled but] Yishbi-benov pursued them. When [David and Avishai] reached Kubi [a border town], they said to each other, "Let's fight him." However, when they reached Bei Trei they said, "Can two cubs kill a full-grown lion? [Yishbi-benov is too strong for us to defeat him in direct combat.] They startled Yishbi-benov, telling him, "Go and find Orpah your mother in the grave; [we have killed her (Rashi)]." When they mentioned his mother's name [telling him of her death], he lost his strength, and they killed him. This [episode of David's close call] is the reason that it says, "Then David's men swore to him saying, 'You shall not go into battle with us any more, so that the light of Israel not be extinguished'" (2 Samuel 21:17).

THREE PEOPLE FOR WHOM THE EARTH SHRANK

[As a follow-up to the account of the earth shrinking for Avishai's sake, the Gemara mentions other persons who experienced a similar miracle.]

The Rabbis taught: There were three persons for whom the earth shrank [to shorten the journey to their destination]. They were: Eliezer, the servant of Abraham; our father Jacob; and Avishai the son of Tzeruiah. The case of Avishai the son of Tzeruiah we just related. [We know that the earth shrank for] Eliezer, the servant of Abraham, because it says, [that on arriving in Aram Naharaim, Eliezer said,] "Now today I came to the well" (Genesis 24:42), implying that he had started his journey [in Canaan] that same day, [a distance that normally takes a long time to complete; hence the earth shrank for him]. [That the earth shrank for] our father Jacob (95b) we know] because it says, "Jacob left Beersheba and went to Charan" (Genesis 28:10). And the next verse says, "He came to a familiar place and spent the night there because the sun had already set" (ibid. v. 11). The first verse says that Jacob reached Charan [which is far outside Eretz Yisrael],[207] whereas the second verse states that he spent the night in Beth El [within the borders of Eretz Yisrael]. [The Gemara resolves the inconsistency:] When Jacob reached Charan, he said to himself: Is it possible that I passed [on my way to Charan] the place [Beth El] where my fathers prayed, and I did not pray there myself? He decided to return to Eretz Yisrael. As soon as he contemplated to go back, the earth shrank, and instantly, "he came to the familiar place" [i.e., Bet El]. [Proof that the earth shrank for Jacob.]

[The Gemara resumes the discussion of how David was punished for being instrumental in the massacre of the *kohanim* of Nob.]

From where do we know that David's descendants were wiped out, [since he requested that his prayer be reversed]? For it says, "When Ataliah, Achaziah's mother, learned that her son was dead, she promptly killed off the entire royal family" (2 Kings 11:1). [The Gemara asks:] But Joash survived [to carry on the Davidic dynasty; so not all descendants were destroyed]? [The Gemara answers:] There, too, [in Nob], one *kohen* named Eviatar survived, as it says, "One son of Achimelech son of Achituv—his name was Eviatar—escaped" (1 Samuel 22:20).

Rav Yehudah said in the name of Rav: If not for the fact that Eviatar son of Achimelech lived on after the massacre, not a single survivor would have remained of David's offspring.

THE DECIMATION OF SANCHERIV'S FORCES

[The Germara returns to the theme of Sancheriv's onslaught against Eretz Yisrael.] We learned in a *Baraita*: The first divisions [of the Assyrian army] crossed the river Jordan swimming, as it says, "It will pass into Judah, flooding as it passes" (Isaiah 8:8). The middle divisions, however, were able to cross marching erect; [by swimming across, the first divisions withdrew so much water that the level of the river was lowered]. For it says, "It reaches to the neck" (ibid.). The last divisions raised clouds of dust with their feet [as they marched across]; indeed, they did not find any water in the river to drink; [the riverbed had dried up by the passage of the second division], until they brought water from someplace else and drank that water. For it says, "I dug wells and drank waters, for the soles of my feet dried up all the rivers" (Isaiah 37:25).

It says, "An angel of God went forth and slew one hundred and eighty-five thousand of the camp of Assyria, and they arose in the morning, and behold, they were all dead corpses" (ibid. v 37:36). R. Abbahu said: These were just the commanders of the legions.

R. Ashi said: This is also borne out by a precise reading of the verse, for it says, "God the Lord of Hosts will send leanness into his fat ones" (ibid. 10:16), meaning, among the "fat ones" of Sancheriv's army [i.e., the commanders, but the number of casualties among the foot soldiers was astronomical (Rashi)].

Ravina said: This is also borne out by the verse, "God sent an angel who destroyed every warrior, commander, and officer in the army of the king of Assyria. Then [Sancheriv] returned in disgrace to his land. As he entered the house of his idol, his own children struck him down by the sword" (2 Chronicles 32:21). [The verse mentions only the slain officers.] From this you can infer [that Sancheriv's army numbered many times one hundred and eighty-five thousand men].

HOW DID THE ANGEL SLAY THE ASSYRIANS?

With what did the angel strike [the Assyrian army]? R. Eliezer said: The angel struck them with his hand, as it says, [at the crossing of the Red Sea,] "And Israel saw *the* great hand" (Exodus 14:31), implying that they saw the hand that was destined to punish Sancheriv.

R. Yehoshua said: The angel struck them with his finger, for it says, "The sorcerers said to Pharaoh, 'It is *the* finger of God!'" (ibid. 14:31), implying that it was the same finger that was destined to punish Sancheriv.

R. Eliezer the son of R. Yose Hagelili said: The Holy One, blessed be He, said to the angel Gabriel: Is your sickle sharpened [and ready to destroy the Assyrian army]? Gabriel replied to God: Master of the universe! It has been sharpened since the six days of creation! As it says, "They fled from the sword, from the sharpened sword" (Isaiah 21:15).

R. Shimon b. Yochai said: The season [when Sancheriv attacked Jerusalem] was the time when the fruits were about to ripen. So the Holy One, blessed be He, said to Gabriel: When you go out to make the fruits ripen,[208] do battle with the Assyrians. For it says, "When he passes through [on his mission to ripen the fruits], he will take you, for he will pass through every morning, by day and by night. It shall be sheer terror to understand this message" (Isaiah 28:19). [It

was so easy to slay the Assyrians that Gabriel did it casually, on his way to ripen the fruits (*Maharsha*).]

R. Papa said: Gabriel's handling of the situation illustrates the popular saying: When you happen to pass by your enemy, make yourself heard to him; [it will unnerve him].

[How did the Assyrians die?] Some say: [Gabriel] breathed into their nostrils, and they died. For it says, "When He blows on them they wither" (ibid. 40:24). R. Yirmeyah b. Abba said: [Gabriel] clapped his hands, and they died, for it says, "I too will pound My hand upon My hand, and I will thereby put My wrath to rest" (Ezekiel 21:22). R. Yitzchak Nafcha said: [Gabriel] opened their ears, so that they heard the song being sung by the *Chayot*, [a category of angels],[209] and as a result they died. For it says, "From Your exaltedness nations have scattered" (Isaiah 33:3).

How many of the Sancheriv's army survived? Rav said: Ten, as it says, "The remnant of the trees of his forest [i.e., Sancheriv's troops] will be few, a child will be able to record them" (ibid. 10:19). What numeral can a child write down? The numeral ten [i.e., the Hebrew letter *yud*, which is just a small dot].

Shmuel said: Nine [soldiers survived]. For it says, "Only gleanings will remain of him, like a picked olive tree, with but two or three olives on the top of the highest branch, or four or five on its branches" (ibid. 17:6), [adding four and five, Shmuel arrives at nine (Rashi)]. R. Yehoshua b. Levi said: Fourteen [soldiers survived]. For it says, "Two, three, four, five" (ibid.); [adding all the numbers in the verse].

R. Yochanan said: Five [men survived, namely,] Sancheriv and his two sons, Nebuchadnezzar and Nebuzaradan. That Nebuzaradan survived we know through an oral tradition, and we know that Nebuchadnezzar survived for it says, [Nebuchanezzar said,] "The form of the fourth is like an angel" (Daniel 3:25).[210] Now, if Nebuchadnezzar never had seen an angel before, how did he know [what an angel looked like]? [Obviously, he *had* seen an angel before, during the rout of Sancheriv's army.]

We know that Sancheriv and his two sons survived, for it says, "It happened that when [Sancheriv] was worshipping in the temple of his idol Nisroch, his sons Adramelech and Sarezer struck him down by the sword" (2 Kings 19:37), [proof that Sancheriv and his two sons survived the debacle at Jerusalem].

THE ASSASSINATION OF SANCHERIV

R. Abbahu said: If the following verse were not expressly written in Scripture, it would be impossible to say it, for it says, "On that day, the Lord will shave with a hired razor those who dwell on the other side of the river, namely, the king of Assyria, his head, and the hair on his legs; his beard will be destroyed, too" (Isaiah 7:20). [No one will dare say such a bizarre thing.]

[The Gemara further develops this metaphoric passage: After Sancheriv's ruin,] the Holy One, blessed be He, came and appeared to him as an old man. [God] said to Sancheriv, "When you go back to the kings of the east and the west whose sons you brought [to Jerusalem] and caused them to be slaughtered, what will you tell them?" Replied Sancheriv, "That is exactly what I am afraid of." He continued, "What shall I do?"

"Go," God replied, (96a) "and disguise yourself."

"How shall I disguise myself?"

"Go and bring me a pair of scissors, and I will shave you."

"Where can I find them?"

"Go to that house [over there; you will find scissors,] and bring them to Me." So Sancheriv went to the house and found a pair of scissors. [Before he entered the house,] some ministering angels appeared to him disguised as men grinding palm kernels. Sancheriv said to them, "Give me a pair of scissors." They replied, "First grind for us a measure of date kernels, then we will give you the scissors."

Sancheriv ground a measure of date kernels, whereupon the angels gave him the scissors.[211] [All this took time, so that] when Sancheriv came and brought the scissors, it had become dark. [God,] in the guise of an old man, said to Sancheriv, "Go and bring a fire, [so that I can see]." So he went and brought a fire. While he was blowing into the fire, the flame set fire to his beard. As a result, he went and shaved both his head *and* his beard, [although initially he had not meant to shave his beard]. And this, they say, is the fulfillment of the phrase, "his beard will be destroyed, too" [not shaved, implying that the beard was destroyed by fire (Rashi)].[212]

R. Papa said: [This anecdote typifies] the popular aphorism: If you singe the hair of an Aramean, and he does not mind, you may even set fire to his beard. You can play even more pranks on him, [and he still will not protest].

[After this experience,] Sancheriv went and found a plank of Noah's ark. "This plank," he said, "must be the great god that saved Noah from the flood!" [He saw himself as another Noah, the lone survivor of the great disaster (Maharal). Speaking to the plank,] he said, "If I go to war and win, I will offer my two sons as a sacrifice to you." His sons overheard what he said, and they killed him. This [is the background] to the verse, "It happened as he was worshipping in the temple of his idol Nisroch that his sons Adarmelech and Sharezer struck him down by the sword" (2 Kings 19:37).

ABRAHAM'S WAR AGAINST THE FOUR KINGS

[The Gemara relates an earlier case where an angel obliterated an enemy.] It says [concerning Abraham's battle against the four kings], "[Abraham] divided [his forces] against them at night [*lailah*]" (Genesis 14:15). R. Yochanan commented: The angel who was appointed to help Abraham was named *lailah* ["night"], for it says, [Job said,] "Perish the day on which I was born, and the night [*lailah*] that announced, 'A male child has been conceived'" (Job 3:3).[213] R. Yitzchak Nafcha said: [*Lailah*] means that nocturnal feats were performed for Abraham [i.e., the stars fought on his behalf]. As it says, "From heaven they fought, the very stars from their orbits did battle with Sisera" (Judges 5:20). Resh Lakish said: The interpretation of the blacksmith [i.e., R. Yitzchak Nafcha] is better than that of the son of the blacksmith [i.e., R. Yochanan].

[In connection with Abraham's war] it says, "[Abraham] hurried after [the invaders] catching up with them in Dan" (Genesis 14:14). R. Yochanan said: When that righteous man [Abraham] reached Dan his strength waned, for he [prophetically] foresaw that his descendants were going to worship idols in Dan. For it says, "[Jeroboam] placed one [of the golden calves] in Beth El and the other one in Dan" (1 Kings 12:29). And that wicked man [Nebuchadnezzar] did not reach the peak of his strength until he reached Dan, for it says, "From Dan is heard the snorting of [Nebuchadnezzar's] horses" (Jeremiah 8:16). [The sin of Jeroboam was the source of Nebuchadnezzar's strength.]

WHY DID NEBUCHADNEZZAR SUCCEED?

R. Zeira said: Although R. Yehudah b. Beteira sent the following message from Netzivin: Be careful with the honor of an elderly scholar who tragically has forgotten his Torah learning [through sickness], and be careful to cut the *veridin*[214] [when slaughtering fowl] in accordance with the ruling of R. Yehudah, and be careful of the honor of [scholars] who are children of ignorant people, for it is from them that Torah knowledge will spring forth;[215] nevertheless, we *do* tell them something like the following: [to teach them that the honor they are receiving is due to some meritorious deed their parents performed].

It says, "You will win, O God, though I may express a grievance to You. Yet I shall present charges against You: Why does the way of the wicked prosper? You have planted them, and they have taken root; they grow, they even bear fruit" (Jeremiah 12:1,2). [Jeremiah asked: Why was Nebuchadnezzar allowed to succeed in conquering Jerusalem?] What answer was Jeremiah given?—"If you race with the foot-runners and they exhaust you, how then can you compete with the horses? If [they exhausted you] in a tranquil land, where you placed your trust, how will you fare in the heights of the Jordan?" (ibid. v. 5); [in other words: you cannot possibly fathom God's ways]. This may be compared to a person who boasted, "I can run a distance of three *parsahs* in front of horses on marshland,

[and they will not catch up with me]." But then he happened upon a person running on foot and ran in front of him just three *mils* on dry land, and was exhausted. [Seeing this,] people said to him, "If you are exhausted from running against a pedestrian, imagine how worn out you would be racing against horses! And if you are so exhausted from running just three *mils*, imagine how worn out you would be if you tried to run three *parsahs*! And if you are tired from running on dry land, how much more tired would you be running on marshland!"

[God said to Jeremiah,] "The same applies to you. If you are astonished at the reward I paid to that wicked [Nebuchanezzar] for the four steps he ran in My honor,[216] imagine how much greater will be the surprise when people see the great reward I will pay to Abraham, Isaac, and Jacob who ran before Me with the vigor of horses" [i.e., they served me ardently]. And this is the meaning of the passage, "When I think of the prophets [Abraham, Isaac, and Jacob], my heart is crushed within me [i.e., I am dumbfounded when I think of the enormous reward that is in store for them], all my bones are shaking; I am like a drunken man, like one overcome by wine, because of God and His holy words" (Jeremiah 23:9).

[The Gemara asks:] What does "the four steps" refer to? It says, "At that time Merodach-baladan son of Baladan, king of Babylonia, sent letters and a gift to Hezekiah, for he had heard that he was ill and had recuperated" (Isaiah 39:1). Now, does it make sense to say that just because he heard that Hezekiah was sick and had recovered, Merodach-baladan sent him letters and a gift? [He was neither his friend nor his ally.]

[The Gemara explains:] Indeed, [it was because of Hezekiah's recovery]. For Merodach-baladan wanted "to inquire about the miracle that had happened in the land" (2 Chronicles 32:31). [What miracle?] R. Yochanan explained: The day on which [the wicked] Achaz[217] died was only two hours long; [it was shortened by ten hours so that there would not be enough time for a state funeral and eulogies (Rashi)]. When Hezekiah fell ill and recovered, the Holy One, blessed be He, restored those ten hours to him. As it says, "Behold, I will cause the shadow on the sundial—which had moved fast on the sundial of Achaz—to move back ten degrees. And the shadow of the sun moved back the ten degrees it had moved ahead" (Isaiah 38:8).

[Perplexed by the unusual length of the day, Merodach-baladan] said to his servants, "What is the meaning of this?" They replied, "Hezekiah was ill and has recovered." Merodach-baladan exclaimed, "If there is such a great man, shouldn't I send him greeting? Write to him as follows: 'Greetings to King Hezekiah! Greetings to the city of Jerusalem! Greetings to the great God!" Nebuchadnezzar was Merodach-baladan's scribe, but at that moment he was not present. When

Nebuchadnezzar came back, he asked [the royal servants], "How did you write the letter?" They told him what they had written. Nebuchanezzar said to them, "You called Him 'the great God,' yet you mention Him last? This is how you should have written: Greetings to the great God! Greetings to the city of Jerusalem! Greetings to King Hezekiah."

The servants said to Nebuchadnezzar, "Let the reader of the letter become the messenger!" [He who gives the advice should carry it out himself. If you don't like the letter, go and retrieve it from the messenger and rewrite it!] [Nebuchadnezzar] ran after the messenger, but when he had taken four steps the angel Gabriel came and stopped him. R. Yochanan remarked: If Gabriel had not stopped him, nothing could have saved the Jewish people. [Had he actually carried out his intention to overtake the messenger, his merit would have been so great that he would have been able to annihilate the Jewish people (Rashi).][218]

A SON HONORS HIS FATHER, A SERVANT HIS MASTER

[The Gemara wonders:] Why was he called [Merodach] Baladan the son of Baladan? [Why is his name the same as his father's?] They said: Baladan [the father] was king, but his face turned into the face of a dog. [As a result, he had to abdicate.] His son, Merodach, succeeded him. [Out of respect] he would sign his documents with his own name and the name of his father, King Baladan [Merodach-baladan]. This is what is meant by the verse, "A son honors his father and a servant his master" (Malachi 1:6). "A son honors his father" is illustrated by what we just said. "A servant his master" is illustrated by the verse [that speaks of Nebuzaradan], "In the fifth month, on the tenth day of the month—which was the nineteenth year of Nebuchadnezzar king of Babylonia—Nebuzaradan, the chief executioner, came; he stood before [Nebuchadnezzar] the king of Babylonia in Jerusalem, and he burned the House of God and the king's palace" (Jeremiah 52:12,13).

(96b) [The above verse states that Nebuzaradan stood before Nebuchadnezzar in Jerusalem. The Gemara asks:] But did Nebuchadnezzar go to Jerusalem? Surely it says that, [when Jerusalem was under siege by Babylonians, King Zedekiah fled, but] "They seized the king and brought him up to the king [Nebuchadnezzar] of Babylonia at Riblah" (2 Kings 25:6). And R. Abahu said that this was Antioch. [So, Nebuchadnezzar was in Antioch, and not in Jerusalem!] R. Chisda and R. Yitzchak b. Avudimi [explained this inconsistency]. One said: An image of Nebuchadnezzar's likeness was engraved on Nebuzaradan's chariot, [so that he felt as if he were standing before Nebuchadnezzar]. The other said: Nebuzaradan was so awestruck by Nebuchadnezzar that it seemed to him as though he were standing before Nebuchadnezzar. [At any rate, Nebuzaradan exemplified the passage "like a servant honors his master."]

THE CONQUEST OF JERUSALEM

Rava said: Nebuchadnezzar sent Nebuzaradan three hundred mules loaded with iron axes that could cut through iron, but they were all shattered on just a single gate of Jerusalem. For it says, "Against one of its gates they beat with all their axes and hammers together, [but it was useless]" (Psalms 74:6). Nebuzaradan wanted to retreat; he said, "I am afraid lest what happened to Sancheriv will happen to me." [God sent an angel to destroy Sancheriv's army.] A heavenly voice proclaimed, "You leaper, son of a leaper, Nebuzaradan, leap into the attack [and conquer Jerusalem]! For the time has come for the Temple to be destroyed and for the Sanctuary to be burned!" Nebuzaradan had a single ax left over. He went and struck the gate with the blunt edge of the ax, and it opened. As it says, [The Psalmist prays:] "May that ax of a wooden thicket be remembered [by God] as though it were brought Above" [and placed before the Heavenly Throne (Rashi)] (Psalms 74:6).

Nebuzaradan marched through the city, killing as he went, until he reached the Sanctuary. When he set it on fire, the Sanctuary rose upward but they pushed it down from Heaven, as it says, "As in a winepress the Lord has trodden the maiden daughter of Jerusalem" (Lamentations 1:15). In his triumph, Nebuzaradan became conceited, when a Heavenly voice came forth and said to him, "You have killed a slain nation; you have burned a burned Sanctuary, you ground flour that was ground already. [It was God Who has decreed Jerusalem's destruction; you have no reason to be proud!]" As it says, "Get a millstone and grind flour; expose your hair and bare a leg, expose a thigh to cross through rivers" (Isaiah 47:2). The verse does not say: "grind wheat" but rather, "grind flour" [i.e., wheat that has already been ground. So, too, Nebuzaradan could defeat Israel only because God had decreed their downfall].

ENEMIES WHO BECAME RIGHTEOUS CONVERTS

The Rabbis taught in a *Baraita*: Naaman [the commander of the army of Aram [Syria][219] was a resident convert.[220] Nebuzaradan was a righteous convert [i.e., a full convert]. Descendants of Sisera [the general of the army of Yavin, king of Canaan][221] learned Torah in Jerusalem [i.e., R. Akiva]. Descendants of Sancheriv taught Torah to the masses. And who were they? Shemaya and Avtalyon.[222] Descendants of Haman studied Torah in B'nei B'rak, and there were even descendants of the wicked Nebuchadnezzar whom the Holy One, blessed be He, tried to bring under the

wings of the *Shechinah*. The ministering angels said to the Holy One, blessed be He, "Master of the universe! Will You bring under the wings of the *Shechinah* the person who destroyed Your House and burned Your Sanctuary?" This is hinted at in the verse, "We would have healed Babylonia, but she is not healed" (Jeremiah 51:19). Ulla said: This refers to Nebuchadnezzar [who would have been healed if his descendants had converted]. R. Shmuel b. Nachmani said: This refers to the rivers of Babylonia [whose brackish water is unfit to drink, and the palm trees along their banks produce bitter-tasting dates (Rashi)].

THEY PERSUADED NEBUCHADNEZZAR TO ATTACK JERUSALEM

Ulla said: Ammon and Moab were evil neighbors of Jerusalem. When they heard that the prophets of Israel were prophesying the destruction of Jerusalem, they sent the following message to Nebuchadnezzar: "Leave Babylonia, and come [to conquer Eretz Yisrael]." Replied Nebuchadnezzar: "I am afraid lest what happened [to Sancheriv] will happen to me." They sent word: "The man is not at home" (Proverbs 7:19), and the word "man" [*ish*] is interpreted to mean the Holy One, blessed be He. [A precedent for this is the verse,] "God is a Man [*ish*] of war" (Exodus 15:3). [Thus, their message was: God will not fight for Israel.] Nebuchadnezzar sent the following reply: "Maybe He is near to them, [and He will come to help them when they repent (Etz Yosef)]." Their answer was: "He has gone on a distant journey" (ibid.); [i.e., their sins are so grave that their God has distanced Himself from them (Etz Yosef)]. Nebuchadnezzar sent the following reply: "They have righteous people who will pray to God and bring Him back." [Ammon and Moab] sent back the reply: "He has taken the bag of silver coins [*kesef*] with Him" (ibid. v. 20); [the righteous Jews have died out].

And "silver" [*kesef*] in this context can refer only to the righteous, as it says, "I acquired her for myself with fifteen silver coins [*kesef*], a *chomer* of barley, and a *lesech* of barley" (Hosea 3:2).[223] Nebuchadnezzar's answer was: "The wicked among them may repent, and they will pray to God for mercy and bring Him back!" Ammon and Moab replied: "God has already set a time for them [telling them that He will not return them before the end of the seventy years of the Babylonian exile (Rashi)], for it says, "He will come home at the appointed time [*kese*]" (Proverbs 7:19). And *kese* in this context can mean only "the appointed time," as for example in the verse, "At the time appointed [*kese*] for our festive day" (Psalms 81:4).

Nebuchadnezzar replied: "It is winter, and I cannot come because of the snow and the rain." They sent to him: "Come by way of the canyons [where you will be sheltered from the elements]." As it says, "Send a messenger to the ruler of the world [Nebuchadnezzar], saying, 'By way of the rocks of the wilderness to the mountain of the daughter of Zion" (Isaiah 16:1). Nebuchadnezzar answered: "If I come I will not have a place to encamp my army [in the area around Jerusalem protected from the rain (Rashi)]." The answer came back: "Their tombs [in the caves around Jerusalem] are better than your palaces." [The prophet Jeremiah foretold that Nebuchadnezzar's army would encamp in those burial caves,] for it says, "At that time, says God, they will remove the bones of the kings of Judah and the bones of its leaders, the bones of its priests and the bones of the prophets and the bones of Jerusalem's inhabitants from their graves, and they will spread them out under the sun and the moon and all the heavenly legions, which they loved and which they worshipped and which they followed" (Jeremiah 8:1,2).

THE ADVENT OF *MASHIACH*

R. Nachman asked R. Yitzchak, "Have you heard when *Bar Nafli* will come?" Replied R. Yitzchak, "Who is *Bar Nafli*?" R. Nachman answered, "*Mashiach*." "Do you call *Mashiach Bar Nafli*?" R. Yitzchak asked. "Yes, I do," R. Nachman retorted, for it says, "On that day I will raise up (97a) the booth of David that is fallen [*hanofelet*]" (Amos 9:11). [*Mashiach* who is a descendant of David will restore the fallen Davidic kingdom. Hence, *Mashiach* is called *Bar Nafli*, son of the fallen one.] R. Yitzchak answered [R. Nachman's question:] This is what R. Yochanan said, "In the generation when the son of David [*Mashiach*] will come, the number of Torah scholars will dwindle, and as for the rest of the people, their eyes will be wearied through anguish and grief. Every day will bring new adversities and harsh decrees. No sooner is one trouble over than another one appears."

The Rabbis taught in a *Baraita*: In the seven-year cycle at the end of which the son of David will come, in the first year, this verse will be fulfilled, "I will make it rain on one town and not on another" (Amos 4:7), [i.e., abundance in one region, famine in another]. In the second year, the arrows of famine will be sent forth" [i.e., there will not be abundance anywhere (Rashi)]. In the third year there will be a great famine; men, women, and children, pious people and men of good deeds will perish, and the Torah will be forgotten by its students [for lack of food (Rashi)]. In the fourth year there will some degree of affluence. In the fifth year there will be great abundance; people will eat, drink, and rejoice; and the Torah will return to its students. In the sixth year there will the sounding [of the shofar heralding the coming of *Mashiach*]. In the seventh year there will be wars [between the heathen nations and the Jews (Rashi)]. At the close of the seventh year [i.e., in the eighth year] the son of David will come.

R. Yosef said: But so many seven-year cycles have passed [with alternating years of famine and plenty], and *Mashiach* has not come! Abaye replied: Was there the sounding [of the shofar] in the sixth year and wars in the seventh? Besides, did [the events] occur in this order?

It was taught in a *Baraita*: R. Yehudah said: In the generation when the son of David will come, the meeting place [of Torah scholars] will be used for immoral purposes, the Galilee will lay waste, the Gavlan will be desolate, the people of the border region will wander from town to town, and not be welcomed. The wisdom of scholars will be unpopular; God-fearing people will be despised, the leaders of the generation will act the way dogs behave,[224] and the truth will have disappeared, as it says, "Truth became lacking, and refraining from evil seemed foolish" (Isaiah 59:15). [The Gemara asks:] What is meant by "and the truth will have disappeared [*ne'ederet*]"? [Surely there will always be Torah scholars who live by the truth!] [The Gemara answers:] In the yeshivah they said: It teaches that [truth] will split into separate groups [*adarim*], and as a result it will disappear. [Honest people will leave the corrupt society and live in isolation (*Maharsha*).] And what is the meaning of "refraining from evil seemed foolish"? In the yeshivah of R. Sheila they said: It means: Whoever turns away from evil will be considered foolish by the general public.

[Speaking of honesty,] Rava said: At first I used to think that there are no honest people in the world, but then one of the Rabbis—R. Tavus, others say, R. Tavyomi was his name—told me that even if they gave him all the treasures in the world, he would not tell a lie. [He told me that he once visited a certain town named Kushta[225] whose people never told a lie, and none of the people there died before his time. He married a woman from there, and had two sons by her. One day, [R. Tavus's] wife was sitting and washing her hair, when her neighbor came and knocked on the door, [asking to speak to her]. Thinking that it would not be proper [to tell her that his wife was washing her hair,] he said to the neighbor, "She is not here." Afterward his two sons died. The townspeople came to him and asked him, "What caused their death?" He told them what had happened. They said to him, "We appeal to you, please leave our town, and do not cause untimely death among us!" [avoiding impropriety is not sufficient grounds for lying].

[After this brief digression the Gemara resumes its discussion of the pre-Messianic era:] We learned in a *Baraita*: R. Nehorai said: In the generation when the son of David will come, young people will humiliate the elderly, yet old people will rise [respectfully] before the young. Daughters will rebel against their mothers; daughters-in-law against their mothers-in-law. The leaders of the generation will act in the way dogs act,[226] and a son will not be ashamed before his father.

We learned in a *Baraita*: R. Nechemiah said: In the generation when the son of David will come, impudence will increase; mutual respect [among people] will wane. The vine will produce its fruit, yet wine will be expensive; [there will be a shortage because everyone wants to become drunk and down excessive amounts of wine (Rashi)]. The entire kingdom [world civilization] will be converted to heresy, and there will be no one to admonish the people [and show them the fallacy of their belief (Etz Yosef)]. [This Baraita] supports R. Yitzchak who said: The son of David will not come until the entire kingdom converts to heresy. Rava said: What verse proves this? "Having turned completely white, it is pure" (Leviticus 13:13).[227]

The Rabbis taught: It says, "God will take up the cause of His people [i.e., He will redeem them] when He sees that their power is gone, and there is no leader or helper" (Deuteronomy 32:36). The son of David will not come until informers abound [i.e., when people who inform on Jews become too successful, God will bring the redemption (Rashi)]. Another explanation: He will not come until students of Torah become few. Another explanation: He will not come until the last penny has gone from the purse. Another explanation: until the Jews give up hope for the redemption, as it says, "and there is no leader or helper," meaning, as if Israel had no Supporter or Helper. This is the premise for a statement by R. Zeira, for whenever R. Zeira found the Rabbis occupied with calculating the time of the coming of Mashiach, he used to say to them, "I beg of you, do not postpone his coming. For we learned in a Baraita: Three things come out of the blue: Mashiach, a found article, and [the bite of] a scorpion. [Therefore, don't try to predict the coming of Mashiach.]

CALCULATING THE TIME OF THE REDEMPTION

R. Katina said: The world will exist for six thousand years, and for one thousand years [i.e., the seventh millennium] it will be desolate, as it says, "God alone will be exalted on that day" (Isaiah 2:11). Abaye said: For two thousand years it will be desolate, for it says, "He will heal us after two days [i.e., two thousand years]; on the third day He will raise us up, and we will live before Him" (Hosea 6:2).

We learned a Baraita that supports R. Katina'a view: Just as the Sabbatical year causes the land to lie fallow one out of seven years, so too the world lies in desolation for one thousand years out of seven millennia, as it says, "God alone will be exalted on that day [i.e., for one thousand years]. And it also says, "A psalm. A song for the day of Sabbath" (Psalms 92:1), meaning the "day" that is totally Sabbath [when all creative activity ceases]. And it says, "For a thousand years in Your eyes are like a bygone yesterday" (Psalms 90:4); [thus "day" in the two preceding verses means a thousand years].

In the yeshivah of Eliyahu it was taught: The world will exist for six thousand years: In the first two thou-sand years there was desolation [the world was without the Torah].[228] The second two thousand years the Torah prospered.[229] The third two thousand years is the Messianic era; [Mashiach will come at some point during those two thousand years]. (97b) But because of our many sins, all those years have elapsed, [and Mashiach did not come at the end of the fourth millennium].

Elijah said to Rav Yehudah, the brother of R. Salla Chasida, "The world will exist not less than eighty-five jubilee cycles [of fifty years; $85 \times 50 = 4,250$ years]. In the final jubilee cycle [or thereafter] the son of David [Mashiach] will come." Rav Yehudah asked Elijah, "[Will he come] at the beginning or at the end [of the last fifty years]?" "I do not know," replied Elijah. Rav Yehudah asked, "Will Mashiach come after the final jubilee has ended, or during the final jubilee?" "I do not know," Elijah replied. R. Ashi said: This is what Elijah answered Rav Yehudah, "Until then, [i.e., the year 4250] do not expect Mashiach; from then on, you may expect him."

R. Chanan b. Tachlifa sent a message to R. Yosef: I met a man who was holding a scroll written in the Hebrew language, in Ashuri letters, [our standard square characters]. I asked him, "Where did you get this scroll?" He replied, "I was hired as a common soldier in the Roman army, and I found it in the storehouses of Rome. And in it was written, 'After four thousand two hundred and ninety-one[230] years from Creation, the world [as we know it] will end, [and a new era will be ushered in]. During some of the years [after 4291] there will be wars of the great sea creatures [i.e., the nations of the world (Maharsha)]; during some of those years there will be the wars of Gog and Magog;[231] and the remaining years [until the year 6000] will be the Messianic era, [when Jews will be free of foreign domination, and Mashiach will have come (Rashi)]. And the Holy One, blessed be He, will renew His world only after seven thousand years." R. Acha the son of Rava said: The scroll stated, "After five thousand years," [not 4,291 years].

We learned in a Baraita: R. Natan said: The following verse pierces and plunges to bottomless depths, [meaning, its intent is unfathomable]: "For there is yet another vision about the appointed time; it will speak of the End, and it will not lie. Though he may tarry, await him, for he will surely come; he will not delay" (Habakkuk 2:3). [Don't accept the date of the redemption] calculated by the Sages on the basis of the passage, "Until a time, and times, and half a time" (Daniel 7:25). And don't [accept the calculation of] R. Simlai based on the verse, "You fed them bread of tears, You made them drink tears in great measure" (Psalms 80:6). And don't [rely on the calculation of] R. Akiva based on the verse, "There will be one more; it is a small one, and then I will shake the heavens and the earth" (Haggai 2:6). In fact, [the three verses do not refer to the redemption but to the era of the second Temple. The prophet announces] that the first Jewish kingdom [i.c., the Hasmonean dynasty] will last seventy years; the second Jewish kingdom [i.e., the Herodian dynasty] will last fifty-two years; and the kingdom of Ben Kosiva [Bar Kochba] will last two-and-a-half years.

[The Gemara asks:] What is meant by "It will speak [yafei'ach] of the End, and it will not lie" (Habakkuk 2:3)? [The Gemara answers:] R. Shmuel b. Nachmani said in the name of R. Yochanan: May the soul of those who calculate the End be tormented [tipach]! Because they say: Since the date of the End that we calculated has arrived and Mashiach did not come, he will never come. Rather you should wait for him, as it says, "Though he may tarry, wait for him" (Habakkuk 2:3). Now you might say: We are awaiting his coming, but God is not awaiting him [i.e., God does not want to bring Mashiach]. Therefore it says, "Therefore, God Himself eagerly awaits [the coming of Mashiach] to grant you favor; and therefore He is exalted to grant you mercy" (Isaiah 30:18). Now you might ask: Since we are awaiting Mashiach, and God is awaiting him, what delays his coming?—The Divine Attribute of Justice delays his coming, [because of our sins]. But since the Attribute of Justice delays his coming, why do we await him?—To receive a reward [for yearning for him]. For it says, "Happy are all who wait for him" (Isaiah 30:18).

THE THIRTY-SIX TZADDIKIM

Abaye said: There are not less than thirty-six righteous people in each generation who merit to behold the sight of the Shechinah [when they enter the World to Come (Yad Ramah)]. For it says, "Happy are all who wait for him [lo]." And the numeric value of lo is thirty-six. [The Gemara asks:] But that is not so! Didn't Rava say that the row before the Holy One, blessed be He, comprises eighteen thousand, as it says, "Surrounding are eighteen thousand" (Ezekiel 40:38)? [The Gemara answers:] That is no difficulty. The thirty-six refers to persons who behold the Shechinah as though through transparent glass, whereas the eighteen thousand refers to persons who behold the Shechinah through tarnished glass. [The Gemara asks:] But are there so many [i.e., thirty-six] who behold the Shechinah clearly? But Chizkiyah said that R. Yirmeyah said in the name of R. Shimon b. Yochai: I have seen people of the highest level [of spirituality], and they are few in number. If they are a thousand, I and my son are among them. If they are a hundred, I and my son are among them. If they are two, they are myself and my son. [Then how could Abaye say that there are never less than thirty-six?] This is no difficulty: The thirty-six refers to those who may enter only with permission, whereas R. Shimon b. Yochai refers to persons who may enter without permission.

IF ALL JEWS REPENT, MASHIACH WILL COME

Rav said: All the [envisioned] dates for the redemption have passed, and now the coming of Mashiach depends only on repentance and good deeds. Shmuel said: It is enough for the mourner to keep his period of mourning, [meaning, Israel's suffering in exile is enough reason for their redemption, even without repentance]. This subject has been debated among Tanna'im: R. Eliezer said: If the Jewish people repent, they will be redeemed; if not, they will not. R. Yehoshua said to R. Eliezer: If they do not repent, they will not be redeemed? Rather, the Holy One, blessed be He, will install a king over them whose decrees will be as harsh as those of Haman, and the Jewish people will repent, and this way God will bring them back to the right path.

It was taught in another Baraita: R. Eliezer said: If the Jewish people repent, they will be redeemed, for it says, "Repent, O wayward children, and I will heal you of your waywardness" (Jeremiah 3:22). R. Yehoshua said to him: But doesn't it say, "For nothing were you sold, and without money will you be redeemed" (Isaiah 52:3)? The phrase, "For nothing were you sold" means [you were exiled] because you worshipped idols [which have no value]; the phrase, "and without money will you be redeemed" means, even without repentance and good deeds. R. Eliezer said to R. Yehoshua: But doesn't it say, "Return to Me, and I will return to you" (Malachi 3:7)? [Implying that first Israel must repent; only then will God redeem them.] R. Yehoshua retorted: But doesn't it say, "I will be your master, I will take you, even one from a city and two from a family, and I will bring you to Zion" (Jeremiah 3:14)? [Implying that God will bring redemption, no matter what, even without the repentance of all the people (Rashi).]

R. Eliezer responded: But doesn't it say, "In stillness and quiet will you be redeemed" (Isaiah 30:15)? [Implying that redemption will come about through voluntary repentance, rather than by repentance induced by suffering (Maharsha).] R. Yehoshua said to R. Eliezer: But doesn't it say, "Thus says God, the Redeemer of Israel, his Holy One, to one who is despised by men, abhorred by nations, the slave of rulers; (98a) kings will see and stand up, nobles also will prostrate themselves" (Isaiah 49:7)? [I.e., Israel will be despised because of its sins; nevertheless, they will be redeemed and "kings will stand up before them": proof that redemption will come without repentance.]

R. Eliezer retorted: But doesn't it say, "If you repent, O Israel, you will return to Me" (Jeremiah 4:1)? [I.e., repentance is a prerequisite for redemption.] R. Yehoshua countered: But it says, "I heard the man clothed in linen, who was above the waters of the river, as he lifted his right hand and his left hand to the heavens and swore by the Life Source of the world that after a period, a period and a half, and when he will have accomplished the breaking of the power of the holy people, then will all these things be fulfilled" (Daniel 12:7); [i.e., after the power of the Jewish people has slumped to its lowest point, their troubles will end, and *Mashiach* will come; thus his coming is not dependent on repentance]. At this R. Eliezer was silent.

PORTENTS OF THE ARRIVAL OF *MASHIACH*

R. Abba also said: There is no clearer sign of the arrival of *Mashiach* than this, as it says, "But you, O mountains of Israel, will give forth your branch and bear your fruit for My people Israel" (Ezekiel 36:8). [The clearest sign that the redemption is imminent is that Eretz Yisrael will produce an abundance of fruit (Rashi).] R. Elazar said: Another clear sign [of the imminent arrival of *Mashiach*] is this, for it says, "For before those days, people had no earning, nor were there earnings from animals; those who traveled back and forth had no peace from the enemy" (Zechariah 8:10), [i.e., poverty, worry, and terror will be rampant]. [The Gemara asks:] What is the meaning of "Those who traveled back and forth had no peace because of the enemy"? Rav said: Even Torah scholars who are promised peace, for it says, "There is abundant peace for those who love Your Torah" (Psalms 119:165) will have no peace from the enemy.

Shmuel said: [*Mashiach* will not come] until all prices are equal; [the prices for grain and wine will be equally low because of the overabundant harvest (Rashi)].

R. Chanina said: The son of David will not come until [food will be so scarce that] a fish will be sought for a sick person, and it cannot be found, as it says, "Then I will make their waters settle and cause their rivers to run like oil" (Ezekiel 32:14); [fish die when the rivers are polluted], and it says, "On that day I will cause the might of the House of Israel to sprout" (ibid. 29:21), [i.e., *Mashiach* will rule].

R. Chama b. Chanina said: *Mashiach* will not come until the degraded kingdom [i.e., Rome] has ceased [to dominate the Jewish people (*Maharsha*)], for it says, "He will cut down the corrupt ones [Rome] with pruning hooks [*mazmeirot*]" (Isaiah 18:5) [with the psalms (*mizmor*) the Jewish people recite in their prayers (*Maharsha*)]. And after that it says, "At that time, an offering will be brought to God, the Master of Legions" (ibid. v. 7).

Zeiri said in the name of R. Chanina: *Mashiach* will not come until there are no arrogant people in Israel. For it says, "For then I will remove from your midst those who delight in your arrogance" (Zephaniah 3:11). And in the next verse it says, "I will leave in your midst a humble and submissive people, and they will take shelter in the Name of God" (ibid. v. 12).

R. Simlai said in the name of R. Elazar b. R. Shimon: *Mashiach* will not come until all the [corrupt] judges and officers are gone from Israel. For it says, "I will turn My hand against you, until I clean away your dross as if with soap . . . then I will restore your judges" (Isaiah 1:25,26). Ulla said: Jerusalem will be redeemed only through charity, for it says, "Zion will be redeemed through justice, and those who return to her, through charity" (ibid. v. 27).

R. Papa said: When there are no more arrogant people, there will be no more *amgushei* [Persian idolatrous priests who oppressed the Jews (Rashi)]. For it says, "I will clean away your dross as if with soap, and I will remove your tin." When there are no more [corrupt] judges [in Israel], the *gazirpatei* [crooked Persian judges] will fade away, for it says, "God has removed your judgments; he has turned away your enemy" (Zepanaiah 3:15).

R. Yochanan said: If you see a generation that slides into poverty, expect *Mashiach*, as it says, "And the impoverished nation You will save" (2 Samuel 22:28). R. Yochanan said: If you see a generation overwhelmed by many troubles like by a river, expect *Mashiach*, as it says, "For trouble will come like a river with the spirit of God devouring it" (Isaiah 59:19); [it will seem as if God Himself wants to destroy them (Rashi)]. And the next verse states, "A redeemer will come to Zion" (ibid. v. 20).

R. Yochanan further said: *Mashiach* will come only in a generation that is either entirely righteous or entirely wicked. He will come in a generation that is entirely righteous, as it says, "And Your people are all righteous, they will inherit the land forever" (ibid. 60:21). He will come in a generation that is entirely wicked, as it says, "He saw that there was no worthy man and was astounded that no one intervened" (Isaiah 59:16), [i.e., no one prayed for them]. And it also says, "For My sake I will do it" (ibid. 48:11).

R. Alexandri said: R. Yehoshua b. Levi pointed out a contradiction: [It says, in regard to the redemption, "I am God, in its [proper] time I will hasten [the coming of *Mashiach*]" (Isaiah 60:22).] On the one hand it says, "In its [proper] time," but on the other hand it says, "I will hasten it" [implying, before its proper time]. [He reconciled the two passages as follows:] If the Jews deserve it, "I will hasten it." If they don't deserve it, "the redemption will come in its proper time."

R. Alexandri said: R. Yehoshua b. Levi pointed out another contradiction: It says, "And Behold! With the clouds of heaven, one like a man came [i.e., *Mashiach*]" (Daniel 7:13), [implying that *Mashiach* will come quickly]. But it also says, "Your king will come to you, a humble man, riding on a donkey" (Zechariah 9:9), [implying that *Mashiach* will come at a slow pace]. [He reconciled the two passages as follows:] If the Jews deserve it, *Mashiach* will come "with the clouds of heaven"; if they don't deserve it, he will come as "a humble man, riding on a donkey."

King Shapur, [king of Persia, contemptuously] said

to Shmuel, "You say that the Messiah will come on a donkey? I will send him my fastest horse." Shmuel countered, "Do you have a horse of a hundred colors?" [implying, your most magnificent horse cannot match the grandeur of *Mashiach*'s donkey].

WHEN WILL *MASHIACH* COME?

R. Yehoshua b. Levi met the prophet Elijah standing at the entrance to R. Shimon b. Yochai's tomb. [R. Yehoshua b. Levi] asked Elijah, "Will I enter the World to Come?" Elijah replied, "If this Lord [the *Shechinah*] desires it." R. Yehoshua b. Levi said, "I saw two people, but I heard the voice of a third person" [Elijah and himself, and the voice of the *Shechinah*]. R. Yehoshua b. Levi asked Elijah, "When will *Mashiach* come?" Elijah repleid, "Go and ask *Mashiach* himself!" "And where is he sitting?" "At the gate of the city of Rome (Gra)." "And by what feature can I recognize him?" "He is sitting among the poor people suffering from *tzaraat* [a leprous disease]. All of them untie and tie their bandages at the same time, but *Mashiach* unties his bandages one by one, for he says: I might be needed any moment, and I don't want to delay my coming [by having to rebandage more than one sore (Rashi)].

R. Yehoshua b. Levi went to *Mashiach* and said, "Peace be upon you, Master and Teacher!" *Mashiach* replied, "Peace be upon you, son of Levi." R. Yehoshua b. Levi asked *Mashiach*, "When are you going to come, master?" "Today," *Mashiach* replied. R. Yehoshua b. Levi went back to Elijah who asked him, "What did *Mashiach* say to you?" R. Yehoshua b. Levi answered, "He said, 'Peace be upon you, son of Levi.'" Elijah said to R. Yehoshua b. Levi, "He has assured you and your father that both of you are destined to enter the World to Come." [Unless you are both completely righteous he would not have greeted you and mentioned your father's name (Rashi).] R. Yehoshua b. Levi then said to Elijah, "He lied to me because he said, 'I am coming today.'" Replied Elijah, "This is what he had in mind, [I will come] 'Today, if you obey his voice!' (Psalms 95:7)."

R. Yose b. Kisma was asked by his students, "When will *Mashiach* come?" He replied, "I am afraid you will ask me for a sign [that will substantiate my prediction]." They said, "We will not ask you for a sign." He told them, "When this gate [of the city of Rome] falls and is rebuilt, falls a second time and is rebuilt, and then falls a third time, and before it will be rebuilt a third time *Mashiach* will come." They said to him, "Teacher, please give us a sign." He countered, "But did you not tell me that you would not ask me for a sign?" They replied, "Even so, [we would like a sign]." He said to them, "Since you insist, [I will give you one]. Let the waters of the cave Pame'as [Banias]²³² turn into blood!" And they did turn into blood.

Lying on his deathbed, R. Yose b. Kisma said to them, "Place my coffin deep [in the ground], **(98b)**

because there will not be a single palm tree in Baby lonia to which a horse of the Persians will not be tied, and there will not be a single coffin in Eretz Yisrael out of which a horse of the Medes will not eat straw, [because in the war of Gog and Magog the armies of Persia and Media will conquer Babylonia. They will dig up the coffins to use as feeding troughs for their horses (Rashi)].

THE BIRTH PANGS OF *MASHIACH*

Rav said: *Mashiach* will not come until the [Roman] empire has extended its reign over the Jews for nine months, as it says, "Therefore, He will deliver them [to their enemies] until the time that a woman in labor gives birth [i.e., nine months], then the rest of [*Mashiach*'s] brothers will return [to Eretz Yisrael], with the [other tribes of the] children of Israel" (Michah 5:2). Ulla said, "Let *Mashiach* come, but let me not see him!" [Ulla had rather not be present during the intense suffering that precedes his coming.] Rabbah too, said: Let *Mashiach* come, but let me not see him!" But R. Yosef said: Let him come, and may I be worthy to sit in the shadow of his donkey's dung." Abbaye asked Rabbah, "Why don't you want to see *Mashiach*'s coming? Is it because you are afraid of the pangs associated with his coming? But we learned in a *Baraita*: R. Elazar was asked by his students: What can a person do to escape the birth pangs of *Mashiach*? And he replied: Let him get involved in the study of Torah and in acts of kindness. And you [Rabbah] practice both Torah study and kindness [to perfection. So what are you afraid of]!" Rabbah replied, "I am afraid that a sin may erase whatever merits I have earned."

This is in line with the teaching of R. Yaakov b. Idi, for R. Yaakov b. Idi pointed out a contradiction: It says, [God promised Jacob,] "I am with you. I will protect you wherever you go" (Genesis 28:5), but then it says, "Jacob was very frightened and distressed" (ibid. 32:8), [in spite of God's promise to protect him], because he was afraid that a sin [may eliminate God's protection].

It is also in line with the following *Baraita*: It says [in the Song the children of Israel sang after crossing the Red Sea], "Until Your people crossed, O God, until the people You gained crossed over" (Exodus 15:16). The phrase "Until Your people crossed, O God" refers to the first time the Jewish people entered into Eretz Yisrael [under Joshua]. The phrase "Until the people You gained crossed over" refers to the second time they entered [when they returned from the Baylonian exile, under Ezra]. [Since both entries appear in the same verse,] it would stand to reason that the Jewish people deserved that a miracle should be performed for them the second time they entered just as it happened the first time they entered, [the Jordan split, the walls of Jericho collapsed].

However, sin was the reason no miracles happened [when they entered under Ezra].

R. Yochanan said likewise: Let *Mashiach* come, but let me not see him. Resh Lakish asked R. Yochanan: Why do you say that? Is it because it says, "When a man flees from a lion and a bear encounters him; and he comes home and leans his hand on the wall and a snake bites him" (Amos 5:19), [so, too, in the Messianic era one calamity will come on the heels of another]? Come, and I will show you that the same thing is happening in everyday life: When a man goes out into his field and runs into a government land surveyor [who decides to truncate his property], it is as though he had run into a lion. When he enters a town and a tax collector confronts him, it is as though he had run into a bear. When he comes home and finds his sons and daughters underfed and famished, it is as though he had been bitten by a snake. [People are facing similar troubles every day; that is no reason to be afraid of the arrival of *Mashiach*.]

Rather, R. Yochanan was afraid because it says, "Ask now and see whether a man has ever given birth. Why then, do I see that every man [*gever*] puts his hands on his loins like a woman in labor, and all faces have turned pale?" (Jeremiah 30:6). [The Gemara expounds:] What is the meaning of "Why do I see every *gever*"? Rava b. Yitzchak said in the name of Rav: This refers to the One to Whom all *gevurah* [power] belongs. [God suffers because He finds it difficult to destroy the idolatrous nations who are His creations (Rashi).] [R. Yochanan did not want to witness this.] What is the meaning of "all faces have turned pale"? R. Yochanan said: It means that the faces of God's heavenly family [the angels] and His earthly family, [the Jewish people, will turn pale] when the Holy One, blessed be He, will say, "These [the gentile nations] are My handiwork, and these [the Jewish people] are My handiwork. How can I destroy these for the sake of those?" [Although they tortured and murdered the Jewish people, they are still God's creatures.] R. Papa said: People have a saying for this: The ox runs and falls, and its master goes and puts a horse at its trough.[233]

MASHIACH'S IDENTITY

R. Giddal said in the name of Rav: The Jewish people is destined to savor the abundance of the era of *Mashiach*. R. Yosef said: That is obvious! Who will savor the era of *Mashiach* [if not the Jews]? Chillek and Billek?[234] [The Gemara explains:] This was said to reject the opinion of R. Hillel who said that there will be no *Mashiach* for the Jewish people [God Himself will redeem them], because they already enjoyed the era of *Mashiach* in the days of Hezekiah, [and all the prophecies about *Mashiach* referred to Hezekiah].

Rav said: The world was created only for David's sake [so that he would sing songs of praise to God].

But Shmuel said: It was created only for Moses [who was destined to receive the Torah]. And R. Yochanan said: It was created only for *Mashiach* [when the world will have reached perfection].

What is *Mashiach*'s name? The yeshivah of R. Shila said: His name is Shiloh, for it says, "until Shiloh comes" (Genesis 49:10). The yeshivah of R. Yannai said: His name is Yinnon, for it says, "May his name endure forever; may his name connote mastery as long as the sun endures [*yinon*]" (Psalms 72:17). The yeshivah of R. Chaninah said: His name is Chaninah [mercy], for it says, "For I will not give you mercy [*chaninah*]" (Jeremiah 16:13).[235] And some say: Menachem ben Chizkiah is his name, for it says, "Because a comforter [*menachem*] to revive my spirit is far from me" (Lamentations 1:16).

Rav Yehudah said in the name of Rav: In the future, the Holy One, blessed be He, will raise another David for the Jewish people [i.e., *Mashiach* who is a descendant of David]. For it says, "They will serve God their Lord and David their king, whom I will raise up for them" (Jeremiah 30:9). It does not say "He raised" [the original David]; rather "I will raise" [i.e., someone else].

R. Papa said to Abaye: But it says, "My servant David *will be* a prince over them forever," (Ezekiel 37:25), [which implies that the original David is the one who will reign over the Jewish people in the future]! [The Gemara answers:] [The two Davids will be] like an emperor and a deputy emperor.

R. Simlai expounded: What is meant by the verse, "Woe to those who yearn for the day of God. Why do you seek the day of God? It is darkness and not light" (Amos 5:18). You can compare it to a rooster and a bat who were waiting for the light of dawn. The rooster said to the bat: I am awaiting the light, because the light is mine. But you [who have no eyes], why should you want the light? [The Jewish people yearn for the day of God, i.e., the redemption, because it will bring them light; but why should the idolators await the day, since for them it will be darkness?]

(99a) In this vein, when a certain heretic asked R. Abahu, "When will the *Mashiach* come?" R. Abahu answered, "When darkness covers those people [i.e., you and those like you]." "You are cursing me!" exclaimed the heretic. R. Abahu replied, "I am only quoting a verse, 'For, behold, darkness may cover the earth and a thick cloud may cover the kingdoms, but upon you God will shine, and His glory will be seen upon you'" (Isaiah 60:2).

THE LENGTH OF
THE MESSIANIC ERA

We learned in a *Baraita*: R. Eliezer said: The Messianic era[236] will last forty years, for it says, "For forty years I will take hold of the generation [and reign over them through *Mashiach*]" (Psalms 95:10). R. Elazar b.

Azariah said: The Messianic era will last seventy years, for it says, "It will be on that day that Tyre will be forgotten for seventy years, like the lifetime of a unique king" (Isaiah 23:15). Now, to which "unique king" does the verse refer? To no one but *Mashiach*.

Rebbi said: The Messianic era will last three generations, for it says, "May they fear you as long as the sun and the moon endure, for a generation and generations" (Psalms 72:5). ["Sun" is an allusion to *Mashiach* (Rashi).][237] R. Hillel said: There will be no *Mashiach* for the Jewish people, [God Himself will redeem Israel and rule over them (Rashi)], because they already enjoyed the era of *Mashiach* during the days of Hezekiah; [R. Hillel thought that Hezekiah was *Mashiach*.] R. Yosef said: May God forgive R. Hillel [for saying so]! When did Hezekiah live? During the time of the first *Bet Hamikdash*. Now Zechariah, prophesying in the days of the second Bet Hamikdash, said, "Rejoice greatly, O daughter of Zion; shout, O daughter of Jerusalem; behold your king is coming to you. He is righteous and victorious, yet humble, riding on a donkey—on a colt, the foal of an ass" (Zechariah 9:9). [Zechariah predicted the coming of *Mashiach* long after the death of Hezekiah, thus Hezekiah could not be *Mashiach*.]

We learned in another *Baraita*: R. Eliezer said: The Messianic era will last forty years. [Proof is:] It says in one verse, [concerning the generation of the Exodus,] "He afflicted you and let you go hungry, and He fed you the *manna*" (Deuteronomy 8:3); and it says elsewhere, "Give us joy as long as You have afflicted us, for the years we have suffered misfortune" (Psalms 90:15). [The Messianic era will last as long as God afflicted the Jews in the Wilderness, namely, forty years.]

R. Dosa said: The Messianic era will last four hundred years. [Proof is:] It says, [regarding the Egyptian exile], "They will be enslaved and oppressed for four hundred years" (Genesis 15:13). And [regarding the Messianic era] it says, "Give us joy as long as you have afflicted us" (Psalms 90:15). [Therefore, like the Egyptian exile, the Messianic era will last four hundred years.]

Rabbi said: The Messianic era will last three hundred and sixty-five years, corresponding to the number of days in the solar year. For it says, "The day of vengeance is in My heart, and the year of My people's redemption arrived" (Isaiah 63:4).[238]

What is the meaning of "The day of vengeance is in My heart"? R. Yochanan said: I have revealed the date of the redemption to My heart; I have not revealed it to My limbs. [God kept it hidden in His "heart" and did not say it aloud so that His "limbs" could hear it.] R. Shimon b. Lakish said: I have revealed the date of the redemption to my heart; I have not revealed it to the ministering angels.

Avimi the son of R. Abahu taught: The Messianic era will last seven thousand years for Israel, for it says,

"As a bridegroom rejoices over his bride, so will God your Lord rejoice over you" (Isaiah 62:5).[239] Rav Yehudah said in the name of Shmuel: The Messianic era will last as long as the time from Creation until now, as it says, "[You and your children will long endure on the land that God swore to your ancestors to give them] as long as the heavens are above the earth" (Deuteronomy 11:21).[240] R. Nachman b. Yitzchak said: As long as from Noah's days until now, as it says, "For this is to Me like the waters of Noah, concerning which I swore . . ." (Isaiah 54:9).[241]

THE REWARDS OF THE MESSIANIC ERA

R. Chiya b. Abba said in the name of R. Yochanan: [All the good things] the prophets prophesied refer only to the Messianic era, but as for the World to Come, "No eye except Yours, O God, has seen that which He will do for one who awaits Him" (Isaiah 64:3). R. Yochanan disagrees with Shmuel, for Shmuel said: There is no difference between this world and that of the Messianic era except [that the Jewish people will be free from] foreign domination.

R. Chiya b. Abba also said in R. Yochanan's name: All the prophets prophesied only [about the reward] for penitents, but the reward for the completely righteous, "no eye except Yours, O God, has seen."

R. Yochanan disagrees with R. Abahu, for R. Abahu said in the name of Rav: The place where penitents stand, [is so sublime], even the righteous cannot attain it. For it says, "Peace, peace to the far and to the near" (Isaiah 57:19). "The far" come before "the near." What is meant by "the far"? One who was far from God before [but repented]. What is meant of "the near"? One who was originally near to God before and is still near now. But R. Yochanan said: "the far" refers to a person who was always far from sin, and "the near" refers to a person who was near sin but is now far away from it. [In R. Yochanan's view the righteous take precedence over the penitents.]

And R. Chiya b. Abba said in the name of R. Yochanan: All the prophets prophesied only about the reward for someone who marries off his daughter to a Torah scholar, and for one who engages in business in partnership with a Torah scholar, [taking him as a silent partner], and for someone who benefits a Torah scholar with his possessions, but the reward for Torah scholars themselves, "no eye, except Yours, O God, has seen." What does "no eye has seen" refer to? R. Yehoshua b. Levi said: It refers to wine that has matured in its grapes since the six days of Creation, [symbolic of secret Torah wisdom]. Resh Lakish said: It refers to Eden, which no eye has ever seen. And if you ask: Where did Adam live [if not in Eden]? He lived in the Garden. And if you ask: But the Garden and Eden are one and the same? Therefore it says, "A river flowed out of Eden to water the Garden" (Genesis

2:10), which shows that Eden and the Garden are different places; [Eden is the World to Come].

CONTEMPT OF THE TORAH

[The Mishnah stated that a person who denies the Divine origin of the Torah does not have a share in the World to Come. From where is this derived?] The Rabbis taught in a *Baraita*: It says, "Since he has shown contempt of God's word and violated His commandment, that person shall be utterly cut off [spiritually]" (Numbers 15:31). This refers to a person who says that the Torah is not from Heaven. Another interpretation is: The passage "Since he has shown contempt of God's word" refers to an *apikoros*.[242] Another interpretation is: The passage "Since he has shown contempt of God's word" refers to a person who acts impudently toward the Torah. "And has violated His commandment" refers to a person who violates the covenant of the flesh [i.e., circumcision]. "He shall be utterly cut off" [*hikaret tikaret*]—the repetition of the word signifies [that the sinner will be cut off twice]: he will be cut off from life in this world [i.e., he will die prematurely], and he will be cut off from life in the World to Come. Based on this, R. Elazar Hamoda'i taught: A person who desecrates sacred property, or disdains the festivals, or violates the covenant of our forefather Abraham [i.e., *milah*], or interprets the Torah contrary to the *halachah*, or humiliates his neighbor in public, although he may have Torah learning and good deeds to his credit, has no share in the World to Come.

We learned in another *Baraita*: It says, "Since he has shown contempt of God's word"—this refers to a person who says that the Torah is not from Heaven. And even if he said that the entire Torah is from Heaven, except for a particular verse, which [he maintains] was said not by God but by Moses himself, he falls into the category of "he has shown contempt of God's word." And even if he said that the entire Torah is from Heaven, except for a single technicality or, except for a specific *kal vachomer* [a logical (*a fortiori*) inference], or except for a specific *gezeirah shava*,[243] he falls into the category of "he has shown contempt of God's word."

It was taught in a *Baraita*: R. Meir used to say: A person who learns Torah but does not teach it to others, falls into the category of "he has shown contempt of God's word." R. Natan said: It refers to anyone who does not heed the Mishnah. R. Nehorai said: It refers to anyone who is able to engage in Torah study but does not. R. Yishmael said: It refers to a person who worships idols. How is [idolatry] suggested in this verse? According to that which was taught in the yeshivah of R. Yishmael: It says, "He has shown contempt of God's word"—this refers to a person who disdains the words spoken by God to Moses at Sinai, namely, "I am God your Lord . . . Do not have any other gods before Me . . ." (Exodus 20:23).

REVIEWING YOUR TORAH LEARNING

R. Yehoshua b. Karchah said: Whoever learns Torah but does not review it is like a person who sows but does not harvest. R. Yehoshua said: Whoever learns Torah and then forgets it is like a woman who gives birth and then buries her child. R. Akiva said: (99b) Sing every day, sing every day! [Review your learning even though you know it "like a song." You will be rewarded to sing for joy in the World to Come (Rashi).] R. Yitzchak b. Avdimi asked: From what verse [is this derived]? For it says, "If a person toils [in the study of Torah, the Torah] will toil for him, for he saddles his mouth to it" (Proverbs 16:26). [This teaches that] a person toils [in the study of Torah] in one place [in this world], and his Torah knowledge toils for him in another place, [before God. The Torah he has learned pleads before God to grant him a more profound understanding of its meaning (Rashi)].

R. Elazar said: Every person is created for toil, as it says, "But man is born for toil" (Job 5:7). Now, I do not know whether he is created for toil by mouth [intellect] or physical toil. When Scripture states "for he saddles his mouth to it," you have to conclude that man is created for toil by mouth. But I still do not know whether he is created for the verbal toil of Torah study or for the verbal toil of secular conversation. However when it says, "Let not this Book of the Torah leave your lips" (Joshua 1:8), you have to say that man is created for the toil of Torah study. And this agrees with Rava's saying: Everyone is created for labor; fortunate are those who merit to be laboring in Torah study.

It says, "He who commits adultery with a woman is devoid of sense" (Proverbs 6:32). Resh Lakish said: This refers to someone who studies Torah occasionally. For it says, "It is good that you store them [Torah teachings] inside you, and that all of them be constantly on your lips" (Proverbs 22:18); [i.e., you should study Torah on a daily basis, and not just once in a while].

MENASHEH RIDICULED THE TORAH

We learned in a *Baraita*: It says, "A person who acts high-handedly [is blaspheming God]" (Numbers 15:30). This refers to [the wicked King] Menasheh the son of Hezekiah, who used to sit and expound Biblical stories and made fun of them. He sneered: Did Moses have nothing better to write in the Torah than "And Lotan's sister was Timna" (Genesis 36:22), or "Timna was a concubine of Eliphaz" (ibid. v. 12), or "Reuben took a walk during the wheat harvest and found mandrakes in the field" (ibid. 30:14)?[244] A Heavenly Voice then proclaimed to Menasheh, "You sit and speak against your brother, you ridicule your mother's son. If you do these things and I remain silent, you will think that I am like you.[245] Well, I will rebuke you and expose your sins before your very eyes" (Psalms 50:21). And concerning Menasheh it was stated in the Prophets, "Woe to those who pull iniquity upon themselves with cords of falsehood, and sin like with the ropes of a wagon" (Isaiah 5:18). [The Gemara asks:] What is meant by "like with the ropes of a wagon"? R. Assi said: [The verse refers to] the *yetzer hara* [evil inclination]: At first the *yetzer hara* is like a spider's thread, but ultimately it is like a rope of a wagon.

[The Gemara asks:] Speaking of the verse, "Lotan's sister was Timna," what indeed is its deeper significance? [The Gemara answers:] Timna was a royal princess, for it says, "Chief Lotan . . . Chief Timna" (Genesis 36:29), and by "chief" an uncrowned ruler is meant. [This is what happened:] Timna wanted to convert and came to Abraham, Isaac, and Jacob, but they did not accept her. Thereupon she became a concubine of Eliphaz, the son of Esau; she reasoned, "It is better to be a maidservant to this [God-fearing] nation than to be a princess to any other nation!" From her descended Amalek who tormented Israel so greatly. Why did this happen? Because they should not have rejected Timna. [Thus the verse that was ridiculed by Menasheh teaches us how highly esteemed Abraham's family was by the royalty of that time.]

[The Gemara explains the second verse that was mocked by Menasheh.] It says, "Reuben took a walk during the wheat harvest." Rava b. R. Yitzchak said in the name of Rav: From here we learn that righteous people do not take what is not theirs. [Reuben went into the fields after they had been harvested, when anyone is allowed to enter and take what he finds (Rashi).] It says, "He found *dudaim* [mandrakes] in the field." What are *dudaim*? Rav said: mandrakes. Levi said: violets. R. Yonatan said: *seviskei* [a certain type of spice (Rashi)].

TORAH STUDY FOR ITS OWN SAKE

R. Alexandri said: Whoever studies Torah for its own sake promotes peace among the heavenly hosts above [the angels], and among the hosts below [men]. For it says, "Or let him take hold of My strength [the Torah], that he may make peace with Me; yea, let him make peace with Me" (Isaiah 27:5), [i.e., peace Above, and peace on earth]. Rav said: [When a person studies Torah for its own sake] it is as if he built the heavenly and earthly palaces. For it says, "I have placed My words in your mouth—and covered you with the shade of My hand—to plant the heavens and lay the foundations of the earth" (ibid. 51:16). R. Yochanan said: [The person who studies Torah for its own sake] also provides protection for the whole world, for it says, "I covered you with the shade of My hand." And Levi said: He even brings the Redemption closer, as it says [in the conclusion of the above-mentioned verse], "and say to Zion: You are My people!" (ibid.).

Resh Lakish said: Whoever teaches Torah to his neighbor's son is regarded by Scripture as though he had "made" that son. For it says [about the people that Abraham and Sarah converted], "And the people they made in Charan" (Genesis 12:5). R. Elazar said: He is considered as if he "made" the words of the Torah, for it says, "If you safeguard the words of this covenant, and you will make them" (Deuteronomy 29:8). [Your students' questions will stimulate you to discover new Torah insights. You thereby discover and "make" new perspectives on the Torah.] Rava said: He is considered as if he "made" himself, as it says, "and you will make them [*otam*]" Do not read *otam* (them), but *atem*, "you" [i.e., "you will create yourself"; in other words, by teaching others you grow yourself].

R. Abahu said: Whoever makes his neighbor perform a mitzvah is considered by Scripture as if he performed the mitzvah himself. For it says, [concerning Moses' staff], "and your staff with which you struck the river [to usher in the Ten Plagues]" (Exodus 17:5). Now did Moses himself strike the river? Surely it was Aaron who struck it! Rather it comes to tell you, that whoever causes his fellow perform a mitzvah is regarded as if he performed it himself. [On God's orders, Moses instructed Aaron to strike the river (Exodus 7:19)].

WHAT IS AN *APIKOROS*?

[The Mishnah listed an *apikoros* among those who have no share in the World to Come. What is an *apikoros*?] Rav and R. Chanina both said: This refers to a person who disdains a Torah scholar. R. Yochanan and R. Yehoshua b. Levi said: This refers to a person who insults his neighbor in front of a Torah scholar. We can understand the statement of [R. Yochanan and R. Yehoshua b. Levi] who say that a person who insults his neighbor in front of a Torah scholar is considered an *apikoros*, for then a person who insults a Torah scholar himself [which is a more reprehensible act] could be considered as one who acts impudently against the Torah. However, according to Rav and R. Chanina who say that a person who insults a Torah scholar himself is considered an *apikoros*, who is meant by "a person who acts impudently against the Torah"? [The Gemara answers:] Rav and R. Chanina had in mind a person like Menasheh the son of Hezekiah, [who disdained Scripture itself].

There are others who taught this dispute as referring to the last part of the *Baraita*, which states: [It says, "For he despised the word of God"]—this refers to a person who acts impudently toward the Torah.] Rav and R. Chanina say that this is a person who insults a Torah scholar himself. R. Yochanan and R. Yehoshua b. Levi say that this is a person who insults his neighbor in front of a Torah scholar. Now, we can understand the view of Rav and R. Chanina who say that a person who insults a Torah scholar himself is considered as "one who acts impudently toward the Torah," for then a person who insults his neighbor in front of a Torah scholar [which is not as insolent an act], may be considered an *apikoros* [a less reprehensible kind of sinner]. However, according to R. Yochanan and R. Yehoshua b. Levi, who say that a person who insults his neighbor in front of a Torah scholar [which would seem not to be as insolent an act] is nevertheless considered one who acts impudently against the Torah, who then is meant by *apikoros*?

[The Gemara answers:] Rav Yosef said: For example, people who say, "What good are the Rabbis? They study Scripture only for themselves, and they study the Oral Law only for themselves!" [They do not realize that the continued existence of the world depends on the Rabbis' Torah study (Rashi).] Abaye challenged R. Yosef: But this [person whom you erroneously rate as an *apikoros*] is also one who acts impudently toward the Torah. For it says, "If not for My covenant [the Torah] day and night, I would not have established the statutes of heaven and earth" (Jeremiah 33:25). [The world endures only because the Torah is studied. A person who claims that the Rabbis' Torah study is of no use is denying an explicit Scriptural passage, and should be included in the category of those who act impudently toward the Torah!]

R. Nachman b. Yitzchak added: [The fact that the righteous of the world benefit others] can be derived also from the verse, "God said, "[If I find in Sodom fifty righteous people], I would spare the whole place on their account" (Genesis 18:26).

[Abaye characterizes an *apikoros* as] a person who sits before his teacher [who is giving a Torah discourse], and when he recalls a teaching on an unrelated subject, says, "We said so and so regarding that matter" instead of saying, "You, Master, said thus." [His lack of respect makes him an *apikoros*.]

Rava said: An example of an *apikoros* are the members of the household of Benjamin the physician who say, "What good are the Rabbis? (100a) They have never permitted us to eat a raven or forbidden to eat a dove; [they have never innovated anything]!"

[Incidentally,] when they would bring a suspected *tereifah*[246] from the house of Benjamin before Rava [for inspection]—if he saw a reason for permitting it to be eaten, he would remark to them, "Look, I am permitting a raven to you!" And if he saw a reason for forbidding it, he would say, "Look, I am forbidding a dove to you!"

R. Papa said: An *apikoros* is a person who says [contemptuously], "O those Rabbis!" R. Papa once forgot himself and, [in the course of a conversation], burst out, ". . . like those Rabbis!" Thereupon he fasted [to atone for using an improper expression].

Levi b. Shmuel and R. Huna b. Chiya were once repairing the mantles of the various scrolls of the yeshivah of Rav Yehudah. When they came to the scroll of the Book of Esther they said to Rav Yehudah, "O, this scroll of Esther [has a lower degree of sanctity]; it doesn't need a mantle, does it?" Rav Yehudah said to them, "This too smacks of disrespect." [They should have asked, "Does it need a mantle?"]

R. Nachman said: An *apikoros* is a person who calls his teacher by his name [instead of saying, "My teacher, Rabbi So-and-so"]. For R. Yochanan said: Why was Geichazi [the servant of the prophet Elisha] punished [with leprosy]? Because he called his master by his name, as it says, "Geichazi said, 'My lord the king! this is the woman and this is her son whom Elisha revived'" (2 Kings 8:5).

R. Yirmeyah was once sitting before R. Zeira and declared: The Holy One, blessed be He, will bring forth a stream from the Holy of Holies, and along the banks of the stream there will be all kinds of delicious fruits. For it says, "All kinds of trees for food will grow up on the banks of the stream. Their leaves will not wither nor their fruit fail; they will yield new fruit every month, because the water for them flows from the Sanctuary. Their fruit will serve for food and their leaves for healing" (Ezekiel 47:12). A certain elderly man in the audience said to R. Yirmeyah, "Well spoken! R. Yochanan said the same thing."

Thereupon R. Yirmeyah said to [his teacher] R. Zeira, "Does such an attitude smack of irreverence? R. Zeira replied: He was merely voicing his support for you; [he was not irreverent]. But if you have heard of something that may be termed irreverent, it is this: R. Yochanan was sitting and expounding: In time to come, the Holy One, blessed be He, will bring precious stones and pearls that are thirty cubits by thirty cubits, and will cut out from them an opening, ten cubits by ten cubits, and He will install them as the gates of Jerusalem. For it says, "I will make your windows of ruby and make your gates of hewn stones" (Isaiah 54:12). A certain student sneered [at R. Yochanan], saying, "We do not find jewels even the size of an egg of a small dove; how will we find stones as huge as the ones you describe!" Some time later the student took a sea voyage and saw ministering angels who were sawing huge precious stones and pearls. "For whom are these stones?" he asked. They replied, "In time to come, the Holy One, blessed be He, will install them in the gates of Jerusalem."

When the student returned home, he found R. Yochanan sitting and expounding. Said the student to R. Yochanan, "My master! Expound! It is fitting for you to expound! The things you expounded I saw with my own eyes!" R. Yochanan said to him, "You good-for-nothing! If you had not seen it yourself, would you not have believed it? You are a person who ridicules the words of the Sages." R. Yochanan set his eyes upon the student, and he turned into a heap of bones. [This was the case of the irreverent student R. Yirmeyah had heard.]

THE HEALTHFUL LEAVES

What is the meaning of [the above-mentioned passage], "their leaves will be for healing *literufah*"? R. Yitzchak b. Avudimi and R. Chisda differ about this. One said: The leaves have the power to open the upper mouth [i.e., to make the mute speak]. The other said: The leaves have the power to open the lower mouth [i.e., the womb] of barren women; [when they eat the leaves they will conceive (Rashi)].[247] R. Yochanan said: The leaves will be taken as actual medicine. [The Gemara asks:] How does R. Yochanan interpret *literufah*? R. Shmuel b. Nachmani said: he sees *literufah* as an acronym for "brightening the faces of Torah scholars." Along these lines R. Yehudah b. R. Simon expounded: Whoever emaciates his face for the sake of Torah study in this world, the Holy One, blessed be He, will make his face radiate in the World to Come [i.e., he will be richly rewarded]. For it says, "His appearance is like Lebanon, excellent like the cedars" (Song of Songs 5:15). R. Tanchum b. Chanilai said: Whoever starves himself for the words of Torah in this world [i.e., studies so diligently that he forgets to eat], the Holy One, blessed be He, will satiate him in the World to Come, as it says, "They will be sated from the abundance of Your house, and from the stream of Your delights You will give them to drink" (Psalms 36:9).

THE REWARD AWAITING
THE RIGHTEOUS

When R. Dimi came [to Babylonia from Eretz Yisrael] he said: In the future the Holy One, blessed be He, will give to every righteous person a full load of His goodness. For it says, "Blessed is the Lord; day by day He loads us [with His goodness], the God of our deliverance, Selah" (Psalms 68:20). Abaye challenged [Rav Dimi]: Is it possible to say this? [How can man receive such infinite goodness? There is no room to absorb it. The whole world is, figuratively speaking, the size of God's span, the distance from the little finger to the thumb (Rashi).] Doesn't it say, "Who measured the waters with the hollow of His hand, and gauged the skies with a span" (Isaiah 40:12)? R. Dimi replied, "Why are you not familiar with the *aggadah*?" [i.e., the homiletical teaching of the Sages], for they say in Eretz Yisrael in the name of Rava b. Mari: In the future the Holy One, blessed be He, will give to every righteous person three hundred and ten worlds, as it says, [the Torah declares,] "That I may grant to those who love me substance [*yesh*], and that I may fill their treasuries" (Proverbs 8:21). Now, the numeric value of *yesh* is three hundred and ten.[248] [This is a metaphor to indicate the monumental reward that is in store for the righteous in the World to Come (Rambam).]

It was taught in a *Baraita*: R. Meir said: With the measure a person measures [for others], God measures for him. [If he donated generously to the poor, God will reward him with equal generosity (Rashi).] For it says, "With a precise measure you will contend with her when you send her away" (Isaiah 27:8), [just as sins are punished measure for measure, so will good deeds be rewarded equitably]. R. Yehoshua said: Is it possible to make such a statement? If a person gives a handful of charity to a poor man in this world, does God give to the donor *His* handful of reward in the World to Come? Doesn't it say, "God gauged the skies with a span" (Isaiah 40:12), [God's "handful" is infinitely greater than the donor's hand]?

R. Meir retorted: But don't you admit this: Which is the greater measure? Is God's measure of goodness greater, or is his measure of retribution greater? (100b) Surely the measure of reward is greater than the measure of punishment, for concerning His measure of goodness it says, "He commanded the skies above, He opened the doors of heaven, and rained manna upon them for food" (Psalms 78:23,24), whereas concerning His measure of punishment it says, "They shall go out and gaze on the corpses of the men who rebelled against Me: Their worms shall not die, not their fire be quenched; they shall be a horror to all flesh" (Isaiah 66:24). Now, when a person puts his finger in a flame in this world it is immediately burned, [how then can the bodies of the dead go on burning forever in the next world]? But just as the Holy One, blessed be He, gives the wicked the strength to receive their punishment, so does He give the righteous the capacity to receive their reward, [immense though it is].

THE BOOK OF BEN SIRA

[The Mishnah listed a person who reads the Apocrypha[249] among those who have no share in the World to Come.]

A Tanna taught: This means the books of the Sadducees.[250] R. Yosef said: It is also forbidden to read the Book of Ben Sira,[251] [because it contains senseless ideas, and reading it is a waste of time (Rashi)]. Abaye said to R. Yosef: What is the reason [for forbidding the Book of Ben Sira? If you say it is because he wrote in it, "Do not strip the skin of a fish even from its gill, because you would spoil the skin, but roast the fish with its skin and eat it with two cakes of bread." [What is wrong with that?] If you object to its plain meaning [that you should not waste the fish's skin], the Torah too says, "You must not destroy its trees" (Deuteronomy 20:19), [you should not needlessly destroy fruit-bearing trees or any food]. If you object to its metaphoric interpretation, [this is worthwhile too,] for it teaches us proper behavior, namely, that one should not cohabit in an unnatural manner. [So there is nothing in this passage that warrants forbidding the Book of Sira.]

Or do you say that the Book of Ben Sira was banned because it says, "A daughter is a false treasure for her father; from worrying about her he cannot sleep at night: in her childhood he worries that she might be seduced; in her puberty, that she may behave promiscuously; when she reaches maturity he worries that she may not marry; when she marries he worries that she may not have children; when she grows old he worries that she should not engage in witchcraft"? But the Rabbis have expressed similar ideas, for they said: It is impossible for the world to exist without both males and females; however, fortunate is he whose children are male, and woe to him whose children are female,"[252] [which parallels the proverb of Ben Sira]. Or do you say that the Book of Ben Sira was banned because it says, "Do not allow sorrow into your heart, for sorrow has killed mighty men"? But King Solomon himself has said this too, "If there is anxiety in a man's heart, let him suppress it [yash'chena]" (Proverbs 12:25).

R. Ammi and R. Assi argue about the meaning of *yash'chena*. One said: It means that he should banish the anxiety from his mind, and the other said it means that he should tell his troubles [yasichena] to others, [who may be able to help him find a solution (Maharsha)]. [Thus, the passage in the Book of Ben Sira teaches a valuable lesson.] Or do you say it was banned because it says, "Prevent crowds from coming into your house, and do not bring everyone into your house." But Rebbi said the same, as we learned in a *Baraita*: Rebbi said: A person should never invite many friends into his house, for it says, "A man with many friends is bound to be harmed" (Proverbs 18:24). [This passage, too, contains an edifying lesson.]

But the ban against the Book of Sira was issued because it says in it, "A thin-bearded man is very wise; a thick-bearded man is a fool. He who blows away the froth from his glass of beer is not thirsty. If someone says, 'What [preserves] shall I have with my bread?' take the bread away from him, [because he is not hungry]." "No one can outsmart a person who has a part in his beard." [It was because of silly sayings such as these that R. Yosef prohibited reading the Book of Ben Sira.]

R. Yosef said: Nevertheless, we may expound on the worthwhile passages in it in public lectures. Passages such as: "A good wife is a precious gift; she is given into the embrace of a God-fearing husband." "An evil woman is a plague to her husband. How shall he rectify the situation? He should divorce her, and he will be cured of his plague." "Fortunate is the husband who has a beautiful wife—[his joy makes it seem as if] he lives twice as long." "Avoid looking at a charming woman, lest you get caught in her trap. Do not turn to her husband to share wine and liquor with him, for many have been destroyed by the looks of a beautiful woman, and numerous are her victims." "Many are the blows sustained by peddlers." [Peddlers deal mostly with housewives, and the suspicious husband beats up the peddler (Rashi).]

"Those that seduce others to immorality are like a spark that ignites a coal; like a coop full of birds so are their houses full of deceit." "Prevent crowds from coming into your house; do not bring everyone into your house." "Although many will inquire after your well-being, nevertheless, reveal your secret to one in a thousand. Guard your words even from the one who lies in your embrace." [Don't share your secrets even with your wife, for she may unintentionally reveal them (Maharsha).] "Do not be distressed by tomorrow's troubles, for you do not know what will happen today; perhaps tomorrow one is no more alive, and it turns out that he was grieving over a world that was not his."

It says [in Proverbs 15:15], "All the days of a poor man are bad," and Ben Sira adds, "His nights, too, for his roof is the lowest, and at the height of the mountain is his vineyard. So the rain from the higher roofs drips on his, [which disturbs his sleep], while the topsoil of his vineyard [he has fertilized] is blown onto the vineyards below."

IRREVERENCE TOWARD THE TORAH

(101a) We learned in a *Baraita*: A person who recites a verse of the Song of Songs and sings it like a [secular] song, and a person who recites a scriptural verse in a banquet hall for the amusement of the guests, brings misfortune to the world. Because then the Torah wears sackcloth, stands before the Holy One, blessed be He, and laments, "Master of the universe! Your children have made a harp out of me for the entertainment of scoffers." God replies, "My daughter! What then should they do when they are eating and drinking?" [The Torah] replied, "Master of the universe! If they are well-versed in Scripture, let them keep busy studying the Torah, the Prophets, and the Writings; if they are proficient in the Mishnah, let them keep busy studying Mishnah, *halachah*, and *aggadah* [i.e., the homiletical teachings of the Sages]; if they are students of Talmud, let them study the laws of Passover on Passover, the laws of *Shavuot* on *Shavuot*, and the laws of *Sukkot* on *Sukkot*." R. Shimon b. Elazar testified in the name of R. Shimon b. Chanania: Whoever recites a verse at the proper time [i.e., at a banquet in honor of a mitzvah] brings good fortune to the world, as it says, "How good is a word spoken at the right time" (Proverbs 15:23).

R. ELIEZER'S FINAL ILLNESS

[The Mishnah listed among those who have no share in the World to Come a person who chants a scriptural verse over a wound in order to heal it.] R. Yochanan said: But only if he spits on the wound, because God's name may not be pronounced over spittle. It was taught: Rav said: [This applies even when the incantation does not contain the Name of God,] like the verse, "When a person is suspected of having the leprous disease, he shall be brought to the *kohen*" (Leviticus 13:9). R. Chanina said: Even like the verse, "He called to Moses" (Leviticus 1:1); [neither of these verses contains any mention of the Name of God or a disease].

Rabbah bar Bar Chanah said: When R. Eliezer fell ill his students came to visit him. He said to them, "There is great anger in the world." [He meant that God was angry at him and made him suffer (Rashi).] They all started to cry, except R. Akiva who laughed. "Why are you laughing?" they asked. "Why are you crying?" R. Akiva retorted. "Is it possible not to weep when we see that a Torah scroll [i.e., R. Eliezer] suffers such pain?" R. Akiva said. "That's why I am laughing! As long as I saw that my master's [R. Eliezer's] wine does not turn sour, and his flax is not smitten, his oil does not turn rancid, and his honey does not spoil, I thought, "Perhaps, God forbid, my master has already received all his reward [for his good deeds] in this world. But now that I see my master in pain, I rejoice." [R. Akiva knew that his master's pain atoned for his shortcomings, and he would receive his full reward in the World to Come.] R. Eliezer then said to R. Akiva, "Akiva! Is there any mitzvah in the Torah that I failed to fulfill?" R. Akiva replied, "Master, you yourself have taught us the verse, 'For there is not one good man on earth who has done good and never sinned'" (Ecclesiastes 7:20).

We learned in a *Baraita*: When R. Eliezer fell ill, four Sages came to visit him: R. Tarfon, R. Yehoshua, R. Elazar b. Azariah, and R. Akiva. R. Tarfon spoke up and said, "You are better for Israel than a drop of rain, for rain is in this world, whereas you [by teaching us Torah] benefit us in this world and in the World to Come." Then R. Yehoshua spoke up and said, "You are better for Israel than the disc of the sun, which gives light only in this world, whereas you give light both in this world and in the World to Come." Then R. Elazar b. Azariah spoke up and said, "You are better for Israel than a father and a mother, for a father and a mother create life in this world, whereas you create life both in this world and the World to Come." But R. Akiva spoke up and said, "Suffering is precious, [for it atones for sins]." Thereupon R. Eliezer said [to his visitors], "Support me, so that I may hear the words of Akiva, my student, who said, 'Suffering is precious.'" Turning to R. Akiva, he said, "Akiva, from where do you derive this?" He replied, "I expound the verse, 'Menasheh was twelve years old when he became king, and he reigned fifty-five years in Jerusalem . . . He did evil in the eyes of God' (2 Kings 21:1,2).

And it says elsewhere, (101b) 'These too are the proverbs of Solomon, which the men of Hezekiah of Judah copied' [Proverbs 25:1], which shows how ardently King Hezekiah, Menasheh's father, promoted the observance of Torah among the people. Now, is it possible that Hezekiah, the King of Judah, taught Torah to the whole world, yet did not teach Torah to Menasheh his son? Rather, for all the trouble Hezekiah took with Menasheh, and for all the effort he put into him, in the end it was only suffering that brought him back to the right path. For it says, 'God spoke to Menasheh and his people, but they would not pay heed, so God brought against them the officers of the army of the King of Assyria, who took Menasheh captive in manacles, bound him in fetters, and led him off to Babylonia. In his distress he entreated the Lord his God and humbled himself greatly before the God of his fathers. He prayed to Him, and He granted his prayer, heard his plea, and returned him to Jerusalem to his kingdom. Then Menasheh knew that God alone is the Lord' [2 Chronicles 33:10–14].'" "From here I infer that suffering is precious," [said R. Akiva].

The Rabbis taught: Three persons offered shrewd arguments,[253] namely: Cain, Esau, and Menasheh. Cain—for it says, [After murdering Abel, Cain was condemned by God to be a restless wanderer. Cain said,] "Is my sin too great to be forgiven?" (Genesis 4:13). Cain said to God: Master of the universe! Is my sin greater than that of the six hundred thousand who will sin against You in the future, and whom You will forgive? [The sin of an entire nation is greater than the sin of an individual.] Esau—for it says, [after Isaac had blessed Jacob,] Esau argued, "Do you have only one blessing, Father?" (Genesis 27:38). Menasheh—at first he appealed to many pagan deities, and in the end he appealed to the God of his fathers.[254]

JEROBOAM, SON OF NEVAT

[The Mishnah said that three kings do not have a share in the World to Come: Jeroboam, Ahab, and Menasheh.] The Rabbis taught: The name Jeroboam [*Yarovam*] signifies that he debased the Jewish nation [*yarov am*]. Another meaning is that "he created discord among the Jewish people [*merivah ba'am*].[255] Another meaning is that "he created discord between Israel and their Father in Heaven, [by introducing idolatry]."

Jeroboam was the son of Nevat. The name Nevat signifies that "he beheld [*nibbat*], but did not see" [he beheld an omen[256] but misinterpreted its significance]. A Tanna taught: Nevat, Michah[257] and Sheva ben Bichri[258] are one and the same person. He was called Nevat because he beheld but did not see. He was called Michah because he was crushed [*mitmachmech*] in the building.[259] And what was his real name? Sheva ben Bichri.

THREE WHO MISINTERPRETED AN OMEN

Our Rabbis taught: Three persons beheld but did not see, [they beheld an omen but did not grasp its significance], namely: Nevat, Achitofel, and the astrologers of Pharaoh. Nevat saw fire coming out of his male organ. He thought that it meant that he would one day be king, but that was not so, for it indicated that Jeroboam would issue from him. Achitofel saw a leprous mark erupt on his male organ. He thought that it meant that he would one day be king, but that was not so, for it indicated that his granddaughter Bathsheba would be the mother of Solomon [who did become king]. The astrologers of Pharaoh—as R. Chama b. R. Chanina said: What is meant by "These are the Waters of Dispute [mei merivah]" (Numbers 20:13)? These are the waters the astrologers of Pharaoh saw but whose meaning they misinterpreted. They saw that Israel's savior [Moses] would be struck through water. [Hoping to kill the Jewish savior,] Pharaoh ordered, "Every boy who is born must be cast into the Nile" (Exodus 1:22). They did not realize, however, that he was to be punished [not literally] by water but rather on account of the Waters of Dispute.[260]

THE SINS OF JEROBOAM

And from where do we know that Jeroboam will not enter the World to Come? For it says, "Thereby the House of Jeroboam incurred guilt—to be annihilated and utterly destroyed from the face of the earth" (1 Kings 13:34); "to be annihilated" implies to be destroyed in this world, "and utterly destroyed" implies to be excluded from the World to Come.

R. Yochanan said: Why did Jeroboam merit to become king? Because he rebuked Solomon. And why was he punished? Because he rebuked Solomon in public. For it says, "The circumstances under which he raised his hand against the king were as follows: Solomon had built up the Millo and repaired the breach of the city of his father, David" (1 Kings 11:27). Jeroboam said to Solomon, "Your father David made breaches in the wall so that Israel might come up to Jerusalem for the Festivals [and enter the city with ease]. You, on the other hand, closed up the breaches in order to levy a toll for Pharaoh's daughter."[261] And what is the meaning of "he raised his hand against the king"? R. Nachman said: Jeroboam took off his tefillin in front of Solomon, [showing contempt of the king]. R. Nachman said: The arrogance that had taken hold of Jeroboam removed him from the World to Come, as it says, "Jeroboam said to himself, 'Now the kingdom may well return to the House of David. If these people still go up to offer sacrifices at the House of God in Jerusalem, the heart of these people will go back to their master Rehoboam of Judah; they will kill me and go back to King Rehoboam of Judah'" (1 Kings 12:26–28).

Jeroboam reasoned: It is a tradition that no one but the kings of the House of Judah may sit in the Temple Court. Now, when the people see Rehoboam sitting and me standing, they will say, "This one [Rehoboam] is the king, and that one [Jeroboam] must be his sub-

ject." And if I will sit too, I will be guilty of treason, and they will execute me and follow Rehoboam. Right away, "the king [Jeroboam] took counsel and made two golden calves. He said to the people, 'You have been going up to Jerusalem long enough. This is your god, O Israel, who brought you up from the land of Egypt!' He set up one [golden calf] in Bethel and placed the other in Dan" (1 Kings 12:26,27).

What is the meaning of, "He took counsel"? R. Yehudah said: [It means that] Jeroboam seated a wicked man next to a righteous one [in the council chamber]. He then said [to his counselors]: "Will you sign your approval of all that I am going to do?" "Yes," they replied. He said to them: "I wish to become king." "Yes," they said. "Will you do all that I tell you?" "Yes," they said. "Even if I command you to worship idols?" At that the rightous member in the council said: "Heaven forbid!" The wicked member of the council [sitting next to the righteous one] said, "Do you really think that a [righteous] man like Jeroboam would worship idols? Of course not. He just wants to put our loyalty to the test, to see whether or not we will accept his commands." [Thereupon the righteous members of the council signed, and when Jeroboam instituted idolatry they could not withdraw their consent (Rashi).]

(102a) And even Achiyah the Shilonite, [the righteous prophet,][262] was misled and signed. [How do we know this?] Because Jehu [king of the northern kingdom of Israel] was a righteous man, for it says, "God said to Jehu, 'Because you have acted well and done what was pleasing to Me, having carried out all that I desired upon the House of Ahab, four generations of your descendants will occupy the throne of Israel'" (2 Kings 10:30). Yet it says in the next verse, "But Jehu was not careful to follow the teachings of the Lord, the God of Israel, with all his heart; he did not turn away from the sins that Jeroboam had caused Israel to commit" (ibid. v. 30,31).[263] Now what caused [the righteous Jehu to leave the golden calves in place? Abaye said: A covenant has been made for the lips, [meaning, any statement, even if it was made unintentionally, may come true.][264] As it says, [Jehu announced,] "Ahab served Baal little; Jehu will serve him much!" Rava said: Jehu saw the signature of Achiya the Shilonite [on Jeroboam's decree] and was misled by it.

[Jeroboam forbade the people to make the pilgrimage to Jerusalem for the three Festivals. With regard to this] it says, "[By preventing] the slaughter [of offerings] the strayers deepened [iniquity], and I will chastise them all" (Hosea 5:2). R. Yochanan explained this: The Holy One, blessed be He, said: They were more stringent than My laws.[265] For I said in the Torah that whoever does not go to Jerusalem [to slaughter offerings on the Festivals merely] violates a positive commandment [and will only be chastised mildly], whereas they said that whoever does go on the pilgrimage will be pierced with the sword.

JEROBOAM AND ACHIYAH
THE SHILONITE

It says, "It happened at the time that Jeroboam was leaving Jerusalem, the prophet Achiya the Shilonite met him on the way. He had put on a new robe, and the two of them were alone in the field" (1 Kings 11:29). A Tanna taught in the name of R. Yose: It was a moment predestined for tragedy, [because at this encounter Achiyah prophesied the division of the united kingdom of the Jewish people].

[The Gemara now cites other teachings by R. Yose regarding momentous events or pivotal places mentioned in Scripture.] "In their hour of doom, they shall perish" (Jeremiah 10:15). A Tanna taught in the name of R. Yose: It was a moment predestined for tragedy. "In an hour of favor I will answer You" (Isaiah 49:8). A Tanna taught in the name of R. Yose: It is a moment predestined for good. "On the day that I make My account, I shall bring their sin to account against them" (Exodus 32:34). A Tanna taught in the name of R. Yose: It is a moment predestined for tragedy. "Rehoboam went to Shechem, for to Shechem all Israel had come to make him king" (1 Kings 12:1). A Tanna taught in the name of R. Yose: Shechem was a place predestined for tragedy; in Shechem they raped Dinah, in Shechem the brothers sold Joseph, in Shechem the kingdom of the House of David was split.

[The Gemara expounds the verse quoted above:] "Jeroboam was leaving Jerusalem." R. Chanina b. Papa said: It means that Jeroboam withdrew from the registry of Jerusalem; [he left Jerusalem for good]. "And Achiyah the Shilonite met him on the way. He had put on a new robe, and the two of them were alone in the field." What is meant by "a new robe"? R. Nachman said: Like a new robe; just as a new robe has no defect, so, too, Jeroboam's Torah knowledge had no defect [i.e., no confusion]. Another explanation: "a new robe" alludes to the fact that Jeroboam and Achiya discovered new insights no ear had ever heard before. What is the meaning of "and the two of them were alone in the field"? Rav Yehudah said in the name of Rav: It means that all the scholars were like grass in the field [i.e., of no consequence] compared to them. And some say: It means that all the reasons for the commandments of the Torah were as plain to them [as a field is to an onlooker].

JEROBOAM SPLIT
THE JEWISH NATION

It says, "Therefore, send gifts to Moreshet-Gath! The houses of Achzib will become a lost cause to the kings of Israel" (Micah 1:4). R. Chanina b. Papa said: [When Jeroboam was crowned as king by the Ten Tribes of Israel,] a heavenly voice cried out and said: [Is this how you repay David?] He who slew the Philistine [Goliath] and thereby gave you possession of [the Philistine city of] Gath. Will you give parting gifts

to his descendants? [I.e., will you revolt against them?] Therefore, the houses of Achziv [i.e., the Ten Tribes] will fall to those who stray after falsehood [achzav]" (Micah 1:14); [i.e., you will be delivered into the hands of heathens whose gods are falsehood].

R. Chinina b. Papa said: Whoever derives pleasure from this world without first reciting a berachah, is considered as if he robbed God and the Community of Israel. For it says, "He who robs his father and mother and says, 'It is no crime,' is a companion to a destructive vandal" (Proverbs 28:24). "His father" can refer only to the Holy One, blessed be He, for it says, "Is He not your Father, your Master?" (Deuteronomy 32:6), and "his mother" can refer only to the Community of Israel [i.e., the Jewish people], for it says, "My son, heed the discipline of your father, and do not forsake the instruction of your mother" (Proverbs 1:8). What is meant by "is a companion to a destructive vandal"? It means that he is a companion to Jeroboam son of Nevat who destroyed the bond that tied Israel to their Father in Heaven.

It says, "Jeroboam caused Israel to stray from God and to commit a great sin" (2 Kings 17:21). R. Chanina said: Like hitting one stick with another and sending it flying, [so did Jeroboam drastically drive the Jews away from God].

JEROBOAM UNWILLING
TO REPENT

R. Oshaia said: Until Jeroboam, Israel suckled from one calf; from then on, from two calves plus the third, original one. R. Yitzchak said: Not a single punishment comes to Israel, that does not contain a small fraction of the first Golden Calf, as it says, "On the day I make My account, I shall bring their sin to account against them" (Exodus 32:24); [meaning: Every punishment that comes upon Israel contains a small amount of the punishment for the Golden Calf]. R. Chanina said: After twenty-four generations the verdict foretold in this verse was paid up, for it says, "He called in my ears in a loud voice, saying, 'The city's accounts draw near, each man with his weapon of destruction in his hand'" (Ezekiel 9:1).[266]

It says, "After this thing, Jeroboam did not turn back from his evil way" (1 Kings 13:33). What does "after this thing" refer to? R. Abba said: After the Holy One, blessed be He, seized Jeroboam by his garment and said to him, "Repent! and I, you and the son of Jesse [David] will stroll together in the Garden of Eden!" Jeroboam replied, "And who will be at the head?" God answered, "The son of Jesse will be at the head." "If so," Jeroboam replied, "I do not want it."

R. Abbahu used to lecture on the subject of the three kings [mentioned in the Mishnah as having no share in the World to Come]. One day he fell ill. [Suspecting that he was being punished for discussing the sins of the three kings,] he undertook not to lecture on this subject anymore. Yet, as soon as he recovered (102b) he began lecturing again. His students said to him, "Didn't you undertake not to lecture about them?" Replied R. Abbahu, "Did they repent [from their evil ways] that I should repent [from publicizing their sins]?"

Rav Ashi once ended his lecture at a point after which comes the Mishnah that deals with the subject of the three kings. He said to his students, "Tomorrow we will begin with the Mishnah concerning our colleagues [i.e., the three kings]. That night, Menasheh appeared to Rav Ashi in his dream and said, "You call us your colleagues and the colleagues of your father? So answer me [this simple question]: From where are you supposed to break the bread over which you recite the *berachah* of *Hamotzi*?" R. Ashi replied, "I don't know." Menasheh said to R. Ashi, "You have not learned this simple law, yet you call us your colleagues!" Replied R. Ashi, "Please teach me this law, and tomorrow I will teach it in your name in the lecture." Menasheh answered, "From the part that is baked into a crust." Said R. Ashi, "Since you are such a great scholar, why did you worship idols?" Menasheh countered, "Had you been living in my time, you would have lifted the bottom of your garment and run after me." [In my time the urge to worship idols was so irresistibly strong, you would have raced like mad to the place of idolatry (Rashi).] The next day R. Ashi started his lecture, "We will begin today's lecture with our teachers," [i.e., the three kings; we must respect them in spite of their sins (Rashi)].

THE WICKEDNESS OF AHAB

[The Mishnah listed Ahab as one of the three kings who do not have a share in the World to Come.] The name Ahab [*Achav*] means: "woe [*ach*] to heaven" and "father [*av*] to idolatry." "Woe to heaven," for it says, "Woe, [*ach*] the trouble that will be born" (Proverbs 17:17). "Father to idolatry," for it says, "As a father has compassion for his children, so has God compassion for those who fear Him" (Psalms 103:13). [Ahab loved idolatry as ardently as a father loves his children (Rashi).]

It says about Ahab, "The least [of his evils] was going in the way of Jeroboam son of Nebat" (1 Kings 16:31). R. Yochanan said: This means that the light sins Ahab committed were equal to the gravest sins committed by Jeroboam. Why then did Scripture make Jeroboam the epitome of sinfulness? Because Jeroboam was the first king to become corrupt.

It says, "Their altars were like heaps upon the furrows of the fields" (Hosea 12:12). R. Yochanan said: There is not a single furrow in Israel on which Ahab did not set up an idol and worship it. And from where do we know that Ahab will not enter the World to Come? For it says, "I will eliminate from the house of Ahab every male offspring, and [Ahab] will be withheld and abandoned in Israel" (1 Kings 21:21)—withheld in this world, and abandoned in the World to Come.

R. Yochanan said: Why did Omri [Ahab's son] deserve to be king? Because he added one fortified city to Eretz Yisrael, as it says, "Then he bought the hill of Samaria from Shemer for two talents of silver; he built a town on the hill and named the town that he built Samaria, after Shemer the owner of the hill" (1 Kings 16:24).

R. Yochanan said: Why did Ahab deserve to be king for twenty-two years? Because he honored the Torah, which was given by means of the twenty-two letters [of the Hebrew alphabet]. For it says, "[Ben Haddad] sent messengers to Ahab inside the city to say to him, 'Thus said Ben Haddad: Your silver and gold are mine, and your beautiful wives and children are mine. . . . Tomorrow at this time I will send my servants to you. They will search your house and the house of your servants, and seize everything that is precious to you and take it away. . . . And Ahab said to the messengers of Ben Haddad, 'Say to my lord the king: All that you first demanded of your servant I shall do, but this thing I cannot do'" (ibid. 20:2–9). What is the meaning of "[that which] is precious to you"? Surely the Torah scroll! [So we see that Ahab showed great respect for the Torah, for he refused to give it up whereas he was willing to relinquish his wives and children (Rashi).]

[The Gemara asks:] How do we know that "[that which] is precious to you" refers to his Torah scroll? Maybe it refers to his idol? [The Gemara answers:] That is not logical. For it says, "All the elders and all the people said to [Ahab], 'Do not obey and do not submit'" (ibid. v. 8). [The Gemara asks:] But perhaps they were shameful elders. [And there is a case where elders were shameful.] For it says, "The advice pleased Absalom and all the elders of Israel" (2 Samuel 17:4), and R. Yosef said that these [elders who plotted against King David] were shameful elders; [perhaps the elders who advised Ahab were corrupt too]? [The Gemara answers:] There [in Absalom's case] it does not say, "and all the people"; however, here [in Ahab's case] it says "and all the people," and it is impossible that there were no righteous men among [the people of Samaria]. For it says, "I will leave in Israel seven thousand—every knee that has not bowed down to Baal and every mouth that has not kissed him" (1 Kings 19:18); [and these righteous men would not have advised Ahab to fight for an idol. Therefore, "that which is precious to you" must refer to his Torah scroll].

R. Nachman said: Ahab was evenly balanced; [his good deeds balanced his bad deeds]. For it says, "God asked, [the Heavenly host] 'Who will entice Ahab so that he will march and fall at Ramot-Gilead?' Then one said thus, and another said thus" (ibid. 22:20).[267] R. Yosef objected to this interpretation: Someone about whom it says, "Indeed, there never was anyone like

Ahab, who committed himself to doing what was displeasing to God, at the instigation of his wife Jezebel" (1 Kings 21:25)—and we have learned in a *Baraita*: Every day Jezebel used to weigh out gold shekels for idols—you say that he was evenly balanced! [No, he was evil to the core!] Rather, Ahab was generous with his money; and because he used to benefit Torah scholars from his wealth, half his sins were forgiven.

[God had asked for a volunteer to lure Ahab to Ramot-Gilead where he was destined to be killed. The verse continues,] "And a certain spirit came forward and stood before God and said, 'I will entice him.' 'How?' God asked him. And he replied, 'I will go out and be a lying spirit in the mouth of all his [false] prophets.' Then God said, 'You will entice, and you will prevail. Go out and do it.'" (1 Kings 22:21,22). What spirit is the verse speaking about? R. Yochanan said: The spirit of Navot the Jezreelite.[268] What is the meaning of "Go out"? [It would have been enough for God to say "Do it."] Ravina said: God said, "Go out of My vicinity." For it says, "One who tells lies shall not live in My house" (Psalms 101:7). [Navot volunteered to be "a lying spirit," and God does not tolerate deception, even for a worthy cause (Yad Ramah).] R. Papa said: People have a saying for it: He who takes vengeance destroys his own house.

It says, "Ahab made an *asheirah* [a tree dedicated to idolatry]. Ahab did more to anger the Lord, the God of Israel, than all the kings of Israel who preceded him" (1 Kings 16:33). R. Yochanan said: This means that he wrote on the doors of Samaria [his capital city]: "Ahab denies the God of Israel." Therefore, he has no share in the God of Israel, [and the World to Come].

It says, "[Jehu] sought out Achaziahu,[269] and they caught him, for he had been hiding in Samaria" (2 Chronicles 22:9). R. Levi said: Achaziahu was busy erasing God's name [from the Torah] and substituting the names of idols. [He was hiding in Samaria, because the people would not have tolerated such an abomination (Rashi).]

MENASHEH EXCLUDED FROM THE WORLD TO COME

[Menasheh is the third of the three kings listed in the Mishnah as having no share in the World to Come.] The name Menasheh signifies that he forgot God [*nashah Yah*]. Another explanation: He was named Menasheh because he caused Israel to be forgotten by their Father in Heaven [*hinshi Yah*]. And from where do we know that he does not enter the World to Come? For it says, "Menasheh was twelve years old when he became king, and he reigned fifty-five years in Jerusalem . . . He did what was displeasing in the eyes of God . . . and made an *asheirah*, as King Ahab of Israel had done" (2 Kings 21:1–3). [The verse compares Menasheh to Ahab]—just as Ahab has no share in the World to Come, so too Menasheh has no share in the World to Come.

R. Yehudah says: Menasheh *does* have a share in the World to Come, for it says, "He prayed to God, and God granted his plea" (2 Chronicles 33:13). R. Yochanan said: Both of them expounded the same verse [to bolster their views], for it says, "I will make them a horror to all the kingdoms of the earth, on account of Menasheh son of Hezekiah" (Jeremiah 15:4). R. Yehudah holds that the verse means: on account of Menasheh who did repent, whereas they [i.e., the other people of Judah] did not repent, [and that is why they will be punished]. The other [the Tanna of the Mishnah] contends (103a) that the verse means: [they will be punished] on account of Menasheh, who did not repent, [and who induced the people of Judah to follow him into sin (Rashi)].

R. Yochanan said: Whoever says that Menasheh has no share in the World to Come weakens the hands of those who want to repent, [when they see that although Menasheh repented he does not have a share in the World to Come, they will have second thoughts]. For a Tanna taught the following *Baraita* before R. Yochanan: Menasheh repented for the last thirty-three years of his life, for it says, "Menasheh was twelve years old when he became king, and he reigned fifty-five years in Jerusalem . . . He made an *asheirah* just as Ahab king of Israel had done" (2 Kings 21:1–3) [i.e., he was wicked for the same number of years that Ahab reigned]. How long did Ahab reign? Twenty-two years. How long did Menasheh reign? Fifty-five years. Subtract from these twenty-two, and there remain thirty-three years [that he showed penitence].

INTERPRETATIONS OF FOUR PUZZLING PASSAGES

R. Yochanan said in the name of R. Shimon b. Yochai: What is the meaning of the passage "[Menasheh prayed to God], and an opening was made for him [*vayechateir*]" (2 Chronicles 33:13)? It should have said, "and He was entreated by him [*vayei'ateir*], and He accepted his prayer."[270] This teaches that the Holy One, blessed be He, made a kind of tunnel [*machteret*] in the heavens in order to [surreptitiously] receive Menasheh with his repentance, on account of [the opposition to Menasheh's admittance on the part of] the Attribute of Strict Justice.[271]

R. Yochanan said further in the name of R. Shimon b. Yochai: What is the meaning of the verse, "In the beginning [*bereishit*] of the reign of Jehoiakim the son of Josiah, king of Judah" (Jeremiah 26:1) and of the verse, "In the beginning [*bereishit*] of the reign of Zedekiah" (ibid. 28:1)? [Usually the expression "in the first year of king So-and-so" is used; why does it say here, "in the beginning"?] Were there then no kings until then? The reason is [that the phrase "in the beginning" recalls Creation, and its use intimates] that the Holy One, blessed be He, wanted to thrust the world back to its primordial formlessness and empti-

ness on account of the wickedness of Jehoiakim. However, when God looked at the people of Jehoiakim's
generation, His anger subsided. [The people, under the
guidance of the Torah scholars, remained faithful to
God.]

Similarly, the Holy One, blessed be He, wanted
to thrust the world back to its primordial formlessness and emptiness on account of the wickedness of
the generation of Zedekiah. However, when God
looked at [the righteousness of] Zedekiah, His anger
subsided. [Since the Torah scholars had been exiled
to Babylonia by Nebuchadnezzar, the people lapsed
into idolatry (Rashi).] [The Gemara objects:] But it
says about Zedekiah, too, "He did what was evil in
the eyes of God" (2 Kings 24:19). [Why do you say
that he was righteous?] [The Gemara answers: His
sin was that] he had the power to oppose [the evil
deeds of his people] but he did not, [but he himself
was righteous].

And R. Yochanan said further in the name of R.
Shimon b. Yochai: What is meant by the verse, "When
a wise man contends with a fool he [the wise man] may
rage and smile, but he will have no satisfaction" (Proverbs 29:9). [The "wise man" symbolizes God; the "fool"
stands for the kings Achaz and Amaziah.] It means that
the Holy One, blessed be He, said: "I became angry at
[the wicked] King Achaz of Judah, and delivered him
into the hands of the kings of Damascus. So he sacrificed to their gods! For it says, "[Achaz] sacrificed to
the gods of Damascus, who were attacking him. He
said, 'Because the gods of the kings of Aram are helping them, I will sacrifice to them so they will help me,'
but they were a cause of downfall for him and for all
Israel" (2 Chronicles 28:23). I smiled upon King
Amaziah [of Judah] and delivered the kings of Edom
into his hands. But he brought their gods [back to
Judah] and bowed down to them! For it says, "It happened that after Amaziah came back after killing the
Edomites and brought the idols of Seirites with him,
that he installed them as his gods. He would bow down
to them and burn incense to them" (ibid. 25:14). [No
matter what God did to induce the kings to repent,
they persisted in their idolatry.] R. Papa said: People
have this saying [about a fool]: "I cried to him, but he
did not realize it; I smiled at him, but he did not realize it. Too bad, he cannot tell the difference between
good and evil."

It says, [when Jerusalem was captured by the
Babylonians,] "All the officers of the king of Babylonia
came and sat in the middle [tavech] gate" (Jeremiah
39:3). R. Yochanan said in the name of R. Shimon b.
Yochai: It was the place where the Sanhedrin decided
[mechatchin] halachot. R. Papa said: There is a popular
saying for it: On the spot where the master used to
hang his weapon there the lowly shepherd hangs his
canteen. [The site where once the Sanhedrin convened
is now a gathering place for Babylonian army person-
nel.]

R. CHISDA
INTERPRETS PASSAGES

R. Chisda said in the name of R. Yirmeyah b. Abba:
What is the meaning of the verse, "I passed by the field
of a lazy man, by the vineyard of a man lacking sense.
It was overgrown with thorns, its surface was covered
with chickweed, and its stone fence lay in ruins" (Proverbs 24:30,31)? "I passed by the field of a lazy man"—
this refers to Achaz; "by a vineyard of a man lacking
sense"—this refers to Menasheh; "it was overgrown
with thorns"—this refers to Amon [the wicked son of
Menasheh]; "its suface was covered with chickweed"—
this refers to Jehoiakim; "and its stone fence lay in
ruins"—this refers to Zedekiah, in whose days the Bet
Hamikdash was destroyed.

R. Chisda also said in the name of R. Yirmeyah b.
Abba: Four classes of sinners will not be privileged to
behold the Shechinah: scoffers, liars, flatterers, and
people who speak evil gossip. Scoffers—for it says, "He
withdrew His hand from scoffers" (Hosea 7:5); liars—
for it says, "He who tells lies shall not live in My house"
(Psalms 101:7); flatterers—for it says, "No flatterer
shall come into His presence" (Job 13:16); people who
speak evil gossip—for it says, "For You are not a God
who desires wickedness; evil cannot abide with You"
(Psalms 5:5), which means: You [God] are righteous;
therefore, an evil one [i.e., one who speaks evil gos-
sip] shall not be allowed in Your dwelling.

THREE BARAITOT ABOUT
WICKED INDIVIDUALS

(103b) The Rabbis taught in a Baraita: Menasheh used
to expound the Book of Leviticus fifty-five different
ways, corresponding to the years of his reign; Ahab
eighty-five ways; Jeroboam one hundred and three
ways.

It was taught in a Baraita: R. Meir used to say:
Absalom has no share in the World to Come, for it says,
"They struck Absalom and killed him" (2 Samuel
18:15). "They struck Absalom" refers to his death in
this world; "and killed him" refers to his losing his
share in the World to Come.

It was taught in a Baraita: R. Shimon b. Elazar
said in the name of R. Yochanan: Achaz and Achziah
[among the kings of Judah], as well as any king of Israel
about whom it says: "He did what was evil in the eyes
of God," will not come to life [at the Resurrection],
but neither are they condemned to Gehinnom [for their
sins].

It says, "Moreover, Menasheh put so many innocent people to death that he filled Jerusalem with blood
from end to end, besides the sin he committed in causing Judah to do what was displeasing to God" (2 Kings
21:16). [What is the meaning of "from end to end"?]
Here [in Babylonia] they explain it to mean that
[Menasheh] killed Isaiah. In Eretz Yisrael they say it
means that every day Menasheh made an idol that was

so heavy that it required a thousand men to carry it, and every day it would kill them all; [the tremendous weight would crush them (Rashi)]. [The Gemara asks:] With whom does the following statement by Rabbah b. Bar Chanah agree? Namely: The soul of a single righteous person is equal to the whole world?—It agrees with the one who said that Menasheh killed Isaiah.

[The Gemara asks:] It says [that Menasheh made] "a graven image" (singular) (2 Chronicles 33:7), and it also says that he made "graven images" (plural) (ibid. v. 19). [How do you explain this inconsistency?] R. Yochanan said: At first he made a graven image that had one face, and in the end he made it with four faces,[272] so that [from whatever direction] the *Shechinah* would enter, it would see it and become infuriated.

HOSPITALITY TO TRAVELERS

We learned in a *Baraita*: R. Natan said: From Gerav to Shiloh is a distance of only three *mils*, [and because of this closeness] the smoke of the fire on the altar of the Bet Hamikdash and the smoke from the sacrifices offered to Michah's idol[273] intermingled. [Seeing this desecration,] the ministering angels tried to drive Michah from the world. But the Holy One, blessed be He, said to the angels: Leave him alone, because his bread is always available for travelers. And it was because of this idol of Michah that the people at the time of the incident of the concubine of Givah[274] were punished. For the Holy One, blessed be He, said to them: You did not protest when My honor was disdained,[275] but when the honor of flesh and blood was disdained [when the concubine of Givah was raped] you did protest.

R. Yochanan said in the name of R. Yose b. Kisma: Giving food to wayfarers is of great importance, for [the failure to do so] turned away two families from Israel [i.e., the nations of Ammon and Moab], for it says, "An Ammonite or Moabite may not enter God's congregation . . . This is because they did not greet you with bread and water when you were on the way out of Egypt" (Deuteronomy 23:2,5). And R. Yochanan said in his own name: [The failure to be hospitable] pushes away those who are near, whereas [offering hospitality] draws near those who are distant, and it causes God to overlook the misdeeds of the wicked, and causes the *Shechinah* to rest even on the prophets of Baal, and an unintentional failure to offer hospitality is considered by God as willful negligence.

[R. Yochanan explains:] "It pushes away those who are near"—(104a) as in the case of Ammon and Moab [whose territories border on Eretz Yisrael].

"It draws near those who are distant"—you can see this from what happened to Jethro, for R. Yochanan said: As a reward for [Jethro's invitation to Moses, saying,] "Call him, and let him have something to eat," (Exodus 2:20) his descendants merited to sit in the Chamber of Hewn Stone [the seat of the Great

Sanhedrin], as it says, "The families of scribes who dwell at Jabez—Tirathites, Shimeathites, and Suchathites. These were the Kenites who descended from Hammath, the father of the house of Rechab" (1 Chronicles 2:55). And elsewhere it says, "The descendants of the Kenite, the father-in-law of Moses, went up with the Judites from the City of Palms to the wilderness of Judah, and they went and settled with the people in the Negeb of Arad" (Judges 1:16). [This proves that the Kenites who are described as "families of scribes," i.e., members of the Sanhedrin, are descendants of Jethro, the father-in-law of Moses. They earned this honor because of Jethro's hospitality.] "It causes God to overlook the misdeeds of the wicked"—as in the case of Michah [whose sin of maintaining an idolatrous shrine was overlooked because he offered food to travelers].[276]

"It causes the *Shechinah* to rest even on the prophets of Baal"—as in the case of the friend of Iddo the prophet, as it says, "While they were sitting at the table, the word of God came to the prophet who had brought him back" (1 Kings 13:20). [A prophet of Baal purported to give Iddo a message from God, telling him to come to his house and have a meal; yet God spoke to the false prophet as a reward for his hospitality.]

"An unintentional failure to offer hospitality is considered by God as willful negligence"—for Rav Yehudah said in the name of Rav: If only Jonathan had given David two loaves of bread [for his getaway,] the people of Nob, the city of priests, would not have been killed, Doeg the Edomite would not have been banished from the World to Come, and Saul and his three sons would not have been killed.[277]

WHY WERE THEY NOT EXCLUDED FROM THE WORLD TO COME?

[The Gemara asks:] Why is [the wicked] Achaz not listed in the Mishnah among those who have no share in the World to Come? R. Yirmeyah b. Abba said: Because he was sandwiched between two righteous men, Jotham and Hezekiah; [he was the son of King Jotham and the father of King Hezekiah, who were both righteous kings]. R. Yosef said: It was because Achaz felt ashamed in the presence of Isaiah, for it says, "God said to Isaiah, 'Go out and meet Achaz, you and your son She'ar Yashuv, at the edge of the channel of the Upper Pool, at the road of the *koveis* field'" (Isaiah 7:3). What does the word *koveis* mean? Some say that Achaz hid [*kavash*] his face and turned away. Others say that Achaz inverted a washer's basket {*koveis*} over his head and turned away, [out of embarrassment].

[The Gemara asks:] Why was the wicked Ammon not listed [as one who is excluded from the World to Come? [The Gemara answers:] Because of the honor of his righteous son Josiah. [The Gemara asks:] If so, let them also not list Menasheh, because of the honor of his righteous father Hezekiah?

[The Gemara answers:] A righteous son can earn merit for a wicked father, but a righteous father cannot earn merit for his wicked son, as it says, "None can save from My hand!" (Deuteronomy 32:39). Abraham cannot save his wicked son Ishmael [from God's punishment]; Isaac cannot save his wicked son Esau; [and by the same token,] Hezekiah cannot save his wicked son Menasheh, and that is why Menasheh is listed in the Mishnah as being excluded from the World to Come. Now, on the basis of this conclusion [that a son can save his wicked father] you can explain that the wicked Achaz, too, is not listed [as having no share in the World to Come] out of consideration of his righteous son Hezekiah's honor. [In other words, the righteous Hezekiah saved his wicked father Achaz.]

[The Gemara asks:] And why did the Mishnah not list Jehoiakim [as one who has no share in the World to Come]? Because of what was taught by R. Chiya b. R. Avuyah who said: [Jehoiakim gained atonement because his body was never buried,] and on his skull was written: "This and still another" [i.e., you suffered one indignity, but another indignity still awaits you (Rashi)].

[The Gemara relates the incident that explains what this means.] The grandfather of R. Pereidah found a skull that was thrown down at the gates of Jerusalem, and on it was written, "This and still another." He buried it, but it came up. He buried it again, but it kept coming up. Then he said: It is the skull of Jehoiakim, about whom it says, "He shall have the burial of a donkey, dragged out and left lying outside the gates of Jerusalem" (Jeremiah 22:19). He said to himself: Still and all, Jehoiakim was a king, and it is not proper to leave his skull in disgrace. So he wrapped the skull in silk and placed it in a chest. When his wife saw the skull, she thought that it was the skull of his first wife whom he could not forget. So she fired the oven and burned it. This is the meaning of the inscription: "This and still another." [A twofold punishment: his skull lying in the street and then being burned. This punishment made sufficient atonement for him that he should have a share in the World to Come.]

HE CARRIED HOSPITALITY
TOO FAR

We learned in a *Baraita*: R. Shimon b. Elazar said: Because Hezekiah sinned by boasting [when he was gravely ill and prayed to God], "I have done what is pleasing to You" (2 Kings 20:3), [he was led to sin again and came to ask,] "What is the sign [that God will heal me]?" (ibid. 20:8).[278] Because he asked, "What is the sign?" he sinned again by inviting idol worshippers to eat at his table.[279] Because he invited idol worshippers to eat at his table, he caused his descendants to go into exile.[280] This supports [the

Amora] Chizkiah's teaching, for Chizkiah said: Whoever invites an idol worshipper into his house and waits on him causes his descendants to go into exile, as it says, "And some of your sons, your own offspring, whom you will have fathered, will be taken to serve as eunuchs in the palace of the king of Babylon" (ibid. 20:18).

[The Gemara describes Hezekiah's extravagant show of hospitality.] It says, "Hezekiah was pleased by their coming, and he showed them his *bet nechot*—the silver, the gold, the spices, and the fragrant oil . . ." (Isaiah 39:2). Rav said: What is the meaning of "his *bet nechot*"? It means that Hezekiah's own wife poured drinks for them.[281] Shmuel said: It means that Hezekiah showed them his treasure house. R. Yochanan said: He showed them weapons that could destroy other weapons; [weapons made of a metal strong enough to smash any weapon].

THE TWO ASTUTE CAPTIVES

The Rabbis taught: It once happened that two men were taken captive on Mount Carmel, and their captor was walking behind them. (104b) One of the captives said to the other, "The camel walking in front of us is blind in one eye; it is carrying two barrels, one of wine, the other of oil; and of the two men leading the camel one is a Jew, the other a gentile." The captor [who had overheard their remarks] said, "Stiff-necked people that you are, from where do you know this?" They replied, "We can tell that the camel is blind in one eye by the grass in front of it. On the side it can see, it eats; on the side it cannot see, it does not eat; [a camel that can see with both eyes eats from both sides]. We can tell that it is carrying two barrels, one of wine and one of oil, because we know that when wine drips it sinks into the ground; whereas when oil drips it floats, [and we noticed that the drops on one side were absorbed in the ground and on the other side remained on the surface]. We could tell that of the two men leading the camel one is a gentile, the other a Jew, because a gentile relieves himself on the road, whereas a Jew relieves himself on the sides of the road [out of modesty]. The captor chased after the camel drivers and found that it was as they had said. So he went and kissed the captives on their heads, brought them to his house, made them a great banquet, and danced before them. He exclaimed, "Blessed be He Who chose the seed of Abraham and gave them of His wisdom; wherever they go they become the princes of their masters!" Then he set them free, and they went home in peace.

EXPOSITIONS OF PASSAGES OF
THE BOOK OF LAMENTATIONS

"She weeps and weeps in the night" (Lamentations 1:2). Why these two weepings? Rabbah said in the name of R. Yochanan: One weeping is for the destruction of the first *Bet Hamikdash* and one for the destruction of the second *Bet Hamikdash*, [which were both destroyed on *Tishah be'Av,* the 9th of Av].

"In the night"—the *Bet Hamikdash* was destroyed because of what happened on the night [of *Tishah b'Av}*. For it says, [after the Spies returned and brought their bad report,] "The entire community broke into loud cries, and the people wept that night" (Numbers 14:1). And Rabbah said in the name of R. Yochanan: That night was the night of *Tishah b'Av*. The Holy One, blessed be He, said to Israel: You wept without cause, therefore I will establish this day for you as a day of weeping for generations to come, [for both Temples were destroyed on *Tishah b'Av*]. Another interpretation of "in the night"—for when a person weeps at night, his voice carries farther than in the day. Another interpretation of "in the night"—for when a person weeps at night, the stars and constellations weep along with him. Another interpretation: For when a person weeps at night, whoever hears it is moved to tears.

It happened that the son of R. Gamliel's neighbor died, and she wept for him at night. Hearing her cry, R. Gamliel cried with her until his eyelashes fell over his eyes. The next day his students noticed it, and they removed her from his neighborhood, [since the weeping was affecting his health].

It says, "Her tears are on her cheeks" (Lamentations 1:2). Rava said in the name of R. Yochanan: Like a woman cries over the death of the husband of her youth, as it says, "Lament—like a maiden girded with sackcloth for the husband of her youth" (Joel 1:8).

"Her adversaries have become her master" (Lamentations 1:5). Rava said in the name of R. Yochanan: Whoever persecutes Israel becomes a leader, as it says, "For he was not wearied the first time the land was distressed, when Assyria exiled the land of Zebulun and the land of Naphtali, but the last time will be severe, by the way of the sea, beyond the Jordan, the region of the nations" (Isaiah 8:23).[282] Rava said in the name of R. Yochanan: Whoever oppresses Israel does not become weary.

"May it never befall you, all who pass along the road" (Lamentations 1:12). Rava said in the name of R. Yochanan: From here we have a source for *kuvlana* from the Torah.[283]

"All who pass along the road." R. Amram said in the name of Rav: [Jerusalem laments:] "They have made me like transgressors of the law," for regarding the destruction of Sodom it says, "And God rained on Sodom and Gomorrah sulphur and fire" (Genesis 19:24); while regarding the destruction of Jerusalem it says, "From on high He sent a fire into my bones" (ibid. 1:13). [Jerusalem laments: I was punished through fire, just as Sodom was.] And it says, "The iniquity of the daughter of my people is greater than the sin of Sodom" (ibid. 4:6).

[The Gemara asks:] Now, if the sin of Jerusalem was greater than that of Sodom, should Jerusalem be treated favorably? [Why was Jerusalem not totally destroyed, as Sodom was?] Rava said in the name of R. Yochanan: There was an extra measure [of suffering] in Jerusalem that Sodom did not have to endure, for concerning Sodom it says, "Only this was the sin of your sister Sodom: arrogance! She and her daughters had plenty of bread and untroubled tranquility; yet she did not support the poor and the needy" (Ezekiel 16:49); whereas regarding Jerusalem it says, "With their own hands, tenderhearted women have cooked their children" (Lamentations 4:10).[284]

"God has trampled [*silah*] all my mighty ones in my midst" (ibid. 1:15)—like a person who says to his friend: This coin has become worthless [*nifselah*]. "All your enemies jeered at you" (ibid. 2:16). Rava said in the name of R. Yochanan: Why did [Jeremiah, the author of Lamentations] place the *pei* before the *ayin*?[285] He did it because of the Spies, who spoke with their mouths what they had not seen with their eyes; [their mouths preceded their eyes].

"They devour My people as they devour food, and do not call upon God" (Psalms 14:4). Rava said in the name of R. Yochanan: Whoever eats the bread of Israel tastes the true taste of bread, and whoever does not eat the bread of Israel does not taste the true taste of bread. [The idolators enjoy the bread they steal from the Jews (Rashi).] "They do not call upon God"—Rav said: This refers to corrupt Jewish judges. And Shmuel said: This refers to teachers of young children [who do not carry out their task scrupulously. It is because of dishonest judges and teachers that the bread of the Jewish people is devoured by their enemies].

SOLOMON'S PORTION IN THE WORLD TO COME

[The Mishnah listed three kings and four commoners who have no portion in the World to Come. The Gemara asks:] Who enumerated them, [since no human being can possibly know this]? R. Ashi said: The Men of the Great Assembly [who had Divine inspiration] enumerated them.

Rav Yehudah said in the name of Rav: They wanted to include one more king [among those who have no share in the World to Come, namely Solomon]. At that moment, the image of his father appeared and prostrated itself before [the Men of the Great Assembly, asking them not to put Solomon on that list,] but they ignored it. Thereupon a fire came down from heaven and licked their benches, but they ignored it. Then a heavenly voice came forth and said to them, "Do you see a man diligent at his work? He will stand before kings [in Gan Eden]; he will not stand before darkened ones [in Gehinnom]" (Proverbs 22:29). He [Solomon] who built the *Bet Hamikdash* before his own house, and that is not all, but My House [the *Bet*

Hamikdash] he built in seven years, while his house he built in thirteen years, [such a man will stand with the righteous kings in Gan Eden, not with the wicked kings in Gehinnom]." But the Men of the Great Assembly ignored even the voice. Thereupon a second heavenly voice came forth and said, "Is it from you [the Men of the Great Assembly] that punishment is meted out, that you despise [Solomon]? Will you choose and not I?" (Job 34:33). Hearing this, they yielded [and did not put Solomon on the list of those that have no share in the World to Come].

The Expounders of Verses used to say: All of them [i.e., all the persons listed in our Mishnah] enter the World to Come. As it says, "Gilead is mine; Menasheh is mine; Ephraim is the stronghold of my head; Judah is my lawgiver; Moab is my washbasin; upon Edom I will cast my lock; Philistia will make overtures of friendship to me" (Psalms 60:9,10). "Gilead is mine"—this is a reference to Ahab who fell in the battle at Ramot Gilead. "Menasheh is mine"—this is a reference to King Menasheh. "Ephraim is the stronghold of my head"—this is a reference to Jeroboam who was descended from the tribe of Ephraim. "Judah is my lawgiver"—this is a reference to Achitofel (**105a**) who was descended from the tribe of Judah. "Moab is my washbasin"—this is a reference to Geichazi, who was stricken with leprosy on account of matters involving washing.[286]

"Upon Edom I will cast my lock"—this is a reference to Doeg the Edomite [who will be "locked up" in Gan Eden]. "Philistia will make overtures of friendship to me [*hitroa'i*]"—the ministering angels said to the Holy One, blessed be He, "Master of the universe! If David who slew the Philistine [Goliath], and who gave possession of the Philistine city of Gath to Your children, will come [and object that You have allowed his enemies Doeg and Achitofel into the World to Come,] what will You say to him?" God replied, "It is my duty to make them friends [*rei'im*] with each other," [meaning, to make the conqueror of the Philistines—David—friends with Doeg and Achitophel (Rashi)].

THE JEWS DEFYING
THE PROPHET

[The Gemara notes that the kings were not the only ones that sinned; the Jews of that time also went astray. The Gemara gives three examples:] It says, "Why is this people—Jerusalem—rebellious with a persistent rebellion?" (Jeremiah 8:5). Rav said: [They acted rebelliously when] the Assembly of Israel [i.e., the Jewish people], gave the prophet Zechariah a crushing retort. The prophet Zechariah said to Israel, "Repent! Think about it; your ancestors who sinned, where are they now? [Dead and gone.]" The Jews snapped back at Zechariah, "And your prophets who did not sin, where are they now? Also dead and gone!" For it says, "Your ancestors, where are they? And the prophets, do

they live forever?" (Zechariah 1:5).[287] The prophet Zechariah replied, "Your ancestors repented and confessed their sins, as it says, 'But the warnings and the decrees with which I charged My servants the prophets overtook your ancestors—did they not?—and in the end they had to admit, 'God has dealt with us according to our ways and our deeds, just as He purposed'" (ibid. v. 6).

[The second example of Israel's defiance of the prophet:] Shmuel said: [The crushing retort was this:] Ten persons came and sat down before [the prophet Ezekiel]. Ezekiel said to them, "Repent." They replied, "A slave whose master has sold him, or a wife whose husband has divorced her, do they have any claim on each other any longer?" [Certainly not! God who sold us to Nebuchadnezzar and thereby divorced us has no further claim on us, and we have no cause to repent.] The Holy One, blessed be He, said to the prophet, "Thus says God, 'Where is the bill of divorce of your mother whom I dismissed? And which of My creditors was it to whom I sold you off? You were only sold off for your sins, and your mother dismissed for your crimes'" (Isaiah 50:1). [Meaning: You were not divorced or sold. When you repent I will take you back.]

And this is what Resh Lakish meant when he said: What is the meaning of the expression "My servant David" and "My servant Nebuchadnezzar"?[288] [Why did God give Nebuchadnezzar the same title as He gave to David?] For it was obvious to Him Who spoke and world was created [i.e., God] that Israel would offer this argument. Therefore, God anticipated them and referred to Nebuchadnezzar as His servant. Because when a servant acquires property, to whom does the servant belong and to whom does the property belong? [Of course, to the master. Therefore, even though the Jews were conquered by Nebuchadnezzar they still belonged to God, for Nebuchadnezzar was God's servant.]

[God rejects the claim of the defiant Jews saying,] "What you have in mind shall never come to pass—when you say, 'We will be like the nations, like the families of the lands, worshipping wood and stone.' As I live—declares the Lord God—I will reign over you with a strong hand and with an outstretched arm, and with overflowing fury!" (Ezekiel 20:32,33). R. Nachman said: I wish that the Merciful One would bring all His wrath upon us already, and thereby redeem us!

[The third example of Israel's defiance of the prophet:] It says, "Let him chastise it to [compel it to do what is] right. Let its God instruct it" (Isaiah 28:26). Rabbah b. Bar Chanah [interpreted this verse as a dialogue, as follows:] The prophet Isaiah said to Israel, "Repent!" They replied, "We are unable to do so. Our evil impulse controls us." Isaiah said to them, "Curb your evil impulse and repent." They retorted, "Let God Who created the evil impulse instruct it [not to entice us]."

BALAAM

[The Mishnah listed four commoners who have no share in the World to Come:] Balaam, Doeg, Achitophel, and Geichazi.

The name Balaam denotes *belo am,* "a man without a people." An alternate explanation of the name Balaam is: *bilah am,* "he confused the people [of Israel]."

R. Yochanan said: Balaam was lame in one of his feet, as it says, "He walked with a limp [*shefi*]" (Numbers 23:3). Samson was lame in both of his legs, for it says, "Dan[289] will be a serpent by the road, slithering [*shefifon*][290] along the path, biting a horse's heels" (Genesis 49:17).

Balaam was blind in one of his eyes, for it says, [Balaam describes himself as,] "The man with the open eye" (Numbers 24:3,15); [only one of his eyes was open; the other was blind].

(105b) It says, "Balaam arose in the morning and saddled his female donkey" (Numbers 22:21). A Tanna taught in the name of R. Shimon b. Elazar: Love disregards the rule of refined conduct, as may be seen from the case of Abraham, as it says, "Abraham got up early in the morning and saddled his donkey" (Genesis 22:3). [Out of his love of God and his eagerness to carry out His command of offering his son Isaac, Abraham saddled his donkey himself, rather than have a servant do it.] Hatred too disregards the rule of refined conduct, as may be seen from Balaam, as it says, "Balaam got up early in the morning, and saddled his female donkey" (Numbers 22:21).

Rav Yehudah said in the name of Rav: A person should make it a practice to engage in the study of Torah or to perform a mitzvah, even if not for its own sake, because from learning Torah and doing a mitzvah for ulterior motives[291] he will eventually come to do it for pure motives. For as a reward for the forty-two offerings that Balak offered up to God[292] he was privileged that Ruth should be his descendant. R. Yose b. Huna said: Ruth was the daughter [i.e., a descendant] of Eglon the grandson of Balak the king of Moab.

[The Gemara digresses:] Rava said to Rabbah b. Mari: It says, [the king's courtiers came to congratulate King David, saying,] "May God grant Solomon a reputation even greater than your own reputation, and may He make his throne even greater than your throne" (1 Kings 1:47). Now, is it good manners to say such a thing to a king? Rabbah b. Mari said to Rava: They did not say, "greater than your own reputation"; what they said was, "something like your reputation." For if you do not say this [then you must translate Judges 5:42 in the following manner,] [Deborah blessed Yael, saying,] "May you be blessed more than the women in the tent." And who are "the women in the tent"? Sarah, Rebeccah, Rachel, and Leah. Now, is it proper to say such a thing? [That Yael should be more blessed than the Matriarchs? Certainly not.] Rather, Deborah wished on Yael, "something like [the blessing bestowed on the Matriarchs]."

[The underlying idea is that it was improper for the courtiers to wish that David's son should outshine him.] This is at odds with R. Yosef b. Choni, for R. Yosef b. Choni said: A man is jealous of everyone except his son and his disciple. His son, as can be seen from the case of Solomon; [for the courtiers wished that David's son should outshine him.] And his disciple, if you prefer, say that it is derived from the following verse, "[Moses] laid his hands on [Joshua his disciple] and commissioned him" (Numbers 27:23), [even though God had commanded Moses to "lean your hand" on him, he laid both "his hands" on him, bestowing all his prophetic powers on his successor Joshua].

BALAAM'S BLESSINGS

[Resuming its discussion of Balaam, the Gemara says:] It says, "God put a thing in Balaam's mouth" (ibid. 23:5). What was this "thing"? R. Elazar said: It was an angel. [God placed Balaam under the control of an angel who prevented him from cursing the Jews (Rashi).] R. Yochanan said: It was a hook [that pulled his mouth shut whenever he tried to utter a curse].

R. Yochanan said: From the blessings of that wicked man [Balaam] you can figure out what he intended to say. He wanted to curse the Jews that they should not have any synagogues or study halls, but he was forced to say, "How good are your tents, Jacob" (ibid. 24:5).[293] He wanted to say: May the *Shechinah* not rest on the Jews, but he was forced to say, "Your dwelling places, O Israel" (ibid.) [which symbolizes the *Bet Hamikdash*]. He meant to say: May Israel's kingdom not endure, but he was forced to say, "They stretch out like streams" (ibid. v. 6); [their kingdom will run on like a stream]. He meant to say: May they have no olive orchards and vineyards, but he was forced to say, "Like gardens by a river."

He tried to say: May their fragrance not spread; instead he was forced to say, "like fragrant aloes planted by God." He tried to say: May they have no kings of impressive stature, but he was forced to say, "like the cedars by the water." He wanted to say: May they not have a king who is the son of a king, but he was forced to say, "May water flow from his wells" [for a longlasting dynasty]. He meant to say: May their king not rule over other nations, but he was forced to say, "and his seed in abundant waters" [a metaphor for the conquest of many nations]. He tried to say: May their kingdom not be strong, but he was forced to say, "May his king be greater than Agag" [a reference to Saul's victory over Agag, King of Amalek]. He intended to say: May their kingdom inspire no fear, but he was forced to say, "May his kingdom be exalted."

R. Abba b. Kahana said: All of Balaam's blessings eventually turned into the curse [he had in mind], except for the curse regarding synagogues and study halls. For it says, "God your Lord transformed his curse to a blessing for you, since God your Lord loves you" (Deuteronomy 23:6); the verse says *curse*, not *curses* [i.e., only one intended curse was transformed into a blessing, that synagogues and *yeshivot* should never disappear from Israel].

R. Shmuel b. Nachmani said in the name of R. Yonatan: What is meant by the verse, "Wounds inflicted by a loved one are faithful, while the kisses of an enemy are deceitful" (Proverbs 27:6)? Better was the curse with which the prophet Achiyah the Shelonite cursed Israel than the blessing with which the wicked Balaam blessed them. Achiyah the Shelonite cursed them, comparing them to a reed, for it says, "God will strike Israel until it sways like a reed in water" (1 Kings 14:15), [because of the sins of Joroboam]. Just as a reed grows in a watery place, and its stem grows back **(106a)** [when it is cut], and it has many roots, and even if all the winds of the world come and blow on it, they cannot budge it from its place, but it sways back and forth in harmony with the winds; and as soon as the winds subside, the reed again stands upright in its place. [The same holds true for Israel.]

However, the wicked Balaam blessed them by comparing them with a cedar. Just as a cedar does not stand in a watery place, and it has only few roots, and its trunk does not grow back once it is cut, and even if all the ordinary winds of the world blow upon it, they cannot budge it from its place, but when the powerful south wind blows upon it, it immediately uproots it and overturns it, [so too should Israel be overturned, according to Balaam's intent]. And the reed surpasses the cedar in yet another respect: The reed has the merit that pens are made from it, to be used to write scrolls of the Torah, the Prophets, and the Writings.

BALAAM'S FINAL WORDS

It says, "When [Balaam] saw the Kenite, he proclaimed his parable" (Numbers 24:21–24). Balaam said to Jethro, "Kenite, were you not with us in giving that advice [to Pharaoh to kill the newborn Jewish boys]? Who placed you among 'the mighty ones' of the world?"[294] And R. Chiya b. Abba said the same teaching in the name of R. Simai: Three persons were involved in giving the advice [to kill the newborn Jewish boys]: Balaam, Job, and Jethro. Balaam who advised Pharaoh to drown the Jewish babies was killed.[295] Job who remained silent [and did not protest] was punished by having to suffer. As for Jethro who [protested against the plan] and then fled [to avoid being killed], his descendants were privileged to sit in the Chamber of the Hewn Stone [in the Temple, as members of the Sanhedrin]. For it says, "The families of the scribes that dwelled at Yabetz—the Tirathites, the Shimeathites, and the Suchatites; they are the Kenites who come from Chammath, father of Beth Rechav" (1 Chronicles 2:55). And it says, "The children of the Kenite, Moses' father-in-law,[296] went up out of the city of palms" (Judges 1:16), [which proves that the Kenites are the descendants of Jethro].

"[Balaam] proclaimed his parable and said, 'Alas! Who can survive God's devastation'" (Numbers 24:23). R. Shimon b. Lakish said: This passage means: Woe to him who claims to be a god. R. Yochanan said: It means: Woe to the nation that will try to hamper the Jews when the Holy One, blessed be He, accomplishes the redemption of His children [the Jewish people]. Who would throw his garment between a lion and a lioness at the time that they mate with one another? [Meaning: Woe to the nation that would try to thwart God's redemption of the Jewish people (Rashi).]

BALAAM'S DEATH

It says, "[In the Jewish campaign against Midian,] along with the other victims, they also killed the five kings of Midian . . . They also killed Balaam son of Beor, by the sword" (Numbers 31:8). [The Gemara asks:] What was Balaam doing there [in Midian]? R. Yochanan said: He had gone to Midian to collect a reward for the twenty-four thousand of Israel whose death he had caused.[297] Mar Zutra b. Toviyah said in the name of Rav: People have a saying for that: "The camel went to demand horns, so they cut off the ears he had." [Balaam's desire for a reward led to his death]. It says, "And Balaam son of Beor, the sorcerer, the children of Israel slew with the sword" (Joshua 13:22).

[The Gemara asks:] Was Balaam just a sorcerer? Why, he was a prophet! [The Gemara answers:] R. Yochanan said: At first he was a prophet, but at the end he was just a sorcerer. [When he began to curse Israel, God took away his prophetic powers, and he became a mere sorcerer (Rashi).] R. Papa said: As a popular saying has it: "She who was the wife of princes and rulers committed adultery with carpenters." [Meaning: Balaam was demoted from prophet to the lowly rank of sorcerer.]

DOEG AND ACHITOPHEL

(106b) R. Yitzchak said: What is the meaning of the passage, "Where is the one who could count? Where is the one who could weigh? Where is the one who could count all these towers?" (Isaiah 33:18). [This verse may be applied to Doeg][298]: Where is the one who can count all the letters in the Torah? [Doeg.] Where is the one who can draw all the inferences in the Torah by means of *kal vachomer* arguments? [Doeg.] Where is the one who can count the towers? [Doeg,] for he counted three hundred fixed laws concerning "a tower that floats in the air."[299]

R. Ami said: Doeg and Achitophel[300] raised four hundred halachic problems concerning "a tower that floats in the air," and not one was solved. Rava remarked: Is raising problems a sign of greatness? Why, in the years of Rav Yehudah all the teaching of the *yeshivot* was in the tractates of the Order of *Nezikin* [Damages], while we study a great deal in all six Orders of the Mishnah, down to the last tractate, *Uktzin*. Rather, we must conclude that the Holy One, blessed be He, desires heart, as it says, "God sees into the heart" (1 Samuel 16:7).

R. Mesharshiya said: Doeg and Achitophel did not really understand the full depth of their halachic studies. Mar Zutra raised an objection to this: It says about Doeg, "Where is the one who can count? Where is the one who can weigh? Where is the one who can count towers?" and you say that Doeg and Achitophel did not clearly understand what they were studying? [The Gemara concludes:] Rather, what R. Mesharshiya meant was that Doeg's and Achitophel's views were not accepted as valid *halachah*. For it says, "God's secret is for those who fear Him" (Psalms 25:14), [God reveals the correct rulings on Torah law only to the God-fearing].

R. Ami said: Doeg did not die until he forgot his learning, for it says, "He will die without instruction, infatuated by his great folly" (Proverbs 5:23). R. Ashi said: He was stricken with leprosy, for it says, "You cut down all those who stray from You" (Psalms 73:27).

R. Yochanan said: Three angels of destruction appeared before Doeg before his death: one that made him forget his learning, one that burned his soul, and another that scattered his ashes in the synagogues and houses of study.

R. Yochanan also said: Doeg and Achitophel did not see each other [i.e., they were not contemporaries]. Doeg lived in the days of Saul, whereas Achitophel lived in the days of David.

R. Yochanan also said: Doeg and Achitophel did not live out half their days. This has also been taught in a *Baraita*: It says, "Those murderous and treacherous men will not live out half their days" (Psalms 55:24). Doeg lived only thirty-four years; Achitophel only thirty-three years.

R. Yochanan said further: At first David called Achitophel his teacher, then his colleague, and ultimately his student. At first David called Achitophel his teacher, as it says, "But it is you—a man of my measure, my mentor and my advisor!" (Psalms 55:14). Subsequently he called him his colleague, as it says, "Sweet was our fellowship; we walked together in God's House" (ibid. v. 15). Ultimately he called him his student, as it says, "My ally in whom I trusted, (107a) who shared my bread,[301] has raised his heel to trample me" (ibid. 41:10).

DAVID AND BATHSHEBA

R. Yehudah said in the name of Rav: A person should never ask to be tested, for David, King of Israel asked to be tested, and he stumbled. David said to God, "Master of the universe! Why do people say in their prayers, 'the God of Abraham, the God of Isaac, and the God of Jacob' and not, 'the God of David'?" God replied, "They [the Patriarchs] were tested by Me [and passed the test], whereas you have not been tested by Me." David said, "Master of the universe! Try me, and test me!" As it says, "Try me, O God, and test me" (Psalms 26:2). God said to David, "I will test you, and I grant you a special privilege. For I did not inform the Patriarchs in advance [of the nature of their tests], whereas I am informing you in advance that I will test you in a matter of adultery." Thereupon, "Late one afternoon, David rose from his couch . . ." (2 Samuel 11:2). R. Yochanan said: He changed his night-couch to a day-couch,[302] forgetting the rule: "There is a small organ in the man; when he satisfies it, it is starved, and when he starves it, it is satisfied."[303] "And he strolled on the roof of the royal palace; and from the roof he saw a woman bathing. The woman was very beautiful" (ibid.).

Bathsheba was washing her hair behind a screen when Satan came to David in the form of a bird. David shot an arrow at it, which tore the screen. Thus Bathsheba was exposed to view, and David saw her. Immediately, "The king sent someone to make inquiries about the woman. He reported, 'She is Bathsheba daughter of Eliam and wife of Uriah the Hittite.' David sent messengers to fetch her; she came to him, and he lay with her—she had just purified herself after her period—and she went home" (ibid. v. 3,4). And that is why David said, "You probed my heart, You searched at night; You tested me, but did not find [me pure]" (Psalms 17:3). [The verse continues,] "My thoughts do not transgress the words of my mouth." David said: I wish that a muzzle had fallen on my mouth, and that I had not said such a thing [as asking to be tested].

Rava expounded: What is meant by the passage, "For the conductor, by David: In God I take refuge. How can you say to me, 'Your mountain was moved by a bird'?" (Psalms 11:1)? David pleaded before the Holy One, blessed be He: Master of the universe! Forgive me for that sin [with Bathsheba] so that people should not say, "Your mountain [i.e., your king] was caused to stray by a mere bird."[304]

Rava expounded: What is the meaning of the verse, "Against You alone have I sinned, and done what is evil in Your sight, so that You are just in Your sentence and right in Your judgment" (ibid. 51:6)? David said to the Holy One, blessed be He: You know full well that had I wished to subdue my evil impulse, I could have done so. However, I said to myself: Let the people not say that the servant got the better of his Master.[305]

Rava expounded: What is the meaning of the passage, "For I was destined for the rib,[306] but my pain is always with me" (Psalms 38:18)? Bathsheba the daughter of Eliam was destined since the six days of creation to be the wife of David, but she came to him with pain [under painful circumstances]. This was also taught in a *Baraita* of the yeshivah of R. Yishmael: Bathsheba the daughter of Eliam was meant to be the wife of David, but he took her before the time was ripe.

Rava expounded: What is the meaning of the verse, "But when I stumble they gleefully gather, the lame gather against me. I know not why; they tore at me and would not be silenced" (Psalms 35:15)? David said to the Holy One, blessed be He: Master of the universe! You know full well that if my enemies were to tear my flesh, my blood would not flow, [because they have humiliated me so greatly].[307] What is more, when they are studying the laws about the four methods of execution, they interrupt their studies and taunt me, saying, "David! If a person seduces a married woman, by what method is he executed?"[308] I said to them, "If a person seduces a married woman he is executed by strangulation, but he has a share in the World to Come; but he who publicly puts his neighbor to shame has no share in the World to Come."

DAVID PRAYS FOR FORGIVENESS

R. Dostai of Biri expounded: To whom may David be compared? To a heathen merchant [who offers his wares bit by bit at a low price]. David pleaded with the Holy One, blessed be He, "Master of the universe! Who can be aware of errors?" (Psalms 19:13). God replied, "Your [unwitting sins] are forgiven." David continued, "Clear me of unknown guilt" (ibid.), and God replied, "Your unknown sins are forgiven." David pressed on, "Also from willful sins spare Your servant" (ibid.). God replied, "Your willful sins are forgiven, too." David continued, "Let them not dominate me; then I will be blameless" (ibid.), meaning "so that the Rabbis will not talk about me." God replied, "You are forgiven." David concluded, "Then I will be clear of grave transgression"—meaning "May my offense [of taking Bathsheba] not be recorded [in Scripture]." God said to David, "That is impossible. If even the letter *yud*, which I removed from the name Sarai [when it was changed to Sarah][309] stood up and protested for many years until Joshua came and I added it to his name, as it says, 'Moses called Hoshea the son of Nun, Joshua [Yehoshua]' [Numbers 13:16], surely it is impossible to erase the entire chapter [of the Bathsheba incident from Scripture]!"

[An alternate exposition,] "Then I will be clear of grave transgression" means that David said to the Holy One, blessed be He, "Forgive me for that sin completely." God replied, "It is already ordained that your son Solomon should say in his wisdom, 'Can a man rake embers into his bosom without burning his clothes? Can a man walk on live coals without scorching his feet? It is the same with one who sleeps with his fellow's wife; none who touches her will go unpunished'" (Proverbs 6:27–29). David said to God, "Am I then totally rejected? [Is there nothing I can do to wipe away my guilt?]" God replied, "Accept suffering upon yourself; [and that will cleanse you]," and he accepted it.

DAVID'S SUFFERING

Rav Yehudah said in Rav's name: For six months David was stricken with leprosy, the *Shechinah* left him, and the Sanhedrin drew away from him. He was stricken with leprosy, for it says, "Purge me with hyssop and I shall be pure; cleanse me, and I shall be whiter than snow" (Psalms 51:9).[310] The *Shechinah* left him, for it says, "Let me again rejoice in Your help; let a vigorous spirit sustain me" (ibid. v. 14). The Sanhedrin drew away from him, for it says, "May those who fear You, those who know Your decrees, turn again to me" (ibid. 119:79). How do we know that his suffering lasted for six months? Because it says, "The length of David's reign over Israel was forty years" (1 Kings 2:11): (107b) "He reigned seven years in Hebron, and he reigned thirty-three years in Jerusalem" (1 Kings 2:11). And it says elswhere, "In Hebron he reigned over Judah seven years and six months" (2 Samuel 5:5). Now, the first verse does not count the six months. [Why not?] Because during those six months he was afflicted with leprosy, [and his reign was impaired].

David prayed to God, "Master of the universe! Forgive me for that sin!" God replied, "You are forgiven." David asked, "Show me a sign of Your favor, that my enemies may see and be frustrated, because You, O God, have given me aid and comfort" (Psalms 86:17). God replied, "During your lifetime I will not make it known publicly that I have forgiven you. However, I shall make it known publicly during the lifetime of your son Solomon."

[How was David's forgiveness made known?]

When Solomon built the *Bet Hamikdash* he tried to bring the Ark into the Holy of Holies, but its gates stuck to each other [and could not be opened]. Solomon recited twenty-four prayers but he was not answered. He said, "O gates! Lift up your heads. Up high, you everlasting doors, so the King of glory may come in! Who is this King of glory? God, mighty and valiant, God valiant in battle. O gates lift up your heads! Lift them up, you everlasting doors, so the King of glory may come in!" (Psalms 24:7–9). Still he was not answered. As soon as he said, "O Lord God, do not reject Your anointed one; remember the loyalty of Your servant David" (2 Chronicles 6:42), he was answered immediately, [and the gates opened]. At that moment, the faces of David's enemies turned black [with humiliation] like the bottom of a pot, and all Israel knew that the Holy One, blessed be He, had forgiven David [for that sin].

GEICHAZI[311]

[The Mishnah listed Geichazi as one of the commoners who have no share in the World to Come.] Geichazi, for it says, "Elisha went to Damascus."[312] Where was Elisha going? R. Yochanan said: He went to Damascus to bring Geichazi back to repentance, but he did not want to repent. Elisha said to Geichazi, "Repent!" Geichazi replied, "[How can I repent?] I learned from you: He who sins and causes others to sin is not given the opportunity to repent, [and I have caused others to sin."

What did Geichazi do [to make others sin]? Some say that he hung a magnet above Jeroboam's idol [i.e., the golden calf he had erected], and thereby suspended [the golden calf] between heaven and earth, [misleading people into thinking that the golden calf had supernatural power and should be worshipped]. Some say that Geichazi engraved the Divine Name in the mouth of the calf, and the calf would proclaim: I am your God . . . and: Do not recognize other gods before Me. And some say that Geichazi drove the rabbis away from Elisha, for it says, "The disciples of the prophets said to Elisha, 'See, the place where we live under your direction is too cramped for us'" (2 Kings 6:1), which proves that until then it was not too cramped. [There was ample space because Geichazi had refused admission to many qualified students.]

The Rabbis taught: Let the left hand push away, but the right hand always draw near, [meaning: When condemning another person you should not rebuff him completely, but you should always suggest a way toward reconciliation,] unlike Elisha who rebuffed Geichazi with both hands,[313] as it says, "Naaman said [to Geichazi], 'Please take two talents [of silver].' He urged him and wrapped two talents of silver . . . Elisha said to Geichazi, 'Where have you been, Geichazi?' He replied, 'Your servant has not gone anywhere.' Elisha then said, 'Did my spirit not go along with you when the man [i.e., Naaman] got down from his chariot to meet you? Is this a time to take money in order to buy clothing, olive groves and vineyards, sheep and oxen, and male and female slaves?'" (2 Kings 5:23).

[The Gemara asks:] Did Geichazi really take that much? He took only money and clothing! R. Yitzchak said: When Naaman came to Elisha, he was sitting and expounding on the chapter of "Eight Reptiles."[314] Naaman, the general of the king of Aram, was a leper. A certain Jewish girl who had been captured from Eretz Yisrael said to him, "If you go to Elisha, he will heal you." When he came to Elisha, Elisha said to him, "Go and immerse seven times in the Jordan River." Naaman retorted, "You are making fun of me!" But his companions urged him, "What have you got to lose? Go and try it."

Naaman immersed in the Jordan and was healed. He then came back to Elisha and brought him as a gift all those things he had, but Elisha did not want to accept it from him, [and Naaman left]. Thereupon, Geichazi went to overtake Naaman, took whatever he took from Naaman, and put it away. When Geichazi came back to Elisha, Elisha saw that leprosy had

erupted on Geichazi's head. "Wicked man," he cried out, "has the time come for you to take the reward for studying the chapter of 'Eight Reptiles' [by taking the eight items mentioned in the verse]? May Naaman's leprosy cling to you and your descendants forever! And as [Geichazi] left his presence, he was snow-white with leprosy" (ibid. v. 27).

It says, "There were four men, lepers, outside the gate" (ibid. 7:3). R. Yochanan said: These were Geichazi and his three sons.

We learned in a *Baraita*: R. Shimon b. Elazar said: When dealing with the carnal impulse, with a child, or with a woman—the left hand should push them away, but the right hand should draw them close.[315]

The Rabbis taught: Elisha became sick on three occasions: once when he incited the bears against the children,[316] once when he pushed Geichazi away with both hands, and the third was the illness of which he died, as it says, "Elisha had been stricken with the illness of which he was to die" (2 Kings 13:14).

Until Abraham there were no signs of old age; whoever saw Abraham said, "This is Isaac," and whoever saw Isaac said, "This is Abraham." Therefore Abraham prayed that he should have visible signs of old age, as it says, "Abraham was old, well advanced in years" (Genesis 24:1). Until the time of Jacob there was no frailty, so he prayed and frailty came into being,[317] as it says, "Joseph was told that his father was sick" (ibid. 48:1). Until the time of Elisha, there was never a sick person who recovered. Then Elisha came and prayed, and he recovered, as it says, "Elisha had been stricken with the illness of which he was to die," [which implies that he had been sick before, but recovered].

THEY HAVE NO SHARE IN THE WORLD TO COME

(107b) [The Mishnah says:] The people of the generation of the Flood have no share in the World to Come, nor will they stand for Judgment, [because they received their punishment through the Flood], for it says, "My spirit will not continue to judge man forever" (Genesis 6:3), which means that there will be neither judgment nor [My] spirit for them.

The people of the generation of the Dispersion have no share in the World to Come, as it says, "God scattered them over the face of the earth" (ibid. 11:8). And it says in the next verse, "It was from there [Babel] that God dispersed them over all the face of the earth" (ibid. 11:9). [The repetition of the phrase implies that] "God scattered them"—in this world; "and God dispersed them"—for the World to Come.

The people of Sodom have no share in the World to Come, for it says, "The people of Sodom were very wicked and sinful against God" (ibid. 13:13)— "Wicked" in this world; "and sinful" for the World to Come. However, they will stand for judgment. R.

Nechemiah said: Neither the people of the generation of the Flood nor the people of Sodom will stand for judgment, for it says, "Therefore the wicked will not stand up [(108a)] in judgment, nor will sinners in the assembly of the righteous" (Psalms 1:5). "Therefore the wicked will not stand up in judgment"—this is a reference to the people of the generation of the Flood; "nor will sinners in the assembly of the righteous"—these are the people of Sodom. They said to R. Nechemiah: The [people of Sodom] will not stand up in the congregation of the righteous, but they will stand for judgment in the congregation of the wicked. [They will be resurrected and brought to judgment like all other sinners (Rashi).]

The Spies have no share in the World to Come, as it says, "The men who had given a bad report about the land thus died before God in the plague" (Numbers 14:37). "They died"—in this world; "in the plague"—for the World to Come.

The people of the generation of the wilderness have no share in the World to Come, nor will they stand for judgment. For it says, "They will end their lives in this desert, and here they will die" (ibid. v. 35), so says R. Akiva. R. Eliezer says: About them it says, "Bring in My devout ones, who made a covenant with Me over sacrifice" (Psalms 50:5). [I.e., the generation of the wilderness that made a covenant with God at Sinai by offering sacrifices will be with God in the World to Come (Rashi).]

The congregation of Korach is not destined to rise up [from the ground], for it says, "The earth covered them over" (Numbers 16:33)—in this world; "and they were lost to the community"—for the World to Come. So says R. Akiva. R. Eliezer says: About them it says, "God deals death and gives life, casts down into the Pit and lifts up" (1 Samuel 2:6).

THE GENERATION OF
THE FLOOD

The Rabbis taught: The people of the generation of the Flood have no share in the World to Come, for it says, "He thus obliterated all existence that had been on the face of the land . . . they were obliterated from the earth" (Genesis 7:23). "He thus obliterated all existence"—in this world; "they were obliterated from the earth"—for the World to Come. So says R. Akiva. R. Yehudah b. Beteira says: They will not come alive at the resurrection, nor will they be judged [at the final Judgment]. For it says, "My spirit will not continue to judge man forever" (ibid. 6:3)—neither judgment nor spirit. Another interpretation: "My spirit will not continue to judge [lo yadon] means that their soul will not return to its sheath [nedon, i.e., their bodies]. R. Menachem b. R. Yose says: Even when the Holy One, blessed be He, restores the souls to the dead bodies [at the Resurrection] their souls will be harmful to them in Gehinnom [i.e., they will not be resurrected,

and their suffering in Gehinnom will increase]. As it says, "You will conceive hay, give birth to straw. Your spirit will devour you like fire" (Isaiah 33:11), [i.e., your soul will destroy your bodies (Rashi)].

WHY WERE THEY PUNISHED
WITH WATER?

The Rabbis taught: The people of the generation of the Flood became arrogant only because of the good God lavished on them. What does it say about them? "Their homes are secure, without fear; they do not feel the rod of God" (Job 21:9), and it says in the next verse, "Their bull breeds and does not fail, their cow calves and never miscarries" (ibid. v. 10). And it says further, "They let their infants run loose like sheep, and their children skip about. They sing to the music of timbrel and lute, and rejoice to the tune of the flute. They live out their days in happiness, their years in pleasure, and go down to the grave calmly" (ibid. 11–13). In their affluence they said to God, 'Leave us alone. We do not want to learn Your ways! What is the Almighty that we should serve Him? What will we gain by praying to Him?'" (ibid. 14,15). They said: Do we need God for anything but a drop of rain? [We don't even need Him for that!] We have rivers and streams to supply our needs. But God said: With the very prosperity [i.e., water] that I lavished on them, they are provoking Me! With that very bounty I shall punish them! As it says, "I Myself am bringing the Flood" (Genesis 6:17).

R. Yose said: The people of the generation of the Flood became arrogant only because of the eyeball, which resembles water [and with which they smugly gazed at their riches]. Therefore God punished them with water, which resembles the eyeball, as it says, "All the wellsprings of the great deep burst forth and the floodgates of the heavens were opened" (Genesis 7:11).

R. Yochanan said: The corruption of the people of the generation of the Flood is described as "great," and [to even the score] they received a punishment that is described as "great." Their corruption is described as "great," for it says, "God saw that man's wickedness on earth was great" (ibid. 6:5). And their punishment is decribed as "great," for it says, "All the wellsprings of the great deep burst forth" (ibid. 7:11). R. Yochanan said: Three of those [hot] springs remained in existence: the whirlpool at Gader, the hot springs of Tiberias, and the great thermal springs at Beiram.

THE PERVERSION OF
THE GENERATION OF
THE FLOOD

It says, "All flesh had perverted its way on earth" (Genesis 6:12). R. Yochanan said: This teaches us that they mated domesticated animal with wild animals, wild animals with domesticated animals, and humans mated with all types of animals. R. Abba b. Kahana said:

[After the Flood] all the animals reverted to mating with their own kind, except the bird *tushlami*, [which continues to mate indiscriminately to this day].

"God said to Noah, 'The end of all flesh has come before Me'" (ibid. v. 13). R. Yochanan said: Come and see how great is the power of robbery, for the people of the generation of the Flood transgressed all laws [i.e., the seven Noachide laws], yet the decree of their punishment was sealed only because they stretched out their hands to commit robbery. For it says, "The world is filled with robbery through them. I will therefore destroy them with the earth" (ibid.). And it says, "Robbery has grown into a rod of evil—neither of themselves, nor of their multitudes, nor of what they amassed, nor is there anyone among them who yearns [for Me]" (Ezekiel 7:11). R. Elazar said: This teaches us that robbery [figuratively] erected itself like a staff, stood before the Holy One, blessed be He, and said to Him: Master of the universe! [There is no good]—either in themselves, nor in their multitudes, nor in what they amassed—nor is there any longing [for God] among them.

In the yeshivah of R. Yishmael they taught: The decree of destruction was passed even on Noah too, but he found favor in the eyes of God. For it says, "[God said,] 'I regret that I created them.' And Noah found favor in God's eyes" (Genesis 6:7,8).[318]

It says, "God regretted that He had made man on earth" (ibid. v. 6). When R. Dimi came [to Babylonia], he said: The Holy One, blessed be He, said: I did a good thing that I prepared graves for them in the earth [i.e., destroy them]. [The Gemara asks:] How is this indicated [in the verse]? It says here [in the above verse], *Vayinachem Hashem*," and it says elsewhere, "He [Joseph] comforted *[vayenachem]* them and spoke kindly to them" (ibid. 50:21). [Thus *vayinachem* denotes that God found comfort in his decision to destroy mankind.]

Some say [that God said]: I did not do well preparing graves for them in the earth, [for they may yet repent]. For it says here, in the present verse, *"Vayinachem Hashem,"* and it says elsewhere, [in response to Moses' plea,] "God reconsidered *[vayinachem]* regarding the evil that He declared He would do to His people" (Exodus 32:14). [Thus *vayinachem* denotes that God regretted having to destroy mankind.]

NOAH'S RIGHTEOUSNESS

It says, "These are the chronicles of Noah: Noah was a righteous man, faultless in his generation" (Genesis 6:9). R. Yochanan said: In his [corrupt] generation he was faultless, but he would not have been considered faultless in [Abraham's] generation. Resh Lakish said: If he was faultless in his [corrupt] generation, he surely would have been righteous if he had lived in [Abraham's] generation.

R. Chanina said: R. Yochanan's interpretation may be illustrated by the following example: A barrel of

wine was stored in a cellar full of vinegar. While the wine is in its place among the vinegar, its good aroma stands out [in comparison to the vinegar]; elsewhere, its aroma does not attract attention. [Similarly, Noah by comparison with his corrupt generation stood out for his righteousness; however, in a righteous generation his virtue would hardly be noticed.] R. Oshaya said: Resh Lakish's interpretation may be illustrated by the following example: A bottle of perfume was lying in a garbage dump. If its pleasant odor stands out among the slime, surely it will attract attention in fragrant surroundings. [So, too, if Noah was righteous even when his generation was evil, he surely would have been upright in a righteous generation.]

THE GREAT FLOOD

It says, "[The Flood] obliterated every organism that had been on the face of the land" (Genesis 7:23). [The Gemara asks:] If man sinned, how did the animals sin? It was taught in the name of R. Yehoshua b. Korcha: You can compare this to a man who set up a wedding canopy for his son and prepared a feast of all kinds of food. A while later his son died [before the wedding took place]. Thereupon the father took apart the wedding canopy, [and discarded the food for the feast], saying: I prepared all this only because of my son. Now that he has died, what do I need a wedding canopy for? So too, the Holy One, blessed be He, said: I created domesticated and wild animals only for the benefit of man. Now that man has sinned, what do I need domesticated and wild animals for? [Therefore the animals were also destroyed in the Flood.] It says, "Everything on dry land died" (ibid. v. 22), but not the fish of the sea.

R. Yose of Caesaria expounded: What is the meaning of the verse, "He glides swiftly on water's surface; may their fate on earth be cursed" (Job 24:18)? This teaches that the righteous Noah used to admonish the people of his generation, saying, "Repent! For if you do not, the Holy One, blessed be He, will bring the Flood upon you, and will make your bodies float on the waters like leather bags! As it says, 'He glides swiftly on water's surface.' And that's not all, but you will be taken as a curse for all future generation, as it says, 'May their fate on earth be cursed.'" [The verse concludes,] "He does not clear the way to the vineyards." This teaches that [Noah warned them about the impending Flood as] they were clearing the paths of their vineyards. The people said to Noah, "[If God is so powerful,] who stops Him from bringing the Flood right now?" Noah replied [in the name of God,] "There is one dove [i.e., righteous person, namely Methuselah] that I must take away from you [before I bring the Flood]." The people replied, (108b) "If so, we will not clear the path of the vineyards" [i.e., we will not follow the straight way, but we will walk on the crooked path of sin, and we will not repent (Rashi)].

Rava expounded: What is meant by the verse, "A torch of scorn to one who is complacent in his thoughts! He is destined to be among those whose feet slip" (Job 12:5)? This teaches that the righteous Noah would admonish his contemporaries and say to them words that are harsh as flames, but they would scorn him. They said to him, "Old man! What is this ark for?" He replied, "The Holy One, blessed be He, is going to bring a flood upon you." They asked, "A flood of what? If He brings a flood of fire, we have something called *alitah* [i.e., a creature that can put out fire and will protect us]. And if He brings a flood of water: if He brings it up from the earth, we have iron plates with which we can cover the earth [to prevent the water from coming up]. And if He brings the water down from the heavens, we have something called *akuv* that will protect us. And some say, it was called *akush* [a highly absorbent sponge that would soak up the rain].

It says, "Seven days passed, and the Flood waters were on the earth" (Genesis 7:10). What was the nature of these seven days [that God postponed the Flood]? Rav said: These were the seven days of mourning for Methuselah. This teaches you that eulogies for the righteous hold back punishment. Another explanation is: The phrase "seven days passed" implies that the Holy One, blessed be He, reversed the natural order of the seven days of Creation. For during the Flood, the sun would rise in the west and set in the east. Another explanation [of the seven days] is: The Holy One, blessed be He, first set aside for them a long period of time [to repent],[319] and afterward he gave them a short period of time, [of seven days as a last chance for repentance]. Yet another explanation: The phrase "seven days passed" teaches that [before the Flood] God gave them a taste of the world to come, so that they would realize what goodness they deprived themselves of, [and thereby their punishment was complete (*Maharsha*)].

It says, "Take seven pairs from every clean animal, each consisting of a male and its mate" (Genesis 7:2). [The Gemara asks:] Do animals have husband–wife [monogamous] relationships? R. Shmuel b. Nachmani said in the name of R. Yonatan: [God wanted Noah to take] only from animals that had not mated with animals of a different species. How could Noah tell? R. Chisda said: He led them past the ark. Those that the ark accepted had certainly not been the object of sin, and whichever the Ark did not accept had certainly been the object of sin. R Abbahu said: Noah took from those animals that came of their own accord.

THE ARK

It says, "Make yourself an ark of *gopher* wood" (Genesis 6:14). What is *gopher*? R. Ada said: The scholars of the yeshivah of R. Shila said: This is *mavligah* wood, and some say it is *gulamish* wood.[320]

"Make a *tzohar* [skylight] for the ark" (ibid. v. 16). R. Yochanan said: The Holy One, blessed be He, said to Noah: Set into the ark precious stones and pearls so that they will light up the ark for you like the noon-time [*tzaharayim*] sun. "Make it slanted so that it is one cubit wide on top" (ibid.). For that way it would last. "Make a bottom, second, and third deck" (ibid.). We learned in a *Baraita*: The bottom deck was for waste matter, the middle deck for animals, and the top deck for people.

AFTER THE FLOOD

It says, "[Noah] sent out the raven. It went back and forth until the water had dried up from the land's surface" (Genesis 8:7). Resh Lakish said: The raven gave Noah a crushing rejoinder. The raven said to Noah, "It seems that your Master [God] hates me, and you, Noah, hate me too. Your Master hates me, [since He commanded you to take into the ark seven pairs of each of the species of clean animals, but only two of each of the species of unclean animals].[321] And you, too, hate me. For when [it comes to sending out a bird] you leave the species of which there are seven, and you send me, one of a species of which there are only two! If the angel of heat or of cold strikes me, [and I die], would not one type of animal become extinct? Or perhaps you desire my mate?" [Noah] replied, "Wicked one! If even relations with the wife who is ordinarily permitted to me are presently prohibited to me, [for God has prohibited cohabitation in the ark], then regarding your mate that is always forbidden to me, is it not certain [that it is forbidden in the ark]?"

"[Noah] then sent the dove from him to see if the water had subsided" (Genesis 8:8). [When he sent out the raven, it does not say "from him."] R. Yirmeyah commented: From here we learn that it is proper for kosher birds to live with the righteous.

"The dove returned to him toward evening, and there was a freshly plucked [*taraf*, also meaning food] olive leaf in its beak" (ibid. v. 11). R. Elazar said: The dove said to the Holy One, blessed be He, "Master of the universe! Let my food be as bitter as an olive, as long as it comes from You, rather than sweet as honey but coming from human beings."[322] How do we know that the word *taraf* denotes food? For it says, "Feed me [*hatrifeini*] my daily portion of bread" (Proverbs 30:8).

CARING FOR THE ANIMALS
IN THE ARK

"Every beast, every land animal, and every bird . . . left the ark by families" (ibid. 8:19). R. Yochanan said: They were by their families, not by themselves. [In the ark, each species was fed separately; not all species from a common trough (Rashi).]

R. Chana b. Bizna said: Eliezer [the servant of Abraham, once] said to Shem [Noah's oldest son], "It says, 'They left the ark by their families.' Now, how were you able to take care of all their individual needs?" Shem said to Eliezer, "Indeed, we had a great deal of trouble in the ark. The animals that are usually fed by day we fed by day, and those that are used to be fed by night we fed by night, [so that we were busy around the clock]. But my father did not know what to feed the *zikita*.[323] One day, he was sitting and cutting up a pomegranate, when a worm dropped out of it, which the *zikita* hungrily ate. From then on, he would knead bran in water for the *zikita*, and when it became wormy, the *zikita* would eat it. Regarding the lion, it was nourished by a fever, [and it therefore did not eat up other animals]. For Rav said: Fever sustains its victim for no less than six days and no more than twelve days. Regarding the *avarshinah*,[324] Father found it lying in its niche inside the ark [instead of coming outside to be fed]. Father said to it: Don't you need food? The *avarchinah* said to Noah: I saw that you were busy, so I said to myself: I will not bother you with feeding me, too. Hearing this, Noah exclaimed: May it be the will of God that you never die! [His blessing was fulfilled] for it says, "I said to myself, 'I will expire with my nest intact; I will live as long as the phoenix'" (Job 29:18).

R. Chanah b. Livai said: Shem, Noah's oldest son, said to Eliezer: When the kings of the east and the west attacked you, what did you do to defeat them?[325] Eliezer said the Shem: The Holy One, blessed be He, took Abraham and placed him at His right hand. We would throw dust at the enemy, which turned into swords; we would throw straw at them, which turned into arrows, [that struck down the enemy]. As it says, "Of David, a psalm: God said to my master [Abraham], 'Sit at My right hand, while I make your enemies your footstool'" (Psalms 110:1). And it says, "Who has aroused [Abraham] from the East, who would proclaim righteousness every step he took? Who has delivered up nations to him and subdued kings before him? The One Who made his sword like dust, his bow like wind-blown straw" (Isaiah 41:2).

THE MIRACLE OF NACHUM ISH GAMZU

Nachum Ish Gamzu had the habit that, whatever would happen to him, he would say, "This, too, is for the best" [*gam zu letovah*]. One day, the Jews wanted to send a gift to Caesar. They said: (109a) With whom should we send the gift? We will send it with Nachum Ish Gamzu because he often has miracles performed for him. When Nachum came to a certain inn, he wanted to stay overnight. "What do you have in that chest?" they asked him. Nachum replied, "I am carrying a gift to Caesar." The guests got up during the night, untied his chest, took all of its contents, and filled it with dirt. When he arrived at Caesar's palace, they opened the chest and found dirt. Caesar angrily shouted, "The

Jews are making fun of me!" They took Nachum out to be killed. Nachum said, "This, too, is for the best [*gam zu letovah*]." Elijah the prophet then came and appeared to the Romans [disguised] like one of them. Elijah said to the Romans, "Perhaps this dirt is from the dirt of our father Abraham, for Abraham would throw dirt at his enemies, and it would turn into swords; he would throw straw, and it would turn into arrows.

[The Romans] tested some of the dirt and found that it was so. There was a certain district that they had been unable to conquer. They threw some of that dirt at the defenders and conquered the district. After their victory they brought Nachum into their treasury and said to him, "Take whatever you want." Nachum filled his chest with gold, and they sent him off with great honor. On his return trip [he stopped at the inn where he had been robbed]. The guests asked him, "What did you bring to the Emperor's palace to be worthy of such honor?" Nachum replied, "Whatever I took from here, I brought there." So the guests took some dirt from their inn and brought it to Caesar. [The Romans tested it and found it to be worthless,] so they executed those people [for trying to dupe them].

THE TOWER OF BABEL

[The Mishnah said:] The generation of the Dispersion has no share in the World to Come. [The Gemara asks:] What did they do wrong? The scholars of the yeshivah of R. Shila said: They said: Let us build a tower, ascend to heaven, and chop an opening in it with axes, so that its water will flow, [and drain out, so that God could not bring another Flood (Etz Yosef)]. They laughed at this explanation in [the *yeshivot* in] Eretz Yisrael: If it is so, they should have built the tower on a mountain [rather than in a valley]![326] [The Gemara answers:] R. Yirmeyah b. Elazar said: They split up into three groups. One group said, "Let us ascend to the top and live there [where no enemy can attack us]." The second group said, "Let us ascend the tower and worship idols." The third group said, "Let us ascend and wage war [against God]." The group that said, "Let us ascend and live there," God dispersed around the world.[327] The group that said, "Let us ascend and wage war," became apes, spirits, demons, and devilish beings. And as for the group that said, "Let us ascend and worship idols," it says, "This was the place where God confused the world's languages" (Genesis 11:9), [to prevent them from forming a universal idolatrous creed (Rashi)].

We learned in a *Baraita*: R. Natan says: The entire generation of the Dispersion had idolatry in mind. For it says here, "They said, 'Come, let us build ourselves a city, and a tower whose top shall reach the sky, and let us make a name [*shem*] for ourselves" (ibid. v. 4). And it says elsewhere, "Do not pronounce the name [*shem*] of another deity" (Exodus 23:13). Just as over there the word *shem* refers to idolatry, so here too. R. Yonatan said: A third of the tower was burned; a third sank into the earth, and one-third is still standing.

THE EVIL OF SODOM

[The Mishnah said:] The people of Sodom have no share in the World to Come. The Rabbis taught: The people of Sodom have no share in the World to Come, as it says, "The people of Sodom were evil and sinful against God, exceedingly so" (Genesis 13:13). They were judged "evil" in this world, and "sinful" in the World to Come. Rav Yehudah said: They were "evil" with their bodies [i.e., promiscuous], and sinful in money matters. They were evil with their bodies, as it says, [Joseph turned down Potiphar's wife proposal to commit adultery, saying,] "How could I do such an evil thing? It would be a sin before God!" (ibid. 39:9), [thus "evil" denotes sexual immorality]. And they were sinful in money matters, as it says, [regarding the refusal to lend money,] "You will have a sin" (Deuteronomy 15:9).

[It says that the people of Sodom were evil and sinful] "against God" (Genesis 13:13)—this refers to blasphemy; "exceedingly so" implies that they sinned intentionally.

We learned in a *Baraita*: The Sodomites were "evil with their money and sinful with their bodies." Evil with their money, for it says, "You may then look unkindly at your impoverished brother" (Deuteronomy 15:9). And they were sinful with their bodies, as it says, [Joseph said,] "It would be a sin before God."

[It says that the Sodomites were evil and sinful] "against God"—this refers to blasphemy; "exceedingly so"—this refers to the Sodomites' shedding of blood, as it says, "Menasheh also shed innocent blood, exceedingly much" (2 Kings 21:16), [hence, when the term "exceedingly" is used regarding the Sodomites it refers also to bloodshed].

The Rabbis taught: The people of Sodom became arrogant only because of the affluence the Holy One, blessed be He, bestowed on them. What does Scripture say about [Sodom in its prosperity]? "There is a land where bread once grew; but its place was transformed resembling fire. It was a place whose stones were sapphires, and it had dust of gold; [it was situated on] a route not known to the buzzard, that the vulture's eye has not seen. Lions' whelps did not traverse it, and lions did not pass over it" (Job 28: 5–8). [The people of Sodom said:] Since Sodom is a land that produces bread, and its dust is gold, why should we tolerate wayfarers who come to us only to drain our wealth. Come let us do away with the practice of [allowing foreigners] to travel in our country. As it says, "A river bursts forth from its normal flow, [and was cast upon the town] that had been forgotten by the wayfarers. They were banished, consigned to [eternal] disgrace" (ibid. v. 4).

[How did the Sodomites discourage travelers from coming?] Rava expounded: What is meant by the verse, "How long will you plot treacherously against a man, will all of you murder with a leaning wall, with a toppled fence?" (Psalms 62:4). This teaches that the Sodomites would look with envy at wealthy wayfarers and would place a rich traveler next to a leaning wall and push the wall down on him, killing him. They would then come and take his money.

Rava expounded: What is meant by the verse, "In the dark they break into houses; by day they shut themselves in; they do not know the light" (Job 24:16)? This teaches that the Sodomites would look with envy at wealthy travelers and would deposit balsam [a fragrant herb] with each traveler for safekeeping, which the travelers would place in their treasure chest. In the evening the Sodomites, like dogs, would come and sniff out the location of the treasure chest. As it says, "They come each evening like growling dogs roaming the city" (Psalms 59:7). [The Sodomites] then would come and burrow there and take the valuables belonging to the traveler. "They let the naked spend the night unclothed, without a garment against the cold" (Job 24:7). "They carry off the donkey of orphans, they exact the ox of a widow as collateral" (ibid. v. 3). "They move boundary markers, they rob a flock and graze it for themselves" (ibid. v. 2). [As for the Sodomites' victim,] "He will be brought to the grave, and lies forever on a mound [of dirt]" (ibid. 21:32).

R. Yose expounded [the verse, "In the dark they break into the houses," at a public lecture in Sepphoris, [explaining how they sniffed out the balsam and found the treasure chests]. That night, three hundred homes were broken into in Sepphoris. The victims came to R. Yose and confronted him, saying, "You have shown the thieves a new method to operate!" R. Yose replied, "Did I know that thieves would come to my lecture?" [Incidentally,] when R. Yose died, the gutters of Sepphoris ran with blood [a metaphor indicating the intense grief the people of Sepphoris felt at R. Yose's passing (Ben Yehoyada)].

THE CROOKED LAWS OF SODOM

The Sodomites said: He who has one ox must graze all the oxen of Sodom for one day. He who has no oxen must graze them for two days. There once was a certain orphan, the son of a widow, [who had no oxen], so the Sodomites gave him oxen to graze. He went and killed the oxen and then said to the Sodomites, (109b) "He who had one ox, let him take one skin [from the dead oxen]. He who had no ox, let him take two skins." [The owners of the dead oxen] said to him, "What kind of absurd nonsense is this?" He said to them, "[I am only applying your policy:] The rule at the end [i.e., the distribution of the skins] should be like the rule at the beginning. Just as the rule at the beginning is that he who has one ox must graze the other oxen for

692

one day, whereas he who has no oxen must graze them for two days; so the rule at the end should be the same: He who had one ox should take one skin, whereas he who had no ox should take two skins!"

In Sodom, a person who crossed the river on the ferry had to pay one *zuz*, while a person who did not cross by ferry [but came a different way] had to pay two *zuz*. If someone had a row of bricks [for sale], every Sodomite would come by and take one brick. [When the owner demanded payment,] each Sodomite would say, "I took just one brick! [You cannot sue me for that.]" [Meanwhile he would lose all his bricks.] If someone spread out garlic or onions to dry, each Sodomite would come by and take one, saying, "I took just one; [so sue me]!"

There were four judges in Sodom: Shakrai, Shakrurai, Zaifai, and Matlei Dina.[328] If a person struck his neighbor's wife and, as a result, she miscarried, the judges would say to the husband: We rule that you should give your wife to the attacker, so that she may become pregnant by him, [and he thereby replaces the unborn child whose death he caused]. If a person cut off the ear of his neighbor's donkey, the judges would say to the owner: Give the donkey to him until the ear grows back. If a person wounded his neighbor, the judges would say to the injured party: Pay your attacker for bleeding you. [Bloodletting was considered to be a healthful and beneficial procedure.] In Sodom, a person that crossed the river on a ferry had to pay four *zuz*; but if he swam across the river, he had to pay eight *zuz*. Once a certain launderer came to Sodom. They said to him, "Pay us four *zuz*; the fare for the ferry." The launderer protested, "[But I did not use the ferry,] I swam across." "In that case," the Sodomites said, "you must pay us eight *zuz*, for you crossed in the water." The launderer refused to pay, so the Sodomites beat him and injured him. The launderer took them to court, but the judge ruled, "You have to pay them a fee for bleeding you and eight *zuz* for swimming across the river!"

ELIEZER IN SODOM

Eliezer, Abraham's servant, once happened to come to Sodom. They beat and injured him. When he took his assailants to court, the Sodomite judge told him, "Pay your attacker a fee, since he let blood for you." Angrily Eliezer took a stick and hit the judge, injuring him. The judge said, "What do you think you are doing?" Eliezer retorted, "The fee you owe me [for letting your blood] give to the man who attacked me [and let my blood]. And as far as my money is concerned, let it stay where it is!"

The Sodomites made a stipulation that anyone who invited a stranger to a wedding feast would be stripped of his garment. There once was a wedding in progress in Sodom, and Eliezer happened to come to Sodom on that day, and since he was a stranger they did not give

him any food. When he wanted to have dinner, Eliezer went [uninvited] to the wedding feast and took a seat at the end of a long table. They said to him, "Who invited you here?" He replied to the one sitting next to him, "You invited me!" The Sodomite said to himself, "[He is lying,] but perhaps the others will hear that I invited him and will strip me of my clothes." So he took his garment and ran outside. Eliezer did the same thing with all of the Sodomites, until they all left the wedding hall, and Eliezer then ate the whole meal himself.

The Sodomites had a certain bed on which they would invite a guest to sleep. When a guest was tall, [and his feet stuck out from the bed,] they cut off his legs. When a guest was short, the Sodomites would stretch him. Eliezer, Abraham's servant happened to come to Sodom. The Sodomites said to him, "Go ahead and sleep on this bed!" Replied Eliezer, "I have vowed since the day my mother died not to sleep in a bed."

Whenever a poor man happened to come to Sodom, each Sodomite would give him a *dinar* on which he had written his name [to be able to identify it later], but they would not sell him any bread. When the poor man starved to death, each Sodomite took back his coin.

There was a certain girl who would give some bread to a poor man [hiding it in a pitcher]. The Sodomites discovered it, and as a punishment they smeared her with honey and placed her on top of the city wall. [Drawn by the honey,] the bees came and killed her. And this is the meaning of the verse, "The outcry of Sodom and Gomorrah is great [*rabbah*]" (Genesis 18:20). Rav Yehudah said in the name of Rav: The Torah hints that Sodom was destroyed because of what they did to the girl [*rivah*].[329]

KORACH

The assembly of Korach has no share in the World to Come. For it says, "The earth then covered them over"—in this world, "and they were lost to the community"—in the World to Come (Numbers 16:33); so says R. Akiva. R. Eliezer says: Scripture says about them, "God deals death and gives life, casts down into the grave and raises up" (1 Samuel 2:6). R. Yehudah b. Beteira says: They are like a lost article that someone is looking for, as it says, "I have strayed like a lost sheep; search for your servant for I have not neglected your commandments" (Psalms 119:176).

[The Gemara expounds on the verse, "Korach son of Yitzhar son Kehat son of Levi took, together with Datan and Abiram, sons of Eliav, and On son of Pelet, the offspring of Reuben" (Numbers 16:1).]

"Korach took . . ." Resh Lakish commented: He took [i.e., bought] a bad deal for himself. He was called Korach, because he caused a bald spot [*korchah*] to be made in Israel, [when he and his followers were swallowed up by the earth]. "Son of Yitzhar" implies that he was a son who stirred up the world against himself with burning anger like the heat of noon [*tzaharayim*]. "Son of Kehat" implies that Korach was a son who disgraced [*hikhah*] his ancestors. "Son of Levi" implies that Korach went down to Gehinnom with his assembly escorting him [*levayah*]. [The Gemara asks:] Why does it not say also "son of Jacob," which would imply: a son who marched [*akav*] himself into Gehinnom?

[The Gemara answers:] R. Shmuel b. R. Yitzchak said: Jacob had pleaded [not to be mentioned among Korach's ancestors], as it says, [Jacob said on his deathbed,] "Let my soul not enter their plot; let my spirit not unite with their meeting" (Genesis 49:6). "Let my soul not enter their plot"—this refers to the Spies; "let my soul not enter their plot"—this refers to the assembly of Korach. "Datan" is one who transgressed the law [*dat*] of God. "Aviram" is one who adamantly [*ibeir*] refused to repent. "And On" refers to one who sat in mourning [*aninut*].[330] "Son of Pelet" implies that miracles [*pelaot*] were performed for On, [for he was saved from Korach's fate]. "Sons of Reuben" implies that On was a son who saw and understood[331] [that Korach's rebellion was wrong, and he withdrew from it].

A WISE WIFE AND A FOOLISH ONE

Rav said: On son of Pelet was saved by his wife. She said to him, "[Why are you joining Korach's rebellion?] What difference does it make to you? No matter who wins, Moses or Korach, either way, you will be only a disciple." On said to his wife, "What shall I do? I was in on their planning sessions and swore that I would join the rebellion, if called." She said [to herself], "I know that Korach's entire assembly are holy men, for it says, 'All the people in the community are holy, every one of them,' [and they would not come close to our tent if I uncovered my hair (Rashi)]" (Numbers 16:3). She said to On, "Stay here, and I will save you!" She then gave him wine to drink and put him to bed inside their tent. She then sat at the entrance of the tent (110a) and loosened her hair. Everyone [of Korach's assembly] who came to summon On and saw her sitting there with her hair uncovered turned around and left, [shocked at her immodest appearance]. In the meantime, the people in Korach's assembly were swallowed up by the earth, [and On was saved by his wife's resourcefulness].

On the other hand, Korach's wife said to him, "See what Moses has done! He himself is king, his brother he appointed High Priest, his brother's sons he has made deputies of the High Priest. If *terumah*[332] is offered, Moses said it should be given to the *kohen*. If the people offer *maaser*,[333] which is given to the Levites, Moses tells you, Levites, to give one tenth of it to the *kohen*.[334] And furthermore, Moses shaved off all your hair [at the inauguration ceremony][335] and made fun of you and treated you like dirt, for he was jealous of your hair."

Korach said to his wife, "But Moses also shaved his hair." She retorted, "Since all the glory belongs to him, it is as if Moses also said, [in the spirit of Samson's words,] 'Let me perish along with the Philistines' [Judges 16:30].[336] And besides, Moses told you, 'Include in your *tzitzit* a thread of blue wool' [Numbers 15:38]. Now, if you think that the thread of blue wool is considered a mitzvah, then take garments made entirely of blue wool and clothe all of your colleagues in the yeshivah." This is the meaning of the verse, "The wisest of women builds her house" (Proverbs 14:1)—this is a reference to the wife of On son of Pelet. "But the foolish one tears it down with her own hands" (ibid.)—this is a refence to Korach's wife.

THE REBELLION

"They had a confrontation with Moses along with two hundred and fifty men from the children of Israel"—they were the most distinguished men of the community who were "chosen for appointed times"—which implies that they knew how to intercalate the year and fix the months in the Jewish calendar.[337] "[They were] men of rank in the community"—they had a good name throughout the world (Numbers 16:2)

"[They demonstrated against Moses and Aaron and declared to them, 'You have gone too far!' . . .] When Moses heard this he threw himself on his face" (ibid. v. 4). [The Gemara asks:] What news did he hear? [The Gemara answers:] R. Shmuel b. Nachmani said in the name of R. Yochanan: He heard that he was suspected of adultery with a married woman, as it says, "There was envy of Moses in the camp" (Psalms 106:16). R. Shmuel b. Yitzchak said: This verse teaches that every husband warned his wife against secluding herself with Moses, for it says, "Moses took his tent and set it up outside the camp" (Exodus 33:7), [so as to avoid further suspicion (Rashi)].

"Moses took the initiative and went to Datan and Aviram" (Numbers 16:25). Resh Lakish said: From here we learn that a person should not be unyielding in a quarrel. [Although Moses had been slandered, he went to Datan and Aviram trying to end the controversy.] For Rav said: Whoever is implacable in a quarrel violates a Biblical prohibition, for it says, "He should not be like Korach and his party" (ibid. 17:5). R. Ashi said: Such a person deserves to be stricken with leprosy. For this verse concludes, "[Elazar did] as God said to him by the hand of Moses" (ibid.), and it says elsewhere [at the Burning Bush], "God said further to Moses, 'Bring your hand to your bosom;' . . . [and when he took it out, his hand was leprous like snow]" (Exodus 4:6); [thus "the hand of Moses" alludes to leprosy].

THE EVIL OF CHALLENGING TORAH AUTHORITIES

R. Yose said: Whoever challenges the sovereignty of the House of David deserves to be bitten by a snake.

For it says, "Adoniahu slaughtered sheep, cattle and fat oxen at the Stone of Zochelet" (1 Kings 1:9), [for a banquet at which he wanted to challenge David's monarchy and take power himself]. And it says elsewhere, ". . . with the venom of those that creep [zochalei] in the dust" (Deuteronomy 32:24), [zochalei, meaning a snake, is seen as cognate to Zochelet, the place where Adoniahu wanted to rebel against David].

R. Chisda said: Whoever challenges his Torah teacher is like one who challenges the Shechinah itself, for it says, "[Datan and Aviram . . . who led a revolution against Moses and Aaron] as part of Korach's rebellion against God" (Numbers 26:9). R. Chama b. R. Chanina said: Whoever quarrels with his teacher is as though he quarreled with the Shechinah, for it says, [when the Jews quarreled with Moses and Aaron about their lack of water], "These are the Waters of Dispute where the children of Israel quarreled with God" (ibid. 20:13), [thus their quarrel with Moses is considered a quarrel with God]. R. Chanina b. Papa said: Whoever finds fault with his teacher [for being too strict (Rashi)] is regarded as if he finds fault with the Shechinah. For it says, [when the Jews complained against Moses and Aaron about not having enough food, Moses said,] "Your complaints are not against us, but against God" (Exodus 16:8). R. Abahu said: Whoever thinks ill of his teacher is regarded as if he thinks ill of the Shechinah, for it says, "The people spoke against God and against Moses" (Numbers 21:5).

KORACH'S WEALTH

King Solomon says, "Here is a sickening evil I have observed under the sun: riches hoarded by their owner to his misfortune" (Ecclesiastes 5:12). Resh Lakish said: This refers to Korach's riches. [Datan and Aviram who were swallowed up by the earth along with their households, their tents,] "and all the yekum at their feet" (Deuteronomy 11:6). R. Elazar said: Yekum refers to a person's wealth, which puts him on his feet. R. Levi said: The keys to Korach's treasure house weighed as much as the load of three hundred white mules,[338] and all those keys and locks were made of leather [rather than metal, and still it took three hundred mules to carry them (Rashi)].

R. Chama b. R. Chanina said: Joseph concealed three treasures in Egypt: One treasure was revealed to Korach, one to Antoninus son of Severus,[339] and one is hidden away for the righteous [to be inherited by them] in the Messianic era.

THE FATE OF KORACH

R. Yochanan said: Korach was neither among those who were swallowed up by the earth nor among those who were burned.[340] Neither among those who were swallowed up, for it says, "[The earth opened its mouth and swallowed them and their households,] and all the

people who were with Korach" (Numbers 16:32), [implying,] but not Korach himself. And Korach was not among those who were burned, for it says, "when the fire annihilated the two hundred and fifty men" (ibid. 26:10), but not Korach himself.

We learned in a Baraita: Korach was among those who were swallowed by the earth, and among those who were burned. [First his soul was burned by a heavenly fire; then his body rolled to where the others stood and was swallowed by the earth (Rashi).] He was among those who were swallowed up, for it says, "The earth opened its mouth and swallowed them and Korach" (ibid. 26:10). And he was also among those who were burned, for it says, "Fire then came down from God, and it consumed the two hundred and fifty men," (ibid. 16:35), and Korach was one of them.

Rava said: What is the meaning of the verse, "Sun and moon stand still on high, as Your arrows fly in brightness" (Habakkuk 3:11)? This teaches that [when the rebels were swallowed up by the earth], the sun and the moon ascended to the heavenly stratum called zevul[341] and said to God, "Master of the universe! If You will render justice for Moses, son of Amram [by punishing Korach and his party] then we will go out and shine. But if not, we will not go out and shine. [They withheld their light,] until God shot arrows at them, saying to them, "For My honor you did not protest, [idolators worship you, disgracing Me, but you do not protest,] but for the honor of flesh and blood you do protest!" Since then [the sun and the moon, protesting against idolatry,] do not shine until they are struck by God's arrows.

Rava expounded: What is meant by the passage, "But if God creates something entirely new, making the earth open its mouth" (Numbers 16:30)? Moses said to the Holy One, blessed be He, "If Gehinnom has already been created, [so that Korach can be sent there,] fine. And if not, let God create it!" [The Gemara asks:] Why did Moses ask for this? If you say that he wanted God actually to create Gehinnom, [that cannot be,] for "there is nothing new under the sun!" (Ecclesiastes 1:9). Rather Moses prayed that the entrance to Gehinnom should be brought up [to the spot where Korach and his party were standing, and they should descend straight into Gehinnom].

THE FATE OF KORACH'S SONS

It says, "But the sons of Korach did not die" (Numbers 26:11). A Tanna taught: They said in the name of R. Yehudah Hanasi: A place was set up high for them in Gehinnom, and they sat on it and sang songs of praise to God. Rabbah b. Bar Chana said: I was once traveling on the road when a certain Arab said to me, "Come, let me show you where Korach and his party were swallowed up." The Arab went and pointed out two cracks in the ground giving out smoke. He took a piece of wool shearings, soaked it in water, stuck it on the point of his spear, and passed it over the cracks, and [the wet wool] was singed. The Arab said to me, "Listen to what you are about to hear." I heard that they were saying, "Moses and his Torah are true, and we are liars!" (110b) The Arab said to Rabbah b. Bar Chanah, "Every thirty days Gehinnom brings them back here, like meat in a pot, and they say, 'Moses and his Torah are true and we are liars!'"

THE GENERATION
OF THE WILDERNESS

[The Mishnah said: The Generation of the Wilderness has no share in the World to Come.] The Rabbis taught in a *Baraita*: For it says, "They will end their lives in this desert, and there they will die" (Numbers 14:35). "They will end their lives"—in this world; "and there they will die"—in the World to Come. And it also says, "Concerning them I swore in anger, they shall never come to My resting place [i.e., the World to Come]" (Psalms 95:11); this is what R. Akiva said. R. Eliezer said: They will enter the World to Come, for it says, "Bring My devout ones, who made a covenant with Me through sacrifice" (ibid. 50:5). Then how do I interpret the verse, "Concerning them I swore in anger, they shall never come to My resting place"? The verse means: In My anger I have sworn, but I take it back. R. Yehoshua b. Korcha said: The verse was said in reference to future generations [that came after the Generation of the Wilderness]. [Thus, the verse,] "Bring My devout ones" refers to the righteous ones of every generation; "who made a covenant with Me"—these are Chananiah, Mishael, and Azariah, who offered their lives to be cast into the fiery furnace; "through sacrifice"—these are R. Akiva and his colleagues who gave their lives to be slaughtered for the sake of the Torah.

R. Shimon b. Menasya said: The Generation of the Wilderness will enter the World to Come, for it says, "And those redeemed by God [i.e., the Generation of the Wilderness] will return, and come to Zion with glad song" (Isaiah 35:10). Rabbah b. Bar Chana said in the name of R. Yochanan: [By excluding the Generation of the Wilderness from access to the World to Come,] Rabbi Akiva has departed from his usual benign attitude, [for he could have expounded the following verse in their favor,] "Go proclaim to Jerusalem: Thus said God: I remember for your sake the kindness of your youth, your love as a bride, how you followed Me in the wilderness, in a land not sown" (Jeremiah 2:2). [R. Akiva could have expounded this verse:] If the people of Jerusalem will enter the World to Come through the merit of the Generation of the Wilderness, then surely [the Generation of the Wilderness itself] will enter the World to Come.

THE FATE OF
THE TEN TRIBES[342]

[The Mishnah says:] The Ten Tribes will not return to Eretz Yisrael, for it says, "[God] exiled them to another land, where they remain even today" (Deuteronomy 29:27)—just as the day goes by and does not return, so the Ten Tribes went and will not return; so says R. Akiva. R. Eliezer says: "even today" implies: Just as the day darkens and then becomes light again [in the morning], so too the Ten Tribes, for whom it is dark now, will one day have light.

[The Gemara comments:] Our Rabbis taught: The Ten Tribes have no share in the World to Come, for it says, "God drove them from their land with anger, rage, and great fury, and He exiled them to another land, where they remain even today." "God drove them from their land"—in this world; "and He exiled them to another land"—in the World to Come—so says Rabbi Akiva. R. Shimon b. Yehudah from the town of Acco says in the name of R. Shimon: If their deeds are like "today," [the day they were exiled, and they do not repent,] they will not return; but if not, [if they do repent,] then they will return [to Eretz Yisrael]. Rabbi says: The Ten Tribes *will* enter the World to Come, for it says, "And in that day, a great shofar will be sounded; and the strayed who are in the land of Assyria and the expelled who are in the land of Egypt will come and worship God in the holy mount, in Jerusalem" (Isaiah 27:13).

Rabbah b. Bar Chana said in the name of R. Yochanan: Rabbi Akiva departed from his usual benign attitude [when he excluded the Ten Tribes from access to the World to Come, for he could have expounded the following verse in their favor,] "Go, make this proclamation toward the north and say: 'Turn back, O rebel Israel'—declares God. 'I will not look on you in anger, for I am compassionate'—declares God; 'I do not bear a grudge forever.'" (Jeremiah 3:12). [R. Akiva could have cited this verse to show that the Ten Tribes *would* return.]

[The Gemara asks:] What was R. Akiva's "usual benign attitude"? It was referred to in a *Baraita*: The minor children of wicked Jews do not enter the World to Come, for it says, "For behold! That day is at hand, burning like an oven. All the arrogant and all the evildoers shall be straw, and the day that is coming—says God of Hosts—shall burn them to ashes and leave of them neither root nor branch" (Malachi 3:19). "Root" in this world, "nor branch" in the World to Come,[343] so says R. Gamliel. R. Akiva said: They *will* enter the world to come,[344] for it says, "God watches over *peta'im*" (Psalms 116:6), and *peta'im* means young children, for in the coastal cities they call a young child *patya*. And it also says, "Hew down the tree and destroy it, but leave the stump with its roots in the ground" (Daniel 4:20), [which R. Akiva interprets to mean that the innocent children of the wicked are not punished for the sins of their parents (Rashi)]; [two examples of R. Akiva's magnanimous outlook].

How then do I interpret, "leave of them neither root nor branch" [which seems to imply the opposite]? It means that God will reward the wicked in this world for any mitzvah—big or small—they fulfilled, [so that they lose their share in the World to Come]. A different interpretation: "root" refers to the soul; "nor branch" refers to the body, [but the children of the wicked merit a share in the World to Come]. But when it comes to the young children of wicked idolators, all agree that they will not enter the World to Come.[345] The Tanna of the *Baraita* derives this teaching from the verse, "You have put an end to all memory of them" (Isaiah 26:14).

DOES A BABY ENTER THE WORLD TO COME?

It was taught: How old must a Jewish child [that died in infancy] be to be eligible to enter the World to Come? R. Chiya and R. Shimon b. Rabbi debated this issue: One said: from birth [i.e., even if it dies at birth]; the other said: from the moment it speaks. The one who says from birth derives it from the verse, "They shall tell of His benificence to people yet to be born" (Psalms 22:32). And the one who says from the moment the child speaks derives it from the verse, "The speaking seed will serve God for generations to come" (ibid. v. 31).

It was taught: Ravina said: [A child is accepted in the World to Come] from conception, for it says, "The seed will serve Him." R. Nachman b. Yitzchak said: from its circumcision, for it says, "From my youth I have been afflicted and near death; I have borne Your dread which devolved upon me [i.e., circumcision]" (ibid. 88:16). A Tanna taught in the name of R. Meir: [A child is accepted in the World to Come] from the moment it says Amen, as it says, "Open the gates and let a righteous nation enter, [a nation] that keeps faith [*shomer emunim*]" (Isaiah 26:2). Do not read *shomer emunim*, "that keeps faith", but *she'omer amen*, "that says Amen." (111a) What does Amen mean? R. Chanina said: It means: God, faithful King.[346]

R. YOCHANAN'S SYMPATHETIC INTERPRETATIONS

It says, "Therefore Sheol[347] has opened wide its gullet and parted its jaws in a measureless gape [*livli chok*]" (Isaiah 5:14). Resh Lakish said: [Sheol parted its jaws] to devour a person who leaves undone even a single law [*chok*].[348] R. Yochanan said: God is not pleased that you say such things about the Jews. Instead, you should interpret the verse in a favorable sense: Even if a person learned no more than a single law [*chok*, he will be saved from Sheol].[349]

It says, "Throughout the land—declares God—two-thirds shall perish and die, and one-third of it shall survive" (Zechariah 13:8). Resh Lakish expounded: This means the third one of Shem's [third son, i.e., Arpachshad who was the ancestor of Abraham. Thus,

only one-third of Israel will survive, and two-thirds will perish (Rashi)]. R. Yochanan said to him: God is not pleased that you say such a thing [about the Jewish people]. Rather, the verse refers a third of all descendants of Noah, [so that all of Israel will survive].

It says, "For I shall be your master. I will take you, one from a city and two from a family, and bring you to Zion" (Jeremiah 3:14). Resh Lakish said: This is meant literally [i.e., only one Jew from a city and two from a family will be redeemed]. R. Yochanan said to him: God is not pleased that you say such a thing about the Jewish people. Rather, the meaning is that even one righteous person from a city will save the entire city, and even two righteous persons from a family will save the entire family.

R. Kahana was sitting in front of Rav and said: The phrase "one from a city and two from a family" is meant literally. Rav said to him: God is not pleased that you say such a thing. Rather, the meaning is that even one righteous person from a city will save the entire city, and even two righteous persons will save the entire family.

Rav noticed that Rav Kahana, [his student,] would groom his hair before coming to sit before him in the study hall. Rav [criticized him for wasting his time on primping,] saying, "You will not be found in the land of the living" (Job 28:13). R. Kahana said, "Are you cursing me?" Rav replied, "No, I am merely quoting a verse that means that the Torah is not found in a person who indulges in the good things of life while studying."

We learned in a *Baraita*: R. Simai said: It says, "I will take you to Myself as a people" (Exodus 6:7), and it says in the next verse, "I will bring you to the land" (ibid. v. 8). By placing the two verses side by side, the Torah compares the Israelites' exodus from Egypt to their coming to Eretz Yisrael. Just as only two out of six hundred thousand lived to come to Eretz Yisrael,[350] so at their exodus from Egypt only two out of every six hundred thousand [survived the Egyptian bondage].[351] Rava said: It will be the same in the Messianic time, [only 1/300,000 Jews will remain at that time (Rashi)]. For it says, "There [Israel] will be humbled as in the days of her youth, as in the days when she came up from Egypt" (Hosea 2:17) [i.e., Israel's numbers will be reduced in the same proportion that they were diminished at the Exodus].

MOSES QUESTIONS GOD'S WAYS

We learned in a *Baraita*: R. Elazar b. R. Yose said: I once visited Alexandria in Egypt and found an old man there who said to me, "Come, let me show you what my ancestors did to your ancestors: some of them they drowned in the sea, some they killed with the sword, and some they crushed [by immuring them in the walls of the] buildings."[352] [R. Yose continued:] And it was because Moses [complained about this] that he was punished, as it says, "Moses returned to God and said, 'O Lord, why do You mistreat Your people? Why did You send me? As soon as I came to Pharaoh to speak in Your name, he made things worse for these people. You have done nothing to help Your people" (Exodus 5:22,23). Thereupon, the Holy One, blessed be He, said to Moses, "Alas for those who are gone and no more to be found!" [i.e., I lament the loss of staunch believers like Abraham, Isaac, and Jacob. Unlike you, Moses, they never questioned My actions (Rashi)]. Many times I revealed Myself to Abraham, Isaac, and Jacob [promising them Eretz Yisrael] under the name *El Shaddai*, yet [although they did not see the fulfillment of these promises,] they never questioned My ways, nor did they ask Me, 'What is Your Name?' [as you did]. I said to Abraham, 'Rise, walk the land, through its length and breadth, for I will give it [all] to you" (Genesis 13:17).

Later on, he looked for a spot to bury his wife Sarah, and could not find one until he bought it for the exorbitant price of four hundred silver *shekels*, and still [although I had promised him this land] he did not question My ways. I said to Isaac, "Sojourn in this land. I will be with you and bless you, since it will be to you and your offspring that I will give all these lands" (ibid. 26:3). Later on, his servants were looking for water and could not find any until they quarreled with the local people, as it says, "The shepherds of Gerar quarreled with Isaac's shepherds, saying, 'The water is ours!'" (ibid. v. 20). Still, he did not question My ways. I said to Jacob, 'I will give to you and your descendants the land upon which you are lying" (ibid. 28:13).

Later on, he looked for a place to pitch his tent and could not find one until he bought it for one hundred *kesitahs* (ibid. 33:19). Still, he did not question My ways, nor did any of the Patriarchs say to Me, 'What is Your name?' On the other hand, right at the start [at the Burning Bush] you asked Me, 'What is your Name?' (Exodus 3:13). And now you are saying to Me, 'You have done nothing to save Your people.' 'Now You will see what I shall do to Pharaoh' (ibid. 6:1), [implying:] The war against Pharaoh [i.e., the Exodus] you will live to see; however you will not live to see the war against the thirty-one kings of Canaan [for you will die before the Jewish people enter Canaan]."

THE DIVINE ATTRIBUTE OF *SLOW TO ANGER*

It says, [after hearing the proclamation of the Thirteen Divine Attributes,] "Moses quickly bowed his head and prostrated himself" (Exodus 34:8). What did Moses see? [i.e., which Attribute so moved him as to make him quickly prostrate himself]? R. Chanina b. Gamla said: Moses saw the Attribute of *Slow to Anger* [and prostrated himself for joy]. And the Rabbis say: He saw the Attribute of *Truth*, [and he bowed because

he was terrified, since the Attribute of Truth demands strict, unmitigated punishment for every sin]. A *Baraita* has been taught that agrees with the one who says that it was the Attribute of *Slow to Anger* that Moses saw, namely: When Moses ascended to Heaven, he found the Holy One, blessed be He, sitting and writing the words *Slow to Anger* in the Torah. Moses said to God, "Master of the universe! Are You slow to anger only at the righteous?" God replied, "I am slow to anger even at the wicked." Moses said to God, "Let the wicked perish!" God said to Moses, "Now you will see that you will need [the Attribute of *Slow to Anger*]."

Later, when Israel sinned [in the episode of the Spies, and God threatened to destroy them, Moses pleaded that they be spared.][353] God said to Moses, "Did you not say to Me, 'You should be slow to anger at the righteous [but not at the wicked]'?" (111b) Moses responded, "Master of the universe! And did You not say to me that You are slow to anger, 'even at the wicked?'" And that is the meaning of the phrase, "Now, O God, is the time for You to exercise even more restraint, as You once declared, 'God is slow to anger, . . .'" (Numbers 14:17,18). [This proves that it was the Attribute of *Slow to Anger* that prompted Moses to prostrate himself with joy.]

R. Chagga once was walking up the steps of the yeshivah when he heard a child reciting the verse, "Your testimonies are indeed enduring; holiness befits Your house, O God, Who are [slow to anger] for many days" (Psalms 93:5).[354] Close to this verse is the psalm beginning with the words, "A prayer of Moses . . ." also said by Moses. R. Chagga said: This proves that it was the Attribute of *Slow to Anger* [that prompted Moses to prostrate himself].

THE WAYWARD CITY

[The Mishnah says:] The inhabitants of a wayward city have no share in the World to Come, as it says, "Lawless men have gone out from your midst and have been successful in leading the city's inhabitants astray" (Deuteronomy 13:14).

(112a) "Destroy [the wayward city] and everything in it" (ibid. v. 15). The Rabbis taught: The words "destroy it" mean to exclude the property of the righteous inhabitants that is outside the city. By contrast, when it says, "and everything in it," it means to include the property of the righteous that is in the city. R. Shimon said: Why did the Torah say that the property of the righteous that is in the city should be destroyed? Because, what caused them to live in that city? Their property! [They stayed there only because they did not want to abandon their property.] Therefore their property is destroyed.

(113a) "At that time Joshua pronounced his oath, saying, 'Cursed be the man before God who undertakes to build this city Jericho: he will lay its foundation at the cost of his firstborn son, and set up its gates at the cost of his youngest" (Joshua 6:26); [i.e., the person who rebuilds the city will lose all his sons]. We learned in a *Baraita*: One may neither build a city on the site of Jericho with the name of another city, nor another city elsewhere with the name of Jericho. As it says, "During [Ahab's] reign, Chiel from the city of Bethel built Jericho. He laid its foundation at the cost of Abiram his firstborn, and set its gates in place at the cost of Seguv his youngest" (1 Kings 16:34) [in fulfillment of Joshua's curse]. We are taught in a *Baraita*: From the death of Aviram, his firstborn son who was wicked, Chiel could not have learned not to build the city, but from the death of [the wicked][355] Seguv, his youngest, he certainly should have learned.

[The Gemara asks:] What did Aviram and Seguv do? [How do we know that they were wicked?] This is what the *Baraita* means to say: From the death of Aviram his firstborn, that wicked man [Chiel] could not have learned; but from the death of Seguv, the wicked [Chiel] should have learned.[356] Now, since it says, "He laid its foundation at the cost of Aviram his firstborn," I know that Seguv was his youngest [for the verse tells us that Joshua's curse was fulfilled]. Why then does it say, "Seguv his youngest"? This teaches that Chiel [had more than two sons,] and he buried them one after another, from Aviram to Seguv, [yet he did not stop rebuilding Jericho].

THE GREAT DROUGHT IN AHAB'S DAYS

Ahab was Chiel's close friend. Ahab and Elijah came to pay a condolence call on Chiel [who was mourning the death of his sons]. Ahab sat and said, "Perhaps the reason [for their deaths] is that when Joshua pronounced his curse [on the person who would rebuild Jericho,] he prohibited: Neither Jericho by another name, nor another city by the name of Jericho." Elijah answered Ahab, "Yes." Ahab said to Elijah, "Now, if even the curse pronounced by Moses has not been fulfilled, for it says, 'Be careful that your heart not be tempted to go astray and worship other gods, bowing down to them. God's anger will then be directed against you, and He will lock up the skies so that there will not be any rain' [Deuteronomy 11:16,17], and although I [Ahab] have set up idols on every single furrow in Israel [i.e., every high place] it has rained so heavily that the downpour prevented me from bowing down to those idols—do you expect me to believe that the curse by Joshua, Moses' student, has been fulfilled?"

Thereupon, "Elijah the Tishbite, a resident of Gilead, told Ahab, 'As the Lord lives, the God of Israel Whom I serve, there will be no dew or rain except by my bidding'" (1 Kings 17:1). Elijah then implored God, and he was given the key to rain [i.e., control over rainfall], after which he got up and left.

"God's word came to [Elijah], saying, 'Leave this place; turn eastward and go into hiding by the brook Kerit, which is east of the Jordan.' The ravens brought him bread and meat every morning, and he drank from the brook'" (ibid. v. 2,6). From where did the ravens get the bread and meat? Rav Yehudah said in the name of Rav: From Ahab's kitchens. "After some time the brook dried up, because there was no rain in the land" (ibid. v. 7). When God saw that there was suffering in the world [because of the drought], it says, "The word of God came to [Elijah], saying, 'Go at once to Tzarfat and stay there; I have designated a widow to feed you.'" (ibid. v. 8). And it says, "After a while, the son of the mistress of the house fell sick" (ibid. v 17).

[When the boy died, Elijah] begged God that He give him the key of resurrection [to enable him to revive the child]. God said to Elijah, "Three keys have not been entrusted to an agent: The key of childbirth, the key of rain, and the key of resurrection. [The key of rain I already gave you, and now you are asking for the key of resurrection, too.] People will say: Two keys are in the hands of the student, and only one is in the hands of the Master! Bring back the key of rain, and take in its place the key of resurrection." [Elijah brought the child back to life, but he gave up the key of rain. As a result, God put an end to the drought,] as it says, "The word of God came to Elijah: "Go, appear before Ahab; then I will send rain upon the earth" (1 Kings 18:1).

A certain Galilean expounded before R. Chisda: Elijah may be compared to a man who locked his gate and then lost his key. [So, too, Elijah; he had the key of rain, locked up the rain, and caused a drought, but he could not unlock it.] R. Yose expounded in Sepphoris: Father Elijah (113b) was a quick-tempered man; [he overreacted to Ahab's blasphemy by bringing on the dreadful drought (Rashi)]. Now, Elijah used to visit R. Yose every day in the *bet midrash*, but [after R. Yose made this disparaging remark about him] he stayed away for three days and did not come to him. When he came, R. Yose said to him, "Why did you not come these last three days?" Elijah replied, "You [insulted me,] calling me a quick-tempered man!" R. Yose retorted, "You showed that you have a bad temper [by staying away for three days for such a trivial reason]."

[The Mishnah said:] It says [concerning the wayward city], "Let nothing that has been banned remain in your hand, [so that God will reverse any display of anger" (Deuteronomy 13:18). As long as the wicked are in the world, God's anger is in the world. [The Gemara asks:] Who are the wicked to whom the Mishnah refers? [The Gemara answers:] R. Yosef said: Thieves.

Our Rabbis taught: When a wicked person enters the world, Divine anger comes to the world, as it says, "Comes the wicked man, comes derision, and with the rogue, contempt" (Proverbs 18:3). When a wicked person perishes from the world [i.e., when he dies], good fortune comes to the world, as it says, "When the wicked perish there are shouts of joy" (Proverbs 11:10). When a righteous person departs from the world, misfortune comes to the world, for it says, "The righteous man perishes, and no one takes it to heart. Pious men are taken away, and no one understands that because of evil [times] the righteous is taken away" (Isaiah 57:1), [to spare him the suffering that is about to come upon the world (Rashi)]. When a righteous person comes into the world, good fortune comes to the world, as it says, "He named him Noah, saying, 'This one will bring us relief from from our work and the anguish of our hands'" (Genesis 5:29).

NOTES

1. *Pesachim* 66a.

2. The part of the dough that goes to the *kohen*; see Numbers 15:20–21.

3. Aaron's nephew, the son of Miriam.

4. An animal that has a lesion or wound that would eventually kill it.

5. The Rabbi used to give his lecture concisely and in a low voice, and the interpreter would repeat it aloud and explain it to the audience.

6. What do the two have in common? Common idolatry, the worship of statues, is easily identifiable. But a tree that is being worshipped, outwardly looks as appealing as any other tree, while in reality it is an object of idolatry. The same holds true for an unworthy judge. To all appearances he seems to be a respectable individual, but internally he is corrupt and leads people astray (Rabbi Chaim Soloveitchik).

7. Since he was an elderly scholar and unable to walk quickly, he was carried, so as not to keep the audience waiting (Rashi).

8. The ceremony of taking off the shoe of the brother of a husband who has died childless, thereby freeing his widow to remarry (Deuteronomy 25:5–9).

9. Deuteronomy 25:3.

10. This is done in order to bring the lunar year into harmony with the solar year.

11. He was called "the Little" because of his great humility.

12. A woman is taken in marriage by money, by marriage contract, or by intercourse (*Kiddushin* 2a).

13. On *Shabbat* it is forbidden to walk a greater distance than two thousand cubits from the edge of town. The *Shabbat* boundary marks the outline of this periphery.

14. Originally the firstborns were assigned to perform the service in the Sanctuary. Then God chose the Levites to replace the firstborns because they did not take part in the worship of the golden calf. Each Levite thus redeemed a firstborn. When a count of the Levites and firstborns was taken, it was found that there were 22,273 firstborns and 22,000 Levites. The 273 firstborns who were in surplus of the available

Levites were to be redeemed at the rate of five shekels per person.

15. Exodus 16:11–13.

16. One who performs the bloodletting procedure; phlebotomy.

17. Jannai was a scion of the non-Davidic Hasmonean dynasty.

18. A man is not allowed to marry two sisters; see Leviticus 18:18. However, if his wife has died, he is allowed to marry her sister.

19. Numbers 13:30.

20. Exodus 2:10.

21. Genesis 26:4.

22. A marginal note in the Gemara notes that in our *Tanach* text this version is not found; however, the Gemara had this variant reading.

23. 1 Samuel 22:18.

24. 1 Samuel 8:11–17.

25. This refers to the episode where Ashmedai, king of the demons, removed Solomon from power, as told in *Gittin* 68a (Rashi).

26. Deuteronomy 21:10–13.

27. There were many Jews present, and all knew the Aramaic script. Now if the writing on the wall had been written in Aramaic script, they could have read it. Yet only Daniel was able to decipher it, which proves that the angel wrote the message not in the Aramaic but in the *Ashurit* script, which was unknown to the Jews at that time, except for Daniel. And since the angel used the superior *Ashurit* script, the Jews adopted it as the script to be used in writing Torah scrolls (Etz Yosef).

28. 1 Kings 1:4,5.

29. Another name for Babylonia (see Genesis 10:10).

30. See Genesis 11:9.

31. The Sabbatical year; see Leviticus 25:1–7.

32. To intercalate means adding an extra month (Adar) in order to bring the lunar year into harmony with the solar year.

33. *Sanhedrin* 18b.

34. See 2 Kings, Chapters 18, 19.

35. Compare Exodus 7:23.

36. About one-third of seventy-one. The *Sanhedrin* is compared to mixed wine, which is one-third wine and two-thirds water.

37. See *Bava Metzia* 85a.

38. This was not part of the warning to the witnesses.

39. A common formula for an oath.

40. Assir Shealtiel was one person.

41. Vayikra Rabbah, 19, *parashat* Metzora.

42. 10 + 10 + 50 = 70.

43. 60 + 6 + 4 = 70.

44. The numeric value of *venoshantem* ["you will have been long in the land"] is 852. If you subtract two years, there are 850 years left, which is the length of time between Israel's entry into Eretz Yisrael in

1273 B.C.E. Because if these two years, the prophecy of *venoshantem* was not fulfilled and, as a consequence, the prophecy of "you will be destroyed" (ibid. v. 26) will not be fulfilled either.

45. The verse is in the feminine, because the subject is God's wisdom [*chochmah*], which in Hebrew has the feminine gender.

46. The people who built the Tower of Babel (Genesis 11:1–8).

47. *Niglu* is in the plural.

48. The Hebrew *kerovim* is plural.

49. Two complex *mesechtot*, dealing with the laws of impurity resulting from *tzora'at* (leprosy) and contact with a corpse. Only after you are proficient in the intricacies of these laws are you ready to study the profound themes of *aggadah*.

50. Metatron is from a root that means guide or guardian; [the Aramaic *natar* means "to guard"] (Aruch).

51. The numeric value of Metatron (314) is the same as that of Shaddai, "the Almighty" (Rashi on Exodus 23:21).

52. The plain meaning is, "do not rebel against him."

53. The censor deleted *keisar*, "Emperor," and replaced it with *kofer*, "heretic" (*Maharsha*).

54. A hard, applelike, yellowish fruit, of the rose family.

55. A priest of the Zoroastrian religion, a religion founded in ancient Persia by Zoroaster. He preached an ethical dualism of opposing forces of Truth and Lie that permeate the entire universe.

56. Ahura Mazda, the deity of light in Zoroastroanism.

57. The spirit of darkness and evil; the antagonist of Ahura Mazda in Zoroastroanism.

58. Leviticus 25:3, 23.

59. Numbers 18:8–20.

60. Deuteronomy 34:6.

61. Leviticus 22:4–6.

62. The verse actually refers to purging vessels that were captured from the Midianites from any taint of forbidden food. R. Abbahu merely said this to pacify the foolish heretic.

63. Compare Isaiah 6:3.

64. Compare Genesis 22:12.

65. The prophet Obadiah, the fourth of the twelve Later Prophets, is the Obadiah who lived in the time of Ahab.

66. Genesis 25:30.

67. For example, like Eglon, King of Moab, who rose respectfully when Ehud told him that he had a message from God (Judges 3:20).

68. For example, like Mesha, King of Moab, who brought his son as a sacrifice to an idol.

69. Genesis 12:14.

70. Sanctification of the Moon.

71. Isaiah 46:3.

72. *Chavilot* is seen here as related to *tachbulot*.

73. After the fall of Jericho, Joshua declared all its valuable objects consecrated to God. However, Achan took some of the forbidden articles, which angered God. At the subsequent battle for the city of Ai, the Israelites were routed. (See Joshua 6:19; 7:1–5).

74. In the war with the Canaanite King of Arad (Numbers 21:1) and in other wars that are not mentioned (Rashi).

75. Although only Achan sinned, all Israel is held responsible, because all Israel is like one body (Malbim).

76. Deuteronomy 3:23.

77. Numbers 25:8.

78. Mount Gerizim and Mount Ebal where the stones were erected are sixty *mils* west of the Jordan (*Sotah* 36a).

79. *Shalom* is one of God's names (*Shabbat* 10b).

80. The *tamid* is the daily continual burnt-offering that was brought day in and day out, one in the morning and one in the afternoon (Numbers 28:1–8).

81. He immediately undertook not to repeat this mistake. The present verse relates that at the second siege of the city of Ai, he spent the night studying Torah (Rashi).

82. Abraham and Sarah lived in the land of Canaan among the Amorites and Hittites. Ezekiel blames Israel's misdeeds on the nefarious influence of these nations (Malbim).

83. Genesis 12:8.

84. In 1 Chronicles 2:6 he is called Dara.

85. Joshua 7:24.

86. Numbers 25:14.

87. He sees Achan as related to *achna*, a kind of snake that forms a circle, connecting its tail to its head (Rashi).

88. The entire incident is cited in Jerusalem Talmud *Chagigah* 2:2.

89. The latter two methods are harsher and are applied for violators of graver sins.

90. The Binding of Isaac.

91. It was the custom to burn the bier and the personal belongings of the king (Rashi).

92. Mentioned in 1 Kings 13:1.

93. 1 Kings 17:22.

94. 2 Kings 4.

95. 2 Kings 5.

96. This is derived from Joshua 1:18.

97. 2 Samuel 3:29.

98. 2 Kings 22:1.

99. See 2 Samuel 3:27.

100. Asahel was killed by Abner; see Samuel 2:23.

101. 1 Samuel 2:19.

102. If a person was chasing someone to kill him, and he could have saved himself by maiming a limb of the pursuer, but killed him instead, he is put to death (*Sanhedrin* 74a).

103. 2 Samuel 17:25; 20:10. Joab was seized with jealous hatred for having been replaced by Amasa and planned to settle the score.

104. Beautiful woman captive; see Deuteronomy 21:10–14.

105. *Bor*, "well," refers to the pitcher of water that was standing beside the head of the sleeping Saul. David could have killed his pursuer Saul, but spared his life (1 Samuel 24:12ff). The *sirah*, "thorn," refers to the time when David could have killed Saul who was asleep in a cave, but was content to cut off the corner of his robe (ibid. v. 4). Abner could have brought about a reconciliation between Saul and David by pointing out David's magnanimous character in sparing Saul's life. Instead, Abner fanned Saul's hatred of David, saying that one of Saul's servants had removed the pitcher, and the robe was torn by a thorn bush (Rashi).

106. E.g., Deuteronomy 21:19.

107. A *yevamah* [a brother's childless widow] must marry the brother, or perform *chalitzah* to be released from this obligation. In the *chalitzah* ceremony the widow takes off the brother's shoe. Joab asked Abner how a one-armed woman would loosen the shoe. When Abner bent down to show how she loosens it with her teeth, Joab stabbed and killed him. David alluded to this when he said, "[Joab] shed blood of war in peacetime, and placed the blood of war . . . on his shoes that are on his feet" (1 Kings 2:5).

108. 2 Samuel 20:10.

109. Leviticus 10:1,2.

110. In the Torah, the word "saying" implies the transmission of a commandment from one generation to the next. This is possible only if children find fathers and mothers who hand the laws to them. Therefore, "saying" implies family life that blossoms in sexual purity, free of adultery (R. Samson Raphael Hirsch).

111. Literally: "flesh whose blood is in its soul."

112. Attributed to Abraham. It contains the proper arrangement of the letters of the Divine name by means of which creation can be achieved.

113. He had in mind the lighting of the candles and the cooking of the food, which are forbidden on *Shabbat* and punishable by death (Rashi).

114. See *Bava Metzia* 59b.

115. *Tirosh*, seen as a contraction of *tehi rosh*, means "you will become the head"; *tirash* means "you will become poor."

116. If a woman is intimate with her husband during the final trimester of pregnancy, it is very beneficial to the child (*Niddah* 38a).

117. The father and the mother must have *one* voice; both must treat him with the same seriousness; both must stand over him in equal authority and share the same ideals and wishes. Only then can they say to themselves that it is not their fault if their son is a failure (R. Samson Raphael Hirsch).

118. The weight of half a *maneh*.

119. "Mountains" is a metaphor for ancestors; see Micah 6:2.

120. See *Sefer Chasidim*, Chapter 369.

121. *Kal vachomer* is a logical, *a fortiori* inference; by a stronger reason, all the more.

122. Jonah 1:1–3.

123. The Torah forbids the eating of worms and insects (Leviticus 11:42).

124. Jonah 3:4.

125. 1 Kings 20:35.

126. The Binding of Isaac on the altar.

127. Abraham considered the entire feast as a sacrifice designed to spread the knowledge of God as the Creator of the universe (Ksav Sofer).

128. The dialogue between Satan and Abraham is couched in verses taken from the Book of Job whose plain meaning is only remotely connected to the subject at hand. Nevertheless, the Sages wanted to make their point in the language of a section of Scripture, as they often do (Maharsha, Iyun Yaakov).

129. According to Maharsha's commentary.

130. *Apikoros* generally denotes a person who denies the existence of God and the truth of the Torah and its beliefs.

131. 1 Kings 21:21–25.

132. 2 Kings 21.

133. Numbers, Chapters 22–24.

134. 1 Samuel 22:9–22.

135. 2 Samuel 17.

136. 2 Kings 5:20.

137. *Terumah* is the first portion of the crop separated and given to a *kohen*. Aaron died in the Wilderness in the fortieth year after the Exodus. The mitzvah to give *terumah* and tithes went into effect only after the Jews entered Eretz Yisrael.

138. A *chaver* is a person who undertook to be stringent in the observance of the laws of *tumah* and *taharah* [ritual cleanness]. The opposite of a *chaver* is an *am haaretz*, someone who is careless in the observance of ritual cleanness.

139. An *am haaretz* is an unlearned, ignorant person; specifically a person who is negligent about observing the laws of *tumah* and *taharah*, Levitical purity and defilement, and the laws of tithing.

140. The plain meaning of the verse is: "You are soon to lie with your fathers, thereupon rise up will the people and go astray."

141. Ezekiel 37:1–14.

142. In the Samaritan Torah scrolls the words "to them," from which R. Gamliel inferred resurrection, are deleted.

143. *Ketubot* 111b.

144. Genesis 2:7.

145. The Rambam in his Commentary on the Mishnah (*Chullin* 126b–127a) confirms the existence of such a creature.

146. An aquatic creature whose blood is used to

produce *techeilet*, the blue dye for the thread in the *tzitzit* fringe (see Numbers 15:38).

147. The Girgashites, descendants of Canaan son of Ham (see Genesis 10:15), and whose rule extended to North Africa.

148. Ishmael was Abraham's oldest son, and Keturah was the wife Abraham took after Sarah's death (Genesis 16:15 and 25:1).

149. The Roman emperor Marcus Aurelius, who became a close friend of Rebbi [R. Yehudah Hanasi].

150. The Holy of Holies, which contained the Holy Ark, was on the west side of the *Bet Hamikdash*, opposite the Western Wall.

151. When the sun sinks beneath the horizon in the west, it seems to be bowing respectfully to the *Shechinah*.

152. If the sun were to set at noon, the change from daylight to darkness would be abrupt. Workers would not know when to stop working, and wayfarers would not have time to look for lodging (Rashi).

153. The order of the segments of the verse has been reversed.

154. According to Shmuel, the Messianic era is not accompanied by changes in the nature of the cosmos.

155. The plain meaning of the phrase is, "Then Moses and the children of Israel were inspired to sing this song," but the use of the future tense indicates that at the resurrection of the dead they will again sing a song.

156. The passage means, "Solomon built a high place. . . . He did not actually worship idols, but since he did not prevent his wives from doing so, it is counted as if he did it himself.

157. Because God created heaven and earth for the sake of the people of Israel, which is destined to inherit the Torah (Rashi).

158. *Nashku*, related to *yishak*, as in "my people will be nourished [*yishak*] by your orders" (Genesis 41:40).

159. A person who works during the day should at least study Torah at night; otherwise the fire of Gehinnom will consume his house (*Maharsha*).

160. R. Elazar has in mind a person who himself is not a Torah scholar and does not study Torah. By supporting Torah scholars he shares in their learning, and the Torah gives life and blessing to those who learn it and to those who support it (*Maharsha*).

161. Gad and Menni are names of pagan deities or the planets Jupiter and Mercury.

162. If the signs of leprosy appear on the walls of a house, the *kohen* examines the walls. If he determines that it is a malignant leprous disease, he orders the house to be demolished (Leviticus 14:33ff). The Mishnah teaches, however, that in a darkened house where the *kohen* cannot properly examine the diseased area, he may disregard it, and there is no need to open the wall to allow light to come in.

163. The world will last six thousand years and will lie desolate for one thousand years. If the righteous who were resurrected in the Messianic era are not buried at the end of the six thousand years, where will they be during the thousand years the world will lie desolate? (Rashi).

164. See Ezekiel 37:1–10. Just as they died again, so will the righteous whom God will resurrect also return to dust.

165. At the Covenant between the Parts (Genesis 15:13) God told Abraham that his descendants would be enslaved for four hundred years (Genesis 15:13). The Ephraimites counted the four hundred years from the Covenant, while in reality, the years of bondage began at the birth of Isaac, thirty years later. As a result of their error, they escaped thirty years before the end of the bondage, and were killed by the people of Gath.

166. The phrase "all around" occurring in both verses establishes the connection between them.

167. Nebuchadnezzer had fashioned some of those bones into cups. When the dead were about to be resurrected, Nebuchadnezzar was trying to drink from one of those bone cups, whereupon the cup struck him on the mouth (Rashi).

168. Chananiah, Mishael, and Azariah.

169. Daniel, Chapter 3.

170. God was hoping that all Israel would refuse to bow down to Nebuchadnezzar's idol.

171. A metaphor for Babylonia, which was known for its many swamps and rivers.

172. They are not mentioned again in Scripture (Rashi).

173. Metaphorically, they died from the pain of watching their fellow Jews being reproached (*Maharsha*).

174. Nebuchadnezzar treated Daniel as an idol.

175. Just as a firebrand is scorched, so were his clothes scorched (Rashi).

176. The reason Joshua gave to Nebuchadnezzar was just an excuse (Rashi).

177. A *kohen*.

178. A *kohen* may not marry an immoral or a divorced woman; see Leviticus 21:7.

179. Also referred to as Bar Kochba, the leader of the revolt against Rome, after the destruction of the second *Bet Hamikdash*.

180. Although our editions of *Tanach* have a Book of Nehemiah, in Talmudic times the Book of Nehemiah was incorporated in the Book of Ezra, and did not appear as a separate book.

181. Every person is assigned an angel that represents him in heaven.

182. The verses beginning with "*Shema Yisrael*" (Deuteronomy 6:4), which are recited as part of the morning and evening prayers.

183. The letter *mem* has two forms. In the middle of a word it is written as an open *mem*; at the end of a word, as a final *mem*, closed on all sides. The *mem* in *lemarbeh* is an exception in that it is written as a final *mem* in the middle of a word.

184. The coming of *Mashiach* will be preceded by a frightful war in which the forces of Gog, the king of Magog, will try to destroy Eretz Yisrael. However, God will wipe out the attacking army, after which *Mashiach* will appear. (See Ezekiel, Chapters 38–39, and Zechariah, Chapter 14.)

185. A question may be asked: But Israel *did* sing a song of praise when they crossed the Red Sea?—The Israelites praised God for their *own* redemption, whereas Jethro was the first to express joy and gratitude to God for a miracle that had occurred to a nation to which he did not belong (Tiferet Shlomoh).

186. Although a convert, Jethro was distressed hearing of the downfall of the Egyptians.

187. Each pair of words counts as two names, for a total of eight names.

188. 2 Kings 15:29.

189. 2 Chronicles 28:20.

190. 2 Kings 17:3.

191. Ibid. 15:19.

192. Isaiah 20:1.

193. Ezra 4:10.

194. Ibid.

195. Ibid.

196. Sancheriv promised the people of Jerusalem that if they surrendered they would not be killed but exiled to "a land that is like your land." He did not boast that the new land would be *better* than Eretz Yisrael.

197. *Trei* is Aramaic for "two" or "double."

198. Leviticus 10:2.

199. He sent his servant Ravshakeh to deliver his scornful message (Isaiah 36:13–20).

200. Opponents of the righteous Hezekiah preferred the wicked Pekach son of Remaliah, ruler of the Northern Kingdom of Israel, and his ally Rezin, king of Aram.

201. See Exodus 14–15 and Joshua 3:16.

202. Before attacking the Kingdom of Judah, the Assyrians had conquered the Ten Tribes of the Northern Kingdom and taken their possessions, which were now part of the spoils.

203. When Saul ordered the massacre of the *kohanim* of the town of Nob (1 Samuel, chapters 21–22), God ordained that the punishment for the massacre should be carried out within a set period. The day Sancheriv wanted to launch his attack on Jerusalem was the last day of that term, and it happened to be the day before Pesach.

204. Orpah was Goliath's mother, thus Yishbi-benob was a brother of Goliath.

205. For reporting to Saul that the *kohanim* had helped David.

206. 1 Samuel 31:6.

207. In the present Syria.

208. Gabriel is in charge of ripening the fruits (Rashi).

209. Mentioned in the first chapter of Ezekiel.

210. The fourth person, the angel Gabriel, who was in the fiery furnace together with Chananiah, Mishael, and Azariah.

211. Sancheriv worked to obtain the scissors, grinding palm kernels, which is usually done in a mill alongside the river. Thus he "hired" the scissors, by doing work "by the side of the river" as predicted in the verse (Isaiah 7:20) (Rashi).

212. This allegory is interpreted to mean that God made Sancheriv a laughingstock. The loss of his hair represents the loss of honor; the destruction of his beard stands for the loss of his kingdom (Maharal).

213. Literally translated the verse reads "*Lailah* announced" as if *lailah* were a living being. This *lailah*, according to R. Yochanan, was the angel that helped Abraham.

214. The main blood vessels in the neck.

215. For example: The illustrious Shemaya and Avtalyon descended from Sancheriv, and the descendants of Haman taught Torah in B'nei B'rak (Rashi).

216. The Gemara will explain this further on.

217. Achaz was Hezekiah's father.

218. The lesson to be learned by scholars who are children of ignorant people is that just as Nebuchadnezzar's success was due to a very small good deed, their parents, too, may have performed a small mitzvah for which they merited to have learned children.

219. See 2 Kings 5:1–19.

220. A gentile who has accepted upon himself to refrain from idol worship.

221. See Judges, Chapters 4 and 5.

222. Two illustrious Sages, mentioned in *Avot* 1:10.

223. The allegory means that God redeemed Israel from Egypt in the merit of the *tzaddikim* who are characterized as *kesef* [silver].

224. A dog always walks ahead of its master, but the master is the one who leads. At a crossroads, the dog looks back to receive direction from the master. In the pre-Messianic times, the leaders will appear to be leading, while in fact, they follow the trend of the masses (R. Elchanan Wasserman).

225. *Kushta* is the Aramaic word for "truth."

226. See footnote 224.

227. The verse refers to *tzaraat*, a leprous disease. A white blotch on the skin is a sign of impurity; but if a person's entire skin has turned white, he is declared pure. So, too, when heresy has swept the whole world, the time for the redemption has come (Rashi).

228. In the year 2000 of Creation, Abraham, at fifty-two years of age, began to spread the belief in God and the fundamental ideas of the Torah (Rashi).

229. The two thousand years from Abraham's fifty-second year until 172 years after the destruction of the second *Bet Hamikdash*. Of course, the Torah did not cease at that point; however, after the death of R. Yehudah Hanasi in 3990, as a result of the dispersion

230. According to the Vilna Gaon: thirty-one.

231. See Ezekiel, Chapters 38 and 39.

232. The source of the Jordan.

233. When the ox recovers, the master finds it difficult to remove the horse. Likewise, when the Jewish people fell into sin, their land was taken over by idolatrous nations. When the Jewish people repent and *Mashiach* comes, it will be difficult for God to eject the idolatrous nations and restore the Jews to their former greatness (Rashi).

234. Fictitious names, like "Tom, Dick, and Harry."

235. The Rebbis found allusions in Scripture that *Mashiach*'s name is similar to their own.

236. The Messianic era lays the groundwork for the Resurrection of the Dead.

237. Generation (singular) denotes one generation; generations (plural) denotes two generations.

238. The verse mentions "day" and "year," which means that for each day in the year the Jews will enjoy a year of redemption in the Messianic era (Rashi).

239. The rejoicing of a bridegroom is seven days, and God's day is a thousand years (see Psalms 90:4).

240. Meaning, as long as the world has already existed. Since they had not been so long in their land, it will be completed in the Messianic era (Rashi).

241. Just as God swore not to bring another flood, so too, He swears that there will be a time—the Messianic era—when He will never be angry with his people.

242. The Gemara will explain this term below.

243. A tradition that similar words in different contexts are meant to clarify one another.

244. Menasheh considered these verses irrelevant.

245. If I do not punish you, you would think that I sanction your behavior.

246. An animal or bird with a defect that will cause its death.

247. Both R. Yitzchak and R. Chisda interpret the word *literufah* as a contraction of *lehatir peh*, "to open the mouth."

248. *Yud* = 10; *shin* = 300.

249. The Apocrypha are books that were not accepted in the Bible, which was closed by the men of the Great Assembly.

250. A heretical sect whose members adhered to the Written Torah but rejected the Oral Torah.

251. The Book of Ben Sira, a collection of proverbs, is one of the books of the Apocrypha.

252. *Bava Batra* 16b.

253. They did not plead for mercy with God but offered unassailable arguments (Rashi).

254. Menasheh cleverly appealed to God only after praying to all the pagan deities. He suggested to God: If You don't save me, You will appear to be as powerless as all the idols I appealed to (Rashi, found only in Ein Yaakov).

255. Jeroboam led the Ten Tribes in their secession from the House of David. This caused civil war.

256. Explained below.

257. Michah lived in the era of the Judges. He built a private idolatrous shrine in his house (Judges 17).

258. Sheva ben Bichri led an unsuccessful revolt against King David (2 Samuel 20).

259. The Midrash says that Pharaoh had the Jewish babies entombed in the bricks of the buildings. When Moses complained to God, He was told that these babies were destined to grow up to become sinners. As proof, Moses was allowed to save a baby that had already been entombed in a brick. The baby grew up to be Michah, the idol worshipper.

260. When the Jews in the Wilderness complained that they were thirsty, Moses gathered the people before a certain rock and addressed them, saying, "Listen now, you rebels." Because of this he was not allowed to enter Eretz Yisrael; see Numbers 20:1–13.

261. When Solomon married Pharaoh's daughter he built a palace for her in the Millo, a large square.

262. 1 Kings 11:29–39.

263. Jehu did not do away with the worship of the two golden calves.

264. In his attempt to wipe out the worship of Baal, Jehu persuaded the Baal worshippers to assemble in the temple of Baal in order to kill them all in one fell swoop. He tricked them by saying, "Ahab served Baal little, Jehu will serve him much!" These words, though spoken as a ruse, somehow had to come true.

265. Literally: "They went deeper."

266. The destruction of Jerusalem, which occurred twenty-four generations after the golden calf, was the last punishment for that sin.

267. This shows that it was difficult to lure Ahab to the place where he was destined to be killed, and that must have been because his good deeds balanced his bad deeds (Rashi).

268. Navot owned a vineyard that Ahab wanted to buy. When Navot refused to sell, Jezebel framed him and had him put to death. See 1 Kings, Chapter 21.

269. Jehu, who rooted out all idol worship, killed Achaziahu, king of Judea, who was a grandson of Ahab.

270. The text actually reads *vayei'ateir*. Since the letters *chet* and *ayin*—being guttural letters—interchange, *vayei'ateir* is expounded as if it would read *vayechateir*.

271. This allegory means that by rights Menasheh's sins were too serious for his repentance to be accepted. But God, in His infinite mercy, sneaked Menasheh into Heaven by a "back door."

272. In an attempt to duplicate the Throne of God, which has four faces (*Maharsha*).

273. When Moses wanted to raise Joseph's coffin from the Nile, he wrote the Divine Name on a plate that he cast into the Nile, whereupon the coffin emerged.

Michah stole the plate and subsequently used it to make the golden calf (*Sotah* 13a). He later fashioned an idol and established a shrine to it in his house (Judges 17).

274. In Judges 19 we are told that a concubine was violated by a group of Benjaminites in the town of Givah. When the tribe of Benjamin refused to punish the wrongdoers, the other tribes took revenge against Benjamin, which led to a bloody civil war in which thousands were killed.

275. You allowed the idolatrous shrine of Michah to operate.

276. See 103b.

277. Fleeing from Saul, David asked Achimelech, the head priest of Nob, for food, which he was given. Doeg who witnessed this, reported it to Saul, who ordered the massacre of the priests of Nob. As a punishment for this cruel act, Saul and his two sons were killed in battle. Had Jonathan given bread to David, these tragedies would have been averted.

278. Because "one sin leads to another sin" (*Avot* 4:2).

279. The idol worshippers were the envoys Merodach-baladan of Babylon sent to Hezekiah to wish him well on his recovery (2 Kings 20:12).

280. 2 Kings 20:17ff.

281. *Bet nechot* means treasure house. He put his wife—his treasure—on view instead of confining her to her quarters, in keeping with the dictates of modesty (*Maharsha*).

282. When the Assyrians exiled the tribes of Zebulun and Naphtali, the people were not overly alarmed, but when Sancheriv would return and uproot the remaining tribes in the northern kingdom, the distress would be felt much more intensely. The land is called the region of the nations, because so many nations desired it.

283. *Kuvlana* is derived from the Aramaic *kaval*, "toward." When relating his misfortune to [*toward*] others, the speaker should add, "My misfortune should never happen to you."

284. In Sodom there was no protracted suffering; the city was destroyed in one fell swoop. By contrast, in Jerusalem the famine was so severe that mothers insanely stooped to eating their children. This additional suffering offset Jerusalem's greater sinfulness, so that it was not completely laid waste (Rashi).

285. The verses of Lamentations are arranged in the order of the *alef-bet*. But in this chapter, and also in chapters 3 and 4, the verse beginning with the letter *pei* (which means mouth) precedes the verse beginning with the *ayin* (which means eye).

286. Geichazi behaved deplorably when the Aramean general Naaman was healed of his leprosy by Elisha, who told him to bathe seven times in the Jordan. (See 2 Kings, Chapter 5.)

287. Rav interprets the passage as a dialogue.

288. 2 Samuel 3:18 and Jeremiah 43:10.

289. Samson was a member of the tribe of Dan.

290. The double *pei* in *shefifon* [*slithering*] alludes to his double lameness (Rashi).

291. Such as fame or honor.

292. Numbers 23:12,14,29,30.

293. Tents are symbolic of synagogues and *yeshivot*.

294. A metaphor for the Sanhedrin, which counted among its members Jethro's descendants.

295. Numbers 31:8.

296. Moses' father-in-law was Jethro.

297. He advised Moab and Midian to have their daughters seduce the Israelites. As a result of their sin, twenty-four thousand Jews died in a plague (Numbers 25:9).

298. Doeg was a great Talmudic scholar, who informed Saul that the priests of Nob had given aid to David, whereupon Saul ordered all the priests put to death for treason. Doeg himself carried out the massacre. For his sins Doeg was denied a share in the World to Come. (See 1 Samuel, chapters 21–22.)

299. He knew three hundred reasons why the upper stroke of the *lamed* should be tilted slightly to the left. Rashi offers this and three other interpretations of this phrase.

300. Like Doeg, Achitophel was an enemy of David who lost his share in the World to Come.

301. I.e., who studied Torah under me, for Torah is compared to bread (Rashi).

302. He had marital relations with his wife during the day instead of at night, so that he should be free of desire during the day (Rashi).

303. The reference is to the male organ. The more he indulges it, the stronger its craving; the less he indulges it, the weaker its craving (Rashi).

304. Satan in the guise of a bird (Rashi).

305. If David had subdued his impulse, he would have passed a test that God had considered him incapable of passing. Thus he would have gotten the better of God.

306. The rib [Adam's rib] alludes to Bathsheba.

307. When a person is humiliated he turns pale since his blood drains from his face.

308. The Gemara in *Shabbat* 56a explains that in David's time, a soldier going out to war gave his wife a conditional *get*, which retroactively would go into effect when the soldier did not return from battle. Since Uriah was killed in the war, Bathsheba was divorced when David met her, so that David did not commit adultery.

309. Genesis 11:29.

310. Hyssop is used in the purification of a *metzora*, a person afflicted with a leprous disease.

311. Elisha's disciple and servant.

312. There is no such verse in Scripture. However, 2 Kings 8:7 states, "Elisha came to Damascus." This is indeed the version in the Ein Yaakov.

313. Naaman, the general of Aram, suffered from leprosy and was healed miraculously by Elisha. He wanted to reward Elisha, but Elisha refused to accept it. After Naaman left, Geichazi ran after him and claimed that Elisha had changed his mind and wanted to accept the gift. Naaman gave Geichazi the gift, which he kept. When Elisha perceived Geichazi's deceit, he cursed him with leprosy.

314. The fourteenth chapter of tractate *Shabbat*.

315. You should not suppress your sexual desire completely, because then you will have no offspring; rather, you should use it in moderation.

316. 2 Kings 23:24.

317. The purpose of frailty in old age was to warn the children of a person's impending death and allow them to travel from their respective homes to be at his bedside (Rashi).

318. The Tanna reads it as one sentence: "I regret that I created them and Noah. And Noah found favor . . ." Noah did not sin, but he was judged according to the majority of his contemporaries who were corrupt (*Maharsha*).

319. Noah built the Ark for one hundred and twenty years during which he exhorted the people to repent.

320. These are species of the cedar family. *Gopher* is commonly translated as cypress.

321. The raven is an unclean bird (Leviticus 11:15).

322. In the ark the dove was fed adequately by Noah, but it preferred the bitter olive leaf that came from God.

323. A small bird or a chameleon.

324. A bird described as *chol*, "phoenix," in Job 29:18.

325. In the war Abraham fought against the four mighty kings (see Genesis, Chapter 14).

326. See Genesis 11:2.

327. See Genesis 11:9.

328. The names mean: Liar, Shocking Liar, Forger, and Perverter of Justice.

329. *Rabbah* can be read as *rivah*.

330. On mourned [i.e., regretted] his participation in the rebellion and was saved.

331. Reuben is seen as a contraction of *reu* "he saw," and *heivin*, "he understood."

332. A portion of the crop given to the *kohen*.

333. The first tithe of the crop, which is given to a Levite.

334. A Levite must give one tenth of the *maaser* he receives to a *kohen* (Numbers 18:26–29).

335. Numbers 8:5–22.

336. Moses was willing to suffer the indignity of being shaven, as long as he could inflict this embarrassment on all the Levites.

337. They knew when to add a month to the year, making it a leap year.

338. This should not be taken literally. The number 300 is often used to indicate a large quantity.

339. The Roman emperor Antoninus, the close friend of R. Yehudah Hanasi.

340. See Numbers 16:32.

341. There are seven heavens. The sun and the moon were in a lower heaven called *rakia* and ascended to the higher heaven called *zevul*.

342. The Ten Tribes of Israel were taken into exile in Assyria (2 Kings 17:6).

343. "Roots" and "branches" are symbolic of children (Rashi).

344. This is an example of R. Akiva's kind attitude.

345. But righteous gentiles and their children have a share in the World to Come (Rashi).

346. The word Amen is formed by the initial letters of the three words *El melech ne'eman*, "God faithful king" (Rashi).

347. Sheol is one of the names of Gehinnom.

348. *Chok* means also "law."

349. He perishes if he did not keep a single law.

350. Only Joshua and Caleb survived of the 600,000 that left Egypt. All the others died in the wilderness as punishment for giving credence to the report of the Spies.

351. Thus the 600,000 that left Egypt were only 1/300,000 of the total Jewish population in Egypt. The others died during the plague of darkness.

352. He may have shown him an ancient chronicle in which these atrocities were recorded (*Maharsha*).

353. Numbers 14:18.

354. Translation according to Rashi.

355. According to Ein Yaakov.

356. Rashi in Ein Yaakov.

‹♦ MAKKOT ♦›

REPAYMENT OF AN
UNSPECIFIC LOAN

(3b) Shmuel said to R. Mattena: Don't settle down in your seat before you explain to me the source for the following ruling of our Rabbis: If someone lends money to his neighbor without specifying the date [for repayment], he is not allowed to demand repayment for at least thirty days, no matter whether the loan was made verbally or against a promissory note. R. Mattena answered: It says, "Be very careful that you do not have an irresponsible idea and say to yourself, 'The seventh year is approaching, and it will be a year of remission [when all debts are cancelled,] you may then look unkindly at your impoverished brother [and not lend him any money]" (Deuteronomy 15:9). Is it not obvious that "the seventh year" is the same as "a year of remission"? [Why does the Torah repeat itself?] It wants to teach us that there is another, similar kind of remission: namely, when a person lends his neighbor some money without specifying the date [for repayment], he may not demand repayment from him for at least thirty days. [Why thirty days?] Because it has been taught [in an unrelated context][1] that thirty days [at the beginning] of a year count as a whole year.

ZOMEMIM, THE
"PLOTTING WITNESSES"

(5b) [The Mishnah says:] It says: "The accused shall be put to death only through the testimony of two or three witnesses" (Deuteronomy 17:6). If the testimony of two witnesses is sufficient to establish the fact, why does the Torah specify three? It is to compare the testimony of two to that of three. Just as three can discredit two as *zomemim*[2] [since they outnumber them] so two can discredit three. And how do we know that two or three can incriminate even a hundred as *zomemim*? Because the verse says, "[two or three] *witnesses*" [indicating that "two or three" are considered the first in a series that may comprise even a hundred]. R. Shimon says [it says "two or three witnesses"] to tell you that just as two are not put to death unless both are proved *zomemim*, so three are not put to death

until all three are proved *zomemim*. R. Akiva said: The third witness is mentioned, not in order to make his punishment more lenient, but in order to deal stringently with him and to make his sentence the same as these. [Meaning: you should not think, since the testimony of two witnesses is sufficient, the evidence of the third is superfluous, and therefore, he should not be punished at all, but you should know that all *zomemim* witnesses form one inseparable unit and must suffer the same punishment (Rashi).] Now, if the Torah punished a person who joined the transgressors as one of the transgressors [i.e., the third *zomem* receives the same punishment as the other two], how much more will it reward the person who joins those who perform the mitzvah the same as those who perform the mitzvah!

A HARMFUL TRIBUNAL?

[The Mishnah says:] A Sanhedrin that condemns a person to death once in seven years is branded a destroyer, [because they should have sought ways of exonerating the defendant]. R. Eliezer b. Azariah said: Once in seventy years. R. Tarfon and R. Akiva said: Had we been on a Sanhedrin, no one would ever have been put to death. Thereupon R. Shimon b. Gamliel remarked: With that attitude they would have increased [the number of] murderers in Israel! [They would eliminate criminals' fear of retribution, so that there would be no deterrent to murder].

THE CITIES OF REFUGE

(9b) Our Rabbis taught: Moses designated three cities on the east bank of the Jordan, and corresponding to them Joshua set aside [three cities] in the land of Canaan, and they were opposite each other like two rows of vines in a vineyard: Hebron in Judah,[3] corresponding to Betzer in the wilderness;[4] Shechem in Mount Ephraim,[5] corresponding to Ramot in Gilead;[6] and Kedesh in Mount Naphtali, corresponding to Golan in Bashan.[7] It says, "Divide the territory of your land into three parts" (Deuteronomy 19:3), which means that the distance from the southern border [of Eretz Yisrael] to Hebron was similar to the distance from Hebron to Shechem; the distance from Hebron to Shechem was similar to that from Shechem to Kedesh; and the distance from Shechem to Kedesh was similar to that from Kedesh to the northern border. [The Gemara asks:] How is it that three cities were needed on the east bank of the Jordan, [for the territory of two tribes] and only three for all of Eretz Yisrael, [for the other ten tribes]? Abaye said: Because in Gilead [which is on the east bank of the Jordan] murder was rampant. (10a) For it says, "Gilead is a city of evildoers, tracked up [akuvah] with blood" (Hosea 6:8). What is meant by akuvah? R. Eliezer explained: It indicates that they tracked down [ekev] their victims to kill them.

Why are [Hebron and Kedesh] situated far from the border [so that an accidental killer at the border would have to run a great distance to reach the nearest refuge city], and the other cities closer to each other? [So that an accidental murderer between Hebron and Shechem and between Shechem and Kedesh could find a refuge city nearby on either side?] Abaye said: Because Shechem was full of murderers, [and therefore a refuge city had to be close by], as it says, "The gangs awaiting a man [to rob] are like a band of priests; they murder on the road to Shechem" (Hosea 6:9). What is meant by the analogy of "like a band of priests"? R. Eliezer said: They formed gangs to commit murder like priests who go in groups to the barns when the terumah[8] is being distributed.

[The Gemara asks:] But were there no more [than six cities of refuge]? Doesn't it say, "Besides the six cities you shall provide an additional forty-two cities" (Numbers 35:6)? Said Abaye: The main six cities afforded asylum in any case, [whether the accidental murderer was aware that it was a city of refuge or not,] whereas the additional cities afforded asylum only if he was aware that it was a city of refuge. [The Gemara asks:] Was Hebron really a city of refuge? Doesn't it say, "They granted Hebron to Caleb as Moses had said"? Abbaye said: Caleb was given only the suburbs of Hebron, as it says, "But the fields of the city and its villages they gave to Caleb son of Yefuneh as his possession" (Joshua 21:12).

TORAH STUDY
AFFORDS PROTECTION

A Tanna taught: If a disciple goes into exile [to a city of refuge], his master is sent into exile along with him, for it says, "[The accidental murderer] would be able to escape to one of these cities and live" (Deuteronomy 4:42), which means that you should provide him with whatever he needs to live, [and Torah study under his master is essential to his spiritual survival]. R. Ze'ira said: From this we infer that a person should not teach the Mishnah to a student who is unworthy, [for even-

tually he will wind up having to go into exile, and his master then must go with him]. R. Yochanan said: If a master goes into exile [to a city of refuge], then the whole yeshivah must go into exile with him. [The Gemara challenges this:] That cannot be correct, for surely R. Yochanan said: From where do we know that the study of Torah provides protection [from evil and wrongdoing]? From the verse, "[Then Moses set aside three cities of refuge . . .] Bezer in the wilderness . . . Ramot . . . and Golan," which is followed by, "This is the Torah that Moses placed before the children of Israel" (Deuteronomy 4:41–45), [meaning, just as the cities of refuge offer protection, so does Torah study. Therefore, a Torah scholar will never have reason to go into exile].

[The Gemara answers:] This contradiction is not difficult to explain: Torah study affords protection only while a scholar is engaged in it, otherwise it does not. Or, if you prefer, you could say that Torah study affords protection from the Angel of Death [but not from having to go into exile], as happened to R. Chisda who was studying Torah and reviewing his studies in the yeshivah. The Angel of Death could not come close to him because he did not stop studying. As a last resort, the Angel of Death sat down atop a cedar in the yard of the yeshivah, and the cedar cracked under him. Startled by the noise, R. Chisda stopped briefly, which gave the Angel of Death the opportunity to overpower him.

MOSES CHERISHED
THE MITZVOT

R. Tanchum b. Chanilai noted: Why was the tribe of Reuben named first in the designation of the cities of refuge, [namely, "the city of Betzer for Reuben"]?[9] Because Reuben was the first one to speak out in rescuing [Joseph from being killed by his brothers], as it says, "Reuben heard these words and tried to rescue Joseph [from his brothers]. 'Let's not kill him,' he said" (Genesis 37:21).

R. Simlai expounded: What is the meaning of the verse, "Moses then set aside three cities on the bank of the Jordan, toward the rising sun" (Deuteronomy 4:41). It means that the Holy One, blessed be He, said to Moses: Make the sun rise for [accidental] murderers. Some say [he expounded like this:] The Holy One, blessed be He, said to Moses, [praising him for designating the cities of refuge]: You made the sun rise for [accidental] murderers.

R. Simlai expounded: What is the meaning of the verse, "A lover of money never has his fill of money, and a lover of a multitude has his fill of wheat" (Ecclesiastes 5:9). "A lover of money never has his fill of money" refers to Moses, our teacher [who loved doing mitzvot as other people love money]. Moses knew that the three cities on the east bank of the Jordan would not assume the status of cities of refuge until the three cities on the other side of the Jordan were designated after his death. Nevertheless, [his love of the *mitzvot* was so great that he wished to fulfill as many as he possibly could]. He said: Since the mitzvah [of designating the three cities of refuge] has come into my reach, I want to fulfill it now [even though the cities were as yet ineffective]!

[Expounding the second part of the passage, R. Simlai said,] "And a lover of a multitude has his fill of wheat" means: Who is fit to teach a multitude of students? He who is filled with the "wheat of Torah" [i.e., he has mastered Scripture, Mishnah, *halachah*, and *aggadah* (Rashi)]. This is similar to the interpretation R. Elazar gave of the verse, "Who can express the mighty acts of God, who can make all of His praise heard?" (Psalms 106:2). This means: Who is fit to proclaim the mighty acts of God? Only a person who is able to make *all* of His praise be heard. But the Rabbis—and some say Rabbah b. Mari—interpreted this passage as follows: He who loves to teach a multitude of students reaps the wheat [of Torah; meaning, he benefits from the stimulating questions the students ask]. Thereupon the eyes of the scholars focused on Rava the son of Rabbah [whom they considered to be a prime example of this quality].

LEARNING TORAH WITH STUDY PARTNERS

R. Ashi said it meant that whoever loves to study among a multitude of fellow students benefits [from the give-and-take of his colleagues]. This is in line with what R. Yose b. Chanina said: What is the meaning of the verse, "A sword against *habaddim*, let them be shown to be fools [*venoalu*]" (Jeremiah 50:36)? It means: May a sword fall upon the necks of Torah scholars who sit by themselves and study separately [*bad b'bad*]; and that's not all, but if they study by themselves they will become fools, [because when they reach faulty conclusions there is no one to set them straight]. For it says here *venoalu*, and elsewhere it says *noalnu*, "for we have been foolish, and we have sinned" (Numbers 12:11) [which proves that *venoalu* means "they will become fools"]. But not only that, but [by studying by themselves] they also commit a sin, for the verse ends, "and we have sinned" (ibid.). Ravina explained the above verse like this: Whoever loves to teach a multitude of students will acquire the grain [of Torah]. This is consistent with what Rabbi said: I learned a great deal from my teachers, I learned more from my colleagues, but from my disciples I learned the most.

TORAH STUDY SURPASSES TEMPLE SERVICE

R. Yehoshua b. Levi said: What is the meaning of the passage, "Our feet stood inside your gates, O Jerusalem" (Psalms 122:2)? It means: How were we able to withstand our enemies in war? Because within the gates of Jerusalem the scholars were engaged in Torah study. R. Yehoshua b. Levi said furthermore: What is the meaning of the verse, "A song of ascents, by David. I rejoiced when they said to me, 'Let us go to the House of God'" (ibid. v. 1)? David said to the Holy One, blessed be He: Master of the universe! I have heard people say, "When will this old man [i.e., David] die, and let his son Solomon come and build us the *Bet Hamikdash* so that we will go up there on the three Pilgrimage Festivals?" And I [David] was happy to hear that. Replied the Holy One, blessed be He, "One day in your courtyards is better than a thousand elsewhere" (ibid. 84:11). The implication is: [God said:] I would rather have one day in which you are studying Torah than a thousand sacrifices that your son Solomon will someday offer to Me on the altar.

THE UNINTENTIONAL MURDERER

We learned in a *Baraita*: R. Eliezer b. Yaakov said: (10b) The word *Miklat* [Refuge] was inscribed on road signs that were posted at every crossroads so that the murderer would know which way to turn [to get to the city of refuge]. Said R. Kahana: What is the Scriptural source for this? It says, "Prepare the way [to the cities of refuge]" (Deuteronomy 19:3). R. Chama b. Chanina introduced his lecture on this subject with the following quotation, "Good and upright is God, therefore He guides sinners on the way" (Psalms 25:8). Now, if He guides sinners [by providing road signs to guide them to the cities of refuge], how much more so the righteous!

R. Shimon b. Lakish opened his discourse on the subject of accidental murderers with the following two verses [to show how Divine justice operates], "If he did not plan to kill his victim, but God caused it to happen, then I will provide a place where the [killer] can find refuge" (Exodus 21:13), and, "As the ancient proverb says, 'Wickedness issues from the wicked'" (1 Samuel 24:13,14). What case does this passage apply to? To two persons, both of whom had committed murder; one accidentally [so that he has to flee to a city of refuge], the other killed intentionally [for which he should receive the death penalty]. There were no witnesses to either of the slayings, [so that both killers escaped punishment]. The Holy One, blessed be He, causes them to meet at the same inn; the one who had killed intentionally [and should receive the death penalty] sits under the stepladder, and the one who had killed accidentally [and should be banished to a city of refuge] comes down the stepladder, falls, and kills [the one under the ladder, and two witnesses saw the incident]. Thus the one who had killed intentionally is slain, [as he should be], and the one who killed by accident is banished to a city of refuge [as he should be].

EIN YAAKOV

Rabbah b. R. Huna said in the name of R. Huna, some say, in the name of R. Elazar: From the Torah, the Prophets, and the Writings it can be derived that [Heaven] guides a person along the way he wants to follow. From the Torah, as it says, "God said to Balaam, 'Do not go with them'" (Numbers 22:12), and then it says, "If the men have come to summon you, set out and go with them" (ibid. v. 20) [Thus once Balaam decided to resist God's will, God steered him on the path he had chosen.] It can be derived from the Prophets, for it says, "I am the Lord your God, Who instructs you for your benefit, Who guides you in the way you choose to go" (Isaiah 48:17). From the Writings, for it says, "If one is drawn to the scoffers, he will [be allowed to] scoff, and if he is drawn to the humble he will find favor" (Proverbs 3:34).

THE MOTHERS OF THE *KOHEN GADOL*

(11a) [It says, "The [accidental] killer is required to live [in the city of refuge] until the High Priest dies. After the High Priest dies, the killer may return to his hereditary land" (Numbers 35:28). [The Mishnah says:] Therefore, the mothers of High Priests used to supply food and clothing [for the exiled murderers in the cities of refuge] so that they would not pray for their sons to die. [The Gemara comments:] What if they would pray, do you think the High Priest would die? Doesn't it say, "As a sparrow must flit and a swallow fly, so an unwarranted curse comes back to the one who utters it" (Proverbs 26:2), [thus a baseless curse is ineffective]?

A certain elderly scholar said: I heard an explanation at a lecture by Rava, that the High Priests [were not without blame, since] they should have prayed for mercy that no accident should happen during their tenure, but they did not; [thus the curse is not baseless]. According to others, the Mishnah reads: [The mothers provided food and clothing] so that the exiled murderers would pray that their sons should *not* die, [and the stream of gifts of food and clothing should continue to flow].

[The Gemara asks:] Does [the High Priest's life] depend on the exiled murderers' prayer? And if they did not pray [for him, do you think] he would die? What could the High Priest have done [to prevent the accidental murder]? As the Babylonian saying goes: Tuviah sinned and Ziggud was punished [an innocent person is punished for someone else's crime].[10] In Eretz Yisrael they put the saying this way: Shechem married Dinah, and Mavgai got the knife.[11] A respected elderly scholar: I heard at a lecture by Rava [that the High Priests were not without blame, for] they should have prayed for mercy that no accident should happen to their generation, but they did not. This is similar to the case of the person who was devoured by a lion some three *parsangs* from the town of R. Yehoshua b.

Levi, and because of that Elijah did not appear to him for three days, [because he failed to pray to avert a mishap like this].

THE CURSE OF A TORAH SCHOLAR

Rav Yehudah said in the name of Rav: A curse of a Torah scholar, even if it was uttered without cause, is fulfilled. From where do we know this? From what happened to Achitofel. [This is what transpired:] When David was digging out the foundations of the *Bet Hamikdash*, the water of the Deep came surging up threatening to flood the world. David asked, "Is there anyone who knows whether it is permitted to write the Divine Name on a shard and cast it into the Deep, so that the water will remain in its place?" [He was concerned that this would cause the Divine Name to be erased, which is forbidden.] When no one answered, David called out, "Whoever knows anything about this and does not tell, may he be suffocated." Hearing this, Achitofel reasoned: If for the sake of restoring peace between husband and wife the Torah said: Let My Name which was written in holiness be erased in water,[12] then surely the Divine Name may be erased to save the whole world from being inundated." "It is permitted," Achitofel exclaimed.

David then wrote the Divine Name on a shard and dropped it into the Deep. Immediately, the water subsided and stayed in its underground domain. Nevertheless it says, "When Achitofel saw that his advice [concerning Absalom's rebellion] had not been followed, he saddled his donkey and went home to his native town. He set his affairs in order, and then he hanged himself" (2 Samuel 17:23). [Thus, David's curse, although unwarranted, was fulfilled.]

R. Abbahu said: The curse of a Torah scholar, even if it was made on condition, is fulfilled. From where do we know this? From [the conditional curse made by] Eli. Eli said to Samuel, "What did He say to you? Keep nothing from me. May unspoken punishments befall you if you do not tell me. Samuel then told him everything, withholding nothing from him" (1 Samuel 3:17). Nevertheless, it says, "But [Samuel's] sons did not follow in his ways" (ibid. 8:3), [Thus Eli's curse, although conditional, was fulfilled.]

(11b) Rav Yehudah said in the name of Rav: If a Torah scholar places someone under a ban, [even a conditional ban], he requires absolution. From where do we know this? From the case of Judah. [For the continuation of this discourse, see *Sotah* 7b.]

THE ERRORS OF JOAB AND ROME'S GUARDIAN ANGEL

(12a) Rav Yehudah said in the name of Rav: Joab made two mistakes at that hour,[13] as it says, "He fled to the tent of God and grabbed the corners of the altar" (1

712

Kings 2:28). His first mistake was that he thought that the corners of the altar provide asylum, whereas in reality only the top of the altar does that; his second mistake was that he thought the altar in Shiloh affords asylum when he grabbed its horns, whereas in reality only the permanent *Bet Hamikdash* does that. Abaye said: He also made a mistake in not realizing that the altar provides sanctuary only to a *kohen* while engaged in the service of the *Bet Hamikdash*, but Joab was not a *kohen*.

Resh Lakish said: In time to come [when God will render His final reckoning with Rome and destroy it], the Guardian Angel of Edom [i.e., Rome] will make three mistakes, as it says, "Who is coming from Edom, with sullied garments from Botzrah?" (Isaiah 63:1). His first mistake will be that he will try to find asylum in Botzrah, while in reality only Betzer provides asylum. His second mistake will be in not realizing that asylum is given only to man, but not to an angel. His third mistake will be not knowing that only accidental murderers receive sanctuary, but he killed intentionally.

THE GREATNESS OF TORAH SCHOLARS

(22b) Rava said: How silly are the people who stand up out of respect for a *sefer Torah* but do not stand up before a great Torah scholar. [That a Torah scholar ranks higher than a *sefer Torah* can be seen in the fact] that the Torah mandates that [a person who is to be flogged] receives forty lashes, but the Rabbis come and [by interpreting the text] reduce it by one [to make it thirty-nine lashes].[14]

THE STRAP USED FOR FLOGGING

(23a) R. Sheshet said in the name of R. Elazar b. Azariah: From where do we derive that the strap [used for flogging] must be made of calf leather? It says, "Forty lashes shall he strike him" (Deuteronomy 25:3), and the next verse reads, "Do not muzzle an ox when it is treading grain."

[The Gemara now cites two unrelated teachings of R. Sheshet in the name of R. Elazar b. Azariah:] R. Sheshet said furthermore in the name of R. Elazar: To disregard the Chol Hamoed [the intermediate days of Pesach and Sukkot, by going to work on them] is the same as worshipping idols, because it says, "Do not make any cast metal idols" (Exodus 34:17), and the next verse says, "Keep the Festival of Matzahs" [and the other Yamim Tovim].

R. Sheshet also said in the name of R. Elazar b. Azariah: Anyone that tells or listens to malicious gossip, and anyone that testifies falsely, deserves to be thrown to the dogs, for it says, "[Do not eat flesh torn off in the field by a predator]. Cast it to the dogs" (Exodus 22:31). And in the next verse says, "Do not accept a false report [i.e., malicious gossip]. Do not join forces with a wicked person to be a corrupt witness."

[Resuming the discussion of the strap:] Two leather strips were running up and down the strap bundle. A Tanna said: One strip was of donkey leather, as a certain Galilean once expounded before R. Chisda: It says, "An ox knows its owner, a donkey its master's trough. Israel does not know, my people takes no thought" (Isaiah 1:3). The Holy One, blessed be He, said: Let the one that recognizes its master's trough [the ox and the donkey] come and inflict punishment [through the straps of calf and donkey leather] on the one that does not recognize his master's trough [a Jew who transgressed].

ABSTAINING FROM SIN IS LIKE DOING A MITZVAH

[The Mishnah says:] All who are liable to *karet* [the punishment of premature death] who were flogged become exempt from their *karet*.[15] For it says, "[Do not go beyond the limit and give him forty lashes] . . . since your brother will then be dishonored in your presence" (Deuteronomy 25:3)—once he has been flogged, he is considered "your brother," [and is no longer liable to *karet*, provided he repented], so says R. Chananiah b. Gamliel. R. Chananiah b. Gamliel said also: If by committing a transgression a person forfeits his soul [through *karet*], a person who performs a mitzvah, how much more should his soul be granted him! R. Shimon said: You can derive this from the source itself [i.e., from the verse that deals with *karet*, rather than derive it from the text dealing with flogging]. For it says there, "Thus whenever anyone does any of these disgusting perversions, the people doing so shall be cut off . . . [i.e., they will be punished by *karet*]" (Leviticus 18:29).

(23b) And [in the introduction to this chapter] it says, "Keep My decrees and laws, which man shall carry out and by which he shall live" (ibid. v. 5). This teaches you that whoever refrains from transgressing[16] is rewarded like one who performs a mitzvah [in that he will be granted life, for it says, "by which he shall live"]. R. Shimon b. Rebbi said: It says, "Be extremely careful not to eat the blood—for the blood, it is the life . . . If you do not eat it, you and your children will have a good life" (Deuteronomy 12:23,25). Now, if a person is rewarded for rejecting something as loathsome as blood, then surely one who refrains from theft and immorality—which people desire and crave—will gain merit for himself, his children, and his grandchildren until the end of time.

R. Chanania b. Akashia says: The Holy One, blessed be He, wished to confer merit upon Israel [so that even a person who merely abstains from sinning should receive a reward]; therefore He gave them Torah and *mitzvot* in abundance, as it says, "God desired, for the sake of its [Israel's] righteousness, that the Torah be expanded and strengthened" (Isaiah 42:21).

HEAVEN AGREES WITH THE EARTHLY BET DIN

[The Gemara says:] R. Yehoshua b. Levi said: Three things were enacted by the worldly Court here on earth, and the Heavenly Court agreed with it. They are: The reading of the Book of Esther [on Purim]; that greeting with the Divine Name, [is not considered "taking God's Name in vain"]; and placing the Levites' tithe in the treasury of the Sanctuary [so that unworthy Levites should not share in it].

The reading of the Book of Esther, as it says, "They confirmed, and the Jews took it upon themselves and their posterity, [to observe Purim in the prescribed manner]" (Esther 9:27): They "confirmed" Above what they had "taken upon themselves" below; [i.e., Heaven agreed with the earthly Court's ruling].

Greeting with the Divine Name, for it says, "Behold, Boaz arrived from Bethlehem. He said to the harvesters, 'God be with you!'" (Ruth 2:4). And it says furthermore, "The angel of God appeared to [Gideon] and said to him, 'God is with you, O mighty hero!'" (Judges 6:12). What is the need for the second verse? So that you should not say that this was Boaz's own idea, and that his action was not approved by Heaven; therefore the Gemara cites the greeting, "God be with you, O mighty hero!" [which was said by an angel, to show that Heaven approved of it].

Placing the Levites' tithe in the treasury of the Sanctuary, as it says, "Bring the full tithe into the storehouse, and let there be food in My House, and thus put Me to the test—said the Lord of hosts. I will surely open the floodgates of the sky for you and pour down blessings on you until there will be no enough" (Malachi 3:20). What is the meaning of "until there will be no enough"? Said Rami b. Rav: It means, until your lips become tired of saying, "Enough, enough!"

THREE DIVINE MANIFESTATIONS

R. Elazar said: The Holy Spirit appeared in three places [at a critical juncture]: at the Court of Shem,[17] at the Court of Samuel, and in the Court of King Solomon. At the Court of Shem, [after Tamar was condemned to death for having been promiscuous], as it says, "Judah recognized [the securities he had given her,] and he said, "She is right. It is from me" (Genesis 38:26). How could he be sure? Maybe just as he had been intimate with her, some other man had lived with her [and fathered her unborn child]? But it was a Heavenly Voice that came forth and said, "I ordained that these two children shall be born who will conquer the world." [The offspring of the union of Judah and Tamar were David and *Mashiach*].

At the Court of Samuel, as it says, "[Samuel said,] 'Here I am! Testify against me, in the presence of God and in the presence of His anointed one: Whose ox have I taken? Whom have I defrauded or whom have I robbed?' . . . He said to them: 'God then is witness,

and His anointed one is witness this day that you have found nothing in my possession.' And He said, 'I am a witness.'" (1 Samuel 12:3–5). [The Gemara asks:] "And He said," shouldn't it be "And *they* said"? [The Gemara answers:] It was a Heavenly Voice that came forth and said, "I am a witness in this matter."

At the Court of Solomon, as it says, "Then the king spoke up, 'Give the live child to her,' he said, 'and do not put it to death; she is its mother'" (1 Kings 3:27). "She is its mother"; how could he be sure? Maybe she was deceiving him? But it was a Heavenly Voice that came forth [at that critical moment] and said, "She is its mother."

Said Rava: How can we be sure that this is so? Maybe Judah had calculated the days and months and found them to tally [with the day he had been intimate with her, so that he had no reason to suspect that she had lived with another man at about the same time]? And Samuel may have thought of all Israel collectively, using the singular [taking "I am a witness" as referring to all Israel], as it says elsewhere, "O Israel, *you are* saved by God an eternal salvation; you will not be ashamed" (Isaiah 45:17). And Solomon, too, [may have rendered his decision by himself] because he saw that one woman was compassionate and the other was not compassionate, [and in none of these cases was there Divine intervention]? We must say therefore that these [cases of Divine manifestations] are known to us by tradition.

DAVID'S ELEVEN FUNDAMENTAL PRINCIPLES

R. Simlai expounded: Six hundred and thirteen *mitzvot* were told to Moses, three hundred and sixty five negative *mitzvot* [things you may not do], corresponding to the number of days in the solar year, and two hundred and forty-eight positive *mitzvot* [things you must do], corresponding to the number of parts of the human body. Said R. Hamenuna: What verse do we have to prove this? It is, "The Torah that Moses commanded us is the heritage of the Congregation of Jacob" (Deuteronomy 33:4). The numeric value of the word Torah is (24a) six hundred and eleven.[18] The commandments "I am God your Lord" and "Do not have any other god before Me" [of the Ten Commandments] we heard from the Almighty Himself [611 + 2 = 613]. David came and condensed [the 613 *mitzvot*] to eleven fundamental principles, as it says, "A Psalm of David. God, who may sojourn in Your tent? Who may dwell on Your Holy Mountain? (1) One who walks in perfect innocence and (2) does what is right, and (3) speaks the truth from his heart; (4) who has no slander on his tongue, (5) who has done his fellow no evil, (6) nor casts disgrace on his close one; (7) in whose eyes a contemptible person is repulsive, (8) but who honors those that fear God; (9) who stands by his oath even to his detriment; (10) who does not lend his money on interest, and (11) takes not a bribe against the innocent. The doer of these shall not falter forever" (Psalms 15).

"One who walks in perfect innocence," that was Abraham, as it says, "Walk before Me and be perfect" (Genesis 17:1). "Who does what is right," someone like Abba Chilkiah.[19] "Speaks truth in his heart" someone like R. Safra.[20] "Who has no slander on his tongue"— that was our Father Jacob, as it says, "[Jacob said to his mother,] 'Suppose my father touches me. He will realize that I am an impostor'" (Genesis 27:12). [If his father discovered the deception, he would have to malign Esau, explaining that he had sold the birthright to him, and that he was entitled to the blessing. This he was unwilling to do (Maharsha)]. "Who has done his fellow no evil" means that he does not go into competition with his fellow craftsman. "Nor casts disgrace on his close one" refers to a person who admonishes his [misbehaving] relatives and thereby makes them his friends (Maharsha). "In whose eyes a contemptible person is repulsive"—that was Hezekiah, king of Judah who dragged his [idolatrous] father's bones on a bed of ropes, [treating his contemptible father with disdain].[21]

"Who honors those that fear God"—that was Jehoshaphat, king of Judah, who, whenever he saw a Torah scholar rose from his seat and embraced and kissed him, calling him, "Father, Father! Rabbi, Rabbi! Teacher, Teacher!" "Who stands by his oath even to his detriment," like R. Yochanan, who once said: I will remain fasting until I come home, [he swore to mortify himself by undertaking a voluntary fast]. "Who does not lend his money on interest," not even interest from an idol worshipper. "He does not take a bribe against the innocent," like R. Yishmael b. R. Yosi.[22]

The verse concludes, "The doer of these shall not falter forever." Whenever R. Gamliel came to this passage he used to cry, saying: Only a person who does all these things shall not falter, but if he does only one of them he will falter! His colleagues said to him: Does it then say: The doer of *all* these things shall not falter? It says, "The doer of these things," meaning, even if he practices only one of these things he will not falter. For if you do not interpret the verse like this, how would you explain [the similar passage], "Do not let yourselves be defiled by any of these acts [of forbidden sexual relations]" (Leviticus 18:24)? Do you mean to say that only a person who committed *all* these perversions becomes defiled, but if he commits only one of them he is not defiled? Surely you must say that if he commits one of these acts he becomes defiled, and likewise here, if he does even one of these virtuous acts [he will not falter].

ISAIAH'S SIX
FUNDAMENTAL PRINCIPLES

Isaiah came and condensed [the 613 *mitzvot*] to six fundamental principles, as it says, "(1) He walks with

righteousness, and (2) speaks with truthfulness; (3) spurns extortionist profits, (4) and shakes off his hands from holding a bribe, (5) he seals his ears from hearing of bloodshed, (6) and he shuts his eyes from seeing evil. He shall dwell in lofty security" (Isaiah 33:15,16). "He walks with righteousness," that is our Father Abraham, as it says, "I have given him special attention so that he will command his children and his household after him . . . doing righteousness and justice" (Genesis 18:19). "He speaks with truthfulness," that is a person who does not make his neighbor angry in public. "He spurns extortionist profits" like, for example, R. Yishmael b. Elisha.[23] "He shakes off his hands from holding a bribe" like, for example, R. Yishmael b. R. Yose.[24] "He seals his ears from hearing of bloodshed" like R. Eliezer b. R. Shimon who never remained silent when he heard a young Torah scholar being maligned, [but spoke up in his defense].[25] "He shuts his eyes from seeing evil" as R. Chiya b. Abba taught; for R. Chiya b. Abba said: This refers to a person who does not gaze at women when they stand washing clothes in the courtyard,[26] and about such a person it says, "He shall dwell in lofty security" (Isaiah 33:16).

MICAH'S THREE
FUNDAMENTAL PRINCIPLES

Micah came and condensed [the 613 *mitzvot*] to three fundamental principles, as it says, "He has told you, O man, what is good, and what God requires of you: (1) Only to do justice, and (2) to love kindness, and (3) to walk humbly with your God" (Micah 6:8). "To do justice" means maintaining justice. "To love kindness" refers to doing acts of kindness. "To walk humbly with your God" means providing for a bride's wedding expenses and burial expenses for the dead. And can we not derive a logical conclusion from this! If, when it comes to things that are not usually done in private the Torah instructs us to "walk humbly," surely this should apply to things that usually are done in a hidden way.

EMUNAH, FAITH, THE SINGLE
ALL-ENCOMPASSING MITZVAH

Finally Isaiah condensed [the 613 *mitzvot*] to two fundamental principles, as it says, "Thus says God, (1) 'Observe justice and (2) perform righteousness'" (Isaiah 56:1). Amos came and condensed them to one principle, as it says, "For thus said God to the House of Israel: Seek Me and live" (Amos 5:4). R. Nachman b. Yitzchak challenged this, saying: Perhaps the passage means: Seek Me by observing the entire Torah and live? But it is Habakkuk who came and boiled down [the 613 *mitzvot*] to one fundamental underlying principle, as it says, "The righteous person shall live through his faith" (Habakuk 2:4) [which means that all the *mitzvot* are included in the mitzvah of *emunah*, faith, the first of the Ten Commandments (*Maharsha*)].

THE PROPHETS REVERSED MOSES' DIRE PREDICTIONS

R. Yose b. R. Chanina said: Moses pronounced four [damaging] decrees on Israel, but four prophets came and called them off. Moses said, "Israel shall thus dwell securely, alone, at the fountain of Jacob" (Deuteronomy 33:28) [meaning: When will Israel dwell securely? When they are as righteous as Jacob (Rashi)]. Amos came and canceled that, as it says, "And I said, 'Lord, God, please refrain! How will Jacob survive, for he is small!'" [meaning, who can be as righteous as Jacob?]. So God relented concerning this. "'It too shall not be,' said the Lord God" (Amos 7:5,6).

Moses said, "And among those nations you will not be tranquil" (Deuteronomy 28:65). But Jeremiah came and said, "Thus said God, 'The people that survived the sword found favor in the wilderness, as I led Israel to its place of tranquility'" (Jeremiah 31:1). Moses said, "God keeps in mind the sins of the fathers to their children and grandchildren, to the third and fourth generation" (Exodus 34:7). Ezekiel came and declared, "The soul that sins—it shall die" (Ezekiel 18:4). Moses said, "You will be lost among the nations" (Leviticus 26:38); but Isaiah came and said, "It shall be on that day that a great shofar will be blown, and those who are lost in the land of Assyria and those cast away in the land of Egypt will come together, and they will prostrate themselves to God on the holy mountain in Jerusalem" (Isaiah 27:13), [thus they will not be lost among the nations].

Rav said: I am afraid of the verse, "You will be lost among the nations." R. Papa objected to Rav's fear, saying: Perhaps this means like a lost object that is looked for by its owner, [and eventually will be found]? As it says, "I have strayed like a lost sheep; seek out Your servant!" (Psalms 119:176). We must say therefore that Rav was upset by the last part of the verse, which reads, "The land of your enemies will consume you" (Leviticus 26:38). Mar Zutra challenged this, saying: Maybe the text means that they will be consumed the way cucumbers and melons are eaten, [where the fruit is eaten but the seeds remain intact; so, too, the seed of Israel will survive the Exile and flourish again (*Maharsha*)].[27]

AKIVA, YOU HAVE COMFORTED US!

On a similar note, it happened, as R. Gamliel, R. Elazar b. Azariah, R. Yehoshua, and R. Akiva were walking on the road, that they heard the loud roar of the Roman crowds in the city of Paltia, from a distance of a hundred and twenty miles. They all began to cry, but R. Akiva was smiling. "Why are you smiling?" they said. "And why are you crying?" replied R. Akiva. They answered, "These idolators who bow down to images and burn incense to idols live in safety and tranquility, whereas our *Bet Hamikdash*, the Footstool of our God, is burned down by fire; (24b) should we not weep?" He retorted, "That's precisely why I am smiling. If this is the reward of people who act against His will, how much greater will be the reward for those who obey Him!" Another time they were going up together to Jerusalem, and just as they came to Har Hatzofim (Mount Scopus) they saw a fox coming out of the place where the Holy of Holies had been located. They began to cry, while R. Akiva smiled. "Why are you smiling?" they asked. "Why are you crying," R. Akiva shot back. They answered, "The place about which the Torah says, 'Any alien who approaches is shall die' (Numbers 1:51) has now become the den of foxes; shouldn't we cry?"

Replied R. Akiva, "That's why I am smiling. For it says, 'I appointed trustworthy witnesses for myself: Uriah the *kohen* and Zechariah son of Jeberechiah' (Isaiah 8:2). Now, what does Uriah the *kohen* have to do with Zechariah? Uriah lived during the time of the first *Bet Hamikdash*, while [the prophet] Zechariah lived during the time of the second *Bet Hamikdash*. But the verse makes the [later] prophecy of Zechariah dependent on the [earlier] prophecy of Uriah. In the [earlier] prophecy in the days of Uriah it says, 'Therefore, because of you, Zion will be plowed over like a field' (Micah 3:12). In Zechariah it says, 'Thus said God, Master of Legions, "Old men and old women will once again sit in the streets of Jerusalem"' (Zechariah 8:4). As long as Uriah's ominous prophecy had not been fulfilled, I was afraid that the prophecy of Zechariah might not be fulfilled; now that Uriah's prophecy has come true, I am sure that Zechariah's prophecy will also come true." At this they said to him, "Akiva, you have comforted us! Akiva, you have comforted us!"

NOTES

1. *Rosh Hashanah* 10b.

2. *Zomemim* are witnesses that have been proven false by the testimony of a second set of witnesses who state that they saw the first set of witnesses at the time of the alleged incident in a place where they could not possibly have witnessed the incident to which they testify. The Torah mandates punishing *zomemim* witnesses by inflicting on them the same punishment they sought to inflict on their victim—be it execution, flogging, or monetary payment (Deuteronomy 19:16–19).

3. Joshua 20:7,8.

4. Deuteronomy 4:43.

5. Joshua 20:7,8.

6. Deuteronomy 4:43.

7. Deuteronomy 4:43.

8. *Terumah* is the first portion of the crop; it is given to the *kohen*.

9. Deuteronomy 4:43.

10. See *Pesachim* 113b.

11. Shechem abducted and raped Jacob's daughter Dinah. Thereupon he persuaded the citizens of the town to submit to circumcision.

12. A suspected adulteress [*sotah*] is made to drink "the bitter curse-bearing" water. A *kohen* writes on a scroll prescribed verses in which the Divine Name appears and dissolves the writing in the water, thereby erasing the Divine Name. If the woman did not commit adultery, the water would not harm her, and domestic peace would be re-established. (See Numbers 5:11–31.)

13. He erred in the interpretation of the verse, "If a person plots against his neighbor to kill him intentionally, then you must even take him from My altar to put him to death" (Exodus 21:14), which is explained to mean: take him from next to My altar, but not from upon the roof of My altar.

14. They interpret the verse to read: Do not go beyond the limit and give him forty lashes. Thus, in effect, no more than thirty-nine lashes could be given.

15. If a person trangressed a commandment that is punishable by *karet*—for example, if he ate *chametz* on Pesach—and he was warned that his transgression is punishable by lashes, he then receives lashes, and thereby is absolved from *karet*.

16. If he has the opportunity to commit a sin, but he refrains from doing it (Bartenura).

17. Shem was no longer alive, but the court was named after him (Rashi).

18. Tav = 400; vav = 6; reish = 200; hei = 5.

19. See *Taanit* 23a, b.

20. A buyer made him an offer for an article while he was reciting the *Shema* and could not interrupt to accept the offer. The anxious buyer raised the offer. After R. Safra finished praying he refused to receive the increased offer, which had been made under misapprehension. (Rashi, quoting She'iltot d'Rav Acha, Vayechi.)

21. *Pesachim* 65b.

22. *Ketubot* 105b.

23. *Ketubot* 105b.

24. *Ketubot* 105b.

25. Defaming a person is tantamount to bloodshed. When he is shamed his blood flows from his face, and he turns pale (*Maharsha*).

26. See *Bava Batra* 57b.

27. An alternate explanation of "The land of your enemies will consume you": When you place a melon in the earth, the melon disintegrates but the seeds sprout. So, too, Israel will survive and reemerge triumphantly from the Exile among the nations.

ᥴᴼ SHEVUOT ᥆ᢣ

ENLARGING JERUSALEM AND THE TEMPLE COURTYARDS

(14a) [The Mishnah says:] They do not add to the city or to the Temple courtyards except with [the approval of] a king, a prophet, the *Urim VeTumim*,[1] and a Sanhedrin of seventy-one members [i.e., the Great Sanhedrin], with [the breads of] two thanksgiving offerings,[2] and with song [i.e., a Song of Thanksgiving, Psalms 100]. The Bet Din walked with the two thanksgiving offerings after them, and all Israel after them. [They walked in this order until they reached the end of the area they wanted to sanctify.]

INTENT IS ALL THAT MATTERS

(15a) We learned in a *Baraita*: With regard to a burnt offering[3] taken from cattle it says, "A fire offering, that is a satisfying aroma to God" (Leviticus 1:9). With regard to a burnt offering of a bird [a dove] it says [similarly], "It is a burnt offering, a fire offering that is a satisfying aroma to God" (ibid. v. 17). This teaches you that it is the same whether you give little [a dove] or a lot [a lamb], as long as you direct your heart to your Father in Heaven.

THE ORCHESTRA OF THE THANKS-OFFERING

(15b) Our Rabbis taught: The Song of Thanksgiving [Psalm 100] was accompanied by *kinor* [a seven-stringed type of guitar], harps, and clanging cymbals, which were played at every corner and at every great stone in Jerusalem. They would recite [Psalm 30, a song for the inauguration of the Temple,] "I will exalt You, God, for You have raised me up from the depths . . ." (Psalms 30:2), and the Song Against Demons [Psalm 91], and others call it the Song Against Plagues. Those who call it Song Against Plagues do so because it says, "nor will any plague come near your tent" (Psalms 91:10). Those who call it Song Against Demons do so because it says, "A thousand [demons] will fall at your side" (ibid. v. 7).[4] This psalm [i.e., Psalm 91] is recited from verse 1 to verse 9 inclusive.

They would then continue with the entire Psalm 3, "A psalm by David, as he fled from Absalom his son."

HEALING BY INCANTATION

R. Yehoshua b. Levi recited the above-mentioned verses before going to sleep. [The Gemara asks:] How could he do that? Didn't he himself say that you are forbidden to heal yourself by quoting Biblical verses, [and he said these verses to drive away demons]? [The Gemara answers:] To protect yourself is different, [it is permitted; only healing through incantation is forbidden]. [The Gemara analyzes:] When R. Yehoshua b. Levi said it is forbidden, he meant where there is already a wound. If there is a wound, is it just forbidden [to heal it through an incantation] and nothing else? Haven't we learned: Whoever utters an incantation over a wound has no share in the World to Come! [This is much more than forbidding it!] [The Gemara answers:] We learned on this subject: R. Yochanan said: They taught this law only if he spits [while reciting the verses],[5] for God's Name may not be mentioned when spitting.[6]

TABERNACLE—SANCTUARY

(16b) We learned in a *Baraita*: R. Elazar said: One verse says, [if a person who has touched a corpse and has not been purified enters the Tabernacle,] "He has contaminated the Tabernacle of God" (Numbers 19:13);[7] and another verse says, "He has contaminated the Sanctuary of God" (ibid. v. 20). If the Tabernacle is mentioned, why mention the Sanctuary; and if the Sanctuary is mentioned, why mention the Tabernacle? If only the Tabernacle was mentioned, I might have thought that for entering the Tabernacle he should be liable [to *karet*], because the Tabernacle was anointed with the anointing oil [and therefore has greater sanctity]; but for entering the Sanctuary [i.e., the *Bet Hamikdash*] he should not be liable. And if only the Sanctuary was mentioned, I might have thought that for entering the Sanctuary he should be liable [to *karet*] because its sanctity is an everlasting sanctity; but for

719

entering the Tabernacle he should not be liable [since it existed only during the wandering in the wilderness]. That is why both Tabernacle and Sanctuary are mentioned.

SEPARATION FROM IMPURITY

(18b) Our Rabbis taught: It says, "You [Moses and Aaron] must separate the Israelites from their impurity" (Leviticus 15:31). R. Yoshia said: From this you can derive a warning to the children of Israel that they should separate themselves from their wives near their periods.[8] And how long before [the onset of the period]? Rabbah said: One *onah* [a day or a night].[9] R. Yochanan said in the name of R. Shimon b. Yochai: He who does not separate from his wife close to her period, even if he has sons like the sons of Aaron, they will die, for it says, "You must separate the Israelites from their impurity . . . This is the law of the woman who has her monthly period," and next to it, "God spoke to Moses right after the death of Aaron's two sons" (Leviticus 16:1). R. Chiya b. Abba said in the name of R. Yochanan: He who separates from his wife close to her period will have male children, for it says, "To make a distinction between the unclean and the clean" (ibid. 11:47) and next to it, "When a woman conceives and gives birth to a boy" (ibid. 12:1). R. Yehoshua b. Levi added: He will have sons worthy to be teachers, for it says, "In order to distinguish between the . . . clean and the unclean, and to teach the children of Israel" (ibid. 10:10,11).

R. Chiya b. Abba said in the name of R. Yochanan: Whoever recites the *Havdalah* over wine at the conclusion of *Shabbat* will have male children, for it says, "In order to distinguish between the holy and the common" (ibid.); [by making *Havdalah* you separate between between *Shabbat* and the weekdays];[10] and elsewhere it says, "To make a distinction between the unclean and the clean" (ibid. 11:47) and next to it, "When a woman conceives and gives birth to a boy" (ibid. 12:1). R. Yehoshua b. Levi said: He will have sons worthy to be teachers, for it says, "In order to distinguish between the holy and the common and to teach the children of Israel."

R. Biyamin b. Yefet said: Whoever sanctifies himself during marital intercourse [by conducting himself with modesty (Rashi)] will have male children, for it says, "You are to sanctify yourselves and you shall become holy" (ibid. 11:44), which is followed by "When a woman conceives and gives birth to a boy" (ibid. 12:1)

"REMEMBER" AND "SAFEGUARD" THE *SHABBAT*

(20b) The words "Remember the Sabbath day" (Exodus 20:8) and "Safeguard the *Shabbat* day" (Deuteronomy 5:12) were proclaimed as a single utterance,[11]

something the human mouth cannot utter and the human ear cannot hear.

IMPARTIAL JUSTICE

(30a) Our Rabbis taught: It says, "The two men shall stand . . . before the judges" (Deuteronomy 19:17). It is a statute that the litigants should stand. R. Yehudah said: I heard that if [the judges] wish to allow them both to sit, they may do so. What is forbidden? They should not make one litigant stand and the other sit; allow one to speak all he wishes, and tell the other to be brief.

Our Rabbis taught: "Judge your fellow fairly" (Leviticus 19:15); the court should not allow one litigant to sit while the other is made to stand; allow one to speak all he wishes, and tell the other to be brief. Another interpretation of "Judge your fellow fairly": Judge everyone by giving him the benefit of the doubt. [When you see a person doing what appears to be wrong, take a favorable view of his action; don't suspect him of wrongdoing (Rashi).] R. Yosef learned: "Judge your fellow fairly"—He who is with you [i.e., "your fellow"] in Torah and *mitzvot*, make an effort to judge him favorably.

(30b) The widow of R. Huna had a case before R. Nachman. He said to himself: What shall I do? If I rise before her, her opponent will be intimidated [and unable to state his case clearly]. If I do not rise before her, [that would be wrong too, for there is a rule that] the wife of a Torah scholar is like a scholar. So he said to his attendant: [When R. Huna's widow is about to enter,] go and make a duck fly over me, so that I will have get up anyhow [and her litigant will think that I got up because of the duck and will not be intimidated].

KEEP AWAY FROM ANYTHING FALSE

Our Rabbis taught: How do we know that a judge should not appoint an advocate for his words? [Meaning: when the judge realizes that he has made a mistake, he should not try to prove himself right by trying to think of other arguments because he is ashamed to admit that he is wrong.] Because it says, "Keep away from anything false" (Exodus 23:7). And how do we know that a judge should not allow an ignorant student to sit before him [to discuss the case at hand, for he may suggest false arguments]? Because it says, "Keep away from anything false." And how do we know that a judge who knows his colleague to be a robber, or a witness who knows his colleague to be a robber [even if the testimony they are about to give is true], should not join with him? Because it says, "Keep away from anything false." And how do we know that a judge who has concluded that the testimony of the witnesses is false should not say: Since the witnesses give evidence, I will decide the case on the basis of their testimony, (31a) and let the guilt be on their heads? Because it says, "Keep away from anything false."

How do we know that if a disciple sitting before his master sees that the poor man is right and the rich man wrong [whereas the master reached the opposite conclusion], he should not remain silent? Because it says, "Keep away from anything false." And how do we know that a disciple who sees his master making a mistake in the law, should not say: I will wait until he finishes, and then I will prove him wrong, and build up another verdict according to my own judgment? Because it says, "Keep away from anything false." And how do we know that a disciple whose master tells him: You know that if I were given a hundred *manehs*, I would not tell a lie, but So-and-so owes me one *maneh*, and I have only one witness to substantiate my claim [and two are needed]. How do we know that the disciple should not join with the witness? Because it says, "Keep away from anything false."

[The Gemara asks:] Is this then derived from, "Keep away from anything false"? Surely this is definitely lying, and the Torah says, "Do not testify as a false witness against your neighbor" (Exodus 20:13)! [The Gemara answers:] The case is, for example, if the master said to his disciple, "I definitely have one witness; and you just stand there in court. You don't have to say anything, so that you will not be telling a lie," [but the debtor will think that you, too, are a witness and will freely admit the debt (Rashi)]; even so it is forbidden, because it says, "Keep away from anything false."

How do we know that if someone has a claim of a hundred *zuz* against his neighbor, he should not say, "I will claim two hundred, so that he will admit a hundred, and be liable for an oath,[12] then I will be able to include in this oath also other claims I have against him [which he totally denied and for which no oath could be imposed]"? Because it says, "Keep away from anything false."

And how do we know that if someone has a claim of a hundred *zuz* against his neighbor and sues for two hundred, the debtor should not say, "I will deny it totally in court, [and not confess even to the one hundred *zuz* I owe him,] but admit it outside the court, so that I would not be liable for an oath, and he may not impose on me an oath and include other claims he has against me"? Because it says, "Keep away from anything false."

And how do we know that if three people have a claim of a hundred *zuz* against one person [and have no witnesses], one should not be the plaintiff, and the other two, the witnesses, in order that they may recover the hundred *zuz* and divide it? Because it says, "Keep away from anything false."

How do we know that, if two come to court, one dressed in rags and the other wearing a cloak worth one hundred *manehs*, the court should say to the rich man, "Either dress like him, or dress him like you, [so that the judges should not be biased in your favor, and the poor man not be intimidated]"? Because it says, "Keep away from anything false."

How do we know that the judge should not hear the words of one litigant before the other litigant arrives? And how do we know that a litigant should not explain his case to the judge before the other litigant arrives? Because it says, "Keep away from anything false."

It says, "He did that which is not good among his people" (Ezekiel 18:18). Rav said: This refers to a person who comes with a power of attorney.[13] Shmuel said: It refers to a person who buys a field whose ownership is being disputed, [and he, being an influential man, relies on his strength to fend off the other claimants (Rashi)].

SACRED AND PROFANE NAMES
(35b) Wherever the term "my Lord" is mentioned in the Torah in connection with Abraham, it refers to God and is sacred, [and may not be erased,] except in the verse, [where Abraham, addressing the leader of the three strangers[14] who appeared at his tent, said,] "My lord, please do not go on past me" (Genesis 18:3) [where "my lord" is secular]. Chanina the son of R. Yehoshua's brother, and R. Elazar b. Azariah in the name of R. Eliezer of Modin, said: This Name ["my Lord"], too, is sacred; [Abraham was addressing God, Who had come to visit him after his circumcision, asking Him not to go away while he was welcoming his guests].

With whom will the following statement agree: Rav Yehudah said in the name of Rav: Hospitality is greater than receiving the *Shechinah*? It agrees with these two [R. Chanina and R. Elazar b. Azariah who said that Abraham was addressing God, asking Him not to go away while he was welcoming his guests. Proof that hospitality takes precedence over receiving the *Shechinah*].

Whenever the term "my Lord" is mentioned in connection with Lot it is secular [and may be erased], except when [Lot said to the two angels], "Please no!" [then turning to God, he said,] "My Lord! I have found favor in Your eyes, and You have been very kind in saving my life" (Genesis 19:18). Lot was speaking to the One Who has the power to kill and to revive, namely, the Holy One, blessed be He.

Whenever the term "my Lord" is mentioned in connection with Nabot[15] it is sacred; in connection with Micah[16] it is secular. R. Eliezer said: The ones in connection with Nabot are all sacred; in connection with Micah, some are secular, and some sacred: the Name beginning with *alef lamed*[17] is secular, *yud hei*[18] is sacred; except the Name *alef lamed* in the verse, "all the days that the House of the Lord was in Shiloh" (Judges 18:31), which is sacred.

Whenever the term "my Lord" is mentioned in connection with Gibeah of Benjamin,[19] it is secular, according to R. Eliezer. R. Yehoshua said it is sacred. R. Eliezer said to him: Does He then promise and not fulfill? [If, as you say, "my Lord" is sacred and refers to God, why did God tell the tribes of Israel to make war against the tribe of Benjamin, and then allow them to be defeated?] R. Yehoshua replied: What He promised He fulfilled, but they only asked whether they should go to war against Benjamin, and which of the tribes should advance first. They did not ask whether they would win or be defeated. In the end, when they inquired [of the *Urim Vetumim*], they approved their action, as it says, "Phinehas son of Elazar son of Aaron ministered before Him in those days, and [inquired of the *Urim Vetumim*,] saying, 'Should I go out again to make war against our kinsmen the children of Benjamin, or should I withdraw?' God answered, 'Go up, for tomorrow I will deliver them into your hands'" (Judges 20:28), [and this promise He fulfilled, for "God routed the Benjaminites before Israel" (ibid. v. 35)].

Whenever the name Solomon is mentioned in the Song of Songs it is sacred [and refers to God; Shlomoh being a contraction of:] the Song to Him to Whom peace belongs,[20] except this, "I have my very own vineyard: you may have the thousand, O Solomon" (Song of Songs 8:12).[21] Solomon may have a thousand for himself; "and two hundred for those that guard its fruit" (ibid.)—namely, the Torah scholars. Some say the following is also secular, "There is Solomon's couch, encircled by sixty warriors" (ibid. 3:7), [because Solomon was terrified of Ashmedai, the king of the demons].[22]

Wherever in Daniel the word "king" is mentioned it is secular, except, "You, O king [Nebuchadnezzar]—to whom the King of kings, Who is the God of Heaven, has given a strong kingdom, power, and honor" (Daniel 2:37). And some say, the following is also sacred, "[Daniel said,] 'My Lord, may this dream be upon your foes, and its interpretation upon your enemies!'" To whom does Daniel say this? Surely not to Nebuchadnezzar, for then he would be cursing Israel who are the enemies of Nebuchadnezzar! [So he must be speaking to God, and the appellation "my Lord" is sacred.] Then what about the first Tanna [who said that the Name is secular, and Daniel was addressing Nebuchadnezzar]? He holds: Are the Jews the only enemies [of Nebuchadnezzar]? Doesn't he have enemies who are heathens? [And when Daniel said to Nebuchadnezzar, "May this dream be upon your foes" he had in mind enemies who are heathens.]

THE GRAVITY OF PERJURY

(38b) Our Sages taught: Concerning the oath of the judges[23]—it also may be said in any language. They say to the defendant: Be aware (39a) that the whole world trembled when the Holy One, blessed be He,

said at Sinai, "Do not take the Name of God your Lord in vain" (Exodus 20:7), [and when you take a false oath you take the Name of God in vain]. And in connection with all transgressions in the Torah it says, *venakkei,* "He will absolve [when you repent]" (ibid. 34:7), but here it says, *lo yenakkei,* "He will not absolve anyone who takes His Name in vain" (ibid. 20:7); [even repentance does not afford forgiveness for a false oath]. And for all the transgressions in the Torah the sinner alone is punished, but here he and his family [will be punished], for it says, "Let not your mouth bring guilt on your flesh" (Ecclesiastes 5:5), and "flesh" means "close relative," as it says, "Do not hide yourself from your *flesh* [i.e., your kin]" (Isaiah 58:7).

And for all the transgressions in the Torah the violator alone is punished, but for swearing falsely he and the whole world [i.e., all Israel] are punished, for it says, "[False] swearing and dishonesty . . . Therefore the land will be destroyed, and all who dwell in it will be enfeebled" (Hosea 4:2,3). But maybe this will happen only if he commits all the crimes [listed in the passage, which also mentions murder, robbery, and adultery]? Let that not enter your mind, for it says, "For due to false oaths the land has become desolate" (Jeremiah 23:10).

And regarding all other transgressions in the Torah, if he merits it, punishment is suspended for two or three generations, but [for swearing falsely] he is punished immediately, as it says, "I send [the curse] forth—says God, Master of Legions—and [the curse] will enter the house of the thief and the house of the one who swears falsely in My Name; and it shall lodge inside his house and consume it to the last timber and stone" (Zechariah 5:4). "I send [the curse] forth—immediately, "and it will enter the house of the thief"—he who "steals the mind" of people [i.e., misleads them], for example, a person whose neighbor does not owe him any money, but he claims that he does, and makes him swear. "And it will enter the house of the one who swears falsely in My Name"—should be taken in its plain sense. "And it shall lodge inside his house and consume it to the last timber and stone"—from this you learn that things [i.e., stones] which neither fire nor water can destroy, a false oath can destroy.

If, [after hearing the judges' admonitions,] he says, "I will not swear," he is dismissed immediately, [for fear that he changes his mind]. But if he said, "I will swear," those who are standing there will say to each other, "Get away from the tents of these evil men" (Numbers 16:26). And when they place him under oath, they say to him, "Be aware that the oath you are about to take is not according to your understanding but according to the understanding of the Almighty, and the understanding of the Bet Din. For this was the case when Moses our Teacher placed Israel under oath. He said to them: You should be aware that I do not place you under oath according to your own minds, but according to the mind of God, and my mind, as it says, "But it is not with you alone that I am making this covenant and this oath [i.e., according to your understanding]. I am making it with those who are standing here with us" (Deuteronomy 29:13).

From here we know that only those who were standing at Mount Sinai were placed under oath. How do we know that the coming generations, and proselytes who were later to be converted [were also placed under oath]? Because the text continues, "and also with those who are not [yet] here with us today" (ibid. v. 14) [meaning, future generations]. From this we know that they were adjured for the commandments they received at Mount Sinai. How do we know that they were adjured for the commandments that were going to be pronounced later, such as the reading of the *Megillah*? Because it says, "The Jews undertook and obligated themselves" (Esther 9:27)—they undertook what they had long ago obligated themselves to do.

WHY IS PERJURY MORE SERIOUS?

The Gemara said earlier: They say to [the defendant]: Be aware that the whole world trembled when the Holy One, blessed be He, said, "Do not take the Name of God, your Lord in vain" (Exodus 20:7). [The Gemara asks:] What is the reason [the earth trembled when this particular commandment was given]? Shall we say because it was given at Sinai? All the Ten Commandments were given at Sinai. The reason must be that [perjury] is more serious. But is it more serious [than the other commandments]? Haven't we learned in a *Baraita*: The following are lenient: positive and negative commandments, except, "Do not take the Name of God your Lord in vain"(Exodus 20:7). [The following are] serious: sins that are punishable by *karet* and death at the hands of the Bet Din, including, "Do not take the Name of God your Lord in vain." [So you see that "Do not take the Name in vain" is the same and not more serious than the sins that are punishable by *karet* or death.]

We must therefore say that [swearing falsely was singled out] because we learned: Concerning all transgressions in the Torah it says, *venakkei*, "He will absolve [when you repent]" (Exodus 34:7), but here [swearing falsely] it says, *lo yenakkei*, "He will not absolve anyone who takes His name in vain" (ibid.). And regarding all transgressions in the Torah doesn't it say, *lo yenakkei*, "He will *not* absolve"? That is needed for R. Elazar's exposition, for we learned: R. Elazar said: [It says *venakkei lo yenakkei*, [literally: "He will absolve, not absolve," which is self-contradictory]. It is impossible to say: "He will absolve" because it already said, "He will not absolve." It is impossible to say: "He will not absolve" because it already said, "He will absolve." How can the two contradictory statements be reconciled? By saying: "He absolves" those who repent, and "He does not absolve" those who do not repent. [But

swearing falsely is more serious than other transgressions, for the Torah says about it, *lo yenakkei*, "God will *not* absolve one who takes His Name in vain" (Exodus 20:7).]

[We learned:] For all transgressions in the Torah he alone is punished, but for swearing falsely both he and his family are punished. [The Gemara asks:] You mean to say that for all transgressions in the Torah his family is not punished? Surely it says, "I will direct My anger against this person *and his family* [for worshipping Molech]"[24] (Leviticus 20:5). And we learned: R. Shimon said: If he sinned, what did his family do wrong? But this shows you in a family where there is a tax collector, all are tax collectors; a robber, all are robbers; because they protect him! [And in the case of other transgressions, too, the whole family is punished, and not just in the case of swearing falsely.]

[The Gemara answers:] In the case of other transgressions the family receives a lighter punishment [than the transgressor himself], but in the case of perjury, the family receives the same punishment as the perjurer. As we learned in a *Baraita*: Rabbi said: [It says about a person who worships Molech,] "I will cut him off [spiritually]" (Leviticus 20:3). Why is this said? Because it says, "I will direct My anger against this man and his family" (ibid. v. 3), I might think the whole family will be cut off, that's why it says, "I will cut *him* off;" to tell you: *him* I will cut off, but not the whole family, [they will receive only a light punishment].

[We learned:] For all transgressions in the Torah he alone is punished, but for swearing falsely he and the whole world [i.e., all of Israel] are punished. [The Gemara asks:] You mean to say that for all transgressions in the Torah, the whole world is not punished? Surely it says, "They will fall over one another" (Leviticus 26:37); one will fall because of the sin of the other; this teaches us that all Israel are responsible for one another, [thus in the case of all transgressions, the whole world, meaning all Israel, is punished, because all Jews are responsible for one another, and required to prevent wrongdoing]? (39b) [The Gemara answers:] There they are punished because they could have prevented the sin by protesting, and they did not protest.

[The Gemara asks:] What is the difference between the wicked of [the transgressor's] family and the wicked of the rest of the world, and the righteous of his family and the righteous of the rest of the world? In the case of other transgressions, he himself receives his own [appropriate] punishment, and the wicked of his family, a severe punishment [because they did not protest], and the wicked of the rest of the world, a light punishment. The righteous, both of his family and the rest of the world are free [although they were able to prevent them, because other transgressions are not as serious as perjury]. In the case of swearing falsely, he and the wicked of his family receive his punishment, and the wicked of the rest of the world, a severe punishment; and the righteous, both of the family and others receive a light punishment [because they were able to prevent it, and did not].

We learned above: If he says, "I will not swear," he is dismissed immediately; but if he says, "I will swear," those who are standing there will say to each other, "Get away from the tents of these evil men." We can understand that the person who swears is committing a wrong, but the claimant who makes him swear, why should he be called evil? [Because the bystanders say "These evil men," meaning both the claimant and the defendant]? [The Gemara answers:] As we learned in a *Baraita*: R. Shimon b. Tarfon said: It says, "The case *between the two* must be decided on the basis of an oath to God" (Exodus 22:10), [the claimant also shares the guilt and is admonished, for if he had provided witnesses when making the loan or had the debtor sign a receipt, there would have been no need for an oath (Rashi)].

NOTES

1. The *Urim VeTumim* were a slip of parchment on which the ineffable four-letter Name of God was written. It was inserted in the folds of the breastplate of the *Kohen Gadol* and was the power that lit up the letters on the breastplate, providing Divine guidance to those making inquiries of it (see Exodus 23:30).

2. A thanksgiving offering consists of an animal to be sacrificed, along with forty loaves of bread, thirty of which are unleavened and ten leavened.

3. *Olah* in Hebrew. This offering was completely burned.

4. This psalm was recited in order to cleanse the unsanctified area of all impure and evil forces (*Maharsha*).

5. They believed that spitting on a wound had the effect of driving away evil spirits.

6. The incantation includes the verse, "I am God Who heals you" (Exodus 15:26). If he spits on a wound while reciting verses, he has no share in the World to Come; but to utter an incantation without spitting is also forbidden. However, to recite verses as a means of protection from mishap is permitted (see *Sanhedrin* 101a).

7. The passage refers to a person who has been contaminated by touching a corpse and enters the Tabernacle or Sanctuary.

8. This section deals with "a woman who has her monthly period" (verse 32).

9. Either a whole day or a whole night. If her period comes during the day, he must separate from the beginning of the day; if during the night, from the beginning of the night (Rashi).

10. In verse 9 the *kohanim* are told not to drink wine when entering the Communion Tent, which implies that you may drink wine when you recite the *Havdalah*.

11. Although the Torah writes these commandments separately, God miraculously combined them at Sinai into one utterance, to tell us that observing the spirit of *Shabbat* goes hand in hand with keeping its laws.

12. If someone admits that part of the claim against him is true, he must take an oath that he owes no more. He is then exempt from paying the part of the claim he denies. However, if he totally denies the claim, no oath can be imposed.

13. He represents the litigant because he loves the legal wrangling. The litigant himself might be willing to compromise, whereas he insists on the full amount of the claim (Rashi).

14. They were actually angels disguised as Arab Bedouins.

15. 1 Kings 21:10,13.

16. Judges 17 and 18.

17. Judges 17:5, 18:5, 10, 24.

18. Judges 18:5, 10, 24.

19. Judges 20:18–28. After the Benjaminites committed the atrocity at Gibeah, the other tribes went to war against them. They inquired of God as to which tribe should lead them in battle. God answered, "Judah should be first." Yet the Benjaminites won the battle.

20. Shlomoh is seen as a contraction of *Shalom Shelo*, "To Whom peace belongs," i.e. God.

21. In an allegorical sense the verse means: God says: From My vineyard (Israel), Solomon may have 1,000 men as soldiers out of every 1,200, and 200 should be left to "guard its fruit," i.e., study the Torah (*Maharsha*).

22. See *Gittin* 68b.

23. The oath of the judges is the oath the judges impose on a defendant who admits the validity of a portion of the claim against him, but denies that he owes the rest.

24. A form of idol worship whereby children are burned as sacrifices.

ᴄᴏ EDUYOT ᴏᴠ

[Unlike the other Tractates, *Eduyot* does not deal with a specific subject but contains a collection of *halachot* and decisions on a variety of topics. *Eduyot* consists of Mishnah alone without Gemara.]

WHY ARE MINORITY OPINIONS RECORDED?

(2a) Mishnah 1:4. [The Mishnah asks:] And why do they record the opinions of Shammai and Hillel when it does not serve any purpose, [in cases where the *halachah* was not decided according to either of them, and they themselves retracted their stated opinions]? [The Mishnah answers:] To teach coming generations that a person should not stubbornly insist that his opinion should prevail, for the fathers of the world [Shammai and Hillel] did not insist that they were right.

Mishnah 1:5. And why do they record the opinion of a single individual among a majority [who disagree with him] when the *halachah* is decided according to the majority? So that if a Bet Din prefers the opinion of the single individual, it may act on the basis of his opinion [and ignore the majority opinion]. And no later Bet Din can overturn the decision of the earlier Bet Din [that acted on the basis of the single individual's opinion] unless it is greater in wisdom [meaning, the head of this Bet Din is greater in wisdom than the head of the earlier Bet Din], and in number [meaning, this Bet Din has more members than the earlier one]. If it was greater in wisdom but not in number, in number but not in wisdom, it may not overturn the decision of the earlier Bet Din; it must be greater both in wisdom and number.

Mishnah 1:6. R. Yehudah said: [Giving a different answer to the question of the previous Mishnah:] If so, [since the *halachah* is decided according to the majority], why do they record the opinion of a single individual among the majority when it serves no purpose? So that if someone says, "I have heard from my teachers that this is the *halachah*, [and not the way the Bet Din ruled,]" he may be told, "What you have heard is the opinion of a single individual, [but he was outvoted by the majority, and the *halachah* is according to the majority view].

HEREDITY

(4a) Mishnah 2:9. R. Akiva used to say: The father imparts to his son good looks, strength, wealth, wisdom, and longevity, and the number of generations before him,[1] which is the appointed end. For it says, "He Who proclaimed the generations from the beginning" (Isaiah 41:4) [i.e., God preordains the fate of future generations]. [For example:] Although it says, "They will be enslaved and oppressed four hundred years" (Genesis 15:13), [and the merit of Abraham's virtue did not save his progeny from Egyptian bondage], Abraham was told, "The fourth generation will return here," (ibid. v. 16) [and because of this promise they were redeemed from Egypt].

THINGS THAT LASTED TWELVE MONTHS

(4b) Mishnah 2:10. He also used to say: There are five things that lasted twelve months: (1) The judgment of the generation of the Flood;[2] (2) the judgment of Job; (3) the judgment of the Egyptians; (4) the judgment of Gog and Magog[3] in time to come will last twelve months; (5) the judgment of the wicked in Gehinnom will continue for twelve months, for it says, "It will be from one month to the same month [a year later]" (Isaiah 66:23).[4]

(7b) Mishnah 5:3. R. Yishmael said: According to Bet Shammai, *Kohelet* [Ecclesiastes] does not render unclean the hands that touch it,[5] [because it is not considered sacred Scripture]; but Bet Hillel holds that it does render the hands unclean, [because Ecclesiastes is considered sacred Scripture].

AKAVYA'S FOUR RULINGS

Mishnah 5:6. Akavya b. Mehalalel testified regarding four things: The Sages said to him, "Akavya, if you retract the four rulings you made [in opposition to the majority], we will appoint you as Head of the Bet Din in Israel [i.e., vice president of the Sanhedrin]. Replied Akavya, "I would rather be called a fool all my life [for rejecting this important office] than that I should become even for one hour a wicked man in the eyes of

God [and repudiate teachings I received from my masters who constituted a majority. And even if I thought that I was permitted to retract my words, I still refuse the offer,] so that people should not say that I reversed myself in order to gain power.

[These are Akavya's four rulings:] (1) He declared unclean the hair that was left over [from an earlier case] of leprosy,[6] and (2) he declared unclean yellow blood,[7] both of which the Sages declared clean. (3) He used to permit the hair of a blemished firstborn[8] animal that had fallen out[9] and was put in a niche in the wall, after which the *kohen* slaughtered it. (8a) But the Sages forbid it. (4) He used to say: A woman convert and a freed maidservant [who are suspected of adultery] are not made to drink the bitter waters [a *sotah* must drink],[10] but the Sages said: They are made to drink the bitter waters. The Sages said to Akavya: [We can prove that we are right,] because Karkemit, a freed maidservant in Jerusalem, was made to drink the bitter waters by Shemaya and Avtalyon. Akavya replied: It was only for show that they made her drink. [They were descendants of converts and wanted to demonstrate that converts are on an equal footing with all Israel.] As a result [of this remark], they excommunicated Akavya [for maligning Shmayah and Avtalyon], and when he died, they stoned his coffin.

R. Yehudah said: God forbid to say that Akavya was excommunicated, for when the Temple Court was closed [on the eve of Pesach when it was filled to capacity with people bringing their Pesach lambs,] there was no one there who equaled Akavya in wisdom and piety. But who then was excommunicated? Eliezer b. Chanoch, who called in question the law concerning the washing of the hands. And when Eliezer b. Chanoch died, the Bet Din sent a stone to be placed on his coffin. This teaches us that whoever is excommunicated and dies while banned, his coffin should be stoned.

AKAVYA AND HIS SON

Mishnah 5:7. On his deathbed Akavya said to his son: Retract the four *halachot* that I declared [in opposition to the Rabbis]. He replied: Why did you not disavow them yourself? Retorted Akavya: I heard them from a majority, and the Sages claimed that they heard [the opposite] from a majority. Therefore I did not want to back out of my position. But you heard [my four rulings] from a single individual [i.e., from me] and you heard [their rulings] from the majority. It is better for you to leave the opinion of the single individual and abide by the ruling of the majority. Replied Akavya's son, "Please, Father, recommend me to your colleagues." "I will not recommend you to them," answered Akavya. "Have I done anything wrong?" the son asked. "No," Akavya replied. "Your own conduct will recommend you, and your own deeds will alienate you."

WHEN ELIJAH WILL COME

(10a) Mishnah 8:7. R. Yehoshua said: I have it by tradition from R. Yochanan b. Zakkai who heard it from his teacher, and his teacher heard it from his teacher as a *halachah* given to Moses from Sinai that Elijah [the harbinger of *Mashiach*] will not come to declare which families are of pure or impure ancestry, but to remove families [of impure lineage] that forced their way into the Jewish community, and to bring in families [of pure lineage] that were forcibly kept out of the Jewish community. [For example:] The family of Bet Tzerifah [which was of pure lineage] was on the other side of the Jordan and Benzion excluded them by force [by announcing that they were of tainted ancestry]. Then there was family [of impure lineage] that Benzion brought in by force [by declaring them to be of pure ancestry]. It is families like these [whose ancestry is known] that Elijah will come to declare pure or impure, to remove from or to bring into the Jewish community.

R. Yehudah said: He will come to bring families into the community but not to remove families from the community [even those brought in by force]. R. Shimon said: [Elijah will come] to settle disputes among the Sages. And the Sages said: He will come, neither to remove nor to bring near, but to make peace in the world, as it says, "Behold, I send you Elijah the prophet before the coming of the great and awesome day of God. He will turn back [to God] the hearts of fathers with their sons, and the hearts of sons with their fathers" (Malachi 3:23,24).

NOTES

1. The son inherits the promised good after the passage of a number of generations, such as the redemption from Egypt, which was promised to Abraham to come about four generations later (Genesis 15:16).

2. Genesis 7:11 and 8:13,14.

3. Ezekiel 38:2ff.

4. And it says in the next verse, "They will go out and see the corpses of the men that rebelled against Me" (Isaiah 66:24).

5. Bet Shammai does not consider Ecclesiastes as Divinely inspired. The Sages ruled that after touching one of the books of *Tanach* you had to wash your hands. The reason is explained in *Shabbat* 14a.

6. A hair had turned white in a leprous white spot, making it unclean (Leviticus 13:3). Then the leprosy was healed, and the man became clean. But the white hair remained until another white spot appeared in the same place. The Sages declared it clean, while Akavyah declared it unclean.

7. Akavya considers it blood of her monthly period, which is unclean; whereas the Sages hold that only red blood is menstrual blood.

8. And was therefore permitted to be slaughtered and eaten by a kohen outside the *Bet Hamikdash*.

9. Cutting the hair or wool of a firstborn animal, even a blemished one, is forbidden. Even hair that has fallen out is forbidden to be used.

10. Because the *kohen* said to the *sotah*, "God will make you into a curse *among your people*" (Numbers 5:21).

✒ AVODAH ZARAH ✑

ROME AND PERSIA CLAIM A REWARD

(2a) R. Chanina b. Papa—some say R. Simlai—lectured: In time to come, the Holy One, blessed be He, will take a Torah scroll in His arm and proclaim, "Whoever has engrossed himself in the study of this Book should come and take his reward." Thereupon all the nations will come running in utter confusion, as it says, "All the nations gathered together" (Isaiah 43:9). The Holy One, blessed be He, will tell them: Don't come to Me in confusion, but let each nation come in (2b) with its scribes, as it says, "And all the kingdoms [leumim] assemble" (ibid.). And the term le'om means "kingdom," as it says, [Rebeccah was told,] "The upperhand will pass from one kingdom to another [le'om mile'om ye'ematz]" (Genesis 25:23).

[The Gemara asks:] Can there be confusion before the Holy One, blessed be He, [to whom everything is absolutely clear and manifest]? [The Gemara answers:] It means that they themselves should not be confused, so that they hear what God is saying to them. The kingdom of Rome will be the first to enter before God [to be judged]. Why does Rome enter first? Because Rome is the most important kingdom. How do we know that it is so important? Because it says, "It[1] will devour the whole earth, trample and crush it" (Daniel 7:23), and R. Yochanan said: This refers to Rome whose power is known all over the world. And how do we know that the most important is the first [to be judged]?

Because R. Chisda said: When a king and a community appear before the Heavenly Court, the king enters first, for it says, [Solomon prayed,] "That He may grant the just due of His servant and of His people Israel" (1 Kings 8:59), [His servant, the king, is mentioned before the people]. And why is this so, [that the king enters first]? If you prefer, you may say that it is not proper for a king to wait outside [while the people are being judged]. Or you may say that the king is judged first, [for fear that if the people were judged first and found guilty, God would hold the king responsible for their shortcomings] and would vent His anger on him. The Holy One, blessed be He, will then ask [Rome], "What have you been busy doing?" They will answer, "Master of the universe! We have created many markets, we have built many bathhouses, we have accumulated a fortune in gold and silver, all for the sake of Israel, to make it possible for them to study the Torah."

The Holy One, blessed be He, will reply, "Fools that you are! All these things you built only to satisfy your own desires. You created markets for the purpose of prostitution; you built bathhouses for your own enjoyment. The silver and gold you amassed is Mine, as it says, 'Silver is Mine, and gold is Mine—says the Lord of Hosts' [Haggai 2:8]. Has anyone of you studied this?" And "this" refers to the Torah, as it says, "This is the Torah that Moses presented before the children of Israel" (Deuteronomy 4:44). At this they will leave deeply depressed.

After Rome has departed, Persia will enter. Why does Persia go next? Because they are second to Rome in importance. How do we know this? Because it says, [Daniel said,] "Then I saw a second, different beast which was like a bear" (Daniel 7:5). And R. Yosef taught that this refers to the Persians who eat and drink voraciously like a bear, are fleshy and overgrown with hair like a bear, and are restless like a bear. The Holy One, blessed be He, will ask them, "What have you been busy with?" They will answer, "Master of the universe! We built many bridges, conquered many great cities, fought many wars, all for the sake of Israel, to enable them to study the Torah."

The Holy One, blessed be He, will answer, "All these things you did only to satisfy your own desires. You built bridges in order to charge tolls, you conquered great cities in order to recruit the population for forced labor. As for waging war, I am the One who fights wars, as it says, 'God is Master of war, His name is God' [Exodus 15:3]. Has anyone of you studied the Torah?" At this they will leave, deeply depressed. But why would the Persians enter after seeing that the Romans failed? They will say to themselves: The Romans destroyed the Bet Hamikdash, whereas we rebuilt it [under King Cyrus of Persia. Therefore, unlike the Romans, we will be judged favorably].

The same thing will happen to every other nation. [The Gemara asks:] But why are Rome and Persia mentioned specifically, and not the other nations? [The Gemara answers:] Because the reign of Rome and Persia will last until the coming of *Mashiach*. But will other nations step forward after seeing the disappointment of the first two? They will say to themselves: Rome and Persia oppressed Israel, but we did not, [therefore, we will be judged kindly].

DIALOGUE BETWEEN GOD AND THE NATIONS

[In the Messianic era] the nations will argue: Master of the universe! Did You then offer us the Torah, and we turned it down? [Why do You blame us for not studying the Torah]? [The Gemara asks:] But how could they say [that God did not offer them the Torah? He *did* offer it to them!]. For it says, "God came from Sinai, shone forth from Seir [i.e., Esau and Rome], appeared from Mount Paran [i.e., Ishmael]" (Deuteronomy 33:2). And it says also, "God came from Teman" (Habakkuk 3:3)? What did He have to do in Seir and Mount Paran? R. Yochanan said: This teaches us that the Holy One, blessed be He, offered the Torah to every nation and language group, but no one accepted it until He offered it to Israel who accepted it. [So you see that God did offer the Torah to the nations.]

We must therefore say that this is what they said: Did we then accept the Torah and not observe it? To which the obvious answer is: So, why did you not accept it? To this they would counter: Master of the universe! Did You then hold the mountain over us like a barrel as you did to Israel, [forcing them to accept it], and did we still reject it? For R. Avdimi b. Chama commented on the passage that relates [that before the Giving of the Torah,] "They stood at the foot of the mountain" (Exodus 19:17) [literally translated: "beneath the mountain"]. He said: This teaches us that God held the mountain over [the children of Israel] like a barrel and threatened, "If you will accept the Torah, fine; but if you do not, here will be your graves; [the mountain will be dropped on you]." [Thus Israel was forced to accept the Torah, the nations argued, but He did not force us to accept it.]

The Holy One, blessed be He, will reply immediately, "Let us take a look at history," as it says, "Let us hear the things that have happened" (Isaiah 43:9). [God will ask the nations,] "There are seven [Noachide] commandments[2] that you did accept. Did you observe them?"

[The Gemara interjects:] And how do we know that the nations did not observe them? Because R. Yosef taught: What is the meaning of the verse, "He stands and makes the earth shake; He looks and makes nations tremble" (Habakkuk 3:6). What did He see? He saw that the nations did not even observe the seven commandments the sons of Noah [i.e., mankind] had

taken upon themselves. Seeing that they did not observe them, He released them from them. [The Gemara asks:] Then they profited [from their disobedience]! Mar the son of Ravina said: (3a) The release from those commandments means that even if they would observe them, they would not receive a reward. [Thus they did not benefit from the release.]

[The Gemara asks:] Is that so? Surely we learned in a *Baraita*: R. Meir used to say: How do we know that even a gentile [who observes the seven Noachide laws] and who engrosses himself in Torah study is equal to a High Priest? For it says, "My laws which *man* shall carry out and by which he shall live" (Leviticus 18:5). It does not say: which a priest, a Levite or Israelite shall carry out and by which he shall live, but "which *man* shall carry out." Proof that even a gentile who engages in Torah study is equal to a High Priest. [The Gemara answers:] We must therefore say that they will not receive as great a reward as someone who does a mitzvah that he is commanded to do, but as someone who does a mitzvah without being commanded. For R. Chanina said: He who does a mitzvah that he is commanded to do ranks higher than someone who does a mitzvah that he is not required to do.[3]

[The Gemara now resumes its account of the dialogue between God and the nations:]

The nations will then say, "Master of the universe! Has Israel who did accept the Torah observed it?" To which the Holy One, blessed be He, will respond, "I can testify that Israel kept the entire Torah." "Master of the universe," the nations will rebut, "can a father testify on behalf of his son? [And Israel is Your son,] for it says, 'Israel is My son, My firstborn' (Exodus 4:22)." The Holy One, blessed be He, will reply, "Let heaven and earth come and testify that Israel observed the whole Torah." They answered, "Master of the universe! Heaven and earth are biased witnesses, for it says, 'If My covenant with the night and the day would not be, [meaning: if the Torah, which is studied day and night, did not exist,] I would not have set up the laws of heaven and earth'" (Jeremiah 33:25); [thus the existence of heaven and earth depends on the Torah].

[The Gemara briefly digresses:] For R. Shimon b. Lakish said: What is meant by the verse, "It was evening, and it was morning, *the sixth day*" (Genesis 1:31)?[4] It teaches us that God made a condition with all of Creation, saying: If Israel accept the Torah [which was given on *the sixth day* of Sivan], fine. If not, I will return you to primordial chaos. [Thus heaven and earth are prejudiced and disqualified as witnesses.]

[The Gemara returns to the dialogue:]

Then the Holy One, blessed be He, will say [to the nations], "Some of your own people will come and testify that Israel observed the whole Torah." Let Nimrod come and testify that Abraham refused to worship idols.[5] Let Laban come and testify that Jacob was above suspicion of theft.[6] Let Potiphar's wife testify that Joseph was above suspicion of immorality. Let

Nebuchadnezzar testify that Chananiah, Mishael, and Azariah did not bow down to an idol. Let Darius come and testify that Daniel never missed a single daily prayer.[7] Let Bildad the Shuchite, Tzofer the Naamite, Elifaz the Temanite, and Elihu ben Berachel the Buzite [the non-Jewish friends of Job] come and testify that Israel observed the whole Torah, as it says, "Let [the nations] bring their witnesses, and they [Israel] will be vindicated" (Isaiah 43:9).

The nations will then petition God, "Master of the universe! Please offer us the Torah once more, and we will observe it." But the Holy One, blessed be He, will answer them, "Fools that you are! He who prepared food on the eve of *Shabbat* [i.e., in this world], will eat on *Shabbat*, [i.e., in the Messianic era], but he who did not prepare food on the eve of *Shabbat*, what will he eat on *Shabbat*? Nevertheless, I have an easy mitzvah, namely *sukkah*. Go ahead and perform it."

[The Gemara digresses:] How can you say that [God offered them the mitzvah of *sukkah*]? Didn't R. Yehoshua b. Levi say: What is meant by "These words which I am commanding you today to do them" (Deuteronomy 6:6)? It means that *today* [in this world] is the time to do the *mitzvot*; they cannot be done tomorrow [in the Messianic times]. *Today* [in this world] is the time to do them, but not the time to be rewarded for them. [How could God offer the nations a mitzvah in Messianic times?] [The Gemara answers:] Because the Holy One, blessed be He, does not deal unfairly with His creatures, [but is responsive to their requests]. And why does He call it "an easy mitzvah"? Because it does not involve any outlay of money.

WHEN GOD WILL LAUGH

[The Gemara resumes the narrative:] Instantly, everyone will get busy and build his *sukkah* on top of his roof. The Holy One, blessed be He, [will test them] by making the sun blaze full force as in the sweltering heat of summer,[8] whereupon every one of them will kick down his *sukkah* and go away [in disgust], as it says, "Let us break the cord of their yokes, shake off their ropes from us, [the yoke of the mitzvah of *sukkah*]" (Psalms 2:3). [The Gemara asks:] But haven't you just said that God does not deal unfairly with His creatures? [Why does He give them such a rigorous test?] [The Gemara answers:] You are right. But with the Jews it also happens occasionally (3b) that the summer lasts until Sukkot, and they, too, are distressed by the heat, [so the test the nations are given is not unfair]. But did not Rava say: If you are distressed, you are exempt from dwelling in the *sukkah*.[9] [So why are the nations condemned for leaving the *sukkah*?] [The Gemara answers:] Granted, the nations would be exempt [because of the heat], but would Jews scornfully kick down the *sukkah* [as the nations did? Certainly not].

The Holy One, blessed be He, then will laugh at [the nations], as it says, "He Who is enthroned in heaven laughs, God mocks at them" (Psalms 2:4). R. Yitzchak said: Only on that day is there laughter for the Holy One, blessed be He.

Some connect this comment of R. Yitzchak with the following teaching: R. Yose said: In time to come [in the Messianic era] the idol worshippers will come and ask to be converted to Judaism. [The Gemara asks:] But do we then accept converts [in the Messianic era]? Surely we learned in a *Baraita*: In the days of *Mashiach* converts will not be accepted, just as converts were not accepted in the days of David and the days of Solomon.[10] [The Gemara answers:] We must therefore say that they will convert by themselves, [but they will not be accepted]. They will put *tefillin* on their heads and arms, attach *tzitzit* to the garments, and affix a *mezuzah* to their doors, but when the war of Gog and Magog will break out[11] they will be asked, "Why have you come?" They will answer, "[To fight] against God and His anointed," as it says, "Why do nations assemble, and regimes talk in vain . . . to conspire against God and His anointed" (Psalms 2:1).

Right away each convert will throw away his mitzvah objects and go away, saying, "Let us break the cord of their yokes" (ibid. v. 3), and the Holy One, blessed be He, will sit and laugh, as it says, "He Who is enthroned in heaven will laugh" (ibid. v. 4). [This is what R. Yitzchak was referring to when he said that only on that day is there laughter for the Holy One, blessed be He.]

Is that so? Didn't Rav Yehudah say in the name of Rav: There are twelve hours in a day. During first three hours God is busy studying the Torah; during the second three He judges the whole world, and when He sees that the world is guilty [and deserves to be destroyed] He rises from the Throne of Justice and sits down on the Throne of Mercy, [and mercifully He decides to spare the world and treat it with leniency]; during the third three hours He feeds the whole world, from the mighty *re'em* [rhinoceros or wild ox] to the smallest insect; during the fourth three hours He plays [and laughs] with the leviathan,[12] as it says, "This leviathan You fashioned to play with" (Psalms 104:26)? [So you see, God *does* engage in playful laughter every day, not just on "that day"!] Said R. Nachman b. Yitzchak: True, He plays and laughs *with* with His creatures [every day], but He does not laugh *at* them, except on that day. [Only on that day God will laugh at their sinful behavior (Rashi).]

R. Acha said to R. Nachman b. Yitzchak: Since the day the *Bet Hamikdash* was destroyed, there is no laughter for the Holy One, blessed be He. How do we know this? Shall we say from the verse, "My Lord God, Master of Legions, declared that day to be for crying and lament" (Isaiah 22:12)? But this refers only to the day [of the destruction of the *Bet Hamikdash*]. But we know it from the verse, "I have long kept silent, I have been still, I have restrained myself, but now I will cry" (ibid. 42:14).

[The Gemara asks: R. Nachman b. Yitzchak said above that during the fourth three hours God plays and laughs with the leviathan. Now that the *Bet Hamikdash* is destroyed and there is no laughter before God,] what does God do during the fourth three hours? [The Gemara answers:] He sits and teaches Torah to the schoolchildren [who died in infancy (Rashi)], for it says, "To whom would He give instruction? To whom would He expound a message? To those newly weaned from milk, just taken away from the breast" (Isaiah 28:9). And before the destruction of the *Bet Hamikdash*, when there was laughter before God, who taught the schoolchildren? If you prefer, say that Metatron[13] taught them, or you could say that God did both [play and laugh with the leviathan and teach schoolchildren].

And what does God do during the night? If you prefer, say that He does the same as in the daytime, or you could say that He rides upon a light cherub and glides through eighteen thousand worlds, as it says, "God's entourage is twice ten thousand, thousands *shin'an*" (Psalms 68:18). Do not read *shin'an* [repeated], but *she'einan*, "that are not there."[14] Or, if you prefer, say: God sits and listens to the songs of the *Chayot* [angels], as it says, "In the day God will command His lovingkindness, even by night His song is with me" (ibid. 42:9).

WHY IS MAN COMPARED TO FISHES?

Rav Yehudah said in the name of Shmuel: What is the meaning of the verse, "You have made man like the fish of the sea" (Habakkuk 1:14). Why is man compared to the fish of the sea? To tell you that just as the fishes of the sea, as soon as they come on dry land, they die, so too man, as soon as he abandons the Torah and the *mitzvot*, he perishes. Another explanation: Just as the fish of the sea die as soon as the sun dries them, so too man, when he is struck by the sun, he dies. This last explanation can be applied to this world or to the World to Come. To this world, in the sense of a saying by R. Chanina who taught: Everything [i.e., all sickness] is in the hands of Heaven, except cold and heat,[15] for it says, "Colds and heat strokes are in the path of the perverse, he who values his life will keep far from them" (Proverbs 22:5).

Or you may say that the explanation applies to the World to Come, in the sense of a saying of R. Shimon b. Lakish who said: There is no Gehinnom in the World to Come [i.e., the Messianic era], but the Holy One, blessed be He, takes the sun out of its case so that it will be intensely hot; the wicked are punished by it, (4a) as it says, "For behold, the day [i.e., the sun] is coming, burning like an oven, when all the wicked people and all the evildoers will be like straw; and that

coming day will burn them up, says God, Master of Legions, so that it will not leave them root or branch" (Malachi 3:19)—no root in this world, and no branch in the World to Come.

The righteous will be healed [by the sun], for it says, "But the sun of righteousness will shine for you who fear My Name, with healing in its rays" (ibid. v. 20). And what is more, the righteous will relish it, as it says, "And you will go out and flourish like calves fattened in the stall" (ibid.). Another explanation: Just as with the fish of the sea, the big swallow the small, so it is with men; if not for the fear of the government, men would swallow each other alive. The same idea is expressed by R. Chanina, the deputy High Priest, who said: Pray for the welfare of the government, because if people did not fear it, a person would swallow his fellow alive.[16]

R. Chinena b. Papa pointed out a contradiction. It says, "We do not find the Almighty overbearing in His strength" (Job 37:23), yet it says, "Great is God and full of power" (Psalms 147:5), and also, "Your right Hand, O God is awesome in power" (Exodus 15:6). This presents no difficulty. The first verse refers to the time of judgment [when God is merciful and does not exercise stern justice]; the other verses refer to the time of war [when God displays His awesome power against His enemies].

PUNISHMENT IN SMALL INSTALLMENTS

R. Abbahu recommended R. Safra to the *Minim* [heretics who were tax collectors], telling them that he was a great Torah scholar. Thereupon they exempted him from paying taxes for thirteen years. One day they ran into R. Safra and asked him [sneeringly], "It says, 'You alone [i.e., Israel] have I singled out of all the families of the earth; that is why I will call you to account for all your iniquities' [Amos 3:2]. If someone is angry, does he let it out on his friend?" R. Safra was silent, unable to answer them. So they tied a scarf around his neck and taunted him. When R. Abbahu came by and found him [being ridiculed] he said to them, "Why do you harass him?" They retorted, "Haven't you told us that he is a great scholar? Well, he cannot explain to us the meaning of this verse!"

R. Abbahu answered, "I told you that he was a Talmudic scholar; did I tell you that he was well-versed in Scripture?" "Then how come *you* are familiar with it?" they asked. "Since we often have dealings with you, [and we know that you like to taunt us with Biblical verses] we apply ourselves to Scripture and familiarize ourselves with it, but the [Babylonian] scholars do not study Scripture thoroughly." "Then will *you* tell us the meaning of the verse?" "I will explain it to you with a parable," he countered. "You can compare it to a man who had loaned money to two people, one of them a friend, the other an enemy. From his friend he will accept payment in small amounts, whereas from his enemy he will demand payment in one lump sum. [So too, God punishes Israel only a little at a time.]

UNCOMPROMISING TRUTH— MERCIFUL JUSTICE

(4b) R. Yosef said: No one should recite the *Mussaf* prayer by himself [without a *minyan*] on the first day of Rosh Hashanah during the first three hours of the day, because, since judgment is then rendered, his deeds may be closely examined and his prayer may be rejected. [The Gemara asks:] If that is so, a congregation should not do it either! [The Gemara answers:] The combined merits of a congregation are greater. If so, you should not recite the *Shemoneh Esrei* of the morning service without a *minyan* either? No, that is not so, since, no doubt, there is a congregation praying at that time,[17] his private prayer will not be rejected. But didn't you say that during the first three hours, the Holy One, blessed be He, is immersed in Torah study, and during the second three He judges the whole world? [How can you say that judgment is rendered in the first three hours?] You may reverse the order, or if you prefer, you do not have to reverse it, [and you can reconcile the inconsistency like this:] While God is immersed in studying the Torah—which is termed "truth" as in, "Buy *truth* and never sell it" (Proverbs 23:23)—He will not overstep the strict letter of the law [but will be stern and uncompromising]; but when He sits in judgment—which is not termed "truth"— God may overstep the strict letter of the law.[18] [Thus, in the first three hours God judges with unmitigated strictness. Therefore, on Rosh Hashanah, you should not pray without a *minyan* during those hours.]

ENCOURAGEMENT FOR *BAALEI TESHUVAH*

R. Yehoshua b. Levi said: What is meant by [the word *today* in, "You shall observe . . . the rules and laws that I am teaching you *today* so that you will do them" (Deuteronomy 7:11)? *Today* [i.e., in this world] is when you should do them; they cannot be done in the World to Come. *Today* is when you should do them, but you will not be rewarded for them today; [the spiritual reward is stored away in the World to Come]. R. Yehoshua b. Levi also said: All the *mitzvot* that the people of Israel do in this world will testify for them in the World to Come, as it says, "Let them bring their witnesses, and they will be vindicated, or else let them hear them say, 'It is the truth'" (Isaiah 43:9). "Let them bring their witnesses" refers to Israel. "Let them hear them say, 'It is the truth'" refers to the idolators.

R. Yehoshua b. Levi also said: The children of Israel made the golden calf, [and the only reason God did not save them from committing this grave sin was] in order to give reassurance to *baalei teshuvah*.[19] [If a

sinner says: "What good is my repentance; my *teshuvah* will never be accepted!" we will show him that God forgave even a sin as grave as worshipping the golden calf (Rashi).] For it says, [God said at Sinai,] "If only their hearts would always remain this way, where they are in such awe of Me" (Deuteronomy 5:26), [proof that they were perfect in their fear of God. But God allowed them to stray and make the golden calf to teach sinners that repentance is effective].

This statement agrees with what R. Yochanan said in the name of R. Shimon b. Yochai: It was not like David to behave the way he did [in connection with Bathsheba], nor was it like Israel [to worship the golden calf]. It was not like David, for it says, [David said] "My heart has died within me" (Psalms 109:22), [meaning, "I conquered my *yetzer hara*"]. Neither was it like Israel [to worship the golden calf], for it says, "If only their hearts would always remain this way." So, why did they commit these acts? (5a) [God ordained it] in order to teach you, that if a person has sinned [and doubts that his repentance will be accepted] you can tell him: Look at the individual [David, whose repentance was accepted]. And if a community commits a sin, you can tell them: Look at the community [of Israel whose sin was forgiven. You, too, will be forgiven].

And both these examples are necessary, for if only the case of David was mentioned, you might have thought that he was forgiven because his transgression was not widely known, but in the case of a community whose sins are public knowledge it might not be so. If, on the other hand, if only the case of a community was mentioned, you might have thought that they are forgiven because the combined merits of a community are greater; but with an individual whose merits are not so great, it is not so. Therefore, both are necessary. This agrees with the following statement by R. Shmuel b. Nachmani who said in the name of R. Yochanan: What is meant by the verse, "The utterance of David the son of Jesse, the utterance of the man who was established on high" (2 Samuel 23:1)? [It means:] The saying of David the son of Jesse, the man who established the principle of *teshuvah*.

R. Shmuel b. Nachmani in the name of R. Yochanan also said: Every mitzvah you do in this world precedes you in the World to Come, as it says, "Your righteous deed will precede you and the glory of God will gather you in [when you die]" (Isaiah 58:8). By the same token, every transgression a person commits clings to him and leads him on the day of judgment, as it says, "They cling to him in the passage of their ways" (Job 6:18). R. Elazar said: His transgression is tied to him like a dog, as it says, "[Joseph] did not listen to [his master's wife]. He would not even lie next to her, to be with her" (Genesis 39:10)—"He would not lie next to her" in this world, [for then he would have] "to be with her" in the World to Come.

AN UNGRATEFUL PEOPLE

Our Rabbis taught: It says, [God said,] "If only their hearts would always remain this way" (Deuteronomy 5:26). Moses said to the children of Israel: You are an ungrateful people, children of an ungrateful ancestor. When the Holy One, blessed be He, said to you, "If only their hearts would always remain this way," you should have said: "*You*, God, please give us such a heart!"[20] You showed your thanklessness when you said [about the wondrous gift of the manna], "We are getting disgusted (5b) with this insubstantial food" (Numbers 21:5). You are children of an ungrateful ancestor, for it says, [Adam said,] "The woman that you gave to be with me—she gave me what I ate from the tree" (Genesis 3:12). [Instead of being grateful to God for giving him a wife, Adam blamed her for his downfall (Rashi).] However, Moses gave this [admonition] to the Israelites only at the end of the forty years [of wandering in the wilderness], as it says, "I led you forty years in the wilderness . . . But until this day, God did not give you a heart to know, eyes to see and ears to hear" (Deuteronomy 29:3,4). Said Rabbah: From this you can learn that it may take forty years to know the mind of your master.

R. Yochanan said in the name of R. Bana'ah: What is the meaning of the verse, "You will be so fortunate to sow upon all waters, sending away the feet of the ox and the donkey" (Isaiah 32:20); [the ox and the donkey symbolize the *yetzer hara,* the evil impulse]. It means this: Fortunate is Israel; when they keep busy learning Torah and doing acts of kindness, they hold sway over their *yetzer hara*, and their *yetzer hara* does not control them. For it says, "You will be so fortunate to sow upon all waters." And "sowing" refers to *tzedakah* [charity], as it says, "Sow for yourselves *tzedakah*, and you will reap according to kindness" (Hosea 10:12). And "water" refers to the Torah, as it says, "Ho, everyone who is thirsty, go to the water" (Isaiah 55:1). The passage "sending away the feet of the ox and the donkey" was expounded by Tanna debei Eliyahu as follows: When it comes to studying the words of the Torah you should buckle down like an ox bearing its yoke and a donkey carrying its burden.

ADAM'S FIRST SUNSET

(8a) Our Rabbis taught: When Adam noticed the days getting gradually shorter,[21] he said, "Woe is me. Perhaps because of my sin the world around me is getting dark and returning to its primordial emptiness and formlessness. So this must be the death to which I have been sentenced from Heaven!" He began fasting and praying for eight days. But when the winter month of Tevet came around, and he observed the days getting longer, he said, "This is the natural way of the world," and made an eight-day holiday. In the following year he celebrated both periods as a holiday. But whereas he established the holidays for the sake of Heaven, his decendants, the heathens, observed them as pagan festivals.

Our Rabbis taught: When Adam, on the day he was created, saw the setting of the sun, he said, "Woe is me. Perhaps it is because of my sin that the world around me is getting dark and returning to its primordial emptiness and formlessness. So this must be the death to which I have been sentenced from Heaven!" So he stayed up all night fasting and crying, and Eve was crying opposite him. However when dawn broke, he said, "This is the natural way of the world." He then roused himself and offered an ox whose horns preceded his hoofs,[22] as it says, "And it shall please God more than a full-grown ox, that has horns and hoofs" (Psalms 69:32).

THE WORLD WILL EXIST 6,000 YEARS

The Tanna debei Eliyahu taught: The world will exist six thousand years: During the first two thousand years it is to be devoid [of Torah]; the next two thousand years are the period of Torah; and the following two thousand years are the era of *Mashiach*, and because of our sins many years of these have elapsed [and *Mashiach* still has not come). [The Gemara asks:] From what point in time do we count the two thousand years of Torah? Do you think from the Giving of the Torah at Sinai? In that case you will find that there are not quite two thousand years from then until now [i.e., until four thousand years after Creation], for if you calculate the years from Creation to the Giving of the Torah [which took place in the year 2448 of Creation], you will find that they are made up of two thousand plus a part of the third [two] thousand; [448 years into the third 2000 years]. We must therefore say that the two thousand years of Torah are calculated from the time that Abraham and Sarah "gathered souls in Haran" (Genesis 12:5), [i.e., converted people to God's cause (Rashi)], for according to tradition Abraham was fifty-two years old at that time.[23] And from Abraham's fifty-second year [i.e., the year 2000] until the Giving of the Torah it is exactly 448 years.

REBBI COUNSELS ANTONINUS[24]

(10a) Antoninus once said to Rebbi: I would like my son Asverus to reign instead of me, and Tiberias to be declared a colony [which would exempt its inhabitants from paying taxes].[25] If I asked for one of these things, it would be approved [by the Senate], but both would not be approved. [Which of the two should I request?] Rebbi [who did not want to give a direct answer so as not to be accused of meddling in government affairs] brought in a man, mounted him on the shoulders of another man, and handed the latter a pigeon. He then told the one who carried his fellow: Tell the fellow on your shoulders to set the bird free.

Antoninus understood this charade to mean that he should ask [the Senate] to appoint his son Asverus to rule in his stead, and that his son then would make Tiberias a tax-free colony.

Another time Antoninus told Rebbi that the Roman officials were getting on his nerves. Rebbi thereupon took him into the garden and picked some radishes, one at the time. Antoninus said to himself: He is advising me to do away with them one at a time, but not to remove them all at once, [for then they might revolt against me]. (10b) But why didn't Rebbi give him straight answers? [Why did he send coded messages?] He thought that the Roman officials might hear of it and cause him trouble. Then why didn't he tell him secretly? Because it says, "A bird of the skies may carry the sound" (Ecclesiastes 10:20); [secrets are bound to be leaked].

Antoninus had a daughter named Girah who committed adultery, so he sent Rebbi an herb named *gargira*,[26] [hinting, *gar Gira*, "Gira has gone astray"]. Rebbi in return sent him some *cusbarta*[27] [hinting: *cus brata*, "Kill your daughter"]. Antoninus then sent some *karti*, leek [hinting, *karet*, "cut off." If I kill my daughter I will be cut off and have no offspring]. Rebbi sent back *chasa*, lettuce [hinting *chas*, "pity," indicating: Have pity on her].

Antoninus used to send Rebbi pieces of gold in a leather bag filled with wheat on top. He said to his servants, "Carry the wheat to Rebbi." [He misled them, so that they should not pilfer the gold pieces]. Rabbi protested, "I don't need it, I have enough gold of my own." Antoninus replied, "Leave it to your heirs, that they leave it to their heirs, for your descendants and those who will follow them will hand it over to those who will come after me," [hinting that future Roman emperors would extort money from the Jews].

ANTONINUS' CLANDESTINE VISITS TO REBBI

Antoninus had a tunnel that led from his house to the house of Rebbi. Every time he visited Rebbi [to learn Torah (Rashi)], he took with him two slaves [as escorts, as befits an emperor]; one he killed at the door of Rebbi's house, and the other he killed when he returned to his own house, [for fear that they would report his clandestine visits to Rebbi]. Antoninus warned Rebbi, "When I visit you, make sure that no one else is present." One day he found R. Chanina b. Chama sitting there, so he said, "Didn't I tell you that no one should be present when I come calling?" Replied Rebbi, "This is not [an ordinary] human being." To which Antoninus retorted, "Then let him tell the servant who is sleeping outside to get up and come in." R. Chanina b. Chama went out and found that the man had been killed. He thought, "What shall I do? Shall I tell him that he is dead? But [the Sages say that] you should not be a bearer of bad tidings. Shall I leave him

there and walk away? I would be humiliating the emperor." So he prayed for the dead man, and he came back to life. He then sent him in. Said Antoninus, "I know full well that even the least one among you can revive the dead; still, when I come calling, I don't want anyone else to be there."

Whenever Antoninus came, he used to wait on Rebbi and serve him food and drink, and when Rebbi wanted to go to bed, Antoninus hunkered down in front of it, saying, "Climb into your bed by stepping on me." "It is not seemly to treat an emperor with disdain," Rebbi answered. "I only wish that I could serve as a mattress to you in the World to Come," Antoninus replied. Once he asked Rebbi, "Will I enter the World to Come?" "Yes," said Rebbi. Antoninus persisted, "But doesn't it say, 'There will be no survivor to the House of Esau' [Obadiah 1:18]?" [Esau symbolizes Rome.] Replied Rebbi, "That refers only to people who act [as ruthlessly as] Esau." Antoninus challenged, "But doesn't it also say, 'There [in Gehinnom] is Edom [i.e., Rome], her kings and all her princes' [Ezekiel 32:29]? Rebbi explained, "It says '*her kings*,' but not '*all* her kings'; it says, 'all her princes' but not 'all her officers.'" We learned the same thing in a *Baraita*: It says, "her kings," but not *all* her kings— this excludes Antoninus the son of Asverus; "all her princes" but not all her officers—this excludes Ketia the son of Shalom.

KETIA'S MARTYRDOM

What is the story of Ketia the son of Shalom? There once was a Roman emperor who hated the Jews. One day he said to the prominent members of his cabinet, [alluding to the Jews in his empire], "If a person has a growth on his foot, should he cut it away and be comfortable, or leave it on and suffer?" They replied, "He should cut it away and be comfortable." Thereupon Ketia the son of Shalom [one of the Roman senators] spoke up and said, "To begin with, you cannot exterminate all of them, for it says, 'For I have scattered you like the four winds [i.e., directions] of heaven'" (Zechariah 2:10). What does this verse imply? If it means that Israel would be scattered to the four corners of the world, then, instead of saying, '*like* the four winds,' it would have said, '*to* the four winds.' It must therefore mean that, just as the world cannot exist without winds, so the world cannot exist without Israel. And what's more, [if you destroy the Jews,] your empire will be called a crippled empire."

The emperor replied, "You have spoken well. However, we have a rule that whoever defeats the emperor in debate is thrown into the furnace. As Ketia was being led away, a Roman matron said about him, "I pity the ship that sails [toward the harbor] without paying the tax," [meaning: I pity you, Ketia. You are giving up your life for the Jews, but since you are not circumcised, you do not have a share in the World to

733

Come[28] (Rashi)]. Hearing this, Ketia cut away his foreskin, exclaiming, "You have paid the tax, you will pass muster and enter Gan Eden." As he was being thrown into the furnace, he exclaimed, "I leave all my possessions to R. Akiva and his colleagues!"

R. Akiva interpreted Ketia's words according to the verse, "[The showbreads] shall be given to Aaron and his sons" (Leviticus 24:9), which is expounded to mean that one-half goes to Aaron and one-half to his sons. A heavenly Voice then exclaimed, "Ketia ben Shalom is destined for eternal life in the World to Come." When Rebbi heard about this he cried, saying, "There are some who earn their portion in the World to Come in one instant; others may earn theirs only after many years!"

Antoninus waited on Rebbi; Adarkan [a great Persian ruler] waited on Rav. When Antoninus died, Rebbi lamented, "The bond of our friendship has been torn apart!" When Adarkan died, Rav lamented, (11a) "The bond of our friendship has been torn apart."

ONKELOS CONVERTS ROMAN SOLDIERS

When Onkelos[29] the son of Kalonymos became a convert to Judaism the Emperor sent a unit of Roman soldiers after him to arrest him, but he won them over by quoting Scriptural verses, so that they, too, converted to Judaism. The Emperor then sent another unit of soldiers after him, ordering them not to speak to him at all. As they were about to take him away, he said to them, "Let me tell you just a simple thing: [In a procession] a low-ranking dignitary carries the torch in front of a high-ranking official, a high-ranking official in front of the senator, the senator in front of the duke, the duke in front of the governor, but does the governor carry a torch in front of the people that follow him?" "No," they replied. "But the Holy One, blessed be He, does carry the light in front of Israel," he countered. For it says, "God went before them . . . as a pillar of fire providing them with light" (Exodus 13:21). Thereupon they, too, converted.

The emperor sent another unit, ordering them not to have any conversation with Onkelos at all. They arrested him, and as they were marching along Onkelos saw a *mezuzah* attached to a doorframe. He placed his hand on it and smiled. "Why are you smiling?" the soldiers asked. He replied, "Everyone knows that a king lives inside the palace, and his guards stand outside to protect him. But when it comes to the Holy One, blessed be He, it is His servants who live inside, while He protects them from the outside. For it says, 'God will guard your departure and your arrival, from this time on forever'" (Psalms 121:8). Thereupon they, too, converted. After that the Emperor gave up and did not send any more soldiers to capture him.

ANTONINUS AND REBBI

It says, "God said [to Rebekkah], 'Two nations [*goyim*] are in your womb'" (Genesis 25:23). Rav Yehudah said in the name of Rav: Don't read *goyim* [nations], but *gei'im* [lords]. This refers to Antoninus [a descendant of Esau] and Rebbi [a descendant of Jacob] on whose tables there was never a lack of lettuce, radish, and cucumber, either in the summer or the winter, and as a Tanna said: Radish is good for dissolving food, lettuce is good for the digestion, cucumbers make the intestines expand. But didn't they teach in the yeshivah of R. Yishmael that cucumbers are called *kishuim* because they are as hard [*kashim*] and harmful to the body as swords? That is no difficulty: that was said of large ones, whereas we are talking about small ones.

R. ELIEZER AND THE *MINIM*

(16b) Our Rabbis taught: When R. Eliezer was arrested on suspicion of belonging to the *minim*, a heretic sect,[30] they brought him up to the platform to be judged. Said the Roman governor to him, "How can a sage like you be involved with such nonsense?" He replied, "I trust the Judge [to be fair]." The governor thought that he had him in mind, while R. Eliezer actually was referring to the Heavenly Judge. So the governor said, "Because you believed that I would judge fairly, by Dimus,[31] you are free to go." When R. Eliezer came home, [he agonized wondering for what failing such a dreadful thing had happened to him (Rashi)]. When his disciples came to comfort him, he did not accept their consolation. Said R. Akiva to him, "Rabbi, please allow me to repeat to you something you have taught me." "Go ahead," said R. Eliezer. "Rabbi," he said, "perhaps you came across one of the teachings of the *minim*, (17a) and you liked it, and that's why you were arrested?" He exclaimed, "Akiva, you have reminded me of something! I was once walking in the upper market of Tzipori [Sepphoris] when I ran into one of the *minim*, named Jacob of Kfar Sekania. He said to me, 'It says in your Torah, "Do not bring a prostitute's fee . . . to the Temple of God your Lord" [Deuteronomy 23:19].[32] May such money be used to build a toilet for the high priest?' And I did not answer him. So he said to me, 'It says, "For they [the idols] were amassed from fees for prostitution, and they shall become prostitutes' fees again" [Micah 1:7]. I was taught that this means: Money that came from a filthy place may be spent on a filthy place.' I liked that explanation very much, and that is why I was arrested on suspicion of being a *min*, for I ignored the admonition, 'Keep yourself far away from her'—which refers to the *minim* 'do not come near the door of her house'—which refers to government circles [Proverbs 5:8]." There are some who apply "Keep yourself far away from her" to both the *minim* and government circles, and "do not come near the door of her house" to a prostitute. And how far should a person keep away? R. Chisda said, "Four cubits."

"The grave has two daughters [that say,] 'Give me, give me!'" (Proverbs 30:15). What is meant by "Give me, give me"? R. Chisda said in the name of Mar Ukva: It is the voice of the two daughters who cry from Gehinnom, calling to this world: Bring, bring! And who are they? *Minut* [heresy], crying out, "Bring me followers of heresy" and the government [crying, "Bring me taxes and tariffs for the king"]. Others say: R. Chisda said in the name of Mar Ukva: It is the voice of Gehinnom crying out, "Bring me the two daughters who cry and call in this world, 'Bring, bring.'"

It says [in reference to apostates who converted to heresy], "All who come to her do not return, nor do they attain the paths of life" (Proverbs 2:19). [The Gemara asks:] But if they do not return, how can they attain the paths of life? [The Gemara answers:] What it means is that even if they repent and turn away from heresy they will not attain the paths of life, [i.e., they will die before long from inner turmoil or the government will execute them (Rashi).

ELAZAR B. DORDIA'S REPENTANCE

Doesn't a person die also when he renounces sins other than heresy? Surely we learned in a *Baraita*: They said about Elazar b. Dordia that there was not a prostitute in the world that he had not visited. Once he heard that there was a prostitute in one of the towns by the sea [whose charms were so great] that she demanded a purse of *dinars* for her services. So he took with him a purse of *dinars* and crossed seven rivers to get to her. As he was with her he told him that even if he repented, his *teshuvah* would never be accepted.

Hearing this he sat between two mountains and cried out, "O, you hills and mountains, please pray for me!" They replied, "How can we pray for you; we need to pray for ourselves, for it says, 'For the mountains will move and the hills will shake'" (Isaiah 54:10). So he cried out, "O, heaven and earth! Please pray for me!" They, too, replied, "How can we pray for you when we need to pray for ourselves, for it says, 'The heavens will dissipate like smoke, and the earth will wear out like a garment' (ibid. 51:6). He then exclaimed, "O, sun and moon, please pray for me!" But they gave the same answer, "How can we pray for you when we ourselves are in need of prayer, for it says, 'Then the moon will be ashamed, and the sun will be abashed'" (ibid. 24:23). He cried out, "O, stars and constellations, please pray for me!" They answered, "How can we pray for you? We need prayers ourselves. For it says, 'All the hosts of heaven will dissolve'" (ibid. 34:4). Finally he said, "I see that it is up to me alone!" He then placed

his head between his knees and wailed bitterly until his soul departed.

Then a heavenly Voice was heard proclaiming: *Rabbi* Elazar b. Dordai is destined for the life of the World to Come! [The Gemara concludes:] So you see that a person who repented of a sin other than heresy also died. [The Gemara answers:] In this case, since he was so deeply involved in immorality it is as if he had been guilty of *minut* [heresy]. When Rebbi heard this story he cried, saying, "There are some who earn eternal life only after many years, yet here is a person who earned it in an instant!" Rebbi also remarked, "Not only that, but he even was called 'Rabbi' [by the heavenly Voice]!"

THE TORAH PROTECTS

R. Chanina and R. Yonatan were walking along the highway when they came to a fork in the road: one road leading to a house of idol worship, the other leading to a house of prostitution. Said one to the other: Let us take the road that leads to the house of idol worship (17b) because the desire to worship idols has been abolished,[33] [and let us not expose ourselves to the seduction of the prostitutes]. The other countered, "No, let us go the way that leads to the house of prostitution, overcome our *yetzer hara*, and be rewarded for it." When they approached the house of prostitution they noticed that the prostitutes withdrew into the house. Said one to the other, "How did you know [that our merit was so great that the prostitutes would withdraw when they saw us coming (Anaf Yosef)]?" The other replied, quoting, "[The Torah] will protect you from immorality, and understanding will safeguard you to rescue you from the way of evil" (Proverbs 2:11,12), [and while we were walking we were discussing Torah thoughts; therefore we were protected (Rashi)].

Our Rabbis taught: When R. Elazar b. Parta and R. Chanina b. Teradyon were arrested [by the Romans], R. Elazar b. Parta said to R. Chanina b. Teradyon: You can be happy, for you have been arrested on one charge; woe is me that I have been arrested on five charges. R. Chanina replied: You can be happy for you have been arrested on five charges but you will be saved; woe is me that I have been arrested on one charge, but I will not be saved, for you involved yourself both in the study of Torah and acts of kindness, whereas I was engaged only in Torah study.

This agrees with R. Huna's opinion, for R. Huna said: He who engages in the study of the Torah alone is as if he had no God [to protect him], for it says, "Israel has gone many days without the true God . . . and without Torah" (2 Chronicles 15:3). What is meant by "without the true God"? It means that a person who engages in the study of the Torah alone is as if he had no God [to protect him]. [The Gemara asks:] But did not R. Chanina involve himself with charitable acts?

735

Surely we learned in a *Baraita*: R. Eliezer b. Yaakov said: A person should not donate money to a charity unless it is supervised by a Torah scholar as great as R. Chanina b. Teradyon [who was a treasurer of a charity fund, so he *was* involved with charity].

[The Gemara answers:] True, he was an honest treasurer, but he did not give charity himself. [The Gemara asks:] But haven't we learned in a *Baraita* that R. Chanina b. Teradyon said: [By mistake] I mixed Purim money [which the poor may use for no other purpose than to buy food for their Purim feast] with general charity funds. [Since I gave the money to the poor without specifying that it was Purim money] I gave them Purim money from my own funds, [proof that he did give charity]. [The Gemara answers:] True, he did indeed give charity, but not as much as he should have.

THE TRIAL OF
R. ELAZAR B. PARTA

When R. Elazar b. Parta was brought to trial [by the Romans] they asked him, "Why have you been teaching the Torah,[34] and why have you been stealing?" He answered, "If a person is a scholar he is not a robber; if he is a robber he is no scholar. And I am neither the one nor the other." "Then why do they call you 'teacher'?" they asked. "I teach weaving," he replied. So they placed two coils [of thread] before him and asked, "Which is the warp and which is the woof?"[35] A miracle happened and a male bee came and sat on the woof, and a female bee came and sat on the warp. "This is the woof, and this is the warp," he answered correctly.[36]

Then they asked him, "Why did you not come to the [idolatrous] assembly at the Meeting House [which the Jews were required to attend]? He replied, "I am an old man, and I was afraid that I would be trampled in the crush." "And how many old people have been trampled till now?" they queried. Again a miracle happened, for on that very day an old man had been trampled to death. "And why did you let your slave go free?" they asked. [The Romans prohibited freeing slaves, because the Torah mandates that Jewish slaves must be set free after six years or in the Jubilee year.] "This never happened," he shot back.

One of them then got up to testify against R. Elazar b. Parta, but Elijah appeared disguised as a Roman senator and said to the false witness, "Leave him alone. Just as miracles occurred in all the other cases, a miracle will happen also in this case, and you will be exposed as a villain." But the false witness paid no attention to Elijah and got up to testify. Just then an urgent letter had to sent to be the emperor, and they appointed this [false witness] to deliver it. On the way, Elijah came and tossed him a distance of four hundred *parsa*, so that he never was heard from again.

THE TRIAL OF R. CHANINA B.
TERADYON

R. Chaninah b. Teradyon [one of the Ten Martyrs][37] was then brought before the judges. They asked him, "Why did you occupy yourself in studying the Torah?"[38] He replied, "The Lord my God commanded me." They immediately sentenced him to be burned, his wife to be killed, and his daughter to be taken to a house of prostitution.

The punishment of burning came on him because he (18a) pronounced the ineffable Name of God as it is written[39] [and not as *Adonai*, as he should have]. [The Gemara asks:] But how could he have done that? Have we not learned: Abba Shaul said: He who pronounces the Name of God as it is written has no share in the World to Come? [The Gemara answers:] He did so in the course of learning, as we are taught in a *Baraita*: It says, "Do not learn *to do* the revolting practices of those nations" (Deuteronomy 18:9), [you may not *do* these practices] but you are allowed to learn about them in order to understand and to teach, [and R. Chanina only did it in order to learn about them]. So why was he punished? Because he pronounced God's ineffable Name in public.

His wife was condemned to be killed because she did not stop him from doing it. From this we can infer that whoever has the power to prevent wrongdoing and does not protest is punished for it.

His daughter was condemned to a house of prostitution, because [of an incident] related by R. Yochanan. He said that once this daughter was walking in front of some Roman aristocrats who remarked, "How elegant are the steps of this girl!" Overhearing this, she immediately made a conscious effort to walk gracefully. And that is what Resh Lakish had in mind when he said: What is meant by the verse, "The iniquity of my heel will surround me" (Psalms 49:6)—The sins a person commits with his heels[40] in this world will surround him [and testify against him] on Judgment Day.

As the three of them were led away they accepted the righteousness of Divine judgment. R. Chanania said, "The deeds of the Mighty One are perfect, for all His ways are just" (Deuteronomy 32:4). His wife continued, "He is a faithful God, never unfair; righteous and moral is He" (ibid.). His daughter followed suit, "Great in counsel and mighty in deed, Your eyes observe all the ways of mankind, so as to repay each man according to his ways and the consequences of his deeds" (Jeremiah 32:19). Said Rava: How great were these righteous people that the appropriate verses came to mind at the precise moment they were accepting the righteousness of Divine judgment.

THE AGONY OF
R. CHANINA B. TERADYON

We learned in a *Baraita*: When R. Yose b. Kisma became sick, R. Chanina b. Teradyon came to visit him.

736

R. Yose b. Kisma said to him, "Chanina my brother, don't you know that the reason this [Roman] empire rules is because Heaven ordained it. For although Rome has laid waste God's Temple, burned His Sanctuary, killed His pious ones, and annihilated His best ones, it still is firmly established. And in spite of this, I hear that you are studying the Torah, hold public meetings, and carry a Torah scroll around with you all the time [in defiance of the Roman prohibition]. R. Chanina replied, "Heaven will have mercy." R. Yose countered, "I am giving you hard facts, and you are saying, 'Heaven will have mercy,' relying on miracles! I would not be surprised if they burned you together with your Torah scroll." "Rabbi," R. Chanina then said, "where do I stand with regard to the World to Come?" [Although he learned Torah constantly he was doubtful.] Replied R. Yose b. Kisma, "Have you done any good deeds?" [For good deeds is what counts.] R. Chanina answered, "I once mistook Purim money for regular *tzedakah* money and distributed from my own money to the poor."[41] "If so," replied R. Yose b. Kisma, "I wish that my share in the World to Come would be like your share, and my lot like yours."

It was said that R. Yose b. Kisma died shortly thereafter. All the Roman aristocrats came to his funeral and eulogized him at a large assembly. When they came back they found R. Chanina b. Teradyon studying the Torah at public gatherings and carrying a Torah scroll around with him. They arrested him, wrapped him in a Torah scroll, and placed bundles of branches around him that they set on fire. They then brought pieces of wool soaked in water and placed them on his heart so that he should not die quickly. His daughter exclaimed, "Father, that I should see you [suffer] like this! [Is that the reward you get for your Torah learning? (Rashi).] He replied, "If I had burned alone, it would be hard for me; but now that I am burned together with a *sefer Torah*, I know that He Who will avenge the suffering of the Torah will avenge my suffering."

His students called out, "Rabbi, what do you see?" He replied, "I see the parchment burning, but the letters are soaring on high!" [Torah scrolls may be burned, but the spirit of the Torah lives on forever (*Maharsha*).] "Open your mouth," they said, "so that the fire should enter your body [and put an end to your agony]." He replied, "Let He Who gave me my soul take it away, but no one should do anything to shorten his life."

The Roman executioner then said to R. Chanina, "Rabbi, if I boost the heat of the flame and take away the pieces of wool, would you bring me to the World to Come?" "Yes, I will," he replied. "Swear it to me," he demanded. He swore. He then stirred up the fire and removed the pieces of wool on R. Chanina's heart, so that his soul quickly left him. The executioner then jumped and threw himself into the fire, whereupon a heavenly Voice exclaimed: R. Chanina b. Teradyon and the executioner have been designated for the World

to Come. When Rebbi heard this he cried and said, "One person earns his share in the World to Come in an instant; another earns it only after many years."

GOD OF MEIR, ANSWER ME!

(18a) Beruriah, the wife of R. Meir, was a daughter of R. Chanina b. Teradyon. She said to her husband, "I am ashamed that my sister is in a house of prostitution."[42] So he took a *tarkav* full of *dinars*, and went to get her released. He said to himself: If she has done nothing wrong, a miracle will happen; but if she has fallen, no miracle will happen to her. Disguised as a Roman horseman he came to her and said, "Give yourself to me." She answered, "I have my menstrual period." "I am willing to wait," he retorted. "But you can find many girls here that are much prettier than me," she said.

He said to himself: That proves that she has not done wrong. No doubt she says the same thing to whoever comes to her. He then went to her guard and said, "Let me take her out of here." The guard replied, "I am afraid of the government." "Take this *tarkav* of *dinars*," R. Meir said. "Use half of it to bribe your superiors, and keep the rest for yourself." "And what shall I do when the half is spent [and they demand more for their silence]?" he asked. R. Meir replied, "Say, 'God of Meir, answer me!' and you will be saved. (18b) "But how can I be sure that this will help?" the guard asked.

R. Meir replied, "I'll show you right now." There were some vicious dogs there. R. Meir taunted them, throwing a clod of earth at them, and when they were poised to pounce on him he said, "God of Meir, answer me!" Instantly the dogs turned around and left him alone. The guard then turned over the girl to him. In the end the authorities found out about it, and the guard was taken to the gallows to be hanged. As he stood there he cried out, "God of Meir, answer me!" They took him down and asked him what he meant, and he told them the whole story. They then engraved the image of R. Meir's on the gate of Rome and announced that whoever saw a person resembling it should turn him in.

One day, some Romans saw him and chased him. He ran away from them and sought refuge in a house of prostitution, [so that his pursuers would not identify him, thinking that a sage like R. Meir would never enter a house of ill repute]. Others say that he happened to see just then a bowl of food cooked by heathens and dipped in one finger and then sucked the other [to mislead his pursuers]. Others say that Elijah the prophet appeared as a prostitute and embraced him [as if he were an old acquaintance]. His pursuers said: This cannot be R. Meir. God forbid! R. Meir would never do a thing like that. He then decided to run away to Babylonia. Others say that he ran away because of the incident with his wife Beruriah [who died under tragic circumstances].

THE PUNISHMENT
FOR SCOFFING

R. Shimon b. Pazi expounded: What is the meaning of the verse, "Praiseworthy is the man who has not walked in the counsel of the wicked, and did not stand in the path of the sinful, and did not sit in the company of scorners" (Psalms 1:1)? If he did not walk there, how could he stand there. And if he did not stand among them, how could he sit among them? And since he did not sit [in the company of scorners] he could not have scorned! The phraseology comes to teach you that if you walk [with the wicked] you will end up standing with them; and if you stand with them, you will ultimately sit with them; and if you sit with them; you will also scorn. And if a person scorns, the following verse will apply to him, "If you have become wise, you have become wise for your own good, and if you have scoffed, you alone will bear responsibility" (Proverbs 9:12). R. Elazar said: He who scoffs will be stricken with affliction, as it says, "So now, do not scoff lest your affliction becomes more severe" (Isaiah 28:22).

Rava used to say to the scholars: Please do not scoff, so that you will not have to endure pain. R. Katina said: Whoever scoffs will have his income slashed, as it says, "He withdraws His hand [that gives sustenance] in the case of scoffers" (Hosea 7:5). R. Shimon b. Lakish said: Whoever scoffs will fall into Gehinnom. R. Oshaia said: He who is arrogant will fall into Gehinnom. R. Chanilai b. Chanilai said: He who scoffs brings destruction on the world, as it says, "So now, do not scoff lest your affliction becomes more severe, for total obliteration have I heard from my Lord, God" (Isaiah 28:22). R. Elazar said: Scoffing is indeed a serious sin since at first it is punished by affliction, but it ends in obliteration, [as stated in the above verse].

R. Shimon b. Pazi expounded the verse, "Praiseworthy is the man who has not walked in the counsel of the wicked" (Psalms 1:1), saying: this refers to a person who has not gone to the theaters and circuses of the idolators; "and did not stand in the path of the sinful" refers to a person who does not attend contests of wild beasts [in Roman arenas]; "and did not sit in the company of scorners" refers to a person who does not attend wrestling matches.[43] Now you might say: Since I do not go to theaters or circuses, and I do not attend contests of wild animals, I will spend my time sleeping. That is why the next verse says, "Rather the Torah of God is his delight, and he studies it day and night" (ibid. v. 2).

R. Shmuel b. Nachmani said in the name of R. Yochanan: "Praiseworthy is the man who has not walked in the counsel of the wicked"—(19a) that is our father Abraham, who did not follow the counsel of the people of the Generation of the Dispersion[44] because that generation was wicked,[45] as it says, "They said, 'Come let us build ourselves a city, and a tower whose top shall reach the sky'" (Genesis 11:4). "And did not stand in the path of the sinful"—Abraham did not stand in the company of the people of Sodom who were sinful, as it says, "The people of Sodom were very wicked, and they sinned against God" (Genesis 13:13). "And did not sit in the company of scorners"—for he did not sit in the gathering of the Philistines, [when he lived among them,][46] because they were scoffers, as it says, "It happened when their hearts became merry that they said, 'Call Samson here and let him entertain us'" (Judges 16:25). [The Philistines ridiculed Samson.]

THE PROPER METHOD
FOR TORAH STUDY

"Praiseworthy is the man who fears God, who greatly desires His commandments" (Psalms 112:1). Does this mean that praiseworthy is the *man* and not the *woman*? R. Amram said in the name of Rav: It means, praiseworthy is he who repents while he is still a vigorous young man. R. Yehoshua b. Levi said: Praiseworthy is he who conquers his evil impulse like a [vigorous] man. "Who greatly desires His commandments" (ibid.) was explained by R. Elazar as follows: "he desires His commandments" but not the reward of His commandments. This is in line with the following aphorism in the Mishnah: Be not like servants who serve their master for the sake of receiving a reward; instead be like servants who serve their master not for the sake of receiving a reward (*Avot* 1:3).

"But his desire is in the Torah of God" (Psalms 1:2). Said Rebbi: A person is most successful in his Torah studies when he learns his favorite tractate, for it says, "But *his desire* is in the Torah of God."

Levi and R. Shimon b. Rebbi once were sitting before Rebbi and expounding portions of Scripture. When the book [they were discussing] was concluded, Levi said: Please bring in the Book of Proverbs, while R. Shimon b. Rebbi said: Please bring in the Book of Psalms. Levi was overruled, and the Book of Psalms was brought in. When they came to the verse, "But his desire is in the Torah of God," Rebbi commented: A person is most successful in his Torah studies when he learns the parts he has a predilection for. To which Levi remarked: Hereby you have given me permission to leave [the lecture, because Psalms is not my favorite subject].

R. Avdimi b. Chama said: When you engage in Torah study, the Holy One, blessed be He, fulfills your desires, as it says, "His desire is [granted if he studies] the Torah of God."

Rava said: In the beginning of this verse the Torah is called "the Torah of God" but after [you have toiled to understand it] it is called your own, since first it says, "His desire is in the *Torah of God*," and the verse continues, "and in *his {own}* Torah he meditates day and night."

Rava also said: You should first study the Torah and meditate in it afterward.[47] For it says "the Torah of God" and then "in *his {own}* Torah he meditates." Rava said furthermore: Go ahead and learn, even though you are liable to forget, and even though you do not understand exactly what it means. For it says, "My soul is shattered with yearning for your ordinances always" (Psalms 119:20). The verse says "shattered"; it does not say "pulverized." [It is enough for the soul to break up the grain (i.e., grasp the general drift), even though it cannot crush it into fine flour, (i.e., understand all the intricate details)].

"He shall be like a tree transplanted alongside brooks of water" (ibid. 1:3). In the yeshivah of R. Yannai they taught: It says "a tree *transplanted*, not "a tree *planted*." Which implies that whoever learns Torah from only one teacher will never be successful; [he has to "transplant" himself to other teachers so as to learn different approaches]. R. Chisda said to his students: I would like to tell you something, but I am afraid you will leave and go elsewhere: Whoever learns Torah from only one teacher will never be successful. They then left him and went to study under Rabbah who explained to them that this saying applies only to probing and analyzing a Talmudic subject [after you are well-versed in relevant text], but when it comes to basic *halachah* it is better to learn from one teacher, so that (**19b**) you don't become confused by the legal terminology [which varies from teacher to teacher].

"Alongside brooks of water" (ibid.)—R. Tanchum b. Chanilai said: This implies that a person should divide his years of study into three parts and devote one-third of them to Scripture, one-third to Mishnah, and one-third to Talmud. [The Gemara asks:] But does a person know how long he is going to live [that he can divide his life span into three]? [The Gemara answers:] What he meant is that you should divide each day into three parts.

"That yields its fruit in its season, and whose leaf never withers" (ibid.). Rava explained: If he yields his fruit in its season, his leaf never withers [meaning: if the student fixes regular times for Torah study, his learning will be of lasting benefit (Rashi)]. Otherwise, the following verse applies both to the student and the teacher, "Not so the wicked; they are like the chaff that the wind blows away" (ibid. v. 4).

R. Abba said in the name of R. Huna, in the name of Rav: It says, "For she has felled many victims; the number of her slain is huge" (Proverbs 7:26). "For she has felled many victims" refers to a rabbinical student who renders decisions before he has reached the age for ordination. "The number of her slain is huge" refers to a rabbinical student who has reached the age of ordination but refuses to render decisions. And what is the age for ordination? When he is forty years old. [The Gemara challenges this:] But Rava decided *halachic* questions, [although he died when he was forty years old]? [The Gemara answers:] [He could render decisions before the age of forty] because there was no one as great in learning as he.

TORAH STUDY WILL MAKE YOU PROSPER

"Whose leaf never withers." R. Acha b. Adda said in the name of Rav, others say: R. Acha b. Abba in the name of Rav Hamnuna, in the name of Rav: Even the small talk of Torah scholars needs to be studied, for it says, "Whose leaf never withers."[48]

R. Yehoshua b. Levi said: The following idea is mentioned in the Torah, repeated in the Prophets and mentioned a third time in the Writings: Whoever occupies himself with Torah study will be successful in all his undertakings. In the Torah, for it says, "If you safeguard the words of this covenant and keep them, you will be successful in all you do" (Deuteronomy 29:8). Repeated in the Prophets, "Let not this Book of the Torah cease from your lips, but recite it day and night, so that you may observe faithfully all that is written in it. Only then will you prosper in your undertakings, and only then will you be successful" (Joshua 1:8). A third time in the Writings, "But his desire is in the Torah of God, and in His Torah he meditates day and night. He shall be like a tree rooted alongside brooks of water, that yield its fruit in its season, and everything he does will succeed" (Psalms 1:2,3).

GUARD YOUR TONGUE FROM EVIL

R. Alexandri once called out, "Who wants life? Who wants life?" A throng of people gathered around him, shouting, "Give us life!" He then recited to them the verse, "Who is the man who is eager for life, who desires years of good fortune? Guard your tongue from evil, and your lips from deceitful speech. Shun evil and do good, seek peace and pursue it" (Psalms 34:13–15). A person might say: I guarded my tongue from evil and my lips from deceitful speech, I may therefore sleep away my days. That is why it says, "Shun evil and do good [*tov*]," and good [*tov*] refers to the Torah, as it says, "For I give you good [*tov*] instruction, do not forsake My Torah" (Proverbs 4:2).

THE *BERACHAH* WE SAY UPON SEEING BEAUTIFUL PEOPLE

(**20a**) It says [concerning the seven Canaanite nations,] "*Lo techaneim,* Do not show them favor" (Deuteronomy 7:2). This is interpreted to mean: Do not find them graceful [*chein*], which supports the opinion of Rav. For Rav said: It is forbidden to say: How beautiful is this idolatress! An objection was raised [from the following incidents]: It happened that R. Shimon b. Gamliel while standing on a step on the Temple Mount saw a heathen woman who was exceptionally beautiful, and he exclaimed: How great are Your works, O God!" (Psalms 104:24). Likewise, when R. Akiva saw the wife of the evil Governor Turnus Rufus, he spat, then laughed, and then wept. He spat, because she originated from a putrid drop [of semen]; he laughed, because he foresaw that she would convert to Judaism and that he would marry her, and he wept, that such beauty should eventually be buried in the earth. [By admiring heathen women, both R. Shimon b. Gamliel and R. Akiva seemed to defy Rav's ruling!] This does not contradict Rav, for the Rabbis were merely praising God. For a Tanna said: When seeing exceptionally beautiful people you should recite the *berachah*, "Who has such in His universe."

THE COWS' SONG OF PRAISE

(24b) It says, [when the Holy Ark was returned from Philistine captivity on a wagon pulled by two cows,] "The cows set out on the direct road [*vayisharnah*]— on the road to Beth-Shemesh" (1 Samuel 6:12). What is the meaning of the word *vayisharnah*? Said R. Yochanan in the name of R. Meir: The cows sang a song [*vayisharnah* is seen as cognate to *shirah*, song]. R. Zutra b. Toviah said in the name of Rav: The cows turned their faces toward the Ark and began to sing. And what did they sing? R. Yochanan said in the name of R. Meir: They sang [the Song of the Sea, beginning with the words], "Moses and the children of Israel then sang this song" (Exodus 15:1). R. Yochanan himself said that they sang, "And you will say on that day, 'Give thanks to God, declare His Name, make His acts known among the peoples; declare that His Name is exalted'" (Isaiah 12:4). R. Shimon b. Lakish said: They sang the "Orphaned" Psalm,[49] "A psalm! Sing to God a new song for He has done wonders; His own right hand and holy arm have helped Him" (Psalm 98). R. Eliezer said: They sang, "God has reigned: Let peoples tremble" (ibid. 99). R. Shmuel b. Nachmani said: They sang, "God has reigned. He has donned grandeur" (ibid. 93). R. Yitzchak Nafcha said: They sang:

Sing, sing, O Ark made of acacia wood,
Rise up in all your splendor,
Covered with gold inside and out,
Ennobled by the Torah scroll you embrace,
Adorned with the jeweled crown of the
    Shechinah.

R. Ashi associated the poem quoted by R. Yitzchak Nafchah with this verse, "When the Ark would journey, Moses said, 'Arise, O God, and let Your foes be scattered . . .'" (Numbers 10:35).

WHEN THE SUN HALTED IN MIDHEAVEN

(25a) It says, [that when Joshua fought against the five mighty kings at Gibeon,] "Then the sun stood still, and the moon stopped, until the people took retribution against their enemies, as is written in the *Sefer Hayashar*, the Book of the Upright" (Joshua 10:13).

What is the Book of the Upright? R. Chiya b. Abba said in the name of R. Yochanan: It is the Book of Abraham, Isaac, and Jacob [i.e., the Book of Genesis] who are described as upright men, as it says, [Balaam wished,] "May my soul die the death of the upright" (Numbers 23:10). And where is it hinted [in Genesis] that the sun would stand still for Joshua, for it says, "as is written in the *Sefer Hayashar*," [i.e., Genesis]?— In the verse, "His [Ephraim's] offspring's fame will fill the nations [with awe]" (Genesis 48:19), [and Joshua belonged to the tribe of Ephraim]. When will Ephraim's fame fill the nations [with awe]? When the sun will stand still for Joshua.

"Thus the sun stood still in midheaven and did not press on to set for a whole day" (Joshua 10:13). [The Gemara asks:] How many hours was that day? R. Yehoshua b. Levi said: Twenty-four hours: The sun moved for six hours and stood still for six hours; again moved six and stood still six; the whole episode lasting twenty-four hours. R. Elazar said: Thirty-six hours: It moved for six hours and stood still for twelve; it again moved for six and stood still for twelve; so that the standstill alone amounted to a full day. R. Shmuel b. Nachmani said: Forty-eight hours: It moved for six hours and stood still for twelve; it then moved for six and stood still for twenty-four; for it says, "It did not press on to set for a whole day," which implies that the previous stoppage did not amount to a whole day.

We learned in a *Baraita*: Just as the sun stood still for Joshua, so did it stand still for Moses [during the war against Sichon].[50] An objection was raised: [Doesn't it say in connection with Joshua,] "Neither before nor since has there ever been such a day" (Joshua 13:14), [then how can you say that the sun stopped also for Moses]? [The Gemara answers:] If you wish you may say that in the case of Moses it stopped for fewer hours, or you may say that in the case of Moses there were no hailstones [as was the case with Joshua] for it says, "While they were fleeing before Israel down the descent from Bet-horon, God hurled huge stones on them from the sky all the way to Azekah, and they perished" (ibid. v. 11).

SKILLED ARCHERS

It says, [in David's lament over the death of Saul and his son Jonathan,] "[We must] teach the children of Judah the archer's bow, as it is recorded in the *Sefer Hayashar*, the Book of the Upright [that Judah's descendants were archers]" (2 Samuel 1:18). What is the Book of the Upright? R. Chiya b. Abba said in the name of R. Yochanan: It is the Book of Abraham, Isaac, and Jacob [i.e., Genesis] who are characterized as upright men, for it says, [Balaam wished,] "May my soul die the death of the upright" (Numbers 23:10). And where is it mentioned [in Genesis that the offspring of Judah were adept at wielding the bow]? In the verse, "Judah, your brothers shall submit to you. Your hand shall be on your enemies' neck" (Genesis 49:8). What kind of warfare requires that the hand is aiming at the [fleeing] enemy's neck?[51] Surely, the bow and arrow. R. Elazar said: [The Book of the Upright] is Deuteronomy, which is here referred to as *Sefer Hayashar* because it contains the passage, "Do what is upright [*hayashar*] and good in God's eyes" (Deuteronomy 6:18). And where is [Judah's skill at handling the bow] alluded to in Deuteronomy? In the [blessing Moses gave to Judah], "May his hands fight his grievance" (ibid. 33:7). What kind of fighting requires both hands? Surely, archery.

R. Shmuel b. Nachmani said: [The Book of the Upright] is the Book of Judges, which is here called *Sefer Hayashar* because it contains the verse, "In those days there was no king in Israel; every man did whatever seemed proper [*hayashar*] in his eyes" (Judges 17:6). And where is [Judah's prowess in archery] mentioned [in the Book of Judges]? In the verse, "So that the generations of the children of Israel would know, to teach them warfare" (ibid. 3:2). Now what kind of warfare needs to be taught? Surely, archery. But how do you know that this verse refers to Judah? From the passage, "Who should go up for us first against the Canaanites, to wage war against them? And God said, 'Judah should go up'" (ibid. 1:1,2).

USE A HEATHEN DOCTOR?

(27b) [R. Yochanan said: When it is doubtful whether a patient will live or die we may not allow a heathen to heal him. However, if he is certain to die we allow a heathen to heal him. The Gemara asked: But the heathen may shorten his life! The Gemara answered: When death is inevitable, a few extra hours of life are not to be considered. Proof is the story of the four lepers[52] outside the gate of Samaria during the siege who decided to defect to the Aramean camp, speculating,] "If we decide to go into the town, what with the famine in the town, we will die there; and if we just sit here, still we die. Come, let us defect to the Aramean camp. If they let us live, we will live, and if they put us to death, we will die" (2 Kings 7:4).

They chose to defect to the Aramean camp, although they might be killed immediately, [whereas by going into the town they would still live a while longer before dying of starvation]. Their defection indicates that [when death is inevitable] no steps should be taken to extend life a short while. An objection was raised from the following: It was taught: You should not have any dealings with the *minim* [heretics];[53] neither are you allowed to be healed by them, even if it means extending life by a few hours.

It once happened that Ben Dama, a nephew of R. Yishmael, was bitten by a snake. Jacob of Kfar Sikania[54] [one of the *minim*] came to heal him, but R. Yishmael did not let him. Ben Dama, however, said, "R. Yishmael, please let him cure me, and I will even

bring you proof from a verse in the Torah that it is permitted." But before he could finish the sentence his soul departed and he died. At this R. Yishmael exclaimed: Ben Dama, you are praiseworthy because your body was pure, and your soul departed in purity. You did not transgress the words of your colleagues who said, "He who breaks down a fence will be bitten by a snake" (Ecclesiastes 10:8), [meaning, a protective fence for the Torah].[55]

[Thus we see that, contrary to what R. Yochanan said above, even in a case where death is a certainty it is forbidden to be cured by a *min*.] [The Gemara answers:] It is different with the heretical teachings of the *minim*, because they are seductive, and the patient may be enticed by them.

The tanna [R. Yishmael] said above: "You did not transgress the words of your colleagues who said, 'He who breaks down a fence will be bitten by a snake.'" [The Gemara asks:] But Ben Dama himself was bitten by a snake! [The Gemara answers:] R. Yishmael referred to a bite of a snake [that strikes those who transgress the words] of the Sages and that can never be cured [but Ben Dama's snake bite was curable and therefore R. Yochanan did not allow him to be healed by the *min*].

[The Gemara asks:] What was the verse Ben Dama wanted to quote [to prove that he may be healed by a *min*]? [The Gemara answers:] "Keep My decrees and laws . . . man shall live by them" (Leviticus 18:5), but not die by them.[56] And R. Yishmael? [In light of this verse, why did he not allow Ben Dama to be healed by the *min*?]—This verse is meant only [when the patient is healed by a *min*] in private, but not in public [where it would cause a desecration of God's Name], as we are taught in the following *Baraita*: R. Yishmael used to say: From where do we know that if they say to a person: "Worship the idol, and we will not kill you," that he may worship it so as not to be killed? Because it says, "Man shall live by them" but not die by them. You might think that he may transgress in public; therefore it says, "You shall not desecrate My holy Name" (Leviticus 22:32).

WHY NEW DECREES ARE NOT EXPLAINED

(35a) [R. Yishmael asked R. Yehoshua why the Sages prohibited cheese made by heathens. R. Yehoshua changed the subject, asking him:] Yishmael, what is the meaning of the verse, "For your love is more delightful than wine" (Song of Songs 1:2)? When R. Dimi came [from Eretz Yisrael to Babylonia] he explained it as follows: The Congregation of Israel said to the Holy One, blessed be He, "Master of the universe! The words of Your beloved ones [the Torah scholars] are more delightful to me than the wine of the Torah, [meaning, the interpretations of the Sages in the Oral Torah are more cherished than the Written Torah].

Why did [R. Yehoshua ask R. Yishmael] precisely about this verse? Said R. Shimon b. Pazi—some say R. Shimon b. Ammi: He hinted at the beginning of the verse, which reads, "Let him give me of the kisses of his mouth" (Ibid.). He meant to say: Yishmael, my brother, press your lips together, and don't be eager for an answer [to the question as to why heathen cheese is forbidden]. Why [did he not want to explain this prohibition]? Said Ulla—some say R. Shmuel b. Abba: It was a new precautionary decree, and we do not give explanations of new decrees.[57] And why not? Because of Ulla's ruling, for Ulla said: When a decree is issued in Eretz Yisrael its reason is not made public until a full year later, for fear that someone might disagree with the reason and disdain the decree. [But now that the reason is undisclosed, everyone will observe the decree, confident that the Rabbis had a valid reason for it (Rashi).]

A TORAH SCHOLAR WHO SHARES HIS KNOWLEDGE

(35b) R. Nachman b. R. Chisda expounded: What is meant by the verse, "Your ointments yields a sweet fragrance" (ibid. v. 3)? To what can a Torah scholar be compared? To a bottle of fragrant oil. When it is uncovered, it gives off an aromatic scent, but when covered its pleasant odor does not spread. [When the Torah scholar teaches others, everyone benefits; when he keeps his knowledge to himself, no one gains.] What is more, [when he teaches others] things that were hidden become revealed to him, as it says, "Therefore the maidens [alamot] love you" (ibid.), which may be read as "The hidden things [alumot] love you." In addition, even the Angel of Death loves him, for the words may be read as "The one in charge of death [al mut] loves you." Moreover, he inherits both world—this world and the World to Come—for the word alamot [maidens] may be read as olamot [worlds], "[both] worlds love you."

DAVID'S CROWN

(44a) R. Huna pointed out the following contradiction: It says, "[The Philistines] had left their gods behind there; David ordered these to be burned" (1 Chronicles 14:12). And it says elsewhere, "[The Philistines] had left their idols there, and David and his men carried them off" (2 Samuel 5:21)! There is no contradiction: The first passage refers to the time before Ittai the Gittite came, the second refers to a time after he came.[58] For it says, "He removed [the idol] Malkam's crown from its head—it weighed a talent of gold and had a precious stone—and it remained over David's head" (2 Samuel 12:30). Now, seeing that it is forbidden to derive benefit from an idol, how could David make use of the crown of an idol? R. Nachman explained: Ittai the Gittite came and abolished it.

[The Gemara asks:] If the crown weighed a talent of gold [about sixty-four pounds], how could David

have put it on? Rav Yehudah explained in the name of Rav: It means that it was worthy of resting on David's head, [not that he actually wore it]. R. Yose b. R. Chanina said: There was a magnet in the crown by which it was suspended above David's head [making it appear that he wore it]. R. Elazar said: It means that there was a precious jewel in the crown worth a talent of gold, [not that it weighed that much].

It says, [David said,] "This came to me because I guarded Your precepts" (Psalms 119:56). What is implied by the word this? David meant to say: As a reward for keeping Your precepts this crown is a testimony on my behalf. What was this testimony? R. Yehoshua b. Levi said: He used to wear the crown in the place of the tefillin, and it fitted him, [proof that he was worthy of it]. [The Gemara asks:] But where did he wear the tefillin [if its place was taken up by the crown]? R. Shmuel b. Yitzchak said: There is enough space on the head to put on two tefillin, [thus he could wear both the tefillin and the crown].

It says, "Then [Jehoiada] brought out the king's son and placed the nezer and the testimony on him" (2 Kings 11:12). Nezer is the crown, but what is the testimony? Rav Yehudah said in the name of Rav: It was a testimony to the house of David that whoever was qualified to be king the crown would fit, but it did not fit an unqualified contender.

It says, "Adonijah son of Haggith[59] exalted himself, saying, 'I will be king!'" (1 Kings 1:5). R. Yehudah said in the name of Rav: He exalted himself, thinking that the crown would fit him, but it did not. "He provided himself with chariot and riders, and fifty men to run before him" (ibid.). What was special about them? It has been taught: All of them had their spleen removed and the soles of their feet scooped [to make them run faster].

DEBATING THE PHILOSOPHERS

(54b) Our Rabbis taught: The philosophers once asked the Elders in Rome, "If your God dislikes idolatry, why does He not abolish it?" The Elders replied, "If the heathens worshipped something the world does not need, He surely would destroy it; but people worship the sun, the moon, stars, and the planets, should He destroy the universe because of fools! The world runs its natural course, and as for the fools who do wrong, they will be held accountable for their misdeeds." Or you could say: Suppose someone stole a measure of wheat and sowed it, should the seed not grow? But the world runs its natural course, and the fools who do wrong will be held accountable. To give you another analogy: Suppose a man had intercourse with his neighbor's wife; by rights she should not conceive. But the world runs its natural course, and the fools who do wrong will be held accountable. In the same vein R. Shimon b. Lakish said: The Holy One, blessed be He, declared: Not only do the wicked use My coin promiscuously, but they force Me to put My stamp in it." [The wicked misuse the God-given power to procreate and force Him to create the embryo that was conceived through adultery.]

A philosopher asked R. Gamliel: "It is written in your Torah, 'God your Lord is [like] a consuming fire, a jealous God' [Deuteronomy 4:24]. Why is He jealous of the worshippers of idols and not of the idol itself?" He replied, "Let me give you a parable. This may be compared to a king who had a son. The son had a dog that he named after his father, and whenever he took an oath he would swear, "By the life of this dog, my father!" When the king hears of this, with whom would he be angry—with the son or the dog? Of course he is angry with his son!"

The philosopher said to R. Gamliel, "You call the idol a dog; but the idol has real power!" "What evidence of its power have you seen?" R. Gamliel retorted. The philosopher replied, "Once a fire broke out in our city. The whole city burned down, only the house of idolatry was spared. [Proof that the idol guarded it]." R. Gamliel responded, "Let me give you a parable. You can compare it to a king against whom one of provinces revolted. When he comes to quell the rebellion, does he fight against the living or the dead? Of course he fights against the living." [The idol is lifeless matter; therefore God does not destroy it.] [The philosopher persisted,] "You call the idol a dog, and you call it a dead thing. In that case, let Him obliterate the idols altogether!"

He replied, "If they worshipped something that is useless, God would certainly wipe it out, but people worship the sun, the moon, stars, planets, brooks, and valleys. Should He destroy His universe because of fools! And so it says, (55a) 'Shall I sweep everything away from the face of the earth?—declares God. Shall I sweep away man and beast? Shall I sweep away the birds of the sky and the fish of the sea, and [all the things that are] stumbling blocks for the wicked?'" (Zephaniah 1:2). This means: Because the wicked stumble over these things [by worshipping them] should He destroy [the sun and the moon, etc.]? Should He destroy mankind because people worship a human being? As it says, "Shall I destroy mankind from the face of the earth?" (ibid. v. 3).

General Agrippas asked R. Gamliel, "It says in your Torah, 'God your Lord is [like] a consuming fire, a jealous God' (Deuteronomy 4:24). [Everyone knows that] a wise man is jealous only of another wise man, a warrior envies only another warrior, and a rich man begrudges only another rich man." [If God is jealous of idols, they must be in a class with Him.] He replied, "I will give you a parable. Suppose a married man takes an additional wife. If the second wife is superior, the first one will not be jealous of her; but if the second wife is inferior, the first wife will be jealous of her." [Therefore God is jealous when people worship contemptible idols.]

A Jew named Zunin said to R. Akiva, "We both know full well that idols are worthless. But how is it that we see people enter the house of idolatry crippled and come out cured? R. Akiva replied with the following parable, "In a city there lived a trustworthy man. All the townspeople used to deposit their money with him without witnesses. One man, however, deposited his money in the presence of witnesses, but on one occasion this man forgot and made a deposit without witnesses. The wife of the trustworthy man said, 'Come, let us deny it.' He answered her, 'Just because this fool acted improperly, shall I ruin my reputation of integrity!'

"The same applies to afflictions and disabilities. When they are sent down on a person, they are placed under oath: You are to come down on this person on such-and-such day and depart on such-and-such day and such-and-such hour and through so-and-so, and by means of such-and-such medicine.' When the time came for the infirmity to leave, the man happened to go to a house of idolatry. The afflictions plead, 'By rights, [since this man visited an idol] we really should not leave him. But because this fool acts in an improper way, shall we break our vow!'" This is what R. Yochanan had in mind when he said: What is the meaning of, [God will send,] "evil and faithful sicknesses" (Deuteronomy 28:59); "evil" in their mission and "faithful" to their oath [to leave at a fixed time, even though the man entered an idolatrous shrine precisely at that moment].

Rava b. R. Yitzchak said to Rav Yehudah: There is a house of idolatry in our town, and whenever there is a drought the idol appears to its priests in a dream and tells them, "Slaughter a human being for me, and I will make it rain." [Why does God allow such things to happen?] Rav Yehudah replied: Rav answered your question, for he taught: What is the meaning of, "When you raise your eyes to the sky and see the sun, moon, stars and other heavenly bodies . . . which God has apportioned [chalak] to all the other nations under the entire heaven" (Deuteronomy 4:19). This teaches you that God made their words [hechelik] slippery, [meaning, God did not prevent them from going astray, but He allowed them to slide into error,] to banish them from the world. This is in line with what R. Shimon b. Lakish said: What is meant by the verse, "If one is drawn to the scoffers, he will scoff, but if one is drawn to the humble, he will find favor" (Proverbs 3:34) This means that if a person comes to defile himself, they open the door for him [i.e., if a person chooses to worship idols, Heaven gives him the means to do so], and if a person comes to purify himself, Heaven will help him [to reach his goal].

NOTES

1. The fourth beast in Daniel's vision as described in Daniel 7:7 symbolized Edom, the progenitor of the

ancient Roman empire and its successor powers in the long exile.

2. Seven commandments were given to all mankind: The command to institute courts of justice, and the prohibitions against blasphemy, idol worship, murder, immorality, robbery, and eating a limb torn off a living animal.

3. The reason is that if a person is commanded to do something he has to overcome an innate impulse to defy authority. If he does it voluntarily, he does not have this rebellious tendency to contend with.

4. The *hei* of *hashishi* is superfluous. It is expounded to mean: Creation will endure only because of *hashishi*, the sixth day, i.e. the sixth day of Sivan on which the Torah was given.

5. The Midrash relates that Nimrod forced Abraham to worship idols. When he refused he was cast into a fiery furnace.

6. Genesis 31:37,38.

7. Daniel 6:1.

8. Sukkot falls in October.

9. *Sukkah* 26a.

10. They converted not out of conviction but because it was fashionable to be Jewish.

11. The War of Gog and Magog is the cataclysmic series of battles that will result in the final redemption and the Messianic era (see Ezekiel, Chapter 39).

12. A mighty sea monster.

13. The name of an angel.

14. By reading *shinan* as *she'einan*, "thousands that are not there," the verse means: God's entourage is twice ten thousand, *less two thousand*, i.e., eighteen thousand (Rashi).

15. It is up to you to protect yourself against catching cold or suffering a heat stroke.

16. *Avot* 3:2.

17. Although not in the same place, since the *Shacharit* prayer must be completed by noon, whereas *Mussaf* may be recited at any time during the day.

18. Truth cannot be bent, whereas judgment can be tempered by mercy.

19. Returnees to Torah observance.

20. They did not ask for a pure heart, because if God gave it to them they would have to thank Him for it, something they did not want to do (Tosafot s.v. *Kefuyei Tova*, 5a).

21. Adam was created in Tishri, which falls at the end of September.

22. All animals were created in their mature form; an ox with full-grown horns. And since the head was created first, the horns preceded the hoofs (Rashi).

23. Abraham was born in 1948 of Creation, so when he was fifty-two years old it was the year 2000.

24. Antoninus is the Roman emperor Marcus Aurelius Antoninus, who was a friend and admirer of Rebbi [R. Yehudah Hanasi]. The period of his reign

was the best that the Jewish people had under Roman rule.

25. Antoninus was a friend of Rebbi and an admirer of the Sages.

26. White mustard.

27. Coriander.

28. She was wrong, of course, because the righteous of the nations of the world *do* have a share in the World to Come (Tosefta *Sanhedrin* 17; Rambam *Hilchot Teshuvah* 3:5; *Yalkut Shimoni, Yeshayah* 429).

29. A nephew of Titus.

30. Probably the early Christians,

31. He swore by the name of his deity (Rashi).

32. The profits earned in an immoral way may not be brought to the *Bet Hamikdash* in fulfillment of a vow or a mitzvah.

33. See *Sanhedrin* 64a.

34. The Romans prohibited teaching the Torah.

35. On a loom, the warp are the threads that run the length of a fabric; the woof are the threads that are inserted into the warp.

36. He realized that miraculously the bees were showing him which was which, because the warp receives the woof, as the female receives from the male.

37. Ten great *Tanna'im* were brutally killed by the Romans, and they are remembered through the prayer *Eileh Ezkera* that is said on Yom Kippur during the *Mussaf* service.

38. Torah study was forbidden by the Romans and punishable by death.

39. Which is forbidden. Only the *Kohen Gadol* during the Yom Kippur service in the *Bet Hamikdash* was allowed to pronounce the Four-Letter Name as it is written.

40. *Mitzvot* that people usually step on with their heels, meaning, they treat them lightly.

41. Purim-money donations may be used by the poor for no other purpose than preparing the festive Purim meal; see above 17a.

42. The Romans had sentenced her to be taken to a brothel; see 17b above.

43. According to Aruch.

44. The people that built the Tower of Babel, whereupon God dispersed humanity over the entire earth (Genesis 11:1–9).

45. The Midrash explains that they planned to ascend to heaven to wage war against God.

46. Genesis 21:34.

47. You should first become thoroughly familiar with the plain meaning of the text and only then study it in depth (Rashi).

48. The rabbis' small talk is compared to a leaf—the least important part of a tree—that does not whither; so, too, their casual conversations have educational value, by the dignified way and the gentle tone of voice in which they express themselves.

49. "Orphaned" because it is anonymous.

50. Numbers 21:21–27.

51. Translation according to Maharsha.

52. Elijah's attendant Geichazi and his three sons.

53. Such as Sadducees and the early Christians.

54. See 17a above.

55. Cautionary rules enacted by the Rabbis to safeguard against transgressions of the law of the Torah itself.

56. This means that one may violate any commandment of the Torah to save a life, with the exception of idolatry, murder, and sexual crimes.

57. Heathen cheese is forbidden for fear that a snake took a bite out of it and left a trace of venom.

58. Since Ittai was a heathen (2 Samuel 15:19) he was able to abolish the idols; therefore, David revoked his first order to have them burned (Rashi).

59. David's fourth son; Haggith was his mother.

✑ HORAYOT ✑

UNFEASIBLE RULINGS

(3b) R. Shimon b. Gamliel and R. Elazar b. Azariah said: No ruling may be imposed on the public unless a majority of the people is able to abide by it. R. Adda b. Abba said: What verse supports this? "You are cursed with a curse, yet you continue to steal from Me, the entire nation" (Malachi 3:9), [the curse—or any decree—is effective only if it encompasses the entire nation or the majority].

DOES ONE TRIBE CONSTITUTE A *KAHAL?*

(5b) From what verse do R. Yehudah and R. Shimon derive that one tribe alone is called *kahal*, "congregation"? Because it says, "Jehoshaphat stood in the *kahal* of Judah and Jerusalem in the Temple of God, before the New Courtyard" (2 Chronicles 20:5); [the tribe Judah alone is called *kahal*]. R. Acha b. Yaakov raised the following objection: What proof is this! Maybe there it is called *kahal* because the tribe Benjamin shared Jerusalem with Judah [and *kahal* refers to two tribes]? But, said R. Acha b. Yaakov, it is derived from, [God promised Jacob,] "Behold—I will make you fruitful and numerous; I will make you a *kahal* [congregation] of nations" (Genesis 48:4).[1] Now, shortly after God made this promise Benjamin was born. So we must conclude that God said [referring to Benjamin]: Another *kahal* will be born to you, [which proves that one tribe is called *kahal*]. Said R. Shaba to R. Kahana: Perhaps the Holy One, blessed be He, meant: When Benjamin is born there will be twelve tribes, so that you could then be called a *kahal* {kahal only applies when there are twelve tribes]? He replied: Do you mean to say that twelve tribes are called a *kahal*, while eleven tribes would not be called a *kahal*? [That is absurd. Therefore, it must be that Benjamin alone is called a *kahal*.]

(6b)R. Acha b. Yaakov said: The tribe of Levi is not called a *kahal*, for it says, "Behold—I will make you fruitful and numerous; I will make you a *kahal* of nations, and I will give this land to your offspring after you as an eternal possession" (Genesis 48:4). Which

implies that he who has possession [in Eretz Yisrael] is called a *kahal*, but not the tribe of Levi [i.e., *kohanim* and Levites] since they do not have a possession in the Land.[2]

AFFLUENT RULERS AND HIGH PRIESTS

(9a) R. Yirmeyah used to say: It says, [in connection with someone who has to bring a sheep as a guilt offering,] "If he cannot afford a sheep or a goat . . . he shall bring two pigeons" (Leviticus 5:7). And later it says, "If he cannot afford two pigeons . . . he shall bring fine flour" (ibid. v. 11). This tell us that [the sliding-scale offering] applies only to a person who is alternately rich and poor [depending on the circumstances], but it excludes a ruler and a High Priest, since they can never be reduced to poverty. Regarding [the affluence of] a ruler it says, "When a ruler sins, and commits from among all the commandments of God his Lord" (Leviticus 4:22), [implying,] that he has no one above him besides God, [thus he must be independently wealthy]. Regarding the High Priest it says, "The *Kohen* who is exalted above his brothers" (ibid. 21:10), meaning, who surpasses his brothers in beauty, strength, wisdom, and wealth. Others say: From where do we know that if the High Priest is poor he must be made wealthier than his brothers? For it says, "Who is exalted above his brothers [*mei'echav*]"—he must be made greater by his brothers.[3]

A SERVANT OF THE PEOPLE

(10a) Our Rabbis taught: "When [*asher*] a ruler sins" (Leviticus 4:22). This excludes a sick man [from being a ruler].[4] [The Gemara asks:] Just because he is sick, should he be removed from office? R. Avdimi b. Chama replied: The exclusion applies to a ruler who was stricken with leprosy, as it says, "God inflicted disease upon the king [Azariah]; he was a leper until the day he died, and he lived in the house of freedom [i.e., an asylum]" (2 Kings 15:5), [implying that he was freed of his royal responsibilities and became a commoner (Rashi)]. Since it says, "he lived in the house of freedom" we understand that until his dethronement [the ruler was not free but] he was a servant [of the people].

The fact that a public official is a servant of the people is illustrated by an incident involving R. Gamliel and R. Yehoshua. They once were traveling aboard a ship. All that R. Gamliel had taken with him was some bread, while R. Yehoshua had taken along bread and flour. When R. Gamliel's bread ran out, he depended on R. Yehoshua's flour. R. Gamliel asked him, "Did you know that we would run into this delay that you took along flour?" R. Yehoshua answered, "There is a star [comet] that appears once every seventy years and leads sailors astray,[5] and I assumed that it might appear and lead us off course." "You possess so much knowledge," R. Gamliel said, "yet you have to sail aboard a ship to make a living!" R. Yehoshua retorted, "Instead of being surprised at me being at sea you should wonder about two of your students who are on land, namely R. Elazar Chisma and R. Yochanan b. Gudgada who are able to figure out how many drops there are in the sea, and yet they have no bread to eat or clothes to wear."

Hearing this, R. Gamliel decided to appoint them as administrators [so that they would earn a decent salary]. When he landed he sent for them, but they did not come; [out of modesty they did not want to accept a post of leadership]. He sent for them a second time, and when they came he said to them, "Do you think that I am offering you leadership? (10b) O no! Servitude is what I am offering you!" as it says, "[The elders advised King Rehoboam,] saying, 'If today you become a servant to this people . . .'" (1 Kings 12:7). [The story illustrates that a ruler is a servant of the people.]

THE RIGHTEOUS AND THE WICKED

R. Nachman b. Chisda expounded: What is meant by the verse, "There is a futility that takes place on earth. Sometimes there are righteous men who are treated as [if they had done] the deeds of the wicked; and there are wicked men who are treated as [if they had done] the deeds of the righteous" (Ecclesiastes 8:14)? It means: Happy are the righteous who are treated *in this world* as the wicked are treated *in the World to Come* [they suffer].[6] Woe to the wicked who are treated *in this world* as the righteous are treated *in the World to Come* [they prosper].[7] Said Rava: Would the righteous object to being rewarded both in this world and the next? [Why can't they have both worlds?] But, said Rava: "Happy are the righteous who are treated *in this world* as the wicked are treated *in this world*" [they prosper], and "woe to the wicked who are treated *in this world* as the righteous are treated *in this world*" [they suffer; thus the wicked suffer both in this world and the next (Etz Yosef)].

R. Papa and R. Huna son of R. Yehoshua once came before Rava. He asked them, "Do you thoroughly understand such-and-such tractate?" "Yes," they replied. "Do you have a good income, [so that you can devote yourselves to studying full-time]?" Rava inquired. "Yes," they replied, "we bought some property [which provides us a livelihood]." Rava exclaimed [applying his own interpretation], "Happy are the righteous who are treated in this world as the wicked are treated in this world [they prosper]."

Rabbah b. Bar Chana said in the name of R. Yochanan: What is the meaning of the verse, "For the ways of God are straight, the righteous walk in them and sinners will stumble over them" (Hosea 14:10)? You can compare it to two men, both of whom roasted their Pesach lamb. One of them ate it with the intention of fulfilling the mitzvah, while the other ate it to gorge himself on a succulent roast. To the one who ate it with the intention of fulfilling the mitzvah we apply the phrase, "the righteous walk in them," while to the one who merely wanted to stuff himself with meat we apply the phrase, "sinners will stumble over them."

ORDER OF PRIORITY

(13a) We learned in a *Baraita*: If a man and his father and his teacher were taken prisoner, [and he was able to ransom only one person] he takes precedence over his teacher [i.e., he should first ransom himself], and his teacher takes precedence over his father, [because his father brought him into this world, whereas his teacher brings him into the World to Come]. But his mother takes precedence over all of them [for captivity is more humiliating for a woman]. A Torah scholar takes precedence over a king of Israel, for if a scholar dies there is no one to replace him; while if a king of Israel dies, every Jew is eligible to become king. A king takes precedence over a High Priest, for it says, "And the king said to [Zadok the High Priest], 'Take with you your master's [i.e., the king's] servants'" (1 Kings 1:33), [thus the king is the High Priest's master]. A High Priest takes precedence over a prophet, for it says, "Let Zadok the priest and Nathan the prophet anoint [Solomon] as king over Israel" (ibid.); Zadok the priest is mentioned before the prophet. And it also says, "Listen now, O Joshua, the High Priest: you and your companions . . ." (Zechariah 3:8).

Lest you think that these companions were ordinary people, the verse continues, "for they are men [worthy] of a *mofet* [miracle]" and the word *mofet* can refer only to a prophet, as it says, "And he [the prophet] gives you a sign or a *mofet*" (Deuteronomy 13:2). A *kohen* takes precedence over a Levite, for it says, "The sons of Amram: Aaron and Moses. Aaron was set apart, to sanctify him as holy of holies" (2 Chronicles 23:13), [and *kohanim* are descendants of Aaron; proof that a *kohen* is superior to a Levite]. A Levite takes precedence over a Yisrael, for it says, "At that time, God set apart the tribe of Levi [from the rest of the Israelites]" (Deuteronomy 10:8).

A Yisrael takes precedence over a bastard, for a Yisrael is of untainted lineage and a bastard is not. A bastard takes precedence over a *natin*,[8] for a bastard was born of Jewish ancestry while a *natin* was not. A *natin* takes precedence over a convert, for the *natin* was raised with us in holiness, while a convert was not. A convert takes precedence over a freed slave, because a slave is included in Noah's curse [when he condemned Canaan to slavery][9] and a convert is not included in the curse.

From what verse is this [order of priority derived]? R. Acha b. R. Chanina said: From the passage, "It [i.e., the Torah] is more precious than [*peninim*] pearls" (Proverbs 3:15), meaning, [a Torah scholar] is more precious than the High Priest who enters the Holy of Holies [*lifnei velifnim*].

We learned in a *Baraita*: R. Shimon b. Yochai said: By rights, a freed slave should take precedence over a convert [rather than the opposite], for the freed slave was raised with us in holiness, and the convert was not; but the freed slave is included in Noah's curse while the convert is not. [Therefore the convert takes precedence.]

The students asked R. Elazar b. R. Tzadok: Why is it that everybody is willing to marry a convert while not everybody is willing to marry a freed slave? He answered: The freed slave is included in Noah's curse, while the convert is not. Another explanation is that as a rule a convert protects her chastity, while a freed slave does not.

The students asked R. Elazar: Why is it that a dog knows its owner and a cat does not? He answered: If a person who eats something from which a mouse has eaten loses his memory, surely the cat that eats the mouse itself [will fail to remember its master].

The students asked R. Elazar: Why are mice being chased by all? Because they are mean by nature. In what way? Rava replied: They gnaw even at clothes [out of sheer destructiveness, for they do not enjoy eating cloth]. (13b) R. Papa replied: [They are so nasty that] they gnaw even at the handle of a pick-ax, [which gives them no pleasure at all].

THINGS THAT STRENGTHEN OR WEAKEN YOUR MEMORY

Our Rabbis taught: Five things make you forget your studies: Eating something from which a mouse or a cat has eaten, eating the heart of an animal, eating olives regularly, drinking what is left over from water that was used for washing, and washing your feet one above the other. Others say: Using your clothes as a pillow will make you forgetful too.

Five things improve your memory: Eating bread baked on coals and, needless to say, eating charcoal

itself; eating a roasted egg without salt; drinking olive oil regularly; drinking wine flavored with spices regularly; and drinking water that is left over from kneading dough. Others say: Dipping your fingers in salt and eating this is also included. "Drinking wine flavored with spices"—this is corroborated by Rava who said: Wine and spices have made me wise. "Drinking olive oil regularly"—R. Yochanan said: Just as eating olives causes you to forget seventy years of learning, so does drinking olive oil restore seventy years of learning. "Dipping your fingers in salt"—Resh Lakish commented: Only one finger. This is the subject of a dispute between *Tanna'im*. R. Yehudah said: One finger but not two; R. Yose said: Two but not three. As a mnemonic to make it easy for you to remember [that they argue about one finger or two] think of the ring finger [which, not counting the thumb, has one finger on its right and two on its left].

A QUESTION OF PROTOCOL

We learned in a *Baraita*: When the *Nasi* [the head of the Sanhedrin] enters [the study hall] all the people rise and do not sit down until he tells them to do so. When the *Av Bet Din* [the leader of the Sanhedrin, second to the *Nasi*] enters, one row on either side [of the center aisle] rises and remains standing until he has taken his seat. When the *Chacham* [third after the *Nasi*] enters, everyone whom he passes rises and sits down [as soon as he has passed] until the *Chacham* is seated. Sons of Torah scholars and Torah scholars who serve the community, may step over the heads of the people [to get to their seats in the front row].[10]

If one of them goes out to answer the call of nature, he may reenter and sit down in his seat [although he disturbs the people over whose heads he has to pass]. Sons of Torah scholars whose father is a *parnas* [leaders of the congregation] may, if they are able to understand the lecture, enter and sit in front of their father with their backs toward the people. However, if they are unable to understand the lecture, they enter and sit down in front of their father with their faces toward the people. R. Elazar b. R. Tzadok said: At festive banquets [the sons of scholars serve as ushers] and are treated as aides [to their fathers].

R. Yochanan said: The above *Baraita* [about the rules concerning who should rise for whom, etc.] was taught in the days of R. Shimon b. Gamliel. At that time R. Shimon b. Gamliel served as *Nasi*, R. Meir served as *Chacham*, and R. Natan as *Av Bet Din*. [Before these new rules were instituted,] whenever R. Shimon b. Gamliel entered everyone rose; likewise when R. Meir and R. Natan entered, everyone rose. Said R. Shimon b. Gamliel: Shouldn't there be a distinction between my office and theirs? [He wanted to safeguard the dignity of the office of *Nasi*; therefore he issued the code of decorum set forth in the above-mentioned *Baraita*.]

749

THE PLAN TO DEPOSE THE NASI

R. Meir and R. Natan were not present on the day [the new code was instituted]. Entering the *bet midrash* on the following day and seeing that the people did not rise for them as usual, they asked, "What has happened?" When told that R. Shimon b. Gamliel had issued the new ruling, R. Meir said to R. Natan, "I am the *Chacham* and you are the *Av Bet Din*; let's get even." "What can we do?" R. Natan wondered. "Let's ask him to give a lecture on tractate *Uktzin*[11] with which he is unfamiliar, and when he is unable to expound on it we will tell him, 'Who can express the mighty acts of God; who can make all of His praise heard' [Psalms 106:2]—who is fit to express 'the mighty acts of God'? Only a person 'who can make *all* of His praise heard.' [And since obviously you are not well-versed in all of the Talmud you are not fit to be the *Nasi*.] We will then depose him, and I will become the *Av Bet Din* and you the *Nasi*."

When R. Jacob b. Korshai overheard their conversation he said to himself, "God forbid! This might cause great embarrassment to the *Nasi*!" So he went and sat down in the upstairs study of R. Shimon b. Gamliel, and loudly expounded on tractate *Uktzin,* over and over again. [Realizing that he was unfamiliar with this tractate, R. Shimon b. Gamliel became suspicious and] said to himself, "What is going on here? Is there anything brewing in the *bet midrash*?" He immediately began studying this tractate in depth and thoroughly familiarized himself with its subject matter.

The next day when R. Meir and R. Natan said to him, "Would you please expound on *Uktzin*?" he gave a lecture on it. After he finished, he said to them, "If I had not reviewed the tractate, you would have humiliated me!" and expelled them from the *bet midrash*. They then went and wrote a number of difficult Gemara questions on a slip of paper, which they threw into the *bet midrash*, [trying to stump R. Shimon b. Gamliel and then depose him. (Rashi)]. Those questions that R. Shimon b. Gamliel could not answer they solved and threw the answers into the *bet midrash* [to show their superior knowledge]. Said R. Yose to the scholars of the *bet midrash*, "The Torah is outside, and we are inside the *bet midrash*; [either they are allowed in, or we will leave]!" [To quell the impending rebellion] R. Gamliel said, "We will allow them to come back, but their punishment will be that none of their halachic rulings will be attributed to them." As a result, statements made by Rabbi Meir were attributed to *acheirim*, "others," and statements by R. Natan were attributed to *yesh omerim*, "some say."

R. Meir and R. Natan were told in their dreams to go and patch things up with R. Shimon b. Gamliel. R. Natan went; R. Meir did not go, for he did not attach any meaning to dreams. When R. Natan came to see him, R. Shimon b. Gamliel remarked caustically, "Your father's lofty position [of *Av Bet Din*] has indeed helped you to become *Av Bet Din*. Did you think his pull would help you to be appointed *Nasi*?"

[The Gemara now focuses on the pseudonym "*acheirim*."] Rabbi taught his son R. Shimon: *Acheirim* say: If it was an exchanged animal[12] (14a) it was not sacrificed. The son asked, "Who are those whose waters we drink but whose names we do not mention?" [Who is the author of the *halachah* you quote by the pseudonym of *acheirim*, "others"?] Rebbi answered, "These are people who wanted to destroy your honor and the honor of your father's house." The son countered, quoting the verse, "Their love, their hate, their jealousy have already perished!" (Ecclesiastes 9:6); [the animosity is over and done with]. Rebbi said to him, "The enemy is gone, but his ruinous actions still exist" (Psalms 9:7); [their names should therefore not be mentioned].

R. Shimon replied, "This applies only in the case where their actions were successful, but in the case of these Rabbis, their actions were not successful; [they did not depose R. Shimon b. Gamliel]." At this, Rebbi taught his son the lesson again, as follows: It was said in the name of R. Meir that if it was an exchanged animal, it was not sacrificed. Rava said: Even Rebbi who was known for his humility used the expression, "It was said in the name of R. Meir" and was reluctant to say explicitly, "R. Meir said."

WIDE-RANGING KNOWLEDGE OR KEEN INTELLIGENCE?

R. Yochanan said: R. Shimon b. Gamliel and the Rabbis differ with regard to the following question: According to one, a scholar who has comprehensive knowledge is superior to a scholar with a brilliant and incisive mind. According to the other, a scholar with a brilliant mind is superior to one who has wide-ranging knowledge. R. Yosef had encyclopedic knowledge of the Talmud; Rabbah was a brilliant and incisive scholar. An inquiry was sent to Eretz Yisrael: Who of these two is preferable [for the post of *rosh yeshivah* of Pumbedita]? The answer came back: A scholar with comprehensive knowledge is preferable, because all the people depend on the owner of the wheat [i.e., a scholar who has the wide-ranging knowledge to answer everyday questions quickly and reliably]. Nevertheless, R. Yosef did not accept the position [in deference to Rabbah]. Rabbah headed the yeshivah for twenty-two years, and after his death R. Yosef served as *rosh yeshivah*.[13] Throughout the years of Rabbah's tenure, R. Yosef [in his modesty] did not call to his house even a cupper[14] [but went to the cupper's place to be bled].

Abaye, Rava, R. Zeira and Rabbah b. Mattena once were studying together when they realized that the time had come to appoint a new *rosh yeshivah* [to the yeshivah of Pumbedita after R. Yosef's death]. They agreed that whoever would make a statement that could not be refuted, should become *rosh yeshivah*. The statements of all of them were disproved except that of Abaye. When Rava saw that Abaye raised his head, he called out to him, "Nachmani, [his nickname], begin [your discourse] and say something. [You are the new *rosh yeshivah*]!"

The question was asked: If you had to choose between R. Zeira and Rabbah b. R. Mattena, which is the superior? R. Zeira was brilliant and asked difficult questions, while Rabbah b. R. Mattena was deliberate but able to arrive at definitive conclusions. So who is preferable? The question remained undecided.

NOTES

1. Jacob was referring to the promise God made in Genesis 35:11.

2. Deuteronomy 18:1,2.

3. *Mei'echav* literally translated means "from his brothers." He should be made greater "from his brothers' wealth."

4. The word *asher* is seen as related to *ashrei*, "happy." Thus a ruler who is unhappy because of illness is unfit to reign.

5. Sailors set course by means of an astrolabe, an instrument that measures the altitude of planets and stars.

6. The righteous are punished in this world for the few sins they committed, and are richly rewarded in the World to Come for their good deeds.

7. The wicked are rewarded with fortune in this world for the few good deeds they did, but they forfeit a share in the World to Come.

8. A descendant of the Gibeonites who deceived Joshua into accepting them as Jews (Joshua 9:23).

9. Genesis 9:25.

10. The people in the audience were seated on the floor.

11. The last and one of the most intricate tractates of the Talmud.

12. In the process of tithing the herd, an animal was mistakenly counted as the tenth.

13. Astrologers had told his mother that he would be *rosh yeshivah* only for two-and-a-half years, and then he would die. He served in that post for two-and-a-half years (*Berachot* 64a).

14. A person who performs bloodletting, a procedure that was thought to be healthful.

↶ ZEVACHIM ↷

GOD OVERLOOKS HIS FRIENDS' SHORTCOMINGS

(41b) In the yeshivah of R. Yishmael it was taught: Why does the Torah mention the diaphragm with the liver and the two kidneys in connection with the bull of the anointed priest,[1] but not in connection with the sin offering for the community for an inadvert violation?[2] You can compare it to a human king who was angry with his friend, but played down his wrongdoing out of his love for him. [In the same way, when the priest—the friend of God—transgresses, God overlooks his shortcoming and mentions his offering in great detail (*Maharsha*).] In the yeshivah of R. Yishmael it was taught in the same vein: Why does the Torah mention the cloth partition in the Sanctuary[3] in connection with the bull of the anointed priest, but not in connection with the sin offering of the community for an inadvertent sin?[4] You can compare this to a human king against whom a province rebelled. If only a minority rebels, his parliament remains in power, but if the majority rebels his parliament cannot stay in power. [In the same way, when the priest—i.e., the minority—sinned, the cloth partition in the Sanctuary is mentioned, but not when the majority transgressed (*Maharsha*).]

THE ALTAR STRADDLES BENJAMIN AND JUDAH

(53b) The south-east corner of the Altar had no base. What is the reason? R. Elazar said: Because that corner was not in the territory of Benjamin. For R. Shmuel b. R. Yitzchak said: The altar extended by one cubit into Judah's territory.[5] R. Levi b. Chama said in R. Chama b. R. Chanina's name: A strip [of the altar] extended from Judah's portion and entered Benjamin's territory. [This was the strip of one cubit width on the east side and on the south side of the altar]. The righteous Benjamin lamented about this every day, wishing that [the entire area of the altar] would be in his territory, as it says, (54a) "[Benjamin] longs for it all day" (Deuteronomy 33:12). Therefore Benjamin was privileged to become a host for the *Shechinah*, as it says, [in Jacob's blessing to Benjamin,] "He dwells between his shoulders" (ibid.), [the *Bet Hamikdash* was built on the highest spot in Benjamin's territory].

SELECTING THE SITE OF THE *BET HAMIKDASH*

(54b) Rava expounded: What is meant by the verse, "[Saul] inquired and said, 'Where are Samuel and David?' Someone said, 'They are in Naiot, in Ramah'" (1 Samuel 19:22)? What does Naiot have to do with Ramah? It means that Samuel and David were in Ramah trying to find the place where the *Bet Hamikdash* should be built.[6] They said: It says, "You must set out and go up to the place that God will choose" (Deuteronomy 17:8); this teaches that the *Bet Hamikdash* was higher than all of Eretz Yisrael, [since you had to go up to get there], and Eretz Yisrael is higher than all other countries. They did not know where that place was, so they took out the Book of Joshua. They found there that regarding the territory of all the tribes it says, "The border went down," "the border went up," and "the border passed"; but with regard to the tribe of Benjamin it says, "the border went up" (Joshua 18:12), but not "it went down."

They then said: This proves that this [Benjamin's territory] is the location of the *Bet Hamikdash*. They thought of building the Temple in Ein Etam, for this is the highest spot, but then they said: let us build it on a slightly lower site [in Jerusalem], for it says, "He dwells between his shoulders" (Deuteronomy 33:12), [and the shoulders are lower than the head; thus it should not be built on the highest spot]. Another reason [why they did not build it at Ein Etam is] that there was a tradition that the Sanhedrin should be located in Judah's territory, while the *Shechinah* [i.e., the *Bet Hamikdash*] should be in Benjamin's territory. They reasoned: If we build the Temple on the highest spot, the Temple and the Sanhedrin will be far apart. Let us build it a little lower, as it says, "He dwells between his shoulders." And it was for this [i.e., for selecting the site of the *Bet Hamikdash*] that Doeg the Edomite envied David.

753

For it says, [David said,] "For the envy of Your House devoured me" (Psalms 69:10). And it says also, "O God, remember unto David all his suffering. How he swore to God and vowed to the Strong of Jacob, '[May misfortune befall me] if I enter the tent of my home, if I go on the bed that is spread for me, if I allow sleep to my eyelids before I find a place for God, resting places for the Strong of Jacob. Behold! We heard of it in Efrat, we found it in the forested field'" (Psalms 132:2–6). "In Efrat" means in the Book of Joshua who descended from Ephraim. "In the forested field" alludes to the territory of Benjamin, about whom it says, "Benjamin is a vicious wolf" (Genesis 49:27), [and a wolf is found in the forest].

THE PRIESTLY GARMENTS
MAKE ATONEMENT

(88b) R. Anani b. Sasson said: Why is the Torah section of the sacrifices placed close to the section of the priestly garments?[7] To teach you that just as sacrifices make atonement, so do the priestly garments make atonement. The linen tunic atones for bloodshed, for it says, "[The brothers] took Joseph's coat. They slaughtered a goat and dipped the coat in the blood" (Genesis 37:31). [It foreshadowed that bloodshed is atoned for by the *kohen*'s tunic [coat] and by immersing in a *mikveh* (Rashi).] The linen pants atoned for immorality, for it says, "Also make linen pants to cover their nakedness" (Exodus 28:42). The turban atoned for arrogance. How do we know this?

Said R. Chanina: Let an article that is high up [on the head] come and atone for haughtiness. The sash atones for impure thoughts of the heart, for the sash was worn [under the armpits] opposite the heart. The breastplate atoned for violations of civil law, as it says, "Make a judgment breastplate" (ibid. v. 15). The *efod* atoned for idolatry, as it says, "Without an *efod* there is [the sin of] *terafim*"[8] (Hosea 3:4). The robe atoned for slander. How do we know this? Said R. Chanina: Let a garment that produces sound [through the gold bells that are attached to the hem of the robe] atone for the sin of the sound [of slander]. The forehead-plate atoned for impudence. It says about the headplate, "[This plate] shall be worn on Aaron's forehead" (ibid. v. 38), and it says about impudence, "You had the forehead [i.e., impudence] of a harlot" (Jeremiah 3:3).

[The Gemara asks:] Is that so? Hasn't R. Yehoshua b. Levi said: For two things we find no atonement through sacrifices; however, we do find an atonement for them through something else. They are: bloodshed and slander. Bloodshed is atoned for by the breaking of the calf's neck,[9] and slander is atoned for by incense. For R. Chanania taught: How do we know that incense atones? Because it says, "[Aaron] offered the incense to atone for the people" (Numbers 17:12). And the yeshivah of R. Yishmael taught likewise: For which sin does the incense atone? For slander. Let that which

is done in secret[10] atone for a wrong [slander] that is committed in secret. So there is a contradiction concerning the atonement for bloodshed and concerning the atonement for slander [for the *Baraita* says that their atonement is through the heifer and incense, not through the tunic and the robe]!

There is no difficulty: bloodshed does not contradict bloodshed. In the one case the murderer is known, [then the tunic atones]; in the other case the murderer is unknown, [then the heifer atones]. [The Gemara asks:] If the murderer is known, he is liable to the death penalty, [and until he is executed the community is not granted atonement]? [The Gemara answers:] It means where he committed murder deliberately but was not warned. [A murderer cannot be condemned to death unless two witnesses warned him not to commit the crime.] Slander too does not contradict slander. Here it was done in secret, [then the incense atones]; there it was done in public, [then the robe atones].

PINCHAS'S ELEVATION
TO PRIESTHOOD

(101b) R. Elazar said in R. Chanina's name: Pinchas was not elevated to priesthood until he killed Zimri, as it says, "It shall be for him and his offspring after him a covenant of eternal priesthood. It is given to him because he zealously took up God's cause" (Numbers 25:13) [This was said after he had slain Zimri.] R. Ashi said: He was not elevated until he made peace between the tribes. For it says, "When Pinchas the priest and the leaders of the assembly and the heads of the thousands of Israel that were with him heard . . ." (Joshua 22:30).[11] And what will R. Ashi do with the verse, "It shall be for him and his offspring after him a covenant of eternal priesthood"? He will say that this was mentioned merely as a blessing [i.e., an announcement that Pinchas would receive the priesthood, but he was not installed as priest until later (Rashi)]. And what will R. Elazar do with the verse, "When Pinchas the priest . . . heard"? He will say that it was a promise that his descendants would inherit his priesthood.

RESPECT THE HEAD OF STATE

(102a) R. Yannai said: You should always be in awe of the ruling monarch, for it says, [Moses said to Pharaoh, announcing the imminent death of the firstborn,] "All your officials will come and bow down to me" (Exodus 11:8), but he did not say this of Pharaoh himself. [Out of respect of the monarchy he did not say, "*You* will come and bow down to me."]. R. Yochanan said: You can derive it from, "The hand of God was upon Elijah, and he bound up his loins and ran before Ahab" (1 Kings 18:46). [Elijah showed respect even for a king as evil as Ahab.]

WHAT PROMPTED JETHRO
TO CONVERT?

(116a) The *Tanna'im* disagree about the interpretation of the following verse, "Moses' father-in-law Jethro heard . . ." (Exodus 18:1). What news did he hear that prompted him to go to Moses and become a convert? R. Yehoshua said: He heard of the war with Amalek,[12] since this is preceded by, "Joshua was thus able to break the ranks of Amalek and his allies with the sword" (ibid. 17:18). R. Elazar Hamodai said: He heard of the giving of the Torah; this inspired him to come to Moses and convert. For when the Holy One, blessed be He, gave to Torah to Israel, the sound of His Voice carried from one end of the earth to the other. All the pagan kings were trembling in their palaces and sang praises [to God], as it says, "In the palace [of each king] all say, 'Glory'" (Psalms 29:9).

They all assembled around the wicked Balaam [the heathen prophet] and asked him: What is this uproarious noise we have heard? Perhaps God is bringing another flood on the world, for it says, "God sat enthroned at the Flood" (ibid. v. 10)? Balaam replied: The verse continues, "God sits enthroned as King forever"—the Holy One, blessed be He, has already sworn that He will not bring another flood on the world; [He will reign as King forever and will never destroy mankind, His subjects]. They said: Perhaps He will not bring a flood of water, but He will bring a flood of fire, as it says, "For God will enter into judgment by fire" (Isaiah 66:16)?

Balaam placated them: He has already sworn that He will not destroy all flesh. They asked: Then what is this clamorous sound we heard? Replied Balaam: He has a precious treasure in His storehouse, which was hidden by Him nine hundred and seventy-four generations before the world was created,[13] and He wants to give it to His children, as it says, "God will give might to His people" (Psalms 29:11), [and "might" signifies the Torah]. To which they all exclaimed, "God will bless His nation with peace!" (ibid.).

R. Eliezer said: [Jethro] heard about the parting of the Sea of Reeds, and that prompted him to come, for it says, "It happened when all the Amorite kings . . . heard that God had dried up the waters of the Jordan for the sake of the children of Israel" (Joshua 5:1), [and the term *heard* is used also in connection with Jethro]. And Rachav the harlot too said to Joshua's messengers, "For we have heard how God dried up the waters of the Sea of Reeds for you when you went forth from Egypt" (ibid. 2:10); [the Parting of the Sea is associated with the word *heard*].

THE *SHECHINAH* RESTED
IN BENJAMIN'S PORTION

(118b) When R. Dimi came [to Babylonia from Eretz Yisrael] he said: The *Shechinah* rested on Israel in three places, namely: in Shiloh, in Nob, in Gibeon,[14] and in the *Bet Hamikdash* [in Jerusalem], and all of these are situated in the territory of Benjamin. For it says [in Moses' blessing of Benjamin], "God hovers over him [Benjamin] all day long" (Deuteronomy 33:12), implying that all "hoverings" [of the *Shechinah*] will be only in the portion of Benjamin. Abaye went and told this to R. Yosef. Said R. Yosef to Abaye: [Keilil [Abaye's father] had only one son, and he is no expert [in *Tanach*]. Doesn't it say, "He abandoned the Tabernacle of Shiloh" (Psalm 78:60), and then it says, "He rejected the tent of Joseph and did not choose the tribe of Ephraim" (ibid. v. 67), [which implies that the Tabernacle was in Joseph's [i.e., Ephraim's] portion, not in Benjamin's]?

Said R. Adda b. Mattena: What is the difficulty? Perhaps [in the Tabernacle] the *Shechinah* was in Benjamin's territory, while the Sanhedrin was in Joseph's [i.e., Ephraim's] portion, as we find in the *Bet Hamikdash* that the *Shechinah* was in Benjamin's portion, whereas the Sanhedrin was in Judah's portion. [The Gemara asks:] How can you compare the two! In the *Bet Hamikdash* the territories of Judah and Benjamin bordered on each other, but did the territories of Benjamin and Ephraim border on each other in Shiloh? [The Gemara answers:] They did indeed border on each other in Shiloh, as R. Chama b. R. Chanina said: A strip extended from Judah's portion and entered Benjamin's portion, and on this the altar was built. The righteous Benjamin lamented about this every day, wishing that the entire area of the altar would be in his portion. So here, in Shiloh, too, a strip extended from Joseph's [i.e., Ephraim's] portion into Benjamin's portion; and that is the meaning of "Taanat Shiloh" (Joshua 16:6) ["The Lament of Shiloh," because regarding the Tabernacle too, Benjamin lamented that not the entire altar was in his portion.]

There is a difference of opinion among *Tanna'im* about this: R. Meir says: "He hovers over him," alludes to the first *Bet Hamikdash*; "all day long" alludes to the second *Bet Hamikdash*; and "He dwells among his shoulders" alludes to the days of *Mashiach* [when the third *Bet Hamikdash* will be built. These are in the portion of Benjamin, but not the Tabernacle of Shiloh, which is in Joseph/Ephraim's portion]. Rabbi said: "He hovers over him" alludes to this world [the *Shechinah* rested in both Temples and in the Tabernacle, and all were in the portion of Benjamin]; "all day long" alludes to the days of *Mashiach*.

HOW LONG DID THE
TABERNACLE STAND?

We learned in a *Baraita*: The Tabernacle in the wilderness lasted thirty-nine years; the Tabernacle at Gilgal lasted fourteen years, namely, the seven years of conquest [of Eretz Yisrael] and the seven years of apportioning the Land [to the tribes]. The Tabernacle of Nob and that of Gibeon lasted fifty-seven years. Thus for Shiloh there are left three hundred and seventy years less [part of] one year.[15]

How do we know that the Tabernacle in the wilderness lasted thirty-nine years? Because a Tanna said: In the first year [after the Exodus] Moses built the Tabernacle; in the second year the Tabernacle was set up and Moses sent out the spies. How do we know that the Tabernacle at Gilgal lasted fourteen years, namely the fourteen years of conquest and the fourteen years of apportioning? Because Caleb said, [at the time the Land was being apportioned,] "I was forty years old when Moses, the servant of God, sent me from Kadesh-Barnea to spy out the land, and I brought him back a report as was in my heart"; and it says, "and now I am eighty-five years old today" (Joshua 14:7, 10).

How old was he when he crossed the Jordan? Seventy-eight years.[16] And he said, "I am eighty-five years old today [at the beginning of the apportioning]." The difference is the seven years it took to conquer the Land. How do we know that there were seven years of apportioning? If you prefer, say, since the conquest took seven years, the apportioning, too, took seven years. And if you prefer, say, because otherwise we cannot explain the verse, "In the fourteenth year after the City was conquered" (Ezekiel 40:1).

How do we know that the Tabernacle at Nob and Gibeon lasted fifty-seven years? Because it says, [when the messenger told Eli that the Ark had been captured that], "As soon as he mentioned the Ark of God, [Eli] fell backwards off his chair . . . and died" (1 Samuel 4:18). Now we learned in a *Baraita*: When Eli the priest died, Shiloh was destroyed, and they moved the Tabernacle to Nob. When Samuel died, Nob was destroyed and they went to Gibeon. And it says, "A long time elapsed from the day that the Ark was housed in Kiriath-jearim, twenty years in all; and the entire House of Israel was drawn to God" (ibid. 7:2).[17] These twenty years were made up as follows: Ten years during which Samuel ruled alone, one year that Saul and Samuel ruled together, two years that Saul reigned by himself, and seven years that David reigned in Hebron, (119a) as it says, "The length of David's reign over Israel was forty years: he reigned seven in Hebron, for it says, (1 Kings 2:11). Now about Solomon it says, "He began to build . . . in the fourth year of his reign" (2 Chronicles 3:2). Thus three hundred and sixty-nine years remain for Shiloh.

SHILOH AND JERUSALEM

We learned in a *Baraita*: It says, "Now you have not yet come to the resting place and the heritage that God your Lord is giving you" (Deuteronomy 12:9). "Resting place" alludes to Shiloh; "heritage" alludes to Jerusalem. And so says the verse, "To Me, My heritage was like a lion in the forest" and it says, "Has My heritage become for Me like a bloodstained bird of

prey?" (Jeremiah 12:8,9); [in both verses "heritage" means Jerusalem]. This is R. Yehudah's opinion. R. Shimon said: "Resting place" alludes to Jerusalem and "heritage" alludes to Shiloh, as it says, "This is My *resting place* place forever and ever, here I will dwell, for I have desired it [i.e., Jerusalem]." And it says, "For God has chosen Zion, He has desired it for His habitation" (Psalms 132:14,13).

We understand the view that "resting place" alludes to Shiloh, for it says "to the resting place and the heritage" [in the correct chronological order, Shiloh followed by Jerusalem]. But according to the one who holds that "resting place" refers to Jerusalem and "heritage" to Shiloh, Moses should have said, [in reverse order] "to the heritage and the resting place" [since Shiloh came before Jerusalem]? This is what he said: Not only have you not reached the *resting place* [Jerusalem], you have not even reached the *heritage* [Shiloh].

NOTES

1. Leviticus 4:9.
2. Leviticus 4:13–21.
3. Leviticus 4:6.
4. Leviticus 4:17 mentions the cloth partition, but not "in the Sanctuary."
5. A strip of one cubit width extended into the territory of Judah. It ran along the eastern and southern sides of the altar, ending one cubit short of the northeast corner and one cubit short of the southwest corner. Thus the southeast corner was in the territory of Judah. This corner had no base, whereas the other three corners did have a base (Rashi).
6. Naiot is seen as related to *na'eh*, "beautiful," meaning, the glorious *Bet Hamikdash*.
7. The section on sacrifices ending in Leviticus 7:28 is followed immediately by the section on priestly clothes.
8. *Terafim* are divining tools of sorcerers.
9. See Deuteronomy 21:1–9.
10. The *kohen* offered the incense on the Golden Altar in the Sanctuary with no one present.
11. After Pinchas settled the controversy among the tribes of Reuben, Gad, and half the tribe of Menasseh and the rest of the tribes he was called "Pinchas the priest" for the first time; [see Joshua, Chapter 22]. Until that time he was referred to as Pinchas son of Elazar son of Aaron.
12. Exodus 17:8–13.
13. From Adam until Moses there were twenty-six generations. Add 974 + 26 = 1,000, which is in line with the verse, "The word He commanded for a thousand generations" (1 Chronicles 16:15) (Rashi).
14. The places where the Tabernacle was situated before the *Bet Hamikdash* was erected in Jerusalem. Nob and Gibeon count as one.

15. From the Exodus until the building of the first *Bet Hamikdash* was 480 years. The years of the Tabernacle add up to 39 + 14 + 57 = 110. Thus the Tabernacle in Shiloh stood 480 – 110 = 370 less part of one year.

16. The spies were sent out in the second year after the Exodus, when Caleb was forty years old. They wan-dered in the wilderness thirty-eight more years. Thus Caleb was 40 + 38 = 78 years old when they crossed the Jordan.

17. The Ark was placed in Kiriath-jearim when it was brought back from the land of the Philistines where it had been four months.

❧ MENACHOT ❧

THE MENORAH

(28b) We learned in a *Baraita*: You should not build a house patterned after the model of the Temple, or a balcony patterned after the Temple balcony, or a courtyard patterned after the Temple courtyard, or a table patterned after the table of the Temple, or a menorah patterned after the menorah of the Temple. But you are allowed to make a menorah with five, six, or eight branches, but not with seven branches [because the golden menorah of the Temple had seven branches], even if it is made of other metals. R. Yose b. R. Yehudah said: You should not make one even of wood, for the Hasmonean kings made a menorah [of wood, after they cleansed the *Bet Hamikdash* in the days of Chanukah]. But the Rabbis said to him: How can you derive a proof from that? The Hasmonean menorah was, in fact, made [not of wood but] of iron bars overlaid with tin. When the Hasmoneans became richer they made one of silver, and when they became still richer they made one of gold.

Shmuel said: The height of the menorah was eighteen handbreadths: three handbreadths for the base and the flower above the base; two handbreaths [above the flower] were left plain [unadorned]. **(29a)** It says, [Solomon made the menorahs,] "with their flowers, lamps, and tongs of gold—*mechalot,* of the finest gold" (2 Chronicles 4:21). What is meant by [the odd term] *mechalot?* R. Ammi said: It implies that [in making the menorahs] they used up all of Solomon's finest gold.[1] For Rav Yehudah said in Rav's name: Solomon made ten *menorot,* and for each he used a thousand talents of gold. They refined the gold in the smelting furnace a thousand times, and as a result, it was reduced from a thousand talents to one talent, [the weight prescribed in the Torah].[2] [The Gemara asks:] Is it possible for gold to shrink that much? Haven't we learned: R. Yose b. R. Yehudah said: It happened that the menorah that was used in the *Bet Hamikdash* was found to be one golden *dinar* heavier than the menorah [in the Tabernacle] made by Moses [which was made of one talent of gold].[3] Thereupon they refined the menorah [of the *Bet Hamikdash*] eighty times in the smelting furnace, and as a result it was

reduced to one talent! [Thus, after refining the menorah eighty times it shrank only one *dinar*!] [The Gemara answers:] Since it had been refined a thousand times in Solomon's days, it did not shrink much more [centuries later].

R. Shmuel b. Nachmani said in the name of R. Yochanan: What is meant by the phrase, *"Aaron shall kindle the lamps on the pure menorah"* (Leviticus 24:4)? It means that a model of the menorah came from the place of purity, [meaning, that a model of the menorah was shown to Moses from Heaven to be reproduced].

It says, "[Arrange the loaves of showbread] *on the pure table"* (ibid. v. 6); this teaches us that they used to lift up the table and display the showbread on it to the people who came to Jerusalem for the Pilgrimage Festivals. They said to them: Look how much God loves you! [The Gemara asks:] How was God's love evident in the showbreads? R. Yehoshua b. Levi answered: A great miracle happened in connection with the showbreads: When they were removed from the table [on *Shabbat*] they were as fresh and warm as when they were placed on it [on the previous *Shabbat*]. For it says, "In order to place hot bread on the day it was taken off [the table]" (1 Samuel 21:7), [indicating that the showbread Achimelech the *kohen* gave to David was still fresh and hot].

THE ARK, THE TABLE, AND THE MENORAH

We learned in a *Baraita*: R. Yose b. R. Yehudah said: An ark of fire and a table of fire and a menorah of fire came down from Heaven [and were shown to Moses]; Moses saw these models and duplicated them, as it says, "Carefully observe the model that you will be shown on the mountain" (Exodus 25:40). [The Gemara asks:] If that is so, would you say then that a fiery model of the entire Tabernacle was shown to Moses, for it says, "You will then be ready to set up the Tabernacle in the proper manner, as you were shown on the mountain" (ibid. 26:30)? [The Gemara answers:] Concerning the Tabernacle it says, "[set it up] in the proper manner" [i.e., according to the instructions you were given]; whereas there [regarding the ark, the table, and the menorah] it says, "the *model* that you will be shown," [implying that an actual image of the ark, table, and menorah was shown to Moses].

R. Chiya b. Abba said in the name of R. Yochanan: The angel Gabriel put on a craftsman's belt[4] and showed Moses the workmanship of the menorah. A Tanna in the yeshivah of R. Yishmael taught: The following things were difficult for Moses to grasp until the Holy One, blessed be He, pointed them out to him with His finger: the menorah, the new moon,[5] and creeping things.[6] [God held up a model of] the menorah, for it says, "*This* is the workmanship of the menorah" (Numbers 8:4).[7] [He showed him a model of] the new moon, as it says, "*This* renewal of the month shall be to you the beginning of New Moons" (Exodus 12:2). [He showed him] creeping things, for it says, "*These* are the creeping things . . . that are unclean to you" (Leviticus 11:29). Others add, [God showed him] also the laws of *shechitah* [the kosher method of slaughtering of animals], for it says, "*This* is what you must do for the altar" (Exodus 29:38).

MOSES MARVELS AT R. AKIVA'S GREATNESS

(29b) Rav Yehudah said in the name of Rav: When Moses ascended on high he found the Holy One, blessed be He, sitting and adding "crowns" [small decorative lines][8] to the letters of the Torah. Said Moses, "Master of the universe! Who has caused You this [extra task]?" Replied God, "Many generations from now there will arise a man named Akiva b. Yosef [i.e., R. Akiva] who will extract piles and piles of laws [from each of these 'crowns']." Said Moses, "Master of the universe! Please allow me to see him." Replied God, "Step back." Moses went and sat eight rows back [in the *bet midrash* of R. Akiva]. When he did not understand the laws being taught he felt disheartened. But at one point they came to a certain subject, and the students asked R. Akiva, "From where do you know this?" and R. Akiva replied, "It is a law that was given to Moses on Sinai.

When Moses heard [that they were quoting him] he was reassured. He then said to Holy One, blessed be He, "Master of the universe ! Since you have a person as great as R. Akiva, why did you give the Torah through me [rather than through him]?" "Be silent!" God replied, "That was My decision." "Master of the universe!" Moses pleaded. "Now that You have shown me R. Akiva's greatness in Torah, show me his reward." "Step back," God replied. Moses stepped back and saw R. Akiva's flesh being weighed in the Roman meat markets.[9] "Master of the universe!" exclaimed Moses. "Is this the reward for learning Torah!" Replied God, "Be silent! That was My decision." [God is rigorously strict with *tzaddikim* in order to raise them to the loftiest heights in the hereafter (Etz Yosef).

GOD OUR GUARDIAN

(33b) R. Chanina said: Come and see how the way of the Holy One, blessed be He, differs from the way of mortal men. According to human rules, the king sits inside the palace, and his servants stand guard for him outside the palace. But with the Holy One, blessed be He, it is not so, for it is His servants that sit inside [their houses], and He watches over them from outside, for it says, "God is your Guardian, God is your protective Shade at your right hand"[10] (Psalms 121:5).

THE *TEFILLIN* OF THE HEAD

(35b) It says, "All the nations of the world will realize that God's name is associated with you, and they will be in awe of you" (Deuteronomy 28:10). R. Eliezer the Great said: This refers to the *tefillin* of the head.[11]

[God said to Moses,] "I will then remove My hand, and you will see My back, but My face will not be seen" (Exodus 33:23). R. Chana b. Bizna said in the name of R. Shimon Chasida: This teaches us that the Holy One, blessed be He, showed Moses the knot of the *tefillin* [which is in the back of the head].

Rav Yehudah said: The knot of the *tefillin* should be placed high up [on the back of the head, and not at the nape of the neck]. And it should face the front so that Israel will be in front and not behind.

THE MITZVAH OF *TZITZIT*

(43b) We learned in a *Baraita*: "These shall be your *tzitzit*, and when you see them, you shall remember all of God's commandments" (Numbers 15:39)—by looking at the [*tzitzit*] you will remember another mitzvah that is dependent on it, namely the reading of the *Shema*. For we learned in a Mishnah: From what time in the morning may the *Shema* be read? From the time you can tell the difference between blue and white, [and the *tzitzit* had white and blue threads]. Another *Baraita* taught: "When you see them, you shall remember all of God's commandments," that is to say: Look at the [*tzitzit*], and you will remind yourself of another mitzvah that is written next to it [in the next verse]. What mitzvah is that? The law regarding *shaatnez* [a forbidden mixture of wool and linen], "Do not wear a forbidden mixture, where wool and linen are together [in a single garment]. Make yourself twisted threads [i.e., *tzitzit*]" (Deuteronomy 22:11,12). We learned in another *Baraita*: "When you see them [the *tzitzit*] you shall remember all of God's commandments"—[This teaches us that] the mitzvah [of *tzitzit*] is equivalent to all other *mitzvot*.[12]

We learned in another *Baraita*: "When you see it [the *tzitzit*], you shall remember all of God's commandments so as to keep them": Looking at the *tzitzit* leads to remembering the *mitzvot*, and remembering them leads to keeping them. R. Shimon b. Yochai said: Whoever is zealous in observing the miztvah of *tzitzit* is worthy of receiving the *Shechinah*, for it says, "When you see it [*oto*, i.e., the *tzitzit*]," and it says, "The Lord your God you shall fear, Him [*oto*] shall you serve" (Deuteronomy 6:13). [The word *oto* (Him or it) occurs in both verses. Since in the latter it refers to God, so too in the verse about *tzitzit* it refers to God (Rashi).]

We learned in a *Baraita*: [One of the threads of the *tzitzit* had to be sky blue].[13] R. Meir said: Why is sky blue the color chosen for the mitzvah of *tzitzit*, rather than any other color Because sky blue resembles the color of the sea, and the sea resembles the sky, and the sky resembles the Divine Throne, as it says, "And under His feet was something like a sapphire brick" (Exodus 24:10), [so that by looking at the *tzitzit* you become mindful of God].

SURROUNDED BY *MITZVOT*
We learned in a *Baraita*: Beloved are Israel, for the Holy One, blessed be He, surrounded them with *mitzvot*: *tefillin* on their heads, *tefillin* on their arms, *tzitzit* on their garments, and *mezuzot* on their doorposts. David said about these *mitzvot*, "Seven times a day I have praise You for Your righteous ordinances" (Psalms 119:164). [*Tefillin* on the head and the arm, four *tzitzit*, and one *mezuzah* makes seven.] And as David entered a bath and saw himself standing naked, he exclaimed, "Woe is me that I stand naked without any *mitzvot* around me!"[14] But when he reminded himself of the *milah* on his flesh he calmed down, and when he came out he sang a song of praise, as it says, "For the conductor; with string music, on the Eighth. A Psalm of David" (Psalms 6:1)—that is, concerning the *milah* [which is performed on the eighth day].[15]

R. Eliezer b. Yaakov said: If a person wears *tefillin* on his head, *tefillin* on his arm, *tzitzit* on his garment, and has a *mezuzah* on his door, it can be taken for granted that he will not sin. For it says, "A three-ply cord[16] is not easily severed" (Ecclesiastes 4:12), and it also says, "An angel of God camps around those who fear Him and rescues them" (Psalms 34:8).

R. Meir used to say: A person should say one hundred *berachot* each day, for it says, "And now, Israel, what [*mah*] does God want of you?" (Deuteronomy 10:12).[17]

HIS *TZITZIT* PROTECTED HIM FROM IMMORALITY
We learned in a *Baraita*: R. Natan said: There is not a single mitzvah in the Torah, even the lightest, whose reward is not enjoyed in this world, and as for its reward in the World to Come, I cannot even guess how infinitely great it is. You can learn this from the mitzvah of *tzitzit*. There was once a man who was very painstaking about the mitzvah of *tzitzit*. He heard of a certain prostitute in one of the towns by the sea who charged four hundred gold *dinars* for her services. He

sent four hundred gold *dinars* and made an appointment to see her. At the set day he came and waited at her door, and the maid came and told her, "The man who sent you four hundred gold *dinars* is here, waiting at the door." "Let him in," she replied.

When he came in she prepared for him seven beds, six of silver and one of gold; and between one bed and the other there were steps of silver, but the last were of gold. She then climbed up to the top bed and lay down on it naked. He too climbed up to sit naked with her, when all of a sudden the four *tzitzit* on his garment struck him across the face; he then slipped off and sat on the floor. She also slipped off and sat on the floor, and said, "By the life of the Roman Emperor, I will not let you go until you tell me what flaw you saw in me." He replied, "I swear! I have never seen a woman as beautiful as you are; but there is one commandment the Lord our God has given us; it is called *tzitzit*, and in connection with it, it says twice, 'I am the Lord your God,'[18] which means, I am the One who will inflict punishment in the future, and I am the One who will give reward in the future. Now [the *tzitzit*] appeared to me as four witnesses [testifying against me]." She said, "I will not let you go until you tell me your name, the name of your town, the name of your teacher, and the name of the school where you studied Torah."

He wrote all this down on a piece of paper and handed it to her. She then got up and divided her possessions into three parts; one-third for the government [so that they should not interfere with her plan to convert]; one-third to be distributed among the poor, and one-third she [sold] and kept the proceeds for herself, except the bedding which she [did not sell]. She then came to the *bet midrash* of R. Chiya and said to him, "Rabbi, please give instructions [to the Bet Din to convert me." "My daughter," he replied, "perhaps you have set your eyes on one of the students?" She then took out the note [the man had given her and told R. Chiya that she was sincere about converting because she came to realize the powerful influence of the mitzvah of *tzitzit* when they struck the man's face (Rashi)]. "Go and enjoy your fortune," R. Chiya replied. The bedding that she had spread out for the man for an immoral purpose she now spread out for him lawfully. This is the reward of the mitzvah in this world; and as for its reward in the World to Come I cannot even guess how infinitely great it is.

WHOEVER PUTS ON *TEFILLIN* WILL LIVE LONG
R. Sheshet said: Whoever does not put on *tefillin* transgresses eight *mitzvot* [because in each of the four verses about the *tefillin* there is a double instruction to place the *tefillin* on the hand and on the head. Neglecting to put on *tefillin* thus involves eight transgressions]. And whoever does not have *tzitzit* attached to his garment transgresses five *mitzvot*.[19] And every *kohen* who does not go up to the platform [to give the priestly

blessing] transgresses three *mitzvot*.[20] And whoever does not have a *mezuzah* on his door transgresses two *mitzvot*, namely, "And write them on the doorpost of your house" (Deuteronomy 6:9) and, "And you shall write them on the doorposts of your house" (ibid. 11:20). Resh Lakish said: Whoever puts on *tefillin* will live long, for it says, (44b) "My Lord, about them [You said], 'They shall live,' and therein is the life of My spirit, may You heal me and cure me" (Isaiah 38:16). [Meaning: Those who carry God's Name when they wear *tefillin* will live (Rashi).]

ISRAEL WILL FLOURISH
IN THE END

[The Gemara creates a moving dialogue between Abraham and God based on Jeremiah 11:15,16.] (53b) R. Yitzchak said: At the time of the destruction of the *Bet Hamikdash*, the Holy One, blessed be He, found Abraham standing in the *Bet Hamikdash*. God said to Abraham, "Why should My [nation] be in My House?" (Jeremiah 11:15). Replied Abraham, "I have come concerning the fate of my children." Said God, "Your children have sinned and therefore were sent into exile." Said Abraham, "Perhaps they only sinned unintentionally?" Replied God, "She carries out her evil designs [purposely]" (ibid.). "But perhaps only a few sinned?" Abraham argued. "With many" (ibid.), God countered. Abraham pleaded, "Still, You should have remembered the covenant of circumcision." God answered, "The sacred flesh is passed away from you" (ibid.), [meaning, they ignored the law of *milah*, which makes their flesh sacred].

"Perhaps if You had waited they would have repented?" Abraham persisted. To which God replied, "When you do your evil deeds, only then do you rejoice, [and you show no remorse]" (ibid.). Hearing this, Abraham put his hands on his head and cried bitterly, "Perhaps, God forbid, there is no hope for them!" A Heavenly Voice then came forth and said, "Verdant olive tree, fair, with choice fruit" (ibid. v. 16); just as the olive tree begins to produce an abundance of beautiful fruit, but only long after it was planted, so will Israel flourish in the end.

R. Yehoshua b. Levi said: Why is Israel compared to an olive tree? To tell you that just as an olive tree does not lose its leaves either in the summer or the winter, so Israel will never be lost either in this world or in the World to Come. R. Yochanan said: Why is Israel compared to an olive tree? To tell you that just as the olive produces its oil only after being crushed, so Israel returns to the right way only after suffering.

THE OIL TYCOON
OF GUSH CHALAV

(85b) "So Joab sent to Tekoa and brought a wise woman from there" (2 Samuel 14:2). Why to Tekoa? Said R. Yochanan: Because in Tekoa they were accus-

tomed to using olive oil; that is why wisdom could be found among them.

Our Rabbis taught: It says, [Moses blessed the tribe of Asher, saying,] "He shall dip his foot in oil" (Deuteronomy 33:24). This refers to the territory of Asher, which gushes forth [olive] oil like a well. The story has been told that once the people of Ludkia needed oil. They appointed a [non-Jewish] agent and instructed him to go to Jerusalem and buy a hundred myriad *manehs* worth of oil. When the agent came to Jerusalem, he was told, "Go to Tyre." When he came to Tyre, he was told, "Go to Gush Chalav [in the territory of Asher]."[21]

In Gush Chalav they told him, "Go to So-and-so in such-and-such field." He went there and found the owner digging up the earth around the olive trees. "I need a hundred myriad worth of oil. Can you fill such an order?" the agent asked. "Certainly. Wait till I finish my work," came the reply. He waited until the owner of the grove finished his work. When he was finished, the owner threw his tools on his back [as a poor worker would] and went on his way, removing the stones from his path as he went, [which led the agent to believe that he was a poor peasant who surely would not be able to supply the large quantity of oil he needed]. The agent said to himself, "Does this man really have a hundred myriad [*manehs*] worth of oil? I suspect that the Jews [who sent me to him] played a trick on me." [Nevertheless, he went along with the grove owner.]

As soon as he got into town, the maidservant of the owner brought out a bowl of hot water and washed the agent's hands and feet. She then brought out for him a golden bowl filled with oil, and he dipped his hands and his feet in it, thereby fulfilling the verse, "He shall dip his foot in oil." After they had eaten and drunk together, the owner measured out to the agent a hundred myriad [*manehs*] worth of oil. Then he asked, "By any chance, do you need more oil?" Replied the agent, "Yes, I do. But I have no more money with me." "Don't worry," said the owner. "If you want to buy more, place your order, and I will go back with you to pick up the money." He then measured out for him another eighteen myriad [*manehs*] worth of oil.

It is said that the agent rented every available horse, mule, camel, and donkey he could find in Eretz Yisrael [to transport the huge shipment]. When he reached his home town, all the townspeople came out to greet and cheer him. He said to them, "Don't praise me. Praise my companion who measured out a hundred myriad [*manehs*] worth of oil, and to whom I still owe eighteen myriad [*manehs*]." [The oil tycoon] exemplifies the passage, "Some pretend to be rich and have nothing, but others act poor and have great wealth" (Proverbs 13:7).

THE MENORAH, A TESTIMONY
TO MANKIND

(86b) "God spoke to Moses: 'Instruct the children of Israel to bring to you clear olive oil from hand-crushed olives" (Leviticus 24:2). R. Shmuel b. Nachmani said: It says "to bring to you" [to show you how much they love you,] but not, "to bring to Me," for I am not in need of light. The table was on the north side and the menorah on the south side [of the Sanctuary, and the golden incense altar stood between the two]. R. Zerika said to R. Elazar: [God said:] I am not in need of food, and I am not in need of light, [for if I needed food and light, I would have put the menorah (lamp) close to the table, the way human beings usually do (Rashi)].

It says, "[Solomon] made narrowing windows for the Temple" (1 Kings 6:4). We learned in a *Baraita*; [The windows were] wide on the outside and narrow on the inside,[22] because God is not in need of light.

"[The menorah shall burn] outside the cloth partition in the Tabernacle" (Leviticus 24:3). [The menorah] is a testimony to mankind that the *Shechinah* rests upon Israel. For how can you say that God is in need of the light [of the menorah], when all the forty years that Israel wandered in the wilderness they traveled only by His light! You must admit therefore that the menorah is a testimony to mankind that the *Shechinah* rests upon Israel. What is the testimony? Said Rava: It is the western lamp of the menorah [i.e., the central lamp whose wick was turned toward the west] into which the same quantity of oil was poured as into the other lamps, yet the *kohen* kindled the others from it and ended with it.[23]

WHAT DO
THE WATCHMEN SAY?

(87a) It says, "Upon your walls, O Jerusalem, I have posted watchmen who shall never be silent by day or by night. 'You [watchmen] who remind God, take no rest!'" (Isaiah 62:6). What do the watchmen say? Rava b. R. Shila said: They say, "You will arise and show Zion mercy, for [there will come] the time to favor her, for the appointed time will have come" (Psalms 102:14). R. Nachman b. Yitzchak said: They say, "God rebuilds Jerusalem; He gathers in the exiles of Israel" (ibid. 147:2). And what did they say before [the destruction of Jerusalem]? "For God has chosen Zion; He has desired it for His habitation" (ibid. 132:13).

THEY WORRY ABOUT THEIR
DAILY BREAD

(103b) R. Chanan said: The verse, "Your life will hang in the balance" (Deuteronomy 28:66) refers to a person who buys grain from year to year. [He has no land of his own, therefore he worries whether he will have the wherewithal to buy grain the next year.] "Day and night you will be terrified" (ibid.) refers to a person who buys grain from week to week. "And you will not be sure of your livelihood" refers to a person who has to rely on the baker [for his daily bread].

THE POOR MAN'S OFFERING

(104b) R. Yitzchak said: Why is the meal offering different in that the term *nefesh* [soul] is used in connection with it?[24] The Holy One, blessed be He, said: Who is it that usually brings a meal offering? A poor man, [because he cannot afford to bring an animal]. I consider his meal offering as if he had offered his soul. R. Yitzchak said also: Why is a meal offering different in that it may be prepared in any of five ways?[25] You can compare it to a human king for whom a friend had prepared a meal. Knowing that his friend was poor [and could afford only inexpensive food], the king said to him, "Prepare it for me in five different ways, so that I will enjoy what you are offering me."

TORAH STUDY IS LIKE
OFFERING A SACRIFICE

(110a) "A song of ascents. Behold, bless God, all you servants of God, who stand in the House of God in the nights" (Psalms 134:1). What is the implication of the phrase, "who stand in the nights"? R. Yochanan said: It refers to the scholars who study the Torah at night; Scripture considers them as if they were performing the service of the *Bet Hamikdash*. It says, [the burnt offerings that are brought in the Temple are] "an everlasting duty upon Israel" (2 Chronicles 2:3). [The Gemara asks: But after the destruction of the Temple the sacrifices ceased! How can they be called everlasting!] R. Giddal said in the name of Rav: It refers to the altar [built in Heaven], where the angel Michael, the great Prince [Israel's guardian angel], stands and brings an offering on it. R. Yochanan said: It refers to the scholars who are engrossed in the study of the laws of the Temple service. Scripture considers it as if the *Bet Hamikdash* was built in their days.

Resh Lakish said: What is implied by the verse, "This is the Torah law of the burnt offering, the meal offering, the sin offering, the inauguration offering, and the peace offering" (Leviticus 7:37)? It teaches us that if a person is busy studying the Torah, it is as though he were offering a burnt offering, a meal offering, a sin offering, and a guilt offering. Said Rava: If so, why does the text say, "*for* the burnt offering, *for* the meal offering"? It should have said, "*a* burnt offering, *a* meal offering"! Rather, said Rava, it means that if a person is busy studying the Torah, he does not need a burnt offering, a meal offering, or a guilt offering. [Thus the verse means: The Torah is for a guilt offering, i.e., it takes the place of a burnt offering, because Torah study atones for our sins.] R. Yitzchak said: What is implied by the passage, "This is the Torah law of the sin offering" (ibid. 6:17) and "This is the Torah law of the guilt offering" (ibid. 7:1)? They teach that whoever is engaged in the study of the laws of the sin offering [in the Order of *Kodashim* (Sacred Things)][26] is as though he were offering a sin offering, and whoever is engaged in the study of the laws of the guilt offering is as though he were offering a guilt offering.

AS LONG AS YOUR INTENTIONS ARE GOOD

[The Mishnah says:] It says regarding the burnt offering of cattle, "A burnt offering, a fire offering, a satisfying aroma to God" (Leviticus 1:9). And regarding the burnt offering of birds it says also, "It is a burnt offering, a fire offering, a satisfying aroma to God" (ibid. v. 17). And concerning the meal offering it says likewise, "a fire offering, a satisfying aroma to God" (ibid. 2:2). This teaches you that no matter whether a person offers much or little, it is all the same, so long as he directs his heart toward Heaven. R. Zeira said: What Biblical verse supports this? The verse, "Sweet is the sleep of the laborer [oveid], whether he eats little or much" (Ecclesiastes 5:11),[27] [meaning: Sweet is the sleep of an oveid, a man who brings a sacrifice, whether it is little or much, it is accepted by God.] R. Ada b. Ahava said: The following verse supports it, "As goods increase so do those who consume them; what advantage then has the owner except what his eyes see" (ibid. v. 10). [Meaning: When sacrifices increase there are many kohanim that eat them; what advantage then does God have, except for beholding the good intentions of those that offer them?]

We learned in a Baraita: R. Shimon b. Azzai said: Come and see what is written in the chapter of the sacrifices. Neither the Divine Attribute (K)El, nor Elo(k)im, but only the Name Hashem, so as not to give heretics an occasion to claim that there are many gods [and one, named so-and-so, wants meal offerings, and another wants cattle or sheep. That is why with all offerings only the Name Hashem is used (Rashi)]. Furthermore, it says about a large ox, "It is a burnt offering, a fire offering, a satisfying aroma to God," and about a meal offering it says likewise, "a fire offering, a satisfying aroma to God," to teach you that no matter whether a person offers much or little, it is all the same, as long as he directs his heart toward Heaven.

Now, lest someone says that God needs the sacrifices for food, it says, "Even were I hungry, I would not tell you, for Mine is the world and all it holds. Do I eat the flesh of bulls?" (Psalms 50:12,13). And it says also, "For Mine is every animal of the forest, the cattle of a thousand mountains. I know every bird in the mountain, the creatures in the field are subject to Me" (ibid. v. 10,11). I did not tell you to sacrifice so that you should say: I will do His will so that He should do my will, [which would be like giving God a bribe]. You do not sacrifice for My sake, but for your own sakes, as it says, "Slaughter it to find favor for yourselves" (Leviticus 19:5).

NOTES

1. *Mechalot is* seen as derived from the root *kalah,* "to finish."

2. Exodus 25:39. A talent is equal to 150 pounds.

3. Exodus 25:39.

4. Craftsmen tied up their clothes with a belt so that they should not get in the way of their work (Rashi).

5. He did not know at what stage in the cycle of the moon the new month should be proclaimed.

6. He did not know which are kosher and which are not.

7. *"This"* implies that God pointed it out to Moses.

8. The crowns, called *taggin,* are three small strokes written in the Torah, *tefillin,* and *mezuzot* on top of the letters *shin, ayin, tet, nun, zayin, gimel, tzadi.*

9. R. Akiva died a martyr's death at the hands of the Romans, who tore off his flesh with sharp-toothed combs.

10. The *mezuzah,* which protects the Jewish home, is affixed to the right doorpost when you enter (Rashi).

11. The knot of the head-*tefillin* is shaped like the letter *dalet,* and the letter *shin* is embossed on the sides of the head-*tefillin.* Thus the greater part of the Divine Name *Shaddai* is contained in the head-*tefillin.*

12. The numeric value of *tzitzit* is 600 (90 + 10 + 90 + 10 + 400 = 600). Add to that 8 threads and 5 knots on each *tzitzit* and you obtain 613, which is the number of all *mitzvot* (Rashi).

13. Numbers 15:21.

14. A bathhouse is exempt from *mezuzah.*

15. Or: *milah* is the eighth mitzvah after the seven previously mentioned; or: *milah* was the first mitzvah given to the Jewish people exclusively, after the seven Noachide *mitzvot* that were given to all mankind (*Maharsha*).

16. Comprised of *tefillin, tzitzit, mezuzah.*

17. The word *mah* is read as *me'ah,* "a hundred"; or *me'ah* is an allusion to the one hundred letters in this verse (Tosafot).

18. It is mentioned twice in Numbers 15:41.

19. Four *mitzvot* in Numbers 15:38 and 39, and the fifth in Deuteronomy 22:12.

20. Two *mitzvot* in Numbers 6:23, and the third in v. 27.

21. Situated northwest of Eretz Yisrael, north of present-day Haifa.

22. Maharsha's version. Ordinary windows are wider on the inside of the building in order to increase the amount of light that enters the house. The windows of the Temple became narrower on the inside, in order to show that the *Bet Hamikdash* did not need any light from the outside but that it radiated the light of holiness to the outside world.

23. Rashi explains that the menorah was kindled in the evening, and by morning the oil in the other lamps had burned out, but the western lamp miracu-

764

lously was still burning and continued to burn the whole day, so that when the lamps were to be kindled in the evening they were kindled from this one. This miracle was the testimony to the world that the *Shechinah* rested upon Israel.

24. Leviticus 2:1.

25. Fine flour; fried in a pan; in a deep pan; unleavened loaves; unleavened wafers.

26. *Kodashim* deals with the laws of the Temple service, sacrifices, and dietary laws.

27. *Oveid*, "laborer," is seen in the sense of "servant, worshipper, a person who brings an offering."

～ CHULLIN ～

MAKING VOWS

(2a) It says, "If you refrain from making vows, you will not sin" (Deuteronomy 23:23), [which implies that making vows is reprehensible]. And it says also, "It is better not to vow at all than to vow and not fulfill" (Ecclesiastes 5:4). And we learned in a *Baraita*: Better than both [i.e., making a vow and paying, and making a vow and not paying,] is not to make a vow at all; this is R. Meir's opinion. R. Yehudah says: Better than both [i.e., making a vow and not paying, and not making any vows] is making a vow and paying it.

SEATING ARRANGEMENT OF THE SANHEDRIN

(5a) It says, "[Ahab] the king of Israel and Jehoshaphat the king of Judah were seated on their thrones, dressed in their robes, at the threshing floor at the gateway of Samaria" (1 Kings 22:10). What is meant by "at the threshing floor"? Do you think it to be taken literally? Surely the gateway of Samaria was not a threshing floor! It can only mean that their seating arrangement was like in the "threshing floor" courtroom, [meaning, just as among the judges of the Sanhedrin there was friendship and trust, so too between Jehoshaphat and Ahab]. For [concerning the seating arrangement in the courtroom] we learned: The Sanhedrin sat in a semicircle in the shape of a threshing floor, so that the judges could see each other [when debating a case, so that they should arrive at a just decision].

It says [that when Elijah was hiding from Ahab], "The ravens brought him bread and meat every morning and every evening" (ibid. 17:6). R. Yehudah explained in the name of Rav [that the ravens brought the meat] from Ahab's kitchen, on orders from God.[1] What is meant by "ravens"? Ravina said: It means real ravens.

WHAT DOES THE WORD "CATTLE" SUGGEST?

It says, "When a man brings an offering to God from cattle" (Leviticus 1:2). The phrase "from cattle" in-cludes people bringing an offering who are [without virtue,] like cattle. From this the Rabbis inferred that we should accept sacrifices even from transgressors in Israel to encourage them to repent, but not from an apostate or from a person who offers wine libations [to idols], or from one who publicly desecrates the *Shabbat*.
(5b) [The Gemara asks:] Is it a general rule that whenever the Torah mentions the word "cattle" it is used in a disparaging sense? But surely it says, "You save both man and beast, O God" (Psalms 36:7), and Rav Yehudah said in the name of Rav: The word "beast" in this verse refers to people who are pure in understanding and behave humbly like cattle. [So you see, the word "cattle" suggests an admirable quality.] [The Gemara answers:] There is a difference. There, [in Psalms 36:7], it says, "man and beast," whereas in our passage it says "cattle" alone [and is used in a negative sense]. [The Gemara asks:] Do you mean to say that whenever it says, "man and beast" it has a commendable overtone? But doesn't it say, "I will sow the House of Israel and the House of Judah the seed of man and the seed of animal" (Jeremiah 31:27). [The seed of man refers to the learned; the seed of animal, to ignorant people; thus "animal" is used in a derogatory sense]? [The Gemara answers:] In this last case, the passage makes a distinction between man and beast, referring to the seed of man separately and the seed of animal separately; [that is why, in this case, "animal" has an unfavorable connotation].

THE RIVER PARTED FOR R. PINCHAS B. YAIR

(7a) The Holy One, blessed be He, does not allow the beasts of the righteous to sin in error. [The following incident illustrates this:] Once, R. Pinchas b. Yair went to ransom captives. On his way he came to the River Ginai. "O, Ginai," he said, "divide your waters for me, so that I can pass through." The river replied, "You are on a mission to do the will of your Creator. I, too, am doing the will of my Creator, [by flowing to the sea].[2] You may or may not accomplish your mission [of ransoming the captives]; I, on the other hand, am surely accomplishing mine [by continuing to flow]." R. Pinchas b. Yair threatened, "If you don't split, I will decree that water will not flow in you ever again." The river split. There was a man with him, carrying wheat [to bake *matzot*] for Pesach, and so R. Pinchas once again commanded the river, "Split for this man; for he is busy doing a mitzvah." The river complied.

There was also an Arab merchant who had come along with them, and so R. Pinchas again ordered the river, "Split also for this man, so that people should not say in astonishment, 'This is how he treats his escorts?'" Thereupon the river split for the Arab too. Exclaimed R. Yosef: Look what a great man R. Pinchas b. Yair is! Why, he is even greater than Moses and the sixty myriad of Israel! For Moses and Israel the Red Sea parted only once, while for R. Pinchas b. Yair the river parted three times! But, on second thought, maybe for R. Pinchas b. Yair it also parted only once, [and he merely spoke to the river to make sure that its waters stayed parted until the two men crossed it]. Say rather that he was just as great as Moses and the sixty myriad of Israel!

R. PINCHAS B. YAIR'S DONKEY

R. Pinchas happened to stop at a certain inn where they placed barley before his donkey, but the donkey did not want to eat it. (7b) They sifted the barley, but the donkey still would not eat it. They then removed all remaining impurities, but it still refused to eat it. R. Pinchas suggested, "Could it be that the barley was not tithed?" So they tithed it, and the donkey ate it. R. Pinchas thereupon exclaimed, "This poor creature is on its way to do the will of the Creator, [helping me ransom the captives], and you wanted to feed it untithed grain!" [All of which proves that God does not allow the beasts of the righteous to sin in error.]

When Rebbi heard that R. Pinchas was coming he went out to meet him. "Would you do me the honor and have a meal with me?" Rebbi asked. "Gladly," R. Pinchas replied. Rebbi's face lit up with delight, [because R. Pinchas was known never to accept invitations to someone else's table]. R. Pinchas said, "You seem to think that [the reason I do not eat at someone else's table is because] I made a vow not to take pleasure from another Jew. Not at all! The Jewish people is a holy nation, [and I really should accept their invitations]. But there are people who want to invite guests but cannot afford it, [and I don't accept their invitations because I don't want to be a burden to them]; while others who can afford to invite guests do not want to, [and when they extend an invitation they don't really mean it. And I don't accept their invitation because] it says, 'Do not eat of a stingy man's food, and do not crave for his delicacies. He is like one keeping accounts; "Eat and drink," he says to you, but he does not really mean it' (Proverbs 23:6,7). But you want to be hospi-

table, and you can afford it, [and that is why I accept your invitation]. However, right now I am in a hurry to perform a mitzvah; but on my way back I will come and visit you."

On his return, he happened to enter [Rebbi's estate] by way of a gate near which he saw some white mules standing. Seeing them, he exclaimed, "With the Angel of Death in this house,[3] how could I dine here?" When Rebbi heard of this he went out to meet him. "I will sell the mules," Rebbi said. R. Pinchas replied, "Do not place a stumbling block before the blind" (Leviticus 19:14); [you are forbidden to keep harmful animals, and so is everyone else. If you sell the mules, you are causing the buyer to transgress]. "I will abandon them." "That would only increase the harm." "I will cut their leg tendons [rendering them unable to kick]." "This would cause pain to the animals, [which is forbidden]." "I will kill them." "You would be causing needless destruction, which is forbidden,"[4] R. Pinchas retorted. But Rebbi continued pressing him [to accept the invitation] when suddenly a mountain sprang up between them, [effectively putting an end to his badgering]. At this Rebbi began to cry and said, "If the righteous have such power while alive, imagine how much power they have after death!"

TZADDIKIM ARE MORE POWERFUL AFTER DEATH

R. Chama b. R. Chanina said: The righteous are more powerful after death than in life, as it says, "Some people were burying a [wicked] man, and just then they saw a [Moabite] troop coming. So they threw the corpse into Elisha's grave. The man's body rolled over and touched the bones of Elisha, and the man came back to life and stood up" (2 Kings 13:21). [During his life, when Elisha wanted to revive the Shunamite's child he prayed and put his mouth on its mouth, his eyes on his eyes and his hands on his hands,[5] whereas after his death, the man was revived just by touching his body. Proof that *tzaddikim* are greater after death than in life.] R. Papa said to Abaye: Perhaps he was brought back to life to fulfill Elijah's blessing, as it says, [Elisha asked Elijah, "May twice as much as your spirit be mine" (ibid. 2:9).

He replied: If it was to fulfill Elijah's blessing, how do you explain the *Baraita* that teaches: [The revived wicked man] only stood up, but did not walk to his house. [If the man was revived to fulfill Elijah's blessing, he should have lived on for some time. Hence he was revived for Elisha's sake, to spare him the disgrace of having to share his grave with a wicked man.] But how then was Elijah's blessing fulfilled? As R. Yochanan said: Elisha healed the leprosy of Naaman,[6] and leprosy is the same as death, as it says, [when Miriam was stricken with leprosy, Moses prayed,] "Let her not be like a corpse" (Numbers 12:12). [Thus by healing Naaman, Elisha, as it were, revived him from the dead, and thereby Elijah's blessing was fulfilled.]

R. Yehoshua b. Levi said: Why are mules called *yeimim*?[7] Because they strike terror [*eimah*] in people. For R. Chanina said: No one ever consulted me about a remedy for a wound caused by a kick of a white mule and recovered. But don't we see people who do recover from it? R. Chanina meant that the wound never healed. But don't we see cases where such wounds did heal? R. Chanina was referring to a wound inflicted by a white-legged mule. [Such wounds never heal.]

R. CHANINA IMMUNE TO WITCHCRAFT

[The Gemara now cites other teachings by R. Chanina:] It says, "There is none beside Him" (Deuteronomy 4:35). R. Chanina said: Even witchcraft [cannot accomplish anything unless God wills it]. A sorceress once tried [to kill R. Chanina through witchcraft by] removing earth from under his feet. He said to her, "No matter how hard you try, you will not succeed, for it says, 'There is none beside Him.'" [The Gemara asks:] But has not R. Yochanan said: Why is witchcraft called *keshafim*?[8] Because it overrides the decrees of the Heavenly Council? [Thus witchcraft *is* effective?] [The Gemara answers:] R. Chanina's case is different; [in his case witchcraft was powerless] because his merits were extraordinarily great, [and that is why God did not allow him to be harmed].

R. Chanina said also: A person does not bruise his finger here on earth unless it was so decreed in Heaven, for it says, "A man's steps are established by God" (Psalms 37:23), and, "A man's steps are decided by God, what does a man know about his own way?" (Proverbs 20:24). R. Elazar said: The blood of a bruise atones like the blood of burnt offering. Rava commented: This applies only if the thumb of the right hand was bruised a second time [before the first bruise was healed], and then only if the person was bruised while he was busy doing a mitzvah.

It was told about R. Pinchas b. Yair that he never said *Hamotzi* over a piece of bread that was not his own [i.e., he never accepted an invitation to a meal, and ever since he was old enough to make responsible decisions he derived no benefit from his father's table.

(9a) Rav Yehudah said in the name of Rav: A Torah scholar should learn three things: writing, *shechitah*, and *milah*.[9] R. Chananiah b. Shelemiah said in the name of Rav: Also how to make the knot for *tefillin*, and the *berachot* that are recited at a wedding ceremony.

IT TAKES FIVE YEARS TO BECOME AN EXPERT

(24a) One verse says, "From twenty-five years of age and up [the Levites shall participate in the work force in the Tabernacle]" (Numbers 8:24), and another verse says, "From thirty years of age and up . . ." (ibid. 4:23). How can the two passages be reconciled? Like this: At the age of twenty-five a Levite enters the work force as a trainee, and at the age of thirty he begins to perform the service. This is the premise for the saying: If a student does not see progress in his studies after five years, he never will. R. Yose says: After three years, for it says, "They were to be educated for three years . . . and teach them the script and language of the Chaldeans" (Daniel 1:5,4). And how does the other [who says: after five years, explain the last two verses]? He would say that the Chaldean language is an exception, for it is easy to learn [and can be mastered in three years]. And R. Yose? He would say that the service in the Tabernacle is different, for it is very difficult [to learn how to dismantle and raise it and to learn the songs and play the instruments that accompany the bringing of the sacrifices (Rashi)].

(24b) It was said of R. Chanina that at the age of eighty he was able to put on and take off his shoes while standing on one foot. R. Chanina explained: The warm baths and the oil with which my mother anointed me have stood me in good stead in my old age.

SCRUPULOUS ABOUT *KASHRUT*

(37b) It says, [Ezekiel said to God,] "Alas, Lord God, my soul has not been defiled; I have never eaten carrion nor meat from a wounded animal from my youth until now, nor has loathsome meat ever come to into my mouth" (Ezekiel 4:14). [This is interpreted as follows:] "My soul has not been defiled," for I did allow impure thoughts to enter my mind during the day, which would bring on impurity during the night. "I have never eaten carrion nor meat from a wounded animal until now," for I have never eaten meat of an animal about which someone said: "Slaughter it! Quick, slaughter it!" [because the animal was about to die and was slaughtered in a hurry before it died]. "Nor has loathsome meat ever come into my mouth," for I did not eat meat of an animal [whose *kashrut* was questionable and] which a rabbi [after careful examination and reflection] declared to be kosher. In the name of R. Natan it was said that it means: I did not eat from an animal from which the priestly gifts were not set aside.

(42a) In the yeshivah of R. Yishmael it was taught: It says, [God said to Moses and Aaron,] "These are the creatures that you may eat" (Leviticus 11:2). The word "these" implies that the Holy One, blessed be He, took hold of one of each species of animal, showed it to Moses, and said to him, "This you may eat, and this you may not eat."

OPEN AND ABOVEBOARD

(44b) We learned in a *Baraita*: If a judge ruled that [a disputed field] belonged to A and not to B, or he declared a thing [ritually] unclean or clean, or forbidden or permissible; and similarly, if witnesses gave evidence in a lawsuit, they are [legally] allowed to buy the thing that was at issue, but the Sages said: Keep away from anything that is offensive or smacks of corruption, [because people may say that the judge ruled in the litigant's favor so that he would sell the item to him at a cheap price (Rashi)].

[If a Torah scholar lost an object, the finder may return it to him even if the scholar cannot give any identifying marks.] Rav Chisda said about this: Who may be considered a Torah scholar? A person who owns an animal that arguably might be either kosher or tereifah,[10] and he decides that it is tereifah [such a person surely will not make any false claims]. R. Chisda said furthermore: To whom does the verse apply, "One who hates gifts will live" (Proverbs 15:27)? To a person who [in a doubtful case] decides that his own animal is tereifah. Mar Zutra lectured in the name of R. Chisda: Whoever studies Scripture and the Mishnah, and, [when in doubt,] decides that his own animal is tereifah, and attends the lectures of Torah scholars [and tries to reconcile conflicting statements in the Mishnah], about him it says, "When you eat the labor of your hands you are praiseworthy, and it is well with you" (Psalms 128:8). R. Zevid said: Such a person deserves to inherit both worlds: this world and the World to Come. "You are praiseworthy" refers to this world, and "it is well with you" refers to the World to Come.

Whenever R. Elazar was sent a gift from the house of the Nasi [Prince] he would not accept it, and whenever he was invited to dine with him he would not go. R. Elazar said to the Nasi, "Don't you want me to live? After all, it says, 'One who hates gifts will live,' [and yet you are trying to offer me a meal]!" Whenever R. Zeira was sent a gift he would not accept it, but whenever he was invited for a meal he did go, for he used to say, "They are honored by the fact that I join them at their meal. [Since they derive pleasure from me, I am not accepting a gift from them.]

WHO BLESSES THE KOHANIM?
(49a) It says, "This is how you must bless the children of Israel" (Numbers 6:23). R. Yishmael said: This verse tells us that the Jewish people receive a blessing through the kohanim, but it does not tell us of any blessing for the kohanim themselves. [Who blesses them?] Since the verse concludes with the words, "and I will bless them," it means that the kohanim bless the Jewish people, and the Holy One, blessed be He, blesses the kohanim. R. Akiva said: We learn from this passage that the Jewish people are blessed by the kohanim, but it does not say that they are blessed by the Almighty! When the verse concludes, "and I will bless them," it means that the kohanim bless the Jew-

ish people, and the Holy One, blessed be He, expresses His approval. But from where does R. Akiva know that the kohanim themselves also receive a blessing? R. Nachman b. Yitzchak said: From the verse, "I will bless those that bless you" (Genesis 12:3). In what way does R. Yishmael show greater partiality toward the kohanim [more so than R. Akiva. After all, R. Akiva, too, derives the blessing for the kohanim from a verse]? R. Yishmael favors the kohanim in that he derives the blessing for both the Jewish people and the kohanim from the same verse, [whereas R. Akiva infers the blessing for the kohanim from a different verse].

ALL HUMAN ORGANS ARE SECURELY ANCHORED
(56b) It says, "He made you and established you [vayechonenecha]" (Deuteronomy 32:6). The word vayechonenecha teaches us that the Holy One, blessed be He, created every human organ attached to a base [konaniot], so that if a person's organ is dislodged he cannot live. We learned in a Baraita: R. Meir used to expound this verse as follows: "He made you and established you"—the Jewish people is a community in which all classes are represented: From their own ranks emerge kohanim, prophets, princes, and kings. As it says, "From them shall come the cornerstones; from them tent pegs; from them bows of combat; and every leader will also come from them" (Zechariah 10:4).

[The following incident illustrates the fact that all human organs are secured in a fixed place:] A Roman once saw a man fall off a roof so that his belly burst open and his intestines stuck out. The Roman then brought the victim's son to the scene, and pretended that he was slaughtering the son. [He hoped that the shock of seeing his son being killed would make the father take a deep breath, which would cause the intestines to be drawn in.] (57a) The father became faint with horror, sighed deeply, and thereby drew in his intestines. The Roman then quickly sewed up his belly.

AN EXPERIMENT WITH ANTS
(57b) It was said about R. Shimon b. Chalafta that he used to conduct experiments. Why did he do that? R. Mesharshia said: [To gain a better understanding of halachah and Torah concepts. For example:] It says, "Lazybones, go to the ant; study its ways and learn! Without leaders, officers, or rulers it lays up its stores during the summer, gathers in its food at the harvest" (Proverbs 6:6–8). So R. Shimon b. Chalafta said to himself: I want to find out if it is true that ants have no ruler [as the verse says]. During midsummer he went to an ant hill and spread his coat over it. He marked the first ant that came out of the ant hill, [to see what the other ants would do to him when they discovered that the explorer ant had deceived them]. The marked ant immediately went back in and re-

ported to the others that shadow had fallen. [Ants avoid the heat and come out only in the shade.] At the news, they all came out. R. Shimon meanwhile had removed his coat, and now the sun was beating down on the unsuspecting ants. [Seeing that they had been misled,] they pounced upon this explorer ant and killed it.

Said R. Shimon b. Chalafta: This tells me that they have no ruler. If they had a ruler, they could not have executed the ant without the ruler's authorization, [and this substantiates the verse in Proverbs]. R. Acha son of Rava said to R. Ashi: [The experiment is inconclusive]. Perhaps the ruler was with them [and participated in the execution of the ant], or the ants were enforcing an existing law [that a deceiver should be sentenced to death], or the incident happened during an interval between the terms of two rulers, [when all laws are suspended,] as it says, "In those days there was no king in Israel; every man did as he pleased" (Judges 17:6); [without a ruler there is anarchy. Thus, R. Shimon b. Chalafta's experiment leaves room for doubt]. We must therefore take Solomon's word for it [when he says that ants have no ruler].

THE DEER WAS BITTEN
BY A SNAKE

Rav Yehudah said: If someone eats three *tiklas*[11] of *chaltit*[12] on an empty stomach, [he will run a high fever, and as a result,] his skin will peel. R. Abbahu said: This actually happened to me when I once ate one *tikla* of *chaltit;*, and if I had not jumped into the water immediately [to cool off from the burning fever], I would have lost my skin. So I applied to myself the verse, "Wisdom preserves the life of him that has it" (Ecclesiastes 7:12).

A question came before to the *Resh Galuta* [the head of Babylonian Jewry][13] about a young deer whose hind legs were broken. Rav examined the area of the juncture of the tendons of the hind legs and declared the deer kosher. He was about to eat from it half-raw when Shmuel said to him, "Aren't you concerned that it may have been bitten by a snake, [and you would be forbidden to eat it because it is dangerous]?" "Then what is the solution?" Rav asked. "Let us put the meat in an oven, and that will bring it to light," Shmuel suggested. When the meat was put in an oven it fell to pieces [proof that the deer was bitten by a snake]. Shmuel applied to Rav the verse, "No harm befalls the righteous" (Proverbs 12:21), and Rav applied to Shmuel the verse, "No secret is hidden from you" (Daniel 4:6).

THE EMPEROR WANTED
TO SEE GOD

(59b) The Roman emperor [Hadrian] once said to R. Yehoshua b. Chananiah, "Your God is compared to a lion, for it says, 'A lion has roared; who will not fear? The Lord God has spoken; who will not prophesy?' (Amos 3:8). What is so remarkable about that? Any hunter can kill a lion!" Replied R. Yehoshua b. Chananiah, "He is not compared to an ordinary lion, but to a lion of Bei Ila'i!" "I want you to show me such a lion," demanded the emperor. "You cannot see it," R. Yehoshua b. Chananiah replied. "I insist that you show it to me!" the emperor commanded. R. Yehoshua b. Chananiah prayed, and the lion emerged from its den. When it was four hundred *parsahs* away [from Rome] it roared once, whereupon all pregnant women miscarried, and the walls of Rome collapsed. When it was three hundred *parsahs* away it roared again, and everyone's teeth fell out, and the emperor himself fell off his throne. "I beg you," he implored, "pray that the lion goes back to its lair!" He prayed and it returned to its lair.

Another time the emperor said to R. Yehoshua b. Chananiah, "I want to see your God." He replied, "You cannot see Him." (60a) "I absolutely must see Him!" the emperor insisted. R. Yehoshua went and directed the emperor to face the sun in midsummer and said to him, "Look up at it." "I cannot," replied the emperor. Said R. Yehoshua, "If you cannot look at the sun, which is only one of the attendants of the Holy One, blessed be He, how do you expect to look at the Divine Presence!"

THE BULL
OF ADAM'S SACRIFICE

Rav Yehudah said: The bull that Adam sacrificed[14] had fully developed horns before it had hoofs,[15] as it says, "It shall please God more than a full-grown bull with horns and hoofs" (Psalms 69:32), and the verse mentions horns before hoofs. This supports the view of R. Yehoshua b. Levi who said: All the animals of creation were created in their full-grown stature,[16] with their approval, and according to the form they chose for themselves. For it says, "Heaven and earth were finished and all their array [*tzeva'am*]" (Genesis 2:1). Do not read *tzeva'am* [their array], but *tzivyonam* [their choice].

NO INTERMINGLING OF SPECIES

R. Chanina b. Papa expounded the verse, "May the glory of God endure forever; let God rejoice in His works" (Psalms 104:31). This verse was said by the angel who supervises the universe. For when the Holy One, blessed be He, commanded the trees to "yield fruit after its kind" (Genesis 1:11), the herbs drew a logical inference: If the Holy One, blessed be He, wished to have vegetation grow haphazardly [and intermingle promiscuously], why did He tell the trees to "yield fruit after its kind"? Furthermore, common sense tells you: If with regard to trees, which by nature do not grow crammed together, [since their branches keep them spaced apart,] the Holy One, blessed be He, commanded that they "yield fruit after its kind," how much more so does this apply to us herbs [which grow packed tightly, exposing them to the danger of mixing with other species]! Immediately each plant came forth after its own kind. Seeing this, the angel that is appointed over the universe declared, "May the glory of God endure forever, may God rejoice in His works [which scrupulously obey His commands]!"

WHY IS THE MOON SMALLER THAN THE SUN?

(60b) R. Shimon b. Pazzi pointed out a contradiction between two verses: One verse says, "And God made the two great lights" (Genesis 1:16), [implying that the sun and the moon were of equal size,] and the verse continues, "the greater light . . . and the smaller light," [indicating that the sun is larger than the moon]. [This is what happened: Originally the sun and the moon were the same size.] The moon then said to the Holy One, blessed be He, "Master of the universe! Is it possible for two kings to wear the same crown? [I should be larger than the sun.]" God answered, "Go and make yourself smaller." "Master of the universe!" pleaded the moon. "Why should I make myself smaller just because I made a legitimate suggestion!" God replied, "Go and rule [shine] by day and by night." "But what good will my light be [during the day]!" moaned the moon. "For what good is a lamp in broad daylight!" God consoled the moon, "Go [and be satisfied,] for Israel will count the days [of the months] and the years according to you." "But it is impossible," said the moon, "to calculate the Jewish calendar without taking into account the solar year,[17] for it says, 'They shall serve as signs [and define] festivals, days, and years'" (ibid. v. 14).

God appeased the moon, saying, "Go [and be satisfied] for the righteous will be named ['the Small'] after you, as we find, Jacob the Small,[18] Shemuel the Small,[19] David the Small.[20] Seeing that the moon was not placated, the Holy One, blessed be He, said, "Bring an atonement for Me because I made the moon smaller." This is what R. Shimon b. Lakish had in mind when he said: Why is the male goat that is offered on the new moon singled out in that it is described as "a sin-offering to God" (Numbers 28:15)? [The words "to God" are not mentioned in connection with sacrifices on other festivals.] Because the Holy One, blessed be He, said, "Let this male goat be an atonement for Me for making the moon smaller."

GOD DESIRES THE PRAYERS OF THE RIGHTEOUS

R. Assi pointed out a contradiction between two verses: One verse says, "[On the third day of Creation,] the earth sent forth vegetation" (Genesis 1:12), whereas another verse, speaking of the sixth day, says, "All the wild plants had not yet sprouted" (ibid. 2:5). This teaches us that the plants began to grow but stopped just as they were about to break through the soil, [thirsting for rain,] until Adam came and prayed for rain for them, and when it rained they sprouted forth. This teaches you that the Holy One, blessed be He, yearns for the prayers of the righteous. [God withheld the rain in order to induce Adam to pray for it.] R. Nachman b. Papa had a garden, and he sowed seeds in it but they did not sprout. He prayed, and immediately it began to rain. He exclaimed: That is what R. Assi has taught, [that God yearns for the prayers of the righteous].

PROOF OF THE DIVINE ORIGIN OF THE TORAH

R. Chanan b. Rava said: [The Torah lists among the animals that may not be eaten] the *shesua* (Deuteronomy 14:7), which is a specific animal that has two backs and two spinal columns. Was Moses then a hunter or an archer [that he would know the characteristics of such a rare animal]? This gives the lie to those who maintain that the Torah was not divinely revealed, [for Moses could not have known the identity and the anatomy of all the animals mentioned in the Torah; only God knows this, and it is He Who enumerated the permitted and forbidden animals].

FORBIDDEN SPECIES OF BIRDS

(63a) Rav Yehudah said: The *shalach*[21] (Leviticus 11:17) is a bird that catches fish from the sea; the *duchifat*[22] is so called because its comb is doubled over, and it was this bird that brought the *shamir* [a tiny worm that could split the hardest stone] to the Bet Hamikdash.[23] Whenever R. Yochanan saw a *shalach* he used to exclaim, "Your judgments are like the vast deep waters" (Psalms 36:7), [meaning: You assigned the *shalach* to carry out Your sentence on fishes that are condemned to death]. Whenever he saw an ant he used to exclaim, "Your righteousness is like the mighty mountains" (ibid.), [for even the minute ant finds its sustenance effortlessly]. R. Yehudah said: *Racham* (Leviticus 11:17) is the vulture. R. Yochanan said: Why is it called *racham*? Because when the *racham* comes, merciful rain [*rachamim*] falls on the world. R. Bibi b. Abaye added: This holds true provided the *racham* perches on something and cries "*sherakrak*" [an imitation of the sound].[24] There is a tradition that when the *racham* will sit on the ground and cry "*sherakrak*," *Mashiach* is on the way, for it says, [about the Messianic era,] "I will whistle to them [*eshrekah*] and gather them" (Zechariah 10:8). R. Adda b. Shimi said to Mar b. R. Idai, "Did not a *racham* once sit down on a ploughed field and cried *sherakrak*, when a stone fell on it and broke its head, [so it was not a harbinger of *Mashiach*]?" "That bird was a liar," he replied; [that's why it was punished].

WISE AND UNWISE WAYS
OF SPENDING MONEY

(84a) R. Yochanan said: (84b) Whoever wants to become rich should raise small cattle. R. Chisda explained: Why does the Torah use the uncommon term *ashterot*, in the expression, "the flocks [*ashterot*] of your sheep and goats" (Deuteronomy 7:13)? Because they enrich [*me'asherot*] their owners.

R. Yochanan also said: If a [wealthy] person inherited money from his father and wants to squander it, he should wear linen garments, use fine glassware, and hire workers and not stay with them. "He should wear linen garments," especially Roman linen [which is very expensive and wears out rapidly]; "use glassware," especially fine crystal [which is expensive and is easily shattered]; "and hire workers and not stay with them," and make them plow with oxen, because the workers can cause a great deal of damage [to the oxen and the crops].

R. Avira gave the following exposition, sometimes in the name of R. Ammi, and sometimes in the name of R. Assi: What is the meaning of the verse, "Good is the man who is gracious and lends, who conducts his affairs with justice" (Psalms 112:5)? A man should always spend less than he can afford on food and drink, spend on clothing as much as he can afford, and when it comes to honoring his wife and taking care of his children he should spend more than he can afford, for they are dependent on him, and he is dependent on "He who spoke and and the universe came into being."

ABRAHAM'S REWARD

(88b) Rava said: Abraham said to God, "I am mere dust and ashes" (Genesis 18:27). As a reward for his humility, his descendants were privileged to receive two *mitzvot*, [one involving ashes, the other involving dust], namely: the mitzvah of the ashes of the Red Cow[25] and the mitzvah of the dust used in the ceremony of a *sotah* [a suspected adulteress].[26] [The Gemara asks:] Why doesn't Rava mention also the mitzvah of covering with dust the blood [of slaughtered fowl and wild animals]?[27] [The Gemara answers:] Because covering the blood is only the performance of a mitzvah but it brings no benefit, [for the slaughtered animal may be eaten even if the blood was not covered. By contrast, the dust of the *sotah* carries the benefit in that it helps to clear the *sotah* of all suspicion, and the ashes of the Red Cow are of benefit because they cleanse a person who has been rendered impure by contact with a corpse].

THE BENEFITS OF *TZITZIT*
AND *TEFILLIN*

Rava said also: The reward Abraham received for saying [to the king of Sodom] (89a) "Not a thread nor a shoestrap! I will not take anything that is yours!" (Genesis 14:23) was that his descendants were given two *mitzvot*, [one involving a thread, the other a strap,] namely, the thread of *techeilet*-blue [of the *tzitzit*],[28] and the strap of the *tefillin*. [The Gemara takes issue with this:] I grant you that the straps of the *tefillin* hold a benefit, for it says, "All the nations of the world will see that God's name is associated with you, and they will be in awe of you" (Deuteronomy 28:10), and we learned in a *Baraita*: R. Eliezer said: This refers to the head-*tefillin*, [thus the *tefillin* benefit the Jewish people in that they trigger awe in the nations]. But of what benefit is the thread of *techeilet* [of the *tzitzit*]?

[The Gemara answers:] We learned in a *Baraita*: R. Meir said: Why is blue singled out from all other colors [as the color of the thread in the *tzitzit*]? Because blue resembles the sea, and the sea resembles heaven, and heaven resembles the color of sapphire, and sapphire resembles the color of the Throne of Glory, as it says, "They saw a vision of the God of Israel, and under His feet was something like a sapphire brick, like the essence of a clear blue sky" (Exodus 24:10),[29] and it also says, "The appearance of a sapphire stone in the likeness of a throne" (Ezekiel 1:26). [Hence, the benefit of the *techeilet* thread is that by looking at it we connect with the higher world of the Throne of Glory.]

[Having mentioned Abraham's encounter with the king of Sodom, the Gemara now derives a lesson from the words Abraham addressed at the king.] R. Abba said: It is very difficult to repent of a theft that has been eaten up, for even perfect *tzaddikim* cannot make restitution for it, as it says, [Abraham said to the king of Sodom,] "I will not take anything that is yours. The only exception is what the young men have eaten" (Genesis 14:24). [Abraham could not return that which had been wrongfully eaten by the young men.]

THE HUMILITY
OF OUR GREAT MEN

R. Yochanan said in the name of R. Elazar b. R. Shimon: Wherever you find a statement by R. Elazar b. R. Yose Hagelili in an *aggadah* strain your ear [to catch every word of it]. R. Elazar b. R. Yose Hagelili said: It says, "It was not because you had greater numbers than all the other nations that God embraced you and chose you" (Deuteronomy 7:7). The Holy One, blessed be He, said to Israel: I love you because even when I bestow greatness on you, you humble yourselves before Me. I bestowed greatness on Abraham, yet he said to Me, "I am mere dust and ashes" (Genesis 18:27). I did the same to Moses and Aaron, but they said, "We are nothing" (Exodus 16:8). I bestowed greatness on David, yet he said, "But I am a worm and not a man"

(Psalms 22:7). But the heathens react differently. I bestowed greatness on Nimrod, and he said, "Come, let us build ourselves a city . . . and let us make a name for ourselves" (Genesis 11:4); on Pharaoh, and he said, "Who is God?" (Exodus 5:2); on Sancheriv, and he said, "Which among all the gods of the lands saved their land from my hand that God should save Jerusalem from my hand?" (2 Kings 18:35); on Nebuchadnezzar, and he said, "I will mount over the tops of the clouds" (Isaiah 14:14); on Hiram the king of Tyre, and he said, "I sit enthroned like God in the heart of the seas" (Ezekiel 28:2).

Rava, others say R. Yochanan, said: The statement Moses and Aaron made shows greater [humility] than that made by Abraham. For Abraham said, "I am mere dust and ashes," whereas Moses and Aaron said, "We are nothing" [which is even less than dust and ashes].

Rava, others say R. Yochanan, also said: The world endures only in the merit of Moses and Aaron, for they said, "We are nothing [mah]," and it says elsewhere, "He suspends the world on nothing [belimah]"[30] (Job 26:7), [for the sake of those who considered themselves as nothing, i.e., Moses and Aaron].

R. Ila'a said: The world continues to exist only in the merit of a person who restrains himself in a fight. For it says, "He suspends the world on belimah [from the verb balam, "to restrain oneself, to close one's mouth"]. R. Abbahu said: In the merit of a person who considers himself as nonexistent, for it says, "Below are the world's arms" (Deuteronomy 33:27) [meaning: The lowly and humble are the arms (pillars) that support the world].

R. Yitzchak said: What is the meaning of the verse, "Indeed, [ha'umnam] in silence speak righteousness; judge mankind with fairness" (Psalms 58:2)? What should you occupy [umanut] yourself with in this world? You should be silent. You might think that you should be silent even when it comes to Torah study? Therefore it says, "Speak righteousness," [and "righteousness" refers to the Torah]. You might think that you are allowed to show off your knowledge of Torah? Therefore it says, "Judge mankind with even-handedness" [i.e., consider everyone as your equal (Iyun Yaakov)].

EXAGGERATIONS

(90b) We learned in a Mishnah: There was a pile of ashes in the middle of the altar, and sometimes the pile contained close to three hundred kor of ashes [an incredible amount].[31] Rava said: It is an exaggeration. R. Ammi said: The Torah, the prophets, and the Sages sometimes speak in exaggerated terms. The Sages speak in exaggerated terms as in the case we just mentioned. The Torah exaggerates as in the phrase, "Great cities fortified to the skies" (Deuteronomy 5:28). The prophets use exaggerations, as in the verse, "The people were playing flutes and rejoicing with great joy; the

ground virtually burst from their noise" (1 Kings 1:40). R. Yitzchak b. Nachmani said in the name of Shmuel: In three places the Sages used exaggerations, namely, regarding the pile of ashes on the altar, the vine, and the curtain [of the *Bet Hamikdash*]. The exaggeration of the pile of ashes was mentioned above; regarding the vine we find the following Mishnah: A golden vine stood at the entrance of the Sanctuary trailing over a supporting trellis, and whoever wanted to donate a [golden] leaf, a [golden] berry, or a [golden] cluster would bring it and hang it on this vine.

R. Elazar b. Tzadok said: It happened once that three hundred *kohanim* were appointed to clear the vine of such offerings [clearly an exaggeration]. About the curtain we learned in a Mishnah: R. Shimon b. Gamliel said in the name of R. Shimon the deputy High Priest: The curtain [at the entrance] of the Sanctuary was a handbreadth thick, and it was woven on seventy-two strands, each strand consisting of twenty-four threads; its length was forty cubits; and its breadth twenty cubits, and it was made up of eighty-two myriad of threads. They used to make two such curtains every year. [When the curtain became unclean] it took three hundred *kohanim* to immerse it; [the number of three hundred *kohanim* is an obvious exaggeration].

JACOB WRESTLING
WITH THE ANGEL

(91a) R. Yehoshua b. Levi said: It says, "Jacob's hip became dislocated as he wrestled with [the angel]"[32] (Genesis 32:26). [How was his hip injured?] It happened in the way that a person holds someone tightly clasped in his arms, and his right hand reaches the other fellow's right thigh.

R. Shmuel b. Nachmani said: The angel appeared to Jacob as a heathen, as a Master said: If a Jew is joined by a heathen on the road, the Jew should let the heathen walk on his right side, [so that his right hand should be nearest to the heathen, enabling him to ward off an attack. Jacob's right thigh, being closest to the angel, sustained the injury]. R. Shmuel b. Acha said in the name of Rava b. Ulla in the presence of R. Papa: The angel appeared to Jacob like a scholar, and a Master said: Whoever walks at the right side of his teacher is a boor. [Thinking that the angel was a scholar, Jacob walked on his left side and was injured on his right hip, which was closest to the angel.] The Rabbis, however, say that the angel came from behind and dislocated both thighs. But how will the Rabbis explain the passage, "as he wrestled with him" [which implies that they grappled face to face]? They interpret it in the sense of the other statement of R. Yehoshua b. Levi who said: This verse teaches that the dust of their feet whirled upward to the Throne of Glory, for it says, "as he wrestled [behei'aveko] with him," and it says, "Clouds are the dust [avak] of His feet" (Nahum 1:3).

HE WANTED TO RETRIEVE SOME SMALL JARS

[After Jacob had taken his family and his possessions across the Jabbok River,] "Jacob remained alone" (Genesis 32:25). R. Elazar said: He remained behind because of some small jars. [Having taken all his possessions across the river, Jacob returned to fetch some small jars.] This shows us that the righteous place a higher value on their money than on their body. Why? Because they do not engage in robbery, [and everything they own is dear to them because it was acquired through honest, hard labor].

A SCHOLAR SHOULD NOT GO OUT ALONE AT NIGHT

"A man wrestled with [Jacob] until the break of dawn" (ibid.). Said R. Yitzchak: From [the fact that Jacob was injured while alone at night] we infer the rule that a scholar should not go out alone at night. R. Abba b. Kahana said: You can derive it from the verse, (91b) "[Naomi said to Ruth: Boaz] will be winnowing barley tonight on the threshing floor" (Ruth 3:2). [Naomi was sure that Boaz would not go home after working until late into night since he would not go out alone at night, but would spend the night resting on the threshing floor] (Rashi).] R. Abbahu said: You can derive it from the verse, "[On the day of the *Akeidah*,] Abraham got up early in the morning and saddled his donkey" (Genesis 22:3). [He did not set out at night, even though he was accompanied by Isaac and the two young men.] The Rabbis said: You can derive it from, "[Jacob said to Joseph,] 'Go now, and see how your brothers and the sheep are doing'" (ibid. 37:14); [go at a time when you can see, namely, during the day]. Rav said: You can derive it from the verse, "[After Jacob's encounter with the angel,] the sun rose for him" (ibid. 32:32). [Jacob left only after the sun had risen, but not before.]

JACOB'S DREAM ON MOUNT MORIAH

R. Akiva said: I once asked R. Gamliel and R. Yehoshua while we were at the meat market of Emmaus where they had gone to buy meat for the wedding banquet of R. Gamliel's son: It says, "The sun rose for him." Did the sun rise just for him? Surely it rose for the whole world! R. Yitzchak replied: It means that the sun that had set for Jacob's sake now rose for him. [Why did the sun rise for Jacob's sake?] For it says, "Jacob left Beer-sheba and headed toward Haran [and he arrived there]" (ibid. 28:10). And next verse says, "He came to a familiar place"[33] (ibid. 11). [Did he come there after he had arrived in Haran?! This is what happened:] When he arrived in Haran he said to himself: Could it be that I passed by [Mount Moriah, the future Temple Mount,] the place where my fathers prayed, and I did

not pray there? He immediately decided to return, but as soon as he thought of going back the earth shrank for him so that he immediately "came to the familiar place." After praying there, he wanted to go back [to Haran], but the Holy One, blessed be He, said: The *tzaddik* has come to My lodging [Mount Moriah]; should he depart without staying overnight? Thereupon the sun set [before its time, for Jacob's sake, so that he should spend the night and pray on the site of the future *Bet Hamikdash*].

It says, "[Preparing to go to sleep, Jacob] took some stones" (ibid.) but it says also, "[Early in the morning,] he took the stone" (ibid. v. 18); [one verse says "stones" (plural), whereas the other says "stone" (singular)]. R. Yitzchak said: This tells us that [when he lay down] all those stones gathered into one place, and each one said: The *tzaddik* should rest his head on me! Thereupon all the stones were fused into one.

GOD LOVES ISRAEL MORE THAN HIS ANGELS

[After wrestling with Jacob, the angel said,] "Let me go, for dawn has broken" (ibid. 32:27). [Jacob] said to him, "Are you a thief or a kidnapper that you are afraid of the morning?" The angel replied, "I am an angel, and since I was created my turn to sing a praise to God has not come until now, [that is why I am asking you to let me go]." This is in line with the view of R. Chananel who said in the name of Rav: Three divisions of ministering angels sing praises to God every day: One division proclaims, "Holy!" The second responds, "Holy!" and the third division shouts out, "Holy is God, Master of Legions!" (Isaiah 6:3).

An objection was raised: We know that the Holy One, blessed be He, has greater love for Israel than for the ministering angels, for Israel sings praises to God every hour, whereas the ministering angels sing praises only once a day. Others say, once a week; and others say, once a month; and others say, once a year; and others say, once in seven years; and others say, once in a jubilee [i.e., fifty years]; and others say, once in eternity. What's more, Israel mentions the name of God [in the *Shema*] after two words, for it says, "Hear Israel, God . . ." (Deuteronomy 6:4), while the ministering angels mention the name of God after three words, as it says, "Holy, holy, holy [is] God, Master of Legions!" (Isaiah 6:3). In addition, the ministering angels do not begin to sing praises in heaven until Israel has sung below on earth, for it says, "When the morning stars sang together," then, "all the heavenly beings shouted for joy" (Job 38:7); ["the morning stars" refers to Israel who are compared to the stars, and "the heavenly beings" are the angels].

[The objection is: How can Rav say that the third division of angels mentions God's name after one word, namely: *Kadosh Hashem*, "Holy [is] God," when Israel mentions His name after two words?] We must therefore say that Rav meant to say: One division of angels says, "Holy"; the second responds, "Holy! Holy!"; and the third says, "Holy, holy, holy, [is] God, Master of Legions!" [thus the angels mention God's name only after three words]. [The Gemara asks:] But what about the praise of *Baruch kevod Hashem*, "Blessed be the glory of God" (Ezekiel 3:12) [where the angels mention God's name after two words, just as Israel does in the *Shema*]? (92a) [The Gemara answers:] *Baruch kevod Hashem* is proclaimed by the *Ophanim* [angels that are part of the Throne of Glory, ranking higher than the ministering angels]. Or you may say: Once permission has been granted, [and the ministering angels did mention God's name after three words], they may then mention His name at their own discretion, [even after two words, and even after one word].

IT IS FORBIDDEN
TO MISLEAD ANYONE

(94a) Shmuel said: It is forbidden to mislead anyone, even gentiles. [The Gemara now cites examples of deceptive practices.] We learned in a *Baraita*: R. Meir used to say: A person should not urge his friend to dine with him when he knows that his friend will not accept the invitation. [He is deceiving his friend into thinking that he really meant to invite him, while he had no intention of doing so.] He should not offer his friend many gifts when he knows that he will not accept them. [This, too, is a form of deception.]

Our Rabbis taught: You should not sell to your neighbor shoes made of the hide of an animal that has died of natural causes, [when he thinks that the hide came from a living animal that was slaughtered, for two reasons: first, because you are misleading him [since the hide of an animal that has died of natural causes is not as durable as the hide of a slaughtered animal], and second, because of the danger [because the animal may have died from a snake bite, and the venom was absorbed in the hide, which may endanger the life of the wearer (Rashi)]. You should not send to your neighbor a barrel of wine with oil floating on the surface [leading him to believe that the entire barrel contains oil]. For it once happened that a man sent his friend a barrel of wine that had oil floating on top. [When the delivery man told the friend that the barrel contained wine] he went and invited some neighbors to share the wine with him. When he discovered oil floating on top he imagined that the barrel was full of oil. Thinking that he had no wine to offer his guests he went and hanged himself [out of shame].[34]

ADVICE FOR DINNER GUESTS

A guest should not give anything from what is set before him to the son and daughter of the host, unless the host gives him permission to do so. For it once hap-

pened during a time of scarcity that a man invited three guests to his house, and he had only three eggs to set before them. When the child of the host came into the room, one of the guests gave him his portion; then the second and third guests gave him their portion. When the father of the child came and saw him stuffing one egg in his mouth and holding two in his hands, he became furious and threw the child to the ground so that he died. When the child's mother saw this she went up on the roof, threw herself down, and died. He too threw himself from the roof and died. R. Eliezer b. Yaakov said: Because of this matter three Jewish souls perished. What is R. Eliezer b. Yaakov telling us [that we did not already know]? It means that the entire story was told by R. Eliezer b. Yaakov.

MITZVOT ARE REWARDED IN
THE HEREAFTER

(142a) [The Mishnah says:] A person should not take the birds' mother along with her young, even for the purpose of [offering them as a sacrifice] to cleanse a leper.[35] Now, think of it, if with regard to such an easy mitzvah, which entails a cost of only an *issar* [a small coin] the Torah says, "[If you do this] you will have it good and will live long" (Deuteronomy 20:7), how much greater will be the reward for the more difficult [and more costly] *mitzvot* in the Torah!

[The Gemara comments:] We learned in a *Baraita*: R. Yaakov said: Whenever the Torah mentions a mitzvah and states its reward right next to it you can infer from it the doctrine of the resurrection of the dead. Next to the mitzvah of honoring your parents it says, "You will live long and have it well" (Deuteronomy 5:16). Next to the mitzvah of sending away the mother bird from the nest it says, "[If you do this] you will have it good and will live long." In light of that, [how do you explain] the case where a man's father said to him, "Go up to the top of the building and bring me down some young birds," and the son went up, sent away the mother bird, and took the birds, [thus fulfilling the *mitzvot* of honoring his father and sending away the mother bird], and on his return he fell and was killed—where is this man's long life, and where is this man's happiness [that the Torah promises as the reward for these *mitzvot*]? We must therefore say that the passage "You will live long" refers to the world that is eternally long [i.e., the World to Come], and "you will have it good" refers to the world that is entirely good [a world where there is neither pain nor suffering, i.e., the World to Come].

[The Gemara asks:] But perhaps such a thing could never happen? [The Gemara answers:] R. Yaakov actually witnessed such an incident. But perhaps this man was thinking sinful thoughts [while fulfilling the two *mitzvot*, and that is why he was punished]? The Holy One, blessed be He, does not count a sinful thought as a sinful deed. But maybe he had idolatry in mind, [and idolatrous thoughts do count as deeds]? For it says, "Thus I will hold the House of Israel to account for their thoughts" (Ezekiel 14:5), which according to R. Acha b. Yaakov refers to idolatry? [Thus the intention of worshipping idols is punishable like the act itself.] This is what R. Yaakov meant to say: If there is a reward for *mitzvot* in this world, then surely that reward should have protected that man from having sinful thoughts and from being harmed; we must therefore say that there is no reward for *mitzvot* in this world; [rather it is stored away and bestowed in the World to Come].

[The Gemara asks:] But did not R. Elazar say that people who are in the process of doing a mitzvah will not come to grief, neither on their way going to the place of the mitzvah nor on their return from it, [yet this person was killed while doing a mitzvah]? [The Gemara answers: The person who climbed up on the roof] must have used a broken ladder, so that harm was inevitable, and in a case where harm is inevitable [you should not rely on a miracle,] for it says, [When told by God to anoint a new king,] "Samuel asked, 'How can I go? If Saul finds out [that I have anointed a new king to replace him] he will kill me'" (1 Samuel 16:2); [Although God had ordered Samuel he hesitated because the mission was perilous.] Said R. Yosef: If Acher[36] had interpreted the verse, [that promises long life and happiness to those who fullfill the *mitzvot*][37] as R. Yaakov, his daughter's son, did, [who said that the reward for *mitzvot* is given in the world to come], he would not have sinned [and become a heretic].

What did Acher see [that made him turn his back on the Torah]? Some say: He saw such an incident [where a person engaged in doing a mitzvah met with an accident and was killed. This made him doubt the truth of the Torah and caused him to become a heretic]. Others say: Acher saw the tongue of R. Chutzpit Hameturgeman lying on a garbage dump.[38] Seeing this he exclaimed, "How dreadful that the mouth that uttered pearls must lick the dust!" But Acher did not know that the passage, "You will have it good" refers to the world that is entirely good, and the passage, "You will live long" refers to the world that is eternally long.

NOTES

1. God said, "I have commanded the ravens to supply you with food" (1 Kings 17:4).

2. Ecclesiastes 1:7.

3. White mules were considered dangerous. Injury by a white mule was usually fatal (Rashi); see *Yoma* 49a.

4. Deuteronomy 20:19.

5. 2 Kings 4:33–35.

6. 2 Kings, Chapter 5.

7. Genesis 36:24.

8. *Keshafim* is seen as a contraction of *makchishin pamalia shel maalah*, "they thwart the Heavenly council."

9. Kosher slaughtering and circumcision.

10. Any animal suffering from a serious disease whose meat is forbidden even if it was ritually slaughtered.

11. The weight of half a *shekel*.

12. A foul substance prepared from the juice of a plant of the parsley family.

13. Exilarch.

14. When Adam realized that night is followed by a new day he gratefully offered a sacrifice to God (*Avodah Zarah* 8a).

15. Ordinarily a calf is born with hoofs, and the horns grow later.

16. Thus the first bull had horns before it had hoofs, since the head came before the legs (Rashi).

17. A lunar month is about 29½ days, and the lunar year, 12 x 29.5, or about 354 days. The solar year comprises 365 days. Thus, the lunar year is about eleven days shorter than the solar year. This means that if in a given year Pesach falls in April, then in the next year it would fall eleven days earlier, and so on, so that Pesach would move from season to season. But the Torah commands that Pesach must be in the spring. Therefore, the lunar calendar is adjusted to the solar year by the periodic insertion of a thirteenth lunar month, Adar II.

18. Amos 7:2.

19. A Tanna, mentioned often in the Gemara (e.g., *Berachot* 28b–29a, *Sanhedrin* 11a).

20. 1 Samuel 17:14.

21. Commonly translated as cormorant, pelican, or heron.

22. Commonly identified as the hoopoe.

23. Since metal tools were forbidden to be used in the building of the *Bet Hamikdash*, the *shamir* served as a cutting instrument in the construction of the Temple (*Gittin* 68b).

24. Compare the English "shriek."

25. Numbers 19:1–22.

26. Numbers 5:11–33.

27. Leviticus 17:13.

28. *Techeilet* is sky-blue wool dyed with the blood of an amphibian called *chilazon*. Today the identity of this animal is not known, so that we do not have the *techeilet* thread in our *tzitzit*. See Numbers 15:38.

29. And whenever God gazes at His Throne He remembers the mitzvah of *tzitzit*, which is equivalent to all the *mitzvot* of the Torah (Rashi).

30. *Belimah* is seen as a contraction of *beli mah*, "without anything."

31. A *kor* equals thirty *se'ah* or about 720 pounds. Thus 300 *kor* weigh about 216,000 pounds.

32. The angel was Samael, the guardian angel of

Esau and the incarnation of Evil. Jacob's wrestling with
the angel foreshadowed the struggle with the forces
of evil that he and his descendants would have from
this time on.

33. Mount Moriah in Jerusalem where Abraham
and Isaac prayed.

34. Translation according to Etz Yosef. Rashi offers a different interpretation.

35. A leper undergoing purification must bring a
sacrifice of two kosher birds (Leviticus 14:4).

36. Acher, "the Other," was the name given to
Elisha b. Abuyah, the great scholar and teacher of R.
Meir, after he became a heretic.

37. Deuteronomy 5:16 and 22:7.

38. He was one of the *Asarah Harugei Malchut*, the
ten *Tanna'im* who were brutally killed by the Romans.

ᥫᥬ ARACHIN ᥫᥬ

HALLEL

(10a) R. Yochanan said in the name of R. Shimon b. Yehotzadak: There are eighteen days on which a person [who is praying by himself, not in a *minyan*,] completes the *Hallel*:[1] the eight days of Sukkot, the eight days of Chanukah, the first day of Pesach and of Shavuot. Outside Eretz Yisrael [where two days of Yom Tov are observed, a person praying by himself completes the *Hallel*] on twenty-one days: The nine days of Sukkot, the eight days of Chanukah, the [first] two days of Pesach, and the two days of Shavuot. [The Gemara asks:] Why is it that on Sukkot we complete the *Hallel* on all days, and on Pesach (10b) we do not do so on all of its days? [The Gemara answers:] On Sukkot the *mussaf* offering of each day is different from that of the day before [the number of bulls offered becomes less from day to day,] whereas the *mussaf* offerings on Pesach are identical each day. [The Gemara asks:] So let *Hallel* be said on *Shabbat* which is different [from weekdays] with its sacrifices? [The Gemara answers:] *Shabbat* is not called a Yom Tov, [and we say *Hallel* only on Yom Tov]. [The Gemara asks:] So let us say the complete *Hallel* on Rosh Chodesh [the New Moon] which is called a Yom Tov? [The Gemara answers:] Rosh Chodesh is not a Yom Tov on which labor is forbidden, as it says, "The song [*Hallel*] will be yours like on the night of the festival's consecration" (Isaiah 30:29). This means that only the night of a Yom Tov that is consecrated [by the prohibition of labor] requires *Hallel*, but a night of a Yom Tov that is not consecrated [by the prohibition of labor, i.e., Rosh Chodesh] does not require *Hallel*. [The Gemara asks:] So let the *Hallel* be said on Rosh Hashanah and Yom Kippur, both of which are called Yom Tov and are sanctified by the prohibition of labor? R. Abbahu suggested the following reason: The ministering angels said to the Holy One, blessed be He: Why don't the Jewish people sing *Hallel* on Rosh Hashanah and Yom Kippur? He answered: Can you imagine that the King sits on the throne of judgment with the books of those destined to live and those destined to die before Him, and the Jewish people should sing *Hallel* before Me? [The Gemara asks:] But how about

Chanukah which is neither a Yom Tov nor is labor prohibited, and yet the *Hallel* is said? [The Gemara answers:] That is because of the miracle [of Chanukah]. Then why is *Hallel* not said on Purim, on which a miracle happened also? R. Yitzchak said: Because we do not sing *Hallel* for a miracle that occurred outside Eretz Yisrael,[2] [and the miracle of Purim happened in Persia]. R. Nachman b. Yitzchak raised an objection: But there is the exodus from Egypt which was a miracle that happened outside Eretz Yisrael, and yet we do say *Hallel* [on Pesach].—There we say *Hallel* because we learned in a *Baraita*: Before the Jews entered Eretz Yisrael, all the lands were appropriate for *Hallel* to be said [if a miracle had happened there, and the Exodus took place before the Jewish people entered Eretz Yisrael]; however, once Israel had entered Eretz Yisrael, no other countries were considered suitable for *Hallel* to be said [for miracles that occurred there, and Purim happened after the Jews entered Eretz Yisrael]. R. Nachman offered a different answer: The reading of the *Megillah* is the *Hallel* of Purim [because it publicizes the miracle and causes everyone to praise God]. Rava said, "I can understand [that *Hallel* is said on Pesach]. For [we are able to say about the exodus from Egypt], 'Give praise, you servants of God'" (Psalms 113:1). [The verse implies that at the moment of deliverance the Jews were servants of God and] no longer servants of Pharaoh. But how can you say about the miracle of Purim, "Give praise, you servants of God"? [The verse implies that at the moment of deliverance they no longer were servants of Achashverosh.] Surely they remained servants of Achashverosh, [even after they were saved from death]!

[The Gemara challenges R. Nachman's opinion:] But according to R. Nachman, who says that the reading of the *Megillah* is the *Hallel*, [of Purim], didn't we learn that once the Children of Israel had entered Eretz Yisrael, all the other lands were no longer appropriate for singing *Hallel* about [and the miracle of Purim happened in Persia]? [The Gemara answers:] After the Jewish people were exiled from Eretz Yisrael, the other lands reverted to their original status. [Accordingly it became permitted once again to say *Hallel* for a miracle that happened there.]

779

IMPROVEMENTS MADE IT WORSE

Our Rabbis taught: There was a flute in the *Bet Hamikdash* that was smooth and thin, it was made of reed, dated back to the days of Moses, and it had a pleasant sound. But when the king ordered it to be plated with gold, its sound was no longer pleasant. When the plating was removed, it sounded again as pleasant as it did before.

There was a cymbal in the *Bet Hamikdash*, made of copper, that dated back to the days of Moses, and it had a pleasant sound. When it became damaged, the Sages sent for craftsmen from Alexandria in Egypt to repair it, but it lost its pleasant sound. As soon as they removed the improvement it sounded again as pleasant as before.

There was a copper mortar in the *Bet Hamikdash* from the days of Moses, and they used it to grind the spices [for the incense mixture]. When it became damaged, the Sages sent for craftsmen from Alexandria to repair it, but it did not mix the spices as well as before. As soon as they removed the improvement it again mixed the spices as well as before. These two utensils [i.e., the cymbal and the mortar] were left over from the first *Bet Hamikdash*, and when they became unserviceable they could not be repaired. Scripture says about them, "They were all made of pure copper" (1 Kings 7:45) and "All their vessels . . . were made from pure copper" (2 Chronicles 4:16). And it says also, "Two vessels of fine gold-colored copper, as splendid as gold" (Ezra 8:27).

R. Shimon b. Gamliel taught: The water of the Shiloah Spring was flowing through a narrow pipe [with a diameter] the size of an *issar* [a small Roman coin, but it supplied all the water that was needed]. The king ordered that it be widened to increase the flow of water, but the water became less instead. When the pipe was narrowed, the water flowed again as before, confirming the message of the verse, "Let not the wise man glorify himself with his wisdom, and let not the strong man glorify himself with his strength" (Jeremiah 9:22), [for his wisdom creates ruin].

THE TEN-STRINGED HARP

(13b) We learned in a Baraita: Rav Yehudah said: The harp of the *Bet Hamikdash* had seven strings, for it says, "In Your presence is the fullness [*sova*] of joy" (Psalms 16:11). Don't read *sova*, (fullness) but *sheva*, (seven). The harp of the days of *Mashiach* has eight strings, as it says, "For the conductor, on the *sheminit*" [i.e., the eighth string] (ibid. 12:1). The harp of the World to Come has ten strings, as it says, "With a ten-stringed instrument and with a lyre, with singing accompanied by a harp" (ibid. 92:4), and it says also, "Give thanks to God with a harp, with a ten-stringed lyre make music to Him. Sing Him a new song, play well with sounds of deep emotion" (ibid. 33:2,3).

EVIL SPEECH

(15a) [The Mishnah says:] We find that a person who maligns [a girl] is punished more severely than one who commits an act [by seducing a girl].[3] And so we also find that the judgment[4] against our ancestors [who griped after receiving the slanderous report of the spies] was sealed only because of their evil speech, as it says, "None of the men . . . who have put Me to the test these ten times[5] shall see the land" (Numbers 14:22).

[The Gemara comments:] We learned in a *Baraita*: R. Elazar b. Parta said: Look how much damage evil speech can do. Consider this: If the spies, who spoke evil of only trees and stones [in Eretz Yisrael] were punished so harshly, how much worse it is if someone speaks evil of his fellow! [The Gemara asks:] How do you know [that the spies were punished for slandering Eretz Yisrael]? Perhaps [they were punished for making a blasphemous statement] as R. Chanina b. Papa explained: The spies made a shocking statement at that time when they said "We cannot attack that people, for it is stronger than we [*mimenu*]" (Numbers 13:31). Do not interpret *mimenu* to mean "than we" but "than He," [the word *mimenu* can mean both "than we" and "than he"]. It is as if they said: Even the Master of the house cannot remove his utensils from there, [meaning: even God Himself cannot expel the people from His land, which is blasphemy]. Rather, said Rabbah in the name of Resh Lakish, it says, "The people who spread the evil report about the land died in a plague before God" (ibid. 14:37), implying that they died just because of the evil report they spread.

TEN REBELLIOUS ACTS

[The above Gemara quoted the verse, "None of the men who have put Me to the test these ten times will see the Land." What ten times does the verse refer to?] R. Yehudah said: Ten times did our forefathers put the Holy One, blessed be He, to the test: twice at the sea, twice because of water, twice because of manna, twice because of quails, once in connection with the golden calf, and once in the Wilderness of Paran.

"Twice at the sea." Once when going down [into the sea], and once when coming up [from the sea]. When going down [they tested God, saying,] "Were there no graves in Egypt that you took us to die in the wilderness?" (Exodus 14:11). When coming up from the sea [they tested God] according to what R. Huna taught, for he said: The Jews of that generation had little faith; as Rabba b. Mari expounded: It says, "They rebelled by the sea, the Red Sea, nevertheless, He saved them for His Name's sake" (Psalms 106:7,8). This teaches that Israel was rebellious at that moment, saying: Just as we are going up on this side, so will the Egyptians go up on the other side. The Holy One, blessed be He, said to the angel in charge of the sea: Cast out the Egyptians on the dry land [so that the Israelites will see that they drowned]! He answered:

Master of the universe! Is there a slave to whom his master gives a gift and then takes it away from him again? [You gave me the Egyptians, and now You are taking them away from me.] Replied the Holy One, blessed be He: "I shall give you afterward one-and-a-half as many of them." [At the Red Sea six hundred Egyptian chariots were drowned, whereas in the days of Deborah, in the battle at Kishon Brook, nine hundred chariots were drowned (Judges 4:13)]. The angel of the Red Sea said: Is there a slave who can lay claim against his master? God answered: The Kishon Brook will be your bond. [Satisfied with this, the angel of the Red Sea] immediately cast the Egyptians on the dry land, as it says, "The Israelites saw the Egyptians dead on the seashore" (Exodus 14:30).

"Twice because of water." First at Marah and then at Refidim. "At Marah" as it says, "They came to Marah, but they could not drink any water there" (ibid. 15:23), and it says, "The people complained to Moses" (ibid. v. 24); "then at Refidim," as it says, "[In Refidim] there was no water for the people to drink" (ibid. 17:1), and then it says, "The people began to quarrel with Moses" (ibid. v. 2).

"Twice because of the manna." Once, as it says, (15b) "Do not go out [to gather the manna on *Shabbat*]" but they did go out (ibid. 16:27). [And the second time, as it says,] "Do not leave over [any manna] until morning" (ibid. 16:19), and they did leave over.

"Twice because of quails." With the first quails,[6] when they complained, "[If we only had died in Egypt,] there at least we could sit by the pots of meat" (ibid. v. 3). With the second quails "The mixed multitude in their midst felt a gluttonous craving and said, 'If only we had meat to eat. . . . We have nothing but this manna to look at!' (Numbers 11:4)."

"In connection with the golden calf," as it is related in the Torah (Exodus 32:1–35).

"In the Wilderness of Paran," as [the story of the spies] is described in the Torah (Numbers 13 and 14).

THE EVILS OF GOSSIP AND SLANDER

R. Yochanan said in the name of R. Yosef b. Zimra: What is the meaning of the verse, "What can He give you, and what can He add to you, O deceitful tongue?" (Psalms 120:3). [What more can God do to stop the tongue from engaging in gossip and slander?] The Holy One, blessed be He, said to the tongue: All parts of the human body are standing upright, only you are lying; all parts of the body are outside; only you are guarded inside. What's more, I surrounded you with two walls, one of bone and one of flesh [the teeth and the lips and cheeks]; "what more can He give you, and what can He add to you, O deceitful tongue!" [The implication is that the tongue is more guarded and protected than all other parts of the body, yet the tongue's ambition is never satisfied.]

R. Yochanan said further in the name of R. Yosef b. Zimra: Spreading evil tales is the same as denying the existence of God, for it says, "May God cut off . . . every tongue that speaks arrogance. . . . They say, 'By our tongues we shall prevail, with lips such as ours, who can be our master?'" (Psalms 12:5).

R. Yochanan also said in the name of R. Yosef b. Zimra: Whoever speaks ill of others will be stricken with leprous plagues, for it says, "He who slanders his neighbor in secret—him I will destroy [*atzmit*]" (ibid. 101:5). And elsewhere [in reference to a leper] it says, *latzemitut*, (Leviticus 25:30), which we translate [in Aramaic] as *lechalutin*, "never-ending." [Since *atzmit* and *latzmitut* are derived from the same root, and the Aramaic term for *atzmit* is used in connection with a leper, the Gemara concludes that a slanderer will be stricken with leprosy.]

Resh Lakish said: What is meant by, "This is the law concerning the leper [*metzora*]" (Leviticus 14:2)? It means: This shall be the law for a person who slanders [*motzi shem ra*. The word *metzora* (leper) is seen as a contraction of *motzi shem ra* (slanderer). Thus, the law of the slanderer is that he shall become a leper.]

Resh Lakish further said: What is the meaning of the verse, "If the snake bites because it was not charmed, then there is no advantage to the charmer's art" (Ecclesiastes 10:11)? At some future time all the animals will come to the snake and say, "The lion attacks and devours [its prey and enjoys it]; the wolf tears and consumes [its prey and enjoys it], but what enjoyment do you derive [from biting a man]? None. You bite a man out of sheer malice. The snake will answer: What enjoyment does the person have who uses his tongue [to malign others]? He too, slanders purely out of malice.

Resh Lakish said also: Whoever slanders makes his sins reach up to heaven, as it says, "They set their mouth against Heaven, and their tongues strut on earth" (Psalms 73:9).

R. Chisda said in the name of Mar Ukva: A person who slanders deserves to be stoned. It says [in connection with talebearing], "He who slanders his neighbor in secret, him I will cut down [*atzmit*]" (ibid. 101:5), and it says elsewhere, "They have cut off [*tzametu*] my life in a pit and threw stones at me" (Lamentations 3:53). [Thus a slanderer deserves to be stoned.]

R. Chisda also said in the name of Mar Ukva: The Holy One, blessed be He, says about a slanderer: He and I cannot live together in the world, as it says, "He who slanders his neighbor in secret—him I will cut down, one with haughty eyes and an expansive heart, him I cannot bear" (Psalms 101:5). Instead of "Him (*oto*) I cannot bear," read, "With him (*itto*) I cannot bear [to be together]." Some say that this refers to arrogant people [rather than slanderers].

R. Chama b. R. Chanina said: What is the remedy for a slanderer? If he is a scholar, he should engage in

Torah study, for it says, "The healing for a tongue is the tree of life" (Proverbs 15:4), and "tongue" here means the evil tongue, as it says, "Their tongue is a like a drawn arrow" (Jeremiah 9:7); and "the tree of life" can mean only the Torah, for it says, "[The Torah] is a tree of life to those who grasp it" (Proverbs 3:18). If the slanderer is an ignorant person, he should become humble, as it says, "He who wants to give up [slandering] should humble himself" (Proverbs 15:4). R. Acha b. Chanina said: If he has slandered already, there is no remedy for him, for King David, in his holy spirit, has cut him off already, as it says, "May God cut off all lips of smooth talk, the tongue that speaks boastfully" (Psalms 12:4). But what should a person do to avoid gossiping? If he is a scholar, he should engage in Torah study, and if he is an ignorant person, he should become humble.

In Eretz Yisrael they said: Gossiping about a third person kills three people: the one who gossips, the one who accepts it, and the one about whom the gossip is told.

R. Chama b. Chanina said: What is meant by the verse, "Death and life are in the hand of the tongue" (Proverbs 18:21)? Does the tongue have "a hand"? It tells you that just as the hand can kill, so can the tongue. You might think that just as the hand can kill only someone that is nearby, so too, the tongue [i.e., slander] can kill only someone that is nearby, that is why the verse says, "Their tongue is like a drawn arrow" (Jeremiah 9:7) [and an arrow kills at a distance]. Then you might think that just as an arrow kills only within forty or fifty cubits, so too, the tongue kills only within forty to fifty cubits. That is why it says, "They set their mouths against Heaven, and their tongues strut on earth" (Psalms 73:9). But since it says already, "They set their mouths against heaven," why was it necessary to state also, "their tongue is like a drawn arrow"? It comes to tell us that the tongue kills like an arrow. But once it says, "Their tongue is like a drawn arrow" why was it necessary to state, "Death and life are in the hand of the tongue?" It agrees with Rava, for Rava said: He who wants to live, can find life through the tongue [by learning Torah]; he who wants to die can find death through the tongue [by slandering others].

WHAT CONSTITUTES GOSSIP?

What constitutes gossip? Rabbah said: For example, if someone says, "There is a fire [burning in the stove] in so-and-so's house.'" Said Abbaye: What is wrong with saying that? He just gave some information [to people who are trying to kindle a fire]! [Rabbah answered: It is wrong] when he said it with a slanderous slant, like, "Where else should there be fire if not in the house of [the wealthy] so-and-so. He is always cooking meat and fish," [implying, that he never shares it with anyone].[7] Rabbah said: Whatever you say in

the presence of the person concerned is not considered gossip. Said Abbaye to him: On the contrary! That constitutes a combination of impudence and gossip! Rabbah replied: I hold with R. Yose, for R. Yose said: I have never said anything behind anyone's back that I would not say in his presence, which proves that saying it in his presence it is not considered gossip.

(16a) Rabbah son of R. Huna said: Repeating a statement a person made in front of three people is not considered gossip. [By stating it in front of three people he indicated that he does not mind if it becomes public knowledge.] Why? [Because he knew that] your friend has a friend, and your friend's friend has a friend, [and eventually the story would spread].

When R. Dimi came from Eretz Yisrael [to Babylonia], he said: What is the meaning of the verse, "If one blesses his friend loudly from early in the morning, it will be considered a curse to him" (Proverbs 27:14)? It refers, for example, to the case of a person who happened to stay in a house where they outdid themselves to make themselves comfortable, and the next morning he goes out into the street and says, "May the Merciful One bless So-and-so, who went all out for me." Whereupon people will come in droves and take advantage of this host. [Although he wants to be hospitable, he does not want to be overrun by visitors (Rashi).]

R. Dimi, the brother of R. Safra, taught: A person should never talk in praise of his neighbor, because by praising him he will end up discrediting him. [He will say, "He is a wonderful person, but he does have one fault . . ."] Some say: R. Dimi, the brother of R. Safra was sick, and R. Safra came to see how he was feeling. R. Dimi said, "May it stand me in good stead that I have kept whatever the Rabbis have decreed." R. Safra replied, "Have you also kept the command: A person should never talk in praise of his neighbor, because by praising him he will end up discrediting him?" He answered: I have not heard it, but if I had heard it, I would have kept it.

SEVEN THINGS THAT CAUSE LEPROSY

R. Shmuel b. Nachmani said in the name of R. Yochanan: Because of seven things the plague of leprosy is brought down on people, namely: slander, bloodshed, false oath, incest, arrogance, robbery, and envy. Because of "slander", for it says, "He who slanders his neighbor in secret, him I will destroy" (Psalms 101:5).[8] Because of "bloodshed," for it says, [after Joab killed Abner, David declared,] "May the house of Joab never be without someone suffering from a discharge, from leprosy . . ." (2 Samuel 3:29). For "a false oath," as it says, "Naaman said, 'Please! Take two talents!'" and it says, "Naaman's leprosy shall therefore cling to you" (2 Kings 5:23 and 27).[9] For "incest," as it says, "God struck Pharaoh . . . with severe plagues because of Abram's wife Sarai" (Genesis 12:17). Because of "arrogance," as it says, "But as he [Uzziah] became strong, his heart became haughty to the point of destructiveness, and he betrayed the Lord his God . . . a leprous growth appeared on his forehead" (2 Chronicles 26:16). Because of "robbery," as it says [concerning a leprous discoloration on a house], "The priest shall give orders that the house be emptied out" (Leviticus 14:36), and a Tanna taught about this: Because he had gathered money that was not his own, the priest comes and scatters it. Because of "envy," as it says, "The owner of the house shall come" (ibid. v. 35), and in the yeshivah of R. Yishmael they commented: This alludes to a person who would reserve his house for himself [and does not let others enjoy his possessions].

WHY IS THE LEPER DIFFERENT?

(16b) R. Shmuel b. Elnadav asked R. Huna, or, as others say, R. Shmuel b. Nadav, the son-in-law of R. Chanina asked R. Chanina; or according to still others, he asked R. Yehoshua b. Levi: In what way is the leper different that the Torah said, "He must remain alone, and his place shall be outside the camp" (Leviticus 13:46)? [His leprosy was caused by slandering through which] he separated a husband from his wife, a man from his neighbor. That is why the Torah says, "He must remain alone." R. Yehoshua b. Levi asked: In what way is the leper different that the Torah said, "[He should bring] two live, clean, birds" (Leviticus 14:4) so that he will become pure again? The Holy One, blessed be He, said: He acted like a babbler, therefore he should offer a babbler [a bird that twitters all the time] as a sacrifice.

REPROOF

We learned in a *Baraita*: It says, "Do not hate your brother in your heart" (Leviticus 19:17). [If it would have said only, "Do not hate your brother," you might think that only hateful acts like] hitting, slapping, or cursing are forbidden. That's why it says, "in your heart." The verse speaks about "hatred in the heart." [The hateful acts are forbidden in Deuteronomy 19:11.] From where do we know that if you see your neighbor doing something improper that you are required to admonish him? Because it says, "You must surely admonish your neighbor" (ibid.). If you admonished him, and he did not accept it, from where do we know that you should admonish him again? Because it says, "You must *surely* admonish him." You might think that you even have to admonish him [publicly] in order to embarrass him. [That is not so.] That's why it says, "Do not bear sin because of him" (ibid.), [do not admonish him if it causes humiliation].

We learned in a *Baraita*: R. Tarfon said: I wonder if there is anyone in this generation who knows how to reprove, [i.e., who will admonish only people who will accept reproof, but not scorners (*Maharsha*)]. For if he admonishes [a scorner] saying, "Remove the splinter from between your eyes," [i.e., "Stop committing such-and-such a sin,"] the scorner would retort, "Remove the beam from between your eyes!" [i.e., "You are guilty of a much greater transgression" (*Maharsha*)]. R. Elazar b. Azariah said: I wonder if there is anyone in this generation who knows how to reprove [without embarrassing the other person (Rashi)]. R. Yochanan b. Nuri said: I call all heaven and earth as witness for myself that often was Akiva b. Yosef [R. Akiva] punished through me because I used to complain about him before R. Gamliel, and he loved me all the more for it, which bears out the verse, "Do not rebuke a scoffer, lest he hate you; rebuke a wise man and he will love you" (Proverbs 9:8).

R. Yehudah son of R. Shimon b. Pazzi asked R. Shimon b. Pazzi: "What is preferable: reproof for the sake of Heaven, or false humility, [where a person alleges that he is not worthy to admonish, while in fact he does not want to arouse the other person's ire (Rashi)]? He answered: Wouldn't you agree that genuine humility is better, for a Master said[10]: Humility is the greatest quality of all? Then, also false humility is better. For R. Yehudah said in the name of Rav: By all means, a person should engage in the study of the Torah and in good deeds, even not for their own sake, because by doing good for ulterior motives, he will eventually come to do good for its own sake. [So you see, false humility will eventually lead to genuine humility.]

Up to what point should reproof be given? Rav said: Until the reprover receives a beating. Shmuel said: Until he is cursed. R. Yochanan said: Until he is shouted at. This question is the subject of a debate by *Tanna'im*: R. Eliezer said: Until he is beaten. R. Yehoshua said: Until he is cursed. Ben Azzai said: Until he is shouted at. All three derived it from the same verse, namely, [Jonathan admonished Saul, saying, "Why should you sin with innocent blood, to kill David for no reason?" Thereupon] "Saul's anger flared up at Jonathan, and he said to him, 'Son of a pervertedly rebellious woman, to your own shame and the shame of your mother's nakedness!'" (1 Samuel 20:30). And then it says, "Saul hurled his spear at him to strike him" (ibid. v. 33). The one who said above "one should give reproof until he receives a beating" said so because it says, "to strike him." [Thus Jonathan gave reproof to the point of being beaten (*Maharsha*)]. The one who said, "until the reprover is cursed" said so because it says, "to your own shame and the shame of your mother's nakedness!" (1 Samuel 20:30). The one who said, "until the reprover is shouted at" said so because it says, "Saul's anger flared up." [The Gemara asks:] But according to the one who says, "until the reprover is shouted at," does the verse not mention also "beating" and "cursing"? [He will answer] that the case of

Jonathan is different. Because of his great love of David, Jonathan risked his life even more [to the point of being beaten and cursed].

DON'T CHANGE YOUR LODGING AND PROFESSION

A boarder who constantly changes his lodging discredits others and himself. [He gives a bad name to the lodging place, and he discredits himself because people will think that he is hard to please.] R. Yehudah said in the name of Rav: From what verse do we derive the rule that a person should not change his lodging? Because it says, "[Abram continued on his travels] until he came to the place where he originally had his tent" (Genesis 13:3).

Rav Yehudah said in the name of Rav: From what verse do we derive that a person should not change his lodging? Because it says [that on his return trip from Egypt, Abaham sojourned at] "the place where his tent had been originally" (Genesis 13:3), [meaning that he stayed in the lodgings he visited on his way to Egypt (Rashi)]. R. Yose b. R. Chanina said: It is derived from [the first part of the verse,] "He proceeded on his journeys" (ibid.) What is the difference? The difference is the case of casual lodging. [The one who derives it from, "the place where his tent had been originally," holds that only a permanent lodging should be revisited, but not a casual lodging. The one who derives it from, "He proceeded on his journeys," maintains that even a casual lodging should be revisited.

R. Yochanan said: From where do we know that a person should not change his occupation and that of his ancestors? For it says, "King Solomon sent for Hiram and brought him down from Tyre. He was the son of a widow of the tribe of Naphtali, and his father had been a Tyrian coppersmith. He was endowed with skill, ability, and talent for executing all work in bronze" (1 Kings 7:13,14); and a Master said: His [paternal grandmother] was of the house of Dan. And it says, [God said concerning Betzalel, the builder of the Tabernacle,] "I have assigned with him Oholiav son of Achisamach of the tribe of Dan [as an assistant]" (Exodus 31:6); [the fact that both Hiram and Oholiav were of the tribe of Dan, and both were builders, proves that Hiram followed his ancestor's profession of craftsman].

TRIVIAL VEXATIONS

[We have learned that afflictions wash away sins (Berachot 5a)]. [The Gemara asks:] What is the most trivial annoyance that might still be considered an affliction [and which will wash away sins]? R. Elazar said: For example, if you had a suit made for yourself, and it does not fit. Rava Ze'ira, or as some say, R. Shmuel b. Nachmani, objected to this, saying: The Sages went much further than that, for they said that

even if you ordered a cup of warmed up wine and they served it chilled, or you ordered chilled wine and they served it warmed, [that too, is considered an affliction], and you mention only the annoyance [of a suit that does not fit]! [Mar b. Ravina said: Even if your shirt got turned inside out, [when you were putting it on]. Rava said: Even as trivial a frustration as putting your hand into your pocket to take out three coins and coming up with only two [is considered an affliction]. But to take out two and coming up with three is not considered an affliction, because it is no trouble to throw one coin back. [The Gemara asks:] What is the practical purpose [of defining the minimum discomfort that qualifies as an affliction]? [The Gemara answers: We want to determine it] because the yeshivah of R. Yishmael taught: Anyone who has not experienced an affliction for forty days has received his world [i.e., he received in this world the tranquility that was set aside for him in the World to Come, but a minor vexation counts as an affliction. Hence the search for the smallest annoyance]. In Eretz Yisrael they said: (17a) Punishment is in store [for anyone who has not experienced an affliction for forty days. Hence the search for the least affliction].

It was taught: R. Eliezer Hagadol said: If the Holy One, blessed be He, wanted to enter into judgment with Abraham, Isaac, or Jacob, not even they could stand before His criticism, [for a wholly righteous person who never sins does not exist]. For it says, "Samuel said to the people, 'And now, stand erect, and I shall enter into judgment with you before God, concerning all the righteous deeds of God that He has done with you and with your forefathers [by not entering into judgment with them]'" (1 Samuel 12:7).

PEOPLE AND THEIR RULER— WHO INFLUENCES WHOM?

It says, "This is the generation of those who seek Him, those who strive for Your Presence [the nation of Jacob], Selah" (Psalms 24:6). R. Yehudah Nesiah[11] and the Rabbis disagree regarding the meaning of this passage. One says: As the leader, so the generation, [i.e., the leader influences his people]. The other says: As the generation, so the leader, [i.e., the people impact on their leader's mindset]. What difference does it make? Do you think that it refers to virtue, so that one Rabbi holds: If the generation is virtuous, so is the leader [since he is influenced by the moral climate of his time]; and the other contends: If the leader is virtuous, so is the generation [since the people are influenced by the ruler's moral leadership]. Then what about King Zedekiah who was virtuous, while his generation was not; and King Jehoiakim who was not virtuous, while his generation was? For R. Yochanan said in the name of R. Shimon b. Yochai: What is the meaning of, "In the beginning of the reign of Jehoiakim son of Josiah, king of Judah" (Jeremiah 26:1)? The Holy

One, blessed be He, wanted to reduce the world to formlessness and emptiness because of [the wicked] Jehoiakim, but when He looked at his generation, His anger subsided [because the generation was virtuous]. And again, the Holy One, blessed be He, wanted to reduce the world to formlessness and emptiness because of the [wicked] generation of Zedekiah, but when He looked at [the righteous] Zedekiah, his anger abated. [Obviously it does not refer to vice and virtue.] Rather, it refers to harshness and gentleness. [One Sage holds that a harsh generation gets a harsh leader, and a good-natured generation will get a gentle ruler, while the other contends that a harsh leader will turn his generation into harsh people, while a gentle leader will transform his generation into gentle people].

THE RETURNEES FROM BABYLONIA MADE SUKKOT

(32b) It says [that upon their return from the Babylonian exile with Ezra], "The entire congregation that had returned from the captivity made sukkot and dwelled in sukkot. The children of Israel had not done so from the days of Joshua son of Nun, and there was very great joy" (Nehemiah 8:17). Is it possible that when David was king they made no sukkot until Ezra came? Rather, the verse [does not refer to tangible sukkot, but it] compares their arrival [in Eretz Yisrael from Babylonia] in the days of Ezra to their arrival [in Eretz Yisrael] in the days of Joshua [after their forty-year wandering in the wilderness, and the word *sukkot* implies that in the days of Ezra they did something they had not done since the days of Joshua, namely]: just as on their arrival in Eretz Yisrael in the days of Joshua they began to count *shemittah* [sabbatical years] and *yovel* [jubilee years] [12] and consecrated walled cities, so too on their arrival in the days of Ezra they began again to count *shemittah* and *yovel* years. And it also says, "The Lord your God will bring you to the Land that your forefathers possessed, and you will possess it" (Deuteronomy 30:5), comparing your possession of the Land to the possession of the Land by your forefathers. Just as your forefathers' possession brought about a renewal of all these things, so will your possession of the land bring about a renewal of all these things.

And the other Tanna [who holds that it does refer to sukkot explains sukkot in a figurative sense:] Ezra asked God to remove from the hearts of the people the passion for idolatry [which had brought about their exile and all their misfortune], and Ezra's merit then shielded them like a sukkah. That is why Scripture

reproached Joshua [for failing to pray for the removal of the craving for idolatry] for in all other verses his name is spelled *Yehoshua*, but here it is written *Yeshua* [the abbreviated form implies Divine displeasure at his failure to pray for the removal of the impulse of idolatry]. Joshua did not pray for it because he thought that the holiness of Eretz Yisrael would be enough to crush the people's impulse toward idolatry].

We can understand that Moses did not pray [for the removal of the passion of idolatry] because, being outside of Eretz Yisrael, he could not count on the merit of the Land to support his plea, but why did Joshua who did have the merit of Eretz Yisrael to bolster his plea, fail to pray [for the removal of the impulse of idolatry]? [That is why Joshua was censured. The reason Joshua did not pray for it is that he thought that the holiness of Eretz Yisrael was enough to crush the people's impulse toward idolatry.]

NOTES

1. The full *Hallel* consists of Psalms 113 through 118. In the shorter version the verses of Psalms 115:1–11 and 116:1–11 are omitted.

2. When the Jews are living in the lands of their enemies their very survival is an ongoing miracle (Iyun Yaakov).

3. He has to pay a hundred *sela* for maligning a girl, whereas if he seduced a girl before she was married, he would have to pay only fifty *sela*.

4. They were not allowed to enter Eretz Yisrael, but were to die during the forty years of wandering (Numbers 14:29–35).

5. This will be explained below.

6. Exodus 16:13.

7. Or, "He always has food cooking in his stove," implying that he is a glutton and a hefty eater (*Maharsha*).

8. "Destroy" in this context alludes to leprosy; see above 15b.

9. After healing the leprosy of Naaman, the commander of the army of Aram, Elisha did not accept any payment. Gechazi, Elisha's attendant, chased after Naaman and greedily asked for gifts which he kept for himself. Naaman asked Gechazi to swear that Elisha had sent him, and he swore falsely. When Elisha found out, he cursed Gechazi with leprosy.

10. *Avodah Zarah* 20b.

11. R. Yehudah HaNasi, the Prince, also called Rebbi.

12. See Leviticus, Chapter 25.

785

✌ TEMURAH ✌

A TIME TO ACT FOR GOD

(14b) R. Yehudah b. Nachman the *meturgeman* (interpreter who explained the lectures) of Resh Lakish gave the following exposition: It says, "God said to Moses, 'Write these words down,'" and the verse continues, "since it is through these words that I have made a covenant with you and Israel" (Exodus 34:27), which comes to teach you that matters you received orally you are not permitted to recite from writing, and that written passages [i.e., verses from the Torah] you are not permitted to recite by heart.[1]

The Tanna of the yeshivah of R. Yishmael taught: It says, "Write down these words," implying that "*these*" words [the words of the Written Torah] you may write down, but laws you received orally you may not write down. [Yet we learned that R. Dimi wanted to write down an oral teaching regarding drink offerings. How could he do that?] The answer was given: Perhaps it is different when it comes to new interpretations [that reconcile contradictory *Baraitot*, and that was what R. Dimi wanted to write down (Rashi)]. For R. Yochanan and Resh Lakish used to look through the book of *Aggadah* on *Shabbat* [so as not to forget the *aggadahs* (Rashi); and *aggadahs* are oral traditions that may not be written down]. They explained their action by citing the verse, "For it is a time to act for God; they have revoked Your Torah" (Psalms 119:126), explaining: [When you are acting for the survival of the Torah] it is better that [one law of the Torah] is broken than that the whole Torah should be forgotten.[2]

THE LAST OF THE *ESHKOLOT*

(15b) When Yosef b. Yo'ezer of Tzereidah and Yosef b. Yochanan of Jerusalem died, the *eshkolot* (grape clusters) came to an end. What is the meant by *eshkolot*? It means: A man who possesses everything. [*Eshkolot* is seen as a contraction of *ish shehakol bo*, "a man who possesses everything" namely, knowledge of Torah, fear of God, and kind deeds (Rashi)]. R. Yehudah said in the name of Shmuel: All the "men of *eshkolot*" who lived from the days of Moses until Yosef b. Yo'ezer learned

Torah as thoroughly as Moses our teacher. From that time on, they did not learn as thoroughly as Moses our teacher.

[The Gemara asks:] But did not Rav Yehudah say in the name of Shmuel: Three thousand *halachot* were forgotten during the period of mourning for Moses? [Then how can you say that the sages that arose after Moses learned as thoroughly as Moses did?] [The Gemara answers:] Those laws that were forgotten were forgotten, but those they learned, they learned [as thoroughly] as Moses our teacher did.

[The Gemara asks:] But haven't we learned in a *Baraita*: After the death of Moses, if those who declared an object unclean were in the majority, the Rabbis declared the object unclean, and if those who declared an object clean were in the majority, the Rabbis declared it clean [which shows that there were differences of opinion soon after the death of Moses; so evidently they did not learn with the same clarity as Moses]? [The Gemara answers:] Their intellectual powers had diminished, [so they could not recall all the laws that were forgotten, therefore they had to settle their differences according to the majority], but the laws they learned, they learned with the same clarity as Moses our teacher did.

THE END OF AN ERA

We learned in a *Baraita*: All the "grape clusters" [i.e., great leaders] that arose in Israel from the days of Moses until the death of Yosef b. Yo'ezer of Tzereidah were free from any *dofi*, "trace of sin." From that time on, a smattering of sin could be detected in them.

[The Gemara asks:] But haven't we learned the following in a *Baraita*? The story is told about a certain chasid [pious man] who groaned while coughing violently. When the doctors were consulted they said that the only remedy was for him to suck warm milk from a goat every morning. They brought a goat and tied it to his bed, and he used to suck milk from it. The next day his friends came to visit him. When they saw the goat they exclaimed, "There is an armed robber in the house,[3] and we should go in to visit him!"

787

[They left immediately. When the *chasid* died] they sat down and reviewed his life and found that he had never sinned except for the fact that he had kept the goat. On his deathbed the *chasid* said, "I know that I have not sinned except that I kept this goat, whereby I transgressed the teaching of my colleagues. For the Rabbis said: You should not raise small cattle in Eretz Yisrael." Small cattle cannot be watched properly and prevented from grazing in other fields. Thus an owner of small cattle is guilty of robbing his neighbor's pasture land. And we have a set rule that whenever the Gemara mentions "a certain chasid" it refers either to R. Yehudah b. Bava or R. Yehudah b. Ila'i. Now these two Rabbis [who, as the Gemara said, are free of any sin] lived many generations after the time of Yosef b. Yo'ezer of Tzereidah. [So you see, that there was no trace of sin *(dofi)* found among the leaders, even after the time of Yosef b. Yo'ezer.] **(16a)** Said R. Yosef: [The word *dofi* here] means dispute, [such as the dispute] about "laying of the hands" [on an animal before it is sacrificed on a Yom Tov.][4] [Thus the Gemara is saying that until the death of Yose b. Yo'ezer there were no disputes about any laws.]

[The Gemara asks:] But does not Yose b. Yo'ezer himself differ regarding the law of the "laying of hands"?[5] [Proof that even in Yose b. Yo'ezer's time there were differences of opinion regarding certain laws.] [The Gemara answers:] When Yose b. Yo'ezer disagreed he was already an old man, and his earlier brilliance had faded.

THE FORGOTTEN *HALACHOT*

[We learned above:] Rav Yehudah said in the name of Rav: Three thousand *halachot* were forgotten during the period of mourning for Moses. [The Gemara elaborates:] They said to Joshua, "Ask [that these forgotten *halachot* should be revealed to you from Heaven]." He replied, "'[The Torah] is not in heaven' (Deuteronomy 30:12), [and from now on all doubts are to be resolved, not by revelation, but by majority vote]." They said to [the prophet] Samuel, "Ask [that Heaven should teach you the forgotten *halachot*]." He replied: It says, "*These* are the *mitzvot*" (Leviticus 27:34), implying [that once these *mitzvot* were given], no prophet has the right to introduce new laws.

Rav Yehudah said in the name of Rav: When Moses left this world to go to Gan Eden he said to Joshua, "Ask me all the laws about which you are in doubt." Replied Joshua, "My Master, have I ever left you and gone elsewhere? [I have no doubts about any law.] Did you not write about me in the Torah, 'His servant, Joshua son of Nun, a youth, would not stir out of the tent' (Exodus 33:11)?" Hearing this, Moses was saddened. [As a punishment for touching a raw nerve in Moses, Joshua] forgot three hundred *halachot*, and all Israel threatened to kill him [unless he told them those laws]. The Holy One, blessed be He, then said to

Joshua, "I cannot tell you these laws; go and keep them busy fighting a war." For it says, "It happened after the death of Moses, servant of God, that God said to Joshua son of Nun, Moses' attendant . . ." (Joshua 1:1). And it says further, "Joshua ordered the marshals of the people, saying, ... 'Prepare provisions for yourselves for within three days you will cross the Jordan to take possession of the land'" (ibid. v. 11).

OTHNIEL RESTORED THE FORGOTTEN TEACHINGS

It has been taught: A thousand and seven hundred *kal vachomer*s,[6] and *gezeirah shavah*s[7] and numeric listings of the Scribes[8] were forgotten during the period of mourning for Moses. Said R. Abbahu: Nevertheless, Othniel[9] son of Kenaz restored these forgotten teachings by dint of his deductive reasoning. For it says, "Othniel son of Kenaz, brother of Caleb, conquered [Kiriat Sefer],[10] so [Caleb] gave him his daughter Achsah as a wife" (Joshua 15:17). And why was she called Achsah? R. Yochanan said: Because whoever saw her became angry [*ka'as*] with his wife, [because Achsah was very beautiful].

[It says in the next verse,] "When [Achsah] came to [Othniel], she urged him to let her ask her father for a field. Then she slid [*vatitznach*] from her donkey [to prostrate herself before Caleb]" (ibid. v. 18). What does the word *vatitznach* mean? Rava said in the name of R. Yitzchak: Achsah said to her father: Just as a donkey when it has no food in its trough immediately cries out [*tzavach*], so too, a woman who has no wheat in her house cries out immediately, as it says, "Caleb said to her, 'What do you want?' She answered, 'Give me a source of blessing, for you have given me an arid land; give me springs of water'" (ibid 18,19), implying, "Give me a man in whom there is nothing but Torah," [since water is the symbol of Torah; and Othniel was a learned but very poor man]. "So he gave her the upper springs and the lower springs" (ibid.). He said to her, "Does a person to whom all the mysteries of the upper and lower worlds are revealed need to ask for food from God?" [Surely not. For a person who studies Torah full-time receives abundant blessings from Heaven.]

WHAT WAS THE NAME OF CALEB'S FATHER?

[The Gemara asks:] But was Caleb the son of Kenaz? [The Gemara above quoted a verse stating that Othniel, the brother of Caleb, was the son of Kenaz.] Wasn't he the son of Jephunneh?[11] [The Gemara answers:] The word Jephunneh alludes to the fact that Caleb turned away [*panah*] from the counsel of the spies. [When the spies maligned Eretz Yisrael, Caleb disassociated himself from them and protested against their slanderous report.][12] [The Gemara is not satisfied with this answer:] But still, was Caleb the son of Kenaz? Wasn't he the son of Chetzron, for it says, "And Caleb the son of Chetzron fathered children by Azubah" (1 Chronicles 2:18). Said Rava: He was a stepson of Kenaz; [Caleb was the son of Kenaz's wife].

GOD FULFILLED OTHNIEL'S WISH

A Tanna taught: Othniel is the same as Jabez (Yavetz).[13] He was called Othniel because God answered him [ana El], and Jabez because he counseled and furthered [ravatz] Torah in Israel. And what was his real name? Yehudah brother of Shimon. And from where do we know that God answered him? Because it says, "Jabez called out to the God of Israel, saying, 'If you bless me and expand my borders, and Your hand is with me, and You keep me from harm, that I not be saddened. . . .' And God granted him that which he requested" (1 Chronicles 4:10).

[The Gemara now expounds the individual segments of this verse:] "If You bless me"—with Torah; "and expand my borders"—with students; "and Your hand is with me"—that I will not forget my studies; "and You keep me from harm"—that I may meet friends like myself; "that I may not be saddened"—that the yetzer hara should not have power over me and discourage me from studying: If You do so, well and good, but if not, I will go with sadness to the grave. Immediately, "God granted his request," [because he passionately wanted to learn Torah].

There is a similar example [of a verse that proves that if you fervently want to learn Torah your wish is granted]. It says, "When the poor man and the moderately wealthy man [i.e., the unlearned man and the man of moderate knowledge] meet, God will enlighten the eyes of both" (Proverbs 29:13). [The Gemara explains:] When a student approaches a teacher and asks him to teach him Torah, then, if he teaches him, God enlightens the eyes of both of them, [for the teacher also needs to learn more], and if not, "The rich man and the pauper meet; God is the Maker of them all" (ibid. 22:2) [which is interpreted to mean:] He who made this one wise can make him a fool, and He who made this one a fool can make him wise. This is how R. Natan interprets the verse.

[Unlike R. Natan who interpreted the above-mentioned verse as referring to a student and a teacher], R. Yehudah Hanasi[14] [interprets it as referring to a poor man who is asking for alms], "If You bless me"—by multiplying and increasing; "and expand my borders"—with son and daughters; "and Your hand is with me"—in business; "and you keep me from harm"—that I have no headache, ear ache or eye ache; "that I may not be saddened"—that the yetzer hara may not have power over me to deter me from studying: If You do this, well and good, but if not, I

will go with sadness to my grave. "And God granted his request." There is a verse that expresses the same idea: "When the poor man and the man of moderate means meet; God will enlighten the eyes of both" (Proverbs 29:13); [the poor man finds relief from his troubles, and the benefactor earns life in the hereafter]. When the poor man approaches the donor and asks him for help; if he helps him, well and good, but if not, "The rich man and the pauper meet; God is the Maker of them all" (ibid. 22:2), [which is interpreted to mean:] He who made this one rich can make him poor, and He who made this one poor can make him rich.

NOTES

1. Tosafot comments that this applies only when you recite verses, like the Shema, on behalf of others with the intention to exempt them.

2. Based on this verse, R. Yehudah Hanasi wrote the Mishnah which is a compilation of all the laws of the Oral Torah. He thereby ensured the survival of the Oral Torah after the destruction of the second Bet Hamikdash when the Jewish people were dispersed all over the world.

3. Small cattle cannot be prevented from grazing in other fields. Thus an owner of small cattle is guilty of robbing someone else's pasture land.

4. This was the first subject about which there was a difference of opinion. Bet Shammai held that is was permitted, whereas Bet Hillel held that it was not permitted. This debate took place after the time of Yose b. Yoezer (Chagigah 15a).

5. Chagigah 15a.

6. A kal vachomer is an a fortiori conclusion from major to minor. For example: If it is forbidden to write on Yom Tov, then surely it is forbidden to write on Shabbat.

7. Similar words in different contexts are meant to clarify one another.

8. For example: Fifteen categories of women exempt their co-wives from chalitzah (Yevamot 2a); thirteen things were taught with reference to a neveilah of a clean bird. The Rabbis used these groupings as a mnemonic aid.

9. The first of the Judges.

10. Kiriat Sefer literally means "the city of the book." Here it is taken to mean that Othniel recaptured the teachings that had been forgotten.

11. Numbers 13:6; Joshua 14:14.

12. Numbers 13:30.

13. 1 Chronicles 2:55.

14. R. Yehudah Hanasi (the Prince) compiled the Mishnah. He is also known as Rebbi.

✣ KERITOT ✣

FATHERLY ADVICE

(6a) R. Mesharshiya said to his sons: When you go to your teacher [to attend his lecture] you should review the Mishnah in advance [so that you are well prepared]. And when you are sitting before your teacher look at his face, for it says, "Your eyes will behold your teacher" (Isaiah 30:20). And when you study your lesson do it by the side of a stream, for just as the stream flows on, so may your learning continue on and on. It is better to be on the trash heaps of Mata Mechasya than in the palaces of Pumbedita, [because the people of Pumbedita are reputed to be robbers].[1] It is better to eat a stinking fish rather than *kutach* [a special dish made of sour milk, bread crusts and salt] that is hard enough to break rocks, [because it closes up the heart].[2]

A HORN AND A FLASK

It says, "Hannah prayed, saying, 'My heart rejoices in God, my horn is exalted in God'" (1 Samuel 2:1). Since Hannah said, "My horn is exalted" and not "My flask is exalted" she prophetically implied that only through a horn will a person become exalted. And so it was: David and Solomon who were anointed as king with a "horn" of oil,[3] their reign lasted a long time. However, Saul and Yehu, who were anointed as king with a flask of oil,[4] their reign did not last a long time.

THE ELEVEN SPICES
OF THE INCENSE

(6b) The Master said: As the grinder would grind [the incense for the *Bet Hamikdash*] the overseer would say, "Grind thoroughly, thoroughly grind." This supports R. Yochanan; for R. Yochanan said: Just as the sound of speaking [while wine is being prepared] is harmful to the wine, so it is beneficial for spices.

R. Yochanan said: Eleven kinds of spices were mentioned to Moses at Sinai. Said R. Huna: In what verse were they mentioned? In the passage, "Take yourself spices—stacte, onycha and galbanum—spices and pure frankincense" (Exodus 30:34). [The Gemara expounds:] "Spices" [in the plural] means two; "stacte, onycha and galbanum" [makes five]; "spices" means another five; "and pure frankincense" which is one, that is together eleven.

REACH OUT TO
NON-OBSERVANT JEWS

R. Chana b. Bizna said in the name of R. Shimon Chasida: A fast in which none of the non-observant Jews participate is no fast. [Non-observant Jews should be invited to join us in our prayers, for eventually they will do *teshuvah*. This idea is symbolized by the *chelbenah* (galbanum)], for *chelbenah* has an unpleasant aroma and yet it was included among the spices of the incense [of the *Bet Hamikdash*]. Abaye said: We derive it from the verse, "He has founded His group upon the earth" (Amos 9:16). [Meaning: Only when all are united is God's rule on earth firmly established].

HONOR YOUR FATHER AND
YOUR MOTHER

(28a) In most places in the Torah the father is mentioned before the mother, [like, "Honor your father and your mother" (Exodus 20:12)]. This may lead you to believe that the honor a son owes his father is greater than the honor he owes his mother; therefore it says, "Every man: Your mother and father shall you revere" (Leviticus 19:3), [where the mother is mentioned before the father,] to teach you that both are equal. But the Sages have said that the father comes before the mother in every respect, because both the son and his mother are required to honor the father. And the same holds true for Torah study. If the son acquired most of his knowledge from his teacher, his teacher comes before his father in all places, [i.e., the son must honor his teacher before honoring his father,[5] because both the son and the father are required to honor the teacher. [But if the father is a Torah scholar, he takes precedence over the teacher.]

NOTES

1. "If a Pumbeditan accompanies you, then change your quarters [so he cannot rob you]" (*Chullin* 127a).
2. *Pesachim* 42a.
3. 1 Samuel 16:13 and 1 Kings 1:39.
4. 1 Samuel 10:1 and 2 Kings 9:3.
5. For example, if a person found two lost objects or animals, one belonging to his teacher, the other to his father, and both need attention, he must take care of his teacher's lost animal before taking care of his father's (*Bava Metzia* 33a).

∽ ME'ILAH ∾

HOW THE ROMAN
DECREE WAS ABOLISHED

(17a) R. Matia b. Cheresh once asked R. Shimon b. Yocha'i in Rome: From where do we know that the blood of swarming animals [like the mole, the mouse and the lizard] is unclean? He replied: Because it says, "These are the unclean ones among the swarming animals" (Leviticus 11:29). His students then said to him: The son of Yocha'i has shown great wisdom, [for this is a fitting answer]. R. Shimon b. Yocha'i replied: I heard this exposition from R. Elazar b. R. Yose.

[The Gemara now relates the events that form the background to R. Elazar's exposition.] For the Roman government once made a decree forbidding the Jews to keep *Shabbat*, circumcise their children, and ordered them to have marital relations with menstruant women. Thereupon R. Reuven b. Istrobeli cut his hair in the Roman style [so that they could not tell that he was a Jew], and went and sat among the Roman [senators]. He said to them, "If you have an enemy, should you make him poor or rich?" They replied, "You should make him poor." He said to them, "If so, let the Jews not work on the Sabbath; that is sure to make them poor, [because they lose a day's income]." They said, "You are right." He retorted, "So, let the decree [forbidden *Shabbat* observance] be annulled." Thereupon they did indeed annul the decree. R. Reuven b. Istrobeli continued, "If you have an enemy, do you want him to be weak or healthy?" "He should be weak," they replied. "If so," he continued, "allow the Jews to circumcise their children when they are eight days old. That will make them weak." [The loss of blood makes them frail.] They said, "You are right," and the decree against *milah* was abolished. Finally he said, "If you have an enemy, do you want him to multiply or to dwindle?" "He should dwindle," they replied. "So forbid them to have marital relations with menstruant women." "You are right," they replied, and the decree was abolished. However, when they later found out that he was a Jew, they reinstated the decrees. The Sages then deliberated as to who should go to Rome to lobby for the cancellation of the decrees.

(17b) [They decided,] "Let R. Shimon b. Yocha'i go, for he has performed many miracles."[1] "And who should escort him?" "R. Elazar son of R. Yose." Said R. Yose [the father of R. Elazar] to the Sages, "If my father Chalafta were still alive, would you have asked to give his son to be executed [by the Romans]?" [Neither can you expect me to send my son. He was afraid that R. Shimon might curse his son, as he explains later. But R. Shimon thought that his refusal was prompted by the fear that his son might be killed by the Romans.] Replied R. Shimon, "If Yocha'i, my father, were still alive, would you have said to him to give his son to be executed [by the Romans]?" [Implying that he too, was risking his life.] Said R. Yose to the Sages, "I will escort R. Shimon, because I am afraid that he will punish [my son Elazar when he says things that displease him]." R. Shimon then pledged not to punish R. Elazar; [so R. Elazar accompanied him]. Nevertheless, he did punish him. For when they were on their way, the following question was put to them: From where do we know that the blood of a swarming animal is unclean? Turning aside, R. Elazar b. R. Yose answered in a whisper, [so that R. Shimon should not notice, for it is improper for a student to answer questions in the presence of an outstanding Torah scholar. But R. Shimon did notice it, and he cursed him[2] (Rashi)]. [Answering the question,] R. Elazar said: It says, [about the swarming animals], "These are the unclean [animals]" (Leviticus 11:29).[3] Said R. Shimon to him, "From the fact that you whispered [your answer] I can see that you are a Torah scholar; nevertheless, the son [R. Elazar] shall not return to the father," [meaning, R. Elazar should die as a punishment for his impudence in answering a question in the presence of a Torah scholar without his permission]. Suddenly Ben Tamalyon [a demon] came to meet them. He said, "Do you want me to come along with you [to help you in your mission]?" Thereupon R. Shimon cried and said, "[Hagar,] the maid of my ancestor [Abraham's] house was worthy to meet an angel three times,[4] and I am not worthy to meet an angel even once. However, let the miracle be performed, no matter how; [even through a demon]." Thereupon Ben Temalyon [the demon] took possession of the Emperor's daughter's body. [She went raving mad, screaming, "Bring me R. Shimon b. Yocha'i!" (Rashi).][5] When R. Shimon arrived [at the Emperor's palace], he called out, "Ben Temalyon, get out! Ben Temalyon, get out!" and as he exclaimed this, the demon left the princess' body. The Emperor told R. Shimon and R. Elazar, "Ask for anything you wish." They were led into the Emperor's treasure chamber and invited to take whatever they desired. They found there the document [containing the decree against the three Jewish practices] and tore it to shreds. It was this visit R. Elazar b. R. Yose was referring to when he said,[6] "[When I was in the treasure chamber in Rome] I saw there [among the plundered vessels of the *Bet Hamikdash*] the *parochet* [curtain] that separates the Holy from the Holy of Holies], which was splattered with the blood [of the bull and the he-goat the *Kohen Gadol* sprinkled on the curtain on Yom Kippur].

NOTES

1. See *Shabbat* 33b.

2. As a result of the curse R. Elazar fell ill with the croup. When R. Yochanan recalled his promise not to invoke punishment on R. Elazar, he prayed for R. Elazar to recover. One of the sailors aboard the ship inadvertently stepped on R. Elazar's neck, whereupon the croup left him and entered the sailor's throat (Rashi, quoting an *aggadah*).

3. This is the incident R. Shimon b. Yocha'i was referring to earlier.

4. It says three times, "And an angel of God said to her" (Genesis 16:9,10,11).

5. Ben Temalyon, the demon, said to R. Shimon: I will enter the Emperor's daughter's body, and she will go mad. They will find no one to heal her until you appear and exorcise me saying, "Get out!" whereupon I will leave her. The Emperor then will do whatever you ask of him. As a sign that I left her body, all the glassware in the palace will shatter (Rashi only in Ein Yaakov).

6. *Yoma* 57a.

ᥩ TAMID ᥩ

RULES OF HYGIENE
AND DECENCY

(27b) R. Shimon b. Gamliel said: Holding back one's bowel movement brings on *hadrokan* [a stomach disorder, dropsy]. Holding back urine brings on jaundice. Rav said to his son Chiya: Take care of your needs morning and evening [at home, even if you do not feel the call of nature], then you will not have to go so far [to the privies in the field when you are away from home]. Rinse a wine glass before you drink, and rinse it again before you put it away. And when you drink water, pour some of it over the rim where your mouth touched before you hand it to your disciple. As it has been taught: A person should not drink water and hand the cup to his disciple unless he first pours some out [in order to clean it]. It once happened that a teacher forgot to pour off some water and handed the cup to his thirsty disciple. The disciple was squeamish and did not want to drink [he did not want to pour some water over the rim of the cup out of respect for his teacher], and so he died of thirst. Then and there they laid down a rule that a person should not drink and pass the cup to his disciple without pouring some out. R. Ashi said: Consequently, if a disciple pours out in the presence of his teacher, this shows no disrespect.

[If you ate something that causes saliva to gather in your mouth] you should not spit out in front of your teacher except when you ate pumkin or groats which are as difficult to digest as molten lead [so, after eating these, don't swallow the saliva, for that is dangerous (Rashi)].

PUNISHED FOR OVERSLEEPING

We have learned elsewhere: The officer of the Temple Mount used to go around to every watch holding burning torches, and if any watchman did not get up and say, "Officer, (28a) officer! I greet you!" it was proof that he was asleep. The officer would tap him with his stick. He was also permitted to singe his clothes. The others would say, "What's that noise in the *Azarah* [the Court of the *Bet Hamikdash*]? That's a Levite crying. He is being beaten and his garments are being singed

because he was asleep at his post." R. Eliezer b. Yaakov said: Once they found my mother's brother asleep, and they singed his clothes. R. Chiya b. Abba said: When R. Yochanan came to this Mishnah he used to say: Happy were the previous generations who punished even people who were overcome by sleep [something they cannot help]; how much more then [did they punish] a person who transgressed deliberately.

ALEXANDER THE GREAT'S
TEN QUESTIONS

(31b) Alexander of Macedonia put ten questions to the elders of the south country. He asked them: Which distance is greater, (32a) from heaven to earth or from east to west? They replied: From east to west. The proof is that when the sun is in the east everyone can look at it [without being blinded], and when it is in the west everyone can look at it [without being blinded, because it is far away], but when the sun is in the middle of the sky no one can look at it [because it is nearer than either east or west]. The Sages, however, say: Both distances are the same, as it says, "For as the heavens are high above the earth, so great is His steadfast love toward those who fear Him. As east is far from west, so far has He removed our sins from us" (Psalms 103:11,12). Now if one of these distances was greater, the verse would not mention both but only the greater one [but since both distances are mentioned, they must be the same]. Then what is the reason why no one can look directly at the sun at high noon, [yet people can look at it when it is in the east or the west]? Because when it is overhead it is perfectly clear, and nothing obstructs its view, [but when it is in the east and the west hills and mountains are in the way].

Alexander asked the Sages: Which was created first: heaven or earth? They replied: Heaven was created first, as it says, "In the beginning God created heaven and earth" (Genesis 1:1). He then asked: Which was created first: light or darkness? They replied: No one knows the answer to this question. [The Gemara asks:] Why didn't they reply that darkness was created first, for it says, "The earth was without form and empty, with darkness on the face of the deep" (ibid. v. 2), followed by, "God said, 'Let there be light'" (ibid. v. 3)? [The Gemara answers:] They thought to themselves: Perhaps next he will ask: what is above and what is below, what is before and what is after [things that are above human understanding]. [The Gemara asks:] If that is the case, they should not have answered the question about heaven either? [The Gemara answers:] At first they thought that he just happened to ask that question [on the spur of the moment], but when they saw that he pursued this line of thinking they thought it over and decided not to answer him so that he should not go on and ask what is above and what is below, what is before and what is after.

Alexander then asked the Sages: Who is called wise? [They answered:] He who considers the outcome of a deed [and is careful to avoid its pitfalls]. He asked: Who is strong? They replied: He who subdues his evil impulse. He asked: Who is a rich man? They replied: He who is happy with his lot.[1] He asked: What should a person do to live? They replied: Let him kill himself [with study and hard work]. What should a person do to kill himself? They replied: Let him "live it up" [and indulge in sensual pleasures]. He said to them: What should a person do to be well-liked? They replied: He should hate to be in charge and govern [because it is impossible for a ruler to please everybody (*Maharsha*)]. He said to them: I have a better answer than yours: He should love to be in charge and govern and use his office to work for the benefit of mankind. [That is what Alexander perceived his mission in life to be.] He said to them: Is it better to live on the sea or on dry land? They answered: It is better to live on dry land, because those that sail the seas are never free from anxiety until they set foot on dry land. He said to them: Which of you is the wisest? They replied: We are all equal, because we all came up with the same answers to your questions. He said to them: Why do you oppose me [by refusing to accept our religion? After all, we are in the majority and we rule over you]. They replied: [The fact that you rule over us does not prove that you are right. For you see,] Satan too, is very powerful [and misleads people all the time]. He said to them: [You are foolish to cling to your faith, for] if I want I can have you all executed by royal decree. They replied: Power is in the hands of the king, but it is not becoming for a king to go back on his word, [and you promised not to harm us if we get the better of you in the debate]. Thereupon he immediately clothed them in purple garments and put chains of gold on their necks.

ALEXANDER IN
THE CITY OF WOMEN

[Alexander the Great] said to the Sages: I want to go to the country of Africa. They told him: You cannot get there, because the Mountains of Darkness are in the way, [and nobody can cross those mountains. On 32b we are told that Gehinnom is behind the Mountains of Darkness]. He replied: That will not stop me from going, and I am asking you to tell me how to get there. They said to him: Take Lybian donkeys that can travel in the dark, and take coils of rope and attach one end of the rope at the place where the darkness begins, so that when you return you can guide yourself by the rope and find your way back [in the dark]. That is what Alexander did, and he set out on his expedition.

He came to a place where there were only women. He wanted to make war with them, but they said to him: If you kill us, people will say that he killed women, and if we defeat you they will call you the king who was defeated by women; [either way you will be the loser]. He said to them: Please let me have some bread. So they brought him gold bread on a gold table. (32b) He said to them: Do people here eat gold bread? They replied: [No, they don't. But we offered you gold bread because we thought] you surely did not come here to eat bread. Don't you have bread back home, that you should come here to ask for bread? [We brought you gold bread because we thought that you wanted our gold and silver.]

When Alexander left that place he wrote on the gate of the city: I, Alexander of Macedonia, was a fool until I came to the city of women in Africa and received advice from the women.

ALEXANDER AT
THE GATE OF GAN EDEN

As he was traveling he sat by a spring and began to eat. He had with him some salted fish, and as they were being washed they gave off a pleasant fragrance; [alternate version: they came back to life]. So he said: This shows that this spring comes from the Garden of Eden. Some say that he took some of the water and washed his face with it; others say that he climbed up the trail that led to the source of the spring until he came to the gate of Gan Eden.

He cried out: Open the gate for me! They replied: "This is the gateway to God—the righteous shall enter through it" (Psalms 118:20). He replied: I am a king! I am an important personage. [If you don't admit me, at least] give me something [from Gan Eden]. They gave him an eyeball. He went and weighed all his silver and gold against it, and it did not weigh as much [as the eyeball]. He said to the Rabbis: How is this possible? They replied: It is the eyeball of a human being, [and the human eye] is never satisfied. [That is why you are not admitted to Gan Eden. Only *tzaddikim* who do not amass worldly goods will enter Gan Eden. (*Maharsha*)]. They took a little dust and covered the eyeball, [meaning: man continues to hoard silver and gold until he is in the grave, covered by dust], and immediately the eyeball was weighed down. And so it says, "As the grave and Gehinnom are not sated, so the eyes of man are not sated" (Proverbs 27:20).

The Tanna debei Eliyahu taught: Gehinnom is above the firmament; some say that it is behind the Mountains of Darkness.

R. Chiya taught: If you study Torah at night, the Divine Presence faces you, as it says, "Arise, cry out at night, in the beginning of the watches! Pour out your heart like water in the presence of God" (Lamentation 2:19), [and the Torah is compared to water].

Rabbi Elazar said in the name of R. Chanina: Torah scholars increase peace in the world, as it says, "And all your children [will be the students of God, and your children [banayich] will have abundant peace" (Isaiah 54:13). Do not read banayich, "your children," but bonayich, "your builders." [The Sages do not want to change the Masoretic text, but to suggest an additional implication—that children are also builders—in this case that the students of Torah are the builders of "abundant peace" (Etz Yosef).

NOTE

1. *Avot* 4:1.

ᕲᕽ NIDDAH ᕽᕲ

THE EMBRYO IN
THE MOTHER'S WOMB

(30b) R. Simlai lectured: What does an embryo look like in its mother's womb? It looks like a folded ledger. Its hands rest on its two temples, its two elbows on its two legs, and its two heels rest against its buttocks. Its head lies between its knees, its mouth is closed and its navel is open, and it eats what its mother eats and drinks what its mother drinks, but it does not defecate because otherwise it would kill its mother. But as soon as it is born, the closed organ [the mouth] opens, and the open one [the navel] closes, for if that would not happen it could not live even one single hour. A light burns above [the embryo's] head, and it looks and sees from one end of the world to the other,[1] as it says, "When His lamp would shine over my head, and I would walk in darkness by His light" (Job 29:3).

And this should not surprise you, for a person sleeping here [in Babylonia] might see Spain in his dream. And a person is never more happy than he is in his pre-natal existence, as it says, "If only I could be as in the earlier months when God would watch over me" (ibid. 29:2). Now which are the days that add up to months and do not add up to years? That can only be the months of pregnancy. The embryo is also taught the entire Torah, for it says, "He taught me and said to me, 'Let My words sustain your heart, observe My commandments and live'" (Proverbs 4:4). And it says also, "When God's mystery was upon my tent" (Job 29:4).

Why do we need an additional verse [to tell us that it is taught the entire Torah]? In case you might say that it was only the prophet who said, ["Observe My commandments and live"], let me give you the following proof: "When God's mystery was upon my tent" [evidence that it was God Who said it]. As soon as it enters the world, an angel comes, slaps it on its mouth, and makes it forget all the Torah completely, as it says, "Sin rests at the door [that opens to life in this world]" (Genesis 4:7). Before it emerges from the womb it is made to take an oath, as it says, "To Me every knee shall kneel and every tongue swear" (Isaiah 45:23). "To

Me every knee shall kneel" refers to the day of dying, about which it says, "All who descend to the dust will kneel before Him" (Psalms 22:30). "Every tongue shall swear" refers to the day of birth, about which it says, "One with clean hands and pure heart; who has not sworn in vain by My soul, and has not sworn deceitfully" (Psalms 24:4).

What is the oath the embryo is made to take? The oath states: Be a *tzaddik* and don't be wicked. And even if everyone says, "You are a *tzaddik*," consider yourself wicked. Always be mindful that the Holy One, blessed be He, is pure and His servants are pure, and that the soul He gave you is pure. If you keep it pure, fine; but if not, I will take it away from you.

THREE PARTNERS IN MAN

(31a) The Rabbis taught: There are three partners in man: The Holy One, blessed be He, his father, and his mother. His father supplies the semen of the white substance out of which are formed the child's bones, sinews, nails, the brain, and the white in his eye. The mother supplies the fluid of the red substance of which is formed the skin, flesh, hair, blood, and the black of his eye; and the Holy One, blessed be He, gives him the spirit and the soul, beauty of features, eyesight, the power of hearing and the ability to speak and to walk, understanding and discernment. When his time to leave this world approaches, the Holy One, blessed be He, takes away His share and leaves the shares of his father and his mother with them. R. Papa noted: This is what people have in mind when they say, "Shake off the salt and throw the flesh to the dog" [If you take away the salt that preserves the flesh, the body is worthless. So, too, if the soul that is the salt of the body is gone, the flesh disintegrates (Rashi).]

GOD'S WONDROUS POWER

R. Chinena b. Papa lectured: What is meant by the verse, "[God] Who performs great deeds that are beyond comprehension, and wonders beyond number"

(Job 9:10)? Consider the contrast between the ability of the Holy One, blessed be He, and that of mortal man. A man will put things in a skin bottle[2] whose slits are tied up and whose opening is on top, and yet it is doubtful whether the things will stay in there or not. By contrast, the Holy One, blessed be He, fashions the embryo in the mother's womb that is open and turned downward, and yet the embryo stays in there.

Another explanation: If a person puts his things on a scale, the heavier they are, the lower the scale descends, but the Holy One, blessed be He, fashioned the woman in a way that the heavier the embryo the higher it rises, [from the lowest chamber at conception it rises steadily to the highest].

R. Yose Hagelili expounded: What is the meaning of the verse, "I thank You, for I am awesomely, wondrously made; Your work is wonderful; I know it very well" (Psalms 139:14)? Consider the contrast between the power of the Holy One, blessed be He, and that of mortal man. If a man puts different seeds into a bed each grows into a different species. By contrast, the Holy One, blessed be He, fashions the embryo in the woman's womb in such a way that [the semen and the ovum] grow into one and the same kind.

UNAWARE OF THE MIRACLE
R. Yosef expounded: What is the intent of the verse, "In that day you will say, 'I give thanks to You, O God, for you were angry with me, and now Your wrath has subsided, and You have comforted me'" (Isaiah 12:1). The verse hints at two people who set out on a business trip when one of them hurt his foot on a thorn [and was forced to cancel his trip]. Angrily he began to curse and blaspheme. Later on when he found out that the ship [on which he had booked passage] had sunk into the sea, he began to praise and extol. That's why it says, "Your anger has subsided and You have comforted me." This agrees with what R. Eliezer said: What is meant by the verse, "God Who *alone* does wondrous things; blessed is His glorious Name forever" (Psalms 72:18,19)? Even the person for whom the miracle is performed is unaware of the miracle; [only God knows it].

QUESTIONS ABOUT MATRIMONY AND CHILDBIRTH
R. Shimon b. Yochai was asked by his students: Why did the Torah mandate that a woman after childbirth should bring a sacrifice? He replied: When she crouches to give birth she swears impulsively that she will never again have intercourse with her husband. The Torah ordained, therefore, that she should bring a sacrifice. And why did the Torah ordain that if she gives birth to a boy the woman is clean after seven days, and if she gives birth to a girl she is clean after fourteen days? When she has a boy with whom all are happy she regrets her oath [not to have intercourse] after seven days; but when she has a girl when everyone is disappointed, she regrets her oath only after fourteen days. And why did the Torah ordain circumcision on the eighth day [and not on the seventh]? So that the guests [at the *brit milah* feast] should not enjoy themselves while the baby's father and mother are not in a happy mood [because they are forbidden to have intercourse until the conclusion of the seventh day].

SHE WILL BE LOVED BY HER HUSBAND
We learned in a *Baraita*: R. Meir used to say: Why did the Torah ordain that the uncleanness of menstruation should last for seven days? Because being in constant contact with his wife, a husband might come to dislike her. Therefore, the Torah ordained: Let her be unclean [even after seeing the slightest bloodstain] for seven days [when intercourse is forbidden] in order that she shall be beloved by her husband like at the time she entered beneath the *chuppah* [the bridal canopy].

A MAN SEARCHES FOR A WIFE
R. Dostai b. R. Yannai was asked by his students: Why does a man go in search of a woman [to marry] and no woman goes in search of a man? You can compare it to the case of a man who lost something. Who searches for what? He who lost the thing goes in search of what he lost. [Adam searches for his rib from which Eve was fashioned.] And why is a man easily appeased and a woman is not easily appeased? He derives his nature from the place from which he was created [from the earth, which is pliable], and she derives hers from the place from which she was created [the rigid bone of a rib]. Why is a woman's voice sweet and a man's voice is not sweet? He derives his voice from the place from which he was created [if you strike the earth it produces a dull sound], and she derives hers from the place from which she was created [when you strike a hollow bone it produces a resonant sound]. And so it says, "Let me hear your voice, for your voice is sweet and your face comely" (Song of Songs 2:14).

WOMEN HAVE SUPERIOR UNDERSTANDING
(45b) R. Chisda said: It says, "God fashioned [*vayiven*] the rib that he had taken from the man into woman" (Genesis 2:22). This teaches us that the Holy One, blessed be He, endowed the women with more under-

standing [*binah*] than the man [*binah* is seen as cognate to *vayiven*].

A GUARANTEED PLACE IN
THE WORLD TO COME

(73a) The Tanna debei Eliyahu teaches: Whoever learns *halachot* [meaning Mishnah and Gemara] every day is guaranteed to have a place in the World to Come, for it says, "*Halichot* of the world are his" (Habakkuk 3:6). Don't read *halichot*; read instead *halachot* [meaning Mishnah, Gemara, and the oral laws handed down to Moses on Sinai (Rashi). If you study these, the World to Come is yours].

NOTES

1. While the embryo is in the womb the *yetzer hara* has no power over it. Therefore it enjoys the primordial pure light that was set aside for the *tzaddikim* (Anaf Yosef).

2. A container made of the skin peeled off the body of an animal, so that the only openings are the cuts at the legs and the tail.

ᴐ UKTZIN ᴑ

GOD WILL BLESS HIS NATION
WITH PEACE

[The Tanna of the final Mishnah of the Talmud points out the heavenly reward that is in store for those who diligently and reverently study the Torah.] (77a) [The Mishnah says:] R. Yehoshua b. Levi said: In the World to Come, the Holy One, blessed be He, will make each *tzaddik* inherit three hundred and ten worlds [meaning: the spiritual delights in the World to Come awaiting those who learn Torah will be 310 times as great as any kind of earthly delight they missed by being immersed in Torah study]. For it says, "I have what [*yesh*] to bequeath to those who love Me, and I shall fill their storehouses" (Proverbs 8:21). [The numeric value of *yesh* is 310.][1]

R. Shimon b. Chalafta said: The Holy One, blessed be He, found no vessel that could hold blessing for Israel except peace, as it says, "God will give might to His nation, God will bless His nation with peace" (Psalms 29:11).

[Tosafot Yom Tov explains: God wants to bestow strength and might on His people. How does He accomplish this? By blessing them with peace. For all the blessings in the world will endure only if there is *shalom. Shalom*, peace, truly is the most fitting ending of the Talmud.]

NOTE
1. *Yud* = 10; *shin* = 300.

ഏ INDEX ൦

INDEX

ABOUT THE TRANSLATOR

Avraham Yaakov Finkel was born in Basel, Switzerland, and lived in The Hague, Netherlands, until 1942, when he was deported to Bergen-Belsen by the Nazis. Mr. Finkel is the author of such books as *The Essential Maimonides, In My Flesh I See God, Contemporary Sages, The Essence of the Holy Days, The Great Chasidic Masters, The Responsa Anthology*, and *The Great Torah Commentators*. Mr. Finkel resides in New York with his wife Suri.